Rivera

The College Board Index of Majors and Graduate Degrees 2001

Rivera

The College Board Index of Majors and Graduate Degrees 2001

Twenty-Third Edition

The College Board
New York

The College Board is a national nonprofit membership association dedicated to preparing, inspiring, and connecting students to college and opportunity. Founded in 1900, the association is composed of more than 3,800 schools, colleges, universities, and other educational organizations. Each year, the College Board serves over three million students and their parents, 22,000 high schools, and 3,500 colleges, through major programs and services in college admission, guidance, assessment, financial aid, enrollment, and teaching and learning. Among its best-known programs are the SAT®, the PSAT/NMSQT™, the Advanced Placement Program®, (AP®), and Pacesetter®. The College Board is committed to the principles of equity and excellence, and that commitment is embodied in all of its programs, services, activities, and concerns.

Editorial inquiries concerning this book should be directed to Guidance Services, The College Board, 45 Columbus Avenue, New York, NY 10023-6992; or telephone 212 713-8120.

Copies of this book are available from your local bookseller or may be ordered from College Board Publications, Two College Way, Forrester Center, WV 25438. The book may also be ordered online through the College Board Store at www.collegeboard.com. The price is $21.95.

Copyright © 2000 by College Entrance Examination Board. All rights reserved. College Board, Advanced Placement Program, AP, College Board Online, Pacesetter, SAT, and the acorn logo are registered trademarks of the College Entrance Examination Board. SAT Learning Center is a trademark owned by the College Entrance Examination Board. PSAT/NMSQT is a joint trademark owned by the College Entrance Examination Board and National Merit Scholarship Corporation. Other products and services may be trademarks of their respective owners. Visit College Board on the Web: www.collegeboard.com.

Library of Congress Catalog Card Number: 80-648202
International Standard Book Number: 0-87447-645-3

Printed in the United States of America

Contents

Preface	1
How to use this book	3
Glossary of special programs	5
Majors by discipline	7
Brief descriptions of majors	13
Majors	49

Special academic programs
- Accelerated program ... 599
- Combined bachelor's/graduate program in:
  - Accounting ... 602
  - Architecture ... 603
  - Business administration ... 603
  - Chemistry ... 604
  - Dentistry ... 604
  - Education ... 605
  - Engineering ... 605
  - Environmental studies ... 606
  - Fine Arts ... 606
  - Forestry ... 607
  - Law ... 607
  - Mathematics ... 607
  - Medicine ... 608
  - Nursing ... 608
  - Occupational therapy ... 609
  - Optometry ... 609
  - Osteopathic medicine ... 609
  - Pharmacy ... 610
  - Physical therapy ... 610
  - Podiatry ... 610
  - Psychology ... 611
  - Social work ... 611
  - Veterinary medicine ... 611
- Combined liberal arts/career program in:
  - Accounting ... 611
  - Architecture ... 613
  - Aviation ... 613
  - Business administration ... 613
  - Computer science ... 616
  - Criminal justice ... 618
  - Education ... 619
  - Engineering ... 621
  - Environmental studies ... 622
  - Forestry ... 624
  - Medical technology ... 624
  - Natural resource management ... 625
  - Nursing ... 625
  - Occupational therapy ... 627
  - Pharmacy ... 628
  - Physical therapy ... 628
  - Physician assistant ... 629
  - Radiology technician ... 629
  - Social work ... 630
- Cooperative education ... 631
- Distance learning ... 636
- Double major ... 641
- Dual enrollment ... 647
- ESL program ... 653
- External degree ... 657
- Honors program ... 658
- Independent study ... 664
- Internship ... 671
- Semester at sea ... 679
- Student-designed major ... 680
- Study abroad ... 683
- Teacher certification ... 689
- United Nations semester ... 693
- Urban semester ... 694
- Visiting/exchange student ... 694
- Washington semester ... 697
- Weekend college ... 699

Colleges in this book ... 703

Alphabetical index of majors ... 723

Dear Friend,

The College Board is dedicated to several key ideas—preparing, inspiring, and connecting students to college and opportunity, while emphasizing equity and excellence. With the College Board's publications, we hope to put a source of college information at your fingertips and help connect you to a college education.

College is a dream for many, a dream worth working hard to achieve. I've been a businessman, a governor, and now the president of the College Board, but nothing makes me prouder than to say that I graduated from college. With perseverance, anyone who desires a college education can attain one. College Board Publications can help you get there.

My best wishes on your journey to success—

Gaston Caperton

Gaston Caperton
President
The College Board

Preface

The College Board Index of Majors and Graduate Degrees, now in its 23rd year, is designed to help students, counselors, and educators to identify colleges that offer particular fields of study at the associate, bachelor's, master's, doctorate, and first-professional levels.

Over 600 majors, listed alphabetically, are included in this book. The colleges and graduate institutions that offer those majors or provide in-depth specialization approximating a major are listed state by state.

The list of majors is based on the 1990 Classification of Instructional Programs (CIP) used by the National Center for Education Statistics, and on data collected for the College Board's Annual Survey of Colleges.

Each year the College Board's annual survey provides colleges with the CIP and asks them to report their majors (even though their own names for majors may not match the CIP names exactly). Colleges can add the names of the majors they offer that do not conform to any major in the CIP. These additional fields (at the undergraduate level) can be found in *The College Board College Handbook* but are not represented in the *Index of Majors*.

In a separate section, there are 61 special academic programs. These are organized alphabetically and include state-by-state listings of colleges offering that program.

To help students who are undecided about a major, two other sections of the *Index of Majors* are of particular use. "Majors by discipline" breaks down each broad discipline into a list of the specific majors offered within it. "Brief descriptions of majors" offers succinct descriptions of the scope of study for each major.

About this book

This edition is based on all-new curriculum and academic program information provided by nearly 3,000 institutions in the College Board's Annual Survey of Colleges 2000–2001. The survey was completed by participating colleges, universities, and graduate institutions in the spring of 2000. The information they supplied was verified with the institutions by a staff of editors to ensure that the data are as complete and accurate as possible. However, program changes occur, and students are urged to contact institutions directly to confirm facts related to their own major of choice.

To be eligible for inclusion, an institution must be accredited by a national accrediting association at the institutional or program level. A complete list of the colleges, universities, and graduate institutions included in the *Index of Majors* can be found at the back of the book, along with an alphabetical index of the majors.

The enormous task of data collection, management, and verification for *The College Board Index of Majors and Graduate Degrees* was directed by Renée Gernand, Director of Information Services; Michael Tuller, Associate Director; and Richard Ziehler, Assistant Director.

collegeboard.com

The College Board has an award-winning Web site that offers continuously updated information to help you with planning, choosing, and applying to college. If you have Internet access, visit the College Board at www.collegeboard.com to find out more about colleges, scholarships, and majors. While you're there, you can also register for the SAT®, visit the SAT Learning Center™, look for scholarships, do a career search, and browse the College Board Store.

We welcome any comments and suggestions that will help us make our publications and services useful to you. Please contact us by mail or telephone: Guidance Services, The College Board, 45 Columbus Avenue, New York, NY 10023-6992; 212 713-8120.

Tom Vanderberg
Editor, Database Publications
Guidance Services

How to use this book

Two of the most important factors in choosing a college are programs of study and location. *The College Board Index of Majors and Graduate Degrees* is designed to help you find colleges that offer what you want to study, where you want to study.

It is important to attend a college that has the major or majors of interest to you. A major (also called a field of study, or a program of study) is an academic field of specialization that students take the majority of courses in during their college studies. Most colleges expect students to take a broad range of courses before declaring a major.

Fields of study

If you already know what you want to study, go right to the list called "Majors" that begins on page 49 and find which colleges offer the major that interests you at the degree level you want. The majors are listed alphabetically, and the schools that offer a major are listed state by state. Some institutions listed here do not offer majors in the traditional sense but do provide in-depth specialization that approximates the course work usually required for a degree.

If you are still exploring options, browse through the list of "Majors by discipline." Here the majors are grouped under broad areas, or disciplines, of study. If you know the broad area in which you are interested—such as health or biological sciences—you can find the specific majors offered in each broad area. If you want to learn more about a specific major, consult "Brief descriptions of majors." The descriptions indicate the scope of the major and, where appropriate, the roles for which the major prepares an individual.

Most of these descriptions are adapted from the 1990 Classification of Instructional Programs (CIP) published by the National Center for Education Statistics; others are derived from descriptions in college catalogs and the data the College Board collects in its Annual Survey of Colleges. These descriptions are generic; the scope of the major at a particular college may be different. You should read the college catalog to determine what a particular major is like at that school.

Levels of study

The levels at which colleges offer specific majors are designated by the following letters found after the college name:

- *C*   Certificate or diploma
- *A*   Associate degree
- *B*   Bachelor's degree
- *T*   Teacher certification
- *M*   Master's degree
- *D*   Doctoral degree
- *F*   First-professional degree
- *W*   Work beyond doctoral or first-professional degree

Undergraduate programs

Undergraduate programs vary in length and may lead to a certificate or diploma, an associate degree, a bachelor's degree, or teacher certification.

Certificate or diploma. These are nondegree offerings below the associate degree and are most often offered in technical and vocational fields of study. They generally lead to employment in an occupational field.

Associate. The associate of arts (AA) or associate of science (AS) degree is granted after completion of a program of study similar to the first two years of a four-year college curriculum. Students who earn an AA or AS often transfer to a four-year college or university where they complete the requirements for a bachelor's degree. The associate in applied science (AAS) is awarded on completion of a technological or vocational program of study.

Bachelor's. Sometimes called baccalaureate degrees, these programs require four or five years of study. The bachelor of arts (BA) and bachelor of science (BS) are the most common baccalaureates, and both include general education courses, a major, and electives. The bachelor of science is more likely to be awarded in the sciences and for professional or technical fields of study. Bachelor of arts degrees are awarded more often in the humanities and arts. However, there are no absolute differences between the degrees, and policies concerning their award vary from college to college.

Teacher certification. *T* next to a major indicates the institution offers specific preparation for teacher certification. All institutions that prepare teachers are accredited by the state; each state sets its own certification standards. Students complete bachelor's degree requirements and state certification requirements; your college adviser will help you prepare a plan of study to meet those twin demands.

A program leading to teacher certification typically involves three types of courses:

- general liberal arts courses
- the major (such as elementary education or mathematics)
- professional education courses, including student teaching

In order to gain certification, most states require candidates to pass an achievement test in the field in which they plan to teach. At some colleges, students who have graduated with a major may complete teacher certification requirements in a fifth year of study.

Graduate programs

Graduate programs vary in length and lead to a master's degree, a doctorate, or a first-professional degree.

Master's. Master of arts (MA) and master of science (MS) programs lead to the first graduate degrees in the liberal arts and sciences. They usually take one to two academic years of study to complete. There are other master's degrees offered, such as the MBA (master of business administration), MLS (master of library science), and MSW (master of social work). See also "Work beyond the doctorate or first-professional degree."

Doctorate. The doctorate degree may be the doctor of philosophy (PhD), awarded in many of the humanities, arts, and sciences, or another degree such as the doctor of education (EdD), or doctor of public health (DPH). Doctorate programs usually consist of course work and independent research culminating in a dissertation or other formal presentation of the results of independent study.

First-professional. First-professional programs are those recognized by the U.S. Department of Education. They require completion of academic prerequisites to become licensed in a recognized profession, at least two years of previous college-level study prior to entering the program, and the total registered time equals at least six academic years. First-professional degrees are awarded in the following fields:

Chiropractic	DC, DCM
Dentistry	DDS, DMD
Divinity/Ministry	BD, MDiv
Law	LLB, JD
Medicine	MD
Optometry	OD
Osteopathic medicine	DO
Pharmacy	BPharm, PharmD
Podiatry	PodD, DP, DPM
Rabbinical/Talmudic studies	MHL, Rav
Veterinary medicine	DVM

Work beyond the doctorate or first-professional degree. Work beyond the doctorate or first-professional degree is advanced graduate study usually consisting of research or other independent pursuits. In some fields, the master's degree is the next highest degree awarded after completion of the first-professional degree. The degrees *M* or *D* listed in this book in the fields of dental specialties, medical specialties, and juridical science are awarded after the first-professional degree has been earned.

Special academic programs. There are 61 special academic programs listed in this section. These programs are described in the glossary. For each program, there is a state-by-state listing of colleges that offer that option.

Colleges in this book

Colleges are listed by state by their characterization of themselves as:

- two-year
- two-year upper division
- three-year
- four-year
- five-year
- graduate

Two-year colleges offer associate degrees and certificates or diplomas. Two-year upper-division institutions and colleges offering three or more years of study usually grant bachelor's degrees. Many of these colleges also offer degrees at the graduate and associate levels. Each college's address is included.

Glossary of special programs

Accelerated program. A program of study completed in less time than is usually required, most often by attending in summer or by carrying extra courses during the regular academic term. Completion of a bachelor's degree program in three years is an example of acceleration.

Combined bachelor's/graduate program. A program to which students are accepted for study at both the undergraduate and graduate levels. The program usually can be completed in less time than two individual programs.

Combined liberal arts/career program. A program of study in which a student typically completes three years of study in a liberal arts field followed by two years of professional/technical study (for example, engineering) at the end of which the student is awarded bachelor of arts and bachelor of science degrees. The combination is sometimes referred to as a 3 + 2 program.

Cooperative education. Also called work-study, this program alternates between semesters (or other periods) of full-time study and full-time employment in related work. Students are paid for their work at the prevailing rate. Five years are required to complete a bachelor's degree program under the cooperative plan, but graduates have the advantage of having completed about a year's practical experience in addition to their studies.

Distance learning. Courses that are broadcast via public or cable stations or the Internet that are viewed in the home (or on campus equipment) for credit.

Double major. Any program of study in which a student completes the requirements of two majors concurrently.

Dual enrollment. A program that lets you enroll in college courses for credit while still enrolled in high school.

ESL program. English as a Second Language is one of the special study options offered on many campuses to help international students improve their English skills.

External degree. A program in which students earn credits toward a college degree through independent study, college courses, proficiency examinations, and personal experience. External degree programs require minimal or no classroom attendance.

Honors program. Any special program for students offering the opportunity for educational enrichment, independent study, acceleration, or some combination of these.

Independent study. An arrangement that allows students to complete some of their college program by studying independently instead of attending scheduled classes and completing group assignments. Typically, students plan programs of study in consultation with a faculty adviser or committee to whom they may report periodically and submit a final report for evaluation.

Internship. Any short-term, supervised work experience, usually related to a student's major field, for which the student earns academic credit. The work can be full- or part-time, on or off campus, paid or unpaid. Student teaching and apprenticeships are examples of internships.

Semester at sea. A program for credit, usually for students with majors in oceanography or marine-related fields, in which students live for part of a semester on a ship, frequently a research vessel. Academic courses are generally taken in conjunction with the sea experience or at separate times during the semester.

Student-designed major. A program that allows a student to construct a major field of study not formally offered by the college. Often nontraditional and interdisciplinary in nature, the major is developed by the student with the approval of a designated college officer or committee.

Study abroad. Any arrangement by which a student completes part of the college program—typically the junior year but frequently only a semester or a summer—studying in another country. A college may operate a campus abroad or it may have a cooperative agreement with some other American college or an institution of the other country.

Teacher certification. A program designed to prepare students to meet the requirements for certification as teachers in elementary and secondary schools.

United Nations semester. A program in which students generally take courses at a college in the New York City metropolitan area while participating in an internship program at the United Nations.

Urban semester. A program for credit in which students of diverse majors spend a semester in a major city, such as Philadelphia, Chicago, New York, Denver, or San Francisco, experiencing the complexities of an urban center through course work, seminars, and/or internships related to their major.

Visiting/exchange student. Any arrangement between a student and a college that permits study for a semester or more at another college without extending the amount of time required for a degree.

Washington semester. A program in which students participate in an internship program with a government agency or department in the Washington, D.C., metropolitan area. Students earn field service credit for their work and frequently take courses at area colleges.

Weekend college. A program that allows students to take a complete course of study and attend classes only on weekends. These programs are generally restricted to a few areas of study at a college and require more than the traditional number of years to complete.

Majors by discipline

Agricultural business/ production
Agribusiness operations
Agricultural business
Agricultural economics
Agricultural food processing
Agricultural mechanization
Agricultural production
Agricultural supplies
Equestrian/equine studies
Farm/ranch management
Greenhouse management
Horticultural services
International agriculture
Landscaping management
Nursery operations
Ornamental horticulture
Turf management

Agricultural sciences
Agricultural animal breeding/genetics
Agricultural animal health
Agricultural animal nutrition
Agricultural animal physiology
Agricultural plant pathology
Agricultural plant physiology
Agricultural sciences
Agronomy/crop science
Animal sciences
Dairy science
Food sciences/technology
Horticulture science
Plant breeding/genetics
Plant protection
Plant sciences
Poultry science
Range science/ management
Soil sciences

Architecture/ related programs
Architecture
Architecture/related programs
Construction/building science
Environmental design
Interior architecture
Landscape architecture
Prearchitecture
Urban/community/ regional planning

Area/ethnic/ cultural studies
African studies
African-American studies
American studies
Area studies
Area/ethnic/cultural studies
Asian studies
Asian-American studies
Canadian studies
Caribbean studies
East Asian studies
Eastern European studies
Ethnic/cultural studies
European studies
Hispanic-American studies
Islamic studies
Jewish/Judaic studies
Latin American studies
Mexican-American studies
Middle Eastern studies
Native American studies
Pacific area studies
Russian/Slavic area studies
South Asian studies
Southeast Asian studies
Western European studies
Women's studies

Biological/life sciences
Behavioral sciences
Biochemistry
Biological immunology
Biological/life science
Biology
Biomedical sciences/ technologies
Biometrics
Biophysics
Biostatistics
Biotechnology research
Botany
Cell biology
Entomology
Evolutionary biology
Genetics, plant/animal
Life sciences
Microbiology /bacteriology
Molecular biology
Natural sciences
Neuroscience
Nutritional sciences
Parasitology
Pathology, human/animal
Pharmacology, human/animal
Physiology, human/ animal
Plant pathology
Plant physiology
Radiation biology
Toxicology
Virology
Zoology

Business
Accounting
Actuarial science
Banking/financial support services
Business
Business administration/ management
Business communications
Business computer facilities operation
Business computer programming
Business economics
Business marketing/ marketing management
Business quantitative methods/management science
Business statistics
Business systems analysis/design
Business systems networking/ telecommunications
Clerical/general office
Construction management
Court reporter
Data entry/information processing
Enterprise management/ operations
Finance/banking
Financial planning
Food management
Hospitality administration/ management
Hotel/motel/restaurant management
Human resources management

Insurance/
    risk management
International business
International business
    marketing
International finance
Investments/securities
Labor/personnel relations
Legal administrative
    assistant
Logistics/materials
    management
Management information
    systems
Management science
Marketing management
Marketing research
Medical administrative
    assistant
Nonprofit/
    public management
Office supervision/
    management
Operations management/
    supervision
Operations research
Organizational behavior
    studies
Public finance
Purchasing/procurement/
    contracts
Real estate
Secretarial/administrative
    services
Taxation
Tourism/
    travel management

Communications
Advertising
Communications
Communications
    technologies
Journalism
Public relations
Radio/television
    broadcasting
Telecommunications

Computer/
information sciences
Computer graphics
Computer programming
Computer science
Computer systems
    analysis
Computer/information
    sciences
Data processing
    technology
Information sciences/
    systems
Software engineering

Conservation/
renewable resources
Conservation/renewable
    resources
Environmental science/
    conservation
Environmental studies
Fisheries/fishing
Forest production/
    processing
Forestry
Natural resources
    management
Wildlife/wildlands
    management

Construction trades
Carpentry
Construction
Construction trades
Construction/building
    technologies
Electrician
Masonry/tile setting
Plumbing/pipefitting
Power/electrical
    transmission

Education
Administration of special
    education
Adult/continuing educa-
    tion administration
Adult/continuing teacher
    education
Agricultural education
Art education
Bilingual/
    bicultural education
Biology education
Business education
Chemistry education
College counseling
Community/junior
    college administration
Comparative/
    international education
Computer education
Counselor education
Curriculum/instruction
Drama/dance teacher
    education
Driver/safety education
Early childhood
    education
Education
Education administration/
    K–12
Education administration/
    supervision
Education of autistic
Education of blind/
    visually handicapped
Education of deaf/hearing
    impaired
Education of emotionally
    handicapped
Education of gifted/
    talented
Education of learning
    disabled
Education of mentally
    handicapped
Education of multiple
    handicapped
Education of physically
    handicapped
Education of speech
    impaired
Education/instructional
    media design
Educational evaluation/
    research
Educational psychology
Educational statistics/
    research methods
Educational supervision
Elementary education
English education
ESL teacher education
Foreign languages
    education
French language teacher
    education
German language
    education
Health education
Health occupations
    education
Higher education
    administration
History education
Home economics
    education
Junior high education
Marketing/distribution
    education
Mathematics education
Music education
Nursing education
Physical education
Physics education
Reading education
Science education
Secondary education
Social/philosophical
    foundations of
    education
Social science education
Social studies education
Spanish language
    education
Special education
Speech education
Speech/theater education
Teacher assistance
Teacher education,
    multiple levels
Technical education
Technology/industrial arts
    education
Trade/industrial education

Engineering

Aerospace/aeronautical/
    astronautical engineering
Agricultural engineering
Architectural engineering
Architectural engineering
    technology
Bioengineering/
    biomedical engineering
Ceramic sciences/
    engineering
Chemical engineering
Civil engineering
Computer engineering
Electrical/electronics/
    communications
    engineering
Engineering
Engineering design
Engineering mechanics
Engineering physics
Engineering science
Engineering/industrial
    management
Environmental health
    engineering
Geological engineering
Geophysical engineering
Industrial/manufacturing
    engineering
Marine engineering/
    naval architecture
Materials engineering
Materials science
Mechanical engineering
Metallurgical engineering
Mining/
    mineral engineering
Nuclear engineering
Ocean engineering
Petroleum engineering
Polymer/
    plastics engineering
Pre-engineering
Software engineering
Systems engineering
Textile sciences/
    engineering

Engineering-related technologies

Architectural engineering
    technology
Automotive technology
Civil engineering/
    civil technology
Construction/building
    technologies
Electrical/electronic
    engineering-related
    technologies
Electromechanical
    instrumentation
Engineering-related
    technologies
Environmental control
    technologies
Industrial production
    technologies
Manufacturing
    technologies
Mechanical engineering
    related technologies
Mining/petroleum
    technologies
Quality control/
    safety technologies
Robotics
Surveying

English

American literature
Comparative literature
Creative writing
English
English composition
English literature
Speech/rhetorical studies
Technical/business
    writing

Foreign languages/ literatures

Arabic
Chinese
Classical/ancient Near
    Eastern languages
Classics
East European languages
East/Southeast Asian
    languages
Foreign languages/
    literatures
Foreign languages/
    translation
French
German
Germanic languages
Greek, ancient
Greek, modern
Hebrew
Italian
Japanese
Latin
Linguistics
Middle Eastern
    languages, other
Portuguese
Romance languages,
    other
Russian
Scandinavian
Slavic languages
South Asian languages
Spanish

Health professions/ related sciences

Acupuncture/
    Oriental medicine
Anatomy
Art therapy
Audiology/
    hearing sciences
Blood bank technology
Cardiovascular
    technology
Clinical laboratory
    science
Clinical/
    medical social work
Communication disorders
Community health services
Cytotechnology
Dance therapy
Dental assistant
Dental hygiene studies
Dental laboratory
    technology
Dental specialties
Diagnostic medical
    sonography
Drug/alcohol abuse
    counseling
Electrocardiograph
    technology
Electrodiagnostic
    technologies
Electroencephalograph
    technology
Emergency medical
    technology
Environmental health
Epidemiology
Health/medical
    biostatistics
Health/medical laboratory
    technologies
Health physics/radiologic
    health
Health professions/
    related sciences
Health system
    administration
Hematology technology
Medical assistant
Medical basic sciences
Medical dietetics
Medical illustrating
Medical laboratory
    assistant
Medical laboratory
    technology
Medical radiologic
    technology
Medical records
    administration
Medical records
    technology
Medical specialties
Medical transcription
Mental health services
Mental health services
    technology

Movement therapy
Music therapy
Nuclear medical
 technology
Nursing
Nursing (post-RN)
Nursing (RN)
Nursing administration
Nursing anesthesiology
Nursing assistant
Occupational health/
 industrial hygiene
Occupational therapy
Occupational therapy
 assistant
Ophthalmic medical
 assistant
Ophthalmic/optometric
 services
Optometric/ophthalmic
 laboratory technology
Orthotics/prosthetics
Perfusion technology
Pharmacy assistant
Physical therapy
Physical therapy assistant
Physician assistant
Predentistry
Premedicine
Prenursing
Preoptometry
Prepharmacy
Prephysical therapy
Preveterinary medicine
Public health
Public health education
Recreational therapy
Rehabilitation/
 therapeutic services
Respiratory therapy
Sign language
 interpretation
Speech pathology
Speech pathology/
 audiology
Surgical/operating room
 technology
Veterinarian assistant
Veterinary specialties

Vocational rehabilitation
 counseling

Home economics
Clothing/apparel/
 textile studies
Consumer resource
 management
Dietetics
Family/
 community studies
Family/
 individual development
Food/nutrition studies
Home economics
Home economics
 business services
Housing studies

Law/legal studies
Legal specialization
Legal studies
Paralegal/legal assistance
Prelaw

Liberal arts/humanities
Liberal arts/humanities
Library science
Library assistant
Library science

Marketing/distribution
Business/personal
 services marketing
Entrepreneurship
Fashion/
 apparel marketing
Financial services
 marketing
Floristry marketing
Food products retailing/
 wholesaling
Health products/
 services marketing
Home/office products
 marketing
Hospitality/
 recreation marketing
Insurance marketing
Marketing/distribution

Retailing/wholesaling
Tourism/travel marketing
Vehicle/petroleum
 products marketing

Mathematics
Applied mathematics
Mathematics
Statistics

Mechanics/repair
Aircraft mechanics
Auto body repair
Diesel mechanics
Electrical/electronics
 equipment repair
Heating/air conditioning/
 refrigeration mechanics
Industrial equipment
 maintenance/repair
Mechanics/repair
Stationary energy sources
 mechanics
Vehicle/mobile equipment
 mechanics

Military technologies
Military technology
 (Air Force)
Military technology
 (Army)
Military technology
 (Coast Guard)
Military technology
 (Merchant Marine)
Military technology
 (Navy/Marines)

Multi/
interdisciplinary
studies
Biological/
 physical sciences
Biopsychology
Environmental studies
Gerontology
Global studies
Historic preservation/
 conservation
International studies

Mathematics/
 computer science
Medieval/
 Renaissance studies
Museum studies
Operations research
Peace/conflict studies
Science/technology/
 society
Systems science/theory

Parks/recreation/
fitness studies
Exercise sciences
Health/physical fitness
Parks/recreation/
 fitness studies
Parks/recreational
 facilities management
Sports fitness
 administration
Sports medicine/
 athletic training

Personal/
miscellaneous
services
Cosmetic services
Culinary arts/related
 services
Funeral services/
 mortuary science
Gaming/sports officiating
Personal services

Philosophy/religion
Philosophy
Philosophy/religion
Religion/religious studies

Physical sciences
Acoustics
Analytical chemistry
Applied physics
Astronomy
Astrophysics
Chemical/atomic physics
Chemistry
Earth/planetary sciences
Elementary particle physics
Geochemistry

Geology
Geophysics/seismology
Inorganic chemistry
Metallurgy
Meteorology
Nuclear physics
Oceanography
Optics
   Organic chemistry
Paleontology
Pharmaceutical/
   medicinal chemistry
Physical sciences
Physical/
   theoretical chemistry
Physics
Plasma/high-temperature
   physics
Polymer chemistry
Solid state/low
   temperature physics
Theoretical/
   mathematical physics

Precision production trades
CAD-CAM/drafting
Graphic/printing
   equipment operation
Leather/upholstery
Precision metal work
Woodworking

Protective services
Corrections
   administration
Criminal justice/
   corrections
Criminal justice/
   law enforcement
   administration
Criminal justice studies
Fire protection
Fire protection/safety
   technology
Fire services
   administration
Firefighting/fire science
Forensic technologies

Law enforcement/
   police science
Protective services
Security/loss prevention

Psychology
Clinical psychology
Cognitive psychology/
   psycholinguistics
Community psychology
Counseling psychology
Developmental/
   child psychology
Experimental psychology
Industrial/organizational
   psychology
Psychobiology/
   physiological
   psychology
Psychology
School psychology
Social psychology

Public administration/ services
Community organization
   services
Human services
Public administration
Public administration/
   services
Public policy analysis
Social work

Science technologies
Biological technology
Nuclear/industrial
   radiologic technologies
Physical sciences
   technologies
Science technologies

Social sciences
Anthropology
Archaeology
Criminology
Demography/
   population studies
Economics
Geography

History
International relations
Political science/
   government
Social sciences
Sociology
Urban studies

Theological studies
Bible studies
Biblical languages/
   literature
Ministerial/
   theological studies
Missionary studies
Pastoral counseling
Religious education
Religious music

Transportation/ materials moving
Air traffic control
Air transportation
Aviation management
Flight attendant
Transportation
   management
Transportation/
   materials moving
Vehicle/
   equipment operation
Water transportation

Visual/performing arts
Acting/directing
Art
Art history/criticism/
   conservation
Arts management
Ceramics
Commercial photography
Conducting
Crafts/folk art/artisanry
Dance
Design/
   visual communications
Drama/theater arts
Drawing

Fashion design/
   illustration
Fiber arts
Film/cinema studies
Film/video/
   cinematography/
   production
Fine arts
Graphic design/
   commercial art/
   illustration
Industrial design
Interior design
Intermedia
Jazz
Metal/jewelry arts
Music
Music business
   management
Music history/literature
Music theory/composition
Music performance
Music, piano/organ
   performance
Music, voice/choral/
   opera performance
Musical theater
Musicology/
   ethnomusicology
Painting
Photography
Playwriting/screenwriting
Printmaking
Sculpture
Studio arts
Technical theater design/
   stagecraft
Theater history/criticism

Vocational home economics
Child care/guidance
Clothing/textile products
   and services
Custodial home services
Home furnishings/
   equipment

Institutional food production
Vocational home economics

First-professional degrees
Chiropractic (DC degree)
Dentistry (DDS or DMD degrees)
Law (JD degree)
Medicine (MD degree)
Optometry (OD degree)
Osteopathic medicine (DO degree)
Pharmacy (BPharm or PharmD)
Podiatry (DPM degree, includes chiropody)
Theological professions (BDiv, MDiv, Rabbinical, or Talmudical)
Veterinary medicine (DVM degree)

Brief descriptions of majors

Accounting. Covers accounting principles/theory, financial accounting, managerial accounting, cost accounting, budget control, tax accounting, auditing, reporting procedures, statement analysis, planning and consulting, business information systems, accounting research methods, professional standards and ethics, and applications to specific for-profit, public, and nonprofit organizations.

Acoustics. The study of sound and the properties and behavior of acoustic wave phenomena under different conditions. Includes instruction in wave theory, energy transformation, vibration phenomena, sound reflection and transmission, scattering and surface wave phenomena, and applications to specific research problems, such as underwater acoustics, crystallography, and health diagnostics.

Acting/directing. Prepares individuals to communicate dramatic information, ideas, and feelings through natural and believable behavior in imaginary circumstances. Includes instruction in voice and acting, speech, movement, improvisation, acting styles, theater history, rehearsal management, scene work, directing, and script interpretation.

Actuarial science. The mathematical and statistical analysis of risk and its application to insurance and other business management problems. Includes instruction in forecasting theory, quantitative and nonquantitative risk measurement, development of risk tables, secondary data analysis, and computer-assisted research methods.

Acupuncture/Oriental medicine. Prepares individuals to be independent practitioners of Oriental and related traditional treatment therapies. Includes instruction in acupuncture, moxibustion, Oriental pharmacology, Oriental medical theory and principles, diagnostic procedures, patient counseling, and related health care arts.

Administration of special education. Principles and techniques of administering educational facilities and programs provided for children or adults with special learning needs.

Adult/continuing education administration. Principles and techniques of administering programs and facilities designed to serve the basic education needs of undereducated adults or the needs of adults seeking further or specialized instruction. Includes instruction in adult education principles, program and facilities planning, personnel management, community and client relations, budgeting and administration, professional standards, and applicable laws and policies.

Adult/continuing teacher education. Prepares individuals to teach adult students in various settings, including basic and remedial education programs, continuing education programs, and programs designed to develop or upgrade specific employment-related knowledge and skills.

Advertising. Describes the creation, execution, transmission, and evaluation of commercial messages concerned with the promotion and sale of products and services. Prepares individuals to function as advertising assistants, technicians, managers, and executives. Includes instruction in advertising theory, marketing strategy, advertising copy/art, layout and production methods, and media relations.

Aerospace/aeronautical/astronautical engineering. Prepares individuals to apply mathematical and scientific principles to the design, development, and operational evaluation of aircraft, space vehicles, and their systems. Also covers applied research on flight characteristics and the development of procedures for launching, guiding, and controlling air and space vehicles.

African studies. Describes the history, society, politics, culture, and economics of Africa, with emphasis on societies south of the Sahara.

African-American studies. Describes the history, society, politics, culture, and economics of the black populations of the Western Hemisphere, with emphasis on the United States and Caribbean. Sometimes called Black studies.

Agribusiness operations. Prepares individuals to apply modern business and economic principles to the production and marketing of agricultural products and services.

Agricultural animal breeding/genetics. Describes the application of genetics to the improvement of agricultural animal health, the development of new animal breeds, and the selective improvement of animal populations.

Agricultural animal health. Describes the scientific principles that affect the prevention and control of diseases in agricultural animals.

Agricultural animal nutrition. Describes the biology and chemistry of proteins, fats, carbohydrates, water, vitamins, and feed additives and their relation to animal health and the production of improved animal products.

Agricultural animal physiology. Application of physiological principles to the study of agricultural animals and production problems. Includes lactation, reproduction, digestion, and growth.

Agricultural business. Prepares individuals to apply modern economic and business principles to the organization, operation, and management of farm and agricultural businesses.

Agricultural economics. Relates modern business and economic principles to the allocation of resources in the production and marketing of agricultural products and services.

Agricultural education. Prepares individuals to teach vocational agriculture at various education levels.

Agricultural engineering. Application of mathematical and scientific principles to the development and evaluation of systems used to produce, process, and store agricultural products; to improve the productivity of agricultural methods; and to develop improved agricultural biological systems.

Agricultural food processing. Prepares individuals to receive, inspect, store, and process agricultural food or products. Instruction covers the characteristics and properties of agricultural products and processing and storage techniques.

Agricultural mechanization. Prepares individuals to sell, select, and service agriculture or agribusiness technical equipment and facilities, including computers, specialized software, power units, machinery, equipment, and utilities.

Agricultural plant pathology. Prepares individuals to recognize diseased plants, identify causal agents, treat disease, and reduce economic loss.

Agricultural plant physiology. Study of the life processes of plants and plant responses to the elements of the physical environment, including nutrition, respiration, growth, photosynthesis, and reproduction.

Agricultural production. Prepares individuals to plan and economically use facilities, natural resources, labor, and capital in the production of plant and animal products.

Agricultural sciences. Describes principles and practices of agricultural research and production. Includes instruction in basic animal, plant, and soil science; animal husbandry and plant cultivation; and soil conservation.

Agricultural supplies. Prepares individuals to sell supplies for agricultural production, provide agricultural services, and purchase and market agricultural products.

Agronomy/crop science. Describes the chemical, physical, and biological relationships of crops and soils. Includes instruction in the growth and behavior of agricultural crops, the breeding of improved and new crop varieties, and the scientific management of soils for maximum plant nutrition and health.

Air traffic control. Prepares individuals to apply technical knowledge and skills to air-traffic management and control, usually with additional training at the FAA Flight Control Center in a cooperative education program. Includes instruction in flight control, the use of radar and electronic scanning devices, plotting of flights, radio communication, interpretation of weather conditions affecting flight, flight instrumentation used by pilots, and maintenance of flight-control center or control-tower logbooks.

Air transportation. Prepares individuals to apply technical knowledge and skills to provide in-flight, ground, and administrative services to the aviation industry.

Aircraft mechanics. Prepares individuals to repair, service, and maintain all aircraft components other than engines, propellers, avionics, and instruments. Includes instruction in layout and fabrication of sheet metal, fabric, wood, and other materials into structural members, parts, and fittings, and replacement of damaged or worn parts such as control cables and hydraulic units.

American literature. The study of the literature and literary development of the United States from the Colonial Era to the present. Includes instruction in period and genre studies, author studies, literary criticism, and regional and oral traditions.

American studies. Describes the history, society, politics, culture, and economics of the United States and its regions.

Analytical chemistry. The study of techniques for analyzing and describing matter, including its precise composition and the interrelationships of elements and compounds. Includes instruction in spectroscopy, chromatography, atomic absorption, photometry, chemical modeling, mathematical analysis, laboratory analysis, and applications to specific research, industrial, and health problems.

Anatomy. The study of the structure and function of living organisms, tissues, organs, and systems. Includes instruction in gross anatomy, histology, ultrastructure, neuroanatomy, microscopy, dissection, electrical and analytical methods, and quantification methods.

Animal sciences. Describes the breeding and husbandry of agricultural animals and the production, processing, and distribution of agricultural animal products.

Anthropology. Describes the systematic and comparative study of human beings and their cultural behavior and institutions. Includes instruction in biological/physical anthropology, primatology, human paleontology and prehistoric archaeology, hominid evolution, anthropological linguistics, ethnography, ethnology, ethnohistory, sociocultural anthropology, and research methods.

Applied mathematics. The application of mathematical principles to the solution of functional area problems, using the knowledge base of the subject or field for which the analytical procedures are being developed. Includes instruction in computer-assisted mathematical analysis and the development of tailored algorithms for solving specific research problems.

Applied physics. Prepares individuals to apply principles of physics and analytical techniques to solving specific problems related to matter and energy. Includes instruction in electricity and magnetism, thermodynamics, mechanics, wave properties, nuclear processes, optics, quantum mechanics, and quantitative methods.

Arabic. Describes the study of the language, literature, and culture of Arabic-speaking peoples, including classic, modern, standard, and related dialects and derivatives.

Archaeology. Describes the systematic study of extinct societies, and the past of living societies, via the excavation, analysis, and interpretation of their artifactual, human, and other remains. Includes instruction in archaeological theory, field and dating methods, conservation, and cultural and physical evolution.

Architectural engineering. Prepares individuals to apply mathematical and scientific principles to the design, development, and operational evaluation of materials, systems, and methods used to construct and equip buildings.

Architectural engineering technology. Prepares individuals to apply basic engineering principles and technical skills in support of architects, engineers, and planners engaged in designing and developing buildings and urban complexes. Includes instruction in design testing procedures, building site analysis, model building and computer graphics, engineering drawing, structural systems testing, and analysis of mechanical and interior systems.

Architecture. Includes instruction in architectural design; architectural history and theory; building structures; site planning; construction; professional responsibilities and standards; and the cultural, social, economic, and environmental issues relating to architectural practice.

Architecture/related programs. Programs describing the principles and methods used to create, adapt, alter, preserve, and control human physical and social surroundings and habitations.

Area studies. The history, society, politics, culture, and economics of a particular geographic region. Colleges that offer area studies may have several area studies majors.

Area/ethnic/cultural studies. Study of the history, society, politics, culture, and economics of a particular geographic region or a particular subset of the population that shares common characteristics, traits, and customs.

Art. Describes the development and practice of art. Includes art appreciation, art history, fundamental principles of design and color, and an introduction to various media and studio techniques.

Art education. Prepares individuals to teach art at various educational levels.

Art history/criticism/conservation. Study of the historical development of art as a social and intellectual phenomenon, the analysis of works of art, and art conservation. Includes instruction in the theory of art, research methods, conservation, and in specific periods, cultures, styles, and themes.

Art therapy. Prepares individuals to help patients use art to overcome physical disabilities, resolve emotional conflicts, and enhance communications with others.

Arts management. Prepares individuals to organize and manage art organizations and facilities. Includes instruction in business and financial management, marketing and fund-raising, personnel management and labor relations, event promotion and management, public relations and arts advocacy, and arts law.

Asian studies. Describes the general history, society, politics, culture, and economics of the continent of Asia, its borderlands, and related island groups.

Asian-American studies. Describes the history, society, politics, culture, and economics of Asian Americans, including immigrants and their descendants from East Asia, South Asia, and Southeast Asia.

Astronomy. Study of matter and energy in the universe. Includes instruction in celestial mechanics, cosmology, and stellar physics, and applications to research on lunar, planetary, solar, stellar, and galactic phenomena.

Astrophysics. Study of the behavior of astronomical phenomena and related physicochemical interactions. Includes instruction in cosmology, plasma, kinetics, stellar physics, convolution and nonequilibrium, radiation transfer theory, non-Euclidian geometries, mathematical modeling, galactic structure theory, and relativistic astronomy.

Audiology/hearing sciences. Scientific study of the anatomy and physiology of the hearing and/or speech organs and their function and malfunction. Includes instruction in bio-acoustics; neuroanatomy of speech, hearing, and language; hearing measurement; communications embryology and congenital defects; hearing aids and related technology; hearing conservation and noise reduction research; and the experimental analysis of hearing, speech, and language disorders.

Auto body repair. Prepares individuals to repair, reconstruct, and finish automobile bodies, fenders, and external features. Includes instruction in all phases of body work preparation and finishing.

Automotive technology. Prepares individuals to apply technical knowledge and skills to repair, service, and maintain all types of automobiles, trucks, vans, and buses. Includes instruction in the diagnosis of malfunctions in and repair of engines; fuel, electrical, cooling, and brake systems; suspension systems.

Aviation management. Prepares individuals to apply technical knowledge and skills to the management of aviation industry operations and services. Includes instruction in airport operations, ground support and flightline operations, passenger and cargo operations, flight safety and security operations, aviation industry regulation, and related business aspects of managing aviation enterprises.

Banking/financial support services. Prepares individuals to perform a wide variety of customer services in banks, insurance agencies, savings and loan companies, and related enterprises. Includes instruction in communications and public relations skills, business equipment operations, and technical skills applicable to the methods and operations of specific financial or insurance services.

Behavioral sciences. Teaches individuals how to observe and measure behavior, apply observations to theoretical models, understand motives and purposes of complex social organisms, and predict what behavior will be under a wide range of circumstances. Includes instruction in anthropology, psychology, geography, history, and sociological issues.

Bible studies. Describes the study of the Bible and its component books from the standpoint of the Christian or Jewish faiths, with an emphasis on understanding and interpreting the theological, doctrinal, and ethical messages contained within it.

Biblical languages/literature. The study of liturgical, scriptural, and historical languages and literatures used by Christianity, Judaism, and other major faiths as vehicles for communicating doctrine, forms of worship, rules, and traditions. Includes instruction in translation techniques, textual analysis and criticism, the study and preservation of ancient manuscripts, and studies of such specific languages as Hebrew, Koine Greek, Biblical Aramaic, and others.

Bilingual/bicultural education. A program in which one learns to teach bilingual/bicultural children or adults.

Biochemistry. Describes the chemical processes of living organisms. Includes instruction in the chemical mechanisms of genetic information storage and transmission, and the chemistry of cells, blood, biological systems and products, and life processes, such as respiration, digestion, and reproduction.

Bioengineering/biomedical engineering. Prepares individuals to apply mathematical and scientific principles to the design, development, and evaluation of biological and health systems and products, such as instrumentation, medical information systems, artificial organs and prostheses, and health management and care delivery systems.

Biological immunology. The study of organismic responses to, and defenses against, invasive foreign substances and parasitical life forms. Includes instruction in the anatomy and physiology of immune systems, autoimmune responses, disease response mechanisms and triggers, antigen receptors, membrane transfer, the histocompatibility complex, immunogenetics, immunochemistry, and immune system regulation.

Biological technology. Prepares individuals to apply scientific principles and technical skills in support of biologists in research and industrial settings. Includes instruction in field research and laboratory methods.

Biological/life sciences. A specialization that draws from the biological and physical sciences.

Biological/physical sciences. Provides a general synthesis of one or more of the biological and physical sciences.

Biology. The scientific study of the structure, function, reproduction, growth, heredity, evolution, behavior, and distribution of living organisms and their relations to their natural environments.

Biology education. Prepares individuals to teach biology at various education levels.

Biomedical sciences/technologies. Interdisciplinary program bridging the life sciences and engineering to prepare individuals for careers in industry (designing and developing instrumentation and systems for use in medical environments, such as diagnostic aids, life-support systems, prosthetic and orthotic devices, and human-machine systems) or government (e.g., at the National Institutes for Health), or for entrance to medical school. Includes instruction in life sciences, biology, chemistry, physics, calculus, biotechnology, principles of design, materials science, and biomechanics.

Biometrics. Describes quantitative measurement methods in the biological sciences; the development of biometrics solutions to specific research problems; and related computer applications. Includes instruction in algebraic analysis, matrix algebra, computer methods, and applications to specific biological subdisciplines.

Biophysics. Describes the application of physics principles to the study of living cells and organisms, including structures and fine structures, bioelectric phenomena, radiation effects, molecular behavior, photosynthesis, membranes, organic thermodynamics, and quantitative analysis and modeling.

Biopsychology. Describes biological links to psychological phenomena, especially the links between biochemical and biophysical activity and the functioning of the central nervous system.

Biostatistics. The application of statistical methods and techniques to the study of living organisms and biological systems. Includes instruction in experimental design and data analysis, projection methods, descriptive statistics, and specific applications to biological subdisciplines.

Biotechnology research. The application of the biological sciences to the development of medical and industrial products and processes, and the methods and equipment used in these procedures. Includes instruction in genetic engineering, cell technology, protein synthesis, applied biology, artificial enzyme production, biomaterial development, and drug therapy mechanisms.

Blood bank technology. Prepares individuals to classify, analyze, and test banked blood under the supervision of a pathologist, physician, or laboratory director. Includes instruction in hematology, blood bank procedures, blood donor selection, blood collection, storage and processing procedures, and topological and compatibility tests.

Botany. Scientific study of plants, related bacteria, fungi, and algae. Includes instruction in the classification, structure, function, reproduction, heredity, evolution, and pathology of plant life, with particular attention to basic processes, such as photosynthesis, plant biochemistry, and plant ecosystems.

Business. Prepares individuals for the world of business, including buying, selling, and producing; business organization; and accounting in profit-making and nonprofit public and private institutions and agencies.

Business administration/management. Prepares individuals to plan, organize, and direct the operations of a firm or organization. Includes instruction in management theory, human resources management and behavior, accounting and other quantitative methods, purchasing and logistics, marketing, and business decision making.

Business communications. Prepares individuals to function in an organization as writers, editors, and/or proofreaders of business or business-related communications.

Business computer facilities operation. Prepares individuals to operate mainframe computers and related peripheral equipment in business settings. Includes instruction in mainframe peripheral equipment operation and monitoring, disk and tape mounting and storage, and printer and related computer facility operations.

Business computer programming. Prepares individuals to apply software theory and programming methods to the solution of business data problems. Includes instruction in designing customized software applications, prototype testing, documentation, input specification, and report generation.

Business economics. The application of economics principles to the analysis of the organization and operation of business enterprises. Includes instruction in monetary theory, banking and financial systems, pricing theory, wage and salary/incentive theory, analysis of markets, and applications of econometrics and quantitative methods to the study of particular businesses and business problems.

Business education. Prepares individuals to teach vocational business at various educational levels.

Business marketing/marketing management. Prepares individuals to manage the process of developing consumer audiences and moving products from producers to consumers. Includes instruction in buyer behavior, marketing research, demand analysis, cost-volume and profit relationships, pricing theory, advertising methods, sales operations and management, consumer relations, and retailing.

Business quantitative methods/management. Describes the application of scientific and mathematical principles to the study of business problems.

Business statistics. The application of mathematical statistics to the description, analysis, and forecasting of business data. Includes instruction in statistical theory and methods, computer applications, data analysis and display, long- and short-term forecasting methods, and marketing performance analysis.

Business systems analysis/design. Prepares individuals to analyze business information needs and prepare specifications for appropriate data system solutions. Includes instruction in information analysis, writing specifications, prototype evaluation, and network application interfaces.

Business systems networking/telecommunications. Prepares individuals to evaluate and resolve business data system hardware and software communication needs. Includes instruction in telecommunications and network theory, hardware and software interfacing, computer network design and evaluation, and computer system facilities and support.

Business/personal services marketing. Prepares individuals to apply marketing concepts in the delivery of services to businesses or individuals.

CAD-CAM/drafting. Prepares individuals to apply technical knowledge and skills to plan and prepare scale pictorial interpretations of engineering and design concepts. Includes instruction in the use of precision drawing instruments, computer-assisted design programs, sketching and illustration, and specification interpretation.

Canadian studies. Study of the history, society, politics, culture, and economics of Canada, including both English- and French-speaking peoples.

Cardiovascular technology. Prepares individuals to perform invasive and noninvasive tests to monitor human heart and circulatory health and to administer prescribed treatment therapies under the supervision of a physician. Includes instruction in the administration of tests such as EKG and phonocardiograms; therapeutic procedures such as cardiac catheterization and Holter monitoring; and equipment preparation and maintenance.

Caribbean studies. Describes the history, society, politics, culture, and economics of the islands in the Caribbean.

Carpentry. Prepares individuals to apply technical knowledge and skills to lay out, fabricate, install, and repair wooden structures and fixtures using hand and power tools. Includes instruction in systems of framing, construction materials, estimating, blueprint reading, and finish carpentry techniques.

Cell biology. The study of the cell as a biological system in plants and animals. Includes instruction in cellular structure and function, biosynthesis, enzyme production, cell communication and nutrition, chromosome organization and function, cell life cycles, and cell pathology.

Ceramic sciences/engineering. Prepares individuals to apply mathematical and scientific principles to the design, development, and operational evaluation of inorganic nonmetallic materials, such as porcelains, cements, industrial ceramics, ceramic superconductors, and abrasives.

Ceramics. Prepares individuals to produce artworks out of clay and similar materials. Includes instruction in hand-built and wheel-thrown techniques, molding, slips and glazes, trimming and decorating, and firing and kiln operation.

Chemical engineering. Prepares individuals to use mathematical and scientific materials in the design, development, and operational evaluation of systems employing chemical processes, such as chemical reactors, electrochemical systems, and heat and mass transfer systems. Covers the analysis of chemical problems such as corrosion, particle abrasion, energy loss, and pollution.

Chemical/atomic physics. The study of the behavior of matter-energy phenomena at the level of atoms and molecules. Includes instruction in chemical physics, atomic forces and structure, fission reactions, molecular orbital theory, molecular bonding, phase equilibria, and quantum theory of solids.

Chemistry. The scientific study of the composition and behavior of matter, including its structure, the processes of chemical change, and the theoretical description and laboratory simulation of these phenomena.

Chemistry education. Prepares individuals to teach chemistry at various education levels.

Child care/guidance. Prepares individuals for employment in institutional and residential family settings, often under the supervision of professional personnel. Includes instruction in child growth and development; play and learning activities; child abuse and neglect prevention; parent-child relationships; and applicable legal regulations.

Chinese. The study of the languages, literatures, and cultures of Chinese-speaking peoples, including dialects, such as Cantonese, Taiwanese, and Mandarin.

Chiropractic (DC). Prepares individuals for professional practice of chiropractic. Includes instruction in chiropractic theory, spinal manipulation therapy, and radiologic diagnosis. May also include principles of neurologic health, nutrition, hydrotherapy, and diet and exercise therapy.

Civil engineering. Prepares individuals to apply mathematical and scientific principles to the design, development, and operational evaluation of structural, load-bearing, material-moving, transportation, water resource, and material control systems.

Civil engineering/civil technology. Prepares individuals to apply basic engineering principles and technical skills in support of civil engineers. Includes instruction in site analysis, structural testing procedures, field and laboratory testing procedures, plan and specification preparation, and test equipment operation and maintenance.

Classical/ancient Near Eastern languages. Instructional programs in such languages and literatures as ancient Egyptian/Egyptology, Coptic, Avestan (Old Persian), Akkadian, Aramaic, Ugaritic, Syriac, Phoenician, Hittite and Hurrian, Sumerian, Luwian, Yemeni, Elamite, Cretan, and Uratian.

Classics. The study of the language, literature, and civilization of the classical Greco-Roman world, including both ancient Greek and Latin.

Clerical/general office. Prepares individuals to provide basic administrative support under the supervision of office managers. Includes instruction in typing, keyboarding, filing, general business correspondence, and office equipment operation.

Clinical laboratory science. Prepares individuals to analyze human body fluids and tissues. Includes instruction in clinical chemistry, microbiology, and immunology; chemical and physical analytic techniques; and data and record systems maintenance.

Clinical psychology. Prepares individuals for the practice of clinical psychology, involving the analysis, diagnosis, and clinical treatment of psychological disorders and behavioral pathologies. Includes instruction in clinical assessment and diagnosis, psychopharmacology, behavior modification, therapeutic intervention, and various therapeutic approaches.

Clinical/medical social work. Prepares individuals for the practice of social work in mental health clinics, hospitals, and community health service organizations. Includes instruction in psychiatric casework, clinical interviewing techniques, therapeutic intervention strategies, psychological test administration, family counseling, and social rehabilitation.

Clothing/apparel/textile studies. The study of contemporary and historical ways of meeting psychological, sociological, economic, and physiological needs relative to clothing and textile products, including techniques of design, production, distribution, marketing, and consumption.

Clothing/textile products and services. Prepares individuals for occupations concerned with clothing, apparel, and textiles management, production, and services. Instruction covers clothing construction, fabric and fabric care, pattern design, principles in clothing construction and selection, fitting and alterations, custom tailoring, clothing maintenance, and textiles testing.

Cognitive psychology/psycholinguistics. The study of the mechanisms and processes of learning and thinking and associated information encoding, decoding, processing, and transmitting systems. Includes instruction in theories of cognition and intelligence, cognitive processes, cybernetics, and psycholinguistics.

College counseling. Describes the organization and provision of counseling, referral, assistance, and administrative services to students in postsecondary educational institutions and adult education facilities and prepares individuals to function as professional counselors in such settings. Includes instruction in applicable laws and policies, residential counseling and services, vocational counseling and placement services, remedial skills counseling, and therapeutic counselor intervention.

Commercial photography. Prepares individuals to use artistic techniques to communicate ideas and information effectively to business and consumer audiences and to record events and people via film, still, and video photography. Includes instruction in specialized camera and equipment operation and maintenance.

Communication disorders. A program that generally describes the principles and practice of identifying and treating disorders of human speech and hearing, and related problems of social communication and health. Includes instruction in developmental and acquired disorders, basic research and clinical methods, and prevention and treatment modalities.

Communications. Study of the creation, transmission, and evaluation of messages. Provides an overview of several types of communication: individual, mass media, journalism, broadcasting, and others.

Communications technologies. Prepares individuals to support communications professionals. Topics covered may include educational media technology, photographic technology, and radio and TV broadcasting technology.

Community health services. Prepares individuals to serve as liaisons between public health and other social services and the recipients of health services. Includes instruction in human health and nutrition, communicable diseases, environmental health, personal hygiene, care of infants, and medications.

Community organization/resources/services. The theories, principles, and practice of organizing communities and neighborhoods for social action, serving as community liaisons to public agencies, and using community resources to furnish information and assistance to all members of a community.

Community psychology. Prepares individuals to apply psychological principles to the analysis of social problems and to implement intervention strategies for addressing these problems. Includes instruction in social ecology, primary and secondary prevention of social pathologies, large-group counseling, creating settings, cultural stress, and the dynamics of social change.

Community/junior college administration. The principles and practice of administration in four-year colleges, universities, and higher education systems and the study of higher education as an object of applied research. Includes instruction in higher education economics and finance; curriculum, faculty, and labor relations; higher education law; college student services; research on higher education; institutional research; and marketing and promotion.

Comparative literature. The study of the literatures of different societies and linguistic groups in comparative perspective, including analyses of cross-cultural influences, national literary styles, the influence of translation, and shared international literary heritage. Includes instruction in the study of literatures in the original languages as well as in English translation.

Comparative/international education. The study of educational practices and institutions within different societies from a comparative perspective and of international educational issues. Includes instruction in comparative research methods, cross-national studies of learning and teaching styles, and international education policy and development.

Computer education. Prepares individuals to teach computer education at various education levels.

Computer engineering. Prepares individuals to apply mathematical and scientific principles to the design, development, and operational evaluation of computer hardware and software systems and related equipment and facilities, and to analyze specific problems in computer applications.

Computer graphics. Prepares individuals to apply principles of hardware and software, and specific computational analysis, programming, mathematical modeling, calculus, linear algebra, differential equations, and probability and statistics.

Computer programming. Prepares individuals to apply the methods and procedures used in designing and writing computer programs to develop solutions to specific operational problems and use requirements, including testing and troubleshooting prototype software packages.

Computer science. An instructional program that describes the scientific and mathematical study of the algorithms used in designing and building computers, and their application to the development and design of actual computing systems. Includes instruction in computer architecture, assembly and programming languages, numerical and computational analysis, computer systems theory, artificial intelligence and cybernetics, and simulation modeling.

Computer systems analysis. Prepares individuals to apply computer programming principles to the design and implementation of large-scale computer applications and networking systems. Includes instruction in system design, user prioritization, system and component optimization, and computer security systems.

Computer/information sciences. An overview of the design, development, and operation of electronic data storage and processing systems, including hardware and software.

Conducting. Prepares individuals to lead bands, choirs, orchestras, and other ensembles in performance. Includes instruction in score analysis and arranging, rehearsal and performance leadership, music coaching, arrangement, and performance planning.

Conservation/renewable resources. A general major that prepares individuals for activities involving the conservation and improvement of natural resources.

Construction. Prepares individuals to apply technical knowledge and skills to the finishing, inspection, and maintenance of structures and related properties.

Construction management. Prepares individuals to manage the construction process. Includes instruction in building site inspection and supervision and supply logistics and procurement.

Construction trades. Programs that prepare individuals to apply technical knowledge and skills in the building, inspecting, and maintaining of structure and related properties.

Construction/building science. Prepares individuals to apply architectural principles and technical knowledge to the construction process. Includes instruction in basic structural principles and techniques, building site inspection and supervision, and plan and specification interpretation.

Construction/building technologies. Prepares individuals to apply basic engineering principles and technical skills in support of engineers, engineering contractors, and other professionals engaged in the construction of buildings and related structures. Includes instruction in basic structural engineering principles and construction techniques, building site inspection and supervision, plan and specification interpretation, and supply logistics and procurement.

Consumer resource management. The study of the processes by which families and households balance needs and wants and maximize the use of available resources. Includes instruction in human behavior, management theory, financial planning, and family consultative services.

Corrections administration. Prepares individuals to apply the theories, principles, and techniques of correctional science to the development, administration, and implementation of procedures for the incarceration, supervision, and rehabilitation of offenders of the law.

Cosmetic services. Prepares individuals to provide a variety of beauty and grooming services.

Counseling psychology. Prepares individuals for the practice of psychological counseling, involving the provision of therapeutic services to individuals and groups experiencing psychological problems. Includes instruction in counseling theory, therapeutic intervention strategies, patient/counselor relationships, testing and assessment methods, and various therapeutic approaches.

Counselor education. Prepares individuals to apply the theories and principles of guidance and counseling to the provision of support for the personal, social, educational, and vocational development of students, and to organize guidance services within elementary, middle, and secondary education institutions. Includes instruction in therapeutic intervention and vocational counseling.

Court reporter. Prepares individuals to record examinations, testimony, judgments or sentences of courts, and other formal legal proceedings by machine shorthand or other procedures. Includes instruction in specialized terminology, procedures and equipment, and professional standards and applicable regulations.

Crafts/folk art/artisanry. The aesthetics, techniques, and creative processes for designing and fashioning objects in one or more of the handcraft or folk art traditions. Prepares individuals to create in these media.

Creative writing. The processes and techniques of original composition in various literary forms, such as short story, poetry, the novel. Includes instruction in technical and editorial skills, criticism, and marketing finished manuscripts.

Criminal justice studies. The study of the criminal justice system, its organizational components and processes, and its legal and public policy contexts. Includes instruction in criminal law and policy, police and correctional systems organization, the administration of justice and the judiciary, and public attitudes regarding criminal justice issues.

Criminal justice/corrections. The principles and procedures for conducting and supervising law enforcement, corrections, and security services.

Criminal justice/law enforcement administration. Prepares individuals to apply the theories and practices of criminal justice to structuring, managing, and controlling criminal justice agencies, including police departments, sheriff's departments, law enforcement divisions and units, and private protection services.

Criminology. The study of crime as a sociopathological phenomenon, the behavior of criminals, and the social institutions evolved to respond to crime. Includes instruction in the psychological and social bases of criminal law and criminal justice systems, penology, and rehabilitation and recidivism.

Culinary arts/related services. Prepares individuals to provide food and beverage services in restaurants, bars, and other commercial establishments. Specialties include baker, pastry chef, bartender, chef, kitchen assistant, and restaurant operations manager.

Curriculum/instruction. Prepares individuals to serve as professional curriculum specialists. Includes curriculum theory, curriculum design and planning, instructional material design and evaluation, curriculum evaluation, and applications to specific subject matter, programs, or educational levels.

Custodial/home services. Prepares individuals for occupations related to commercial housekeeping and cleaning operations and for providing housekeeping services to paying clients and homebound individuals.

Cytotechnology. Prepares individuals to perform oncological and related pathological analyses of human tissue samples under the supervision of a pathologist. Includes instruction in pathology laboratory procedures, equipment operation and maintenance, and slide and tissue sample preparation.

Dairy science. The biological theories and principles that apply to the production and management of dairy animals and the production of milk products.

Dance. Prepares individuals to express ideas, feelings, and/or inner visions through the performance of one or more of the dance disciplines, including ballet, modern, jazz, ethnic, and folk dance. Includes the study and analysis of dance as a cultural phenomenon and instruction in choreography, dance history and criticism, and dance production.

Dance therapy. Prepares individuals to employ dance as a tool to assist patients in overcoming physical disabilities, resolving emotional conflicts, and enhancing communication with others.

Data entry/information processing. Prepares individuals to support business information operations by using computer equipment to enter, process, and retrieve data for a wide variety of administrative purposes. Includes instruction in using basic business software and hardware, business computer networking, and principles of desktop publishing.

Data processing technology. Prepares individuals to use computers and associated software packages to perform a variety of tasks, including text processing, number processing, graphics, and data base management.

Demography/population studies. The systematic study of population models and phenomena and related issues of social structure and behavior. Includes instruction in mortality and fertility, migration, mathematical and statistical analysis of population data, and applications to economics and government planning.

Dental assistant. Prepares individuals to assist a dentist or dental hygienist. Includes instruction in chairside assistance, patient preparation, dental office functions and laboratory procedures, and dental radiography.

Dental hygiene studies. Prepares individuals to provide tooth cleaning and related oral health therapies, either independently or in collaboration with dentists. Includes instruction in basic preventive oral health care, dental hygiene therapy, patient examination and counseling, dental radiography, and local anesthesia.

Dental laboratory technology. Prepares individuals

to make and repair dental prostheses and restorative appliances as prescribed by a dentist. Includes instruction in complete and partial denture construction, crown and fixed bridge fabrication, and customized porcelain and acrylic restorations.

Dental specialties. Advanced study by dentists or other medical doctors in dental practice specialties and related sciences such as oral biology, endodontics, orthodontics, pediatrics, periodontics, dental immunology, and dental pathology.

Dentistry (DDS or DMD). Prepares individuals for professional practice of dentistry. Includes instruction in the prevention, diagnosis, and treatment of diseases and abnormalities of the teeth and gums and related parts of the oral cavity; study of related anatomical and physiological principles, professional ethics and standards, and supervised clinical practice.

Design/visual communications. The theories and techniques for effectively communicating ideas and information and packaging products for business and consumer audiences.

Developmental/child psychology. The study of the psychological growth and development of individuals from infancy through adulthood. Includes instruction in cognitive, perceptual, emotional, and personality development; the effects of biological maturation on behavior; testing and assessment methods; and the psychology of aging.

Diagnostic medical sonography. Prepares individuals to perform diagnostic and monitoring procedures using acoustic energy, under the supervision of a physician. Includes instruction in patient preparation, ultrasound testing and examination procedures, sonogram evaluation, and equipment operation.

Diesel mechanics. Prepares individuals to apply technical knowledge and skills to repair, service, and maintain diesel engines in vehicles, such as automobiles, buses, ships, trucks, railroad locomotives, and construction equipment, as well as stationary diesel engines in electrical generators and related equipment.

Dietetics. Program that describes the provision of nutritional services, menu planning, and diet consultation for individuals, families, and institutions. Includes instruction in planning and directing food service activities, diet and nutrition analysis and plan formulation, food preparation management, client education, and related services.

Drama/dance education. Prepares individuals to teach drama and/or dance at various education levels.

Drama/theater arts. The study of dramatic works and their performance. Includes instruction in major works of dramatic literature, dramatic styles, and the principles of organizing and producing dramatic productions.

Drawing. Prepares individuals to express emotions, ideas, or inner visions through representation by lines made on a surface. Includes instruction in eye-hand coordination, value, shape, perspective, figure and still-life drawing, and the use of such media as pen and ink, pencil, charcoal, pastel, and brush.

Driver/safety education. Prepares individuals to teach driver and safety education programs at various education levels.

Drug/alcohol abuse counseling. Prepares individuals to counsel drug users, addicts, family members, and associates, using various strategies and treatments. Includes instruction in outreach, patient education, therapeutic intervention methods, and diagnostic procedures. Also covers liaison with community health, law enforcement, social, and legal services.

Early childhood education. Prepares individuals to teach all relevant subject matter to students ranging in age from infancy through 8 years (grade 3), depending on state regulations.

Earth/planetary sciences. Study of the earth and other planets as comprehensive physical systems incorporating solids, liquids, and gases, as well as exhibiting interactions with other systems. Includes instruction in planetary evolution, gravitational physics, volcanism and crustal movement, orbital mechanics, and radiation physics.

East Asian studies. The history, society, politics, culture, and economics of East Asia, including China, Japan, Korea, Mongolia, and Eastern Central Asia, Taiwan, and Tibet.

East European languages. Study of Eastern European languages other than Russian or Slavic languages, such as Finnish, Hungarian, Estonian, Latvian, and Lithuanian.

East/Southeast Asian languages. Study of languages other than Chinese or Japanese, such as Korean, Tibetan, Mongolian, Tagalog, Thai, Laotian, Vietnamese, Cambodian, Indonesian Malay, and Burmese.

Eastern European studies. The history, society, politics, culture, and economics of Eastern Europe, including the Balkans, Czech Republic, Hungary, Poland,

Romania, the European portions of the former USSR and its constituent republics, and the former East Germany.

Ecology. The study of ecological systems and the physical interactions among system components. Includes instruction in population biology, large and small ecosystems, environmental factors affecting organisms, evolution and extinction, and symbiotic relationships.

Economics. The study of the production, conservation, and allocation of resources in conditions of scarcity, together with the organizational frameworks related to these processes. Includes instruction in economic theory, micro- and macroeconomics, comparative economic systems, money and banking systems, and quantitative analytical methods.

Education. Includes instruction in the theory and practice of learning and teaching, the basic principles of educational psychology, the planning and administration of educational activities, and the social foundations of education.

Education administration/K–12. Prepares individuals to serve as principals or other administrators at these levels. Includes instruction in program planning, personnel management, community relations, budgeting, and professional standards.

Education administration/supervision. The study of the principles and techniques of administering a wide variety of schools and other education organizations and facilities and supervising education personnel.

Education of autistic. The design and provision of educational services for children or adults who are autistic. Includes instruction in identifying students with autism, developing education plans, teaching and supervising, counseling, and applicable laws and policies.

Education of blind/visually handicapped. The design and provision of educational services for children or adults with visual disabilities that adversely affect their educational performance. Includes instruction in identifying visually handicapped students, developing education plans, counseling, and applicable laws and regulations.

Education of deaf/hearing impaired. The design and provision of educational services for children or adults with hearing impairments that adversely affect their educational performance. Includes instruction in identifying hearing impaired students, developing individual education plans, counseling, and applicable laws and regulations.

Education of emotionally handicapped. The design and provision of educational services for children or adults with mental disabilities that adversely affect their educational performance. Includes instruction in identifying mentally handicapped students, developing individual education plans, teaching and supervising, counseling, and applicable laws and policies.

Education of gifted/talented. The design and provision of educational services for children or adults exhibiting exceptional intellectual, psychomotor, or artistic talent, or potential, or who exhibit exceptional maturity or social leadership. Includes instruction in identifying gifted and talented students, developing individual education plans, teaching and supervising, counseling, and applicable laws and policies.

Education of learning disabled. The design and provision of educational services for children or adults with specific learning disabilities that adversely affect their educational performance. Includes instruction in identifying specific learning disabled students, developing education plans, counseling, and applicable laws and regulations.

Education of mentally handicapped. The design and provision of educational services for children or adults with mental disabilities that adversely affect their performance. Includes instruction in identifying mentally handicapped students, developing education plans, counseling, and applicable laws and regulations.

Education of multiple handicapped. The design and provision of educational services for children or adults with multiple disabilities that adversely affect their educational performance. Includes instruction in identifying multiple handicapped students, developing education plans, counseling, and applicable laws and regulations.

Education of physically handicapped. The design and provision of educational services for children or adults with physical disabilities that adversely affect their educational performance. Includes instruction in identifying physically disabled students, developing education plans, counseling, and applicable laws and regulations.

Education of speech impaired. The design and provision of educational services for children or adults with speech impairments that adversely affect their educational performance. Includes instruction in identifying speech-impaired students, developing education plans, counseling, and applicable laws and regulations.

Education/instructional media design. The principles and techniques used in developing instructional materials and related educational resources in such media as film, video, text, art, and software. Includes instruction in the techniques specific to various media; the behavioral principles applicable to using various media; the design, testing, and production of instructional materials; and the management of media facilities and programs.

Educational evaluation/research. The principles and procedures used in gathering information about educational programs, personnel, and methods, and the analysis of such information for planning purposes. Includes instruction in evaluation theory, research design and planning, data analysis and interpretation, and related economic and policy issues.

Educational psychology. The application of psychology to the study of teachers and learners, the nature and effects of various learning environments, and the psychological effects of various methods, resources, organization, and nonschool experience on the educational process. Includes instruction in learning theory, human growth and development, research methods, and psychological evaluation.

Educational statistics/research methods. The application of statistics to the analysis and solution of educational research problems and the development of technical designs for research studies. Includes instruction in mathematical statistics, computer applications, instrument design, and research methodologies.

Educational supervision. Prepares individuals to supervise school instructional and support personnel. Includes instruction in the principles of staffing and organization, the supervision of learning activities, personnel relations, and administration.

Educational testing/measurement. The principles and procedures used in designing, implementing, and evaluating tests and other mechanisms that evaluate student progress and assess the performance of specific teaching tools, strategies, and curricula. Includes instruction in psychometric measurement, instrument design, and data analysis and interpretation.

Electrical/electronic engineering-related technologies. Prepares individuals to apply basic engineering principles and technical skills in support of engineering, research, and industrial applications of electricity, lasers, and computers. Programs prepare students to become computer engineering, communications, and laser and optical technicians.

Electrical/electronics/communications engineering. Prepares individuals to apply mathematical and scientific principles to the design, development, and operational evaluation of electrical, electronics, and related communications systems and their components, including electrical power generation systems, and to analyze such problems as superconduction, wave propagation, energy storage and retrieval, and reception and amplification.

Electrician. Prepares individuals to apply technical knowledge and skills to operate, maintain, and repair electrical and electronic equipment. Includes instruction in electrical circuitry, simple gearing, linkages and lubrication of machines and appliances, and the use of testing equipment.

Electrocardiograph technology. Prepares individuals to perform examinations of electromotive variations in human heart activity using an electrocardiograph machine, under the supervision of a physician. Includes instruction in patient preparation and equipment operation and maintenance.

Electrodiagnostic technologies. Prepares individuals to record and study the electrical activity of the brain. Instruction covers taking medical history, operating equipment, studying brain patterns, managing the laboratory and patients, and maintaining equipment.

Electroencephalograph technology. Prepares individuals to perform examinations of electromotive variations in human brain activity using an electroencephalograph machine, under the supervision of a physician. Includes instruction in patient preparation and equipment operation and maintenance.

Electromechanical instrumentation. Prepares individuals to support engineers engaged in developing industrial systems that rely on electrical power. Prepares students to become biomedical, computer maintenance, electromechanical, instrumentation, or robotics technicians.

Electronics/electrical equipment repair. Prepares individuals to apply technical knowledge and skills to the adjustment, maintenance, part replacement, and repair of electronic and electrical tools and equipment.

Elementary education. Prepares individuals to teach students in kindergarten through grade 8. Instruction covers all subject matter taught in elementary school.

Elementary particle physics. The study of the basic constituents of subatomic matter and energy and the forces governing fundamental processes. Includes instruction in quantum theory, field theory, single-particle systems, perturbation and scattering theory, quarks, and methods for detecting particle emission and absorption.

Emergency medical technology. Prepares individuals to perform initial medical diagnosis, treatment, and comprehensive care in medical crises, under the supervision of a coordinating physician. Includes instruction in diagnosis, anesthetics, obstetrics, and basic surgical procedures.

Engineering. Prepares individuals to apply mathematical and scientific principles to solve a wide variety of practical problems in industry, business, and commerce.

Engineering design. Prepares individuals to coordinate dissimilar systems to carry out single functions, plan engineering projects involving multiple tasks, evaluate procedures, resolve specification and requirement conflicts, and choose among competing solutions.

Engineering mechanics. The application of the mathematical and scientific principles of classical mechanics to the analysis and evaluation of the behavior of structures, forces, and materials. Includes instruction in statistics, kinetics, dynamics, celestial mechanics, stress and failure, and electromagnetism.

Engineering physics. The application of the mathematical and scientific principles of physics to the analysis and evaluation of engineering problems. Includes instruction in high- and low-temperature phenomena, superconductivity, applied thermodynamics, molecular and particle physics, and space science research.

Engineering science. The application of mathematical and scientific principles to the analysis and evaluation of engineering problems, including applied research in human behavior, statistics, biology, chemistry, the earth and planetary sciences, atmospherics and meteorology, and computer applications.

Engineering/industrial management. The planning and operation of organizations, including budgeting, quality control, resource allocation and utilization, product production and distribution, human resource management, systems and plant maintenance, scheduling, and storage.

Engineering-related technologies. Prepares individuals to apply basic engineering principles and technical skills in support of engineering projects.

English. Study of the literature and culture of English-speaking peoples and the history and structure of the English language.

English composition. Covers English vocabulary; principles of grammar, morphology, syntax and semantics; and techniques of selecting, developing, combining, and expressing ideas in appropriate written forms.

English education. Prepares individuals to teach English grammar, composition, and literature at various education levels.

English literature. Study of the literature of the peoples of the British Commonwealth. Includes instruction in period and genre studies, author studies, country and regional specializations, literary criticism, and folkloric traditions.

Enterprise management/operations. Prepares individuals to develop, own, and operate businesses.

Entomology. The study of insects, including life cycles, morphology, physiology, ecology, taxonomy, population dynamics, genetics, and ecosystem relations. Includes instruction in the control of insects.

Entrepreneurship. Prepares individuals in marketing techniques applicable to developing business enterprises.

Environmental control technologies. The basic engineering principles and technical skills needed to support professionals engaged in environmental protection. Includes instruction in energy management, solar technology, water quality and wastewater treatment, environmental and pollution control, heating, air conditioning, and refrigeration technology.

Environmental design. Study of total environments and living systems, both indoor and outdoor. Includes instruction in relating the structural, aesthetic, and social concerns affecting life and work to the needs of clients and the constraints of the site.

Environmental health. Prepares public health specialists to monitor environmental health hazards and to manage environmental health programs. Includes instruction in environmental and genetic toxicology; biohazard research, testing, and evaluation procedures; and the study of applicable regulations.

Environmental health engineering. The design, development, and operational evaluation of systems for controlling contained living environments and for monitoring and controlling factors in the external natural environment. Includes instruction in pollution control, waste and hazardous materials disposal, conservation, and life support.

Environmental science/conservation. The study of the biological and physical aspects of the environment. Includes instruction in the conservation and/or improvement of natural resources, such as air, soil, water, land, fish, and wildlife, as well as methods of controlling environmental pollution.

Environmental studies. Program that generally describes the effects of human activities on the environment from the perspectives of the natural and engineering sciences, social sciences, and humanities. Includes instruction in environmental, natural, and social sciences; biology, chemistry and geology; environmental economics; and regional, national, and global environmental problems.

Epidemiology. The scientific study of the distribution of disease in human populations, patterns in the life cycles of infectious diseases, and methods of preventing disease outbreaks and promoting population health.

Equestrian/equine studies. Prepares individuals to care for horses and equipment, to train horses, and to manage horse training, breeding, and housing.

ESL teacher education. The principles and practice of teaching English to students who are not proficient in it or who do not speak, read, or write English.

Ethnic/cultural studies. Study of the history, society, politics, culture, and economics of subsets of the population sharing common racial characteristics. Colleges that offer ethnic and cultural studies may have several majors in this area.

European studies. The history, society, politics, culture, and economics of the European continent and its borderlands.

Evolutionary biology. The scientific study of the generation of organismic traits and of shared traits across taxonomic classifications and the refinement of related theory and experimental methods. Includes instruction in the process of heredity, genetic mutation and variation, ecological determinants of species survival and adaptation, population genetics, developmental biology, and paleontology.

Exercise sciences. The scientific study of the anatomy, physiology, biochemistry, and biophysics of human movement and applications to exercise and therapeutic rehabilitation. Includes instruction in biomechanics, motor development and coordination, and diagnostic and rehabilitative methods and equipment.

Experimental psychology. The study of behavior under experimental conditions and the analysis of controlled behavioral responses. Includes instruction in learning theory, research design and experimental methods, psychological measurement, statistical methods, and analysis of cognitive and behavioral variables.

Family/community studies. The study of cultural, social, and technological influences on families in changing societies, including family programs and support services.

Family/individual development. The study of the developmental and behavioral characteristics of the individual, within the context of the family, from infancy through old age.

Farm/ranch management. Prepares individuals to manage a farm or ranch. Includes instruction in computer-assisted management analysis, accounting, taxes, production, financing, government programs, and contracts.

Fashion/apparel marketing. Prepares individuals to perform marketing tasks specifically applicable to all segments of the apparel and fashion industry.

Fashion design/illustration. Prepares individuals to apply artistic principles and techniques to the design of commercial apparel and accessories. Includes instruction in the illustration of fashion concepts, apparel and accessory design, computer-assisted design, labor and cost analysis, and principles of management.

Fiber arts. Prepares individuals to express emotions, ideas, or inner visions by constructing artworks from woven or nonwoven fabrics and fibrous materials. Includes instruction in weaving techniques and loom operation; nonwoven techniques, such as knitting, coiling, netting, and crocheting; quilting; and dyeing and pigmentation.

Film/cinema studies. The study of the history, development, theory, and criticism of the film/video arts, as well as the basic principles of filmmaking and film production.

Film/video/cinematography/production. Prepares individuals to communicate dramatic information, ideas, and feelings through making and producing films and videos. Includes instruction in the theory of film and film technology, production, directing, and editing.

Finance/banking. Prepares individuals to plan, manage, and analyze the financial and monetary performance of business enterprises, banking institutions, or other organizations. Includes instruction in accounting, financial instruments, capital planning, funds acquisition, and investment and portfolio management.

Financial management/services. Prepares individuals to provide financial or banking services to individuals or institutions.

Financial planning. Prepares individuals to plan and manage the financial interests and growth of individuals and institutions. Includes instruction in portfolio management, investment management, estate planning, insurance, tax planning, and strategic investing.

Financial services marketing. Prepares individuals in marketing techniques applicable to banks, credit unions, and other financial institutions.

Fine arts. Prepares creative artists in the visual and plastic media. Includes instruction in the traditional fine arts (drawing, painting, sculpture, printmaking) and/or modern media (ceramics, textiles, intermedia, photography); theory of art; color theory; composition and perspective; anatomy; managing a studio; and art portfolio marketing.

Fire protection. Prepares individuals to perform firefighting and related services.

Fire protection/safety technology. Prepares individuals to apply fire prevention and control skills to reducing fire risk, loss limitation, supervising substance removal, conducting fire investigations, and advising on safety procedures and fire prevention policies.

Fire services administration. Prepares individuals to structure and manage fire departments, fire prevention services, fire inspection and investigation offices, and ancillary rescue services.

Firefighting/fire science. Prepares individuals to be firefighters. Includes instruction in firefighting equipment operation and maintenance, principles of fire science and combustible substances, methods of control, handling hazardous materials, and fire rescue procedures.

Fisheries/fishing. The study of the husbandry of fish populations for recreational, ecological, and commercial purposes, and the management of marine life resources and fisheries. Includes instruction in principles of aquatic and marine biology, fishing production and management operations, and monitoring water quality.

Flight attendant. Prepares individuals to apply technical knowledge and skills to the performance of a variety of personal services conducive to the safety and comfort of airline passengers during flight, including verifying tickets, explaining the use of safety equipment, providing passenger services, and responding to in-flight emergencies.

Floristry marketing. Prepares individuals to perform marketing tasks specifically applicable to the floristry industry.

Food management. Program that describes principles and procedures essential for quality in food production and presentation, in institutional or commercial settings. Students learn to identify food service industry standards of quality, trends, and customer expectations. Includes instruction in production, menu planning and merchandising, marketing, restaurant operations, purchasing, receiving and storage, cost control, accounting, and personnel management.

Food products retailing/wholesaling. Prepares individuals in marketing techniques applicable to food supply and grocery wholesaling and retailing.

Food sciences/technology. The biological, chemical, physical, and engineering principles and practices involved in converting agricultural products to forms suitable for direct human consumption or storage, and the solution of problems relating to product transportation, storage, and marketing.

Food/nutrition studies. The study of the role of food and nutrition in individual and family health and of food production, preparation, and service. Includes instruction in food consumption, nutrition, and the organization and administration of food systems.

Foreign languages/literatures. The study of multiple foreign languages and literatures.

Foreign languages/translation. Prepares individuals to translate written documents or to consecutively or simultaneously interpret oral communications. Includes instruction in translating and/or interpreting from a foreign language into English, from English into another language, or between two foreign languages.

Foreign languages education. Prepares individuals to teach foreign language programs at various education levels.

Forensic technologies. Prepares individuals to conduct crime scene and laboratory analyses of evidentiary materials, including human remains, under the supervision of a pathologist, forensic scientist, or other law enforcement personnel. Includes instruction in the principles of pathology, laboratory technology and procedures, dusting and fingerprinting, and reconstructive analysis.

Forest production/processing. Prepares individuals to assist engineers, chemists, or forest product scientists in the measurement, analysis, testing, and processing of harvested raw forest materials, and in the selection, grading, and marketing of forest products.

Forestry. Prepares individuals to manage and develop forests for economic, recreational, and ecological purposes. Includes instruction in forest-related sciences, mapping, statistics, harvesting and production technology, and resource protection.

French. The study of the language, literature, and culture of French-speaking peoples, including related languages and dialects, such as Creole, Provençal, and Walloon.

French language teacher education. Prepares individuals to teach French language programs at various education levels.

Funeral services/mortuary science. Prepares individuals to supervise and perform the embalming and cremation of human corpses, to provide funeral and burial services, and to sell funerary equipment.

Gaming/sports officiating. Prepares individuals to supervise and conduct gaming operations and to officiate at sports events.

Genetics, plant/animal. The study of biological inheritance and variation in organisms and of the mechanisms of gene behavior. Includes instruction in molecular genetics, mutation, cloning, breeding, genetic biochemistry and biophysics, and gene transference and modification.

Geochemistry. The study of the chemical properties and behavior of the silicates and other substances forming, and formed by, geomorphological processes of the earth and other planets. Includes instruction in chemical thermodynamics, equilibria in silicate systems, atomic bonding, isotropic fractionation, and geochemical modeling.

Geography. The study of the spatial distribution and interrelationships of people, natural resources, and plant and animal life. Includes instruction in historical, political, cultural, economic, and physical geography; cartographic methods; remote sensing; and applications to such areas as land-use planning and development studies.

Geological engineering. Prepares individuals to apply mathematical and geological principles to the analysis of engineering problems, including the geological evaluation of construction sites, the analysis of geological forces acting on structures and systems, and the analysis of potential natural resource recovery sites.

Geology. The study of the earth, the forces acting upon it, and the behavior of the solids, liquids, and gases comprising it. Includes instruction in historical geology, geomorphology, sedimentology, the chemistry of rocks and soils, stratigraphy, geostatistics, volcanology, and glaciology.

Geophysical engineering. Prepares individuals to apply mathematical, geophysical, and planetary principles to the analysis and evaluation of engineering problems, including gravitational and magnetic forces, time and space factors, and celestial mass and motion.

Geophysics/seismology. The study of the physics of solids and its application to the study of the earth and other planets. Includes instruction in gravimetry, seismology, earthquake forecasting, magnetometry, electrical properties of solid bodies, plate tectonics, thermodynamics, and remote sensing.

German. The study of the language, literature, and culture of German-speaking peoples, including related dialects, such as Low German, Swiss-German, and Old or Middle German.

German language education. Prepares individuals to teach German language programs at various education levels.

Germanic languages. Programs in Germanic languages, such as Yiddish, Dutch, Flemish, Old German, Frisian, Gothic, and Saxon.

Gerontology. The study of the aging process in individuals and human populations, using the knowledge and methodologies of the social sciences, psychology, and the biological and health sciences.

Global studies. Program that examines world patterns of interaction and the trend toward increasing interdependence of nations and peoples through cross-cultural comparisons. Includes instruction in anthropology, foreign cultures, economics, geography, and politics.

Graphic design/commercial art/illustration. Prepares individuals to use artistic techniques to communicate information effectively to business and consumer audiences via illustrations and other forms of printed media. Includes instruction in concept design and such techniques as engraving, etching, lithography, offset, painting, collage, and computer graphics.

Graphic/printing equipment operation. Prepares individuals to apply technical knowledge and skills to plan and execute visual images and print products using mechanical, electronic, and digital graphic and printing equipment.

Greek, ancient. The study of the language, literature, and culture of ancient and medieval Greece, including archaic Greece, classical Greece, the Hellenistic world, and Byzantium.

Greek, modern. The study of the language, literature, and culture of modern Greece, generally comprising the period from the fall of Byzantium in 1453 to the present.

Greenhouse management. Prepares individuals to produce commercial plant species in controlled environments and to manage commercial and experimental greenhouse operations.

Health education. Prepares individuals to teach health education programs at various education levels.

Health occupations education. Programs that prepare individuals to teach specific vocational health occupation programs at various education levels.

Health physics/radiologic health. The study of the scientific measurement of radiation levels and dosages affecting human beings. Includes instruction in radiation dosimetry; the health effects of natural and human-made radiation; operation and maintenance of testing and monitoring equipment; and applicable standards and regulations pertaining to radiation emissions.

Health products/services marketing. Prepares individuals in marketing techniques specifically applicable to the health care supplies and services industry.

Health professions/related sciences. Programs that prepare individuals to provide health care, do related research, or provide support services.

Health system administration. Prepares physicians and other professionals to plan and manage health care systems and service networks. Includes instruction in planning and coordination, business and financial management, fund-raising and marketing, public relations, human resources management, and health law.

Health/medical biostatistics. The advanced study of the health applications of statistical models and analytical techniques. Includes instruction in descriptive and inferential studies of human populations and the human organism and its biological components.

Health/medical laboratory technologies. Prepares individuals to perform diagnostic and analytical laboratory procedures that support medical research and practice.

Health/physical fitness. Programs that describe the study of human physiology and behavior as applied to sports, and the leadership and management of physical fitness and sports services.

Heating/air conditioning/refrigeration mechanics. Prepares individuals to apply technical knowledge and skills to repair, install, and service heating, air conditioning, and refrigeration systems. Includes instruction in diagnostic techniques, the use of testing equipment, and the principles of mechanics, electricity, and electronics.

Hebrew. The study of the language, literature, and culture of Hebrew-speaking peoples, including premodern and modern Hebrew dialects and derivatives.

Hematology technology. Prepares individuals to test and analyze blood samples under the supervision of a laboratory director or physician. Includes instruction in laboratory procedures and hematology; conducting quantitative, qualitative, and coagulation tests on cellular and plasma blood components; and equipment operation and maintenance.

Higher education administration. The study of the principles and practices of administration in colleges, universities, and higher education systems. Includes instruction in higher education economics and finance, curriculum, faculty and labor relations, student services, institutional research, and marketing and promotion.

Hispanic-American studies. The history, society, politics, culture, and economics of Hispanic Americans in the United States, including Mexican Americans, Puerto Ricans, Cuban Americans, and other groups.

Historic preservation/conservation. The architectural design principles and building techniques used in historic structures and environments, and the process of saving and restoring old buildings and districts for contemporary use and enjoyment. Includes instruction in architectural history, building conservation techniques, real estate, land use, and tax laws and codes.

History. The study and interpretation of the past, including the gathering, recording, synthesizing, and analyzing of evidence and theories about past events. Includes instruction in historiography, historical research methods, and studies of specific periods.

History education. Prepares individuals to teach history at various education levels.

Home economics. The study of the relationship between people and aspects of their environment, such as food, clothing, housing, and finances.

Home economics business services. Programs that cover the relationship between the economic environment and the home and family.

Home economics education. Prepares individuals to teach vocational home economics at various education levels.

Home furnishings/equipment. Prepares individuals to advise and assist clients in selecting and installing home furnishings. Includes instruction in selecting and purchasing home furnishings and equipment, and in floral design, accessory construction, textiles, and upholstery.

Home/office products marketing. Prepares individuals in marketing techniques applicable to hardware, building materials and equipment, and household supplies.

Horticultural services. Prepares individuals to produce, process, and market plants, shrubs, and trees used principally for ornamental, recreational, and aesthetic purposes and to establish and manage horticultural enterprises.

Horticulture science. Study of the cultivation of garden and ornamental plants, such as fruits, vegetables, flowers, and nursery crops. Includes instruction in specific types of plants, plant breeding, landscaping, and the management of crops throughout the plant life cycle.

Hospitality administration/management. Prepares individuals to serve as general managers of hospitality operations. Includes instruction in the management and operation of the travel and tourism, hotel and lodging, food services, and recreation facilities; hospitality marketing strategies; and management of franchise operations.

Hospitality/recreation marketing. Prepares individuals in marketing techniques applicable to a wide variety of hospitality and leisure industry settings.

Hotel/motel/restaurant management. Prepares individuals to manage facilities that provide food and/or lodging services to the traveling public. Includes instruction in purchasing and storage of supplies, facilities design, personnel management, marketing and sales promotion strategies, and convention and event management.

Housing studies. The study of the social, economic, and aesthetic aspects of housing and other environments. Includes instruction in planning, designing, furnishing, and equipping households and in the behavioral, developmental, public policy, and cultural issues related to households.

Human resources management. Prepares individuals to manage the development of human capital in organizations and to provide related services to individuals and groups. Includes instruction in personnel policies, sex roles, civil rights, human resources law and regulations, motivation and compensation systems, recruitment and selection, and job training programs.

Human services. Programs that prepare individuals to help those in need of assistance through support, advocacy, mediation, or care. Students learn how to interview clients, collect information, implement treatment plans, consult with other workers and agencies, solve problems, and advocate for clients.

Industrial design. Prepares individuals to use artistic techniques to communicate information to business and consumer audiences via the creation of forms, shapes, and packaging for manufactured products. Includes instruction in designing in a wide variety of media, prototype construction, and product structure and performance criteria.

Industrial equipment maintenance/repair. Prepares individuals to apply technical knowledge and skills to maintain and repair industrial machinery and equipment, such as cranes, pumps, engines and motors, conveyor systems, and production machinery.

Industrial production technologies. Prepares individuals to apply basic engineering principles and technical skills in support of engineers and other professionals engaged in developing and using industrial manufacturing systems and processes. Includes instruction in design and prototype testing, instrument calibration, and diagnosis and repair.

Industrial/manufacturing engineering. Prepares individuals to apply mathematical and scientific principles to the design, development, and operational evaluation of integrated systems for managing industrial production processes, including efficiency engineering, logistics and material flow, industrial quality control, automation, and cost analysis.

Industrial/organizational psychology. The study of individual and group behavior in organizational settings. Includes instruction in group behavior and organizational theory, reward/punishment structures, human-machine interactions, motivation dynamics, and job testing and assessment.

Information sciences/systems. The study and development of electronic systems for transmitting information via signalling networks and of information transmission from the point of generation to reception and interpretation. Includes instruction in information systems design and provider capacity and requirements analysis.

Inorganic chemistry. The scientific study of the elements and their compounds, other than the hydrocarbons and their derivatives. Includes instruction in the characterization and synthesis of noncarbon molecules, including structure and bonding, conductivity, and reactive properties; and research techniques such as spectroscopy, X-ray diffraction, and photoelectron analysis.

Institutional food production. Prepares individuals to manage and supervise institutional food service operations, including school food and other government-regulated food services. Includes instruction in management, purchasing and storage, food preparation, diet and menu planning, sanitation, and safety.

Insurance marketing. Prepares individuals in marketing techniques specifically applicable to the insurance industry.

Insurance/risk management. Prepares individuals to manage risk in organizational settings and to provide risk-aversion services to businesses and individuals. Includes instruction in risk theory, casualty insurance and general liability, property insurance, employee benefits, social and health insurance, loss adjustment, underwriting, and pension planning.

Interdisciplinary studies. Majors that combine one or more distinct disciplines.

Interior architecture. Study of the practice of interior architecture—the processes and techniques of designing living, work, and leisure indoor environments. Includes instruction in building design and structural systems, heating and cooling systems, safety and health standards, and interior design principles.

Interior design. Prepares individuals to apply artistic principles and techniques to the planning, designing, equipping, and furnishing of residential and commercial interior spaces. Includes instruction in drafting, principles of interior lighting and acoustics, furniture and furnishings, textiles, and building codes.

Intermedia. Prepares individuals to express emotions, ideas, or inner visions in either two or three dimensions, through simultaneous use of a variety of materials and media.

International agriculture. The application of agricultural principles to problems of global food production and distribution and to the study of the agricultural systems of other nations.

International business. Prepares individuals to manage international business operations. Includes instruction in the principles and processes of export sales, trade controls, monetary issues, and international business policy.

International business marketing. Prepares individuals in marketing techniques for enterprises engaged in exporting or importing goods and services in world markets. Includes instruction in international trade controls, foreign trade operations, locating markets, negotiation practices, and monetary issues.

International finance. Prepares individuals to manage international financial operations and related currency transactions. Includes instruction in international banking, international monetary and financial policy, money and capital markets, foreign exchange, risk analysis, and international cash flow operations.

International relations. The study of international politics and institutions and the conduct of diplomacy and foreign policy. Includes instruction in international relations theory, foreign policy analysis, national security and strategic studies, international law, and the comparative study of specific countries and regions.

International studies. Multi- and interdisciplinary program that examines peoples, events, movements, institutions, societies, cultures, and issues. Includes instruction in history; international economics, law, and politics; foreign languages; sociology; anthropology; and political geography.

Investments/securities. Prepares individuals to manage assets placed in capital markets and to understand related technical operations. Includes instruction in security analysis, debt and equity analysis, investment strategies, securities markets, computer-assisted research, portfolio management and performance analysis, and applications to specific investment problems and business situations.

Islamic studies. The study of the history, society, politics, culture, and economics of the Islamic peoples.

Italian. The study of the language, literature, and culture of Italian-speaking peoples, including dialects and related languages, such as Sicilian, Friulian, and Sardinian.

Japanese. The study of the language, literature, and culture of Japanese-speaking peoples.

Jazz. The study of the jazz musical tradition, including history, forms, and performance. Instruction may cover performance (instrumental or voice) andarranging/composition.

Jewish/Judaic studies. The study of the history, society, politics, culture, and economics of the Jewish people.

Journalism. The study of the methods and techniques for gathering, processing, and delivering news. Includes instruction in newswriting and editing, reporting, journalism law and policy, professional standards and ethics, and journalism history and research.

Junior high education. Prepares individuals to teach students in the middle, intermediate, or junior high grades, which may include grades 4 through 9, depending on the school system or state regulations. Includes preparation to teach a comprehensive curriculum or specific subject matter.

Labor/personnel relations. The study of employee-management interactions and the management of issues and disputes regarding working conditions and worker benefit packages. Includes instruction in labor history, policies and strategies of the labor movement, union organization, labor-management negotiation, labor law and contract interpretation, labor economics, welfare and benefit packages, grievance procedures, and labor policy issues.

Landscape architecture. Prepares individuals for the practice of landscape architecture. Includes instruction in site planning and engineering, environmental impact, garden and landscape art and design, horticulture, and applicable regulations.

Landscaping management. Prepares individuals to procure, plant, and maintain grounds and indoor and outdoor ornamental plants. Includes instruction in equipment maintenance and facilities management.

Latin. The study of the language, literature, and culture of the ancient and Medieval Latin-speaking peoples, including Classical Roman Latin, related ancient Italic dialects and languages, and Medieval Latin and its derivatives.

Latin American studies. The history, society, politics, culture, and economics of Mexico, the Caribbean, and Central and South America.

Law (JD). Prepares individuals for the practice of law and for advanced study in jurisprudence. Includes instruction in the theory and practice of the legal system, including the statutory, administrative, and judicial components of civil and criminal law.

Law enforcement/police science. Prepares individuals to perform the duties of police and public security officers, including patrol and investigative activities, traffic and crowd control and public relations, evidence collection and management, basic crime prevention methods, and weapon and equipment operation and maintenance.

Leather/upholstery. Prepares individuals to apply technical knowledge and skills to fabricate and repair all types of upholstery and leather goods.

Legal administrative assistant. Prepares individuals to perform the duties of special assistants and/or personal secretaries for lawyers, judges, and legal counsels. Includes instruction in business and legal communications, filing systems and records management, legal terminology and research methods, and professional standards and legal requirements.

Legal specialization. Advanced programs of study that prepare attorneys and law school graduates for advanced technical specialization in legal research and practice.

Legal studies. Programs that describe the theory, history, and application of the rules of conduct by which societal relations are formally structured and adjudicated.

Liberal arts/humanities. The study of the humanities (literature, the arts, and philosophy), history, foreign languages, social sciences, mathematics, and natural sciences. Study of the liberal arts and humanities prepares students to develop general knowledge and reasoning ability rather than specific skills. Many two-year colleges offer a major in liberal arts and humanities as preparation for transfer to a four-year college.

Library assistant. Prepares individuals to assist professional librarians. Includes instruction in the principles and procedures of library operation; library resources and services; acquisition, cataloging, storage, and display systems; and discovery and retrieval of materials.

Library science. Includes instruction in the knowledge and skills required to develop, organize, store, retrieve, administer, and facilitate the use of collections of information in such formats as books, documents, manuscripts, machine-readable databases, and filmed and recorded materials.

Linguistics. The study of language and the relationships among languages. Includes instruction in psycholinguistics, anthropological linguistics, historical linguistics, mathematical linguistics, grammatical theory, philosophy of language, sociolinguistics, and language and culture studies.

Logistics/materials management. Prepares individuals to manage and coordinate the logistical functions in an enterprise, including acquisitions, internal allocation of resources, and the handling and delivery of output. Includes instruction in acquisitions and purchasing, and resource estimation and allocation.

Management information systems. Prepares individuals to develop and manage data systems and related facilities for processing and retrieving internal business information. Includes instruction in cost and accounting information systems, management control systems, and computer facilities and equipment operation and maintenance.

Management science. The application of mathematical, programming, and operations research techniques to the analysis of problems of business organization and performance. Includes instruction in optimization theory, stochastic and dynamic modeling, operations analysis, and the design and testing of prototype systems and evaluation models.

Manufacturing technologies. Prepares individuals to apply technical knowledge of manufacturing processes and equipment to achieve the most efficient and safe methods of productivity. Includes instruction in manufacturing and construction technology, industrial and mechanical technology, electronics and computer technology, manufacturing analysis and planning, economics, and mathematics.

Marine/aquatic biology. The study of marine organisms and their environmefts. Includes instruction in freshwater and saltwater organisms; physiological and anatomical marine adaptations, ocean and freshwater ecologies; and marine microbiology, mammalogy, and botany.

Marine engineering/naval architecture. Prepares individuals to apply mathematical and scientific principles to the design, development, and operational evaluation of vessels operating on or under the water, and to analyze related engineering problems, such as corrosion, stress, safety and life support, communications and sensing, and environmental hazards.

Marketing management. Prepares individuals to provide for and manage the movement of goods and services from producer to consumer.

Marketing research. Prepares individuals to provide analytical descriptions of consumer behavior patterns and market environments to marketing managers and other business decisionmakers. Includes instruction in survey research methods, research design, new product test marketing, exploratory marketing, and consumer needs and preference analysis.

Marketing/distribution. Prepares individuals to plan and execute, at the operational or direct sales level, the promotion and distribution of ideas, goods, and services in order to create exchanges that satisfy individual and organization objectives.

Marketing/distribution education. Prepares individuals to teach vocational marketing operations and/or marketing and distributive education programs at various education levels.

Masonry/tile setting. Prepares individuals to lay or set brick, concrete block, hard tile, marble, and related materials, using trowels, levels, hammers, chisels, and other hand tools.

Materials engineering. Prepares individuals to apply mathematical and scientific principles to the design, development, and evaluation of materials and related processes used in manufacturing. Includes instruction in the synthesis of new industrial materials and the analysis of materials requirements and specifications.

Materials science. The application of mathematical and scientific principles to the analysis and evaluation of the characteristics and behavior of solids, including internal structure, chemical properties, and transport and energy flow properties.

Mathematics. The analysis of quantities, magnitudes, forms, and their relationships, using symbolic logic and language. Includes instruction in algebra, calculus, functional analysis, geometry, number theory, logic, topology, and other specializations.

Mathematics education. Prepares individuals to teach mathematics at various education levels.

Mathematics/computer science. A general synthesis of mathematics and computer science or a specialization that draws from mathematics and computer science.

Mechanical engineering. Prepares individuals to apply mathematical and scientific principles to the design, development, and evaluation of physical systems used in manufacturing, including machine tools, stationary power units, self-propelled vehicles, and hydraulic and electric systems.

Mechanical engineering-related technologies. Prepares individuals to apply basic engineering principles and technical skills in support of engineers and other professionals engaged in developing mechanical systems. Includes instruction in specific technologies, such as aeronautical/aerospace, automotive, and mechanical engineering.

Mechanics/repair. Prepares individuals to apply technical knowledge and skills in the adjustment, maintenance, part replacement, and repair of tools, equipment, and machines.

Medical administrative assistant. Prepares individuals to provide administrative assistance to physicians, health service administrators, and other health professionals.

Medical assistant. Prepares individuals to support physicians by providing assistance during patient examination, treatment, and monitoring; by keeping health record information; and by performing other practice-related duties.

Medical basic sciences. Advanced research in the disciplines that support the clinical practice of medicine.

Medical dietetics. Prepares individuals to plan and administer special diets in clinical situations, in consultation with physicians. Includes instruction in the principles of medical nutrition and the management of health care facility food services.

Medical illustrating. Prepares individuals to demonstrate medical facts by the creation of illustrations, such as drawings, models, photographs, and films. Includes instruction in illustrating live treatment situations as well as working from data, notes, and samples.

Medical laboratory assistant. Prepares individuals to support laboratory directors and technicians by performing routine clinical laboratory procedures and clerical tasks.

Medical laboratory technology. Prepares individuals to perform general medical laboratory procedures and routines, under the supervision of a physician. Includes instruction in equipment operation and maintenance, test procedures, and record keeping.

Medical radiologic technology. Prepares individuals to perform diagnostic examinations and administer therapeutic procedures using X-rays and related radiations, under the supervision of a radiologist. Includes instruction in conducting CAT scans, xeroradiography, and thermography.

Medical records administration. Prepares individuals to supervise and manage the preparation, storage, and use of medical records and related information systems. Includes instruction in the legal and technical aspects of medical records and the design and management of secure data systems.

Medical records technology. Prepares individuals to classify medical information and prepare records, under the supervision of a medical records administrator. Includes instruction in medical records science and terminology, record classification, indexing, and computer operations.

Medical specialties. Scientific study, by residents and other medical doctors, of specialized fields and related clinical research. Includes instruction in fields such as pediatrics, anesthesiology, obstetrics, gynecology, oncology, surgery, radiology, internal medicine, neurology, clinical pathology, and psychiatry.

Medical transcription. Prepares individuals to execute verbatim medical minutes, reports, and orders. Includes instruction in dictation, analysis of written notes and visual evidence, computer and transcription machine operation, formal medical correspondence, and report formats.

Medicine (MD). Prepares individuals for the professional practice of medicine.

Medieval/Renaissance studies. Study of the medieval and Renaissance periods in European and Mediterranean history from the perspective of various disciplines in the humanities and social sciences, such as history, archaeology, art, and music.

Mental health services. Prepares individuals to provide counseling and support services related to the care and treatment of persons with mental, emotional, or behavioral disorders.

Mental health services technology. Prepares individuals to assist psychiatrists, psychologists, nurses, and other mental health personnel in patient care and treatment. Includes instruction in interviewing patients, recording data, taking vital signs, supervising administration of routine medication, and assisting in examinations and treatment procedures.

Metal/jewelry arts. Prepares individuals to fashion artwork from gems and other stones and precious metals.

Includes instruction in gemology, metalsmithing, stonecutting, metal casting and molding, and design.

Metallurgical engineering. Prepares individuals to apply mathematical and metallurgical principles to the design, development, and operational evaluation of metal components of structural, power, transmission, and moving systems, and to analyze such engineering problems as stress, alloy behavior, and electromagnetic and thermodynamic characteristics.

Metallurgy. Scientific study of the chemical and physical properties of metals and related compounds in their solid, liquid, and gaseous states, together with applications to industrial problems. Includes instruction in X-ray diffraction, metallurgical microscopy, solid-state physics, molecular bonding, electrodynamics of metals, elasticity and mechanical properties, and processing behavior.

Meteorology. Study of the composition and behavior of the atmosphere surrounding the earth and other planets, the effect of the earth's atmosphere on terrestrial weather, and related problems of environment and climate. Includes instruction in atmospheric chemistry and physics, atmospheric dynamics, climatology and climate change, weather simulation, weather forecasting, climate modeling and mathematical theory, and studies of specific phenomena, such as clouds, weather systems, storms, and precipitation patterns.

Mexican-American studies. Describes the history, society, politics, culture, and economics of Mexican Americans.

Microbiology/bacteriology. The study of microorganisms, including bacteria and viruses, as distinguished from the cellular components of larger organisms. Includes instruction in the ecological behavior of microorganisms, their anatomy and physiology, pathogenesis, and microbe evolution and mutation.

Middle Eastern languages, other. Middle Eastern languages and literatures other than Arabic and Hebrew, including Farsi (Iranian), Turkish, Berber, and Armenian.

Middle Eastern studies. The history, society, politics, culture, and economics of the Fertile Crescent, Arabic-speaking North Africa, Anatolia, the Caucasus, Iran, the Arabian Peninsula, and the Indo-Soviet borderlands of Central Asia.

Military technologies. Prepares individuals to undertake advanced and specialized leadership and technical responsibilities in the armed services and related national security organizations. Includes instruction in weapons systems and technology, communications, intelligence, management, logistics, and strategy.

Mining/mineral engineering. Prepares individuals to apply mathematical and scientific principles to the design, development, and operational evaluation of mineral extraction, processing, and refining systems, including open pit and shaft mines, prospecting and site analysis, and mineral processing and refining methods.

Mining/petroleum technologies. Programs that prepare individuals to apply basic principles of engineering and technical skills in support of engineers and other professionals engaged in locating and extracting mineral and petroleum resources.

Ministerial/theological studies. Prepares individuals for the professional study and practice of theology and ministry.

Missionary studies. The theory and practice of Christian or other religious outreach, social service, and proselytization.

Molecular biology. The study of the molecular structures and processes that underlie the storage and transmission of genetic information, energy transfer, hormone generation, and such basic life processes as development, growth, and aging.

Movement therapy. Prepares individuals to employ hands-on repatterning and verbal instruction as a tool to assist patients in overcoming physical disabilities, resolving emotional conflicts, and enhancing communication with others. Includes instruction in physiological patterning/cognitive-motor functioning, movement analysis and performance, and psychological/emotional expression.

Museum studies. Prepares individuals to develop, organize, conserve, and retrieve artifacts, exhibits, and collections in museums and galleries and to assume curatorial positions in museums. Includes instruction in institutional management, acquisition, exhibit design, and conservation.

Music. The study and appreciation of music and music performance. Includes instruction in principles of harmony, musical notation, musical styles, the historical development of music, and the fundamentals of various musical instruments.

Music business management. Prepares individuals to organize and manage music operations, facilities, and personnel. Includes instruction in business and financial management, personnel management and labor relations, event promotion, and music products merchandising.

Music education. Prepares individuals to teach music and music appreciation at various education levels.

Music history/literature. The study of the historical evolution of music as a social and intellectual phenomenon, the development of musical instruments and techniques, and the analysis and criticism of musical literature. Includes instruction in music history research methods, aesthetic analysis of musical compositions, and the study of specific periods, cultural traditions, styles, and themes.

Music performance. Prepares individuals to master musical instruments and become solo and/or ensemble performers. Includes instruction on one or more specific instruments.

Music theory/composition. The study of techniques of creating and arranging music. Includes instruction in aural theory, melody, counterpoint, complex harmony, improvisation, instrumentation, and electronic and computer applications.

Music therapy. Prepares individuals to employ music as a tool to assist patients in overcoming physical disabilities, resolving emotional conflicts, and enhancing communication with others. Includes instruction in leading and monitoring individual and group musical activities with patients.

Music, piano/organ performance. Prepares individuals to master the piano, organ, or related keyboard instruments and become solo, ensemble, and/or accompanist performers. Includes instruction in ensemble playing, accompanying, and keyboard and pedal skills.

Music, voice/choral/opera performance. Prepares individuals to master the human voice and become solo and/or ensemble performers in concert, choir, opera, or other media. Includes instruction in voice pedagogy, diction, vocal physiology and exercise, expressive movement, repertoire, and recital.

Musical theater. Provides training in acting, vocal music, speech, movement, and dance. Instruction includes study of musical theater forms, such as cabaret and experimental musical theater.

Musicology/ethnomusicology. The study of the forms, methods, and functions of music in Western and non-Western societies and cultures. Includes instruction in music theory and musicological research methods, and studies of specific cultural styles, such as jazz, folk music, rock, and the music of non-Western cultures.

Native American studies. Describes the history, society, politics, culture, and economics of the original inhabitants of the Western Hemisphere, including American Indians, Aleuts, and Eskimos.

Natural resources management. Prepares individuals to conserve and/or improve natural resources such as air, soil, water, land, fish, and wildlife for economic and recreational purposes.

Natural sciences. Broad program providing sound foundation in sciences and mathematics to prepare for careers in medicine and research. Includes instruction in biology, chemistry, earth science, mathematics, geography, and physics.

Neuroscience. The study of the anatomy, physiology, biophysics, biochemistry, and molecular biology of neuron cells and biological nervous systems. Includes instruction in neurological signaling, neuroanatomy and brain research, neuropharmacology, and neuropsychological research.

Nonprofit/public management. Prepares individuals to manage the business affairs of nonprofit corporations, including foundations, education institutions, and other such organizations as well as public and governmental agencies. Includes instruction in business management, public administration, accounting and financial management, taxation, and business law.

Nuclear engineering. Prepares individuals to apply mathematical and scientific principles to the design, development, and operational evaluation of systems for controlling and manipulating nuclear energy, including nuclear power plant design, fission and fusion reactor design, and safety systems design.

Nuclear medical technology. Prepares individuals to administer radioactive isotopes via injections and to measure glandular and other bodily activity by means of in vitro and in vivo detection and specimen testing. Includes instruction in equipment operation and maintenance, and materials storage and safety.

Nuclear physics. The study of the properties and behavior of atomic nuclei. Includes instruction in nuclear reaction theory, quantum mechanics, nuclear fission and fusion, strong and weak atomic forces, photon and electron reactions, and statistical methods.

Nuclear/industrial radiologic technologies. Prepares individuals to apply scientific principles and technical skills in support of design, testing, and operations procedures related to the industrial use of radioisotopes and nuclear energy.

Nursery operations. Prepares individuals to produce turf, shrubs, and trees for the purpose of transplanting or propagation. Includes instruction in enterprise management.

Nursing. Prepares students to care for those who are ill; to rehabilitate, counsel, and educate patients; and to work as part of a health care team in many settings. Instruction includes the humanities, natural sciences, nursing theory, and clinical practice. Nursing programs may prepare students for different licenses [see Nursing (RN) and Nursing, practical, below].

Nursing (post-RN). Any of several special post-RN programs that provide training in such areas as adult health, family practice, maternal/child health, midwifery, nursing science, pediatric nursing, and public health.

Nursing (RN). The study of the theories, techniques, and procedures for promoting health and providing care for the sick or disabled. Includes instruction in the administration of medication, assisting a physician during treatment and examination, and planning education for health maintenance. The major prepares students to take the licensure exam for registered nurses.

Nursing administration. Prepares registered nurses to manage nursing personnel and services in hospitals and other health care delivery agencies.

Nursing anesthesiology. Prepares registered nurses to administer anesthetics and provide care for patients before, during, and after anesthesia.

Nursing assistant. Prepares individuals to perform routine nursing-related services to patients in hospitals or long-term care facilities, under the training and supervision of a registered nurse or licensed practical nurse.

Nursing education. Prepares individuals to teach nursing, educate patients, and develop nursing staffs. Includes instruction in curriculum development and practicums in which students teach nursing at the undergraduate or graduate levels.

Nursing, practical. Prepares individuals to assist in providing general nursing care under the direction of a registered nurse, physician, or dentist. Includes instruction in taking patient vital signs, applying sterile dressings, patient health education, and assisting in examinations and treatment.

Nutritional sciences. The study of the biological processes by which organisms ingest, digest, and use the chemical compounds vital to survival that cannot be synthesized by the organism itself. Includes instruction in nutritional biochemistry and biophysics, anatomy and physiology of digestive systems, environmental and behavioral aspects of nutrition, and studies of the nutritional problems of specific organisms.

Occupational health/industrial hygiene. Prepares public health specialists to monitor and evaluate health standards related to industrial and commercial work places and locations. Includes instruction in occupational health and safety standards and regulations; test and monitoring equipment operation and maintenance; and industrial toxicology.

Occupational therapy. Prepares individuals to employ self-care, work, and play activities as therapeutic regimes for patients in order to increase independent functioning, enhance development, and assist recovery from disabilities.

Occupational therapy assistant. Prepares individuals to support occupational therapists by providing assistance during patient examinations, treatment, and monitoring; by keeping patient and related health record information; and by performing a wide range of practice-related duties.

Ocean engineering. Prepares individuals to apply mathematical and scientific principles to the design, development, and operational evaluation of systems that operate within coastal or ocean environments. Includes the design of systems for working in underwater environments and the analysis of related problems, such as the action of water on physical systems and people, tidal forces, and wave motion.

Oceanography. The study of the oceans and associated phenomena, including the land/water and water/atmosphere boundaries. Includes instruction in physical oceanography, marine chemistry and geology, and applications to specific research problems, such as coastal erosion, seawater corrosion and reactive behavior, and seafloor volcanism.

Office supervision/management. Prepares individuals to supervise and manage the operations and personnel of business offices. Includes instruction in labor relations, budgeting, scheduling, records management, security, office facilities design, and public relations.

Operations management/supervision. Prepares individuals to manage and direct the physical and/or technical functions of firms or organizations, particularly those relating to development, production, and manufacturing. Includes instruction in manufacturing and production systems, industrial labor relations, systems analysis, productivity analysis and cost control, and materials planning.

Operations research. Program that describes the development and application of complex mathematical or simulation models to solve problems involving operational systems, where the system concerned is subject to human intervention. Includes instruction in advanced multivariate analysis, application of judgment and statistical tests, optimization theory and techniques, resource allocation theory, mathematical modeling, control theory, statistical analysis, and application to specific research problems.

Ophthalmic medical assistant. Prepares individuals to support ophthalmologists by providing assistance during patient examinations, treatment, and monitoring, and by keeping patient and related health record information.

Ophthalmic/optometric services. Prepares individuals to assist ophthalmologists and/or optometrists in providing clinical services. Instruction may cover filling prescriptions, dispensing optical supplies, grinding lenses, patient counseling, vision testing, and diagnosis.

Optics. The study of light energy, including its structure, properties, and behavior under different conditions. Includes instruction in wave theory and mechanics, electromagnetic theory, physical optics, laser theory, coherence and chaotic light, nonlinear optics, and harmonic generation.

Optometric/ophthalmic laboratory technology. Prepares individuals to make prescription lenses and related visual aid equipment, under the supervision of an optician or optometrist. Includes instruction in optical laboratory procedures, principles of vision optics, lens grinding and polishing, contact lens fabrication, and glasses construction.

Optometry (OD). Prepares individuals for the professional practice of optometry. Describes the principles and techniques of examining, diagnosing, and treating conditions of the visual system. Includes instruction in prescribing glasses and contact lenses, corrective therapies, patient counseling, physician referral, and ethics and professional standards.

Organic chemistry. The study of the properties and behavior of hydrocarbon compounds and their derivatives. Includes instruction in molecular conversion and synthesis, the molecular structure of living cells and systems, the mutual reactivity of organic and inorganic compounds in combination, and the spectroscopic analysis of hydrocarbon compounds.

Organizational behavior studies. The study of the behavior and motivations of individuals functioning in organized groups and its application to business and industrial settings. Includes instruction in organization theory, industrial and organizational psychology, social psychology, sociology of organizations, and reinforcement and incentive theory.

Ornamental horticulture. Prepares individuals to produce flowers, foliage, and related plant materials in fields and greenhouses for ornamental purposes, and to arrange, package, and market these materials. Includes instruction in enterprise management.

Orthotics/prosthetics. Prepares individuals, under the supervision of a physician and in consultation with therapists, to make and fit orthoses and prostheses. Includes instruction in design, crafting, and production techniques; properties of materials; anatomy and physiology; and patient counseling.

Osteopathic medicine (DO). Prepares individuals for the professional practice of osteopathy, a system of holistic diagnosis and treatment of health problems. Includes instruction in allopathic methods, spinal manipulation, musculoskeletal and nervous system influence on body health, promoting natural defense mechanisms, and the interrelation of the various body systems.

Pacific area studies. The history, society, politics, culture, and economics of Australia, New Zealand, and the Pacific Islands, excluding the Philippines, Taiwan, and Japan.

Painting. Prepares individuals to express emotions, ideas, or inner visions by the application of paints and related chemical color substances to canvases or other materials. Includes instruction in color and color mixing, surface preparation, composition, oil, acrylic and watercolor media, and painting techniques.

Paleontology. The study of extinct life forms and associated fossil remains, and the reconstruction and analysis of ancient life forms, ecosystems, and geologic processes. Includes instruction in sedimentation and fossilization processes, fossil chemistry, evolutionary biology and paleobiology, field and laboratory research methods, and in such specific subjects as paleoecology, paleoclimatology, and invertebrate and vertebrate paleontology.

Paralegal/legal assistance. Prepares individuals to perform research, drafting, record keeping, and related administrative functions under the supervision of an attorney. Includes instruction in legal research, drafting legal documents, pleading, and court procedures.

Parasitology. The study of organisms living on or within biological hosts, their behavioral interactions with host organisms, and defenses against parasitical infestations. Includes instruction in parasitical evolution and community behavior, parasite metabolism, immunization processes, and drug development and reactions.

Parks/recreation/fitness studies. Study of the principles underlying recreational and leisure activities and the practices involved in providing indoor and outdoor recreational facilities and services to the general public.

Parks/recreational facilities management. Prepares individuals to develop and manage park and other indoor and outdoor recreation and leisure facilities. Includes instruction in supervising support personnel, health and safety standards, public relations, and basic business and marketing principles.

Pastoral counseling. Prepares ordained ministers, priests, rabbis, and other religious leaders in the principles and methods of clinical pastoral counseling, marriage and family therapy, youth ministry, outreach and evangelism, and ministry to special populations.

Pathology, human/animal. The study of the nature, causes, and development of human and animal diseases and the mechanisms of disease infestation and transfer. Includes instruction in human and animal pathobiology, disease morphology and biochemistry, physiology of disease and cell injury, and immunopathology.

Peace/conflict studies. The study of the origins, resolution, and prevention of international and intergroup conflicts. Includes instruction in peace research methods and related social scientific and psychological knowledge bases.

Perfusion technology. Prepares individuals to operate heart-lung machines and monitor patient conditions under the direct supervision of a surgeon. Includes instruction in patient examination and preparation, equipment operation and maintenance, anesthesia, and operating room procedures.

Personal services. Programs that prepare individuals to provide a variety of services to consumers, businesses, and industries.

Petroleum engineering. Prepares individuals to apply mathematical and scientific principles to the design, development, and operational evaluation of systems for locating, extracting, processing, and refining crude petroleum and natural gas.

Pharmaceutical/medicinal chemistry. Scientific study of the structural and reactive properties of natural and synthetic compounds intended for applications to human or animal medicine, pharmaceutical industrial uses, or treatment of plant disease. Includes instruction in molecular synthesis, drug design, properties of natural organic compounds, cosmetic chemistry, chemical manufacturing systems, drug behavior and host metabolism, and specific applications to health and industrial problems.

Pharmacology, human/animal. The study of the therapeutic and toxic effects of drugs on living tissues and entire organisms. Includes instruction in pharmacodynamic behavior, drug metabolism, chemical pharmacology, therapeutic applications, and chemical profile analysis.

Pharmacy (BPharm, PharmD). Prepares individuals to practice pharmacy. Includes instruction in the principles of medicinal chemistry; drug behavior; drug metabolism; mixing, preparing, and dispensing prescription medications; and pharmacy management.

Pharmacy assistant. Prepares individuals to support pharmacists by providing assistance during patient consultation, counter dispensing operations, and prescription preparation, and by keeping patient and related health record information.

Philosophy. The study of ideas and their logical structure, including arguments and investigations about abstract and real phenomena. Includes instruction in logic, ethics, aesthetics, epistemology, metaphysics, symbolism, and the history of philosophy.

Philosophy/religion. Study of the modes, methods, and types of logical inquiry, and of organized systems of belief and related practices.

Photography. The principles and techniques of communicating information, ideas, and feelings through the creation of images on photographic film or plates. Includes instruction in camera and equipment operation, developing, light and composition, color and special effects, and photographic art and history.

Physical education. Prepares individuals to teach physical education programs and/or to coach sports at various education levels.

Physical sciences. The study of inanimate objects, processes of matter and energy, and associated phenomena.

Physical sciences technologies. Prepares individuals to apply scientific principles and technical skills in support of physical science research and development projects.

Physical therapy. Prepares individuals, upon referral by a physician, to evaluate patients and plan and carry out treatment programs to prevent or remediate physical dysfunction, relieve pain, and prevent further disability. Includes instruction in kinesiology and evaluation of skeletal, neurological, and cardiovascular disorders.

Physical therapy assistant. Prepares individuals to support physical therapists by providing assistance during patient examinations, treatment, and monitoring.

Physical/theoretical chemistry. The study of the theoretical properties of matter and the relation of physical forces and phenomena to the chemical structure and behavior of molecules and other compounds. Includes instruction in reaction theory, computer simulation of structures and actions, transition theory, statistical mechanics, phase studies, quantum chemistry, and surface properties.

Physician assistant. Prepares individuals to manage the treatment of patients with routine or chronic health problems, in consultation with a physician or under indirect supervision. Includes instruction in patient interviewing and history taking, laboratory testing and analysis, administration of medications, minor surgery, and prescribing routine drugs.

Physics. The study of matter and energy and the formulation and testing of the laws governing the behavior of the matter-energy continuum. Includes instruction in classical and modern physics, electricity and magnetism, thermodynamics, mechanics, wave properties, nuclear processes, relativity and quantum theory, and quantitative and laboratory methods.

Physics education. Prepares individuals to teach physics at various education levels.

Physiology, human/animal. The study of organismic and systemic function and behavior in humans and animals, including such processes as respiration, circulation, digestion, excretion, and reproduction.

Plant breeding/genetics. The theories and principles underlying plant breeding, development, and mutation, including hybridization and differential selection for plant improvement.

Plant pathology. The causes, development, and treatment of plant diseases. Includes instruction in the nature and behavior of disease causal agents, the chemistry and physics of basic pathogens, disease host behaviors, and the analysis of disease control.

Plant physiology. The study of plant functions and life processes, including such metabolic processes as photosynthesis, respiration, assimilation, and transpiration; and plant systems, including reproduction, digestion, and anatomy.

Plant protection. The principles and practices of controlling and preventing economic loss caused by plant pests. Includes instruction in entomology, plant pathology, weed science, crop science, and environmental toxicology.

Plant sciences. The theories and principles involved in the production and management of plants for food, feed, fiber, and soil conservation.

Plasma/high-temperature physics. The study of the properties and behavior of matter at high temperatures, where molecular and atomic structures are in a disassociated ionic or electronic state.

Playwriting/screenwriting. Principles and techniques for communicating dramatic information, ideas, and feelings through the composition of written works for the theater and/or film. Includes instruction in creative writing craft; scene writing; stage and/or camera instructions; and script development, reading, and editing.

Plumbing/pipefitting. Prepares individuals to apply technical knowledge and skills to lay out, assemble, install, and maintain piping fixtures and systems for steam, hot water, heating, cooling, drainage, lubricating, sprinkling, and industrial processing systems.

Podiatry, podiatric medicine (DPM). Prepares individuals for the practice of podiatric medicine. Includes instruction in the principles and procedures used in the observation, diagnosis, care, and treatment of disease, injury, deformity, or other anomalies of the human foot.

Political science/government. The study of political institutions and behavior. Includes instruction in political philosophy, political theory, comparative government and politics, parties and interest groups, public opinion, and political research methods.

Polymer chemistry. The study of synthesized macromolecules and their interactions with other substances. Includes instruction in molecular bonding theory, polymerization, properties and behavior of unstable compounds, the development of tailored polymers, and transition phenomena.

Polymer/plastics engineering. Prepares individuals to apply mathematical and scientific principles to the design, development, and operational evaluation of synthesized macromolecular compounds. Includes instruction in the development of industrial materials with tailored properties, the design of lightweight structural components, the use of liquid or solid polymers, and the analysis and control of polymerization processes.

Portuguese. The study of the language, literature, and culture of Portuguese-speaking peoples, including the Luso-Brazilian and African dialects.

Poultry science. Prepares individuals to apply the theories and principles of poultry science to the management and production of poultry.

Power/electrical transmission. Prepares individuals to apply technical knowledge and skills to install, operate, maintain, and repair residential, commercial, and industrial electrical systems and the power lines that transmit electricity from the source of generation to the place of consumption.

Prearchitecture. Prepares individuals for admission to a four- or five-year bachelor's program in architecture.

Precision metal work. A program that prepares individuals to practice one or more metal work trades, such as welding, machine tool work, sheet metal work, and tool and die making.

Precision production trades. Prepares individuals to use technical knowledge and skills to create products using precision craftsmanship or technical illustration.

Predentistry. Prepares individuals for admission to a first-professional program in dentistry. A predentistry program includes English, chemistry, biology, and physics in addition to the undergraduate major, which can be in any challenging field.

Pre-engineering. Prepares individuals for admission to a four-year engineering program.

Prelaw. A four-year program, in virtually any major, that prepares individuals for admission to a professional law program.

Premedicine. A four-year program, in virtually any major, that prepares individuals for admission to a professional medical program. Students must complete five year-long math courses and English composition.

Prenursing. Generally a two-year program, prepares individuals for admission to professional RN (registered nurse), VN (vocational nurse), or dental hygienist program. Includes instruction in anatomy, physiology, microbiology, chemistry, and nutrition.

Preoptometry. A program of study in any of a wide range of majors that prepares individuals for admission to a professional optometry program. Any broad-based undergraduate program that includes many science and mathematics courses is preparation for study of optometry at the professional level.

Prepharmacy. Prepares individuals for admission to a professional pharmacy program.

Prephysical therapy. Prepares individuals for admission to a professional program in physical therapy.

Preveterinary medicine. Prepares individuals for admission to a professional program in veterinary medicine. Students take courses in language, social sciences, humanities, mathematics, chemistry, biological sciences, and physical sciences in addition to their major.

Printmaking. Prepares individuals to render art concepts onto surfaces and transfer images, via ink or dyes, onto paper or fabric. Includes instruction in monochrome and color printing; tonality; chemistry; and such techniques as serigraphy, lithography, intaglio, woodcut, stencil, and etching.

Protective services. A program that describes the principles and procedures for providing police, fire, and other safety services, and for managing penal institutions.

Psychobiology/physiological psychology. The study of the biological bases of psychological functioning. Includes instruction in functional neuroanatomy, neural system development, memory storage and retrieval, cognition and perception, behavior, and experimental design.

Psychology. The study of individual and collective behavior. Covers the physical and environmental bases of behavior and the analysis and treatment of behavior problems and disorders. Includes instruction in the principles of the various subfields of psychology, research methods, and psychological assessment and testing methods.

Public administration. Prepares individuals to serve as managers in the executive arms of local, state, and federal government. Includes instruction in the management of public policy, in executive-legislative relations, public budgetary processes and financial management, administrative law, public personnel management, professional ethics, and research methods.

Public administration/services. Prepares individuals to analyze, manage, and deliver public programs and services.

Public finance. Prepares individuals to manage the financial assets and budgets of public sector organizations. Includes instruction in public trusts and investments; the laws and procedures used to plan, prepare, and administer public agency budgets; and the preparation and analysis of public budget projections and policies.

Public health. Prepares specialists to monitor and evaluate potential and actual environmental health hazards, and to plan and manage environmental health programs. Includes instruction in environmental and genetic toxicology, biohazard research, testing and evaluation procedures, and environmental and health law regulations.

Public health education. Prepares specialists to provide education and information to populations affected by or at-risk of disease outbreak and health hazards. Includes instruction in public relations and public health campaign management.

Public policy analysis. The systematic analysis of public policy issues and decision-making processes. Includes instruction in the role of economic and political factors in public decision making and policy formation, microeconomic analysis of policy issues, resource allocation and decision modeling, cost/benefit analysis, and statistical methods.

Public relations. The methods and techniques used in communicating image-oriented corporate and sponsor messages to various audiences, promoting client interests, and managing client-media relations.

Purchasing/procurement/contracts. Prepares individuals to manage the process by which a firm or organization contracts for goods and services to support its operations and contracts to sell goods and services to other firms or organizations. Includes instruction in contract law, negotiations, buying procedures, cost and price analysis, vendor relations, contract administration, and auditing and inspection.

Quality control/safety technologies. Prepares individuals to apply basic engineering principles and technical skills in support of engineers and other professionals engaged in maintaining consistent manufacturing and construction standards. Includes instruction in quality control systems management principles, technical standards, testing and inspection procedures, and equipment operation and maintenance.

Radiation biology. The study of the effects of radiation on organisms and biological systems. Includes instruction in particle physics, ionization, cellular and organismic repair systems, genetic and pathological effects of radiation, and the measurement of radiation dosages.

Radio/television broadcasting. The methods and techniques used to plan, produce, and direct entertainment and informational programs in the broadcast media. Prepares individuals to function as professional announcers, directors, and producers. Includes instruction in scheduling, film and tape editing, on- and off-camera/microphone techniques, sound mixing, and broadcast law policies and regulations.

Range science/management. The principles and practices involved in studying and managing rangelands, arid regions, grasslands, and other areas of low productivity. Includes instruction in livestock grazing, social science, ecology, and hydrology.

Reading education. Prepares individuals to diagnose reading problems and to teach reading at various education levels.

Real estate. Prepares individuals to develop, buy, sell, appraise, and manage real property. Includes instruction in land-use development policy, real estate law and marketing procedures, agency management, brokerage, property inspection and appraisal, real estate investing, leased and rental properties, and commercial real estate.

Recreational therapy. Prepares individuals to plan, organize, and direct medically approved programs of leisure activity to promote patient physical and mental health and functioning. Includes instruction in volunteer and staff supervision, patient evaluation and monitoring, behavioral therapy, and recreation program and predischarge planning.

Rehabilitation/therapeutic services. Programs that prepare individuals to provide assistance in stabilizing and/or improving diagnosed health problems, through art, music, movement, or other means.

Religion/religious studies. The study of the nature of religious beliefs and specific religious and quasi-religious systems. Includes instruction in phenomenology; the sociology, psychology, literature, and art of religion; mythology; scriptural and textural studies; religious history and politics; and studies of particular faith communities and their behaviors.

Religious education. The theory and practice of providing educational services to members of faith communities. Includes instruction in planning and teaching lessons, organizing and supervising instructional activities, designing and developing instructional materials, and administering religious education programs and facilities.

Religious music. The history, theory, composition, and performance of music for religious or sacred purposes. Prepares individuals for religious musical vocations, such as choir director, cantor, organist, and chanter.

Respiratory therapy. Prepares individuals to perform therapeutic and life-support procedures using respiratory equipment, under the supervision of a physician. Includes instruction in administering inhalants, monitoring heart-lung machines and other intensive care therapies, anesthesia, emergency procedures, and equipment operation and maintenance.

Retailing/wholesaling. Programs that prepare individuals to sell or market items or services.

Robotics. Prepares individuals to apply basic engineering principles and technical skills in support of engineers and other professionals engaged in developing and using robots. Includes instruction in design and operational testing and in system maintenance and repair procedures.

Romance languages, other. The languages, literatures, and cultures of peoples who speak languages other than French, Italian, Portuguese, and Spanish, which are descended from Latin dialects and their modern derivatives.

Russian. The study of the language, literature, and culture of Russian-speaking peoples.

Russian/Slavic studies. The history, society, politics, culture, and economics of the Slavic peoples of Europe, including Russia.

Scandinavian. The study of the languages, literatures, and cultures of Scandinavian people, including Danish, Icelandic, Norwegian, Swedish, and Old Norse.

Scandinavian studies. The history, society, politics, culture, and economics of Northern Europe and the Baltic, including Denmark, Finland, Iceland, Norway, and Sweden.

School psychology. Prepares individuals to apply principles of clinical and counseling psychology to the diagnosis and treatment of student behavioral problems. Includes instruction in child and/or adolescent development; learning theory; testing, observation, and other procedures for assessing educational, personality, and motor skill development; therapeutic intervention strategies; and school psychological services planning.

Science education. Prepares individuals to teach general science programs, or a combination of biology and physical science, at various education levels.

Science technologies. Programs that prepare individuals to apply scientific principles and technical skills in support of scientific research and development.

Science/technology/society. Covers the social and public policy ramifications of science and technology, the relationship of science and engineering to public policy, and the social and ethical dimensions of scientific and technological enterprises.

Sculpture. Prepares individuals to create three-dimensional artworks. Includes instruction in the analysis of form in space; round and relief concepts; composition; such media as clay, plaster, wood, stone, and metal; and such techniques as carving, welding, and casting.

Secondary education. Prepares individuals to teach students in the secondary grades, which may include grades 7 through 12, depending on the school system or state regulations. Includes training to teach a comprehensive curriculum and/or specific subject matter.

Secretarial/administrative services. Prepares individuals to perform the duties of administrative assistants and/or secretaries and stenographers. Includes instruction in business communications, word processing and data entry, office machines operation, office procedures, filing, and records management.

Security/loss prevention. Prepares individuals to perform routine inspection, patrol, and crime prevention services for private clients. Includes instruction in the provision of personal protection as well as property security.

Sign language interpretation. Prepares individuals to interpret oral speech for the hearing impaired. Includes instruction in American Sign Language or other deaf languages, finger spelling, orientation to deaf culture, and interpreting from signing to voice as well as from voice to signing.

Slavic languages. Study of Byelorussian, Bulgarian, Czech, Polish, Serbo-Croatian, Old Slavonic, Ukrainian, or other Slavic languages.

Social psychology. The scientific study of individual behavior in group contexts, and of group behavior and associated phenomena. Includes instruction in learning theory, group theory and dynamics, sex roles, attitude formation, and criminal behavior and other social pathologies.

Social science education. Prepares individuals to teach specific social science subjects and programs at various education levels.

Social sciences. The study of human social behavior and institutions. Students use many methodologies, including scientific method, to analyze complex behavioral patterns in a search for the underlying forces that determine how that behavior will become manifest. A major in the social sciences may blend study of several specific social sciences, such as economics and anthropology.

Social studies education. Prepares individuals to teach general social studies programs at various education levels.

Social work. Prepares individuals for social welfare administration and counseling, including the study of organized means of providing basic support services for vulnerable individuals and groups. Covers social welfare policy, casework planning, social counseling and intervention strategies, and administrative procedures and regulations.

Social/philosophical foundations of education. The systematic study of education as a social and cultural institution and the educational process as an object of humanistic inquiry. Includes instruction in such subjects as the philosophy, history, and sociology of education; the economics and politics of education; and educational policy studies.

Sociology. The systematic study of social institutions and relationships. Includes instruction in social theory, sociological research methods, social organization and structure, social stratification, dynamics of social change, family structure, and deviance and control.

Software engineering. Prepares individuals to apply mathematical and scientific principles to the design, implementation, validation, and management of computer software for mainframe and personal computers. Includes instruction in programming methodology; procedural, data, and control abstraction; and specifications, design methods, and testing.

Soil sciences. The scientific classification and study of soils and soil properties. Includes instruction in soil chemistry, physics, biology, fertility, morphogenesis, mineralogy and hydrology, and conservation and management.

Solid-state/low-temperature physics. The scientific study of solids and related states of matter at low energy levels, including liquids and dense gases. Includes instruction in statistical mechanics, quantum theory, low-temperature phenomena, electron theory of metals, magnetism and superconductivity, equilibria and dynamics of liquids, and quantitative modeling.

South Asian languages. The study of the languages, literatures, and cultures of peoples of South Asia, including such languages as Hindu, Urdu, Bengali, Punjabi, and the Dravidian group, and ancestral languages, such as Sanskrit, Pali, and Bactrian.

South Asian studies. The history, society, politics, culture, and economics of the peoples of the Indian subcontinent and the Indian Ocean, including Bangladesh, Bhutan, India, Nepal, Pakistan, Sri Lanka, and the Maldive Islands.

Southeast Asian studies. The history, society, politics, cultures and economics of the Southeast Asian Peninsula and the Indonesian and Philippine archipelagoes, including Burma, Cambodia, Indonesia, Laos, Malaysia, the Philippines, Singapore, Thailand, and Vietnam.

Spanish. The study of the language, literature, and culture of Spanish-speaking peoples, including related or derived dialects and languages, such as Catalan, Castilian, and various Latin American dialects.

Spanish language education. Prepares individuals to teach Spanish language at various education levels.

Special education. The design and provision of teaching and other educational services to children or adults with special learning needs or disabilities. Includes instruction in diagnosing learning disabilities, developing individual education plans, teaching and supervising special education students, special education counseling, and applicable laws and policies.

Speech education. Prepares individuals to teach speech and language arts at various education levels.

Speech pathology. Prepares individuals to provide therapeutic care to persons with physical or behavioral disorders that affect speaking or comprehension. Includes instruction in identifying and assessing speech and language disorders; structure and development of aphasia; psychosocial and educational effects of speech/language disorders; and the planning and management of patient therapy.

Speech pathology/audiology. Prepares individuals to provide therapeutic care to persons with hearing and related communication disorders. Includes instruction in the principles of audiology, the structure and development of hearing and communications disorders, the identification and assessment of speech disorders and hearing loss, psychosocial and educational effects of speech and hearing disorders, and the planning and management of patient therapy.

Speech/rhetorical studies. The study of interpersonal communication from the scientific/behavioral and humanistic perspectives. Includes instruction in the theory and physiology of speech, the structure and analysis of argument and other types of public speech, the social role of speech, oral interpretation of literature, and the relation of speech to nonverbal and other forms of message exchange.

Speech/theater education. Prepares individuals to teach speech, communication, and theater at various education levels.

Sports/fitness administration. Prepares individuals to apply business, coaching, and physical education principles to the organization, administration, and management of athletic programs and teams, fitness/rehabilitation facilities, and sport recreation services. Includes instruction in program planning and development; business and financial management; sales, marketing, and recruitment; and applicable health and safety standards.

Sports medicine/athletic training. Prepares individuals to prevent and treat athletic injuries, to perform related rehabilitative therapy, and to manage the provision of health and treatment services to athletes. Includes instruction in basic sports medicine, dietetics, movement and motivation sciences, preventive and treatment remedies, equipment maintenance, clinic management, and patient education and counseling.

Stationary energy sources mechanics. Prepares individuals to install, operate, and maintain large power sources for such purposes as generating electricity, pumping, and heating.

Statistics. The mathematical theory and proofs forming the basis of probability and inference, and their applications to the collection, analysis, and description of data. Includes instruction in statistical theory, experimental analysis, sampling techniques, and survey research.

Studio arts. Prepares individuals to function as creative artists. Includes instruction in traditional fine arts (drawing, painting, sculpture, painting) and modern media (ceramics, textiles, intermedia, photography).

Surgical/operating room technology. Prepares individuals to perform general technical support tasks in the operating room before, during, and after surgery. Includes instruction in preoperation patient and surgical team preparation, handling surgical instruments, supply inventory maintenance, sterilization and cleaning of equipment, and operating room safety procedures.

Surveying. Prepares individuals to apply mathematic and scientific principles to the delineation, determination, planning, and positioning of land tracts, land and water boundaries, land contours and features; and preparation of related maps, charts, and reports. Includes instruction in applied geodesy (determining the size and shape of the earth and position of exact points on its surface), computer graphics, photointerpretation, plane and geodetic surveying, measuring, traversing, survey equipment operation and maintenance, instrument calibration, and basic cartography.

Systems engineering. Prepares individuals to apply mathematical and scientific principles to the design, development, and operational evaluation of total systems solutions to a wide variety of engineering problems, including the integration of human, physical, energy, communications, management, and information requirements, and the application of analytical methods to specific situations.

Systems science/theory. A multidisciplinary approach to the analysis and solution of complex problems using data and models from the natural, social, technological, behavioral, and life sciences.

Taxation. Prepares individuals to provide tax advice and management services to individuals and corporations. Includes instruction in tax law and regulations, tax record systems, individual and corporate income taxation, partnerships and fiduciary relationships, estates and trusts, property depreciation, and capital gains and losses.

Teacher assistance. Prepares individuals to assist teachers in regular classroom settings or to instruct and supervise special student populations, such as bilingual/bicultural students, special education students, and adult learners. Includes instruction in techniques of general classroom supervision and in assisting with lessons.

Teacher education, multiple levels. Prepares individuals to teach students at more than one education level, such as a combined program in elementary/secondary, early childhood/ elementary/middle school, or junior high/high school education.

Technical education. Prepares individuals to teach specific vocational education programs.

Technical theater design/stagecraft. Prepares individuals to apply artistic, technical, and dramatic principles and techniques to the communication of dramatic information, ideas, and feelings. Includes instruction in set and lighting design, theater acoustics, property management, costume design, and technical direction and production.

Technical/business writing. The methods and skills needed for writing and editing scientific, technical, and business papers and monographs.

Technology/industrial arts education. Prepares individuals to teach technology education/industrial arts programs at various education levels.

Telecommunications. Prepares individuals to apply technical knowledge to analyze and evaluate the production, storage, and transmission of messages via radio, TV, cable, telephone, and other emerging electronic communications technologies. Explores their structures, economics, and effects in contemporary society. Includes instruction in information technologies, telecommunication media arts, and multichannel and broadcast management.

Textile sciences/engineering. Prepares individuals to apply mathematical and scientific principles to the design, development, and operational evaluation of systems to test and manufacture fibers and fiber products, both synthetic and natural; to develop new and improved fibers and textiles; and to analyze related engineering problems, such as molecular synthesis, chemical manufacturing, and strength and stress.

Theater history/criticism. Study of the literature, history, and analysis of theatrical productions and theater methods and organization. Includes instruction in the themes and archetypes in dramatic literature; the history of acting, directing, and technical theater; and specific historical and cultural styles and traditions.

Theological professions (BDiv, MDiv, Rabbinical, Talmudical). A professional program that prepares individuals for ordination as ministers, priests, or rabbis. Includes instruction in the theology, history, and writings of a particular faith.

Theological studies. The study of the beliefs and doctrines of a particular religious faith from the point of view of that faith. Includes instruction in systematic theology, historical theology, moral theology, doctrinal studies, dogmatics, apologetics, and applications to specific questions of ecclesiastical policy and religious life.

Theoretical/mathematical physics. The scientific and mathematical formulation and evaluation of the physical laws governing, and models describing, matter-energy phenomena. Includes instruction in classical and quantum theory, relativity theory, field theory, vector and coordinate analysis, wave and particle theory, and statistical theory and analysis.

Tourism/travel management. Prepares individuals to manage travel-related enterprises and conventions and/or tour services. Includes instruction in travel agency management; tour, convention, and event planning; travel industry operations and procedures; tourism marketing and promotion strategies; and travel industry law.

Tourism/travel marketing. Prepares individuals to market various travel and tourism settings.

Toxicology. The scientific study of the nature, identification, and characteristics of poisons, toxic substances, and exogenous chemical agents and their effect on biological organisms. Includes instruction in environmental biology, chemico-physiological mechanisms, genetic toxicology, and the development of toxic defenses and antidotes.

Trade/industrial education. Prepares individuals to teach specific vocational trades and industry programs at various education levels.

Transportation management. Program explores major modes of transportation—their characteristics, functions, and inherent advantages—to prepare individuals for management positions with shipper, carrier, or government agencies involved in transportation. Includes instruction in transportation and logistics, public transport management, private carrier management, and physical distribution management.

Transportation/materials moving. Prepares individuals to apply technical knowledge and skills to move people or materials, via air or ground.

Turf management. Prepares individuals to develop, manage, and maintain ornamental or recreational grassed areas; to prepare and maintain athletic playing surfaces; and to produce turf for transplantation.

Urban studies. The application of social science principles to the study of urban institutions and the forces influencing urban social and political life. Includes instruction in the development and evolution of urban areas, urban sociology, principles of urban and social planning, and the politics and economics of urban government and services.

Urban/regional/community planning. Prepares individuals to apply principles of planning and analysis to the development and improvement of urban areas or surrounding regions, including the development of master plans, the design of urban services systems, and the economic and policy issues related to planning and plan implementation.

Vehicle/equipment operation. Prepares individuals to apply technical knowledge and skills to operate commercial and construction vehicles and mobile equipment.

Vehicle/mobile equipment mechanics. Prepares individuals to apply technical knowledge and skills to maintain and repair aircraft, land vehicles, ships, construction equipment, and portable power equipment.

Vehicle/petroleum products marketing. Prepares individuals to perform marketing tasks applicable to the vehicular sales and retail petroleum industries.

Veterinarian assistant. Prepares individuals to assist veterinarians and veterinary technicians by restraining animals, feeding, and general patient care; keeping animal and health record information; and performing a wide range of practice-related duties.

Veterinary medicine (DVM). Prepares individuals for the independent professional practice of veterinary medicine. Includes instruction in observation, diagnosis, care, and treatment of illness, disease, injury, and deformity in animals.

Veterinary specialties. The scientific study of the clinical specializations and supporting applied sciences related to the practice of veterinary medicine. Includes instruction in veterinary anatomy, physiology, pharmacology, pathology, toxicology, preventive medicine, immunology; large animal and small animal surgery and medicine; and animal nutrition.

Virology. The scientific study of viruses, a group of parasitical subcellular biologic entities. Includes viral classification, genetic effects of viral infestations, viral genomes and phenomes, viral applications in genetic research and engineering, and the development of antiviral drugs and other therapies.

Visual/performing arts. A program that prepares individuals in one or more of the visual artistic media or performing disciplines.

Vocational home economics. Prepares individuals for working in or managing businesses related to child care, clothing, and apparel; institutional food preparation; home furnishings installation, custodial services, and related services.

Vocational rehabilitation counseling. Prepares individuals, under the supervision of physicians or psychologists, to assist patients in coping with physical and/or mental disabilities that affect work. Includes instruction in vocational counseling, patient evaluation and monitoring, administering psychological and psychomotor tests, and planning training programs.

Water transportation. Prepares individuals to apply technical knowledge and skills to perform such water-related tasks as diving, fishing, operating ships, and repairing ships.

Western European studies. The history, society, politics, culture, and economics of the Western European peoples, including the Alpine region, the British Isles, France, the Iberian Peninsula, Italy, the Low Countries, and Germany.

Wildlife/wildlands management. Covers the principles and practices of the conservation and management of wildlands and wildlife resources for aesthetic, ecological, and recreational uses.

Women's studies. A program covering historical, social, political, cultural, and economic perspectives on women as individuals and social actors. Programs add to existing knowledge about women and also generate new perspectives on what is already known about human history and culture.

Woodworking. Prepares individuals to apply technical knowledge and skills to lay out and shape stock; assemble wooden articles; mark, saw, carve, and sand wooden products; repair wooden articles; and use a variety of hand and power tools.

Zoology. The scientific study of animals, including their structure, reproduction, growth, heredity, evolution, behavior, and distribution.

Majors

Accounting

Alabama
Alabama Agricultural and Mechanical University *B, M*
Alabama State University *B*
Athens State University *B*
Auburn University at Montgomery *B*
Auburn University *B, M*
Bessemer State Technical College *C, A*
Birmingham-Southern College *B*
Calhoun Community College *A*
Chattahoochee Valley Community College *A*
Faulkner University *B*
Harry M. Ayers State Technical College *A*
Huntingdon College *B*
J. F. Drake State Technical College *C, A*
Jacksonville State University *B*
Jefferson State Community College *A*
Lawson State Community College *A*
Oakwood College *A, B*
Samford University *B, M*
South College *A*
Southern Union State Community College *A*
Sparks State Technical College *A*
Spring Hill College *B, M*
Talladega College *B*
Troy State University Montgomery *B*
Troy State University *B*
Tuskegee University *B*
University of Alabama
   Birmingham *B, M*
   Huntsville *C, B, M*
University of Alabama *B, M, D*
University of Mobile *B*
University of Montevallo *B*
University of North Alabama *B*
University of South Alabama *B, M*
University of West Alabama *A, B*
Wallace State Community College at Hanceville *A*

Alaska
Alaska Pacific University *B*
University of Alaska
   Anchorage *A, B*
   Fairbanks *A, B*
   Southeast *C*

Arizona
Arizona State University *B, M*
Central Arizona College *C, A*
DeVry Institute of Technology Phoenix *B*
Eastern Arizona College *C*
Gateway Community College *C, A*
Glendale Community College *A*
Grand Canyon University *B*
Mesa Community College *A*
Mohave Community College *C, A*
Northern Arizona University *B*
Northland Pioneer College *C, A*
Paradise Valley Community College *C, A*
Phoenix College *A*
Pima Community College *C, A*
Prescott College *B*
Rio Salado College *C, A*
Scottsdale Community College *C, A*
University of Arizona *B, M*
University of Phoenix *C, B*
Yavapai College *A*

Arkansas
Arkansas State University *B*
Arkansas Tech University *B*
Garland County Community College *A*
Harding University *B*
Henderson State University *B*
Hendrix College *B, M*
John Brown University *B*
Lyon College *B*
Northwest Arkansas Community College *A*
Ouachita Baptist University *B*
Southern Arkansas University *B*
University of Arkansas
   Little Rock *B*
   Monticello *B*
   Pine Bluff *B*
University of Arkansas *B, M*
University of Central Arkansas *B*
University of the Ozarks *B*
Westark College *A*

California
Allan Hancock College *C, A*
American River College *C, A*
Armstrong University *B, M*
Azusa Pacific University *B*
Bakersfield College *A*
Barstow College *C, A*
Butte College *C, A*
Cabrillo College *C, A*
California College for Health Sciences *A, B*
California Lutheran University *B*
California State Polytechnic University: Pomona *B*
California State University
   Bakersfield *B*
   Chico *B, M*
   Dominguez Hills *B*
   Fresno *B*
   Fullerton *B, M*
   Hayward *B, M*
   Long Beach *B*
   Los Angeles *B, M*
   Northridge *M*
   Sacramento *M*
   Stanislaus *B*
Canada College *C, A*
Cerritos Community College *A*
Chabot College *A*
Chaffey Community College *C, A*
Chapman University *B*
Citrus College *C*
City College of San Francisco *C, A*
Claremont McKenna College *B*
Coastline Community College *C, A*
College of Marin: Kentfield *A*
College of San Mateo *C, A*
College of the Canyons *C, A*
College of the Desert *A*
College of the Sequoias *C*
College of the Siskiyous *C, A*
Columbia College *C*
Compton Community College *C, A*
Concordia University *B*
Crafton Hills College *C*
Cuyamaca College *C, A*
Cypress College *C, A*
De Anza College *C, A*
DeVry Institute of Technology
   Pomona *B*
   West Hills *B*
Diablo Valley College *C, A*
East Los Angeles College *A*
Empire College *C, A*
Evergreen Valley College *C*
Foothill College *C, A*
Fresno City College *C, A*
Fresno Pacific University *B*
Gavilan Community College *C*
Glendale Community College *C, A*
Golden Gate University *C, B, M*
Golden West College *C, A*
Grossmont Community College *C, A*
Heald Business College
   Fresno *C, A*
   Santa Rosa *C, A*
Humphreys College *A, B*
Irvine Valley College *C, A*
John F. Kennedy University *C*
Kings River Community College *C, A*
La Sierra University *B, M*
Lake Tahoe Community College *C, A*
Las Positas College *C*
Lincoln University *B*
Long Beach City College *C, A*
Los Angeles Harbor College *C, A*
Los Angeles Mission College *A*
Los Angeles Pierce College *C, A*
Los Angeles Southwest College *A*
Los Angeles Trade and Technical College *C, A*
Los Angeles Valley College *C*
Los Medanos College *C, A*
Loyola Marymount University *B*
Marymount College *A*
Master's College *B*
Mendocino College *C, A*
Merced College *A*
MiraCosta College *C, A*
Mission College *A*
Modesto Junior College *C, A*
Monterey Peninsula College *C, A*
Moorpark College *C, A*
Mount St. Mary's College *A, B*
Mount San Antonio College *C, A*
Napa Valley College *A*
National University *B, M*
Ohlone College *C, A*
Orange Coast College *C, A*
Pacific Union College *B*
Palo Verde College *C, A*
Palomar College *C, A*
Pasadena City College *C, A*
Pepperdine University *B*
Point Loma Nazarene University *C, B*
Rio Hondo College *A*
Riverside Community College *C, A*
Sacramento City College *C, A*
Saddleback College *A*
St. Mary's College of California *B*
San Bernardino Valley College *C, A*
San Diego City College *C, A*
San Diego Mesa College *C, A*
San Diego Miramar College *A*
San Diego State University *C, B, M*
San Francisco State University *B, M*
San Joaquin Delta College *A*
San Jose City College *C, A*
San Jose State University *B, M*
Santa Ana College *C, A*
Santa Barbara City College *C, A*
Santa Clara University *B*
Santa Monica College *B*
Santa Rosa Junior College *C*
Shasta College *A*
Sierra College *A*
Solano Community College *C, A*
Southwestern College *C, A*
Taft College *C, A*
University of La Verne *B*
University of Redlands *B*
University of San Diego *B*
University of San Francisco *B*
University of Southern California *B, M*
Vanguard University of Southern California *B*
Ventura College *C, A*
West Hills Community College *A*
West Los Angeles College *C, A*
West Valley College *A*
Yuba College *C*

Colorado
Adams State College *B*
Aims Community College *A*
Arapahoe Community College *A*
Colorado Christian University *B*
Colorado Mountain College
   Alpine Campus *C, A*
   Spring Valley Campus *C, A*
   Timberline Campus *C, A*
Colorado State University *B*
Community College of Aurora *C, A*
Community College of Denver *C, A*
Fort Lewis College *B*
Front Range Community College *C, A*
Lamar Community College *A*
Mesa State College *B*
Metropolitan State College of Denver *B*
Morgan Community College *A*
Northeastern Junior College *A*
Pikes Peak Community College *C, A*
Pueblo Community College *A*
Red Rocks Community College *C, A*
Regis University *B*
Trinidad State Junior College *A*
University of Colorado
   Boulder *B, M*
   Colorado Springs *B*
   Denver *M*
University of Denver *B, M*
University of Southern Colorado *B*
Western State College of Colorado *B*

Connecticut
Albertus Magnus College *B*
Asnuntuck Community-Technical College *A*
Briarwood College *A*
Capital Community College *A*
Central Connecticut State University *B*
Eastern Connecticut State University *B, M*
Fairfield University *B*
Gateway Community College *A*
Housatonic Community-Technical College *A*
Manchester Community-Technical College *C, A*
Middlesex Community-Technical College *A*
Mitchell College *A*
Naugatuck Valley Community-Technical College *C, A*
Northwestern Connecticut Community-Technical College *A*
Norwalk Community-Technical College *A*
Quinebaug Valley Community College *A*
Quinnipiac University *B, M*
Sacred Heart University *A, B*
Southern Connecticut State University *B*
Teikyo Post University *A, B*
Three Rivers Community-Technical College *C, A*
Tunxis Community College *C, A*
University of Bridgeport *B, M*
University of Connecticut *B*
University of Hartford *B*
University of New Haven *B, M*
Western Connecticut State University *B, M*

Delaware
Delaware State University *B*
Delaware Technical and Community College
   Owens Campus *C, A*
   Stanton/Wilmington Campus *C, A*
   Terry Campus *C, A*
Goldey-Beacom College *A, B*
University of Delaware *B, M*
Wesley College *B*
Wilmington College *B*

District of Columbia
American University *B, M*
Catholic University of America *B, M*
Gallaudet University *B*
George Washington University *B, M, D*
Georgetown University *B*
Howard University *B*

Accounting

Southeastern University *A, B, M*
University of the District of Columbia *B*

Florida
Barry University *B*
Bethune-Cookman College *B*
Brevard Community College *C*
Broward Community College *C, A*
Central Florida Community College *A*
Clearwater Christian College *B*
Daytona Beach Community
 College *C, A*
Edison Community College *C, A*
Edward Waters College *B*
Flagler College *B*
Florida Agricultural and Mechanical
 University *B*
Florida Atlantic University *B, M*
Florida Community College at
 Jacksonville *A*
Florida Gulf Coast University *C, B*
Florida Institute of Technology *M*
Florida International University *B, M*
Florida Memorial College *B*
Florida Metropolitan University
 Orlando College North *A, B*
Florida National College *A*
Florida Southern College *B*
Florida State University *B, M*
Gulf Coast Community College *C, A*
Hillsborough Community College *C, A*
Indian River Community College *A*
International College *A, B*
Jacksonville University *B, M*
Jones College *A, B*
Keiser College *A*
Lynn University *B*
Manatee Community College *A*
Miami-Dade Community College *C, A*
Northwood University
 Florida Campus *A, B*
Nova Southeastern University *B, M*
Palm Beach Atlantic College *B*
Palm Beach Community College *A*
Pensacola Junior College *C, A*
Polk Community College *A*
St. Leo University *B*
St. Petersburg Junior College *C, A*
St. Thomas University *B*
Santa Fe Community College *C, A*
South College: Palm Beach Campus *A*
South Florida Community College *C, A*
Stetson University *B, M*
University of Central Florida *B, M*
University of Florida *B, M*
University of Miami *C, B, M, D*
University of North Florida *B, M*
University of South Florida *B, M*
University of Tampa *B*
University of West Florida *B, M*
Valencia Community College *A*
Warner Southern College *B*

Georgia
Abraham Baldwin Agricultural
 College *A*
Albany State University *B*
Atlanta Metropolitan College *A*
Augusta State University *B*
Bainbridge College *A*
Berry College *B, M*
Brenau University *B, M*
Chattahoochee Technical Institute *C, A*
Clark Atlanta University *B*
Clayton College and State University *B*
Coastal Georgia Community College *A*
Columbus State University *B, M*
Columbus Technical Institute *C*
Darton College *C, A*
DeKalb Technical Institute *C, A*
DeVry Institute of Technology
 Alpharetta *B*
 Atlanta *B*
Emory University *B*
Fort Valley State University *B*
Gainesville College *A*

Georgia College and State University *B*
Georgia Military College *A*
Georgia Southern University *B, M*
Georgia Southwestern State
 University *A, B*
Georgia State University *B, M, D*
Gwinnett Technical Institute *C, A*
Kennesaw State University *B, M*
LaGrange College *B*
Mercer University *B, M*
Middle Georgia College *A*
Morehouse College *B*
Morris Brown College *B*
North Georgia College & State
 University *B*
Oglethorpe University *B*
Reinhardt College *B*
Savannah State University *B*
Savannah Technical Institute *A*
Shorter College *B*
South Georgia College *A*
State University of West Georgia *B*
Thomas College *B*
University of Georgia *B, M*
Valdosta State University *B, M*
Waycross College *A*

Hawaii
Brigham Young University
 Hawaii *B*
Chaminade University of Honolulu *B*
Hawaii Pacific University *A, B*
University of Hawaii
 Hawaii Community College *A*
 Hilo *B*
 Kapiolani Community
  College *C, A*
 Kauai Community College *C, A*
 Leeward Community College *A*
 Manoa *B, M*
 Maui Community College *A*
 West Oahu *B*
 Windward Community
  College *C, A*

Idaho
Albertson College of Idaho *B*
Boise State University *B, M*
College of Southern Idaho *A*
Eastern Idaho Technical College *C, A*
Idaho State University *B*
Lewis-Clark State College *B*
Northwest Nazarene University *B*
Ricks College *A*
University of Idaho *B, M*

Illinois
Augustana College *B*
Barat College *B*
Benedictine University *B*
Black Hawk College
 East Campus *C, A*
Black Hawk College *C, A*
Blackburn College *B*
Bradley University *B, M*
Carl Sandburg College *C, A*
Chicago State University *B*
City Colleges of Chicago
 Harold Washington College *C, A*
 Kennedy-King College *C, A*
 Malcolm X College *A*
 Olive-Harvey College *C, A*
 Wright College *C, A*
College of DuPage *C, A*
College of Lake County *C, A*
Concordia University *B*
Danville Area Community College *C, A*
De Paul University *B, M*
DeVry Institute of Technology
 Addison *B*
 Chicago *B*
Dominican University *B, M*
Eastern Illinois University *B*
Elgin Community College *C, A*
Elmhurst College *B, M*
Eureka College *B*

Governors State University *B, M*
Greenville College *B*
Highland Community College *C, A*
Illinois College *B*
Illinois Eastern Community Colleges
 Olney Central College *A*
Illinois State University *B, M*
Illinois Wesleyan University *B*
John A. Logan College *C, A*
John Wood Community College *A*
Joliet Junior College *C, A*
Judson College *B*
Kankakee Community College *C, A*
Kaskaskia College *C, A*
Kishwaukee College *C, A*
Lewis University *B*
Lewis and Clark Community College *A*
Lincoln Land Community College *A*
Loyola University of Chicago *B, M*
MacCormac College *A*
MacMurray College *B*
McHenry County College *C, A*
McKendree College *B*
Millikin University *B*
Monmouth College *B, T*
Moraine Valley Community College *C*
Morton College *A*
National-Louis University *C, B*
North Central College *B*
North Park University *B*
Northeastern Illinois University *B, M*
Northern Illinois University *B, M*
Northwestern Business College *A*
Northwestern University *D*
Oakton Community College *C, A*
Olivet Nazarene University *B*
Parkland College *C, A*
Prairie State College *C*
Quincy University *A, B*
Rend Lake College *A*
Richland Community College *A*
Robert Morris College: Chicago *C, A*
Rock Valley College *C, A*
Rockford College *B*
Roosevelt University *B, M*
St. Augustine College *C, A*
St. Xavier University *C, B*
Sauk Valley Community College *C, A*
Shawnee Community College *A*
Southern Illinois University
 Carbondale *B, M*
 Edwardsville *B, M*
Southwestern Ilinois College *A*
Trinity Christian College *B*
Trinity International University *B*
Triton College *C, A*
University of Chicago *M, D*
University of Illinois
 Chicago *B, M*
 Springfield *B, M*
 Urbana-Champaign *B, M, D*
University of St. Francis *B*
Waubonsee Community College *C, A*
Western Illinois University *B, M*
William Rainey Harper College *C, A*

Indiana
Ancilla College *C*
Anderson University *B*
Ball State University *B*
Bethel College *B*
Butler University *B*
Franklin College *B*
Goshen College *B*
Grace College *B*
Indiana Institute of Technology *A, B*
Indiana State University *B*
Indiana University
 Bloomington *B, M*
 East *A, B*
 Kokomo *B*
 Northwest *B, M*
 South Bend *B, M*
 Southeast *B*

Indiana University--Purdue University
 Indiana University-Purdue
  University Fort Wayne *C, B, M*
 Indiana University-Purdue
  University Indianapolis *M*
Indiana Wesleyan University *A, B*
International Business College *C, A*
Ivy Tech State College
 Central Indiana *A*
 Columbus *C, A*
 Eastcentral *C, A*
 Kokomo *C, A*
 Lafayette *C, A*
 Northcentral *C, A*
 Northeast *C, A*
 Northwest *C, A*
 Southcentral *C, A*
 Southeast *C, A*
 Southwest *C, A*
 Wabash Valley *C, A*
 Whitewater *C, A*
Manchester College *A, B, M*
Marian College *A, B*
Michiana College *C, A*
Oakland City University *A*
Purdue University
 Calumet *B*
 North Central Campus *A, B*
Purdue University *B*
Saint Mary's College *B*
St. Joseph's College *B*
St. Mary-of-the-Woods College *A, B*
Taylor University *B*
Tri-State University *A, B*
University of Evansville
University of Indianapolis *B, M*
University of Notre Dame *B, M*
University of St. Francis *A, B*
University of Southern Indiana *B, M*
Valparaiso University *B*
Vincennes University *A*

Iowa
American Institute of Business *C, A*
Briar Cliff College *B*
Buena Vista University *B*
Central College *B*
Clarke College *B*
Coe College *B*
Des Moines Area Community
 College *C, A*
Dordt College *B*
Drake University *B*
Graceland University *B*
Grand View College *B*
Hawkeye Community College *C, A*
Iowa Central Community College *A*
Iowa State University *B*
Iowa Wesleyan College *B*
Kirkwood Community College *C, A*
Loras College *B*
Luther College *B*
Marshalltown Community College *A*
Marycrest International University *B*
Morningside College *B*
Mount Mercy College *B*
Muscatine Community College *A*
Northeast Iowa Community
 College *C, A*
Northwestern College *B*
St. Ambrose University *B, M*
Scott Community College *A*
Simpson College *B*
Southeastern Community College
 North Campus *B*
Southwestern Community College *A*
University of Dubuque *A, B*
University of Iowa *B, M, D*
University of Northern Iowa *B*
Upper Iowa University *B*
Waldorf College *A*
Wartburg College *C, B*
Western Iowa Tech Community
 College *C, A*
William Penn University *B*

Kansas
Allen County Community College A
Baker University B
Benedictine College A, B
Bethany College B
Bethel College B
Butler County Community College A
Central Christian College A, B
Coffeyville Community College A
Colby Community College A
Dodge City Community College C
Emporia State University B
Fort Hays State University B
Hutchinson Community College A
Independence Community College A
Johnson County Community College A
Kansas City Kansas Community
    College A
Kansas State University A, B, M
Kansas Wesleyan University A, B
McPherson College B
MidAmerica Nazarene University B
Pittsburg State University B, M
Pratt Community College C, A
St. Mary College B
Seward County Community
    College C, A
Tabor College B, M
University of Kansas B, M
Washburn University of Topeka B
Wichita State University B, M

Kentucky
Asbury College B
Ashland Community College A
Bellarmine College B
Brescia University C, B
Campbellsville University A, B
Cumberland College B, T
Eastern Kentucky University B
Georgetown College B
Kentucky State University B
Kentucky Wesleyan College B
Lexington Community College A
Lindsey Wilson College B
Maysville Community College A
Morehead State University B
Murray State University B
National Business College A
Northern Kentucky University B, M
Owensboro Community College A
Paducah Community College A
Pikeville College B
Prestonsburg Community College A
Spalding University B
Thomas More College A, B
Transylvania University B
Union College A, B
University of Kentucky B, M
University of Louisville B
Western Kentucky University B, M

Louisiana
Delgado Community College A
Dillard University B
Louisiana State University
    Shreveport B
Louisiana State University and
    Agricultural and Mechanical
    College B, M, D
Louisiana Tech University B, M
Loyola University New Orleans B
McNeese State University B
Nicholls State University B
Northwestern State University A, B
Nunez Community College C, A
Our Lady of Holy Cross College B
Southeastern Louisiana University B
Southern University
    New Orleans B
    Shreveport A
Southern University and Agricultural and
    Mechanical College B, M
Tulane University B
University of Louisiana at Lafayette B
University of Louisiana at Monroe B
University of New Orleans B, M
Xavier University of Louisiana B

Maine
Andover College A
Beal College B
Husson College A, B
Mid-State College C, A
St. Joseph's College B
Thomas College A, B
University of Maine
    Machias A, B
    Presque Isle B
University of Maine B
University of Southern Maine B

Maryland
Allegany College A
Anne Arundel Community College C, A
Baltimore City Community College A
Carroll Community College C, A
Charles County Community
    College C, A
Chesapeake College C, A
Columbia Union College A, B
Community College of Baltimore County
    Catonsville C, A
    Essex C, A
Frederick Community College A
Frostburg State University B
Hagerstown Community College A
Harford Community College C, A
Loyola College in Maryland B
Montgomery College
    Germantown Campus A
    Rockville Campus A
    Takoma Park Campus A
Morgan State University B
Mount St. Mary's College B
Prince George's Community
    College C, A
Salisbury State University B
Towson University B
University of Baltimore M
University of Maryland
    College Park B
    Eastern Shore B
Villa Julie College A, B
Wor-Wic Community College C, A

Massachusetts
American International College B
Assumption College C, A, B, M
Atlantic Union College A, B
Babson College B
Bay Path College A, B
Bay State College A
Becker College A
Bentley College B, M
Boston College B
Boston University B
Bridgewater State College B
Bristol Community College A
Cape Cod Community College A
Clark University B
Elms College B
Fisher College C, A
Fitchburg State College B, M
Gordon College B
Greenfield Community College C, A
Holyoke Community College C, A
Lasell College B
Marian Court College C, A
Massachusetts Bay Community
    College C, A
Massachusetts College of Liberal Arts B
Massasoit Community College A
Merrimack College B
Middlesex Community College A
Mount Ida College A
Mount Wachusett Community College C
Newbury College A
Nichols College B
North Shore Community College A
Northeastern University A, B, M

Northern Essex Community
    College C, A
Roxbury Community College A
Salem State College B
Springfield Technical Community
    College C, A
Stonehill College B, M
Suffolk University C, B, M
University of Massachusetts
    Amherst B, M
    Dartmouth B
Western New England College B, M
Westfield State College B

Michigan
Adrian College A
Alma College B
Alpena Community College A
Andrews University B
Aquinas College B, T
Baker College
    of Auburn Hills A, B
    of Cadillac C, A, B
    of Jackson C, A, B
    of Mount Clemens C, A, B
    of Muskegon C, A, B
    of Owosso A, B
    of Port Huron C, A, B
Bay de Noc Community College C, A
Calvin College B
Central Michigan University B
Cleary College A, B
Cornerstone College and Grand Rapids
    Baptist Seminary B
Davenport College of Business A, B
Delta College A
Detroit College of Business A, B
Eastern Michigan University B, M
Ferris State University B, M
Glen Oaks Community College C
Gogebic Community College A
Grand Rapids Community College A
Grand Valley State University B, M
Great Lakes College C, A
Henry Ford Community College A
Hillsdale College B
Hope College B
Jackson Community College C, A
Kalamazoo Valley Community
    College C, A
Kellogg Community College C, A
Kettering University B
Kirtland Community College A
Lake Michigan College A
Lake Superior State University A, B
Lansing Community College A
Macomb Community College C, A
Madonna University B
Marygrove College C, A
Michigan State University B, M, D
Mid Michigan Community College A
Monroe County Community
    College C, A
Montcalm Community College A
Mott Community College A
Muskegon Community College A
North Central Michigan College C, A
Northern Michigan University B
Northwestern Michigan College A
Northwood University A, B
Oakland Community College C, A
Oakland University B, M
Olivet College B
Rochester College B
Saginaw Valley State University B, M
St. Clair County Community College A
Schoolcraft College C, A
Siena Heights University A, B
Southwestern Michigan College A
Spring Arbor College B
Suomi College B
University of Detroit Mercy B
University of Michigan
    Flint B
University of Michigan M

Walsh College of Accountancy and
    Business Administration B, M
Washtenaw Community College A
Wayne State University B
West Shore Community College A
Western Michigan University B, M

Minnesota
Alexandria Technical College A
Anoka-Ramsey Community College A
Augsburg College B
Bemidji State University B
Central Lakes College A
Century Community and Technical
    College A
College of St. Benedict B
College of St. Catherine: St. Paul
    Campus B
College of St. Scholastica B
Concordia College: Moorhead B
Concordia University: St. Paul B
Dakota County Technical College C
Gustavus Adolphus College B
Hennepin Technical College C, A
Inver Hills Community College C, A
Itasca Community College C, A
Lake Superior College: A Community
    and Technical College C, A
Metropolitan State University B
Minneapolis Community and Technical
    College C, A
Minnesota State College - Southeast
    Technical C, A
Minnesota State University, Mankato B
Moorhead State University B
National American University
    St. Paul B
North Hennepin Community College A
Northland Community & Technical
    College C, A
Northwestern College B
Pine Technical College C
Ridgewater College: A Community and
    Technical College C, A
St. Cloud State University B, M
St. Cloud Technical College C, A
St. John's University B
St. Mary's University of Minnesota B
St. Paul Technical College C, A
South Central Technical College A
Southwest State University A, B
University of Minnesota
    Crookston A, B
    Duluth B
    Twin Cities C, B
University of St. Thomas C, B, M
Winona State University B

Mississippi
Alcorn State University B
Belhaven College C, B
Copiah-Lincoln Community College A
Delta State University B, M
Itawamba Community College C
Jackson State University B, M
Mary Holmes College A
Millsaps College B, M
Mississippi College C, B, M
Mississippi Delta Community College A
Mississippi Gulf Coast Community
    College
    Jackson County Campus A
    Jefferson Davis Campus A
    Perkinston A
Mississippi State University B, M
Mississippi University for Women B
Mississippi Valley State University B
Northwest Mississippi Community
    College A
University of Mississippi B, M, D
University of Southern Mississippi B, M

Missouri
Avila College B
Central Methodist College B
Central Missouri State University B, M

51

Accounting

College of the Ozarks B
Culver-Stockton College B
DeVry Institute of Technology
   Kansas City B
Drury University B
East Central College C, A
Evangel University A, B
Fontbonne College B
Hannibal-LaGrange College B
Lincoln University B
Lindenwood University B
Longview Community College C, A
Maple Woods Community College C, A
Maryville University of Saint Louis B, M
Missouri Baptist College B
Missouri Southern State College A, B
Missouri Valley College B
Missouri Western State College B
Moberly Area Community College A
Northwest Missouri State
   University B, M
Ozarks Technical Community College A
Park University B
Penn Valley Community College C, A
Rockhurst University C, B
St. Charles County Community
   College C, A
St. Louis University B, M, D
Southeast Missouri State University B
Southwest Baptist University A, B
Southwest Missouri State
   University B, M
St. Louis Community College
   St. Louis Community College at
      Florissant Valley C
   St. Louis Community College at
      Forest Park C, A
   St. Louis Community College at
      Meramec C, A
State Fair Community College A
Stephens College B
Three Rivers Community College A
Truman State University B, M
University of Missouri
   Columbia B, M, D
   Kansas City B, M
   St. Louis B, M
Washington University B
Webster University C, B
Westminster College B
William Jewell College B
William Woods University B

Montana
Carroll College B
Flathead Valley Community
   College C, A
Montana State University
   Billings C, A, B
   Bozeman M
   College of Technology-Great
      Falls C, A
Montana Tech of the University of
   Montana: College of Technology A
Montana Tech of the University of
   Montana A, B
Rocky Mountain College B
University of Great Falls A, B
University of Montana-Missoula B, M

Nebraska
Bellevue University B
Central Community College C, A
College of Saint Mary A
Concordia University B
Creighton University B
Doane College B
Hastings College B
Lincoln School of Commerce C, A
Metropolitan Community College C, A
Mid Plains Community College Area A
Midland Lutheran College A, B
Northeast Community College A
Southeast Community College
   Lincoln Campus A
Union College A

University of Nebraska
   Lincoln B, M
   Omaha B, M

Nevada
Community College of Southern
   Nevada A
University of Nevada
   Las Vegas B, M
   Reno B, M
Western Nevada Community
   College C, A

New Hampshire
Antioch New England Graduate
   School M
Daniel Webster College C
Franklin Pierce College B
Hesser College A, B
McIntosh College C, A
New England College B
New Hampshire College C, A, B, M
New Hampshire Community Technical
   College
   Berlin A
   Claremont A
   Laconia C, A
   Manchester C, A
   Nashua C, A
   Stratham C, A
New Hampshire Technical Institute C, A
Plymouth State College of the University
   System of New Hampshire B
Rivier College A, B, M
St. Anselm College B
University of New Hampshire B, M

New Jersey
Atlantic Cape Community College C, A
Bergen Community College A
Berkeley College A
Bloomfield College B
Brookdale Community College A
Burlington County College C, A
Caldwell College B, M
Camden County College A
Centenary College B, M
College of St. Elizabeth C
Cumberland County College C, A
Essex County College C, A
Fairleigh Dickinson University B, M
Georgian Court College B
Gloucester County College C, A
Hudson County Community College A
Kean University B
Mercer County Community College A
Middlesex County College A
Monmouth University B
New Jersey City University M
Ocean County College C
Passaic County Community College A
Ramapo College of New Jersey B
Raritan Valley Community College A
Rider University B, M
Rowan University B

Rutgers
   The State University of New Jersey:
      Camden College of Arts and
      Sciences B
   The State University of New Jersey:
      Camden Graduate Campus M
   The State University of New Jersey:
      Douglass College B
   The State University of New Jersey:
      Livingston College B
   The State University of New Jersey:
      Newark College of Arts and
      Sciences B
   The State University of New Jersey:
      Newark Graduate Campus M
   The State University of New Jersey:
      Rutgers College B
   The State University of New Jersey:
      University College Camden B
   The State University of New Jersey:
      University College New
      Brunswick B
   The State University of New Jersey:
      University College Newark B
St. Peter's College B, M
Salem Community College A
Seton Hall University B, M
Sussex County Community College C, A
The College of New Jersey B
Thomas Edison State College C, A, B
Union County College A
Warren County Community College C, A
William Paterson University of New
   Jersey B

New Mexico
Albuquerque Technical-Vocational
   Institute C, A
Clovis Community College A
College of Santa Fe A, B
College of the Southwest B
Eastern New Mexico University
   Roswell Campus C
Eastern New Mexico University B
New Mexico Highlands University B
New Mexico Junior College A
New Mexico State University
   Carlsbad C
New Mexico State University B, M
Northern New Mexico Community
   College C, A
San Juan College A
Santa Fe Community College C, A
University of New Mexico M
Western New Mexico University B

New York
Adelphi University B, M
Adirondack Community College A
Alfred University B
Berkeley College of New York City A
Berkeley College A, B
Briarcliffe College C
Broome Community College A
Bryant & Stratton Business Institute
   Albany A
   Syracuse A
Canisius College B, M
Cayuga County Community
   College C, A

City University of New York
   Baruch College B, M, D
   Borough of Manhattan Community
      College A
   Bronx Community College A
   Brooklyn College B, M
   Hostos Community College A
   Hunter College B
   Kingsborough Community
      College A
   La Guardia Community College A
   Lehman College B, M
   Medgar Evers College B
   New York City Technical
      College A
   Queens College B, M
   Queensborough Community
      College A
   York College B
Clarkson University B
Clinton Community College A
College of St. Rose B, M
Columbia-Greene Community
   College C, A
Concordia College B
Corning Community College C, A
D'Youville College B
Daemen College C, B
DeVry Institute of Technology
   New York B
Dominican College of Blauvelt B
Dowling College B
Dutchess Community College C, A
Elmira College B
Finger Lakes Community College A
Five Towns College A
Fordham University B, M
Fulton-Montgomery Community
   College A
Genesee Community College C, A
Hartwick College B
Herkimer County Community College A
Hilbert College A, B
Hofstra University B, M
Houghton College B
Hudson Valley Community College C, A
Iona College B
Ithaca College B
Jamestown Business College A
Jamestown Community College A
Jefferson Community College C, A
Keuka College B
Le Moyne College B
Long Island University
   Brooklyn Campus B, M
   C. W. Post Campus B, M
   Southampton College B
Manhattan College B
Maria College A
Marist College A
Marymount College B
Marymount Manhattan College B
Mercy College C, B
Mohawk Valley Community
   College C, A
Molloy College B
Monroe College A, B
Monroe Community College A
Mount St. Mary College C, B
Nassau Community College A
Nazareth College of Rochester B
New York Institute of
   Technology A, B, M
New York University A, B, M, D
Niagara County Community
   College C, A
Niagara University B
Nyack College B
Onondaga Community College A
Orange County Community College A
Pace University:
   Pleasantville/Briarcliff C, A, B, M, D
Pace University C, A, B, M, D
Regents College B
Roberts Wesleyan College B

Rochester Institute of
  Technology A, B, M
Rockland Community College A
St. Bonaventure University B
St. Francis College B
St. John Fisher College B
St. John's University A, B, M
St. Thomas Aquinas College B
Schenectady County Community
  College A
Siena College B, M, T
St. Joseph's College
  St. Joseph's College: Suffolk
    Campus B
  St. Joseph's College B
State University of New York
  Albany B, M
  Binghamton B, M
  Buffalo B, M, D
  College at Brockport B
  College at Fredonia B
  College at Geneseo B
  College at Old Westbury B
  College at Oneonta B
  College at Plattsburgh B
  College of Agriculture and
    Technology at Cobleskill A
  College of Agriculture and
    Technology at Morrisville A
  College of Technology at Alfred A
  College of Technology at Canton A
  College of Technology at Delhi A
  Farmingdale C
  Institute of Technology at
    Utica/Rome B, M
  New Paltz B, M
  Oswego B, M
Suffolk County Community College A
Syracuse University B, M
Technical Career Institutes A
Tompkins-Cortland Community
  College C, A
Touro College C, A, B, M
Ulster County Community College A
Union College M
Utica College of Syracuse University B
Wagner College B
Westchester Business Institute C, A
Westchester Community College C, A
Wood Tobe-Coburn School A

North Carolina
Alamance Community College C, A
Appalachian State University B, M
Asheville Buncombe Technical
  Community College A
Barton College B
Beaufort County Community College A
Belmont Abbey College B
Bennett College B
Caldwell Community College and
  Technical Institute A
Campbell University B
Cape Fear Community College A
Catawba Valley Community
  College C, A
Cecils College C, A
Central Carolina Community College A
Central Piedmont Community College A
Cleveland Community College A
Coastal Carolina Community College A
Craven Community College A
Davidson County Community
  College C, A
Durham Technical Community
  College A
East Carolina University B, M
Edgecombe Community College A
Elizabeth City State University B
Elon College B
Fayetteville State University B
Fayetteville Technical Community
  College A
Forsyth Technical Community College A
Gardner-Webb University B

Gaston College A
Greensboro College B
Guilford College B
Guilford Technical Community
  College C, A
Halifax Community College A
High Point University B
James Sprunt Community College A
Johnson C. Smith University B
Johnston Community College A
Lenoir Community College A
Lenoir-Rhyne College B
Mars Hill College B
Martin Community College C, A
Mayland Community College A
Meredith College B
Methodist College B
Mitchell Community College A
Montgomery Community College A
Mount Olive College A, B
Nash Community College A
North Carolina Agricultural and
  Technical State University B
North Carolina Central University B
North Carolina State University B, M
North Carolina Wesleyan College B
Pfeiffer University B
Piedmont Community College A
Pitt Community College A
Queens College B
Randolph Community College A
Richmond Community College C, A
Rockingham Community College A
Rowan-Cabarrus Community
  College C, A
St. Augustine's College B
Salem College B
Sampson Community College A
Sandhills Community College C, A
South Piedmont Community
  College C, A
Southwestern Community College C, A
Surry Community College A
Tri-County Community College A
University of North Carolina
  Asheville B
  Chapel Hill B, M, D
  Charlotte B, M
  Greensboro B, M
  Pembroke B
  Wilmington B, M
Vance-Granville Community College A
Wake Forest University B, M
Wake Technical Community College A
Wayne Community College A
Western Carolina University B, M
Western Piedmont Community
  College A
Wilkes Community College C, A
Wilson Technical Community College A
Wingate University B
Winston-Salem State University B

North Dakota
Dickinson State University B
Jamestown College B
Minot State University: Bottineau
  Campus A
Minot State University B
North Dakota State College of Science A
North Dakota State University B
University of Mary A, B
University of North Dakota B

Ohio
Ashland University B
Baldwin-Wallace College C, B
Belmont Technical College A
Bluffton College B
Bowling Green State University
  Firelands College C, A
Bowling Green State University B, M
Capital University B
Case Western Reserve
  University B, M, D
Cedarville College B

Central Ohio Technical College A
Central State University B
Cincinnati State Technical and
  Community College A
Circleville Bible College B
Clark State Community College C, A
Cleveland State University B, M
College of Mount St. Joseph A, B
Columbus State Community
  College C, A
David N. Myers College B
Davis College C, A
DeVry Institute of Technology
  Columbus B
Defiance College A, B
Edison State Community College C, A
Franciscan University of
  Steubenville A, B
Franklin University A, B
Heidelberg College B
Hocking Technical College C, A
Jefferson Community College A
John Carroll University B
Kent State University
  Ashtabula Regional Campus A
  Stark Campus B
  Trumbull Campus A
  Tuscarawas Campus A
Kent State University C, B, M, D
Lake Erie College B
Lakeland Community College C, A
Lima Technical College A
Lorain County Community College C, A
Malone College B
Marietta College B
Marion Technical College C, A
Miami University
  Hamilton Campus C, A
  Middletown Campus C, A
  Oxford Campus B, M
Miami-Jacobs College C, A
Mount Union College B
Mount Vernon Nazarene College B
Muskingum Area Technical College C, A
Muskingum College B
North Central State College A
Northwest State Community
  College C, A
Northwestern College A
Notre Dame College of Ohio C, B
Ohio Dominican College C, B
Ohio Northern University B
Ohio State University
  Columbus Campus B, M, D
Ohio University A, B, M
Ohio Valley Business College A
Ohio Wesleyan University B
Otterbein College B
Owens Community College
  Findlay Campus C, A
  Toledo C, A
Shawnee State University A
Sinclair Community College A
Southern Ohio College A
Southern State Community College A
Stark State College of Technology A
Terra Community College A
Tiffin University A, B
University of Akron
  Wayne College A
University of Akron A, B, M
University of Cincinnati
  Clermont College C, A
  Raymond Walters College C, A
University of Cincinnati B, D
University of Dayton B
University of Findlay A, B
University of Rio Grande A, B
University of Toledo A, B, M
Ursuline College C, B
Walsh University A, B
Washington State Community College A
Wilberforce University B
Wilmington College B
Wittenberg University B

Wright State University B
Xavier University B
Youngstown State University A, B, M

Oklahoma
Cameron University B
Connors State College A
East Central University B
Eastern Oklahoma State College A
Langston University B
Northeastern Oklahoma Agricultural and
  Mechanical College C, A
Northeastern State University B
Northern Oklahoma College A
Northwestern Oklahoma State
  University B
Oklahoma Baptist University B
Oklahoma Christian University of
  Science and Arts B
Oklahoma City University B, M
Oklahoma Panhandle State University B
Oklahoma State University
  Oklahoma City A
  Okmulgee A
Oklahoma State University B, M
Oral Roberts University B
Redlands Community College A
Rogers State University A
Rose State College A
St. Gregory's University A, B
Southeastern Oklahoma State
  University B
Southern Nazarene University B
Southwestern Oklahoma State
  University B
Tulsa Community College A
University of Central Oklahoma B
University of Oklahoma B
University of Science and Arts of
  Oklahoma B
University of Tulsa C, B, M

Oregon
Central Oregon Community College A
Chemeketa Community College A
Clackamas Community College C, A
Eastern Oregon University B
Lane Community College C, A
Linfield College B
Linn-Benton Community College C, A
Mount Hood Community College C, A
Oregon Institute of Technology B
Portland Community College C, A
Portland State University C
Southern Oregon University B
University of Oregon B, M, D
University of Portland B
Western Baptist College B

Pennsylvania
Albright College B
Allentown College of St. Francis de
  Sales B
Alvernia College A, B
Beaver College B
Bloomsburg University of
  Pennsylvania B, M
Bucknell University B, M
Bucks County Community College A
Butler County Community College A
Cabrini College B
California University of
  Pennsylvania A, B
Cambria-Rowe Business College C, A
Carlow College B
Cedar Crest College C, B
Central Pennsylvania College A
Chatham College B
Chestnut Hill College A, B
Cheyney University of Pennsylvania B
Churchman Business School A
Clarion University of Pennsylvania C, B
College Misericordia B
Community College of Allegheny
  County C, A
Community College of Beaver County A

Community College of Philadelphia A
Delaware County Community College C, A
Delaware Valley College B
Drexel University B, M
Duquesne University B
Eastern College B
Elizabethtown College B
Franklin and Marshall College B
Gannon University A, B
Geneva College B, T
Grove City College B, M
Gwynedd-Mercy College A, B
Harrisburg Area Community College C, A
Holy Family College B
ICS Center for Degree Studies A
Immaculata College C, A, B
Indiana University of Pennsylvania B
Juniata College B
King's College A, B, M
Kutztown University of Pennsylvania B
La Roche College B
La Salle University A, B
Lackawanna Junior College C
Laurel Business Institute A
Lebanon Valley College of Pennsylvania C, A, B
Lehigh Carbon Community College C, A
Lehigh University B
Lincoln University B
Lock Haven University of Pennsylvania B
Luzerne County Community College C, A
Lycoming College B
Manor College A
Mansfield University of Pennsylvania A, B
Marywood University B
Mercyhurst College C, A, B
Messiah College B
Montgomery County Community College C, A
Moravian College B
Mount Aloysius College A, B
Muhlenberg College B
Neumann College C, B
Northampton County Area Community College C, A
Peirce College A
Penn State
  Erie, The Behrend College B
  Harrisburg B
  University Park B
Pennsylvania College of Technology A
Philadelphia University C, A, B, M
Pittsburgh Technical Institute A
Point Park College C, A, B
Reading Area Community College C, A
Robert Morris College B, M
Rosemont College B
St. Francis College B
St. Joseph's University C, A, B, M
St. Vincent College C, B
Sawyer School C, A
Seton Hill College B
Shippensburg University of Pennsylvania B
Slippery Rock University of Pennsylvania M
South Hills School of Business & Technology A
Susquehanna University B
Temple University B, M, D
Thiel College A, B
Tri-State Business Institute A
University of Pennsylvania A, B, M, D
University of Pittsburgh
  Greensburg B
  Johnstown B
  Titusville A
University of Pittsburgh B
University of Scranton B, M
Villanova University B
Washington and Jefferson College A, B
Waynesburg College B
West Chester University of Pennsylvania B, M
Westminster College B
Westmoreland County Community College A
Widener University B, M
Wilkes University B
Wilson College A, B
York College of Pennsylvania B
Yorktowne Business Institute A

Puerto Rico
American University of Puerto Rico A, B
Atlantic College A, B
Bayamon Central University B, M
Caribbean University A, B
Colegio Universitario del Este C, A, B
Huertas Junior College A
Inter American University of Puerto Rico
  Aguadilla Campus A, B
  Arecibo Campus A, B
  Barranquitas Campus A, B
  Bayamon Campus A, B
  Fajardo Campus A, B
  Guayama Campus A, B
  Metropolitan Campus A, B, M
  San German Campus B, M
National College of Business and Technology A
Pontifical Catholic University of Puerto Rico B, M
Ramirez College of Business and Technology A
Technological College of San Juan C, A
Turabo University A, B, M
Universidad Metropolitana B, M
University of Puerto Rico
  Aguadilla B
  Arecibo Campus A, B
  Cayey University College B
  Humacao University College A, B
  Ponce University College B
  Rio Piedras Campus B, M
  Utuado A
University of the Sacred Heart B

Rhode Island
Bryant College B, M
Community College of Rhode Island C, A
Johnson & Wales University A, B, M
Providence College B
Rhode Island College B
Roger Williams University A, B
Salve Regina University B, M
University of Rhode Island B, M

South Carolina
Aiken Technical College C, A
Anderson College B
Benedict College B
Central Carolina Technical College A
Charleston Southern University B, M
Chesterfield-Marlboro Technical College A
Clemson University B, M
Coastal Carolina University B
Coker College B
College of Charleston B, M
Columbia College B
Converse College B
Florence-Darlington Technical College A
Francis Marion University B
Furman University B
Greenville Technical College A
Lander University B
Midlands Technical College C, A
Newberry College B
Orangeburg-Calhoun Technical College C, A
Piedmont Technical College C, A
Presbyterian College B
South Carolina State University B
Southern Wesleyan University B
Spartanburg Technical College A
Tri-County Technical College A
Trident Technical College A
University of South Carolina
  Aiken B
University of South Carolina B, M
Voorhees College B
Wofford College B
York Technical College C, A

South Dakota
Augustana College B
Black Hills State University B
Dakota Wesleyan University B
Huron University A, B
Kilian Community College A
Mount Marty College A, B
Northern State University B
Sinte Gleska University A
Southeast Technical Institute A
University of South Dakota B, M
Western Dakota Technical Institute A

Tennessee
Belmont University B, M
Bethel College B
Carson-Newman College B
Chattanooga State Technical Community College A
Christian Brothers University B
Columbia State Community College A
Cumberland University B
David Lipscomb University B
Draughons Junior College of Business: Nashville A
East Tennessee State University B, M
Freed-Hardeman University B
Hiwassee College A
Knoxville Business College A
Lambuth University B
Lee University B
Lincoln Memorial University B
Middle Tennessee State University B, M
Milligan College B
Nashville State Technical Institute A
Northeast State Technical Community College C
Pellissippi State Technical Community College A
Rhodes College M
Roane State Community College A
Shelby State Community College C
Southern Adventist University A, B, M
Tennessee State University A, B
Tennessee Technological University B
Tennessee Wesleyan College B
Trevecca Nazarene University B
Tusculum College B
Union University B, T
University of Memphis B, M
University of Tennessee
  Chattanooga M
  Knoxville B, M
  Martin B, M
Walters State Community College A

Texas
Alvin Community College A
Amarillo College C, A
Amber University B
Angelina College A
Angelo State University M
Austin Community College A
Baylor University B, M
Blinn College A
Brazosport College A
Brookhaven College A
Coastal Bend College A
College of the Mainland A
Collin County Community College District C
Dallas Baptist University B, M
DeVry Institute of Technology
  Irving B
Del Mar College A
East Texas Baptist University B
Eastfield College C, A
El Paso Community College C, A
Galveston College C, A
Grayson County College C, A
Hardin-Simmons University B
Houston Baptist University B, M
Houston Community College System A
Howard College C, A
Howard Payne University B
Huston-Tillotson College B
Kilgore College C, A
Lamar State College at Orange C, A
Lamar State College at Port Arthur C, A
Lamar University B
LeTourneau University B
Lee College C, A
Lon Morris College A
Lubbock Christian University B
McMurry University B
Midland College C, A
Midwestern State University B, M
Mountain View College A
Navarro College C, A
North Lake College A
Northeast Texas Community College A
Northwood University: Texas Campus A, B
Our Lady of the Lake University of San Antonio B
Palo Alto College A
Paris Junior College A
Prairie View A&M University B
Rice University M
Richland College A
St. Edward's University C, B
St. Mary's University B, M
St. Philip's College A
Sam Houston State University B, M
San Antonio College A
San Jacinto College
  North C, A
Schreiner College B
Southern Methodist University B, M
Southwest Texas State University B, M
Southwestern Adventist University B
Southwestern Assemblies of God University B
Southwestern University B
Stephen F. Austin State University B, M
Sul Ross State University B
Tarleton State University B
Tarrant County College A
Texas A&M International University B, M
Texas A&M University
  Commerce B, M
  Corpus Christi B, M
  Kingsville B, M
  Texarkana B, M
Texas A&M University B, M, D
Texas Christian University B, M
Texas Lutheran University B
Texas Southern University B, M
Texas State Technical College
  Harlingen C
  Sweetwater C, A
Texas Tech University B, M
Texas Wesleyan University B, M
Texas Woman's University B
Trinity University B, M
Trinity Valley Community College C, A
University of Houston
  Clear Lake B, M
  Downtown B
  Victoria B
University of Houston B, M, D
University of Mary Hardin-Baylor B
University of North Texas B, M, D
University of St. Thomas B, M

University of Texas
   Arlington B, M, D
   Austin B, M, D
   Brownsville B
   Dallas B, M, D
   El Paso B, M
   Pan American B
   San Antonio B, M
   Tyler B
   of the Permian Basin B, M
Vernon Regional Junior College A
Victoria College C, A
Weatherford College C, A
West Texas A&M University B, M
Western Texas College C, A
Wiley College B

Utah
Brigham Young University B, M
College of Eastern Utah C
Dixie State College of Utah A
LDS Business College C, A
Mountain West College C, A
Salt Lake Community College A
Snow College A
Southern Utah University B, M
University of Utah B, M
Utah State University B, M
Utah Valley State College C, A
Weber State University B, M
Westminster College B

Vermont
Castleton State College B
Champlain College A, B
College of St. Joseph in Vermont A, B
Johnson State College C, A, B
Lyndon State College B
Norwich University B
St. Michael's College B
Southern Vermont College A, B
Trinity College of Vermont A, B
Vermont Technical College A

Virginia
Averett College B
Blue Ridge Community College A
Bridgewater College B
Central Virginia Community
   College C, A
Christopher Newport University B
College of William and Mary M
Danville Community College A
ECPI College of Technology C, A
Eastern Mennonite University B
Ferrum College B
George Mason University B, M
Germanna Community College A
Hampton University B
J. Sargeant Reynolds Community
   College C, A
James Madison University B, M
John Tyler Community College A
Liberty University B
Longwood College B
Lord Fairfax Community College A
Lynchburg College B
Mountain Empire Community College A
National Business College A, B
New River Community College A
Norfolk State University B
Northern Virginia Community College A
Old Dominion University B, M
Patrick Henry Community College A
Piedmont Virginia Community
   College A
Radford University B
Randolph-Macon College B
Shenandoah University B
Southwest Virginia Community
   College A
Thomas Nelson Community College A
Tidewater Community College A
University of Richmond B
University of Virginia's College at
   Wise B

University of Virginia M
Virginia Commonwealth
   University C, B, M
Virginia Highlands Community
   College C, A
Virginia Polytechnic Institute and State
   University B, M
Virginia State University B
Virginia Union University B
Virginia Western Community College A
Washington and Lee University B
Wytheville Community College A

Washington
Bellevue Community College C, A
Big Bend Community College A
Central Washington University B
Centralia College C
City University C, B, M
Clark College C, A
Columbia Basin College A
Eastern Washington University B
Edmonds Community College C, A
Everett Community College C, A
Gonzaga University B
Grays Harbor College C, A
Green River Community College C, A
Highline Community College C
Lake Washington Technical College C, A
Lower Columbia College C, A
Olympic College C, A
Pacific Lutheran University B
Peninsula College A
Pierce College C, A
Renton Technical College C, A
St. Martin's College B
Seattle Central Community College C, A
Seattle Pacific University C, B, T
Seattle University B, M
Shoreline Community College C, A
Skagit Valley College C, A
South Puget Sound Community
   College C, A
South Seattle Community College C, A
Spokane Community College A
Spokane Falls Community College A
Tacoma Community College C
University of Washington B, M
Walla Walla Community College C, A
Washington State University B, M
Wenatchee Valley College A
Western Washington University B
Whatcom Community College A
Whitworth College B
Yakima Valley Community College C, A

West Virginia
Alderson-Broaddus College B
Bethany College B
Bluefield State College B
College of West Virginia A, B
Concord College B
Davis and Elkins College A, B
Fairmont State College A, B
Glenville State College B
Marshall University B
Ohio Valley College A
Potomac State College of West Virginia
   University A
Southern West Virginia Community and
   Technical College A
University of Charleston A, B
West Liberty State College B
West Virginia Northern Community
   College A
West Virginia State College A, B
West Virginia University B, M
West Virginia Wesleyan College B
Wheeling Jesuit University B, M

Wisconsin
Blackhawk Technical College A
Bryant & Stratton College A
Cardinal Stritch University B
Carroll College B
Carthage College B

Chippewa Valley Technical College A
Concordia University Wisconsin B
Gateway Technical College C
Lakeland College B, M
Lakeshore Technical College A
Madison Area Technical College C, A
Marian College of Fond du Lac B
Marquette University B
Milwaukee Area Technical College A
Moraine Park Technical College C, A
Mount Mary College B
Mount Senario College B
Nicolet Area Technical College A
Northeast Wisconsin Technical
   College A
Northland College B
St. Norbert College B
Silver Lake College B
Southwest Wisconsin Technical
   College C, A
University of Wisconsin
   Eau Claire B
   Green Bay B
   La Crosse B
   Madison B, M, D
   Milwaukee B
   Oshkosh B
   Parkside B
   Platteville B
   River Falls B
   Stevens Point B
   Superior B
   Whitewater B, M
Viterbo University B
Waukesha County Technical College A
Western Wisconsin Technical College A
Wisconsin Indianhead Technical
   College A

Wyoming
Casper College C, A
Central Wyoming College C, A
Eastern Wyoming College A
Laramie County Community
   College C, A
Sheridan College A
University of Wyoming B
Western Wyoming Community
   College A

Acting/directing

California
Allan Hancock College C
American Conservatory Theater M
American Film Institute Center for
   Advanced Film and Television
   Studies M
California Institute of the Arts M
California State University
   Fullerton M
   Hayward B
   Long Beach B, M
Gavilan Community College A
Grossmont Community College C, A
Irvine Valley College A
Monterey Peninsula College A
Pepperdine University B
San Diego State University M
Santa Barbara City College A
Santa Rosa Junior College C
University of Southern California B, M

Connecticut
University of Connecticut B

District of Columbia
Howard University B

Florida
Florida State University B
Jacksonville University B

Hawaii
Hawaii Pacific University C

Illinois
Barat College B
Columbia College B
De Paul University M
Monmouth College B
Rockford College B

Indiana
University of Evansville B
Vincennes University A

Iowa
Maharishi University of Management B
University of Iowa M
University of Northern Iowa B

Kansas
Central Christian College A
Seward County Community College A

Louisiana
Dillard University B

Maryland
University of Maryland
   Baltimore County B

Massachusetts
Boston University B, M
Clark University B
Emerson College B
Hampshire College B
Northeastern University A, B
Salem State College B
Simon's Rock College of Bard B

Minnesota
Minnesota State University, Mankato B
Moorhead State University B
University of Minnesota
   Duluth B

Missouri
Webster University B

New Hampshire
Franklin Pierce College B

New Jersey
Centenary College B
Rowan University B
Rutgers
   The State University of New Jersey:
      Mason Gross School of the
      Arts B, M
   The State University of New Jersey:
      New Brunswick Graduate
      Campus M

New York
American Academy of Dramatic Arts
   American Academy of Dramatic
      Arts A
Bard College B
City University of New York
   City College B
Ithaca College B
Long Island University
   C. W. Post Campus B
Marymount College B
New York University B, M
Niagara University B
Sarah Lawrence College B, M
State University of New York
   College at Fredonia B
   New Paltz B
   Purchase B

North Carolina
Greensboro College B
University of North Carolina
   Greensboro B, M

Ohio
Kent State University
   Stark Campus B
Kent State University B, M
Ohio University B, M
University of Akron M
Youngstown State University B

Acting/directing

Oklahoma
Southeastern Oklahoma State
 University *B*

Pennsylvania
Allentown College of St. Francis de
 Sales *B*
Carnegie Mellon University *B*
Northampton County Area Community
 College *A*
Seton Hill College *B*
University of the Arts *B*

Texas
Baylor University *B, M*
Blinn College *C, A*
Lon Morris College *A*
Southern Methodist University *M*
Texas Tech University *B, M*
Trinity University *B*

Utah
Brigham Young University *B*

Vermont
Johnson State College *B*
Marlboro College *B*

Washington
Cornish College of the Arts *B*
Eastern Washington University *B*
North Seattle Community College *C, A*
Western Washington University *B*

Wisconsin
University of Wisconsin
 Madison *B, M*
Viterbo University *B*

Actuarial science

California
Master's College *B*

Connecticut
Central Connecticut State University *B*
University of Connecticut *B*
University of Hartford *B*

Florida
Florida State University *B*

Georgia
Georgia State University *B, M*

Illinois
Bradley University *B*
Roosevelt University *B*
St. Xavier University *B*
University of Illinois
 Urbana-Champaign *B*
University of St. Francis *B*

Indiana
Ball State University *B, M*
Butler University *B*
Indiana University
 Northwest *B*
Vincennes University *A*

Iowa
Buena Vista University *B*
Drake University *B*
University of Iowa *B, M*

Kentucky
Bellarmine College *B*

Maryland
Frostburg State University *B*

Massachusetts
Boston University *M*

Michigan
Central Michigan University *B*
Eastern Michigan University *B*
Ferris State University *B*
University of Michigan
 Flint *B*

Minnesota
University of Minnesota
 Twin Cities *B*
University of St. Thomas *B*

Missouri
Central Missouri State University *B*
Maryville University of Saint Louis *B*
Missouri Valley College *B*

Nebraska
University of Nebraska
 Kearney *B*
 Lincoln *B, M*

New Hampshire
Plymouth State College of the University
 System of New Hampshire *B*

New Jersey
Rider University *B*
St. Peter's College *A, B, M*
Sussex County Community College *C*

New York
City University of New York
 Baruch College *B*
 City College *B*
College of Insurance *B, M*
New York University *B*
Utica College of Syracuse University *B*

North Carolina
North Carolina Central University *B*

North Dakota
Jamestown College *B*
North Dakota State University *B*

Ohio
Bowling Green State University *B*
Ohio State University
 Columbus Campus *B*
Ohio University *B*

Oklahoma
University of Central Oklahoma *B*

Pennsylvania
Harrisburg Area Community College *A*
Lebanon Valley College of
 Pennsylvania *B*
Lincoln University *B*
Lycoming College *B*
Mansfield University of Pennsylvania *B*
Mercyhurst College *B*
Penn State
 University Park *B*
Seton Hill College *B*
Temple University *B, M*
Thiel College *B*
University of Pennsylvania *B, M*

Rhode Island
Bryant College *B*

Tennessee
Southern Adventist University *B*

Utah
Brigham Young University *B*

Wisconsin
Carroll College *B*
University of Wisconsin
 Madison *M*

Acupuncture/Oriental medicine

Washington
Bastyr University *B, M*

Administration of special education

Arkansas
University of Central Arkansas *M*

California
Azusa Pacific University *M*
California Lutheran University *M*
California State University
 Bakersfield *M*
 Fresno *M*
 Fullerton *M*
 Los Angeles *M*
 Northridge *M*
Fresno Pacific University *M, T*
Mount St. Mary's College *M*
University of California
 Berkeley *T*
University of San Diego *M*
University of Southern California *M, D*

District of Columbia
Gallaudet University *M, D*
Howard University *M*

Florida
Barry University *M*
Florida Agricultural and Mechanical
 University *M*

Georgia
Columbus State University *B*

Illinois
Benedictine University *M*
University of Illinois
 Springfield *M*

Indiana
Ball State University *T*
Indiana State University *M*
Purdue University
 Calumet *B, T*

Iowa
University of Iowa *M, D*

Kansas
Fort Hays State University *M*

Kentucky
Murray State University *M, T*

Louisiana
Northwestern State University *T*

Massachusetts
American International College *B*
Eastern Nazarene College *M, T*
Lesley College *M, T*

Minnesota
St. Cloud State University *M*
Winona State University *M, T*

Missouri
Lindenwood University *M*
University of Missouri
 Columbia *D*

New Hampshire
Rivier College *M*

New Jersey
Monmouth University *M*

New Mexico
New Mexico Highlands University *M*

New York
Columbia University
 Teachers College *M, D*

North Carolina
Appalachian State University *B*
University of North Carolina
 Greensboro *M, D*

Ohio
Kent State University *M, D*
Ohio State University
 Columbus Campus *M*
University of Akron *M*
University of Cincinnati *M, D*
Walsh University *B*
Wright State University *M*
Youngstown State University *M*

Oklahoma
Northeastern State University *M*

Oregon
Western Oregon University *T*

Pennsylvania
La Salle University *B, T*
Marywood University *M, T*

Puerto Rico
Inter American University of Puerto Rico
 Metropolitan Campus *D*

South Carolina
Furman University *M*

South Dakota
University of South Dakota *D*

Texas
Texas A&M International
 University *M, T*
Texas Woman's University *M*

Vermont
Johnson State College *M*

Virginia
Virginia Polytechnic Institute and State
 University *B, D*

Washington
Whitworth College *B, M, T*

West Virginia
Marshall University *M*

Adult/continuing education administration

Alaska
University of Alaska
 Anchorage *M*

Arizona
University of Phoenix *M*

California
Biola University *B*
San Francisco State University *M*

Florida
Florida State University *M, D*
Nova Southeastern University *D*

Idaho
University of Idaho *M*

Illinois
Northern Illinois University *M, D*

Indiana
Ball State University *D, T*
Purdue University
 Calumet *B, T*

Iowa
Drake University *M, D, T*
Iowa State University *M, D*
University of Iowa *M, D*

Louisiana
Northwestern State University *T*

Maine
University of Southern Maine *M*

Massachusetts
Harvard University *M, D*
Suffolk University *M*

Michigan
Michigan State University *M, D*

Mississippi
University of Southern Mississippi *M*

Missouri
University of Missouri
 Columbia *M, D*

New Hampshire
University of New Hampshire *M*

New York
Adelphi University *M*
City University of New York
    Lehman College *M, T*
Columbia University
    Teachers College *M, D*
Cornell University *B*
Fordham University *M, D*
State University of New York
    College at Buffalo *M*

North Carolina
East Carolina University *M*
North Carolina Agricultural and
    Technical State University *M*
North Carolina State University *M, D*

Ohio
Ohio State University
    Columbus Campus *M*
Wittenberg University *B*

Oklahoma
Oklahoma State University *M, D*
University of Oklahoma *M, D*

Oregon
Oregon State University *M*

Pennsylvania
Penn State
    University Park *M, D*
University of Pennsylvania *M*

South Carolina
University of South Carolina *M*

South Dakota
University of South Dakota *M, D*

Tennessee
Tusculum College *M*

Texas
Texas A&M University
    Kingsville *M*
University of the Incarnate Word *M*

Washington
Eastern Washington University *M*
Western Washington University *M*

West Virginia
Marshall University *M*

Wisconsin
Milwaukee Area Technical College *C*
University of Wisconsin
    Madison *M, D*

Adult/continuing teacher education

Alabama
Auburn University *B*
Troy State University
    Montgomery *M*
University of South Alabama *D*
University of West Alabama *M*

Arkansas
University of Arkansas
    Little Rock *M*
University of Arkansas *M, D*

California
Biola University *B*
Patten College *B*
San Francisco State University *M*
Whittier College *T*

Colorado
Colorado Christian University *B*

Delaware
Delaware State University *M*

District of Columbia
George Washington University *M*

Florida
Florida Agricultural and Mechanical
    University *M*
Florida International University *M, D*
University of South Florida *M*

Georgia
Georgia State University *B, M, D*
University of Georgia *M, D*

Illinois
National-Louis University *M, D*
Northeastern Illinois University *B, M*

Indiana
Ball State University *M*
Indiana University--Purdue University
    Indiana University-Purdue
        University Indianapolis *M*

Iowa
Marycrest International University *M*

Kansas
Kansas State University *M, D*

Kentucky
Morehead State University *M*

Maine
University of Southern Maine *M*

Maryland
Coppin State College *M*

Massachusetts
Boston University *M, T*

Michigan
Northern Michigan University *B*
University of Michigan *M*
Wayne State University *M*
Western Michigan University *B*

Minnesota
Ridgewater College: A Community and
    Technical College *A*
University of Minnesota
    Twin Cities *M*

Missouri
Central Missouri State University *M, T*
University of Missouri
    Kansas City *M*
    St. Louis *M*

Nebraska
University of Nebraska
    Lincoln *M*

Nevada
University of Nevada
    Las Vegas *B, M*

New Jersey
Rutgers
    The State University of New Jersey:
    New Brunswick Graduate
        Campus *M, D*

New Mexico
University of New Mexico *M*

New York
Elmira College *M*
State University of New York
    College at Buffalo *M*
Syracuse University *M, D*

North Carolina
North Carolina Agricultural and
    Technical State University *M*
North Carolina State University *M*
University of North Carolina
    Greensboro *M*

Ohio
Cleveland State University *M, D*
Ohio University *M*

Oklahoma
Oklahoma State University *M, D*
University of Central Oklahoma *M*

Pennsylvania
Cheyney University of Pennsylvania *M*
Indiana University of Pennsylvania *M*
Temple University *M*

Texas
Southwest Texas State University *M*
Texas A&M University
    Commerce *M*
Texas A&M University *B, M*
University of North Texas *M, D*

Virginia
James Madison University *M*
Virginia Commonwealth
    University *C, M*

Washington
Eastern Washington University *M*
Seattle University *M*
Western Washington University *M*

Wisconsin
University of Wisconsin
    Madison *M, D*

Advertising

Alabama
Spring Hill College *B*
University of Alabama *B, M*

Arizona
Northern Arizona University *B*

Arkansas
Harding University *B*
University of Arkansas
    Little Rock *B*

California
Art Center College of Design *B*
California Lutheran University *B*
California State University
    Fullerton *B, M*
    Hayward *B*
Chapman University *B*
College of San Mateo *A*
Irvine Valley College *A*
Los Angeles Southwest College *A*
Mount San Antonio College *A*
Orange Coast College *A*
Palomar College *C, A*
Pepperdine University *B*
San Diego State University *B*
San Jose State University *B*
Santa Ana College *C, A*
University of San Francisco *B*

Colorado
Adams State College *B*
Trinidad State Junior College *A*
University of Colorado
    Boulder *B*
University of Denver *M*
University of Southern Colorado *B*

Connecticut
Middlesex Community-Technical
    College *C*
Quinnipiac University *B*

Delaware
Delaware Technical and Community
    College
        Terry Campus *A*

District of Columbia
University of the District of Columbia *A*

Florida
Art Institute
    of Fort Lauderdale *A, B*
Barry University *B*
Florida Southern College *B*
Florida State University *B*
Gulf Coast Community College *A*
Manatee Community College *A*
Northwood University
    Florida Campus *A*
University of Central Florida *B*
University of Florida *B*
University of Miami *B*

Georgia
Clark Atlanta University *B*
University of Georgia *B*

Hawaii
Hawaii Pacific University *B*

Illinois
American Academy of Art *A, B*
Columbia College *B*
Concordia University *B*
Danville Area Community College *A*
Northwestern University *M*
Parkland College *A*
Richland Community College *A*
University of Illinois
    Urbana-Champaign *B, M*
University of St. Francis *B*

Indiana
Ball State University *B*
Franklin College *B*
Indiana State University *B*
Vincennes University *A*

Iowa
Clarke College *B*
Drake University *B*
Iowa Lakes Community College *A*
Iowa State University *B*
St. Ambrose University *B*

Kansas
Independence Community College *A*
Pittsburg State University *B*
University of Kansas *B*

Kentucky
Murray State University *B, M*
University of Kentucky *B*
Western Kentucky University *B*

Massachusetts
Babson College *B*
Emerson College *B, M*
Endicott College *B*
Mount Ida College *A*
Salem State College *B*
Suffolk University *M*
Western New England College *B*

Michigan
Bay de Noc Community College *C*
Central Michigan University *B*
Ferris State University *C, B*
Grand Valley State University *B*
Lansing Community College *A*
Michigan State University *B, M*
North Central Michigan College *C*
Northwood University *A*
Schoolcraft College *A*
Western Michigan University *B*

Minnesota
Concordia College: Moorhead *B*
Hennepin Technical College *C, A*
Moorhead State University *B*
St. Cloud State University *B*
St. Cloud Technical College *C, A*
Winona State University *B*

Mississippi
Jackson State University *M*
Mississippi Delta Community College *A*
University of Southern Mississippi *B*

Missouri
Drury University *B*
Southeast Missouri State University *B*

Advertising

St. Louis Community College
    St. Louis Community College at
        Florissant Valley *A*
Stephens College *B*
University of Missouri
    Columbia *B*
Washington University *B*
Webster University *B*

Nebraska
Hastings College *B*
Northeast Community College *A*
University of Nebraska
    Kearney *B*
    Lincoln *B*
    Omaha *B*

Nevada
University of Nevada
    Reno *B*

New Hampshire
Franklin Pierce College *B*
New England College *B*
New Hampshire College *B*

New Jersey
Fairleigh Dickinson University *B*
Rider University *B*
Rowan University *B*
Thomas Edison State College *B*

New Mexico
Santa Fe Community College *A*

New York
City University of New York
    Baruch College *B*
    City College *B*
    New York City Technical
        College *A*
Fashion Institute of Technology *A, B*
Iona College *B*
Marist College *B*
Medaille College *B*
New York Institute of Technology *B, M*
Onondaga Community College *A*
Pace University *B*
School of Visual Arts *B*
Syracuse University *B, M*

North Carolina
Alamance Community College *C*
Appalachian State University *B*
Campbell University *B*
Central Piedmont Community College *A*
Guilford Technical Community
    College *A*
Halifax Community College *A*

Ohio
Bowling Green State University *B*
Columbus College of Art and Design *B*
Kent State University
    Stark Campus *B*
Kent State University *B*
Marietta College *B*
Ohio University *B*
Wilmington College *B*
Xavier University *A, B*
Youngstown State University *B*

Oklahoma
Oklahoma Christian University of
    Science and Arts *B*
Oklahoma City University *B*
Southeastern Oklahoma State
    University *B*
University of Central Oklahoma *B*
University of Oklahoma *B*

Oregon
University of Oregon *B, M*

Pennsylvania
California University of Pennsylvania *B*
Community College of Beaver County *A*
Duquesne University *B*
Gannon University *B*

Mercyhurst College *B*
Penn State
    University Park *B, M*
Point Park College *B*
University of the Arts *B*
Waynesburg College *B*

Puerto Rico
University of Puerto Rico
    Carolina Regional College *A, B*
University of the Sacred Heart *B*

Rhode Island
Johnson & Wales University *A*

South Carolina
Greenville Technical College *C*
University of South Carolina *B*

South Dakota
Southeast Technical Institute *A*

Tennessee
Chattanooga State Technical Community
    College *A*
Union University *B*
University of Tennessee
    Knoxville *B*

Texas
Abilene Christian University *B*
Amarillo College *A*
Lamar University *B*
Palo Alto College *A*
Sam Houston State University *B*
Southern Methodist University *B*
Southwest Texas State University *B*
Texas A&M University
    Commerce *B*
Texas Christian University *B*
Texas Tech University *B*
University of Houston *B*
University of North Texas *B*
University of Texas
    Austin *B, M, D*
West Texas A&M University *B*

Utah
Brigham Young University *B*
Southern Utah University *B*

Vermont
Champlain College *A, B*

Virginia
Hampton University *B*

Washington
Seattle Central Community College *C, A*
Washington State University *B*

West Virginia
Bethany College *B*
Concord College *B*
West Virginia State College *A*

Wisconsin
Marquette University *B, M*

Aerospace/aeronautical/astronautical engineering

Alabama
Auburn University *B, M, D*
Tuskegee University *B*
University of Alabama *B, M*

Arizona
Arizona State University *B, M, D*
Embry-Riddle Aeronautical University
    Prescott Campus *B*
University of Arizona *B, M, D*

California
Allan Hancock College *A*
California Institute of
    Technology *B, M, D*
California Polytechnic State University:
    San Luis Obispo *B, M*

California State Polytechnic University:
    Pomona *B*
California State University
    Long Beach *B, M*
    Northridge *M*
Foothill College *A*
Merced College *A*
San Diego State University *B, M*
San Jose State University *B, M*
Stanford University *M, D*
University of California
    Davis *B*
    Irvine *B*
    Los Angeles *B, M, D*
    San Diego *B, M, D*
University of Southern
    California *B, M, D*

Colorado
United States Air Force Academy *B*
University of Colorado
    Boulder *B, M, D*
    Colorado Springs *M*

District of Columbia
George Washington University *M, D*

Florida
Embry-Riddle Aeronautical
    University *B, M*
Florida Institute of Technology *B, M, D*
University of Central Florida *B, M*
University of Florida *B, M, D*
University of Miami *B*

Georgia
Georgia Institute of Technology *B, M, D*

Hawaii
University of Hawaii
    Honolulu Community College *A*

Illinois
Illinois Institute of Technology *B*
Parkland College *A*
University of Illinois
    Urbana-Champaign *B, M, D*

Indiana
Purdue University *B, M, D*
University of Notre Dame *B, M, D*

Iowa
Iowa State University *B, M, D*

Kansas
University of Kansas *B, M, D*
Wichita State University *B, M, D*

Maryland
Prince George's Community College *A*
United States Naval Academy *B*
University of Maryland
    College Park *B, M, D*
    Eastern Shore *B*

Massachusetts
Boston University *B, M, D*
Massachusetts Institute of
    Technology *B, M, D*
Worcester Polytechnic Institute *B, M*

Michigan
University of Michigan *B, M, D*
Western Michigan University *B*

Minnesota
Northland Community & Technical
    College *A*
University of Minnesota
    Twin Cities *B, M, D*

Mississippi
Mississippi State University *B, M*

Missouri
East Central College *A*
St. Louis University *B*
University of Missouri
    Rolla *B, M, D*

New Hampshire
Daniel Webster College *A*

New Jersey
Rutgers
    The State University of New Jersey:
        College of Engineering *B*
    The State University of New Jersey:
        New Brunswick Graduate
        Campus *M, D*

New York
City University of New York
    Bronx Community College *A*
Clarkson University *B*
Cornell University *M, D*
New York Institute of Technology *B*
Polytechnic University
    Long Island Campus *M, D*
Polytechnic University *M*
Rensselaer Polytechnic Institute *B, M, D*
Rochester Institute of Technology *B*
State University of New York
    Buffalo *B, M, D*
Syracuse University *B, M, D*
United States Military Academy *B*

North Carolina
North Carolina State University *B, M, D*
St. Augustine's College *B*

North Dakota
North Dakota State University *B*

Ohio
Case Western Reserve
    University *B, M, D*
Kent State University
    Stark Campus *B*
Kent State University *B*
Ohio State University
    Columbus Campus *B, M, D*
University of Cincinnati *B, M, D*
University of Dayton *M, D*

Oklahoma
Oklahoma State University
    Oklahoma City *A*
Southeastern Oklahoma State
    University *B*
University of Oklahoma *B, M, D*

Pennsylvania
Gettysburg College *B*
Lock Haven University of
    Pennsylvania *B*
Penn State
    University Park *B, M, D*

Tennessee
University of Tennessee
    Knoxville *B, M, D*

Texas
Alvin Community College *C, A*
LeTourneau University *B*
Rice University *M, D*
Texas A&M University *B, M, D*
University of Houston *M, D*
University of Texas
    Arlington *B, M, D*
    Austin *B, M, D*

Utah
Utah State University *B*

Virginia
University of Virginia *B*
Virginia Polytechnic Institute and State
    University *B, M, D*

Washington
University of Washington *B, M, D*

West Virginia
West Virginia University *B, M, D*

African studies

California
Palomar College C
San Diego City College A
San Francisco State University B
Stanford University B
University of California
　Los Angeles M

Connecticut
Connecticut College B
Trinity College B
Yale University B, M

District of Columbia
Howard University B, M, D

Florida
Florida International University B
Manatee Community College A
University of Miami B

Georgia
Clark Atlanta University M, D
Emory University B
Morris Brown College B
Oxford College of Emory University B

Illinois
University of Illinois
　Urbana-Champaign M

Iowa
Luther College B
University of Iowa B

Kansas
University of Kansas B

Louisiana
Dillard University B

Maine
Bowdoin College B

Massachusetts
Brandeis University B
Hampshire College B
Harvard College B
Mount Holyoke College B
Tufts University M
Wellesley College B

Michigan
Lansing Community College A
Oakland University B
University of Michigan B
Western Michigan University B

Minnesota
Carleton College B
University of Minnesota
　Twin Cities B

Missouri
University of Missouri
　St. Louis C
Washington University B

New Hampshire
Dartmouth College B

New Jersey
Bloomfield College B
Rutgers
　The State University of New Jersey:
　　Douglass College B
　The State University of New Jersey:
　　Livingston College B
　The State University of New Jersey:
　　Newark College of Arts and
　　Sciences B
　The State University of New Jersey:
　　Rutgers College B
　The State University of New Jersey:
　　University College New
　　Brunswick B

New York
Bard College B
Barnard College B
City University of New York
　Brooklyn College B
　Queens College B
Colgate University B
Columbia University
　Columbia College B
　Graduate School M, D
　School of General Studies B
Cornell University B, M
Fordham University B
Hobart and William Smith Colleges B
Hofstra University B
Nassau Community College A
St. Lawrence University B
Sarah Lawrence College B
State University of New York
　Binghamton B
　Stony Brook B
Vassar College B

North Carolina
University of North Carolina
　Chapel Hill B

Ohio
Antioch College B
College of Wooster B
Kent State University
　Stark Campus B
Ohio State University
　Columbus Campus B, M
Ohio University B, M
University of Toledo B

Pennsylvania
Bryn Mawr College B
Lehigh University B
University of Pennsylvania B

South Carolina
Claflin University B

Texas
Southwest Texas State University B

Vermont
Marlboro College B

African-American studies

Arizona
Arizona State University B

California
California State University
　Dominguez Hills B
　Fresno B
　Fullerton B
　Hayward B
　Long Beach C, B
　Los Angeles B
　Northridge B
City College of San Francisco A
Claremont McKenna College B
Contra Costa College A
De Anza College C, A
East Los Angeles College A
Fresno City College A
Los Angeles Southwest College A
Loyola Marymount University B
Merritt College A
Pitzer College B
Pomona College B
San Diego City College A
San Diego Mesa College A
San Diego State University B
San Francisco State University B
San Jose State University B
Santa Ana College A
Santa Barbara City College A
Scripps College B
Solano Community College A
Sonoma State University B
Southwestern College A
Stanford University B
University of California
　Berkeley B, D
　Davis B
　Irvine B
　Los Angeles B, M
　Riverside B
　Santa Barbara B
University of Southern California B
Ventura College A

Colorado
Metropolitan State College of Denver B
University of Colorado
　Boulder B
University of Northern Colorado B

Connecticut
Trinity College B
Wesleyan University B
Yale University B, M, D

District of Columbia
Howard University B

Florida
Florida Agricultural and Mechanical
　University B
University of Miami B
University of South Florida B

Georgia
Clark Atlanta University M
Emory University B, M, D
Georgia State University B
Mercer University B
Morehouse College B
Morris Brown College B
Oxford College of Emory University B
University of Georgia B

Illinois
Chicago State University B
City Colleges of Chicago
　Kennedy-King College A
　Olive-Harvey College A
De Paul University B
Dominican University B
Eastern Illinois University B
Knox College B
Northwestern University B
Roosevelt University B
University of Illinois
　Chicago B

Indiana
Earlham College B
Indiana State University B
Indiana University
　Bloomington B
　Northwest B
Purdue University B

Iowa
Coe College B
Luther College B
University of Iowa B, M

Kansas
University of Kansas B

Kentucky
University of Louisville B

Maine
Bates College B
Bowdoin College B
Colby College B

Maryland
Morgan State University B, M, D
University of Maryland
　Baltimore County B
　College Park B

Massachusetts
Amherst College B
Boston University M
Brandeis University B
College of the Holy Cross B
Hampshire College B
Harvard College B
Harvard University M
Mount Holyoke College B
Northeastern University B
Simmons College B
Simon's Rock College of Bard B
Smith College B
Tufts University B
University of Massachusetts
　Amherst B, M, D
　Boston B
Wellesley College B

Michigan
Eastern Michigan University B
University of Michigan B
Wayne State University B
Western Michigan University B

Minnesota
Carleton College B
University of Minnesota
　Twin Cities B

Missouri
Washington University B

Nebraska
University of Nebraska
　Omaha B

New Hampshire
Dartmouth College B

New Jersey
Bloomfield College B
Richard Stockton College of New
　Jersey C
Rowan University B
Rutgers
　The State University of New Jersey:
　　Camden College of Arts and
　　Sciences B
　The State University of New Jersey:
　　Douglass College B
　The State University of New Jersey:
　　Livingston College B
　The State University of New Jersey:
　　Newark College of Arts and
　　Sciences B
　The State University of New Jersey:
　　Rutgers College B
　The State University of New Jersey:
　　University College Camden B
　The State University of New Jersey:
　　University College New
　　Brunswick B
Seton Hall University B
William Paterson University of New
　Jersey B

New Mexico
University of New Mexico B

New York
Audrey Cohen College A, B
City University of New York
　Brooklyn College B
　City College B
　College of Staten Island B
　Hunter College B
　Lehman College B
　York College B
Columbia University
　Columbia College B
　Graduate School M
　School of General Studies B
Cornell University B, M
Eugene Lang College/New School
　University B
Fordham University B
Hamilton College B
Hobart and William Smith Colleges B
Manhattanville College B
New York University B, M
Sarah Lawrence College B

African-American studies

State University of New York
  Albany *B, M*
  Binghamton *B*
  Buffalo *B*
  College at Brockport *B*
  College at Cortland *B*
  College at Geneseo *B*
  College at Oneonta *B*
  New Paltz *B*
  Stony Brook *B*
Syracuse University *B*

North Carolina
Duke University *B*
St. Augustine's College *B*
University of North Carolina
  Chapel Hill *B*
  Charlotte *B*

Ohio
Antioch College *B*
College of Wooster *B*
Denison University *B*
Kent State University *B*
Miami University
  Oxford Campus *B*
Oberlin College *B*
Ohio State University
  Columbus Campus *B, M*
Ohio University *B*
Ohio Wesleyan University *B*
University of Cincinnati *B*
Youngstown State University *B*

Oklahoma
Oklahoma State University *C*
University of Oklahoma *B*
University of Tulsa *C*

Pennsylvania
Franklin and Marshall College *B*
Gettysburg College *B*
Lincoln University *B*
Penn State
  University Park *B*
Temple University *B, M, D*
University of Pennsylvania *B*
University of Pittsburgh *B*

Rhode Island
Brown University *B*
Providence College *B*
Rhode Island College *B*
University of Rhode Island *B*

South Carolina
Claflin University *B*
University of South Carolina *B*

Tennessee
University of Tennessee
  Knoxville *B*
Vanderbilt University *B*

Texas
Southern Methodist University *B*

Vermont
Goddard College *B*
Marlboro College *B*

Virginia
College of William and Mary *B*
University of Virginia *B*

Wisconsin
Marquette University *B*
University of Wisconsin
  Madison *B, M*

Agribusiness operations

Alabama
Alabama Agricultural and Mechanical
  University *B, M*
Wallace State Community College at
  Hanceville *C, A*

Arizona
Eastern Arizona College *A*
Mesa Community College *A*

Arkansas
Arkansas State University *B*
University of Arkansas *B*

California
Allan Hancock College *C, A*
Bakersfield College *A*
College of the Redwoods *A*
San Joaquin Delta College *C, A*
Santa Clara University *M*
Santa Rosa Junior College *C, A*
Shasta College *C, A*
Ventura College *C, A*

Delaware
Delaware Technical and Community
  College
    Owens Campus *C, A*
University of Delaware *B*

Florida
Florida Agricultural and Mechanical
  University *B*
Indian River Community College *A*
Miami-Dade Community College *A*

Georgia
South Georgia College *A*

Hawaii
University of Hawaii
  Hilo *B*

Idaho
Ricks College *A*

Illinois
Black Hawk College *C, A*
Danville Area Community College *A*
Illinois State University *B, M*
Kishwaukee College *A*
Lincoln Land Community College *A*
Parkland College *A*

Iowa
Des Moines Area Community College *C*
Dordt College *B*
Iowa State University *B*
Iowa Western Community College *A*
North Iowa Area Community College *A*

Kansas
Colby Community College *A*
Cowley County Community
  College *C, A*
Dodge City Community College *C, A*
McPherson College *B*
MidAmerica Nazarene University *B*

Kentucky
Midway College *B*
Morehead State University *A*
Murray State University *B*

Louisiana
Nicholls State University *B*

Maryland
University of Maryland
  College Park *B, M, D*
  Eastern Shore *B*

Michigan
Delta College *A*

Minnesota
Ridgewater College: A Community and
  Technical College *A*
Southwest State University *C, A, B*
University of Minnesota
  Crookston *A, B*

Mississippi
Hinds Community College *A*
Mississippi State University *B*
Northwest Mississippi Community
  College *A*

Missouri
College of the Ozarks *B*
Crowder College *A*
Mineral Area College *C, A*

Nebraska
Nebraska College of Technical
  Agriculture *A*
Northeast Community College *A*

New Mexico
Eastern New Mexico University *B*

New York
Cornell University *B*

North Carolina
North Carolina State University *B*
Wayne Community College *A*

North Dakota
Bismarck State College *A*
North Dakota State College of Science *A*

Ohio
Clark State Community College *A*
Owens Community College
  Toledo *A*
Wilmington College *B*

Oklahoma
Northern Oklahoma College *A*
Oklahoma State University *B*
Redlands Community College *A*
Western Oklahoma State College *A*

Pennsylvania
Delaware Valley College *B*
Penn State
  Abington *A*
  Altoona *A*
  Berks *A*
  Delaware County *A*
  Erie, The Behrend College *A*
  Fayette *A*
  Hazleton *A*
  Mont Alto *A*
  New Kensington *A*
  Schuylkill - Capital College *A*
  Shenango *A*
  University Park *B*
  Wilkes-Barre *A*
  Worthington Scranton *A*
  York *A*

South Carolina
Clemson University *B*
South Carolina State University *B, M*

South Dakota
Western Dakota Technical Institute *A*

Tennessee
Middle Tennessee State University *B*
Motlow State Community College *A*
Tennessee Technological University *B*

Texas
Abilene Christian University *B*
Angelo State University *B*
Palo Alto College *C, A*
Southwest Texas State University *B*
Stephen F. Austin State University *B*
Sul Ross State University *B, M*
Texas A&M University
  Kingsville *B*
Texas A&M University *B, M, D*
Texas State Technical College
  Harlingen *C, A*

Utah
Brigham Young University *B*
Snow College *C, A*
Utah State University *M*

Vermont
Vermont Technical College *A*

Washington
Columbia Basin College *A*

Wisconsin
Southwest Wisconsin Technical
  College *A*
University of Wisconsin
  Madison *B*
  Platteville *B*
Western Wisconsin Technical College *A*

Wyoming
Casper College *A*
Central Wyoming College *A*
Eastern Wyoming College *A*

Agricultural animal breeding/genetics

California
Modesto Junior College *A*

Illinois
John Wood Community College *C, A*
Kishwaukee College *C, A*

Iowa
Iowa State University *M, D*

Mississippi
Hinds Community College *A*

New York
Cornell University *B, M, D*

Ohio
Lake Erie College *B*

Oklahoma
Northeastern Oklahoma Agricultural and
  Mechanical College *A*
Oklahoma State University *M, D*

Texas
Tarleton State University *B*
Texas A&M University *M, D*

Virginia
College of William and Mary *B*

Agricultural animal health

California
Los Angeles Pierce College *A*

Colorado
Colorado Mountain College
  Spring Valley Campus *A*

Idaho
University of Idaho *B, M, D*

Massachusetts
North Shore Community College *A*

Nebraska
Nebraska College of Technical
  Agriculture *A*
University of Nebraska
  Lincoln *M*

New York
Cornell University *B*

Oklahoma
Oklahoma State University *M*

Texas
Sul Ross State University *A, B*

Agricultural animal nutrition

Georgia
University of Georgia *D*

Illinois
Joliet Junior College *C*

Iowa
Iowa State University *M, D*

Agricultural business

New York
Cornell University *B, M, D*

North Carolina
North Carolina State University *M, D*

Oklahoma
Oklahoma State University *D*

Texas
Texas A&M University *M, D*

Agricultural animal physiology

Idaho
University of Idaho *D*

New York
Cornell University *B*

North Carolina
North Carolina State University *M, D*

Utah
Snow College *A*

Agricultural business

Alabama
Alabama Agricultural and Mechanical University *B*
Central Alabama Community College *A*
Enterprise State Junior College *A*
James H. Faulkner State Community College *A*
Jefferson State Community College *A*
Northeast Alabama Community College *A*
Northwest-Shoals Community College *C*

Arizona
Arizona Western College *A*
Central Arizona College *C, A*

Arkansas
Arkansas State University
  Beebe Branch *A*
Arkansas Tech University *B*
Southern Arkansas University *B*
Westark College *A*

California
Butte College *C, A*
California Polytechnic State University:
  San Luis Obispo *B*
California State Polytechnic University:
  Pomona *B*
California State University
  Chico *B*
  Fresno *B*
College of the Desert *A*
College of the Redwoods *C*
College of the Sequoias *C*
Imperial Valley College *C, A*
Kings River Community College *C, A*
Los Angeles Pierce College *C, A*
Merced College *A*
MiraCosta College *C, A*
Modesto Junior College *A*
Mount San Antonio College *A*
Riverside Community College *A*
San Diego State University *B*
San Joaquin Delta College *A*
Santa Rosa Junior College *C*
Shasta College *A*
University of California
  Davis *B*
West Hills Community College *A*
Yuba College *C*

Colorado
Colorado State University *B*
Fort Lewis College *B*
Lamar Community College *A*
Northeastern Junior College *C*

Delaware
Delaware State University *B*
University of Delaware *B*

Florida
Florida Southern College *B*
Hillsborough Community College *C, A*
Indian River Community College *A*
Pensacola Junior College *A*
South Florida Community College *A*

Georgia
Abraham Baldwin Agricultural College *A*
Gainesville College *C*
South Georgia College *A*
University of Georgia *B*

Idaho
College of Southern Idaho *C, A*

Illinois
Black Hawk College
  East Campus *C, A*
Black Hawk College *A*
Carl Sandburg College *A*
Highland Community College *A*
Illinois Eastern Community Colleges
  Wabash Valley College *A*
John A. Logan College *A*
John Wood Community College *A*
Kaskaskia College *C, A*
Kishwaukee College *C, A*
Lake Land College *C*
Lewis and Clark Community College *C, A*
Lincoln Land Community College *A*
Parkland College *C, A*
Rend Lake College *A*
Richland Community College *A*
Shawnee Community College *A*

Iowa
American Institute of Business *A*
Des Moines Area Community College *A*
Hawkeye Community College *A*
Marshalltown Community College *A*
North Iowa Area Community College *A*
Northeast Iowa Community College *A*
Southeastern Community College
  North Campus *A*
Southwestern Community College *A*
Waldorf College *A*

Kansas
Central Christian College *A*
Coffeyville Community College *A*
Cowley County Community College *C, A*
Dodge City Community College *A*
Fort Hays State University *B*
Garden City Community College *A*
Hutchinson Community College *C, A*
Independence Community College *A*
Kansas State University *B, M*
MidAmerica Nazarene University *B*
Pratt Community College *C, A*
Seward County Community College *A*

Kentucky
Berea College *B*
Henderson Community College *C*
Lindsey Wilson College *A*
Owensboro Community College *A*

Louisiana
Louisiana State University and Agricultural and Mechanical College *B*
Louisiana Tech University *B*
University of Louisiana at Monroe *B*

Maine
University of Maine *B*

Michigan
Andrews University *A, B*
Delta College *A*
Michigan State University *C, B*

Minnesota
Northland Community & Technical College *A*
Ridgewater College: A Community and Technical College *C, A*
Southwest State University *C*
University of Minnesota
  Crookston *A, B*
  Twin Cities *B*

Mississippi
Alcorn State University *B*
Mississippi Delta Community College *A*
Mississippi State University *M*

Missouri
Central Missouri State University *B*
College of the Ozarks *B*
Mineral Area College *C, A*
Missouri Valley College *B*
Northwest Missouri State University *B*
Southeast Missouri State University *B*
Southwest Missouri State University *B*
State Fair Community College *A*
Three Rivers Community College *A*
University of Missouri
  Columbia *B*

Montana
Dawson Community College *C, A*
Miles Community College *A*
Montana State University
  Bozeman *A*
  Northern *A*
Rocky Mountain College *B*

Nebraska
Central Community College *C, A*
Nebraska College of Technical Agriculture *A*
Northeast Community College *A*
University of Nebraska
  Kearney *B*
  Lincoln *B*

New Hampshire
University of New Hampshire *B*

New Jersey
County College of Morris *A*
Rutgers
  The State University of New Jersey:
  Cook College *B*

New Mexico
New Mexico State University *B*

New York
Cornell University *B*
State University of New York
  College of Agriculture and Technology at Cobleskill *A, B*
  College of Agriculture and Technology at Morrisville *A*
  College of Technology at Alfred *A*

North Carolina
James Sprunt Community College *A*
North Carolina Agricultural and Technical State University *B*
North Carolina State University *B*
Surry Community College *A*

North Dakota
Dickinson State University *A, B*
Lake Region State College *C, A*
North Dakota State College of Science *A*

Ohio
Northwestern College *C, A*
Ohio State University
  Columbus Campus *B*
Owens Community College
  Toledo *C, A*
Terra Community College *A*
Wilmington College *B*

Oklahoma
Eastern Oklahoma State College *C, A*
Langston University *B*
Northeastern Oklahoma Agricultural and Mechanical College *A*
Northwestern Oklahoma State University *B*
Oklahoma Panhandle State University *B*
Oklahoma State University *B*
Redlands Community College *A*
Rogers State University *A*

Oregon
Chemeketa Community College *C*
Eastern Oregon University *B*
Linn-Benton Community College *A*
Oregon State University *B*

Pennsylvania
Penn State
  Beaver *A*
  Dubois *A*
  McKeesport *A*
  University Park *A*

Puerto Rico
University of Puerto Rico
  Mayaguez Campus *B*

South Dakota
Dakota Wesleyan University *B*
South Dakota State University *B*
Western Dakota Technical Institute *A*

Tennessee
Columbia State Community College *A*
Freed-Hardeman University *B*
Hiwassee College *A*
Jackson State Community College *A*
University of Tennessee
  Knoxville *B*
  Martin *B*

Texas
Hill College *A*
Howard College *A*
Lubbock Christian University *A, B*
Navarro College *A*
Sam Houston State University *M*
South Plains College *A*
Tarleton State University *B*
Texas A&M University
  Commerce *M*
  Kingsville *B, M*
Texas A&M University *B, M*
Texas Tech University *B*
Trinity Valley Community College *A*
Weatherford College *C, A*
West Texas A&M University *B*

Utah
Brigham Young University *B*
Snow College *A*
Southern Utah University *B*
Utah State University *B*

Vermont
Vermont Technical College *A*

Virginia
Lord Fairfax Community College *A*

Washington
Columbia Basin College *A*
Highline Community College *A*
Skagit Valley College *A*
Spokane Community College *A*
Walla Walla Community College *C, A*
Washington State University *B, M*
Yakima Valley Community College *C, A*

Wisconsin
Moraine Park Technical College *C*
Northeast Wisconsin Technical College *A*
Southwest Wisconsin Technical College *A*
University of Wisconsin
  Madison *B*
  River Falls *B*

Agricultural business

Wyoming
Central Wyoming College *A*
Laramie County Community College *A*
Northwest College *A*
Sheridan College *C, A*
University of Wyoming *B*

Agricultural economics

Alabama
Auburn University *B, M, D*
Tuskegee University *M*

Arizona
University of Arizona *B, M*

Arkansas
University of Arkansas *M*

California
San Joaquin Delta College *A*
University of California
 Davis *B, M, D*

Colorado
Colorado State University *B, M, D*

Connecticut
University of Connecticut *B, M, D*

Delaware
University of Delaware *B, M*

Florida
University of Florida *B, M, D*

Georgia
University of Georgia *B, M, D*

Idaho
University of Idaho *B, M*

Illinois
Black Hawk College *C*

Indiana
Purdue University *A, B, M, D*

Iowa
Iowa State University *M, D*

Kansas
Coffeyville Community College *A*
Garden City Community College *A*
Kansas State University *B, M, D*

Kentucky
Eastern Kentucky University *A*
University of Kentucky *M, D*

Louisiana
Louisiana State University and
 Agricultural and Mechanical
 College *M, D*
Southern University and Agricultural and
 Mechanical College *B*

Maine
University of Maine *B, M*

Maryland
University of Maryland
 College Park *C, B, M, D*

Michigan
Michigan State University *B, M, D*

Minnesota
Northland Community & Technical
 College *A*
Ridgewater College: A Community and
 Technical College *A*
Southwest State University *C*
University of Minnesota
 Twin Cities *B, M, D*

Mississippi
Mississippi State University *B, M, D*
Northwest Mississippi Community
 College *A*

Missouri
Central Missouri State University *B*
Truman State University *B*
University of Missouri
 Columbia *B, M, D*

Nebraska
University of Nebraska
 Lincoln *B, M, D*

Nevada
University of Nevada
 Reno *B, M*

New Jersey
Rutgers
 The State University of New Jersey:
 New Brunswick Graduate
 Campus *M*

New Mexico
New Mexico State University *M*

New York
Cornell University *M*

North Carolina
North Carolina Agricultural and
 Technical State University *M*
North Carolina State University *B, M*

North Dakota
North Dakota State University *B, M*

Ohio
Ohio State University
 Columbus Campus *B, M, D*

Oklahoma
Eastern Oklahoma State College *A*
Langston University *B*
Northeastern Oklahoma Agricultural and
 Mechanical College *A*
Oklahoma State University *B*

Oregon
Eastern Oregon University *B*
Oregon State University *B, M, D*

Puerto Rico
University of Puerto Rico
 Mayaguez Campus *M*

South Carolina
Clemson University *B, M, D*

South Dakota
South Dakota State University *B*

Tennessee
Hiwassee College *A*
University of Tennessee
 Knoxville *M, D*

Texas
Lubbock Christian University *B*
Prairie View A&M University *M*
Tarleton State University *B*
Texas A&M University
 Commerce *B, M*
Texas A&M University *B, M, D*
Texas Tech University *B, M, D*

Utah
Southern Utah University *B*
Utah State University *B, M*

Vermont
University of Vermont *B, M*

Virginia
Virginia Polytechnic Institute and State
 University *B, M, D*

Washington
Washington State University *B, M, D*

Wisconsin
University of Wisconsin
 Madison *B, M, D*
 Platteville *B*

Wyoming
Eastern Wyoming College *A*
University of Wyoming *M*

Agricultural education

Arizona
University of Arizona *B, M*

Arkansas
Arkansas State University *B, M, T*
Southern Arkansas University *B, T*
University of Arkansas
 Pine Bluff *B, T*
University of Arkansas *B, M*

California
California Polytechnic State University:
 San Luis Obispo *B, T*
California State Polytechnic University:
 Pomona *T*
California State University
 Chico *T*
 Fresno *M*
University of California
 Davis *T*

Colorado
Colorado State University *B, T*

Connecticut
University of Connecticut *B, T*

Delaware
University of Delaware *B, T*

Florida
University of Florida *B, M, D*

Georgia
Fort Valley State University *B, T*
University of Georgia *B, M*

Idaho
University of Idaho *B, M, T*

Illinois
Southern Illinois University
 Carbondale *M*
University of Illinois
 Urbana-Champaign *B, M, T*

Indiana
Purdue University *A*
Vincennes University *A*

Iowa
Iowa State University *B, M, D, T*

Kansas
Colby Community College *A*
Kansas State University *B*
Wichita State University *T*

Kentucky
Morehead State University *B*
Murray State University *B, T*
Western Kentucky University *B, M*

Louisiana
Southern University and Agricultural and
 Mechanical College *B*

Maryland
University of Maryland
 Eastern Shore *B*

Minnesota
Ridgewater College: A Community and
 Technical College *A*
University of Minnesota
 Twin Cities *B, M, T*

Mississippi
Mississippi State University *B, M, T*
Northwest Mississippi Community
 College *A*

Missouri
Central Missouri State University *B, T*

Northwest Missouri State
 University *B, M, T*
Southwest Missouri State University *B*
University of Missouri
 Columbia *B*

Montana
Miles Community College *A*
Montana State University
 Bozeman *B, M, T*

Nebraska
University of Nebraska
 Lincoln *B, M*

Nevada
University of Nevada
 Reno *B*

New Mexico
New Mexico State University *B, M*

New York
Cornell University *B, T*
State University of New York
 Oswego *T*

North Carolina
North Carolina Agricultural and
 Technical State University *B, M, T*
North Carolina State University *M, T*

North Dakota
North Dakota State University *B, M, T*

Ohio
Ohio State University
 Columbus Campus *B, M, D*
Wilmington College *B*

Oklahoma
East Central University *B*
Eastern Oklahoma State College *A*
Northeastern Oklahoma Agricultural and
 Mechanical College *A*
Oklahoma Panhandle State University *B*
Oklahoma State University *B, M, D, T*

Oregon
Oregon State University *M*

Pennsylvania
Delaware Valley College *T*
Penn State
 University Park *M, D*

South Carolina
Clemson University *B, M*

South Dakota
South Dakota State University *B, M*

Tennessee
Tennessee Technological University *B, T*
University of Tennessee
 Knoxville *B, M, T*
 Martin *B, T*

Texas
Prairie View A&M University *M*
Sam Houston State University *M, T*
Southwest Texas State University *M, T*
Stephen F. Austin State University *T*
Tarleton State University *B, M, T*
Texas A&M University
 Commerce *M, T*
 Kingsville *B, M*
Texas A&M University *B, M, D*
Texas Tech University *M*

Utah
Snow College *A*
Utah State University *B*

Vermont
University of Vermont *T*

Washington
Washington State University *B, T*

West Virginia
West Virginia University *B, M, T*

Wisconsin
University of Wisconsin
　　Madison B, M, T
　　Platteville B, T
　　River Falls B, M, T

Wyoming
Casper College A
Eastern Wyoming College A
Northwest College A
University of Wyoming B

Agricultural engineering

Alabama
Auburn University M
Northeast Alabama Community
　　College A

Arizona
University of Arizona B, M, D

Arkansas
University of Arkansas B, M

California
California State Polytechnic University:
　　Pomona B
Imperial Valley College C, A
University of California
　　Davis B, M, D

Colorado
Colorado State University B, M, D

Delaware
University of Delaware B

Florida
University of Florida B, M, D

Georgia
Abraham Baldwin Agricultural
　　College A
Atlanta Metropolitan College A
Fort Valley State University B
Georgia Perimeter College A
Middle Georgia College A
University of Georgia B, M, D

Hawaii
University of Hawaii
　　Manoa B, M

Idaho
College of Southern Idaho A
North Idaho College A
University of Idaho B, M, D

Illinois
Judson College B
Parkland College A
University of Illinois
　　Urbana-Champaign B, M, D

Indiana
Purdue University B, M, D
Vincennes University A

Iowa
Iowa State University B, M, D

Kansas
Kansas State University B, M, D

Kentucky
University of Kentucky B, M, D

Louisiana
Louisiana State University and
　　Agricultural and Mechanical
　　College B

Maine
University of Maine B, M

Maryland
Anne Arundel Community College A

Michigan
Michigan State University B, M, D

Minnesota
Concordia College: Moorhead B
University of Minnesota
　　Twin Cities B, M, D

Mississippi
Mississippi Gulf Coast Community
　　College
　　Perkinston A
Mississippi State University B

Missouri
University of Missouri
　　Columbia B, M, D

Nebraska
University of Nebraska
　　Lincoln B, M

New Jersey
Rutgers
　　The State University of New Jersey:
　　　　College of Engineering B
　　The State University of New Jersey:
　　　　Cook College B
　　The State University of New Jersey:
　　　　New Brunswick Graduate
　　　　Campus M

New Mexico
New Mexico State University B

New York
Cornell University B, M, D
State University of New York
　　College of Agriculture and
　　　　Technology at Cobleskill A, B
　　College of Agriculture and
　　　　Technology at Morrisville A

North Carolina
North Carolina Agricultural and
　　Technical State University B
North Carolina State University B, M, D
St. Augustine's College B

North Dakota
North Dakota State University B, M

Ohio
Ohio State University
　　Columbus Campus B, M, D

Oklahoma
Northeastern Oklahoma Agricultural and
　　Mechanical College A
Oklahoma State University B, M, D

Oregon
Oregon State University M, D

Pennsylvania
Lock Haven University of
　　Pennsylvania B
Penn State
　　University Park C, B, M, D

South Carolina
Clemson University B, M, D

South Dakota
South Dakota State University B, M

Tennessee
Hiwassee College A
Tennessee Technological University B
University of Tennessee
　　Knoxville B, M, D

Texas
Kilgore College A
Texas A&M University B, M, D

Utah
Utah State University B, M, D

Washington
Washington State University B

Wisconsin
University of Wisconsin
　　Madison B, M, D
　　River Falls B

Agricultural food processing

California
Modesto Junior College A
Napa Valley College C, A

Hawaii
University of Hawaii
　　Hawaii Community College A

Illinois
Kishwaukee College A
Richland Community College A
University of Illinois
　　Urbana-Champaign B

Iowa
Iowa State University M, D

Kansas
Garden City Community College A
Kansas State University B, M, D

Kentucky
Murray State University B, M

Michigan
Michigan State University B

Minnesota
University of Minnesota
　　Crookston B

New York
Cornell University B

North Carolina
Bladen Community College C
North Carolina State University A
Southeastern Community College A

Ohio
Ohio State University
　　Columbus Campus B

Oregon
Mount Hood Community College A

Puerto Rico
University of Puerto Rico
　　Mayaguez Campus M

Rhode Island
Johnson & Wales University A

Texas
Texas A&M University M, D
Texas State Technical College
　　Waco C

Washington
Highline Community College A

Wisconsin
Moraine Park Technical College C, A

Wyoming
Casper College A

Agricultural mechanization

California
Bakersfield College A
Butte College C, A
California Polytechnic State University:
　　San Luis Obispo B
College of the Desert C, A
College of the Sequoias C
Imperial Valley College A
Kings River Community College C
Merced College C, A
Modesto Junior College C, A
Mount San Antonio College C, A
San Joaquin Delta College C, A
Shasta College A
West Hills Community College C, A
Yuba College C

Colorado
Northeastern Junior College C, A

Georgia
Fort Valley State University B

Idaho
Boise State University A
Lewis-Clark State College A
Ricks College C, A

Illinois
Black Hawk College C, A
Kishwaukee College C, A
Lake Land College C, A
Parkland College A
Southern Illinois University
　　Carbondale M
University of Illinois
　　Urbana-Champaign B

Indiana
Purdue University A, B

Iowa
Hawkeye Community College A
Iowa Lakes Community College C
Iowa State University B
Kirkwood Community College A
North Iowa Area Community College A

Kansas
Garden City Community College A
Hutchinson Community College C, A
Kansas State University B
Pratt Community College C, A

Kentucky
Eastern Kentucky University B
Murray State University B

Michigan
Michigan State University C

Minnesota
Central Lakes College C
South Central Technical College A

Mississippi
Hinds Community College C
Northwest Mississippi Community
　　College A

Missouri
Northwest Missouri State University B
University of Missouri
　　Columbia B

Montana
Miles Community College A
Montana State University
　　Bozeman B

Nebraska
Nebraska College of Technical
　　Agriculture A
Northeast Community College A
University of Nebraska
　　Lincoln B, M

New York
State University of New York
　　College of Agriculture and
　　　　Technology at Morrisville A

North Carolina
Beaufort County Community College A
North Carolina State University A

North Dakota
Lake Region State College C
North Dakota State University B, M

Ohio
Northwestern College C, A

Agricultural mechanization

Oklahoma
Cameron University *B*
Oklahoma State University *M*

Oregon
Lane Community College *C, A*
Portland Community College *A*

Pennsylvania
Penn State
   Erie, The Behrend College *B*
   University Park *B*

Puerto Rico
University of Puerto Rico
   Mayaguez Campus *B*

South Carolina
Clemson University *B*

South Dakota
South Dakota State University *B*

Texas
Sam Houston State University *B, M*
Southwest Texas State University *B*
Stephen F. Austin State University *B*
Tarleton State University *B*

Utah
Utah State University *C, A*

Washington
Centralia College *A*
Walla Walla Community College *C, A*
Washington State University *B*
Yakima Valley Community College *A*

Wisconsin
Madison Area Technical College *C, A*
Moraine Park Technical College *C*
Southwest Wisconsin Technical
   College *C*
Wisconsin Indianhead Technical
   College *C*

Wyoming
Casper College *A*

Agricultural plant pathology

Arizona
University of Arizona *M, D*

California
University of California
   Davis *M, D*
   Riverside *M, D*

New Jersey
Rutgers
   The State University of New Jersey:
     Cook College *B*
   The State University of New Jersey:
     New Brunswick Graduate
     Campus *M, D*

New Mexico
New Mexico State University *B, M*

New York
Cornell University *B, M, D*

North Carolina
North Carolina State University *M, D*

North Dakota
North Dakota State University *M, D*

Oklahoma
Oklahoma State University *M, D*

South Carolina
Clemson University *B, M*

South Dakota
South Dakota State University *M*

Tennessee
University of Tennessee
   Knoxville *M*

Texas
Texas A&M University *M, D*

Washington
Washington State University *B*

Agricultural plant physiology

Delaware
University of Delaware *B*

New Jersey
Rutgers
   The State University of New Jersey:
     New Brunswick Graduate
     Campus *M, D*

North Carolina
North Carolina State University *M, D*

Agricultural production

Alabama
Auburn University *B, M, D*
Central Alabama Community College *A*
Gadsden State Community College *C*
Northwest-Shoals Community College *C*

Arizona
Prescott College *B, M*

Arkansas
University of Arkansas
   Pine Bluff *M*
University of Arkansas *M*

California
Butte College *A*
San Joaquin Delta College *A*
Shasta College *A*

Colorado
Lamar Community College *A*
Northeastern Junior College *C, A*

Connecticut
University of Connecticut *B*

Florida
South Florida Community College *A*

Hawaii
University of Hawaii
   Manoa *B*

Idaho
Ricks College *A*

Illinois
Black Hawk College
   East Campus *C, A*
Black Hawk College *C, A*
Carl Sandburg College *C*
Illinois Eastern Community Colleges
   Wabash Valley College *A*
John Wood Community College *C*
Joliet Junior College *C, A*
Kishwaukee College *C*
Lake Land College *A*
Richland Community College *A*

Indiana
Purdue University *D*

Iowa
Hawkeye Community College *A*
Iowa Lakes Community College *A*
Iowa State University *M, D*
Kirkwood Community College *A*
Muscatine Community College *A*
North Iowa Area Community College *A*
Southeastern Community College
   North Campus *A*
Western Iowa Tech Community
   College *C*

Kansas
Barton County Community College *C, A*
Cowley County Community
   College *C, A*
Garden City Community College *A*
Pratt Community College *C, A*

Kentucky
Western Kentucky University *A*

Maine
University of Maine *B*

Massachusetts
University of Massachusetts
   Amherst *A*

Minnesota
Alexandria Technical College *C, A*
Ridgewater College: A Community and
   Technical College *C*
University of Minnesota
   Crookston *B*

Montana
Dawson Community College *C*

Nebraska
Central Community College *C*
Nebraska College of Technical
   Agriculture *A*
Northeast Community College *A*

North Carolina
Bladen Community College *C*
North Carolina State University *A*
Wayne Community College *A*

Ohio
Ohio State University
   Columbus Campus *B*
Southern State Community College *A*
Wilmington College *B*

Oklahoma
Northeastern Oklahoma Agricultural and
   Mechanical College *A*
Oklahoma State University *M*

Puerto Rico
University of Puerto Rico
   Utuado *A*

South Dakota
Western Dakota Technical Institute *A*

Texas
Angelo State University *B*
Central Texas College *C, A*
Odessa College *C, A*
Southwest Texas State University *B, T*
Stephen F. Austin State University *B*
Texas A&M University
   Corpus Christi *M*
Texas Tech University *B*

Vermont
Sterling College *A, B*

Virginia
Virginia Polytechnic Institute and State
   University *A, B, M*

Washington
Columbia Basin College *A*
Spokane Community College *A*
Walla Walla Community College *C, A*
Washington State University *B*
Yakima Valley Community College *C, A*

Wyoming
Central Wyoming College *C, A*
Sheridan College *A*

Agricultural sciences

Alabama
Auburn University *B*
Calhoun Community College *A*
Central Alabama Community College *A*
Chattahoochee Valley Community
   College *A*
James H. Faulkner State Community
   College *A*
Northeast Alabama Community
   College *A*
Northwest-Shoals Community College *C*

Alaska
University of Alaska
   Fairbanks *B*

Arizona
Arizona Western College *C, A*
Central Arizona College *C, A*
Cochise College *A*
Eastern Arizona College *A*
Prescott College *B*
University of Arizona *B*

Arkansas
Arkansas State University *B, M*
Southern Arkansas University *B*
University of Arkansas
   Monticello *B*
   Pine Bluff *B*

California
Butte College *C, A*
California Polytechnic State University:
   San Luis Obispo *M*
California State Polytechnic University:
   Pomona *B, M*
California State University
   Chico *B*
Cerritos Community College *A*
College of the Desert *A*
College of the Sequoias *C, A*
Cuesta College *C, A*
Imperial Valley College *A*
Kings River Community College *A*
Los Angeles Pierce College *C, A*
Merced College *A*
Modesto Junior College *C, A*
Riverside Community College *A*
San Joaquin Delta College *C, A*
Santa Rosa Junior College *C*
Shasta College *A*
Sierra College *C, A*
University of California
   Berkeley *M, D*
Ventura College *A*
West Hills Community College *A*

Colorado
Colorado State University *B, M*
Lamar Community College *A*

Connecticut
University of Connecticut *B, M, D*

Delaware
Delaware State University *B*
University of Delaware *A, B*

Florida
Broward Community College *A*
Chipola Junior College *A*
Florida Agricultural and Mechanical
   University *B, M*
Indian River Community College *A*
Pensacola Junior College *A*
Polk Community College *A*
South Florida Community College *A*

Georgia
Abraham Baldwin Agricultural
   College *A*
Andrew College *A*
Atlanta Metropolitan College *A*
Clayton College and State University *A*

Dalton State College A
Darton College A
East Georgia College A
Floyd College A
Fort Valley State University B
Gainesville College A
Georgia Perimeter College A
South Georgia College A
Waycross College A
Young Harris College A

Hawaii
University of Hawaii
 Hawaii Community College C, A
 Hilo B
 Windward Community College C

Idaho
College of Southern Idaho A
North Idaho College A
Ricks College C
University of Idaho B

Illinois
Black Hawk College A
Highland Community College A
Illinois State University B
Kishwaukee College A
Lake Land College A
Lewis and Clark Community College A
Lincoln Land Community College A
Shawnee Community College A
Southern Illinois University
 Carbondale B
University of Illinois
 Urbana-Champaign B
Western Illinois University B

Indiana
Purdue University A, B, M
Vincennes University A

Iowa
Dordt College A, B
Hawkeye Community College A
Maharishi University of Management B
Marshalltown Community College A

Kansas
Allen County Community College C, A
Barton County Community College A
Butler County Community College A
Central Christian College A
Coffeyville Community College A
Colby Community College A
Cowley County Community College A
Fort Hays State University B
Garden City Community College A
Hutchinson Community College A
Pratt Community College A
Seward County Community College A

Kentucky
Berea College B
Morehead State University B
Murray State University B, M
University of Kentucky B
Western Kentucky University B, M, T

Louisiana
McNeese State University B
Southern University and Agricultural and Mechanical College B
University of Louisiana at Lafayette B

Maine
University of Maine B, M

Maryland
University of Maryland
 College Park B
 Eastern Shore B, M

Massachusetts
Hampshire College B

Michigan
Hillsdale College B
Michigan State University B

St. Clair County Community College A

Minnesota
Ridgewater College: A Community and Technical College A
University of Minnesota
 Twin Cities B, M

Mississippi
Alcorn State University B, M
Mississippi Delta Community College A
Mississippi State University B

Missouri
Crowder College A
Lincoln University A, B
Northwest Missouri State
 University B, M
Southeast Missouri State University B
Southwest Missouri State University B
Truman State University B
University of Missouri
 Columbia B

Montana
Miles Community College A
Montana State University
 Northern A

New Hampshire
University of New Hampshire B

New Jersey
Rutgers
 The State University of New Jersey: Cook College B, T

New Mexico
Eastern New Mexico University A
New Mexico Junior College A
New Mexico State University
 Carlsbad A
New Mexico State University B, M
Western New Mexico University A

New York
Cornell University B
State University of New York
 College of Agriculture and Technology at Cobleskill A
 College of Agriculture and Technology at Morrisville A
 College of Technology at Alfred A

North Carolina
North Carolina Agricultural and Technical State University B, M
North Carolina State University A
Sandhills Community College A

North Dakota
Lake Region State College A
Williston State College C, A

Ohio
Ohio State University
 Columbus Campus B, M, D

Oklahoma
Cameron University B
Connors State College A
Eastern Oklahoma State College A
Langston University B
Murray State College A
Northern Oklahoma College A
Northwestern Oklahoma State University B
Oklahoma State University B, M
Redlands Community College A

Oregon
Central Oregon Community College A
Chemeketa Community College A
Oregon State University B, M

Pennsylvania
Penn State
 University Park C, B

South Carolina
Clemson University M

South Dakota
South Dakota State University A, B

Tennessee
Austin Peay State University B
Tennessee State University B, M
University of Tennessee
 Knoxville B
 Martin B
Walters State Community College A

Texas
Angelina College A
Blinn College A
Central Texas College C, A
Coastal Bend College A
Hardin-Simmons University B
Hill College A
Howard College A
Kilgore College A
Lubbock Christian University A, B
Navarro College C, A
North Central Texas College A
Odessa College A
Palo Alto College A
Panola College A
Paris Junior College A
Prairie View A&M University B
Sam Houston State University B, M
South Plains College A
Southwest Texas State University B
Stephen F. Austin State University B, M
Tarleton State University B, M
Texas A&M University
 Commerce B, M
Texas A&M University B, M
Texas Tech University B, M
Tyler Junior College A
West Texas A&M University B, M
Western Texas College A

Utah
Southern Utah University A

Vermont
University of Vermont B

Virginia
College of William and Mary B
Ferrum College B
Virginia State University B

Washington
Clark College A
Walla Walla Community College C, A
Washington State University B
Yakima Valley Community College A

West Virginia
Potomac State College of West Virginia University A
West Virginia University M, D

Wisconsin
Southwest Wisconsin Technical College A
University of Wisconsin
 Platteville B
 River Falls B

Wyoming
Casper College A
Central Wyoming College A
Eastern Wyoming College A
Laramie County Community College A
Northwest College A
Sheridan College A
University of Wyoming B

Agricultural supplies

Arizona
Glendale Community College C

California
Modesto Junior College A

Colorado
Aims Community College C, A

Illinois
Carl Sandburg College C
John Wood Community College C
Joliet Junior College C, A
Kishwaukee College A

Iowa
Iowa Lakes Community College A
Kirkwood Community College A
Muscatine Community College A
Southeastern Community College
 North Campus A
Western Iowa Tech Community College C, A

Kansas
Barton County Community College C, A

Michigan
St. Clair County Community College C, A

Texas
Sul Ross State University C, A
Texas A&M University B

Wisconsin
Madison Area Technical College C

Wyoming
University of Wyoming B

Agronomy/crop science

Alabama
Alabama Agricultural and Mechanical University B
Auburn University B, M, D

Arizona
Prescott College B, M

Arkansas
University of Arkansas B, M, D

California
Butte College C, A
California State Polytechnic University:
 Pomona B
California State University
 Chico B
 Fresno B, M
Merced College A
Modesto Junior College A
San Joaquin Delta College A
Sierra College C, A
University of California
 Davis B, M
Ventura College C, A
West Hills Community College A

Colorado
Colorado State University B, M, D
Lamar Community College A

Connecticut
University of Connecticut B

Delaware
University of Delaware B

Florida
Florida Agricultural and Mechanical University B
University of Florida M, D

Georgia
University of Georgia B, M, D

Hawaii
University of Hawaii
 Hilo B

Idaho
Ricks College C
University of Idaho B

Agronomy/crop science

Illinois
Richland Community College *A*
University of Illinois
 Urbana-Champaign *B, M, D*

Indiana
Purdue University *A, B, M, D*

Iowa
Des Moines Area Community College *C*
Iowa State University *B*

Kansas
Colby Community College *A*
Garden City Community College *A*
Kansas State University *B, M, D*
McPherson College *B*

Kentucky
Murray State University *B*
University of Kentucky *B, M, D*

Louisiana
Louisiana State University and
 Agricultural and Mechanical
 College *M, D*

Maryland
University of Maryland
 College Park *B, M, D*

Michigan
Michigan State University *B, M, D*

Minnesota
Ridgewater College: A Community and
 Technical College *C, A*
Southwest State University *B*
University of Minnesota
 Crookston *A, B*
 Twin Cities *M, D*

Mississippi
Alcorn State University *B*
Mississippi State University *B, M, D*

Missouri
College of the Ozarks *B*
Northwest Missouri State University *B*
Southeast Missouri State University *B*
Southwest Missouri State University *B*
Truman State University *B*
University of Missouri
 Columbia *M, D*

Nebraska
Northeast Community College *A*
University of Nebraska
 Lincoln *B, M, D*

New Hampshire
University of New Hampshire *B*

New Jersey
Rutgers
 The State University of New Jersey:
 Cook College *B*

New Mexico
New Mexico State University *B, M, D*

New York
Cornell University *B*
State University of New York
 College of Agriculture and
 Technology at Cobleskill *A*
 College of Technology at Alfred *A*

North Carolina
North Carolina State University *B, M, D*

North Dakota
North Dakota State University *B, M*

Ohio
Ohio State University
 Agricultural Technical Institute *A*
 Columbus Campus *B*
Wilmington College *B*

Oklahoma
Cameron University *B*
Eastern Oklahoma State College *A*
Northeastern Oklahoma Agricultural and
 Mechanical College *A*
Oklahoma Panhandle State University *B*
Oklahoma State University *B, M, D*

Oregon
Eastern Oregon University *B*
Oregon State University *B, M, D*

Pennsylvania
Delaware Valley College *B*
Penn State
 University Park *C, B, M, D*

Puerto Rico
University of Puerto Rico
 Mayaguez Campus *B, M*

South Carolina
Clemson University *M, D*

South Dakota
South Dakota State University *B, M, D*

Tennessee
Tennessee Technological University *B*
University of Tennessee
 Martin *B*

Texas
Stephen F. Austin State University *B*
Tarleton State University *B*
Texas A&M University
 Commerce *M*
 Kingsville *M*
Texas A&M University *B, M, D*
Texas Tech University *B, D*

Utah
Brigham Young University *B, M*
Dixie State College of Utah *A*
Utah State University *B*

Virginia
Virginia Polytechnic Institute and State
 University *B, M, D*

Washington
Highline Community College *A*
Washington State University *B, M, D*
Yakima Valley Community College *C, A*

Wisconsin
Chippewa Valley Technical College *A*
University of Wisconsin
 Madison *B, M, D*
 Platteville *B*
 River Falls *B*

Wyoming
University of Wyoming *M, D*

Air Force

Alabama
Community College of the Air Force *A*

Idaho
University of Idaho *B*

North Carolina
Methodist College *A, B*

Pennsylvania
La Salle University *C, B*
West Chester University of
 Pennsylvania *C*

Tennessee
Tennessee State University *B*

Virginia
Mary Baldwin College *T*

Washington
Pierce College *A*

Air traffic control

Alabama
Community College of the Air Force *A*

Alaska
University of Alaska
 Anchorage *A*

California
Cuyamaca College *A*
Mount San Antonio College *A*

Connecticut
Gateway Community College *A*

Michigan
Western Michigan University *B*

Minnesota
Inver Hills Community College *A*

New Hampshire
Daniel Webster College *B*

New Jersey
Thomas Edison State College *A, B*

North Dakota
University of North Dakota *B*

Ohio
Kent State University *B*

Utah
Dixie State College of Utah *C*

Air transportation

Alaska
University of Alaska
 Anchorage *A*
 Fairbanks *A*

Arizona
Cochise College *A*
Embry-Riddle Aeronautical University
 Prescott Campus *B*

Arkansas
Henderson State University *B*

California
Chabot College *A*
City College of San Francisco *C, A*
College of San Mateo *C, A*
Cuyamaca College *A*
Cypress College *C, A*
Glendale Community College *C*
Long Beach City College *C, A*
Mount San Antonio College *A*
Orange Coast College *C, A*
Pacific Union College *B*
Palomar College *C, A*
San Diego Mesa College *C*
Santa Rosa Junior College *C*

Colorado
Aims Community College *C, A*
Arapahoe Community College *C*
Colorado Northwestern Community
 College *A*
Metropolitan State College of Denver *B*

Connecticut
Three Rivers Community-Technical
 College *A*
University of New Haven *B*

Delaware
Delaware State University *B*
Wilmington College *B*

District of Columbia
University of the District of
 Columbia *A, B*

Florida
Broward Community College *A*
Embry-Riddle Aeronautical
 University *A, B, M*
Florida Institute of Technology *B, M*
Florida Memorial College *B*
Jacksonville University *B*
Miami-Dade Community College *A*
Palm Beach Community College *A*

Illinois
Lewis University *B*
Lincoln Land Community College *A*
Southern Illinois University
 Carbondale *A*
University of Illinois
 Urbana-Champaign *C*

Indiana
Purdue University *B*

Iowa
Iowa Central Community College *A*
Iowa Lakes Community College *A*
University of Dubuque *B*

Kansas
Central Christian College *A*
Hesston College *A*
Kansas State University *A, B*

Kentucky
Eastern Kentucky University *B*
Northern Kentucky University *A*

Louisiana
Louisiana Tech University *B*
University of Louisiana at Monroe *B*

Maryland
Community College of Baltimore County
 Catonsville *C, A*

Massachusetts
North Shore Community College *A*

Michigan
Andrews University *B*
Concordia College *B*
Cornerstone College and Grand Rapids
 Baptist Seminary *A, B*
Lansing Community College *A*
Northwestern Michigan College *A*
Oakland Community College *A*
Western Michigan University *B*

Minnesota
Vermilion Community College *A*

Mississippi
Delta State University *B, M*

Missouri
St. Louis University *B*
St. Louis Community College
 St. Louis Community College at
 Meramec *C*

Montana
Rocky Mountain College *B*

Nebraska
University of Nebraska
 Kearney *B*
 Omaha *B*

New Hampshire
Daniel Webster College *B*

New Jersey
Cumberland County College *A*
Mercer County Community College *A*
Raritan Valley Community College *A*

New Mexico
Eastern New Mexico University
 Roswell Campus *A*
San Juan College *A*

New York
Adelphi University *B*
Dowling College *B*
Schenectady County Community
 College *A*

North Dakota
University of North Dakota B, T

Ohio
Kent State University C, B

Oklahoma
Oklahoma City Community College A
Rose State College A
Southeastern Oklahoma State
   University B
University of Oklahoma B
Western Oklahoma State College A

Oregon
Lane Community College A
Mount Hood Community College A

Pennsylvania
Community College of Allegheny
   County A
Community College of Beaver County A
Lehigh Carbon Community College A
Luzerne County Community College A

Puerto Rico
Inter American University of Puerto Rico
   Bayamon Campus B

Tennessee
Middle Tennessee State University B

Texas
Baylor University B
LeTourneau University B
Navarro College C, A
Palo Alto College A
Texas Southern University B
Texas State Technical College
   Waco C, A

Utah
Dixie State College of Utah A
Salt Lake Community College A
Westminster College B

Virginia
Northern Virginia Community College A

Washington
Big Bend Community College A
Central Washington University B
Green River Community College A
Highline Community College C, A

West Virginia
College of West Virginia A
Fairmont State College B

Wisconsin
Concordia University Wisconsin B
Gateway Technical College A

Wyoming
Casper College A

Aircraft mechanics

Alabama
Community College of the Air Force A

Alaska
University of Alaska
   Anchorage C, A
   Fairbanks C, A

Arizona
Cochise College A
Pima Community College C, A

California
Chaffey Community College A
City College of San Francisco C, A
College of San Mateo C, A
Cypress College C, A
Gavilan Community College C, A
Glendale Community College C, A
Kings River Community College C
Long Beach City College C, A
Merced College A

Mount San Antonio College A
Orange Coast College C, A
Sacramento City College C, A
San Bernardino Valley College C
San Diego Miramar College C, A
Shasta College C, A
Solano Community College C, A
West Los Angeles College C, A

Colorado
Colorado Northwestern Community
   College C, A
Community College of Denver C
Westwood College of Aviation
   Technology A

Connecticut
Housatonic Community-Technical
   College A
Quinebaug Valley Community College A

Florida
Embry-Riddle Aeronautical University A

Georgia
Atlanta Metropolitan College A
Clayton College and State University A
Georgia Southwestern State University A

Hawaii
University of Hawaii
   Honolulu Community College C, A

Idaho
Idaho State University C, A

Illinois
Lewis University C, A, B
Lincoln Land Community College A
Moody Bible Institute B
Rock Valley College A
Southern Illinois University
   Carbondale A, B
Southwestern Illinois College C, A
University of Illinois
   Urbana-Champaign C

Indiana
Ivy Tech State College
   Wabash Valley A
Vincennes University A

Iowa
Hawkeye Community College A
Indian Hills Community College A
Iowa Western Community College A

Kansas
Cowley County Community
   College C, A
Kansas State University A
Pratt Community College A

Maryland
Chesapeake College C, A
Frederick Community College C, A

Massachusetts
Middlesex Community College A

Michigan
Baker College
   of Muskegon B
Lansing Community College A
Macomb Community College C, A
Northern Michigan University A
Oakland Community College A
Southwestern Michigan College C, A
Wayne County Community College C
Western Michigan University B

Minnesota
Minnesota State College - Southeast
   Technical C
Northland Community & Technical
   College C, A

Mississippi
Hinds Community College C

Missouri
Maple Woods Community College C, A

New Hampshire
New Hampshire Community Technical
   College
   Nashua A

New Jersey
Cumberland County College A

New Mexico
Eastern New Mexico University
   Roswell Campus A

New York
College of Aeronautics A, B
Mohawk Valley Community College A
State University of New York
   Farmingdale C, A

North Carolina
Guilford Technical Community
   College A
Wayne Community College A

Ohio
Cincinnati State Technical and
   Community College C, A
Columbus State Community College A

Oklahoma
Southeastern Oklahoma State
   University B

Oregon
Lane Community College C, A
Portland Community College C, A

Pennsylvania
Pittsburgh Institute of Aeronautics A

South Carolina
Greenville Technical College A
Trident Technical College A

Texas
Amarillo College C, A
Houston Community College System C
LeTourneau University B
St. Philip's College A
South Plains College A
Tarrant County College C, A
Texas State Technical College
   Harlingen C, A
   Sweetwater C, A
   Waco C, A

Utah
Salt Lake Community College C, A
Utah State University A, B

Virginia
Hampton University A
Northern Virginia Community College A

Washington
Big Bend Community College A
Everett Community College C, A
South Seattle Community College C, A
Spokane Community College A
Walla Walla College C, A

Wisconsin
Blackhawk Technical College C
Gateway Technical College C

American literature

California
California State University
   Bakersfield B, M
   Hayward B
Pitzer College B
San Joaquin Delta College A
University of California
   San Diego B, M, D
   Santa Cruz B, D
University of Southern California B

Whittier College B

Colorado
Fort Lewis College B

District of Columbia
George Washington University M, D

Florida
Eckerd College B
Miami-Dade Community College A
New College of the University of South
   Florida B

Idaho
Boise State University B

Illinois
Lincoln Land Community College A
Northwestern University B
Richland Community College A

Indiana
Indiana University--Purdue University
   Indiana University-Purdue
      University Fort Wayne B
Purdue University
   Calumet B
University of Evansville B

Iowa
University of Iowa B, M, T

Kansas
Independence Community College A

Maine
Bowdoin College B
University of Maine
   Fort Kent B

Maryland
Johns Hopkins University D

Massachusetts
Assumption College B
Clark University M
Hampshire College B
Harvard College B
Simmons College B
Tufts University B, M, D

Michigan
Lansing Community College A
Michigan State University B, M, D

Minnesota
Concordia College: Moorhead B
St. Cloud State University B
St. Mary's University of Minnesota B

Missouri
St. Louis University M, D
Washington University B, M, D

Montana
Miles Community College A

New Jersey
Rowan University B
Stevens Institute of Technology B

New York
Bard College B
City University of New York
   Baruch College B
   Brooklyn College B
   Hunter College M
Columbia University
   Graduate School M, D
Eugene Lang College/New School
   University B
Manhattanville College B
New York University B, M, D
St. Lawrence University B
Sarah Lawrence College B
United States Military Academy B

Ohio
College of Wooster B
Miami University
   Oxford Campus B

Wittenberg University *B*

Pennsylvania
California University of Pennsylvania *B*
Gettysburg College *B*
Holy Family College *B, T*
Immaculata College *B*
La Salle University *B*
University of Pittsburgh
    Johnstown *B*
West Chester University of
    Pennsylvania *B*
Westminster College *B, T*

Rhode Island
Brown University *B, M, D*

Texas
Texas A&M University
    Commerce *B*
University of North Texas *D*

Vermont
Bennington College *B*
Castleton State College *B*
Marlboro College *B*
Middlebury College *B*

Virginia
Longwood College *B, M, T*

Washington
Everett Community College *A*
Evergreen State College *B*
North Seattle Community College *C, A*

West Virginia
Concord College *B*

Wisconsin
Marquette University *D, T*

American studies

Alabama
Faulkner University *B*
Huntingdon College *B*
University of Alabama *B, M*

Arkansas
Harding University *B*
University of Arkansas *B*

California
California State University
    Chico *B*
    Fullerton *B, M*
Chapman University *B*
Claremont McKenna College *B*
Foothill College *C, A*
Los Angeles Valley College *A*
Mills College *B*
Mount St. Mary's College *B*
Occidental College *B*
Pepperdine University *M*
Pitzer College *B*
Pomona College *B*
Riverside Community College *A*
San Diego State University *B*
San Francisco State University *B*
Scripps College *B*
Stanford University *B*
University of California
    Berkeley *B*
    Davis *B*
    Santa Cruz *B*
University of Southern California *B*

Colorado
University of Colorado
    Boulder *B*

Connecticut
Connecticut College *B*
Fairfield University *B, M*
St. Joseph College *B*
Trinity College *B, M*
Wesleyan University *B*

Western Connecticut State University *B*
Yale University *B, M, D*

District of Columbia
American University *B*
George Washington University *B, M, D*
Georgetown University *B*
Trinity College *B*

Florida
Eckerd College *B*
Florida State University *B, M*
Manatee Community College *A*
Miami-Dade Community College *A*
Stetson University *B*
University of Miami *B*
University of South Florida *B, M*

Georgia
Emory University *M, D*
Oglethorpe University *B*
Oxford College of Emory University *B*
Wesleyan College *B*

Hawaii
University of Hawaii
    Manoa *B, M, D*
    West Oahu *B*

Idaho
Idaho State University *B*
University of Idaho *B*

Illinois
De Paul University *B*
Dominican University *B*
Elmhurst College *B*
Knox College *B*
Lake Forest College *B*
Lewis University *B*
Millikin University *B*
Northwestern University *B*
Roosevelt University *B*

Indiana
Franklin College *B*
Indiana University
    Bloomington *D*
    South Bend *A*
Indiana University--Purdue University
    Indiana University-Purdue
        University Fort Wayne *C*
University of Notre Dame *B, M*
Valparaiso University *B*
Vincennes University *A*

Iowa
Coe College *B*
Marycrest International University *A, B*
University of Iowa *B, M, D*
University of Northern Iowa *B*

Kansas
University of Kansas *B, M, D*

Kentucky
Lindsey Wilson College *B*
Thomas More College *B*

Louisiana
Tulane University *B*

Maine
Bates College *B*
Colby College *B*
University of New England *B*
University of Southern Maine *M*

Maryland
Anne Arundel Community College *A*
Goucher College *B*
Howard Community College *A*
Johns Hopkins University *B*
University of Maryland
    Baltimore County *B*
    College Park *B, M, D*
    Eastern Shore *M*
Washington College *B*

Massachusetts
Amherst College *B*
Boston College *M*
Boston University *B, M, D*
Brandeis University *B, M, D*
Elms College *B*
Hampshire College *B*
Harvard College *B*
Harvard University *D*
Mount Holyoke College *B*
Pine Manor College *B*
Smith College *B*
Stonehill College *B*
Tufts University *B, M*
University of Massachusetts
    Boston *B, M*
    Lowell *B*
Wellesley College *B*
Western New England College *B, T*
Wheaton College *B*
Williams College *B*

Michigan
Albion College *B*
Hillsdale College *B*
Siena Heights University *B*
University of Michigan
    Dearborn *B*
    Flint *M*
University of Michigan *B, M, D*
Wayne State University *B*
Western Michigan University *B*

Minnesota
Carleton College *B*
Moorhead State University *B*
St. Cloud State University *B*
St. Olaf College *B*
University of Minnesota
    Twin Cities *B, M, D*

Mississippi
Mississippi College *B*
Mississippi Delta Community College *A*
University of Southern Mississippi *B*

Missouri
St. Louis University *B, M, D*
Southeast Missouri State University *B*
University of Missouri
    Kansas City *B*
Washington University *B, M*

Nebraska
Creighton University *B*
Midland Lutheran College *B*

New Hampshire
Franklin Pierce College *B*
Keene State College *B*
New Hampshire College *B*

New Jersey
Bergen Community College *C*
College of St. Elizabeth *B*
Ramapo College of New Jersey *B*
Rider University *B*
Rowan University *B*
Rutgers
    The State University of New Jersey:
        Douglass College *B*
    The State University of New Jersey:
        Livingston College *B*
    The State University of New Jersey:
        Newark College of Arts and
        Sciences *B*
    The State University of New Jersey:
        Rutgers College *B*
    The State University of New Jersey:
        University College New
        Brunswick *B*
St. Peter's College *B*

New Mexico
University of New Mexico *B, M, D*

New York
Bard College *B*

Barnard College *B*
City University of New York
    Brooklyn College *B*
    College of Staten Island *B*
    Lehman College *B*
    Queens College *B*
College of New Rochelle *B*
College of St. Rose *B*
Columbia University
    School of General Studies *B*
Cornell University *B*
Dominican College of Blauvelt *B*
Elmira College *B*
Eugene Lang College/New School
    University *B*
Fordham University *B*
Fulton-Montgomery Community
    College *A*
Hamilton College *B*
Hobart and William Smith Colleges *B*
Hofstra University *B*
Manhattanville College *B*
Marist College *B*
Marymount College *B*
Nazareth College of Rochester *B*
New York University *B, M, D*
St. John's University *B*
Sarah Lawrence College *B*
Siena College *B, T*
Skidmore College *B*
State University of New York
    Buffalo *B, M, D*
    College at Fredonia *B*
    College at Geneseo *B*
    College at Old Westbury *B*
    Oswego *B*
Syracuse University *B*
Union College *B*
Vassar College *B*
Wells College *B*

North Carolina
High Point University *B*
Meredith College *B*
Montreat College *B*
Salem College *B*
University of North Carolina
    Chapel Hill *B*
    Pembroke *B*
Wingate University *B*

Ohio
Antioch College *B*
Ashland University *B*
Bowling Green State University *B, M, D*
Case Western Reserve
    University *B, M, D*
Cedarville College *B*
Kent State University
    Stark Campus *B*
Kent State University *B*
Miami University
    Oxford Campus *B*
Mount Union College *B*
Mount Vernon Nazarene College *B*
Oberlin College *B*
University of Dayton *B*
University of Rio Grande *B*
University of Toledo *B*
Ursuline College *B*
Wittenberg University *B*
Youngstown State University *B*

Oklahoma
Northeastern State University *M*
Southern Nazarene University *B*

Oregon
Oregon State University *B*
Reed College *B*
Willamette University *B*

Pennsylvania
Albright College *B*
Bucks County Community College *A*
Cabrini College *B*
California University of Pennsylvania *B*

Dickinson College B
Franklin and Marshall College B
Gettysburg College B
Lafayette College B
Lebanon Valley College of
    Pennsylvania B
Lehigh University B, M
Lycoming College B
Muhlenberg College B
Penn State
    Abington B
    Altoona B
    Delaware County B
    Harrisburg B, M
    University Park B
Rosemont College B
St. Francis College B
St. Joseph's University C
Temple University B
University of Pennsylvania A, B, M, D
University of Pittsburgh
    Bradford B
    Greensburg B
    Johnstown B
West Chester University of
    Pennsylvania B

Rhode Island
Brown University B, M, D
Providence College B
Salve Regina University B

South Carolina
Claflin University B

Tennessee
Cumberland University B
David Lipscomb University B
Freed-Hardeman University B
King College B, T
Rhodes College B
Tennessee Wesleyan College B
University of Tennessee
    Knoxville B
University of the South B
Vanderbilt University B

Texas
Baylor University B, M
Howard Payne University B
Our Lady of the Lake University of San
    Antonio B
Southwest Texas State University B
Southwestern University B
University of Texas
    Austin B, M, D
    Dallas B
    San Antonio B

Utah
Brigham Young University B
Utah State University B, M

Vermont
Burlington College B
College of St. Joseph in Vermont B
Goddard College B
Marlboro College B
Middlebury College B
St. Michael's College B

Virginia
College of William and Mary B, M, D
George Mason University B
Mary Washington College B
Shenandoah University B
University of Richmond B
Virginia Wesleyan College B

Washington
Everett Community College A
Evergreen State College B
North Seattle Community College C, A
Olympic College A
Washington State University B, M, D
Western Washington University B
Whitworth College B

Wyoming
University of Wyoming B, M

Analytical chemistry

Florida
Florida State University B, M, D

Illinois
Governors State University M

Iowa
Iowa State University M, D

Massachusetts
Harvard College B
Massachusetts College of Pharmacy and
    Health Sciences M, D
Mount Holyoke College M
Tufts University M, D
Worcester Polytechnic Institute B, M

Missouri
Crowder College A

New Jersey
Stevens Institute of Technology M, D

New York
Columbia University
    Graduate School M, D
Sarah Lawrence College B
State University of New York
    College of Environmental Science
    and Forestry M, D

North Carolina
University of North Carolina
    Chapel Hill M, D

Pennsylvania
Mercyhurst College B

Texas
Texas State Technical College
    Harlingen A
University of North Texas M, D

Utah
University of Utah M, D

Wisconsin
Marquette University M, D
University of Wisconsin
    Madison M

Anatomy

Alabama
Auburn University M

Arizona
University of Arizona M, D

Arkansas
University of Arkansas
    for Medical Sciences M, D

California
Citrus College A
Crafton Hills College A
Loma Linda University M, D
San Joaquin Delta College A
University of California
    Irvine D
    Los Angeles M, D
    San Francisco D
University of Southern California M, D

Colorado
Colorado State University M, D

District of Columbia
Georgetown University D
Howard University M, D

Florida
Broward Community College A
University of Miami D

Georgia
Georgia Military College A
Medical College of Georgia D
University of Georgia M

Hawaii
University of Hawaii
    Manoa M, D

Idaho
Lewis-Clark State College B

Illinois
Loyola University of Chicago M, D
Northwestern University M, D
Parkland College A
University of Illinois
    Chicago M, D

Indiana
Indiana State University T
Indiana University--Purdue University
    Indiana University-Purdue
    University Indianapolis M, D

Iowa
University of Iowa M, D

Kansas
Seward County Community College A

Louisiana
Louisiana State University Medical
    Center M, D
Tulane University M, D

Maryland
Uniformed Services University of the
    Health Sciences D
University of Maryland
    Baltimore M, D

Massachusetts
Boston University M, D
Hampshire College B
Harvard University M, D
Tufts University D

Michigan
Michigan State University M, D
University of Michigan M, D
Wayne State University M, D

Minnesota
Minnesota State University, Mankato B
University of Minnesota
    Twin Cities M

Mississippi
University of Mississippi
    Medical Center M, D

Missouri
St. Louis University M, D

New York
Columbia University
    Graduate School M, D
State University of New York
    Buffalo M, D
    Stony Brook M, D
    Upstate Medical University M, D
University of Rochester M, D

North Carolina
Duke University B, M, D
East Carolina University D
University of North Carolina
    Chapel Hill M, D

North Dakota
University of North Dakota M, D

Ohio
Case Western Reserve University D
Ohio State University
    Columbus Campus M, D
University of Cincinnati D
Wright State University M

Oregon
Oregon Health Sciences University M, D

Pennsylvania
MCP Hahnemann University M, D
Penn State
    College of Medicine, Milton S.
    Hershey Medical Center M, D
University of Pennsylvania M, D

Puerto Rico
University of Puerto Rico
    Medical Sciences Campus M, D

South Dakota
University of South Dakota M, D

Tennessee
University of Tennessee
    Memphis M, D

Texas
Texas A&M University M, D
Texas Tech University Health Science
    Center M, D
University of Texas
    Medical Branch at Galveston M, D

Utah
Brigham Young University M, D

Vermont
University of Vermont D

Virginia
Virginia Commonwealth
    University C, M, D

Washington
Eastern Washington University B

Wisconsin
Medical College of Wisconsin M, D
University of Wisconsin
    Madison M, D

Animal sciences

Alabama
Alabama Agricultural and Mechanical
    University B, M
Auburn University B, M, D
Northeast Alabama Community
    College A
Tuskegee University B, M

Alaska
University of Alaska
    Fairbanks B

Arizona
Arizona Western College A
University of Arizona B, M, D

Arkansas
Arkansas State University B
University of Arkansas B, M, D

California
Bakersfield College A
Butte College C, A
California Polytechnic State University:
    San Luis Obispo B
California State Polytechnic University:
    Pomona B
California State University
    Chico B
    Fresno B
College of the Redwoods C, A
College of the Sequoias C
College of the Siskiyous A
Kings River Community College C
Los Angeles Pierce College C, A
Merced College A
Modesto Junior College A
Moorpark College C, A
Mount San Antonio College C, A
San Joaquin Delta College A
Santa Rosa Junior College C
Sierra College C, A
University of California
    Davis B, M, D

Ventura College C, A
West Hills Community College C, A

Colorado
Colorado State University B, M, D
Lamar Community College A

Connecticut
University of Connecticut A, B, M

Delaware
University of Delaware B, M, D

Florida
Florida Agricultural and Mechanical
  University B
University of Florida B, M, D

Georgia
Abraham Baldwin Agricultural
  College A
Berry College B
Fort Valley State University B
Middle Georgia College A
University of Georgia B, M, D

Hawaii
University of Hawaii
  Hilo B
  Manoa B, M

Idaho
Ricks College C, A
University of Idaho B, M, D

Illinois
Black Hawk College
  East Campus C
Southern Illinois University
  Carbondale B, M
University of Illinois
  Urbana-Champaign B, M, D

Indiana
Purdue University B, M, D

Iowa
Des Moines Area Community College C
Dordt College B
Hawkeye Community College A
Iowa State University B
Waldorf College A

Kansas
Butler County Community College A
Central Christian College A
Coffeyville Community College A
Colby Community College A
Garden City Community College A
Kansas State University B, M, D
McPherson College B
Seward County Community College A

Kentucky
Murray State University B
University of Kentucky B, M, D

Louisiana
Louisiana Tech University B

Maine
University of Maine B, M

Maryland
University of Maryland
  College Park B, M, D

Massachusetts
Becker College A
Berkshire Community College C
Hampshire College B
Mount Ida College A, B
North Shore Community College C
University of Massachusetts
  Amherst B, M, D

Michigan
Andrews University B
Michigan State University C, B, M, D

Minnesota
South Central Technical College A

University of Minnesota
  Crookston A, B
  Twin Cities B, M, D

Mississippi
Alcorn State University B
Mississippi State University B
Northwest Mississippi Community
  College A

Missouri
College of the Ozarks B
Northwest Missouri State University B
Southeast Missouri State University B
Southwest Missouri State University B
Truman State University B
University of Missouri
  Columbia B, M, D

Montana
Montana State University
  Bozeman B, M

Nebraska
Northeast Community College A
University of Nebraska
  Lincoln B, M, D

Nevada
University of Nevada
  Reno B, M

New Hampshire
University of New
  Hampshire A, B, M, D

New Jersey
Rutgers
  The State University of New Jersey:
    Cook College B
  The State University of New Jersey:
    New Brunswick Graduate
    Campus M, D

New Mexico
New Mexico State University B, M, D

New York
Cornell University B, M, D
Medaille College A
State University of New York
  College of Agriculture and
    Technology at Cobleskill A, B
  College of Agriculture and
    Technology at Morrisville A
  College of Environmental Science
    and Forestry B, M, D
  College of Technology at Alfred A
  College of Technology at Delhi A

North Carolina
James Sprunt Community College A
North Carolina Agricultural and
  Technical State University B, M
North Carolina State University B, M, D
Sampson Community College C

North Dakota
North Dakota State University B, M, D

Ohio
Ohio State University
  Columbus Campus B, M, D
Wilmington College B

Oklahoma
Cameron University B
Eastern Oklahoma State College A
Langston University B
Northeastern Oklahoma Agricultural and
  Mechanical College A
Oklahoma Panhandle State University B
Oklahoma State University B, M

Oregon
Linn-Benton Community College A
Oregon State University B, M, D

Pennsylvania
Delaware Valley College B
Harcum College A

Penn State
  University Park C, B, M, D

Puerto Rico
University of Puerto Rico
  Arecibo Campus A
  Mayaguez Campus B, M
  Utuado A

Rhode Island
University of Rhode Island B

South Carolina
Clemson University B

South Dakota
South Dakota State University B, M, D

Tennessee
Hiwassee College A
Middle Tennessee State University B
Tennessee State University B, M
Tennessee Technological University B
University of Tennessee
  Knoxville B, M, D
  Martin B

Texas
Abilene Christian University B
Angelo State University B, M
Central Texas College C
Lubbock Christian University B
Palo Alto College C, A
Prairie View A&M University M
Sam Houston State University B
Southwest Texas State University B
Stephen F. Austin State University B
Sul Ross State University B, M
Tarleton State University B
Texas A&M University
  Commerce B, M
  Kingsville B, M
Texas A&M University B, M, D
Texas Tech University B, M, D
Western Texas College A

Utah
Brigham Young University B, M
Snow College A
Southern Utah University A
Utah State University C, B, M, D

Vermont
Sterling College A
University of Vermont B, M, D

Virginia
Blue Ridge Community College C, A
Virginia Polytechnic Institute and State
  University B, M, D

Washington
Highline Community College A
Pierce College A
Washington State University B, M, D

West Virginia
West Virginia University B, M

Wisconsin
Chippewa Valley Technical College A
Madison Area Technical College A
St. Norbert College B
University of Wisconsin
  Madison B, M, D
  Platteville B
  River Falls B

Wyoming
Casper College A
Central Wyoming College A
Eastern Wyoming College A
Northwest College A
Sheridan College A
University of Wyoming B, M, D

Anthropology

Alabama
Auburn University B
University of Alabama
  Birmingham B, M
University of Alabama B, M
University of South Alabama B

Alaska
University of Alaska
  Anchorage B
  Fairbanks B, M, D

Arizona
Arizona State University B, M, D
Cochise College A
Eastern Arizona College A
Northern Arizona University B, M
Pima Community College A
Prescott College B
University of Arizona B, M, D

Arkansas
Hendrix College B
University of Arkansas B, M

California
Bakersfield College A
Biola University B
Cabrillo College A
California State Polytechnic University:
  Pomona B
California State University
  Bakersfield B
  Chico C, B, M
  Dominguez Hills B
  Fresno B
  Fullerton B, M
  Hayward B, M
  Long Beach B, M
  Los Angeles B, M
  Monterey Bay B
  Northridge B
  Sacramento B, M
  Stanislaus B
Canada College A
Cerritos Community College A
Chaffey Community College A
Chapman University B
College of the Desert A
Crafton Hills College A
Cypress College A
De Anza College A
Diablo Valley College A
East Los Angeles College A
Foothill College A
Fresno City College A
Gavilan Community College A
Glendale Community College A
Golden West College A
Humboldt State University B
Imperial Valley College A
Irvine Valley College A
Long Beach City College C, A
Los Medanos College A
Merced College A
Mills College B
Monterey Peninsula College A
Occidental College B
Ohlone College C, A
Orange Coast College A
Pitzer College B
Pomona College B
Riverside Community College A
Saddleback College A
St. Mary's College of California B
San Diego City College A
San Diego Miramar College A
San Diego State University B
San Francisco State University B, M
San Joaquin Delta College A
San Jose State University B
Santa Ana College A
Santa Barbara City College A

Anthropology

Santa Clara University *B*
Santa Rosa Junior College *A*
Scripps College *B*
Sonoma State University *B, M*
Southwestern College *A*
Stanford University *B, M, D*
University of California
    Berkeley *B, M, D*
    Davis *B, M, D*
    Irvine *B*
    Los Angeles *B, M, D*
    Riverside *B, M, D*
    San Diego *B, D*
    Santa Barbara *B, M*
    Santa Cruz *B, M, D*
University of La Verne *B*
University of Redlands *B*
University of San Diego *B*
University of Southern
    California *B, M, D*
Vanguard University of Southern
    California *B*
Ventura College *A*
West Los Angeles College *C, A*
Westmont College *B*
Whittier College *B*

Colorado
Colorado College *B*
Colorado State University *B, M*
Fort Lewis College *B*
Metropolitan State College of
    Denver *B, T*
University of Colorado
    Boulder *B, M, D*
    Colorado Springs *B*
    Denver *B, M*
University of Denver *B, M*
Western State College of Colorado *B*

Connecticut
Central Connecticut State University *B*
Connecticut College *B*
Trinity College *B*
University of Connecticut *B, M, D*
Wesleyan University *B, M*
Western Connecticut State University *B*
Yale University *B, M, D*

Delaware
University of Delaware *B*

District of Columbia
American University *B, M, D*
Catholic University of America *B, M, D*
George Washington University *B, M*
Howard University *B*
University of the District of Columbia *B*

Florida
Broward Community College *A*
Eckerd College *B*
Florida Atlantic University *B, M*
Florida State University *B, M, D*
Gulf Coast Community College *A*
Indian River Community College *A*
Manatee Community College *A*
Miami-Dade Community College *A*
New College of the University of South
    Florida *B*
Palm Beach Community College *A*
Pensacola Junior College *A*
Rollins College *B*
Santa Fe Community College *A*
University of Central Florida *B*
University of Florida *B, M, D*
University of Miami *B*
University of South Florida *B, M, D*

Georgia
Agnes Scott College *B*
Atlanta Metropolitan College *A*
Berry College *B*
East Georgia College *A*
Emory University *B, D*
Gainesville College *A*
Georgia Perimeter College *A*

Georgia Southern University *B*
Georgia State University *B, M*
Oxford College of Emory University *B*
State University of West Georgia *B*
Thomas College *B*
University of Georgia *B, M, D*
Valdosta State University *B*

Hawaii
Hawaii Pacific University *B*
University of Hawaii
    Hilo *B*
    Manoa *B, M, D*
    West Oahu *B*

Idaho
Albertson College of Idaho *B*
Boise State University *B*
College of Southern Idaho *A*
Idaho State University *B, M*
North Idaho College *A*
University of Idaho *B, M*

Illinois
Benedictine University *T*
Black Hawk College
    East Campus *A*
Chicago State University *B*
Illinois State University *B*
Judson College *B*
Knox College *B*
Lake Forest College *B*
Lincoln Land Community College *A*
Loyola University of Chicago *B*
Morton College *A*
National-Louis University *B*
North Park University *B*
Northeastern Illinois University *B*
Northern Illinois University *B, M*
Northwestern University *B, M, D*
Parkland College *A*
Principia College *B*
Richland Community College *A*
Rockford College *B*
Southern Illinois University
    Carbondale *B, M, D*
    Edwardsville *B*
Southwestern Illinois College *A*
Triton College *A*
University of Chicago *B, M, D*
University of Illinois
    Chicago *B, M, D*
    Urbana-Champaign *B, M, D*
Wheaton College *B*

Indiana
Ball State University *B, M*
Butler University *B*
DePauw University *B*
Goshen College *B*
Indiana State University *B, T*
Indiana University
    Bloomington *B, M, D*
Indiana University--Purdue University
    Indiana University-Purdue
        University Fort Wayne *B*
    Indiana University-Purdue
        University Indianapolis *B*
Saint Mary's College *B*
University of Evansville *B*
University of Indianapolis *B*
University of Notre Dame *B*
Vincennes University *A*

Iowa
Cornell College *B, T*
Drake University *B*
Grinnell College *B*
Iowa State University *B, M*
Luther College *B*
University of Iowa *B, M, D, T*
University of Northern Iowa *B*

Kansas
Kansas City Kansas Community
    College *A*
Kansas State University *B*

University of Kansas *B, M, D*
Washburn University of Topeka *B*
Wichita State University *B, M*

Kentucky
Centre College *B*
Eastern Kentucky University *B*
Northern Kentucky University *B*
University of Kentucky *B, M, D*
University of Louisville *B*
Western Kentucky University *B, T*

Louisiana
Louisiana State University and
    Agricultural and Mechanical
    College *B, M*
Tulane University *B, M, D*
University of Louisiana at Lafayette *B*
University of New Orleans *B*

Maine
Bates College *B*
Bowdoin College *B*
Colby College *B*
University of Maine *B*
University of Southern Maine *B*

Maryland
Community College of Baltimore County
    Essex *A*
Johns Hopkins University *B, D*
St. Mary's College of Maryland *B*
University of Maryland
    College Park *B, M*

Massachusetts
Amherst College *B*
Boston University *B, M, D*
Brandeis University *B, M, D*
Bridgewater State College *B*
Hampshire College *B*
Harvard College *B*
Harvard University *M, D*
Massachusetts Institute of Technology *B*
Mount Holyoke College *B*
Northeastern University *B, M*
Simon's Rock College of Bard *B*
Smith College *B*
Tufts University *B*
University of Massachusetts
    Amherst *B, M, D*
    Boston *B*
Wellesley College *B*
Wheaton College *B*
Williams College *B*

Michigan
Albion College *B*
Central Michigan University *B*
Eastern Michigan University *B*
Grand Valley State University *B*
Kalamazoo College *B, T*
Kellogg Community College *A*
Lansing Community College *A*
Michigan State University *B, M, D*
Oakland University *B*
Olivet College *B*
University of Michigan
    Dearborn *B*
    Flint *B*
University of Michigan *B, M, D*
Wayne State University *B, M, D*
Western Michigan University *B, M*

Minnesota
Carleton College *B*
Crown College *A*
Gustavus Adolphus College *B*
Hamline University *B*
Macalester College *B*
Minnesota State University, Mankato *B*
Moorhead State University *B*
St. Cloud State University *B*
University of Minnesota
    Duluth *B*
    Twin Cities *B, M, D*

Mississippi
Millsaps College *B*
Mississippi State University *B*
University of Mississippi *B, M*
University of Southern Mississippi *B, M*

Missouri
Drury University *B*
Southeast Missouri State University *B*
Southwest Missouri State University *B*
University of Missouri
    Columbia *B, M, D*
    St. Louis *B*
Washington University *B, M, D*
Webster University *B*
Westminster College *B*

Montana
Rocky Mountain College *B, T*
University of Montana-Missoula *B, M*

Nebraska
Creighton University *B*
University of Nebraska
    Lincoln *B, M*

Nevada
University of Nevada
    Las Vegas *B, M, D*
    Reno *B, M, D*

New Hampshire
Dartmouth College *B*
Franklin Pierce College *B*
Plymouth State College of the University
    System of New Hampshire *B*
University of New Hampshire *B*

New Jersey
Drew University *B*
Fairleigh Dickinson University *B*
Monmouth University *B*
Montclair State University *B, M*
Princeton University *B, M, D*
Richard Stockton College of New
    Jersey *B*
Rowan University *B*
Rutgers
    The State University of New Jersey:
        Douglass College *B*
    The State University of New Jersey:
        Livingston College *B*
    The State University of New Jersey:
        New Brunswick Graduate
        Campus *M, D*
    The State University of New Jersey:
        Newark College of Arts and
        Sciences *B*
    The State University of New Jersey:
        Rutgers College *B*
    The State University of New Jersey:
        University College New
        Brunswick *B*
Seton Hall University *B*
Thomas Edison State College *B*

New Mexico
Eastern New Mexico University *B, M*
New Mexico Highlands University *B*
New Mexico State University *B, M*
San Juan College *A*
University of New Mexico *B, M, D*

New York
Adelphi University *B*
Bard College *B*
Barnard College *B*
City University of New York
    Brooklyn College *B*
    College of Staten Island *B*
    Graduate School and University
        Center *D*
    Hunter College *B, M*
    Lehman College *B*
    Queens College *B*
    York College *B*
Colgate University *B*

Columbia University
    Columbia College *B*
    Graduate School *M, D*
    Teachers College *M, D*
Cornell University *B, M, D*
Dowling College *B*
Elmira College *B*
Eugene Lang College/New School
    University *B*
Fordham University *B*
Hamilton College *B*
Hartwick College *B*
Hobart and William Smith Colleges *B*
Hofstra University *B*
Ithaca College *B*
Long Island University
    Brooklyn Campus *B*
Nazareth College of Rochester *B*
New York University *B, M, D*
Pace University:
    Pleasantville/Briarcliff *T*
Pace University *B, T*
St. John Fisher College *B*
St. John's University *B*
St. Lawrence University *B*
Sarah Lawrence College *B*
Skidmore College *B*
State University of New York
    Albany *B, M, D*
    Binghamton *B, M, D*
    Buffalo *B, M, D*
    College at Brockport *B*
    College at Buffalo *B*
    College at Cortland *B*
    College at Geneseo *B, T*
    College at Oneonta *B*
    College at Plattsburgh *B*
    College at Potsdam *B*
    New Paltz *B*
    Oswego *B*
    Purchase *B*
    Stony Brook *B, M, D*
Syracuse University *B, M, D*
Union College *B*
University of Rochester *B*
Utica College of Syracuse University *B*
Vassar College *B*
Wells College *B*

North Carolina

Appalachian State University *B*
Belmont Abbey College *B*
Davidson College *B*
Duke University *B, M, D*
East Carolina University *B, M*
Elon College *B*
North Carolina State University *B*
North Carolina Wesleyan College *B*
University of North Carolina
    Chapel Hill *B, M, D*
    Charlotte *B*
    Greensboro *B*
    Wilmington *B*
Wake Forest University *B, M*
Western Carolina University *B*

North Dakota

North Dakota State University *B, M*
University of North Dakota *B*

Ohio

Antioch College *B*
Case Western Reserve
    University *B, M, D*
Cleveland State University *B, M*
Denison University *B*
Franciscan University of Steubenville *B*
Heidelberg College *B*
Kent State University
    Stark Campus *B*
Kent State University *B, M*
Kenyon College *B*
Miami University
    Middletown Campus *A*
    Oxford Campus *B*
Oberlin College *B*

Ohio State University
    Columbus Campus *B, M, D*
Ohio University *B*
Ohio Wesleyan University *B*
University of Akron *B*
University of Cincinnati *B, M*
University of Dayton *B*
University of Toledo *B*
Wright State University *B*
Youngstown State University *B*

Oklahoma

University of Oklahoma *B, M, D*
University of Tulsa *B, M*

Oregon

Central Oregon Community College *A*
Chemeketa Community College *A*
Eastern Oregon University *B, T*
Lewis & Clark College *B*
Linfield College *B*
Oregon State University *B, M*
Portland State University *B, M, D*
Reed College *B*
Southern Oregon University *B*
University of Oregon *B, M, D*

Pennsylvania

Bloomsburg University of
    Pennsylvania *B*
Bryn Mawr College *B*
Bucknell University *B*
California University of Pennsylvania *B*
Carlow College *B*
Clarion University of Pennsylvania *B*
Dickinson College *B*
Drexel University *B*
Edinboro University of Pennsylvania *B*
Elizabethtown College *B*
Franklin and Marshall College *B*
Gettysburg College *B*
Haverford College *B, T*
Indiana University of Pennsylvania *B*
Juniata College *B*
Kutztown University of Pennsylvania *B*
Lafayette College *B*
Lehigh University *B*
Lock Haven University of
    Pennsylvania *B*
Lycoming College *B*
Mansfield University of
    Pennsylvania *B, T*
Mercyhurst College *B*
Millersville University of
    Pennsylvania *B*
Muhlenberg College *B*
Penn State
    University Park *B, M, D*
St. Vincent College *B*
Slippery Rock University of
    Pennsylvania *B, T*
Swarthmore College *B*
Temple University *B, M*
University of Pennsylvania *A, B, M, D*
University of Pittsburgh
    Greensburg *B*
University of Pittsburgh *B, M, D*
Ursinus College *B*
West Chester University of
    Pennsylvania *B*

Puerto Rico

Inter American University of Puerto Rico
    Metropolitan Campus *B*
University of Puerto Rico
    Rio Piedras Campus *B*

Rhode Island

Brown University *B, M, D*
Rhode Island College *B*
Salve Regina University *B*
University of Rhode Island *B*

South Carolina

College of Charleston *B*
University of South Carolina *B, M*

South Dakota

University of South Dakota *B*

Tennessee

Middle Tennessee State University *B*
Rhodes College *B*
University of Memphis *B, M*
University of Tennessee
    Knoxville *B, M, D*
University of the South *B*
Vanderbilt University *B, M, D*

Texas

Baylor University *B*
Galveston College *A*
Midland College *A*
Rice University *B, M, D*
Southern Methodist University *B, M, D*
Southwest Texas State University *B*
Southwestern University *B*
Texas A&M University
    Commerce *B*
    Kingsville *B*
Texas A&M University *B, M, D*
Texas Tech University *B, M*
Trinity University *B*
University of Houston
    Clear Lake *B*
University of Houston *B, M*
University of North Texas *B*
University of Texas
    Arlington *B, M*
    Austin *B, M, D*
    Dallas *B*
    El Paso *B*
    Pan American *B*
    San Antonio *B, M*

Utah

Brigham Young University *B, M*
Snow College *A*
University of Utah *B, M, D*
Utah State University *B*

Vermont

Bennington College *B*
Johnson State College *B*
Marlboro College *B*
Middlebury College *B*
University of Vermont *B*

Virginia

College of William and Mary *B, M*
George Mason University *B*
James Madison University *B*
Longwood College *B, T*
Mary Washington College *B*
Radford University *B*
Sweet Briar College *B*
University of Virginia's College at
    Wise *T*
University of Virginia *B, M, D*
Virginia Commonwealth University *B*
Washington and Lee University *B*

Washington

Central Washington University *B*
Centralia College *A*
Eastern Washington University *B*
Everett Community College *A*
Evergreen State College *B*
Highline Community College *A*
Lower Columbia College *A*
Pacific Lutheran University *B*
University of Washington *B, M, D*
Washington State University *B, M, D*
Western Washington University *B, M, T*
Whitman College *B*

West Virginia

Marshall University *B*

Wisconsin

Beloit College *B*
Lawrence University *B, T*
Marquette University *B, T*
Ripon College *B*

University of Wisconsin
    Madison *B, M, D*
    Milwaukee *B, M, D*
    Oshkosh *B*
    Parkside *B*
    River Falls *T*

Wyoming

Casper College *A*
Laramie County Community College *A*
University of Wyoming *B, M*
Western Wyoming Community
    College *A*

Applied mathematics

Alabama

Auburn University *B, M*
Oakwood College *B*
University of Alabama
    Birmingham *D*
    Huntsville *D*
University of Alabama *M, D*

Arizona

Northern Arizona University *B*
University of Arizona *M, D*

Arkansas

University of Arkansas
    Little Rock *B, M*

California

California Institute of Technology *B, D*
California State University
    Chico *B*
    Fullerton *M*
    Hayward *B, M*
    Long Beach *B, M*
    Los Angeles *B, M*
    Northridge *B, M*
    Stanislaus *B*
Chapman University *B*
College of the Sequoias *A*
Harvey Mudd College *B*
Mount St. Mary's College *B*
Ohlone College *C*
Pacific Union College *B, T*
San Diego City College *A*
San Diego Miramar College *A*
San Diego State University *M*
San Francisco State University *B*
San Jose State University *B*
Santa Clara University *C, M*
University of California
    Berkeley *B, D*
    Davis *M, D*
    Los Angeles *B*
    Riverside *M*
    San Diego *B, M*
    Santa Barbara *B, M*
    Santa Cruz *B, M*
University of Southern California *M, D*

Colorado

Colorado School of Mines *B*
University of Colorado
    Boulder *B, M, D*
    Colorado Springs *B, M*
    Denver *B, M, D*

Connecticut

University of Connecticut *B*
Yale University *B*

District of Columbia

George Washington University *B, M*

Florida

Florida Institute of Technology *B, M, D*
Florida International University *B, M*
Florida State University *B, M, D*
University of Central Florida *M, D*
University of Miami *B*
University of North Florida *M*
University of West Florida *B, M*

Georgia
Armstrong Atlantic State University B, T
Brenau University B
Columbus State University B
Georgia Institute of Technology B, M
Georgia Military College A
Georgia State University B, M, D
University of Georgia M
Valdosta State University B

Idaho
University of Idaho B

Illinois
Elgin Community College A
Millikin University B, T
National-Louis University B
North Central College A
North Park University B
Northeastern Illinois University M
Northwestern University B, M, D
Trinity International University B
University of Chicago B
University of Illinois
    Urbana-Champaign M

Indiana
Franklin College B
Goshen College B
Indiana University
    South Bend B
Indiana University--Purdue University
    Indiana University-Purdue
        University Fort Wayne M
Oakland City University B
Purdue University
    Calumet B, M
Saint Mary's College B, T
St. Joseph's College B
University of Evansville B
University of Notre Dame M

Iowa
Grand View College B
Iowa State University M, D
University of Iowa D
William Penn University B

Kansas
Independence Community College A

Kentucky
Asbury College B
Bellarmine College B, T
Brescia University B
Institute of Electronic Technology A
University of Kentucky M

Louisiana
Nicholls State University M
Tulane University M

Maryland
Johns Hopkins University B, D
Loyola College in Maryland B
Towson University M
University of Maryland
    Baltimore County M, D
    College Park M, D

Massachusetts
Clark University B
Hampshire College B
Harvard College B
Harvard University M, D
Salem State College B
Tufts University B, M
University of Massachusetts
    Amherst M
    Boston B
    Lowell A, B
Worcester Polytechnic Institute B, M

Michigan
Ferris State University B
Kettering University B
Lansing Community College A
Michigan State University B, M, D
Oakland University D
University of Detroit Mercy B
University of Michigan B, M, D
Wayne State University M
Western Michigan University B, M, D

Minnesota
Concordia College: Moorhead B
Metropolitan State University B
Moorhead State University B
University of Minnesota
    Duluth M
Winona State University B

Mississippi
Mississippi State University D

Missouri
Maryville University of Saint Louis B
Missouri Southern State College B
St. Louis University B
Truman State University B
University of Missouri
    Columbia M
    Rolla B, M
    St. Louis B, D
Washington University B

Montana
Montana Tech of the University of
    Montana B
University of Montana-Missoula B, M, D
Western Montana College of The
    University of Montana B

Nebraska
Creighton University B

Nevada
University of Nevada
    Las Vegas B

New Hampshire
Franklin Pierce College B
Keene State College B
Plymouth State College of the University
    System of New Hampshire B
University of New Hampshire B

New Jersey
Bloomfield College B
New Jersey Institute of Technology B, M
Princeton University D
Rutgers
    The State University of New Jersey:
        Newark College of Arts and
        Sciences B
    The State University of New Jersey:
        University College Newark B
Stevens Institute of Technology B, M, D

New Mexico
New Mexico Institute of Mining and
    Technology B, M

New York
Barnard College B
City University of New York
    Brooklyn College B, M
    Hunter College M
    Queens College B
Columbia University
    Fu Foundation School of
        Engineering and Applied
        Science B, M, D
    School of General Studies B
Cornell University D
Hofstra University M
Long Island University
    C. W. Post Campus M
New York University M
Rensselaer Polytechnic Institute M
Rochester Institute of
    Technology A, B, M
St. Thomas Aquinas College B
Siena College B, T
State University of New York
    Albany B
    Farmingdale A, B
    Institute of Technology at
        Utica/Rome B
    Oswego B
    Stony Brook B, M, D
University of Rochester B, M

North Carolina
Elizabeth City State University B
Johnson C. Smith University B
North Carolina Agricultural and
    Technical State University M
North Carolina State University B, M, D
St. Augustine's College B
University of North Carolina
    Chapel Hill B
    Charlotte M, D
Western Carolina University M

Ohio
Bowling Green State University B
Case Western Reserve
    University B, M, D
Kent State University
    Stark Campus B
Kent State University B, M, D
Ohio State University
    Columbus Campus M, D
Ohio University B
University of Akron B, M
University of Dayton B, M
Wright State University M

Oklahoma
East Central University B
Oklahoma City Community College A
University of Central Oklahoma B, M
University of Tulsa B

Oregon
University of Oregon M, D

Pennsylvania
California University of Pennsylvania B
Carnegie Mellon University B, M, D
Geneva College B
Indiana University of Pennsylvania B
La Roche College B
La Salle University B, T
Lehigh University M, D
Robert Morris College B
University of Pittsburgh
    Greensburg B
University of Pittsburgh B, M
Ursinus College B
Widener University B

Puerto Rico
Inter American University of Puerto Rico
    San German Campus B
Turabo University B
University of Puerto Rico
    Mayaguez Campus M

Rhode Island
Brown University B, M, D
Salve Regina University B
University of Rhode Island D

South Carolina
Charleston Southern University B
Coastal Carolina University B
Limestone College B
University of South Carolina
    Aiken B

Tennessee
Bethel College B
University of Tennessee
    Chattanooga B

Texas
Baylor University B
Lamar University B
Rice University B, M, D
Southern Methodist University M
Southwestern Adventist University B
Texas A&M University B
University of Houston
    Downtown B
University of Houston B, M
University of Texas
    Arlington D
    Austin M, D
    Dallas B, M, D
    El Paso B

Utah
Utah State University D
Weber State University B

Virginia
Hampden-Sydney College B
Hampton University B, M
Longwood College B, T
Mary Baldwin College B
Old Dominion University M, D
Radford University M
University of Virginia's College at
    Wise T
University of Virginia B, M, D

Washington
Seattle University B
University of Washington B, M, D
Western Washington University B

West Virginia
Alderson-Broaddus College B
West Virginia State College B

Wisconsin
University of Wisconsin
    Milwaukee B
    Stout B

Applied physics

Alabama
Alabama Agricultural and Mechanical
    University D

Alaska
University of Alaska
    Fairbanks B

California
California Institute of Technology B, D
Stanford University M, D
University of California
    Davis B
    San Diego B, M, D

Connecticut
Yale University B

Georgia
Georgia Institute of Technology B, M
Georgia Military College A
South Georgia College A

Indiana
University of Notre Dame B

Kansas
Central Christian College A

Massachusetts
Harvard College B
Northeastern University B
University of Massachusetts
    Boston M

Michigan
Kettering University B
University of Michigan M, D

Minnesota
University of Minnesota
    Duluth B
Winona State University B

Nevada
University of Nevada
    Las Vegas B

Applied physics

New Jersey
New Jersey Institute of Technology B, M, D
Rutgers
 The State University of New Jersey: Newark College of Arts and Sciences B
Stevens Institute of Technology B

New York
Columbia University
 Fu Foundation School of Engineering and Applied Science B, M, D
Pace University: Pleasantville/Briarcliff C
Pace University C
Rensselaer Polytechnic Institute B
State University of New York College at Geneseo B

North Dakota
University of North Dakota B

Ohio
College of Mount St. Joseph B
Kent State University B
Ohio University B
Xavier University B

Oregon
Linfield College B

Pennsylvania
Grove City College B
Indiana University of Pennsylvania B
Shippensburg University of Pennsylvania B

Texas
St. Philip's College A
University of Texas
 Arlington D
 Austin M

Virginia
Christopher Newport University B, M
George Mason University M

Arabic

California
University of California
 Berkeley M, D
 Los Angeles B

District of Columbia
Catholic University of America M, D
Georgetown University B, M, D

Georgia
Oxford College of Emory University B

Illinois
University of Chicago B

Maryland
Johns Hopkins University B

Massachusetts
Harvard College B
Harvard University D
Mount Holyoke College B
Simon's Rock College of Bard B

Michigan
Michigan State University B
University of Michigan B, M
Wayne State University B

Minnesota
University of Minnesota
 Twin Cities M

Missouri
Washington University B, M

New York
Columbia University
 Graduate School M, D
State University of New York
 Binghamton B

Ohio
Ohio State University
 Columbus Campus B

Texas
University of Texas
 Austin B, M, D

Utah
Brigham Young University B, M

Washington
University of Washington B

Archaeology

Arizona
Pima Community College C, A

California
California State University
 Hayward B
Fresno City College C
Imperial Valley College C
Merced College A
Palomar College C, A
University of California
 Berkeley M
 Los Angeles M, D
 San Diego B

Colorado
Fort Lewis College B

Connecticut
Norwalk Community-Technical College C
Wesleyan University B
Yale University B, M

District of Columbia
George Washington University B

Florida
Gulf Coast Community College A

Illinois
Richland Community College A
Southwestern Illinois College A
Wheaton College B

Indiana
Ball State University M
Indiana University
 Bloomington D
University of Evansville B
University of Indianapolis B

Kansas
University of Kansas B

Massachusetts
Boston University B, M, D
Bridgewater State College B
Harvard College B
Tufts University B
Wellesley College B

Michigan
Michigan Technological University M
University of Michigan M, D

Minnesota
Hamline University B
University of Minnesota
 Twin Cities M, D

Missouri
Washington University B, M, D

New Hampshire
Franklin Pierce College B

New Jersey
Princeton University M, D

New York
Bard College B
City University of New York
 Hunter College B
Columbia University
 Columbia College B
Cornell University B, M
Hamilton College B
New York University M
State University of New York
 Albany B, M
 Buffalo M, D

North Carolina
Appalachian State University B
Brevard College B
University of North Carolina
 Chapel Hill B, M, D

Ohio
College of Wooster B
Hocking Technical College A
Kent State University B, M
Oberlin College B
University of Cincinnati M, D

Pennsylvania
Bryn Mawr College B, M, D
Haverford College B
Mercyhurst College B
University of Pennsylvania M, D

Rhode Island
Brown University B, M, D

Texas
Baylor University B
University of Texas
 Austin B

Utah
Weber State University C, A

Virginia
Washington and Lee University B

Washington
Western Washington University B

Wisconsin
University of Wisconsin
 La Crosse B

Architectural engineering

Alabama
Auburn University B, M

California
California State University
 Fullerton B
East Los Angeles College A
San Joaquin Delta College A
University of Southern California B, M

Colorado
University of Colorado
 Boulder B

District of Columbia
University of the District of Columbia A

Florida
Miami-Dade Community College A
University of Miami B

Hawaii
University of Hawaii
 Honolulu Community College A

Illinois
City Colleges of Chicago
 Olive-Harvey College C, A
Illinois Institute of Technology B
Lincoln Land Community College A
Parkland College A

Kansas
Central Christian College A
Independence Community College A
Kansas State University B, M
Pratt Community College A

University of Kansas B, M

Massachusetts
Harvard College B
Tufts University B

Mississippi
Holmes Community College A

Nebraska
University of Nebraska
 Lincoln B

New Jersey
Union County College A

North Carolina
North Carolina Agricultural and Technical State University B, M

Ohio
Columbus State Community College A

Oklahoma
Oklahoma State University B, M

Pennsylvania
Drexel University B
Lock Haven University of Pennsylvania B
Penn State
 University Park B, M, D

Rhode Island
New England Institute of Technology B

Tennessee
Tennessee State University B

Texas
University of Texas
 Austin B, M

Vermont
Vermont Technical College A

Virginia
John Tyler Community College A

Wisconsin
Milwaukee Area Technical College A
Milwaukee School of Engineering B, M

Wyoming
University of Wyoming B

Architectural engineering technology

Alabama
Lawson State Community College C, A
Northeast Alabama Community College A

Alaska
University of Alaska
 Anchorage A

Arizona
Mesa Community College A
University of Advancing Computer Technology A, B

California
Allan Hancock College A
Chabot College A
Chaffey Community College C, A
City College of San Francisco A
College of the Desert C, A
Contra Costa College A
Cuyamaca College A
East Los Angeles College A
Golden West College C, A
Long Beach City College C, A
Los Angeles Harbor College C, A
Los Angeles Trade and Technical College C, A
Modesto Junior College C, A
Mount San Antonio College C, A
Orange Coast College C, A
San Joaquin Delta College C, A

Santa Monica College *C, A*
Sierra College *C, A*
Ventura College *A*

Colorado
Arapahoe Community College *C, A*
Denver Technical College: A Division of
    DeVry University *A*
Front Range Community College *C, A*
Pikes Peak Community College *A*
Pueblo Community College *C, A*

Connecticut
Capital Community College *A*
Norwalk Community-Technical
    College *A*
Three Rivers Community-Technical
    College *C, A*
University of Hartford *B*

Delaware
Delaware Technical and Community
    College
        Owens Campus *A*
        Stanton/Wilmington Campus *A*
        Terry Campus *A*

Florida
Daytona Beach Community College *A*
Florida Community College at
    Jacksonville *A*
Gulf Coast Community College *A*
Hillsborough Community College *A*
Miami-Dade Community College *A*
St. Petersburg Junior College *A*
Seminole Community College *A*

Georgia
Southern Polytechnic State University *B*

Hawaii
University of Hawaii
    Hawaii Community College *C*

Idaho
Ricks College *A*

Illinois
Joliet Junior College *C, A*
Lincoln Land Community College *A*
Oakton Community College *A*
Southern Illinois University
    Carbondale *A*
William Rainey Harper College *C, A*

Indiana
Indiana State University *A*
Indiana University--Purdue University
    Indiana University-Purdue
        University Fort Wayne *A, B*
    Indiana University-Purdue
        University Indianapolis *B*
Purdue University
    North Central Campus *A*
Purdue University *A, B*

Iowa
Iowa Western Community College *A*
University of Northern Iowa *B*
Western Iowa Tech Community
    College *A*

Kansas
Independence Community College *A*
Kansas City Kansas Community
    College *C, A*

Kentucky
Eastern Kentucky University *B*
Lexington Community College *A*

Louisiana
Delgado Community College *A*
Louisiana State University and
    Agricultural and Mechanical
    College *B*

Maryland
Montgomery College
    Rockville Campus *A*

Massachusetts
Fitchburg State College *B*
Franklin Institute of Boston *A*
Massasoit Community College *A*
Wentworth Institute of Technology *A, B*

Michigan
Andrews University *A*
Baker College
    of Auburn Hills *A*
    of Mount Clemens *A*
    of Muskegon *A*
    of Owosso *A*
Delta College *A*
Ferris State University *A*
Monroe County Community
    College *C, A*
Oakland Community College *A*

Minnesota
Anoka-Ramsey Community College *A*
Lake Superior College: A Community
    and Technical College *C, A*
St. Cloud Technical College *C, A*

Mississippi
Mississippi Delta Community College *A*
University of Southern Mississippi *B*

Missouri
Central Missouri State University *A, B*
Lincoln University *B*
Mineral Area College *C, A*
St. Louis Community College
    St. Louis Community College at
        Meramec *A*

Nebraska
Southeast Community College
    Lincoln Campus *A*

New Hampshire
New Hampshire Technical Institute *A*

New Jersey
Brookdale Community College *C*
Essex County College *A*
Mercer County Community College *C, A*
Thomas Edison State College *A, B*
Union County College *A*

New Mexico
Eastern New Mexico University
    Roswell Campus *A*

New York
City University of New York
    New York City Technical
        College *A*
Dutchess Community College *A*
Erie Community College
    South Campus *A*
Finger Lakes Community College *A*
Institute of Design and Construction *A*
New York Institute of Technology *A, B*
Orange County Community College *A*
State University of New York
    College of Technology at
        Alfred *A, B*
    College of Technology at Delhi *A*
    Farmingdale *A*
Suffolk County Community College *A*

North Carolina
Cape Fear Community College *A*
Catawba Valley Community College *A*
Central Carolina Community College *A*
Central Piedmont Community College *A*
Coastal Carolina Community College *A*
Durham Technical Community
    College *C, A*
Forsyth Technical Community College *A*
Gaston College *A*
Nash Community College *A*
Pitt Community College *A*
Roanoke-Chowan Community College *A*
Sandhills Community College *A*
Wake Technical Community
    College *C, A*

Wilkes Community College *A*

North Dakota
North Dakota State College of Science *A*

Ohio
Bowling Green State University *B*
Cincinnati State Technical and
    Community College *A*
Columbus State Community College *A*
Lakeland Community College *C*
Owens Community College
    Toledo *A*
Sinclair Community College *A*
Stark State College of Technology *A*
Terra Community College *C, A*
University of Toledo *A*

Oklahoma
Oklahoma State University
    Oklahoma City *A*

Oregon
Mount Hood Community College *C, A*

Pennsylvania
Butler County Community College *A*
Community College of Beaver County *A*
Community College of Philadelphia *A*
Delaware County Community College *A*
Harrisburg Area Community
    College *C, A*
Northampton County Area Community
    College *A*
Penn State
    Fayette *A*
    University Park *C*
    Worthington Scranton *A*
Pennsylvania College of Technology *A*
Pennsylvania Institute of Technology *A*

South Carolina
Greenville Technical College *C, A*
Midlands Technical College *A*
Spartanburg Technical College *A*
Trident Technical College *C, A*

South Dakota
Southeast Technical Institute *A*

Tennessee
Nashville State Technical Institute *A*
University of Memphis *B*

Texas
Abilene Christian University *A*
Del Mar College *A*
Midland College *A*
Southwest Texas State University *B*
Tarrant County College *C, A*
Texas Tech University *B*
University of Houston *B*

Vermont
Vermont Technical College *A, B*

Virginia
Central Virginia Community College *A*
J. Sargeant Reynolds Community
    College *C, A*
John Tyler Community College *A*
New River Community College *A*
Norfolk State University *A*
Northern Virginia Community College *A*
Virginia Western Community College *A*

Washington
Everett Community College *C*
Spokane Community College *A*
Spokane Falls Community College *C, A*

West Virginia
Bluefield State College *A, B*
Fairmont State College *A, B*

Wisconsin
Madison Area Technical College *A*
Northeast Wisconsin Technical
    College *A*
Waukesha County Technical College *A*

Wisconsin Indianhead Technical
    College *A*

Architecture

Alabama
Auburn University *B*
Tuskegee University *B*

Arizona
Arizona State University *B, M, D*
Pima Community College *C*
University of Arizona *B, M*

Arkansas
University of Arkansas *B*

California
California College of Arts and Crafts *B*
California Polytechnic State University:
    San Luis Obispo *B*
California State Polytechnic University:
    Pomona *B, M*
Chabot College *A*
Los Angeles Harbor College *A*
Riverside Community College *C, A*
San Bernardino Valley College *A*
San Diego Mesa College *C, A*
Southern California Institute of
    Architecture *B, M*
University of California
    Berkeley *B, M, D*
    Los Angeles *M, D*
University of San Francisco *B*
University of Southern California *B, M*

Colorado
University of Colorado
    Boulder *B*
    Denver *M*

Connecticut
Connecticut College *B*
Yale University *B, M*

District of Columbia
Catholic University of America *B, M*
Howard University *B*
University of the District of Columbia *B*

Florida
Broward Community College *A*
Florida Agricultural and Mechanical
    University *B, M*
Florida Atlantic University *B*
Florida International University *B, M*
Santa Fe Community College *A*
Seminole Community College *A*
South Florida Community College *A*
University of Florida *B, M, D*
University of Miami *B, M*
University of South Florida *M*

Georgia
Georgia Institute of Technology *B, M, D*
Middle Georgia College *A*
Morehouse College *B*
Morris Brown College *B*
Savannah College of Art and
    Design *B, M*
Southern Polytechnic State University *B*

Hawaii
University of Hawaii
    Manoa *B, M*

Idaho
University of Idaho *B, M*

Illinois
Illinois Institute of Technology *B, M, D*
Lincoln Land Community College *A*
Southern Illinois University
    Carbondale *B*
Triton College *A*
University of Illinois
    Chicago *B, M*
    Urbana-Champaign *B, M*

75

Architecture

Indiana
Ball State University B, M
Goshen College B
University of Notre Dame B, M

Iowa
Iowa State University B, M

Kansas
Central Christian College A
Kansas State University B, M
University of Kansas B, M

Kentucky
University of Kentucky B

Louisiana
Louisiana State University and
 Agricultural and Mechanical
 College B, M
Louisiana Tech University B
Southern University and Agricultural and
 Mechanical College B
Tulane University B
University of Louisiana at Lafayette B

Maine
University of Maine
 Augusta A, B

Maryland
Howard Community College A
Morgan State University M
University of Maryland
 College Park B, M

Massachusetts
Boston Architectural Center B, M
Harvard University M
Massachusetts College of Art B
Massachusetts Institute of
 Technology M, D
Smith College B
Wellesley College B
Wentworth Institute of Technology B

Michigan
Andrews University B
Cranbrook Academy of Art M
Eastern Michigan University B
Lawrence Technological University B, M
Oakland Community College A
University of Detroit Mercy B, M
University of Michigan B, M, D

Minnesota
University of Minnesota
 Twin Cities B, M

Mississippi
Mississippi State University B, M

Missouri
Drury University B
Washington University B, M

Montana
Montana State University
 Bozeman M

Nebraska
University of Nebraska
 Lincoln B, M

Nevada
University of Nevada
 Las Vegas B, M

New Jersey
Brookdale Community College A
New Jersey Institute of Technology B, M
Princeton University B, M, D

New Mexico
University of New Mexico B, M

New York
Barnard College B
City University of New York
 City College B

Columbia University
 Columbia College B
 Graduate School M
 School of General Studies B
Cooper Union for the Advancement of
 Science and Art B
Cornell University B, M
Hobart and William Smith Colleges B
New York Institute of Technology B
Parsons School of Design M
Pratt Institute B, M
Rensselaer Polytechnic Institute B, M
State University of New York
 Buffalo B, M
 College of Agriculture and
  Technology at Morrisville A
Syracuse University B, M

North Carolina
Central Carolina Community College A
Guilford Technical Community
 College C, A
Nash Community College A
North Carolina State University B, M
University of North Carolina
 Charlotte B, M
Wake Technical Community
 College C, A

North Dakota
North Dakota State University B

Ohio
Bryant & Stratton College A
Kent State University
 Stark Campus B
Kent State University B, M
Miami University
 Oxford Campus M
Ohio State University
 Columbus Campus B, M
University of Cincinnati B, M

Oklahoma
Oklahoma State University
 Oklahoma City A
Oklahoma State University B, M
University of Oklahoma B, M

Oregon
Chemeketa Community College A
Portland State University B
University of Oregon B, M

Pennsylvania
Carnegie Mellon University B, M, D
Drexel University B
Harrisburg Area Community College A
Lehigh University B
Penn State
 University Park B, M
Philadelphia University B
Temple University B
University of Pennsylvania M, D

Puerto Rico
Universidad Politecnica de Puerto
 Rico B
University of Puerto Rico
 Rio Piedras Campus M

Rhode Island
Roger Williams University B

South Carolina
Clemson University B, M

Tennessee
Tennessee State University B
University of Tennessee
 Knoxville B, M

Texas
Baylor University B
Brazosport College A
El Paso Community College A
Galveston College A
Palo Alto College A
Prairie View A&M University B

Rice University B, M, D
Texas A&M University M, D
Texas Tech University B, M
University of Houston B, M
University of Texas
 Arlington B, M
 Austin B, M
 San Antonio B, M

Utah
University of Utah B, M

Vermont
Bennington College B
Norwich University M

Virginia
Hampton University B
Northern Virginia Community College A
University of Virginia B, M
Virginia Polytechnic Institute and State
 University B, M

Washington
University of Washington B, M
Washington State University B, M

Wisconsin
Milwaukee Area Technical College A
University of Wisconsin
 Milwaukee B, M, D

Architecture/related programs

Alabama
Lawson State Community College C, A
Northeast Alabama Community
 College A

Arizona
Phoenix College C
Yavapai College C, A

Arkansas
Westark College A

California
East Los Angeles College A
Fresno City College C, A
Glendale Community College C, A
Golden West College C, A
Los Angeles Harbor College A
MiraCosta College C, A
Modesto Junior College C, A
Saddleback College C, A
San Diego Mesa College C, A
San Joaquin Delta College C
Santa Rosa Junior College C
University of California
 Irvine B, M, D

Colorado
Denver Technical College: A Division of
 DeVry University A

Connecticut
Three Rivers Community-Technical
 College C, A

Florida
Art Institute
 of Fort Lauderdale A, B
Broward Community College A
Miami-Dade Community College C, A
Tallahassee Community College A

Georgia
Floyd College A

Illinois
City Colleges of Chicago
 Wright College C, A
Illinois Eastern Community Colleges
 Lincoln Trail College A
Kishwaukee College A
Monmouth College B
University of Illinois
 Chicago B

William Rainey Harper College A

Indiana
Ball State University B
Indiana State University A

Iowa
Cornell College B
Des Moines Area Community College C

Kansas
Central Christian College A
Garden City Community College A
Independence Community College C, A
Kansas City Kansas Community
 College C, A
University of Kansas B

Maine
Central Maine Technical College A

Maryland
University of Maryland
 Eastern Shore B

Massachusetts
Franklin Institute of Boston C, A
Harvard University M, D
Wentworth Institute of Technology B

Michigan
Baker College
 of Owosso A
Ferris State University A
Henry Ford Community College A
Monroe County Community
 College C, A
North Central Michigan College C, A
Northern Michigan University A
St. Clair County Community College A
Washtenaw Community College A

Minnesota
Hennepin Technical College C, A
Northland Community & Technical
 College C, A
South Central Technical College A

Missouri
Washington University B, M

New Hampshire
Keene State College B
University of New Hampshire A

New Jersey
Essex County College A
New Jersey Institute of Technology M

New York
Cornell University B
Genesee Community College A
New York Institute of Technology A, B
Onondaga Community College A
State University of New York
 Buffalo B
 College of Technology at Alfred A

North Carolina
Durham Technical Community
 College C, A
Fayetteville Technical Community
 College A
Guilford Technical Community
 College C, A
Wake Technical Community
 College C, A

Ohio
Bryant & Stratton College A
Central Ohio Technical College C, A
Columbus State Community College A
Kent State University
 Stark Campus B
Terra Community College C, A
University of Toledo A

Oklahoma
Eastern Oklahoma State College A
Oklahoma State University
 Oklahoma City C, A

Oklahoma State University *B, M*

Pennsylvania
Lehigh University *B*
Luzerne County Community
  College *C, A*
Philadelphia University *B*
Triangle Tech
  DuBois Campus *A*

South Carolina
Greenville Technical College *C, A*

South Dakota
Southeast Technical Institute *A*

Texas
El Paso Community College *A*
Texas A&M University *M*

Utah
Salt Lake Community College *A*

Vermont
Bennington College *M*
Norwich University *B*

Virginia
John Tyler Community College *C, A*
New River Community College *A*
Thomas Nelson Community College *A*

Washington
Highline Community College *A*
Washington State University *B*

Wisconsin
Northeast Wisconsin Technical
  College *A*

Area studies

Alabama
University of South Alabama *B*

Alaska
University of Alaska
  Fairbanks *B, M*

Arizona
Prescott College *B, M*

California
University of California
  Berkeley *B*

Colorado
United States Air Force Academy *B*

Connecticut
Trinity College *B*

District of Columbia
George Washington University *M*

Florida
New College of the University of South
  Florida *B*
Rollins College *B*

Hawaii
Hawaii Pacific University *B*

Idaho
University of Idaho *B*

Illinois
Lake Forest College *B*
University of Chicago *M*

Kentucky
Georgetown College *B*

Louisiana
University of Louisiana at Lafayette *D*

Maine
University of Maine
  Fort Kent *B*

Maryland
Johns Hopkins University *B*

Massachusetts
Bridgewater State College *B*
Hampshire College *B*
Harvard College *B*

Michigan
Eastern Michigan University *B*
Kalamazoo College *B*

Minnesota
University of Minnesota
  Twin Cities *B*

Mississippi
University of Mississippi *B, M*

Missouri
Washington University *B*
William Jewell College *B*

New Hampshire
University of New Hampshire *B*

New Mexico
College of Santa Fe *B*
New Mexico Highlands University *M*

New York
Alfred University *B*
Bard College *B*
Cornell University *B*
Eugene Lang College/New School
  University *B*
Iona College *B*
Marymount College *B*
Regents College *B*
Sarah Lawrence College *B*

Oklahoma
Oklahoma State University *C*

Pennsylvania
Bucknell University *B*
Drexel University *B*
Gannon University *B*
Swarthmore College *B*
University of Pittsburgh *M*

Tennessee
Maryville College *B*

Texas
El Paso Community College *A*
Southern Methodist University *B*

Utah
Brigham Young University *B, M*
Utah State University *B*

Vermont
Burlington College *B*
Marlboro College *B*

Virginia
College of William and Mary *B*
Emory & Henry College *B*
University of Virginia *B*

Washington
Western Washington University *B*

West Virginia
University of Charleston *B*

Wisconsin
St. Norbert College *B*

Area/ethnic/cultural studies

Arizona
Prescott College *B, M*

California
Azusa Pacific University *B*
Biola University *B, M, D*
California State University
  Fullerton *B*
  Sacramento *B*
Chabot College *A*
City College of San Francisco *A*
Loyola Marymount University *B*
Pomona College *B*
Riverside Community College *A*
Sacramento City College *A*
San Francisco State University *M*
Santa Barbara City College *A*
Solano Community College *A*
University of California
  Irvine *B, M, D*
Whittier College *B*
Yuba College *A*

Colorado
Fort Lewis College *B*

Connecticut
Trinity College *B*
University of Connecticut *M*

Delaware
University of Delaware *M*

District of Columbia
Gallaudet University *B*

Florida
Eckerd College *B*
Polk Community College *A*

Georgia
Andrew College *A*
Toccoa Falls College *B, M*

Hawaii
Hawaii Pacific University *B*

Idaho
Boise State University *B*

Indiana
Manchester College *B*
St. Mary-of-the-Woods College *B*
Valparaiso University *B*

Iowa
Cornell College *B*

Kansas
Wichita State University *B*

Kentucky
Thomas More College *A, B*

Maine
University of Maine
  Fort Kent *B*
University of Southern Maine *B, M*

Maryland
Towson University *B*

Massachusetts
Boston College *B*
Boston University *B, M*
Hampshire College *B*
Harvard College *B*
Northeastern University *B*
Tufts University *M*

Minnesota
Bethel College *B*
Hamline University *B*
Minnesota State University, Mankato *B*

Mississippi
University of Mississippi *B*

Missouri
University of Missouri
  Columbia *B*
Washington University *B*

New Mexico
New Mexico Highlands University *M*

New York
Bard College *B*
Barnard College *B*
City University of New York
  Hunter College *B*
Cornell University *B*
Eugene Lang College/New School
  University *B*
Iona College *B*
Sage Junior College of Albany *A*
St. Francis College *B*
Sarah Lawrence College *B*
Skidmore College *B*
State University of New York
  College at Oneonta *B*
  Empire State College *A, B*

North Carolina
Appalachian State University *M*
East Carolina University *M*
University of North Carolina
  Greensboro *B*

Ohio
Antioch College *B*
Bowling Green State University *B*
Youngstown State University *B*

Oklahoma
Oklahoma State University *C*
University of Oklahoma *B*

Oregon
Central Oregon Community College *A*
Pacific University *B*

Pennsylvania
Dickinson College *B*
Gettysburg College *B*
Immaculata College *C, D*

Rhode Island
Brown University *B*

South Carolina
Columbia International University *B*
Wofford College *B*

South Dakota
Sinte Gleska University *B*

Utah
Salt Lake Community College *A*

Vermont
Burlington College *B*
Goddard College *B, M*
Marlboro College *B*

Virginia
Emory & Henry College *B*
George Mason University *D*
Old Dominion University *M*
University of Richmond *B*

Washington
Evergreen State College *B*
North Seattle Community College *C, A*
Washington State University *B*
Western Washington University *B*

Army

Alabama
Calhoun Community College *A*

Colorado
Red Rocks Community College *C*

Georgia
Georgia Military College *A*
Savannah State University *C*

Idaho
University of Idaho *B*

Iowa
Marshalltown Community College *A*

Louisiana
Northwestern State University *C*

New York
Canisius College *C*

North Carolina
Methodist College *A, B*

Pennsylvania
La Salle University C, B
Mercyhurst College B
West Chester University of Pennsylvania C
Widener University B

South Carolina
Wofford College C

Texas
El Paso Community College A
University of Texas
    Pan American B

Virginia
Mary Baldwin College T

Washington
Eastern Washington University B
Pierce College A

Wisconsin
Ripon College B

Art

Alabama
Alabama State University B, T
Athens State University B
Auburn University at Montgomery B
Birmingham-Southern College B, T
Calhoun Community College A
Huntingdon College B, T
Jacksonville State University B
James H. Faulkner State Community College A
Northeast Alabama Community College A
Northwest-Shoals Community College A
Samford University B
Troy State University B
University of Alabama
    Huntsville B
University of Mobile B, T
University of Montevallo B, T
University of South Alabama B
Wallace State Community College at Hanceville A

Alaska
University of Alaska
    Anchorage B
    Fairbanks B
    Southeast B

Arizona
Arizona State University M
Eastern Arizona College A
Grand Canyon University B
Northern Arizona University B
Phoenix College A
Pima Community College A
South Mountain Community College A
University of Arizona M

Arkansas
Arkansas State University B, M
Arkansas Tech University B
Harding University B
Henderson State University B
Hendrix College B
Lyon College B
Southern Arkansas University B
University of Arkansas
    Little Rock B, M
    Monticello B
University of Arkansas B, M
University of Central Arkansas B
University of the Ozarks B
Westark College A

California
Allan Hancock College A
Art Center College of Design B
Azusa Pacific University B
Biola University B
Cabrillo College A
California Baptist University B
California Institute of the Arts C, B
California Lutheran University B
California State Polytechnic University: Pomona B
California State University
    Bakersfield B
    Chico B, M
    Fresno B, M
    Fullerton B
    Hayward B
    Long Beach B, M
    Los Angeles B
    Monterey Bay B
    Northridge B, M
    Sacramento B, M
Canada College A
Cerritos Community College A
Cerro Coso Community College A
Chabot College A
Chaffey Community College A
Chapman University B, M
Claremont McKenna College B
College of Notre Dame B
College of the Canyons A
College of the Sequoias A
Columbia College A
Compton Community College A
Concordia University B
Crafton Hills College A
Cypress College A
De Anza College A
East Los Angeles College A
Foothill College C, A
Fresno City College A
Gavilan Community College A
Golden West College A
Humboldt State University B, M
Imperial Valley College A
Irvine Valley College A
Kings River Community College A
La Sierra University B
Lake Tahoe Community College C, A
Los Angeles Harbor College A
Los Angeles Mission College A
Los Angeles Southwest College A
Los Angeles Valley College A
Mendocino College C, A
Mills College B
MiraCosta College A
Mission College C, A
Modesto Junior College A
Monterey Peninsula College A
Mount San Jacinto College A
Occidental College B
Palomar College C, A
Pepperdine University B
Pitzer College B
Point Loma Nazarene University B
Pomona College B
Riverside Community College C, A
Saddleback College A
St. Mary's College of California B
San Diego Miramar College A
San Diego State University B, M
San Francisco Art Institute B, M
San Francisco State University B
San Jose City College C
San Jose State University M
Santa Barbara City College A
Santa Clara University B
Santa Rosa Junior College C, A
Shasta College A
Sierra College C, A
Skyline College A
Southwestern College C, A
Stanford University B, M, D
Taft College A
University of California
    Berkeley B, M
    Irvine B, M
    Los Angeles B, M
    Santa Barbara B
    Santa Cruz B
University of La Verne B
University of Redlands B
University of San Diego B
University of Southern California B
University of the Pacific B
West Hills Community College A
West Los Angeles College C, A
West Valley College A
Westmont College B
Whittier College B

Colorado
Adams State College B, M
Colorado Christian University B
Colorado Mountain College
    Alpine Campus A
    Spring Valley Campus A
    Timberline Campus A
Colorado State University B
Fort Lewis College B
Lamar Community College A
Metropolitan State College of Denver B
Morgan Community College A
Red Rocks Community College A
University of Denver B
University of Northern Colorado B, M, T
University of Southern Colorado B, T
Western State College of Colorado B

Connecticut
Albertus Magnus College B
Central Connecticut State University B
Eastern Connecticut State University B
Naugatuck Valley Community-Technical College A
Norwalk Community-Technical College A
Sacred Heart University A, B
Southern Connecticut State University B, M
Trinity College B
University of Hartford M
University of New Haven B
Western Connecticut State University B
Yale University B

Delaware
Delaware State University B
University of Delaware B

District of Columbia
American University B
Catholic University of America B, M, T
Corcoran College of Art and Design B
Georgetown University B
Howard University B, M

Florida
Broward Community College A
Eckerd College B
Florida Atlantic University B
Florida Southern College B
Florida State University B, M
Gulf Coast Community College A
Hillsborough Community College A
Indian River Community College A
Jacksonville University B, M
New College of the University of South Florida B
Palm Beach Atlantic College B, T
Pensacola Junior College A
Polk Community College A
Stetson University B
University of Central Florida B
University of Miami B, M
University of North Florida B
University of South Florida B, M
University of Tampa B
University of West Florida B

Georgia
Agnes Scott College B
Albany State University B
Atlanta College of Art B
Berry College B
Brenau University B
Clayton College and State University A
Columbus State University B
East Georgia College A
Georgia College and State University B
Georgia Military College A
Georgia Perimeter College A
Georgia Southern University B
Georgia Southwestern State University B
LaGrange College B
Macon State College A
Mercer University B, T
Morris Brown College B
North Georgia College & State University B
Oglethorpe University B
Piedmont College B
State University of West Georgia B
University of Georgia B, M, D
Young Harris College A

Hawaii
Brigham Young University
    Hawaii B
University of Hawaii
    Hilo B
    Manoa B

Idaho
Albertson College of Idaho B
Boise State University B, M
College of Southern Idaho A
Idaho State University A, B, M
Ricks College A
University of Idaho B, M

Illinois
Augustana College B
Black Hawk College
    East Campus A
Chicago State University B
City Colleges of Chicago
    Harold Washington College A
College of Lake County A
Columbia College B
Concordia University B, T
Dominican University B
Eastern Illinois University B, M, T
Elgin Community College A
Elmhurst College B, T
Eureka College B
Governors State University B, M
Greenville College B, T
Highland Community College C, A
Illinois College B
Illinois State University B, M, T
Illinois Wesleyan University B
John A. Logan College A
John Wood Community College A
Joliet Junior College A
Judson College B
Kankakee Community College A
Kishwaukee College A
Knox College B
Lewis University B, T
Loyola University of Chicago B
MacMurray College B
McHenry County College A
McKendree College B, T
Millikin University B, T
Monmouth College B, T
North Central College B
North Park University B
Northeastern Illinois University B
Northern Illinois University B, M
Olivet Nazarene University B, T
Parkland College A
Quincy University A, B, T
Richland Community College A
Rockford College B
Sauk Valley Community College A
Southern Illinois University
    Carbondale B, M
    Edwardsville B, M
Southwestern Illinois College A
Springfield College in Illinois A
Trinity Christian College B
Trinity International University M

Triton College *A*
University of Illinois
    Springfield *B*
Western Illinois University *B*
Wheaton College *B*
William Rainey Harper College *A*

Indiana
Ball State University *B, M*
Bethel College *B*
Earlham College *B*
Goshen College *B*
Grace College *B*
Hanover College *B*
Indiana State University *B, T*
Indiana University
    Northwest *B*
    South Bend *B*
Manchester College *A, B, T*
Marian College *A, B*
Oakland City University *B*
Purdue University *B, M*
Saint Mary's College *B*
Taylor University *B*
University of Evansville *B*
University of Indianapolis *B, M*
University of St. Francis *B*
University of Southern Indiana *B*
Valparaiso University *B, T*
Wabash College *B*

Iowa
Briar Cliff College *B*
Buena Vista University *B, T*
Central College *B, T*
Clarke College *A, B, T*
Coe College *B*
Cornell College *B, T*
Dordt College *B*
Drake University *B*
Grand View College *B*
Grinnell College *B*
Iowa State University *B*
Loras College *B*
Luther College *B*
Maharishi University of
    Management *A, B, M*
Marycrest International University *A, B*
Morningside College *B*
Mount Mercy College *B*
North Iowa Area Community College *A*
Northwestern College *B, T*
Simpson College *B*
University of Iowa *B, T*
University of Northern Iowa *B, M*
Upper Iowa University *B*
Waldorf College *A, B*
Wartburg College *B, T*

Kansas
Allen County Community College *A*
Bethany College *B, T*
Bethel College *B, T*
Butler County Community College *A*
Central Christian College *A*
Coffeyville Community College *A*
Cowley County Community College *A*
Dodge City Community College *A*
Emporia State University *B, T*
Fort Hays State University *B*
Garden City Community College *A*
Independence Community College *A*
Kansas City Kansas Community
    College *A*
Kansas State University *B, M*
McPherson College *B, T*
Newman University *B*
Ottawa University *B, T*
Pittsburg State University *B, M, T*
St. Mary College *B*
Seward County Community College *A*
Sterling College *B*
Wichita State University *B, M, T*

Kentucky
Bellarmine College *B, T*

Brescia University *B*
Campbellsville University *B*
Centre College *B*
Cumberland College *B, T*
Kentucky Wesleyan College *B, T*
Lindsey Wilson College *B*
Pikeville College *B*
Thomas More College *A, B*

Louisiana
Centenary College of Louisiana *B, T*
Delgado Community College *A*
Dillard University *B*
Louisiana State University
    Shreveport *B*
Louisiana Tech University *B, M*
Loyola University New Orleans *B*
McNeese State University *B*
Nicholls State University *B*
Northwestern State University *B, M*
Southeastern Louisiana University *B*
Tulane University *M*
University of Louisiana at Monroe *B*
Xavier University of Louisiana *B*

Maine
Bates College *B*
Colby College *B*
Maine College of Art *B*
University of Maine
    Augusta *A, B*
    Presque Isle *A, B*
University of Southern Maine *B*

Maryland
Allegany College *A*
Baltimore City Community College *A*
Charles County Community College *A*
College of Notre Dame of Maryland *B*
Frederick Community College *A*
Goucher College *B*
Hood College *B*
Howard Community College *A*
Loyola College in Maryland *B*
St. Mary's College of Maryland *B*
Salisbury State University *B, T*
Towson University *B, M, T*
University of Maryland
    Baltimore County *B*
    Eastern Shore *B*
Washington College *B*
Western Maryland College *B*

Massachusetts
Anna Maria College *B*
Berkshire Community College *A*
Bridgewater State College *B*
Bristol Community College *A*
Clark University *B*
Framingham State College *M*
Hampshire College *B*
Harvard College *B*
Massachusetts Bay Community
    College *C*
Montserrat College of Art *B*
Mount Holyoke College *B*
Mount Ida College *A, B*
Mount Wachusett Community College *A*
Northeastern University *B*
Regis College *B*
School of the Museum of Fine Arts *B, M*
Simon's Rock College of Bard *B*
Smith College *B, M*
Springfield College *B*
University of Massachusetts
    Amherst *M*
    Boston *B*
Westfield State College *B*

Michigan
Adrian College *A, B, T*
Alma College *B, T*
Andrews University *B*
Calvin College *B, T*
Central Michigan University *B, M*
Concordia College *B, T*
Eastern Michigan University *B, M, T*

Gogebic Community College *A*
Grand Valley State University *B*
Henry Ford Community College *A*
Hillsdale College *B*
Kalamazoo College *B, T*
Kellogg Community College *A*
Lake Michigan College *A*
Lansing Community College *A*
Madonna University *A, B, T*
Marygrove College *B, T*
Michigan State University *B, M*
Mott Community College *A*
Northern Michigan University *B, T*
Northwestern Michigan College *A*
Olivet College *B, T*
Saginaw Valley State University *B*
Siena Heights University *A, B*
Spring Arbor College *B*
Suomi College *B*
University of Michigan *B, M*
Wayne State University *B, M*
Western Michigan University *B, M, T*

Minnesota
Augsburg College *B*
Bemidji State University *B*
College of St. Benedict *B*
Concordia College: Moorhead *B*
Concordia University: St. Paul *B*
Gustavus Adolphus College *B*
Minneapolis College of Art and
    Design *M*
Minnesota State University,
    Mankato *B, M*
Northland Community & Technical
    College *A*
Ridgewater College: A Community and
    Technical College *A*
St. Cloud State University *B, M*
St. John's University *B*
St. Olaf College *B*
Southwest State University *B, T*
University of Minnesota
    Duluth *B, M*
    Twin Cities *M, D*
Winona State University *B*

Mississippi
Belhaven College *B, T*
Hinds Community College *A*
Mississippi College *B, M*
Mississippi Gulf Coast Community
    College
        Jefferson Davis Campus *A*
Tougaloo College *B*
William Carey College *B*

Missouri
Central Missouri State University *B, M*
College of the Ozarks *B*
Columbia College *B*
Crowder College *A*
Culver-Stockton College *B, T*
Drury University *B, T*
East Central College *A*
Fontbonne College *B, M, T*
Hannibal-LaGrange College *B*
Jefferson College *A*
Lincoln University *B*
Lindenwood University *M*
Missouri Valley College *B*
Missouri Western State College *B*
Northwest Missouri State University *B*
Park University *B*
Southeast Missouri State University *B*
Southwest Baptist University *B*
Southwest Missouri State University *B*
Truman State University *B*
University of Missouri
    Columbia *B, M*
    Kansas City *B, M*
Webster University *B, M*
William Jewell College *B*
William Woods University *B*

Montana
Carroll College *A*
Montana State University
    Billings *B*
    Bozeman *B, T*
Rocky Mountain College *B*
University of Great Falls *B, T*
University of Montana-Missoula *B, M*
Western Montana College of The
    University of Montana *B, T*

Nebraska
Bellevue University *B*
Chadron State College *B*
Creighton University *B*
Dana College *B*
Doane College *B*
Hastings College *B*
Midland Lutheran College *B, T*
Nebraska Wesleyan University *B*
Northeast Community College *A*
Peru State College *B*
University of Nebraska
    Kearney *B, M, T*
    Lincoln *B*
Wayne State College *B, M, T*

Nevada
Community College of Southern
    Nevada *A*
University of Nevada
    Las Vegas *B, M*
    Reno *B*

New Hampshire
Colby-Sawyer College *B, T*
Franklin Pierce College *B*
Keene State College *B*
New England College *B*
Plymouth State College of the University
    System of New Hampshire *B*
White Pines College *B*

New Jersey
Brookdale Community College *A*
Caldwell College *B*
College of St. Elizabeth *B, T*
Essex County College *A*
Fairleigh Dickinson University *B*
Felician College *B*
Georgian Court College *B, T*
Gloucester County College *A*
Kean University *B*
Monmouth University *B*
Montclair State University *B, M, T*
New Jersey City University *B, T*
Ocean County College *A*
Richard Stockton College of New
    Jersey *B*
Rowan University *C, B*
Rutgers
    The State University of New Jersey:
        Camden College of Arts and
        Sciences *B, T*
    The State University of New Jersey:
        Douglass College *B*
    The State University of New Jersey:
        Livingston College *B*
    The State University of New Jersey:
        Mason Gross School of the
        Arts *B*
    The State University of New Jersey:
        New Brunswick Graduate
        Campus *M*
    The State University of New Jersey:
        Newark College of Arts and
        Sciences *B, T*
    The State University of New Jersey:
        Rutgers College *B*
    The State University of New Jersey:
        University College Camden *B, T*
    The State University of New Jersey:
        University College New
        Brunswick *B*
Sussex County Community College *A*
Thomas Edison State College *B*

William Paterson University of New Jersey B

New Mexico
Eastern New Mexico University A, B
New Mexico State University Alamogordo A
New Mexico State University B, M
Northern New Mexico Community College A
San Juan College A
University of New Mexico B, M

New York
Adirondack Community College A
Bard College B
Cayuga County Community College A
City University of New York
    Brooklyn College M
    City College B
    College of Staten Island B
    Hunter College M
    Kingsborough Community College A
    Lehman College M
    Queensborough Community College A
Colgate University B
Daemen College B, T
Dowling College B, T
Elmira College B
Fordham University B
Fulton-Montgomery Community College A
Hartwick College B
Herkimer County Community College A
Houghton College B
Ithaca College B
Long Island University
    C. W. Post Campus B, M
    Southampton College B
Molloy College B
Nazareth College of Rochester B, T
Onondaga Community College A
Pace University:
    Pleasantville/Briarcliff B, T
Pace University B, T
Parsons School of Design C, A, B, T
Roberts Wesleyan College B
St. John's University B
St. Thomas Aquinas College B, T
Sarah Lawrence College B
School of Visual Arts B, M
State University of New York
    Albany B, M
    College at Brockport B
    College at Fredonia B
    College at Plattsburgh B
    College at Potsdam B
    New Paltz B, T
    Oswego B
Vassar College B
Westchester Community College A

North Carolina
Appalachian State University B
Brevard College A, B
College of the Albemarle A
Davidson College B
East Carolina University B, M
Elizabeth City State University B
Elon College B
Greensboro College B, T
Guilford College B
High Point University B
Louisburg College A
Mars Hill College B, T
Meredith College B
Methodist College B
North Carolina Agricultural and Technical State University B, T
North Carolina Central University B
St. Augustine's College B
Sandhills Community College A
Southeastern Community College A

University of North Carolina
    Asheville B, T
    Charlotte B
    Greensboro B, M, T
Warren Wilson College B
Western Carolina University B
Wingate University B

North Dakota
Dickinson State University B, T
Minot State University: Bottineau Campus A
Minot State University B, T
North Dakota State University B
Valley City State University B

Ohio
Ashland University A
Baldwin-Wallace College B
Bluffton College B
Bowling Green State University B, M
Capital University B
Cleveland State University B, T
College of Mount St. Joseph A, B, T
Defiance College B, T
Kent State University
    Stark Campus B
Kenyon College B
Malone College B
Miami University
    Oxford Campus B, M, T
Mount Union College B
Mount Vernon Nazarene College B
Muskingum College B
Ohio Dominican College B, T
Ohio Northern University B
Ohio State University
    Columbus Campus B, M
Ohio University B, M
Otterbein College B
University of Akron B
University of Dayton B
University of Findlay B
University of Rio Grande A, B, T
University of Toledo B
Ursuline College B
Wilmington College B
Wittenberg University B
Wright State University B
Xavier University B
Youngstown State University B

Oklahoma
Cameron University B
Connors State College A
East Central University B, T
Langston University B
Northeastern State University B
Northern Oklahoma College A
Oklahoma Baptist University B, T
Oklahoma Christian University of Science and Arts B
Oklahoma City University B
Oklahoma State University B
Oral Roberts University B
Redlands Community College A
Rose State College A
Seminole State College A
Southeastern Oklahoma State University B
University of Central Oklahoma B
University of Oklahoma B, M
University of Science and Arts of Oklahoma B, T
University of Tulsa B, M
Western Oklahoma State College A

Oregon
Chemeketa Community College A
George Fox University B
Lewis & Clark College B
Linfield College B
Linn-Benton Community College A
Marylhurst University C, B
Oregon State University B
Pacific University B

Southern Oregon University B, T
University of Oregon B
Western Oregon University B
Willamette University B

Pennsylvania
Allegheny College B
Bucknell University B
Carlow College B
Cedar Crest College B
Cheyney University of Pennsylvania B
Clarion University of Pennsylvania B
Community College of Allegheny County A
Community College of Philadelphia A
Edinboro University of Pennsylvania B, M
Elizabethtown College B
Gettysburg College B
Harrisburg Area Community College A
Holy Family College B
Indiana University of Pennsylvania B
Kutztown University of Pennsylvania B
Lehigh University B
Lock Haven University of Pennsylvania B
Mansfield University of Pennsylvania B, T
Marywood University C
Mercyhurst College B
Messiah College B
Millersville University of Pennsylvania B
Moravian College B, T
Penn State
    University Park B, M
Seton Hill College B, T
Shippensburg University of Pennsylvania B
Slippery Rock University of Pennsylvania B
Susquehanna University B
Temple University B
Thiel College B
University of Pennsylvania A, B, M, D
Washington and Jefferson College B
Waynesburg College B
Westminster College B
Wilkes University B
York College of Pennsylvania B

Puerto Rico
University of Puerto Rico
    Mayaguez Campus B
    Rio Piedras Campus B

Rhode Island
Community College of Rhode Island A
University of Rhode Island B

South Carolina
Anderson College B
Benedict College B
Claflin University B
Coker College B, T
Columbia College B
Francis Marion University B
Furman University B, T
Lander University B
Newberry College B
North Greenville College A
Presbyterian College B
Winthrop University B

South Dakota
Augustana College B
Black Hills State University B
Dakota Wesleyan University B
Northern State University B
South Dakota State University B
University of South Dakota B, M

Tennessee
Austin Peay State University B
Belmont University B
Carson-Newman College B, T
Columbia State Community College A

Fisk University B
Freed-Hardeman University B, T
Lambuth University B
LeMoyne-Owen College B
Maryville College B
Middle Tennessee State University B
Rhodes College B, T
Roane State Community College A
Southern Adventist University B
Tennessee Technological University T
Union University B, T
University of Memphis B, M
University of Tennessee
    Chattanooga B, T
    Knoxville B, M
    Martin B
Walters State Community College A

Texas
Abilene Christian University B
Alvin Community College A
Amarillo College A
Angelina College A
Angelo State University B, T
Austin College B
Austin Community College A
Baylor University B
Brazosport College A
Central Texas College A
Dallas Baptist University B
Del Mar College A
El Paso Community College A
Galveston College A
Grayson County College A
Hardin-Simmons University B
Hill College A
Howard College A
Howard Payne University T
Kilgore College A
Lamar University B
Lon Morris College A
McMurry University B, T
Midland College A
Midwestern State University B
Mountain View College C, A
Navarro College C, A
Northeast Texas Community College A
Our Lady of the Lake University of San Antonio B
Palo Alto College A
Panola College A
Rice University B
St. Philip's College A
Sam Houston State University B, M
San Jacinto College
    North A
Schreiner College B
Southwest Texas State University B, T
Southwestern University B, T
Stephen F. Austin State University B, M, T
Sul Ross State University B, M
Tarleton State University B
Texas A&M University
    Commerce B, M
    Corpus Christi T
Texas Christian University T
Texas College B
Texas Lutheran University B
Texas Tech University B, M, D
Texas Wesleyan University B
Texas Woman's University M, T
Trinity University B
Trinity Valley Community College A
University of Houston
    Clear Lake B
University of Houston B
University of Mary Hardin-Baylor B, T
University of Texas
    Arlington B
    Austin B
    El Paso B, M
    San Antonio B, M
    Tyler B
University of the Incarnate Word B

Wayland Baptist University *B*
West Texas A&M University *B, M*
Western Texas College *A*
Wharton County Junior College *A*

Utah
Brigham Young University *B*
Dixie State College of Utah *A*
Salt Lake Community College *A*
Snow College *A*
University of Utah *B, M*
Utah State University *B, M*
Weber State University *B*
Westminster College *B*

Vermont
Bennington College *M*
Castleton State College *B*
Green Mountain College *B*
Johnson State College *B*
Marlboro College *B*
St. Michael's College *B*

Virginia
Averett College *B, T*
Bluefield College *B*
Bridgewater College *B*
Christopher Newport University *B*
Eastern Mennonite University *B*
Emory & Henry College *B, T*
Ferrum College *B*
George Mason University *B*
James Madison University *B, T*
Longwood College *B, T*
Lynchburg College *B*
Mary Baldwin College *B*
Norfolk State University *B*
Old Dominion University *B*
Radford University *B, M*
Roanoke College *B, T*
University of Virginia's College at Wise *B, T*
University of Virginia *B*
Virginia Intermont College *B*
Virginia Polytechnic Institute and State University *B*
Virginia Union University *B*
Virginia Wesleyan College *B*

Washington
Central Washington University *B, M*
Eastern Washington University *B, M, T*
Everett Community College *A*
Evergreen State College *B*
Highline Community College *A*
Lower Columbia College *A*
North Seattle Community College *C*
Pacific Lutheran University *B*
Seattle Pacific University *B*
Seattle University *B*
University of Puget Sound *B, T*
University of Washington *B, M*
Walla Walla College *B*
Washington State University *B, M*
Western Washington University *B, T*
Whitworth College *B, T*

West Virginia
Concord College *B*
Davis and Elkins College *B*
Shepherd College *B*
University of Charleston *B*
West Virginia University *B, M, T*

Wisconsin
Alverno College *B*
Cardinal Stritch University *A, B*
Carroll College *B*
Carthage College *B*
Concordia University Wisconsin *B*
Lakeland College *B*
Marian College of Fond du Lac *B*
Mount Mary College *B*
Northland College *B, T*
Ripon College *B, T*
St. Norbert College *B, T*
Silver Lake College *B*

University of Wisconsin
 Eau Claire *B*
 Green Bay *B*
 La Crosse *B*
 Madison *B, M*
 Milwaukee *B, M, D*
 Oshkosh *B*
 Parkside *B*
 Platteville *B*
 River Falls *B*
 Stevens Point *B*
 Whitewater *B, T*
Viterbo University *B*
Wisconsin Lutheran College *B*

Wyoming
Casper College *A*
Central Wyoming College *C, A*
Eastern Wyoming College *A*
Sheridan College *A*
University of Wyoming *B, M*
Western Wyoming Community College *A*

Art education

Alabama
Alabama State University *B*
Birmingham-Southern College *B, T*
Huntingdon College *B, T*
University of Alabama
 Birmingham *B, M*

Arizona
Arizona State University *B, T*
Eastern Arizona College *A*
Grand Canyon University *B*
Northern Arizona University *B, T*
Prescott College *B, M*
University of Arizona *B, M*

Arkansas
Arkansas State University *B, T*
Arkansas Tech University *B*
Harding University *B, M, T*
Henderson State University *B, M, T*
Ouachita Baptist University *B, T*
Southern Arkansas University *B, T*
University of Arkansas
 Monticello *B*
 Pine Bluff *B, T*
University of Central Arkansas *T*
University of the Ozarks *B, T*
Williams Baptist College *B*

California
Azusa Pacific University *B, T*
California Baptist University *B, T*
California Lutheran University *B, T*
California State Polytechnic University:
 Pomona *T*
California State University
 Bakersfield *B, T*
 Chico *T*
 Dominguez Hills *T*
 Fullerton *B, T*
 Long Beach *B, T*
 Northridge *B, T*
Cuesta College *C, A*
Humboldt State University *T*
Mount St. Mary's College *T*
Occidental College *T*
San Francisco State University *B, T*
San Jose State University *T*
Sonoma State University *T*
University of San Francisco *M*
University of the Pacific *T*
Westmont College *T*

Colorado
Adams State College *B, M, T*
Colorado State University *T*
Fort Lewis College *T*
Metropolitan State College of Denver *B, T*
University of Denver *B*

Western State College of Colorado *T*

Connecticut
Central Connecticut State University *B, M*
Southern Connecticut State University *B, M, T*

Delaware
Delaware State University *B*

District of Columbia
Gallaudet University *B, T*
George Washington University *M, T*
Howard University *B*
Trinity College *M*
University of the District of Columbia *B*

Florida
Flagler College *B*
Florida Agricultural and Mechanical University *B, M*
Florida Atlantic University *M*
Florida International University *B, M, T*
Florida Southern College *B*
Florida State University *B, M, D, T*
Jacksonville University *B, M, T*
Palm Beach Atlantic College *B, T*
Palm Beach Community College *A*
Stetson University *B, T*
University of Central Florida *B, M*
University of Florida *B, M*
University of North Florida *B*
University of South Florida *B, M*
University of West Florida *B, T*

Georgia
Armstrong Atlantic State University *B, M, T*
Atlanta Metropolitan College *A*
Berry College *B*
Brenau University *B*
Clark Atlanta University *B*
Columbus State University *B, M*
Gainesville College *A*
Georgia College and State University *B, T*
Georgia Southern University *B, M, T*
Georgia Southwestern State University *B, M*
Georgia State University *B, M*
LaGrange College *B*
Mercer University *T*
North Georgia College & State University *B, M*
Piedmont College *B, T*
Reinhardt College *B*
Shorter College *B, T*
State University of West Georgia *B, M*
University of Georgia *B, M, D, T*
Valdosta State University *B, M*
Young Harris College *A*

Hawaii
Brigham Young University Hawaii *B, T*
University of Hawaii Manoa *B, T*

Idaho
Boise State University *B, M, T*
Northwest Nazarene University *B*
University of Idaho *B, M, T*

Illinois
Augustana College *B, T*
Blackburn College *B, T*
Bradley University *B*
Chicago State University *B*
City Colleges of Chicago
 Olive-Harvey College *A*
Columbia College *M*
Dominican University *T*
Elmhurst College *B*
Greenville College *B, T*
Illinois College *T*
John A. Logan College *A*
Kankakee Community College *A*

Lewis University *T*
Loyola University of Chicago *T*
McKendree College *T*
Moraine Valley Community College *A*
North Central College *B, T*
North Park University *T*
Northern Illinois University *B, M, T*
Northwestern University *B, T*
Olivet Nazarene University *B, T*
Parkland College *A*
Quincy University *A, B, T*
Rockford College *T*
Sauk Valley Community College *A*
School of the Art Institute of Chicago *B, M*
Trinity Christian College *B, T*
University of Illinois
 Chicago *B*
 Urbana-Champaign *B, M, D, T*
Wheaton College *T*

Indiana
Anderson University *B, T*
Ball State University *B*
Goshen College *B*
Grace College *B*
Indiana State University *B, M, T*
Indiana University
 Bloomington *B, M*
Indiana University--Purdue University
 Indiana University-Purdue
  University Indianapolis *B, M, T*
Indiana Wesleyan University *B, T*
Oakland City University *B*
St. Mary-of-the-Woods College *B*
Taylor University *B*
University of Evansville *T*
University of Indianapolis *B, M, T*
University of St. Francis *B*
University of Southern Indiana *B, T*
Vincennes University *A*

Iowa
Briar Cliff College *B*
Buena Vista University *B, T*
Central College *T*
Clarke College *B, T*
Cornell College *B, T*
Dordt College *B*
Drake University *M*
Graceland University *T*
Iowa State University *T*
Iowa Wesleyan College *B*
Loras College *B*
Luther College *B*
Morningside College *B*
Mount Mercy College *T*
Northwestern College *T*
St. Ambrose University *B, T*
Simpson College *B*
University of Iowa *B, M, D, T*
Wartburg College *B, T*

Kansas
Baker University *B, T*
Bethany College *B*
Bethel College *T*
Colby Community College *A*
Emporia State University *B*
Garden City Community College *A*
Independence Community College *A*
Kansas State University *B, T*
Kansas Wesleyan University *B, T*
McPherson College *B, T*
Ottawa University *B, T*
Pittsburg State University *B, T*
University of Kansas *B, M, T*
Wichita State University *B, M*

Kentucky
Asbury College *B, T*
Berea College *B, T*
Brescia University *B, T*
Campbellsville University *B*
Cumberland College *B, T*
Eastern Kentucky University *B*

Kentucky State University *B*
Morehead State University *M*
Murray State University *B, T*
Northern Kentucky University *B, T*
Spalding University *B*
Thomas More College *B*
Transylvania University *B, T*
University of Kentucky *B, M*
Western Kentucky University *B, M*

Louisiana
Centenary College of Louisiana *B, T*
Dillard University *B*
Louisiana State University
    Shreveport *B*
Louisiana Tech University *B*
McNeese State University *T*
Nicholls State University *B*
Northwestern State University *B, M, T*
Southeastern Louisiana University *B*
University of Louisiana at Monroe *B*
Xavier University of Louisiana *B, T*

Maine
Maine College of Art *T*
University of Maine *B*
University of Southern Maine *B, T*

Maryland
College of Notre Dame of Maryland *T*
Columbia Union College *B*
Community College of Baltimore County
    Catonsville *A*
    Essex *A*
Maryland Institute College of
    Art *B, M, T*
Montgomery College
    Germantown Campus *A*
    Rockville Campus *A*
    Takoma Park Campus *A*
St. Mary's College of Maryland *T*
Towson University *B, M*
University of Maryland
    College Park *B, T*
    Eastern Shore *B*

Massachusetts
Anna Maria College *B, T*
Boston University *B, M*
Bridgewater State College *M, T*
Elms College *T*
Fitchburg State College *M*
Framingham State College *T*
Massachusetts College of Art *B, M*
Montserrat College of Art *T*
Northeastern University *B*
School of the Museum of Fine
    Arts *B, M, T*
Springfield College *B*
Tufts University *M, T*
University of Massachusetts
    Dartmouth *B, M*
Westfield State College *B, T*

Michigan
Adrian College *B, T*
Albion College *B, T*
Alma College *T*
Andrews University *M*
Aquinas College *B, T*
Calvin College *B*
Central Michigan University *B, M*
Concordia College *B, T*
Eastern Michigan University *B, M, T*
Gogebic Community College *A*
Grand Valley State University *T*
Kellogg Community College *A*
Lansing Community College *A*
Michigan State University *B, M*
Northern Michigan University *B, M, T*
University of Michigan
    Dearborn *B*
    Flint *B, T*
University of Michigan *B*
Wayne State University *B, M, T*
Western Michigan University *B, M*

Minnesota
Augsburg College *T*
Bemidji State University *T*
Bethel College *B*
College of St. Benedict *B, T*
College of St. Catherine: St. Paul
    Campus *B, M, T*
Concordia College: Moorhead *B, T*
Concordia University: St. Paul *B, T*
Gustavus Adolphus College *T*
Hamline University *B*
Minnesota State University,
    Mankato *B, M, T*
Moorhead State University *B, M, T*
Northwestern College *B*
Ridgewater College: A Community and
    Technical College *A*
St. John's University *B, T*
St. Olaf College *T*
Southwest State University *B, T*
University of Minnesota
    Duluth *B*
    Twin Cities *B, M, T*
Winona State University *B, T*

Mississippi
Coahoma Community College *A*
Delta State University *T*
Mississippi College *B, M*
Mississippi Delta Community College *A*
Mississippi Gulf Coast Community
    College
    Jefferson Davis Campus *A*
    Perkinston *A*
Mississippi University for Women *B, T*
Northwest Mississippi Community
    College *A*
University of Mississippi *B, M, T*
University of Southern Mississippi *M*
William Carey College *M*

Missouri
Avila College *T*
Central Missouri State University *B, T*
College of the Ozarks *B, T*
Columbia College *T*
Culver-Stockton College *B, T*
Evangel University *B*
Fontbonne College *B*
Hannibal-LaGrange College *B*
Lincoln University *B, T*
Lindenwood University *B, M*
Maryville University of Saint
    Louis *B, M, T*
Missouri Southern State College *B, T*
Missouri Western State College *B*
Northwest Missouri State
    University *B, M, T*
Park University *T*
Southeast Missouri State University *B*
Southwest Baptist University *B, T*
Southwest Missouri State University *B*
Truman State University *M, T*
University of Missouri
    Columbia *B*
Washington University *B, M, T*
William Woods University *B, T*

Montana
Montana State University
    Billings *B, T*
    Bozeman *T*
Rocky Mountain College *B, T*
University of Great Falls *B, T*
University of Montana-Missoula *T*
Western Montana College of The
    University of Montana *B, T*

Nebraska
Concordia University *T*
Creighton University *T*
Dana College *B*
Doane College *T*
Hastings College *B, M, T*
Midland Lutheran College *B, T*
Peru State College *B, T*
Union College *T*
University of Nebraska
    Kearney *B, M, T*
    Lincoln *B, T*

Nevada
University of Nevada
    Reno *B*

New Hampshire
Colby-Sawyer College *B, T*
Notre Dame College *B, M*
Plymouth State College of the University
    System of New Hampshire *B, T*
Rivier College *B, T*
University of New Hampshire *B, T*

New Jersey
Caldwell College *T*
College of St. Elizabeth *T*
Kean University *B, M*
Monmouth University *B, T*
New Jersey City University *M, T*
Richard Stockton College of New
    Jersey *B*
Rowan University *B, M*
Rutgers
    The State University of New Jersey:
    New Brunswick Graduate
    Campus *M, D*
The College of New Jersey *B, T*

New Mexico
New Mexico Highlands University *B*
University of New Mexico *B, M*
Western New Mexico University *B*

New York
Adelphi University *B, M*
Alfred University *M, T*
City University of New York
    Brooklyn College *B*
    City College *B, T*
    Hunter College *M*
    Lehman College *M*
    Queens College *M, T*
    York College *T*
College of New Rochelle *B, M, T*
College of St. Rose *B, M, T*
Columbia University
    Teachers College *M, D*
Dowling College *B*
Elmira College *B, T*
Eugene Lang College/New School
    University *T*
Fordham University *T*
Fulton-Montgomery Community
    College *A*
Hofstra University *B, T*
Long Island University
    C. W. Post Campus *B, M*
    Southampton College *B, T*
Manhattanville College *M, T*
Marymount College *B, T*
Marymount Manhattan College *B, T*
Nazareth College of Rochester *B, M, T*
New York Institute of Technology *B, T*
New York State College of Ceramics at
    Alfred University *B, M*
New York University *M, D, T*
Pace University:
    Pleasantville/Briarcliff *B, M, T*
Pace University *B, M, T*
Pratt Institute *B, M*
Roberts Wesleyan College *B, T*
Rochester Institute of Technology *M*
St. John's University *B, T*
St. Lawrence University *T*
St. Thomas Aquinas College *B, T*
School of Visual Arts *B, T*
State University of New York
    College at Buffalo *B, M, T*
    New Paltz *B, M, T*
    Oswego *M*
Syracuse University *B, M, T*

North Carolina
Appalachian State University *B, M, T*
Barton College *B, T*
Cleveland Community College *A*
East Carolina University *B, M*
Greensboro College *B, T*
High Point University *B, T*
Lenoir Community College *A*
Lenoir-Rhyne College *B, T*
Mars Hill College *B, T*
Meredith College *B, T*
Methodist College *B, T*
North Carolina Central University *B*
Sandhills Community College *A*
University of North Carolina
    Charlotte *B*
    Greensboro *B*
    Pembroke *B, T*
Western Carolina University *B, T*
Wingate University *B, T*
Winston-Salem State University *B*

North Dakota
Dickinson State University *B, T*
Minot State University *B, T*
University of North Dakota *B, T*
Valley City State University *B, T*

Ohio
Ashland University *B, T*
Baldwin-Wallace College *B*
Bluffton College *B*
Bowling Green State University *B*
Capital University *T*
Case Western Reserve University *B, M*
Central State University *B*
College of Mount St. Joseph *B, T*
Defiance College *B, T*
Hiram College *T*
Kent State University
    Stark Campus *B*
Kent State University *B, M*
Malone College *B*
Miami University
    Oxford Campus *B, M, T*
Mount Union College *T*
Mount Vernon Nazarene College *B, T*
Notre Dame College of Ohio *T*
Ohio Dominican College *D*
Ohio Northern University *T*
Ohio State University
    Columbus Campus *M, D*
Ohio University *B, T*
Ohio Wesleyan University *B*
Otterbein College *B*
Shawnee State University *T*
University of Akron *M*
University of Cincinnati *B, M, T*
University of Dayton *B, M, T*
University of Findlay *B, T*
University of Rio Grande *B, T*
University of Toledo *B, M, T*
Wilberforce University *T*
Wilmington College *B*
Wittenberg University *B*
Wright State University *B, M, T*
Xavier University *M, T*
Youngstown State University *B, M, T*

Oklahoma
Cameron University *B, T*
Eastern Oklahoma State College *A*
Northeastern Oklahoma Agricultural and
    Mechanical College *A*
Northeastern State University *B*
Oklahoma Baptist University *B, T*
Oklahoma Christian University of
    Science and Arts *B, T*
Oklahoma City University *B*
Oral Roberts University *B, T*
Southeastern Oklahoma State
    University *B, T*
Southwestern Oklahoma State
    University *B, M, T*
University of Central Oklahoma *B*
University of Tulsa *M, T*

Oregon
Linfield College T
Portland State University T
Southern Oregon University T

Pennsylvania
Beaver College B, M, T
Carlow College B, M, T
Edinboro University of
  Pennsylvania B, T
Indiana University of
  Pennsylvania B, M, T
Kutztown University of
  Pennsylvania B, M, T
Lincoln University B, T
Lycoming College T
Mansfield University of
  Pennsylvania B, M, T
Marywood University B, M, T
Mercyhurst College T
Messiah College B, T
Millersville University of
  Pennsylvania B, M, T
Moore College of Art and Design B, T
Moravian College T
Penn State
  University Park B, M, D
St. Vincent College B
Seton Hill College B, T
Temple University B, M
University of the Arts M
Wilkes University T

Puerto Rico
Escuela de Artes Plasticas de Puerto
  Rico B
Inter American University of Puerto Rico
  San German Campus B
Pontifical Catholic University of Puerto
  Rico B, T

Rhode Island
Rhode Island College B, M

South Carolina
Anderson College B, T
Claflin University B
Coker College B, T
Columbia College B
Converse College T
Francis Marion University B
Furman University T
Lander University B, M, T
Limestone College B
South Carolina State University B, T
University of South Carolina B, M
Winthrop University M, T

South Dakota
Augustana College B, T
Black Hills State University B, T
Dakota State University B, T
Dakota Wesleyan University B, T
Northern State University B, T
South Dakota State University B
University of South Dakota T

Tennessee
Belmont University B, M, T
Bethel College T
Cumberland University B
Freed-Hardeman University T
Lambuth University B, T
Lincoln Memorial University B, T
Maryville College B, T
Middle Tennessee State University B
Roane State Community College A
Tusculum College B, T
Union University B, T
University of Tennessee
  Chattanooga B
  Knoxville B, T
  Martin B, T

Texas
Abilene Christian University B, T
Baylor University B, T
Del Mar College A
Hardin-Simmons University B, T
Houston Baptist University B
Howard Payne University T
Kilgore College A
Lamar University T
Lubbock Christian University B
McMurry University T
Schreiner College T
Southwest Texas State University T
Southwestern University T
Tarleton State University B, T
Texas A&M University
  Commerce B
  Corpus Christi T
  Kingsville B, M
Texas Christian University B, T
Texas Lutheran University T
Texas Tech University M
Texas Wesleyan University T
Texas Woman's University M
University of Dallas B, T
University of Houston
  Clear Lake T
University of Houston M
University of Mary Hardin-Baylor T
University of North Texas B, M, D, T
University of Texas
  Arlington T
  Austin M
  Pan American B, T
  San Antonio T
Wayland Baptist University T
West Texas A&M University T

Utah
Brigham Young University B, M
Weber State University B

Vermont
Castleton State College B, T
Goddard College T
Johnson State College B
St. Michael's College B, M
University of Vermont B, T

Virginia
Averett College B, T
Bridgewater College T
Hollins University T
Longwood College B, T
Northern Virginia Community College A
Virginia Commonwealth
  University B, M
Virginia Intermont College B, T
Virginia Wesleyan College B, T

Washington
Central Washington University B, T
North Seattle Community College C
Pacific Lutheran University T
Seattle Pacific University B
Western Washington University B, M, T
Whitworth College B, T

West Virginia
Concord College B, T
Fairmont State College B
Glenville State College B
Shepherd College T
West Liberty State College B
West Virginia State College B
West Virginia Wesleyan College B

Wisconsin
Alverno College B, T
Beloit College B, T
Cardinal Stritch University B, T
Carroll College B, T
Lawrence University T
Marian College of Fond du Lac B, T
Mount Mary College B, T
Mount Senario College T
St. Norbert College T
Silver Lake College B, T
University of Wisconsin
  Green Bay T
  La Crosse B, T
  Madison B, M, T
  Milwaukee B, M
  Parkside T
  Platteville B
  River Falls B, T
  Stout B, T
  Superior B, T
  Whitewater B
Viterbo University B, T

Art history/criticism/conservation

Alabama
Birmingham-Southern College B
Chattahoochee Valley Community
  College A
University of Alabama
  Birmingham B, M
University of Alabama B, M
University of South Alabama B

Arizona
Arizona State University B
Northern Arizona University B
University of Arizona B, M, D

Arkansas
University of Arkansas
  Little Rock B

California
Art Center College of Design M
California College of Arts and Crafts M
California State University
  Chico B
  Dominguez Hills B
  Fullerton M
  Hayward B
  Long Beach B, M
  Northridge B, M
Chapman University B
De Anza College C, A
Dominican University of California B
Foothill College C, A
Gavilan Community College A
Grossmont Community College A
Los Angeles Southwest College A
Los Angeles Valley College A
Loyola Marymount University B
Mills College B
MiraCosta College A
Occidental College B
Pacific Union College B
Pitzer College B
Pomona College B
San Diego City College A
San Diego State University B, M
San Francisco State University M
San Jose State University B, M
Santa Barbara City College A
Santa Clara University B
Scripps College B
Sonoma State University B
University of California
  Berkeley B, M, D
  Davis B, M
  Irvine B, M
  Los Angeles B, M, D
  Riverside B, M
  San Diego B
  Santa Barbara B, M, D
University of Redlands B
University of Southern
  California B, M, D
University of the Pacific B
Whittier College B

Colorado
Colorado College B
Colorado State University B
University of Colorado
  Boulder B, M
University of Denver B, M
Western State College of Colorado B

Connecticut
Albertus Magnus College B
Connecticut College B
St. Joseph College B
Southern Connecticut State
  University B, M
Trinity College B
University of Connecticut B
University of Hartford B
Wesleyan University B
Yale University B, M, D

Delaware
University of Delaware B, M, D

District of Columbia
American University B, M
Catholic University of America B
Gallaudet University B
George Washington University B, M, D
Georgetown University B
Howard University B, M
Trinity College B

Florida
Florida International University B
Florida State University B, M, D
Jacksonville University B
Palm Beach Community College A
Rollins College B
University of Florida B, M
University of Miami B, M
University of South Florida M
University of West Florida B

Georgia
Berry College B
Emory University B, M, D
Georgia State University M
Oxford College of Emory University B
Piedmont College B
Savannah College of Art and
  Design B, M
University of Georgia B, M
Wesleyan College B

Hawaii
University of Hawaii
  Manoa M

Illinois
Augustana College B
Barat College B
Bradley University B
De Paul University B
Dominican University B
Knox College B
Lake Forest College B
Loyola University of Chicago B
North Park University B
Northern Illinois University B
Northwestern University B, M, D
Principia College B
Richland Community College A
Rockford College B
Roosevelt University B
School of the Art Institute of Chicago M
University of Chicago B, M, D
University of Illinois
  Chicago B, M, D
  Urbana-Champaign B, M, D

Indiana
DePauw University B
Hanover College B
Indiana State University M
Indiana University
  Bloomington B, M, D
Indiana University--Purdue University
  Indiana University-Purdue
    University Indianapolis B
Indiana Wesleyan University B
Marian College B

Art history/criticism/conservation

University of Evansville *B*
University of Notre Dame *B, M*

Iowa
Clarke College *A, B, T*
Drake University *B*
Loras College *B*
University of Iowa *B, M, D*
University of Northern Iowa *B*
Waldorf College *A, B*

Kansas
Baker University *B*
University of Kansas *B, M, D*
Wichita State University *B*

Kentucky
Berea College *B*
University of Kentucky *B, M, T*
University of Louisville *B, M, D*

Louisiana
Louisiana State University and Agricultural and Mechanical College *M*
Tulane University *B*
University of New Orleans *B*

Maine
Bowdoin College *B*
Colby College *B*
University of Maine *B*
University of Southern Maine *B*

Maryland
College of Notre Dame of Maryland *B*
Montgomery College
    Rockville Campus *A*
Western Maryland College *B*

Massachusetts
Assumption College *B*
Boston College *B*
Boston University *B, M, D*
Brandeis University *B*
Clark University *B*
College of the Holy Cross *B*
Framingham State College *B*
Hampshire College *B*
Harvard College *B*
Harvard University *D*
Massachusetts College of Art *B*
Massachusetts College of Liberal Arts *B*
Mount Holyoke College *B*
Salem State College *B*
Simmons College *B*
Simon's Rock College of Bard *B*
Smith College *B*
Stonehill College *B*
Tufts University *B, M*
University of Massachusetts
    Amherst *B, M*
    Dartmouth *B*
Wellesley College *B*
Wheaton College *B*
Williams College *B, M*

Michigan
Andrews University *B*
Aquinas College *B*
Calvin College *B*
Eastern Michigan University *B*
Hope College *B, T*
Kalamazoo College *B*
Kendall College of Art and Design *B*
Michigan State University *B, M*
Oakland University *B*
University of Michigan *B, M, D*
Wayne State University *B, M*
Western Michigan University *B*

Minnesota
Augsburg College *B*
Carleton College *B*
College of St. Catherine: St. Paul Campus *B*
Concordia College: Moorhead *B*
Gustavus Adolphus College *B*
Hamline University *B*
Macalester College *B*
Minnesota State University, Mankato *B*
Moorhead State University *B*
St. Cloud State University *B*
St. Olaf College *B*
University of Minnesota
    Duluth *B*
    Morris *B*
    Twin Cities *B, M, D*
University of St. Thomas *B, M*

Mississippi
Millsaps College *B, T*
University of Mississippi *B, M, T*

Missouri
Kansas City Art Institute *B*
Lindenwood University *B, M*
Missouri Western State College *B*
St. Louis University *B*
Truman State University *B*
University of Missouri
    Kansas City *B, M*
    St. Louis *B*
Washington University *B, M, D*
Webster University *B*

Montana
University of Montana-Missoula *B*

Nebraska
Hastings College *B*
University of Nebraska
    Kearney *B*
    Lincoln *B*
    Omaha *B*

Nevada
University of Nevada
    Reno *B*

New Hampshire
Dartmouth College *B*
Franklin Pierce College *B*
New England College *B*
Plymouth State College of the University System of New Hampshire *B*
University of New Hampshire *B*

New Jersey
Drew University *B*
Georgian Court College *B*
Kean University *B*
Monmouth University *B*
Princeton University *B, D*
Rowan University *B*
Rutgers
    The State University of New Jersey: Camden College of Arts and Sciences *B*
    The State University of New Jersey: Douglass College *B*
    The State University of New Jersey: Livingston College *B*
    The State University of New Jersey: New Brunswick Graduate Campus *M, D*
    The State University of New Jersey: Newark College of Arts and Sciences *B*
    The State University of New Jersey: Rutgers College *B*
    The State University of New Jersey: University College Camden *B*
    The State University of New Jersey: University College New Brunswick *B*
Seton Hall University *B*

New Mexico
University of New Mexico *B, M, D*

New York
Adelphi University *B*
Alfred University *B*
Bard College *B, M*
Barnard College *B*
Canisius College *B*
City University of New York
    Brooklyn College *B, M*
    City College *B, M*
    Graduate School and University Center *D*
    Hunter College *B, M*
    Lehman College *B, M*
    Queens College *B, M*
    York College *B*
Colgate University *B*
College of New Rochelle *B, T*
Columbia University
    Columbia College *B*
    Graduate School *M, D*
    School of General Studies *B*
Cornell University *B, D*
Fordham University *B*
Hamilton College *B*
Hartwick College *B*
Hobart and William Smith Colleges *B*
Hofstra University *B*
Ithaca College *B*
Long Island University
    C. W. Post Campus *B, M*
Manhattanville College *B*
Marymount College *B*
Nazareth College of Rochester *B*
New York University *B, M, D*
Pace University:
    Pleasantville/Briarcliff *A, B*
Pace University *A, B*
Parsons School of Design *M*
Pratt Institute *B, M*
Sarah Lawrence College *B*
Skidmore College *B*
State University of New York
    Binghamton *B, M, D*
    Buffalo *B, M*
    College at Buffalo *B, M*
    College at Fredonia *B*
    College at Geneseo *B*
    College at Oneonta *B*
    College at Potsdam *B*
    New Paltz *B*
    Purchase *B, M*
    Stony Brook *B, M, D*
Syracuse University *B, M*
University of Rochester *B*
Wells College *B*

North Carolina
Brevard College *B*
Duke University *B, D*
East Carolina University *B*
Meredith College *B*
Queens College *B*
Salem College *B*
University of North Carolina
    Chapel Hill *B, M, D*
    Greensboro *B*
    Wilmington *B*
Wake Forest University *B*

Ohio
Baldwin-Wallace College *B*
Bowling Green State University *B*
Case Western Reserve University *B, M, D*
College of Wooster *B*
Denison University *B*
Hiram College *B*
John Carroll University *B*
Kent State University *B, M*
Kenyon College *B*
Lourdes College *A, B*
Miami University
    Oxford Campus *B*
Notre Dame College of Ohio *B*
Oberlin College *B*
Ohio State University
    Columbus Campus *B, M, D*
Ohio University *B, M*
Ohio Wesleyan University *B*
University of Akron *B*
University of Cincinnati *C, B, M*
University of Dayton *B*
University of Toledo *B*
Ursuline College *B*
Wittenberg University *B*
Wright State University *B*
Youngstown State University *B*

Oklahoma
Oklahoma City University *M*
Rogers State University *A*
St. Gregory's University *A*
University of Oklahoma *B, M*
University of Tulsa *B*

Oregon
Portland State University *B*
Reed College *B*
University of Oregon *M, D*
Willamette University *B*

Pennsylvania
Allegheny College *B*
Beaver College *B*
Bloomsburg University of Pennsylvania *B, M*
Bryn Mawr College *B, M, D*
Bucknell University *B*
California University of Pennsylvania *B*
Carlow College *B*
Chatham College *B*
Chestnut Hill College *A, B*
Eastern College *B*
Edinboro University of Pennsylvania *B*
Franklin and Marshall College *B*
Gettysburg College *B*
Haverford College *B*
Immaculata College *A*
Juniata College *B*
La Salle University *B*
Lycoming College *B*
Mansfield University of Pennsylvania *B*
Marywood University *C*
Messiah College *B*
Moravian College *B*
Muhlenberg College *B*
Penn State
    University Park *B, M, D*
Rosemont College *B*
St. Vincent College *B*
Seton Hill College *B*
Susquehanna University *B*
Swarthmore College *B*
Temple University *B, M, D*
University of Pennsylvania *A, B, M, D*
University of Pittsburgh *B, M, D*
Villanova University *B*
Washington and Jefferson College *B*

Puerto Rico
University of Puerto Rico
    Rio Piedras Campus *B*

Rhode Island
Brown University *B, M, D*
Providence College *B*
Rhode Island College *B*
University of Rhode Island *B*

South Carolina
College of Charleston *B*
Converse College *B*
Furman University *B*
University of South Carolina *B, M*
Winthrop University *B*
Wofford College *B*

Tennessee
Lambuth University *B*
Rhodes College *B*
Tennessee State University *B*
University of Memphis *B, M*
University of Tennessee
    Knoxville *B*
University of the South *B*

Texas
Baylor University *B*
Lamar University *M*

Lon Morris College *A*
Rice University *B, M*
Southern Methodist University *B, M*
Southwestern University *B*
Texas A&M University
    Commerce *M, D*
Texas Christian University *B, M*
Texas Tech University *B*
Texas Woman's University *B, M*
Trinity University *B*
University of Dallas *B*
University of Houston *B*
University of North Texas *B, M*
University of Texas
    Arlington *B*
    Austin *B, M, D*

Utah
Brigham Young University *B, M*
Dixie State College of Utah *A*
University of Utah *B, M*

Vermont
Marlboro College *B*
Middlebury College *B*
University of Vermont *B*

Virginia
George Mason University *B*
Hollins University *B*
James Madison University *B*
Longwood College *B*
Mary Baldwin College *B*
Mary Washington College *B*
Old Dominion University *B*
Randolph-Macon College *B*
Randolph-Macon Woman's College *B*
Sweet Briar College *B*
University of Richmond *B*
University of Virginia *M, D*
Virginia Commonwealth
    University *B, M, D*
Washington and Lee University *B*

Washington
Eastern Washington University *B*
University of Washington *B, M, D*
Western Washington University *B*
Whitman College *B*

Wisconsin
Beloit College *B*
Lawrence University *B*
University of Wisconsin
    Madison *B, M, D*
    Milwaukee *B, M*
    Parkside *B*
    Superior *B, M*
    Whitewater *B, T*

Art therapy

Alabama
Spring Hill College *B*

Arkansas
Harding University *B*
University of Central Arkansas *B*

California
College of Notre Dame *M*

Colorado
Naropa University *M*

Connecticut
Albertus Magnus College *B, M*

District of Columbia
George Washington University *M*

Florida
University of Tampa *C*

Georgia
Piedmont College *B*

Illinois
Barat College *B*
Millikin University *B*
School of the Art Institute of Chicago *M*
Southern Illinois University
    Edwardsville *M*
University of Illinois
    Chicago *M*

Indiana
Goshen College *B*
St. Mary-of-the-Woods College *B*
University of Indianapolis *B*

Iowa
Grand View College *C*

Kansas
Emporia State University *M*
Pittsburg State University *B*

Kentucky
University of Louisville *M*

Massachusetts
Anna Maria College *B*
Elms College *B*
Emmanuel College *B*
Endicott College *B*
Springfield College *B, M*

Michigan
Andrews University *B*
Marygrove College *B*

Missouri
Avila College *B*

New Jersey
Brookdale Community College *A*
Caldwell College *C*

New York
College of New Rochelle *B, M, T*
Herkimer County Community College *A*
Hofstra University *M*
Long Island University
    C. W. Post Campus *B, M*
Nazareth College of Rochester *M*
New York University *M*
Pratt Institute *M*
Russell Sage College *B*
St. Thomas Aquinas College *B*

Ohio
Bowling Green State University *B*
Capital University *B*
Ursuline College *M*

Oregon
Marylhurst University *M*

Pennsylvania
Beaver College *B*
Chestnut Hill College *C*
MCP Hahnemann University *M*
Marywood University *B, M*
Mercyhurst College *B*
Seton Hill College *B, M*

South Carolina
Converse College *B*

Texas
University of Houston
    Clear Lake *C*

Vermont
Norwich University *M*

Wisconsin
Alverno College *B, T*
Marian College of Fond du Lac *B*
Mount Mary College *B, M*
University of Wisconsin
    Superior *B, M*

Arts management

Alabama
Spring Hill College *B*

Arizona
Northern Arizona University *B*

California
California State University
    Dominguez Hills *M*
    Hayward *B*
Golden Gate University *M*
Santa Rosa Junior College *C*
Skyline College *C*
University of the Pacific *B*

Delaware
Delaware State University *B*

District of Columbia
American University *B, M*
Howard University *B*

Florida
Florida State University *M*

Georgia
Brenau University *B*
Georgia College and State University *B*
Piedmont College *B*

Illinois
Benedictine University *B*
Columbia College *B, M*
Elmhurst College *B*
Millikin University *B*
Quincy University *A, B*
Roosevelt University *B, M*
School of the Art Institute of Chicago *M*
University of Illinois
    Springfield *M*

Indiana
Butler University *B*
Indiana University
    Bloomington *M*

Iowa
Buena Vista University *B*
Luther College *B*
Upper Iowa University *B*
Wartburg College *B*

Kansas
Kansas Wesleyan University *B*

Kentucky
Bellarmine College *B*
University of Kentucky *B, T*

Louisiana
Dillard University *B*
Southeastern Louisiana University *B*
University of New Orleans *M*

Maryland
Goucher College *M*

Massachusetts
Simmons College *B*

Michigan
Adrian College *B*
Aquinas College *B*
Bay de Noc Community College *C*
Eastern Michigan University *B*
University of Michigan *M*

Minnesota
St. Mary's University of Minnesota *B, M*

Missouri
Culver-Stockton College *B*

Nebraska
Bellevue University *B*
Creighton University *B*

New Hampshire
Franklin Pierce College *B*

New Mexico
College of Santa Fe *B*

New York
City University of New York
    Baruch College *B*
    Lehman College *B*
Columbia University
    Teachers College *M*
Concordia College *B*
Herkimer County Community College *A*
Ithaca College *B*
Long Island University
    C. W. Post Campus *B*
    Southampton College *B*
Marymount Manhattan College *C*
New York University *M*
Pratt Institute *M*
State University of New York
    Buffalo *M*
    Purchase *C*
Wagner College *B*

North Carolina
Bennett College *B*
Brevard College *B*
Catawba College *B*
Pfeiffer University *B*
Salem College *B*
University of North Carolina
    Pembroke *B*

Ohio
Baldwin-Wallace College *B*
Notre Dame College of Ohio *B*
University of Cincinnati *M*
University of Findlay *B*
Ursuline College *B*
Wright State University *B*

Oklahoma
Oklahoma City University *B, M*

Oregon
University of Oregon *M*

Pennsylvania
Cabrini College *B*
Carnegie Mellon University *M*
Chatham College *B*
Drexel University *M*
Gettysburg College *B*
Marywood University *B*
Mercyhurst College *B*
Point Park College *B*
Seton Hill College *B*
University of Pennsylvania *M*
Waynesburg College *B*

Puerto Rico
Turabo University *M*

South Carolina
College of Charleston *B*
Newberry College *B*

South Dakota
University of South Dakota *B*

Texas
El Paso Community College *C*
Southern Methodist University *M*
Texas A&M University
    Commerce *B*
Texas Tech University *M*

Vermont
Green Mountain College *B*
Johnson State College *B*

Virginia
Mary Baldwin College *B*
Randolph-Macon College *B*
Shenandoah University *B, M*

West Virginia
University of Charleston *B*

Wisconsin
Lakeland College *B*
University of Wisconsin
    Madison *M*
    Stevens Point *B*

Viterbo University B

Asian studies

Alabama
Samford University B
University of Alabama B

Alaska
University of Alaska
    Fairbanks B

Arizona
Pima Community College A

California
Cabrillo College A
California State University
    Chico B
    Long Beach M
    Sacramento B
Claremont McKenna College B
Cypress College A
Loyola Marymount University B
Occidental College B
Pepperdine University B
Pitzer College B
Pomona College B
San Diego State University B, M
San Francisco State University B, M
Scripps College B
University of California
    Berkeley B, M, D
    Los Angeles M
    Riverside B
    Santa Barbara B, M
University of Redlands B
University of San Francisco M

Colorado
Colorado College B
Fort Lewis College B
University of Colorado
    Boulder B
University of Denver B

Connecticut
Connecticut College B
Trinity College B

Florida
Florida State University B, M
Miami-Dade Community College A
University of Florida B

Georgia
Emory University B
Oxford College of Emory University B

Hawaii
University of Hawaii
    Manoa B, M
    West Oahu B

Illinois
Augustana College B
Lake Forest College B
Northwestern University B
University of Illinois
    Urbana-Champaign B, M

Indiana
Earlham College B
Indiana University
    Bloomington M, D

Iowa
University of Iowa B, M
University of Northern Iowa B

Louisiana
Dillard University B
Tulane University B

Maine
Bowdoin College B

Maryland
Johns Hopkins University B

Massachusetts
Amherst College B
College of the Holy Cross B
Hampshire College B
Harvard College B
Mount Holyoke College B
Northeastern University B
Tufts University B
Wellesley College B
Wheaton College B
Williams College B

Michigan
University of Michigan B
Wayne State University B
Western Michigan University B

Minnesota
Carleton College B
Hamline University B
St. Olaf College B

Missouri
Washington University B

Montana
University of Montana-Missoula B

Nevada
University of Nevada
    Las Vegas B

New Hampshire
Dartmouth College B

New Jersey
Seton Hall University B, M

New Mexico
University of New Mexico B

New York
Bard College B
City University of New York
    City College B
Colgate University B
Columbia University
    School of General Studies B
Cornell University B, M
Hamilton College B
Hobart and William Smith Colleges B
Hofstra University B
Manhattanville College B
St. John's University B
St. Lawrence University B
Sarah Lawrence College B
Skidmore College B
State University of New York
    Albany B
Vassar College B

North Carolina
Duke University B
St. Andrews Presbyterian College B
University of North Carolina
    Chapel Hill B

Ohio
Bowling Green State University B
Case Western Reserve University B
Ohio University B
University of Cincinnati C, B
University of Findlay B
University of Toledo B

Oklahoma
Oklahoma City University B
Oklahoma State University C

Oregon
University of Oregon B, M

Pennsylvania
Gettysburg College B
Lehigh University B
Swarthmore College B
Temple University B
University of Pittsburgh C

Rhode Island
Brown University B

South Carolina
Furman University B

Tennessee
University of Tennessee
    Knoxville B

Texas
Baylor University B
Rice University B
Southwest Texas State University B
Trinity University B
University of Texas
    Austin B, M

Utah
Brigham Young University B
University of Utah B
Utah State University B

Vermont
Marlboro College B
Middlebury College B
St. Michael's College B
University of Vermont B

Virginia
Mary Baldwin College B

Washington
Central Washington University B
Evergreen State College B
Gonzaga University B
North Seattle Community College C, A
University of Puget Sound B
Washington State University B
Whitman College B

Wisconsin
Carthage College B
University of Wisconsin
    Madison B

Asian-American studies

California
California State University
    Hayward B
    Long Beach C
De Anza College C, A
Pitzer College B
Pomona College B
San Francisco State University B, M
Scripps College B
Southwestern College A
University of California
    Berkeley B
    Irvine B
    Los Angeles B, M
    Riverside B
University of Southern California B

Georgia
Oxford College of Emory University A

Massachusetts
Hampshire College B
Harvard College B

New York
Sarah Lawrence College B

Oklahoma
Oklahoma State University C

Pennsylvania
Gettysburg College B

Washington
North Seattle Community College C
University of Washington B

Astronomy

Arizona
Northern Arizona University B
University of Arizona B, M, D

California
California Institute of Technology B, D
Compton Community College A
De Anza College A
Diablo Valley College A
Gavilan Community College A
Golden West College A
Ohlone College C, A
Orange Coast College A
Palomar College C, A
Pomona College B
Riverside Community College A
Saddleback College A
San Bernardino Valley College A
San Diego State University B, M
San Francisco State University B
San Joaquin Delta College A
Southwestern College A
University of California
    Berkeley M, D
    Los Angeles M, D
    Santa Cruz D
University of Southern California B

Connecticut
Connecticut College B
Wesleyan University B, M
Yale University B, M, D

Delaware
University of Delaware B

District of Columbia
Howard University M, D

Florida
Florida Institute of Technology B
Santa Fe Community College A
University of Florida B, M, D

Georgia
Georgia State University D
University of Georgia B
Valdosta State University B
Young Harris College A

Hawaii
University of Hawaii
    Hilo B
    Manoa M, D

Idaho
North Idaho College A

Illinois
Kishwaukee College A
Morton College A
Parkland College A
Southwestern Ilinois College A
University of Chicago M, D
University of Illinois
    Urbana-Champaign B, M, D

Indiana
Ball State University B
Indiana University
    Bloomington B, M, D
Valparaiso University B

Iowa
Drake University B
University of Iowa B, M

Kansas
Benedictine College B
University of Kansas B

Maryland
Johns Hopkins University B, D
University of Maryland
    College Park B, M, D

Massachusetts
Amherst College *B*
Boston University *B, M, D*
Hampshire College *B*
Harvard College *B*
Harvard University *M, D*
Mount Holyoke College *B*
Simon's Rock College of Bard *B*
Smith College *B*
Tufts University *B*
University of Massachusetts
    Amherst *B, M, D*
Wellesley College *B*
Wheaton College *B*
Williams College *B*

Michigan
Bay de Noc Community College *A*
Central Michigan University *B*
University of Michigan *B, M, D*

Minnesota
Minnesota State University, Mankato *B*
University of Minnesota
    Twin Cities *B*

Nebraska
University of Nebraska
    Lincoln *M, D*

New Hampshire
Dartmouth College *B*

New Jersey
Middlesex County College *A*
Rutgers
    The State University of New Jersey:
    New Brunswick Graduate
    Campus *M, D*

New Mexico
New Mexico Institute of Mining and
    Technology *B*
New Mexico State University *M, D*

New York
Barnard College *B*
Colgate University *B*
Columbia University
    Columbia College *B*
    Graduate School *M, D*
    School of General Studies *B*
Cornell University *B, M, D*
Sarah Lawrence College *B*
State University of New York
    Stony Brook *B*
University of Rochester *B*
Vassar College *B*

Ohio
Case Western Reserve
    University *B, M, D*
Mount Union College *B*
Ohio State University
    Columbus Campus *B, M, D*
Ohio University *B*
Ohio Wesleyan University *B*
Wilmington College *B*
Youngstown State University *B*

Oklahoma
Tulsa Community College *A*
University of Oklahoma *B*

Pennsylvania
Eastern College *B*
Gettysburg College *B*
Haverford College *B*
Lycoming College *B*
Penn State
    University Park *B*
Swarthmore College *B*
University of Pennsylvania *B, M, D*
University of Pittsburgh *M, D*
Villanova University *B*
West Chester University of
    Pennsylvania *B*

Rhode Island
Brown University *B*

Tennessee
Vanderbilt University *M*

Texas
Lon Morris College *A*
Rice University *M, D*
University of Texas
    Austin *B, M, D*

Utah
Snow College *A*

Vermont
Bennington College *B*
Marlboro College *B*

Virginia
University of Virginia *B, M, D*

Washington
Everett Community College *A*
Highline Community College *A*
Lower Columbia College *A*
University of Washington *B, M, D*
Western Washington University *B*
Whitman College *B*

Wisconsin
University of Wisconsin
    La Crosse *B*
    Madison *B, M, D*

Wyoming
University of Wyoming *B*

Astrophysics

Alaska
University of Alaska
    Fairbanks *M, D*

California
San Francisco State University *B*
University of California
    Berkeley *B*
    Los Angeles *B*
    Santa Cruz *D*

Colorado
University of Colorado
    Boulder *M, D*

Connecticut
Connecticut College *B*
Yale University *B*

Florida
Florida Institute of Technology *B*

Georgia
Agnes Scott College *B*

Illinois
Northwestern University *B*
University of Chicago *M, D*

Indiana
Indiana University
    Bloomington *B, D*

Iowa
Iowa State University *M, D*
University of Iowa *M, D*

Massachusetts
Boston University *B*
Harvard College *B*
Harvard University *D*
Tufts University *M, D*
Williams College *B*

Michigan
Michigan State University *B*
University of Michigan *B*

Minnesota
University of Minnesota
    Twin Cities *B, M, D*

New Jersey
Princeton University *B, M, D*

New Mexico
New Mexico Institute of Mining and
    Technology *B, M, D*
University of New Mexico *B*

New York
Colgate University *B*
Columbia University
    Columbia College *B*
    Graduate School *M, D*
    School of General Studies *B*

Oklahoma
University of Oklahoma *B*

Oregon
University of Oregon *M, D*

Pennsylvania
Swarthmore College *B*
Villanova University *B*

Texas
Texas Christian University *B*
University of North Texas *M*

Vermont
Marlboro College *B*

Wisconsin
University of Wisconsin
    Madison *B, M, D*

Audiology/hearing sciences

Alabama
University of Alabama *M*
University of Montevallo *B, M, T*

Colorado
University of Northern Colorado *B, M*

District of Columbia
Gallaudet University *D*

Florida
Nova Southeastern University *D*
Polk Community College *A*
University of Florida *D*

Idaho
Idaho State University *M*

Illinois
Northern Illinois University *B, M*
Northwestern University *B*

Indiana
Ball State University *M*
Indiana University
    Bloomington *B*
Indiana University--Purdue University
    Indiana University-Purdue
    University Fort Wayne *B*

Iowa
University of Iowa *B*
University of Northern Iowa *M*

Kansas
University of Kansas
    Medical Center *M, D*
University of Kansas *M, D*

Kentucky
Murray State University *M*

Louisiana
Louisiana State University Medical
    Center *M*

Massachusetts
Boston University *M, D*
Emerson College *B, M*
Massachusetts Institute of Technology *D*
Northeastern University *M*

Michigan
Central Michigan University *M, D*
Wayne State University *M*

Minnesota
Moorhead State University *B*

Mississippi
University of Southern Mississippi *B*

Missouri
Washington University *M, D*

New Jersey
Camden County College *C*
Seton Hall University *D*
The College of New Jersey *M*

New York
Adelphi University *B*
City University of New York
    Lehman College *M*
Columbia University
    Teachers College *D*
Hofstra University *M*
State University of New York
    Buffalo *M*
    College at Plattsburgh *B, M*
    New Paltz *B, M*
Syracuse University *M, D*

North Carolina
University of North Carolina
    Chapel Hill *M*

Ohio
Cleveland State University *B, M*
Kent State University
    Stark Campus *B*
Kent State University *M, D*
Ohio State University
    Columbus Campus *B, M, D*
Ohio University *B*

Oregon
Portland State University *B, M*

Pennsylvania
California University of Pennsylvania *M*
Thiel College *B*

Puerto Rico
University of Puerto Rico
    Medical Sciences Campus *M*

Rhode Island
University of Rhode Island *M*

South Dakota
Northern State University *B, T*

Tennessee
University of Tennessee
    Knoxville *B, M, D*

Texas
Lamar University *M*
Stephen F. Austin State University *B, T*
Texas Tech University *B*
University of Houston *M*
University of North Texas *M*
University of Texas
    Tyler *B*

Utah
Brigham Young University *B*
University of Utah *B, M*

Virginia
James Madison University *M*

Washington
University of Washington *M, D*

Wisconsin
University of Wisconsin
    Oshkosh *M*

Wyoming
University of Wyoming *M*

Auto body repair

Alabama
Bevill State Community College *A*
Gadsden State Community College *C*
George C. Wallace State Community College
  Dothan *C, A*
  Selma *C*
Harry M. Ayers State Technical College *C*
Lawson State Community College *C*
Northwest-Shoals Community College *C*
Reid State Technical College *C*
Shelton State Community College *C, A*
Sparks State Technical College *C*
Wallace State Community College at Hanceville *C, A*

Arizona
Arizona Western College *C*
Mesa Community College *C*

Arkansas
North Arkansas College *C*

California
Allan Hancock College *C, A*
Cerritos Community College *A*
Cerro Coso Community College *C, A*
Chabot College *A*
Chaffey Community College *C, A*
College of Marin: Kentfield *C, A*
College of the Sequoias *C, A*
College of the Siskiyous *C, A*
Columbia College *C*
Compton Community College *C, A*
Contra Costa College *C, A*
Cuesta College *C, A*
Cuyamaca College *A*
Cypress College *C, A*
East Los Angeles College *C*
Fresno City College *C, A*
Gavilan Community College *C*
Golden West College *C, A*
Imperial Valley College *C, A*
Los Angeles Pierce College *C, A*
Los Angeles Trade and Technical College *C, A*
Mendocino College *C, A*
Merced College *C, A*
MiraCosta College *C, A*
Modesto Junior College *C, A*
Mount San Jacinto College *C*
Palomar College *C, A*
Pasadena City College *C, A*
Porterville College *C, A*
Riverside Community College *C, A*
Santa Barbara City College *C, A*
Santa Monica College *C, A*
Santa Rosa Junior College *C*
Solano Community College *C, A*
Southwestern College *C, A*
West Hills Community College *C, A*
Yuba College *C*

Colorado
Aims Community College *C, A*
Arapahoe Community College *C*
Mesa State College *C, A*
Morgan Community College *A*
Pikes Peak Community College *C, A*
Pueblo Community College *C, A*
Trinidad State Junior College *C, A*

Florida
Central Florida Community College *C*
Daytona Beach Community College *C*
South Florida Community College *C*

Georgia
Athens Area Technical Institute *C*
Dalton State College *C, A*
Floyd College *A*

Hawaii
University of Hawaii
  Hawaii Community College *C, A*
  Honolulu Community College *A*
  Kauai Community College *C, A*
  Maui Community College *A*

Idaho
Boise State University *C, A*
College of Southern Idaho *C, A*
Idaho State University *C, A*
Lewis-Clark State College *A*
North Idaho College *C, A*

Illinois
Black Hawk College *C, A*
Carl Sandburg College *C, A*
City Colleges of Chicago
  Kennedy-King College *C*
College of Lake County *C*
Highland Community College *C*
Illinois Eastern Community Colleges
  Olney Central College *A*
John A. Logan College *C, A*
Joliet Junior College *C, A*
Kaskaskia College *C, A*
Kishwaukee College *C, A*
Lake Land College *C*
Parkland College *C*
Prairie State College *C*
Waubonsee Community College *C*

Indiana
Vincennes University *A*

Iowa
Des Moines Area Community College *C, A*
Hawkeye Community College *C*
Indian Hills Community College *C, A*
Iowa Lakes Community College *C*
Kirkwood Community College *C*
Northeast Iowa Community College *C*
Scott Community College *A*
Southeastern Community College
  North Campus *C*
Southwestern Community College *C*
Western Iowa Tech Community College *C, A*

Kansas
Butler County Community College *C, A*
Central Christian College *A*
Hutchinson Community College *C, A*

Maryland
Harford Community College *C*

Michigan
Alpena Community College *C*
Andrews University *B*
Bay de Noc Community College *C*
Ferris State University *A*
Kirtland Community College *C*
Mott Community College *A*
Northern Michigan University *C*
Oakland Community College *C, A*
Washtenaw Community College *C, A*

Minnesota
Central Lakes College *C, A*
Dakota County Technical College *C, A*
Dunwoody Institute *A*
Hennepin Technical College *C, A*
Inver Hills Community College *A*
Lake Superior College: A Community and Technical College *C*
Minnesota State College - Southeast Technical *C*
Northland Community & Technical College *C, A*
Ridgewater College: A Community and Technical College *C*
St. Cloud Technical College *C, A*
St. Paul Technical College *C*
South Central Technical College *A*

Mississippi
Coahoma Community College *C*
East Central Community College *C*
Hinds Community College *C*
Itawamba Community College *C*
Mississippi Gulf Coast Community College
  Jefferson Davis Campus *C*
  Perkinston *C*
Northeast Mississippi Community College *C*
Northwest Mississippi Community College *C*

Missouri
Ranken Technical College *A*

Montana
Montana State University
  Billings *C*
  College of Technology-Great Falls *C*
Montana Tech of the University of Montana *A*

Nebraska
Central Community College *C, A*
Metropolitan Community College *C, A*
Mid Plains Community College Area *C*
Northeast Community College *A*
Southeast Community College
  Milford Campus *A*

New Hampshire
New Hampshire Community Technical College
  Nashua *A*

New Mexico
San Juan College *C, A*

New York
Erie Community College
  South Campus *A*
State University of New York
  College of Technology at Alfred *A*

North Carolina
Blue Ridge Community College *C*
Caldwell Community College and Technical Institute *C*
Cape Fear Community College *C*
Cleveland Community College *C*
Coastal Carolina Community College *C, A*
Craven Community College *C*
Edgecombe Community College *C*
Fayetteville Technical Community College *C*
Forsyth Technical Community College *C*
Guilford Technical Community College *C*
Haywood Community College *C*
Mayland Community College *C*
Montgomery Community College *C*
Sandhills Community College *C*
South Piedmont Community College *C*
Surry Community College *C, A*
Tri-County Community College *C*
Wilkes Community College *C*

North Dakota
Bismarck State College *C, A*

Ohio
Owens Community College
  Toledo *C, A*

Oklahoma
Oklahoma State University
  Okmulgee *A*
Western Oklahoma State College *A*

Oregon
Clackamas Community College *C, A*
Lane Community College *C, A*
Linn-Benton Community College *C*
Portland Community College *C, A*

Pennsylvania
Delaware County Community College *C*
Education America
  Vale Technical Institute *A*
Pennsylvania College of Technology *C*

Rhode Island
New England Institute of Technology *C, A*

South Carolina
Greenville Technical College *C*
Horry-Georgetown Technical College *A*
Technical College of the Lowcountry *C, A*

South Dakota
Southeast Technical Institute *A*
Western Dakota Technical Institute *C*

Tennessee
Chattanooga State Technical Community College *C*
Southern Adventist University *C*

Texas
Amarillo College *C*
Central Texas College *C, A*
Del Mar College *C*
Eastfield College *C, A*
Grayson County College *C*
Hill College *C, A*
Houston Community College System *C*
Howard College *C*
St. Philip's College *C, A*
San Jacinto College
  North *C, A*
South Plains College *A*
Tarrant County College *C, A*
Texas State Technical College
  Harlingen *C, A*
  Sweetwater *C*
  Waco *C, A*
Trinity Valley Community College *C*

Utah
Dixie State College of Utah *C, A*
Salt Lake Community College *A*
Utah Valley State College *A*
Weber State University *C, A*

Virginia
Danville Community College *C*
Northern Virginia Community College *C*
Piedmont Virginia Community College *C*

Washington
Columbia Basin College *A*
Green River Community College *C, A*
Lake Washington Technical College *C, A*
Lower Columbia College *C, A*
Renton Technical College *C, A*
South Seattle Community College *C, A*
Spokane Community College *A*
Walla Walla Community College *C, A*

Wisconsin
Chippewa Valley Technical College *C*
Lakeshore Technical College *C*
Madison Area Technical College *C*
Milwaukee Area Technical College *C*
Moraine Park Technical College *C*
Northeast Wisconsin Technical College *C*
Southwest Wisconsin Technical College *C*
Waukesha County Technical College *C*
Wisconsin Indianhead Technical College *C*

Wyoming
Laramie County Community College *C, A*

Automotive technology

Alabama
Gadsden State Community College *C*
George C. Wallace State Community College
    Selma *C*
J. F. Drake State Technical College *C*
John M. Patterson State Technical College *A*
Northwest-Shoals Community College *C*
Wallace State Community College at Hanceville *C, A*

Alaska
University of Alaska
    Anchorage *C, A*
    Southeast *C, A*

Arizona
Arizona Western College *A*
Central Arizona College *C, A*
Eastern Arizona College *C, A*
Gateway Community College *C, A*
Glendale Community College *C, A*
Yavapai College *C, A*

Arkansas
Arkansas State University *A*
North Arkansas College *C*
Westark College *C, A*

California
Allan Hancock College *C, A*
American River College *A*
Bakersfield College *A*
Butte College *C, A*
Chabot College *C, A*
Chaffey Community College *C, A*
Columbia College *A*
Compton Community College *C, A*
Cypress College *C, A*
East Los Angeles College *C, A*
Fresno City College *C, A*
Golden West College *C, A*
Los Angeles Harbor College *C, A*
MiraCosta College *C, A*
Modesto Junior College *C, A*
Mount San Jacinto College *C, A*
Palo Verde College *C, A*
Rio Hondo College *C, A*
Riverside Community College *C, A*
Saddleback College *C*
San Bernardino Valley College *C, A*
Santa Ana College *C, A*
Santa Barbara City College *C, A*
Shasta College *C, A*
Sierra College *C, A*
Skyline College *C, A*
Ventura College *C, A*

Colorado
Arapahoe Community College *C, A*
Front Range Community College *C, A*
Mesa State College *C, A*
Morgan Community College *C, A*
Northeastern Junior College *C, A*
Otero Junior College *C*
Pikes Peak Community College *C, A*
Pueblo Community College *C, A*
Red Rocks Community College *C, A*
Trinidad State Junior College *C, A*

Connecticut
Gateway Community College *A*
Naugatuck Valley Community-Technical College *C, A*

Florida
Brevard Community College *C*
Broward Community College *A*
Central Florida Community College *C, A*
Florida Community College at Jacksonville *A*
Indian River Community College *A*
New England Institute of Technology *A*
Pensacola Junior College *A*
Seminole Community College *C, A*
South Florida Community College *C*

Georgia
Athens Area Technical Institute *C*
Chattahoochee Technical Institute *C, A*
Columbus Technical Institute *C*
DeKalb Technical Institute *A*
Gwinnett Technical Institute *C, A*
Savannah Technical Institute *A*
Waycross College *A*

Hawaii
University of Hawaii
    Hawaii Community College *C, A*
    Honolulu Community College *A*
    Kauai Community College *C, A*
    Maui Community College *A*

Idaho
Boise State University *C, A*
College of Southern Idaho *A*
Eastern Idaho Technical College *C, A*
Idaho State University *C*
North Idaho College *C, A*

Illinois
Black Hawk College
    East Campus *C, A*
Black Hawk College *C, A*
City Colleges of Chicago
    Kennedy-King College *C, A*
College of DuPage *C, A*
Elgin Community College *C, A*
Highland Community College *C, A*
Kankakee Community College *C, A*
Kaskaskia College *C, A*
Kishwaukee College *C, A*
Lewis and Clark Community College *A*
McHenry County College *C, A*
Moraine Valley Community College *C, A*
Oakton Community College *C, A*
Parkland College *A*
Prairie State College *C, A*
Rock Valley College *C, A*
Southeastern Illinois College *C, A*
Southern Illinois University
    Carbondale *A*
Spoon River College *A*
Triton College *C, A*
Waubonsee Community College *C, A*

Indiana
Ivy Tech State College
    Central Indiana *C, A*
    Eastcentral *C, A*
    Kokomo *C, A*
    Lafayette *C, A*
    Northcentral *C, A*
    Northeast *C, A*
    Northwest *C, A*
    Southcentral *C, A*
    Southwest *C, A*
    Wabash Valley *C, A*
Vincennes University *A*

Iowa
Des Moines Area Community College *C, A*
Indian Hills Community College *A*
Iowa Central Community College *A*
Iowa Lakes Community College *C*
North Iowa Area Community College *A*
Northeast Iowa Community College *C, A*
Scott Community College *A*
Western Iowa Tech Community College *C, A*

Kansas
Barton County Community College *C, A*
Butler County Community College *C, A*
Central Christian College *A*
Hutchinson Community College *C, A*
Johnson County Community College *C, A*
McPherson College *A*
Pittsburg State University *C, A, B*

Kentucky
Hazard Community College *A*

Louisiana
Delgado Community College *C, A*

Maine
Eastern Maine Technical College *C, A*
Washington County Technical College *C*

Maryland
Community College of Baltimore County
    Catonsville *C, A*
Harford Community College *C*
Montgomery College
    Rockville Campus *C*

Massachusetts
Franklin Institute of Boston *A, B*
Massachusetts Bay Community College *A*
Middlesex Community College *A*
Mount Wachusett Community College *C, A*

Michigan
Alpena Community College *C, A*
Andrews University *B*
Baker College
    of Muskegon *A*
Bay de Noc Community College *C, A*
Ferris State University *A*
Glen Oaks Community College *C*
Gogebic Community College *C, A*
Henry Ford Community College *C, A*
Kalamazoo Valley Community College *C, A*
Kirtland Community College *C*
Macomb Community College *C, A*
Mid Michigan Community College *C*
Northern Michigan University *C, A*
Northwestern Michigan College *A*
Wayne County Community College *C*

Minnesota
Anoka-Ramsey Community College *A*
Central Lakes College *C, A*
Dakota County Technical College *C, A*
Dunwoody Institute *A*
Hennepin Technical College *C, A*
Hibbing Community College: A Technical and Community College *C*
Lake Superior College: A Community and Technical College *C, A*
Mesabi Range Community and Technical College *C, A*
Minneapolis Community and Technical College *C*
Minnesota State College - Southeast Technical *C*
North Hennepin Community College *A*
Northland Community & Technical College *C, A*
Pine Technical College *C, A*
Ridgewater College: A Community and Technical College *C*
Rochester Community and Technical College *C*
St. Cloud Technical College *C, A*
St. Paul Technical College *C*
South Central Technical College *A*

Mississippi
East Mississippi Community College *C*
Mississippi Gulf Coast Community College
    Jefferson Davis Campus *C*
Northeast Mississippi Community College *C*

Missouri
Central Missouri State University *A*
Ozarks Technical Community College *A*
Ranken Technical College *A*

Montana
Dawson Community College *A*
Montana State University
    Billings *C*
Montana Tech of the University of Montana *A*

Nebraska
Metropolitan Community College *C, A*
Mid Plains Community College Area *C, A*
Northeast Community College *A*

Nevada
Community College of Southern Nevada *A*
Western Nevada Community College *C, A*

New Hampshire
New Hampshire Community Technical College
    Berlin *C, A*
    Laconia *A*
    Manchester *C, A*
    Nashua *A*
    Stratham *C, A*

New Jersey
Brookdale Community College *C, A*
Burlington County College *A*
Gloucester County College *A*
Middlesex County College *A*

New Mexico
Albuquerque Technical-Vocational Institute *C*
Dona Ana Branch Community College of New Mexico State University *C, A*
New Mexico Junior College *C, A*
San Juan College *C, A*
Western New Mexico University *C, A*

New York
Columbia-Greene Community College *A*
Corning Community College *C, A*
Erie Community College
    South Campus *A*
Fulton-Montgomery Community College *C, A*
Monroe Community College *A*
Onondaga Community College *A*
Rockland Community College *A*
State University of New York
    College of Agriculture and Technology at Morrisville *A*
    College of Technology at Alfred *A*
    College of Technology at Canton *C, A*
    Farmingdale *A*
Suffolk County Community College *A*
Westchester Community College *A*

North Carolina
Asheville Buncombe Technical Community College *C, A*
Beaufort County Community College *A*
Bladen Community College *C*
Blue Ridge Community College *C*
Caldwell Community College and Technical Institute *C*
Cape Fear Community College *A*
Catawba Valley Community College *C, A*
Central Carolina Community College *A*
Coastal Carolina Community College *A*
Craven Community College *C, A*
Davidson County Community College *C*
Durham Technical Community College *A*
Guilford Technical Community College *C, A*
Lenoir Community College *C, A*
Martin Community College *C, A*
Montgomery Community College *A*
Pitt Community College *C, A*
Randolph Community College *A*
Rowan-Cabarrus Community College *C*
Sandhills Community College *C, A*

South Piedmont Community College *C*
Southwestern Community College *A*
Surry Community College *C, A*
Wilkes Community College *A*
Wilson Technical Community College *C*

North Dakota
Bismarck State College *C, A*
Williston State College *A*

Ohio
Cincinnati State Technical and
 Community College *A*
Columbus State Community College *A*
Muskingum Area Technical College *A*
Northwestern College *C, A*
Owens Community College
 Toledo *A*
Stark State College of Technology *A*
Terra Community College *C, A*
University of Akron *A*

Oklahoma
Oklahoma State University
 Okmulgee *A*

Oregon
Central Oregon Community
 College *C, A*
Chemeketa Community College *A*
Clackamas Community College *A*
Lane Community College *C, A*
Linn-Benton Community College *C, A*
Mount Hood Community College *A*
Portland Community College *C, A*

Pennsylvania
Delaware County Community College *C*
Education America
 Vale Technical Institute *A*
Johnson Technical Institute *A*
Lehigh Carbon Community College *C, A*
Luzerne County Community College *A*

Puerto Rico
University of Puerto Rico
 Carolina Regional College *A, B*

South Carolina
Aiken Technical College *A*
Florence-Darlington Technical
 College *C, A*
Greenville Technical College *A*
Orangeburg-Calhoun Technical
 College *A*
Spartanburg Technical College *C, A*
Trident Technical College *C, A*
York Technical College *A*

South Dakota
Southeast Technical Institute *A*
Western Dakota Technical Institute *C, A*

Tennessee
Nashville State Technical Institute *A*
Northeast State Technical Community
 College *C, A*
Pellissippi State Technical Community
 College *A*
Southern Adventist University *C*

Texas
Amarillo College *C, A*
Angelina College *C*
Brazosport College *C, A*
Central Texas College *C, A*
Eastfield College *C, A*
El Paso Community College *C*
Houston Community College
 System *C, A*
Lamar State College at Port Arthur *C, A*
Midland College *C, A*
St. Philip's College *C, A*
South Plains College *A*
Tarrant County College *C, A*
Texas State Technical College
 Harlingen *C*
 Waco *A*
Trinity Valley Community College *C*

Utah
Dixie State College of Utah *C, A*
Salt Lake Community College *A*
Weber State University *C, A, B*

Vermont
Vermont Technical College *A*

Virginia
Blue Ridge Community College *C*
Eastern Shore Community College *C*
J. Sargeant Reynolds Community
 College *C*
John Tyler Community College *C*
New River Community College *A*
Northern Virginia Community
 College *C, A*
Southwest Virginia Community
 College *C*

Washington
Clark College *C, A*
Columbia Basin College *A*
Grays Harbor College *A*
Lake Washington Technical College *C, A*
Peninsula College *A*
Skagit Valley College *C, A*
Spokane Community College *C, A*
Spokane Falls Community College *C, A*
Walla Walla Community College *C, A*
Wenatchee Valley College *C, A*
Western Washington University *B*
Yakima Valley Community College *A*

Wisconsin
Gateway Technical College *C*
Lakeshore Technical College *C*
Milwaukee Area Technical College *A*
Nicolet Area Technical College *C*
Northeast Wisconsin Technical
 College *C*
Southwest Wisconsin Technical
 College *C*
Waukesha County Technical College *A*
Western Wisconsin Technical College *C*

Wyoming
Casper College *C, A*
Central Wyoming College *C, A*
Western Wyoming Community
 College *C, A*

Aviation management

Alabama
Auburn University *B*

Alaska
University of Alaska
 Anchorage *A*

Arizona
Embry-Riddle Aeronautical University
 Prescott Campus *B*

California
Cypress College *A*
San Bernardino Valley College *A*

Connecticut
Naugatuck Valley Community-Technical
 College *A*

Delaware
Delaware State University *B*
Wilmington College *B*

Florida
Broward Community College *A*
Embry-Riddle Aeronautical University *B*
Florida Community College at
 Jacksonville *A*
Florida Institute of Technology *A, B, M*
Jacksonville University *B*
Lynn University *B*
Miami-Dade Community College *A*

Hawaii
University of Hawaii
 Honolulu Community College *A*

Illinois
Lewis University *C, B*
Lincoln Land Community College *A*
Southern Illinois University
 Carbondale *B*

Iowa
University of Dubuque *B*

Louisiana
Southern University
 Shreveport *A*

Maryland
Community College of Baltimore County
 Catonsville *C, A*

Massachusetts
Bridgewater State College *B*

Michigan
Baker College
 of Muskegon *A, B*
Northern Michigan University *A*
Oakland Community College *A*
Western Michigan University *B*

Minnesota
Inver Hills Community College *A*
Lake Superior College: A Community
 and Technical College *A*
Minnesota State University, Mankato *B*
Northland Community & Technical
 College *C, A*
Vermilion Community College *A*
Winona State University *A*

Missouri
Central Missouri State University *M*
St. Louis University *A, B*

Montana
Rocky Mountain College *B*

New Hampshire
Daniel Webster College *A, B*

New Jersey
Mercer County Community College *A*

New York
Dowling College *B, M*
St. Francis College *B*
State University of New York
 Farmingdale *B*

North Carolina
Caldwell Community College and
 Technical Institute *A*
Guilford Technical Community
 College *C, A*
Lenoir Community College *A*

North Dakota
University of North Dakota *B*

Ohio
Kent State University *B*
Ohio University *B*
Sinclair Community College *A*

Oklahoma
Southern Nazarene University *B*
Tulsa Community College *A*
Western Oklahoma State College *A*

Oregon
Portland Community College *A*

Pennsylvania
Community College of Allegheny
 County *A*
Community College of Beaver County *A*
Lehigh Carbon Community College *A*
Luzerne County Community College *A*
Marywood University *B*
Robert Morris College *B*

Puerto Rico
Inter American University of Puerto Rico
 Bayamon Campus *B*

Tennessee
Middle Tennessee State University *M*

Texas
LeTourneau University *B*
Midland College *C*

Utah
Dixie State College of Utah *A*
Westminster College *B*

Virginia
Averett College *B*
Hampton University *B*

West Virginia
College of West Virginia *A*
Fairmont State College *B*
Salem-Teikyo University *B*

Banking/financial support services

Alabama
Chattahoochee Valley Community
 College *A*
George C. Wallace State Community
 College
 Selma *C*
Jefferson State Community College *A*
Northeast Alabama Community
 College *A*
Northwest-Shoals Community College *C*
Snead State Community College *C*
Talladega College *B*
University of Alabama *B, M, D*
Wallace State Community College at
 Hanceville *A*

Arizona
Arizona Western College *A*
Gateway Community College *A*
Phoenix College *A*
Pima Community College *C, A*
Rio Salado College *A*

Arkansas
Northwest Arkansas Community
 College *A*
Westark College *A*

California
Cabrillo College *A*
California State University
 Bakersfield *B*
 Dominguez Hills *B*
 Northridge *B*
Canada College *A*
Cerritos Community College *A*
Chabot College *A*
Compton Community College *C, A*
Diablo Valley College *A*
Fresno City College *C, A*
Imperial Valley College *C, A*
Long Beach City College *C, A*
Los Angeles Southwest College *A*
Los Angeles Valley College *A*
Merced College *A*
Mission College *A*
Mount San Antonio College *C, A*
National University *M*
Palomar College *C, A*
Pasadena City College *C, A*
Porterville College *C, A*
Riverside Community College *A*
San Francisco State University *B*
San Joaquin Delta College *C*
San Jose City College *A*
Solano Community College *C, A*
Yuba College *C*

Colorado
Arapahoe Community College *C, A*

Community College of Aurora *C, A*
Lamar Community College *A*
Pueblo Community College *C, A*

Connecticut
Housatonic Community-Technical
  College *C*
Sacred Heart University *A*

Delaware
Delaware Technical and Community
  College
    Owens Campus *A*
    Stanton/Wilmington Campus *A*
    Terry Campus *C, A*

District of Columbia
Southeastern University *M*

Florida
Daytona Beach Community College *A*
Florida Community College at
  Jacksonville *C*
Gulf Coast Community College *A*
Indian River Community College *A*
Miami-Dade Community College *A*
Pensacola Junior College *A*
Santa Fe Community College *A*
Seminole Community College *A*
Tallahassee Community College *A*
University of Miami *M*
University of North Florida *B*

Georgia
Chattahoochee Technical Institute *C*
Mercer University *M*
South Georgia College *A*

Hawaii
Hawaii Pacific University *B*
University of Hawaii
  Windward Community
    College *C, A*

Illinois
Black Hawk College *C, A*
Carl Sandburg College *A*
City Colleges of Chicago
  Harold Washington College *C, A*
De Paul University *B*
Illinois Eastern Community Colleges
  Lincoln Trail College *C, A*
John A. Logan College *A*
Lewis and Clark Community College *A*
Prairie State College *C*
Rock Valley College *C, A*
Sauk Valley Community College *C*
Southwestern Illinois College *A*
Waubonsee Community College *C, A*
William Rainey Harper College *C, A*

Indiana
Indiana State University *B*
Manchester College *B*
University of Evansville *A*
University of Indianapolis *A*
Vincennes University *A*

Iowa
American Institute of Business *A*
Drake University *B*
Kirkwood Community College *A*
North Iowa Area Community College *A*
Northeast Iowa Community College *A*

Kansas
Dodge City Community College *C, A*
Kansas City Kansas Community
  College *A*
Seward County Community College *C*

Kentucky
Ashland Community College *A*
Elizabethtown Community College *A*
Hopkinsville Community College *A*
Midway College *B*
Northern Kentucky University *B*
Paducah Community College *A*
Southeast Community College *A*

Louisiana
Southern University
  Shreveport *A*

Maine
Husson College *B*

Maryland
Baltimore City Community College *C*
Frederick Community College *C, A*
Montgomery College
  Germantown Campus *A*
  Takoma Park Campus *A*
Wor-Wic Community College *C, A*

Massachusetts
Berkshire Community College *A*
Bristol Community College *A*
Massachusetts Bay Community
  College *C*
New England College of Finance *C, A*
Suffolk University *B, M*

Michigan
Central Michigan University *B*
Delta College *A*
Mid Michigan Community College *A*
Monroe County Community
  College *C, A*
Oakland Community College *A*

Minnesota
University of Minnesota
  Twin Cities *C*

Mississippi
East Mississippi Community College *A*
Jackson State University *B*
Mississippi Gulf Coast Community
  College
    Jefferson Davis Campus *A*
    Perkinston *A*

Missouri
East Central College *C*
Southeast Missouri State University *B*
St. Louis Community College
  St. Louis Community College at
    Florissant Valley *A*
  St. Louis Community College at
    Forest Park *A*
  St. Louis Community College at
    Meramec *A*
State Fair Community College *A*

Nebraska
University of Nebraska
  Omaha *A*

Nevada
Community College of Southern
  Nevada *A*

New Jersey
Bergen Community College *A*
Bloomfield College *B*
Camden County College *A*
Gloucester County College *A*
St. Peter's College *B*
Thomas Edison State College *A, B*
Union County College *A*

New Mexico
Albuquerque Technical-Vocational
  Institute *C, A*
Clovis Community College *A*
Eastern New Mexico University
  Roswell Campus *C, A*
New Mexico Junior College *A*
New Mexico State University
  Alamogordo *C*
  Carlsbad *C*
San Juan College *A*

New York
Adirondack Community College *A*
Dominican College of Blauvelt *B*
Erie Community College
  City Campus *A*
  South Campus *A*
Fordham University *M*
Hilbert College *A*
Hofstra University *B, M*
Mohawk Valley Community
  College *C, A*
Monroe Community College *A*
New York Institute of Technology *B, M*
Onondaga Community College *A*
Pace University:
  Pleasantville/Briarcliff *B, M*
Pace University *B, M*
Suffolk County Community College *C*

North Carolina
Alamance Community College *A*
Appalachian State University *B*
Fayetteville Technical Community
  College *A*
Johnson C. Smith University *B*
North Carolina Central University *B*
Southeastern Community College *A*

North Dakota
North Dakota State College of Science *A*

Ohio
Defiance College *B*
Jefferson Community College *A*
Kent State University
  Trumbull Campus *A*
Lorain County Community College *A*
Shawnee State University *A*
Sinclair Community College *A*
University of Akron *A*
Washington State Community College *A*

Oklahoma
Connors State College *C, A*
Oklahoma City Community College *C*

Oregon
Chemeketa Community College *C, A*
University of Oregon *M, D*

Pennsylvania
Bucks County Community College *A*
California University of Pennsylvania *B*
Community College of Allegheny
  County *C, A*
Community College of Beaver County *A*
Delaware County Community
  College *C, A*
La Salle University *A, B*
Lackawanna Junior College *A*
Lebanon Valley College of
  Pennsylvania *C*
Northampton County Area Community
  College *A*
Penn State
  University Park *C*
Pittsburgh Technical Institute *A*
Point Park College *A*
Reading Area Community College *C, A*
Westmoreland County Community
  College *A*

Puerto Rico
Caribbean University *A*
Universidad Metropolitana *C, B*
University of Puerto Rico
  Mayaguez Campus *B*
  Rio Piedras Campus *B*

Rhode Island
Providence College *B*

South Carolina
Midlands Technical College *A*

Tennessee
Fisk University *B*
Pellissippi State Technical Community
  College *C*
University of Memphis *B*

Texas
College of the Mainland *A*
Houston Community College
  System *C, A*
Northeast Texas Community College *A*
Palo Alto College *A*
University of North Texas *B, M, D*
University of Texas
  Arlington *B, D*

Utah
Salt Lake Community College *A*
Utah Valley State College *C, A*

Virginia
Averett College *B*
Dabney S. Lancaster Community
  College *C*
J. Sargeant Reynolds Community
  College *C*
Lord Fairfax Community College *C*
Southwest Virginia Community
  College *C*
Tidewater Community College *A*
University of Richmond *C*

Washington
Gonzaga University *B*
Renton Technical College *C*
Spokane Falls Community College *C, A*

West Virginia
College of West Virginia *A*
Fairmont State College *A, B*
Marshall University *B*
Southern West Virginia Community and
  Technical College *A*
West Liberty State College *B*
West Virginia Northern Community
  College *A*
West Virginia State College *A, B*

Wisconsin
Gateway Technical College *A*
Milwaukee Area Technical College *A*
University of Wisconsin
  Whitewater *M*

Wyoming
Sheridan College *A*
Western Wyoming Community
  College *A*

Behavioral sciences

Alabama
Athens State University *B*

Arizona
Prescott College *B, M*

Arkansas
Arkansas Tech University *B*

California
California Baptist University *B*
California State University
  Bakersfield *M*
  Monterey Bay *B*
College of Notre Dame *B*
Concordia University *B*
La Sierra University *B*
MiraCosta College *A*
Modesto Junior College *A*
San Diego City College *A*
Santa Rosa Junior College *A*
University of California
  Davis *D*
  San Diego *D*
University of La Verne *B*

Colorado
Colorado Mountain College
  Spring Valley Campus *A*
Metropolitan State College of Denver *B*
University of Colorado
  Denver *D*

Behavioral sciences

Connecticut
Northwestern Connecticut Community-Technical College *A*

Idaho
Lewis-Clark State College *A*

Illinois
Barat College *B*
National-Louis University *B*

Indiana
Vincennes University *A*

Iowa
Cornell College *B*

Kansas
Garden City Community College *A*
Sterling College *B*

Maine
University of Maine Presque Isle *B*
University of Southern Maine *B*

Massachusetts
Berkshire Community College *A*
Cape Cod Community College *A*
Hampshire College *B*
Harvard College *B*

Michigan
Spring Arbor College *B*

Minnesota
College of St. Scholastica *B*

Nebraska
Concordia University *B*
Northeast Community College *A*

New Hampshire
Antioch New England Graduate School *M*
College for Lifelong Learning *B*
Franklin Pierce College *B*

New Jersey
Drew University *B*

New York
Adirondack Community College *A*
City University of New York John Jay College of Criminal Justice *B*
Concordia College *B*
Fulton-Montgomery Community College *A*
New York Institute of Technology *B, M*
Polytechnic University *M*
State University of New York Health Science Center at Brooklyn *D*

North Dakota
Dickinson State University *B, T*

Ohio
Ursuline College *B*
Wright State University *M*

Oklahoma
Mid-America Bible College *B*
St. Gregory's University *B*
Seminole State College *A*
Southern Nazarene University *B*

Pennsylvania
Delaware County Community College *A*
Franklin and Marshall College *B*
Gettysburg College *B*
Mount Aloysius College *A, B*
Point Park College *B*
York College of Pennsylvania *B*

South Dakota
Dakota Wesleyan University *B*
Mount Marty College *B*

Tennessee
King College *B, T*

Tennessee Wesleyan College *B*

Utah
Southern Utah University *B*

Vermont
Green Mountain College *B*

Wisconsin
Beloit College *B*
University of Wisconsin Madison *B*

Bible studies

Alabama
Faulkner University *B*
Oakwood College *A*
Samford University *A*

Alaska
Alaska Bible College *C, A, B*

Arizona
Grand Canyon University *B*
Southwestern College *C, A, B*

Arkansas
Central Baptist College *B*
Ouachita Baptist University *B*
Williams Baptist College *B*

California
Azusa Pacific University *B, M*
Biola University *B, M*
Fresno Pacific University *B*
Hope International University *B*
LIFE Bible College *A, B*
Master's College *B*
Pacific Union College *A*
Patten College *C, A*
San Jose Christian College *C, A, B*
Simpson College *C, A, B*
Vanguard University of Southern California *B, M*

Colorado
Colorado Christian University *C, B*
Nazarene Bible College *A, B*

District of Columbia
Catholic University of America *M, D*

Florida
Clearwater Christian College *B*
Florida Baptist Theological College *A, B*
Florida Christian College *A, B*
Florida College *B*
Hobe Sound Bible College *C, A, B*
Southeastern College of the Assemblies of God *B*
Warner Southern College *B*

Georgia
Atlanta Christian College *B*
Covenant College *B*
Emmanuel College *B*
Toccoa Falls College *B*

Idaho
Boise Bible College *A, B*

Illinois
Judson College *B*
Lincoln Christian College and Seminary *A, B, M*
Moody Bible Institute *B, M*
North Park University *B*
Olivet Nazarene University *B*
Trinity International University *B*
Wheaton College *B*

Indiana
Anderson University *B, M*
Bethel College *A, B*
Grace College *A, B*
Indiana Wesleyan University *A, B*
University of Evansville *B*

Iowa
Emmaus Bible College *C, A, B*
Faith Baptist Bible College and Theological Seminary *C, A, B, M*
Waldorf College *A*

Kansas
Barclay College *A, B*
Central Christian College *A, B*
Hesston College *A*
Manhattan Christian College *C, A, B*

Kentucky
Asbury College *B*
Campbellsville University *B*
Clear Creek Baptist Bible College *C, A, B*
Kentucky Christian College *B*
Mid-Continent College *C, B*
St. Catharine College *C, A*

Maryland
Washington Bible College *C, A, B, M, T*

Massachusetts
Atlantic Union College *A*
Boston College *M*
Boston University *M, D*
Gordon College *B*

Michigan
Calvin College *B*
Cornerstone College and Grand Rapids Baptist Seminary *C, A, B, M*
Grace Bible College *A, B*
Reformed Bible College *A, B*
Rochester College *B*
William Tyndale College *C, B*

Minnesota
Bethel College *B*
Concordia University: St. Paul *B*
Crown College *C, A, B*
Minnesota Bible College *A*
North Central University *C*
Northwestern College *C, A, B*

Mississippi
Belhaven College *C, B*
Blue Mountain College *B*
Magnolia Bible College *B*
Wesley College *B*

Missouri
Berean University *A, B, M*
Evangel University *B*
Hannibal-LaGrange College *B*
Ozark Christian College *C, A, B*
St. Louis Christian College *B*
Southwest Baptist University *B*

Nebraska
Grace University *C, A, B, M*

New Jersey
Drew University *M, D*

New York
Houghton College *B*
Nyack College *B, M*

North Carolina
Montreat College *B*

North Dakota
Trinity Bible College *A, B*

Ohio
Cedarville College *C*
Lourdes College *A, B*
Malone College *B*
Pontifical College Josephinum *M*

Oklahoma
Mid-America Bible College *B*
Oklahoma Baptist University *B*
Oklahoma Christian University of Science and Arts *B*
Oklahoma City University *B*
Oral Roberts University *B, M*

Southwestern College of Christian Ministries *B*

Oregon
Eugene Bible College *C, B*
George Fox University *B*
Multnomah Bible College *B, M*
Northwest Christian College *B*
Western Baptist College *B*

Pennsylvania
Eastern College *B*
Geneva College *A, B*
Lancaster Bible College *C, A, B, M*
Messiah College *B*
Philadelphia College of Bible *C, A, B, M*
Valley Forge Christian College *C, A, B*

Puerto Rico
Bayamon Central University *M*

Rhode Island
Providence College *M*

South Carolina
Charleston Southern University *B*
Columbia International University *C, A, B*

Tennessee
Crichton College *C, B*
David Lipscomb University *M*
Freed-Hardeman University *B, M*
Hiwassee College *A*
Johnson Bible College *A, B, M*
King College *B*
Lee University *B*
Tennessee Temple University *A, B*
Tennessee Wesleyan College *B*
Trevecca Nazarene University *M*
Union University *B*
University of the South *M, D*

Texas
Abilene Christian University *B, M*
Arlington Baptist College *C, B*
Dallas Baptist University *A, B*
Hardin-Simmons University *B*
Howard Payne University *B*
Institute for Christian Studies *B*
Lubbock Christian University *B, M*
San Jacinto College North *A*
Southwestern Assemblies of God University *B*

Virginia
Bluefield College *B*
Eastern Mennonite University *C, B*

Washington
Puget Sound Christian College *C, A, B*

Biblical languages/literature

Arkansas
Harding University *B*
Ouachita Baptist University *B*

California
Master's College *B*

Colorado
Colorado Christian University *B*

Florida
Florida Christian College *B*

Georgia
Toccoa Falls College *B*

Idaho
Northwest Nazarene University *B*

Illinois
Concordia University *B*
Lincoln Christian College and Seminary *M*

North Park University *B*
Trinity International University *D*
University of Chicago *B*

Indiana
Taylor University *B*

Maryland
Washington Bible College *M*

Massachusetts
Boston University *M, D*

Michigan
Concordia College *B*
Cornerstone College and Grand Rapids Baptist Seminary *B*
University of Michigan *B*
William Tyndale College *B*

Minnesota
Concordia University: St. Paul *B*
North Central University *B*

Mississippi
Magnolia Bible College *B*
Wesley College *B*

New York
Nyack College *M*

Oklahoma
Oral Roberts University *B, M*

Oregon
Eugene Bible College *B*
Multnomah Bible College *B*

Pennsylvania
Philadelphia College of Bible *B*

South Carolina
Columbia International University *B*

Tennessee
Carson-Newman College *B*
David Lipscomb University *B*
Milligan College *B*
Tennessee Temple University *B*
Union University *B*

Texas
Arlington Baptist College *B*
Baylor University *B*
Howard Payne University *B*
Institute for Christian Studies *B*
Southwestern Assemblies of God University *B*

Washington
Walla Walla College *B*

Bilingual/bicultural education

Arizona
Mesa Community College *C*
Northern Arizona University *M, T*
Prescott College *B, M*
University of Arizona *M*
University of Phoenix *M*

California
Butte College *A*
California Baptist University *T*
California Lutheran University *M*
California State University
 Bakersfield *M*
 Chico *T*
 Fullerton *M*
 Hayward *T*
 Long Beach *T*
 Monterey Bay *M*
 Northridge *M*
 Sacramento *B, M, T*
 San Marcos *T*
 Stanislaus *B*
Cerritos Community College *A*
Compton Community College *C, A*

Contra Costa College *A*
Fresno City College *A*
Fresno Pacific University *M, T*
Imperial Valley College *A*
Loyola Marymount University *M*
National University *M, T*
Pacific Oaks College *T*
Point Loma Nazarene University *T*
Sacramento City College *C, A*
San Diego City College *A*
San Diego State University *M, T*
San Francisco State University *M, T*
Santa Barbara City College *C*
University of California
 Irvine *M*
 Los Angeles *M, D*
 Riverside *T*
 San Diego *M*
 Santa Cruz *M*
University of La Verne *T*
University of San Diego *M, T*
University of San Francisco *M, D, T*
University of the Pacific *T*
Ventura College *A*

Colorado
Colorado Mountain College
 Spring Valley Campus *A*
 Timberline Campus *A*
Fort Lewis College *T*
University of Colorado
 Boulder *M, D*
University of Northern Colorado *M*

Connecticut
Fairfield University *M, T*
Quinebaug Valley Community College *C*
Southern Connecticut State University *M*

Delaware
University of Delaware *M*

Idaho
Albertson College of Idaho *T*
Boise State University *B, T*
College of Southern Idaho *A*

Illinois
Chicago State University *M, T*
Columbia College *M*
Northeastern Illinois University *B, M*
Western Illinois University *B*

Indiana
Ball State University *T*

Massachusetts
Boston University *B, M, T*
Eastern Nazarene College *M, T*
Elms College *B, M, T*
Fitchburg State College *B*
University of Massachusetts
 Boston *M*
Wheelock College *B*

Michigan
Calvin College *B, T*
Eastern Michigan University *B, T*
Saginaw Valley State University *T*
Wayne State University *M, T*

Minnesota
College of St. Scholastica *T*
University of Minnesota
 Twin Cities *M*
Winona State University *B, T*

Missouri
St. Louis Christian College *A, B*

New Jersey
Georgian Court College *T*
Montclair State University *T*
New Jersey City University *T*
Rider University *B, T*
Rutgers
 The State University of New Jersey:
 New Brunswick Graduate Campus *M, T*

Seton Hall University *M*

New Mexico
College of Santa Fe *B*
Santa Fe Community College *A*
Western New Mexico University *T*

New York
Bank Street College of Education *M*
City University of New York
 Brooklyn College *B, M*
 City College *B, M, T*
 Hunter College *M, T*
 La Guardia Community College *A*
 Lehman College *M, T*
 York College *T*
Columbia University
 Teachers College *M*
D'Youville College *B, T*
Hofstra University *M*
Long Island University
 Brooklyn Campus *M*
 C. W. Post Campus *M*
Marist College *T*
Pace University:
 Pleasantville/Briarcliff *B*
Pace University *B*
St. John's University *B, M, T*
State University of New York
 Albany *M*
 Buffalo *M, T*
 College at Brockport *M, T*
 College at Buffalo *M*
 College at Old Westbury *B, T*
 New Paltz *T*
Touro College *C*

Ohio
University of Findlay *B, M, T*

Oregon
Chemeketa Community College *A*
Eastern Oregon University *T*
Western Oregon University *T*

Pennsylvania
Immaculata College *M*
La Salle University *B, M*
Lebanon Valley College of Pennsylvania *B, T*

Puerto Rico
Inter American University of Puerto Rico
 Metropolitan Campus *B, M*
Turabo University *M*
Universidad Metropolitana *B*
University of the Sacred Heart *B*

Rhode Island
Rhode Island College *B*

Tennessee
Union University *B, T*

Texas
Del Mar College *A*
East Texas Baptist University *T*
McMurry University *T*
Richland College *A*
St. Edward's University *B, T*
Southern Methodist University *M*
Southwest Texas State University *M, T*
Sul Ross State University *M*
Texas A&M International University *B, M, T*
Texas A&M University
 Commerce *B*
 Corpus Christi *T*
 Kingsville *B, M, D*
Texas Southern University *M*
Texas Tech University *M*
Texas Wesleyan University *B, M, T*
University of Houston
 Clear Lake *T*
University of Houston *M*
University of North Texas *M*

University of Texas
 Arlington *T*
 Brownsville *M*
 Pan American *M, T*
 San Antonio *M*
West Texas A&M University *T*

Utah
Weber State University *B*

Washington
Central Washington University *M, T*
Heritage College *B, M*
Renton Technical College *C, A*
University of Washington *M*
Walla Walla Community College *A*
Washington State University *T*

Wisconsin
Alverno College *T*
Marquette University *T*
Mount Mary College *B*

Biochemistry

Alabama
Auburn University *B*
Oakwood College *B*
Samford University *B*
Spring Hill College *B*
University of Alabama
 Birmingham *D*

Arizona
Arizona State University *B*
Grand Canyon University *B*
University of Arizona *B, M, D*

Arkansas
Harding University *B*
John Brown University *B*
University of Arkansas
 for Medical Sciences *M, D*

California
Azusa Pacific University *B*
Biola University *B*
California Institute of Technology *D*
California Lutheran University *B*
California Polytechnic State University:
 San Luis Obispo *B*
California State University
 Bakersfield *B*
 Chico *B*
 Fullerton *B*
 Hayward *B, M*
 Long Beach *B, M*
 Los Angeles *B, M*
 Northridge *B*
College of Notre Dame *B*
La Sierra University *B*
Loma Linda University *M, D*
Loyola Marymount University *B*
Mills College *C, B*
Mount St. Mary's College *B*
Occidental College *B*
Pacific Union College *B*
Pepperdine University *B*
Pitzer College *B*
Point Loma Nazarene University *B*
Pomona College *B*
St. Mary's College of California *B*
San Francisco State University *B, M*
Stanford University *D*
University of California
 Berkeley *M, D*
 Davis *B, M, D*
 Los Angeles *B, M, D*
 Riverside *B, M, D*
 San Diego *B, D*
 San Francisco *D*
 Santa Barbara *B, M, D*
 Santa Cruz *D*
University of San Francisco *B*
University of Southern California *B*
University of the Pacific *B*

Biochemistry

Colorado
Colorado College B
Colorado State University B, M, D
Fort Lewis College B
Regis University B
University of Colorado
  Boulder B
  Health Sciences Center D
University of Denver B

Connecticut
Connecticut College B
Quinnipiac University B
Sacred Heart University C, B
St. Joseph College B, M, T
Trinity College B
University of Connecticut M, D
Wesleyan University B, D
Yale University B, M, D

Delaware
University of Delaware B, M, D

District of Columbia
Catholic University of America B
George Washington University M
Georgetown University B, D
Howard University M, D
Trinity College B

Florida
Florida Institute of Technology B
Florida State University B
Stetson University B
University of Florida M, D
University of Miami B, M, D
University of Tampa B
University of West Florida B

Georgia
Agnes Scott College B
Berry College B
LaGrange College B
Medical College of Georgia D
Spelman College B
University of Georgia B, M, D

Hawaii
University of Hawaii
  Manoa M, D

Idaho
Idaho State University B
University of Idaho B, M, D

Illinois
Benedictine University B
Bradley University B
Chicago State University B
Dominican University B
Finch University of Health Sciences/The
  Chicago Medical School M, D
Knox College B
Lewis University B
Loyola University of Chicago D
Morton College A
North Central College B
Northwestern University B, M, D
Rockford College B
University of Chicago M, D
University of Illinois
  Chicago B, M, D
  Urbana-Champaign B, M, D

Indiana
Indiana University
  Bloomington B, M, D
Indiana University--Purdue University
  Indiana University-Purdue
    University Indianapolis M, D
Manchester College B
Purdue University B, M, D
St. Joseph's College A, B
University of Notre Dame B, M, D

Iowa
Coe College B
Cornell College B
Iowa State University B, M, D
Maharishi University of Management B
Simpson College B
University of Iowa B, M, D
University of Northern Iowa B
Wartburg College B

Kansas
Benedictine College B
Kansas State University B, M, D
Southwestern College B
University of Kansas B, M, D

Kentucky
Asbury College B
Centre College B
Murray State University B
Western Kentucky University B

Louisiana
Centenary College of Louisiana B
Louisiana State University
  Shreveport B
Louisiana State University Medical
  Center M, D
Louisiana State University and
  Agricultural and Mechanical
  College B, M, D
Tulane University B
Xavier University of Louisiana B

Maine
Bates College B
Bowdoin College B
Colby College B
University of Maine B, M, D

Maryland
Columbia Union College B
Hood College B
Johns Hopkins University B
Mount St. Mary's College B
Uniformed Services University of the
  Health Sciences
University of Maryland
  Baltimore County B, D
  Baltimore D
  College Park B, M, D
Western Maryland College B

Massachusetts
American International College B
Boston College B
Boston University B, M, D
Brandeis University B, M, D
Bridgewater State College B
Clark University B
College of the Holy Cross B
Hampshire College B
Harvard College B
Harvard University M, D
Merrimack College B
Mount Holyoke College B
Northeastern University B
Regis College B
Simmons College B
Smith College B
Suffolk University B
Tufts University D
University of Massachusetts
  Amherst M, D
  Boston B
Wellesley College B
Wheaton College B
Worcester Polytechnic Institute B, M

Michigan
Alma College B
Andrews University B
Calvin College B
Eastern Michigan University B
Hope College B, T
Madonna University B
Michigan State University B, M, D
Northern Michigan University B, M
Oakland University B
Olivet College B, T
Saginaw Valley State University B
Spring Arbor College B
University of Detroit Mercy B
University of Michigan
  Dearborn B
University of Michigan B, M
Wayne State University M, D
Western Michigan University B

Minnesota
Bethel College B
College of St. Catherine: St. Paul
  Campus B
College of St. Scholastica B
Gustavus Adolphus College B
Mayo Graduate School D
Minnesota State University, Mankato B
University of Minnesota
  Duluth B
  Twin Cities B, M, D

Mississippi
Mississippi State University B, M
University of Mississippi
  Medical Center M, D
University of Mississippi B

Missouri
St. Louis University D
University of Missouri
  Columbia B, M, D
  Rolla B
  St. Louis C
William Jewell College B

Montana
Montana State University
  Bozeman M, D
University of Montana-Missoula M, D

Nebraska
Nebraska Wesleyan University B
University of Nebraska
  Lincoln B, M, D

Nevada
University of Nevada
  Reno B, M, D

New Hampshire
Dartmouth College B, D
St. Anselm College B
University of New Hampshire B, M, D

New Jersey
Bloomfield College B
Drew University B
Fairleigh Dickinson University B
Georgian Court College B
Montclair State University B
Ramapo College of New Jersey B
Richard Stockton College of New
  Jersey B
Rider University B
Rowan University B
Rutgers
  The State University of New Jersey:
    Camden College of Arts and
    Sciences B
  The State University of New Jersey:
    Cook College B
  The State University of New Jersey:
    Douglass College B
  The State University of New Jersey:
    Livingston College B
  The State University of New Jersey:
    New Brunswick Graduate
    Campus M, D
  The State University of New Jersey:
    Rutgers College B
  The State University of New Jersey:
    University College Camden B
  The State University of New Jersey:
    University College New
    Brunswick B
St. Peter's College B
Seton Hall University B
Stevens Institute of Technology B, M, D

New Mexico
New Mexico Institute of Mining and
  Technology B, M
New Mexico State University B
University of New Mexico B

New York
Adelphi University B, M
Albany Medical College M, D
Barnard College B
Canisius College B
City University of New York
  Brooklyn College B, M
  City College B, M, D
  College of Staten Island B
  Graduate School and University
    Center D
  Hunter College M
  Lehman College B
  Queens College B, M
Colgate University B
College of Mount St. Vincent B
College of St. Rose B
Columbia University
  Columbia College B
  Graduate School M, D
Cornell University B, M, D
Elmira College B
Hamilton College B
Hartwick College B
Hobart and William Smith Colleges B
Hofstra University B
Iona College B
Ithaca College B
Keuka College B
Manhattan College B, T
Manhattanville College B
Marist College B
Nazareth College of Rochester B
New York University B, M, D
Niagara University B
Pace University:
  Pleasantville/Briarcliff B
Pace University B
Rensselaer Polytechnic Institute B, M
Roberts Wesleyan College B
Rochester Institute of Technology B
Rockefeller University D
Russell Sage College B
St. Bonaventure University B
Sarah Lawrence College B
Skidmore College B
State University of New York
  Albany B, M, D
  Binghamton B
  Buffalo B, M, D
  College at Fredonia B
  College at Geneseo B
  College at Plattsburgh B
  College of Environmental Science
    and Forestry B, M, D
  Health Science Center at
    Brooklyn D
  Stony Brook B, D
  Upstate Medical University M, D
Syracuse University B
Union College B
University of Rochester B, M, D
Vassar College B
Wells College B

North Carolina
Duke University M, D
East Carolina University B, D
Lenoir-Rhyne College B, T
North Carolina State University B, M, D
Queens College B
University of North Carolina
  Chapel Hill M, D
Wake Forest University D

North Dakota
Jamestown College B
North Dakota State University M, D
University of North Dakota M, D

Ohio
Case Western Reserve University *B, M, D*
College of Mount St. Joseph *B*
College of Wooster *B*
Denison University *B*
Kent State University *M, D*
Kenyon College *B*
Marietta College *B*
Miami University
   Oxford Campus *B*
Mount Vernon Nazarene College *B*
Notre Dame College of Ohio *B*
Oberlin College *B*
Ohio Northern University *B*
Ohio State University
   Columbus Campus *B, M, D*
Ohio University *B*
Ohio Wesleyan University *B*
Otterbein College *B*
University of Cincinnati *D*
University of Dayton *B*
Wilmington College *B*
Wittenberg University *B*
Wright State University *M*

Oklahoma
Oklahoma Christian University of Science and Arts *B*
Oklahoma City University *B*
Oklahoma State University *B, M, D*
Oral Roberts University *B*
Southern Nazarene University *B*
University of Oklahoma *B*

Oregon
Lewis & Clark College *B*
Oregon Graduate Institute *M, D*
Oregon Health Sciences University *M, D*
Oregon State University *M, D*
Reed College *B*
University of Oregon *B*

Pennsylvania
Albright College *B*
Alvernia College *B*
Bucknell University *B*
Carnegie Mellon University *B, D*
Cedar Crest College *B*
Chatham College *B*
Chestnut Hill College *B*
College Misericordia *B*
Dickinson College *B*
Duquesne University *B*
East Stroudsburg University of Pennsylvania *B*
Eastern College *B*
Edinboro University of Pennsylvania *B*
Elizabethtown College *B*
Gettysburg College *B*
Grove City College *B*
Holy Family College *B*
Immaculata College *B*
Indiana University of Pennsylvania *B*
Juniata College *B*
La Salle University *B*
Lafayette College *B*
Lebanon Valley College of Pennsylvania *B*
Lehigh University *B*
MCP Hahnemann University *M, D*
Mansfield University of Pennsylvania *B*
Mercyhurst College *B*
Messiah College *B*
Muhlenberg College *B*
Penn State
   College of Medicine, Milton S. Hershey Medical Center *M, D*
   University Park *B*
Philadelphia University *B*
Rosemont College *B*
St. Vincent College *B*
Seton Hill College *B*
Susquehanna University *B*
Swarthmore College *B*
Temple University *B*
Thomas Jefferson University: College of Health Professions *D*
University of Pennsylvania *A, B, M, D*
University of Scranton *A, M*
University of the Sciences in Philadelphia *B*
Ursinus College *B*
West Chester University of Pennsylvania *B*
Westminster College *B*
Wilkes University *B*

Puerto Rico
University of Puerto Rico
   Medical Sciences Campus *M, D*

Rhode Island
Brown University *B, M, D*
Providence College *B*
University of Rhode Island *M, D*

South Carolina
Clemson University *B, M, D*
College of Charleston *B*
Converse College *B*
Furman University *B*

South Dakota
South Dakota State University *B*
University of South Dakota *M, D*

Tennessee
David Lipscomb University *B*
King College *B*
Lee University *B*
Maryville College *B*
Rhodes College *B*
Roane State Community College *A*
Southern Adventist University *B*
Tennessee State University *B*
Tennessee Technological University *B*
University of Tennessee
   Knoxville *B, M, D*
   Memphis *M, D*
Vanderbilt University *D*

Texas
Abilene Christian University *B*
Baylor University *B*
Houston Baptist University *B*
Rice University *B, M, D*
St. Edward's University *B*
St. Mary's University *B*
Schreiner College *B*
Southern Methodist University *B*
Southwest Texas State University *M*
Texas A&M University *B, M, D*
Texas Christian University *B*
Texas Tech University Health Science Center *M, D*
Texas Tech University *B*
Texas Wesleyan University *B*
Trinity University *B*
University of Dallas *B*
University of Houston *B, M, D*
University of North Texas *B, M, D*
University of Texas
   Arlington *B*
   Austin *B, M, D*
   Medical Branch at Galveston *M, D*
   Southwestern Medical Center at Dallas *M, D*

Utah
Brigham Young University *B, M, D*
Snow College *A*
University of Utah *M, D*
Utah State University *M, D*

Vermont
Bennington College *B*
Castleton State College *B*
Marlboro College *B*
Middlebury College *B*
Norwich University *B*
St. Michael's College *B*
University of Vermont *B, M, D*

Virginia
Averett College *B*
Eastern Mennonite University *B*
Hampden-Sydney College *B*
Mary Baldwin College *B*
Old Dominion University *B*
Roanoke College *B*
Sweet Briar College *B*
University of Richmond *B*
University of Virginia *D*
Virginia Commonwealth University *C, M, D*
Virginia Polytechnic Institute and State University *B, M*

Washington
Eastern Washington University *B*
Gonzaga University *B*
Seattle Pacific University *B*
Seattle University *B*
University of Washington *B, M, D*
Washington State University *B, M, D*
Western Washington University *B*

West Virginia
Bethany College *B*
West Virginia University *M, D*

Wisconsin
Beloit College *B*
Lawrence University *B*
Marquette University *B*
Medical College of Wisconsin *M, D*
Ripon College *B*
University of Wisconsin
   Eau Claire *B*
   Madison *B, M, D*
   Parkside *B*
Viterbo University *B*

Bioengineering/biomedical engineering

Alabama
University of Alabama
   Birmingham *M, D*

Arizona
Arizona State University *B, M, D*
University of Arizona *M, D*

Arkansas
University of Arkansas for Medical Sciences *A*

California
California State University
   Long Beach *B*
   Sacramento *M*
College of the Canyons *A*
Napa Valley College *C, A*
University of California
   Berkeley *B, M, D*
   Davis *B, M, D*
   Irvine *M, D*
   San Diego *B, M, D*
   San Francisco *M, D*
University of Southern California *B, M, D*

Connecticut
Hartford Graduate Center *M*
Trinity College *B*
University of Connecticut *M, D*
University of Hartford *B*
Yale University *B*

Delaware
University of Delaware *M, D*

District of Columbia
Catholic University of America *B, M, D*

Florida
Florida International University *B*
Florida State University *B*
Keiser College *A*
South Florida Community College *A*
University of Florida *M, D*
University of Miami *B, M, D*

Georgia
Georgia Institute of Technology *M, D*
Mercer University *B, M*
University of Georgia *B, M*

Idaho
University of Idaho *B, M*

Illinois
Northwestern University *B, M, D*
Parkland College *A*
University of Illinois
   Chicago *B, M, D*
   Urbana-Champaign *B*

Indiana
Indiana University--Purdue University
   Indiana University-Purdue University Indianapolis *M*
Rose-Hulman Institute of Technology *M*

Iowa
Iowa State University *M, D*
University of Iowa *B, M, D*

Kentucky
Madisonville Community College *A*
University of Kentucky *M, D*

Louisiana
Louisiana State University and Agricultural and Mechanical College *B, M*
Louisiana Tech University *B, D*
Tulane University *B, M, D*

Maryland
Howard Community College *C, A*
Johns Hopkins University *B, M, D*
Montgomery College
   Rockville Campus *A*

Massachusetts
Berkshire Community College *A*
Boston University *B, M, D*
Harvard College *B*
Massachusetts Institute of Technology *M, D*
Northern Essex Community College *C, A*
Tufts University *M*
Western New England College *B*
Worcester Polytechnic Institute *B, M, D*

Michigan
Schoolcraft College *A*
University of Michigan *M, D*
Wayne State University *M, T*

Minnesota
University of Minnesota
   Twin Cities *M, D*

Mississippi
Mississippi State University *B, M*

Missouri
St. Louis University *B*
Washington University *B, M, D*

Nebraska
University of Nebraska
   Lincoln *B*

Nevada
University of Nevada
   Reno *M, D*

New Jersey
New Jersey Institute of Technology *M*
Rutgers
   The State University of New Jersey: College of Engineering *B*
   The State University of New Jersey: New Brunswick Graduate Campus *M, D*
Stevens Institute of Technology *B*

Bioengineering/biomedical engineering

New York
Columbia University
    Fu Foundation School of
        Engineering and Applied
        Science *B, M, D*
New York Institute of Technology *B*
Rensselaer Polytechnic Institute *B, M, D*
State University of New York
    Buffalo *M, D*
    Stony Brook *M, D*
Syracuse University *B, M, D*
Touro College *C*
University of Rochester *B, M, D*

North Carolina
Duke University *B, M, D*

North Dakota
North Dakota State University *B*

Ohio
Case Western Reserve
    University *B, M, D*
Ohio State University
    Columbus Campus *M, D*
University of Akron *B, M, D*
University of Toledo *B*
Wright State University *B, M*

Oklahoma
Oral Roberts University *B*

Oregon
Oregon Graduate Institute *M, D*

Pennsylvania
Carnegie Mellon University *B, M, D*
Cedar Crest College *B*
Drexel University *M, D*
Gettysburg College *B*
Lock Haven University of
    Pennsylvania *B*
Penn State
    College of Medicine, Milton S.
        Hershey Medical Center *M, D*
    University Park *M, D*
Temple University *B*
University of Pennsylvania *B, M, D*
University of Pittsburgh *B, M, D*

Rhode Island
Brown University *B, M, D*
University of Rhode Island *B*

South Carolina
Clemson University *M, D*

Tennessee
University of Memphis *M*
University of Tennessee
    Memphis *M, D*
Vanderbilt University *B, M, D*

Texas
Rice University *B, M, D*
Texas A&M University *B, M, D*
University of Houston *M*
University of Texas
    Arlington *M, D*
    Austin *M, D*
    Southwestern Medical Center at
        Dallas *M, D*

Utah
University of Utah *M, D*

Vermont
University of Vermont *M*
Vermont Technical College *A*

Virginia
University of Virginia *M, D*
Virginia Commonwealth
    University *B, M, D*
Virginia Polytechnic Institute and State
    University *B, M, D*

Washington
University of Washington *M, D*
Walla Walla College *B*

Wisconsin
Marquette University *B, M, D*
Milwaukee School of Engineering *B*
University of Wisconsin
    Madison *B, M, D*

Biological immunology

California
Stanford University *D*
University of California
    Berkeley *M, D*
    Davis *M, D*
    Los Angeles *M, D*

Illinois
University of Chicago *M, D*

Indiana
Indiana University--Purdue University
    Indiana University-Purdue
        University Indianapolis *M, D*

Iowa
University of Iowa *D*

Maine
University of Southern Maine *M*

Michigan
University of Michigan *D*

Minnesota
Mayo Graduate School *D*

Missouri
Washington University *D*

New York
Albany Medical College *M, D*
Cornell University *B, M, D*
State University of New York
    Health Science Center at
        Brooklyn *D*

North Carolina
North Carolina State University *M, D*
University of North Carolina
    Chapel Hill *M, D*

Ohio
Ohio State University
    Columbus Campus *M, D*

Texas
University of North Texas *M*
University of Texas
    Southwestern Medical Center at
        Dallas *M, D*

Utah
Brigham Young University *M*

Washington
University of Washington *M, D*

West Virginia
West Virginia University *M, D*

Biological technology

Alabama
Auburn University *B*
Northwest-Shoals Community College *A*

California
California Lutheran University *B*
De Anza College *C, A*
Foothill College *C, A*
MiraCosta College *C, A*
San Diego City College *A*
Skyline College *A*
University of California
    Davis *B*

Colorado
Community College of Aurora *C*

Connecticut
Quinnipiac University *B*
University of New Haven *A, B*

Delaware
Delaware Technical and Community
    College
        Stanton/Wilmington Campus *A*

Florida
Barry University *B*

Indiana
Indiana State University *B*

Iowa
Indian Hills Community College *A*

Kansas
Kansas City Kansas Community
    College *C, A*

Massachusetts
Assumption College *B*
Massachusetts Bay Community
    College *A*
Middlesex Community College *C, A*
North Shore Community College *A*
Northeastern University *A, B*

Minnesota
St. Cloud State University *B*

Missouri
University of Missouri
    St. Louis *C*

Montana
Montana State University
    College of Technology-Great
        Falls *A*

Nebraska
Central Community College *C, A*

New Hampshire
New Hampshire Community Technical
    College
        Manchester *A*
University of New Hampshire *B*

New Jersey
County College of Morris *A*
Mercer County Community College *A*
Middlesex County College *A*

New York
City University of New York
    York College *B*
Manhattan College *M*
Monroe Community College *A*
Rochester Institute of Technology *B*
State University of New York
    College of Agriculture and
        Technology at Cobleskill *A*
    College of Agriculture and
        Technology at Morrisville *A*
    College of Technology at Alfred *A*

Ohio
Lakeland Community College *A*

Oregon
Portland Community College *A*

Pennsylvania
Penn State
    University Park *B*
Thomas Jefferson University: College of
    Health Professions *B*

Texas
Collin County Community College
    District *C, A*
Texas State Technical College
    Sweetwater *A*

Utah
Weber State University *C, A*

Vermont
Vermont Technical College *A*

Washington
Shoreline Community College *A*

West Virginia
Salem-Teikyo University *B, M*

Wisconsin
Madison Area Technical College *A*

Biological/life sciences

Alabama
Shelton State Community College *A*
Tuskegee University *T*
University of North Alabama *B*

Arizona
Grand Canyon University *B*
Mohave Community College *A*
Prescott College *B, M*

Arkansas
Henderson State University *B*
Philander Smith College *B*
University of Arkansas
    for Medical Sciences *M, D*

California
Azusa Pacific University *B*
Butte College *A*
California Baptist University *B*
California State Polytechnic University:
    Pomona *M*
College of the Canyons *A*
Compton Community College *A*
Crafton Hills College *A*
Fresno City College *A*
Fresno Pacific University *B*
Gavilan Community College *A*
Grossmont Community College *A*
Imperial Valley College *A*
Loma Linda University *B*
Long Beach City College *A*
Master's College *T*
MiraCosta College *A*
Pitzer College *B*
Sacramento City College *A*
Santa Barbara City College *A*
Santa Rosa Junior College *A*
Taft College *A*
University of the Pacific *T*
Yuba College *A*

Colorado
Adams State College *B*
Colorado Mountain College
    Timberline Campus *A*
Colorado State University *B*
Fort Lewis College *B*
Trinidad State Junior College *A*
University of Southern Colorado *B, T*

Connecticut
Connecticut College *B*
Mitchell College *A*
Northwestern Connecticut
    Community-Technical College *A*
Quinnipiac University *B*
St. Joseph College *B*
Southern Connecticut State
    University *B, T*
University of Connecticut *M, D*

Florida
Nova Southeastern University *B*
Polk Community College *A*
South Florida Community College *A*

Georgia
Albany State University *B*
Andrew College *A*
Clayton College and State University *A*
Dalton State College *A*
Gainesville College *A*
Reinhardt College *A*
Young Harris College *A*

Hawaii
University of Hawaii
  Manoa *M, D*

Idaho
College of Southern Idaho *A*
Ricks College *A*

Illinois
Black Hawk College
  East Campus *A*
Chicago State University *M*
City Colleges of Chicago
  Richard J. Daley College *C, A*
John Wood Community College *A*
Kankakee Community College *A*
Kishwaukee College *A*
Lake Land College *A*
Lewis University *B, T*
Morton College *A*
North Park University *B*
Northwestern University *B, T*
Olivet Nazarene University *B, T*
Parkland College *A*
Richland Community College *A*
Sauk Valley Community College *A*
Southwestern Illinois College *A*
University of Chicago *B, M, D*
William Rainey Harper College *A*

Indiana
Ancilla College *A*
Goshen College *B*
Indiana University
  Bloomington *B*
Manchester College *B, T*
University of Evansville *B*
Vincennes University *A*

Iowa
Iowa Wesleyan College *B*
North Iowa Area Community College *A*
University of Northern Iowa *B*
Upper Iowa University *B*

Kansas
Baker University *T*
Butler County Community College *A*
Central Christian College *A*
Coffeyville Community College *A*
Cowley County Community College *A*
Garden City Community College *A*
Hutchinson Community College *A*
Independence Community College *A*
Kansas State University *B*
MidAmerica Nazarene University *B*
Seward County Community College *A*
Wichita State University *T*

Kentucky
Midway College *B*

Louisiana
Louisiana State University
  Shreveport *B*
McNeese State University *B*
Nunez Community College *A*

Maine
College of the Atlantic *B*
Husson College *B*
University of Maine
  Fort Kent *B*
  Presque Isle *B*
University of New England *B*

Maryland
Chesapeake College *A*
Howard Community College *A*
Morgan State University *B*
University of Maryland
  Eastern Shore *B, M*

Massachusetts
Anna Maria College *B, M*
Berkshire Community College *A*
Cape Cod Community College *A*
Clark University *B*
Hampshire College *B*

Harvard College *B*
Massachusetts Bay Community
  College *A*
Middlesex Community College *A*
Northeastern University *B, M, D*
Tufts University *B, M, D*

Michigan
Calvin College *B*
Northern Michigan University *T*
West Shore Community College *A*
Western Michigan University *M, D, T*

Minnesota
Concordia University: St. Paul *B*
Crown College *B*
Moorhead State University *B, T*
Northland Community & Technical
  College *A*
Winona State University *B, T*

Mississippi
Holmes Community College *A*
University of Mississippi *B*

Missouri
Crowder College *A*
Fontbonne College *B*
Lincoln University *B*
Lindenwood University *B*
Missouri Southern State College *B, T*
Rockhurst University *B*
University of Missouri
  Rolla *B, T*
  St. Louis *B*
Washington University *B, D*

Montana
Miles Community College *A*
Stone Child College *A*
University of Montana-Missoula *B, M*

Nebraska
Hastings College *B, T*
University of Nebraska
  Lincoln *B, M, D*

New Hampshire
Antioch New England Graduate
  School *M*
Dartmouth College *B*
Franklin Pierce College *B*
Keene State College *B, T*
New Hampshire Technical Institute *A*
Rivier College *B*
University of New Hampshire *B*

New Jersey
Brookdale Community College *A*
Felician College *B*
Rowan University *C, B*

New Mexico
New Mexico Highlands University *M*
Western New Mexico University *B*

New York
Adirondack Community College *A*
Bard College *B*
Concordia College *B*
Cornell University *B*
Corning Community College *A*
Finger Lakes Community College *A*
Fordham University *B*
Iona College *B*
Jefferson Community College *A*
Keuka College *B, T*
New York Institute of Technology *B*
New York University *B, M, D*
Niagara University *B*
Rochester Institute of Technology *A*
State University of New York
  College of Environmental Science
    and Forestry *B*
  Upstate Medical University *M, D*
Union College *B*
United States Military Academy *B*
University of Rochester *B*

North Carolina
Brevard College *B*
East Carolina University *D*

North Dakota
Mayville State University *T*
Minot State University: Bottineau
  Campus *A*
Minot State University *T*
University of Mary *T*

Ohio
Ashland University *B, T*
Cleveland State University *B, M, D, T*
Defiance College *B, T*
Denison University *B*
Hiram College *B, T*
Kent State University
  Stark Campus *A*
Ohio Dominican College *D*
Ohio University
  Zanesville Campus *A*
Otterbein College *B*
Ursuline College *B*
Washington State Community College *A*
Wittenberg University *B*
Youngstown State University *B, M*

Oklahoma
Eastern Oklahoma State College *A*
Northern Oklahoma College *A*
Oklahoma State University *B, M, D*
Seminole State College *A*
University of Oklahoma *M*

Oregon
Central Oregon Community College *A*
Southern Oregon University *B*
University of Portland *B*
Western Baptist College *B*

Pennsylvania
Community College of Allegheny
  County *A*
La Salle University *B, T*
Muhlenberg College *B*
Penn State
  College of Medicine, Milton S.
    Hershey Medical Center *M, D*
  University Park *B, M*
Philadelphia University *B*
Swarthmore College *B*

Puerto Rico
Caribbean University *B*
Inter American University of Puerto Rico
  Barranquitas Campus *B*
University of Puerto Rico
  Arecibo Campus *A*
  Mayaguez Campus *B*

Rhode Island
Community College of Rhode Island *A*

Tennessee
David Lipscomb University *B*
Lee University *B*
Roane State Community College *A*
University of Tennessee
  Knoxville *M, D*

Texas
Central Texas College *A*
Concordia University at Austin *B, T*
LeTourneau University *B*
Texas Wesleyan University *B*
Tyler Junior College *A*
University of Texas
  El Paso *M*
  Medical Branch at Galveston *M, D*
Wayland Baptist University *B*
Western Texas College *A*

Vermont
Bennington College *B*
Marlboro College *B*
Middlebury College *B*

Virginia
Central Virginia Community College *A*
George Mason University *D*
Germanna Community College *A*
Lord Fairfax Community College *A*
Mountain Empire Community College *A*
Tidewater Community College *A*
Virginia Polytechnic Institute and State
  University *D*

Washington
Centralia College *A*
Everett Community College *A*
Evergreen State College *B*
Highline Community College *A*
Lower Columbia College *A*
Olympic College *A*

West Virginia
Davis and Elkins College *B*

Wisconsin
Carthage College *T*
Concordia University Wisconsin *B, T*
Mount Senario College *T*

Wyoming
Casper College *A*
Central Wyoming College *A*
Western Wyoming Community
  College *A*

Biological/physical sciences

Alabama
Calhoun Community College *A*
Faulkner University *B*
Talladega College *B*
University of Alabama
  Birmingham *B*
University of South Alabama *M, D*

Alaska
University of Alaska
  Anchorage *B*
  Fairbanks *B, M*

Arizona
Arizona State University *M*
Arizona Western College *A*
Central Arizona College *A*
Northland Pioneer College *A*
Prescott College *B, M*

Arkansas
Southern Arkansas University *B*
University of Central Arkansas *B*

California
American River College *A*
California Lutheran University *B*
Cerro Coso Community College *C, A*
College of the Siskiyous *A*
Foothill College *A*
Fresno City College *A*
Glendale Community College *A*
Golden West College *A*
Harvey Mudd College *B*
Master's College *B*
Porterville College *A*
Santa Monica College *A*
Solano Community College *A*
University of California
  Los Angeles *M, D*
  Santa Barbara *B*
University of La Verne *B*
University of the Pacific *B*
West Hills Community College *A*

Colorado
Colorado Mountain College
  Alpine Campus *A*
  Spring Valley Campus *A*
  Timberline Campus *A*
Morgan Community College *A*

Biological/physical sciences

University of Colorado
   Boulder *M*
   Denver *M*

Connecticut
Albertus Magnus College *B*

District of Columbia
Trinity College *B*

Florida
Florida Southern College *B*
Palm Beach Community College *A*
University of North Florida *B*
University of South Florida *B*

Georgia
Atlanta Metropolitan College *A*
Spelman College *B*
University of Georgia *B*
Young Harris College *A*

Idaho
Lewis-Clark State College *B*
Northwest Nazarene University *B*

Illinois
Black Hawk College *A*
Blackburn College *B, T*
College of DuPage *A*
College of Lake County *A*
Kankakee Community College *A*
Kishwaukee College *A*
Lake Forest College *B*
Lincoln Land Community College *A*
McHenry County College *A*
Moraine Valley Community College *A*
National-Louis University *B*
North Central College *B, T*
Olivet Nazarene University *B, T*
Prairie State College *A*
St. Xavier University *B*
Shawnee Community College *A*
Southern Illinois University
   Carbondale *D*
Triton College *A*
Waubonsee Community College *A*

Indiana
Indiana State University *B, M, T*
Indiana University
   Bloomington *M*
   East *B*
Purdue University *B*
University of Southern Indiana *A, B*
Valparaiso University *A*

Iowa
Briar Cliff College *B*
Clarke College *B*
Grinnell College *B*
Marycrest International University *A, B*
St. Ambrose University *B*
University of Northern Iowa *B, M*
William Penn University *B*

Kansas
Benedictine College *B, T*
Central Christian College *A*
Fort Hays State University *B*
Kansas City Kansas Community
   College *A*
Pratt Community College *A*
Sterling College *B*
University of Kansas
   Medical Center *M, D*
University of Kansas *B*

Kentucky
Alice Lloyd College *B*
Berea College *T*
Brescia University *B*
St. Catharine College *A*

Louisiana
Delgado Community College *A*
Louisiana State University and
   Agricultural and Mechanical
   College *M*

Maine
St. Joseph's College *B*
University of Maine *B, M*

Maryland
Baltimore City Community College *A*
Cecil Community College *C, A*
Charles County Community College *A*
Johns Hopkins University *B, D*
Montgomery College
   Germantown Campus *A*
   Rockville Campus *A*
   Takoma Park Campus *A*
Towson University *B*
Villa Julie College *B*
Washington College *B*

Massachusetts
Anna Maria College *B*
Brandeis University *B*
Elms College *B*
Hampshire College *B*
Harvard University *B*
Simon's Rock College of Bard *B*
Springfield College *B*
University of Massachusetts
   Amherst *B*
Wellesley College *B*
Wheaton College *B*
Worcester Polytechnic Institute *B, M, D*
Worcester State College *B*

Michigan
Andrews University *B, M*
Concordia College *B, T*
Eastern Michigan University *B, M*
Grand Valley State University *B*
Hope College *B*
Lake Michigan College *A*
Lansing Community College *A*
Madonna University *A, B*
Michigan State University *B, M*
Northern Michigan University *B, T*
Rochester College *A*
Saginaw Valley State University *B*
University of Michigan
   Flint *B, T*

Minnesota
College of St. Benedict *B*
Concordia University: St. Paul *B*
Metropolitan State University *B*
Minnesota State University, Mankato *B*
St. John's University *B*
University of Minnesota
   Twin Cities *B*
Winona State University *B, T*

Mississippi
Delta State University *B, M*
Mary Holmes College *A*
Mississippi College *M*
Mississippi State University *B*
Rust College *B*

Missouri
Maryville University of Saint Louis *B*
Missouri Valley College *B*
Southeast Missouri State
   University *B, M*
Southwest Missouri State University *M*
St. Louis Community College
   St. Louis Community College at
     Meramec *A*
Washington University *B, M, D*

Montana
Carroll College *B*
Montana Tech of the University of
   Montana *B*
Stone Child College *A*

Nebraska
Nebraska Wesleyan University *B*
University of Nebraska
   Omaha *B*

New Hampshire
Keene State College *B*
St. Anselm College *B, T*

New Jersey
Drew University *B*
Fairleigh Dickinson University *B, M*
Gloucester County College *A*
Rutgers
   The State University of New Jersey:
     Camden College of Arts and
     Sciences *B*
   The State University of New Jersey:
     University College Camden *B*

New Mexico
New Mexico Institute of Mining and
   Technology *B, M, D*
Northern New Mexico Community
   College *A*

New York
Alfred University *B*
City University of New York
   Baruch College *B*
   Brooklyn College *B, M*
   Lehman College *B*
   Queens College *B*
Colgate University *B*
Columbia University
   Graduate School *M, D*
Corning Community College *A*
Fulton-Montgomery Community
   College *A*
Hofstra University *B*
Le Moyne College *B*
Manhattanville College *B*
North Country Community College *A*
Rensselaer Polytechnic Institute *B, M, D*
St. Thomas Aquinas College *B, T*
Sarah Lawrence College *B*
State University of New York
   Buffalo *B, M, D*
   College at Potsdam *B, T*
   College of Agriculture and
     Technology at Cobleskill *A*
   College of Environmental Science
     and Forestry *B, M, D*
   College of Technology at Alfred *A*
   Empire State College *A, B*
Touro College *B*
Union College *B, M*

North Carolina
Brevard College *A, B*
Cape Fear Community College *A*
Chowan College *B*
Mars Hill College *B*
North Carolina Central University *B*
Southeastern Community College *A*
Wayne Community College *A*

North Dakota
North Dakota State University *B*
University of Mary *B*

Ohio
Bowling Green State University
   Firelands College *A*
Clark State Community College *A*
Defiance College *B, T*
Heidelberg College *B*
Jefferson Community College *A*
Kent State University *B*
Lorain County Community College *A*
Lourdes College *A, B*
University of Akron *B*
Ursuline College *B*
Walsh University *B*
Wilberforce University *B*
Wittenberg University *B*
Wright State University *D*
Youngstown State University *B*

Oklahoma
Eastern Oklahoma State College *A*
Northeastern Oklahoma Agricultural and
   Mechanical College *A*
Oklahoma City University *B*

Oregon
Portland State University *B, M*
Reed College *B*
Southern Oregon University *B*

Pennsylvania
Beaver College *B*
Bloomsburg University of
   Pennsylvania *B, T*
Butler County Community College *A*
California University of Pennsylvania *B*
Carnegie Mellon University *B*
Chatham College *B*
Clarion University of Pennsylvania *B, T*
Delaware County Community College *A*
Drexel University *B*
East Stroudsburg University of
   Pennsylvania *B, M*
Edinboro University of Pennsylvania *B*
Geneva College *B, T*
Gettysburg College *B*
Juniata College *B*
King's College *B, T*
Kutztown University of
   Pennsylvania *B, T*
La Salle University *B*
Lehigh University *B*
Lock Haven University of
   Pennsylvania *B*
Luzerne County Community College *A*
Penn State
   Abington *B*
   Altoona *A*
   Beaver *A*
   Berks *B*
   Dubois *A*
   Erie, The Behrend College *B*
   Lehigh Valley *B*
   McKeesport *A*
   New Kensington *A*
   Shenango *A*
   University Park *B*
Philadelphia University *B*
University of Pittsburgh *B*
Villanova University *A, B*

Puerto Rico
Bayamon Central University *B*
University of Puerto Rico
   Carolina Regional College *A*
   Humacao University College *A*

Rhode Island
Brown University *B*
Community College of Rhode Island *A*

South Carolina
Erskine College *B*
North Greenville College *B*

South Dakota
Black Hills State University *B*

Tennessee
Bethel College *B*
Christian Brothers University *B*
David Lipscomb University *B*
East Tennessee State University *B, T*
Middle Tennessee State University *B*
Tennessee State University *B*

Texas
Central Texas College *A*
College of the Mainland *A*
Galveston College *A*
Hill College *A*
Navarro College *A*
North Central Texas College *A*
Palo Alto College *A*
San Antonio College *A*
Southwest Texas State University *M*
Stephen F. Austin State University *B, M*
Texas A&M University
   Commerce *B, M*

Texas Christian University B, M
Texas Tech University B
University of Houston
    Downtown B
University of Texas
    Austin M, D
    Dallas M
    El Paso B
    Medical Branch at Galveston M
    Pan American M
    San Antonio B
Wayland Baptist University M

Utah

Dixie State College of Utah A
Salt Lake Community College A

Vermont

Bennington College B
Castleton State College B
Lyndon State College B
Marlboro College B

Virginia

College of William and Mary M, D
Danville Community College A
J. Sargeant Reynolds Community
    College A
Lord Fairfax Community College A
Mary Baldwin College B
New River Community College A
Northern Virginia Community College A
Paul D. Camp Community College A
Southside Virginia Community
    College A
Tidewater Community College A
University of Virginia M
Virginia Commonwealth
    University C, B, M
Virginia Highlands Community
    College A
Virginia Intermont College B
Virginia Polytechnic Institute and State
    University M, D
Virginia Wesleyan College B
Virginia Western Community College A
Wytheville Community College A

Washington

Centralia College A
Columbia Basin College A
Pacific Lutheran University C, B
Seattle University B
University of Puget Sound B, T
University of Washington M, D
Washington State University B
Western Washington University B

West Virginia

Bluefield State College A, B
College of West Virginia B
Marshall University B, M
Shepherd College T

Wisconsin

Lawrence University B
Madison Area Technical College A
Mount Mary College B
Mount Senario College B
Northland College B, T
St. Norbert College B
University of Wisconsin
    Green Bay B
    Madison M
    River Falls B, T
    Stevens Point B, T
    Superior B

Wyoming

Laramie County Community College A
Northwest College A

Biology

Alabama

Alabama Agricultural and Mechanical
    University B, M
Alabama State University B, M
Athens State University B
Auburn University at Montgomery B
Auburn University B
Birmingham-Southern College B, T
Chattahoochee Valley Community
    College A
Faulkner University B
Huntingdon College B, T
Jacksonville State University B, M
James H. Faulkner State Community
    College A
Lawson State Community College A
Northeast Alabama Community
    College A
Oakwood College B
Samford University B
Southern Union State Community
    College A
Spring Hill College B, T
Stillman College B
Talladega College B
Troy State University B
Tuskegee University B, M, T
University of Alabama
    Birmingham B, M, D
    Huntsville B, M
University of Alabama B, M, D
University of Mobile B, T
University of Montevallo B, T
University of North Alabama B
University of South Alabama B, M
University of West Alabama B, T

Alaska

University of Alaska
    Anchorage B, M
    Fairbanks B, M, D
    Southeast B

Arizona

Arizona State University B, M, D
Arizona Western College A
Cochise College A
Eastern Arizona College A
Glendale Community College A
Grand Canyon University B
Northern Arizona University B, M, D, T
Prescott College B, M
South Mountain Community College A
University of Arizona B

Arkansas

Arkansas State University
    Beebe Branch A
Arkansas State University B, M
Arkansas Tech University B
Harding University B
Henderson State University B
Hendrix College B
John Brown University B
Lyon College B
Ouachita Baptist University B
Philander Smith College B
Phillips Community College of the
    University of Arkansas A
Southern Arkansas University B
University of Arkansas
    Little Rock B
    Monticello A
    Pine Bluff B
University of Arkansas B, M, D
University of Central Arkansas B, M
University of the Ozarks B
Westark College A
Williams Baptist College B

California

Allan Hancock College A
Azusa Pacific University B
Bakersfield College A
Barstow College A
Biola University B
Cabrillo College A
California Baptist University B
California Institute of Technology B, D
California Lutheran University B
California Polytechnic State University:
    San Luis Obispo B, M
California State Polytechnic University:
    Pomona B
California State University
    Bakersfield B
    Chico B, M
    Dominguez Hills B, M
    Fresno B, M
    Fullerton B, M
    Hayward B, M
    Long Beach B, M
    Los Angeles B, M
    Northridge B, M
    Sacramento B, M
    San Marcos B
    Stanislaus B
Canada College A
Cerritos Community College A
Chabot College A
Chaffey Community College A
Chapman University B
Citrus College A
City College of San Francisco A
Claremont McKenna College B
College of Marin: Kentfield A
College of Notre Dame B
College of San Mateo A
College of the Canyons A
College of the Desert A
College of the Siskiyous A
Columbia College A
Compton Community College A
Concordia University B
Contra Costa College A
Crafton Hills College A
Cuesta College C, A
De Anza College A
Diablo Valley College A
Dominican University of California B
Foothill College A
Glendale Community College A
Golden West College A
Harvey Mudd College B
Holy Names College B
Humboldt State University B, M
Irvine Valley College A
Kings River Community College A
La Sierra University B
Las Positas College A
Loma Linda University M, D
Long Beach City College A
Los Angeles Southwest College A
Los Angeles Valley College A
Los Medanos College A
Loyola Marymount University B
Marymount College A
Master's College B
Mendocino College A
Merced College A
Mills College B
MiraCosta College A
Mission College A
Monterey Peninsula College A
Moorpark College A
Mount St. Mary's College B
Mount San Antonio College A
Occidental College B, M
Ohlone College C, A
Orange Coast College A
Pacific Union College B
Palomar College C, A
Pasadena City College C, A
Pepperdine University B
Pitzer College B
Point Loma Nazarene University B
Pomona College B
Porterville College A
Riverside Community College A
Saddleback College A
St. Mary's College of California B
San Bernardino Valley College A
San Diego City College A
San Diego Mesa College A
San Diego Miramar College A
San Diego State University B, M, D
San Francisco State University B, M
San Joaquin Delta College A
San Jose City College A
San Jose State University B, M
Santa Ana College A
Santa Barbara City College A
Santa Clara University B
Santa Monica College A
Scripps College B
Sierra College A
Solano Community College A
Sonoma State University B, M
Southwestern College A
Stanford University B, M, D
University of California
    Berkeley M, D
    Davis B
    Irvine B, M, D
    Los Angeles B, M, D
    Riverside B, M, D
    San Diego B, D
    Santa Barbara B, M, D
    Santa Cruz B, D
University of La Verne B
University of Redlands B
University of San Diego B
University of San Francisco B, M
University of Southern California B
University of the Pacific B, M
Vanguard University of Southern
    California B
Ventura College C, A
Victor Valley College A
West Hills Community College A
West Los Angeles College C, A
West Valley College A
Westmont College B
Whittier College B, M

Colorado

Adams State College B
Colorado Christian University B
Colorado College B
Colorado Mountain College
    Alpine Campus A
    Spring Valley Campus A
    Timberline Campus A
Fort Lewis College B
Lamar Community College A
Mesa State College A, B
Metropolitan State College of
    Denver B, T
Otero Junior College A
Red Rocks Community College A
Regis University B
Trinidad State Junior College A
United States Air Force Academy B
University of Colorado
    Boulder B, M, D
    Colorado Springs B
    Denver B, M
University of Denver B, M, D
University of Northern
    Colorado B, M, D, T
University of Southern Colorado B, T
Western State College of Colorado B

Connecticut

Albertus Magnus College B
Central Connecticut State
    University B, M
Connecticut College B
Eastern Connecticut State University B
Fairfield University B
Quinnipiac University B
Sacred Heart University A, B
St. Joseph College B, M, T

Southern Connecticut State
  University B, M, T
Trinity College B
University of Bridgeport B
University of Connecticut B
University of Hartford B, M
University of New Haven A, B
Wesleyan University B, D
Western Connecticut State
  University B, M
Yale University B, M, D

Delaware
Delaware State University B, M
University of Delaware B, M, D
Wesley College B

District of Columbia
American University B, M
Catholic University of America B, T
Gallaudet University B
George Washington University B, M, D
Georgetown University B, M, D
Howard University B, M, D
Trinity College B
University of the District of
  Columbia B, T

Florida
Barry University B, M, T
Bethune-Cookman College B
Broward Community College A
Chipola Junior College A
Clearwater Christian College B
Eckerd College B
Edward Waters College B
Florida Agricultural and Mechanical
  University B, M
Florida Atlantic University B, M
Florida Gulf Coast University B
Florida Institute of Technology B, D
Florida International University B, M, D
Florida Memorial College B
Florida Southern College B
Florida State University B, M, D
Gulf Coast Community College A
Indian River Community College A
Jacksonville University B, M, D
Manatee Community College A
Miami-Dade Community College A
New College of the University of South
  Florida B
Palm Beach Atlantic College B, T
Palm Beach Community College A
Pensacola Junior College A
Rollins College B
St. Leo University B
St. Thomas University B
Stetson University B
University of Central Florida B, M
University of Miami B, M, D
University of North Florida B
University of South Florida B, D
University of Tampa A, B, T
University of West Florida B, M
Warner Southern College B

Georgia
Abraham Baldwin Agricultural
  College A
Agnes Scott College B
Armstrong Atlantic State University B, T
Atlanta Metropolitan College A
Augusta State University B
Berry College B, T
Brenau University B
Brewton-Parker College A, B
Clark Atlanta University B, M, D
Clayton College and State University A
Coastal Georgia Community College A
Columbus State University B
Covenant College B
Darton College A
East Georgia College A
Emory University B, D
Floyd College A

Fort Valley State University B
Georgia College and State
  University B, M
Georgia Institute of Technology B, M, D
Georgia Military College A
Georgia Perimeter College A
Georgia Southern University B, M
Georgia Southwestern State University B
Georgia State University B, M, D
Kennesaw State University B
LaGrange College B
Mercer University B
Morehouse College B
Morris Brown College B
North Georgia College & State
  University B
Oglethorpe University B
Oxford College of Emory University B
Paine College B
Piedmont College B
Reinhardt College B
Savannah State University B
Shorter College B
South Georgia College A
Spelman College B
State University of West Georgia B
Thomas College B
University of Georgia B
Valdosta State University B
Waycross College A
Wesleyan College B, T
Young Harris College A

Hawaii
Brigham Young University
  Hawaii B
Chaminade University of Honolulu B
Hawaii Pacific University B
University of Hawaii
  Hilo B
  Manoa B

Idaho
Albertson College of Idaho B
Boise State University B, M, T
College of Southern Idaho A
Idaho State University A, B, M, D
Lewis-Clark State College B
North Idaho College A
Northwest Nazarene University B
Ricks College A
University of Idaho B, M

Illinois
Augustana College B
Barat College B
Benedictine University B, T
Black Hawk College
  East Campus A
Blackburn College B
Bradley University B, M, T
Chicago State University B, T
City Colleges of Chicago
  Harold Washington College A
  Kennedy-King College C
  Malcolm X College A
  Olive-Harvey College A
Concordia University B, T
Danville Area Community College A
De Paul University B, M, T
Dominican University B
Eastern Illinois University B, M, T
Elmhurst College B, T
Eureka College B, T
Governors State University B
Greenville College B, T
Highland Community College A
Illinois College B
Illinois Institute of Technology M, D
Illinois State University B, M, D, T
Illinois Wesleyan University B
John A. Logan College A
Joliet Junior College A
Judson College B
Kankakee Community College A
Knox College B

Lake Forest College B
Lewis University B, T
Lewis and Clark Community College A
Lincoln Land Community College A
Loyola University of Chicago B, M
MacMurray College B
McKendree College B, T
Millikin University B, T
Monmouth College B, T
National-Louis University B
North Central College B, T
North Park University B
Northeastern Illinois University B, M
Northern Illinois University B, M, D, T
Northwestern University B, M, D
Olivet Nazarene University B, T
Parkland College A
Principia College B, T
Quincy University A, B, T
Rend Lake College A
Richland Community College A
Rockford College B
Roosevelt University B, M
St. Xavier University B
Sauk Valley Community College A
Southern Illinois University
  Carbondale B, M
  Edwardsville B, M
Southwestern Ilinois College A
Springfield College in Illinois A
Trinity Christian College B, T
Trinity International University B
Triton College A
University of Illinois
  Chicago B, M, D
  Springfield B, M
  Urbana-Champaign B, M, D
University of St. Francis B
Western Illinois University B, M
Wheaton College B

Indiana
Anderson University B
Ball State University B, M
Bethel College A, B
Butler University B
DePauw University B
Earlham College B
Franklin College B
Goshen College B
Grace College B
Hanover College B
Indiana State University B, M, D, T
Indiana University
  Bloomington B, M
  East B
  Kokomo B
  Northwest B, T
  South Bend A, B
  Southeast B
Indiana University--Purdue University
  Indiana University-Purdue
    University Fort Wayne A, B, M
  Indiana University-Purdue
    University Indianapolis B, M
Indiana Wesleyan University A, B
Manchester College B, T
Marian College B, T
Oakland City University B
Purdue University
  Calumet B, M
  North Central Campus A, B
Purdue University B, M, D
Saint Mary's College B, T
St. Joseph's College B
St. Mary-of-the-Woods College B
Taylor University B
Tri-State University B
University of Evansville B
University of Indianapolis B, M
University of Notre Dame B, M, D
University of St. Francis B
University of Southern Indiana B
Valparaiso University A, B, T
Vincennes University A

Wabash College B

Iowa
Briar Cliff College B
Buena Vista University B, T
Central College B, T
Clarke College B, T
Coe College B
Cornell College B, T
Dordt College B
Drake University B, M
Graceland University B, T
Grand View College B
Grinnell College B, T
Hawkeye Community College A
Iowa State University B
Iowa Wesleyan College B
Iowa Western Community College A
Loras College B
Luther College B
Maharishi University of Management B
Marshalltown Community College A
Marycrest International University A, B
Morningside College B
Mount Mercy College B, T
North Iowa Area Community College A
Northwestern College B, T
St. Ambrose University B
Simpson College B
University of Dubuque B, T
University of Iowa B, M, D, T
University of Northern Iowa B, M
Upper Iowa University B
Waldorf College A
Wartburg College B, T
William Penn University B

Kansas
Allen County Community College A
Baker University B, T
Barton County Community College A
Benedictine College B, T
Bethany College B, T
Bethel College B, T
Central Christian College A
Coffeyville Community College A
Colby Community College A
Dodge City Community College A
Emporia State University B, M, T
Fort Hays State University B, M
Garden City Community College A
Hutchinson Community College A
Independence Community College A
Kansas City Kansas Community
  College A
Kansas State University B, M, D
Kansas Wesleyan University B, T
McPherson College B, T
MidAmerica Nazarene University B
Newman University B
Ottawa University B
Pittsburg State University B, M, T
Pratt Community College A
St. Mary College B
Seward County Community College A
Southwestern College B
Sterling College B
Tabor College B
University of Kansas B, M, D
Washburn University of Topeka B
Wichita State University B, M

Kentucky
Alice Lloyd College B
Asbury College B, T
Bellarmine College B, T
Berea College B, T
Brescia University B
Campbellsville University B
Centre College B
Cumberland College B, T
Eastern Kentucky University B, M
Georgetown College B
Kentucky State University B
Kentucky Wesleyan College B, T
Lindsey Wilson College A, B, T

Midway College *B*
Morehead State University *B, M, T*
Murray State University *B, M, T*
Northern Kentucky University *B*
Pikeville College *B, T*
Spalding University *B*
Thomas More College *B*
Transylvania University *B, T*
Union College *B*
University of Kentucky *B, M, D*
University of Louisville *B, M*
Western Kentucky University *B, M, T*

Louisiana
Centenary College of Louisiana *B, T*
Dillard University *B*
Louisiana State University and Agricultural and Mechanical College *B*
Louisiana Tech University *B, M*
Loyola University New Orleans *B*
Nicholls State University *B*
Northwestern State University *B*
Our Lady of Holy Cross College *B, T*
Southeastern Louisiana University *B, M*
Southern University
  New Orleans *B*
  Shreveport *A*
Southern University and Agricultural and Mechanical College *B, M*
University of Louisiana at Lafayette *B, M*
University of Louisiana at Monroe *B, M*
University of New Orleans *B, M*
Xavier University of Louisiana *B*

Maine
Bates College *B*
Bowdoin College *B*
Colby College *B*
Husson College *B*
St. Joseph's College *B*
University of Maine
  Augusta *B*
  Farmington *B*
  Fort Kent *B*
  Machias *B*
  Presque Isle *B*
University of Maine *B, M, D*
University of New England *B*
University of Southern Maine *B*

Maryland
Allegany College *A*
Bowie State University *B*
Charles County Community College *A*
College of Notre Dame of Maryland *B*
Columbia Union College *B*
Community College of Baltimore County
  Essex *A*
Coppin State College *B*
Frederick Community College *A*
Frostburg State University *B, T*
Goucher College *B*
Hagerstown Community College *A*
Harford Community College *A*
Hood College *B, T*
Johns Hopkins University *B, D*
Loyola College in Maryland *B*
Morgan State University *B*
Mount St. Mary's College *B*
St. Mary's College of Maryland *B*
Salisbury State University *B, T*
Towson University *B, M, T*
University of Maryland
  Baltimore County *B, M, D*
  College Park *B*
  Eastern Shore *B*
Villa Julie College *A, B*
Washington College *B, T*
Western Maryland College *B*

Massachusetts
American International College *B*
Amherst College *B*
Anna Maria College *B, M*
Assumption College *B*
Atlantic Union College *B*
Bay Path College *B*
Berkshire Community College *A*
Boston College *B, M, D*
Boston University *B, M, D*
Brandeis University *B*
Bridgewater State College *B, M*
Clark University *B, M, D*
College of the Holy Cross *B*
Curry College *B*
Eastern Nazarene College *B*
Elms College *B*
Emmanuel College *B*
Fitchburg State College *B, M*
Framingham State College *B*
Gordon College *B*
Hampshire College *B*
Harvard College *B, T*
Harvard University *M, D*
Massachusetts College of Liberal Arts *B*
Massachusetts Institute of Technology *B, D*
Merrimack College *B*
Mount Holyoke College *B*
Northeastern University *A, B, M, D*
Pine Manor College *A, B*
Regis College *B*
Salem State College *B*
Simmons College *B*
Simon's Rock College of Bard *B*
Smith College *B, M, D*
Springfield College *B*
Springfield Technical Community College *A*
Stonehill College *B*
Suffolk University *B*
Tufts University *B, M, D*
University of Massachusetts
  Amherst *B, M, D*
  Boston *B, M*
  Dartmouth *B, M*
  Lowell *B, M*
Wellesley College *B*
Western New England College *B, T*
Westfield State College *B*
Wheaton College *B*
Williams College *B*
Worcester Polytechnic Institute *B, M*
Worcester State College *B*

Michigan
Adrian College *A, B, T*
Albion College *B, T*
Alma College *B, T*
Alpena Community College *A*
Andrews University *B, M*
Aquinas College *B, T*
Calvin College *B, T*
Central Michigan University *B, M*
Concordia College *B, T*
Cornerstone College and Grand Rapids Baptist Seminary *B, T*
Eastern Michigan University *B, M*
Ferris State University *B*
Gogebic Community College *A*
Grand Valley State University *B*
Hillsdale College *B*
Hope College *B, T*
Kalamazoo College *B, T*
Kellogg Community College *A*
Lake Michigan College *A*
Lake Superior State University *B, T*
Lansing Community College *A*
Madonna University *B, T*
Marygrove College *B, T*
Michigan State University *B, M*
Michigan Technological University *B, M, D, T*
Mid Michigan Community College *A*
Northern Michigan University *B, M, T*
Oakland University *B, M, T*
Olivet College *B, T*
Saginaw Valley State University *B*
Siena Heights University *A, B*
Spring Arbor College *B*
University of Detroit Mercy *B, M*
University of Michigan
  Dearborn *B*
  Flint *B, M, T*
University of Michigan *B, M, D, T*
Wayne State University *B, M, D*
Western Michigan University *B, M, D, T*

Minnesota
Augsburg College *B*
Bemidji State University *B, M*
Bethel College *B*
Carleton College *B*
College of St. Benedict *B*
College of St. Catherine: St. Paul Campus *B*
College of St. Scholastica *B*
Concordia College: Moorhead *B*
Gustavus Adolphus College *B*
Hamline University *B*
Macalester College *B, T*
Metropolitan State University *B*
Minnesota State University, Mankato *B, M*
Moorhead State University *B*
Northland Community & Technical College *A*
Northwestern College *B*
Ridgewater College: A Community and Technical College *A*
St. Cloud State University *B, M*
St. John's University *B*
St. Mary's University of Minnesota *B*
St. Olaf College *B, T*
Southwest State University *B, T*
University of Minnesota
  Duluth *B, M*
  Morris *B*
  Twin Cities *B*
University of St. Thomas *B*
Winona State University *B, T*

Mississippi
Alcorn State University *B, M*
Belhaven College *B, T*
Blue Mountain College *B*
Delta State University *B, T*
East Central Community College *A*
Hinds Community College *A*
Jackson State University *B, M*
Mary Holmes College *A*
Millsaps College *B, T*
Mississippi College *B, M*
Mississippi Delta Community College *A*
Mississippi Gulf Coast Community College
  Jefferson Davis Campus *A*
  Perkinston *A*
Mississippi State University *B, M, D*
Mississippi University for Women *B, T*
Mississippi Valley State University *B*
Rust College *B*
Tougaloo College *B*
University of Mississippi *B, M, D, T*
University of Southern Mississippi *B, M, D*
William Carey College *B, T*

Missouri
Avila College *B*
Central Methodist College *B*
Central Missouri State University *B, M*
College of the Ozarks *B*
Crowder College *A*
Culver-Stockton College *B, T*
Drury University *B*
East Central College *A*
Evangel University *B*
Fontbonne College *T*
Hannibal-LaGrange College *B*
Jefferson College *A*
Lincoln University *B*
Lindenwood University *B*
Maryville University of Saint Louis *B*
Mineral Area College *A*
Missouri Baptist College *B*
Missouri Southern State College *B, T*
Missouri Valley College *B*
Missouri Western State College *B, T*
Northwest Missouri State University *B, M*
Park University *B*
Rockhurst University *B*
St. Louis University *B, M, D*
Southeast Missouri State University *B, M*
Southwest Baptist University *B*
Southwest Missouri State University *B, M*
St. Louis Community College
  St. Louis Community College at Florissant Valley *A*
  St. Louis Community College at Forest Park *A*
Stephens College *B*
Three Rivers Community College *A*
Truman State University *B, M*
University of Missouri
  Columbia *B, M, D*
  Kansas City *B, M*
  St. Louis *B, M, D*
Washington University *B, M, D*
Webster University *B*
Westminster College *B*
William Jewell College *B, T*
William Woods University *B, T*

Montana
Carroll College *B, T*
Little Big Horn College *A*
Miles Community College *A*
Montana State University
  Billings *B*
  Bozeman *B, M, D*
  Northern *A, B*
Montana Tech of the University of Montana *B*
Rocky Mountain College *B, T*
University of Great Falls *B*
University of Montana-Missoula *B*
Western Montana College of The University of Montana *B*

Nebraska
Chadron State College *B*
College of Saint Mary *B, T*
Concordia University *B, T*
Creighton University *B*
Dana College *B*
Doane College *B*
Hastings College *B*
Midland Lutheran College *B, T*
Nebraska Wesleyan University *B*
Northeast Community College *A*
Union College *B*
University of Nebraska
  Kearney *B, M, T*
  Lincoln *B, M, D*
  Omaha *B, M*
Wayne State College *B, T*

Nevada
University of Nevada
  Las Vegas *B, M, D*
  Reno *B, M, D*
Western Nevada Community College *A*

New Hampshire
Antioch New England Graduate School *C, M*
Colby-Sawyer College *B, T*
Dartmouth College *B, D*
Franklin Pierce College *B*
Keene State College *B, T*
New England College *B, T*
Notre Dame College *B*
Plymouth State College of the University System of New Hampshire *B*
Rivier College *B, M, T*
St. Anselm College *B, T*
Thomas More College of Liberal Arts *B*

Biology

University of New Hampshire
 Manchester *A*
University of New Hampshire *B, M*

New Jersey
Atlantic Cape Community College *A*
Bloomfield College *B*
Brookdale Community College *A*
Caldwell College *B*
College of St. Elizabeth *B, T*
Drew University *B*
Essex County College *A*
Fairleigh Dickinson University *B, M*
Felician College *B*
Georgian Court College *B, M, T*
Gloucester County College *A*
Kean University *B*
Monmouth University *B*
Montclair State University *B, M, T*
New Jersey City University *B*
New Jersey Institute of
 Technology *B, M, D*
Ramapo College of New Jersey *B*
Raritan Valley Community College *A*
Richard Stockton College of New
 Jersey *B*
Rider University *B*
Rowan University *B*
Rutgers
 The State University of New Jersey:
  Camden College of Arts and
  Sciences *B, T*
 The State University of New Jersey:
  Camden Graduate Campus *M*
 The State University of New Jersey:
  Cook College *B, T*
 The State University of New Jersey:
  Douglass College *B, T*
 The State University of New Jersey:
  Livingston College *B, T*
 The State University of New Jersey:
  Newark College of Arts and
  Sciences *B, T*
 The State University of New Jersey:
  Newark Graduate Campus *M*
 The State University of New Jersey:
  Rutgers College *B, T*
 The State University of New Jersey:
  University College Camden *B, T*
 The State University of New Jersey:
  University College New
  Brunswick *B, T*
 The State University of New Jersey:
  University College Newark *T*
St. Peter's College *B*
Salem Community College *A*
Seton Hall University *B, M*
Sussex County Community College *A*
The College of New Jersey *B, T*
Thomas Edison State College *A, B*
Union County College *A*
Warren County Community College *A*
William Paterson University of New
 Jersey *B, M*

New Mexico
College of Santa Fe *A, B*
College of the Southwest *B*
Eastern New Mexico University *B, M*
New Mexico Highlands University *B, M*
New Mexico Institute of Mining and
 Technology *B, M*
New Mexico Junior College *A*
New Mexico State University *B, M, D*
San Juan College *A*
University of New Mexico *B, M, D*
Western New Mexico University *B*

New York
Adelphi University *B, M*
Adirondack Community College *A*
Alfred University *B*
Bard College *B*
Barnard College *B*
Canisius College *B*

City University of New York
 Baruch College *B*
 Brooklyn College *B, M*
 City College *B, M, D, T*
 College of Staten Island *B, T*
 Graduate School and University
  Center *D*
 Hunter College *B, M*
 Kingsborough Community
  College *A*
 Lehman College *B, M*
 Medgar Evers College *A, B*
 Queens College *B, M*
 Queensborough Community
  College *A*
 York College *B*
Clarkson University *B*
Colgate University *B*
College of Mount St. Vincent *B, T*
College of New Rochelle *B, T*
College of St. Rose *B*
Columbia University
 Columbia College *B*
 Graduate School *M, D*
 School of General Studies *B*
Concordia College *B, T*
Cornell University *B*
D'Youville College *B*
Daemen College *B, T*
Dominican College of Blauvelt *B*
Dowling College *B, T*
Elmira College *B, T*
Fordham University *B, M, D*
Fulton-Montgomery Community
 College *A*
Hamilton College *B*
Hartwick College *B, T*
Hobart and William Smith Colleges *B*
Hofstra University *B, M*
Houghton College *B*
Iona College *B*
Ithaca College *B, T*
Keuka College *B, T*
Le Moyne College *B*
Long Island University
 Brooklyn Campus *B, M*
 C. W. Post Campus *B, M*
 Southampton College *B*
Manhattan College *B*
Manhattanville College *B*
Marist College *B, T*
Marymount College *B, T*
Marymount Manhattan College *B*
Medaille College *B*
Mercy College *B*
Molloy College *B*
Monroe Community College *A*
Mount St. Mary College *B, T*
Nazareth College of Rochester *B*
New York Institute of Technology *B*
New York University *A, B, M, D*
Niagara University *B*
Pace University:
 Pleasantville/Briarcliff *B, T*
Pace University *B, T*
Regents College *B*
Rensselaer Polytechnic Institute *B, M, D*
Roberts Wesleyan College *B*
Rochester Institute of Technology *A, B*
Rockefeller University *D*
Russell Sage College *B, T*
St. Bonaventure University *B, T*
St. Francis College *B, T*
St. John Fisher College *B*
St. John's University *B, M, D*
St. Lawrence University *B, T*
St. Thomas Aquinas College *B, T*
Sarah Lawrence College *B*
Siena College *B, T*
Skidmore College *B*
St. Joseph's College
 St. Joseph's College: Suffolk
  Campus *B, T*
 St. Joseph's College *B*

State University of New York
 Albany *B, M, D*
 Binghamton *B, M, D*
 Buffalo *B, M, D*
 College at Brockport *B, M, T*
 College at Buffalo *B, M*
 College at Cortland *B*
 College at Fredonia *B, M, T*
 College at Geneseo *B, M, T*
 College at Old Westbury *B, T*
 College at Oneonta *B, M*
 College at Plattsburgh *B, M*
 College at Potsdam *B, T*
 College of Agriculture and
  Technology at Morrisville *A*
 College of Environmental Science
  and Forestry *B, M, D*
 New Paltz *B, M, T*
 Oswego *B*
 Purchase *B*
 Stony Brook *B, M*
Suffolk County Community College *A*
Syracuse University *B, M, D*
Touro College *B*
Union College *B*
University of Rochester *B, M, D*
Utica College of Syracuse University *B*
Vassar College *B*
Wagner College *B, T*
Wells College *B*

North Carolina
Appalachian State University *B, M*
Barber-Scotia College *B*
Barton College *B*
Belmont Abbey College *B*
Bennett College *B*
Brevard College *B*
Campbell University *B*
Catawba College *B, T*
Chowan College *B*
Davidson College *B*
Duke University *B*
East Carolina University *B, M*
Elizabeth City State University *B*
Elon College *B*
Fayetteville State University *B*
Gardner-Webb University *B*
Greensboro College *B, T*
Guilford College *B*
Guilford Technical Community
 College *A*
High Point University *B*
Johnson C. Smith University *B*
Lees-McRae College *B, T*
Louisburg College *A*
Mars Hill College *B, T*
Meredith College *B*
Methodist College *A, B, T*
Mount Olive College *A, B*
North Carolina Agricultural and
 Technical State University *B, M*
North Carolina Central University *B, M*
North Carolina State University *B*
North Carolina Wesleyan College *B*
Peace College *B*
Pfeiffer University *B*
Queens College *B*
St. Andrews Presbyterian College *B*
St. Augustine's College *B*
Salem College *B*
Sandhills Community College *A*
Shaw University *B*
University of North Carolina
 Asheville *B, T*
 Chapel Hill *B, M, D*
 Charlotte *B, M, D*
 Greensboro *B, M, T*
 Pembroke *B*
 Wilmington *B, M, T*
Wake Forest University *B, M, D*
Warren Wilson College *B*
Western Carolina University *B, M*
Western Piedmont Community
 College *A*

Wingate University *B*
Winston-Salem State University *B*

North Dakota
Dickinson State University *B, T*
Jamestown College *B*
Mayville State University *B, T*
Minot State University: Bottineau
 Campus *A*
Minot State University *B, T*
North Dakota State University *B, T*
University of Mary *B*
University of North Dakota *B, M, D, T*
Valley City State University *B*

Ohio
Antioch College *B*
Ashland University *B*
Baldwin-Wallace College *B, T*
Bluffton College *B*
Bowling Green State University *B, M, D*
Capital University *B*
Case Western Reserve
 University *B, M, D*
Cedarville College *B, T*
Central State University *B*
Cincinnati State Technical and
 Community College *A*
College of Mount St. Joseph *B, T*
College of Wooster *B*
Defiance College *B, T*
Denison University *B*
Franciscan University of Steubenville *B*
Heidelberg College *B*
Hiram College *B*
John Carroll University *B, M*
Kent State University
 Stark Campus *B*
Kent State University *B, M, T*
Kenyon College *B*
Lake Erie College *B*
Lorain County Community College *A*
Lourdes College *A, B*
Malone College *B*
Marietta College *B*
Miami University
 Oxford Campus *B, T*
Mount Union College *B*
Mount Vernon Nazarene College *B*
Muskingum College *B*
Notre Dame College of Ohio *B, T*
Oberlin College *B*
Ohio Dominican College *B, D*
Ohio Northern University *B*
Ohio State University
 Columbus Campus *B*
Ohio University *B*
Ohio Wesleyan University *B*
Otterbein College *B*
Owens Community College
 Toledo *A*
Shawnee State University *B*
Terra Community College *A*
University of Akron *B, M*
University of Cincinnati
 Raymond Walters College *A*
University of Cincinnati *B, M, D, T*
University of Dayton *B, M, D*
University of Findlay *B*
University of Rio Grande *A, B, T*
University of Toledo *B, M, D*
Ursuline College *B*
Walsh University *B*
Wilberforce University *B*
Wilmington College *B*
Wittenberg University *B*
Wright State University *B, M*
Xavier University *B*
Youngstown State University *B, M*

Oklahoma
Cameron University *B*
Carl Albert State College *A*
Connors State College *A*
East Central University *B*
Eastern Oklahoma State College *A*

Langston University *B*
Northeastern Oklahoma Agricultural and Mechanical College *A*
Northeastern State University *B*
Northwestern Oklahoma State University *B*
Oklahoma Baptist University *B, T*
Oklahoma Christian University of Science and Arts *B*
Oklahoma City Community College *A*
Oklahoma City University *B*
Oklahoma Panhandle State University *B*
Oklahoma State University *B*
Oral Roberts University *B*
Redlands Community College *A*
Rogers State University *A*
Rose State College *A*
St. Gregory's University *A, B*
Southeastern Oklahoma State University *B*
Southern Nazarene University *B*
Southwestern Oklahoma State University *B*
University of Central Oklahoma *B, M*
University of Science and Arts of Oklahoma *B*
University of Tulsa *B, M, D*
Western Oklahoma State College *A*

Oregon
Central Oregon Community College *A*
Chemeketa Community College *A*
Concordia University *B, T*
Eastern Oregon University *B, T*
George Fox University *B, T*
Lewis & Clark College *B*
Linfield College *B*
Linn-Benton Community College *A*
Oregon State University *B*
Pacific University *B*
Portland State University *B, M*
Reed College *B*
Southern Oregon University *B, T*
University of Oregon *B, M, D*
University of Portland *B, T*
Western Oregon University *B*
Willamette University *B*

Pennsylvania
Albright College *B, T*
Allegheny College *B*
Allentown College of St. Francis de Sales *B*
Alvernia College *B*
Beaver College *B*
Bloomsburg University of Pennsylvania *B, M, T*
Bryn Athyn College of the New Church *B*
Bryn Mawr College *B, M, D*
Bucknell University *B, M*
Bucks County Community College *A*
Butler County Community College *A*
Cabrini College *B*
California University of Pennsylvania *B, M*
Carlow College *B*
Carnegie Mellon University *B, D*
Cedar Crest College *B*
Chatham College *B*
Chestnut Hill College *B*
Cheyney University of Pennsylvania *B*
Clarion University of Pennsylvania *B, M, T*
College Misericordia *B*
Community College of Allegheny County *A*
Community College of Beaver County *A*
Delaware Valley College *B*
Dickinson College *B*
Drexel University *B, M, D*
Duquesne University *B, M*
East Stroudsburg University of Pennsylvania *B, M*
Eastern College *B*
Edinboro University of Pennsylvania *B, M, T*
Elizabethtown College *B*
Franklin and Marshall College *B*
Gannon University *B*
Geneva College *B*
Gettysburg College *B*
Grove City College *B*
Gwynedd-Mercy College *B*
Harrisburg Area Community College *A*
Haverford College *B, T*
Holy Family College *B, T*
Immaculata College *B*
Indiana University of Pennsylvania *B, M, T*
Juniata College *B*
King's College *B, T*
Kutztown University of Pennsylvania *B, T*
La Roche College *B*
La Salle University *B, T*
Lafayette College *B*
Lebanon Valley College of Pennsylvania *B, T*
Lehigh University *B*
Lincoln University *B*
Lock Haven University of Pennsylvania *B*
Lycoming College *B*
Mansfield University of Pennsylvania *B, T*
Marywood University *B*
Mercyhurst College *B*
Messiah College *B*
Millersville University of Pennsylvania *B, M, T*
Montgomery County Community College *A*
Moravian College *B, T*
Muhlenberg College *B, T*
Neumann College *B, T*
Northampton County Area Community College *A*
Penn State
   Erie, The Behrend College *B*
   University Park *B, M, D*
Pennsylvania College of Technology *A*
Philadelphia University *B*
Point Park College *B*
Reading Area Community College *A*
Rosemont College *B*
St. Francis College *B*
St. Joseph's University *A, B, M*
St. Vincent College *B*
Seton Hill College *B, T*
Shippensburg University of Pennsylvania *B, M, T*
Slippery Rock University of Pennsylvania *B, T*
Susquehanna University *B, T*
Swarthmore College *B*
Temple University *B, M, D*
Thiel College *B*
University of Pennsylvania *A, B, M, D*
University of Pittsburgh
   Bradford *B, T*
   Greensburg *B*
   Johnstown *B*
University of Pittsburgh *B, M, D*
University of Scranton *B, T*
University of the Sciences in Philadelphia *B*
Ursinus College *B, T*
Villanova University *B, M*
Washington and Jefferson College *B*
Waynesburg College *B*
West Chester University of Pennsylvania *B, M*
Westminster College *B*
Widener University *B*
Wilkes University *B*
Wilson College *B*
York College of Pennsylvania *A, B, T*

Puerto Rico
Bayamon Central University *B*
Caribbean University *B*
Inter American University of Puerto Rico
   Aguadilla Campus *B*
   Arecibo Campus *B*
   Barranquitas Campus *B*
   Bayamon Campus *B*
   Guayama Campus *B*
   Metropolitan Campus *B*
   San German Campus *B*
Pontifical Catholic University of Puerto Rico *B*
Turabo University *B*
Universidad Metropolitana *B*
University of Puerto Rico
   Aguadilla *A*
   Cayey University College *B*
   Humacao University College *B*
   Mayaguez Campus *B, M*
   Medical Sciences Campus *D*
   Ponce University College *A*
   Rio Piedras Campus *B, M, D*
University of the Sacred Heart *B*

Rhode Island
Brown University *B, M, D*
Providence College *B, T*
Rhode Island College *B, M*
Roger Williams University *A, B*
Salve Regina University *B*
University of Rhode Island *B*

South Carolina
Anderson College *B, T*
Benedict College *B*
Charleston Southern University *B*
Claflin University *B*
Clemson University *B*
Coastal Carolina University *B*
Coker College *B, T*
College of Charleston *B, T*
Columbia College *B*
Converse College *B*
Erskine College *B*
Francis Marion University *B*
Furman University *B, T*
Lander University *B, T*
Limestone College *B*
Morris College *B*
Newberry College *B, T*
Presbyterian College *B, T*
South Carolina State University *B*
Southern Wesleyan University *B, T*
The Citadel *B*
University of South Carolina
   Aiken *B*
   Spartanburg *B*
University of South Carolina *B, M, D*
Voorhees College *B*
Winthrop University *B, M*
Wofford College *B, T*

South Dakota
Augustana College *B, T*
Black Hills State University *B*
Dakota State University *B*
Dakota Wesleyan University *B*
Mount Marty College *B*
Northern State University *B*
Sinte Gleska University *A*
South Dakota State University *B, M*
University of South Dakota *B, M, D*

Tennessee
Austin Peay State University *B, M*
Belmont University *B, T*
Bethel College *B, T*
Carson-Newman College *B, T*
Christian Brothers University *B*
Columbia State Community College *A*
Crichton College *B*
Cumberland University *A, B*
David Lipscomb University *B*
Dyersburg State Community College *A*
East Tennessee State University *B, M*
Fisk University *B, M*
Freed-Hardeman University *B, T*
Hiwassee College *A*
King College *B, T*
Lambuth University *B*
Lane College *B*
LeMoyne-Owen College *B*
Lincoln Memorial University *B, T*
Maryville College *B*
Middle Tennessee State University *B, M*
Milligan College *B*
Motlow State Community College *A*
Rhodes College *B, T*
Southern Adventist University *B*
Tennessee State University *B, M*
Tennessee Technological University *B, M, T*
Tennessee Temple University *B*
Tennessee Wesleyan College *B, T*
Trevecca Nazarene University *B*
Tusculum College *B*
Union University *B, T*
University of Memphis *B, M, D*
University of Tennessee
   Chattanooga *B*
   Knoxville *B*
   Martin *B*
University of the South *B*
Walters State Community College *A*

Texas
Abilene Christian University *B*
Alvin Community College *A*
Amarillo College *A*
Angelina College *A*
Angelo State University *B, M, T*
Austin College *B*
Austin Community College *A*
Baylor University *B, M, D*
Blinn College *A*
Brazosport College *A*
Cedar Valley College *A*
Central Texas College *A*
Coastal Bend College *A*
College of the Mainland *A*
Concordia University at Austin *B*
Dallas Baptist University *B*
Del Mar College *A*
East Texas Baptist University *B*
El Paso Community College *A*
Galveston College *A*
Grayson County College *A*
Hardin-Simmons University *B*
Hill College *A*
Houston Baptist University *B*
Howard College *A*
Howard Payne University *B, T*
Huston-Tillotson College *B*
Jarvis Christian College *B*
Kilgore College *A*
Lamar State College at Orange *A*
Lamar University *B, M*
LeTourneau University *B*
Lon Morris College *A*
Lubbock Christian University *B*
McMurry University *B, T*
Midland College *A*
Midwestern State University *B, M*
Navarro College *A*
Northeast Texas Community College *A*
Odessa College *A*
Our Lady of the Lake University of San Antonio *B*
Palo Alto College *A*
Panola College *A*
Paris Junior College *A*
Paul Quinn College *B*
Prairie View A&M University *B, M*
Rice University *B, M, D*
St. Edward's University *B, T*
St. Mary's University *B*
St. Philip's College *A*
Sam Houston State University *B, M*
San Jacinto College
   North *A*

Schreiner College B, T
South Plains College A
Southern Methodist University B, M, D
Southwest Texas State
    University B, M, T
Southwestern Adventist University B, T
Southwestern University B, T
Stephen F. Austin State
    University B, M, T
Sul Ross State University B, M, T
Tarleton State University B, M
Texas A&M International University B
Texas A&M University
    Commerce B, M
    Corpus Christi B, M, T
    Kingsville B, M
    Texarkana T
Texas A&M University B, M, D
Texas Christian University B, M, T
Texas College B
Texas Lutheran University B
Texas Southern University B, M
Texas Tech University B, M, D
Texas Wesleyan University B
Texas Woman's University B, M, T
Trinity University B
Trinity Valley Community College A
University of Dallas B
University of Houston
    Clear Lake B, M
University of Houston B, M, D
University of Mary Hardin-Baylor B, T
University of North Texas B, M, D
University of St. Thomas B
University of Texas
    Arlington B, M
    Austin B, M, D
    Brownsville B, M
    Dallas B, M, D
    El Paso B, M, D
    Pan American B, M, T
    San Antonio B, M
    Tyler B
    of the Permian Basin B, M
University of the Incarnate Word B, M
Wayland Baptist University B
West Texas A&M University B, M
Western Texas College A
Wharton County Junior College A
Wiley College B

Utah
Dixie State College of Utah A
Salt Lake Community College A
Snow College A
Southern Utah University B, T
University of Utah B, M, D
Utah State University B, M, D
Westminster College B

Vermont
Bennington College B
Castleton State College B
Goddard College B
Green Mountain College B
Johnson State College B
Marlboro College B
Middlebury College B
Norwich University B
St. Michael's College B
Trinity College of Vermont B
University of Vermont B, M, D

Virginia
Averett College B, T
Bluefield College B
Bridgewater College B
Christopher Newport University B
College of William and Mary B, M
Eastern Mennonite University B
Emory & Henry College B, T
Ferrum College B
George Mason University B, M
Germanna Community College A
Hampden-Sydney College B
Hampton University B, M
Hollins University B
James Madison University B, M, T
Liberty University B, T
Longwood College B, T
Lynchburg College B
Mary Baldwin College B
Mary Washington College B
Norfolk State University B, T
Old Dominion University B, M
Piedmont Virginia Community
    College A
Radford University B
Randolph-Macon College B
Randolph-Macon Woman's College B
Roanoke College B, T
St. Paul's College B
Shenandoah University B
Sweet Briar College B
University of Richmond B, M, T
University of Virginia's College at
    Wise B, T
University of Virginia B, M, D
Virginia Commonwealth
    University B, M
Virginia Intermont College B
Virginia Military Institute B
Virginia Polytechnic Institute and State
    University B, M, D, T
Virginia State University B, M
Virginia Union University B
Virginia Wesleyan College B
Washington and Lee University B

Washington
Central Washington University B, M
Eastern Washington University B, M, T
Everett Community College A
Evergreen State College B
Gonzaga University B
Heritage College B
Lower Columbia College A
Pacific Lutheran University B
St. Martin's College B
Seattle Pacific University B, T
Seattle University B
University of Puget Sound B, T
University of Washington B
Walla Walla College B, M
Washington State University B, M
Western Washington University B, M, T
Whitman College B
Whitworth College B, T

West Virginia
Alderson-Broaddus College B
Bethany College B
Concord College B
Davis and Elkins College B
Fairmont State College B
Glenville State College B
Marshall University B, M
Potomac State College of West Virginia
    University A
Salem-Teikyo University B
Shepherd College B
University of Charleston B
West Liberty State College B
West Virginia State College B
West Virginia University Institute of
    Technology B
West Virginia University B, M, D, T
West Virginia Wesleyan College B
Wheeling Jesuit University B

Wisconsin
Alverno College B, T
Beloit College B, T
Cardinal Stritch University B
Carroll College B
Carthage College B, T
Concordia University Wisconsin B
Lakeland College B
Lawrence University B
Marian College of Fond du Lac B
Marquette University B, M, D
Mount Mary College B
Mount Senario College B, T
Northland College B
Ripon College B
St. Norbert College B, T
Silver Lake College B, T
University of Wisconsin
    Eau Claire B, M
    Green Bay B
    La Crosse B
    Madison B, T
    Milwaukee B, M, D
    Oshkosh B
    Parkside B
    Platteville B, T
    River Falls B
    Stevens Point B, M
    Superior B
    Whitewater B, T
Viterbo University B
Wisconsin Lutheran College B

Wyoming
Casper College A
Central Wyoming College A
Eastern Wyoming College A
Laramie County Community College A
Northwest College A
Sheridan College A
University of Wyoming B
Western Wyoming Community
    College A

Biology teacher education

Alabama
Alabama Agricultural and Mechanical
    University B, M
Athens State University B
Birmingham-Southern College T
Faulkner University B
Huntingdon College T
Oakwood College B
Talladega College T
Tuskegee University B
University of Alabama B

Alaska
University of Alaska
    Southeast M

Arizona
Arizona State University B, T
Grand Canyon University B
Northern Arizona University B, M, T
Prescott College B, M
University of Arizona B, M

Arkansas
Arkansas State University B, M, T
Arkansas Tech University B
Harding University B, M, T
Henderson State University B, M, T
John Brown University B, T
Ouachita Baptist University B, T
Philander Smith College B
Southern Arkansas University B, T
University of Central Arkansas T
University of the Ozarks B, T

California
California State Polytechnic University:
    Pomona T
California State University
    Chico T
    Long Beach T
Concordia University B
Humboldt State University T
Loyola Marymount University M
Master's College T
Pacific Union College T
San Diego State University B
San Francisco State University B, T
University of the Pacific T

Colorado
Adams State College B, T
Colorado State University T
Fort Lewis College T
University of Southern Colorado T
Western State College of Colorado T

Connecticut
Central Connecticut State University B
Fairfield University T
Quinnipiac University B, M
St. Joseph College T
Southern Connecticut State
    University B, M, T

Delaware
Delaware State University B, M
University of Delaware B, T

District of Columbia
Catholic University of America B

Florida
Barry University T
Bethune-Cookman College B, T
Florida Agricultural and Mechanical
    University T
Florida Institute of Technology B, M
Gulf Coast Community College A
St. Leo University B, T
St. Thomas University B, T
Southeastern College of the Assemblies
    of God B, T
Stetson University B, T
University of West Florida B, T

Georgia
Agnes Scott College T
Armstrong Atlantic State University T
Brewton-Parker College B
Columbus State University B, M
Georgia College and State
    University M, T
North Georgia College & State
    University B, M
Wesleyan College T

Hawaii
Brigham Young University
    Hawaii B, T
University of Hawaii
    Manoa B, T

Idaho
Boise State University T
Northwest Nazarene University B

Illinois
Augustana College B, T
Barat College B
Chicago State University B, T
Concordia University B, T
Dominican University T
Eastern Illinois University B, T
Elmhurst College B
Eureka College T
Governors State University B, T
Greenville College B
Illinois College T
Lake Land College A
Loyola University of Chicago T
MacMurray College B, T
McKendree College B, T
North Central College B, T
North Park University T
Northwestern University B, T
Olivet Nazarene University B, T
Quincy University T
Rockford College T
Roosevelt University B
Trinity Christian College B, T
Trinity International University B, T
University of Illinois
    Chicago T
    Urbana-Champaign B, M, T
University of St. Francis T
Wheaton College T

Indiana
Ball State University T

Butler University *T*
Franklin College *T*
Goshen College *B*
Grace College *B*
Indiana State University *B, T*
Indiana University
    Bloomington *B, T*
    Northwest *B*
    South Bend *B, T*
    Southeast *B*
Indiana University--Purdue University
    Indiana University-Purdue
        University Fort Wayne *B, T*
Indiana Wesleyan University *T*
Manchester College *B, T*
Purdue University
    Calumet *B*
St. Mary-of-the-Woods College *B*
Taylor University *B*
University of Evansville *T*
University of Indianapolis *B, T*
University of Southern Indiana *B, T*
Valparaiso University *B*
Vincennes University *A*

Iowa
Buena Vista University *B, T*
Central College *T*
Clarke College *B, T*
Cornell College *B, T*
Dordt College *B*
Drake University *M*
Graceland University *B*
Iowa State University *T*
Iowa Wesleyan College *B*
Loras College *T*
Luther College *B*
Morningside College *B*
Northwestern College *T*
St. Ambrose University *B, T*
University of Iowa *B, T*
Wartburg College *T*
William Penn University *B*

Kansas
Baker University *T*
Benedictine College *T*
Bethany College *B*
Bethel College *T*
Central Christian College *A*
Colby Community College *A*
Emporia State University *T*
Garden City Community College *A*
Independence Community College *A*
McPherson College *B, T*
MidAmerica Nazarene University *B, T*
Newman University *T*
Ottawa University *T*
Pittsburg State University *B*
St. Mary College *T*
Tabor College *B, T*
University of Kansas *B, T*

Kentucky
Campbellsville University *B*
Cumberland College *B, T*
Kentucky State University *B*
Murray State University *B, M, T*
Pikeville College *B, T*
Transylvania University *B, T*
Union College *M*

Louisiana
Centenary College of Louisiana *B, T*
Dillard University *B*
Louisiana State University
    Shreveport *B*
McNeese State University *T*
Nicholls State University *B*
Northwestern State University *B, T*
Southern University and Agricultural and
    Mechanical College *B*
University of New Orleans *B*
Xavier University of Louisiana *B, T*

Maine
College of the Atlantic *B, T*

Husson College *B, T*
St. Joseph's College *B*
University of Maine
    Farmington *B*
    Machias *B*
    Presque Isle *B*
University of New England *B, T*
University of Southern Maine *T*

Maryland
Salisbury State University *B*
University of Maryland
    Eastern Shore *B*

Massachusetts
Assumption College *T*
Bridgewater State College *M, T*
Elms College *T*
Fitchburg State College *B, M, T*
Framingham State College *B, T*
Harvard College *T*
Merrimack College *T*
Northeastern University *M*
Tufts University *T*
University of Massachusetts
    Dartmouth *T*
Western New England College *T*
Westfield State College *B, T*
Worcester State College *T*

Michigan
Albion College *B, T*
Alma College *T*
Andrews University *M, T*
Calvin College *B*
Central Michigan University *B, M*
Concordia College *B, T*
Eastern Michigan University *B, T*
Grand Valley State University *T*
Michigan Technological University *T*
Northern Michigan University *B, M, T*
University of Detroit Mercy *M*
Western Michigan University *B*

Minnesota
Augsburg College *T*
Bemidji State University *T*
Bethel College *B*
College of St. Catherine: St. Paul
    Campus *T*
College of St. Scholastica *T*
Concordia College: Moorhead *T*
Concordia University: St. Paul *B, T*
Gustavus Adolphus College *T*
Minnesota State University,
    Mankato *B, M, T*
Moorhead State University *B, T*
Northland Community & Technical
    College *A*
St. Cloud State University *M, T*
St. Olaf College *T*
Southwest State University *B, T*
University of Minnesota
    Morris *T*
University of St. Thomas *T*
Winona State University *B, T*

Mississippi
Blue Mountain College *B*
Delta State University *B*
Mississippi College *M*
Mississippi State University *T*
Mississippi Valley State University *B, T*
University of Mississippi *B, T*

Missouri
Avila College *T*
Central Missouri State University *B, T*
College of the Ozarks *B, T*
Lindenwood University *M*
Maryville University of Saint
    Louis *B, M, T*
Missouri Baptist College *T*
Missouri Southern State College *B, T*
Missouri Valley College *T*
Northwest Missouri State
    University *B, T*

Rockhurst University *B*
Southwest Missouri State University *B*
Truman State University *M, T*
University of Missouri
    Columbia *B*
    St. Louis *T*
Washington University *B, M, T*

Montana
Montana State University
    Billings *B, T*
    Bozeman *T*
Rocky Mountain College *B, T*
University of Great Falls *B, T*
University of Montana-Missoula *T*
Western Montana College of The
    University of Montana *B, T*

Nebraska
College of Saint Mary *B, T*
Concordia University *T*
Creighton University *T*
Dana College *B*
Doane College *T*
Hastings College *B, M, T*
Midland Lutheran College *B, T*
Peru State College *B, T*
Union College *T*
University of Nebraska
    Kearney *T*
    Lincoln *B, T*

New Hampshire
Antioch New England Graduate
    School *M*
Colby-Sawyer College *B, T*
Keene State College *B, T*
New England College *B, T*
Notre Dame College *B, M*
Plymouth State College of the University
    System of New Hampshire *B, T*
Rivier College *B, T*
St. Anselm College *T*
University of New Hampshire *T*

New Jersey
Fairleigh Dickinson University *M*
Monmouth University *B, T*
Richard Stockton College of New
    Jersey *B*
Rowan University *T*
St. Peter's College *T*
The College of New Jersey *B, T*

New Mexico
New Mexico Institute of Mining and
    Technology *M*

New York
Alfred University *M, T*
Canisius College *B, M, T*
City University of New York
    Brooklyn College *B*
    City College *B*
    College of Staten Island *M*
    Lehman College *M*
    Queens College *T*
    York College *T*
Colgate University *M*
College of St. Rose *B, T*
Columbia University
    Teachers College *M, D*
D'Youville College *B, M, T*
Dowling College *B*
Elmira College *B, T*
Fordham University *M, T*
Hofstra University *B, M, T*
Houghton College *B, T*
Ithaca College *B, T*
Keuka College *B*
Long Island University
    C. W. Post Campus *B, M, T*
    Southampton College *T*
Manhattan College *T*
Marymount College *B, T*
Marymount Manhattan College *B, T*
Molloy College *B*

Nazareth College of Rochester *T*
New York Institute of Technology *B, T*
New York University *B, M, T*
Niagara University *B, T*
Pace University:
    Pleasantville/Briarcliff *B, M, T*
Pace University *B, M, T*
St. Francis College *B*
St. John Fisher College *B, T*
St. John's University *B, M, T*
St. Thomas Aquinas College *B, T*
Siena College *T*
State University of New York
    Binghamton *M*
    Buffalo *T*
    College at Brockport *M, T*
    College at Buffalo *B, M*
    College at Fredonia *B, T*
    College at Geneseo *B, M, T*
    College at Old Westbury *B*
    College at Oneonta *B, M, T*
    College at Plattsburgh *B, M*
    College at Potsdam *B, M*
    College of Environmental Science
        and Forestry *B, T*
    New Paltz *B, M, T*
    Oswego *B, M*
    Stony Brook *T*
Syracuse University *B, M, T*
Vassar College *T*
Wagner College *T*
Wells College *T*

North Carolina
Campbell University *B, T*
Cleveland Community College *A*
Greensboro College *B, T*
Lees-McRae College *T*
Lenoir Community College *A*
Lenoir-Rhyne College *B, T*
Louisburg College *A*
Mars Hill College *T*
Meredith College *T*
Methodist College *A, B, T*
Montreat College *T*
North Carolina Agricultural and
    Technical State University *B, T*
St. Augustine's College *B, T*
Sandhills Community College *A*
Shaw University *B, T*
University of North Carolina
    Greensboro *B, M, T*
    Pembroke *B, T*
    Wilmington *T*
Wake Forest University *M, T*
Western Carolina University *M, T*
Wingate University *B, T*

North Dakota
Dickinson State University *B, T*
Jamestown College *B*
Mayville State University *B, T*
Minot State University *B, T*
North Dakota State University *B, T*
University of Mary *B*
University of North Dakota *B, T*
Valley City State University *B, T*

Ohio
Baldwin-Wallace College *T*
Bluffton College *B*
Bowling Green State University *B*
Case Western Reserve University *T*
Cedarville College *T*
College of Mount St. Joseph *T*
Defiance College *B, T*
Hiram College *T*
John Carroll University *T*
Kent State University
    Stark Campus *B*
Kent State University *T*
Malone College *B*
Miami University
    Oxford Campus *B, M, T*
Mount Union College *T*
Mount Vernon Nazarene College *T*

Biology teacher education

Ohio Dominican College D
Otterbein College B
Shawnee State University B, T
University of Akron B
University of Dayton B, M, T
University of Findlay B, T
University of Rio Grande B, T
University of Toledo B, T
Wilmington College B
Xavier University B, M, T
Youngstown State University B, M

Oklahoma
Cameron University B
East Central University T
Eastern Oklahoma State College A
Northeastern State University B
Oklahoma Baptist University B, T
Oklahoma State University M, D
Southern Nazarene University B
University of Central Oklahoma B
University of Tulsa T

Oregon
Concordia University B, M, T
George Fox University B, M, T
Linfield College T
Oregon State University M
Portland State University T
Southern Oregon University T
University of Portland T
Western Baptist College B
Western Oregon University T

Pennsylvania
Allentown College of St. Francis de Sales T
Alvernia College B
Bucknell University T
Cabrini College B, T
California University of Pennsylvania B, T
Carlow College T
Carnegie Mellon University T
Chatham College M, T
Chestnut Hill College T
Clarion University of Pennsylvania B, T
College Misericordia B, T
Delaware Valley College T
Dickinson College T
Duquesne University B, M, T
Elizabethtown College T
Gannon University T
Gettysburg College T
Grove City College B, T
Gwynedd-Mercy College T
Holy Family College B, M, T
Juniata College B, T
King's College T
La Roche College B
La Salle University B, T
Lebanon Valley College of Pennsylvania T
Lock Haven University of Pennsylvania B, T
Lycoming College T
Mansfield University of Pennsylvania B, T
Marywood University T
Mercyhurst College B
Messiah College T
Moravian College T
Point Park College B
St. Vincent College T
Seton Hill College B, T
Shippensburg University of Pennsylvania T
Thiel College B
University of Pittsburgh
    Bradford B
    Johnstown B, T
Washington and Jefferson College T
Waynesburg College B, T
Westminster College T
Widener University T
Wilkes University M, T
Wilson College T
York College of Pennsylvania B, T

Puerto Rico
Inter American University of Puerto Rico
    Arecibo Campus B
    Barranquitas Campus B
    Fajardo Campus B, T
    Metropolitan Campus B
Universidad Metropolitana B

Rhode Island
Rhode Island College B
Salve Regina University B

South Carolina
Anderson College B, T
Claflin University B
Coker College B, T
Columbia College B
Furman University T
Limestone College B
Morris College B, T
South Carolina State University B, T
The Citadel M
Wofford College T

South Dakota
Augustana College B, T
Black Hills State University B, T
Dakota State University B, T
Huron University B
Mount Marty College B
Northern State University T
South Dakota State University B
University of South Dakota T

Tennessee
Belmont University T
Christian Brothers University B, M, T
Crichton College B
Cumberland University B
David Lipscomb University B, T
Freed-Hardeman University T
Lambuth University T
Lincoln Memorial University B, T
Maryville College B, T
Middle Tennessee State University M, T
Southern Adventist University B
Tennessee Temple University B
Tennessee Wesleyan College B, T
Trevecca Nazarene University B, T
Union University B, T
University of Tennessee
    Martin B, T

Texas
Abilene Christian University B, T
Baylor University B, T
Del Mar College A
East Texas Baptist University B
Hardin-Simmons University B, T
Houston Baptist University T
Howard Payne University T
Lamar University T
LeTourneau University B
Lubbock Christian University B
McMurry University T
St. Mary's University T
Schreiner College T
Southwest Texas State University M, T
Tarleton State University M, T
Texas A&M International University B, T
Texas A&M University
    Commerce B
    Kingsville T
Texas Christian University T
Texas Lutheran University T
Texas Wesleyan University B, T
University of Dallas T
University of Houston
    Clear Lake T
University of Houston T
University of Mary Hardin-Baylor T
University of Texas
    Arlington T
    San Antonio T
Wayland Baptist University T
West Texas A&M University T

Utah
Brigham Young University B, M
Utah State University B
Weber State University B

Vermont
Castleton State College B, T
Johnson State College B
St. Michael's College B

Virginia
Averett College B, T
Bridgewater College T
Christopher Newport University T
Hampton University B
Hollins University T
Liberty University B
Longwood College B, T
Radford University T
St. Paul's College T
University of Virginia's College at Wise T
Virginia Intermont College B, T
Virginia Wesleyan College T

Washington
Central Washington University B, T
Heritage College B
Seattle Pacific University B
University of Washington M, T
Washington State University T
Western Washington University B, T
Whitworth College B, T

West Virginia
Alderson-Broaddus College T
Concord College B, T
Fairmont State College B
Glenville State College B
Shepherd College T
University of Charleston B
West Liberty State College B
Wheeling Jesuit University T

Wisconsin
Alverno College B, T
Cardinal Stritch University B, T
Carroll College B, T
Carthage College T
Lakeland College T
Marian College of Fond du Lac B, T
Mount Mary College B, T
Mount Senario College T
Northland College T
St. Norbert College T
University of Wisconsin
    Green Bay T
    La Crosse B, T
    Platteville B
    River Falls T
    Superior B, T
    Whitewater B
Viterbo University B, T

Biomedical sciences/ technologies

Alabama
Northwest-Shoals Community College A

California
California State University
    Hayward B
Cerritos Community College A
East Los Angeles College C
San Diego Miramar College A
San Francisco State University M
University of California
    San Diego M, D

Florida
Barry University M
Hillsborough Community College A
Nova Southeastern University M

Illinois
Chicago State University M

Maine
Kennebec Valley Technical College A

Maryland
Howard Community College C, A

Massachusetts
Franklin Institute of Boston A
Worcester Polytechnic Institute M, D

Michigan
University of Michigan B

Nebraska
Creighton University M, D

New Jersey
Thomas Edison State College B
University of Medicine and Dentistry of New Jersey
    School of Health Related Professions C, M, D

New York
Touro College C

North Carolina
Catawba College B
University of North Carolina
    Chapel Hill M, D

Ohio
Wright State University D

Pennsylvania
Community College of Allegheny County A
Delaware County Community College C, A
Drexel University M, D
Lock Haven University of Pennsylvania B

Puerto Rico
Inter American University of Puerto Rico
    Bayamon Campus B

South Dakota
Southeast Technical Institute A

Texas
Baylor University M, D
St. Philip's College A
Texas A&M University B
Texas State Technical College
    Harlingen A
University of Mary Hardin-Baylor B

Vermont
Norwich University B
Vermont Technical College A

Virginia
ECPI College of Technology C, A

West Virginia
Marshall University M, D
Ohio Valley College A

Biometrics

California
University of California
    Berkeley M, D
University of Southern California M, D

Colorado
University of Colorado
    Health Sciences Center M, D

Louisiana
Louisiana State University Medical Center M, D

Michigan
University of Michigan B, M
Nebraska
University of Nebraska
 Lincoln M
New Jersey
Rutgers
 The State University of New Jersey:
  Cook College B
 The State University of New Jersey:
  Douglass College B
 The State University of New Jersey:
  Livingston College B
 The State University of New Jersey:
  Rutgers College B
 The State University of New Jersey:
  University College New
  Brunswick B
New York
Columbia University
 Graduate School M, D
Cornell University B, M, D
State University of New York
 Albany M, D
 College of Environmental Science
  and Forestry M, D
North Carolina
Duke University M
Texas
University of Texas
 Arlington D
 San Antonio M
Wisconsin
University of Wisconsin
 Madison M

Biophysics

Alabama
University of Alabama
 Birmingham D
California
California Institute of Technology D
La Sierra University B
Pacific Union College B
Pitzer College B
Stanford University M, D
University of California
 Berkeley M, D
 Davis D
 San Diego B, M, D
 San Francisco D
University of San Francisco B
Colorado
University of Colorado
 Health Sciences Center M, D
Connecticut
University of Connecticut B, M, D
District of Columbia
Georgetown University M, D
Hawaii
University of Hawaii
 Manoa M, D
Idaho
University of Idaho B, M, D
Illinois
Finch University of Health Sciences/The
 Chicago Medical School M, D
Loyola University of Chicago D
Northwestern University B
University of Chicago M, D
University of Illinois
 Urbana-Champaign B, M, D

Indiana
Indiana University--Purdue University
 Indiana University-Purdue
  University Indianapolis M, D
University of Notre Dame M, D
University of Southern Indiana B
Iowa
Iowa State University B, M, D
University of Iowa M, D
Louisiana
Centenary College of Louisiana B
Maryland
Johns Hopkins University B, D
University of Maryland
 Baltimore M, D
Massachusetts
Boston University M, D
Brandeis University M, D
Hampshire College B
Harvard College B
Harvard University M, D
Suffolk University B
Tufts University D
Michigan
Andrews University B
University of Michigan B, D
Wayne State University D
Minnesota
St. Mary's University of Minnesota B
University of Minnesota
 Twin Cities M, D
Missouri
University of Missouri
 Rolla B
Washington University B, D
New York
City University of New York
 Brooklyn College B, M
Columbia University
 Columbia College B
 Graduate School M, D
Rensselaer Polytechnic Institute B, M
Rockefeller University D
St. Lawrence University B
State University of New York
 Albany D
 Buffalo B, M, D
 College at Geneseo B
 Stony Brook M, D
Syracuse University D
University of Rochester B, M, D
North Carolina
University of North Carolina
 Chapel Hill M, D
Ohio
Case Western Reserve University D
Ohio State University
 Columbus Campus B, M, D
Wittenberg University B
Oklahoma
Oklahoma City University B
Southwestern Oklahoma State
 University B
Oregon
Oregon State University M, D
Pennsylvania
Carnegie Mellon University B, D
University of Pennsylvania B, M, D
University of Scranton B
Ursinus College B
Westminster College B
Rhode Island
Brown University B, M, D

Tennessee
University of Tennessee
 Memphis M, D
Vanderbilt University D
Texas
Texas A&M University M
University of Houston B
University of Texas
 Southwestern Medical Center at
  Dallas M, D
Virginia
Hampden-Sydney College B
University of Virginia D
Washington
University of Washington M, D
Walla Walla College B
Wisconsin
Medical College of Wisconsin M, D
University of Wisconsin
 Madison M, D

Biopsychology

California
University of California
 Riverside B
Connecticut
Quinnipiac University B
Illinois
University of Chicago M, D
Iowa
Morningside College B
Massachusetts
College of the Holy Cross B
Hampshire College B
Michigan
Grand Valley State University B
University of Michigan B
Missouri
Washington University B
Nebraska
Nebraska Wesleyan University B
New Jersey
Rider University B
Rutgers
 The State University of New Jersey:
  New Brunswick Graduate
  Campus D
New York
Barnard College B
Hamilton College B
State University of New York
 New Paltz B
Vassar College B
Ohio
Wittenberg University B
Pennsylvania
Albright College B
Franklin and Marshall College B
Philadelphia University B
Westminster College B
Wilson College B
Texas
University of North Texas M
Vermont
Bennington College B
Virginia
Northern Virginia Community College A
Wisconsin
Ripon College B

Biostatistics

Alabama
University of Alabama
 Birmingham M, D
California
Loma Linda University M
University of California
 Berkeley M, D
 Los Angeles M, D
District of Columbia
Georgetown University M
Hawaii
University of Hawaii
 Manoa D
Iowa
University of Iowa M, D
Louisiana
Tulane University M, D
Massachusetts
Boston University M, D
University of Massachusetts
 Boston B
Michigan
University of Michigan M, D
Western Michigan University M
Minnesota
University of Minnesota
 Twin Cities B, M, D
New York
Columbia University
 Graduate School D
Cornell University B
State University of New York
 Albany M, D
 Buffalo M
 College of Environmental Science
  and Forestry M, D
North Carolina
University of North Carolina
 Chapel Hill B, M, D
Ohio
Case Western Reserve University M, D
Ohio State University
 Columbus Campus D
Pennsylvania
Penn State
 College of Medicine, Milton S.
  Hershey Medical Center M
Texas
Southwestern Adventist University B
Vermont
University of Vermont M
Virginia
Virginia Commonwealth
 University M, D
Washington
University of Washington M, D
Wisconsin
Medical College of Wisconsin D

Biotechnology research

California
California State Polytechnic University:
 Pomona B
California State University
 Hayward C
Contra Costa College C
Foothill College C, A
Ohlone College C
San Francisco State University B

Santa Barbara City College *A*
Skyline College *A*
Solano Community College *C*

Colorado
Red Rocks Community College *A*

Connecticut
Quinnipiac University *B*
University of Connecticut *M*

Delaware
University of Delaware *B*

Florida
Florida Institute of Technology *M*

Iowa
Des Moines Area Community College *A*

Maine
University of Southern Maine *B*

Maryland
Baltimore City Community College *A*
Montgomery College
 Germantown Campus *A*
 Takoma Park Campus *A*
Villa Julie College *A*

Massachusetts
Assumption College *B*
Massachusetts Institute of
 Technology *M, D*
Merrimack College *B*
Middlesex Community College *C, A*
Springfield Technical Community
 College *A*
Worcester Polytechnic Institute *B, M, D*
Worcester State College *B, M*

Michigan
Michigan State University *D*
Mid Michigan Community College *A*
University of Michigan *C*
Wayne State University *M*

Minnesota
Minnesota State University, Mankato *B*
St. Cloud State University *B*

Mississippi
Mississippi Gulf Coast Community
 College
 Jefferson Davis Campus *A*

Missouri
University of Missouri
 St. Louis *C*

Montana
Montana State University
 Bozeman *B*
 College of Technology-Great
 Falls *A*

Nebraska
University of Nebraska
 Omaha *B*

New Hampshire
New Hampshire Community Technical
 College
 Stratham *C, A*
Plymouth State College of the University
 System of New Hampshire *B*

New Jersey
Rutgers
 The State University of New Jersey:
 Cook College *B*
 The State University of New Jersey:
 Douglass College *B*
William Paterson University of New
 Jersey *B, M*

New York
Manhattan College *M*
Rochester Institute of Technology *B*

State University of New York
 College at Fredonia *B*
 College of Environmental Science
 and Forestry *B, M, D*

North Carolina
Alamance Community College *A*

North Dakota
North Dakota State University *B*

Ohio
Lakeland Community College *A*

Oklahoma
Oklahoma City Community College *A*

Oregon
Oregon State University *B*

Pennsylvania
East Stroudsburg University of
 Pennsylvania *B*
Elizabethtown College *B*
Lehigh University *M, D*
MCP Hahnemann University *M, D*
Thomas Jefferson University: College of
 Health Professions *B*

Puerto Rico
University of Puerto Rico
 Mayaguez Campus *B*

Texas
Stephen F. Austin State University *M*

Utah
Brigham Young University *B, M, D*
Dixie State College of Utah *A*

Vermont
Vermont Technical College *A*

Virginia
Blue Ridge Community College *C*

Washington
Seattle Central Community College *A*
Shoreline Community College *A*

West Virginia
West Liberty State College *B*

Wisconsin
University of Wisconsin
 River Falls *B*

Blood bank technology

Florida
Brevard Community College *C*

Indiana
Indiana University
 Northwest *C*

Massachusetts
Massasoit Community College *C*

New Mexico
Albuquerque Technical-Vocational
 Institute *C*

North Carolina
Duke University *C*

Ohio
Lakeland Community College *C*

South Dakota
Western Dakota Technical Institute *C*

Wisconsin
Chippewa Valley Technical College *C*

Botany

Alabama
Auburn University *B, M, D*

Alaska
University of Alaska
 Fairbanks *M*

Arizona
Arizona State University *B, M, D*
Northern Arizona University *B*

Arkansas
Arkansas State University
 Beebe Branch *A*
Arkansas State University *B*
University of Arkansas *B*

California
California State Polytechnic University:
 Pomona *B*
California State University
 Chico *M*
 Long Beach *B*
 Stanislaus *B*
Cerritos Community College *A*
Citrus College *A*
Compton Community College *A*
Humboldt State University *B*
Riverside Community College *A*
San Francisco State University *B*
San Joaquin Delta College *A*
San Jose State University *B*
Santa Ana College *A*
Southwestern College *A*
University of California
 Berkeley *M, D*
 Davis *B, M, D*
 Riverside *B, M, D*
Ventura College *A*
West Hills Community College *A*

Colorado
Adams State College *B*
Colorado State University *B, M, D*

Connecticut
Connecticut College *B, M*
Southern Connecticut State University *B*
University of Connecticut *M, D*

District of Columbia
George Washington University *M, D*

Florida
Pensacola Junior College *A*
Santa Fe Community College *A*
University of Florida *B, M, D*
University of South Florida *M*

Georgia
Georgia Military College *A*
University of Georgia *B, M, D*

Hawaii
University of Hawaii
 Manoa *B, M, D*

Idaho
College of Southern Idaho *A*
Idaho State University *B*
North Idaho College *A*
Ricks College *A*
University of Idaho *B, M, D*

Illinois
Rend Lake College *A*
St. Xavier University *B*
Southern Illinois University
 Carbondale *B, M, D*
University of Illinois
 Urbana-Champaign *B, M, D*

Indiana
Ball State University *B*
Indiana University
 Bloomington *M, D*
Purdue University *B, M, D*
Vincennes University *A*

Iowa
Iowa State University *B, M, D*
Marshalltown Community College *A*

Kansas
Independence Community College *A*
Pratt Community College *A*
Seward County Community College *A*
University of Kansas *M, D*

Kentucky
Thomas More College *B, T*

Louisiana
Louisiana State University and
 Agricultural and Mechanical
 College *M, D*

Maine
College of the Atlantic *B*
University of Maine *B, M, D*

Maryland
University of Maryland
 College Park *M, D*

Massachusetts
Hampshire College *B*
Harvard College *B*
University of Massachusetts
 Amherst *M, D*

Michigan
Andrews University *B*
Eastern Michigan University *B*
Michigan State University *B, M, D*
Northern Michigan University *B*
University of Michigan *B, M, D*

Minnesota
Minnesota State University, Mankato *B*
St. Cloud State University *B*

Mississippi
Mary Holmes College *A*

Missouri
East Central College *A*
Mineral Area College *A*
Northwest Missouri State University *B*
Washington University *D*

Montana
University of Montana-Missoula *B*

New Hampshire
Antioch New England Graduate
 School *M*
University of New Hampshire *M, D*

New Jersey
New Jersey Institute of Technology *B*
Rowan University *B*
Rutgers
 The State University of New Jersey:
 Camden College of Arts and
 Sciences *B*
 The State University of New Jersey:
 Cook College *B*
 The State University of New Jersey:
 Douglass College *B*
 The State University of New Jersey:
 Livingston College *B*
 The State University of New Jersey:
 Newark College of Arts and
 Sciences *B*
 The State University of New Jersey:
 Rutgers College *B*
 The State University of New Jersey:
 University College Camden *B*
 The State University of New Jersey:
 University College New
 Brunswick *B*

New Mexico
Western New Mexico University *B*

New York
Cornell University *M, D*
State University of New York
 College of Environmental Science
 and Forestry *B, M, D*

North Carolina
Duke University *M, D*
Mars Hill College *B*
North Carolina State University *M, D*

North Dakota
North Dakota State University *B, M, D*

Ohio
Kent State University
 Stark Campus *B*
Kent State University *B, M, D*
Miami University
 Oxford Campus *B, M, D*
Ohio State University
 Columbus Campus *B, M, D*
Ohio University *B, M, D*
Ohio Wesleyan University *B*
University of Akron *B*
Wittenberg University *B*

Oklahoma
Oklahoma State University *B, M*
Southeastern Oklahoma State
 University *B*
University of Oklahoma *B, M, D*

Oregon
Oregon State University *B*

Pennsylvania
California University of Pennsylvania *B*
Juniata College *B*

South Carolina
Clemson University *M*

Tennessee
University of Tennessee
 Knoxville *B, M, D*

Texas
Hill College *A*
Southwest Texas State University *B*
Texas A&M University *B, M, D*
University of North Texas *M*
University of Texas
 Austin *B, M, D*

Utah
Brigham Young University *B, M, D*
Dixie State College of Utah *A*
Snow College *A*
Southern Utah University *B*
Utah State University *B, M*
Weber State University *B*

Vermont
Marlboro College *B*
University of Vermont *B, M, D*

Washington
Centralia College *A*
Eastern Washington University *B*
University of Washington *B, M, D*
Washington State University *M, D*

Wisconsin
University of Wisconsin
 Madison *B, M, D*

Wyoming
University of Wyoming *B, M, D*

Business

Alabama
Alabama Agricultural and Mechanical
 University *B*
Auburn University at Montgomery *B, M*
Birmingham-Southern College *B*
Central Alabama Community
 College *C, A*
Enterprise State Junior College *A*
Faulkner University *B*
Huntingdon College *B*
Jacksonville State University *B*
Jefferson State Community College *A*
Marion Military Institute *A*
Northeast Alabama Community
 College *A*
Reid State Technical College *C*
Shelton State Community College *C, A*
South College *A*
Stillman College *B*
Talladega College *B*
Troy State University *B*
University of Mobile *B, M*
University of Montevallo *B*
University of South Alabama *B*
Wallace State Community College at
 Hanceville *A*

Alaska
University of Alaska
 Anchorage *C, A*
 Fairbanks *C, A, B*
 Southeast *B*

Arizona
American Indian College of the
 Assemblies of God *A*
Arizona State University *B*
Arizona Western College *C, A*
Central Arizona College *A*
Dine College *A*
Gateway Community College *A*
Glendale Community College *C, A*
Northern Arizona University *B, M*
Northland Pioneer College *A*
Paradise Valley Community
 College *C, A*
Phoenix College *A*
Prescott College *B, M*
Rio Salado College *C, A*
Scottsdale Community College *C, A*
University of Arizona *B*

Arkansas
Arkansas State University
 Beebe Branch *A*
 Mountain Home *A*
Mississippi County Community
 College *C, A*
North Arkansas College *A*
Phillips Community College of the
 University of Arkansas *A*
Southern Arkansas University *A*
University of Arkansas
 Little Rock *B*
 Monticello *B*
University of Arkansas *B*
Westark College *A*
Williams Baptist College *B*

California
Allan Hancock College *A*
Azusa Pacific University *B*
Barstow College *C, A*
Biola University *B*
Butte College *C, A*
Cabrillo College *C, A*
California College for Health
 Sciences *C, A, B*
California Lutheran University *B*
California Polytechnic State University:
 San Luis Obispo *M*
California State University
 Bakersfield *B*
 Dominguez Hills *B*
 Fresno *B, M*
 Fullerton *M*
 Hayward *B*
 Long Beach *B*
 Los Angeles *B, M*
 Monterey Bay *B*
 Sacramento *B, M*
 Stanislaus *B*
Canada College *C, A*
Cerritos Community College *A*
Chabot College *A*
Citrus College *A*
Coastline Community College *C, A*
College of Marin: Kentfield *A*
College of Notre Dame *B*
College of San Mateo *C, A*
College of the Canyons *A*
College of the Desert *A*
College of the Redwoods *A*
College of the Sequoias *A*
Columbia College *A*
Compton Community College *C*
Concordia University *B*
Cuesta College *C, A*
Cypress College *A*
Diablo Valley College *C*
Dominican University of California *B*
Fresno City College *C, A*
Fresno Pacific University *B*
Gavilan Community College *C, A*
Glendale Community College *A*
Golden Gate University *B, M*
Golden West College *C, A*
Grossmont Community College *C, A*
Humboldt State University *B*
Humphreys College *A, B*
Irvine Valley College *A*
John F. Kennedy University *C*
Lake Tahoe Community College *A*
Lincoln University *B, M*
Long Beach City College *C, A*
Los Angeles Harbor College *C, A*
Los Angeles Pierce College *C, A*
Los Angeles Southwest College *A*
Los Angeles Trade and Technical
 College *A*
Los Angeles Valley College *C, A*
Master's College *B*
Mendocino College *A*
Merced College *A*
Merritt College *C, A*
Mills College *B*
Mission College *C, A*
Modesto Junior College *A*
Monterey Peninsula College *A*
Mount St. Mary's College *B*
Mount San Antonio College *A*
Napa Valley College *A*
National Hispanic University *B*
National University *B, M*
Ohlone College *A*
Orange Coast College *C, A*
Pacific Union College *B*
Palomar College *A*
Pasadena City College *A*
Porterville College *A*
Rio Hondo College *C*
Riverside Community College *C, A*
Sacramento City College *A*
Saddleback College *A*
St. Mary's College of California *M*
San Diego City College *C, A*
San Diego Mesa College *C, A*
San Joaquin Delta College *C, A*
San Jose City College *C*
Santa Ana College *A*
Santa Barbara City College *C, A*
Santa Monica College *C, A*
Shasta College *A*
Sierra College *A*
Southwestern College *A*
Taft College *A*
University of Judaism *B*
University of La Verne *B*
University of Redlands *B*
University of San Diego *M*
University of San Francisco *B*
University of the Pacific *M*
Vanguard University of Southern
 California *B*
Ventura College *C, A*
Victor Valley College *C, A*
West Hills Community College *C, A*
West Los Angeles College *A*
West Valley College *A*
Westmont College *B*
Whittier College *B*
Yuba College *A*

Colorado
Adams State College *B*
Colorado Mountain College
 Alpine Campus *C, A*
 Spring Valley Campus *C, A*
 Timberline Campus *C, A*
Community College of Aurora *C, A*
Denver Technical College: A Division of
 DeVry University *A*
Fort Lewis College *B*
Front Range Community College *C, A*
Lamar Community College *A*
Morgan Community College *A*
Red Rocks Community College *A*
Regis University *B*
Trinidad State Junior College *A*
University of Denver *B, M*
University of Southern Colorado *B*

Connecticut
Briarwood College *A*
Eastern Connecticut State University *B*
Housatonic Community-Technical
 College *C, A*
Quinnipiac University *B, M*
Sacred Heart University *A, B*
Teikyo Post University *A, B*
University of Bridgeport *B, M*
University of Connecticut *B, M, D*
Western Connecticut State
 University *B, M*

Delaware
Delaware Technical and Community
 College
 Owens Campus *C, A*
 Stanton/Wilmington Campus *C, A*
 Terry Campus *C, A*
Goldey-Beacom College *M*
Wilmington College *B*

District of Columbia
American University *B, M*
Catholic University of America *B*
Gallaudet University *B*
Southeastern University *A, B*

Florida
Barry University *B*
Broward Community College *A*
Edison Community College *A*
Flagler College *B*
Florida Metropolitan University
 Orlando College North *A, B*
Florida Southern College *M*
Hillsborough Community College *A*
Jacksonville University *B*
Lake City Community College *A*
Lake-Sumter Community College *C, A*
Manatee Community College *A*
Palm Beach Atlantic College *B*
Palm Beach Community College *A*
Pensacola Junior College *A*
Polk Community College *A*
St. Thomas University *M*
South Florida Community College *A*
Tallahassee Community College *A*
University of Central Florida *B, M*
University of Florida *B, M, D*
University of Miami *C, M*
University of North Florida *M*
University of South Florida *B, M*

Georgia
Agnes Scott College *B*
Albany State University *M*
Andrew College *A*
Atlanta Christian College *A, B*
Bainbridge College *A*
Clayton College and State University *B*
Columbus State University *B, M*
Covenant College *B*
Dalton State College *A*
Darton College *C, A*
Emory University *B*
Floyd College *A*
Fort Valley State University *B*

Business

Gainesville College A
Georgia College and State
    University B, M
Georgia Military College A
Georgia Perimeter College A
Georgia Southwestern State University B
LaGrange College B
Macon State College C, A
Middle Georgia College C, A
Oxford College of Emory University B
Paine College B
Reinhardt College A, B
South Georgia College C, A
State University of West Georgia M
Thomas College A, B, M
Truett-McConnell College A
University of Georgia B
Waycross College C
Young Harris College A

Hawaii
Chaminade University of Honolulu A, B
Hawaii Pacific University A, B
University of Hawaii
    Hilo B
    Kapiolani Community College A
    Manoa B
    Maui Community College C, A

Idaho
Albertson College of Idaho B
College of Southern Idaho A
Idaho State University A
Lewis-Clark State College B

Illinois
Augustana College B
Barat College B
Benedictine University B, T
Black Hawk College
    East Campus A
Career Colleges of Chicago A
City Colleges of Chicago
    Malcolm X College A
    Olive-Harvey College C, A
    Richard J. Daley College C, A
Concordia University B
De Paul University B, M
Elmhurst College B
Eureka College B
Greenville College B
Highland Community College C, A
Illinois College B
John Wood Community College A
Judson College B
Kishwaukee College A
Lake Forest College B
Lake Land College A
Lewis University B
Lewis and Clark Community College A
Lincoln Land Community College A
MacCormac College A
McKendree College B
Moraine Valley Community
    College C, A
Morton College A
North Central College B
North Park University B, M
Northeastern Illinois University B
Northern Illinois University B
Olivet Nazarene University B
Parkland College A
Quincy University A, B
Rend Lake College A
Richland Community College A
Rock Valley College C, A
Rockford College B
Roosevelt University B, M
St. Augustine College A
St. Xavier University B
Sauk Valley Community College A
Shawnee Community College A
Southern Illinois University
    Carbondale B, M, D
    Edwardsville B
Southwestern Ilinois College A

Springfield College in Illinois A
Trinity Christian College B
University of Chicago M, D
University of Illinois
    Chicago B
    Springfield B
William Rainey Harper College C, A

Indiana
Anderson University A
Ball State University B
Bethel College A
Franklin College B
Goshen College B
Indiana University
    Bloomington C, B, M, D
    Northwest A, B, M
    South Bend A, B
    Southeast A, B
Indiana University--Purdue University
    Indiana University-Purdue
        University Fort Wayne A, B, M
    Indiana University-Purdue
        University Indianapolis C, B, M
International Business College B
Manchester College A, B
Marian College A, B
Oakland City University A, B
Purdue University
    Calumet A, B
    North Central Campus C, A, B
St. Mary-of-the-Woods College A, B
University of Indianapolis A, B
University of Notre Dame B
University of St. Francis B
University of Southern Indiana B, M
Valparaiso University B
Vincennes University A

Iowa
American Institute of Business C, A
Briar Cliff College B
Buena Vista University B
Coe College B
Des Moines Area Community College A
Dordt College A, B
Drake University B
Grand View College B
Hawkeye Community College A
Iowa Wesleyan College B
Loras College B
Luther College B
Maharishi University of Management M
Marshalltown Community College A
Marycrest International University B
Mount Mercy College B
North Iowa Area Community College A
Northeast Iowa Community College A
St. Ambrose University B
Southeastern Community College
    North Campus A
    South Campus A
Southwestern Community College A
University of Northern Iowa B
Upper Iowa University A, B
Waldorf College B

Kansas
Baker University B, T
Barclay College B
Barton County Community College A
Central Christian College A, B
Cloud County Community College A
Coffeyville Community College A
Colby Community College A
Cowley County Community College A
Dodge City Community College A
Fort Hays State University B
Garden City Community College A
Hesston College A
Hutchinson Community College A
Independence Community College A
Kansas City Kansas Community
    College A
Kansas State University M
Kansas Wesleyan University A, B, M

McPherson College T
MidAmerica Nazarene
    University A, B, M
Newman University B
Pittsburg State University B
St. Mary College B
Seward County Community
    College C, A
Southwestern College B
Tabor College B
University of Kansas B, M, D
Washburn University of Topeka B

Kentucky
Asbury College B
Berea College B
Brescia University A, B, M
Campbellsville University A, B
Eastern Kentucky University B, M
Kentucky State University B
Kentucky Wesleyan College B
Maysville Community College A
Morehead State University M
Murray State University B
National Business College C, A
Owensboro Community College A
St. Catharine College A
Spalding University A, B
Transylvania University B
University of Kentucky B, M, D
University of Louisville M
Western Kentucky University M

Louisiana
Centenary College of Louisiana B
Dillard University B
Louisiana State University
    Eunice A
Loyola University New Orleans B, M
Nicholls State University B
Northwestern State University A, B
Tulane University A

Maine
Eastern Maine Technical College A
Husson College B, M
Maine Maritime Academy B, M
St. Joseph's College B
Thomas College A
University of Maine
    Fort Kent A, B
    Machias A, B
    Presque Isle B
University of Maine B
University of New England B

Maryland
Allegany College C, A
Anne Arundel Community College C, A
Baltimore City Community College A
Carroll Community College A
Cecil Community College C, A
Chesapeake College A
College of Notre Dame of Maryland B
Community College of Baltimore County
    Catonsville C, A
Harford Community College A
Loyola College in Maryland B
Mount St. Mary's College B
University of Baltimore B, M
University of Maryland
    College Park B, M, D
Washington College B
Wor-Wic Community College C, A

Massachusetts
American International College M
Anna Maria College B, M
Assumption College A, B, M
Babson College B
Bay Path College B
Berkshire Community College A
Bridgewater State College B
Clark University B, M
Dean College C, A
Eastern Nazarene College B
Greenfield Community College A

Hampshire College B
Harvard University D
Holyoke Community College A
Marian Court College C, A
Merrimack College B
New England College of Finance A
Nichols College M
Northern Essex Community College A
Quincy College C, A
Springfield Technical Community
    College A
Suffolk University B, M
University of Massachusetts
    Lowell A
Western New England College B

Michigan
Andrews University A
Baker College
    of Cadillac A
    of Jackson B
    of Muskegon A
    of Owosso A
Bay de Noc Community College C
Calvin College B
Central Michigan University B
Cleary College A, B
Concordia College B
Davenport College of Business A, B
Delta College A
Eastern Michigan University B
Ferris State University A, B
Glen Oaks Community College A
Gogebic Community College C, A
Grace Bible College A, B
Grand Rapids Community College C, A
Great Lakes College A
Henry Ford Community College A
Hillsdale College B
Jackson Community College C, A
Kirtland Community College C
Lake Superior State University A, B
Lansing Community College A
Macomb Community College C, A
Madonna University A, B
Marygrove College A, B
Mott Community College C, A
North Central Michigan College C, A
Northern Michigan University A, B, T
Northwestern Michigan College A
Northwood University A
Oakland University B
Olivet College B
Saginaw Valley State University B
St. Clair County Community
    College C, A
Schoolcraft College C, A
Siena Heights University A, B
Southwestern Michigan College C, A
Suomi College B
University of Detroit Mercy B
Walsh College of Accountancy and
    Business Administration B
Wayne State University B, M
West Shore Community College A

Minnesota
Augsburg College B
Bethel College B
Concordia College: Moorhead B
Crown College A, B
Gustavus Adolphus College B
Mesabi Range Community and Technical
    College A
Minneapolis Community and Technical
    College C, A
Minnesota State University, Mankato B
Moorhead State University B
National American University
    St. Paul A, B
Northland Community & Technical
    College A
Pine Technical College A
Ridgewater College: A Community and
    Technical College A

Rochester Community and Technical
  College *A*
St. Cloud State University *B*
Winona State University *B, M*

Mississippi
Belhaven College *M*
Blue Mountain College *B*
Coahoma Community College *A*
Delta State University *B*
East Central Community College *A*
Mary Holmes College *A*
Mississippi Gulf Coast Community
  College
  Jefferson Davis Campus *A*
  Perkinston *A*
University of Mississippi *B*

Missouri
College of the Ozarks *B*
Crowder College *A*
Drury University *B*
East Central College *C, A*
Evangel University *B*
Fontbonne College *B, M*
Hannibal-LaGrange College *B*
Jefferson College *A*
Lindenwood University *M*
Longview Community College *A*
Maple Woods Community College *A*
Maryville University of Saint Louis *B, M*
Mineral Area College *C, A*
Missouri Southern State College *A*
Northwest Missouri State University *B*
Park University *B, M*
Penn Valley Community College *A*
Rockhurst University *B*
St. Louis University *B*
Southwest Baptist University *A*
Southwest Missouri State University
  West Plains Campus *A*
Southwest Missouri State University *B*
St. Louis Community College
  St. Louis Community College at
    Forest Park *A*
  St. Louis Community College at
    Meramec *C, A*
University of Missouri
  Columbia *B, M, D*
  Kansas City *B, M*
  St. Louis *B*
Webster University *B, M*

Montana
Carroll College *A*
Dawson Community College *A*
Flathead Valley Community
  College *C, A*
Little Big Horn College *A*
Miles Community College *A*
Montana State University
  Billings *A, B*
  Bozeman *B*
Montana Tech of the University of
  Montana *A, B*
Rocky Mountain College *B*
Stone Child College *A*
University of Montana-Missoula *B*
Western Montana College of The
  University of Montana *A, B*

Nebraska
Clarkson College *B, M*
Creighton University *M*
Hastings College *B*
Metropolitan Community College *A*
Mid Plains Community College Area *A*
Midland Lutheran College *B, T*
Nebraska Wesleyan University *B*
Northeast Community College *A*
University of Nebraska
  Omaha *B, M*

Nevada
Community College of Southern
  Nevada *A*
University of Nevada
  Reno *B*
Western Nevada Community
  College *C, A*

New Hampshire
College for Lifelong Learning *A*
Daniel Webster College *B*
Franklin Pierce College *B*
Hesser College *A*
Keene State College *B*
New Hampshire College *B*
New Hampshire Community Technical
  College
  Berlin *A*
  Claremont *A*
  Stratham *C, A*
Notre Dame College *B*
St. Anselm College *B*
University of New Hampshire *B, M*

New Jersey
Bloomfield College *B*
Brookdale Community College *A*
Burlington County College *A*
Essex County College *C, A*
Felician College *B*
Gloucester County College *A*
Mercer County Community College *C, A*
Ocean County College *A*
Passaic County Community
  College *C, A*
Raritan Valley Community College *C*
Richard Stockton College of New
  Jersey *B*
Rowan University *C, B*
Rutgers
  The State University of New Jersey:
    New Brunswick Graduate
    Campus *M*
St. Peter's College *C*
Salem Community College *A*
Stevens Institute of Technology *B*
The College of New Jersey *B*
Union County College *A*
Warren County Community College *C, A*

New Mexico
Clovis Community College *A*
College of Santa Fe *A, B, M*
Eastern New Mexico University
  Roswell Campus *C, A*
New Mexico Junior College *A*
New Mexico State University
  Alamogordo *A*
  Carlsbad *A*
New Mexico State University *A, B*
Northern New Mexico Community
  College *A*
Western New Mexico University *B, M*

New York
Adirondack Community College *A*
Audrey Cohen College *B, M*
Berkeley College of New York City *B*
Berkeley College *B*
Cayuga County Community
  College *C, A*
City University of New York
  Baruch College *B, M*
  Bronx Community College *A*
  City College *B*
  College of Staten Island *A, B*
  Hostos Community College *A*
  Medgar Evers College *A, B*
  Queensborough Community
    College *A*
College of Insurance *B*
College of Mount St. Vincent *A, B*
College of New Rochelle *B, T*
Columbia-Greene Community College *C*
Concordia College *A*
Cornell University *D*
D'Youville College *B*
Daemen College *T*
Finger Lakes Community College *A*
Fordham University *B, M*
Fulton-Montgomery Community
  College *A*
Herkimer County Community
  College *C, A*
Houghton College *B*
Hudson Valley Community College *A*
Interboro Institute *A*
Iona College *M*
Ithaca College *B*
Long Island University
  Brooklyn Campus *A, B, M*
  Southampton College *B*
Manhattan College *B*
Maria College *A*
Marymount College *B*
Medaille College *B*
Mercy College *C*
Monroe Community College *A*
Nazareth College of Rochester *B, M*
New York University *A, B, M, D*
Niagara County Community College *A*
Niagara University *A, B*
North Country Community College *A*
Nyack College *B*
Onondaga Community College *A*
Orange County Community College *A*
Pace University:
  Pleasantville/Briarcliff *C, A, B, M, D*
Pace University *C, A, B, M, D*
Regents College *A, B*
Rochester Institute of
  Technology *A, B, M*
Rockland Community College *A*
St. John's University *A*
St. Thomas Aquinas College *B*
Schenectady County Community
  College *C, A*
Skidmore College *B*
St. Joseph's College
  St. Joseph's College: Suffolk
    Campus *C*
  St. Joseph's College *C, B*
State University of New York
  Albany *B, M*
  College at Buffalo *B*
  College at Cortland *B*
  College at Plattsburgh *B*
  College of Agriculture and
    Technology at Cobleskill *A*
  College of Agriculture and
    Technology at Morrisville *A*
  Empire State College *A, B*
  Institute of Technology at
    Utica/Rome *B, M*
  Maritime College *B*
  Purchase *C*
Suffolk County Community College *A*
Syracuse University *B*
Tompkins-Cortland Community
  College *A*
Touro College *A, B*
Ulster County Community College *C, A*
Westchester Community College *C*

North Carolina
Alamance Community College *C, A*
Appalachian State University *B*
Beaufort County Community College *A*
Blue Ridge Community College *A*
Brevard College *A, B*
Campbell University *A, B, M*
Carteret Community College *A*
Coastal Carolina Community College *A*
Davidson County Community
  College *C, A*
Gardner-Webb University *B, M*
Johnson C. Smith University *B*
Lenoir-Rhyne College *B, M*
Louisburg College *A*
Mars Hill College *B*
North Carolina Agricultural and
  Technical State University *B*
Pfeiffer University *B*
Piedmont Community College *A*
St. Andrews Presbyterian College *B*
Surry Community College *A*
Wake Forest University *B*
Wake Technical Community College *A*
Wayne Community College *A*
Wingate University *B*

North Dakota
Dickinson State University *B*
Trinity Bible College *A, B*

Ohio
Ashland University *A, B, M*
Belmont Technical College *A*
Bluffton College *B*
Bowling Green State University
  Firelands College *A*
Bowling Green State University *B*
Capital University *B*
Central State University *B*
Circleville Bible College *A*
Clark State Community College *A*
David N. Myers College *B*
Davis College *A*
Defiance College *A, B, T*
Jefferson Community College *A*
Kent State University
  Ashtabula Regional Campus *C, A*
  East Liverpool Regional Campus *A*
  Stark Campus *A*
  Trumbull Campus *A*
Kent State University *C, B, M, D*
Lima Technical College *A*
Lorain County Community College *A*
Lourdes College *C, A, B*
Marion Technical College *C, A*
Miami University
  Middletown Campus *A*
  Oxford Campus *B*
Muskingum College *B*
North Central State College *A*
Northwest State Community College *A*
Ohio State University
  Columbus Campus *B, M, D*
Ohio University
  Lancaster Campus *A*
Ohio University *B*
Ohio Valley Business College *A*
Otterbein College *B*
Shawnee State University *B*
Sinclair Community College *C, A*
Southern State Community College *A*
Stark State College of Technology *A*
Terra Community College *A*
Tiffin University *A*
Union Institute *B*
University of Akron
  Wayne College *A*
University of Akron *A*
University of Cincinnati
  Clermont College *C, A*
  Raymond Walters College *C, A*
University of Dayton *B*
University of Findlay *A, B*
Walsh University *A, B*
Washington State Community College *A*
Xavier University *A, B*
Youngstown State University *A, B, M*

Oklahoma
Carl Albert State College *A*
Connors State College *A*
East Central University *B*
Eastern Oklahoma State College *A*
Mid-America Bible College *B*
Northeastern Oklahoma Agricultural and
  Mechanical College *A*
Northeastern State University *B*
Northern Oklahoma College *A*
Oklahoma Baptist University *B*
Oklahoma Christian University of
  Science and Arts *B, T*
Oklahoma City Community College *A*
Oklahoma City University *B, M*
Oklahoma State University
  Oklahoma City *C, A*

Oklahoma State University B, M, D
Rogers State University A
Rose State College C, A
St. Gregory's University A, B
Southern Nazarene University B, M
Southwestern Oklahoma State University B, M
Tulsa Community College A
University of Science and Arts of Oklahoma B, T
Western Oklahoma State College A

Oregon
Clatsop Community College A
Concordia University B
Eastern Oregon University B, T
Lewis & Clark College B
Linfield College B
Linn-Benton Community College A
Marylhurst University B, M
Mount Hood Community College C, A
Portland Community College A
Portland State University B, M
Southern Oregon University B
University of Oregon B, M, D
Western Baptist College B
Western Oregon University B

Pennsylvania
Allentown College of St. Francis de Sales B, M
Beaver College B
Bucks County Community College A
Butler County Community College A
Cambria-Rowe Business College A
Community College of Beaver County A
Community College of Philadelphia A
Delaware County Community College A
Drexel University B
Duquesne University B, M
Franklin and Marshall College B
Gannon University C
Geneva College A, B, M, T
Harcum College A
Harrisburg Area Community College C
ICS Center for Degree Studies A
Immaculata College C
Indiana University of Pennsylvania M
La Salle University B
Lackawanna Junior College A
Lebanon Valley College of Pennsylvania C
Lehigh University B
Lycoming College B
Marywood University C
Mercyhurst College A, B
Montgomery County Community College C, A
Northampton County Area Community College A
Peirce College A, B
Penn State
    Abington A, B
    Altoona A, B
    Beaver A
    Berks A, B
    Delaware County A, B
    Dubois A, B
    Erie, The Behrend College A
    Fayette A, B
    Harrisburg B
    Hazleton A, B
    Lehigh Valley A, B
    McKeesport A
    Mont Alto A, B
    New Kensington A
    Schuylkill - Capital College A, B
    Shenango A, B
    University Park C, A, B
    Wilkes-Barre A
    Worthington Scranton A, B
    York A, B
Philadelphia University B, M
Reading Area Community College C, A
St. Francis College B
St. Joseph's University C, A, B, M
Seton Hill College B
Shippensburg University of Pennsylvania B
Susquehanna University B
Temple University B, M
University of Pittsburgh
    Johnstown C, B
    Titusville A
University of Pittsburgh B
Valley Forge Military College A
Villanova University B
Waynesburg College A, B
West Chester University of Pennsylvania M
Wilson College B
York College of Pennsylvania A, B, T

Puerto Rico
American University of Puerto Rico B
Bayamon Central University A, B, M
Huertas Junior College A
ICPR Junior College A
Inter American University of Puerto Rico
    Barranquitas Campus B
    Fajardo Campus A, B
Pontifical Catholic University of Puerto Rico B, M
Ramirez College of Business and Technology A
Universidad Metropolitana B
Universidad Politecnica de Puerto Rico B
University of Puerto Rico
    Bayamon University College A, B
    Cayey University College B
    Rio Piedras Campus B, M

Rhode Island
Bryant College M
Community College of Rhode Island A
New England Institute of Technology B
Providence College C, A, B
Rhode Island College B
University of Rhode Island M, D

South Carolina
Charleston Southern University B, M
Converse College B
Denmark Technical College A
Greenville Technical College C, A
North Greenville College B
Orangeburg-Calhoun Technical College A
Piedmont Technical College C, A
Southern Wesleyan University A, M
Technical College of the Lowcountry C, A
Trident Technical College A
University of South Carolina
    Aiken B
York Technical College A

South Dakota
Augustana College B
Dakota State University A, B
Dakota Wesleyan University A, B
Northern State University B
Sinte Gleska University A

Tennessee
Austin Peay State University B
Belmont University B
Carson-Newman College B, T
Christian Brothers University B
Columbia State Community College A
Cumberland University A, B, M
David Lipscomb University B
Freed-Hardeman University B
Hiwassee College A
Lambuth University B
Lane College B
Lee University B
Lincoln Memorial University B, M, T
Martin Methodist College B
Middle Tennessee State University B
Pellissippi State Technical Community College A
Roane State Community College A
Tennessee Technological University B, M
Tennessee Temple University B
University of Tennessee
    Knoxville
    Martin M
Walters State Community College A

Texas
Amarillo College C, A
Amber University B, M
Angelo State University B
Austin College B
Baylor University B
Blinn College A
Brazosport College A
Cedar Valley College A
Central Texas College C, A
Coastal Bend College A
College of the Mainland A
Concordia University at Austin B
East Texas Baptist University B
Eastfield College A
El Paso Community College C, A
Grayson County College A
Howard College C, A
Howard Payne University T
Kilgore College A
Lamar State College at Orange A
Lamar University B, M
LeTourneau University B
Lon Morris College A
Lubbock Christian University B
McMurry University B
Midland College C, A
Midwestern State University B
Navarro College A
North Central Texas College A
Odessa College A
Our Lady of the Lake University of San Antonio M
Panola College A
Paris Junior College A
Rice University B
St. Mary's University B
San Jacinto College
    North C
Southern Methodist University B, M
Southwestern Assemblies of God University A, B
Southwestern University B
Stephen F. Austin State University B, M
Sul Ross State University B
Tarleton State University B, T
Tarrant County College A
Temple College C, A
Texas A&M University
    Commerce B, M
    Kingsville B
    Texarkana B
Texas Christian University M
Texas Lutheran University B
Texas Southern University B
Texas Tech University B, M, D
Tyler Junior College A
University of Houston
    Clear Lake B
    Downtown B
    Victoria M
University of Houston M, D
University of Mary Hardin-Baylor B
University of North Texas B, M, D
University of St. Thomas B
University of Texas
    Austin B, M, D
    Brownsville B
    Dallas B, M
    El Paso M
    Pan American B, M
    San Antonio M
    Tyler B
University of the Incarnate Word B, M
Vernon Regional Junior College C, A
Weatherford College C, A
West Texas A&M University B
Western Texas College A

Utah
Brigham Young University B
Dixie State College of Utah A
LDS Business College A
Salt Lake Community College A
Snow College C, A
Utah State University B
Utah Valley State College C, A, B
Westminster College B

Vermont
Castleton State College A, B
Champlain College A, B
College of St. Joseph in Vermont B
Community College of Vermont C, A
Johnson State College B
Southern Vermont College A
Vermont Technical College A

Virginia
Blue Ridge Community College C
Bluefield College B
Central Virginia Community College A
Christopher Newport University B
Danville Community College A
George Mason University B
Germanna Community College A
Hollins University B
J. Sargeant Reynolds Community College A
John Tyler Community College A
Longwood College B
Lord Fairfax Community College C, A
Mountain Empire Community College A
National Business College A, B
Norfolk State University B, T
Piedmont Virginia Community College C, A
Richard Bland College A
Shenandoah University C
Southwest Virginia Community College A
Sweet Briar College C
University of Virginia B
Virginia Commonwealth University M, D
Virginia Polytechnic Institute and State University D
Virginia Wesleyan College B

Washington
Everett Community College C, A
Henry Cogswell College B
Heritage College C, B
Highline Community College C, A
Lower Columbia College C, A
North Seattle Community College A
Pierce College C, A
South Puget Sound Community College C, A
South Seattle Community College A
Spokane Community College C, A
Spokane Falls Community College C, A
Tacoma Community College C
Walla Walla College B
Western Washington University B
Whatcom Community College C, A
Whitworth College B
Yakima Valley Community College C, A

West Virginia
Alderson-Broaddus College A, B
Bluefield State College A
College of West Virginia A, B
Concord College B
Davis and Elkins College B
Fairmont State College A, B
Glenville State College B
Marshall University A, B, M
Potomac State College of West Virginia University A
Shepherd College A
Southern West Virginia Community and Technical College A

West Liberty State College B
West Virginia Northern Community College A
West Virginia State College A, B
West Virginia University Institute of Technology B
West Virginia University B, M
Wheeling Jesuit University M

Wisconsin

Bryant & Stratton College A
Cardinal Stritch University A, B
Carthage College B
Chippewa Valley Technical College A
Concordia University Wisconsin B
Marian College of Fond du Lac B, M
Milwaukee School of Engineering B
Mount Senario College B
Northeast Wisconsin Technical College A
Northland College B
Ripon College B
St. Norbert College B
University of Wisconsin
    Eau Claire B
    Green Bay B
    La Crosse B
    Madison B, M, D
    Parkside B
    Platteville B
    Superior B
Viterbo University B

Wyoming

Casper College A
Central Wyoming College A
Eastern Wyoming College A
Laramie County Community College A
Northwest College A
Sheridan College A
Western Wyoming Community College A

Business administration/management

Alabama

Alabama Agricultural and Mechanical University B, M
Alabama State University A, B
Athens State University B
Auburn University at Montgomery B
Auburn University B, M, D
Bevill State Community College A
Birmingham-Southern College M
Calhoun Community College A
Central Alabama Community College A
Chattahoochee Valley Community College B
Concordia College B
Enterprise State Junior College A
Faulkner University A, B
George C. Wallace State Community College
    Selma C, A
Huntingdon College B
Jacksonville State University B, M
James H. Faulkner State Community College A
Lawson State Community College A
Northeast Alabama Community College A
Northwest-Shoals Community College A
Oakwood College B
Samford University B, M
Snead State Community College A
South College B
Spring Hill College A, B, M
Troy State University
    Dothan B, M
    Montgomery A, B, M
Troy State University B, M
Tuskegee University B

University of Alabama
    Birmingham B, M
    Huntsville B, M
University of Alabama B, M
University of Mobile B
University of Montevallo B
University of North Alabama B, M
University of South Alabama B, M
University of West Alabama B

Alaska

Alaska Pacific University A, B, M
University of Alaska
    Anchorage C, A, B, M
    Fairbanks A, B, M

Arizona

Arizona State University B, M, D
Arizona Western College C, A
Central Arizona College C, A
Cochise College A
DeVry Institute of Technology
    Phoenix B
Dine College A
Eastern Arizona College A
Glendale Community College C, A
Grand Canyon University B, M
Mesa Community College A
Mohave Community College C, A
Northern Arizona University B, M
Northland Pioneer College C, A
Phoenix College C, A
Pima Community College C, A
Prescott College B, M
Rio Salado College C, A
South Mountain Community College C, A
Southwestern College A
University of Arizona M, D
University of Phoenix A, B, M
Yavapai College C, A

Arkansas

Arkansas State University
    Beebe Branch A
Arkansas State University B, M
Arkansas Tech University B
Central Baptist College A
Harding University B
Henderson State University B, M
John Brown University B
Lyon College B
Northwest Arkansas Community College A
Ouachita Baptist University B
Philander Smith College B
Phillips Community College of the University of Arkansas A
Southern Arkansas University Tech A
Southern Arkansas University B
University of Arkansas
    Little Rock B, M
    Monticello B
    Pine Bluff B
University of Arkansas B, M, D
University of Central Arkansas B, M
University of the Ozarks A, B
Westark College C, A

California

Allan Hancock College C, A
Armstrong University B, M
Azusa Pacific University B, M
Bakersfield College A
Barstow College C, A
Butte College A
Cabrillo College A
California Baptist University B
California Lutheran University B, M
California Maritime Academy B
California Polytechnic State University: San Luis Obispo B
California State Polytechnic University: Pomona M

California State University
    Bakersfield B, M
    Chico B, M
    Dominguez Hills B, M
    Fresno B, M
    Fullerton B
    Hayward B, M
    Long Beach M
    Los Angeles B, M
    Monterey Bay B
    Northridge B, M
    San Marcos B, M
    Stanislaus B, M
Canada College C, A
Cerritos Community College A
Cerro Coso Community College C, A
Chaffey Community College C, A
Chapman University B, M
City College of San Francisco A
Claremont McKenna College B
Coastline Community College C, A
College of Notre Dame B, M
College of the Canyons C, A
College of the Siskiyous C, A
Columbia College C, A
Compton Community College C, A
Concordia University B
Crafton Hills College C, A
Cuyamaca College C, A
Cypress College A
De Anza College C, A
DeVry Institute of Technology
    Fremont B
    Long Beach B
    Pomona B
    West Hills B
Diablo Valley College C, A
Dominican University of California M
East Los Angeles College A
Evergreen Valley College C
Foothill College A
Fresno City College A
Fresno Pacific University M
Golden Gate University A, B, M, D
Golden West College C, A
Grossmont Community College C, A
Heald Business College
    Fresno C, A
    Santa Rosa C, A
Holy Names College B, M
Hope International University B
Humboldt State University B, M
Humphreys College A, B
Imperial Valley College A
Irvine Valley College C, A
John F. Kennedy University B
La Sierra University B, M
Lincoln University B, M
Long Beach City College C, A
Los Angeles Harbor College C, A
Los Angeles Mission College A
Los Angeles Southwest College A
Los Angeles Trade and Technical College A
Loyola Marymount University B, M
Marymount College A
Master's College B
Mendocino College C, A
Menlo College B
Merced College A
MiraCosta College C, A
Mission College A
Modesto Junior College A
Monterey Peninsula College A
Moorpark College C, A
Mount St. Mary's College B
Mount San Antonio College C, A
Mount San Jacinto College C, A
Pacific Union College B
Palo Verde College C, A
Palomar College A
Patten College B
Pepperdine University B, M
Point Loma Nazarene University C, B
Porterville College A

Riverside Community College C, A
Saddleback College C, A
St. Mary's College of California B, M
San Bernardino Valley College C, A
San Diego City College A
San Diego Mesa College C, A
San Diego Miramar College A
San Diego State University C, B, M
San Francisco State University M
San Joaquin Delta College C, A
San Jose State University B, M
Santa Ana College A
Santa Barbara City College C, A
Santa Clara University M
Santa Monica College C, A
Santa Rosa Junior College A
Shasta College A
Sierra College C, A
Simpson College B
Skyline College C, A
Solano Community College C, A
Sonoma State University B, M
Southwestern College A
Stanford University M, D
Taft College A
United States International University B, M, D
University of California
    Berkeley B, M, D
    Davis M
    Irvine M, D
    Los Angeles M, D
    Riverside B, M
University of La Verne A, B, M
University of Redlands B
University of San Diego B, M
University of San Francisco B, M
University of Southern California B, M, D
University of the Pacific B
Vanguard University of Southern California B
Ventura College A
West Hills Community College C, A
West Los Angeles College C, A
West Valley College C, A
Yuba College C

Colorado

Adams State College B
Arapahoe Community College C, A
Colorado Christian University B, M
Colorado Mountain College
    Alpine Campus A
    Spring Valley Campus C, A
    Timberline Campus A
Colorado State University B, M
Colorado Technical University B, M
Community College of Aurora C, A
Community College of Denver C, A
Denver Technical College: A Division of DeVry University B
Fort Lewis College B
Front Range Community College C, A
Lamar Community College A
Mesa State College B, M
Metropolitan State College of Denver B
Northeastern Junior College A
Otero Junior College A
Pikes Peak Community College A
Pueblo Community College C, A
Red Rocks Community College C, A
Regis University B
Trinidad State Junior College A
University of Colorado
    Boulder B, M, D
    Colorado Springs B, M
    Denver B, M
University of Denver B
University of Northern Colorado B
University of Southern Colorado M
Western State College of Colorado B

Connecticut

Albertus Magnus College C, A, B, M

113

Business administration/management

Asnuntuck Community-Technical College A
Briarwood College A
Capital Community College C, A
Central Connecticut State University B, M
Fairfield University B, M
Gateway Community College A
Hartford Graduate Center M
Housatonic Community-Technical College A
Manchester Community-Technical College A
Middlesex Community-Technical College A
Mitchell College A
Naugatuck Valley Community-Technical College C, A
Northwestern Connecticut Community-Technical College A
Quinebaug Valley Community College C, A
Quinnipiac University B, M
Sacred Heart University B, M
St. Joseph College B
Southern Connecticut State University B, M
Teikyo Post University A, B
Three Rivers Community-Technical College C, A
Tunxis Community College C, A
University of Bridgeport C, A, M
University of Connecticut B
University of Hartford B, M
University of New Haven A, B, M
Western Connecticut State University B, M
Yale University M, D

Delaware
Delaware State University M
Delaware Technical and Community College
    Owens Campus C, A
    Terry Campus C, A
Goldey-Beacom College A, B, M
University of Delaware B, M
Wesley College A, B
Wilmington College M

District of Columbia
Gallaudet University B
George Washington University B, M, D
Georgetown University B, M
Howard University B, M
Southeastern University A, B, M
Trinity College B, M
University of the District of Columbia B, M

Florida
Barry University B, M
Bethune-Cookman College B
Brevard Community College A
Broward Community College A
Central Florida Community College A
Chipola Junior College A
Clearwater Christian College B
Daytona Beach Community College A
Eckerd College B
Edward Waters College B
Embry-Riddle Aeronautical University A, B, M
Flagler College B
Florida Agricultural and Mechanical University B, M
Florida Atlantic University B, M, D
Florida Community College at Jacksonville A
Florida Gulf Coast University B, M
Florida Institute of Technology B, M
Florida International University B, M, D
Florida Keys Community College A
Florida Memorial College B
Florida Metropolitan University
    Orlando College North A, B, M
Florida National College A
Florida Southern College B
Florida State University B, M, D
Gulf Coast Community College A
Hillsborough Community College A
Indian River Community College A
International College A, B, M
Jacksonville University B, M
Jones College A, B
Lake City Community College A
Lake-Sumter Community College A
Manatee Community College A
Miami-Dade Community College A
Northwood University
    Florida Campus A, B
Nova Southeastern University B, M, D
Palm Beach Atlantic College B, M
Palm Beach Community College A
Pasco-Hernando Community College C, A
Pensacola Junior College A
Polk Community College A
Rollins College M
St. Leo University B, M
St. Petersburg Junior College A
St. Thomas University B, M
Santa Fe Community College A
South College: Palm Beach Campus A, B
South Florida Community College A
Southeastern College of the Assemblies of God B
Stetson University B, M
Tallahassee Community College A
Tampa Technical Institute A
University of Central Florida B, M, D
University of Miami B, M, D
University of North Florida B
University of South Florida B, M, D
University of Tampa B, M
University of West Florida M
Valencia Community College A
Warner Southern College B

Georgia
Abraham Baldwin Agricultural College A
Albany State University B
American InterContinental University A, B, M
Atlanta Christian College B
Atlanta Metropolitan College A
Augusta State University B, M
Berry College B, M
Brewton-Parker College A, B
Clark Atlanta University B, M
Clayton College and State University A, B
Columbus State University B, M
Columbus Technical Institute C
Darton College A
DeVry Institute of Technology
    Alpharetta B
    Atlanta B
East Georgia College A
Emmanuel College A, B
Emory University B
Fort Valley State University B
Gainesville College A
Georgia Institute of Technology B, M, D
Georgia Military College A
Georgia Perimeter College A
Georgia Southern University B, M
Georgia Southwestern State University B, M
Georgia State University B, M, D
Herzing College of Business and Technology A
Kennesaw State University B, M
LaGrange College A
Macon State College C
Mercer University B, M
Middle Georgia College A
Morehouse College B
Morris Brown College B
North Georgia College & State University B
Oglethorpe University M
Piedmont College B
Shorter College B, M
South Georgia College A
State University of West Georgia B
Toccoa Falls College B
University of Georgia B, M, D
Valdosta State University A, B, M
Waycross College A
Wesleyan College C, B

Hawaii
Brigham Young University
    Hawaii B
Chaminade University of Honolulu M
Hawaii Pacific University A, B, M
University of Hawaii
    Hilo B
    Manoa B, M
    West Oahu B

Idaho
Albertson College of Idaho B
Boise State University M
College of Southern Idaho A
Eastern Idaho Technical College A
Idaho State University A, B, M
Lewis-Clark State College B
North Idaho College A
Northwest Nazarene University B, M
Ricks College A

Illinois
Augustana College B
Barat College B
Benedictine University C, A, M
Black Hawk College C, A
Blackburn College B
Bradley University B, M
Carl Sandburg College A
Chicago State University B
City Colleges of Chicago
    Harold Washington College A
    Harry S. Truman College A
    Kennedy-King College A
    Malcolm X College A
    Olive-Harvey College A
    Wright College C, A
College of DuPage C, A
College of Lake County C, A
Columbia College B
De Paul University B, M
DeVry Institute of Technology
    Addison B
    Chicago B
Dominican University B, M
Eastern Illinois University M
Elgin Community College C, A
Elmhurst College C, B
Eureka College B
Governors State University B, M
Greenville College B
Highland Community College A
Illinois College B
Illinois Institute of Technology M
Illinois State University B, M
Illinois Wesleyan University B
John A. Logan College A
Joliet Junior College A
Judson College B
Kankakee Community College C, A
Kaskaskia College C, A
Kendall College A, B
Lake Forest Graduate School of Management M
Lewis University B, M
Lewis and Clark Community College A
Lincoln Christian College and Seminary B
Lincoln Land Community College C, A
Loyola University of Chicago B, M
MacCormac College A
MacMurray College A, B
McHenry County College C, A
McKendree College B
Millikin University B
Monmouth College B, T
Moraine Valley Community College A
Morton College A
National-Louis University C, B, M
North Central College M
North Park University B, M
Northeastern Illinois University B, M
Northern Illinois University M
Northwestern Business College A
Northwestern University M
Oakton Community College A
Olivet Nazarene University B, M
Parkland College A
Principia College B
Quincy University A, B, M
Rend Lake College A
Robert Morris College: Chicago C, A, B
Rock Valley College C, A
Rockford College B, M
Roosevelt University B, M
St. Augustine College A
St. Xavier University M
Sauk Valley Community College C, A
Southeastern Illinois College A
Southern Illinois University
    Carbondale B, M
    Edwardsville M
Southwestern Illinois College A
Trinity Christian College B
Triton College C, A
University of Illinois
    Chicago M, D
    Springfield B, M
    Urbana-Champaign B, M, D
University of St. Francis B, M
Waubonsee Community College C, A
Western Illinois University B, M

Indiana
Ancilla College A
Anderson University B, M
Ball State University A, B, M
Bethel College B, M
Butler University B, M
Earlham College B
Goshen College B
Grace College B
Hanover College B
ITT Technical Institute
    Indianapolis M
Indiana Institute of Technology A, B, M
Indiana State University B, M
Indiana University
    Bloomington B, M, D
    East A, B
    Kokomo A, B, M
    Northwest B, M
    South Bend B, M
    Southeast M
Indiana University--Purdue University Indiana University-Purdue University Fort Wayne A, M
Indiana Wesleyan University A, B
Ivy Tech State College
    Central Indiana C, A
    Columbus C, A
    Eastcentral C, A
    Kokomo C, A
    Lafayette C, A
    Northcentral C, A
    Northeast C, A
    Northwest C, A
    Southcentral C, A
    Southeast C, A
    Southwest C, A
    Wabash Valley C, A
    Whitewater A
Manchester College A, B
Oakland City University A
Purdue University
    Calumet B, M
Purdue University B, M, D
Saint Mary's College B

Business administration/management

St. Joseph's College *B*
St. Mary-of-the-Woods College *B*
Taylor University *A, B*
Tri-State University *A, B*
University of Evansville *B*
University of Indianapolis *A, B*
University of Notre Dame *M*
University of St. Francis *M*
University of Southern Indiana *B*
Valparaiso University *B*
Vincennes University *A*

Iowa
American Institute of Business *C, A*
Buena Vista University *B*
Central College *B, T*
Clarke College *A, B, M*
Coe College *B*
Des Moines Area Community College *A*
Drake University *M*
Graceland University *B*
Grand View College *B*
Indian Hills Community College *A*
Iowa Central Community College *A*
Iowa State University *B, M*
Iowa Wesleyan College *B*
Kirkwood Community College *A*
Loras College *B*
Luther College *B*
Maharishi University of Management *A, B, M*
Marshalltown Community College *A*
Marycrest International University *B*
Morningside College *B*
Mount Mercy College *B*
North Iowa Area Community College *A*
Northeast Iowa Community College *A*
Northwestern College *B*
St. Ambrose University *B, M, D*
Simpson College *B*
University of Dubuque *A, B, M*
University of Iowa *B*
University of Northern Iowa *B, M*
Upper Iowa University *B*
Waldorf College *A, B*
Wartburg College *C, B*
Western Iowa Tech Community College *A*
William Penn University *B*

Kansas
Allen County Community College *A*
Baker University *M*
Benedictine College *A, B, M*
Bethany College *B*
Bethel College *B*
Butler County Community College *C, A*
Central Christian College *A, B*
Coffeyville Community College *A*
Cowley County Community College *A*
Emporia State University *B, M*
Fort Hays State University *B, M*
Independence Community College *A*
Johnson County Community College *A*
Kansas City Kansas Community College *A*
Kansas State University *B*
Manhattan Christian College *B*
McPherson College *B*
MidAmerica Nazarene University *B, M*
Newman University *B*
Ottawa University *B*
Pittsburg State University *M*
Pratt Community College *C, A*
St. Mary College *B, M*
Seward County Community College *A*
Southwestern College *B*
Sterling College *B*
Tabor College *B*
University of Kansas *M*
Washburn University of Topeka *B, M*
Wichita State University *B, M*

Kentucky
Alice Lloyd College *B*
Ashland Community College *A*
Bellarmine College *B, M*
Campbellsville University *A, B*
Cumberland College *B, T*
Eastern Kentucky University *B*
Georgetown College *B*
Henderson Community College *A*
Hopkinsville Community College *A*
Kentucky Christian College *B*
Kentucky State University *B*
Lexington Community College *A*
Lindsey Wilson College *A, B*
Madisonville Community College *A*
Maysville Community College *A*
Midway College *A, B*
Morehead State University *B*
Murray State University *A, B, M*
National Business College *C, A*
Northern Kentucky University *A, B, M*
Owensboro Community College *A*
Owensboro Junior College of Business *C, A*
Paducah Community College *A*
Pikeville College *A, B*
St. Catharine College *A*
Somerset Community College *A*
Southeast Community College *A*
Thomas More College *A, B, M*
Union College *A, B*
University of Louisville *B*
Western Kentucky University *A, B*

Louisiana
Bossier Parish Community College *A*
Centenary College of Louisiana *B, M*
Delgado Community College *C, A*
Dillard University *B*
Louisiana State University
 Alexandria *A*
 Shreveport *B, M*
Louisiana State University and Agricultural and Mechanical College *B, M, D*
Louisiana Tech University *B, M, D*
Loyola University New Orleans *B, M*
McNeese State University *B, M*
Nicholls State University *A, B, M*
Northwestern State University *B, M*
Nunez Community College *A*
Our Lady of Holy Cross College *B*
Remington College - Education America, Inc. *A*
Southeastern Louisiana University *B, M*
Southern University
 New Orleans *B*
 Shreveport *A*
Southern University and Agricultural and Mechanical College *B*
Tulane University *B*
University of Louisiana at Lafayette *B, M*
University of Louisiana at Monroe *B, M*
University of New Orleans *B, M*
Xavier University of Louisiana *B*

Maine
Andover College *A*
Beal College *C, A*
Central Maine Technical College *A*
Eastern Maine Technical College *A*
Husson College *A, B, M*
Kennebec Valley Technical College *A*
Maine Maritime Academy *B*
Mid-State College *A*
St. Joseph's College *B*
Southern Maine Technical College *A*
Thomas College *B, M*
University of Maine
 Augusta *A, B*
 Fort Kent *A, B*
 Machias *B*
 Presque Isle *B*
University of Maine *B, M*
University of New England *B*
University of Southern Maine *A, B, M*

Maryland
Allegany College *A*
Baltimore City Community College *A*
Bowie State University *B, M*
Charles County Community College *C, A*
Chesapeake College *C*
Columbia Union College *B*
Community College of Baltimore County
 Catonsville *A*
 Essex *C, A*
Frederick Community College *A*
Frostburg State University *B, M*
Goucher College *B*
Hagerstown Community College *A*
Harford Community College *C, A*
Hood College *B, M*
Howard Community College *C, A*
Loyola College in Maryland *M*
Montgomery College
 Germantown Campus *C, A*
 Rockville Campus *C, A*
 Takoma Park Campus *C, A*
Morgan State University *B, M*
Mount St. Mary's College *M*
Prince George's Community College *A*
Salisbury State University *B, M*
Towson University *B*
University of Baltimore *M*
University of Maryland
 College Park *B, M*
 Eastern Shore *B*
 University College *M*
Villa Julie College *A, B*
Western Maryland College *B*
Wor-Wic Community College *A*

Massachusetts
American International College *A, B, M*
Anna Maria College *A, B, M*
Assumption College *A, B, M*
Atlantic Union College *B*
Babson College *B, M*
Bay Path College *A, B*
Bay State College *A*
Becker College *A, B*
Bentley College *A, B, M*
Berkshire Community College *A*
Boston College *B, M*
Boston University *B, M, D*
Bridgewater State College *B*
Bristol Community College *A*
Bunker Hill Community College *C, A*
Cape Cod Community College *A*
Clark University *B, M*
Curry College *B*
Dean College *A*
Eastern Nazarene College *A, B*
Elms College *B*
Emmanuel College *B*
Endicott College *A, B*
Fisher College *C, A*
Fitchburg State College *B, M*
Framingham State College *B, M*
Gordon College *B*
Greenfield Community College *A*
Harvard University *M, D*
Holyoke Community College *A*
Lasell College *B*
Lesley College *B, M*
Massachusetts Bay Community College *C, A*
Massachusetts College of Liberal Arts *B*
Massachusetts Institute of Technology *M, D*
Massachusetts Maritime Academy *C, B*
Massasoit Community College *A*
Merrimack College *A, B*
Middlesex Community College *A*
Mount Ida College *A, B*
Mount Wachusett Community College *A*
New England College of Finance *A*
Newbury College *A, B*
Nichols College *A, B, M*
North Shore Community College *A*
Northeastern University *A, B, M*
Northern Essex Community College *A*
Pine Manor College *A, B*
Regis College *B*
Roxbury Community College *A*
Salem State College *B, M*
Simmons College *B, M*
Springfield College *B*
Springfield Technical Community College *A*
Stonehill College *B*
Suffolk University *B, M*
University of Massachusetts
 Amherst *B, M, D*
 Boston *B, M*
 Dartmouth *B, M*
 Lowell *B, M*
Western New England College *B, M*
Westfield State College *B*
Worcester Polytechnic Institute *B, M*
Worcester State College *B*

Michigan
Adrian College *A, B, T*
Alma College *B*
Alpena Community College *A*
Andrews University *B, M*
Aquinas College *B, M, T*
Baker College
 of Auburn Hills *A, B*
 of Cadillac *A, B*
 of Jackson *A*
 of Mount Clemens *A, B, M*
 of Muskegon *A, B, M*
 of Owosso *A, B*
 of Port Huron *A, B*
Bay de Noc Community College *C, A*
Calvin College *B*
Central Michigan University *B, M*
Cleary College *A, B*
Cornerstone College and Grand Rapids Baptist Seminary *B*
Davenport College of Business *A, B*
Detroit College of Business *A, B*
Eastern Michigan University *B, M, T*
Ferris State University *A, B*
Glen Oaks Community College *C*
Gogebic Community College *A*
Grand Rapids Community College *A*
Grand Valley State University *B, M*
Great Lakes College *A, B*
Hillsdale College *B*
Hope College *B, T*
Kalamazoo Valley Community College *C, A*
Kellogg Community College *C, A*
Kettering University *B*
Kirtland Community College *A*
Lake Michigan College *A*
Lake Superior State University *A, B, M*
Lansing Community College *A*
Lawrence Technological University *B, M*
Macomb Community College *C, A*
Madonna University *B, M*
Marygrove College *B*
Michigan State University *B, M, D*
Michigan Technological University *B*
Mid Michigan Community College *A*
Monroe County Community College *C, A*
Montcalm Community College *A*
North Central Michigan College *C, A*
Northern Michigan University *B*
Northwestern Michigan College *A*
Northwood University *A, B, M*
Oakland Community College *A*
Oakland University *M*
Olivet College *B*
Rochester College *B*
Saginaw Valley State University *B, M*
St. Clair County Community College *A*
Schoolcraft College *A*
Southwestern Michigan College *C, A*

Spring Arbor College B, M
Suomi College B
University of Detroit Mercy B, M
University of Michigan
    Dearborn B, M
    Flint B, M
University of Michigan B, M, D
Walsh College of Accountancy and Business Administration B
Western Michigan University B, M, T
William Tyndale College B

Minnesota
Anoka-Ramsey Community College A
Augsburg College B
Bemidji State University B
Bethel College B
Central Lakes College A
Century Community and Technical College A
College of St. Benedict B
College of St. Catherine: St. Paul Campus B, M
College of St. Scholastica B, M
Crown College A, B
Hamline University B
Hibbing Community College: A Technical and Community College A
Inver Hills Community College A
Itasca Community College A
Metropolitan State University B, M
Minneapolis Community and Technical College C, A
Minnesota State University, Mankato B
Moorhead State University B, M
National American University St. Paul B
North Central University B
North Hennepin Community College A
Northwestern College B
St. Cloud State University B, M
St. Cloud Technical College C, A
St. John's University B
St. Mary's University of Minnesota B, M
Southwest State University A, B, M
University of Minnesota
    Crookston A, B
    Duluth B, M
    Morris B
    Twin Cities C, B, M, D
University of St. Thomas B, M
Winona State University B, M

Mississippi
Alcorn State University B, M
Belhaven College C, B, M
Blue Mountain College B
Copiah-Lincoln Community College A
Delta State University B, M
Holmes Community College A
Jackson State University M, D
Mary Holmes College A
Millsaps College B, M
Mississippi College B, M
Mississippi Gulf Coast Community College
    Jackson County Campus A
    Perkinston A
Mississippi State University B, M, D
Mississippi University for Women B
Mississippi Valley State University B
Northwest Mississippi Community College A
Rust College A, B
University of Mississippi B, M, D
University of Southern Mississippi B, M
William Carey College B, M

Missouri
Avila College B, M
Central Methodist College B
Central Missouri State University B, M
College of the Ozarks B
Columbia College A, B, M
Culver-Stockton College B
DeVry Institute of Technology Kansas City B
Drury University M
East Central College A
Evangel University B
Hannibal-LaGrange College B
Harris Stowe State College B
Lincoln University B, M
Lindenwood University B, M
Longview Community College A
Maple Woods Community College C, A
Maryville University of Saint Louis B, M
Missouri Baptist College C, A, B
Missouri Southern State College B
Missouri Valley College B
Missouri Western State College A, B
Northwest Missouri State University M
Ozarks Technical Community College C, A
Penn Valley Community College C, A
Rockhurst University B, M
St. Charles County Community College C, A
St. Louis University B, M, D
Southeast Missouri State University B, M
Southwest Baptist University B, M
Southwest Missouri State University B, M
St. Louis Community College
    St. Louis Community College at Florissant Valley A
Stephens College B, M
Truman State University B
University of Missouri
    Columbia B
    St. Louis C, M
Washington University B, M, D
Webster University B, M
Westminster College B
William Jewell College B
William Woods University B, M

Montana
Carroll College B
Little Big Horn College A
Miles Community College A
Montana State University
    Billings A, B
    College of Technology-Great Falls A
    Northern A, B
Montana Tech of the University of Montana A, B
Rocky Mountain College B
University of Great Falls A, B
University of Montana-Missoula B, M
Western Montana College of The University of Montana A

Nebraska
Bellevue University B, M
Central Community College C, A
Chadron State College B, M
Clarkson College B, M
College of Saint Mary C, A, B
Concordia University B
Dana College B
Doane College B, M
Hastings College B
Lincoln School of Commerce A
Metropolitan Community College A
Midland Lutheran College B
Nebraska Wesleyan University B
Northeast Community College A
Peru State College B
Southeast Community College
    Lincoln Campus A
Union College A, B
University of Nebraska
    Kearney B, M
    Lincoln B, M, D
Wayne State College B, M, T

Nevada
Community College of Southern Nevada C, A
University of Nevada
    Las Vegas M
    Reno M

New Hampshire
Antioch New England Graduate School M
Colby-Sawyer College B
Dartmouth College M
Franklin Pierce College B
Hesser College A
McIntosh College A
New England College B
New Hampshire College A, B, M
New Hampshire Community Technical College
    Berlin C, A
    Laconia C, A
    Manchester C, A
    Nashua A
    Stratham C, A
New Hampshire Technical Institute A
Plymouth State College of the University System of New Hampshire B, M
Rivier College A, B, M
University of New Hampshire Manchester A, B
University of New Hampshire A, B

New Jersey
Atlantic Cape Community College A
Berkeley College A
Bloomfield College B
Brookdale Community College A
Burlington County College A
Caldwell College B
Camden County College A
Centenary College B
College of St. Elizabeth C, B, M
County College of Morris A
Cumberland County College A
DeVry Institute A
Essex County College A
Fairleigh Dickinson University B, M
Felician College B
Georgian Court College B, M
Gloucester County College A
Hudson County Community College A
Kean University B
Mercer County Community College C, A
Middlesex County College A
Monmouth University M
Montclair State University B, M
New Jersey City University B
New Jersey Institute of Technology B, M
Ocean County College A
Passaic County Community College C
Ramapo College of New Jersey B, M
Raritan Valley Community College C
Richard Stockton College of New Jersey B
Rider University A, B, M
Rowan University M
Rutgers
    The State University of New Jersey: Camden College of Arts and Sciences B
    The State University of New Jersey: Camden Graduate Campus M
    The State University of New Jersey: Douglass College B
    The State University of New Jersey: Livingston College B
    The State University of New Jersey: Newark College of Arts and Sciences B
    The State University of New Jersey: Newark Graduate Campus M, D
    The State University of New Jersey: Rutgers College B
    The State University of New Jersey: University College Camden B
    The State University of New Jersey: University College New Brunswick B
    The State University of New Jersey: University College Newark B
St. Peter's College A, B, M
Salem Community College A
Seton Hall University C, B, M
Stevens Institute of Technology M
Sussex County Community College A
The College of New Jersey B
Thomas Edison State College C, A, B, M
Union County College A
William Paterson University of New Jersey B, M

New Mexico
Albuquerque Technical-Vocational Institute C, A
Clovis Community College A
College of Santa Fe A, B, M
College of the Southwest B
Dona Ana Branch Community College of New Mexico State University C, A
Eastern New Mexico University B, M
New Mexico Highlands University B, M
New Mexico Institute of Mining and Technology A, B
New Mexico Junior College A
New Mexico State University M, D
Northern New Mexico Community College C, A
San Juan College A
Santa Fe Community College A
University of New Mexico B, M
Western New Mexico University B, M

New York
Adelphi University B, M
Adirondack Community College A
Alfred University B, M
Audrey Cohen College B, M
Berkeley College of New York City A, B
Berkeley College A, B
Briarcliffe College A, B
Bryant & Stratton Business Institute
    Albany A
    Syracuse A
Canisius College M
Cayuga County Community College A
City University of New York
    Baruch College B, M
    Borough of Manhattan Community College A
    Brooklyn College B
    College of Staten Island B
    Graduate School and University Center D
    Kingsborough Community College A
    La Guardia Community College A
    Lehman College B
    Queensborough Community College A
    York College B
Clarkson University B, M
Clinton Community College A

Business administration/management

College of Mount St. Vincent *B*
College of St. Rose *B, M*
Columbia University
    Graduate School *M, D*
Columbia-Greene Community College *A*
Concordia College *A, B*
Corning Community College *A*
D'Youville College *B*
Daemen College *B*
DeVry Institute of Technology
    New York *B*
Dowling College *C, B, M*
Dutchess Community College *A*
Elmira College *B*
Erie Community College
    City Campus *A*
    North Campus *A*
    South Campus *A*
Finger Lakes Community College *A*
Five Towns College *A, B*
Fordham University *B, M*
Fulton-Montgomery Community
    College *A*
Genesee Community College *A*
Hartwick College *B*
Herkimer County Community College *A*
Hilbert College *A, B*
Hudson Valley Community College *A*
Iona College *A, B*
Ithaca College *B*
Jamestown Business College *A*
Jamestown Community College *A*
Jefferson Community College *C, A*
Katharine Gibbs School
    New York *A*
Keuka College *B*
Le Moyne College *B, M*
Long Island University
    Brooklyn Campus *B, M*
    C. W. Post Campus *B, M*
    Southampton College *B*
Manhattan College *M*
Manhattanville College *B*
Marist College *B, M*
Marymount College *B*
Marymount Manhattan College *B*
Medaille College *B, M*
Mercy College *B*
Mohawk Valley Community
    College *C, A*
Molloy College *B*
Monroe College *A, B*
Mount St. Mary College *C, B, M*
Nassau Community College *C, A*
New York Institute of
    Technology *A, B, M*
New York University *B, M, D*
Niagara County Community College *A*
Niagara University *M*
North Country Community College *A*
Nyack College *A, B*
Orange County Community College *A*
Rensselaer Polytechnic Institute *B, M, D*
Roberts Wesleyan College *B*
Rochester Institute of
    Technology *A, B, M*
Rockland Community College *A*
Russell Sage College *B*
Sage Junior College of Albany *A*
St. Bonaventure University *M*
St. Francis College *A, B*
St. John Fisher College *B, M*
St. John's University *A, B, M*
St. Thomas Aquinas College *B, M*
Schenectady County Community
    College *A*
St. Joseph's College
    St. Joseph's College: Suffolk
      Campus *B*
    St. Joseph's College *B*

State University of New York
    Albany *B, M*
    Binghamton *M*
    Buffalo *B, M, D*
    College at Brockport *B*
    College at Buffalo *B*
    College at Fredonia *B*
    College at Old Westbury *B*
    College at Plattsburgh *B*
    College of Agriculture and
      Technology at Cobleskill *A*
    College of Agriculture and
      Technology at Morrisville *A*
    College of Technology at Alfred *A*
    College of Technology at Canton *A*
    College of Technology at
      Delhi *A, B*
    Empire State College *M*
    Farmingdale *C, A*
    Institute of Technology at
      Utica/Rome *B, M*
    Maritime College *B*
    New Paltz *B, M*
    Oswego *B, M*
    Stony Brook *M*
Suffolk County Community College *A*
Syracuse University *B, M, D*
Tompkins-Cortland Community
    College *C, A*
Touro College *A, B*
Trocaire College *A*
Ulster County Community College *A*
Union College *M*
United States Military Academy *B*
University of Rochester *M, D*
Utica College of Syracuse University *B*
Villa Maria College of Buffalo *A*
Wagner College *B, M*
Westchester Business Institute *C, A*
Westchester Community College *A*

North Carolina
Alamance Community College *C, A*
Appalachian State University *M*
Asheville Buncombe Technical
    Community College *A*
Barber-Scotia College *B*
Barton College *B*
Beaufort County Community College *A*
Belmont Abbey College *B*
Bennett College *B*
Bladen Community College *A*
Brevard College *B*
Brunswick Community College *A*
Caldwell Community College and
    Technical Institute *A*
Campbell University *B, M*
Cape Fear Community College *A*
Catawba College *B*
Catawba Valley Community
    College *C, A*
Cecils College *A*
Central Carolina Community College *A*
Central Piedmont Community College *A*
Chowan College *B*
Cleveland Community College *A*
College of the Albemarle *A*
Craven Community College *A*
Duke University *M, D*
Durham Technical Community
    College *A*
East Carolina University *B, M*
Edgecombe Community College *A*
Elizabeth City State University *B*
Elon College *B, M*
Fayetteville State University *B, M*
Fayetteville Technical Community
    College *A*
Forsyth Technical Community College *A*
Gardner-Webb University *B, M*
Gaston College *A*
Guilford College *B*
Guilford Technical Community
    College *A*
Halifax Community College *A*

Haywood Community College *C, A*
High Point University *M*
James Sprunt Community College *A*
Johnson C. Smith University *B*
Johnston Community College *A*
Lees-McRae College *B*
Louisburg College *A*
Mars Hill College *B*
Martin Community College *C, A*
Mayland Community College *A*
Meredith College *B, M*
Methodist College *A, B*
Mitchell Community College *A*
Montgomery Community College *C, A*
Montreat College *B, M*
Mount Olive College *A, B*
Nash Community College *A*
North Carolina Agricultural and
    Technical State University *B*
North Carolina Central University *B, M*
North Carolina State University *B*
North Carolina Wesleyan College *B*
Peace College *B*
Pfeiffer University *B, M*
Piedmont Community College *A*
Pitt Community College *A*
Queens College *B, M*
Randolph Community College *A*
Richmond Community College *C, A*
Roanoke-Chowan Community College *A*
Rockingham Community College *A*
Rowan-Cabarrus Community
    College *C, A*
St. Andrews Presbyterian College *B*
St. Augustine's College *B*
Salem College *B*
Sampson Community College *A*
Sandhills Community College *A*
Shaw University *A, B*
South Piedmont Community
    College *C, A*
Southeastern Community College *A*
Southwestern Community College *C, A*
Surry Community College *A*
Tri-County Community College *A*
University of North Carolina
    Asheville *B*
    Chapel Hill *B, M, D*
    Charlotte *B, M*
    Greensboro *B, M*
    Pembroke *B, M*
    Wilmington *B, M*
Vance-Granville Community College *A*
Wake Forest University *M*
Warren Wilson College *B*
Wayne Community College *A*
Western Carolina University *B, M*
Western Piedmont Community
    College *A*
Wilkes Community College *A*
Wilson Technical Community
    College *C, A*
Wingate University *M*

North Dakota
Bismarck State College *A*
Dickinson State University *B*
Jamestown College *B*
Lake Region State College *C, A*
Mayville State University *A, B*
Minot State University: Bottineau
    Campus *C, A*
Minot State University *B, T*
North Dakota State College of Science *A*
North Dakota State University *B, M*
University of Mary *A, B, M*
University of North Dakota *B, M*
Valley City State University *B*

Ohio
Antioch College *B*
Ashland University *B, M*
Baldwin-Wallace College *B*
Bluffton College *B*
Bowling Green State University *B, M*
Capital University *B, M*

Case Western Reserve
    University *B, M, D*
Cedarville College *B*
Central Ohio Technical College *A*
Central State University *B*
Chatfield College *A*
Cincinnati State Technical and
    Community College *A*
Cleveland State University *M, D*
College of Mount St. Joseph *A, B*
Columbus State Community
    College *C, A*
David N. Myers College *B*
Davis College *A*
DeVry Institute of Technology
    Columbus *B*
Defiance College *A, B, M*
Edison State Community College *A*
Franciscan University of
    Steubenville *A, B, M*
Franklin University *A, B, M*
Heidelberg College *B, M*
Hiram College *B*
Hocking Technical College *A*
ITT Technical Institute
    Youngstown *A*
John Carroll University *B, M*
Kent State University
    Stark Campus *B*
    Trumbull Campus *A*
    Tuscarawas Campus *A*
Kent State University *B, M, D*
Lake Erie College *B*
Lakeland Community College *C, A*
Lima Technical College *A*
Lourdes College *C, A, B*
Malone College *B, M*
Miami University
    Hamilton Campus *A*
    Middletown Campus *C, A*
    Oxford Campus *B, M*
Mount Union College *B*
Mount Vernon Nazarene College *A, B*
Muskingum Area Technical College *A*
North Central State College *C, A*
Northwest State Community College *A*
Northwestern College *A*
Notre Dame College of Ohio *C, A, B*
Ohio Dominican College *C, B*
Ohio Northern University *B*
Ohio State University
    Columbus Campus *M, D*
Ohio University
    Chillicothe Campus *A, B*
    Southern Campus at Ironton *A, B*
Ohio University *A, B, M*
Otterbein College *B*
Owens Community College
    Toledo *A*
Sinclair Community College *A*
Terra Community College *A*
Tiffin University *A, B, M*
University of Akron
    Wayne College *A*
University of Akron *B, M*
University of Cincinnati
    Clermont College *A*
    Raymond Walters College *A*
University of Cincinnati *C, B, M, D*
University of Dayton *B, M*
University of Findlay *B, M*
University of Rio Grande *A, B*
University of Toledo *A, B, M*
Ursuline College *B*
Walsh University *A, B, M*
Washington State Community College *A*
Wilberforce University *B*
Wilmington College *B*
Wittenberg University *B*
Wright State University *B, M*
Xavier University *A, B, M*
Youngstown State University *A, B, M*

Oklahoma
Cameron University *B, M*

Business administration/management

Connors State College A
East Central University B
Eastern Oklahoma State College A
Langston University B
Murray State College A
Northeastern Oklahoma Agricultural and Mechanical College A
Northeastern State University B, M
Northern Oklahoma College A
Northwestern Oklahoma State University B
Oklahoma Baptist University B
Oklahoma Christian University of Science and Arts B
Oklahoma City University B, M
Oklahoma Panhandle State University A, B
Oklahoma State University
    Oklahoma City C, A
    Okmulgee A
Oklahoma State University B, M, D
Oral Roberts University B, M
Redlands Community College A
Rogers State University A
Rose State College C, A
St. Gregory's University A
Seminole State College A
Southeastern Oklahoma State University B, M
Southern Nazarene University A, B, M
Tulsa Community College A
University of Central Oklahoma B, M
University of Oklahoma B, M, D
University of Science and Arts of Oklahoma B
University of Tulsa C, M
Western Oklahoma State College A

Oregon
Central Oregon Community College A
Chemeketa Community College A
Concordia University B
Eastern Oregon University B
George Fox University M
Lane Community College C
Marylhurst University B, M
Northwest Christian College B
Oregon Graduate Institute C, M
Oregon Institute of Technology B
Oregon State University B, M
Pacific University B
Portland Community College A
Portland State University B, D
Southern Oregon University B
University of Oregon B, M, D
University of Portland B, M
Western Baptist College A, B
Willamette University B, M

Pennsylvania
Albright College B
Allentown College of St. Francis de Sales B, M
Alvernia College B
Beaver College C, B
Bloomsburg University of Pennsylvania B, M
Bucknell University B, M
Bucks County Community College A
Butler County Community College A
Cabrini College B
California University of Pennsylvania A, B, M
Cambria-Rowe Business College A
Carlow College B
Carnegie Mellon University B, M, D
Cedar Crest College B
Chatham College B, M
Chestnut Hill College A, B
Cheyney University of Pennsylvania B
Churchman Business School A
Clarion University of Pennsylvania A, B, M
College Misericordia B
Community College of Allegheny County C, A
Community College of Beaver County A
Community College of Philadelphia C, A
Delaware County Community College A
Delaware Valley College C, A, B
Drexel University M, D
East Stroudsburg University of Pennsylvania B
Eastern College B, M
Edinboro University of Pennsylvania A, B
Elizabethtown College C, A, B
Gannon University A, B, M
Gettysburg College B
Grove City College B
Gwynedd-Mercy College A, B
Harrisburg Area Community College C, A
Holy Family College C, B
Immaculata College B, M
Indiana University of Pennsylvania A, B, M
Juniata College B
King's College A, B
Kutztown University of Pennsylvania B
La Roche College C, B
La Salle University A, B, M
Lackawanna Junior College A
Lebanon Valley College of Pennsylvania A, B, M
Lehigh Carbon Community College C, A
Lehigh University M
Lincoln University B
Luzerne County Community College C, A
Lycoming College B
Manor College A
Mansfield University of Pennsylvania A, B
Marywood University B, M
Mercyhurst College B
Messiah College B
Millersville University of Pennsylvania B
Montgomery County Community College A
Moravian College B, M
Mount Aloysius College A, B
Muhlenberg College B
Neumann College C, B
Northampton County Area Community College A
Peirce College A, B
Penn State
    Erie, The Behrend College B, M
    Harrisburg B
    University Park C, B, M, D
Pennsylvania College of Technology A, B
Pennsylvania Institute of Technology A
Philadelphia College of Bible B
Philadelphia University A, B, M
Pittsburgh Technical Institute A
Point Park College C, A, B, M
Reading Area Community College A
Robert Morris College A, B, M
Rosemont College B
St. Francis College C, B, M
St. Joseph's University A, B, M
St. Vincent College C, B
Sawyer School A
Seton Hill College B
Shippensburg University of Pennsylvania B
Slippery Rock University of Pennsylvania B
South Hills School of Business & Technology A
Susquehanna University B
Temple University B, M, D
Thiel College B
Tri-State Business Institute A
University of Pennsylvania C, A, B, M, D
University of Pittsburgh
    Bradford B
    Greensburg B
University of Pittsburgh M, D
University of Scranton A, B, M
Ursinus College B
Villanova University B, M
Washington and Jefferson College C, A, B
Waynesburg College B, M
West Chester University of Pennsylvania B, M
Westminster College B
Westmoreland County Community College C, A
Widener University A, B, M
Wilkes University B, M
Wilson College A, B
York College of Pennsylvania B, M
Yorktowne Business Institute A

Puerto Rico
American University of Puerto Rico B
Atlantic College A, B
Bayamon Central University B, M
Caribbean University A, B
Colegio Universitario del Este C, A
Columbia College A, B
Huertas Junior College A
Humacao Community College A
ICPR Junior College C, A
Inter American University of Puerto Rico
    Aguadilla Campus A, B
    Arecibo Campus A, B
    Barranquitas Campus A, B
    Bayamon Campus A, B
    Fajardo Campus B
    Guayama Campus B
    Metropolitan Campus A, B, M
    San German Campus A, B, M
Pontifical Catholic University of Puerto Rico B, M
Turabo University A, B, M
Universidad Metropolitana B, M
Universidad Politecnica de Puerto Rico B, M
University of Puerto Rico
    Aguadilla A, B
    Arecibo Campus A, B
    Bayamon University College A, B
    Carolina Regional College B
    Cayey University College B
    Humacao University College A, B
    Mayaguez Campus B, M
    Ponce University College A, B
    Rio Piedras Campus B, M
    Utuado A
University of the Sacred Heart B

Rhode Island
Bryant College B, M
Community College of Rhode Island C, A
Johnson & Wales University A, B
Providence College B, M
Rhode Island College B
Roger Williams University B
Salve Regina University A, B, M
University of Rhode Island B

South Carolina
Aiken Technical College C, A
Anderson College B
Benedict College B
Charleston Southern University B, M
Chesterfield-Marlboro Technical College A
Claflin University B
Clemson University B, M
Coastal Carolina University B
Coker College B
College of Charleston B
Columbia College B
Erskine College B
Florence-Darlington Technical College C
Francis Marion University B, M
Furman University B
Lander University B
Limestone College A, B
Midlands Technical College A
Morris College B
Newberry College B
North Greenville College B
Piedmont Technical College C
Presbyterian College B
South Carolina State University B
Southern Wesleyan University B
Spartanburg Technical College A
Technical College of the Lowcountry C
The Citadel B, M
Tri-County Technical College C, A
Trident Technical College A
University of South Carolina
    Aiken B
    Spartanburg B
University of South Carolina B, M, D
Voorhees College B
Winthrop University B, M
York Technical College A

South Dakota
Augustana College B
Black Hills State University B
Dakota State University A, B, T
Huron University A, B
Kilian Community College A
Mount Marty College A, B
Northern State University B
Sinte Gleska University A, B
Southeast Technical Institute A
University of South Dakota B, M

Tennessee
Austin Peay State University A
Belmont University M
Bethel College B
Carson-Newman College B
Christian Brothers University B
Cleveland State Community College A
Columbia State Community College C
Crichton College B
David Lipscomb University B
Draughons Junior College of Business: Nashville A
Dyersburg State Community College A
East Tennessee State University B, M
Fisk University B
Freed-Hardeman University B
Hiwassee College A
Jackson State Community College A
King College B
Knoxville Business College A
Lambuth University B
LeMoyne-Owen College B
Lee University B
Maryville College B
Middle Tennessee State University C, B, M
Milligan College B
Motlow State Community College A
Nashville State Technical Institute A
Northeast State Technical Community College A
Pellissippi State Technical Community College A
Rhodes College B, T
Roane State Community College A
Shelby State Community College A
Southern Adventist University B, M
Tennessee State University B, M
Tennessee Temple University A, B
Tennessee Wesleyan College B
Trevecca Nazarene University B, M
Tusculum College B, M
Union University B, M
University of Memphis B, M, D
University of Tennessee
    Chattanooga B, M
    Knoxville B, M, D
    Martin B
Vanderbilt University D

Volunteer State Community College A

Texas
Abilene Christian University B, M
Alvin Community College A
Amber University B, M
Angelina College A
Angelo State University B, M
Austin Community College A
Baylor University B, M
Brazosport College C, A
Brookhaven College A
Central Texas College C, A
Coastal Bend College A
College of the Mainland A
Collin County Community College District C, A
Concordia University at Austin B
Dallas Baptist University A, B, M
DeVry Institute of Technology Irving B
Del Mar College A
East Texas Baptist University B
Eastfield College A
El Paso Community College C, A
Galveston College C, A
Hardin-Simmons University B, M
Hill College A
Houston Baptist University B, M
Howard Payne University B
Huston-Tillotson College B
Jarvis Christian College B
Lamar State College at Orange C
Lamar State College at Port Arthur A
Lamar University B
LeTourneau University B, M
Lee College C, A
McMurry University B
Midland College C, A
Midwestern State University B, M
Navarro College C, A
North Lake College A
Northeast Texas Community College C, A
Northwood University: Texas Campus A, B
Our Lady of the Lake University of San Antonio B, M
Palo Alto College A
Paris Junior College A
Prairie View A&M University M
Rice University B, M, D
Richland College A
St. Edward's University B, M, T
St. Mary's University M
St. Philip's College A
Sam Houston State University B, M
San Antonio College A
San Jacinto College North C, A
Schreiner College B
South Plains College A
Southwest Texas State University B, M, T
Southwestern Adventist University B, M
Southwestern Assemblies of God University A, B
Stephen F. Austin State University B, M
Sul Ross State University B, M
Tarleton State University B, M
Tarrant County College C, A
Texas A&M International University B, M
Texas A&M University
 Commerce B, M
 Corpus Christi B, M
 Galveston B
 Kingsville M
 Texarkana B, M
Texas A&M University M, D
Texas Christian University B, M, T
Texas College B
Texas Southern University M
Texas Tech University B
Texas Wesleyan University B, M
Texas Woman's University B, M, T
Trinity University B
Trinity Valley Community College A
Tyler Junior College C, A
University of Dallas M
University of Houston
 Clear Lake B, M
 Downtown B
 Victoria B, T
University of Houston M, D
University of Mary Hardin-Baylor B, M
University of North Texas B, M
University of St. Thomas B, M
University of Texas
 Arlington B, M, D
 Austin B, D
 Brownsville B, M
 Dallas M, D
 El Paso B, M
 San Antonio B, M
 Tyler B, M
 of the Permian Basin M
University of the Incarnate Word B, M
Victoria College C, A
Wayland Baptist University A, B, M
West Texas A&M University B, M
Western Texas College A
Wharton County Junior College A
Wiley College B

Utah
Brigham Young University B, M
College of Eastern Utah A
Dixie State College of Utah A, B
LDS Business College A
Mountain West College C, A
Salt Lake Community College A
Snow College A
Southern Utah University B
University of Utah B, M, D
Utah State University B, M
Weber State University B
Westminster College B, M

Vermont
Castleton State College B
Champlain College A, B
College of St. Joseph in Vermont A, B
Goddard College B
Green Mountain College B
Johnson State College A, B
Lyndon State College A, B
Norwich University B
St. Michael's College B, M
Southern Vermont College B
Trinity College of Vermont A, B
University of Vermont B, M
Vermont Technical College A

Virginia
Averett College B, M
Blue Ridge Community College A
Bluefield College B
Bridgewater College B
Central Virginia Community College A
Christopher Newport University B
College of William and Mary B, M
Dabney S. Lancaster Community College A
Danville Community College A
Eastern Mennonite University B, M
Eastern Shore Community College A
Ferrum College B
George Mason University B, M
Germanna Community College A
Hampton University B, M
J. Sargeant Reynolds Community College C, A
James Madison University B, M
Liberty University B, M
Longwood College B
Lord Fairfax Community College A
Lynchburg College B, M
Mary Baldwin College B
Mary Washington College B
Mountain Empire Community College A
National Business College A, B
New River Community College A
Northern Virginia Community College A
Old Dominion University B, M, D
Patrick Henry Community College A
Paul D. Camp Community College A
Piedmont Virginia Community College A
Radford University B, M
Regent University M
Roanoke College B
St. Paul's College B
Shenandoah University B, M
Southside Virginia Community College C, A
Southwest Virginia Community College A
Thomas Nelson Community College A
Tidewater Community College A
University of Richmond B, M
University of Virginia's College at Wise B
University of Virginia M, D
Virginia Commonwealth University B, M, D
Virginia Highlands Community College A
Virginia Intermont College B
Virginia Polytechnic Institute and State University M
Virginia State University B
Virginia Union University B
Virginia Wesleyan College B
Virginia Western Community College A
Washington and Lee University B
Wytheville Community College A

Washington
Antioch University Seattle M
Bellevue Community College A
Central Washington University B
Centralia College A
City University C, A, B, M
Clark College C, A
Eastern Washington University B, M
Edmonds Community College C, A
Everett Community College C, A
Evergreen State College B
Gonzaga University B, M
Grays Harbor College C, A
Heritage College C, B
Highline Community College C, A
Lower Columbia College A
Pacific Lutheran University B, M
Peninsula College A
Pierce College C, A
St. Martin's College B, M
Seattle Pacific University C, B, M
Seattle University B, M
Shoreline Community College A
Skagit Valley College C, A
Spokane Community College C, A
Spokane Falls Community College C, A
University of Puget Sound B
University of Washington B, M, D
Walla Walla College B
Walla Walla Community College A
Washington State University B, M, D
Wenatchee Valley College A
Western Washington University B, M
Whatcom Community College A
Whitworth College B
Yakima Valley Community College C, A

West Virginia
Alderson-Broaddus College A, B
Bluefield State College B
College of West Virginia C, A, B
Concord College B
Davis and Elkins College A, B
Fairmont State College B
Glenville State College B
Marshall University B, M
Ohio Valley College B
Potomac State College of West Virginia University A
Salem-Teikyo University B
Shepherd College B
University of Charleston A, B, M
West Liberty State College B
West Virginia Northern Community College A
West Virginia State College A, B
West Virginia University Parkersburg B
West Virginia University Institute of Technology A, B
West Virginia University B
West Virginia Wesleyan College B, M
Wheeling Jesuit University B

Wisconsin
Alverno College B
Beloit College B
Cardinal Stritch University A, B, M
Carroll College B
Carthage College B
Concordia University Wisconsin B
Lakeland College B, M
Lakeshore Technical College A
Madison Area Technical College A
Marian College of Fond du Lac B, M
Marquette University B, M
Milwaukee Area Technical College A
Milwaukee School of Engineering B
Mount Mary College B
Mount Senario College B
Nicolet Area Technical College A
Northeast Wisconsin Technical College A
Northland College B
St. Norbert College B
Silver Lake College B
University of Wisconsin
 Eau Claire B, M
 Green Bay B, M
 La Crosse B, M
 Madison B, M, D
 Milwaukee M
 Oshkosh M
 Parkside M
 Platteville B
 River Falls B
 Stevens Point B
 Stout B
 Superior B
 Whitewater B, M
Viterbo University B
Western Wisconsin Technical College A
Wisconsin Lutheran College B

Wyoming
Casper College A
Central Wyoming College A
Eastern Wyoming College A
Laramie County Community College A
Northwest College A
Sheridan College A
University of Wyoming B, M

Business communications

California
Chapman University B
Golden Gate University C
Holy Names College B
Pepperdine University B
Point Loma Nazarene University B
Saddleback College C

Connecticut
Quinnipiac University B

District of Columbia
University of the District of Columbia A

Florida
Barry University M
Florida State University B
Gulf Coast Community College A

Business communications

Georgia
Brenau University *B*
South Georgia College *A*

Hawaii
Hawaii Pacific University *B*

Illinois
Roosevelt University *B, M*
Waubonsee Community College *C*

Kansas
MidAmerica Nazarene University *B*

Maine
University of Maine
    Presque Isle *B*

Maryland
Villa Julie College *A*

Massachusetts
Assumption College *B*
Babson College *B*
Bentley College *B, M*
Emerson College *B, M*
Suffolk University *M*

Michigan
Calvin College *B*
Central Michigan University *B*
Western Michigan University *B*

Minnesota
College of St. Scholastica *B*
University of St. Thomas *C, B, M*

Mississippi
Mississippi College *B*

Missouri
Rockhurst University *B*

Montana
Montana Tech of the University of
    Montana *A*
Western Montana College of The
    University of Montana *B*

Nebraska
Creighton University *B*
Hastings College *B*

New Hampshire
Antioch New England Graduate
    School *M*

New York
Audrey Cohen College *B*
City University of New York
    Baruch College *B*

North Carolina
Elon College *B*

North Dakota
University of Mary *B*

Ohio
College of Mount St. Joseph *B*
Marietta College *B*
University of Akron *B*

Oklahoma
University of Central Oklahoma *B*

Oregon
Marylhurst University *B, M*

Pennsylvania
Chestnut Hill College *B*
Grove City College *B*
King's College *B*
La Salle University *B*
Marywood University *C*
Thiel College *B*

Puerto Rico
Pontifical Catholic University of Puerto
    Rico *B*

South Dakota
Augustana College *B*

Tennessee
Christian Brothers University *B*
David Lipscomb University *B*

Texas
Houston Community College System *C*
Lubbock Christian University *B*
Southwestern Adventist University *B*

Virginia
Dabney S. Lancaster Community
    College *A*

Wisconsin
Madison Area Technical College *C, A*

Business computer facilities operation

California
Barstow College *C, A*
Chaffey Community College *C*
College of San Mateo *C, A*
College of the Desert *C, A*
Compton Community College *A*
Diablo Valley College *A*
Los Angeles Trade and Technical
    College *C, A*
Los Angeles Valley College *A*
MiraCosta College *C, A*
Mission College *A*
Pasadena City College *A*
Shasta College *A*
Victor Valley College *A*
West Hills Community College *A*
Yuba College *C*

Colorado
Colorado Mountain College
    Alpine Campus *C, A*
    Spring Valley Campus *C, A*
    Timberline Campus *C*
Otero Junior College *C, A*

Florida
New England Institute of Technology *A*

Georgia
Abraham Baldwin Agricultural
    College *A*
Chattahoochee Technical Institute *C*
Darton College *A*
South Georgia College *C, A*

Illinois
Black Hawk College *C*
Eastern Illinois University *B*
MacCormac College *C, A*
Parkland College *C*
Prairie State College *C*
Triton College *C*

Iowa
Indian Hills Community College *C*
Kirkwood Community College *C*
Western Iowa Tech Community
    College *C, A*

Kansas
Johnson County Community College *A*
Pratt Community College *A*

Kentucky
Paducah Community College *A*

Massachusetts
Bunker Hill Community College *A*

Michigan
Bay de Noc Community College *C*
Lake Superior State University *A*
Monroe County Community College *C*

Minnesota
Dakota County Technical College *C, A*
St. Cloud Technical College *C, A*
St. Paul Technical College *C, A*
Winona State University *B*

Missouri
Central Missouri State University *B*
Penn Valley Community College *C, A*
St. Louis Community College
    St. Louis Community College at
        Florissant Valley *A*

Nebraska
Lincoln School of Commerce *C*
Mid Plains Community College
    Area *C, A*

New Hampshire
New Hampshire Community Technical
    College
    Claremont *A*
    Nashua *A*

New Jersey
Camden County College *C*
Mercer County Community College *C*

New Mexico
New Mexico Junior College *C, A*

New York
City University of New York
    Borough of Manhattan Community
        College *A*
    La Guardia Community College *A*
    Lehman College *C*
    Queensborough Community
        College *A*

North Carolina
Piedmont Community College *C*
Wake Technical Community College *A*

Ohio
Kent State University
    Trumbull Campus *A*

Oklahoma
Eastern Oklahoma State College *A*

Pennsylvania
Community College of Beaver County *A*
Community College of Philadelphia *C*
Delaware County Community College *A*
Immaculata College *C*
Laurel Business Institute *A*
Mercyhurst College *C*
Peirce College *C, A, B*
Pennsylvania College of Technology *C*

Puerto Rico
Pontifical Catholic University of Puerto
    Rico *B*

Tennessee
Hiwassee College *A*
Knoxville Business College *A*

Texas
Del Mar College *C, A*
El Paso Community College *C*
Midland College *C, A*
Southwest Texas State University *B*
Texas State Technical College
    Sweetwater *C*

Utah
LDS Business College *C*
Salt Lake Community College *C, A*
Southern Utah University *A*

Vermont
Champlain College *A, B*
College of St. Joseph in Vermont *B*

Virginia
ECPI College of Technology *C, A*
J. Sargeant Reynolds Community
    College *C*

Washington
Clark College *A*
Renton Technical College *C, A*
Yakima Valley Community College *C*

Wisconsin
Moraine Park Technical College *C*

Business computer programming

Alabama
Enterprise State Junior College *A*
George C. Wallace State Community
    College
    Selma *A*
Northwest-Shoals Community
    College *C, A*
Sparks State Technical College *A*

Alaska
University of Alaska
    Anchorage *A*

Arizona
Central Arizona College *A*
DeVry Institute of Technology
    Phoenix *B*
Gateway Community College *C*
Mesa Community College *A*

Arkansas
Garland County Community
    College *C, A*
Henderson State University *B*
Southern Arkansas University
    Tech *A*

California
Bakersfield College *A*
Barstow College *A*
Butte College *C, A*
Canada College *A*
Cerritos Community College *A*
Chabot College *A*
Chaffey Community College *C, A*
City College of San Francisco *A*
College of the Siskiyous *C, A*
Compton Community College *A*
Contra Costa College *A*
De Anza College *C, A*
DeVry Institute of Technology
    Fremont *B*
    Long Beach *B*
    Pomona *B*
    West Hills *B*
Diablo Valley College *A*
Evergreen Valley College *A*
Grossmont Community College *C, A*
Irvine Valley College *C, A*
Los Angeles Harbor College *C, A*
Los Angeles Pierce College *C, A*
Los Angeles Southwest College *A*
Los Angeles Valley College *C, A*
Merced College *A*
Mission College *A*
Moorpark College *A*
Mount San Antonio College *C*
Pasadena City College *A*
Saddleback College *C*
San Diego City College *C, A*
Shasta College *A*
Ventura College *A*
Victor Valley College *A*
West Hills Community College *A*

Colorado
Denver Technical College: A Division of
    DeVry University *A*

Connecticut
Norwalk Community-Technical
    College *A*
Sacred Heart University *M*
Three Rivers Community-Technical
    College *A*
Tunxis Community College *C, A*

Florida
Edison Community College *C*
Gulf Coast Community College *A*

Indian River Community College *A*
Miami-Dade Community College *A*
Palm Beach Community College *A*
Pasco-Hernando Community College *A*
Seminole Community College *A*
Valencia Community College *A*

Georgia
Abraham Baldwin Agricultural
 College *A*
Atlanta Metropolitan College *A*
Chattahoochee Technical Institute *C, A*
Dalton State College *C, A*
Darton College *A*
Georgia College and State University *B*
Macon State College *A*
South Georgia College *A*

Idaho
Idaho State University *C, A*
North Idaho College *A*

Illinois
Black Hawk College *A*
City Colleges of Chicago
 Wright College *C, A*
College of DuPage *C, A*
College of Lake County *A*
Elgin Community College *A*
Kankakee Community College *A*
Kaskaskia College *A*
Kishwaukee College *A*
McHenry County College *C, A*
Moraine Valley Community
 College *C, A*
National-Louis University *C*
Northwestern Business College *A*
Parkland College *A*
Prairie State College *C, A*
Robert Morris College: Chicago *C, A*
Southern Illinois University
 Carbondale *A, B*
Southwestern Ilinois College *C, A*
Triton College *C, A*
Waubonsee Community College *C, A*
William Rainey Harper College *C, A*

Indiana
Indiana Wesleyan University *A, B*
Purdue University
 North Central Campus *A*

Iowa
Des Moines Area Community College *A*
Indian Hills Community College *A*
Kirkwood Community College *A*
Luther College *B*
Marycrest International University *B*
Northeast Iowa Community College *A*
Scott Community College *A*
Southeastern Community College
 North Campus *C*
 South Campus *C*
Southwestern Community College *A*
Western Iowa Tech Community
 College *A*

Kansas
Barton County Community College *C, A*
Central Christian College *A*
Johnson County Community
 College *C, A*
Kansas City Kansas Community
 College *C, A*
Seward County Community
 College *C, A*

Kentucky
Paducah Community College *A*

Louisiana
Southern University
 New Orleans *A*
 Shreveport *A*

Maine
Husson College *B*

Maryland
Community College of Baltimore County
 Catonsville *C, A*
Harford Community College *C*
Montgomery College
 Germantown Campus *A*
 Takoma Park Campus *A*

Massachusetts
Bay Path College *B*
Cape Cod Community College *A*
North Shore Community College *C*
Roxbury Community College *A*

Michigan
Baker College
 of Cadillac *A*
 of Muskegon *A, B*
 of Port Huron *A*
Cleary College *A, B*
Grand Rapids Community College *A*
Lansing Community College *A*
Macomb Community College *C, A*
Mid Michigan Community College *A*
Monroe County Community
 College *C, A*
Mott Community College *C*
North Central Michigan College *A*
Washtenaw Community College *A*

Minnesota
Alexandria Technical College *A*
Dakota County Technical College *C, A*
NEI College of Technology *A*
St. Cloud Technical College *C, A*
St. Paul Technical College *C, A*
Winona State University *B*

Mississippi
Copiah-Lincoln Community College *A*
East Central Community College *A*
Northwest Mississippi Community
 College *A*

Missouri
East Central College *A*
Longview Community College *C, A*
Maple Woods Community College *C, A*
Southwest Missouri State University
 West Plains Campus *A*
St. Louis Community College
 St. Louis Community College at
 Florissant Valley *A*
 St. Louis Community College at
 Meramec *C, A*

Montana
Montana Tech of the University of
 Montana *B*

Nebraska
Lincoln School of Commerce *A*
Mid Plains Community College Area *C*

New Hampshire
Antioch New England Graduate
 School *M*
Hesser College *A*
New Hampshire Community Technical
 College
 Nashua *A*

New Jersey
Bergen Community College *A*
Burlington County College *C*
Camden County College *C*
DeVry Institute *A*
Middlesex County College *C*
Passaic County Community
 College *C, A*

New Mexico
New Mexico Junior College *A*
Northern New Mexico Community
 College *C*

New York
Columbia-Greene Community
 College *C, A*
Fulton-Montgomery Community
 College *A*
State University of New York
 College of Agriculture and
 Technology at Cobleskill *A*
 College of Agriculture and
 Technology at Morrisville *A*
Westchester Business Institute *C, A*

North Carolina
Alamance Community College *A*
Asheville Buncombe Technical
 Community College *A*
Beaufort County Community College *A*
Brunswick Community College *C, A*
Caldwell Community College and
 Technical Institute *C, A*
Campbell University *A*
Central Carolina Community College *A*
Coastal Carolina Community College *A*
College of the Albemarle *A*
Craven Community College *A*
Davidson County Community College *C*
Durham Technical Community
 College *C, A*
Edgecombe Community College *A*
Fayetteville Technical Community
 College *A*
Forsyth Technical Community College *A*
Gaston College *A*
Guilford Technical Community
 College *A*
Haywood Community College *C, A*
Mitchell Community College *A*
Piedmont Community College *A*
Pitt Community College *A*
Roanoke-Chowan Community
 College *C, A*
Sampson Community College *A*
Sandhills Community College *A*
South Piedmont Community
 College *A*
Surry Community College *C, A*
Wake Technical Community
 College *C, A*
Wilkes Community College *C, A*
Wilson Technical Community College *A*

North Dakota
North Dakota State College of Science *A*

Ohio
Cincinnati State Technical and
 Community College *A*
DeVry Institute of Technology
 Columbus *B*
Kent State University
 Stark Campus *B*
 Trumbull Campus *A*
Kent State University *C, B*
Lorain County Community College *A*
Marion Technical College *C, A*
Miami University
 Middletown Campus *C, A*
Miami-Jacobs College *C, A*
North Central State College *A*
Northwestern College *A*
Owens Community College
 Findlay Campus *A*
Southern State Community College *A*
University of Akron
 Wayne College *A*
University of Akron *A*
University of Cincinnati
 Raymond Walters College *A*

Oklahoma
Oklahoma Baptist University *B*
Oklahoma State University
 Oklahoma City *A*
St. Gregory's University *A*
Tulsa Community College *A*

Oregon
Chemeketa Community College *A*
Linn-Benton Community College *A*
Portland Community College *A*

Pennsylvania
Community College of Beaver County *A*
Community College of Philadelphia *A*
Delaware County Community College *A*
Grove City College *B*
Manor College *A*
Mount Aloysius College *A*
Pennsylvania College of Technology *A*
York College of Pennsylvania *A, B*

Puerto Rico
Colegio Universitario del Este *A*
ICPR Junior College *A*
University of Puerto Rico
 Aguadilla *A*

South Carolina
Greenville Technical College *A*
York Technical College *A*

South Dakota
Southeast Technical Institute *A*

Tennessee
Pellissippi State Technical Community
 College *A*

Texas
Eastfield College *A*
Hill College *A*
Richland College *A*
Texas State Technical College
 Harlingen *A*
Tyler Junior College *A*

Utah
LDS Business College *A*
Mountain West College *C, A*
Southern Utah University *A*

Vermont
Champlain College *A, B*

Virginia
ECPI College of Technology *C, A*

Washington
Peninsula College *A*
Renton Technical College *C, A*
Skagit Valley College *A*
South Puget Sound Community
 College *C, A*
Spokane Community College *C, A*
Spokane Falls Community College *C*

West Virginia
Davis and Elkins College *B*
Potomac State College of West Virginia
 University *A*

Wisconsin
Chippewa Valley Technical College *A*
Gateway Technical College *A*
Milwaukee School of Engineering *B*
Moraine Park Technical College *A*
St. Norbert College *B*

Business economics

Alabama
Alabama Agricultural and Mechanical
 University *B*
Alabama State University *B*
Auburn University at Montgomery *B*
Auburn University *B, M, D*
Jacksonville State University *B*
Talladega College *B*
Troy State University *B*
University of Alabama
 Birmingham *B*
University of Alabama *B, M, D*
University of Mobile *B*
University of North Alabama *B*
University of South Alabama *B*

Alaska
University of Alaska
 Fairbanks *B*

Business economics

Arizona
Northern Arizona University *B*
University of Arizona *B*

Arkansas
Arkansas State University *B*
Arkansas Tech University *B*
Hendrix College *B*
University of Arkansas
    Little Rock *B*
University of Arkansas *B*
University of Central Arkansas *B*

California
Barstow College *A*
California Lutheran University *B*
California Polytechnic State University:
    San Luis Obispo *B, M*
California State University
    Fullerton *B*
    Hayward *B, M*
    Long Beach *B*
    Northridge *B*
Chapman University *B*
Claremont McKenna College *B*
College of the Desert *A*
College of the Redwoods *A*
East Los Angeles College *A*
Mills College *B*
San Joaquin Delta College *A*
University of California
    Los Angeles *B*
    Riverside *B*
    Santa Barbara *B*
    Santa Cruz *B*
University of La Verne *B*
University of San Diego *B*
Ventura College *A*

Connecticut
Albertus Magnus College *B*
Quinnipiac University *B*
Southern Connecticut State University *B*
University of Bridgeport *B*
University of New Haven *B*

Delaware
University of Delaware *M, D*

Florida
Barry University *B*
Florida Agricultural and Mechanical
    University *B*
Jacksonville University *B*
Stetson University *B*
University of Central Florida *B, M*
University of North Florida *B*
University of South Florida *B, M*
University of Tampa *B*
Valencia Community College *A*

Georgia
Clark Atlanta University *B*
Columbus State University *B, M*
Georgia College and State University *B*
Georgia Institute of Technology *B, M, D*
Georgia Southern University *B*
Georgia State University *M*
Kennesaw State University *B, M*
Mercer University *B*
Morehouse College *B*
Morris Brown College *B*
Oglethorpe University *B*
South Georgia College *A*
State University of West Georgia *B*
University of Georgia *B, M, D*
Valdosta State University *B*

Hawaii
Hawaii Pacific University *A, B*

Idaho
Boise State University *B*

Illinois
Barat College *B*
Benedictine University *B*
Bradley University *B*
De Paul University *B, M*
Loyola University of Chicago *B*
Millikin University *B*
Northwestern University *D*
Rockford College *B*
Roosevelt University *B*
Southern Illinois University
    Carbondale *B*
    Edwardsville *B*
University of Chicago *M, D*
Western Illinois University *B*
Wheaton College *B*

Indiana
Anderson University *B*
Indiana University
    Southeast *B*
Indiana University--Purdue University
    Indiana University-Purdue
        University Fort Wayne *B*
Indiana Wesleyan University *B*
Taylor University *B*
University of Evansville *B*
University of Indianapolis *B*

Iowa
Buena Vista University *B*
Luther College *B*
Morningside College *B*
North Iowa Area Community
    College *C, A*
Northwestern College *B*
Simpson College *B*
University of Iowa *B*

Kansas
Bethany College *B*
Central Christian College *A, B*
Seward County Community College *A*
Washburn University of Topeka *B*

Kentucky
Bellarmine College *B*
Eastern Kentucky University *B*
Kentucky State University *B*
Midway College *B*
Morehead State University *B*
Murray State University *B*
National Business College *A*
Thomas More College *A, B*
University of Kentucky *B*
University of Louisville *B*
Western Kentucky University *B*

Louisiana
Dillard University *B*
Louisiana State University
    Shreveport *B*
Louisiana State University and
    Agricultural and Mechanical
    College *B*
Louisiana Tech University *B*
Loyola University New Orleans *B*
Nicholls State University *B*
Southern University
    New Orleans *B*
Southern University and Agricultural and
    Mechanical College *B*
University of Louisiana at Lafayette *B*
University of Louisiana at Monroe *B*
University of New Orleans *B, M, D*
Xavier University of Louisiana *B*

Maine
Husson College *B*
St. Joseph's College *B*
University of Maine
    Farmington *B*
University of Maine *B*

Maryland
Allegany College *C, A*

Massachusetts
American International College *B*
Assumption College *B*
Babson College *B*
Bay Path College *B*
Bentley College *B*
Nichols College *B*
Stonehill College *B*
Suffolk University *M*

Michigan
Andrews University *B, M*
Eastern Michigan University *B*
Lake Superior State University *B*
Michigan Technological University *B, M*
Northwood University *B*
Olivet College *B*
Saginaw Valley State University *B, M*
Spring Arbor College *B*
University of Detroit Mercy *B, M*
Western Michigan University *B*

Minnesota
Winona State University *B*

Mississippi
Jackson State University *B*
University of Mississippi *B, M, D*
University of Southern Mississippi *B*

Missouri
Fontbonne College *B*
Lincoln University *B*
Northwest Missouri State University *B*
Park University *B*
St. Louis University *B, D*
Southeast Missouri State University *B*
University of Missouri
    St. Louis *C*
Washington University *B*

Montana
Carroll College *B*
Montana State University
    Billings *B*
Rocky Mountain College *B*

Nebraska
Hastings College *B*
University of Nebraska
    Lincoln *B*
    Omaha *B*

Nevada
University of Nevada
    Las Vegas *B, M*
    Reno *B, M*

New Hampshire
New Hampshire College *B*
Plymouth State College of the University
    System of New Hampshire *B*

New Jersey
Bloomfield College *B*
Fairleigh Dickinson University *B, M*
Monmouth University *B*
Rider University *B*
St. Peter's College *B*
Seton Hall University *B*
William Paterson University of New
    Jersey *B*

New Mexico
Eastern New Mexico University *B*
New Mexico State University *B, M*
Western New Mexico University *B*

New York
Audrey Cohen College *B*
Canisius College *B*
City University of New York
    Baruch College *B*
    Brooklyn College *B*
Elmira College *B*
Fordham University *B, M*
Ithaca College *B*
Manhattan College *B*
Mohawk Valley Community
    College *C, A*
New York University *B, M, D*
Pace University:
    Pleasantville/Briarcliff *B, M, D*
Pace University *B, M, D*
Siena College *B, T*
State University of New York
    Buffalo *D*
    College at Oneonta *B, M*
    College at Potsdam *B*
    College of Technology at Canton *A*
Touro College *B*
Union College *B*
Utica College of Syracuse University *B*
Wagner College *B*

North Carolina
Appalachian State University *B*
Greensboro College *B*
Lenoir-Rhyne College *B*
Meredith College *B*
North Carolina Agricultural and
    Technical State University *B*
North Carolina State University *B*
University of North Carolina
    Charlotte *B, M*
    Wilmington *B*
Western Carolina University *B*
Winston-Salem State University *B*

North Dakota
Dickinson State University *A*

Ohio
Bowling Green State University *B*
Cleveland State University *B*
College of Wooster *B*
David N. Myers College *B*
Kent State University *B, M*
Miami University
    Oxford Campus *B*
Muskingum College *B*
Notre Dame College of Ohio *B*
Ohio State University
    Columbus Campus *B*
Ohio University *B*
Ohio Wesleyan University *B*
Otterbein College *B*
Tiffin University *B*
University of Akron *B, M*
University of Cincinnati
    Raymond Walters College *A*
Wilberforce University *B*
Wittenberg University *B*
Wright State University *B, M*
Xavier University *B, M*

Oklahoma
East Central University *B*
Oklahoma City University *B, M*
Oklahoma State University *B*
Tulsa Community College *A*
University of Central Oklahoma *B*
University of Oklahoma *B*

Oregon
Eastern Oregon University *B*
George Fox University *B*

Pennsylvania
Bloomsburg University of
    Pennsylvania *B*
California University of Pennsylvania *B*
Carnegie Mellon University *B*
Clarion University of Pennsylvania *B*
Drexel University *B*
Grove City College *B*
Kutztown University of Pennsylvania *B*
La Salle University *B*
Lehigh University *B, M, D*
Messiah College *B*
Penn State
    Erie, The Behrend College *B*
    University Park *C, B*
Robert Morris College *B*
Rosemont College *B*
Seton Hill College *B*
University of Pittsburgh
    Johnstown *B*
Ursinus College *B*
Villanova University *B*

West Chester University of
  Pennsylvania B, M
Westminster College B
Widener University B
York College of Pennsylvania B

Puerto Rico

Inter American University of Puerto Rico
  Bayamon Campus B
Pontifical Catholic University of Puerto
  Rico B
Universidad Metropolitana B
University of Puerto Rico
  Bayamon University College A, B
  Mayaguez Campus B
  Rio Piedras Campus B, M

Rhode Island

Brown University B, M
Providence College B
Rhode Island College B
Salve Regina University M

South Carolina

Francis Marion University B
South Carolina State University B
University of South Carolina
  Aiken B
University of South Carolina B
Wofford College B

Tennessee

Belmont University B
Carson-Newman College B
David Lipscomb University B
East Tennessee State University B
Freed-Hardeman University B
Lincoln Memorial University B
Middle Tennessee State University B
Tennessee State University B
Tennessee Technological University B
University of Memphis B
University of Tennessee
  Knoxville M, D
  Martin B

Texas

Baylor University B, M
Dallas Baptist University B
Houston Baptist University B
Lamar University B
McMurry University B
Midland College A
Sam Houston State University B
Southwest Texas State University B
Stephen F. Austin State University B
Texas A&M International University B
Texas A&M University
  Commerce B
  Kingsville B
Tyler Junior College A
University of Mary Hardin-Baylor B
University of North Texas B
University of Texas
  Arlington B, D
  Dallas M, D
  El Paso B, M
  Pan American B
  San Antonio B, M
  Tyler B
West Texas A&M University B

Utah

Snow College C, A
Utah State University M, D
Weber State University B
Westminster College B

Virginia

Bridgewater College B
Christopher Newport University B
Hampden-Sydney College B
James Madison University B
Mary Baldwin College B
Old Dominion University B
Randolph-Macon College B
Southwest Virginia Community
  College A

Virginia Commonwealth
  University B, M
Virginia Polytechnic Institute and State
  University B
Virginia State University B, M
Wytheville Community College A

Washington

Gonzaga University B
Seattle Pacific University B, T
Seattle University B
Washington State University B

West Virginia

Concord College B
Marshall University B
Potomac State College of West Virginia
  University A
West Liberty State College B
West Virginia University B, M, D

Wisconsin

Beloit College B
Marquette University B
Mount Senario College B
University of Wisconsin
  Superior B
  Whitewater B

Wyoming

Northwest College A
University of Wyoming B, M, D

Business education

Alabama

Alabama Agricultural and Mechanical
  University B, M
Chattahoochee Valley Community
  College A
James H. Faulkner State Community
  College A
Lawson State Community College A
Oakwood College B

Arizona

Arizona State University B, T
Eastern Arizona College A
Northern Arizona University T

Arkansas

Arkansas State University B, M, T
Arkansas Tech University B
Henderson State University B, T
Ouachita Baptist University B, T
Philander Smith College B
Southern Arkansas University B, T
University of Arkansas
  Monticello B
  Pine Bluff B, T
University of Central Arkansas M, T
University of the Ozarks B, T

California

Azusa Pacific University B, T
California Baptist University B, T
California State University
  Bakersfield B, T
  Chico T
  Dominguez Hills T
  Fullerton T
  Northridge B, T
Fresno Pacific University T
Humboldt State University T
Merritt College C, A
Mount St. Mary's College T
Pacific Union College B, T
San Jose State University T

Colorado

Adams State College B, T
Colorado Mountain College
  Alpine Campus A
Colorado State University T
Fort Lewis College T

Connecticut

Central Connecticut State
  University B, M
Sacred Heart University B, M, T

Delaware

Delaware State University B

District of Columbia

University of the District of Columbia B

Florida

Bethune-Cookman College B, T
Florida Agricultural and Mechanical
  University B, M
Gulf Coast Community College A
Manatee Community College A
Palm Beach Community College A
University of Central Florida B, M
University of South Florida B, M

Georgia

Albany State University M
Armstrong Atlantic State University B, T
Atlanta Christian College A, B
Atlanta Metropolitan College A
Brewton-Parker College A, B
Darton College A
East Georgia College A
Gainesville College A
Georgia Southern University B, M, T
Georgia Southwestern State
  University B, M
Middle Georgia College A
South Georgia College A
State University of West Georgia B, M
University of Georgia B, M, T
Valdosta State University B, M

Hawaii

Brigham Young University
  Hawaii B, T
University of Hawaii
  Manoa T

Idaho

Boise State University B
College of Southern Idaho A
North Idaho College A
Ricks College A
University of Idaho B, M, T

Illinois

Chicago State University B
Eastern Illinois University B, T
Illinois State University B, T
John A. Logan College A
McKendree College B, T
National-Louis University C
Parkland College A
Southern Illinois University
  Carbondale B
Trinity Christian College B, T
University of Illinois
  Urbana-Champaign B

Indiana

Ball State University B, M, T
Bethel College B
Grace College B
Indiana State University B, M, T
Indiana Wesleyan University B
Oakland City University B
Saint Mary's College T
University of Indianapolis B, T
University of St. Francis B
University of Southern Indiana B, T
Vincennes University A

Iowa

Buena Vista University B, T
Central College T
Dordt College B
Drake University M
Grand View College B, T
Morningside College B
Mount Mercy College T
Northwestern College T

St. Ambrose University B, T
University of Northern Iowa B, M

Kansas

Baker University T
Bethany College B
Butler County Community College A
Central Christian College A
Colby Community College A
Emporia State University B, M, T
Fort Hays State University B, T
Garden City Community College A
McPherson College B, T
MidAmerica Nazarene University B, T
Tabor College B, T
Washburn University of Topeka B

Kentucky

Cumberland College B, T
Eastern Kentucky University B
Morehead State University B
Murray State University B, T
Northern Kentucky University B, T
Spalding University B
Thomas More College B
Union College B
Western Kentucky University B, M

Louisiana

McNeese State University T
Nicholls State University B
Northwestern State University B, M, T
Our Lady of Holy Cross College B
Southern University and Agricultural and
  Mechanical College B

Maine

Husson College B, T
Thomas College B
University of Maine
  Machias B

Maryland

Frostburg State University B, T
Montgomery College
  Germantown Campus A
  Rockville Campus A
Morgan State University B, M
Prince George's Community College A
University of Maryland
  Eastern Shore B

Massachusetts

American International College T
Bristol Community College A
Holyoke Community College A
Northern Essex Community College A
Salem State College B
Suffolk University B, M, T
University of Massachusetts
  Dartmouth T
Westfield State College B, T

Michigan

Central Michigan University B, M
Cornerstone College and Grand Rapids
  Baptist Seminary B, T
Eastern Michigan University B, M
Ferris State University B
Northern Michigan University B, T
Siena Heights University B, T
University of Michigan
  Dearborn B
Western Michigan University B

Minnesota

College of St. Catherine: St. Paul
  Campus B
Concordia College: Moorhead B
Minnesota State University,
  Mankato M, T
Northland Community & Technical
  College A
Ridgewater College: A Community and
  Technical College A
University of Minnesota
  Twin Cities B, M, T
Winona State University B, M, T

Business education

Mississippi
Blue Mountain College B
Coahoma Community College A
Delta State University B
Hinds Community College A
Jackson State University B
Mary Holmes College A
Mississippi College B, M
Mississippi Delta Community College A
Mississippi Gulf Coast Community College
    Jefferson Davis Campus A
    Perkinston A
Mississippi State University B, T
Northwest Mississippi Community College A
Rust College B
University of Mississippi T
University of Southern Mississippi B

Missouri
Avila College T
Central Missouri State University B, M, T
College of the Ozarks B, T
Columbia College T
Evangel University B
Hannibal-LaGrange College B
Lincoln University B, T
Lindenwood University B, M
Missouri Baptist College T
Missouri Southern State College B, T
Northwest Missouri State University B, M, T
Rockhurst University B
Southwest Baptist University T
Southwest Missouri State University B
University of Missouri
    St. Louis T

Montana
Miles Community College A
Montana State University
    Billings B, T
University of Montana-Missoula T
Western Montana College of The University of Montana B, T

Nebraska
Chadron State College M
Concordia University T
Dana College B
Doane College B
Hastings College B, M, T
Mid Plains Community College Area A
Midland Lutheran College B, T
Northeast Community College A
Union College T
University of Nebraska
    Kearney B, M, T
    Lincoln B, T
    Omaha B, T

Nevada
University of Nevada
    Reno B

New Jersey
Monmouth University T
Montclair State University B, M, T
Rider University B, T
Rowan University C
St. Peter's College T

New Mexico
Eastern New Mexico University B
University of New Mexico B
Western New Mexico University B

New York
Alfred University M, T
Canisius College B, M, T
City University of New York
    Lehman College B, M, T
Concordia College B, T
D'Youville College B, M, T
Dowling College B
Fulton-Montgomery Community College A
Hofstra University B, T
Le Moyne College T
Long Island University
    Brooklyn Campus B, M, T
Nazareth College of Rochester B, M, T
New York Institute of Technology B, T
New York University M, D
Niagara University B, T
Pace University:
    Pleasantville/Briarcliff B, M, T
Pace University B, M, T
St. Bonaventure University T
St. Francis College B, T
Siena College T
State University of New York
    College at Buffalo B, M, T
    College at Oneonta B, T
    Oswego B, T
Utica College of Syracuse University B

North Carolina
Appalachian State University B, M, T
Cleveland Community College A
East Carolina University B
Elizabeth City State University B, T
Fayetteville State University B, T
Lenoir-Rhyne College B, T
Meredith College T
North Carolina Agricultural and Technical State University B
North Carolina Central University M
St. Augustine's College B, T
Sandhills Community College A
University of North Carolina
    Greensboro M, T
Winston-Salem State University B

North Dakota
Dickinson State University B, T
Mayville State University B, T
Minot State University: Bottineau Campus A
Minot State University B, T
University of North Dakota B, M, T
Valley City State University B, T

Ohio
Ashland University B, M, T
Baldwin-Wallace College T
Bluffton College B
Bowling Green State University B, M
Capital University T
College of Mount St. Joseph T
Defiance College B, T
Kent State University
    Stark Campus B
Kent State University B, M
Mount Union College T
Mount Vernon Nazarene College B, T
Ohio University B, T
University of Akron M
University of Findlay B, T
University of Rio Grande B, T
University of Toledo B, M, T
Walsh University B
Wilmington College B
Wright State University B, M, T
Xavier University M, T
Youngstown State University B, M

Oklahoma
East Central University B
Eastern Oklahoma State College A
Langston University B
Northeastern Oklahoma Agricultural and Mechanical College A
Northwestern Oklahoma State University B, T
Oklahoma Christian University of Science and Arts B, T
Oklahoma City University B
Oklahoma Panhandle State University B
Oral Roberts University B, T
Southeastern Oklahoma State University B, T
Southern Nazarene University B
Southwestern Oklahoma State University T
University of Central Oklahoma B

Oregon
Portland State University T
Western Baptist College B

Pennsylvania
Bloomsburg University of Pennsylvania B, M, T
Community College of Philadelphia A
Delaware Valley College T
Geneva College B, T
Gwynedd-Mercy College B, T
Indiana University of Pennsylvania B, M, T
Mercyhurst College T
Reading Area Community College A
Robert Morris College B, M
St. Joseph's University B, M
Shippensburg University of Pennsylvania B, T
Temple University B, T

Puerto Rico
American University of Puerto Rico B, T
Caribbean University B, T
Inter American University of Puerto Rico
    Metropolitan Campus M
    San German Campus M
Pontifical Catholic University of Puerto Rico B, T
University of Puerto Rico
    Mayaguez Campus T

Rhode Island
Johnson & Wales University T

South Carolina
South Carolina State University B, T
University of South Carolina M
Winthrop University B, M, T

South Dakota
Black Hills State University B
Dakota State University B, T
Dakota Wesleyan University B, T
Northern State University M, T

Tennessee
Lee University B
Lincoln Memorial University B, T
Middle Tennessee State University B, M, T
Union University B, T
University of Tennessee
    Knoxville B, T
    Martin B, T

Texas
Abilene Christian University B, T
Baylor University B, T
East Texas Baptist University B
Houston Baptist University T
Howard Payne University T
Lamar University T
LeTourneau University B
Lubbock Christian University B
McMurry University T
St. Mary's University B, T
Southwest Texas State University T
Southwestern Adventist University B
Tarleton State University B, T
Texas A&M International University T
Texas A&M University
    Commerce T
    Corpus Christi T
    Kingsville T
Texas Christian University T
Texas Lutheran University T
Texas Tech University M
Texas Wesleyan University B, T
University of Mary Hardin-Baylor T
University of North Texas M, T
Wayland Baptist University T
West Texas A&M University T

Utah
Snow College C, A
Southern Utah University T
Utah State University B, M, D
Weber State University B

Virginia
Bluefield College B
James Madison University B, T
Norfolk State University B, T
Old Dominion University M
St. Paul's College B
University of Virginia's College at Wise T
Virginia Intermont College B, T
Virginia State University B

Washington
Central Washington University B, M, T
Eastern Washington University B, M, T
North Seattle Community College C, A
Renton Technical College C, A
Walla Walla College B

West Virginia
Concord College B, T
Fairmont State College B
Glenville State College B
Shepherd College T

Wisconsin
Concordia University Wisconsin B, T
Lakeland College B
Marian College of Fond du Lac T
Mount Mary College B, T
Northland College T
University of Wisconsin
    Superior B, T
    Whitewater B, T

Wyoming
Central Wyoming College A
Eastern Wyoming College A
University of Wyoming B

Business marketing/marketing management

Alabama
Alabama Agricultural and Mechanical University B
Alabama State University B
Auburn University at Montgomery B
Auburn University B
Birmingham-Southern College B
Faulkner University B
Huntingdon College B
Jacksonville State University B
Spring Hill College B
University of Alabama
    Birmingham B
    Huntsville B
University of Alabama B
University of Mobile B
University of North Alabama B
University of South Alabama B

Alaska
University of Alaska
    Anchorage B

Arizona
Arizona Western College C, A
Grand Canyon University B
Mesa Community College A
Phoenix College C, A
University of Arizona B
University of Phoenix C, B

Arkansas
Arkansas State University B
Harding University B
University of Arkansas
    Little Rock B

University of Arkansas B
University of the Ozarks B

California
Armstrong University B, M
Butte College C, A
California College for Health
  Sciences A, B
California State University
  Chico B
  Fresno B
  Fullerton B, M
City College of San Francisco A
Compton Community College C
Concordia University B
Crafton Hills College C
De Anza College C, A
Fashion Institute of Design and
  Merchandising A
Golden Gate University B, M
Lake Tahoe Community College C, A
Modesto Junior College A
National University M
Pacific Union College B
Saddleback College C, A
San Diego Miramar College A
San Diego State University B, M
Santa Barbara City College C, A
University of La Verne B
University of San Francisco B
Ventura College A
Yuba College C

Colorado
Aims Community College C, A
Arapahoe Community College C, A
Community College of Aurora A
Community College of Denver C, A
Metropolitan State College of Denver B
Pikes Peak Community College C
University of Colorado
  Boulder B, M
  Denver M

Connecticut
Central Connecticut State University B
Fairfield University B
Middlesex Community-Technical
  College A
Northwestern Connecticut
  Community-Technical College A
Norwalk Community-Technical
  College A
Quinnipiac University B, M
Sacred Heart University B
Southern Connecticut State University B
University of Bridgeport B
University of Connecticut B
University of New Haven B
Western Connecticut State University B

Delaware
Delaware State University B
Delaware Technical and Community
  College
    Owens Campus C, A
    Stanton/Wilmington Campus C, A
    Terry Campus C, A
Goldey-Beacom College B

District of Columbia
American University B, M
Georgetown University B

Florida
Barry University B
Brevard Community College A
Daytona Beach Community College A
Edison Community College C, A
Florida Atlantic University B
Florida International University B
Florida Metropolitan University
  Orlando College North A, B
Florida Southern College B
Florida State University B
Gulf Coast Community College A
Jacksonville University B, M

Northwood University
  Florida Campus B
Palm Beach Atlantic College B
Palm Beach Community College A
St. Petersburg Junior College A
Santa Fe Community College A
Seminole Community College C
South Florida Community College A
Stetson University B
University of Central Florida B
University of Florida B, M
University of Miami B
University of North Florida B
University of South Florida B
University of Tampa B
Valencia Community College A
Warner Southern College B

Georgia
Augusta State University B
Berry College B
Brenau University B
Brewton-Parker College B
Clayton College and State
  University C, A, B
Coastal Georgia Community
  College C, A
Columbus State University B
Dalton State College A
DeKalb Technical Institute A
Emory University B
Fort Valley State University B
Georgia College and State University B
Georgia Southern University B
Georgia State University B, M, D
Gwinnett Technical Institute C, A
Kennesaw State University B
Mercer University B, M
Middle Georgia College A
Morehouse College B
South Georgia College A
State University of West Georgia B
Thomas College B
University of Georgia B

Hawaii
Chaminade University of Honolulu A, B
Hawaii Pacific University B
University of Hawaii
  Hawaii Community College C, A
  Hilo B
  Manoa B
  West Oahu B

Idaho
Boise State University B
College of Southern Idaho A
Eastern Idaho Technical College C, A
Idaho State University C
Ricks College C, A
University of Idaho B

Illinois
Augustana College B
Barat College B
Benedictine University B, M
Bradley University B
Columbia College B
De Paul University M
Eastern Illinois University B
Elmhurst College B
Illinois State University B
John Wood Community College A
Loyola University of Chicago B
MacCormac College A
Millikin University B
Morton College A
North Central College B
North Park University B
Northern Illinois University B
Olivet Nazarene University B
Quincy University A, B
Rock Valley College C, A
Rockford College B
Roosevelt University B, M
St. Xavier University M

Sauk Valley Community College C, A
Southern Illinois University
  Carbondale B
Trinity Christian College B
Triton College C, A
University of Illinois
  Chicago B
Western Illinois University B
William Rainey Harper College C, A

Indiana
Anderson University B
Ball State University B
Franklin College B
Goshen College B
Indiana Institute of Technology B
Indiana State University B
Indiana University
  Kokomo B
  South Bend B
Indiana University--Purdue University
  Indiana University-Purdue
    University Fort Wayne B
Indiana Wesleyan University B
Marian College B
Purdue University
  North Central Campus A
Taylor University B
University of Evansville B
University of Notre Dame B
University of Southern Indiana B
Valparaiso University B

Iowa
Buena Vista University B
Clarke University B
Des Moines Area Community College A
Hawkeye Community College A
Iowa State University B
Kirkwood Community College A
Loras College B
Luther College B
Morningside College B
Northeast Iowa Community College A
Northwestern College B
St. Ambrose University B
Southwestern Community College A
University of Iowa B
University of Northern Iowa B
Wartburg College B

Kansas
Emporia State University B
Fort Hays State University B
Kansas City Kansas Community
  College A
Newman University B
Pittsburg State University M
Washburn University of Topeka B
Wichita State University B

Kentucky
Eastern Kentucky University B
Hazard Community College A
Kentucky State University B
Morehead State University B
Murray State University B
University of Kentucky B
University of Louisville B
Western Kentucky University B

Louisiana
Louisiana State University and
  Agricultural and Mechanical
    College B, M, D
Louisiana Tech University B
Loyola University New Orleans B
Nicholls State University B
Southeastern Louisiana University B
Southern University and Agricultural and
  Mechanical College B
University of Louisiana at Lafayette B
University of Louisiana at Monroe B
University of New Orleans B
Xavier University of Louisiana B

Maine
Husson College B
St. Joseph's College B
Thomas College B
University of Maine
  Machias B

Maryland
Charles County Community
  College C, A
Hagerstown Community College A
Morgan State University B
Prince George's Community
  College C, A
University of Maryland
  College Park B

Massachusetts
Assumption College B
Babson College B
Boston University B
Bridgewater State College B
Emerson College M
Endicott College B
Fitchburg State College B
Greenfield Community College C
Lasell College B
Massasoit Community College A
Newbury College A, B
Nichols College B
North Shore Community College A
Northeastern University A, B
Northern Essex Community College A
Springfield Technical Community
  College A
Suffolk University B, M
University of Massachusetts
  Amherst B
  Dartmouth B
Worcester Polytechnic Institute M

Michigan
Adrian College B
Baker College
  of Cadillac A
  of Muskegon A, B
  of Port Huron A, B
Central Michigan University B
Cleary College B
Davenport College of Business A, B
Delta College A
Detroit College of Business A, B
Eastern Michigan University B
Ferris State University C, B
Grand Rapids Community College A
Grand Valley State University B, M
Hillsdale College B
Kettering University B
Kirtland Community College A
Lansing Community College A
Michigan State University B, M, D
Mid Michigan Community College A
Muskegon Community College A
Oakland University B
Rochester College B
University of Detroit Mercy B
University of Michigan
  Flint B
Wayne State University B
West Shore Community College A
Western Michigan University B

Minnesota
Alexandria Technical College C, A
Anoka-Ramsey Community College A
Augsburg College B
Century Community and Technical
  College A
Mesabi Range Community and Technical
  College C, A
Minneapolis Community and Technical
  College C, A
Moorhead State University B
National American University
  St. Paul B
Northwestern College B

St. Cloud State University *B*
St. Mary's University of Minnesota *B*
University of Minnesota
  Twin Cities *B*
University of St. Thomas *B, M*
Winona State University *B*

Mississippi
Delta State University *B*
Mississippi College *B*
Mississippi Gulf Coast Community
  College
    Jackson County Campus *A*
    Perkinston *A*
Mississippi State University *B*
University of Mississippi *B*
University of Southern Mississippi *B*

Missouri
Central Missouri State University *B*
Maryville University of Saint Louis *B, M*
Missouri Baptist College *B*
Missouri Southern State College *B*
Missouri Western State College *B*
Rockhurst University *B*
St. Charles County Community
  College *A*
St. Louis University *B, M, D*
Southwest Missouri State University *B*
Three Rivers Community College *A*
University of Missouri
  St. Louis *C, B*

Montana
Flathead Valley Community College *A*
Montana State University
  Billings *B*
Montana Tech of the University of
  Montana *B*

Nebraska
Creighton University *B*
Hastings College *B*
Lincoln School of Commerce *A*
Southeast Community College
  Lincoln Campus *A*
University of Nebraska
  Lincoln *B*
  Omaha *B*

Nevada
University of Nevada
  Las Vegas *B*
  Reno *B*

New Hampshire
Franklin Pierce College *B*
Hesser College *A*
McIntosh College *A*
New Hampshire Community Technical
  College
    Manchester *C, A*
New Hampshire Technical Institute *A*
Plymouth State College of the University
  System of New Hampshire *B*
Rivier College *M*

New Jersey
Brookdale Community College *A*
Camden County College *A*
Cumberland County College *A*
Fairleigh Dickinson University *B*
Kean University *B*
Monmouth University *B*
Passaic County Community College *A*
Richard Stockton College of New
  Jersey *B*
Rowan University *B*

Rutgers
  The State University of New Jersey:
    Camden College of Arts and
    Sciences *B*
  The State University of New Jersey:
    Douglass College *B*
  The State University of New Jersey:
    Livingston College *B*
  The State University of New Jersey:
    Newark College of Arts and
    Sciences *B*
  The State University of New Jersey:
    Rutgers College *B*
  The State University of New Jersey:
    University College Camden *B*
  The State University of New Jersey:
    University College New
    Brunswick *B*
  The State University of New Jersey:
    University College Newark *B*
Seton Hall University *B*
The College of New Jersey *B*

New Mexico
College of the Southwest *B*
Eastern New Mexico University *B*
New Mexico State University *B*
Western New Mexico University *B*

New York
Adirondack Community College *A*
Broome Community College *A*
Bryant & Stratton Business Institute
  Syracuse *A*
City University of New York
  Kingsborough Community
    College *A*
  New York City Technical
    College *A*
  York College *B*
Clarkson University *B*
Dominican College of Blauvelt *B*
Dowling College *B*
Elmira College *B*
Five Towns College *A*
Herkimer County Community College *A*
Ithaca College *B*
Jamestown Business College *A*
Long Island University
  Brooklyn Campus *B*
  C. W. Post Campus *M*
  Southampton College *B*
Monroe Community College *A*
New York Institute of Technology *B, M*
Pace University:
  Pleasantville/Briarcliff *B, M*
Pace University *B, M*
Regents College *B*
Rochester Institute of
  Technology *A, B, M*
Sage Junior College of Albany *A*
St. John Fisher College *B*
St. Thomas Aquinas College *B, M*
Siena College *B, M, T*
State University of New York
  Albany *M*
  College at Old Westbury *B*
  College at Plattsburgh *B*
  College of Technology at Alfred *A*
Suffolk County Community
  College *C, A*
Touro College *B*
Westchester Community College *A*

North Carolina
East Carolina University *B*
Meredith College *B*
North Carolina Agricultural and
  Technical State University *B*
Southwestern Community College *A*
University of North Carolina
  Chapel Hill *D*
  Charlotte *B*
  Wilmington *B*
Western Carolina University *B*

North Dakota
Mayville State University *A*
Minot State University: Bottineau
  Campus *C, A*
University of North Dakota *B*
Williston State College *C, A*

Ohio
Ashland University *B*
Bowling Green State University
  Firelands College *C*
Cedarville University *B*
Cincinnati State Technical and
  Community College *A*
Cleveland State University *B, M*
David N. Myers College *B*
Defiance College *B*
Edison State Community College *A*
Franklin University *B*
Kent State University
  Stark Campus *B*
Kent State University *B, M, D*
Lima Technical College *A*
Marion Technical College *C, A*
Miami University
  Oxford Campus *B, M*
North Central State College *C*
Northwest State Community College *A*
Northwestern College *A*
Notre Dame College of Ohio *C, B*
Stark State College of Technology *A*
Terra Community College *A*
Tiffin University *B*
University of Akron
  Wayne College *A*
University of Akron *B, M*
University of Dayton *B*
University of Findlay *B*
University of Toledo *M*
Ursuline College *B*
Walsh University *A, B*
Washington State Community College *A*
Wright State University *B, M*
Xavier University *B, M*
Youngstown State University *A, B, M*

Oklahoma
Connors State College *A*
East Central University *B*
Northeastern State University *B*
Oklahoma Baptist University *B*
Oklahoma City University *B, M*
Oklahoma State University
  Oklahoma City *A*
Oklahoma State University *B, M, D*
Oral Roberts University *B*
Southern Nazarene University *B*
University of Central Oklahoma *B*
University of Oklahoma *B*
University of Tulsa *B*

Oregon
Oregon State University *B*
Southern Oregon University *B*
University of Portland *B*

Pennsylvania
Allentown College of St. Francis de
  Sales *B*
Beaver College *B*
Bucks County Community College *A*
California University of Pennsylvania *B*
Cedar Crest College *C*
Chestnut Hill College *B*
Clarion University of Pennsylvania *B*
College Misericordia *B*
Community College of Allegheny
  County *A*
Delaware County Community College *A*
Delaware Valley College *B*
Drexel University *B, M*
Duquesne University *B*
Gannon University *B*
Grove City College *B*
ICS Center for Degree Studies *A*
Immaculata College *A*

King's College *A, B*
Kutztown University of Pennsylvania *B*
La Salle University *B*
Lebanon Valley College of
  Pennsylvania *C*
Lehigh University *B*
Mansfield University of Pennsylvania *B*
Marywood University *B*
Mercyhurst College *B*
Messiah College *B*
Montgomery County Community
  College *A*
Neumann College *B*
Northampton County Area Community
  College *A*
Penn State
  Erie, The Behrend College *B*
  University Park *B*
Philadelphia University *B*
Robert Morris College *B, M*
St. Francis College *B*
St. Joseph's University *C, A, B, M*
Shippensburg University of
  Pennsylvania *B*
South Hills School of Business &
  Technology *A*
Susquehanna University *B*
Temple University *B, M, D*
University of Pennsylvania *A, B, M, D*
University of Pittsburgh *B*
University of Scranton *B*
Villanova University *B*
York College of Pennsylvania *B*

Puerto Rico
Bayamon Central University *B, M*
Colegio Universitario del Este *C, A, B*
ICPR Junior College *A*
Inter American University of Puerto Rico
  Aguadilla Campus *B*
  Metropolitan Campus *B, M*
Pontifical Catholic University of Puerto
  Rico *B*
Turabo University *B, M*
Universidad Metropolitana *A, B, M*
University of Puerto Rico
  Aguadilla *A, B*
  Bayamon University College *A, B*
  Ponce University College *B*
University of the Sacred Heart *M*

Rhode Island
Bryant College *B, M*
Community College of Rhode
  Island *C, A*
Johnson & Wales University *A, B, M*
University of Rhode Island *B*

South Carolina
Anderson College *B*
Central Carolina Technical College *A*
Charleston Southern University *B, M*
Coastal Carolina University *B*
Greenville Technical College *A*
University of South Carolina *B*

South Dakota
Black Hills State University *B*
Dakota State University *B*
Huron University *B*
Western Dakota Technical Institute *A*

Tennessee
Belmont University *B*
Christian Brothers University *B*
Freed-Hardeman University *B*
Lambuth University *B*
Middle Tennessee State University *B*
Southern Adventist University *B*
Trevecca Nazarene University *B*
University of Memphis *B*
University of Tennessee
  Martin *B*

Texas
Abilene Christian University *B*
Baylor University

Brazosport College C, A
Brookhaven College A
College of the Mainland A
Dallas Baptist University B, M
Del Mar College A
East Texas Baptist University B
Galveston College C, A
Hardin-Simmons University B
Houston Community College
  System C, A
Howard Payne University B
Huston-Tillotson College B
Lamar University B
LeTourneau University B
McMurry University B
Northwood University: Texas Campus B
Our Lady of the Lake University of San
  Antonio B
Prairie View A&M University B
St. Mary's University B
Sam Houston State University B
Southern Methodist University B
Southwest Texas State University B
Stephen F. Austin State University B
Sul Ross State University B
Tarleton State University B
Texas A&M International University B
Texas A&M University
  Commerce B
  Corpus Christi B
  Texarkana B
Texas A&M University B
Texas Christian University B
Texas Tech University B
Texas Woman's University B
Trinity University B
Tyler Junior College C, A
University of Houston
  Clear Lake B
University of Houston B, M, D
University of Mary Hardin-Baylor B
University of North Texas B, M, D
University of Texas
  Arlington B, D
  Austin B, D
  Brownsville B
  Dallas B, M, D
  El Paso B
  San Antonio B
  Tyler B
Vernon Regional Junior College A
Weatherford College C, A
West Texas A&M University B

Utah
Brigham Young University B
University of Utah B, M
Utah State University B
Weber State University B
Westminster College B

Vermont
Castleton State College B
Champlain College A, B

Virginia
Averett College B
Christopher Newport University B
George Mason University B
J. Sargeant Reynolds Community
  College A
James Madison University B
Longwood College B
Old Dominion University B
Radford University B
Virginia State University B

Washington
Centralia College C
City University C, B, M
Eastern Washington University B, T
Edmonds Community College A
Everett Community College C, A
Green River Community College A
Seattle University B
Shoreline Community College A

Spokane Community College C, A
Washington State University B

West Virginia
Concord College B
Davis and Elkins College B
Glenville State College B
Marshall University B
University of Charleston A, B
West Virginia University B
West Virginia Wesleyan College B

Wisconsin
Cardinal Stritch University C
Carthage College B
Lakeland College B, M
Lakeshore Technical College A
University of Wisconsin
  Eau Claire B
  Milwaukee B
  Stout B
  Superior B
Viterbo University B
Waukesha County Technical College A

Wyoming
Central Wyoming College A
University of Wyoming B
Western Wyoming Community
  College A

Business quantitative methods/management science

Alabama
University of Alabama B, M, D

Arkansas
University of Central Arkansas B

California
California State University
  Fullerton M
  Hayward M
  Long Beach C, B
  Northridge B, M
  Stanislaus B
Fresno City College C, A
University of Judaism M
University of Southern California M

Colorado
Northeastern Junior College A

District of Columbia
American University B, M
George Washington University M, D
University of the District of Columbia A

Florida
Keiser College A
University of Miami M
University of West Florida B

Georgia
Columbus Technical Institute C
Dalton State College A
Georgia College and State University B
State University of West Georgia B

Hawaii
University of Hawaii
  Manoa B

Illinois
Eastern Illinois University B
John Wood Community College C, A

Indiana
Valparaiso University B

Iowa
Iowa State University B
University of Iowa M, D

Kentucky
Elizabethtown Community College A

Maine
St. Joseph's College B

Massachusetts
Babson College B
Suffolk University B

Michigan
Aquinas College M
Walsh College of Accountancy and
  Business Administration M

Minnesota
St. Cloud State University B
Southwest State University C
University of St. Thomas M
Winona State University B

Missouri
St. Louis Community College
  St. Louis Community College at
    Meramec C, A

Nebraska
University of Nebraska
  Lincoln B

Nevada
Community College of Southern
  Nevada A

New Hampshire
Antioch New England Graduate
  School M

New Jersey
Fairleigh Dickinson University M

New Mexico
New Mexico Highlands University B

New York
Iona College M
Niagara County Community
  College C, A
Orange County Community College A
Polytechnic University
  Long Island Campus M
Rochester Institute of
  Technology C, B, M

North Carolina
Barton College B
University of North Carolina
  Chapel Hill D

North Dakota
North Dakota State University M
University of Mary M

Ohio
Cleveland State University B
Franklin University B
John Carroll University B
Kent State University
  East Liverpool Regional Campus A
Wright State University M
Xavier University M

Oklahoma
Oklahoma State University M

Oregon
University of Oregon B

Pennsylvania
Duquesne University B
La Salle University B
Lehigh University M
Penn State
  University Park B
Philadelphia University M
Temple University B, M, D

Puerto Rico
Inter American University of Puerto Rico
  Guayama Campus B
University of Puerto Rico
  Rio Piedras Campus B, M

Tennessee
Belmont University B

University of Tennessee
  Knoxville M

Washington
Gonzaga University B
North Seattle Community College A
Washington State University B

West Virginia
Concord College B

Wisconsin
University of Wisconsin
  Madison M, D
  Stout M

Business statistics

Colorado
University of Denver B

District of Columbia
Southeastern University B

Florida
University of Miami M

Georgia
South Georgia College A

Massachusetts
Babson College B

Michigan
Olivet College B
Western Michigan University B

Minnesota
Winona State University A

New York
Manhattan College B
Syracuse University M

Ohio
Bowling Green State University B, M

Pennsylvania
La Salle University B
Temple University B, M, D

Puerto Rico
University of Puerto Rico
  Rio Piedras Campus B

Tennessee
University of Tennessee
  Knoxville B, M

Texas
Baylor University B
University of Texas
  Arlington D

Utah
Brigham Young University B

Business systems analysis/design

California
Barstow College A
California State University
  Northridge B, M
Canada College C, A
Cerritos Community College A
Irvine Valley College C, A
Saddleback College C

Connecticut
Norwalk Community-Technical
  College A

District of Columbia
Howard University B

Florida
Gulf Coast Community College A
St. Petersburg Junior College A
Tallahassee Community College C

Business systems analysis/design

University of Miami *B, M*

Georgia
Columbus State University *B*

Illinois
Danville Area Community College *A*
Illinois Eastern Community Colleges
　Lincoln Trail College *C, A*
MacCormac College *C, A*
Southern Illinois University
　Carbondale *B*
William Rainey Harper College *C, A*

Iowa
Des Moines Area Community College *A*
Western Iowa Tech Community
　College *C*

Kentucky
Northern Kentucky University *C*

Louisiana
University of Louisiana at Monroe *B*

Maine
Husson College *B*

Maryland
Montgomery College
　Germantown Campus *A*

Massachusetts
Cape Cod Community College *C, A*

Michigan
Baker College
　of Mount Clemens *A*

Minnesota
St. Cloud State University *B*

Missouri
Penn Valley Community College *C*
St. Louis Community College
　St. Louis Community College at
　　Meramec *A*

New Hampshire
Antioch New England Graduate
　School *M*
McIntosh College *C*

New Jersey
St. Peter's College *A*

New Mexico
New Mexico State University *B*

New York
City University of New York
　Baruch College *M*
State University of New York
　College of Agriculture and
　　Technology at Cobleskill *A*

North Carolina
Cape Fear Community College *A*
Coastal Carolina Community College *A*
South Piedmont Community
　College *C, A*
Wilson Technical Community
　College *C, A*

Ohio
Kent State University
　Stark Campus *B*
Kent State University *B, D*
Southern Ohio College *A*
University of Findlay *B*

Oklahoma
Oklahoma Baptist University *B*

Pennsylvania
Delaware County Community College *C*
Pennsylvania College of Technology *B*
Shippensburg University of
　Pennsylvania *B*

Tennessee
University of Tennessee
　Knoxville *B*

Texas
Brookhaven College *A*
San Antonio College *A*
Texas A&M University
　Commerce *B*
Texas A&M University *M, D*

Vermont
Champlain College *A, B*

Virginia
ECPI College of Technology *C, A*

Washington
Antioch University Seattle *M*

West Virginia
Marshall University *B*

Wyoming
Central Wyoming College *A*

Business systems networking/telecommunications

Alabama
Community College of the Air Force *A*
ITT Technical Institute
　Birmingham *A*

Arizona
Glendale Community College *A*
ITT Technical Institute
　Phoenix *A*
Mesa Community College *A*
Thunderbird, The American Graduate
　School of International
　Management *M*

California
Butte College *C, A*
California State University
　Hayward *C, B, M*
Chaffey Community College *C*
Coastline Community College *C*
DeVry Institute of Technology
　Fremont *B*
　Long Beach *B*
　Pomona *B*
　West Hills *B*
Golden Gate University *C, B, M*
Irvine Valley College *C, A*
National University *M*
Saddleback College *C*

Colorado
Colorado Mountain College
　Spring Valley Campus *A*
Front Range Community College *C*
ITT Technical Institute
　Thornton *A*
Pikes Peak Community College *C, A*

Connecticut
Manchester Community-Technical
　College *A*
Naugatuck Valley Community-Technical
　College *C*

Florida
Edison Community College *C*
ITT Technical Institute
　Ft. Lauderdale *A*
　Jacksonville *A*
　Maitland *A*
　Miami *A*
　Tampa *A*
New England Institute of Technology *C*
St. Petersburg Junior College *C, A*
Seminole Community College *C*
South Florida Community College *C, A*

Georgia
DeVry Institute of Technology
　Alpharetta *B*
　Atlanta *B*

Idaho
Eastern Idaho Technical College *A*
ITT Technical Institute
　Boise *A*

Illinois
Black Hawk College *C*
College of Lake County *C, A*
De Paul University *M*
DeVry Institute of Technology
　Addison *B*
Elgin Community College *C*
ITT Technical Institute
　Burr Ridge *A*
　Matteson *C*
Illinois State University *B*
Lake Land College *A*
McHenry County College *C*
Moraine Valley Community
　College *C, A*
Parkland College *C, A*
Robert Morris College: Chicago *C, A*
Roosevelt University *M*
Sauk Valley Community College *C*
Southeastern Illinois College *A*
Waubonsee Community College *C*

Indiana
ITT Technical Institute
　Fort Wayne *A*
　Indianapolis *A*
　Newburgh *A*

Iowa
Iowa Central Community College *A*
North Iowa Area Community College *A*
Northeast Iowa Community College *A*

Kansas
Johnson County Community College *A*

Kentucky
ITT Technical Institute
　Louisville *A*
Owensboro Junior College of Business *A*

Louisiana
Bossier Parish Community College *A*

Maryland
Carroll Community College *C, A*
Howard Community College *C, A*
Montgomery College
　Germantown Campus *C, A*
Morgan State University *B*
University of Maryland
　University College *M*

Massachusetts
Cape Cod Community College *C, A*
Franklin Institute of Boston *C*
Middlesex Community College *C, A*

Michigan
Alpena Community College *A*
Baker College
　of Cadillac *A*
　of Mount Clemens *A*
　of Muskegon *C, A*
　of Owosso *A*
　of Port Huron *A*
Grand Rapids Community College *C*
Lansing Community College *A*

Minnesota
Alexandria Technical College *A*
Central Lakes College *C, A*
St. Cloud Technical College *C, A*
University of Minnesota
　Twin Cities *B*

Mississippi
Northwest Mississippi Community
　College *A*

Missouri
ITT Technical Institute
　Arnold *A*
　Earth City *A*
Webster University *M*

Montana
Montana Tech of the University of
　Montana *A*

Nebraska
ITT Technical Institute
　Omaha *A*
University of Nebraska
　Kearney *B*

New Hampshire
Franklin Pierce College *B*
McIntosh College *A*
New Hampshire Community Technical
　College
　Nashua *C, A*

New Jersey
Cumberland County College *C, A*
Mercer County Community College *C, A*
Ocean County College *C*
Stevens Institute of Technology *M, D*

New Mexico
Albuquerque Technical-Vocational
　Institute *C, A*
ITT Technical Institute
　Albuquerque *A*

New York
City University of New York
　Borough of Manhattan Community
　　College *A*
Herkimer County Community College *A*
Hudson Valley Community College *A*
Iona College *M*
Niagara County Community College *A*
Onondaga Community College *A*
Polytechnic University *M*
Rochester Institute of Technology *B*
Schenectady County Community
　College *A*
State University of New York
　College of Agriculture and
　　Technology at Cobleskill *A*
　Institute of Technology at
　　Utica/Rome *B*
Syracuse University *M*
Tompkins-Cortland Community
　College *A*

North Carolina
Central Carolina Community College *A*
Cleveland Community College *C, A*
College of the Albemarle *A*
Craven Community College *A*
Haywood Community College *C, A*
Pitt Community College *A*
South Piedmont Community
　College *C, A*
Southwestern Community College *A*
Wilkes Community College *C, A*

North Dakota
Bismarck State College *A*
Lake Region State College *C, A*

Ohio
Cincinnati State Technical and
　Community College *A*
ITT Technical Institute
　Dayton *A*
　Norwood *A*
　Strongsville *A*
　Youngstown *A*
Kent State University *B, M*
Lima Technical College *A*
Miami-Jacobs College *C, A*
Owens Community College
　Toledo *A*

Oklahoma
Northeastern State University *B*

128

Oregon
ITT Technical Institute
　Portland *A*
Portland Community College *C*

Pennsylvania
Bucks County Community College *A*
Community College of Allegheny
　County *C*
Delaware County Community College *A*
ITT Technical Institute
　Monroeville *A*
Peirce College *C, A, B*
Pennsylvania College of Technology *B*
Reading Area Community College *A*

Tennessee
David Lipscomb University *B*
ITT Technical Institute
　Knoxville *A*
　Memphis *A*
　Nashville *A*
Tusculum College *B*

Texas
Central Texas College *C, A*
Collin County Community College
　District *C, A*
Eastfield College *C, A*
ITT Technical Institute
　Arlington *A*
　Houston North *A*
　Houston South *A*
　Houston *A*
　Richardson *A*
　San Antonio *A*
Texas Tech University *M*
University of Dallas *M*

Utah
ITT Technical Institute
　Murray *A*
Weber State University *B*

Vermont
Champlain College *A, B*

Virginia
Christopher Newport University *B*
ECPI College of Technology *C, A*
ITT Technical Institute
　Norfolk *A*
　Richmond *A*
J. Sargeant Reynolds Community
　College *C*
Tidewater Community College *A*

Washington
Centralia College *C*
Clark College *C, A*
ITT Technical Institute
　Bothell *A*
　Seattle *A*
　Spokane *A*
Renton Technical College *C, A*

Wisconsin
Gateway Technical College *A*
ITT Technical Institute
　Greenfield *A*
Northeast Wisconsin Technical
　College *A*
Southwest Wisconsin Technical
　College *A*
University of Wisconsin
　Stout *B*

Wyoming
Eastern Wyoming College *A*

Business/personal services marketing

Alabama
Lawson State Community College *C*

Arkansas
Phillips Community College of the
　University of Arkansas *A*

California
California College for Health
　Sciences *A, B*
California State University
　Hayward *B, M*
Compton Community College *A*
Merced College *A*
Saddleback College *C, A*
Skyline College *C, A*

Colorado
Northeastern Junior College *A*
Pikes Peak Community College *C*

Connecticut
Norwalk Community-Technical
　College *A*
Tunxis Community College *C, A*

Florida
Broward Community College *A*
Florida National College *A*
Pensacola Junior College *A*
St. Thomas University *B, M*

Georgia
Emory University *B*

Illinois
Danville Area Community College *A*
Greenville College *B*
Kankakee Community College *A*
Oakton Community College *C*
Richland Community College *A*
William Rainey Harper College *C, A*

Indiana
Indiana State University *B*
Vincennes University *A*

Iowa
Faith Baptist Bible College and
　Theological Seminary *A, B*

Kansas
Garden City Community College *A*
Independence Community College *C, A*
Seward County Community
　College *A*

Kentucky
Murray State University *B, M*
Owensboro Community College *A*

Maine
Andover College *A*
Husson College *B*
St. Joseph's College *B*
University of Maine
　Machias *A, B*

Maryland
Baltimore City Community College *A*

Massachusetts
Babson College *B*

Michigan
Kalamazoo Valley Community
　College *C, A*
Oakland Community College *C*
Schoolcraft College *A*

Minnesota
Dakota County Technical College *C, A*
Inver Hills Community College *A*
Itasca Community College *A*
University of Minnesota
　Crookston *A, B*

Missouri
Lindenwood University *M*

Nebraska
Lincoln School of Commerce *A*
Northeast Community College *A*

New Hampshire
Rivier College *M*

New Jersey
Union County College *A*

New York
Adirondack Community College *A*
Audrey Cohen College *B*
Bryant & Stratton Business Institute
　Syracuse *C, A*
City University of New York
　Baruch College *B*
Clinton Community College *A*
Jefferson Community College *A*
Medaille College *B*
Rochester Institute of Technology *B, M*

North Carolina
Belmont Abbey College *B*
Sampson Community College *A*

Ohio
Ashland University *B*
Defiance College *B*
Hocking Technical College *A*
Kent State University
　East Liverpool Regional Campus *A*
　Stark Campus *B*
Wilmington College *B*

Oregon
Northwest Christian College *B*

Pennsylvania
Central Pennsylvania College *A*
Cheyney University of Pennsylvania *B*
La Salle University *A, B*
Lehigh Carbon Community College *A*
Tri-State Business Institute *A*
York College of Pennsylvania *B*

Rhode Island
Providence College *B*

Texas
Central Texas College *C, A*
St. Mary's University *B*
South Plains College *A*

Utah
Salt Lake Community College *A*

Washington
Columbia Basin College *A*
Edmonds Community College *C*
Everett Community College *A*

Wisconsin
Chippewa Valley Technical College *A*
Gateway Technical College *A*

CAD-CAM/drafting

Alabama
Bessemer State Technical College *C, A*
Bevill State Community College *A*
Calhoun Community College *C, A*
Central Alabama Community College *A*
Faulkner University *A*
Gadsden State Community College *C*
George C. Wallace State Community
　College
　Dothan *C, A*
　Selma *A*
Harry M. Ayers State Technical
　College *A*
ITT Technical Institute
　Birmingham *A*
J. F. Drake State Technical College *C, A*
Jefferson Davis Community College *C*
John M. Patterson State Technical
　College *C, A*
Lawson State Community College *C, A*
Northwest-Shoals Community
　College *C, A*
Shelton State Community College *C, A*
Southern Union State Community
　College *A*
Sparks State Technical College *A*
Wallace State Community College at
　Hanceville *C, A*

Alaska
University of Alaska
　Anchorage *C, A*
　Fairbanks *C*

Arizona
Arizona Western College *C, A*
Central Arizona College *C*
Cochise College *A*
Eastern Arizona College *C, A*
Glendale Community College *C, A*
ITT Technical Institute
　Phoenix *A*
　Tucson *A*
Mesa Community College *C*
Northland Pioneer College *C*
Pima Community College *C, A*
Universal Technical Institute *A*

Arkansas
Arkansas State University
　Beebe Branch *A*
ITT Technical Institute
　Little Rock *A*
Northwest Arkansas Community
　College *A*
Phillips Community College of the
　University of Arkansas *C, A*
Southern Arkansas University
　Tech *C, A*
Westark College *C, A*

California
American River College *A*
Bakersfield College *A*
Barstow College *C*
Butte College *C, A*
Cabrillo College *C*
Cerritos Community College *A*
Cerro Coso Community College *C, A*
Chabot College *C, A*
Chaffey Community College *C, A*
Citrus College *C, A*
City College of San Francisco *C, A*
College of San Mateo *C, A*
College of the Canyons *C, A*
College of the Desert *C, A*
College of the Redwoods *C, A*
College of the Sequoias *C*
Compton Community College *C, A*
Contra Costa College *C, A*
Cuyamaca College *C, A*
De Anza College *C, A*
Diablo Valley College *C, A*
Don Bosco Technical Institute *A*
East Los Angeles College *C*
Evergreen Valley College *A*
Fresno City College *C, A*
Glendale Community College *C, A*
Golden West College *C, A*
ITT Technical Institute
　Anaheim *A*
　Lathrop *A*
　Oxnard *A*
　Rancho Cordova *A*
　San Bernardino *A*
　San Diego *A*
　Sylmar *A*
　Torrance *A*
　West Covina *A*
Irvine Valley College *C, A*
Las Positas College *C, A*
Long Beach City College *C, A*
Los Angeles Harbor College *C, A*
Los Angeles Pierce College *C, A*
Los Angeles Southwest College *C, A*
Los Angeles Trade and Technical
　College *C, A*
Los Angeles Valley College *C*
Merced College *A*

CAD-CAM/drafting

MiraCosta College C, A
Mission College C, A
Modesto Junior College A
Monterey Peninsula College C, A
Mount San Antonio College C, A
Napa Valley College C, A
Ohlone College C, A
Orange Coast College C, A
Pacific Union College A, B
Palomar College C, A
Pasadena City College C, A
Porterville College C, A
Rio Hondo College A
Riverside Community College C, A
Sacramento City College C, A
Saddleback College C, A
San Diego City College C, A
San Joaquin Delta College A
San Jose City College A
Santa Ana College C, A
Santa Barbara City College C, A
Santa Monica College C, A
Sierra College C, A
Solano Community College C, A
Southwestern College C
Taft College A
Ventura College C, A
West Valley College C, A

Colorado
Aims Community College C
Community College of Aurora A
Community College of Denver C
Denver Technical College: A Division of DeVry University A
Front Range Community College C, A
ITT Technical Institute
   Thornton A
Otero Junior College C
Pikes Peak Community College C
Pueblo Community College C, A
Red Rocks Community College C, A
Technical Trades Institute A
Trinidad State Junior College A

Connecticut
Capital Community College C
Gateway Community College C
Naugatuck Valley Community-Technical College C, A
Three Rivers Community-Technical College C, A

Delaware
Delaware Technical and Community College
   Stanton/Wilmington Campus A

Florida
Art Institute
   of Fort Lauderdale A, B
Brevard Community College A
Central Florida Community College A
Daytona Beach Community College A
Florida Community College at
   Jacksonville A
ITT Technical Institute
   Ft. Lauderdale A
   Jacksonville A
   Maitland A
   Tampa A
Indian River Community College A
Keiser College A
New England Institute of Technology A
Palm Beach Community College A
Pasco-Hernando Community College A
Pensacola Junior College A
Polk Community College C
Santa Fe Community College A
Seminole Community College C
South Florida Community College C, A
Valencia Community College A

Georgia
Athens Area Technical Institute C
Atlanta Metropolitan College A
Bainbridge College C, A
Chattahoochee Technical Institute C
Clayton College and State University A
Coastal Georgia Community College C, A
Dalton State College C, A
Darton College A
DeKalb Technical Institute C
Gwinnett Technical Institute A
Middle Georgia College C
Waycross College A

Hawaii
University of Hawaii
   Hawaii Community College A
   Honolulu Community College A
   Maui Community College A

Idaho
Boise State University A
College of Southern Idaho C, A
ITT Technical Institute
   Boise A
Idaho State University C, A
Lewis-Clark State College A, B
North Idaho College C, A
Ricks College A

Illinois
Black Hawk College C, A
Carl Sandburg College C, A
City Colleges of Chicago
   Harold Washington College C
College of DuPage C, A
College of Lake County C, A
Danville Area Community College C
Highland Community College C
ITT Technical Institute
   Hoffman Estates A
   Matteson A
Illinois Eastern Community Colleges
   Lincoln Trail College A
John A. Logan College C, A
John Wood Community College A
Joliet Junior College A
Kankakee Community College C, A
Kaskaskia College C, A
Kishwaukee College A
Lake Land College C
Lewis and Clark Community College A
Moraine Valley Community College C
Morton College C, A
Oakton Community College A
Parkland College C
Prairie State College C
Rend Lake College A
Robert Morris College: Chicago C, A
Sauk Valley Community College C, A
Shawnee Community College C, A
Southwestern Illinois College C, A
Triton College C, A
Waubonsee Community College C
William Rainey Harper College C

Indiana
ITT Technical Institute
   Fort Wayne A
   Indianapolis A
Indiana State University A
Indiana University--Purdue University
   Indiana University-Purdue
     University Fort Wayne C, A
   Indiana University-Purdue
     University Indianapolis A
Ivy Tech State College
   Central Indiana C, A
   Columbus C, A
   Eastcentral A
   Kokomo C, A
   Lafayette C, A
   Northcentral C, A
   Northeast C, A
   Northwest C, A
   Southcentral C, A
   Southwest A
   Wabash Valley A
Oakland City University C, A

Purdue University A, B
Tri-State University A, B
Vincennes University A

Iowa
Clinton Community College A
Des Moines Area Community College C, A
Hamilton Technical College A
Hawkeye Community College A
Indian Hills Community College A
Iowa Central Community College C, A
Iowa Lakes Community College A
Kirkwood Community College C, A
Marshalltown Community College A
Southeastern Community College
   North Campus C, A
Southwestern Community College C, A
Waldorf College A

Kansas
Allen County Community College A
Barton County Community College A
Butler County Community College C, A
Central Christian College A
Cowley County Community College C, A
Garden City Community College A
Hutchinson Community College A
Independence Community College C, A
Johnson County Community College C, A
Kansas City Kansas Community College C, A

Kentucky
Eastern Kentucky University A
ITT Technical Institute
   Louisville A
Kentucky State University A
Murray State University A
Western Kentucky University A

Louisiana
Bossier Parish Community College C, A
Delgado Community College A
McNeese State University A
Nunez Community College C, A
Southern University
   Shreveport C

Maine
Central Maine Technical College A
Southern Maine Technical College C, A

Maryland
Anne Arundel Community College C
Baltimore City Community College C, A
Carroll Community College C, A
Charles County Community College C
Chesapeake College C, A
Community College of Baltimore County
   Catonsville C, A
   Essex C, A
Frederick Community College C, A
Harford Community College C
Howard Community College C, A
Montgomery College
   Germantown Campus C, A
   Rockville Campus A
Prince George's Community College C, A

Massachusetts
Bristol Community College C
Franklin Institute of Boston C, A
Greenfield Community College C
ITT Technical Institute
   Framingham A
Massachusetts Bay Community College C
Massasoit Community College C
Middlesex Community College C, A
North Shore Community College C
Northeastern University M
Northern Essex Community College A
Roxbury Community College A

Springfield Technical Community College C

Michigan
Alpena Community College A
Baker College
   of Auburn Hills A
   of Mount Clemens A
   of Muskegon A
   of Owosso A
Bay de Noc Community College A
Ferris State University A
Glen Oaks Community College C
Gogebic Community College A
Grand Rapids Community College C, A
Henry Ford Community College A
ITT Technical Institute
   Grand Rapids A
   Troy A
Jackson Community College C, A
Kalamazoo Valley Community College C, A
Kellogg Community College A
Kirtland Community College C
Lake Michigan College C, A
Lake Superior State University C, A
Lansing Community College A
Macomb Community College C, A
Mid Michigan Community College C
Monroe County Community College C, A
Montcalm Community College C, A
Mott Community College C, A
Muskegon Community College C, A
North Central Michigan College C
Northern Michigan University B
Northwestern Michigan College A
Oakland Community College C, A
St. Clair County Community College C, A
Schoolcraft College C, A
Southwestern Michigan College C, A
Washtenaw Community College C, A
Western Michigan University B

Minnesota
Alexandria Technical College C, A
Central Lakes College C
Dunwoody Institute A
Hennepin Technical College C, A
Hibbing Community College: A Technical and Community College C, A
Lake Superior College: A Community and Technical College A
Minnesota State College - Southeast Technical C, A
Northland Community & Technical College C, A
Ridgewater College: A Community and Technical College C, A
Rochester Community and Technical College C
St. Cloud Technical College C, A
St. Paul Technical College C
South Central Technical College A

Mississippi
Copiah-Lincoln Community College A
East Central Community College A
East Mississippi Community College A
Hinds Community College C, A
Holmes Community College A
Itawamba Community College C
Meridian Community College A
Mississippi Gulf Coast Community College
   Jackson County Campus A
   Jefferson Davis Campus C, A
   Perkinston A
Northwest Mississippi Community College A

Missouri
Central Missouri State University A, B
Crowder College A

East Central College *C, A*
ITT Technical Institute
  Earth City *A*
Lincoln University *A*
Longview Community College *A*
Mineral Area College *A*
Missouri Southern State College *C, A*
Moberly Area Community College *C, A*
Penn Valley Community College *A*
Southeast Missouri State University *C*
Southwest Missouri State University *B*
St. Louis Community College
  St. Louis Community College at
    Florissant Valley *C, A*
  St. Louis Community College at
    Forest Park *A*
Three Rivers Community College *A*

Montana
Montana State University
  Billings *C, A*
  Northern *A, B*
Montana Tech of the University of
  Montana: College of Technology *A*
Montana Tech of the University of
  Montana *A*

Nebraska
Central Community College *C, A*
ITT Technical Institute
  Omaha *A*
Metropolitan Community College *C, A*
Mid Plains Community College
  Area *C, A*
Northeast Community College *A*
Southeast Community College
  Lincoln Campus *A*
  Milford Campus *A*

Nevada
Community College of Southern
  Nevada *C, A*
ITT Technical Institute
  Henderson *A*
Western Nevada Community
  College *C, A*

New Hampshire
Keene State College *A, B*
New Hampshire Community Technical
  College
    Berlin *A*
    Manchester *A*
    Nashua *C, A*
    Stratham *C, A*

New Jersey
Bergen Community College *C*
Brookdale Community College *C, A*
Burlington County College *C, A*
Camden County College *C, A*
County College of Morris *C*
Cumberland County College *C*
Gloucester County College *A*
Mercer County Community College *C*
Middlesex County College *C*
Thomas Edison State College *A, B*

New Mexico
Albuquerque Technical-Vocational
  Institute *C, A*
Clovis Community College *A*
Dona Ana Branch Community College of
  New Mexico State University *C, A*
Eastern New Mexico University
  Roswell Campus *C, A*
ITT Technical Institute
  Albuquerque *A*
New Mexico Junior College *C, A*
New Mexico State University
  Alamogordo *C*
Northern New Mexico Community
  College *C, A*
San Juan College *A*
Santa Fe Community College *A*
Western New Mexico University *A*

New York
Adirondack Community College *C, A*
City University of New York
  New York City Technical
    College *A*
  Queensborough Community
    College *A*
Corning Community College *C*
Dutchess Community College *C*
Erie Community College
  South Campus *A*
Genesee Community College *C, A*
Hudson Valley Community College *A*
ITT Technical Institute
  Getzville *A*
Institute of Design and Construction *A*
Mohawk Valley Community
  College *C, A*
Niagara County Community
  College *C, A*
Onondaga Community College *C*
Orange County Community College *C*
State University of New York
  College of Agriculture and
    Technology at Morrisville *A*
  College of Technology at Alfred *A*
  College of Technology at Canton *C*
  College of Technology at
    Delhi *C, A*
Suffolk County Community College *A*
Ulster County Community College *C, A*
Westchester Community College *C*

North Carolina
Alamance Community College *C, A*
Appalachian State University *B*
Asheville Buncombe Technical
  Community College *A*
Beaufort County Community College *A*
Blue Ridge Community College *C, A*
Caldwell Community College and
  Technical Institute *C, A*
Cape Fear Community College *A*
Catawba Valley Community College *C*
Central Carolina Community College *A*
College of the Albemarle *A*
Davidson County Community College *C*
Durham Technical Community
  College *C, A*
Edgecombe Community College *C*
Forsyth Technical Community College *A*
Gaston College *C*
Lenoir Community College *A*
Mitchell Community College *C, A*
Piedmont Community College *C*
Richmond Community College *C*
Rockingham Community College *C*
Rowan-Cabarrus Community College *A*
Sandhills Community College *C, A*
South Piedmont Community College *A*
Surry Community College *C, A*
Wake Technical Community
  College *C, A*
Wilson Technical Community College *A*

Ohio
Belmont Technical College *C*
Bryant & Stratton College *A*
Cincinnati State Technical and
  Community College *A*
Clark State Community College *A*
Edison State Community College *C*
Hocking Technical College *C, A*
ITT Technical Institute
  Dayton *A*
  Norwood *A*
  Strongsville *A*
  Youngstown *A*
Jefferson Community College *A*
Kent State University
  Tuscarawas Campus *A*
Lakeland Community College *C*
Lima Technical College *C*
Miami University
  Hamilton Campus *C*
  Middletown Campus *C*
  Oxford Campus *C*
Muskingum Area Technical College *A*
North Central State College *C, A*
Northwest State Community College *A*
Owens Community College
  Toledo *A*
Shawnee State University *A*
Sinclair Community College *A*
Southern Ohio College *A*
Southern State Community College *A*
Terra Community College *C*
University of Akron
  Wayne College *A*
University of Akron *A*
University of Rio Grande *A*
Youngstown State University *A*

Oklahoma
Cameron University *A*
Connors State College *C, A*
Langston University *A*
Northeastern Oklahoma Agricultural and
  Mechanical College *A*
Northern Oklahoma College *A*
Oklahoma City Community College *A*
Oklahoma State University
  Oklahoma City *A*
  Okmulgee *A*
Redlands Community College *A*
Rose State College *A*
Tulsa Community College *A*
Western Oklahoma State College *A*

Oregon
Central Oregon Community
  College *C, A*
Chemeketa Community College *A*
Clackamas Community College *A*
ITT Technical Institute
  Portland *A*
Lane Community College *C, A*
Linn-Benton Community College *A*
Portland Community College *C, A*

Pennsylvania
Butler County Community College *A*
California University of
  Pennsylvania *A, B*
Community College of Allegheny
  County *C, A*
Community College of Beaver County *A*
Community College of Philadelphia *C, A*
Delaware County Community
  College *C, A*
Harrisburg Area Community College *C*
ITT Technical Institute
  Mechanicsburg *A*
  Monroeville *A*
  Pittsburgh *A*
Johnson Technical Institute *A*
Lehigh Carbon Community College *C, A*
Luzerne County Community
  College *C, A*
Montgomery County Community
  College *A*
Northampton County Area Community
  College *A*
Penn State
  University Park *C*
Pennsylvania College of Technology *B*
Pittsburgh Technical Institute *A*
Triangle Tech
  DuBois Campus *A*
  Pittsburgh Campus *A*
Westmoreland County Community
  College *A*

Puerto Rico
Turabo University *C*

Rhode Island
Johnson & Wales University *A*
New England Institute of Technology *A*

South Carolina
Aiken Technical College *C*
Central Carolina Technical College *A*
Chesterfield-Marlboro Technical
  College *C*
Florence-Darlington Technical
  College *C, A*
Greenville Technical College *C*
Horry-Georgetown Technical College *C*
ITT Technical Institute
  Greenville *A*
Midlands Technical College *C, A*
Orangeburg-Calhoun Technical
  College *A*
Piedmont Technical College *A*
Spartanburg Technical College *C*
Technical College of the Lowcountry *C*
Tri-County Technical College *A*
Trident Technical College *C*
York Technical College *A*

South Dakota
Black Hills State University *A*
Southeast Technical Institute *A*
Western Dakota Technical Institute *A*

Tennessee
Chattanooga State Technical Community
  College *C*
ITT Technical Institute
  Knoxville *A*
  Memphis *A*
  Nashville *A*
Northeast State Technical Community
  College *C, A*
Pellissippi State Technical Community
  College *C, A*

Texas
Abilene Christian University *A*
Alvin Community College *C, A*
Amarillo College *C, A*
Austin Community College *C, A*
Brazosport College *C, A*
Central Texas College *C, A*
Coastal Bend College *A*
College of the Mainland *A*
Collin County Community College
  District *C, A*
Del Mar College *C, A*
Eastfield College *C, A*
El Paso Community College *C, A*
Grayson County College *C, A*
Hill College *C, A*
Houston Community College
  System *C, A*
Howard College *C*
ITT Technical Institute
  Arlington *A*
  Austin *A*
  Houston North *A*
  Houston South *A*
  Houston *A*
  Richardson *A*
  San Antonio *A*
Kilgore College *A*
LeTourneau University *A*
Lee College *C, A*
Midland College *A*
Mountain View College *A*
Navarro College *C, A*
North Central Texas College *A*
Odessa College *C, A*
Paris Junior College *A*
Prairie View A&M University *B*
St. Philip's College *C, A*
Sam Houston State University *B*
San Antonio College *A*
San Jacinto College
  North *C, A*
South Plains College *A*
Tarrant County College *C, A*
Temple College *C, A*
Texas Southern University *B*

CAD-CAM/drafting

Texas State Technical College
    Harlingen *A*
    Sweetwater *C, A*
    Waco *C, A*
Trinity Valley Community College *C, A*
Tyler Junior College *C, A*
Vernon Regional Junior College *C, A*
Victoria College *C, A*
Wharton County Junior College *A*

Utah
College of Eastern Utah *C*
Dixie State College of Utah *C, A*
ITT Technical Institute
    Murray *A*
Salt Lake Community College *A*
Southern Utah University *A*
Utah State University *A*
Utah Valley State College *A*
Weber State University *A*

Virginia
Central Virginia Community College *C*
Dabney S. Lancaster Community
    College *C, A*
Danville Community College *A*
Eastern Shore Community College *C*
ITT Technical Institute
    Norfolk *A*
J. Sargeant Reynolds Community
    College *C*
Lord Fairfax Community College *C*
Mountain Empire Community College *A*
New River Community College *A*
Northern Virginia Community
    College *C, A*
Patrick Henry Community College *A*
Paul D. Camp Community College *A*
Southside Virginia Community
    College *C, A*
Southwest Virginia Community
    College *C*
Thomas Nelson Community College *A*
Tidewater Community College *A*
Virginia Highlands Community
    College *C, A*
Wytheville Community College *C, A*

Washington
Big Bend Community College *C*
Centralia College *C, A*
Clark College *C, A*
Columbia Basin College *C*
Everett Community College *C, A*
Green River Community College *A*
Highline Community College *A*
ITT Technical Institute
    Bothell *A*
    Seattle *A*
    Spokane *A*
Lake Washington Technical College *C, A*
North Seattle Community College *A*
Olympic College *C, A*
Renton Technical College *C*
Seattle Central Community College *A*
Shoreline Community College *C, A*
South Puget Sound Community
    College *C, A*
South Seattle Community College *C, A*
Spokane Falls Community College *C, A*
Yakima Valley Community College *A*

West Virginia
Fairmont State College *B*
Southern West Virginia Community and
    Technical College *A*
West Virginia State College *A*
West Virginia University Institute of
    Technology *A*

Wisconsin
Blackhawk Technical College *A*
Chippewa Valley Technical College *A*
Gateway Technical College *C*
Herzing College *A, B*
ITT Technical Institute
    Greenfield *A*
Lakeshore Technical College *A*
Madison Area Technical College *C*
Milwaukee Area Technical College *C*
Moraine Park Technical College *C, A*
Northeast Wisconsin Technical
    College *A*
Southwest Wisconsin Technical
    College *A*
Waukesha County Technical
    College *C, A*
Wisconsin Indianhead Technical
    College *C, A*

Wyoming
Casper College *A*
Sheridan College *C, A*

Canadian studies

Indiana
Franklin College *B*

Maine
University of Maine
    Fort Kent *B*

New York
St. Lawrence University *B*
State University of New York
    College at Plattsburgh *B*

Utah
Brigham Young University *B*

Vermont
Marlboro College *B*
University of Vermont *B*

Virginia
George Mason University *B*

Washington
University of Washington *B*
Western Washington University *B*

Cardiovascular technology

Alabama
Community College of the Air Force *A*

Arkansas
University of Arkansas
    for Medical Sciences *A*

California
Butte College *A*
Grossmont Community College *C, A*

Florida
Barry University *B*
Broward Community College *A*
Edison Community College *A*
Hillsborough Community College *C*

Illinois
Benedictine University *M*
William Rainey Harper College *A*

Indiana
Indiana University--Purdue University
    Indiana University-Purdue
    University Indianapolis *C*

Louisiana
Southern University
    Shreveport *A*

Maine
Southern Maine Technical College *A*

Maryland
Howard Community College *C, A*

Massachusetts
Northeastern University *B*

Michigan
Oakland Community College *A*

Nebraska
Nebraska Methodist College of Nursing
    and Allied Health *A, B*

New York
Molloy College *A*

North Carolina
Caldwell Community College and
    Technical Institute *C, A*

Ohio
University of Toledo *A*

Pennsylvania
Gwynedd-Mercy College *A*
Pennsylvania College of Technology *A*
Thomas Jefferson University: College of
    Health Professions *B*

South Dakota
Southeast Technical Institute *A*

Tennessee
Northeast State Technical Community
    College *A*

Virginia
Northern Virginia Community College *C*

Washington
Spokane Community College *A*

Caribbean studies

California
Pitzer College *B*

Florida
Florida State University *B*
Rollins College *B*

Georgia
Emory University *B*

Illinois
Northwestern University *B*

Maryland
Johns Hopkins University *B*

Massachusetts
Northeastern University *B*

Michigan
University of Michigan *B*

New Hampshire
Dartmouth College *B*

New Jersey
Rutgers
    The State University of New Jersey:
        Douglass College *B*
    The State University of New Jersey:
        Livingston College *B*
    The State University of New Jersey:
        Rutgers College *B*
    The State University of New Jersey:
        University College New
        Brunswick *B*

New York
City University of New York
    Brooklyn College *B*
    City College *B*
New York University *M*
St. Francis College *B*
State University of New York
    Albany *B, M*
    Binghamton *B*

Carpentry

Alabama
Calhoun Community College *C*
Central Alabama Community College *C*
Gadsden State Community College *C*
Harry M. Ayers State Technical
    College *C*
John M. Patterson State Technical
    College *C*
Lawson State Community College *C*
Northwest-Shoals Community College *C*
Reid State Technical College *C*
Southern Union State Community
    College *A*
Sparks State Technical College *C*

Alaska
University of Alaska
    Southeast *C, A*

Arizona
Central Arizona College *C*
Eastern Arizona College *C*
Gateway Community College *C, A*
Northland Pioneer College *C, A*

Arkansas
North Arkansas College *C*

California
Bakersfield College *A*
College of the Sequoias *C*
Fresno City College *C, A*
Long Beach City College *C, A*
Los Angeles Trade and Technical
    College *C, A*
Palomar College *C, A*
Pasadena City College *C, A*
Porterville College *C, A*
San Joaquin Delta College *C, A*
Santa Ana College *C, A*
Shasta College *A*
Sierra College *C, A*

Colorado
Community College of Aurora *A*
Red Rocks Community College *C, A*
Trinidad State Junior College *C*

Florida
Brevard Community College *C*
Indian River Community College *C*
South Florida Community College *C*

Hawaii
University of Hawaii
    Hawaii Community College *C, A*
    Honolulu Community College *C, A*
    Kauai Community College *C, A*
    Maui Community College *A*

Idaho
Idaho State University *A*
North Idaho College *C, A*
Ricks College *A*

Illinois
Black Hawk College *A*
Southwestern Ilinois College *C, A*
Triton College *C, A*

Indiana
Ivy Tech State College
    Central Indiana *C, A*
    Lafayette *C, A*
    Northcentral *C, A*
    Northwest *C, A*
    Southwest *C, A*
Oakland City University *C*
Vincennes University *A*

Iowa
Des Moines Area Community College *A*
Indian Hills Community College *C*
Iowa Central Community College *C*
Kirkwood Community College *C*
Maharishi University of Management *C*
Northeast Iowa Community College *C*
Southwestern Community College *C*
Western Iowa Tech Community
    College *C*

Kansas
Central Christian College *A*

Hutchinson Community College C, A

Louisiana
Nunez Community College C

Maine
Southern Maine Technical College A

Maryland
Cecil Community College C, A

Michigan
Bay de Noc Community College C
Great Lakes College C, A
Jackson Community College C, A
Lansing Community College C, A
Northern Michigan University C

Minnesota
Alexandria Technical College C
Hennepin Technical College C, A
Lake Superior College: A Community and Technical College C, A
Mesabi Range Community and Technical College A
Minnesota State College - Southeast Technical C, A
Ridgewater College: A Community and Technical College C
Rochester Community and Technical College C
St. Cloud Technical College C
St. Paul Technical College C

Mississippi
Coahoma Community College C
Hinds Community College C
Mississippi Gulf Coast Community College
  Jefferson Davis Campus C
  Perkinston C
Southwest Mississippi Community College C

Missouri
Ranken Technical College A
St. Louis Community College
  St. Louis Community College at Forest Park A

Montana
Little Big Horn College C
Miles Community College A
Salish Kootenai College C

Nebraska
Central Community College C
Mid Plains Community College Area C, A

Nevada
Western Nevada Community College A

New Mexico
Albuquerque Technical-Vocational Institute C
San Juan College C, A

New York
Fulton-Montgomery Community College A
Hudson Valley Community College A
Mohawk Valley Community College C
State University of New York
  College of Technology at Alfred A
  College of Technology at Delhi C, A

North Carolina
Alamance Community College C
Asheville Buncombe Technical Community College C
Bladen Community College C
Blue Ridge Community College C
Cape Fear Community College C
Cleveland Community College C
College of the Albemarle C
Davidson County Community College C
Fayetteville Technical Community College C
Forsyth Technical Community College C
Guilford Technical Community College C
Piedmont Community College C
Pitt Community College C
Rowan-Cabarrus Community College C
Vance-Granville Community College C

North Dakota
Bismarck State College C, A

Oklahoma
Northeastern Oklahoma Agricultural and Mechanical College A

Oregon
Clackamas Community College C

Pennsylvania
Community College of Allegheny County C
Delaware County Community College C
Johnson Technical Institute A
Pennsylvania College of Technology C
Triangle Tech
  DuBois Campus A
Williamson Free School of Mechanical Trades C

Rhode Island
New England Institute of Technology C, A

South Carolina
Greenville Technical College C
Technical College of the Lowcountry C

South Dakota
Western Dakota Technical Institute C

Texas
Brazosport College C, A
Howard College C
North Lake College A
Odessa College C, A
Paris Junior College A
St. Philip's College A

Utah
College of Eastern Utah C, A
Salt Lake Community College A
Utah Valley State College A

Virginia
J. Sargeant Reynolds Community College C

Washington
Columbia Basin College A
Grays Harbor College C, A
Green River Community College A
Seattle Central Community College C, A
Spokane Community College C, A
Walla Walla Community College C, A

Wisconsin
Chippewa Valley Technical College C
Gateway Technical College C
Milwaukee Area Technical College C
Western Wisconsin Technical College C
Wisconsin Indianhead Technical College C

Cell biology

Alabama
Huntingdon College B
University of Alabama
  Birmingham D

Arizona
University of Arizona B

California
California Institute of Technology D
California State University
  Fresno B
  Long Beach B
  Northridge B
Pomona College B
San Diego State University B, D
San Francisco State University B, M
Stanford University D
University of California
  Davis B, D
  Irvine D
  Los Angeles B, M, D
  San Diego B
  San Francisco D
  Santa Barbara B, M, D
  Santa Cruz B, D
University of Southern California M, D

Colorado
Fort Lewis College B
University of Colorado
  Boulder B, M, D
  Health Sciences Center D

Connecticut
Connecticut College B
Quinnipiac University M
University of Connecticut M, D
Yale University M, D

District of Columbia
Catholic University of America M, D
Georgetown University D

Florida
Florida Institute of Technology B, M
University of Miami D

Georgia
Medical College of Georgia D
University of Georgia B, M, D

Illinois
Loyola University of Chicago D
Northwestern University B, M, D
University of Chicago M, D
University of Illinois
  Urbana-Champaign B

Indiana
Ball State University B
University of Indianapolis B

Iowa
Iowa State University M, D
University of Iowa M, D

Kansas
University of Kansas M, D

Kentucky
Western Kentucky University B

Louisiana
Louisiana State University Medical Center M, D
Tulane University B, M, D

Maine
Colby College B
University of Maine B

Maryland
Uniformed Services University of the Health Sciences D
University of Maryland
  Baltimore County D
  Baltimore M, D

Massachusetts
Boston University B
Brandeis University M, D
Hampshire College B
Harvard College B
Harvard University M, D
Tufts University D
University of Massachusetts
  Amherst M, D

Michigan
University of Michigan B, M, D

Minnesota
Southwest State University B
University of Minnesota
  Duluth B
  Twin Cities B, M, D
Winona State University B

Missouri
St. Louis University D
Southwest Missouri State University B
University of Missouri
  Kansas City M
Washington University D

New Hampshire
Dartmouth College B
University of New Hampshire B

New Jersey
Rowan University B
Rutgers
  The State University of New Jersey: Camden College of Arts and Sciences B
  The State University of New Jersey: Cook College B
  The State University of New Jersey: Douglass College B
  The State University of New Jersey: Livingston College B
  The State University of New Jersey: New Brunswick Graduate Campus M, D
  The State University of New Jersey: Rutgers College B
  The State University of New Jersey: University College Camden B
  The State University of New Jersey: University College New Brunswick B

New York
Albany Medical College M, D
Bard College B
Columbia University
  Graduate School M, D
Long Island University
  Brooklyn Campus M
New York University M, D
Rockefeller University D
State University of New York
  Albany M, D
  College of Environmental Science and Forestry B, M, D
  Stony Brook M, D
University of Rochester B

North Carolina
Duke University M, D
Methodist College A, B
University of North Carolina
  Chapel Hill M, D

North Dakota
North Dakota State University D

Ohio
Case Western Reserve University D
Kent State University M, D
Ohio State University
  Columbus Campus M, D
Ohio University B
University of Akron B

Oklahoma
Northeastern State University B

Oregon
Oregon Health Sciences University M, D
Oregon State University D

Pennsylvania
Bucknell University B
Carnegie Mellon University B
Juniata College B
Lock Haven University of Pennsylvania B
MCP Hahnemann University M, D
Mansfield University of Pennsylvania B

Cell biology

Penn State
College of Medicine, Milton S. Hershey Medical Center M, D
Thomas Jefferson University: College of Health Professions D
University of Pennsylvania M, D
West Chester University of Pennsylvania B

Rhode Island
Brown University B, M, D

Tennessee
Vanderbilt University M, D

Texas
Texas A&M University Commerce B
Texas A&M University B
Texas Tech University B
University of Texas
Dallas M, D
Medical Branch at Galveston M, D

Utah
Brigham Young University M, D

Vermont
Bennington College B
Johnson State College B
Marlboro College B
University of Vermont M, D

Virginia
University of Virginia D

Washington
University of Washington M, D
Western Washington University B

Wisconsin
Marquette University D, T
Medical College of Wisconsin M, D
University of Wisconsin
Madison M
Superior B

Ceramic sciences/engineering

Illinois
Parkland College A
University of Illinois Urbana-Champaign B

Iowa
Iowa State University B

Massachusetts
Massachusetts Institute of Technology D

Missouri
East Central College A
University of Missouri Rolla B, M, D

New Jersey
Rutgers
The State University of New Jersey: College of Engineering B
The State University of New Jersey: New Brunswick Graduate Campus M, D

New Mexico
New Mexico Institute of Mining and Technology B

New York
New York State College of Ceramics at Alfred University B, M, D

Ohio
Case Western Reserve University M, D
Hocking Technical College A
Ohio State University Columbus Campus B

Pennsylvania
Lock Haven University of Pennsylvania B

Puerto Rico
University of Puerto Rico Ponce University College A

South Carolina
Clemson University B, M, D

Washington
University of Washington B

Ceramics

Alabama
University of Alabama M

Arizona
Arizona State University B, M

California
Butte College C, A
California College of Arts and Crafts B, M
California State University
Fullerton B, M
Hayward B
Long Beach B, M
Northridge B, M
Chabot College A
De Anza College C, A
Glendale Community College C
Grossmont Community College A
Monterey Peninsula College A
Palomar College A
Pasadena City College C, A
San Francisco Art Institute B, M
Santa Rosa Junior College C
Ventura College A
West Los Angeles College C, A

Colorado
Adams State College B
Colorado State University B

Connecticut
University of Hartford B, M

District of Columbia
George Washington University M

Florida
Barry University B
University of Miami B

Georgia
LaGrange College B
University of Georgia B

Illinois
Barat College B
Richland Community College A
Rockford College B
School of the Art Institute of Chicago B, M

Indiana
Ball State University B
University of Evansville B
Vincennes University A

Iowa
University of Iowa B, M

Kansas
Allen County Community College A
Pratt Community College A
Seward County Community College A
University of Kansas B, M

Maine
Maine College of Art B

Maryland
Maryland Institute College of Art B

Massachusetts
Massachusetts College of Art B, M

School of the Museum of Fine Arts B, M
Simon's Rock College of Bard B
University of Massachusetts Dartmouth B

Michigan
Center for Creative Studies: College of Art and Design B
Cranbrook Academy of Art M
Grand Valley State University B
Henry Ford Community College A
Northern Michigan University B
Oakland Community College A
Siena Heights University B
Suomi College B
University of Michigan B
Western Michigan University B

Minnesota
Minnesota State University, Mankato B
Moorhead State University B

Missouri
Kansas City Art Institute B
Lindenwood University M
Washington University B, M
Webster University B

New Hampshire
Plymouth State College of the University System of New Hampshire B

New Jersey
Rowan University B
Rutgers
The State University of New Jersey: Mason Gross School of the Arts B, M

New York
Columbia University Teachers College M, D
New York State College of Ceramics at Alfred University B, M, T
Parsons School of Design C, A, B, T
Pratt Institute B, M
Rochester Institute of Technology A, B, M
State University of New York College at Fredonia B
New Paltz B, M
Syracuse University B, M

North Carolina
Haywood Community College A
Montgomery Community College C, A

Ohio
Bowling Green State University B
Cleveland Institute of Art B
Columbus College of Art and Design B
Ohio State University Columbus Campus B
Ohio University B, M
Shawnee State University B
University of Akron B
Wittenberg University B
Youngstown State University B

Oklahoma
University of Oklahoma B

Oregon
Pacific Northwest College of Art B
University of Oregon B, M

Pennsylvania
Beaver College B
Immaculata College A
Mercyhurst College B
Moore College of Art and Design B
Seton Hill College B
Temple University B, M
University of the Arts B, M

Rhode Island
Providence College B
Rhode Island College B
Salve Regina University B

Tennessee
Union University B

Texas
McMurry University B
Sam Houston State University M
Texas A&M University Commerce B, M
Texas Woman's University B, M
University of Dallas M, T
University of North Texas B, M
University of Texas
Arlington B
El Paso B
San Antonio B, M
Western Texas College A

Utah
Brigham Young University M
Dixie State College of Utah A

Vermont
Bennington College B, M
Marlboro College B

Virginia
Lord Fairfax Community College C
Virginia Intermont College B

Washington
University of Washington B, M
Western Washington University B

West Virginia
West Virginia State College B
West Virginia Wesleyan College B

Wisconsin
University of Wisconsin Madison B

Chemical engineering

Alabama
Auburn University B, M, D
Northeast Alabama Community College A
Tuskegee University B
University of Alabama Huntsville B, M
University of Alabama B, M, D
University of South Alabama B, M

Arizona
Arizona State University B, M, D
University of Arizona B, M, D

Arkansas
University of Arkansas B, M

California
California Institute of Technology B, M, D
California State Polytechnic University: Pomona B
California State University
Long Beach B
Northridge B, M
San Jose State University B, M
Stanford University B, M, D
University of California
Berkeley B, M, D
Davis B
Irvine B, M, D
Los Angeles B, M, D
Riverside B, M, D
San Diego B, M, D
Santa Barbara B, M, D
University of Southern California B, M, D

Colorado
Colorado School of Mines B, M, D
Colorado State University B, M, D
National Technological University M
University of Colorado Boulder B, M, D

Connecticut
Fairfield University *B*
University of Connecticut *B, M, D*
University of Hartford *B*
University of New Haven *A, B*
Yale University *B, M, D*

Delaware
University of Delaware *B, M, D*

District of Columbia
Howard University *B, M*

Florida
Brevard Community College *A*
Florida Agricultural and Mechanical
 University *B, M, D*
Florida Institute of Technology *B, M, D*
Florida International University *B*
Florida State University *B, M, D*
Miami-Dade Community College *A*
Pensacola Junior College *A*
University of Florida *B, M, D*
University of South Florida *B, M, D*

Georgia
Georgia Institute of Technology *B, M, D*
Middle Georgia College *A*
Morris Brown College *B*

Idaho
College of Southern Idaho *A*
North Idaho College *A*
Ricks College *A*
University of Idaho *B, M, D*

Illinois
Illinois Institute of Technology *B, M, D*
Northwestern University *B, M, D*
Parkland College *A*
University of Illinois
 Chicago *B, M, D*
 Urbana-Champaign *B, M, D*

Indiana
Purdue University *B, M, D*
Rose-Hulman Institute of
 Technology *B, M*
Tri-State University *B*
University of Notre Dame *B, M, D*
Vincennes University *A*

Iowa
Iowa State University *B, M, D*
University of Iowa *B, M, D*

Kansas
Independence Community College *A*
Kansas State University *B, M, D*
University of Kansas *B, M*

Kentucky
University of Kentucky *B, M, D*
University of Louisville *B, M, D*

Louisiana
Louisiana State University and
 Agricultural and Mechanical
 College *B, M, D*
Louisiana Tech University *B*
Tulane University *B, M, D*
University of Louisiana at
 Lafayette *B, M*

Maine
University of Maine *B, M, D*

Maryland
Frederick Community College *A*
Johns Hopkins University *B, M, D*
Montgomery College
 Rockville Campus *A*
University of Maryland
 Baltimore County *B, M, D*
 College Park *B, M, D*

Massachusetts
Harvard College *B*
Harvard University *D*

Massachusetts Institute of
 Technology *B, M, D*
Northeastern University *B, M, D*
Tufts University *B, M, D*
University of Massachusetts
 Amherst *B, M, D*
 Lowell *B, M*
Worcester Polytechnic Institute *B, M, D*

Michigan
Calvin College *B*
Michigan State University *B, M, D*
Michigan Technological
 University *B, M, D, T*
University of Detroit Mercy *B, M, D*
University of Michigan *B, M, D*
Wayne State University *B, M, D*
Western Michigan University *B*

Minnesota
University of Minnesota
 Duluth *B*
 Twin Cities *B, M, D*
Winona State University *B*

Mississippi
Mississippi State University *B, M*
University of Mississippi *B*

Missouri
East Central College *A*
University of Missouri
 Columbia *B, M, D*
 Rolla *B, M, D*
Washington University *B, M, D*

Montana
Montana State University
 Bozeman *B, M*

Nebraska
University of Nebraska
 Lincoln *B, M*

Nevada
University of Nevada
 Reno *B, M, D*

New Hampshire
University of New Hampshire *B, M, D*

New Jersey
Essex County College *A*
New Jersey Institute of
 Technology *B, M, D*
Princeton University *B, M, D*
Rowan University *B*
Rutgers
 The State University of New Jersey:
  College of Engineering *B*
 The State University of New Jersey:
  New Brunswick Graduate
  Campus *M, D*
Seton Hall University *B*
Stevens Institute of Technology *B, M, D*

New Mexico
New Mexico Institute of Mining and
 Technology *B*
New Mexico State University *B, M*
University of New Mexico *B, M*

New York
City University of New York
 Bronx Community College *A*
 City College *B, M, D*
 Graduate School and University
  Center *D*
Clarkson University *B, M, D*
Columbia University
 Fu Foundation School of
  Engineering and Applied
  Science *B, M, D*
Cooper Union for the Advancement of
 Science and Art *B, M*
Cornell University *B, M, D*
Elmira College *B*
Finger Lakes Community College *A*
Manhattan College *B, M*

New York University *B*
Pace University:
 Pleasantville/Briarcliff *B*
Pace University *B*
Polytechnic University *B, M, D*
Rensselaer Polytechnic Institute *B, M, D*
State University of New York
 Buffalo *B, M, D*
 College of Environmental Science
  and Forestry *B, M, D*
 Stony Brook *B*
Suffolk County Community College *A*
Syracuse University *B, M, D*
United States Military Academy *B*
University of Rochester *B, M*

North Carolina
Cape Fear Community College *A*
North Carolina Agricultural and
 Technical State University *B*
North Carolina State University *B, M, D*
St. Augustine's College *B*

North Dakota
University of North Dakota *B, M*

Ohio
Case Western Reserve
 University *B, M, D*
Cleveland State University *B, M, D*
Lorain County Community College *A*
Ohio State University
 Columbus Campus *B, M, D*
Ohio University *B, M, D*
University of Akron *B, M, D*
University of Cincinnati *B, M, D*
University of Dayton *B, M*
University of Toledo *B, M*
Washington State Community College *A*
Wilberforce University *B*
Xavier University *B*
Youngstown State University *B, M*

Oklahoma
Northeastern Oklahoma Agricultural and
 Mechanical College *A*
Oklahoma State University *B, M, D*
University of Oklahoma *B, M, D*
University of Tulsa *B, M, D*

Oregon
Oregon State University *B, M, D*

Pennsylvania
Bucknell University *B, M*
Carnegie Mellon University *B, M, D*
Drexel University *B, M, D*
Gannon University *B*
Geneva College *B*
Gettysburg College *B*
Lafayette College *B*
Lehigh University *B, M, D*
Lock Haven University of
 Pennsylvania *B*
Penn State
 University Park *C, B, M, D*
Seton Hill College *B*
University of Pennsylvania *B, M, D*
University of Pittsburgh *B, M, D*
Villanova University *B, M*
Widener University *B, M*

Puerto Rico
University of Puerto Rico
 Mayaguez Campus *B, M, D*
 Ponce University College *A*

Rhode Island
Brown University *B, M, D*
University of Rhode Island *B, M, D*

South Carolina
Clemson University *B, M, D*
Lander University *B*
University of South Carolina *B, M, D*

South Dakota
South Dakota School of Mines and
 Technology *B, M*

Tennessee
Christian Brothers University *B*
Tennessee Technological
 University *B, M, D*
University of Tennessee
 Knoxville *B, M, D*
Vanderbilt University *B, M, D*

Texas
Houston Baptist University *B*
Kilgore College *A*
Lamar University *B*
Prairie View A&M University *B*
Rice University *B, M, D*
Texas A&M University
 Kingsville *B, M*
Texas A&M University *B, M, D*
Texas Tech University *B, M, D*
University of Houston *B, M, D*
University of Texas
 Austin *B, M, D*

Utah
Brigham Young University *B, M, D*
Salt Lake Community College *A*
Snow College *A*
Southern Utah University *A*
University of Utah *B, M, D*

Virginia
Hampton University *B*
University of Virginia *B, M, D*
Virginia Commonwealth University *B*
Virginia Polytechnic Institute and State
 University *B, M, D*
Washington and Lee University *B*

Washington
Lower Columbia College *A*
University of Washington *B, M, D*
Walla Walla College *B*
Washington State University *B, M, D*

West Virginia
West Virginia University Institute of
 Technology *B*
West Virginia University *B, M, D*

Wisconsin
Milwaukee Area Technical College *A*
University of Wisconsin
 Madison *B, M, D*
Viterbo University *B*

Wyoming
Laramie County Community College *A*
University of Wyoming *B, M, D*

Chemical/atomic physics

California
University of California
 San Diego *B*

Colorado
University of Colorado
 Boulder *D*

District of Columbia
Catholic University of America *B*

Florida
Florida State University *M, D*

Illinois
University of Illinois
 Urbana-Champaign *D*

Indiana
University of Notre Dame *M*

Kentucky
Centre College *B*

Massachusetts
Harvard College *B*
Harvard University *M, D*

Chemical/atomic physics

Michigan
Michigan State University B, D

Minnesota
St. Mary's University of Minnesota B
University of Minnesota
  Twin Cities M, D

Nevada
University of Nevada
  Reno D

New York
Columbia University
  Columbia College B
  Graduate School M, D

Ohio
Kent State University M, D, T
Ohio State University
  Columbus Campus M, D

Tennessee
Maryville College B
Union University B

Texas
Rice University B
University of North Texas M, D

Utah
University of Utah D

Virginia
Norfolk State University M

Wisconsin
Marquette University M, D
University of Wisconsin
  Madison M, D

Chemistry

Alabama
Alabama Agricultural and Mechanical
  University B, M
Alabama State University B
Athens State University B
Auburn University B, M, D
Birmingham-Southern College B, T
Calhoun Community College A
Chattahoochee Valley Community
  College A
Huntingdon College B, T
Jacksonville State University B
James H. Faulkner State Community
  College A
Lawson State Community College A
Northeast Alabama Community
  College A
Oakwood College B
Samford University B
Southern Union State Community
  College A
Spring Hill College B, T
Stillman College B
Talladega College B
Troy State University B
Tuskegee University B, M
University of Alabama
  Birmingham B, M, D
  Huntsville B, M
University of Alabama B, M, D
University of Mobile B
University of Montevallo B, T
University of North Alabama B
University of South Alabama B
University of West Alabama B, T

Alaska
University of Alaska
  Anchorage B
  Fairbanks B, M

Arizona
Arizona State University B, M, D
Arizona Western College A
Cochise College A

Eastern Arizona College A
Grand Canyon University B
Northern Arizona University B, M, T
Phoenix College A
South Mountain Community College A
University of Arizona B, M, D

Arkansas
Arkansas State University B, M
Arkansas Tech University B
Harding University B
Henderson State University B
Hendrix College B
John Brown University B
Lyon College B
Ouachita Baptist University B
Philander Smith College B
Phillips Community College of the
  University of Arkansas A
Southern Arkansas University B
University of Arkansas
  Little Rock B, M
  Monticello B
  Pine Bluff B
University of Arkansas B, M, D
University of Central Arkansas B
University of the Ozarks B
Westark College A

California
Allan Hancock College A
Azusa Pacific University B
Bakersfield College A
Cabrillo College A
California Institute of Technology B, D
California Lutheran University B
California Polytechnic State University:
  San Luis Obispo B, M
California State Polytechnic University:
  Pomona B, M
California State University
  Bakersfield B
  Chico C, B
  Dominguez Hills B
  Fresno B, M
  Fullerton B, M
  Hayward B, M
  Long Beach B, M
  Los Angeles B, M
  Northridge B, M
  Sacramento B, M
  San Marcos B
  Stanislaus B
Canada College A
Cerritos Community College A
Chaffey Community College A
Chapman University B
Citrus College A
City College of San Francisco A
Claremont McKenna College B
College of San Mateo A
College of the Desert A
College of the Siskiyous A
Columbia College A
Compton Community College A
Contra Costa College A
Crafton Hills College A
Cuesta College C, A
Cypress College A
De Anza College A
East Los Angeles College A
Foothill College A
Fresno City College A
Gavilan Community College A
Glendale Community College A
Golden West College A
Grossmont Community College C, A
Harvey Mudd College B
Humboldt State University B
Irvine Valley College A
La Sierra University B
Las Positas College A
Long Beach City College C, A
Los Angeles Southwest College A
Los Angeles Valley College A
Los Medanos College A

Loyola Marymount University B
Merced College A
Mills College B
MiraCosta College A
Mission College A
Monterey Peninsula College A
Moorpark College A
Mount St. Mary's College B
Occidental College B
Ohlone College C, A
Orange Coast College A
Pacific Union College B
Palomar College C, A
Pepperdine University B
Pitzer College B
Point Loma Nazarene University B
Pomona College B
Porterville College A
Riverside Community College A
Saddleback College A
St. Mary's College of California B
San Bernardino Valley College A
San Diego City College A
San Diego Mesa College C, A
San Diego Miramar College A
San Diego State University B, M, D
San Francisco State University B, M
San Joaquin Delta College A
San Jose State University B, M
Santa Ana College A
Santa Barbara City College A
Santa Clara University B
Santa Monica College A
Santa Rosa Junior College A
Scripps College B
Sierra College A
Solano Community College A
Sonoma State University B
Southwestern College C, A
Stanford University B, M, D
University of California
  Berkeley B, M, D
  Davis B, M, D
  Irvine B, M, D
  Los Angeles B, M, D
  Riverside B, M, D
  San Diego B, D
  Santa Barbara B, M, D
  Santa Cruz B, M, D
University of La Verne C, B
University of Redlands B
University of San Diego B
University of San Francisco B, M
University of Southern
  California B, M, D
University of the Pacific B, M, D
Vanguard University of Southern
  California B
Ventura College A
West Hills Community College A
West Los Angeles College C, A
West Valley College A
Westmont College B
Whittier College B

Colorado
Adams State College B
Colorado College B
Colorado Mountain College
  Spring Valley Campus A
Colorado School of Mines B, M, D
Colorado State University B, M, D
Fort Lewis College B
Metropolitan State College of Denver B
Otero Junior College A
Red Rocks Community College A
Regis University B
Trinidad State Junior College A
United States Air Force Academy B
University of Colorado
  Boulder B, M, D
  Colorado Springs B
  Denver B, M
University of Denver B, M, D

University of Northern
  Colorado B, M, D, T
University of Southern Colorado B, T
Western State College of Colorado B

Connecticut
Central Connecticut State
  University B, M
Connecticut College B
Fairfield University B
Quinnipiac University B
Sacred Heart University A, B, M
St. Joseph College B, M, T
Southern Connecticut State
  University B, M
Trinity College B
University of Connecticut B, M, D
University of Hartford B
University of New Haven A, B
Wesleyan University B, M, D
Western Connecticut State University B
Yale University B, M, D

Delaware
Delaware State University B, M
University of Delaware B, M, D

District of Columbia
American University B, M, D
Catholic University of
  America B, M, D, T
Gallaudet University B
George Washington University B, M, D
Georgetown University B, M, D
Howard University B, M, D
Trinity College B
University of the District of Columbia B

Florida
Barry University B
Bethune-Cookman College B
Broward Community College A
Eckerd College B
Florida Agricultural and Mechanical
  University B, M
Florida Atlantic University B, M
Florida Institute of Technology B, M, D
Florida International University B, M, D
Florida Southern College B
Florida State University B, M, D
Gulf Coast Community College A
Indian River Community College A
Jacksonville University B
Manatee Community College A
Miami-Dade Community College A
New College of the University of South
  Florida B
Palm Beach Community College A
Pensacola Junior College A
Rollins College B
St. Thomas University B
Santa Fe Community College A
Stetson University B
University of Central Florida B, M
University of Florida B, M, D
University of Miami B, M, D
University of North Florida B
University of South Florida B, M, D
University of Tampa A, B, T
University of West Florida B

Georgia
Abraham Baldwin Agricultural
  College A
Agnes Scott College B
Albany State University B
Armstrong Atlantic State University B, T
Atlanta Metropolitan College A
Augusta State University B
Berry College B, T
Clark Atlanta University B, M, D
Clayton College and State University A
Columbus State University B
Covenant College B
Dalton State College A
Darton College A
East Georgia College A

Emory University *B, D*
Floyd College *A*
Fort Valley State University *B*
Gainesville College *A*
Georgia College and State University *B*
Georgia Institute of Technology *B, M, D*
Georgia Military College *A*
Georgia Perimeter College *A*
Georgia Southern University *B*
Georgia Southwestern State University *B*
Georgia State University *B, M, D*
Kennesaw State University *B*
LaGrange College *B*
Mercer University *B*
Middle Georgia College *A*
Morehouse College *B*
Morris Brown College *B*
North Georgia College & State University *B*
Oglethorpe University *B*
Oxford College of Emory University *B*
Paine College *B*
Piedmont College *B*
Savannah State University *B*
Shorter College *B*
South Georgia College *A*
Spelman College *B*
State University of West Georgia *B*
University of Georgia *B, M, D*
Valdosta State University *B*
Waycross College *A*
Wesleyan College *B, T*
Young Harris College *A*

Hawaii
Brigham Young University
    Hawaii *B*
Chaminade University of Honolulu *B*
University of Hawaii
    Hilo *B*
    Manoa *B, M, D*

Idaho
Albertson College of Idaho *B*
Boise State University *B, T*
College of Southern Idaho *A*
Idaho State University *A, B, M*
Lewis-Clark State College *B*
North Idaho College *A*
Northwest Nazarene University *B*
Ricks College *A*
University of Idaho *B, M, D*

Illinois
Augustana College *B, T*
Barat College *B*
Benedictine University *B, T*
Black Hawk College
    East Campus *A*
Blackburn College *B*
Bradley University *B, M, T*
Chicago State University *B, T*
City Colleges of Chicago
    Harold Washington College *A*
    Kennedy-King College *A*
    Olive-Harvey College *A*
Concordia University *B, T*
Danville Area Community College *A*
De Paul University *B, M, T*
Dominican University *B*
Eastern Illinois University *B, M, T*
Elmhurst College *B, T*
Eureka College *B*
Governors State University *B*
Greenville College *B, T*
Highland Community College *A*
Illinois College *B*
Illinois Institute of Technology *B, M, D*
Illinois State University *B, M, T*
Illinois Wesleyan University *B*
John A. Logan College *A*
Joliet Junior College *A*
Judson College *B*
Kishwaukee College *A*
Knox College *B*
Lake Forest College *B*

Lewis University *B, T*
Lincoln Land Community College *A*
Loyola University of Chicago *B, M, D*
MacMurray College *B*
McKendree College *B*
Millikin University *B, T*
Monmouth College *B, T*
Morton College *A*
North Central College *B, T*
North Park University *B*
Northeastern Illinois University *B, M*
Northern Illinois University *B, M, D, T*
Northwestern University *B, M, D*
Olivet Nazarene University *B, T*
Parkland College *A*
Principia College *B*
Quincy University *A, B*
Rend Lake College *A*
Rockford College *B*
Roosevelt University *B*
St. Xavier University *B*
Sauk Valley Community College *A*
Southern Illinois University
    Carbondale *B, M, D*
    Edwardsville *B, M*
Southwestern Ilinois College *A*
Springfield College in Illinois *A*
Trinity Christian College *B, T*
Trinity International University *B*
Triton College *A*
University of Chicago *B, M, D*
University of Illinois
    Chicago *B, M, D*
    Springfield *B*
    Urbana-Champaign *B, M, D*
Western Illinois University *B, M*
Wheaton College *B, T*

Indiana
Anderson University *B*
Ball State University *B, M*
Bethel College *A, B*
Butler University *B, M*
DePauw University *B*
Earlham College *B*
Franklin College *B*
Goshen College *B*
Grace College *B*
Hanover College *B*
Indiana State University *B, M, T*
Indiana University
    Bloomington *B, M, D*
    Northwest *B, T*
    South Bend *A, B*
    Southeast *B*
Indiana University--Purdue University
    Indiana University-Purdue
        University Fort Wayne *A, B, M*
    Indiana University-Purdue
        University Indianapolis *B, M*
Indiana Wesleyan University *A, B*
Manchester College *B, T*
Marian College *B, T*
Purdue University
    Calumet *B*
Purdue University *B, M, D*
Rose-Hulman Institute of Technology *B*
Saint Mary's College *B, T*
St. Joseph's College *B*
Taylor University *B*
Tri-State University *B*
University of Evansville *B*
University of Indianapolis *A, B*
University of Notre Dame *B, M, D*
University of St. Francis *B*
University of Southern Indiana *B*
Valparaiso University *B, T*
Vincennes University *A*
Wabash College *B*

Iowa
Briar Cliff College *B*
Buena Vista University *B, T*
Central College *B, T*
Clarke College *B, T*
Coe College *B*

Cornell College *B, T*
Dordt College *B*
Drake University *B*
Graceland University *B, T*
Grinnell College *B*
Iowa State University *B, M, D*
Iowa Wesleyan College *B*
Loras College *B*
Luther College *B*
Maharishi University of
    Management *A, B*
Morningside College *B*
North Iowa Area Community College *A*
Northwestern College *B, T*
St. Ambrose University *B*
Simpson College *B*
University of Iowa *B, M, D, T*
University of Northern Iowa *B, M*
Upper Iowa University *B*
Waldorf College *A*
Wartburg College *B, T*

Kansas
Allen County Community College *A*
Baker University *B, T*
Benedictine College *B*
Bethany College *B, T*
Bethel College *B, T*
Butler County Community College *A*
Central Christian College *A*
Coffeyville Community College *A*
Colby Community College *A*
Dodge City Community College *A*
Emporia State University *B, T*
Fort Hays State University *B*
Garden City Community College *A*
Independence Community College *A*
Kansas City Kansas Community
    College *A*
Kansas State University *B, M, D*
Kansas Wesleyan University *B, T*
McPherson College *B, T*
MidAmerica Nazarene University *B*
Newman University *B*
Pittsburg State University *B, M, T*
Pratt Community College *A*
St. Mary College *B*
Seward County Community College *A*
Southwestern College *B*
Tabor College *B*
University of Kansas *B, M, D*
Washburn University of Topeka *B*
Wichita State University *B, M, D, T*

Kentucky
Asbury College *B*
Bellarmine College *B, T*
Berea College *B, T*
Brescia University *B*
Campbellsville University *B*
Centre College *B*
Cumberland College *B, T*
Eastern Kentucky University *B, M*
Georgetown College *B, T*
Kentucky State University *B*
Kentucky Wesleyan College *B, T*
Lindsey Wilson College *A*
Morehead State University *B*
Murray State University *B, M, T*
Northern Kentucky University *B, T*
Pikeville College *B*
Spalding University *B*
Thomas More College *A, B*
Transylvania University *B, T*
Union College *B*
University of Kentucky *B, M, D*
University of Louisville *B, M, D*
Western Kentucky University *B, M, T*

Louisiana
Centenary College of Louisiana *B, T*
Dillard University *B*
Louisiana State University
    Shreveport *B*

Louisiana State University and
    Agricultural and Mechanical
    College *B, M, D*
Louisiana Tech University *B, M*
Loyola University New Orleans *B*
McNeese State University *B, M*
Nicholls State University *B*
Northwestern State University *B*
Our Lady of Holy Cross College *T*
Southeastern Louisiana University *B*
Southern University
    New Orleans *B*
    Shreveport *A*
Southern University and Agricultural and
    Mechanical College *B, M*
Tulane University *B, M, D*
University of Louisiana at Lafayette *B*
University of Louisiana at Monroe *B, M*
University of New Orleans *B, M, D*
Xavier University of Louisiana *B*

Maine
Bates College *B*
Bowdoin College *B*
Colby College *B*
University of Maine *B, M, D*
University of Southern Maine *B*

Maryland
Allegany College *A*
College of Notre Dame of Maryland *B*
Columbia Union College *B*
Community College of Baltimore County
    Essex *A*
Coppin State College *B*
Frederick Community College *A*
Frostburg State University *B, T*
Goucher College *B, T*
Hagerstown Community College *A*
Harford Community College *A*
Hood College *B, T*
Johns Hopkins University *B, D*
Loyola College in Maryland *B*
Morgan State University *B*
Mount St. Mary's College *B*
St. Mary's College of Maryland *B*
Salisbury State University *B, T*
Towson University *B*
United States Naval Academy *B*
University of Maryland
    Baltimore County *B, M, D*
    College Park *B, M, D*
    Eastern Shore *B*
Villa Julie College *A, B*
Washington College *B, T*
Western Maryland College *B*

Massachusetts
American International College *B*
Amherst College *B*
Assumption College *B*
Atlantic Union College *B*
Boston College *B, M, D*
Boston University *B, M, D*
Brandeis University *B, M, D*
Bridgewater State College *B, M*
Clark University *B, M, D*
College of the Holy Cross *B*
Curry College *B*
Eastern Nazarene College *B*
Elms College *B*
Emmanuel College *B*
Fitchburg State College *B*
Framingham State College *B*
Gordon College *B*
Hampshire College *B*
Harvard College *B*
Harvard University *M, D*
Massachusetts College of Liberal Arts *B*
Massachusetts College of Pharmacy and
    Health Sciences *B, M*
Massachusetts Institute of
    Technology *B, D*
Mount Holyoke College *B, M*
Northeastern University *B, M, D*
Regis College *B*

Salem State College *B*
Simmons College *B*
Simon's Rock College of Bard *B*
Smith College *B*
Springfield Technical Community
  College *A*
Stonehill College *B*
Suffolk University *B*
Tufts University *B*
University of Massachusetts
  Amherst *B, M, D*
  Boston *B, M*
  Dartmouth *B, M*
  Lowell *B, M, D*
Wellesley College *B*
Western New England College *B, T*
Wheaton College *B*
Williams College *B*
Worcester Polytechnic Institute *B, M, D*
Worcester State College *B*

Michigan
Adrian College *A, B, T*
Albion College *B, T*
Alma College *B, T*
Andrews University *B*
Aquinas College *B, T*
Calvin College *B, T*
Central Michigan University *B, M*
Eastern Michigan University *B*
Gogebic Community College *A*
Grand Valley State University *B*
Hillsdale College *B*
Hope College *B, T*
Kalamazoo College *B, T*
Kellogg Community College *A*
Kettering University *B*
Lake Michigan College *A*
Lake Superior State University *A, B*
Lansing Community College *A*
Lawrence Technological University *B*
Madonna University *B, T*
Marygrove College *B, T*
Michigan State University *B, M, D*
Michigan Technological
  University *B, M, D, T*
Mid Michigan Community College *A*
Northern Michigan University *A, B, M*
Oakland University *B, M, T*
Olivet College *B, T*
Saginaw Valley State University *B*
Siena Heights University *A, B*
Spring Arbor College *B*
University of Detroit Mercy *B, M*
University of Michigan
  Dearborn *B*
  Flint *B, T*
University of Michigan *B, M, D, T*
Wayne State University *B, M, D*
Western Michigan University *B, M, T*

Minnesota
Augsburg College *B*
Bemidji State University *B, M*
Bethel College *B*
Carleton College *B*
College of St. Benedict *B*
College of St. Catherine: St. Paul
  Campus *B*
College of St. Scholastica *B*
Concordia College: Moorhead *B*
Gustavus Adolphus College *B*
Hamline University *B*
Macalester College *B, T*
Minnesota State University,
  Mankato *B, M*
Moorhead State University *B*
Ridgewater College: A Community and
  Technical College *A*
St. Cloud State University *B*
St. John's University *B*
St. Mary's University of Minnesota *B*
St. Olaf College *B, T*
Southwest State University *B*

University of Minnesota
  Duluth *B, M*
  Morris *B*
  Twin Cities *B, M, D*
University of St. Thomas *B*
Winona State University *B*

Mississippi
Alcorn State University *B*
Belhaven College *B*
Blue Mountain College *B*
Copiah-Lincoln Community College *A*
Delta State University *B, T*
East Central Community College *A*
Hinds Community College *A*
Jackson State University *B, M*
Mary Holmes College *A*
Millsaps College *B, T*
Mississippi College *B, M*
Mississippi State University *B, M, D*
Mississippi University for Women *B, T*
Mississippi Valley State University *B*
Rust College *B*
Tougaloo College *B*
University of Mississippi *B, M, D, T*
University of Southern
  Mississippi *B, M, D*
William Carey College *B*

Missouri
Avila College *B*
Central Methodist College *B*
Central Missouri State University *B*
College of the Ozarks *B*
Crowder College *A*
Culver-Stockton College *B*
Drury University *B, T*
East Central College *A*
Evangel University *B*
Lincoln University *B*
Lindenwood University *B*
Maryville University of Saint Louis *B*
Missouri Baptist College *B*
Missouri Southern State College *B, T*
Missouri Western State College *B, T*
Northwest Missouri State University *B*
Park University *B*
Rockhurst University *B*
St. Louis University *B, M*
Southeast Missouri State University *B*
Southwest Baptist University *B*
Southwest Missouri State
  University *B, M*
St. Louis Community College
  St. Louis Community College at
    Florissant Valley *A*
  St. Louis Community College at
    Forest Park *A*
Three Rivers Community College *A*
Truman State University *B*
University of Missouri
  Columbia *B, M, D*
  Kansas City *B, M*
  Rolla *B, M, D, T*
  St. Louis *B, M, D*
Washington University *B, M, D*
Westminster College *B*
William Jewell College *B, T*

Montana
Carroll College *B, T*
Montana State University
  Billings *B*
  Bozeman *B, M, D, T*
  Northern *A, B*
Montana Tech of the University of
  Montana *B*
Rocky Mountain College *B, T*
University of Great Falls *B*
University of Montana-Missoula *B, M, D*
Western Montana College of The
  University of Montana *B*

Nebraska
Chadron State College *B*
College of Saint Mary *B, T*

Concordia University *B, T*
Creighton University *B*
Dana College *B*
Doane College *B*
Hastings College *B*
Midland Lutheran College *B, T*
Nebraska Wesleyan University *B*
Northeast Community College *A*
Union College *B*
University of Nebraska
  Kearney *B, T*
  Lincoln *B, M, D*
  Omaha *B*
Wayne State College *B, T*

Nevada
University of Nevada
  Las Vegas *B, M*
  Reno *B, M, D*

New Hampshire
Dartmouth College *B, D*
Keene State College *B*
Plymouth State College of the University
  System of New Hampshire *B*
Rivier College *B, T*
St. Anselm College *B, T*
University of New Hampshire *B, M, D*

New Jersey
Atlantic Cape Community College *A*
Bloomfield College *B*
Brookdale Community College *A*
Caldwell College *B*
College of St. Elizabeth *B, T*
Drew University *B*
Essex County College *A*
Fairleigh Dickinson University *B, M*
Georgian Court College *B, T*
Gloucester County College *A*
Hudson County Community College *A*
Kean University *B*
Middlesex County College *A*
Monmouth University *B*
Montclair State University *B, M*
New Jersey City University *B*
New Jersey Institute of Technology *B, M*
Princeton University *B, M, D*
Ramapo College of New Jersey *B*
Raritan Valley Community College *A*
Richard Stockton College of New
  Jersey *B*
Rider University *B*
Rowan University *B*
Rutgers
  The State University of New Jersey:
    Camden College of Arts and
    Sciences *B, T*
  The State University of New Jersey:
    Camden Graduate Campus *M*
  The State University of New Jersey:
    Cook College *B*
  The State University of New Jersey:
    Douglass College *B*
  The State University of New Jersey:
    Livingston College *B*
  The State University of New Jersey:
    New Brunswick Graduate
    Campus *M, D, T*
  The State University of New Jersey:
    Newark College of Arts and
    Sciences *B*
  The State University of New Jersey:
    Newark Graduate Campus *M*
  The State University of New Jersey:
    Rutgers College *B*
  The State University of New Jersey:
    University College Camden *B, T*
  The State University of New Jersey:
    University College New
    Brunswick *B*
St. Peter's College *B*
Salem Community College *A*
Seton Hall University *B, M, D, T*
Stevens Institute of Technology *B, M, D*
Sussex County Community College *A*

The College of New Jersey *B, T*
Thomas Edison State College *A, B*
Union County College *A*
Warren County Community College *A*
William Paterson University of New
  Jersey *B*

New Mexico
College of Santa Fe *A*
Eastern New Mexico University *B, M*
New Mexico Highlands University *B, M*
New Mexico Institute of Mining and
  Technology *B, M, D*
New Mexico Junior College *A*
New Mexico State University *B, M, D*
San Juan College *A*
University of New Mexico *B, M, D*
Western New Mexico University *B*

New York
Adelphi University *B, M*
Adirondack Community College *A*
Alfred University *B*
Bard College *B*
Barnard College *B*
Canisius College *B*
City University of New York
  Brooklyn College *B, M*
  City College *B, M, D, T*
  College of Staten Island *B, T*
  Graduate School and University
    Center *D*
  Hunter College *B*
  Kingsborough Community
    College *A*
  Lehman College *B*
  Queens College *B, M*
  Queensborough Community
    College *A*
  York College *B*
Clarkson University *B, M, D*
Colgate University *B*
College of Mount St. Vincent *B, T*
College of New Rochelle *B, T*
College of St. Rose *B*
Columbia University
  Columbia College *B*
  Graduate School *M, D*
  School of General Studies *B*
Cornell University *B, D*
Daemen College *B, T*
Elmira College *B, T*
Fordham University *B, M, D*
Hamilton College *B*
Hartwick College *B, T*
Hobart and William Smith Colleges *B*
Hofstra University *B*
Houghton College *B*
Hudson Valley Community College *A*
Iona College *B*
Ithaca College *B, T*
Le Moyne College *B*
Long Island University
  Brooklyn Campus *B, M*
  C. W. Post Campus *B*
  Southampton College *B*
Manhattan College *B*
Manhattanville College *B*
Marist College *B, T*
Marymount College *B, T*
Monroe Community College *A*
Mount St. Mary College *B, T*
Nazareth College of Rochester *B*
New York University *B, M, D*
Niagara University *B*
Pace University:
  Pleasantville/Briarcliff *B, T*
Pace University *B, T*
Polytechnic University *B, M, D*
Regents College *B*
Rensselaer Polytechnic Institute *B, M, D*
Rochester Institute of
  Technology *A, B, M*
Russell Sage College *B, T*
St. Bonaventure University *B, T*
St. John Fisher College *B*

St. John's University B, M
St. Lawrence University B, T
St. Thomas Aquinas College B, T
Siena College B, T
Skidmore College B
St. Joseph's College
    St. Joseph's College B
State University of New York
    Albany B, M, D
    Binghamton B, M, D
    Buffalo B, M, D
    College at Brockport B, T
    College at Buffalo B, M
    College at Cortland B
    College at Fredonia B, M, T
    College at Geneseo B, T
    College at Old Westbury B, T
    College at Oneonta B, M
    College at Plattsburgh B, M
    College at Potsdam B, T
    College of Agriculture and
      Technology at Morrisville A
    College of Environmental Science
      and Forestry B, M, D
    College of Technology at Alfred A
    New Paltz B, M, T
    Oswego B, M
    Purchase B
    Stony Brook B, M, D, T
Syracuse University B, M, D
Touro College B
Union College B
United States Military Academy B
University of Rochester B, M, D
Utica College of Syracuse University B
Vassar College B, M
Wagner College B, T
Wells College B

North Carolina
Appalachian State University B, M
Barton College B
Bennett College B
Campbell University B
Catawba College B, T
Davidson College B
Duke University B, M, D
East Carolina University B, M
Elizabeth City State University B
Elon College B
Fayetteville State University B
Gardner-Webb University B
Greensboro College B
Guilford College B
Guilford Technical Community
    College A
High Point University B
Johnson C. Smith University B
Lenoir-Rhyne College B
Louisburg College A
Mars Hill College B, T
Meredith College B
Methodist College A, B, T
North Carolina Agricultural and
  Technical State University B, M
North Carolina Central University B, M
North Carolina State University B, M, D
North Carolina Wesleyan College B
Pfeiffer University B
St. Andrews Presbyterian College B
St. Augustine's College B
Salem College B
Sandhills Community College A
Shaw University B
University of North Carolina
    Asheville B, T
    Chapel Hill B, M, D
    Charlotte B, M
    Greensboro B, M, T
    Pembroke B
    Wilmington B, M, T
Wake Forest University B, M, D
Warren Wilson College B
Western Carolina University B, M
Wingate University B

Winston-Salem State University B

North Dakota
Bismarck State College A
Dickinson State University B, T
Jamestown College B
Mayville State University B, T
Minot State University: Bottineau
    Campus A
Minot State University B, T
North Dakota State
    University B, M, D, T
University of North Dakota B, M, D
Valley City State University B

Ohio
Antioch College B
Ashland University B
Baldwin-Wallace College B, T
Bluffton College B
Bowling Green State University B, M
Capital University B
Case Western Reserve
    University B, M, D
Cedarville College B, T
Central State University B
Cleveland State University B, M, D, T
College of Mount St. Joseph B, T
College of Wooster B
Defiance College B, T
Denison University B
Franciscan University of Steubenville B
Heidelberg College B
Hiram College B
Jefferson Community College A
John Carroll University B, M
Kent State University
    Stark Campus B
Kent State University B, M, D, T
Kenyon College B
Lake Erie College B
Lorain County Community College A
Lourdes College A, B
Malone College B
Marietta College B
Miami University
    Middletown Campus A
    Oxford Campus B, M, D, T
Mount Union College B
Mount Vernon Nazarene College B
Muskingum College B
Notre Dame College of Ohio B, T
Oberlin College B
Ohio Dominican College C, A, B, T
Ohio Northern University B
Ohio State University
    Columbus Campus B, M, D
Ohio University B, M, D
Ohio Wesleyan University B
Otterbein College B
Shawnee State University B
Terra Community College A
University of Akron B, M, D
University of Cincinnati
    Raymond Walters College A
University of Cincinnati B, M, D
University of Dayton B, M
University of Rio Grande A, B, T
University of Toledo B, M, D
Walsh University B
Wilberforce University B
Wilmington College B
Wittenberg University B
Wright State University B, M
Xavier University B
Youngstown State University B, M

Oklahoma
Cameron University B
Connors State College A
East Central University B, T
Eastern Oklahoma State College A
Langston University B
Northeastern Oklahoma Agricultural and
    Mechanical College A
Northeastern State University B

Northern Oklahoma College A
Northwestern Oklahoma State
    University B
Oklahoma Baptist University B, T
Oklahoma Christian University of
    Science and Arts B
Oklahoma City Community College A
Oklahoma City University B
Oklahoma Panhandle State University B
Oklahoma State University B, M, D
Oral Roberts University B
Redlands Community College A
Rogers State University A
Rose State College A
Southeastern Oklahoma State
    University B
Southern Nazarene University B
Southwestern Oklahoma State
    University B
Tulsa Community College A
University of Central Oklahoma B
University of Oklahoma B, M, D
University of Science and Arts of
    Oklahoma B
University of Tulsa B, M

Oregon
Central Oregon Community College A
Chemeketa Community College A
Concordia University B
Eastern Oregon University B, T
George Fox University B, T
Lewis & Clark College B
Linfield College B
Oregon State University B, M, D
Pacific University B
Portland State University B, M
Reed College B
Southern Oregon University B
University of Oregon B, M, D
University of Portland B
Western Oregon University B
Willamette University B

Pennsylvania
Albright College B, T
Allegheny College B
Allentown College of St. Francis de
    Sales B
Alvernia College B
Beaver College B
Bloomsburg University of
    Pennsylvania B, T
Bryn Mawr College B, M, D
Bucknell University B, M
Bucks County Community College A
Cabrini College B
California University of Pennsylvania B
Carlow College B
Carnegie Mellon University B, M, D
Cedar Crest College B
Chatham College B
Chestnut Hill College A, B
Cheyney University of Pennsylvania B
Clarion University of Pennsylvania B, T
College Misericordia B
Community College of Allegheny
    County A
Delaware Valley College B
Dickinson College B
Drexel University B, M, D
Duquesne University B, M, D
East Stroudsburg University of
    Pennsylvania B
Eastern College B
Edinboro University of
    Pennsylvania B, T
Elizabethtown College B
Franklin and Marshall College B
Gannon University B
Geneva College B, T
Gettysburg College B
Grove City College B
Harrisburg Area Community College A
Haverford College B, T
Holy Family College B, T

Immaculata College B
Indiana University of
    Pennsylvania B, M, T
Juniata College B
King's College B, T
Kutztown University of
    Pennsylvania B, T
La Roche College B
La Salle University B
Lafayette College B
Lebanon Valley College of
    Pennsylvania B
Lehigh University B, M, D
Lincoln University B
Lock Haven University of
    Pennsylvania B
Lycoming College B
Mansfield University of
    Pennsylvania B, T
Mercyhurst College B
Messiah College B
Millersville University of
    Pennsylvania B, T
Moravian College B, T
Muhlenberg College B, T
Northampton County Area Community
    College A
Penn State
    Erie, The Behrend College B
    University Park B, M, D
Philadelphia University B
Reading Area Community College A
Rosemont College B
St. Francis College B
St. Joseph's University A, B, M
St. Vincent College B
Seton Hill College B, T
Shippensburg University of
    Pennsylvania B, T
Slippery Rock University of
    Pennsylvania B, T
Susquehanna University B, T
Swarthmore College B
Temple University B, M, D
Thiel College B
University of Pennsylvania A, B, M, D
University of Pittsburgh
    Bradford B, T
    Johnstown B
University of Pittsburgh B, M, D
University of Scranton B, M, T
University of the Sciences in
    Philadelphia B
Ursinus College B, T
Villanova University B, M, D
Washington and Jefferson College B
Waynesburg College B
West Chester University of
    Pennsylvania B, M
Westminster College B
Widener University B
Wilkes University B
Wilson College B
York College of Pennsylvania A, B

Puerto Rico
Bayamon Central University B
Inter American University of Puerto Rico
    Arecibo Campus B
    Metropolitan Campus B
    San German Campus B
Pontifical Catholic University of Puerto
    Rico B, M
Turabo University B
Universidad Metropolitana B
University of Puerto Rico
    Cayey University College B
    Mayaguez Campus B, M
    Rio Piedras Campus B, M, D
University of the Sacred Heart B

Rhode Island
Brown University B, M, D
Providence College B, M, T
Rhode Island College B
Roger Williams University A, B

Chemistry

Salve Regina University *B*
University of Rhode Island *B, M, D*

South Carolina
Benedict College *B*
Charleston Southern University *B*
Claflin University *B*
Clemson University *B, M, D*
Coastal Carolina University *B*
Coker College *B, T*
College of Charleston *B, T*
Columbia College *B*
Converse College *B*
Erskine College *B*
Francis Marion University *B*
Furman University *B, M, T*
Lander University *B, T*
Limestone College *B*
Newberry College *B*
Presbyterian College *B, T*
South Carolina State University *B*
Southern Wesleyan University *B*
The Citadel *B*
University of South Carolina
    Aiken *B*
    Spartanburg *B*
University of South Carolina *B, M, D*
Winthrop University *B*
Wofford College *B, T*

South Dakota
Augustana College *B, T*
Black Hills State University *B*
Dakota State University *B*
Mount Marty College *B*
Northern State University *B*
South Dakota School of Mines and Technology *B*
South Dakota State University *B, M, D*
University of South Dakota *B, M*

Tennessee
Austin Peay State University *B*
Belmont University *B, T*
Bethel College *B*
Carson-Newman College *B, T*
Christian Brothers University *B*
Columbia State Community College *A*
Crichton College *B*
Cumberland University *A, B*
David Lipscomb University *B*
East Tennessee State University *B, M*
Fisk University *B, M*
Freed-Hardeman University *B*
Hiwassee College *A*
King College *B, T*
Lambuth University *B*
Lane College *B*
LeMoyne-Owen College *B*
Lee University *B*
Lincoln Memorial University *B, T*
Maryville College *B, T*
Middle Tennessee State University *B, M, D*
Milligan College *B*
Rhodes College *B, T*
Roane State Community College *A*
Southern Adventist University *B*
Tennessee State University *B, M*
Tennessee Technological University *B, M, T*
Tennessee Wesleyan College *B, T*
Trevecca Nazarene University *B*
Union University *B, T*
University of Memphis *B, M, D*
University of Tennessee
    Chattanooga *B*
    Knoxville *B, M, D*
    Martin *B*
University of the South *B*
Vanderbilt University *B, M, D*

Texas
Abilene Christian University *B*
Amarillo College *A*
Angelina College *A*
Austin College *B*
Baylor University *B, M, D*
Blinn College *A*
Brazosport College *A*
Central Texas College *A*
Coastal Bend College *A*
College of the Mainland *A*
Del Mar College *A*
East Texas Baptist University *B*
El Paso Community College *A*
Galveston College *A*
Grayson County College *A*
Hardin-Simmons University *B*
Hill College *A*
Houston Baptist University *B*
Howard College *A*
Howard Payne University *B, T*
Huston-Tillotson College *B*
Jarvis Christian College *B*
Kilgore College *A*
Lamar University *B, M*
LeTourneau University *B*
Lon Morris College *A*
Lubbock Christian University *B*
McMurry University *B, T*
Midland College *A*
Midwestern State University *B*
Navarro College *A*
Northeast Texas Community College *A*
Odessa College *A*
Our Lady of the Lake University of San Antonio *B*
Palo Alto College *A*
Panola College *A*
Paris Junior College *A*
Prairie View A&M University *B, M*
Rice University *B, M, D*
St. Edward's University *B, T*
St. Mary's University *B*
St. Philip's College *A*
Sam Houston State University *B, M*
San Jacinto College
    North *A*
Schreiner College *B*
South Plains College *A*
Southern Methodist University *B, M*
Southwest Texas State University *B, M, T*
Southwestern Adventist University *B, T*
Southwestern University *B, T*
Stephen F. Austin State University *B, M, T*
Sul Ross State University *B*
Tarleton State University *B, T*
Texas A&M International University *B*
Texas A&M University
    Commerce *B, M*
    Corpus Christi *B, T*
    Kingsville *B, M*
Texas A&M University *B, M, D*
Texas Christian University *B, M, D, T*
Texas Lutheran University *B*
Texas Southern University *B, M*
Texas Tech University *B, M, D*
Texas Wesleyan University *B*
Texas Woman's University *B, M, T*
Trinity University *B*
Trinity Valley Community College *A*
Tyler Junior College *A*
University of Dallas *B*
University of Houston
    Clear Lake *B, M*
    Downtown *B*
University of Houston *B, M, D*
University of Mary Hardin-Baylor *B, T*
University of North Texas *B, M, D*
University of St. Thomas *B*
University of Texas
    Arlington *B, M, D*
    Austin *B, M, D*
    Dallas *B, M, D*
    El Paso *B, M*
    Pan American *B, T*
    San Antonio *B, M*
    Tyler *B*
    of the Permian Basin *B*
University of the Incarnate Word *B*
Wayland Baptist University *B*
West Texas A&M University *B, M, T*
Wharton County Junior College *A*
Wiley College *B*

Utah
Brigham Young University *B, M, D*
Dixie State College of Utah *A*
Salt Lake Community College *A*
Snow College *A*
Southern Utah University *B, T*
University of Utah *B, M, D*
Utah State University *B, M, D*
Weber State University *B*
Westminster College *B*

Vermont
Bennington College *B*
Castleton State College *A*
Marlboro College *B*
Middlebury College *B*
Norwich University *B*
St. Michael's College *B*
University of Vermont *B, M, D*

Virginia
Averett College *B, T*
Bluefield College *B*
Bridgewater College *B*
College of William and Mary *B, M*
Eastern Mennonite University *B*
Emory & Henry College *B, T*
Ferrum College *B*
George Mason University *B, M*
Hampden-Sydney College *B*
Hampton University *B, M*
Hollins University *B*
James Madison University *B, T*
Longwood College *B, T*
Lynchburg College *B*
Mary Baldwin College *B*
Mary Washington College *B*
Norfolk State University *B*
Old Dominion University *B, M*
Piedmont Virginia Community College *A*
Radford University *B*
Randolph-Macon College *B*
Randolph-Macon Woman's College *B*
Roanoke College *B, T*
Shenandoah University *B*
Sweet Briar College *B*
University of Richmond *B, T*
University of Virginia's College at Wise *B, T*
University of Virginia *B, M, D*
Virginia Commonwealth University *B, M, D*
Virginia Military Institute *B*
Virginia Polytechnic Institute and State University *B, M, D, T*
Virginia State University *B*
Virginia Union University *B*
Virginia Wesleyan College *B*
Washington and Lee University *B*

Washington
Central Washington University *B, M*
Centralia College *A*
Eastern Washington University *B, T*
Everett Community College *A*
Evergreen State College *B*
Gonzaga University *B*
Lower Columbia College *A*
Pacific Lutheran University *B*
St. Martin's College *B*
Seattle Pacific University *B, T*
Seattle University *B*
University of Puget Sound *B, T*
University of Washington *B, M, D*
Walla Walla College *B*
Washington State University *B, M, D*
Western Washington University *B, M, T*
Whitman College *B*
Whitworth College *B, T*

West Virginia
Alderson-Broaddus College *B*
Bethany College *B*
Concord College *B*
Davis and Elkins College *B*
Fairmont State College *B*
Glenville State College *B*
Marshall University *B, M*
Potomac State College of West Virginia University *A*
Shepherd College *B*
University of Charleston *B*
West Liberty State College *B*
West Virginia State College *B*
West Virginia University Institute of Technology *B*
West Virginia University *B, M, D, T*
West Virginia Wesleyan College *B*
Wheeling Jesuit University *B*

Wisconsin
Alverno College *B, T*
Beloit College *B*
Cardinal Stritch University *B*
Carroll College *B*
Carthage College *B, T*
Lakeland College *B*
Lawrence University *B*
Marian College of Fond du Lac *B*
Marquette University *B, M, D, T*
Mount Mary College *B*
Mount Senario College *B, T*
Northland College *B*
Ripon College *B, T*
St. Norbert College *B, T*
Silver Lake College *T*
University of Wisconsin
    Eau Claire *B*
    Green Bay *B*
    La Crosse *B*
    Madison *B, M, D*
    Milwaukee *B, M, D*
    Oshkosh *B*
    Parkside *B*
    Platteville *B, T*
    River Falls *B*
    Stevens Point *B, T*
    Superior *B, T*
    Whitewater *B, T*
Viterbo University *B*
Wisconsin Lutheran College *B*

Wyoming
Casper College *A*
Laramie County Community College *A*
Northwest College *A*
University of Wyoming *B, M, D*
Western Wyoming Community College *A*

Chemistry teacher education

Alabama
Alabama Agricultural and Mechanical University *B, M*
Athens State University *B*
Birmingham-Southern College *T*
Faulkner University *B*
Huntingdon College *T*
Oakwood College *B*
Talladega College *T*
University of Alabama *B*

Arizona
Arizona State University B, T
Grand Canyon University B
Northern Arizona University B, T
University of Arizona B, M

Arkansas
Arkansas State University B, M, T
Arkansas Tech University B
Harding University B, T
John Brown University B, T
Ouachita Baptist University B, T
Southern Arkansas University B, T
University of Central Arkansas T
University of the Ozarks B, T

California
Azusa Pacific University T
California State Polytechnic University:
   Pomona T
California State University
   Long Beach T
San Diego State University B
San Francisco State University B, T
University of the Pacific T

Colorado
Adams State College B, T
Colorado State University T
Fort Lewis College T
University of Southern Colorado T
Western State College of Colorado T

Connecticut
Central Connecticut State University B
Fairfield University T
Quinnipiac University B, M
St. Joseph College T
Southern Connecticut State
   University B, M, T

Delaware
University of Delaware B, T

District of Columbia
Catholic University of America B

Florida
Bethune-Cookman College B, T
Florida Agricultural and Mechanical
   University T
Florida Institute of Technology B, M
Gulf Coast Community College A
St. Thomas University B, T
Stetson University B, T
University of West Florida B, T

Georgia
Agnes Scott College T
Armstrong Atlantic State University T
Columbus State University B
North Georgia College & State
   University B, M
Wesleyan College T

Hawaii
University of Hawaii
   Manoa B, T

Idaho
Boise State University T
Northwest Nazarene University B

Illinois
Augustana College B, T
Chicago State University B, T
Concordia University B, T
Dominican University T
Elmhurst College B
Governors State University B, T
Greenville College B
Illinois College T
Judson College B, T
Lewis University T
Loyola University of Chicago T
North Central College B, T
North Park University T
Northwestern University B, T
Olivet Nazarene University B, T
Rockford College T
Roosevelt University B
Trinity Christian College B, T
University of Illinois
   Chicago B
   Urbana-Champaign B, M, T
Wheaton College T

Indiana
Ball State University T
Butler University T
Franklin College B
Goshen College B
Indiana State University B, T
Indiana University
   Bloomington B, T
   Northwest B
   South Bend B, T
Indiana University--Purdue University
   Indiana University-Purdue
      University Fort Wayne B, T
Indiana Wesleyan University T
Manchester College B, T
Purdue University
   Calumet B
Taylor University B
University of Evansville T
University of Indianapolis B, T
University of St. Francis B
University of Southern Indiana B, T
Valparaiso University B
Vincennes University A

Iowa
Buena Vista University B, T
Central College T
Clarke College B, T
Cornell College B, T
Dordt College B
Drake University M
Graceland University T
Iowa State University T
Iowa Wesleyan College B
Loras College T
Luther College B
Morningside College B
Northwestern College T
St. Ambrose University B, T
University of Iowa B, T
Wartburg College T
William Penn University B

Kansas
Baker University T
Benedictine College T
Bethany College B
Bethel College T
Colby Community College A
Garden City Community College A
Independence Community College A
McPherson College B, T
MidAmerica Nazarene University B, T
Ottawa University T
Pittsburg State University B
St. Mary College T
Tabor College B, T
University of Kansas B, T

Kentucky
Campbellsville University B
Cumberland College B, T
Murray State University B, M, T
Transylvania University B, T
Union College M

Louisiana
Centenary College of Louisiana B, T
Dillard University B
Louisiana State University
   Shreveport B
McNeese State University T
Nicholls State University B
Northwestern State University B, T
Our Lady of Holy Cross College T
Southern University and Agricultural and
   Mechanical College B
University of New Orleans B
Xavier University of Louisiana B, T

Maine
St. Joseph's College B
University of New England B, T
University of Southern Maine T

Maryland
Salisbury State University B

Massachusetts
Assumption College T
Boston University B
Bridgewater State College M, T
Elms College T
Framingham State College B, T
Harvard College T
Merrimack College T
Northeastern University M
Salem State College M
Tufts University T
University of Massachusetts
   Dartmouth T
Western New England College T
Worcester State College T

Michigan
Albion College B, T
Alma College T
Calvin College B
Central Michigan University B, M
Eastern Michigan University B, T
Grand Valley State University T
Michigan State University B
Michigan Technological University T
Northern Michigan University B, M, T
Western Michigan University B

Minnesota
Augsburg College T
Bethel College B
College of St. Scholastica T
Concordia College: Moorhead T
Gustavus Adolphus College T
Minnesota State University,
   Mankato B, T
Moorhead State University B, T
St. Cloud State University T
St. Olaf College T
Southwest State University B, T
University of Minnesota
   Morris T
University of St. Thomas T
Winona State University B, T

Mississippi
Blue Mountain College B
Delta State University T
Mississippi State University T
University of Mississippi B, T

Missouri
Avila College T
Central Missouri State University B, T
College of the Ozarks B, T
Lindenwood University M
Maryville University of Saint
   Louis B, M, T
Missouri Baptist College T
Missouri Southern State College B, T
Missouri Western State College T
Northwest Missouri State
   University B, T
Rockhurst University B
Southwest Missouri State University B
Truman State University M, T
University of Missouri
   Columbia B
   St. Louis T
Washington University B, M, T

Montana
Montana State University
   Billings B, T
   Bozeman T
Rocky Mountain College B, T
University of Great Falls B, T
University of Montana-Missoula T
Western Montana College of The
   University of Montana B, T

Nebraska
College of Saint Mary B, T
Concordia University T
Creighton University T
Dana College B
Doane College T
Hastings College B, M, T
Midland Lutheran College B, T
Nebraska Wesleyan University B
Peru State College T
Union College T
University of Nebraska
   Kearney B
   Lincoln T

New Hampshire
Keene State College B, T
Rivier College B, T
St. Anselm College T
University of New Hampshire T

New Jersey
Monmouth University B, T
Rowan University T
St. Peter's College T
The College of New Jersey B, T

New Mexico
New Mexico Institute of Mining and
   Technology M

New York
Alfred University M, T
Canisius College B, M, T
City University of New York
   Brooklyn College B
   City College T
   Queens College T
   York College T
Colgate University M
College of St. Rose B, T
Columbia University
   Teachers College M, D
D'Youville College M, T
Dowling College B
Elmira College B, T
Fordham University M, T
Hofstra University B, M, T
Houghton College B, T
Ithaca College B, T
Long Island University
   C. W. Post Campus B, T
   Southampton College T
Manhattan College B, T
Marymount College B, T
Nazareth College of Rochester T
New York Institute of Technology B, T
New York University B, M, T
Niagara University B, T
Pace University:
   Pleasantville/Briarcliff B, M, T
Pace University B, M, T
St. John Fisher College B, T
St. John's University B, M, T
St. Thomas Aquinas College B, T
Siena College T
State University of New York
   Binghamton M
   Buffalo T
   College at Brockport M, T
   College at Buffalo B, M
   College at Fredonia B, M, T
   College at Geneseo B, M
   College at Old Westbury B
   College at Oneonta B, M, T
   College at Plattsburgh B, M
   College at Potsdam B, M
   College of Environmental Science
      and Forestry T
   New Paltz B, M, T
   Oswego B, M
Syracuse University B, M, T
Vassar College T
Wagner College T

Wells College *T*

North Carolina
Catawba College *T*
Lenoir Community College *A*
Lenoir-Rhyne College *B, T*
Louisburg College *A*
Mars Hill College *T*
Meredith College *T*
Methodist College *A, B, T*
North Carolina Agricultural and Technical State University *B, T*
North Carolina Central University *B, M*
Sandhills Community College *A*
University of North Carolina
    Charlotte *B*
    Greensboro *B, M, T*
    Wilmington *T*
Wake Forest University *M, T*

North Dakota
Dickinson State University *B, T*
Jamestown College *B*
Mayville State University *B, T*
Minot State University *B, T*
North Dakota State University *B, T*
University of North Dakota *B, T*
Valley City State University *B, T*

Ohio
Baldwin-Wallace College *T*
Bluffton College *B*
Bowling Green State University *B, M*
Case Western Reserve University *T*
Cedarville College *T*
College of Mount St. Joseph *T*
Defiance College *B, T*
Hiram College *T*
John Carroll University *T*
Kent State University
    Stark Campus *B*
Kent State University *T*
Malone College *B*
Miami University
    Oxford Campus *B, T*
Mount Union College *T*
Ohio Dominican College *D*
Otterbein College *B*
Shawnee State University *B, T*
University of Akron *B*
University of Dayton *B, M, T*
University of Findlay *T*
University of Rio Grande *B, T*
University of Toledo *B, T*
Wilmington College *B*
Xavier University *B, M, T*
Youngstown State University *B, M*

Oklahoma
Cameron University *B*
East Central University *T*
Eastern Oklahoma State College *A*
Northeastern State University *B*
Oklahoma Baptist University *B, T*
Oklahoma State University *M, D*
Southern Nazarene University *B*
University of Central Oklahoma *B*
University of Tulsa *B, T*

Oregon
Concordia University *B, M, T*
George Fox University *B, M, T*
Linfield College *T*
Oregon State University *M*
Portland State University *T*
University of Portland *T*
Western Oregon University *T*

Pennsylvania
Allentown College of St. Francis de Sales *T*
Alvernia College *B*
Bucknell University *T*
Cabrini College *B, T*
California University of Pennsylvania *B, T*
Carnegie Mellon University *T*
Chatham College *M, T*
Chestnut Hill College *T*
Clarion University of Pennsylvania *B, T*
Delaware Valley College *T*
Dickinson College *T*
Duquesne University *B, M, T*
Elizabethtown College *T*
Gannon University *T*
Gettysburg College *T*
Grove City College *B, T*
Holy Family College *B, M, T*
Juniata College *B, T*
King's College *T*
La Roche College *B*
La Salle University *B, T*
Lebanon Valley College of Pennsylvania
Lock Haven University of Pennsylvania *B, T*
Lycoming College *T*
Mansfield University of Pennsylvania *B, T*
Mercyhurst College *B*
Messiah College *T*
Moravian College *T*
St. Vincent College *T*
Seton Hill College *B, T*
Shippensburg University of Pennsylvania *T*
Thiel College *B*
University of Pittsburgh
    Bradford *B*
    Johnstown *B, T*
Washington and Jefferson College *T*
Waynesburg College *B, T*
Westminster College *T*
Widener University *T*
Wilkes University *M, T*
Wilson College *T*

Puerto Rico
Inter American University of Puerto Rico
    Arecibo Campus *B*
    Metropolitan Campus *B*

Rhode Island
Rhode Island College *B*
Salve Regina University *B*

South Carolina
Coker College *B, T*
Columbia College *B*
Furman University *T*
South Carolina State University *B, T*
Wofford College *T*

South Dakota
Black Hills State University *B, T*
Dakota State University *B, T*
Mount Marty College *B*
Northern State University *T*
South Dakota State University *B*

Tennessee
Belmont University *T*
Christian Brothers University *B, M, T*
Cumberland University *B*
David Lipscomb University *B, T*
Lambuth University *T*
Lincoln Memorial University *B, T*
Maryville College *B, T*
Southern Adventist University *B*
Tennessee Wesleyan College *B, T*
Trevecca Nazarene University *B, T*
Union University *B, T*
University of Tennessee
    Martin *B, T*

Texas
Abilene Christian University *B, T*
Angelo State University *T*
Baylor University *B, T*
East Texas Baptist University *B*
Hardin-Simmons University *B, T*
Houston Baptist University *T*
Howard Payne University *T*
Lamar University *T*
LeTourneau University *B*
Lubbock Christian University *B*
McMurry University *T*
St. Mary's University *T*
Southwest Texas State University *M, T*
Texas A&M University
    Commerce *B*
    Kingsville *T*
Texas Christian University *T*
Texas Lutheran University *T*
Texas Wesleyan University *B, T*
University of Dallas *T*
University of Houston
    Clear Lake *T*
University of Houston *T*
University of Mary Hardin-Baylor *T*
University of Texas
    Arlington *T*
    San Antonio *T*
Wayland Baptist University *T*
West Texas A&M University *T*

Utah
Brigham Young University *B*
Utah State University *B*
Weber State University *B*

Vermont
Castleton State College *B, T*
St. Michael's College *B*

Virginia
Bridgewater College *T*
Hampton University *B*
Hollins University *T*
Longwood College *B, T*
Radford University *T*
University of Virginia's College at Wise *T*
Virginia Wesleyan College *T*

Washington
Central Washington University *B, T*
Heritage College *B*
Washington State University *T*
Western Washington University *B, T*
Whitworth College *B, T*

West Virginia
Alderson-Broaddus College *T*
Concord College *B, T*
Fairmont State College *B*
Glenville State College *B*
Shepherd College *T*
West Liberty State College *B*
Wheeling Jesuit University *T*

Wisconsin
Alverno College *T*
Cardinal Stritch University *B, T*
Carroll College *B, T*
Carthage College *T*
Lakeland College *T*
Lawrence University *T*
Marian College of Fond du Lac *B, T*
Mount Mary College *B, T*
Northland College *T*
St. Norbert College *T*
University of Wisconsin
    Green Bay *T*
    La Crosse *B, T*
    Platteville *B*
    River Falls *T*
    Superior *B, T*
Viterbo University *B, T*

Child care/guidance

Alabama
Gadsden State Community College *C*
Harry M. Ayers State Technical College *C*
Jefferson State Community College *A*
Northwest-Shoals Community College *C*
Reid State Technical College *C*
Snead State Community College *C*
Wallace State Community College at Hanceville *A*

Alaska
University of Alaska
    Anchorage *C, A*
    Fairbanks *C, A*
    Southeast *C, A*

Arizona
Arizona Western College *C, A*
Eastern Arizona College *C, A*
Glendale Community College *C*
Northland Pioneer College *C, A*
Phoenix College *C, A*
Pima Community College *C, A*

Arkansas
Arkansas State University *M*
Harding University *B*
Henderson State University *A*
Southern Arkansas University Tech *C, A*
University of Central Arkansas *A, M*

California
American River College *C, A*
Barstow College *C, A*
Butte College *A*
Cabrillo College *C, A*
California State University
    Bakersfield *B*
    Fullerton *B*
    Long Beach *C*
    Northridge *B*
    Sacramento *B*
Canada College *C, A*
Cerro Coso Community College *C, A*
Chabot College *A*
Chaffey Community College *C, A*
College of the Canyons *C, A*
College of the Desert *C, A*
College of the Sequoias *C, A*
College of the Siskiyous *C, A*
Compton Community College *C, A*
Cuyamaca College *C, A*
Foothill College *C, A*
Fresno City College *C, A*
Glendale Community College *A*
Grossmont Community College *C, A*
Imperial Valley College *C, A*
Kings River Community College *C*
Las Positas College *C, A*
Los Angeles Harbor College *C, A*
Los Angeles Southwest College *C, A*
Los Medanos College *C, A*
Merritt College *C, A*
MiraCosta College *C, A*
Modesto Junior College *C, A*
Moorpark College *C, A*
Ohlone College *A*
Orange Coast College *C, A*
Palomar College *C, A*
Porterville College *C, A*
Rio Hondo College *C*
Riverside Community College *C, A*
Sacramento City College *C, A*
Saddleback College *C*
San Bernardino Valley College *C*
San Diego City College *C, A*
San Diego Mesa College *C*
San Joaquin Delta College *C, A*
Santa Rosa Junior College *C*
Shasta College *A*
Sierra College *A*
Southwestern College *A*
University of California
    Davis *M*
University of La Verne *C, B*
Ventura College *C, A*
Victor Valley College *C, A*
West Valley College *C, A*

Colorado
Aims Community College *C, A*
Arapahoe Community College *A*

Child care/guidance

Colorado Northwestern Community
  College C, A
Community College of Aurora C, A
Front Range Community College C, A
Lamar Community College A
Pikes Peak Community College C, A
Pueblo Community College A

Connecticut
Briarwood College C, A
Gateway Community College C
Housatonic Community-Technical
  College C, A
Mitchell College A

Delaware
Delaware Technical and Community
  College
    Owens Campus C, A
    Stanton/Wilmington Campus C, A
    Terry Campus C, A
University of Delaware B, T

District of Columbia
Gallaudet University B

Florida
Brevard Community College C
Broward Community College A
Central Florida Community College C
Chipola Junior College C, A
Daytona Beach Community
  College C, A
Gulf Coast Community College A
Hillsborough Community College C
Indian River Community College C
Miami-Dade Community College C
Palm Beach Community College A
Pasco-Hernando Community College C
Pensacola Junior College A
Polk Community College A
St. Petersburg Junior College C
Santa Fe Community College A
Seminole Community College A
South Florida Community College C, A

Georgia
Abraham Baldwin Agricultural
  College A
Athens Area Technical Institute C
Chattahoochee Technical Institute C, A
Darton College A
Fort Valley State University B
Gainesville College A
Macon State College A
Middle Georgia College A
Spelman College B
Waycross College A

Hawaii
University of Hawaii
  Honolulu Community College C, A

Idaho
Boise State University C, A
College of Southern Idaho C, A
Idaho State University C, A
Lewis-Clark State College C, A
Ricks College A

Illinois
Black Hawk College C, A
Carl Sandburg College A
City Colleges of Chicago
  Harold Washington College C
  Malcolm X College C, A
  Olive-Harvey College A
College of DuPage C, A
College of Lake County A
Elgin Community College C
Eureka College B
Highland Community College C, A
Illinois Eastern Community Colleges
  Wabash Valley College A
John Wood Community College A
Kaskaskia College A
Kishwaukee College A
Lake Land College C, A

Lewis and Clark Community College A
McHenry County College C, A
Moraine Valley Community College A
Parkland College C, A
Prairie State College C, A
Rock Valley College C, A
Southeastern Illinois College A
Southwestern Ilinois College C, A
Triton College C, A
Waubonsee Community College C, A
William Rainey Harper College C, A

Indiana
Ivy Tech State College
  Central Indiana C, A
  Eastcentral A
  Kokomo A
  Northeast C, A
  Whitewater A
St. Joseph's College A
Vincennes University A

Iowa
Des Moines Area Community
  College C, A
Hawkeye Community College A
Indian Hills Community College C, A
Iowa Western Community College A
Kirkwood Community College C, A
Marshalltown Community College C, A
Muscatine Community College C
Northeast Iowa Community College C
Southeastern Community College
  North Campus A
Western Iowa Tech Community
  College C, A

Kansas
Allen County Community College C
Barton County Community College C, A
Butler County Community College C, A
Central Christian College A
Coffeyville Community College A
Colby Community College A
Cowley County Community College A
Dodge City Community College C, A
Garden City Community College A
Hutchinson Community College C
Independence Community College C, A
Johnson County Community College A
Kansas City Kansas Community
  College C, A
Pittsburg State University B

Kentucky
Eastern Kentucky University A
Midway College A
Murray State University A
St. Catharine College C, A

Louisiana
Nicholls State University A
Northwestern State University B
Southern University
  Shreveport A
University of Louisiana at Monroe A

Maine
Andover College C, A
Southern Maine Technical College C, A
University of Maine B

Maryland
Anne Arundel Community College A
Carroll Community College C, A
Charles County Community
  College C, A
Chesapeake College C, A
Frederick Community College A
Montgomery College
  Germantown Campus C
  Rockville Campus C, A
Prince George's Community
  College C, A
Villa Julie College A

Massachusetts
Bristol Community College A

Fisher College A
Holyoke Community College A
Massachusetts Bay Community
  College C, A
Massasoit Community College A
Middlesex Community College C
Mount Wachusett Community
  College C, A
Northern Essex Community College A
Wheelock College B, M

Michigan
Baker College
  of Muskegon C
  of Owosso A
Bay de Noc Community College A
Central Michigan University B
Delta College C, A
Ferris State University A
Gogebic Community College C
Grand Rapids Community College A
Kellogg Community College C
Lake Superior State University A, B
Lansing Community College A
Macomb Community College A
Madonna University C, A, B, T
Mid Michigan Community College C, A
Monroe County Community College A
Montcalm Community College C, A
Mott Community College A
Oakland Community College C, A
St. Clair County Community College A
Schoolcraft College C, A
Wayne County Community College C

Minnesota
Alexandria Technical College C
Central Lakes College C
Inver Hills Community College A
Minneapolis Community and Technical
  College A
Minnesota State College - Southeast
  Technical C, A
Pine Technical College C
Rochester Community and Technical
  College A
St. Cloud Technical College C, A
St. Paul Technical College C, A

Mississippi
Hinds Community College A
Itawamba Community College A
Mary Holmes College A
Meridian Community College A
Mississippi Gulf Coast Community
  College
    Perkinston C

Missouri
Central Missouri State University A
Jefferson College A
Mineral Area College C
Moberly Area Community College C, A
Northwest Missouri State University C
Penn Valley Community College C, A
Southeast Missouri State University A
St. Louis Community College
  St. Louis Community College at
    Florissant Valley A
  St. Louis Community College at
    Forest Park A

Montana
Dawson Community College C
Little Big Horn College A
Montana State University
  Billings A
Western Montana College of The
  University of Montana C

Nebraska
Central Community College C, A
Metropolitan Community College C, A
Northeast Community College A
Southeast Community College
  Lincoln Campus A
Wayne State College B

Nevada
Western Nevada Community
  College C, A

New Hampshire
College for Lifelong Learning C
Hesser College A
Keene State College A, B, T
New Hampshire Community Technical
  College
    Claremont C
    Laconia C
    Nashua C
    Stratham C, A

New Jersey
County College of Morris C
Hudson County Community
  College C, A
Ocean County College C, A
Sussex County Community College C
Thomas Edison State College A, B

New Mexico
Albuquerque Technical-Vocational
  Institute A
Dona Ana Branch Community College of
  New Mexico State University C
Eastern New Mexico University
  Roswell Campus A
Eastern New Mexico University A
San Juan College C

New York
Broome Community College C, A
City University of New York
  College of Staten Island C
  La Guardia Community College A
Dutchess Community College C, A
Erie Community College
  City Campus A
Genesee Community College C
Hudson Valley Community College A
Jamestown Community College C
Medaille College B
Nassau Community College A
Orange County Community College A
Rockland Community College C
Sage Junior College of Albany A
St. John Fisher College C
State University of New York
  College of Agriculture and
    Technology at Cobleskill A
  Purchase C
Tompkins-Cortland Community
  College A
Utica College of Syracuse University B
Westchester Community College C, A

North Carolina
Asheville Buncombe Technical
  Community College C, A
Blue Ridge Community College A
Cape Fear Community College A
Central Carolina Community
  College C, A
Central Piedmont Community College A
Cleveland Community College C, A
Coastal Carolina Community
  College C, A
Craven Community College C, A
Halifax Community College C
Haywood Community College C, A
Johnston Community College C, A
Mayland Community College C
Montgomery Community College A
Nash Community College A
Pitt Community College A
Richmond Community College C, A
Sandhills Community College A
South Piedmont Community
  College C, A
Southeastern Community College A
Southwestern Community College A
Surry Community College A
Vance-Granville Community
  College C, A

143

Child care/guidance

Wayne Community College A
Wilkes Community College C, A
Wilson Technical Community
 College C, A

North Dakota
Lake Region State College C, A
North Dakota State University B, M

Ohio
Edison State Community College A
Hocking Technical College C, A
Jefferson Community College C
Kent State University B, T
Lakeland Community College A
Lourdes College A, B
Mount Vernon Nazarene College A
Muskingum Area Technical College A
Ohio University A
Sinclair Community College C, A
University of Toledo C
Youngstown State University A, B

Oklahoma
Connors State College C, A
Murray State College A
Northeastern Oklahoma Agricultural and
 Mechanical College A
Oklahoma City Community
 College C, A
Oklahoma State University B
Redlands Community College A
Rose State College A
Tulsa Community College C, A
Western Oklahoma State College A

Oregon
Central Oregon Community College C
Chemeketa Community College A
Clatsop Community College C
Lane Community College C, A
Linn-Benton Community College A
Portland Community College C, A

Pennsylvania
Central Pennsylvania College A
Community College of Allegheny
 County C, A
Community College of Beaver County A
Community College of Philadelphia A
Gannon University M
Harrisburg Area Community College C
Laurel Business Institute A
Luzerne County Community
 College C, A
Northampton County Area Community
 College C, A
Penn State
 University Park C
Pennsylvania College of Technology A
Reading Area Community College C, A
Seton Hill College C, B
Westmoreland County Community
 College C, A

Puerto Rico
University of Puerto Rico
 Rio Piedras Campus B

South Carolina
Aiken Technical College C
Chesterfield-Marlboro Technical
 College C
Denmark Technical College C
Florence-Darlington Technical
 College C
Greenville Technical College C
Midlands Technical College C
Orangeburg-Calhoun Technical
 College C
Piedmont Technical College C
South Carolina State University B
Technical College of the
 Lowcountry C, A
Tri-County Technical College C
Trident Technical College C, A
York Technical College C

South Dakota
Kilian Community College C, A

Tennessee
Belmont University B
Trevecca Nazarene University A
University of Tennessee
 Knoxville M
Walters State Community College A

Texas
Abilene Christian University A, B
Alvin Community College C, A
Amarillo College C, A
Austin Community College C, A
Central Texas College C, A
Coastal Bend College C, A
College of the Mainland A
Collin County Community College
 District C, A
Del Mar College C, A
Eastfield College C, A
El Paso Community College C, A
Houston Community College
 System C, A
Howard College C
Kilgore College C
Lamar State College at Port Arthur C, A
Midland College C, A
Navarro College A
Odessa College C, A
San Antonio College C, A
San Jacinto College
 North C, A
South Plains College A
Tarrant County College C, A
Trinity Valley Community College C, A
Tyler Junior College C, A
University of North Texas B
Vernon Regional Junior College C
Weatherford College C, A

Utah
College of Eastern Utah A
Dixie State College of Utah A
Salt Lake Community College C, A
Snow College A
Weber State University A

Virginia
Central Virginia Community College C
Danville Community College C
J. Sargeant Reynolds Community
 College C, A
John Tyler Community College C, A
Lord Fairfax Community College C
Southwest Virginia Community
 College C
Virginia Polytechnic Institute and State
 University B
Virginia Western Community College A

Washington
Centralia College C, A
Clark College C, A
Columbia Basin College C, A
Edmonds Community College C, A
Everett Community College A
Highline Community College C, A
Lake Washington Technical College C, A
North Seattle Community College C, A
Peninsula College A
Pierce College A
Renton Technical College C
Shoreline Community College C
Walla Walla Community College C
Yakima Valley Community College C, A

West Virginia
Fairmont State College A
Shepherd College A
West Virginia Northern Community
 College C

Wisconsin
Blackhawk Technical College C
Gateway Technical College A
Lakeshore Technical College C
Madison Area Technical College A
Milwaukee Area Technical College A
Nicolet Area Technical College C, A
Northeast Wisconsin Technical
 College C
Silver Lake College A
Southwest Wisconsin Technical
 College C, A
Waukesha County Technical College A
Western Wisconsin Technical College A
Wisconsin Indianhead Technical
 College C

Chinese

California
Cabrillo College A
California State University
 Long Beach C
Claremont McKenna College B
Monterey Institute of International
 Studies C
National Hispanic University C, B
Pitzer College B
Pomona College B
San Francisco State University B, M
San Jose State University B
Scripps College B
Stanford University B, M, D
University of California
 Berkeley B, M, D
 Davis B
 Irvine B
 Los Angeles B
 Riverside B
 Santa Barbara B
University of Southern
 California B, M, D

Colorado
University of Colorado
 Boulder B, M

Connecticut
Connecticut College B
Fairfield University B
Yale University B

District of Columbia
George Washington University B
Georgetown University B

Hawaii
University of Hawaii
 Manoa B, M, D

Idaho
Ricks College A

Indiana
Butler University B
Indiana University
 Bloomington M, D
St. Mary-of-the-Woods College B

Iowa
Grinnell College B
University of Iowa B, T

Maine
Bates College B

Maryland
Johns Hopkins University B
University of Maryland
 College Park B

Massachusetts
Harvard College B
Simon's Rock College of Bard B
Tufts University B
University of Massachusetts
 Amherst B, M
Wellesley College B
Williams College B

Michigan
Michigan State University B
University of Michigan M, D

Minnesota
Augsburg College B
University of Minnesota
 Twin Cities B, M, D

Missouri
Washington University B, M, D

Montana
University of Montana-Missoula B

New Hampshire
Dartmouth College B

New Jersey
Rutgers
 The State University of New Jersey:
  Douglass College B
 The State University of New Jersey:
  Livingston College B
 The State University of New Jersey:
  Rutgers College B
 The State University of New Jersey:
  University College New
  Brunswick B
Seton Hall University T

New York
Bard College B
City University of New York
 Hunter College B
Columbia University
 Graduate School M, D
Cornell University B
Hamilton College B
State University of New York
 Albany B

Ohio
Ohio State University
 Columbus Campus B

Oregon
Pacific University B
Portland State University B
Reed College B
University of Oregon B

Pennsylvania
Haverford College T
Lincoln University B
Swarthmore College B
University of Pittsburgh B, M

Rhode Island
Brown University B

Texas
Trinity University B

Utah
Brigham Young University B, M
University of Utah B

Vermont
Bennington College B
Middlebury College B

Washington
Central Washington University B
Pacific Lutheran University B
University of Puget Sound T
University of Washington B

Wisconsin
University of Wisconsin
 Madison B, M, D

Chiropractic (D.C.)

California
Cleveland Chiropractic College of Los
 Angeles F
Life Chiropractic College West F
Los Angeles College of Chiropractic F

Palmer College of Chiropractic-West *F*
Georgia
Life College *F*
Illinois
National College of Chiropractic: Chiropractic Professions *F*
Iowa
Palmer College of Chiropractic *F*
Minnesota
Northwestern College of Chiropractic *F*
Missouri
Cleveland Chiropractic College of Kansas City *F*
Logan College of Chiropractic *F*
New York
New York Chiropractic College *F*
Oregon
Western States Chiropractic College *F*
South Carolina
Sherman College of Straight Chiropractic *F*
Texas
Parker College of Chiropractic *F*
Texas Chiropractic College *F*

Civil engineering

Alabama
Alabama Agricultural and Mechanical University *B*
Auburn University *B, M, D*
University of Alabama
   Birmingham *B, M, D*
   Huntsville *B, M*
University of Alabama *M, D*
University of South Alabama *B*
Alaska
University of Alaska
   Anchorage *B, M*
   Fairbanks *B, M*
Arizona
Arizona State University *B, M, D*
Arizona Western College *A*
Central Arizona College *A*
Northern Arizona University *B*
University of Arizona *B, M, D*
Arkansas
University of Arkansas *B, M*
California
California Institute of Technology *B, M, D*
California Polytechnic State University: San Luis Obispo *B*
California State Polytechnic University: Pomona *B*
California State University
   Chico *B*
   Fresno *B, M*
   Fullerton *B, M*
   Long Beach *B, M*
   Los Angeles *B, M*
   Northridge *B, M*
   Sacramento *B, M*
City College of San Francisco *C, A*
East Los Angeles College *A*
Loyola Marymount University *B, M*
San Diego State University *B, M*
San Francisco State University *B*
San Joaquin Delta College *C*
San Jose State University *B, M*
Santa Ana College *C, A*
Santa Clara University *B, M*
Shasta College *A*
Stanford University *B, M, D*
University of California
   Berkeley *B, M, D*
   Davis *B*
   Irvine *B, M, D*
   Los Angeles *B, M, D*
University of Southern California *B, M, D*
University of the Pacific *B*
Colorado
Colorado State University *B, M, D*
United States Air Force Academy *B*
University of Colorado
   Boulder *B, M, D*
   Denver *B, M, D*
Connecticut
United States Coast Guard Academy *B*
University of Connecticut *B, M, D*
University of Hartford *B, M*
University of New Haven *A, B*
Delaware
University of Delaware *B, M, D*
District of Columbia
Catholic University of America *B, M, D*
George Washington University *B, M, D*
Howard University *B, M*
University of the District of Columbia *A, B*
Florida
Broward Community College *A*
Edison Community College *A*
Embry-Riddle Aeronautical University *B*
Florida Agricultural and Mechanical University *B, M*
Florida Atlantic University *M*
Florida Institute of Technology *B, M, D*
Florida International University *B, M, D*
Florida State University *B, M, D*
Manatee Community College *A*
Miami-Dade Community College *A*
Pensacola Junior College *A*
Tallahassee Community College *A*
University of Central Florida *B, M, D*
University of Florida *B, M, D*
University of Miami *B, M, D*
University of North Florida *B*
University of South Florida *B, M, D*
Georgia
Armstrong Atlantic State University *A*
Georgia Institute of Technology *B, M, D*
Middle Georgia College *A*
Morris Brown College *B*
Hawaii
University of Hawaii
   Manoa *B, M, D*
Idaho
Boise State University *B*
College of Southern Idaho *A*
North Idaho College *A*
Ricks College *A*
University of Idaho *B, M, D*
Illinois
Bradley University *B, M*
Illinois Institute of Technology *B, M, D*
Lake Land College *A*
Lincoln Land Community College *A*
Northwestern University *B, M, D*
Parkland College *A*
Southern Illinois University
   Carbondale *B, M*
   Edwardsville *B, M*
University of Illinois
   Chicago *B, M, D*
   Urbana-Champaign *B, M, D*
Indiana
Indiana Institute of Technology *B*
Purdue University
   Calumet *A*
Purdue University *B, M, D*
Rose-Hulman Institute of Technology *B, M*
Tri-State University *B*
University of Evansville *B*
University of Notre Dame *B, M, D*
Valparaiso University *B*
Vincennes University *A*
Iowa
Iowa State University *B, M, D*
University of Iowa *B, M, D*
Kansas
Independence Community College *A*
Kansas State University *B, M, D*
University of Kansas *B, M, D*
Kentucky
University of Kentucky *B, M, D*
University of Louisville *B, M, D*
Louisiana
Louisiana State University and Agricultural and Mechanical College *B, M, D*
Louisiana Tech University *B*
Southern University and Agricultural and Mechanical College *B*
Tulane University *B, M, D*
University of Louisiana at Lafayette *B, M*
University of New Orleans *B*
Maine
University of Maine *B, M, D*
Maryland
Johns Hopkins University *B, M, D*
Montgomery College
   Rockville Campus *A*
Morgan State University *B*
University of Maryland
   Baltimore County *M, D*
   College Park *B, M, D*
Massachusetts
Harvard University *D*
Massachusetts Institute of Technology *B, M, D*
Merrimack College *B*
Northeastern University *B, M, D*
Tufts University *B, M*
University of Massachusetts
   Amherst *B, M, D*
   Dartmouth *B*
   Lowell *B, M*
Worcester Polytechnic Institute *B, M, D*
Michigan
Calvin College *B*
Lawrence Technological University *B*
Michigan State University *B, M, D*
Michigan Technological University *B, M, D, T*
University of Detroit Mercy *B, M*
University of Michigan *B, M, D*
Wayne State University *B, M, D*
Western Michigan University *B, M*
Minnesota
Concordia College: Moorhead *B*
St. Cloud Technical College *C, A*
University of Minnesota
   Twin Cities *C, B, M, D*
Mississippi
Mississippi State University *B, M*
University of Mississippi *B*
Missouri
East Central College *A*
University of Missouri
   Columbia *B, M, D*
   Kansas City *B, M*
   Rolla *B, M, D*
   St. Louis *B*
Washington University *B, M, D*
Montana
Carroll College *B*
Montana State University
   Bozeman *B, M*
Montana Tech of the University of Montana *B*
Nebraska
Southeast Community College
   Milford Campus *A*
University of Nebraska
   Lincoln *B, M*
   Omaha *B, M*
Nevada
University of Nevada
   Las Vegas *B, M, D*
   Reno *B, M, D*
New Hampshire
University of New Hampshire *B, M, D*
New Jersey
Essex County College *A*
Middlesex County College *A*
New Jersey Institute of Technology *B, M, D*
Ocean County College *C*
Princeton University *B, M, D*
Rowan University *B*
Rutgers
   The State University of New Jersey: College of Engineering *B*
   The State University of New Jersey: New Brunswick Graduate Campus *M, D*
Seton Hall University *B*
Stevens Institute of Technology *B, M, D*
New Mexico
New Mexico State University *B, M*
University of New Mexico *B, M*
New York
City University of New York
   City College *B, M, D*
   College of Staten Island *A*
   Graduate School and University Center *D*
Clarkson University *B, M, D*
Columbia University
   Fu Foundation School of Engineering and Applied Science *B, M, D*
Cooper Union for the Advancement of Science and Art *B, M*
Cornell University *B*
Manhattan College *B, M*
New York University *B*
Pace University *B*
Polytechnic University
   Long Island Campus *B, M, D*
Polytechnic University *B, M, D*
Rensselaer Polytechnic Institute *B, M, D*
State University of New York
   Buffalo *B, M, D*
   College of Environmental Science and Forestry *B, M, D*
Syracuse University *B, M, D*
Union College *B*
United States Military Academy *B*
North Carolina
Central Carolina Community College *A*
Duke University *B, M, D*
Fayetteville Technical Community College *A*
Guilford Technical Community College *C, A*
Johnston Community College *A*
North Carolina Agricultural and Technical State University *B*
North Carolina State University *B, M, D*
St. Augustine's College *B*
University of North Carolina
   Charlotte *B, M*

North Dakota
North Dakota State University B, M
University of North Dakota B, M

Ohio
Belmont Technical College A
Case Western Reserve
  University B, M, D
Cleveland State University B, M, D
Columbus State Community College A
Ohio Northern University B
Ohio State University
  Columbus Campus B, M, D
Ohio University B, M
Owens Community College
  Toledo A
University of Akron B, M, D
University of Cincinnati B, M, D
University of Dayton B, M
University of Toledo B, M
Wilberforce University B
Youngstown State University B, M

Oklahoma
Oklahoma State University
  Oklahoma City A
Oklahoma State University B, M, D
University of Oklahoma B, M, D

Oregon
Oregon Institute of Technology B
Oregon State University B, M, D
Portland State University B, M, D
University of Portland B, M

Pennsylvania
Bucknell University B, M
Carnegie Mellon University B, M, D
Drexel University B, M, D
Geneva College B
Gettysburg College B
Lafayette College B
Lehigh University B, M, D
Lock Haven University of
  Pennsylvania B
Messiah College B
Penn State
  Harrisburg B
  University Park B, M, D
Temple University B, M
University of Pennsylvania B, M, D
University of Pittsburgh C, B, M, D
Villanova University B, M
Widener University B, M

Puerto Rico
Caribbean University B
Universidad Politecnica de Puerto
  Rico B, M
University of Puerto Rico
  Mayaguez Campus B, M, D
  Ponce University College A

Rhode Island
Brown University B, M, D
University of Rhode Island B, M, D

South Carolina
Clemson University B, M, D
The Citadel B
University of South Carolina B, M, D

South Dakota
South Dakota School of Mines and
  Technology B, M
South Dakota State University B

Tennessee
Chattanooga State Technical Community
  College A
Christian Brothers University B
Tennessee State University B
Tennessee Technological
  University B, M, D
University of Memphis B, M
University of Tennessee
  Knoxville B, M, D
Vanderbilt University B, M, D

Texas
Houston Baptist University B
Kilgore College A
Lamar University B
Prairie View A&M University B
Rice University B, M, D
Texas A&M University
  Kingsville B, M
Texas A&M University B, M, D
Texas Tech University B, M, D
University of Houston B, M, D
University of Texas
  Arlington B, M, D
  Austin B, M, D
  El Paso B, M
  San Antonio B, M

Utah
Brigham Young University B, M, D
Salt Lake Community College A
Snow College A
University of Utah B, M, D
Utah State University B, M, D

Vermont
Norwich University B
University of Vermont B, M, D
Vermont Technical College A

Virginia
John Tyler Community College A
Northern Virginia Community College A
Old Dominion University B
University of Virginia B, M, D
Virginia Military Institute B
Virginia Polytechnic Institute and State
  University B, M, D

Washington
Centralia College A
Gonzaga University B
St. Martin's College B
Seattle University B
Shoreline Community College A
University of Washington B, M, D
Washington State University B, M, D
Yakima Valley Community College A

West Virginia
Potomac State College of West Virginia
  University A
West Virginia University Institute of
  Technology B
West Virginia University B, M, D

Wisconsin
Chippewa Valley Technical College A
Marquette University B, M, D
Milwaukee Area Technical College A
Northeast Wisconsin Technical
  College A
University of Wisconsin
  Madison B, M, D
  Milwaukee B
  Platteville B

Wyoming
University of Wyoming B, M, D

Civil engineering/civil technology

Alabama
Alabama Agricultural and Mechanical
  University B
Community College of the Air Force A
Gadsden State Community College C, A

Arizona
Eastern Arizona College A
Phoenix College A

Arkansas
University of Arkansas
  Little Rock A, B

California
Allan Hancock College A
Butte College C, A
California Institute of Technology M, D
California State University
  Long Beach B
Chabot College A
City College of San Francisco C, A
San Joaquin Delta College C
Santa Ana College C, A
Santa Rosa Junior College C, A
Shasta College C, A
Southwestern College A
Ventura College A

Colorado
Front Range Community College C, A
Metropolitan State College of Denver B
Pueblo Community College A
Trinidad State Junior College C, A
University of Southern Colorado B

Connecticut
Capital Community College A
Central Connecticut State University B
Three Rivers Community-Technical
  College A

Delaware
Delaware State University B
Delaware Technical and Community
  College
  Owens Campus A
  Stanton/Wilmington Campus A
  Terry Campus C, A

Florida
Broward Community College A
Daytona Beach Community College A
Florida Agricultural and Mechanical
  University B
Florida Community College at
  Jacksonville A
Gulf Coast Community College A
Manatee Community College A
Miami-Dade Community College A
Pensacola Junior College A
Tallahassee Community College A
Valencia Community College A

Georgia
Georgia Southern University B
Savannah State University B
Southern Polytechnic State University B

Idaho
Idaho State University A

Illinois
Black Hawk College A
Bradley University B
College of Lake County C, A
Parkland College C

Indiana
Indiana University--Purdue University
  Indiana University-Purdue
    University Fort Wayne A
  Indiana University-Purdue
    University Indianapolis A
Purdue University
  North Central Campus A
University of Southern Indiana A
Vincennes University A

Iowa
Des Moines Area Community College A
Hawkeye Community College A
Iowa Western Community College A

Kansas
Independence Community College A
Johnson County Community College A
Kansas State University A

Kentucky
Murray State University A, B
Western Kentucky University B

Louisiana
Delgado Community College A
Louisiana Tech University B

Maine
Central Maine Technical College A
University of Maine B

Maryland
Community College of Baltimore County
  Catonsville C, A
Montgomery College
  Rockville Campus A

Massachusetts
Bristol Community College A
Massasoit Community College A
Merrimack College B
Northeastern University B
Northern Essex Community College C
Springfield Technical Community
  College A
University of Massachusetts
  Lowell A, B
Wentworth Institute of Technology B

Michigan
Ferris State University A
Lansing Community College A
Macomb Community College C, A
Michigan Technological University A

Minnesota
Dunwoody Institute A
Lake Superior College: A Community
  and Technical College A
Rochester Community and Technical
  College A
St. Cloud Technical College C, A
St. Paul Technical College C
South Central Technical College A

Mississippi
Hinds Community College A
Northwest Mississippi Community
  College C, A

Missouri
Mineral Area College C, A
Missouri Western State College A, B
St. Louis Community College
  St. Louis Community College at
    Florissant Valley A
Three Rivers Community College A

Montana
Montana State University
  Northern A, B

Nebraska
Metropolitan Community College C, A
Southeast Community College
  Milford Campus A
University of Nebraska
  Omaha B

New Hampshire
University of New Hampshire A, B

New Jersey
Brookdale Community College C
Essex County College A
Gloucester County College A
Mercer County Community College A
Middlesex County College A
Ocean County College A
Thomas Edison State College A, B
Union County College A

New York
Broome Community College A
City University of New York
  College of Staten Island A
  New York City Technical
    College A
Columbia University
  Fu Foundation School of
    Engineering and Applied
    Science B

Cornell University *M, D*
Erie Community College
  North Campus *A*
Hudson Valley Community College *A*
Mohawk Valley Community College *A*
Monroe Community College *C, A*
Nassau Community College *A*
Rochester Institute of Technology *B*
State University of New York
  College of Technology at Alfred *A*
  College of Technology at Canton *A*
  Institute of Technology at
    Utica/Rome *B*
Westchester Community College *A*

North Carolina
Asheville Buncombe Technical
  Community College *A*
Central Carolina Community College *A*
Central Piedmont Community College *A*
Fayetteville Technical Community
  College *A*
Gaston College *A*
Guilford Technical Community
  College *C, A*
Sandhills Community College *A*
University of North Carolina
  Charlotte *B*
Wake Technical Community College *A*

North Dakota
North Dakota State College of Science *A*

Ohio
Cincinnati State Technical and
  Community College *A*
Clark State Community College *A*
Columbus State Community College *A*
Lakeland Community College *A*
Owens Community College
  Toledo *A*
Sinclair Community College *A*
Stark State College of Technology *A*
University of Akron *A*
University of Toledo *A*
Youngstown State University *A, B*

Oklahoma
Oklahoma State University
  Oklahoma City *A*
Tulsa Community College *C, A*

Oregon
Chemeketa Community College *A*
Linn-Benton Community College *C*
Mount Hood Community College *A*
Portland Community College *C, A*

Pennsylvania
Butler County Community College *A*
Community College of Allegheny
  County *A*
ICS Center for Degree Studies *A*
Penn State
  Harrisburg *B*
Pennsylvania College of Technology *A*
Pennsylvania Institute of Technology *A*
Point Park College *A, B*
Temple University *A*
University of Pittsburgh
  Johnstown *B*

Puerto Rico
University of Puerto Rico
  Bayamon University College *A*
  Ponce University College *A*

South Carolina
Central Carolina Technical College *A*
Florence-Darlington Technical College *A*
Francis Marion University *B*
Horry-Georgetown Technical College *A*
Midlands Technical College *A*
South Carolina State University *B*
Spartanburg Technical College *A*
Trident Technical College *C, A*

South Dakota
Southeast Technical Institute *A*

Tennessee
Nashville State Technical Institute *A*
Pellissippi State Technical Community
  College *A*

Texas
Houston Community College System *A*
Kilgore College *A*
San Antonio College *A*
University of Houston
  Downtown *B*
University of Houston *B*

Vermont
Vermont Technical College *A*

Virginia
Central Virginia Community College *A*
J. Sargeant Reynolds Community
  College *C, A*
Lord Fairfax Community College *A*
Northern Virginia Community
  College *C, A*
Tidewater Community College *A*
Virginia Western Community College *A*

Washington
Big Bend Community College *A*
Centralia College *A*
Everett Community College *C*
Highline Community College *A*
Shoreline Community College *A*
South Seattle Community College *A*
Spokane Community College *A*
Walla Walla Community College *C, A*

West Virginia
Bluefield State College *A, B*
Fairmont State College *A, B*
West Virginia University Institute of
  Technology *A*

Wisconsin
Chippewa Valley Technical College *A*
Gateway Technical College *A*
Madison Area Technical College *A*
Moraine Park Technical College *A*
Northeast Wisconsin Technical
  College *A*

Classical/ancient Near Eastern languages

California
University of California
  Berkeley *B*

Colorado
Naropa University *C, M*

Connecticut
Yale University *B, M, D*

Delaware
University of Delaware *B*

District of Columbia
Catholic University of America *M, D*

Illinois
University of Chicago *B, M, D*
Wheaton College *B*

Massachusetts
Harvard College *B*
Harvard University *M, D*

Michigan
University of Michigan *B*
Wayne State University *B, M*

Missouri
St. Louis University *B*

Montana
Carroll College *B*

New Jersey
Rutgers
  The State University of New Jersey:
    Newark College of Arts and
    Sciences *B*

New York
Columbia University
  Columbia College *B*
New York University *B*
State University of New York
  Binghamton *B*

Ohio
Ohio Wesleyan University *B*

Texas
University of Texas
  Austin *B, M, D*

Utah
Brigham Young University *B*

Washington
Seattle Pacific University *B*
University of Washington *M*

Classics

Alabama
Samford University *B*
University of Alabama *B*

Arizona
University of Arizona *B, M*

Arkansas
University of Arkansas *B*

California
California State University
  Long Beach *B*
Claremont McKenna College *B*
Loyola Marymount University *B*
Pitzer College *B*
Pomona College *B*
St. Mary's College of California *B*
San Diego State University *B*
San Francisco State University *B, M*
Santa Clara University *B*
Scripps College *B*
Stanford University *B, M, D*
University of California
  Berkeley *B, M, D*
  Davis *B, M*
  Irvine *B, M, D*
  Los Angeles *B, M, D*
  Riverside *B*
  San Diego *B*
  Santa Barbara *B, M, D*
University of Southern
  California *B, M, D*
University of the Pacific *B*

Colorado
Colorado College *B*
University of Colorado
  Boulder *B, M, D*

Connecticut
Albertus Magnus College *B*
Connecticut College *B*
Trinity College *B*
University of Connecticut *B*
Wesleyan University *B*
Yale University *B, M, D*

Delaware
University of Delaware *B*

District of Columbia
Catholic University of America *B, M*
George Washington University *B*
Georgetown University *B*
Howard University *B*

Florida
Florida State University *B, M, D*
New College of the University of South
  Florida *B*
Rollins College *B*
University of Florida *B, M*
University of South Florida *B, M*

Georgia
Agnes Scott College *B*
Emory University *B*
Georgia State University *B*
Oxford College of Emory University *B*
University of Georgia *B, M*

Hawaii
University of Hawaii
  Manoa *B, M*

Idaho
University of Idaho *B*

Illinois
Augustana College *B, T*
Knox College *B*
Loyola University of Chicago *B, M, D*
Monmouth College *B, T*
North Central College *B*
Northwestern University *B, M, D*
Rockford College *B*
Southern Illinois University
  Carbondale *B*
University of Chicago *B, M, D*
University of Illinois
  Chicago *B*
  Urbana-Champaign *B, M*
Wheaton College *B*

Indiana
Ball State University *B*
DePauw University *B*
Earlham College *B*
Hanover College *B*
University of Evansville *B*
University of Notre Dame *B*
Valparaiso University *B, T*
Wabash College *B*

Iowa
Coe College *B*
Cornell College *B*
Grinnell College *B*
Loras College *B*
Luther College *B*
University of Iowa *B, M, D*

Kansas
University of Kansas *B, M*

Kentucky
Asbury College *B*
Centre College *B*
University of Kentucky *B, M*

Louisiana
Centenary College of Louisiana *B*
Loyola University New Orleans *B*
Tulane University *B*

Maine
Bates College *B*
Bowdoin College *B*
Colby College *B*
University of Southern Maine *B*

Maryland
College of Notre Dame of Maryland *B*
Johns Hopkins University *B, D*
Loyola College in Maryland *B*
University of Maryland
  Baltimore County *B*
  College Park *B, M*

Massachusetts
Amherst College *B*
Assumption College *B*
Boston College *B*
Boston University *B, M, D*
Brandeis University *B*
Clark University *B*
College of the Holy Cross *B*

Classics

Harvard College *B*
Harvard University *D*
Hellenic College/Holy Cross *B*
Mount Holyoke College *B*
Regis College *B*
Smith College *B*
Tufts University *B, M*
University of Massachusetts
    Amherst *B, M*
    Boston *B*
Wellesley College *B*
Wheaton College *B*
Williams College *B*

Michigan
Calvin College *B*
Hillsdale College *B*
Hope College *B*
Kalamazoo College *B*
University of Michigan *B, M, D*
Wayne State University *B, M*

Minnesota
Carleton College *B*
College of St. Benedict *B*
Concordia College: Moorhead *B*
Gustavus Adolphus College *B*
Macalester College *B*
St. John's University *B*
St. Olaf College *B*
University of Minnesota
    Twin Cities *B, M, D*
University of St. Thomas *B*

Mississippi
Millsaps College *B, T*
University of Mississippi *B, M*

Missouri
St. Louis University *B*
Truman State University *B*
University of Missouri
    Columbia *B, M, D*
Washington University *B, M*

Montana
University of Montana-Missoula *B*

Nebraska
Creighton University *B*
University of Nebraska
    Lincoln *B, M*

New Hampshire
Dartmouth College *B*
St. Anselm College *B*
University of New Hampshire *B*

New Jersey
Drew University *B*
Montclair State University *B*
Princeton University *B, M, D*
Richard Stockton College of New
  Jersey *B*
Rutgers
    The State University of New Jersey:
      Douglass College *B*
    The State University of New Jersey:
      Livingston College *B*
    The State University of New Jersey:
      New Brunswick Graduate
      Campus *M, D, B*
    The State University of New Jersey:
      Rutgers College *B*
    The State University of New Jersey:
      University College New
      Brunswick *B*
St. Peter's College *B*
Seton Hall University *B*

New Mexico
University of New Mexico *B*

New York
Bard College *B*
Barnard College *B*
City University of New York
    Brooklyn College *B, M*
    Graduate School and University
      Center *M, D*
    Queens College *B*
Colgate University *B*
College of New Rochelle *B, T*
Columbia University
    Columbia College *B*
    Graduate School *M, D*
    School of General Studies *B*
Cornell University *B, M, D*
Elmira College *B*
Fordham University *B, M, D*
Hamilton College *B*
Hobart and William Smith Colleges *B*
Hofstra University *B*
Jewish Theological Seminary of
  America *D*
Manhattanville College *B*
New York University *B, M, D*
St. Bonaventure University *B*
Sarah Lawrence College *B*
Siena College *B*
Skidmore College *B*
State University of New York
    Albany *B, M*
    Binghamton *B*
    Buffalo *B, M, D*
Syracuse University *B, M*
Union College *B*

North Carolina
Davidson College *B*
Duke University *B, M, D*
University of North Carolina
    Asheville *B, T*
    Chapel Hill *B, M, D*
    Greensboro *B*
Wake Forest University *B*

Ohio
Case Western Reserve University *B*
College of Wooster *B*
Denison University *B*
Franciscan University of Steubenville *B*
Hiram College *B*
Kent State University
    Stark Campus *B*
Kent State University *B, M*
Kenyon College *B*
Miami University
    Oxford Campus *B*
Oberlin College *B*
Ohio State University
    Columbus Campus *B, M, D*
Ohio University *B*
Ohio Wesleyan University *B*
University of Akron *B*
University of Cincinnati *B, M, D*
University of Toledo *B, M*
Wright State University *B*
Xavier University *B*

Oklahoma
University of Oklahoma *B*
University of Tulsa *C, B*

Oregon
Reed College *B*
University of Oregon *B, M*
Willamette University *B*

Pennsylvania
Bryn Mawr College *B, M, D*
Bucknell University *B*
Dickinson College *B*
Duquesne University *B*
Franklin and Marshall College *B*
Gettysburg College *B*
Haverford College *B*
La Salle University *B*
Lehigh University *B*
Moravian College *B*
Muhlenberg College *B*
Penn State
    Lehigh Valley *B*
    University Park *B*
Swarthmore College *B*
Temple University *B*
University of Pennsylvania *A, B, M, D*
University of Pittsburgh *B, M, D*
University of Scranton *B*
Villanova University *B*
Westminster College *B*

Rhode Island
Brown University *B, M, D*
University of Rhode Island *B*

South Carolina
College of Charleston *B, T*
University of South Carolina *B*

Tennessee
Rhodes College *B, T*
University of Tennessee
    Chattanooga *B*
    Knoxville *B*
Vanderbilt University *B, M, D*

Texas
Austin College *B*
Baylor University *B*
Rice University *B*
Southwestern University *B*
Texas Tech University *M*
Trinity University *B*
University of Dallas *B*
University of Houston *B*
University of Texas
    Arlington *B*
    Austin *B, M, D*

Utah
Brigham Young University *B*
University of Utah *B*

Vermont
Marlboro College *B*
Middlebury College *B*
St. Michael's College *B*
University of Vermont *B, M*

Virginia
Christendom College *B*
College of William and Mary *B*
George Mason University *B*
Hampden-Sydney College *B*
Hollins University *B*
Mary Washington College *B*
Randolph-Macon College *B*
Randolph-Macon Woman's College *B*
Sweet Briar College *B*
University of Richmond *B, T*
University of Virginia *B, M, D*
Washington and Lee University *B*

Washington
Pacific Lutheran University *B*
Seattle Pacific University *B*
University of Puget Sound *B*
University of Washington *B, M, D*
Washington State University *B*
Western Washington University *B*
Whitman College *B*

Wisconsin
Beloit College *B*
Lawrence University *B, T*
Marquette University *B*
Ripon College *B*
University of Wisconsin
    Madison *B, M, D*
    Milwaukee *B*

Clerical/general office

Alabama
Community College of the Air Force *A*
Gadsden State Community College *C*
George C. Wallace State Community
  College
    Selma *C*
James H. Faulkner State Community
  College *C*
Lawson State Community College *C*
Northwest-Shoals Community College *C*
Sparks State Technical College *A*
Wallace State Community College at
  Hanceville *C, A*

Alaska
University of Alaska
    Anchorage *C*

Arizona
Arizona Western College *C, A*
Cochise College *C, A*
Dine College *C, A*
Eastern Arizona College *C*
Mesa Community College *A*
Paradise Valley Community
  College *C, A*
Phoenix College *C*
Pima Community College *C*

Arkansas
Garland County Community College *C*

California
Allan Hancock College *A*
American River College *A*
Bakersfield College *A*
Barstow College *C, A*
Canada College *C, A*
Cerritos Community College *A*
Cerro Coso Community College *C, A*
Chabot College *A*
Chaffey Community College *C*
Citrus College *C, A*
City College of San Francisco *A*
Coastline Community College *C*
College of San Mateo *A*
College of the Desert *A*
College of the Redwoods *C*
College of the Sequoias *C, A*
College of the Siskiyous *C, A*
Columbia College *C*
Compton Community College *C, A*
Contra Costa College *A*
Crafton Hills College *C, A*
Cypress College *C, A*
East Los Angeles College *A*
Empire College *C*
Evergreen Valley College *A*
Fresno City College *C, A*
Gavilan Community College *C*
Golden West College *C, A*
Heald Business College
    Fresno *C, A*
    Santa Rosa *C, A*
Humphreys College *C, A, B*
Imperial Valley College *C, A*
Kings River Community College *C*
Lake Tahoe Community College *C, A*
Long Beach City College *C, A*
Los Angeles Harbor College *C, A*
Los Angeles Mission College *C, A*
Los Angeles Southwest College *A*
Los Angeles Trade and Technical
  College *C, A*
Los Angeles Valley College *A*
Merced College *A*
MiraCosta College *C, A*
Mission College *A*
Modesto Junior College *C*
Monterey Peninsula College *C, A*
Mount St. Mary's College *A*
Mount San Antonio College *C, A*
Mount San Jacinto College *C*
Ohlone College *C, A*
Orange Coast College *C, A*
Palo Verde College *C, A*
Palomar College *C, A*
Pasadena City College *C, A*
Porterville College *A*

Rio Hondo College *A*
Sacramento City College *C, A*
Saddleback College *C*
San Bernardino Valley College *C*
San Diego City College *C, A*
San Diego Mesa College *C, A*
San Diego Miramar College *A*
San Joaquin Delta College *C, A*
San Jose City College *C, A*
Santa Monica College *C, A*
Santa Rosa Junior College *C*
Shasta College *A*
Sierra College *C, A*
Skyline College *C, A*
Solano Community College *A*
Southwestern College *A*
Taft College *A*
Ventura College *C, A*
West Hills Community College *A*
West Valley College *A*
Yuba College *C*

Colorado
Adams State College *B*
Lamar Community College *C*
Northeastern Junior College *C*
Pikes Peak Community College *C*
Pueblo Community College *C, A*
Trinidad State Junior College *C*

Connecticut
Briarwood College *C*
Gateway Community College *C, A*
Naugatuck Valley Community-Technical College *C*
Northwestern Connecticut Community-Technical College *C*
Quinebaug Valley Community College *C*

Delaware
Delaware Technical and Community College
    Owens Campus *C, A*
    Stanton/Wilmington Campus *A*

Florida
Brevard Community College *C*
Broward Community College *A*
Gulf Coast Community College *C, A*
Hillsborough Community College *C*
Miami-Dade Community College *A*
Pensacola Junior College *C*
Polk Community College *C*
Santa Fe Community College *A*
Seminole Community College *C*
South Florida Community College *C*
Valencia Community College *C, A*

Georgia
Abraham Baldwin Agricultural College *A*
Atlanta Metropolitan College *A*
Chattahoochee Technical Institute *C*
Clayton College and State University *C, A*
Dalton State College *C, A*
Darton College *C*
Georgia Military College *A*
Gwinnett Technical Institute *C*
Herzing College of Business and Technology *A*
Macon State College *C, A*
Middle Georgia College *C*
Morris Brown College *B*
South Georgia College *A*

Hawaii
University of Hawaii
    Kauai Community College *C, A*
    Leeward Community College *C, A*
    Windward Community College *C, A*

Idaho
College of Southern Idaho *C*
Eastern Idaho Technical College *C*

Illinois
City Colleges of Chicago
    Kennedy-King College *C*
    Wright College *C*
Elgin Community College *C*
Highland Community College *C*
John A. Logan College *C*
John Wood Community College *C*
Joliet Junior College *A*
Kankakee Community College *C*
Kaskaskia College *C*
Kishwaukee College *C, A*
Lake Land College *C*
Lewis and Clark Community College *A*
MacCormac College *C*
Morton College *C*
Robert Morris College: Chicago *C, A*
Rock Valley College *C, A*
Sauk Valley Community College *C*
Southeastern Illinois College *C*
Southwestern Ilinois College *C, A*
Waubonsee Community College *C*
William Rainey Harper College *C*

Indiana
Ancilla College *C*
Indiana Wesleyan University *A*
Purdue University
    North Central Campus *A*
Vincennes University *A*

Iowa
American Institute of Business *A*
Des Moines Area Community College *C*
Dordt College *A*
Hawkeye Community College *C*
Iowa Lakes Community College *C*
Iowa Western Community College *C*
Kirkwood Community College *C*
Marshalltown Community College *C*
North Iowa Area Community College *C*
Northeast Iowa Community College *C*
Southeastern Community College
    North Campus *C, A*
    South Campus *C*

Kansas
Allen County Community College *C*
Butler County Community College *C, A*
Coffeyville Community College *A*
Colby Community College *C*
Cowley County Community College *C, A*
Independence Community College *C, A*
Kansas City Kansas Community College *C, A*
Pratt Community College *C, A*
Seward County Community College *C, A*
Washburn University of Topeka *C, A*

Kentucky
Ashland Community College *A*
Kentucky Christian College *A*
National Business College *A*
Owensboro Community College *A*
Owensboro Junior College of Business *C, A*

Louisiana
Nunez Community College *C*

Maine
Andover College *C, A*
Husson College *A*
University of Maine
    Machias *A, B*

Maryland
Charles County Community College *C*
Community College of Baltimore County
    Catonsville *A*
Montgomery College
    Takoma Park Campus *C*

Massachusetts
Berkshire Community College *A*
Bristol Community College *C*
Cape Cod Community College *C, A*
Holyoke Community College *C*
Marian Court College *C, A*
Massasoit Community College *C*
Middlesex Community College *C*
Northern Essex Community College *C*
Springfield Technical Community College *C*

Michigan
Baker College
    of Auburn Hills *C*
    of Cadillac *C*
    of Jackson *C*
    of Mount Clemens *C*
    of Muskegon *C*
    of Owosso *C, A*
    of Port Huron *C*
Bay de Noc Community College *C*
Delta College *C, A*
Great Lakes College *C*
Henry Ford Community College *A*
Kellogg Community College *C*
Kirtland Community College *C*
Mid Michigan Community College *C*
Monroe County Community College *C, A*
North Central Michigan College *C, A*
Oakland Community College *A*
St. Clair County Community College *C, A*
Wayne County Community College *C*
West Shore Community College *C, A*

Minnesota
Alexandria Technical College *C*
Central Lakes College *C*
Hennepin Technical College *C, A*
Hibbing Community College: A Technical and Community College *C, A*
Itasca Community College *C*
Lake Superior College: A Community and Technical College *C*
Minnesota State College - Southeast Technical *C*
Northland Community & Technical College *C*
Pine Technical College *C*
Ridgewater College: A Community and Technical College *C*
Rochester Community and Technical College *C, A*
St. Cloud Technical College *C, A*
St. Paul Technical College *C*
Winona State University *B*

Mississippi
Itawamba Community College *C, A*
Southwest Mississippi Community College *C, A*

Missouri
Crowder College *A*
Hannibal-LaGrange College *A*
Jefferson College *C*
Longview Community College *C*
Maple Woods Community College *C*
Mineral Area College *C, A*
Moberly Area Community College *C, A*
Penn Valley Community College *C*
St. Louis Community College
    St. Louis Community College at Meramec *A*
Three Rivers Community College *C*

Montana
Little Big Horn College *C*
Miles Community College *C, A*
Montana State University
    Billings *C*
    College of Technology-Great Falls *A*
Montana Tech of the University of Montana *A*
Stone Child College *C, A*

Nebraska
Lincoln School of Commerce *C*
Mid Plains Community College Area *A*
Southeast Community College
    Lincoln Campus *A*
University of Nebraska
    Kearney *B*

Nevada
Western Nevada Community College *A*

New Hampshire
McIntosh College *C*
New Hampshire Community Technical College
    Claremont *C*

New Jersey
Gloucester County College *C, A*
Katharine Gibbs School
    Gibbs College *A*
Raritan Valley Community College *C*
Salem Community College *C*
Sussex County Community College *C*

New Mexico
College of Santa Fe *A*
Dona Ana Branch Community College of New Mexico State University *C*
New Mexico State University
    Alamogordo *C*
    Carlsbad *C*

New York
Adirondack Community College *C, A*
Cayuga County Community College *C*
Corning Community College *C*
Erie Community College
    City Campus *C*
    North Campus *C*
    South Campus *C*
Fulton-Montgomery Community College *C*
Herkimer County Community College *A*
Niagara County Community College *C, A*
North Country Community College *C, A*
Onondaga Community College *C, A*
Schenectady County Community College *C*
Trocaire College *C*
Westchester Business Institute *C, A*

North Carolina
Asheville Buncombe Technical Community College *C, A*
Carteret Community College *A*
Central Carolina Community College *A*
Cleveland Community College *A*
College of the Albemarle *C*
Edgecombe Community College *A*
Forsyth Technical Community College *C, A*
Gaston College *C*
Halifax Community College *A*
Johnston Community College *A*
Mayland Community College *C*
Roanoke-Chowan Community College *A*
Rockingham Community College *A*
Sampson Community College *A*
South Piedmont Community College *C, A*
Southeastern Community College *A*
Surry Community College *C, A*
Western Piedmont Community College *A*
Wilson Technical Community College *C*

North Dakota
Bismarck State College *C, A*
Minot State University: Bottineau Campus *C*
North Dakota State College of Science *C*

Ohio
Belmont Technical College *C, A*
Bowling Green State University
    Firelands College *C*

Clerical/general office

Cincinnati State Technical and
 Community College *A*
Columbus State Community
 College *C, A*
Davis College *C*
Edison State Community College *C*
Hocking Technical College *C, A*
Jefferson Community College *C*
Kent State University
 Trumbull Campus *A*
 Tuscarawas Campus *A*
Marion Technical College *C, A*
Miami University
 Hamilton Campus *C, A*
 Middletown Campus *C, A*
Miami-Jacobs College *C, A*
Northwest State Community
 College *C, A*
Northwestern College *C*
Ohio Valley Business College *A*
Owens Community College
 Toledo *C*
Southern State Community College *C*
Stark State College of Technology *C*
Terra Community College *A*
University of Akron *A*
University of Cincinnati
 Raymond Walters College *C, A*
University of Findlay *A*
University of Toledo *C*
Youngstown State University *A*

Oklahoma
Eastern Oklahoma State College *A*
Oklahoma City Community College *A*
Redlands Community College *A*
Seminole State College *A*
Tulsa Community College *C*

Oregon
Central Oregon Community College *C*
Chemeketa Community College *C*
Clackamas Community College *C*
Lane Community College *C*
Linn-Benton Community College *C*

Pennsylvania
Bucks County Community College *C, A*
Butler County Community College *A*
Churchman Business School *C*
Clarion University of Pennsylvania *C*
Community College of Philadelphia *C, A*
Lackawanna Junior College *C*
Laurel Business Institute *A*
Lehigh Carbon Community College *A*
Manor College *C, A*
Mercyhurst College *C*
Montgomery County Community
 College *A*
Newport Business Institute *A*
Pennsylvania College of Technology *A*
Reading Area Community College *C, A*
South Hills School of Business &
 Technology *A*

Puerto Rico
American University of Puerto Rico *B*
Atlantic College *C*
Caribbean University *A*
Colegio Universitario del Este *C, A*
Humacao Community College *C*
Pontifical Catholic University of Puerto
 Rico *A*
Ramirez College of Business and
 Technology *A*
Universidad Metropolitana *C*
University of Puerto Rico
 Aguadilla *A*

Rhode Island
Community College of Rhode Island *C*

South Carolina
Aiken Technical College *C*
Chesterfield-Marlboro Technical
 College *C, A*

Florence-Darlington Technical
 College *C*
Orangeburg-Calhoun Technical
 College *C*
Piedmont Technical College *C*
Technical College of the Lowcountry *C*
Tri-County Technical College *C*
Trident Technical College *C*
York Technical College *C*

South Dakota
Northern State University *C, A, B*
Sinte Gleska University *A*
Western Dakota Technical Institute *C*

Tennessee
Chattanooga State Technical Community
 College *A*
Knoxville Business College *A*
Lincoln Memorial University *A, B*
Roane State Community College *C, A*

Texas
Alvin Community College *C, A*
Amarillo College *A*
Angelina College *C, A*
Blinn College *A*
Central Texas College *C*
Coastal Bend College *A*
College of the Mainland *A*
Collin County Community College
 District *A*
El Paso Community College *C, A*
Galveston College *C, A*
Grayson County College *C, A*
Hill College *A*
Houston Community College System *C*
Howard College *C, A*
Kilgore College *C*
Lee College *C, A*
Midland College *C, A*
Mountain View College *C*
North Central Texas College *A*
Panola College *C*
San Antonio College *C, A*
San Jacinto College
 North *C, A*
Tarrant County College *C*
Texas A&M University
 Commerce *B*
Texas Southern University *B*
Texas State Technical College
 Harlingen *C*
 Sweetwater *C, A*
Tyler Junior College *C*
Vernon Regional Junior College *C*
Victoria College *C*
Weatherford College *C, A*

Virginia
Central Virginia Community College *C*
Dabney S. Lancaster Community
 College *C*
ECPI College of Technology *C, A*
Eastern Shore Community College *C, A*
Germanna Community College *C*
J. Sargeant Reynolds Community
 College *C*
Lord Fairfax Community College *C*
Mountain Empire Community College *A*
National Business College *A*
Patrick Henry Community College *C*
Piedmont Virginia Community
 College *C, A*
Southside Virginia Community
 College *C*
Tidewater Community College *C*
Wytheville Community College *C*

Washington
Big Bend Community College *C*
Centralia College *C, A*
Clark College *A*
Everett Community College *C, A*
Green River Community College *C, A*
Highline Community College *C, A*
Lower Columbia College *A*

North Seattle Community College *C*
Olympic College *C*
Pierce College *C, A*
Renton Technical College *C, A*
Shoreline Community College *C*
Skagit Valley College *C*
South Puget Sound Community
 College *C, A*
Spokane Community College *C, A*
Walla Walla Community College *C, A*

West Virginia
Concord College *A*
Fairmont State College *C*
Glenville State College *A*

Wisconsin
Blackhawk Technical College *A*
Chippewa Valley Technical College *C*
Gateway Technical College *C*
Lakeshore Technical College *C*
Madison Area Technical College *C*
Nicolet Area Technical College *C*
Southwest Wisconsin Technical
 College *C*
University of Wisconsin
 Whitewater *B*
Western Wisconsin Technical College *C*

Wyoming
Eastern Wyoming College *C*

Clinical laboratory science

Alabama
Central Alabama Community College *A*
Enterprise State Junior College *A*
James H. Faulkner State Community
 College *A*
Troy State University *B*
Tuskegee University *B*
University of Alabama
 Birmingham *B, M*
University of Alabama *B*
University of South Alabama *B*

Arizona
Arizona State University *B*
Phoenix College *A*
University of Arizona *B, M*

Arkansas
Arkansas State University *A, B*
Arkansas Tech University *B*
Henderson State University *B*
John Brown University *B*
Phillips Community College of the
 University of Arkansas *A*
University of Arkansas
 for Medical Sciences *B*

California
California State University
 Bakersfield *B*
 Dominguez Hills *M*
City College of San Francisco *C, A*
Empire College *A*
Loma Linda University *A, B*
San Francisco State University *B*

Connecticut
Quinnipiac University *B*
Sacred Heart University *A, B*
University of Connecticut *B*
University of Hartford *B*
University of New Haven *B*
Western Connecticut State University *B*

Delaware
University of Delaware *B*
Wesley College *B*

District of Columbia
Catholic University of America *B*
Howard University *B*

Florida
Florida Atlantic University *B*

Florida Gulf Coast University *B*
Florida International University *B, M*
Florida Memorial College *B*
Manatee Community College *A*
Miami-Dade Community College *A*
Stetson University *B*
University of Central Florida *B*
University of Miami *B*
University of South Florida *B*

Georgia
Armstrong Atlantic State University *B*
Augusta State University *B*
Clayton College and State University *A*
Georgia Southern University *B*
Georgia State University *B*
Oglethorpe University *B*
Savannah State University *B*
Waycross College *A*

Hawaii
University of Hawaii
 Manoa *B*

Idaho
Idaho State University *B*

Illinois
Bradley University *B*
Eastern Illinois University *B*
Finch University of Health Sciences/The
 Chicago Medical School *M*
Illinois College *B*
Illinois State University *B*
National-Louis University *B*
North Park University *B*
Northern Illinois University *B*
Quincy University *A, B*
University of Illinois
 Chicago *B, M*
 Springfield *B*
Western Illinois University *B*

Indiana
Calumet College of St. Joseph *B*
Indiana University
 Southeast *B*
Indiana University--Purdue University
 Indiana University-Purdue
 University Indianapolis *B*
Manchester College *B*
Purdue University
 Calumet *B*
Purdue University *B, M*
St. Joseph's College *B*
Valparaiso University *B*

Iowa
Dordt College *B*
Graceland University *B*
Northwestern College *B*
Simpson College *B*
University of Iowa *B*
Wartburg College *B*

Kansas
University of Kansas
 Medical Center *B*
Wichita State University *B*

Kentucky
Campbellsville University *B*
Eastern Kentucky University *B*
Hazard Community College *A*
Kentucky State University *B*
Morehead State University *B*
Murray State University *B*
Spalding University *B*
University of Kentucky *B*
University of Louisville *B*
Western Kentucky University *B*

Louisiana
Louisiana State University
 Alexandria *A*
Louisiana State University Medical
 Center *B, M*
Louisiana Tech University *B*

University of Louisiana at Monroe *B*
University of New Orleans *B*

Maine
University of Maine *B, M*
University of New England *B*

Maryland
Salisbury State University *B*

Massachusetts
American International College *B*
Atlantic Union College *B*
Fitchburg State College *B*
Laboure College *C, A*
Massasoit Community College *A*
Northeastern University *A, B, M*
Salem State College *B*
Springfield College *B*
Stonehill College *B*
University of Massachusetts
    Amherst *B*
    Boston *B*
    Dartmouth *B*

Michigan
Andrews University *A, B, M*
Calvin College *B*
Central Michigan University *B*
Eastern Michigan University *B*
Ferris State University *B*
Gogebic Community College *A*
Grand Valley State University *B*
Lake Superior State University *B*
Lansing Community College *A*
Madonna University *B*
Michigan State University *B, M*
Michigan Technological University *B, T*
Northern Michigan University *C, A, B*
Oakland University *B*
Saginaw Valley State University *B*
University of Michigan
    Flint *B*
Wayne State University *C, B, M*

Minnesota
Bemidji State University *B*
College of St. Catherine: St. Paul
    Campus *B*
College of St. Scholastica *B*
Concordia College: Moorhead *B*
Moorhead State University *B*
St. Cloud State University *B*
St. Mary's University of Minnesota *B*

Mississippi
Alcorn State University *B*
Copiah-Lincoln Community College *A*
Delta State University *B*
Mississippi Gulf Coast Community
    College
        Perkinston *A*
Mississippi State University *B*
Rust College *B*
University of Mississippi
    Medical Center *B*
University of Mississippi *B*
University of Southern Mississippi *B, M*

Missouri
Central Missouri State University *B*
Culver-Stockton College *B*
Lincoln University *B*
Lindenwood University *B*
Maryville University of Saint Louis *B*
Northwest Missouri State University *B*
Rockhurst University *B*
St. Louis University *B*
Southwest Missouri State University *B*
University of Missouri
    St. Louis *B*
William Jewell College *B*

Montana
University of Montana-Missoula *B*

Nevada
University of Nevada
    Las Vegas *B*

New Jersey
College of St. Elizabeth *B*
Fairleigh Dickinson University *B, M*
Felician College *B*
Kean University *B*
Monmouth University *B*
Ramapo College of New Jersey *B*
Rutgers
    The State University of New Jersey:
        Newark College of Arts and
        Sciences *B*
St. Peter's College *B*
University of Medicine and Dentistry of
    New Jersey
    School of Health Related
        Professions *C, B*

New Mexico
Eastern New Mexico University *B*

New York
City University of New York
    College of Staten Island
    York College *B*
Elmira College *B*
Hartwick College *B*
Hudson Valley Community College *A*
Iona College *B*
Keuka College *B*
Long Island University
    C. W. Post Campus *B*
Mercy College *B*
Mount St. Mary College *B*
Nassau Community College *A*
Orange County Community College *A*
Pace University:
    Pleasantville/Briarcliff *B*
Pace University *B*
St. Francis College *B*
State University of New York
    Albany *B*
    Buffalo *B, M*
    College at Brockport *B*
    College at Plattsburgh *B*
    Health Science Center at Stony
        Brook *B*
    Stony Brook *B*
    Upstate Medical University *B*
Westchester Community College *A*

North Carolina
Catawba College *B*
Durham Technical Community
    College *A*
East Carolina University *B*
High Point University *B*
Lenoir-Rhyne College *B*
Salem College *B*
University of North Carolina
    Chapel Hill *B*
    Charlotte *B*
    Greensboro *B*
    Pembroke *B*
    Wilmington *B*
Western Carolina University *B*
Winston-Salem State University *B*

North Dakota
Bismarck State College *A*
Jamestown College *B*
North Dakota State University *B*
University of Mary *B*
University of North Dakota *B, M*

Ohio
Cincinnati State Technical and
    Community College *A*
College of Mount St. Joseph *B*
Malone College *B*
Miami University
    Oxford Campus *B*
Ohio State University
    Columbus Campus *B*
Ohio University *B*
University of Akron *B*
University of Cincinnati
    Clermont College *A*
University of Cincinnati *B*
Walsh University *B*
Wright State University *B*

Oklahoma
Oklahoma Christian University of
    Science and Arts *B*
Oklahoma Panhandle State University *B*
Oklahoma State University *B*
Oral Roberts University *B*
University of Central Oklahoma *B*

Oregon
Oregon State University *B*

Pennsylvania
Albright College *B*
Alvernia College *B*
Bloomsburg University of
    Pennsylvania *B*
Cabrini College *B*
Carlow College *C*
Cheyney University of Pennsylvania *B*
Elizabethtown College *B*
Gannon University *B*
Gwynedd-Mercy College *B*
Indiana University of Pennsylvania *B*
King's College *B*
Lock Haven University of
    Pennsylvania *B*
MCP Hahnemann University *A, B*
Mansfield University of Pennsylvania *B*
Marywood University *B*
Mercyhurst College *B*
Messiah College *B*
Reading Area Community College *A*
Seton Hill College *B*
Thomas Jefferson University: College of
    Health Professions *C, B*
University of Pennsylvania *M, D*
University of Pittsburgh *B*
University of Scranton *B*
Washington and Jefferson College *B*
Wilkes University *B*

Puerto Rico
Inter American University of Puerto Rico
    Metropolitan Campus *B*
    San German Campus *C, B*
Pontifical Catholic University of Puerto
    Rico *B*
University of Puerto Rico
    Arecibo Campus *T*
    Medical Sciences Campus *B, M*

Rhode Island
Rhode Island College *B*
Salve Regina University *B, M*
University of Rhode Island *B, M*

South Carolina
Anderson College *A*
Francis Marion University *B*
Lander University *B*
University of South Carolina *B*
Winthrop University *B*

South Dakota
Augustana College *B*
Mount Marty College *B*
University of South Dakota *B*

Tennessee
Austin Peay State University *B*
Carson-Newman College *B*
East Tennessee State University *B*
King College *B*
Lincoln Memorial University *B*
Southern Adventist University *B*
Tusculum College *B*
University of Tennessee
    Knoxville *B*

Texas
Amarillo College *A*
Angelo State University *B*
Austin Community College *A*
Baylor University *B*
Del Mar College *A*
Grayson County College *A*
Howard Payne University *B*
Lamar University *B*
LeTourneau University *B*
Midwestern State University *B*
Navarro College *C*
Odessa College *A*
Prairie View A&M University *B*
St. Mary's University *B*
Sam Houston State University *B*
Southwest Texas State University *B*
Stephen F. Austin State University *B*
Tarleton State University *B*
Texas A&M University
    Corpus Christi *B*
Texas State Technical College
    Waco *A*
Texas Woman's University *B*
University of Houston *B*
University of Mary Hardin-Baylor *B*
University of North Texas *B*
University of Texas
    Arlington *B*
    Austin *B*
    El Paso *B*
    Medical Branch at Galveston *B*
    Pan American *B*
    San Antonio *B*
    Southwestern Medical Center at
        Dallas *B*
    Tyler *B*
University of the Incarnate Word *B*
West Texas A&M University *B*

Utah
Brigham Young University *B*
Snow College *A*
Weber State University *B*

Vermont
University of Vermont *B, M*

Virginia
Averett College *B*
Bridgewater College *B*
Eastern Mennonite University *B*
Emory & Henry College *B*
George Mason University *B*
Mary Baldwin College *B*
Norfolk State University *B*
Northern Virginia Community College *C*
Old Dominion University *B*
Roanoke College *B*
University of Virginia's College at
    Wise *B*
Virginia Commonwealth
    University *B, M*

Washington
University of Washington *B, M*

West Virginia
Concord College *B*
Marshall University *B*
West Liberty State College *B*
West Virginia University *B, M*

Wisconsin
Marian College of Fond du Lac *B*
Marquette University *B*
University of Wisconsin
    Madison *B*
    Milwaukee *B, M*
    Stevens Point *B*

Wyoming
University of Wyoming *B*

Clinical psychology

Alabama
Alabama Agricultural and Mechanical University *M*
Auburn University *M, D*
University of Alabama *D*

Alaska
University of Alaska
    Anchorage *M*

California
Antioch Southern California
    Los Angeles *M*
    Santa Barbara *M*
Azusa Pacific University *M, D*
Biola University *B, M, D*
California Lutheran University *M*
California School of Professional
    Psychology
    Alameda *D*
    San Diego *D*
California State University
    Bakersfield *M*
    Fullerton *M*
    Hayward *M*
    Stanislaus *M*
Fielding Institute *M, D*
John F. Kennedy University *M*
La Sierra University *B*
Loma Linda University *D*
Pacific Graduate School of
    Psychology *D*
Pepperdine University *B, M*
San Diego State University *D*
San Francisco State University *M*
San Jose State University *M*
United States International University *D*
University of California
    Los Angeles *M, D*
    Santa Cruz *B*
University of La Verne *D*
Vanguard University of Southern
    California *M*
Wright Institute *D*

Colorado
University of Denver *D*
Western State College of Colorado *B*

Connecticut
University of Hartford *M, D*

Delaware
University of Delaware *M, D*

District of Columbia
American University *D*
Catholic University of America *M, D*
Gallaudet University *D*
George Washington University *D*
University of the District of Columbia *M*

Florida
Barry University *M*
Carlos Albizu University *D*
Florida Institute of Technology *D*
Florida State University *B, M, D*
Nova Southeastern University *D*
University of Central Florida *M*
University of Miami *M, D*

Georgia
Emory University *D*
Toccoa Falls College *B*

Idaho
Idaho State University *D*

Illinois
Adler School of Professional
    Psychology *D*
Benedictine University *M*
Chicago School of Professional
    Psychology *D*
De Paul University *M, D*
Eastern Illinois University *M*
Finch University of Health Sciences/The
    Chicago Medical School *D*
Loyola University of Chicago *M, D*
Northwestern University *D*
Roosevelt University *B, M, D*
Wheaton College *M, D*

Indiana
Indiana State University *M, D*
Purdue University
    Calumet *B*
University of Evansville *B*
University of Indianapolis *M, D*
Valparaiso University *M*

Iowa
University of Iowa *D*
Upper Iowa University *B*

Kansas
Pittsburg State University *M*
University of Kansas *D*
Washburn University of Topeka *M*

Kentucky
Eastern Kentucky University *M*
Morehead State University *M*
Murray State University *M*
Spalding University *M, D*
University of Kentucky *M, D*
University of Louisville *M, D*

Maine
Husson College *B*
University of Maine *D*

Maryland
Loyola College in Maryland *M, D*
Uniformed Services University of the
    Health Sciences *D*

Massachusetts
American International College *M*
Bridgewater State College *B*
Clark University *D*
Massachusetts School of Professional
    Psychology *D*
Suffolk University *M, D*
Tufts University *B*
University of Massachusetts
    Boston *D*
    Dartmouth *M*
Westfield State College *M*

Michigan
Center for Humanistic Studies *M*
Central Michigan University *M, D*
University of Detroit Mercy *M, D*
University of Michigan
    Flint *B*

Mississippi
Jackson State University *D*

Missouri
University of Missouri
    Columbia *M, D*
Washington University *M, D*

New Hampshire
Antioch New England Graduate
    School *M, D*
Franklin Pierce College *B*

New Jersey
Fairleigh Dickinson University *M*
Rutgers
    The State University of New Jersey:
    New Brunswick Graduate
    Campus *D*
Seton Hall University *D*

New York
Adelphi University *M, D*
City University of New York
    Brooklyn College *B*
    City College *D*
    Graduate School and University
    Center *D*
    Queens College *M*
Columbia University
    Teachers College *D*
Fordham University *M, D*
Hofstra University *D*
Long Island University
    Brooklyn Campus *D*
    C. W. Post Campus *D*
New York University *D*
Nyack College *M*
Pace University:
    Pleasantville/Briarcliff *M*
Pace University *M*
St. John's University *M, D*
State University of New York
    Albany *M, D*
    Binghamton *D*
    Buffalo *D*
    Stony Brook *M, D*
Syracuse University *M, D*
University of Rochester *D*

North Carolina
Duke University *D*
East Carolina University *M*
University of North Carolina
    Chapel Hill *M, D*
    Charlotte *M*
Western Carolina University *M*

Ohio
Bowling Green State University *M, D*
Case Western Reserve University *D*
Kent State University *M, D*
Ohio University *M, D*
Union Institute *D*
University of Dayton *M*
Wright State University *D*
Xavier University *D*

Oklahoma
University of Tulsa *M, D*

Oregon
George Fox University *M, D*
Pacific University *M, D*

Pennsylvania
Bryn Mawr College *M, D*
Chestnut Hill College *M, D*
Edinboro University of Pennsylvania *M*
Immaculata College *D*
Indiana University of Pennsylvania *D*
La Salle University *B, D*
MCP Hahnemann University *M, D*
Mansfield University of Pennsylvania *M*
Millersville University of
    Pennsylvania *M*
Moravian College *B*
Temple University *M, D*
West Chester University of
    Pennsylvania *M*
Widener University *D*

Puerto Rico
Inter American University of Puerto Rico
    Metropolitan Campus *M*
Pontifical Catholic University of Puerto
    Rico *M*
University of Puerto Rico
    Rio Piedras Campus *M, D*

Rhode Island
University of Rhode Island *D*

South Carolina
Francis Marion University *M*
University of South Carolina
    Aiken *M*
University of South Carolina *D*

South Dakota
University of South Dakota *D*

Tennessee
Crichton College *B*
University of Tennessee
    Knoxville *B*
Vanderbilt University *M, D*

Texas
Abilene Christian University *M*
Baylor University *M, D*
Houston Baptist University *M*
Midwestern State University *M*
Our Lady of the Lake University of San
    Antonio *M*
St. Mary's University *M*
Sam Houston State University *M*
Southern Methodist University *M*
Texas A&M University *D*
Texas Tech University *D*
University of Houston
    Clear Lake *M*
University of Houston *D*
University of North Texas *M, D*
University of Texas
    El Paso *M*
    Southwestern Medical Center at
    Dallas *M, D*
    Tyler *M*
    of the Permian Basin *M*

Utah
Brigham Young University *D*

Vermont
College of St. Joseph in Vermont *M*
Marlboro College *B*
St. Michael's College *M*

Virginia
Averett College *B*
College of William and Mary *D*
Norfolk State University *D*
Old Dominion University *D*
Regent University *M, D*
University of Virginia *D*
Virginia Commonwealth
    University *M, D*

Washington
Antioch University Seattle *M*
Eastern Washington University *M*
Seattle Pacific University *D*
University of Washington *D*

West Virginia
Marshall University *M*

Wisconsin
Marquette University *M, D*

Clinical/medical social work

Alabama
Southern Union State Community
    College *A*

Arizona
Arizona Western College *A*

Arkansas
Arkansas Tech University *B*

California
California State University
    Fresno *B, M*
East Los Angeles College *C*
Loma Linda University *M*

Michigan
Calvin College *B*

Mississippi
University of Southern Mississippi *M*

Montana
Dawson Community College *A*

Nebraska
Central Community College *C, A*

New Mexico
New Mexico Highlands University *M*

Pennsylvania
Clarion University of Pennsylvania *A, B*

University of Pittsburgh *C*
Widener University *M, D*

South Dakota
University of South Dakota *B*

Texas
Baylor University *B*

Washington
Tacoma Community College *C*

Wisconsin
Concordia University Wisconsin *B*

Clothing/apparel/textile studies

Alabama
Alabama Agricultural and Mechanical University *B, M*
Auburn University *B, M, D*
John M. Patterson State Technical College *C*
University of Alabama *B, M*

Arizona
Mesa Community College *A*

Arkansas
University of Arkansas Pine Bluff *B*
University of Arkansas *B*
University of Central Arkansas *B*

California
California State Polytechnic University: Pomona *B*
California State University
 Long Beach *B*
 Northridge *B*
Cerritos Community College *A*
Chabot College *A*
Chaffey Community College *C*
Compton Community College *A*
Fresno City College *C, A*
Glendale Community College *A*
Los Angeles Mission College *A*
Los Angeles Trade and Technical College *C, A*
Mendocino College *C*
Modesto Junior College *A*
Mount San Antonio College *A*
Pacific Union College *A, B*
Sacramento City College *C, A*
Saddleback College *C*
San Francisco State University *B*
Santa Rosa Junior College *C*
University of California Davis *B, M*

Colorado
Art Institute of Colorado *A*
Colorado State University *B, M*

Connecticut
University of Connecticut *M*

Delaware
Delaware State University *B*

Florida
Florida Community College at Jacksonville *A*
Florida State University *B, M*

Georgia
Georgia Southern University *B*
Morris Brown College *B*
Savannah College of Art and Design *B, M*
University of Georgia *B, M, D*

Hawaii
University of Hawaii Manoa *B*

Idaho
Ricks College *A*
University of Idaho *B*

Illinois
International Academy of Merchandising and Design *A, B*
Joliet Junior College *A*
Northern Illinois University *B*
Southern Illinois University Carbondale *B*
University of Illinois Urbana-Champaign *B, M*

Indiana
Indiana State University *B*
Indiana University Bloomington *B, M*
Purdue University *B, M, D*
Vincennes University *A*

Iowa
Iowa State University *B, M, D*
University of Northern Iowa *B*

Kansas
Kansas State University *B, M*
Pittsburg State University *B, T*

Kentucky
Kentucky State University *B*
Murray State University *B*
University of Kentucky *B*
Western Kentucky University *B*

Louisiana
Southern University and Agricultural and Mechanical College *B*

Massachusetts
Framingham State College *B*

Michigan
Delta College *A*
Eastern Michigan University *M*
Marygrove College *A, B*
Michigan State University *B, M*

Minnesota
Concordia College: Moorhead *B*
Minnesota State University, Mankato *B, M*
University of Minnesota Twin Cities *B*

Mississippi
Mississippi University for Women *B*
University of Southern Mississippi *B*

Missouri
Central Missouri State University *B*
Southeast Missouri State University *B*
Southwest Missouri State University *B*
University of Missouri Columbia *B, M*

Nebraska
University of Nebraska
 Kearney *B*
 Lincoln *B, M*
 Omaha *B*

New Mexico
New Mexico State University *B*

New York
Cornell University *B, M*
Marymount College *B*
State University of New York
 College at Buffalo *B*
 College at Oneonta *B*
Syracuse University *B, M*

North Carolina
Appalachian State University *B*
Bennett College *B*
East Carolina University *B*
North Carolina Agricultural and Technical State University *B*

University of North Carolina Greensboro *B, M, D*

North Dakota
North Dakota State University *B*

Ohio
Bluffton College *B*
Bowling Green State University *B, M*
Kent State University *B*
Miami University Oxford Campus *M*
Ohio State University Columbus Campus *B, M, D*
Ohio University *B*
University of Akron *A, B*
Youngstown State University *B*

Oklahoma
East Central University *B*
Langston University *B*
Northeastern State University *B*
Oklahoma State University *B, M*
University of Central Oklahoma *B, M*

Oregon
Art Institute of Portland *A, B*

Pennsylvania
Albright College *B*
Cheyney University of Pennsylvania *B*
Immaculata College *B*
Mercyhurst College *B*
Philadelphia University *B, M*

Rhode Island
Johnson & Wales University *A*
University of Rhode Island *B, M*

South Carolina
Tri-County Technical College *A*

Tennessee
Carson-Newman College *B*
Freed-Hardeman University *B*
Hiwassee College *A*
Lambuth University *B*
Middle Tennessee State University *B*
Shelby State Community College *C*
Tennessee State University *B*
University of Tennessee Knoxville *B*

Texas
Baylor University *B*
Lamar University *B*
Navarro College *C, A*
Texas A&M University Kingsville *B*
Texas Christian University *B*
Texas Southern University *M*
Texas Tech University *B, M, D*
Texas Woman's University *B, M, D*
University of North Texas *B, M*
University of Texas Austin *B*

Utah
Salt Lake Community College *C*
Snow College *A*
Southern Utah University *A*

Virginia
Regent University *D*
Virginia Polytechnic Institute and State University *B, M, D*

Washington
Seattle Pacific University *B, T*
Washington State University *B, M*

West Virginia
Fairmont State College *A*

Wisconsin
University of Wisconsin
 Madison *B, M*
 Stout *B*

Wyoming
University of Wyoming *B*

Clothing/textile products and services

Alabama
Alabama Agricultural and Mechanical University *B, M*
Community College of the Air Force *A*
Lawson State Community College *C*
Shelton State Community College *A*

Arizona
Mesa Community College *A*

California
Butte College *A*
College of the Desert *C, A*
Fashion Institute of Design and Merchandising San Francisco *A*
Fashion Institute of Design and Merchandising *A*
Fresno City College *A*
Long Beach City College *C, A*
Merced College *A*
Orange Coast College *C, A*
Sacramento City College *C, A*
Saddleback College *C, A*
Sierra College *C, A*

Colorado
Art Institute of Colorado *A*

District of Columbia
University of the District of Columbia *B*

Florida
Art Institute of Fort Lauderdale *A*
Gulf Coast Community College *A*
Santa Fe Community College *A*

Idaho
Ricks College *A*

Illinois
College of DuPage *C, A*

Indiana
Indiana State University *B, M*
Vincennes University *A*

Iowa
Des Moines Area Community College *C, A*
Hawkeye Community College *A*

Kansas
Johnson County Community College *A*
Pittsburg State University *B*

Kentucky
Murray State University *B*

Maryland
University of Maryland Eastern Shore *B*

Michigan
Eastern Michigan University *M*
Northern Michigan University *C*
Wayne State University *B, M*
Western Michigan University *B*

Minnesota
College of St. Catherine: St. Paul Campus *B*

Mississippi
Hinds Community College *C*

Missouri
Penn Valley Community College *A*

North Carolina
Appalachian State University *B*
North Carolina Central University *B*

153

Clothing/textile products and services (continued)

North Dakota
North Dakota State University B
Ohio
Youngstown State University B
Oklahoma
Oklahoma State University B, M
Pennsylvania
Moore College of Art and Design B
Philadelphia University C, A, B
South Carolina
Technical College of the Lowcountry C
Tennessee
University of Tennessee
 Knoxville M
Texas
St. Philip's College C, A
Utah
Snow College A
Washington
Seattle Pacific University B
West Virginia
Fairmont State College A
Wisconsin
Madison Area Technical College A
Waukesha County Technical College C

Coast Guard

Maine
Maine Maritime Academy C
Massachusetts
Massachusetts Maritime Academy B

Cognitive psychology/psycholinguistics

California
California State University
 Stanislaus B
University of California
 Los Angeles B
 San Diego B, D
 Santa Cruz B, D
Connecticut
Yale University B
Delaware
University of Delaware M, D
District of Columbia
George Washington University D
Georgia
Emory University D
University of Georgia B
Illinois
Northwestern University B
Iowa
University of Iowa D
Kansas
University of Kansas B
Louisiana
Tulane University B
Massachusetts
Hampshire College B
Harvard College B
Simon's Rock College of Bard B
Tufts University B, M, D
Wellesley College B
Michigan
University of Michigan B

New Hampshire
Antioch New England Graduate
 School D
New Jersey
Kean University M
Rutgers
 The State University of New Jersey:
  New Brunswick Graduate
  Campus D
New York
City University of New York
 Graduate School and University
  Center D
Columbia University
 Graduate School M, D
 Teachers College M, D
Sarah Lawrence College B
State University of New York
 Albany M, D
 Binghamton D
 Buffalo D
University of Rochester B
Oregon
George Fox University B
Pennsylvania
Carnegie Mellon University B
Temple University D
West Chester University of
 Pennsylvania B
Rhode Island
Brown University B, M, D
Tennessee
Vanderbilt University B
Texas
University of Texas
 Dallas M
Vermont
Marlboro College B
Virginia
Washington and Lee University B

College counseling

California
University of Southern California M
Colorado
University of Northern Colorado D
University of Southern Colorado M
Connecticut
Central Connecticut State University M
Southern Connecticut State University M
Delaware
University of Delaware M
Florida
University of Florida M, D
Illinois
Western Illinois University M
Indiana
Indiana University
 Bloomington M
Iowa
Iowa State University T
St. Ambrose University M, T
University of Northern Iowa M
Kentucky
Eastern Kentucky University M
Western Kentucky University M
Louisiana
Nicholls State University M
Maine
University of Southern Maine M

Maryland
Johns Hopkins University M
Massachusetts
Northeastern University M
Springfield College M
Michigan
Michigan State University M
Minnesota
Minnesota State University, Mankato M
Ridgewater College: A Community and
 Technical College A
Mississippi
Jackson State University B
Montana
University of Montana-Missoula M, D
New Hampshire
Rivier College M
New Jersey
The College of New Jersey B, M
New York
City University of New York
 Hunter College M
Columbia University
 Teachers College M
Fordham University M, D
Long Island University
 C. W. Post Campus M
St. Bonaventure University M
North Carolina
University of North Carolina
 Charlotte M
 Greensboro M, D
Western Carolina University M
Ohio
Bowling Green State University M
Miami University
 Oxford Campus M
Ohio State University
 Columbus Campus M, D
University of Dayton M
Oklahoma
Oklahoma State University M, D
Pennsylvania
Duquesne University M
Eastern College M
Indiana University of Pennsylvania M
Kutztown University of
 Pennsylvania B, M
Lehigh University M, D
Shippensburg University of
 Pennsylvania M
Villanova University M
Puerto Rico
Inter American University of Puerto Rico
 Metropolitan Campus M
South Carolina
University of South Carolina M
Texas
Trinity Valley Community College A
Vermont
Johnson State College M
Virginia
Longwood College M
Washington
Seattle University M

Commercial photography

Alabama
Bessemer State Technical College C
Community College of the Air Force A

Arizona
Northern Arizona University B
California
Academy of Art College C, A, B, M
Allan Hancock College A
Art Center College of Design B
Butte College A
California State University
 Fullerton M
Compton Community College C
Diablo Valley College A
East Los Angeles College C
Lake Tahoe Community College C
Long Beach City College C, A
Modesto Junior College A
Otis College of Art and Design B
Pasadena City College C, A
Sacramento City College C, A
Saddleback College A
Santa Monica College A
Solano Community College C, A
Ventura College C, A
Colorado
Art Institute
 of Colorado A
Colorado Mountain College
 Spring Valley Campus A
Connecticut
Paier College of Art C, A
Florida
Art Institute
 of Fort Lauderdale A
Ringling School of Art and Design B
Georgia
Art Institute
 of Atlanta A
Atlanta College of Art B
Gwinnett Technical Institute A
Illinois
College of DuPage C, A
Judson College B
Prairie State College C, A
Iowa
Hawkeye Community College A
Louisiana
Tulane University B, M
Maryland
Harford Community College C
Montgomery College
 Rockville Campus A
Massachusetts
Simon's Rock College of Bard B
Michigan
Center for Creative Studies: College of
 Art and Design B
Oakland Community College C, A
Washtenaw Community College A
Minnesota
Ridgewater College: A Community and
 Technical College C, A
Nebraska
Metropolitan Community College A
Nevada
Community College of Southern
 Nevada A
New Hampshire
White Pines College B
New Jersey
Middlesex County College A
New York
City University of New York
 La Guardia Community
  College C, A
Fashion Institute of Technology A

Mohawk Valley Community
    College C, A
Parsons School of Design C, A, B, T
Pratt Institute B
Rochester Institute of Technology B, M
Rockland Community College A
School of Visual Arts B
Syracuse University B

North Carolina
Alamance Community College C
Randolph Community College A

Ohio
Ohio Institute of Photography and
    Technology A
University of Akron A

Oklahoma
University of Central Oklahoma B

Pennsylvania
Antonelli Institute of Art and
    Photography A
Community College of Philadelphia A
Northampton County Area Community
    College C
Pittsburgh Technical Institute A

Texas
Amarillo College A
El Paso Community College A
Houston Community College
    System C, A
Kilgore College A
Midland College A
North Central Texas College A
Odessa College A
Texas A&M University
    Commerce B

Virginia
Northern Virginia Community College A
Virginia Intermont College B

Washington
Art Institute of Seattle A
Seattle Central Community College A

Wisconsin
Madison Area Technical College A

Wyoming
Northwest College A

Communication disorders

Alabama
Alabama Agricultural and Mechanical
    University M
Auburn University B, M

Arizona
Arizona State University B, D
University of Arizona B, M, D

California
Biola University B
California State University
    Chico B, M
    Fresno B, M
San Diego State University B, M, D
University of the Pacific B, M

Colorado
University of Colorado
    Boulder B, M, D

District of Columbia
Howard University M, D

Georgia
University of Georgia B, M, D

Illinois
Southern Illinois University
    Carbondale B, M, D
Western Illinois University B, M

Kansas
Kansas State University B
University of Kansas B

Kentucky
Murray State University B, M

Louisiana
Nicholls State University B
Southeastern Louisiana University M

Maine
University of Maine B, M

Massachusetts
Boston University B, M
Bridgewater State College B, M
Emerson College B, M, D
University of Massachusetts
    Amherst B, M, D

Michigan
Calvin College B
Northern Michigan University B, M
Wayne State University B, M, D

Minnesota
Minnesota State University,
    Mankato B, M
St. Cloud State University B, M
University of Minnesota
    Duluth B, M, T
    Twin Cities M, D

Mississippi
Jackson State University M

Missouri
Rockhurst University B, M
Southeast Missouri State University M
Truman State University B, M

New York
College of St. Rose B, M, T
State University of New York
    College at Fredonia B
    New Paltz B, M
Syracuse University B

North Carolina
Western Carolina University B, M

Ohio
Bowling Green State University B, M, D
Case Western Reserve
    University B, M, D
University of Akron B, M

Pennsylvania
Edinboro University of Pennsylvania B
West Chester University of
    Pennsylvania M

Rhode Island
University of Rhode Island B

South Carolina
Winthrop University B

South Dakota
Augustana College B
University of South Dakota B, M

Texas
Baylor University B, M
Our Lady of the Lake University of San
    Antonio B, M
Southwest Texas State University B, M
University of Houston B
University of Texas
    Austin B, M, D
    Dallas D
    Pan American B, M
West Texas A&M University B, M

Vermont
University of Vermont B, M, T

Virginia
Longwood College B, T
Radford University B

Washington
Eastern Washington University B, M, T

Wisconsin
University of Wisconsin
    Madison B, M, D
    Milwaukee B, M
    Oshkosh B
    River Falls B, M

Communications

Alabama
Auburn University at Montgomery B
Community College of the Air Force A
Enterprise State Junior College A
Huntingdon College B
Jacksonville State University B
Jefferson State Community College A
Oakwood College B
Southern Union State Community
    College A
Spring Hill College B
Stillman College B
University of Alabama
    Birmingham B
University of Mobile B
University of Montevallo M
University of South Alabama B, M

Alaska
University of Alaska
    Fairbanks B, M
    Southeast B

Arizona
Arizona State University B, M, D
Cochise College A
Grand Canyon University B
Phoenix College A
Prescott College B, M
South Mountain Community College C
University of Arizona B, M, D

Arkansas
Harding University B
Ouachita Baptist University B
Southern Arkansas University B
University of Arkansas
    Little Rock B, M
    Pine Bluff B
University of Arkansas B, M
University of the Ozarks B

California
Azusa Pacific University B
Barstow College A
Biola University B
California Baptist University B
California Lutheran University B
California State Polytechnic University:
    Pomona B
California State University
    Bakersfield B
    Chico B, M
    Dominguez Hills B
    Fresno B, M
    Fullerton B, M
    Hayward B
    Monterey Bay B
    Northridge M
    Sacramento B, M
    San Marcos B
    Stanislaus B
Chaffey Community College A
Chapman University B
Citrus College A
College of Marin: Kentfield A
College of Notre Dame B
College of the Desert A
College of the Sequoias A
College of the Siskiyous A
Concordia University B
Cuesta College C, A
De Anza College A

Fashion Institute of Design and
    Merchandising A
Foothill College C, A
Fresno City College A
Fresno Pacific University B
Gavilan Community College A
ITT Technical Institute
    Oxnard A
La Sierra University B
Loyola Marymount University B, M
Marymount College A
Master's College B
Menlo College B
Merced College A
Mills College B
MiraCosta College A
Modesto Junior College C, A
Monterey Peninsula College A
Moorpark College A
Pacific Union College B
Pasadena City College C, A
Pepperdine University B, M
Point Loma Nazarene University B
St. Mary's College of California B
San Bernardino Valley College C, A
San Diego State University B, M
Santa Ana College C, A
Santa Barbara City College A
Santa Clara University B
Santa Rosa Junior College C
Shasta College A
Sierra College A
Simpson College B
Sonoma State University B
Stanford University B, M, D
United States International University B
University of California
    Los Angeles B
    San Diego B, M, D
    Santa Barbara B, M, D
University of La Verne B
University of San Diego B
University of San Francisco B
University of Southern
    California B, M, D
University of the Pacific B
Vanguard University of Southern
    California B
Ventura College A
Westmont College B

Colorado
Adams State College B
Colorado Christian University B
Fort Lewis College B
Lamar Community College A
Metropolitan State College of Denver B
Red Rocks Community College A
Regis University B
University of Colorado
    Boulder B, M, D
    Colorado Springs B, M
    Denver B, M
University of Denver B
University of Northern Colorado B, M, T
University of Southern Colorado B
Western State College of Colorado B

Connecticut
Albertus Magnus College B
Asnuntuck Community-Technical
    College A
Briarwood College A
Central Connecticut State University B
Eastern Connecticut State University B
Fairfield University B
Middlesex Community-Technical
    College A
Quinnipiac University B, M
Sacred Heart University A, B
Southern Connecticut State University B
University of Bridgeport B
University of Connecticut B, M, D
University of Hartford B, M
University of New Haven A, B
Western Connecticut State University B

155

Communications

Delaware
University of Delaware B, M
Wesley College B
Wilmington College B

District of Columbia
American University B
Catholic University of America B
Gallaudet University B
George Washington University B
Howard University B, M, D
Trinity College B

Florida
Art Institute
    of Fort Lauderdale A
Barry University B, M
Clearwater Christian College B
Edward Waters College B
Embry-Riddle Aeronautical University B
Flagler College B
Florida Atlantic University B, M
Florida Institute of Technology B, M
Florida International University B, M
Florida Southern College B
Florida State University B, M, D
Gulf Coast Community College A
Jacksonville University B
Lake City Community College A
Lynn University B
Palm Beach Atlantic College B
Polk Community College A
Rollins College M
St. Thomas University B
South Florida Community College A
Southeastern College of the Assemblies
    of God B
Stetson University B
University of Central Florida B, M
University of Florida M, D
University of Miami B, M
University of North Florida B
University of South Florida B, M
University of Tampa B
University of West Florida B, M
Warner Southern College B

Georgia
Abraham Baldwin Agricultural
    College A
Andrew College A
Augusta State University B
Berry College B
Clark Atlanta University B
Columbus State University B
Emmanuel College B
Floyd College A
Georgia Southern University B
Georgia State University M
Kennesaw State University B
Mercer University B, M
Morris Brown College B
Oglethorpe University B
Reinhardt College B
Savannah State University B
Shorter College B
South Georgia College A
Toccoa Falls College B
Valdosta State University B
Wesleyan College B
Young Harris College A

Hawaii
Brigham Young University
    Hawaii A
Chaminade University of Honolulu B
Hawaii Pacific University B
University of Hawaii
    Hilo B
    Manoa B, M, D

Idaho
Boise State University B, T
College of Southern Idaho A
Idaho State University A, B, M
Lewis-Clark State College B
North Idaho College A

Northwest Nazarene University B
Ricks College A
University of Idaho B

Illinois
Augustana College B
Barat College B
Benedictine University B
Bradley University B
Concordia University B
Danville Area Community College A
De Paul University B, M
Dominican University B
Elmhurst College B
Eureka College B
Governors State University B, M
Illinois State University M
John Wood Community College A
Judson College B
Kendall College B
Kishwaukee College A
Lake Forest College B
Lewis University B
Lincoln Land Community College A
Loyola University of Chicago B, T
McKendree College B
Millikin University B
Monmouth College B, T
Moody Bible Institute B
North Central College B
North Park University B
Northwestern University B, M, D
Olivet Nazarene University B
Parkland College A
Rend Lake College A
Roosevelt University B
St. Xavier University B
Sauk Valley Community College A
Southwestern Illinois College A
Trinity Christian College B
Trinity International University B
University of Illinois
    Springfield B, M
    Urbana-Champaign D
University of St. Francis B
Western Illinois University B, M
Wheaton College B, T

Indiana
Bethel College B
DePauw University B
Goshen College B
Grace College B
Hanover College B
Indiana State University B, M
Indiana University
    Bloomington B, M, D
    East B
    Kokomo B
    Northwest B
    Southeast B
Indiana University--Purdue University
    Indiana University-Purdue
        University Fort Wayne B, M
    Indiana University-Purdue
        University Indianapolis B
Indiana Wesleyan University A, B
Manchester College B, T
Marian College B
Purdue University
    Calumet B, M
    North Central Campus C
Purdue University B, M, D
Saint Mary's College B
St. Joseph's College B
Taylor University B
Tri-State University A, B
University of Evansville B
University of Indianapolis B
University of St. Francis B
University of Southern Indiana A, B
Valparaiso University B

Iowa
Buena Vista University B
Central College B

Clarke College B
Dordt College B
Drake University B
Grand View College B
Iowa Wesleyan College B
Loras College B
Luther College B
Marycrest International University B
Morningside College B
Northwestern College B
St. Ambrose University B
Simpson College B
University of Dubuque B, M
University of Iowa B, M, D, T
University of Northern Iowa B, M
Upper Iowa University B
Waldorf College A, B
Wartburg College T

Kansas
Baker University B, T
Barton County Community College A
Bethany College B
Bethel College B
Central Christian College A
Coffeyville Community College A
Cowley County Community College A
Emporia State University B
Fort Hays State University B, M
Garden City Community College A
Hutchinson Community College A
Independence Community College A
Kansas State University B, M
Kansas Wesleyan University B, T
McPherson College B
MidAmerica Nazarene University B, T
Newman University B
Ottawa University B
Pittsburg State University B, M, T
Pratt Community College A
St. Mary College B
Seward County Community College A
Southwestern College B
Sterling College B
Tabor College B
Washburn University of Topeka B
Wichita State University B, M

Kentucky
Bellarmine College B
Campbellsville University B
Cumberland College B
Henderson Community College A
Kentucky Mountain Bible College B
Kentucky Wesleyan College B
Mid-Continent College B
Midway College B
Morehead State University B, M
Murray State University B, M
Paducah Community College A
Spalding University B
Thomas More College A, B
University of Kentucky B, M, D
University of Louisville B
Western Kentucky University B, M

Louisiana
Centenary College of Louisiana B
Dillard University B
Loyola University New Orleans B, M
Southeastern Louisiana University B
Tulane University B
University of Louisiana at
    Lafayette B, M
University of Louisiana at Monroe M
University of New Orleans B, M

Maine
St. Joseph's College B
University of Maine
    Presque Isle A, B
University of Maine B
University of Southern Maine B

Maryland
Allegany College A
Anne Arundel Community College A

Bowie State University M
Charles County Community College A
College of Notre Dame of Maryland B
Columbia Union College B
Community College of Baltimore County
    Catonsville A
Coppin State College B
Frederick Community College A
Frostburg State University B
Goucher College B
Hood College B
Loyola College in Maryland B
Salisbury State University B
Towson University B, M
University of Baltimore B
University of Maryland
    College Park D
    Eastern Shore B
Villa Julie College A
Western Maryland College B

Massachusetts
American International College B
Assumption College C
Atlantic Union College B
Bay Path College B
Becker College A
Boston College B
Boston University B, M
Bridgewater State College B, M
Bristol Community College A
Cape Cod Community College A
Clark University B, M
Curry College B
Dean College A
Eastern Nazarene College B
Emerson College B, M
Emmanuel College B
Endicott College B
Fitchburg State College B, M
Framingham State College B
Gordon College B
Hampshire College B
Massachusetts Bay Community
    College C, A
Merrimack College B
Middlesex Community College A
Mount Ida College A
Newbury College A
Pine Manor College B
Regis College B
Salem State College B
Simmons College B, M
Stonehill College B
Suffolk University B, M
University of Massachusetts
    Amherst B, M, D

Michigan
Adrian College A, B, T
Albion College B, T
Alma College B
Andrews University B, M
Aquinas College B, T
Baker College
    of Jackson A
Bay de Noc Community College C
Calvin College B
Concordia College B
Grand Valley State University B, M
Henry Ford Community College A
Hope College B
Lansing Community College A
Madonna University A, B, T
Michigan State University B, M, D
Northern Michigan University B
Oakland University B
Olivet College B
Saginaw Valley State University B
Schoolcraft College A
Siena Heights University B
Spring Arbor College B
University of Detroit Mercy B
University of Michigan
    Dearborn B
    Flint B, T

University of Michigan *B, M, D*
Wayne State University *B, M, D*
Western Michigan University *B, M*

Minnesota
Augsburg College *B*
Bethel College *B, M*
College of St. Benedict *B*
College of St. Catherine: St. Paul
 Campus *B*
College of St. Scholastica *B*
Concordia College: Moorhead *B*
Concordia University: St. Paul *B*
Gustavus Adolphus College *B*
Hamline University *B*
Lake Superior College: A Community
 and Technical College *C*
Macalester College *B*
Metropolitan State University *B*
Moorhead State University *B*
Northland Community & Technical
 College *A*
Northwestern College *B*
Ridgewater College: A Community and
 Technical College *A*
St. Cloud State University *B, M*
St. John's University *B*
Southwest State University *B*
University of Minnesota
 Duluth *B*
 Morris *B*
University of St. Thomas *B*
Winona State University *B*

Mississippi
Belhaven College *B*
Jackson State University *B*
Mary Holmes College *A*
Mississippi College *B, M*
Mississippi Delta Community College *A*
Mississippi Gulf Coast Community
 College
  Perkinston *A*
Mississippi State University *B*
Mississippi University for Women *B*
Mississippi Valley State University *B*
Rust College *B*
University of Southern
 Mississippi *B, M, D*
William Carey College *B*

Missouri
Avila College *B*
Central Methodist College *B*
Central Missouri State University *B, M*
College of the Ozarks *B*
Crowder College *A*
Culver-Stockton College *B*
Drury University *B, M*
East Central College *A*
Evangel University *A, B*
Fontbonne College *B*
Hannibal-LaGrange College *B*
Jefferson College *A*
Lindenwood University *B, M*
Maryville University of Saint Louis *B*
Mineral Area College *A*
Missouri Baptist College *B*
Missouri Southern State College *B*
Missouri Valley College *B*
Missouri Western State College *T*
Northwest Missouri State University *B*
Park University *B*
Rockhurst University *B*
St. Louis University *A, B, M*
Southwest Baptist University *B*
Southwest Missouri State
 University *B, M*
St. Louis Community College
 St. Louis Community College at
  Florissant Valley *A*
 St. Louis Community College at
  Forest Park *A*
 St. Louis Community College at
  Meramec *A*
Stephens College *B*

University of Missouri
 Columbia *B, M, D*
 Kansas City *B, M*
 St. Louis *B*
Webster University *C, B, M*

Montana
Carroll College *A, B, T*
Miles Community College *A*
Montana State University
 Billings *B*
 Northern *B*
Montana Tech of the University of
 Montana *B, M*
Rocky Mountain College *A*
University of Great Falls *B*
University of Montana-Missoula *B, M*

Nebraska
Bellevue University *B*
College of Saint Mary *A, B*
Concordia University *B*
Dana College *B*
Doane College *B*
Hastings College *B*
Midland Lutheran College *B*
Nebraska Wesleyan University *B*
University of Nebraska
 Kearney *B*
 Lincoln *B*
 Omaha *B, M*
Wayne State College *B, M, T*

Nevada
Community College of Southern
 Nevada *A*
University of Nevada
 Las Vegas *B, M*
 Reno *B, M*

New Hampshire
Antioch New England Graduate
 School *M*
Colby-Sawyer College *B*
Franklin Pierce College *B*
Hesser College *A*
New England College *B*
New Hampshire College *B*
Plymouth State College of the University
 System of New Hampshire *B*
Rivier College *B*
St. Anselm College *C*
University of New Hampshire
 Manchester *B*
University of New Hampshire *B*

New Jersey
Bloomfield College *B*
Burlington County College *A*
Caldwell College *C, B*
Centenary College *B*
College of St. Elizabeth *B*
Fairleigh Dickinson University *B, M*
Gloucester County College *A*
Kean University *B*
Middlesex County College *A*
Monmouth University *B, M*
New Jersey City University *B*
New Jersey Institute of Technology *B, M*
Passaic County Community College *A*
Ramapo College of New Jersey *B*
Raritan Valley Community College *A*
Richard Stockton College of New
 Jersey *B*
Rider University *B*
Rowan University *B*

Rutgers
 The State University of New Jersey:
  Cook College *B*
 The State University of New Jersey:
  Douglass College *B*
 The State University of New Jersey:
  Livingston College *B*
 The State University of New Jersey:
  New Brunswick Graduate
  Campus *M, D*
 The State University of New Jersey:
  Rutgers College *B*
 The State University of New Jersey:
  University College New
  Brunswick *B*
St. Peter's College *B*
Seton Hall University *B, M*
The College of New Jersey *B*
Thomas Edison State College *B*
Union County College *A*
William Paterson University of New
 Jersey *B, M*

New Mexico
College of Santa Fe *B*
Eastern New Mexico University *B, M*
New Mexico Highlands University *B*
New Mexico Junior College *A*
New Mexico State University *B, M*
San Juan College *A*

New York
Adelphi University *B*
Adirondack Community College *C, A*
Alfred University *B*
Audrey Cohen College *A, B*
Broome Community College *A*
Canisius College *B*
City University of New York
 Brooklyn College *B*
 City College *B*
 College of Staten Island *B*
 Hunter College *B*
 Lehman College *B*
 Queens College *B, M*
College of Mount St. Vincent *B*
College of New Rochelle *B, M, T*
College of St. Rose *B, M*
Columbia University
 Teachers College *M, D*
Cornell University *B, M, D*
Dominican College of Blauvelt *B*
Dutchess Community College *A*
Erie Community College
 South Campus *A*
Fashion Institute of Technology *A*
Finger Lakes Community College *A*
Five Towns College *A, B*
Fordham University *B, M*
Fulton-Montgomery Community
 College *A*
Genesee Community College *A*
Hamilton College *B*
Hofstra University *B*
Houghton College *B*
Iona College *B, M*
Ithaca College *B, M*
Jamestown Community College *A*
Keuka College *B*
Long Island University
 Southampton College *B*
Manhattan College *B*
Marist College *B*
Marymount College *B*
Marymount Manhattan College *B*
Medaille College *B*
Mohawk Valley Community College *C*
Molloy College *B*
Monroe Community College *A*
Mount St. Mary College *B, T*
Nassau Community College *A*
New York Institute of
 Technology *A, B, M*
New York University *B, M, D*
Niagara University *B*
Nyack College *B*

Orange County Community College *A*
Pace University:
 Pleasantville/Briarcliff *B*
Pace University *B*
Polytechnic University *C*
Regents College *B*
Rensselaer Polytechnic Institute *B, M, D*
Roberts Wesleyan College *B*
Rochester Institute of Technology *A, B*
Rockland Community College *A*
Russell Sage College *B*
Sage Junior College of Albany *A*
St. Francis College *B*
St. John's University *B*
St. Thomas Aquinas College *B*
St. Joseph's College
 St. Joseph's College: Suffolk
  Campus *B*
State University of New York
 Albany *B, M*
 Buffalo *B, M, D*
 College at Brockport *B, M*
 College at Buffalo *B*
 College at Fredonia *B*
 College at Geneseo *B*
 College at Old Westbury *B*
 College at Oneonta *B*
 College at Plattsburgh *B*
 Institute of Technology at
  Utica/Rome *B*
 New Paltz *B*
 Oswego *B*
Suffolk County Community College *A*
Syracuse University *B, M*
Tompkins-Cortland Community
 College *A*
Touro College *B*
Ulster County Community College *A*
Westchester Community College *A*

North Carolina
Appalachian State University *B*
Barton College *B*
Belmont Abbey College *B*
Bennett College *B*
Catawba College *B*
Chowan College *A*
East Carolina University *B*
Elon College *B*
Gardner-Webb University *B*
Johnson C. Smith University *B*
Lenoir-Rhyne College *B*
Louisburg College *A*
Mars Hill College *B*
Meredith College *T*
Methodist College *A, B*
Mount Olive College *B*
North Carolina Agricultural and
 Technical State University *B*
North Carolina State University *B*
Peace College *B*
Pfeiffer University *B*
Queens College *B*
St. Augustine's College *B*
Salem College *B*
Sandhills Community College *C*
University of North Carolina
 Chapel Hill *B, M, D*
 Charlotte *B*
 Pembroke *B*
Wake Forest University *B, M*
Western Carolina University *B*
Wingate University *B*
Winston-Salem State University *B*

North Dakota
Dickinson State University *B, T*
Jamestown College *B*
North Dakota State University *B, M*
University of Mary *B*
University of North Dakota *B, M*

Ohio
Antioch College *B*
Ashland University *B*
Baldwin-Wallace College *C, B*

Bluffton College *B*
Bowling Green State University *B*
Capital University *B*
Cedarville College *B*
Cleveland State University *B, M*
College of Mount St. Joseph *A, B, T*
College of Wooster *B*
Defiance College *B*
Denison University *B*
Franciscan University of Steubenville *B*
Franklin University *B*
Heidelberg College *B*
Hiram College *B*
John Carroll University *B, M*
Kent State University
    Stark Campus *B*
Kent State University *B, M, D*
Lake Erie College *B*
Malone College *B*
Marietta College *B*
Miami University
    Middletown Campus *A*
    Oxford Campus *B, T*
Mount Union College *B, T*
Mount Vernon Nazarene College *B*
Notre Dame College of Ohio *B, T*
Ohio Dominican College *C, B*
Ohio Northern University *B*
Ohio State University
    Columbus Campus *B, M, D*
Ohio University
    Southern Campus at Ironton *A*
Ohio University *B*
Otterbein College *B*
Shawnee State University *A*
Sinclair Community College *A*
Union Institute *B*
University of Akron *B, M*
University of Cincinnati *B, M, T*
University of Dayton *B, M*
University of Findlay *B*
University of Rio Grande *A, B*
University of Toledo *B*
Walsh University *B*
Wilmington College *B*
Wright State University *B*
Youngstown State University *B*

Oklahoma
Cameron University *B*
Connors State College *A*
East Central University *B*
Langston University *B*
Northeastern Oklahoma Agricultural and
    Mechanical College *A*
Northeastern State University *M*
Oklahoma Baptist University *B*
Oklahoma Christian University of
    Science and Arts *B*
Oklahoma City University *B*
Oklahoma Panhandle State University *B*
Oklahoma State University *B, M*
Oral Roberts University *B*
Southeastern Oklahoma State
    University *B*
Southern Nazarene University *A, B*
Southwestern Oklahoma State
    University *B*
University of Central Oklahoma *B*
University of Oklahoma *B, M, D*
University of Science and Arts of
    Oklahoma *B*
University of Tulsa *B*

Oregon
Central Oregon Community College *A*
George Fox University *B*
Lewis & Clark College *B*
Linfield College *B*
Marylhurst University *B*
Multnomah Bible College *B*
Northwest Christian College *B*
Pacific University *B*
Southern Oregon University *B*
University of Portland *B, M*
Western Baptist College *B*
Western Oregon University *B*

Pennsylvania
Allegheny College *B*
Allentown College of St. Francis de
    Sales *B*
Alvernia College *B*
Beaver College *C, B*
Bloomsburg University of
    Pennsylvania *B, M, T*
Bucks County Community College *A*
Cabrini College *B*
California University of
    Pennsylvania *B, M*
Carlow College *B, T*
Carnegie Mellon University *B*
Cedar Crest College *B*
Central Pennsylvania College *A*
Chatham College *B*
Chestnut Hill College *C*
Cheyney University of
    Pennsylvania *B, T*
Clarion University of Pennsylvania *B, M*
College Misericordia *B*
Delaware County Community College *A*
Delaware Valley College *B*
Drexel University *B*
Duquesne University *B, M*
East Stroudsburg University of
    Pennsylvania *B*
Eastern College *B*
Edinboro University of
    Pennsylvania *B, M*
Elizabethtown College *B*
Gannon University *B, T*
Geneva College *B, T*
Gettysburg College *B*
Grove City College *B*
Holy Family College *B*
Indiana University of
    Pennsylvania *B, M, T*
Juniata College *B*
King's College *B*
Kutztown University of
    Pennsylvania *B, T*
La Roche College *B*
La Salle University *A, B, M*
Lebanon Valley College of
    Pennsylvania *C*
Lincoln University *B*
Lock Haven University of
    Pennsylvania *B*
Lycoming College *B*
Mansfield University of Pennsylvania *B*
Marywood University *M*
Mercyhurst College *B*
Messiah College *B*
Millersville University of
    Pennsylvania *B*
Montgomery County Community
    College *A*
Muhlenberg College *B*
Neumann College *B, T*
Penn State
    Erie, The Behrend College *B*
    Harrisburg *B*
    Lehigh Valley *B*
    University Park *B, M, D*
    Wilkes-Barre *A*
Point Park College *B*
Robert Morris College *B, M*
St. Francis College *B*
St. Vincent College *B*
Sawyer School *A*
Seton Hill College *C, B*
Shippensburg University of
    Pennsylvania *M*
Slippery Rock University of
    Pennsylvania *B*
Susquehanna University *B*
Temple University *B, M, D*
Thiel College *B*
University of Pennsylvania *A, B, M, D*
University of Pittsburgh
    Bradford *B*
    Greensburg *B*
    Johnstown *B*
University of Pittsburgh *B*
University of Scranton *B, T*
Ursinus College *B*
Villanova University *B*
Waynesburg College *B*
West Chester University of
    Pennsylvania *B, M*
Widener University *B*
Wilkes University *B*
Wilson College *A, B*
York College of Pennsylvania *A, B*

Puerto Rico
American University of Puerto Rico *A, B*
Inter American University of Puerto Rico
    Bayamon Campus *B*
Pontifical Catholic University of Puerto
    Rico *B*
Universidad Metropolitana *B*
University of Puerto Rico
    Rio Piedras Campus *B, M*
University of the Sacred Heart *B*

Rhode Island
Bryant College *B*
Johnson & Wales University *A*
Providence College *B*
Rhode Island College *B*
Roger Williams University *A, B*
University of Rhode Island *B*

South Carolina
Anderson College *B*
Clemson University *B, M*
Coker College *B*
College of Charleston *B*
Columbia International University *B*
Francis Marion University *B*
Furman University *B*
Newberry College *B*
North Greenville College *B*
University of South Carolina
    Aiken *B*
    Spartanburg *B*

South Dakota
Augustana College *B*
Dakota Wesleyan University *B*
South Dakota State University *B, M*

Tennessee
Belmont University *B*
Carson-Newman College *B*
David Lipscomb University *B*
Freed-Hardeman University *B*
Hiwassee College *A*
Lambuth University *B*
Lane College *B*
Lee University *B*
Lincoln Memorial University *B*
Milligan College *B*
Roane State Community College *A*
Tennessee State University *B*
Tennessee Technological University *B*
Tennessee Temple University *B*
Trevecca Nazarene University *B*
Union University *B, T*
University of Tennessee
    Chattanooga *B*
    Knoxville *M, D*
Vanderbilt University *B*

Texas
Amarillo College *A*
Angelo State University *B*
Austin College *B*
Baylor University *B, M*
Blinn College *A*
Brazosport College *B*
Coastal Bend College *A*
Concordia University at Austin *B*
Dallas Baptist University *B*
El Paso Community College *A*
Galveston College *A*
Hardin-Simmons University *B*
Hill College *A*
Houston Baptist University *B*
Howard Payne University *B, T*
Huston-Tillotson College *B*
Kilgore College *A*
Lamar University *B*
Lubbock Christian University *B*
McMurry University *B, T*
Midland College *A*
Navarro College *B*
Our Lady of the Lake University of San
    Antonio *B*
Palo Alto College *A*
Panola College *A*
St. Edward's University *B*
St. Mary's University *B, M, T*
South Plains College *A*
Southern Methodist University *B*
Southwestern Adventist University *B*
Southwestern Assemblies of God
    University *A*
Southwestern University *B, T*
Stephen F. Austin State
    University *B, M, T*
Sul Ross State University *B*
Tarleton State University *B*
Texas A&M International University *B*
Texas A&M University
    Commerce *B*
    Corpus Christi *B*
    Kingsville *B*
Texas Christian University *B, M, T*
Texas Lutheran University *B*
Texas Southern University *B, M*
Texas Wesleyan University *B*
Trinity University *B*
Trinity Valley Community College *A*
University of Houston
    Clear Lake *B*
    Victoria *B*
University of Houston *M*
University of Mary Hardin-Baylor *B*
University of North Texas *B, M*
University of St. Thomas *B*
University of Texas
    Arlington *B*
    El Paso *M*
    Pan American *A, B, T*
University of the Incarnate Word *B, M*
Weatherford College *A*
West Texas A&M University *M*

Utah
Brigham Young University *B, M*
Dixie State College of Utah *A*
Salt Lake Community College *A*
Southern Utah University *B*
University of Utah *M, D*
Utah State University *M*
Westminster College *B, M*

Vermont
Castleton State College *A, B*
Champlain College *A, B*
College of St. Joseph in Vermont *B*
Lyndon State College *A, B*
Norwich University *B*
Southern Vermont College *B*

Virginia
Bridgewater College *B*
Christopher Newport University *B*
Eastern Mennonite University *B*
Emory & Henry College *B*
Hollins University *B*
James Madison University *B*
Liberty University *B*
Longwood College *B*
Lord Fairfax Community College *A*
Lynchburg College *B*
Mary Baldwin College *B*
Norfolk State University *B, M*
Northern Virginia Community College *A*
Radford University *B*

Randolph-Macon Woman's College *B*
Regent University *M, D*
St. Paul's College *B*
Shenandoah University *B*
University of Virginia's College at Wise *B*
Virginia Polytechnic Institute and State University *B*
Virginia Wesleyan College *B*

Washington
Eastern Washington University *B, M, T*
Everett Community College *A*
Grays Harbor College *A*
Green River Community College *C*
Highline Community College *A*
Lower Columbia College *A*
Pacific Lutheran University *B*
Seattle Pacific University *B*
Seattle University *B*
Skagit Valley College *A*
University of Puget Sound *B, T*
University of Washington *B, M, D*
Walla Walla College *B*
Washington State University *B, M*
Western Washington University *B*
Whitworth College *B, T*

West Virginia
Alderson-Broaddus College *B*
Bethany College *B*
Concord College *B*
Davis and Elkins College *B*
Fairmont State College *B*
Marshall University *B, M*
Salem-Teikyo University *A, B*
Shepherd College *B*
West Liberty State College *B*
West Virginia State College *A, B*
West Virginia University *B, M*
West Virginia Wesleyan College *B*

Wisconsin
Alverno College *B, T*
Cardinal Stritch University *B*
Carroll College *B*
Carthage College *B*
Concordia University Wisconsin *B*
Marian College of Fond du Lac *B*
Marquette University *B, M*
Moraine Park Technical College *A*
Mount Mary College *B*
St. Norbert College *B*
University of Wisconsin
 Eau Claire *B*
 Green Bay *B*
 La Crosse *B*
 Madison *B, M, D*
 Milwaukee *B, M*
 Oshkosh *B*
 Parkside *B*
 Platteville *B*
 Stevens Point *B, M*
 Superior *B, M*
 Whitewater *B, M*
Wisconsin Lutheran College *B*

Wyoming
Casper College *A*
Eastern Wyoming College *A*
Northwest College *A*
Sheridan College *A*
University of Wyoming *B, M*
Western Wyoming Community College *A*

Communications technologies

Alabama
Alabama Agricultural and Mechanical University *B*
Community College of the Air Force *A*
Gadsden State Community College *A*
Jefferson State Community College *A*

Alaska
Prince William Sound Community College *C, A*

Arizona
Glendale Community College *A*
Northland Pioneer College *C, A*

Arkansas
Arkansas Tech University *M*

California
Bakersfield College *A*
Barstow College *C*
Butte College *C, A*
Chabot College *C, A*
City College of San Francisco *A*
College of San Mateo *C, A*
Golden Gate University *C, B*
Los Angeles Southwest College *A*
Los Angeles Trade and Technical College *C, A*
Los Angeles Valley College *C*
Moorpark College *A*
Mount San Antonio College *C, A*
Napa Valley College *C, A*
Palomar College *C, A*
Pasadena City College *C, A*
Rio Hondo College *A*
San Diego City College *A*
San Jose City College *C, A*
Santa Monica College *A*
Skyline College *C, A*
Solano Community College *A*
Southwestern College *C, A*
Ventura College *A*
Yuba College *C*

Colorado
Art Institute of Colorado *A*
Pikes Peak Community College *C, A*

Connecticut
Manchester Community-Technical College *C*
Naugatuck Valley Community-Technical College *C*
Norwalk Community-Technical College *A*

Florida
Art Institute of Fort Lauderdale *B*
ITT Technical Institute Maitland *B*
Miami-Dade Community College *A*
South Florida Community College *A*

Georgia
Clark Atlanta University *B*
University of Georgia *B*
Valdosta State University *B*

Illinois
Black Hawk College *A*
College of DuPage *C, A*
Columbia College *B*
Governors State University *M*
Northwestern University *M*
Parkland College *A*
Southwestern Illinois College *C, A*

Indiana
Ball State University *B*
Ivy Tech State College Northcentral *A*
St. Mary-of-the-Woods College *B*

Iowa
Iowa Central Community College *A*
Kirkwood Community College *A*
Marshalltown Community College *A*
Scott Community College *A*
Waldorf College *A, B*

Kansas
Coffeyville Community College *A*
Hutchinson Community College *A*

Kansas City Kansas Community College *C, A*

Kentucky
Asbury College *B*
Murray State University *B, M*

Maryland
Anne Arundel Community College *A*
Bowie State University *B*
Frederick Community College *A*
Harford Community College *A*
Villa Julie College *B*

Massachusetts
Bay Path College *B*
Bristol Community College *C*
Fitchburg State College *B*
Mount Wachusett Community College *A*
Newbury College *A*
Northeastern University *A*
Northern Essex Community College *A*
Springfield Technical Community College *A*
Worcester State College *B*

Michigan
Andrews University *B*
Eastern Michigan University *B*
Ferris State University *A, B*
Kalamazoo Valley Community College *C, A*
Kellogg Community College *A*
Lansing Community College *A*
Macomb Community College *C, A*
Oakland Community College *A*
Saginaw Valley State University *M*
Schoolcraft College *A*
Western Michigan University *B*

Minnesota
Dakota County Technical College *C*
Hennepin Technical College *C, A*
Inver Hills Community College *A*
NEI College of Technology *A*
Northwestern College *B*
St. Cloud Technical College *C, A*
Winona State University *B*

Mississippi
Hinds Community College *A*
Jackson State University *B*
Northwest Mississippi Community College *A*

Missouri
Evangel University *B*
Fontbonne College *B*
Ranken Technical College *A*

Montana
Miles Community College *A*

Nebraska
Central Community College *C, A*
Hastings College *B*

New Hampshire
Franklin Pierce College *B*

New Jersey
Bergen Community College *C*
Brookdale Community College *A*
County College of Morris *A*
Mercer County Community College *A*
Ocean County College *A*
Rowan University *B*

New Mexico
Santa Fe Community College *A*

New York
Cayuga County Community College *A*
City University of New York
 Queens College *B*
 Queensborough Community College *A*
Five Towns College *A, B*
Fulton-Montgomery Community College *A*

Genesee Community College *A*
Herkimer County Community College *A*
Hofstra University *B*
Monroe Community College *A*
New York University *M, D*
Rochester Institute of Technology *B, M*
St. John's University *A, B*
State University of New York Institute of Technology at Utica/Rome *B*
Syracuse University *M, D*

North Carolina
Belmont Abbey College *B*
Chowan College *B*
Wilkes Community College *A*

Ohio
Bowling Green State University Firelands College *A*
Cedarville College *B*
Columbus State Community College *A*
Kent State University *C, B, M, D*
Owens Community College Toledo *A*
University of Akron *B*

Oklahoma
Langston University *B*
Oklahoma State University Oklahoma City *A*
Oklahoma State University *M*
Rogers State University *A*
Southern Nazarene University *B*
Tulsa Community College *A*

Oregon
Lane Community College *C, A*
Portland Community College *C*

Pennsylvania
California University of Pennsylvania *B*
Chatham College *C, B, M*
Chestnut Hill College *C, B, M*
Cheyney University of Pennsylvania *B*
Community College of Allegheny County *A*
Community College of Beaver County *A*
Duquesne University *B, M*
East Stroudsburg University of Pennsylvania *A, B*
Gannon University *B*
Immaculata College *A*
Luzerne County Community College *A*
Northampton County Area Community College *C, A*
Point Park College *B*
St. Vincent College *B*
Seton Hill College *B*
Westmoreland County Community College *A*
Widener University *B*

Puerto Rico
American University of Puerto Rico *B*
Inter American University of Puerto Rico Bayamon Campus *A*
University of Puerto Rico
 Arecibo Campus *A, B*
 Humacao University College *A*

Rhode Island
Salve Regina University *B*

South Carolina
Trident Technical College *C, A*

Tennessee
Nashville State Technical Institute *A*
Southern Adventist University *A*
Tennessee Technological University *B*
Trevecca Nazarene University *B*

Texas
Abilene Christian University *B*
Amarillo College *A*
Coastal Bend College *A*
Collin County Community College District *C, A*

Communications technologies

Eastfield College *A*
El Paso Community College *A*
Houston Community College
 System *C, A*
Richland College *A*
St. Philip's College *A*
Southwest Texas State University *B*
Tarrant County College *A*
Texas A&M University
 Commerce *M*
Texas State Technical College
 Harlingen *A*
 Sweetwater *A*
Texas Tech University *B*

Utah
Dixie State College of Utah *A*
University of Utah *B*

Vermont
Champlain College *A, B*
Lyndon State College *B*

Virginia
ECPI College of Technology *C, A*
George Mason University *M*
J. Sargeant Reynolds Community
 College *C*
Virginia Western Community College *A*

Washington
Eastern Washington University *B*
Spokane Falls Community College *A*
University of Washington *M*

West Virginia
Bluefield State College *A*
Southern West Virginia Community and
 Technical College *A*
West Virginia State College *A*

Wisconsin
Milwaukee Area Technical College *A*
University of Wisconsin
 Superior *B, M*

Community health services

Alaska
University of Alaska
 Fairbanks *C, A*

Arizona
Northland Pioneer College *C*
Pima Community College *C*

Arkansas
University of Arkansas *M*

California
California College for Health
 Sciences *M*
California State University
 Bakersfield *B*
 Chico *B*
 Dominguez Hills *B*
 Fresno *B*
East Los Angeles College *A*
Santa Rosa Junior College *C*

Delaware
Delaware State University *B*

Florida
University of Florida *B, M*

Georgia
Armstrong Atlantic State
 University *B, M*

Hawaii
University of Hawaii
 Kapiolani Community College *A*

Illinois
Kishwaukee College *A*
Lake Land College *A*
Northern Illinois University *B*

Indiana
Indiana State University *B*

Iowa
University of Northern Iowa *B*

Kentucky
Eastern Kentucky University *B*
Western Kentucky University *B, M*

Maine
University of Maine
 Farmington *B*
 Presque Isle *B*

Maryland
Harford Community College *A*

Massachusetts
Greenfield Community College *C, A*
Mount Wachusett Community College *C*
Springfield College *B, M*
Worcester State College *B*

Michigan
Bay de Noc Community College *A*
University of Michigan
 Flint *B*
University of Michigan *M*
Wayne State University *C, M*
Western Michigan University *B*

Minnesota
Alexandria Technical College *C*
Bemidji State University *B*
Minnesota State University,
 Mankato *B, M*
Moorhead State University *B*
St. Cloud State University *B*

Missouri
St. Louis University *M*

Montana
Montana State University
 Billings *M*

Nebraska
University of Nebraska
 Lincoln *B*

New Jersey
Seton Hall University *C*

New York
City University of New York
 Brooklyn College *M*
 Hunter College *M*
 Kingsborough Community
  College *A*
 Lehman College *M*
 York College *B*
Erie Community College
 City Campus *A*
Ithaca College *B*
Long Island University
 Brooklyn Campus *M*
Marymount College *B*
St. John Fisher College *C*
St. Joseph's College
 St. Joseph's College: Suffolk
  Campus *B*
 St. Joseph's College *B*
Suffolk County Community College *A*

North Carolina
North Carolina Central University *B*
University of North Carolina
 Pembroke *B*

Ohio
Cleveland State University *M*
Kent State University *B, M*
Ohio State University
 Columbus Campus *B*
Ohio University
 Southern Campus at Ironton *A*
Ohio University *B, M*
University of Toledo *B*
Youngstown State University *B*

Oklahoma
University of Central Oklahoma *B*

Pennsylvania
Community College of Allegheny
 County *A*
La Salle University *B*
West Chester University of
 Pennsylvania *B*

Puerto Rico
Inter American University of Puerto Rico
 Barranquitas Campus *B*

Rhode Island
Providence College *B*

South Carolina
Morris College *B*

Tennessee
University of Tennessee
 Knoxville *B*

Texas
Baylor University *B*
Lamar University *B*
Prairie View A&M University *B*
Sam Houston State University *B*
Southwest Texas State University *B*
Texas A&M University *B*
Texas Tech University *B*
Texas Woman's University *B, M*
University of North Texas *B, M*
University of Texas
 Austin *B*
 Medical Branch at Galveston *M*
 San Antonio *B*
Vernon Regional Junior College *C*

Utah
Brigham Young University *B*

Virginia
James Madison University *B*
Old Dominion University *M*

Washington
Central Washington University *B*
Eastern Washington University *B*
Edmonds Community College *C, A*
Shoreline Community College *A*
Western Washington University *B*

West Virginia
Salem-Teikyo University *B*
Shepherd College *A*
West Virginia University *M*

Wisconsin
University of Wisconsin
 La Crosse *B*
Western Wisconsin Technical College *A*

Community organization/resources/services

Alabama
Alabama State University *A, B*
Samford University *A*

Alaska
University of Alaska
 Fairbanks *B*

Arizona
Prescott College *B*

Arkansas
Southern Arkansas University *B*

California
California State University
 Dominguez Hills *B*
Humphreys College *B*
Merritt College *C, A*
National University *M*
University of California
 Davis *M*

Connecticut
Manchester Community-Technical
 College *C, A*
University of Hartford *B*

Hawaii
University of Hawaii
 Honolulu Community College *C, A*

Illinois
Lincoln Land Community College *A*
North Park University *M*
Southern Illinois University
 Carbondale *M*

Indiana
Indiana University
 South Bend *M*

Iowa
Iowa Central Community College *A*
Kirkwood Community College *A*
Marshalltown Community College *A*

Kentucky
Henderson Community College *A*
Murray State University *M*

Massachusetts
Springfield College *B, M*
University of Massachusetts
 Boston *B*
Worcester State College *M*

Michigan
Aquinas College *B*
Central Michigan University *B*
Kellogg Community College *C*
University of Michigan *D*

Minnesota
Bemidji State University *B*
Winona State University *B*

Mississippi
Delta State University *M*

Missouri
Rockhurst University *B*
St. Louis University *B*

Nebraska
University of Nebraska
 Omaha *B*

New Hampshire
Antioch New England Graduate
 School *M*

New Jersey
Thomas Edison State College *A, B*

New Mexico
University of New Mexico *A, B*

New York
Audrey Cohen College *A, B*
City University of New York
 Brooklyn College *B*
Cornell University *B*
Dominican College of Blauvelt *C*
Genesee Community College *A*
Hudson Valley Community College *A*
Mohawk Valley Community College *A*
State University of New York
 Empire State College *A, B*
Suffolk County Community College *A*
Ulster County Community College *A*
Westchester Community College *C, A*

Ohio
University of Akron *A*
University of Cincinnati *B*
University of Findlay *A*

Oklahoma
East Central University *B, M*

Oregon
Chemeketa Community College *A*
Clackamas Community College *C, A*
Lane Community College *A*

Pennsylvania
California University of Pennsylvania A
Mercyhurst College C
St. Joseph's University M

Rhode Island
Providence College B

Tennessee
Cleveland State Community College A
Cumberland University M
University of Tennessee
  Chattanooga B

Texas
Abilene Christian University M
Texas A&M University B
University of North Texas M

Vermont
Goddard College B

Virginia
Emory & Henry College B
J. Sargeant Reynolds Community
  College A

Community psychology

Alabama
Troy State University
  Dothan M
Troy State University M

Alaska
University of Alaska
  Fairbanks M

California
San Francisco State University C
University of La Verne D

Colorado
Adams State College M

Connecticut
Southern Connecticut State University M
University of New Haven M

District of Columbia
Catholic University of America M
George Washington University M

Florida
Florida Agricultural and Mechanical
  University M

Illinois
Roosevelt University M

Kansas
Pittsburg State University B

Maine
University of Maine
  Fort Kent B
University of New England B

Maryland
Bowie State University B

Massachusetts
Hampshire College B
University of Massachusetts
  Lowell M

Minnesota
St. Cloud State University M

Montana
Montana State University
  Billings M

New Hampshire
Antioch New England Graduate
  School M, D

New Jersey
Fairleigh Dickinson University B, M

New York
Audrey Cohen College A, B

City University of New York
  Kingsborough Community
    College A
College of New Rochelle M
Hofstra University M, D
New York University D

Ohio
Kent State University M
University of Akron M

Oregon
Western Baptist College B

Pennsylvania
Holy Family College B
MCP Hahnemann University M
Mansfield University of Pennsylvania M
Penn State
  Harrisburg M
Widener University B

Puerto Rico
University of Puerto Rico
  Rio Piedras Campus M

South Carolina
Francis Marion University M

Tennessee
Southern Adventist University M
Vanderbilt University D

Texas
Lamar University M
St. Mary's University M, D

Vermont
Burlington College B
Trinity College of Vermont M

Virginia
Norfolk State University M

West Virginia
Fairmont State College B

Community/junior college administration

California
California Lutheran University M

Illinois
Chicago State University M
Northeastern Illinois University M

Indiana
Ball State University M, D
Indiana State University M

Iowa
University of Iowa M, D

Kansas
Pittsburg State University M

Massachusetts
Springfield College D

Michigan
Central Michigan University M

Minnesota
University of Minnesota
  Twin Cities M

New Jersey
Rowan University M

New York
Columbia University
  Teachers College M, D
State University of New York
  Buffalo M, D

North Carolina
North Carolina State University M, D
Western Carolina University M

Oklahoma
Northeastern State University M

South Carolina
Clemson University M

Texas
Texas A&M University
  Commerce M, D

Virginia
George Mason University D

Comparative literature

Arizona
Prescott College B, M
University of Arizona M, D

Arkansas
University of Arkansas M, D

California
California State University
  Fullerton B, M
  Long Beach B
  Northridge B
Chapman University M
College of the Desert A
Fresno Pacific University B
Glendale Community College A
Long Beach City College C, A
Mills College B, M
Occidental College B
San Diego State University B
San Francisco State University B, M
Stanford University B, M, D
University of California
  Berkeley B, M, D
  Davis B, M, D
  Irvine B, M, D
  Los Angeles M, D
  Riverside B, M, D
  San Diego M, D
  Santa Barbara B, M, D
  Santa Cruz B
University of Judaism B
University of La Verne B
University of Southern
  California B, M, D
Whittier College B

Colorado
Colorado College B
University of Colorado
  Boulder M, D

Connecticut
Sacred Heart University B
Trinity College B
University of Connecticut M, D
Yale University B, M, D

Delaware
University of Delaware B

District of Columbia
Catholic University of America M, D
Georgetown University B

Florida
Eckerd College B

Georgia
Emory University B, D
Oxford College of Emory University B
University of Georgia B, M, D

Idaho
Lewis-Clark State College B

Illinois
De Paul University B
Kendall College B
McKendree College B
Millikin University B, T
Northeastern Illinois University M
Northwestern University B, M, D
Parkland College A
Roosevelt University B, M
University of Chicago M, D

University of Illinois
  Urbana-Champaign B, M, D

Indiana
Indiana University
  Bloomington B, M, D
Indiana University--Purdue University
  Indiana University-Purdue
    University Fort Wayne B
Manchester College A
University of Evansville B

Iowa
Graceland University B
Loras College B
University of Iowa B, M, D

Louisiana
Louisiana State University and
  Agricultural and Mechanical
  College M, D

Maine
University of Maine
  Fort Kent B

Maryland
Johns Hopkins University B, D
University of Maryland
  College Park M, D

Massachusetts
Brandeis University B
Clark University B
Hampshire College B
Harvard College B
Harvard University M, D
Massachusetts College of Liberal Arts B
Massachusetts Institute of Technology B
Simmons College B, M
Simon's Rock College of Bard B
Smith College B
Tufts University B, M, D
University of Massachusetts
  Amherst B, M, D
Wellesley College B
Williams College B

Michigan
Hillsdale College B
Michigan State University M
University of Michigan B, M, D
Wayne State University M

Minnesota
University of Minnesota
  Twin Cities B, M, D
University of St. Thomas B

Missouri
Washington University B, M, D

Montana
University of Montana-Missoula B

Nebraska
Wayne State College B

New Hampshire
Dartmouth College B

New Jersey
Bloomfield College B
Montclair State University M
Princeton University B, M, D
Ramapo College of New Jersey B
Rutgers
  The State University of New Jersey:
    Douglass College B
  The State University of New Jersey:
    Livingston College B
  The State University of New Jersey:
    New Brunswick Graduate
    Campus M, D
  The State University of New Jersey:
    Rutgers College B
  The State University of New Jersey:
    University College New
    Brunswick B

New Mexico
University of New Mexico *B, M*

New York
Bard College *B*
Barnard College *B*
City University of New York
    Baruch College *B*
    Brooklyn College *B*
    City College *B*
    Graduate School and University
      Center *M, D*
    Lehman College *B*
    Queens College *B*
Columbia University
    Columbia College *B*
    School of General Studies *B*
Cornell University *B, D*
Eugene Lang College/New School
    University *B*
Fordham University *B*
Hamilton College *B*
Hobart and William Smith Colleges *B*
Hofstra University *B*
New York University *B, M, D*
Sarah Lawrence College *B*
State University of New York
    Binghamton *B, M, D*
    Buffalo *M, D*
    College at Geneseo *B*
    Stony Brook *B*
University of Rochester *B, M*

North Carolina
Brevard College *B*
Duke University *M, D*
University of North Carolina
    Chapel Hill *B, M, D*

North Dakota
North Dakota State University *M*

Ohio
Case Western Reserve University *B, M*
College of Wooster *B*
Kent State University *M*
Miami University
    Oxford Campus *B*
Oberlin College *B*
Ohio State University
    Columbus Campus *B, M*
Ohio Wesleyan University *B*
Otterbein College *B*
Terra Community College *A*
University of Cincinnati *B, M, D, T*
University of Dayton *B*
University of Toledo *B*
Wilberforce University *B, T*
Wittenberg University *B*

Oklahoma
East Central University *B*
University of Central Oklahoma *B, M*

Oregon
Chemeketa Community College *A*
Reed College *B*
University of Oregon *B, M, D*
Willamette University *B*

Pennsylvania
Bryn Mawr College *B*
Cedar Crest College *B*
Gettysburg College *B*
Haverford College *B, T*
Immaculata College *B*
La Salle University *B*
Penn State
    Harrisburg *B*
    New Kensington *A*
    University Park *B, M, D*
Seton Hill College *B*
Swarthmore College *B*
University of Pennsylvania *A, B, M, D*
West Chester University of
    Pennsylvania *B*

Puerto Rico
University of Puerto Rico
    Rio Piedras Campus *B, M*

Rhode Island
Brown University *B, M, D*
University of Rhode Island *B*

South Carolina
University of South Carolina *M, D*

Tennessee
University of Tennessee
    Knoxville *B*
University of the South *B*
Vanderbilt University *M, D*

Texas
University of North Texas *B*
University of Texas
    Arlington *D*
    Austin *M, D*
    Dallas *B*
    El Paso *B, M*

Utah
Brigham Young University *B, M*
University of Utah *M, D*

Vermont
Bennington College *B*
Burlington College *B*
Johnson State College *B*
Marlboro College *B*

Virginia
Lynchburg College *B*
Randolph-Macon Woman's College *B*
University of Virginia *B*

Washington
Evergreen State College *B*
Gonzaga University *B*
Pacific Lutheran University *B*
University of Washington *B, M, D*
Western Washington University *B*
Whitworth College *B, T*

West Virginia
Alderson-Broaddus College *B*

Wisconsin
Beloit College *B*
University of Wisconsin
    Madison *B, M, D*
    Milwaukee *B*

Comparative/international education

District of Columbia
American University *M*
George Washington University *M*
Howard University *M*

Florida
Florida International University *M*
Florida State University *M, D*
Lynn University *D*

Indiana
Indiana University
    Bloomington *M*

Massachusetts
Boston University *M*
Endicott College *M*
Lesley College *M*

Missouri
Missouri Southern State College *B*

New York
Columbia University
    Teachers College *M, D*
New York University *M, D*
State University of New York
    Albany *M, D*
    Buffalo *M, D*

Ohio
Ohio State University
    Columbus Campus *M*

Virginia
University of Virginia *M, D*

Computer engineering

Alabama
Auburn University *B, M, D*
University of Alabama
    Huntsville *B, M, D*
University of South Alabama *B*

Arizona
Arizona State University *B*
DeVry Institute of Technology
    Phoenix *B*
Northern Arizona University *B*
University of Arizona *B*

Arkansas
University of Arkansas *B, M*

California
California Institute of Technology *B*
California Polytechnic State University:
    San Luis Obispo *B*
California State University
    Chico *B*
    Fresno *B*
    Long Beach *B, M*
    Northridge *B, M*
    Sacramento *B*
Compton Community College *A*
De Anza College *A*
Diablo Valley College *C, A*
San Diego State University *B*
San Jose State University *B, M*
Santa Ana College *C, A*
Santa Barbara City College *C, A*
Santa Clara University *C, B, M, D*
University of California
    Davis *B*
    Irvine *B, M, D*
    Los Angeles *B*
    San Diego *B, M, D*
    Santa Barbara *M, D*
    Santa Cruz *B, M, D*
University of Southern
    California *B, M, D*
University of the Pacific *B*

Colorado
Colorado Technical University *B, M*
National Technological University *M*
University of Colorado
    Boulder *B*
    Colorado Springs *B*
University of Denver *M*

Connecticut
Fairfield University *B, M*
Trinity College *B*
University of Bridgeport *B, M*
University of Connecticut *B, M, D*
University of Hartford *B*

Delaware
University of Delaware *B*

District of Columbia
Catholic University of America *B*
George Washington University *B, M, D*

Florida
Brevard Community College *A*
Broward Community College *A*
Daytona Beach Community College *A*
Embry-Riddle Aeronautical University *B*
Florida Atlantic University *B, M*
Florida Institute of Technology *B, M, D*
Florida International University *B, M*
Florida State University *B*
Hillsborough Community College *A*
Keiser College *A*
Manatee Community College *A*
Pensacola Junior College *A*
South Florida Community College *A*
University of Central Florida *B, M, D*
University of Florida *B, M, D*
University of Miami *B*
University of South Florida *B, M, D*
University of West Florida *B*

Georgia
Armstrong Atlantic State University *A*
DeKalb Technical Institute *A*
Georgia Institute of Technology *B*
Mercer University *B, M*
Middle Georgia College *A*

Hawaii
University of Hawaii
    Honolulu Community College *A*

Idaho
College of Southern Idaho *A*
University of Idaho *B, M*

Illinois
Bradley University *B*
Dominican University *B*
Illinois Institute of Technology *B, M*
Northwestern University *B, M, D*
Parkland College *A*
Southern Illinois University
    Edwardsville *B*
University of Illinois
    Chicago *B*
    Urbana-Champaign *B*

Indiana
Indiana Institute of Technology *B*
Indiana University--Purdue University
    Indiana University-Purdue
      University Indianapolis *B*
Purdue University
    Calumet *B*
Purdue University *B*
Rose-Hulman Institute of Technology *B*
University of Evansville *B*
University of Notre Dame *B, M, D*

Iowa
Iowa State University *B, M, D*
University of Iowa *B, M, D*

Kansas
Kansas State University *B*
University of Kansas *B, M*
Wichita State University *B*

Kentucky
Bellarmine College *B*
University of Louisville *B, M*

Louisiana
Grantham College of Engineering *A, B*
Louisiana State University and
    Agricultural and Mechanical
    College *B*
Tulane University *B, M, D*
University of Louisiana at
    Lafayette *B, M, D*

Maine
Southern Maine Technical College *A*
University of Maine *B*

Maryland
Johns Hopkins University *B, M, D*
University of Maryland
    Baltimore County *B*
    College Park *B*

Massachusetts
Berkshire Community College *A*
Boston University *B, M, D*
Eastern Nazarene College *B*
Franklin Institute of Boston *A*
Harvard College *B*
Harvard University *D*
Merrimack College *B*
Northeastern University *B, M*

Stonehill College *B*
Suffolk University *B*
Tufts University *B, M, D*
University of Massachusetts
 Amherst *B, M, D*
 Dartmouth *B*
 Lowell *M*
Worcester Polytechnic Institute *B, M*

Michigan
Detroit College of Business *A, B*
Eastern Michigan University *B*
Kettering University *B*
Lake Superior State University *B*
Michigan State University *B*
Oakland University *B, M*
University of Detroit Mercy *B*
University of Michigan
 Dearborn *M*
University of Michigan *B, M, D*
Wayne State University *M, D*
Western Michigan University *B, M*

Minnesota
Mesabi Range Community and Technical College *A*
University of Minnesota
 Duluth *B*
 Twin Cities *B, M*

Mississippi
Copiah-Lincoln Community College *A*
Jackson State University *B*
Mississippi State University *B, M, D*

Missouri
DeVry Institute of Technology
 Kansas City *B*
St. Louis University *B*
University of Missouri
 Columbia *B, M, D*
 Rolla *B, M, D*
Washington University *B, M, D*

Montana
Montana State University
 Bozeman *B*
Montana Tech of the University of Montana *B*

Nebraska
University of Nebraska
 Lincoln *B*
 Omaha *B*

Nevada
University of Nevada
 Las Vegas *B*
 Reno *M, D*

New Hampshire
New Hampshire Community Technical College
 Nashua *A*
University of New Hampshire *B, M, D*

New Jersey
New Jersey Institute of Technology *B, M, D*
Ocean County College *C*
Princeton University *B, M, D*
Rutgers
 The State University of New Jersey: College of Engineering *B*
 The State University of New Jersey: New Brunswick Graduate Campus *M, D*
Seton Hall University *B*
Stevens Institute of Technology *B, M, D*

New Mexico
New Mexico State University
 Alamogordo *C, A*
University of New Mexico *B*

New York
City University of New York
 Queensborough Community College *A*
Clarkson University *B*
Columbia University
 Fu Foundation School of Engineering and Applied Science *B, M, D*
Manhattan College *M*
New York Institute of Technology *B, M*
New York University *B*
Onondaga Community College *A*
Pace University *B*
Polytechnic University
 Long Island Campus *B*
Polytechnic University *B*
Rensselaer Polytechnic Institute *B, M, D*
Rochester Institute of Technology *B, M*
State University of New York
 Binghamton *M*
 Buffalo *B*
 New Paltz *B, M*
 Stony Brook *B*
Syracuse University *B, M, D*
United States Military Academy *B*

North Carolina
Cape Fear Community College *A*
Central Carolina Community College *A*
College of the Albemarle *A*
Davidson County Community College *C, A*
Johnson C. Smith University *B*
North Carolina State University *B, M, D*
Southwestern Community College *A*
Surry Community College *A*
University of North Carolina
 Charlotte *B*

North Dakota
North Dakota State University *B*

Ohio
Case Western Reserve University *B, M, D*
Ohio Northern University *B*
Ohio State University
 Columbus Campus *B*
Ohio University *B*
University of Akron *B, M*
University of Cincinnati *B, M, D*
University of Dayton *B*
University of Toledo *B*
Wright State University *B, M, D*

Oklahoma
Oklahoma State University
 Oklahoma City *C, A*
Oklahoma State University *B, M, D*
Oral Roberts University *B*
University of Oklahoma *B*

Oregon
Oregon Graduate Institute *M, D*
Oregon State University *B, M, D*
Portland State University *B*
University of Portland *B*

Pennsylvania
Bucknell University *B*
Carnegie Mellon University *B, M, D*
Drexel University *B*
Elizabethtown College *B*
Gannon University *B, M*
Gettysburg College *B*
Lehigh University *B, M*
Lock Haven University of Pennsylvania *B*
Penn State
 Erie, The Behrend College *A, B*
 University Park *B, D*
University of Pennsylvania *B, M, D*
University of Pittsburgh *B*
University of Scranton *M*
Villanova University *B, M*
Widener University *M*

Puerto Rico
University of Puerto Rico
 Mayaguez Campus *B*
 Ponce University College *A*

Rhode Island
Brown University *B*
New England Institute of Technology *A*
University of Rhode Island *B*

South Carolina
Clemson University *B, M, D*
Horry-Georgetown Technical College *A*
Lander University *B*
University of South Carolina *B, M, D*
York Technical College *A*

South Dakota
South Dakota School of Mines and Technology *B, M*

Tennessee
Chattanooga State Technical Community College *A*
Christian Brothers University *B*
University of Memphis *B*
Vanderbilt University *B*

Texas
Amarillo College *A*
LeTourneau University *B*
Rice University *B, M, D*
St. Mary's University *B, M*
Southern Methodist University *B, M, D*
Texas A&M University
 Kingsville *B, M*
Texas A&M University *B, M, D*
Texas Tech University *B*
University of Houston
 Clear Lake *B, M*
University of Houston *B*
University of Texas
 Arlington *B, M, D*
 Dallas *B, M, D*
 El Paso *M, D*
 San Antonio *B, M*

Utah
Brigham Young University *B*
Salt Lake Community College *A*
University of Utah *B*
Utah State University *B*

Vermont
Vermont Technical College *A, B*

Virginia
Christopher Newport University *B*
ECPI College of Technology *C, A*
George Mason University *M*
New River Community College *A*
Old Dominion University *B*
Virginia Polytechnic Institute and State University *B, M, D*
Wytheville Community College *A*

Washington
Eastern Washington University *B*
Gonzaga University *B*
Pacific Lutheran University *B*
Renton Technical College *A*
University of Washington *B, M*
Washington State University *B*

West Virginia
West Virginia University *B, D*

Wisconsin
Marquette University *B*
Milwaukee School of Engineering *B*
University of Wisconsin
 Madison *B, M, D*
 Parkside *B*

Computer graphics

Alabama
Huntingdon College *B*

Arizona
ITT Technical Institute
 Phoenix *A*
Northland Pioneer College *C, A*
Phoenix College *A*
University of Advancing Computer Technology *A, B*

Arkansas
Garland County Community College *C, A*
Westark College *C*

California
Art Institutes International
 San Francisco *A, B*
California Institute of the Arts *B, M*
California Lutheran University *B*
California State University
 Monterey Bay *B*
Chaffey Community College *C*
College of the Canyons *C, A*
Cypress College *C*
Foothill College *C, A*
Gavilan Community College *C, A*
ITT Technical Institute
 Rancho Cordova *A*
 Sylmar *A*
 West Covina *A*
Los Angeles Southwest College *C, A*
MiraCosta College *C, A*
Modesto Junior College *C, A*
Ohlone College *C, A*
Orange Coast College *C, A*
Saddleback College *C*
Santa Ana College *C*
Santa Barbara City College *C*
Santa Rosa Junior College *C*

Colorado
Art Institute of Colorado *A*
ITT Technical Institute
 Thornton *A*
Morgan Community College *C*
Pueblo Community College *A*

Florida
Art Institute of Fort Lauderdale *A, B*
ITT Technical Institute
 Tampa *A*
Indian River Community College *A*
International Fine Arts College *A*
Jacksonville University *B*
Keiser College *A*
Ringling School of Art and Design *B*
Seminole Community College *A*
Tallahassee Community College *A*

Georgia
Atlanta College of Art *B*
Savannah College of Art and Design *M*

Hawaii
University of Hawaii
 Honolulu Community College *A*

Idaho
College of Southern Idaho *A*
ITT Technical Institute
 Boise *A*

Illinois
American Academy of Art *A, B*
Columbia College *B*
Dominican University *B*
Elgin Community College *C, A*
International Academy of Merchandising and Design *A*
Parkland College *A*
Triton College *C, A*

Indiana
ITT Technical Institute
 Indianapolis *B*
Purdue University *A, B*
Taylor University *B*
Vincennes University *A*

Iowa
Des Moines Area Community College *A*
Marycrest International University *B*

Computer graphics

University of Dubuque *B*

Louisiana
Bossier Parish Community College *C, A*

Maine
Southern Maine Technical College *A*

Maryland
Carroll Community College *C, A*
Community College of Baltimore County
    Catonsville *A*
Montgomery College
    Rockville Campus *A*

Massachusetts
Bristol Community College *C*
Hampshire College *B*
Harvard College *B*
Mount Wachusett Community College *A*
Newbury College *A*
Northern Essex Community College *A*
Simon's Rock College of Bard *B*
Springfield College *B*

Michigan
Baker College
    of Auburn Hills *A*
    of Muskegon *A*
    of Owosso *A*
Center for Creative Studies: College of
    Art and Design *A*
Eastern Michigan University *C*
Jackson Community College *C, A*
Kalamazoo Valley Community
    College *A*

Minnesota
Hennepin Technical College *C, A*
St. Cloud Technical College *C, A*

Mississippi
Meridian Community College *A*

Missouri
St. Charles County Community
    College *A*
St. Louis University *B*

Montana
Miles Community College *A*

Nevada
Community College of Southern
    Nevada *C, A*

New Hampshire
Franklin Pierce College *B*
White Pines College *B*

New Jersey
Bloomfield College *B*
Camden County College *A*
Cumberland County College *C*
Essex County College *C*
Gloucester County College *C, A*
Middlesex County College *A*
Seton Hall University *C*
Sussex County Community College *C, A*

New Mexico
Dona Ana Branch Community College of
    New Mexico State University *A*
New Mexico Junior College *A*

New York
Briarcliffe College *C*
College of Aeronautics *B*
Columbia-Greene Community College *C*
Corning Community College *C, A*
Jamestown Community College *C*
New York Institute of Technology *B*
Pratt Institute *B, M*
Rochester Institute of Technology *B, M*
Rockland Community College *A*
State University of New York
    College of Technology at Alfred *A*
Suffolk County Community College *A*
Syracuse University *B, M*
Westchester Business Institute *C, A*

North Carolina
Alamance Community College *C*
Guilford Technical Community
    College *C*
University of North Carolina
    Chapel Hill *M, D*
Wake Technical Community College *A*

North Dakota
Dickinson State University *A*

Ohio
Columbus State Community College *A*
Davis College *A*
Edison State Community College *A*
Kent State University
    Ashtabula Regional Campus *C*
Kent State University *C*
Ohio Institute of Photography and
    Technology *A*
Ohio Northern University *B*
Terra Community College *A*

Oklahoma
Oklahoma State University
    Okmulgee *A*

Oregon
ITT Technical Institute
    Portland *A*
Linn-Benton Community College *A*

Pennsylvania
Beaver College *C*
Bucks County Community College *A*
La Salle University *B*
Pittsburgh Technical Institute *A*

South Carolina
Aiken Technical College *C*

Tennessee
ITT Technical Institute
    Knoxville *A*

Texas
Amarillo College *C, A*
Central Texas College *C*
Midland College *C, A*
Schreiner College *B*
Texas State Technical College
    Harlingen *A*
Trinity Valley Community College *C, A*
University of Mary Hardin-Baylor *B*

Utah
College of Eastern Utah *C, A*
Dixie State College of Utah *C, A*
Salt Lake Community College *A*

Vermont
Champlain College *A, B*

Virginia
Central Virginia Community College *C*
Lord Fairfax Community College *C*
New River Community College *A*

Washington
Clark College *A*
Everett Community College *A*
Evergreen State College *B*
Green River Community College *C*
ITT Technical Institute
    Seattle *A*

Computer programming

Alabama
Athens State University *B*
Calhoun Community College *A*
Enterprise State Junior College *C*
J. F. Drake State Technical College *A*
John M. Patterson State Technical
    College *C, A*
Northwest-Shoals Community College *A*
Sparks State Technical College *A*
Wallace State Community College at
    Hanceville *A*

Arizona
Central Arizona College *C, A*
Eastern Arizona College *C*
Mohave Community College *C*
South Mountain Community College *C*
University of Advancing Computer
    Technology *A, B*

Arkansas
Northwest Arkansas Community
    College *A*
University of Arkansas
    Little Rock *A*
Westark College *C, A*

California
Barstow College *C, A*
California Lutheran University *B*
Canada College *A*
Cerritos Community College *A*
Chabot College *A*
City College of San Francisco *C, A*
Claremont McKenna College *B*
College of Marin: Kentfield *A*
College of the Redwoods *C*
Columbia College *A*
Crafton Hills College *C, A*
Cypress College *C*
De Anza College *C, A*
East Los Angeles College *A*
Evergreen Valley College *C*
Foothill College *C, A*
Fresno City College *A*
Gavilan Community College *C*
Grossmont Community College *C, A*
Irvine Valley College *C, A*
Los Angeles Mission College *C*
Los Angeles Pierce College *C, A*
Los Angeles Southwest College *A*
Merced College *A*
MiraCosta College *C, A*
Modesto Junior College *A*
Ohlone College *C, A*
Pasadena City College *C, A*
Point Loma Nazarene University *C*
Riverside Community College *C, A*
Saddleback College *C, A*
San Diego Mesa College *C, A*
San Joaquin Delta College *C, A*
San Jose City College *C, A*
Santa Ana College *A*
Santa Monica College *C, A*
Santa Rosa Junior College *C*
Sierra College *A*
Solano Community College *C, A*
Sonoma State University *B*
Southwestern College *C, A*
Ventura College *A*
Victor Valley College *C*
West Valley College *C, A*

Colorado
Denver Technical College: A Division of
    DeVry University *A, B*
Red Rocks Community College *C, A*
Technical Trades Institute *A*
Trinidad State Junior College *A*
University of Southern Colorado *B*

Connecticut
Asnuntuck Community-Technical
    College *C*
Capital Community College *C*
Naugatuck Valley Community-Technical
    College *A*
Northwestern Connecticut
    Community-Technical College *C, A*
Norwalk Community-Technical
    College *A*

Delaware
Delaware Technical and Community
    College
        Owens Campus *A*
        Stanton/Wilmington Campus *A*
        Terry Campus *A*

District of Columbia
Southeastern University *A, B, M*

Florida
Brevard Community College *A*
Broward Community College *A*
Central Florida Community College *A*
Daytona Beach Community College *A*
Edison Community College *A*
Florida Community College at
    Jacksonville *A*
Florida Keys Community College *A*
Florida National College *A*
Gulf Coast Community College *A*
Hillsborough Community College *A*
Indian River Community College *A*
Keiser College *A*
Lake City Community College *A*
Lake-Sumter Community College *A*
Manatee Community College *A*
New England Institute of Technology *A*
Palm Beach Community College *A*
Pasco-Hernando Community College *A*
Pensacola Junior College *A*
Santa Fe Community College *A*
Seminole Community College *A*
South Florida Community College *A*
Tallahassee Community College *C, A*
Valencia Community College *A*

Georgia
Abraham Baldwin Agricultural
    College *C*
Athens Area Technical Institute *C, A*
Chattahoochee Technical Institute *C, A*
Columbus State University *A, B*
Columbus Technical Institute *C*
Darton College *A*
DeKalb Technical Institute *A*
Georgia Southwestern State
    University *A, B*
Gwinnett Technical Institute *A*
Kennesaw State University *B*
Macon State College *A*
Savannah Technical Institute *A*
South Georgia College *A*
Valdosta State University *B*
Waycross College *A*

Idaho
North Idaho College *A*

Illinois
Black Hawk College
    East Campus *A*
City Colleges of Chicago
    Olive-Harvey College *C, A*
Danville Area Community College *C, A*
De Paul University *B, M*
Highland Community College *A*
Joliet Junior College *A*
Kaskaskia College *A*
Lincoln Land Community College *C, A*
McKendree College *B*
Northwestern Business College *A*
Parkland College *A*
Prairie State College *A*
Richland Community College *A*
Rock Valley College *C*
Sauk Valley Community College *A*
Southeastern Illinois College *A*
Southwestern Illinois College *A*
University of St. Francis *B*
William Rainey Harper College *C, A*

Indiana
Indiana State University *B*
Indiana University
    East *A*
    Southeast *A*

Computer programming

Indiana University--Purdue University
    Indiana University-Purdue University Fort Wayne *C, A, B*
Purdue University
    Calumet *B*
St. Joseph's College *A*
Tri-State University *A*
University of Evansville *B*
Vincennes University *A*

Iowa
American Institute of Business *A*
Buena Vista University *B*
Des Moines Area Community College *A*
Iowa Lakes Community College *A*
Iowa Western Community College *A*
Luther College *B*
Northeast Iowa Community College *A*
Southeastern Community College
    North Campus *A*
Southwestern Community College *A*
Western Iowa Tech Community
    College *A*

Kansas
Benedictine College *B, T*
Coffeyville Community College *A*
Independence Community College *C, A*
Kansas City Kansas Community
    College *A*
Kansas State University *M*
McPherson College *B*
Seward County Community
    College *C, A*

Kentucky
Murray State University *B*

Louisiana
Nunez Community College *A*

Maine
Andover College *C, A*
Eastern Maine Technical College *C*
Husson College *A, B*
University of Maine
    Fort Kent *B*

Maryland
Charles County Community College *A*
Columbia Union College *A*
Community College of Baltimore County
    Catonsville *A*
    Essex *A*
Harford Community College *C*
Montgomery College
    Germantown Campus *C, A*
    Rockville Campus *C, A*
    Takoma Park Campus *C*
Prince George's Community
    College *C, A*
University of Maryland
    College Park *M*
Wor-Wic Community College *C, A*

Massachusetts
Atlantic Union College *A*
Berkshire Community College *C, A*
Bristol Community College *A*
Clark University *B*
Fitchburg State College *C*
Franklin Institute of Boston *A*
Massachusetts College of Liberal Arts *B*
Massasoit Community College *A*
Mount Wachusett Community College *A*
Newbury College *A*
North Shore Community College *A*
Northern Essex Community College *A*
Tufts University *B*
Wentworth Institute of Technology *C*

Michigan
Baker College
    of Auburn Hills *A*
    of Cadillac *A*
    of Jackson *A*
    of Mount Clemens *A*
    of Muskegon *A*
    of Owosso *A*
    of Port Huron *A*
Calvin College *B*
Cleary College *B*
Delta College *A*
Grand Rapids Community College *A*
Grand Valley State University *B*
Jackson Community College *C, A*
Kalamazoo Valley Community
    College *A*
Kellogg Community College *C, A*
Lansing Community College *A*
Macomb Community College *C, A*
Monroe County Community College *A*
Northern Michigan University *B*
Oakland Community College *A*
Schoolcraft College *A*
Southwestern Michigan College *A*
Washtenaw Community College *A*

Minnesota
Alexandria Technical College *A*
Dakota County Technical College *C, A*
Hennepin Technical College *C, A*
Inver Hills Community College *A*
Lake Superior College: A Community
    and Technical College *C, A*
Mesabi Range Community and Technical
    College *A*
Minneapolis Community and Technical
    College *A*
NEI College of Technology *C*
National American University
    St. Paul *A, B*
St. Cloud Technical College *C, A*
St. Paul Technical College *C, A*
South Central Technical College *A*
Winona State University *B*

Mississippi
Copiah-Lincoln Community College *A*
East Central Community College *A*
East Mississippi Community College *A*
Holmes Community College *A*
Itawamba Community College *A*
Jackson State University *B*
Mary Holmes College *A*
Meridian Community College *A*
Mississippi Delta Community College *A*
Northwest Mississippi Community
    College *A*

Missouri
East Central College *C, A*
Jefferson College *A*
Missouri Southern State College *C, A, B*
St. Charles County Community
    College *A*
St. Louis Community College
    St. Louis Community College at
        Florissant Valley *A*
    St. Louis Community College at
        Forest Park *A*

Montana
Montana State University
    Northern *A*
University of Montana-Missoula *B*

Nebraska
Lincoln School of Commerce *A*
Metropolitan Community College *A*
Midland Lutheran College *B*
Northeast Community College *A*
Peru State College *B*
Southeast Community College
    Milford Campus *A*

Nevada
Community College of Southern
    Nevada *A*
Western Nevada Community College *A*

New Hampshire
Daniel Webster College *C*
Hesser College *A*
New Hampshire Community Technical
    College
    Laconia *C, A*
    Manchester *C*
    Stratham *C, A, D*

New Jersey
Atlantic Cape Community College *A*
Essex County College *A*
Middlesex County College *A*
Ocean County College *C*
Raritan Valley Community College *C, A*
St. Peter's College *C, A, B*

New Mexico
Clovis Community College *A*
New Mexico Institute of Mining and
    Technology *B, M, D*
New Mexico Junior College *A*

New York
Briarcliffe College *C*
Cayuga County Community College *C*
City University of New York
    Borough of Manhattan Community
        College *A*
    Brooklyn College *B*
    La Guardia Community College *A*
    Queensborough Community
        College *C, A*
College of St. Rose *C*
Corning Community College *A*
Dominican College of Blauvelt *C*
Finger Lakes Community College *A*
Fulton-Montgomery Community
    College *A*
Medaille College *B*
Mohawk Valley Community
    College *C, A*
Nassau Community College *A*
Pace University:
    Pleasantville/Briarcliff *C*
Pace University *C*
Regents College *A, B*
Rochester Institute of
    Technology *A, B, M*
Rockland Community College *A*
Schenectady County Community
    College *C, A*
State University of New York
    College at Buffalo *B*
    College of Agriculture and
        Technology at Cobleskill *A*
    Farmingdale *A*
    Purchase *C*
Westchester Business Institute *C, A*
Wood Tobe-Coburn School *A*

North Carolina
Alamance Community College *C, A*
Beaufort County Community College *A*
Belmont Abbey College *B*
Bladen Community College *C, A*
Blue Ridge Community College *A*
Brunswick Community College *A*
Catawba Valley Community
    College *C, A*
Central Carolina Community College *A*
Cleveland Community College *C, A*
College of the Albemarle *A*
Davidson County Community
    College *A*
Durham Technical Community
    College *C, A*
Edgecombe Community College *A*
Fayetteville Technical Community
    College *A*
Gaston College *C, A*
Guilford Technical Community
    College *A*
Johnston Community College *A*
Lenoir Community College *A*
Mayland Community College *C*
Mitchell Community College *C, A*
Piedmont Community College *A*
Roanoke-Chowan Community College *A*
Rowan-Cabarrus Community
    College *C, A*
Sandhills Community College *C, A*
South Piedmont Community College *A*
Southwestern Community College *A*
Surry Community College *A*
Wake Technical Community
    College *C, A*
Wilson Technical Community College *A*

North Dakota
North Dakota State College of Science *A*

Ohio
Belmont Technical College *A*
Bowling Green State University
    Firelands College *A*
Bryant & Stratton College *A*
Central Ohio Technical College *C, A*
Cincinnati State Technical and
    Community College *A*
Cleveland Institute of Electronics *C*
Columbus State Community
    College *C, A*
Edison State Community College *C, A*
Kent State University
    Ashtabula Regional Campus *A*
    East Liverpool Regional Campus *A*
    Stark Campus *B*
    Trumbull Campus *A*
Kent State University *B*
Marion Technical College *A*
Miami-Jacobs College *C, A*
North Central State College *A*
Northwest State Community College *A*
Owens Community College
    Findlay Campus *A*
    Toledo *C, A*
Stark State College of Technology *A*
Tiffin University *A*
University of Akron *A, B*
University of Cincinnati
    Clermont College *A*
    Raymond Walters College *C, A*
Washington State Community College *A*
Youngstown State University *A, B*

Oklahoma
Eastern Oklahoma State College *A*
Northeastern Oklahoma Agricultural and
    Mechanical College *C, A*
Northwestern Oklahoma State
    University *B*
Oklahoma City Community College *A*
Oklahoma State University
    Oklahoma City *C, A*
    Okmulgee *A*
Oklahoma State University *B*
Rogers State University *C, A*
St. Gregory's University *A*
Tulsa Community College *C, A*
Western Oklahoma State College *A*

Oregon
Chemeketa Community College *A*
Lane Community College *A*
Linn-Benton Community College *A*
Southern Oregon University *B*

Pennsylvania
Beaver College *B*
Bucks County Community College *C, A*
Butler County Community College *A*
California University of
    Pennsylvania *A, B*
Delaware County Community College *A*
Delaware Valley College *C*
Gwynedd-Mercy College *A*
La Salle University *A, B, M*

Laurel Business Institute *A*
Mercyhurst College *C*
Philadelphia University *B*
Pittsburgh Technical Institute *A*
Reading Area Community College *A*
Sawyer School *C*
Temple University *B, M, D*
Tri-State Business Institute *A*
Westminster College *B*
Westmoreland County Community College *A*
York College of Pennsylvania *A*

Puerto Rico
American University of Puerto Rico *A*
Atlantic College *A*
Colegio Universitario del Este *A*
Huertas Junior College *A*
Humacao Community College *A*
National College of Business and Technology *A*
Pontifical Catholic University of Puerto Rico *A*
Ramirez College of Business and Technology *A*
Universidad Metropolitana *C, A, B*

Rhode Island
Community College of Rhode Island *C, A*
Johnson & Wales University *A*
New England Institute of Technology *A*

South Carolina
Aiken Technical College *C*
Central Carolina Technical College *A*
Charleston Southern University *A*
Greenville Technical College *A*
Limestone College *A, B*
Orangeburg-Calhoun Technical College *A*
Piedmont Technical College *C*
Tri-County Technical College *A*
Trident Technical College *A*
York Technical College *A*

South Dakota
Kilian Community College *A*
South Dakota School of Mines and Technology *B*
Southeast Technical Institute *A*

Tennessee
Chattanooga State Technical Community College *A*
Roane State Community College *A*
Southern Adventist University *M*
Tennessee State University *B*

Texas
Alvin Community College *C, A*
Amarillo College *C, A*
Angelina College *A*
Austin Community College *A*
Brazosport College *C, A*
Brookhaven College *A*
Central Texas College *C, A*
Coastal Bend College *A*
College of the Mainland *A*
Collin County Community College District *C, A*
Del Mar College *C, A*
Eastfield College *A*
El Paso Community College *A*
Galveston College *A*
Grayson County College *A*
Hill College *A*
Houston Community College System *C, A*
LeTourneau University *B*
Lee College *C, A*
Midland College *A*
Odessa College *A*
Palo Alto College *A*
San Antonio College *A*
San Jacinto College
  North *C, A*

Southwest Texas State University *M*
Tarrant County College *C, A*
Temple College *C, A*
Texas Christian University *M*
Texas State Technical College
  Harlingen *A*
  Waco *A*
Trinity Valley Community College *C, A*
Weatherford College *A*
Western Texas College *A*

Utah
Mountain West College *A*

Vermont
Champlain College *A, B*

Virginia
Danville Community College *A*
ECPI College of Technology *C, A*
J. Sargeant Reynolds Community College *C, A*
John Tyler Community College *A*
Lord Fairfax Community College *A*
National Business College *A*
New River Community College *A*
Northern Virginia Community College *A*
Patrick Henry Community College *A*
Piedmont Virginia Community College *C, A*

Washington
City University *C, B*
Clark College *C, A*
Columbia Basin College *A*
Edmonds Community College *C*
Evergreen State College *B*
North Seattle Community College *C, A*
Olympic College *A*
Renton Technical College *A*
Skagit Valley College *A*
South Seattle Community College *C, A*
Walla Walla College *A*
Western Washington University *B*

West Virginia
Potomac State College of West Virginia University *A*
West Virginia State College *A*
West Virginia University Institute of Technology *B*
Wheeling Jesuit University *B*

Wisconsin
Blackhawk Technical College *A*
Chippewa Valley Technical College *A*
Madison Area Technical College *A*
Milwaukee Area Technical College *A*
Nicolet Area Technical College *A*
Northeast Wisconsin Technical College *A*
Southwest Wisconsin Technical College *A*
Western Wisconsin Technical College *A*
Wisconsin Indianhead Technical College *A*

Computer science

Alabama
Alabama State University *B*
Auburn University *B*
Bessemer State Technical College *C, A*
Bevill State Community College *A*
Birmingham-Southern College *B*
Huntingdon College *B*
Lawson State Community College *C, A*
Northeast Alabama Community College *A*
Oakwood College *B*
Samford University *B*
Shelton State Community College *C*

Alaska
University of Alaska
  Anchorage *B*
  Fairbanks *B, M*

Arizona
Arizona State University *B, M, D*
Arizona Western College *C*
Cochise College *A*
Grand Canyon University *B*
Mesa Community College *A*
Mohave Community College *C*
Paradise Valley Community College *C*

Arkansas
Harding University *B*
Lyon College *B*
Ouachita Baptist University *B*
Philander Smith College *B*
University of Central Arkansas *B*

California
California Institute of Technology *B, M, D*
California Lutheran University *B*
California State Polytechnic University:
  Pomona *B, M*
California State University
  Bakersfield *B*
  Fresno *B, M*
  Fullerton *B, M*
  Hayward *B, M*
  Long Beach *B, M*
  Sacramento *B, M*
  San Marcos *B, M*
Chabot College *A*
College of Notre Dame *B*
College of the Canyons *C, A*
Columbia College *C*
Cuesta College *C, A*
De Anza College *A*
Foothill College *A*
Fresno City College *C, A*
Fresno Pacific University *B*
Kings River Community College *A*
La Sierra University *B*
Lake Tahoe Community College *C, A*
Las Positas College *A*
Los Angeles Pierce College *C, A*
Los Angeles Southwest College *C, A*
Los Medanos College *C*
Loyola Marymount University *M*
Master's College *B*
Merced College *A*
MiraCosta College *A*
Mission College *A*
Modesto Junior College *A*
Napa Valley College *C*
National University *B, M*
Palomar College *C, A*
Pepperdine University *B*
Point Loma Nazarene University *B*
Pomona College *B*
Riverside Community College *A*
Saddleback College *A*
San Bernardino Valley College *C, A*
San Diego State University *B, M*
San Francisco State University *B, M*
San Joaquin Delta College *C, A*
San Jose State University *B, M*
Santa Ana College *C, A*
Santa Barbara City College *C, A*
Santa Monica College *C*
Scripps College *B*
Sierra College *A*
Skyline College *A*
Stanford University *M, D*
University of California
  Los Angeles *B*
  Riverside *B, M, D*
  San Diego *B, M, D*
  Santa Cruz *B, D*
University of San Diego *B*
University of Southern California *B, M, D*
University of the Pacific *B*

Westmont College *B*

Colorado
Colorado School of Mines *B*
Colorado Technical University *B, M, D*
Fort Lewis College *B*
Lamar Community College *A*
Metropolitan State College of Denver *B*
Regis University *B*
Technical Trades Institute *A*
Trinidad State Junior College *A*
University of Colorado
  Boulder *B, M, D*
  Colorado Springs *B, M, D*
  Denver *B, M*
University of Denver *B, M*

Connecticut
Central Connecticut State University *B*
Fairfield University *B*
Hartford Graduate Center *M*
Quinnipiac University *B, M*
Sacred Heart University *B*
Trinity College *B*

Delaware
Delaware State University *B*
Delaware Technical and Community College
  Terry Campus *A*

District of Columbia
American University *B, M*
Gallaudet University *B*
Georgetown University *B*
University of the District of Columbia *A, B*

Florida
Barry University *B, T*
Broward Community College *A*
Edward Waters College *B*
Embry-Riddle Aeronautical University *B*
Florida Atlantic University *B, M, D*
Florida Institute of Technology *B, M, D*
Florida Memorial College *B*
Florida Southern College *B*
Florida State University *C, B, M, D*
Gulf Coast Community College *A*
Hillsborough Community College *A*
Nova Southeastern University *B, M, D*
St. Thomas University *B*
Stetson University *B*
University of Miami *B, M*
University of West Florida *B, M*

Georgia
Albany State University *B*
Atlanta Metropolitan College *A*
Berry College *B*
Clayton College and State University *A*
Coastal Georgia Community College *A*
Columbus State University *A, B, M*
Emory University *B*
Georgia Perimeter College *A*
Georgia Southwestern State University *B, M*
Georgia State University *B, M*
LaGrange College *B*
Mercer University *B*
Middle Georgia College *A*
Oxford College of Emory University *A*
Piedmont College *B*
Savannah State University *B*
State University of West Georgia *B*
Valdosta State University *B*
Young Harris College *A*

Hawaii
Brigham Young University
  Hawaii *A, B*
Chaminade University of Honolulu *B*
Hawaii Pacific University *B*

Idaho
Albertson College of Idaho *B*
Boise State University *B, M*
College of Southern Idaho *A*

Idaho State University *B*
Ricks College *A*

Illinois
Augustana College *B*
Barat College *B*
Benedictine University *B*
Bradley University *B*
Concordia University *B*
Dominican University *B*
Elmhurst College *B*
Eureka College *B*
Governors State University *B, M*
Greenville College *B*
Highland Community College *A*
John Wood Community College *A*
Judson College *B*
Lake Forest College *B*
Lewis University *B*
Lewis and Clark Community College *A*
MacCormac College *C, A*
MacMurray College *B*
McKendree College *B*
Monmouth College *B*
Northwestern University *B, M, D*
Olivet Nazarene University *B*
Parkland College *A*
Principia College *B*
Quincy University *A, B*
Richland Community College *A*
Rockford College *B*
Roosevelt University *C, B, M*
St. Xavier University *B*
Southwestern Illinois College *C, A*
Springfield College in Illinois *A*
Triton College *A*
University of Chicago *M, D*
University of Illinois
    Urbana-Champaign *M*
University of St. Francis *B*
Wheaton College *B*
William Rainey Harper College *A*

Indiana
Anderson University *B*
Bethel College *A*
DePauw University *B*
Earlham College *B*
Franklin College *B*
Indiana Institute of Technology *B*
Indiana State University *B*
Indiana University
    East *A*
Indiana University--Purdue University
    Indiana University-Purdue
        University Fort Wayne *A, B, M*
Manchester College *A, B*
Marian College *A*
Oakland City University *C, A, B*
Purdue University
    Calumet *B*
Rose-Hulman Institute of Technology *B*
Taylor University *B*
Tri-State University *B*
University of Indianapolis *B*
Valparaiso University *B*
Vincennes University *A*

Iowa
Buena Vista University *B*
Clarke College *B*
Coe College *B*
Dordt College *B*
Drake University *B*
Graceland University *B*
Grand View College *B*
Grinnell College *B*
Iowa Wesleyan College *B*
Loras College *B*
Luther College *B*
Maharishi University of Management *M*
Marycrest International
    University *A, B, M*
Morningside College *B*
Mount Mercy College *B*
North Iowa Area Community College *A*

Northwestern College *B*
St. Ambrose University *B*
Simpson College *B*
University of Iowa *B, M, D*
University of Northern Iowa *B*

Kansas
Allen County Community College *A*
Baker University *B*
Butler County Community College *A*
Dodge City Community College *A*
Garden City Community College *A*
Kansas Wesleyan University *A, B, T*
McPherson College *T*
Pittsburg State University *B*
Seward County Community College *A*
Southwestern College *B*
Tabor College *B*

Kentucky
Bellarmine College *B*
Centre College *B*
Kentucky State University *B*
Kentucky Wesleyan College *B*
Murray State University *B*
Northern Kentucky University *B*
Pikeville College *A, B*

Louisiana
Dillard University *B*
Grantham College of Engineering *A, B*
Louisiana State University
    Shreveport *B*
Louisiana State University and
    Agricultural and Mechanical
    College *B, D*
Louisiana Tech University *B, M*
McNeese State University *B*
Nicholls State University *B*
Southeastern Louisiana University *B*
Southern University
    Shreveport *A*
Southern University and Agricultural and
    Mechanical College *B, M*
Tulane University *B, M, D*
University of Louisiana at
    Lafayette *B, M, D*
University of Louisiana at Monroe *B*
University of New Orleans *B, M*

Maine
Andover College *A*
Bowdoin College *B*
Colby College *B*
Mid-State College *C*
Southern Maine Technical College *A*
University of Maine
    Farmington *B*
    Fort Kent *A*
University of Southern Maine *B, M*

Maryland
Allegany College *A*
Anne Arundel Community College *A*
Baltimore City Community College *A*
College of Notre Dame of Maryland *B*
Community College of Baltimore County
    Catonsville *A*
Coppin State College *B*
Frederick Community College *A*
Goucher College *B*
Hagerstown Community College *A*
Harford Community College *A*
Howard Community College *A*
Johns Hopkins University *B*
Montgomery College
    Rockville Campus *A*
Morgan State University *B*
Mount St. Mary's College *B*
Prince George's Community College *A*
St. Mary's College of Maryland *B*
Salisbury State University *B*
Towson University *B, M*
University of Maryland
    Baltimore County *B, M, D*

Massachusetts
Amherst College *B*
Bay Path College *B*
Berkshire Community College *A*
Boston College *B*
Brandeis University *B, M, D*
Bridgewater State College *B, M*
Bunker Hill Community College *C, A*
Cape Cod Community College *A*
Eastern Nazarene College *B*
Fitchburg State College *B, M*
Framingham State College *B*
Hampshire College *B*
Harvard College *B*
Massachusetts Bay Community
    College *A*
Massachusetts Institute of
    Technology *B, M, D*
Merrimack College *B*
Middlesex Community College *A*
Mount Holyoke College *B*
Newbury College *A*
North Shore Community College *A*
Northeastern University *B, M, D*
Northern Essex Community
    College *C, A*
Quincy College *C, A*
Simon's Rock College of Bard *B*
Smith College *B*
Springfield Technical Community
    College *A*
Stonehill College *B*
Suffolk University *B*
Tufts University *B*
University of Massachusetts
    Amherst *B, M, D*
    Boston *M, D*
    Lowell *B, M, D*
Wentworth Institute of Technology *B*
Western New England College *B*
Wheaton College *B*
Williams College *B*
Worcester Polytechnic Institute *B*

Michigan
Albion College *B*
Alma College *B*
Baker College
    of Mount Clemens *B*
    of Owosso *A, B*
    of Port Huron *A, B*
Calvin College *B*
Central Michigan University *B*
Grand Valley State University *B*
Hillsdale College *B*
Kettering University *B*
Lawrence Technological University *B*
Mid Michigan Community College *A*
Northern Michigan University *B*
University of Detroit Mercy *B, M*
University of Michigan
    Flint *B*
University of Michigan *B*
Western Michigan University *B, M, D*

Minnesota
Bemidji State University *B*
Bethel College *B*
Carleton College *B*
College of St. Benedict *B*
Fond Du Lac Tribal and Community
    College *A*
Gustavus Adolphus College *B*
Hamline University *B*
Lake Superior College: A Community
    and Technical College *A*
Metropolitan State University *B*
Minnesota State University,
    Mankato *B, M*
Moorhead State University *B*
Ridgewater College: A Community and
    Technical College *A*
St. Cloud State University *B, M*
St. John's University *B*

University of Minnesota
    Duluth *B, M*
    Morris *B*
    Twin Cities *C, B*
Winona State University *B*

Mississippi
Belhaven College *C, B*
Coahoma Community College *A*
Holmes Community College *A*
Millsaps College *B, T*
Mississippi College *B, M*
Rust College *B*

Missouri
Central Methodist College *B*
College of the Ozarks *B*
Columbia College *B*
Drury University *B*
Lindenwood University *B*
Missouri Southern State College *A, B*
Park University *B*
Southwest Baptist University *A, B*
University of Missouri
    Rolla *B, M, D*
    St. Louis *B*
Webster University *B*
William Jewell College *B*

Montana
Carroll College *A, T*
Montana State University
    Billings *B*
    Bozeman *B, M*
Montana Tech of the University of
    Montana *B*
Rocky Mountain College *B*
University of Great Falls *A, B*
University of Montana-Missoula *B*

Nebraska
Concordia University *B, T*
Dana College *B*
Doane College *B*
Mid Plains Community College Area *A*
Midland Lutheran College *B*
Nebraska Wesleyan University *B*
Peru State College *B*
Union College *B*
University of Nebraska
    Lincoln *B, M, D*
    Omaha *B, M*

Nevada
University of Nevada
    Las Vegas *B, M, D*
    Reno *B, M*

New Hampshire
Antioch New England Graduate
    School *M*
Daniel Webster College *B*
Dartmouth College *B*
Franklin Pierce College *B*
Keene State College *B*
New Hampshire Community Technical
    College
    Nashua *C, A*
Plymouth State College of the University
    System of New Hampshire *B*
Rivier College *C, A, B, M*
St. Anselm College *B*

New Jersey
Brookdale Community College *A*
Caldwell College *B*
Cumberland County College *A*
Fairleigh Dickinson University *B, M*
Gloucester County College *A*
Hudson County Community College *A*
Monmouth University *B, M*
New Jersey Institute of
    Technology *B, M, D*
Ocean County College *A*
Princeton University *B, M, D*
Ramapo College of New Jersey *B*
Raritan Valley Community College *A*

Computer science

167

Computer science

Richard Stockton College of New Jersey B
Rowan University B
Rutgers
   The State University of New Jersey: Camden College of Arts and Sciences B
   The State University of New Jersey: Cook College B
   The State University of New Jersey: Douglass College B
   The State University of New Jersey: Livingston College B
   The State University of New Jersey: Newark College of Arts and Sciences B
   The State University of New Jersey: Rutgers College B
   The State University of New Jersey: University College Camden B
   The State University of New Jersey: University College New Brunswick B
   The State University of New Jersey: University College Newark B
St. Peter's College B
Stevens Institute of Technology B, M, D
Thomas Edison State College C, A, B
Union County College A

New Mexico
College of Santa Fe B
Dona Ana Branch Community College of New Mexico State University A
New Mexico Institute of Mining and Technology B, M, D
New Mexico State University
   Alamogordo C
   Carlsbad A

New York
Adirondack Community College A
Alfred University B
Barnard College B
Canisius College B
Cayuga County Community College A
City University of New York
   Baruch College B, M
   Bronx Community College A
   City College B
   College of Staten Island A, B, M, D
   La Guardia Community College A
   Medgar Evers College A
Clarkson University B, M
Clinton Community College A
Colgate University B
Columbia University
   Columbia College B
   School of General Studies B
Columbia-Greene Community College A
Corning Community College A
Dowling College B
Dutchess Community College A
Finger Lakes Community College A
Fordham University B
Fulton-Montgomery Community College A
Herkimer County Community College A
Hobart and William Smith Colleges B
Hofstra University B, M
Houghton College B
Iona College B
Ithaca College B
Jamestown Community College A
Jefferson Community College A
Manhattan College B
Marist College B
Medaille College B
Monroe Community College A
Mount St. Mary College C, B, T
Nassau Community College A
New York Institute of Technology B
New York University B, M, D
Niagara County Community College A
Niagara University C, B
Nyack College B

Onondaga Community College A
Pace University:
   Pleasantville/Briarcliff B, M
Pace University B, M
Polytechnic University B, M, D
Rensselaer Polytechnic Institute B, M, D
Roberts Wesleyan College B
Rochester Institute of Technology B, M
Russell Sage College B
St. Bonaventure University B
St. John Fisher College B
St. Lawrence University B
Siena College C, B
St. Joseph's College
   St. Joseph's College: Suffolk Campus B
State University of New York
   Binghamton B, M, D
   Buffalo B, M, D
   College of Agriculture and Technology at Cobleskill A
   College of Agriculture and Technology at Morrisville A
   College of Technology at Alfred A
   Farmingdale A
   New Paltz B, M
   Oswego B
   Stony Brook B, M, D
Suffolk County Community College A
Syracuse University B, M
Tompkins-Cortland Community College A
United States Military Academy B
Vassar College B
Wagner College B
Wells College B
Westchester Business Institute C, A
Westchester Community College A

North Carolina
Barber-Scotia College B
Brevard College B
East Carolina University B, M
Elon College B
High Point University B
Mars Hill College B
Meredith College B
Methodist College A, B
North Carolina State University M, D
St. Augustine's College B
Sandhills Community College A
Shaw University B
University of North Carolina
   Asheville B
   Charlotte B, M
   Pembroke B
Wake Forest University B, M
Western Carolina University B

North Dakota
Dickinson State University B, T
Jamestown College B
Minot State University B
North Dakota State University B, M, D
University of North Dakota B, M

Ohio
Ashland University B
Baldwin-Wallace College B
Bluffton College B
Bowling Green State University B
Capital University B
Case Western Reserve University B
Cedarville College B
Central State University B
College of Mount St. Joseph A, B
Defiance College A, B
Franciscan University of Steubenville B
Franklin University A, B, M
Heidelberg College B
Hiram College B
Jefferson Community College A
John Carroll University B
Kent State University
   Stark Campus B
Kent State University B, M, D

Lourdes College C
Malone College B
Marietta College B
Mount Union College B
Muskingum Area Technical College A
Muskingum College B
Ohio Dominican College C, B
Ohio State University
   Columbus Campus B, M, D
Ohio University
   Southern Campus at Ironton A
Ohio University B
Ohio Wesleyan University B
Otterbein College B
Owens Community College
   Toledo A
RETS Tech Center A
Southern Ohio College A
Stark State College of Technology A
University of Dayton B
University of Findlay A, B
University of Rio Grande A, B
University of Toledo B
Wilmington College B
Xavier University B
Youngstown State University B

Oklahoma
Cameron University B
Eastern Oklahoma State College A
Murray State College A
Northeastern State University B
Oklahoma Baptist University B
Oklahoma Christian University of Science and Arts B
Oklahoma City Community College A
Oklahoma City University B, M
Oklahoma State University B, M, D
Oral Roberts University B
Redlands Community College A
Seminole State College A
Southwestern Oklahoma State University B
University of Central Oklahoma B
University of Science and Arts of Oklahoma B
University of Tulsa C, B, M, D

Oregon
Central Oregon Community College A
Eastern Oregon University B
Lewis & Clark College B
Linfield College B
Linn-Benton Community College A
Oregon Graduate Institute M, D
Oregon Institute of Technology B
Southern Oregon University B
University of Portland B
Western Baptist College B
Western Oregon University B
Willamette University B

Pennsylvania
Allegheny College B
Allentown College of St. Francis de Sales B
Bryn Mawr College B
Bucknell University B
Bucks County Community College A
Carlow College B
Carnegie Mellon University B
Chestnut Hill College B
Dickinson College B
Drexel University B, M, D
Duquesne University B
Elizabethtown College B
Geneva College B
Gettysburg College B
Juniata College B
King's College B
La Salle University B, M
Lebanon Valley College of Pennsylvania B
Lehigh Carbon Community College A
Lehigh University B, M, D

Lock Haven University of Pennsylvania B
Mansfield University of Pennsylvania B
Moravian College B
Muhlenberg College B
Pennsylvania Institute of Technology A
Philadelphia University C, B, M
Seton Hill College C, B
Susquehanna University B
Tri-State Business Institute A
University of Pittsburgh B, M, D
Waynesburg College A, B
Westminster College B, T
Westmoreland County Community College C, A

Puerto Rico
Huertas Junior College A
Inter American University of Puerto Rico
   Aguadilla Campus C, A, B
   Arecibo Campus A, B
   Barranquitas Campus A, B
   Bayamon Campus A, B
   Metropolitan Campus D
   San German Campus B
Universidad Metropolitana A, B
University of Puerto Rico
   Mayaguez Campus B, M
   Rio Piedras Campus B
University of the Sacred Heart B

Rhode Island
Brown University B, M, D
Johnson & Wales University A
New England Institute of Technology A, B
Providence College B
Rhode Island College B
Roger Williams University A, B

South Carolina
Benedict College B
Claflin University B
Clemson University B, M
College of Charleston B
Francis Marion University B
Furman University B
Presbyterian College B
Wofford College B

South Dakota
Augustana College B
Dakota State University B, T
Huron University B
Sinte Gleska University B
South Dakota School of Mines and Technology B, M
South Dakota State University B

Tennessee
Belmont University B
Carson-Newman College B
Christian Brothers University B
David Lipscomb University B
Dyersburg State Community College A
Freed-Hardeman University B
King College B
Lane College B
LeMoyne-Owen College B
Maryville College B
Middle Tennessee State University B, M
Milligan College B
Motlow State Community College C
Roane State Community College A
Southern Adventist University A, B
Tennessee Technological University B
University of Memphis B
University of Tennessee
   Knoxville B, M, D
   Martin B
University of the South B

Texas
Abilene Christian University B
Alvin Community College C, A
Angelo State University B
Baylor University B, M

Central Texas College C, A
Coastal Bend College A
Concordia University at Austin B
Dallas Baptist University B
Del Mar College A
El Paso Community College A
Galveston College A
Hill College C, A
Huston-Tillotson College B
LeTourneau University B
Lon Morris College A
McMurry University B
Panola College A
St. Edward's University C, B, T
St. Mary's University B
South Plains College A
Southern Methodist
  University C, B, M, D
Southwest Texas State
  University B, M, T
Southwestern Adventist University B
Tarleton State University B, T
Texas A&M University
  Commerce B, M
Texas A&M University B, M, D
Texas College B
Texas Lutheran University B
Texas Southern University B
Texas State Technical College
  Waco A
Texas Tech University M
Texas Wesleyan University B
University of Houston
  Clear Lake B, M
University of Houston B, M, D
University of Mary Hardin-Baylor B
University of Texas
  Dallas M
  El Paso M
  Pan American B, M, T
  Tyler B, M
  of the Permian Basin B
Western Texas College A
Wiley College B

Utah
Brigham Young University B, M, D
Dixie State College of Utah A, B
Salt Lake Community College A
Snow College A
University of Utah B, M, D
Weber State University B
Westminster College B

Vermont
Burlington College C
Lyndon State College A
Marlboro College B
Middlebury College B
Norwich University B
St. Michael's College B
University of Vermont B, M

Virginia
Averett College B
Bluefield College B
Bridgewater College B
Christopher Newport University B, M
Danville Community College A
ECPI College of Technology C, A
Eastern Mennonite University B
Emory & Henry College B
Ferrum College B
Hampton University B, M
Hollins University B
J. Sargeant Reynolds Community
  College A
Longwood College B, T
Mary Baldwin College B
Mary Washington College B
National Business College A
Northern Virginia Community College A
Old Dominion University B, M, D
Piedmont Virginia Community
  College A
Radford University B

Roanoke College B
Sweet Briar College B
University of Richmond B
Virginia Military Institute B
Virginia Wesleyan College B
Washington and Lee University B

Washington
Centralia College A
Eastern Washington University B, M, T
Everett Community College A
Gonzaga University B
Grays Harbor College C
Henry Cogswell College B
Lower Columbia College A
North Seattle Community College C, A
Olympic College A
Pacific Lutheran University B
Renton Technical College C, A
St. Martin's College B
Seattle University B
University of Puget Sound B, T
University of Washington B
Walla Walla College B
Walla Walla Community College C, A
Washington State University B, M, D
Western Washington University B
Whatcom Community College A
Whitworth College B, T

West Virginia
Alderson-Broaddus College A, B
College of West Virginia A, B
Concord College B
Davis and Elkins College A, B
Fairmont State College B
Glenville State College A, B
Salem-Teikyo University B
West Virginia University Institute of
  Technology B
West Virginia University B, M, D
West Virginia Wesleyan College B
Wheeling Jesuit University B

Wisconsin
Beloit College B
Carthage College B
Marquette University B
Northland College B
Ripon College B
Silver Lake College B, T
University of Wisconsin
  Green Bay B
  La Crosse B, T
  Milwaukee B
  Oshkosh B
  Parkside B
  Platteville B
  Superior B
Viterbo University T

Wyoming
Casper College A
Central Wyoming College A

Computer systems analysis

Alabama
James H. Faulkner State Community
  College C, A

Arizona
Mohave Community College C
Paradise Valley Community College C

Arkansas
University of Arkansas M

California
Cerritos Community College A
College of Marin: Kentfield A
De Anza College A
Glendale Community College C
Irvine Valley College C, A
San Bernardino Valley College C, A

San Diego City College A
University of California
  San Diego B, M, D

Colorado
Art Institute
  of Colorado A
Colorado Mountain College
  Timberline Campus A
Colorado Technical University B, M, D
Denver Technical College: A Division of
  DeVry University A, B
Technical Trades Institute A

Connecticut
Norwalk Community-Technical
  College A

Delaware
Delaware Technical and Community
  College
  Owens Campus A
  Stanton/Wilmington Campus A
  Terry Campus A

District of Columbia
George Washington University B
Southeastern University A, B, M

Florida
Brevard Community College A
Broward Community College A
Florida Community College at
  Jacksonville A
Gulf Coast Community College A
Indian River Community College A
Palm Beach Community College A
Seminole Community College A
University of Miami B

Georgia
Georgia Southwestern State University B

Illinois
De Paul University M
Parkland College C, A
William Rainey Harper College A

Indiana
Indiana University--Purdue University
  Indiana University-Purdue
    University Fort Wayne C

Iowa
Des Moines Area Community College A
Marshalltown Community College A
Northeast Iowa Community College A
St. Ambrose University B

Kansas
Independence Community College C, A
Kansas State University A
Pittsburg State University B

Kentucky
Murray State University B
Owensboro Junior College of Business A

Maine
Husson College B
Mid-State College A
St. Joseph's College C
University of Maine
  Fort Kent B

Maryland
Baltimore City Community College A
Frederick Community College A
Prince George's Community College A

Massachusetts
Clark University B
Harvard College B
Mount Ida College A
Northeastern University M
Wentworth Institute of Technology C
Worcester Polytechnic Institute B, M

Michigan
Baker College
  of Muskegon B

Lansing Community College A
Oakland Community College A
Saginaw Valley State University B
University of Detroit Mercy B

Minnesota
Hennepin Technical College C, A
Mesabi Range Community and Technical
  College A
NEI College of Technology A
Pine Technical College C, A
Winona State University B

Missouri
Missouri Southern State College B
Rockhurst University C, B
St. Louis Community College
  St. Louis Community College at
    Florissant Valley A
  St. Louis Community College at
    Forest Park A

Montana
Montana Tech of the University of
  Montana B

New Hampshire
McIntosh College A

New Mexico
Clovis Community College A
San Juan College A

New York
City University of New York
  Baruch College M
Elmira College B
Medaille College B
Rochester Institute of Technology M
State University of New York
  College of Agriculture and
    Technology at Cobleskill A
  Institute of Technology at
    Utica/Rome B
Westchester Business Institute C, A

North Carolina
Durham Technical Community
  College C, A
Mayland Community College A
Southeastern Community College A
Western Piedmont Community
  College A

Ohio
Cincinnati State Technical and
  Community College A
Jefferson Community College A
Kent State University
  Stark Campus A
Kent State University B, M, D
Miami University
  Middletown Campus A
  Oxford Campus B, M
University of Akron C, B
University of Cincinnati M
University of Dayton B
University of Findlay B

Oklahoma
Eastern Oklahoma State College A
Oklahoma Baptist University B
Oklahoma City Community College A

Oregon
Lane Community College A

Pennsylvania
Carnegie Mellon University B
Drexel University B
Grove City College B
Laurel Business Institute A
Mercyhurst College B

Rhode Island
New England Institute of
  Technology A, B

South Carolina
Midlands Technical College C

Computer systems analysis

South Dakota
South Dakota School of Mines and Technology *B*

Tennessee
Motlow State Community College *C*

Texas
El Paso Community College *A*
Texas State Technical College
　Harlingen *A*
University of Houston *B*
University of North Texas *M*
University of Texas
　El Paso *B*

Utah
LDS Business College *A*

Vermont
Champlain College *A, B*
Vermont Technical College *A, B*

Virginia
Blue Ridge Community College *C*
ECPI College of Technology *C, A*
John Tyler Community College *A*

Washington
Grays Harbor College *C*
North Seattle Community College *C, A*
Renton Technical College *C*
Whatcom Community College *A*

West Virginia
Marshall University *B*

Wisconsin
Bryant & Stratton College *A*
Carthage College *B*
Lakeshore Technical College *A*
Southwest Wisconsin Technical College *A*
University of Wisconsin
　Whitewater *B*

Wyoming
Central Wyoming College *C, A*

Computer teacher education

Arkansas
University of Central Arkansas *T*

California
California State University
　Sacramento *T*
Fresno Pacific University *M*
United States International University *M, D*

Connecticut
Western Connecticut State University *M*

District of Columbia
Trinity College *M*

Florida
Barry University *M*
Florida Institute of Technology *B, M*
Nova Southeastern University *M*
Stetson University *B, T*

Illinois
Concordia University *B, M, T*
De Paul University *B, T*
University of Illinois
　Urbana-Champaign *B, M, T*

Indiana
Ball State University *T*
Franklin College *T*
Indiana State University *T*
Indiana Wesleyan University *T*
University of Indianapolis *T*

Iowa
Clarke College *B, T*
Loras College *T*
Morningside College *M*

Kansas
Benedictine College *T*
Emporia State University *T*
Independence Community College *A*
McPherson College *B, T*
Ottawa University *T*
Pittsburg State University *B, T*
St. Mary College *T*

Kentucky
Spalding University *M*

Louisiana
Xavier University of Louisiana *M*

Maine
Thomas College *M*

Massachusetts
Lesley College *M, T*
Worcester State College *T*

Michigan
Central Michigan University *B*
Eastern Michigan University *B, T*
Grand Valley State University *T*
Michigan Technological University *T*
Northern Michigan University *B, T*

Minnesota
Minnesota State University,
　Mankato *B, T*
University of Minnesota
　Morris *T*

Mississippi
Mississippi College *M*
Mississippi State University *T*

Missouri
Fontbonne College *M*
Missouri Southern State College *B, T*
Northwest Missouri State University *M, T*
Webster University *M*

Montana
Montana State University
　Billings *T*
Western Montana College of The University of Montana *T*

Nebraska
College of Saint Mary *B, T*
Concordia University *T*
Doane College *B*
Hastings College *M*
Peru State College *B, T*
Union College *T*
University of Nebraska
　Lincoln *B, T*

Nevada
University of Nevada
　Las Vegas *B*

New Hampshire
University of New Hampshire *T*

New Jersey
Monmouth University *T*
Rowan University *T*
St. Peter's College *M, T*

New Mexico
New Mexico Institute of Mining and Technology *M*

New York
Adelphi University *M*
College of Mount St. Vincent *T*
Columbia University
　Teachers College *M*
Hofstra University *T*
Long Island University
　C. W. Post Campus *M*
Manhattan College *B, T*
Nazareth College of Rochester *M*
Russell Sage College *T*
State University of New York
　Albany *B, M, T*
　College at Buffalo *M*

North Carolina
University of North Carolina
　Greensboro *B, T*

North Dakota
Dickinson State University *B, T*
Mayville State University *B, T*

Ohio
Ashland University *M, T*
Baldwin-Wallace College *T*
Bluffton College *B*
Bowling Green State University *B, M*
Kent State University
　Stark Campus *B*
Mount Union College *T*
University of Dayton *M*
Youngstown State University *B, T*

Oklahoma
Eastern Oklahoma State College *A*
Southwestern Oklahoma State University *T*
University of Central Oklahoma *B*

Oregon
Western Oregon University *T*

Pennsylvania
California University of Pennsylvania *M*
University of Pennsylvania *M*
University of Pittsburgh
　Bradford *B*

South Dakota
Dakota State University *B, T*

Tennessee
Johnson Bible College *M*

Texas
Abilene Christian University *B, T*
Baylor University *B, T*
East Texas Baptist University *B*
Hardin-Simmons University *B, T*
Lamar University *T*
LeTourneau University *B*
McMurry University *T*
St. Mary's University *T*
Southwest Texas State University *M, T*
Texas A&M University
　Commerce *M, T*
　Corpus Christi *T*
Texas Christian University *T*
University of Houston
　Clear Lake *T*
University of Houston *T*
University of Mary Hardin-Baylor *T*
University of North Texas *M*
University of Texas
　San Antonio *T*
Wayland Baptist University *T*
West Texas A&M University *T*

Vermont
St. Michael's College *M*

Virginia
Bridgewater College *T*
Hollins University *T*
Shenandoah University *M*

Washington
Gonzaga University *M*
Heritage College *B*
Whitworth College *B, T*

Wisconsin
Alverno College *T*
Cardinal Stritch University *M, T*
Lawrence University *T*
Northland College *T*
St. Norbert College *T*
University of Wisconsin
　La Crosse *B, T*
　Whitewater *B, T*

Viterbo University *B, T*

Computer/information sciences

Alabama
Alabama Agricultural and Mechanical University *B, M*
Alabama State University *B*
Athens State University *B*
Bessemer State Technical College *C, A*
Bevill State Community College *A*
Birmingham-Southern College *B*
Calhoun Community College *C, A*
Central Alabama Community College *C, A*
Chattahoochee Valley Community College *A*
Community College of the Air Force *A*
Enterprise State Junior College *A*
Faulkner University *A*
Gadsden State Community College *C, A*
George C. Wallace State Community College
　Dothan *C, A*
　Selma *C, A*
Jacksonville State University *B*
James H. Faulkner State Community College *A*
Jefferson State Community College *A*
Northeast Alabama Community College *A*
Northwest-Shoals Community College *A*
Oakwood College *A, B*
Reid State Technical College *A*
Shelton State Community College *C*
Snead State Community College *A*
South College *A*
Southern Union State Community College *A*
Stillman College *B*
Talladega College *B*
Troy State University
　Dothan *B*
　Montgomery *A, B, M*
Troy State University *B*
Tuskegee University *B*
University of Alabama
　Birmingham *B, M, D*
　Huntsville *B, M, D*
University of Alabama *B, M, D*
University of Mobile *B*
University of North Alabama *B*
University of South Alabama *B, M*

Alaska
University of Alaska
　Fairbanks *B, M*
　Southeast *C, A*

Arizona
Arizona Western College *C, A*
Central Arizona College *C, A*
Cochise College *A*
DeVry Institute of Technology
　Phoenix *B*
Dine College *A*
Embry-Riddle Aeronautical University
　Prescott Campus *B*
Gateway Community College *C, A*
Grand Canyon University *B*
ITT Technical Institute
　Tucson *A*
Mesa Community College *A*
Mohave Community College *A*
Northern Arizona University *B*
Northland Pioneer College *C, A*
Paradise Valley Community College *C, A*
Phoenix College *A*
Pima Community College *A*
Prescott College *B, M*
Rio Salado College *C, A*
Scottsdale Community College *C, A*

South Mountain Community
    College C, A
University of Arizona B, M, D
University of Phoenix M
Yavapai College C, A

Arkansas
Arkansas State University
    Beebe Branch A
    Mountain Home C
Arkansas State University B, M
Arkansas Tech University B
Garland County Community
    College C, A
Harding University B
Henderson State University B
Hendrix College B
ITT Technical Institute
    Little Rock A
Northwest Arkansas Community
    College A
Southern Arkansas University B
University of Arkansas
    Little Rock B, M
    Monticello B
    Pine Bluff B
University of Arkansas B, M, D
University of Central Arkansas B
University of the Ozarks B
Westark College A

California
Allan Hancock College C, A
Azusa Pacific University B
Barstow College C, A
Biola University B
Butte College C, A
Cabrillo College A
California Lutheran University B
California Polytechnic State University:
    San Luis Obispo B, M
California State Polytechnic University:
    Pomona B, M
California State University
    Bakersfield B
    Chico B, M
    Dominguez Hills B, M
    Fresno B, M
    Fullerton B, M
    Hayward B, M
    Long Beach B, M
    Los Angeles B
    Monterey Bay B
    Northridge B, M
    Sacramento B, M
    San Marcos B
    Stanislaus B
Canada College C, A
Cerritos Community College A
Cerro Coso Community College C, A
Chabot College A
Chaffey Community College C, A
Chapman University B, M
Citrus College C, A
City College of San Francisco C, A
Claremont McKenna College B
Coastline Community College C, A
College of Marin: Kentfield A
College of Notre Dame B
College of San Mateo C, A
College of the Canyons A
College of the Desert C, A
College of the Redwoods C, A
College of the Sequoias C
College of the Siskiyous C, A
Columbia College C, A
Compton Community College C, A
Contra Costa College A
Crafton Hills College C, A
Cypress College C, A
De Anza College A
DeVry Institute of Technology
    Fremont B
    Long Beach B
    West Hills B
Diablo Valley College C

East Los Angeles College A
Evergreen Valley College A
Foothill College C, A
Fresno City College C, A
Fresno Pacific University B
Gavilan Community College C, A
Glendale Community College C, A
Golden Gate University C, B, M
Golden West College A
Grossmont Community College C, A
Harvey Mudd College B
Heald Business College
    Santa Rosa C, A
Humphreys College A, B
ITT Technical Institute
    Anaheim A
    Hayward A
    Lathrop A
    Rancho Cordova A
    San Bernardino A
    San Diego A
    Santa Clara A
    Sylmar A
    Torrance A
    West Covina A
Imperial Valley College A
Irvine Valley College C, A
Kings River Community College A
Lake Tahoe Community College C
Las Positas College C, A
Lincoln University B
Los Angeles Harbor College C, A
Los Angeles Mission College A
Los Angeles Pierce College C, A
Los Angeles Southwest College A
Los Angeles Trade and Technical
    College C, A
Los Medanos College C
Loyola Marymount University B
Master's College B
Mendocino College C, A
Merced College A
Merritt College C, A
Mills College B, M
MiraCosta College C, A
Mission College C
Modesto Junior College A
Monterey Peninsula College C, A
Moorpark College A
Mount San Jacinto College A
Napa Valley College A
National Hispanic University B
Orange Coast College C, A
Oxnard College A
Pacific Union College B
Palo Verde College C
Palomar College C, A
Pepperdine University B
Pomona College B
Porterville College A
Riverside Community College C, A
Sacramento City College C, A
Saddleback College C, A
San Diego City College C, A
San Diego Miramar College A
San Diego State University B, M
San Francisco State University B
San Joaquin Delta College C, A
San Jose City College A
San Jose State University B, M
Santa Ana College C, A
Santa Barbara City College C, A
Santa Monica College C
Shasta College A
Sierra College A
Skyline College C, A
Solano Community College A
Sonoma State University B
Southwestern College C, A
Stanford University B, M, D
Taft College A

University of California
    Berkeley B, M, D
    Davis B, M, D
    Irvine B, M, D
    Los Angeles B, M, D
    Riverside B, M, D
    San Diego B, M, D
    Santa Barbara B
    Santa Cruz B, M, D
University of La Verne B
University of Redlands B
University of San Diego B
University of San Francisco B, M
University of Southern
    California B, M, D
University of the Pacific B
Ventura College C, A
Victor Valley College A
West Hills Community College A
West Valley College C, A
Yuba College A

Colorado
Adams State College B
Colorado Christian University B
Colorado School of Mines B
Colorado State University B, M, D
Colorado Technical University B, M, D
Community College of Aurora C, A
Community College of Denver C, A
Lamar Community College C
Mesa State College B
Metropolitan State College of Denver B
National Technological University M
Otero Junior College C, A
Pueblo Community College C, A
Red Rocks Community College C, A
Regis University B
Technical Trades Institute A
Trinidad State Junior College A
United States Air Force Academy B
University of Colorado
    Boulder B, M, D
    Colorado Springs B
    Denver M
University of Denver B
University of Southern Colorado B

Connecticut
Asnuntuck Community-Technical
    College A
Capital Community College A
Central Connecticut State University B
Eastern Connecticut State University B
Fairfield University B
Hartford Graduate Center M
Housatonic Community-Technical
    College C, A
Mitchell College A
Naugatuck Valley Community-Technical
    College A
Quinebaug Valley Community
    College C, A
Quinnipiac University B, M
Sacred Heart University B, M
Southern Connecticut State University B
Teikyo Post University B
Three Rivers Community-Technical
    College A
Trinity College B
University of Bridgeport B, M
University of Hartford B, M
University of New Haven A, B, M
Wesleyan University B, M
Western Connecticut State University B
Yale University B, M, D

Delaware
Delaware State University B
Delaware Technical and Community
    College
    Owens Campus C, A
    Stanton/Wilmington Campus A
    Terry Campus A
Goldey-Beacom College A, B
University of Delaware B, M, D

District of Columbia
Catholic University of America B
Gallaudet University B
George Washington University B, M
Southeastern University M
University of the District of
    Columbia C, A, B

Florida
Barry University B, T
Bethune-Cookman College B
Broward Community College A
Central Florida Community College A
Chipola Junior College A
Daytona Beach Community College A
Eckerd College B
Edison Community College A
Embry-Riddle Aeronautical University B
Florida Agricultural and Mechanical
    University B
Florida Atlantic University B, M, D
Florida Gulf Coast University B
Florida International University B, M, D
Florida Memorial College B
Florida Metropolitan University
    Orlando College North A, B
Florida State University B, M, D
Gulf Coast Community College A
Hillsborough Community College A
Indian River Community College A
International College A, B
Jacksonville University B
Jones College A, B
Keiser College A
Lake City Community College A
Manatee Community College A
Miami-Dade Community College C, A
Northwood University
    Florida Campus A, B
Nova Southeastern University B, M, D
Palm Beach Community College A
Pensacola Junior College A
Polk Community College A
Rollins College B
St. Leo University B
St. Petersburg Junior College C
St. Thomas University B
Seminole Community College A
South College: Palm Beach Campus A
South Florida Community College A
Stetson University B
University of Central Florida B, M, D
University of Florida B, M
University of Miami C, B, M
University of North Florida B, M
University of Tampa A, B
University of West Florida B

Georgia
Abraham Baldwin Agricultural
    College A
Albany State University B
Armstrong Atlantic State University B
Atlanta Metropolitan College A
Augusta State University B
Clark Atlanta University B, M
Clayton College and State University B
Columbus State University B
Covenant College B
Dalton State College A
Darton College A
DeKalb Technical Institute C, A
DeVry Institute of Technology
    Alpharetta B
Emory University M
Floyd College A
Fort Valley State University B
Gainesville College A
Georgia College and State University B
Georgia Institute of Technology B, M, D
Georgia Southern University B
Georgia Southwestern State
    University B, M
Georgia State University B, M, D
Kennesaw State University B
LaGrange College B

171

Computer/information sciences

Mercer University *B*
Morehouse College *B*
Morris Brown College *B*
North Georgia College & State
   University *B*
Savannah State University *B*
Savannah Technical Institute *C, A*
Shorter College *B*
South Georgia College *A*
Southern Polytechnic State
   University *B, M*
Spelman College *B*
State University of West Georgia *B*
Truett-McConnell College *A*
University of Georgia *B, M, D*
Valdosta State University *B*
Waycross College *A*
Young Harris College *A*

Hawaii
Brigham Young University
   Hawaii *B*
Chaminade University of Honolulu *A, B*
Hawaii Pacific University *B*
University of Hawaii
   Hilo *B*
   Honolulu Community College *A*
   Leeward Community College *C, A*
   Manoa *B, M, D*

Idaho
Albertson College of Idaho *B*
Boise State University *B, M, T*
Idaho State University *B*
North Idaho College *A*
Northwest Nazarene University *B*
Ricks College *A*
University of Idaho *B, M, D*

Illinois
Barat College *B*
Benedictine University *B*
Black Hawk College
   East Campus *A*
Blackburn College *B*
Bradley University *B*
Career Colleges of Chicago *C*
Carl Sandburg College *A*
Chicago State University *B*
City Colleges of Chicago
   Harold Washington College *A*
   Harry S. Truman College *A*
   Kennedy-King College *C, A*
   Olive-Harvey College *C, A*
Concordia University *B*
Danville Area Community College *A*
De Paul University *C, B, M, D*
DeVry Institute of Technology
   Addison *B*
Dominican University *B*
Eureka College *B*
Governors State University *B, M*
Greenville College *B*
Highland Community College *A*
Illinois College *B*
Illinois Eastern Community Colleges
   Frontier Community College *C, A*
   Lincoln Trail College *A*
Illinois Institute of Technology *C, M, D*
Illinois Wesleyan University *B*
John A. Logan College *A*
John Wood Community College *A*
Joliet Junior College *C, A*
Judson College *B*
Knowledge Systems Institute *C, M*
Knox College *B*
Lake Land College *C, A*
Lewis University *B*
Lewis and Clark Community College *A*
Lincoln Land Community College *C, A*
Loyola University of Chicago *B, M*
MacCormac College *A*
MacMurray College *B*
McKendree College *B*
Monmouth College *B*
Morton College *C, A*

North Central College *B, M*
Northeastern Illinois University *B, M*
Northern Illinois University *B, M*
Northwestern Business College *A*
Oakton Community College *A*
Olivet Nazarene University *B*
Parkland College *C, A*
Quincy University *A, B*
Rend Lake College *A*
Richland Community College *A*
Rock Valley College *C, A*
Rockford College *B*
Roosevelt University *B, M*
St. Augustine College *C, A*
St. Xavier University *B*
Sauk Valley Community College *A*
Southern Illinois University
   Carbondale *B, M*
   Edwardsville *B, M*
Southwestern Ilinois College *C, A*
Trinity Christian College *B*
Trinity International University *B*
Triton College *C, A*
University of Chicago *B*
University of Illinois
   Chicago *B*
   Springfield *B, M*
   Urbana-Champaign *B, M, D*
University of St. Francis *B*
Western Illinois University *B, M*
William Rainey Harper College *A*

Indiana
Ancilla College *A*
Anderson University *B*
Ball State University *B, M*
Bethel College *A*
Butler University *B*
Calumet College of St. Joseph *A, B*
Goshen College *B*
Grace College *B*
Hanover College *B*
Indiana Institute of Technology *A, B*
Indiana State University *B*
Indiana University
   Bloomington *B, M, D*
   East *A*
   South Bend *A, B*
   Southeast *B*
Indiana University--Purdue University
   Indiana University-Purdue
     University Fort Wayne *C, A, B*
   Indiana University-Purdue
     University Indianapolis *B, M*
Indiana Wesleyan University *A, B*
International Business College *C, A*
Ivy Tech State College
   Central Indiana *A*
   Columbus *A*
   Eastcentral *C, A*
   Kokomo *C, A*
   Lafayette *C, A*
   Northcentral *C, A*
   Northeast *C, A*
   Northwest *C, A*
   Southcentral *C, A*
   Southeast *C, A*
   Southwest *A*
   Wabash Valley *C, A*
   Whitewater *C, A*
Manchester College *A, B*
Michiana College *B*
Oakland City University *C, A, B*
Purdue University
   Calumet *B*
Purdue University *B, M, D*
St. Joseph's College *B*
St. Mary-of-the-Woods College *B*
Taylor University *B*
Tri-State University *B*
University of Evansville *B*
University of Indianapolis *B*
University of Notre Dame *B*
University of Southern Indiana *B*
Valparaiso University *B*

Vincennes University *A*

Iowa
Briar Cliff College *B*
Buena Vista University *B*
Central College *B*
Clarke College *B*
Cornell College *B*
Des Moines Area Community
   College *C, A*
Dordt College *B*
Drake University *B*
Emmaus Bible College *B*
Graceland University *B*
Grand View College *B*
Indian Hills Community College *C, A*
Iowa State University *B, M, D*
Iowa Wesleyan College *B*
Loras College *B*
Luther College *B*
Maharishi University of
   Management *B, M*
Marshalltown Community College *C, A*
Marycrest International University *B*
Morningside College *B*
Mount Mercy College *B*
Northeast Iowa Community College *C*
Northwestern College *B*
St. Ambrose University *C, B*
Simpson College *B*
Southwestern Community College *C*
University of Dubuque *B*
University of Iowa *B, M, D*
University of Northern Iowa *B*
Waldorf College *A, B*
Wartburg College *B*
William Penn University *B*

Kansas
Allen County Community College *A*
Baker University *B*
Barton County Community College *A*
Bethany College *B*
Butler County Community College *C, A*
Central Christian College *A*
Coffeyville Community College *A*
Dodge City Community College *A*
Emporia State University *B*
Fort Hays State University *B*
Garden City Community College *A*
Hesston College *A*
Hutchinson Community College *A*
Independence Community College *C, A*
Kansas City Kansas Community
   College *C, A*
Kansas State University *B, M, D*
Kansas Wesleyan University *A, B*
MidAmerica Nazarene University *B*
Pittsburg State University *B, T*
Seward County Community
   College *C, A*
Southwestern College *B*
Sterling College *B*
University of Kansas *B, M, D*
Washburn University of Topeka *A, B*
Wichita State University *B, M*

Kentucky
Asbury College *B*
Bellarmine College *B*
Campbellsville University *A, B*
Cumberland College *B*
Eastern Kentucky University *B*
Georgetown College *B*
Henderson Community College *C*
Kentucky State University *B*
Lindsey Wilson College *A*
Midway College *A*
Murray State University *B*
Owensboro Junior College of
   Business *C, A*
Paducah Community College *A*
St. Catharine College *A*
Southeast Community College *A*
Spalding University *B*
Thomas More College *A, B*

Transylvania University *B*
University of Kentucky *B, M, D*
University of Louisville *M*
Western Kentucky University *B, M*

Louisiana
Bossier Parish Community College *A*
Dillard University *B*
Grantham College of Engineering *A, B*
ITT Technical Institute
   St. Rose *A*
Louisiana State University
   Alexandria *A*
   Eunice *A*
Loyola University New Orleans *B*
McNeese State University *B*
Our Lady of Holy Cross College *T*
Southern University
   Shreveport *A*
Tulane University *B, M, D*
Xavier University of Louisiana *B*

Maine
Andover College *A*
Southern Maine Technical College *A*
Thomas College *A, B*
University of Maine
   Augusta *A, B*
   Fort Kent *B*
University of Maine *B, M*

Maryland
Allegany College *A*
Anne Arundel Community College *C, A*
Baltimore City Community College *A*
Bowie State University *B, M*
Carroll Community College *C, A*
Chesapeake College *A*
College of Notre Dame of Maryland *B*
Columbia Union College *B*
Community College of Baltimore County
   Catonsville *C, A*
   Essex *C, A*
Frederick Community College *A*
Frostburg State University *B, M*
Hagerstown Community College *A*
Harford Community College *C, A*
Hood College *B, M*
Johns Hopkins University *B*
Loyola College in Maryland *B*
Montgomery College
   Germantown Campus *A*
   Rockville Campus *A*
   Takoma Park Campus *C, A*
Morgan State University *B*
Prince George's Community
   College *C, A*
Towson University *B, M*
United States Naval Academy *B*
University of Baltimore *B*
University of Maryland
   Baltimore County *B, M, D*
   College Park *B, M, D*
   Eastern Shore *B, M*
Villa Julie College *A, B*
Wor-Wic Community College *C, A*

Massachusetts
Assumption College *B*
Atlantic Union College *A, B*
Babson College *B*
Bay Path College *B*
Bay State College *A*
Becker College *C, A*
Berkshire Community College *C, A*
Boston College *B*
Boston University *B, M, D*
Bristol Community College *A*
Cape Cod Community College *A*
Clark University *B*
Elms College *C, B*
Fisher College *C, A*
Fitchburg State College *B*
Framingham State College *B*
Franklin Institute of Boston *C, A*
Gordon College *B*

Greenfield Community College A
Hampshire College B
Harvard College B
Holyoke Community College A
Marian Court College A
Massachusetts Bay Community
   College A
Massachusetts College of Liberal Arts B
Massasoit Community College C, A
Merrimack College A
Mount Wachusett Community
   College C, A
Newbury College A
North Shore Community College A
Northeastern University B, M, D
Northern Essex Community College A
Roxbury Community College C, A
Salem State College B
Simmons College B
Springfield College B
Suffolk University B, M
Tufts University B
University of Massachusetts
   Boston B
   Dartmouth B, M
Wellesley College B
Wentworth Institute of Technology B
Western New England College B
Westfield State College B
Wheaton College B
Worcester Polytechnic Institute B, M, D
Worcester State College B

Michigan
Albion College B, T
Alma College B
Alpena Community College C, A
Andrews University B, M
Aquinas College B
Baker College
   of Auburn Hills A
   of Cadillac A
   of Jackson A
   of Mount Clemens A, B
   of Muskegon B
   of Owosso B
   of Port Huron A, B
Calvin College B
Central Michigan University B, M
Cleary College A, B
Cornerstone College and Grand Rapids
   Baptist Seminary B
Davenport College of Business A, B
Delta College A
Eastern Michigan University B, M
Ferris State University C, B
Glen Oaks Community College C
Gogebic Community College A
Grand Rapids Community College C, A
Grand Valley State University B
Great Lakes College C, A
Henry Ford Community College A
Hope College B, T
ITT Technical Institute
   Grand Rapids A
   Troy A
Kalamazoo College B
Lake Superior State University A
Lansing Community College A
Lawrence Technological University B
Macomb Community College C, A
Madonna University A, B, T
Marygrove College C, B
Michigan State University B, M, D
Michigan Technological
   University B, M, T
Monroe County Community
   College C, A
Montcalm Community College A
Mott Community College A
Muskegon Community College C, A
North Central Michigan College A
Northern Michigan University A, B, T
Northwood University A, B
Oakland Community College A

Oakland University B, M
Olivet College B
Saginaw Valley State University B, T
Siena Heights University A, B
Southwestern Michigan College C, A
Spring Arbor College B
University of Detroit Mercy B, M
University of Michigan
   Dearborn A
University of Michigan B, M, D
Walsh College of Accountancy and
   Business Administration B
Washtenaw Community College A
Wayne State University C, B, M, D

Minnesota
Augsburg College B
Bemidji State University B, M
Bethel College B
College of St. Catherine: St. Paul
   Campus B
College of St. Scholastica B
Concordia College: Moorhead B
Crown College C, A, B
Gustavus Adolphus College B
Hamline University B
Hennepin Technical College C, A
Lake Superior College: A Community
   and Technical College C, A
Macalester College B
Mesabi Range Community and Technical
   College A
Minnesota State University, Mankato B
Moorhead State University B
NEI College of Technology A
National American University
   St. Paul A
North Hennepin Community College A
Northland Community & Technical
   College A
Ridgewater College: A Community and
   Technical College C, A
Rochester Community and Technical
   College A
St. Cloud State University B
St. Cloud Technical College C, A
St. Mary's University of Minnesota B
Southwest State University B
University of Minnesota
   Twin Cities M, D
University of St. Thomas B
Winona State University B

Mississippi
Alcorn State University M
Copiah-Lincoln Community College A
East Central Community College A
East Mississippi Community
   College C, A
Hinds Community College A
Holmes Community College C, A
Itawamba Community College A
Jackson State University B, M
Mary Holmes College A
Mississippi College C, B
Mississippi Gulf Coast Community
   College
      Jefferson Davis Campus A
      Perkinston A
Mississippi State University B, M, D
Mississippi Valley State University B
Northwest Mississippi Community
   College A
University of Mississippi B
University of Southern Mississippi B, M

Missouri
Avila College B
Central Methodist College B
Central Missouri State University B
College of the Ozarks B
Columbia College A, B
Crowder College A
DeVry Institute of Technology
   Kansas City B
Drury University B

East Central College A
Evangel University B
Fontbonne College B
Hannibal-LaGrange College B
Jefferson College A
Lincoln University A
Lindenwood University B
Longview Community College A
Maple Woods Community College A
Mineral Area College A
Missouri Baptist College B
Missouri Southern State University A, B
Missouri Valley College B
Missouri Western State College B
Moberly Area Community College C, A
Northwest Missouri State University B
Ozarks Technical Community College A
Park University B
Penn Valley Community College C, A
Ranken Technical College A
Rockhurst University B
St. Charles County Community
   College C, A
St. Louis University A, B
Southeast Missouri State University A, B
Southwest Baptist University B
Southwest Missouri State University B
St. Louis Community College
   St. Louis Community College at
      Florissant Valley A
   St. Louis Community College at
      Forest Park A
   St. Louis Community College at
      Meramec C, A
State Fair Community College A
Truman State University B
University of Missouri
   Columbia B, M, D
   Kansas City B, M
   Rolla B, M, D
   St. Louis B
Washington University B, M, D
Webster University B, M
Westminster College B
William Woods University B

Montana
Dawson Community College A
Miles Community College A
Montana State University
   Billings C, A, B
   College of Technology-Great
      Falls C, A
   Northern A, B
Montana Tech of the University of
   Montana: College of Technology A
Montana Tech of the University of
   Montana B
Rocky Mountain College C, A, B
Salish Kootenai College C, A
University of Great Falls A, B
University of Montana-Missoula M

Nebraska
Central Community College C, A
College of Saint Mary C, A, B
Concordia University B
Creighton University B
Doane College B
Mid Plains Community College Area A
Midland Lutheran College B
Nebraska Wesleyan University B
Peru State College B
University of Nebraska
   Kearney B
   Omaha B, M
Wayne State College B

Nevada
ITT Technical Institute
   Henderson A
University of Nevada
   Reno B
Western Nevada Community College A

New Hampshire
Antioch New England Graduate
   School M
College for Lifelong Learning C, A
Daniel Webster College B
Franklin Pierce College B
Keene State College A, B
McIntosh College C, A
New Hampshire College C, A, B
New Hampshire Community Technical
   College
      Berlin A
      Laconia C, A
      Manchester A
      Nashua C, A
New Hampshire Technical Institute C, A
St. Anselm College B
University of New
   Hampshire A, B, M, D

New Jersey
Atlantic Cape Community College A
Bergen Community College C
Bloomfield College B
Brookdale Community College A
Caldwell College C, B
Camden County College C, A
Centenary College B
College of St. Elizabeth C, B
Drew University B
Essex County College C, A
Fairleigh Dickinson University B, M
Felician College B
Gloucester County College C, A
Kean University B
Mercer County Community College C
Middlesex County College A
Monmouth University C, B, M
Montclair State University B, M
New Jersey City University B
New Jersey Institute of
   Technology B, M, D
Ocean County College A
Passaic County Community College A
Raritan Valley Community College A
Richard Stockton College of New
   Jersey B
Rider University B
Rowan University B
Rutgers
   The State University of New Jersey:
   New Brunswick Graduate
   Campus M, D
St. Peter's College B
Salem Community College C, A
Seton Hall University B
Stevens Institute of Technology B, M, D
Sussex County Community College C, A
The College of New Jersey B
Thomas Edison State College C, A, B
Union County College A
Warren County Community College C, A
William Paterson University of New
   Jersey B

New Mexico
Clovis Community College A
College of Santa Fe B
Eastern New Mexico University
   Roswell Campus A
Eastern New Mexico University B
New Mexico Highlands University B
New Mexico Institute of Mining and
   Technology B, M, D
New Mexico Junior College C, A
New Mexico State University
   Carlsbad A
New Mexico State University B, M, D
Northern New Mexico Community
   College A
San Juan College A
Santa Fe Community College A
University of New Mexico B, M, D
Western New Mexico University B

Computer/information sciences

New York
Adelphi University *B*
Adirondack Community College *A*
Alfred University *B*
Briarcliffe College *C, A*
Broome Community College *A*
Bryant & Stratton Business Institute
    Albany *A*
    Syracuse *C, A*
Cayuga County Community College *A*
City University of New York
    Baruch College *B, M*
    Borough of Manhattan Community College *A*
    Brooklyn College *B, M*
    City College *B*
    College of Staten Island *A, B, M, D*
    Graduate School and University Center *D*
    Hunter College *B, M*
    John Jay College of Criminal Justice *B*
    Kingsborough Community College *A*
    La Guardia Community College *A*
    Lehman College *B*
    Medgar Evers College *A*
    New York City Technical College *A*
    Queens College *B, M*
    Queensborough Community College *A*
Clinton Community College *A*
Colgate University *B*
College of Mount St. Vincent *B*
College of St. Rose *C, B*
Columbia University
    Fu Foundation School of Engineering and Applied Science *B, M, D*
    School of General Studies *B*
Columbia-Greene Community College *A*
Cornell University *B, M, D*
Corning Community College *C, A*
DeVry Institute of Technology
    New York *B*
Dominican College of Blauvelt *C, B*
Dowling College *B*
Dutchess Community College *A*
Erie Community College
    North Campus *A*
Finger Lakes Community College *C, A*
Fordham University *B*
Fulton-Montgomery Community College *A*
Hamilton College *B*
Hartwick College *B*
Herkimer County Community College *A*
Hobart and William Smith Colleges *B*
Hofstra University *B, M*
Iona College *C, B, M*
Ithaca College *B*
Jamestown Business College *A*
Jamestown Community College *A*
Jefferson Community College *A*
Long Island University
    Brooklyn Campus *B, M*
    C. W. Post Campus *A, B*
Manhattan College *B*
Manhattanville College *B*
Marist College *B*
Marymount College *B*
Marymount Manhattan College *C*
Medaille College *B*
Mercy College *C, B*
Mohawk Valley Community College *A*
Molloy College *B*
Monroe College *A, B*
Monroe Community College *A*
Mount St. Mary College *C, B, T*
Nassau Community College *A*
New York Institute of Technology *B, M*
New York University *B, M, D*
Niagara County Community College *A*
Niagara University *C, B*
Onondaga Community College *A*
Orange County Community College *A*
Pace University:
    Pleasantville/Briarcliff *B, M*
Pace University *B, M*
Polytechnic University
    Long Island Campus *B, M, D*
Polytechnic University *B, M*
Regents College *B*
Rensselaer Polytechnic Institute *B, M, D*
Roberts Wesleyan College *B*
Rochester Institute of Technology *A, B, M*
St. Bonaventure University *B*
St. Francis College *A*
St. John Fisher College *B*
St. John's University *C, B*
St. Thomas Aquinas College *B*
Sarah Lawrence College *B*
Schenectady County Community College *A*
Skidmore College *B*
State University of New York
    Albany *B, M, D*
    Binghamton *B, M*
    Buffalo *B, M, D*
    College at Brockport *B, M*
    College at Buffalo *B*
    College at Fredonia *B*
    College at Geneseo *B*
    College at Old Westbury *B*
    College at Oneonta *B*
    College at Plattsburgh *B*
    College at Potsdam *B*
    College of Agriculture and Technology at Cobleskill *A*
    College of Agriculture and Technology at Morrisville *A*
    College of Technology at Alfred *A*
    College of Technology at Canton *A*
    Institute of Technology at Utica/Rome *B, M*
    Oswego *B*
    Purchase *C*
Suffolk County Community College *C, A*
Syracuse University *B, M, D*
Technical Career Institutes *A*
Tompkins-Cortland Community College *A*
Touro College *B*
Trocaire College *C, A*
Ulster County Community College *A*
Union College *B, M*
United States Military Academy *B*
University of Rochester *B, M, D*
Utica College of Syracuse University *B*
Vassar College *B*
Villa Maria College of Buffalo *A*
Westchester Business Institute *C, A*
Westchester Community College *A*

North Carolina
Barton College *B*
Bennett College *B*
Bladen Community College *C, A*
Brunswick Community College *A*
Carteret Community College *C, A*
Catawba College *B*
Central Piedmont Community College *A*
College of the Albemarle *A*
Davidson County Community College *A*
Duke University *B, M, D*
Edgecombe Community College *A*
Elizabeth City State University *B*
Elon College *B*
Fayetteville State University *B*
Gardner-Webb University *B*
Guilford Technical Community College *A*
Halifax Community College *C, A*
High Point University *B*
Johnson C. Smith University *B*
Lenoir-Rhyne College *B*
Louisburg College *A*
Methodist College *A, B*
Mount Olive College *B*
North Carolina Agricultural and Technical State University *B, M*
North Carolina Central University *B*
North Carolina State University *B*
Pfeiffer University *B*
St. Augustine's College *B*
Sampson Community College *A*
Sandhills Community College *C, A*
Shaw University *B*
South Piedmont Community College *A*
Southwestern Community College *A*
University of North Carolina
    Charlotte *D*
    Greensboro *B, M*
    Pembroke *B*
    Wilmington *B*
Wake Technical Community College *C, A*
Western Carolina University *B*
Wilson Technical Community College *A*
Winston-Salem State University *B*

North Dakota
Dickinson State University *B, T*
Jamestown College *B*
Lake Region State College *C, A*
Minot State University: Bottineau Campus *A*
Minot State University *B*
North Dakota State College of Science *A*
North Dakota State University *B*
University of North Dakota *B, M*
Valley City State University *B*
Williston State College *C, A*

Ohio
Antioch College *B*
Baldwin-Wallace College *C*
Bluffton College *B*
Bowling Green State University *B, M*
Bryant & Stratton College *A*
Capital University *B*
Case Western Reserve University *B, M, D*
Cedarville College *B*
Cincinnati State Technical and Community College *A*
Cleveland State University *B, M*
College of Wooster *B*
DeVry Institute of Technology
    Columbus *B*
Defiance College *A, B*
Denison University *B*
Edison State Community College *C, A*
Franciscan University of Steubenville *B*
Heidelberg College *B*
Hiram College *B*
Hocking Technical College *A*
Jefferson Community College *A*
John Carroll University *B*
Kent State University
    East Liverpool Regional Campus *A*
    Stark Campus *B*
    Tuscarawas Campus *A*
Kent State University *B*
Lima Technical College *A*
Lorain County Community College *A*
Marietta College *B*
Marion Technical College *C, A*
Miami University
    Middletown Campus *A*
Miami-Jacobs College *C, A*
Mount Union College *B*
Mount Vernon Nazarene College *B*
Muskingum Area Technical College *A*
Muskingum College *B*
North Central State College *C, A*
Northwestern College *A*
Oberlin College *B*
Ohio Northern University *B*
Ohio State University
    Columbus Campus *B, M, D*
Ohio University *B*
Ohio Valley Business College *A*
Ohio Wesleyan University *B*
Otterbein College *B*
Owens Community College
    Toledo *C, A*
RETS Tech Center *A*
Shawnee State University *A*
Sinclair Community College *A*
University of Akron *A, B, M*
University of Cincinnati
    Raymond Walters College *A*
University of Cincinnati *B, M, T*
University of Dayton *B, M*
University of Findlay *B*
University of Rio Grande *A, B*
University of Toledo *A, B*
Walsh University *B*
Wilberforce University *B*
Wilmington College *B*
Wittenberg University *B*
Wright State University *B, M, D*
Youngstown State University *A, B*

Oklahoma
Cameron University *A, B*
Connors State College *C, A*
East Central University *B*
Eastern Oklahoma State College *A*
Langston University *B*
Murray State College *A*
Northeastern Oklahoma Agricultural and Mechanical College *A*
Northern Oklahoma College *A*
Northwestern Oklahoma State University *B*
Oklahoma Baptist University *B*
Oklahoma Christian University of Science and Arts *B*
Oklahoma City Community College *A*
Oklahoma City University *B, M*
Oklahoma Panhandle State University *B*
Oklahoma State University
    Oklahoma City *A*
    Okmulgee *A*
Oklahoma State University *B, M, D*
Oral Roberts University *B*
Redlands Community College *A*
Rose State College *A*
St. Gregory's University *B*
Southeastern Oklahoma State University *B*
Southern Nazarene University *B*
Southwestern Oklahoma State University *B*
Tulsa Community College *C, A*
University of Central Oklahoma *B*
University of Oklahoma *B, M, D*
University of Tulsa *B*
Western Oklahoma State College *A*

Oregon
Central Oregon Community College *A*
Chemeketa Community College *A*
Eastern Oregon University *B*
George Fox University *B*
Lewis & Clark College *B*
Linn-Benton Community College *A*
Mount Hood Community College *C, A*
Oregon Graduate Institute *C, M, D*
Oregon State University *B, M, D*
Pacific University *B*
Portland State University *B, M*
Southern Oregon University *B*
University of Oregon *B, M, D*

Pennsylvania
Albright College *B*
Allegheny College *B*
Allentown College of St. Francis de Sales *B, M*
Alvernia College *B*
Beaver College *C, B*
Bloomsburg University of Pennsylvania *B*
Bucknell University *B*
Bucks County Community College *A*

Butler County Community College *A*
Cabrini College *B*
California University of Pennsylvania *B*
Carlow College *B*
Carnegie Mellon University *B, M, D*
Cedar Crest College *C, B*
Central Pennsylvania College *A*
Chatham College *B*
Cheyney University of Pennsylvania *B*
Churchman Business School *C*
Clarion University of Pennsylvania *B*
College Misericordia *B*
Community College of Beaver County *A*
Community College of Philadelphia *A*
Delaware County Community College *A*
Delaware Valley College *C, A, B*
Drexel University *M*
East Stroudsburg University of
  Pennsylvania *B, M*
Edinboro University of
  Pennsylvania *A, B*
Gannon University *B*
Gettysburg College *B*
Gwynedd-Mercy College *B*
Harrisburg Area Community
  College *C, A*
Holy Family College *C, B*
ICS Center for Degree Studies *A*
Immaculata College *B*
Indiana University of Pennsylvania *B*
Johnson Technical Institute *A*
King's College *A, B*
Kutztown University of
  Pennsylvania *B, M*
La Roche College *B*
La Salle University *B, M*
Lackawanna Junior College *A*
Lafayette College *B*
Lehigh University *B, M, D*
Lincoln University *B*
Lock Haven University of
  Pennsylvania *B*
Luzerne County Community College *A*
Lycoming College *B*
Mansfield University of
  Pennsylvania *A, B*
Marywood University *B, M*
Messiah College *B*
Millersville University of
  Pennsylvania *A, B*
Montgomery County Community
  College *A*
Moravian College *B*
Mount Aloysius College *A*
Muhlenberg College *B*
Neumann College *C*
Northampton County Area Community
  College *A*
Peirce College *C, A, B*
Penn State
  Erie, The Behrend College *B*
  Harrisburg *B, M*
  University Park *B, D*
  York *A*
Pennsylvania College of Technology *A*
Philadelphia University *C, B*
Pittsburgh Technical Institute *C*
Point Park College *C, A, B*
Robert Morris College *B, M*
Rosemont College *M*
St. Francis College *B*
St. Joseph's University *C, A, B, M*
St. Vincent College *C, B*
Sawyer School *C*
Seton Hill College *C, B*
Shippensburg University of
  Pennsylvania *B, M*
Slippery Rock University of
  Pennsylvania *B*
South Hills School of Business &
  Technology *A*
Swarthmore College *B*
Thiel College *B*
Tri-State Business Institute *A*
University of Pennsylvania *B, M, D*
University of Pittsburgh
  Bradford *A, B*
  Johnstown *B*
University of Scranton *A, B*
Ursinus College *B*
Villanova University *B, M*
Waynesburg College *B*
West Chester University of
  Pennsylvania *B, M*
Westminster College *B*
Widener University *B*
Wilkes University *B*
York College of Pennsylvania *B, M*
Yorktowne Business Institute *A*

Puerto Rico
Bayamon Central University *A, B*
Caribbean University *A, B*
ICPR Junior College *A*
Inter American University of Puerto Rico
  Arecibo Campus *A, B*
  Barranquitas Campus *A, B*
  Bayamon Campus *A, B*
  Fajardo Campus *A*
  Metropolitan Campus *A, B*
  San German Campus *B*
Technological College of San Juan *C, A*
Universidad Metropolitana *B*
University of Puerto Rico
  Arecibo Campus *A, B*
  Bayamon University College *A, B*
  Mayaguez Campus *B, M*
  Ponce University College *A, B*
  Rio Piedras Campus *B*

Rhode Island
Bryant College *A, B*
Johnson & Wales University *A*
New England Institute of
  Technology *A, B*
Providence College *B*
Roger Williams University *A, B*
University of Rhode Island *B, M*

South Carolina
Benedict College *B*
Claflin University *B*
Clemson University *B, M, D*
Coastal Carolina University *B*
College of Charleston *B*
Converse College *B*
Denmark Technical College *C*
Francis Marion University *B*
Furman University *B*
Lander University *B*
Limestone College *A, B*
South Carolina State University *B*
Spartanburg Technical College *C, A*
Technical College of the
  Lowcountry *C, A*
The Citadel *B*
Tri-County Technical College *C, A*
University of South Carolina
  Spartanburg *B*
University of South Carolina *B, M, D*
Voorhees College *B*
Winthrop University *B*
Wofford College *B*
York Technical College *C*

South Dakota
Dakota State University *B, M*
Kilian Community College *A*
Mount Marty College *B*
South Dakota School of Mines and
  Technology *B, M*
South Dakota State University *B, T*
Southeast Technical Institute *A*
University of South Dakota *B, M*

Tennessee
Austin Peay State University *B*
Carson-Newman College *B*
Columbia State Community College *A*
David Lipscomb University *B*
Draughons Junior College of Business:
  Nashville *A*
East Tennessee State University *B, M*
Fisk University *B*
Freed-Hardeman University *B*
Hiwassee College *A*
Jackson State Community College *A*
Knoxville Business College *A*
Lambuth University *B*
Maryville College *B*
Middle Tennessee State University *B*
Milligan College *B*
Nashville State Technical Institute *A*
Northeast State Technical Community
  College *A*
Rhodes College *B*
Roane State Community College *A*
Tennessee State University *B*
Tennessee Technological University *B*
Tennessee Wesleyan College *B*
Trevecca Nazarene University *A, B*
Tusculum College *B*
Union University *B, T*
University of Tennessee
  Chattanooga *B, M*
  Knoxville *B, M, D*
University of the South *B*
Vanderbilt University *B, M, D*
Walters State Community College *A*

Texas
Abilene Christian University *B*
Amarillo College *C, A*
Angelina College *A*
Angelo State University *B*
Blinn College *A*
Brazosport College *A*
Cedar Valley College *A*
Central Texas College *C, A*
Coastal Bend College *A*
College of the Mainland *A*
Collin County Community College
  District *C, A*
Dallas Baptist University *B*
Del Mar College *A*
East Texas Baptist University *B*
Eastfield College *A*
El Paso Community College *C, A*
Galveston College *A*
Grayson County College *C, A*
Hardin-Simmons University *B*
Hill College *C, A*
Houston Baptist University *B*
Houston Community College
  System *C, A*
Howard College *C, A*
Howard Payne University *B, T*
Huston-Tillotson College *B*
Jarvis Christian College *B*
Kilgore College *A*
Lamar State College at Orange *C, A*
Lamar State College at Port Arthur *C, A*
Lamar University *B*
LeTourneau University *B*
Lee College *C, A*
McMurry University *B*
Midland College *A*
Midwestern State University *B, M*
Mountain View College *A*
Navarro College *C, A*
North Central Texas College *A*
North Lake College *A*
Northeast Texas Community
  College *C, A*
Northwood University: Texas
  Campus *A, B*
Palo Alto College *A*
Panola College *A*
Paul Quinn College *B*
Prairie View A&M University *B*
Rice University *B*
Richland College *A*
St. Edward's University *B, T*
St. Mary's University *B, M*
Sam Houston State University *B, M*
San Antonio College *C, A*
San Jacinto College
  North *C, A*
Schreiner College *B*
South Plains College *A*
Southern Methodist University *B, M, D*
Southwest Texas Junior College *A*
Southwest Texas State University *B, M*
Southwestern Adventist University *B*
Southwestern University *B, T*
Stephen F. Austin State
  University *B, M, T*
Sul Ross State University *B*
Tarleton State University *B, T*
Tarrant County College *C, A*
Texas A&M University
  Commerce *B*
  Corpus Christi *B, M*
Texas A&M University *B, M, D*
Texas Christian University *B, T*
Texas Lutheran University *B*
Texas Southern University *B*
Texas State Technical College
  Sweetwater *A*
  Waco *A*
Texas Tech University *B, M, D*
Texas Wesleyan University *B*
Texas Woman's University *B, T*
Trinity University *B*
Trinity Valley Community College *C, A*
Tyler Junior College *C, A*
University of Dallas *B*
University of Houston
  Clear Lake *B, M*
  Downtown *B*
  Victoria *B, T*
University of Houston *B, M, D*
University of Mary Hardin-Baylor *B*
University of North Texas *B, D*
University of Texas
  Arlington *M, D*
  Austin *B, M, D*
  Dallas *B, M, D*
  El Paso *B, M*
  San Antonio *B, M, D*
  Tyler *B, M*
Weatherford College *C, A*
West Texas A&M University *B*
Western Texas College *A*

Utah
Brigham Young University *B, M, D*
College of Eastern Utah *C*
LDS Business College *A*
Salt Lake Community College *C, A*
Snow College *A*
Southern Utah University *B*
University of Utah *B, M, D*
Utah State University *B, M*
Utah Valley State College *C, A, B*
Weber State University *A, B*

Vermont
Bennington College *B*
Castleton State College *B*
Champlain College *A, B*
College of St. Joseph in Vermont *A, B*
Johnson State College *A, B*
Lyndon State College *A, B*
Marlboro College *B*
Middlebury College *B*
Norwich University *B*
St. Michael's College *B*

Virginia
Averett College *B*
Blue Ridge Community College *C, A*
Bluefield College *B*
Christopher Newport University *B*
College of William and Mary *B, M, D*
Dabney S. Lancaster Community
  College *A*
Danville Community College *A*
ECPI College of Technology *C, A*
Eastern Mennonite University *B*
Eastern Shore Community College *C, A*
George Mason University *B, M*

Computer/information sciences

Germanna Community College A
Hampton University B
Hollins University B, M
J. Sargeant Reynolds Community
    College A
James Madison University B, M
John Tyler Community College A
Liberty University B
Longwood College B, T
Lord Fairfax Community College A
Lynchburg College B
Mary Baldwin College B
National Business College A
New River Community College A
Norfolk State University B
Northern Virginia Community College A
Old Dominion University B, M, D
Patrick Henry Community College A
Paul D. Camp Community College A
Piedmont Virginia Community
    College C, A
Radford University B
Randolph-Macon College B
Roanoke College B
St. Paul's College B
Southside Virginia Community
    College C, A
Southwest Virginia Community
    College A
Thomas Nelson Community College A
Tidewater Community College A
University of Virginia's College at
    Wise B
University of Virginia B, M, D
Virginia Commonwealth
    University B, M
Virginia Highlands Community
    College A
Virginia Polytechnic Institute and State
    University B, M, D
Virginia Union University B
Virginia Western Community College A
Washington and Lee University B

Washington
Bellevue Community College A
Big Bend Community College A
Central Washington University B
City University M
Clark College C, A
Columbia Basin College A
Edmonds Community College A
Everett Community College C, A
Evergreen State College B
Grays Harbor College A
Heritage College C, A, B
Highline Community College A
Lower Columbia College A
North Seattle Community College C, A
Olympic College A
Pacific Lutheran University B
Peninsula College A
Renton Technical College C
St. Martin's College B
Seattle Pacific University B, T
Shoreline Community College C, A
Skagit Valley College C, A
South Seattle Community College C, A
Spokane Falls Community College C, A
Tacoma Community College A
University of Puget Sound B, T
University of Washington B, M, D
Walla Walla College B
Walla Walla Community College C, A
Wenatchee Valley College C, A
Western Washington University B
Whitworth College B, T

West Virginia
Alderson-Broaddus College B
Bethany College B
Bluefield State College A, B
College of West Virginia A, B
Concord College B
Fairmont State College B
Glenville State College B

Marshall University B
Potomac State College of West Virginia
    University A
Salem-Teikyo University B
Shepherd College B
Southern West Virginia Community and
    Technical College A
University of Charleston A, B
West Virginia State College A
West Virginia University Institute of
    Technology B
West Virginia University M
West Virginia Wesleyan College B
Wheeling Jesuit University B

Wisconsin
Alverno College T
Cardinal Stritch University B
Carroll College B
Carthage College B
Chippewa Valley Technical College A
Lakeland College B
Lakeshore Technical College A
Lawrence University B
Madison Area Technical College A
Marquette University C, B
Milwaukee Area Technical College A
Nicolet Area Technical College A
Northeast Wisconsin Technical
    College C, A
Northland College B
Ripon College B
St. Norbert College B
University of Wisconsin
    Eau Claire B
    Madison B, M, D
    Milwaukee M
    Parkside B
    River Falls B
    Stevens Point B
    Superior B
    Whitewater B, T
Viterbo University B
Waukesha County Technical College A

Wyoming
Central Wyoming College A
Sheridan College A
University of Wyoming B, M, D
Western Wyoming Community
    College A

Conducting

Alabama
Alabama Agricultural and Mechanical
    University B

Alaska
University of Alaska
    Fairbanks M

Arizona
Grand Canyon University B
University of Arizona M

California
Azusa Pacific University M
California State University
    Long Beach B, M
Chapman University B
San Francisco Conservatory of Music M
San Francisco State University M
University of Southern California M, D

Colorado
University of Colorado
    Boulder M, D

Connecticut
University of Hartford M, D

District of Columbia
Catholic University of America M, D
Howard University B

Florida
Florida State University M
University of Miami M, D

Illinois
Roosevelt University B

Indiana
Butler University M
Indiana University
    Bloomington B
Valparaiso University M

Iowa
Drake University M
University of Iowa M

Kansas
University of Kansas M, D

Kentucky
Campbellsville University B

Louisiana
Loyola University New Orleans B, M

Maryland
Johns Hopkins University: Peabody
    Conservatory of Music M, D
Johns Hopkins University B, M, D

Massachusetts
Boston Conservatory M

Michigan
Calvin College B
Michigan State University M
University of Michigan D

Minnesota
Concordia College: Moorhead B

Missouri
Hannibal-LaGrange College B
University of Missouri
    Kansas City M, D
Webster University M

New Jersey
Rider University M

New York
Columbia University
    Teachers College M, D
Eastman School of Music of the
    University of Rochester M, D
Ithaca College M
Manhattan School of Music M, D
Mannes College of Music B, M
University of Rochester M, D

North Carolina
Brevard College A, B

Ohio
Bowling Green State University M
Cleveland Institute of Music B, M
Kent State University
    Stark Campus B
Kent State University M
Oberlin College B, M
Ohio University M
University of Cincinnati B, M, D

Oklahoma
University of Oklahoma M, D

Oregon
Portland State University M

Pennsylvania
Carnegie Mellon University M
Mercyhurst College B
Penn State
    University Park M
Temple University M

South Carolina
Columbia College B
University of South Carolina M, D

Texas
Arlington Baptist College B
Baylor University M
Concordia University at Austin B, T
Sam Houston State University M
Southern Methodist University M
Texas Christian University M
University of Houston D

Utah
Brigham Young University M

Virginia
Shenandoah University M

Washington
University of Washington M, D

Wisconsin
University of Wisconsin
    Madison B, M

Conservation/renewable resources

Alaska
Alaska Pacific University B, M
University of Alaska
    Fairbanks A

Arizona
Dine College A
Prescott College B, M
University of Arizona M, D

California
Butte College C, A
California State University
    Monterey Bay B
College of the Desert A
Mendocino College C, A
Shasta College C, A
Sierra College C
University of California
    Berkeley M
    Santa Cruz D
Ventura College A

Colorado
Colorado Mountain College
    Timberline Campus A
Colorado Northwestern Community
    College A
University of Denver B

Connecticut
University of Connecticut B, M

Florida
Polk Community College A
Rollins College B

Georgia
Young Harris College A

Idaho
North Idaho College A

Illinois
Joliet Junior College C

Iowa
Upper Iowa University B

Kansas
Hutchinson Community College A
Seward County Community College A

Louisiana
Tulane University B
University of Louisiana at Lafayette B

Maine
College of the Atlantic B, M
Unity College B
University of Maine
    Machias B, T
University of Maine B

Maryland
Frostburg State University *M*
Harford Community College *A*
University of Maryland
  College Park *B*
  Eastern Shore *M, D*

Massachusetts
Berkshire Community College *A*
Clark University *B, M*
Massachusetts Maritime Academy *C*

Michigan
Northern Michigan University *B*

Minnesota
Itasca Community College *A*
University of Minnesota
  Crookston *A*
  Twin Cities *M, D*
Vermilion Community College *A*

Montana
Salish Kootenai College *A*

Nebraska
Bellevue University *B*
Nebraska College of Technical
  Agriculture *A*

New Hampshire
Antioch New England Graduate
  School *M*
University of New Hampshire *B*

New Mexico
Northern New Mexico Community
  College *A*

New York
Cornell University *B*
Finger Lakes Community College *C, A*
Long Island University
  C. W. Post Campus *B*
State University of New York
  College of Agriculture and
    Technology at Cobleskill *A, B*
  College of Agriculture and
    Technology at Morrisville *A*
  College of Environmental Science
    and Forestry *B, M, D*

North Carolina
North Carolina State University *B*

Ohio
Hocking Technical College *A*
Kent State University
  Stark Campus *B*
Kent State University *B*
Muskingum College *B*
Ohio State University
  Columbus Campus *B*

Oklahoma
Murray State College *A*

Pennsylvania
Beaver College *M*
Penn State
  University Park *M, D*

South Dakota
Sinte Gleska University *C, A*

Texas
Texas A&M University
  Corpus Christi *M*
Texas Tech University *B*

Utah
Brigham Young University *B, M, D*

Vermont
Goddard College *B, M*
Johnson State College *B*
Sterling College *A, B*

Virginia
Mountain Empire Community College *A*

Washington
Grays Harbor College *C*
Washington State University *B*

Wisconsin
University of Wisconsin
  Madison *M, D*
  River Falls *B*
  Stevens Point *B, M*

Construction

Alabama
Northwest-Shoals Community College *C*

Arizona
Eastern Arizona College *C*
Gateway Community College *C*
Northland Pioneer College *C*
Pima Community College *A*
Yavapai College *C, A*

Arkansas
John Brown University *A, B*

California
Allan Hancock College *C*
Butte College *C, A*
California Polytechnic State University:
  San Luis Obispo *B*
California State University
  Fresno *B*
Chabot College *A*
City College of San Francisco *A*
College of San Mateo *C*
College of the Desert *A*
College of the Redwoods *C, A*
Compton Community College *C*
Diablo Valley College *C*
Fresno City College *C, A*
Modesto Junior College *C, A*
Orange Coast College *C, A*
Palomar College *C, A*
Pasadena City College *C, A*
Porterville College *C*
Saddleback College *C*
San Francisco State University *C*
San Joaquin Delta College *C, A*
Santa Monica College *A*
Sierra College *A*
Ventura College *C, A*
Victor Valley College *C, A*
West Valley College *C, A*

Colorado
Arapahoe Community College *C, A*
Pikes Peak Community College *C, A*

Delaware
Delaware Technical and Community
  College
    Terry Campus *A*

Florida
Brevard Community College *C, A*
Indian River Community College *C*
Lake City Community College *C*
Miami-Dade Community College *A*
Palm Beach Community College *A*
Pensacola Junior College *A*
Santa Fe Community College *A*
South Florida Community College *A*
Tallahassee Community College *A*

Georgia
Gwinnett Technical Institute *C, A*

Illinois
College of DuPage *A*
Oakton Community College *A*
Parkland College *C, A*
Southwestern Illinois College *A*
Triton College *A*
Waubonsee Community College *C*

Indiana
Indiana State University *B*

Oakland City University *C*
Purdue University *A, B*
Vincennes University *A*

Iowa
Iowa Lakes Community College *C*
Kirkwood Community College *C, A*
Southeastern Community College
  North Campus *A*

Kansas
Central Christian College *A*
Hutchinson Community College *C, A*

Kentucky
Northern Kentucky University *B*

Maine
Central Maine Technical College *C, A*
Southern Maine Technical College *A*

Maryland
Montgomery College
  Rockville Campus *A*
University of Maryland
  Eastern Shore *B*

Massachusetts
Cape Cod Community College *C*
Wentworth Institute of Technology *B*

Michigan
Delta College *A*
Ferris State University *C, B*
Gogebic Community College *A*
Jackson Community College *C, A*
Lansing Community College *C, A*
Northern Michigan University *C, A, B*
Oakland Community College *C, A*

Minnesota
Hennepin Technical College *C, A*
Inver Hills Community College *A*
Minnesota State University, Mankato *B*
University of Minnesota
  Twin Cities *B*

Mississippi
Mississippi Delta Community College *A*
Northeast Mississippi Community
  College *C*

Missouri
Longview Community College *C, A*

Montana
Miles Community College *A*

Nebraska
Central Community College *C*
Metropolitan Community College *C, A*
Mid Plains Community College
  Area *C, A*

Nevada
Western Nevada Community College *A*

New Hampshire
New Hampshire Community Technical
  College
    Laconia *C, A*
    Manchester *A*

New Jersey
Raritan Valley Community College *A*

New Mexico
Albuquerque Technical-Vocational
  Institute *A*
Northern New Mexico Community
  College *C, A*

New York
Erie Community College
  City Campus *C, A*
Fulton-Montgomery Community
  College *A*
Herkimer County Community College *A*
Hudson Valley Community College *A*
Institute of Design and Construction *A*
Orange County Community College *C*

State University of New York
  College of Agriculture and
    Technology at Morrisville *A*
  College of Environmental Science
    and Forestry *B*
  College of Technology at Alfred *A*
  College of Technology at Canton *C*
Suffolk County Community College *A*
Tompkins-Cortland Community
  College *C, A*

North Carolina
Blue Ridge Community College *C*
Cleveland Community College *C*
Haywood Community College *C, A*
Wilkes Community College *C, A*

Ohio
Columbus State Community College *A*
Jefferson Community College *A*

Oklahoma
Oklahoma State University *B*
University of Central Oklahoma *B*

Oregon
Chemeketa Community College *A*
Lane Community College *C, A*

Pennsylvania
Community College of Allegheny
  County *C, A*
Delaware County Community College *C*
Johnson Technical Institute *A*
Luzerne County Community
  College *C, A*
Penn State
  University Park *C*
Westmoreland County Community
  College *C*
Williamson Free School of Mechanical
  Trades *A*

Puerto Rico
Technological College of San Juan *C*

South Carolina
Aiken Technical College *C*
Denmark Technical College *C*
Trident Technical College *C*

Texas
Brazosport College *C, A*
Del Mar College *C, A*
Houston Community College System *C*
Odessa College *C, A*
St. Philip's College *A*
San Jacinto College
  North *C, A*
Texas A&M University
  Commerce *B*
Texas State Technical College
  Waco *A*

Utah
Snow College *C, A*
Utah Valley State College *C, A*
Weber State University *A, B*

Virginia
John Tyler Community College *C*

Washington
Olympic College *C, A*
Spokane Falls Community College *C*
Wenatchee Valley College *A*

Wisconsin
Gateway Technical College *C*
University of Wisconsin
  Platteville *B*
Western Wisconsin Technical College *C*
Wisconsin Indianhead Technical
  College *C*

Wyoming
Casper College *C, A*

Construction management

Arizona
Northern Arizona University B
Rio Salado College C, A

California
Cabrillo College C, A
California State University
 Chico B
 Fresno B
 Hayward C
City College of San Francisco A
Saddleback College C, A
Santa Rosa Junior College C
University of Southern California M

Colorado
Front Range Community College C, A
University of Denver B, M

Connecticut
Central Connecticut State University B

Delaware
Delaware Technical and Community College
 Stanton/Wilmington Campus A

Florida
Florida International University B
Hillsborough Community College A
Tallahassee Community College A

Georgia
Gwinnett Technical Institute A

Idaho
Boise State University B

Illinois
Roosevelt University M
Southwestern Illinois College C, A
Triton College C, A

Indiana
Purdue University B
Vincennes University A

Iowa
Indian Hills Community College A
Southeastern Community College
 North Campus A

Kansas
Central Christian College A
Pittsburg State University B

Kentucky
Murray State University B

Louisiana
Louisiana State University and Agricultural and Mechanical College B

Maine
University of Maine C, B

Maryland
Community College of Baltimore County
 Catonsville C, A
Montgomery College
 Rockville Campus C, A

Massachusetts
Cape Cod Community College C
Wentworth Institute of Technology B

Michigan
Andrews University M
Eastern Michigan University B
Ferris State University B
Northern Michigan University B
Oakland Community College C, A
Western Michigan University B

Minnesota
Inver Hills Community College A
Minnesota State University, Mankato B
Moorhead State University B
North Hennepin Community College A
University of Minnesota
 Twin Cities B

Nebraska
University of Nebraska
 Lincoln B

Nevada
University of Nevada
 Las Vegas B

New Mexico
Albuquerque Technical-Vocational Institute A

New York
Herkimer County Community College A
Mohawk Valley Community College A
Polytechnic University C, M
Pratt Institute B

North Dakota
North Dakota State University B

Ohio
Columbus State Community College A

Pennsylvania
Lehigh Carbon Community College A

South Dakota
South Dakota State University B

Texas
Texas A&M University M

Vermont
Vermont Technical College A

Washington
Spokane Falls Community College A

Construction trades

Alabama
Bessemer State Technical College C, A
Community College of the Air Force A
George C. Wallace State Community College
 Selma C
Northwest-Shoals Community College C
Shelton State Community College C
Wallace State Community College at Hanceville C, A

Alaska
University of Alaska
 Fairbanks A
 Southeast C, A

Arizona
Central Arizona College A
Cochise College C
Gateway Community College C, A
Northland Pioneer College C, A

California
Butte College C, A
College of the Sequoias C, A
Cuesta College C, A
Diablo Valley College C
Don Bosco Technical Institute A
Fresno City College C, A
Los Angeles Pierce College C, A
Saddleback College C, A
San Diego Mesa College C, A
San Jose City College C, A
Santa Rosa Junior College C, A

Colorado
Arapahoe Community College C
Community College of Denver A
Red Rocks Community College C, A
Trinidad State Junior College C, A

Florida
Seminole Community College C

Hawaii
University of Hawaii
 Honolulu Community College C, A

Idaho
Boise State University C

Illinois
Black Hawk College A
Joliet Junior College C, A
Lincoln Land Community College C
Parkland College C
Southwestern Ilinois College C, A
Triton College C, A

Indiana
Ivy Tech State College
 Central Indiana C, A
 Eastcentral C, A
 Kokomo C, A
 Northeast C, A
 Northwest C, A
 Wabash Valley C, A
 Whitewater C, A
Oakland City University C
Purdue University
 North Central Campus A
Vincennes University A

Iowa
Des Moines Area Community College C
Iowa Western Community College C, A
North Iowa Area Community College A

Kansas
Central Christian College A
Garden City Community College A
Kansas City Kansas Community College C

Maine
Eastern Maine Technical College C, A
Southern Maine Technical College A

Maryland
Cecil Community College C, A

Michigan
Gogebic Community College C
Jackson Community College C, A
Macomb Community College C
Northern Michigan University A, B

Minnesota
Hennepin Technical College C, A
Lake Superior College: A Community and Technical College C, A
North Hennepin Community College C, A
Ridgewater College: A Community and Technical College C
St. Cloud Technical College C

Mississippi
Meridian Community College C
Mississippi Gulf Coast Community College
 Perkinston A
Northeast Mississippi Community College C

Missouri
East Central College C, A

Montana
Flathead Valley Community College A
Miles Community College A

Nebraska
Central Community College C
Northeast Community College A
Southeast Community College
 Milford Campus A

New Hampshire
New Hampshire Community Technical College
 Berlin A
 Manchester A

New Mexico
Clovis Community College C, A

New York
City University of New York
 New York City Technical College A
Erie Community College
 North Campus A
Fulton-Montgomery Community College A
Onondaga Community College A
State University of New York
 College of Technology at Delhi C, A

North Carolina
Cape Fear Community College C
Durham Technical Community College C
Piedmont Community College C
Pitt Community College A
Roanoke-Chowan Community College C
Vance-Granville Community College C

North Dakota
North Dakota State College of Science A

Ohio
Jefferson Community College A
Ohio State University
 Agricultural Technical Institute A

Oklahoma
Northeastern Oklahoma Agricultural and Mechanical College A
Oklahoma City Community College A
Western Oklahoma State College A

Oregon
Chemeketa Community College A
Lane Community College C, A

Pennsylvania
Community College of Allegheny County C, A
Triangle Tech
 DuBois Campus A
Williamson Free School of Mechanical Trades C, A

South Carolina
Technical College of the Lowcountry C
Trident Technical College C

South Dakota
Sinte Gleska University A

Texas
Abilene Christian University A
Central Texas College C, A
Howard College C
Midland College C
San Jacinto College
 North C, A
Texas State Technical College
 Harlingen C, A

Utah
College of Eastern Utah C, A
Salt Lake Community College A

Vermont
Vermont Technical College A

Virginia
Lord Fairfax Community College C
Piedmont Virginia Community College C

Washington
Peninsula College C
Renton Technical College C

West Virginia
Fairmont State College A

Wisconsin
Chippewa Valley Technical College C
Milwaukee Area Technical College C

Western Wisconsin Technical College C

Wyoming
Laramie County Community
    College C, A

Construction/building science

Alabama
Auburn University B, M
Shelton State Community College C
Tuskegee University B

Arizona
Arizona State University B
Northern Arizona University B
Yavapai College C, A

Arkansas
John Brown University A, B

California
Fresno City College C, A
University of Southern California M

Colorado
Trinidad State Junior College C, A

Florida
Broward Community College A
Hillsborough Community College A
Indian River Community College A
Lake City Community College C
Pensacola Junior College A
South Florida Community College A

Hawaii
University of Hawaii
    Honolulu Community College A

Illinois
Joliet Junior College C, A
Lincoln Land Community College A
Parkland College C, A
Southwestern Illinois College C, A

Indiana
Purdue University
    Calumet B
Vincennes University A

Kansas
Central Christian College A
Pittsburg State University B

Kentucky
Murray State University B

Maine
Eastern Maine Technical College C, A
Southern Maine Technical College A

Maryland
Community College of Baltimore County
    Catonsville C, A
University of Maryland
    Eastern Shore B

Massachusetts
Cape Cod Community College C
Massachusetts Institute of
    Technology M, D
Wentworth Institute of Technology A, B

Michigan
Baker College
    of Jackson A
Monroe County Community
    College C, A
Northern Michigan University B
Washtenaw Community College A

Minnesota
Hennepin Technical College C, A
North Hennepin Community College A
Ridgewater College: A Community and
    Technical College C

Missouri
Washington University B, M

New York
Fulton-Montgomery Community
    College A
Rensselaer Polytechnic Institute B, M
State University of New York
    College of Agriculture and
        Technology at Morrisville A
    College of Environmental Science
        and Forestry B, M
    College of Technology at Delhi A

North Carolina
Durham Technical Community
    College C

Ohio
Columbus State Community College A
University of Akron B
University of Toledo A

Oklahoma
Oklahoma State University
    Oklahoma City A
    Okmulgee A
Oklahoma State University B
University of Oklahoma B, M
Western Oklahoma State College A

Pennsylvania
Johnson Technical Institute A

Rhode Island
New England Institute of Technology A

South Carolina
Clemson University B, M
Greenville Technical College C, A
Technical College of the
    Lowcountry C, A

Texas
Texas A&M University B, M
Texas State Technical College
    Harlingen C, A

Virginia
John Tyler Community College C
Lord Fairfax Community College C
Northern Virginia Community College C
Virginia Polytechnic Institute and State
    University B, M, D

Washington
Clark College C, A
University of Washington B, M

Construction/building technologies

Alabama
Jefferson State Community College C, A
John M. Patterson State Technical
    College C
Lawson State Community College C
Northwest-Shoals Community College C
Tuskegee University B

Arizona
Arizona State University B, M
Northern Arizona University B
Pima Community College C, A

California
Butte College C, A
California State University
    Long Beach B
College of the Desert C
College of the Redwoods A
Compton Community College C, A
Diablo Valley College C
Don Bosco Technical Institute A
Riverside Community College A
Saddleback College C
San Bernardino Valley College C
San Joaquin Delta College C

Santa Rosa Junior College C
Shasta College C, A
Sierra College A
Southwestern College C, A

Colorado
Colorado State University B
Red Rocks Community College C, A
Trinidad State Junior College A

Connecticut
Central Connecticut State University B
Norwalk Community-Technical
    College C, A

Delaware
Delaware Technical and Community
    College
    Terry Campus A

Florida
Daytona Beach Community College A
Florida Agricultural and Mechanical
    University B
Florida Community College at
    Jacksonville A
Florida International University B, M
Gulf Coast Community College A
Indian River Community College A
Lake City Community College C
Manatee Community College A
Palm Beach Community College A
Pensacola Junior College A
St. Petersburg Junior College C, A
Seminole Community College A
Tallahassee Community College A
University of Florida B, M
University of North Florida B
Valencia Community College A

Georgia
Georgia Institute of Technology B
Georgia Southern University B
Southern Polytechnic State
    University B, M

Idaho
Boise State University B
Idaho State University A
Ricks College A

Illinois
College of Lake County C, A
Joliet Junior College C, A
Oakton Community College A
Rock Valley College C, A
Southern Illinois University
    Carbondale A
    Edwardsville B
Southwestern Illinois College C, A
Triton College C, A

Indiana
Indiana State University B
Indiana University--Purdue University
    Indiana University-Purdue
        University Fort Wayne B
Purdue University
    Calumet B
Tri-State University A
Vincennes University A

Iowa
Southeastern Community College
    North Campus A

Kansas
Central Christian College A
Kansas City Kansas Community
    College C, A
Kansas State University B
Pittsburg State University B, M

Louisiana
University of Louisiana at Monroe B

Maine
Eastern Maine Technical College C, A
Southern Maine Technical College A

Maryland
Community College of Baltimore County
    Catonsville C, A

Massachusetts
Cape Cod Community College C
Fitchburg State College B
Northeastern University A

Michigan
Baker College
    of Mount Clemens A
Delta College A
Kalamazoo Valley Community
    College C
Lake Superior State University A
Lawrence Technological University A
Macomb Community College C
Mott Community College A
Northern Michigan University B
Washtenaw Community College A
Western Michigan University B

Minnesota
Hennepin Technical College C, A
Inver Hills Community College A
Lake Superior College: A Community
    and Technical College C, A
Moorhead State University B
St. Cloud Technical College C, A

Missouri
Central Missouri State University A, B
Crowder College A
Mineral Area College C, A
Ozarks Technical Community College C
Southwest Missouri State University B

Montana
Montana State University
    Bozeman B

Nebraska
University of Nebraska
    Lincoln B
    Omaha B

Nevada
University of Nevada
    Las Vegas B

New Hampshire
New Hampshire Community Technical
    College
    Manchester C, A
University of New Hampshire A

New Jersey
Essex County College A
Ocean County College C
Thomas Edison State College A, B

New Mexico
Western New Mexico University C, A

New York
Dutchess Community College A
Fulton-Montgomery Community
    College A
Herkimer County Community College A
Mohawk Valley Community College C
Monroe Community College A
Onondaga Community College A
State University of New York
    College of Environmental Science
        and Forestry B, M
    College of Technology at Alfred A
    College of Technology at Canton A
    College of Technology at Delhi A
    Farmingdale A, B
Suffolk County Community College A
Technical Career Institutes A

North Carolina
Cape Fear Community College C
Durham Technical Community
    College C
Vance-Granville Community College C

Construction/building technologies

Western Piedmont Community College *A*

North Dakota
North Dakota State College of Science *A*
North Dakota State University *B*

Ohio
Bowling Green State University *B, M*
Cincinnati State Technical and Community College *A*
Clark State Community College *A*
Columbus State Community College *A*
Jefferson Community College *A*
Lakeland Community College *C*
Ohio State University
 Columbus Campus *B*
Stark State College of Technology *A*
Terra Community College *C, A*
University of Akron
 Wayne College *A*
University of Akron *A*
University of Toledo *A, B*

Oklahoma
Oklahoma State University
 Oklahoma City *C, A*
 Okmulgee *A*
Oklahoma State University *B*
Western Oklahoma State College *A*

Oregon
Chemeketa Community College *A*
Clackamas Community College *C, A*
Lane Community College *C, A*
Portland Community College *C, A*

Pennsylvania
Community College of Allegheny County *C*
Community College of Philadelphia *A*
Delaware County Community College *A*
Harrisburg Area Community College *C, A*
Lehigh Carbon Community College *A*
Pennsylvania College of Technology *A, B*

Puerto Rico
University of Puerto Rico
 Bayamon University College *A*

Rhode Island
New England Institute of Technology *A*

South Carolina
Aiken Technical College *C*
Greenville Technical College *A*
Piedmont Technical College *C, A*
Technical College of the Lowcountry *C, A*
Trident Technical College *C*

Tennessee
Nashville State Technical Institute *A*

Texas
Howard College *C*
Midland College *C*
St. Philip's College *C, A*
San Jacinto College
 North *C, A*
Southwest Texas State University *B*
Texas A&M University
 Commerce *B*
Texas State Technical College
 Harlingen *A*
University of Houston *B*
University of North Texas *B*

Utah
Brigham Young University *B*
Salt Lake Community College *C, A*

Vermont
Vermont Technical College *A*

Virginia
J. Sargeant Reynolds Community College *A*

John Tyler Community College *C*
Lord Fairfax Community College *C*
Norfolk State University *B*
Piedmont Virginia Community College *A*

Washington
Central Washington University *B*
Eastern Washington University *B*
Edmonds Community College *C, A*
Spokane Community College *C, A*
Washington State University *B*

West Virginia
Fairmont State College *A, B*

Wisconsin
Northeast Wisconsin Technical College *C*
University of Wisconsin
 Stout *B*
Waukesha County Technical College *C*

Wyoming
Casper College *A*

Consumer resource management

Alabama
University of Alabama *B, M*

Arizona
Arizona State University *B, M*
Arizona Western College *A*
University of Arizona *B, M, D*

California
Allan Hancock College *A*
California State University
 Fresno *B*
 Long Beach *B*
College of the Redwoods *C*
College of the Sequoias *C*
College of the Siskiyous *C, A*
Glendale Community College *A*
Los Angeles Harbor College *A*
Los Angeles Mission College *A*
Los Angeles Southwest College *A*
Ohlone College *C, A*
Pacific Union College *A*
Palomar College *C, A*
Sacramento City College *C, A*
Saddleback College *C*
San Bernardino Valley College *A*

Colorado
Colorado State University *B, M*

Connecticut
University of Connecticut *B*

Delaware
University of Delaware *B*

Florida
Florida State University *B, M*
Palm Beach Community College *A*

Georgia
University of Georgia *B*

Hawaii
University of Hawaii
 Manoa *B*

Illinois
Bradley University *B, T*
Southern Illinois University
 Carbondale *B*
University of Illinois
 Urbana-Champaign *B, M, D*

Indiana
Indiana State University *B, M*
Purdue University *B*

Iowa
Iowa State University *B*

Kansas
Kansas State University *B*

Kentucky
University of Kentucky *B*

Louisiana
Louisiana Tech University *B*
Southeastern Louisiana University *B*

Maine
Husson College *B*

Maryland
University of Maryland
 Eastern Shore *B*

Massachusetts
Framingham State College *B, M*
University of Massachusetts
 Amherst *B*

Michigan
Andrews University *B*
Central Michigan University *B*
Eastern Michigan University *B*
Madonna University *B*
Michigan State University *B, M*
Western Michigan University *B*

Minnesota
Minnesota State University,
 Mankato *B, M*
St. Olaf College *B, T*
University of Minnesota
 Twin Cities *B, M, D*

Mississippi
Mississippi College *B*
University of Southern Mississippi *M*

Missouri
Fontbonne College *B*
Southeast Missouri State University *B*
University of Missouri
 Columbia *B, M*

Nebraska
University of Nebraska
 Lincoln *B, M*
 Omaha *B*

New Mexico
New Mexico State University *M*

New York
City University of New York
 Queens College *B*
Cornell University *B, M, D*
State University of New York
 College at Oneonta *B*
Syracuse University *B, M*

North Dakota
North Dakota State University *B*

Ohio
Baldwin-Wallace College *B*
Bowling Green State University *B*
Kent State University *B, T*
Ohio State University
 Columbus Campus *B, M, D*

Oklahoma
Oklahoma State University *B, M, D*
Southern Nazarene University *A, B*

Oregon
George Fox University *B*
Oregon State University *M, D*

Pennsylvania
Immaculata College *B*
Indiana University of Pennsylvania *B*
Mercyhurst College *B*

South Dakota
South Dakota State University *B*

Tennessee
David Lipscomb University *B*
Freed-Hardeman University *B*

Lambuth University *B*
Middle Tennessee State University *B*
Tennessee State University *B*
University of Memphis *B, M*

Texas
Southwest Texas State University *B*
Texas Tech University *D*
Texas Woman's University *B*

Utah
University of Utah *B*
Utah State University *B, M, D*

Vermont
University of Vermont *B*

Virginia
Norfolk State University *B*

Washington
Seattle Pacific University *B, T*

Wisconsin
Mount Mary College *B*
University of Wisconsin
 Madison *B, M*

Corrections administration

Alabama
Troy State University *B, M*

Arizona
Central Arizona College *C, A*
Eastern Arizona College *A*
Northland Pioneer College *C, A*

California
California State University
 Hayward *B*
College of the Redwoods *C*
Fresno City College *C, A*
Gavilan Community College *C, A*
Grossmont Community College *C, A*
Imperial Valley College *C, A*
Sacramento City College *C, A*
Santa Ana College *C*

Colorado
Pueblo Community College *A*

District of Columbia
University of the District of Columbia *A*

Florida
Gulf Coast Community College *C*
Hillsborough Community College *C*
Lake City Community College *C*
Seminole Community College *C*
South Florida Community College *C*
Valencia Community College *C*

Idaho
Ricks College *A*

Illinois
City Colleges of Chicago
 Harold Washington College *A*
Elgin Community College *A*
Triton College *C*

Indiana
Vincennes University *A*

Iowa
Kirkwood Community College *C, A*
Simpson College *B*

Kansas
Cowley County Community College *A*
Kansas City Kansas Community College *A*

Kentucky
Eastern Kentucky University *A, B*

Louisiana
Bossier Parish Community College *A*

Maryland
Baltimore City Community College C, A
Community College of Baltimore County
  Catonsville C, A
Coppin State College M
University of Baltimore C
Wor-Wic Community College A

Massachusetts
Bristol Community College C
Holyoke Community College C

Michigan
Alpena Community College C, A
Ferris State University M
Glen Oaks Community College C
Gogebic Community College C
Kellogg Community College C, A
Kirtland Community College A
Lake Michigan College A
Marygrove College C, A
Northwestern Michigan College C
Oakland Community College C, A
St. Clair County Community College C
Schoolcraft College A
Washtenaw Community College A

Minnesota
Lake Superior College: A Community
  and Technical College C
Northland Community & Technical
  College A
Winona State University B

Missouri
College of the Ozarks B
Longview Community College C, A
Penn Valley Community College C, A
St. Louis University B

Nevada
Community College of Southern
  Nevada A
Western Nevada Community
  College C, A

New Hampshire
Hesser College A

New Jersey
Burlington County College C
Middlesex County College A

New Mexico
University of New Mexico B

New York
Herkimer County Community College C
Monroe Community College C, A
Westchester Community College A

Ohio
Belmont Technical College A
Clark State Community College A
Columbus State Community College A
Hocking Technical College A
Lakeland Community College C, A
Lima Technical College A
Tiffin University B
University of Akron B
Xavier University A
Youngstown State University A, B, M

Oklahoma
Langston University B
Western Oklahoma State College A

Oregon
Clackamas Community College C, A
Western Oregon University M

Pennsylvania
Bucks County Community College A
Community College of Allegheny
  County A
York College of Pennsylvania A, B

Puerto Rico
Universidad Metropolitana B

Rhode Island
Community College of Rhode Island A
Salve Regina University M

Texas
Alvin Community College C
Amarillo College A
Central Texas College C
Coastal Bend College C, A
El Paso Community College C, A
Hardin-Simmons University B
St. Mary's University M
Sam Houston State University B
Southwest Texas State University B
Stephen F. Austin State University B
University of Texas
  Brownsville B
Weatherford College A
Western Texas College A

Utah
Weber State University B

Virginia
Southwest Virginia Community
  College A

Washington
Spokane Community College C, A
Tacoma Community College A
Walla Walla Community College A

West Virginia
Bluefield State College A

Wisconsin
Moraine Park Technical College A

Cosmetic services

Alabama
Calhoun Community College C
Gadsden State Community College C
George C. Wallace State Community
  College
    Dothan C
Harry M. Ayers State Technical
  College C
J. F. Drake State Technical College C
John M. Patterson State Technical
  College C
Northwest-Shoals Community College C
Reid State Technical College C
Shelton State Community College C
Wallace State Community College at
  Hanceville C

Arizona
Northland Pioneer College C, A

California
Allan Hancock College C, A
Butte College C, A
College of the Sequoias C, A
Compton Community College C, A
Contra Costa College A
Fashion Institute of Design and
  Merchandising A
Gavilan Community College C, A
Glendale Community College A
Golden West College C, A
Los Medanos College C
Merced College C
MiraCosta College C, A
Napa Valley College C
Riverside Community College C, A
Sacramento City College C, A
Saddleback College C
San Jose City College C, A
Santa Ana College C, A
Santa Barbara City College C, A
Skyline College C, A
Solano Community College C, A

Colorado
Lamar Community College C
Northeastern Junior College C
Trinidad State Junior College C, A

Florida
Brevard Community College C
Central Florida Community College C
Daytona Beach Community College C
Indian River Community College C
Lake City Community College C
Pasco-Hernando Community College C
Pensacola Junior College C
Seminole Community College C
South Florida Community College C

Georgia
Chattahoochee Technical Institute C
Columbus Technical Institute C
DeKalb Technical Institute C
Waycross College A

Hawaii
University of Hawaii
  Honolulu Community College C, A

Idaho
Idaho State University C

Illinois
Black Hawk College C
Danville Area Community College C, A
Highland Community College C
Illinois Eastern Community Colleges
  Olney Central College C
John A. Logan College C, A
Kaskaskia College C
Lake Land College C
Southwestern Ilinois College C
Waubonsee Community College C

Indiana
Ivy Tech State College
  Wabash Valley C
Vincennes University A

Iowa
Southeastern Community College
  North Campus C

Kansas
Barton County Community College C, A
Cowley County Community
  College C, A
Garden City Community College C
Johnson County Community College C

Massachusetts
Greenfield Community College C, A
North Shore Community College C
Springfield Technical Community
  College C, A

Michigan
Gogebic Community College A
Kirtland Community College C
Lansing Community College A
Montcalm Community College C, A
Northern Michigan University C
Oakland Community College C, A

Minnesota
Century Community and Technical
  College C
Minneapolis Community and Technical
  College C
Minnesota State College - Southeast
  Technical C, A
Northland Community & Technical
  College A
St. Paul Technical College C, A

Mississippi
Coahoma Community College C
Holmes Community College C
Mississippi Gulf Coast Community
  College
    Perkinston C

New Jersey
Ocean County College C

New Mexico
Albuquerque Technical-Vocational
  Institute A
New Mexico Junior College C, A
Northern New Mexico Community
  College C, A

North Carolina
Alamance Community College C
Beaufort County Community College C
Bladen Community College C
Blue Ridge Community College C
Brunswick Community College C, A
Caldwell Community College and
  Technical Institute C
Cape Fear Community College C
Central Carolina Community College A
Coastal Carolina Community
  College C, A
College of the Albemarle C
Craven Community College C
Davidson County Community College C
Edgecombe Community College C
Fayetteville Technical Community
  College C
Guilford Technical Community
  College C
Haywood Community College C, A
James Sprunt Community College C
Johnston Community College C
Lenoir Community College C
Martin Community College C
Mayland Community College C, A
Mitchell Community College C
Nash Community College C
Piedmont Community College C, A
Pitt Community College C
Rockingham Community College C
Sampson Community College A
Sandhills Community College C, A
Southeastern Community College C
Vance-Granville Community College C
Wayne Community College C
Wilson Technical Community College C

Oregon
Mount Hood Community College A

Pennsylvania
Community College of Allegheny
  County A

South Carolina
Denmark Technical College C
Florence-Darlington Technical
  College C
Technical College of the
  Lowcountry C, A
Trident Technical College C

Texas
Central Texas College C
Del Mar College C
Grayson County College A
Houston Community College System C
Lamar State College at Port Arthur C, A
Lee College C
Northeast Texas Community
  College C, A
Odessa College C, A
Panola College C
San Jacinto College
  North C, A
Trinity Valley Community College C
Vernon Regional Junior College C
Weatherford College C, A

Utah
College of Eastern Utah A
Salt Lake Community College A

Washington
Everett Community College A
Lake Washington Technical College C
Olympic College C, A
Renton Technical College C
Seattle Central Community College C, A

Shoreline Community College C
Spokane Community College C, A
Walla Walla Community College C, A

Wisconsin
Chippewa Valley Technical College C
Gateway Technical College C
Madison Area Technical College A
Moraine Park Technical College C
Nicolet Area Technical College C
Southwest Wisconsin Technical College C
Wisconsin Indianhead Technical College C

Wyoming
Eastern Wyoming College C, A
Sheridan College A

Counseling psychology

Alabama
Alabama Agricultural and Mechanical University M
Auburn University D
Northwest-Shoals Community College A
Samford University B
Troy State University Montgomery M
Troy State University M
University of North Alabama M

Alaska
Alaska Pacific University M

Arizona
Northern Arizona University M
Prescott College B, M
Southwestern College B
University of Phoenix M

Arkansas
Arkansas State University M
University of Central Arkansas M

California
California Baptist University M
California State University
    Bakersfield M
    Chico T
    Fullerton M
    Hayward M
    Long Beach M
    Stanislaus M
Chapman University M
College of Notre Dame M
Compton Community College A
Dominican University of California M
East Los Angeles College A
Holy Names College M
Hope International University M
John F. Kennedy University M
Loyola Marymount University B, M
Mount St. Mary's College M
National University M, T
Pacific Oaks College B, M
Santa Clara University M
United States International University M
University of California Santa Barbara M, D
University of La Verne M

Colorado
Adams State College M
Naropa University M
University of Denver M, D
University of Northern Colorado M, D
Western State College of Colorado B

Connecticut
Asnuntuck Community-Technical College A
Southern Connecticut State University M
University of Hartford M

District of Columbia
George Washington University M

Howard University M

Florida
Carlos Albizu University M
Nova Southeastern University M
Palm Beach Atlantic College M
Rollins College M
St. Thomas University M
University of Florida D
University of Miami M, D
University of North Florida M

Georgia
Atlanta Christian College B
Clark Atlanta University M, D
Georgia State University D
Toccoa Falls College B
University of Georgia D
Valdosta State University M

Hawaii
Chaminade University of Honolulu M

Illinois
Adler School of Professional Psychology M
Chicago State University M
Governors State University M
Lewis University M
Loyola University of Chicago M, D
Northwestern University M
Roosevelt University M
St. Xavier University C, M
Trinity International University M
University of Illinois Springfield M

Indiana
Ball State University M, D
Grace College M
Indiana State University M, D
Indiana Wesleyan University A, B, M
Manchester College B
University of St. Francis M
Valparaiso University M

Iowa
Morningside College B
University of Iowa D

Kansas
Central Christian College A
Kansas Wesleyan University B
Pittsburg State University B, M, T
University of Kansas M, D

Kentucky
Kentucky Christian College B
Lindsey Wilson College B

Louisiana
Louisiana Tech University D
Nicholls State University M
Southern University and Agricultural and Mechanical College M

Maine
University of Maine M, D

Maryland
Bowie State University M
Columbia Union College B
Frostburg State University M
Loyola College in Maryland M
University of Baltimore M

Massachusetts
Anna Maria College B, M
Assumption College M
Boston University D
Cambridge College M
Clark University M, D
Eastern Nazarene College M
Fitchburg State College M
Framingham State College M
Lesley College B, M
Northeastern University M, D
Salem State College M
Simon's Rock College of Bard B

Springfield College M
Suffolk University M
Tufts University M
University of Massachusetts Amherst D
Westfield State College M

Michigan
Michigan State University M, D
Western Michigan University M, D
William Tyndale College B

Minnesota
Bethel College M
Minnesota State University, Mankato M
Ridgewater College: A Community and Technical College A
St. Cloud State University M
St. Mary's University of Minnesota M
University of St. Thomas M, D

Mississippi
Mississippi College M
University of Southern Mississippi M, D
William Carey College M

Missouri
Avila College M
Central Missouri State University M
Lindenwood University M
Northwest Missouri State University M
Southeast Missouri State University M
University of Missouri Columbia M, D
    Kansas City M, D
Webster University M

Montana
University of Great Falls B, M

Nebraska
Doane College M
Wayne State College B

Nevada
University of Nevada Las Vegas M

New Hampshire
Antioch New England Graduate School M, D
Notre Dame College M
Rivier College M

New Jersey
Caldwell College M
Centenary College M
College of St. Elizabeth M
Georgian Court College M
Monmouth University M
New Jersey City University M
Rider University M
Rutgers
    The State University of New Jersey: New Brunswick Graduate Campus M
Seton Hall University D

New Mexico
New Mexico State University D
University of New Mexico D

New York
Adelphi University M, D
Audrey Cohen College A, B
City University of New York Brooklyn College M
College of New Rochelle M
Columbia University Teachers College M, D
Fordham University M, D
Marist College M
New York University D
Pace University: Pleasantville/Briarcliff M
Pace University M
St. Bonaventure University M

State University of New York
    Albany D
    Buffalo D
    Oswego M

North Carolina
Appalachian State University B, M
Catawba College B
Gardner-Webb University M

North Dakota
Trinity Bible College B
University of North Dakota D

Ohio
Circleville Bible College B
Franciscan University of Steubenville M
Heidelberg College M
John Carroll University M
University of Akron M, D
University of Cincinnati Raymond Walters College C
Walsh University B, M
Wright State University M

Oklahoma
East Central University M
Northeastern State University M
Northwestern Oklahoma State University M
Southeastern Oklahoma State University M
Southern Nazarene University M
University of Central Oklahoma M
University of Oklahoma D
University of Tulsa M

Oregon
George Fox University M
Lewis & Clark College M
Oregon State University M, D

Pennsylvania
Beaver College M
Chatham College M
Chestnut Hill College C, M, D
Gannon University M, D
Geneva College B
Holy Family College M
Immaculata College B, M, D
Indiana University of Pennsylvania M
Kutztown University of Pennsylvania B, M
La Salle University M
MCP Hahnemann University M
Marywood University M
Penn State
    Harrisburg B
    University Park D
Rosemont College M
Seton Hill College M
Temple University M, D
University of Scranton M
Villanova University M
West Chester University of Pennsylvania M

Puerto Rico
Inter American University of Puerto Rico Metropolitan Campus M

Rhode Island
Salve Regina University M

South Carolina
Columbia International University M
Lander University B

South Dakota
Sinte Gleska University B

Tennessee
Crichton College B
Johnson Bible College M
Lee University B, M
Southern Adventist University M
Trevecca Nazarene University M
University of Memphis D

University of Tennessee
    Knoxville M

Texas
Abilene Christian University M
Amber University M
Angelo State University M
Dallas Baptist University M
Lamar University M
Midwestern State University M
Our Lady of the Lake University of San
    Antonio M, D
Prairie View A&M University M
St. Mary's University M, D
Southern Methodist University M
Southwest Texas State University M
Stephen F. Austin State University M
Tarleton State University B, M
Texas A&M International University M
Texas A&M University
    Commerce B, M, D
    Kingsville M
    Texarkana M
Texas A&M University D
Texas Tech University M, D
Texas Woman's University M, D
University of Houston
    Victoria M
University of Houston D
University of Mary Hardin-Baylor M
University of North Texas B, M, D
University of Texas
    Tyler M
West Texas A&M University M

Vermont
Burlington College B
College of St. Joseph in Vermont M
Goddard College M
Johnson State College M
Marlboro College B

Virginia
Eastern Mennonite University M
Liberty University M
Longwood College M
Regent University D
Virginia Commonwealth
    University M, D

Washington
Central Washington University M
City University M
Eastern Washington University M
Evergreen State College B
Gonzaga University M
Pacific Lutheran University M
St. Martin's College M
Western Washington University M

West Virginia
Marshall University B, M

Wisconsin
Marquette University D
University of Wisconsin
    Madison M, D
    Whitewater M
Viterbo University B

Counselor education

Alabama
Alabama Agricultural and Mechanical
    University B, M
Alabama State University M
Auburn University at Montgomery M
Auburn University M, D, T
Jacksonville State University M
Troy State University
    Montgomery M
Troy State University M
Tuskegee University M
University of Alabama
    Birmingham M
University of Alabama M, D

University of Montevallo M
University of North Alabama M
University of South Alabama M, D, T
University of West Alabama M

Alaska
University of Alaska
    Anchorage M
    Fairbanks M

Arizona
Arizona State University M, D
Northern Arizona University M
Prescott College B, M
University of Arizona M, D
University of Phoenix M

Arkansas
Arkansas State University M, T
Henderson State University M
John Brown University M
Southern Arkansas University M
University of Arkansas
    Little Rock M
University of Arkansas M, D
University of Central Arkansas M

California
Azusa Pacific University M
Barstow College A
California Lutheran University M
California Polytechnic State University:
    San Luis Obispo M
California State University
    Bakersfield M
    Chico T
    Dominguez Hills M
    Fresno M
    Hayward M, T
    Long Beach M
    Northridge M
    Sacramento M, T
    Stanislaus M
Chapman University M, T
Fresno Pacific University M, T
Humboldt State University T
La Sierra University M
Mount St. Mary's College M
Point Loma Nazarene University M
San Diego State University M, T
San Francisco State University M
San Jose State University M
Sonoma State University M
University of California
    Berkeley T
    Santa Barbara M
University of La Verne M
University of Redlands M
University of San Diego M
University of San Francisco T
University of Southern California M, D
Whittier College M

Colorado
Adams State College M
University of Colorado
    Colorado Springs M
    Denver M
University of Northern Colorado M, D, T
University of Southern Colorado M

Connecticut
Central Connecticut State University M
Fairfield University M
St. Joseph College M
Southern Connecticut State University M
University of Bridgeport M
University of Hartford M, T
Western Connecticut State University M

Delaware
University of Delaware M
Wilmington College M

District of Columbia
Catholic University of America M, D
Gallaudet University M
George Washington University M, D

Howard University M
Trinity College M
University of the District of Columbia M

Florida
Barry University M
Carlos Albizu University M
Florida Atlantic University M
Florida Gulf Coast University M
Florida International University M
Florida State University M, D
Nova Southeastern University M
St. Thomas University M
Stetson University M
University of Central Florida M
University of Florida D
University of North Florida M
University of South Florida M

Georgia
Albany State University M
Augusta State University M
Clark Atlanta University M, D
Columbus State University M
Fort Valley State University M
Georgia Southern University M, T
Georgia State University D
University of Georgia M

Hawaii
University of Hawaii
    Manoa M

Idaho
Boise State University M, D
Idaho State University M, D
Northwest Nazarene University M
University of Idaho M

Illinois
Bradley University M
Chicago State University M
Concordia University M
De Paul University M
Eastern Illinois University M
Governors State University M
Loyola University of Chicago D
Northeastern Illinois University M
Northern Illinois University M, D
Northwestern University M, D
Roosevelt University M
Western Illinois University M

Indiana
Ball State University T
Butler University M
Indiana University
    Bloomington M, D
    South Bend M
    Southeast M
Indiana University--Purdue University
    Indiana University-Purdue
        University Fort Wayne M
    Indiana University-Purdue
        University Indianapolis M
Purdue University
    Calumet M
University of St. Francis M

Iowa
Buena Vista University M
Drake University M
Iowa State University M, T
University of Iowa M, D
University of Northern Iowa M

Kansas
Central Christian College A
Emporia State University M
Fort Hays State University M
Independence Community College A
Kansas State University M, D
Pittsburg State University M
University of Kansas M
Wichita State University M

Kentucky
Eastern Kentucky University M

Morehead State University M
Murray State University M
Spalding University M
University of Kentucky M, D
University of Louisville M, D
Western Kentucky University M

Louisiana
Louisiana State University and
    Agricultural and Mechanical
    College M
Louisiana Tech University M
Loyola University New Orleans M
McNeese State University M, T
Northwestern State University M, T
Our Lady of Holy Cross College M
Southeastern Louisiana University M
Southern University and Agricultural and
    Mechanical College M
University of Louisiana at Lafayette M
University of Louisiana at Monroe M
University of New Orleans M, D
Xavier University of Louisiana M

Maine
University of Maine M, D
University of Southern Maine M

Maryland
Bowie State University M
Frostburg State University M
Loyola College in Maryland M
University of Maryland
    College Park M, D, T
    Eastern Shore M
Western Maryland College M

Massachusetts
Boston College M, D
Boston University M, D, T
Bridgewater State College M, T
Fitchburg State College M
Lesley College T
Northeastern University M
Salem State College M
Springfield College M
University of Massachusetts
    Boston M
Westfield State College M

Michigan
Andrews University M, D
Central Michigan University M
Eastern Michigan University M
Michigan State University M, D
Oakland University M, D
Siena Heights University M
University of Detroit Mercy M
Wayne State University M, D
Western Michigan University M, D

Minnesota
Minnesota State University, Mankato M
Moorhead State University M
Ridgewater College: A Community and
    Technical College A
St. Cloud State University M
Winona State University M

Mississippi
Delta State University M
Jackson State University M
Mississippi College M
Mississippi State University M, T
University of Southern Mississippi B, M

Missouri
Central Missouri State University M
Lincoln University M
Lindenwood University M
Northwest Missouri State
    University M, T
St. Louis University M, D
Southeast Missouri State University M
Southwest Missouri State University M
Stephens College M
Truman State University M

University of Missouri
   Columbia *M, D*
   Kansas City *M*
   St. Louis *M*

Montana

Montana State University
   Billings *M*
   Northern *M*
University of Great Falls *D*
University of Montana-Missoula *M, D*

Nebraska

Chadron State College *M*
Creighton University *M*
University of Nebraska
   Kearney *M, T*
   Omaha *M*

Nevada

University of Nevada
   Las Vegas *M*
   Reno *M, D*

New Hampshire

Antioch New England Graduate
  School *M*
Notre Dame College *M*
Plymouth State College of the University
  System of New Hampshire *M*
Rivier College *M*
University of New Hampshire *M*

New Jersey

Kean University *M*
Monmouth University *M*
Montclair State University *M*
Rider University *M*
Rowan University *M*
Seton Hall University *M*
The College of New Jersey *M*

New Mexico

College of Santa Fe *M*
College of the Southwest *M*
Eastern New Mexico University *M*
New Mexico Highlands University *M*
New Mexico State University *M, D*
University of New Mexico *M, D, T*
Western New Mexico University *M, T*

New York

Alfred University *M*
Canisius College *M, T*
City University of New York
   Brooklyn College *M*
   College of Staten Island *M*
   Hunter College *M*
   Queens College *M*
College of New Rochelle *M*
College of St. Rose *C, M*
Columbia University
   Teachers College *M*
Hofstra University *M, T*
Long Island University
   Brooklyn Campus *M*
   C. W. Post Campus *M*
Manhattan College *M*
New York University *M, D*
Niagara University *M*
St. John's University *M, T*
St. Lawrence University *M*
State University of New York
   Albany *M*
   Buffalo *M, D, T*
   College at Brockport *M*
   College at Buffalo *M*
   College at Oneonta *M*
   College at Plattsburgh *M, T*
   Oswego *M*
Syracuse University *M, D*
University of Rochester *M*

North Carolina

Appalachian State University *M*
Campbell University *M*
East Carolina University *M, T*
Gardner-Webb University *M*
Lenoir-Rhyne College *M*
North Carolina Agricultural and
  Technical State University *M*
North Carolina Central University *M*
North Carolina State University *M, D*
University of North Carolina
   Chapel Hill *M*
   Charlotte *M*
   Greensboro *M, D*
   Pembroke *M, T*
Wake Forest University *M, T*

North Dakota

North Dakota State University *M*
University of North Dakota *M, D*

Ohio

Bowling Green State University *M*
Cleveland State University *M, D*
Heidelberg College *M*
John Carroll University *C, M*
Kent State University *M*
Malone College *M*
Ohio State University
   Columbus Campus *M, D*
Ohio University *M, D*
University of Akron *M, D*
University of Cincinnati *M, D*
University of Dayton *M*
University of Toledo *M, D, T*
Wright State University *M*
Xavier University *M*
Youngstown State University *M*

Oklahoma

East Central University *M, T*
Northeastern State University *M*
Northwestern Oklahoma State
  University *M, T*
Oklahoma State University *M, D*
Southeastern Oklahoma State
  University *M, T*
Southwestern Oklahoma State
  University *M, T*
University of Central Oklahoma *M*
University of Oklahoma *M*

Oregon

Lewis & Clark College *M*
Oregon State University *M, D*
Portland State University *M, T*
University of Oregon *M, D*

Pennsylvania

Bucknell University *M*
California University of
  Pennsylvania *M, T*
Duquesne University *M*
Eastern College *M*
Edinboro University of Pennsylvania *M*
Gwynedd-Mercy College *M*
Indiana University of Pennsylvania *M, D*
Kutztown University of
  Pennsylvania *B, M*
Lehigh University *M, D*
Marywood University *M, T*
Millersville University of
  Pennsylvania *M*
Penn State
   University Park *M, D*
Philadelphia College of Bible *M*
Shippensburg University of
  Pennsylvania *M, T*
Slippery Rock University of
  Pennsylvania *M*
University of Pennsylvania *M, D, T*
University of Scranton *M*
Villanova University *M*
West Chester University of
  Pennsylvania *M*
Westminster College *M*

Puerto Rico

Bayamon Central University *M*
Inter American University of Puerto Rico
   Metropolitan Campus *M*
   San German Campus *M*
Pontifical Catholic University of Puerto
  Rico *M*
Turabo University *M*
University of Puerto Rico
   Rio Piedras Campus *M, D*

Rhode Island

Providence College *M*
Rhode Island College *M*
University of Rhode Island *M*

South Carolina

Clemson University *M*
South Carolina State University *M*
The Citadel *M*
University of South Carolina *M, D*
Winthrop University *M, T*

South Dakota

Northern State University *M*
South Dakota State University *M*
University of South Dakota *M, D*

Tennessee

Austin Peay State University *M*
Carson-Newman College *M*
East Tennessee State University *M, T*
Lincoln Memorial University *M*
Middle Tennessee State University *M*
Tennessee State University *M*
Tennessee Technological University *M*
University of Memphis *M, D*
University of Tennessee
   Chattanooga *M*
   Knoxville *M*
   Martin *M*

Texas

Abilene Christian University *M, T*
Angelo State University *M*
Dallas Baptist University *M*
Hardin-Simmons University *M*
Houston Baptist University *B, M*
Lamar University *M*
Midwestern State University *M*
Our Lady of the Lake University of San
  Antonio *M*
Prairie View A&M University *M*
Sam Houston State University *M, T*
Southwest Texas State University *M, T*
Stephen F. Austin State University *M*
Sul Ross State University *M*
Tarleton State University *B, M, T*
Texas A&M International
  University *M, T*
Texas A&M University
   Corpus Christi *M, T*
   Kingsville *M*
Texas Tech University *M, D*
Texas Woman's University *M*
University of Houston
   Clear Lake *M*
   Victoria *M*
University of Houston *M*
University of Mary Hardin-Baylor *M*
University of North Texas *B, M, D, T*
University of Texas
   Brownsville *M*
   El Paso *M*
   Pan American *M*
   San Antonio *M*
   of the Permian Basin *M*
West Texas A&M University *M, T*

Utah

Brigham Young University *M, D*

Vermont

Goddard College *M*
Johnson State College *M*
Lyndon State College *M*
University of Vermont *M, T*

Virginia

College of William and Mary *M, D*
George Mason University *M*
Hampton University *M*
James Madison University *M*
Longwood College *M*
Lynchburg College *M*
Old Dominion University *M*
Radford University *M*
University of Virginia *M, D*
Virginia Commonwealth University *M*
Virginia State University *M*

Washington

Central Washington University *M, T*
City University *M*
Eastern Washington University *M*
Gonzaga University *M*
Heritage College *M*
St. Martin's College *M*
Seattle Pacific University *M*
Seattle University *M*
University of Puget Sound *M*
Western Washington University *B, M*
Whitworth College *B, M, T*

West Virginia

Marshall University *B, M*
West Virginia University *M, D*

Wisconsin

Concordia University Wisconsin *M*
University of Wisconsin
   Madison *M, D*
   Oshkosh *M*
   Platteville *M*
   River Falls *M*
   Stout *M*
   Superior *M*
   Whitewater *M*

Court reporter

Alabama

Gadsden State Community College *A*
James H. Faulkner State Community
  College *A*

Arizona

Gateway Community College *C, A*
Northland Pioneer College *C, A*
Pima Community College *C, A*

California

Butte College *C, A*
Cerritos Community College *C, A*
Chabot College *A*
City College of San Francisco *C, A*
College of Marin: Kentfield *C, A*
College of the Redwoods *C*
Cypress College *C, A*
Humphreys College *C, A, B*
San Diego State University *C*
Shasta College *C*
West Valley College *A*

Florida

Brevard Community College *A*
Broward Community College *A*
Daytona Beach Community College *A*
Florida Metropolitan University
  Orlando College North *A*
Miami-Dade Community College *A*
Pensacola Junior College *A*

Illinois

Career Colleges of Chicago *A*
Illinois Eastern Community Colleges
  Wabash Valley College *C*
MacCormac College *A*
Triton College *A*

Iowa

American Institute of Business *A*

Maryland

Villa Julie College *A*

Massachusetts

Massachusetts Bay Community
  College *A*
Massasoit Community College *A*

Springfield Technical Community
   College A

Michigan
Central Michigan University B
Lansing Community College A
Oakland Community College C, A

Mississippi
Mississippi Gulf Coast Community
   College
     Jefferson Davis Campus A
     Perkinston A
Northwest Mississippi Community
   College A
University of Mississippi B

Missouri
St. Louis Community College
   St. Louis Community College at
      Meramec A
State Fair Community College A

Montana
Montana Tech of the University of
   Montana A

New Mexico
Albuquerque Technical-Vocational
   Institute C, A

New York
State University of New York
   College of Technology at Alfred A

North Carolina
Guilford Technical Community
   College C, A
Lenoir Community College A

Ohio
Clark State Community College A
Stark State College of Technology A

Oklahoma
Rogers State University A
Rose State College A

Pennsylvania
Central Pennsylvania College A
Community College of Allegheny
   County C, A
Manor College C, A

Puerto Rico
National College of Business and
   Technology A

Rhode Island
Johnson & Wales University A, B

South Carolina
Midlands Technical College A

Tennessee
Chattanooga State Technical Community
   College A

Texas
Alvin Community College C, A
Amarillo College C, A
Austin Community College C, A
Del Mar College A
El Paso Community College A
Houston Community College
   System C, A
Northwood University: Texas
   Campus A, B
San Antonio College C

Washington
Green River Community College A

Wisconsin
Gateway Technical College A
Lakeshore Technical College A
Madison Area Technical College A
Wisconsin Indianhead Technical
   College A

Crafts/folk art/artisanry

Arizona
Prescott College B, M

California
California State University
   Northridge B
College of the Siskiyous A
Fresno City College C, A
Palomar College A
Pasadena City College A
San Joaquin Delta College A
Santa Ana College C

Georgia
North Georgia College & State
   University B

Illinois
University of Illinois
   Urbana-Champaign B

Indiana
Goshen College B
Indiana University--Purdue University
   Indiana University-Purdue
      University Fort Wayne B

Kansas
Allen County Community College A

Massachusetts
Bridgewater State College B
Fitchburg State College B
Merrimack College B

Michigan
Northern Michigan University A

Montana
Western Montana College of The
   University of Montana B

New York
Fulton-Montgomery Community
   College A
Mohawk Valley Community College A
New York University M
Rochester Institute of
   Technology A, B, M

Ohio
Cleveland Institute of Art B
Kent State University
   Stark Campus B
Kent State University B, M
University of Akron B

Pennsylvania
Kutztown University of Pennsylvania B
University of the Arts B

Texas
University of North Texas B, M

Vermont
Goddard College B

Virginia
Southwest Virginia Community
   College C
Virginia Commonwealth University B

Washington
North Seattle Community College C, A

Creative writing

Alabama
University of Alabama M

Alaska
University of Alaska
   Anchorage M
   Fairbanks M

Arizona
Arizona State University M

Prescott College B, M
University of Arizona B, M

Arkansas
Arkansas Tech University B
University of Arkansas M

California
Antioch Southern California
   Los Angeles M
Barstow College A
California College of Arts and Crafts M
California State University
   Chico B
   Hayward B
   Long Beach B, M
   Los Angeles M
   Monterey Bay B
   Northridge B
Chapman University M
Dominican University of California B
Foothill College A
Fresno Pacific University B
Grossmont Community College A
Mills College M
Orange Coast College A
Otis College of Art and Design M
Pepperdine University B
Pitzer College B
St. Mary's College of California M
San Diego State University M
San Francisco State University B, M
San Joaquin Delta College A
University of California
   Irvine M
   Riverside B
   San Diego B
   Santa Cruz B
University of Redlands B
University of San Francisco M
University of Southern California B, M

Colorado
Colorado College B
Colorado State University M
Naropa University B, M
University of Colorado
   Boulder B
University of Denver B, M, D
University of Southern Colorado B

Connecticut
Sacred Heart University B
Southern Connecticut State
   University B
Trinity College B, M

District of Columbia
American University M
Gallaudet University B

Florida
Eckerd College B
Florida International University M
Florida State University B, M, D
St. Leo University B
University of Florida M
University of Miami B
University of Tampa A, B
University of West Florida B

Georgia
Agnes Scott College B
Emory University B
Georgia State University M
Kennesaw State University B
Oxford College of Emory University B

Idaho
Albertson College of Idaho B
Boise State University B, D
Lewis-Clark State College B
University of Idaho M

Illinois
Augustana College B
Columbia College B, M
Knox College B

McKendree College B
Millikin University B, T
North Central College B
Northwestern University B
Richland Community College A
Roosevelt University M
School of the Art Institute of Chicago M
Southern Illinois University
   Carbondale M

Indiana
Bethel College A
Indiana State University B, M
Indiana University
   Bloomington M
Indiana University--Purdue University
   Indiana University-Purdue
      University Fort Wayne B
Indiana Wesleyan University B
Manchester College A
Purdue University
   Calumet B
Saint Mary's College B
St. Joseph's College B
University of Evansville B

Iowa
Maharishi University of Management B
University of Iowa B, M

Kansas
Independence Community College A
Pittsburg State University B
Wichita State University M

Louisiana
Louisiana State University and
   Agricultural and Mechanical
   College M
Loyola University New Orleans B
McNeese State University M

Maine
University of Maine
   Farmington B
University of Southern Maine B

Maryland
Goucher College B
Johns Hopkins University B, M
Loyola College in Maryland B
University of Maryland
   College Park M

Massachusetts
Boston University M
Bridgewater State College B
Emerson College B, M
Endicott College B
Hampshire College B
Harvard College B
Massachusetts College of Liberal Arts B
Merrimack College B
Simon's Rock College of Bard B
University of Massachusetts
   Amherst M
Wheaton College B

Michigan
Grand Valley State University B
Michigan State University M
Northern Michigan University B, M
Siena Heights University B
University of Michigan B, M
Western Michigan University M

Minnesota
Bethel College B
Hamline University M
Macalester College B
Minnesota State University, Mankato M
Moorhead State University M
Northwestern College B
St. Cloud State University B
St. Mary's University of Minnesota B
Southwest State University B
University of Minnesota
   Twin Cities M

Creative writing

University of St. Thomas *B*
Winona State University *B*

Missouri
Fontbonne College *B*
Kansas City Art Institute *B*
Rockhurst University *C*
Southwest Missouri State University *B*
Stephens College *B*
University of Missouri
    Kansas City *B*
    St. Louis *C*
Washington University *B, M*

Montana
Carroll College *A, B*
Miles Community College *A*
Rocky Mountain College *A*
University of Montana-Missoula *B, M*

Nebraska
University of Nebraska
    Omaha *B*
Wayne State College *B*

Nevada
University of Nevada
    Las Vegas *M*

New Hampshire
Dartmouth College *B*
Franklin Pierce College *B*
New England College *B*
Plymouth State College of the University System of New Hampshire *B*
Rivier College *B, M*
University of New Hampshire *M*

New Jersey
Bloomfield College *B*
Rider University *B*

New Mexico
College of Santa Fe *B*
Institute of American Indian Arts *A*
University of New Mexico *B*

New York
Bard College *B, M*
City University of New York
    Baruch College *B*
    Brooklyn College *B*
    City College *M*
    Lehman College *M*
Columbia University
    School of General Studies *B*
Eugene Lang College/New School University *B*
Fordham University *B*
Hamilton College *B*
Houghton College *B*
Long Island University
    Brooklyn Campus *M*
    Southampton College *B, M*
Manhattan College *B*
Marymount College *B*
New York University *B, M*
Pratt Institute *B*
St. Lawrence University *B*
Sarah Lawrence College *B, M*
State University of New York
    Albany *D*
    New Paltz *B*
    Oswego *B*
    Purchase *B*
Syracuse University *M*

North Carolina
Brevard College *B*
Lenoir-Rhyne College *B*
North Carolina State University *B*
St. Andrews Presbyterian College *B*
University of North Carolina
    Greensboro *M*
    Wilmington *M*
Warren Wilson College *B*

North Dakota
Dickinson State University *B*

Ohio
Antioch College *B*
Ashland University *B*
Bowling Green State University *B, M*
College of Wooster *B*
Denison University *B*
Hiram College *B*
Kent State University *B*
Miami University
    Oxford Campus *B, M*
Oberlin College *B*
Ohio Northern University *B*
Ohio University *B*
Ohio Wesleyan University *B*
University of Cincinnati *M, D*
Wittenberg University *B*

Oklahoma
Oklahoma Christian University of Science and Arts *B*
Oklahoma State University *B*
Southeastern Oklahoma State University *B*
University of Central Oklahoma *M*

Oregon
Eastern Oregon University *B, T*
Linfield College *B*
Pacific University *B*
Portland State University *M*
Reed College *B*
University of Oregon *M*

Pennsylvania
Bryn Mawr College *B*
California University of Pennsylvania *B*
Carlow College *B*
Carnegie Mellon University *B*
Eastern College *B*
Gettysburg College *B*
Immaculata College *A*
La Salle University *B*
Seton Hill College *B, M*
Susquehanna University *B*
Temple University *B*
University of Pittsburgh
    Johnstown *B*
University of Pittsburgh *C, B*
Waynesburg College *B*
Westminster College *B, T*

Rhode Island
Brown University *B, M*
Roger Williams University *B*

South Carolina
Anderson College *B*
Columbia College *B*
University of South Carolina *M*

South Dakota
Dakota Wesleyan University *B*

Tennessee
University of Memphis *M*

Texas
St. Edward's University *B*
Southern Methodist University *B*
Southwest Texas State University *M*
Texas A&M University
    Commerce *B*
University of Houston *B, M, D*
University of Texas
    Austin *M*
    El Paso *M*

Utah
University of Utah *M*

Vermont
Bennington College *B, M*
Burlington College *B*
Goddard College *B, M*
Green Mountain College *B*
Johnson State College *B*
Marlboro College *B*
Middlebury College *B*
Norwich University *M*

Southern Vermont College *B*

Virginia
Christopher Newport University *B*
George Mason University *M*
Hollins University *M*
Old Dominion University *M*
Randolph-Macon Woman's College *B*
Sweet Briar College *B*
University of Virginia *M*
Virginia Commonwealth University *M*

Washington
Everett Community College *A*
Evergreen State College *B*
North Seattle Community College *C, A*
Pacific Lutheran University *B*
Seattle University *B*
Western Washington University *B*
Whitworth College *B, T*

West Virginia
Alderson-Broaddus College *B*
Concord College *B*
West Virginia State College *B*

Wisconsin
Beloit College *B*
Cardinal Stritch University *B*
Carroll College *B*
Lakeland College *B*
Northland College *B*
University of Wisconsin
    Parkside *B*
    Whitewater *B, T*
Viterbo University *B*

Criminal justice studies

Alabama
Auburn University at Montgomery *B, M*
Central Alabama Community College *C, A*
Chattahoochee Valley Community College *C, A*
Community College of the Air Force *A*
Faulkner University *A, B*
Jacksonville State University *B, M*
Lawson State Community College *A*
Northwest-Shoals Community College *A*
Troy State University
    Dothan *B*
Troy State University *B*
University of Alabama *B, M*

Arizona
Arizona State University *B, M, D*
Arizona Western College *A*
Central Arizona College *A*
Grand Canyon University *B*
Northern Arizona University *B, M*
Northland Pioneer College *A*
Pima Community College *A*
Scottsdale Community College *A*

Arkansas
Arkansas State University
    Mountain Home *A*
Southern Arkansas University *B*
University of Arkansas
    Little Rock *B*
    Monticello *A*
University of Arkansas *B*

California
California Baptist University *B*
California State University
    Bakersfield *B*
    Long Beach *B, M*
    Los Angeles *B, M*
Chapman University *B*
Citrus College *A*
College of the Redwoods *C*
College of the Sequoias *A*
Golden West College *C, A*
Los Angeles Mission College *C, A*

Modesto Junior College *A*
National University *B, M*
Pacific Union College *B*
Riverside Community College *A*
Saddleback College *C*
San Diego Miramar College *A*
San Francisco State University *B*
Sierra College *A*
Ventura College *C, A*
West Valley College *A*
Yuba College *A*

Colorado
Colorado Mountain College
    Spring Valley Campus *A*
Community College of Aurora *A*
Red Rocks Community College *A*
Trinidad State Junior College *A*
Western State College of Colorado *B*

Connecticut
Briarwood College *A*
Sacred Heart University *B*
Three Rivers Community-Technical College *C, A*
University of Hartford *B*
University of New Haven *M*

Delaware
Delaware State University *B*
Delaware Technical and Community College
    Owens Campus *A*
    Terry Campus *A*
University of Delaware *B*
Wilmington College *B*

District of Columbia
American University *B, M*
George Washington University *B, M*

Florida
Broward Community College *A*
Central Florida Community College *A*
Edison Community College *A*
Florida Agricultural and Mechanical University *B*
Florida Atlantic University *B*
Florida Gulf Coast University *B*
Florida International University *B*
Florida Southern College *B*
Florida State University *B, M, D*
Gulf Coast Community College *A*
Hillsborough Community College *A*
Indian River Community College *A*
Lake City Community College *A*
Manatee Community College *A*
Miami-Dade Community College *C, A*
Polk Community College *A*
St. Thomas University *B*
University of Central Florida *B, M*
University of Florida *B*
University of North Florida *B, M*
University of South Florida *B, M*
University of West Florida *B, M*

Georgia
Armstrong Atlantic State University *A, B, M*
Augusta State University *A, B*
Brewton-Parker College *A*
Chattahoochee Technical Institute *C, A*
Clark Atlanta University *M*
Columbus State University *C, A, B*
Darton College *A*
East Georgia College *A*
Gainesville College *A*
Georgia Military College *A*
Georgia Southern University *B*
Georgia State University *M*
Macon State College *A*
Reinhardt College *A*
South Georgia College *A*
Thomas College *B*
University of Georgia *B*
Young Harris College *A*

Criminal justice studies

Hawaii
University of Hawaii
    Hawaii Community College *A*
    Honolulu Community College *A*

Idaho
Idaho State University *A*
Lewis-Clark State College *B*
North Idaho College *A*
University of Idaho *B*

Illinois
Carl Sandburg College *C*
Governors State University *B, M*
Illinois State University *B, M*
John A. Logan College *A*
Lewis and Clark Community College *A*
Lincoln Land Community College *A*
Loyola University of Chicago *B, M*
McKendree College *B*
Northeastern Illinois University *B*
Olivet Nazarene University *B*
Parkland College *A*
Quincy University *A, B*
Rend Lake College *A*
Rockford College *B*
Roosevelt University *B*
St. Xavier University *B*
Sauk Valley Community College *A*
University of Illinois
    Chicago *B, M, D*

Indiana
Anderson University *A, B*
Ball State University *A, B*
Butler University *B*
Grace College *B*
Indiana State University *B, M*
Indiana University
    Bloomington *B, M, D*
    East *A*
    Kokomo *A, B*
    Northwest *A, B*
    South Bend *A, B*
Indiana University--Purdue University
    Indiana University-Purdue
        University Fort Wayne *A, B*
    Indiana University-Purdue
        University Indianapolis *A, B*
Indiana Wesleyan University *A, B*
Manchester College *A*
Oakland City University *A, B*
St. Joseph's College *B*
Tri-State University *A, B*
University of Evansville *B*

Iowa
Briar Cliff College *B*
Buena Vista University *B*
Graceland University *B*
Grand View College *B*
Iowa Wesleyan College *B*
Morningside College *B*
St. Ambrose University *B, M, T*
Simpson College *B*
Southeastern Community College
    South Campus *A*
University of Dubuque *B*
William Penn University *B*

Kansas
Bethany College *B*
Butler County Community College *A*
Fort Hays State University *B*
Kansas Wesleyan University *A, B*
Washburn University of Topeka *A, B*
Wichita State University *B, M*

Kentucky
Bellarmine College *B*
Campbellsville University *A*
Kentucky State University *B*
Lindsey Wilson College *B*
Murray State University *A, B*
Pikeville College *B*
Thomas More College *B*
Union College *B*

Louisiana
Dillard University *B*
Louisiana State University
    Alexandria *A*
    Eunice *A*
    Shreveport *B*
Southeastern Louisiana University *B*
University of Louisiana at Lafayette *B*
University of Louisiana at Monroe *B, M*

Maine
Andover College *A*
Husson College *B*
University of Maine
    Fort Kent *A*
    Presque Isle *A*
University of Southern Maine *B*

Maryland
Allegany College *A*
Chesapeake College *A*
Frederick Community College *A*
Montgomery College
    Rockville Campus *A*
Prince George's Community
    College *C, A*
University of Baltimore *B, M*
University of Maryland
    Eastern Shore *B*

Massachusetts
American International College *B, M*
Anna Maria College *B*
Becker College *A, B*
Berkshire Community College *A*
Bristol Community College *A*
Bunker Hill Community College *C, A*
Curry College *B*
Dean College *A*
Endicott College *B*
Fisher College *B*
Fitchburg State College *B, M*
Lasell College *B*
Mount Ida College *A, B*
Mount Wachusett Community
    College *C, A*
North Shore Community College *A*
Northeastern University *A, B, M*
Northern Essex Community College *A*
Quincy College *A*
Stonehill College *B*
Suffolk University *M*
University of Massachusetts
    Boston *A*
    Lowell *M*

Michigan
Adrian College *A, B*
Calvin College *B*
Kirtland Community College *A*
Lansing Community College *A*
Madonna University *C, A, B*
Michigan State University *B, M*
Northern Michigan University *A, B*
Saginaw Valley State University *B*
Schoolcraft College *A*
Siena Heights University *A, B*
University of Detroit Mercy *B, M*
Wayne State University *B, M*
Western Michigan University *B*

Minnesota
Bemidji State University *A, B*
Concordia University: St. Paul *B*
Gustavus Adolphus College *B*
Hamline University *B*
Metropolitan State University *B*
Moorhead State University *B*
Northland Community & Technical
    College *A*
Northwestern College *B*
Ridgewater College: A Community and
    Technical College *A*
St. Cloud State University *B, M*
St. Mary's University of Minnesota *B*
Vermilion Community College *A*
Winona State University *B*

Mississippi
Alcorn State University *B*
Delta State University *B, M*
Hinds Community College *A*
Itawamba Community College *A*
Jackson State University *B, M*
Mississippi Gulf Coast Community
    College
    Perkinston *A*
Mississippi Valley State University *B*
University of Southern Mississippi *B, M*

Missouri
Central Methodist College *B*
Drury University *M*
East Central College *A*
Harris Stowe State College *B*
Lindenwood University *B*
Longview Community College *A*
Maple Woods Community College *A*
Mineral Area College *C, A*
Missouri Baptist College *B*
Missouri Western State College *B*
Penn Valley Community College *A*
Southeast Missouri State
    University *B, M*
St. Louis Community College
    St. Louis Community College at
        Forest Park *C*
    St. Louis Community College at
        Meramec *A*
Truman State University *B*

Montana
University of Great Falls *A, B, M*

Nebraska
University of Nebraska
    Kearney *B*
    Omaha *B*
Wayne State College *B*

Nevada
Community College of Southern
    Nevada *C, A*

New Hampshire
College for Lifelong Learning *B*
Franklin Pierce College *B*
McIntosh College *A*

New Jersey
Bloomfield College *B*
Brookdale Community College *A*
Cumberland County College *A*
Essex County College *A*
Hudson County Community College *A*
Monmouth University *B, M*
New Jersey City University *M*
Richard Stockton College of New
    Jersey *B*
Rowan University *B*
Rutgers
    The State University of New Jersey:
        Camden College of Arts and
        Sciences *B*
    The State University of New Jersey:
        Newark College of Arts and
        Sciences *B*
    The State University of New Jersey:
        University College Camden *B*
    The State University of New Jersey:
        University College Newark *B*
Seton Hall University *B*
Thomas Edison State College *A, B*
Union County College *C, A*
Warren County Community College *A*

New Mexico
Albuquerque Technical-Vocational
    Institute *A*
Clovis Community College *A*
College of the Southwest *B*
Eastern New Mexico University
    Roswell Campus *A*
Eastern New Mexico University *B*
New Mexico Junior College *A*
New Mexico State University
    Alamogordo *A*
New Mexico State University *A, B, M*
Northern New Mexico Community
    College *A*
Santa Fe Community College *A*

New York
Alfred University *B*
Broome Community College *C, A*
Canisius College *C, B*
City University of New York
    Graduate School and University
        Center *D*
    John Jay College of Criminal
        Justice *B, M, D*
Columbia-Greene Community College *A*
Corning Community College *A*
Elmira College *B*
Fordham University *B, M, D*
Fulton-Montgomery Community
    College *C, A*
Herkimer County Community College *A*
Hilbert College *A, B*
Keuka College *B*
Long Island University
    C. W. Post Campus *B*
Marist College *B*
Medaille College *B*
Mercy College *C, B*
Mohawk Valley Community College *A*
Molloy College *B*
Monroe Community College *A*
New York Institute of Technology *B*
Niagara University *B, M*
North Country Community College *A*
Onondaga Community College *A*
Orange County Community College *A*
Rockland Community College *A*
Russell Sage College *B*
St. Francis College *A*
State University of New York
    Albany *B, M, D*
    College at Brockport *B*
    College at Buffalo *B, M*
    College at Fredonia *B*
    College at Plattsburgh *B*
    College at Potsdam *B*
Tompkins-Cortland Community
    College *C, A*
Utica College of Syracuse University *B*

North Carolina
Alamance Community College *A*
Appalachian State University *B*
Belmont Abbey College *B*
Campbell University *B*
Cape Fear Community College *A*
Carteret Community College *A*
Central Carolina Community College *A*
East Carolina University *B*
Elon College *B*
Fayetteville State University *B*
Guilford College *B*
Haywood Community College *A*
High Point University *B*
Lees-McRae College *B*
Methodist College *A, B*
Mount Olive College *B*
North Carolina Central University *B, M*
North Carolina State University *B*
North Carolina Wesleyan College *B*
Pfeiffer University *B*
Piedmont Community College *B*
Rowan-Cabarrus Community College *A*
St. Augustine's College *B*
Shaw University *A, B*
South Piedmont Community
    College *C, A*
Southwestern Community College *A*
University of North Carolina
    Charlotte *B, M*
    Pembroke *B*
    Wilmington *B*
Western Carolina University *B*
Wilson Technical Community College *A*

North Dakota
Dickinson State University B
Jamestown College B
Minot State University M
University of North Dakota B

Ohio
Baldwin-Wallace College B
Bowling Green State University B
Central Ohio Technical College A
Kent State University
    Ashtabula Regional Campus B
    Stark Campus B
    Trumbull Campus A
Kent State University B, M
Lourdes College A, B
Marion Technical College A
Mount Vernon Nazarene College B
North Central State College A
Ohio Dominican College C, B
Ohio Northern University B
Ohio University
    Chillicothe Campus B
    Southern Campus at Ironton B
Union Institute B
University of Cincinnati
    Clermont College A
University of Cincinnati B, M, D
University of Dayton B
University of Toledo B
Wilmington College B
Xavier University A, B, M
Youngstown State University A, B, M

Oklahoma
Cameron University A, B
East Central University B
Eastern Oklahoma State College A
Mid-America Bible College B
Northeastern Oklahoma Agricultural and Mechanical College A
Northeastern State University B, M
Oklahoma City University B
Rogers State University A
Rose State College A
Southern Nazarene University B
Tulsa Community College A
University of Tulsa C

Oregon
Chemeketa Community College C, A
Lane Community College A
Portland State University B, M
Southern Oregon University B
University of Portland B

Pennsylvania
Allentown College of St. Francis de Sales B
Bloomsburg University of Pennsylvania B
Bucks County Community College A
Butler County Community College A
Community College of Beaver County A
Duquesne University B
Edinboro University of Pennsylvania B
Gannon University B
Geneva College B
King's College A, B
Kutztown University of Pennsylvania B
La Roche College B
La Salle University A, B
Lackawanna Junior College A
Lincoln University B
Lycoming College B
Montgomery County Community College A
Moravian College B
Mount Aloysius College A, B
Penn State
    Abington B
    Altoona A, B
    Harrisburg B
    Schuylkill - Capital College B
    University Park B, M, D
Point Park College B
St. Francis College B
Shippensburg University of Pennsylvania C, B, M
Temple University B, M, D
Thiel College B
University of Scranton A
Valley Forge Military College A
West Chester University of Pennsylvania B, M
Westminster College B

Puerto Rico
Inter American University of Puerto Rico
    Aguadilla Campus B
    Arecibo Campus B
    Fajardo Campus B
    Metropolitan Campus B, M
Turabo University M

Rhode Island
Rhode Island College B
Roger Williams University A, B

South Carolina
Charleston Southern University B
Chesterfield-Marlboro Technical College C
Florence-Darlington Technical College A
Horry-Georgetown Technical College A
Midlands Technical College C, A
Orangeburg-Calhoun Technical College A
Piedmont Technical College A
Spartanburg Methodist College A
Technical College of the Lowcountry A

South Dakota
Dakota Wesleyan University A, B
Huron University B
Kilian Community College A
University of South Dakota B

Tennessee
Hiwassee College A
Lane College B
Tennessee State University B, M
University of Tennessee
    Knoxville B

Texas
Angelo State University B
Austin Community College C, A
Blinn College C, A
Coastal Bend College A
Dallas Baptist University B
Del Mar College A
Eastfield College C, A
El Paso Community College A
Galveston College C, A
Hill College A
Lamar University B, M
Lon Morris College A
Navarro College A
North Central Texas College A
Our Lady of the Lake University of San Antonio C
Paul Quinn College B
Prairie View A&M University B
St. Edward's University B
St. Mary's University B, M
Sam Houston State University B, M
San Jacinto College
    North C, A
Southwestern Adventist University B
Stephen F. Austin State University B
Sul Ross State University B
Tarleton State University B, M
Tarrant County College A
Texas A&M International University B, M
Texas A&M University
    Commerce B
    Texarkana B
Texas Christian University B
University of Houston
    Downtown B
University of Mary Hardin-Baylor B
University of North Texas B
University of Texas
    Arlington B, M
    El Paso B
    San Antonio B
    Tyler B
    of the Permian Basin B
Vernon Regional Junior College C, A
Wayland Baptist University B

Utah
Dixie State College of Utah A
Salt Lake Community College A
Weber State University A, B

Vermont
Castleton State College A, B
Champlain College A, B
Norwich University B

Virginia
Averett College B
Blue Ridge Community College C
Dabney S. Lancaster Community College A
Ferrum College B
J. Sargeant Reynolds Community College A
Longwood College M
Radford University B, M
Roanoke College B
University of Richmond B
University of Virginia's College at Wise B
Virginia Wesleyan College B

Washington
Gonzaga University B
Peninsula College A
Pierce College A
St. Martin's College B
Shoreline Community College A
Spokane Community College C
Tacoma Community College C
Walla Walla Community College A
Yakima Valley Community College A

West Virginia
Bluefield State College B
College of West Virginia A, B
Fairmont State College B
Marshall University B, M
Potomac State College of West Virginia University A
Salem-Teikyo University B
West Liberty State College B
West Virginia State College A, B
Wheeling Jesuit University B

Wisconsin
Carthage College B
Concordia University Wisconsin B
Mount Senario College B
University of Wisconsin
    Madison B, M
    Milwaukee B, M
    Superior B
Viterbo University B

Wyoming
Eastern Wyoming College A

Criminal justice/corrections

Alabama
Alabama State University B
Athens State University B
Calhoun Community College A
Central Alabama Community College C, A
Jacksonville State University B
James H. Faulkner State Community College A
Northwest-Shoals Community College A
Troy State University M
University of Alabama
    Birmingham B, M
University of South Alabama B
Wallace State Community College at Hanceville A

Alaska
University of Alaska
    Anchorage B
    Fairbanks B

Arizona
Central Arizona College C, A
Phoenix College A
Pima Community College C
Prescott College B, M

Arkansas
Garland County Community College A
Harding University B
University of Arkansas
    Little Rock M
University of Arkansas B

California
California Lutheran University B
California State University
    Bakersfield B
    Fullerton B
    Hayward B
    Sacramento B, M
Chaffey Community College C, A
Chapman University B, M
College of San Mateo C, A
College of the Canyons C, A
College of the Redwoods C
College of the Siskiyous A
Compton Community College C
De Anza College A
Fresno City College C, A
Gavilan Community College C, A
Kings River Community College C, A
Las Positas College A
Los Angeles Harbor College A
Los Angeles Southwest College A
Modesto Junior College C, A
Napa Valley College C, A
Sacramento City College C, A
Saddleback College C
San Diego State University A, B
San Joaquin Delta College C, A
San Jose City College C, A
Santa Ana College A
Santa Barbara City College C, A
Santa Rosa Junior College C, A
Sierra College A
Solano Community College C, A
Southwestern College C, A
Taft College A
University of La Verne B
Ventura College A
West Hills Community College C, A
West Los Angeles College C, A
Yuba College A

Colorado
Northeastern Junior College A
Otero Junior College A
Red Rocks Community College C, A
Trinidad State Junior College A
University of Colorado
    Denver M

Connecticut
Briarwood College A
Manchester Community-Technical College C, A
Mitchell College A, B
Naugatuck Valley Community-Technical College C, A
Norwalk Community-Technical College A
Sacred Heart University B
Teikyo Post University B
Tunxis Community College A
University of New Haven B

Criminal justice/corrections

Florida
Bethune-Cookman College *B*
Brevard Community College *A*
Broward Community College *A*
Central Florida Community College *C*
Daytona Beach Community
  College *C, A*
Edward Waters College *B*
Florida Community College at
  Jacksonville *A*
Florida Memorial College *B*
Gulf Coast Community College *C, A*
Hillsborough Community College *A*
Lake City Community College *C*
Manatee Community College *A*
Miami-Dade Community College *C, A*
Palm Beach Community College *C, A*
Pasco-Hernando Community College *C*
Pensacola Junior College *A*
Polk Community College *C, A*
St. Petersburg Junior College *C, A*
University of Central Florida *B*
University of West Florida *B*

Georgia
Albany State University *M*
Atlanta Metropolitan College *A*
Clayton College and State University *A*
Dalton State College *A*
Floyd College *A*
Fort Valley State University *B*
Georgia Military College *A*
Georgia State University *B*
LaGrange College *A, B*
Mercer University *B*
Morris Brown College *B*
North Georgia College & State
  University *B*
Savannah State University *B*
South Georgia College *A*
State University of West Georgia *B*
Valdosta State University *B*
Waycross College *A*

Hawaii
Chaminade University of
  Honolulu *A, B, M*
University of Hawaii
  Honolulu Community College *A*
  Maui Community College *A*
  West Oahu *B*

Idaho
Boise State University *A, B, M*
Lewis-Clark State College *B*

Illinois
Black Hawk College *C, A*
Chicago State University *B, M*
City Colleges of Chicago
  Harold Washington College *C, A*
  Wright College *C, A*
College of DuPage *C*
Joliet Junior College *C, A*
Kankakee Community College *A*
Lewis University *B*
MacMurray College *A, B*
Moraine Valley Community
  College *C, A*
Prairie State College *C, A*
Richland Community College *A*
St. Xavier University *M*
Sauk Valley Community College *A*
Spoon River College *A*
Triton College *C, A*
University of Illinois
  Springfield *B*
William Rainey Harper College *C, A*

Indiana
Ancilla College *A*
Indiana State University *B*
Manchester College *A*
Purdue University
  Calumet *A*
St. Joseph's College *B*
University of Indianapolis *A, B*

Vincennes University *A*

Iowa
Buena Vista University *B*
Indian Hills Community College *A*
Iowa Wesleyan College *B*
Iowa Western Community College *A*
Kirkwood Community College *C, A*
Loras College *B*
Mount Mercy College *B*
Simpson College *B*
Southeastern Community College
  North Campus *A*
Waldorf College *A*

Kansas
Barton County Community College *C, A*
Central Christian College *A*
Colby Community College *A*
Cowley County Community
  College *C, A*
Dodge City Community College *A*
Garden City Community College *A*
Independence Community College *A*
Newman University *B*
Pittsburg State University *B*
Seward County Community
  College *C, A*
Southwestern College *B*
Washburn University of Topeka *B, M*

Kentucky
Murray State University *B*
St. Catharine College *A*

Louisiana
Bossier Parish Community College *A*
Loyola University New Orleans *B*
McNeese State University *B*

Maine
Andover College *A*
St. Joseph's College *B*
Southern Maine Technical College *A*
University of Maine
  Fort Kent *A*

Maryland
Allegany College *C, A*
Chesapeake College *C, A*
Community College of Baltimore County
  Catonsville *C, A*
Coppin State College *B, M*
Hagerstown Community College *C, A*
Harford Community College *A*
Howard Community College *A*
Wor-Wic Community College *A*

Massachusetts
Anna Maria College *B, M*
Bay Path College *A, B*
Becker College *B*
Berkshire Community College *A*
Cape Cod Community College *A*
Dean College *A*
Holyoke Community College *A*
Mount Ida College *A, B*
Northeastern University *A, B, M*
Roxbury Community College *A*
Salem State College *B*
Westfield State College *B, M*

Michigan
Alpena Community College *A*
Baker College
  of Cadillac *C, A*
  of Muskegon *C, A*
Concordia College *B, T*
Delta College *A*
Ferris State University *C, B*
Gogebic Community College *A*
Grand Valley State University *B*
Jackson Community College *C, A*
Kellogg Community College *A*
Kirtland Community College *C*
Lake Superior State University *A, B*
Mid Michigan Community College *A*
Montcalm Community College *C, A*

Muskegon Community College *C*
North Central Michigan College *A*
Northern Michigan University *C*
Olivet College *B*
St. Clair County Community
  College *C, A*
University of Michigan
  Flint *B, M*
Washtenaw Community College *A*
West Shore Community College *C, A*

Minnesota
Minnesota State University,
  Mankato *B, M*
Moorhead State University *B*
Northland Community & Technical
  College *A*
St. Cloud State University *B*
Vermilion Community College *A*
Winona State University *B*

Mississippi
Coahoma Community College *A*
Hinds Community College *A*

Missouri
Drury University *B, M*
Hannibal-LaGrange College *B*
Missouri Valley College *B*
St. Charles County Community
  College *A*
St. Louis University *B*
Southeast Missouri State University *B*
Southwest Baptist University *B*

Montana
University of Great Falls *A, B*

Nebraska
Central Community College *C, A*
Chadron State College *B*
Hastings College *B*
Midland Lutheran College *B*
Northeast Community College *A*
University of Nebraska
  Omaha *M, D*

Nevada
Community College of Southern
  Nevada *A*
University of Nevada
  Las Vegas *B, M*

New Hampshire
Franklin Pierce College *B*
McIntosh College *A*
St. Anselm College *B*

New Jersey
Caldwell College *B*
Centenary College *B*
Gloucester County College *A*
Hudson County Community College *A*
Middlesex County College *A*
New Jersey City University *B*
Raritan Valley Community College *A*
Rowan University *B*
Salem Community College *A*
Sussex County Community College *A*
Warren County Community College *A*

New Mexico
College of Santa Fe *B*
Dona Ana Branch Community College of
  New Mexico State University *A*
Eastern New Mexico University *B*
New Mexico Junior College *A*
San Juan College *A*
Western New Mexico University *A, B*

New York
Adirondack Community College *A*
Broome Community College *A*
Cayuga County Community
  College *C, A*
City University of New York
  John Jay College of Criminal
  Justice *B*
Clinton Community College *A*

College of St. Rose *B*
Dutchess Community College *A*
Elmira College *B*
Finger Lakes Community College *C, A*
Herkimer County Community College *A*
Hudson Valley Community College *A*
Long Island University
  C. W. Post Campus *M*
Molloy College *B*
Orange County Community College *A*
Pace University:
  Pleasantville/Briarcliff *B*
Pace University *B*
Roberts Wesleyan College *B*
Rochester Institute of Technology *B*
St. Thomas Aquinas College *B*
State University of New York
  College at Brockport *B*
  Oswego *B*
Suffolk County Community College *A*
Ulster County Community College *A*
Westchester Community College *A*

North Carolina
Alamance Community College *A*
Barber-Scotia College *B*
Beaufort County Community College *A*
Central Carolina Community College *A*
Chowan College *B*
Coastal Carolina Community
  College *C, A*
College of the Albemarle *A*
Durham Technical Community
  College *C, A*
Edgecombe Community College *A*
Gaston College *A*
Guilford Technical Community
  College *A*
Halifax Community College *A*
James Sprunt Community College *A*
Johnson C. Smith University *B*
Lenoir Community College *A*
Louisburg College *A*
Mayland Community College *A*
Mitchell Community College *C, A*
Randolph Community College *A*
Richmond Community College *A*
Sampson Community College *A*
Sandhills Community College *A*
Southeastern Community College *A*
Surry Community College *A*
Tri-County Community College *A*
Vance-Granville Community College *A*
Western Piedmont Community
  College *A*

North Dakota
Minot State University *B*

Ohio
Cedarville College *B*
Central Ohio Technical College *A*
Columbus State Community College *A*
Defiance College *A, B*
Edison State Community College *A*
Hocking Technical College *A*
Jefferson Community College *A*
Kent State University
  East Liverpool Regional Campus *A*
  Stark Campus *B*
Lima Technical College *A*
Muskingum Area Technical College *A*
Northwest State Community College *A*
Ohio University
  Chillicothe Campus *B*
  Eastern Campus *B*
  Zanesville Campus *B*
Ohio University *B*
Owens Community College
  Toledo *A*
Terra Community College *C*
University of Findlay *A, B*
University of Toledo *A*
Wilmington College *B*
Youngstown State University *A, B, M*

189

Criminal justice/corrections

Oklahoma
East Central University *B*
Eastern Oklahoma State College *A*
Oklahoma City Community College *A*
Redlands Community College *A*
Seminole State College *A*
Southwestern Oklahoma State
  University *B*
University of Central Oklahoma *B*

Oregon
Central Oregon Community College *A*
Chemeketa Community College *A*
Lane Community College *C*
Linn-Benton Community College *C, A*
Southern Oregon University *B*
Western Oregon University *B*

Pennsylvania
Bucks County Community College *A*
Central Pennsylvania College *A*
Chestnut Hill College *A, B*
Community College of Allegheny
  County *A*
Delaware County Community
  College *C, A*
Holy Family College *B*
La Salle University *B*
Lehigh Carbon Community College *C, A*
Mercyhurst College *B*
Seton Hill College *B*
University of Pittsburgh
  Bradford *B*
  Greensburg *B*
University of Scranton *B*
Widener University *B, M*
York College of Pennsylvania *A, B*

Puerto Rico
Caribbean University *B*
Colegio Universitario del Este *A, B*
Inter American University of Puerto Rico
  Barranquitas Campus *B*
University of Puerto Rico
  Carolina Regional College *A*
University of the Sacred Heart *B*

South Carolina
Anderson College *A*
Benedict College *B*
Central Carolina Technical College *C, A*
Charleston Southern University *B*
Chesterfield-Marlboro Technical
  College *C*
Coker College *B*
Denmark Technical College *C, A*
Greenville Technical College *A*
Orangeburg-Calhoun Technical
  College *C*
South Carolina State University *B*
Spartanburg Methodist College *A*
The Citadel *B*
Trident Technical College *A*
Voorhees College *B*

South Dakota
Mount Marty College *B*
Northern State University *B*
Sinte Gleska University *B*

Tennessee
Draughons Junior College of Business:
  Nashville *A*
East Tennessee State University *B, M*
Roane State Community College *A*
Shelby State Community College *C, A*
Walters State Community College *A*

Texas
Abilene Christian University *B*
Alvin Community College *C, A*
Amarillo College *A*
Angelina College *A*
Central Texas College *C, A*
Hill College *C, A*
Jarvis Christian College *B*
McMurry University *B*
Midland College *C, A*
Midwestern State University *B*
Navarro College *C, A*
Northeast Texas Community College *A*
Palo Alto College *A*
Sam Houston State University *D*
San Jacinto College
  North *C*
South Plains College *A*
Southwest Texas State University *B, M*
Sul Ross State University *B*
Texas A&M University
  Commerce *B*
  Corpus Christi *B*
Texas Wesleyan University *B*
Texas Woman's University *B*
Trinity Valley Community College *C, A*
Tyler Junior College *C, A*
University of Houston
  Victoria *B*
University of North Texas *B*
University of Texas
  Pan American *B, M*
Victoria College *C, A*
Western Texas College *A*
Wiley College *A, B*

Utah
Snow College *A*

Vermont
Castleton State College *A, B*
Champlain College *A, B*
Southern Vermont College *A, B*
Trinity College of Vermont *B*

Virginia
Christopher Newport University *B*
Mountain Empire Community College *A*
St. Paul's College *B*
Tidewater Community College *A*
Virginia Highlands Community
  College *C*
Virginia Wesleyan College *B*
Wytheville Community College *C*

Washington
Central Washington University *B*
Centralia College *C, A*
Eastern Washington University *B*
Everett Community College *A*
Grays Harbor College *C, A*
Highline Community College *A*
Olympic College *A*
Shoreline Community College *A*
Skagit Valley College *C, A*
Tacoma Community College *A*

West Virginia
Fairmont State College *A, B*
Marshall University *B, M*
Shepherd College *A*
West Virginia Northern Community
  College *A*
West Virginia University
  Parkersburg *C, A*

Wisconsin
Concordia University Wisconsin *B*
Gateway Technical College *A*
Northeast Wisconsin Technical
  College *A*
University of Wisconsin
  Eau Claire *B*
  Oshkosh *B*
Viterbo University *B*

Wyoming
Casper College *A*
Central Wyoming College *A*
Western Wyoming Community
  College *A*

Criminal justice/law enforcement administration

Alabama
Auburn University *B*
George C. Wallace State Community
  College
  Selma *A*
Jefferson Davis Community College *A*
Northwest-Shoals Community College *C*
Troy State University *M*
University of North Alabama *B, M*
University of South Alabama *B*

Arizona
Arizona Western College *A*
Eastern Arizona College *A*
Glendale Community College *C, A*
Pima Community College *C*
University of Arizona *B*
Yavapai College *C, A*

Arkansas
Northwest Arkansas Community
  College *A*

California
California State University
  Chico *B*
  Hayward *B*
College of the Redwoods *C, A*
Crafton Hills College *C, A*
Cuesta College *C, A*
De Anza College *A*
Diablo Valley College *C*
Fresno City College *C, A*
Gavilan Community College *C*
Glendale Community College *A*
Golden West College *C, A*
Imperial Valley College *C, A*
Irvine Valley College *C, A*
Lake Tahoe Community College *C, A*
Long Beach City College *C, A*
Mendocino College *A*
Modesto Junior College *A*
Monterey Peninsula College *C, A*
National University *B*
Ohlone College *C, A*
Palo Verde College *A*
Palomar College *C, A*
San Bernardino Valley College *C, A*
San Diego Miramar College *C, A*
San Jose State University *B, M*
Santa Monica College *C, A*
Skyline College *C, A*
Sonoma State University *B*
Southwestern College *C, A*

Colorado
Aims Community College *A*
Arapahoe Community College *C, A*
Colorado Northwestern Community
  College *C, A*
Community College of Aurora *A*
Mesa State College *A*
Metropolitan State College of Denver *B*
Pikes Peak Community College *C, A*
Pueblo Community College *A*
Trinidad State Junior College *A*

Connecticut
Asnuntuck Community-Technical
  College *A*
Central Connecticut State University *M*
Northwestern Connecticut
  Community-Technical College *A*
Norwalk Community-Technical
  College *A*
Sacred Heart University *B, M*
University of New Haven *B*
Western Connecticut State
  University *B, M*

Delaware
Delaware Technical and Community
  College
  Stanton/Wilmington Campus *A*

District of Columbia
George Washington University *M*
University of the District of Columbia *A*

Florida
Edison Community College *A*
Florida Atlantic University *M*
Florida International University *M*
Gulf Coast Community College *A*
Hillsborough Community College *A*
Lake City Community College *C*
Lake-Sumter Community College *A*
Lynn University *M*
Pasco-Hernando Community College *A*
Pensacola Junior College *A*
Seminole Community College *C, A*
South Florida Community College *A*
Tallahassee Community College *A*
Valencia Community College *A*

Georgia
Clayton College and State University *A*
Columbus State University *B, M*
Georgia College and State University *B*
Georgia Military College *A*
South Georgia College *A*

Hawaii
Hawaii Pacific University *A, B*
University of Hawaii
  Hawaii Community College *A*
  Honolulu Community College *A*

Idaho
Boise State University *A, B*
College of Southern Idaho *A*
Ricks College *A*

Illinois
Bradley University *B*
Carl Sandburg College *A*
City Colleges of Chicago
  Harold Washington College *C, A*
Danville Area Community College *A*
Joliet Junior College *C, A*
Kaskaskia College *C, A*
Lewis University *M*
Lincoln Land Community College *C, A*
Richland Community College *A*
Rock Valley College *A*
Southeastern Illinois College *C, A*
Southern Illinois University
  Carbondale *B, M*
Triton College *C*
Western Illinois University *B, M*

Indiana
Purdue University
  Calumet *B*
University of Indianapolis *A, B*
Vincennes University *A*

Iowa
Des Moines Area Community College *A*
Indian Hills Community College *A*
Iowa Lakes Community College *A*
Southeastern Community College
  North Campus *A*
Western Iowa Tech Community
  College *A*

Kansas
Central Christian College *A*
Cowley County Community
  College *C, A*
Garden City Community College *A*
Kansas City Kansas Community
  College *C, A*
Seward County Community College *A*

Kentucky
Campbellsville University *B*
Kentucky Wesleyan College *B*
University of Louisville *B, M*

Louisiana
Nicholls State University A, B
Southern University
    Shreveport C, A

Maine
Andover College A
Husson College B
Southern Maine Technical College A
University of Maine
    Augusta A, B
    Fort Kent A
    Presque Isle A, B

Maryland
Anne Arundel Community College C, A
Baltimore City Community College A
Cecil Community College C, A
Community College of Baltimore County
    Catonsville C, A
Montgomery College
    Rockville Campus A
University of Baltimore C
Wor-Wic Community College C, A

Massachusetts
Anna Maria College M
Bay Path College A, B
Becker College B
Berkshire Community College A
Boston University M
Cape Cod Community College A
Dean College A
Massachusetts Bay Community
    College A
Middlesex Community College A
Newbury College A
Northeastern University B, M
Salem State College B
University of Massachusetts
    Lowell A, B
Western New England College B, M
Westfield State College B, M

Michigan
Alpena Community College A
Calvin College B
Grand Valley State University B, M
Kalamazoo Valley Community
    College A
Kirtland Community College A
Lansing Community College A
Mott Community College C, A
Muskegon Community College A
Northwestern Michigan College A
Oakland Community College C, A
St. Clair County Community
    College C, A
Suomi College A
Washtenaw Community College A
West Shore Community College A

Minnesota
Inver Hills Community College A
Northland Community & Technical
    College A
Rochester Community and Technical
    College A
Southwest State University B
Vermilion Community College A
Winona State University B

Mississippi
Mississippi College B, M
Mississippi Delta Community College A
Mississippi Gulf Coast Community
    College
        Jefferson Davis Campus A
Mississippi Valley State University M

Missouri
Central Missouri State University B, M
College of the Ozarks B
Columbia College A, B, M
Culver-Stockton College B
Hannibal-LaGrange College B
Lincoln University A, B
Longview Community College C, A
Maple Woods Community College C, A
Missouri Southern State College A, B
Park University B
Penn Valley Community College C, A
St. Charles County Community
    College A
St. Louis University B
St. Louis Community College
    St. Louis Community College at
        Forest Park C
University of Missouri
    Kansas City B, M

Montana
Flathead Valley Community College A
University of Great Falls B

Nebraska
Peru State College B

New Hampshire
Franklin Pierce College B
Hesser College B
McIntosh College A
New Hampshire Technical Institute A
Notre Dame College B

New Jersey
Essex County College A
Kean University B
Middlesex County College A
Rutgers
    The State University of New Jersey:
        Livingston College B
    The State University of New Jersey:
        Rutgers College B
    The State University of New Jersey:
        University College New
        Brunswick B
Salem Community College A
Thomas Edison State College A, B

New Mexico
New Mexico State University
    Carlsbad A
Western New Mexico University C, B

New York
Adirondack Community College A
City University of New York
    John Jay College of Criminal
        Justice B
Columbia-Greene Community College A
Corning Community College A
Erie Community College
    City Campus A
    North Campus A
Finger Lakes Community College C, A
Genesee Community College C, A
Herkimer County Community College A
Iona College B, M
Jefferson Community College C, A
Mohawk Valley Community College A
Monroe Community College C
Nassau Community College A
Niagara County Community College A
Rochester Institute of Technology B
St. John's University C, A, B, M
Schenectady County Community
    College A
State University of New York
    College of Technology at
        Canton A, B
        Farmingdale C, A

North Carolina
Alamance Community College A
Barton College B
Beaufort County Community College A
College of the Albemarle A
Craven Community College A
Elizabeth City State University B
Forsyth Technical Community College A
Johnston Community College A
Roanoke-Chowan Community College A
Rockingham Community College A
Wilson Technical Community College C

Ohio
Ashland University A, B
Bluffton College B
Bowling Green State University
    Firelands College A
Central Ohio Technical College A
Clark State Community College A
Columbus State Community College A
Kent State University
    Stark Campus B
Lima Technical College A
Marion Technical College A
North Central State College A
Terra Community College C
Tiffin University A, B
University of Akron
    Wayne College A
University of Akron A
University of Findlay B
Youngstown State University A, B, M

Oklahoma
Eastern Oklahoma State College A
Northern Oklahoma College A
Oklahoma City University M
Redlands Community College A
Southeastern Oklahoma State
    University B
University of Central Oklahoma M

Oregon
Central Oregon Community College A
Chemeketa Community College A
Portland Community College A
Southern Oregon University B

Pennsylvania
Alvernia College B
Chestnut Hill College A, B
Delaware Valley College B
Harrisburg Area Community College A
Lehigh Carbon Community College A
Mansfield University of
    Pennsylvania A, B
Marywood University B
Mercyhurst College B, M
Northampton County Area Community
    College A
Penn State
    Fayette B
Reading Area Community College A
University of Pittsburgh
    Greensburg B
    Titusville C
Villanova University M
Waynesburg College B

Puerto Rico
Colegio Universitario del Este B
Inter American University of Puerto Rico
    Guayama Campus B

Rhode Island
Johnson & Wales University A, B
Salve Regina University A, B, M

South Carolina
Aiken Technical College A
Charleston Southern University B
Lander University B
Morris College B
Technical College of the Lowcountry A
University of South Carolina
    Spartanburg B
University of South Carolina B, M

Tennessee
Lambuth University B
Middle Tennessee State University B, M
Tennessee State University M
University of Memphis B, M
University of Tennessee
    Chattanooga B, M
    Martin B

Texas
Abilene Christian University B
Alvin Community College C, A
Central Texas College C, A
Collin County Community College
    District C, A
Concordia University at Austin B
Grayson County College A
Hill College C, A
Howard College C
Howard Payne University B
Kilgore College A
Lamar State College at Port Arthur A
Midland College A
St. Edward's University B
Sam Houston State University M
South Plains College A
Southwest Texas State University M
Sul Ross State University M
Texas A&M University
    Commerce B
Texas Southern University B, M
Trinity Valley Community College C, A
University of Texas
    of the Permian Basin M
West Texas A&M University B
Western Texas College A
Wharton County Junior College A

Virginia
Bluefield College B
Central Virginia Community College A
Danville Community College A
Hampton University B
Mountain Empire Community College A
New River Community College A
Northern Virginia Community
    College C, A
Shenandoah University B
Thomas Nelson Community College A
Virginia Commonwealth
    University C, B, M
Virginia Wesleyan College B

Washington
Bellevue Community College A
City University C, B, M
Columbia Basin College A
Eastern Washington University B
Everett Community College A
Lower Columbia College A
Seattle University B
Spokane Community College A
Spokane Falls Community College C, A
Washington State University B, M

West Virginia
Fairmont State College A, B

Wisconsin
Carroll College B
Marian College of Fond du Lac B
University of Wisconsin
    Parkside B
    Platteville B

Wyoming
Central Wyoming College A
University of Wyoming B
Western Wyoming Community
    College A

Criminology

Alabama
Alabama State University M
Auburn University B
Enterprise State Junior College C

Arizona
Central Arizona College A

Arkansas
Arkansas State University B

California
Bakersfield College A
California Lutheran University B

California State University
   Bakersfield *B*
   Fresno *B, M*
   Stanislaus *B*
Chabot College *B*
Fresno City College *C, A*
Porterville College *C, A*
San Diego State University *B*
San Francisco State University *B*
San Jose State University *M*
University of California
   Irvine *B, D*
University of La Verne *B*
University of Southern California *M*
West Hills Community College *A*

Colorado
Adams State College *B*
Regis University *B*
Trinidad State Junior College *A*
University of Southern Colorado *B*

Connecticut
Central Connecticut State University *B*
Mitchell College *A*

Delaware
University of Delaware *M, D*

District of Columbia
Gallaudet University *B*

Florida
Barry University *B*
Florida State University *B, M, D*
Gulf Coast Community College *A*
Lake City Community College *A*
Manatee Community College *A*
St. Leo University *B*
St. Thomas University *B, M*
University of Miami *B*
University of Tampa *B*

Georgia
Clark Atlanta University *B*
Clayton College and State University *A*
Darton College *A*
East Georgia College *A*
Georgia Military College *A*
Morris Brown College *B*
South Georgia College *A*
Valdosta State University *B*

Hawaii
Chaminade University of Honolulu *A, B*

Idaho
Ricks College *A*

Illinois
Dominican University *B*
Kishwaukee College *A*
Roosevelt University *B*

Indiana
Ancilla College *A*
Ball State University *B*
Franklin College *B*
Indiana State University *B, M*
Indiana Wesleyan University *B*
University of Evansville *B*
Valparaiso University *B*

Iowa
North Iowa Area Community College *A*
University of Northern Iowa *B*
Upper Iowa University *B*

Kansas
MidAmerica Nazarene University *B*

Kentucky
Union College *B*

Louisiana
Dillard University *B*

Maine
Husson College *B*
University of Southern Maine *B*

Maryland
Howard Community College *A*
University of Maryland
   College Park *B, M, D*
   Eastern Shore *B*

Massachusetts
American International College *B, M*
Bridgewater State College *B*
Northeastern University *B, M*
Suffolk University *B, M*

Michigan
Central Michigan University *B*
Eastern Michigan University *B, M*

Minnesota
Hamline University *B*
Minnesota State University, Mankato *B*
Ridgewater College: A Community and
   Technical College *A*
St. Cloud State University *B, M*
University of Minnesota
   Duluth *B*
   Twin Cities *B*
University of St. Thomas *B*
Winona State University *B*

Missouri
College of the Ozarks *B*
Drury University *B*
Evangel University *B*
Lindenwood University *B*
University of Missouri
   St. Louis *B, M, D*

Nebraska
Midland Lutheran College *B*

Nevada
University of Nevada
   Reno *B*

New Jersey
The College of New Jersey *B*

New York
City University of New York
   John Jay College of Criminal
     Justice *B*
College of St. Rose *B*
Iona College *B*
Keuka College *B*
Medaille College *B*
Niagara University *B*
St. Joseph's College
   St. Joseph's College: Suffolk
     Campus *C*
   St. Joseph's College *C*
State University of New York
   College at Old Westbury *B*

North Carolina
Barber-Scotia College *B*
Belmont Abbey College *B*
Chowan College *B*

Ohio
Capital University *B*
Kent State University *B*
Ohio State University
   Columbus Campus *B*
Ohio University *B*

Oklahoma
East Central University *B, M*
Northeastern Oklahoma Agricultural and
   Mechanical College *A*
University of Oklahoma *B*

Oregon
Southern Oregon University *B*

Pennsylvania
Albright College *B*
Butler County Community College *A*
Indiana University of
   Pennsylvania *A, B, M, D*
La Salle University *B*
Mercyhurst College *B*

Reading Area Community College *A*
St. Joseph's University *B, M*
Seton Hill College *B*
University of Pennsylvania *M, D*
University of Pittsburgh
   Greensburg *B*

Puerto Rico
Caribbean University *B*
Colegio Universitario del Este *A*
Inter American University of Puerto Rico
   Metropolitan Campus *B*
Pontifical Catholic University of Puerto
   Rico *B, M*
Turabo University *B*

South Carolina
The Citadel *B*

South Dakota
Dakota Wesleyan University *A*

Texas
Jarvis Christian College *B*
North Central Texas College *A*
Panola College *A*
South Plains College *A*
Texas A&M University
   Commerce *B*
University of Texas
   Dallas *B*
   of the Permian Basin *B*
Wharton County Junior College *A*

Utah
University of Utah *C*

Vermont
Castleton State College *B*
Champlain College *A, B*

Virginia
Christopher Newport University *B*
Old Dominion University *B*

Wisconsin
Marquette University *B*
Mount Senario College *B*

Culinary arts/related services

Alabama
James H. Faulkner State Community
   College *C, A*

Alaska
University of Alaska
   Anchorage *A*
   Fairbanks *C, A*

Arizona
Arizona Western College *C*
Pima Community College *A*
Scottsdale Community College *C, A*

California
Bakersfield College *A*
Chaffey Community College *C*
Columbia College *A*
Cypress College *C, A*
Diablo Valley College *C*
Glendale Community College *C, A*
Grossmont Community College *C*
Lake Tahoe Community College *A*
Long Beach City College *A*
Los Angeles Mission College *C, A*
Modesto Junior College *C*
San Francisco State University *B*
San Joaquin Delta College *C, A*
Santa Barbara City College *C, A*
Santa Rosa Junior College *C*

Colorado
Art Institute
   of Colorado *A, B*
Community College of Aurora *A*
Community College of Denver *A*

Mesa State College *C, A*
Pueblo Community College *C, A*

Connecticut
Asnuntuck Community-Technical
   College *C, A*
Manchester Community-Technical
   College *C*
Naugatuck Valley Community-Technical
   College *C*
Norwalk Community-Technical
   College *C*

Delaware
Delaware Technical and Community
   College
     Stanton/Wilmington Campus *C, A*

District of Columbia
University of the District of Columbia *A*

Florida
Art Institute
   of Fort Lauderdale *C, A*
Brevard Community College *C*
Central Florida Community College *A*
Florida Community College at
   Jacksonville *A*
Gulf Coast Community College *A*
Indian River Community College *C, A*
New England Institute of Technology *A*
Palm Beach Community College *C*
Pensacola Junior College *C, A*
South Florida Community College *C*
Valencia Community College *A*

Georgia
Art Institute
   of Atlanta *A*
Gwinnett Technical Institute *C, A*

Hawaii
University of Hawaii
   Kapiolani Community College *A*
   Kauai Community College *C, A*

Idaho
Boise State University *C, A*
College of Southern Idaho *C, A*
North Idaho College *C*
Ricks College *A*

Illinois
Black Hawk College *C, A*
City Colleges of Chicago
   Malcolm X College *A*
College of DuPage *C, A*
College of Lake County *C*
Elgin Community College *C, A*
Joliet Junior College *C, A*
Kaskaskia College *C, A*
Kendall College *C, A*
Lincoln Land Community College *C, A*
Moraine Valley Community
   College *C, A*
Southwestern Ilinois College *C, A*
Triton College *C, A*
University of Illinois
   Urbana-Champaign *B*
William Rainey Harper College *C, A*

Indiana
Oakland City University *C, A*
Vincennes University *A*

Iowa
Des Moines Area Community College *A*
Iowa Western Community College *A*
Kirkwood Community College *C, A*
Scott Community College *A*

Kentucky
Paducah Community College *A*

Louisiana
Bossier Parish Community College *C*
Nicholls State University *A, B*
Nunez Community College *C, A*

Maine
Central Maine Technical College *C*
Eastern Maine Technical College *C, A*
Southern Maine Technical College *A*
Washington County Technical College *C*

Maryland
Allegany College *A*
Baltimore International College *C, A*

Massachusetts
Berkshire Community College *C*
Bristol Community College *C*
Bunker Hill Community College *C*
Holyoke Community College *C*
Massasoit Community College *C, A*
Newbury College *A, B*
North Shore Community College *A*

Michigan
Baker College
   of Muskegon *A*
Bay de Noc Community College *C*
Grand Rapids Community College *A*
Henry Ford Community College *C, A*
Lansing Community College *A*
Macomb Community College *C, A*
Monroe County Community
   College *C, A*
Mott Community College *A*
Northern Michigan University *C, A, B*
Northwestern Michigan College *A*
Oakland Community College *C, A*
Schoolcraft College *C, A*
Washtenaw Community College *C, A*
West Shore Community College *C, A*

Minnesota
Dakota County Technical College *C, A*
Hibbing Community College: A
   Technical and Community College *A*
St. Cloud Technical College *C*
St. Paul Technical College *C*
South Central Technical College *A*

Mississippi
Hinds Community College *C, A*
Mississippi Gulf Coast Community
   College
     Jefferson Davis Campus *C*
Mississippi University for Women *B*

Missouri
Ozarks Technical Community
   College *C, A*
St. Louis Community College
   St. Louis Community College at
     Florissant Valley *A*
   St. Louis Community College at
     Forest Park *A*

Montana
Montana State University
   Billings *C*
University of Montana-Missoula *A*

Nebraska
Metropolitan Community College *C, A*
Southeast Community College
   Lincoln Campus *A*

Nevada
Community College of Southern
   Nevada *A*
University of Nevada
   Las Vegas *B*

New Hampshire
McIntosh College *C*
New Hampshire College *A*
New Hampshire Community Technical
   College
     Berlin *C, A*
     Laconia *C, A*
University of New Hampshire *A*

New Jersey
Atlantic Cape Community College *A*
Bergen Community College *C, A*
Brookdale Community College *A*
Burlington County College *C*
Hudson County Community College *C*
Mercer County Community College *C, A*
Middlesex County College *C*
Union County College *A*

New Mexico
Albuquerque Technical-Vocational
   Institute *C*
Dona Ana Branch Community College of
   New Mexico State University *C*

New York
Adirondack Community College *C, A*
Culinary Institute of America *A, B*
Erie Community College
   City Campus *A*
   North Campus *A*
Five Towns College *A*
Mohawk Valley Community
   College *C, A*
Monroe Community College *C, A*
New York Institute of Technology *A*
Niagara County Community College *A*
Onondaga Community College *C, A*
Rockland Community College *C*
Schenectady County Community
   College *C, A*
State University of New York
   College of Agriculture and
     Technology at Cobleskill *C, A*
   College of Technology at Alfred *A*
Westchester Community College *A*

North Carolina
Alamance Community College *C, A*
College of the Albemarle *C*
Guilford Technical Community
   College *C, A*
Lenoir Community College *C, A*
Piedmont Community College *C*
Sandhills Community College *A*
South Piedmont Community College *C*
Southwestern Community College *A*
Wake Technical Community College *A*

Ohio
Bowling Green State University *B*
Cincinnati State Technical and
   Community College *C, A*
Columbus State Community College *A*
Hocking Technical College *C, A*
Muskingum Area Technical College *A*
Sinclair Community College *C, A*
University of Akron *C, A*

Oklahoma
Northeastern Oklahoma Agricultural and
   Mechanical College *A*
Oklahoma State University
   Okmulgee *A*

Oregon
Central Oregon Community College *C*
Lane Community College *C, A*
Linn-Benton Community College *A*
Portland Community College *C*

Pennsylvania
Art Institute
   of Philadelphia *A*
Bucks County Community College *A*
Butler County Community College *C, A*
Community College of Allegheny
   County *C, A*
Community College of Beaver County *A*
Community College of Philadelphia *A*
Drexel University *B*
Harrisburg Area Community
   College *C, A*
Immaculata College *A, B*
Indiana University of Pennsylvania *C*
Mercyhurst College *A, B*
Northampton County Area Community
   College *C*
Pennsylvania College of
   Technology *C, A*
Pennsylvania Institute of Culinary Arts *A*
Reading Area Community College *A*
Westmoreland County Community
   College *C, A*
Yorktowne Business Institute *A*

Puerto Rico
Colegio Universitario del Este *C*

Rhode Island
Johnson & Wales University *A, B*

South Carolina
Denmark Technical College *C*
Greenville Technical College *C, A*
Technical College of the Lowcountry *C*
Trident Technical College *C, A*

Tennessee
Nashville State Technical Institute *A*

Texas
Central Texas College *C, A*
Del Mar College *C, A*
El Paso Community College *C, A*
Galveston College *C, A*
Houston Community College System *C*
Odessa College *C, A*
St. Philip's College *C, A*
San Jacinto College
   North *C, A*
Texas State Technical College
   Harlingen *A*
   Waco *C, A*
Trinity Valley Community College *C*

Utah
Salt Lake Community College *A*
Utah Valley State College *C, A*

Vermont
New England Culinary Institute *A*

Virginia
J. Sargeant Reynolds Community
   College *A*
Northern Virginia Community College *C*
Tidewater Community College *C, A*

Washington
Art Institute of Seattle *A*
Clark College *C, A*
Edmonds Community College *C, A*
Lake Washington Technical College *C, A*
Olympic College *C, A*
Pierce College *C*
Renton Technical College *C, A*
Seattle Central Community College *A*
Skagit Valley College *C, A*
South Puget Sound Community
   College *C, A*
South Seattle Community College *C, A*
Spokane Community College *A*
Spokane Falls Community College *C*

West Virginia
Shepherd College *A*
West Virginia Northern Community
   College *C, A*
West Virginia University Institute of
   Technology *A*

Wisconsin
Blackhawk Technical College *A*
Madison Area Technical College *C, A*
Milwaukee Area Technical College *A*
Moraine Park Technical College *A*
Nicolet Area Technical College *A*
Southwest Wisconsin Technical
   College *C, A*
Waukesha County Technical College *A*
Western Wisconsin Technical College *A*
Wisconsin Indianhead Technical
   College *C*

Curriculum/instruction

Alabama
Alabama Agricultural and Mechanical
   University *B, M*
Auburn University *D*

Arizona
Arizona State University *M, D*
Northern Arizona University *M, D*
Prescott College *B, M*
University of Phoenix *M*

Arkansas
University of Arkansas
   Pine Bluff *B*
University of Arkansas *D*

California
Azusa Pacific University *M*
California Lutheran University *M*
California Polytechnic State University:
   San Luis Obispo *M*
California State University
   Bakersfield *M*
   Chico *M*
   Dominguez Hills *M*
   Fresno *M*
   Fullerton *M*
   Hayward *M*
   Los Angeles *M*
   Northridge *M*
   Sacramento *M*
   Stanislaus *M*
Chapman University *M*
Concordia University *M*
Dominican University of California *M*
Fresno Pacific University *M*
La Sierra University *M, D*
National University *M*
Point Loma Nazarene University *M*
St. Mary's College of California *M*
San Diego State University *M, T*
Sonoma State University *M*
Stanford University *M, D*
University of California
   Riverside *M, D*
   San Diego *M*
   Santa Cruz *M*
University of La Verne *M*
University of San Diego *M*
University of San Francisco *D*
University of Southern California *M, D*
University of the Pacific *B, M, D*

Colorado
Colorado Christian University *M*
University of Colorado
   Boulder *M, D*
   Colorado Springs *M*
   Denver *M*
University of Denver *M, D*

Connecticut
Fairfield University *M*
University of Connecticut *M, D, T*
Western Connecticut State University *M*

Delaware
Delaware State University *M*
University of Delaware *M, D*

District of Columbia
Catholic University of America *D*
George Washington University *M, D*
Howard University *M*
Trinity College *M*

Florida
Florida Atlantic University *M, D*
Florida Gulf Coast University *B*
Florida International University *M, D*
University of Central Florida *M, D*
University of Florida *M, D*
University of South Florida *B, M, D*
University of West Florida *M, D*

Curriculum/instruction

Georgia
Clark Atlanta University *M*
Columbus State University *M*
Covenant College *M*
Georgia Southern University *D*

Hawaii
University of Hawaii
    Manoa *D*

Idaho
Boise State University *M, D*
Northwest Nazarene University *M*

Illinois
Benedictine University *M*
Bradley University *M*
Chicago State University *M, T*
Concordia University *M*
De Paul University *M*
Governors State University *M*
Illinois State University *M, D*
Loyola University of Chicago *M, D*
National-Louis University *M*
North Central College *M*
Northern Illinois University *M, D*
Quincy University *M*
St. Xavier University *M*
Southern Illinois University
    Carbondale *M, D*
University of Illinois
    Chicago *D*
University of St. Francis *M*

Indiana
Anderson University *M*
Ball State University *M, T*
Indiana State University *M, D*
Indiana University
    Bloomington *D*
Purdue University *D*
University of Indianapolis *M*
Valparaiso University *M*

Iowa
Buena Vista University *B*
Dordt College *M*
Drake University *M, D, T*
Iowa State University *M, D*
University of Iowa *M, D*

Kansas
Emporia State University *M*
Kansas State University *D*
Pittsburg State University *B, M*
St. Mary College *M*
Tabor College *M*
University of Kansas *M, D*
Washburn University of Topeka *M*
Wichita State University *M*

Kentucky
Campbellsville University *M*
Morehead State University *M*
Spalding University *M*
Union College *M*
University of Kentucky *M*

Louisiana
Louisiana State University and
    Agricultural and Mechanical
    College *D*
Louisiana Tech University *M, D*
Nicholls State University *M*
Our Lady of Holy Cross College *M*
Southeastern Louisiana University *M*
University of Louisiana at Lafayette *M*
University of Louisiana at Monroe *D*
University of New Orleans *M, D*
Xavier University of Louisiana *M*

Maine
University of Southern Maine *M*

Maryland
Coppin State College *M*
Frostburg State University *M*
Hood College *M*
Loyola College in Maryland *M*
University of Maryland
    Baltimore County *T*
    College Park *M, D, T*
Western Maryland College *M*

Massachusetts
American International College *M*
Atlantic Union College *M*
Boston College *M, D*
Boston University *M, D*
Framingham State College *M*
Gordon College *M*
Harvard University *M, D*
Lesley College *M, T*
Northeastern University *M*
Tufts University *M*
University of Massachusetts
    Lowell *M*
Wheelock College *M*

Michigan
Andrews University *M, D*
Calvin College *M, T*
Eastern Michigan University *M*
Michigan State University *M, D*
University of Detroit Mercy *M*
Wayne State University *D*

Minnesota
Bemidji State University *M*
College of St. Scholastica *M*
Minnesota State University,
    Mankato *M, T*
Moorhead State University *M*
St. Cloud State University *M*
University of Minnesota
    Twin Cities *M*
University of St. Thomas *M, D*
Winona State University *B, M, T*

Mississippi
Mississippi University for Women *M*
University of Mississippi *M*
University of Southern Mississippi *M*

Missouri
Central Missouri State University *M, T*
Lindenwood University *M*
St. Louis University *M, D*
University of Missouri
    Columbia *M, D*
    Kansas City *M*
    St. Louis *M*
Washington University *M*
William Woods University *M*

Montana
University of Great Falls *D*
University of Montana-Missoula *M, D*

Nebraska
Concordia University *M*
Doane College *M*
University of Nebraska
    Kearney *M*
    Lincoln *M, D*

Nevada
University of Nevada
    Las Vegas *B, M, D, T*
    Reno *D*

New Hampshire
Antioch New England Graduate
    School *M*
Keene State College *M*
Notre Dame College *M*
Rivier College *M*
University of New Hampshire *D*

New Jersey
Caldwell College *M*
Rider University *M*
Rowan University *M*
Seton Hall University *M*

New Mexico
College of the Southwest *M*
New Mexico Highlands University *M*
New Mexico State University *D*
University of New Mexico *D, T*

New York
Bank Street College of Education *M*
City University of New York
    Hunter College *M*
Columbia University
    Teachers College *M, D*
Fordham University *M, D*
Jewish Theological Seminary of
    America *M, D*
Long Island University
    C. W. Post Campus *B, M*
Manhattanville College *M*
Medaille College *M*
Mercy College *M*
Pace University:
    Pleasantville/Briarcliff *M*
Pace University *M*
Roberts Wesleyan College *M*
St. John's University *D, T*
State University of New York
    Albany *M, D*
Syracuse University *M, D*
University of Rochester *M, D*

North Carolina
Appalachian State University *B*
Campbell University *M*
North Carolina State University *M, D*
University of North Carolina
    Chapel Hill *M, D*
    Greensboro *D*
    Wilmington *M*

Ohio
Ashland University *M, T*
Cleveland State University *M*
John Carroll University *M*
Kent State University
    Ashtabula Regional Campus *M*
Kent State University *M, D*
Malone College *M*
Miami University
    Oxford Campus *M*
Mount Vernon Nazarene College *M*
Ohio University *M, D*
Otterbein College *M*
University of Cincinnati *M, D*
University of Toledo *M, D*
Wright State University *M*
Youngstown State University *M*

Oklahoma
Northeastern State University *M*
Oklahoma State University *M, D*
Oral Roberts University *M*
Southern Nazarene University *M*
University of Central Oklahoma *B*
University of Oklahoma *M, D*

Oregon
Concordia University *M*
George Fox University *M*
Portland State University *M, D*
Western Oregon University *M, T*

Pennsylvania
Bloomsburg University of
    Pennsylvania *M*
Bucknell University *M*
Community College of Philadelphia *A*
Gannon University *M*
Immaculata College *M*
Lehigh University *D*
Lock Haven University of
    Pennsylvania *M*
Neumann College *M*
Penn State
    University Park *M, D*
Temple University *M*
University of Pennsylvania *M*
Westminster College *M*

Puerto Rico
Inter American University of Puerto Rico
    Metropolitan Campus *M, D*
Pontifical Catholic University of Puerto
    Rico *M*
Turabo University *M*
University of Puerto Rico
    Rio Piedras Campus *M, D*

Rhode Island
Rhode Island College *M*

South Carolina
University of South Carolina *D*
Winthrop University *T*

South Dakota
South Dakota State University *M*
University of South Dakota *D*

Tennessee
Austin Peay State University *M*
Carson-Newman College *M*
Freed-Hardeman University *B, M, T*
Lincoln Memorial University *M*
Middle Tennessee State University *M, T*
Southern Adventist University *M*
Tennessee State University *M, D*
Tennessee Technological University *M*
Tennessee Temple University *M*
Trevecca Nazarene University *M*
University of Memphis *M, D*
University of Tennessee
    Knoxville *M, D*
Vanderbilt University *M, D*

Texas
Angelo State University *M*
Baylor University *M, D*
Concordia University at Austin *M*
Midwestern State University *M*
Our Lady of the Lake University of San
    Antonio *M*
Prairie View A&M University *M*
Texas A&M University
    Commerce *D*
    Corpus Christi *M, T*
Texas A&M University *B, M, D*
Texas Southern University *B, M, D*
Texas Tech University *M, D*
University of Houston
    Clear Lake *M*
University of Houston *M, D*
University of North Texas *D*
University of Texas
    Arlington *M*
    Austin *M, D*
    El Paso *M*
    Pan American *T*
    San Antonio *M*
    Tyler *B, M*
West Texas A&M University *M*

Utah
Utah State University *B, M, D*

Vermont
Castleton State College *B, M, T*
Johnson State College *M*
Lyndon State College *M*
St. Michael's College *M*
University of Vermont *M, D, T*

Virginia
Averett College *M*
College of William and Mary *M*
George Mason University *M*
Longwood College *M*
Lynchburg College *M*
Radford University *M*
University of Virginia *M, D*
Virginia Commonwealth University *M*
Virginia Polytechnic Institute and State
    University *M, D*
Virginia State University *M*

Washington
City University *M*
Eastern Washington University *M*
Gonzaga University *M*
Seattle Pacific University *M*

Seattle University *M*
University of Puget Sound *M*
University of Washington *D*
Walla Walla College *M*

West Virginia
West Virginia University *D*

Wisconsin
Concordia University Wisconsin *M*
Mount Mary College *M*
University of Wisconsin
    Madison *M, D*
    Milwaukee *M*
    Superior *M*

Custodial/home services

Alabama
Central Alabama Community College *A*

California
American River College *A*
Bakersfield College *A*
Chabot College *A*
Cypress College *C*
Long Beach City College *C, A*
MiraCosta College *C*
Mission College *A*

Florida
Indian River Community College *C*
Pensacola Junior College *C*
South Florida Community College *C*

Illinois
College of DuPage *C*
Elgin Community College *C*

Massachusetts
North Shore Community College *C, A*

Michigan
Bay de Noc Community College *C*

New Mexico
Dona Ana Branch Community College of
    New Mexico State University *A*

North Dakota
North Dakota State University *B*

Pennsylvania
Community College of Allegheny
    County *C*

Texas
Stephen F. Austin State University *B*

Washington
Pierce College *C*
Renton Technical College *C*
Tacoma Community College *C*

Wisconsin
Waukesha County Technical College *C*

Cytotechnology

Alabama
Community College of the Air Force *A*
Oakwood College *B*
Shelton State Community College *A*
University of Alabama
    Birmingham *B*

Arkansas
University of Arkansas
    for Medical Sciences *B*

California
California State University
    Dominguez Hills *M*
Loma Linda University *C, B*

Connecticut
University of Connecticut *B*

Florida
Barry University *B*
University of Miami *B*

Illinois
Augustana College *B*
Illinois College *B*

Indiana
Indiana University
    Bloomington *B*
Indiana University--Purdue University
    Indiana University-Purdue
        University Indianapolis *C, A, B*

Iowa
Luther College *B*

Kansas
University of Kansas
    Medical Center *B*

Kentucky
University of Louisville *B*

Massachusetts
American International College *B*

Michigan
Eastern Michigan University *B*
Northern Michigan University *B*
Wayne State University *B*

Minnesota
Minnesota State University, Mankato *B*
Moorhead State University *B*
St. Mary's University of Minnesota *B*
Winona State University *B*

Mississippi
University of Mississippi
    Medical Center *B*

Missouri
Rockhurst University *B*
University of Missouri
    St. Louis *B*

New Jersey
Bloomfield College *B*
Felician College *B*
Monmouth University *B*
St. Peter's College *B*
Thomas Edison State College *B*
University of Medicine and Dentistry of
    New Jersey
        School of Health Related
            Professions *C, B*

New York
College of St. Rose *B*
Long Island University
    Brooklyn Campus *B*
St. John's University *B*
State University of New York
    Health Science Center at
        Brooklyn *B*
    Health Science Center at Stony
        Brook *B*
    Oswego *B*
    Stony Brook *B*
    Upstate Medical University *B*

North Carolina
Central Piedmont Community College *C*
University of North Carolina
    Chapel Hill *C*

North Dakota
University of North Dakota *B*

Ohio
Notre Dame College of Ohio *B*
University of Akron *B*

Pennsylvania
Slippery Rock University of
    Pennsylvania *B*
Thiel College *B*
Thomas Jefferson University: College of
    Health Professions *C, B*

Puerto Rico
University of Puerto Rico
    Medical Sciences Campus *C*

Rhode Island
Salve Regina University *B*

Tennessee
University of Tennessee
    Memphis *B*

Texas
University of North Texas *B*

West Virginia
Alderson-Broaddus College *B*
Marshall University *B*

Wisconsin
Marian College of Fond du Lac *B*

Dairy science

California
California Polytechnic State University:
    San Luis Obispo *B*
College of the Sequoias *C*
Los Angeles Pierce College *C, A*
Modesto Junior College *A*
West Hills Community College *C, A*

Florida
University of Florida *M*

Georgia
University of Georgia *B, M*

Idaho
University of Idaho *B*

Iowa
Iowa State University *B*
Northeast Iowa Community College *C*

Minnesota
Ridgewater College: A Community and
    Technical College *C*
University of Minnesota
    Crookston *A*

Mississippi
Northwest Mississippi Community
    College *A*

New Hampshire
University of New Hampshire *A, B*

New York
Cornell University *B*
State University of New York
    College of Agriculture and
        Technology at Cobleskill *A*
    College of Agriculture and
        Technology at Morrisville *A*
    College of Technology at Alfred *A*

Ohio
Ohio State University
    Agricultural Technical Institute *A*
    Columbus Campus *M, D*

Pennsylvania
Delaware Valley College *B*

South Carolina
Clemson University *B, M*

South Dakota
South Dakota State University *B, M*

Texas
Texas A&M University *B, M, D*

Utah
Utah State University *C, A, B, M*

Vermont
Vermont Technical College *A*

Virginia
Virginia Polytechnic Institute and State
    University *B, M*

Washington
Skagit Valley College *A*

Wisconsin
Lakeshore Technical College *C*
Southwest Wisconsin Technical
    College *C*
University of Wisconsin
    Madison *B, M, D*

Dance

Alabama
Birmingham-Southern College *B*
Huntingdon College *B, T*
University of Alabama *B*

Arizona
Arizona State University *B, M*
Prescott College *B, M*
University of Arizona *B*

California
Allan Hancock College *C, A*
Cabrillo College *A*
California Institute of the Arts *C, B, M*
California State University
    Fresno *B*
    Fullerton *B*
    Hayward *B*
    Long Beach *B, M*
    Los Angeles *B*
    Northridge *B*
Chabot College *A*
Chaffey Community College *A*
Chapman University *B*
Compton Community College *A*
Cypress College *A*
Fresno City College *C, A*
Glendale Community College *C, A*
Golden West College *A*
Grossmont Community College *C, A*
Irvine Valley College *A*
Lake Tahoe Community College *A*
Long Beach City College *A*
Loyola Marymount University *B*
Mills College *B, M*
MiraCosta College *A*
Monterey Peninsula College *A*
Mount San Jacinto College *A*
Orange Coast College *A*
Palomar College *C, A*
Pitzer College *B*
Pomona College *B*
Saddleback College *A*
St. Mary's College of California *B*
San Diego State University *B*
San Francisco State University *B*
San Jose State University *B, M*
Santa Ana College *C, A*
Santa Monica College *A*
Santa Rosa Junior College *C*
Scripps College *B*
Southwestern College *A*
University of California
    Irvine *B, M*
    Los Angeles *B, M*
    Riverside *B, M, D*
    San Diego *B*
    Santa Barbara *B*
    Santa Cruz *C, B*
Westmont College *B*

Colorado
Colorado College *B*
Colorado State University *B*
Naropa University *C, B*
University of Colorado
    Boulder *B, M*

Connecticut
Connecticut College *B*
Naugatuck Valley Community-Technical
    College *A*
Trinity College *B*
University of Hartford *B*

Dance

Wesleyan University B

District of Columbia
American University M
George Washington University B
Howard University B

Florida
Florida International University B
Florida State University B, M
Jacksonville University B
Miami-Dade Community College A
Palm Beach Community College A
Polk Community College A
University of Florida B
University of South Florida B

Georgia
Brenau University B
Emory University B

Hawaii
University of Hawaii
    Manoa B, M

Idaho
Ricks College A
University of Idaho B

Illinois
Barat College B
Columbia College B
Northwestern University B
Rockford College B
Southern Illinois University
    Edwardsville B
University of Illinois
    Urbana-Champaign B, M

Indiana
Ball State University B
Butler University B
Indiana University
    Bloomington B, M
Vincennes University A

Iowa
University of Iowa B, M

Kansas
University of Kansas B

Louisiana
Centenary College of Louisiana B, T

Maryland
Charles County Community College A
Goucher College B
Montgomery College
    Rockville Campus A
Towson University B, T
University of Maryland
    Baltimore County B
    College Park B, M

Massachusetts
Boston Conservatory B, M
Dean College A
Emerson College B
Hampshire College B
Mount Holyoke College B
Simon's Rock College of Bard B
Smith College B, M
University of Massachusetts
    Amherst B

Michigan
Alma College B
Eastern Michigan University B
Hope College B, T
Lansing Community College A
Marygrove College B, T
University of Michigan B, M, T
Wayne State University B, T
Western Michigan University B

Minnesota
Gustavus Adolphus College B
St. Olaf College B
University of Minnesota
    Twin Cities B
Winona State University A

Mississippi
Belhaven College B
University of Southern Mississippi B

Missouri
Lindenwood University B
Southwest Missouri State University B
Stephens College B
University of Missouri
    Kansas City B
Washington University B
Webster University B

Montana
University of Montana-Missoula B

Nebraska
University of Nebraska
    Lincoln B, M

Nevada
University of Nevada
    Las Vegas B

New Hampshire
Antioch New England Graduate
    School C, M
Franklin Pierce College B

New Jersey
Middlesex County College A
Montclair State University B
Rowan University B
Rutgers
    The State University of New Jersey:
        Douglass College B
    The State University of New Jersey:
        Livingston College B
    The State University of New Jersey:
        Mason Gross School of the
        Arts B
    The State University of New Jersey:
        New Brunswick Graduate
        Campus M
    The State University of New Jersey:
        Rutgers College B
    The State University of New Jersey:
        University College New
        Brunswick B

New Mexico
University of New Mexico B

New York
Adelphi University B
Bard College B
Barnard College B
City University of New York
    Hunter College B, M
    Lehman College B
    Queens College B
    Queensborough Community
        College A
Columbia University
    Columbia College B
    School of General Studies B
    Teachers College M
Cornell University B
Fordham University B
Hamilton College B
Hobart and William Smith Colleges B
Hofstra University B
Juilliard School B
Long Island University
    Brooklyn Campus B
    C. W. Post Campus B
Marymount Manhattan College B
New York University B, M, D
Sarah Lawrence College B, M
Skidmore College B
State University of New York
    Buffalo B
    College at Brockport B, M, T
    College at Potsdam B
    Purchase B, M
Wells College B

North Carolina
Duke University C
East Carolina University B
Lees-McRae College B
Louisburg College A
Meredith College B, T
North Carolina School of the Arts B
University of North Carolina
    Charlotte B, T
    Greensboro B, M, T

Ohio
Antioch College B
Baldwin-Wallace College B
Case Western Reserve University M
College of Wooster B
Denison University B
Kent State University
    Stark Campus A
Kent State University B
Kenyon College B
Lake Erie College B
Oberlin College B
Ohio State University
    Columbus Campus B, M
Ohio University B
Ohio Wesleyan University B
Sinclair Community College A
University of Akron B
University of Cincinnati B
Wittenberg University B
Wright State University B

Oklahoma
Oklahoma City University B
University of Central Oklahoma B
University of Oklahoma B, M

Oregon
Reed College B
University of Oregon B, M

Pennsylvania
Allentown College of St. Francis de
    Sales B
Cedar Crest College B
Dickinson College B
La Roche College B
Mercyhurst College B
Muhlenberg College B
Point Park College B
Slippery Rock University of
    Pennsylvania B
Temple University B, M, D
University of the Arts C, B

Rhode Island
Roger Williams University A, B

South Carolina
Coker College B
Columbia College B
Winthrop University B

Tennessee
Columbia State Community College C
University of Tennessee
    Martin B

Texas
Kilgore College A
Lamar University B
Midland College A
Sam Houston State University B, M
Southern Methodist University B, M
Southwest Texas State University B
Stephen F. Austin State University B, T
Texas Christian University B, M, T
Texas Tech University B
Texas Woman's University B, M, D, T
Tyler Junior College A

University of North Texas B
University of Texas
    Austin B
University of the Incarnate Word B
West Texas A&M University B

Utah
Brigham Young University B
Dixie State College of Utah A
Snow College A
University of Utah B, M
Utah State University B
Weber State University B

Vermont
Bennington College B
Johnson State College B
Marlboro College B
Middlebury College B

Virginia
George Mason University B, M
Hollins University B
Longwood College T
Radford University B
Randolph-Macon Woman's College B
Shenandoah University B, M
Sweet Briar College B
Virginia Commonwealth University B
Virginia Intermont College B

Washington
Cornish College of the Arts B
Evergreen State College B
University of Washington B, M

West Virginia
Marshall University B

Wisconsin
Alverno College T
University of Wisconsin
    Madison B, M
    Milwaukee B
    Stevens Point B
    Whitewater B, T

Wyoming
Western Wyoming Community
    College A

Dance therapy

California
University of California
    Los Angeles M

Colorado
Naropa University C, B, M

Illinois
Barat College B
Columbia College M

New Hampshire
Antioch New England Graduate
    School M

New York
City University of New York
    Hunter College B, M
Pratt Institute M

Pennsylvania
MCP Hahnemann University M
Mercyhurst College B

Wisconsin
University of Wisconsin
    Madison B, M

Data entry/information processing

Alabama
Bessemer State Technical College C
James H. Faulkner State Community
    College C, A

Data entry/information processing

Lawson State Community College *A*
Northwest-Shoals Community College *A*

Arizona
Central Arizona College *A*
Gateway Community College *C*
Paradise Valley Community
  College *C, A*
Phoenix College *C*
Scottsdale Community College *C*
South Mountain Community
  College *C, A*
Yavapai College *C, A*

Arkansas
Arkansas State University
  Beebe Branch *A*
Phillips Community College of the
  University of Arkansas *C, A*
Southern Arkansas University
  Tech *C*
Westark College *C, A*

California
Allan Hancock College *C, A*
Bakersfield College *A*
Barstow College *C, A*
Butte College *C, A*
Cabrillo College *C, A*
California State University
  Fullerton *B, M*
Canada College *C, A*
Cerro Coso Community College *A*
Chabot College *C, A*
Chaffey Community College *C*
City College of San Francisco *C, A*
Coastline Community College *A*
College of the Canyons *C*
College of the Desert *C, A*
College of the Redwoods *A*
College of the Sequoias *C*
Columbia College *C*
Compton Community College *C, A*
Cypress College *C, A*
Diablo Valley College *A*
East Los Angeles College *C, A*
Evergreen Valley College *A*
Fresno City College *C*
Gavilan Community College *C*
Golden West College *C, A*
Grossmont Community College *C, A*
Humphreys College *C, A, B*
Imperial Valley College *C, A*
Irvine Valley College *C, A*
Kings River Community College *C*
Los Angeles Harbor College *C, A*
Los Angeles Southwest College *A*
Los Angeles Valley College *C, A*
MiraCosta College *C*
Ohlone College *C, A*
Orange Coast College *C, A*
Riverside Community College *C, A*
Saddleback College *C*
San Diego City College *C, A*
San Diego Mesa College *C, A*
San Joaquin Delta College *A*
San Jose City College *A*
Santa Barbara City College *C, A*
Santa Rosa Junior College *C*
Shasta College *C, A*
Sierra College *C, A*
Solano Community College *A*
West Hills Community College *A*
West Valley College *C, A*

Colorado
Community College of Aurora *A*
Community College of Denver *C*
Morgan Community College *C*
Pikes Peak Community College *C*
Pueblo Community College *C, A*
Red Rocks Community College *C, A*

Connecticut
Briarwood College *C, A*
Gateway Community College *C*

Middlesex Community-Technical
  College *C*
Naugatuck Valley Community-Technical
  College *C*
Northwestern Connecticut
  Community-Technical College *C*
Norwalk Community-Technical
  College *C, A*
Quinebaug Valley Community
  College *C, A*
Three Rivers Community-Technical
  College *A*

Delaware
Delaware Technical and Community
  College
    Owens Campus *C, A*
    Stanton/Wilmington Campus *C, A*
    Terry Campus *C, A*

District of Columbia
University of the District of
  Columbia *C, A*

Florida
Daytona Beach Community
  College *C, A*
Florida Community College at
  Jacksonville *C*
Indian River Community College *A*
Lake-Sumter Community College *A*
Pasco-Hernando Community College *C*
St. Petersburg Junior College *C, A*
Santa Fe Community College *A*
Tallahassee Community College *C*
Valencia Community College *A*

Georgia
Abraham Baldwin Agricultural
  College *A*
DeKalb Technical Institute *C*
Gwinnett Technical Institute *A*
Macon State College *C, B*
South Georgia College *A*
Valdosta State University *A, B*
Waycross College *A*

Hawaii
University of Hawaii
  Kapiolani Community
    College *C, A*

Idaho
Eastern Idaho Technical College *C, A*

Illinois
Black Hawk College
  East Campus *C, A*
Black Hawk College *C, A*
City Colleges of Chicago
  Malcolm X College *C, A*
College of Lake County *C, A*
Danville Area Community College *C*
Elgin Community College *C*
Illinois Eastern Community Colleges
  Frontier Community College *C, A*
  Lincoln Trail College *C, A*
  Olney Central College *C, A*
  Wabash Valley College *C, A*
John A. Logan College *C*
John Wood Community College *C, A*
Joliet Junior College *C, A*
Kankakee Community College *C*
Kaskaskia College *A*
Kishwaukee College *C*
Lake Land College *C*
Lincoln Land Community College *C, A*
MacCormac College *C*
McHenry County College *C*
Morton College *C*
National-Louis University *C*
Parkland College *A*
Prairie State College *C*
Rend Lake College *A*
Sauk Valley Community College *A*
Shawnee Community College *C*
Southeastern Illinois College *A*
Triton College *C, A*

Waubonsee Community College *C, A*
William Rainey Harper College *C*

Indiana
Grace College *A*
Oakland City University *C, A*
Vincennes University *A*

Iowa
American Institute of Business *A*
Des Moines Area Community College *C*
Hawkeye Community College *C*
Kirkwood Community College *C, A*
Northeast Iowa Community College *C*

Kansas
Allen County Community College *C*
Central Christian College *A*
Colby Community College *A*
Cowley County Community
  College *C, A*
Independence Community College *C, A*
Pratt Community College *C, A*
Seward County Community
  College *C, A*
Washburn University of Topeka *A*

Kentucky
Murray State University *A*
National Business College *A*
Paducah Community College *A*

Louisiana
Nunez Community College *C*
Southern University
  Shreveport *A*

Maine
Andover College *A*
Central Maine Technical College *C, A*
Husson College *A*
Southern Maine Technical College *A*

Maryland
Baltimore City Community College *C, A*
Community College of Baltimore County
  Catonsville *C, A*
Hagerstown Community College *C, A*
Montgomery College
  Germantown Campus *A*
  Takoma Park Campus *C*
Prince George's Community
  College *C, A*
Villa Julie College *A*

Massachusetts
Franklin Institute of Boston *C*
Holyoke Community College *C, A*
Middlesex Community College *C, A*
Mount Wachusett Community College *C*
North Shore Community College *C, A*
Northern Essex Community College *A*
Roxbury Community College *A*
Springfield Technical Community
  College *C*

Michigan
Baker College
  of Auburn Hills *A*
  of Muskegon *A*
  of Owosso *B*
  of Port Huron *A*
Cornerstone College and Grand Rapids
  Baptist Seminary *A*
Davenport College of Business *A*
Gogebic Community College *A*
Lake Superior State University *A*
Lansing Community College *A*
Macomb Community College *C, A*
Monroe County Community
  College *C, A*
Montcalm Community College *C, A*
Mott Community College *A*
North Central Michigan College *C*
Northwestern Michigan College *A*
Oakland Community College *C, A*
St. Clair County Community College *A*
West Shore Community College *A*

Minnesota
Alexandria Technical College *C, A*
Hennepin Technical College *C, A*
Itasca Community College *A*
Lake Superior College: A Community
  and Technical College *C*
Mesabi Range Community and Technical
  College *C, A*
Minnesota State College - Southeast
  Technical *C*
Northland Community & Technical
  College *C*
Pine Technical College *C*
St. Cloud Technical College *C*
St. Paul Technical College *C, A*

Mississippi
Copiah-Lincoln Community College *A*
Mary Holmes College *A*
Mississippi Gulf Coast Community
  College
    Jackson County Campus *A*
    Jefferson Davis Campus *A*
    Perkinston *A*
Northwest Mississippi Community
  College *A*

Missouri
Baptist Bible College *A*
East Central College *C, A*
Longview Community College *C, A*
Maple Woods Community College *C, A*
Penn Valley Community College *C, A*
St. Louis Community College
  St. Louis Community College at
    Florissant Valley *C, A*
  St. Louis Community College at
    Meramec *C, A*
State Fair Community College *A*

Montana
Flathead Valley Community College *A*
Western Montana College of The
  University of Montana *A*

Nebraska
Mid Plains Community College Area *C*

Nevada
Western Nevada Community
  College *C, A*

New Hampshire
Hesser College *C, A*
New Hampshire Community Technical
  College
    Berlin *C*
    Nashua *C*

New Jersey
Berkeley College *C*
Brookdale Community College *A*
County College of Morris *C*
Essex County College *A*
Gloucester County College *A*
Salem Community College *A*
The College of New Jersey *B*
Thomas Edison State College *C*
Warren County Community College *C*

New Mexico
Clovis Community College *A*
New Mexico Junior College *C, A*
New Mexico State University
  Alamogordo *C*
Santa Fe Community College *A*

New York
Berkeley College of New York City *C*
Briarcliffe College *A*
City University of New York
  Bronx Community College *A*
  Hostos Community College *C*
  Lehman College *C*
  Medgar Evers College *A*
  Queensborough Community
    College *C*
Clinton Community College *C, A*

Data entry/information processing

Columbia-Greene Community College *C, A*
Dutchess Community College *C*
Fulton-Montgomery Community College *A*
Herkimer County Community College *C, A*
Hudson Valley Community College *C, A*
Jamestown Community College *C*
Jefferson Community College *C, A*
Niagara County Community College *A*
Orange County Community College *C, A*
Pace University: Pleasantville/Briarcliff *A*
Pace University *A*
St. Joseph's College
St. Joseph's College: Suffolk Campus *C*
State University of New York
College of Agriculture and Technology at Morrisville *C, A*
College of Technology at Alfred *A*
Suffolk County Community College *C*
Tompkins-Cortland Community College *A*
Trocaire College *C*
Ulster County Community College *A*
Westchester Business Institute *C, A*

North Carolina
Bladen Community College *A*
Cecils College *A*
East Carolina University *B*
Halifax Community College *A*
Piedmont Community College *A*
Vance-Granville Community College *A*
Western Piedmont Community College *A*

North Dakota
Bismarck State College *C, A*
Mayville State University *A*

Ohio
Bowling Green State University
Firelands College *C*
Central Ohio Technical College *C*
Columbus State Community College *C, A*
David N. Myers College *A, B*
Kent State University
Ashtabula Regional Campus *A*
Trumbull Campus *A*
Marion Technical College *C*
Miami University
Middletown Campus *C*
Miami-Jacobs College *A*
Northwest State Community College *C, A*
Northwestern College *C, A*
Sinclair Community College *C*
Southern State Community College *C*
Terra Community College *C*
University of Akron
Wayne College *C, A*
University of Akron *A*
University of Cincinnati
Clermont College *A*
Raymond Walters College *C*
Youngstown State University *A*

Oklahoma
Northeastern Oklahoma Agricultural and Mechanical College *A*
Oklahoma State University
Oklahoma City *C*
Rogers State University *A*
St. Gregory's University *A*
Tulsa Community College *A*
Western Oklahoma State College *A*

Oregon
Chemeketa Community College *A*
Portland Community College *C, A*

Pennsylvania
Bucks County Community College *C*
Butler County Community College *A*
C.H.I/RETS Campus *C*
California University of Pennsylvania *A*
Community College of Beaver County *C, A*
Lackawanna Junior College *C*
Montgomery County Community College *A*
Peirce College *C, A, B*
Pennsylvania College of Technology *A*
Reading Area Community College *C, A*
Robert Morris College *A*
South Hills School of Business & Technology *C*

Puerto Rico
American University of Puerto Rico *B*
Colegio Universitario del Este *A*
Huertas Junior College *C*
ICPR Junior College *C*
National College of Business and Technology *A*
Turabo University *A*
Universidad Metropolitana *C, A, B*

Rhode Island
Johnson & Wales University *A*

South Carolina
Aiken Technical College *C*
Central Carolina Technical College *C*
Chesterfield-Marlboro Technical College *C, A*
Denmark Technical College *C*
Florence-Darlington Technical College *C*
Horry-Georgetown Technical College *C*
Orangeburg-Calhoun Technical College *C*
Tri-County Technical College *C*
Trident Technical College *C*
York Technical College *C*

Tennessee
Austin Peay State University *A*
Chattanooga State Technical Community College *C*
Hiwassee College *A*
Northeast State Technical Community College *C*
Pellissippi State Technical Community College *A*
Shelby State Community College *C*

Texas
Alvin Community College *C*
Amarillo College *C*
Austin Community College *C*
Brazosport College *C, A*
Brookhaven College *A*
Cedar Valley College *A*
Central Texas College *C*
Coastal Bend College *A*
College of the Mainland *C, A*
Eastfield College *A*
El Paso Community College *C*
Galveston College *C*
Grayson County College *A*
Hill College *C, A*
Jacksonville College *C*
Midland College *A*
Navarro College *A*
North Central Texas College *A*
North Lake College *A*
Palo Alto College *A*
Paris Junior College *A*
San Antonio College *C*
San Jacinto College
North *C, A*
Southwest Texas Junior College *A*
Temple College *A*
Texas State Technical College
Harlingen *C, A*
Texas Wesleyan University *B*
Trinity Valley Community College *C, A*
Vernon Regional Junior College *C, A*
Weatherford College *C*

Utah
Salt Lake Community College *A*

Virginia
Dabney S. Lancaster Community College *C*
ECPI College of Technology *C, A*
Germanna Community College *C*
J. Sargeant Reynolds Community College *C*
Mountain Empire Community College *C*
National Business College *C*
New River Community College *A*
Northern Virginia Community College *C*
Virginia Western Community College *A*

Washington
Big Bend Community College *A*
Centralia Community College *C, A*
Clark College *C, A*
Green River Community College *C, A*
Lower Columbia College *C, A*
North Seattle Community College *A*
Seattle Central Community College *C*
South Seattle Community College *A*
Spokane Community College *C, A*

West Virginia
College of West Virginia *C*
Fairmont State College *A*
Glenville State College *B*
Shepherd College *A*
West Virginia Northern Community College *C*
West Virginia University Parkersburg *A*

Wisconsin
Blackhawk Technical College *C, A*
Chippewa Valley Technical College *A*
Lakeshore Technical College *A*
Madison Area Technical College *C*
Moraine Park Technical College *A*
Northeast Wisconsin Technical College *C, A*
Southwest Wisconsin Technical College *C*
Western Wisconsin Technical College *A*

Wyoming
Laramie County Community College *A*
Western Wyoming Community College *C, A*

Data processing technology

Alabama
Chattahoochee Valley Community College *C*
Community College of the Air Force *A*
Harry M. Ayers State Technical College *C, A*
J. F. Drake State Technical College *A*
John M. Patterson State Technical College *C*
Northwest-Shoals Community College *C, A*
Wallace State Community College at Hanceville *A*

Arizona
Arizona Western College *C*
Central Arizona College *A*
Eastern Arizona College *C*
Mohave Community College *C*
Northland Pioneer College *C, A*
Pima Community College *C*

Arkansas
Arkansas State University *B*
University of Arkansas *B*
University of Central Arkansas *B*

California
Bakersfield College *A*
Barstow College *C*
Cabrillo College *A*
Cerritos Community College *A*
Chabot College *C, A*
College of the Redwoods *C*
Compton Community College *C, A*
Cypress College *C, A*
Fresno City College *C, A*
Gavilan Community College *C*
Heald Business College
Fresno *C, A*
Los Angeles Mission College *C*
Los Angeles Valley College *C, A*
Monterey Peninsula College *C, A*
Mount San Antonio College *C, A*
Pacific Union College *B*
Pasadena City College *C, A*
Porterville College *C*
San Diego City College *C, A*
San Joaquin Delta College *A*
Santa Ana College *C, A*
Santa Monica College *C, A*
Sierra College *A*
Skyline College *C, A*
Ventura College *A*
Victor Valley College *C*
Yuba College *C*

Colorado
Colorado Mountain College
Alpine Campus *C*
Spring Valley Campus *C*
Denver Technical College: A Division of DeVry University *A, B*
Red Rocks Community College *C, A*

Connecticut
Norwalk Community-Technical College *A*
Three Rivers Community-Technical College *C*
University of New Haven *B*

Delaware
Delaware Technical and Community College
Owens Campus *C, A*
Stanton/Wilmington Campus *A*
Terry Campus *A*

Florida
Broward Community College *A*
Florida Community College at Jacksonville *C, A*
Florida Keys Community College *C*
Florida Metropolitan University
Orlando College North *A*
Gulf Coast Community College *C*
Hillsborough Community College *C*
Indian River Community College *C*
Keiser College *A*
Miami-Dade Community College *C*
Pasco-Hernando Community College *C*
Santa Fe Community College *A*
Seminole Community College *C*
South Florida Community College *C*
Tallahassee Community College *C*

Georgia
Abraham Baldwin Agricultural College *A*
Clayton College and State University *C, A*
Columbus State University *C*
Dalton State College *C, A*
Darton College *A*
South Georgia College *C*
Waycross College *C*

Hawaii
Hawaii Pacific University *A*
University of Hawaii
Kapiolani Community College *C, A*

Illinois
Black Hawk College
 East Campus *A*
Chicago State University *B*
City Colleges of Chicago
 Harold Washington College *C, A*
 Olive-Harvey College *C, A*
Highland Community College *A*
Kishwaukee College *C*
Lewis and Clark Community College *A*
Lincoln Land Community College *A*
Oakton Community College *C, A*
Parkland College *A*
Sauk Valley Community College *C, A*
Southwestern Ilinois College *A*
Spoon River College *C, A*
Triton College *C, A*
William Rainey Harper College *C, A*

Indiana
Indiana State University *B, M*
Indiana University
 Northwest *C, A, B*
Indiana University--Purdue University
 Indiana University-Purdue
  University Fort Wayne *C*
Purdue University
 North Central Campus *A*
Purdue University *A, B*
Tri-State University *A*

Iowa
American Institute of Business *A*
Dordt College *A*
Northeast Iowa Community College *A*
Southeastern Community College
 North Campus *C, A*

Kansas
Colby Community College *A*
Dodge City Community College *C, A*
Hutchinson Community College *A*
Independence Community College *C, A*
Kansas City Kansas Community
 College *C, A*
Seward County Community
 College *C, A*

Kentucky
Henderson Community College *A*
Kentucky State University *A*
Lexington Community College *A*
Maysville Community College *A*
Owensboro Junior College of
 Business *C, A*
Southeast Community College *A*
Thomas More College *A, B*
Western Kentucky University *A*

Louisiana
Delgado Community College *A*
Louisiana State University
 Alexandria *A*
McNeese State University *A*

Maine
Andover College *C, A*
Husson College *A*

Maryland
Allegany College *C*
Cecil Community College *C, A*
Community College of Baltimore County
 Catonsville *C, A*
Howard Community College *C, A*
Montgomery College
 Germantown Campus *A*
Wor-Wic Community College *C*

Massachusetts
Bay Path College *B*
Berkshire Community College *C, A*
Franklin Institute of Boston *C*
Springfield Technical Community
 College *A*

Michigan
Baker College
 of Auburn Hills *A*
 of Jackson *A*
 of Mount Clemens *A*
 of Muskegon *A*
 of Port Huron *A*
Bay de Noc Community College *C*
Detroit College of Business *C*
Gogebic Community College *A*
Grand Rapids Community College *C, A*
Jackson Community College *C, A*
Kalamazoo Valley Community
 College *A*
Lansing Community College *A*
Montcalm Community College *A*
Mott Community College *C*
Muskegon Community College *C, A*
North Central Michigan College *A*
St. Clair County Community
 College *C, A*
Schoolcraft College *C*
Washtenaw Community College *A*
West Shore Community College *C, A*

Minnesota
Hennepin Technical College *C, A*
Lake Superior College: A Community
 and Technical College *C*
St. Cloud Technical College *C*
Winona State University *B*

Mississippi
Copiah-Lincoln Community College *C*
East Central Community College *A*
Hinds Community College *C, A*
Jackson State University *B*
Mississippi Gulf Coast Community
 College
  Jefferson Davis Campus *A*
Northwest Mississippi Community
 College *A*
Southwest Mississippi Community
 College *C, A*
University of Southern Mississippi *B*

Missouri
Jefferson College *A*
St. Louis Community College
 St. Louis Community College at
  Florissant Valley *C, A*
 St. Louis Community College at
  Forest Park *C, A*
 St. Louis Community College at
  Meramec *C, A*

Montana
Little Big Horn College *A*
Miles Community College *A*
Montana Tech of the University of
 Montana: College of Technology *A*
Montana Tech of the University of
 Montana *A*
Stone Child College *A*

Nebraska
Mid Plains Community College Area *A*
Northeast Community College *C*

Nevada
Community College of Southern
 Nevada *A*
Western Nevada Community College *C*

New Hampshire
New Hampshire Community Technical
 College
  Laconia *C, A*
  Nashua *C, A*

New Jersey
Atlantic Cape Community College *A*
Brookdale Community College *A*
Burlington County College *C, A*
Essex County College *C*
Gloucester County College *A*
Rowan University *C, B*
St. Peter's College *A*

Salem Community College *A*
Stevens Institute of Technology *M, D*

New Mexico
Albuquerque Technical-Vocational
 Institute *C, A*
Dona Ana Branch Community College of
 New Mexico State University *A*
New Mexico State University
 Carlsbad *C*
San Juan College *A*

New York
Adirondack Community College *C, A*
Cayuga County Community
 College *C, A*
City University of New York
 Bronx Community College *A*
 Hostos Community College *A*
 Kingsborough Community
  College *A*
 La Guardia Community College *A*
 New York City Technical
  College *A*
 Queensborough Community
  College *A*
College of St. Rose *C*
Columbia-Greene Community College *A*
Five Towns College *C, A*
Fulton-Montgomery Community
 College *A*
Genesee Community College *C*
Herkimer County Community College *A*
Hudson Valley Community College *C, A*
Iona College *C*
Jamestown Business College *A*
New York Institute of Technology *A*
Onondaga Community College *C*
Orange County Community College *A*
Pace University:
 Pleasantville/Briarcliff *A, B*
Pace University *A, B*
Rockland Community College *C, A*
St. John's University *A*
State University of New York
 College of Agriculture and
  Technology at Cobleskill *A*
 College of Technology at Alfred *A*
 College of Technology at Delhi *C*
 Farmingdale *C, A*
 Purchase *C*
Tompkins-Cortland Community
 College *A*
Westchester Business Institute *C, A*

North Carolina
Caldwell Community College and
 Technical Institute *A*
Haywood Community College *A*
James Sprunt Community College *A*
Lenoir Community College *C, A*
Western Piedmont Community
 College *A*

North Dakota
Lake Region State College *C, A*

Ohio
Belmont Technical College *C*
Cincinnati State Technical and
 Community College *A*
Davis College *A*
Jefferson Community College *C, A*
Kent State University *C*
Miami-Jacobs College *A*
Northwest State Community College *C*
Ohio Valley Business College *A*
RETS Tech Center *C*
Shawnee State University *A*
University of Akron *A*
University of Toledo *A*
Washington State Community College *A*
Youngstown State University *A*

Oklahoma
Cameron University *A*
Connors State College *C, A*

Oklahoma City Community College *A*
Oklahoma State University
 Oklahoma City *C, A*

Oregon
Lane Community College *A*

Pennsylvania
Bucks County Community College *A*
Delaware County Community College *A*
Gannon University *C*
Harrisburg Area Community
 College *C, A*
Johnson Technical Institute *A*
Laurel Business Institute *A*
Mercyhurst College *C*
Montgomery County Community
 College *A*
Northampton County Area Community
 College *A*
Reading Area Community College *A*
St. Francis College *A*
Sawyer School *C*
University of Pittsburgh
 Titusville *C*
Yorktowne Business Institute *A*

Puerto Rico
Colegio Universitario del Este *A, B*
Humacao Community College *C*

Rhode Island
Community College of Rhode Island *A*

South Carolina
Aiken Technical College *A*
Chesterfield-Marlboro Technical
 College *C, A*
Florence-Darlington Technical College *A*
Horry-Georgetown Technical
 College *C, A*
Midlands Technical College *A*
Orangeburg-Calhoun Technical
 College *C, A*
Piedmont Technical College *C, A*
Spartanburg Technical College *A*
Technical College of the
 Lowcountry *C, A*
Tri-County Technical College *A*
Trident Technical College *C, A*

South Dakota
Kilian Community College *A*
Sinte Gleska University *A*

Tennessee
Northeast State Technical Community
 College *C*

Texas
Alvin Community College *C*
Angelina College *C, A*
Austin Community College *C*
Brazosport College *C, A*
Central Texas College *C, A*
Coastal Bend College *A*
Collin County Community College
 District *C*
Eastfield College *A*
El Paso Community College *C*
Galveston College *C*
Hill College *C, A*
Howard College *C*
Lee College *C, A*
Midland College *A*
North Central Texas College *A*
Paris Junior College *C, A*
St. Philip's College *C*
San Jacinto College
 North *C, A*
South Plains College *A*
Southwest Texas Junior College *A*
Stephen F. Austin State University *B*
Temple College *C, A*
Texas State Technical College
 Waco *C, A*
Trinity Valley Community College *A*
Tyler Junior College *C*

199

Data processing technology

University of Texas
   El Paso *B*
Vernon Regional Junior College *C, A*
Weatherford College *C, A*
Western Texas College *C, A*
Wharton County Junior College *A*

Utah
Dixie State College of Utah *A*
LDS Business College *A*
Salt Lake Community College *C*
Southern Utah University *A*

Vermont
Burlington College *C*

Virginia
ECPI College of Technology *C, A*
Eastern Mennonite University *A*
J. Sargeant Reynolds Community
   College *C, A*
Lord Fairfax Community College *C*
Mountain Empire Community College *C*
Virginia Highlands Community
   College *A*

Washington
Centralia College *A*
Columbia Basin College *A*
Edmonds Community College *A*
Lake Washington Technical College *C, A*
Lower Columbia College *C, A*
North Seattle Community College *C, A*
Peninsula College *A*
Pierce College *C, A*
Renton Technical College *C*
Shoreline Community College *C, A*
South Puget Sound Community
   College *C, A*
Spokane Community College *C, A*
Tacoma Community College *C*
Walla Walla College *B*
Walla Walla Community College *C, A*
Whatcom Community College *C, A*
Yakima Valley Community College *C*

West Virginia
Potomac State College of West Virginia
   University *A*
West Virginia Northern Community
   College *C, A*

Wisconsin
Lakeshore Technical College *A*
Moraine Park Technical College *A*
Northeast Wisconsin Technical
   College *A*
Southwest Wisconsin Technical
   College *C*
Wisconsin Indianhead Technical
   College *A*

Wyoming
Casper College *A*
Central Wyoming College *C, A*
Western Wyoming Community
   College *C, A*

Demography/population studies

California
Long Beach City College *C, A*
University of California
   Berkeley *M, D*
University of Southern California *M*

District of Columbia
Georgetown University *M*

Florida
Florida State University *C, M*

Kansas
Coffeyville Community College *A*

Louisiana
Tulane University *M, D*

Massachusetts
Hampshire College *B*

Michigan
University of Michigan *D*

New Jersey
Princeton University *M, D*

New York
State University of New York
   Albany *B, M*

North Carolina
Western Carolina University *B*

Ohio
Bowling Green State University *M*

Pennsylvania
University of Pennsylvania *M, D*

Puerto Rico
University of Puerto Rico
   Medical Sciences Campus *M*

Rhode Island
Brown University *B*

Wisconsin
University of Wisconsin
   Madison *M, D*

Dental assistant

Alabama
Calhoun Community College *C, A*
Community College of the Air Force *A*
James H. Faulkner State Community
   College *C, A*
Northwest-Shoals Community College *A*
Wallace State Community College at
   Hanceville *C, A*

Alaska
University of Alaska
   Anchorage *C, A*

Arizona
Phoenix College *A*
Pima Community College *C*

California
Allan Hancock College *C, A*
Bakersfield College *A*
California State University
   Dominguez Hills *B*
Cerritos Community College *C, A*
Chaffey Community College *C, A*
Citrus College *C, A*
City College of San Francisco *C, A*
College of San Mateo *C, A*
College of the Redwoods *C*
Contra Costa College *A*
Cypress College *C, A*
Diablo Valley College *A*
Foothill College *C, A*
Kings River Community College *C, A*
Merced College *C, A*
Modesto Junior College *A*
Monterey Peninsula College *C, A*
Orange Coast College *C, A*
Palomar College *C, A*
Pasadena City College *C, A*
Rio Hondo College *A*
Sacramento City College *C, A*
San Diego Mesa College *C, A*
San Jose City College *A*
Santa Rosa Junior College *A*

Colorado
Front Range Community College *C*
Pikes Peak Community College *C, A*
Pueblo Community College *C, A*

Connecticut
Briarwood College *C, A*
Tunxis Community College *C*

Florida
Brevard Community College *C*
Broward Community College *C*
Daytona Beach Community College *C*
Edison Community College *C*
Gulf Coast Community College *C*
Indian River Community College *C*
Palm Beach Community College *C*
Pasco-Hernando Community College *C*
Pensacola Junior College *C*
Santa Fe Community College *C*
Tallahassee Community College *C*

Georgia
Brewton-Parker College *A*

Hawaii
University of Hawaii
   Kapiolani Community
   College *C, A*

Idaho
Boise State University *C*
College of Southern Idaho *A*
Eastern Idaho Technical College *C*

Illinois
Black Hawk College *C*
Elgin Community College *C*
John A. Logan College *C*
Kaskaskia College *C*
Lewis and Clark Community College *C*
Morton College *C*
Parkland College *C*
Rock Valley College *C*
Shawnee Community College *A*

Indiana
Indiana University
   Northwest *C*
   South Bend *C*
Indiana University--Purdue University
   Indiana University-Purdue
     University Fort Wayne *C*
   Indiana University-Purdue
     University Indianapolis *C*
Ivy Tech State College
   Lafayette *C, A*
University of Southern Indiana *A*

Iowa
Des Moines Area Community College *C*
Hawkeye Community College *C*
Iowa Western Community College *C*
Kirkwood Community College *C, A*
Marshalltown Community College *C*
Northeast Iowa Community College *C*
Scott Community College *C*
Western Iowa Tech Community
   College *C*

Kansas
Dodge City Community College *C, A*

Kentucky
Elizabethtown Community College *A*
Hazard Community College *A*

Maine
University of Maine
   Augusta *A*

Maryland
Montgomery College
   Takoma Park Campus *C, A*

Massachusetts
Massasoit Community College *C*
Middlesex Community College *C, A*
Mount Ida College *C, A*
Northeastern University *A, B*
Northern Essex Community College *C*
Springfield Technical Community
   College *C*

Michigan
Bay de Noc Community College *C*
Delta College *C, A*
Grand Rapids Community College *A*
Lake Michigan College *C, A*
Mott Community College *A*
Northwestern Michigan College *A*
Washtenaw Community College *C*
Wayne County Community College *C*

Minnesota
Dakota County Technical College *C*
Hennepin Technical College *C, A*
Hibbing Community College: A
   Technical and Community College *A*
Rochester Community and Technical
   College *C*
St. Cloud Technical College *C, A*
South Central Technical College *A*

Mississippi
Hinds Community College *C, A*

Missouri
East Central College *C, A*
St. Louis Community College
   St. Louis Community College at
     Forest Park *A*

Montana
Montana State University
   College of Technology-Great
     Falls *C*
Salish Kootenai College *A*

Nebraska
Central Community College *C, A*
Metropolitan Community College *C*
Mid Plains Community College Area *C*
Southeast Community College
   Lincoln Campus *C*

New Hampshire
New Hampshire Technical Institute *C*

New Jersey
Camden County College *C, A*
Essex County College *C*
Union County College *C*
University of Medicine and Dentistry of
   New Jersey
   School of Health Related
     Professions *C, A*

New York
Monroe Community College *C*
New York University *C*

North Carolina
Alamance Community College *C*
Asheville Buncombe Technical
   Community College *C*
Brunswick Community College *C*
Cape Fear Community College *C*
Central Piedmont Community College *C*
Coastal Carolina Community College *A*
Fayetteville Technical Community
   College *C*
Guilford Technical Community
   College *C*
Rowan-Cabarrus Community College *C*
University of North Carolina
   Chapel Hill *C*
Wake Technical Community College *C*
Western Piedmont Community
   College *C*
Wilkes Community College *C*

North Dakota
North Dakota State College of Science *C*

Ohio
Jefferson Community College *C, A*
Lima Technical College *A*
Ohio Valley Business College *A*

Oklahoma
Rose State College *C, A*

Oregon
Central Oregon Community College *C*
Chemeketa Community College *A*
Lane Community College *C*
Linn-Benton Community College *C*

Portland Community College *C*

Pennsylvania
Community College of Allegheny County *C*
Community College of Philadelphia *C*
Harcum College *C, A*
Harrisburg Area Community College *C*
Luzerne County Community College *C*
Manor College *A*
Median School of Allied Health Careers *C*
Northampton County Area Community College *C*
West Chester University of Pennsylvania *B*
Westmoreland County Community College *C*
Yorktowne Business Institute *A*

Puerto Rico
Huertas Junior College *A*
Ramirez College of Business and Technology *A*
University of Puerto Rico Medical Sciences Campus *A*

Rhode Island
Community College of Rhode Island *C*

South Carolina
Aiken Technical College *C*
Florence-Darlington Technical College *C*
Greenville Technical College *C*
Horry-Georgetown Technical College *C*
Midlands Technical College *C*
Spartanburg Technical College *A*
Tri-County Technical College *C*
Trident Technical College *C*
York Technical College *C*

Tennessee
East Tennessee State University *C*
Roane State Community College *A*
Volunteer State Community College *C*

Texas
Amarillo College *C*
Del Mar College *C, A*
El Paso Community College *C, A*
Grayson County College *C*
Houston Community College System *C*
Lon Morris College *C*
Tarrant County College *C*
Texas State Technical College
    Harlingen *A*
    Waco *C*
University of North Texas *B*

Virginia
J. Sargeant Reynolds Community College *C*
Wytheville Community College *C*

Washington
Columbia Basin College *C*
Highline Community College *A*
Lake Washington Technical College *C, A*
Renton Technical College *C*
South Puget Sound Community College *C, A*
Spokane Community College *C, A*

Wisconsin
Blackhawk Technical College *C*
Chippewa Valley Technical College *C*
Concordia University Wisconsin *C*
Gateway Technical College *C*
Lakeshore Technical College *C*
Madison Area Technical College *C*
Moraine Park Technical College *C*
Northeast Wisconsin Technical College *C*
Waukesha County Technical College *C*
Western Wisconsin Technical College *C*

Wyoming
Sheridan College *C*

Western Wyoming Community College *A*

Dental hygiene studies

Alabama
Northwest-Shoals Community College *A*
Wallace State Community College at Hanceville *A*

Alaska
University of Alaska
    Anchorage *A*

Arizona
Northern Arizona University *B*
Phoenix College *A*
Pima Community College *A*
Rio Salado College *A*

Arkansas
University of Arkansas for Medical Sciences *A, B*
Westark College *A*

California
Cabrillo College *C, A*
Cerritos Community College *C, A*
Chabot College *C, A*
Cypress College *C, A*
Diablo Valley College *C, A*
Foothill College *A*
Fresno City College *A*
Loma Linda University *B*
Pasadena City College *C, A*
Riverside Community College *A*
Sacramento City College *C, A*
Santa Rosa Junior College *C, A*
Taft College *A*
University of California
    San Francisco *B*
University of Southern California *B*
West Los Angeles College *C, A*

Colorado
Colorado Northwestern Community College *A*
Community College of Denver *A*
Pueblo Community College *A*
University of Colorado
    Health Sciences Center *B*

Connecticut
Tunxis Community College *A*
University of Bridgeport *A, B*
University of New Haven *A, B*

Delaware
Delaware Technical and Community College
    Stanton/Wilmington Campus *A*
    Terry Campus *A*

District of Columbia
Howard University *C*

Florida
Brevard Community College *A*
Broward Community College *A*
Edison Community College *A*
Florida Community College at Jacksonville *A*
Gulf Coast Community College *A*
Indian River Community College *A*
Manatee Community College *A*
Miami-Dade Community College *A*
Palm Beach Community College *A*
Pasco-Hernando Community College *A*
Pensacola Junior College *A*
Polk Community College *A*
St. Petersburg Junior College *A*
Santa Fe Community College *A*
Tallahassee Community College *A*
Valencia Community College *A*

Georgia
Abraham Baldwin Agricultural College *A*

Armstrong Atlantic State University *A, B*
Athens Area Technical Institute *A*
Brewton-Parker College *A*
Clayton College and State University *A*
Darton College *A*
Floyd College *A*
Gainesville College *A*
Georgia Perimeter College *A*
Macon State College *A*
Medical College of Georgia *B, M*
Middle Georgia College *A*
Valdosta State University *A*
Waycross College *A*

Hawaii
University of Hawaii
    Kapiolani Community College *A*
    Manoa *B*

Idaho
College of Southern Idaho *A*
Idaho State University *B*

Illinois
City Colleges of Chicago
    Kennedy-King College *A*
Lake Land College *A*
Lewis and Clark Community College *A*
Parkland College *A*
Prairie State College *A*
Southern Illinois University
    Carbondale *A, B*
William Rainey Harper College *A*

Indiana
Indiana University
    Bloomington *A, B*
    Northwest *A*
    South Bend *A*
Indiana University--Purdue University
    Indiana University-Purdue University Fort Wayne *A*
    Indiana University-Purdue University Indianapolis *A*
University of Southern Indiana *A, B*
Vincennes University *A*

Iowa
Des Moines Area Community College *A*
Hawkeye Community College *A*
Iowa Western Community College *A*
Kirkwood Community College *A*

Kansas
Colby Community College *A*
Johnson County Community College *A*
Wichita State University *A, B*

Kentucky
Henderson Community College *C*
Lexington Community College *A*
Prestonsburg Community College *A*
University of Louisville *A, B*
Western Kentucky University *A, B*

Louisiana
Louisiana State University Medical Center *A, B*
Southern University
    Shreveport *A*
University of Louisiana at Monroe *A, B*

Maine
University of Maine
    Augusta *A, B*
University of New England *A, B*

Maryland
Allegany College *A*
Baltimore City Community College *A*
Charles County Community College *A*
University of Maryland
    Baltimore *B, M*
Villa Julie College *A*

Massachusetts
Bristol Community College *A*
Cape Cod Community College *A*
Middlesex Community College *A*

Northeastern University *A, B*
Springfield Technical Community College *A*

Michigan
Baker College
    of Port Huron *A*
Delta College *A*
Ferris State University *A*
Grand Rapids Community College *A*
Kalamazoo Valley Community College *A*
Kellogg Community College *A*
Lansing Community College *A*
Mott Community College *A*
Oakland Community College *A*
University of Detroit Mercy *B*
University of Michigan *B, M*

Minnesota
Century Community and Technical College *A*
Lake Superior College: A Community and Technical College *A*
Minnesota State University, Mankato *A*
Rochester Community and Technical College *A*
St. Cloud Technical College *A*
University of Minnesota
    Twin Cities *C, B*

Mississippi
Meridian Community College *A*
Mississippi Delta Community College *A*
University of Mississippi
    Medical Center *B*

Missouri
Missouri Southern State College *A*
St. Louis Community College
    St. Louis Community College at Forest Park *A*
University of Missouri
    Kansas City *B, M*

Nebraska
Central Community College *C, A*

Nevada
Community College of Southern Nevada *A*

New Hampshire
New Hampshire Technical Institute *A*

New Jersey
Bergen Community College *A*
Camden County College *A*
Essex County College *A*
Middlesex County College *A*
Thomas Edison State College *B*
Union County College *A*
University of Medicine and Dentistry of New Jersey
    School of Health Related Professions *C, A, B*

New Mexico
University of New Mexico *A, B*

New York
Broome Community College *A*
City University of New York
    Hostos Community College *A*
    New York City Technical College *A*
Erie Community College
    North Campus *A*
Hudson Valley Community College *A*
Monroe Community College *A*
New York University *A*
Onondaga Community College *A*
Orange County Community College *A*
State University of New York
    Farmingdale *A*

North Carolina
Asheville Buncombe Technical Community College *A*

Dental hygiene studies

Cape Fear Community College *A*
Catawba Valley Community College *A*
Central Piedmont Community College *A*
Coastal Carolina Community College *A*
Fayetteville Technical Community
 College *A*
Guilford Technical Community
 College *A*
University of North Carolina
 Chapel Hill *C, B*
Wayne Community College *A*

North Dakota
North Dakota State College of Science *A*

Ohio
Columbus State Community College *A*
Lakeland Community College *A*
Lorain County Community College *A*
Ohio State University
 Columbus Campus *B*
Owens Community College
 Toledo *A*
Shawnee State University *A*
Sinclair Community College *A*
Stark State College of Technology *A*
University of Cincinnati
 Raymond Walters College *A*
Youngstown State University *A*

Oklahoma
Rose State College *A*
Tulsa Community College *A*
Western Oklahoma State College *A*

Oregon
Lane Community College *A*
Mount Hood Community College *A*
Oregon Health Sciences University *B*
Oregon Institute of Technology *A, B*
Portland Community College *A*

Pennsylvania
California University of Pennsylvania *B*
Community College of Philadelphia *A*
Harcum College *A*
Harrisburg Area Community College *A*
Luzerne County Community College *A*
Manor College *A*
Montgomery County Community
 College *A*
Northampton County Area Community
 College *A*
Pennsylvania College of
 Technology *A, B*
University of Pittsburgh *C, B*
West Chester University of
 Pennsylvania *B*
Westmoreland County Community
 College *A*

Puerto Rico
University of Puerto Rico
 Medical Sciences Campus *A*

Rhode Island
Community College of Rhode Island *A*
University of Rhode Island *B*

South Carolina
Central Carolina Technical College *C*
Florence-Darlington Technical College *A*
Greenville Technical College *A*
Horry-Georgetown Technical College *A*
Midlands Technical College *A*
Orangeburg-Calhoun Technical
 College *C*
Piedmont Technical College *C*
Tri-County Technical College *C*
Trident Technical College *C, A*
York Technical College *A*

South Dakota
University of South Dakota *A, B*

Tennessee
Chattanooga State Technical Community
 College *A*
Columbia State Community College *A*

East Tennessee State University *A*
Hiwassee College *A*
Southern Adventist University *A*
Tennessee State University *A, B*
University of Tennessee
 Memphis *B*

Texas
Amarillo College *A*
Blinn College *C, A*
Coastal Bend College *A*
Collin County Community College
 District *A*
Del Mar College *A*
El Paso Community College *A*
Howard College *A*
Midwestern State University *B*
Tarrant County College *A*
Texas State Technical College
 Harlingen *A*
Texas Woman's University *B*
Tyler Junior College *A*
Wharton County Junior College *A*

Utah
Dixie State College of Utah *A*
Salt Lake Community College *A*
Weber State University *A, B*

Vermont
University of Vermont *A*

Virginia
Lord Fairfax Community College *A*
Northern Virginia Community College *A*
Old Dominion University *B, M*
Virginia Commonwealth University *B*
Virginia Highlands Community
 College *A*
Virginia Western Community College *A*
Wytheville Community College *A*

Washington
Clark College *A*
Eastern Washington University *B*
Lake Washington Technical College *A*
Pierce College *A*
Shoreline Community College *A*
University of Washington *B*
Yakima Valley Community College *A*

West Virginia
West Liberty State College *A, B*
West Virginia University Institute of
 Technology *A*
West Virginia University *B, M*

Wisconsin
Blackhawk Technical College *A*
Chippewa Valley Technical College *A*
Gateway Technical College *A*
Madison Area Technical College *A*
Marquette University *B*
Milwaukee Area Technical College *A*
Northeast Wisconsin Technical
 College *A*
Waukesha County Technical College *A*
Western Wisconsin Technical College *A*

Wyoming
Laramie County Community College *A*
Sheridan College *A*
University of Wyoming *B*

Dental laboratory technology

Alabama
Community College of the Air Force *A*

Arizona
Pima Community College *A*

California
City College of San Francisco *C, A*
Cypress College *A*
Diablo Valley College *C, A*
Merced College *A*

Pasadena City College *C, A*
Riverside Community College *C, A*

Florida
Florida National College *A*
Indian River Community College *A*

Georgia
Atlanta Metropolitan College *A*
Gwinnett Technical Institute *A*

Idaho
Idaho State University *A*

Illinois
Southern Illinois University
 Carbondale *A*
Triton College *C, A*

Indiana
Indiana University--Purdue University
 Indiana University-Purdue
 University Fort Wayne *A*

Iowa
Kirkwood Community College *A*

Kentucky
Lexington Community College *A*

Louisiana
Louisiana State University Medical
 Center *A, B*

Massachusetts
Boston University *B*
Middlesex Community College *A*

Michigan
Bay de Noc Community College *C*

New Jersey
Union County College *A*

New York
City University of New York
 New York City Technical
 College *A*
Erie Community College
 South Campus *A*
New York University *M*

North Carolina
Durham Technical Community
 College *C, A*

Ohio
Columbus State Community College *A*

Oregon
Portland Community College *C, A*

Pennsylvania
West Chester University of
 Pennsylvania *B*

Texas
Howard College *C, A*
Texas State Technical College
 Harlingen *C, A*

Virginia
J. Sargeant Reynolds Community
 College *C, A*

West Virginia
West Virginia State College *A*

Wisconsin
Milwaukee Area Technical College *A*

Dental specialties

Alabama
University of Alabama
 Birmingham *M*

California
Loma Linda University *M, D*
University of California
 Los Angeles *M, D*
University of Southern California *M, D*

Connecticut
University of Connecticut *M*

Florida
University of Florida *M, D*

Georgia
Medical College of Georgia *D*

Illinois
City Colleges of Chicago
 Olive-Harvey College *A*
Southern Illinois University
 Edwardsville *C*
University of Illinois
 Chicago *M*

Indiana
Indiana University--Purdue University
 Indiana University-Purdue
 University Indianapolis *M, D*

Iowa
University of Iowa *M*
Waldorf College *A*

Kentucky
Henderson Community College *C*
University of Kentucky *M*
University of Louisville *M*

Maryland
University of Maryland
 Baltimore *M, D*

Massachusetts
Boston University *M, D*
Harvard University *M, D*

Michigan
University of Michigan *M, D*

Minnesota
University of Minnesota
 Twin Cities *M, D*

Missouri
St. Louis University *M*
University of Missouri
 Kansas City *M, D*

New York
Columbia University
 Graduate School *M*
State University of New York
 Buffalo *M, D*
University of Rochester *M*

North Carolina
University of North Carolina
 Chapel Hill *M*

Ohio
Ohio State University
 Columbus Campus *M*

Oregon
Oregon Health Sciences University *M*

Pennsylvania
University of Pittsburgh *M, D*

Washington
University of Washington *M*

West Virginia
West Virginia University *M*

Wisconsin
Marquette University *M, D*

Dentistry (D.D.S. or D.M.D.)

Alabama
University of Alabama at Birmingham:
 School of Dentistry *F*

California
Loma Linda University: School of
 Dentistry *F*

Design/visual communications

University of California Los Angeles:
School of Dentistry *F*
University of California San Francisco:
School of Dentistry *F*
University of Southern California: School
of Dentistry *F*
University of the Pacific: School of
Dentistry *F*

Colorado
University of Colorado Health Sciences
Center: School of Dentistry *F*

Connecticut
University of Connecticut: School of
Dentistry *F*

District of Columbia
Howard University: College of
Dentistry *F*

Florida
University of Florida: College of
Dentistry *F*

Georgia
Medical College of Georgia: School of
Dentistry *F*

Illinois
Northwestern University: Dental
School *F*
Southern Illinois University: School of
Dentistry *F*
University of Illinois at Chicago: College
of Dentistry *F*

Indiana
Indiana University School of Dentistry *F*

Iowa
University of Iowa College of
Dentistry *F*

Kentucky
University of Kentucky: College of
Dentistry *F*
University of Louisville: School of
Dentistry *F*

Louisiana
Louisiana State University Medical
Center: School of Dentistry *F*

Maryland
University of Maryland at Baltimore:
School of Dentistry *F*

Massachusetts
Boston University Goldman School of
Dental Medicine *F*
Harvard School of Dental Medicine *F*
Tufts University: School of Dental
Medicine *F*

Michigan
University of Detroit Mercy: School of
Dentistry *F*
University of Michigan: School of
Dentistry *F*

Minnesota
University of Minnesota Twin Cities:
School of Dentistry *F*

Mississippi
University of Mississippi Medical
Center: School of Dentistry *F*

Missouri
University of Missouri Kansas City:
School of Dentistry *F*

Nebraska
Creighton University: School of
Dentistry *F*
University of Nebraska Medical Center:
College of Dentistry *F*

New Jersey
University of Medicine and Dentistry of
New Jersey
New Jersey Dental School *F*

New York
Columbia University
School of Dental and Oral
Surgery *F*
New York University: College of
Dentistry *F*
State University of New York Health
Sciences Center at Stony Brook:
School of Dentistry *F*
State University of New York at Buffalo:
School of Dentistry *F*

North Carolina
University of North Carolina at Chapel
Hill: School of Dentistry *F*

Ohio
Case Western Reserve University: School
of Dentistry *F*
Ohio State University Columbus
Campus: College of Dentistry *F*

Oklahoma
University of Oklahoma Health Sciences
Center: College of Dentistry *F*

Oregon
Oregon Health Sciences University:
School of Dentistry *F*

Pennsylvania
Temple University: School of
Dentistry *F*
University of Pennsylvania: School of
Dental Medicine *F*
University of Pittsburgh: School of
Dental Medicine *F*

Puerto Rico
University of Puerto Rico Medical
Sciences Campus: School of
Dentistry *F*

South Carolina
Medical University of South Carolina:
College of Dental Medicine *F*

Tennessee
Meharry Medical College: School of
Dentistry *F*
University of Tennessee Memphis:
College of Dentistry *F*

Texas
Texas A&M University: Baylor College
of Dentistry *F*
University of Texas Health Sciences
Center-Dental Branch *F*

Virginia
Virginia Commonwealth University:
School of Dentistry *F*

Washington
University of Washington: School of
Dentistry *F*

West Virginia
West Virginia University: School of
Dentistry *F*

Wisconsin
Marquette University: School of
Dentistry *F*

Design/visual communications

Alabama
Auburn University *B*

Arizona
Northern Arizona University *B*
Pima Community College *A*

Arkansas
John Brown University *B*

California
Academy of Art College *A, B, M*
Allan Hancock College *A*
Art Center College of Design *B, M*
Art Institutes International
San Francisco *A, B*
California State University
Chico *B*
Long Beach *B*
Chaffey Community College *C, A*
Mount San Antonio College *A*
Otis College of Art and Design *B*
Saddleback College *C, A*
University of California
Berkeley *M*
Davis *B*
Los Angeles *B, M*

Colorado
Art Institute
of Colorado *A, B*
Colorado Mountain College
Spring Valley Campus *A*
Front Range Community College *C*
Pikes Peak Community College *C, A*

Connecticut
Central Connecticut State University *B*
Northwestern Connecticut
Community-Technical College *A*
Paier College of Art *C, B*
Sacred Heart University *B*
University of Hartford *M*

District of Columbia
American University *B*
Howard University *B*

Florida
International Academy of Merchandising
and Design *A, B*
Jacksonville University *B*
Ringling School of Art and Design *B*
Stetson University *B*

Georgia
Atlanta College of Art *B*
DeKalb Technical Institute *C*

Illinois
American Academy of Art *A, B*
Black Hawk College *A*
City Colleges of Chicago
Harold Washington College *A*
Wright College *C, A*
College of DuPage *C, A*
Columbia College *B*
Elgin Community College *C, A*
Illinois Institute of Technology *M, D*
International Academy of Merchandising
and Design *B*
Judson College *B*
Moraine Valley Community College *A*
Northwestern University *M*
Parkland College *A*
Prairie State College *A*
School of the Art Institute of
Chicago *B, M*
Southern Illinois University
Carbondale *B*
Waubonsee Community College *C, A*

Indiana
Ball State University *B*
Bethel College *A, B*
International Business College *C, A*
Ivy Tech State College
Columbus *A*
Northcentral *A*
Southcentral *A*
Southwest *A*
Wabash Valley *A*
Purdue University *B*
University of Indianapolis *B*
University of Notre Dame *B, M*

Iowa
Dordt College *B*
Iowa State University *B, M*
Maharishi University of Management *B*

Kansas
Cowley County Community College *A*
University of Kansas *B, M*

Louisiana
Delgado Community College *A*

Maryland
Maryland College of Art and
Design *C, A*
Maryland Institute College of Art *B*
Villa Julie College *B*

Massachusetts
Emmanuel College *B*
Endicott College *B*
Hampshire College *B*
Harvard College *B*
Massachusetts College of Art *B, M*
Montserrat College of Art *B*
Northern Essex Community College *A*
Simon's Rock College of Bard *B*
University of Massachusetts
Dartmouth *B, M*

Michigan
Cranbrook Academy of Art *M*
Kendall College of Art and Design *B*
Saginaw Valley State University *B*
Suomi College *B*
University of Michigan *B*

Minnesota
Central Lakes College *C*
College of Visual Arts *B*
Minneapolis College of Art and
Design *B*
University of Minnesota
Twin Cities *B*
Winona State University *B*

Missouri
Maryville University of Saint Louis *B*
Southwest Missouri State University *B*
Washington University *B, M*
William Woods University *B*

New Hampshire
Franklin Pierce College *B*
Rivier College *A, B*

New Jersey
Kean University *B*
Union County College *C, A*

New Mexico
New Mexico State University
Alamogordo *A*
Northern New Mexico Community
College *A*

New York
Daemen College *B*
Eugene Lang College/New School
University *B*
New York State College of Ceramics at
Alfred University *B, T*
Pace University:
Pleasantville/Briarcliff *C, A*
Pace University *C, A*
Parsons School of Design *C, A, B, M, T*
Pratt Institute *M*
Rochester Institute of Technology *A, B*
School of Visual Arts *B, M*
State University of New York
Farmingdale *B*

North Carolina
Duke University *B*
Mount Olive College *B*
North Carolina Central University *B*
Peace College *B*

Ohio
Bowling Green State University *B*

203

Design/visual communications

Edison State Community College *A*
Kent State University *B, M*
Ohio Institute of Photography and Technology *A*
Ohio State University
    Columbus Campus *B*
Ohio University *B*
University of Cincinnati
    Raymond Walters College *A*
University of Cincinnati *M*
University of Dayton *B*
Ursuline College *B*

Oklahoma
Oral Roberts University *B*
University of Oklahoma *B*

Oregon
Chemeketa Community College *A*
Portland State University *B*

Pennsylvania
Art Institute
    of Pittsburgh *A*
California University of Pennsylvania *A*
Carnegie Mellon University *B*
Drexel University *B*
Harrisburg Area Community College *A*
Marywood University *C, B*
Seton Hill College *B*
University of the Arts *B*

Puerto Rico
Escuela de Artes Plasticas de Puerto Rico *B*

South Carolina
Clemson University *B*
Winthrop University *M*

Texas
Amarillo College *C, A*
Howard Payne University *B*
St. Edward's University *B*
Texas A&M University
    Commerce *B*
Texas State Technical College
    Harlingen *A*
Texas Woman's University *B, M*
University of Texas
    Austin *B*

Utah
Salt Lake Community College *A*
Weber State University *B*

Virginia
Radford University *B*
Virginia Commonwealth University *M*

Washington
Cornish College of the Arts *B*
Evergreen State College *B*
Shoreline Community College *C, A*
Yakima Valley Community College *A*

West Virginia
Bethany College *B*
Fairmont State College *A*
Shepherd College *A, B*

Wisconsin
Madison Area Technical College *A*
University of Wisconsin
    Madison *B*

Wyoming
Northwest College *A*

Developmental/child psychology

Arizona
South Mountain Community College *A*

Arkansas
University of Central Arkansas *B*

California
California State University
    Bakersfield *B*
    Hayward *M*
    Sacramento *B*
    Stanislaus *B*
Citrus College *C*
Palo Verde College *A*
Saddleback College *A*
San Francisco State University *M*
San Jose State University *M*
University of California
    Riverside *B*
    Santa Cruz *B, D*

Connecticut
Connecticut College *B*
Mitchell College *B*

District of Columbia
Catholic University of America *M, D*
George Washington University *D*

Florida
Florida International University *D*
Manatee Community College *A*

Georgia
Georgia Military College *A*
State University of West Georgia *B, M*
University of Georgia *D*

Illinois
City Colleges of Chicago
    Harold Washington College *A*
Loyola University of Chicago *M, D*
National-Louis University *B*

Indiana
Purdue University
    Calumet *B*

Iowa
University of Iowa *D*
Waldorf College *A*

Kansas
Central Christian College *A*
University of Kansas *B, M, D*

Kentucky
Lindsey Wilson College *M*

Maryland
University of Maryland
    Baltimore County *D*
    College Park *M, D*

Massachusetts
Becker College *B*
Fitchburg State College *B*
Hampshire College *B*
Harvard College *B*
Northeastern University *M*
Pine Manor College *B*
Simon's Rock College of Bard *B*
Suffolk University *B*
Tufts University *B, M, D*
Wheelock College *B, M*

Michigan
University of Detroit Mercy *B*

Minnesota
University of Minnesota
    Twin Cities *B, M, D*

New Hampshire
Antioch New England Graduate School *M, D*
Colby-Sawyer College *B*
New Hampshire College *B*
Plymouth State College of the University System of New Hampshire *B*

New Jersey
Gloucester County College *A*
Rowan University *M*

Rutgers
    The State University of New Jersey:
    New Brunswick Graduate Campus *D*

New York
Adelphi University *M, D*
Audrey Cohen College *A, B*
City University of New York
    Graduate School and University Center *D*
Columbia University
    Teachers College *M, D*
Cornell University *B, M, D*
Fulton-Montgomery Community College *A*
Sarah Lawrence College *B*
State University of New York
    Albany *M, D*
University of Rochester *D*
Utica College of Syracuse University *B*

North Carolina
University of North Carolina
    Chapel Hill *M, D*

Ohio
Bowling Green State University *M, D*
Case Western Reserve University *D*
University of Akron *D*

Oklahoma
Northeastern State University *B*
Redlands Community College *C*

Pennsylvania
Seton Hill College *B*
Temple University *M, D*

Tennessee
Maryville College *B*
Vanderbilt University *M, D*

Texas
Houston Baptist University *B*
University of Houston *D*
University of Texas
    Dallas *M*
University of the Incarnate Word *M*

Vermont
Bennington College *B*
Marlboro College *B*

Virginia
Christopher Newport University *B*
Longwood College *B*
Radford University *M*

Washington
Eastern Washington University *B, M, T*
Western Washington University *B*

Diagnostic medical sonography

Alabama
Northwest-Shoals Community College *A*
Wallace State Community College at Hanceville *A*

Arizona
Arizona Western College *A*
Gateway Community College *C, A*

California
Foothill College *C*
Orange Coast College *C, A*

Colorado
Community College of Denver *C*

Connecticut
Gateway Community College *A*

Delaware
Delaware Technical and Community College
    Stanton/Wilmington Campus *A*

District of Columbia
George Washington University *B*

Florida
Barry University *B*
Brevard Community College *C*
Broward Community College *A*
Florida Community College at Jacksonville *A*
Hillsborough Community College *C, A*
Polk Community College *A*
Valencia Community College *A*

Georgia
Medical College of Georgia *B, M*

Hawaii
University of Hawaii
    Kapiolani Community College *A*

Illinois
City Colleges of Chicago
    Wright College *A*
Kaskaskia College *C*
Triton College *A*

Indiana
Indiana University
    Bloomington *B*
University of Southern Indiana *A*

Kansas
Fort Hays State University *B*
University of Kansas
    Medical Center *C*

Louisiana
Delgado Community College *A*
Southern University
    Shreveport *A*

Maryland
Montgomery College
    Rockville Campus *A*

Massachusetts
Bunker Hill Community College *C*
Massasoit Community College *C*
Middlesex Community College *C, A*
Springfield Technical Community College *A*

Michigan
Jackson Community College *C, A*
Lansing Community College *A*
Mott Community College *A*
Oakland Community College *A*

Minnesota
College of St. Catherine-Minneapolis *C, A*
St. Cloud Technical College *C, A*

Missouri
Penn Valley Community College *C*

Nebraska
Nebraska Methodist College of Nursing and Allied Health *A, B*

New Hampshire
New Hampshire Technical Institute *C*

New Jersey
Bergen Community College *A*
Gloucester County College *A*
Sussex County Community College *A*
University of Medicine and Dentistry of New Jersey
    School of Health Related Professions *C, B*

New York
Hudson Valley Community College *C*
Rochester Institute of Technology *C, B*
State University of New York
    Health Science Center at Brooklyn *B*
Trocaire College *C*

North Carolina
Forsyth Technical Community College *A*
Pitt Community College *A*

Ohio
Central Ohio Technical College *C, A*

Oregon
Oregon Health Sciences University *C*

Pennsylvania
Community College of Allegheny County *A*
South Hills School of Business & Technology *C, A*
Thomas Jefferson University: College of Health Professions *B*

Puerto Rico
Colegio Universitario del Este *C, A*

South Carolina
Greenville Technical College *C*

Texas
Collin County Community College District *C*
Del Mar College *C, A*
El Paso Community College *C*
Houston Community College System *C*
St. Philip's College *C*
Tyler Junior College *C, A*

Utah
Weber State University *B*

Virginia
Southwest Virginia Community College *C*
Tidewater Community College *C*

Washington
Bellevue Community College *A*
Seattle University *B*

West Virginia
College of West Virginia *A, B*

Wisconsin
Chippewa Valley Technical College *A*

Diesel mechanics

Alabama
Harry M. Ayers State Technical College *C*
John M. Patterson State Technical College *C*
Sparks State Technical College *C*
Wallace State Community College at Hanceville *C, A*

Alaska
University of Alaska
 Anchorage *C, A*
 Southeast *C, A*

Arizona
Central Arizona College *C, A*
Universal Technical Institute *C, A*

California
Allan Hancock College *C, A*
Cerritos Community College *C*
Golden West College *A*
Merced College *C, A*
San Bernardino Valley College *C, A*
Southwestern College *C*

Colorado
Northeastern Junior College *C, A*
Trinidad State Junior College *C, A*

Georgia
DeKalb Technical Institute *C*

Hawaii
University of Hawaii
 Hawaii Community College *C, A*
 Honolulu Community College *C, A*

Idaho
College of Southern Idaho *C, A*
Eastern Idaho Technical College *C, A*
Idaho State University *C, A*
North Idaho College *C, A*

Illinois
Black Hawk College
 East Campus *C*
Black Hawk College *C, A*
Danville Area Community College *A*
Illinois Eastern Community Colleges
 Wabash Valley College *A*
John A. Logan College *C*
Kishwaukee College *C, A*
Parkland College *A*
Sauk Valley Community College *A*
Southeastern Illinois College *C, A*

Indiana
Oakland City University *C, A*
Vincennes University *A*

Iowa
Des Moines Area Community College *C, A*
Northeast Iowa Community College *C*
Scott Community College *A*
Western Iowa Tech Community College *A*

Kansas
Barton County Community College *C*
Pittsburg State University *B*

Maine
Washington County Technical College *C*

Massachusetts
Massasoit Community College *C, A*

Michigan
Oakland Community College *C, A*

Minnesota
Alexandria Technical College *C, A*
Central Lakes College *C*
Dakota County Technical College *C*
Hibbing Community College: A Technical and Community College *C*
Lake Superior College: A Community and Technical College *C*
St. Cloud Technical College *C, A*
St. Paul Technical College *C*

Mississippi
Itawamba Community College *C*
Northeast Mississippi Community College *C*

Montana
Montana State University
 Billings *C*
University of Montana-Missoula *A*

Nebraska
Central Community College *C, A*
Mid Plains Community College Area *C, A*
Northeast Community College *A*
Southeast Community College
 Milford Campus *A*

New Hampshire
New Hampshire Community Technical College
 Berlin *A*

New Mexico
Albuquerque Technical-Vocational Institute *C*
San Juan College *C, A*

New York
State University of New York
 College of Agriculture and Technology at Cobleskill *A*
 College of Agriculture and Technology at Morrisville *A*
 College of Technology at Alfred *A*

North Carolina
Caldwell Community College and Technical Institute *C*
Cape Fear Community College *C*
Coastal Carolina Community College *C, A*
Forsyth Technical Community College *C*
Guilford Technical Community College *C, A*
Johnston Community College *C, A*
Wilkes Community College *C, A*
Wilson Technical Community College *C*

North Dakota
Lake Region State College *C, A*
Williston State College *A*

Ohio
Northwestern College *C, A*
Owens Community College
 Toledo *A*

Oklahoma
Oklahoma State University
 Okmulgee *A*
Western Oklahoma State College *A*

Oregon
Lane Community College *C, A*
Linn-Benton Community College *C, A*
Portland Community College *C, A*

Pennsylvania
Delaware County Community College *C*
Johnson Technical Institute *A*

South Carolina
Greenville Technical College *C*

South Dakota
Southeast Technical Institute *A*
Western Dakota Technical Institute *C*

Texas
Angelina College *C, A*
Central Texas College *C, A*
College of the Mainland *C, A*
Del Mar College *C, A*
Houston Community College System *C*
North Central Texas College *A*
St. Philip's College *C, A*
San Jacinto College
 North *C, A*
South Plains College *A*
Texas State Technical College
 Waco *A*

Utah
College of Eastern Utah *A*
Salt Lake Community College *C*
Weber State University *A*

Virginia
J. Sargeant Reynolds Community College *C*
New River Community College *C*
Southwest Virginia Community College *C*

Washington
Centralia College *A*
Clark College *C, A*
Columbia Basin College *A*
Grays Harbor College *A*
Lake Washington Technical College *C, A*
Peninsula College *A*
Skagit Valley College *C, A*
Spokane Community College *A*

Wisconsin
Blackhawk Technical College *A*
Chippewa Valley Technical College *C*
Northeast Wisconsin Technical College *C*
Western Wisconsin Technical College *C*

Wyoming
Casper College *C, A*
Sheridan College *C, A*

Dietetics

Alabama
Alabama Agricultural and Mechanical University *B, M, D*

Arizona
Arizona Western College *C*
Central Arizona College *C, A*

Arkansas
Harding University *B*
Ouachita Baptist University *B*
University of Arkansas
 for Medical Sciences *C*
University of Central Arkansas *B*

California
Allan Hancock College *C*
Chaffey Community College *C, A*
Compton Community College *A*
Grossmont Community College *C, A*
Long Beach City College *C, A*
Point Loma Nazarene University *B*
San Bernardino Valley College *C, A*
San Francisco State University *B*
Santa Ana College *C, A*
Santa Rosa Junior College *C*
University of California
 Berkeley *B*
 Davis *B*

Colorado
University of Northern Colorado *B*

Connecticut
Briarwood College *A*
Middlesex Community-Technical College *A*
University of Connecticut *B*
University of New Haven *B, M*

Delaware
University of Delaware *B*

Florida
Florida Community College at Jacksonville *A*
Florida International University *B, M, D*
Florida State University *B, M*
Palm Beach Community College *A*
Pensacola Junior College *A*

Georgia
University of Georgia *B*

Idaho
College of Southern Idaho *A*

Illinois
Dominican University *B*
Olivet Nazarene University *B*
William Rainey Harper College *C, A*

Indiana
Ball State University *A, B*
Vincennes University *A*

Iowa
Iowa State University *B, M*
Kirkwood Community College *C*
University of Northern Iowa *B*

Kansas
Kansas State University *B*

Kentucky
Berea College *B*
Eastern Kentucky University *M*
Murray State University *A, B*
Western Kentucky University *B*

Louisiana
Delgado Community College *A*
Louisiana State University and Agricultural and Mechanical College *B*
Louisiana Tech University *B, M*
Nicholls State University *B*
University of Louisiana at Lafayette *B*

Dietetics

Maine
Southern Maine Technical College *A*
Washington County Technical College *A*

Maryland
University of Maryland
 College Park *B*

Massachusetts
Framingham State College *B, M*
Laboure College *C, A*

Michigan
Andrews University *B*
Central Michigan University *B*
Eastern Michigan University *B*
Michigan State University *B, M, D*
Northern Michigan University *B*
Wayne State University *B*

Minnesota
Concordia College: Moorhead *B*
Minnesota State University, Mankato *B*
St. John's University *B*
University of Minnesota
 Crookston *A*

Missouri
Central Missouri State University *B*
College of the Ozarks *B*
Fontbonne College *B*
Southwest Missouri State University *B*

Nebraska
University of Nebraska
 Kearney *B*
 Omaha *B*

New Hampshire
Keene State College *B*
University of New Hampshire *A*

New Jersey
Middlesex County College *A*

New York
Broome Community College *C*
City University of New York
 La Guardia Community College *A*
D'Youville College *B, M*
Dutchess Community College *A*
Rochester Institute of Technology *B*
Rockland Community College *A*
State University of New York
 College at Buffalo *B*
 College at Oneonta *B*
 College of Agriculture and
  Technology at Morrisville *A*
Suffolk County Community College *A*
Syracuse University *B*
Westchester Community College *A*

North Carolina
East Carolina University *B*
Lenoir Community College *C, A*
Meredith College *C*
Western Carolina University *B*

North Dakota
North Dakota State University *B*
University of North Dakota *B*

Ohio
Bowling Green State University *B*
Cincinnati State Technical and
 Community College *C, A*
Columbus State Community College *A*
Hocking Technical College *A*
Kent State University *B*
Miami University
 Oxford Campus *B*
Muskingum Area Technical College *A*
Notre Dame College of Ohio *B*
Ohio University *B*
Sinclair Community College *C, A*
University of Akron *B, M*
University of Cincinnati
 Raymond Walters College *A*
University of Dayton *B*

Youngstown State University *A, B*

Oklahoma
Northeastern State University *B*
Oklahoma State University
 Okmulgee *A*

Oregon
Central Oregon Community College *C*

Pennsylvania
Gannon University *C, B*
Indiana University of Pennsylvania *B*
Marywood University *B, M*
Mercyhurst College *B*
Messiah College *B*
Seton Hill College *B*
University of Pittsburgh *B*

Puerto Rico
University of Puerto Rico
 Rio Piedras Campus *B*

Rhode Island
University of Rhode Island *B*

Tennessee
Carson-Newman College *B*
Tennessee Technological University *B*
University of Tennessee
 Martin *B*

Texas
Abilene Christian University *B*
St. Philip's College *A*
Tarleton State University *B*
Texas Christian University *B*
Texas Tech University *B*
Texas Woman's University *B*
University of Texas
 Pan American *B*
 Southwestern Medical Center at
  Dallas *B*

Utah
Brigham Young University *B*

Vermont
University of Vermont *B*

Virginia
James Madison University *B*

Washington
Central Washington University *B*
Shoreline Community College *A*
Spokane Community College *A*
Washington State University *M*

West Virginia
Marshall University *B*

Wisconsin
Milwaukee Area Technical College *A*
Mount Mary College *B, M*
University of Wisconsin
 Stevens Point *B*
 Stout *B*
Viterbo University *B*

Drama/dance teacher education

Alabama
Birmingham-Southern College *T*
Huntingdon College *T*

Arizona
Grand Canyon University *B*
Northern Arizona University *T*
University of Arizona *B*

Arkansas
Ouachita Baptist University *B, T*
University of the Ozarks *B, T*

California
California State University
 Long Beach *T*
San Diego State University *B*

San Francisco State University *B, T*
University of the Pacific *T*

District of Columbia
Catholic University of America *B*
George Washington University *T*

Florida
Flagler College *B*
Jacksonville University *B*
Stetson University *B, T*

Georgia
Brenau University *B*
University of Georgia *B*

Hawaii
University of Hawaii
 Manoa *B, T*

Illinois
Barat College *B*
Greenville College *B*
Loyola University of Chicago *T*
North Park University *T*
Rockford College *T*

Indiana
Indiana State University *T*
Indiana University--Purdue University
 Indiana University-Purdue
  University Fort Wayne *B*
Vincennes University *A*

Iowa
Buena Vista University *B, T*
Central College *T*
Clarke College *B, T*
Dordt College *B*
Graceland University *T*
Luther College *B*
University of Iowa *T*

Kansas
St. Mary College *T*
Southwestern College *B*

Louisiana
Centenary College of Louisiana *B, T*

Maryland
Community College of Baltimore County
 Essex *A*
University of Maryland
 College Park *B*

Massachusetts
Boston University *B, M*
Bridgewater State College *B, T*
Emerson College *B, M*
Tufts University *T*

Michigan
Eastern Michigan University *B, T*

Minnesota
Minnesota State University, Mankato *B*
St. Cloud State University *T*
Southwest State University *B, T*
Winona State University *B, T*

Missouri
Avila College *T*
Lindenwood University *M*
Washington University *B, M, T*
William Jewell College *T*

Montana
Rocky Mountain College *B, T*
University of Montana-Missoula *T*
Western Montana College of The
 University of Montana *T*

Nebraska
Dana College *B*
Hastings College *B, T*
University of Nebraska
 Lincoln *B*

New Jersey
Rowan University *T*

New York
Columbia University
 Teachers College *M*
New York University *M, D, T*

North Carolina
East Carolina University *B*
Greensboro College *B, T*
Lees-McRae College *T*
Meredith College *B, T*
University of North Carolina
 Charlotte *B*
 Greensboro *B, M, T*

North Dakota
Dickinson State University *B, T*

Ohio
Ashland University *B, T*
Baldwin-Wallace College *T*
Bowling Green State University *B, M*
Kent State University
 Stark Campus *B*
Kent State University *T*
Miami University
 Oxford Campus *T*
Ohio State University
 Columbus Campus *M*
University of Findlay *T*
Youngstown State University *B*

Oklahoma
East Central University *B, T*
Eastern Oklahoma State College *A*

Oregon
Portland State University *T*
University of Portland *T*

Pennsylvania
Point Park College *B*

Rhode Island
Salve Regina University *B*

South Carolina
Columbia College *B*
Furman University *T*
South Carolina State University *B, T*

South Dakota
Black Hills State University *T*
University of South Dakota *T*

Texas
Abilene Christian University *B, T*
Angelo State University *T*
Baylor University *B, T*
East Texas Baptist University *B*
Hardin-Simmons University *B, T*
Howard Payne University *T*
Lamar University *T*
McMurry University *T*
Southwest Texas State University *T*
Texas A&M University
 Commerce *T*
 Kingsville *T*
Texas Christian University *T*
University of Dallas *T*
University of Houston *T*
West Texas A&M University *T*

Utah
Brigham Young University *B*
Weber State University *B*

Vermont
Castleton State College *B, T*
Johnson State College *B*
St. Michael's College *B*

Virginia
Christopher Newport University *T*
Longwood College *T*
Virginia Highlands Community
 College *A*

Washington
Central Washington University *B, M, T*
North Seattle Community College *C*

Washington State University *T*
Western Washington University *B, T*
Whitworth College *B, T*

Wisconsin
Alverno College *T*
University of Wisconsin
   Green Bay *T*
   Whitewater *B*

Drama/theater arts

Alabama
Alabama State University *B*
Auburn University *B*
Birmingham-Southern College *B*
Calhoun Community College *A*
Huntingdon College *B, T*
Jacksonville State University *B*
Northwest-Shoals Community College *C*
Samford University *B*
Shelton State Community College *C, A*
Spring Hill College *B*
University of Alabama
   Birmingham *B*
University of Alabama *B*
University of Mobile *B*
University of Montevallo *B, T*
University of South Alabama *B*

Alaska
University of Alaska
   Anchorage *B*
   Fairbanks *B*

Arizona
Arizona State University *B, M, D*
Arizona Western College *A*
Eastern Arizona College *A*
Grand Canyon University *B*
Northern Arizona University *B, T*
Pima Community College *A*
Prescott College *B, M*
University of Arizona *B, M*

Arkansas
Arkansas State University *B*
Arkansas Tech University *B*
Harding University *B*
Henderson State University *B*
Hendrix College *B*
Lyon College *B*
Ouachita Baptist University *B*
Southern Arkansas University *B*
University of Arkansas
   Little Rock *B*
University of Arkansas *B, M*
University of the Ozarks *B*

California
Allan Hancock College *C*
American River College *A*
Barstow College *A*
California Institute of the Arts *C, B, M*
California Lutheran University *B*
California State Polytechnic University:
   Pomona *B*
California State University
   Bakersfield *B*
   Chico *B*
   Dominguez Hills *B*
   Fresno *B*
   Fullerton *B, M*
   Hayward *B*
   Long Beach *B, M*
   Monterey Bay *B*
   Northridge *B, M*
   Sacramento *B, M*
   Stanislaus *B*
Canada College *A*
Cerritos Community College *A*
Chabot College *A*
Chaffey Community College *A*
Chapman University *B*
Claremont McKenna College *B*
College of the Sequoias *A*

College of the Siskiyous *A*
Compton Community College *A*
Concordia University *B*
Contra Costa College *A*
Crafton Hills College *A*
Cypress College *C, A*
Diablo Valley College *A*
East Los Angeles College *A*
Foothill College *A*
Fresno City College *A*
Fresno Pacific University *B*
Gavilan Community College *A*
Glendale Community College *C*
Golden West College *A*
Humboldt State University *B, M*
Irvine Valley College *A*
Kings River Community College *A*
Lake Tahoe Community College *C, A*
Las Positas College *A*
Long Beach City College *A*
Los Angeles Southwest College *A*
Loyola Marymount University *B*
Mendocino College *A*
Merced College *A*
MiraCosta College *A*
Modesto Junior College *A*
Monterey Peninsula College *A*
Moorpark College *A*
Mount San Jacinto College *A*
Occidental College *B*
Ohlone College *A*
Orange Coast College *A*
Palomar College *A*
Pepperdine University *B*
Pitzer College *B*
Point Loma Nazarene University *B*
Pomona College *B*
Riverside Community College *A*
Sacramento City College *A*
Saddleback College *A*
St. Mary's College of California *B*
San Diego City College *A*
San Diego Mesa College *A*
San Diego State University *B, M*
San Francisco State University *B, M*
San Jose State University *B, M*
Santa Ana College *C, A*
Santa Clara University *B*
Santa Monica College *A*
Santa Rosa Junior College *C, A*
Scripps College *B*
Shasta College *C, A*
Solano Community College *A*
Sonoma State University *B*
Southwestern College *A*
Stanford University *B, M, D*
University of California
   Berkeley *B, M, D*
   Davis *B, M, D*
   Irvine *B, M*
   Los Angeles *B, M, D*
   Riverside *B*
   San Diego *B, M*
   Santa Barbara *B, M, D*
   Santa Cruz *C, B*
University of La Verne *B*
University of San Diego *M*
University of Southern California *B*
University of the Pacific *B*
Vanguard University of Southern
   California *B*
Ventura College *C, A*
West Valley College *A*
Westmont College *B*
Whittier College *B, M*

Colorado
Adams State College *B*
Colorado Christian University *B*
Colorado College *B*
Colorado Mountain College
   Spring Valley Campus *A*
Colorado State University *B*
Fort Lewis College *B*
Naropa University *C, B*

Otero Junior College *A*
Red Rocks Community College *A*
University of Colorado
   Boulder *B, M, D*
University of Denver *B*
University of Northern Colorado *B, T*
Western State College of Colorado *B*

Connecticut
Central Connecticut State University *B*
Connecticut College *B*
Southern Connecticut State University *B*
Trinity College *B*
University of Connecticut *B, M*
University of Hartford *B*
Wesleyan University *B*
Western Connecticut State University *B*
Yale University *B, M, D*

Delaware
Delaware State University *B*
University of Delaware *M*

District of Columbia
American University *B*
Catholic University of America *B, M, T*
Gallaudet University *B*
George Washington University *B, M*
University of the District of Columbia *B*

Florida
Barry University *B*
Broward Community College *A*
Chipola Junior College *A*
Eckerd College *B*
Flagler College *B*
Florida Agricultural and Mechanical
   University *B*
Florida Atlantic University *B, M*
Florida Gulf Coast University *B*
Florida International University *B*
Florida Southern College *B*
Florida State University *B, M, D*
Gulf Coast Community College *A*
Indian River Community College *A*
Jacksonville University *B*
Miami-Dade Community College *A*
Palm Beach Atlantic College *B*
Palm Beach Community College *A*
Pensacola Junior College *A*
Rollins College *B*
Stetson University *B*
University of Central Florida *B*
University of Florida *B, M*
University of Miami *B*
University of South Florida *B*
University of West Florida *B*
Valencia Community College *A*

Georgia
Agnes Scott College *B*
Albany State University *B*
Andrew College *A*
Armstrong Atlantic State University *B*
Berry College *B*
Brenau University *B*
Clark Atlanta University *B*
Darton College *A*
Emory University *B*
Gainesville College *A*
Georgia College and State University *B*
Georgia Perimeter College *A*
Georgia Southern University *B*
Georgia State University *B*
LaGrange College *B*
Macon State College *B*
Middle Georgia College *A*
Morehouse College *B*
Morris Brown College *B*
Piedmont College *B*
Shorter College *B*
Spelman College *B*
State University of West Georgia *B*
University of Georgia *B, M, D*
Valdosta State University *B*
Young Harris College *A*

Hawaii
Brigham Young University
   Hawaii *A*
University of Hawaii
   Manoa *B, M, D*

Idaho
Albertson College of Idaho *B*
Boise State University *B*
College of Southern Idaho *A*
Idaho State University *B, M*
Lewis-Clark State College *B*
Ricks College *A*
University of Idaho *B, M*

Illinois
Augustana College *B*
Barat College *B*
Bradley University *B, T*
City Colleges of Chicago
   Harold Washington College *A*
   Kennedy-King College *C, A*
Columbia College *B*
De Paul University *B, M*
Dominican University *B*
Eastern Illinois University *B, T*
Elmhurst College *B*
Eureka College *B*
Illinois State University *B, M, T*
Illinois Wesleyan University *B*
Judson College *B*
Kishwaukee College *A*
Knox College *B*
Lewis University *B, T*
Lincoln Land Community College *A*
Loyola University of Chicago *B*
Millikin University *B*
National-Louis University *B*
North Central College *B*
North Park University *B*
Northeastern Illinois University *M*
Northern Illinois University *B, M*
Northwestern University *B, M, D*
Parkland College *A*
Principia College *B*
Rockford College *B*
Roosevelt University *B, M*
Sauk Valley Community College *A*
Southern Illinois University
   Carbondale *B, M*
   Edwardsville *B*
Southwestern Illinois College *A*
Triton College *A*
University of Illinois
   Chicago *B, M*
   Urbana-Champaign *B, M, D*
Western Illinois University *B, M*

Indiana
Anderson University *B*
Ball State University *B*
Bethel College *B*
Butler University *B*
Earlham College *B*
Franklin College *B*
Goshen College *B*
Hanover College *B*
Indiana State University *B, M, T*
Indiana University
   Bloomington *B, M, D*
   Northwest *B*
   South Bend *B*
Indiana University--Purdue University
   Indiana University-Purdue
     University Fort Wayne *B*
Marian College *A, B*
Purdue University *B, M*
Saint Mary's College *B*
Taylor University *B*
University of Evansville *B*
University of Indianapolis *B*
University of Notre Dame *B*
Valparaiso University *B, T*
Vincennes University *A*
Wabash College *B*

Drama/theater arts

Iowa
Briar Cliff College B
Buena Vista University B, T
Central College B
Clarke College A, B, T
Coe College B
Cornell College B, T
Dordt College B
Drake University B, T
Graceland University B, T
Grand View College B
Grinnell College B
Maharishi University of Management B
Morningside College B
North Iowa Area Community College A
St. Ambrose University B
Simpson College B
University of Iowa B, M, T
University of Northern Iowa B
Waldorf College A, B

Kansas
Baker University B, T
Benedictine College B, T
Bethel College T
Butler County Community College A
Central Christian College B
Coffeyville Community College A
Colby Community College A
Emporia State University B
Garden City Community College A
Independence Community College A
Kansas City Kansas Community College A
Kansas State University B
Kansas Wesleyan University B, T
McPherson College B, T
Ottawa University B, T
Pittsburg State University B
Pratt Community College A
St. Mary College B
Seward County Community College A
Southwestern College B
Sterling College B
Tabor College B
University of Kansas B, M, D
Washburn University of Topeka B
Wichita State University B

Kentucky
Campbellsville University B
Centre College B
Cumberland College B
Eastern Kentucky University B
Georgetown College B
Morehead State University B
Murray State University B, T
Northern Kentucky University B
Thomas More College A, B
Transylvania University B
Union College B
University of Kentucky B, M, T
University of Louisville B, M
Western Kentucky University B, T

Louisiana
Bossier Parish Community College A
Centenary College of Louisiana B
Dillard University B
Louisiana State University and Agricultural and Mechanical College B, M, D
Loyola University New Orleans B
McNeese State University B
Southern University and Agricultural and Mechanical College B
Tulane University B, M
University of New Orleans B, M

Maine
Bates College B
Colby College B
University of Maine Farmington B
University of Maine B, M
University of Southern Maine B

Maryland
Charles County Community College A
Community College of Baltimore County Essex A
Frederick Community College A
Goucher College B
Howard Community College A
Morgan State University B
St. Mary's College of Maryland B
Towson University B, M
University of Maryland Baltimore County B
College Park B, M, D
Washington College B
Western Maryland College B

Massachusetts
Berkshire Community College A
Boston College B
Brandeis University B, M
Bridgewater State College B
Bristol Community College A
Clark University B
College of the Holy Cross B
Dean College A
Emerson College B, M
Fitchburg State College B
Hampshire College B
Massachusetts Bay Community College A
Massachusetts College of Liberal Arts B
Middlesex Community College A
Mount Holyoke College B
Northeastern University B
Pine Manor College A
Regis College B
Simon's Rock College of Bard B
Smith College B
Springfield Technical Community College A
Suffolk University B
University of Massachusetts Amherst B, M
Boston B
Wellesley College B
Westfield State College B
Williams College B

Michigan
Adrian College A, B
Albion College B, T
Alma College B
Calvin College B
Central Michigan University B
Eastern Michigan University B, M
Grand Valley State University B
Henry Ford Community College A
Hillsdale College B
Hope College B, T
Kalamazoo College B, T
Kellogg Community College A
Lake Michigan College A
Lansing Community College A
Michigan State University B, M, D
Mid Michigan Community College A
Northern Michigan University B
Saginaw Valley State University B
Schoolcraft College A
Siena Heights University B
University of Detroit Mercy B
University of Michigan Flint B
University of Michigan B, M, D, T
Wayne State University B, M, D
Western Michigan University B, T

Minnesota
Augsburg College B
Bemidji State University B
Bethel College B
College of St. Benedict B
College of St. Catherine: St. Paul Campus B
Concordia College: Moorhead B
Concordia University: St. Paul B
Gustavus Adolphus College B
Hamline University B
Macalester College B, T
Minnesota State University, Mankato B, M
Moorhead State University B
North Central University B
Northwestern College B
St. Cloud State University B
St. John's University B
St. Mary's University of Minnesota B
St. Olaf College B
Southwest State University B
University of Minnesota Duluth B
Morris B
Twin Cities B, M, D
University of St. Thomas B
Winona State University B

Mississippi
Belhaven College B
Blue Mountain College B
Hinds Community College A
Jackson State University B
Millsaps College B, T
Mississippi University for Women B
University of Mississippi B, M
University of Southern Mississippi B, M
William Carey College B

Missouri
Avila College B
Central Methodist College B
Central Missouri State University B, M
College of the Ozarks B
Culver-Stockton College B
Drury University B
Evangel University A, B
Fontbonne College B, T
Hannibal-LaGrange College B
Lindenwood University B
Missouri Southern State College B, T
Missouri Valley College B
Northwest Missouri State University B
Rockhurst University B
St. Louis University B
Southeast Missouri State University B
Southwest Baptist University B
Southwest Missouri State University B, M
St. Louis Community College
  St. Louis Community College at Florissant Valley A
Stephens College B
Truman State University B
University of Missouri Columbia B, M, D
Kansas City B, M
Washington University B, M
Webster University B
William Jewell College B
William Woods University B

Montana
Carroll College B
Rocky Mountain College B
University of Montana-Missoula B, M
Western Montana College of The University of Montana B

Nebraska
Chadron State College B
Concordia University B
Creighton University B
Doane College B
Hastings College B, D
Midland Lutheran College B, T
Nebraska Wesleyan University B
Northeast Community College A
University of Nebraska Kearney B, T
Lincoln B, M
Omaha B, M
Wayne State College B, T

Nevada
University of Nevada Las Vegas B, M
Reno B

New Hampshire
Dartmouth College B
Franklin Pierce College B
Keene State College B
New England College B
Plymouth State College of the University System of New Hampshire B
University of New Hampshire B

New Jersey
Bloomfield College B
Brookdale Community College A
Cumberland County College A
Drew University B
Essex County College A
Gloucester County College A
Kean University B
Middlesex County College A
Montclair State University B, M
Ocean County College A
Raritan Valley Community College A
Rider University B
Rowan University B
Rutgers
  The State University of New Jersey: Camden College of Arts and Sciences B, T
  The State University of New Jersey: Douglass College B
  The State University of New Jersey: Livingston College B
  The State University of New Jersey: Mason Gross School of the Arts B, M
  The State University of New Jersey: New Brunswick Graduate Campus M
  The State University of New Jersey: Newark College of Arts and Sciences B
  The State University of New Jersey: Rutgers College B
  The State University of New Jersey: University College Camden B, T
  The State University of New Jersey: University College New Brunswick B
Thomas Edison State College B
Union County College A
William Paterson University of New Jersey B

New Mexico
College of Santa Fe B
Eastern New Mexico University B
New Mexico State University B
San Juan College A
University of New Mexico B, M

New York
Adelphi University B
Adirondack Community College A
Alfred University B
Barnard College B
City University of New York
  Brooklyn College B, M
  City College B
  College of Staten Island B
  Graduate School and University Center D
  Hunter College B, M
  Lehman College B
  Queens College B
  Queensborough Community College A
  York College B
Colgate University B
Columbia University
  Columbia College B
  School of General Studies B
Cornell University B

Dowling College *B*
Elmira College *B*
Finger Lakes Community College *A*
Five Towns College *B*
Fordham University *B*
Fulton-Montgomery Community
 College *A*
Genesee Community College *A*
Hamilton College *B*
Hartwick College *B*
Hobart and William Smith Colleges *B*
Hofstra University *B*
Ithaca College *B*
Juilliard School *B*
Long Island University
 Brooklyn Campus *B*
 C. W. Post Campus *B, M*
Manhattanville College *B*
Marymount College *B*
Marymount Manhattan College *B*
Mount St. Mary College *B*
Nazareth College of Rochester *B*
New York University *B, M, D*
Niagara University *B*
Pace University:
 Pleasantville/Briarcliff *A, B*
Pace University *A, B*
Rockland Community College *A*
Russell Sage College *B*
St. Lawrence University *B*
Sarah Lawrence College *B, M*
Schenectady County Community
 College *A*
Skidmore College *B*
State University of New York
 Albany *B, M*
 Binghamton *B, M*
 College at Brockport *B*
 College at Buffalo *B*
 College at Fredonia *B*
 College at Geneseo *B*
 College at Oneonta *B*
 College at Plattsburgh *B*
 College at Potsdam *B*
 New Paltz *B*
 Oswego *B*
 Stony Brook *B, M*
Suffolk County Community College *A*
Syracuse University *B, M*
Utica College of Syracuse University *B*
Vassar College *B*
Wagner College *B*
Wells College *B*
Westchester Community College *A*

North Carolina
Barton College *B*
Brevard College *B*
Campbell University *B*
Catawba College *B, T*
Chowan College *B*
College of the Albemarle *A*
Duke University *B*
East Carolina University *B*
Elon College *B*
Fayetteville State University *B*
Greensboro College *B, T*
Guilford College *B*
Guilford Technical Community
 College *A*
High Point University *B*
Lees-McRae College *B, T*
Lenoir-Rhyne College *B, T*
Louisburg College *A*
Meredith College *B, T*
North Carolina Agricultural and
 Technical State University *B*
North Carolina Central University *B*
North Carolina School of the Arts *B*
North Carolina Wesleyan College *B*
Pfeiffer University *B*
Queens College *B*
Shaw University *B*
Southeastern Community College *A*

University of North Carolina
 Asheville *B, T*
 Chapel Hill *B, M*
 Charlotte *B, T*
 Greensboro *B, M*
 Wilmington *B*
Wake Forest University *B*
Western Carolina University *B*
Wilkes Community College *A*

North Dakota
Dickinson State University *B*
Jamestown College *B*
Minot State University *B*
North Dakota State University *B, M*
Trinity Bible College *B*
University of North Dakota *B, M*

Ohio
Antioch College *B*
Ashland University *B*
Baldwin-Wallace College *B*
Bowling Green State University *B, M, D*
Case Western Reserve University *B*
Cleveland State University *B*
College of Wooster *B*
Denison University *B*
Hiram College *B, T*
Kent State University
 Stark Campus *B*
Kent State University *B, M*
Kenyon College *B*
Marietta College *B*
Miami University
 Oxford Campus *B, M*
Mount Union College *B*
Mount Vernon Nazarene College *B*
Muskingum College *B*
Oberlin College *B*
Ohio Northern University *B*
Ohio State University
 Columbus Campus *B, M, D*
Ohio University *B, M*
Ohio Wesleyan University *B*
Otterbein College *B*
Sinclair Community College *A*
University of Akron *B, M*
University of Cincinnati *B, M*
University of Dayton *B*
University of Findlay *B*
University of Toledo *B*
Wilmington College *B*
Wright State University *B*
Youngstown State University *B*

Oklahoma
Cameron University *B*
East Central University *B*
Eastern Oklahoma State College *A*
Northeastern Oklahoma Agricultural and
 Mechanical College *A*
Northeastern State University *B*
Northwestern Oklahoma State
 University *B*
Oklahoma Baptist University *B, T*
Oklahoma City University *B, M*
Oral Roberts University *B*
St. Gregory's University *A, B*
Tulsa Community College *A*
University of Central Oklahoma *B*
University of Oklahoma *B, M*
University of Science and Arts of
 Oklahoma *B*
University of Tulsa *B*

Oregon
Concordia University *B*
Eastern Oregon University *B*
Lewis & Clark College *B*
Linfield College *B*
Mount Hood Community College *A*
Pacific University *B*
Portland State University *B, M*
Reed College *B*
Southern Oregon University *B, T*
University of Oregon *B, M, D*

University of Portland *B, M*
Western Oregon University *B*
Willamette University *B*

Pennsylvania
Allegheny College *B*
Allentown College of St. Francis de
 Sales *B*
Beaver College *B*
Bloomsburg University of
 Pennsylvania *B*
Bucknell University *B*
Bucks County Community College *A*
California University of Pennsylvania *B*
Carnegie Mellon University *B, M*
Cedar Crest College *B*
Chatham College *B*
Cheyney University of Pennsylvania *B*
Clarion University of Pennsylvania *B*
Community College of Allegheny
 County *A*
Community College of Philadelphia *A*
Dickinson College *B*
Duquesne University *B*
East Stroudsburg University of
 Pennsylvania *B*
Edinboro University of Pennsylvania *B*
Franklin and Marshall College *B*
Gannon University *B*
Gettysburg College *B*
Harrisburg Area Community College *A*
Indiana University of Pennsylvania *B*
King's College *B*
Kutztown University of Pennsylvania *B*
Lehigh University *B*
Lock Haven University of
 Pennsylvania *B*
Lycoming College *B*
Mansfield University of Pennsylvania *B*
Marywood University *B*
Messiah College *B*
Muhlenberg College *B*
Penn State
 University Park *B, M*
Point Park College *B*
St. Vincent College *B*
Seton Hill College *B*
Slippery Rock University of
 Pennsylvania *B*
Susquehanna University *B*
Swarthmore College *B*
Temple University *B, M*
University of Pennsylvania *A, B*
University of Pittsburgh
 Johnstown *B*
University of Pittsburgh *B, M, D*
University of Scranton *B*
University of the Arts *B*
Villanova University *M*
West Chester University of
 Pennsylvania *B*
Westminster College *B, T*
Wilkes University *B*

Puerto Rico
University of Puerto Rico
 Rio Piedras Campus *B*
University of the Sacred Heart *B*

Rhode Island
Brown University *B, M*
Community College of Rhode Island *A*
Providence College *B*
Rhode Island College *B, M*
Roger Williams University *A, B*
Salve Regina University *B*
University of Rhode Island *B*

South Carolina
Charleston Southern University *B*
Coastal Carolina University *B*
Coker College *B*
College of Charleston *B*
Converse College *B*
Francis Marion University *B*
Furman University *B, T*

Newberry College *B*
North Greenville College *A*
Presbyterian College *B*
South Carolina State University *B*
University of South Carolina *B, M*
Winthrop University *B*

South Dakota
Augustana College *B*
Black Hills State University *B*
University of South Dakota *B, M*

Tennessee
Belmont University *B, T*
Bethel College *B*
David Lipscomb University *B*
Freed-Hardeman University *B, T*
Lambuth University *B*
Maryville College *B*
Middle Tennessee State University *B*
Rhodes College *B*
Roane State Community College *A*
Tennessee State University *B*
Trevecca Nazarene University *B*
Union University *B, T*
University of Memphis *B, M*
University of Tennessee
 Chattanooga *B*
 Knoxville *B, M*
 Martin *B*
Vanderbilt University *B*
Walters State Community College *A*

Texas
Abilene Christian University *B*
Alvin Community College *A*
Amarillo College *A*
Angelina College *A*
Austin Community College *A*
Baylor University *B, M*
Brazosport College *A*
College of the Mainland *A*
Del Mar College *A*
East Texas Baptist University *B*
El Paso Community College *A*
Galveston College *A*
Grayson County College *A*
Hardin-Simmons University *B*
Howard College *A*
Howard Payne University *B, T*
Kilgore College *A*
Lamar University *B, M*
Lee College *A*
Lon Morris College *A*
McMurry University *B, T*
Midland College *A*
Midwestern State University *B*
Navarro College *A*
Northeast Texas Community College *A*
Our Lady of the Lake University of San
 Antonio *B*
Panola College *A*
Paris Junior College *A*
Prairie View A&M University *B*
St. Edward's University *B, T*
St. Philip's College *A*
Sam Houston State University *B*
San Jacinto College
 North *A*
South Plains College *A*
Southern Methodist University *B, M*
Southwest Texas State
 University *B, M, T*
Southwestern University *B, T*
Stephen F. Austin State
 University *B, M, T*
Sul Ross State University *B*
Tarleton State University *B*
Texas A&M University
 Commerce *B, M*
 Corpus Christi *T*
 Kingsville *B, T*
Texas A&M University *B*
Texas Christian University *B, T*
Texas Lutheran University *B*
Texas Tech University *B, M, D*

Texas Wesleyan University *B*
Texas Woman's University *B, M, T*
Trinity University *B*
Trinity Valley Community College *A*
Tyler Junior College *A*
University of Dallas *B*
University of Houston *B, M*
University of North Texas *B, M*
University of St. Thomas *B*
University of Texas
   Arlington *B*
   Austin *B, M, D*
   El Paso *B, M*
   Pan American *B, M, T*
   Tyler *B*
University of the Incarnate Word *B*
Wayland Baptist University *B*
West Texas A&M University *B*
Western Texas College *A*
Wharton County Junior College *A*

Utah
Brigham Young University *B, M, D*
Dixie State College of Utah *A*
Southern Utah University *B*
University of Utah *B, M, D*
Utah State University *B, M*
Weber State University *B*

Vermont
Bennington College *B*
Castleton State College *B*
Johnson State College *B*
Marlboro College *B*
Middlebury College *B*
St. Michael's College *B*
University of Vermont *B*

Virginia
Averett College *B, T*
Bluefield College *B*
Christopher Newport University *B*
College of William and Mary *B*
Emory & Henry College *B*
Ferrum College *B*
George Mason University *B*
Hampton University *B*
Hollins University *B*
James Madison University *B, T*
Longwood College *B, T*
Lynchburg College *B*
Mary Baldwin College *B*
Mary Washington College *B*
Old Dominion University *B*
Radford University *B*
Randolph-Macon College *B*
Randolph-Macon Woman's College *B*
Roanoke College *B, T*
Shenandoah University *B*
Sweet Briar College *B*
University of Richmond *B*
University of Virginia's College at
   Wise *B, T*
University of Virginia *B, M*
Virginia Commonwealth
   University *B, M*
Virginia Intermont College *B*
Virginia Polytechnic Institute and State
   University *B, M*
Virginia Union University *B*
Virginia Wesleyan College *B*
Washington and Lee University *B*

Washington
Central Washington University *B*
Centralia College *A*
Eastern Washington University *B, T*
Everett Community College *A*
Evergreen State College *B*
Gonzaga University *B*
Highline Community College *A*
Lower Columbia College *A*
North Seattle Community College *C, A*
Pacific Lutheran University *B*
St. Martin's College *B*
Seattle Pacific University *B, T*

Seattle University *B*
University of Puget Sound *B, T*
University of Washington *B, M, D*
Washington State University *B, M*
Western Washington University *B, M*
Whitman College *B*

West Virginia
Alderson-Broaddus College *B*
Bethany College *B*
Davis and Elkins College *B*
Fairmont State College *B*
Marshall University *B*
West Virginia University *B, M*
West Virginia Wesleyan College *B*

Wisconsin
Alverno College *T*
Beloit College *B*
Cardinal Stritch University *B*
Carroll College *B*
Carthage College *B, T*
Lakeland College *B*
Lawrence University *B, T*
Marquette University *B, T*
Ripon College *B, T*
University of Wisconsin
   Eau Claire *B*
   Green Bay *B*
   La Crosse *B*
   Madison *B, M, D*
   Milwaukee *B*
   Parkside *B*
   Platteville *B*
   Stevens Point *B*
   Superior *B, M*
Viterbo University *B, T*

Wyoming
Casper College *A*
Central Wyoming College *A*
Laramie County Community College *A*
University of Wyoming *B*
Western Wyoming Community
   College *A*

Drawing

Alabama
Birmingham-Southern College *B*

Arizona
Arizona State University *B, M*

California
Academy of Art College *C, A, B, M*
Biola University *B*
California College of Arts and
   Crafts *B, M*
California Institute of the Arts *C, B, M*
California State University
   Fullerton *B, M*
   Hayward *B*
   Long Beach *B, M*
   Northridge *B, M*
Chabot College *A*
Grossmont Community College *A*
Monterey Peninsula College *A*
Otis College of Art and Design *B, M*
Pasadena City College *A*
San Francisco Art Institute *B, M*
Santa Rosa Junior College *C*
Solano Community College *A*
University of San Francisco *B*

Colorado
Adams State College *B*
Colorado State University *B*
Naropa University *C, B*

Connecticut
University of Hartford *B*

Florida
Art Institute
   of Fort Lauderdale *A*

Georgia
Atlanta College of Art *B*
Georgia Military College *A*
Georgia State University *B, M*
LaGrange College *B*
University of Georgia *B*

Idaho
Northwest Nazarene University *B*

Illinois
American Academy of Art *A, B*
City Colleges of Chicago
   Olive-Harvey College *A*
Lewis University *B*
Rend Lake College *A*
Richland Community College *A*
Rockford College *B*
School of the Art Institute of
   Chicago *B, M*

Indiana
Ball State University *B*
Indiana University--Purdue University
   Indiana University-Purdue
   University Fort Wayne *B*
University of Evansville *B*
Vincennes University *A*

Iowa
Drake University *B*
University of Iowa *B, M*

Kansas
Allen County Community College *A*
Central Christian College *A*
Pratt Community College *A*

Maine
Maine College of Art *B*

Maryland
Maryland College of Art and Design *A*
Maryland Institute College of Art *B*

Massachusetts
Boston University *B*
Hampshire College *B*
Montserrat College of Art *B*
School of the Museum of Fine Arts *B, M*
Simon's Rock College of Bard *B*

Michigan
Center for Creative Studies: College of
   Art and Design *B*
Lansing Community College *A*
Lawrence Technological University *B*
Northern Michigan University *B*
Siena Heights University *B*
University of Michigan *B*

Minnesota
College of Visual Arts *B*
Minneapolis College of Art and
   Design *B*
Minnesota State University, Mankato *B*
Moorhead State University *B*

Mississippi
Mississippi University for Women *B*

Missouri
Kansas City Art Institute *B*
Lindenwood University *B, M*
University of Missouri
   St. Louis *B*
Washington University *B, M*
Webster University *B*

New Hampshire
Plymouth State College of the University
   System of New Hampshire *B*
Rivier College *B*

New Jersey
Rowan University *B*
Rutgers
   The State University of New Jersey:
   Mason Gross School of the
   Arts *B, M*

New York
Bard College *B*
City University of New York
   Brooklyn College *M*
   Queens College *B*
New York State College of Ceramics at
   Alfred University *B, M, T*
Parsons School of Design *C, A, B, T*
Pratt Institute *B, M*
Rochester Institute of Technology *A, B*
Sarah Lawrence College *B*
School of Visual Arts *B, M*
State University of New York
   Albany *B, M*
   College at Fredonia *B*

North Carolina
Brevard College *A, B*

Ohio
Bowling Green State University *B*
Cleveland Institute of Art *B*
Kent State University *B, M*
Lourdes College *A*
Ohio State University
   Columbus Campus *B*
Ohio University *B*
Shawnee State University *B*
University of Akron *B*
Wittenberg University *B*

Oregon
Pacific Northwest College of Art *B*
Portland State University *B*
University of Oregon *B, M*

Pennsylvania
Carnegie Mellon University *B*
Immaculata College *A*
Mercyhurst College *B*
Moore College of Art and Design *B*
Seton Hill College *B*

Puerto Rico
University of Puerto Rico
   Rio Piedras Campus *B*

Rhode Island
Providence College *B*
Rhode Island College *B*

South Carolina
Anderson College *B*

Tennessee
Carson-Newman College *B*
Union University *B*

Texas
Sam Houston State University *M*
Stephen F. Austin State University *M*
University of North Texas *B, M*
University of Texas
   El Paso *B*
   San Antonio *B, M*
Western Texas College *A*

Utah
Dixie State College of Utah *A*

Vermont
Bennington College *B, M*
Burlington College *B*
Marlboro College *B*

Virginia
Virginia Intermont College *B*

Washington
Cornish College of the Arts *B*
North Seattle Community College *C*
Western Washington University *B*

West Virginia
Marshall University *B, M*
West Virginia State College *B*
West Virginia Wesleyan College *B*

Wisconsin
Milwaukee Institute of Art & Design *B*

Driver/safety education

Alabama
University of Montevallo B, M, T
Florida
University of Tampa T
Georgia
University of Georgia M
Indiana
Indiana State University T
Iowa
Iowa State University T
William Penn University B
Kansas
Emporia State University T
Louisiana
Northwestern State University T
Mississippi
Mississippi State University T
Missouri
Missouri Baptist College T
Missouri Western State College T
Nebraska
Chadron State College T
Peru State College T
New Hampshire
Keene State College A
North Carolina
North Carolina Agricultural and Technical State University B, M, T
Oklahoma
Northeastern State University C
Southeastern Oklahoma State University T
Southwestern Oklahoma State University T
University of Central Oklahoma B
Pennsylvania
Lock Haven University of Pennsylvania T
West Chester University of Pennsylvania C
South Dakota
Northern State University T
Texas
Lamar University T
Southwest Texas State University T
Texas A&M University Commerce B
Virginia
Bridgewater College T
University of Virginia's College at Wise T
West Virginia
Glenville State College B

Drug/alcohol abuse counseling

Alabama
Gadsden State Community College A
Wallace State Community College at Hanceville A
Arizona
Pima Community College C, A
Rio Salado College C, A
California
Allan Hancock College C
Butte College C, A
California State University Hayward C
College of San Mateo C, A
College of the Redwoods C
Cypress College C
East Los Angeles College C
Fresno City College C, A
Glendale Community College C
Imperial Valley College C, A
Loma Linda University M
Mendocino College C, A
Merced College C, A
Modesto Junior College C
Mount San Jacinto College C, A
Saddleback College C
San Diego City College C, A
San Jose City College C, A
United States International University C
Connecticut
Asnuntuck Community-Technical College A
Capital Community College A
Gateway Community College C, A
Housatonic Community-Technical College A
Manchester Community-Technical College A
Middlesex Community-Technical College A
Naugatuck Valley Community-Technical College A
Northwestern Connecticut Community-Technical College A
Norwalk Community-Technical College A
Three Rivers Community-Technical College A
Tunxis Community College A
Delaware
Delaware Technical and Community College
  Stanton/Wilmington Campus A
  Terry Campus A
Florida
Florida Community College at Jacksonville A
St. Petersburg Junior College A
Illinois
City Colleges of Chicago
  Harold Washington College C, A
College of DuPage C, A
College of Lake County C, A
Elgin Community College C
Governors State University M
Moraine Valley Community College C
National-Louis University C, B, M
Oakton Community College C
Prairie State College A
Roosevelt University M
Triton College C, A
Waubonsee Community College C
Indiana
Indiana University--Purdue University
  Indiana University-Purdue University Fort Wayne C
Iowa
Des Moines Area Community College C
Iowa Western Community College A
Southeastern Community College
  North Campus A
  South Campus A
Kansas
Dodge City Community College A
Kansas City Kansas Community College A
Pittsburg State University M
Louisiana
Southern University
  Shreveport C, A
University of Louisiana at Monroe M
Maine
University of Maine
  Augusta C
University of Southern Maine M
Maryland
Community College of Baltimore County
  Essex C
Howard Community College A
Wor-Wic Community College C, A
Massachusetts
Middlesex Community College C
North Shore Community College C, A
Northern Essex Community College C
Springfield College M
Michigan
Lake Superior State University A
University of Detroit Mercy A, B
Washtenaw Community College A
Wayne County Community College C
Wayne State University C
Minnesota
College of St. Catherine-Minneapolis C, A
Mesabi Range Community and Technical College C, A
Minneapolis Community and Technical College C, A
Ridgewater College: A Community and Technical College A
St. Cloud State University B, M
University of Minnesota
  Twin Cities C
Missouri
Missouri Valley College B
St. Charles County Community College A
Montana
Dawson Community College A
Flathead Valley Community College A
Little Big Horn College A
Stone Child College A
University of Great Falls C, A
Nebraska
Bellevue University B
New Hampshire
New Hampshire Technical Institute A
New Jersey
Mercer County Community College C
New Mexico
Northern New Mexico Community College A
New York
Broome Community College A
Columbia University
  School of Nursing C
Columbia-Greene Community College C
Corning Community College A
Dutchess Community College C
Erie Community College
  City Campus A
Finger Lakes Community College A
Hudson Valley Community College A
Marymount Manhattan College C
Medaille College C
Mohawk Valley Community College A
New York Institute of Technology M
New York University M, D
St. Joseph's College
  St. Joseph's College: Suffolk Campus C
Suffolk County Community College A
Tompkins-Cortland Community College A
Ulster County Community College A
Westchester Community College C, A
North Carolina
East Carolina University M
Guilford Technical Community College A
Sandhills Community College A
Southwestern Community College A
North Dakota
Minot State University B
Ohio
Columbus State Community College A
North Central State College C
University of Akron C
University of Toledo A
Wright State University M
Oklahoma
Oklahoma State University
  Oklahoma City A
Oregon
Chemeketa Community College A
Lane Community College A
Oregon Health Sciences University C
Portland Community College C, A
Pennsylvania
Alvernia College C, B
Community College of Allegheny County C
Community College of Philadelphia C
MCP Hahnemann University A, B
Northampton County Area Community College C
St. Vincent College C
Rhode Island
Community College of Rhode Island A
South Dakota
Kilian Community College A
University of South Dakota B
Tennessee
Cleveland State Community College C
Shelby State Community College C
Texas
Alvin Community College C, A
Amarillo College C, A
Angelina College A
Central Texas College C, A
Eastfield College C, A
El Paso Community College A
Galveston College C, A
Grayson County College C, A
Howard College C, A
Lamar State College at Port Arthur C, A
Lee College C, A
Midland College C, A
Odessa College A
St. Mary's University M
Virginia
J. Sargeant Reynolds Community College C
Northern Virginia Community College C, A
Washington
Clark College C, A
Lower Columbia College A
Peninsula College A
Pierce College C, A
Seattle University C
Tacoma Community College C
Wenatchee Valley College C, A
Yakima Valley Community College C, A
Wisconsin
Chippewa Valley Technical College A
Gateway Technical College C
Moraine Park Technical College A
Viterbo University C
Waukesha County Technical College A

Early childhood education

Alabama
Alabama Agricultural and Mechanical University B, M, T
Alabama State University A, B, M, T
Athens State University B
Auburn University B, M, D, T
Birmingham-Southern College B, T
Calhoun Community College A
Concordia College B
Huntingdon College B, T
Jacksonville State University B, M, T
James H. Faulkner State Community College A
Lawson State Community College A
Northwest-Shoals Community College A
Samford University B, M, T
Shelton State Community College C
Spring Hill College B, M
Troy State University Dothan B, M, T
Troy State University B, M, T
Tuskegee University B, T
University of Alabama Birmingham B, M, D, T
University of Alabama B, M
University of Mobile B, M, T
University of Montevallo B, M, T
University of North Alabama B, M
University of South Alabama B, M, T
University of West Alabama B, M, T

Alaska
University of Alaska
Fairbanks C, A
Southeast C, A, B, T

Arizona
Arizona State University B
Central Arizona College A
Northern Arizona University B, M, T
Pima Community College C, A
Prescott College B, M
Scottsdale Community College C, A
South Mountain Community College C
University of Arizona B, M

Arkansas
Arkansas State University B, M, T
Arkansas Tech University A, B
Harding University B, T
Henderson State University M, T
John Brown University B
Ouachita Baptist University B, T
Southern Arkansas University B, T
University of Arkansas
Little Rock B, M
Pine Bluff B
University of Central Arkansas M, T
University of the Ozarks B, T
Williams Baptist College B

California
Allan Hancock College C, A
Butte College C, A
California Baptist University B, T
California College for Health Sciences A
California Lutheran University B, M
California State University
Bakersfield B, M
Chico B
Fresno M
Long Beach T
Northridge M
Sacramento B, M, T
Stanislaus B
Canada College C, A
Cerritos Community College A
Chabot College C, A
Chaffey Community College C, A
College of the Redwoods A
College of the Sequoias C
Concordia University B
Crafton Hills College C, A
Cuesta College C, A
De Anza College C, A
East Los Angeles College C
Foothill College C, A
Fresno City College C, A
Gavilan Community College C
Glendale Community College C, A
Hope International University A
Imperial Valley College C, A
Irvine Valley College C, A
Kings River Community College C, A
Lake Tahoe Community College C, A
Los Angeles Southwest College A
Marymount College A
Merced College C, A
Merritt College C, A
Mills College B, T
MiraCosta College C, A
Mount St. Mary's College A
Mount San Jacinto College C, A
Napa Valley College C, A
Ohlone College C, A
Orange Coast College C, A
Pacific Oaks College B, M
Pacific Union College A, B
Palomar College C, A
Pasadena City College C, A
Patten College A, B
Riverside Community College C, A
Saddleback College C, A
San Diego Mesa College C, A
San Diego Miramar College A
San Francisco State University T
San Joaquin Delta College C
San Jose City College C, A
San Jose State University M
Santa Ana College C, A
Santa Barbara City College C, A
Santa Rosa Junior College C
Shasta College A
Sierra College C, A
Solano Community College C, A
Sonoma State University M, T
Southwestern College C
Taft College C, A
University of California
Santa Barbara M
University of La Verne B, M, T
Ventura College C, A
West Hills Community College A
West Valley College A
Whittier College B, T
Yuba College C

Colorado
Colorado Mountain College
Alpine Campus A
Community College of Aurora A
Community College of Denver C, A
Fort Lewis College T
Metropolitan State College of Denver T
Naropa University C, B
Northeastern Junior College C, A
Otero Junior College C
Pueblo Community College A
Red Rocks Community College A
University of Colorado
Denver M
University of Northern Colorado M, T

Connecticut
Asnuntuck Community-Technical College C, A
Capital Community College C, A
Central Connecticut State University B, M
Connecticut College T
Eastern Connecticut State University B, M, T
Gateway Community College C, A
Housatonic Community-Technical College A
Manchester Community-Technical College A
Mitchell College A, B
Naugatuck Valley Community-Technical College A
Northwestern Connecticut Community-Technical College C, A
Norwalk Community-Technical College C, A
Sacred Heart University A, B, M, T
St. Joseph College M, T
Teikyo Post University C, A
Three Rivers Community-Technical College C, A
University of Hartford B, M, T

Delaware
Delaware State University B
Delaware Technical and Community College
Stanton/Wilmington Campus C, A
University of Delaware B, T
Wilmington College A, B

District of Columbia
Catholic University of America B, M, T
Gallaudet University B, T
George Washington University M
Howard University M
Trinity College M, T
University of the District of Columbia B, T

Florida
Barry University B, M, T
Brevard Community College A
Broward Community College A
Central Florida Community College C, A
Florida Atlantic University M
Florida Gulf Coast University B, T
Florida International University M
Florida Southern College B
Florida State University C, B, M, D, T
Indian River Community College A
Lynn University A, B
Manatee Community College A
Miami-Dade Community College C, A
Nova Southeastern University B
Palm Beach Community College A
Pensacola Junior College A
Polk Community College A
St. Petersburg Junior College A
Santa Fe Community College C, A
Southeastern College of the Assemblies of God B, T
Tallahassee Community College A
University of Central Florida B
University of Florida M
University of Miami M

Georgia
Agnes Scott College T
Albany State University B, M, T
Armstrong Atlantic State University B
Atlanta Christian College B
Atlanta Metropolitan College A
Augusta State University B, M
Berry College B, M, T
Brenau University B, M, T
Brewton-Parker College B
Columbus State University B, M
DeKalb Technical Institute C
Gainesville College A
Georgia College and State University B, M, T
Georgia Southern University B, M, T
Georgia Southwestern State University B, M, T
Georgia State University B, M, D
Kennesaw State University B, M
LaGrange College B
Morris Brown College B
North Georgia College & State University B, M
Oglethorpe University B, M, T
Paine College B
Piedmont College B, M, T
Reinhardt College B
Savannah State University B
Spelman College B, T
State University of West Georgia B, M
Thomas College B
Toccoa Falls College B, T
University of Georgia B, M, D, T
Valdosta State University B, M
Wesleyan College B, M, T

Hawaii
Chaminade University of Honolulu B, T
University of Hawaii
Hawaii Community College C, A
Honolulu Community College C, A
Kauai Community College C, A
Manoa B, T

Idaho
Boise State University T
Idaho State University B, T
North Idaho College A
Ricks College A

Illinois
Bradley University B, T
Chicago State University B, M, T
City Colleges of Chicago
Harold Washington College C, A
Kennedy-King College A
Malcolm X College A
Columbia College B
Concordia University B, M, T
De Paul University C, B, T
Dominican University T
Eastern Illinois University B
Elmhurst College B, M
Governors State University B, M, T
Greenville College B
Highland Community College C, A
Illinois College B, T
Illinois State University B, T
John A. Logan College A
Joliet Junior College A
Judson College B, T
Kankakee Community College A
Kendall College C, A, B, T
Kishwaukee College A
Lewis and Clark Community College C, A
Loyola University of Chicago M, D, T
National-Louis University B, M, T
North Park University B, M
Northeastern Illinois University B
Northern Illinois University B, M, T
Oakton Community College A
Olivet Nazarene University B, T
Parkland College A
Rend Lake College A
Roosevelt University B, M
St. Augustine College C, A
St. Xavier University M
Southern Illinois University
Carbondale B
Edwardsville B
Southwestern Illinois College A
Spoon River College A
Triton College C, A
University of Illinois
Urbana-Champaign B
William Rainey Harper College C, A

Indiana
Ball State University B, M, D, T
Bethel College A
Butler University B, T
Goshen College B, T
Indiana State University A, B, M, T
Indiana University
Bloomington B, T
South Bend
Indiana University--Purdue University
Indiana University-Purdue University Fort Wayne A
Indiana University-Purdue University Indianapolis A
Indiana Wesleyan University T
Manchester College A

Early childhood education

Marian College A, B, T
Purdue University
    Calumet A
Purdue University B, M
St. Mary-of-the-Woods College A, B, T
Taylor University A
Vincennes University A

Iowa
Central College T
Clarke College B, M, T
Des Moines Area Community College A
Drake University B
Graceland University T
Iowa Lakes Community College A
Iowa State University B, T
Iowa Wesleyan College B
Kirkwood Community College A
Luther College B
Morningside College B, M
Mount Mercy College T
North Iowa Area Community College A
Northeast Iowa Community College C
Northwestern College T
St. Ambrose University B, T
Simpson College B, T
University of Iowa M
University of Northern Iowa B, M
Waldorf College A
Wartburg College T
William Penn University B

Kansas
Bethel College T
Butler County Community College A
Central Christian College A
Coffeyville Community College A
Emporia State University M, T
Garden City Community College A
Hesston College A
Independence Community College A
Kansas City Kansas Community
    College C, A
Kansas Wesleyan University A
McPherson College B, T
Pittsburg State University B, T
Pratt Community College A
Seward County Community College A

Kentucky
Campbellsville University B
Cumberland College B, M, T
Hazard Community College A
Hopkinsville Community College A
Kentucky State University B
Mid-Continent College B
Morehead State University B
Murray State University B
Northern Kentucky University B, M, T
Owensboro Community College A
Spalding University B, M, T
University of Kentucky B, T
University of Louisville M
Western Kentucky University M

Louisiana
Centenary College of Louisiana B, T
Delgado Community College A
Dillard University B, T
Louisiana Tech University B
McNeese State University B, M, T
Nicholls State University M
Northwestern State University B, M, T
Nunez Community College A
Southern University
    Shreveport A
Southern University and Agricultural and
    Mechanical College B
University of Louisiana at Monroe B
Xavier University of Louisiana B, T

Maine
Andover College C, A
Eastern Maine Technical College C, A
St. Joseph's College B
University of Maine
    Farmington B

University of New England B
Washington County Technical
    College C, A

Maryland
Baltimore City Community College C, A
Bowie State University B, T
Charles County Community
    College C, A
College of Notre Dame of Maryland B
Columbia Union College A, B, T
Community College of Baltimore County
    Catonsville A
    Essex C, A
Coppin State College B
Frederick Community College A
Frostburg State University B, T
Hagerstown Community College A
Howard Community College C, A
Montgomery College
    Germantown Campus A
    Rockville Campus A
    Takoma Park Campus A
Prince George's Community
    College C, A
St. Mary's College of Maryland T
Salisbury State University B
Towson University B, M, T
University of Maryland
    College Park B
Villa Julie College A, B, T

Massachusetts
American International College B, M
Anna Maria College B, M, T
Bay Path College C, A, B
Bay State College A
Becker College C, A, B, T
Berkshire Community College C, A
Boston College B, M, T
Boston University B, M, T
Bridgewater State College B, M, T
Bunker Hill Community College C
Cape Cod Community College C, A
Curry College B
Dean College A
Eastern Nazarene College A, B, M, T
Elms College B, M, T
Endicott College C, A, B
Fisher College C, A
Fitchburg State College B, M, T
Framingham State College B, M, T
Gordon College B
Greenfield Community College A
Hampshire College B
Holyoke Community College A
Lasell College B
Lesley College B, M, T
Massachusetts College of Liberal Arts T
Massasoit Community College C, A
Middlesex Community College C, A
Mount Ida College A, B, T
Mount Wachusett Community College A
North Shore Community College A
Northeastern University B
Northern Essex Community College A
Pine Manor College T
Quincy College C, A
Roxbury Community College A
Salem State College B, M
Simmons College B, M
Springfield College B, M, T
Springfield Technical Community
    College A
Stonehill College B
Tufts University B, M, T
Wellesley College T
Westfield State College B, M, T
Wheaton College T
Wheelock College B, M
Worcester State College B, M, T

Michigan
Adrian College A, T
Alma College T

Baker College
    of Muskegon A
Calvin College B, T
Central Michigan University M
Ferris State University A
Glen Oaks Community College C, A
Gogebic Community College A
Grace Bible College B
Hillsdale College B
Madonna University B, T
Marygrove College C, B, M, T
Monroe County Community
    College C, A
Muskegon Community College C
North Central Michigan College C, A
Northern Michigan University A, B, T
Oakland Community College A
Oakland University M, D
Saginaw Valley State University M
Spring Arbor College T
University of Detroit Mercy M
University of Michigan
    Dearborn B
    Flint B, T
Washtenaw Community College A
Wayne State University M
Western Michigan University M
William Tyndale College A

Minnesota
Augsburg College B, T
Bethel College B
College of St. Catherine: St. Paul
    Campus B, T
College of St. Scholastica T
Concordia University: St. Paul B, T
Crown College A, B, T
Martin Luther College B
Minnesota State University, Mankato M
Moorhead State University B, M, T
Northwestern College B
St. Cloud State University M
St. Cloud Technical College C, A
St. Mary's University of Minnesota B
Southwest State University B, T
University of Minnesota
    Crookston A, B
    Duluth B, T
    Twin Cities B, M
Winona State University B, M, T

Mississippi
Coahoma Community College A
Jackson State University B, T
Mary Holmes College C, A
Mississippi State University T
Rust College A, B
Tougaloo College A
University of Mississippi B

Missouri
Central Missouri State University T
Culver-Stockton College T
East Central College A
Evangel University A, B, T
Fontbonne College B
Hannibal-LaGrange College B
Harris Stowe State College B, T
Jefferson College A
Lindenwood University B
Maryville University of Saint
    Louis B, M, T
Mineral Area College C
Missouri Baptist College B, T
Missouri Southern State College B, T
Missouri Valley College T
Northwest Missouri State
    University B, M, T
Park University B
St. Charles County Community
    College C, A
Southeast Missouri State University B, T
Southwest Baptist University T
Southwest Missouri State University B

St. Louis Community College
    St. Louis Community College at
        Florissant Valley A
Stephens College B, T
University of Missouri
    Columbia B
    Kansas City M
    St. Louis B, M, T
Washington University M
Webster University B, M, T
William Jewell College T
William Woods University B, T

Montana
Dawson Community College C, A
Montana State University
    Billings B, M
University of Great Falls A
Western Montana College of The
    University of Montana C, A

Nebraska
College of Saint Mary A, B, T
Concordia University B, M, T
Midland Lutheran College B, T
Northeast Community College C, A
Peru State College B, T
University of Nebraska
    Kearney B, T

Nevada
University of Nevada
    Las Vegas B

New Hampshire
Antioch New England Graduate
    School M
College for Lifelong Learning A, B
Hesser College A
Keene State College A, B, T
McIntosh College C, A
New Hampshire Community Technical
    College
        Berlin C, A
        Laconia C, A
        Manchester C, A, T
        Nashua C, A
New Hampshire Technical Institute C, A
Notre Dame College A, B
Plymouth State College of the University
    System of New Hampshire B, T
Rivier College C, A, B, M, T
University of New Hampshire M

New Jersey
Bergen Community College A
Brookdale Community College A
College of St. Elizabeth T
Cumberland County College C, A
Essex County College A
Hudson County Community
    College C, A
Kean University B, M
New Jersey City University B, M
Passaic County Community College A
Raritan Valley Community College A
Rider University B
Rowan University B

Rutgers
   The State University of New Jersey: Camden College of Arts and Sciences *T*
   The State University of New Jersey: Douglass College *T*
   The State University of New Jersey: Livingston College *T*
   The State University of New Jersey: New Brunswick Graduate Campus *M, D, T*
   The State University of New Jersey: Newark College of Arts and Sciences *T*
   The State University of New Jersey: Rutgers College *T*
   The State University of New Jersey: University College Camden *T*
   The State University of New Jersey: University College New Brunswick *T*
   The State University of New Jersey: University College Newark *T*
Salem Community College *C, A*
Seton Hall University *B, T*
The College of New Jersey *B, T*
Union County College *A*
Warren County Community College *C*

New Mexico
Eastern New Mexico University *B*
New Mexico State University *B*
Northern New Mexico Community College *A*
San Juan College *C, A*
University of New Mexico *B*
Western New Mexico University *C, A*

New York
Adelphi University *M*
Bank Street College of Education *M*
Barnard College *T*
Cayuga County Community College *A*
City University of New York
   Baruch College *B*
   Borough of Manhattan Community College *A*
   Brooklyn College *B, M, T*
   City College *B, M, T*
   Hostos Community College *A*
   Hunter College *B, T*
   Kingsborough Community College *A*
   Lehman College *M, T*
   Queens College *B, M, T*
College of Mount St. Vincent *T*
College of St. Rose *M, T*
Columbia University
   Teachers College *M, D*
Corning Community College *C*
Dutchess Community College *C, A*
Eugene Lang College/New School University *T*
Fulton-Montgomery Community College *A*
Herkimer County Community College *A*
Hofstra University *M, T*
Jamestown Community College *C*
Jefferson Community College *A*
Long Island University
   Brooklyn Campus *B, M*
Manhattan College *B, T*
Manhattanville College *M, T*
Maria College *A*
Marymount Manhattan College *B, T*
Monroe Community College *C*
Nassau Community College *A*
Nazareth College of Rochester *M, T*
New York University *A, B, M, T*
Onondaga Community College *C*
Pace University:
   Pleasantville/Briarcliff *A, B, T*
Pace University *A, B, T*
Sarah Lawrence College *M*
Schenectady County Community College *C, A*
St. Joseph's College
   St. Joseph's College: Suffolk Campus *B, M, T*
St. Joseph's College *B, T*
State University of New York
   College at Buffalo *B, T*
   College at Fredonia *B, T*
   College at Geneseo *T*
   College at Old Westbury *T*
   College at Oneonta *B, M, T*
   College of Agriculture and Technology at Cobleskill *A*
   College of Technology at Canton *A*
   New Paltz *M, T*
Suffolk County Community College *A*
Syracuse University *B, M, T*
Tompkins-Cortland Community College *A*
Trocaire College *A*
Vassar College *T*
Villa Maria College of Buffalo *A*
Wagner College *B, T*

North Carolina
Alamance Community College *C, A*
Appalachian State University *M*
Beaufort County Community College *A*
Bennett College *B*
Bladen Community College *C*
Caldwell Community College and Technical Institute *A*
Campbell University *M*
Catawba Valley Community College *C, A*
Central Carolina Community College *C, A*
Cleveland Community College *A*
College of the Albemarle *C*
Davidson County Community College *C, A*
Duke University *C*
Durham Technical Community College *C, A*
East Carolina University *B*
Edgecombe Community College *C, A*
Fayetteville Technical Community College *A*
Forsyth Technical Community College *A*
Gaston College *C, A*
Greensboro College *B, T*
Guilford Technical Community College *C, A*
Halifax Community College *A*
High Point University *B, T*
Johnson C. Smith University *B, T*
Lenoir Community College *C, A*
Lenoir-Rhyne College *M, T*
Louisburg College *A*
Martin Community College *C, A*
Mayland Community College *C, A*
Meredith College *T*
Mitchell Community College *A*
Montgomery Community College *C, A*
Nash Community College *A*
North Carolina Agricultural and Technical State University *B, T*
North Carolina Central University *B, T*
Pitt Community College *A*
Roanoke-Chowan Community College *A*
Rockingham Community College *C, A*
Rowan-Cabarrus Community College *A*
Salem College *M*
Sampson Community College *C, A*
Sandhills Community College *A*
Southwestern Community College *A*
Surry Community College *C, A*
University of North Carolina
   Chapel Hill *B, M*
   Charlotte *B, M*
   Greensboro *B, M, D, T*
   Pembroke *B*
   Wilmington *B*
Vance-Granville Community College *C, A*
Wake Technical Community College *C, A*
Warren Wilson College *B, T*
Western Carolina University *B, T*
Wilson Technical Community College *C, A*

North Dakota
Dickinson State University *B, T*
Jamestown College *B*
Mayville State University *A, T*
University of Mary *B, M, T*
University of North Dakota *B, M, T*

Ohio
Ashland University *B, M, T*
Baldwin-Wallace College *B*
Bluffton College *B*
Bowling Green State University *B*
Capital University *B*
Cedarville College *B*
Central Ohio Technical College *A*
Central State University *B*
Chatfield College *A*
Circleville Bible College *A*
Clark State Community College *A*
Cleveland State University *B*
College of Mount St. Joseph *A, B, T*
Columbus State Community College *A*
Defiance College *B*
Edison State Community College *A*
Franciscan University of Steubenville *C, A*
Hiram College *T*
John Carroll University *M, T*
Kent State University
   Ashtabula Regional Campus *A*
   Stark Campus *B*
Kent State University *B, M*
Lakeland Community College *A*
Lima Technical College *C, A*
Lorain County Community College *A*
Lourdes College *B*
Malone College *B*
Marietta College *B*
Miami University
   Oxford Campus *T*
Mount Union College *B, T*
Mount Vernon Nazarene College *B, T*
Muskingum College *B, T*
North Central State College *A*
Notre Dame College of Ohio *B, T*
Ohio Dominican College *A, D*
Ohio Northern University *B, T*
Ohio University
   Zanesville Campus *B*
Ohio University *B, D, T*
Ohio Wesleyan University *B*
Otterbein College *B*
Owens Community College
   Findlay Campus *A*
   Toledo *A*
Shawnee State University *T*
Southern State Community College *A*
Stark State College of Technology *A*
Terra Community College *A*
University of Akron *B, T*
University of Cincinnati
   Clermont College *A*
University of Cincinnati *B, M, T*
University of Dayton *B, M, T*
University of Findlay *B*
University of Rio Grande *A*
University of Toledo *B, M, T*
Walsh University *B*
Wilmington College *B*
Wright State University *B, M, T*
Xavier University *A, B*
Youngstown State University *B, M*

Oklahoma
Cameron University *B*
Carl Albert State College *C*
Connors State College *A*
East Central University *B, T*
Northeastern Oklahoma Agricultural and Mechanical College *C, A*
Northeastern State University *B, M*
Northwestern Oklahoma State University *B, T*
Oklahoma Baptist University *B, T*
Oklahoma Christian University of Science and Arts *B, T*
Oklahoma State University *B, M, D, T*
Oral Roberts University *B, T*
Rose State College *A*
Southeastern Oklahoma State University *B, T*
Southern Nazarene University *B, M*
Southwestern Oklahoma State University *M, T*
University of Central Oklahoma *B, M*
University of Oklahoma *B, T*
University of Science and Arts of Oklahoma *B*

Oregon
Central Oregon Community College *A*
Chemeketa Community College *A*
Clatsop Community College *C*
Concordia University *B, M, T*
Eastern Oregon University *B, M*
Mount Hood Community College *A*
Portland State University *T*
University of Portland *T*
Western Oregon University *M, T*
Willamette University *M*

Pennsylvania
Alvernia College *B*
Beaver College *B, M, T*
Bloomsburg University of Pennsylvania *B, M, T*
Bucknell University *B, T*
Bucks County Community College *A*
Butler County Community College *A*
Cabrini College *B, T*
California University of Pennsylvania *A, B, M, T*
Carlow College *B, M, T*
Carnegie Mellon University *T*
Central Pennsylvania College *A*
Chatham College *M, T*
Chestnut Hill College *B, M, T*
Cheyney University of Pennsylvania *B, T*
Clarion University of Pennsylvania *B, T*
College Misericordia *B, T*
Community College of Beaver County *C, A*
Delaware County Community College *A*
Duquesne University *B, M, T*
East Stroudsburg University of Pennsylvania *B, T*
Edinboro University of Pennsylvania *A, B, T*
Elizabethtown College *B*
Gannon University *A, B*
Grove City College *B*
Gwynedd-Mercy College *T*
Harcum College *A*
Harrisburg Area Community College *A*
Holy Family College *B, T*
Immaculata College *T*
Indiana University of Pennsylvania *B, M, T*
Juniata College *B, T*
King's College *B, T*
Kutztown University of Pennsylvania *B, T*
La Roche College *M*
Lehigh Carbon Community College *A*
Lincoln University *B, M, T*
Lock Haven University of Pennsylvania *B, T*
Manor College *A*
Mansfield University of Pennsylvania *B, T*
Marywood University *M, T*
Mercyhurst College *A, B*
Messiah College *B, T*

Millersville University of
  Pennsylvania *T*
Montgomery County Community
  College *A*
Mount Aloysius College *A, B*
Neumann College *B*
Philadelphia College of Bible *B, T*
Point Park College *A, B, T*
Reading Area Community College *A*
Rosemont College *T*
St. Vincent College *T*
Seton Hill College *B, T*
Shippensburg University of
  Pennsylvania *T*
Susquehanna University *B, T*
Temple University *M*
University of Pittsburgh *T*
University of Scranton *B*
Valley Forge Christian College *A, B*
West Chester University of
  Pennsylvania *B, T*
Widener University *B, M, T*
York College of Pennsylvania *C*

Puerto Rico

Bayamon Central University *B, M*
Colegio Universitario del Este *B*
Inter American University of Puerto Rico
  Aguadilla Campus *B*
  Arecibo Campus *B*
  Barranquitas Campus *B*
  Fajardo Campus *B, T*
  Guayama Campus *B*
  Metropolitan Campus *B*
  San German Campus *B*
Pontifical Catholic University of Puerto
  Rico *B, M*
Universidad Metropolitana *B*
University of Puerto Rico
  Bayamon University College *B*
  Rio Piedras Campus *M*

Rhode Island

Community College of Rhode Island *A*
Rhode Island College *B, M*
Salve Regina University *B*

South Carolina

Anderson College *B, T*
Benedict College *B*
Charleston Southern University *M*
Clemson University *B, T*
Coastal Carolina University *B, M, T*
Coker College *B, T*
College of Charleston *M*
Columbia College *B, T*
Columbia International
  University *B, M, T*
Converse College *B, M, T*
Erskine College *B, T*
Francis Marion University *B, M, T*
Furman University *B, M, T*
Lander University *B, T*
Morris College *B, T*
Newberry College *B, T*
North Greenville College *B, T*
Presbyterian College *B, T*
South Carolina State University *B, M*
Southern Wesleyan University *B, T*
Spartanburg Technical College *A*
University of South Carolina
  Aiken *B*
  Spartanburg *B, M, T*
University of South Carolina *M, D*
Voorhees College *B*
Winthrop University *B, T*
York Technical College *C, A*

South Dakota

Black Hills State University *B, T*
Northern State University *B, T*
South Dakota State University *B*

Tennessee

Austin Peay State University *T*
Belmont University *B, T*
Carson-Newman College *B*

Chattanooga State Technical Community
  College *A*
Columbia State Community
  College *C, A*
Crichton College *B*
David Lipscomb University *B, T*
East Tennessee State University *M, T*
Johnson Bible College *A, B, T*
Lee University *B, T*
Lincoln Memorial University *B, T*
Middle Tennessee State University *B, T*
Milligan College *B, T*
Roane State Community College *A*
Shelby State Community College *A*
Southern Adventist University *B*
Tennessee State University *B*
Tennessee Technological
  University *B, M, T*
Tennessee Temple University *B, T*
Tusculum College *B, T*
Union University *B, T*
University of Memphis *B, T*
University of Tennessee
  Knoxville *B, T*
  Martin *B, T*
Vanderbilt University *B, M, D, T*

Texas

Alvin Community College *C, A*
Angelo State University *B*
Baylor University *T*
Brookhaven College *A*
Concordia University at Austin *B, T*
Dallas Baptist University *B, M, T*
Del Mar College *A*
Hardin-Simmons University *C, B, T*
Houston Baptist University *B*
Howard Payne University *T*
Lamar University *T*
Sam Houston State University *M, T*
Southwest Texas State University *M, T*
Southwestern University *T*
Stephen F. Austin State University *M*
Texas A&M International
  University *B, M, T*
Texas A&M University
  Commerce *B, M*
  Corpus Christi *M, T*
  Kingsville *M*
  Texarkana *T*
Texas College *A*
Texas Southern University *M*
Texas Tech University *M*
Texas Wesleyan University *B, M, T*
Texas Woman's University *M, D, T*
Trinity Valley Community College *C, A*
University of Houston
  Clear Lake *M, T*
University of Houston *M*
University of Mary Hardin-Baylor *T*
University of North Texas *B, M, T*
University of Texas
  Arlington *T*
  Pan American *M, T*
  San Antonio *T*
  Tyler *M*
  of the Permian Basin *M*
University of the Incarnate Word *B, M*
Wayland Baptist University *T*
West Texas A&M University *T*
Western Texas College *C, A*

Utah

Brigham Young University *B*
College of Eastern Utah *A*
Dixie State College of Utah *A*
Salt Lake Community College *A*
Utah State University *B*
Weber State University *B, T*
Westminster College *B*

Vermont

Bennington College *B*
Champlain College *A, B, T*
College of St. Joseph in Vermont *B*
Goddard College *B*

Johnson State College *M*
Lyndon State College *B*
Middlebury College *T*
Trinity College of Vermont *B, T*
University of Vermont *B, T*

Virginia

Averett College *B*
Bluefield College *B*
Dabney S. Lancaster Community
  College *C*
Eastern Mennonite University *T*
Eastern Shore Community College *C*
Germanna Community College *C*
Hampton University *B*
Hollins University *T*
James Madison University *M, T*
John Tyler Community College *C, A*
Longwood College *B, T*
New River Community College *C*
Norfolk State University *B, M, T*
Northern Virginia Community
  College *C, A*
Old Dominion University *M*
Radford University *T*
St. Paul's College *T*
Southwest Virginia Community
  College *A*
Thomas Nelson Community
  College *C, A*
Tidewater Community College *C, A*
University of Richmond *B, T*

Washington

Bellevue Community College *C, A*
Central Washington University *B, T*
Centralia College *C, A*
Clark College *C, A*
Eastern Washington University *M, T*
Everett Community College *A*
Grays Harbor College *C, A*
Green River Community College *A*
Heritage College *C, A, B*
North Seattle Community College *A*
Olympic College *C, A*
Pierce College *A*
Renton Technical College *C, A*
Seattle Central Community College *C*
Shoreline Community College *A*
Skagit Valley College *C, A*
South Puget Sound Community
  College *C, A*
Spokane Falls Community College *A*
Walla Walla College *A*
Walla Walla Community College *C*
Washington State University *T*
Wenatchee Valley College *C, A*
Western Washington University *T*
Whatcom Community College *C, A*
Yakima Valley Community College *A*

West Virginia

Concord College *B, T*
Fairmont State College *B*
Glenville State College *B*
Marshall University *B, M*
Shepherd College *T*
West Liberty State College *B*
West Virginia State College *B*

Wisconsin

Alverno College *A, T*
Beloit College *T*
Cardinal Stritch University *B, T*
Carroll College *B*
Concordia University Wisconsin *B, T*
Lakeland College *B*
Marian College of Fond du Lac *B, T*
Marquette University *B*
Milwaukee Area Technical College *C*
Mount Mary College *B, T*
Mount Senario College *B, T*
St. Norbert College *T*
Silver Lake College *B, T*

University of Wisconsin
  Green Bay *T*
  La Crosse *T*
  Madison *B, T*
  Oshkosh *M*
  Parkside *T*
  Platteville *B, T*
  River Falls *T*
  Stevens Point *B, T*
  Stout *B, T*
  Whitewater *B, T*

Wyoming

Casper College *A*
Sheridan College *C*
Western Wyoming Community
  College *A*

Earth/planetary sciences

Alaska

University of Alaska
  Fairbanks *B*

Arizona

Northern Arizona University *B, T*
Prescott College *B, M*
University of Arizona *M, D*

Arkansas

University of Arkansas *B*

California

California Institute of Technology *B, D*
California State University
  Chico *B*
  Dominguez Hills *B*
  Los Angeles *B*
  Monterey Bay *B*
  Northridge *B*
  Stanislaus *B*
Cerritos Community College *A*
Chaffey Community College *A*
College of the Redwoods *C, A*
Columbia College *A*
Los Angeles Valley College *A*
Merced College *A*
Ohlone College *C*
Stanford University *B, M*
University of California
  Berkeley *B*
  Irvine *M, D*
  Los Angeles *B*
  San Diego *B, D*
  Santa Cruz *B, M, D*

Colorado

Adams State College *B*
Colorado State University *B, M, D*
University of Colorado
  Boulder *M, D*
University of Northern Colorado *B, M, T*

Connecticut

Central Connecticut State
  University *B, M*
Southern Connecticut State University *B*
Wesleyan University *B, M*
Western Connecticut State
  University *B, M*

Delaware

University of Delaware *B, T*

Florida

Florida Institute of Technology *M*

Georgia

Mercer University *B*
State University of West Georgia *B*

Idaho

Boise State University *B*
University of Idaho *M*

Illinois

Augustana College *B, T*

Black Hawk College
  East Campus A
City Colleges of Chicago
  Olive-Harvey College A
Concordia University B
Morton College A
Northeastern Illinois University B, M
Parkland College A
Richland Community College A

Indiana
Ball State University M
DePauw University B
Indiana State University M, T
University of Indianapolis B
Vincennes University A

Iowa
Drake University B
Iowa State University B, M, D
University of Dubuque B

Kansas
Emporia State University B, T

Kentucky
Murray State University B, T

Louisiana
Tulane University B

Maryland
Frostburg State University B, T
Johns Hopkins University B
Towson University B

Massachusetts
Boston University B
Bridgewater State College B
Fitchburg State College B
Hampshire College B
Harvard College B
Harvard University M, D
Massachusetts Institute of
  Technology B, M, D
Tufts University T
University of Massachusetts
  Amherst B

Michigan
Adrian College A, B, T
Central Michigan University B
Eastern Michigan University B
Michigan State University B
Northern Michigan University B, T
University of Michigan
  Flint B, T
University of Michigan D
Western Michigan University B, M

Minnesota
St. Cloud State University B
Winona State University B, T

Missouri
Central Missouri State University B
Southeast Missouri State
  University B, M
University of Missouri
  Kansas City B
Washington University B, M, D

Montana
Montana State University
  Bozeman B, M

Nebraska
Midland Lutheran College T
University of Nebraska
  Kearney B, T

New Hampshire
Dartmouth College B
University of New Hampshire B

New Jersey
Kean University B

Rutgers
  The State University of New Jersey:
    Cook College T
  The State University of New Jersey:
    Newark College of Arts and
    Sciences T
  The State University of New Jersey:
    University College Newark T

New York
Adelphi University B, M
Alfred University T
City University of New York
  City College B
  Queens College B
Columbia University
  Columbia College B
  Graduate School M, D
Hofstra University B
Sarah Lawrence College B
State University of New York
  Albany B
  College at Brockport B, T
  College at Buffalo B
  College at Cortland B
  College at Fredonia B
  College at Geneseo T
  College at Oneonta B, M
  College at Potsdam T
  New Paltz B
  Oswego T
  Stony Brook B, M, D, T
Suffolk County Community College A

North Carolina
North Carolina Central University M
University of North Carolina
  Charlotte B, T

North Dakota
Minot State University B, T
North Dakota State University B, T

Ohio
Ashland University B, T
Central State University B
Kent State University B
Mount Union College T
Muskingum College B
Wilmington College B
Wittenberg University B
Wright State University M
Youngstown State University B

Oregon
Western Oregon University B

Pennsylvania
Bloomsburg University of
  Pennsylvania B, T
California University of
  Pennsylvania B, M
Clarion University of Pennsylvania B, T
East Stroudsburg University of
  Pennsylvania B
Edinboro University of
  Pennsylvania B, T
Gannon University B, T
Indiana University of Pennsylvania B, T
La Salle University B
Lock Haven University of
  Pennsylvania B, T
Mansfield University of Pennsylvania T
Millersville University of
  Pennsylvania B, M, T
Penn State
  University Park B, M, D
Shippensburg University of
  Pennsylvania B, T
Slippery Rock University of
  Pennsylvania B, T
West Chester University of
  Pennsylvania B
Wilkes University B

South Carolina
Furman University B
University of South Carolina M

South Dakota
University of South Dakota B

Tennessee
Tennessee Temple University B

Texas
Baylor University B, M
Lamar University B
Stephen F. Austin State University T
Texas A&M University
  Commerce B, M
  Corpus Christi T
Texas A&M University B
Texas Tech University B, M, D
University of Houston B
University of Texas
  El Paso B
  of the Permian Basin B
West Texas A&M University T

Utah
Brigham Young University B, M

Virginia
George Mason University B
Norfolk State University T

Washington
Central Washington University B
Centralia College A
Eastern Washington University B, T
Pacific Lutheran University B
Western Washington University B

Wisconsin
Northland College B, T
University of Wisconsin
  Green Bay B
  Madison B
  River Falls B, T

East Asian studies

Arizona
University of Arizona B, M, D

California
Pitzer College B
Stanford University B, M
University of California
  Davis B
  Irvine B, M, D
  Los Angeles B
  Santa Cruz B
University of Southern California B, M

Connecticut
Wesleyan University B
Yale University B, M

District of Columbia
George Washington University B, M

Florida
Eckerd College B

Illinois
University of Chicago M, D

Indiana
DePauw University B
Indiana University
  Bloomington B, M
Valparaiso University B

Maine
Bates College B
Colby College B

Maryland
Johns Hopkins University B

Massachusetts
Boston University B
Hampshire College B
Harvard College B
Harvard University M, D
Simmons College B

Tufts University B, M
Wellesley College B

Michigan
Oakland University B
University of Michigan B, M
Wayne State University B

Minnesota
Augsburg College B
Hamline University B
Macalester College B
St. Cloud State University B
University of Minnesota
  Twin Cities B, M
University of St. Thomas B

Missouri
University of Missouri
  St. Louis C
Washington University B, M

New Jersey
Princeton University B, M, D
Rutgers
  The State University of New Jersey:
    Douglass College B
  The State University of New Jersey:
    Livingston College B
  The State University of New Jersey:
    Rutgers College B
  The State University of New Jersey:
    University College New
    Brunswick B

New York
City University of New York
  Queens College B
Columbia University
  Columbia College B
  Graduate School M, D
  School of General Studies B
Cornell University B, M, D
Hamilton College B
New York University B
St. John's University M
Sarah Lawrence College B
State University of New York
  Albany B
United States Military Academy B

Ohio
College of Wooster B
Denison University B
Oberlin College B
Ohio State University
  Columbus Campus B
Ohio Wesleyan University B
Wittenberg University B

Oregon
Lewis & Clark College B
Willamette University B

Pennsylvania
Bryn Mawr College B
Bucknell University B
Dickinson College B
Gettysburg College B
Haverford College B, T
Penn State
  University Park B
University of Pennsylvania B, M, D
University of Pittsburgh M
Ursinus College B

Rhode Island
Brown University B

Tennessee
Vanderbilt University B

Vermont
Middlebury College B

Virginia
College of William and Mary B
Emory & Henry College B
Mary Baldwin College B

University of Virginia *M*
Washington and Lee University *B*

Washington
Seattle University *B*
University of Washington *M*
Western Washington University *B*

East European languages

Massachusetts
Harvard College *B*
Harvard University *D*

New Jersey
Princeton University *B, M, D*

North Carolina
University of North Carolina
   Chapel Hill *M, D*

Pennsylvania
La Salle University *B*

Washington
University of Washington *B*

East/Southeast Asian languages

Arizona
Arizona State University *B*

California
University of California
   Berkeley *B, M*
   Los Angeles *B, M, D*
University of Southern
   California *B, M, D*

Colorado
University of Colorado
   Boulder *M*

Connecticut
Yale University *M, D*

Florida
University of Florida *B*

Hawaii
University of Hawaii
   Manoa *B, M, D*

Illinois
University of Chicago *B, M, D*

Indiana
Indiana University
   Bloomington *B*

Kansas
University of Kansas *B, M*

Maine
Bates College *B*

Massachusetts
Amherst College *B*
Harvard College *B*
Harvard University *D*
Smith College *B*

Michigan
Michigan State University *B*
University of Michigan *M, D*

Missouri
Washington University *B, M*

New Hampshire
Dartmouth College *B*

New Jersey
Rutgers
   The State University of New Jersey:
     Douglass College *B*
   The State University of New Jersey:
     Livingston College *B*
   The State University of New Jersey:
     Rutgers College *B*
   The State University of New Jersey:
     University College New
     Brunswick *B*

New York
Columbia University
   Columbia College *B*
   Graduate School *M, D*
Cornell University *B*

Ohio
Ohio State University
   Columbus Campus *M, D*

Oregon
University of Oregon *M*

Utah
Brigham Young University *B, M*

Washington
University of Washington *B, M, D*

Wisconsin
Beloit College *B*

Eastern European studies

California
California State University
   Fullerton *B*
San Diego State University *B*

Colorado
University of Colorado
   Boulder *B*

Connecticut
Connecticut College *B*
Wesleyan University *B*

Florida
Florida State University *B, M*

Georgia
Emory University *B*
Oxford College of Emory University *B*

Iowa
University of Iowa *B*

Massachusetts
Harvard College *B*
Tufts University *B, M*
Wellesley College *B*

Michigan
University of Michigan *B*

Minnesota
Augsburg College *B*
Hamline University *B*

New Jersey
Rutgers
   The State University of New Jersey:
     Douglass College *B*
   The State University of New Jersey:
     Livingston College *B*
   The State University of New Jersey:
     Rutgers College *B*
   The State University of New Jersey:
     University College New
     Brunswick *B*
Seton Hall University *C*

New York
Bard College *B*
Columbia University
   Columbia College *B*
   Graduate School *M, D*
State University of New York
   Albany *B*

North Carolina
University of North Carolina
   Chapel Hill *B*

Ohio
Kent State University *B*
Ohio State University
   Columbus Campus *B, M*
University of Cincinnati *C*

Oklahoma
Oklahoma State University *C*

Pennsylvania
California University of Pennsylvania *B*
La Salle University *B, M*
University of Pittsburgh *C*

Vermont
Marlboro College *B*
University of Vermont *B*

Washington
University of Washington *B*

Ecology

Alabama
Tuskegee University *B, M*

Arizona
Prescott College *B, M*
University of Arizona *B, M, D*

California
California Polytechnic State University:
   San Luis Obispo *B*
California State University
   Fresno *B*
Gavilan Community College *A*
Irvine Valley College *A*
Orange Coast College *A*
San Diego State University *B, D*
San Francisco State University *B, M*
University of California
   Berkeley *M, D*
   Davis *M, D*
   San Diego *B*
   Santa Barbara *B*
   Santa Cruz *B, D*

Colorado
Colorado State University *M, D*
Naropa University *B*

Connecticut
University of Connecticut *B, M, D*
University of New Haven *B, M*
Wesleyan University *B, M*

Delaware
Wesley College *B*

Florida
Florida Institute of Technology *B, M*
University of Florida *M, D*
University of Miami *B*
University of West Florida *B*

Georgia
University of Georgia *B, M, D*

Idaho
Idaho State University *B*
Ricks College *C, A*

Illinois
Greenville College *B*
University of Chicago *M, D*
University of Illinois
   Urbana-Champaign *B*

Indiana
Indiana University
   Bloomington *M, D*

Iowa
Iowa State University *B, M, D*
Maharishi University of Management *B*
University of Dubuque *B*

Kansas
University of Kansas *M, D*

Kentucky
Eastern Kentucky University *B*
Morehead State University *B*

Louisiana
Tulane University *B, M, D*

Maine
College of the Atlantic *B, M*
Unity College *B*
University of Maine
   Farmington *B*
   Machias *B*

Maryland
Frostburg State University *M*
Towson University *B*
University of Maryland
   Eastern Shore *B*

Massachusetts
Berkshire Community College *A*
Boston University *B*
Hampshire College *B*
Harvard College *B*
Simon's Rock College of Bard *B*
Tufts University *B, M*

Michigan
Eastern Michigan University *B*
Michigan Technological University *B*
Northern Michigan University *B*
University of Michigan
   Dearborn *B*
University of Michigan *B, M*

Minnesota
Hamline University *B*
Minnesota State University, Mankato *B*
St. Cloud State University *B*
St. Mary's University of Minnesota *B*
Southwest State University *B*
University of Minnesota
   Twin Cities *B, M, D*

New Hampshire
Antioch New England Graduate
   School *M*
Franklin Pierce College *B*
University of New Hampshire *B*

New Jersey
Caldwell College *C*
Princeton University *B, M, D*
Richard Stockton College of New
   Jersey *B*
Rutgers
   The State University of New Jersey:
     Camden College of Arts and
     Sciences *B*
   The State University of New Jersey:
     Cook College *B*
   The State University of New Jersey:
     Douglass College *B*
   The State University of New Jersey:
     Livingston College *B*
   The State University of New Jersey:
     New Brunswick Graduate
     Campus *M, D*
   The State University of New Jersey:
     Rutgers College *B*
   The State University of New Jersey:
     University College Camden *B*
   The State University of New Jersey:
     University College New
     Brunswick *B*

New York
Columbia University
   Graduate School *D*
Columbia-Greene Community College *A*

Ecology

Concordia College *B*
Cornell University *B, M, D*
Iona College *B*
St. John's University *B*
State University of New York
   Albany *M*
   College of Environmental Science
     and Forestry *B, M, D*
   Stony Brook *M, D*
University of Rochester *B*

North Carolina
Appalachian State University *B*
Brevard College *B*
North Carolina State University *M*
University of North Carolina
   Chapel Hill *M, D*

Ohio
Kent State University *M, D, T*
Ohio State University
   Columbus Campus *B, M, D*
University of Akron *B*

Oklahoma
Oklahoma State University *M, D*
Rose State College *A*

Oregon
University of Oregon *M, D*

Pennsylvania
California University of Pennsylvania *B*
Carlow College *B*
East Stroudsburg University of
   Pennsylvania *B*
Juniata College *B*
Lock Haven University of
   Pennsylvania *B*
Penn State
   University Park *M, D*
Slippery Rock University of
   Pennsylvania *M*
University of Pittsburgh *B*
West Chester University of
   Pennsylvania *B*
Westminster College *B*

Rhode Island
Brown University *D*

Tennessee
University of Tennessee
   Knoxville *M, D*

Texas
Baylor University *M*
University of North Texas *M, D*
University of Texas
   Austin *B*

Utah
Brigham Young University *M, D*
Dixie State College of Utah *A*
Utah State University *B, M, D*

Vermont
Goddard College *B*
Marlboro College *B*

Virginia
Averett College *B*
Lynchburg College *B*
Old Dominion University *D*

Washington
Evergreen State College *B*
University of Washington *B, M, D*
Western Washington University *B*

West Virginia
Salem-Teikyo University *B*

Wisconsin
Northland College *B*

Economics

Alabama
Alabama State University *B*
Auburn University *B*
Birmingham-Southern College *B*
Jacksonville State University *B*
Lawson State Community College *A*
Talladega College *B*
Tuskegee University *B*
University of Alabama
   Birmingham *B*
University of Alabama *B, M, D*
University of South Alabama *B*

Alaska
University of Alaska
   Anchorage *B*
   Fairbanks *B, M*

Arizona
Arizona State University *B, M, D*
Northern Arizona University *B*
University of Arizona *B, M, D*

Arkansas
Arkansas State University *B*
Arkansas Tech University *B*
Harding University *B*
Hendrix College *B*
Lyon College *B*
Ouachita Baptist University *B*
University of Arkansas
   Little Rock *B*
University of Arkansas *M, D*
University of Central Arkansas *B*
Westark College *A*

California
Bakersfield College *A*
Cabrillo College *A*
California Institute of Technology *B*
California Lutheran University *B*
California Polytechnic State University:
   San Luis Obispo *B*
California State Polytechnic University:
   Pomona *B, M*
California State University
   Bakersfield *B*
   Chico *B*
   Dominguez Hills *B*
   Fresno *B, M*
   Fullerton *B, M*
   Hayward *B, M*
   Long Beach *B, M*
   Los Angeles *B, M*
   Northridge *B*
   Sacramento *B, M*
   San Marcos *B*
   Stanislaus *B*
Cerritos Community College *A*
Chaffey Community College *A*
Chapman University *B*
Claremont McKenna College *B*
Crafton Hills College *A*
Cypress College *A*
De Anza College *A*
Diablo Valley College *A*
East Los Angeles College *A*
Foothill College *A*
Gavilan Community College *A*
Glendale Community College *A*
Golden Gate University *B, M*
Golden West College *A*
Grossmont Community College *A*
Humboldt State University *B*
Irvine Valley College *A*
Long Beach City College *C, A*
Los Angeles Valley College *A*
Loyola Marymount University *B*
Marymount College *A*
Merced College *A*
MiraCosta College *A*
Monterey Peninsula College *A*
Occidental College *B*
Ohlone College *A*
Orange Coast College *A*
Palomar College *C, A*
Pepperdine University *B*
Pitzer College *B*
Point Loma Nazarene University *B*
Pomona College *B*
Riverside Community College *A*
Saddleback College *A*
St. Mary's College of California *B*
San Diego State University *B, M*
San Francisco State University *B, M*
San Jose State University *B, M*
Santa Ana College *A*
Santa Barbara City College *A*
Santa Clara University *B*
Santa Rosa Junior College *A*
Scripps College *B*
Sonoma State University *B*
Southwestern College *A*
Stanford University *B, M, D*
University of California
   Berkeley *B, M, D*
   Davis *B, M, D*
   Irvine *B, M, D*
   Los Angeles *B, M, D*
   Riverside *B, M, D*
   San Diego *B, D*
   Santa Barbara *B, M, D*
   Santa Cruz *B, M, D*
University of Redlands *B*
University of San Diego *B*
University of San Francisco *B, M*
University of Southern
   California *B, M, D*
University of the Pacific *B*
Ventura College *A*
West Los Angeles College *C, A*
Westmont College *B*

Colorado
Adams State College *B*
Colorado College *B*
Colorado School of Mines *B, M, D*
Colorado State University *B, M, D*
Fort Lewis College *B*
Metropolitan State College of
   Denver *B, T*
Red Rocks Community College *A*
Regis University *B*
United States Air Force Academy *B*
University of Colorado
   Boulder *B, M, D*
   Colorado Springs *B*
   Denver *B, M*
University of Denver *B, M*
University of Northern Colorado *B*
Western State College of Colorado *B*

Connecticut
Albertus Magnus College *B*
Central Connecticut State University *B*
Connecticut College *B*
Eastern Connecticut State University *B*
Fairfield University *B*
Quinnipiac University *B*
Sacred Heart University *A, B*
St. Joseph College *B*
Trinity College *B, M*
University of Connecticut *B, M, D*
University of Hartford *B*
University of New Haven *B*
Wesleyan University *B, M*
Western Connecticut State University *B*
Yale University *B, M, D*

Delaware
University of Delaware *B*
Wesley College *B*

District of Columbia
American University *B, M, D*
Catholic University of America *B, M, D*
Gallaudet University *B*
George Washington University *B, M, D*
Georgetown University *B, D*
Howard University *B, M, D*
Southeastern University *B, M*
Trinity College *B*
University of the District of Columbia *B*

Florida
Barry University *B*
Broward Community College *A*
Eckerd College *B*
Florida Agricultural and Mechanical
   University *B*
Florida Atlantic University *B, M*
Florida International University *B, M, D*
Florida Southern College *B*
Florida State University *B, M, D*
Gulf Coast Community College *A*
Jacksonville University *B*
Miami-Dade Community College *A*
New College of the University of South
   Florida *B*
Pensacola Junior College *A*
Rollins College *B*
Stetson University *B*
University of Central Florida *B*
University of Florida *B, M, D*
University of Miami *B, M, D*
University of North Florida *B*
University of South Florida *B*
University of Tampa *A, B*
University of West Florida *B*

Georgia
Agnes Scott College *B*
Armstrong Atlantic State University *B*
Atlanta Metropolitan College *A*
Berry College *B*
Brewton-Parker College *A*
Clark Atlanta University *B, M*
Covenant College *B*
Emory University *B, D*
Fort Valley State University *B*
Georgia Military College *A*
Georgia Southern University *B*
Georgia State University *B, M, D*
Kennesaw State University *B*
Mercer University *B*
Middle Georgia College *A*
Morehouse College *B*
Oglethorpe University *B*
Oxford College of Emory University *B*
Shorter College *B*
South Georgia College *A*
Spelman College *B*
State University of West Georgia *B*
University of Georgia *B*
Valdosta State University *B*

Hawaii
Chaminade University of Honolulu *B*
Hawaii Pacific University *B*
University of Hawaii
   Hilo *B*
   Manoa *B, M, D*
   West Oahu *B*

Idaho
Albertson College of Idaho *B*
Boise State University *B, T*
College of Southern Idaho *A*
Idaho State University *B*
Ricks College *A*
University of Idaho *B, M*

Illinois
Augustana College *B*
Barat College *B*
Benedictine University *B, T*
Black Hawk College
   East Campus *A*
Bradley University *B*
Chicago State University *B*
De Paul University *B, M*
Dominican University *B*
Eastern Illinois University *B, M*
Elmhurst College *B*
Illinois College *B*
Illinois State University *B, M*

Illinois Wesleyan University B
John Wood Community College A
Kishwaukee College A
Knox College B
Lake Forest College B
Lake Land College A
Lewis University B
Lincoln Land Community College A
Loyola University of Chicago B
McKendree College B
Monmouth College B, T
Morton College A
National-Louis University B
North Central College B
North Park University B
Northeastern Illinois University B
Northern Illinois University B, M
Northwestern University B, M, D
Olivet Nazarene University B
Parkland College A
Principia College B
Richland Community College A
Rockford College B
Roosevelt University B, M
Sauk Valley Community College A
Southern Illinois University
    Carbondale B, M, D
    Edwardsville B, M
Southwestern Illinois College A
Triton College A
University of Chicago B, M, D
University of Illinois
    Chicago B, M, D
    Springfield B
    Urbana-Champaign B, M, D
Western Illinois University B, M
Wheaton College B

Indiana
Ball State University B, M
Butler University B
DePauw University B
Earlham College B
Franklin College B
Goshen College B
Hanover College B
Indiana State University B, M, T
Indiana University
    Bloomington B, M, D
    Northwest B
    South Bend A, B
    Southeast B
Indiana University--Purdue University
    Indiana University-Purdue
        University Fort Wayne B
    Indiana University-Purdue
        University Indianapolis B, M
Indiana Wesleyan University A, B
Manchester College B
Marian College T
Purdue University M, D
Rose-Hulman Institute of Technology B
Saint Mary's College B
St. Joseph's College B
Taylor University B
University of Evansville B
University of Indianapolis B
University of Notre Dame B, M, D
University of Southern Indiana B
Valparaiso University B, T
Vincennes University A
Wabash College B

Iowa
Buena Vista University B, T
Central College B, T
Coe College B
Cornell College B, T
Drake University B
Graceland University B, T
Grinnell College B
Iowa State University B, M, D
Loras College B
Luther College B
Morningside College B
Northwestern College B

St. Ambrose University B, T
Simpson College B
University of Iowa B, D, T
University of Northern Iowa B
Waldorf College A
Wartburg College B, T

Kansas
Allen County Community College A
Baker University B
Benedictine College B
Bethany College B
Butler County Community College A
Central Christian College A
Coffeyville Community College A
Dodge City Community College A
Emporia State University B
Fort Hays State University B
Independence Community College A
Kansas City Kansas Community
    College A
Kansas State University B, M, D
Pittsburg State University B
Seward County Community College A
University of Kansas B, M, D
Washburn University of Topeka B
Wichita State University B, M

Kentucky
Bellarmine College B
Berea College B
Campbellsville University B
Centre College B
Cumberland College B
Eastern Kentucky University B
Murray State University B, M
Northern Kentucky University B
Thomas More College A, B
Transylvania University B
University of Kentucky B, M, D
University of Louisville B
Western Kentucky University B, M, T

Louisiana
Centenary College of Louisiana B
Dillard University B
Louisiana State University and
    Agricultural and Mechanical
    College B, M, D
Loyola University New Orleans B
Nicholls State University B
Southern University
    New Orleans B
Tulane University B, M, D
University of New Orleans B

Maine
Bates College B
Bowdoin College B
Colby College B
University of Maine B, M
University of Southern Maine B

Maryland
Allegany College A
College of Notre Dame of Maryland B
Community College of Baltimore County
    Essex A
Frederick Community College A
Frostburg State University B
Goucher College B
Hood College B
Johns Hopkins University B, D
Loyola College in Maryland B
Morgan State University B, M
Mount St. Mary's College B
St. Mary's College of Maryland B
Salisbury State University B
Towson University B
United States Naval Academy B
University of Maryland
    Baltimore County B
    College Park B, M, D
Washington College B, T
Western Maryland College B

Massachusetts
American International College B
Amherst College B
Assumption College B
Babson College B
Boston College B, M, D
Boston University B, M, D
Brandeis University B
Bridgewater State College B
Clark University B, M, D
College of the Holy Cross B
Emmanuel College B
Fitchburg State College B
Framingham State College B
Gordon College B
Hampshire College B
Harvard College B
Harvard University M, D
Massachusetts Institute of
    Technology B, M, D
Merrimack College B
Mount Holyoke College B
Nichols College B
Northeastern University B, M, D
Regis College B
Salem State College B
Simmons College B
Simon's Rock College of Bard B
Smith College B
Stonehill College B
Suffolk University B, M
Tufts University B, M
University of Massachusetts
    Amherst B, M, D
    Boston B
    Dartmouth B
    Lowell B
Wellesley College B
Western New England College B
Westfield State College B
Wheaton College B
Williams College B, M
Worcester State College B

Michigan
Adrian College A, B, T
Albion College B
Alma College B, T
Andrews University B
Aquinas College B, T
Calvin College B
Central Michigan University B, M
Eastern Michigan University B, M
Grand Valley State University B
Hillsdale College B
Hope College B, T
Kalamazoo College B, T
Michigan State University B, M, D
Northern Michigan University B, T
Oakland University B
Olivet College B
Saginaw Valley State University B
University of Detroit Mercy B, M
University of Michigan
    Dearborn B
    Flint B, T
University of Michigan B, M, D, T
Wayne State University B, M, D
Western Michigan University B, M, D

Minnesota
Augsburg College B
Bemidji State University B
Bethel College B
Carleton College B
College of St. Benedict B
College of St. Catherine: St. Paul
    Campus B
College of St. Scholastica B
Concordia College: Moorhead B
Gustavus Adolphus College B
Hamline University B
Macalester College B
Metropolitan State University B
Minnesota State University,
    Mankato B, M

Moorhead State University B
Ridgewater College: A Community and
    Technical College A
St. Cloud State University B, M
St. John's University B
St. Olaf College B
University of Minnesota
    Duluth B
    Morris B
    Twin Cities B, M, D
University of St. Thomas B
Winona State University B

Mississippi
Alcorn State University B
Jackson State University B
Mary Holmes College A
Millsaps College B, T
Mississippi State University B, M
Rust College B
Tougaloo College B
University of Mississippi B

Missouri
Central Methodist College B
Central Missouri State University B, M
Drury University B
East Central College A
Lindenwood University B
Missouri Southern State College B
Missouri Valley College B
Missouri Western State College B
Northwest Missouri State University B
Park University B
Rockhurst University B
St. Louis University B, M, D
Southeast Missouri State University B
Southwest Missouri State University B
Three Rivers Community College A
Truman State University B
University of Missouri
    Columbia B, M, D
    Kansas City B, M
    Rolla B, T
    St. Louis B, M
Washington University B, M, D
Westminster College B
William Jewell College B

Montana
Montana State University
    Bozeman B, M
Rocky Mountain College B
University of Montana-Missoula B, M

Nebraska
Creighton University B
Doane College B
Hastings College B
Midland Lutheran College B
Nebraska Wesleyan University B
University of Nebraska
    Kearney B
    Lincoln B, M, D
    Omaha B, M

New Hampshire
Dartmouth College B
Franklin Pierce College B
Keene State College B
Plymouth State College of the University
    System of New Hampshire B
St. Anselm College B, T
University of New Hampshire B, M, D

New Jersey
Bloomfield College B
College of St. Elizabeth B
Drew University B
Fairleigh Dickinson University B
Kean University B
Monmouth University B
Montclair State University B, M
New Jersey City University B
Princeton University B, M, D
Ramapo College of New Jersey B

Economics

Richard Stockton College of New Jersey *B*
Rider University *B*
Rowan University *B*
Rutgers
   The State University of New Jersey: Camden College of Arts and Sciences *B*
   The State University of New Jersey: Douglass College *B*
   The State University of New Jersey: Livingston College *B*
   The State University of New Jersey: New Brunswick Graduate Campus *M, D*
   The State University of New Jersey: Newark College of Arts and Sciences *B*
   The State University of New Jersey: Rutgers College *B*
   The State University of New Jersey: University College Camden *B*
   The State University of New Jersey: University College New Brunswick *B*
   The State University of New Jersey: University College Newark *B*
St. Peter's College *B*
Seton Hall University *B*
The College of New Jersey *B*
Thomas Edison State College *B*

New Mexico
New Mexico State University *B*
San Juan College *A*
University of New Mexico *B, M, D*

New York
Adelphi University *B*
Alfred University *B*
Bard College *B*
Barnard College *B*
Canisius College *B*
City University of New York
   Baruch College *B, M*
   Brooklyn College *B, M*
   City College *B, M*
   College of Staten Island *B*
   Graduate School and University Center *D*
   Hunter College *B, M*
   Lehman College *B*
   Queens College *B, M*
   York College *B*
Clarkson University *B*
Colgate University *B*
College of Mount St. Vincent *B*
College of New Rochelle *B, T*
Columbia University
   Columbia College *B*
   Graduate School *M, D*
   School of General Studies *B*
   Teachers College *M, D*
Cornell University *B, M, D*
Dominican College of Blauvelt *B*
Dowling College *B*
Elmira College *B*
Eugene Lang College/New School University *B*
Fordham University *B, M, D*
Hamilton College *B*
Hartwick College *B*
Hobart and William Smith Colleges *B*
Hofstra University *B*
Iona College *B, M*
Ithaca College *B*
Le Moyne College *B*
Long Island University
   Brooklyn Campus *B, M*
   C. W. Post Campus *B*
Manhattan College *B*
Marist College *B*
Marymount College *B*
Nazareth College of Rochester *B*
New York Institute of Technology *B*
New York University *B, M, D*

Pace University: Pleasantville/Briarcliff *B, T*
Pace University *B, T*
Regents College *B*
Rensselaer Polytechnic Institute *B, M, D*
Rochester Institute of Technology *B*
St. Francis College *B*
St. John Fisher College *B*
St. John's University *B, M*
St. Lawrence University *B*
Sarah Lawrence College *B*
Siena College *B*
Skidmore College *B*
State University of New York
   Albany *B, M, D*
   Binghamton *B, M, D*
   Buffalo *B, M, D*
   College at Buffalo *B*
   College at Cortland *B*
   College at Fredonia *B*
   College at Geneseo *B, T*
   College at Oneonta *B*
   College at Plattsburgh *B*
   College at Potsdam *B*
   Empire State College *A, B*
   New Paltz *B*
   Oswego *B*
   Purchase *C, B*
   Stony Brook *B, M, D*
Suffolk County Community College *A*
Syracuse University *B, M, D*
Touro College *B*
Union College *B*
United States Military Academy *B*
University of Rochester *B, M, D*
Utica College of Syracuse University *B*
Vassar College *B*
Wells College *B*

North Carolina
Appalachian State University *B*
Belmont Abbey College *B*
Campbell University *B*
Davidson College *B*
Duke University *B, M, D*
East Carolina University *B, M*
Elon College *B*
Guilford College *B*
Johnson C. Smith University *B*
Lenoir-Rhyne College *B, T*
Meredith College *B*
North Carolina State University *B, M, D*
Pfeiffer University *B*
Salem College *B*
University of North Carolina
   Asheville *B, T*
   Chapel Hill *B, M, D*
   Charlotte *B*
   Greensboro *B, M, T*
   Wilmington *B*
Wake Forest University *B*
Warren Wilson College *B*
Wingate University *B*

North Dakota
North Dakota State University *B*
University of North Dakota *B, M*

Ohio
Antioch College *B*
Ashland University *B*
Baldwin-Wallace College *B*
Bluffton College *B*
Bowling Green State University *B, M*
Capital University *B*
Case Western Reserve University *B*
Central State University *B*
Cleveland State University *B, M*
College of Wooster *B*
Denison University *B*
Franciscan University of Steubenville *B*
Heidelberg College *B*
Hiram College *B, T*
John Carroll University *B*
Kent State University
   Stark Campus *B*

Kent State University *B, M, D*
Kenyon College *B*
Marietta College *B*
Miami University
   Oxford Campus *B, M*
Mount Union College *B*
Muskingum College *B*
Notre Dame College of Ohio *B, T*
Oberlin College *B*
Ohio Dominican College *B*
Ohio State University
   Columbus Campus *B, M, D*
Ohio University *B, M*
Ohio Wesleyan University *B*
Otterbein College *B*
University of Akron *B, M*
University of Cincinnati
   Raymond Walters College *A*
University of Cincinnati *C, B, M, D, T*
University of Dayton *B*
University of Findlay *B*
University of Toledo *B, M*
Wilberforce University *B*
Wilmington College *B*
Wittenberg University *B*
Wright State University *B, M*
Xavier University *B*
Youngstown State University *B, M*

Oklahoma
Langston University *B*
Oklahoma City University *B*
Oklahoma State University *B, M, D*
Tulsa Community College *A*
University of Central Oklahoma *B, M*
University of Oklahoma *B, M, D*
University of Science and Arts of Oklahoma *B*
University of Tulsa *B*

Oregon
Central Oregon Community College *A*
Chemeketa Community College *A*
George Fox University *B*
Lewis & Clark College *B*
Linfield College *B*
Linn-Benton Community College *A*
Oregon State University *B, M, D*
Pacific University *B*
Portland State University *B, M, D*
Reed College *B*
Southern Oregon University *B*
University of Oregon *B, M, D*
Western Oregon University *B*
Willamette University *B*

Pennsylvania
Albright College *B*
Allegheny College *B*
Bloomsburg University of Pennsylvania *B*
Bryn Mawr College *B*
Bucknell University *B*
California University of Pennsylvania *B*
Carnegie Mellon University *B, D*
Chatham College *B*
Chestnut Hill College *B*
Cheyney University of Pennsylvania *B*
Clarion University of Pennsylvania *B*
Dickinson College *B*
Duquesne University *B*
East Stroudsburg University of Pennsylvania *B*
Eastern College *B*
Edinboro University of Pennsylvania *B*
Elizabethtown College *B*
Franklin and Marshall College *B*
Gettysburg College *B*
Grove City College *B*
Haverford College *B, T*
Holy Family College *B*
Immaculata College *B*
Indiana University of Pennsylvania *B*
Juniata College *B*
King's College *B*
La Salle University *B*

Lafayette College *B*
Lebanon Valley College of Pennsylvania *B*
Lehigh University *B, M, D*
Lincoln University *B*
Lock Haven University of Pennsylvania *B*
Lycoming College *B*
Mansfield University of Pennsylvania *B, T*
Messiah College *B*
Millersville University of Pennsylvania *B, T*
Moravian College *B*
Muhlenberg College *B*
Penn State
   University Park *B, M, D*
Philadelphia University *B, M*
Robert Morris College *B*
Rosemont College *B*
St. Francis College *B*
St. Joseph's University *B*
St. Vincent College *B*
Seton Hill College *B*
Shippensburg University of Pennsylvania *B, T*
Slippery Rock University of Pennsylvania *B, T*
Susquehanna University *B*
Swarthmore College *B*
Temple University *B, M, D*
University of Pennsylvania *A, B, M, D*
University of Pittsburgh
   Bradford *B*
   Johnstown *B*
University of Pittsburgh *B, M, D*
University of Scranton *B*
Ursinus College *B*
Villanova University *B*
Washington and Jefferson College *B*
Westminster College *B*
Widener University *B*
Wilkes University *B*
Wilson College *B*
York College of Pennsylvania *B*

Puerto Rico
Turabo University *B*
University of Puerto Rico
   Cayey University College *B*
   Mayaguez Campus *B*
   Rio Piedras Campus *B, M*

Rhode Island
Brown University *B, M, D*
Bryant College *B*
Providence College *B*
Rhode Island College *B*
Salve Regina University *B*
University of Rhode Island *B, D*

South Carolina
Benedict College *B*
Charleston Southern University *B*
Clemson University *B, M*
College of Charleston *B*
Converse College *B*
Francis Marion University *B*
Furman University *B*
Newberry College *B*
Presbyterian College *B*
University of South Carolina
   Aiken *B*
University of South Carolina *B, M, D*
Wofford College *B*

South Dakota
Augustana College *B, T*
Northern State University *B*
South Dakota State University *B, M, T*
University of South Dakota *B*

Tennessee
Belmont University *B*
Carson-Newman College *B*
Columbia State Community College *A*
East Tennessee State University *B*

Hiwassee College A
Maryville College B, T
Middle Tennessee State
    University B, M, D
Rhodes College B
Roane State Community College A
Tennessee Technological University B
Union University B, T
University of Memphis B, M
University of Tennessee
    Chattanooga B
    Knoxville B, M, D
    Martin B
University of the South B
Vanderbilt University B, M, D

Texas
Austin College B
Baylor University B, M
College of the Mainland A
Galveston College A
Hardin-Simmons University B
Houston Baptist University B
Lamar University B
Lon Morris College A
Midland College A
Midwestern State University B
Palo Alto College A
Prairie View A&M University B, M
Rice University B, M, D
St. Edward's University B, T
St. Mary's University M
St. Philip's College A
Southern Methodist University B, M, D
Southwest Texas State University B, T
Southwestern University B
Tarleton State University B, T
Texas A&M University
    Commerce B, M
Texas A&M University B, M, D
Texas Christian University B, M, T
Texas Lutheran University B
Texas Tech University B, M, D
Texas Woman's University B, T
Trinity University B
University of Dallas B, T
University of Houston B, M, D
University of Mary Hardin-Baylor B
University of North Texas B, M
University of St. Thomas B
University of Texas
    Arlington B, M, T
    Austin B, M, D
    Dallas B
    El Paso B, M
    of the Permian Basin B
West Texas A&M University B
Western Texas College A

Utah
Brigham Young University B, M
Dixie State College of Utah A
Snow College A
University of Utah B, M, D
Utah State University B, M, D
Weber State University B

Vermont
Marlboro College B
Middlebury College B
Norwich University B
St. Michael's College B
University of Vermont B

Virginia
Bridgewater College B
Christopher Newport University B
College of William and Mary B
Eastern Mennonite University B
Emory & Henry College B
George Mason University B, M, D
Hampden-Sydney College B
Hampton University B
Hollins University B
James Madison University B
Liberty University A

Longwood College B
Lynchburg College B
Mary Baldwin College B
Mary Washington College B
Norfolk State University B
Old Dominion University B, M
Radford University B, M
Randolph-Macon College B
Randolph-Macon Woman's College B
Roanoke College B, T
Sweet Briar College B
University of Richmond B
University of Virginia's College at
    Wise B, T
University of Virginia B, M, D
Virginia Commonwealth
    University C, B, M
Virginia Military Institute B
Virginia Polytechnic Institute and State
    University B, M, D
Washington and Lee University B

Washington
Central Washington University B
Eastern Washington University B, T
Everett Community College A
Evergreen State College B
Gonzaga University B
Highline Community College A
Lower Columbia College A
Pacific Lutheran University B
Seattle University B, M
University of Puget Sound B, T
University of Washington B, M, D
Washington State University B, M, D
Western Washington University B, T
Whitman College B
Whitworth College B, T

West Virginia
Bethany College B
Marshall University B
Potomac State College of West Virginia
    University A
Shepherd College B
West Virginia State College B
West Virginia University B
West Virginia Wesleyan College B

Wisconsin
Beloit College B
Carthage College B, T
Concordia University Wisconsin B
Lakeland College B
Lawrence University B, T
Marquette University B, M
Northland College B, T
Ripon College B
St. Norbert College B, T
University of Wisconsin
    Eau Claire B
    Green Bay B
    La Crosse B, T
    Madison B, M, D
    Milwaukee B, M, D
    Oshkosh B
    Parkside B
    Platteville B
    River Falls B, T
    Stevens Point B, T
    Superior B
    Whitewater B, T

Wyoming
Casper College A
Central Wyoming College A
Eastern Wyoming College A
Laramie County Community College A
Western Wyoming Community
    College A

Education

Alabama
Alabama Agricultural and Mechanical
    University B, M
Athens State University B
Birmingham-Southern College B
Calhoun Community College A
Central Alabama Community College A
Faulkner University B
Lawson State Community College A
Northwest-Shoals Community College A
Shelton State Community College A
Talladega College B
Troy State University
    Montgomery M
Troy State University M
Tuskegee University B, T
University of Alabama
    Birmingham D, T
Wallace State Community College at
    Hanceville A

Alaska
University of Alaska
    Southeast M

Arizona
Arizona Western College A
Central Arizona College C, A
Cochise College A
Dine College A
Grand Canyon University B, M
Phoenix College A
Prescott College B, M
University of Arizona M, D

Arkansas
Central Baptist College A
Henderson State University B, M, T
John Brown University B, M, T
Ouachita Baptist University B
Philander Smith College B
Phillips Community College of the
    University of Arkansas A
University of Arkansas
    Pine Bluff B, M, T
University of Arkansas M
University of Central Arkansas M
University of the Ozarks B
Westark College A
Williams Baptist College B

California
Allan Hancock College C, A
Armstrong University A
Azusa Pacific University B, M, D
Barstow College C, A
Biola University B, M, T
Butte College A
California Baptist University B, M
California Lutheran University B, M
California Polytechnic State University:
    San Luis Obispo M
California State Polytechnic University:
    Pomona M
California State University
    Bakersfield M, T
    Chico M
    Dominguez Hills M
    Fresno B, M
    Hayward M
    Los Angeles M
    Monterey Bay B, M
    Sacramento B, M
    San Marcos B
    Stanislaus B
Chaffey Community College A
Chapman University M
College of the Canyons A
College of the Siskiyous A
Columbia College C
Concordia University B, T
Cypress College A
Fielding Institute D

Holy Names College M
Humphreys College A
John F. Kennedy University M
Los Angeles Southwest College A
Loyola Marymount University M
Master's College B
Merced College A
Merritt College A
Mills College B
Napa Valley College A
National University M, T
Occidental College T
Pacific Union College M
Pepperdine University B, M
Point Loma Nazarene University M
Porterville College A
Riverside Community College A
St. Mary's College of California M
San Diego State University M, D, T
Santa Rosa Junior College A
Simpson College M, T
Sonoma State University M
Southwestern College A
Stanford University M, D
University of California
    Berkeley M, D
    Davis M, D, T
    Irvine D
    Los Angeles M, D
    Riverside M, D
    Santa Barbara M, D
    Santa Cruz M
University of La Verne B, M, T
University of Redlands M
University of San Diego B, M, D
University of Southern
    California B, M, D
University of the Pacific B
Vanguard University of Southern
    California M, T
Ventura College A
West Hills Community College A
Whittier College B, M, T

Colorado
Adams State College B, M, T
Colorado Christian University B
Colorado Mountain College
    Alpine Campus A
    Spring Valley Campus A
    Timberline Campus A
Fort Lewis College T
Lamar Community College A
Morgan Community College A
Otero Junior College A
Regis University B
Trinidad State Junior College A
University of Colorado
    Boulder T
    Colorado Springs M
University of Southern Colorado B
Western State College of Colorado T

Connecticut
Central Connecticut State
    University B, M
Eastern Connecticut State University M
Northwestern Connecticut
    Community-Technical College C, A
Sacred Heart University B, M
St. Joseph College M, T
Southern Connecticut State
    University B, T
Teikyo Post University C, A, T
Trinity College B, T
University of Connecticut M, T
University of Hartford B
University of New Haven M
Western Connecticut State University M

Delaware
Delaware State University B
University of Delaware B, T
Wesley College B, M
Wilmington College D

221

District of Columbia
American University *D*
Catholic University of America *B, M*
Gallaudet University *B*
Howard University *M, D*
Trinity College *M*

Florida
Barry University *B*
Broward Community College *A*
Chipola Junior College *A*
Daytona Beach Community College *A*
Edward Waters College *B*
Flagler College *B*
Florida Institute of Technology *B, M, D*
Florida Southern College *B*
Indian River Community College *A*
Jacksonville University *B*
Lake City Community College *A*
Manatee Community College *A*
Nova Southeastern University *B, M, D*
Pensacola Junior College *A*
Polk Community College *A*
Rollins College *T*
St. Leo University *M*
South Florida Community College *A*
Stetson University *B, M*
University of Central Florida *B*
University of Miami *M, D*
University of South Florida *B, M, D*

Georgia
Abraham Baldwin Agricultural
 College *A*
Andrew College *A*
Atlanta Metropolitan College *A*
Brenau University *B*
Brewton-Parker College *A*
Clark Atlanta University *B*
Clayton College and State University *A*
Dalton State College *A*
Darton College *A*
Emory University *M, D*
Floyd College *A*
Gainesville College *A*
Georgia College and State University *M*
Georgia Military College *A*
Georgia Perimeter College *A*
Georgia Southwestern State
 University *M*
Kennesaw State University *B*
LaGrange College *B, M*
Middle Georgia College *A*
Morehouse College *B*
Oxford College of Emory University *B*
Reinhardt College *A*
South Georgia College *A*
State University of West Georgia *B, T*
Toccoa Falls College *B*
Truett-McConnell College *A*
University of Georgia *M*
Valdosta State University *T*
Waycross College *A*
Young Harris College *A*

Hawaii
Brigham Young University
 Hawaii *B*
University of Hawaii
 Hilo *T*

Idaho
Albertson College of Idaho *T*
Boise State University *B, M*
Idaho State University *M*
Lewis-Clark State College *B, T*
North Idaho College *A*
Ricks College *A*
University of Idaho *B, M, D*

Illinois
Augustana College *B*
Barat College *B, M*
Chicago State University *B*
City Colleges of Chicago
 Kennedy-King College *A*
Columbia College *M*
Concordia University *B, T*
Danville Area Community College *A*
De Paul University *B*
Dominican University *M*
Elmhurst College *B*
Governors State University *M*
Greenville College *B*
Highland Community College *A*
John Wood Community College *A*
Kankakee Community College *A*
Kaskaskia College *A*
Kishwaukee College *A*
Knox College *B*
Lake Forest College *B*
Lake Land College *A*
Lewis and Clark Community College *A*
Lincoln Land Community College *A*
McKendree College *B, T*
Millikin University *B, T*
Monmouth College *B, T*
Moody Bible Institute *B*
Moraine Valley Community College *C*
National-Louis University *M*
North Central College *B, T*
North Park University *M*
Northwestern University *B*
Olivet Nazarene University *M*
Parkland College *A*
Principia College *B*
Quincy University *M*
Rend Lake College *A*
Richland Community College *A*
Rockford College *B, M*
St. Xavier University *C, B, M*
Sauk Valley Community College *A*
Southern Illinois University
 Carbondale *D*
Southwestern Ilinois College *A*
Trinity Christian College *B, T*
Trinity International University *D*
Triton College *A*
University of Chicago *M, D*
University of Illinois
 Urbana-Champaign *D*
University of St. Francis *B*
William Rainey Harper College *A*

Indiana
Anderson University *B*
Calumet College of St. Joseph *B*
Earlham College *B*
Franklin College *B*
Goshen College *B*
Indiana State University *B, M*
Indiana University
 Bloomington *B, M, D, T*
 Southeast *B, T*
Indiana University--Purdue University
 Indiana University-Purdue
 University Fort
 Wayne *A, B, M, T*
Manchester College *B, T*
Purdue University
 Calumet *B, T*
Purdue University *B, M, D, T*
St. Mary-of-the-Woods College *B*
University of Evansville *B*
University of Indianapolis *B*
University of Southern Indiana *B*
Valparaiso University *M*
Vincennes University *A*

Iowa
Buena Vista University *B, T*
Clarke College *B, M, T*
Coe College *B*
Cornell College *B, T*
Dordt College *B*
Drake University *D*
Grand View College *B*
Hawkeye Community College *A*
Iowa State University *M, D*
Iowa Wesleyan College *B*
Iowa Western Community College *A*
Loras College *B*
Luther College *B*
Maharishi University of
 Management *A, M*
Marshalltown Community College *A*
Marycrest International University *B, M*
Morningside College *B, M*
North Iowa Area Community College *A*
Northeast Iowa Community College *A*
Northwestern College *B, T*
St. Ambrose University *B, T*
Simpson College *B*
Southwestern Community College *A*
University of Dubuque *M*
University of Northern Iowa *D*
Upper Iowa University *B*
Waldorf College *A*
William Penn University *B*

Kansas
Baker University *M*
Barton County Community College *C, A*
Bethany College *B, T*
Central Christian College *A*
Cloud County Community College *A*
Coffeyville Community College *A*
Colby Community College *A*
Cowley County Community College *A*
Dodge City Community College *A*
Garden City Community College *A*
Hutchinson Community College *A*
Independence Community College *C, A*
McPherson College *B, T*
MidAmerica Nazarene University *M*
Pittsburg State University *B*
Pratt Community College *A*
St. Mary College *M*
Seward County Community College *A*
Southwestern College *B, M*
Sterling College *B*
Tabor College *B, T*
Washburn University of Topeka *B*

Kentucky
Bellarmine College *B, M*
Berea College *B*
Campbellsville University *B*
Kentucky State University *B*
Madisonville Community College *A*
Northern Kentucky University *B*
Spalding University *B, M, T*
Thomas More College *B*
University of Kentucky *M, D*
Western Kentucky University *M*

Louisiana
Centenary College of Louisiana *M*
Dillard University *B*
Louisiana State University
 Shreveport *M*
Louisiana State University and
 Agricultural and Mechanical
 College *C, M*
Louisiana Tech University *M*
McNeese State University *M*
Northwestern State University *M*
Our Lady of Holy Cross College *M*
Xavier University of Louisiana *B*

Maine
St. Joseph's College *B*
University of Maine
 Fort Kent *B*
 Machias *A*
 Presque Isle *B*
University of Maine *B, M*
University of New England *B, M, T*

Maryland
Anne Arundel Community College *A*
Baltimore City Community College *A*
Carroll Community College *A*
Chesapeake College *A*
College of Notre Dame of Maryland *B*
Columbia Union College *A, B*
Community College of Baltimore County
 Catonsville *A*
Coppin State College *B, M*
Frostburg State University *M*
Hagerstown Community College *A*
Harford Community College *A*
Loyola College in Maryland *M*
Montgomery College
 Germantown Campus *A*
 Rockville Campus *A*
 Takoma Park Campus *A*
Salisbury State University *M*
University of Maryland
 Baltimore County *B, M, T*
 Eastern Shore *B*
Washington College *T*
Western Maryland College *M, T*

Massachusetts
Anna Maria College *B, T*
Assumption College *B*
Boston University *B, M, D, T*
Bunker Hill Community College *C, A*
Cambridge College *M*
Cape Cod Community College *A*
Clark University *M*
Curry College *B, M*
Eastern Nazarene College *B, M, T*
Elms College *B, M*
Emmanuel College *B, M, T*
Fitchburg State College *B, M, T*
Gordon College *M*
Hampshire College *B*
Harvard University *M, D*
Lesley College *B, M, D*
Massachusetts College of Liberal
 Arts *B, M, T*
Mount Holyoke College *B*
Mount Ida College *A, B, T*
Northeastern University *B, T*
Salem State College *B, M*
Simmons College *B, M*
Smith College *B, M*
Springfield College *M*
Stonehill College *B*
Suffolk University *B, M, T*
Tufts University *M*
University of Massachusetts
 Amherst *B, M, D*
 Boston *D*
Western New England College *T*
Westfield State College *B, T*
Worcester State College *M*

Michigan
Adrian College *B*
Alpena Community College *A*
Andrews University *M, D*
Aquinas College *M*
Calvin College *B, M, T*
Gogebic Community College *A*
Grand Valley State University *M, T*
Hillsdale College *B*
Kalamazoo Valley Community
 College *A*
Kirtland Community College *A*
Lake Michigan College *A*
Lansing Community College *A*
Northern Michigan University *M*
Northwestern Michigan College *A*
Oakland University *M, D*
Olivet College *M, T*
St. Clair County Community College *A*
Spring Arbor College *M, T*
Suomi College *A*
University of Detroit Mercy *B, M*
University of Michigan
 Dearborn *B, M, T*
 Flint *M*
University of Michigan *M, D*
West Shore Community College *A*
Western Michigan University *B, M, D*

Minnesota
Bethel College *M*
College of St. Benedict *B*
College of St. Catherine: St. Paul
 Campus *B*
Concordia College: Moorhead *B, T*
Concordia University: St. Paul *B, M*

Fond Du Lac Tribal and Community College A
Hamline University B, M, D
Itasca Community College A
Minnesota State University, Mankato B, M
Moorhead State University B, T
North Hennepin Community College A
Northland Community & Technical College A
Ridgewater College: A Community and Technical College A
St. John's University B
St. Mary's University of Minnesota M, D
St. Olaf College B
Southwest State University M
University of Minnesota
    Duluth M
    Morris B, T
    Twin Cities M, D
Winona State University B, M, T

Mississippi
Coahoma Community College A
Copiah-Lincoln Community College A
Delta State University D
East Central Community College A
Jackson State University B, T
Mary Holmes College A
Mississippi Delta Community College A
Mississippi Gulf Coast Community College
    Jefferson Davis Campus A
    Perkinston A
Mississippi State University D
Mississippi University for Women B
Northwest Mississippi Community College A
Tougaloo College B, T
University of Mississippi D
University of Southern Mississippi D
Wesley College C

Missouri
Avila College M, T
Central Methodist College M
Columbia College B, M
Crowder College A
Drury University B, M
East Central College A
Evangel University A, B
Fontbonne College B
Hannibal-LaGrange College B
Jefferson College A
Lindenwood University B, M
Maryville University of Saint Louis B, M, T
Missouri Southern State College B
Park University M
St. Louis Christian College B
St. Louis University B
Southwest Baptist University M
St. Louis Community College
    St. Louis Community College at Meramec A
Stephens College B
Three Rivers Community College A
University of Missouri
    Columbia B
    Kansas City B, M, D
    St. Louis B, M, D
Washington University B, M, D, T
Webster University B, T
William Woods University B, T

Montana
Miles Community College A
Montana State University
    Billings B, M, T
    Bozeman M, D
    Northern B
Rocky Mountain College B, T
University of Montana-Missoula M, D
Western Montana College of The University of Montana A, T

Nebraska
Concordia University B, M, T
Dana College B
Doane College M
Mid Plains Community College Area A
Midland Lutheran College B, T
Northeast Community College A
Peru State College B, M, T
University of Nebraska
    Kearney B, M, T
    Lincoln B

New Hampshire
Franklin Pierce College B
Keene State College B, T
New Hampshire Technical Institute A
Rivier College C, A, B, M, T

New Jersey
Atlantic Cape Community College A
Brookdale Community College A
Caldwell College B
College of St. Elizabeth M
Essex County College A
Fairleigh Dickinson University B
Georgian Court College M
Gloucester County College A
Middlesex County College A
Monmouth University B, M
Montclair State University M, D
Richard Stockton College of New Jersey T
Rider University B
Rowan University B, M
St. Peter's College M
Salem Community College A
Seton Hall University M
Union County College A
Warren County Community College A
William Paterson University of New Jersey A

New Mexico
College of Santa Fe B
Eastern New Mexico University M
New Mexico Junior College A
New Mexico State University
    Alamogordo A
    Carlsbad A
New Mexico State University M
San Juan College A
Santa Fe Community College A
University of New Mexico M, D
Western New Mexico University B, M

New York
Alfred University B, M
Audrey Cohen College A, B
Barnard College T
Canisius College M
City University of New York
    Brooklyn College B, M
    Medgar Evers College A
    Queens College M
Colgate University B, M
College of Mount St. Vincent B
College of St. Rose B, T
Columbia-Greene Community College C
Concordia College B
Cornell University B, M, D
D'Youville College B, T
Dominican College of Blauvelt B, T
Dowling College B
Eugene Lang College/New School University T
Fordham University T
Fulton-Montgomery Community College A
Houghton College B
Iona College M
Jewish Theological Seminary of America M, D
Keuka College B, T
Long Island University
    Brooklyn Campus B
Manhattan College B

Medaille College B, T
Molloy College B, M, T
Nazareth College of Rochester M, T
Niagara University B, M, T
St. Lawrence University M
St. Thomas Aquinas College B, M, T
Sarah Lawrence College M
St. Joseph's College
    St. Joseph's College: Suffolk Campus B, T
    St. Joseph's College B
State University of New York
    Buffalo M
    College at Brockport M
    College at Buffalo B
    College at Cortland B
    College at Fredonia B, M, T
    Empire State College A, B
    Oswego M
Touro College M
University of Rochester M, D
Villa Maria College of Buffalo A
Wagner College B, M

North Carolina
Appalachian State University B, D
Barber-Scotia College B
Barton College B
Beaufort County Community College A
Belmont Abbey College B
Bladen Community College A
Campbell University A, B, M, T
Carteret Community College A
Central Carolina Community College A
Chowan College B
Coastal Carolina Community College A
College of the Albemarle A
Edgecombe Community College A
Elon College B
Gardner-Webb University B, M
Greensboro College B, T
James Sprunt Community College A
Lenoir Community College A
Lenoir-Rhyne College B, M, T
Louisburg College A
Mars Hill College B, T
Martin Community College A
Mayland Community College C, A
Methodist College A, B
Montgomery Community College A
Mount Olive College A
Nash Community College A
North Carolina Agricultural and Technical State University B, T
North Carolina State University B, M, D
Roanoke-Chowan Community College A
Sampson Community College A
South Piedmont Community College C, A
Southwestern Community College A
Surry Community College A
University of North Carolina
    Chapel Hill M
    Greensboro M, D
Vance-Granville Community College A
Wake Forest University B
Warren Wilson College B, T

North Dakota
Jamestown College B
Mayville State University B
Minot State University: Bottineau Campus A
Minot State University B, T
North Dakota State College of Science A
North Dakota State University B
University of Mary B, M
University of North Dakota M

Ohio
Antioch College B
Baldwin-Wallace College B, M
Bluffton College B, M
Capital University B
Central State University B, M
Circleville Bible College B

College of Mount St. Joseph M
Defiance College B, M, T
Denison University B
Edison State Community College A
Heidelberg College M
Hiram College B
Kent State University
    Stark Campus B
    Trumbull Campus A
Kent State University B, M, D
Lake Erie College M
Marietta College B, M
Muskingum College M
Northwest State Community College A
Ohio State University
    Columbus Campus B, M, D
Ohio University
    Eastern Campus M
Ohio University M, D
Otterbein College B
Shawnee State University B, T
Terra Community College A
Union Institute B, D
University of Akron B, M, D
University of Cincinnati
    Raymond Walters College A
University of Dayton B, M
University of Rio Grande B, M, T
Ursuline College B, T
Walsh University M
Washington State Community College A
Wilmington College B
Wittenberg University B
Xavier University B, M, T
Youngstown State University B, M

Oklahoma
Cameron University B, M, T
Connors State College A
Langston University B
Northeastern Oklahoma Agricultural and Mechanical College A
Northeastern State University B, M
Northwestern Oklahoma State University B, M
Oklahoma City University B, M
Oklahoma State University B, M, D, T
Oral Roberts University M
Redlands Community College A
St. Gregory's University A, B
Seminole State College A
Southeastern Oklahoma State University B
Southern Nazarene University B
Southwestern Oklahoma State University M
Tulsa Community College A
University of Central Oklahoma B, M
University of Science and Arts of Oklahoma B
University of Tulsa M, T

Oregon
Central Oregon Community College A
Chemeketa Community College C
Concordia University B, M, T
Eastern Oregon University B
George Fox University B, M, T
Lewis & Clark College M
Linfield College B, T
Linn-Benton Community College C, A
Oregon State University M, D
Pacific University B, M, T
Portland State University M
Southern Oregon University B, T
University of Oregon B
University of Portland M
Western Baptist College B
Western Oregon University B, M

Pennsylvania
Alvernia College B
Beaver College B, M
Bryn Athyn College of the New Church A, B
Bucknell University B, M

Education

223

Education

Bucks County Community College A
Butler County Community College A
Cabrini College B, M
California University of
   Pennsylvania A, B
College Misericordia B, M
Community College of Beaver County A
Community College of Philadelphia A
Duquesne University B, M, T
Gannon University B
Grove City College B
Holy Family College M
Juniata College B
Kutztown University of Pennsylvania M
La Salle University B, M, T
Lackawanna Junior College A
Lehigh Carbon Community College A
Lehigh University M, D
Lincoln University B, M
Luzerne County Community College A
Mansfield University of Pennsylvania M
Mercyhurst College B
Neumann College M
Northampton County Area Community
   College A
Philadelphia College of Bible M
Reading Area Community College A
Robert Morris College B, M
St. Francis College M
St. Joseph's University M
Seton Hill College B, M, T
Swarthmore College B
University of Pennsylvania B, M, D, T
University of Pittsburgh
   Greensburg B
University of Pittsburgh M, D, T
Villanova University M
Westminster College B, M
York College of Pennsylvania B

Puerto Rico

Caribbean University M
Inter American University of Puerto Rico
   Barranquitas Campus B
   Fajardo Campus B
   Guayama Campus A, B
   San German Campus B
Pontifical Catholic University of Puerto
   Rico A, B, M
University of Puerto Rico
   Bayamon University College A
   Carolina Regional College A
   Ponce University College A
   Utuado A, B
University of the Sacred Heart B

Rhode Island

Brown University B, M, T
Community College of Rhode Island A
Johnson & Wales University D, T
Providence College B
Rhode Island College M
University of Rhode Island M, D

South Carolina

Charleston Southern University B, M
Chesterfield-Marlboro Technical
   College A
Columbia College B, T
Converse College B, T
Erskine College B, T
Lander University B, T
Limestone College B
Newberry College B
Southern Wesleyan University M
Technical College of the Lowcountry C
The Citadel B, T
University of South Carolina
   Aiken B

South Dakota

Black Hills State University B, M, T
Dakota State University B, T
Dakota Wesleyan University B
Kilian Community College A
Sinte Gleska University A, B, M

Tennessee

Austin Peay State University M
Belmont University M
Bethel College M
Carson-Newman College B, T
Cumberland University B, M
David Lipscomb University B, M, T
Dyersburg State Community College A
Hiwassee College A
Lambuth University B
LeMoyne-Owen College B
Lee University B, M
Lincoln Memorial University B, T
Maryville College B
Milligan College B, M
Motlow State Community College A
Nashville State Technical Institute C
Roane State Community College A
Shelby State Community College A
Tennessee State University B
Tennessee Technological University B
Tennessee Temple University A
Tennessee Wesleyan College B, T
Tusculum College M
Union University B, M, T
University of Memphis M
University of Tennessee
   Knoxville B, D
Walters State Community College A

Texas

Abilene Christian University B, M, T
Amarillo College A
Angelina College A
Arlington Baptist College B
Baylor University B, M
Brazosport College A
Cedar Valley College A
Central Texas College A
Coastal Bend College A
Collin County Community College
   District A
Concordia University at Austin B, M, T
Dallas Baptist University B, M, T
Grayson County College A
Hill College A
Houston Baptist University B, M
Howard College A
Howard Payne University B
Huston-Tillotson College B
Jarvis Christian College B
Kilgore College A
Lamar State College at Orange A
Lon Morris College A
Lubbock Christian University B
Midwestern State University B
Navarro College C, A
Odessa College A
Our Lady of the Lake University of San
   Antonio M
Panola College A
Paris Junior College A
St. Edward's University B
St. Philip's College A
Schreiner College T
South Plains College A
Southwestern Assemblies of God
   University A, M
Southwestern University B, T
Tarleton State University B, T
Texas A&M International University M
Texas A&M University
   Commerce M, D
   Kingsville B, M
Texas Christian University M, T
Texas Wesleyan University B, T
Trinity Valley Community College A
University of Dallas B, T
University of Houston
   Victoria B
University of St. Thomas B, M
University of Texas
   Arlington M
   El Paso M
University of the Incarnate Word B, M

Wayland Baptist University M
West Texas A&M University M
Western Texas College A

Utah

Brigham Young University B, M
Salt Lake Community College A
Snow College A
Southern Utah University B, M
University of Utah M
Utah Valley State College A
Westminster College B, M

Vermont

Bennington College B
Castleton State College B, M, T
Champlain College A, B
College of St. Joseph in Vermont M
Community College of Vermont C, A
Goddard College B
Green Mountain College B
Johnson State College B, M
Lyndon State College M
Norwich University M
St. Michael's College M
Trinity College of Vermont M
University of Vermont B, M, T

Virginia

Bluefield College B
Central Virginia Community College A
Christopher Newport University B, M
Eastern Mennonite University A, M
Eastern Shore Community College A
George Mason University D
Germanna Community College A
Hampton University B
Hollins University M, T
James Madison University M
Liberty University B
Longwood College B, T
Lord Fairfax Community College A
Mary Baldwin College M, T
Mountain Empire Community College A
New River Community College A
Norfolk State University M
Paul D. Camp Community College A
Piedmont Virginia Community
   College A
Radford University M
Regent University M, D
Shenandoah University M
Southside Virginia Community
   College A
Southwest Virginia Community
   College A
Sweet Briar College C
Tidewater Community College A
University of Richmond T
University of Virginia M, D
Virginia Commonwealth
   University C, M, T
Virginia Highlands Community
   College A
Virginia Polytechnic Institute and State
   University M, D
Virginia Wesleyan College T
Virginia Western Community College A
Wytheville Community College A

Washington

Centralia College A
City University T
Clark College A
Eastern Washington University B, T
Everett Community College A
Gonzaga University M
Grays Harbor College A
Heritage College B, M
Highline Community College A
Lower Columbia College A
North Seattle Community College C, A
St. Martin's College M
Seattle Pacific University B, M, D
University of Washington M, D, T
Walla Walla College B

Washington State University B, M, D, T
Wenatchee Valley College A
Western Washington University B, T
Whatcom Community College A
Whitworth College B, M, T

West Virginia

Alderson-Broaddus College B
Bethany College B
Bluefield State College A
College of West Virginia A
Concord College B, T
Davis and Elkins College B
Fairmont State College B
Glenville State College B
Marshall University B, M
Potomac State College of West Virginia
   University A
Salem-Teikyo University B, M
West Virginia State College B
West Virginia University D

Wisconsin

Alverno College B, M
Cardinal Stritch University B, M
Carroll College B, M
Carthage College B, M, T
Concordia University Wisconsin B
Lakeland College M
Marian College of Fond du Lac B, M
Marquette University M, D
Mount Mary College B
Mount Senario College B
Ripon College B
St. Norbert College T
Silver Lake College M
University of Wisconsin
   Green Bay M
   Madison M, D
   Milwaukee B
   Platteville M
   Stevens Point M
   Stout M
   Superior M
   Whitewater B, M, T
Viterbo University B

Wyoming

Casper College A
Laramie County Community College A
Northwest College A
Sheridan College A
University of Wyoming M, D
Western Wyoming Community
   College A

Education administration/ K-12

Alabama

Alabama Agricultural and Mechanical
   University B, M

Alaska

University of Alaska
   Southeast M

Arizona

Prescott College B, M

Arkansas

Arkansas State University M, T
Arkansas Tech University M
Harding University M
Henderson State University M
Philander Smith College B

California

California State University
   Fullerton M
San Francisco State University M
Simpson College T
United States International
   University M, T
University of San Diego M

Education administration/supervision

Colorado
University of Denver D

Connecticut
Sacred Heart University T

District of Columbia
George Washington University M

Florida
Broward Community College A
Edward Waters College B
Nova Southeastern University M
University of Miami M

Georgia
Columbus State University B
LaGrange College B
State University of West Georgia M

Hawaii
Chaminade University of Honolulu B

Illinois
Kendall College A, B
National-Louis University D
Rockford College B, M
Roosevelt University M, D

Indiana
Ball State University B
Indiana University
  Northwest M
Indiana University--Purdue University
  Indiana University-Purdue
    University Fort Wayne M
Purdue University
  Calumet B
University of Indianapolis B

Iowa
Buena Vista University B
Clarke College M
University of Iowa M, D
University of Northern Iowa M

Kansas
Baker University M
Central Christian College A
Pittsburg State University M
Washburn University of Topeka M

Kentucky
Eastern Kentucky University M
Murray State University M, T
Spalding University M, T
Union College B, M
University of Louisville M, D
Western Kentucky University M

Louisiana
Centenary College of Louisiana M
Southern University and Agricultural and
  Mechanical College M

Maine
University of Southern Maine M

Massachusetts
Bridgewater State College T
Eastern Nazarene College M, T
Emmanuel College M
Harvard University M, D
Springfield College M
Westfield State College M

Michigan
Central Michigan University M
Michigan State University M, D
Saginaw Valley State University M
University of Detroit Mercy M, T

Minnesota
Minnesota State University, Mankato M
Moorhead State University B
St. Cloud State University M
University of St. Thomas B, M, D
Winona State University M, T

Mississippi
University of Mississippi M

Missouri
Central Methodist College B
Crowder College A
Drury University B, M
Lincoln University M
Lindenwood University M
Maryville University of Saint Louis M, T
Northwest Missouri State University M
Southeast Missouri State University M
Southwest Missouri State University M
University of Missouri
  Kansas City M
  St. Louis M
Washington University M

Montana
Rocky Mountain College B, T
University of Montana-Missoula M, D

Nebraska
Chadron State College M
Creighton University M
Midland Lutheran College B
University of Nebraska
  Kearney M
Wayne State College M

New Hampshire
Antioch New England Graduate
  School M
Rivier College M
University of New Hampshire M

New Jersey
Rider University M
Rowan University B, M
Rutgers
  The State University of New Jersey:
    New Brunswick Graduate
      Campus M, D

New York
Bank Street College of Education M
City University of New York
  Brooklyn College B, M, T
Columbia University
  Teachers College M, D
Fordham University M, D
Jewish Theological Seminary of
  America M, D
Long Island University
  C. W. Post Campus M
Manhattan College B, T
St. Bonaventure University B
State University of New York
  New Paltz M

North Carolina
Belmont Abbey College B
College of the Albemarle A
East Carolina University M
Fayetteville State University B
Pfeiffer University B
University of North Carolina
  Chapel Hill M
  Charlotte M
  Greensboro M, D
  Pembroke B, M, T
Western Carolina University M

North Dakota
Mayville State University B
University of Mary M

Ohio
Baldwin-Wallace College B
John Carroll University C, M, T
Kent State University
  Stark Campus B
Kent State University M, D
Miami University
  Oxford Campus M
Ohio State University
  Columbus Campus M, D
University of Akron M
University of Findlay M
Washington State Community College A
Youngstown State University M, D

Oklahoma
Northwestern Oklahoma State
  University T
Oklahoma Baptist University B
Oklahoma State University B, M, D, T
Southeastern Oklahoma State
  University M
Southern Nazarene University M

Oregon
Concordia University M
Lewis & Clark College M
Portland State University M

Pennsylvania
Alvernia College B
Bucknell University M, T
Cabrini College T
California University of
  Pennsylvania M, T
Clarion University of Pennsylvania M
Duquesne University M
Edinboro University of Pennsylvania M
Lancaster Bible College B
Marywood University M, T
Millersville University of
  Pennsylvania M
Shippensburg University of
  Pennsylvania M, T
Villanova University M
Westminster College M

Puerto Rico
Inter American University of Puerto Rico
  Barranquitas Campus B

Rhode Island
Providence College M
Rhode Island College M

South Carolina
Charleston Southern University M
Columbia College B, T

South Dakota
Dakota State University B
Northern State University B
University of South Dakota M, D

Tennessee
David Lipscomb University M
Lincoln Memorial University B, M, T
Roane State Community College A
Tennessee Wesleyan College B, T
Vanderbilt University M, D

Texas
Dallas Baptist University M
Midwestern State University M
Our Lady of the Lake University of San
  Antonio M
Schreiner College C
Tarleton State University B, M
Texas A&M University
  Commerce B, M
  Corpus Christi M, T
  Kingsville B
Texas Christian University C, M
University of Houston M
University of Mary Hardin-Baylor M
University of North Texas M, D
University of Texas
  Pan American M, D
University of the Incarnate Word B

Utah
Brigham Young University D

Vermont
Johnson State College M
St. Michael's College M
University of Vermont T

Virginia
Liberty University M
Longwood College M
Radford University B, M
Virginia Polytechnic Institute and State
  University D, T

Washington
Eastern Washington University M
University of Puget Sound M
Western Washington University M
Whitworth College B, M

Wisconsin
Marian College of Fond du Lac M
Northland College B
University of Wisconsin
  Superior M

Wyoming
Western Wyoming Community
  College A

Education administration/supervision

Alabama
Alabama Agricultural and Mechanical
  University M
Alabama State University M
Auburn University at Montgomery M
Auburn University M, D
Community College of the Air
  Force C, A
Jacksonville State University M, T
Samford University B, M, T
Troy State University
  Dothan M
  Montgomery M
Troy State University M
University of Alabama
  Birmingham M, D, T
University of Alabama M, D
University of Montevallo M, T
University of North Alabama M
University of South Alabama M, D
University of West Alabama M

Alaska
University of Alaska
  Anchorage M

Arizona
Arizona State University M, D
Northern Arizona University M, D
Prescott College B
University of Arizona M, D
University of Phoenix M

Arkansas
Arkansas State University D, T
Harding University M
Henderson State University M
University of Arkansas
  Little Rock M, D
University of Arkansas M, D
University of Central Arkansas M

California
Azusa Pacific University M
Barstow College A
California Baptist University M, T
California Lutheran University M
California Polytechnic State University:
  San Luis Obispo M
California State University
  Bakersfield M
  Chico T
  Dominguez Hills M
  Fresno M, D
  Fullerton M
  Hayward M, T
  Long Beach M, T
  Los Angeles M
  Northridge M
  Sacramento M
  San Marcos M
  Stanislaus M
Chaffey Community College C
Chapman University M, T
Concordia University
Fresno Pacific University M
La Sierra University M, D

Education administration/supervision

Loyola Marymount University *M, T*
Mills College *D*
Mount St. Mary's College *M*
National University *M, T*
Pepperdine University *M, D*
Point Loma Nazarene University *M*
St. Mary's College of California *M*
San Diego State University *M, T*
San Francisco State University *T*
San Jose State University *M, T*
Santa Clara University *C, M*
Sonoma State University *M*
Stanford University *M, D*
United States International
   University *M, D, T*
University of California
   Berkeley *T*
   Irvine *D*
   Los Angeles *M, D*
   Riverside *M, D, T*
University of Judaism *M*
University of La Verne *C, M, D*
University of San Diego *M, D*
University of San Francisco *M, D, T*
University of the Pacific *M, D*
Whittier College *T*

Colorado
University of Colorado
   Boulder *D*
   Denver *M, D*
University of Denver *M, D*
University of Northern Colorado *M, D, T*

Connecticut
Fairfield University *M*
Sacred Heart University *B, M, T*
University of Bridgeport *D*
University of Connecticut *M, D*
University of Hartford *M, D, T*
University of New Haven *M*

Delaware
University of Delaware *M, D*
Wesley College *M*
Wilmington College *M*

District of Columbia
American University *M, D*
Catholic University of America *M, D*
Gallaudet University *M*
George Washington University *M*
Howard University *M*
Trinity College *M*
University of the District of Columbia *M*

Florida
Florida Agricultural and Mechanical
   University *M*
Florida Atlantic University *M, D*
Florida Gulf Coast University *B*
Florida International University *M, D*
Florida State University *M, D*
Nova Southeastern University *D*
Stetson University *M*
University of Central Florida *M, D*
University of Florida *M, D*
University of North Florida *M, D*
University of South Florida *B, M, D*

Georgia
Albany State University *M*
Augusta State University *M*
Clark Atlanta University *M, D*
Columbus State University *M*
Covenant College *M*
Georgia College and State
   University *M, T*
Georgia Southern University *M, D, T*
Georgia State University *M, D*
State University of West Georgia *M*
University of Georgia *M, D*
Valdosta State University *M*

Hawaii
University of Hawaii
   Manoa *M, D*

Idaho
Idaho State University *D*
University of Idaho *B, M, D*

Illinois
Benedictine University *M*
Bradley University *M*
Chicago State University *M*
Concordia University *M*
De Paul University *M*
Dominican University *M*
Eastern Illinois University *M*
Governors State University *M*
Illinois State University *M, D*
Lewis University *M*
Loyola University of Chicago *M, D*
National-Louis University *M*
North Central College *M*
Northeastern Illinois University *M*
Northern Illinois University *M, D*
Quincy University *M*
Roosevelt University *C, M, D*
St. Xavier University *M*
Southern Illinois University
   Carbondale *M, D*
   Edwardsville *M*
University of Illinois
   Chicago *M, D*
   Urbana-Champaign *M, D, T*
Western Illinois University *M*

Indiana
Ball State University *B, M, D, T*
Butler University *M*
Indiana State University *M, D*
Indiana University
   Bloomington *M, D*
Indiana University--Purdue University
   Indiana University-Purdue
      University Fort Wayne *M*
   Indiana University-Purdue
      University Indianapolis *M*
Purdue University *M, D*

Iowa
Buena Vista University *B*
Clarke College *M*
Drake University *M, D*
Iowa State University *M, D*
University of Iowa *M, D*
University of Northern Iowa *M*

Kansas
Benedictine College *M*
Emporia State University *M*
Kansas State University *M, D*
Pittsburg State University *M*
University of Kansas *M*
Wichita State University *M, D*

Kentucky
Cumberland College *M*
Murray State University *B, M, T*
Spalding University *M, D, T*
Union College *M*

Louisiana
Centenary College of Louisiana *M*
Louisiana State University and
   Agricultural and Mechanical
   College *M*
Louisiana Tech University *D*
McNeese State University *B, M, T*
Nicholls State University *M*
Northwestern State University *M, T*
Our Lady of Holy Cross College *M*
Southeastern Louisiana University *M*
University of Louisiana at Lafayette *M*
University of Louisiana at Monroe *M, D*
University of New Orleans *M, D*
Xavier University of Louisiana *M*

Maine
University of Maine *M, D*
University of Southern Maine *M*

Maryland
Bowie State University *M*
College of Notre Dame of Maryland *M*
Coppin State College *M*
Frostburg State University *M*
Hood College *M*
Loyola College in Maryland *M*
Morgan State University *M, D*
Salisbury State University *M*
University of Maryland
   College Park *M, D, T*
Western Maryland College *M*

Massachusetts
American International College *M*
Atlantic Union College *M*
Boston College *M, D*
Boston University *M, D*
Bridgewater State College *M, T*
Cambridge College *M*
Eastern Nazarene College *M, T*
Elms College *M*
Emmanuel College *M*
Fitchburg State College *M*
Framingham State College *M*
Harvard University *M, D*
Lesley College *M, T*
Salem State College *M*
Springfield College *M*
Suffolk University *M*
University of Massachusetts
   Boston *M*
   Lowell *M, D*
Westfield State College *M*
Wheelock College *M*

Michigan
Central Michigan University *M, D*
Detroit College of Business *A, B*
Eastern Michigan University *M, D*
Madonna University *M*
Marygrove College *M*
Northern Michigan University *M*
Oakland University *M, D*
Saginaw Valley State University *M*
University of Detroit Mercy *M*
University of Michigan
   Flint *M*
Wayne State University *D*
Western Michigan University *M, D*

Minnesota
Bemidji State University *M*
Minnesota State University, Mankato *M*
Moorhead State University *M*
St. Cloud State University *M, D, T*
St. Mary's University of Minnesota *M*
University of Minnesota
   Twin Cities *M, D*
University of St. Thomas *M, D*
Winona State University *M, T*

Mississippi
Delta State University *M*
Jackson State University *M, D*
Mississippi College *M*
Mississippi State University *M, T*
University of Mississippi *M, D*
University of Southern Mississippi *M*
William Carey College *M*

Missouri
Central Missouri State University *M*
Lindenwood University *M*
Northwest Missouri State University *M*
St. Louis University *M, D*
Southwest Baptist University *M*
Southwest Missouri State University *M*
University of Missouri
   Columbia *M, D*
   Kansas City *M*
   St. Louis *M*
William Woods University *M*

Montana
University of Great Falls *D*
University of Montana-Missoula *M, D*

Nebraska
Concordia University *M, T*
Doane College *M*
University of Nebraska
   Kearney *M*
   Lincoln *B, M, D, T*
   Omaha *M, D*

Nevada
University of Nevada
   Las Vegas *M, D*
   Reno *M, D*

New Hampshire
Antioch New England Graduate
   School *M*
Keene State College *M*
Plymouth State College of the University
   System of New Hampshire *M*
Rivier College *M*
University of New Hampshire
   Manchester *M*
University of New Hampshire *D*

New Jersey
Caldwell College *M*
Georgian Court College *M*
Kean University *M*
Monmouth University *M*
Montclair State University *M*
New Jersey City University *C, M*
Rider University *M*
Rowan University *M, D*
Rutgers
   The State University of New Jersey:
      New Brunswick Graduate
      Campus *M, D*
St. Peter's College *M*
Seton Hall University *M, D*
The College of New Jersey *M*

New Mexico
College of the Southwest *M*
New Mexico Highlands University *M*
New Mexico State University *M, D*
University of New Mexico *M, D, T*
Western New Mexico University *M*

New York
Bank Street College of Education *M*
Canisius College *M*
City University of New York
   Baruch College *M*
   Brooklyn College *B, M, T*
   City College *M*
   College of Staten Island *T*
   Queens College *C*
College of New Rochelle *M*
College of St. Rose *M, T*
Columbia University
   Teachers College *M, D*
Dowling College *C, D, T*
Fordham University *M, D*
Hofstra University *M, D, T*
Iona College *M*
Long Island University
   Brooklyn Campus *M*
   C. W. Post Campus *M*
Manhattan College *M*
New York University *M, D*
Niagara University *M*
Pace University:
   Pleasantville/Briarcliff *M*
Pace University *M*
St. Bonaventure University *M*
St. John's University *M, D, T*
St. Lawrence University *M*
State University of New York
   Albany *M, D*
   Binghamton *D*
   Buffalo *M, D, T*
   College at Brockport *M*
   College at Buffalo *C*
   College at Fredonia *T*
   College at Plattsburgh *M, T*
   New Paltz *M, D*
   Oswego *M*
Syracuse University *M, D*
Touro College *C, M*

University of Rochester M, D

North Carolina
Campbell University M
East Carolina University D
Fayetteville State University M
Gardner-Webb University M
North Carolina Agricultural and
 Technical State University M
North Carolina Central University M
North Carolina State University M, D
University of North Carolina
 Chapel Hill D
 Charlotte C, D
 Greensboro M, D
 Wilmington M
Western Carolina University M, D

North Dakota
North Dakota State University M
University of Mary M
University of North Dakota M, D

Ohio
Ashland University M, D, T
Bowling Green State University M, D
Cleveland State University B, M, D
Franciscan University of Steubenville M
John Carroll University C, M
Kent State University M, D
Malone College M
Miami University
 Oxford Campus D
Ohio State University
 Columbus Campus M, D
Ohio University M, D
University of Akron M, D
University of Cincinnati M, D
University of Dayton M, D, T
University of Findlay M
University of Toledo M, D, T
Ursuline College M
Wright State University M
Xavier University M, T
Youngstown State University M, D

Oklahoma
East Central University M, T
Northeastern State University M
Northwestern Oklahoma State
 University M
Oklahoma State University M, D
Oral Roberts University M
Southeastern Oklahoma State
 University M
Southwestern Oklahoma State
 University M
University of Central Oklahoma M
University of Oklahoma M, D, T

Oregon
Concordia University M
Lewis & Clark College M
Portland State University D, T
University of Oregon M, D

Pennsylvania
Beaver College M
Bucknell University M
Carlow College M
Cheyney University of Pennsylvania M
Duquesne University M, D
Edinboro University of Pennsylvania M
Immaculata College M, D
Indiana University of Pennsylvania D
La Roche College C
Lehigh University M, D
Marywood University T
Penn State
 University Park C, M, D
Philadelphia College of Bible M
St. Joseph's University M
Temple University M, D
University of Pittsburgh M, D
University of Scranton M
Westminster College M
Widener University M, D

Puerto Rico
Bayamon Central University M
Caribbean University M
Inter American University of Puerto Rico
 Metropolitan Campus M, D
 San German Campus M
Pontifical Catholic University of Puerto
 Rico M
Turabo University M
Universidad Metropolitana M
University of Puerto Rico
 Rio Piedras Campus M, D

Rhode Island
Providence College M
Rhode Island College M

South Carolina
Charleston Southern University M
Clemson University M
Columbia International University M
Furman University M
South Carolina State University D
The Citadel M
University of South Carolina M, D
Winthrop University M, T

South Dakota
South Dakota State University M
University of South Dakota M, D

Tennessee
Austin Peay State University M
East Tennessee State University M, D, T
Freed-Hardeman University B, M, T
Lincoln Memorial University M
Middle Tennessee State University M, T
Southern Adventist University M
Tennessee Technological University M
Tennessee Temple University M
Trevecca Nazarene University M, D
University of Memphis M, D
University of Tennessee
 Chattanooga M

Texas
Abilene Christian University M, T
Angelo State University M
Baylor University M, D
Houston Baptist University M
Lamar University M
Lubbock Christian University M
Midwestern State University M
Prairie View A&M University M
St. Mary's University M
Sam Houston State University M
Schreiner College M
Southwest Texas State University M, T
Sul Ross State University M
Tarleton State University B, M, D, T
Texas A&M International
 University M, T
Texas A&M University
 Commerce M, D
 Corpus Christi M, D, T
 Kingsville M
Texas A&M University M, D
Texas Christian University M, T
Texas Southern University M, D
Texas Tech University M, D
Texas Woman's University M, T
Trinity University M
University of Houston
 Clear Lake M
 Victoria M
University of Houston M, D
University of Mary Hardin-Baylor M
University of North Texas M, D
University of Texas
 Arlington M
 Austin M, D
 Brownsville M
 El Paso M, D
 Pan American M, D
 San Antonio M, D
 Tyler M
 of the Permian Basin M

West Texas A&M University M, T

Utah
Brigham Young University M, D
University of Utah M, D

Vermont
Castleton State College M
Goddard College B
Johnson State College M
St. Michael's College M
University of Vermont M, D, T

Virginia
College of William and Mary M, D
George Mason University M
James Madison University M, T
Liberty University M, D
Longwood College M
Lynchburg College M
Old Dominion University M
Radford University M
Regent University M, T
University of Virginia M, D
Virginia Commonwealth University M
Virginia State University M

Washington
Central Washington University M, T
City University C, M
Eastern Washington University M
Gonzaga University M
Heritage College M
Pacific Lutheran University M
Seattle Pacific University M, D
Seattle University M
University of Washington M, D
Walla Walla College M
Western Washington University M
Whitworth College M

West Virginia
Marshall University M
West Virginia University M, D

Wisconsin
Cardinal Stritch University M, D
Concordia University Wisconsin M
Marian College of Fond du Lac M
University of Wisconsin
 Madison M, D
 Milwaukee M, T
 Superior M

Education of autistic

Kansas
University of Kansas M, D

Massachusetts
Emerson College B, M

Missouri
Fontbonne College B

North Carolina
University of North Carolina
 Greensboro M

Ohio
Xavier University T
Youngstown State University B, M

Puerto Rico
Bayamon Central University M

Education of blind/visually handicapped

Arkansas
University of Arkansas
 Little Rock M
University of Arkansas B

California
San Francisco State University T

Florida
Florida State University B, M, T

Massachusetts
Boston College M

Michigan
Eastern Michigan University B, T
Western Michigan University B

Mississippi
Jackson State University B

Missouri
Lindenwood University M

New York
Columbia University
 Teachers College M, D
Dominican College of Blauvelt B, T

North Carolina
Appalachian State University M

Ohio
Ohio State University
 Columbus Campus M, D
University of Toledo B, T

Oklahoma
Northeastern State University M

Oregon
Portland State University T

Pennsylvania
Kutztown University of Pennsylvania B
University of Pittsburgh T

Puerto Rico
Inter American University of Puerto Rico
 Barranquitas Campus B

South Dakota
Northern State University B, T

Education of deaf/hearing impaired

Alabama
University of Alabama B, M

Arkansas
University of Arkansas
 Little Rock A, B, M

California
California State University
 Los Angeles M
 Northridge M
 Stanislaus B
Saddleback College C, A
San Diego Mesa College A
San Francisco State University T
San Jose State University T

Connecticut
Northwestern Connecticut
 Community-Technical College A

District of Columbia
Gallaudet University B, M, D

Florida
Flagler College B

Georgia
Georgia Perimeter College C, A
Georgia State University M

Idaho
Idaho State University M

Illinois
MacMurray College B, T
Northwestern University B

Indiana
Indiana State University M

Kansas
University of Kansas M, D

Wichita State University *T*
Kentucky
Eastern Kentucky University *B*
Louisiana
Dillard University *B*
Southern University and Agricultural and Mechanical College *B*
Maryland
Western Maryland College *M*
Massachusetts
Boston College *B*
Boston University *B, M, T*
Elms College *B, M, T*
Emerson College *B, M*
Smith College *M*
Michigan
Calvin College *B, T*
Eastern Michigan University *B, T*
Grand Valley State University *T*
Mississippi
Jackson State University *B*
University of Southern Mississippi *B*
Missouri
Fontbonne College *B*
Washington University *M*
Nebraska
University of Nebraska
  Lincoln *B, M*
  Omaha *M*
New Jersey
Kean University *B*
The College of New Jersey *B, M, T*
William Paterson University of New Jersey *M*
New York
Canisius College *M, T*
City University of New York
  Brooklyn College *B, M*
  Hunter College *M*
Columbia University
  Teachers College *M, D*
Elmira College *B, T*
Hofstra University *T*
Ithaca College *B, M, T*
Marymount Manhattan College *B, T*
Nazareth College of Rochester *T*
New York University *B, T*
Pace University:
  Pleasantville/Briarcliff *B*
Pace University *B*
Rochester Institute of Technology *M*
State University of New York
  College at Cortland *B, T*
  New Paltz *B, M, T*
North Carolina
Barton College *B*
Lenoir-Rhyne College *B, M, T*
University of North Carolina
  Greensboro *B*
North Dakota
Minot State University *B, M, T*
Ohio
Cincinnati State Technical and Community College *C, A*
Kent State University *B, M, D*
Ohio State University
  Columbus Campus *M, D*
University of Cincinnati *M, D*
University of Toledo *B, T*
Oklahoma
University of Science and Arts of Oklahoma *B*
University of Tulsa *B, T*
Oregon
Lewis & Clark College *M*
Western Oregon University *T*

Pennsylvania
Bloomsburg University of Pennsylvania *M*
Duquesne University *B*
Indiana University of Pennsylvania *B, T*
University of Pittsburgh *T*
South Carolina
Converse College *B, T*
South Dakota
Augustana College *B, M, T*
Northern State University *B, T*
Tennessee
Lambuth University *B, T*
Tennessee Temple University *B*
University of Tennessee
  Knoxville *B, T*
Texas
Abilene Christian University *T*
Eastfield College *A*
Lamar University *M, D*
Texas Christian University *B, T*
Texas Woman's University *M, T*
University of the Incarnate Word *M*
Virginia
Hampton University *M*
Longwood College *M*
Wisconsin
University of Wisconsin
  Milwaukee *T*

Education of emotionally handicapped

Arizona
Grand Canyon University *B, T*
Arkansas
Arkansas State University *M, T*
California
California Lutheran University *M*
California State University
  Los Angeles *M*
  Northridge *M*
Fresno Pacific University *M, T*
Sonoma State University *M*
District of Columbia
George Washington University *M, D*
Trinity College *M*
Florida
Florida International University *B, T*
Florida State University *B, M, T*
Nova Southeastern University *M*
University of South Florida *B, M*
University of West Florida *B, T*
Georgia
Columbus State University *B, M*
Georgia College and State University *M, T*
North Georgia College & State University *M*
State University of West Georgia *B, M*
Idaho
Lewis-Clark State College *T*
Illinois
Barat College *B*
Benedictine University *B, M, T*
Bradley University *B, T*
Chicago State University *M*
Greenville College *T*
MacMurray College *B, T*
National-Louis University *M*
Trinity Christian College *B, T*
University of St. Francis *B*
Indiana
Ball State University *T*
Indiana State University *B, T*

University of Evansville *B, M*
University of St. Francis *T*
Valparaiso University *M*
Iowa
Loras College *B*
University of Iowa *M*
Kansas
University of Kansas *M, D*
Wichita State University *T*
Louisiana
Dillard University *B*
Maine
University of Maine
  Farmington *B*
Massachusetts
American International College *B, M*
Northeastern University *M*
Michigan
Central Michigan University *B, M*
Eastern Michigan University *B, M*
Grand Valley State University *T*
Hope College *B, T*
Saginaw Valley State University *T*
University of Detroit Mercy *B, M*
Western Michigan University *B*
Minnesota
Bethel College *M*
Moorhead State University *B, T*
University of St. Thomas *M*
Winona State University *B, T*
Mississippi
Mississippi State University *T*
Missouri
Avila College *B, T*
Fontbonne College *B*
Harris Stowe State College *T*
Lindenwood University *M*
University of Missouri
  Kansas City *M*
Nebraska
University of Nebraska
  Omaha *B, M*
New Hampshire
Keene State College *M, T*
Notre Dame College *M*
Rivier College *M*
New York
Bank Street College of Education *M*
City University of New York
  Brooklyn College *B, M*
  City College *B, M, T*
  Lehman College *M*
Columbia University
  Teachers College *M, D*
Dominican College of Blauvelt *B, T*
Fordham University *M*
Manhattan College *M*
Nazareth College of Rochester *T*
New York University *M, T*
State University of New York
  College at Buffalo *B, M*
  New Paltz *M*
North Carolina
Appalachian State University *M*
East Carolina University *B*
Greensboro College *B, T*
North Carolina Central University *M*
University of North Carolina
  Charlotte *M*
  Greensboro *M*
  Wilmington *B*
Western Carolina University *M*
North Dakota
University of Mary *M*
Ohio
Central State University *B*

Kent State University *B, M, D*
University of Akron *M*
University of Cincinnati *M, D*
University of Findlay *T*
University of Toledo *B, T*
Walsh University *B*
Wright State University *M*
Youngstown State University *B, M*
Oklahoma
University of Central Oklahoma *B, M*
Pennsylvania
Indiana University of Pennsylvania *M, T*
La Salle University *B, T*
Rhode Island
Rhode Island College *B, M*
South Carolina
Converse College *T*
South Carolina State University *B, T*
South Dakota
Augustana College *B, T*
Northern State University *B, T*
Tennessee
Johnson Bible College *B, T*
Lambuth University *B, T*
Texas
Texas Woman's University *M*
West Texas A&M University *T*
Vermont
St. Michael's College *M*
Virginia
Eastern Mennonite University *T*
Longwood College *M*
Radford University *T*
University of Virginia's College at Wise *T*
West Virginia
Fairmont State College *B*
Wisconsin
Silver Lake College *B, T*
University of Wisconsin
  Oshkosh *M*

Education of gifted/talented

Arizona
Grand Canyon University *M*
Arkansas
Arkansas State University *M, T*
Arkansas Tech University *M*
Southern Arkansas University *M*
University of Arkansas
  Little Rock *M*
University of Central Arkansas *M*
California
California State University
  Los Angeles *M*
  Northridge *M*
  Sacramento *M*
Saddleback College *C*
San Diego State University *C*
Colorado
University of Denver *M, D*
Delaware
Delaware State University *B*
Florida
Jacksonville University *B*
St. Leo University *B*
University of South Florida *M*
Georgia
Georgia State University *M*
University of Georgia *D*

Idaho
Lewis-Clark State College T

Illinois
Chicago State University M
Northeastern Illinois University M

Indiana
Ball State University T
Indiana State University M

Iowa
Morningside College M
University of Northern Iowa M

Kansas
University of Kansas M, D
Wichita State University T

Louisiana
Dillard University B
Northwestern State University B, M, T
University of Louisiana at Lafayette M

Michigan
Central Michigan University M

Minnesota
University of St. Thomas M

Mississippi
Jackson State University B
Mississippi State University T
Mississippi University for Women M
William Carey College M

Missouri
Drury University B, M
Fontbonne College B
Harris Stowe State College T
Maryville University of Saint Louis M, T
University of Missouri
    Columbia M, D

Nebraska
University of Nebraska
    Kearney M, T

New York
College of New Rochelle M
Columbia University
    Teachers College M, D
Manhattanville College M, T

North Carolina
Catawba College B, T
Lenoir-Rhyne College T
University of North Carolina
    Charlotte M
    Greensboro M

Ohio
Ashland University M, T
Kent State University B, M
Ohio University M
Wright State University M
Youngstown State University M

Oklahoma
Northeastern State University M
Oklahoma City University M

Oregon
University of Oregon M

Pennsylvania
Bloomsburg University of
    Pennsylvania M
Widener University M

South Carolina
Converse College T

South Dakota
Northern State University B, T

Texas
Hardin-Simmons University C, M
Texas A&M International
    University M, T
University of Houston M

University of Texas
    Pan American M, T

Vermont
Johnson State College M

Virginia
Eastern Mennonite University M
Norfolk State University M

Washington
Eastern Washington University T
Whitworth College M

West Virginia
Fairmont State College B
Marshall University B, M
West Virginia State College B

Wisconsin
Carthage College M

Education of learning disabled

Arizona
Grand Canyon University B, T

Arkansas
University of Central Arkansas M

California
California Lutheran University M
California State Polytechnic University:
    Pomona T
California State University
    Dominguez Hills M, T
    Long Beach T
    Los Angeles M
    Northridge M
Holy Names College M, T
San Jose State University M
Sonoma State University M, T
University of California
    Riverside T
University of La Verne M, T
University of San Francisco T

District of Columbia
American University M
Trinity College M

Florida
Bethune-Cookman College B, T
Flagler College B
Florida International University B, T
Florida Southern College B
Florida State University B, M, T
Jacksonville University B, M, T
Lynn University M
Nova Southeastern University M
Palm Beach Atlantic College B
Stetson University M
University of South Florida B, M
University of West Florida B, T

Georgia
Armstrong Atlantic State
    University B, M, T
Augusta State University M
Columbus State University B, M
Georgia College and State
    University M, T
Georgia State University M
Mercer University B, T
North Georgia College & State
    University M
State University of West Georgia M

Illinois
Barat College B
Benedictine University B, M, T
Bradley University B, M
Chicago State University M
De Paul University M
Elmhurst College B
Greenville College T
MacMurray College B, T

National-Louis University M
Northwestern University B
Rockford College M
St. Xavier University M
Trinity Christian College B, T
University of St. Francis B

Indiana
Ball State University T
Indiana State University B, M, T
University of Evansville B, M
University of Indianapolis T
University of St. Francis T

Iowa
Iowa State University T
Morningside College B, M
Northwestern College T
University of Iowa M

Kansas
Bethany College T
Pittsburg State University B
University of Kansas M, D
Washburn University of Topeka M
Wichita State University T

Kentucky
Brescia University B, T

Louisiana
Dillard University B

Maine
University of Maine
    Farmington B

Massachusetts
American International College M, D
Assumption College M

Michigan
Aquinas College B
Calvin College M, T
Central Michigan University M
Grand Valley State University M, T
Hope College B, T
Madonna University B, M, T
Saginaw Valley State University B, M, T
University of Detroit Mercy M

Minnesota
Moorhead State University B, M, T
University of Minnesota
    Duluth T
University of St. Thomas M
Winona State University B, M, T

Mississippi
Jackson State University B

Missouri
Avila College B, T
Culver-Stockton College T
Fontbonne College B
Harris Stowe State College T
Northwest Missouri State
    University B, M, T
Southwest Missouri State University M
University of Missouri
    Columbia M, D
    Kansas City M

Nebraska
University of Nebraska
    Kearney B, M, T
    Omaha M

New Hampshire
Keene State College M, T
New England College B, T
Notre Dame College M
Rivier College M

New Jersey
Fairleigh Dickinson University M
Rowan University M
William Paterson University of New
    Jersey M

New York
City University of New York
    Brooklyn College B, M, T
Columbia University
    Teachers College M, D
Fordham University M
Manhattanville College M, T
Nazareth College of Rochester T
State University of New York
    College at Geneseo M
Syracuse University M

North Carolina
Appalachian State University M
East Carolina University B
Fayetteville State University M
Greensboro College B, T
Salem College M, T
University of North Carolina
    Chapel Hill M
    Charlotte M
    Pembroke B, T
Western Carolina University M

North Dakota
Minot State University M
University of Mary M

Ohio
Ashland University B, M, T
Baldwin-Wallace College B, M
Capital University T
College of Mount St. Joseph T
Hiram College T
Kent State University B, M, D
Malone College B, M
Notre Dame College of Ohio M, T
Ohio University B, T
University of Akron B, M, T
University of Cincinnati M, D
University of Dayton B, T
University of Findlay B, T
University of Toledo B, T
Wittenberg University B
Wright State University B, M, T
Youngstown State University B, M

Oklahoma
Northeastern State University B
Northwestern Oklahoma State
    University B, T
Oklahoma Baptist University B, T
Southwestern Oklahoma State
    University B, T
University of Central Oklahoma B, M
University of Oklahoma B, T

Oregon
University of Oregon M, D
University of Portland T
Western Oregon University T

Pennsylvania
Indiana University of Pennsylvania M
Marywood University T

Puerto Rico
Inter American University of Puerto Rico
    Metropolitan Campus B

Rhode Island
Rhode Island College M

South Carolina
Francis Marion University M
Furman University B, M
South Carolina State University B, T
Southern Wesleyan University B, T

South Dakota
Augustana College B, T
Northern State University B, T

Tennessee
Johnson Bible College B, T

Texas
Texas Woman's University M
West Texas A&M University T

Education of learning disabled

Utah
Southern Utah University B, T

Virginia
Hampton University B
Longwood College M
Radford University T
University of Virginia's College at Wise T

West Virginia
Concord College B, T
Davis and Elkins College B
Glenville State College B
Marshall University B, M
West Virginia Wesleyan College B
Wheeling Jesuit University T

Wisconsin
Carthage College B, T
Silver Lake College B, T
University of Wisconsin
    Eau Claire B, M
    Madison B, M, D, T
    Oshkosh M
    Superior M
    Whitewater B, T

Education of mentally handicapped

Alabama
Tuskegee University B, T

Alaska
Prince William Sound Community College C, A

Arkansas
University of Central Arkansas M
University of the Ozarks B

California
California Lutheran University M
California State University Northridge M
Fresno Pacific University M, T
San Francisco State University T
Sonoma State University M

Colorado
Adams State College M

Florida
Edward Waters College B
Flagler College B
Florida International University B, T
Florida State University B, M, T
Nova Southeastern University M
University of South Florida B, M
University of West Florida B, T

Georgia
Augusta State University B, M
Columbus State University B, M
Georgia College and State University M, T
North Georgia College & State University B, M
State University of West Georgia B, M

Idaho
Lewis-Clark State College T

Illinois
Bradley University B, T
Chicago State University B, M
Greenville College T
Trinity Christian College B, T

Indiana
Ball State University T
Indiana State University B, M, T
Manchester College B, T
University of Evansville B, M
Valparaiso University M

Iowa
Iowa State University T
Loras College B
Morningside College B, M
Northwestern College T
University of Iowa M
University of Northern Iowa B

Kansas
University of Kansas M, D
Wichita State University T

Kentucky
Brescia University B

Louisiana
Dillard University B
Nicholls State University M
Northwestern State University B, T

Maine
University of Maine Farmington B

Massachusetts
American International College B, M

Michigan
Calvin College B, T
Central Michigan University B
Eastern Michigan University B, T
Grand Valley State University M, T
University of Detroit Mercy B, M
Western Michigan University B

Minnesota
Moorhead State University B, T
University of St. Thomas M
Winona State University B, T

Mississippi
Jackson State University B
Mississippi State University T

Missouri
Avila College B, T
Fontbonne College B
Harris Stowe State College T
Lindenwood University M
Northwest Missouri State University B, M, T
Southwest Missouri State University M

Nebraska
University of Nebraska
    Kearney B, M, T
    Omaha M

New Hampshire
Keene State College M, T

New Jersey
William Paterson University of New Jersey M

New York
City University of New York
    Brooklyn College B, M, T
    City College B, M, T
    Lehman College M
Columbia University Teachers College M, D
Dominican College of Blauvelt B, T
Fordham University M
Manhattan College M
Nazareth College of Rochester T
State University of New York
    College at Buffalo B, M
    College at Geneseo M, T
    New Paltz M

North Carolina
Appalachian State University M
East Carolina University B, M
Greensboro College B, T
North Carolina Central University M
Shaw University B, T
University of North Carolina
    Charlotte B, M
    Greensboro M
    Pembroke B, T
    Wilmington B

Western Carolina University M

North Dakota
Minot State University B, M, T
University of Mary B

Ohio
Bluffton College B
Central State University B
Hiram College T
Kent State University B, M, D
University of Cincinnati M, D
University of Dayton B, T
University of Findlay T
University of Toledo B, T
Walsh University B
Wright State University B, M
Youngstown State University B

Oklahoma
East Central University B, T
Northwestern Oklahoma State University B, T
Oklahoma Baptist University B, T
St. Gregory's University A
Southwestern Oklahoma State University B, T
University of Central Oklahoma B, M
University of Oklahoma B, T

Oregon
Western Oregon University T

Pennsylvania
California University of Pennsylvania M
Indiana University of Pennsylvania M, T
Kutztown University of Pennsylvania B
La Salle University B, T
University of Pittsburgh T

Puerto Rico
Inter American University of Puerto Rico Metropolitan Campus B

Rhode Island
Rhode Island College B, M

South Carolina
Converse College M, T
Furman University B, M
South Carolina State University B, T
Southern Wesleyan University B, T

South Dakota
Augustana College B, T
Northern State University B, T

Tennessee
Johnson Bible College B, T
Lambuth University B, T

Texas
Angelina College A
Texas A&M University Kingsville M
Texas Woman's University M
West Texas A&M University T

Virginia
Eastern Mennonite University T
Longwood College M
Radford University T
University of Virginia's College at Wise T

West Virginia
Alderson-Broaddus College T
Concord College B, T
Fairmont State College B
Glenville State College B
Marshall University B, M
West Liberty State College B
West Virginia State College B

Wisconsin
Carthage College B, T
Silver Lake College B, T
University of Wisconsin
    Eau Claire B, M
    Oshkosh M

Education of multiple handicapped

Alabama
University of Alabama M

Arkansas
Arkansas State University M, T

California
California State Polytechnic University: Pomona T
California State University
    Dominguez Hills T
    Long Beach T
    Los Angeles M
San Francisco State University T
San Jose State University M, T
Sonoma State University M

District of Columbia
Gallaudet University B, M, T

Florida
Flagler College B
Nova Southeastern University M

Georgia
Georgia State University M
State University of West Georgia B, M

Idaho
Lewis-Clark State College T

Illinois
National-Louis University M

Indiana
Ball State University T
Indiana State University B, T
University of Evansville B, M

Iowa
Clarke College M
Iowa State University T
Morningside College B, M
Northwestern College T
University of Iowa M

Kansas
University of Kansas M, D

Kentucky
Brescia University B

Maine
University of Maine M

Massachusetts
Boston College M

Minnesota
Winona State University B, T

Mississippi
Jackson State University B
Mississippi State University T

Missouri
Fontbonne College B
Lindenwood University M

Nebraska
University of Nebraska Kearney B, M, T

New Jersey
Gloucester County College A

New York
City University of New York Brooklyn College B, M, T
Dominican College of Blauvelt M
Iona College B, T
Nazareth College of Rochester T
Syracuse University M, D

North Carolina
Appalachian State University M
University of North Carolina Greensboro M

North Dakota
Minot State University *M*

Ohio
Ashland University *M, T*
College of Mount St. Joseph *T*
Kent State University *B, M, D*
Ohio Dominican College *B*
Ohio State University
    Columbus Campus *M, D*
Ohio University *B, T*
Sinclair Community College *A*
University of Akron *B, M, T*
University of Findlay *T*
University of Toledo *B, T*
Walsh University *B*
Wright State University *B, M, T*
Youngstown State University *B*

Oklahoma
University of Central Oklahoma *M*

Oregon
Portland State University *T*
University of Oregon *M, D*
Western Oregon University *T*

Pennsylvania
Marywood University *T*

Puerto Rico
Inter American University of Puerto Rico
    Metropolitan Campus *B*

Rhode Island
Rhode Island College *B, M*

South Dakota
Northern State University *B, T*

Tennessee
Johnson Bible College *B, T*
Lambuth University *B, T*

Virginia
Norfolk State University *M*
Radford University *T*
Virginia Commonwealth University *M*

Washington
Yakima Valley Community College *C*

Education of physically handicapped

Alabama
University of Alabama *M*

Arkansas
University of Central Arkansas *B, M*

California
California State Polytechnic University:
    Pomona *T*
California State University
    Los Angeles *M*
    Northridge *M*
    Sacramento *T*
Fresno Pacific University *M, T*
San Francisco State University *T*
San Jose State University *T*

Florida
Flagler College *B*

Georgia
Georgia State University *M*
State University of West Georgia *B, M*

Idaho
Lewis-Clark State College *T*

Indiana
Ball State University *T*

Iowa
University of Iowa *M*

Massachusetts
Springfield College *M, T*

Michigan
Eastern Michigan University *B, T*

Minnesota
University of St. Thomas *M*
Winona State University *B, T*

Mississippi
Jackson State University *B*

Missouri
Fontbonne College *B*
Lindenwood University *M*

Nebraska
University of Nebraska
    Kearney *B, M, T*

New Jersey
William Paterson University of New
    Jersey *M*

New York
City University of New York
    Brooklyn College *B, M, T*
    Lehman College *M*
Columbia University
    Teachers College *M, D*
State University of New York
    College at Buffalo *B, M*

North Carolina
Appalachian State University *M*

North Dakota
University of Mary *B*

Ohio
Bluffton College *B*
Kent State University *B, M, D*
Ohio State University
    Columbus Campus *M, D*
University of Cincinnati *M, D*
University of Toledo *B, T*
Wright State University *M*

Oklahoma
East Central University *B, T*

Oregon
Western Oregon University *T*

Pennsylvania
California University of Pennsylvania *M*
Cheyney University of Pennsylvania *T*
Indiana University of Pennsylvania *B*
La Salle University *B, T*
University of Pittsburgh *T*

Puerto Rico
University of Puerto Rico
    Bayamon University College *A, B*

Rhode Island
Rhode Island College *B*

South Dakota
Augustana College *B, T*
Northern State University *B, T*

Tennessee
Johnson Bible College *B, T*
Lambuth University *B, T*

Texas
Texas Woman's University *M*
West Texas A&M University *T*

West Virginia
Marshall University *B, M*

Education of speech impaired

Alabama
Alabama Agricultural and Mechanical
    University *B, T*
University of Alabama *M*

Arkansas
University of Central Arkansas *M*

California
California State University
    Chico *C, T*
    Long Beach *T*
    Northridge *B, M*
San Francisco State University *B, M, D*
San Jose State University *T*
University of Redlands *B, M*
University of San Francisco *M*

Georgia
Armstrong Atlantic State
    University *B, M, T*
Georgia State University *M*
Valdosta State University *B, M*

Illinois
Northwestern University *B*

Indiana
Ball State University *T*
Indiana State University *B, T*

Kansas
Wichita State University *T*

Kentucky
Eastern Kentucky University *B, M*
Murray State University *B, M, T*
Western Kentucky University *B*

Louisiana
Louisiana Tech University *B*
Southeastern Louisiana University *B*
Southern University and Agricultural and
    Mechanical College *B, M*

Maine
University of Maine
    Farmington *B*

Massachusetts
Emerson College *B, M, D*

Michigan
Calvin College *B, T*
Eastern Michigan University *B, T*
Wayne State University *B, T*

Mississippi
Jackson State University *B*

Missouri
Fontbonne College *B, M*
Truman State University *B, M*

Nebraska
University of Nebraska
    Kearney *B, M, T*
    Lincoln *M*
    Omaha *B, M, T*

New Jersey
Kean University *B, M*
William Paterson University of New
    Jersey *M*

New Mexico
New Mexico State University *B*

New York
City University of New York
    Brooklyn College *B, M, T*
Columbia University
    Teachers College *M, D*
Elmira College *B, T*
Hofstra University *M, T*
Ithaca College *B, M, T*
Long Island University
    C. W. Post Campus *B, M*
Mercy College *T*
Nazareth College of Rochester *M, T*
New York University *B, T*
Pace University:
    Pleasantville/Briarcliff *B*
Pace University *B*
St. John's University *B, T*

State University of New York
    College at Fredonia *B, M, T*
    College at Geneseo *T*
    New Paltz *B, M, T*

North Carolina
Appalachian State University *M*
University of North Carolina
    Greensboro *M*

North Dakota
Minot State University *B, M, T*

Ohio
Kent State University *T*
University of Akron *B, M, T*
University of Toledo *B, T*

Oklahoma
Northeastern State University *B*
University of Central Oklahoma *B*
University of Tulsa *B, T*

Oregon
Portland State University *T*

Pennsylvania
Bloomsburg University of
    Pennsylvania *B, M, T*
Indiana University of Pennsylvania *B*
Kutztown University of Pennsylvania *B*
West Chester University of
    Pennsylvania *B, M, T*

Puerto Rico
Inter American University of Puerto Rico
    Metropolitan Campus *B*
Turabo University *B*

South Carolina
Columbia College *B*

South Dakota
Augustana College *B, T*

Tennessee
Lambuth University *B, T*

Texas
Baylor University *B*
El Paso Community College *A*
University of Texas
    Pan American *T*

Virginia
Hampton University *M*

West Virginia
Marshall University *B, M*

Wisconsin
University of Wisconsin
    Madison *M, D, T*
    River Falls *B, T*
    Whitewater *M*

Education/instructional media design

Alabama
Alabama State University *M*
Auburn University *M, T*
Jacksonville State University *M*
University of South Alabama *M, D*

Arizona
Arizona State University *M, D*

Arkansas
Arkansas Tech University *M*
Southern Arkansas University *M*
University of Arkansas
    Little Rock *M*
University of Arkansas *M*

California
California State University
    Chico *B, M*
San Diego State University *M, T*
San Francisco State University *M*

Education/instructional media design

San Jose State University *M*

Colorado
University of Northern Colorado *M, T*

Connecticut
Central Connecticut State University *M*
Fairfield University *M*
University of Connecticut *D, T*

District of Columbia
Gallaudet University *M*

Florida
Nova Southeastern University *M*
University of Central Florida *M*

Georgia
Georgia College and State
 University *M, T*
Georgia Southern University *M, T*
Georgia State University *M, D*
State University of West Georgia *M*
University of Georgia *M, D, T*

Hawaii
University of Hawaii
 Manoa *M*

Idaho
Idaho State University *M*
University of Idaho *B*

Illinois
National-Louis University *M*
Northern Illinois University *M, D*
Southern Illinois University
 Edwardsville *M*

Indiana
Indiana State University *B, M, T*

Iowa
Clarke College *M*
Iowa State University *T*
University of Iowa *M, D*
University of Northern Iowa *M*

Kansas
Emporia State University *M*

Louisiana
Northwestern State University *M*

Maryland
Towson University *M*
Western Maryland College *M*

Massachusetts
Boston University *M, T*
Bridgewater State College *M, T*
Harvard University *M, D*
University of Massachusetts
 Boston *M*

Michigan
Wayne State University *M, D*

Minnesota
College of St. Scholastica *M, T*
St. Cloud State University *M*

Mississippi
Jackson State University *M*
University of Southern Mississippi *M*

Missouri
Webster University *B*

Nebraska
University of Nebraska
 Omaha *B, T*

New Jersey
Georgian Court College *M*
Kean University *M*
Richard Stockton College of New
 Jersey *M*

New York
Columbia University
 Teachers College *M, D*
Rochester Institute of Technology *M*

State University of New York
 Albany *M*
Syracuse University *M, D*

North Carolina
Appalachian State University *M*
East Carolina University *M*
North Carolina Agricultural and
 Technical State University *M*
North Carolina Central University *M*
University of North Carolina
 Chapel Hill *M*
 Charlotte *M*
 Wilmington *M*
Western Carolina University *M*

Ohio
John Carroll University *M*
Kent State University *C, M*
Miami University
 Oxford Campus *M*
Ohio State University
 Columbus Campus *M, D*
University of Akron *M, D*
University of Toledo *M*

Oklahoma
Northwestern Oklahoma State
 University *M*
University of Central Oklahoma *B, M*

Oregon
Portland Community College *C*
Portland State University *M, T*

Pennsylvania
Bloomsburg University of
 Pennsylvania *M*
Duquesne University *M*
Lehigh University *M, D*
Marywood University *M, T*
Wilkes University *M*

Puerto Rico
Bayamon Central University *A, B*
University of the Sacred Heart *M*

South Carolina
University of South Carolina *M*

Tennessee
East Tennessee State University *M, T*
Lincoln Memorial University *M*
University of Memphis *C*

Texas
Prairie View A&M University *M*
Texas A&M University
 Corpus Christi *M, T*
Texas A&M University *M*
Texas Tech University *M, D*
University of Houston
 Clear Lake *M*
University of Houston *M*
University of North Texas *M*
West Texas A&M University *M*

Utah
Utah State University *M, D*

Virginia
James Madison University *M, T*
Longwood College *M*
Radford University *M*

Washington
City University *M*
Eastern Washington University *M*

Wisconsin
University of Wisconsin
 La Crosse *M*

Educational evaluation/research

California
California State University
 Fresno *M*

San Diego State University *M, T*
University of California
 Berkeley *T*

Colorado
University of Colorado
 Boulder *D*

District of Columbia
Catholic University of America *D*

Florida
Florida State University *M, D*
University of South Florida *M*

Georgia
Clark Atlanta University *M*

Iowa
University of Iowa *M, D*

Kentucky
University of Kentucky *D*

Massachusetts
Boston College *M, D*
Northeastern University *M*

Michigan
Michigan State University *D*
Wayne State University *M, D*

Missouri
University of Missouri
 Kansas City *M*

New Jersey
Rowan University *M*

New York
Columbia University
 Teachers College *M, D*

North Carolina
North Carolina State University *M, D*
University of North Carolina
 Greensboro *M, D*

Ohio
Ohio University *M, D*
University of Dayton *M*
University of Toledo *M*

Pennsylvania
Bucknell University *M*

Puerto Rico
University of Puerto Rico
 Rio Piedras Campus *M*

South Carolina
University of South Carolina *M, D*

South Dakota
University of South Dakota *M, D*

Texas
Texas Christian University *M*
University of the Incarnate Word *M*

Educational psychology

Alabama
University of Alabama *M, D*

Arizona
Arizona State University *M, D*
Northern Arizona University *D*
Prescott College *B, M*
University of Arizona *M, D*

California
Azusa Pacific University *M*
California Lutheran University *M*
California State University
 Dominguez Hills *T*
 Hayward *M, T*
 Long Beach *M*
 Northridge *M*
Chapman University *M, T*
Fresno Pacific University *M, T*

La Sierra University *M*
Loyola Marymount University *M*
St. Mary's College of California *M*
University of California
 Riverside *M, D*
 Santa Barbara *M, D*
University of San Francisco *M, D*
University of Southern California *D, T*
University of the Pacific *M, D, T*

Colorado
University of Colorado
 Boulder *M, D*
 Denver *M*
University of Denver *M, D*
University of Northern Colorado *M, D*

Connecticut
Eastern Connecticut State University *M*
University of Connecticut *M, D, T*

Delaware
University of Delaware *B, M, T*

District of Columbia
Catholic University of America *D*
Howard University *M*

Florida
Florida State University *M, D*
University of Florida *M, D*

Georgia
Georgia State University *M, D*
State University of West Georgia *M*
University of Georgia *M, D*
Valdosta State University *M*

Hawaii
University of Hawaii
 Manoa *M, D*

Idaho
Idaho State University *M*

Illinois
Loyola University of Chicago *M, D*
National-Louis University *M, D*
Northern Illinois University *M, D*
Southern Illinois University
 Carbondale *M, D*
University of Illinois
 Urbana-Champaign *M, D*

Indiana
Indiana State University *M*
Indiana University
 Bloomington *M, D*

Iowa
Iowa State University *T*
University of Iowa *M, D*

Kansas
Fort Hays State University *M*
Kansas State University *D*
Pittsburg State University *A, B, D*
University of Kansas *M, D*
Wichita State University *M*

Kentucky
University of Kentucky *M, D*

Louisiana
Louisiana Tech University *M*
Nicholls State University *M*

Maine
University of Southern Maine *M*

Maryland
St. Mary's College of Maryland *B*
University of Maryland
 College Park *M, D, T*

Massachusetts
American International College *M*
Boston College *D*
Harvard University *M, D*
Northeastern University *M*
Tufts University *M, T*

Michigan
Eastern Michigan University *M*
Michigan State University *M, D*
University of Michigan *D*
Wayne State University *M, D*

Minnesota
University of Minnesota
  Duluth *M*
  Twin Cities *M, D*

Mississippi
Alcorn State University *B*
Mississippi State University *B, M, D*
University of Mississippi *M, D*

Nebraska
University of Nebraska
  Kearney *M*
  Lincoln *M, D*
  Omaha *M*

Nevada
University of Nevada
  Las Vegas *M, D*

New Jersey
Kean University *M*
Montclair State University *M*
New Jersey City University *M*
Rowan University *M, T*
Rutgers
  The State University of New Jersey:
    New Brunswick Graduate
    Campus *M, D*

New Mexico
University of New Mexico *M, D*

New York
City University of New York
  Brooklyn College *M*
  Graduate School and University
    Center *D*
College of St. Rose *M*
Columbia University
  Teachers College *M, D*
Eugene Lang College/New School
  University *B*
Long Island University
  Brooklyn Campus *M*
Marist College *M*
New York University *M, D*
Rochester Institute of Technology *M*
State University of New York
  Buffalo *M, D*
  College at Plattsburgh *M, T*
Syracuse University *M, D*
Touro College *M*

North Carolina
University of North Carolina
  Chapel Hill *M*

Ohio
John Carroll University *M*
Kent State University *M, D*
Miami University
  Oxford Campus *M*
Ohio State University
  Columbus Campus *M, D*
University of Dayton *M*
University of Toledo *M*

Oklahoma
Northwestern Oklahoma State
  University *M*
University of Oklahoma *M, D*

Oregon
University of Oregon *M, D*

Pennsylvania
Duquesne University *M*
Edinboro University of Pennsylvania *M*
Indiana University of Pennsylvania *M*
Lehigh University *M, D*
Marywood University *T*

Penn State
  University Park *M, D*
Temple University *M, D*
University of Pittsburgh *M, D*

Puerto Rico
Pontifical Catholic University of Puerto
  Rico *M*

Rhode Island
Rhode Island College *M*

South Dakota
University of South Dakota *M, D*

Tennessee
Motlow State Community College *A*
Tennessee State University *D*
Tennessee Technological University *M*
University of Memphis *M, D*
University of Tennessee
  Knoxville *M, D*
Vanderbilt University *M, D*

Texas
Baylor University *M, D*
Southwest Texas State University *M, T*
Texas A&M University
  Commerce *M, D*
Texas A&M University *M, D*
Texas Tech University *M, D*
University of Houston *M*
University of Mary Hardin-Baylor *M*
University of North Texas *M, D*
University of Texas
  Austin *M, D*
  El Paso *M*
  Pan American *M*

Utah
Brigham Young University *B, M, D*
University of Utah *M, D*

Virginia
College of William and Mary *M, D*
James Madison University *M*
University of Virginia *M, D*
Virginia Polytechnic Institute and State
  University *D*

West Virginia
West Virginia University *M, D*

Wisconsin
University of Wisconsin
  Eau Claire *M*
  Madison *M, D*
  Milwaukee *M*
  Whitewater *M*

Educational statistics/research methods

Alabama
University of Alabama *D*

California
Stanford University *M, D*

Colorado
University of Northern Colorado *M, D*

Florida
Florida State University *M, D*
University of Florida *M, D*
University of Miami *M, D*

Georgia
Georgia State University *M, D*
University of Georgia *D*

Indiana
Indiana State University *M*

Iowa
University of Iowa *M, D*

Maryland
University of Maryland
  College Park *M, D, T*

Massachusetts
Northeastern University *M*

Michigan
University of Detroit Mercy *M*

New Jersey
Rutgers
  The State University of New Jersey:
    New Brunswick Graduate
    Campus *M, D*

New York
Columbia University
  Teachers College *M*
Fordham University *M, D*
Hofstra University *M, D*
State University of New York
  Albany *M, D*
  Buffalo *M, D*

North Carolina
University of North Carolina
  Greensboro *M, D*

North Dakota
University of North Dakota *M*

Ohio
Ohio State University
  Columbus Campus *M, D*
Ohio University *M, D*

Oklahoma
Oklahoma State University *M, D*

Pennsylvania
Bucknell University *B*
West Chester University of
  Pennsylvania *M*

Texas
University of North Texas *D*

Educational supervision

Alabama
Alabama State University *M*
University of Alabama *D*

Arkansas
University of Central Arkansas *M*

California
California Lutheran University *M*
California State University
  Stanislaus *M*
National University *M, T*
St. Mary's College of California *M*

Connecticut
Central Connecticut State University *M*
Fairfield University *M*

Delaware
University of Delaware *M, D*
Wesley College *M*

District of Columbia
George Washington University *M*
Howard University *M*
University of the District of Columbia *M*

Florida
Stetson University *M*

Georgia
Clark Atlanta University *M, D*
Columbus State University *M*
Valdosta State University *M*

Idaho
Northwest Nazarene University *M*

Illinois
De Paul University *M*
National-Louis University *D*
University of Illinois
  Chicago *M*
University of St. Francis *M*

Indiana
Indiana State University *M, D*

Kansas
Wichita State University *T*

Kentucky
Murray State University *M, T*
Union College *M*
University of Louisville *D*

Louisiana
Centenary College of Louisiana *M*
Nicholls State University *M*
Northwestern State University *T*

Maine
University of Maine *M*

Maryland
Johns Hopkins University *M*
Morgan State University *M, D*
Salisbury State University *M*

Massachusetts
American International College *M*
Harvard University *M, D*
Springfield College *M*

Michigan
Central Michigan University *D*
Wayne State University *M*

Minnesota
Bethel College *M*
Minnesota State University, Mankato *M*
Winona State University *M, T*

Mississippi
Jackson State University *M*

Missouri
Lindenwood University *M*

Nebraska
University of Nebraska
  Kearney *M*

New Hampshire
Antioch New England Graduate
  School *M*
University of New Hampshire *M*

New Jersey
Caldwell College *C, M*
Georgian Court College *M*

New York
City University of New York
  Baruch College *M*
  Brooklyn College *M*
Columbia University
  Teachers College *M, D*
Fordham University *M, D*
New York University *M, T*
State University of New York
  Albany *D*
  Buffalo *M, D*
  New Paltz *M*

North Carolina
Appalachian State University *M*
East Carolina University *M*
Fayetteville State University *M*
North Carolina Agricultural and
  Technical State University *M*
North Carolina Central University *M*
University of North Carolina
  Greensboro *M, D*
Western Carolina University *M*

Ohio
Baldwin-Wallace College *M*
John Carroll University *M*
Kent State University *M*
Otterbein College *M*
University of Akron *M, T*
University of Cincinnati *M, D*
University of Dayton *M, D*
University of Toledo *T*
Wright State University *M*

233

Youngstown State University M, D
Oklahoma
Northeastern State University M
Oklahoma State University M, D
University of Oklahoma M, D
Pennsylvania
Carlow College M
Delaware Valley College M
Lehigh University M, D
Marywood University T
St. Joseph's University M
Shippensburg University of
  Pennsylvania T
Villanova University M
Puerto Rico
Inter American University of Puerto Rico
  Metropolitan Campus M
South Carolina
Clemson University M
Furman University M
The Citadel M
Winthrop University T
Tennessee
David Lipscomb University M
Tennessee State University M
Tennessee Technological University M
Texas
Abilene Christian University M, T
Angelo State University M
Lamar University M
Our Lady of the Lake University of San
  Antonio M
Prairie View A&M University M
Sam Houston State University M
Southwestern Assemblies of God
  University B
Sul Ross State University M
Tarleton State University B, T
Texas A&M International University T
Texas A&M University
  Commerce D
  Kingsville M
Texas Tech University M
Texas Woman's University M
University of Houston
  Victoria M
University of North Texas M
University of Texas
  Brownsville M
  El Paso M
  Pan American M
  of the Permian Basin M
Utah
Brigham Young University D
Vermont
Johnson State College M
Virginia
Longwood College M
Radford University M
Washington
Central Washington University M, T
Seattle University D
Western Washington University M
West Virginia
Marshall University M
Wisconsin
University of Wisconsin
  Oshkosh M
  River Falls M
  Superior M

Educational testing/measurement

California
California State University
  Northridge M
Stanford University M, D
Delaware
University of Delaware M, D
Georgia
Georgia State University M
University of Georgia M, D
Indiana
Indiana State University M
Indiana University
  Bloomington D
Iowa
Iowa State University M
University of Iowa M, D
Kentucky
University of Louisville D
Massachusetts
American International College M
Harvard University M, D
Tufts University M
Michigan
Michigan State University M, D
New Jersey
Rutgers
  The State University of New Jersey:
    New Brunswick Graduate
    Campus M, D
New York
Columbia University
  Teachers College M, D
Fordham University M, D
State University of New York
  Albany M, D
  Buffalo M, D
Syracuse University M, D
North Carolina
University of North Carolina
  Greensboro M, D
Ohio
Kent State University M, D
Ohio State University
  Columbus Campus M, D
Pennsylvania
University of Pennsylvania M, D
South Carolina
University of South Carolina M
Texas
Sul Ross State University M
University of Texas
  Pan American M
West Texas A&M University T

Electrical/electronic engineering-related technologies

Alabama
Alabama Agricultural and Mechanical
  University B
Calhoun Community College A
Central Alabama Community College A
Community College of the Air Force A
Gadsden State Community College C, A
Harry M. Ayers State Technical
  College C, A
ITT Technical Institute
  Birmingham A, B
Jacksonville State University B
James H. Faulkner State Community
  College C
John M. Patterson State Technical
  College A
Lawson State Community College C, A
Northwest-Shoals Community College A
Reid State Technical College A
Sparks State Technical College A
Alaska
University of Alaska
  Anchorage C, A
Arizona
Central Arizona College C, A
Cochise College A
DeVry Institute of Technology
  Phoenix A, B
Glendale Community College A
ITT Technical Institute
  Phoenix A, B
  Tucson A
Northland Pioneer College C, A
Pima Community College C, A
Arkansas
Arkansas State University
  Beebe Branch A
  Mountain Home C, A
Arkansas State University A
Arkansas Tech University C, A
Garland County Community College A
ITT Technical Institute
  Little Rock A
Mississippi County Community
  College A
North Arkansas College C, A
Northwest Arkansas Community
  College A
Phillips Community College of the
  University of Arkansas C
Southern Arkansas University
  Tech C, A
University of Arkansas
  Little Rock A, B
Westark College A
California
Allan Hancock College C, A
Barstow College C
Butte College C, A
California State University
  Long Beach B
Cerritos Community College C, A
Cerro Coso Community College C, A
Chabot College A
City College of San Francisco C, A
College of San Mateo C, A
College of the Canyons A
College of the Redwoods C
College of the Sequoias C, A
Compton Community College C, A
Cuyamaca College A
DeVry Institute of Technology
  Fremont A, B
  Long Beach A, B
  Pomona A, B
Don Bosco Technical Institute A
Evergreen Valley College C
Foothill College C, A
ITT Technical Institute
  Anaheim A, B
  Hayward A
  Lathrop A
  Oxnard A
  Rancho Cordova A, B
  San Bernardino A
  San Diego A, B
  Santa Clara A
  Sylmar A
  Torrance A
  West Covina A
Irvine Valley College C, A
Los Angeles Harbor College C, A
Los Angeles Southwest College C, A
Los Angeles Trade and Technical
  College C, A
Los Angeles Valley College C, A
Merced College A
Moorpark College C, A
Mount San Antonio College C, A
Napa Valley College C, A
Ohlone College C, A
Orange Coast College C, A
Pacific Union College A, B
Riverside Community College C, A
Saddleback College C
San Bernardino Valley College C, A
San Diego City College C, A
San Joaquin Delta College C, A
San Jose City College C
Santa Clara University C
Santa Monica College C, A
Santa Rosa Junior College C, A
Shasta College A
Sierra College C, A
Solano Community College C, A
Southwestern College C, A
Taft College A
University of San Diego B
Ventura College A
Victor Valley College C, A
West Valley College C, A
Yuba College C
Colorado
Aims Community College A
Arapahoe Community College C, A
Colorado Technical University A, B
Community College of Aurora A
Community College of Denver C, A
Denver Technical College: A Division of
  DeVry University A, B
Front Range Community College C, A
ITT Technical Institute
  Thornton A, B
Mesa State College C, A
Metropolitan State College of Denver B
Pikes Peak Community College C, A
Pueblo Community College C, A
Red Rocks Community College C, A
University of Southern Colorado B
Connecticut
Capital Community College A
Gateway Community College A
Naugatuck Valley Community-Technical
  College A
Northwestern Connecticut
  Community-Technical College C
Norwalk Community-Technical
  College A
Three Rivers Community-Technical
  College A
University of Hartford A, B
Delaware
Delaware State University B
Delaware Technical and Community
  College
  Owens Campus A
  Stanton/Wilmington Campus C, A
  Terry Campus A
District of Columbia
University of the District of Columbia A
Florida
Brevard Community College C, A
Daytona Beach Community College A
Embry-Riddle Aeronautical University B
Florida Agricultural and Mechanical
  University B
Florida Community College at
  Jacksonville A
Gulf Coast Community College A
Hillsborough Community College A

Electrical/electronic engineering-related technologies

ITT Technical Institute
   Ft. Lauderdale *A, B*
   Jacksonville *A, B*
   Maitland *A*
   Miami *A*
   Tampa *A, B*
Indian River Community College *A*
Lake City Community College *A*
Manatee Community College *A*
Miami-Dade Community College *C, A*
Palm Beach Community College *A*
Pensacola Junior College *A*
St. Petersburg Junior College *A*
Santa Fe Community College *A*
Seminole Community College *A*
South Florida Community College *A*
Tampa Technical Institute *A, B*
University of Central Florida *B*
Valencia Community College *A*

Georgia
Athens Area Technical Institute *A*
Bainbridge College *A*
Chattahoochee Technical Institute *A*
Clayton College and State
   University *C, A*
Columbus Technical Institute *C, A*
DeKalb Technical Institute *C, A*
DeVry Institute of Technology
   Alpharetta *A, B*
   Atlanta *A, B*
Fort Valley State University *A, B*
Georgia Southern University *B*
Herzing College of Business and
   Technology *A*
Savannah State University *B*
Savannah Technical Institute *A*
Southern Polytechnic State University *B*

Hawaii
University of Hawaii
   Hawaii Community College *A*
   Honolulu Community College *C, A*

Idaho
Eastern Idaho Technical College *C, A*
ITT Technical Institute
   Boise *A, B*
Idaho State University *C, A*
Lewis-Clark State College *A*
Ricks College *A*

Illinois
Bradley University *B*
College of DuPage *C, A*
College of Lake County *C, A*
DeVry Institute of Technology
   Addison *A, B*
   Chicago *A, B*
Elgin Community College *C, A*
Highland Community College *A*
ITT Technical Institute
   Burr Ridge *A*
   Hoffman Estates *A, B*
Illinois Eastern Community Colleges
   Wabash Valley College *A*
John Wood Community College *A*
Joliet Junior College *C, A*
Kaskaskia College *A*
Kishwaukee College *C, A*
Lincoln Land Community College *C, A*
McHenry County College *C, A*
Moraine Valley Community College *C*
Oakton Community College *C, A*
Parkland College *C, A*
Prairie State College *C, A*
Rock Valley College *C, A*
Roosevelt University *B*
Shawnee Community College *A*
Southern Illinois University
   Carbondale *A, B*
Waubonsee Community College *C, A*
William Rainey Harper College *C, A*

Indiana
ITT Technical Institute
   Fort Wayne *A*
   Indianapolis *A, B*
   Newburgh *A*
Indiana State University *B, M*
Indiana University--Purdue University
   Indiana University-Purdue
     University Fort Wayne *A, B*
   Indiana University-Purdue
     University Indianapolis *A, B*
Ivy Tech State College
   Central Indiana *A*
   Columbus *C, A*
   Eastcentral *C, A*
   Kokomo *C, A*
   Lafayette *C, A*
   Northcentral *C, A*
   Northeast *C, A*
   Northwest *C, A*
   Southcentral *C, A*
   Southeast *A*
   Southwest *C, A*
   Wabash Valley *A*
   Whitewater *A*
Oakland City University *A*
Purdue University
   Calumet *B*
   North Central Campus *A*
Purdue University *A, B*
University of Southern Indiana *A*
Vincennes University *A*

Iowa
Clinton Community College *A*
Des Moines Area Community College *A*
Hamilton Technical College *A, B*
Hawkeye Community College *A*
Indian Hills Community College *A*
Iowa Western Community College *A*
Kirkwood Community College *A*
Northeast Iowa Community College *A*
Southeastern Community College
   North Campus *A*
Southwestern Community College *A*
Western Iowa Tech Community
   College *A*

Kansas
Allen County Community College *C*
Johnson County Community College *A*
Kansas City Kansas Community
   College *C, A*
Kansas State University *A, B*
Pittsburg State University *B*
Washburn University of Topeka *A*
Wichita State University *A*

Kentucky
Henderson Community College *A*
ITT Technical Institute
   Louisville *A*
Institute of Electronic Technology *A*
Kentucky State University *A*
Lexington Community College *A*
Maysville Community College *A*
Murray State University *A, B*
Northern Kentucky University *B*
Owensboro Community College *A*
Western Kentucky University *B*

Louisiana
Delgado Community College *A*
Grantham College of Engineering *A, B*
ITT Technical Institute
   St. Rose *A*
Louisiana Tech University *B*
McNeese State University *A, B*
Northwestern State University *A, B*
Remington College - Education America,
   Inc. *A*
Southern University
   Shreveport *A*
Southern University and Agricultural and
   Mechanical College *A, B*

Maine
Eastern Maine Technical College *A*
Kennebec Valley Technical College *A*
Southern Maine Technical College *A*
University of Maine *B*

Maryland
Baltimore City Community College *A*
Cecil Community College *C, A*
Charles County Community
   College *C, A*
Chesapeake College *C*
Frederick Community College *C, A*
Hagerstown Community College *C, A*
Harford Community College *C, A*
Howard Community College *C, A*
Montgomery College
   Germantown Campus *C, A*
   Rockville Campus *A*
Prince George's Community
   College *C, A*
University of Maryland
   Eastern Shore *B*

Massachusetts
Berkshire Community College *A*
Bristol Community College *A*
Bunker Hill Community College *C, A*
Franklin Institute of Boston *C, A*
Holyoke Community College *A*
ITT Technical Institute
   Framingham *A*
Massachusetts Bay Community
   College *C, A*
Massasoit Community College *A*
Mount Wachusett Community
   College *C, A*
Northeastern University *A, B*
Northern Essex Community
   College *C, A*
Springfield Technical Community
   College *A*
University of Massachusetts
   Dartmouth *B*
   Lowell *A, B*
Wentworth Institute of Technology *A, B*

Michigan
Andrews University *A*
Baker College
   of Mount Clemens *A*
   of Muskegon *A, B*
   of Owosso *A*
Bay de Noc Community College *C, A*
Central Michigan University *B*
Ferris State University *A, B*
Glen Oaks Community College *C*
Grand Rapids Community College *A*
Great Lakes College *C, A*
Henry Ford Community College *A*
ITT Technical Institute
   Grand Rapids *A*
   Troy *A*
Jackson Community College *C, A*
Kalamazoo Valley Community
   College *C, A*
Kellogg Community College *C, A*
Lake Michigan College *A*
Lake Superior State University *A, B*
Lansing Community College *A*
Lawrence Technological University *A*
Macomb Community College *C, A*
Michigan Technological University *A, B*
Monroe County Community College *A*
Montcalm Community College *A*
Mott Community College *A*
Muskegon Community College *C, A*
Northern Michigan University *B*
Northwestern Michigan College *C*
Oakland Community College *C, A*
St. Clair County Community
   College *C, A*
Schoolcraft College *A*
Southwestern Michigan College *C, A*
Washtenaw Community College *A*
Wayne County Community College *C*
Wayne State University *B*
West Shore Community College *A*

Minnesota
Anoka-Ramsey Community College *A*
Hennepin Technical College *C, A*
Lake Superior College: A Community
   and Technical College *C, A*
Minnesota State University, Mankato *B*
NEI College of Technology *A*
North Hennepin Community College *A*
Ridgewater College: A Community and
   Technical College *C, A*
Rochester Community and Technical
   College *A*
St. Cloud Technical College *C, A*
St. Paul Technical College *C*
South Central Technical College *A*

Mississippi
Coahoma Community College *A*
Copiah-Lincoln Community
   College *C, A*
East Central Community College *A*
Hinds Community College *A*
Itawamba Community College *A*
Mississippi Delta Community College *A*
Mississippi Gulf Coast Community
   College
     Jackson County Campus *A*
     Jefferson Davis Campus *A*
     Perkinston *A*
Northwest Mississippi Community
   College *A*
University of Southern Mississippi *B*

Missouri
Central Missouri State University *A, B*
Crowder College *C, A*
DeVry Institute of Technology
   Kansas City *A, B*
East Central College *A*
ITT Technical Institute
   Arnold *A*
   Earth City *A, B*
Lincoln University *A*
Longview Community College *A*
Maple Woods Community College *C, A*
Mineral Area College *C, A*
Missouri Western State College *A, B*
Moberly Area Community College *C, A*
Ozarks Technical Community
   College *C, A*
Penn Valley Community College *C, A*
St. Charles County Community
   College *A*
Southeast Missouri State University *C, B*
Southwest Missouri State University *B*
St. Louis Community College
   St. Louis Community College at
     Florissant Valley *A*
   St. Louis Community College at
     Forest Park *A*
   St. Louis Community College at
     Meramec *A*
State Fair Community College *A*

Montana
Montana State University
   Bozeman *B*
   Northern *A, B*

Nebraska
Central Community College *C, A*
ITT Technical Institute
   Omaha *A*
Metropolitan Community College *C, A*
Northeast Community College *A*
Southeast Community College
   Lincoln Campus *A*
University of Nebraska
   Omaha *B*

Nevada
Community College of Southern
   Nevada *A*

Electrical/electronic engineering-related technologies

ITT Technical Institute
    Henderson *A*
Western Nevada Community
    College *C, A*

New Hampshire
Keene State College *A, B*
New Hampshire Community Technical
    College
    Manchester *A*
    Nashua *A*
New Hampshire Technical Institute *A*
University of New Hampshire
    Manchester *B*
University of New Hampshire *B*

New Jersey
Atlantic Cape Community College *A*
Bergen Community College *A*
Brookdale Community College *C*
Burlington County College *A*
Camden County College *A*
County College of Morris *A*
DeVry Institute *A, B*
Essex County College *A*
Hudson County Community
    College *C, A*
Mercer County Community College *C, A*
Middlesex County College *A*
Passaic County Community College *A*
Salem Community College *C*
Thomas Edison State College *C, A, B*

New Mexico
Albuquerque Technical-Vocational
    Institute *C, A*
Dona Ana Branch Community College of
    New Mexico State University *C, A*
ITT Technical Institute
    Albuquerque *A, B*
New Mexico State University
    Alamogordo *A*
    Carlsbad *A*
Northern New Mexico Community
    College *C, A*
San Juan College *A*

New York
Adirondack Community College *A*
Briarcliffe College *C, A*
Broome Community College *A*
Cayuga County Community
    College *C, A*
City University of New York
    Bronx Community College *A*
    College of Staten Island *A*
    New York City Technical
        College *A*
    Queensborough Community
        College *A*
Clinton Community College *A*
College of Aeronautics *A, B*
Corning Community College *A*
DeVry Institute of Technology
    New York *A, B*
Dutchess Community College *A*
Erie Community College
    North Campus *A*
Fulton-Montgomery Community
    College *A*
Genesee Community College *A*
Hudson Valley Community College *A*
ITT Technical Institute
    Albany *A*
    Getzville *A*
    Liverpool *A*
Jamestown Community College *A*
Mohawk Valley Community College *A*
Monroe Community College *C, A*
Nassau Community College *A*
New York Institute of Technology *A, B*
Niagara County Community College *A*
Onondaga Community College *A*
Orange County Community College *A*
Regents College *A, B*
Rochester Institute of
    Technology *A, B, M*
Rockland Community College *A*
Schenectady County Community
    College *A*
State University of New York
    College at Buffalo *B*
    College of Agriculture and
        Technology at Morrisville *A*
    College of Technology at
        Alfred *A, B*
    College of Technology at Canton *A*
        Farmingdale *C, A, B*
    Institute of Technology at
        Utica/Rome *B*
Technical Career Institutes *A*
Tompkins-Cortland Community
    College *C, A*
Westchester Community College *C, A*

North Carolina
Asheville Buncombe Technical
    Community College *A*
Beaufort County Community College *A*
Bladen Community College *C, A*
Blue Ridge Community College *C, A*
Brunswick Community College *C, A*
Caldwell Community College and
    Technical Institute *A*
Cape Fear Community College *A*
Catawba Valley Community College *A*
Central Carolina Community College *A*
Central Piedmont Community College *A*
Cleveland Community College *C, A*
College of the Albemarle *C, A*
Craven Community College *C, A*
Davidson County Community College *C*
Durham Technical Community
    College *C, A*
East Carolina University *B*
Edgecombe Community College *C, A*
Fayetteville Technical Community
    College *A*
Forsyth Technical Community College *A*
Guilford Technical Community
    College *C, A*
Halifax Community College *A*
Haywood Community College *A*
Johnston Community College *A*
Lenoir Community College *A*
Mitchell Community College *C, A*
Montgomery Community College *A*
Nash Community College *A*
Pitt Community College *A*
Randolph Community College *A*
Richmond Community College *A*
Rowan-Cabarrus Community College *A*
South Piedmont Community College *A*
Southeastern Community College *A*
Southwestern Community College *A*
Surry Community College *C, A*
University of North Carolina
    Charlotte *B*
Vance-Granville Community
    College *C, A*
Wake Technical Community
    College *C, A*
Western Carolina University *B*
Wilkes Community College *C, A*
Wilson Technical Community
    College *C, A*

North Dakota
North Dakota State College of Science *A*

Ohio
Bowling Green State University
    Firelands College *A*
Bowling Green State University *B*
Bryant & Stratton College *A, B*
Cincinnati State Technical and
    Community College *A*
Clark State Community College *C*
Cleveland Institute of Electronics *C, A*
Cleveland State University *B*
Columbus State Community College *A*
DeVry Institute of Technology
    Columbus *A, B*
Edison State Community College *A*
Hocking Technical College *A*
ITT Technical Institute
    Dayton *A*
    Norwood *A*
    Strongsville *A*
    Youngstown *A*
Jefferson Community College *A*
Kent State University
    Ashtabula Regional Campus *A*
    Trumbull Campus *A*
    Tuscarawas Campus *A*
Kent State University *B*
Lakeland Community College *C, A*
Lima Technical College *A*
Miami University
    Hamilton Campus *A*
    Middletown Campus *C, A, B*
    Oxford Campus *A*
Muskingum Area Technical College *A*
North Central State College *A*
Northwest State Community College *C*
Ohio Northern University *B*
Ohio University *A*
Owens Community College
    Findlay Campus *A*
Shawnee State University *A, B*
Sinclair Community College *A*
Southern State Community College *A*
Stark State College of Technology *A*
Terra Community College *A*
University of Akron
    Wayne College *A*
University of Akron *A, B*
University of Cincinnati
    Clermont College *A*
University of Dayton *B*
University of Toledo *A, B*
Washington State Community College *A*
Youngstown State University *A, B*

Oklahoma
Cameron University *A*
Oklahoma City Community College *A*
Oklahoma State University
    Oklahoma City *A*
    Okmulgee *A*
Oklahoma State University *B*
Redlands Community College *C, A*
Rogers State University *A*
Rose State College *C, A*
Southeastern Oklahoma State
    University *B*
Tulsa Community College *C, A*

Oregon
Central Oregon Community College *C*
Chemeketa Community College *A*
ITT Technical Institute
    Portland *A*
Lane Community College *A*
Linn-Benton Community College *A*
Oregon Institute of Technology *A, B*
Portland Community College *A*

Pennsylvania
Butler County Community College *A*
C.H.I/RETS Campus *A*
California University of
    Pennsylvania *A, B*
Community College of Allegheny
    County *C, A*
Community College of Beaver County *A*
Community College of Philadelphia *C, A*
Delaware County Community College *A*
Edinboro University of Pennsylvania *A*
Electronic Institutes: Middletown *A*
Harrisburg Area Community
    College *C, A*
ICS Center for Degree Studies *A*
ITT Technical Institute
    Mechanicsburg *A*
    Monroeville *A*
    Pittsburgh *A*
Lehigh Carbon Community College *C, A*
Luzerne County Community
    College *C, A*
Montgomery County Community
    College *A*
Northampton County Area Community
    College *A*
Peirce College *C, A, B*
Penn State
    Altoona *A*
    Beaver *A*
    Berks *A*
    Dubois *A*
    Erie, The Behrend College *A, B*
    Fayette *A*
    Harrisburg *B*
    Hazleton *A*
    Lehigh Valley *B*
    New Kensington *A*
    Schuylkill - Capital College *A*
    Shenango *A*
    University Park *C, B*
    Wilkes-Barre *A, B*
    York *A*
Pennsylvania College of Technology *A*
Pennsylvania Institute of Technology *A*
Pittsburgh Institute of Aeronautics *A*
Pittsburgh Technical Institute *A*
Point Park College *A, B*
Reading Area Community College *A*
Temple University *C, A*
University of Pittsburgh
    Johnstown *B*
Westmoreland County Community
    College *A*

Puerto Rico
Inter American University of Puerto Rico
    Aguadilla Campus *B*
    Bayamon Campus *B*
    Metropolitan Campus *B*
National College of Business and
    Technology *A*
Technological College of San Juan *A*
University of Puerto Rico
    Aguadilla *A, B*
    Bayamon University College *A*
    Humacao University College *A*

Rhode Island
Community College of Rhode
    Island *C, A*
Johnson & Wales University *A, B*
New England Institute of Technology *A*

South Carolina
Aiken Technical College *A*
Chesterfield-Marlboro Technical
    College *C, A*
Florence-Darlington Technical College *A*
Francis Marion University *B*
Greenville Technical College *A*
ITT Technical Institute
    Greenville *A*
Midlands Technical College *A*
Orangeburg-Calhoun Technical
    College *A*
Piedmont Technical College *A*
South Carolina State University *B*
Spartanburg Technical College *A*
Technical College of the Lowcountry *C*
Tri-County Technical College *A*
Trident Technical College *A*
York Technical College *A*

South Dakota
South Dakota State University *B*
Southeast Technical Institute *A*

Tennessee
Columbia State Community College *A*
ITT Technical Institute
    Knoxville *A, B*
    Memphis *A*
    Nashville *A, B*
Motlow State Community College *A*
Nashville State Technical Institute *A*

Northeast State Technical Community College C, A
Pellissippi State Technical Community College A
University of Memphis B

Texas
Amarillo College C, A
Angelina College A
Austin Community College C, A
Brazosport College C, A
Brookhaven College A
College of the Mainland A
Collin County Community College District C, A
DeVry Institute of Technology Irving A, B
Del Mar College A
Eastfield College C, A
El Paso Community College C, A
Grayson County College A
Hill College C, A
Houston Community College System C, A
ITT Technical Institute
  Arlington A
  Austin A
  Houston North A
  Houston South A
  Houston A
  Richardson A
  San Antonio A
Lamar State College at Port Arthur C, A
LeTourneau University B
Lee College A
McMurry University B
Midland College C, A
Mountain View College A
North Central Texas College A
North Lake College A
Paris Junior College A
Prairie View A&M University B
Richland College A
St. Philip's College A
Sam Houston State University B
San Antonio College C, A
San Jacinto College
  North C, A
Tarrant County College A
Texas State Technical College
  Harlingen A
  Sweetwater C, A
  Waco C, A
Texas Tech University B
Tyler Junior College A
University of Houston Downtown B
University of Houston B, M
University of North Texas B
Victoria College A
Weatherford College C, A
Wharton County Junior College A

Utah
Brigham Young University M
ITT Technical Institute Murray A, B
Salt Lake Community College A
Snow College A
Utah State University B
Utah Valley State College A
Weber State University A, B

Vermont
Vermont Technical College A

Virginia
Blue Ridge Community College A
Central Virginia Community College A
Dabney S. Lancaster Community College C, A
ECPI College of Technology C, A
ITT Technical Institute
  Norfolk A
  Richmond A
J. Sargeant Reynolds Community College C, A
John Tyler Community College A
Lord Fairfax Community College A
Mountain Empire Community College A
New River Community College A
Norfolk State University A, B
Northern Virginia Community College C, A
Paul D. Camp Community College A
Piedmont Virginia Community College A
Southside Virginia Community College C, A
Virginia Highlands Community College A
Virginia Western Community College A
Wytheville Community College A

Washington
Central Washington University B
Centralia College A
Clark College A
Columbia Basin College A
Eastern Washington University B
Edmonds Community College C, A
Green River Community College A
Highline Community College A
ITT Technical Institute
  Bothell A
  Seattle A, B
  Spokane A
Lake Washington Technical College C, A
Lower Columbia College A
North Seattle Community College A
Peninsula College A
Pierce College C, A
Renton Technical College C, A
Skagit Valley College A
South Puget Sound Community College C, A
Spokane Community College C, A
Spokane Falls Community College C, A
Walla Walla College A, B
Western Washington University B

West Virginia
Bluefield State College A, B
College of West Virginia A
Corinthian Schools: National Institute of Technology A
Fairmont State College A, B
Marshall University B
Potomac State College of West Virginia University A
Shepherd College A
West Virginia Northern Community College A
West Virginia State College A
West Virginia University Parkersburg A
West Virginia University Institute of Technology A, B

Wisconsin
Blackhawk Technical College A
Chippewa Valley Technical College A
Gateway Technical College A
Herzing College A
ITT Technical Institute Greenfield A, B
Lakeshore Technical College A
Milwaukee Area Technical College A
Milwaukee School of Engineering A, B
Northeast Wisconsin Technical College A
Southwest Wisconsin Technical College A
Western Wisconsin Technical College A

Wyoming
Casper College A

Electrical/electronics/communications engineering

Alabama
Alabama Agricultural and Mechanical University B
Auburn University B, M, D
Lawson State Community College A
Northwest-Shoals Community College C, A
Tuskegee University B, M
University of Alabama
  Birmingham B, M, D
  Huntsville B, M, D
University of Alabama B, M, D
University of South Alabama B, M
Wallace State Community College at Hanceville A

Alaska
University of Alaska Fairbanks B, M

Arizona
Arizona State University B, M, D
Embry-Riddle Aeronautical University Prescott Campus B
Northern Arizona University B
University of Arizona B, M, D

Arkansas
Arkansas State University Mountain Home C, A
Arkansas Tech University B
John Brown University B
University of Arkansas M

California
California Institute of Technology B, M, D
California Polytechnic State University: San Luis Obispo B, M
California State Polytechnic University: Pomona B, M
California State University
  Chico B, M
  Fresno B
  Fullerton B, M
  Long Beach B, M
  Los Angeles B, M
  Northridge B, M
  Sacramento B, M
City College of San Francisco C, A
Cogswell Polytechnic College B
College of the Canyons C, A
College of the Redwoods A
Cuesta College C, A
De Anza College A
DeVry Institute of Technology West Hills A, B
East Los Angeles College A
Los Angeles Harbor College C, A
Los Angeles Southwest College C, A
Loyola Marymount University B, M
Merritt College C, A
Modesto Junior College A
Saddleback College C
San Diego State University B, M
San Francisco State University B
San Jose State University B, M
Santa Clara University B, M, D
Stanford University B, M, D
University of California
  Berkeley B, M, D
  Davis B
  Irvine B, M, D
  Los Angeles B, M, D
  Riverside B, M, D
  San Diego B, M, D
  Santa Barbara B, M, D
University of San Diego B
University of Southern California B, M, D
University of the Pacific B

Colorado
Colorado State University B, M, D
Colorado Technical University B, M
Denver Technical College: A Division of DeVry University A, B
National Technological University M
United States Air Force Academy B
University of Colorado
  Boulder B, M, D
  Colorado Springs B, M, D
  Denver B, M
University of Denver B, M

Connecticut
Fairfield University B
Hartford Graduate Center M
Trinity College B
United States Coast Guard Academy B
University of Bridgeport M
University of Connecticut B, M, D
University of Hartford B, M
University of New Haven A, B, M
Yale University B, M, D

Delaware
University of Delaware B, M, D

District of Columbia
Catholic University of America B, M, D
George Washington University B, M, D
Howard University B, M, D
University of the District of Columbia B

Florida
Broward Community College A
Florida Agricultural and Mechanical University B, M, D
Florida Atlantic University B, M, D
Florida Institute of Technology B, M, D
Florida International University B, M, D
Florida State University B, M, D
Gulf Coast Community College A
Hillsborough Community College C, A
Indian River Community College A
Jacksonville University B
Miami-Dade Community College A
Palm Beach Community College A
Pensacola Junior College A
Seminole Community College C, A
South Florida Community College C, A
University of Central Florida B, M, D
University of Florida B, M, D
University of Miami B, M, D
University of North Florida B
University of South Florida B, M, D
University of West Florida B

Georgia
DeKalb Technical Institute A
Georgia Institute of Technology B, M, D
Mercer University B, M
Middle Georgia College A
Thomas College A

Hawaii
University of Hawaii Manoa B, M, D

Idaho
Boise State University B
College of Southern Idaho A
North Idaho College A
Ricks College A
University of Idaho B, M, D

Illinois
Bradley University B, M
City Colleges of Chicago Olive-Harvey College C, A
Dominican University B
Illinois Institute of Technology B, M, D
Joliet Junior College C, A
Northern Illinois University B, M
Northwestern University B, M, D
Parkland College A
Sauk Valley Community College C, A

Southern Illinois University
   Carbondale *B, M*
   Edwardsville *B, M*
University of Illinois
   Chicago *B, M, D*
   Urbana-Champaign *B, M, D*

Indiana
Indiana Institute of Technology *B*
Indiana University--Purdue University
   Indiana University-Purdue
      University Fort Wayne *B*
   Indiana University-Purdue
      University Indianapolis *B, M*
Purdue University
   Calumet *B*
Purdue University *B, M, D*
Rose-Hulman Institute of
   Technology *B, M*
Tri-State University *B*
University of Evansville *B*
University of Notre Dame *B, M, D*
Valparaiso University *B*

Iowa
Dordt College *B*
Iowa State University *B, M, D*
Maharishi University of Management *B*
Northeast Iowa Community College *A*
Southeastern Community College
   North Campus *A*
University of Iowa *B, M, D*

Kansas
Allen County Community College *C, A*
Kansas State University *B, M, D*
University of Kansas *B, M, D*
Wichita State University *B, M, D*

Kentucky
Institute of Electronic Technology *A*
Northern Kentucky University *B*
University of Kentucky *B, M, D*
University of Louisville *B, M*

Louisiana
Grantham College of Engineering *A, B*
Louisiana State University and
   Agricultural and Mechanical
   College *B, M, D*
Louisiana Tech University *B*
Southern University and Agricultural and
   Mechanical College *B*
Tulane University *B, M, D*
University of Louisiana at Lafayette *B*
University of New Orleans *B*

Maine
Kennebec Valley Technical College *A*
Southern Maine Technical College *A*
University of Maine *B, M*
University of New England *A*
University of Southern Maine *B*

Maryland
Anne Arundel Community College *C*
Charles County Community College *A*
Johns Hopkins University *B, M, D*
Loyola College in Maryland *B*
Morgan State University *B*
United States Naval Academy *B*
University of Maryland
   Baltimore County *M, D*
   College Park *B, M, D*
Wor-Wic Community College *A*

Massachusetts
Berkshire Community College *A*
Boston University *B, M, D*
Fitchburg State College *B*
Franklin Institute of Boston *A*
Massachusetts Institute of
   Technology *B, M, D*
Merrimack College *B*
Northeastern University *B, M, D*
Suffolk University *B*
Tufts University *B, M, D*

University of Massachusetts
   Amherst *B*
   Dartmouth *B, M, D*
   Lowell *B, M, D*
Wentworth Institute of Technology *B*
Western New England College *B, M*
Worcester Polytechnic Institute *B, M, D*

Michigan
Calvin College *B*
Grand Valley State University *B*
Kettering University *B*
Lake Superior State University *B*
Lawrence Technological University *B*
Michigan State University *B, M, D*
Michigan Technological
   University *B, M, D, T*
Monroe County Community College *A*
Oakland University *B, M*
Saginaw Valley State University *B*
University of Detroit Mercy *B, M, D*
University of Michigan
   Dearborn *B, M*
University of Michigan *B, M, D*
Wayne State University *B, M, D*
Western Michigan University *B, M*

Minnesota
Concordia College: Moorhead *B*
Minnesota State College - Southeast
   Technical *C, A*
Minnesota State University,
   Mankato *B, M*
St. Cloud State University *B*
South Central Technical College *A*
University of Minnesota
   Duluth *B*
   Twin Cities *C, B, M, D*

Mississippi
Holmes Community College *A*
Jackson State University *B*
Meridian Community College *A*
Mississippi State University *B, M, D*
University of Mississippi *B*

Missouri
East Central College *A*
Ozarks Technical Community College *A*
St. Louis University *B, M*
University of Missouri
   Columbia *B, M, D*
   Kansas City *B, M*
   Rolla *B, M, D*
   St. Louis *B*
Washington University *B, M, D*

Montana
Montana State University
   Bozeman *B, M*

Nebraska
Southeast Community College
   Milford Campus *A*
University of Nebraska
   Lincoln *B, M*
   Omaha *B*

Nevada
Community College of Southern
   Nevada *C, A*
University of Nevada
   Las Vegas *B, M, D*
   Reno *B, M, D*

New Hampshire
New Hampshire Community Technical
   College
      Nashua *A*
University of New Hampshire *B, M*

New Jersey
Essex County College *A*
Monmouth University *M*
New Jersey Institute of
   Technology *B, M, D*
Ocean County College *C*
Princeton University *B, M, D*

Rowan University *B*
Rutgers
   The State University of New Jersey:
      College of Engineering *B*
   The State University of New Jersey:
      New Brunswick Graduate
      Campus *M, D*
Seton Hall University *B*
Stevens Institute of Technology *B, M, D*

New Mexico
Dona Ana Branch Community College of
   New Mexico State University *C, A*
New Mexico Institute of Mining and
   Technology *B*
New Mexico State University *B, M*
University of New Mexico *B, M*

New York
Alfred University *B, M*
Cayuga County Community College *A*
City University of New York
   City College *B, M, D*
   College of Staten Island *A*
   Graduate School and University
      Center *D*
Clarkson University *B, M, D*
Columbia University
   Fu Foundation School of
      Engineering and Applied
      Science *B, M, D*
Cooper Union for the Advancement of
   Science and Art *B*
Cornell University *B, M, D*
DeVry Institute of Technology
   New York *A, B*
Finger Lakes Community College *A*
Fulton-Montgomery Community
   College *C, A*
Hofstra University *B*
Manhattan College *B, M*
New York Institute of
   Technology *A, B, M*
New York University *B*
Onondaga Community College *A*
Pace University:
   Pleasantville/Briarcliff *B*
Pace University *B*
Polytechnic University
   Long Island Campus *B, M, D*
Polytechnic University *B, M, D*
Rensselaer Polytechnic Institute *B, M, D*
Rochester Institute of Technology *B, M*
State University of New York
   Binghamton *B, M, D*
   Buffalo *B, M, D*
   College of Agriculture and
      Technology at Morrisville *A*
   Maritime College *B*
   New Paltz *B, M*
   Stony Brook *B, M, D*
Suffolk County Community College *A*
Syracuse University *B, M, D*
Union College *B, M*
United States Military Academy *B*
University of Rochester *B, M, D*
Utica College of Syracuse University *B*

North Carolina
Alamance Community College *A*
Appalachian State University *B*
Beaufort County Community College *A*
Blue Ridge Community College *A*
Cape Fear Community College *A*
College of the Albemarle *A*
Davidson County Community
   College *C, A*
Duke University *B, M, D*
Durham Technical Community
   College *C, A*
Edgecombe Community College *A*
Guilford Technical Community
   College *C, A*
Mayland Community College *A*
Mitchell Community College *C, A*
Nash Community College *A*

North Carolina Agricultural and
   Technical State University *B, M, D*
North Carolina State University *B, M, D*
Richmond Community College *A*
Rockingham Community College *A*
Southwestern Community College *A*
University of North Carolina
   Charlotte *B, M, D*
Vance-Granville Community
   College *C, A*

North Dakota
North Dakota State University *B, M*
University of North Dakota *B, M*

Ohio
Belmont Technical College *A*
Case Western Reserve
   University *B, M, D*
Cedarville College *B*
Central Ohio Technical College *C, A*
Cleveland State University *B, M, D*
Columbus State Community College *A*
Edison State Community College *A*
Hocking Technical College *A*
Kent State University
   Ashtabula Regional Campus *A*
   Trumbull Campus *A*
Marion Technical College *A*
Ohio Northern University *B*
Ohio State University
   Columbus Campus *B, M, D*
Ohio University *B, M, D*
RETS Tech Center *C, A*
University of Akron *B, M, D*
University of Cincinnati *B, M, D*
University of Dayton *B, M, D*
University of Toledo *B, M*
Washington State Community College *A*
Wilberforce University *B*
Wright State University *B, M*
Youngstown State University *B, M*

Oklahoma
Oklahoma Christian University of
   Science and Arts *B*
Oklahoma State University
   Oklahoma City *A*
Oklahoma State University *B, M, D*
Oral Roberts University *B*
Rogers State University *A*
University of Oklahoma *B, M, D*
University of Tulsa *B, M*

Oregon
Chemeketa Community College *A*
George Fox University *B*
Oregon Graduate Institute *M, D*
Oregon State University *B*
Portland State University *B*
University of Portland *B, M*

Pennsylvania
Bucknell University *B, M*
Carnegie Mellon University *B, M, D*
Drexel University *B, M, D*
Gannon University *B, M*
Geneva College *B*
Gettysburg College *B*
Grove City College *B*
Lafayette College *B*
Lehigh Carbon Community College *A*
Lehigh University *B, M, D*
Lock Haven University of
   Pennsylvania *B*
Penn State
   Berks *B*
   Erie, The Behrend College *A, B*
   Harrisburg *B, M*
   University Park *B, M, D*
Pittsburgh Institute of Aeronautics *A*
Reading Area Community College *A*
Temple University *B, M*
University of Pennsylvania *B, M, D*
University of Pittsburgh *B, M, D*
University of Scranton *A, B*
Villanova University *B, M*

Widener University *B, M*
Wilkes University *B, M*

Puerto Rico
Columbia College *A*
Inter American University of Puerto Rico
 Bayamon Campus *B*
Turabo University *B*
Universidad Politecnica de Puerto
 Rico *B*
University of Puerto Rico
 Mayaguez Campus *B, M*

Rhode Island
Brown University *B, M, D*
Johnson & Wales University *A, B*
University of Rhode Island *B, M, D*

South Carolina
Clemson University *B, M, D*
Greenville Technical College *A*
Horry-Georgetown Technical College *A*
Technical College of the
 Lowcountry *C, A*
The Citadel *B*
University of South Carolina *B, M, D*

South Dakota
South Dakota School of Mines and
 Technology *B, M*
South Dakota State University *B*

Tennessee
Christian Brothers University *B*
Columbia State Community College *C*
Motlow State Community College *C*
Tennessee State University *B*
Tennessee Technological
 University *B, M, D*
University of Memphis *B, M*
University of Tennessee
 Knoxville *B, M, D*
Vanderbilt University *B, M, D*

Texas
Abilene Christian University *B*
Baylor University *B*
Del Mar College *A*
Houston Baptist University *B*
Lamar University *B*
LeTourneau University *B*
Prairie View A&M University *B*
Rice University *B, M, D*
St. Mary's University *B, M*
Southern Methodist University *B, M, D*
Texas A&M University
 Kingsville *B, M*
Texas A&M University *B, M, D*
Texas Tech University *B, M, D*
University of Houston *B, M, D*
University of Texas
 Arlington *B, M, D*
 Austin *B, M, D*
 Dallas *B, M, D*
 El Paso *B, M*
 Pan American *B*
 San Antonio *B, M*

Utah
Brigham Young University *B, M, D*
Salt Lake Community College *A*
Snow College *C, A*
University of Utah *B, M, D*
Utah State University *B, M, D*
Utah Valley State College *A*

Vermont
Norwich University *B*
University of Vermont *B, M, D*
Vermont Technical College *A*

Virginia
ECPI College of Technology *C, A*
George Mason University *B, M*
Hampton University *B*
John Tyler Community College *A*
Norfolk State University *B*
Old Dominion University *B*

Southwest Virginia Community
 College *A*
Thomas Nelson Community College *A*
University of Virginia *B, M, D*
Virginia Commonwealth University *B*
Virginia Military Institute *B*
Virginia Polytechnic Institute and State
 University *B, M, D*

Washington
Gonzaga University *B*
Henry Cogswell College *B*
Renton Technical College *C, A*
Seattle Pacific University *B*
Seattle University *B*
Skagit Valley College *C, A*
University of Washington *B, M, D*
Walla Walla College *B*
Washington State University *B, M, D*

West Virginia
College of West Virginia *A*
Potomac State College of West Virginia
 University *A*
West Virginia State College *A*
West Virginia University Institute of
 Technology *B*
West Virginia University *B, M, D*

Wisconsin
Blackhawk Technical College *A*
Marquette University *B, M, D*
Milwaukee School of Engineering *B*
University of Wisconsin
 Madison *B, M, D*
 Milwaukee *B*
 Platteville *B*

Wyoming
University of Wyoming *B, M, D*
Western Wyoming Community
 College *C, A*

Electrician

Alabama
George C. Wallace State Community
 College
 Dothan *C, A*
J. F. Drake State Technical College *C*
Sparks State Technical College *A*

California
Allan Hancock College *C*
Diablo Valley College *C*
Foothill College *C*
Fresno City College *C, A*
Modesto Junior College *C, A*

Florida
Brevard Community College *C*
Central Florida Community College *C*
South Florida Community College *C*

Georgia
Chattahoochee Technical Institute *C*

Hawaii
University of Hawaii
 Honolulu Community College *C, A*
 Kauai Community College *C, A*

Idaho
Idaho State University *C*

Illinois
Black Hawk College *A*
Danville Area Community College *C*
John Wood Community College *C, A*
Prairie State College *C, A*
Sauk Valley Community College *C*
Southwestern Illinois College *C, A*
Waubonsee Community College *C*

Indiana
Ivy Tech State College
 Central Indiana *C, A*
 Kokomo *C, A*
 Lafayette *C*
 Northcentral *C, A*
 Northeast *C, A*
 Northwest *C, A*
 Southwest *C, A*
 Wabash Valley *C, A*
Oakland City University *C*

Iowa
Iowa Central Community College *A*

Kansas
Pittsburg State University *C*

Maine
Eastern Maine Technical College *C*
Washington County Technical College *C*

Massachusetts
Franklin Institute of Boston *C, A*

Michigan
Kellogg Community College *C, A*
Northern Michigan University *A*

Minnesota
Dunwoody Institute *C, A*
Hennepin Technical College *C, A*
Hibbing Community College: A
 Technical and Community College *C*
Lake Superior College: A Community
 and Technical College *C, A*
Ridgewater College: A Community and
 Technical College *C*
St. Cloud Technical College *C, A*
St. Paul Technical College *C*

Mississippi
Itawamba Community College *A*
Mississippi Gulf Coast Community
 College
 Jefferson Davis Campus *C*

Nebraska
Mid Plains Community College Area *C*
Northeast Community College *A*

Nevada
Western Nevada Community College *A*

New Hampshire
New Hampshire Community Technical
 College
 Laconia *C, A*

New Mexico
Albuquerque Technical-Vocational
 Institute *C*
Dona Ana Branch Community College of
 New Mexico State University *A*
Northern New Mexico Community
 College *C, A*

New York
Dutchess Community College *A*
State University of New York
 College of Technology at Canton *C*

North Carolina
Beaufort County Community College *C*
Blue Ridge Community College *C*
Cleveland Community College *C*
Coastal Carolina Community College *A*
Haywood Community College *C, A*
Johnston Community College *C*
Pitt Community College *A*
Rockingham Community College *C*
Southwestern Community College *C*
Tri-County Community College *A*
Vance-Granville Community College *C*

North Dakota
North Dakota State College of Science *A*

Oregon
Central Oregon Community College *C*

Lane Community College *A*

Pennsylvania
Delaware County Community College *C*
Luzerne County Community College *A*
Triangle Tech
 DuBois Campus *A*

South Carolina
Trident Technical College *A*

South Dakota
Western Dakota Technical Institute *A*

Tennessee
Northeast State Technical Community
 College *C, A*

Texas
Brazosport College *C, A*
St. Philip's College *C, A*
Texas State Technical College
 Waco *C*

Utah
Dixie State College of Utah *C*
Salt Lake Community College *A*

Virginia
Central Virginia Community College *C*
Virginia Highlands Community
 College *C*

Washington
Big Bend Community College *A*

Wisconsin
Gateway Technical College *C*
Northeast Wisconsin Technical
 College *C*

Electrocardiograph technology

California
De Anza College *C*
East Los Angeles College *A*

Colorado
Denver Technical College: A Division of
 DeVry University *A*

Massachusetts
Middlesex Community College *C*
North Shore Community College *C*

Michigan
Baker College
 of Auburn Hills *A*
Monroe County Community College *C*

Minnesota
North Hennepin Community College *A*

New York
Niagara County Community College *C*

Ohio
Cincinnati State Technical and
 Community College *C*
Columbus State Community College *C*
University of Toledo *C*

South Carolina
Tri-County Technical College *C*

Virginia
Southwest Virginia Community
 College *C*

Electrodiagnostic technologies

Alabama
Central Alabama Community College *A*

California
Orange Coast College *C, A*
San Joaquin Delta College *A*

Electrodiagnostic technologies

Florida
Miami-Dade Community College *A*
Santa Fe Community College *A*

Kansas
Newman University *B*

Pennsylvania
Carlow College *C*

Washington
Spokane Community College *A*

Wisconsin
Western Wisconsin Technical College *A*

Electroencephalograph technology

Arizona
Phoenix College *C*

California
California College for Health Sciences *A*
Orange Coast College *C, A*

Illinois
Black Hawk College *A*
Springfield College in Illinois *A*

Iowa
Kirkwood Community College *A*

Maryland
Harford Community College *A*

North Carolina
Southwestern Community College *A*

Electromechanical instrumentation

Alabama
Community College of the Air Force *A*
Jefferson State Community College *C, A*
John M. Patterson State Technical College *A*
Northwest-Shoals Community College *A*

Alaska
University of Alaska
 Anchorage *A*

Arizona
Gateway Community College *C, A*
Mesa Community College *A*
Pima Community College *C, A*

Arkansas
John Brown University *A*
North Arkansas College *A*
Phillips Community College of the University of Arkansas *C, A*
Southern Arkansas University Tech *A*
University of Arkansas for Medical Sciences *A*

California
Chabot College *A*
City College of San Francisco *A*
Foothill College *C, A*
Long Beach City College *C, A*
Los Angeles Southwest College *A*
Los Angeles Trade and Technical College *C, A*
Moorpark College *A*
Ohlone College *C, A*
Pasadena City College *C, A*
San Diego City College *A*

Colorado
Colorado Northwestern Community College *A*
Pikes Peak Community College *A*

Delaware
Delaware Technical and Community College
 Stanton/Wilmington Campus *A*
 Terry Campus *A*

District of Columbia
University of the District of Columbia *B*

Florida
Keiser College *A*
Miami-Dade Community College *A*
New England Institute of Technology *C, A*

Georgia
Athens Area Technical Institute *A*
Chattahoochee Technical Institute *A*
Clayton College and State University *A*
Savannah Technical Institute *A*

Illinois
Black Hawk College *C, A*
College of DuPage *C, A*
College of Lake County *C, A*
Elgin Community College *A*
ITT Technical Institute
 Matteson *A*
Joliet Junior College *C, A*
Moraine Valley Community College *C, A*
Parkland College *C, A*
Southwestern Illinois College *C, A*
Waubonsee Community College *C, A*
William Rainey Harper College *C*

Indiana
Indiana University--Purdue University
 Indiana University-Purdue University Indianapolis *A*
Ivy Tech State College
 Wabash Valley *A*
Oakland City University *A*
Purdue University
 North Central Campus *A*

Iowa
Southwestern Community College *A*
Western Iowa Tech Community College *A*

Kansas
Kansas City Kansas Community College *C, A*

Kentucky
Institute of Electronic Technology *A*
Western Kentucky University *B*

Louisiana
Delgado Community College *A*
McNeese State University *A*

Maryland
Allegany College *A*
Montgomery College
 Germantown Campus *C, A*
 Rockville Campus *A*
Prince George's Community College *A*

Massachusetts
Bristol Community College *A*
Franklin Institute of Boston *A*
Massachusetts Bay Community College *A*
Massasoit Community College *A*
Northern Essex Community College *C, A*
Springfield Technical Community College *C, A*

Michigan
Bay de Noc Community College *C*
Grand Rapids Community College *A*
Great Lakes College *C, A*
Kellogg Community College *C, A*
Lake Michigan College *A*
Lake Superior State University *B*
Lansing Community College *A*
Michigan Technological University *A*
Muskegon Community College *A*
Oakland Community College *C, A*
Schoolcraft College *A*
Washtenaw Community College *A*
Wayne State University *B*

Minnesota
Lake Superior College: A Community and Technical College *C, A*
St. Cloud Technical College *C, A*
St. Paul Technical College *A*

Mississippi
Hinds Community College *A*
Holmes Community College *A*
Mississippi Delta Community College *A*

Missouri
Ranken Technical College *A*

New Hampshire
New Hampshire Community Technical College
 Nashua *A*

New Jersey
Brookdale Community College *C*
Burlington County College *C*
Camden County College *A*
Salem Community College *A*
Union County College *A*

New Mexico
San Juan College *A*

New York
City University of New York
 College of Staten Island *A*
College of Aeronautics *A, B*
Erie Community College
 City Campus *C*
 North Campus *A*
 South Campus *A*
Genesee Community College *A*
Regents College *B*
Rochester Institute of Technology *A*
State University of New York
 College at Buffalo *B*
 College of Technology at Alfred *A, B*

North Carolina
Caldwell Community College and Technical Institute *A*
Cape Fear Community College *A*
Central Carolina Community College *A*
Craven Community College *A*
Halifax Community College *A*
Pitt Community College *A*
Randolph Community College *C*
Richmond Community College *A*
South Piedmont Community College *A*
Wake Technical Community College *A*
Wilkes Community College *C, A*

Ohio
Central Ohio Technical College *A*
Cincinnati State Technical and Community College *A*
Columbus State Community College *A*
Hocking Technical College *A*
Jefferson Community College *A*
Lorain County Community College *A*
Marion Technical College *A*
Shawnee State University *A*
Sinclair Community College *A*
Terra Community College *C, A*

Oklahoma
Northeastern Oklahoma Agricultural and Mechanical College *A*
Western Oklahoma State College *A*

Oregon
Chemeketa Community College *A*
Clackamas Community College *C, A*

Pennsylvania
Butler County Community College *A*
California University of Pennsylvania *A*
Community College of Allegheny County *C, A*
Community College of Beaver County *A*
Community College of Philadelphia *A*
Delaware County Community College *A*
Edinboro University of Pennsylvania *A*
Lehigh Carbon Community College *C, A*
Luzerne County Community College *C*
Northampton County Area Community College *A*
Peirce College *C, A, B*
Penn State
 Altoona *B*
 Berks *B*
 Dubois *A*
 New Kensington *B*
 Schuylkill - Capital College *A*
 University Park *C*
 Wilkes-Barre *B*
Pennsylvania College of Technology *A*
Pittsburgh Technical Institute *A*
University of Pennsylvania *B*
Westmoreland County Community College *A*

Puerto Rico
Technological College of San Juan *C, A*
University of Puerto Rico
 Bayamon University College *A*

Rhode Island
Community College of Rhode Island *C, A*

South Carolina
Aiken Technical College *A*
Denmark Technical College *A*
Florence-Darlington Technical College *A*
Midlands Technical College *C*
Orangeburg-Calhoun Technical College *A*
South Carolina State University *B*
Spartanburg Technical College *A*
Tri-County Technical College *A*

South Dakota
Southeast Technical Institute *A*

Tennessee
Cleveland State Community College *C*

Texas
Amarillo College *C*
Angelina College *C, A*
Brazosport College *C, A*
Brookhaven College *A*
Eastfield College *A*
Lee College *A*
Richland College *A*
San Jacinto College
 North *C, A*
Tarrant County College *A*
Texas State Technical College
 Harlingen *A*
 Sweetwater *C, A*
 Waco *C, A*
University of North Texas *B, M*

Vermont
Vermont Technical College *B*

Virginia
ECPI College of Technology *C, A*
J. Sargeant Reynolds Community College *C*
John Tyler Community College *A*
Tidewater Community College *A*
Virginia Highlands Community College *C*

Washington
Columbia Basin College *A*
Edmonds Community College *C, A*
Lake Washington Technical College *C, A*
South Seattle Community College *A*

Spokane Community College *A*
Tacoma Community College *C*
Walla Walla College *B*
Walla Walla Community College *C, A*
Yakima Valley Community College *A*

Wisconsin
Blackhawk Technical College *A*
Chippewa Valley Technical College *A*
Gateway Technical College *A*
Lakeshore Technical College *A*
Milwaukee Area Technical College *A*
Moraine Park Technical College *A*
Northeast Wisconsin Technical College *A*
Southwest Wisconsin Technical College *A*
Waukesha County Technical College *A*
Wisconsin Indianhead Technical College *A*

Electronics/electrical equipment repair

Alabama
Bessemer State Technical College *C, A*
Bevill State Community College *A*
Calhoun Community College *C, A*
Community College of the Air Force *A*
George C. Wallace State Community College
    Dothan *C, A*
Harry M. Ayers State Technical College *A*
J. F. Drake State Technical College *C, A*
John M. Patterson State Technical College *C, A*
Northwest-Shoals Community College *C*
Reid State Technical College *A*
Snead State Community College *C*
Wallace State Community College at Hanceville *C, A*

Alaska
University of Alaska
    Anchorage *C, A*

Arizona
Gateway Community College *A*
Mohave Community College *C, A*
Northland Pioneer College *C*

Arkansas
Westark College *C*

California
Allan Hancock College *C, A*
Cerritos Community College *A*
Chabot College *A*
Chaffey Community College *C, A*
Coastline Community College *C, A*
College of the Redwoods *C*
Cypress College *C, A*
Diablo Valley College *C*
East Los Angeles College *C*
Empire College *C*
Fresno City College *C, A*
Las Positas College *C, A*
Long Beach City College *C, A*
Los Angeles Harbor College *C, A*
Los Angeles Mission College *C, A*
Los Angeles Trade and Technical College *C, A*
Los Medanos College *C, A*
Mendocino College *C, A*
Modesto Junior College *C, A*
Mount San Antonio College *C, A*
Orange Coast College *C, A*
Palomar College *C, A*
Sacramento City College *C, A*
Saddleback College *C*
San Bernardino Valley College *C, A*
San Jose City College *A*
Sierra College *C, A*
Yuba College *C*

Colorado
Arapahoe Community College *C*
Community College of Denver *C, A*
Red Rocks Community College *C, A*
Technical Trades Institute *A*
Westwood College of Aviation Technology *A*

Connecticut
Gateway Community College *C*

Florida
Brevard Community College *C*
Chipola Junior College *C*
Embry-Riddle Aeronautical University *A*
Lake City Community College *C, A*
New England Institute of Technology *A*
Seminole Community College *C*

Georgia
Athens Area Technical Institute *C*
Chattahoochee Technical Institute *C*
Clayton College and State University *C, A*
Coastal Georgia Community College *C, A*
Dalton State College *C, A*
Darton College *A*
DeKalb Technical Institute *C*
Gwinnett Technical Institute *A*
Macon State College *A*
Waycross College *A*

Hawaii
University of Hawaii
    Hawaii Community College *A*
    Honolulu Community College *A*

Idaho
Boise State University *C, A*
College of Southern Idaho *C*
Idaho State University *C*
Lewis-Clark State College *A, B*

Illinois
City Colleges of Chicago
    Wright College *C, A*
College of DuPage *C, A*
College of Lake County *C*
Danville Area Community College *A*
Elgin Community College *C*
Illinois Eastern Community Colleges
    Lincoln Trail College *A*
John A. Logan College *C, A*
Joliet Junior College *C*
Kankakee Community College *C, A*
Lincoln Land Community College *C, A*
Prairie State College *C*
Rend Lake College *A*
Richland Community College *A*
Sauk Valley Community College *C*
Southwestern Illinois College *C, A*
Spoon River College *A*
Triton College *C, A*
Waubonsee Community College *C*
William Rainey Harper College *C, A*

Indiana
Vincennes University *A*

Iowa
Des Moines Area Community College *A*
Hawkeye Community College *A*
Indian Hills Community College *C*
Kirkwood Community College *C, A*
Northeast Iowa Community College *A*
Southwestern Community College *C, A*
Western Iowa Tech Community College *C*

Kansas
Allen County Community College *A*
Butler County Community College *A*
Dodge City Community College *C, A*
Hutchinson Community College *A*
Johnson County Community College *A*
Pittsburg State University *C*

Louisiana
Delgado Community College *A*
Nunez Community College *C, A*

Maine
Central Maine Technical College *A*
Southern Maine Technical College *A*

Maryland
Howard Community College *C, A*
Montgomery College
    Rockville Campus *A*

Massachusetts
Bunker Hill Community College *C, A*
Franklin Institute of Boston *C*

Michigan
Baker College
    of Cadillac *A*
Bay de Noc Community College *C*
Delta College *A*
Grand Rapids Community College *C, A*
Jackson Community College *C, A*
Lansing Community College *A*
Macomb Community College *C*
Northern Michigan University *A*
Northwestern Michigan College *A*
Oakland Community College *C, A*
Schoolcraft College *C*
Washtenaw Community College *A*

Minnesota
Hennepin Technical College *C, A*
Lake Superior College: A Community and Technical College *C, A*
Minnesota State College - Southeast Technical *C, A*
NEI College of Technology *A*
Northland Community & Technical College *C, A*
St. Cloud Technical College *C, A*
St. Paul Technical College *C*

Mississippi
East Mississippi Community College *C*
Hinds Community College *A*
Mississippi Delta Community College *C*
Mississippi Gulf Coast Community College
    Perkinston *A*

Missouri
East Central College *C, A*
Moberly Area Community College *C, A*
Ranken Technical College *A*
St. Charles County Community College *A*

Montana
Miles Community College *C, A*
Montana State University
    Northern *A, B*

Nebraska
Metropolitan Community College *C*
Mid Plains Community College
    Area *A*
Northeast Community College *A*
Southeast Community College
    Milford Campus *A*

New Hampshire
New Hampshire Community Technical College
    Manchester *A*
    Nashua *A*

New Jersey
Gloucester County College *C, A*
Raritan Valley Community College *A*

New Mexico
Clovis Community College *C, A*
Dona Ana Branch Community College of New Mexico State University *C, A*
Eastern New Mexico University
    Roswell Campus *C, A*
Western New Mexico University *A*

New York
City University of New York
    New York City Technical College *A*
College of Aeronautics *A, B*
Erie Community College
    South Campus *A*
Hudson Valley Community College *A*
Mohawk Valley Community College *C, A*
State University of New York
    College of Technology at Alfred *A*
    College of Technology at Canton *C*
Technical Career Institutes *C, A*

North Carolina
Alamance Community College *A*
Asheville Buncombe Technical Community College *C*
Cape Fear Community College *A*
Catawba Valley Community College *C*
Central Piedmont Community College *A*
Coastal Carolina Community College *C, A*
College of the Albemarle *C*
Davidson County Community College *C, A*
Durham Technical Community College *C, A*
Fayetteville Technical Community College *A*
Forsyth Technical Community College *C*
Gaston College *C*
Johnston Community College *C*
Lenoir Community College *C*
Piedmont Community College *C, A*
Pitt Community College *C*
Richmond Community College *C*
Rockingham Community College *A*
Sandhills Community College *C*
South Piedmont Community College *C*
Surry Community College *A*
Tri-County Community College *A*
Vance-Granville Community College *C, A*
Wake Technical Community College *C, A*
Wilson Technical Community College *C, A*

North Dakota
Bismarck State College *A*
Lake Region State College *A*

Ohio
Cleveland Institute of Electronics *C, A*
Columbus State Community College *A*
Edison State Community College *A*
Jefferson Community College *A*
North Central State College *A*
Ohio University *A*
Owens Community College
    Toledo *A*
Stark State College of Technology *A*

Oklahoma
Rogers State University *A*
Tulsa Community College *A*
Western Oklahoma State College *A*

Oregon
Central Oregon Community College *C, A*
Clackamas Community College *C, A*
Lane Community College *A*
Mount Hood Community College *A*

Pennsylvania
Community College of Allegheny County *A*
Community College of Beaver County *A*
Delaware County Community College *C*
Johnson Technical Institute *A*
Lehigh Carbon Community College *A*
Luzerne County Community College *C*
Northampton County Area Community College *C, A*

Electronics/electrical equipment repair

Pittsburgh Institute of Aeronautics A

Puerto Rico
Huertas Junior College C, A
Technological College of San Juan C

Rhode Island
New England Institute of Technology C, A

South Carolina
Aiken Technical College C
Central Carolina Technical College C
Chesterfield-Marlboro Technical College C
Denmark Technical College A
Florence-Darlington Technical College C
Greenville Technical College A
Horry-Georgetown Technical College A
Midlands Technical College C
Orangeburg-Calhoun Technical College A
Piedmont Technical College C, A
Technical College of the Lowcountry C
Tri-County Technical College C
Trident Technical College C
York Technical College A

South Dakota
Southeast Technical Institute A
Western Dakota Technical Institute A

Texas
Alvin Community College C, A
Amarillo College C, A
Angelina College C, A
Austin Community College A
Central Texas College C, A
Collin County Community College District C, A
Del Mar College C, A
El Paso Community College C, A
Grayson County College A
Houston Community College System C
Kilgore College C
Lee College C, A
Midland College A
Odessa College C, A
St. Philip's College C, A
San Jacinto College
    North C, A
South Plains College A
Tarrant County College C
Temple College A
Texas State Technical College
    Harlingen C
    Sweetwater C
    Waco C, A
Vernon Regional Junior College C, A

Utah
College of Eastern Utah C
Salt Lake Community College A
Utah Valley State College A

Virginia
ECPI College of Technology C, A
Eastern Shore Community College C, A
Mountain Empire Community College A
Northern Virginia Community College C, A
Paul D. Camp Community College A
Southwest Virginia Community College C
Thomas Nelson Community College C
Virginia Highlands Community College C

Washington
Centralia College A
Edmonds Community College C
Lower Columbia College C
North Seattle Community College A
Olympic College A
Peninsula College A
Renton Technical College C, A
Skagit Valley College C, A

Spokane Community College A

West Virginia
West Virginia Northern Community College A

Wisconsin
Blackhawk Technical College A
Chippewa Valley Technical College C, A
Gateway Technical College C
Herzing College A, B
Lakeshore Technical College C
Madison Area Technical College C, A
Moraine Park Technical College C, A
Southwest Wisconsin Technical College A
Waukesha County Technical College C, A
Western Wisconsin Technical College C
Wisconsin Indianhead Technical College C, A

Wyoming
Eastern Wyoming College C
Western Wyoming Community College C, A

Elementary education

Alabama
Alabama Agricultural and Mechanical University B, M, T
Alabama State University B, M, T
Athens State University B
Auburn University at Montgomery B, M
Auburn University B, M, D, T
Birmingham-Southern College B, T
Calhoun Community College A
Chattahoochee Valley Community College A
Concordia College B
Faulkner University B, T
Huntingdon College B, T
Jacksonville State University B, M, T
James H. Faulkner State Community College A
Northeast Alabama Community College A
Northwest-Shoals Community College A
Oakwood College B
Samford University B, M, T
Spring Hill College B, M
Stillman College B, T
Troy State University
    Dothan B, M, T
    Montgomery M
Troy State University B, M, T
Tuskegee University B, T
University of Alabama
    Birmingham B, M
    Huntsville C, B, T
University of Alabama B, M, D
University of Mobile B, T
University of Montevallo B, M, T
University of North Alabama B, M
University of South Alabama B, M, D, T
University of West Alabama B, M, T

Alaska
Alaska Pacific University B, M
University of Alaska
    Anchorage B, T
    Fairbanks M
    Southeast B, T

Arizona
American Indian College of the Assemblies of God B
Arizona State University B, M, D
Eastern Arizona College A
Gateway Community College A
Grand Canyon University B, M, T
Northern Arizona University B, M
Prescott College B, M
Southwestern College B, T
University of Arizona B, M

Arkansas
Arkansas State University B, M, T
Arkansas Tech University B, M
Harding University B, M, T
Henderson State University B, M, T
Hendrix College T
John Brown University B
Ouachita Baptist University B, T
Philander Smith College B
Southern Arkansas University B, M, T
University of Arkansas
    Little Rock B, M, T
    Monticello B, M
    Pine Bluff B, M
University of Arkansas B, M, D
University of Central Arkansas M, T
University of the Ozarks B, T
Westark College A
Williams Baptist College B

California
Allan Hancock College C, A
Azusa Pacific University B, T
Barstow College C, A
Biola University B, T
California Baptist University B, T
California Lutheran University B, M
California Polytechnic State University: San Luis Obispo T
California State University
    Bakersfield B, M
    Chico T
    Dominguez Hills M, T
    Fullerton T
    Hayward T
    Long Beach M, T
    Los Angeles M
    Monterey Bay B
    Northridge M
    Sacramento M, T
    San Marcos T
Chapman University T
College of Notre Dame M, T
Concordia University B, T
Cypress College A
Fresno Pacific University B, T
Holy Names College T
Hope International University B, M, T
Humboldt State University B, T
Imperial Valley College A
La Sierra University B, M
Loyola Marymount University C, M, T
Master's College B, T
Mills College T
Mount St. Mary's College B
National University T
Occidental College T
Pacific Oaks College T
Pacific Union College B, M, T
Patten College T
Point Loma Nazarene University T
St. Mary's College of California T
San Diego State University M, T
San Francisco State University M, T
San Jose State University M
Simpson College B, T
Sonoma State University M, T
United States International University T
University of California
    Riverside T
    Santa Barbara T
    Santa Cruz M
University of La Verne B, M, T
University of Redlands B, T
University of San Francisco T
University of Southern California B
University of the Pacific B, T
Vanguard University of Southern California T
Westmont College B, T
Whittier College T

Colorado
Adams State College B, M, T
Colorado College M
Colorado State University T

Fort Lewis College T
Metropolitan State College of Denver T
Otero Junior College A
University of Colorado
    Boulder T
    Colorado Springs T
University of Denver B
University of Northern Colorado M, D, T
University of Southern Colorado C, T
Western State College of Colorado T

Connecticut
Central Connecticut State University B, M
Connecticut College M, T
Eastern Connecticut State University B, M, T
Quinnipiac University B, M
Sacred Heart University B, M, T
St. Joseph College M, T
Southern Connecticut State University B, M, T
Trinity College B, T
University of Bridgeport M, T
University of Connecticut B, T
University of Hartford B, M, T
University of New Haven M
Western Connecticut State University B, M

Delaware
Delaware State University B
University of Delaware B, T
Wesley College B
Wilmington College B, M

District of Columbia
American University B, M, T
Catholic University of America B, M, T
Gallaudet University B, T
George Washington University M
Trinity College M, T
University of the District of Columbia B, T

Florida
Barry University B, M, T
Bethune-Cookman College B, T
Broward Community College A
Clearwater Christian College B
Flagler College B
Florida Agricultural and Mechanical University B, M
Florida Atlantic University B, M
Florida Baptist Theological College B
Florida Christian College B
Florida College B
Florida Gulf Coast University B, M, T
Florida International University B, M, T
Florida Memorial College B, T
Florida Southern College B
Florida State University B, M, D, T
Gulf Coast Community College A
Hillsborough Community College A
Hobe Sound Bible College B, T
Indian River Community College A
Jacksonville University B, M, T
Lynn University B
Manatee Community College A
Miami-Dade Community College A
Nova Southeastern University B, M
Palm Beach Atlantic College B, M, T
Palm Beach Community College A
Pensacola Junior College A
Rollins College B, M, T
St. Leo University B, T
St. Thomas University B, M, T
Southeastern College of the Assemblies of God B, T
Stetson University B, M
University of Central Florida B, M
University of Florida B, M
University of Miami B, M
University of North Florida B, M
University of South Florida B, M
University of Tampa B, T

University of West Florida B, T
Warner Southern College B

Georgia
Agnes Scott College T
Armstrong Atlantic State
   University B, M, T
Atlanta Christian College B
Atlanta Metropolitan College A
Clark Atlanta University B
Columbus State University B, M
Covenant College B, T
Emmanuel College B
Emory University B
Fort Valley State University B, M, T
Gainesville College A
Georgia Southwestern State
   University B, M, T
Kennesaw State University B, M
LaGrange College B
Macon State College A
Mercer University B, M, T
Middle Georgia College A
Morehouse College B
Morris Brown College B
North Georgia College & State
   University B, M
Oglethorpe University B, M, T
Reinhardt College B
Shorter College B, T
State University of West Georgia B, M
Toccoa Falls College B, T
University of Georgia D, T
Valdosta State University M

Hawaii
Brigham Young University
   Hawaii B, T
Chaminade University of Honolulu B, T
University of Hawaii
   Hilo T
   Manoa B, M, T

Idaho
Albertson College of Idaho B
Boise State University B, T
College of Southern Idaho A
Idaho State University B, T
Lewis-Clark State College B, T
North Idaho College A
Northwest Nazarene University B, M
Ricks College A
University of Idaho B, M, T

Illinois
Augustana College B, T
Barat College B
Benedictine University B, M, T
Black Hawk College
   East Campus A
Blackburn College B, T
Bradley University B, T
Chicago State University B, M, T
City Colleges of Chicago
   Harold Washington College C, A
   Kennedy-King College A
Columbia College M
Concordia University B, T
De Paul University B, T
Dominican University T
Eastern Illinois University B, M
Elmhurst College B
Eureka College B
Governors State University B, T
Greenville College T
Illinois College B, T
Illinois State University B, T
Illinois Wesleyan University B
John A. Logan College A
Joliet Junior College A
Judson College B
Kankakee Community College A
Kishwaukee College A
Knox College T
Lake Forest College T
Lewis University B

Lincoln Land Community College A
Loyola University of Chicago B, T
MacMurray College B, T
McKendree College B, T
Millikin University B, T
Monmouth College B, T
National-Louis University B, M, T
North Central College B, T
North Park University B, M
Northeastern Illinois University B, T
Northern Illinois University B, M, T
Olivet Nazarene University B, M, T
Parkland College A
Principia College B, T
Quincy University A, B, T
Rend Lake College A
Rockford College B, M
Roosevelt University B, M
St. Xavier University M
Sauk Valley Community College A
Southern Illinois University
   Carbondale B
   Edwardsville B, M
Southwestern Illinois College A
Springfield College in Illinois A
Trinity Christian College B, T
Trinity International University B, T
University of Illinois
   Chicago B
   Urbana-Champaign B, M, D, T
University of St. Francis B, M, T
Western Illinois University B, M
Wheaton College B, T

Indiana
Ancilla College A
Anderson University B, T
Ball State University B, M, D, T
Bethel College B
Butler University B, M
DePauw University B
Franklin College B
Goshen College B
Grace College B
Hanover College B, T
Indiana State University B, M, D, T
Indiana University
   Bloomington B, M, D, T
   East B
   Kokomo B, M
   Northwest B, M, T
   South Bend B, M, T
   Southeast B, M
Indiana University--Purdue University
   Indiana University-Purdue
      University Fort Wayne B, M, T
   Indiana University-Purdue
      University Indianapolis B, M, T
Indiana Wesleyan University B, M, T
Manchester College B, T
Marian College B
Oakland City University B
Purdue University
   Calumet B, M, T
   North Central Campus B, M, T
Purdue University B, M, D
Saint Mary's College B, T
St. Joseph's College B
St. Mary-of-the-Woods College B, T
Taylor University B
Tri-State University B, T
University of Evansville B
University of Indianapolis B, M, T
University of St. Francis B, M
University of Southern Indiana B, M
Valparaiso University B, T
Vincennes University A

Iowa
Briar Cliff College B
Buena Vista University B, T
Central College B, T
Clarke College B, M, T
Coe College B
Cornell College B, T
Dordt College B, T

Drake University B, M
Emmaus Bible College B
Faith Baptist Bible College and
   Theological Seminary B, T
Graceland University B, T
Grand View College B, T
Grinnell College T
Iowa State University B, M, T
Iowa Wesleyan College B
Loras College B
Luther College B
Maharishi University of Management B
Marshalltown Community College A
Marycrest International University B, M
Morningside College B, M
Mount Mercy College B
Northwestern College B, T
St. Ambrose University B, T
Simpson College B, T
University of Dubuque B, T
University of Iowa B, M, D, T
University of Northern Iowa B, M
Upper Iowa University B, T
Wartburg College B, T
William Penn University B

Kansas
Baker University B, T
Barclay College B
Benedictine College B, T
Bethany College B, T
Bethel College B, T
Butler County Community College A
Central Christian College A
Coffeyville Community College A
Colby Community College A
Dodge City Community College A
Emporia State University B, M
Fort Hays State University B, M, T
Garden City Community College A
Independence Community College A
Kansas City Kansas Community
   College A
Kansas State University B, M, T
Kansas Wesleyan University B, T
McPherson College B
MidAmerica Nazarene University B, T
Newman University B, T
Ottawa University B, T
Pittsburg State University B, M, T
Pratt Community College A
St. Mary College B, T
Southwestern College B, M, T
Sterling College B
Tabor College B
University of Kansas B, T
Washburn University of Topeka B
Wichita State University B, M, T

Kentucky
Alice Lloyd College B
Asbury College B, T
Bellarmine College B, M, T
Berea College B, T
Brescia University B, T
Campbellsville University B
Centre College B, T
Cumberland College B, M, T
Eastern Kentucky University B, M
Georgetown College B, M
Kentucky Christian College B, T
Kentucky State University B
Kentucky Wesleyan College B
Lindsey Wilson College B, T
Mid-Continent College B
Midway College B
Morehead State University B, M, T
Murray State University B, M, T
Northern Kentucky University B, M, T
Pikeville College B, T
Spalding University B, M, T
Thomas More College B
Transylvania University B, T
Union College B, M, T
University of Kentucky B, M, T
University of Louisville M

Western Kentucky University B, M, T

Louisiana
Centenary College of Louisiana B, M, T
Dillard University B, T
Louisiana State University
   Shreveport B
Louisiana State University and
   Agricultural and Mechanical
   College B
Louisiana Tech University B
Loyola University New Orleans B, M
McNeese State University B, M, T
Nicholls State University B, M
Northwestern State University B, M, T
Our Lady of Holy Cross College B
Southeastern Louisiana University B
Southern University
   New Orleans B
Southern University and Agricultural and
   Mechanical College B, M
University of Louisiana at Lafayette B
University of Louisiana at Monroe B, M
University of New Orleans B
Xavier University of Louisiana B, T

Maine
College of the Atlantic B, T
Husson College B, T
St. Joseph's College B
University of Maine
   Farmington B
   Fort Kent B, T
   Machias B
   Presque Isle B
University of Maine B, M
University of New England B, T
University of Southern Maine T

Maryland
Allegany College A
Anne Arundel Community College A
Bowie State University B, M, T
Cecil Community College A
Charles County Community College A
Chesapeake College A
College of Notre Dame of Maryland B
Columbia Union College B, T
Community College of Baltimore County
   Catonsville A
Coppin State College B
Frostburg State University B, M, T
Goucher College B, T
Howard Community College A
Loyola College in Maryland B, T
Montgomery College
   Germantown Campus A
   Takoma Park Campus A
Morgan State University B, M, T
Mount St. Mary's College B, M, T
Prince George's Community College A
St. Mary's College of Maryland T
Salisbury State University B
Towson University B, M, T
University of Maryland
   College Park B
Villa Julie College A, B, T
Washington Bible College B, T
Western Maryland College M, T

Massachusetts
American International College B, M
Anna Maria College B, M, T
Assumption College B
Atlantic Union College B
Bay Path College B
Becker College A, B, T
Boston College B, M, T
Boston University B, M, T
Brandeis University T
Bridgewater State College B, M, T
Bristol Community College A
Cambridge College M
Clark University M
Curry College B
Eastern Nazarene College B, M, T

Elms College *B, M, T*
Emmanuel College *B, M, T*
Endicott College *B, M*
Fitchburg State College *B, M, T*
Framingham State College *B, M, T*
Gordon College *B*
Hampshire College *B*
Hellenic College/Holy Cross *B*
Lasell College *B*
Lesley College *B, M, T*
Massachusetts College of Liberal Arts *T*
Merrimack College *M, T*
Northeastern University *B*
Pine Manor College *T*
Regis College *M*
Salem State College *B, M*
Simmons College *B, M*
Smith College *M*
Springfield College *B, M, T*
Springfield Technical Community College *A*
Stonehill College *B*
Suffolk University *M, T*
Tufts University *M*
University of Massachusetts
 Boston *M*
 Dartmouth *T*
Wellesley College *T*
Western New England College *T*
Westfield State College *M*
Wheaton College *T*
Wheelock College *B, M*
Worcester State College *B, M, T*

Michigan
Adrian College *B, T*
Albion College *T*
Alma College *B*
Andrews University *B, M, T*
Aquinas College *B, T*
Calvin College *B, T*
Central Michigan University *B, M*
Concordia College *B, T*
Eastern Michigan University *B, M, T*
Gogebic Community College *A*
Grace Bible College *B*
Grand Valley State University *M, T*
Hillsdale College *B*
Hope College *B, T*
Kellogg Community College *A*
Lake Superior State University *B*
Lansing Community College *A*
Madonna University *B, T*
Marygrove College *T*
Michigan State University *B*
Mid Michigan Community College *A*
Northern Michigan University *B, M, T*
Oakland University *B*
Olivet College *T*
Saginaw Valley State University *B, M*
Schoolcraft College *A*
Siena Heights University *B, M, T*
Spring Arbor College *T*
University of Detroit Mercy *B, M, T*
University of Michigan
 Dearborn *T*
 Flint *B, T*
University of Michigan *B*
Wayne State University *B, M, T*
Western Michigan University *B, M, T*

Minnesota
Augsburg College *B, T*
Bemidji State University *B, M, T*
Bethel College *B*
College of St. Benedict *B*
College of St. Catherine: St. Paul Campus *B, M, T*
College of St. Scholastica *B, T*
Concordia College: Moorhead *B, T*
Concordia University: St. Paul *B, T*
Crown College *B*
Gustavus Adolphus College *B*
Hamline University *B, T*
Martin Luther College *B*

Minnesota State University, Mankato *B, M, T*
Moorhead State University *B, M, T*
North Central University *B*
Northland Community & Technical College *A*
Northwestern College *B*
Ridgewater College: A Community and Technical College *A*
St. Cloud State University *B, M, T*
St. John's University *B*
St. Mary's University of Minnesota *B*
Southwest State University *B, T*
University of Minnesota
 Duluth *B, T*
 Morris
 Twin Cities *B, M, T*
University of St. Thomas *B, M, T*
Winona State University *B, M, T*

Mississippi
Alcorn State University *B, M*
Belhaven College *B, M, T*
Blue Mountain College *B*
Coahoma Community College *A*
Copiah-Lincoln Community College *A*
Delta State University *B, M*
Hinds Community College *A*
Holmes Community College *A*
Itawamba Community College *A*
Jackson State University *M, D, T*
Mary Holmes College *A*
Millsaps College *B, T*
Mississippi College *B, M, T*
Mississippi Delta Community College *A*
Mississippi Gulf Coast Community College
 Jefferson Davis Campus *A*
 Perkinston *A*
Mississippi State University *B, M, T*
Mississippi University for Women *B, T*
Mississippi Valley State University *B, M, T*
Northwest Mississippi Community College *A*
Rust College *B*
Tougaloo College *B, T*
University of Mississippi *B, T*
University of Southern Mississippi *B*
William Carey College *B, M*

Missouri
Avila College *B, T*
Baptist Bible College *B*
Central Methodist College *B, M*
Central Missouri State University *B, M, T*
College of the Ozarks *B, T*
Columbia College *T*
Crowder College *A*
Culver-Stockton College *B, T*
Drury University *B, T*
East Central College *A*
Evangel University *B, T*
Fontbonne College *B*
Hannibal-LaGrange College *B*
Harris Stowe State College *B, T*
Jefferson College *A*
Lincoln University *B, M*
Lindenwood University *B*
Maryville University of Saint Louis *B, M, T*
Mineral Area College *A*
Missouri Baptist College *B, T*
Missouri Southern State College *B, T*
Missouri Valley College *B, T*
Missouri Western State College *B*
Northwest Missouri State University *B, M, T*
Ozark Christian College *A*
Park University *B*
Rockhurst University *B*
Southeast Missouri State University *B, M, T*
Southwest Baptist University *B, T*

Southwest Missouri State University *B, M*
St. Louis Community College
 St. Louis Community College at Meramec *A*
Stephens College *B, T*
Truman State University *M, T*
University of Missouri
 Columbia *B*
 Kansas City *B*
 St. Louis *B, M, T*
Washington University *B, M, T*
Webster University *B, T*
Westminster College *B, T*
William Jewell College *B, T*
William Woods University *B, T*

Montana
Carroll College *B*
Miles Community College *A*
Montana State University
 Billings *B, T*
 Bozeman *B, T*
 Northern *B, M, T*
Rocky Mountain College *B, T*
Salish Kootenai College *A*
Stone Child College *A*
University of Great Falls *B, M, T*
University of Montana-Missoula *B*
Western Montana College of The University of Montana *B, T*

Nebraska
Chadron State College *B, M*
College of Saint Mary *B, T*
Concordia University *B, M, T*
Creighton University *B*
Dana College *B*
Doane College *B*
Grace University *A*
Mid Plains Community College Area *A*
Midland Lutheran College *B, T*
Nebraska Wesleyan University *B*
Northeast Community College *A*
Peru State College *B, T*
Union College *B, T*
University of Nebraska
 Kearney *B, M, T*
 Lincoln *B, T*
 Omaha *B, M, T*
Wayne State College *B, M*

Nevada
University of Nevada
 Las Vegas *B, T*
 Reno *B, M, T*

New Hampshire
Colby-Sawyer College *B, T*
Dartmouth College *T*
Franklin Pierce College *B*
Keene State College *B, T*
New England College *B, T*
Notre Dame College *B, M*
Plymouth State College of the University System of New Hampshire *B, M, T*
Rivier College *B, M, T*
University of New Hampshire Manchester *M, T*
University of New Hampshire *M*

New Jersey
Brookdale Community College *A*
Caldwell College *B, T*
Centenary College *T*
College of St. Elizabeth *B, T*
Essex County College *A*
Fairleigh Dickinson University *M*
Felician College *B, T*
Georgian Court College *B, T*
Kean University *B, M*
Monmouth University *M*
New Jersey City University *B, T*
Raritan Valley Community College *A*
Richard Stockton College of New Jersey *B*
Rider University *B, T*

Rowan University *B, M*
Rutgers
 The State University of New Jersey: Camden College of Arts and Sciences *T*
 The State University of New Jersey: Douglass College *T*
 The State University of New Jersey: Livingston College *T*
 The State University of New Jersey: New Brunswick Graduate Campus *M, D, T*
 The State University of New Jersey: Newark College of Arts and Sciences *T*
 The State University of New Jersey: Rutgers College *T*
 The State University of New Jersey: University College Camden *T*
 The State University of New Jersey: University College New Brunswick *T*
 The State University of New Jersey: University College Newark *T*
St. Peter's College *B, T*
Seton Hall University *B, M, T*
The College of New Jersey *B, M, T*
William Paterson University of New Jersey *B, M*

New Mexico
College of Santa Fe *B*
College of the Southwest *B, T*
Eastern New Mexico University *B*
New Mexico Highlands University *A, B, T*
New Mexico Junior College *A*
New Mexico State University *B*
Northern New Mexico Community College *A*
University of New Mexico *B, M*
Western New Mexico University *B, M, T*

New York
Adelphi University *B, M, T*
Alfred University *B, M, T*
Bank Street College of Education *M*
Barnard College *T*
Canisius College *B, M, T*
City University of New York
 Baruch College *B, M*
 Brooklyn College *B, M, T*
 City College *B, M, T*
 College of Staten Island *M*
 Hunter College *B, M, T*
 Kingsborough Community College *A*
 Lehman College *M, T*
 Medgar Evers College *B, T*
 Queens College *B, M, T*
College of Mount St. Vincent *T*
College of New Rochelle *M*
College of St. Rose *B, M, T*
Columbia University
 School of General Studies *T*
 Teachers College *M, D*
Concordia College *B, T*
Corning Community College *A*
D'Youville College *B, M, T*
Daemen College *B, T*
Dominican College of Blauvelt *B, T*
Dowling College *B, M, T*
Dutchess Community College *A*
Elmira College *B, M, T*
Eugene Lang College/New School University *T*
Fordham University *M, T*
Fulton-Montgomery Community College *A*
Hobart and William Smith Colleges *T*
Hofstra University *A, B, M, T*
Houghton College *B, T*
Iona College *B, M, T*
Jefferson Community College *A*
Keuka College *B, T*
Le Moyne College *M, T*

Long Island University
    Brooklyn Campus *B, M*
    C. W. Post Campus *B, M*
    Southampton College *B, M*
Manhattan College *B, T*
Manhattanville College *M, T*
Marist College *B, T*
Marymount College *B, T*
Marymount Manhattan College *B, T*
Medaille College *B, T*
Mercy College *T*
Molloy College *B, M, T*
Mount St. Mary College *M*
Nazareth College of Rochester *M, T*
New York Institute of Technology *B, M*
New York University *B, M, D, T*
Niagara University *B, M, T*
Nyack College *B*
Pace University:
    Pleasantville/Briarcliff *B, M, T*
Pace University *B, M, T*
Roberts Wesleyan College *B, T*
Rockland Community College *A*
Russell Sage College *B, M, T*
Sage Junior College of Albany *A*
St. Bonaventure University *B, M*
St. Francis College *B, T*
St. John Fisher College *B, T*
St. John's University *B, M, T*
St. Thomas Aquinas College *B, M, T*
Sarah Lawrence College *M*
Schenectady County Community
    College *A*
Skidmore College *T*
St. Joseph's College
    St. Joseph's College: Suffolk
        Campus *B, T*
    St. Joseph's College *B, T*
State University of New York
    Binghamton *M*
    Buffalo *M, D, T*
    College at Brockport *B, M, T*
    College at Buffalo *B, M, T*
    College at Cortland *M*
    College at Fredonia *B, M, T*
    College at Geneseo *B, M, T*
    College at Old Westbury *B, T*
    College at Oneonta *B, M, T*
    College at Plattsburgh *B, M*
    College at Potsdam *B, M, T*
    New Paltz *B, M, T*
    Oswego *B, M, T*
Syracuse University *B, M, T*
Ulster County Community College *A*
University of Rochester *M*
Vassar College *T*
Wagner College *B, M, T*
Wells College *T*

North Carolina
Appalachian State University *B, M, T*
Barber-Scotia College *B*
Barton College *B*
Belmont Abbey College *B*
Bennett College *B*
Campbell University *B, M, T*
Catawba College *B, M, T*
Chowan College *B, T*
Cleveland Community College *A*
East Carolina University *B, M*
Elizabeth City State University *B, T*
Elon College *B, M, T*
Fayetteville State University *M*
Gardner-Webb University *B, M*
Greensboro College *B, T*
Guilford College *B, T*
Guilford Technical Community
    College *A*
High Point University *B, T*
James Sprunt Community College *A*
John Wesley College *B*
Johnson C. Smith University *B, T*
Lees-McRae College *T*
Lenoir Community College *C, A*
Lenoir-Rhyne College *B, M, T*
Louisburg College *A*
Mars Hill College *B, T*
Martin Community College *A*
Meredith College *T*
Methodist College *A, B, T*
Montreat College *B, T*
North Carolina Agricultural and
    Technical State University *B, M, T*
North Carolina Central
    University *B, M, T*
North Carolina Wesleyan College *B*
Pfeiffer University *B, T*
Pitt Community College *A*
Queens College *B, M, T*
St. Andrews Presbyterian College *B, T*
St. Augustine's College *B, T*
Salem College *M, T*
Sandhills Community College *A*
Shaw University *B, T*
Southeastern Community College *A*
University of North Carolina
    Asheville *T*
    Chapel Hill *B, M*
    Charlotte *B, M*
    Greensboro *B, M*
    Pembroke *B, M, T*
    Wilmington *B, M*
Wake Forest University *B*
Warren Wilson College *B, T*
Western Carolina University *B, M, T*
Wingate University *B, M, T*
Winston-Salem State University *B*

North Dakota
Dickinson State University *B, T*
Jamestown College *B*
Mayville State University *B, T*
Minot State University: Bottineau
    Campus *A*
Minot State University *B, M, T*
North Dakota State University *B, T*
Trinity Bible College *B, T*
University of Mary *B, M, T*
University of North Dakota *B, M, T*
Valley City State University *B, T*

Ohio
Antioch College *T*
Baldwin-Wallace College *B*
Bluffton College *B*
Bowling Green State University
    Firelands College *A*
Bowling Green State University *B, M*
Capital University *B*
Cedarville College *B*
Central State University *B*
Circleville Bible College *B*
Cleveland State University *B, T*
College of Mount St. Joseph *B, T*
College of Wooster *B*
Defiance College *B, T*
Franciscan University of
    Steubenville *B, M*
Heidelberg College *T*
Hiram College *B, T*
John Carroll University *B, M, T*
Kent State University
    Stark Campus *B*
Kent State University *T*
Lake Erie College *B*
Lorain County Community College *A*
Lourdes College *B*
Malone College *B*
Marietta College *B*
Miami University
    Middletown Campus *B*
    Oxford Campus *B, M*
Mount Vernon Nazarene College *B, T*
Muskingum College *B, M, T*
Notre Dame College of Ohio *B, T*
Ohio Dominican College *B, D*
Ohio Northern University *B, T*
Ohio State University
    Columbus Campus *M, T*
Ohio University
    Chillicothe Campus *B*
    Eastern Campus *B*
    Lancaster Campus *A*
    Southern Campus at Ironton *B, M*
    Zanesville Campus *B*
Ohio University *B, M, D, T*
Ohio Wesleyan University *B*
Otterbein College *B*
Owens Community College
    Toledo *C*
Shawnee State University *T*
University of Akron *B, M, D, T*
University of Cincinnati *B, M, D, T*
University of Findlay *B, M, T*
University of Rio Grande *B, T*
University of Toledo *B, M, T*
Ursuline College *B*
Walsh University *B*
Washington State Community College *A*
Wilmington College *B*
Wittenberg University *B*
Wright State University *B, M, T*
Xavier University *M, T*
Youngstown State University *B, M*

Oklahoma
Cameron University *B, T*
Carl Albert State College *A*
Connors State College *A*
East Central University *B, M, T*
Eastern Oklahoma State College *A*
Langston University *B, M*
Mid-America Bible College *B*
Murray State College *A*
Northeastern Oklahoma Agricultural and
    Mechanical College *A*
Northeastern State University *B*
Northern Oklahoma College *A*
Northwestern Oklahoma State
    University *B, M, T*
Oklahoma Baptist University *B, T*
Oklahoma Christian University of
    Science and Arts *B, T*
Oklahoma City University *B, M*
Oklahoma Panhandle State University *B*
Oklahoma State University *B, M, D, T*
Oral Roberts University *B, T*
Rogers State University *A*
Rose State College *A*
Seminole State College *A*
Southeastern Oklahoma State
    University *B, M, T*
Southern Nazarene University *B, M*
Southwestern Oklahoma State
    University *B, M, T*
University of Central Oklahoma *B, M*
University of Oklahoma *B, T*
University of Science and Arts of
    Oklahoma *B*
University of Tulsa *B, T*
Western Oklahoma State College *A*

Oregon
Chemeketa Community College *A*
Concordia University *B, M, T*
Eastern Oregon University *B, M*
George Fox University *B, M, T*
Lewis & Clark College *M*
Linfield College *B, T*
Linn-Benton Community College *A*
Northwest Christian College *B*
Oregon State University *M*
Portland State University *T*
Southern Oregon University *M, T*
University of Portland *B, M, T*
Western Baptist College *B*
Western Oregon University *B, T*
Willamette University *M*

Pennsylvania
Albright College *T*
Allentown College of St. Francis de
    Sales *B, M*
Alvernia College *B*
Beaver College *B, M, T*
Bloomsburg University of
    Pennsylvania *B, M, T*
Bucknell University *B, M, T*
Butler County Community College *A*
Cabrini College *B, T*
California University of
    Pennsylvania *B, M, T*
Carlow College *B, T*
Carnegie Mellon University *T*
Cedar Crest College *B, T*
Chatham College *M, T*
Chestnut Hill College *B, M, T*
Cheyney University of
    Pennsylvania *B, M, T*
Clarion University of Pennsylvania *B, T*
College Misericordia *B*
Community College of Allegheny
    County *A*
Duquesne University *B, M, T*
East Stroudsburg University of
    Pennsylvania *B, M, T*
Eastern College *B, T*
Edinboro University of
    Pennsylvania *B, M, T*
Elizabethtown College *B*
Gannon University *B*
Geneva College *B, T*
Gettysburg College *T*
Grove City College *B, T*
Gwynedd-Mercy College *B, T*
Harrisburg Area Community College *A*
Holy Family College *B, M, T*
Immaculata College *T*
Indiana University of
    Pennsylvania *B, M, D, T*
Juniata College *B, T*
King's College *B, T*
Kutztown University of
    Pennsylvania *B, M, T*
La Roche College *B*
La Salle University *B, T*
Lancaster Bible College *B*
Lebanon Valley College of
    Pennsylvania *B, T*
Lehigh University *M, D*
Lincoln University *B, M, T*
Lock Haven University of
    Pennsylvania *B, T*
Lycoming College *T*
Manor College *A*
Mansfield University of
    Pennsylvania *B, M, T*
Marywood University *B, M, T*
Mercyhurst College *B, T*
Messiah College *B, T*
Millersville University of
    Pennsylvania *B, M, T*
Montgomery County Community
    College *A*
Moravian College *B, T*
Muhlenberg College *T*
Neumann College *B*
Penn State
    Delaware County *B*
    Harrisburg *B*
    University Park *B*
Philadelphia College of Bible *B, T*
Point Park College *B, T*
Reading Area Community College *A*
Rosemont College *T*
St. Francis College *B*
St. Joseph's University *B, M*
St. Vincent College *T*
Seton Hill College *B, M, T*
Shippensburg University of
    Pennsylvania *B, M, T*
Slippery Rock University of
    Pennsylvania *B, M, T*
Susquehanna University *B, T*
Temple University *B, M*
Thiel College *T*
University of Pennsylvania *A, B, M*
University of Pittsburgh
    Johnstown *B, T*
University of Pittsburgh *T*

University of Scranton B, M
Valley Forge Christian College B
Villanova University B
Waynesburg College B, T
West Chester University of
    Pennsylvania B, M, T
Westminster College B, M, T
Widener University B, M, T
Wilkes University B, M, T
Wilson College B
York College of Pennsylvania B, T

Puerto Rico
American University of Puerto Rico B, T
Bayamon Central University B, M
Caribbean University B, T
Inter American University of Puerto Rico
    Aguadilla Campus B
    Arecibo Campus B
    Barranquitas Campus B
    Fajardo Campus B, T
    Guayama Campus B
    Metropolitan Campus B, M
    San German Campus B
Pontifical Catholic University of Puerto
    Rico B, T
Turabo University B
Universidad Metropolitana B
University of Puerto Rico
    Aguadilla B
    Arecibo Campus A, B
    Cayey University College B, T
    Humacao University College B
    Ponce University College B
    Rio Piedras Campus B, M
University of the Sacred Heart B

Rhode Island
Providence College B
Rhode Island College B, M, T
Roger Williams University T
Salve Regina University T
University of Rhode Island B

South Carolina
Anderson College B, T
Benedict College B
Charleston Southern University M
Claflin University B
Clemson University B, M, T
Coastal Carolina University B, M, T
Coker College B, T
College of Charleston B, M, T
Columbia College B, M, T
Columbia International
    University B, M, T
Converse College B, M, T
Erskine College B, T
Francis Marion University M
Furman University B, M, T
Lander University B, M, T
Limestone College B
Morris College B, T
Newberry College B, T
North Greenville College B, T
Presbyterian College B, T
South Carolina State University B, M
Southern Wesleyan University B, T
University of South Carolina
    Aiken B, M, T
    Spartanburg B, M, T
University of South Carolina M, D
Voorhees College B
Winthrop University B, M, T

South Dakota
Augustana College B, M, T
Black Hills State University B, T
Dakota State University B, T
Dakota Wesleyan University B, T
Huron University B
Mount Marty College B
Northern State University B, M, T
Sinte Gleska University B
University of South Dakota B, M, T

Tennessee
Aquinas College B, T
Austin Peay State University M, T
Belmont University B, T
Bethel College B, T
Carson-Newman College B, M, T
Christian Brothers University B, M, T
Columbia State Community College A
Crichton College B
Cumberland University B, T
David Lipscomb University B, T
East Tennessee State University B, M, T
Fisk University B, T
Freed-Hardeman University B, T
Hiwassee College A
Johnson Bible College A, B, T
King College T
Lambuth University B, T
Lee University B, T
Lincoln Memorial University B, T
Maryville College B, T
Milligan College B, T
Motlow State Community College A
Roane State Community College A
Southern Adventist University B
Tennessee State University M, T
Tennessee Technological University M
Tennessee Temple University B, M, T
Tennessee Wesleyan College B, T
Trevecca Nazarene University B, M, T
Tusculum College B, T
Union University B, T
University of Memphis B, T
University of Tennessee
    Chattanooga M
    Knoxville T
    Martin B, T
Vanderbilt University B, M, D, T

Texas
Abilene Christian University B, M, T
Amarillo College A
Angelina College A
Angelo State University B
Arlington Baptist College B
Austin College M
Baylor University T
Brazosport College A
Coastal Bend College A
College of the Mainland A
Concordia University at Austin B, T
Dallas Baptist University B, M
East Texas Baptist University B
El Paso Community College A
Galveston College A
Grayson County College A
Hardin-Simmons University B, T
Houston Baptist University B, M
Howard Payne University B, T
Huston-Tillotson College T
Jarvis Christian College B
Lamar University M, T
LeTourneau University B
Lubbock Christian University B, M
McMurry University B
Midwestern State University B
Navarro College A
Our Lady of the Lake University of San
    Antonio T
Paul Quinn College B
Prairie View A&M University M
St. Edward's University T
St. Mary's University B, T
Sam Houston State University M, T
Schreiner College T
Southern Methodist University T
Southwest Texas State
    University B, M, T
Southwestern Adventist University B, M
Southwestern Assemblies of God
    University B
Southwestern University B, T
Stephen F. Austin State University M, T
Sul Ross State University B, T
Tarleton State University B, M, T

Texas A&M International
    University B, M, T
Texas A&M University
    Commerce B, M, D, T
    Corpus Christi M, T
    Kingsville B
    Texarkana M, T
Texas Christian University B, M, T
Texas College B
Texas Lutheran University B, T
Texas Tech University M
Texas Wesleyan University B, M, T
Texas Woman's University M
Trinity University B, M
Trinity Valley Community College A
University of Dallas B, T
University of Houston
    Victoria M
University of Houston M, T
University of Mary Hardin-Baylor B, T
University of North Texas B, M, D, T
University of Texas
    Arlington M, T
    Brownsville M
    Pan American B, M, T
    San Antonio M, T
    Tyler T
    of the Permian Basin M
University of the Incarnate Word B
Wayland Baptist University B, T
West Texas A&M University M, T
Wharton County Junior College A
Wiley College B

Utah
Brigham Young University B, M
Dixie State College of Utah A
Salt Lake Community College A
Snow College A
Southern Utah University B, T
University of Utah B
Utah State University B, M, D
Weber State University B, M, T
Westminster College B

Vermont
Bennington College B
Castleton State College B, M, T
Champlain College A, B, T
College of St. Joseph in Vermont B, M
Goddard College B
Green Mountain College B, T
Johnson State College B, M
Lyndon State College B
Middlebury College T
Norwich University T
St. Michael's College B, M
Trinity College of Vermont B, T
University of Vermont B, T

Virginia
Averett College T
Bluefield College B
Bridgewater College T
Christopher Newport University T
College of William and Mary T
Eastern Mennonite University T
George Mason University M
Hampton University B, M
Hollins University T
James Madison University M, T
Liberty University B, M
Longwood College B, T
Mary Baldwin College T
Mary Washington College T
Old Dominion University M
Radford University T
Randolph-Macon College T
Randolph-Macon Woman's College T
St. Paul's College T
Shenandoah University C
University of Richmond T
University of Virginia's College at
    Wise T
Virginia Intermont College B, T
Virginia Wesleyan College T

Washington
Central Washington University B, M, T
Eastern Washington University B, M, T
Evergreen State College M
Gonzaga University T
Pacific Lutheran University B
Puget Sound Christian College A
St. Martin's College B, T
Walla Walla College B, T
Western Washington University M, T
Whitworth College B, M, T

West Virginia
Alderson-Broaddus College B
Bethany College B
Bluefield State College B
College of West Virginia A
Concord College B, T
Davis and Elkins College B
Fairmont State College B
Glenville State College B
Marshall University B, M
Ohio Valley College B
Potomac State College of West Virginia
    University A
Salem-Teikyo University B, M, T
Shepherd College B, T
University of Charleston B
West Liberty State College B
West Virginia State College B
West Virginia University
    Parkersburg B
West Virginia University M, T
West Virginia Wesleyan College B
Wheeling Jesuit University T

Wisconsin
Alverno College B, T
Beloit College T
Cardinal Stritch University B, T
Carroll College B, T
Carthage College B, T
Concordia University Wisconsin B, T
Lakeland College B
Lawrence University T
Marian College of Fond du Lac B, T
Marquette University B
Mount Mary College B, T
Mount Senario College B, T
Northland College B, T
Ripon College B, T
St. Norbert College B, T
Silver Lake College B, T
University of Wisconsin
    Eau Claire B, M
    Green Bay B, T
    La Crosse B, M, T
    Madison B, T
    Oshkosh B, M, T
    Parkside T
    Platteville B, T
    River Falls B, M, T
    Stevens Point B, M, T
    Superior M
    Whitewater B, T
Viterbo University B, T
Wisconsin Lutheran College B

Wyoming
Casper College A
Central Wyoming College A
Eastern Wyoming College A
Laramie County Community College A
Northwest College A
Sheridan College A
University of Wyoming B
Western Wyoming Community
    College A

Elementary particle physics

Massachusetts
Harvard College B
Tufts University M, D

New York
Columbia University
 Graduate School *M, D*

Wisconsin
University of Wisconsin
 Madison *M, D*

Emergency medical technology

Alabama
Bessemer State Technical College *C*
Calhoun Community College *C*
Central Alabama Community College *A*
Enterprise State Junior College *A*
Faulkner University *A*
Gadsden State Community College *A*
George C. Wallace State Community
 College
   Dothan *C, A*
James H. Faulkner State Community
 College *A*
Lawson State Community College *A*
Lurleen B. Wallace Junior College *C, A*
Northeast Alabama Community
 College *A*
Northwest-Shoals Community College *C*
University of Alabama
 Birmingham *C*
University of South Alabama *C*
Wallace State Community College at
 Hanceville *C, A*

Alaska
University of Alaska
 Anchorage *A*

Arizona
Arizona Western College *C*
Central Arizona College *C, A*
Cochise College *A*
Eastern Arizona College *C, A*
Glendale Community College *C*
Northland Pioneer College *A*
Phoenix College *C, A*
Pima Community College *C, A*
Scottsdale Community College *C, A*
Yavapai College *C*

Arkansas
Arkansas State University *A*
Garland County Community
 College *A*
North Arkansas College *A*
Northwest Arkansas Community
 College *C, A*
University of Arkansas
 for Medical Sciences *C, A*
Westark College *C, A*

California
Allan Hancock College *C*
Bakersfield College *A*
Barstow College *C*
Butte College *A*
California State University
 Chico *C*
Citrus College *C*
College of the Canyons *C*
College of the Desert *C*
College of the Sequoias *C*
Columbia College *C*
Compton Community College *C, A*
Crafton Hills College *C, A*
East Los Angeles College *C*
Foothill College *A*
Imperial Valley College *C*
Loma Linda University *B*
Los Medanos College *C, A*
Modesto Junior College *C*
Mount San Antonio College *C, A*
Palomar College *C, A*
Riverside Community College *A*
Saddleback College *C*
San Joaquin Delta College *C, A*

Santa Rosa Junior College *C*
Skyline College *C*
Southwestern College *C, A*
Ventura College *A*
Victor Valley College *C*

Colorado
Aims Community College *C*
Arapahoe Community College *C, A*
Front Range Community College *C*
Morgan Community College *C*
Northeastern Junior College *C, A*
Pikes Peak Community College *C, A*
Red Rocks Community College *A*

Connecticut
Capital Community College *C, A*
Naugatuck Valley Community-Technical
 College *C*
Three Rivers Community-Technical
 College *C*

Delaware
Delaware Technical and Community
 College
   Owens Campus *A*
   Stanton/Wilmington Campus *A*
   Terry Campus *A*

District of Columbia
George Washington University *B*

Florida
Brevard Community College *C, A*
Broward Community College *C, A*
Central Florida Community College *C, A*
Daytona Beach Community
 College *C, A*
Edison Community College *C, A*
Florida Community College at
 Jacksonville *C, A*
Florida Keys Community College *C*
Gulf Coast Community College *C, A*
Hillsborough Community College *C, A*
Indian River Community College *C, A*
Lake City Community College *C, A*
Lake-Sumter Community College *A*
Miami-Dade Community College *A*
Palm Beach Community College *C, A*
Pasco-Hernando Community
 College *C, A*
Pensacola Junior College *C, A*
Polk Community College *C*
St. Petersburg Junior College *C, A*
Santa Fe Community College *C, A*
Seminole Community College *C, A*
South Florida Community College *C*
Tallahassee Community College *C, A*
Valencia Community College *C, A*

Georgia
Clayton College and State University *C*
Dalton State College *A*
Darton College *C, A*
DeKalb Technical Institute *C*
Floyd College *A*
Gainesville College *A*
Gwinnett Technical Institute *C*
Macon State College *A*
Valdosta State University *A*
Waycross College *A*

Hawaii
University of Hawaii
 Kapiolani Community
  College *C, A*

Idaho
College of Southern Idaho *C*
Ricks College *A*

Illinois
Black Hawk College *C*
City Colleges of Chicago
 Malcolm X College *C*
College of DuPage *C*
Elgin Community College *C*

Illinois Eastern Community Colleges
 Frontier Community College *C*
John A. Logan College *C*
Kankakee Community College *C, A*
McHenry County College *C, A*
Moraine Valley Community College *C*
Parkland College *C*
Prairie State College *C*
Rend Lake College *A*
Southeastern Illinois College *C*
Southwestern Ilinois College *C, A*
William Rainey Harper College *C*

Indiana
Ball State University *A*
Indiana University
 Bloomington *A*
Indiana University--Purdue University
 Indiana University-Purdue
  University Indianapolis *A*
Ivy Tech State College
 Kokomo *A*
 Southwest *A*
 Wabash Valley *A*
University of St. Francis *A*

Iowa
Hawkeye Community College *A*
Iowa Central Community College *C, A*
Kirkwood Community College *A*
North Iowa Area Community College *A*
Northeast Iowa Community College *A*
Southeastern Community College
 North Campus *A*
Southwestern Community College *C*
Western Iowa Tech Community
 College *A*

Kansas
Allen County Community College *A*
Barton County Community College *C, A*
Coffeyville Community College *A*
Dodge City Community College *C*
Hutchinson Community College *C, A*
Independence Community College *C, A*
Johnson County Community
 College *C, A*
Kansas City Kansas Community
 College *C, A*

Kentucky
Eastern Kentucky University *C, A*

Louisiana
Bossier Parish Community College *A*
Delgado Community College *A*
Nicholls State University *A*
Nunez Community College *C, A*
University of Louisiana at Lafayette *A*

Maine
Eastern Maine Technical College *C*
Kennebec Valley Technical College *A*

Maryland
Anne Arundel Community College *C, A*
Baltimore City Community College *C, A*
Charles County Community College *A*
Chesapeake College *C*
Community College of Baltimore County
 Essex *C, A*
Frederick Community College *C, A*
Howard Community College *C, A*
University of Maryland
 Baltimore County *B, M*

Massachusetts
Cape Cod Community College *C, A*
Greenfield Community College *C*
Laboure College *A*
Massachusetts Bay Community
 College *C*
North Shore Community College *C*
Springfield College *B*

Michigan
Baker College
 of Mount Clemens *C*
 of Muskegon *C, A*
Davenport College of Business *C, A*
Delta College *C*
Great Lakes College *C, A*
Henry Ford Community College *C, A*
Jackson Community College *C, A*
Kalamazoo Valley Community
 College *C*
Kellogg Community College *C, A*
Lansing Community College *A*
Macomb Community College *C, A*
Montcalm Community College *A*
Mott Community College *A*
Oakland Community College *A*
Schoolcraft College *C*
Wayne County Community College *C*

Minnesota
Century Community and Technical
 College *A*
Inver Hills Community College *A*
Lake Superior College: A Community
 and Technical College *C*
Mesabi Range Community and Technical
 College *C*
St. Cloud Technical College *C*
South Central Technical College *A*
University of Minnesota
 Duluth *C*

Mississippi
East Mississippi Community College *C*
Hinds Community College *C, A*
Mississippi Delta Community College *A*
Mississippi Gulf Coast Community
 College
  Jefferson Davis Campus *C, A*
  Perkinston *A*
University of Mississippi
 Medical Center *C*

Missouri
Crowder College *C*
East Central College *C, A*
Jefferson College *C*
Missouri Southern State College *C*
Moberly Area Community College *C*
Penn Valley Community College *A*
Southwest Baptist University *A*
St. Louis Community College
 St. Louis Community College at
  Forest Park *A*
 St. Louis Community College at
  Meramec *A*
Three Rivers Community College *C*

Montana
Montana State University
 College of Technology-Great
  Falls *A*
University of Montana-Missoula *A*

Nebraska
Creighton University *C, A, B*
Nebraska Methodist College of Nursing
 and Allied Health *C, A*
Northeast Community College *A*

Nevada
Community College of Southern
 Nevada *A*

New Hampshire
New Hampshire Technical Institute *A*

New Jersey
Essex County College *A*
University of Medicine and Dentistry of
 New Jersey
  School of Health Related
   Professions *C, A*

New Mexico
Dona Ana Branch Community College of
 New Mexico State University *C, A*

Eastern New Mexico University
  Roswell Campus C, A
New Mexico Junior College A
University of New Mexico C, B

New York
Broome Community College A
City University of New York
  Borough of Manhattan Community
    College A
  La Guardia Community College A
Corning Community College A
Dutchess Community College A
Erie Community College
  South Campus C
Finger Lakes Community College C
Fulton-Montgomery Community
  College A
Herkimer County Community College A
Hudson Valley Community College C
Rochester Institute of Technology C
Rockland Community College A
Westchester Community College C, A

North Carolina
Asheville Buncombe Technical
  Community College A
Catawba Valley Community College A
Coastal Carolina Community College A
College of the Albemarle C
Davidson County Community College A
Gaston College A
Guilford Technical Community
  College C, A
Montgomery Community College A
Randolph Community College A
Rockingham Community College A
Sandhills Community College A
Southwestern Community College A
Tri-County Community College C
Wake Technical Community
  College C, A
Western Carolina University B
Wilson Technical Community College A

Ohio
Belmont Technical College C, A
Cincinnati State Technical and
  Community College C
Clark State Community College A
Columbus State Community
  College C, A
Hocking Technical College A
Jefferson Community College A
Lakeland Community College C
Lima Technical College A
Lorain County Community College C
Shawnee State University A
Sinclair Community College A
University of Cincinnati
  Raymond Walters College A
University of Toledo C, A
Youngstown State University C, A

Oklahoma
Oklahoma City Community
  College C, A
Redlands Community College A
Western Oklahoma State College A

Oregon
Central Oregon Community College A
Chemeketa Community College A
Clackamas Community College C
Clatsop Community College C, A
Lane Community College C, A
Linn-Benton Community College C
Oregon Health Sciences University C
Portland Community College C, A

Pennsylvania
California University of Pennsylvania A
Delaware County Community College A
Harrisburg Area Community
  College C, A
Lackawanna Junior College C, A
Lehigh Carbon Community College C, A

Luzerne County Community College A
MCP Hahnemann University C, A, B, M
University of Pittsburgh
  Johnstown A

Puerto Rico
Inter American University of Puerto Rico
  Aguadilla Campus C
Universidad Metropolitana C

South Carolina
Greenville Technical College A
Piedmont Technical College C

South Dakota
University of South Dakota B, M

Tennessee
Jackson State Community College C
Northeast State Technical Community
  College C
Roane State Community College A
Shelby State Community College A
Volunteer State Community College C

Texas
Alvin Community College A
Amarillo College C, A
Angelina College C, A
Blinn College C
Collin County Community College
  District C
Del Mar College C
El Paso Community College C
Galveston College C
Grayson County College C, A
Houston Community College System C
Lee College C, A
Midland College C
Navarro College A
North Central Texas College A
Odessa College C, A
San Jacinto College
  North C, A
Tarleton State University B
Tarrant County College C, A
Texas State Technical College
  Harlingen C
  Sweetwater C, A
Trinity Valley Community College C
Tyler Junior College C, A
University of North Texas B
Weatherford College C, A
Western Texas College C, A

Utah
Brigham Young University B
Dixie State College of Utah C, A
Snow College C, A
Weber State University A

Virginia
Hampton University B
John Tyler Community College C
Mountain Empire Community College C
Northern Virginia Community College A
Tidewater Community College A

Washington
Central Washington University B
Columbia Basin College A
North Seattle Community College C
Spokane Community College C, A
Spokane Falls Community College C
Tacoma Community College A

Wisconsin
Blackhawk Technical College C
Chippewa Valley Technical College C
Gateway Technical College C
Madison Area Technical College C, A
Nicolet Area Technical College C
Western Wisconsin Technical College C
Wisconsin Indianhead Technical
  College C

Wyoming
Sheridan College C, A

Engineering

Alabama
Central Alabama Community College A
Chattahoochee Valley Community
  College A
Lawson State Community College A
Northeast Alabama Community
  College A
Shelton State Community College A
Talladega College B
University of Alabama
  Huntsville M
University of Alabama M
Wallace State Community College at
  Hanceville A

Arizona
Arizona Western College A
Central Arizona College A
Mesa Community College A
Phoenix College A
University of Arizona B

Arkansas
Arkansas State University B
Arkansas Tech University B
Harding University B
John Brown University B
University of Arkansas M, D
Westark College A

California
Allan Hancock College A
California Institute of Technology B
California Polytechnic State University:
  San Luis Obispo M
California State Polytechnic University:
  Pomona M
California State University
  Long Beach M
  Los Angeles B
  Northridge B, M
  Sacramento B
Chabot College A
Chaffey Community College A
Citrus College A
City College of San Francisco A
College of San Mateo A
College of the Canyons A
College of the Sequoias A
College of the Siskiyous A
Contra Costa College A
Cypress College A
De Anza College A
Diablo Valley College C, A
East Los Angeles College A
Foothill College A
Fresno City College A
Harvey Mudd College B, M
Imperial Valley College A
Long Beach City College C, A
Los Angeles Pierce College A
Los Angeles Southwest College C, A
Merced College A
Mission College A
Modesto Junior College A
Mount San Antonio College A
Palomar College A
Pepperdine University B
Riverside Community College C, A
Saddleback College A
San Diego City College C, A
San Diego Mesa College A
San Diego State University M, D
San Francisco State University M
San Joaquin Delta College A
San Jose State University M
Santa Ana College C, A
Santa Barbara City College A
Santa Clara University B, M
Santa Rosa Junior College A
Scripps College B
Shasta College A
Sierra College A

Stanford University B, M
Taft College A
University of California
  Davis M, D
  Irvine B, M, D
  Los Angeles B, M, D
  Santa Barbara B, M, D
University of the Pacific B
Ventura College C, A
West Hills Community College A
West Los Angeles College C, A
West Valley College A

Colorado
Colorado School of Mines B
Trinidad State Junior College A
United States Air Force Academy B
University of Colorado
  Boulder M
  Colorado Springs M
  Denver M
University of Denver B

Connecticut
Fairfield University B
Trinity College B
Tunxis Community College A
University of Hartford B
University of New Haven M

District of Columbia
George Washington University B, M, D

Florida
Brevard Community College A
Broward Community College A
Chipola Junior College A
Daytona Beach Community College A
Edison Community College A
Gulf Coast Community College A
Hillsborough Community College A
Indian River Community College A
Lake City Community College A
Manatee Community College A
Miami-Dade Community College C
Palm Beach Community College A
Pensacola Junior College A
Polk Community College A
South Florida Community College A
Tallahassee Community College A
University of Central Florida M
University of Miami M, D
University of South Florida B, M, D

Georgia
Andrew College A
Clark Atlanta University B
Dalton State College A
Darton College A
Gainesville College A
Georgia Military College A
Morehouse College B
Reinhardt College A
Spelman College B
Young Harris College A

Idaho
Idaho State University B
North Idaho College A
Ricks College A
University of Idaho B, M

Illinois
City Colleges of Chicago
  Harold Washington College A
  Olive-Harvey College C, A
College of Lake County A
Danville Area Community College A
Eastern Illinois University B
Highland Community College A
Illinois College B
Illinois Institute of Technology C, M, D
John Wood Community College A
Kankakee Community College A
Kaskaskia College A
Kishwaukee College A
Lake Land College A
Lincoln Land Community College A

Engineering

MacMurray College *B*
McHenry County College *A*
Monmouth College *B*
Northwestern University *B*
Oakton Community College *A*
Olivet Nazarene University *B*
Parkland College *A*
Rend Lake College *A*
Richland Community College *A*
Sauk Valley Community College *A*
Southern Illinois University
    Carbondale *M, D*
Southwestern Illinois College *A*
Triton College *A*
University of Illinois
    Urbana-Champaign *B, M*
Waubonsee Community College *A*
Wheaton College *B*
William Rainey Harper College *A*

Indiana
Bethel College *B*
Indiana University--Purdue University
    Indiana University-Purdue
        University Fort Wayne *B*
    Indiana University-Purdue
        University Indianapolis *A*
Purdue University
    Calumet *B, M*
Purdue University *B, M*
Taylor University *B*
University of Evansville *B*
University of Notre Dame *M*
Vincennes University *A*

Iowa
Cornell College *B*
Dordt College *B*
Iowa Wesleyan College *B*
Kirkwood Community College *A*
Maharishi University of Management *B*
Marshalltown Community College *A*
North Iowa Area Community College *A*
Waldorf College *A*

Kansas
Barton County Community College *A*
Butler County Community College *A*
Central Christian College *A*
Coffeyville Community College *A*
Colby Community College *A*
Cowley County Community College *A*
Dodge City Community College *A*
Garden City Community College *A*
Hutchinson Community College *A*
Independence Community College *A*
Kansas City Kansas Community
    College *A*
Pratt Community College *A*
Seward County Community College *A*

Kentucky
Brescia University *A*
Murray State University *B*

Louisiana
Dillard University *B*
Louisiana Tech University *D*
McNeese State University *B, M*
Tulane University *B*

Maine
University of Maine *B, M*

Maryland
Allegany College *A*
Anne Arundel Community College *A*
Baltimore City Community College *A*
Charles County Community College *A*
College of Notre Dame of Maryland *B*
Columbia Union College *A*
Community College of Baltimore County
    Catonsville *A*
    Essex *A*
Frederick Community College *A*
Hagerstown Community College *A*
Harford Community College *A*
Howard Community College *A*
Johns Hopkins University *B*
Loyola College in Maryland *B, M*
Montgomery College
    Germantown Campus *A*
    Rockville Campus *A*
    Takoma Park Campus *A*
Morgan State University *M, D*
Prince George's Community College *A*
United States Naval Academy *B*
University of Maryland
    Baltimore County *B*
    College Park *B, M*

Massachusetts
Berkshire Community College *A*
Boston University *B, M*
Bristol Community College *A*
Cape Cod Community College *A*
Emmanuel College *B*
Harvard College *B*
Harvard University *D*
Holyoke Community College *A*
Massachusetts Maritime Academy *B*
Merrimack College *B*
Mount Ida College *A*
North Shore Community College *A*
Northeastern University *B, M*
Springfield Technical Community
    College *A*
Tufts University *B*
Wellesley College *B*
Worcester Polytechnic Institute *B, M*

Michigan
Alpena Community College *A*
Andrews University *B*
Calvin College *B*
Ferris State University *A*
Gogebic Community College *A*
Grand Valley State University *M*
Kalamazoo Valley Community
    College *A*
Kettering University *B*
Kirtland Community College *A*
Lake Michigan College *A*
Lake Superior State University *A*
Lansing Community College *A*
Lawrence Technological University *M*
Michigan State University *B*
Michigan Technological
    University *B, M, D, T*
Mid Michigan Community College *A*
Oakland Community College *A*
Schoolcraft College *A*
University of Detroit Mercy *B, M*
University of Michigan
    Dearborn *B*
University of Michigan *B, M, D*
Washtenaw Community College *A*
Wayne State University *T*
Western Michigan University *B, M, D*

Minnesota
Anoka-Ramsey Community College *A*
Augsburg College *B*
Concordia College: Moorhead *B*
Itasca Community College *A*
Minnesota State University,
    Mankato *B, M*
Northland Community & Technical
    College *A*
Rochester Community and Technical
    College *A*
University of Minnesota
    Twin Cities *C*
Winona State University *B*

Mississippi
Copiah-Lincoln Community College *A*
East Central Community College *A*
Hinds Community College *A*
Holmes Community College *A*
Mary Holmes College *A*
Mississippi Delta Community College *A*
Mississippi Gulf Coast Community
    College
        Perkinston *A*
Mississippi State University *D*
University of Mississippi *B*

Missouri
Crowder College *A*
East Central College *A*
Hannibal-LaGrange College *A*
Jefferson College *A*
Longview Community College *A*
Maple Woods Community College *A*
Mineral Area College *A*
Missouri Southern State College *B*
Moberly Area Community College *A*
Penn Valley Community College *A*
St. Charles County Community
    College *A*
Southwest Missouri State University
    West Plains Campus *A*
St. Louis Community College
    St. Louis Community College at
        Florissant Valley *A*
    St. Louis Community College at
        Forest Park *A*
    St. Louis Community College at
        Meramec *C, A*
University of Missouri
    Columbia *M*
Washington University *B, M, D*

Montana
Miles Community College *A*
Montana State University
    Bozeman *D*
Montana Tech of the University of
    Montana *A, B, M*

Nebraska
Union College *A*
University of Nebraska
    Lincoln *M, D*

Nevada
University of Nevada
    Reno *D*

New Hampshire
Dartmouth College *M, D*
University of New Hampshire *B*

New Jersey
Brookdale Community College *A*
Cumberland County College *A*
Essex County College *A*
Georgian Court College *B*
Gloucester County College *A*
Monmouth University *M*
New Jersey Institute of Technology *B, M*
Ocean County College *A*
Rowan University *B, M*
Stevens Institute of Technology *B*
The College of New Jersey *B, T*
Union County College *A*

New Mexico
Albuquerque Technical-Vocational
    Institute *A*
New Mexico Highlands University *B*
New Mexico Institute of Mining and
    Technology *B*
New Mexico Junior College *A*
New Mexico State University
    Carlsbad *A*
New Mexico State University *D*
San Juan College *A*
Santa Fe Community College *A*
University of New Mexico *A, B, D*

New York
Adirondack Community College *A*
Alfred University *B*
City University of New York
    Borough of Manhattan Community
        College *A*
Clarkson University *B*
Cooper Union for the Advancement of
    Science and Art *B*
Cornell University *B*
Dominican College of Blauvelt *B*
Erie Community College
    North Campus *A*
Finger Lakes Community College *A*
Fulton-Montgomery Community
    College *A*
Hudson Valley Community College *A*
Jamestown Community College *A*
Mohawk Valley Community College *A*
Nassau Community College *A*
Niagara University *A*
Orange County Community College *A*
Pace University *B*
Rensselaer Polytechnic Institute *B, M, D*
Rochester Institute of Technology *A*
St. Thomas Aquinas College *B*
State University of New York
    College of Agriculture and
        Technology at Morrisville *A*
    College of Technology at Alfred *A*
    Maritime College *B*
    Stony Brook *M*
Ulster County Community College *A*
University of Rochester *B*
Westchester Community College *C, A*

North Carolina
Brevard College *A*
Cleveland Community College *A*
Elon College *B*
Guilford Technical Community
    College *A*
Johnson C. Smith University *B*
Lenoir Community College *A*
Louisburg College *A*
North Carolina Agricultural and
    Technical State University *M*
North Carolina State University *M*
Shaw University *B*
University of North Carolina
    Charlotte *M*
Western Piedmont Community
    College *A*

North Dakota
North Dakota State University *B, M, D*

Ohio
Case Western Reserve University *B, M*
Edison State Community College *A*
Jefferson Community College *A*
Lorain County Community College *A*
Muskingum College *B*
Oberlin College *B*
Ohio State University
    Columbus Campus *B, M, D*
Owens Community College
    Toledo *A*
University of Akron *B, M*
University of Cincinnati *B, M, D*
University of Dayton *B, M, D*
Washington State Community College *A*
Wittenberg University *B*
Wright State University *M*
Youngstown State University *B, M*

Oklahoma
Connors State College *A*
Eastern Oklahoma State College *A*
Northeastern Oklahoma Agricultural and
    Mechanical College *A*
Oklahoma City Community College *A*
Oklahoma State University *B, M, D*
Oral Roberts University *B*
Redlands Community College *A*
Rogers State University *A*
St. Gregory's University *A*
Tulsa Community College *A*
University of Oklahoma *B, M, D*
Western Oklahoma State College *A*

Oregon
Chemeketa Community College *A*
George Fox University *B*

Linn-Benton Community College *A*

Pennsylvania
Beaver College *B*
Bucks County Community College *A*
Butler County Community College *A*
Chatham College *B*
Community College of Philadelphia *A*
Delaware County Community College *A*
Drexel University *M*
Elizabethtown College *B*
Gannon University *M*
Geneva College *A, B*
Gettysburg College *B*
Harrisburg Area Community College *A*
Lafayette College *B*
Lebanon Valley College of
 Pennsylvania *B*
Lehigh Carbon Community College *A*
Lincoln University *B*
Lock Haven University of
 Pennsylvania *B*
Messiah College *B*
Northampton County Area Community
 College *A*
Pittsburgh Institute of Aeronautics *A*
Reading Area Community College *A*
St. Francis College *B*
St. Vincent College *B*
Seton Hill College *B*
Swarthmore College *B*
Temple University *B, D*
University of Pittsburgh
 Greensburg *B*
University of Pittsburgh *B, M*
Valley Forge Military College *A*
Westminster College *B*
Widener University *A, B*
York College of Pennsylvania *A*

Puerto Rico
University of Puerto Rico
 Mayaguez Campus *B*
 Ponce University College *A*

Rhode Island
Brown University *B, M, D*
Community College of Rhode Island *A*
Providence College *B*
Roger Williams University *A, B*

South Carolina
Anderson College *A*
Lander University *B*
Presbyterian College *B*

South Dakota
South Dakota State University *M*

Tennessee
Columbia State Community College *A*
David Lipscomb University *B*
Maryville College *B*
Southern Adventist University *A*
Tennessee State University *B, M*
University of Memphis *D*
University of Tennessee
 Chattanooga *B, M*
 Martin *B*
Walters State Community College *A*

Texas
Amarillo College *A*
Baylor University *B*
Brazosport College *A*
Central Texas College *A*
Coastal Bend College *A*
College of the Mainland *A*
Del Mar College *A*
El Paso Community College *A*
Galveston College *A*
Grayson County College *A*
Hill College *A*
Houston Baptist University *B*
Kilgore College *A*
Lamar University *M, D*
LeTourneau University *B*
Lubbock Christian University *B*

Navarro College *A*
Odessa College *A*
Palo Alto College *A*
Panola College *A*
Prairie View A&M University *M*
St. Mary's University *M*
South Plains College *A*
Southern Methodist University *B, M*
Texas A&M University
 Kingsville *M*
Texas A&M University *M, D*
Texas Christian University *B*
Texas Tech University *B, M, D*
Trinity Valley Community College *A*
Tyler Junior College *A*
University of Houston *M, D*
University of Texas
 El Paso *B, M*
 Tyler *B, M*
Western Texas College *A*
Wharton County Junior College *A*

Utah
Dixie State College of Utah *A*
Salt Lake Community College *A*
Snow College *A*
Southern Utah University *A*

Vermont
St. Michael's College *B*

Virginia
Danville Community College *A*
Hampton University *B*
J. Sargeant Reynolds Community
 College *A*
Mary Baldwin College *B*
Piedmont Virginia Community
 College *A*
Southwest Virginia Community
 College *A*
Thomas Nelson Community College *A*
Tidewater Community College *A*
University of Virginia *B*
Virginia Western Community College *A*

Washington
Centralia College *A*
Clark College *A*
Everett Community College *C, A*
Gonzaga University *B*
Grays Harbor College *A*
Highline Community College *A*
Lower Columbia College *A*
Olympic College *A*
Seattle Pacific University *B*
Shoreline Community College *A*
South Seattle Community College *A*
University of Washington *B, M*
Walla Walla College *B*
Washington State University *M*
Whitworth College *B*

West Virginia
College of West Virginia *A*
Marshall University *M*
Shepherd College *A*
West Virginia University
 Parkersburg *A*
West Virginia University *M, D*

Wisconsin
Beloit College *B*
Milwaukee School of Engineering *M*
University of Wisconsin
 Madison *B*
 Milwaukee *M, D*

Wyoming
Casper College *A*
Laramie County Community College *A*
Northwest College *A*
Sheridan College *A*
Western Wyoming Community
 College *A*

| Engineering design |

California
Compton Community College *C*

Michigan
Western Michigan University *B*

Minnesota
Dunwoody Institute *A*

New York
College of Aeronautics *A*

Ohio
Edison State Community College *A*
Washington State Community College *A*

Oklahoma
Cameron University *B*
Langston University *A*
Northeastern State University *B*

Oregon
Chemeketa Community College *A*

South Carolina
Trident Technical College *C*

Washington
Olympic College *C, A*
Western Washington University *B*

| Engineering mechanics |

Alabama
University of Alabama *M, D*

Arizona
Central Arizona College *A*
University of Arizona *M, D*

California
California State University
 Northridge *B, M*
City College of San Francisco *C, A*
East Los Angeles College *A*
University of California
 San Diego *B, M, D*
University of Southern California *B, M*

Colorado
Colorado School of Mines *M*
United States Air Force Academy *B*

Florida
University of Florida *M, D*

Georgia
Georgia Institute of Technology *M, D*

Idaho
Idaho State University *M*

Illinois
Parkland College *A*
University of Illinois
 Urbana-Champaign *B, M, D*

Indiana
Purdue University
 Calumet *B*

Iowa
Iowa State University *M, D*
Southeastern Community College
 North Campus *A*

Kentucky
University of Kentucky *M, D*

Maryland
Johns Hopkins University *B, M, D*

Massachusetts
Boston University *M*
Worcester Polytechnic Institute *B, M*

Michigan
Michigan State University *B, M, D*
Michigan Technological University *M, D*

University of Michigan *M*
Washtenaw Community College *A*

Minnesota
Winona State University *B*

Mississippi
Mississippi State University *M*

Missouri
East Central College *A*
University of Missouri
 Rolla *B, M, D*

Nebraska
University of Nebraska
 Lincoln *M*

New Jersey
Rutgers
 The State University of New Jersey:
 New Brunswick Graduate
 Campus *M, D*

New Mexico
New Mexico Institute of Mining and
 Technology *B, M*

New York
Columbia University
 Fu Foundation School of
 Engineering and Applied
 Science *B, M, D*
New York University *B*
Rensselaer Polytechnic Institute *B, M, D*

Ohio
Case Western Reserve University *M, D*
Cleveland State University *M*
Muskingum College *B*
Ohio State University
 Columbus Campus *M, D*
University of Cincinnati *B, M, D*
University of Dayton *M*

Oklahoma
Northeastern Oklahoma Agricultural and
 Mechanical College *A*

Pennsylvania
Gettysburg College *B*
Lehigh University *B*
Lock Haven University of
 Pennsylvania *B*
Penn State
 University Park *C, M*
Widener University *M*

South Carolina
Clemson University *M, D*

Texas
Texas A&M University *M, D*
University of Texas
 Arlington *M*
 Austin *M, D*

Utah
University of Utah *M*

Virginia
University of Virginia *M*
Virginia Commonwealth University *B*
Virginia Polytechnic Institute and State
 University *M, D*

Wisconsin
University of Wisconsin
 Madison *B, M, D*
Waukesha County Technical College *A*

| Engineering physics |

Alabama
Samford University *B*

Arizona
Northern Arizona University *B*
University of Arizona *B*

Arkansas
Arkansas State University
  Mountain Home C
Arkansas Tech University B
Ouachita Baptist University B
Southern Arkansas University B

California
California Institute of Technology B
Loyola Marymount University B
Point Loma Nazarene University B
Santa Clara University B
University of California
  Berkeley B
  San Diego B, M, D
University of the Pacific B
Westmont College B

Colorado
Colorado School of Mines B, M, D
University of Colorado
  Boulder B

Connecticut
Connecticut College B
Yale University B, M, D

Florida
Embry-Riddle Aeronautical University B
Jacksonville University B

Idaho
Northwest Nazarene University B

Illinois
Augustana College B
Bradley University B
Parkland College A
University of Illinois
  Chicago B
  Urbana-Champaign B

Indiana
Taylor University B

Iowa
Loras College B
Morningside College B
St. Ambrose University B
University of Northern Iowa B

Kansas
University of Kansas B

Kentucky
Murray State University B, M

Maine
University of Maine B

Maryland
Morgan State University B

Massachusetts
Brandeis University B
Eastern Nazarene College B
Harvard College B
Merrimack College B
Tufts University B
University of Massachusetts
  Boston B
Worcester Polytechnic Institute B, M

Michigan
Hope College B
Oakland University B
University of Michigan B

Minnesota
Bemidji State University B
St. Mary's University of Minnesota B

Mississippi
Mississippi College B

Missouri
East Central College A
Southeast Missouri State University B
Washington University B, M, D

Nebraska
University of Nebraska
  Omaha B

Nevada
University of Nevada
  Reno B

New Hampshire
Dartmouth College B

New Jersey
Stevens Institute of Technology M, D

New York
Barnard College B
Columbia University
  Fu Foundation School of
   Engineering and Applied
   Science M, D
Cornell University B
New York University B
Rensselaer Polytechnic Institute B, M, D
State University of New York
  Buffalo B
Syracuse University B
United States Military Academy B

North Carolina
Elon College B

North Dakota
North Dakota State University B

Ohio
Case Western Reserve University B
John Carroll University B
Miami University
  Oxford Campus B
Ohio State University
  Columbus Campus B
Wright State University B

Oklahoma
Northeastern State University B
Oklahoma Christian University of
  Science and Arts B
Oral Roberts University B
Southwestern Oklahoma State
  University B
University of Oklahoma B, M, D
University of Tulsa B

Oregon
Oregon State University B

Pennsylvania
Elizabethtown College B
Gettysburg College B
Lehigh University B
Lock Haven University of
  Pennsylvania B
University of Pittsburgh B

Rhode Island
Brown University B

South Dakota
Augustana College B
South Dakota State University B

Tennessee
Christian Brothers University B
University of Tennessee
  Knoxville B

Texas
Abilene Christian University B
Texas A&M University M
Texas Tech University B

Utah
Weber State University B

Vermont
University of Vermont M

Virginia
University of Virginia M, D
Washington and Lee University B

West Virginia
West Virginia Wesleyan College B

Wisconsin
University of Wisconsin
  Platteville B

Engineering science

Arizona
Arizona State University M, D

California
California Institute of Technology M, D
California Polytechnic State University:
  San Luis Obispo B
California State University
  Fullerton B
Stanford University M
University of California
  Berkeley B, M, D
  San Diego B

Colorado
Colorado State University B
United States Air Force Academy B

Connecticut
Gateway Community College A
Hartford Graduate Center M
Manchester Community-Technical
  College A
Norwalk Community-Technical
  College A
Yale University B

District of Columbia
George Washington University M, D

Florida
Manatee Community College A
University of Florida B, M
University of Miami B

Idaho
Idaho State University D

Illinois
Benedictine University B
College of DuPage A
Northwestern University B
Principia College B

Indiana
Manchester College B

Iowa
Iowa State University B

Kansas
Garden City Community College A

Louisiana
Louisiana State University and
  Agricultural and Mechanical
  College M, D
Tulane University B
University of New Orleans M, D

Massachusetts
Berkshire Community College A
Boston University D
Greenfield Community College A
Harvard College B
Harvard University M, D
Massachusetts Maritime Academy B
Merrimack College A
Middlesex Community College A
North Shore Community College A
Northern Essex Community College A
Tufts University B

Michigan
Glen Oaks Community College A
University of Michigan
  Flint B
University of Michigan B
Washtenaw Community College A

Mississippi
University of Mississippi M, D

Missouri
Washington University B, M, D

Montana
Montana Tech of the University of
  Montana B, M

Nebraska
Metropolitan Community College A

New Hampshire
Daniel Webster College A
Dartmouth College B

New Jersey
Camden County College A
County College of Morris A
Gloucester County College A
Hudson County Community College A
Mercer County Community College A
Middlesex County College A
New Jersey Institute of Technology B, M
Passaic County Community College A
Raritan Valley Community College A
Rutgers
  The State University of New Jersey:
   College of Engineering B
The College of New Jersey B

New Mexico
New Mexico Institute of Mining and
  Technology B, M
University of New Mexico B

New York
Adirondack Community College A
Broome Community College A
City University of New York
  Borough of Manhattan Community
   College A
  College of Staten Island A, B
  Queensborough Community
   College C
Clarkson University M, D
Columbia-Greene Community College A
Corning Community College A
Dutchess Community College A
Finger Lakes Community College A
Fulton-Montgomery Community
  College A
Genesee Community College A
Hofstra University B
Hudson Valley Community College A
Jefferson Community College A
Monroe Community College A
New York State College of Ceramics at
  Alfred University B
Onondaga Community College A
Pace University:
  Pleasantville/Briarcliff B
Rensselaer Polytechnic Institute B, M, D
Rochester Institute of Technology A
State University of New York
  Buffalo M
  College of Agriculture and
   Technology at Morrisville A
  College of Technology at Alfred A
  College of Technology at Canton A
  College of Technology at Delhi A
  Stony Brook B
Suffolk County Community College A
Tompkins-Cortland Community
  College A
University of Rochester B
Westchester Community College A

Ohio
Case Western Reserve
  University B, M, D
Franciscan University of Steubenville B
Jefferson Community College A
University of Cincinnati M, D
University of Toledo M, D
Wright State University B, M

Oklahoma
Oklahoma State University *B*

Pennsylvania
Gettysburg College *B*
Lock Haven University of
  Pennsylvania *B*
Penn State
  Harrisburg *M*
  University Park *B, M*
Pennsylvania College of Technology *A*
Valley Forge Military College *A*
Wilkes University *B*

Tennessee
David Lipscomb University *B*
University of Tennessee
  Knoxville *B, M, D*
Vanderbilt University *B*

Texas
Abilene Christian University *B*
St. Mary's University *B*
Trinity University *B*
University of Houston *M, D*

Virginia
George Mason University *M*
Sweet Briar College *B*
Virginia Polytechnic Institute and State
  University *B*

Washington
Pacific Lutheran University *B*
Washington State University *D*

Engineering-related technologies

Alabama
Alabama Agricultural and Mechanical
  University *B*
Community College of the Air Force *A*
Enterprise State Junior College *A*
Jacksonville State University *B*
Lawson State Community College *A*
Northwest-Shoals Community College *A*
Snead State Community College *C, A*

Alaska
University of Alaska
  Anchorage *B*

Arizona
Arizona Western College *A*
Central Arizona College *A*
Gateway Community College *A*
Glendale Community College *A*
South Mountain Community College *A*

Arkansas
Arkansas State University *A, B*
Phillips Community College of the
  University of Arkansas *A*
Southern Arkansas University
  Tech *C, A*

California
Allan Hancock College *A*
American River College *A*
Bakersfield College *A*
Barstow College *A*
Butte College *A*
Cabrillo College *A*
California Maritime Academy *B*
California Polytechnic State University:
  San Luis Obispo *B*
California State Polytechnic University:
  Pomona *B*
California State University
  Long Beach *B*
Canada College *A*
Cerritos Community College *A*
Cerro Coso Community College *C, A*
Chabot College *A*
Chaffey Community College *A*
Citrus College *A*

City College of San Francisco *C, A*
College of Marin: Kentfield *A*
College of San Mateo *A*
College of the Desert *A*
College of the Siskiyous *C, A*
Compton Community College *A*
Contra Costa College *A*
Cuyamaca College *A*
Cypress College *A*
Diablo Valley College *C, A*
Don Bosco Technical Institute *A*
East Los Angeles College *C, A*
Evergreen Valley College *A*
Gavilan Community College *A*
Glendale Community College *C, A*
Golden West College *C, A*
Los Angeles Harbor College *A*
Los Angeles Trade and Technical
  College *C, A*
Los Angeles Valley College *A*
Merced College *A*
Mission College *A*
Modesto Junior College *C, A*
Mount San Antonio College *A*
Mount San Jacinto College *A*
Pacific Union College *A, B*
Pasadena City College *C, A*
Riverside Community College *C, A*
San Bernardino Valley College *A*
San Diego City College *C, A*
San Joaquin Delta College *C, A*
San Jose City College *A*
Santa Barbara City College *A*
Shasta College *A*
Solano Community College *A*
Taft College *A*
Ventura College *A*
West Hills Community College *A*

Colorado
Aims Community College *A*
Community College of Denver *C, A*
Pueblo Community College *C, A*
Red Rocks Community College *C, A*

Connecticut
Asnuntuck Community-Technical
  College *A*
Capital Community College *A*
Central Connecticut State University *B*
Fairfield University *M*
Gateway Community College *A*
Middlesex Community-Technical
  College *A*
Naugatuck Valley Community-Technical
  College *C, A*
Norwalk Community-Technical
  College *A*
Three Rivers Community-Technical
  College *A*
University of Hartford *B*

Delaware
Delaware State University *B*
Delaware Technical and Community
  College
    Owens Campus *A*
    Stanton/Wilmington Campus *C*
    Terry Campus *C, A*
University of Delaware *B*

Florida
Brevard Community College *C, A*
Daytona Beach Community College *A*
Embry-Riddle Aeronautical University *B*
Hillsborough Community College *A*
Indian River Community College *A*
Manatee Community College *A*
Miami-Dade Community College *A*
Polk Community College *A*
Seminole Community College *A*

Georgia
Atlanta Metropolitan College *A*
Chattahoochee Technical Institute *A*
Clayton College and State University *A*
Gainesville College *A*

Valdosta State University *A*
Waycross College *A*
Young Harris College *A*

Hawaii
University of Hawaii
  Honolulu Community College *C, A*
  Maui Community College *A*

Illinois
Black Hawk College *C, A*
Danville Area Community College *A*
Highland Community College *A*
Kishwaukee College *C, A*
Lincoln Land Community College *A*
Moraine Valley Community
  College *C, A*
Southern Illinois University
  Carbondale *B*
Triton College *C, A*
Wheaton College *B*
William Rainey Harper College *C, A*

Indiana
Indiana University--Purdue University
  Indiana University-Purdue
    University Fort Wayne *C, A, B*
Ivy Tech State College
  Northwest *A*
Purdue University
  Calumet *B*
University of Southern Indiana *B*
Vincennes University *A*

Iowa
Des Moines Area Community College *A*
University of Northern Iowa *B*
William Penn University *B*

Kansas
Central Christian College *A*
Coffeyville Community College *A*
Cowley County Community College *A*
Kansas City Kansas Community
  College *C, A*
Kansas State University *B*
McPherson College *B*
Pittsburg State University *B, M*

Kentucky
Ashland Community College *A*
Institute of Electronic Technology *A*
Kentucky Wesleyan College *B*
Lexington Community College *A*
Murray State University *B, M*
Northern Kentucky University *M*

Louisiana
Northwestern State University *A, B*

Maine
Central Maine Technical College *A*
Eastern Maine Technical College *A*
Kennebec Valley Technical College *A*
Maine Maritime Academy *B*

Maryland
Charles County Community
  College *C, A*
Chesapeake College *C, A*
Harford Community College *A*
Montgomery College
  Rockville Campus *A*
  Takoma Park Campus *A*
University of Maryland
  Eastern Shore *B*

Massachusetts
Franklin Institute of Boston *A*
Massachusetts Maritime Academy *B*
Northeastern University *A, B*
Roxbury Community College *A*
Wentworth Institute of Technology *A, B*

Michigan
Andrews University *A, B*
Grand Rapids Community College *A*
Henry Ford Community College *A*
Lake Superior State University *A*

Lansing Community College *A*
Macomb Community College *C, A*
Michigan Technological University *A*
Mott Community College *A*
Muskegon Community College *A*
North Central Michigan College *A*
Northwestern Michigan College *A*
St. Clair County Community
  College *C, A*
Southwestern Michigan College *A*
Wayne State University *M, D*
West Shore Community College *A*

Minnesota
Alexandria Technical College *A*
Lake Superior College: A Community
  and Technical College *A*
Minnesota State University, Mankato *B*
NEI College of Technology *A*
North Hennepin Community College *A*
St. Cloud State University *B*

Mississippi
Mississippi Delta Community College *A*
University of Southern Mississippi *M*

Missouri
Missouri Southern State College *A*
St. Louis Community College
  St. Louis Community College at
    Forest Park *A*

Montana
Miles Community College *A*
Montana Tech of the University of
  Montana: College of Technology *A*
Montana Tech of the University of
  Montana *A*

Nebraska
University of Nebraska
  Omaha *B*
Wayne State College *B, T*

New Hampshire
New Hampshire Community Technical
  College
    Berlin *A*
    Claremont *A*

New Jersey
Brookdale Community College *A*
Camden County College *A*
County College of Morris *A*
Essex County College *A*
New Jersey Institute of Technology *B*
The College of New Jersey *B, T*
Thomas Edison State College *A, B*

New Mexico
New Mexico State University *A, B*
Northern New Mexico Community
  College *A*

New York
Adirondack Community College *A*
City University of New York
  Bronx Community College *A*
  New York City Technical
    College *A, B*
  Queensborough Community
    College *A*
College of Aeronautics *A, B*
Corning Community College *A*
Fulton-Montgomery Community
  College *A*
Hudson Valley Community College *A*
Jamestown Community College *A*
Manhattan College *M*
New York Institute of Technology *B*
Orange County Community College *C*
Regents College *A, B*
Rochester Institute of Technology *A, B*

Engineering/industrial management

State University of New York
    College at Buffalo *B, M*
    College of Agriculture and
        Technology at Morrisville *A*
    College of Technology at Alfred *A*
    College of Technology at Canton *A*
Tompkins-Cortland Community
    College *A*
Westchester Community College *C, A*

North Carolina
Central Piedmont Community College *A*
Davidson County Community
    College *C, A*
East Carolina University *B*
Forsyth Technical Community College *A*
Gaston College *A*
Guilford Technical Community
    College *A*
Mayland Community College *C*
Wake Technical Community College *A*
Wayne Community College *A*
Wilkes Community College *A*
Wilson Technical Community College *A*

North Dakota
North Dakota State College of Science *A*

Ohio
Bryant & Stratton College *A, B*
Central State University *B*
Cincinnati State Technical and
    Community College *C, A*
Cleveland Institute of Electronics *C, A*
Edison State Community College *A*
Kent State University
    Ashtabula Regional Campus *A, B*
    Trumbull Campus *A*
    Tuscarawas Campus *A*
Lima Technical College *A*
Marion Technical College *A*
Miami University
    Oxford Campus *A*
Northwest State Community College *A*
Owens Community College
    Toledo *A*
Shawnee State University *A, B*
Sinclair Community College *A*
Terra Community College *C, A*
University of Akron *A*
University of Dayton *B*
Washington State Community College *A*
Youngstown State University *A, B*

Oklahoma
Murray State College *A*
Northeastern Oklahoma Agricultural and
    Mechanical College *A*
Oklahoma State University
    Oklahoma City *A*
Oklahoma State University *B*
Rogers State University *A*
Southwestern Oklahoma State
    University *A*
Tulsa Community College *A*

Oregon
Portland Community College *A*

Pennsylvania
Bucks County Community College *A*
Community College of Allegheny
    County *C, A*
Community College of Beaver County *A*
Delaware County Community College *A*
Lebanon Valley College of
    Pennsylvania *A*
Lehigh Carbon Community College *A*
Montgomery County Community
    College *A*
Penn State
    University Park *C*
Pennsylvania College of
    Technology *C, A*
Pittsburgh Institute of Aeronautics *A*
Pittsburgh Technical Institute *C*
Point Park College *A, B*

Reading Area Community College *A*
Slippery Rock University of
    Pennsylvania *B*

Puerto Rico
Caribbean University *A*
University of Puerto Rico
    Arecibo Campus *A, B*
    Bayamon University College *A, B*

Rhode Island
Community College of Rhode Island *A*
New England Institute of Technology *B*
Rhode Island College *B*

South Carolina
Charleston Southern University *B*
Spartanburg Technical College *A*
Trident Technical College *C, A*
York Technical College *A*

Tennessee
Austin Peay State University *B*
East Tennessee State University *B, M*
Jackson State Community College *A*
Northeast State Technical Community
    College *A*
Tennessee Technological University *B*
Walters State Community College *A*

Texas
Angelina College *A*
Grayson County College *A*
Hill College *A*
LeTourneau University *B*
North Central Texas College *A*
Richland College *A*
San Antonio College *A*
San Jacinto College
    North *C, A*
Southwest Texas State University *B*
Tarleton State University *B*
Texas A&M University
    Commerce *B, M*
    Kingsville *B*
Texas A&M University *B*
Texas Southern University *B*
Texas Tech University *B*
University of Houston
    Downtown *B*
West Texas A&M University *B, M*

Utah
Brigham Young University *M*
Utah State University *B*
Weber State University *A, B*

Vermont
Vermont Technical College *A, B*

Virginia
Dabney S. Lancaster Community
    College *A*
Germanna Community College *A*
Northern Virginia Community College *A*
Patrick Henry Community College *A*
Virginia Highlands Community
    College *A*
Virginia State University *B*

Washington
Bellevue Community College *A*
Clark College *A*
Columbia Basin College *A*
Everett Community College *C, A*
Highline Community College *A*
North Seattle Community College *A*
Peninsula College *A*
Shoreline Community College *A*
Skagit Valley College *A*
South Seattle Community College *A*
Western Washington University *B*
Yakima Valley Community College *A*

West Virginia
Potomac State College of West Virginia
    University *A*
Salem-Teikyo University *B*

West Virginia University
    Parkersburg *A*
West Virginia University Institute of
    Technology *A, B*

Wisconsin
Blackhawk Technical College *A*
Moraine Park Technical College *A*
Silver Lake College *B*
Southwest Wisconsin Technical
    College *A*

Wyoming
Laramie County Community
    College *C, A*
Sheridan College *A*
Western Wyoming Community
    College *A*

Engineering/industrial management

California
Claremont McKenna College *B*
Loyola Marymount University *M*
Santa Clara University *C, M*
University of Southern California *M*
University of the Pacific *B*

Colorado
Fort Lewis College *B*
National Technological University *M*
University of Colorado
    Boulder *M*

District of Columbia
Catholic University of America *M*
George Washington University *M, D*

Florida
Florida Institute of Technology *M*
Florida International University *M*
Hillsborough Community College *A*
Palm Beach Community College *A*
Tallahassee Community College *A*
University of Miami *B*
University of South Florida *M*

Georgia
Mercer University *B, M*

Idaho
Idaho State University *B*
University of Idaho *M*

Illinois
Bradley University *B*
Northern Illinois University *M*
Northwestern University *B, M, D*
University of Illinois
    Chicago *B*

Indiana
Purdue University
    Calumet *B, T*
Rose-Hulman Institute of Technology *M*
Tri-State University *B*

Kansas
Kansas State University *M*
University of Kansas *M*
Wichita State University *M*

Louisiana
University of Louisiana at Lafayette *M*
University of New Orleans *C, M*

Maryland
Johns Hopkins University *M*
University of Maryland
    Baltimore County *M*
    Eastern Shore *B*

Massachusetts
Massachusetts Maritime Academy *B*
Northeastern University *M*
University of Massachusetts
    Amherst *M*
Western New England College *M*

Worcester Polytechnic Institute *B, M*

Michigan
Kettering University *M*
Lake Superior State University *B*
Lawrence Technological University *B*
Oakland University *M*
University of Detroit Mercy *M*
University of Michigan
    Dearborn *M*
    Flint *B*
Wayne State University *M*
Western Michigan University *B, M*

Missouri
St. Louis University *B*
University of Missouri
    Rolla *B, M, D*

Montana
Montana State University
    Bozeman *M*

New Jersey
New Jersey Institute of Technology *M, D*
Princeton University *B, M, D*

New York
College of Aeronautics *B*
Columbia University
    Fu Foundation School of
        Engineering and Applied
        Science *B*
New York Institute of Technology *B*
Rensselaer Polytechnic Institute *B, M, D*
Rochester Institute of Technology *M*
Syracuse University *B*
United States Merchant Marine
    Academy *B*

North Carolina
Cape Fear Community College *A*
Haywood Community College *A*
Mitchell Community College *A*
North Carolina Agricultural and
    Technical State University *B*
North Carolina State University *M, D*
Pitt Community College *A*

Ohio
David N. Myers College *B*
Edison State Community College *A*
Miami University
    Oxford Campus *B*
University of Dayton *B*

Oklahoma
Oklahoma State University *B, M, D*
University of Tulsa *M*

Oregon
Portland State University *M*
University of Portland *B*

Pennsylvania
Cheyney University of Pennsylvania *B*
Drexel University *M*
Grove City College *B*
Wilkes University *B*
York College of Pennsylvania *B*

Puerto Rico
University of Puerto Rico
    Mayaguez Campus *B*

South Dakota
South Dakota State University *M*

Tennessee
University of Tennessee
    Chattanooga *B, M*
Vanderbilt University *M*

Texas
LeTourneau University *B*
St. Mary's University *M*
Southern Methodist University *M, D*
Texas A&M University
    Kingsville *B, M*

253

Engineering/industrial management

Texas State Technical College
    Harlingen *A*
Texas Tech University *M*
University of Houston *M*

Utah
Brigham Young University *M*
Utah Valley State College *B*

Vermont
University of Vermont *B*

Washington
St. Martin's College *M*
Washington State University *M*

Wisconsin
Marquette University *M*
Milwaukee School of Engineering *M*
Northeast Wisconsin Technical
    College *A*

English

Alabama
Alabama Agricultural and Mechanical
    University *B*
Alabama State University *B*
Athens State University *B*
Auburn University at Montgomery *B*
Auburn University *B, M, D, T*
Birmingham-Southern College *B, T*
Calhoun Community College *A*
Faulkner University *B, T*
Huntingdon College *B, T*
Jacksonville State University *B, M*
James H. Faulkner State Community
    College *A*
Oakwood College *B*
Samford University *B*
Spring Hill College *B, T*
Stillman College *B*
Talladega College *B*
Troy State University
    Dothan *B, T*
    Montgomery *B*
Troy State University *B*
Tuskegee University *B*
University of Alabama
    Birmingham *B, M*
    Huntsville *B, M*
University of Alabama *B, M, D*
University of Mobile *B, T*
University of Montevallo *B, M, T*
University of North Alabama *B, M*
University of South Alabama *B, M*
University of West Alabama *B, T*

Alaska
University of Alaska
    Anchorage *B, M*
    Fairbanks *B, M*

Arizona
Arizona State University *B, M, D*
Arizona Western College *A*
Cochise College *A*
Eastern Arizona College *A*
Grand Canyon University *B*
Mohave Community College *A*
Northern Arizona University *B, M, T*
Prescott College *B, M*
University of Arizona *B, M, D*

Arkansas
Arkansas State University
    Beebe Branch *A*
Arkansas State University *B, M*
Arkansas Tech University *B*
Harding University *B*
Henderson State University *B*
Hendrix College *B*
Lyon College *B*
Ouachita Baptist University *B*
Philander Smith College *B*
Southern Arkansas University *B*

University of Arkansas
    Little Rock *B*
    Monticello *B*
    Pine Bluff *B*
University of Arkansas *B, M, D*
University of Central Arkansas *B*
University of the Ozarks *B, T*
Westark College *A*
Williams Baptist College *B*

California
Allan Hancock College *A*
Azusa Pacific University *B*
Bakersfield College *A*
Barstow College *A*
Biola University *B*
Butte College *A*
Cabrillo College *A*
California Baptist University *B*
California Institute of Technology *B*
California Lutheran University *B*
California Polytechnic State University:
    San Luis Obispo *B, M*
California State Polytechnic University:
    Pomona *B, M*
California State University
    Bakersfield *B, M*
    Chico *B, M*
    Dominguez Hills *B, M*
    Fresno *B*
    Fullerton *B, M*
    Hayward *B, M*
    Long Beach *B, M, T*
    Los Angeles
    Monterey Bay *B*
    Northridge *B, M*
    Sacramento *B, M*
    San Marcos *B*
    Stanislaus *B, M*
Canada College *A*
Cerritos Community College *A*
Chabot College *A*
Chaffey Community College *A*
Chapman University *B, M*
Citrus College *A*
Claremont McKenna College *B*
College of Notre Dame *B, M*
College of San Mateo *A*
College of the Canyons *A*
College of the Desert *A*
College of the Sequoias *A*
College of the Siskiyous *A*
Columbia College *A*
Compton Community College *A*
Concordia University *B*
Contra Costa College *A*
Crafton Hills College *A*
Cypress College *A*
De Anza College *A*
Diablo Valley College *A*
Dominican University of California *B*
Foothill College *A*
Fresno City College *A*
Fresno Pacific University *B*
Gavilan Community College *A*
Glendale Community College *A*
Golden West College *A*
Grossmont Community College *C, A*
Holy Names College *B, M*
Humboldt State University *B, M*
Imperial Valley College *A*
Kings River Community College *A*
La Sierra University *B, M*
Lake Tahoe Community College *A*
Long Beach City College *A*
Los Angeles Mission College *A*
Los Angeles Southwest College *A*
Los Angeles Valley College *A*
Loyola Marymount University *B, M*
Marymount College *A*
Master's College *B*
Mendocino College *A*
Merced College *A*
Merritt College *A*
Mills College *B, M*

MiraCosta College *A*
Modesto Junior College *A*
Monterey Peninsula College *A*
Mount St. Mary's College *B*
Napa Valley College *A*
Occidental College *B*
Ohlone College *A*
Orange Coast College *A*
Pacific Union College *B*
Palo Verde College *A*
Pepperdine University *B*
Pitzer College *B*
Pomona College *B*
Porterville College *B*
Riverside Community College *A*
Saddleback College *A*
St. John's Seminary College *B*
St. Mary's College of California *B*
San Diego City College *A*
San Diego Miramar College *A*
San Diego State University *B, M*
San Francisco State University *B, M*
San Joaquin Delta College *A*
San Jose State University *B, M*
Santa Ana College *A*
Santa Barbara City College *A*
Santa Clara University *B*
Santa Monica College *A*
Santa Rosa Junior College *A*
Scripps College *B*
Simpson College *B*
Skyline College *A*
Solano Community College *A*
Sonoma State University *B, M*
Southwestern College *A*
Stanford University *B, M, D*
Taft College *A*
United States International University *B*
University of California
    Berkeley *B, M, D*
    Davis *B, M, D*
    Irvine *B, M, D*
    Los Angeles *B, M, D*
    Riverside *B, M, D*
    San Diego *B*
    Santa Barbara *B, M, D*
University of La Verne *B*
University of Redlands *B*
University of San Diego *B*
University of San Francisco *B*
University of Southern California *B, D*
University of the Pacific *B*
Vanguard University of Southern
    California *B*
Ventura College *A*
West Los Angeles College *C, A*
West Valley College *A*
Westmont College *B*
Whittier College *B*

Colorado
Adams State College *B*
Colorado Christian University *B*
Colorado College *B*
Colorado Mountain College
    Alpine Campus *A*
    Spring Valley Campus *A*
    Timberline Campus *A*
Colorado State University *B, M*
Fort Lewis College *B*
Lamar Community College *A*
Mesa State College *A, B*
Metropolitan State College of
    Denver *B, T*
Red Rocks Community College *A*
Regis University *B*
United States Air Force Academy *B*
University of Colorado
    Boulder *B, M, D*
    Colorado Springs *B, M*
    Denver *B, M*
University of Denver *B, M, D*
University of Northern Colorado *B, M, T*
University of Southern Colorado *B, T*
Western State College of Colorado *B*

Connecticut
Albertus Magnus College *B*
Central Connecticut State
    University *B, M*
Connecticut College *B*
Eastern Connecticut State University *B*
Fairfield University *B*
Northwestern Connecticut
    Community-Technical College *A*
Quinnipiac University *B*
Sacred Heart University *A, B*
St. Joseph College *B, T*
Southern Connecticut State
    University *B, M*
Teikyo Post University *B*
Trinity College *B, M*
University of Connecticut *B, M, D*
University of Hartford *B*
University of New Haven *B*
Wesleyan University *B*
Western Connecticut State
    University *B, M*
Yale University *B, M, D*

Delaware
Delaware State University *B*
University of Delaware *B, M, D*
Wesley College *B*

District of Columbia
American University *B, M*
Catholic University of
    America *B, M, D, T*
Gallaudet University *B*
George Washington University *B*
Georgetown University *B, M*
Howard University *B, M, D*
Trinity College *B*
University of the District of
    Columbia *A, B*

Florida
Barry University *B*
Bethune-Cookman College *B*
Broward Community College *A*
Clearwater Christian College *B*
Flagler College *B*
Florida Agricultural and Mechanical
    University *B*
Florida Atlantic University *B, M*
Florida Gulf Coast University *B*
Florida International University *B, M*
Florida Memorial College *B*
Florida Southern College *B*
Florida State University *C, B, M, D*
Gulf Coast Community College *A*
Indian River Community College *A*
Jacksonville University *B*
Lynn University *B*
Manatee Community College *A*
Miami-Dade Community College *A*
Palm Beach Atlantic College *B, T*
Palm Beach Community College *A*
Pensacola Junior College *A*
Polk Community College *A*
Rollins College *B*
St. Leo University *B*
St. Thomas University *B*
Southeastern College of the Assemblies
    of God *B*
Stetson University *B, M*
University of Central Florida *B, M*
University of Florida *B, M, D*
University of Miami *B, M, D*
University of North Florida *B, M*
University of South Florida *B, M, D*
University of Tampa *A, B, T*
Warner Southern College *B*

Georgia
Abraham Baldwin Agricultural
    College *A*
Agnes Scott College *B*
Albany State University *B*
Armstrong Atlantic State University *B, T*
Atlanta Metropolitan College *A*

Augusta State University *B*
Berry College *B, T*
Brenau University *B*
Clark Atlanta University *B, M*
Clayton College and State University *A*
Columbus State University *B*
Covenant College *B*
Dalton State College *A*
Darton College *A*
East Georgia College *A*
Emmanuel College *B*
Floyd College *A*
Fort Valley State University *B*
Gainesville College *A*
Georgia College and State
  University *B, M, T*
Georgia Perimeter College *A*
Georgia Southern University *B, M*
Georgia Southwestern State University *B*
Georgia State University *B, M, D*
Kennesaw State University *B*
LaGrange College *B*
Mercer University *B, T*
Middle Georgia College *A*
Morehouse College *B*
Morris Brown College *B*
North Georgia College & State
  University *B*
Oglethorpe University *B*
Oxford College of Emory University *B*
Paine College *B*
Piedmont College *B*
Savannah State University *B*
Shorter College *B, T*
South Georgia College *A*
Spelman College *B*
State University of West Georgia *B*
Thomas College *B*
Toccoa Falls College *B*
University of Georgia *B, M, D*
Valdosta State University *B, M*
Waycross College *A*
Wesleyan College *B, T*
Young Harris College *A*

Hawaii

Brigham Young University
  Hawaii *B*
Chaminade University of Honolulu *B*
Hawaii Pacific University *B*
University of Hawaii
  Hilo *B*
  Manoa *B, M, D*
  West Oahu *B*

Idaho

Albertson College of Idaho *B*
Boise State University *M, D*
College of Southern Idaho *A*
Idaho State University *A, B, M, D*
Lewis-Clark State College *B*
North Idaho College *A*
Northwest Nazarene University *B*
Ricks College *A*
University of Idaho *B, M*

Illinois

Augustana College *B*
Barat College *B*
Benedictine University *B, T*
Black Hawk College
  East Campus *A*
Black Hawk College *C, A*
Blackburn College *B, T*
Bradley University *B, M, T*
Chicago State University *B, M, T*
City Colleges of Chicago
  Harold Washington College *A*
  Kennedy-King College *A*
Concordia University *B*
De Paul University *B, M, T*
Dominican University *B*
Eastern Illinois University *B, M, T*
Elmhurst College *B, T*
Eureka College *B, T*
Governors State University *B, M*

Greenville College *B, T*
Illinois College *B*
Illinois State University *B, M, D, T*
Illinois Wesleyan University *B*
John A. Logan College *A*
Joliet Junior College *A*
Judson College *B*
Kishwaukee College *A*
Knox College *B*
Lake Forest College *B*
Lewis University *B, T*
Lewis and Clark Community College *A*
Lincoln Land Community College *A*
Loyola University of Chicago *B, M, D*
MacMurray College *B*
McKendree College *B*
Monmouth College *B, T*
Morton College *A*
National-Louis University *B*
North Central College *B, T*
North Park University *B*
Northeastern Illinois University *B, M*
Northern Illinois University *B, M, D, T*
Northwestern University *B, M, D*
Olivet Nazarene University *B, T*
Parkland College *A*
Principia College *B, T*
Quincy University *A, B, T*
Rend Lake College *A*
Richland Community College *A*
Rockford College *B*
Roosevelt University *B, M*
St. Xavier University *C, B, M*
Sauk Valley Community College *A*
Southern Illinois University
  Carbondale *B, M, D*
  Edwardsville *B, M*
Southwestern Ilinois College *A*
Spoon River College *A*
Springfield College in Illinois *A*
Trinity Christian College *B, T*
Trinity International University *B*
Triton College *A*
University of Chicago *B, M, D*
University of Illinois
  Chicago *B, M, D*
  Springfield *B, M*
  Urbana-Champaign *B, M, D*
University of St. Francis *B*
Western Illinois University *B, M*
Wheaton College *B*
William Rainey Harper College *A*

Indiana

Anderson University *B*
Ball State University *B, M, D, T*
Bethel College *B*
Butler University *B, M*
Earlham College *B*
Franklin College *B*
Goshen College *B*
Grace College *B*
Hanover College *B*
Indiana State University *M*
Indiana University
  Bloomington *B, M, D*
  East *B*
  Kokomo *B*
  Northwest *B, T*
  South Bend *B*
  Southeast *B*
Indiana University--Purdue University
  Indiana University-Purdue
    University Fort Wayne *B, M*
  Indiana University-Purdue
    University Indianapolis *B, M*
Indiana Wesleyan University *A, B*
Manchester College *B, T*
Marian College *B, T*
Oakland City University *B*
Purdue University
  Calumet *B*
  North Central Campus *B*
Purdue University *B, M, D*
Saint Mary's College *B, T*

St. Joseph's College *B*
St. Mary-of-the-Woods College *B*
Taylor University *B*
University of Evansville *B*
University of Indianapolis *B, M*
University of Notre Dame *B, M, D*
University of St. Francis *B*
University of Southern Indiana *B*
Valparaiso University *B, M, T*
Vincennes University *A*
Wabash College *B*

Iowa

Briar Cliff College *B*
Buena Vista University *B, T*
Central College *B, T*
Clarke College *A, B, T*
Coe College *B*
Cornell College *B, T*
Dordt College *B*
Drake University *B*
Graceland University *T*
Grand View College *B*
Grinnell College *B*
Iowa State University *B, M, D*
Iowa Wesleyan College *B*
Loras College *B*
Luther College *B*
Maharishi University of
  Management *A, B, M*
Marshalltown Community College *A*
Marycrest International University *A, B*
Morningside College *B*
Mount Mercy College *B, T*
North Iowa Area Community College *A*
Northwestern College *B*
St. Ambrose University *B, T*
Simpson College *B*
University of Dubuque *B, T*
University of Iowa *B, M, D, T*
University of Northern Iowa *B, M*
Upper Iowa University *B*
Waldorf College *A*
Wartburg College *B, T*
William Penn University *B*

Kansas

Baker University *B, T*
Barton County Community College *A*
Benedictine College *B, T*
Bethany College *B*
Bethel College *B, T*
Central Christian College *A*
Coffeyville Community College *A*
Colby Community College *A*
Cowley County Community College *A*
Emporia State University *B, M, T*
Fort Hays State University *B, M*
Garden City Community College *A*
Hutchinson Community College *A*
Independence Community College *A*
Kansas City Kansas Community
  College *A*
Kansas State University *B, M*
Kansas Wesleyan University *B, T*
McPherson College *B, T*
MidAmerica Nazarene University *B*
Newman University *B*
Ottawa University *B*
Pittsburg State University *B, M, T*
Pratt Community College *A*
St. Mary College *B*
Seward County Community College *A*
Southwestern College *B*
Sterling College *B*
Tabor College *B*
University of Kansas *B, M, D*
Washburn University of Topeka *B*
Wichita State University *B, M, T*

Kentucky

Alice Lloyd College *B*
Asbury College *B, T*
Bellarmine College *B, T*
Berea College *B, T*
Brescia University *B*

Campbellsville University *B*
Centre College *B*
Cumberland College *B, T*
Eastern Kentucky University *B, M*
Georgetown College *B, T*
Kentucky State University *B*
Kentucky Wesleyan College *B, T*
Lindsey Wilson College *A, B, T*
Midway College *B*
Morehead State University *B, M*
Murray State University *B, M, T*
Northern Kentucky University *B*
Pikeville College *B*
Spalding University *B*
Thomas More College *A, B*
Transylvania University *B, T*
Union College *B*
University of Kentucky *B, M, D*
University of Louisville *B*
Western Kentucky University *B, M, T*

Louisiana

Centenary College of Louisiana *B, T*
Dillard University *B*
Louisiana State University
  Shreveport *B*
Louisiana State University and
  Agricultural and Mechanical
  College *B, M, D*
Louisiana Tech University *B, M*
Loyola University New Orleans *B*
McNeese State University *B, M*
Nicholls State University *B*
Northwestern State University *B, M*
Our Lady of Holy Cross College *B*
Southeastern Louisiana University *B, M*
Southern University
  New Orleans *B*
Southern University and Agricultural and
  Mechanical College *B*
Tulane University *B, M, D*
University of Louisiana at
  Lafayette *B, M, D*
University of Louisiana at Monroe *B, M*
University of New Orleans *B, M*
Xavier University of Louisiana *B*

Maine

Bates College *B*
Bowdoin College *B*
Colby College *B*
St. Joseph's College *B*
University of Maine
  Augusta *B*
  Farmington *B*
  Fort Kent *B*
  Machias *B*
  Presque Isle *B*
University of Maine *B, M*
University of New England *B*
University of Southern Maine *B*

Maryland

Allegany College *A*
Bowie State University *B*
College of Notre Dame of Maryland *B*
Columbia Union College *B*
Community College of Baltimore County
  Essex *A*
Coppin State College *B*
Frederick Community College *A*
Frostburg State University *B, T*
Goucher College *B*
Hood College *B, T*
Johns Hopkins University *B*
Loyola College in Maryland *B*
Morgan State University *B, M*
Mount St. Mary's College *B, T*
St. Mary's College of Maryland *B*
Salisbury State University *B, M, T*
Towson University *B*
United States Naval Academy *B*
University of Baltimore *B*

English

University of Maryland
    Baltimore County B
    College Park B, M, D, T
    Eastern Shore B
Villa Julie College B
Washington College B, M, T
Western Maryland College B

Massachusetts
American International College B
Amherst College B
Anna Maria College B
Assumption College B
Atlantic Union College B
Bay Path College B
Bentley College B
Berkshire Community College A
Boston College B, M, D
Boston University B, M, D
Brandeis University B, M, D
Bridgewater State College B, M
Clark University B, M
College of the Holy Cross B
Curry College B
Eastern Nazarene College B
Elms College B
Emmanuel College B
Fitchburg State College B, M
Framingham State College B, M
Gordon College B
Hampshire College B
Harvard College B, T
Harvard University M, D
Massachusetts College of Liberal Arts B
Massachusetts Institute of Technology B
Merrimack College B
Mount Holyoke College B
Nichols College B
Northeastern University B, M, D
Pine Manor College A, B
Regis College B
Roxbury Community College A
St. John's Seminary College B
Salem State College B, M
Simmons College B, M
Simon's Rock College of Bard B
Smith College B
Springfield College B
Stonehill College B
Suffolk University B
Tufts University B, M, D
University of Massachusetts
    Amherst B, M, D
    Boston B, M
    Dartmouth B
    Lowell B
Wellesley College B
Western New England College B
Westfield State College B, M
Wheaton College B
Williams College B
Worcester State College B

Michigan
Adrian College A, B, T
Albion College B, T
Alma College B, T
Andrews University B, M
Aquinas College B, T
Calvin College B, T
Central Michigan University B, M
Concordia College B, T
Cornerstone College and Grand Rapids Baptist Seminary B, T
Eastern Michigan University B
Grand Valley State University B
Hillsdale College B
Hope College B, T
Kalamazoo College B, T
Kellogg Community College C, A
Lake Michigan College A
Lake Superior State University B, T
Lansing Community College A
Madonna University A, B, T
Marygrove College B, T
Michigan State University B, M, D

Michigan Technological University B, D
Northern Michigan University B, M, T
Oakland University B, M
Olivet College B, T
Rochester College B
Saginaw Valley State University B
Siena Heights University B
Spring Arbor College B
University of Detroit Mercy B
University of Michigan
    Dearborn B
    Flint B, T
University of Michigan B, M, D, T
Wayne State University B, M, D
Western Michigan University B, M, D, T
William Tyndale College B

Minnesota
Augsburg College B
Bemidji State University B, M
Bethel College B
Carleton College B
College of St. Benedict B
College of St. Catherine: St. Paul Campus B
College of St. Scholastica B
Concordia College: Moorhead B, T
Concordia University: St. Paul B
Crown College B
Gustavus Adolphus College B
Hamline University B
Macalester College B, T
Metropolitan State University B
Minnesota State University, Mankato B, M
Moorhead State University B
North Central University B
Northland Community & Technical College A
Northwestern College B
St. Cloud State University B, M
St. John's University B
St. Mary's University of Minnesota B
St. Olaf College B
Southwest State University B, T
University of Minnesota
    Duluth B, M
    Morris B
    Twin Cities B, M, D
University of St. Thomas B, M
Winona State University B, M

Mississippi
Alcorn State University B
Belhaven College B
Blue Mountain College B
Delta State University B, T
Hinds Community College A
Jackson State University B, M
Mary Holmes College A
Millsaps College B, T
Mississippi College B, M
Mississippi Delta Community College A
Mississippi State University B, M
Mississippi University for Women B, T
Mississippi Valley State University B
Rust College B
Tougaloo College B
University of Mississippi B, M, D, T
University of Southern Mississippi B, M, D
William Carey College B, T

Missouri
Avila College B
Central Methodist College B
Central Missouri State University B, M
College of the Ozarks B
Columbia College B
Crowder College A
Culver-Stockton College B, T
Drury University B, T
East Central College A
Evangel University B
Fontbonne College B, T
Hannibal-LaGrange College B

Lindenwood University B
Maryville University of Saint Louis B
Mineral Area College A
Missouri Baptist College B
Missouri Southern State College B, T
Missouri Valley College B
Missouri Western State College B
Northwest Missouri State University B, M
Park University B
Rockhurst University B
St. Louis University B, M
Southeast Missouri State University B, M
Southwest Baptist University B, T
Southwest Missouri State University B, M
Stephens College B
Three Rivers Community College A
Truman State University B, M
University of Missouri
    Columbia B, M, D
    Kansas City B, M
    Rolla B, T
    St. Louis B, M
Washington University B, M, D
Webster University C, B
Westminster College B
William Jewell College B, T
William Woods University B, T

Montana
Carroll College A, B, T
Miles Community College A
Montana State University
    Billings B
    Bozeman B, M, T
    Northern B
Rocky Mountain College B, T
University of Great Falls B
University of Montana-Missoula B
Western Montana College of The University of Montana B

Nebraska
Bellevue University B
Chadron State College B
College of Saint Mary B, T
Concordia University B, D
Creighton University B, M
Dana College B
Doane College B
Hastings College B
Midland Lutheran College B, T
Nebraska Wesleyan University B
Northeast Community College A
Peru State College B, T
Union College B
University of Nebraska
    Kearney B, M, T
    Lincoln B, M, D
    Omaha B, M
Wayne State College B, M, T

Nevada
Community College of Southern Nevada A
University of Nevada
    Las Vegas B, M, D
    Reno B, M, D

New Hampshire
Colby-Sawyer College B, T
Dartmouth College B
Franklin Pierce College B
Keene State College B
New England College B, T
New Hampshire College B
New Hampshire Technical Institute A
Notre Dame College B
Plymouth State College of the University System of New Hampshire B
Rivier College B, M, T
St. Anselm College B, T
Thomas More College of Liberal Arts B

University of New Hampshire Manchester B
University of New Hampshire B, M, D

New Jersey
Bloomfield College B
Brookdale Community College A
Caldwell College B
Centenary College B
College of St. Elizabeth B, T
Drew University B, M, D
Fairleigh Dickinson University B, M
Felician College B, M
Georgian Court College B, T
Gloucester County College A
Kean University B
Monmouth University B
Montclair State University B, T
New Jersey City University B
Passaic County Community College A
Princeton University B, M, D
Richard Stockton College of New Jersey B
Rider University B
Rowan University B
Rutgers
    The State University of New Jersey: Camden College of Arts and Sciences B, T
    The State University of New Jersey: Camden Graduate Campus M
    The State University of New Jersey: Douglass College B, T
    The State University of New Jersey: Livingston College B, T
    The State University of New Jersey: New Brunswick Graduate Campus M, D
    The State University of New Jersey: Newark College of Arts and Sciences B, T
    The State University of New Jersey: Newark Graduate Campus M
    The State University of New Jersey: Rutgers College B, T
    The State University of New Jersey: University College Camden B, T
    The State University of New Jersey: University College New Brunswick B, T
    The State University of New Jersey: University College Newark B, T
St. Peter's College B
Salem Community College A
Seton Hall University B, M, T
Stevens Institute of Technology B
Sussex County Community College A
The College of New Jersey B, M, T
Thomas Edison State College B
Warren County Community College A
William Paterson University of New Jersey B, M

New Mexico
College of Santa Fe A, B
College of the Southwest B
Eastern New Mexico University B, M
New Mexico Highlands University B
New Mexico State University B, M
San Juan College A
University of New Mexico B, M, D
Western New Mexico University B

New York
Adelphi University M
Alfred University B
Bard College B
Barnard College B
Canisius College B

City University of New York
   Baruch College *B*
   Brooklyn College *B, M*
   City College *B, M, T*
   College of Staten Island *B, M, T*
   Graduate School and University Center *D*
   Hunter College *M*
   Lehman College *B, M*
   Queens College *B, M*
   York College *B*
Colgate University *B*
College of Mount St. Vincent *A, B, T*
College of New Rochelle *B, T*
College of St. Rose *B, M*
Columbia University
   Columbia College *B*
   Graduate School *M, D*
   School of General Studies *B*
Concordia College *B, T*
Cornell University *B, M, D, T*
D'Youville College *B*
Daemen College *B, T*
Dominican College of Blauvelt *B*
Dowling College *B, T*
Elmira College *B, T*
Eugene Lang College/New School University *B*
Fordham University *B, M, D*
Fulton-Montgomery Community College *A*
Hamilton College *B*
Hartwick College *B, T*
Hilbert College *B*
Hobart and William Smith Colleges *B*
Hofstra University *B*
Houghton College *B*
Iona College *B, M*
Ithaca College *B, T*
Keuka College *B*
Le Moyne College *B*
Long Island University
   Brooklyn Campus *B, M*
   C. W. Post Campus *B, M*
   Southampton College *B*
Manhattanville College *B*
Marist College *B, T*
Marymount College *B, T*
Marymount Manhattan College *B*
Mercy College *B*
Molloy College *B*
Mount St. Mary College *B, T*
Nazareth College of Rochester *B*
New York Institute of Technology *B*
New York University *B, M, D*
Niagara University *B*
Nyack College *B*
Pace University:
   Pleasantville/Briarcliff *B, T*
Pace University *B, T*
Regents College *B*
Roberts Wesleyan College *B*
Russell Sage College *B, T*
St. Bonaventure University *B, T*
St. Francis College *B, T*
St. John Fisher College *B*
St. John's University *B, M, D*
St. Thomas Aquinas College *B, T*
Sarah Lawrence College *B*
Siena College *B, T*
Skidmore College *B*
St. Joseph's College
   St. Joseph's College: Suffolk Campus *B, T*
   St. Joseph's College *B, T*

State University of New York
   Albany *B, M, D*
   Binghamton *B, M, D*
   Buffalo *B, M*
   College at Brockport *B, M, T*
   College at Buffalo *B, M*
   College at Cortland *B*
   College at Fredonia *B, M, T*
   College at Geneseo *B, T*
   College at Old Westbury *B*
   College at Oneonta *B, M*
   College at Plattsburgh *B*
   College at Potsdam *B, M, T*
   New Paltz *B, M, T*
   Oswego *B, M*
   Purchase *B*
   Stony Brook *B, M, D, T*
Syracuse University *B, M, D*
Touro College *B*
Union College *B*
United States Military Academy *B*
University of Rochester *B, M, D*
Utica College of Syracuse University *B*
Vassar College *B*
Wagner College *B, T*
Wells College *B*

North Carolina
Appalachian State University *B, M*
Barton College *B, T*
Belmont Abbey College *B*
Bennett College *B*
Brevard College *A, B*
Campbell University *B*
Catawba College *B, T*
Chowan College *B*
Davidson College *B*
Duke University *B, D*
East Carolina University *B, M*
Elizabeth City State University *B*
Elon College *B, T*
Fayetteville State University *B*
Gardner-Webb University *B*
Greensboro College *B, T*
Guilford College *B, T*
High Point University *B*
Johnson C. Smith University *B*
Lees-McRae College *B*
Lenoir-Rhyne College *B*
Louisburg College *A*
Mars Hill College *B, T*
Meredith College *B*
Montreat College *B*
Mount Olive College *B*
North Carolina Agricultural and Technical State University *B, M, T*
North Carolina Central University *B, M*
North Carolina State University *B, M*
North Carolina Wesleyan College *B*
Peace College *B*
Pfeiffer University *B*
Queens College *B*
St. Andrews Presbyterian College *B*
St. Augustine's College *B*
Salem College *B*
Sandhills Community College *A*
Shaw University *B*
University of North Carolina
   Asheville *B, T*
   Chapel Hill *B, M, D, T*
   Charlotte *B, M*
   Greensboro *B, M, D, T*
   Pembroke *B, M*
   Wilmington *B, M, T*
Wake Forest University *B, M*
Warren Wilson College *B*
Western Carolina University *B, M*
Wingate University *B*
Winston-Salem State University *B*

North Dakota
Dickinson State University *B, T*
Jamestown College *B*
Mayville State University *B*
Minot State University: Bottineau Campus *A*

Minot State University *B, T*
North Dakota State University *B, M*
University of Mary *B, T*
University of North Dakota *B, M, D, T*
Valley City State University *B*

Ohio
Antioch College *B*
Ashland University *B*
Baldwin-Wallace College *B, T*
Bowling Green State University *B, M, D*
Capital University *B*
Case Western Reserve University *B, M, D*
Cedarville College *B, T*
Central State University *B*
Cleveland State University *B, M, T*
College of Mount St. Joseph *B, T*
College of Wooster *B*
Defiance College *B, T*
Denison University *B*
Franciscan University of Steubenville *B*
Heidelberg College *B*
Hiram College *B*
John Carroll University *B, M*
Kent State University
   Stark Campus *B*
Kent State University *B, M, D, T*
Kenyon College *B*
Lake Erie College *B*
Lourdes College *A, B*
Malone College *B*
Marietta College *B*
Miami University
   Middletown Campus *A*
   Oxford Campus *B, M, D, T*
Mount Union College *B*
Mount Vernon Nazarene College *B*
Muskingum College *B*
Notre Dame College of Ohio *B, T*
Oberlin College *B*
Ohio Dominican College *B, D*
Ohio Northern University *B*
Ohio State University
   Columbus Campus *B, M, D*
Ohio University *B, M, D*
Ohio Wesleyan University *B*
Otterbein College *B*
Owens Community College
   Toledo *A*
Pontifical College Josephinum *B*
Shawnee State University *B*
Terra Community College *A*
University of Akron *B, M*
University of Cincinnati *B, M, D, T*
University of Dayton *B, M*
University of Findlay *B*
University of Rio Grande *B, T*
University of Toledo *B, M, D*
Ursuline College *B*
Walsh University *B*
Wilberforce University *B*
Wilmington College *B*
Wittenberg University *B*
Wright State University *B, M*
Xavier University *A, B, M*
Youngstown State University *B, M*

Oklahoma
Cameron University *B, M*
Carl Albert State College *A*
Connors State College *A*
East Central University *B*
Eastern Oklahoma State College *A*
Langston University *B*
Mid-America Bible College *B*
Murray State College *A*
Northeastern Oklahoma Agricultural and Mechanical College *A*
Northeastern State University *B*
Northern Oklahoma College *A*
Northwestern Oklahoma State University *B*
Oklahoma Baptist University *B, T*
Oklahoma Christian University of Science and Arts *B, T*

Oklahoma City University *B*
Oklahoma Panhandle State University *B*
Oklahoma State University *B, M, D*
Oral Roberts University *B*
Rogers State University *A*
Rose State College *A*
St. Gregory's University *A, B*
Southeastern Oklahoma State University *B*
Southern Nazarene University *B*
Southwestern Oklahoma State University *B*
Tulsa Community College *A*
University of Oklahoma *B, M, D*
University of Science and Arts of Oklahoma *B, T*
University of Tulsa *B, M, D*
Western Oklahoma State College *A*

Oregon
Central Oregon Community College *A*
Chemeketa Community College *A*
Concordia University *B*
Eastern Oregon University *B, T*
George Fox University *B*
Lewis & Clark College *B*
Linfield College *B*
Oregon State University *B, M*
Pacific University *B*
Portland State University *B, M*
Reed College *B*
Southern Oregon University *B, T*
University of Oregon *B, M, D*
University of Portland *B*
Western Baptist College *B*
Western Oregon University *B*
Willamette University *B*

Pennsylvania
Albright College *B, T*
Allegheny College *B*
Allentown College of St. Francis de Sales *B*
Alvernia College *B*
Beaver College *B, M*
Bloomsburg University of Pennsylvania *B, T*
Bryn Athyn College of the New Church *A, B*
Bryn Mawr College *B*
Bucknell University *B, M*
Butler County Community College *A*
Cabrini College *B*
California University of Pennsylvania *B, M*
Carlow College *B*
Carnegie Mellon University *B*
Cedar Crest College *B*
Chatham College *B*
Chestnut Hill College *B*
Cheyney University of Pennsylvania *B*
Clarion University of Pennsylvania *B, M, T*
College Misericordia *B*
Community College of Allegheny County *A*
Delaware Valley College *B*
Dickinson College *B*
Drexel University *B*
Duquesne University *B, M, D*
East Stroudsburg University of Pennsylvania *B*
Edinboro University of Pennsylvania *B, T*
Elizabethtown College *B*
Franklin and Marshall College *B*
Gannon University *B, M*
Geneva College *B, T*
Gettysburg College *B*
Grove City College *B*
Gwynedd-Mercy College *B*
Haverford College *B, T*
Holy Family College *B, T*
Immaculata College *B*
Indiana University of Pennsylvania *B, M, D*

Juniata College *B*
King's College *B*
Kutztown University of
    Pennsylvania *B, M, T*
La Roche College *B*
La Salle University *B, T*
Lafayette College *B*
Lebanon Valley College of
    Pennsylvania *B, T*
Lehigh University *B, M, D*
Lincoln University *B*
Lock Haven University of
    Pennsylvania *B*
Lycoming College *B*
Mansfield University of
    Pennsylvania *A, B, T*
Marywood University *B*
Mercyhurst College *B*
Messiah College *B*
Millersville University of
    Pennsylvania *B, M, T*
Moravian College *B, T*
Muhlenberg College *B, T*
Neumann College *B, T*
Penn State
    Abington *B*
    Altoona *B*
    Delaware County *B*
    Erie, The Behrend College *B*
    University Park *B, M, D*
Point Park College *B*
Robert Morris College *B*
Rosemont College *B*
St. Francis College *B*
St. Joseph's University *B*
St. Vincent College *B*
Seton Hill College *B, T*
Shippensburg University of
    Pennsylvania *B, M, T*
Slippery Rock University of
    Pennsylvania *B, M, T*
Susquehanna University *B, T*
Swarthmore College *B*
Temple University *B, M, D*
Thiel College *B*
University of Pennsylvania *A, B, M, D*
University of Pittsburgh
    Bradford *B, T*
    Greensburg *B*
University of Pittsburgh *C, M, D*
University of Scranton *B, T*
Ursinus College *B, T*
Villanova University *B, M*
Washington and Jefferson College *B*
Waynesburg College *B*
West Chester University of
    Pennsylvania *M*
Westminster College *B, M, T*
Widener University *B*
Wilkes University *B*
Wilson College *B*
York College of Pennsylvania *B, T*

Puerto Rico
Bayamon Central University *B*
Inter American University of Puerto Rico
    Metropolitan Campus *B*
    San German Campus *B*
Pontifical Catholic University of Puerto
    Rico *B*
University of Puerto Rico
    Cayey University College *B*
    Mayaguez Campus *B, M*
    Rio Piedras Campus *B, M*
University of the Sacred Heart *B*

Rhode Island
Brown University *B, M, D*
Bryant College *B*
Providence College *B, T*
Rhode Island College *B, M*
Salve Regina University *B*
University of Rhode Island *B, M, D*

South Carolina
Anderson College *B, T*
Benedict College *B*
Charleston Southern University *B*
Clemson University *B, M*
Coastal Carolina University *B*
Coker College *B*
College of Charleston *B, M, T*
Columbia College *B*
Converse College *B*
Erskine College *B, T*
Francis Marion University *B*
Furman University *B, T*
Lander University *B*
Limestone College *B*
Morris College *B*
Newberry College *B, T*
Presbyterian College *B, T*
South Carolina State University *B*
Southern Wesleyan University *B, T*
The Citadel *B, M*
University of South Carolina
    Aiken *B*
    Spartanburg *B*
University of South Carolina *B, M, D*
Voorhees College *B*
Winthrop University *B, M*
Wofford College *B, T*

South Dakota
Augustana College *B, T*
Black Hills State University *B*
Dakota State University *B*
Dakota Wesleyan University *B*
Mount Marty College *B*
Northern State University *B*
South Dakota State University *B, M*
University of South Dakota *B, M, D*

Tennessee
Austin Peay State University *B, M*
Belmont University *B, T*
Bethel College *B, T*
Carson-Newman College *B, T*
Christian Brothers University *B*
Crichton College *B*
Cumberland University *B*
David Lipscomb University *B*
Dyersburg State Community College *A*
East Tennessee State University *B, M, T*
Fisk University *B*
Freed-Hardeman University *B, T*
Hiwassee College *C*
King College *B, T*
Lambuth University *B*
Lane College *B*
LeMoyne-Owen College *B*
Lee University *B*
Lincoln Memorial University *B, T*
Maryville College *B, T*
Middle Tennessee State
    University *B, M, D*
Milligan College *B, T*
Rhodes College *B, T*
Roane State Community College *A*
Southern Adventist University *B*
Tennessee State University *B, M*
Tennessee Technological
    University *B, M, T*
Tennessee Temple University *B*
Tennessee Wesleyan College *B, T*
Trevecca Nazarene University *B*
Tusculum College *B*
Union University *B, T*
University of Memphis *B, M*
University of Tennessee
    Chattanooga *B, M, T*
    Knoxville *B, M, D*
    Martin *B*
University of the South *B*
Vanderbilt University *B, M, D*
Walters State Community College *A*

Texas
Abilene Christian University *B, T*
Amarillo College *A*
Angelina College *A*
Angelo State University *B, M*
Austin College *B*
Baylor University *B, M, D*
Blinn College *A*
Brazosport College *A*
Coastal Bend College *A*
Concordia University at Austin *B, T*
Dallas Baptist University *B*
Del Mar College *A*
East Texas Baptist University *B*
El Paso Community College *A*
Galveston College *A*
Hardin-Simmons University *B, M*
Hill College *A*
Houston Baptist University *B*
Howard College *A*
Howard Payne University *B, T*
Jarvis Christian College *B*
Lamar University *B, M*
LeTourneau University *B*
Lon Morris College *A*
Lubbock Christian University *B*
McMurry University *B*
Midland College *A*
Midwestern State University *B, M*
Navarro College *A*
Northeast Texas Community College *A*
Our Lady of the Lake University of San
    Antonio *B, M*
Palo Alto College *A*
Panola College *A*
Paris Junior College *A*
Prairie View A&M University *B, M*
Rice University *B, M, D*
St. Edward's University *B, T*
St. Mary's University *B, M*
Sam Houston State University *B, M*
San Jacinto College
    North *A*
Schreiner College *B*
Southern Methodist University *B, M*
Southwest Texas State
    University *B, M*
Southwestern Adventist University *B, T*
Southwestern University *B, T*
Stephen F. Austin State
    University *B, M, T*
Sul Ross State University *B, M, T*
Tarleton State University *B, M, T*
Texas A&M International
    University *B, M, T*
Texas A&M University
    Commerce *B, M*
    Corpus Christi *B, M, T*
    Kingsville *B, M*
    Texarkana *B, T*
Texas A&M University *B, M, D*
Texas Christian University *B, M, D, T*
Texas College *B*
Texas Lutheran University *B*
Texas Tech University *B, M, D*
Texas Wesleyan University *B*
Texas Woman's University *B, M, T*
Trinity University *B*
Trinity Valley Community College *A*
Tyler Junior College *A*
University of Dallas *B, M, D*
University of Houston
    Clear Lake *B, M*
    Downtown *B*
    Victoria *B, T*
University of Houston *B, M, D*
University of Mary Hardin-Baylor *B, T*
University of North Texas *B, M, D*
University of St. Thomas *B*
University of Texas
    Arlington *B, M, D*
    Austin *B, M, D*
    Brownsville *B, M*
    El Paso *B, M*
    Pan American *B, M, T*
    San Antonio *B, M*
    Tyler *B, M*
    of the Permian Basin *B, M*
University of the Incarnate Word *B, M*
Wayland Baptist University *B*
West Texas A&M University *B, M*
Western Texas College *A*
Wharton County Junior College *A*
Wiley College *B*

Utah
Brigham Young University *B, M*
Dixie State College of Utah *A*
Snow College *A*
Southern Utah University *B, T*
University of Utah *C, B, M, D*
Utah State University *B, M*
Weber State University *B*
Westminster College *B*

Vermont
Bennington College *B*
Burlington College *B*
Castleton State College *B*
College of St. Joseph in Vermont *B*
Goddard College *B*
Green Mountain College *B*
Johnson State College *B*
Lyndon State College *B*
Marlboro College *B*
Middlebury College *B*
Norwich University *B*
St. Michael's College *B*
Southern Vermont College *B*
University of Vermont *B, M*

Virginia
Averett College *B*
Bluefield College *B*
Bridgewater College *B*
Christendom College *B*
Christopher Newport University *B*
College of William and Mary *B*
Eastern Mennonite University *B*
Emory & Henry College *B, T*
Ferrum College *B*
George Mason University *B*
Hampden-Sydney College *B*
Hampton University *M*
Hollins University *B*
James Madison University *B, M, T*
Liberty University *B, T*
Longwood College *B, M, T*
Mary Baldwin College *B*
Mary Washington College *B*
Norfolk State University *B*
Old Dominion University *B, M*
Radford University *B, M*
Randolph-Macon College *B*
Randolph-Macon Woman's College *B*
Roanoke College *B, T*
St. Paul's College *B*
Shenandoah University *B*
Sweet Briar College *B*
University of Richmond *B, M, T*
University of Virginia's College at
    Wise *B, T*
University of Virginia *B, M, D*
Virginia Commonwealth
    University *B, M*
Virginia Intermont College *B*
Virginia Military Institute *B*
Virginia Polytechnic Institute and State
    University *B, M, T*
Virginia State University *B, M*
Virginia Union University *B*
Virginia Wesleyan College *B*
Washington and Lee University *B*

Washington
Central Washington University *B, M*
Centralia College *A*
Eastern Washington University *B, M, T*
Everett Community College *A*
Evergreen State College *B*
Gonzaga University *B, M*
Heritage College *B*
Highline Community College *A*
Lower Columbia College *A*
North Seattle Community College *C, A*
Pacific Lutheran University *B*

St. Martin's College *B*
Seattle Pacific University *B, T*
Seattle University *B*
University of Puget Sound *B, T*
University of Washington *B, M, D*
Walla Walla College *B*
Washington State University *B, M, D*
Western Washington University *B, M*
Whitman College *B*
Whitworth College *B, T*

West Virginia
Alderson-Broaddus College *B*
Bethany College *B*
Concord College *B*
Davis and Elkins College *B*
Fairmont State College *B*
Glenville State College *B*
Marshall University *B, M*
Potomac State College of West Virginia University *A*
Shepherd College *B, T*
University of Charleston *B*
West Liberty State College *B*
West Virginia State College *B*
West Virginia University *B, M, D, T*
West Virginia Wesleyan College *B*
Wheeling Jesuit University *B*

Wisconsin
Alverno College *B, T*
Beloit College *B*
Cardinal Stritch University *B*
Carroll College *B*
Carthage College *B, T*
Concordia University Wisconsin *T*
Lakeland College *B*
Lawrence University *B*
Marian College of Fond du Lac *B, T*
Marquette University *B, M, D, T*
Mount Mary College *B*
Mount Senario College *B, T*
Northland College *B*
Ripon College *B, T*
St. Norbert College *B, T*
Silver Lake College *B, T*
University of Wisconsin
  Eau Claire *B, M*
  Green Bay *B*
  La Crosse *B*
  Madison *B, M, D*
  Milwaukee *B, M, D*
  Oshkosh *B*
  Parkside *B*
  Platteville *B*
  River Falls *B, M*
  Stevens Point *B, M, T*
  Superior *B*
  Whitewater *B, T*
Viterbo University *B*
Wisconsin Lutheran College *B*

Wyoming
Casper College *A*
Central Wyoming College *A*
Eastern Wyoming College *A*
Laramie County Community College *A*
Northwest College *A*
Sheridan College *A*
University of Wyoming *B, M*
Western Wyoming Community College *A*

English composition

Arizona
Grand Canyon University *B*
Prescott College *B, M*

Arkansas
John Brown University *B*

California
California State University
  Chico *C*
  Long Beach *B*
  Los Angeles *M*
Chapman University *M*
Glendale Community College *A*
Humboldt State University *M*
Irvine Valley College *A*
Pitzer College *B*
San Francisco State University *C, M*
Stanford University *B*
University of California
  San Diego *B*

Colorado
University of Colorado
  Denver *B*
University of Southern Colorado *B*

Connecticut
Quinnipiac University *B*
Sacred Heart University *B*
Southern Connecticut State University *M*

Florida
Florida Southern College *B*
Gulf Coast Community College *A*
University of Miami *M*
University of West Florida *B, M*

Idaho
Lewis-Clark State College *B*

Illinois
Illinois State University *M*
National-Louis University *M*
Northeastern Illinois University *B, M*
Northwestern University *B*
Richland Community College *A*
University of Illinois
  Urbana-Champaign *B*

Indiana
DePauw University *B*
Indiana State University *B*
Indiana University
  Bloomington *B*
  South Bend *A, B*
Indiana University--Purdue University
  Indiana University-Purdue University Fort Wayne *B*
Purdue University
  Calumet *B*
University of Evansville *B*

Iowa
Graceland University *B, T*
Loras College *B*
Luther College *B*
University of Iowa *B*
Wartburg College *B*

Kansas
Butler County Community College *A*
Independence Community College *A*

Kentucky
University of Louisville *D*

Maryland
Johns Hopkins University *B*

Massachusetts
Emerson College *M*
Wheaton College *B*

Michigan
Eastern Michigan University *B*

Minnesota
Concordia College: Moorhead *B*
Metropolitan State University *B*
St. Cloud State University *B*
Winona State University *B*

Mississippi
East Central Community College *A*

Missouri
Crowder College *A*
Lincoln University *B*

Montana
Miles Community College *A*

Nevada
University of Nevada
  Reno *B*

New Jersey
Rowan University *B*
Salem Community College *A*
The College of New Jersey *B*

New York
Bard College *B*
Manhattan College *B*
Manhattanville College *B*

North Dakota
Minot State University *B*
North Dakota State University *M*

Ohio
Mount Union College *B*
Ohio Northern University *B*
Otterbein College *B*
University of Toledo *B*

Oklahoma
Oral Roberts University *B*
Redlands Community College *A*
University of Central Oklahoma *B, M*

Pennsylvania
Carnegie Mellon University *D*
La Roche College *B*
La Salle University *B*
University of Pittsburgh
  Greensburg *B*
University of Pittsburgh *B*

Tennessee
Union University *B, T*
University of Tennessee
  Knoxville *B*

Texas
Baylor University *B*
Huston-Tillotson College *B*
St. Philip's College *A*
Texas A&M University
  Commerce *B*
University of North Texas *B*

Utah
Snow College *A*

Vermont
Burlington College *B*
Marlboro College *B*

Virginia
University of Virginia's College at Wise *T*

Washington
North Seattle Community College *C, A*
Western Washington University *B*

West Virginia
Concord College *B*

Wisconsin
Marquette University *B*
Viterbo University *B*

English education

Alabama
Alabama Agricultural and Mechanical University *B, M*
Athens State University *B*
Auburn University *B*
Birmingham-Southern College *T*
Faulkner University *B*
Huntingdon College *T*
Jacksonville State University *B, M*
Oakwood College *B*
Talladega College *T*
Troy State University
  Dothan *B, M*
University of Alabama *B*
University of Mobile *B, M, T*

Alaska
University of Alaska
  Anchorage *M*

Arizona
Arizona State University *B, T*
Grand Canyon University *B*
Northern Arizona University *T*
Prescott College *B, M*
University of Arizona *B, M, D*

Arkansas
Arkansas State University *B, M, T*
Arkansas Tech University *B, M*
Harding University *B, M, T*
Henderson State University *B, M, T*
John Brown University *B, T*
Ouachita Baptist University *B, T*
Philander Smith College *B*
Southern Arkansas University *B, T*
University of Arkansas
  Monticello *B*
  Pine Bluff *B, M, T*
University of Arkansas *B*
University of Central Arkansas *M, T*
University of the Ozarks *B, T*
Williams Baptist College *B*

California
Azusa Pacific University *T*
California Baptist University *B, T*
California Lutheran University *B, T*
California Polytechnic State University:
  San Luis Obispo *B, T*
California State Polytechnic University:
  Pomona *T*
California State University
  Bakersfield *B, T*
  Chico *T*
  Dominguez Hills *T*
  Fullerton *T*
  Long Beach *T*
  Northridge *B, T*
  Sacramento *T*
Concordia University *B, T*
Fresno Pacific University *B, T*
Hope International University *B*
Humboldt State University *T*
Los Angeles Southwest College *A*
Loyola Marymount University *M*
Master's College *T*
Mills College *T*
Mount St. Mary's College *T*
Occidental College *T*
Pacific Union College *T*
San Diego State University *B*
San Francisco State University *B, T*
San Jose State University *T*
Simpson College *B, T*
Sonoma State University *T*
University of San Francisco *T*
University of the Pacific *T*
Westmont College *T*

Colorado
Adams State College *B, T*
Colorado State University *T*
Metropolitan State College of Denver *T*
University of Colorado
  Boulder *T*
  Colorado Springs *T*
University of Denver *B*
University of Southern Colorado *T*
Western State College of Colorado *T*

Connecticut
Central Connecticut State
  University *B, M*
Fairfield University *T*
Quinnipiac University *B, M*

Sacred Heart University B, M, T
Southern Connecticut State
  University B, M, T

Delaware
Delaware State University B
University of Delaware B, T
Wesley College B

District of Columbia
Catholic University of America B, M
George Washington University M, T
Howard University B
Trinity College M

Florida
Barry University T
Bethune-Cookman College B, T
Flagler College B
Florida Agricultural and Mechanical
  University B, M
Florida Atlantic University B
Florida International University B, M, T
Florida State University B, M, D, T
Hobe Sound Bible College B, T
Nova Southeastern University M
St. Leo University B, T
St. Thomas University B, T
Southeastern College of the Assemblies
  of God B, T
Stetson University B, T
University of Central Florida B, M
University of Florida M
University of South Florida B, M
University of West Florida B, T
Warner Southern College B

Georgia
Agnes Scott College M, T
Albany State University M
Armstrong Atlantic State
  University B, M, T
Berry College B
Brewton-Parker College B
Clark Atlanta University B
Columbus State University B, M
Covenant College B, T
Fort Valley State University B, T
Gainesville College A
Georgia College and State
  University M, T
Georgia Southern University B, M, T
Georgia Southwestern State
  University B, M
Georgia State University M, D
Kennesaw State University B
LaGrange College T
Mercer University M, T
North Georgia College & State
  University B, M
Piedmont College T
Shorter College M
Toccoa Falls College B, T
University of Georgia B, M, T
Valdosta State University M, T
Wesleyan College T

Hawaii
Brigham Young University
  Hawaii B
University of Hawaii
  Manoa B, T

Idaho
Albertson College of Idaho B
Boise State University M, T
Lewis-Clark State College B, T
Northwest Nazarene University B
University of Idaho M

Illinois
Augustana College B, T
Barat College B, T
Blackburn College B, T
Chicago State University B
Columbia College M
Concordia University B, T
Dominican University T
Elmhurst College B
Eureka College T
Governors State University B, M, T
Greenville College B, T
Illinois College T
Judson College B, T
Lewis University T
Loyola University of Chicago T
MacMurray College B, T
McKendree College B, T
National-Louis University M
North Central College B, T
North Park University T
Northwestern University B, T
Olivet Nazarene University B, T
Quincy University T
Rockford College T
Roosevelt University B
St. Xavier University M
Southern Illinois University
  Carbondale B
Trinity Christian College B, T
Trinity International University B, T
University of Illinois
  Chicago B
  Urbana-Champaign B, M, T
University of St. Francis T
Wheaton College T

Indiana
Anderson University B, T
Ball State University T
Bethel College B
Butler University T
Franklin College B, T
Goshen College B
Grace College B
Indiana State University B, M, T
Indiana University
  Bloomington B, T
  Northwest B
  South Bend B
  Southeast B
Indiana University--Purdue University
  Indiana University-Purdue
    University Fort Wayne B, T
  Indiana University-Purdue
    University Indianapolis B, T
Indiana Wesleyan University B, T
Manchester College B, T
Oakland City University B
Purdue University
  Calumet B
St. Mary-of-the-Woods College B
Taylor University B
Tri-State University B, T
University of Evansville T
University of Indianapolis B, M, T
University of St. Francis B
University of Southern Indiana B, T
Valparaiso University B
Vincennes University A

Iowa
Buena Vista University B, T
Central College T
Clarke College B, T
Cornell College B, T
Dordt College B
Drake University M, T
Graceland University T
Grand View College B, T
Iowa State University T
Iowa Wesleyan College B
Loras College T
Luther College B
Morningside College B
Northwestern College T
St. Ambrose University B, T
University of Iowa B, M, D, T
Wartburg College T
William Penn University B

Kansas
Baker University T
Benedictine College T
Bethany College B
Bethel College T
Colby Community College A
Emporia State University B
Independence Community College A
Kansas Wesleyan University B, T
McPherson College B, T
MidAmerica Nazarene University B, T
Newman University T
Ottawa University B, T
Pittsburg State University B, T
St. Mary College T
Southwestern College B, T
Tabor College B, T
University of Kansas B, T
Washburn University of Topeka B

Kentucky
Campbellsville University B
Cumberland College B, T
Kentucky State University B
Murray State University B, M, T
Pikeville College B, T
Thomas More College B
Transylvania University B, T
Union College B
Western Kentucky University M

Louisiana
Centenary College of Louisiana B, T
Dillard University B
Louisiana State University
  Shreveport B
McNeese State University T
Nicholls State University B
Northwestern State University B, M, T
Our Lady of Holy Cross College B
Southeastern Louisiana University B
Southern University and Agricultural and
  Mechanical College B
University of Louisiana at Monroe B
University of New Orleans B, M
Xavier University of Louisiana B, M, T

Maine
St. Joseph's College B
University of Maine
  Farmington B
  Machias B
  Presque Isle B
University of Maine M
University of New England T
University of Southern Maine T

Maryland
College of Notre Dame of Maryland T
Columbia Union College B
Frostburg State University B, T
Mount St. Mary's College B, T
Salisbury State University B
University of Maryland
  College Park B
  Eastern Shore B

Massachusetts
Assumption College T
Boston University B, M, T
Bridgewater State College M, T
Elms College B, M, T
Fitchburg State College B, M, T
Framingham State College B, M, T
Harvard College T
Merrimack College T
Northeastern University B
Salem State College M
Smith College M
Springfield College B
Tufts University M, T
University of Massachusetts
  Dartmouth T
Western New England College T
Westfield State College B, T
Worcester State College M, T

Michigan
Albion College B, T
Alma College T
Andrews University M, T
Calvin College B
Central Michigan University B
Concordia College B, T
Eastern Michigan University B, T
Ferris State University B
Grand Valley State University T
Lansing Community College A
Michigan State University M
Northern Michigan University B, M, T
Saginaw Valley State University T
University of Michigan B, D
Wayne State University B, M, T

Minnesota
Augsburg College T
Bemidji State University M, T
Bethel College B
College of St. Benedict T
College of St. Catherine: St. Paul
  Campus B, T
College of St. Scholastica T
Concordia College: Moorhead T
Crown College B, T
Gustavus Adolphus College T
Minnesota State University,
  Mankato B, M, T
Moorhead State University B, T
Northwestern College B
Ridgewater College: A Community and
  Technical College A
St. Cloud State University M, T
St. John's University T
St. Mary's University of Minnesota B
St. Olaf College T
University of Minnesota
  Duluth B
  Morris T
  Twin Cities T
University of St. Thomas T
Winona State University B, M, T

Mississippi
Blue Mountain College B
Coahoma Community College A
Delta State University B, M
Mississippi College M
Mississippi Delta Community College A
Mississippi Gulf Coast Community
  College
    Jefferson Davis Campus A
Mississippi State University T
Mississippi Valley State University B, T
Rust College B
University of Mississippi B, T
William Carey College M

Missouri
Central Missouri State
  University B, M, T
College of the Ozarks B, T
Columbia College T
Culver-Stockton College T
Evangel University B
Fontbonne College B
Hannibal-LaGrange College B
Harris Stowe State College T
Lincoln University B, T
Maryville University of Saint
  Louis B, M, T
Missouri Baptist College T
Missouri Southern State College B, T
Missouri Valley College T
Missouri Western State College B
Northwest Missouri State
  University B, M, T
Park University T
Rockhurst University B
Southeast Missouri State University B
Southwest Baptist University T
Southwest Missouri State University B
Truman State University M, T
University of Missouri
  St. Louis T
William Jewell College T
William Woods University B

Montana

Montana State University
    Billings *B, T*
    Bozeman *T*
Rocky Mountain College *B, T*
University of Great Falls *B, T*
University of Montana-Missoula *T*
Western Montana College of The
    University of Montana *B, T*

Nebraska

Chadron State College *M*
College of Saint Mary *B, T*
Concordia University *T*
Creighton University *T*
Dana College *B*
Doane College *T*
Hastings College *B, M, T*
Mid Plains Community College Area *A*
Midland Lutheran College *B, T*
Peru State College *B, T*
Union College *T*
University of Nebraska
    Kearney *B, M, T*
    Lincoln *B, T*

Nevada

University of Nevada
    Reno *B*

New Hampshire

Colby-Sawyer College *B, T*
Franklin Pierce College *T*
Keene State College *T*
New England College *B, T*
Notre Dame College *B, M*
Plymouth State College of the University
    System of New Hampshire *B, T*
Rivier College *B, M, T*
St. Anselm College *T*
University of New Hampshire
    Manchester *M*
University of New Hampshire *B, T*

New Jersey

Caldwell College *T*
Centenary College *T*
College of St. Elizabeth *T*
Fairleigh Dickinson University *M*
Monmouth University *B, T*
Richard Stockton College of New
    Jersey *B*
Rider University *B, T*
Rowan University *B, M*
Rutgers
    The State University of New Jersey:
        Douglass College *T*
    The State University of New Jersey:
        Livingston College *T*
    The State University of New Jersey:
        New Brunswick Graduate
        Campus *M, D, T*
    The State University of New Jersey:
        Rutgers College *T*
    The State University of New Jersey:
        University College New
        Brunswick *T*
St. Peter's College *T*
The College of New Jersey *B, T*

New Mexico

College of the Southwest *B, T*
New Mexico Highlands University *B*

New York

Adelphi University *B, M*
Alfred University *M, T*
Canisius College *B, M, T*
City University of New York
    Brooklyn College *B, M*
    City College *B*
    Hunter College *B, M*
    Lehman College *M*
    Queens College *M, T*
    York College *T*
Colgate University *M*
College of St. Rose *B, T*
Columbia University
    Teachers College *M, D*
D'Youville College *B, M, T*
Dowling College *B*
Elmira College *B, T*
Fordham University *M, T*
Hofstra University *B, M, T*
Houghton College *B, T*
Ithaca College *B, T*
Keuka College *B, T*
Le Moyne College *T*
Long Island University
    C. W. Post Campus *B, M, T*
    Southampton College *T*
Manhattan College *B, T*
Manhattanville College *M, T*
Marist College *B, T*
Marymount Manhattan College *B, T*
Molloy College *B*
Nazareth College of Rochester *T*
New York Institute of Technology *B, T*
New York University *B, M, D, T*
Niagara University *B, T*
Pace University:
    Pleasantville/Briarcliff *B, M, T*
Pace University *B, M, T*
Roberts Wesleyan College *B, T*
St. Bonaventure University *M*
St. Francis College *B, T*
St. John Fisher College *B, T*
St. John's University *B, M, T*
St. Lawrence University *T*
St. Thomas Aquinas College *B, T*
Sarah Lawrence College *M*
Siena College *T*
State University of New York
    Albany *B, M, T*
    Binghamton *M*
    Buffalo *M, D, T*
    College at Brockport *B, M, T*
    College at Buffalo *B, M*
    College at Cortland *B, M, T*
    College at Fredonia *B, M, T*
    College at Geneseo *B, M, T*
    College at Oneonta *B, T*
    College at Plattsburgh *B, M*
    College at Potsdam *B, M, T*
    New Paltz *B, M, T*
    Oswego *M*
Syracuse University *B, M, D, T*
University of Rochester *M, D*
Utica College of Syracuse University *B*
Vassar College *T*
Wells College *T*

North Carolina

Appalachian State University *B, M, T*
Barton College *T*
Belmont Abbey College *T*
Bennett College *B, T*
Campbell University *B, T*
Catawba College *T*
Chowan College *B, T*
Davidson College *T*
East Carolina University *B, M*
Elizabeth City State University *B, T*
Fayetteville State University *B, T*
Gardner-Webb University *B, M*
Greensboro College *B, T*
Johnson C. Smith University *B*
Lees-McRae College *T*
Lenoir Community College *A*
Lenoir-Rhyne College *B, T*
Louisburg College *A*
Mars Hill College *B, T*
Meredith College *T*
Methodist College *A, B, T*
Montreat College *T*
North Carolina Agricultural and
    Technical State University *B, M, T*
North Carolina Central University *B, M*
North Carolina State University *T*
Queens College *T*
St. Augustine's College *B, T*
Sandhills Community College *A*
Shaw University *B, T*
University of North Carolina
    Charlotte *B, M*
    Greensboro *B, M, T*
    Pembroke *B, M, T*
    Wilmington *T*
Wake Forest University *M, T*
Western Carolina University *B, M, T*
Wingate University *B, T*

North Dakota

Dickinson State University *B, T*
Jamestown College *B*
Mayville State University *B, T*
Minot State University *B, T*
North Dakota State University *B, T*
University of Mary *B*
University of North Dakota *B, T*
Valley City State University *B, T*

Ohio

Ashland University *B, T*
Baldwin-Wallace College *T*
Bluffton College *B*
Bowling Green State University *B*
Capital University *T*
Case Western Reserve University *T*
Cedarville College *B, T*
Central State University *B*
College of Mount St. Joseph *T*
Defiance College *B, T*
Hiram College *T*
John Carroll University *T*
Kent State University
    Stark Campus *B*
Kent State University *M, T*
Malone College *B*
Miami University
    Oxford Campus *B, M, T*
Mount Union College *T*
Mount Vernon Nazarene College *B, T*
Ohio Dominican College *D*
Ohio Northern University *B, T*
Ohio University *B, T*
Otterbein College *B*
University of Akron *M*
University of Dayton *B, M, T*
University of Findlay *B, T*
University of Rio Grande *B, T*
University of Toledo *B, T*
Walsh University *B*
Wilberforce University *T*
Wilmington College *B*
Wittenberg University *B*
Wright State University *B, M, T*
Xavier University *M, T*
Youngstown State University *B, M*

Oklahoma

Cameron University *B, T*
East Central University *B, T*
Eastern Oklahoma State College *A*
Mid-America Bible College *B*
Northeastern Oklahoma Agricultural and
    Mechanical College *A*
Northeastern State University *B*
Northwestern Oklahoma State
    University *B, T*
Oklahoma Baptist University *B, T*
Oklahoma Christian University of
    Science and Arts *B, T*
Oklahoma City University *B*
Oral Roberts University *B, T*
Southeastern Oklahoma State
    University *B, T*
Southern Nazarene University *B, M*
Southwestern Oklahoma State
    University *B, M, T*
University of Central Oklahoma *B*
University of Tulsa *T*

Oregon

Concordia University *B, M, T*
George Fox University *B, M, T*
Linfield College *T*
Oregon State University *M*
Portland State University *T*
Southern Oregon University *T*
University of Portland *T*
Western Baptist College *B*

Pennsylvania

Allentown College of St. Francis de
    Sales *M, T*
Alvernia College *B*
Beaver College *B, M, T*
Bucknell University *T*
Cabrini College *B, T*
California University of
    Pennsylvania *B, T*
Carlow College *T*
Carnegie Mellon University *T*
Chatham College *M, T*
Chestnut Hill College *T*
Clarion University of Pennsylvania *B, T*
College Misericordia *B, T*
Delaware Valley College *T*
Dickinson College *T*
Duquesne University *B, T*
East Stroudsburg University of
    Pennsylvania *B, T*
Eastern College *B, T*
Elizabethtown College *T*
Gannon University *M, T*
Gettysburg College *T*
Grove City College *B, T*
Gwynedd-Mercy College *T*
Holy Family College *B, T*
Immaculata College *T*
Indiana University of
    Pennsylvania *B, M, T*
Juniata College *B, T*
King's College *T*
La Roche College *B*
La Salle University *B, T*
Lebanon Valley College of
    Pennsylvania *T*
Lincoln University *B, T*
Lock Haven University of
    Pennsylvania *B, T*
Lycoming College *T*
Mansfield University of
    Pennsylvania *B, T*
Marywood University *T*
Mercyhurst College *B*
Messiah College *T*
Millersville University of
    Pennsylvania *B, M, T*
Moravian College *T*
Penn State
    Harrisburg *B*
Philadelphia College of Bible *B, T*
Point Park College *B*
Robert Morris College *T*
St. Joseph's University *B*
St. Vincent College *T*
Seton Hill College *B, T*
Temple University *B, M, T*
Thiel College *B*
University of Pennsylvania *M, D*
University of Pittsburgh
    Bradford *B*
    Johnstown *B, T*
Villanova University *T*
Washington and Jefferson College *T*
Waynesburg College *T*
West Chester University of
    Pennsylvania *B, T*
Westminster College *B, T*
Widener University *M, T*
Wilkes University *M, T*
Wilson College *T*
York College of Pennsylvania *B, T*

Puerto Rico

Bayamon Central University *B*
Caribbean University *B, T*
Inter American University of Puerto Rico
    Barranquitas Campus *B, T*
    Guayama Campus *B*
    Metropolitan Campus *B, M*

English education

Pontifical Catholic University of Puerto Rico *B, T*
Turabo University *B, M*
Universidad Metropolitana *B*
University of Puerto Rico
 Mayaguez Campus *M*

Rhode Island
Providence College *B*
Rhode Island College *B, M*
Salve Regina University *B*

South Carolina
Anderson College *B, T*
Charleston Southern University *M, T*
Claflin University *B*
Coker College *B, T*
Columbia College *B*
Furman University *T*
Lander University *M, T*
Limestone College *B*
Morris College *B, T*
South Carolina State University *B, T*
The Citadel *M*
University of South Carolina
 Aiken *B, T*
Voorhees College *B*
Wofford College *T*

South Dakota
Augustana College *B, T*
Black Hills State University *B, T*
Dakota State University *B, T*
Dakota Wesleyan University *B, T*
Mount Marty College *B*
Northern State University *B, M, T*
South Dakota State University *B*
University of South Dakota *B, T*

Tennessee
Belmont University *T*
Bethel College *B, T*
Christian Brothers University *B, M, T*
Crichton College *B*
Cumberland University *B*
David Lipscomb University *B, T*
Freed-Hardeman University *T*
Lambuth University *T*
Lee University *B*
Lincoln Memorial University *B, T*
Maryville College *B, T*
Southern Adventist University *B*
Tennessee Technological University *B*
Tennessee Temple University *B*
Tennessee Wesleyan College *B, T*
Trevecca Nazarene University *B, T*
Tusculum College *B, T*
Union University *B, T*
University of Tennessee
 Chattanooga *B, T*
 Knoxville *T*
 Martin *B, T*
Vanderbilt University *M, D*

Texas
Abilene Christian University *B, T*
Baylor University *B, T*
Del Mar College *A*
East Texas Baptist University *B*
Hardin-Simmons University *B, T*
Houston Baptist University *T*
Howard Payne University *T*
Lamar University *T*
LeTourneau University *B*
Lubbock Christian University *B*
McMurry University *T*
Prairie View A&M University *M*
St. Edward's University *B, T*
St. Mary's University *T*
Schreiner College *T*
Southwest Texas State University *M, T*
Tarleton State University *M, T*
Texas A&M International
 University *B, M, T*
Texas A&M University
 Commerce *T*
 Corpus Christi *T*

Texas Christian University *T*
Texas Lutheran University *T*
Texas Wesleyan University *B, M, T*
University of Dallas *T*
University of Houston
 Clear Lake *T*
University of Houston *T*
University of Mary Hardin-Baylor *T*
University of Texas
 Arlington *T*
 San Antonio *T*
Wayland Baptist University *T*
West Texas A&M University *T*

Utah
Brigham Young University *B, M*
Southern Utah University *B*
Weber State University *B*

Vermont
Castleton State College *B, T*
College of St. Joseph in Vermont *B*
Goddard College *B*
Johnson State College *B*
Lyndon State College *B*
St. Michael's College *B*
University of Vermont *B, M, T*

Virginia
Averett College *B, T*
Bridgewater College *T*
Christopher Newport University *T*
Eastern Mennonite University *T*
Emory & Henry College *M*
Hampton University *B*
Hollins University *T*
Liberty University *B*
Longwood College *B, T*
Lynchburg College *M*
Radford University *T*
St. Paul's College *T*
University of Virginia's College at
 Wise *T*
Virginia Intermont College *B, T*
Virginia Wesleyan College *T*

Washington
Central Washington University *B, M, T*
North Seattle Community College *C*
Pacific Lutheran University *T*
Seattle Pacific University *B, T*
Washington State University *T*
Western Washington University *B, T*
Whitworth College *B, M, T*

West Virginia
Alderson-Broaddus College *T*
Concord College *B, T*
Fairmont State College *B*
Glenville State College *B*
Shepherd College *T*
West Liberty State College *B*
West Virginia State College *B*
West Virginia Wesleyan College *B*
Wheeling Jesuit University *T*

Wisconsin
Alverno College *B, T*
Cardinal Stritch University *B, T*
Carroll College *B, T*
Carthage College *T*
Lakeland College *T*
Lawrence University *T*
Mount Mary College *B, T*
Mount Senario College *B, T*
Northland College *T*
St. Norbert College *T*
University of Wisconsin
 Green Bay *T*
 La Crosse *B, T*
 Madison *M*
 Parkside *T*
 Platteville *B, T*
 River Falls *T*
 Superior *B, T*
 Whitewater *B*
Viterbo University *B, T*

English literature

Arizona
Arizona Western College *A*

California
California State University
 Bakersfield *B, M*
 Dominguez Hills *B, M*
 Hayward *B*
 Northridge *B*
Irvine Valley College *A*
Pitzer College *B*
Point Loma Nazarene University *B*
Saddleback College *A*
Stanford University *B*
University of California
 San Diego *B, M, D*
 Santa Cruz *B*
University of Redlands *B*
University of Southern California *B*
Whittier College *B*

Colorado
Fort Lewis College *B*

Connecticut
Trinity College *B*

District of Columbia
Gallaudet University *B*
George Washington University *M, D*
Trinity College *B*

Florida
Barry University *B*
Eckerd College *B*
New College of the University of South Florida *B*

Georgia
Morris Brown College *B*

Idaho
Boise State University *B*

Illinois
North Central College *B*
Northwestern University *B*
Richland Community College *A*

Indiana
DePauw University *B*
Indiana State University *M*
Indiana University--Purdue University
 Indiana University-Purdue
 University Fort Wayne *B*
University of Evansville *B*

Iowa
Maharishi University of Management *B*
Marshalltown Community College *A*
University of Iowa *B, M, T*

Maine
Bowdoin College *B*
University of Maine
 Farmington *B*
 Fort Kent *B*

Maryland
Johns Hopkins University *D*

Massachusetts
Assumption College *B*
Clark University *M*
Fitchburg State College *B*
Hampshire College *B*
Harvard College *B*
Roxbury Community College *A*
Simmons College *B, M*
Simon's Rock College of Bard *B*
Tufts University *B, M, D*

Michigan
Eastern Michigan University *M*
University of Michigan *D*

Minnesota
Bethel College *B*

Concordia College: Moorhead *B*
St. Cloud State University *B*
St. Mary's University of Minnesota *B*

Mississippi
Jackson State University *B*

Missouri
St. Louis University *M, D*
Washington University *B, M, D*

New Jersey
Rowan University *B*

New Mexico
College of Santa Fe *B*

New York
Bard College *B*
City University of New York
 Baruch College *B*
 Brooklyn College *B*
 Graduate School and University
 Center *D*
Columbia University
 Graduate School *M, D*
 School of General Studies *B*
Elmira College *B, T*
Eugene Lang College/New School
 University *B*
Hamilton College *B*
Hofstra University *M*
Mercy College *B*
New York University *B, M, D*
St. Bonaventure University *M*
St. Lawrence University *B*
Sarah Lawrence College *B*
United States Military Academy *B*

North Carolina
Duke University *B*
Fayetteville State University *B*
North Carolina State University *B*
University of North Carolina
 Chapel Hill *D*

Ohio
College of Wooster *B*
Kent State University *M*
Miami University
 Oxford Campus *B*
University of Cincinnati *B, M, D, T*

Oklahoma
Southeastern Oklahoma State
 University *B*

Oregon
Central Oregon Community College *A*
University of Oregon *B*

Pennsylvania
California University of Pennsylvania *B*
Gannon University *M*
Gettysburg College *B*
Holy Family College *B, T*
Immaculata College *B*
La Salle University *B*
University of Pennsylvania *A, B, M, D*
University of Pittsburgh
 Johnstown *B*
University of Pittsburgh *B*
University of Scranton *M*
West Chester University of
 Pennsylvania *B*
Westminster College *B, T*

Rhode Island
Brown University *B, M, D*
Roger Williams University *A, B*

Texas
Texas A&M University
 Commerce *B*
University of North Texas *D*

Utah
Southern Utah University *B*

Vermont
Bennington College *B*
Marlboro College *B*
Middlebury College *B*

Virginia
George Mason University *M*
Longwood College *B, M, T*

Washington
Everett Community College *A*
Evergreen State College *B*

West Virginia
Concord College *B*

Wisconsin
Marquette University *D, T*

Enterprise management/operations

Alabama
Chattahoochee Valley Community College *A*

Alaska
University of Alaska Anchorage *C, A*

Arizona
Eastern Arizona College *C, A*
Gateway Community College *C*
Northland Pioneer College *C*
Rio Salado College *C*
University of Arizona *B*

California
Azusa Pacific University *M*
Cabrillo College *C, A*
California State University
 Dominguez Hills *B*
 Hayward *B, M*
Coastline Community College *A*
College of Marin: Kentfield *C, A*
College of San Mateo *C, A*
Compton Community College *C, A*
Cuyamaca College *A*
Lake Tahoe Community College *C, A*
Los Angeles Trade and Technical College *A*
Los Medanos College *C, A*
Mendocino College *A*
Merced College *A*
Mount San Antonio College *C, A*
Mount San Jacinto College *C*
Pasadena City College *A*
Santa Monica College *C, A*
Shasta College *A*
Solano Community College *C, A*
Southwestern College *C, A*
Yuba College *C*

Colorado
Colorado Northwestern Community College *A*
Northeastern Junior College *A*

Connecticut
Quinnipiac University *B*

District of Columbia
Gallaudet University *B*
Trinity College *M*

Florida
Florida Keys Community College *C*

Georgia
Darton College *A*
Gwinnett Technical Institute *C*
Southern Polytechnic State University *B, M*

Idaho
Northwest Nazarene University *B*

Illinois
Black Hawk College *C, A*
De Paul University *M*
Elgin Community College *C*
Kishwaukee College *C*
McHenry County College *C*
Moraine Valley Community College *A*
Northwestern Business College *A*
Parkland College *C*
Prairie State College *C*
Waubonsee Community College *C, A*
William Rainey Harper College *C, A*

Kansas
Central Christian College *A, B*
Pratt Community College *C, A*

Kentucky
Morehead State University *A*
St. Catharine College *A*

Louisiana
Southern University
 Shreveport *A*

Maine
Maine Maritime Academy *A, B*

Massachusetts
Middlesex Community College *C*
Northeastern University *B*
Springfield Technical Community College *A*
Suffolk University *M*
University of Massachusetts
 Lowell *B*

Michigan
Baker College
 of Port Huron *A*
Ferris State University *C, B*
Gogebic Community College *A*
Lansing Community College *C*
Mid Michigan Community College *A*
North Central Michigan College *C*
Northern Michigan University *B*
Oakland Community College *A*
Schoolcraft College *A*

Minnesota
Alexandria Technical College *C*
St. Cloud Technical College *C, A*
University of St. Thomas *C, B, M*

Missouri
Missouri Valley College *A*
Three Rivers Community College *A*

Nebraska
University of Nebraska
 Omaha *B*

Nevada
University of Nevada
 Reno *B*

New Jersey
Bergen Community College *C*
Burlington County College *C*
Mercer County Community College *C*
Stevens Institute of Technology *B*
Thomas Edison State College *A, B*
Warren County Community College *C, A*

New York
Corning Community College *A*
Erie Community College
 City Campus *C*
 North Campus *C*
 South Campus *C*
Herkimer County Community College *C, A*
Medaille College *C, B*

Ohio
Kent State University
 Trumbull Campus *A*
Kent State University *C*
Lakeland Community College *C*
University of Akron *A*
University of Findlay *B*
Xavier University *B, M*

Oklahoma
Northeastern Oklahoma Agricultural and Mechanical College *A*
Rose State College *A*

Oregon
Portland Community College *C*

Pennsylvania
Bucks County Community College *A*
Central Pennsylvania College *A*
Community College of Allegheny County *C, A*
Delaware County Community College *C, A*
Drexel University *B*
Northampton County Area Community College *C, A*
Philadelphia University *B*
Reading Area Community College *C, A*
Temple University *B*
West Chester University of Pennsylvania *M*

Puerto Rico
ICPR Junior College *A*
University of Puerto Rico
 Rio Piedras Campus *B*

South Carolina
Florence-Darlington Technical College *A*
Morris College *B*
Voorhees College *B*

South Dakota
Black Hills State University *B*

Tennessee
Southern Adventist University *M*
Tusculum College *B*

Texas
Baylor University *B*
Brookhaven College *A*
Collin County Community College District *C*
Galveston College *C, A*
Midland College *C, A*
Palo Alto College *A*
Richland College *A*
St. Mary's University *B*
Tarrant County College *A*

Vermont
Lyndon State College *A, B*

Virginia
J. Sargeant Reynolds Community College *C*
Northern Virginia Community College *C*

Washington
Lake Washington Technical College *C*
Washington State University *B*

West Virginia
Potomac State College of West Virginia University *A*
Southern West Virginia Community and Technical College *A*
West Virginia Wesleyan College *B*

Wisconsin
Gateway Technical College *C*
Madison Area Technical College *C*
Moraine Park Technical College *C*
University of Wisconsin
 Platteville *B*

Wyoming
University of Wyoming *B*

Entomology

Alabama
Auburn University *B, M, D*

Arizona
University of Arizona *M, D*

Arkansas
University of Arkansas *M, D*

California
California State University
 Stanislaus *B*
San Jose State University *B*
University of California
 Berkeley *B*
 Davis *B, M, D*
 Riverside *B, M, D*

Colorado
Colorado State University *M, D*

Connecticut
University of Connecticut *M, D*

Delaware
University of Delaware *B, M*

Florida
University of Florida *B, M, D*

Georgia
University of Georgia *B, M, D*

Hawaii
University of Hawaii
 Manoa *B, M, D*

Idaho
University of Idaho *B, M, D*

Illinois
University of Illinois
 Urbana-Champaign *B, M, D*

Indiana
Purdue University *B, M, D*

Iowa
Iowa State University *B, M, D*

Kansas
Kansas State University *M, D*
University of Kansas *M, D*

Kentucky
University of Kentucky *M, D*

Louisiana
Louisiana State University and Agricultural and Mechanical College *M, D*

Maine
University of Maine *B, M*

Maryland
University of Maryland
 College Park *M, D*

Massachusetts
Harvard College *B*
University of Massachusetts
 Amherst *M, D*

Michigan
Michigan State University *B, M, D*

Minnesota
University of Minnesota
 Twin Cities *M, D*

Mississippi
Mississippi State University *M, D*

Missouri
University of Missouri
 Columbia *M, D*

Montana
Montana State University
 Bozeman *M*

Nebraska
University of Nebraska
 Lincoln *M, D*

New Hampshire
Antioch New England Graduate School *M*

Entomology

New Jersey
Rutgers
  The State University of New Jersey:
    New Brunswick Graduate
    Campus *M, D*

New York
Cornell University *B, M, D*
State University of New York
  College of Environmental Science
    and Forestry *B, M, D*

North Carolina
North Carolina State University *B, M, D*

North Dakota
North Dakota State University *M, D*

Ohio
Ohio State University
  Columbus Campus *B, M, D*

Oklahoma
Eastern Oklahoma State College *A*
Oklahoma State University *B, M, D*

Oregon
Chemeketa Community College *A*
Oregon State University *B, M, D*

Pennsylvania
Penn State
  University Park *M, D*

South Carolina
Clemson University *M, D*

South Dakota
South Dakota State University *M*

Tennessee
University of Tennessee
  Knoxville *M, D*

Texas
Texas A&M University *B, M, D*
Texas Tech University *M*

Utah
Brigham Young University *B, M, D*

Virginia
Virginia Polytechnic Institute and State
  University *M, D*

Washington
Washington State University *B, M, D*

Wisconsin
University of Wisconsin
  Madison *B, M, D*

Wyoming
University of Wyoming *B, M, D*

Entrepreneurship

Arkansas
University of Central Arkansas *A*

California
California State University
  Fresno *B*
  Hayward *B, M*
  Monterey Bay *B*
Chaffey Community College *C, A*
Golden Gate University *M*
Golden West College *C, A*
Las Positas College *C, A*
Los Medanos College *C, A*
MiraCosta College *C, A*
Monterey Peninsula College *A*
Ohlone College *C, A*
Riverside Community College *C, A*
Saddleback College *C*
San Francisco State University *B*
Santa Ana College *A*
Santa Barbara City College *A*
Santa Rosa Junior College *C*
Southwestern College *C, A*

Colorado
Community College of Aurora *C, A*
Lamar Community College *C*
Northeastern Junior College *C, A*
Red Rocks Community College *C*

Connecticut
Central Connecticut State University *B*
Gateway Community College *C, A*
Middlesex Community-Technical
  College *C*
University of Hartford *B*

District of Columbia
Southeastern University *A, B*

Florida
Brevard Community College *C*
Florida State University *B*
Jacksonville University *B*
Lynn University *B*
St. Petersburg Junior College *C*
University of Miami *B, M*

Georgia
DeKalb Technical Institute *C*
Kennesaw State University *M*
Reinhardt College *A, B*

Hawaii
Hawaii Pacific University *B*

Idaho
College of Southern Idaho *A*
North Idaho College *A*

Illinois
Barat College *B*
College of DuPage *C*
Millikin University *B*
Trinity Christian College *B*
Triton College *C*
William Rainey Harper College *C, A*

Indiana
Goshen College *B*

Iowa
Buena Vista University *B*
Des Moines Area Community
  College *C, A*
Northeast Iowa Community College *C*

Kansas
Allen County Community College *A*
Independence Community College *C, A*
Johnson County Community
  College *C, A*
Seward County Community College *C*
Wichita State University *B*

Maine
Andover College *A*
Husson College *B*
Thomas College *B*

Massachusetts
American International College *B*
Babson College *B*
Bristol Community College *C*
Endicott College *B*
Northeastern University *B*
Northern Essex Community College *A*
Suffolk University *M*

Michigan
Baker College
  of Jackson *A*
  of Muskegon *A*
  of Owosso *A*
  of Port Huron *A*
Detroit College of Business *A, B, M*
Northern Michigan University *B*
Suomi College *B*
Washtenaw Community College *C*

Minnesota
St. Cloud State University *C*

Mississippi
Mary Holmes College *C*

Missouri
Drury University *B, M*
Missouri Southern State College *B*

Montana
Miles Community College *A*
Montana Tech of the University of
  Montana *B*

Nebraska
College of Saint Mary *C*
Northeast Community College *A*

New Hampshire
Antioch New England Graduate
  School *M*
Hesser College *A*
McIntosh College *C, A*
New England College *B*
New Hampshire Community Technical
  College
    Berlin *C*
New Hampshire Technical Institute *C*

New Jersey
Burlington County College *A*
Fairleigh Dickinson University *B*
Middlesex County College *A*

New Mexico
New Mexico Junior College *A*

New York
Broome Community College *A*
Bryant & Stratton Business Institute
  Syracuse *A*
Canisius College *C, B*
City University of New York
  Baruch College *B*
  Borough of Manhattan Community
    College *A*
  Kingsborough Community
    College *A*
Corning Community College *A*
Interboro Institute *A*
Pace University:
  Pleasantville/Briarcliff *C*
Pace University *C*
Rensselaer Polytechnic Institute *B, M, D*
Sage Junior College of Albany *A*
State University of New York
  College of Technology at
    Alfred *C, A*
Syracuse University *B*

North Carolina
Central Carolina Community College *C*
Edgecombe Community College *C*

North Dakota
University of North Dakota *B*

Ohio
Central Ohio Technical College *A*
Cincinnati State Technical and
  Community College *C*
Davis College *C*
Kent State University
  East Liverpool Regional Campus *A*
Kent State University *C*
Lourdes College *A, B*
Ohio University *B*
Sinclair Community College *A*
University of Findlay *A, B*
University of Toledo *B*

Oklahoma
Eastern Oklahoma State College *A*

Oregon
Concordia University *B*
Mount Hood Community College *A*

Pennsylvania
Bucks County Community College *C*
Central Pennsylvania College *A*
Chatham College *B*
Gettysburg College *B*
Harrisburg Area Community College *C*
Laurel Business Institute *A*
Luzerne County Community College *C*
Muhlenberg College *B*
Penn State
  University Park *C*
Seton Hill College *B*
University of Pennsylvania *B, M*
University of Pittsburgh
  Titusville *C*

Puerto Rico
Universidad Metropolitana *A, B*

Rhode Island
Community College of Rhode Island *C*
Johnson & Wales University *A, B*

South Carolina
Aiken Technical College *C*
Columbia College *B*
York Technical College *C*

South Dakota
Black Hills State University *B*

Texas
Central Texas College *C*
Howard Payne University *B*
St. Mary's University *B*
University of Houston *B*
University of North Texas *B*

Utah
Brigham Young University *B*

Vermont
College of St. Joseph in Vermont *A*

Virginia
Hampton University *B*

Washington
Clark College *A*
Columbia Basin College *A*
Grays Harbor College *C*
Henry Cogswell College *C*
Highline Community College *A*
North Seattle Community College *C*
Pacific Lutheran University *B*
Peninsula College *C*
Pierce College *C*
Spokane Falls Community College *A*

Environmental control technologies

Alabama
Community College of the Air Force *A*
Gadsden State Community College *C, A*
George C. Wallace State Community
  College
    Dothan *C, A*
James H. Faulkner State Community
  College *C, A*
Northwest-Shoals Community College *A*
Samford University *M*
University of Mobile *B*

Arizona
Arizona Western College *C*
Central Arizona College *C, A*
Gateway Community College *C, A*
Northland Pioneer College *C*
Pima Community College *C, A*

Arkansas
Southern Arkansas University
  Tech *A*
Westark College *A*

California
Allan Hancock College *C, A*
Butte College *A*
Chaffey Community College *C, A*
City College of San Francisco *C*
College of the Canyons *C*

De Anza College C, A
Long Beach City College C, A
Los Angeles Trade and Technical
 College C, A
Merced College C, A
Merritt College C, A
Orange Coast College C, A
Palomar College C, A
San Diego City College C, A
San Diego Mesa College C, A
Sierra College C
Southwestern College C
University of California
 Riverside B
Ventura College C, A

Colorado
Arapahoe Community College C, A
Colorado Mountain College
 Timberline Campus A
Community College of Denver C, A
Front Range Community College C, A
Mesa State College A, B
Pikes Peak Community College A
Red Rocks Community College C, A

Connecticut
Middlesex Community-Technical
 College C
Naugatuck Valley Community-Technical
 College C, A
Norwalk Community-Technical
 College A
Three Rivers Community-Technical
 College A
University of New Haven A

Delaware
Delaware Technical and Community
 College
  Owens Campus A
  Stanton/Wilmington Campus A

District of Columbia
University of the District of Columbia A

Florida
Chipola Junior College A
Daytona Beach Community College C
Florida International University B, M
Palm Beach Community College C, A
Pensacola Junior College A
Santa Fe Community College C, A
Valencia Community College A

Idaho
Boise State University C

Illinois
Black Hawk College C, A
Bradley University B
City Colleges of Chicago
 Wright College C, A
College of Lake County C
Kishwaukee College C, A
Waubonsee Community College C, A

Indiana
Indiana State University B

Iowa
Clinton Community College C, A
Iowa Lakes Community College A
Kirkwood Community College C, A
Muscatine Community College C, A
Scott Community College C, A

Kansas
Johnson County Community
 College C, A
Kansas City Kansas Community
 College C, A
Kansas State University B

Kentucky
Lexington Community College A
Murray State University A, B
Western Kentucky University B

Louisiana
Nunez Community College C, A

Maine
Southern Maine Technical College A

Maryland
Charles County Community College C

Massachusetts
Cape Cod Community College C
Holyoke Community College A
Massachusetts Bay Community
 College A
Massachusetts Maritime Academy B
Northeastern University A
Northern Essex Community College C
Springfield Technical Community
 College C, A
Suffolk University B
University of Massachusetts
 Lowell M
Wentworth Institute of Technology B

Michigan
Baker College
 of Owosso A
Delta College A
Eastern Michigan University B
Ferris State University A, B
Grand Rapids Community College A
Henry Ford Community College A
Kalamazoo Valley Community
 College C, A
Lake Superior State University A, B
Lansing Community College A
Mid Michigan Community College C
Northern Michigan University A, B
Oakland Community College C, A
Schoolcraft College A

Minnesota
Dunwoody Institute A
St. Cloud Technical College C, A
St. Paul Technical College C
Vermilion Community College A

Mississippi
Copiah-Lincoln Community College C
Hinds Community College A
Mississippi Gulf Coast Community
 College
 Jackson County Campus A
Mississippi Valley State University B, M

Missouri
Central Missouri State University A
Maple Woods Community College A
University of Missouri
 St. Louis C

Montana
Montana State University
 Northern A

Nevada
Community College of Southern
 Nevada A

New Jersey
Burlington County College C
Mercer County Community College C, A
Middlesex County College A
Ocean County College A
Salem Community College C, A
Thomas Edison State College A, B

New Mexico
New Mexico Junior College C, A
San Juan College A

New York
City University of New York
 New York City Technical
 College A
Mohawk Valley Community College A
Monroe Community College A
New York Institute of
 Technology A, B, M

State University of New York
 College of Technology at Canton A
Ulster County Community College A
Westchester Community College A

North Carolina
Pitt Community College A
South Piedmont Community
 College C, A
Wake Technical Community College A

Ohio
Cincinnati State Technical and
 Community College A
Columbus State Community
 College C, A
Kent State University
 Ashtabula Regional Campus A
 Tuscarawas Campus A
Kent State University C
Muskingum Area Technical College A
Ohio University
 Chillicothe Campus A
Ohio University A
Owens Community College
 Findlay Campus C, A
 Toledo A
Shawnee State University B
Stark State College of Technology A
Terra Community College C, A
University of Toledo A

Oklahoma
Oklahoma State University
 Oklahoma City C, A
Rose State College A
Tulsa Community College C, A
University of Tulsa M

Oregon
Clackamas Community College C, A
Lane Community College A
Linn-Benton Community College C, A
Mount Hood Community College C, A

Pennsylvania
Butler County Community College A
California University of Pennsylvania A
Community College of Allegheny
 County A
Community College of Philadelphia A
Delaware County Community College A
Penn State
 Harrisburg M
 University Park M
Pennsylvania College of Technology A
St. Joseph's University M
Temple University A
Westmoreland County Community
 College A

Puerto Rico
Universidad Metropolitana C
University of Puerto Rico
 Aguadilla A

South Carolina
Aiken Technical College C
Central Carolina Technical College A
Greenville Technical College C, A
Technical College of the Lowcountry C

Tennessee
Middle Tennessee State University B
Pellissippi State Technical Community
 College A
Roane State Community College C

Texas
Collin County Community College
 District C, A
El Paso Community College C, A
Lamar State College at Port Arthur C, A
San Jacinto College
 North C, A
Tarrant County College C, A

Texas State Technical College
 Harlingen A
 Waco C, A

Virginia
Lord Fairfax Community College A

Washington
Columbia Basin College A
Green River Community College C, A
Shoreline Community College A

Wisconsin
Milwaukee Area Technical College A
Milwaukee School of Engineering M
Moraine Park Technical College A

Environmental design

Alabama
Auburn University B

Arizona
Scottsdale Community College C, A
Yavapai College C, A

California
Art Center College of Design B, M
City College of San Francisco A
Otis College of Art and Design B
University of California
 Los Angeles M

Colorado
University of Colorado
 Boulder B
 Denver M, D

Connecticut
Yale University M

Indiana
Ball State University B

Massachusetts
Conway School of Landscape Design M
Hampshire College B
Harvard University M
University of Massachusetts
 Amherst B

Michigan
Michigan State University M
University of Michigan B, M

Minnesota
Alexandria Technical College C
Northland Community & Technical
 College C, A
University of Minnesota
 Twin Cities B

Missouri
Ranken Technical College A
Washington University M

Montana
Montana State University
 Bozeman B

New Jersey
Rutgers
 The State University of New Jersey:
 Cook College B
Thomas Edison State College A, B

New Mexico
University of New Mexico B

New York
Cornell University B
Parsons School of Design B
State University of New York
 Albany B
 Buffalo B
 College of Environmental Science
 and Forestry B, M
Suffolk County Community College A
Syracuse University B, M

North Carolina
North Carolina State University *B*

North Dakota
North Dakota State University *B*

Ohio
Bowling Green State University *B*
Kent State University *B, M*
Miami University
 Oxford Campus *B*
Ohio State University
 Columbus Campus *B, M*

Oklahoma
Northeastern Oklahoma Agricultural and Mechanical College *A*
University of Oklahoma *B*

Pennsylvania
Delaware Valley College *C, B*
University of Pennsylvania *A, B, M*

Puerto Rico
University of Puerto Rico
 Rio Piedras Campus *B*

Texas
Texas A&M University *B*
University of Houston *B*

Virginia
Virginia Polytechnic Institute and State University *D*

Environmental health

Alabama
University of Alabama
 Birmingham *D*

Arkansas
University of Arkansas
 Little Rock *B*
 for Medical Sciences *M*

California
California State University
 Fresno *B*
 Hayward *B*
Las Positas College *C, A*
Loma Linda University *M*
San Diego State University *M*
San Jose State University *B*
University of California
 Berkeley *B*
 Los Angeles *M, D*
University of Southern California *M, D*

Colorado
Colorado State University *B, M, D*

Delaware
Delaware State University *B*

Florida
Brevard Community College *C*
University of Miami *B*

Georgia
University of Georgia *B, M*

Idaho
Boise State University *B*

Illinois
Illinois State University *B*

Indiana
Indiana State University *B*

Iowa
Iowa Wesleyan College *B*
University of Iowa *M, D*

Kentucky
Murray State University *B, M*

Louisiana
Tulane University *M, D*

Maine
University of New England *B*
University of Southern Maine *B*

Massachusetts
Anna Maria College *M*
Boston University *M, D*

Michigan
Central Michigan University *B*
Ferris State University *B*
Oakland University *B*
University of Michigan
 Flint *B*
University of Michigan *M, D*

Minnesota
University of Minnesota
 Twin Cities *M, D*
Vermilion Community College *A*

Mississippi
Mississippi Valley State University *B, M*

Missouri
Crowder College *A*
Missouri Southern State College *A, B*

New Hampshire
Antioch New England Graduate School *M*

New Jersey
Richard Stockton College of New Jersey *B*
Rutgers
 The State University of New Jersey:
  Cook College *B*

New York
City University of New York
 Queensborough Community College *A*
 York College *B*
New York University *M, D*
State University of New York
 Albany *M, D*
University of Rochester *M*

North Carolina
Durham Technical Community College *C, A*
East Carolina University *B, M*
University of North Carolina
 Chapel Hill *M, D*
Western Carolina University *B*

Ohio
Bowling Green State University *B*
Case Western Reserve University *M, D*
Ohio University *B*
University of Findlay *B*
Wright State University *B*

Oklahoma
East Central University *B*

Oregon
Oregon State University *B, M*

Pennsylvania
Gannon University *C*
Indiana University of Pennsylvania *B*
University of Pittsburgh *C, M, D*
West Chester University of Pennsylvania *B*

Puerto Rico
University of Puerto Rico
 Medical Sciences Campus *M*

South Carolina
University of South Carolina *M, D*

Tennessee
East Tennessee State University *B, M*
Roane State Community College *A*

Texas
Brazosport College *C, A*

Utah
Brigham Young University *B*

Washington
University of Washington *B, M*

Wisconsin
University of Wisconsin
 Eau Claire *B, M*

Environmental health engineering

Alabama
University of Alabama
 Birmingham *D*

Arizona
University of Arizona *M, D*

Arkansas
Northwest Arkansas Community College *A*
University of Arkansas *M*

California
California State University
 Chico *C*
College of the Canyons *A*
San Diego State University *B*
University of California
 Irvine *B, M*
 Riverside *B, M, D*
University of Southern California *B, M, D*

Colorado
United States Air Force Academy *B*
University of Colorado
 Boulder *B*

Connecticut
University of Connecticut *M, D*
University of Hartford *M*
University of New Haven *M*

Delaware
University of Delaware *B*

Florida
Florida Institute of Technology *M*
Florida International University *M*
University of Central Florida *B, M, D*
University of Florida *B, M, D*
University of Miami *B*
University of South Florida *M*

Georgia
Georgia Institute of Technology *M, D*
Mercer University *B, M*

Idaho
Idaho State University *M*
University of Idaho *M*

Illinois
Illinois Institute of Technology *B, M, D*
University of Illinois
 Urbana-Champaign *M, D*

Indiana
Rose-Hulman Institute of Technology *M*
University of Notre Dame *B*

Iowa
University of Iowa *M, D*

Kansas
University of Kansas *M, D*

Louisiana
Louisiana State University and Agricultural and Mechanical College *B*

Massachusetts
Harvard College *B*
Massachusetts Institute of Technology *M, D*
Northeastern University *M*

Suffolk University *B*
Tufts University *B, M*
University of Massachusetts
 Amherst *M*

Michigan
Michigan State University *D*
Michigan Technological University *B, M, D, T*
University of Michigan *B, M, D*
Wayne State University *M*
Western Michigan University *B*

Missouri
University of Missouri
 Rolla *M*

Montana
Montana State University
 Bozeman *M*
Montana Tech of the University of Montana *B, M*

Nebraska
University of Nebraska
 Lincoln *M*

Nevada
University of Nevada
 Reno *B, M, D*

New Hampshire
University of New Hampshire *B*

New Jersey
New Jersey Institute of Technology *M, D*
Rutgers
 The State University of New Jersey:
  New Brunswick Graduate Campus *M, D*

New Mexico
Albuquerque Technical-Vocational Institute *A*
New Mexico Institute of Mining and Technology *B, M*
New Mexico State University *M*
University of New Mexico *M*

New York
Columbia University
 Fu Foundation School of Engineering and Applied Science *B, M, D*
Manhattan College *B, M*
New York University *B*
Pace University *B*
Polytechnic University *M*
Rensselaer Polytechnic Institute *B*
Syracuse University *B, M*

North Dakota
North Dakota State University *M*

Ohio
Marietta College *B*
University of Akron *A*
University of Findlay *B*

Oklahoma
University of Oklahoma *B, M, D*

Oregon
University of Portland *B*

Pennsylvania
Drexel University *B, M, D*
Duquesne University *B*
Gannon University *B*
Gettysburg College *B*
Penn State
 Harrisburg *B*
 University Park *B, M, D*
Temple University *B, M*
Villanova University *M*

Tennessee
Vanderbilt University *M, D*

Texas
Lamar University *M*

Environmental science/conservation

Palo Alto College C, A
Southern Methodist University B
Texas Tech University B, M
University of Houston M, D
University of Texas
    Arlington M, D
    Austin M
    El Paso M, D

Utah
Utah State University B, M, D

Virginia
John Tyler Community College A
Old Dominion University B

Washington
Seattle University B
Washington State University M

Wisconsin
Milwaukee School of Engineering M

Wyoming
University of Wyoming M

Environmental science/conservation

Alabama
Alabama Agricultural and Mechanical University B
Auburn University B
Northwest-Shoals Community College C, A
Samford University B
Spring Hill College B
Tuskegee University B, M
University of Alabama
    Huntsville C
University of West Alabama B

Alaska
Alaska Pacific University B, M
University of Alaska
    Fairbanks B

Arizona
Arizona Western College A
Dine College A
Northern Arizona University B
Prescott College B, M
University of Arizona B
University of Phoenix C

Arkansas
Arkansas State University D
John Brown University B
University of Arkansas
    Pine Bluff B
University of Arkansas B
University of Central Arkansas B
University of the Ozarks B

California
California Polytechnic State University:
    San Luis Obispo B
California State University
    Chico B
    Fullerton M
    Hayward B
    Monterey Bay B
    Sacramento B
    Stanislaus B
Chapman University B
College of the Desert A
Columbia College A
Dominican University of California B
Fresno City College C, A
Fresno Pacific University B
Irvine Valley College C, A
Loyola Marymount University B, M
Mills College B
Modesto Junior College C, A
Moorpark College A
Mount San Antonio College A
National University M

Riverside Community College A
Saddleback College A
San Diego State University B
San Francisco State University M
San Joaquin Delta College A
San Jose State University M
Santa Barbara City College C, A
Santa Rosa Junior College C, A
Sonoma State University B
University of California
    Berkeley M, D
    Davis B
    Irvine M, D
    Riverside B
    Santa Barbara
    Santa Cruz B, D
University of La Verne C, B
University of Redlands B
University of San Francisco B, M
University of Southern California B
Whittier College B

Colorado
Adams State College B
Colorado College B
Colorado Mountain College
    Timberline Campus A
Metropolitan State College of Denver B
Naropa University C, B, M
Trinidad State Junior College A
University of Colorado
    Boulder B
    Denver M

Connecticut
Central Connecticut State University B
Connecticut College B
Gateway Community College A
Middlesex Community-Technical College A
Sacred Heart University B
Teikyo Post University B
University of Connecticut B, M, D
University of New Haven A, B, M
Wesleyan University B, M

Delaware
University of Delaware B
Wesley College B

District of Columbia
American University B, M
George Washington University B
Trinity College B
University of the District of Columbia B

Florida
Central Florida Community College A
Florida Atlantic University M
Florida Gulf Coast University B
Florida Institute of Technology B, M, D
Florida International University B, M
Florida Southern College B
Gulf Coast Community College A
Hillsborough Community College A
Jacksonville University B
Miami-Dade Community College A
Pensacola Junior College A
St. Leo University B
Seminole Community College A
Stetson University B
University of Florida B
University of Miami B
University of South Florida B
University of Tampa B

Georgia
Berry College B
Brenau University B
Columbus State University M
Mercer University B
Shorter College B
Thomas College B
University of Georgia M
Valdosta State University B

Hawaii
Hawaii Pacific University B

University of Hawaii
    Manoa B

Idaho
College of Southern Idaho A
University of Idaho B, M

Illinois
Augustana College B
Bradley University B, M
De Paul University B
Dominican University B
Monmouth College B
Northeastern Illinois University B
Principia College B
Quincy University A, B
Southern Illinois University
    Edwardsville B
University of Illinois
    Springfield M
    Urbana-Champaign M, D
University of St. Francis B
Wheaton College B

Indiana
Ball State University M
Bethel College B
Goshen College B
Indiana University
    Bloomington B, M, D
    Northwest C
Manchester College B
Purdue University B, M
St. Joseph's College B
Taylor University B
Tri-State University B
University of Evansville B
University of Indianapolis B
University of Notre Dame B
University of St. Francis B
Valparaiso University B
Vincennes University A

Iowa
Central College B
Dordt College B
Iowa State University B
Marycrest International University B
Morningside College B
Muscatine Community College A
Northwestern College B
Simpson College B
University of Dubuque B
University of Iowa B
University of Northern Iowa M

Kansas
Pittsburg State University B
Tabor College B
Wichita State University M

Kentucky
Georgetown College B
Midway College B
University of Kentucky B

Louisiana
Louisiana State University
    Shreveport B
Louisiana State University and Agricultural and Mechanical College B, M
Louisiana Tech University B
McNeese State University B, M
Southern University and Agricultural and Mechanical College M
Tulane University B

Maine
Colby College B
College of the Atlantic B
St. Joseph's College B
Unity College B
University of Maine
    Farmington B
    Machias B, T
    Presque Isle B
University of New England B

Maryland
Frostburg State University B, M
Harford Community College C, A
Howard Community College A
University of Maryland
    College Park B, M
    Eastern Shore B, M, D
Washington College B

Massachusetts
Anna Maria College M
Assumption College B
Berkshire Community College A
Boston University B, M
Bristol Community College A
Cape Cod Community College C, A
College of the Holy Cross B
Curry College B
Fitchburg State College B
Harvard College B
Holyoke Community College A
Massachusetts Maritime Academy B
Merrimack College B
Quincy College C, A
Roxbury Community College A
Simmons College B
Springfield College B
Suffolk University A
University of Massachusetts
    Amherst B
    Lowell B
Western New England College B
Westfield State College B
Wheaton College B
Worcester Polytechnic Institute B

Michigan
Adrian College A, B
Albion College B
Aquinas College B
Calvin College B
Lake Superior State University A, B
Lansing Community College A
Michigan State University B, M, D
Mid Michigan Community College A
Northern Michigan University B
Olivet College B
Schoolcraft College A
University of Michigan
    Dearborn B
University of Michigan B, M, D
Western Michigan University B

Minnesota
Bemidji State University B, M
Bethel College B
Fond Du Lac Tribal and Community College A
Gustavus Adolphus College B
Itasca Community College A
Minnesota State University,
    Mankato B, M
St. Cloud State University B, M
University of Minnesota
    Twin Cities B, M, D
Vermilion Community College A
Winona State University B

Mississippi
Jackson State University M, D

Missouri
Central Methodist College B
Maryville University of Saint Louis B
St. Charles County Community College A
St. Louis University B
University of Missouri
    Columbia D
Washington University B
Westminster College B

Montana
Miles Community College A
Montana State University
    Billings B
    Bozeman B, M, D

Environmental science/conservation

Rocky Mountain College B
Salish Kootenai College B
University of Montana-Missoula M
Western Montana College of The University of Montana B

Nebraska

Bellevue University B
Creighton University B
Dana College B
Midland Lutheran College B
University of Nebraska
   Lincoln B, M

Nevada

University of Nevada
   Las Vegas B, M, D
   Reno B, M
Western Nevada Community College A

New Hampshire

Antioch New England Graduate School M
Colby-Sawyer College B
Dartmouth College B
Franklin Pierce College B
New England College B
Plymouth State College of the University System of New Hampshire B, M
University of New Hampshire B, M, D

New Jersey

Bloomfield College B
Caldwell College C
Fairleigh Dickinson University B
Montclair State University M
New Jersey Institute of Technology B, M, D
Ramapo College of New Jersey B
Raritan Valley Community College A
Richard Stockton College of New Jersey B
Rider University B
Rowan University M
Rutgers
   The State University of New Jersey: Cook College B
   The State University of New Jersey: Douglass College B
   The State University of New Jersey: New Brunswick Graduate Campus M, D
   The State University of New Jersey: Newark College of Arts and Sciences B
   The State University of New Jersey: Newark Graduate Campus M, D
Thomas Edison State College A, B
Warren County Community College A
William Paterson University of New Jersey B

New Mexico

Albuquerque Technical-Vocational Institute A
College of Santa Fe B
College of the Southwest B
New Mexico Highlands University B, M
New Mexico Institute of Mining and Technology B
New Mexico State University
   Carlsbad A
New Mexico State University B
Northern New Mexico Community College C, A

New York

Bard College M
Barnard College B
City University of New York
   Graduate School and University Center D
   Kingsborough Community College A
   Medgar Evers College B
   Queens College B
Colgate University B

Columbia University
   Columbia College B
   School of General Studies B
Concordia College B
Cornell University B, M, D
Elmira College B
Finger Lakes Community College C, A
Fulton-Montgomery Community College A
Ithaca College B
Long Island University
   C. W. Post Campus B, M
Marist College B
Molloy College B
Pace University:
   Pleasantville/Briarcliff B, M
Pace University B, M
Polytechnic University
   Long Island Campus B
Polytechnic University B
Rensselaer Polytechnic Institute B
Rochester Institute of Technology B, M
St. Bonaventure University B
St. John's University B
State University of New York
   Binghamton B
   College at Brockport B
   College at Oneonta B
   College at Plattsburgh B
   College of Agriculture and Technology at Cobleskill A
   College of Agriculture and Technology at Morrisville A
   College of Environmental Science and Forestry B, M, D
   College of Technology at Alfred A
   Maritime College B
   Purchase B
Syracuse University B
Tompkins-Cortland Community College A
Trocaire College A
United States Military Academy B
Wells College B

North Carolina

Beaufort County Community College A
Belmont Abbey College B
Blue Ridge Community College C, A
Catawba College B
Duke University B, M, D
Elon College B
Meredith College B
Montreat College B
North Carolina Central University B
North Carolina State University B
North Carolina Wesleyan College B
Shaw University B
Southeastern Community College A
University of North Carolina
   Asheville B
   Chapel Hill B, M, D
   Wilmington B
Wake Technical Community College A
Warren Wilson College B
Wilson Technical Community College A

Ohio

Antioch College B
Ashland University B
Columbus State Community College A
Defiance College B
Denison University B
Hocking Technical College A
Kent State University
   Ashtabula Regional Campus C, A
   Stark Campus B
Kent State University B
Marietta College B
Miami University
   Oxford Campus M
Mount Vernon Nazarene College B
Muskingum College B
Oberlin College B
Ohio Northern University B

Ohio State University
   Agricultural Technical Institute A
   Columbus Campus B, M, D
Otterbein College B
University of Cincinnati M, D
University of Findlay A, B
University of Toledo B
Youngstown State University B

Oklahoma

Eastern Oklahoma State College A
Northeastern State University B
Oklahoma Christian University of Science and Arts B
Oklahoma State University B, M, D
St. Gregory's University B
Southeastern Oklahoma State University B
Southern Nazarene University B
University of Tulsa B

Oregon

Eastern Oregon University B
Marylhurst University B
Oregon Graduate Institute M, D
Oregon Institute of Technology B
Oregon State University B
Portland State University B, D
Southern Oregon University B
University of Oregon B, M
Willamette University B

Pennsylvania

Albright College B
Allegheny College B
Allentown College of St. Francis de Sales B
Beaver College M
Bryn Mawr College B
Bucknell University B
Cabrini College B
California University of Pennsylvania B
Chatham College C, B
Chestnut Hill College C, B
Clarion University of Pennsylvania B
Delaware Valley College B
Dickinson College B
Drexel University B, M, D
Eastern College B
Edinboro University of Pennsylvania B
Elizabethtown College B
Gannon University B, M
Gettysburg College B
Harrisburg Area Community College A
Immaculata College B
Indiana University of Pennsylvania B
Juniata College B
King's College B
Kutztown University of Pennsylvania B
La Salle University B
Lehigh University M, D
Lock Haven University of Pennsylvania B
Mansfield University of Pennsylvania B
Marywood University B
Messiah College B
Muhlenberg College B
Penn State
   Altoona B
   University Park C, B
Philadelphia University B
Point Park College B
St. Joseph's University B
St. Vincent College B
Shippensburg University of Pennsylvania B, M
Slippery Rock University of Pennsylvania B
Susquehanna University B
Temple University B
Thiel College B
University of Pennsylvania B
University of Pittsburgh
   Greensburg B
University of Scranton B

University of the Sciences in Philadelphia B
Waynesburg College B
Widener University B
Wilson College B

Puerto Rico

Bayamon Central University B
Inter American University of Puerto Rico
   Bayamon Campus B
Pontifical Catholic University of Puerto Rico B
Turabo University M
Universidad Metropolitana B
University of Puerto Rico
   Rio Piedras Campus B

Rhode Island

Brown University B, M
Salve Regina University B
University of Rhode Island B, M, D

South Carolina

Charleston Southern University B
College of Charleston M
Furman University B

South Dakota

Black Hills State University B
Mount Marty College B
Sinte Gleska University A

Tennessee

Lincoln Memorial University B
Maryville College B
Tennessee Technological University B
Tusculum College B
University of Tennessee
   Chattanooga B, M
   Martin B

Texas

Abilene Christian University B
Baylor University B, M
Coastal Bend College A
Concordia University at Austin B
Lamar University B, M
Lubbock Christian University B
McMurry University B
Midland College C, A
Midwestern State University B
Sam Houston State University B
Southern Methodist University B
Southwest Texas State University B, M
Stephen F. Austin State University B, M
Sul Ross State University B
Tarleton State University M
Texas A&M International University B
Texas A&M University
   Commerce B
   Corpus Christi B, M
Texas A&M University B
Texas State Technical College
   Harlingen A
University of Houston
   Clear Lake B, M
University of North Texas M, D
University of Texas
   Dallas M
   San Antonio M
University of the Incarnate Word B
West Texas A&M University B, M

Utah

Brigham Young University B
Dixie State College of Utah A
Snow College A

Vermont

Bennington College B
Castleton State College B
Johnson State College B
Marlboro College B
Middlebury College B
Norwich University B
Southern Vermont College A, B
Sterling College A, B
University of Vermont B

Vermont Technical College A

Virginia
Averett College B
Christopher Newport University B, M
Eastern Mennonite University B
Emory & Henry College B
Ferrum College B
George Mason University D
Longwood College M
Mary Washington College B
Roanoke College B, T
St. Paul's College B
Shenandoah University B
University of Virginia's College at Wise B
University of Virginia B, M, D
Virginia Intermont College B
Virginia Polytechnic Institute and State University B

Washington
Centralia College A
Everett Community College A
Evergreen State College B, M
Heritage College B
Seattle University B
Skagit Valley College A
University of Washington B
Washington State University B, M, D
Western Washington University B, M

West Virginia
Alderson-Broaddus College B
College of West Virginia A
Davis and Elkins College B
Glenville State College A
Marshall University B, M
Salem-Teikyo University B
Shepherd College B
University of Charleston B
West Virginia Wesleyan College B
Wheeling Jesuit University B

Wisconsin
Alverno College B
Carroll College B
Northland College B
St. Norbert College B
University of Wisconsin
    Green Bay B, M
    Madison M, D
    Platteville B

Environmental studies

Alabama
Birmingham-Southern College B
Northwest-Shoals Community College A

Alaska
Alaska Pacific University B, M
University of Alaska
    Southeast B

Arizona
Northern Arizona University B
Prescott College B, M

Arkansas
University of Arkansas B
Westark College A

California
Azusa Pacific University B
California State University
    Fullerton M
    Hayward B
    Monterey Bay B
Chaffey Community College A
National University M
Occidental College B
Pitzer College B
Pomona College B
Saddleback College A
San Diego State University C
Santa Rosa Junior College A
United States International University B
University of California
    Berkeley B
    Riverside B
University of Southern California B
University of the Pacific B

Colorado
Colorado College B
Colorado Mountain College
    Timberline Campus A
Metropolitan State College of Denver B
Naropa University C, B, M
University of Colorado
    Boulder B
University of Denver B

Connecticut
Connecticut College B
Sacred Heart University B
Wesleyan University C
Yale University M, D

District of Columbia
American University B, M
George Washington University B, M

Florida
Eckerd College B
Florida State University B
New College of the University of South Florida B
Rollins College B
Stetson University B

Georgia
Brenau University B
Mercer University B
Oxford College of Emory University B
Piedmont College B
Shorter College B

Hawaii
Hawaii Pacific University B

Illinois
Elmhurst College B
Lake Forest College B
Roosevelt University B
Wheaton College B

Indiana
Earlham College B
Goshen College B
Manchester College B
St. Mary-of-the-Woods College M
University of Evansville B

Iowa
Central College B
Cornell College B
Dordt College B
Maharishi University of Management B, M
Morningside College B
St. Ambrose University B
University of Dubuque B
University of Iowa B

Kansas
McPherson College B
University of Kansas M, D

Louisiana
Centenary College of Louisiana B
Xavier University of Louisiana B

Maine
Bates College B
Bowdoin College B
Colby College B
College of the Atlantic B, M
Unity College B
University of Maine
    Presque Isle B
University of New England B
University of Southern Maine B

Maryland
Johns Hopkins University B
Towson University B
Washington College B

Massachusetts
Berkshire Community College A
Boston University B, M
Cape Cod Community College A
Clark University B
Fitchburg State College B
Hampshire College B
Harvard College B
Massachusetts Maritime Academy B
Mount Holyoke College B
Northeastern University B
Springfield College B
Wellesley College B
Worcester Polytechnic Institute B

Michigan
Northern Michigan University B

Minnesota
Bethel College B
Concordia College: Moorhead B
Gustavus Adolphus College B
Hamline University B
Macalester College B
Minnesota State University, Mankato B
University of Minnesota
    Duluth B
University of St. Thomas B
Vermilion Community College B
Winona State University B

Missouri
Drury University B
Maryville University of Saint Louis B
St. Charles County Community College A
Southeast Missouri State University B
Stephens College B
University of Missouri
    Kansas City B
    St. Louis C
Washington University B
Webster University B
Westminster College B

Montana
Carroll College B
University of Montana-Missoula B, M
Western Montana College of The University of Montana B

Nebraska
Dana College B
Doane College B
University of Nebraska
    Lincoln B
    Omaha B

Nevada
University of Nevada
    Las Vegas B

New Hampshire
Antioch New England Graduate School M, D
Dartmouth College B
Franklin Pierce College B
New Hampshire Community Technical College
    Berlin A
St. Anselm College B

New Jersey
Ramapo College of New Jersey B
Richard Stockton College of New Jersey B
Sussex County Community College A
Thomas Edison State College B

New Mexico
College of Santa Fe B
New Mexico Institute of Mining and Technology B

New York
Alfred University B
Bard College M
Canisius College B
City University of New York
    Queens College B
Colgate University B
College of St. Rose B
Columbia University
    School of General Studies B
Elmira College B
Finger Lakes Community College A
Fulton-Montgomery Community College A
Hobart and William Smith Colleges B
Hudson Valley Community College A
Ithaca College B
Long Island University
    C. W. Post Campus B
Marist College B
Rensselaer Polytechnic Institute M, D
St. John's University B
St. Lawrence University B
Sarah Lawrence College B
Siena College B
State University of New York
    College at Brockport B
    College at Fredonia B
    College of Agriculture and Technology at Cobleskill A
    College of Agriculture and Technology at Morrisville A
    College of Environmental Science and Forestry B, M, D
Suffolk County Community College A
Syracuse University B
University of Rochester B
Wells College B

North Carolina
Brevard College B
Elon College B
Montreat College B
North Carolina Central University B
Pfeiffer University B
St. Andrews Presbyterian College B

Ohio
Antioch College B
Bowling Green State University B
Capital University B
Case Western Reserve University B
Cleveland State University B
Columbus State Community College A
Defiance College B
Hiram College B
John Carroll University B
Lake Erie College B
Lourdes College B
Marietta College B
Ohio Northern University B
Ohio University M
Ohio Wesleyan University B
Otterbein College B
University of Findlay B
University of Toledo B
Ursuline College B
Wittenberg University B
Youngstown State University B

Oklahoma
Eastern Oklahoma State College A
Oklahoma State University B, M, D
Southeastern Oklahoma State University B

Oregon
Lewis & Clark College B
Oregon Graduate Institute M, D
Southern Oregon University B
University of Portland B
Willamette University B

Pennsylvania
Allegheny College B
Allentown College of St. Francis de Sales B

Environmental studies

Beaver College B, M
Bucknell University B
Chatham College B
Dickinson College B
Gettysburg College B
Grove City College T
Juniata College B
Mansfield University of Pennsylvania B
Neumann College B
Thiel College B
University of Pittsburgh
 Johnstown B
University of Pittsburgh B
Ursinus College B

Puerto Rico
Inter American University of Puerto Rico
 San German Campus M
Pontifical Catholic University of Puerto
 Rico B

Rhode Island
Brown University B, M
Providence College B

South Carolina
Charleston Southern University B

Tennessee
Maryville College B
Tusculum College B

Texas
Baylor University M
Lamar University B
Lubbock Christian University B
Midland College A
Texas A&M University
 Commerce B
Texas State Technical College
 Harlingen A
University of Houston
 Clear Lake B, M
University of St. Thomas B
University of Texas
 Austin M
University of the Incarnate Word B

Utah
Dixie State College of Utah A
Salt Lake Community College A
University of Utah B
Utah State University M

Vermont
Goddard College B
Green Mountain College B
Johnson State College B
Marlboro College B
St. Michael's College B
Sterling College A, B
University of Vermont B

Virginia
Averett College B
Bluefield College B
College of William and Mary B
Eastern Mennonite University B
Emory & Henry College B
Randolph-Macon College B
Roanoke College B
Southwest Virginia Community
 College A
Virginia Commonwealth University C
Washington and Lee University B

Washington
Evergreen State College B, M
Western Washington University B
Whitman College B

West Virginia
Bethany College B
College of West Virginia A, B
Davis and Elkins College B
Shepherd College B
West Virginia Wesleyan College B

Wisconsin
Alverno College B
Carroll College B
Northland College B
Ripon College B
University of Wisconsin
 Green Bay B, M
 Madison B, M

Epidemiology

Alabama
University of Alabama
 Birmingham D

Arizona
University of Arizona M, D

California
Loma Linda University M, D
San Diego State University M
University of California
 Berkeley D
 Davis M, D
 Los Angeles M, D

Connecticut
Yale University M, D

District of Columbia
George Washington University D
Georgetown University M

Florida
University of Miami M, D

Georgia
Emory University D

Iowa
University of Iowa M, D

Louisiana
Tulane University M, D

Maryland
University of Maryland
 Baltimore M, D

Massachusetts
Boston University M, D

Michigan
Michigan State University M
University of Michigan M, D

Minnesota
University of Minnesota
 Twin Cities M, D

New York
State University of New York
 Albany B, M, D
 Buffalo M, D

North Carolina
East Carolina University B
University of North Carolina
 Chapel Hill M, D

Ohio
Case Western Reserve University M, D

Pennsylvania
University of Pennsylvania M, D
University of Pittsburgh M, D

Puerto Rico
University of Puerto Rico
 Medical Sciences Campus M

South Carolina
University of South Carolina M, D

Texas
Texas A&M University M

Washington
University of Washington M

Wisconsin
Medical College of Wisconsin M

Equestrian/equine studies

Arizona
Scottsdale Community College A

California
College of the Sequoias C
Merced College A
Moorpark College A
Mount San Antonio College C
Santa Rosa Junior College C, A
Shasta College C, A
Sierra College C, A

Colorado
Colorado State University B
Lamar Community College C, A
Northeastern Junior College A
Pikes Peak Community College C

Connecticut
Teikyo Post University C, A, B

Idaho
College of Southern Idaho A

Illinois
Black Hawk College
 East Campus C, A
Black Hawk College A
Parkland College C, A

Indiana
St. Mary-of-the-Woods College A, B

Iowa
Kirkwood Community College A

Kansas
Colby Community College A
Dodge City Community College C, A

Kentucky
Midway College A, B
Murray State University B
University of Louisville C, B

Massachusetts
Mount Ida College A, B
University of Massachusetts
 Amherst A

Michigan
Michigan State University C

Minnesota
University of Minnesota
 Crookston B

Missouri
Truman State University B
William Woods University B, M

Montana
Dawson Community College A
Rocky Mountain College B

New Hampshire
University of New Hampshire A, B

New Jersey
Centenary College A, B

New York
State University of New York
 College of Agriculture and
  Technology at Cobleskill A
 College of Agriculture and
  Technology at Morrisville A, B

North Carolina
Martin Community College C, A

Ohio
Hocking Technical College A
Lake Erie College B
Ohio State University
 Agricultural Technical Institute A
 Columbus Campus B
Ohio University
 Southern Campus at Ironton A
Ohio University A
Otterbein College B
University of Findlay A, B

Oklahoma
Connors State College C, A
Northeastern Oklahoma Agricultural and
 Mechanical College A
Redlands Community College A
Rogers State University C, A

Oregon
Linn-Benton Community College A

Pennsylvania
Delaware Valley College A, B
Wilson College B

Rhode Island
Johnson & Wales University A, B

Texas
Central Texas College C
North Central Texas College A
Sul Ross State University B
Tarleton State University B
Weatherford College A

Virginia
Averett College B
J. Sargeant Reynolds Community
 College C
Lord Fairfax Community College C
Virginia Intermont College B

West Virginia
Salem-Teikyo University B, M

Wyoming
Central Wyoming College C, A
Laramie County Community College A
Northwest College C, A

ESL teacher education

Alabama
University of Alabama
 Huntsville C
University of Alabama M

Alaska
Alaska Bible College B

Arizona
Arizona State University M
Grand Canyon University M
Northern Arizona University M
University of Arizona M, D

California
Azusa Pacific University M
California State University
 Dominguez Hills M
 Fullerton M, T
 Hayward M
 Long Beach T
 Los Angeles M
College of Marin: Kentfield C, A
Fresno Pacific University M
Holy Names College C, M
Long Beach City College C, A
Loyola Marymount University M
Monterey Institute of International
 Studies M
San Francisco State University M
San Jose State University M
United States International
 University B, M, D
University of California
 Los Angeles M
 San Diego M
University of San Francisco M
University of Southern California M
University of the Pacific T

Colorado
Fort Lewis College T

Connecticut
Central Connecticut State University *M*
Norwalk Community-Technical College *C*

Delaware
University of Delaware *B, M, T*

District of Columbia
American University *M*
Catholic University of America *B*
George Washington University *A*
Georgetown University *M*

Florida
Florida State University *C*
Hobe Sound Bible College *B, T*
Lynn University *C*
Nova Southeastern University *M*
Tallahassee Community College *C*
University of Central Florida *M*
University of Miami *B*

Georgia
Georgia State University *M*

Hawaii
Brigham Young University Hawaii *B*
Hawaii Pacific University *B*
University of Hawaii Manoa *B, M, T*

Idaho
Boise State University *T*
University of Idaho *M*

Illinois
Lincoln Christian College and Seminary *C*
Moody Bible Institute *B*
Southern Illinois University Carbondale *M*
University of Illinois Urbana-Champaign *M*

Indiana
Ball State University *D, T*
Goshen College *B*

Iowa
Iowa State University *T*
Northwestern College *T*
University of Iowa *B, M, D*
University of Northern Iowa *B, M*

Kansas
McPherson College *T*

Kentucky
Murray State University *B, M, T*

Maryland
University of Maryland Baltimore County *M*

Massachusetts
Boston University *M, T*
Eastern Nazarene College *B, M, T*
Elms College *B, M, T*
Salem State College *M*
Simmons College *B, M*
University of Massachusetts Boston *M*

Michigan
Andrews University *B, M, T*
Central Michigan University *M*
Michigan State University *M*

Minnesota
Hamline University *B*
Macalester College *T*
Minnesota State University, Mankato *T*
Moorhead State University *B, T*
Northwestern College *B*
University of Minnesota
  Duluth *T*
  Twin Cities *M, T*

Mississippi
University of Mississippi *M*

Missouri
Central Missouri State University *C, M, T*
Missouri Southern State College *B*
Webster University *B*

Montana
Carroll College *B*

Nebraska
Doane College *B, T*
University of Nebraska Kearney *B, T*

New Hampshire
Notre Dame College *M*

New Jersey
Fairleigh Dickinson University *M*
Montclair State University *T*
New Jersey City University *T*
Rider University *B, T*
Rutgers
  The State University of New Jersey: Camden College of Arts and Sciences *T*
  The State University of New Jersey: New Brunswick Graduate Campus *M, T*
  The State University of New Jersey: University College Camden *T*
Seton Hall University *M*
The College of New Jersey *M, T*

New Mexico
College of Santa Fe *B*
Western New Mexico University *B*

New York
City University of New York
  Brooklyn College *B, M*
  Hunter College *M*
  Queens College *M, T*
College of New Rochelle *M*
Columbia University Teachers College *M, D*
Hofstra University *M*
Le Moyne College *T*
Long Island University
  Brooklyn Campus *M*
  C. W. Post Campus *M*
Manhattanville College *M*
Mercy College *T*
Nazareth College of Rochester *M*
New York University *M, D, T*
Nyack College *B*
St. John's University *M, T*
State University of New York
  Albany *M*
  Buffalo *M, T*
  New Paltz *M, T*
  Stony Brook *M, T*

North Carolina
Meredith College *M*
University of North Carolina Charlotte *M*

Ohio
Bowling Green State University *B*
Cedarville College *T*
Kent State University *M, T*
Ohio Dominican College *B, D*
Ohio State University Columbus Campus *M*
University of Dayton *B, M, T*
University of Findlay *B, M, T*
University of Toledo *M, T*

Oklahoma
Langston University *M*
Oklahoma Christian University of Science and Arts *B, T*
Oklahoma City University *M*
Oral Roberts University *M*

Oregon
Eastern Oregon University *B, T*
Portland State University *M*
Western Oregon University *M, T*

Pennsylvania
Penn State University Park *M*
Temple University *M*
University of Pennsylvania *M*
University of Pittsburgh *T*
West Chester University of Pennsylvania *M*

Puerto Rico
American University of Puerto Rico *B, T*
Inter American University of Puerto Rico
  Fajardo Campus *B, T*
  Metropolitan Campus *B, M*
  San German Campus *M*
National College of Business and Technology *A*
Pontifical Catholic University of Puerto Rico *B, M, T*
Turabo University *M*
University of Puerto Rico
  Humacao University College *B*
  Mayaguez Campus *T*

Rhode Island
Rhode Island College *M*

South Carolina
Columbia International University *C, A*

Tennessee
Carson-Newman College *M*
Johnson Bible College *B, T*
Maryville College *B, T*
Union University *B, T*

Texas
Houston Baptist University *B, T*
Lamar University *T*
McMurry University *T*
San Antonio College *C*
Texas A&M University
  Commerce *T*
  Corpus Christi *T*
Texas Christian University *B, M, T*
Texas Wesleyan University *M*
University of Texas
  Arlington *T*
  San Antonio *M, T*
West Texas A&M University *T*

Utah
Brigham Young University *B, M, T*
Snow College *A*

Vermont
St. Michael's College *M*

Virginia
Liberty University *B*
Shenandoah University *C*

Washington
Central Washington University *T*
City University *C, M*
Eastern Washington University *M, T*
Gonzaga University *M*
Seattle Pacific University *M*
Seattle University *M*
University of Washington *B, T*
Washington State University *T*
Western Washington University *C*
Whitworth College *B, M, T*

Wisconsin
Cardinal Stritch University *M, D, T*
St. Norbert College *T*

Ethnic/cultural studies

Arizona
Prescott College *B, M*

California
Cabrillo College *A*
California State Polytechnic University: Pomona *B*
California State University
  Hayward *B*
  Monterey Bay *B*
College of San Mateo *A*
Compton Community College *A*
De Anza College *C, A*
Foothill College *A*
Fresno Pacific University *B*
Grossmont Community College *A*
Los Angeles Valley College *A*
Loyola Marymount University *B*
Mills College *B*
MiraCosta College *A*
Monterey Peninsula College *A*
Pitzer College *B*
Riverside Community College *A*
Saddleback College *A*
San Francisco State University *M*
Santa Ana College *A*
University of California
  Berkeley *B, M, D*
  Riverside *B*
  San Diego *B, D*
  Santa Cruz *B*

Colorado
Fort Lewis College *B*
University of Colorado Boulder *B*
University of Denver *B*

Connecticut
Trinity College *B*

District of Columbia
Catholic University of America *D*

Hawaii
University of Hawaii Manoa *B*

Idaho
Boise State University *B*

Illinois
National-Louis University *B*

Indiana
Goshen College *B*
Indiana University Northwest *B*
Indiana University--Purdue University
  Indiana University-Purdue University Fort Wayne *C*
Manchester College *B*

Iowa
Cornell College *B*

Kansas
Central Christian College *A*

Maine
University of Maine Fort Kent *B*

Maryland
Johns Hopkins University *B*
Washington College *B*

Massachusetts
Hampshire College *B*
Harvard College *B*
Simmons College *B*
Simon's Rock College of Bard *B*

Minnesota
Metropolitan State University *B*
Minnesota State University, Mankato *B*
St. Olaf College *B*

Missouri
Washington University *B*

Ethnic/cultural studies (continued)

Nevada
University of Nevada
   Reno B

New Jersey
Ramapo College of New Jersey B
Richard Stockton College of New
   Jersey C

New York
Audrey Cohen College A, B
Bard College B
Cornell University B
Eugene Lang College/New School
   University B
Nyack College B
Sarah Lawrence College B

Ohio
Bowling Green State University B
Kent State University B
Ohio State University
   Columbus Campus B, M, D
University of Cincinnati
   Raymond Walters College C

Oregon
Chemeketa Community College A
University of Oregon B

Pennsylvania
Penn State
   University Park B
University of Pennsylvania B

Texas
Brazosport College A
University of Texas
   Austin B

Vermont
Burlington College B
Goddard College B, M
Marlboro College B

Virginia
Bridgewater College B
College of William and Mary B

Washington
Evergreen State College B
North Seattle Community College C
University of Washington B
Western Washington University B

Wisconsin
University of Wisconsin
   La Crosse C

European studies

Alabama
Huntingdon College B

California
Chapman University B
Loyola Marymount University B
Pepperdine University B
Pitzer College B
San Diego State University B
Scripps College B
University of California
   Los Angeles B

Colorado
Fort Lewis College B

Connecticut
Connecticut College B

District of Columbia
George Washington University B

Florida
Florida State University B

Hawaii
University of Hawaii
   West Oahu B

Indiana
Valparaiso University B

Iowa
University of Northern Iowa B

Kansas
University of Kansas B

Kentucky
Georgetown College B

Massachusetts
Amherst College B
Brandeis University B
Harvard College B
Tufts University B, M
Wellesley College B

Michigan
Hillsdale College B
Western Michigan University B

Minnesota
Hamline University B
University of Minnesota
   Morris B
   Twin Cities B

Missouri
University of Missouri
   St. Louis C
Washington University B, M

Nebraska
University of Nebraska
   Lincoln B

New Mexico
University of New Mexico B

New York
Bard College B
Barnard College B
Canisius College C, B
Cornell University B
Eugene Lang College/New School
   University B
Hobart and William Smith Colleges B
New York University B, M
Sarah Lawrence College B

North Carolina
Queens College B

Ohio
Ohio University B
University of Toledo B
Wittenberg University B

Pennsylvania
California University of Pennsylvania B
Carnegie Mellon University B
Chatham College B
St. Joseph's University C

Rhode Island
Brown University B

South Carolina
University of South Carolina B

Tennessee
Vanderbilt University B

Texas
Howard Payne University B
Southern Methodist University B
Southwest Texas State University B
Trinity University B

Utah
Brigham Young University B

Vermont
Goddard College B
Marlboro College B
Middlebury College B
University of Vermont B

Virginia
College of William and Mary B

Emory & Henry College B

Washington
Gonzaga University B
Seattle Pacific University B
University of Washington B

Evolutionary biology

California
San Diego State University B
University of California
   Davis B
   San Diego B

Florida
University of West Florida B

Illinois
Northwestern University B
University of Chicago M, D

Louisiana
Tulane University B, M, D

Massachusetts
Harvard College B
Harvard University M, D
University of Massachusetts
   Amherst M, D

Missouri
Washington University D

New Hampshire
Antioch New England Graduate
   School M
Dartmouth College B
University of New Hampshire B

New Jersey
Rutgers
   The State University of New Jersey:
     Camden College of Arts and
     Sciences B
   The State University of New Jersey:
     Cook College B
   The State University of New Jersey:
     Douglass College B
   The State University of New Jersey:
     Livingston College B
   The State University of New Jersey:
     Rutgers College B
   The State University of New Jersey:
     University College Camden B
   The State University of New Jersey:
     University College New
     Brunswick B

New York
Columbia University
   Graduate School D
   School of General Studies B
Cornell University B, M, D

Pennsylvania
Lehigh University M, D

Exercise sciences

Alabama
Auburn University B
Huntingdon College B
Jacksonville State University B
Samford University B

Arizona
Arizona State University B, M, D
Northern Arizona University B

Arkansas
University of Arkansas M, D

California
California State University
   Chico B
   Fresno A
   Hayward B, M

Chapman University B
Concordia University B
La Sierra University B
MiraCosta College C
Occidental College B
Orange Coast College C, A
Santa Ana College A
Santa Barbara City College A
University of California
   Davis B, M
University of Southern
   California B, M, D
University of the Pacific M
Vanguard University of Southern
   California B

Colorado
Adams State College B
Colorado State University B, M
Fort Lewis College B
Metropolitan State College of Denver B
University of Colorado
   Boulder B, M, D
University of Northern Colorado B, T
Western State College of Colorado B, T

Connecticut
Central Connecticut State University B
Manchester Community-Technical
   College A
Southern Connecticut State
   University B, M, T

Delaware
University of Delaware B, M, D

District of Columbia
George Washington University B, M

Florida
Barry University B, M
Florida State University M, D
Santa Fe Community College A
Stetson University B, T
University of Florida B, M, D
University of Miami B, M
University of West Florida B
Warner Southern College B

Georgia
Columbus State University B
Darton College A
East Georgia College A
Georgia Southern University B, M
Georgia State University D
Piedmont College B
Valdosta State University B

Hawaii
Brigham Young University
   Hawaii B
University of Hawaii
   Manoa B

Idaho
Albertson College of Idaho B
Boise State University M
University of Idaho B

Illinois
Concordia University B
Elmhurst College B
North Central College B
Northeastern Illinois University M
William Rainey Harper College A

Indiana
DePauw University B
Indiana State University B
Indiana University
   Bloomington D
University of Evansville B
University of Southern Indiana B
Vincennes University A

Iowa
Buena Vista University B
Central College B
Clarke College B

Dordt College *B*
Iowa Wesleyan College *B*
Loras College *B*
Maharishi University of Management *A*
Morningside College *B*
North Iowa Area Community College *A*
Northwestern College *B*
University of Iowa *B, M, D*

Kansas
Kansas State University *B, M*

Kentucky
Campbellsville University *B*
Murray State University *B*
Thomas More College *A*
University of Louisville *M*

Louisiana
Centenary College of Louisiana *B*
Tulane University *B*

Maryland
Community College of Baltimore County
    Essex *A*
Towson University *B*

Massachusetts
Becker College *B*
Boston University *B, M*
Bridgewater State College *B*
Fitchburg State College *B*
Gordon College *B*
Hampshire College *B*
Lasell College *B*
Mount Ida College *A*
Northeastern University *B, M*
Smith College *M*
Springfield College *B, M*
University of Massachusetts
    Amherst *B, M, D*
Westfield State College *B*

Michigan
Adrian College *B*
Alma College *B*
Calvin College *B*
Central Michigan University *M*
Hope College *B*
Lake Superior State University *B*
Michigan State University *D*
Northern Michigan University *M*
Oakland Community College *C, A*
Oakland University *M*
University of Michigan *B, D*

Minnesota
College of St. Scholastica *B*
Concordia College: Moorhead *B*
Hamline University *B*
Minnesota State University, Mankato *B*
St. Cloud State University *M*
University of Minnesota
    Duluth *B*
Winona State University *B*

Mississippi
Mississippi University for Women *B*
University of Mississippi *B, M*

Missouri
Drury University *B*
Missouri Western State College *B*
St. Louis University *B*
Truman State University *B*

Montana
Rocky Mountain College *B*
University of Montana-Missoula *B*

Nebraska
Concordia University *B*
Creighton University *B*
Nebraska Wesleyan University *B*
University of Nebraska
    Lincoln *B*

Nevada
University of Nevada
    Las Vegas *B, M*

New Hampshire
Colby-Sawyer College *B*
New England College *B*
New Hampshire Community Technical
    College
    Manchester *C, A*
Notre Dame College *B*
Plymouth State College of the University
    System of New Hampshire *B*
Rivier College *B*
University of New Hampshire *B*

New Jersey
Bergen Community College *C*
County College of Morris *A*
Gloucester County College *A*
Ocean County College *C*
Rutgers
    The State University of New Jersey:
    Cook College *B*
    The State University of New Jersey:
    Douglass College *B*
    The State University of New Jersey:
    Livingston College *B*
    The State University of New Jersey:
    Rutgers College *B*
    The State University of New Jersey:
    University College New
    Brunswick *B*

New York
Adelphi University *B, M*
Hofstra University *B*
Ithaca College *B, M*
Long Island University
    Brooklyn Campus *B*
Orange County Community College *A*
Skidmore College *B*
State University of New York
    Buffalo *B, M, D*

North Carolina
Appalachian State University *M*
Brevard College *B*
Campbell University *B*
Chowan College *B*
East Carolina University *B, M*
Elon College *B*
High Point University *B*
Louisburg College *A*
Meredith College *B*
St. Andrews Presbyterian College *B*
Wake Forest University *B, M*

North Dakota
Mayville State University *B*
North Dakota State University *B*

Ohio
Baldwin-Wallace College *B*
Bowling Green State University *B*
Cedarville College *B*
Cincinnati State Technical and
    Community College *C*
Defiance College *B*
Kent State University
    Stark Campus *B*
Kent State University *B, M, D*
Malone College *B*
Miami University
    Oxford Campus *B, M*
Mount Union College *B*
Mount Vernon Nazarene College *B*
Ohio State University
    Columbus Campus *B*
Ohio University *B, M*
University of Toledo *B, M*
Youngstown State University *B*

Oklahoma
East Central University *B*
Northeastern State University *B*
Oklahoma Baptist University *B*
Oral Roberts University *B*
Southern Nazarene University *B*
University of Tulsa *B*

Oregon
Central Oregon Community College *A*
Linfield College *B*
Oregon State University *B*
Pacific University *B*
University of Oregon *B, M, D*
Willamette University *B*

Pennsylvania
Bloomsburg University of
    Pennsylvania *M*
Butler County Community College *A*
Cabrini College *B*
East Stroudsburg University of
    Pennsylvania *B*
Immaculata College *B*
Messiah College *B*
West Chester University of
    Pennsylvania *M*

Puerto Rico
Inter American University of Puerto Rico
    San German Campus *D*

South Carolina
Anderson College *B*
Erskine College *B, T*
Furman University *B*
Lander University *B*
University of South Carolina
    Aiken *B*
University of South Carolina *B, M, D*

South Dakota
Augustana College *B*

Tennessee
Belmont University *B*
Bethel College *B*
David Lipscomb University *B*
Middle Tennessee State University *M*
Southern Adventist University *B*
Tennessee Wesleyan College *B*
Trevecca Nazarene University *B*
Union University *B*
University of Memphis *B, M*
University of Tennessee
    Chattanooga *B*
    Knoxville *B*

Texas
Abilene Christian University *B*
Austin College *B, M*
Blinn College *A*
Hardin-Simmons University *B*
McMurry University *B*
Midwestern State University *B, M*
St. Edward's University *B, T*
St. Mary's University *B, T*
Schreiner College *B*
Southwest Texas State University *B, T*
Tarleton State University *B*
Tyler Junior College *A*
University of Houston *B*
University of Texas
    Austin *M, D*
    Brownsville *B*
    of the Permian Basin *B*

Utah
Brigham Young University *B, M, D*
Weber State University *B*

Vermont
Castleton State College *B*
Johnson State College *B*

Virginia
Liberty University *B*
Longwood College *B*

Washington
Bastyr University *B*
Centralia College *A*
Eastern Washington University *B*
Seattle Pacific University *B*
University of Puget Sound *B*
Washington State University *B, M*
Western Washington University *B*

West Virginia
Alderson-Broaddus College *B*
Davis and Elkins College *B*
West Liberty State College *B*
West Virginia University *B, M*

Wisconsin
Carthage College *B*
University of Wisconsin
    Eau Claire *B*
    La Crosse *B, M*
    Milwaukee *B, M*

Wyoming
University of Wyoming *B*

Experimental psychology

California
California State University
    Stanislaus *B*
La Sierra University *B*
Pomona College *B*
San Francisco State University *M*
University of California
    Santa Cruz *B, D*

Connecticut
University of Hartford *M*

District of Columbia
American University *D*
Catholic University of America *M, D*

Florida
Embry-Riddle Aeronautical University *B*
Florida Atlantic University *D*
Florida State University *B, M, D*

Illinois
De Paul University *M, D*
Loyola University of Chicago *D*
Millikin University *B*

Indiana
Indiana State University *M*
University of Evansville *B*

Iowa
University of Iowa *D*

Kansas
University of Kansas *D*
Wichita State University *D*

Kentucky
University of Kentucky *M, D*
University of Louisville *M, D*

Maine
University of Maine *M, D*

Maryland
Johns Hopkins University *B*

Massachusetts
Harvard College *B*
Tufts University *B, M, D*

Missouri
University of Missouri
    Columbia *M, D*

New Hampshire
Franklin Pierce College *B*

New Jersey
Fairleigh Dickinson University *M*

New York
City University of New York
    Graduate School and University
    Center *D*
Columbia University
    Graduate School *M, D*
Fordham University *D*

Experimental psychology

Long Island University
  C. W. Post Campus *M*
New York University *D*
St. John's University *M*
Sarah Lawrence College *B*
State University of New York
  Buffalo *D*
  Stony Brook *M, D*
Syracuse University *M, D*

North Carolina
Duke University *M, D*
University of North Carolina
  Chapel Hill *M, D*

Ohio
Bowling Green State University *M, D*
Case Western Reserve University *D*
Kent State University *M, D*
Ohio University *M, D*
University of Dayton *M*

Oklahoma
Northeastern State University *B*
University of Central Oklahoma *M*

Oregon
Oregon Health Sciences University *M, D*

Pennsylvania
Mansfield University of Pennsylvania *M*
Moravian College *B*
Temple University *M, D*

Rhode Island
University of Rhode Island *D*

South Carolina
University of South Carolina *B, M, D*

Texas
Southern Methodist University *M, D*
Texas Tech University *M, D*
University of North Texas *M, D*
University of Texas
  Arlington *D*
  El Paso *M*

Vermont
Goddard College *B*
Marlboro College *B*

Virginia
Longwood College *B*

Washington
Central Washington University *M*
Eastern Washington University *M*

Wisconsin
University of Wisconsin
  Madison *B, M, D*
  Oshkosh *M*

Family/community studies

Alabama
Alabama Agricultural and Mechanical
  University *B*

Arkansas
John Brown University *B*

California
California State University
  Northridge *B*
Diablo Valley College *C*
Fresno City College *C*
Grossmont Community College *C, A*
Loyola Marymount University *M*
Merritt College *C, A*
Modesto Junior College *A*
Monterey Peninsula College *A*
Sacramento City College *C, A*
Santa Ana College *A*
University of California
  Davis *M*

Delaware
University of Delaware *B, M, D*

Florida
University of Florida *B, M*

Illinois
College of Lake County *C*
Olivet Nazarene University *B, T*
Shawnee Community College *A*

Indiana
Goshen College *B*
Indiana State University *B*

Iowa
Iowa State University *B*
University of Northern Iowa *B, M*

Kentucky
Murray State University *B*

Maryland
University of Maryland
  College Park *B, M*

Massachusetts
Hampshire College *B*

Michigan
Adrian College *B, T*
Michigan State University *M*
Northern Michigan University *B*

Mississippi
University of Mississippi *B*

New Hampshire
University of New Hampshire *B*

New York
State University of New York
  College at Plattsburgh *B*

North Carolina
Campbell University *B*
North Carolina Agricultural and
  Technical State University *B*
University of North Carolina
  Greensboro *B, M, D, T*

North Dakota
North Dakota State University *B, M*

Ohio
Bowling Green State University *B*
Kent State University *B, M*
Lima Technical College *A*
Mount Vernon Nazarene College *A*
Ohio State University
  Columbus Campus *B, M, D*
Ohio University *B, M*
University of Akron *A*
Ursuline College *B*

Oklahoma
Oklahoma Christian University of
  Science and Arts *B*
Oklahoma State University *B, M, D*

Pennsylvania
MCP Hahnemann University *M, D*
Messiah College *B*
Penn State
  University Park *C*
Seton Hill College *B*

Tennessee
Carson-Newman College *B, T*
Tennessee Technological University *B*
University of Tennessee
  Knoxville *B, M*

Texas
Lamar University *B*
Our Lady of the Lake University of San
  Antonio *M*
Prairie View A&M University *B*
University of Houston *B*

Utah
Brigham Young University *M, D*

Snow College *C, A*
University of Utah *B, M*

Vermont
University of Vermont *B*

Virginia
Liberty University *B*

Wisconsin
University of Wisconsin
  Madison *M, D*

Wyoming
University of Wyoming *B, M*

Family/individual development

Alabama
Auburn University *B, M, D*
Oakwood College *B*
Samford University *B*
University of Alabama *B, M*

Arizona
Arizona State University *D*
Central Arizona College *C, A*
Pima Community College *C, A*
University of Arizona *B*

Arkansas
University of Arkansas
  Pine Bluff *B*
University of Arkansas *B*
Westark College *A*

California
Azusa Pacific University *M*
California Polytechnic State University:
  San Luis Obispo *B*
California State University
  Bakersfield *B, M*
  Dominguez Hills *M*
  Northridge *B, M*
Hope International University *B*
Loma Linda University *M*
Long Beach City College *C, A*
Merced College *A*
Moorpark College *A*
Pacific Oaks College *M*
Point Loma Nazarene University *B*
Solano Community College *C*
University of California
  Davis *B, D*
University of La Verne *M*

Colorado
Colorado State University *B, M*

Connecticut
Mitchell College *A, B*
Trinity College *B*
University of Connecticut *B, M, D*

Delaware
University of Delaware *B*

District of Columbia
George Washington University *D*
University of the District of Columbia *B*

Florida
Florida State University *B, M*
Nova Southeastern University *D*
University of Florida *M, D*

Georgia
Fort Valley State University *B*
Georgia Southern University *B*
University of Georgia *B, M, D*

Hawaii
Hawaii Pacific University *B*
University of Hawaii
  Manoa *B*

Idaho
Ricks College *A*

University of Idaho *B*

Illinois
City Colleges of Chicago
  Harold Washington College *A*
Northern Illinois University *B, M*
University of Illinois
  Urbana-Champaign *B, M, D*

Indiana
Anderson University *B*
Indiana State University *B, M*
Purdue University *B, M, D*
St. Mary-of-the-Woods College *C, A, B*

Iowa
Iowa State University *M, D*

Kansas
Kansas State University *B, M, T*

Kentucky
Berea College *B*
Eastern Kentucky University *B*
Kentucky State University *B*
Murray State University *B*
University of Kentucky *B, M*

Louisiana
Louisiana State University and
  Agricultural and Mechanical
  College *B*
Louisiana Tech University *B*
Northwestern State University *B*
Southern University and Agricultural and
  Mechanical College *B*
University of Louisiana at Lafayette *B*
University of Louisiana at Monroe *M, D*

Maine
University of Maine *M*

Massachusetts
Bay Path College *B*
Hampshire College *B*
Hellenic College/Holy Cross *B*
Springfield College *M*

Michigan
Central Michigan University *B*
Concordia College *B*
Eastern Michigan University *C, B*
Kalamazoo Valley Community
  College *C, A*
Michigan State University *D*
Wayne State University *C, B, M*
Western Michigan University *B*

Minnesota
Bethel College *B*
Concordia College: Moorhead *B*
Minnesota State University, Mankato *B*
Northwestern College *B*
University of Minnesota
  Twin Cities *B*

Mississippi
Mississippi College *M*
Mississippi University for Women *B, T*
University of Southern Mississippi *B*

Missouri
Central Missouri State University *B*
Missouri Baptist College *B*
Northwest Missouri State University *B*
Southeast Missouri State University *B*
Southwest Missouri State University *B*
University of Missouri
  Columbia *B, M*

Nebraska
Grace University *B*
University of Nebraska
  Kearney *B*
  Lincoln *M*

Nevada
University of Nevada
  Reno *B, M*

Fashion design/illustration

New Hampshire
University of New Hampshire *B, M*

New Jersey
Atlantic Cape Community College *A*
Kean University *M*
Seton Hall University *B, M*
Sussex County Community College *C*

New Mexico
New Mexico State University *B*

New York
Cornell University *B, M, D*
Fulton-Montgomery Community
   College *A*
Ithaca College *C*
Sage Junior College of Albany *A*
State University of New York
   College at Oneonta *B*
   Oswego *B*
Syracuse University *B, M, D*

North Carolina
Appalachian State University *B*
East Carolina University *B, M*
Meredith College *B*
North Carolina Agricultural and
   Technical State University *B*
North Carolina Central University *B*
University of North Carolina
   Charlotte *B*
   Greensboro *B, M, D*
Western Carolina University *B*

North Dakota
North Dakota State University *B*

Ohio
Ashland University *B*
Bowling Green State University *B, M*
Kent State University *B, M, T*
Miami University
   Oxford Campus *B, M, T*
Northwest State Community College *A*
Ohio State University
   Columbus Campus *B, M, D*
Ohio University *B, M*
Terra Community College *A*
University of Akron *B, M*
Wright State University *M*

Oklahoma
Langston University *B*
Northeastern State University *B*
Oklahoma Christian University of
   Science and Arts *B*
Oklahoma State University *B, M*
St. Gregory's University *A*
University of Central Oklahoma *B, M*

Oregon
Chemeketa Community College *A*
Clackamas Community College *C*
Northwest Christian College *M*
Oregon State University *B, M, D*

Pennsylvania
Indiana University of Pennsylvania *B*
Penn State
   Altoona *A, B*
   Dubois *A, B*
   Fayette *A, B*
   Mont Alto *A, B*
   Schuylkill - Capital College *A*
   Shenango *A, B*
   University Park *C, A, B, M, D*
   Worthington Scranton *A, B*
St. Joseph's University *M*
Seton Hill College *B*
University of Pittsburgh *B, M*

Rhode Island
Community College of Rhode
   Island *C, A*
University of Rhode Island *B, M*

South Carolina
Benedict College *B*

South Carolina State University *M*
Spartanburg Technical College *C*

South Dakota
South Dakota State University *B*

Tennessee
East Tennessee State University *B, T*
Freed-Hardeman University *B*
Lee University *B*
Southern Adventist University *B*
Tennessee State University *B*
University of Tennessee
   Knoxville *M*
   Martin *B*
Vanderbilt University *B*

Texas
Abilene Christian University *B*
Baylor University *B*
Brazosport College *C, A*
El Paso Community College *A*
Galveston College *A*
Southwest Texas State University *B*
Stephen F. Austin State University *B*
Texas A&M University
   Kingsville *B*
Texas Tech University *B, M, D*
Texas Woman's University *B, M, D*
University of North Texas *B, M*
University of Texas
   Arlington *B*
   Austin *B, M, D*

Utah
Brigham Young University *M, D*
Southern Utah University *B*
University of Utah *B*
Utah State University *B, M, D*
Weber State University *B*

Vermont
Southern Vermont College *A*
University of Vermont *B, M*

Virginia
Radford University *B*
Virginia Polytechnic Institute and State
   University *B, M, D*

Washington
Seattle Pacific University *M*
Washington State University *B, M*

Wisconsin
Moraine Park Technical College *C, A*
University of Wisconsin
   Madison *B, M, D*
   Stout *B, M*

Wyoming
Eastern Wyoming College *A*
University of Wyoming *B*

Farm/ranch management

Arizona
Central Arizona College *C*

Arkansas
University of Arkansas
   Monticello *A*

Colorado
Colorado Northwestern Community
   College *C*
Colorado State University *B*
Lamar Community College *C*
Morgan Community College *C*
Northeastern Junior College *C, A*
Otero Junior College *C*
Pueblo Community College *C*
Trinidad State Junior College *C*

Florida
University of Florida *B*

Georgia
Fort Valley State University *B*

Idaho
Boise State University *C*
Eastern Idaho Technical College *C*
Idaho State University *C*

Illinois
Lincoln Land Community College *A*

Indiana
Purdue University *B*

Iowa
Hawkeye Community College *A*
Iowa State University *B, M*
North Iowa Area Community College *A*

Kansas
Allen County Community College *A*
Butler County Community College *A*
Colby Community College *A*
Cowley County Community
   College *C, A*
Dodge City Community College *C, A*
Garden City Community College *A*
Hutchinson Community College *A*
McPherson College *B*
Seward County Community College *A*

Minnesota
Alexandria Technical College *C*
Ridgewater College: A Community and
   Technical College *C*
St. Cloud Technical College *C*
Southwest State University *C*

Mississippi
Mississippi Delta Community College *A*

Missouri
Crowder College *A*
Northwest Missouri State
   University *C, B*

Montana
Miles Community College *A*

Nebraska
Central Community College *C, A*
Northeast Community College *A*

Nevada
University of Nevada
   Reno *B*

New York
Cornell University *B*

North Dakota
Dickinson State University *A*

Ohio
Ohio State University
   Columbus Campus *B*
University of Findlay *B*
Wilmington College *B*

Oklahoma
Eastern Oklahoma State College *A*
Langston University *B*
Northeastern Oklahoma Agricultural and
   Mechanical College *C, A*
Redlands Community College *C, A*

Pennsylvania
Penn State
   University Park *C*

Rhode Island
Johnson & Wales University *A*

South Carolina
Clemson University *B*

South Dakota
Western Dakota Technical Institute *A*

Texas
Central Texas College *C, A*
Navarro College *A*
North Central Texas College *A*
Northeast Texas Community College *C*
Sam Houston State University *B*

Southwest Texas State University *B*
Tarleton State University *B*
Texas A&M University *B*
Texas Christian University *C*
Texas State Technical College
   Harlingen *C, A*
Trinity Valley Community College *C, A*
Tyler Junior College *C, A*
Vernon Regional Junior College *C, A*
Weatherford College *C, A*
Wharton County Junior College *A*

Utah
Snow College *A*

Vermont
Sterling College *B*

Virginia
Virginia Highlands Community
   College *C*

Washington
Big Bend Community College *C*

West Virginia
West Virginia University *B, M, D*

Wisconsin
Chippewa Valley Technical College *C*
Lakeshore Technical College *C*
Northeast Wisconsin Technical
   College *A*
Southwest Wisconsin Technical
   College *C*
Wisconsin Indianhead Technical
   College *C*

Wyoming
Eastern Wyoming College *A*
Sheridan College *A*
University of Wyoming *B*

Fashion design/illustration

Alabama
Alabama Agricultural and Mechanical
   University *B, M*
Wallace State Community College at
   Hanceville *A*

Arkansas
Harding University *B*

California
Academy of Art College *C, A, B, M*
Allan Hancock College *C, A*
Art Institutes International
   San Francisco *A, B*
Brooks College *A*
Butte College *C, A*
California College of Arts and Crafts *B*
Chaffey Community College *C, A*
College of the Desert *C*
College of the Sequoias *C*
Diablo Valley College *C, A*
Fashion Institute of Design and
   Merchandising
   San Francisco *A*
Fashion Institute of Design and
   Merchandising *A*
Los Angeles Southwest College *A*
Los Angeles Trade and Technical
   College *A*
Modesto Junior College *C, A*
Orange Coast College *C, A*
Otis College of Art and Design *C, B*
Palomar College *C, A*
Saddleback College *C, A*
San Joaquin Delta College *C, A*
Santa Rosa Junior College *C, A*
Solano Community College *C*
University of San Francisco *B*
Ventura College *C, A*
West Hills Community College *C*
West Valley College *C, A*

Fashion design/illustration

Colorado
Art Institute
  of Colorado A

Connecticut
University of New Haven A, B

Delaware
University of Delaware B

Florida
Art Institute
  of Fort Lauderdale A
Florida State University B, M
International Academy of Merchandising
  and Design A, B
International Fine Arts College A
Lynn University B
Manatee Community College A
Miami-Dade Community College A
Santa Fe Community College A

Georgia
American InterContinental
  University A, B
Morris Brown College B
Savannah College of Art and
  Design B, M

Hawaii
University of Hawaii
  Honolulu Community College C, A

Idaho
Ricks College A

Illinois
Columbia College B
Dominican University B
International Academy of Merchandising
  and Design A, B
School of the Art Institute of Chicago B
William Rainey Harper College C, A

Indiana
Ball State University B
Indiana State University B
Vincennes University A

Iowa
Iowa State University B

Kansas
Central Christian College A
Kansas State University B

Maryland
Baltimore City Community College C, A

Massachusetts
Bay State College A
Lasell College B
Massachusetts College of Art B
Mount Ida College A, B

Michigan
Adrian College B
Central Michigan University B
Delta College A
Western Michigan University B

Minnesota
University of Minnesota
  Twin Cities B

Missouri
Lindenwood University B
Stephens College B
Washington University B, M

New Jersey
Brookdale Community College A
Burlington County College A
Centenary College B

New York
Eugene Lang College/New School
  University B
Fashion Institute of Technology A, B
Marist College B
Marymount College B

Pace University:
  Pleasantville/Briarcliff C
Pace University C
Parsons School of Design A, B, T
Pratt Institute B
State University of New York
  College at Buffalo B
Syracuse University B, M
Wood Tobe-Coburn School A

North Carolina
Mars Hill College B
Meredith College B

Ohio
Columbus College of Art and Design B
Davis College A
Kent State University
  Stark Campus B
Kent State University B
Ohio Institute of Photography and
  Technology C, A
Sinclair Community College A
University of Cincinnati B
Ursuline College B

Oklahoma
Northeastern Oklahoma Agricultural and
  Mechanical College A
Oklahoma State University B

Oregon
Art Institute
  of Portland A, B
George Fox University B
Oregon State University B

Pennsylvania
Art Institute
  of Philadelphia A
  of Pittsburgh A
Bradley Academy for the Visual Arts A
California University of Pennsylvania A
Drexel University B, M
Harcum College A
Philadelphia University C, B

Puerto Rico
Pontifical Catholic University of Puerto
  Rico A

South Carolina
Greenville Technical College C

Tennessee
Hiwassee College A

Texas
Baylor University B
El Paso Community College A
Houston Community College
  System C, A
Texas Tech University B
Texas Woman's University B, M
University of North Texas B, M
University of the Incarnate Word B

Utah
Brigham Young University B
Salt Lake Community College C

Virginia
Virginia Commonwealth University B

Washington
Art Institute of Seattle A

West Virginia
Davis and Elkins College A, B

Wisconsin
Mount Mary College B
University of Wisconsin
  Madison B, M
Waukesha County Technical College A

Fashion/apparel marketing

Alabama
Alabama Agricultural and Mechanical
  University B, M
Auburn University B
Wallace State Community College at
  Hanceville A

Arizona
Mesa Community College A
Northern Arizona University B
Phoenix College C
Scottsdale Community College C, A

Arkansas
Harding University B
University of Central Arkansas B

California
American River College C, A
Brooks College A
Butte College C, A
California State University
  Long Beach B
Canada College C, A
Chaffey Community College C, A
City College of San Francisco C, A
College of San Mateo C, A
College of the Desert C
College of the Sequoias C
Evergreen Valley College A
Fashion Institute of Design and
  Merchandising
    San Francisco A
Fashion Institute of Design and
  Merchandising A
Fresno City College C, A
Las Positas College C
Los Angeles Trade and Technical
  College C, A
Los Angeles Valley College C, A
Marymount College A
Modesto Junior College C, A
Mount San Antonio College C, A
Orange Coast College C, A
Pacific Union College B
Palomar College C, A
Pasadena City College C, A
Saddleback College C, A
San Diego Mesa College C, A
San Francisco State University B
San Joaquin Delta College C, A
Santa Ana College A
Santa Rosa Junior College C
Shasta College A
Sierra College C, A
Solano Community College A
Ventura College C, A
West Valley College C, A
Yuba College C

Colorado
Art Institute
  of Colorado A

Connecticut
Asnuntuck Community-Technical
  College A
Briarwood College A
Gateway Community College A
Tunxis Community College C, A
University of Bridgeport A, B

Delaware
University of Delaware B

District of Columbia
Howard University B
University of the District of Columbia A

Florida
Brevard Community College A
Gulf Coast Community College A
International Fine Arts College A
Lynn University A, B
Miami-Dade Community College A

Santa Fe Community College A

Georgia
Abraham Baldwin Agricultural
  College A
American InterContinental
  University A, B
Brenau University B
Clark Atlanta University B
Gwinnett Technical Institute A
Middle Georgia College C, A
Morris Brown College B
University of Georgia B

Hawaii
University of Hawaii
  Honolulu Community College C, A

Idaho
Ricks College A

Illinois
Black Hawk College C, A
Chicago State University B
College of DuPage A
Dominican University B
John A. Logan College A
Joliet Junior College A
Kaskaskia College A
Olivet Nazarene University B
Triton College C, A
University of Illinois
  Urbana-Champaign B
Waubonsee Community College C
William Rainey Harper College C, A

Indiana
Indiana State University B

Iowa
Des Moines Area Community
  College C, A
Hawkeye Community College A
Kirkwood Community College C, A
North Iowa Area Community College A

Kentucky
Eastern Kentucky University B
Murray State University B

Louisiana
Louisiana State University and
  Agricultural and Mechanical
  College B
University of Louisiana at Lafayette B

Maine
Thomas College A

Maryland
Baltimore City Community College A
University of Maryland
  Eastern Shore B

Massachusetts
Bay State College A
Fisher College C, A
Lasell College B
Massasoit Community College C
Middlesex Community College A
Mount Ida College A, B
Newbury College A
University of Massachusetts
  Amherst B

Michigan
Adrian College B
Central Michigan University B
Eastern Michigan University B
Grand Rapids Community College A
Lansing Community College A
Northwood University A, B
Oakland Community College A

Minnesota
Alexandria Technical College C, A
College of St. Catherine: St. Paul
  Campus B
Ridgewater College: A Community and
  Technical College C

Rochester Community and Technical
    College C, A
South Central Technical College A

Mississippi
Delta State University B
Hinds Community College A
Holmes Community College A
Mississippi Gulf Coast Community
    College
        Jackson County Campus A
        Jefferson Davis Campus A
        Perkinston A
Northwest Mississippi Community
    College A

Missouri
Central Missouri State University A
Lincoln University B
Lindenwood University B
Penn Valley Community College A
Southeast Missouri State University B
St. Louis Community College
    St. Louis Community College at
        Florissant Valley A
Stephens College B

Montana
University of Montana-Missoula A

Nebraska
Northeast Community College A
University of Nebraska
    Omaha B

New Hampshire
Hesser College A
New Hampshire College C, A, B

New Jersey
Berkeley College A
Brookdale Community College A
Middlesex County College A

New Mexico
Dona Ana Branch Community College of
    New Mexico State University A

New York
Berkeley College of New York City A
Berkeley College A
City University of New York
    Kingsborough Community
        College A
    New York City Technical
        College A
Erie Community College
    City Campus A
Fashion Institute of Technology A, B
Genesee Community College A
Herkimer County Community College A
Laboratory Institute of Merchandising B
Marist College B
Monroe Community College C, A
Nassau Community College A
Parsons School of Design A, B
Sage Junior College of Albany A
State University of New York
    College at Buffalo B
    College at Oneonta B
Wood Tobe-Coburn School A

North Carolina
Central Piedmont Community College A
Meredith College B

North Dakota
Lake Region State College C, A
North Dakota State University B

Ohio
Ashland University B
Bowling Green State University B
Davis College A
Kent State University
    Stark Campus B
Kent State University B
Mount Vernon Nazarene College B

Owens Community College
    Toledo A
University of Akron A
Ursuline College B
Youngstown State University B

Oklahoma
Northeastern State University B
Oklahoma State University B, M
Tulsa Community College C, A
University of Central Oklahoma B

Oregon
George Fox University B

Pennsylvania
Art Institute
    of Philadelphia A
    of Pittsburgh A
Bradley Academy for the Visual Arts A
Community College of Philadelphia C, A
Immaculata College A, B
Indiana University of Pennsylvania B
Marywood University C
Mercyhurst College B
Philadelphia University B, M
Westmoreland County Community
    College A

Rhode Island
Community College of Rhode Island A
Johnson & Wales University A
University of Rhode Island B

South Carolina
Greenville Technical College C
Midlands Technical College C
South Carolina State University B

South Dakota
South Dakota State University B

Tennessee
David Lipscomb University B
Draughons Junior College of Business:
    Nashville A
Freed-Hardeman University B
Lambuth University B
O'More College of Design A, B
University of Tennessee
    Martin B

Texas
Abilene Christian University B
Alvin Community College C, A
Austin Community College C, A
Brookhaven College A
Cedar Valley College A
El Paso Community College C, A
Houston Community College
    System C, A
Midland College A
Northwood University: Texas
    Campus A, B
Palo Alto College C, A
Sam Houston State University B
South Plains College A
Southwest Texas State University B
Stephen F. Austin State University B
Tarleton State University B
Tarrant County College C, A
Texas Tech University B
Texas Woman's University B, M, D
University of North Texas B
University of the Incarnate Word B

Utah
Brigham Young University B
Dixie State College of Utah C, A
Salt Lake Community College C
Utah State University B
Utah Valley State College C, A
Weber State University A

Virginia
Bridgewater College B
J. Sargeant Reynolds Community
    College C, A

Virginia Polytechnic Institute and State
    University B

Washington
Art Institute of Seattle A
Central Washington University B
Highline Community College A
Pierce College A
Seattle Central Community College A

West Virginia
Davis and Elkins College A, B
Fairmont State College A
Marshall University B
Shepherd College A

Wisconsin
Madison Area Technical College A
Milwaukee Area Technical College A
Mount Mary College B
Northeast Wisconsin Technical
    College A
Western Wisconsin Technical College A

Fiber arts

Arizona
Arizona State University B, M

California
Academy of Art College C, A, B, M
California College of Arts and
    Crafts B, M
California State University
    Long Beach B, M
University of California
    Davis M

Colorado
Colorado State University B

Georgia
Savannah College of Art and
    Design B, M
University of Georgia B

Illinois
Barat College B
School of the Art Institute of
    Chicago B, M

Indiana
Vincennes University A

Kansas
University of Kansas B, M

Maryland
Maryland Institute College of Art B

Massachusetts
Massachusetts College of Art B, M
University of Massachusetts
    Dartmouth B

Michigan
Center for Creative Studies: College of
    Art and Design B
Cranbrook Academy of Art M
Northern Michigan University B
Suomi College B
University of Michigan B

Minnesota
Minnesota State University, Mankato B

Missouri
Kansas City Art Institute B
Lindenwood University M

New Jersey
Rowan University B

New Mexico
Northern New Mexico Community
    College C, A

New York
Parsons School of Design C, A, B, T

State University of New York
    College at Buffalo B
Syracuse University B, M

North Carolina
Haywood Community College A
North Carolina State University B

Ohio
Bowling Green State University B, M
Cleveland Institute of Art B
Kent State University B
Lourdes College A
University of Akron B

Oregon
University of Oregon B, M

Pennsylvania
Moore College of Art and Design B
Philadelphia University B, M
Temple University B, M
University of the Arts B

Rhode Island
Rhode Island College B

Texas
Texas Woman's University B, M
University of North Texas B, M

Washington
University of Washington B, M
Western Washington University B

West Virginia
West Virginia State College B

Wisconsin
University of Wisconsin
    Madison B

Film/cinema studies

California
Allan Hancock College A
Chapman University B, M
Diablo Valley College A
Long Beach City College A
Orange Coast College A
Palomar College C, A
Pitzer College B
San Francisco Art Institute B, M
San Francisco State University B, M
Santa Barbara City College A
University of California
    Berkeley B
    Irvine B
    Los Angeles B
    Santa Barbara B
    Santa Cruz C, B
University of Southern
    California B, M, D

Colorado
Colorado College B
University of Colorado
    Boulder B

Connecticut
Trinity College B
University of Hartford B
Wesleyan University B
Yale University B

District of Columbia
American University B, M
Howard University M

Florida
University of Miami B, M

Georgia
Emory University B, M
Georgia State University B
Oxford College of Emory University B

Illinois
Columbia College B

Film/cinema studies

Northwestern University *B, M, D*
Southern Illinois University
    Carbondale *M*
Indiana
Indiana State University *B*
Indiana University
    South Bend *A*
Iowa
Maharishi University of Management *B*
University of Iowa *B, M, D*
Kansas
Pittsburg State University *B*
Massachusetts
Clark University *B*
Emerson College *B*
Hampshire College *B*
Harvard College *B*
Massachusetts College of Art *B, M*
Michigan
Calvin College *B*
University of Michigan *B*
Wayne State University *B*
Minnesota
Moorhead State University *B*
University of Minnesota
    Twin Cities *B*
Missouri
Webster University *B*
Nebraska
University of Nebraska
    Lincoln *B*
Nevada
University of Nevada
    Las Vegas *B*
New Hampshire
Dartmouth College *B*
Keene State College *B*
New Jersey
Rowan University *B*
Rutgers
    The State University of New Jersey:
    Mason Gross School of the
    Arts *B*
New Mexico
University of New Mexico *B*
New York
Bard College *B*
City University of New York
    Brooklyn College *B, M*
    City College *B, M*
    College of Staten Island *B, M*
    Hunter College *B*
    Queens College *B*
Columbia University
    Columbia College *B*
    School of General Studies *B*
Fordham University *B*
Ithaca College *B*
Long Island University
    C. W. Post Campus *B*
New York University *B, M, D*
Sarah Lawrence College *B*
School of Visual Arts *B*
State University of New York
    Binghamton *B*
    Stony Brook *B*
University of Rochester *B*
North Carolina
University of North Carolina
    Greensboro *B, M*
Ohio
Bowling Green State University *B*
Denison University *B*
Wright State University *B*

Pennsylvania
Allentown College of St. Francis de
    Sales *B*
La Salle University *B*
Penn State
    University Park *B, M*
Temple University *B, M*
University of Pittsburgh *C, B*
Rhode Island
Rhode Island College *B*
Tennessee
University of Tennessee
    Knoxville *B*
Texas
Sam Houston State University *B, M*
Southern Methodist University *B*
Utah
Brigham Young University *B, M, D*
University of Utah *B*
Vermont
Burlington College *C, B*
Marlboro College *B*
Wisconsin
University of Wisconsin
    Madison *B*
    Milwaukee *B*
Viterbo University *B*

Film/video/cinematography/production

Arizona
Scottsdale Community College *A*
California
Academy of Art College *C, A, B, M*
Allan Hancock College *C*
American Film Institute Center for
    Advanced Film and Television
    Studies *M*
Art Center College of Design *B, M*
Biola University *B*
California College of Arts and
    Crafts *B, M*
California Institute of the Arts *C, B, M*
California State University
    Long Beach *B*
Chapman University *B, M*
City College of San Francisco *A*
Cogswell Polytechnical College *B*
College of San Mateo *A*
De Anza College *C, A*
Diablo Valley College *A*
Grossmont Community College *C, A*
Los Angeles Valley College *C*
Master's College *B*
Modesto Junior College *A*
Moorpark College *A*
Orange Coast College *A*
Pitzer College *B*
San Francisco Art Institute *B, M*
University of California
    Los Angeles *M, D*
    Santa Barbara *B*
    Santa Cruz *B*
University of Southern California *B, M*
Vanguard University of Southern
    California *B*
Colorado
Art Institute
    of Colorado *A*
Connecticut
University of Hartford *B*
District of Columbia
American University *M*

Florida
Florida Metropolitan University
    Orlando College North *A*
Florida State University *B, M*
International Fine Arts College *B*
Miami-Dade Community College *A*
Palm Beach Community College *A*
University of Central Florida *B*
University of Miami *B*
Valencia Community College *A*
Georgia
American InterContinental
    University *A, B*
Art Institute
    of Atlanta *A*
Atlanta College of Art *B*
Savannah College of Art and
    Design *B, M*
Illinois
Columbia College *B, M*
Northwestern University *B, M, D*
School of the Art Institute of
    Chicago *B, M*
University of Illinois
    Chicago *M*
Iowa
University of Iowa *B, M*
Kansas
Southwestern College *B*
Maine
Southern Maine Technical College *C, A*
Maryland
University of Maryland
    Baltimore County *B*
Villa Julie College *A, B*
Massachusetts
Boston University *B, M*
Emerson College *B*
Fitchburg State College *B*
Hampshire College *B*
Harvard College *B*
Massachusetts College of Art *B, M*
School of the Museum of Fine Arts *B, M*
Simon's Rock College of Bard *B*
Suffolk University *B*
Michigan
Lansing Community College *A*
Northern Michigan University *B*
Oakland Community College *C, A*
Minnesota
Minneapolis College of Art and
    Design *B*
Minneapolis Community and Technical
    College *A*
Moorhead State University *B*
Missouri
Kansas City Art Institute *B*
Webster University *B*
Montana
Montana State University
    Bozeman *B*
New Jersey
Bloomfield College *B*
Cumberland County College *A*
Fairleigh Dickinson University *B*
Rutgers
    The State University of New Jersey:
    Mason Gross School of the
    Arts *B, M*
Union County College *A*
New Mexico
College of Santa Fe *B*
New York
Bard College *B, M*

City University of New York
    Brooklyn College *M*
    City College *B, M*
    Hunter College *M*
Five Towns College *A, B*
Ithaca College *B*
New York Institute of Technology *M*
New York State College of Ceramics at
    Alfred University *B, M, T*
New York University *B, M*
Pratt Institute *B*
Rochester Institute of
    Technology *A, B, M*
School of Visual Arts *B*
State University of New York
    Buffalo *M*
    Purchase *B*
Syracuse University *B, M*
North Carolina
North Carolina School of the Arts *B*
Ohio
Columbus College of Art and Design *B*
Kent State University *B*
Ohio University *B, M*
University of Findlay *B*
Oklahoma
University of Oklahoma *B*
Pennsylvania
Art Institute
    of Pittsburgh *A*
Bucks County Community College *A*
Drexel University *B*
La Salle University *B*
Point Park College *B*
University of the Arts *B*
Rhode Island
New England Institute of Technology *A*
South Carolina
Trident Technical College *C*
York Technical College *C*
Tennessee
Pellissippi State Technical Community
    College *A*
Southern Adventist University *B*
Texas
El Paso Community College *C, A*
North Lake College *A*
South Plains College *A*
Texas State Technical College
    Waco *A*
University of Texas
    Arlington *B*
Vermont
Burlington College *C, B*
Champlain College *A, B*
Marlboro College *B*
Middlebury College *B*
Virginia
J. Sargeant Reynolds Community
    College *C*
Washington
Art Institute of Seattle *A*
Evergreen State College *B*
Shoreline Community College *A*
Wisconsin
Milwaukee Area Technical College *A*
University of Wisconsin
    Madison *B*
    Oshkosh *B*

Finance/banking

Alabama
Alabama Agricultural and Mechanical
    University *B, M*
Alabama State University *B*

Finance/banking

Auburn University at Montgomery *B*
Auburn University *B*
Birmingham-Southern College *B*
Huntingdon College *B*
Jacksonville State University *B*
James H. Faulkner State Community
 College *A*
Oakwood College *B*
Spring Hill College *B*
Talladega College *B*
Troy State University
 Montgomery *B*
Tuskegee University *B*
University of Alabama
 Birmingham *B*
 Huntsville *B*
University of Mobile *B*
University of Montevallo *B*
University of North Alabama *B*
University of South Alabama *B*

Alaska
University of Alaska
 Anchorage *B*

Arizona
Arizona State University *B*
Grand Canyon University *B*
Mohave Community College *C, A*
Northern Arizona University *B*
Pima Community College *C*
Scottsdale Community College *C*
University of Arizona *B*
University of Phoenix *C*

Arkansas
Arkansas State University *B*
Mississippi County Community
 College *C, A*
University of Arkansas
 Little Rock *B*
University of Arkansas *B*
University of Central Arkansas *B*

California
Armstrong University *B, M*
California Lutheran University *B*
California State Polytechnic University:
 Pomona *B*
California State University
 Chico *B*
 Fresno *B*
 Hayward *B, M*
 Long Beach *B*
 Los Angeles *B, M*
 Northridge *M*
Golden Gate University *C, B, M*
La Sierra University *B, M*
Lake Tahoe Community College *A*
Modesto Junior College *A*
National University *M*
Pacific Union College *B*
San Francisco State University *B*
San Joaquin Delta College *C*
San Jose State University *B*
Santa Clara University *B*
Southwestern College *A*
Vanguard University of Southern
 California *B*

Colorado
Adams State College *B*
Colorado State University *B*
Fort Lewis College *B*
Metropolitan State College of Denver *B*
University of Colorado
 Boulder *B, M, D*
 Colorado Springs *B*
 Denver *M*
University of Denver *B, M*
University of Southern Colorado *B*

Connecticut
Central Connecticut State University *B*
Fairfield University *B, M*
Naugatuck Valley Community-Technical
 College *A*

Norwalk Community-Technical
 College *A*
Quinnipiac University *B, M*
Sacred Heart University *B*
Southern Connecticut State University *B*
Teikyo Post University *B*
University of Bridgeport *B, M*
University of Connecticut *B*
University of Hartford *B*
University of New Haven *B, M*

Delaware
Delaware State University *B*
University of Delaware *B*
Wilmington College *B*

District of Columbia
American University *B, M*
Catholic University of America *B, M*
George Washington University *B, M*
Georgetown University *B*
Howard University *B*
University of the District of Columbia *B*

Florida
Broward Community College *A*
Edison Community College *A*
Florida Atlantic University *B*
Florida Community College at
 Jacksonville *A*
Florida Gulf Coast University *B*
Florida International University *B, M*
Florida Southern College *B*
Florida State University *B, M*
Jacksonville University *B, M*
Northwood University
 Florida Campus *A, B*
Palm Beach Community College *A*
St. Thomas University *B*
South College: Palm Beach Campus *B*
South Florida Community College *A*
Stetson University *B*
University of Central Florida *B*
University of Florida *B, M*
University of Miami *B*
University of North Florida *B, M*
University of South Florida *B*
University of Tampa *B*
University of West Florida *B*

Georgia
Augusta State University *B*
Berry College *B*
Brenau University *B*
Clark Atlanta University *B, M*
Columbus State University *B, M*
Emory University *B*
Georgia Southern University *B*
Georgia State University *B, M, D*
Kennesaw State University *M*
Mercer University *B, M*
Morehouse College *B*
North Georgia College & State
 University *B*
Reinhardt College *A, B*
South Georgia College *A*
State University of West Georgia *B*
University of Georgia *B*
Valdosta State University *B*

Hawaii
Hawaii Pacific University *A, B*
University of Hawaii
 Hilo *B*
 Manoa *B*

Idaho
Boise State University *B*
College of Southern Idaho *A*
Idaho State University *B*
Northwest Nazarene University *B*
Ricks College *A*
University of Idaho *B*

Illinois
Augustana College *B*
Barat College *B*
Benedictine University *B*

Bradley University *B*
Chicago State University *B*
Danville Area Community College *A*
Eastern Illinois University *B*
Elmhurst College *B*
Eureka College *B*
Governors State University *B*
Illinois College *B*
Illinois State University *B*
Lewis University *B*
Loyola University of Chicago *B*
Millikin University *B*
Morton College *A*
North Central College *B*
North Park University *B*
Northeastern Illinois University *B*
Northern Illinois University *B*
Northwestern University *D*
Olivet Nazarene University *B*
Roosevelt University *B, M*
St. Xavier University *M*
Southern Illinois University
 Carbondale *B*
University of Chicago *M, D*
University of Illinois
 Chicago *B*
 Urbana-Champaign *B, M, D*
University of St. Francis *B*
Western Illinois University *B*
William Rainey Harper College *C, A*

Indiana
Anderson University *B*
Ball State University *B*
Butler University *B*
Franklin College *B*
Goshen College *B*
Indiana Institute of Technology *B*
Indiana State University *B*
Indiana University
 South Bend *A, B*
 Southeast *B*
Indiana Wesleyan University *B*
Marian College *A, B*
Purdue University
 Calumet *B*
Saint Mary's College *B*
St. Joseph's College *B*
University of Evansville *B*
University of Notre Dame *B*
University of Southern Indiana *B*
Valparaiso University *B*
Vincennes University *A*

Iowa
American Institute of Business *A*
Buena Vista University *B*
Clarke College *B*
Drake University *B*
Iowa State University *B*
Loras College *B*
Marycrest International University *B*
Northwestern College *B*
St. Ambrose University *B*
University of Iowa *B, D*
University of Northern Iowa *B*
Waldorf College *A, B*
Wartburg College *B*

Kansas
Central Christian College *A*
Emporia State University *B*
Hutchinson Community College *A*
McPherson College *B*
Pittsburg State University *B*
Tabor College *B*
Wichita State University *B*

Kentucky
Eastern Kentucky University *B*
Murray State University *B*
Southeast Community College *A*
University of Kentucky *B*
University of Louisville *B*
Western Kentucky University *B*

Louisiana
Centenary College of Louisiana *B*
Dillard University *B*
Louisiana State University
 Shreveport *B*
Louisiana State University and
 Agricultural and Mechanical
 College *B, M, D*
Louisiana Tech University *B*
Loyola University New Orleans *B*
McNeese State University *B*
Nicholls State University *B*
Southeastern Louisiana University *B*
Southern University
 Shreveport *C, A*
Tulane University *B*
University of Louisiana at Lafayette *B*
University of Louisiana at Monroe *B*
University of New Orleans *B*

Maine
Eastern Maine Technical College *A*
Husson College *B*
Thomas College *B*
University of Maine *B*

Maryland
College of Notre Dame of Maryland *B*
Loyola College in Maryland *M*
Morgan State University *B, M*
Mount St. Mary's College *B*
University of Maryland
 College Park *B*

Massachusetts
American International College *B*
Babson College *B*
Bentley College *B, M*
Boston College *B, M, D*
Boston University *B, M*
Bridgewater State College *B*
Clark University *M*
Fitchburg State College *B*
Lasell College *B*
Massachusetts Bay Community
 College *C*
Massachusetts College of Liberal Arts *B*
Merrimack College *B*
Newbury College *A*
Nichols College *B*
Northeastern University *A, B, M*
Northern Essex Community
 College *C, A*
Salem State College *B*
Simmons College *B*
Springfield Technical Community
 College *A*
Stonehill College *B*
Suffolk University *B, M*
University of Massachusetts
 Dartmouth *B*
Western New England College *B, M*
Westfield State College *B*

Michigan
Central Michigan University *B*
Davenport College of Business *C*
Detroit College of Business *A, B*
Eastern Michigan University *B*
Ferris State University *B*
Grand Valley State University *B, M*
Jackson Community College *C, A*
Kettering University *B*
Lake Michigan College *A*
Macomb Community College *C, A*
Michigan State University *B, M, D*
Mott Community College *A*
North Central Michigan College *A*
Northern Michigan University *B*
Northwood University *A, B*
Oakland University *B*
Olivet College *B*
Saginaw Valley State University *B, M*
University of Michigan
 Flint *B, M*
Wayne State University *B*

279

Finance/banking

Western Michigan University *B*

Minnesota
Alexandria Technical College *C, A*
Augsburg College *B*
Concordia University: St. Paul *B*
Metropolitan State University *B*
Minnesota State University, Mankato *B*
Moorhead State University *B*
Northwestern College *B*
St. Cloud State University *B*
St. Cloud Technical College *C, A*
University of St. Thomas *B*
Winona State University *B*

Mississippi
Delta State University *B*
Hinds Community College *A*
Mississippi State University *B*
University of Mississippi *B*
University of Southern Mississippi *B*

Missouri
Avila College *B*
Central Missouri State University *B*
Culver-Stockton College *B*
Fontbonne College *B*
Lindenwood University *B, M*
Mineral Area College *C, A*
Missouri Southern State College *B*
Northwest Missouri State University *B*
Rockhurst University *B*
St. Louis University *B, M, D*
Southwest Missouri State University *B*
University of Missouri
    Columbia *B*
    St. Louis *B*
Washington University *B*
Webster University *M*

Montana
Carroll College *B*
Montana State University
    Billings *B*

Nebraska
Creighton University *B*
University of Nebraska
    Lincoln *B*
    Omaha *B*

Nevada
University of Nevada
    Las Vegas *B*
    Reno *B*

New Hampshire
Franklin Pierce College *B*
New England College *B*
New Hampshire College *B*
Plymouth State College of the University System of New Hampshire *B*
University of New Hampshire *B*

New Jersey
Bloomfield College *B*
Fairleigh Dickinson University *B, M*
Gloucester County College *A*
Kean University *B*
Monmouth University *B*
Passaic County Community College *C*
Rider University *B*
Rowan University *B*

Rutgers
    The State University of New Jersey: Camden College of Arts and Sciences *B*
    The State University of New Jersey: Douglass College *B*
    The State University of New Jersey: Livingston College *B*
    The State University of New Jersey: Newark College of Arts and Sciences *B*
    The State University of New Jersey: Rutgers College *B*
    The State University of New Jersey: University College Camden *B*
    The State University of New Jersey: University College New Brunswick *B*
    The State University of New Jersey: University College Newark *B*
St. Peter's College *A*
Seton Hall University *B*
The College of New Jersey *B*
Thomas Edison State College *C, A, B*

New Mexico
Eastern New Mexico University *B*
New Mexico Highlands University *B*
New Mexico State University *B*

New York
Adelphi University *B, M*
Canisius College *B*
City University of New York
    Baruch College *B, M, D*
Clarkson University *B*
Clinton Community College *C*
College of Insurance *M*
Concordia College *B*
Dowling College *C, B*
Fordham University *B, M*
Fulton-Montgomery Community College *A*
Hudson Valley Community College *A*
Iona College *B*
Ithaca College *B*
Long Island University
    C. W. Post Campus *B, M*
Manhattan College *B*
Manhattanville College *B*
New York University *B, M, D*
Orange County Community College *A*
Pace University:
    Pleasantville/Briarcliff *A, B, M, D*
Pace University *A, B, M, D*
Regents College *B*
Rochester Institute of Technology *B, M*
St. Bonaventure University *B*
St. John Fisher College *B*
St. John's University *B, M*
St. Thomas Aquinas College *B*
Siena College *B, T*
State University of New York
    Albany *B, M*
    College at Old Westbury *B*
    College at Plattsburgh *B*
    College of Agriculture and Technology at Cobleskill *A*
    College of Technology at Alfred *A*
    Institute of Technology at Utica/Rome *B*
    New Paltz *B*
    Oswego *B*
Suffolk County Community College *A*
Syracuse University *B, M*
Ulster County Community College *C, A*
Wagner College *B*

North Carolina
Appalachian State University *B*
Barton College *B*
Catawba Valley Community College *C, A*
Forsyth Technical Community College *A*
Lenoir-Rhyne College *B*
Mars Hill College *B*

Meredith College *B*
North Carolina Agricultural and Technical State University *B*
Southwestern Community College *A*
University of North Carolina
    Chapel Hill *D*
    Greensboro *B*
    Wilmington *B*
Wake Forest University *B*
Western Carolina University *B*
Wilson Technical Community College *A*

North Dakota
Dickinson State University *B*
Minot State University *B*
University of North Dakota *B*

Ohio
Ashland University *B*
Baldwin-Wallace College *B*
Case Western Reserve University *M, D*
Cedarville College *B*
Central State University *B*
Cincinnati State Technical and Community College *A*
Cleveland State University *B, D*
David N. Myers College *B*
Defiance College *B*
Franklin University *B*
John Carroll University *B*
Kent State University
    Stark Campus *B*
Kent State University *C, B, D*
Lima Technical College *A*
Miami University
    Middletown Campus *A*
    Oxford Campus *B, M*
Mount Vernon Nazarene College *B*
Northwest State Community College *A*
Ohio State University
    Columbus Campus *B*
Ohio University *B*
Otterbein College *B*
Shawnee State University *A*
Terra Community College *A*
Tiffin University *B*
University of Akron *B, M*
University of Cincinnati *B, M, D*
University of Dayton *B*
University of Findlay *A, B*
University of Toledo *B, M*
Walsh University *A, B*
Wilberforce University *B*
Wright State University *M*
Youngstown State University *A, B, M*

Oklahoma
Connors State College *A*
East Central University *B*
Northeastern Oklahoma Agricultural and Mechanical College *C*
Northeastern State University *B*
Oklahoma Baptist University *B*
Oklahoma City Community College *C, A*
Oklahoma State University *B, M*
Oral Roberts University *B*
Rogers State University *C*
Southeastern Oklahoma State University *B*
Southern Nazarene University *B*
Tulsa Community College *A*
University of Central Oklahoma *B*
University of Oklahoma *B*
University of Tulsa *C, B*

Oregon
Linfield College *B*
University of Oregon *B*
University of Portland *B*

Pennsylvania
Allentown College of St. Francis de Sales *B*
Beaver College *B*
Bucks County Community College *A*
Cabrini College *B*

Central Pennsylvania College *A*
Chestnut Hill College *B*
Drexel University *B, M*
Duquesne University *B*
Gannon University *B*
ICS Center for Degree Studies *A*
Indiana University of Pennsylvania *B*
King's College *B, M*
Kutztown University of Pennsylvania *B*
La Roche College *B*
La Salle University *B*
Lackawanna Junior College *A*
Lehigh University *B*
Lincoln University *B*
Marywood University *M*
Mercyhurst College *B*
Penn State
    Erie, The Behrend College *B*
    Harrisburg
    University Park *B*
Philadelphia University *B, M*
Robert Morris College *B, M*
St. Francis College *B*
St. Joseph's University *C, A, B, M*
St. Vincent College *B*
Seton Hill College *B*
Shippensburg University of Pennsylvania *B*
Susquehanna University *B*
Temple University *B, M, D*
University of Pennsylvania *B, M, D*
University of Pittsburgh
    Johnstown
University of Pittsburgh *B*
University of Scranton *B, M*
Villanova University *B*
Waynesburg College *B*
Westminster College *B*
Widener University *B*
York College of Pennsylvania *B*

Puerto Rico
Inter American University of Puerto Rico
    Bayamon Campus *B*
    Metropolitan Campus *B, M*
    San German Campus *B, M*
Pontifical Catholic University of Puerto Rico *B*
University of Puerto Rico
    Aguadilla *B*
    Arecibo Campus *A, B*
    Bayamon University College *A, B*
    Ponce University College *B*
    Rio Piedras Campus *B, M*

Rhode Island
Bryant College *B, M*
Johnson & Wales University *A, B*
Rhode Island College *B*
University of Rhode Island *B*

South Carolina
Charleston Southern University *B, M*
Coastal Carolina University *B*
Converse College *B*
Francis Marion University *B*
University of South Carolina
    Aiken *B*
University of South Carolina *B*
Wofford College *B*

South Dakota
Northern State University *B*
Southeast Technical Institute *A*

Tennessee
Belmont University *B*
Christian Brothers University *B*
Cleveland State Community College *C*
East Tennessee State University *B*
Freed-Hardeman University *B*
Middle Tennessee State University *B*
Roane State Community College *A*
Tennessee Technological University *B*
Union University *B, T*
University of Memphis *B, M*

University of Tennessee
    Knoxville *B*
    Martin *B*

Texas
Amarillo College *A*
Angelo State University *B*
Baylor University *B*
Coastal Bend College *A*
Dallas Baptist University *B*
Del Mar College *C, A*
El Paso Community College *A*
Hardin-Simmons University *B*
Houston Baptist University *B*
Lamar University *B*
McMurry University *B*
Midwestern State University *B*
Northwood University: Texas
    Campus *A, B*
Our Lady of the Lake University of San
    Antonio *M*
Prairie View A&M University *B*
Sam Houston State University *B*
Southern Methodist University *B*
Southwest Texas State University *B*
Stephen F. Austin State University *B*
Sul Ross State University *B*
Tarleton State University *B*
Texas A&M International University *B*
Texas A&M University
    Corpus Christi *B*
    Kingsville *B*
    Texarkana *B*
Texas A&M University *B, M, D*
Texas Christian University *B*
Texas Tech University *B*
Texas Wesleyan University *B*
Trinity University *B*
University of Dallas *M*
University of Houston
    Clear Lake *B, M*
University of Houston *B*
University of Mary Hardin-Baylor *B*
University of North Texas *B, M, D*
University of St. Thomas *B*
University of Texas
    Arlington *B*
    Austin *B, D*
    Brownsville *B*
    El Paso *B*
    Pan American *B*
    San Antonio *B, M*
    of the Permian Basin *B*
West Texas A&M University *B, M*

Utah
Brigham Young University *B*
University of Utah *B, M*
Utah State University *B*
Weber State University *B*
Westminster College *B*

Vermont
Castleton State College *B*
College of St. Joseph in Vermont *B*

Virginia
Blue Ridge Community College *A*
Central Virginia Community College *A*
Christopher Newport University *B*
Dabney S. Lancaster Community
    College *C*
George Mason University *B*
Hampton University *B*
James Madison University *B*
Longwood College *B*
Old Dominion University *B*
Radford University *B*
Virginia Highlands Community
    College *C*
Virginia Polytechnic Institute and State
    University *B*
Virginia Union University *B*

Washington
Eastern Washington University *B*
Seattle University *B, M*
Washington State University *B*
Western Washington University *B*

West Virginia
Bethany College *B*
Concord College *B*
Fairmont State College *A*
University of Charleston *B*
West Virginia University *B*
West Virginia Wesleyan College *B*

Wisconsin
Concordia University Wisconsin *B*
Madison Area Technical College *A*
Marian College of Fond du Lac *B*
Marquette University *B*
University of Wisconsin
    Eau Claire *B*
    La Crosse *B*
    Madison *M, D*
    Milwaukee *B*
    Oshkosh *B*
    Platteville *B*
    Whitewater *B*
Western Wisconsin Technical College *A*
Wisconsin Indianhead Technical
    College *A*

Wyoming
University of Wyoming *B, M*

Financial management/services

Alabama
Central Alabama Community
    College *C, A*
Community College of the Air Force *A*
Enterprise State Junior College *A*
Faulkner University *B*
Southern Union State Community
    College *C, A*
Troy State University *B*
University of South Alabama *B*
Wallace State Community College at
    Hanceville *A*

Arizona
University of Arizona *B*

Arkansas
University of Arkansas *B*
Westark College *A*

California
American River College *A*
Bakersfield College *A*
Barstow College *C*
California State University
    Fullerton *B*
Chapman University *B*
City College of San Francisco *C, A*
College of the Desert *C, A*
John F. Kennedy University *C*
Moorpark College *A*
San Diego State University *B, M*
San Joaquin Delta College *C, A*
Shasta College *A*
Sierra College *A*
Ventura College *A*

Colorado
Community College of Denver *C, A*
Pueblo Community College *C, A*
Red Rocks Community College *C, A*

Connecticut
Central Connecticut State
    University *B, M*
Quinnipiac University *B, M*
Western Connecticut State University *B*

Delaware
Goldey-Beacom College *A, B*

District of Columbia
Southeastern University *A, B*

Florida
Florida Southern College *B*
Florida State University *C*
Hillsborough Community College *A*
Lake-Sumter Community College *A*
Manatee Community College *A*
Seminole Community College *A*
Tallahassee Community College *A*
Warner Southern College *B*

Idaho
Idaho State University *B*

Illinois
Benedictine University *M*
City Colleges of Chicago
    Harold Washington College *C, A*
De Paul University *B, M*
Northern Illinois University *M*
Oakton Community College *C, A*
Quincy University *A, B*
Triton College *A*
William Rainey Harper College *C, A*

Indiana
Indiana Institute of Technology *A, B*
Indiana State University *B*
Indiana University--Purdue University
    Indiana University-Purdue
        University Fort Wayne *B*

Iowa
Drake University *B*

Kansas
Fort Hays State University *B*
Kansas State University *B*
Washburn University of Topeka *B*

Kentucky
Morehead State University *B*
Western Kentucky University *B*

Maine
Husson College *B*
University of Maine
    Augusta *A, B*

Massachusetts
Babson College *B*
Boston University *B, M*
Bristol Community College *A*
Merrimack College *C*
New England College of Finance *C*
Suffolk University *M*
University of Massachusetts
    Amherst *B*

Michigan
Baker College
    of Muskegon *A, B*
Cleary College *B*
Detroit College of Business *B*
Ferris State University *B*
Hillsdale College *B*
Kirtland Community College *A*
Lansing Community College *A*
University of Detroit Mercy *B*
Walsh College of Accountancy and
    Business Administration *B, M*

Minnesota
Minnesota State University, Mankato *B*
National American University
    St. Paul *B*
St. Cloud State University *B*
St. Cloud Technical College *C, A*

Missouri
Truman State University *B*

Nebraska
Hastings College *B*
University of Nebraska
    Lincoln *B*

New Hampshire
Franklin Pierce College *B*

New Jersey
Monmouth University *B*
Stevens Institute of Technology *B*

New Mexico
College of the Southwest *B*

New York
City University of New York
    La Guardia Community College *A*
Finger Lakes Community College *A*
Iona College *M*
Ithaca College *B*
Long Island University
    Brooklyn Campus *B*
Medaille College *C, B*
Monroe Community College *A*
Pace University:
    Pleasantville/Briarcliff *B, M, D*
Pace University *B, M, D*
Polytechnic University *M*
St. Thomas Aquinas College *B, M*
State University of New York
    Oswego *B*
Touro College *A, B*

North Carolina
Central Piedmont Community College *A*
East Carolina University *B*
University of North Carolina
    Charlotte *B*

Ohio
Ashland University *B, M*
Bowling Green State University *B*
Cincinnati State Technical and
    Community College *A*
Columbus State Community College *A*
Edison State Community College *A*
Kent State University
    Stark Campus *B*
Kent State University *C*
Lima Technical College *A*
North Central State College *A*
Notre Dame College of Ohio *C, B*
Owens Community College
    Toledo *A*
Terra Community College *A*
University of Akron *A, B, M*
Wittenberg University *B*
Wright State University *M*
Xavier University *B, M*

Oklahoma
Oklahoma City University *B, M*
Southwestern Oklahoma State
    University *B*

Oregon
Concordia University *B*
Portland Community College *A*
Western Baptist College *B*

Pennsylvania
Clarion University of Pennsylvania *B*
Community College of Allegheny
    County *C, A*
Grove City College *B*
La Salle University *B*
Luzerne County Community
    College *C, A*
Mercyhurst College *B*
Penn State
    University Park *C*
Reading Area Community College *C, A*

Puerto Rico
Inter American University of Puerto Rico
    Barranquitas Campus *B*
University of Puerto Rico
    Carolina Regional College *A, B*

Rhode Island
Bryant College *B, M*
Providence College *B*

South Carolina
Clemson University *B*

Financial management/services

South Dakota
Dakota Wesleyan University *B*
Huron University *B*
Southeast Technical Institute *A*

Tennessee
Nashville State Technical Institute *A*

Texas
Abilene Christian University *B*
Baylor University *B*
Grayson County College *A*
Houston Community College
    System *C, A*
Howard Payne University *B*
Navarro College *A*
Texas A&M University
    Commerce *B*
Texas Christian University *B*
University of Houston
    Downtown *B*
University of Houston *M, D*
University of Texas
    Dallas *M, D*
    Pan American *B*
    Tyler *B*

Utah
Brigham Young University *B*
Utah State University *B*
Weber State University *B*

Virginia
Bridgewater College *B*
Southwest Virginia Community
    College *C*
Thomas Nelson Community College *C*

Washington
City University *C, B*
Pacific Lutheran University *B*

West Virginia
Marshall University *B*

Wisconsin
Northeast Wisconsin Technical
    College *A*
Southwest Wisconsin Technical
    College *A*
University of Wisconsin
    Madison *B*
    Platteville *B*

Wyoming
Laramie County Community
    College *C, A*

Financial planning

California
San Diego State University *B, M*

Connecticut
Manchester Community-Technical
    College *C*
Naugatuck Valley Community-Technical
    College *C*

Georgia
Georgia State University *M*

Illinois
John Wood Community College *A*
St. Xavier University *M*

Iowa
Des Moines Area Community College *C*

Maryland
Howard Community College *C, A*

Massachusetts
Bentley College *M*
Lasell College *B*
Merrimack College *C*
New England College of Finance *C*

Michigan
Central Michigan University *B*
Northern Michigan University *B*

Minnesota
Minnesota State University, Mankato *B*

New Jersey
Seton Hall University *M*

New York
Pace University:
    Pleasantville/Briarcliff *M*
Pace University *M*

Ohio
Defiance College *B*
Youngstown State University *B*

Pennsylvania
American College *M*
Marywood University *B*

Texas
Baylor University *B*
University of Dallas *M*

Washington
City University *C, M*

West Virginia
Marshall University *B*

Wisconsin
Waukesha County Technical College *A*

Financial services marketing

Arkansas
Westark College *C*

Colorado
Community College of Aurora *C, A*
Northeastern Junior College *A*

Florida
Broward Community College *A*
Polk Community College *A*
St. Thomas University *B*

Illinois
Governors State University *B*
William Rainey Harper College *C, A*

Indiana
Indiana State University *B*

Iowa
Grand View College *C*

Kansas
Hutchinson Community College *A*

Kentucky
Henderson Community College *C*

Maine
Husson College *B*

Minnesota
Minnesota State University, Mankato *B*

Missouri
Missouri Southern State College *B*

New Jersey
Ramapo College of New Jersey *A, B*

New York
College of Mount St. Vincent *B*
Jefferson Community College *A*
Medaille College *B*
Pace University:
    Pleasantville/Briarcliff *B, M, D*
Pace University *B, M, D*

North Carolina
Western Piedmont Community
    College *A*

Ohio
Columbus State Community College *A*

Pennsylvania
American College *M*
Central Pennsylvania College *A*
Community College of Philadelphia *A*

South Dakota
Southeast Technical Institute *A*

Washington
Highline Community College *A*

Fine arts

Alabama
Faulkner University *B*
James H. Faulkner State Community
    College *A*
Northwest-Shoals Community College *A*
Troy State University *B*
University of North Alabama *B*

Alaska
University of Alaska
    Fairbanks *B*

Arizona
Arizona Western College *A*
Cochise College *A*
Dine College *A*
Mohave Community College *C, A*
Northern Arizona University *B*
Prescott College *B, M*

Arkansas
University of Arkansas *B*

California
Academy of Art College *C, A, B, M*
Art Center College of Design *B, M*
Azusa Pacific University *B*
Barstow College *A*
Butte College *A*
California Baptist University *B*
California Institute of the Arts *M*
California State University
    Chico *B, M*
    Fullerton *M*
    Monterey Bay *B*
Chaffey Community College *A*
Citrus College *A*
City College of San Francisco *A*
College of Marin: Kentfield *A*
College of San Mateo *A*
College of the Desert *A*
Golden West College *A*
Irvine Valley College *A*
John F. Kennedy University *M*
La Sierra University *B*
Lake Tahoe Community College *A*
Las Positas College *A*
Los Medanos College *A*
Marymount College *A*
Merced College *A*
Mills College *B*
Modesto Junior College *A*
Moorpark College *A*
Mount St. Mary's College *B*
Ohlone College *A*
Orange Coast College *A*
Otis College of Art and Design *B, M*
Pacific Union College *B*
Pepperdine University *B*
Pomona College *B*
Sacramento City College *A*
Saddleback College *A*
San Diego City College *A*
San Diego Mesa College *A*
San Diego Miramar College *A*
San Diego State University *M*
San Francisco Art Institute *B, M*
San Joaquin Delta College *A*
San Jose City College *A*
Santa Monica College *A*

Shasta College *A*
Sierra College *A*
Solano Community College *A*
Stanford University *B*
University of California
    Berkeley *M*
    Davis *M*
    Irvine *B*
University of Southern California *M, D*
Ventura College *C, A*
Victor Valley College *A*

Colorado
Adams State College *B*
Colorado Mountain College
    Alpine Campus *A*
Colorado State University *M*
Naropa University *C, B*
University of Colorado
    Boulder *B, M*
    Denver *B*

Connecticut
Asnuntuck Community-Technical
    College *A*
Central Connecticut State University *B*
Eastern Connecticut State University *B*
Housatonic Community-Technical
    College *A*
Middlesex Community-Technical
    College *A*
Norwalk Community-Technical
    College *A*
Paier College of Art *C, B*
Quinebaug Valley Community College *A*
St. Joseph College *B*
Trinity College *B*
University of Bridgeport *B*
University of Hartford *B, M*
Yale University *M*

Delaware
University of Delaware *B, M*

District of Columbia
American University *B*
Corcoran College of Art and Design *B*
George Washington University *B*

Florida
Eckerd College *B*
Flagler College *B*
Jacksonville University *B*
Miami-Dade Community College *A*
New College of the University of South
    Florida *B*
Palm Beach Community College *A*
Ringling School of Art and Design *B*
Stetson University *B*
University of Tampa *B, T*

Georgia
Abraham Baldwin Agricultural
    College *A*
Armstrong Atlantic State University *B, T*
Atlanta College of Art *B*
Atlanta Metropolitan College *A*
Berry College *B*
Brewton-Parker College *A*
Clark Atlanta University *B*
Georgia Southwestern State University *B*
Kennesaw State University *B*
Morehouse College *B*
Reinhardt College *B*
Spelman College *B*
Young Harris College *A*

Hawaii
Brigham Young University
    Hawaii *B*

Idaho
Lewis-Clark State College *B*
University of Idaho *M*

Illinois
American Academy of Art *A, B*
Barat College *B*

City Colleges of Chicago
    Kennedy-King College *A*
    Olive-Harvey College *A*
Columbia College *B*
Dominican University *B*
Illinois College *B*
Lake Land College *A*
Lewis and Clark Community College *A*
Lincoln Land Community College *A*
National-Louis University *B*
North Park University *B*
Parkland College *A*
Quincy University *A, B*
Rend Lake College *A*
Rockford College *B*
St. Xavier University *B*
Sauk Valley Community College *A*
Southwestern Illinois College *A*
William Rainey Harper College *A*

Indiana
Ancilla College *A*
Ball State University *B*
Indiana State University *M*
Indiana University
    Bloomington *B, M*
    East *A, B*
    South Bend *A, B*
    Southeast *B*
Indiana University--Purdue University
    Indiana University-Purdue
      University Fort Wayne *B*
    Indiana University-Purdue
      University Indianapolis *B*
Saint Mary's College *B*
St. Mary-of-the-Woods College *B*
University of St. Francis *M*
Vincennes University *A*

Iowa
Clarke College *B*
Drake University *B*
Maharishi University of
    Management *A, B, M*
Marshalltown Community College *A*
University of Northern Iowa *B, M*
Upper Iowa University *B*

Kansas
Allen County Community College *A*
Bethel College *B*
Coffeyville Community College *A*
Independence Community College *A*
Pratt Community College *A*
Seward County Community College *A*
Washburn University of Topeka *B*

Kentucky
Eastern Kentucky University *B*
Georgetown College *B, T*
Northern Kentucky University *B*
Thomas More College *B*
University of Kentucky *B*

Louisiana
Centenary College of Louisiana *B*
Dillard University *B*
Loyola University New Orleans *B*
Southern University and Agricultural and
    Mechanical College *B*
University of Louisiana at Lafayette *B*

Maine
Maine College of Art *B, M*
University of Maine
    Presque Isle *B*
University of Maine *B*
University of Southern Maine *B*

Maryland
Community College of Baltimore County
    Essex *A*
Frostburg State University *B, T*
Goucher College *B*
Maryland College of Art and
    Design *C, A*
Maryland Institute College of Art *B, M*

Montgomery College
    Germantown Campus *A*
Morgan State University *B*
Mount St. Mary's College *A*
University of Maryland
    Baltimore County *B*
    College Park *M*
Villa Julie College *A*

Massachusetts
Amherst College *B*
Anna Maria College *B*
Brandeis University *B*
Bridgewater State College *B*
Bristol Community College *C*
Curry College *B*
Elms College *B*
Hampshire College *B*
Harvard College *B*
Harvard University *M, D*
Massachusetts College of Art *B, M*
Merrimack College *B*
Montserrat College of Art *B*
Northeastern University *A, B*
School of the Museum of Fine Arts *B, M*
Simon's Rock College of Bard *B*
Smith College *M*
Springfield Technical Community
    College *A*
Stonehill College *B*
Suffolk University *C, B*
Tufts University *B*
University of Massachusetts
    Lowell *B*
Wheaton College *B*

Michigan
Andrews University *B*
Calvin College *B*
Center for Creative Studies: College of
    Art and Design *B*
Kendall College of Art and Design *B*
Lake Superior State University *B*
Marygrove College *B*
Oakland Community College *A*
Olivet College *B*
St. Clair County Community College *A*
Schoolcraft College *A*
University of Michigan *B, M*

Minnesota
Bethel College *B*
College of Visual Arts *B*
Hamline University *B, M*
Minnesota State University, Mankato *B*
Northland Community & Technical
    College *A*
St. Cloud State University *B*
St. Mary's University of Minnesota *B*
St. Olaf College *B*
Winona State University *B*

Mississippi
Belhaven College *B*
East Central Community College *A*
Mississippi Delta Community College *A*
Mississippi State University *M*
Mississippi University for Women *B*
Mississippi Valley State University *B*

Missouri
Avila College *B*
Columbia College *B*
East Central College *A*
Hannibal-LaGrange College *B*
Lindenwood University *B, M*
St. Louis Community College
    St. Louis Community College at
      Forest Park *A*
    St. Louis Community College at
      Meramec *A*
Three Rivers Community College *A*
University of Missouri
    St. Louis *C, B*
Washington University *B, M*
William Woods University *B, T*

Montana
Montana State University
    Northern *B*
University of Montana-Missoula *B, M*
Western Montana College of The
    University of Montana *B*

Nebraska
Midland Lutheran College *B*
University of Nebraska
    Kearney *B, M, T*
    Lincoln *B, M*

Nevada
Community College of Southern
    Nevada *A*
University of Nevada
    Las Vegas *B, M*

New Hampshire
Franklin Pierce College *B*
New Hampshire Community Technical
    College
      Laconia *A*
Notre Dame College *B*
Plymouth State College of the University
    System of New Hampshire *B*
Rivier College *B*
St. Anselm College *B*
University of New Hampshire *B*
White Pines College *B*

New Jersey
Bloomfield College *B*
Caldwell College *B*
Essex County College *A*
Fairleigh Dickinson University *B*
Felician College *B*
Monmouth University *B*
New Jersey City University *B, M*
Ramapo College of New Jersey *B*
Rider University *B*
Rowan University *B*
St. Peter's College *B*
The College of New Jersey *B*

New Mexico
Clovis Community College *A*
College of Santa Fe *B*
College of the Southwest *B*
New Mexico Highlands University *B*
New Mexico Junior College *A*
New Mexico State University *B, M*
Northern New Mexico Community
    College *A*
Western New Mexico University *B*

New York
Alfred University *B*
Bard College *B, M*
City University of New York
    City College *B*
    Hunter College *B*
    Kingsborough Community
      College *A*
    La Guardia Community College *A*
    Lehman College *B, M*
Columbia-Greene Community College *A*
Cooper Union for the Advancement of
    Science and Art *C, B*
Fashion Institute of Technology *A*
Finger Lakes Community College *A*
Fordham University *B*
Fulton-Montgomery Community
    College *A*
Herkimer County Community College *A*
Hofstra University *B*
Ithaca College *B*
Long Island University
    C. W. Post Campus *M*
    Southampton College *B*
Manhattanville College *B*
Mannes College of Music *B, M*
Marist College *B*
Marymount College *B*
Mohawk Valley Community College *A*
Monroe Community College *A*

Nassau Community College *A*
New York Institute of Technology *B*
New York State College of Ceramics at
    Alfred University *B, M, T*
New York University *B, M, D*
Niagara County Community College *A*
Pace University:
    Pleasantville/Briarcliff *A*
Pace University *A*
Parsons School of Design *C, A, B, T*
Pratt Institute *B, M*
Rensselaer Polytechnic Institute *B, M*
Roberts Wesleyan College *B*
Rochester Institute of
    Technology *A, B, M*
Rockland Community College *A*
Sage Junior College of Albany *A*
St. John's University *B*
St. Lawrence University *B*
Sarah Lawrence College *B*
School of Visual Arts *B, M*
State University of New York
    Buffalo *B, M*
    College at Brockport *B*
    College at Cortland *B*
    Empire State College *A, B*
Suffolk County Community College *A*
Syracuse University *B, M*

North Carolina
Brevard College *A, B*
Central Piedmont Community College *A*
Lenoir Community College *A*
Methodist College *B*
Mitchell Community College *A*
Mount Olive College *A, B*
North Carolina Central University *B*
Rockingham Community College *A*
Wingate University *B*
Winston-Salem State University *B*

North Dakota
Dickinson State University *B*
Jamestown College *B*

Ohio
Ashland University *B*
Capital University *B*
College of Mount St. Joseph *B*
Columbus College of Art and Design *B*
Kent State University
    Stark Campus
Kent State University *B, M*
Lake Erie College *B*
Lorain County Community College *A*
Lourdes College *A, B*
Notre Dame College of Ohio *B*
Ohio Northern University *B*
Ohio State University
    Columbus Campus *B, M*
Shawnee State University *B*
Sinclair Community College *A*
University of Akron *A, B*
University of Cincinnati *C, B, M*
University of Dayton *B*
University of Rio Grande *B*
University of Toledo *B*
Wilberforce University *B*
Xavier University *B*
Youngstown State University *B*

Oklahoma
Cameron University *B*
East Central University *B*
Northeastern Oklahoma Agricultural and
    Mechanical College *A*
Oklahoma State University *B*
University of Tulsa *M*

Oregon
Central Oregon Community College *A*
Eastern Oregon University *B*
Lewis & Clark College *B*
Marylhurst University *B*
Pacific Northwest College of Art *C, B*
Reed College *B*
University of Oregon *B, M*

Fine arts

Willamette University *B*

Pennsylvania
Beaver College *B*
Bucks County Community College *A*
California University of Pennsylvania *B*
Carnegie Mellon University *B, M*
Cedar Crest College *B*
Chestnut Hill College *B*
Community College of Allegheny
 County *A*
Dickinson College *B*
Edinboro University of Pennsylvania *M*
Gettysburg College *B*
Haverford College *B*
La Salle University *B*
Lafayette College *B*
Lehigh Carbon Community College *C, A*
Lock Haven University of
 Pennsylvania *B*
Lycoming College *B*
Montgomery County Community
 College *A*
Moore College of Art and Design *B*
Penn State
 Altoona *B*
Seton Hill College *B*
University of Pennsylvania *C, A, B, M*
University of the Arts *B, M*
West Chester University of
 Pennsylvania *B*
Wilkes University *B*
Wilson College *B*
York College of Pennsylvania *B*

Puerto Rico
Pontifical Catholic University of Puerto
 Rico *B*
University of Puerto Rico
 Rio Piedras Campus *B*

Rhode Island
Rhode Island College *B*

South Carolina
Charleston Southern University *B*
Clemson University *B, M*
Converse College *B*
Winthrop University *B*

Tennessee
Bethel College *B*
Cumberland University *B*
East Tennessee State University *B, M, T*
King College *B*
Milligan College *B*
Tennessee Technological University *B*
University of the South *B*
Vanderbilt University *B*

Texas
Alvin Community College *A*
College of the Mainland *A*
El Paso Community College *C*
Houston Baptist University *B*
Lon Morris College *A*
Paris Junior College *A*
St. Edward's University *B*
St. Philip's College *A*
Tarleton State University *B*
Texas A&M University
 Commerce *M*
 Kingsville *B, M, T*
Texas Christian University *B, M*
University of North Texas *B, M, D*
University of Texas
 of the Permian Basin *B*

Utah
Southern Utah University *T*
Utah State University *M*
Weber State University *B*

Vermont
Bennington College *B, M*
Burlington College *B*
Goddard College *B*
Green Mountain College *B*

Johnson State College *B, M*
Marlboro College *B*

Virginia
Christopher Newport University *B*
College of William and Mary *B*
Ferrum College *B*
Hampden-Sydney College *B*
James Madison University *M*
John Tyler Community College *C, A*
Longwood College *B, T*
Norfolk State University *B, T*
Northern Virginia Community College *A*
Radford University *B, M*
Regent University *M*
Roanoke College *B*
Tidewater Community College *A*
Virginia Intermont College *B*
Virginia Wesleyan College *B*

Washington
Central Washington University *B, M*
Centralia College *A*
Cornish College of the Arts *B*
Everett Community College *A*
Evergreen State College *B*
Lower Columbia College *A*
North Seattle Community College *C*
Seattle Pacific University *B, T*
Seattle University *B*
Western Washington University *B*

West Virginia
Bethany College *B*
Marshall University *B, M*
West Virginia State College *A, B*

Wisconsin
Cardinal Stritch University *B*
Mount Senario College *B, T*
Northland College *B*
University of Wisconsin
 Madison *M*
 Oshkosh *B*
Viterbo University *B*

Wyoming
Laramie County Community College *A*
University of Wyoming *B*

Fire protection

Alabama
Wallace State Community College at
 Hanceville *A*

Arizona
Arizona Western College *A*

Arkansas
Garland County Community College *A*
Southern Arkansas University
 Tech *A*

California
Chabot College *C, A*
Fresno City College *C, A*
Mount San Jacinto College *C, A*
San Diego Miramar College *C, A*
Santa Ana College *A*
Shasta College *C, A*

Florida
Polk Community College *A*
St. Petersburg Junior College *C*

Hawaii
University of Hawaii
 Honolulu Community College *A*

Illinois
Black Hawk College *A*
Joliet Junior College *C, A*
Lewis and Clark Community College *A*
Moraine Valley Community
 College *C, A*
Southwestern Illinois College *C, A*

Iowa
Des Moines Area Community College *A*

Kansas
Kansas City Kansas Community
 College *C, A*

Maine
Southern Maine Technical College *A*

Maryland
Montgomery College
 Rockville Campus *A*

Massachusetts
Berkshire Community College *A*
Massachusetts Maritime Academy *C*

Michigan
Kalamazoo Valley Community
 College *C, A*
Madonna University *C, A, B*

Minnesota
North Hennepin Community College *A*

Missouri
Jefferson College *C, A*
Penn Valley Community College *A*

New Hampshire
New Hampshire Community Technical
 College
 Laconia *A*

New Jersey
Thomas Edison State College *A, B*
Union County College *C, A*

New Mexico
New Mexico Junior College *C, A*

New York
Broome Community College *C, A*
City University of New York
 John Jay College of Criminal
 Justice *M*
Corning Community College *C, A*
Rockland Community College *A*
Suffolk County Community College *A*

North Carolina
Alamance Community College *C*
Central Piedmont Community College *A*
Coastal Carolina Community
 College *C, A*
Davidson County Community College *A*
Durham Technical Community
 College *C, A*
Wilson Technical Community College *A*

Oklahoma
Oklahoma State University
 Oklahoma City *A*

Oregon
Chemeketa Community College *A*

Pennsylvania
Bucks County Community College *A*
Community College of Allegheny
 County *A*

Texas
Amarillo College *A*
Galveston College *C, A*
Howard College *C*
Midland College *A*
Trinity Valley Community College *C, A*
Tyler Junior College *C, A*
West Texas A&M University *B*

Washington
Edmonds Community College *C, A*
Yakima Valley Community College *A*

Wisconsin
Madison Area Technical College *C, A*
Milwaukee Area Technical College *A*
Waukesha County Technical College *A*

Fire protection/safety technology

Alabama
Community College of the Air Force *A*

Alaska
University of Alaska
 Anchorage *A*
 Fairbanks *C, A*

Arizona
Arizona Western College *A*
Central Arizona College *C*
Cochise College *A*

California
Allan Hancock College *C, A*
American River College *A*
Bakersfield College *A*
Barstow College *C, A*
Butte College *C, A*
California State University
 Los Angeles *B*
City College of San Francisco *C, A*
Cogswell Polytechnical College *B*
College of San Mateo *C, A*
College of the Desert *A*
Columbia College *C, A*
Compton Community College *C*
Fresno City College *C*
Glendale Community College *C, A*
Long Beach City College *C, A*
Mission College *C, A*
Monterey Peninsula College *C, A*
Rio Hondo College *A*
San Joaquin Delta College *C, A*
Santa Ana College *A*
Santa Rosa Junior College *C*
Shasta College *A*
Sierra College *C, A*
Victor Valley College *C, A*

Colorado
Aims Community College *A*
Arapahoe Community College *C*
Pikes Peak Community College *A*

Connecticut
Capital Community College *A*
Naugatuck Valley Community-Technical
 College *A*
Norwalk Community-Technical
 College *A*
Three Rivers Community-Technical
 College *A*
University of New Haven *A, B, M*

Delaware
Delaware Technical and Community
 College
 Stanton/Wilmington Campus *A*

Florida
Edison Community College *A*
Indian River Community College *C, A*
Miami-Dade Community College *C, A*
Pensacola Junior College *A*
Santa Fe Community College *A*

Georgia
Georgia Military College *A*
Georgia Perimeter College *A*
Savannah Technical Institute *A*

Hawaii
University of Hawaii
 Honolulu Community College *C, A*

Idaho
Boise State University *C*
College of Southern Idaho *A*
Idaho State University *A*

Illinois
College of DuPage *C, A*
College of Lake County *A*
Elgin Community College *C, A*

Firefighting/fire science

John Wood Community College *C*
Kankakee Community College *C*
Kishwaukee College *C, A*
Lincoln Land Community College *C, A*
Moraine Valley Community
 College *C, A*
Parkland College *C, A*
Prairie State College *C, A*
Waubonsee Community College *C, A*

Indiana
Vincennes University *A*

Iowa
Kirkwood Community College *C, A*

Kansas
Hutchinson Community College *A*
Kansas City Kansas Community
 College *C, A*

Kentucky
Eastern Kentucky University *C, A, B*

Louisiana
Delgado Community College *A*
Louisiana State University
 Eunice *C, A*

Maine
Southern Maine Technical College *A*

Maryland
Community College of Baltimore County
 Catonsville *C, A*
Montgomery College
 Rockville Campus *C, A*

Massachusetts
Berkshire Community College *A*
Bunker Hill Community College *A*
Cape Cod Community College *A*
Massachusetts Maritime Academy *C*
Massasoit Community College *C*
Middlesex Community College *A*
Mount Wachusett Community College *A*
North Shore Community College *A*
Springfield Technical Community
 College *A*
Worcester Polytechnic Institute *M*

Michigan
Delta College *A*
Kellogg Community College *C, A*
Lake Superior State University *A, B*
Mott Community College *A*

Mississippi
Hinds Community College *A*
Mississippi Gulf Coast Community
 College
 Jefferson Davis Campus *A*
 Perkinston *A*

Missouri
East Central College *A*
Ozarks Technical Community College *A*
Penn Valley Community College *C, A*
St. Louis Community College
 St. Louis Community College at
  Florissant Valley *A*
 St. Louis Community College at
  Forest Park *C, A*

Nebraska
Southeast Community College
 Lincoln Campus *A*
University of Nebraska
 Lincoln *A*

Nevada
Community College of Southern
 Nevada *A*
Western Nevada Community
 College *C, A*

New Hampshire
New Hampshire Community Technical
 College
 Berlin *C, A*
 Laconia *A*

New Jersey
Camden County College *A*
Mercer County Community College *C, A*
New Jersey City University *B*
Ocean County College *C, A*
Sussex County Community College *C*
Thomas Edison State College *A, B*

New Mexico
Albuquerque Technical-Vocational
 Institute *A*
Eastern New Mexico University
 Roswell Campus *A*
San Juan College *A*

New York
City University of New York
 John Jay College of Criminal
  Justice *B, M*
Corning Community College *A*
Monroe Community College *A*
Onondaga Community College *C, A*
Rockland Community College *A*

North Carolina
Cleveland Community College *C, A*
Coastal Carolina Community
 College *C, A*
College of the Albemarle *A*
Gaston College *A*
Rockingham Community College *A*
Rowan-Cabarrus Community College *A*
Wilson Technical Community College *A*

Ohio
Lorain County Community College *A*
Sinclair Community College *A*
University of Akron *A*

Oklahoma
Oklahoma State University
 Oklahoma City *A*
Oklahoma State University *B*
Tulsa Community College *A*

Oregon
Chemeketa Community College *A*
Portland Community College *C, A*

Pennsylvania
Community College of Allegheny
 County *A*
Community College of Philadelphia *A*
Delaware County Community College *A*
Harrisburg Area Community
 College *C, A*
Luzerne County Community
 College *C, A*
Montgomery County Community
 College *A*
Westmoreland County Community
 College *C, A*

Puerto Rico
University of the Sacred Heart *B*

Rhode Island
Providence College *A, B*

Texas
Amarillo College *C, A*
College of the Mainland *A*
Collin County Community College
 District *A*
Del Mar College *A*
El Paso Community College *A*
Galveston College *C, A*
Houston Community College
 System *C, A*
Midland College *A*
Navarro College *C, A*
Odessa College *C, A*
San Antonio College *A*

South Plains College *A*
Tarrant County College *C, A*
West Texas A&M University *B*

Virginia
Northern Virginia Community
 College *C, A*

Washington
Bellevue Community College *A*
Pierce College *A*
Spokane Falls Community College *C*

West Virginia
Shepherd College *A*

Wisconsin
Blackhawk Technical College *A*
Moraine Park Technical College *C*
Northeast Wisconsin Technical
 College *A*

Fire services administration

Alabama
Jefferson State Community College *A*
Northwest-Shoals Community College *A*

California
Cogswell Polytechnical College *B*
Fresno City College *C*
Santa Ana College *A*

Connecticut
Gateway Community College *A*
Norwalk Community-Technical
 College *A*
University of New Haven *B*

District of Columbia
University of the District of
 Columbia *A, B*

Georgia
Macon State College *A*

Hawaii
University of Hawaii
 Honolulu Community College *A*

Idaho
Lewis-Clark State College *A*

Illinois
Black Hawk College *A*
College of DuPage *C*
Moraine Valley Community College *C*
Southern Illinois University
 Carbondale *B*

Kansas
Kansas City Kansas Community
 College *C, A*

Maine
Southern Maine Technical College *A*

Massachusetts
Berkshire Community College *A*
Cape Cod Community College *C*
Salem State College *B*

New Hampshire
New Hampshire Community Technical
 College
 Laconia *A*
Rivier College *B*

New York
Erie Community College
 South Campus *A*
Schenectady County Community
 College *A*

Oregon
Eastern Oregon University *B*
Western Oregon University *B*

Pennsylvania
Northampton County Area Community
 College *C, A*

South Carolina
Greenville Technical College *A*

Texas
Hill College *C, A*

Virginia
Hampton University *B*
Northern Virginia Community
 College *C, A*
Thomas Nelson Community College *A*

Washington
Olympic College *C, A*
South Puget Sound Community
 College *A*
Spokane Community College *A*
Wenatchee Valley College *A*

Firefighting/fire science

Alabama
Calhoun Community College *A*
Central Alabama Community
 College *C, A*
Chattahoochee Valley Community
 College *C, A*
Northwest-Shoals Community College *A*

Arizona
Arizona Western College *A*
Glendale Community College *C, A*
Mohave Community College *C, A*
Northland Pioneer College *C, A*
Phoenix College *C, A*
Pima Community College *A*
Scottsdale Community College *C, A*
Yavapai College *C, A*

Arkansas
Northwest Arkansas Community
 College *A*
Southern Arkansas University
 Tech *A*

California
Allan Hancock College *C*
Cabrillo College *C, A*
Chabot College *C, A*
College of the Sequoias *C*
College of the Siskiyous *C, A*
Compton Community College *A*
Crafton Hills College *C, A*
East Los Angeles College *C*
Fresno City College *C, A*
Imperial Valley College *C, A*
Lake Tahoe Community College *C, A*
Las Positas College *A*
Los Angeles Harbor College *C, A*
Los Medanos College *C, A*
Merced College *C, A*
Modesto Junior College *A*
Mount San Antonio College *C, A*
Palo Verde College *C, A*
Palomar College *C, A*
Pasadena City College *A*
Porterville College *C*
Riverside Community College *C, A*
Santa Ana College *A*
Santa Monica College *C, A*
Santa Rosa Junior College *A*
Sierra College *C, A*
Solano Community College *C, A*
Southwestern College *C, A*

Colorado
Aims Community College *C*

Connecticut
University of New Haven *B, M*

District of Columbia
University of the District of Columbia *A*

285

Firefighting/fire science

Florida
Brevard Community College C, A
Broward Community College A
Central Florida Community College A
Daytona Beach Community
 College C, A
Florida Community College at
 Jacksonville A
Gulf Coast Community College A
Hillsborough Community College C, A
Lake-Sumter Community College A
Manatee Community College A
Palm Beach Community College A
Pasco-Hernando Community College C
Pensacola Junior College C, A
Polk Community College A
St. Petersburg Junior College A
Seminole Community College C, A
University of Florida B
Valencia Community College A

Hawaii
University of Hawaii
 Honolulu Community College C, A

Illinois
Carl Sandburg College C, A
City Colleges of Chicago
 Harold Washington College A
College of DuPage C
Illinois Eastern Community Colleges
 Frontier Community College C
John Wood Community College A
Joliet Junior College C
Kankakee Community College C
Kishwaukee College C, A
McHenry County College C, A
Moraine Valley Community College C
Oakton Community College C, A
Richland Community College A
Rock Valley College A
Southeastern Illinois College C
Southwestern Illinois College C, A
Triton College C, A
Waubonsee Community College C
William Rainey Harper College C, A

Iowa
Iowa Western Community College A
Northeast Iowa Community College A

Kansas
Barton County Community College C
Butler County Community College C, A
Dodge City Community College A
Johnson County Community College A
Kansas City Kansas Community
 College C, A

Maine
Eastern Maine Technical College A
Southern Maine Technical College A

Maryland
Charles County Community College A
Montgomery College
 Rockville Campus A

Massachusetts
Anna Maria College B
Berkshire Community College A
Bristol Community College A
Cape Cod Community College A
Massachusetts Maritime Academy C
Massasoit Community College A
Springfield Technical Community
 College C

Michigan
Delta College A
Grand Rapids Community College A
Henry Ford Community College A
Kalamazoo Valley Community
 College C, A
Kellogg Community College C
Kirtland Community College A
Lansing Community College A
Macomb Community College C, A
Mid Michigan Community College A
Oakland Community College C, A
Schoolcraft College C, A

Minnesota
Lake Superior College: A Community
 and Technical College A

Mississippi
Meridian Community College A

Missouri
Central Missouri State University M
Three Rivers Community College C

Montana
Miles Community College C

Nevada
Community College of Southern
 Nevada A

New Hampshire
New Hampshire Community Technical
 College
 Berlin A
 Laconia A

New Jersey
Burlington County College A
Essex County College A
Middlesex County College A

New Mexico
Dona Ana Branch Community College of
 New Mexico State University A
New Mexico State University
 Alamogordo A
 Carlsbad C, A

New York
Corning Community College C
Schenectady County Community
 College C

North Carolina
Alamance Community College A
Tri-County Community College C

Ohio
Cleveland State University B
Columbus State Community College A
Hocking Technical College A
Lakeland Community College C, A
Owens Community College
 Toledo C, A
Stark State College of Technology A

Oklahoma
Oklahoma State University
 Oklahoma City A
Western Oklahoma State College A

Oregon
Central Oregon Community College A
Chemeketa Community College A
Mount Hood Community College C, A

Pennsylvania
Holy Family College B
Mercyhurst College C

Rhode Island
Community College of Rhode Island A

Tennessee
Volunteer State Community College C

Texas
Blinn College C, A
Collin County Community College
 District C
Houston Community College System C
Midland College A
Odessa College C, A
South Plains College A
Texas A&M University
 Commerce C
Trinity Valley Community College C, A
Vernon Regional Junior College C

Utah
Utah Valley State College C, A

Virginia
J. Sargeant Reynolds Community
 College C, A
Lord Fairfax Community College C
Southwest Virginia Community
 College C
Tidewater Community College A
Virginia Highlands Community
 College C
Virginia Western Community College C

Washington
Skagit Valley College A
South Puget Sound Community
 College C, A
Spokane Community College A
Walla Walla Community College A

Wisconsin
Chippewa Valley Technical College A
Gateway Technical College A
Moraine Park Technical College C
Waukesha County Technical College C

Wyoming
Casper College A

Fisheries/fishing

Alabama
Auburn University B, M, D

Alaska
University of Alaska
 Fairbanks B, M, D

Arkansas
University of Arkansas
 Pine Bluff B, M

California
College of the Redwoods C, A
Humboldt State University B
University of California
 Davis B

Colorado
Colorado State University B, M, D
Trinidad State Junior College C, A

Delaware
Delaware State University B

Florida
University of Florida M, D

Georgia
University of Georgia B

Idaho
College of Southern Idaho A
North Idaho College A
University of Idaho B, M, D

Illinois
Lake Land College A

Iowa
Iowa State University M, D

Kansas
Pittsburg State University B

Kentucky
Kentucky State University M
Murray State University B

Louisiana
Louisiana State University and
 Agricultural and Mechanical
 College M

Maine
Unity College B

Maryland
Frostburg State University B, M

Massachusetts
Massachusetts Maritime Academy C

Michigan
Lake Superior State University B
Michigan State University B, M, D
Mid Michigan Community College A
Northern Michigan University M
University of Michigan B, M

Minnesota
University of Minnesota
 Twin Cities B, M, D
Vermilion Community College A

Mississippi
Mississippi Gulf Coast Community
 College
 Jefferson Davis Campus C
 Perkinston A

Missouri
East Central College A

Montana
Miles Community College A

Nebraska
University of Nebraska
 Lincoln B

New Jersey
Rutgers
 The State University of New Jersey:
 Cook College B

New Mexico
New Mexico State University B

New York
Cornell University B
State University of New York
 College of Agriculture and
  Technology at Cobleskill A
 College of Agriculture and
  Technology at Morrisville A
 College of Environmental Science
  and Forestry B, M, D

North Carolina
Brunswick Community College A
Haywood Community College A
North Carolina State University B

North Dakota
Minot State University: Bottineau
 Campus A
North Dakota State University B
University of North Dakota B

Ohio
Hocking Technical College A
Ohio State University
 Columbus Campus B

Oklahoma
Southeastern Oklahoma State
 University B

Oregon
Central Oregon Community College A
Clatsop Community College C
Mount Hood Community College A
Oregon State University B, M, D

Pennsylvania
Mansfield University of Pennsylvania B

Rhode Island
University of Rhode Island B, M

South Carolina
Clemson University B, M

South Dakota
South Dakota State University B, M

Tennessee
Lincoln Memorial University B
Tennessee Technological University B

Food sciences/technology

Texas
Texas A&M University
 Galveston *B*
Texas A&M University *B, M, D*
Texas Tech University *B*

Vermont
University of Vermont *B, M*

Virginia
Virginia Polytechnic Institute and State University *M, D*

Washington
Heritage College *C, A*
Highline Community College *A*
Peninsula College *A*
University of Washington *B, M, D*

West Virginia
Bluefield State College *A*

Wisconsin
Northland College *B*

Flight attendant

California
Chabot College *A*
Cypress College *C, A*
Mount San Antonio College *A*
Orange Coast College *C, A*
San Bernardino Valley College *C*

Louisiana
University of Louisiana at Monroe *A*

New Jersey
Mercer County Community College *A*

North Carolina
Asheville Buncombe Technical Community College *C, A*

Ohio
Cincinnati State Technical and Community College *C*

Washington
Spokane Falls Community College *C*

Floristry marketing

California
Modesto Junior College *C*

Illinois
Kishwaukee College *C, A*

Minnesota
Rochester Community and Technical College *A*

New Jersey
Bergen Community College *C*

North Carolina
Johnston Community College *C, A*
Randolph Community College *C*

Ohio
Ohio State University
 Agricultural Technical Institute *A*

Oklahoma
Oklahoma State University
 Oklahoma City *C*

Oregon
Mount Hood Community College *C, A*

Washington
Lake Washington Technical College *C, A*

Wisconsin
Gateway Technical College *A*

Food management

Alabama
Community College of the Air Force *A*

Alaska
University of Alaska
 Fairbanks *C, A*

California
Cabrillo College *C, A*
Chaffey Community College *C, A*
Columbia College *A*
Compton Community College *C, A*
Contra Costa College *A*
Cypress College *A*
Diablo Valley College *A*
Mission College *C, A*
Modesto Junior College *A*
Mount San Antonio College *C, A*
Orange Coast College *C, A*
Pasadena City College *C, A*

Colorado
Pueblo Community College *C, A*
Red Rocks Community College *C, A*

Connecticut
Asnuntuck Community-Technical College *C, A*
Manchester Community-Technical College *A*
Naugatuck Valley Community-Technical College *A*
Norwalk Community-Technical College *A*

Delaware
Delaware Technical and Community College
 Stanton/Wilmington Campus *A*

Florida
Indian River Community College *A*
Palm Beach Community College *A*

Hawaii
University of Hawaii
 Hawaii Community College *A*

Illinois
Dominican University *B*

Kansas
Washburn University of Topeka *A*

Maryland
Baltimore International College *A, B*
Prince George's Community College *C*

Massachusetts
Berkshire Community College *A*
Newbury College *A*

Michigan
Baker College
 of Muskegon *A*
Ferris State University *C, A*
Henry Ford Community College *A*

Minnesota
Dakota County Technical College *C, A*

Missouri
St. Louis Community College
 St. Louis Community College at Meramec *C*

Nebraska
University of Nebraska
 Omaha *B*

New Hampshire
Hesser College *A*
University of New Hampshire *A*

New Jersey
Gloucester County College *A*
Middlesex County College *C, A*

New York
Fulton-Montgomery Community College *A*
Monroe Community College *C, A*
New York University *B, M, D*
Onondaga Community College *A*
Rochester Institute of Technology *B, M*
State University of New York
 College of Agriculture and Technology at Morrisville *A*
Syracuse University *B*

North Carolina
Appalachian State University *B*
Sandhills Community College *C, A*
Wake Technical Community College *A*

Ohio
Columbus State Community College *A*
Kent State University
 Stark Campus *B*
Sinclair Community College *C*

Pennsylvania
Bucks County Community College *A*
Indiana University of Pennsylvania *B*
Seton Hill College *B*

Rhode Island
Johnson & Wales University *A, B*

Tennessee
Shelby State Community College *C, A*
University of Tennessee
 Knoxville *M*

Texas
El Paso Community College *C, A*
St. Philip's College *A*
Texas State Technical College
 Harlingen *C, A*

Vermont
New England Culinary Institute *B*

Virginia
Southwest Virginia Community College *C*

West Virginia
Fairmont State College *A*

Wisconsin
Milwaukee Area Technical College *C*
Nicolet Area Technical College *A*
Western Wisconsin Technical College *A*

Food products retailing/wholesaling

California
College of the Canyons *C*
Modesto Junior College *A*

Hawaii
University of Hawaii
 Maui Community College *A*

Indiana
Vincennes University *A*

Iowa
Kirkwood Community College *C, A*

Kansas
Seward County Community College *C, A*

Kentucky
National Business College *A*

Massachusetts
Becker College *C*
Newbury College *A*

Michigan
Ferris State University *C*
Western Michigan University *B*

New Hampshire
University of New Hampshire *A*

New Jersey
Bergen Community College *A*
Brookdale Community College *A*
Gloucester County College *A*
St. Peter's College *C*

New York
Fulton-Montgomery Community College *A*
Rochester Institute of Technology *B*

North Carolina
Central Piedmont Community College *A*

Ohio
Ohio State University
 Agricultural Technical Institute *A*

Pennsylvania
St. Joseph's University *C, A, B, M*

Rhode Island
Johnson & Wales University *A, B*

Texas
El Paso Community College *C, A*

Washington
Green River Community College *C*
South Seattle Community College *A*

Food sciences/technology

Alabama
Alabama Agricultural and Mechanical University *B, M, D*

Arizona
Prescott College *B, M*

Arkansas
University of Arkansas *B, M, D*

California
California Polytechnic State University:
 San Luis Obispo *B*
California State University
 Fresno *B*
Fresno City College *C, A*
Kings River Community College *C*
Mission College *C, A*
Modesto Junior College *C, A*
San Joaquin Delta College *A*
University of California
 Davis *B, M, D*

Colorado
Colorado State University *B*

Delaware
University of Delaware *B, M*

Florida
University of Florida *B, M, D*

Georgia
University of Georgia *B, M, D*

Hawaii
University of Hawaii
 Manoa *M*

Idaho
College of Southern Idaho *A*
University of Idaho *B*

Illinois
City Colleges of Chicago
 Malcolm X College *A*
Illinois Institute of Technology *M*
University of Illinois
 Urbana-Champaign *B, M, D*

Indiana
Purdue University *B, M, D*

Iowa
Iowa State University *M, D*

Food sciences/technology

Kansas
Kansas State University B, M, D

Kentucky
Murray State University B
University of Kentucky B

Louisiana
Louisiana State University and Agricultural and Mechanical College B, M, D

Maine
Eastern Maine Technical College C, A
University of Maine B, M, D

Maryland
University of Maryland
 College Park B, M, D
 Eastern Shore M

Massachusetts
Berkshire Community College C
Framingham State College B, M
North Shore Community College A
University of Massachusetts
 Amherst B, M, D

Michigan
Michigan State University B, M, D
Western Michigan University B

Minnesota
Minnesota State University, Mankato B
University of Minnesota
 Twin Cities B, M, D

Mississippi
Hinds Community College A
Mississippi State University B, M, D
Northwest Mississippi Community College A

Missouri
University of Missouri
 Columbia B, M, D

Nebraska
University of Nebraska
 Lincoln B, M, D

New Jersey
Rutgers
 The State University of New Jersey: Cook College B
 The State University of New Jersey: Douglass College B
 The State University of New Jersey: New Brunswick Graduate Campus M, D
 The State University of New Jersey: University College New Brunswick B

New York
Cornell University B
Fulton-Montgomery Community College A

North Carolina
North Carolina State University B, M, D

North Dakota
North Dakota State University B, M, D

Ohio
Ohio State University
 Columbus Campus B, M, D

Oklahoma
Eastern Oklahoma State College A
Oklahoma State University M

Oregon
Oregon State University B, M, D

Pennsylvania
Delaware Valley College C, B
Penn State
 University Park C, B, M, D

Puerto Rico
University of Puerto Rico
 Mayaguez Campus M
 Utuado A

South Carolina
Clemson University B, D
Greenville Technical College C, A

Tennessee
Hiwassee College A
University of Tennessee
 Knoxville B, M, D

Texas
Sul Ross State University B
Texas A&M University
 Commerce B
 Kingsville B, M
Texas A&M University B, M, D
Texas Tech University B, M

Utah
Brigham Young University B, M
Snow College A
Utah State University B, M, D

Vermont
University of Vermont M

Virginia
Virginia Polytechnic Institute and State University B, M

Washington
Pierce College C
Washington State University M, D

Wisconsin
Northeast Wisconsin Technical College A
University of Wisconsin
 Madison B, M, D
 River Falls B

Wyoming
University of Wyoming M

Food/nutrition studies

Alabama
Alabama Agricultural and Mechanical University B
Auburn University B
Jacksonville State University B
Oakwood College B
Tuskegee University B, M
University of Alabama B, M
Wallace State Community College at Hanceville C, A

Arizona
Central Arizona College C
Mesa Community College A

Arkansas
Ouachita Baptist University B
University of Arkansas B
University of Central Arkansas B

California
Bakersfield College A
California Polytechnic State University: San Luis Obispo B
California State Polytechnic University: Pomona B
California State University
 Chico B, M
 Fresno B
 Long Beach B, M
 Los Angeles B
 Northridge B
Chapman University B, M
City College of San Francisco C, A
College of the Desert A
College of the Sequoias C
Fresno City College C, A
Glendale Community College A
Kings River Community College C
Long Beach City College C, A
Los Angeles Mission College A
Merritt College C
Modesto Junior College A
Ohlone College C
Orange Coast College C, A
Pacific Union College A, B
Riverside Community College A
Saddleback College C, A
San Diego State University B, M
San Joaquin Delta College C, A
San Jose State University M
Santa Ana College C, A
Santa Rosa Junior College C
Southwestern College C
University of California
 Berkeley B
 Davis B
Ventura College A

Colorado
Art Institute
 of Colorado A, B
Colorado State University B, M, D

Connecticut
Gateway Community College A
St. Joseph College B, M
University of Bridgeport M

Delaware
Delaware State University B
University of Delaware B, M

District of Columbia
Gallaudet University B
University of the District of Columbia B

Florida
Broward Community College A
Florida State University B, M
Hillsborough Community College A
Miami-Dade Community College A
Pensacola Junior College C

Georgia
Fort Valley State University B
Georgia Southern University B
Georgia State University B, M
Morris Brown College B
University of Georgia B, M, D

Hawaii
University of Hawaii
 Hawaii Community College C, A

Idaho
Idaho State University B
Ricks College A
University of Idaho B

Illinois
Dominican University B
Eastern Illinois University M
Loyola University of Chicago B
Morton College A
Northern Illinois University B, M
Rend Lake College C, A
Shawnee Community College C, A
Southern Illinois University
 Carbondale B, M
University of Illinois
 Urbana-Champaign B, M, D
William Rainey Harper College A

Indiana
Ball State University A, B
Indiana State University B, M
Marian College B
Purdue University
 North Central Campus C
Purdue University B, M, D
Vincennes University A

Iowa
Iowa State University B, M, D
University of Northern Iowa B

Kansas
Kansas State University B, M, D
Pittsburg State University B, T
Seward County Community College A

Kentucky
Berea College B
Eastern Kentucky University B
Murray State University B
Spalding University T
University of Kentucky B, M
Western Kentucky University B, T

Louisiana
Southern University and Agricultural and Mechanical College B

Maine
Southern Maine Technical College A
University of Maine B, M, D
Washington County Technical College A

Maryland
Morgan State University B
University of Maryland
 College Park B
 Eastern Shore B

Massachusetts
Framingham State College B, M
Hampshire College B
University of Massachusetts
 Amherst B

Michigan
Andrews University B, M
Central Michigan University B, M
Eastern Michigan University B
Madonna University B
Marygrove College B
Michigan State University B, M
Northern Michigan University B
Wayne State University B, M, D
Western Michigan University B

Minnesota
College of St. Benedict B
College of St. Catherine: St. Paul Campus B
Concordia College: Moorhead B
Minnesota State University, Mankato B, M
University of Minnesota
 Crookston A
 Twin Cities B

Mississippi
Alcorn State University B
University of Southern Mississippi B, M, D

Missouri
College of the Ozarks B
Northwest Missouri State University B
St. Louis University B, M
Southeast Missouri State University B
University of Missouri
 Columbia B, M

Nebraska
University of Nebraska
 Kearney B
 Lincoln B, M
 Omaha B
Wayne State College B

Nevada
University of Nevada
 Reno B, M

New Hampshire
University of New Hampshire B

New Jersey
College of St. Elizabeth B, M

New Mexico
New Mexico State University B
University of New Mexico B, M

288

New York
Adirondack Community College *C, A*
City University of New York
　Brooklyn College *B, M*
　Hunter College *B, M*
　Lehman College *B, M*
Cornell University *B, M, D*
D'Youville College *B, M*
Fulton-Montgomery Community
　College *C, A*
Long Island University
　C. W. Post Campus *B*
Marymount College *B*
New York University *B, M, D*
Rockland Community College *A*
State University of New York
　Buffalo *M*
　College at Buffalo *B*
　College at Oneonta *B*
　College at Plattsburgh *B*
　College of Agriculture and
　　Technology at Cobleskill *A*
　College of Agriculture and
　　Technology at Morrisville *A*
　Farmingdale *A*
Suffolk County Community College *A*
Syracuse University *B, M, D*
Westchester Community College *A*

North Carolina
Appalachian State University *B*
Bennett College *B*
Campbell University *B*
Central Piedmont Community College *A*
East Carolina University *B, M*
Meredith College *B*
North Carolina Agricultural and
　Technical State University *B, M*
North Carolina Central University *B*
University of North Carolina
　Chapel Hill *B*
　Greensboro *B, M, D*

North Dakota
North Dakota State University *B, M*

Ohio
Ashland University *B*
Bluffton College *B*
Bowling Green State University *B, M*
Case Western Reserve
　University *B, M, D*
Kent State University *B, M*
Miami University
　Oxford Campus *B, M*
Ohio State University
　Columbus Campus *B, M, D*
Ohio University *B, M*
Sinclair Community College *A*
University of Akron *B*
University of Cincinnati *B, M*
University of Dayton *B*
Youngstown State University *A, B*

Oklahoma
Langston University *B*
Northeastern State University *B*
Oklahoma State University *B, M, D*
University of Central Oklahoma *B, M*

Oregon
George Fox University *B*
Oregon State University *B, M, D*

Pennsylvania
Butler County Community College *A*
Cheyney University of Pennsylvania *B*
Delaware Valley College *B*
Edinboro University of Pennsylvania *B*
Harrisburg Area Community College *A*
Immaculata College *B, M, T*
Indiana University of Pennsylvania *B, M*
Mercyhurst College *B*
Penn State
　University Park *C, B, M, D*
Seton Hill College *B*

Puerto Rico
University of Puerto Rico
　Rio Piedras Campus *B*

Rhode Island
University of Rhode Island *B, M, D*

South Carolina
South Carolina State University *B*
Winthrop University *B, M*

South Dakota
Mount Marty College *B*
South Dakota State University *B*

Tennessee
Carson-Newman College *B*
David Lipscomb University *B*
East Tennessee State University *M*
Hiwassee College *A*
Lambuth University *B*
Middle Tennessee State University *B*
Shelby State Community College *A*
Tennessee State University *B*
Tennessee Technological University *B*
University of Memphis *M*
University of Tennessee
　Knoxville *B, M*

Texas
Baylor University *B*
Lamar University *B*
Palo Alto College *C, A*
Prairie View A&M University *B*
Sam Houston State University *B*
Southwest Texas State University *B*
Stephen F. Austin State University *B*
Texas A&M University
　Kingsville *B*
Texas Christian University *B*
Texas Southern University *M*
Texas State Technical College
　Harlingen *C, A*
Texas Tech University *B, M, D*
Texas Woman's University *B, M*
University of Houston *B*
University of Texas
　Austin *B, M*

Utah
Brigham Young University *B, M*
Dixie State College of Utah *A*
Snow College *A*
University of Utah *M*
Utah State University *B, M, D*

Vermont
University of Vermont *B, M*

Virginia
Radford University *B*
Virginia Polytechnic Institute and State
　University *B, M, D*

Washington
Central Washington University *B*
Highline Community College *A*
Seattle Pacific University *B, T*
Shoreline Community College *A*
South Seattle Community College *A*
Washington State University *B*

West Virginia
Fairmont State College *A*
Marshall University *B*

Wisconsin
Madison Area Technical College *A*
Northeast Wisconsin Technical
　College *C*
University of Wisconsin
　Madison *B, M, D*
　Stevens Point *M*
　Stout *B, M*
Viterbo University *B*

Wyoming
University of Wyoming *B*

Foreign language/translation

Arizona
Pima Community College *C*

California
College of the Canyons *A*

Florida
Gulf Coast Community College *A*
University of Central Florida *B*

Georgia
East Georgia College *A*

Michigan
Western Michigan University *B*

Missouri
Central Methodist College *B*
Missouri Southern State College *B*

Nebraska
University of Nebraska
　Kearney *B*

New Jersey
Union County College *C*

New York
Bard College *B*
City University of New York
　Brooklyn College *B*

Ohio
Kent State University
　Stark Campus *B*
Walsh University *B*
Wittenberg University *B*

Oklahoma
Oklahoma City Community College *A*

Oregon
Lewis & Clark College *B*

Pennsylvania
University of Pittsburgh *C*

Puerto Rico
University of Puerto Rico
　Rio Piedras Campus *M*

South Carolina
College of Charleston *M*

Utah
Brigham Young University *B*
Dixie State College of Utah *A*

Vermont
Bennington College *B*
Marlboro College *B*

Virginia
Shenandoah University *C*

Washington
Western Washington University *B*

Wisconsin
University of Wisconsin
　Madison *B, M, D*

Foreign languages education

Alabama
Auburn University *B*
Birmingham-Southern College *T*
University of Alabama *B*
University of Mobile *B, T*

Alaska
University of Alaska
　Fairbanks *C, A, B*

Arizona
Arizona State University *B, T*
Northern Arizona University *T*
Prescott College *B, M*
University of Arizona *B, M*

Arkansas
Arkansas Tech University *B*
Harding University *B, M, T*
Ouachita Baptist University *B, T*
Southern Arkansas University *B, T*
University of Arkansas *B*
University of Central Arkansas *M, T*

California
Azusa Pacific University *T*
California Baptist University *B, T*
California Lutheran University *B, T*
California State University
　Bakersfield *B, T*
　Chico *M*
　Long Beach *T*
　Northridge *B, T*
　Sacramento *T*
Humboldt State University *T*
Los Angeles Southwest College *A*
Mount St. Mary's College *T*
Occidental College *T*
San Francisco State University *B, T*
Sonoma State University *T*
University of the Pacific *T*

Colorado
Colorado State University *T*
Metropolitan State College of Denver *T*
University of Colorado
　Boulder *T*
University of Denver *B*
University of Southern Colorado *T*

Connecticut
Central Connecticut State
　University *B, M*
Fairfield University *T*
Quinnipiac University *B, M*

Delaware
Delaware State University *B*
University of Delaware *B, T*

District of Columbia
George Washington University *M, T*

Florida
Bethune-Cookman College *B, T*
Flagler College *B*
Florida International University *B, M, T*
Florida State University *B, M, D, T*
Stetson University *B, T*
University of Central Florida *B*
University of Florida *M*
University of South Florida *B, M*

Georgia
Agnes Scott College *T*
Berry College *T*
Fort Valley State University *B, T*
Georgia Southwestern State
　University *B, M, T*
Kennesaw State University *B*
Mercer University *T*
North Georgia College & State
　University *M*
State University of West Georgia *B, M*
University of Georgia *B, M*

Hawaii
University of Hawaii
　Manoa *B, T*

Idaho
University of Idaho *M*

Illinois
Augustana College *B, T*
Kishwaukee College *A*
North Park University *T*
Northwestern University *B, T*
Rockford College *T*
University of Illinois
　Chicago *B*
　Urbana-Champaign *B, M, T*

Indiana
Ball State University T
Butler University T
Goshen College B
Grace College B
Indiana State University B, M, T
Indiana University
    South Bend B, T
Indiana University--Purdue University
    Indiana University-Purdue
        University Fort Wayne T
Manchester College B, T
St. Mary-of-the-Woods College B
University of Evansville T
University of Indianapolis B, T
University of Southern Indiana B, T
Vincennes University A

Iowa
Clarke College B, T
Dordt College B
Drake University M
Graceland University T
Iowa State University T
Luther College B
Morningside College B
St. Ambrose University B, T
University of Iowa B, M, T

Kansas
Benedictine College T
Bethel College T
Emporia State University B
McPherson College B, T
MidAmerica Nazarene University B, T
Pittsburg State University B, T
Southwestern College B, T
University of Kansas B, T
Washburn University of Topeka B

Kentucky
Murray State University B, M, T
Transylvania University B, T
University of Louisville M
Western Kentucky University M

Louisiana
Centenary College of Louisiana B, T
Dillard University B
McNeese State University T
Nicholls State University B
University of Louisiana at Monroe B
University of New Orleans B

Maine
University of Maine
    Presque Isle B
University of Southern Maine T

Maryland
College of Notre Dame of Maryland T
University of Maryland
    College Park B, T

Massachusetts
Assumption College T
Boston University M, T
Framingham State College T
Northeastern University B
Tufts University M, T
University of Massachusetts
    Dartmouth T
Westfield State College T

Michigan
Albion College B, T
Andrews University M, T
Lansing Community College A
Northern Michigan University B, T
University of Michigan
    Dearborn B
Wayne State University M, T

Minnesota
Bethel College B
College of St. Benedict T
College of St. Catherine: St. Paul
    Campus B
Gustavus Adolphus College T
Minnesota State University,
    Mankato B, M, T
St. John's University T
St. Mary's University of Minnesota B
St. Olaf College T
University of Minnesota
    Morris T
    Twin Cities M
Winona State University B, T

Mississippi
Blue Mountain College B
Delta State University T
Mississippi State University T
University of Mississippi B, T
University of Southern Mississippi M

Missouri
Central Methodist College B
Central Missouri State University B, T
College of the Ozarks B, T
Evangel University B
Missouri Southern State College B, T
Rockhurst University B
Southeast Missouri State University B
Southwest Missouri State University B
Truman State University M, T
University of Missouri
    Columbia B
William Jewell College T

Montana
Montana State University
    Billings B, T
University of Montana-Missoula T

Nebraska
Creighton University T
Dana College B
Doane College T
Hastings College B, M, T
Union College T
University of Nebraska
    Kearney B, M, T
    Lincoln B, T

Nevada
University of Nevada
    Reno B

New Hampshire
Franklin Pierce College T
Keene State College T
Rivier College B, M, T
University of New Hampshire T

New Jersey
Caldwell College T
Monmouth University B, T
Richard Stockton College of New
    Jersey B
Rider University B, T
Rowan University T
Rutgers
    The State University of New Jersey:
        Douglass College T
    The State University of New Jersey:
        Livingston College T
    The State University of New Jersey:
        New Brunswick Graduate
        Campus M, D, T
    The State University of New Jersey:
        Rutgers College T
    The State University of New Jersey:
        University College New
        Brunswick T
    The State University of New Jersey:
        University College Newark T
St. Peter's College T
The College of New Jersey B, T

New Mexico
New Mexico Highlands University B

New York
Adelphi University B, M
Canisius College B, M, T
City University of New York
    Brooklyn College B, M
    City College B, T
    College of Staten Island T
    Hunter College B, M
    Lehman College M
    Queens College M, T
College of Mount St. Vincent T
Columbia University
    Teachers College M, D
D'Youville College M, T
Dowling College B
Elmira College B, T
Fordham University T
Houghton College B, T
Ithaca College B, T
Le Moyne College T
Long Island University
    C. W. Post Campus B, T
Manhattan College B, T
Manhattanville College M, T
Nazareth College of Rochester T
New York University B, M, T
Pace University:
    Pleasantville/Briarcliff B, M, T
Pace University B, M, T
St. Bonaventure University T
St. John Fisher College B
St. John's University B, T
St. Thomas Aquinas College B, T
State University of New York
    Albany B, M, T
    Buffalo M, D, T
    College at Buffalo B, T
    College at Cortland B, M, T
    College at Fredonia B, T
    College at Old Westbury B, T
    College at Oneonta B, T
    New Paltz B, M, T
University of Rochester M
Vassar College T
Wells College T

North Carolina
Appalachian State University B, M, T
Barton College T
Davidson College T
Gardner-Webb University B
Lenoir-Rhyne College B, T
Meredith College T
Methodist College A, B, T
North Carolina Agricultural and
    Technical State University B, T
North Carolina Central University B
North Carolina State University T
University of North Carolina
    Greensboro B, M, T

North Dakota
Dickinson State University B, T
Minot State University B
University of North Dakota B, T

Ohio
Bowling Green State University B
Hiram College T
Kent State University
    East Liverpool Regional Campus A
    Stark Campus B
Kent State University T
Mount Union College T
Ohio University B, T
Otterbein College B
University of Dayton B, M, T
University of Toledo B, T
Walsh University B
Wilmington College B
Wittenberg University B
Wright State University B, T
Youngstown State University B, M, T

Oklahoma
Oklahoma Baptist University B, T
Oklahoma City University B
Oral Roberts University B, T
Southeastern Oklahoma State
    University B, T
University of Central Oklahoma B
University of Oklahoma B, T
University of Tulsa T

Oregon
Linfield College T
University of Oregon M, T
University of Portland T
Western Oregon University T

Pennsylvania
Chatham College M, T
Clarion University of Pennsylvania B, T
Dickinson College T
Duquesne University T
East Stroudsburg University of
    Pennsylvania B, T
Gannon University T
Immaculata College T
Juniata College B, T
King's College T
La Salle University B, T
Lincoln University B, T
Lock Haven University of
    Pennsylvania B, T
Lycoming College T
Mansfield University of
    Pennsylvania B, T
Millersville University of
    Pennsylvania B, M, T
Moravian College T
St. Joseph's University B
St. Vincent College T
Seton Hill College B, T
Temple University B, M, T
Thiel College B
University of Pennsylvania M
Ursinus College B
Washington and Jefferson College T
West Chester University of
    Pennsylvania B, M, T
Westminster College B, T
Widener University M

Rhode Island
Providence College B
Rhode Island College B, M

South Carolina
Charleston Southern University B
Columbia College B
Converse College T
Erskine College B, T
Furman University T

South Dakota
Northern State University B, T
University of South Dakota B, T

Tennessee
Lee University B
Maryville College B, T
Middle Tennessee State University M, T
Union University B, T
University of Tennessee
    Chattanooga B, T
    Knoxville T

Texas
Abilene Christian University B, T
Baylor University B, T
Del Mar College A
Houston Baptist University T
Lamar University T
Lubbock Christian University B
Texas Christian University T
Texas Lutheran University T
University of Houston M, T
University of Texas
    Austin M, D
West Texas A&M University T

Utah
Brigham Young University B, M
Southern Utah University B

Vermont
Castleton State College *B, T*
St. Michael's College *B*
University of Vermont *B, M, T*

Virginia
Christopher Newport University *T*
Eastern Mennonite University *T*
Longwood College *T*
Radford University *T*
University of Virginia's College at Wise *T*
Virginia Wesleyan College *T*

Washington
Central Washington University *B*
Pacific Lutheran University *T*
Western Washington University *B, T*
Whitworth College *B, T*

West Virginia
Wheeling Jesuit University *T*

Wisconsin
Cardinal Stritch University *B, T*
Carthage College *M, T*
Lawrence University *T*
Mount Mary College *B, T*
University of Wisconsin
    Madison *T*
Viterbo University *B, T*

Foreign languages/literatures

Alabama
Auburn University at Montgomery *B*
Community College of the Air Force *A*
University of North Alabama *B*

Alaska
University of Alaska
    Anchorage *B*
    Fairbanks *B*

Arizona
Cochise College *A*
Eastern Arizona College *A*
University of Arizona *B*

Arkansas
Arkansas Tech University *B*
Westark College *A*

California
Cabrillo College *A*
California Lutheran University *B*
California State University
    Monterey Bay *B*
College of the Sequoias *A*
Crafton Hills College *A*
Diablo Valley College *A*
Fresno City College *A*
Glendale Community College *A*
Golden West College *A*
Imperial Valley College *A*
Kings River Community College *A*
Long Beach City College *C, A*
Los Angeles Southwest College *A*
MiraCosta College *A*
Modesto Junior College *A*
Monterey Peninsula College *A*
Pitzer College *B*
Pomona College *B*
Saddleback College *A*
St. Mary's College of California *B*
San Diego City College *A*
San Diego Mesa College *A*
Santa Ana College *A*
Santa Monica College *A*
Scripps College *B*
Solano Community College *A*
University of California
    Los Angeles *M, D*
    Riverside *B*
    San Diego *B*
University of the Pacific *B*
West Valley College *A*
Whittier College *B*

Colorado
Colorado State University *M*
Fort Lewis College *B*
Metropolitan State College of Denver *B, T*
University of Northern Colorado *M, T*
University of Southern Colorado *B*

Connecticut
Central Connecticut State University *B*
Southern Connecticut State University *B, M*
Trinity College *B*
University of Hartford *B*

Delaware
University of Delaware *B, M*

District of Columbia
George Washington University *B*
Howard University *M*

Florida
Bethune-Cookman College *B*
Broward Community College *A*
Eckerd College *B*
Gulf Coast Community College *A*
Indian River Community College *A*
Miami-Dade Community College *A*
New College of the University of South Florida *B*
Polk Community College *A*
Rollins College *B*
South Florida Community College *A*
Stetson University *B*
University of Miami *M, D*
University of Tampa *A*

Georgia
Atlanta Metropolitan College *A*
Clark Atlanta University *B, M*
Georgia Perimeter College *A*
Mercer University *T*
North Georgia College & State University *B, M*
Oxford College of Emory University *B*
South Georgia College *A*
University of Georgia *B, M, D*
Young Harris College *A*

Hawaii
University of Hawaii
    Manoa *B, D*

Idaho
College of Southern Idaho *A*
Idaho State University *A*
North Idaho College *A*
Northwest Nazarene University *B*
University of Idaho *B*

Illinois
City Colleges of Chicago
    Harold Washington College *A*
    Kennedy-King College *A*
    Olive-Harvey College *A*
De Paul University *T*
Eastern Illinois University *B, T*
Greenville College *B*
Illinois State University *M*
Kishwaukee College *A*
Knox College *B*
Lincoln Land Community College *A*
Northwestern University *B, T*
Olivet Nazarene University *B*
Principia College *B*
Rend Lake College *A*
Rockford College *B*
Roosevelt University *B, M*
Sauk Valley Community College *A*
Southern Illinois University
    Carbondale *B, M*
    Edwardsville *B*
Southwestern Illinois College *A*
Triton College *A*

Indiana
Goshen College *B*
Grace College *B*
Indiana State University *M*
Indiana University
    Bloomington *B, M, D*
Manchester College *B, T*
Purdue University
    Calumet *B*
Purdue University *B, M, D*
University of Evansville *B*
Vincennes University *A*

Iowa
Cornell College *B*
Graceland University *B*
St. Ambrose University *B*

Kansas
Barton County Community College *A*
Butler County Community College *A*
Coffeyville Community College *A*
Cowley County Community College *A*
Emporia State University *B, T*
Fort Hays State University *B*
Hutchinson Community College *A*
Independence Community College *A*
Kansas City Kansas Community College *A*
Kansas State University *B, M*
Kansas Wesleyan University *B*
McPherson College *B, T*
MidAmerica Nazarene University *B*
Seward County Community College *A*
Southwestern College *B*

Kentucky
Bellarmine College *B*
Murray State University *B, M*

Louisiana
Centenary College of Louisiana *B, T*

Maine
University of Maine
    Fort Kent *B*
University of Maine *B*
University of Southern Maine *B*

Maryland
Frostburg State University *B*
Mount St. Mary's College *B*
St. Mary's College of Maryland *B*
University of Maryland
    Baltimore County *B*

Massachusetts
Assumption College *B*
Boston University *B*
Brandeis University *M, D*
Cape Cod Community College *A*
Clark University *B*
Elms College *B*
Gordon College *B*
Harvard College *B*
Massachusetts Institute of Technology *B*
Merrimack College *B*
Northeastern University *B*
Simon's Rock College of Bard *B*
Stonehill College *B*
Suffolk University *B*
Tufts University *B, M*
University of Massachusetts
    Lowell *B*
Wellesley College *B*

Michigan
Albion College *T*
Lake Michigan College *A*
Lansing Community College *A*
Northern Michigan University *T*
Oakland University *B*
Wayne State University *D*
Western Michigan University *B, T*

Minnesota
Minnesota State University, Mankato *B*
Moorhead State University *B*
Northland Community & Technical College *A*
St. Olaf College *B, T*
University of Minnesota
    Morris *B*
    Twin Cities *B*
Winona State University *B*

Mississippi
Delta State University *B*
Mississippi College *B*
Mississippi State University *B, M*
University of Southern Mississippi *B*

Missouri
Central Methodist College *B*
Mineral Area College *A*
Three Rivers Community College *A*
University of Missouri
    Columbia *D*
    Kansas City *M*
Washington University *B, M, D*
Webster University *B*

Montana
Miles Community College *A*
Montana State University
    Bozeman *B*
University of Montana-Missoula *B*

Nebraska
Hastings College *B*
University of Nebraska
    Lincoln *M, D*

Nevada
University of Nevada
    Las Vegas *M*
    Reno *M*

New Jersey
Monmouth University *B*
Richard Stockton College of New Jersey *B*
Rowan University *B*
St. Peter's College *B*
Seton Hall University *B*
Thomas Edison State College *B*

New Mexico
New Mexico State University *B*
San Juan College *A*
University of New Mexico *B*

New York
Adelphi University *B*
Alfred University *B*
Bard College *B*
City University of New York
    Hunter College *B*
College of Mount St. Vincent *M*
Cornell University *B*
Elmira College *B*
Eugene Lang College/New School University *B*
Hamilton College *B*
Iona College *B, M*
Ithaca College *B*
Jewish Theological Seminary of America *B, M, D*
Long Island University
    Brooklyn Campus *B*
Manhattanville College *B*
New York University *B, M, D*
Orange County Community College *A*
Regents College *B*
St. Lawrence University *B, T*
St. Thomas Aquinas College *B, T*
Sarah Lawrence College *B*
St. Joseph's College
    St. Joseph's College *B, T*
State University of New York
    College at Brockport *B*
    Purchase *B*
    Stony Brook *D*
Syracuse University *B, D*
Touro College *B*
Union College *B*

University of Rochester *B*
Wells College *B*

North Carolina
Elon College *B*
Gardner-Webb University *B*
High Point University *B*
Winston-Salem State University *B*

North Dakota
Minot State University *T*
University of North Dakota *B*

Ohio
Antioch College *B*
College of Wooster *B*
Kent State University
  Stark Campus *B*
Kent State University *B, M*
Kenyon College *B*
Lake Erie College *B*
University of Dayton *B*
Wright State University *B*
Youngstown State University *B*

Oklahoma
Oklahoma Baptist University *B, T*
Western Oklahoma State College *A*

Oregon
Central Oregon Community College *A*
Chemeketa Community College *A*
Lewis & Clark College *B*
Pacific University *B*
Portland State University *B, M*
Southern Oregon University *B*
University of Oregon *B, M, D*

Pennsylvania
California University of Pennsylvania *B*
Carnegie Mellon University *D*
Cedar Crest College *B*
Community College of Allegheny
  County *A*
Duquesne University *B*
Edinboro University of Pennsylvania *B*
Gannon University *B*
Immaculata College *B*
Juniata College *B*
La Salle University *B, T*
Lebanon Valley College of
  Pennsylvania *B, T*
Mercyhurst College *B*
Rosemont College *B*
Seton Hill College *C, B, T*
University of Pennsylvania *M, D*
Westminster College *B*
Wilson College *B*
York College of Pennsylvania *A*

Puerto Rico
University of Puerto Rico
  Rio Piedras Campus *B*

South Carolina
Converse College *B*
Newberry College *B*
Winthrop University *B*

South Dakota
Augustana College *B*

Tennessee
Austin Peay State University *B*
East Tennessee State University *B, T*
King College *B*
Lambuth University *B*
Lee University *B*
Middle Tennessee State University *B*
Southern Adventist University *B*
University of Memphis *B*
University of Tennessee
  Knoxville *M, D*
Vanderbilt University *B, M, D*

Texas
Blinn College *A*
Brazosport College *A*
Central Texas College *A*
Del Mar College *A*
El Paso Community College *A*
Hill College *A*
Howard College *A*
Lee College *A*
Midland College *A*
Odessa College *A*
Palo Alto College *A*
Panola College *A*
Paris Junior College *A*
San Jacinto College
  North *A*
Southern Methodist University *B*
Texas A&M University *M*
Texas Tech University *M*
Western Texas College *A*

Utah
Brigham Young University *B*
Snow College *A*
Southern Utah University *B, T*
University of Utah *M, D*

Vermont
Castleton State College *B*
Marlboro College *B*
St. Michael's College *B*

Virginia
George Mason University *B, M*
James Madison University *B, T*
Old Dominion University *B*
Radford University *B*
Sweet Briar College *B*
University of Virginia's College at
  Wise *B*
Virginia Commonwealth University *B*
Virginia Military Institute *B*
Virginia Polytechnic Institute and State
  University *B*
Virginia Wesleyan College *B*

Washington
Everett Community College *A*
Evergreen State College *B*
Highline Community College *A*
Washington State University *B, M*
Whitworth College *B, T*

West Virginia
Davis and Elkins College *B*
Marshall University *B*
West Virginia University *B, M, T*

Wisconsin
Beloit College *B*
Carthage College *B*
Ripon College *B, T*
University of Wisconsin
  Milwaukee *M*
Viterbo University *B*

Wyoming
Casper College *A*
Eastern Wyoming College *A*
Northwest College *A*
Western Wyoming Community
  College *A*

Forensic technologies

Alabama
University of Alabama
  Birmingham *M*

Arizona
Scottsdale Community College *C*

California
Moorpark College *C, A*
National University *M*

Connecticut
Tunxis Community College *C*
University of New Haven *B, M*

District of Columbia
George Washington University *M*

Florida
Florida International University *M*
St. Petersburg Junior College *C, A*
Santa Fe Community College *A*
University of Central Florida *B*

Illinois
University of Illinois
  Chicago *M*

Indiana
Indiana University
  Bloomington *M*

Iowa
Iowa Western Community College *C, A*

Kentucky
Eastern Kentucky University *B*

Massachusetts
Massachusetts Bay Community
  College *A*

Michigan
Michigan State University *B*
Oakland Community College *C, A*

Minnesota
Hamline University *C*

Mississippi
University of Mississippi *B*

Missouri
College of the Ozarks *B*

New Mexico
New Mexico State University
  Alamogordo *A*

New York
City University of New York
  John Jay College of Criminal
    Justice *B, M*
Herkimer County Community College *A*
Hudson Valley Community College *A*
State University of New York
  College at Buffalo *B*
Tompkins-Cortland Community
  College *A*

Oklahoma
University of Central Oklahoma *B*

Pennsylvania
York College of Pennsylvania *A*

Puerto Rico
University of Puerto Rico
  Ponce University College *B*

Texas
Baylor University *B*

Virginia
New River Community College *A*

Washington
Bellevue Community College *C*

West Virginia
Marshall University *M*
Southern West Virginia Community and
  Technical College *C, A*

Forest production/processing

Alabama
Alabama Agricultural and Mechanical
  University *B*
Lurleen B. Wallace Junior College *A*
Northwest-Shoals Community College *C*

Florida
Pensacola Junior College *A*

Idaho
University of Idaho *M, D*

Iowa
Iowa State University *B, M, D*

Maine
University of Maine *B*

Maryland
Allegany College *C*

Michigan
Michigan State University *M, D*
Michigan Technological University *C*

Minnesota
University of Minnesota
  Twin Cities *B*
Vermilion Community College *A*

Mississippi
Mississippi State University *D*

New Hampshire
University of New Hampshire *A*

New York
State University of New York
  College of Environmental Science
    and Forestry *B, M, D*

North Carolina
Haywood Community College *A*
Montgomery Community College *A*
North Carolina State University *B*
Southeastern Community College *A*
Wayne Community College *A*

Ohio
Hocking Technical College *C*

Oklahoma
Northeastern Oklahoma Agricultural and
  Mechanical College *A*

Oregon
Oregon State University *B, M, D*

Pennsylvania
Penn State
  Mont Alto *A*
  University Park *C, B*
Pennsylvania College of Technology *A*

South Carolina
Orangeburg-Calhoun Technical
  College *A*

Texas
Panola College *A*

Virginia
Mountain Empire Community College *C*
Virginia Polytechnic Institute and State
  University *B, M, D*

Washington
Green River Community College *A*
Spokane Community College *A*
University of Washington *B*

Wisconsin
University of Wisconsin
  Madison *B, M, D*

Forestry

Alabama
Alabama Agricultural and Mechanical
  University *B*
Auburn University *B, M, D*
Chattahoochee Valley Community
  College *A*
James H. Faulkner State Community
  College *A*
Northeast Alabama Community
  College *A*
Northwest-Shoals Community College *C*
Samford University *B*
Tuskegee University *B*

Alaska
University of Alaska
 Fairbanks *B*

Arizona
Eastern Arizona College *A*
Northern Arizona University *B, M, D*

Arkansas
University of Arkansas
 Monticello *B, M*

California
Bakersfield College *A*
Citrus College *C*
College of the Redwoods *C, A*
College of the Siskiyous *A*
Columbia College *C, A*
Cypress College *A*
Humboldt State University *B*
Kings River Community College *A*
Modesto Junior College *C, A*
Mount San Antonio College *C, A*
Riverside Community College *A*
Sierra College *A*
University of California
 Berkeley *B, M*

Colorado
Colorado State University *B, M, D*
Front Range Community College *C*

Connecticut
Yale University *M, D*

Florida
Gulf Coast Community College *A*
Lake City Community College *A*
Miami-Dade Community College *A*
Pensacola Junior College *A*
University of Florida *B, M, D*

Georgia
Abraham Baldwin Agricultural
 College *A*
Andrew College *A*
Atlanta Metropolitan College *A*
Clayton College and State University *A*
Dalton State College *A*
Darton College *A*
Gainesville College *A*
Georgia Perimeter College *A*
University of Georgia *B, M, D*
Waycross College *C, A*
Young Harris College *A*

Idaho
College of Southern Idaho *A*
North Idaho College *A*
Ricks College *A*
University of Idaho *B, M, D*

Illinois
Joliet Junior College *C*
Shawnee Community College *A*
Southeastern Illinois College *A*
Southern Illinois University
 Carbondale *B, M*
University of Illinois
 Urbana-Champaign *B, M*

Indiana
Purdue University *B, M, D*
Vincennes University *A*

Iowa
Cornell College *B*
Iowa State University *B, M, D*
Iowa Wesleyan College *B*
Marshalltown Community College *A*

Kansas
Colby Community College *A*
Garden City Community College *A*
Hutchinson Community College *A*

Kentucky
University of Kentucky *B, M*

Louisiana
Louisiana State University and
 Agricultural and Mechanical
 College *B, M, D*
Louisiana Tech University *B*
Southern University and Agricultural and
 Mechanical College *B*
University of Louisiana at Monroe *C, A*

Maine
Unity College *B*
University of Maine
 Fort Kent *A*
University of Maine *B, M*

Maryland
Allegany College *A*

Massachusetts
Harvard University *M*
North Shore Community College *A*
University of Massachusetts
 Amherst *B, M, D*

Michigan
Michigan State University *B, M, D*
Michigan Technological
 University *A, B, M, D*
University of Michigan *M*
Western Michigan University *B*

Minnesota
Itasca Community College *A*
Rochester Community and Technical
 College *A*
University of Minnesota
 Twin Cities *B, M, D*
Vermilion Community College *A*

Mississippi
Holmes Community College *A*
Mississippi Delta Community College *A*
Mississippi Gulf Coast Community
 College
 Perkinston *A*
Mississippi State University *B, M*

Missouri
East Central College *A*
University of Missouri
 Columbia *B, M, D*

Montana
Miles Community College *A*
Salish Kootenai College *A*
University of Montana-Missoula *B, M, D*

Nebraska
University of Nebraska
 Lincoln *D*

Nevada
University of Nevada
 Reno *B*

New Hampshire
New Hampshire Community Technical
 College
 Berlin *A*
University of New Hampshire *B*

New Jersey
Rutgers
 The State University of New Jersey:
 Cook College *B*
Thomas Edison State College *A, B*

New Mexico
Northern New Mexico Community
 College *A*

New York
Fulton-Montgomery Community
 College *A*
Jamestown Community College *A*
Jefferson Community College *C*
State University of New York
 College of Environmental Science
 and Forestry *A, B, M, D*

North Carolina
Brevard College *B*
Catawba College *B*
College of the Albemarle *A*
Duke University *M, D*
Haywood Community College *A*
High Point University *B*
Lees-McRae College *B*
North Carolina State University *M, D*
Sandhills Community College *A*
Wake Forest University *B, M*

North Dakota
Minot State University: Bottineau
 Campus *C, A*
North Dakota State University *B*

Ohio
Hocking Technical College *A*
Miami University
 Oxford Campus *B, M*
Ohio State University
 Columbus Campus *B*

Oklahoma
Eastern Oklahoma State College *A*
Northeastern Oklahoma Agricultural and
 Mechanical College *A*
Oklahoma State University *B, M*

Oregon
Central Oregon Community College *A*
Chemeketa Community College *A*
Mount Hood Community College *C, A*
Oregon State University *M, D*

Pennsylvania
Albright College *B*
Franklin and Marshall College *B*
Gettysburg College *B*
Lebanon Valley College of
 Pennsylvania *B*
Muhlenberg College *B*
Penn State
 University Park *B, M, D*

South Carolina
Clemson University *B, M, D*
Horry-Georgetown Technical College *A*
Presbyterian College *B*

Tennessee
Hiwassee College *A*
University of Tennessee
 Knoxville *B, M*
University of the South *B*

Texas
Baylor University *B*
Panola College *C*
Stephen F. Austin State
 University *B, M, D*
Texas A&M University *B, M, D*

Utah
Dixie State College of Utah *A*
Snow College *A*
Utah State University *B, M, D*

Vermont
Sterling College *A*
University of Vermont *B, M*

Virginia
Dabney S. Lancaster Community
 College *A*
Virginia Polytechnic Institute and State
 University *B*
Washington and Lee University *B*

Washington
Centralia College *A*
Heritage College *C, A*
Highline Community College *A*
Spokane Community College *A*
University of Washington *B, M, D*
Washington State University *B*

West Virginia
Glenville State College *A*
Marshall University *B*
Potomac State College of West Virginia
 University *A*
West Virginia University *B, M, D*

Wisconsin
Beloit College *B*
Northland College *B*
University of Wisconsin
 Oshkosh *B*
 Stevens Point *B*

Wyoming
Casper College *A*
Northwest College *A*

French

Alabama
Alabama State University *B*
Auburn University *B, M*
Birmingham-Southern College *B, T*
Jacksonville State University *B*
Oakwood College *B*
Samford University *B*
Spring Hill College *T*
University of Alabama
 Birmingham *B*
 Huntsville *B*
University of Alabama *B, M*
University of Montevallo *B*
University of South Alabama *B*

Arizona
Arizona State University *B, M*
Northern Arizona University *B, T*
University of Arizona *B, M, D*

Arkansas
Arkansas State University *B*
Harding University *B*
Hendrix College *B*
Ouachita Baptist University *B*
University of Arkansas
 Little Rock *B*
University of Arkansas *B, M*
University of Central Arkansas *B*

California
Cabrillo College *A*
California Lutheran University *B*
California State University
 Chico *B*
 Dominguez Hills *B*
 Fresno *B*
 Fullerton *B, M*
 Hayward *B*
 Long Beach *B, M*
 Los Angeles *B, M*
 Northridge *B*
 Sacramento *B, M*
 Stanislaus *B*
Canada College *A*
Cerritos Community College *A*
Chabot College *A*
Chaffey Community College *A*
Chapman University *B*
Citrus College *A*
Claremont McKenna College *B*
College of Notre Dame *B*
College of San Mateo *A*
College of the Desert *A*
College of the Siskiyous *A*
Compton Community College *A*
Crafton Hills College *A*
Cypress College *A*
De Anza College *A*
East Los Angeles College *C*
Foothill College *A*
Glendale Community College *A*
Golden West College *A*
Grossmont Community College *C, A*
Humboldt State University *B*
Imperial Valley College *A*
Irvine Valley College *A*
Long Beach City College *C, A*

Los Angeles Southwest College A
Los Angeles Valley College A
Loyola Marymount University B
Mendocino College A
Merced College A
Merritt College A
Mills College B
MiraCosta College A
Modesto Junior College A
Monterey Institute of International
  Studies C
Mount St. Mary's College B
Occidental College B
Ohlone College A
Orange Coast College A
Pacific Union College B
Pepperdine University B
Pitzer College B
Pomona College B
Riverside Community College A
St. Mary's College of California B
San Diego City College A
San Diego Mesa College A
San Diego Miramar College A
San Diego State University B, M
San Francisco State University B, M
San Joaquin Delta College A
San Jose State University B, M
Santa Barbara City College A
Santa Clara University B
Santa Monica College A
Scripps College B
Solano Community College A
Sonoma State University B
Southwestern College A
Stanford University B, M, D
University of California
  Berkeley B, M, D
  Davis B, M, D
  Irvine B, M, D
  Los Angeles B, M, D
  Riverside B, M, D
  San Diego B, M
  Santa Barbara B, M, D
  Santa Cruz B, D
University of La Verne B
University of Redlands B
University of San Diego B
University of San Francisco B
University of Southern
  California B, M, D
University of the Pacific B
Ventura College A
West Los Angeles College C, A
Westmont College B
Whittier College B

Colorado
Colorado College B
Colorado State University B
Red Rocks Community College A
Regis University B
University of Colorado
  Boulder B, M, D
  Denver B
University of Denver B, M
University of Northern Colorado B, T
Western State College of Colorado B

Connecticut
Albertus Magnus College B
Central Connecticut State
  University B, M
Connecticut College B, M
Fairfield University B
Sacred Heart University C, A
St. Joseph College B, T
Southern Connecticut State University B
Trinity College B
University of Connecticut B, M, D
University of Hartford B
Wesleyan University B
Yale University B, M, D

Delaware
Delaware State University B

University of Delaware B, M, T

District of Columbia
American University B, M
Catholic University of
  America B, M, D, T
Gallaudet University B
George Washington University B
Georgetown University B
Howard University B, M, D
Trinity College B
University of the District of Columbia B

Florida
Barry University B
Eckerd College B
Florida Agricultural and Mechanical
  University B
Florida Atlantic University B, M
Florida International University B
Florida State University B, M, D
Jacksonville University B
Manatee Community College A
Miami-Dade Community College A
New College of the University of South
  Florida B
Rollins College B
Stetson University B
University of Central Florida B
University of Florida B, M
University of Miami B
University of South Florida B, M

Georgia
Agnes Scott College B
Albany State University B
Augusta State University B
Berry College B, T
Clark Atlanta University B
Clayton College and State University A
Columbus State University B
Emory University B, D
Georgia College and State
  University B, T
Georgia Southern University B
Georgia Southwestern State University B
Georgia State University B, M
Kennesaw State University B
Mercer University B
Morehouse College B
Morris Brown College B
North Georgia College & State
  University B
Oxford College of Emory University B
Shorter College B, T
South Georgia College A
Spelman College B
State University of West Georgia B
University of Georgia B, M
Valdosta State University B
Young Harris College A

Hawaii
University of Hawaii
  Manoa B, M

Idaho
Boise State University B
Idaho State University A, B
Ricks College A
University of Idaho B, M

Illinois
Augustana College B, T
Bradley University B, T
City Colleges of Chicago
  Harold Washington College A
De Paul University B
Dominican University B
Elmhurst College B, T
Greenville College B
Illinois College B
Illinois State University B, T
Illinois Wesleyan University B
Kishwaukee College A
Knox College B
Lake Forest College B

Loyola University of Chicago B
MacMurray College B
Millikin University B, T
Monmouth College B, T
North Central College B, T
North Park University B
Northeastern Illinois University B
Northern Illinois University B, M, T
Northwestern University B, M, D
Olivet Nazarene University B, T
Parkland College A
Principia College B, T
Rend Lake College A
Richland Community College A
Rockford College B
St. Xavier University B
Southern Illinois University
  Carbondale B
Springfield College in Illinois A
Triton College A
University of Chicago B
University of Illinois
  Chicago B, M
  Urbana-Champaign B, M, D
Western Illinois University B
Wheaton College B

Indiana
Anderson University B
Ball State University B, T
Butler University B
DePauw University B
Earlham College B
Franklin College B
Goshen College B
Grace College B
Hanover College B
Indiana State University B, M
Indiana University
  Bloomington B, M, D
  Northwest
    South Bend A, B
    Southeast B
Indiana University--Purdue University
  Indiana University-Purdue
    University Fort Wayne A, B
  Indiana University-Purdue
    University Indianapolis B
Manchester College B, T
Marian College B, T
Purdue University
  Calumet B
Saint Mary's College B, T
St. Mary-of-the-Woods College B
Taylor University B
University of Evansville B
University of Indianapolis B
University of Notre Dame B, M
University of Southern Indiana B
Valparaiso University B, T
Vincennes University A
Wabash College B

Iowa
Central College B, T
Clarke College B, T
Coe College B
Cornell College B, T
Drake University B
Grinnell College B
Iowa State University B
Loras College B
Luther College B
Maharishi University of Management A
Morningside College B
St. Ambrose University B, T
Simpson College B
University of Iowa B, M, D, T
University of Northern Iowa B, M
Wartburg College B, T

Kansas
Baker University B, T
Benedictine College B, T
Butler County Community College A
Independence Community College A

Pittsburg State University B, T
Pratt Community College A
Southwestern College B
University of Kansas B, M, D
Washburn University of Topeka B
Wichita State University B

Kentucky
Asbury College B, T
Berea College B, T
Centre College B
Eastern Kentucky University B
Georgetown College B, T
Kentucky Wesleyan College B
Morehead State University B
Murray State University B, T
Northern Kentucky University B
Transylvania University B, T
University of Kentucky B, M
University of Louisville B
Western Kentucky University B, T

Louisiana
Centenary College of Louisiana B, T
Dillard University B
Louisiana State University
  Shreveport B
Louisiana State University and
  Agricultural and Mechanical
  College B, M, D
Louisiana Tech University B
Loyola University New Orleans B
McNeese State University B
Nicholls State University B
Southeastern Louisiana University B
Southern University
  New Orleans B
Southern University and Agricultural and
  Mechanical College B
Tulane University B, M
University of Louisiana at Lafayette M
University of Louisiana at Monroe B
University of New Orleans B
Xavier University of Louisiana B

Maine
Bates College B
Bowdoin College B
Colby College B
University of Maine
  Fort Kent B
  Presque Isle B
University of Maine B, M
University of Southern Maine B

Maryland
College of Notre Dame of Maryland B
Community College of Baltimore County
  Catonsville A
Frostburg State University T
Goucher College B
Hood College B, T
Johns Hopkins University B, D
Loyola College in Maryland B
Mount St. Mary's College B
Salisbury State University B, T
Towson University B, T
University of Maryland
  Baltimore County B
  College Park B, M, D
Washington College B, T
Western Maryland College B

Massachusetts
Amherst College B
Assumption College B
Atlantic Union College B
Boston College B, M, D
Boston University B, M, D
Brandeis University B, M, D
Bridgewater State College B
Clark University B
College of the Holy Cross B
Eastern Nazarene College B
Framingham State College B
Gordon College B
Harvard College B

Harvard University D
Mount Holyoke College B
Northeastern University B
Regis College B
Roxbury Community College A
Simmons College B, M
Smith College B
Suffolk University B
Tufts University B, M
University of Massachusetts
    Amherst B, M
    Boston B
    Dartmouth B
Wellesley College B
Wheaton College B
Williams College B

Michigan
Adrian College A, B, T
Albion College B, T
Alma College B, T
Andrews University B
Aquinas College B, T
Calvin College B, T
Central Michigan University B
Eastern Michigan University B, M
Grand Valley State University B
Hillsdale College B
Hope College B, T
Kalamazoo College B, T
Lansing Community College A
Madonna University B, T
Michigan State University B, M, D
Michigan Technological University C
Northern Michigan University B, T
Oakland University B, T
Saginaw Valley State University B
University of Michigan
    Dearborn B
    Flint B, T
University of Michigan B, M, D
Wayne State University B, M
Western Michigan University B, T

Minnesota
Augsburg College B
Bemidji State University B
Carleton College B
College of St. Benedict B
College of St. Catherine: St. Paul
    Campus B
Concordia College: Moorhead B, T
Gustavus Adolphus College B
Hamline University B
Macalester College B, T
Minnesota State University,
    Mankato B, M
St. Cloud State University B
St. John's University B
St. Mary's University of Minnesota B
St. Olaf College B, T
University of Minnesota
    Morris B
    Twin Cities B, M, D
University of St. Thomas B
Winona State University B

Mississippi
Blue Mountain College B
Millsaps College B, T
Mississippi College B
Mississippi University for Women T
University of Mississippi B, M, D

Missouri
Central Methodist College B
Central Missouri State University B, T
College of the Ozarks B
Drury University B, T
East Central College A
Lincoln University B
Lindenwood University B
Missouri Southern State College B
Missouri Western State College B, T
Northwest Missouri State University B
Rockhurst University B
St. Louis University B, M
Southeast Missouri State University B
Southwest Missouri State University B
Truman State University B
University of Missouri
    Columbia B, M
    Kansas City B
    St. Louis B
Washington University B, M, D
Webster University B
Westminster College B
William Jewell College B
William Woods University B

Montana
Carroll College B, T
Montana State University
    Bozeman T
    Northern B
Rocky Mountain College A
University of Montana-Missoula B, M

Nebraska
Creighton University B
Doane College B
Nebraska Wesleyan University B
Union College B
University of Nebraska
    Kearney B, M, T
    Lincoln B
    Omaha B

Nevada
University of Nevada
    Las Vegas B
    Reno B

New Hampshire
Dartmouth College B
Keene State College B
Plymouth State College of the University
    System of New Hampshire B
Rivier College B, M, T
St. Anselm College C, B
University of New Hampshire B

New Jersey
Bloomfield College B
Caldwell College B
College of St. Elizabeth B, T
Drew University B
Fairleigh Dickinson University B
Georgian Court College B, T
Montclair State University B, M, T
Richard Stockton College of New
    Jersey B
Rider University B
Rutgers
    The State University of New Jersey:
        Camden College of Arts and
        Sciences B, T
    The State University of New Jersey:
        Douglass College B, T
    The State University of New Jersey:
        Livingston College B, T
    The State University of New Jersey:
        New Brunswick Graduate
        Campus M, D, T
    The State University of New Jersey:
        Newark College of Arts and
        Sciences B, T
    The State University of New Jersey:
        Rutgers College B, T
    The State University of New Jersey:
        University College Camden B, T
    The State University of New Jersey:
        University College New
        Brunswick B, T
    The State University of New Jersey:
        University College Newark T
Seton Hall University B, T

New Mexico
University of New Mexico B, M, D

New York
Adelphi University B
Alfred University B
Bard College B
Barnard College B
Canisius College B
City University of New York
    Brooklyn College B, M
    City College B, T
    Graduate School and University
        Center D
    Hunter College B, M
    Lehman College B
    Queens College B, M
    York College B
Colgate University B
College of Mount St. Vincent B, T
College of New Rochelle B, T
Columbia University
    Columbia College B
    Graduate School M, D
    School of General Studies B
Cornell University B, T
Daemen College B, T
Elmira College B, T
Fordham University B, M, D
Hamilton College B
Hartwick College B, T
Hobart and William Smith Colleges B
Hofstra University B
Houghton College B
Iona College B
Ithaca College B, T
Le Moyne College B
Long Island University
    C. W. Post Campus B
Manhattan College B
Manhattanville College B
Marist College B, T
Marymount College B, T
Molloy College B
Nazareth College of Rochester B
New York University B, M, D
Niagara University B
Orange County Community College A
Pace University:
    Pleasantville/Briarcliff T
Pace University B
Russell Sage College T
St. Bonaventure University B
St. John Fisher College B
St. John's University B
St. Lawrence University B, T
St. Thomas Aquinas College B
Sarah Lawrence College B
Siena College B, T
Skidmore College B
State University of New York
    Albany B, M, D
    Binghamton B, M
    Buffalo B, M, D
    College at Brockport B, T
    College at Buffalo B
    College at Cortland B
    College at Fredonia B, T
    College at Geneseo B, T
    College at Oneonta B
    College at Plattsburgh B
    College at Potsdam B, T
    New Paltz B, T
    Oswego B
    Stony Brook B, T
Syracuse University B, M
United States Military Academy B
University of Rochester B, M
Vassar College B
Wells College B

North Carolina
Appalachian State University B
Campbell University B
Catawba College B
Davidson College B
Duke University B, M, D
East Carolina University B
Elon College B
Gardner-Webb University B
Greensboro College B
Guilford College B, T
High Point University B
Lenoir-Rhyne College B, T
Meredith College B
Methodist College A, B, T
North Carolina Agricultural and
    Technical State University B, T
North Carolina Central University B
North Carolina State University B
Queens College B
St. Augustine's College B
Salem College B
University of North Carolina
    Asheville B, T
    Chapel Hill T
    Charlotte B
    Greensboro B, T
    Wilmington B, T
Wake Forest University B
Western Carolina University B

North Dakota
Minot State University B, T
North Dakota State University B
University of North Dakota B, T

Ohio
Ashland University B
Baldwin-Wallace College B, T
Bowling Green State University B, M
Capital University B
Case Western Reserve University B, M
Cleveland State University B
College of Wooster B
Denison University B
Franciscan University of Steubenville B
Hiram College B, T
John Carroll University B
Kent State University
    Stark Campus B
Kent State University B, M
Kenyon College B
Lake Erie College B
Lourdes College A, B
Marietta College B
Miami University
    Oxford Campus B, M, T
Mount Union College B
Muskingum College B
Oberlin College B
Ohio Northern University B
Ohio State University
    Columbus Campus B, M, D
Ohio University B, M
Ohio Wesleyan University B
Otterbein College B
Owens Community College
    Toledo A
University of Akron B, M
University of Cincinnati B, M, D, T
University of Dayton B
University of Toledo B, M
Walsh University B
Wittenberg University B
Wright State University B
Xavier University A, B
Youngstown State University B

Oklahoma
Northeastern State University B
Oklahoma Baptist University B, T
Oklahoma City University B
Oklahoma State University B
Oral Roberts University B
Tulsa Community College A
University of Central Oklahoma B
University of Oklahoma B, M, D
University of Tulsa B
Western Oklahoma State College A

Oregon
Lewis & Clark College B
Linfield College B
Oregon State University B
Pacific University B
Portland State University B, M

French

Reed College B
University of Oregon B, M
University of Portland T
Western Oregon University T
Willamette University B

Pennsylvania
Albright College B, T
Allegheny College B
Bloomsburg University of
  Pennsylvania B, T
Bryn Mawr College B, M
Bucknell University B
Cabrini College B
California University of Pennsylvania B
Carnegie Mellon University B
Cedar Crest College B
Chatham College B
Chestnut Hill College A, B
Cheyney University of Pennsylvania B
Clarion University of Pennsylvania B, T
Dickinson College B
East Stroudsburg University of
  Pennsylvania B
Eastern College B
Elizabethtown College B
Franklin and Marshall College B
Gettysburg College B
Grove City College B, T
Haverford College B, T
Holy Family College B, T
Immaculata College C, A, B
Indiana University of Pennsylvania B
Juniata College B
King's College B, T
Kutztown University of
  Pennsylvania B, T
La Salle University B, T
Lafayette College B
Lebanon Valley College of
  Pennsylvania B, T
Lehigh University B
Lincoln University B
Lock Haven University of
  Pennsylvania B
Lycoming College B
Mansfield University of
  Pennsylvania B, T
Marywood University B
Mercyhurst College B
Messiah College B
Millersville University of
  Pennsylvania B, M, T
Moravian College B, T
Muhlenberg College B, T
Penn State
  University Park B, M, D
Rosemont College B
St. Francis College B
St. Joseph's University B
Seton Hill College T
Shippensburg University of
  Pennsylvania B, T
Slippery Rock University of
  Pennsylvania B
Susquehanna University B, T
Swarthmore College B
Temple University B
Thiel College B
University of Pennsylvania A, B, M
University of Pittsburgh B, M, D
University of Scranton B, T
Ursinus College B, T
Villanova University B
Washington and Jefferson College B
West Chester University of
  Pennsylvania B, M
Westminster College B
Widener University B
Wilkes University B

Puerto Rico
Pontifical Catholic University of Puerto
  Rico B

University of Puerto Rico
  Mayaguez Campus B
  Rio Piedras Campus B
University of the Sacred Heart B

Rhode Island
Brown University B, M, D
Providence College B, T
Rhode Island College B, M
Salve Regina University B
University of Rhode Island B

South Carolina
Claflin University B
Clemson University B
Coker College B
College of Charleston B, T
Columbia College B
Converse College B
Erskine College B
Francis Marion University B
Furman University B, T
Newberry College B
Presbyterian College B, T
South Carolina State University B
The Citadel B
University of South Carolina
  Spartanburg B
University of South Carolina B, M
Wofford College B, T

South Dakota
Augustana College B, T
Northern State University B
South Dakota State University B
University of South Dakota B

Tennessee
Belmont University B, T
Carson-Newman College B, T
David Lipscomb University B
Fisk University B
King College B, T
Lee University B
Milligan College B
Rhodes College B, T
Tennessee State University B
Tennessee Technological University B, T
Union University B, T
University of Tennessee
  Chattanooga B
  Knoxville B, M
  Martin B
University of the South B
Vanderbilt University B, M, D

Texas
Abilene Christian University B
Angelo State University B, T
Austin College B
Baylor University B
Blinn College A
Coastal Bend College A
Hardin-Simmons University B
Houston Baptist University B
Kilgore College A
Lamar University B
Midland College A
Paris Junior College A
Rice University B, M, D
St. Mary's University B
Sam Houston State University B
South Plains College A
Southern Methodist University B
Southwest Texas State University B, T
Southwestern University B, T
Stephen F. Austin State University B, T
Texas A&M University B
Texas Christian University B, T
Texas Tech University B, M
Trinity University B
University of Dallas B
University of Houston B, M
University of North Texas B, M
University of St. Thomas B

University of Texas
  Arlington B, M
  Austin B, M, D
  El Paso B
  San Antonio B

Utah
Brigham Young University B, M
Snow College A
Southern Utah University B
University of Utah B, M
Utah State University B
Weber State University B

Vermont
Bennington College B
Marlboro College B
Middlebury College B
St. Michael's College B
University of Vermont B, M

Virginia
Bridgewater College B
Christendom College B
Christopher Newport University B
College of William and Mary B
Eastern Mennonite University B
Emory & Henry College B, T
Ferrum College B
George Mason University B
Hampden-Sydney College B
Hollins University B
Longwood College B, T
Lynchburg College B
Mary Baldwin College B
Mary Washington College B
Norfolk State University T
Randolph-Macon College B
Randolph-Macon Woman's College B
Roanoke College B, T
Sweet Briar College B
University of Richmond B, T
University of Virginia's College at
  Wise B, T
University of Virginia B, M, D
Virginia Wesleyan College B
Washington and Lee University B

Washington
Central Washington University B
Centralia College A
Eastern Washington University B, M, T
Everett Community College A
Evergreen State College B
Gonzaga University B
Highline Community College A
Pacific Lutheran University B
Seattle Pacific University B
Seattle University B
University of Puget Sound B, T
University of Washington B
Walla Walla College B
Washington State University B
Western Washington University B, T
Whitman College B
Whitworth College B, T

West Virginia
Bethany College B
Davis and Elkins College B
Fairmont State College B
Marshall University B
Potomac State College of West Virginia
  University A
Wheeling Jesuit University B

Wisconsin
Beloit College B
Cardinal Stritch University B
Carthage College B, T
Lawrence University B
Marquette University B
Mount Mary College B, T
Ripon College B, T
St. Norbert College B, T

University of Wisconsin
  Eau Claire B
  Green Bay B
  La Crosse B
  Madison B, M, D
  Milwaukee B
  Oshkosh B
  Parkside B
  River Falls B
  Stevens Point B, T
  Whitewater B, T

Wyoming
Casper College A
University of Wyoming B, M
Western Wyoming Community
  College A

Funeral services/mortuary science

Alabama
Jefferson State Community College A

Arkansas
Arkansas State University
  Mountain Home A

California
Cypress College C, A
San Francisco College of Mortuary
  Science A

Colorado
Arapahoe Community College A

Connecticut
Briarwood College A

District of Columbia
University of the District of Columbia A

Florida
Lynn University A
Miami-Dade Community College A
St. Petersburg Junior College A

Georgia
Gupton Jones College of Funeral
  Service C, A

Illinois
Carl Sandburg College A
City Colleges of Chicago
  Malcolm X College A
Morton College A
Southern Illinois University
  Carbondale A, B

Indiana
Vincennes University A

Iowa
Marshalltown Community College A
North Iowa Area Community College A

Kansas
Kansas City Kansas Community
  College C, A

Louisiana
Delgado Community College A

Maryland
Community College of Baltimore County
  Catonsville C, A

Massachusetts
Mount Ida College A, B

Michigan
Ferris State University A
Gogebic Community College A
Schoolcraft College A
Wayne State University B

Minnesota
University of Minnesota
  Twin Cities B

Mississippi
University of Southern Mississippi *B*

Missouri
St. Louis Community College
   St. Louis Community College at Forest Park *A*

New Jersey
Hudson County Community College *A*
Mercer County Community College *C, A*

New York
American Academy McAllister Institute of Funeral Service *C, A*
City University of New York
   La Guardia Community College *A*
Fulton-Montgomery Community College *A*
Hudson Valley Community College *A*
Nassau Community College *A*
St. John's University *B*
State University of New York
   College of Technology at Canton *A*

North Carolina
Fayetteville Technical Community College *C, A*
Forsyth Technical Community College *C*

Ohio
Cincinnati College of Mortuary Science *A, B*
Xavier University *B*

Oklahoma
University of Central Oklahoma *C, B*

Oregon
Mount Hood Community College *A*

Pennsylvania
Gannon University *A, B*
Luzerne County Community College *A*
Northampton County Area Community College *A*
Pittsburgh Institute of Mortuary Science *C, A*
Point Park College *A, B*
Thiel College *B*

South Carolina
Florence-Darlington Technical College *A*
Greenville Technical College *A*

Tennessee
John A. Gupton College *C, A*

Texas
Amarillo College *A*
Commonwealth Institute of Funeral Service *C, A*
San Antonio College *A*

Virginia
John Tyler Community College *A*

Washington
Spokane Falls Community College *A*

Wisconsin
Milwaukee Area Technical College *A*

Gaming/sports officiating

Arizona
Mohave Community College *C*

California
San Francisco State University *B*

Iowa
Marshalltown Community College *A*
North Iowa Area Community College *A*

Kansas
Central Christian College *A, B*

Maine
University of Southern Maine *C*

Minnesota
Central Lakes College *C*

Texas
Southwestern Adventist University *B*

Genetics, plant/animal

Arizona
University of Arizona *M, D*

California
California Institute of Technology *D*
Stanford University *M, D*
University of California
   Berkeley *B, M, D*
   Davis *B, M, D*
   Los Angeles *M, D*
   Riverside *D*
   San Francisco *D*

Connecticut
University of Connecticut *M, D*
Yale University *M, D*

District of Columbia
George Washington University *M, D*
Howard University *M, D*

Georgia
University of Georgia *B, M, D*

Hawaii
University of Hawaii
   Manoa *M, D*

Illinois
University of Chicago *M, D*
University of Illinois
   Chicago *D*
   Urbana-Champaign *B*

Indiana
Ball State University *B*
Indiana University
   Bloomington *D*
Indiana University--Purdue University
   Indiana University-Purdue University Indianapolis *M, D*

Iowa
Iowa State University *B, M, D*
University of Iowa *D*

Kansas
Kansas State University *M, D*
University of Kansas *B, M, D*

Louisiana
Louisiana State University Medical Center *M, D*
Tulane University *M, D*

Maryland
University of Maryland
   Baltimore *M, D*

Massachusetts
Hampshire College *B*
Harvard University *M, D*
Simon's Rock College of Bard *B*
Tufts University *M, D*

Michigan
Michigan State University *D*
University of Michigan *M, D*

Minnesota
Minnesota State University, Mankato *B*
St. Cloud State University *B*
University of Minnesota
   Twin Cities *M, D*

Mississippi
Mississippi State University *M*

Missouri
University of Missouri
   Columbia *D*
Washington University *D*

New Hampshire
Dartmouth College *B*
University of New Hampshire *M, D*

New Jersey
Rutgers
   The State University of New Jersey: Camden College of Arts and Sciences *B*
   The State University of New Jersey: Cook College *B*
   The State University of New Jersey: Douglass College *B*
   The State University of New Jersey: Livingston College *B*
   The State University of New Jersey: Rutgers College *B*
   The State University of New Jersey: University College Camden *B*
   The State University of New Jersey: University College New Brunswick *B*

New York
Albany Medical College *M, D*
Cornell University *B, M, D*
Rockefeller University *D*
State University of New York
   Albany *D*
   College of Environmental Science and Forestry *B, M, D*
   Stony Brook *M, D*
University of Rochester *D*

North Carolina
North Carolina State University *M, D*
University of North Carolina
   Chapel Hill *M, D*
Wake Forest University *D*

Ohio
Case Western Reserve University *D*
Ohio State University
   Columbus Campus *B, M, D*
Ohio Wesleyan University *B*
Wittenberg University *B*

Oregon
Oregon State University *M, D*
University of Oregon *M, D*

Pennsylvania
Carnegie Mellon University *B*
Penn State
   University Park *M, D*
Thomas Jefferson University: College of Health Professions *D*
University of Pennsylvania *M, D*

South Carolina
Clemson University *B, M*

Texas
Texas A&M University *B, M, D*
University of Texas
   Medical Branch at Galveston *M, D*
   Southwestern Medical Center at Dallas *M, D*

Utah
Brigham Young University *M, D*
Dixie State College of Utah *A*

Vermont
Marlboro College *B*

Virginia
Virginia Commonwealth University *M, D*
Virginia Polytechnic Institute and State University *D*

Washington
University of Washington *M, D*
Washington State University *B, M, D*

West Virginia
West Virginia University *M, D*

Wisconsin
University of Wisconsin
   Madison *M, D*

Geochemistry

Arizona
Northern Arizona University *B*

California
California Institute of Technology *B, D*
Pomona College *B*
San Francisco State University *B*
University of California
   Los Angeles *M, D*

Colorado
Colorado School of Mines *M, D*

Florida
University of Miami *B*

Maine
Colby College *B*

Massachusetts
Bridgewater State College *B*
Hampshire College *B*
Harvard College *B*

Michigan
Grand Valley State University *B*
Hope College *B*

Missouri
University of Missouri
   Rolla *B, M, D*

Montana
Montana Tech of the University of Montana *M*

Nevada
University of Nevada
   Reno *M, D*

New Mexico
New Mexico Institute of Mining and Technology *M, D*

New York
Columbia University
   Columbia College *B*
   School of General Studies *B*
State University of New York
   Albany *M, D*
   College at Cortland *B*
   College at Fredonia *B*
   College at Geneseo *B*
   Oswego *B*

North Dakota
North Dakota State University *B*

Oregon
University of Oregon *M, D*

Rhode Island
Brown University *B, M, D*

Texas
University of Texas
   Dallas *M, D*

Utah
Snow College *A*

Geography

Alabama
Auburn University *B*
Jacksonville State University *B*
Samford University *B*
University of Alabama *B, M*
University of North Alabama *B*
University of South Alabama *B*

Geography

Alaska
University of Alaska
  Fairbanks *B*

Arizona
Arizona State University *B, M, D*
Northern Arizona University *B, M, T*
University of Arizona *B, M, D*

Arkansas
Arkansas State University *B*
University of Arkansas *B, M*
University of Central Arkansas *B*
Westark College *A*

California
Bakersfield College *A*
Cabrillo College *A*
California State Polytechnic University:
  Pomona *B*
California State University
  Chico *B, M*
  Dominguez Hills *B*
  Fresno *B, M*
  Fullerton *B, M*
  Hayward *B, M*
  Long Beach *B, M*
  Los Angeles *B, M*
  Northridge *B*
  Sacramento *B*
  Stanislaus *B*
Canada College *A*
Cerritos Community College *A*
Chabot College *A*
Chaffey Community College *A*
College of the Canyons *A*
College of the Desert *A*
Compton Community College *A*
Contra Costa College *A*
Crafton Hills College *A*
Cypress College *A*
De Anza College *A*
Diablo Valley College *A*
East Los Angeles College *A*
Foothill College *A*
Fresno City College *A*
Gavilan Community College *A*
Grossmont Community College *A*
Humboldt State University *B*
Irvine Valley College *A*
Long Beach City College *C, A*
Los Angeles Southwest College *A*
Los Angeles Valley College *A*
Merced College *A*
MiraCosta College *A*
Ohlone College *C, A*
Orange Coast College *A*
Riverside Community College *A*
Saddleback College *A*
San Bernardino Valley College *A*
San Diego City College *A*
San Diego Miramar College *A*
San Diego State University *B, M, D*
San Francisco State University *B, M*
San Jose State University *B, M*
Santa Ana College *A*
Santa Barbara City College *A*
Santa Rosa Junior College *A*
Sonoma State University *B*
Southwestern College *A*
University of California
  Berkeley *B, M, D*
  Davis *B, M, D*
  Los Angeles *B, M, D*
  Riverside *B, M, D*
  Santa Barbara *B, M, D*
University of Southern
  California *B, M, D*
Ventura College *A*
West Hills Community College *A*
West Los Angeles College *C, A*

Colorado
United States Air Force Academy *B*
University of Colorado
  Boulder *B, M, D*
  Colorado Springs *B*
  Denver *B*
University of Denver *B, M, D*
University of Northern Colorado *B, T*

Connecticut
Central Connecticut State
  University *B, M*
Southern Connecticut State University *B*
University of Connecticut *B, M*

Delaware
University of Delaware *B, M*

District of Columbia
George Washington University *B, M*
University of the District of Columbia *B*

Florida
Broward Community College *A*
Florida Atlantic University *B, M*
Florida State University *B, M, D*
Jacksonville University *B*
Palm Beach Community College *A*
Pensacola Junior College *A*
Stetson University *B*
University of Florida *B, M, D*
University of Miami *B, M*
University of South Florida *B, M*
University of Tampa *A*

Georgia
Atlanta Metropolitan College *A*
Georgia Southern University *B*
Georgia State University *B, M*
State University of West Georgia *B*
University of Georgia *B, M, D*

Hawaii
University of Hawaii
  Hilo *B*
  Manoa *B, M, D*

Idaho
College of Southern Idaho *A*
Ricks College *A*
University of Idaho *B, M, D*

Illinois
Augustana College *B, T*
Chicago State University *B, M, T*
Concordia University *B*
De Paul University *B, T*
Eastern Illinois University *B*
Elmhurst College *B, T*
Illinois State University *B, T*
Lincoln Land Community College *A*
Morton College *A*
Northeastern Illinois University *B, M*
Northern Illinois University *B, M*
Northwestern University *B*
Parkland College *A*
Richland Community College *A*
Roosevelt University *B*
Southern Illinois University
  Carbondale *B, M, D*
  Edwardsville *B, M*
Southwestern Ilinois College *A*
Triton College *A*
University of Chicago *B, M*
University of Illinois
  Chicago *B, M*
  Urbana-Champaign *B, M, D*
Western Illinois University *B, M*

Indiana
Ball State University *B*
DePauw University *B*
Indiana State University *B, M, D, T*
Indiana University
  Bloomington *B, M, D*
  Southeast *B*
Indiana University--Purdue University
  Indiana University-Purdue
    University Indianapolis *B*
Valparaiso University *B, T*

Vincennes University *A*

Iowa
Graceland University *T*
North Iowa Area Community College *A*
University of Iowa *B, M, D, T*
University of Northern Iowa *B, M*

Kansas
Allen County Community College *A*
Kansas State University *B, M, D*
Pittsburg State University *B, T*
Seward County Community College *A*
University of Kansas *B, M, D*

Kentucky
Eastern Kentucky University *B*
Morehead State University *B*
Murray State University *B, M, T*
Northern Kentucky University *B*
University of Kentucky *B, M, D*
University of Louisville *B*
Western Kentucky University *A, B, M, T*

Louisiana
Louisiana State University
  Shreveport *B*
Louisiana State University and
  Agricultural and Mechanical
  College *B, M, D*
Louisiana Tech University *B*
Nicholls State University *A*
University of Louisiana at Monroe *B*
University of New Orleans *B, M*

Maine
University of Maine
  Farmington *B*
University of Southern Maine *B*

Maryland
Community College of Baltimore County
  Essex *A*
Frostburg State University *B*
Johns Hopkins University *B, D*
Salisbury State University *B, T*
Towson University *B, M*
University of Maryland
  Baltimore County *B*
  College Park *B, M, D*

Massachusetts
Boston University *B, M, D*
Bridgewater State College *B*
Clark University *B, M, D*
Fitchburg State College *B*
Framingham State College *B*
Hampshire College *B*
Mount Holyoke College *B*
Salem State College *B, M*
Simon's Rock College of Bard *B*
University of Massachusetts
  Amherst *B, M*
  Boston *B*
Worcester State College *B*

Michigan
Aquinas College *B, T*
Calvin College *B, T*
Central Michigan University *B*
Eastern Michigan University *B, M*
Grand Valley State University *B*
Lake Michigan College *A*
Lansing Community College *A*
Michigan State University *B, M, D*
Northern Michigan University *B, T*
University of Michigan
  Flint *B*
University of Michigan *B*
Wayne State University *B, M*
Western Michigan University *B, M*

Minnesota
Alexandria Technical College *C, A*
Bemidji State University *B*
Gustavus Adolphus College *B*
Macalester College *B*
Minnesota State University,
  Mankato *B, M*
St. Cloud State University *B, M*
University of Minnesota
  Duluth *B*
  Twin Cities *B, M, D*
University of St. Thomas *B*
Winona State University *A*

Mississippi
University of Southern Mississippi *B, M*

Missouri
Central Missouri State University *B*
East Central College *A*
Northwest Missouri State University *B*
Southeast Missouri State University *B*
Southwest Missouri State University *B*
Three Rivers Community College *A*
University of Missouri
  Columbia *B, M*
  Kansas City *B*

Montana
University of Montana-Missoula *B, M*

Nebraska
Bellevue University *B*
Concordia University *B, T*
University of Nebraska
  Kearney *B, T*
  Lincoln *B, M, D*
  Omaha *B, M*
Wayne State College *B, T*

Nevada
University of Nevada
  Reno *B, M*

New Hampshire
Dartmouth College *B*
Keene State College *B*
Plymouth State College of the University
  System of New Hampshire *B*
University of New Hampshire *B*

New Jersey
Montclair State University *B*
Rowan University *B*
Rutgers
  The State University of New Jersey:
    Cook College *B*
  The State University of New Jersey:
    Douglass College *B*
  The State University of New Jersey:
    Livingston College *B*
  The State University of New Jersey:
    New Brunswick Graduate
    Campus *M, D*
  The State University of New Jersey:
    Rutgers College *B*
  The State University of New Jersey:
    University College New
    Brunswick *B*
William Paterson University of New
  Jersey *B*

New Mexico
New Mexico State University *B, M*
University of New Mexico *B, M*

New York
City University of New York
  Hunter College *B, M*
  Lehman College *B*
Colgate University *B*
Hofstra University *B*
Long Island University
  C. W. Post Campus *B*
Regents College *B*

State University of New York
  Albany *B, M*
  Binghamton *B, M*
  Buffalo *B, M, D*
  College at Buffalo *B*
  College at Cortland *B*
  College at Geneseo *B, T*
  College at Oneonta *B*
  College at Plattsburgh *B*
  New Paltz *B*
Syracuse University *B, M, D*
United States Military Academy *B*
Vassar College *B*

North Carolina
Appalachian State University *B*
East Carolina University *B, M*
Fayetteville State University *B*
North Carolina Central University *B*
University of North Carolina
  Chapel Hill *B, M, D*
  Charlotte *B, M*
  Greensboro *B, M, T*
  Wilmington *B*
Western Carolina University *B*

North Dakota
University of North Dakota *B, M, T*

Ohio
Bowling Green State University *B*
Kent State University
  Stark Campus *B*
Kent State University *B, M, D*
Miami University
  Middletown Campus *A*
  Oxford Campus *B, M*
Ohio State University
  Columbus Campus *B, M, D*
Ohio University *B, M*
Ohio Wesleyan University *B*
University of Akron *B, M*
University of Cincinnati *B, M, D, T*
University of Toledo *B, M*
Wittenberg University *B*
Wright State University *B*
Youngstown State University *B*

Oklahoma
Langston University *B*
Northeastern State University *B*
Oklahoma State University *B, M*
Tulsa Community College *A*
University of Central Oklahoma *B*
University of Oklahoma *B, M, D*

Oregon
Central Oregon Community College *A*
Chemeketa Community College *A*
Oregon State University *B, M, D*
Portland State University *B, M*
Southern Oregon University *B*
University of Oregon *B, M, D*
Western Oregon University *B*

Pennsylvania
Bloomsburg University of
  Pennsylvania *B*
Bucknell University *B*
California University of
  Pennsylvania *B, M*
Cheyney University of Pennsylvania *B*
Clarion University of Pennsylvania *B*
East Stroudsburg University of
  Pennsylvania *B*
Edinboro University of Pennsylvania *B*
Indiana University of Pennsylvania *B, M*
Kutztown University of Pennsylvania *B*
Lock Haven University of
  Pennsylvania *B, T*
Mansfield University of
  Pennsylvania *A, B, T*
Millersville University of
  Pennsylvania *B, T*
Penn State
  University Park *B, M, D*

Shippensburg University of
  Pennsylvania *B, T*
Slippery Rock University of
  Pennsylvania *B, T*
Temple University *M*
University of Pittsburgh
  Johnstown *B*
University of Pittsburgh *C*
Villanova University *B*
West Chester University of
  Pennsylvania *B, M*

Puerto Rico
University of Puerto Rico
  Rio Piedras Campus *B*

Rhode Island
Rhode Island College *B*

South Carolina
University of South Carolina *B, M, D*

South Dakota
South Dakota State University *B, M, T*

Tennessee
Columbia State Community College *A*
East Tennessee State University *B, M*
University of Memphis *B, M*
University of Tennessee
  Knoxville *B, M, D*
  Martin *B*

Texas
Baylor University *B*
Del Mar College *A*
Galveston College *A*
Houston Community College
  System *C, A*
Sam Houston State University *B*
Southwest Texas State
  University *B, M, D, T*
Stephen F. Austin State University *B, T*
Texas A&M University
  Commerce *B, M*
Texas A&M University *B, M, D*
Texas Tech University *B, M*
University of North Texas *B, M*
University of Texas
  Arlington *T*
  Austin *B, M, D*
  Dallas *B*
  San Antonio *B*
West Texas A&M University *B, T*
Western Texas College *A*

Utah
Brigham Young University *B, M*
Salt Lake Community College *A*
Snow College *A*
University of Utah *B, M, D*
Utah State University *B, M*
Weber State University *B*

Vermont
Middlebury College *B*
University of Vermont *B, M*

Virginia
Emory & Henry College *B*
George Mason University *B, M*
James Madison University *B, T*
Longwood College *T*
Mary Washington College *B*
Old Dominion University *B*
Radford University *B*
Virginia Polytechnic Institute and State
  University *B, M*

Washington
Central Washington University *B*
Eastern Washington University *B, T*
Everett Community College *A*
Highline Community College *A*
University of Washington *B, M, D*
Western Washington University *B, M, T*

West Virginia
Concord College *B*

Marshall University *B, M*
West Virginia University *B, M, D*

Wisconsin
Carroll College *B*
Carthage College *B, T*
University of Wisconsin
  Eau Claire *B*
  La Crosse *B, T*
  Madison *B, M, D*
  Milwaukee *B, M, D*
  Oshkosh *B*
  Parkside *B*
  Platteville *B, T*
  River Falls *B, T*
  Stevens Point *B, T*
  Whitewater *B, T*

Wyoming
Casper College *A*
University of Wyoming *B, M*
Western Wyoming Community
  College *A*

Geological engineering

Alabama
Auburn University *B*

Alaska
University of Alaska
  Fairbanks *B, M*

Arizona
University of Arizona *B*

California
University of Southern California *M*

Colorado
Colorado School of Mines *B, M, D*

Idaho
North Idaho College *A*
University of Idaho *B, M*

Illinois
University of Illinois
  Chicago *D*

Massachusetts
Harvard College *B*

Michigan
Michigan Technological
  University *B, M, D, T*

Minnesota
University of Minnesota
  Twin Cities *B, M, D*

Mississippi
University of Mississippi *B*

Missouri
East Central College *A*
University of Missouri
  Rolla *B, M, D*

Montana
Montana Tech of the University of
  Montana *B, M*

Nevada
University of Nevada
  Reno *B, M*

New Jersey
Rutgers
  The State University of New Jersey:
  Newark College of Arts and
  Sciences *B*

New Mexico
New Mexico State University *B*

New York
Columbia University
  Fu Foundation School of
  Engineering and Applied
  Science *B, M, D*

North Dakota
University of North Dakota *B*

Oklahoma
Northeastern Oklahoma Agricultural and
  Mechanical College *A*
University of Oklahoma *B, M, D*
University of Tulsa *B, M*

Pennsylvania
Drexel University *M*

Rhode Island
Brown University *B*

South Dakota
South Dakota School of Mines and
  Technology *B, M, D*

Utah
Brigham Young University *B*
University of Utah *B, M, D*

Wisconsin
University of Wisconsin
  Madison *B, M, D*

Geology

Alabama
Auburn University *B, M*
University of Alabama *B, M, D*
University of North Alabama *B*
University of South Alabama *B*

Alaska
University of Alaska
  Fairbanks *B, M, D*

Arizona
Arizona State University *B, M, D*
Arizona Western College *A*
Eastern Arizona College *A*
Northern Arizona University *B, M*
Prescott College *B, M*
University of Arizona *B, M, D*

Arkansas
Arkansas Tech University *B*
University of Arkansas
  Little Rock *B*
University of Arkansas *B, M*

California
Bakersfield College *A*
California Institute of Technology *B, D*
California Lutheran University *B*
California State Polytechnic University:
  Pomona *B*
California State University
  Bakersfield *B, M*
  Chico *B, M*
  Dominguez Hills *B*
  Fresno *B, M*
  Fullerton *B*
  Hayward *B, M*
  Long Beach *B, M*
  Los Angeles *B, M*
  Northridge *B, M*
  Sacramento *B*
  Stanislaus *B*
Cerritos Community College *A*
Chaffey Community College *A*
College of San Mateo *A*
College of the Canyons *A*
College of the Desert *A*
College of the Siskiyous *A*
Compton Community College *A*
Crafton Hills College *A*
Cypress College *A*
De Anza College *A*
Diablo Valley College *A*
East Los Angeles College *A*
Foothill College *A*
Gavilan Community College *A*
Golden West College *A*
Grossmont Community College *A*

Geology

Humboldt State University *B*
Irvine Valley College *A*
Loma Linda University *B, M*
Los Angeles Southwest College *A*
Los Angeles Valley College *A*
MiraCosta College *A*
Moorpark College *A*
Occidental College *B*
Ohlone College *C, A*
Orange Coast College *A*
Palomar College *A*
Pomona College *B*
Riverside Community College *A*
Saddleback College *A*
San Bernardino Valley College *A*
San Diego City College *A*
San Diego State University *B, M*
San Francisco State University *B, M*
San Joaquin Delta College *A*
San Jose State University *B, M*
Santa Ana College *A*
Santa Barbara City College *A*
Santa Monica College *A*
Scripps College *B*
Sierra College *A*
Sonoma State University *B*
Southwestern College *A*
Stanford University *B, M, D*
University of California
    Berkeley *B, M, D*
    Davis *B, M, D*
    Los Angeles *B, M, D*
    Riverside *B, M, D*
    Santa Barbara *B, M, D*
    Santa Cruz *B, D*
University of Southern
    California *B, M, D*
University of the Pacific *B*
Ventura College *A*
West Hills Community College *A*
West Los Angeles College *C, A*
West Valley College *A*

Colorado
Adams State College *B*
Colorado College *B*
Colorado Mountain College
    Spring Valley Campus *A*
Colorado School of Mines *M, D*
Colorado State University *B, M, T*
Fort Lewis College *B*
Red Rocks Community College *A*
University of Colorado
    Boulder *B, M, D*
    Denver *B*
Western State College of Colorado *B, T*

Connecticut
Eastern Connecticut State University *B*
University of Connecticut *B, M, D*
Wesleyan University *B*
Yale University *B, M, D*

Delaware
University of Delaware *B, M, D*

District of Columbia
George Washington University *B, M, D*

Florida
Florida Atlantic University *B, M*
Florida International University *B, M, D*
Florida State University *B, M, D*
Gulf Coast Community College *A*
Miami-Dade Community College *A*
Pensacola Junior College *A*
University of Florida *B, M, D*
University of Miami *B*
University of South Florida *B, M, D*

Georgia
Atlanta Metropolitan College *A*
Clayton College and State University *A*
Columbus State University *B*
East Georgia College *A*
Gainesville College *A*
Georgia Perimeter College *A*
Georgia Southern University *B*
Georgia Southwestern State University *B*
Georgia State University *B, M*
Middle Georgia College *A*
Oxford College of Emory University *B*
State University of West Georgia *B*
University of Georgia *B, M, D*

Hawaii
University of Hawaii
    Hilo *B*
    Manoa *B*

Idaho
Boise State University *B, M*
College of Southern Idaho *A*
Idaho State University *A, B, M*
Lewis-Clark State College *B*
North Idaho College *A*
Ricks College *A*
University of Idaho *B, M, D*

Illinois
Augustana College *B, T*
Bradley University *B, T*
Eastern Illinois University *B*
Highland Community College *A*
Illinois State University *B*
Northern Illinois University *B, M, D*
Northwestern University *B, M, D*
Olivet Nazarene University *B*
Parkland College *A*
Southern Illinois University
    Carbondale *B, M, D*
Triton College *A*
University of Illinois
    Chicago *B, M*
    Urbana-Champaign *B, M, D*
Western Illinois University *B*
Wheaton College *B, T*

Indiana
Ball State University *B, M*
DePauw University *B*
Earlham College *B*
Hanover College *B*
Indiana State University *B, M, D, T*
Indiana University
    Bloomington *B, M, D*
    Northwest *B*
Indiana University--Purdue University
    Indiana University-Purdue
        University Fort Wayne *B*
    Indiana University-Purdue
        University Indianapolis *B, M*
Purdue University *B, M, D*
University of Notre Dame *B*
University of Southern Indiana *B*
Valparaiso University *B*
Vincennes University *A*

Iowa
Cornell College *B, T*
Iowa State University *B, M, D*
University of Iowa *B, M, D, T*
University of Northern Iowa *B*

Kansas
Fort Hays State University *B, M*
Kansas State University *B, M*
University of Kansas *B, M, D*
Wichita State University *A, B*

Kentucky
Eastern Kentucky University *B, M*
Morehead State University *B*
Murray State University *B, T*
Northern Kentucky University *B, T*
University of Kentucky *B, M, D*
Western Kentucky University *B*

Louisiana
Centenary College of Louisiana *B, T*
Louisiana State University and
    Agricultural and Mechanical
    College *B, M, D*
Louisiana Tech University *B*
Nicholls State University *B*
Tulane University *B, M, D*
University of Louisiana at
    Lafayette *B, M*
University of Louisiana at Monroe *B, M*
University of New Orleans *B, M*

Maine
Bates College *B*
Bowdoin College *B*
Colby College *B*
University of Maine
    Farmington *B*
    Presque Isle *B*
University of Maine *B, M, D*
University of Southern Maine *B*

Maryland
Johns Hopkins University *B, D*
University of Maryland
    College Park *B, M, D*

Massachusetts
Amherst College *B*
Boston College *B, M*
Boston University *B, M, D*
Bridgewater State College *B*
Hampshire College *B*
Harvard University *M, D*
Mount Holyoke College *B*
Northeastern University *B*
Salem State College *B*
Smith College *B*
Tufts University *B*
University of Massachusetts
    Amherst *B, M, D*
Wellesley College *B*
Williams College *B*

Michigan
Albion College *B, T*
Calvin College *B, T*
Central Michigan University *B*
Eastern Michigan University *B*
Grand Valley State University *B*
Hope College *B*
Lake Michigan College *A*
Lake Superior State University *B, T*
Michigan State University *B, M, D*
Michigan Technological
    University *B, M, D, T*
University of Michigan *B, M*
Wayne State University *B, M*
Western Michigan University *B, M, D*

Minnesota
Bemidji State University *B*
Carleton College *B*
Gustavus Adolphus College *B*
Macalester College *B, T*
Ridgewater College: A Community and
    Technical College *A*
University of Minnesota
    Duluth *B, M*
    Morris *B*
    Twin Cities *B, M, D*
University of St. Thomas *B*
Winona State University *B*

Mississippi
Hinds Community College *A*
Millsaps College *B, T*
Mississippi State University *B, M*
University of Mississippi *B*
University of Southern Mississippi *B, M*

Missouri
Central Missouri State University *B*
East Central College *A*
Northwest Missouri State University *B*
St. Louis University *B*
Southeast Missouri State University *B*
Southwest Missouri State University *B*
University of Missouri
    Columbia *B, M, D*
    Kansas City *B, M*
    Rolla *B, M, D*

Montana
Montana Tech of the University of
    Montana *M*
Rocky Mountain College *B*
University of Montana-Missoula *B, M, D*
Western Montana College of The
    University of Montana *B*

Nebraska
University of Nebraska
    Lincoln *B, M, D*
    Omaha *B*

Nevada
University of Nevada
    Las Vegas *B, M, D*
    Reno *B, M, D*

New Hampshire
Antioch New England Graduate
    School *M*
Dartmouth College *D*
Keene State College *B*
University of New Hampshire *B, M, D*

New Jersey
Montclair State University *B, M, T*
New Jersey City University *B*
Princeton University *B, M, D*
Richard Stockton College of New
    Jersey *B*
Rider University *B*
Rutgers
    The State University of New Jersey:
        Cook College *B*
    The State University of New Jersey:
        Douglass College *B*
    The State University of New Jersey:
        Livingston College *B*
    The State University of New Jersey:
        New Brunswick Graduate
        Campus *M, D*
    The State University of New Jersey:
        Newark College of Arts and
        Sciences *B*
    The State University of New Jersey:
        Rutgers College *B*
    The State University of New Jersey:
        University College New
        Brunswick *B*

New Mexico
Eastern New Mexico University *B*
New Mexico Institute of Mining and
    Technology *B, M, D*
New Mexico State University *B, M*
San Juan College *A*
University of New Mexico *B, M, D*

New York
Adirondack Community College *A*
Alfred University *B*
City University of New York
    Brooklyn College *B, M*
    City College *B*
    Graduate School and University
        Center *D*
    Hunter College *B*
    Lehman College *B*
    Queens College *B, M*
    York College *B*
Colgate University *B*
Columbia University
    Columbia College *B*
    Graduate School *M, D*
    School of General Studies *B*
Concordia College *B*
Cornell University *B, M, D*
Hamilton College *B*
Hartwick College *B*
Hobart and William Smith Colleges *B*
Hofstra University *B*
Long Island University
    C. W. Post Campus *B*
Regents College *B*
Rensselaer Polytechnic Institute *B, M, D*
St. Lawrence University *B, T*

Sarah Lawrence College *B*
Skidmore College *B*
State University of New York
  Albany *B, M, D*
  Binghamton *B, M, D*
  Buffalo *B, M, D*
  College at Brockport *B*
  College at Buffalo *B*
  College at Cortland *B*
  College at Fredonia *B, T*
  College at Geneseo *B, T*
  College at Oneonta *B*
  College at Plattsburgh *B*
  College at Potsdam *B*
  New Paltz *B, M, T*
  Oswego *B*
  Stony Brook *B*
Suffolk County Community College *A*
Syracuse University *B, M, D*
Union College *B*
University of Rochester *B, M, D*
Vassar College *B*

North Carolina
Duke University *B, M, D*
East Carolina University *B, M*
Elizabeth City State University *B*
Guilford College *B*
North Carolina State University *B*
University of North Carolina
  Chapel Hill *B, M, D*
  Charlotte *B*
  Wilmington *B, M*
Western Carolina University *B*

North Dakota
North Dakota State University *B*
University of North Dakota *B, M, D, T*

Ohio
Ashland University *B*
Baldwin-Wallace College *B*
Bowling Green State University *B, M*
Case Western Reserve
  University *B, M, D*
Central State University *B*
Cleveland State University *B*
College of Wooster *B*
Denison University *B*
Kent State University
  Stark Campus *B*
Kent State University *B, M, D*
Marietta College *B*
Miami University
  Oxford Campus *B, M, D*
Mount Union College *B*
Muskingum College *B*
Oberlin College *B*
Ohio State University
  Columbus Campus *B, M, D*
Ohio University *B, M*
Ohio Wesleyan University *B*
University of Akron *B, M*
University of Cincinnati *B, M, D, T*
University of Dayton *B*
University of Toledo *B, M*
Wilmington College *B*
Wittenberg University *B*
Wright State University *B, M*
Youngstown State University *B*

Oklahoma
Northeastern Oklahoma Agricultural and
  Mechanical College *A*
Oklahoma State University *B, M*
Tulsa Community College *A*
University of Oklahoma *B, M, D*
University of Tulsa *B, M, D*

Oregon
Central Oregon Community College *A*
Chemeketa Community College *A*
Oregon State University *B, M, D*
Portland State University *B, M*
Southern Oregon University *B*
University of Oregon *B, M, D*

Pennsylvania
Allegheny College *B*
Bloomsburg University of
  Pennsylvania *B*
Bryn Mawr College *B, M, D*
Bucknell University *B*
California University of Pennsylvania *B*
Clarion University of Pennsylvania *B*
Dickinson College *B*
Edinboro University of Pennsylvania *B*
Franklin and Marshall College *B*
Haverford College *B*
Juniata College *B*
Kutztown University of Pennsylvania *B*
La Salle University *B*
Lafayette College *B*
Lock Haven University of
  Pennsylvania *B*
Mansfield University of Pennsylvania *B*
Mercyhurst College *B*
Millersville University of
  Pennsylvania *B*
Moravian College *B*
Penn State
  University Park *B, M, D*
Slippery Rock University of
  Pennsylvania *B*
Temple University *B, M*
University of Pennsylvania *A, B, M, D*
University of Pittsburgh
  Bradford *B*
  Johnstown *B*
University of Pittsburgh *B, M, D*
West Chester University of
  Pennsylvania *B*

Puerto Rico
University of Puerto Rico
  Mayaguez Campus *B, M*

Rhode Island
Brown University *B, M, D*
University of Rhode Island *B*

South Carolina
Charleston Southern University *B*
Clemson University *B, M*
College of Charleston *B*
University of South Carolina *B, M, D*

South Dakota
South Dakota School of Mines and
  Technology *B, M, D*

Tennessee
Austin Peay State University *B*
East Tennessee State University *B*
Middle Tennessee State University *B*
Tennessee Technological University *B*
University of Memphis *B, M*
University of Tennessee
  Chattanooga *B*
  Knoxville *B, M, D*
  Martin *B*
University of the South *B*
Vanderbilt University *B, M*

Texas
Abilene Christian University *B*
Amarillo College *A*
Baylor University *B, M, D*
Central Texas College *A*
Coastal Bend College *A*
Del Mar College *A*
El Paso Community College *A*
Galveston College *A*
Grayson County College *A*
Hardin-Simmons University *B*
Hill College *A*
Lamar University *B*
Midland College *A*
Midwestern State University *B*
Odessa College *A*
Palo Alto College *A*
Panola College *A*
Rice University *B, M, D*
St. Mary's University *B, T*
Sam Houston State University *B*
Southern Methodist University *B, M, D*
Stephen F. Austin State University *B, M*
Sul Ross State University *B, M*
Tarleton State University *B*
Texas A&M University
  Commerce *B*
  Corpus Christi *B, T*
  Kingsville *B, M, T*
Texas A&M University *B, M, D*
Texas Christian University *B, M*
Texas Tech University *B*
Trinity University *B*
Tyler Junior College *A*
University of Houston *B, M, D*
University of Texas
  Arlington *B, M*
  Austin *B, M, D*
  Dallas *B, M, D*
  El Paso *B, M, D*
  San Antonio *B, M*
  of the Permian Basin *B, M*
West Texas A&M University *B*
Western Texas College *A*

Utah
Brigham Young University *B, M*
Dixie State College of Utah *A*
Salt Lake Community College *A*
Snow College *A*
Southern Utah University *B*
University of Utah *B, M, D*
Utah State University *B, M*
Weber State University *B*

Vermont
Castleton State College *B*
Middlebury College *B*
Norwich University *B*
University of Vermont *B, M*

Virginia
College of William and Mary *B*
George Mason University *B*
James Madison University *B*
Mary Washington College *B*
Old Dominion University *B, M*
Radford University *B*
Virginia Polytechnic Institute and State
  University *B, M, D*
Washington and Lee University *B*

Washington
Central Washington University *B, M*
Eastern Washington University *B, M*
Everett Community College *A*
Evergreen State College *B*
Highline Community College *A*
University of Puget Sound *B, T*
University of Washington *B, M, D*
Washington State University *B, M, D*
Western Washington University *B, M, T*
Whitman College *B*

West Virginia
Marshall University *B*
Potomac State College of West Virginia
  University *A*
West Virginia University *B, M, D*

Wisconsin
Beloit College *B*
Lawrence University *B*
St. Norbert College *B*
University of Wisconsin
  Eau Claire *B*
  Madison *B, M, D*
  Milwaukee *B, M, D*
  Oshkosh *B*
  Parkside *B*
  River Falls *B*

Wyoming
Casper College *A*
University of Wyoming *B, M, D*
Western Wyoming Community
  College *A*

Geophysical engineering

Arizona
Arizona Western College *A*
University of Arizona *M, D*

California
Stanford University *M, D*

Colorado
Colorado School of Mines *B, M, D*

Massachusetts
Harvard College *B*
Tufts University *B, M*

Missouri
East Central College *A*

Montana
Montana Tech of the University of
  Montana *B, M*

New York
Columbia University
  Fu Foundation School of
    Engineering and Applied
    Science *M, D*

Oklahoma
University of Tulsa *B, M*

Utah
University of Utah *B, M, D*

Virginia
Radford University *M*

Geophysics/seismology

Alaska
University of Alaska
  Fairbanks *M, D*

California
California Institute of Technology *B, D*
California State University
  Northridge *B*
Occidental College *B*
San Francisco State University *B*
Stanford University *B, M, D*
University of California
  Berkeley *B, M, D*
  Los Angeles *B, M, D*
  Riverside *B*
  Santa Barbara *B, M*
  Santa Cruz *B, D*
University of the Pacific *B*

Colorado
Colorado School of Mines *M, D*
University of Colorado
  Boulder *D*

Delaware
University of Delaware *B*

Hawaii
University of Hawaii
  Manoa *B, M, D*

Idaho
Boise State University *B, M*
Idaho State University *M*
University of Idaho *M*

Illinois
University of Chicago *B, M, D*

Kansas
Kansas State University *B*

Louisiana
University of New Orleans

Massachusetts
Boston College *B, M*
Harvard College *B*

Geophysics/seismology

Michigan
Eastern Michigan University B
Hope College B
Michigan Technological University B, M
Western Michigan University B

Minnesota
University of Minnesota
   Twin Cities B, M, D

Missouri
St. Louis University B, M, D
University of Missouri
   Rolla B, M, D

Montana
Montana Tech of the University of
   Montana M

Nevada
University of Nevada
   Reno B, M, D

New Mexico
New Mexico Institute of Mining and
   Technology B, M, D

New York
Columbia University
   Columbia College B
   Graduate School M, D
   School of General Studies B
St. Lawrence University B
State University of New York
   College at Fredonia B
   College at Geneseo B

North Carolina
North Carolina State University B

Ohio
Ohio State University
   Columbus Campus B, M, D
University of Akron B, M

Oklahoma
University of Oklahoma B, M

Oregon
Oregon State University M, D

South Carolina
University of South Carolina B

Tennessee
University of Memphis D

Texas
Baylor University B
Southern Methodist University B, M, D
Texas A&M University B, M, D
Texas Tech University B
University of Houston B, M, D
University of Texas
   Austin B
   Dallas M, D
   El Paso B, M

University of Alabama
   Birmingham B
   Huntsville B
University of Alabama B, M
University of South Alabama B

Arizona
Arizona State University B, M
Northern Arizona University B, T
University of Arizona B, M

Arkansas
Harding University B
Hendrix College B
University of Arkansas B, M
University of Central Arkansas B

California
Bakersfield College A
Cabrillo College A
California Lutheran University B
California State University
   Chico B
   Fresno B
   Fullerton B, M
   Long Beach B, M
   Northridge B
   Sacramento B, M
Cerritos Community College A
Chabot College A
Chaffey Community College A
Citrus College A
Claremont McKenna College B
College of San Mateo A
College of the Desert A
Compton Community College A
Cypress College A
De Anza College A
Foothill College A
Golden West College A
Grossmont Community College C, A
Long Beach City College C, A
Los Angeles Valley College A
Loyola Marymount University B
Merced College A
Mills College B
MiraCosta College A
Modesto Junior College A
Monterey Institute of International
   Studies C
Orange Coast College A
Pepperdine University B
Pitzer College B
Pomona College B
Riverside Community College A
St. Mary's College of California B
San Diego Mesa College A
San Diego State University B
San Francisco State University B, M
San Joaquin Delta College A
San Jose State University B
Santa Barbara City College A
Santa Monica College A
Scripps College B
Solano Community College A
Sonoma State University B
Stanford University B, M, D
University of California
   Berkeley B, M, D
   Davis B, M, D
   Irvine B, M, D
   Los Angeles B, M
   Riverside B, M, D
   San Diego B, M
   Santa Barbara B, M, D
   Santa Cruz B, D
University of La Verne B
University of Redlands B
University of San Francisco C
University of Southern
   California B, M, D
University of the Pacific B
Ventura College A

Colorado
Colorado College B

Colorado State University B
Red Rocks Community College A
University of Colorado
   Boulder B, M
   Denver B
University of Denver B, M
University of Northern Colorado B, T

Connecticut
Central Connecticut State University B
Connecticut College B
Fairfield University B
Southern Connecticut State University B
Trinity College B
University of Connecticut B, M, D
University of Hartford B
Wesleyan University B
Yale University B, M, D

Delaware
University of Delaware B, M, T

District of Columbia
American University B
Catholic University of America B, M, T
Gallaudet University B
George Washington University B
Georgetown University B, M, D
Howard University B

Florida
Eckerd College B
Florida Atlantic University B, M
Florida International University B
Florida State University B, M
Manatee Community College A
Miami-Dade Community College A
New College of the University of South
   Florida B
Rollins College B
Stetson University B
University of Florida B, M, D
University of Miami B
University of South Florida B

Georgia
Agnes Scott College B
Berry College B, T
Clark Atlanta University B
Emory University B
Georgia Southern University B
Georgia State University B, M
Mercer University B
Morehouse College B
Oxford College of Emory University B
South Georgia College A
University of Georgia B, M

Hawaii
University of Hawaii
   Manoa B, M

Idaho
Boise State University B
Idaho State University A, B
Ricks College A
University of Idaho B, M

Illinois
Augustana College B, T
Bradley University B, T
City Colleges of Chicago
   Harold Washington College A
De Paul University B
Elmhurst College B, T
Illinois College B
Illinois State University B, T
Illinois Wesleyan University B
Knox College B
Lake Forest College B
Loyola University of Chicago B
Millikin University B
North Central College B, T
Northern Illinois University B, M, T
Northwestern University B, D
Parkland College A
Principia College B
Richland Community College A

Rockford College B
Southern Illinois University
   Carbondale B
Triton College A
University of Chicago B
University of Illinois
   Chicago B, M
   Urbana-Champaign B, M, D
Wheaton College B

Indiana
Anderson University B
Ball State University B, T
Butler University B
DePauw University B
Earlham College B
Goshen College B
Grace College B
Hanover College B
Indiana State University B, M
Indiana University
   Bloomington B, M, D
   South Bend A, B
Indiana University--Purdue University
   Indiana University-Purdue
     University Fort Wayne A, B
   Indiana University-Purdue
     University Indianapolis B
Manchester College B, T
Marian College B, T
University of Evansville B
University of Indianapolis B
University of Notre Dame B, M
University of Southern Indiana B
Valparaiso University B, T
Vincennes University A
Wabash College B

Iowa
Central College B, T
Coe College B
Cornell College B, T
Dordt College B
Drake University B
Graceland University B, T
Grinnell College B
Iowa State University B
Loras College B
Luther College B
St. Ambrose University B, T
Simpson College B
University of Iowa B, M, D, T
University of Northern Iowa B, M
Waldorf College A
Wartburg College B, T

Kansas
Baker University B, T
Bethel College B, T
Kansas Wesleyan University B
University of Kansas B, M, D
Washburn University of Topeka B

Kentucky
Berea College B, T
Centre College B
Eastern Kentucky University B
Georgetown College B, T
Kentucky Wesleyan College B
Murray State University B, T
University of Kentucky B, M
University of Louisville B, M
Western Kentucky University B, T

Louisiana
Centenary College of Louisiana B, T
Dillard University B
Louisiana State University and
   Agricultural and Mechanical
   College B
Loyola University New Orleans B
Tulane University B, M, D
Xavier University of Louisiana B

Maine
Bates College B
Bowdoin College B

Colby College *B*
University of Maine *B*

Maryland
Community College of Baltimore County
  Catonsville *A*
Hood College *B*
Johns Hopkins University *B, D*
Loyola College in Maryland *B*
Mount St. Mary's College *B*
Towson University *B, T*
University of Maryland
  Baltimore County *B*
  College Park *B, M, D*
Washington College *B, T*
Western Maryland College *B*

Massachusetts
Amherst College *B*
Boston College *B*
Boston University *B*
Brandeis University *B, M, D*
College of the Holy Cross *B*
Gordon College *B*
Harvard College *B*
Harvard University *M, D*
Mount Holyoke College *B*
Northeastern University *B*
Regis College *B*
Simon's Rock College of Bard *B*
Smith College *B*
Tufts University *B, M*
University of Massachusetts
  Amherst *B, M, D*
  Boston *B*
Wellesley College *B*
Wheaton College *B*
Williams College *B*

Michigan
Adrian College *A, B, T*
Albion College *B, T*
Alma College *B, T*
Andrews University *B*
Aquinas College *B, T*
Calvin College *B, T*
Central Michigan University *B*
Eastern Michigan University *B*
Grand Valley State University *B*
Hillsdale College *B*
Hope College *B, T*
Kalamazoo College *B, T*
Lansing Community College *A*
Michigan State University *B, M, D*
Michigan Technological University *C*
Northern Michigan University *B, T*
Oakland University *B, T*
University of Michigan
  Flint *B, T*
University of Michigan *B, M, D, T*
Wayne State University *B, M*
Western Michigan University *B, T*

Minnesota
Augsburg College *B*
Bemidji State University *B*
Carleton College *B*
College of St. Benedict *B*
Concordia College: Moorhead *B, T*
Gustavus Adolphus College *B*
Hamline University *B*
Macalester College *B, T*
Minnesota State University,
  Mankato *B, M*
St. Cloud State University *B*
St. John's University *B*
St. Olaf College *B, T*
University of Minnesota
  Morris *B*
  Twin Cities *B, M, D*
University of St. Thomas *B*
Winona State University *B*

Mississippi
Millsaps College *B, T*
University of Mississippi *B, M*

Missouri
Central Methodist College *B*
Central Missouri State University *B, T*
College of the Ozarks *B*
Drury University *B, T*
Missouri Southern State College *B*
Missouri Western State College *T*
St. Louis University *B*
Southeast Missouri State University *B*
Southwest Missouri State University *B*
Truman State University *B*
University of Missouri
  Columbia *B, M*
  Kansas City *B*
  St. Louis *B*
Washington University *B, M, D*
Webster University *B*

Montana
Montana State University
  Bozeman *T*
University of Montana-Missoula *B, M*

Nebraska
Concordia University *B, T*
Creighton University *B*
Dana College *B*
Doane College *B*
Hastings College *B*
Nebraska Wesleyan University *B*
Union College *B*
University of Nebraska
  Kearney *B, M, T*
  Lincoln *B*
  Omaha *B*

Nevada
University of Nevada
  Las Vegas *B*
  Reno *B*

New Hampshire
Dartmouth College *B*
Keene State College *B*
St. Anselm College *C*
University of New Hampshire *B*

New Jersey
Drew University *B*
Georgian Court College *T*
Montclair State University *B, T*
Princeton University *B, M, D*
Rider University *B*
Rutgers
  The State University of New Jersey:
    Camden College of Arts and
    Sciences *B, T*
  The State University of New Jersey:
    Douglass College *B, T*
  The State University of New Jersey:
    Livingston College *B, T*
  The State University of New Jersey:
    New Brunswick Graduate
    Campus *M, D*
  The State University of New Jersey:
    Newark College of Arts and
    Sciences *B, T*
  The State University of New Jersey:
    Rutgers College *B, T*
  The State University of New Jersey:
    University College Camden *B, T*
  The State University of New Jersey:
    University College New
    Brunswick *B, T*
  The State University of New Jersey:
    University College Newark *T*
Seton Hall University *T*

New Mexico
University of New Mexico *B, M*

New York
Alfred University *B*
Bard College *B*
Barnard College *B*
Canisius College *B*
City University of New York
  Brooklyn College *B*
  Graduate School and University
    Center *M, D*
  Hunter College *B*
  Lehman College *B*
  Queens College *B*
Colgate University *B*
Columbia University
  Columbia College *B*
  Graduate School *M, D*
  School of General Studies *B*
Cornell University *B, T*
Fordham University *B*
Hamilton College *B*
Hartwick College *B, T*
Hofstra University *B*
Ithaca College *B, T*
Long Island University
  C. W. Post Campus *B*
Nazareth College of Rochester *B*
New York University *B, M, D*
Orange County Community College *A*
Rensselaer Polytechnic Institute *B*
St. John Fisher College *B*
St. Lawrence University *B, T*
Sarah Lawrence College *B*
Skidmore College *B*
State University of New York
  Binghamton *B*
  Buffalo *B, M*
  New Paltz *B, T*
  Oswego *B*
  Stony Brook *T*
Syracuse University *B, M*
United States Military Academy *B*
University of Rochester *B, M*
Vassar College *B*
Wells College *B*

North Carolina
Davidson College *B*
Duke University *B, M*
East Carolina University *B*
Guilford College *B, T*
Lenoir-Rhyne College *B, T*
Methodist College *A*
Salem College *B*
University of North Carolina
  Asheville *B, T*
  Chapel Hill *B, M, D, T*
  Charlotte *B*
  Greensboro *B, T*
Wake Forest University *B*
Western Carolina University *B*

North Dakota
Dickinson State University *B, T*
Minot State University *B, T*
North Dakota State University *B*
University of North Dakota *B, T*

Ohio
Baldwin-Wallace College *B, T*
Bowling Green State University *B, M*
Case Western Reserve University *B*
Cleveland State University *B*
College of Wooster *B*
Denison University *B*
Heidelberg College *B*
Hiram College *B, T*
John Carroll University *B*
Kent State University
  Stark Campus *B*
Kent State University *B, M*
Kenyon College *B*
Lake Erie College *B*
Miami University
  Oxford Campus *B, T*
Mount Union College *B*
Muskingum College *B*
Oberlin College *B*
Ohio State University
  Columbus Campus *B, M, D*
Ohio University *B, M*
Ohio Wesleyan University *B*
University of Akron *B*
University of Cincinnati *B, T*
University of Dayton *B*
University of Toledo *B, M*
Wittenberg University *B*
Wright State University *B*
Xavier University *A, B*
Youngstown State University *B*

Oklahoma
Northeastern State University *B*
Oklahoma Baptist University *B, T*
Oklahoma City University *B*
Oklahoma State University *B*
Oral Roberts University *B*
Tulsa Community College *A*
University of Central Oklahoma *B*
University of Oklahoma *B, M*
University of Tulsa *B*

Oregon
Lewis & Clark College *B*
Linfield College *B*
Oregon State University *B*
Pacific University *B*
Portland State University *B, M*
Reed College *B*
University of Oregon *B, M, D*
University of Portland *T*
Western Oregon University *T*
Willamette University *B*

Pennsylvania
Allegheny College *B*
Bloomsburg University of
  Pennsylvania *B*
Bryn Mawr College *B*
Bucknell University *B*
California University of Pennsylvania *B*
Carnegie Mellon University *B*
Chestnut Hill College *B*
Dickinson College *B*
East Stroudsburg University of
  Pennsylvania *B*
Edinboro University of
  Pennsylvania *B*
Elizabethtown College *B*
Franklin and Marshall College *B*
Gettysburg College *B*
Haverford College *B, T*
Immaculata College *C, A, B*
Indiana University of Pennsylvania *B, M*
Juniata College *B*
Kutztown University of
  Pennsylvania *B, T*
La Salle University *B*
Lafayette College *B*
Lebanon Valley College of
  Pennsylvania *B, T*
Lehigh University *B*
Lock Haven University of
  Pennsylvania *B, T*
Lycoming College *B*
Mansfield University of
  Pennsylvania *B, T*
Messiah College *B*
Millersville University of
  Pennsylvania *B, M, T*
Moravian College *B, T*
Muhlenberg College *B, T*
Penn State
  University Park *B, M, D*
Rosemont College *B*
St. Joseph's University *B*
Susquehanna University *B*
Swarthmore College *B*
Temple University *B*
University of Pennsylvan
University of Pittsburgh
University of Scranton
Ursinus College *B, T*
Villanova University
Washington and Jeff
West Chester Unive
  Pennsylvania *B*
Westminster Coll

German

Widener University *B*
Wilkes University *B*

Rhode Island
Brown University *B, M, D*
University of Rhode Island *B*

South Carolina
Clemson University *B*
College of Charleston *B, T*
Converse College *B*
Furman University *B, T*
Presbyterian College *B, T*
The Citadel *B*
University of South Carolina *B, M*
Wofford College *B*

South Dakota
Augustana College *B, T*
Northern State University
South Dakota State University *B*
University of South Dakota *B*

Tennessee
Belmont University *B*
Carson-Newman College *B, T*
David Lipscomb University *B*
Rhodes College *B, T*
Tennessee Technological University *B, T*
University of Tennessee
    Knoxville *M*
University of the South *B*
Vanderbilt University *B, M, D*

Texas
Angelo State University *B, T*
Austin College *B*
Baylor University *B*
Blinn College *A*
Coastal Bend College *A*
Hardin-Simmons University *B*
Kilgore College *A*
Paris Junior College *A*
Rice University *B, M, D*
St. Mary's University *B*
Sam Houston State University *B*
Southern Methodist University *B*
Southwest Texas State University *B, T*
Southwestern University *B*
Texas A&M University
    Commerce *B*
Texas A&M University *B*
Texas Lutheran University *B*
Texas Tech University *B, M*
[...] University *B*
[...] of Dallas *B*
[...] Houston *B, M*
[...] North Texas *B*

Mary Washington College *B*
Randolph-Macon College *B*
Randolph-Macon Woman's College *B*
Sweet Briar College *B*
University of Richmond *B, T*
University of Virginia *B, M, D*
Virginia Wesleyan College *B*
Washington and Lee University *B*

Washington
Central Washington University *B*
Centralia College *A*
Eastern Washington University *B, T*
Everett Community College *A*
Gonzaga University *B*
Highline Community College *A*
Pacific Lutheran University *B*
Seattle Pacific University *B*
Seattle University *B*
University of Puget Sound *B, T*
University of Washington *B, M, D*
Walla Walla College *B*
Washington State University *B*
Western Washington University *B, T*
Whitman College *B*

West Virginia
Bethany College *B*
Marshall University *B*

Wisconsin
Beloit College *B*
Carthage College *B, T*
Lakeland College *B*
Lawrence University *B*
Marian College of Fond du Lac *B*
Marquette University *B*
Ripon College *B, T*
St. Norbert College *B, T*
University of Wisconsin
    Eau Claire *B*
    Green Bay *B*
    La Crosse *B*
    Madison *B, M, D*
    Milwaukee *B*
    Oshkosh *B*
    Parkside *B*
    Platteville *B*
    River Falls *B*
    Stevens Point *B, T*
    Whitewater *B, T*

Wyoming
Casper College *A*
University of Wyoming *B, M*

German language teacher education

Alabama
Birmingham-Southern College *T*
University of Alabama *B*

Arizona
Arizona State University *B, T*
Northern Arizona University *B, T*
University of Arizona *B, M*

California
California State University
    Chico *T*
    Fullerton *T*
    Long Beach *T*
Humboldt State University *T*
San Diego State University *B*
San Francisco State University *B, T*
San Jose State University *T*
University of the Pacific *T*

Colorado
Colorado State University *T*

Connecticut
Central Connecticut State University *B*
Fairfield University *T*

Delaware
University of Delaware *B, T*

Florida
Stetson University *B, T*

Georgia
Agnes Scott College *T*
Georgia Southern University *B, M, T*

Hawaii
University of Hawaii
    Manoa *B, T*

Idaho
Boise State University *T*

Illinois
Augustana College *B, T*
Elmhurst College *B*
Illinois College *T*
Loyola University of Chicago *T*
North Park University *T*
Northwestern University *B, T*
Rockford College *T*
University of Illinois
    Chicago *B*
    Urbana-Champaign *B, M, T*
Wheaton College *T*

Indiana
Anderson University *B, T*
Ball State University *T*
Goshen College *B*
Grace College *B*
Indiana State University *B, T*
Indiana University
    Bloomington *B, T*
    South Bend *B, T*
Indiana University--Purdue University
    Indiana University-Purdue
        University Fort Wayne *B, T*
    Indiana University-Purdue
        University Indianapolis *B, T*
Manchester College *B, T*
University of Evansville *T*
University of Indianapolis *T*
University of Southern Indiana *B, T*
Valparaiso University *B*

Iowa
Central College *T*
Cornell College *B, T*
Dordt College *B*
Drake University *M, T*
Graceland University *T*
Iowa State University *T*
Loras College *T*
Luther College *B*
St. Ambrose University *B, T*
University of Iowa *B, T*
Wartburg College *T*

Kansas
Baker University *T*
Bethel College *T*

Kentucky
Murray State University *B, M, T*

Louisiana
Centenary College of Louisiana *B, T*
Dillard University *B*

Maryland
Towson University *T*

Massachusetts
Harvard College *T*
Tufts University *T*

Michigan
Albion College *B, T*
Calvin College *B*
Central Michigan University *B*
Eastern Michigan University *B, T*
Grand Valley State University *T*
Northern Michigan University *B, M, T*
Western Michigan University *B*

Minnesota
Augsburg College *T*
Bemidji State University *T*
College of St. Benedict *T*
Concordia College: Moorhead *T*
Gustavus Adolphus College *T*
Minnesota State University,
    Mankato *B, M, T*
St. Cloud State University *T*
St. John's University *T*
St. Olaf College *T*
University of Minnesota
    Duluth *B*
    Morris *T*
University of St. Thomas *T*
Winona State University *B, T*

Mississippi
Mississippi State University *T*
University of Mississippi *B, T*

Missouri
Central Missouri State University *B, T*
College of the Ozarks *B, T*
Southwest Missouri State University *B*
University of Missouri
    Columbia *B*
    St. Louis *T*
Washington University *B, M, T*

Montana
University of Montana-Missoula *T*

Nebraska
Creighton University *T*
Dana College *B*
Doane College *T*
Hastings College *B, M, T*
Midland Lutheran College *B, T*
University of Nebraska
    Kearney *B*
    Lincoln *B, T*

New Hampshire
University of New Hampshire *T*

New Jersey
Fairleigh Dickinson University *M*
Rider University *B*

New York
Canisius College *B, M, T*
City University of New York
    Queens College *T*
Fordham University *M, T*
Hofstra University *B, T*
Ithaca College *B, T*
New York University *B, T*
St. John Fisher College *B, T*
State University of New York
    Buffalo *T*
    New Paltz *B, T*
    Oswego *B*
Vassar College *T*
Wells College *T*

North Carolina
East Carolina University *B*
Lenoir-Rhyne College *B, T*
University of North Carolina
    Charlotte *B*
    Greensboro *B, T*
Wake Forest University *M, T*
Western Carolina University *B, T*

North Dakota
Dickinson State University *B, T*
Minot State University *B, T*
North Dakota State University *B, T*
University of North Dakota *B, T*

Ohio
Baldwin-Wallace College *T*
Bowling Green State University *B*
Hiram College *T*
Kent State University
    Stark Campus *B*
Kent State University *T*

Miami University
    Oxford Campus *B, T*
Mount Union College *T*
Ohio University *B*
University of Dayton *B, M, T*
University of Toledo *B, T*
Xavier University *M, T*
Youngstown State University *B, M, T*

Oklahoma
Oklahoma Baptist University *B, T*
Oklahoma City University *B*
University of Central Oklahoma *B*
University of Tulsa *T*

Oregon
Eastern Oregon University *B, T*
Linfield College *T*
Portland State University *T*
University of Portland *T*
Western Oregon University *T*

Pennsylvania
Bucknell University *T*
California University of
    Pennsylvania *B, T*
Chestnut Hill College *T*
Dickinson College *T*
Duquesne University *B, T*
Gettysburg College *T*
Juniata College *B, T*
La Salle University *B, T*
Lebanon Valley College of
    Pennsylvania *T*
Lock Haven University of
    Pennsylvania *B, T*
Lycoming College *T*
Mansfield University of
    Pennsylvania *B, T*
Messiah College *T*
Moravian College *T*
Villanova University *T*
Washington and Jefferson College *T*
Westminster College *T*
Widener University *T*
Wilkes University *T*

South Carolina
Furman University *T*

South Dakota
Augustana College *B, T*
South Dakota State University *B*
University of South Dakota *T*

Tennessee
David Lipscomb University *B, T*
University of Tennessee
    Martin *B, T*

Texas
Baylor University *B, T*
Hardin-Simmons University *B, T*
Southwest Texas State University *M, T*
Texas Lutheran University *T*
University of Dallas *T*
University of Houston *T*
University of Texas
    Arlington *M, T*
    San Antonio *T*

Utah
Brigham Young University *B*
Weber State University *B*

Virginia
Bridgewater College *T*
Christopher Newport University *T*
Eastern Mennonite University *T*
Hollins University *T*
Longwood College *B, T*
Radford University *T*
Virginia Wesleyan College *T*

Washington
Central Washington University *B, T*
Pacific Lutheran University *B*
Western Washington University *B, T*
Whitworth College *T*

Wisconsin
Carthage College *T*
Lakeland College *B*
Lawrence University *T*
St. Norbert College *T*
University of Wisconsin
    Green Bay *T*
    La Crosse *B, T*
    Madison *M*
    Parkside *T*
    Platteville *B, T*
    River Falls *T*
    Whitewater *B*

Germanic languages

California
Humboldt State University *B*
University of California
    Berkeley *B*
    Los Angeles *M, D*

Illinois
University of Chicago *B, M, D*

Massachusetts
Harvard College *B*

Michigan
Calvin College *B*
University of Michigan
    Flint *B*

Minnesota
University of Minnesota
    Twin Cities *M, D*

New York
Columbia University
    Graduate School *M, D*
Cornell University *M, D*
State University of New York
    Stony Brook *B, M, D*

North Carolina
University of North Carolina
    Chapel Hill *M, D*

Ohio
University of Cincinnati *M, D*

Oklahoma
Western Oklahoma State College *A*

Tennessee
University of Tennessee
    Knoxville *B*

Texas
University of Texas
    Austin *M, D*

Wisconsin
University of Wisconsin
    Madison *B*

Gerontology

Alabama
Shelton State Community College *C*
Spring Hill College *C*
University of South Alabama *C*

Arizona
Phoenix College *C*
Pima Community College *A*
University of Arizona *M*

Arkansas
University of Arkansas
    Little Rock *A, M*
    Pine Bluff *B*
Westark College *A*

California
American River College *C, A*
California College for Health Sciences *C*
California State University
    Chico *C*
    Dominguez Hills *B*
    Long Beach *M*
    Los Angeles *B*
    Sacramento *B*
    Stanislaus *B*
Chaffey Community College *C, A*
Coastline Community College *C*
MiraCosta College *A*
Saddleback College *C*
San Diego State University *C, B*
San Francisco State University *M*
San Jose State University *M*
University of Southern
    California *B, M, D*

Colorado
Community College of Denver *C*
Naropa University *M*
Red Rocks Community College *C*
University of Colorado
    Colorado Springs *C*
University of Denver *M*
University of Northern Colorado *B, M*

Connecticut
Manchester Community-Technical
    College *C*
Naugatuck Valley Community-Technical
    College *C, A*
Quinnipiac University *B*

Florida
Bethune-Cookman College *B*
Florida State University *C*
Lynn University *C, B, M*
St. Petersburg Junior College *C*
University of South Florida *B*

Illinois
City Colleges of Chicago
    Wright College *C, A*
Concordia University *M*
Dominican University *C, B*
Eastern Illinois University *M*
Kendall College *C, A, B*
McKendree College *B*
Northeastern Illinois University *M*
Roosevelt University *B, M*
Western Illinois University *M*

Indiana
Ancilla College *C*
Ball State University *M*
Indiana University
    East *C*
Indiana University--Purdue University
    Indiana University-Purdue
        University Fort Wayne *C*
Manchester College *A*
Purdue University
    Calumet *B*
St. Mary-of-the-Woods College *C, A*
Vincennes University *A*

Iowa
Briar Cliff College *C*

Kansas
Central Christian College *A*
University of Kansas *M, D*
Washburn University of Topeka *A*
Wichita State University *B, M*

Kentucky
Thomas More College *A*
University of Kentucky *D*

Louisiana
University of Louisiana at Monroe *M*
University of New Orleans *C*

Maryland
Sojourner-Douglass College *B*
Towson University *B*
Villa Julie College *A*

Massachusetts
Assumption College *C*
Cape Cod Community College *C*
College of the Holy Cross *B*
Hampshire College *B*
Holyoke Community College *C*
Springfield College *B, M*
University of Massachusetts
    Boston *B, D*

Michigan
Aquinas College *A*
Eastern Michigan University *C*
Lansing Community College *A*
Madonna University *C, A, B*
Mott Community College *A*
Oakland Community College *C, A*
Siena Heights University *A*
University of Michigan *M, D*
Wayne County Community College *C*
Wayne State University *C*

Minnesota
Minnesota State University, Mankato *M*
St. Cloud State University *M*
Winona State University *A*

Mississippi
East Central Community College *A*

Missouri
Central Missouri State University *M*
Southwest Missouri State University *B*
St. Louis Community College
    St. Louis Community College at
        Forest Park *C*
University of Missouri
    St. Louis *C, M*
Webster University *M*

Nebraska
University of Nebraska
    Omaha *B, M*

Nevada
University of Nevada
    Las Vegas *C*

New Hampshire
New Hampshire Community Technical
    College
    Laconia *C, A*
    Manchester *C, A*
    Stratham *C, A*
New Hampshire Technical Institute *C*
Notre Dame College *M*

New Jersey
Caldwell College *C*
College of St. Elizabeth *C*
Gloucester County College *C*
Ocean County College *A*
Richard Stockton College of New
    Jersey *C*
Seton Hall University *C*
Thomas Edison State College *B*
Union County College *C, A*

New York
Alfred University *B*
Broome Community College *A*
Canisius College *C*
City University of New York
    Brooklyn College *B, M*
    Hostos Community College *A*
    La Guardia Community College *A*
    York College *B*
College of New Rochelle *M*
Columbia University
    School of Nursing *M*
Genesee Community College *C*
Hofstra University *M*
Ithaca College *C*
Long Island University
    C. W. Post Campus *M*
    Southampton College *M*
Marymount Manhattan College *C*
Mercy College *C*

Gerontology

St. John Fisher College *C*
St. Joseph's College
   St. Joseph's College *C*
Touro College *M*
Utica College of Syracuse
   University *C, B*

North Carolina
Appalachian State University *M*
Sandhills Community College *C, A*
Shaw University *B*
Southeastern Community College *A*
University of North Carolina
   Charlotte *M*

Ohio
Bowling Green State University *B*
Case Western Reserve University *B*
College of Mount St. Joseph *A, B*
Columbus State Community College *A*
John Carroll University *B*
Kent State University
   Stark Campus *B*
Kent State University *B, M*
Lourdes College *C, A, B*
Miami University
   Oxford Campus *M*
Ohio Dominican College *C, A*
Sinclair Community College *C*
University of Akron
   Wayne College *C*
University of Cincinnati
   Clermont College *C*
University of Findlay *C*

Oklahoma
Connors State College *C, A*
Oklahoma State University *C*
Rogers State University *A*

Oregon
Chemeketa Community College *A*
Clackamas Community College *C*
Mount Hood Community College *C*
Portland Community College *C, A*

Pennsylvania
Alvernia College *C*
California University of
   Pennsylvania *A, B*
Cedar Crest College *C*
Chatham College *C*
Chestnut Hill College *C, B*
Community College of Philadelphia *C*
Duquesne University *M*
Gannon University *C*
Gwynedd-Mercy College *C*
King's College *A, B*
La Roche College *C*
Lincoln University *C*
Mercyhurst College *B*
Millersville University of
   Pennsylvania *A*
Reading Area Community College *A*
University of Pittsburgh
   Bradford *C*
University of Scranton *A, B*
West Chester University of
   Pennsylvania *B, M*

Puerto Rico
Pontifical Catholic University of Puerto
   Rico *A, B*
Universidad Metropolitana *B*
University of Puerto Rico
   Medical Sciences Campus *C, M*

South Carolina
Coastal Carolina University *C*
Greenville Technical College *C*
Lander University *C*
Midlands Technical College *C*

Texas
Abilene Christian University *M*
Baylor University *M*
Stephen F. Austin State University *B*
University of North Texas *B*

University of Texas
   Medical Branch at Galveston *M*

Utah
University of Utah *M*
Weber State University *B*

Virginia
Lynchburg College *C*
Northern Virginia Community College *A*
Virginia Commonwealth University *M*

Washington
Central Washington University *B*
Heritage College *C*

Wisconsin
Mount Mary College *M*

Global studies

California
California State University
   Monterey Bay *B*

Connecticut
Sacred Heart University *B*

Indiana
Manchester College *B*

Iowa
Marycrest International University *B*
University of Iowa *B*

Kansas
Bethel College *B*

Massachusetts
Assumption College *B*
Hampshire College *B*
Northeastern University *B*

Missouri
Rockhurst University *B*

New York
Sage Junior College of Albany *A*
St. Lawrence University *B*
Sarah Lawrence College *B*

North Carolina
Wake Technical Community College *A*

Ohio
Wittenberg University *B*

Pennsylvania
Chatham College *B*
Gettysburg College *B*

South Carolina
Piedmont Technical College *A*

Texas
Prairie View A&M University *B*

Vermont
Marlboro College *B*

Washington
Pacific Lutheran University *B*

Wisconsin
Ripon College *B*
University of Wisconsin
   Madison *B, M*

Graphic design/ commercial art/illustration

Alabama
Alabama State University *B*
Bessemer State Technical College *C*
Calhoun Community College *A*
Community College of the Air Force *A*
James H. Faulkner State Community
   College *A*
Oakwood College *A*
Samford University *B*

Arizona
Arizona State University *B*
Eastern Arizona College *A*
Glendale Community College *A*
Grand Canyon University *B*
Northern Arizona University *B*
Phoenix College *C, A*
Pima Community College *C, A*
Yavapai College *C, A*

Arkansas
Arkansas Tech University *B*
Garland County Community College *A*
Harding University *B*
John Brown University *B*
Northwest Arkansas Community
   College *A*
Ouachita Baptist University *B*
Southern Arkansas University
   Tech *A*

California
Academy of Art College *C, A, B, M*
Allan Hancock College *A*
Art Center College of Design *B, M*
Biola University *B*
Brooks College *A*
Butte College *A*
California College of Arts and
   Crafts *B, M*
California Institute of the Arts *C, B, M*
California Lutheran University *B*
California Polytechnic State University:
   San Luis Obispo *B*
California State University
   Fresno *B*
   Fullerton *B*
   Hayward *B*
   Long Beach *B*
   Northridge *B*
Cerro Coso Community College *C*
Chabot College *A*
Chaffey Community College *C, A*
Chapman University *B*
City College of San Francisco *C, A*
College of San Mateo *C, A*
College of the Redwoods *C, A*
College of the Sequoias *C*
Compton Community College *C, A*
Cuyamaca College *C, A*
Cypress College *A*
De Anza College *C, A*
Evergreen Valley College *A*
Fashion Institute of Design and
   Merchandising *A*
Foothill College *C, A*
Glendale Community College *C, A*
Golden West College *C, A*
La Sierra University *B*
Las Positas College *A*
Long Beach City College *A*
Los Angeles Pierce College *A*
Los Angeles Southwest College *A*
Los Angeles Trade and Technical
   College *A*
Los Angeles Valley College *C, A*
Los Medanos College *C, A*
Merced College *C, A*
MiraCosta College *C, A*
Mission College *C, A*
Modesto Junior College *C, A*
Moorpark College *C, A*
Orange Coast College *A*
Otis College of Art and Design *C, B*
Pacific Union College *A*
Palomar College *C, A*
Pasadena City College *C, A*
Point Loma Nazarene University *B*
Porterville College *C, A*
Riverside Community College *C, A*
Saddleback College *C, A*
San Bernardino Valley College *C, A*
San Diego City College *C, A*
San Diego State University *B*
Santa Ana College *A*
Santa Barbara City College *C, A*

Santa Monica College *A*
Santa Rosa Junior College *C, A*
Shasta College *A*
Solano Community College *A*
Southwestern College *A*
University of San Francisco *B*
University of the Pacific *B*
Ventura College *C*
West Hills Community College *C, A*

Colorado
Arapahoe Community College *C, A*
Art Institute
   of Colorado *A, B*
Colorado Mountain College
   Spring Valley Campus *C, A*
Colorado State University *B*
Community College of Denver *C, A*
Red Rocks Community College *A*
Rocky Mountain College of Art &
   Design *A*
Trinidad State Junior College *C, A*
University of Denver *B*
Western State College of Colorado *B*

Connecticut
Central Connecticut State University *B*
Housatonic Community-Technical
   College *C, A*
Manchester Community-Technical
   College *C, A*
Mitchell College *A*
Northwestern Connecticut
   Community-Technical College *C, A*
Norwalk Community-Technical
   College *C, A*
Paier College of Art *C, B*
Quinebaug Valley Community College *C*
Sacred Heart University *B*
Tunxis Community College *C, A*
University of Bridgeport *B*
University of Hartford *B*
University of New Haven *C, A, B*
Western Connecticut State University *B*

Delaware
University of Delaware *B*

District of Columbia
Corcoran College of Art and Design *B*
Gallaudet University *B*
George Washington University *M*

Florida
Art Institute
   of Fort Lauderdale *C, A, B*
Brevard Community College *A*
Daytona Beach Community College *A*
Flagler College *B*
Florida Agricultural and Mechanical
   University *B*
Florida Community College at
   Jacksonville *A*
Florida Keys Community College *A*
Florida Metropolitan University
   Orlando College North *A*
Florida Southern College *B*
Indian River Community College *A*
International Academy of Merchandising
   and Design *A*
International Fine Arts College *A*
Jacksonville University *B*
Lake-Sumter Community College *A*
Lynn University *B*
Manatee Community College *A*
Miami-Dade Community College *A*
Palm Beach Community College *A*
Pensacola Junior College *A*
Ringling School of Art and Design *B*
St. Petersburg Junior College *A*
Santa Fe Community College *A*
Stetson University *B*
Tampa Technical Institute *A*
University of Florida *B*
University of Miami *C, B*
University of Tampa *B*
Valencia Community College *A*

Graphic design/commercial art/illustration

Georgia
American InterContinental
 University *A, B*
Art Institute
 of Atlanta *A, B*
Atlanta College of Art *B*
Brenau University *B*
Darton College *A*
DeKalb Technical Institute *C*
LaGrange College *B*
Savannah College of Art and
 Design *B, M*
University of Georgia *B*

Hawaii
Brigham Young University
 Hawaii *A*
University of Hawaii
 Honolulu Community College *C, A*

Idaho
Boise State University *B*
North Idaho College *A*
Northwest Nazarene University *B*

Illinois
American Academy of Art *A, B*
Barat College *B*
Chicago State University *B*
City Colleges of Chicago
 Harold Washington College *A*
 Kennedy-King College *C, A*
Columbia College *B*
Dominican University *B*
Highland Community College *C, A*
International Academy of Merchandising
 and Design *A, B*
Judson College *B*
Lewis University *B*
Millikin University *B*
North Park University *B*
Oakton Community College *A*
Robert Morris College: Chicago *C, A*
Southern Illinois University
 Carbondale *A*
Trinity Christian College *B*
University of Illinois
 Chicago *B, M*
 Urbana-Champaign *B*

Indiana
Anderson University *B*
Ball State University *B*
Goshen College *B*
Grace College *B*
Indiana State University *B*
Indiana University
 Bloomington *B, M*
Indiana University--Purdue University
 Indiana University-Purdue
  University Fort Wayne *A, B*
Oakland City University *B*
University of Evansville *B*
University of Indianapolis *B*
University of St. Francis *A, B*
Valparaiso University *B*
Vincennes University *A*

Iowa
Buena Vista University *B*
Clarke College *B*
Des Moines Area Community College *A*
Dordt College *B*
Drake University *B*
Graceland University *B*
Grand View College *B*
Hawkeye Community College *A*
Iowa State University *B, M*
Marycrest International University *B*
Morningside College *B*
St. Ambrose University *B*
Simpson College *B*
Upper Iowa University *B*
Wartburg College *B*

Kansas
Cowley County Community College *A*
Johnson County Community College *A*
Kansas City Kansas Community
 College *A*
Pittsburg State University *B*
Pratt Community College *A*
Tabor College *B*
University of Kansas *B, M*
Wichita State University *B*

Kentucky
Brescia University *B*
Northern Kentucky University *B*
Western Kentucky University *B*

Louisiana
Louisiana Tech University *B*
Loyola University New Orleans *B*

Maine
Maine College of Art *B*
University of Maine
 Augusta *A*

Maryland
Anne Arundel Community College *C*
Carroll Community College *C, A*
Columbia Union College *B*
Frostburg State University *B*
Maryland College of Art and Design *A*
Maryland Institute College of Art *B*
Montgomery College
 Rockville Campus *A*
Prince George's Community College *A*
University of Baltimore *M*
University of Maryland
 Baltimore County *B*
Villa Julie College *A*
Western Maryland College *B*

Massachusetts
Becker College *C, A*
Boston University *B, M*
Bridgewater State College *B*
Bunker Hill Community College *C, A*
Elms College *B*
Endicott College *C, A, B*
Fitchburg State College *B*
Greenfield Community College *A*
Holyoke Community College *C*
Massachusetts College of Art *B, M*
Massasoit Community College *A*
Middlesex Community College *C, A*
Montserrat College of Art *B*
Mount Ida College *A, B*
Newbury College *A*
North Shore Community College *C*
Northeastern University *A, B*
Northern Essex Community
 College *C, A*
Salem State College *B*
Simmons College *B*
Simon's Rock College of Bard *B*
Smith College *D*
Springfield Technical Community
 College *A*
Suffolk University *C, B*
University of Massachusetts
 Dartmouth *B*

Michigan
Alma College *B*
Baker College
 of Auburn Hills *A*
 of Mount Clemens *A*
 of Muskegon *A*
 of Owosso *A*
 of Port Huron *A*
Center for Creative Studies: College of
 Art and Design *B*
Central Michigan University *B*
Cranbrook Academy of Art *M*
Delta College *A*
Ferris State University *A, B*
Grand Valley State University *B*
Henry Ford Community College *A*
Kalamazoo Valley Community
 College *C, A*
Kellogg Community College *A*
Kendall College of Art and Design *B*
Lansing Community College *A*
Macomb Community College *C, A*
Marygrove College *C*
Mid Michigan Community College *A*
Muskegon Community College *C, A*
Northern Michigan University *A, B*
Northwestern Michigan College *A*
Oakland Community College *C, A*
Olivet College *B*
St. Clair County Community College *A*
Schoolcraft College *A*
Siena Heights University *B*
University of Michigan *B*
Western Michigan University *B*

Minnesota
Alexandria Technical College *C*
Bemidji State University *B*
Central Lakes College *C*
College of Visual Arts *B*
Dakota County Technical College *C, A*
Inver Hills Community College *A*
Mesabi Range Community and Technical
 College *C*
Minneapolis College of Art and
 Design *B*
Minnesota State University, Mankato *B*
Moorhead State University *B*
North Hennepin Community College *A*
Northwestern College *A, B*
St. Cloud State University *B*
St. Cloud Technical College *C*
St. Mary's University of Minnesota *B*
St. Paul Technical College *C*
University of Minnesota
 Duluth *B*
 Twin Cities *C, B*
Winona State University *B*

Mississippi
Hinds Community College *A*
Mississippi College *B*
Mississippi Gulf Coast Community
 College
 Perkinston *A*
Mississippi University for Women *B*
Northwest Mississippi Community
 College *A*

Missouri
Avila College *B*
Central Missouri State University *B*
College of the Ozarks *B*
Kansas City Art Institute *B*
Maryville University of Saint Louis *B*
Missouri Southern State College *B*
Missouri Western State College *B*
Penn Valley Community College *A*
St. Charles County Community
 College *A*
Southwest Baptist University *B*
St. Louis Community College
 St. Louis Community College at
  Florissant Valley *A*
 St. Louis Community College at
  Meramec *A*
Truman State University *B*
University of Missouri
 St. Louis *B*
Washington University *B, M*
Webster University *B*
William Woods University *B*

Montana
Western Montana College of The
 University of Montana *A*

Nebraska
Central Community College *C, A*
Concordia University *B*
Creighton University *B*
Doane College *B*
Metropolitan Community College *A*
Midland Lutheran College *B*
Southeast Community College
 Milford Campus *A*
Union College *B*
University of Nebraska
 Kearney *B*
Wayne State College *B*

Nevada
Community College of Southern
 Nevada *A*

New Hampshire
Colby-Sawyer College *B*
Franklin Pierce College *B*
Keene State College *B*
New Hampshire Community Technical
 College
 Berlin *C, A*
 Laconia *C, A*
 Manchester *C, A*
Notre Dame College *B*
Plymouth State College of the University
 System of New Hampshire *B*
Rivier College *B*
White Pines College *B*

New Jersey
Bergen Community College *C, A*
Brookdale Community College *A*
Centenary College *B*
County College of Morris *A*
Cumberland County College *A*
Essex County College *A*
Felician College *B*
Gloucester County College *C, A*
Mercer County Community College *A*
Middlesex County College *A*
Monmouth University *B*
Ocean County College *C*
Rowan University *B*
Rutgers
 The State University of New Jersey:
  Mason Gross School of the
  Arts *B*
 The State University of New Jersey:
  Newark College of Arts and
  Sciences *B*
Seton Hall University *B*
Sussex County Community College *C, A*
The College of New Jersey *B*
Union County College *A*

New Mexico
Clovis Community College *A*
New Mexico Highlands University *B*
New Mexico Junior College *C, A*
San Juan College *A*

New York
Adelphi University *B*
Briarcliffe College *A*
City University of New York
 Bronx Community College *A*
 City College *B*
 Kingsborough Community
  College *A*
College of St. Rose *B*
Daemen College *B*
Dutchess Community College *A*
Eugene Lang College/New School
 University *B*
Finger Lakes Community College *A*
Fulton-Montgomery Community
 College *A*
Genesee Community College *A*
Long Island University
 C. W. Post Campus *B*
 Southampton College *B*
Marymount Manhattan College *C*
Mohawk Valley Community
 College *C, A*
Monroe Community College *A*
Nassau Community College *A*
New York Institute of Technology *B, M*
New York State College of Ceramics at
 Alfred University *B, T*
New York University *B, M*

307

Graphic design/commercial art/illustration

Onondaga Community College A
Parsons School of Design C, A, B, T
Pratt Institute A, B, M
Rochester Institute of
  Technology A, B, M
Rockland Community College C, A
Sage Junior College of Albany A
St. John's University B
St. Thomas Aquinas College B
School of Visual Arts B, M
State University of New York
  College at Buffalo B
  College at Fredonia B
  College of Agriculture and
    Technology at Cobleskill A
  Farmingdale C, A
  New Paltz B
  Oswego B
Suffolk County Community College A
Syracuse University B, M
Tompkins-Cortland Community
  College A
Ulster County Community College C, A
Villa Maria College of Buffalo A
Westchester Business Institute C, A
Westchester Community College C
Wood Tobe-Coburn School C

North Carolina
Campbell University B
Catawba Valley Community College A
Central Piedmont Community College A
Chowan College B
Gaston College C
Guilford Technical Community
  College C, A
Halifax Community College A
James Sprunt Community College A
Johnston Community College A
Lenoir Community College C
Meredith College B
North Carolina State University B, M
Pitt Community College A
Randolph Community College A
South Piedmont Community College A
Southwestern Community College A

North Dakota
Bismarck State College C, A
Dickinson State University A

Ohio
Ashland University B
Central State University B
Clark State Community College A
Cleveland Institute of Art B
College of Mount St. Joseph C, A, B
Columbus College of Art and Design B
Davis College C, A
Defiance College B
Edison State Community College A
Kent State University
  Stark Campus A
Kent State University B, M
Lakeland Community College A
Marietta College B
Ohio Institute of Photography and
  Technology C, A
Ohio Northern University B
Ohio University B
Owens Community College
  Toledo A
Sinclair Community College A
Terra Community College A
University of Akron A, B
University of Cincinnati
  Raymond Walters College C, A
University of Cincinnati B
University of Dayton B
University of Findlay B
Wittenberg University B
Youngstown State University B

Oklahoma
Northeastern Oklahoma Agricultural and
  Mechanical College A
Northeastern State University B
Oklahoma City Community College A
Oklahoma State University
  Okmulgee A
Oklahoma State University B
Oral Roberts University B
Redlands Community College C
Rogers State University C, A
Southwestern Oklahoma State
  University B
University of Central Oklahoma B

Oregon
Art Institute
  of Portland A, B
Lane Community College C, A
Mount Hood Community College A
Pacific Northwest College of Art C, B
Portland Community College A
Portland State University B

Pennsylvania
Antonelli Institute of Art and
  Photography A
Art Institute
  of Philadelphia A
  of Pittsburgh A
Beaver College C, B
Bradley Academy for the Visual Arts A
Bucks County Community College A
Butler County Community College A
Cabrini College B
California University of Pennsylvania B
Carnegie Mellon University B
Chatham College B
Community College of Allegheny
  County C, A
Delaware County Community College A
Drexel University B
Harrisburg Area Community
  College C, A
Kutztown University of Pennsylvania B
La Roche College B
Lehigh Carbon Community College A
Luzerne County Community
  College C, A
Montgomery County Community
  College A
Moore College of Art and Design B
Moravian College B
Northampton County Area Community
  College A
Penn State
  University Park B
Pennsylvania College of
  Technology A, B
Philadelphia University B
Pittsburgh Technical Institute A
Seton Hill College B
Temple University B, M
University of the Arts B
Waynesburg College B
Westmoreland County Community
  College A
York College of Pennsylvania B

Puerto Rico
Atlantic College A, B
Ramirez College of Business and
  Technology A
University of Puerto Rico
  Carolina Regional College A, B

Rhode Island
Salve Regina University B

South Carolina
Anderson College B
Clemson University B
Coker College B
Greenville Technical College C
Midlands Technical College A
Piedmont Technical College C
Trident Technical College A

South Dakota
Black Hills State University B
South Dakota State University B
Southeast Technical Institute A

Tennessee
Belmont University B
Chattanooga State Technical Community
  College A
David Lipscomb University B
Lambuth University B
Nashville State Technical Institute A
O'More College of Design B
Roane State Community College C, A
Southern Adventist University B
Union University B
University of Tennessee
  Knoxville B
  Martin B

Texas
Abilene Christian University B
Amarillo College C, A
Brookhaven College A
Coastal Bend College A
Collin County Community College
  District C, A
El Paso Community College A
Grayson County College C, A
Hill College A
Houston Community College
  System C, A
Lamar University B
Lubbock Christian University B
Midland College A
Navarro College A
Sam Houston State University B
San Antonio College A
Schreiner College B
South Plains College A
Southwest Texas State University B, T
Stephen F. Austin State University M
Texas A&M University
  Commerce B, M
Texas Christian University B
Texas State Technical College
  Harlingen A
  Waco C, A
Texas Tech University B
Texas Woman's University B, M
Tyler Junior College C, A
University of Houston M
University of North Texas B, M
University of Texas
  Arlington B
West Texas A&M University B

Utah
Brigham Young University B
Salt Lake Community College C, A
Weber State University B

Vermont
Castleton State College B
Champlain College A, B
Lyndon State College A, B

Virginia
Central Virginia Community College A
Hampton University B
Longwood College B
Mary Baldwin College B
Northern Virginia Community College A
Thomas Nelson Community College A
Tidewater Community College A
Virginia Commonwealth University B
Virginia Intermont College A, B
Virginia Western Community College A

Washington
Art Institute of Seattle C, A
Central Washington University B
Centralia College A
Clark College C, A
Columbia Basin College A
Cornish College of the Arts B
Eastern Washington University B
Everett Community College A
Henry Cogswell College B
Highline Community College A
Pacific Lutheran University B
Shoreline Community College C, A
Skagit Valley College C, A
Spokane Falls Community College C, A
University of Washington B, M
Western Washington University B
Whatcom Community College A

West Virginia
Concord College B
Fairmont State College B
Marshall University B
West Liberty State College B
West Virginia State College B
West Virginia Wesleyan College B

Wisconsin
Carthage College B
Concordia University Wisconsin B
Gateway Technical College A
Madison Area Technical College A
Milwaukee Area Technical College A
Milwaukee Institute of Art & Design B
Mount Mary College B
St. Norbert College B
Silver Lake College A
University of Wisconsin
  Madison B
  Platteville B
  Stout B
Viterbo University B
Western Wisconsin Technical College A

Wyoming
Laramie County Community College A
Northwest College A

Graphic/printing equipment operation

Alabama
Alabama Agricultural and Mechanical
  University B
Bessemer State Technical College C
Community College of the Air Force A
J. F. Drake State Technical College C, A
John M. Patterson State Technical
  College C, A
University of Alabama B, M

Arizona
Pima Community College C, A

Arkansas
Arkansas State University B
Phillips Community College of the
  University of Arkansas A

California
Allan Hancock College A
American River College A
Bakersfield College A
Butte College A
California Polytechnic State University:
  San Luis Obispo B
City College of San Francisco A
Don Bosco Technical Institute A
Fashion Institute of Design and
  Merchandising A
Fresno City College C, A
Las Positas College A
Los Angeles Trade and Technical
  College C, A
Mission College C, A
Modesto Junior College C, A
Moorpark College A
Palomar College C, A
Rio Hondo College A
Riverside Community College C, A
Sacramento City College C, A
Saddleback College C
San Joaquin Delta College A
Ventura College A

Colorado
Aims Community College C, A
Community College of Aurora A
Community College of Denver C, A

Connecticut
Central Connecticut State University B
Gateway Community College C

District of Columbia
University of the District of Columbia A, B

Florida
Art Institute of Fort Lauderdale A, B
Florida Community College at Jacksonville A
Miami-Dade Community College C, A
Palm Beach Community College A

Georgia
Chattahoochee Technical Institute C
Columbus Technical Institute C
Darton College A
DeKalb Technical Institute C
Georgia Southern University B

Hawaii
University of Hawaii Honolulu Community College A

Idaho
Idaho State University A
Lewis-Clark State College A

Illinois
College of DuPage C, A
College of Lake County C
Elgin Community College C
Moraine Valley Community College C
Parkland College A
Prairie State College C
Triton College C, A
Waubonsee Community College C

Indiana
Ball State University A
Vincennes University A

Iowa
Clinton Community College A
Des Moines Area Community College C, A
Iowa Western Community College A
Kirkwood Community College A
Western Iowa Tech Community College C, A

Kansas
Hutchinson Community College C, A
Kansas City Kansas Community College C, A
Pittsburg State University B

Kentucky
Eastern Kentucky University A
Murray State University A

Maine
Central Maine Technical College A

Maryland
Montgomery College Rockville Campus A

Massachusetts
Northern Essex Community College C
Springfield Technical Community College C, A

Michigan
Alpena Community College C, A
Andrews University A, B
Baker College of Muskegon A
Bay de Noc Community College C
Gogebic Community College C
Grand Rapids Community College A
Henry Ford Community College A
Lansing Community College A
Macomb Community College C, A
Muskegon Community College A
Northern Michigan University B
Oakland Community College C, A
Southwestern Michigan College A
Washtenaw Community College A
Western Michigan University B

Minnesota
Central Lakes College C
Dakota County Technical College C, A
Dunwoody Institute A
Hennepin Technical College C, A
Mesabi Range Community and Technical College C, A
St. Cloud Technical College C
St. Paul Technical College C
South Central Technical College A

Mississippi
Hinds Community College C, A
Mississippi Delta Community College C
Northwest Mississippi Community College C, A

Missouri
Central Missouri State University A, B
College of the Ozarks B
East Central College C, A
Evangel University A
Moberly Area Community College C, A
Ozarks Technical Community College C, A
St. Louis Community College
  St. Louis Community College at Florissant Valley A
  St. Louis Community College at Forest Park A

Montana
Miles Community College A

Nebraska
Central Community College C, A
Metropolitan Community College C, A
Southeast Community College Lincoln Campus C

Nevada
Community College of Southern Nevada C, A

New Hampshire
New Hampshire Community Technical College
  Berlin C, A
  Laconia C, A

New Jersey
Bergen Community College C
Burlington County College A
Kean University B

New Mexico
Albuquerque Technical-Vocational Institute C, A

New York
City University of New York New York City Technical College A
Erie Community College South Campus A
Fulton-Montgomery Community College C, A
Mohawk Valley Community College C
Rochester Institute of Technology A, B, M

North Carolina
Alamance Community College C
Appalachian State University B
Chowan College A, B
Forsyth Technical Community College C
Lenoir Community College A

North Dakota
North Dakota State College of Science C, A

Ohio
Cincinnati State Technical and Community College A
Columbus State Community College A
Lourdes College A

Oklahoma
Northeastern Oklahoma Agricultural and Mechanical College A
Northeastern State University B

Oregon
Chemeketa Community College A
Linn-Benton Community College A
Mount Hood Community College C, A
Portland Community College C, A

Pennsylvania
Bucks County Community College A
California University of Pennsylvania A, B
Delaware County Community College C
Luzerne County Community College A
Montgomery County Community College A
Northampton County Area Community College C
Pennsylvania College of Technology A
Westmoreland County Community College A

Puerto Rico
University of Puerto Rico Carolina Regional College A

South Carolina
Midlands Technical College C
Trident Technical College C

South Dakota
Southeast Technical Institute A

Texas
Central Texas College C, A
College of the Mainland C
Eastfield College C, A
Houston Community College System C, A
Lee College C, A
Midland College A
Navarro College A
South Plains College A
Southwest Texas State University B
Tarrant County College A
Texas A&M University Commerce B
Texas State Technical College Waco C, A
Tyler Junior College C, A

Utah
Dixie State College of Utah C, A
Salt Lake Community College A
Utah Valley State College C, A

Virginia
Dabney S. Lancaster Community College C, A
Danville Community College A
J. Sargeant Reynolds Community College C
John Tyler Community College C
Virginia Intermont College A

Washington
Clark College C, A
Edmonds Community College C
Everett Community College A
Lake Washington Technical College C
Seattle Central Community College A
Shoreline Community College C, A
Walla Walla College C, A, B

West Virginia
Fairmont State College B
West Virginia University Institute of Technology A

Wisconsin
Gateway Technical College C
Lakeshore Technical College C
Madison Area Technical College C, A
Milwaukee Area Technical College A
Moraine Park Technical College A
Northeast Wisconsin Technical College C
Waukesha County Technical College A
Western Wisconsin Technical College C, A

Greek, ancient

Alabama
Samford University B

California
Master's College B
San Diego State University B
Santa Clara University B
University of California
  Berkeley B, M
  Davis B
  Los Angeles B, M
  Santa Cruz B, D

Colorado
University of Denver B

Connecticut
Yale University B

District of Columbia
Howard University B

Florida
Florida State University B, M

Georgia
Oxford College of Emory University B
University of Georgia B, M

Illinois
Augustana College B
Concordia University B
Loyola University of Chicago B
Monmouth College B
Moody Bible Institute B
North Central College B
Rockford College B
University of Chicago B

Indiana
Butler University B
DePauw University B
Indiana University Bloomington B, M, D
University of Notre Dame B
Wabash College B

Iowa
University of Iowa B, M

Kentucky
Asbury College B

Louisiana
Tulane University B, M

Maryland
Washington Bible College M

Massachusetts
Amherst College B
Boston College B, M
Boston University B
Harvard College B
Smith College B
Tufts University B
Wellesley College B

Michigan
Calvin College B
Concordia College B
University of Michigan B, M, D, T

Greek, ancient

Minnesota
Concordia University: St. Paul *B*
Macalester College *B*
University of Minnesota
    Twin Cities *B, M, D*
University of St. Thomas *B*

Missouri
St. Louis University *B*
Washington University *B, M*

Nebraska
Creighton University *B*
University of Nebraska
    Lincoln *B*

New Hampshire
Dartmouth College *B*
St. Anselm College *C*
University of New Hampshire *B*

New Jersey
Rutgers
    The State University of New Jersey:
      Douglass College *B*
    The State University of New Jersey:
      Livingston College *B*
    The State University of New Jersey:
      Rutgers College *B*
    The State University of New Jersey:
      University College New
      Brunswick *B*

New York
Bard College *B*
City University of New York
    Brooklyn College *B*
    Hunter College *B*
    Lehman College *B*
    Queens College *B*
Columbia University
    Graduate School *M, D*
Elmira College *B*
Fordham University *B, M, D*
Hamilton College *B*
New York University *B*
Sarah Lawrence College *B*
Syracuse University *B, M*
Vassar College *B*

North Carolina
Duke University *B*
University of North Carolina
    Chapel Hill *B, M, D*
Wake Forest University *B*

Ohio
John Carroll University *B*
Miami University
    Oxford Campus *B*
Oberlin College *B*
Ohio University *B*
University of Akron *B*
Wright State University *B*

Oregon
Multnomah Bible College *B*
University of Oregon *B*

Pennsylvania
Bryn Mawr College *B, M, D*
Dickinson College *B*
Duquesne University *B*
Franklin and Marshall College *B*
Haverford College *B*
Swarthmore College *B*
University of Scranton *B*
Ursinus College *B, T*

Rhode Island
Brown University *B, M, D*

South Carolina
Furman University *B*

Tennessee
Union University *B*
University of Tennessee
    Knoxville *B*

University of the South *B*

Texas
Baylor University *B*
Rice University *B*
University of Dallas *B*
University of Texas
    Austin *B*

Utah
Brigham Young University *B*

Vermont
Marlboro College *B*
Middlebury College *B*
University of Vermont *B, M*

Virginia
Hampden-Sydney College *B*
Randolph-Macon College *B*
Randolph-Macon Woman's College *B*
Sweet Briar College *B*
University of Richmond *B*

Washington
University of Washington *B*

Wisconsin
Lawrence University *B, T*
University of Wisconsin
    Madison *B, M*

Greek, modern

California
Loyola Marymount University *B*

Connecticut
Connecticut College *B*

District of Columbia
Catholic University of America *B, M, D*
Howard University *B*

Georgia
Oxford College of Emory University *B*

Iowa
Luther College *B*

Louisiana
Tulane University *B*

Maryland
Johns Hopkins University *B*

Massachusetts
Boston University *B*
Harvard College *B*

Michigan
Calvin College *B*
University of Michigan *B*

Minnesota
St. Olaf College *B*

Montana
University of Montana-Missoula *B*

New Hampshire
University of New Hampshire *B*

New York
Bard College *B*
City University of New York
    Brooklyn College *M*
    Queens College *B*
Colgate University *B*
Columbia University
    Graduate School *M, D*
Fordham University *B*
New York University *B*

Ohio
College of Wooster *B*
Ohio State University
    Columbus Campus *B*

Pennsylvania
Gettysburg College *B*

South Carolina
University of South Carolina *B*

Tennessee
Rhodes College *B*
University of the South *B*

Virginia
College of William and Mary *B*

Greenhouse management

California
Los Angeles Pierce College *C*

Illinois
College of DuPage *C*
Joliet Junior College *C, A*
Kishwaukee College *C, A*
Southwestern Illinois College *A*
Triton College *C, A*
William Rainey Harper College *C, A*

Maine
Southern Maine Technical College *C, A*

Massachusetts
North Shore Community College *A*

Michigan
Bay de Noc Community College *C*

Minnesota
University of Minnesota
    Crookston *A*

Nebraska
Central Community College *C*
Nebraska College of Technical
    Agriculture *A*

New Hampshire
University of New Hampshire *A*

New York
State University of New York
    College of Agriculture and
      Technology at Cobleskill *A*
    College of Technology at Alfred *A*

North Carolina
Alamance Community College *C*
Carteret Community College *C*
Johnston Community College *C*
Pitt Community College *C*

North Dakota
Minot State University: Bottineau
    Campus *C, A*

Ohio
Ohio State University
    Agricultural Technical Institute *A*

Pennsylvania
Westmoreland County Community
    College *A*

South Dakota
Southeast Technical Institute *A*

Tennessee
Walters State Community College *A*

Texas
Western Texas College *C, A*

Vermont
Vermont Technical College *A*

Virginia
Lord Fairfax Community College *C*

Washington
Spokane Community College *A*

Health education

Alabama
Alabama State University *B, T*

Auburn University *B*
Jacksonville State University *B*
Lawson State Community College *A*
University of Alabama
    Birmingham *B, M, T*
University of Alabama *B, M, D*
University of South Alabama *B, T*

Arizona
Glendale Community College *C*
University of Arizona *B*

Arkansas
Arkansas State University *B, T*
Harding University *B, T*
Ouachita Baptist University *B, T*
University of Arkansas
    Little Rock *B*
University of Central Arkansas *B, M, T*

California
Azusa Pacific University *T*
California College for Health Sciences *C*
California State University
    Chico *T*
    Dominguez Hills *T*
    Fullerton *T*
    Long Beach *M, T*
    Northridge *B, T*
    Sacramento *T*
Columbia College *C*
San Diego State University *B*
San Francisco State University *B, M, T*
San Jose State University *T*

Connecticut
Southern Connecticut State
    University *B, T*
Western Connecticut State University *B*

Delaware
Delaware State University *B*
University of Delaware *B, T*

District of Columbia
Howard University *B*
University of the District of Columbia *B*

Florida
Florida International University *B, M, T*
Florida State University *B, M*
Gulf Coast Community College *A*
Manatee Community College *A*
Palm Beach Community College *A*
Tallahassee Community College *A*
University of West Florida *B, M, T*

Georgia
Augusta State University *M*
Brewton-Parker College *A, B*
Clark Atlanta University *B*
Georgia College and State
    University *B, M, T*
Georgia Perimeter College *A*
Georgia Southwestern State
    University *B, M, T*
Kennesaw State University *B*
Morris Brown College *B*
South Georgia College *A*
University of Georgia *M, D*
Valdosta State University *B*

Hawaii
University of Hawaii
    Manoa *B, T*

Idaho
Idaho State University *B, M, T*
Lewis-Clark State College *B, T*
Northwest Nazarene University *B*
Ricks College *A*

Illinois
Chicago State University *B*
Eastern Illinois University *B, T*
Illinois State University *B, T*
North Park University *T*

Southern Illinois University
　Carbondale B, M, D
　Edwardsville B
Western Illinois University B, M

Indiana
Anderson University B, T
Ball State University B
Butler University T
Franklin College T
Indiana State University B, M, T
Indiana University
　Bloomington B, M, D, T
Indiana University--Purdue University
　Indiana University-Purdue
　　University Indianapolis B, M
Indiana Wesleyan University T
Manchester College B, T
University of Indianapolis T
University of St. Francis B
Vincennes University A

Iowa
Central College T
Dordt College B
Drake University T
Graceland University T
Iowa State University B, T
Iowa Wesleyan College B
Northwestern College T
St. Ambrose University B, T
University of Iowa T
University of Northern Iowa B, M
Upper Iowa University B
Wartburg College T
William Penn University B

Kansas
Benedictine College T
Bethany College B
Bethel College T
Emporia State University B, T
Garden City Community College A
Independence Community College A
McPherson College T
MidAmerica Nazarene University B, T
Ottawa University T
Pittsburg State University B, T
Tabor College B, T
University of Kansas B, T
Washburn University of Topeka B
Wichita State University T

Kentucky
Campbellsville University B
Cumberland College B, T
Morehead State University B
Murray State University B, T
Union College M
University of Kentucky B
Western Kentucky University B

Louisiana
Centenary College of Louisiana B, T
Dillard University B
McNeese State University B, M
Nicholls State University B
Northwestern State University T

Maine
University of Maine
　Farmington B
　Presque Isle B

Maryland
Allegany College A
Community College of Baltimore County
　Essex A
Morgan State University B
Prince George's Community College A
University of Maryland
　College Park B, M, D, T
　Eastern Shore B

Massachusetts
Boston University M, T
Bridgewater State College B, M, T
Curry College B

Northeastern University B
Springfield College B, M, T
Westfield State College B, T
Worcester State College M, T

Michigan
Adrian College B, T
Alma College T
Central Michigan University B, M
Ferris State University B
Michigan State University M, D
Northern Michigan University B, M, T
Wayne State University M, T
Western Michigan University B

Minnesota
Augsburg College B, T
Bemidji State University T
Bethel College B
Concordia College: Moorhead T
Gustavus Adolphus College T
Hamline University B
Minnesota State University,
　Mankato B, M
Moorhead State University B, T
Northland Community & Technical
　College A
Ridgewater College: A Community and
　Technical College A
Southwest State University B, T
University of Minnesota
　Duluth B
University of St. Thomas B, T
Winona State University B, M, T

Mississippi
Coahoma Community College A
Jackson State University B, M
Mary Holmes College A
Mississippi Delta Community College A
Mississippi State University T
Mississippi University for Women M
Tougaloo College B

Missouri
College of the Ozarks T
Culver-Stockton College T
Lindenwood University B
Missouri Baptist College B, T
Missouri Southern State College B
Southwest Baptist University T
Truman State University M, T

Montana
Montana State University
　Billings B, T
　Bozeman T
Rocky Mountain College B, T
University of Montana-Missoula T
Western Montana College of The
　University of Montana B, T

Nebraska
Concordia University T
University of Nebraska
　Kearney B, T
　Lincoln B, T
　Omaha B, T

Nevada
University of Nevada
　Las Vegas B
　Reno B

New Hampshire
Keene State College T
Plymouth State College of the University
　System of New Hampshire B, M, T

New Jersey
Montclair State University B, M, T
Rowan University C, B
Seton Hall University B, M, T
The College of New Jersey B, M
Thomas Edison State College B
William Paterson University of New
　Jersey B

New Mexico
University of New Mexico B, M, T
Western New Mexico University B

New York
Adelphi University M
City University of New York
　Brooklyn College B, M
　Hunter College B, M, T
　Lehman College B, M, T
　Queens College T
　York College B, T
College of Mount St. Vincent B, T
Columbia University
　Teachers College M, D
Corning Community College A
Fulton-Montgomery Community
　College A
Hofstra University B, M, T
Ithaca College B, T
Long Island University
　C. W. Post Campus B, T
Manhattan College B, T
New York University M, D, T
St. Joseph's College
　St. Joseph's College: Suffolk
　　Campus C
State University of New York
　College at Brockport B, M, T
　College at Cortland B, M, T
　Oswego T
Syracuse University B

North Carolina
Appalachian State University B, M, T
Cleveland Community College A
East Carolina University B, M
Elon College B, T
Fayetteville State University B, T
Gardner-Webb University B
Johnson C. Smith University B
Lenoir Community College A
North Carolina Central University B
North Carolina State University T
Sandhills Community College A
University of North Carolina
　Greensboro B, T
　Pembroke B, T

North Dakota
Dickinson State University B, T
Mayville State University B, T
Valley City State University B, T

Ohio
Ashland University B, T
Baldwin-Wallace College B, T
Bluffton College B
Bowling Green State University B
Capital University T
Cedarville College T
Central State University B
College of Mount St. Joseph B, T
Defiance College B, T
Kent State University
　Stark Campus B
Kent State University B, M, T
Malone College B
Miami University
　Oxford Campus B, M, T
Mount Union College T
Mount Vernon Nazarene College B, T
Ohio Northern University B, T
Ohio State University
　Columbus Campus M, D
Ohio University B, T
Otterbein College B
University of Akron M
University of Cincinnati B, M, T
University of Findlay B, T
University of Rio Grande B, T
University of Toledo B, M, D, T
Wilmington College B
Youngstown State University B, M, T

Oklahoma
East Central University T

Eastern Oklahoma State College A
Northeastern Oklahoma Agricultural and
　Mechanical College A
Northeastern State University B
Northwestern Oklahoma State
　University B, T
Oklahoma Baptist University B, T
Oklahoma City University B
Oklahoma State University M, D
Oral Roberts University B, T
Southeastern Oklahoma State
　University B, M, T
Southwestern Oklahoma State
　University B, M, T
University of Central Oklahoma B

Oregon
Chemeketa Community College A
Concordia University B, M, T
George Fox University B, M, T
Linfield College T
Oregon State University M
Portland State University B, M, T
University of Portland T
Western Oregon University T

Pennsylvania
Beaver College M
Bucks County Community College A
East Stroudsburg University of
　Pennsylvania B, T
Gettysburg College T
Lincoln University B, T
Lock Haven University of
　Pennsylvania B, T
Penn State
　Harrisburg M
　University Park M, D
St. Joseph's University M
Slippery Rock University of
　Pennsylvania B
Temple University B, M
University of Pennsylvania M
Ursinus College B, T
West Chester University of
　Pennsylvania B, M, B

Puerto Rico
Colegio Universitario del Este B

Rhode Island
Rhode Island College B, M

South Carolina
South Carolina State University B, T
University of South Carolina M

South Dakota
Dakota State University B, T
Mount Marty College B
Northern State University M
University of South Dakota M

Tennessee
Austin Peay State University B, T
Belmont University T
Bethel College B
East Tennessee State University B
Freed-Hardeman University T
Lambuth University T
Lincoln Memorial University B, T
Maryville College B, T
Middle Tennessee State University B
Tennessee Technological
　University B, M, T
University of Tennessee
　Knoxville M, D, T
Vanderbilt University M

Texas
Abilene Christian University B, T
Baylor University B, M, T
Del Mar College A
Hardin-Simmons University B, T
Kilgore College A
Lamar University T
Prairie View A&M University M
Sam Houston State University M, T

Health education

Southwest Texas State University M, T
Texas A&M University
  Commerce M, T
  Kingsville B
Texas A&M University B, M, D
Texas Christian University T
Texas Woman's University D, T
University of Houston
  Clear Lake T
University of Houston B, M
University of North Texas B, M, T
University of Texas
  Arlington T
  Austin M, D
  El Paso M
  Pan American B, M, T
  San Antonio T
  Tyler M, T
West Texas A&M University M

Utah
Brigham Young University B
Snow College A
University of Utah B, M, D
Utah State University B

Vermont
Johnson State College B

Virginia
Averett College B, T
George Mason University B, M
Hampton University B
James Madison University M, T
Liberty University B
Longwood College B, T
Lynchburg College B
Norfolk State University B
Radford University B, T
University of Virginia's College at
  Wise T
Virginia Commonwealth University B

Washington
Central Washington University B, T
Eastern Washington University B, T
Pacific Lutheran University T
Renton Technical College C, A
Western Washington University B, T
Whitworth College B, T

West Virginia
Concord College B
Shepherd College T
West Liberty State College B
West Virginia State College B
West Virginia Wesleyan College B

Wisconsin
Carroll College T
Ripon College T
University of Wisconsin
  La Crosse B, M, T
  Platteville T
  River Falls T
  Superior T

Wyoming
University of Wyoming B

Health occupations teacher education

Alabama
Lawson State Community College A

California
Crafton Hills College C, A

Florida
Palm Beach Community College A

Georgia
Columbus State University M

Illinois
North Park University T

University of Illinois
  Chicago M

Iowa
University of Iowa B, T

Kentucky
Cumberland College B, T
University of Louisville B, T

Maine
University of Maine
  Presque Isle B

Michigan
Michigan Technological University T

Minnesota
Gustavus Adolphus College T
Minnesota State University, Mankato B
Winona State University B, M, T

New York
City University of New York
  Brooklyn College B
New York Institute of
  Technology A, B, T
State University of New York
  College at Brockport M
  College at Buffalo B, M
  Oswego B

North Carolina
North Carolina State University M

Ohio
Bowling Green State University B
Youngstown State University B, M

Pennsylvania
Lock Haven University of
  Pennsylvania B, T

Tennessee
Belmont University B, T

Texas
Southwest Texas State University M, T
Texas A&M University
  Commerce M
Texas A&M University M, D
University of Houston M, D
University of Texas
  Southwestern Medical Center at
  Dallas B

Washington
Western Washington University B

Wisconsin
University of Wisconsin
  La Crosse B, M, T

Health physics/radiologic health

Arkansas
University of Central Arkansas B

California
University of California
  Los Angeles M, D

Colorado
National Technological University M

Florida
Gulf Coast Community College A

Georgia
Georgia Institute of Technology M

Illinois
Illinois Institute of Technology M
University of St. Francis B

Indiana
University of St. Francis A

Massachusetts
Massachusetts College of Pharmacy and
  Health Sciences B
Northern Essex Community College A

Michigan
Delta College A
University of Michigan M
Wayne State University M

Nevada
University of Nevada
  Las Vegas B, M

New Jersey
New Jersey Institute of Technology M
Thomas Edison State College A, B

New York
Monroe Community College A

Oregon
Oregon State University B

Pennsylvania
Bloomsburg University of
  Pennsylvania B
University of Pittsburgh C

Puerto Rico
Colegio Universitario del Este C

South Carolina
Francis Marion University B

Tennessee
Roane State Community College C

Texas
Texas A&M University B
University of Texas
  Medical Branch at Galveston B

Virginia
Central Virginia Community College A

Wisconsin
University of Wisconsin
  Madison M, D

Wyoming
Casper College A

Health products/services marketing

California
Saddleback College C

Connecticut
Asnuntuck Community-Technical
  College A

Indiana
Indiana State University B

Michigan
Northwood University A, B

Pennsylvania
Carlow College B

Puerto Rico
Universidad Metropolitana B

Health professions/related sciences

Alabama
Auburn University B, M, D
Chattahoochee Valley Community
  College A
Community College of the Air Force A
Faulkner University A
University of South Alabama B

Arizona
Grand Canyon University B, M
Phoenix College A
Prescott College B, M

Arkansas
Northwest Arkansas Community
  College A
Southern Arkansas University
  Tech C
University of Arkansas
  Little Rock B

California
Barstow College A
Butte College A
Cabrillo College A
California College for Health Sciences B
California State University
  Bakersfield B
  Chico B
  Dominguez Hills B
  Fresno B
  Hayward B
  Los Angeles B, M
  Northridge B, M
Chapman University B, M
Citrus College A
College of the Canyons A
Columbia College A
Compton Community College A
Concordia University B
Crafton Hills College C, A
Diablo Valley College A
East Los Angeles College C
Fresno City College C, A
Irvine Valley College A
Mendocino College C, A
Mission College A
Mount St. Mary's College A, B
Riverside Community College A
Samuel Merritt College B
San Joaquin Delta College A
San Jose State University B, M
University of California
  Irvine M, D
University of La Verne B
Ventura College A
Whittier College B

Colorado
Colorado Mountain College
  Alpine Campus A
Colorado Technical University B, M
Trinidad State Junior College C, A

Connecticut
Briarwood College C, A
Northwestern Connecticut
  Community-Technical College C
Quinebaug Valley Community College C
Quinnipiac University B, M
University of Hartford B, M

Delaware
Delaware Technical and Community
  College
    Owens Campus C
    Stanton/Wilmington Campus C
    Terry Campus A

District of Columbia
George Washington University M
Howard University D

Florida
Barry University M
Brevard Community College C
Central Florida Community College A
Edison Community College A
Florida Atlantic University B
Jones College B
Lake City Community College C, A
Lynn University A
Miami-Dade Community College A
St. Petersburg Junior College C, A
University of Central Florida M
University of Miami B
University of North Florida B, M

Georgia
Albany State University B

Health professions/related sciences

Armstrong Atlantic State University *B, M*
Augusta State University *A*
Bainbridge College *A*
Brewton-Parker College *A*
Columbus State University *B*
Covenant College *A*
Emmanuel College *A, B*
Emory University *A*
Gainesville College *A*
Georgia Perimeter College *A*
Macon State College *A*
Middle Georgia College *A*
Morris Brown College *B*
Shorter College *B*
South Georgia College *A*

Idaho
Boise State University *B*
College of Southern Idaho *C, A*
Ricks College *A*

Illinois
Benedictine University *B*
Black Hawk College *C, A*
City Colleges of Chicago
  Richard J. Daley College *C, A*
College of DuPage *C, A*
College of Lake County *C*
Finch University of Health Sciences/The Chicago Medical School *M, D*
John Wood Community College *A*
Kishwaukee College *C, A*
Lewis and Clark Community College *A*
Moraine Valley Community College *C, A*
Rend Lake College *A*
St. Xavier University *M*
Southern Illinois University Carbondale *B*
Southwestern Ilinois College *C, A*
University of Illinois Springfield *B, M*

Indiana
Ball State University *M*
Calumet College of St. Joseph *B*
Indiana State University *M*
Indiana University Bloomington *B, M*
Purdue University *B, M, D*
University of Evansville *B, M*
University of Southern Indiana *B*

Iowa
Cornell College *B*
Grand View College *B*
Northeast Iowa Community College *A*
St. Ambrose University *B*
Scott Community College *C, A*
University of Northern Iowa *B*
Waldorf College *A*

Kansas
Central Christian College *A*
Coffeyville Community College *A*
Garden City Community College *A*
Hutchinson Community College *A*
Kansas City Kansas Community College *A*
Pratt Community College *A*
Seward County Community College *C, A*
Wichita State University *B, M*

Louisiana
Dillard University *B*
Tulane University *M, D*

Maine
Kennebec Valley Technical College *A*
University of Southern Maine *B*

Maryland
Columbia Union College *A, B*
Towson University *B, M, T*
University of Maryland Eastern Shore *B, M*

Villa Julie College *A*

Massachusetts
Bay Path College *B*
Becker College *A, B*
Boston University *M, D*
Bunker Hill Community College *C*
Greenfield Community College *C*
Lasell College *A*
Massachusetts College of Pharmacy and Health Sciences *B*
Middlesex Community College *C*
Mount Ida College *A*
Northeastern University *A, B, M, D*
Pine Manor College *A*
Roxbury Community College *C*
Worcester State College *B*

Michigan
Albion College *T*
Andrews University *B*
Baker College
  of Cadillac *C, A, B*
  of Jackson *A*
Central Michigan University *B*
Grand Valley State University *B, M*
Madonna University *B*
Marygrove College *A*
Northern Michigan University *T*
Southwestern Michigan College *C, A*
University of Michigan Flint *B*
University of Michigan *B, M, D*
Western Michigan University *B, T*

Minnesota
College of St. Catherine-Minneapolis *C*
College of St. Scholastica *B*
Minneapolis Community and Technical College *C*
Minnesota State University, Mankato *B*
North Hennepin Community College *A*
Northland Community & Technical College *A*
Pine Technical College *A*
Rochester Community and Technical College *A*
University of Minnesota Crookston *B*
University of St. Thomas *B*
Winona State University *B*

Mississippi
Alcorn State University *B*
Holmes Community College *A*
Jackson State University *B*
William Carey College *B*

Missouri
East Central College *A*
Fontbonne College *T*
Maryville University of Saint Louis *B*
Mineral Area College *A*
St. Charles County Community College *A*
Stephens College *B*
Truman State University *B*

Montana
Montana State University
  College of Technology-Great Falls *A*
Montana Tech of the University of Montana *A, B*
University of Great Falls *A*

Nebraska
Central Community College *C, A*
Dana College *B*
Doane College *B*
Union College *A, B*

Nevada
University of Nevada Las Vegas *B*

New Hampshire
New Hampshire Community Technical College
  Berlin *A*

New Jersey
New Jersey City University *B, M*
Raritan Valley Community College *A*
St. Peter's College *C, B*
University of Medicine and Dentistry of New Jersey
  School of Health Related Professions *C, A, B, M, D*

New Mexico
Albuquerque Technical-Vocational Institute *C*
Western New Mexico University *A, B*

New York
Adirondack Community College *A*
Alfred University *B*
City University of New York
  Brooklyn College *B, M*
  Hunter College *M*
  Medgar Evers College *A*
  Queensborough Community College *A*
College of Mount St. Vincent *B, M*
Columbia University
  Teachers College *M, D*
Fulton-Montgomery Community College *A*
Ithaca College *B, M*
Long Island University
  Brooklyn Campus *B, M*
New York University *C*
Onondaga Community College *A*
St. Joseph's College
  St. Joseph's College: Suffolk Campus *C, B*
State University of New York
  College at Brockport *B*
  College at Cortland *B*
  College of Agriculture and Technology at Morrisville *A*
  Health Science Center at Brooklyn *B*
  Health Science Center at Stony Brook *B*
Touro College *B*
Villa Maria College of Buffalo *C, A*

North Carolina
Bennett College *B*
Brevard College *B*
Carolinas College of Health Sciences *C, A*
Lenoir Community College *A*
Mars Hill College *B*
Meredith College *B*

North Dakota
Minot State University: Bottineau Campus *A*

Ohio
Columbus State Community College *A*
Davis College *A*
Kent State University
  Stark Campus *B*
Kent State University *B*
Marion Technical College *C*
Ohio State University
  Columbus Campus *M, D*
RETS Tech Center *A*
Union Institute *B*
University of Cincinnati
  Raymond Walters College *A*
University of Findlay *B*
Ursuline College *B*
Wittenberg University *B*
Youngstown State University *A, B*

Oklahoma
St. Gregory's University *B*
Southern Nazarene University *B*

Southwestern Oklahoma State University *B*
Tulsa Community College *A*
University of Central Oklahoma *M*

Oregon
Chemeketa Community College *A*
Lane Community College *A*
Oregon Institute of Technology *B*
Western Baptist College *B*

Pennsylvania
Bloomsburg University of Pennsylvania *A*
Bucks County Community College *A*
California University of Pennsylvania *B*
Carlow College *B*
Community College of Allegheny County *C, A*
Delaware County Community College *A*
Duquesne University *B, M*
Elizabethtown College *B*
Gwynedd-Mercy College *A*
Immaculata College *A*
Juniata College *B*
La Roche College *M*
La Salle University *A, B*
Lock Haven University of Pennsylvania *B*
MCP Hahnemann University *A, B, M*
Manor College *A*
Mansfield University of Pennsylvania *A, B*
Median School of Allied Health Careers *C*
Point Park College *A, B*
Sawyer School *A*
University of Pennsylvania *C, B, M, D*
University of Pittsburgh *C, B*
University of Scranton *B*
Ursinus College *B*
West Chester University of Pennsylvania *B*
Widener University *B*
York College of Pennsylvania *A, B*

Puerto Rico
Colegio Universitario del Este *A*
University of Puerto Rico
  Medical Sciences Campus *B*

Rhode Island
University of Rhode Island *B*

South Carolina
Clemson University *B*
Erskine College *B*
York Technical College *C*

South Dakota
Augustana College *B*
Dakota State University *A, B*

Tennessee
Cumberland University *A, B*
East Tennessee State University *A, B*
Motlow State Community College *A*
Southern Adventist University *B*
Volunteer State Community College *A*

Texas
Baylor University *B, M*
Central Texas College *C, A*
College of the Mainland *A*
LeTourneau University *B*
Panola College *A*
Paris Junior College *A*
Southwest Texas State University *B, M*
Southwestern Adventist University *A, B*
Texas A&M University
  Commerce *B*
  Corpus Christi *B*
University of Houston *B, M, D*
University of North Texas *B, M*

Health professions/related sciences

University of Texas
    Medical Branch at Galveston *M*
    Pan American *B*
    San Antonio *B*
    Tyler *B*

Utah
Brigham Young University *M*
University of Utah *M*

Vermont
Castleton State College *A, B*
Champlain College *A, B*
Community College of Vermont *A*
Goddard College *B*

Washington
City University *M*
Everett Community College *C, A*
Highline Community College *A*
Lower Columbia College *A*
Renton Technical College *C*
University of Washington *M*
Walla Walla College *B*

West Virginia
College of West Virginia *B, M*
West Virginia University Institute of
    Technology *A, B*
West Virginia University *B, M*

Wisconsin
Beloit College *B*
Marquette University *B*
University of Wisconsin
    Milwaukee *B*

Wyoming
Eastern Wyoming College *A*
Northwest College *A*
Sheridan College *A*
University of Wyoming *B*
Western Wyoming Community
    College *A*

Health system administration

Alabama
Auburn University *B*
Community College of the Air Force *A*
University of Alabama
    Birmingham *M, D*

Alaska
University of Alaska
    Fairbanks *A*
    Southeast *A*

Arizona
Arizona State University *M*
Gateway Community College *C, A*
University of Arizona *B*

Arkansas
Harding University *B*
University of Arkansas
    Little Rock *M*

California
Azusa Pacific University *M*
Barstow College *C*
California College for Health Sciences *B*
California State University
    Bakersfield *M*
    Chico *B*
    Dominguez Hills *B*
    Hayward *M*
    Northridge *M*
Chapman University *M*
Imperial Valley College *C, A*
Loma Linda University *M*
Mount St. Mary's College *B*
National College *B, M*
St. Mary's College of California *M*
San Jose State University *M*
University of California
    Berkeley *D*

University of La Verne *C, B, M*
University of San Francisco *M*
University of Southern California *M*

Colorado
Community College of Denver *C*
Denver Technical College: A Division of
    DeVry University *B*
Metropolitan State College of Denver *B*
Naropa University *M*
University of Colorado
    Denver *M*

Connecticut
Quinnipiac University *B, M*
Sacred Heart University *M*
University of Connecticut *B*
University of New Haven *M*
Western Connecticut State University *M*

District of Columbia
George Washington University *D*
Southeastern University *A, B, M*

Florida
Barry University *M*
Broward Community College *A*
Florida Agricultural and Mechanical
    University *A*
Florida Atlantic University *B*
Florida Institute of Technology *M*
Florida International University *B, M*
Florida State University *C*
Lynn University *C, B, M*
Miami-Dade Community College *A*
Nova Southeastern University *M*
Pensacola Junior College *A*
Polk Community College *A*
St. Leo University *B*
University of Central Florida *B*
University of Florida *M, D*
University of Miami *B*
University of North Florida *M*
University of South Florida *M*
University of Tampa *C, M*

Georgia
Armstrong Atlantic State
    University *B, M*
Columbus State University *B, M*
Georgia Institute of Technology *M*
Georgia Southern University *M*
Georgia State University *M, D*
Macon State College *B*
Mercer University *M*

Hawaii
University of Hawaii
    Hawaii Community College *C*
    West Oahu *B*

Idaho
College of Southern Idaho *A*
Idaho State University *B*

Illinois
Benedictine University *B*
Governors State University *B, M*
National-Louis University *B*
Roosevelt University *B, M*
Southern Illinois University
    Carbondale *B*
University of Illinois
    Springfield *M*
University of St. Francis *M*

Indiana
Goshen College *B*
Indiana State University *B*
Indiana University
    Bloomington *B*
    Northwest *A, B*
    South Bend *B*
Indiana University--Purdue University
    Indiana University-Purdue
        University Fort Wayne *B*
    Indiana University-Purdue
        University Indianapolis *B, M*

Purdue University
    North Central Campus *A*
University of Evansville *M*

Iowa
Des Moines Area Community College *A*
Indian Hills Community College *A*
Iowa Lakes Community College *A*
St. Ambrose University *M*
University of Iowa *M, D*
University of Osteopathic Medicine and
    Health Sciences
        Des Moines University -
        Osteopathic Medical Center *B, M*
Upper Iowa University *B*

Kansas
University of Kansas
    Medical Center *B*
University of Kansas *M*
Wichita State University *B*

Kentucky
Eastern Kentucky University *B*
University of Kentucky *B, M*
Western Kentucky University *B*

Louisiana
Tulane University *M, D*
University of Louisiana at Lafayette *M*
University of New Orleans *M*

Maine
St. Joseph's College *M*
University of New England *B*
University of Southern Maine *M*

Maryland
Baltimore City Community College *C, A*
Columbia Union College *B*

Massachusetts
Assumption College *C*
Bay Path College *A, B*
Boston University *M*
Emmanuel College *M*
Framingham State College *M*
Lasell College *B*
Newbury College *B*
Northeastern University *B*
Simmons College *M*
Springfield College *B, M*
Stonehill College *B*
University of Massachusetts
    Lowell *M*

Michigan
Baker College
    of Mount Clemens *B*
    of Muskegon *B*
    of Owosso *B*
Central Michigan University *M*
Concordia College *B*
Davenport College of Business *B*
Detroit College of Business *B*
Eastern Michigan University *B*
Ferris State University *B*
Lansing Community College *A*
Oakland Community College *C, A*
University of Detroit Mercy *M*
University of Michigan
    Dearborn *B*
    Flint *B, M*
University of Michigan *M, D*
Wayne State University *C, M*

Minnesota
Concordia College: Moorhead *B*
Moorhead State University *M*
St. Mary's University of Minnesota *B, M*
University of Minnesota
    Twin Cities *M*
University of St. Thomas *M*
Winona State University *B*

Mississippi
Jackson State University *B*
Mississippi College *M*

Mississippi Gulf Coast Community
    College
        Jackson County Campus *C*
University of Mississippi *D*

Missouri
Avila College *M*
Lindenwood University *B*
Maryville University of Saint Louis *B*
St. Louis University *M, D*
Southeast Missouri State University *M*
Southwest Missouri State University *M*
University of Missouri
    Columbia *M*
Webster University *B, M*

Montana
Montana State University
    Billings *B, M*
    Bozeman *B*
University of Great Falls *B*

Nebraska
Central Community College *C, A*
Clarkson College *B, M*
Creighton University *B, M*

Nevada
University of Nevada
    Las Vegas *B*

New Hampshire
University of New Hampshire *B, M*

New Jersey
College of St. Elizabeth *M*
Essex County College *A*
Rutgers
    The State University of New Jersey:
        Newark Graduate Campus *M*
Seton Hall University *C, M*
Thomas Edison State College *B*

New York
City University of New York
    Baruch College *M*
    Brooklyn College *B, M*
    Lehman College *B*
D'Youville College *M*
Dominican College of Blauvelt *B*
Herkimer County Community College *A*
Hofstra University *M*
Iona College *M*
Ithaca College *B*
Long Island University
    Brooklyn Campus *B, M*
    C. W. Post Campus *B, M*
New York University *A, M*
Rochester Institute of Technology *M*
St. Francis College *B*
St. John's University *B*
St. Joseph's College
    St. Joseph's College *B*
State University of New York
    College at Fredonia *B*
    Health Science Center at Stony
        Brook *M*
    Institute of Technology at
        Utica/Rome *B*
Union College *M*

North Carolina
Duke University *M*
Meredith College *M*
Pfeiffer University *B, M*
University of North Carolina
    Chapel Hill *B, M, D*
    Charlotte *M*
Western Carolina University *B*

Ohio
Bowling Green State University *B*
College of Mount St. Joseph *B*
David N. Myers College *C, B*
Franklin University *B*
Heidelberg College *B*
Kent State University
    Stark Campus *B*

314

Ohio State University
  Columbus Campus M
Ohio University B
Shawnee State University B
University of Cincinnati B, M
University of Findlay M
Ursuline College B
Wilberforce University B
Wright State University M
Xavier University M

Oklahoma
Langston University B
Northeastern State University B

Oregon
Chemeketa Community College A
Concordia University B
Oregon State University B, M

Pennsylvania
Beaver College C, B
Community College of Allegheny
  County C
Duquesne University B
Harrisburg Area Community College A
King's College C, B, M
Lebanon Valley College of
  Pennsylvania C
Manor College C, A
Marywood University M
Median School of Allied Health
  Careers C
Neumann College C
Peirce College A, B
Penn State
  Harrisburg B, M
  University Park B, M, D
Philadelphia University C
Robert Morris College B, M
St. Joseph's University C, A, B, M
Seton Hill College B
Temple University M
University of Pennsylvania B, M, D
University of Pittsburgh M, D
University of Scranton A, B, M
West Chester University of
  Pennsylvania B, M
Widener University M, D
Wilkes University M
York College of Pennsylvania B, M

Puerto Rico
University of Puerto Rico
  Medical Sciences Campus M

Rhode Island
Providence College C, A, B
Salve Regina University M
University of Rhode Island B

South Carolina
Greenville Technical College C, A
Lander University B
Tri-County Technical College C
University of South Carolina M

South Dakota
Augustana College B
Black Hills State University B
University of South Dakota B

Tennessee
Carson-Newman College B
Southern Adventist University B, M
Tennessee State University B
Tennessee Wesleyan College B
University of Memphis M

Texas
Baylor University M
Dallas Baptist University B
Galveston College A
Houston Baptist University B
Howard Payne University B
Our Lady of the Lake University of San
  Antonio M
Southwest Texas State University B, M

Southwestern Adventist University B
Texas A&M University
  Commerce B
Texas Woman's University M
Trinity University M
University of Houston
  Clear Lake B, M
University of Mary Hardin-Baylor M
University of North Texas M
University of Texas
  Arlington M
  El Paso B
  Medical Branch at Galveston B
  Southwestern Medical Center at
    Dallas B

Utah
LDS Business College A
Weber State University B

Virginia
Mary Baldwin College B
Norfolk State University B
Shenandoah University C
Virginia Commonwealth
  University B, M, D

Washington
Eastern Washington University B
Highline Community College A
North Seattle Community College C
University of Washington M
Washington State University M

West Virginia
College of West Virginia B
Davis and Elkins College A, B
Fairmont State College B
Marshall University M
Wheeling Jesuit University B

Wisconsin
Cardinal Stritch University B
Northeast Wisconsin Technical
  College A
University of Wisconsin
  Eau Claire B
  Madison M
Viterbo University B

Health/medical biostatistics

California
University of California
  Los Angeles M, D

Iowa
University of Iowa M, D

Louisiana
Tulane University M, D

New York
State University of New York
  Albany B, M
  Buffalo M

North Carolina
University of North Carolina
  Chapel Hill M, D

Pennsylvania
University of Pittsburgh M, D

Puerto Rico
University of Puerto Rico
  Medical Sciences Campus M

South Carolina
University of South Carolina M, D

Health/medical laboratory technologies

Alabama
Auburn University B

Community College of the Air Force A

Arizona
Arizona Western College A

Arkansas
Arkansas State University
  Beebe Branch A
Phillips Community College of the
  University of Arkansas A
Westark College A

California
City College of San Francisco C, A
Orange Coast College C, A
Pacific Union College B

Connecticut
Quinnipiac University C
University of Bridgeport B
University of Connecticut B

Florida
Broward Community College A
Indian River Community College A
Keiser College A
Miami-Dade Community College A
Polk Community College A

Georgia
Armstrong Atlantic State University B
Athens Area Technical Institute C, A
Atlanta Metropolitan College A
Darton College A
Gainesville College A
Waycross College A

Illinois
Barat College B
John A. Logan College A
Moraine Valley Community College A
Southwestern Ilinois College A

Indiana
Indiana University
  Northwest C
Indiana Wesleyan University A, B
Purdue University
  North Central Campus A
Saint Mary's College B
St. Mary-of-the-Woods College B
Vincennes University A

Iowa
Briar Cliff College B
North Iowa Area Community College A

Kansas
Seward County Community
  College C, A

Louisiana
Southern University
  Shreveport A

Maryland
Villa Julie College A

Massachusetts
Boston University B
North Shore Community College C
University of Massachusetts
  Lowell B

Michigan
Aquinas College B
Great Lakes College C
Michigan State University B
Oakland Community College C, A

Minnesota
Lake Superior College: A Community
  and Technical College A

Mississippi
Meridian Community College A
Mississippi Gulf Coast Community
  College
  Perkinston A

Montana
University of Montana-Missoula A

Nebraska
Union College B
University of Nebraska
  Kearney B

New Hampshire
University of New Hampshire B

New Jersey
Felician College A, B
Monmouth University B

New Mexico
New Mexico State University
  Alamogordo A

New York
New York Institute of Technology B
St. Thomas Aquinas College B
State University of New York
  Upstate Medical University B
Suffolk County Community College A

North Carolina
Cape Fear Community College C
Cleveland Community College C
Elon College B
Sampson Community College C

North Dakota
Dickinson State University B

Ohio
Columbus State Community College A
Kent State University B
Ohio Northern University B
Youngstown State University B

Oklahoma
East Central University B
Southeastern Oklahoma State
  University B
Tulsa Community College C, A

Oregon
Portland Community College A

Pennsylvania
College Misericordia B
Community College of Allegheny
  County A
Delaware County Community College C
Lycoming College B
MCP Hahnemann University A, B
Montgomery County Community
  College A
Reading Area Community College A
Seton Hill College B
University of Pittsburgh C

Rhode Island
Community College of Rhode Island C

South Carolina
Aiken Technical College C
Greenville Technical College A
Spartanburg Technical College A

South Dakota
South Dakota State University B

Tennessee
Lee University B
Roane State Community College A

Texas
Midland College A
Navarro College A
University of North Texas B
University of Texas
  El Paso B
  Pan American B

Vermont
University of Vermont B, M

Virginia
Northern Virginia Community College A
Thomas Nelson Community College A

Health/medical laboratory technologies

Washington
Shoreline Community College A
Walla Walla College B

Wisconsin
Chippewa Valley Technical College A
Moraine Park Technical College A

Health/physical fitness

Alabama
Calhoun Community College A
Chattahoochee Valley Community College A
Huntingdon College B, T
Lawson State Community College A
Northeast Alabama Community College A
Northwest-Shoals Community College C
Samford University B
Troy State University B
University of Alabama
  Birmingham D

Arizona
Arizona Western College A
Eastern Arizona College A
Grand Canyon University B
Northern Arizona University B
Pima Community College A
University of Arizona M
Yavapai College A

Arkansas
Arkansas State University B
Harding University B
John Brown University B
Ouachita Baptist University B
University of Arkansas B

California
California Baptist University B
California State Polytechnic University:
  Pomona B
California State University
  Fresno A
  Hayward B, M
  Long Beach M
  Sacramento M
  Stanislaus B
Chaffey Community College C
Chapman University B
Columbia College A
Cypress College C
East Los Angeles College A
Humboldt State University B
Imperial Valley College A
Irvine Valley College C, A
La Sierra University B
Lake Tahoe Community College A
Long Beach City College A
Merced College A
Modesto Junior College A
Palomar College A
Pepperdine University B
Point Loma Nazarene University B
Saddleback College A
St. Mary's College of California B, M
San Diego City College C, A
San Diego Miramar College A
San Diego State University B, M
San Jose State University B, M
Santa Barbara City College C
University of San Francisco B
University of the Pacific B, T
West Los Angeles College C, A
Yuba College C

Colorado
Adams State College B, M
Colorado Mountain College
  Timberline Campus A
Front Range Community College C, A
Mesa State College B
Trinidad State Junior College A

University of Colorado
  Boulder B, M, D

Connecticut
Central Connecticut State University B
Mitchell College A

Delaware
Delaware State University B
University of Delaware B, M

District of Columbia
American University B

Florida
Barry University B
Florida Atlantic University B, M
Gulf Coast Community College A
Nova Southeastern University B
Palm Beach Community College A
St. Petersburg Junior College C
University of West Florida B, M

Georgia
Albany State University B
Armstrong Atlantic State University B, T
Darton College A
East Georgia College A
Georgia Southern University B
Georgia State University B, M
Middle Georgia College A
North Georgia College & State University B, M
South Georgia College A
State University of West Georgia B, M
Valdosta State University B
Young Harris College A

Hawaii
Brigham Young University
  Hawaii B
University of Hawaii
  Manoa B

Idaho
Boise State University B, M
College of Southern Idaho A
North Idaho College A
Northwest Nazarene University B

Illinois
Chicago State University B, M, T
Elmhurst College B
Greenville College B, T
Illinois College B
John Wood Community College A
Judson College B, T
Kishwaukee College A
McHenry County College C
Monmouth College B, T
Southern Illinois University
  Edwardsville B, M
Southwestern Illinois College A
Trinity International University B
University of Illinois
  Chicago B, M, D, T
  Urbana-Champaign B, M, D
Wheaton College B

Indiana
Anderson University B
Franklin College B
Goshen College B
Indiana State University B, T
Indiana Wesleyan University B
Taylor University B
Tri-State University B
University of Evansville B
Vincennes University A

Iowa
Cornell College B, T
Dordt College B
Graceland University B, T
Iowa State University B, M
Iowa Wesleyan College B
Luther College B
Northwestern College B, T
St. Ambrose University B

University of Iowa M, D
William Penn University B

Kansas
Benedictine College B
Bethel College B
Central Christian College A
Coffeyville Community College A
Dodge City Community College A
Garden City Community College A
Kansas City Kansas Community College A
Kansas Wesleyan University B, T
McPherson College B, T
Ottawa University B
Pittsburg State University B, M, T
Seward County Community College A
Sterling College B
Tabor College B
University of Kansas B

Kentucky
Asbury College B
Campbellsville University B
Cumberland College B
Kentucky Wesleyan College B, T
Murray State University B
University of Kentucky M, D

Louisiana
Centenary College of Louisiana B, T
Louisiana State University
  Shreveport B
Louisiana Tech University B
Nicholls State University B
University of Louisiana at Monroe B

Maine
Husson College B
St. Joseph's College B
University of Maine
  Presque Isle B

Maryland
Anne Arundel Community College A
Chesapeake College C
Columbia Union College B
Community College of Baltimore County
  Catonsville A
  Essex A
Howard Community College A
Western Maryland College B, M

Massachusetts
Becker College B
Berkshire Community College C
Bridgewater State College B, M
Cape Cod Community College A
Dean College A
Eastern Nazarene College B
Fitchburg State College B
Greenfield Community College C
Mount Ida College A
Northeastern University B
Springfield College B, M
Westfield State College B

Michigan
Adrian College B, T
Alma College T
Andrews University B
Aquinas College B
Calvin College B, T
Central Michigan University B, M
Eastern Michigan University B, M
Grand Valley State University B
Henry Ford Community College C, A
Lake Michigan College A
Lake Superior State University A
Michigan State University D
Northern Michigan University B, T
Olivet College B
Spring Arbor College B
Western Michigan University B

Minnesota
Bemidji State University B
Bethel College B

Concordia College: Moorhead B
Concordia University: St. Paul B
Gustavus Adolphus College B
Hamline University B
Minnesota State University, Mankato B
Moorhead State University B
Ridgewater College: A Community and Technical College A
St. Cloud State University B, M
St. Mary's University of Minnesota C
Southwest State University B
University of St. Thomas B, M
Winona State University B, T

Mississippi
Mississippi University for Women B, T
Mississippi Valley State University B, T
University of Mississippi T
University of Southern Mississippi B
William Carey College B

Missouri
College of the Ozarks B
Culver-Stockton College T
East Central College A
Missouri Southern State College B, T
Missouri Western State College T
Southwest Baptist University B, T
Southwest Missouri State University M
Three Rivers Community College A
Truman State University B
University of Missouri
  Kansas City B

Montana
Miles Community College A
Montana State University
  Bozeman B, M
Rocky Mountain College B, T
University of Great Falls A, B
University of Montana-Missoula B

Nebraska
Concordia University B, T
Dana College B
Hastings College B
Nebraska Wesleyan University B
Northeast Community College A
Union College B
Wayne State College B, T

Nevada
University of Nevada
  Las Vegas B

New Hampshire
Hesser College A
Plymouth State College of the University System of New Hampshire B

New Jersey
Camden County College C
County College of Morris C
Gloucester County College A
Middlesex County College A
Rowan University B
Salem Community College A

New Mexico
Albuquerque Technical-Vocational Institute C
New Mexico Highlands University B
San Juan College C
Santa Fe Community College A

New York
City University of New York
  Lehman College M
  Queens College B
Finger Lakes Community College A
Fulton-Montgomery Community College A
Genesee Community College A
Herkimer County Community College A
Ithaca College B, M, T
Long Island University
  C. W. Post Campus M
Monroe Community College A

Nassau Community College *A*
Niagara County Community College *A*
State University of New York
    College at Buffalo *B*
    College at Potsdam *B*
Suffolk County Community College *A*
Syracuse University *B*

North Carolina
Brevard College *B*
Catawba College *B*
Chowan College *B, T*
East Carolina University *B, M*
Elon College *B*
Greensboro College *B, T*
Lenoir-Rhyne College *B, T*
Mars Hill College *B*
North Carolina Agricultural and
    Technical State University *B, T*
St. Augustine's College *B*
Sandhills Community College *A*
Shaw University *B*
University of North Carolina
    Chapel Hill *B, M, T*
    Charlotte *B*
    Wilmington *B*
Wake Forest University *B, M*

North Dakota
Dickinson State University *B, T*
Mayville State University *B*
North Dakota State University *M, D*

Ohio
Baldwin-Wallace College *B*
Bluffton College *B*
Bowling Green State University *M*
Capital University *B*
Cedarville College *B*
Central State University *B*
Defiance College *B, T*
Malone College *B*
Miami University
    Oxford Campus *B, T*
Mount Vernon Nazarene College *B, T*
Ohio Northern University *B*
Ohio State University
    Columbus Campus *B, M, D*
Ohio University *B, M*
Otterbein College *B*
Sinclair Community College *A*
University of Akron *B, M*
University of Dayton *B*
University of Findlay *B, T*
Youngstown State University *B*

Oklahoma
Cameron University *B*
Connors State College *A*
East Central University *B, T*
Eastern Oklahoma State College *A*
Northeastern Oklahoma Agricultural and
    Mechanical College *C, A*
Northeastern State University *B*
Northwestern Oklahoma State
    University *B*
Oklahoma Baptist University *B, T*
Oklahoma City University *B*
Oklahoma Panhandle State University *B*
Oklahoma State University *B, M*
Oral Roberts University *B*
Rose State College *A*
Seminole State College *A*
University of Oklahoma *B, M*
University of Science and Arts of
    Oklahoma *B, T*
Western Oklahoma State College *A*

Oregon
Central Oregon Community College *A*
Eastern Oregon University *B*
Lane Community College *C, A*
Linfield College *B*
Oregon State University *B*
Southern Oregon University *B, T*

Pennsylvania
Bloomsburg University of
    Pennsylvania *B*
Bucks County Community College *A*
Butler County Community College *A*
Eastern College *B*
Indiana University of Pennsylvania *B, M*
Lincoln University *B*
Lock Haven University of
    Pennsylvania *B*
Marywood University *B*
Messiah College *B*
Northampton County Area Community
    College *A*
Penn State
    University Park *B*
Pennsylvania College of Technology *A*
Philadelphia College of Bible *B*
Slippery Rock University of
    Pennsylvania *B, M*
West Chester University of
    Pennsylvania *M*

Puerto Rico
Universidad Metropolitana *B*
University of the Sacred Heart *B*

South Carolina
Anderson College *B, T*
Benedict College *B*
Charleston Southern University *B*
Erskine College *B, T*
Furman University *B, M, T*
Limestone College *B*
Technical College of the Lowcountry *C*
University of South Carolina *M, D*
Voorhees College *B*

South Dakota
Augustana College *B, T*
Black Hills State University *B*
Dakota State University *B*
South Dakota State University *B, M, T*

Tennessee
Austin Peay State University *B, M*
Belmont University *B, T*
Carson-Newman College *B, T*
Columbia State Community College *A*
David Lipscomb University *B*
East Tennessee State University *B, M, T*
Freed-Hardeman University *B, T*
Lambuth University *B*
Lee University *B*
Lincoln Memorial University *B, T*
Middle Tennessee State
    University *B, M, D*
Milligan College *B, T*
Tennessee Wesleyan College *B, T*
Trevecca Nazarene University *B, T*
Tusculum College *B*
Union University *B, T*
University of Tennessee
    Knoxville *B, M, D*
    Martin *B*
Walters State Community College *A*

Texas
Abilene Christian University *B*
Alvin Community College *A*
Amarillo College *A*
Angelo State University *M*
Baylor University *B*
Concordia University at Austin *T*
Del Mar College *A*
East Texas Baptist University *B*
El Paso Community College *A*
Hill College *A*
Houston Community College
    System *C, A*
Howard College *A*
Kilgore College *A*
Lamar University *B, M*
LeTourneau University *B*
Lee College *A*
Northeast Texas Community College *A*
Prairie View A&M University *B*
St. Edward's University *B, T*
St. Philip's College *A*
Sam Houston State University *B*
South Plains College *A*
Southwest Texas State
    University *B, M, T*
Southwestern Adventist
    University *A, B, T*
Stephen F. Austin State University *B, T*
Sul Ross State University *B, T*
Tarleton State University *D*
Texas A&M International
    University *B, T*
Texas A&M University
    Commerce *B*
    Corpus Christi *B*
Texas A&M University *B, M, D*
Texas Lutheran University *B, T*
Texas Tech University *B, M*
Texas Wesleyan University *B, M*
Texas Woman's University *B, M, D, T*
Trinity Valley Community College *A*
Tyler Junior College *A*
University of Houston
    Clear Lake *B, M*
University of Houston *M*
University of Mary Hardin-Baylor *B*
University of North Texas *B, M*
University of Texas
    Arlington *B*
    Austin *B*
    El Paso *B, M*
    Pan American *B, M, T*
    San Antonio *B*
    of the Permian Basin *B, T*
West Texas A&M University *B*
Western Texas College *A*

Utah
Brigham Young University *B, M*
University of Utah *B, M, D*
Weber State University *B*

Vermont
Castleton State College *B*
Johnson State College *B*

Virginia
Averett College *B*
Bridgewater College *B*
Christopher Newport University *B*
College of William and Mary *B*
Emory & Henry College *B, T*
George Mason University *B*
James Madison University *B, M, T*
Longwood College *B, T*
Lynchburg College *B*
Norfolk State University *B*
Northern Virginia Community College *C*
University of Virginia's College at
    Wise *T*
Virginia Intermont College *B, T*

Washington
Central Washington University *M*
Eastern Washington University *B*
Everett Community College *A*
Grays Harbor College *C*
Highline Community College *A*
Pacific Lutheran University *B*
Renton Technical College *C, A*
Seattle Pacific University *M*
Western Washington University *B, T*
Whitworth College *B*

West Virginia
Marshall University *B*
Shepherd College *B, T*
West Virginia University *B*
West Virginia Wesleyan College *B*

Wisconsin
University of Wisconsin
    Platteville *B, T*
    Stevens Point *B, T*

Heating/air conditioning/refrigeration mechanics

Alabama
Bessemer State Technical College *C*
Bevill State Community College *A*
Calhoun Community College *C, A*
Community College of the Air Force *A*
George C. Wallace State Community
    College
    Selma *C*
Harry M. Ayers State Technical
    College *A*
J. F. Drake State Technical College *C*
John M. Patterson State Technical
    College *C, A*
Northwest-Shoals Community
    College *C, A*
Shelton State Community College *C, A*
Southern Union State Community
    College *A*
Wallace State Community College at
    Hanceville *C, A*

Alaska
University of Alaska
    Anchorage *C, A*

Arizona
Arizona Western College *C, A*
Eastern Arizona College *C*
Gateway Community College *C, A*
Mohave Community College *C, A*
Pima Community College *C, A*
Universal Technical Institute *C, A*

Arkansas
North Arkansas College *C*

California
Cerro Coso Community College *C, A*
Citrus College *C, A*
College of San Mateo *C, A*
College of the Desert *C, A*
College of the Sequoias *C, A*
Cypress College *C, A*
Diablo Valley College *C*
Foothill College *C*
Fresno City College *C, A*
Long Beach City College *C, A*
Los Angeles Trade and Technical
    College *C, A*
Modesto Junior College *C, A*
Mount San Antonio College *C, A*
Orange Coast College *C, A*
Riverside Community College *C, A*
Sacramento City College *C, A*
San Bernardino Valley College *C, A*
San Diego City College *C, A*
San Jose City College *C, A*
Shasta College *C, A*
Southwestern College *C*

Colorado
Community College of Aurora *A*
Red Rocks Community College *C, A*
Technical Trades Institute *C, A*

Delaware
Delaware Technical and Community
    College
    Owens Campus *C, A*
    Stanton/Wilmington Campus *A*

District of Columbia
University of the District of Columbia *C*

Florida
Brevard Community College *C, A*
Central Florida Community College *C*
Chipola Junior College *C*
Daytona Beach Community College *C*
Hillsborough Community College *A*
Indian River Community College *C, A*
Miami-Dade Community College *A*
New England Institute of Technology *A*
Santa Fe Community College *C*

Heating/air conditioning/refrigeration mechanics

Seminole Community College *C*
South Florida Community College *C*

Georgia
Athens Area Technical Institute *C*
Bainbridge College *C*
Chattahoochee Technical Institute *C*
Darton College *A*
DeKalb Technical Institute *C*
Georgia Southwestern State University *A*
Waycross College *A*

Hawaii
University of Hawaii
    Honolulu Community College *C, A*

Idaho
Boise State University *C, A*
College of Southern Idaho *C, A*
Lewis-Clark State College *A*
North Idaho College *C, A*

Illinois
Black Hawk College *C, A*
City Colleges of Chicago
    Kennedy-King College *C, A*
College of DuPage *C, A*
College of Lake County *C, A*
Elgin Community College *C, A*
Illinois Eastern Community Colleges
    Lincoln Trail College *C, A*
John A. Logan College *C*
Joliet Junior College *C*
Kankakee Community College *C, A*
Lake Land College *C*
Lincoln Land Community College *C*
Moraine Valley Community College *C*
Morton College *A*
Oakton Community College *C, A*
Prairie State College *C*
Rend Lake College *C*
Sauk Valley Community College *C, A*
Southeastern Illinois College *C*
Southwestern Illinois College *C*
Triton College *C, A*
Waubonsee Community College *C, A*
William Rainey Harper College *C, A*

Indiana
Oakland City University *C, A*

Iowa
Des Moines Area Community
    College *C, A*
Hawkeye Community College *C*
Indian Hills Community College *C*
North Iowa Area Community College *A*
Northeast Iowa Community College *C*
Scott Community College *A*
Western Iowa Tech Community
    College *C, A*

Kansas
Pittsburg State University *C*

Louisiana
Delgado Community College *C*
Nunez Community College *C, A*

Maine
Eastern Maine Technical College *C, A*
Southern Maine Technical College *C, A*
Washington County Technical College *C*

Maryland
Cecil Community College *C, A*
Chesapeake College *C*

Massachusetts
Massachusetts Maritime Academy *C*
Massasoit Community College *A*
Springfield Technical Community
    College *C*

Michigan
Grand Rapids Community College *C, A*
Henry Ford Community College *C, A*
Jackson Community College *C, A*
Kellogg Community College *C, A*
Lansing Community College *A*
Macomb Community College *C, A*
Mid Michigan Community College *C, A*
Mott Community College *C, A*
Northern Michigan University *C, A*
Oakland Community College *A*
Washtenaw Community College *A*
Wayne County Community College *C*

Minnesota
Dunwoody Institute *A*
Hennepin Technical College *C, A*
Hibbing Community College: A
    Technical and Community College *C*
Minnesota State College - Southeast
    Technical *C, A*
St. Cloud Technical College *C, A*
South Central Technical College *C, A*

Mississippi
East Central Community College *C*
Hinds Community College *C*
Holmes Community College *A*
Itawamba Community College *C*
Mississippi Delta Community College *A*
Mississippi Gulf Coast Community
    College
    Jefferson Davis Campus *C*
    Perkinston *C*
Northwest Mississippi Community
    College *C, A*
Southwest Mississippi Community
    College *C*

Missouri
East Central College *C, A*
Jefferson College *C, A*
Maple Woods Community College *C, A*
Penn Valley Community College *C, A*
Ranken Technical College *A*

Montana
Montana State University
    Billings *A*

Nebraska
Central Community College *C, A*
Metropolitan Community College *C, A*
Mid Plains Community College
    Area *C, A*
Northeast Community College *A*
Southeast Community College
    Milford Campus *A*

Nevada
Community College of Southern
    Nevada *C, A*
Western Nevada Community College *A*

New Hampshire
New Hampshire Community Technical
    College
    Manchester *C, A*

New Jersey
Middlesex County College *A*
Raritan Valley Community College *A*

New Mexico
Albuquerque Technical-Vocational
    Institute *C*
Dona Ana Branch Community College of
    New Mexico State University *C, A*

New York
City University of New York
    New York City Technical
    College *A*
Dutchess Community College *C*
Erie Community College
    North Campus *C*
Hudson Valley Community College *A*
Jamestown Community College *A*
Mohawk Valley Community College *C*
Monroe Community College *C, A*
Niagara County Community College *C*
State University of New York
    College of Technology at Alfred *A*
    College of Technology at Canton *C*
    College of Technology at
    Delhi *C, A*
Technical Career Institutes *C, A*

North Carolina
Alamance Community College *C, A*
Asheville Buncombe Technical
    Community College *C, A*
Blue Ridge Community College *C*
Brunswick Community College *C*
Caldwell Community College and
    Technical Institute *C, A*
Cape Fear Community College *C*
Catawba Valley Community College *C*
Central Piedmont Community College *A*
Cleveland Community College *C*
Coastal Carolina Community
    College *C, A*
College of the Albemarle *C*
Craven Community College *C, A*
Davidson County Community College *C*
Forsyth Technical Community College *C*
Gaston College *C*
Guilford Technical Community
    College *C*
Haywood Community College *C*
Johnston Community College *C, A*
Lenoir Community College *C*
Martin Community College *C, A*
Mitchell Community College *C*
Piedmont Community College *C*
Pitt Community College *C*
Roanoke-Chowan Community
    College *C*
Rockingham Community College *C*
Rowan-Cabarrus Community College *C*
South Piedmont Community
    College *C, A*
Southeastern Community College *C*
Southwestern Community College *C*
Tri-County Community College *C*
Vance-Granville Community College *C*
Wake Technical Community College *C*
Wilson Technical Community College *C*

North Dakota
Bismarck State College *C, A*
North Dakota State College of
    Science *C, A*

Ohio
Belmont Technical College *C, A*
Cincinnati State Technical and
    Community College *C, A*
Columbus State Community
    College *C, A*
North Central State College *A*
Northwestern College *C, A*
Owens Community College
    Toledo *C*
RETS Tech Center *C*
Sinclair Community College *C, A*
Stark State College of Technology *A*
Terra Community College *C, A*
Washington State Community College *A*

Oklahoma
Oklahoma State University
    Oklahoma City *C, A*
    Okmulgee *A*
Tulsa Community College *A*

Oregon
Lane Community College *C, A*
Linn-Benton Community College *C, A*
Portland Community College *C, A*

Pennsylvania
C.H.I/RETS Campus *C*
Community College of Allegheny
    County *C, A*
Lehigh Carbon Community College *C, A*
Northampton County Area Community
    College *C*
Pennsylvania College of
    Technology *A, B*
Reading Area Community College *C*
Triangle Tech
    Pittsburgh Campus *C, A*
Westmoreland County Community
    College *A*

Puerto Rico
Huertas Junior College *C, A*

Rhode Island
New England Institute of
    Technology *C, A*

South Carolina
Aiken Technical College *C*
Central Carolina Technical College *C*
Florence-Darlington Technical
    College *C, A*
Greenville Technical College *C*
Horry-Georgetown Technical College *A*
Midlands Technical College *C, A*
Piedmont Technical College *C, A*
Spartanburg Technical College *C, A*
Technical College of the
    Lowcountry *C, A*
Tri-County Technical College *A*
Trident Technical College *C*
York Technical College *A*

South Dakota
Southeast Technical Institute *A*

Tennessee
Chattanooga State Technical Community
    College *C*

Texas
Alvin Community College *A*
Austin Community College *C, A*
Brazosport College *C, A*
Cedar Valley College *A*
Central Texas College *C, A*
Coastal Bend College *C, A*
College of the Mainland *C, A*
Del Mar College *C, A*
Eastfield College *C, A*
El Paso Community College *C, A*
Grayson County College *C, A*
Hill College *C, A*
Houston Community College System *C*
Lamar State College at Port Arthur *C, A*
Lee College *C, A*
Midland College *C, A*
Odessa College *C, A*
Paris Junior College *A*
St. Philip's College *C, A*
San Jacinto College
    North *C, A*
South Plains College *A*
Texas State Technical College
    Harlingen *C, A*
    Sweetwater *C*
    Waco *C, A*
Trinity Valley Community College *C*
Tyler Junior College *C, A*
Western Texas College *C*
Wharton County Junior College *C*

Utah
Salt Lake Community College *C, A*
Utah Valley State College *A*

Virginia
Central Virginia Community College *C*
Danville Community College *A*
John Tyler Community College *C*
Mountain Empire Community College *C*
New River Community College *C*
Northern Virginia Community
    College *C, A*
Patrick Henry Community College *C*
Piedmont Virginia Community
    College *C*
Southside Virginia Community
    College *C*

Southwest Virginia Community
College *C*
Thomas Nelson Community College *C*
Tidewater Community College *C*
Virginia Highlands Community
College *C*

Washington
North Seattle Community College *A*
Renton Technical College *C, A*
Spokane Community College *A*
Spokane Falls Community College *C*
Walla Walla Community College *C, A*
Wenatchee Valley College *C, A*

West Virginia
West Virginia Northern Community
College *A*

Wisconsin
Chippewa Valley Technical College *A*
Gateway Technical College *A*
Milwaukee Area Technical College *A*
Moraine Park Technical College *C*
Northeast Wisconsin Technical
College *A*
Waukesha County Technical College *C*
Western Wisconsin Technical
College *C, A*
Wisconsin Indianhead Technical
College *C*

Wyoming
Eastern Wyoming College *C, A*

Hebrew

California
Master's College *B*
University of California
Berkeley *M, D*
Los Angeles *B*

Connecticut
Fairfield University *B*

District of Columbia
Catholic University of America *M, D*

Illinois
Concordia University *B*
Moody Bible Institute *B*
University of Chicago *B*

Maryland
Washington Bible College *M*

Massachusetts
Harvard College *B*
Harvard University *D*

Michigan
Concordia College *B*
University of Michigan *B*

Minnesota
Carleton College *B*
Concordia University: St. Paul *B*
University of Minnesota
Twin Cities *B*

Missouri
Washington University *B, M*

New York
City University of New York
Brooklyn College *B*
Hunter College *B*
Lehman College *B*
Queens College *B*
Columbia University
Graduate School *M, D*
Cornell University *B*
Hofstra University *B*
New York University *B, M, D*
State University of New York
Binghamton *B*
Touro College *B*

Ohio
Ohio State University
Columbus Campus *B*

Oregon
University of Oregon *B*

Pennsylvania
Temple University *B*

Rhode Island
Brown University *B*

Tennessee
Union University *B*

Texas
University of Texas
Austin *B, M, D*

Washington
University of Washington *B*

Wisconsin
University of Wisconsin
Madison *B, M, D*
Milwaukee *B*

Hematology technology

Colorado
Pikes Peak Community College *C*

Florida
New England Institute of Technology *C*

New Mexico
Albuquerque Technical-Vocational
Institute *C*

New York
Westchester Community College *A*

Ohio
Columbus State Community College *C*

Pennsylvania
Lackawanna Junior College *A*

Higher education administration

Alabama
University of Alabama *M, D*

Arizona
Arizona State University *M, D*
University of Arizona *M, D*

Arkansas
University of Arkansas
Little Rock *D*
University of Arkansas *M, D*

California
Azusa Pacific University *M, D*
California State University
Stanislaus *M*
San Diego State University *M, T*
San Jose State University *M*

Colorado
Colorado State University *M*
University of Denver *M, D*

Connecticut
Sacred Heart University *T*
University of Connecticut *M, D, T*

District of Columbia
George Washington University *M, D*

Florida
Barry University *M*
Florida State University *M, D*
Nova Southeastern University *D*
University of Florida *D*
University of Miami *M, D*

Georgia
Georgia Southern University *M*
University of Georgia *D*

Illinois
Loyola University of Chicago *M, D*
Northeastern Illinois University *M*
Southern Illinois University
Carbondale *M, D*

Indiana
Ball State University *M, D*
Indiana State University *M*
Indiana University
Bloomington *D*
Purdue University *D*

Iowa
Iowa State University *M, D*
Maharishi University of Management *M*
University of Iowa *M, D*

Kansas
Pittsburg State University *M*
University of Kansas *M*

Kentucky
University of Kentucky *M, D*
University of Louisville *M, T*

Maine
University of Southern Maine *M*

Massachusetts
Boston College *M, D*
Springfield College *D*
Suffolk University *M*

Michigan
Michigan State University *M, D*
Wayne State University *D*

Minnesota
Minnesota State University, Mankato *M*

Mississippi
University of Mississippi *M*
University of Southern Mississippi *D*

Missouri
Central Missouri State University *M*
St. Louis University *M, D*

Montana
University of Montana-Missoula *M, D*

New Jersey
Rowan University *M*
Seton Hall University *D*

New York
Canisius College *M*
City University of New York
Baruch College *M*
Columbia University
Teachers College *M, D*
Fordham University *M, D*
New York University *M, D*
State University of New York
Albany *M, D*
Buffalo *M, D*
College at Brockport *M*
College at Buffalo *M*
New Paltz *D*
Syracuse University *M, D*
University of Rochester *M, D*

North Carolina
Campbell University *M*
Fayetteville State University *M*
North Carolina State University *M, D*
University of North Carolina
Greensboro *M*

Ohio
Bowling Green State University *D*
Kent State University *M, D*
Ohio State University
Columbus Campus *M, D*
Ohio University
Zanesville Campus *M*

University of Akron *M, T*
University of Toledo *M, D, T*

Oklahoma
Oklahoma State University *M, D*
University of Oklahoma *M, D*

Oregon
Portland State University *D*

Pennsylvania
Penn State
University Park *M, D*
University of Pennsylvania *M, D*
Villanova University *M*
Widener University *D*

Puerto Rico
Inter American University of Puerto Rico
Metropolitan Campus *M*
San German Campus *M*

South Carolina
University of South Carolina *D*

South Dakota
University of South Dakota *M, D*

Tennessee
University of Memphis *D*
Vanderbilt University *M, D*

Texas
Dallas Baptist University *M*
Tarleton State University *D*
Texas A&M University
Commerce *M, D*
Kingsville *M, D*
Texas Southern University *D*
Texas Tech University *M, D*
University of Houston *D*
University of North Texas *D*
University of Texas
San Antonio *M*
Tyler *M*

Vermont
University of Vermont *M, D, T*

Virginia
University of Virginia *D*
Virginia Polytechnic Institute and State
University *M, D*

Washington
Western Washington University *M*

West Virginia
Marshall University *M*

Wisconsin
Concordia University Wisconsin *M*

Hispanic-American studies

Arizona
Arizona State University *B*
University of Arizona *B, M*

California
California State University
Fullerton *B*
Hayward *B*
Long Beach *B*
Cerritos Community College *A*
City College of San Francisco *A*
Contra Costa College *A*
De Anza College *C, A*
Fresno City College *A*
Imperial Valley College *A*
Loyola Marymount University *B*
Mills College *B*
Pitzer College *B*
San Diego Mesa College *A*
San Francisco State University *B*
Santa Ana College *A*
Santa Barbara City College *A*
Scripps College *B*
Sonoma State University *B*

University of California
    Berkeley *B*
    Los Angeles *B*
    Riverside *B*
University of San Diego *B*
Ventura College *A*

Colorado
Adams State College *B*
Metropolitan State College of Denver *B*
University of Northern Colorado *B*

Connecticut
Connecticut College *B*

Illinois
University of Illinois
    Chicago *M*

Indiana
Goshen College *B*

Maine
University of Southern Maine *B*

Maryland
Johns Hopkins University *B*

Massachusetts
Boston College *B*
Hampshire College *B*
Northeastern University *B*

Michigan
University of Michigan *B*

Minnesota
St. Olaf College *B*
University of Minnesota
    Twin Cities *B*

New Hampshire
Dartmouth College *B*

New Jersey
Rutgers
    The State University of New Jersey:
      Douglass College *B*
    The State University of New Jersey:
      Livingston College *B*
    The State University of New Jersey:
      Newark College of Arts and
      Sciences *B*
    The State University of New Jersey:
      Rutgers College *B*
    The State University of New Jersey:
      University College New
      Brunswick *B*

New Mexico
Western New Mexico University *B*

New York
Bard College *B*
City University of New York
    Brooklyn College *B*
Columbia University
    Columbia College *B*
    School of General Studies *B*
Eugene Lang College/New School
    University *B*
Hobart and William Smith Colleges *B*
Mount St. Mary College *B*
Sarah Lawrence College *B*

Pennsylvania
Bryn Mawr College *B*

Puerto Rico
Pontifical Catholic University of Puerto
    Rico *B*

Rhode Island
Brown University *B, M, D*

Texas
Palo Alto College *A*
University of Texas
    El Paso *B*
    San Antonio *B, M*

Virginia
Sweet Briar College *B*

Washington
University of Washington *B*
Yakima Valley Community College *A*

Historic preservation/conservation

Delaware
University of Delaware *B, M*

District of Columbia
George Washington University *M*

Georgia
Georgia State University *M*
Savannah College of Art and
    Design *B, M*
University of Georgia *M*

Illinois
School of the Art Institute of Chicago *M*

Indiana
Ball State University *M*

Kentucky
University of Kentucky *M*

Maryland
Goucher College *B, M*

Massachusetts
Boston University *M*
Harvard College *B*

Michigan
Eastern Michigan University *C, M*

New York
Columbia University
    Graduate School *M*
Cornell University *M*

North Carolina
Randolph Community College *C, A*

Ohio
Ursuline College *B*

Oregon
University of Oregon *M*

Pennsylvania
Bucks County Community College *C*

Rhode Island
Roger Williams University *B*
Salve Regina University *B*

South Carolina
College of Charleston *B*

Texas
University of Texas
    Austin *D*

Utah
University of Utah *M*

Vermont
University of Vermont *M*

Virginia
Mary Washington College *B*

History

Alabama
Alabama State University *B, M*
Athens State University *B*
Auburn University at Montgomery *B*
Auburn University *B, M, D*
Birmingham-Southern College *B, T*
Community College of the Air Force *A*
Faulkner University *B*
Huntingdon College *B, T*
Jacksonville State University *B, M*
Lawson State Community College *A*
Oakwood College *B*
Samford University *B*
Spring Hill College *B, T*
Stillman College *B*
Talladega College *B, T*
Troy State University
    Dothan *B*
    Montgomery *A, B*
Troy State University *B*
Tuskegee University *B*
University of Alabama
    Birmingham *B, M*
    Huntsville *B, M*
University of Alabama *B, M, D*
University of Mobile *B, T*
University of Montevallo *B, T*
University of North Alabama *B*
University of South Alabama *B, M*
University of West Alabama *B, T*

Alaska
University of Alaska
    Anchorage *B*
    Fairbanks *B*

Arizona
Arizona State University *B, M, D*
Cochise College *A*
Eastern Arizona College *A*
Grand Canyon University *B*
Northern Arizona University *B, M, D, T*
Prescott College *M*
South Mountain Community College *A*
University of Arizona *B, M, D*

Arkansas
Arkansas State University
    Beebe Branch *A*
Arkansas State University *B, M*
Arkansas Tech University *B*
Harding University *B*
Henderson State University *B*
Hendrix College *B*
John Brown University *B*
Lyon College *B*
Ouachita Baptist University *B*
Southern Arkansas University *B*
University of Arkansas
    Little Rock *B, M*
    Monticello *B*
    Pine Bluff *B*
University of Arkansas *B, M, D*
University of Central Arkansas *B, M*
University of the Ozarks *B*
Westark College *A*
Williams Baptist College *B*

California
Azusa Pacific University *B*
Bakersfield College *A*
Biola University *B*
Cabrillo College *A*
California Baptist University *B*
California Institute of Technology *B*
California Lutheran University *B*
California Polytechnic State University:
    San Luis Obispo *B*
California State Polytechnic University:
    Pomona *B*
California State University
    Bakersfield *B, M*
    Chico *B, M*
    Dominguez Hills *B*
    Fresno *B, M*
    Fullerton *B, M*
    Hayward *B, M*
    Long Beach *B, M*
    Los Angeles *B, M*
    Northridge *B*
    Sacramento *B, M*
    San Marcos *B*
    Stanislaus *B, M*
Canada College *A*
Cerritos Community College *A*
Chabot College *A*
Chaffey Community College *A*
Chapman University *B*
Claremont McKenna College *B*
College of Notre Dame *B*
College of the Canyons *A*
College of the Desert *A*
Compton Community College *A*
Concordia University *B*
Contra Costa College *A*
Crafton Hills College *A*
Cypress College *A*
De Anza College *A*
Diablo Valley College *A*
Dominican University of California *B*
East Los Angeles College *A*
Foothill College *A*
Fresno City College *A*
Fresno Pacific University *B*
Gavilan Community College *A*
Glendale Community College *A*
Golden West College *A*
Grossmont Community College *A*
Holy Names College *B*
Humboldt State University *B*
Irvine Valley College *A*
La Sierra University *B*
Long Beach City College *C, A*
Los Angeles Southwest College *A*
Los Angeles Valley College *A*
Loyola Marymount University *B*
Marymount College *A*
Master's College *B*
Merced College *A*
Mills College *B*
MiraCosta College *A*
Monterey Peninsula College *A*
Mount St. Mary's College *B*
Occidental College *B*
Ohlone College *A*
Orange Coast College *A*
Pacific Union College *B*
Palo Verde College *A*
Pepperdine University *B, M*
Pitzer College *B*
Point Loma Nazarene University *B*
Pomona College *B*
Riverside Community College *A*
Saddleback College *A*
St. Mary's College of California *B*
San Diego City College *A*
San Diego Miramar College *A*
San Diego State University *B, M*
San Francisco State University *B, M*
San Jose State University *B, M*
Santa Ana College *A*
Santa Barbara City College *A*
Santa Clara University *B*
Santa Monica College *A*
Scripps College *B*
Simpson College *B*
Solano Community College *A*
Sonoma State University *B, M*
Southwestern College *A*
Stanford University *B, M, D*
University of California
    Berkeley *B, M, D*
    Davis *B, M, D*
    Irvine *B, M, D*
    Los Angeles *B, M, D*
    Riverside *B, M, D*
    San Diego *B, M, D*
    Santa Barbara *B, M, D*
    Santa Cruz *B, M, D*
University of La Verne *B*
University of Redlands *B*
University of San Diego *B, M*
University of San Francisco *B*
University of Southern
    California *B, M, D*
University of the Pacific *B*
Vanguard University of Southern
    California *B*
Ventura College *A*
West Los Angeles College *C, A*
West Valley College *A*

Westmont College B
Whittier College B

Colorado

Adams State College B
Colorado Christian University B
Colorado College B
Colorado State University B, M, D
Fort Lewis College B
Lamar Community College A
Mesa State College B
Metropolitan State College of
  Denver B, T
Otero Junior College A
Red Rocks Community College A
Regis University B
United States Air Force Academy B
University of Colorado
  Boulder B, M, D
  Colorado Springs B, M
  Denver B, M
University of Denver B, M
University of Northern Colorado B, M, T
University of Southern Colorado B
Western State College of Colorado B

Connecticut

Albertus Magnus College B
Central Connecticut State
  University B, M
Connecticut College B
Eastern Connecticut State University B
Fairfield University B
Quinnipiac University B
Sacred Heart University B
St. Joseph College B, T
Southern Connecticut State
  University B, M
Teikyo Post University B
Trinity College B, M
University of Connecticut B, M, D
University of Hartford B
University of New Haven B
Wesleyan University B
Western Connecticut State
  University B, M
Yale University B, M, D

Delaware

Delaware State University B
University of Delaware B, M, D
Wesley College B

District of Columbia

American University B, M, D
Catholic University of
  America B, M, D, T
Gallaudet University B
George Washington University B, M, D
Georgetown University B, D
Howard University B, M, D
Trinity College B
University of the District of
  Columbia A, B

Florida

Barry University B
Bethune-Cookman College B
Broward Community College A
Clearwater Christian College B
Eckerd College B
Edward Waters College B
Flagler College B
Florida Agricultural and Mechanical
  University B
Florida Atlantic University B, M
Florida Gulf Coast University B
Florida International University B, M, D
Florida Southern College B
Florida State University B, M, D
Gulf Coast Community College A
Indian River Community College A
Jacksonville University B
Lynn University B
Manatee Community College A
Miami-Dade Community College A

New College of the University of South
  Florida B
Palm Beach Atlantic College B, T
Palm Beach Community College A
Pensacola Junior College A
Rollins College B
St. Leo University B
St. Thomas University B
Stetson University B
University of Central Florida B, M
University of Florida B, M, D
University of Miami B, M, D
University of North Florida B, M
University of South Florida B, M
University of Tampa A, B
University of West Florida B, M
Warner Southern College B

Georgia

Abraham Baldwin Agricultural
  College A
Agnes Scott College B
Albany State University B
Andrew College A
Armstrong Atlantic State
  University B, M, T
Atlanta Metropolitan College A
Augusta State University B
Berry College B, T
Brenau University B
Brewton-Parker College A, B
Clark Atlanta University B, M
Clayton College and State University A
Columbus State University B
Covenant College B
Dalton State College A
Darton College A
East Georgia College A
Emmanuel College B
Emory University B, M, D
Gainesville College A
Georgia College and State
  University B, M, T
Georgia Military College A
Georgia Perimeter College A
Georgia Southern University B, M
Georgia Southwestern State University B
Georgia State University B, M, D
Kennesaw State University B
LaGrange College B
Mercer University B, T
Middle Georgia College A
Morehouse College B
Morris Brown College B
North Georgia College & State
  University B
Oglethorpe University B
Oxford College of Emory University B
Paine College B
Piedmont College B
Savannah State University B
Shorter College B, T
South Georgia College A
Spelman College B
State University of West Georgia B, M
Thomas College B
University of Georgia B, M, D
Valdosta State University B, M
Waycross College A
Wesleyan College B, T

Hawaii

Brigham Young University
  Hawaii B
Chaminade University of Honolulu B
Hawaii Pacific University B
University of Hawaii
  Hilo B
  Manoa B, M, D
  West Oahu B

Idaho

Albertson College of Idaho B
Boise State University B, M, T
College of Southern Idaho A
Idaho State University A, B

Lewis-Clark State College B
North Idaho College A
Northwest Nazarene University B
Ricks College A
University of Idaho B, M, D

Illinois

Augustana College B, T
Barat College B
Benedictine University B, T
Black Hawk College
  East Campus A
Blackburn College B, T
Bradley University B, T
Chicago State University B, M
City Colleges of Chicago
  Kennedy-King College A
Concordia University B
Danville Area Community College A
De Paul University B, M, T
Dominican University B
Eastern Illinois University B, M, T
Elmhurst College B, T
Eureka College B, T
Highland Community College A
Illinois College B
Illinois State University B, M, T
Illinois Wesleyan University B
John A. Logan College A
John Wood Community College A
Joliet Junior College A
Judson College B
Kendall College B
Kishwaukee College A
Knox College B
Lake Forest College B
Lewis University B, T
Lewis and Clark Community College A
Lincoln Land Community College A
Loyola University of Chicago B, M, D, T
MacMurray College B
McKendree College B
Millikin University B, T
Monmouth College B, T
Morton College A
North Central College B, T
North Park University B
Northeastern Illinois University B, M
Northern Illinois University B, M, D
Northwestern University B, M, D
Olivet Nazarene University B, T
Parkland College A
Principia College B, T
Quincy University A, B, T
Rend Lake College A
Richland Community College A
Rockford College B
Roosevelt University B, M
St. Xavier University B
Sauk Valley Community College A
Southern Illinois University
  Carbondale B, M, D
  Edwardsville B, M
Southwestern Illinois College A
Springfield College in Illinois A
Trinity Christian College B, T
Trinity International University B
Triton College A
University of Chicago B, M, D
University of Illinois
  Chicago B, M, D
  Springfield B, M
  Urbana-Champaign B, M, D
University of St. Francis B
Western Illinois University B, M
Wheaton College B

Indiana

Ancilla College A
Anderson University B
Ball State University B, M
Bethel College B
Butler University B, M
DePauw University B
Earlham College B
Franklin College B

Goshen College B
Hanover College B
Indiana State University B, M, T
Indiana University
  Bloomington B, M, D
  East B
  Northwest B
  South Bend A, B
  Southeast B
Indiana University--Purdue University
  Indiana University-Purdue
    University Fort Wayne A, B
  Indiana University-Purdue
    University Indianapolis B, M
Indiana Wesleyan University A, B
Manchester College B, T
Marian College B
Oakland City University A, B
Purdue University
  Calumet B
Purdue University B, M, D
Saint Mary's College B, T
St. Joseph's College B
St. Mary-of-the-Woods College B
Taylor University B
University of Evansville B
University of Indianapolis B, M
University of Notre Dame B, M, D
University of St. Francis B
University of Southern Indiana B
Valparaiso University B, M, T
Vincennes University A
Wabash College B

Iowa

Briar Cliff College B
Buena Vista University B, T
Central College B, T
Clarke College A, B, T
Coe College B
Cornell College B, T
Dordt College B
Drake University B
Graceland University B, T
Grand View College B
Grinnell College B
Iowa State University B, M, D
Iowa Wesleyan College B
Loras College B
Luther College B
Marycrest International University A, B
Morningside College B
Mount Mercy College B, T
North Iowa Area Community College A
Northwestern College B
St. Ambrose University B, T
Simpson College B
University of Iowa B, M, D, T
University of Northern Iowa B, M
Waldorf College A
Wartburg College B, T
William Penn University B

Kansas

Allen County Community College A
Baker University B, T
Benedictine College B, T
Bethany College B, T
Bethel College B, T
Butler County Community College A
Central Christian College A
Coffeyville Community College A
Colby Community College A
Emporia State University B, M
Fort Hays State University B, M
Independence Community College A
Kansas City Kansas Community
  College A
Kansas State University B, M, D
Kansas Wesleyan University B, T
McPherson College B, T
MidAmerica Nazarene University B
Newman University B
Ottawa University B, T
Pittsburg State University B, M, T
Pratt Community College A

St. Mary College *B*
Southwestern College *B*
Sterling College *B*
Tabor College *B*
University of Kansas *B, M, D*
Washburn University of Topeka *B*
Wichita State University *B, M, T*

Kentucky
Alice Lloyd College *B*
Asbury College *B*
Bellarmine College *B, T*
Berea College *B, T*
Brescia University *B*
Campbellsville University *B*
Centre College *B*
Cumberland College *B, T*
Eastern Kentucky University *B, M*
Georgetown College *B, T*
Kentucky Christian College *B*
Kentucky State University *B*
Kentucky Wesleyan College *B, T*
Lindsey Wilson College *B, T*
Morehead State University *B*
Murray State University *B, M, T*
Northern Kentucky University *B*
Pikeville College *B*
Spalding University *B*
Thomas More College *A, B*
Transylvania University *B, T*
Union College *B*
University of Kentucky *B, M, D*
University of Louisville *B, M*
Western Kentucky University *B, M, T*

Louisiana
Centenary College of Louisiana *B, T*
Dillard University *B*
Louisiana State University
  Shreveport *B*
Louisiana State University and
  Agricultural and Mechanical
  College *B, M, D*
Louisiana Tech University *B, M*
Loyola University New Orleans *B*
McNeese State University *B*
Nicholls State University *B*
Northwestern State University *M*
Our Lady of Holy Cross College *B*
Southeastern Louisiana University *B, M*
Southern University
  New Orleans *B*
Southern University and Agricultural and
  Mechanical College *B, M*
Tulane University *B, M, D*
University of Louisiana at
  Lafayette *B, M*
University of Louisiana at Monroe *B, M*
University of New Orleans *B, M*
Xavier University of Louisiana *B*

Maine
Bates College *B*
Bowdoin College *B*
Colby College *B*
St. Joseph's College *B*
University of Maine
  Farmington *B*
  Machias *B*
  Presque Isle *B*
University of Maine *B, M, D*
University of Southern Maine *B*

Maryland
Allegany College *A*
Bowie State University *B*
Charles County Community College *A*
College of Notre Dame of Maryland *B*
Columbia Union College *B*
Community College of Baltimore County
  Essex *A*
Coppin State College *B*
Frederick Community College *A*
Frostburg State University *B*
Goucher College *B*
Hood College *B, T*

Johns Hopkins University *B, D*
Loyola College in Maryland *B*
Morgan State University *B, M, D*
Mount St. Mary's College *B*
St. Mary's College of Maryland *B*
Salisbury State University *B, M, T*
Towson University *B*
United States Naval Academy *B*
University of Baltimore *B*
University of Maryland
  Baltimore County *B, M*
  College Park *B, M, D*
  Eastern Shore *B*
Washington College *B, M, T*
Western Maryland College *B*

Massachusetts
American International College *B*
Amherst College *B*
Anna Maria College *B*
Assumption College *B*
Atlantic Union College *B*
Bay Path College *B*
Bentley College *B*
Boston College *B, M, D*
Boston University *B, M, D*
Brandeis University *B, M, D*
Bridgewater State College *B, M*
Clark University *B, M, D*
College of the Holy Cross *B*
Curry College *B*
Eastern Nazarene College *B*
Elms College *B*
Emmanuel College *B*
Fitchburg State College *B, M*
Framingham State College *B, M*
Gordon College *B*
Hampshire College *B*
Harvard College *B*
Harvard University *M, D*
Massachusetts College of Liberal Arts *B*
Massachusetts Institute of Technology *B*
Merrimack College *B*
Mount Holyoke College *B*
Nichols College *B*
Northeastern University *B, M, D*
Pine Manor College *A*
Regis College *B*
St. John's Seminary College *B*
Salem State College *B, M*
Simmons College *B*
Smith College *B*
Springfield College *B*
Stonehill College *B*
Suffolk University *B*
Tufts University *B, M, T*
University of Massachusetts
  Amherst *B, M, D*
  Boston *B, M*
  Dartmouth *B*
  Lowell *B*
Wellesley College *B*
Western New England College *B*
Westfield State College *B, M*
Wheaton College *B*
Williams College *B*
Worcester State College *B*

Michigan
Adrian College *A, B, T*
Albion College *B, T*
Alma College *B, T*
Andrews University *B, M*
Aquinas College *B, T*
Calvin College *B, T*
Central Michigan University *B, M, D*
Cornerstone College and Grand Rapids
  Baptist Seminary *B, T*
Eastern Michigan University *C, B, M*
Grand Valley State University *B*
Hillsdale College *B*
Hope College *B, T*
Kalamazoo College *B, T*
Kellogg Community College *B*
Lake Michigan College *A*
Lake Superior State University *B, T*

Lansing Community College *A*
Madonna University *B, T*
Marygrove College *B, T*
Michigan State University *B, M, D*
Michigan Technological University *B*
Northern Michigan University *B, M, T*
Oakland University *B, M, T*
Olivet College *B, T*
Rochester College *B*
Saginaw Valley State University *B*
Siena Heights University *B*
Spring Arbor College *B*
University of Detroit Mercy *B*
University of Michigan
  Dearborn *B*
  Flint *B, T*
University of Michigan *B, M, D, T*
Wayne State University *C, B, M, D*
Western Michigan University *B, M, D, T*
William Tyndale College *B*

Minnesota
Augsburg College *B*
Bemidji State University *B*
Bethel College *B*
Carleton College *B*
College of St. Benedict *B*
College of St. Catherine: St. Paul
  Campus *B*
College of St. Scholastica *B*
Concordia College: Moorhead *B*
Concordia University: St. Paul *B*
Crown College *B*
Gustavus Adolphus College *B*
Hamline University *B*
Macalester College *B*
Metropolitan State University *B*
Minnesota State University,
  Mankato *B, M*
Moorhead State University *B*
Northwestern College *B*
Ridgewater College: A Community and
  Technical College *A*
St. Cloud State University *B, M*
St. John's University *B*
St. Mary's University of Minnesota *B*
St. Olaf College *B, T*
Southwest State University *B*
University of Minnesota
  Duluth *B*
  Morris *B*
  Twin Cities *B, M, D*
University of St. Thomas *B*
Winona State University *B*

Mississippi
Alcorn State University *B*
Belhaven College *B, T*
Blue Mountain College *B*
Delta State University *B*
Hinds Community College *A*
Jackson State University *B, M, D*
Millsaps College *B, T*
Mississippi College *B, M*
Mississippi Delta Community College *A*
Mississippi State University *B, M, D*
Mississippi University for Women *B, T*
Mississippi Valley State University *B*
Tougaloo College *B*
University of Mississippi *B, M, D, T*
University of Southern
  Mississippi *B, M, D*
William Carey College *B*

Missouri
Avila College *B*
Central Methodist College *B*
Central Missouri State University *B, M*
College of the Ozarks *B*
Columbia College *B*
Crowder College *A*
Culver-Stockton College *B*
Drury University *B, T*
East Central College *A*
Evangel University *B*
Fontbonne College *B, T*

Hannibal-LaGrange College *B*
Lincoln University *B, M*
Lindenwood University *B*
Maryville University of Saint Louis *B*
Missouri Baptist College *B*
Missouri Southern State College *B, T*
Missouri Valley College *B*
Missouri Western State College *B, T*
Northwest Missouri State
  University *B, M*
Park University *B*
Rockhurst University *B*
St. Louis University *B, M, D*
Southeast Missouri State
  University *B, M*
Southwest Baptist University *B*
Southwest Missouri State
  University *B, M*
Stephens College *B*
Three Rivers Community College *A*
Truman State University *B, M*
University of Missouri
  Columbia *B, M, D*
  Kansas City *B, M*
  Rolla *B*
  St. Louis *B, M*
Washington University *B, M, D*
Webster University *B*
Westminster College *B*
William Jewell College *B*
William Woods University *B*

Montana
Carroll College *B, T*
Montana State University
  Billings *B*
  Bozeman *B, M, T*
Rocky Mountain College *B, T*
University of Great Falls *B, T*
University of Montana-Missoula *B, M*
Western Montana College of The
  University of Montana *T*

Nebraska
Chadron State College *B*
Concordia University *B, T*
Creighton University *B*
Dana College *B*
Doane College *B*
Hastings College *B*
Midland Lutheran College *B, T*
Nebraska Wesleyan University *B*
Union College *B*
University of Nebraska
  Kearney *B, M, T*
  Lincoln *B, M, D*
  Omaha *B, M*
Wayne State College *B, M, T*

Nevada
University of Nevada
  Las Vegas *B, M, D*
  Reno *B, M, D*

New Hampshire
Dartmouth College *B*
Franklin Pierce College *B*
Keene State College *B*
Notre Dame College *B*
Plymouth State College of the University
  System of New Hampshire *B*
Rivier College *B*
St. Anselm College *B, T*
University of New Hampshire
  Manchester *B*
University of New Hampshire *B, M, D*

New Jersey
Atlantic Cape Community College *A*
Bloomfield College *B*
Caldwell College *B*
Centenary College *B*
College of St. Elizabeth *B*
Drew University *B*
Fairleigh Dickinson University *B*
Felician College *B*
Georgian Court College *B*

Gloucester County College A
Kean University B
Monmouth University B, M
Montclair State University B
New Jersey City University B
New Jersey Institute of Technology B
Princeton University B, M, D
Ramapo College of New Jersey B
Richard Stockton College of New Jersey B
Rider University B
Rowan University B
Rutgers
   The State University of New Jersey: Camden College of Arts and Sciences B
   The State University of New Jersey: Camden Graduate Campus M
   The State University of New Jersey: Douglass College B
   The State University of New Jersey: Livingston College B
   The State University of New Jersey: New Brunswick Graduate Campus M, D
   The State University of New Jersey: Newark College of Arts and Sciences B
   The State University of New Jersey: Newark Graduate Campus M
   The State University of New Jersey: Rutgers College B
   The State University of New Jersey: University College Camden B
   The State University of New Jersey: University College New Brunswick B
   The State University of New Jersey: University College Newark B
St. Peter's College B
Salem Community College A
Seton Hall University B, T
Stevens Institute of Technology B
The College of New Jersey B, T
Thomas Edison State College B
William Paterson University of New Jersey B

New Mexico
College of the Southwest B
Eastern New Mexico University B
New Mexico Highlands University B
New Mexico State University B, M
San Juan College A
University of New Mexico B, M, D
Western New Mexico University B

New York
Adelphi University B
Adirondack Community College A
Alfred University B
Bard College B
Barnard College B
Canisius College B
City University of New York
   Baruch College B
   Brooklyn College B, M
   City College B, M, T
   College of Staten Island B
   Graduate School and University Center D
   Hunter College B, M
   Lehman College B, M
   Queens College B, M
   Queensborough Community College A
   York College B
Clarkson University B
Colgate University B
College of Mount St. Vincent A, B, T
College of New Rochelle B, T
College of St. Rose B, M

Columbia University
   Columbia College B
   Graduate School M, D
   School of General Studies B
   Teachers College M, D
Concordia College B, T
Cornell University B, M, D
D'Youville College B
Daemen College B
Dominican College of Blauvelt B
Dowling College B
Elmira College B, T
Eugene Lang College/New School University B
Fordham University B, M, D
Fulton-Montgomery Community College A
Hamilton College B
Hartwick College B
Hobart and William Smith Colleges B
Hofstra University B
Houghton College B
Iona College B, M
Ithaca College B
Jewish Theological Seminary of America D
Keuka College B, T
Le Moyne College B
Long Island University
   Brooklyn Campus B
   C. W. Post Campus B, M
   Southampton College B, T
Manhattan College B
Manhattanville College B
Marist College B, T
Marymount College B
Marymount Manhattan College B
Mercy College B
Molloy College B
Monroe Community College A
Mount St. Mary College B, T
Nazareth College of Rochester B, T
New York University B, M, D
Niagara University B
Nyack College B
Pace University:
   Pleasantville/Briarcliff B, T
Pace University B, T
Polytechnic University M
Regents College B
Roberts Wesleyan College B
Russell Sage College B, T
St. Bonaventure University B
St. Francis College B
St. John Fisher College B
St. John's University B, M, D
St. Lawrence University B
St. Thomas Aquinas College B, T
Sarah Lawrence College B
Siena College B, T
Skidmore College B
St. Joseph's College
   St. Joseph's College: Suffolk Campus B
   St. Joseph's College B
State University of New York
   Albany B, M, D
   Binghamton B, M, D
   Buffalo B, M, D
   College at Brockport B, M, T
   College at Buffalo B, M
   College at Cortland B, M
   College at Fredonia B
   College at Geneseo B, T
   College at Oneonta B, M
   College at Plattsburgh B, M
   College at Potsdam B, T
   Empire State College A, B
   New Paltz B
   Oswego B, M
   Purchase B
   Stony Brook B, M, D
Suffolk County Community College A
Syracuse University B, M, D
Touro College B

Union College B
United States Military Academy B
University of Rochester B, M, D
Utica College of Syracuse University B
Vassar College B
Wagner College B
Wells College B

North Carolina
Appalachian State University B, M
Barton College B
Belmont Abbey College B
Brevard College B
Campbell University B
Catawba College B, T
Chowan College B
Davidson College B
Duke University B, M, D
East Carolina University B, M
Elizabeth City State University B
Elon College B, T
Fayetteville State University B
Gardner-Webb University B
Greensboro College B, T
Guilford College B, T
High Point University B
Johnson C. Smith University B
Lees-McRae College B
Lenoir-Rhyne College B, T
Louisburg College A
Mars Hill College B, T
Meredith College B
Methodist College A, B
Montreat College B
Mount Olive College B
North Carolina Agricultural and Technical State University B, M, T
North Carolina Central University B, M
North Carolina State University B, M
North Carolina Wesleyan College B
Pfeiffer University B
Queens College B
St. Andrews Presbyterian College B
St. Augustine's College B
Salem College B
Sandhills Community College A
University of North Carolina
   Asheville B, T
   Chapel Hill B, M, D
   Charlotte B, M, T
   Greensboro B, M, T
   Pembroke B
   Wilmington B, M, T
Wake Forest University B, M
Warren Wilson College B
Western Carolina University B, M
Wingate University B
Winston-Salem State University B

North Dakota
Dickinson State University B, T
Jamestown College B
Minot State University: Bottineau Campus A
Minot State University B, T
North Dakota State University B, M, T
University of North Dakota B, M, D, T
Valley City State University B

Ohio
Antioch College B
Ashland University B
Baldwin-Wallace College B
Bluffton College B
Bowling Green State University B, M, D
Capital University B
Case Western Reserve University B, M, D
Cedarville College B
Central State University B
Cleveland State University B, M, T
College of Mount St. Joseph B, T
College of Wooster B
Defiance College B, T
Denison University B
Franciscan University of Steubenville B

Heidelberg College B
Hiram College B, T
John Carroll University B, M
Kent State University
   Stark Campus B
Kent State University B, M, D
Kenyon College B
Lake Erie College B
Lourdes College A, B
Malone College B
Marietta College B
Miami University
   Middletown Campus A
   Oxford Campus B, M
Mount Union College B
Mount Vernon Nazarene College B
Muskingum College B
Notre Dame College of Ohio B, T
Oberlin College B
Ohio Dominican College B, T
Ohio Northern University B
Ohio State University
   Columbus Campus B, M, D
Ohio University
   Southern Campus at Ironton A
Ohio University B, M, D
Ohio Wesleyan University B
Otterbein College B
Shawnee State University B, T
University of Akron B, M, D
University of Cincinnati B, M, D, T
University of Dayton B
University of Findlay B, T
University of Toledo B, M, D
Ursuline College B
Walsh University B
Wilmington College B
Wittenberg University B
Wright State University B, M
Xavier University A, B, M
Youngstown State University B, M

Oklahoma
Cameron University B, M
Connors State College A
East Central University B
Eastern Oklahoma State College A
Langston University B
Murray State College A
Northeastern Oklahoma Agricultural and Mechanical College A
Northeastern State University B
Northwestern Oklahoma State University B
Oklahoma Baptist University B
Oklahoma Christian University of Science and Arts B
Oklahoma City Community College A
Oklahoma City University B
Oklahoma Panhandle State University B
Oklahoma State University B, M, D
Oral Roberts University B
Redlands Community College A
Rogers State University A
Rose State College A
St. Gregory's University B
Southeastern Oklahoma State University B
Southern Nazarene University B
Southwestern Oklahoma State University B
Tulsa Community College A
University of Central Oklahoma B, M
University of Oklahoma B, M, D
University of Science and Arts of Oklahoma B
University of Tulsa B, M
Western Oklahoma State College A

Oregon
Central Oregon Community College A
Chemeketa Community College A
Eastern Oregon University B, T
George Fox University B, T
Lewis & Clark College B
Linfield College B

Multnomah Bible College *B*
Oregon State University *B*
Pacific University *B*
Portland State University *B, M*
Reed College *B*
Southern Oregon University *B*
University of Oregon *B, M, D*
University of Portland *B*
Western Oregon University *B*
Willamette University *B*

Pennsylvania
Albright College *B*
Allegheny College *B*
Allentown College of St. Francis de Sales *B*
Alvernia College *B*
Beaver College *B*
Bloomsburg University of Pennsylvania *B*
Bryn Mawr College *B*
Bucknell University *B*
Cabrini College *B*
California University of Pennsylvania *B*
Carlow College *B*
Carnegie Mellon University *B, M, D*
Cedar Crest College *B*
Chatham College *B*
Chestnut Hill College *C, A, B*
Clarion University of Pennsylvania *B*
College Misericordia *B*
Dickinson College *B*
Drexel University *B*
Duquesne University *B, M*
East Stroudsburg University of Pennsylvania *B, M*
Eastern College *B*
Edinboro University of Pennsylvania *B*
Elizabethtown College *B*
Franklin and Marshall College *B*
Gannon University *B*
Geneva College *B, T*
Gettysburg College *B*
Grove City College *B*
Gwynedd-Mercy College *B*
Haverford College *B, T*
Holy Family College *B, T*
Immaculata College *B*
Indiana University of Pennsylvania *B, M*
Juniata College *B*
King's College *B*
Kutztown University of Pennsylvania *B*
La Roche College *B*
La Salle University *B, T*
Lafayette College *B*
Lebanon Valley College of Pennsylvania *B, T*
Lehigh University *B, M, D*
Lincoln University *B*
Lock Haven University of Pennsylvania *B*
Lycoming College *B*
Mansfield University of Pennsylvania *B, T*
Mercyhurst College *B*
Messiah College *B*
Millersville University of Pennsylvania *B, M, T*
Moravian College *B*
Muhlenberg College *B, T*
Penn State
   Abington *B*
   Erie, The Behrend College *B*
   University Park *B, M, D*
Point Park College *B*
Rosemont College *B*
St. Francis College *B*
St. Joseph's University *B*
St. Vincent College *B*
Seton Hill College *B, T*
Shippensburg University of Pennsylvania *B, M, T*
Slippery Rock University of Pennsylvania *B, M, T*
Susquehanna University *B*
Swarthmore College *B*
Temple University *B, M, D*
Thiel College *B*
University of Pennsylvania *A, B, M, D*
University of Pittsburgh
   Bradford *B, T*
   Greensburg *B*
   Johnstown *B*
University of Pittsburgh *B, M, D*
University of Scranton *B, M*
Ursinus College *B*
Villanova University *B, M*
Washington and Jefferson College *B*
Waynesburg College *B*
West Chester University of Pennsylvania *B, M*
Westminster College *B, M*
Widener University *B*
Wilkes University *B*
Wilson College *B*
York College of Pennsylvania *B*

Puerto Rico
Inter American University of Puerto Rico
   Metropolitan Campus *B*
   San German Campus *B*
Pontifical Catholic University of Puerto Rico *B*
University of Puerto Rico
   Mayaguez Campus *B*
   Rio Piedras Campus *B, M, D*
University of the Sacred Heart *B*

Rhode Island
Brown University *B, M, D*
Bryant College *B*
Providence College *B, M, T*
Rhode Island College *B, M*
Roger Williams University *A, B*
Salve Regina University *B*
University of Rhode Island *B, M*

South Carolina
Anderson College *B, T*
Benedict College *B*
Charleston Southern University *B*
Claflin University *B*
Clemson University *B, M*
Coastal Carolina University *B*
Coker College *B, T*
College of Charleston *B, M, T*
Columbia College *B*
Converse College *B*
Erskine College *B*
Francis Marion University *B*
Furman University *B, T*
Lander University *B, T*
Limestone College *B*
Morris College *B*
Newberry College *B, T*
Presbyterian College *B, T*
South Carolina State University *B*
Southern Wesleyan University *B*
The Citadel *B, M*
University of South Carolina
   Aiken *B*
   Spartanburg *B*
University of South Carolina *B, M, D*
Winthrop University *B, M*
Wofford College *B*

South Dakota
Augustana College *B, T*
Black Hills State University *B*
Dakota Wesleyan University *B*
Mount Marty College *B*
Northern State University *B*
South Dakota State University *B*
University of South Dakota *B, M*

Tennessee
Austin Peay State University *B*
Belmont University *B, T*
Bethel College *B*
Carson-Newman College *B, T*
Christian Brothers University *B*
Columbia State Community College *A*
Crichton College *B*
Cumberland University *A, B*
David Lipscomb University *B*
East Tennessee State University *B, M*
Fisk University *B*
Freed-Hardeman University *B, T*
Hiwassee College *A*
King College *B, T*
Lambuth University *B*
Lane College *B*
LeMoyne-Owen College *B*
Lee University *B*
Lincoln Memorial University *B, T*
Maryville College *B, T*
Middle Tennessee State University *B, M, D*
Milligan College *B, T*
Rhodes College *B, T*
Roane State Community College *A*
Southern Adventist University *B*
Tennessee State University *B, M*
Tennessee Technological University *B, T*
Tennessee Temple University *B*
Tennessee Wesleyan College *B*
Trevecca Nazarene University *B, T*
Tusculum College *B*
Union University *B, T*
University of Memphis *B, M, D*
University of Tennessee
   Chattanooga *B*
   Knoxville *B, M, D*
   Martin *B*
University of the South *B*
Vanderbilt University *B, M, D*

Texas
Abilene Christian University *B, M*
Angelo State University *B, M, T*
Austin College *B*
Baylor University *B, M*
Blinn College *A*
Brazosport College *A*
Coastal Bend College *A*
College of the Mainland *A*
Concordia University at Austin *B, T*
Dallas Baptist University *B*
Del Mar College *A*
East Texas Baptist University *B*
El Paso Community College *A*
Galveston College *A*
Hardin-Simmons University *B, M*
Houston Baptist University *B*
Howard Payne University *B, T*
Jarvis Christian College *B*
Kilgore College *A*
Lamar University *B, M*
LeTourneau University *B*
Lon Morris College *A*
McMurry University *B, T*
Midland College *A*
Midwestern State University *B, M*
Northeast Texas Community College *A*
Our Lady of the Lake University of San Antonio *B*
Palo Alto College *A*
Panola College *A*
Paris Junior College *A*
Prairie View A&M University *B*
Rice University *B, M, D*
St. Edward's University *B, T*
St. Mary's University *B, M*
St. Philip's College *A*
Sam Houston State University *B, M*
San Jacinto College
   North *A*
Schreiner College *B*
South Plains College *A*
Southern Methodist University *B, M, D*
Southwest Texas State University *B, M*
Southwestern Adventist University *B, T*
Southwestern University *B, T*
Stephen F. Austin State University *B, M, T*
Sul Ross State University *B, M, T*
Tarleton State University *B, M, T*
Texas A&M International University *B, M, T*
Texas A&M University
   Commerce *B, M*
   Corpus Christi *B, T*
   Kingsville *B, M*
   Texarkana *B, T*
Texas A&M University *B, M, D*
Texas Christian University *B, M, D, T*
Texas College *B*
Texas Lutheran University *B*
Texas Southern University *B, M*
Texas Tech University *B, M, D*
Texas Wesleyan University *B*
Texas Woman's University *B, M, T*
Trinity University *B*
Tyler Junior College *A*
University of Dallas *B*
University of Houston
   Clear Lake *B, M*
   Victoria *B*
University of Houston *B, M, D*
University of Mary Hardin-Baylor *B, T*
University of North Texas *B, M, D*
University of St. Thomas *B*
University of Texas
   Arlington *B, M, D*
   Austin *B, M, D*
   Brownsville *B, M*
   Dallas *B*
   El Paso *B, M, D*
   Pan American *B, M*
   San Antonio *B, M*
   Tyler *B, M*
   of the Permian Basin *B, M*
University of the Incarnate Word *B*
Wayland Baptist University *B*
West Texas A&M University *B, M, T*
Western Texas College *A*
Wharton County Junior College *A*
Wiley College *B*

Utah
Brigham Young University *B, M, D*
Dixie State College of Utah *A*
Snow College *A*
Southern Utah University *B, T*
University of Utah *B, M, D*
Utah State University *B, M*
Weber State University *B*
Westminster College *B*

Vermont
Bennington College *B*
Burlington College *B*
Castleton State College *B*
College of St. Joseph in Vermont *B*
Goddard College *B*
Green Mountain College *B*
Johnson State College *B*
Marlboro College *B*
Middlebury College *B*
Norwich University *B*
St. Michael's College *B*
University of Vermont *B, M*

Virginia
Averett College *B, T*
Bluefield College *B*
Bridgewater College *B*
Christendom College *B*
Christopher Newport University *B*
College of William and Mary *B, M, D*
Eastern Mennonite University *B*
Emory & Henry College *B, T*
Ferrum College *B*
George Mason University *B, M*
Hampden-Sydney College *B*
Hampton University *B*
Hollins University *B*
James Madison University *B, M, T*
Liberty University *B, T*
Longwood College *B, T*
Lynchburg College *B*
Mary Baldwin College *B*

Mary Washington College *B*
Norfolk State University *B*
Old Dominion University *B, M*
Radford University *B*
Randolph-Macon College *B*
Randolph-Macon Woman's College *B*
Roanoke College *B, T*
Shenandoah University *B*
Sweet Briar College *B*
University of Richmond *B, M, T*
University of Virginia's College at Wise *B, T*
University of Virginia *B, M, D*
Virginia Commonwealth University *B, M*
Virginia Intermont College *B*
Virginia Military Institute *B*
Virginia Polytechnic Institute and State University *B, M*
Virginia State University *B, M*
Virginia Union University *B*
Virginia Wesleyan College *B*
Washington and Lee University *B*

Washington
Central Washington University *B, M*
Centralia College *A*
Eastern Washington University *B, M, T*
Everett Community College *A*
Evergreen State College *B*
Gonzaga University *B*
Highline Community College *A*
Lower Columbia College *A*
Pacific Lutheran University *B*
St. Martin's College *B*
Seattle Pacific University *B, T*
Seattle University *B*
University of Puget Sound *B, T*
University of Washington *B, M, D*
Walla Walla College *B*
Washington State University *B, M, D*
Western Washington University *B, M, T*
Whitman College *B*
Whitworth College *B, T*

West Virginia
Alderson-Broaddus College *B*
Bethany College *B*
Concord College *B*
Davis and Elkins College *B*
Fairmont State College *B*
Glenville State College *B*
Marshall University *B, M*
Potomac State College of West Virginia University *A*
Shepherd College *B*
University of Charleston *B*
West Liberty State College *B*
West Virginia State College *B*
West Virginia University Institute of Technology *B*
West Virginia University *B, M, D*
West Virginia Wesleyan College *B*
Wheeling Jesuit University *B*

Wisconsin
Alverno College *B, T*
Beloit College *B*
Cardinal Stritch University *B*
Carroll College *B*
Carthage College *B, T*
Concordia University Wisconsin *B, T*
Lakeland College *B*
Lawrence University *B*
Marian College of Fond du Lac *B*
Marquette University *B, M, D, T*
Mount Mary College *B*
Mount Senario College *B, T*
Northland College *B, T*
Ripon College *B, T*
St. Norbert College *B, T*
Silver Lake College *B, T*

University of Wisconsin
   Eau Claire *B, M*
   Green Bay *B*
   La Crosse *B, T*
   Madison *B, M, D*
   Milwaukee *B, M*
   Oshkosh *B*
   Parkside *B*
   Platteville *B, T*
   River Falls *B*
   Stevens Point *B, M, T*
   Superior *B, T*
   Whitewater *B, T*
Wisconsin Lutheran College *B*

Wyoming
Casper College *A*
Eastern Wyoming College *A*
Laramie County Community College *A*
Northwest College *A*
University of Wyoming *B, M*
Western Wyoming Community College *A*

History teacher education

Alabama
Alabama Agricultural and Mechanical University *B, M*
Athens State University *B*
Birmingham-Southern College *T*
Faulkner University *B*
Huntingdon College *T*
Oakwood College *B*
University of Alabama *B*

Arizona
Arizona State University *B, T*
Grand Canyon University *B*
Northern Arizona University *B, T*
University of Arizona *B, M*

Arkansas
Harding University *B, M, T*
University of Central Arkansas *T*

California
Azusa Pacific University *T*
California State University
   Chico *T*
Concordia University *B*
Loyola Marymount University *M*
Master's College *T*
Pacific Union College *T*
University of San Diego *M*
University of the Pacific *T*

Colorado
Adams State College *B, T*
Fort Lewis College *T*
University of Southern Colorado *T*

Connecticut
Central Connecticut State University *B*
Fairfield University *T*
Quinnipiac University *B, M*
St. Joseph College *T*
Southern Connecticut State University *B, T*

Delaware
University of Delaware *B, T*

District of Columbia
Catholic University of America *B*

Florida
Barry University *T*
Flagler College *B*
Florida Agricultural and Mechanical University *T*
St. Leo University *B, T*
St. Thomas University *B, T*
Stetson University *B, T*
University of West Florida *B, T*

Georgia
Agnes Scott College *T*

Armstrong Atlantic State University *M, T*
Brewton-Parker College *B*
Columbus State University *B, M*
Covenant College *B, T*
Mercer University *M, T*
North Georgia College & State University *B, M*
Piedmont College *T*
Toccoa Falls College *B, T*
Valdosta State University *T*
Wesleyan College *T*

Hawaii
University of Hawaii
   Manoa *B, T*

Idaho
Boise State University *T*
Northwest Nazarene University *B*

Illinois
Augustana College *B, T*
Chicago State University *B, T*
Concordia University *B, T*
Dominican University *T*
Elmhurst College *B*
Eureka College *T*
Greenville College *B*
Illinois College *T*
John A. Logan College *A*
Lewis University *T*
MacMurray College *B, T*
McKendree College *B, T*
North Central College *B, T*
North Park University *T*
Northwestern University *B, T*
Olivet Nazarene University *B, T*
Quincy University *T*
Rockford College *T*
Roosevelt University *B*
Trinity Christian College *B, T*
Trinity International University *B, T*
University of Illinois
   Chicago *B, M*
University of St. Francis *T*
Wheaton College *T*

Indiana
Ball State University *T*
Butler University *T*
Franklin College *T*
Goshen College *B*
Indiana State University *B, T*
Indiana University--Purdue University
Indiana University-Purdue University Fort Wayne *B*
Manchester College *B, T*
Taylor University *B*
University of Evansville *T*
University of Indianapolis *B, M, T*
University of Southern Indiana *B, T*
Valparaiso University *B*
Vincennes University *A*

Iowa
Buena Vista University *B, T*
Central College *T*
Clarke College *B, T*
Cornell College *B, T*
Dordt College *B*
Drake University *M, T*
Graceland University *T*
Iowa State University *T*
Loras College *T*
Luther College *B*
Morningside College *B*
Northwestern College *T*
St. Ambrose University *B, T*
University of Iowa *B, T*
Wartburg College *B, T*
William Penn University *B*

Kansas
Baker University *T*
Benedictine College *T*
Bethany College *B*

Bethel College *T*
Garden City Community College *A*
Independence Community College *A*
McPherson College *B, T*
Ottawa University *T*
Pittsburg State University *B, T*
St. Mary College *T*
Tabor College *B, T*

Kentucky
Campbellsville University *B*
Cumberland College *B, T*
Kentucky State University *B*
Murray State University *B, M, T*
Transylvania University *B, T*
Union College *M*

Louisiana
Dillard University *B*
University of New Orleans *M*
Xavier University of Louisiana *M*

Maine
St. Joseph's College *B*
University of Maine
   Machias *B*
   Presque Isle *B*
University of New England *B, T*
University of Southern Maine *T*

Maryland
College of Notre Dame of Maryland *T*
Salisbury State University *B*

Massachusetts
Assumption College *T*
Bridgewater State College *M, T*
Elms College *M, T*
Fitchburg State College *B, M, T*
Framingham State College *B, M, T*
Harvard College *T*
Merrimack College *T*
Northeastern University *M*
Salem State College *M*
Tufts University *T*
University of Massachusetts
   Dartmouth *T*
Western New England College *T*
Westfield State College *B, M, T*
Worcester State College *M, T*

Michigan
Albion College *B, T*
Alma College *T*
Andrews University *M, T*
Calvin College *B*
Central Michigan University *B*
Concordia College *B, T*
Eastern Michigan University *B, T*
Grand Valley State University *T*
Michigan State University *M*
Northern Michigan University *B, M, T*
Saginaw Valley State University *T*
Western Michigan University *B*

Minnesota
Bemidji State University *T*
Bethel College *B*
Concordia College: Moorhead *T*
Concordia University: St. Paul *B, T*
Crown College *B, T*
Minnesota State University,
   Mankato *B, M, T*
Moorhead State University *B, T*
St. Cloud State University *M, T*
St. Mary's University of Minnesota *B*
St. Olaf College *T*
University of Minnesota
   Morris *T*
Winona State University *B, T*

Mississippi
Mississippi College *M*

Missouri
Avila College *T*
College of the Ozarks *B, T*
Culver-Stockton College *T*

Fontbonne College *B*
Maryville University of Saint
   Louis *B, M, T*
Missouri Baptist College *T*
Northwest Missouri State
   University *M, T*
Southwest Baptist University *T*
Southwest Missouri State University *B*
Truman State University *M, T*
Washington University *B, M, T*

Montana

Montana State University
   Billings *B, T*
   Bozeman *T*
Rocky Mountain College *B, T*
University of Great Falls *B, T*
University of Montana-Missoula *T*
Western Montana College of The
   University of Montana *B, T*

Nebraska

Concordia University *T*
Creighton University *T*
Dana College *B*
Doane College *T*
Hastings College *B, M, T*
Midland Lutheran College *B, T*
Peru State College *B, T*
Union College *T*
University of Nebraska
   Kearney *B*
   Lincoln *B, T*

New Hampshire

Keene State College *B, T*
Notre Dame College *B, M*
Rivier College *B, T*
St. Anselm College *T*
University of New Hampshire *T*

New Jersey

Caldwell College *T*
Monmouth University *B, T*
New Jersey Institute of Technology *M*
Rider University *B*
Rowan University *T*
St. Peter's College *T*
The College of New Jersey *B, T*

New York

Canisius College *B, M, T*
City University of New York
   Brooklyn College *B*
   City College *B*
   Lehman College *M*
   Queens College *T*
   York College *T*
College of St. Rose *T*
Columbia University
   Teachers College *M, D*
D'Youville College *B, M, T*
Elmira College *B, T*
Fordham University *M, T*
Long Island University
   C. W. Post Campus *B, M, T*
   Southampton College *T*
Manhattan College *B, T*
Marist College *B, T*
Molloy College *B*
Nazareth College of Rochester *T*
New York University *B, M, T*
Pace University:
   Pleasantville/Briarcliff *B, M, T*
Pace University *B, M, T*
Roberts Wesleyan College *B*
St. John Fisher College *B, T*
St. Thomas Aquinas College *B, T*
State University of New York
   College at Brockport *M, T*
   College at Geneseo *B, M, T*
   College at Oneonta *B, M, T*
   New Paltz *B, M, T*
   Oswego *B*
Vassar College *T*
Wells College *T*

North Carolina

Appalachian State University *M*
Campbell University *B, T*
East Carolina University *M*
Gardner-Webb University *B*
Lenoir Community College *A*
Louisburg College *A*
Mars Hill College *T*
Meredith College *T*
Montreat College *T*
North Carolina Agricultural and
   Technical State University *B, T*
North Carolina Central University *B, M*
Queens College *T*
Sandhills Community College *A*
University of North Carolina
   Charlotte *B*
   Greensboro *B, M, T*
   Wilmington *T*
Wake Forest University *T*
Wingate University *B, T*

North Dakota

Dickinson State University *B, T*
Jamestown College *B*
Mayville State University *B, T*
Minot State University *B, T*
North Dakota State University *B, T*
University of North Dakota *B, T*
Valley City State University *B, T*

Ohio

Baldwin-Wallace College *B*
Bluffton College *B*
Bowling Green State University *B, M*
Case Western Reserve University *T*
Cedarville College *B*
College of Mount St. Joseph *T*
Defiance College *B, T*
Hiram College *T*
John Carroll University *T*
Kent State University
   Stark Campus *B*
Kent State University *T*
Malone College *B*
Miami University
   Oxford Campus *M, T*
Mount Union College *T*
Ohio University *B*
Otterbein College *B*
Shawnee State University *B, T*
University of Akron *T*
University of Dayton *B, M, T*
University of Findlay *B, T*
University of Rio Grande *B, T*
University of Toledo *B, T*
Wilmington College *B*
Xavier University *M, T*
Youngstown State University *B, M*

Oklahoma

Cameron University *B*
East Central University *B, T*
Eastern Oklahoma State College *A*
Northeastern State University *B*
Oklahoma City University *B*
Oklahoma State University *M, D*
Southern Nazarene University *B*
Southwestern Oklahoma State
   University *B, T*
University of Central Oklahoma *B*
University of Tulsa *T*

Oregon

Concordia University *B, M, T*
Linfield College *T*
University of Portland *T*
Western Baptist College *B*
Western Oregon University *T*

Pennsylvania

Alvernia College *B*
Chatham College *M, T*
College Misericordia *B, T*
Elizabethtown College *T*
Gettysburg College *T*
Grove City College *B, T*
King's College *T*
La Salle University *B, T*
Lebanon Valley College of
   Pennsylvania *T*
Lock Haven University of
   Pennsylvania *B, T*
Lycoming College *T*
Mansfield University of
   Pennsylvania *B, T*
Mercyhurst College *B*
St. Vincent College *T*
Seton Hill College *B, T*
Thiel College *B*
University of Pittsburgh
   Bradford *B*
Villanova University *T*
Washington and Jefferson College *T*
Waynesburg College *B, T*
Westminster College *T*
Widener University *T*
Wilkes University *M*
York College of Pennsylvania *B, T*

Puerto Rico

Inter American University of Puerto Rico
   Metropolitan Campus *B*
Turabo University *B*
Universidad Metropolitana *B*
University of Puerto Rico
   Mayaguez Campus *T*

Rhode Island

Rhode Island College *B*
Salve Regina University *B*

South Carolina

Anderson College *B*
Coker College *B, T*
Columbia College *B*
Furman University *T*
Lander University *B, T*
Morris College *B, T*
South Carolina State University *B, T*

South Dakota

Augustana College *B, T*
Black Hills State University *B, T*
Dakota State University *B, T*
Huron University *B*
Mount Marty College *B*
Northern State University *T*
South Dakota State University *B*
University of South Dakota *B, T*

Tennessee

Belmont University *T*
Bethel College *B, T*
Christian Brothers University *B, M, T*
Cumberland University *B*
David Lipscomb University *B, T*
Lambuth University *T*
Lee University *B*
Lincoln Memorial University *B, T*
Maryville College *B, T*
Southern Adventist University *B*
Tennessee Temple University *B*
Tennessee Wesleyan College *B, T*
Trevecca Nazarene University *B, T*
Tusculum College *B, T*
Union University *B, T*
University of Tennessee
   Martin *B, T*

Texas

Abilene Christian University *B, T*
Baylor University *B, T*
Del Mar College *A*
East Texas Baptist University *B*
Hardin-Simmons University *B, T*
Houston Baptist University *B*
Howard Payne University *T*
Lamar University *T*
LeTourneau University *B*
Lubbock Christian University *B*
McMurry University *T*
St. Mary's University *T*
Schreiner College *T*
Southwest Texas State University *M, T*
Texas A&M International
   University *B, T*
Texas A&M University
   Commerce *T*
   Corpus Christi *T*
   Kingsville *T*
Texas Christian University *T*
Texas Lutheran University *T*
Texas Wesleyan University *B, T*
University of Dallas *T*
University of Houston
   Clear Lake *T*
University of Houston *T*
University of Mary Hardin-Baylor *T*
University of Texas
   Arlington *T*
   San Antonio *T*
Wayland Baptist University *T*
West Texas A&M University *T*

Utah

Brigham Young University *B*
Weber State University *B*

Vermont

Castleton State College *B, T*
College of St. Joseph in Vermont *B*
Johnson State College *B*
St. Michael's College *B*

Virginia

Averett College *B, T*
Bridgewater College *T*
Christopher Newport University *M, T*
Hampton University *B*
Hollins University *T*
Liberty University *B*
Longwood College *B, T*
Radford University *T*
University of Virginia's College at
   Wise *T*
Virginia Intermont College *B, T*
Virginia Wesleyan College *T*

Washington

Central Washington University *B, T*
Heritage College *B*
Washington State University *T*
Western Washington University *B, T*
Whitworth College *B, T*

West Virginia

Fairmont State College *B*
Glenville State College *B*
Wheeling Jesuit University *T*

Wisconsin

Alverno College *B, T*
Cardinal Stritch University *B, T*
Carroll College *B, T*
Carthage College *T*
Lakeland College *B, T*
Lawrence University *T*
Marian College of Fond du Lac *B, T*
Mount Mary College *B, T*
Mount Senario College *T*
Northland College *T*
St. Norbert College *T*
University of Wisconsin
   Green Bay *T*
   La Crosse *B, T*
   Platteville *B*
   River Falls *T*
   Superior *B, T*
   Whitewater *B*

Wyoming

Western Wyoming Community
   College *A*

Home economics

Alabama

Alabama Agricultural and Mechanical
   University *B*

Jacksonville State University *B*
James H. Faulkner State Community
 College *A*
Northeast Alabama Community
 College *A*
Oakwood College *B*
University of Alabama *B, M*
University of Montevallo *B, T*
University of North Alabama *B*

Arizona
Phoenix College *A*
South Mountain Community College *A*

Arkansas
Harding University *B, T*
Henderson State University
Ouachita Baptist University *B*
University of Arkansas *B, M*
University of Central Arkansas *B, M*

California
Allan Hancock College *A*
American River College *C, A*
Bakersfield College *A*
Butte College *C, A*
Cabrillo College *C, A*
California State University
 Long Beach *B*
 Los Angeles *B, M*
 Northridge *B, M*
 Sacramento *B*
Canada College *A*
Cerritos Community College *A*
Chaffey Community College *C, A*
City College of San Francisco *A*
College of the Sequoias *A*
College of the Siskiyous *C, A*
Compton Community College *A*
Fresno City College *A*
Glendale Community College *A*
Long Beach City College *C, A*
Los Angeles Valley College *A*
Master's College *B*
Merced College *A*
Modesto Junior College *A*
Monterey Peninsula College *A*
Moorpark College *A*
Mount San Antonio College *A*
Orange Coast College *A*
Pacific Union College *B*
Point Loma Nazarene University *B*
Riverside Community College *A*
Sacramento City College *C, A*
Saddleback College *C, A*
San Francisco State University *B, M*
San Joaquin Delta College *A*
Santa Monica College *C, A*
Shasta College *A*
Sierra College *A*
Skyline College *C, A*
Solano Community College *C, A*
Ventura College *C, A*

Colorado
Colorado State University *B*

Connecticut
St. Joseph College *B, T*

Delaware
University of Delaware *B*

District of Columbia
Gallaudet University *B*
University of the District of Columbia *B*

Florida
Chipola Junior College *A*
Florida State University *B, D*
Gulf Coast Community College *A*
Miami-Dade Community College *C*
Palm Beach Community College *A*
Polk Community College *A*

Georgia
Abraham Baldwin Agricultural
 College *A*
Atlanta Metropolitan College *A*
Clayton College and State University *A*
Dalton State College *A*
East Georgia College *A*
Fort Valley State University *B*
Georgia Perimeter College *A*
Middle Georgia College *A*
University of Georgia *M*

Hawaii
University of Hawaii
 Manoa *B*

Idaho
Idaho State University *B*
Ricks College *A*
University of Idaho *B, M*

Illinois
Eastern Illinois University *B, M, T*
Illinois State University *B, M, T*
Kishwaukee College *A*
Lake Land College *A*
Olivet Nazarene University *B, T*
Western Illinois University *B*

Indiana
Ball State University *B, M*
Indiana State University *B, M*
Purdue University *B, M, D*
Vincennes University *A*

Iowa
Iowa State University *B, M*
Marshalltown Community College *A*
North Iowa Area Community College *A*

Kansas
Barton County Community College *A*
Coffeyville Community College *A*
Colby Community College *A*
Cowley County Community College *A*
Garden City Community College *A*
Hutchinson Community College *A*
Kansas City Kansas Community
 College *A*
Kansas State University *B, D*
Pittsburg State University *B, T*
Pratt Community College *A*

Kentucky
Berea College *B, T*
Morehead State University *A, B*
Murray State University *B, M*

Louisiana
Louisiana State University and
 Agricultural and Mechanical
 College *M, D*
Louisiana Tech University *M*
McNeese State University *B*
Nicholls State University *B*
Northwestern State University *B*
Southern University and Agricultural and
 Mechanical College *B*
University of Louisiana at Lafayette *M*
University of Louisiana at Monroe *B*

Maryland
University of Maryland
 Eastern Shore *B*

Massachusetts
Atlantic Union College *B*
Framingham State College *B, M*

Michigan
Central Michigan University *B, M*
Eastern Michigan University *M*
Ferris State University *B*
Lansing Community College *A*
Madonna University *B, T*
Michigan State University *B*
Western Michigan University *B, T*

Minnesota
College of St. Catherine: St. Paul
 Campus *B*
Concordia College: Moorhead *B*
Minnesota State University,
 Mankato *B, M*
University of Minnesota
 Twin Cities *B, M, D*

Mississippi
Alcorn State University *B*
Delta State University *B*
Hinds Community College *A*
Mississippi Delta Community College *A*
Mississippi State University *B*
University of Southern Mississippi *B*

Missouri
Central Missouri State University *B*
College of the Ozarks *B*
East Central College *A*
Fontbonne College *B*
Southeast Missouri State University *M*
University of Missouri
 Columbia *D*

Montana
Little Big Horn College *A*
Miles Community College *A*
Montana State University
 Bozeman *B, M*

Nebraska
Central Community College *C, A*
Chadron State College *B*
University of Nebraska
 Kearney *B*
 Lincoln *M, D*
 Omaha *B*
Wayne State College *B, T*

New Hampshire
Keene State College *B*

New Jersey
College of St. Elizabeth *T*
Montclair State University *B, M, T*

New Mexico
Eastern New Mexico University *B*
University of New Mexico *B, M, D*

New York
City University of New York
 Queens College *B, M*
Marymount College *B*
State University of New York
 College at Oneonta *B*

North Carolina
Appalachian State University *B, M*
Bennett College *B*
Campbell University *B, T*
Meredith College *B*
North Carolina Agricultural and
 Technical State University *B, T*
North Carolina Central University *B, M*
University of North Carolina
 Greensboro *B, M, T*

Ohio
Bluffton College *B*
Kent State University *B*
Mount Vernon Nazarene College *A, B*
Ohio State University
 Columbus Campus *B, M, D*
University of Akron *B*
Youngstown State University *B*

Oklahoma
Connors State College *A*
East Central University *B*
Langston University *B*
Northeastern State University *B*
Oklahoma State University *B, M, D*
Rose State College *A*
University of Central Oklahoma *B*

Oregon
Chemeketa Community College *A*
George Fox University *B*
Linn-Benton Community College *A*

Pennsylvania
Drexel University *M*
Immaculata College *A, B*
Seton Hill College *B, T*

Puerto Rico
Pontifical Catholic University of Puerto
 Rico *B*
University of Puerto Rico
 Rio Piedras Campus *B, M*

South Carolina
South Carolina State University *B*

South Dakota
South Dakota State University *M*

Tennessee
David Lipscomb University *B*
East Tennessee State University *B, T*
Freed-Hardeman University *B*
Hiwassee College *A*
Middle Tennessee State University *M*
Tennessee State University *B, M*
Tennessee Technological University *B, T*
University of Memphis *B, M*
University of Tennessee
 Chattanooga *B*
 Knoxville *B, M, D*
 Martin *B, M*

Texas
Abilene Christian University *B*
Baylor University *B*
Brazosport College *A*
Coastal Bend College *A*
Lamar State College at Port Arthur *A*
Lamar University *B, M*
Panola College *A*
Prairie View A&M University *M*
Sam Houston State University *B, M*
South Plains College *A*
Southwest Texas State University *B*
Stephen F. Austin State University *B, M*
Tarleton State University *B, T*
Texas A&M University
 Kingsville *B, M*
Texas Tech University *B*
Texas Woman's University *B, T*
Tyler Junior College *A*
University of Texas
 Austin *B*

Utah
Brigham Young University *B*
Snow College *A*
Southern Utah University *B, T*
Utah State University *M*

Virginia
Bridgewater College *B*
Norfolk State University *B*

Washington
Central Washington University *B, M*
Highline Community College *A*
Washington State University *B*

West Virginia
Fairmont State College *B*
Marshall University *B, M*
Shepherd College *B*
West Virginia University *B, M, T*

Wisconsin
Mount Mary College *B*
University of Wisconsin
 Madison *B, M*

Home economics business services

California
California State University
 Northridge *B*

Georgia
University of Georgia *B*

Home economics business services

Illinois
Northern Illinois University *M*

Indiana
Indiana State University *B*

Louisiana
Nicholls State University *B*

Nebraska
University of Nebraska
 Kearney *B*

Ohio
Kent State University *T*

Oklahoma
Connors State College *A*

South Carolina
South Carolina State University *B*

Texas
University of North Texas *B*

Virginia
Virginia State University *B*

Home economics education

Alabama
Alabama Agricultural and Mechanical
 University *B, M*
Jacksonville State University *B*
Northeast Alabama Community
 College *A*
Oakwood College *B*
University of Alabama *B*

Arizona
Arizona State University *B, T*
Phoenix College *A*
University of Arizona *B*

Arkansas
Harding University *B, M, T*
Ouachita Baptist University *B, T*
University of Arkansas
 Pine Bluff *T*
University of Arkansas *B*
University of Central Arkansas *B, M, T*

California
California State Polytechnic University:
 Pomona *T*
California State University
 Dominguez Hills *T*
 Long Beach *B, T*
 Northridge *B, T*
 Sacramento *T*
Master's College *T*
Pacific Union College *T*
Point Loma Nazarene University *B*
Saddleback College *C, A*
San Francisco State University *B, M, T*

Colorado
Colorado State University *T*

Connecticut
St. Joseph College *T*

Delaware
University of Delaware *B, T*

District of Columbia
Gallaudet University *B, T*

Florida
Florida International University *B, M, T*
Florida State University *B, M*

Georgia
Berry College *B*
Fort Valley State University *B, T*
Georgia Southern University *B, T*
University of Georgia *B, M*

Hawaii
University of Hawaii
 Manoa *B, T*

Idaho
Idaho State University *B, T*
Ricks College *A*
University of Idaho *B, T*

Illinois
Olivet Nazarene University *B, T*
University of Illinois
 Urbana-Champaign *M*

Indiana
Ball State University *B*
Indiana State University *B, M, T*
Vincennes University *A*

Iowa
Iowa State University *B, M, D, T*

Kansas
Colby Community College *A*
Kansas State University *B*
Pittsburg State University *B, T*

Kentucky
Berea College *B, T*
Eastern Kentucky University *B*
Morehead State University *B*
Murray State University *B, T*
Western Kentucky University *B*

Louisiana
McNeese State University *T*
Northwestern State University *B, M, T*

Maryland
University of Maryland
 Eastern Shore *B*

Massachusetts
Framingham State College *B, M, T*

Michigan
Central Michigan University *B*
Eastern Michigan University *B, T*
Ferris State University *B*
Michigan State University *B, M*
Northern Michigan University *B*
Western Michigan University *B*

Minnesota
College of St. Catherine: St. Paul
 Campus *B, T*
Concordia College: Moorhead *T*
Minnesota State University,
 Mankato *B, M, T*
University of Minnesota
 Twin Cities *M, T*

Mississippi
Mississippi State University *T*
Northwest Mississippi Community
 College *A*

Missouri
Central Missouri State
 University *B, M, T*
Fontbonne College *B*
Northwest Missouri State
 University *B, T*
Southeast Missouri State
 University *B, M*
Southwest Missouri State University *B*

Montana
Montana State University
 Bozeman *T*

Nebraska
Concordia University *T*
University of Nebraska
 Kearney *B, T*

Nevada
University of Nevada
 Reno *B*

New Hampshire
Keene State College *T*

New Jersey
St. Peter's College *T*

New Mexico
New Mexico State University *B*
University of New Mexico *B*

New York
City University of New York
 Brooklyn College *B*
 Queens College *B, M, T*
Marymount College *B, T*
State University of New York
 College at Oneonta *B, M, T*

North Carolina
Appalachian State University *B, T*
Campbell University *B, T*
East Carolina University *B*
Meredith College *T*
North Carolina Agricultural and
 Technical State University *B, T*
North Carolina Central University *B, M*
University of North Carolina
 Greensboro *B, M, D, T*
Western Carolina University *B, T*

North Dakota
North Dakota State University *B, M, T*

Ohio
Ashland University *B, T*
Bluffton College *B*
Bowling Green State University *B*
Kent State University *B, M, T*
Miami University
 Oxford Campus *M*
Mount Vernon Nazarene College *B, T*
Ohio State University
 Columbus Campus *M, D*
University of Akron *M*
Youngstown State University *B, M*

Oklahoma
East Central University *B*
Langston University *B*
Northeastern State University *B*
University of Central Oklahoma *B*

Oregon
George Fox University *B, M, T*
Oregon State University *M*

Pennsylvania
Immaculata College *T*
Indiana University of
 Pennsylvania *B, M, T*
Marywood University *B, T*
Seton Hill College *B, T*

Puerto Rico
Pontifical Catholic University of Puerto
 Rico *B, T*
University of Puerto Rico
 Rio Piedras Campus *B, M*

South Carolina
South Carolina State University *B, T*
Winthrop University *B, M, T*

South Dakota
South Dakota State University *B*

Tennessee
Carson-Newman College *B*
University of Tennessee
 Knoxville *B, M, T*
 Martin *B, T*

Texas
Abilene Christian University *B, T*
Lamar University *T*
Prairie View A&M University *M*
Sam Houston State University *M, T*
Texas A&M University
 Kingsville *B*
Texas Tech University *M, D*

University of the Incarnate Word *B*

Utah
Brigham Young University *B*
Snow College *A*
Utah State University *B*

Vermont
University of Vermont *T*

Virginia
Bridgewater College *B*
Virginia Polytechnic Institute and State
 University *B, T*

Washington
Central Washington University *B, T*
Washington State University *T*

West Virginia
Fairmont State College *B*
Shepherd College *T*

Wisconsin
Mount Mary College *B, T*
University of Wisconsin
 Madison *B, M, T*
 Stevens Point *B, T*
 Stout *B, M, T*

Wyoming
University of Wyoming *B*

Home furnishings/equipment

Alabama
Jefferson State Community College *A*
John M. Patterson State Technical
 College *C*
Wallace State Community College at
 Hanceville *A*

California
Long Beach City College *C, A*
Modesto Junior College *C, A*
Santa Rosa Junior College *C*
Solano Community College *A*

Colorado
Technical Trades Institute *A*

Florida
Hillsborough Community College *A*

Georgia
Abraham Baldwin Agricultural
 College *A*

Illinois
Black Hawk College *A*
College of DuPage *C, A*
Joliet Junior College *A*
Prairie State College *A*

Indiana
Vincennes University *A*

Iowa
Hawkeye Community College *A*
Kirkwood Community College *A*
Scott Community College *C*

Kansas
Johnson County Community College *A*
Pittsburg State University *B*

Kentucky
Eastern Kentucky University *A*
Murray State University *B*

Massachusetts
Holyoke Community College *A*

Michigan
Bay de Noc Community College *C*
Grand Rapids Community College *A*

North Carolina
Appalachian State University *B*

Horticulture science

Ohio
Youngstown State University B

Oregon
Portland Community College C

Texas
St. Philip's College C
University of North Texas B

West Virginia
Fairmont State College A

Wisconsin
Waukesha County Technical College A

Home/office products marketing

Indiana
Vincennes University A

North Carolina
High Point University B

Wisconsin
Madison Area Technical College A

Horticultural services

Alabama
James H. Faulkner State Community College C
Northwest-Shoals Community College C
Wallace State Community College at Hanceville C

Arizona
Glendale Community College C
Mesa Community College A

Arkansas
Mississippi County Community College C, A

California
Bakersfield College A
Butte College C, A
California Polytechnic State University: San Luis Obispo B
College of San Mateo C, A
College of the Sequoias C
Diablo Valley College C
Los Angeles Pierce College C, A
Merced College C, A
Mount San Antonio College C, A
San Joaquin Delta College A
Santa Barbara City College C
Shasta College C
Ventura College A
Victor Valley College C

Colorado
Front Range Community College C, A
Naropa University B

Connecticut
Naugatuck Valley Community-Technical College C, A
University of Connecticut A

Delaware
Delaware Technical and Community College
 Owens Campus C, A

Florida
Miami-Dade Community College A
Pensacola Junior College A

Georgia
Darton College A
Georgia Perimeter College A
University of Georgia B, M, D

Idaho
Boise State University C, A
Ricks College C

Illinois
Black Hawk College
 East Campus C, A
Black Hawk College C, A
College of DuPage C
Illinois Eastern Community Colleges
 Wabash Valley College A
Joliet Junior College C, A
Kishwaukee College C, A
McHenry County College C, A
Rend Lake College A
Richland Community College A
Shawnee Community College C, A
Southwestern Ilinois College C, A
William Rainey Harper College C, A

Indiana
Vincennes University A

Iowa
Des Moines Area Community College A
Hawkeye Community College A
Iowa State University B, M, D

Kansas
Coffeyville Community College A
Dodge City Community College A

Kentucky
Murray State University A
St. Catharine College A

Massachusetts
Cape Cod Community College C
North Shore Community College A
University of Massachusetts
 Amherst A

Michigan
Andrews University A

Minnesota
Dakota County Technical College C, A
Pine Technical College C
University of Minnesota
 Crookston A

Mississippi
Mississippi Delta Community College A
Northwest Mississippi Community College A

Missouri
College of the Ozarks B
Southeast Missouri State University B
State Fair Community College A

Nebraska
Central Community College C, A
Metropolitan Community College C, A
Nebraska College of Technical Agriculture A
Northeast Community College A
University of Nebraska
 Lincoln D

New Hampshire
University of New Hampshire A

New Jersey
Bergen Community College A

New York
State University of New York
 College of Agriculture and Technology at Cobleskill A, B
 College of Agriculture and Technology at Morrisville A
 College of Technology at Alfred A
 College of Technology at Delhi A
Suffolk County Community College C, A

North Carolina
Alamance Community College C, A
Blue Ridge Community College A
Carteret Community College C
Fayetteville Technical Community College A
Forsyth Technical Community College A
Haywood Community College C, A
Johnston Community College C
Mayland Community College C, A
North Carolina State University B
Sampson Community College A
Surry Community College C, A
Tri-County Community College C
Western Piedmont Community College A
Wilkes Community College C, A

North Dakota
Minot State University: Bottineau Campus C, A
North Dakota State University B, M

Ohio
Clark State Community College A
Ohio State University
 Columbus Campus B, M, D

Oklahoma
Eastern Oklahoma State College A
Oklahoma State University
 Oklahoma City C, A
Oklahoma State University B, M

Oregon
Mount Hood Community College C, A

Pennsylvania
Chatham College C
Community College of Allegheny County A
Luzerne County Community College C, A
Mercyhurst College C
Penn State
 University Park C
Temple University A
Westmoreland County Community College A
Williamson Free School of Mechanical Trades C, A

Puerto Rico
University of Puerto Rico
 Mayaguez Campus M

South Carolina
Clemson University B, M
Piedmont Technical College C
Technical College of the Lowcountry C, A
Trident Technical College C, A

South Dakota
Southeast Technical Institute A

Tennessee
Tennessee Technological University B

Texas
Central Texas College C
Collin County Community College District A
Houston Community College System A
Midland College C
Richland College A
Stephen F. Austin State University B
Tarleton State University B
Tarrant County College C, A
Texas A&M University B, M, D
Texas Tech University B, M
Trinity Valley Community College C, A
Western Texas College C, A

Utah
Salt Lake Community College C

Vermont
University of Vermont B
Vermont Technical College A

Virginia
J. Sargeant Reynolds Community College A
Lord Fairfax Community College A
Tidewater Community College A
Virginia Western Community College A

Washington
Clark College A
Edmonds Community College C
Highline Community College A
Lake Washington Technical College C, A
Skagit Valley College A
South Puget Sound Community College C, A
Spokane Community College A

Wisconsin
Gateway Technical College A
Madison Area Technical College A
Northeast Wisconsin Technical College C

Horticulture science

Alabama
Auburn University B, M, D
Northwest-Shoals Community College C

Arizona
Cochise College C

Arkansas
University of Arkansas B, M

California
California State Polytechnic University: Pomona B
California State University
 Fresno B
Diablo Valley College C
Golden West College C, A
Kings River Community College C
Los Angeles Pierce College C, A
Merritt College C, A
University of California
 Davis M
West Hills Community College C, A

Colorado
Colorado State University B, M, D

Connecticut
University of Connecticut B

Florida
Florida Southern College B
Pensacola Junior College A
University of Florida B, M, D

Georgia
Berry College B
Floyd College A
Fort Valley State University A, B

Hawaii
University of Hawaii
 Hilo B
 Manoa B, M, D

Idaho
Ricks College A
University of Idaho B

Illinois
Black Hawk College
 East Campus C
Danville Area Community College A
Kishwaukee College A
Richland Community College A
University of Illinois
 Urbana-Champaign B
William Rainey Harper College C, A

Indiana
Purdue University A, B, M, D
Vincennes University A

Kansas
Coffeyville Community College A
Kansas State University B, M, D

Louisiana
Louisiana State University and Agricultural and Mechanical College M, D

Horticulture science

Southeastern Louisiana University B
Maryland
University of Maryland
 College Park B, M, D
Massachusetts
Becker College C
Cape Cod Community College C
North Shore Community College A
Michigan
Michigan State University B, M, D
St. Clair County Community
 College C, A
Minnesota
Central Lakes College C, A
University of Minnesota
 Twin Cities M, D
Mississippi
Mississippi State University B, M, D
Missouri
College of the Ozarks B
East Central College C, A
Northwest Missouri State University B
Southeast Missouri State University B
Southwest Missouri State University B
St. Louis Community College
 St. Louis Community College at
  Meramec C, A
University of Missouri
 Columbia M, D
Montana
Montana State University
 Bozeman B
Nebraska
Nebraska College of Technical
 Agriculture C, A
University of Nebraska
 Lincoln B, M
New Hampshire
University of New Hampshire A, B
New Jersey
Rutgers
 The State University of New Jersey:
  Cook College B
Thomas Edison State College A, B
New Mexico
New Mexico State University B, M
New York
City University of New York
 Bronx Community College A
Cornell University M, D
State University of New York
 College of Agriculture and
  Technology at Cobleskill A, B
 College of Agriculture and
  Technology at Morrisville A
 College of Technology at Alfred A
 College of Technology at Delhi A
North Carolina
Alamance Community College C, A
Catawba Valley Community
 College C, A
Central Piedmont Community
 College C, A
Haywood Community College A
Johnston Community College C
Lenoir Community College C, A
North Carolina State University B, M, D
Rockingham Community College C, A
North Dakota
North Dakota State University B, M
Ohio
Owens Community College
 Toledo C, A
Oklahoma
Cameron University B

Eastern Oklahoma State College A
Oklahoma State University
 Oklahoma City C, A
Oklahoma State University B, M
Tulsa Community College A
Oregon
Central Oregon Community College A
Chemeketa Community College A
Oregon State University B, M, D
Pennsylvania
Community College of Allegheny
 County A
Delaware Valley College B
Penn State
 University Park B, M, D
Temple University B
Puerto Rico
University of Puerto Rico
 Mayaguez Campus B, M
 Utuado A
South Carolina
Clemson University B, M
Horry-Georgetown Technical College A
Trident Technical College A
South Dakota
South Dakota State University B
Tennessee
Hiwassee College A
Tennessee Technological University B
Texas
Grayson County College C
Midland College C
Richland College A
Sam Houston State University B
Southwest Texas State University B, T
Stephen F. Austin State University B
Texas A&M University B, M, D
Texas Tech University B, M
Utah
Brigham Young University B, M
Dixie State College of Utah A
Salt Lake Community College C
Utah State University B, M, D
Vermont
Vermont Technical College A
Virginia
Northern Virginia Community College A
Virginia Polytechnic Institute and State
 University B, M, D
Virginia Western Community College A
Washington
Clark College A
Washington State University B, M, D
West Virginia
Potomac State College of West Virginia
 University A
West Virginia Northern Community
 College A
Wisconsin
Blackhawk Technical College C
Gateway Technical College A
University of Wisconsin
 Madison B, M, D
 River Falls B

Hospitality administration/management

Alabama
James H. Faulkner State Community
 College C, A
Jefferson State Community College A
Shelton State Community College C
Tuskegee University B

Alaska
Alaska Pacific University C
Arizona
Scottsdale Community College C, A
Arkansas
Arkansas Tech University B
Garland County Community
 College C, A
North Arkansas College C
California
Chaffey Community College C
College of the Redwoods C, A
Columbia College C, A
Golden Gate University M
MiraCosta College C, A
Monterey Peninsula College A
San Diego Mesa College C, A
San Francisco State University B
San Jose State University B
Santa Rosa Junior College C
Skyline College C, A
University of San Francisco B
Colorado
Arapahoe Community College A
Colorado Mountain College
 Alpine Campus A
Metropolitan State College of Denver B
Connecticut
Norwalk Community-Technical
 College A
Three Rivers Community-Technical
 College C, A
University of New Haven M
Delaware
Delaware State University B
Delaware Technical and Community
 College
 Owens Campus A
District of Columbia
Howard University B
Florida
Brevard Community College A
Broward Community College A
Central Florida Community College A
Daytona Beach Community College A
Edison Community College A
Florida Community College at
 Jacksonville A
Florida International University B, M
Florida State University B
Hillsborough Community College A
Indian River Community College A
Lynn University B, M
Palm Beach Community College A
Polk Community College A
St. Thomas University B
South Florida Community College A
University of Central Florida B
Valencia Community College A
Georgia
Abraham Baldwin Agricultural
 College A
Hawaii
University of Hawaii
 Kauai Community College C, A
 Manoa B, M
Illinois
City Colleges of Chicago
 Harold Washington College C, A
Lewis and Clark Community College A
Lincoln Land Community College A
MacCormac College C, A
Northwestern Business College A
Roosevelt University C, B, M
Southwestern Ilinois College C, A
Triton College C, A
Waubonsee Community College C
William Rainey Harper College C, A

Indiana
Indiana Institute of Technology B
Indiana University--Purdue University
 Indiana University-Purdue
  University Fort Wayne B
International Business College C, A
Ivy Tech State College
 Northeast C, A
 Northwest C, A
Purdue University A
Vincennes University A
Iowa
Des Moines Area Community College A
University of Northern Iowa B
Kansas
Butler County Community College A
Kentucky
University of Kentucky B
Louisiana
Delgado Community College A
Southern University
 Shreveport A
University of New Orleans B
Maine
Andover College C, A
Husson College M
Mid-State College C, A
Southern Maine Technical College A
Thomas College B
University of Maine
 Machias B
Maryland
Allegany College A
Baltimore City Community College A
Montgomery College
 Rockville Campus C, A
Massachusetts
Berkshire Community College A
Boston University B
Endicott College B
Holyoke Community College A
Massachusetts Bay Community
 College C, A
Middlesex Community College C, A
Mount Ida College A, B
Newbury College B
University of Massachusetts
 Amherst B, M
Michigan
Baker College
 of Mount Clemens A
 of Muskegon A
 of Owosso A
 of Port Huron A
Central Michigan University B
Eastern Michigan University B
Great Lakes College A
Jackson Community College C, A
Lake Michigan College C, A
Minnesota
National American University
 St. Paul B
Winona State University B
Mississippi
Delta State University B
Missouri
East Central College C, A
St. Louis University B
Nevada
Community College of Southern
 Nevada A
University of Nevada
 Las Vegas B, M, D
 Reno B
New Hampshire
McIntosh College C
New Hampshire College B

Hospitality/recreation marketing

New Hampshire Community Technical College
  Berlin *C, A*
New Hampshire Technical Institute *A*

New Jersey
Atlantic Cape Community College *C, A*
Essex County College *A*
Ocean County College *C*

New Mexico
Albuquerque Technical-Vocational Institute *C, A*
Dona Ana Branch Community College of New Mexico State University *A*

New York
Cornell University *B, M, D*
New York University *M*
Niagara University *B*
Rochester Institute of Technology *A, B, M*
Rockland Community College *A*
State University of New York
  College at Buffalo *B*
  College at Oneonta *B*
  College of Agriculture and Technology at Cobleskill *A*
Syracuse University *B*
Villa Maria College of Buffalo *A*

North Carolina
Barber-Scotia College *B*
Cape Fear Community College *A*
Western Carolina University *B*

Ohio
Bowling Green State University *B*
Central State University *B*
Columbus State Community College *C, A*
Jefferson Community College *A*
Kent State University
  Stark Campus *B*
Kent State University *B*
Lakeland Community College *A*
North Central State College *A*
Ohio State University,
  Columbus Campus *B*
Owens Community College
  Toledo *A*
Tiffin University *A, B*
University of Akron
  Wayne College *A*
University of Akron *A*
University of Cincinnati
  Clermont College *A*
University of Findlay *B*
Youngstown State University *A, B*

Oklahoma
Oklahoma State University *M*
Tulsa Community College *A*

Oregon
Central Oregon Community College *A*
Chemeketa Community College *A*
Mount Hood Community College *C, A*
Southern Oregon University *B*

Pennsylvania
Butler County Community College *A*
ICS Center for Degree Studies *A*
Mercyhurst College *A, B*
Peirce College *A, B*
Penn State
  Beaver *A*
  Berks *A*
  University Park *B, M*
Robert Morris College *B*
Seton Hill College *A*
Temple University *B, M*
Yorktowne Business Institute *A*

Puerto Rico
Colegio Universitario del Este *C, A*
National College of Business and Technology *A*

Rhode Island
Johnson & Wales University *A, B, M*

South Carolina
Technical College of the Lowcountry *C*
University of South Carolina *B, M*

Tennessee
Belmont University *B*

Texas
Austin Community College *A*
Central Texas College *C, A*
Galveston College *C*
Huston-Tillotson College *B*
St. Philip's College *A*
Stephen F. Austin State University *B*
Tarrant County College *C, A*
University of Dallas *M*
University of North Texas *B, M*

Utah
Utah Valley State College *C, A*

Vermont
Champlain College *A, B*
Johnson State College *B*
Southern Vermont College *A, B*

Virginia
J. Sargeant Reynolds Community College *A*
National Business College *A*
Southwest Virginia Community College *C*

Washington
South Puget Sound Community College *C, A*
South Seattle Community College *A*
Yakima Valley Community College *C, A*

West Virginia
Concord College *B*
Davis and Elkins College *B*
West Virginia Northern Community College *A*

Wisconsin
Lakeland College *B*
Madison Area Technical College *A*
Milwaukee Area Technical College *A*
Nicolet Area Technical College *A*
University of Wisconsin
  Stout *M*
Waukesha County Technical College *A*
Wisconsin Indianhead Technical College *A*

Wyoming
Sheridan College *C, A*

Hospitality/recreation marketing

Alabama
Alabama Agricultural and Mechanical University *B*

Arizona
Northland Pioneer College *C*
Pima Community College *A*

Arkansas
Garland County Community College *C, A*

California
American River College *A*
City College of San Francisco *A*
College of the Canyons *C*
Cypress College *C, A*
Glendale Community College *A*
Los Angeles Trade and Technical College *A*
Los Angeles Valley College *A*
Monterey Peninsula College *A*
Orange Coast College *C, A*
Pasadena City College *A*
Riverside Community College *A*
San Francisco State University *B*
United States International University *B*

Colorado
Colorado Mountain College
  Alpine Campus *A*
Community College of Aurora *C*
Metropolitan State College of Denver *B*

Connecticut
Manchester Community-Technical College *C, A*

District of Columbia
Howard University *B*

Florida
Brevard Community College *A*
Miami-Dade Community College *A*
Northwood University
  Florida Campus *A, B*
Pensacola Junior College *A*
St. Thomas University *B*

Georgia
Floyd College *A*
Savannah State University *B*

Hawaii
University of Hawaii
  Kapiolani Community College *C, A*

Illinois
Lincoln Land Community College *C, A*
Moraine Valley Community College *C*
Parkland College *C, A*
William Rainey Harper College *C, A*

Indiana
Indiana University--Purdue University
  Indiana University-Purdue University Fort Wayne *A*
Vincennes University *A*

Iowa
American Institute of Business *A*

Kansas
Butler County Community College *C, A*

Louisiana
Northwestern State University *B*

Maine
Andover College *C, A*
Husson College *B*
Mid-State College *C, A*
University of Maine
  Machias *A, B*

Maryland
Montgomery College
  Rockville Campus *A*

Massachusetts
Bay State College *A*
Roxbury Community College *A*

Michigan
Ferris State University *C, B*
Lansing Community College *A*
Northwood University *A, B*
Siena Heights University *A, B*

Minnesota
University of Minnesota
  Crookston *A, B*

Mississippi
Northwest Mississippi Community College *A*

Missouri
East Central College *A*

Nevada
Community College of Southern Nevada *A*

New Hampshire
New Hampshire Community Technical College
  Laconia *C, A*
New Hampshire Technical Institute *C, A*
University of New Hampshire *B*

New Jersey
Burlington County College *A*
Cumberland County College *A*

New York
Finger Lakes Community College *A*
Rochester Institute of Technology *M*
State University of New York
  College at Buffalo *B*
  College of Agriculture and Technology at Cobleskill *A*
Tompkins-Cortland Community College *A*
Villa Maria College of Buffalo *A*

North Carolina
Wake Technical Community College *A*

Ohio
Columbus State Community College *B*
Ohio State University
  Columbus Campus *B*
Owens Community College
  Toledo *C, A*
University of Akron *A*
University of Findlay *B*
Youngstown State University *A, B*

Oklahoma
Oklahoma State University
  Okmulgee *A*
Tulsa Community College *A*

Oregon
Central Oregon Community College *A*

Pennsylvania
Butler County Community College *C, A*
Laurel Business Institute *C*
Montgomery County Community College *A*
Pittsburgh Technical Institute *A*
Robert Morris College *M*
Sawyer School *A*
Yorktowne Business Institute *A*

Rhode Island
Johnson & Wales University *B*

South Carolina
Technical College of the Lowcountry *C, A*

South Dakota
Sinte Gleska University *B*

Texas
Central Texas College *C*
El Paso Community College *C, A*
Galveston College *C*

Vermont
Champlain College *A, B*
College of St. Joseph in Vermont *B*

Washington
Highline Community College *A*
Lake Washington Technical College *C, A*
Skagit Valley College *A*

West Virginia
Bluefield State College *A*
Concord College *B*

Wisconsin
Chippewa Valley Technical College *A*
Madison Area Technical College *A*
Nicolet Area Technical College *A*
Northeast Wisconsin Technical College *A*

Hotel/motel/restaurant management

Alabama
Auburn University B
Community College of the Air Force A
James H. Faulkner State Community College C, A

Alaska
Alaska Pacific University C

Arizona
Central Arizona College C, A
Cochise College A
Northern Arizona University B
Pima Community College A
Scottsdale Community College C, A

Arkansas
North Arkansas College C, A
Phillips Community College of the University of Arkansas A

California
California State Polytechnic University: Pomona B
Chaffey Community College C, A
City College of San Francisco C, A
College of the Canyons C
College of the Desert C
Columbia College C, A
Compton Community College C, A
Cypress College A
Diablo Valley College A
Golden Gate University C, B
Lake Tahoe Community College C, A
Long Beach City College C, A
Los Angeles Trade and Technical College A
MiraCosta College C, A
Mission College A
Monterey Peninsula College C, A
Orange Coast College C, A
Oxnard College A
San Bernardino Valley College C, A
San Diego Mesa College C, A
San Francisco State University B
Santa Barbara City College C, A
United States International University B

Colorado
Colorado Mountain College
    Alpine Campus A
Colorado State University B
Metropolitan State College of Denver B
University of Denver B, M
Western State College of Colorado B

Connecticut
Briarwood College A
Gateway Community College A
Manchester Community-Technical College A
Naugatuck Valley Community-Technical College A
Norwalk Community-Technical College A
University of New Haven C, A, B

Delaware
Delaware Technical and Community College
    Owens Campus A
    Stanton/Wilmington Campus C, A
University of Delaware B

District of Columbia
Howard University B

Florida
Bethune-Cookman College B
Broward Community College A
Daytona Beach Community College A
Florida Community College at Jacksonville A
Florida Southern College B
Gulf Coast Community College A
Hillsborough Community College A
Keiser College A
Lynn University B
Miami-Dade Community College A
Northwood University
    Florida Campus A, B
Pensacola Junior College A
Polk Community College A

Georgia
Gainesville College A
Georgia Southern University B
Georgia State University B, M
Gwinnett Technical Institute A
Morris Brown College B

Hawaii
Brigham Young University
    Hawaii B
University of Hawaii
    Hawaii Community College C
    Kapiolani Community College A

Idaho
College of Southern Idaho A
Lewis-Clark State College A

Illinois
Black Hawk College C, A
Chicago State University B
City Colleges of Chicago
    Harold Washington College C, A
College of DuPage C, A
John Wood Community College A
Joliet Junior College C, A
Kendall College A, B
Lewis and Clark Community College A
Lexington College A
Oakton Community College C, A
Parkland College C, A
Triton College C, A
William Rainey Harper College C, A

Indiana
Indiana University--Purdue University
    Indiana University-Purdue University Fort Wayne A
    Indiana University-Purdue University Indianapolis A
Purdue University
    Calumet B
    North Central Campus A
Purdue University B, M
University of Indianapolis A, B
Vincennes University A

Iowa
American Institute of Business A
Des Moines Area Community College A
Iowa Lakes Community College A
Iowa State University B, M, D
Iowa Western Community College A
Kirkwood Community College A

Kansas
Central Christian College A
Colby Community College A
Cowley County Community College A
Kansas State University B, M
Washburn University of Topeka A

Kentucky
Berea College B
Western Kentucky University B

Louisiana
Southern University
    Shreveport A
University of Louisiana at Lafayette B

Maine
Andover College C, A
Beal College A
Husson College B
Mid-State College C, A
Southern Maine Technical College A
University of Maine
    Augusta A
    Machias B

Maryland
Allegany College A
Anne Arundel Community College C, A
Baltimore International College A, B
Harford Community College A
Montgomery College
    Rockville Campus A
Prince George's Community College C
University of Maryland
    Eastern Shore B
Wor-Wic Community College C, A

Massachusetts
Bay Path College A, B
Bay State College A
Becker College B
Boston University B
Bunker Hill Community College C, A
Cape Cod Community College A
Endicott College B
Fisher College A
Lasell College B
Marian Court College C, A
Massasoit Community College A
Newbury College A
Northeastern University A
Northern Essex Community College A
Quincy College A

Michigan
Bay de Noc Community College C
Central Michigan University B
Davenport College of Business A, B
Ferris State University C, A, B
Grand Rapids Community College A
Henry Ford Community College A
Jackson Community College C, A
Lansing Community College A
Michigan State University B, M
Mid Michigan Community College A
Muskegon Community College A
Northern Michigan University A, B
Northwestern Michigan College A
Northwood University A, B
Oakland Community College A
Schoolcraft College A
Siena Heights University A, B
Washtenaw Community College A

Minnesota
Alexandria Technical College C, A
University of Minnesota
    Crookston A, B

Mississippi
Coahoma Community College A
Meridian Community College A
Mississippi Gulf Coast Community College
    Jefferson Davis Campus A
    Perkinston A
Northwest Mississippi Community College A
University of Southern Mississippi B

Missouri
Central Missouri State University B
College of the Ozarks B
East Central College C, A
Jefferson College A
Southwest Missouri State University B
St. Louis Community College
    St. Louis Community College at Forest Park C, A
University of Missouri
    Columbia B

Montana
Flathead Valley Community College A

Nevada
Community College of Southern Nevada C, A

New Hampshire
Hesser College A
New Hampshire College B
New Hampshire Community Technical College
    Laconia C, A
New Hampshire Technical Institute C, A
University of New Hampshire B

New Jersey
Atlantic Cape Community College A
Bergen Community College A
Burlington County College C
County College of Morris A
Katharine Gibbs School
    Gibbs College A
Mercer County Community College A
Middlesex County College A
Passaic County Community College A
Thomas Edison State College A, B

New Mexico
New Mexico State University B

New York
Broome Community College A
Bryant & Stratton Business Institute
    Syracuse A
Canisius College B
City University of New York
    New York City Technical College A, B
Clinton Community College A
Cornell University B, M, D
Dutchess Community College A
Erie Community College
    City Campus A
Finger Lakes Community College A
Genesee Community College A
Jefferson Community College C, A
Katharine Gibbs School
    New York A
Keuka College B
Mohawk Valley Community College C, A
Monroe College A
Monroe Community College A
Nassau Community College A
New York Institute of Technology B
New York University B, M
Onondaga Community College A
Rochester Institute of Technology A, B, M
St. John's University B
Schenectady County Community College C
State University of New York
    College at Plattsburgh B
    College of Agriculture and Technology at Cobleskill A
    College of Agriculture and Technology at Morrisville A
    College of Technology at Delhi A
Suffolk County Community College A
Tompkins-Cortland Community College A
Trocaire College C, A

North Carolina
Appalachian State University B
Asheville Buncombe Technical Community College A
Cape Fear Community College A
Central Piedmont Community College A
East Carolina University B
North Carolina Wesleyan College B
Sandhills Community College A
Southwestern Community College A
Wake Technical Community College A
Wilkes Community College C, A

North Dakota
Bismarck State College C, A
North Dakota State University B

Ohio
Ashland University B

Bowling Green State University B
Cincinnati State Technical and
   Community College A
Columbus State Community College A
Hocking Technical College A
Kent State University
   Stark Campus B
North Central State College A
Sinclair Community College C, A
Tiffin University B
University of Akron A
Youngstown State University A, B

Oklahoma
Langston University B
Northeastern Oklahoma Agricultural and
   Mechanical College A
Oklahoma State University B
University of Central Oklahoma B

Oregon
Chemeketa Community College A
Lane Community College C, A
Southern Oregon University B

Pennsylvania
Bucks County Community College C, A
Central Pennsylvania College A
Cheyney University of Pennsylvania B
Community College of Allegheny
   County C
Community College of Philadelphia A
Delaware County Community
   College C, A
Drexel University B
East Stroudsburg University of
   Pennsylvania B
Harrisburg Area Community College A
Indiana University of Pennsylvania B
Lebanon Valley College of
   Pennsylvania B
Lehigh Carbon Community College A
Luzerne County Community
   College C, A
Marywood University B
Mercyhurst College B
Montgomery County Community
   College A
Northampton County Area Community
   College A
Peirce College A, B
Pennsylvania Institute of Culinary Arts A
Pittsburgh Technical Institute A
Westmoreland County Community
   College A
Widener University B
Yorktowne Business Institute A

Puerto Rico
Colegio Universitario del Este B
ICPR Junior College C, A
Inter American University of Puerto Rico
   Aguadilla Campus B
National College of Business and
   Technology A
Universidad Metropolitana A
University of Puerto Rico
   Carolina Regional College A, B

Rhode Island
Johnson & Wales University A, B

South Carolina
Greenville Technical College C
Horry-Georgetown Technical College A
Technical College of the Lowcountry C
Trident Technical College A

South Dakota
Black Hills State University A, B
South Dakota State University B

Tennessee
Hiwassee College A
Knoxville Business College A
Pellissippi State Technical Community
   College A

University of Tennessee
   Knoxville B
Walters State Community College A

Texas
Central Texas College C, A
Collin County Community College
   District C, A
Del Mar College A
El Paso Community College A
Houston Community College
   System C, A
Northwood University: Texas
   Campus A, B
St. Philip's College A
Texas Tech University B, M
University of Houston B, M
University of North Texas B, M
Wiley College B

Utah
Dixie State College of Utah C, A

Vermont
Champlain College A, B
College of St. Joseph in Vermont B
Johnson State College B
New England Culinary Institute A
Southern Vermont College A, B

Virginia
J. Sargeant Reynolds Community
   College A
James Madison University B
Northern Virginia Community
   College C, A
Southwest Virginia Community
   College C
Tidewater Community College C, A
Virginia Polytechnic Institute and State
   University B, M, D
Virginia State University B

Washington
Highline Community College C, A
Spokane Community College A
Washington State University B
Yakima Valley Community College C, A

West Virginia
Bluefield State College A
Concord College B
West Virginia Northern Community
   College A
West Virginia State College A

Wisconsin
Chippewa Valley Technical College A
Milwaukee Area Technical College A
Mount Mary College B
University of Wisconsin
   Stout B

Housing studies

Alabama
Auburn University B

Arkansas
University of Arkansas B

California
California State University
   Northridge B
San Francisco State University B
Santa Rosa Junior College C

Florida
Florida State University B, M
Miami-Dade Community College A

Georgia
University of Georgia B, M, D

Illinois
Olivet Nazarene University B

Indiana
Indiana State University M

Iowa
Iowa State University B
University of Northern Iowa B

Kentucky
Eastern Kentucky University B
Murray State University B
Western Kentucky University B

Michigan
Michigan State University M, D

Minnesota
Minnesota State University, Mankato B
University of Minnesota
   Twin Cities B

Missouri
Southeast Missouri State University B
Southwest Missouri State University B
University of Missouri
   Columbia B, M

Nebraska
University of Nebraska
   Kearney B

Nevada
University of Nevada
   Reno B

New York
Cornell University B, M, D

North Carolina
Appalachian State University B
Campbell University B
University of North Carolina
   Greensboro B

Ohio
Miami University
   Oxford Campus B

Oklahoma
Oklahoma State University M, D

Oregon
Oregon State University B

Tennessee
Tennessee Technological University B
University of Tennessee
   Knoxville M

Texas
Texas Christian University B
Texas Tech University M
University of North Texas B

Virginia
Virginia Polytechnic Institute and State
   University B, M, D

Human resources management

Alabama
Auburn University at Montgomery B
Auburn University B
Birmingham-Southern College B
Community College of the Air Force A
Faulkner University B, M
Troy State University
   Dothan M
   Montgomery B, M
Troy State University M
Tuskegee University M
University of Alabama B, M, D

Arizona
University of Arizona B
University of Phoenix C

Arkansas
Harding University B
University of Central Arkansas B

California
Antioch Southern California
   Santa Barbara M
Azusa Pacific University M
California State Polytechnic University:
   Pomona B
California State University
   Chico B
   Dominguez Hills B
   Fresno B
   Hayward C, B, M
   Long Beach B
   Los Angeles B
   Northridge B, M
   Stanislaus B
Cerritos Community College A
Chapman University M
City College of San Francisco A
College of Marin: Kentfield A
Dominican University of California B
Fresno Pacific University B
Holy Names College B
La Sierra University M
Loyola Marymount University B
National University B, M
San Diego State University M
San Francisco State University B
San Jose State University B
Santa Rosa Junior College C
Simpson College B
University of San Francisco M
Ventura College A
Yuba College C

Colorado
Arapahoe Community College C
Colorado Technical University B, M
University of Colorado
   Boulder B
   Colorado Springs B

Connecticut
University of New Haven B

Delaware
Delaware State University B
Delaware Technical and Community
   College
   Owens Campus A
   Terry Campus A
Wilmington College B, M

District of Columbia
American University B, M
Catholic University of America B, M
George Washington University D
Southeastern University M
Trinity College M

Florida
Barry University M
Eckerd College B
Florida Atlantic University B
Florida Institute of Technology M
Florida International University B
Florida Southern College B
Florida State University B
Nova Southeastern University M
Rollins College M
St. Leo University B
St. Thomas University M
University of Miami C, B, M
University of North Florida M
Valencia Community College A

Georgia
Georgia Southwestern State University B
Georgia State University B, M, D
Kennesaw State University M
Macon State College A
University of Georgia M

Hawaii
Hawaii Pacific University B, M
University of Hawaii
   Manoa B

Human resources management

Idaho
Boise State University *B*
Idaho State University *B, M*
University of Idaho *B*

Illinois
Barat College *B*
Benedictine University *M*
De Paul University *B, M*
Governors State University *B*
Illinois Institute of Technology *M*
Joliet Junior College *C*
Kendall College *B*
Kishwaukee College *A*
Lake Land College *A*
Lewis University *B*
Loyola University of Chicago *B, M*
Millikin University *B*
Moraine Valley Community College *C, A*
National-Louis University *M*
Northeastern Illinois University *B, M*
Rockford College *B*
Roosevelt University *B, M*
St. Xavier University *M*
Trinity Christian College *B*
University of Illinois Urbana-Champaign *M, D*
Western Illinois University *B*
William Rainey Harper College *C, A*

Indiana
Bethel College *B*
Indiana Institute of Technology *B*
Indiana State University *B, M*
Oakland City University *B*
Purdue University
 Calumet *B*
 North Central Campus *C, A, B*
St. Mary-of-the-Woods College *B*
University of Evansville *B*
University of St. Francis *B*

Iowa
Briar Cliff College *B*
Loras College *B*
Maharishi University of Management *A, B, D*
University of Iowa *B, D*

Kansas
Central Christian College *A*
MidAmerica Nazarene University *B*
Pittsburg State University *B, M*
Southwestern College *B*
Wichita State University *B*

Louisiana
Louisiana Tech University *B*

Maine
Thomas College *B*
University of Maine Augusta *C*

Maryland
Community College of Baltimore County Essex *C*
Montgomery College Germantown Campus *A*
Towson University *M*
University of Maryland College Park *B*

Massachusetts
American International College *B, M*
Assumption College *C*
Bay Path College *B*
Boston College *B*
Brandeis University *M*
Emerson College *M*
Emmanuel College *M*
Fitchburg State College *M*
Framingham State College *M*
Marian Court College *C, A*
Newbury College *A*
Nichols College *B*
Northeastern University *A, B*
Springfield College *M*

Michigan
Baker College
 of Muskegon *A*
 of Owosso *A, B*
 of Port Huron *A*
Central Michigan University *B, M*
Cleary College *B*
Concordia College *B*
Davenport College of Business *B*
Eastern Michigan University *B, M*
Ferris State University *B*
Grand Valley State University *B*
Lansing Community College *A*
Marygrove College *M*
Michigan State University *B, M, D*
Oakland University *B*

Minnesota
Crown College *B*
Inver Hills Community College *A*
Lake Superior College: A Community and Technical College *C*
Metropolitan State University *B*
Minnesota State University, Mankato *B*
St. Paul Technical College *C, A*
University of St. Thomas *B, M*
Winona State University *B*

Mississippi
University of Southern Mississippi *B*

Missouri
Central Missouri State University *B*
Lindenwood University *B, M*
Northwest Missouri State University *B*
Rockhurst University *B*
St. Louis University *B*
Southeast Missouri State University *B*
University of Missouri St. Louis *C*
Washington University *B, M*
Webster University *B, M*

Montana
Montana State University Billings *B*
Montana Tech of the University of Montana *A*
Western Montana College of The University of Montana *A*

Nebraska
Bellevue University *B*
Doane College *B*
Hastings College *B*
University of Nebraska Omaha *B*

Nevada
University of Nevada
 Las Vegas *B*
 Reno *B*

New Hampshire
Antioch New England Graduate School *M*
New Hampshire College *C*
New Hampshire Technical Institute *A*
Plymouth State College of the University System of New Hampshire *B*
Rivier College *M*

New Jersey
Bloomfield College *B*
Fairleigh Dickinson University *M*
Rider University *B, M*
Rowan University *B*
Rutgers
 The State University of New Jersey:
 New Brunswick Graduate Campus *M*
Seton Hall University *M*
Thomas Edison State College *C, A, B*

New Mexico
Eastern New Mexico University *B*
University of New Mexico *B*

New York
City University of New York Baruch College *B, M*
Herkimer County Community College *A*
Iona College *M*
Le Moyne College *B*
Long Island University Brooklyn Campus *B, M*
Medaille College *C, B*
New York Institute of Technology *B, M*
Pace University: Pleasantville/Briarcliff *C*
Pace University *C*
Regents College *B*
Roberts Wesleyan College *B, M*
Rochester Institute of Technology *A, M*
St. John Fisher College *B*
St. Joseph's College
 St. Joseph's College: Suffolk Campus *C, B*
 St. Joseph's College *B*
State University of New York Oswego *B*
Suffolk County Community College *A*
Syracuse University *M*

North Carolina
Barton College *B*
Davidson County Community College *C, A*
Guilford Technical Community College *C*
High Point University *B*
Meredith College *B*
Mount Olive College *B*
North Carolina State University *B*
Peace College *B*
Western Carolina University *M*

North Dakota
Valley City State University *B*

Ohio
Baldwin-Wallace College *C*
Bowling Green State University Firelands College *C*
Bowling Green State University *B*
Central Ohio Technical College *A*
Columbus State Community College *A*
David N. Myers College *B*
Defiance College *B*
Franklin University *B*
Kent State University *B, M*
Lakeland Community College *C*
Lorain County Community College *A*
Lourdes College *B*
Marietta College *B*
Marion Technical College *A*
Miami University Oxford Campus *B*
Northwest State Community College *A*
Notre Dame College of Ohio *B*
Ohio State University Columbus Campus *B, M, D*
Ohio University *B*
Tiffin University *B*
University of Akron *B, M*
University of Cincinnati *M*
University of Findlay *B*
Ursuline College *B*
Wright State University *B*
Xavier University *B, M*

Oklahoma
Langston University *B*
Northeastern State University *B*
Oklahoma State University *B*
Southwestern Oklahoma State University *B*
Tulsa Community College *C, A*
University of Central Oklahoma *B*

Oregon
George Fox University *B*
University of Oregon *D*

Pennsylvania
Alvernia College *A, B*
Beaver College *B*
Cabrini College *B*
California University of Pennsylvania *B*
Cedar Crest College *C*
Chestnut Hill College *B*
College Misericordia *M*
Community College of Allegheny County *C, A*
Community College of Beaver County *A*
Drexel University *B*
Duquesne University *B*
Gannon University *C*
Indiana University of Pennsylvania *B*
King's College *B*
Kutztown University of Pennsylvania *B*
La Roche College *M*
La Salle University *B*
Lebanon Valley College of Pennsylvania *C*
Lincoln University *B*
Manor College *C*
Mansfield University of Pennsylvania *B*
Messiah College *B*
Penn State University Park *C*
Philadelphia University *C, B*
Point Park College *B*
Reading Area Community College *C, A*
Robert Morris College *B*
St. Francis College *M*
Seton Hill College *B*
Susquehanna University *B*
University of Pennsylvania *B, M*
University of Scranton *B, M*
West Chester University of Pennsylvania *M*
Widener University *B, M*

Puerto Rico
Bayamon Central University *B*
Inter American University of Puerto Rico
 Bayamon Campus *B*
 Guayama Campus *B*
 Metropolitan Campus *M*
 San German Campus *B, M*
Turabo University *B*
Universidad Metropolitana *B*
University of Puerto Rico
 Humacao University College *B*
 Rio Piedras Campus *B*
University of the Sacred Heart *M*

Rhode Island
Rhode Island College *B*
Salve Regina University *M*

South Carolina
Clemson University *M*
Southern Wesleyan University *B*
University of South Carolina *M*

South Dakota
Black Hills State University *B*
Huron University *B*

Tennessee
Freed-Hardeman University *B*
Tennessee Wesleyan College *B*
University of Tennessee Knoxville *M, D*
Vanderbilt University *B, M, D*

Texas
Abilene Christian University *B*
Baylor University *B*
Houston Baptist University *M*
Houston Community College System *C, A*
Lamar University *B*
Our Lady of the Lake University of San Antonio *B*
St. Mary's University *B*
Tarleton State University *B*

Texas A&M University
   Commerce *B*
   Texarkana *B*
University of Dallas *M*
University of Houston
   Clear Lake *M*
University of Houston *B*
University of North Texas *B, M, D*
University of Texas
   Arlington *M*
   Austin *M*
   Pan American *B*
   San Antonio *B*
Vernon Regional Junior College *A*
Weatherford College *C, A*

Utah
Salt Lake Community College *A*
University of Utah *M*
Utah State University *B, M*
Weber State University *B*
Westminster College *B*

Virginia
Bluefield College *B*
University of Richmond *C*

Washington
Big Bend Community College *C*
Eastern Washington University *B*
Pacific Lutheran University *B*
Pierce College *C*
Washington State University *B*
Western Washington University *B*

West Virginia
Concord College *B*
Ohio Valley College *B*
University of Charleston *M*

Wisconsin
Cardinal Stritch University *C*
Marian College of Fond du Lac *B*
Marquette University *B, M*
Silver Lake College *B*
University of Wisconsin
   Madison *B*
   Milwaukee *B*
   Oshkosh *B*
   Parkside *B*
   Platteville *B*
   Stout *M*
   Whitewater *B*
Viterbo University *B*

Human services

Alabama
Northwest-Shoals Community College *A*
Troy State University
   Montgomery *M*
Troy State University *B*

Alaska
Alaska Pacific University *B*
Prince William Sound Community
   College *A*
University of Alaska
   Anchorage *A, B*
   Fairbanks *B*

Arizona
Northland Pioneer College *C*
Prescott College *B, M*

Arkansas
Henderson State University *B*

California
Allan Hancock College *C, A*
California State University
   Dominguez Hills *B*
   Fullerton *B*
   Monterey Bay *B*
Canada College *A*
Columbia College *C*
Cypress College *C, A*
Fielding Institute *M*
Fresno City College *C, A*
Holy Names College *B*
Hope International University *B*
Modesto Junior College *C, A*
Mount St. Mary's College *M*
Saddleback College *C*
San Bernardino Valley College *C, A*

Colorado
Colorado State University *C*
Community College of Denver *C, A*
Metropolitan State College of Denver *B*

Connecticut
Albertus Magnus College *B*
Asnuntuck Community-Technical
   College *C, A*
Housatonic Community-Technical
   College *A*
Middlesex Community-Technical
   College *A*
Mitchell College *A*
Naugatuck Valley Community-Technical
   College *C, A*
Northwestern Connecticut
   Community-Technical College *A*
Norwalk Community-Technical
   College *A*
Quinebaug Valley Community College *A*
Three Rivers Community-Technical
   College *A*
Tunxis Community College *C, A*
University of Bridgeport *B*

District of Columbia
George Washington University *B, M*

Florida
Brevard Community College *A*
Central Florida Community College *A*
Edison Community College *A*
Florida Community College at
   Jacksonville *A*
Florida Gulf Coast University *B*
Hillsborough Community College *A*
Indian River Community College *A*
Palm Beach Community College *A*
Pasco-Hernando Community College *A*
St. Leo University *B*
St. Thomas University *B*

Georgia
Darton College *A*
LaGrange College *B*

Hawaii
Hawaii Pacific University *B*
University of Hawaii
   Honolulu Community College *A*
   Maui Community College *A*

Idaho
College of Southern Idaho *C*
North Idaho College *A*
University of Idaho *M*

Illinois
Carl Sandburg College *C*
College of DuPage *C, A*
Danville Area Community College *A*
Elmhurst College *B*
Kendall College *A, B*
Millikin University *B*
National-Louis University *B, M*
Oakton Community College *C*
Parkland College *A*
Rock Valley College *C, A*
Roosevelt University *M*
Sauk Valley Community College *C*
Southeastern Illinois College *A*
University of Illinois
   Springfield *M*

Indiana
Bethel College *B*
Indiana Institute of Technology *B*
Indiana University
   East *A*
Indiana University--Purdue University
   Indiana University-Purdue
     University Fort Wayne *A*
St. Mary-of-the-Woods College *B*

Iowa
Des Moines Area Community College *A*
Graceland University *B*
Grand View College *B*
Iowa Western Community College *A*
North Iowa Area Community College *A*
Northeast Iowa Community College *A*
Upper Iowa University *B*
Waldorf College *A*

Kansas
Independence Community College *A*
Ottawa University *B*
Washburn University of Topeka *C, A, B*

Kentucky
Bellarmine College *B*
Hazard Community College *A*
Pikeville College *B*

Louisiana
Southern University
   Shreveport *A*

Maine
University of Maine
   Augusta *A, B*
   Fort Kent *A*
   Machias *B*
   Presque Isle *B*

Maryland
Carroll Community College *C, A*
Charles County Community
   College *C, A*
Chesapeake College *C*
Frederick Community College *A*
University of Baltimore *B*
University of Maryland
   Baltimore County *M, D*

Massachusetts
Assumption College *B*
Becker College *A, B*
Berkshire Community College *A*
Brandeis University *M*
Bristol Community College *A*
Cape Cod Community College *A*
Fitchburg State College *B*
Framingham State College *M*
Holyoke Community College *C*
Lasell College *B*
Lesley College *B*
Massachusetts Bay Community
   College *C, A*
Mount Ida College *A*
Northeastern University *B*
Simmons College *B*
Springfield College *B, M*
University of Massachusetts
   Boston *B, M*

Michigan
Adrian College *A, B*
Baker College
   of Cadillac *A*
   of Jackson *A*
   of Mount Clemens *A*
   of Muskegon *A, B*
Grace Bible College *A, B*
Lake Superior State University *B*
Suomi College *B*

Minnesota
Fond Du Lac Tribal and Community
   College *A*
Inver Hills Community College *A*
Itasca Community College *A*
Mesabi Range Community and Technical
   College *A*
Metropolitan State University *B*
Minneapolis Community and Technical
   College *C, A*
Moorhead State University *M*
Pine Technical College *A*
St. Mary's University of Minnesota *B*
Winona State University *B*

Missouri
Central Methodist College *B*
Central Missouri State University *M*
Fontbonne College *B*
Hannibal-LaGrange College *B*
Lindenwood University *B*
Longview Community College *C, A*
Mineral Area College *C, A*
Missouri Baptist College *B*
Park University *B*
St. Charles County Community
   College *A*
Southwest Baptist University *B*

Montana
Flathead Valley Community College *A*
Miles Community College *A*
Salish Kootenai College *B*
Stone Child College *A*
University of Great Falls *A, B, M*

Nebraska
College of Saint Mary *B*
Doane College *B*
Hastings College *B*
Midland Lutheran College *B*

New Hampshire
Antioch New England Graduate
   School *M*
Hesser College *A*
New England College *M*
New Hampshire Community Technical
   College
   Berlin *C, A*
   Claremont *A*
   Laconia *C, A*
   Manchester *C, A*
   Nashua *C, A*
New Hampshire Technical Institute *C, A*
Plymouth State College of the University
   System of New Hampshire *B*

New Jersey
Essex County College *A*
Hudson County Community College *A*
Mercer County Community College *A*
Ocean County College *A*
Passaic County Community College *A*
Rider University *M*
Sussex County Community College *C*
Thomas Edison State College *A, B*

New Mexico
Northern New Mexico Community
   College *A*
San Juan College *C, A*
Santa Fe Community College *A*

New York
Audrey Cohen College *A, B*
Broome Community College *A*
City University of New York
   Borough of Manhattan Community
     College *A*
   New York City Technical
     College *A, B*
Clinton Community College *A*
Columbia University
   School of General Studies *B*
Columbia-Greene Community College *A*
Cornell University *B, M, D*
Corning Community College *A*
Finger Lakes Community College *A*
Fulton-Montgomery Community
   College *A*
Herkimer County Community College *A*
Hilbert College *B*
Jamestown Community College *A*
Jefferson Community College *A*
Medaille College *C, B*

Human services

Monroe Community College *C, A*
Mount St. Mary College *B*
New York University *A*
Niagara County Community College *A*
Onondaga Community College *A*
Pace University *B*
Rockland Community College *A*
Russell Sage College *B*
St. John's University *B, M*
Schenectady County Community
    College *A*
State University of New York
    College of Technology at Alfred *A*
    College of Technology at Canton *A*
    Oswego *M*
Suffolk County Community College *A*
Tompkins-Cortland Community
    College *A*
Touro College *A*
Westchester Community College *C, A*

North Carolina
Beaufort County Community College *A*
Central Carolina Community College *A*
Elon College *B*
Halifax Community College *A*
Lenoir Community College *A*
Mitchell Community College *A*
Montreat College *B*
Sandhills Community College *A*
South Piedmont Community
    College *C, A*
Wake Technical Community College *A*
Wayne Community College *A*
Wingate University *B*

Ohio
Bowling Green State University
    Firelands College *A*
Central Ohio Technical College *A*
Chatfield College *A*
Cincinnati State Technical and
    Community College *C*
David N. Myers College *B*
Edison State Community College *A*
John Carroll University *M*
Kent State University
    Ashtabula Regional Campus *A*
Lakeland Community College *C, A*
Marion Technical College *A*
Mount Vernon Nazarene College *A*
Ohio University
    Zanesville Campus *B*
Ohio University *A*
Stark State College of Technology *A*
University of Akron
    Wayne College *A*
University of Akron *A*
University of Cincinnati
    Clermont College *A*

Oregon
Chemeketa Community College *A*

Pennsylvania
Drexel University *M*
La Roche College *B*
Lackawanna Junior College *A*
Lincoln University *B, M*
Montgomery County Community
    College *A*
Mount Aloysius College *A*
St. Joseph's University *A*
Seton Hill College *B*
University of Scranton *A, B*
Villanova University *B*

Puerto Rico
Turabo University *M*

South Carolina
Aiken Technical College *A*
Anderson College *B*
Denmark Technical College *A*
Greenville Technical College *C, A*

South Dakota
Black Hills State University *B*

Sinte Gleska University *B*

Tennessee
Bethel College *B*
Hiwassee College *B*
Martin Methodist College *B*
Maryville College *B*
Milligan College *B*
Tennessee Wesleyan College *B*

Texas
Angelina College *A*
McMurry University *B*
St. Edward's University *M*
San Antonio College *A*
South Plains College *A*
Texas Southern University *B*
Texas Woman's University *B, M*
Tyler Junior College *C, A*

Utah
Salt Lake Community College *C*

Vermont
Burlington College *B*
Champlain College *A, B*
College of St. Joseph in Vermont *B*
Southern Vermont College *A*
Trinity College of Vermont *A, B*

Virginia
Blue Ridge Community College *A*
Central Virginia Community College *C*
John Tyler Community College *A*
New River Community College *C, A*
Northern Virginia Community College *A*
Southside Virginia Community
    College *C, A*
Southwest Virginia Community
    College *C*
Virginia Highlands Community
    College *C, A*
Virginia Wesleyan College *B*
Virginia Western Community College *A*

Washington
Central Washington University *B*
Columbia Basin College *A*
Everett Community College *A*
Grays Harbor College *A*
Seattle Central Community College *A*
Skagit Valley College *A*
Western Washington University *B*

West Virginia
Salem-Teikyo University *B*
West Virginia Northern Community
    College *C, A*

Wisconsin
Gateway Technical College *A*
Marian College of Fond du Lac *B*
Southwest Wisconsin Technical
    College *A*
University of Wisconsin
    Oshkosh *B*
    Superior *M*

Wyoming
Central Wyoming College *A*

Industrial design

Alabama
Auburn University *B, M*

Arizona
Arizona State University *B, M*
Yavapai College *C, A*

California
Academy of Art College *C, A, B, M*
Art Center College of Design *B, M*
California College of Arts and Crafts *B*
California State University
    Long Beach *B, M*
College of the Sequoias *C*

ITT Technical Institute
    San Bernardino *B*
Los Angeles Pierce College *C, A*
San Francisco State University *B*
University of San Francisco *B*

Colorado
Art Institute
    of Colorado *B*
Metropolitan State College of Denver *B*

Connecticut
University of Bridgeport *B*

Florida
Art Institute
    of Fort Lauderdale *A, B*

Georgia
Georgia Institute of Technology *B*
Morris Brown College *B*
Savannah College of Art and Design *M*

Illinois
University of Illinois
    Chicago *B, M*
    Urbana-Champaign *B*

Indiana
ITT Technical Institute
    Fort Wayne *B*
Oakland City University *A, B*
Purdue University *B*

Kansas
University of Kansas *B, M*

Louisiana
University of Louisiana at Lafayette *B*

Massachusetts
Massachusetts College of Art *B*
Wentworth Institute of Technology *B*

Michigan
Center for Creative Studies: College of
    Art and Design *B*
Cranbrook Academy of Art *M*
Henry Ford Community College *A*
Kendall College of Art and Design *B*
Macomb Community College *C, A*
Northern Michigan University *A, B*
Oakland Community College *A*
University of Michigan *B*
Western Michigan University *B*

Minnesota
St. Cloud Technical College *C, A*

Missouri
College of the Ozarks *B*

New Hampshire
University of New Hampshire *M*

New York
Pratt Institute *B, M*
Rochester Institute of
    Technology *A, B, M*
Syracuse University *B, M*

North Carolina
North Carolina State University *M*

Ohio
Cleveland Institute of Art *B*
Columbus College of Art and Design *B*
Kent State University *B*
Notre Dame College of Ohio *B*
Ohio State University
    Columbus Campus *B, M*
University of Cincinnati *B*

Oklahoma
Oklahoma State University
    Oklahoma City *C, A*

Oregon
Portland Community College *C, A*

Pennsylvania
Art Institute
    of Philadelphia *A*
    of Pittsburgh *A*
California University of Pennsylvania *B*
Carnegie Mellon University *B*
Northampton County Area Community
    College *A*
Philadelphia University *B*
University of the Arts *B, M*

Puerto Rico
Ramirez College of Business and
    Technology *A*

Texas
Texas A&M University
    Commerce *B*

Utah
Brigham Young University *B*
ITT Technical Institute
    Murray *B*

Virginia
Lord Fairfax Community College *C*
Virginia Polytechnic Institute and State
    University *B*

Washington
Art Institute of Seattle *A*
University of Washington *B, M*
Western Washington University *B*

Wisconsin
Milwaukee Institute of Art & Design *B*
Western Wisconsin Technical College *A*

Industrial equipment maintenance/repair

Alabama
Community College of the Air Force *A*
Gadsden State Community College *C, A*
Harry M. Ayers State Technical
    College *C*
John M. Patterson State Technical
    College *C, A*
Northwest-Shoals Community College *C*
Snead State Community College *C*
University of West Alabama *A*

Alaska
University of Alaska
    Anchorage *C, A*

Arizona
Central Arizona College *A*

Arkansas
Arkansas Tech University *C, A*
Phillips Community College of the
    University of Arkansas *A*
Southern Arkansas University
    Tech *A*
University of Arkansas
    Monticello *A*
Westark College *C*

California
Allan Hancock College *C*
Cabrillo College *C, A*
Fresno City College *C, A*
Long Beach City College *C, A*
Merced College *C, A*
Pacific Union College *B*

Colorado
Pueblo Community College *C, A*
Red Rocks Community College *C*

Delaware
Delaware Technical and Community
    College
    Terry Campus *C, A*

Florida
Miami-Dade Community College *A*

Georgia
Athens Area Technical Institute C
Chattahoochee Technical Institute C
Coastal Georgia Community College C
Columbus Technical Institute C
Georgia Southwestern State University A
Waycross College A

Idaho
Boise State University C, A
Lewis-Clark State College A
North Idaho College A

Illinois
Black Hawk College C
College of Lake County C, A
Danville Area Community College A
Illinois Eastern Community Colleges
　Olney Central College A
　Wabash Valley College C
John A. Logan College C, A
John Wood Community College C
Kankakee Community College C, A
Kaskaskia College C, A
Lake Land College C
Moraine Valley Community College C
Prairie State College C
Richland Community College A
Southeastern Illinois College A
Southwestern Ilinois College C, A
Triton College C, A
Waubonsee Community College A
William Rainey Harper College C

Indiana
Ivy Tech State College
　Central Indiana C, A
　Columbus C, A
　Eastcentral C, A
　Kokomo C, A
　Lafayette C, A
　Northcentral C, A
　Northeast C, A
　Northwest C, A
　Southcentral C, A
　Southeast C, A
　Southwest C, A
　Wabash Valley C, A
　Whitewater C, A
Vincennes University A

Iowa
Des Moines Area Community College A
Hawkeye Community College C
Marshalltown Community College A
Muscatine Community College A

Maine
Washington County Technical College C

Michigan
Ferris State University A, B
Great Lakes College C, A
Jackson Community College C
Kellogg Community College C, A
Lansing Community College A
Muskegon Community College C
Southwestern Michigan College C, A

Minnesota
Hennepin Technical College C, A
Inver Hills Community College A
Mesabi Range Community and Technical College C
NEI College of Technology A
St. Cloud Technical College C

Mississippi
East Central Community College C
Hinds Community College C
Meridian Community College C
Mississippi Delta Community College C
Mississippi Gulf Coast Community College
　Jackson County Campus A
　Jefferson Davis Campus C

Missouri
Jefferson College A
Maple Woods Community College A
Moberly Area Community College C, A
Ranken Technical College A

Montana
Montana State University
　Billings C

Nebraska
Central Community College C, A
Metropolitan Community College A
Northeast Community College A
Southeast Community College
　Milford Campus A

New Hampshire
New Hampshire Community Technical College
　Nashua A

New Jersey
Cumberland County College A

New York
State University of New York
　College of Agriculture and Technology at Cobleskill A

North Carolina
Alamance Community College C, A
Bladen Community College C
Blue Ridge Community College C
Brunswick Community College C, A
Caldwell Community College and Technical Institute A
Cape Fear Community College C
Central Carolina Community College A
Craven Community College A
Davidson County Community College C
Durham Technical Community College C
Guilford Technical Community College C, A
Halifax Community College C, A
Mayland Community College C
Mitchell Community College A
Nash Community College C
Richmond Community College C
Roanoke-Chowan Community College A
Rockingham Community College C
Rowan-Cabarrus Community College C
Sampson Community College C, A
Vance-Granville Community College C
Wake Technical Community College C, A
Wilson Technical Community College C

Ohio
Jefferson Community College A
Stark State College of Technology A

Oregon
Chemeketa Community College A

Pennsylvania
Johnson Technical Institute A
Pennsylvania College of Technology C, A
Reading Area Community College A
Westmoreland County Community College A

South Carolina
Aiken Technical College C
Central Carolina Technical College C
Greenville Technical College C
Piedmont Technical College C
Spartanburg Technical College A
Tri-County Technical College A
Trident Technical College C, A
York Technical College A

South Dakota
Southeast Technical Institute A
Western Dakota Technical Institute A

Tennessee
Northeast State Technical Community College C, A

Texas
Amarillo College C, A
Grayson County College A
Texas State Technical College
　Harlingen C
　Waco C, A

Utah
Utah Valley State College C, A
Weber State University A

Virginia
John Tyler Community College C
New River Community College C
Piedmont Virginia Community College C
Southside Virginia Community College C
Southwest Virginia Community College C
Thomas Nelson Community College C
Tidewater Community College A
Virginia Highlands Community College C

Washington
Big Bend Community College A
Lake Washington Technical College C
Lower Columbia College A
Spokane Community College A

West Virginia
West Virginia Northern Community College C

Wisconsin
Chippewa Valley Technical College A
Gateway Technical College C
Lakeshore Technical College C
Madison Area Technical College C
Moraine Park Technical College C
Northeast Wisconsin Technical College A
Waukesha County Technical College C
Western Wisconsin Technical College C
Wisconsin Indianhead Technical College C

Wyoming
Western Wyoming Community College C, A

Industrial production technologies

Alabama
Alabama Agricultural and Mechanical University B, M
Central Alabama Community College A
Community College of the Air Force A
Jacksonville State University B
John M. Patterson State Technical College A
University of West Alabama B

Alaska
University of Alaska
　Anchorage A

Arizona
Arizona Western College C, A
Northland Pioneer College C, A
Pima Community College A

Arkansas
Arkansas State University
　Beebe Branch A
Mississippi County Community College A
Phillips Community College of the University of Arkansas C
Southern Arkansas University
　Tech A
Southern Arkansas University A, B
University of Arkansas
　Little Rock A
　Pine Bluff A, B
Westark College B

California
American River College A
Bakersfield College A
Barstow College C, A
Butte College A
California Polytechnic State University:
　San Luis Obispo B
California State University
　Chico B
　Long Beach B
　Los Angeles B
City College of San Francisco C, A
Don Bosco Technical Institute A
Fashion Institute of Design and Merchandising A
Gavilan Community College C, A
Long Beach City College C, A
Los Angeles Pierce College C, A
Los Angeles Trade and Technical College C, A
Merced College A
MiraCosta College C, A
Mount San Antonio College A
Orange Coast College C, A
Pacific Union College B, M
Pasadena City College C, A
Riverside Community College A
San Diego City College C, A
San Francisco State University B
Sierra College A
Solano Community College A
Southwestern College C, A
Taft College A
University of San Diego B
Ventura College A
West Hills Community College A

Colorado
Colorado State University B
Front Range Community College C
Metropolitan State College of Denver B

Connecticut
Central Connecticut State University B
Manchester Community-Technical College A
Naugatuck Valley Community-Technical College A
University of New Haven B

Delaware
Delaware Technical and Community College
　Stanton/Wilmington Campus A

Florida
Art Institute
　of Fort Lauderdale A, B
Miami-Dade Community College A
Pensacola Junior College C
University of West Florida B
Valencia Community College A

Georgia
Georgia Southern University B
Middle Georgia College A
Southern Polytechnic State University B

Idaho
Eastern Idaho Technical College C
Lewis-Clark State College A
Ricks College A
University of Idaho B

Illinois
Black Hawk College C, A
Bradley University B
College of DuPage C, A
Eastern Illinois University B, M
Elgin Community College A
Illinois Eastern Community Colleges
　Wabash Valley College A

Industrial production technologies

Illinois State University B, M, T
John Wood Community College A
Joliet Junior College C, A
Kaskaskia College C, A
Lewis and Clark Community College A
McHenry County College C
Moraine Valley Community College C
Northern Illinois University B
Oakton Community College A
Parkland College C, A
Prairie State College C, A
Rend Lake College C, A
Richland Community College A
Southern Illinois University
    Carbondale B, M
Western Illinois University B, M
William Rainey Harper College C, A

Indiana
Indiana State University B, M
Indiana University--Purdue University
    Indiana University-Purdue
        University Fort Wayne A, B
International Business College A
Purdue University
    North Central Campus A
Purdue University B
Tri-State University A

Iowa
Kirkwood Community College C, A
Northeast Iowa Community College A
Southeastern Community College
    North Campus A
University of Northern Iowa B, M, D
William Penn University B

Kansas
Allen County Community College C, A
Butler County Community College C, A
Garden City Community College A
Hutchinson Community College A
Johnson County Community
    College C, A
Kansas State University A
McPherson College B
Pittsburg State University B

Kentucky
Berea College B
Morehead State University A, B
Murray State University B, M
Northern Kentucky University A, B
Western Kentucky University B

Louisiana
Bossier Parish Community College C, A
Southeastern Louisiana University A, B
University of Louisiana at Lafayette A, B

Maine
University of Southern Maine B

Massachusetts
Berkshire Community College A
Massachusetts Maritime Academy B
University of Massachusetts
    Lowell M

Michigan
Andrews University A
Baker College
    of Muskegon B
Bay de Noc Community College A
Central Michigan University B
Eastern Michigan University B, M
Ferris State University A, B
Grand Rapids Community College C, A
Henry Ford Community College A
Kalamazoo Valley Community
    College C, A
Kellogg Community College C, A
Kirtland Community College A
Lansing Community College C, A
Macomb Community College C, A
Monroe County Community
    College C, A
Montcalm Community College A

Mott Community College A
Muskegon Community College C, A
Northwestern Michigan College A
Oakland Community College C, A
Saginaw Valley State University B
St. Clair County Community
    College C, A
Schoolcraft College A
University of Detroit Mercy B
Wayne State University B
Western Michigan University B

Minnesota
Bemidji State University B
Dunwoody Institute A
Moorhead State University B
Ridgewater College: A Community and
    Technical College C, A
St. Cloud Technical College C
St. Mary's University of Minnesota B

Mississippi
Alcorn State University B
Copiah-Lincoln Community
    College C, A
Mississippi Gulf Coast Community
    College
        Perkinston A
Mississippi State University B
Mississippi Valley State University B
University of Southern Mississippi B

Missouri
Central Missouri State University B, M
College of the Ozarks B
Crowder College A
Missouri Western State College A
Southwest Missouri State University
    West Plains Campus A
Southwest Missouri State University B
St. Louis Community College
    St. Louis Community College at
        Florissant Valley A
Three Rivers Community College A

Montana
Montana State University
    Northern A, B

Nebraska
Central Community College C, A
Chadron State College B
Peru State College B
University of Nebraska
    Lincoln A
    Omaha B
Wayne State College B

Nevada
Community College of Southern
    Nevada A
Western Nevada Community College A

New Jersey
Bergen Community College A
Burlington County College A
Camden County College C, A
County College of Morris A
Cumberland County College C, A
Gloucester County College A
Kean University B
Thomas Edison State College A, B

New Mexico
Albuquerque Technical-Vocational
    Institute C, A
Eastern New Mexico University B
San Juan College C, A

New York
Broome Community College A
City University of New York
    College of Staten Island C, A
    Queensborough Community
        College C, A
Clinton Community College A
Corning Community College A

Erie Community College
    City Campus A
    North Campus A
    South Campus A
Fulton-Montgomery Community
    College A
Hudson Valley Community College A
Mohawk Valley Community
    College C, A
Monroe Community College A
New York Institute of Technology B
Rochester Institute of Technology M
Schenectady County Community
    College C, A
State University of New York
    College at Buffalo B, M
    College at Fredonia B
    College of Technology at Canton A
    Institute of Technology at
        Utica/Rome B
Technical Career Institutes C, A

North Carolina
Alamance Community College C, A
Appalachian State University B, M
Blue Ridge Community College A
Cape Fear Community College A
Catawba Valley Community College A
Central Piedmont Community College A
East Carolina University B, M
Elizabeth City State University B
Gaston College A
Lenoir Community College A
Martin Community College C, A
North Carolina Agricultural and
    Technical State University B, M
Randolph Community College C
University of North Carolina
    Charlotte B
Wake Technical Community
    College C, A
Wayne Community College A
Western Carolina University B, M

North Dakota
Bismarck State College C, A
North Dakota State College of
    Science C, A
University of North Dakota B, M

Ohio
Cincinnati State Technical and
    Community College A
Clark State Community College A
Columbus State Community College A
Edison State Community College A
Hocking Technical College A
Kent State University
    Trumbull Campus A
    Tuscarawas Campus A
Kent State University B, M
Lakeland Community College C, A
Lima Technical College A
Lorain County Community College A
North Central State College C, A
Northwest State Community
    College C, A
Ohio Northern University B
Ohio University A
Owens Community College
    Findlay Campus A
Sinclair Community College C, A
Stark State College of Technology A
Terra Community College C, A
University of Akron A
University of Cincinnati
    Clermont College A
University of Dayton B
University of Toledo A

Oklahoma
Northeastern Oklahoma Agricultural and
    Mechanical College A
Northeastern State University B
Southeastern Oklahoma State
    University B

Southwestern Oklahoma State
    University B
Tulsa Community College A

Oregon
Central Oregon Community College A
Chemeketa Community College A
Lane Community College C, A
Linn-Benton Community College A
Mount Hood Community College A
Oregon Institute of Technology B
Portland Community College C, A

Pennsylvania
Butler County Community College A
California University of Pennsylvania A
Cheyney University of Pennsylvania B
Community College of Philadelphia A
Delaware County Community College A
Edinboro University of Pennsylvania A
Harrisburg Area Community
    College C, A
ICS Center for Degree Studies A
Lackawanna Junior College A
Lehigh Carbon Community College C, A
Mercyhurst College C
Millersville University of
    Pennsylvania B
Northampton County Area Community
    College C
Penn State
    Altoona A
    Berks A
    Dubois A
    Erie, The Behrend College A
    Fayette A
    Hazleton A
    McKeesport A
    New Kensington A
    Schuylkill - Capital College A
    Shenango A
    University Park B
    Wilkes-Barre A
    York A
Pennsylvania College of
    Technology A, B
Reading Area Community College A
Westmoreland County Community
    College C, A

Puerto Rico
Caribbean University B
University of Puerto Rico
    Bayamon University College A
    Ponce University College A

Rhode Island
Rhode Island College B, M

South Carolina
Clemson University M, D
South Carolina State University B
Trident Technical College C, A

South Dakota
Western Dakota Technical Institute C

Tennessee
Cleveland State Community College A
Middle Tennessee State University B, M
Northeast State Technical Community
    College A
Tennessee Technological University B
Walters State Community College C

Texas
Abilene Christian University B
Angelina College C, A
Brookhaven College A
Grayson County College C, A
Hill College C, A
Houston Community College
    System C, A
Lamar State College at Orange A
Lamar University B
Midland College A
Navarro College C, A
North Central Texas College A

Prairie View A&M University *B*
Richland College *A*
Sam Houston State University *B, M*
Southwest Texas State University *B, M*
Sul Ross State University *B, M*
Tarleton State University *B, T*
Tarrant County College *C, A*
Texas A&M University
  Commerce *B, M*
Texas Southern University *B*
Texas State Technical College
  Harlingen *C, A*
  Sweetwater *C, A*
  Waco *A*
University of Houston *B, M*
University of North Texas *B*
University of Texas
  Tyler *B*
West Texas A&M University *B, M*

Utah
Brigham Young University *B*
Utah State University *B, M*
Weber State University *C, A, B*

Virginia
Blue Ridge Community College *C*
Dabney S. Lancaster Community
  College *A*
J. Sargeant Reynolds Community
  College *C*

Washington
Everett Community College *A*
Grays Harbor College *C, A*
Shoreline Community College *A*
South Seattle Community College *A*
Walla Walla College *B*
Western Washington University *B*

West Virginia
Fairmont State College *A, B*
West Virginia State College *B*
West Virginia University
  Parkersburg *A*

Wisconsin
Chippewa Valley Technical College *A*
Gateway Technical College *A*
Lakeshore Technical College *C*
Milwaukee Area Technical College *A*
Moraine Park Technical College *A*
Northeast Wisconsin Technical
  College *A*
University of Wisconsin
  Platteville *M*
  Stout *B*
Western Wisconsin Technical College *A*
Wisconsin Indianhead Technical
  College *C*

Industrial/manufacturing engineering

Alabama
Auburn University *B, M, D*
University of Alabama
  Huntsville *B, M, D*
University of Alabama *B, M*

Alaska
University of Alaska
  Anchorage *M*
  Fairbanks *M*

Arizona
Arizona State University *B, M, D*
Central Arizona College *C, A*
Pima Community College *A*
University of Arizona *B, M*

Arkansas
University of Arkansas *B, M*

California
California Polytechnic State University:
  San Luis Obispo *B*

California State Polytechnic University:
  Pomona *B*
California State University
  Hayward *B*
  Long Beach *B*
  Los Angeles *B*
  Northridge *B, M*
City College of San Francisco *C, A*
Cuesta College *C, A*
East Los Angeles College *A*
MiraCosta College *C, A*
San Jose State University *M*
Santa Ana College *C, A*
Santa Barbara City College *A*
Stanford University *B, M, D*
University of California
  Berkeley *B, M, D*
  San Diego *M, D*
University of San Diego *B*
University of Southern
  California *B, M, D*

Colorado
University of Southern Colorado *B*

Connecticut
Fairfield University *B*
Manchester Community-Technical
  College *A*
University of Bridgeport *M*
University of Connecticut *B*
University of Hartford *B*
University of New Haven *A, B, M*

District of Columbia
George Washington University *M*

Florida
Art Institute
  of Fort Lauderdale *A, B*
Florida Agricultural and Mechanical
  University *B*
Florida International University *M*
Florida State University *B, M, D*
Hillsborough Community College *A*
Miami-Dade Community College *A*
Pensacola Junior College *A*
University of Central Florida *B, M, D*
University of Miami *B, M, D*
University of South Florida *B, M, D*

Georgia
Georgia Institute of Technology *B, M, D*
Mercer University *B*
Morris Brown College *B*

Idaho
University of Idaho *B, M*

Illinois
Bradley University *B, M*
Illinois Institute of Technology *M*
Lincoln Land Community College *C, A*
Northern Illinois University *B, M*
Northwestern University *B*
Parkland College *A*
Rend Lake College *A*
Richland Community College *A*
Southern Illinois University
  Edwardsville *B*
University of Illinois
  Chicago *B, M, D*
  Urbana-Champaign *B, M, D*

Indiana
Indiana Institute of Technology *B*
Purdue University
  Calumet *B, T*
Purdue University *B, M, D*
University of Evansville *B*

Iowa
Iowa State University *B, M, D*
St. Ambrose University *B*
Southeastern Community College
  North Campus *A*
University of Iowa *B, M, D*

Kansas
Allen County Community College *C, A*
Kansas State University *B, M, D*
Wichita State University *B, M, D*

Kentucky
University of Kentucky *M*
University of Louisville *B, M, D*

Louisiana
Louisiana State University and
  Agricultural and Mechanical
  College *B, M*
Louisiana Tech University *B*

Maryland
Morgan State University *B*

Massachusetts
Boston University *B, M, D*
Fitchburg State College *B*
Northeastern University *B, M, D*
Tufts University *B*
University of Massachusetts
  Amherst *B, M, D*
Wentworth Institute of Technology *B*
Western New England College *B*
Worcester Polytechnic Institute *B, M, D*

Michigan
Central Michigan University *B*
Grand Valley State University *B*
Kettering University *B, M*
Lake Superior State University *A*
Monroe County Community
  College *C, A*
University of Michigan
  Dearborn *B, M*
University of Michigan *B, M, D*
Wayne State University *B, M, D*
Western Michigan University *B, M, D*

Minnesota
Concordia College: Moorhead *B*
St. Cloud State University *B*
University of Minnesota
  Duluth *B*
  Twin Cities *M, D*

Mississippi
Jackson State University *B*
Mississippi State University *B, M*

Missouri
Central Missouri State University *M*
East Central College *C, A*
University of Missouri
  Columbia *B, M, D*

Montana
Montana State University
  Bozeman *B, M*
  Northern *A*

Nebraska
University of Nebraska
  Lincoln *B, M*
  Omaha *B*

New Jersey
New Jersey Institute of
  Technology *B, M, D*
Rutgers
  The State University of New Jersey:
    College of Engineering *B*
  The State University of New Jersey:
    New Brunswick Graduate
    Campus *M, D*

New Mexico
New Mexico State University *B, M*
University of New Mexico *M*

New York
Cayuga County Community College *A*
Columbia University
  Fu Foundation School of
    Engineering and Applied
    Science *B, M, D*
Cornell University *B*

Hofstra University *B*
New York Institute of Technology *B*
Pace University *B*
Polytechnic University *M*
Rensselaer Polytechnic Institute *B, M, D*
Rochester Institute of Technology *B, M*
State University of New York
  Binghamton *M*
  Buffalo *B, M, D*
Syracuse University *M*

North Carolina
Cape Fear Community College *A*
Edgecombe Community College *A*
Martin Community College *C, A*
North Carolina Agricultural and
  Technical State University *B, M*
North Carolina State University *B, M, D*
St. Augustine's College *B*
Western Piedmont Community
  College *A*
Wilson Technical Community College *A*

North Dakota
North Dakota State University *B, M*

Ohio
Central Ohio Technical College *A*
Cleveland State University *B, M, D*
Edison State Community College *A*
Jefferson Community College *A*
Kent State University
  Trumbull Campus *A*
Kent State University *B*
Lorain County Community College *A*
Marion Technical College *A*
Miami University
  Oxford Campus *B*
Muskingum College *B*
Ohio State University
  Columbus Campus *B, M, D*
Ohio University *B, M*
University of Cincinnati *B, M, D*
University of Toledo *B, M*
Washington State Community College *A*
Youngstown State University *B, M*

Oklahoma
Northeastern Oklahoma Agricultural and
  Mechanical College *A*
Oklahoma State University *B, M, D*
Tulsa Community College *A*
University of Oklahoma *B, M, D*

Oregon
Chemeketa Community College *C, A*
Clackamas Community College *C*
Oregon State University *B, M, D*
Portland State University *M*

Pennsylvania
Drexel University *B*
Elizabethtown College *B*
Geneva College *B*
Lehigh University *B, M, D*
Penn State
  University Park *B, M, D*
Reading Area Community College *A*
University of Pittsburgh *B, M, D*

Puerto Rico
Caribbean University *B*
Inter American University of Puerto Rico
  Bayamon Campus *B*
Turabo University *B*
Universidad Politecnica de Puerto
  Rico *B, M*
University of Puerto Rico
  Mayaguez Campus *B*
  Ponce University College *A*

Rhode Island
University of Rhode Island *B, M, D*

South Carolina
Clemson University *B, M, D*

South Dakota
South Dakota School of Mines and
  Technology B

Tennessee
Hiwassee College A
Tennessee Technological
  University B, M, D
University of Memphis B, M
University of Tennessee
  Knoxville B, M

Texas
Houston Baptist University B
Lamar University B
Midwestern State University B
St. Mary's University B, M
Southwest Texas State University B
Texas A&M University
  Kingsville B, M
Texas A&M University B, M, D
Texas Tech University B, M, D
University of Houston B, M, D
University of Texas
  Arlington B, M, D
  Austin M, D
  Dallas B, M
  El Paso B, M
  Pan American B

Utah
Brigham Young University B, M, D
Snow College A

Virginia
ECPI College of Technology C, A
Virginia Polytechnic Institute and State
  University B, M, D

Washington
Pierce College A
Seattle University B
Shoreline Community College A
University of Washington B
Washington State University B
Western Washington University B

West Virginia
West Virginia University Institute of
  Technology B
West Virginia University B, M, D

Wisconsin
Blackhawk Technical College A
Marquette University B, M, D
Milwaukee School of Engineering B
University of Wisconsin
  Madison B, M, D
  Milwaukee B
  Platteville B
  Stout B

Industrial/organizational psychology

Alabama
Alabama Agricultural and Mechanical
  University M

Arkansas
University of Arkansas
  Little Rock M

California
Antioch Southern California
  Santa Barbara M
California School of Professional
  Psychology
    Alameda D
    San Diego M, D
California State University
  Hayward B
  Long Beach M
College of Notre Dame B
John F. Kennedy University M
Pepperdine University B
Point Loma Nazarene University B
San Diego State University M
San Francisco State University M
United States International
  University M, D

Connecticut
University of New Haven M

District of Columbia
George Washington University D

Florida
Carlos Albizu University M
Florida Institute of Technology M, D
University of Central Florida M
University of West Florida M

Illinois
Adler School of Professional
  Psychology M
De Paul University B, M, D
Elmhurst College M
Roosevelt University M
St. Xavier University B

Indiana
Purdue University
  Calumet B
University of Evansville B

Iowa
Morningside College B

Louisiana
Louisiana Tech University M

Maine
Husson College B
University of Maine
  Fort Kent B

Maryland
University of Baltimore M

Massachusetts
Bridgewater State College B
Fitchburg State College B
Springfield College M

Michigan
Central Michigan University M, D
Northern Michigan University B
University of Detroit Mercy B, M

Minnesota
Minnesota State University, Mankato M

Missouri
St. Louis University B

Nebraska
Nebraska Wesleyan University B
University of Nebraska
  Omaha M

New Hampshire
Antioch New England Graduate
  School M

New Jersey
Bloomfield College C
Fairleigh Dickinson University M
Rutgers
  The State University of New Jersey:
    New Brunswick Graduate
      Campus D

New York
City University of New York
  Baruch College M, D
  Brooklyn College B, M
  Graduate School and University
    Center D
Columbia University
  Teachers College M, D
Hofstra University M
Ithaca College B
Jamestown Community College C
New York University M, D
State University of New York
  Albany M, D

North Carolina
High Point University B
University of North Carolina
  Charlotte M

Ohio
Bowling Green State University M, D
Ohio State University
  Columbus Campus M, D
Ohio University M, D
University of Akron D
Wright State University M, D

Oklahoma
Northeastern State University B
University of Tulsa M, D

Oregon
Western Baptist College B

Pennsylvania
California University of Pennsylvania B
La Salle University B
Lincoln University B
MCP Hahnemann University M
Moravian College B
West Chester University of
  Pennsylvania M

Puerto Rico
Inter American University of Puerto Rico
  Metropolitan Campus M
University of Puerto Rico
  Rio Piedras Campus M

South Carolina
Clemson University M, D

Tennessee
Middle Tennessee State University B
University of Tennessee
  Knoxville M, D

Texas
Abilene Christian University B
Angelo State University M
Lamar University M
St. Mary's University M
Texas A&M University D
University of Houston D
University of North Texas M
University of the Incarnate Word B

Vermont
Goddard College M

Virginia
Averett College B
Christopher Newport University M
Longwood College B
Old Dominion University D

Washington
City University M

Wisconsin
University of Wisconsin
  Oshkosh M

Information sciences/systems

Alabama
Alabama State University B
Faulkner University B
Northwest-Shoals Community College A
Oakwood College B

Alaska
University of Alaska
  Anchorage A

Arizona
Arizona Western College C
Cochise College A
Eastern Arizona College C, A
Northern Arizona University B
Phoenix College A
Prescott College B, M

Scottsdale Community College C, A
South Mountain Community
  College C, A

Arkansas
University of Central Arkansas B

California
Allan Hancock College A
Azusa Pacific University B
California Baptist University B
California Lutheran University B
California State Polytechnic University:
  Pomona B
California State University
  Bakersfield B
  Chico B
  Fresno B
  Fullerton B, M
  Hayward B, M
  Long Beach B
  Los Angeles B
  Monterey Bay B
  Stanislaus B
Chabot College A
Chapman University B
College of the Canyons C, A
Compton Community College C
Cypress College A
DeVry Institute of Technology
  Pomona B
Empire College C
Fresno City College C, A
Humboldt State University B
Kings River Community College C, A
La Sierra University B
Los Angeles Harbor College A
Master's College A
Merced College A
Mission College C, A
Moorpark College C, A
National University B
Ohlone College C, A
Orange Coast College C, A
Pacific Union College A, B
Palomar College A
San Diego City College A
San Diego State University B, M
San Joaquin Delta College C
Santa Barbara City College C, A
Santa Clara University B
Santa Monica College C, A
Santa Rosa Junior College C
Sierra College A
Skyline College C, A
Southwestern College A
United States International University B
University of California
  San Diego B
University of San Francisco B
University of the Pacific B
Ventura College C, A
West Hills Community College C

Colorado
Colorado Mountain College
  Alpine Campus A
Community College of Aurora C, A
Community College of Denver C, A
Denver Technical College: A Division of
  DeVry University A, B
Fort Lewis College B
Lamar Community College A
Regis University M
University of Colorado
  Colorado Springs B
  Denver M
University of Denver M
University of Southern Colorado B

Connecticut
Gateway Community College C, A
Manchester Community-Technical
  College C, A
Middlesex Community-Technical
  College C, A

Information sciences/systems

Northwestern Connecticut
Community-Technical College *A*
Norwalk Community-Technical
College *C, A*
Sacred Heart University *M*
Three Rivers Community-Technical
College *A*
University of Hartford *B*

Delaware
Delaware State University *B*
Delaware Technical and Community
College
Owens Campus *A*
Stanton/Wilmington Campus *A*
Terry Campus *A*

District of Columbia
American University *B, M*
Gallaudet University *B*
George Washington University *B, M*
Southeastern University *M*

Florida
Barry University *B*
Bethune-Cookman College *B*
Broward Community College *A*
Daytona Beach Community College *A*
Florida Community College at
Jacksonville *A*
Florida Institute of Technology *B, M*
Florida International University *B*
Hillsborough Community College *A*
Jacksonville University *B*
Lake City Community College *A*
Miami-Dade Community College *C, A*
Northwood University
Florida Campus *B*
Nova Southeastern University *D*
Palm Beach Atlantic College *B*
Palm Beach Community College *A*
Pensacola Junior College *A*
Polk Community College *A*
St. Petersburg Junior College *C*
Seminole Community College *A*
South College: Palm Beach Campus *B*
Stetson University *B*
Tampa Technical Institute *A*
University of Miami *M*

Georgia
American InterContinental
University *A, B, M*
Atlanta Metropolitan College *A*
Brewton-Parker College *B*
Columbus State University *B*
Darton College *A*
DeVry Institute of Technology
Atlanta *B*
Fort Valley State University *B*
Georgia College and State University *B*
Herzing College of Business and
Technology *A*
Kennesaw State University *B, M*
Mercer University *B, M*
Piedmont College *B*
Reinhardt College *B*
Savannah State University *B*
University of Georgia *M*
Valdosta State University *B*

Hawaii
Brigham Young University
Hawaii *B*
Hawaii Pacific University *M*
University of Hawaii
Honolulu Community College *A*

Idaho
Boise State University *B, M*
Idaho State University *B, M*
Lewis-Clark State College *C, A*

Illinois
Barat College *B*
Chicago State University *B*
City Colleges of Chicago
Harold Washington College *C, A*
Danville Area Community College *A*
De Paul University *C, B, M*
DeVry Institute of Technology
Chicago *B*
Dominican University *B, M*
Elmhurst College *B*
Highland Community College *A*
Illinois College *B*
John A. Logan College *C, A*
John Wood Community College *A*
Joliet Junior College *A*
MacCormac College *C, A*
National-Louis University *C, B*
Olivet Nazarene University *B*
Rockford College *B*
Roosevelt University *C, B, M*
Southwestern Illinois College *A*
Trinity Christian College *B*
University of St. Francis *B*
William Rainey Harper College *C, A*

Indiana
Ancilla College *C, A*
Anderson University *B*
Bethel College *B*
Franklin College *B*
Goshen College *B*
Indiana Institute of Technology *A, B*
Indiana State University *B*
Indiana University
Kokomo *B*
Indiana University--Purdue University
Indiana University-Purdue
University Fort Wayne *A, B*
Purdue University
Calumet *A, B*
Taylor University *A*
University of Indianapolis *A, B*

Iowa
American Institute of Business *A*
Buena Vista University *B*
Central College *B*
Des Moines Area Community College *A*
Dordt College *B*
Graceland University *B*
Grand View College *C*
Simpson College *B*
Southeastern Community College
South Campus *C*
University of Iowa *B, M, D*
University of Northern Iowa *B*
Waldorf College *A, B*
Wartburg College *C, B*

Kansas
Central Christian College *A*
Emporia State University *B*
Independence Community College *C, A*
Kansas State University *B*
MidAmerica Nazarene University *B*
Newman University *A, B*
St. Mary College *B*
Southwestern College *B*

Kentucky
Ashland Community College *A*
Elizabethtown Community College *A*
Madisonville Community College *A*
Murray State University *B*
Northern Kentucky University *B*
Owensboro Community College *A*
Owensboro Junior College of Business *A*
Thomas More College *A, B*

Louisiana
Louisiana State University
Shreveport *M*
Louisiana State University and
Agricultural and Mechanical
College *M*
Loyola University New Orleans *B*
Northwestern State University *A, B*
Nunez Community College *C, A*
Tulane University *A, B*
Xavier University of Louisiana *B*

Maine
Eastern Maine Technical College *C*
Husson College *A*
University of Maine
Machias *A*

Maryland
Allegany College *A*
Baltimore City Community College *A*
Bowie State University *M*
Cecil Community College *C, A*
Charles County Community
College *C, A*
Chesapeake College *C*
Columbia Union College *B*
Frederick Community College *A*
Montgomery College
Germantown Campus *A*
Rockville Campus *A*
Takoma Park Campus *A*
Morgan State University *B*
Prince George's Community
College *C, A*
University of Maryland
Baltimore County *B, M, D*
Villa Julie College *B, M*

Massachusetts
American International College *B*
Assumption College *B*
Babson College *B*
Bay Path College *B*
Bentley College *B, M*
Berkshire Community College *C, A*
Boston College *B*
Bristol Community College *C, A*
Cape Cod Community College *A*
Endicott College *A*
Harvard College *B*
Massachusetts Bay Community
College *C, A*
Massachusetts College of Liberal Arts *B*
Mount Wachusett Community College *C*
North Shore Community College *A*
Northeastern University *M*
Northern Essex Community College *A*
Springfield College *B*
Suffolk University *B*
Tufts University *B*
University of Massachusetts
Lowell *A, B*
Westfield State College *B*
Worcester Polytechnic Institute *B, M*

Michigan
Alpena Community College *C, A*
Andrews University *B*
Baker College
of Auburn Hills *A*
of Owosso *A*
of Port Huron *A, B*
Calvin College *B*
Detroit College of Business *A, B*
Eastern Michigan University *B, M*
Ferris State University *B, M*
Grand Valley State University *B, M*
Lake Michigan College *A*
Lawrence Technological University *M*
Mott Community College *A*
Northwestern Michigan College *A*
Oakland Community College *A*
Schoolcraft College *A*
University of Michigan *M, D*
Wayne State University *B*
Western Michigan University *B*

Minnesota
Alexandria Technical College *A*
Anoka-Ramsey Community College *A*
Augsburg College *C*
Century Community and Technical
College *C, A*
College of St. Catherine: St. Paul
Campus *A*
Concordia University: St. Paul *B*
Crown College *C, A, B*
Hennepin Technical College *C, A*
Metropolitan State University *B*
Minnesota State University, Mankato *B*
NEI College of Technology *A*
National American University
St. Paul *A*
St. Cloud Technical College *C, A*
University of Minnesota
Crookston *A, B*
Twin Cities *C*
Winona State University *B*

Mississippi
Belhaven College *B*
Jackson State University *B*

Missouri
Central Missouri State University *M*
Culver-Stockton College *B*
Fontbonne College *B*
Lincoln University *B*
Missouri Southern State College *A, B*
Missouri Western State College *B*
Northwest Missouri State University *B*
Rockhurst University *B*
University of Missouri
Kansas City *B*
Rolla *M*
William Jewell College *B*

Montana
Little Big Horn College *A*
Montana State University
Billings *B*
Montana Tech of the University of
Montana *B*
Stone Child College *A*
Western Montana College of The
University of Montana *A*

Nebraska
Chadron State College *B*
Doane College *B*
Lincoln School of Commerce *C*
Metropolitan Community College *A*
Nebraska Wesleyan University *B*
Southeast Community College
Lincoln Campus *C, A*
Union College *A, B*
University of Nebraska
Kearney *B*
Wayne State College *B*

Nevada
Community College of Southern
Nevada *A*

New Hampshire
Daniel Webster College *A, B*
Franklin Pierce College *B*
McIntosh College *C*
New Hampshire Community Technical
College
Nashua *A*
Stratham *C, A*
Plymouth State College of the University
System of New Hampshire *B*

New Jersey
Burlington County College *C, A*
Caldwell College *C, B*
DeVry Institute *A*
Essex County College *C*
Fairleigh Dickinson University *M*
Mercer County Community College *C*
Monmouth University *C*
New Jersey Institute of
Technology *B, M, D*
Ocean County College *C*
Ramapo College of New Jersey *B*

Information sciences/systems

Rutgers
- The State University of New Jersey: Camden College of Arts and Sciences *B*
- The State University of New Jersey: Newark College of Arts and Sciences *B*
- The State University of New Jersey: University College Camden *B*
- The State University of New Jersey: University College Newark *B*

St. Peter's College *C, A, B*
Salem Community College *C, A*
Seton Hall University *C, M*
Stevens Institute of Technology *M, D*

New Mexico
Albuquerque Technical-Vocational Institute *C, A*
New Mexico Highlands University *B*
New Mexico State University
- Alamogordo *A*
- Carlsbad *A*

San Juan College *A*

New York
Briarcliffe College *C*
Canisius College *B*
Cayuga County Community College *C*
City University of New York
- Baruch College *B*
- Brooklyn College *B, M*
- New York City Technical College *A*
- Queensborough Community College *A*
- York College *B*

College of St. Rose *C, B*
Columbia University
- Fu Foundation School of Engineering and Applied Science *M, D*

Dominican College of Blauvelt *B*
Erie Community College
- City Campus *A*
- North Campus *A*
- South Campus *A*

Finger Lakes Community College *C, A*
Fordham University *B*
Fulton-Montgomery Community College *A*
Genesee Community College *A*
Hartwick College *B*
Ithaca College *B*
Jefferson Community College *C, A*
Long Island University
- Brooklyn Campus *B*
- C. W. Post Campus *A, B, M*

Manhattan College *B*
Marist College *B, M*
Marymount College *C, B*
Medaille College *B*
Mercy College *B*
Molloy College *B*
New York University *B*
Niagara University *C, B*
Pace University:
- Pleasantville/Briarcliff *C, A*

Pace University *C, A*
Regents College *B*
Rochester Institute of Technology *B, M*
Russell Sage College *B*
Sage Junior College of Albany *A*
St. John's University *C, B*
Siena College *C*
State University of New York
- Albany *B, M, D*
- College at Brockport *B*
- College at Buffalo *B*
- College at Old Westbury *B*
- College of Agriculture and Technology at Cobleskill *A*
- Farmingdale *C, A*
- Oswego *B*
- Stony Brook *B*

Syracuse University *B, M, D*

Union College *B*
United States Military Academy *B*
Westchester Business Institute *C, A*
Westchester Community College *C, A*

North Carolina
Alamance Community College *A*
Appalachian State University *B*
Beaufort County Community College *A*
Blue Ridge Community College *A*
Campbell University *B*
Catawba Valley Community College *A*
Central Carolina Community College *C, A*
Central Piedmont Community College *A*
Cleveland Community College *C, A*
College of the Albemarle *A*
Durham Technical Community College *C, A*
Fayetteville Technical Community College *A*
Martin Community College *C, A*
Meredith College *B*
Mitchell Community College *C, A*
Nash Community College *A*
North Carolina Central University *M*
North Carolina Wesleyan College *B*
Rockingham Community College *C, A*
Rowan-Cabarrus Community College *C, A*
Sampson Community College *A*
Sandhills Community College *C, A*
South Piedmont Community College *A*
Surry Community College *A*
Tri-County Community College *A*
University of North Carolina
- Chapel Hill *M*

Vance-Granville Community College *A*

North Dakota
Jamestown College *B*
Mayville State University *B*
Minot State University: Bottineau Campus *A*
University of Mary *B*

Ohio
Baldwin-Wallace College *B*
Case Western Reserve University *M, D*
Cincinnati State Technical and Community College *A*
Clark State Community College *C*
College of Mount St. Joseph *A, B*
Columbus State Community College *A*
David N. Myers College *C, B*
Kent State University
- Stark Campus *B*

Kent State University *B, D*
Lakeland Community College *C, A*
Marietta College *B*
Miami-Jacobs College *C, A*
Muskingum Area Technical College *A*
Notre Dame College of Ohio *B*
Ohio Dominican College *B*
Ohio State University
- Columbus Campus *B*

Ohio University *B*
Shawnee State University *B*
Terra Community College *A*
Tiffin University *B*
University of Cincinnati *M, D*
University of Dayton *B*
University of Findlay *B*
University of Toledo *M*
Wilberforce University *B*
Youngstown State University *A, B*

Oklahoma
Northwestern Oklahoma State University *B*
Oklahoma Baptist University *B*
Oklahoma Christian University of Science and Arts *B*
Oklahoma City University *M*
Oklahoma Panhandle State University *B*
Oklahoma State University *B*

Southeastern Oklahoma State University *B*
University of Central Oklahoma *B*
Western Oklahoma State College *A*

Oregon
Lane Community College *C*

Pennsylvania
Bucks County Community College *A*
California University of Pennsylvania *A, B*
Carnegie Mellon University *B, M*
Cedar Crest College *C, B*
Clarion University of Pennsylvania *B*
College Misericordia *B*
Community College of Allegheny County *A*
Community College of Beaver County *A*
Delaware County Community College *A*
Drexel University *B, M, D*
Gannon University *B*
Harcum College *A*
Immaculata College *C, B*
La Salle University *A, B, M*
Lehigh Carbon Community College *C, A*
Lehigh University *B*
Lock Haven University of Pennsylvania *B*
Mansfield University of Pennsylvania *A, B*
Messiah College *B*
Montgomery County Community College *C, A*
Moravian College *B*
Muhlenberg College *B*
Penn State
- Abington *B*
- Altoona *A*
- Beaver *B*
- Berks *A, B*
- Delaware County *B*
- Dubois *A*
- Fayette *A*
- Hazleton *A*
- Lehigh Valley *A, B*
- McKeesport *B*
- Mont Alto *A*
- New Kensington *A, B*
- Schuylkill - Capital College *A*
- Shenango *A*
- University Park *B*
- Wilkes-Barre *A*
- Worthington Scranton *A*
- York *A*

Philadelphia University *C, B*
Robert Morris College *M*
Seton Hill College *C, B*
Shippensburg University of Pennsylvania *M*
Slippery Rock University of Pennsylvania *B*
Susquehanna University *B*
Temple University *B, M*
Thiel College *A, B*
Tri-State Business Institute *A*
University of Pittsburgh
- Greensburg *B*

University of Pittsburgh *B, M, D*
University of Scranton *B*
Westmoreland County Community College *C*
Widener University *A, B*
Wilkes University *B*
York College of Pennsylvania *B, M*

Puerto Rico
Humacao Community College *A*
Inter American University of Puerto Rico
- Barranquitas Campus *B*
- Bayamon Campus *B*
- Metropolitan Campus *D*

National College of Business and Technology *A*
Universidad Metropolitana *B*

University of Puerto Rico
- Mayaguez Campus *B*

University of the Sacred Heart *B*

Rhode Island
Johnson & Wales University *B*
Salve Regina University *B, M*

South Carolina
Charleston Southern University *B*
Claflin University *B*
Clemson University *B*
College of Charleston *B*
Orangeburg-Calhoun Technical College *C*
Spartanburg Methodist College *A*
Trident Technical College *A*
Wofford College *C*

South Dakota
Dakota State University *A, B, M*

Tennessee
Belmont University *B, M*
Chattanooga State Technical Community College *C, A*
David Lipscomb University *B*
Freed-Hardeman University *B*
Lee University *B*
Middle Tennessee State University *B*
Tusculum College *B*
University of Tennessee
- Knoxville *M*

Texas
Amarillo College *C, A*
Brookhaven College *A*
Central Texas College *C, A*
Collin County Community College District *C, A*
DeVry Institute of Technology
- Irving *B*

El Paso Community College *C, A*
Galveston College *C, A*
Houston Baptist University *M*
Howard Payne University *B*
Lamar University *M*
LeTourneau University *B*
Lee College *C, A*
Lubbock Christian University *B*
Midland College *C, A*
Palo Alto College *A*
Panola College *C, A*
St. Philip's College *A*
Southwestern Adventist University *A, B, T*
Texas A&M International University *B*
Texas A&M University
- Commerce *B*
- Corpus Christi *B*

Texas State Technical College
- Harlingen *A*
- Sweetwater *A*
- Waco *C, A*

Texas Wesleyan University *B*
University of Houston
- Victoria *B*

University of Houston *B*
University of Mary Hardin-Baylor *B, M, T*
University of North Texas *M, D*
University of Texas
- Dallas *B*
- Pan American *B*

Victoria College *C, A*

Utah
College of Eastern Utah *C*
LDS Business College *A*
Salt Lake Community College *A*
Snow College *A*
Utah State University *B, M*
Weber State University *B*
Westminster College *B, M*

Vermont
Champlain College *A, B*
College of St. Joseph in Vermont *B*

Johnson State College A, B
University of Vermont B

Virginia
Blue Ridge Community College A
Central Virginia Community College A
Danville Community College C
ECPI College of Technology C, A
Eastern Mennonite University B
Ferrum College B
George Mason University M
J. Sargeant Reynolds Community
  College A
James Madison University B
Roanoke College B
Shenandoah University C
Thomas Nelson Community College A
University of Richmond C, A
Virginia Commonwealth University C, B
Virginia Polytechnic Institute and State
  University B, M
Wytheville Community College A

Washington
Big Bend Community College C, A
Centralia College A
City University C
Clark College C
Eastern Washington University B
Edmonds Community College C
Everett Community College C, A
Green River Community College C, A
North Seattle Community College C, A
Olympic College C, A
Renton Technical College C
Skagit Valley College A
South Puget Sound Community
  College C, A
South Seattle Community College C, A
Walla Walla Community College C, A
Wenatchee Valley College A
Yakima Valley Community College A

West Virginia
Alderson-Broaddus College B
Marshall University B, M
University of Charleston A, B
West Liberty State College B
West Virginia Northern Community
  College A
West Virginia Wesleyan College B

Wisconsin
Cardinal Stritch University B, M
Milwaukee Area Technical College A
Milwaukee School of Engineering B
Northland College B
University of Wisconsin
  Green Bay B
  Madison B, M, D
  Parkside B
  Superior B
Wisconsin Indianhead Technical
  College A

Wyoming
Laramie County Community College A
Sheridan College A
University of Wyoming B

Inorganic chemistry

Florida
Florida State University B, M, D

Iowa
Iowa State University M, D

Kansas
Pratt Community College A

Maryland
Johns Hopkins University B

Massachusetts
Hampshire College B
Harvard College B

Mount Holyoke College M
Tufts University M, D
Worcester Polytechnic Institute B, M

New Jersey
Stevens Institute of Technology M, D

New York
Columbia University
  Graduate School M, D
Fordham University M
Sarah Lawrence College B
State University of New York
  Albany D

North Carolina
University of North Carolina
  Chapel Hill M, D

Oregon
University of Oregon M, D

Texas
University of North Texas M, D

Utah
University of Utah M, D

Vermont
Bennington College B

Wisconsin
Marquette University M, D

Institutional food production

Alabama
Community College of the Air Force A
Enterprise State Junior College A
Gadsden State Community College C
Shelton State Community College C
Wallace State Community College at
  Hanceville C, A

Arizona
Arizona Western College A
Phoenix College C, A

Arkansas
Southern Arkansas University
  Tech C

California
American River College A
Bakersfield College A
California State University
  Long Beach C
Cerritos Community College A
Chaffey Community College C
College of the Redwoods C
College of the Sequoias C
Contra Costa College A
Cypress College C, A
Diablo Valley College C
Fresno City College C, A
Long Beach City College C, A
Los Angeles Mission College A
Los Angeles Trade and Technical
  College C, A
Merced College A
Modesto Junior College C
Palomar College C, A
San Joaquin Delta College A
Santa Rosa Junior College C
Shasta College A
Sierra College C, A
Southwestern College C
Yuba College C

Colorado
Arapahoe Community College A
Art Institute
  of Colorado A, B
Front Range Community College C, A
Pikes Peak Community College A
Pueblo Community College A

Connecticut
Gateway Community College C, A
Manchester Community-Technical
  College A
University of New Haven A

Florida
Gulf Coast Community College A
Miami-Dade Community College A
Pensacola Junior College A

Georgia
Abraham Baldwin Agricultural
  College A
Darton College A
Georgia Military College A

Hawaii
University of Hawaii
  Honolulu Community College C, A
  Kapiolani Community
    College C, A

Idaho
Idaho State University C, A
Ricks College A

Illinois
City Colleges of Chicago
  Malcolm X College A
John Wood Community College C
William Rainey Harper College C, A

Indiana
Marian College B

Iowa
Des Moines Area Community College C
Indian Hills Community College C, A
Iowa Western Community College A
Kirkwood Community College C, A

Kansas
Barton County Community College C
Johnson County Community
  College C, A

Kentucky
Eastern Kentucky University A
Murray State University A

Louisiana
Delgado Community College A

Maine
Eastern Maine Technical College C
Southern Maine Technical College A
Washington County Technical
  College C, A

Maryland
Montgomery College
  Rockville Campus C, A

Michigan
Andrews University A
Bay de Noc Community College C
Eastern Michigan University M
Ferris State University C, A
Grand Rapids Community College A
Henry Ford Community College A
Lansing Community College A
Madonna University B
Montcalm Community College C, A
Mott Community College A
Oakland Community College A

Minnesota
Alexandria Technical College C

Mississippi
Copiah-Lincoln Community College A
Hinds Community College C, A
Mississippi Gulf Coast Community
  College
    Perkinston C

Missouri
Penn Valley Community College C

St. Louis Community College
  St. Louis Community College at
    Forest Park A

Nebraska
Central Community College C, A
Metropolitan Community College C, A
Southeast Community College
  Lincoln Campus A

New Jersey
Brookdale Community College A

New Mexico
Albuquerque Technical-Vocational
  Institute C

New York
City University of New York
  La Guardia Community College A
Erie Community College
  North Campus A
Fulton-Montgomery Community
  College A
Mohawk Valley Community College A
Rochester Institute of Technology B, M
Rockland Community College A
State University of New York
  College of Technology at Delhi A
Tompkins-Cortland Community
  College A
Westchester Community College A

North Carolina
Asheville Buncombe Technical
  Community College A
Cape Fear Community College A
Johnston Community College C
Wilkes Community College C, A

North Dakota
North Dakota State College of Science A

Ohio
Cincinnati State Technical and
  Community College C
Kent State University B
Notre Dame College of Ohio B
Sinclair Community College C, A

Oklahoma
Oklahoma State University B, M

Pennsylvania
Bucks County Community College A
Butler County Community College A
Community College of Allegheny
  County C, A
Community College of Philadelphia C, A
Harrisburg Area Community
  College C, A
Immaculata College B
Luzerne County Community
  College C, A
Montgomery County Community
  College A
Penn State
  University Park C
Pennsylvania College of Technology A
Seton Hill College B
Westmoreland County Community
  College A

South Carolina
Horry-Georgetown Technical College A
South Carolina State University B

Texas
Collin County Community College
  District C
El Paso Community College A
Hill College A
Houston Community College
  System C, A
Lamar University B
St. Philip's College A
Sam Houston State University B
San Jacinto College
  North C, A

Institutional food production (continued)

Tarrant County College *A*
Texas State Technical College
   Harlingen *C, A*
   Waco *C, A*
Texas Woman's University *M*

Virginia
J. Sargeant Reynolds Community
   College *C, A*
Northern Virginia Community College *A*

Washington
North Seattle Community College *C*
Renton Technical College *C*
Yakima Valley Community College *C*

West Virginia
Fairmont State College *A*

Wisconsin
Blackhawk Technical College *A*
Gateway Technical College *A*
Northeast Wisconsin Technical
   College *C*
Southwest Wisconsin Technical
   College *C, A*
Waukesha County Technical College *C*
Western Wisconsin Technical College *C*

Insurance marketing

Alabama
Enterprise State Junior College *A*
Wallace State Community College at
   Hanceville *A*

California
City College of San Francisco *A*
Fresno City College *C, A*
Pasadena City College *C*
San Francisco State University *B*

Colorado
Community College of Aurora *C*
Northeastern Junior College *A*

District of Columbia
Howard University *B*

Florida
Florida Community College at
   Jacksonville *A*

Illinois
Richland Community College *A*
William Rainey Harper College *C, A*

Indiana
Ball State University *B*
Indiana State University *B*
Vincennes University *A*

Iowa
Drake University *B*
Kirkwood Community College *A*

Kansas
Dodge City Community College *C, A*

Maine
Husson College *B*

Michigan
Bay de Noc Community College *C*
Lansing Community College *A*
Olivet College *B*

New York
College of Insurance *C*
New York Institute of Technology *A*
Westchester Community College *C*

North Carolina
Central Piedmont Community College *A*
Edgecombe Community College *C*
Fayetteville Technical Community
   College *A*
Lenoir Community College *C*
Sampson Community College *C*

North Dakota
North Dakota State College of Science *A*

Ohio
Youngstown State University *A, B*

Oklahoma
Oklahoma City Community College *C*
Tulsa Community College *C, A*

Pennsylvania
La Salle University *A, B*

Puerto Rico
Caribbean University *A*

Texas
University of North Texas *B, M*

Washington
Highline Community College *A*

Insurance/risk management

Alabama
Wallace State Community College at
   Hanceville *A*

California
Fresno City College *C, A*
Long Beach City College *C, A*
Los Angeles Southwest College *A*
Merced College *A*
San Francisco State University *B*
Santa Ana College *C, A*

Colorado
Community College of Aurora *C*

Connecticut
University of Connecticut *B*
University of Hartford *B, M*

District of Columbia
Howard University *B*

Florida
Daytona Beach Community College *C*
Florida Community College at
   Jacksonville *C*
Florida International University *B*
Florida State University *B*
Miami-Dade Community College *C*
University of Florida *B, M*

Georgia
Georgia State University *B, M, D*
University of Georgia *B*

Illinois
Bradley University *B*
Illinois State University *B*
Illinois Wesleyan University *B*
Roosevelt University *B*
William Rainey Harper College *C, A*

Indiana
Ball State University *B*
Indiana State University *B*

Iowa
Kirkwood Community College *A*

Kansas
Hutchinson Community College *A*

Kentucky
Eastern Kentucky University *B*
Thomas More College *B*

Louisiana
University of Louisiana at Lafayette *B*

Massachusetts
Northeastern University *B*

Michigan
Ferris State University *C*
Lansing Community College *A*
Oakland Community College *C, A*

Olivet College *B*
Western Michigan University *B*

Minnesota
Minnesota State University, Mankato *B*
St. Cloud State University *B*
University of Minnesota
   Twin Cities *B*
University of St. Thomas *M*

Mississippi
Delta State University *B*
Mississippi State University *B*
University of Mississippi *B*

Missouri
Southwest Missouri State University *B*

New Jersey
Thomas Edison State College *A, B*

New York
College of Insurance *A, B, M*
Hudson Valley Community College *A*
Nassau Community College *C*
Onondaga Community College *A*
Pace University:
   Pleasantville/Briarcliff *M*
Pace University *M*
Suffolk County Community College *A*

North Carolina
Appalachian State University *B*
Central Piedmont Community College *A*
Fayetteville Technical Community
   College *A*

Ohio
Bowling Green State University *B*
Ohio State University
   Columbus Campus *B*

Oklahoma
Oklahoma City Community College *C*
Tulsa Community College *C, A*
University of Central Oklahoma *B*

Pennsylvania
Community College of Allegheny
   County *C*
Gannon University *B*
La Salle University *B*
Mercyhurst College *B*
Penn State
   University Park *B*
Pittsburgh Technical Institute *A*
Temple University *B, M, D*
University of Pennsylvania *B, M, D*

South Carolina
Limestone College *A*
University of South Carolina *B*

Tennessee
University of Memphis *B*

Texas
Baylor University *B*
Houston Community College
   System *C, A*
University of North Texas *B, M, D*

Virginia
J. Sargeant Reynolds Community
   College *C*

Washington
Seattle University *B*
Washington State University *B*

Wisconsin
Chippewa Valley Technical College *C*
Madison Area Technical College *A*
University of Wisconsin
   La Crosse *B*
   Madison *B, M, D*
Waukesha County Technical College *A*

Interdisciplinary studies

Alabama
Alabama Agricultural and Mechanical
   University *B*
Birmingham-Southern College *B*
Huntingdon College *B*
Northeast Alabama Community
   College *A*
Northwest-Shoals Community College *A*
Snead State Community College *A*
Spring Hill College *B*
Stillman College *B*
Troy State University *B*
University of Alabama
   Huntsville *M, D*
University of Alabama *B, M, D*
University of South Alabama *B*

Alaska
Alaska Bible College *B*
University of Alaska
   Anchorage *B, M*
   Fairbanks *A, B, M, D*

Arizona
Arizona State University *B*
Pima Community College *A*
Prescott College *B, M*
University of Arizona *B*

Arkansas
Arkansas Tech University *M*
Hendrix College *B*
John Brown University *B*
Westark College *A*

California
California State University
   Bakersfield *B*
   Chico *B, M*
   Fullerton *B, M*
   Hayward *B, M*
   Long Beach *M*
   Los Angeles *B*
   Monterey Bay *B*
Chabot College *A*
Claremont McKenna College *B*
Compton Community College *A*
De Anza College *A*
Dominican University of California *B*
Holy Names College *B*
Hope International University *B*
John F. Kennedy University *M*
Master's College *B*
Monterey Institute of International
   Studies *M*
Mount San Jacinto College *A*
National University *B*
Palo Verde College *A*
Pepperdine University *B*
Pomona College *B*
Saddleback College *A*
San Diego State University *B, M*
Sonoma State University *B, M*
Thomas Aquinas College *B*
United States International University *A*
University of California
   Berkeley *B*
   Irvine *B, M, D*
University of Southern California *B*
University of the Pacific *B*
Vanguard University of Southern
   California *B*

Colorado
Colorado College *B*
Naropa University *B*
Pikes Peak Community College *C*
Red Rocks Community College *A*
University of Colorado
   Boulder *B*
   Colorado Springs *B*
University of Northern
   Colorado *B, M, D*

Interdisciplinary studies

Connecticut
Central Connecticut State University B
Eastern Connecticut State University B
Naugatuck Valley Community-Technical College A
Trinity College B
University of Connecticut B
University of Hartford B
Wesleyan University B

Delaware
University of Delaware B, M, D

District of Columbia
American University B, M
George Washington University B, M
Georgetown University B
Trinity College B

Florida
Brevard Community College A
Clearwater Christian College A
Eckerd College B
Florida Atlantic University D
Florida Institute of Technology B
Hillsborough Community College A
New College of the University of South Florida B
Polk Community College A
Southeastern College of the Assemblies of God B
University of Miami D
University of South Florida B
University of West Florida B
Valencia Community College A

Georgia
Agnes Scott College B
Berry College B
Covenant College B
Georgia State University B, M
Morehouse College B
Oxford College of Emory University B
Piedmont College B
University of Georgia B
Waycross College A
Wesleyan College B

Hawaii
Brigham Young University Hawaii B
Chaminade University of Honolulu A, B
University of Hawaii Manoa B

Idaho
Boise State University M
Idaho State University B, M
Ricks College A
University of Idaho B, M

Illinois
Barat College B
Black Hawk College C, A
Columbia College B, M
De Paul University M
Governors State University B
Greenville College B
Illinois College B
Illinois Eastern Community Colleges
    Frontier Community College A
    Lincoln Trail College A
    Olney Central College A
Illinois Institute of Technology B
Knox College B
Millikin University B
Monmouth College B
Moraine Valley Community College A
Parkland College A
Roosevelt University B
Sauk Valley Community College A
Shimer College B
Southern Illinois University Carbondale B
Trinity International University M
Triton College A
University of Chicago B
Wheaton College B, M

Indiana
DePauw University B
Goshen College B
Manchester College B
Purdue University B
St. Mary-of-the-Woods College B
University of Notre Dame M, D

Iowa
Briar Cliff College B
Coe College B
Cornell College B
Grinnell College B
Hawkeye Community College A
Iowa State University B, M
Kirkwood Community College A
Luther College B
Morningside College B
Mount Mercy College B
St. Ambrose University B
University of Iowa B, M, D

Kansas
Kansas State University A
McPherson College B
Newman University B
St. Mary College B
Southwestern College B

Kentucky
Alice Lloyd College B
Berea College B
Maysville Community College A
University of Kentucky B
University of Louisville M
Western Kentucky University B, M

Louisiana
Centenary College of Louisiana B

Maine
Bowdoin College B
College of the Atlantic M
Unity College B
University of Maine
    Augusta B
    Farmington B
    Fort Kent B

Maryland
Bowie State University B
Cecil Community College A
Charles County Community College A
Frostburg State University M
Goucher College B
Loyola College in Maryland B
Mount St. Mary's College B
St. John's College B, M
St. Mary's College of Maryland B
Towson University B
University of Baltimore B
University of Maryland
    Baltimore County B
    College Park B
    University College B
Villa Julie College B
Washington College B
Wor-Wic Community College A

Massachusetts
Amherst College B
Anna Maria College B
Assumption College B
Bay Path College B
Boston College B
Boston University B, M, D
Brandeis University B
Cambridge College M
Clark University B, M, D
Emmanuel College B
Fitchburg State College B
Gordon College B
Hampshire College B
Harvard College B
Lasell College B
Lesley College M
Massachusetts College of Liberal Arts B
North Shore Community College A
Northeastern University B
Regis College B
Simon's Rock College of Bard B
Stonehill College B
Suffolk University B
Tufts University B, M, D
University of Massachusetts
    Amherst B
    Boston B
    Dartmouth B
Wheaton College B

Michigan
Albion College B
Bay de Noc Community College A
Calvin College B
Central Michigan University B
Eastern Michigan University B, M
Hope College B
Lake Superior State University B
Lawrence Technological University B
Marygrove College A, B
Northern Michigan University B
Oakland University B
Olivet College B
Rochester College B
University of Michigan B, M
Wayne State University B, M, D
Western Michigan University B

Minnesota
Augsburg College B
Bethel College B
Carleton College B
College of St. Benedict B
College of St. Catherine: St. Paul Campus B
Concordia University: St. Paul B
Gustavus Adolphus College B
Hamline University B
Inver Hills Community College A
Macalester College B
Martin Luther College B
Metropolitan State University B
Minnesota State University, Mankato M
Moorhead State University B
Northland Community & Technical College A
St. Cloud State University M
St. John's University B
St. Mary's University of Minnesota B, M
St. Olaf College B
Southwest State University B
University of Minnesota
    Duluth B
    Morris B
    Twin Cities B, M, D
Vermilion Community College A
Winona State University B

Mississippi
Mississippi State University B

Missouri
College of the Ozarks B
Columbia College A, B
Missouri Baptist College B
Missouri Western State College B
University of Missouri
    Columbia B
    Kansas City B, D
    St. Louis B
Washington University B
Webster University B
William Jewell College B
William Woods University B

Montana
Little Big Horn College A
Montana State University Bozeman B
University of Montana-Missoula D

Nebraska
Creighton University M
Dana College B
Doane College B
Hastings College B
University of Nebraska
    Kearney B
    Omaha B
Wayne State College B

Nevada
University of Nevada Las Vegas B

New Hampshire
Antioch New England Graduate School M
Daniel Webster College B
Dartmouth College B
Franklin Pierce College B
Keene State College B
New Hampshire Community Technical College Nashua A
Notre Dame College B, M
Plymouth State College of the University System of New Hampshire B
University of New Hampshire B

New Jersey
Bloomfield College B
County College of Morris A
Mercer County Community College C
Monmouth University B
Princeton University B
Richard Stockton College of New Jersey B
Rutgers
    The State University of New Jersey: Camden College of Arts and Sciences B
    The State University of New Jersey: Cook College B
    The State University of New Jersey: Douglass College B
    The State University of New Jersey: Livingston College B
    The State University of New Jersey: New Brunswick Graduate Campus D
    The State University of New Jersey: Newark College of Arts and Sciences B
    The State University of New Jersey: Rutgers College B
    The State University of New Jersey: University College Camden B
    The State University of New Jersey: University College New Brunswick B
    The State University of New Jersey: University College Newark B

New Mexico
Dona Ana Branch Community College of New Mexico State University A
New Mexico Institute of Mining and Technology A, B
New Mexico State University Alamogordo A
New Mexico State University A, B, M, D
Western New Mexico University M

New York
Alfred University B
Bard College B
City University of New York
    Baruch College B
    Queens College B
Clarkson University B
Columbia University
    Columbia College B
    Teachers College M, D
Cornell University B
Elmira College B
Eugene Lang College/New School University B
Hamilton College B
Hartwick College B

Interdisciplinary studies

Herkimer County Community College *A*
Hobart and William Smith Colleges *B*
Hofstra University *B, M*
Jamestown Community College *A*
Long Island University
    C. W. Post Campus *M*
Marist College *B*
Marymount College *B*
Marymount Manhattan College *B*
Molloy College *B*
Mount St. Mary College *B, T*
New York Institute of Technology *B*
New York University *B, M*
Nyack College *B*
Orange County Community College *A*
Rensselaer Polytechnic Institute *M, D*
Rochester Institute of
    Technology *A, B, M*
Russell Sage College *B*
St. Francis College *B*
St. John Fisher College *B*
St. Lawrence University *B*
Skidmore College *B*
State University of New York
    Binghamton *B*
    College at Brockport *B*
    College at Buffalo *B, M*
    College at Fredonia *B, M*
    College at Oneonta *B*
    New Paltz *B*
    Purchase *B*
    Stony Brook *B*
United States Military Academy *B*
University of Rochester *B*
Vassar College *B*
Wells College *B*

North Carolina
Appalachian State University *B*
Brevard College *B*
Catawba College *B*
Chowan College *B*
Davidson College *B*
East Carolina University *M, D*
Greensboro College *B*
Johnston Community College *A*
Lees-McRae College *B*
Methodist College *B*
North Carolina State University *B*
Salem College *B*
Western Piedmont Community
    College *A*

North Dakota
Mayville State University *B*
University of North Dakota *B*
Valley City State University *B*
Williston State College *C, A*

Ohio
Bowling Green State University
    Firelands College *A*
Bowling Green State University *B, M, D*
Capital University *B*
Chatfield College *A*
Edison State Community College *A*
Franklin University *B*
John Carroll University *B*
Kent State University *B*
Lourdes College *B*
Miami University
    Middletown Campus *A*
    Oxford Campus *B*
Mount Union College *B*
Ohio Dominican College *A, B*
Ohio State University
    Columbus Campus *M*
Ohio University
    Zanesville Campus *B*
Ohio University *M, D*
Ohio Wesleyan University *B*
Owens Community College
    Toledo *A*
Terra Community College *A*
Union Institute *B, D*
University of Cincinnati *M, D*

University of Dayton *M*
University of Toledo *B*
Youngstown State University *B*

Oklahoma
Cameron University *A, B*
Connors State College *A*
Oklahoma Baptist University *B*
Oklahoma Christian University of
    Science and Arts *B*
Oklahoma State University *M*
Oral Roberts University *B*
Southern Nazarene University *B*

Oregon
Chemeketa Community College *A*
Concordia University *B*
Eastern Oregon University *B*
George Fox University *B*
Marylhurst University *B, M*
Northwest Christian College *A, B*
Oregon State University *M*
Portland State University *B*
Reed College *B, M*
Southern Oregon University *B*
University of Portland *B*
Western Baptist College *B*

Pennsylvania
Allegheny College *B*
Alvernia College *A*
Bryn Athyn College of the New
    Church *A, B*
Bucknell University *B, M*
Chatham College *B*
Franklin and Marshall College *B*
Gettysburg College *B*
Holy Family College *B*
Juniata College *B*
Lackawanna Junior College *C*
Lafayette College *B*
Lehigh University *B, M, D*
Lock Haven University of
    Pennsylvania *M*
Marywood University *B, D*
Penn State
    Harrisburg *B*
    University Park *B, M, D*
Rosemont College *B*
Seton Hill College *B*
Temple University *B*
University of Pittsburgh *C, B, M*
Villanova University *B*
York College of Pennsylvania *B*

Puerto Rico
University of Puerto Rico
    Rio Piedras Campus *B*
University of the Sacred Heart *B*

South Carolina
Aiken Technical College *A*
Coastal Carolina University *B*
Florence-Darlington Technical College *A*
Lander University *B*
Midlands Technical College *C, A*
North Greenville College *B*
Trident Technical College *A*
University of South Carolina
    Aiken *B*
    Spartanburg *B*

South Dakota
Augustana College *B*
Sinte Gleska University *B*
South Dakota School of Mines and
    Technology *B*
University of South Dakota *M*

Tennessee
Austin Peay State University *B, T*
Carson-Newman College *B*
East Tennessee State University *B, M, T*
Lambuth University *B*
Lane College *B*
Martin Methodist College *B*
Rhodes College *B*
Tennessee Technological University *B, T*

Tennessee Temple University *A, B*
Tennessee Wesleyan College *B, T*
Tusculum College *B*
University of Memphis *B*
University of Tennessee
    Martin *B*
Vanderbilt University *B, M, D*
Walters State Community College *A*

Texas
Abilene Christian University *B, M, T*
Amber University *B, M*
Angelo State University *M*
Austin College *B*
Baylor University *B*
Brazosport College *A*
Central Texas College *B*
Coastal Bend College *A*
Concordia University at Austin *B*
Dallas Baptist University *B, M*
Howard Payne University *B, T*
Lamar University *B*
LeTourneau University *B*
Lubbock Christian University *B*
Midland College *A*
Midwestern State University *B*
Odessa College *A*
Prairie View A&M University *B*
Sam Houston State University *B*
Southwest Texas State University *M*
Stephen F. Austin State University *B, M*
Sul Ross State University *B*
Tarleton State University *B, T*
Texas A&M International University *M*
Texas A&M University
    Commerce *B*
    Corpus Christi *B, M*
    Kingsville *B*
    Texarkana *B, M*
Texas A&M University *B*
Texas Tech University *B, M*
Texas Wesleyan University *B*
Texas Woman's University *B*
Tyler Junior College *A*
University of Dallas *B*
University of Houston
    Downtown *B*
    Victoria *B, M, T*
University of Houston *B*
University of Mary Hardin-Baylor *B*
University of North Texas *B, M*
University of Texas
    Arlington *B, M*
    Brownsville *B*
    Dallas *B, M*
    El Paso *B, M*
    Pan American *B*
    San Antonio *B*
    Tyler *B, M*
University of the Incarnate Word *B, M*
West Texas A&M University *B, M*

Utah
Utah State University *M*

Vermont
Bennington College *B*
Burlington College *B*
Castleton State College *B*
Community College of Vermont *A*
Goddard College *M*
Johnson State College *B*
Marlboro College *B*
Norwich University *M*
Sterling College *A, B*

Virginia
College of William and Mary *B*
Emory & Henry College *B*
George Mason University *B, M*
Hollins University *B, M*
Liberty University *B, T*
Norfolk State University *B*
Patrick Henry Community College *A*
Radford University *B*
Sweet Briar College *B*

Thomas Nelson Community College *A*
University of Richmond *B*
University of Virginia's College at
    Wise *B*
Virginia Highlands Community
    College *A*
Virginia Polytechnic Institute and State
    University *B*
Virginia State University *M*
Virginia Union University *B*
Virginia Wesleyan College *B*

Washington
Central Washington University *B, M*
Eastern Washington University *B, M*
Evergreen State College *B*
Gonzaga University *B, M*
Heritage College *A, B*
University of Puget Sound *B*
University of Washington *B*
Washington State University *D*
Western Washington University *B, M*
Whitworth College *B*

West Virginia
Bethany College *B*
College of West Virginia *B*
Concord College *B*
Fairmont State College *B*
Glenville State College *B*
West Virginia State College *A*
West Virginia University *B*

Wisconsin
Beloit College *B*
Marquette University *B, M, D*
Northland College *B*
Silver Lake College *B*
University of Wisconsin
    Milwaukee *B, D*
    Parkside *B*
Wisconsin Lutheran College *B*

Wyoming
Sheridan College *A*
University of Wyoming *B, M*

Interior architecture

Alabama
Auburn University *B*

Arizona
Arizona State University *B, M*
Phoenix College *A*

California
California College of Arts and Crafts *B*
California State University
    Long Beach *B*
University of San Francisco *B*

Colorado
University of Colorado
    Denver *M*

Connecticut
University of Bridgeport *B*
University of New Haven *A, B*

Florida
Florida International University *B*
Palm Beach Community College *A*

Idaho
University of Idaho *B*

Illinois
Columbia College *M*
Harrington Institute of Interior
    Design *C, A, B*
School of the Art Institute of Chicago *B*
Triton College *C, A*

Iowa
Iowa State University *B, M*

Kansas
Central Christian College *A*

Kansas State University B
Louisiana
Delgado Community College A
Louisiana State University and
  Agricultural and Mechanical
  College B
Louisiana Tech University B
University of Louisiana at Lafayette B
Maryland
Community College of Baltimore County
  Catonsville C, A
Harford Community College C, A
University of Maryland
  Eastern Shore B
Massachusetts
Bay Path College A
Boston Architectural Center B, M
Newbury College A
Pine Manor College B
Michigan
Central Michigan University B
Lansing Community College A
Lawrence Technological University B
Michigan State University B
Northern Michigan University B
Mississippi
University of Southern Mississippi B
Missouri
Southeast Missouri State University B
St. Louis Community College
  St. Louis Community College at
    Meramec A
Washington University M
Nebraska
Metropolitan Community College A
Nevada
University of Nevada
  Las Vegas B
New York
Cornell University B
Onondaga Community College A
Parsons School of Design B
Suffolk County Community College A
Villa Maria College of Buffalo A
North Carolina
Cape Fear Community College A
Ohio
Bowling Green State University B
Kent State University B
Ohio State University
  Columbus Campus B
Oklahoma
University of Oklahoma B
Oregon
University of Oregon B, M
Pennsylvania
Indiana University of Pennsylvania B
La Roche College B
Northampton County Area Community
  College A
South Carolina
Converse College B
Texas
Lamar University B
St. Philip's College A
Sam Houston State University B
Southwest Texas State University B
Stephen F. Austin State University B
Texas A&M University
  Kingsville B, M
Texas Tech University B
University of Houston B
University of North Texas B, M

University of Texas
  Arlington B
  San Antonio B
Utah
LDS Business College A
Virginia
Longwood College B
Washington
Seattle Pacific University B
Spokane Falls Community College A
Washington State University B, M
Wisconsin
University of Wisconsin
  Madison M

Interior design

Alabama
Northwest-Shoals Community College C
University of Alabama B
Wallace State Community College at
  Hanceville A
Arizona
Mesa Community College A
Northern Arizona University B
Phoenix College A
Scottsdale Community College A
University of Advancing Computer
  Technology A, B
Arkansas
Harding University B
California
Academy of Art College C, A, B, M
Allan Hancock College A
American River College A
Art Center College of Design B, M
Bakersfield College A
Brooks College A
California State University
  Chico B
  Fresno B
  Long Beach B, M
  Sacramento B
Canada College C, A
Cerritos Community College A
Chaffey Community College C, A
City College of San Francisco A
College of the Desert A
College of the Sequoias C
Contra Costa College A
Cuesta College C, A
Fashion Institute of Design and
  Merchandising
    San Francisco A
Fashion Institute of Design and
  Merchandising A
Las Positas College C, A
Los Angeles Harbor College A
Los Angeles Mission College C, A
Marymount College A
Modesto Junior College C, A
Monterey Peninsula College C, A
Moorpark College C, A
Mount San Antonio College C, A
Ohlone College C, A
Orange Coast College C, A
Pacific Union College A, B
Palomar College C, A
Saddleback College C, A
San Diego State University B
San Joaquin Delta College C, A
San Jose State University B
Santa Rosa Junior College C
Sierra College C
Solano Community College C, A
Southwestern College C, A
University of San Francisco B
Ventura College A
West Valley College C, A

Colorado
Arapahoe Community College C, A
Art Institute
  of Colorado B
Colorado State University B
Rocky Mountain College of Art &
  Design B
Technical Trades Institute A
Connecticut
Paier College of Art C, B
University of New Haven C, A, B
Delaware
Delaware Technical and Community
  College
    Terry Campus A
District of Columbia
George Washington University M
Howard University B
Florida
Art Institute
  of Fort Lauderdale C, A, B
Broward Community College A
Daytona Beach Community College A
Florida Community College at
  Jacksonville A
Florida International University B
Florida State University B, M
Indian River Community College A
International Academy of Merchandising
  and Design A, B
International Fine Arts College A
Palm Beach Community College A
Ringling School of Art and Design B
Seminole Community College A
University of Florida B
Georgia
American InterContinental
  University A, B
Art Institute
  of Atlanta B
Atlanta College of Art B
Brenau University B
Georgia Southern University B
Gwinnett Technical Institute A
Savannah College of Art and
  Design B, M
University of Georgia B
Valdosta State University B
Hawaii
Chaminade University of Honolulu B
Idaho
Ricks College A
University of Idaho B
Illinois
Columbia College B, M
Harrington Institute of Interior
  Design C, A, B
International Academy of Merchandising
  and Design B
Joliet Junior College A
Prairie State College A
Southern Illinois University
  Carbondale B
Triton College C, A
William Rainey Harper College A
Indiana
Indiana State University B
Indiana University
  Bloomington B, M
Indiana University--Purdue University
  Indiana University-Purdue
    University Fort Wayne A
  Indiana University-Purdue
    University Indianapolis A
Ivy Tech State College
  Northcentral A
  Southwest C, A
Marian College A
Purdue University B

Vincennes University A
Iowa
Drake University B
Hawkeye Community College A
University of Northern Iowa B
Kansas
Kansas State University B
University of Kansas B, M
Kentucky
Murray State University B
University of Kentucky B
University of Louisville B
Louisiana
Northwestern State University B
Maryland
Anne Arundel Community College A
Community College of Baltimore County
  Catonsville C, A
Harford Community College A
Maryland Institute College of Art C, B
Montgomery College
  Rockville Campus A
University of Maryland
  Eastern Shore B
Massachusetts
Atlantic Union College B
Bay Path College C
Becker College C, A
Boston Architectural Center B
Endicott College C, A, B
Massachusetts Bay Community
  College C
Mount Ida College A, B
Newbury College A
Suffolk University C, B, M
University of Massachusetts
  Amherst B
Wentworth Institute of Technology B
Michigan
Adrian College A
Baker College
  of Auburn Hills A
  of Mount Clemens A
  of Muskegon A
  of Owosso A
Center for Creative Studies: College of
  Art and Design B
Cranbrook Academy of Art M
Delta College A
Eastern Michigan University B
Henry Ford Community College A
Kendall College of Art and Design B
Lawrence Technological University B
Macomb Community College C, A
Michigan State University M
University of Michigan B
Western Michigan University B
Minnesota
Alexandria Technical College C, A
Dakota County Technical College C, A
Minnesota State University, Mankato B
University of Minnesota
  Twin Cities B
Mississippi
Mississippi College B
Mississippi Gulf Coast Community
  College
    Perkinston A
Mississippi University for Women B
Missouri
Central Missouri State University B
Maryville University of Saint Louis B
William Woods University B
New Hampshire
Hesser College A
New Hampshire Community Technical
  College
    Manchester C

Interior design

New Jersey
Berkeley College A
Brookdale Community College A
Centenary College A, B
Kean University B

New York
Broome Community College C
Cornell University B, M
Dowling College B
Fashion Institute of Technology A, B
Institute of Design and Construction A
Marymount College C, B
Monroe Community College C, A
Nassau Community College C, A
New York Institute of Technology B
New York School of Interior
 Design C, A, B, M
Onondaga Community College A
Pace University:
 Pleasantville/Briarcliff C
Pace University C
Parsons School of Design C, A, B, T
Pratt Institute B, M
Rochester Institute of
 Technology A, B, M
Sage Junior College of Albany A
School of Visual Arts B
Suffolk County Community College A
Syracuse University B, M
Villa Maria College of Buffalo A

North Carolina
Campbell University B
Cape Fear Community College A
Central Piedmont Community College A
East Carolina University B
Halifax Community College C, A
High Point University B
Meredith College B
Randolph Community College A
Salem College B
University of North Carolina
 Greensboro B, M, T
Western Carolina University B
Western Piedmont Community
 College A

North Dakota
North Dakota State University B

Ohio
Ashland University B
Bowling Green State University B
Cleveland Institute of Art B
College of Mount St. Joseph C, A, B
Columbus College of Art and Design B
Davis College A
Kent State University
 Stark Campus B
Kent State University B
Mount Vernon Nazarene College B
Ohio State University
 Columbus Campus B, M
Ohio University B
University of Akron B
University of Cincinnati B
Ursuline College B

Oklahoma
Oklahoma Christian University of
 Science and Arts B
Oklahoma State University B
Tulsa Community College C, A
University of Central Oklahoma B, M

Oregon
Art Institute
 of Portland A, B
George Fox University B
Marylhurst University B
Portland Community College C, A

Pennsylvania
Antonelli Institute of Art and
 Photography A
Art Institute
 of Philadelphia A
 of Pittsburgh A
Beaver College B
Bradley Academy for the Visual Arts A
Drexel University B, M
Harcum College A
La Roche College B
Mercyhurst College B
Philadelphia University B
Seton Hill College B

Puerto Rico
University of Puerto Rico
 Carolina Regional College A

Rhode Island
New England Institute of Technology A

South Carolina
Anderson College B
Converse College B

South Dakota
South Dakota State University B

Tennessee
Carson-Newman College B
Lambuth University B
Middle Tennessee State University B
O'More College of Design B
Pellissippi State Technical Community
 College A
University of Tennessee
 Knoxville B, M
 Martin B

Texas
Abilene Christian University B
Amarillo College C, A
Baylor University B
El Paso Community College C, A
Houston Community College
 System C, A
St. Philip's College C
Texas A&M University
 Kingsville B
University of Houston B
University of North Texas B, M
University of Texas
 Arlington B
 Austin B
University of the Incarnate Word B

Utah
Brigham Young University B
Dixie State College of Utah A
LDS Business College A
Salt Lake Community College C
Utah State University B
Weber State University A

Virginia
Bridgewater College B
J. Sargeant Reynolds Community
 College C
Lord Fairfax Community College C
Mary Baldwin College B
Northern Virginia Community College A
Tidewater Community College A
Virginia Commonwealth University B

Washington
Art Institute of Seattle C, A
Bellevue Community College A
Cornish College of the Arts B
Spokane Falls Community College C, A

West Virginia
Fairmont State College A
University of Charleston B

Wisconsin
Concordia University Wisconsin B
Gateway Technical College A
Madison Area Technical College A
Milwaukee Area Technical College A
Milwaukee Institute of Art & Design B
Mount Mary College B
University of Wisconsin
 Madison B
 Stevens Point B
Waukesha County Technical College A
Western Wisconsin Technical College A

Intermedia

Arizona
Arizona State University B, M
University of Advancing Computer
 Technology A, B

California
Academy of Art College C, A, B, M
Ohlone College C, A
San Francisco Art Institute B, M

Colorado
Art Institute
 of Colorado A

Connecticut
Naugatuck Valley Community-Technical
 College A

Florida
Art Institute
 of Fort Lauderdale A

Georgia
Art Institute
 of Atlanta A, B
Atlanta College of Art B
Augusta State University B
University of Georgia B

Illinois
American Academy of Art A, B
Columbia College B
International Academy of Merchandising
 and Design A

Iowa
Maharishi University of
 Management B, M
St. Ambrose University B
University of Iowa M

Louisiana
Tulane University C, B

Maryland
Maryland Institute College of Art B

Massachusetts
Hampshire College B
Massachusetts College of Art B, M
School of the Museum of Fine Arts B, M
University of Massachusetts
 Dartmouth B

Michigan
University of Michigan B

Minnesota
Moorhead State University B

New Jersey
Ramapo College of New Jersey B
Union County College A

New York
Bard College B
Fulton-Montgomery Community
 College C, A
New York Institute of Technology C
New York State College of Ceramics at
 Alfred University B, M, T
Rochester Institute of Technology B

Oregon
Pacific University B

Pennsylvania
Eastern College B
Indiana University of
 Pennsylvania B, M, D

Puerto Rico
University of Puerto Rico
 Rio Piedras Campus B

South Carolina
Benedict College B

Vermont
Bennington College M

Washington
Art Institute of Seattle A
Highline Community College A
Western Washington University B

Wisconsin
University of Wisconsin
 Milwaukee B

International agriculture

California
Kings River Community College C
University of California
 Davis B, M

Idaho
University of Idaho B

Illinois
Kishwaukee College A

Iowa
Iowa State University B

Kansas
MidAmerica Nazarene University B

New York
Cornell University B, M

Oregon
Oregon State University B

Utah
Utah State University B

Vermont
Sterling College B

Virginia
Eastern Mennonite University B

Wyoming
University of Wyoming B

International business

Alabama
Auburn University B
Birmingham-Southern College B
Huntingdon College B
Samford University B
Spring Hill College B
University of Mobile B

Arizona
Cochise College A
Gateway Community College C, A
Grand Canyon University B
Paradise Valley Community
 College C, A
Pima Community College A
Rio Salado College C, A
Scottsdale Community College C, A
South Mountain Community
 College C, A
Thunderbird, The American Graduate
 School of International
 Management M

Arkansas
Arkansas State University B
Harding University B
Northwest Arkansas Community
 College A

International business

California
Antioch Southern California
  Santa Barbara M
Armstrong University B, M
Azusa Pacific University M
California State Polytechnic University:
  Pomona B
California State University
  Dominguez Hills B
  Fresno B
  Fullerton B
  Hayward M
  Long Beach C, B
  Los Angeles B, M
  Monterey Bay B
Claremont McKenna College B
Coastline Community College C
Compton Community College C
Foothill College C, A
Golden Gate University C, B, M
Grossmont Community College C, A
Irvine Valley College C, A
Lincoln University B, M
Loyola Marymount University B
Monterey Institute of International
  Studies M
Monterey Peninsula College C, A
Mount St. Mary's College B
National University M
Orange Coast College C, A
Pacific Union College B
Palomar College C, A
Pepperdine University B, M
St. Mary's College of California B
San Diego State University B, M
San Francisco State University B
San Jose City College C
San Jose State University B
Southwestern College C, A
United States International
  University B, M, D
University of La Verne B
University of San Diego M
University of San Francisco B
Vanguard University of Southern
  California B

Colorado
Arapahoe Community College C, A
Fort Lewis College B
University of Colorado
  Boulder B
  Denver M
University of Denver B, M

Connecticut
Albertus Magnus College B
Central Connecticut State
  University B, M
Fairfield University B
Quinnipiac University B
Sacred Heart University B
Teikyo Post University B
University of Bridgeport B, M
University of New Haven B
Yale University M

Delaware
Goldey-Beacom College B

District of Columbia
American University B, M
George Washington University B, M
Georgetown University B
Howard University B
Southeastern University B, M

Florida
Barry University B
Bethune-Cookman College B
Brevard Community College A
Broward Community College A
Eckerd College B
Edison Community College A
Florida Atlantic University B
Florida International University B, M
Florida Southern College B
Florida State University B
Jacksonville University B, M
Lynn University B, M
Northwood University
  Florida Campus A, B
Nova Southeastern University M, D
Palm Beach Atlantic College B
Rollins College B
St. Thomas University B, M
Stetson University B
University of Miami C, M
University of North Florida B
University of Tampa B

Georgia
Georgia Southern University B
Georgia State University M
Kennesaw State University M
LaGrange College B
Mercer University B, M
Savannah State University B
University of Georgia B, M
Wesleyan College B

Hawaii
Brigham Young University
  Hawaii B
Chaminade University of Honolulu B
Hawaii Pacific University B
University of Hawaii
  Manoa B, D
  West Oahu B

Idaho
Albertson College of Idaho B
Boise State University B
Lewis-Clark State College B
Northwest Nazarene University B

Illinois
Augustana College B
Benedictine University B
Black Hawk College C
Bradley University B
City Colleges of Chicago
  Harold Washington College A
De Paul University M
Dominican University B
Elmhurst College B
Governors State University B
Illinois State University B
Illinois Wesleyan University B
Judson College B
MacCormac College A
McHenry County College C
Millikin University B
North Central College B
North Park University B
Oakton Community College C, A
Olivet Nazarene University B
Parkland College C
Roosevelt University B, M
St. Xavier University B, M
Triton College A
William Rainey Harper College C, A

Indiana
Franklin College B
Goshen College B
Grace College B
Saint Mary's College B
St. Joseph's College B
Taylor University B
University of Evansville B
University of Indianapolis B
Valparaiso University B

Iowa
Buena Vista University B
Central College B
Clarke College B
Cornell College B
Graceland University B
Iowa State University B
Iowa Wesleyan College B
Loras College B
Luther College B
Marycrest International University B
St. Ambrose University B
Simpson College B
Wartburg College B

Kansas
Baker University B
Emporia State University B
McPherson College B
St. Mary College B
Wichita State University B

Kentucky
Bellarmine College B

Louisiana
Louisiana State University and
  Agricultural and Mechanical
  College B
Loyola University New Orleans B

Maine
Husson College B
Maine Maritime Academy B
St. Joseph's College B
Thomas College B

Maryland
College of Notre Dame of Maryland B
Frederick Community College A
Loyola College in Maryland M
Mount St. Mary's College B
University of Maryland
  University College M

Massachusetts
American International College B
Assumption College B
Babson College B, M
Bay Path College B
Boston University B
Brandeis University M
Elms College B
Emerson College M
Endicott College B
Hampshire College B
Merrimack College B
Middlesex Community College C
Newbury College A, B
Northeastern University B
Northern Essex Community College A
Suffolk University B, M

Michigan
Adrian College B
Alma College B
Aquinas College B
Central Michigan University B, M
Davenport College of Business B
Detroit College of Business B
Eastern Michigan University B, M
Ferris State University C, B
Grand Valley State University B
Lansing Community College A
Madonna University B, M
Marygrove College B
Michigan Technological University C
Mott Community College A
Northwood University A, B
Olivet College B
Saginaw Valley State University B

Minnesota
Augsburg College B
College of St. Catherine: St. Paul
  Campus B
College of St. Scholastica B
Concordia College: Moorhead B
Gustavus Adolphus College B
Hamline University B
Metropolitan State University B
Minnesota State University, Mankato B
Moorhead State University B
National American University
  St. Paul B
Northwestern College B
St. Cloud State University B
University of Minnesota
  Twin Cities B
University of St. Thomas B, M
Winona State University A

Mississippi
University of Mississippi B

Missouri
Avila College B
Lindenwood University B
Maryville University of Saint Louis M
Missouri Southern State College B
Northwest Missouri State University B
St. Louis University B, M, D
St. Louis Community College
  St. Louis Community College at
  Forest Park A
University of Missouri
  St. Louis C, B, M
Webster University B, M
William Jewell College B

Montana
University of Montana-Missoula B

Nebraska
Creighton University B
Hastings College B
University of Nebraska
  Lincoln B

Nevada
University of Nevada
  Reno B

New Hampshire
Franklin Pierce College B
Hesser College A
New Hampshire College B, M, D

New Jersey
Berkeley College A
Brookdale Community College A
Caldwell College C, B
Fairleigh Dickinson University M
Ramapo College of New Jersey B
Rider University B
St. Peter's College A, B, M
Seton Hall University C, M
The College of New Jersey B
Thomas Edison State College A, B

New Mexico
Albuquerque Technical-Vocational
  Institute C, A
New Mexico State University B

New York
Berkeley College of New York City A, B
Berkeley College A, B
Broome Community College A
Canisius College C
City University of New York
  Baruch College M
Concordia College B
D'Youville College B, M
Daemen College M
Dominican College of Blauvelt B
Dowling College B
Elmira College B
Erie Community College
  City Campus A
Fordham University B, M
Hofstra University B, M
Hudson Valley Community College A
Iona College B, M
Ithaca College B
Long Island University
  C. W. Post Campus M
Manhattan College B
Monroe Community College A
New York Institute of Technology M
New York University B, M, D
Pace University:
  Pleasantville/Briarcliff B, M, D
Pace University B, M, D
Regents College B

349

Rochester Institute of
  Technology C, B, M
St. John Fisher College B
State University of New York
  College at Brockport B
  Farmingdale C
  New Paltz B, M
Syracuse University M
Tompkins-Cortland Community
  College A
Touro College M
Union College M
Westchester Community College A

North Carolina
Campbell University B
Central Piedmont Community College A
Gardner-Webb University B
High Point University B, M
Lenoir-Rhyne College B
Mars Hill College B
Meredith College B
North Carolina State University B
St. Andrews Presbyterian College B
Salem College B
University of North Carolina
  Charlotte B
Western Carolina University B

North Dakota
Minot State University B

Ohio
Baldwin-Wallace College M
Bowling Green State University B
Cedarville College B
Central State University B
Cincinnati State Technical and
  Community College A
Cleveland State University B
Hiram College B
Hocking Technical College C
Kent State University M
Lake Erie College B
Lourdes College B
Marietta College B
Mount Union College B
Mount Vernon Nazarene College B
North Central State College C
Notre Dame College of Ohio B
Ohio Dominican College B
Ohio Northern University B
Ohio State University
  Columbus Campus B
Ohio University B
Ohio Wesleyan University B
Tiffin University B
University of Akron B, M
University of Cincinnati
  Raymond Walters College C
University of Cincinnati M, D
University of Dayton B
University of Findlay B
University of Rio Grande B
University of Toledo M
Wittenberg University B
Wright State University M
Xavier University M

Oklahoma
Northeastern State University B
Oklahoma Baptist University B
Oklahoma City University B, M
Oklahoma State University B
Oral Roberts University B
University of Oklahoma B
University of Tulsa B

Oregon
Concordia University B
Linfield College B
Oregon State University B
Portland State University M
University of Portland B

Pennsylvania
Beaver College B

California University of Pennsylvania B
Cedar Crest College C
Chatham College B
Clarion University of Pennsylvania B
Dickinson College B
Drexel University B
Duquesne University B
Elizabethtown College B
Gannon University B
Grove City College B
Harrisburg Area Community College C
Holy Family College B
Immaculata College B
Juniata College B
King's College B
Kutztown University of Pennsylvania B
La Roche College B
La Salle University B
Lebanon Valley College of
  Pennsylvania B
Manor College A
Mansfield University of Pennsylvania B
Marywood University B
Messiah College B
Neumann College B
Peirce College A, B
Penn State
  University Park C
Philadelphia University B, M
Point Park College M
St. Joseph's University M
Seton Hill College B
Temple University B, M
Thiel College B
University of Pennsylvania B, M, D
University of Pittsburgh M
University of Scranton B, M
Villanova University B
Waynesburg College B
Westminster College B
Widener University B

Puerto Rico
Pontifical Catholic University of Puerto
  Rico B
University of Puerto Rico
  Rio Piedras Campus M

Rhode Island
Bryant College M
Johnson & Wales University B, M
Providence College B
Rhode Island College B
Roger Williams University B
University of Rhode Island B

South Carolina
Clemson University B
Converse College B
North Greenville College B
University of South Carolina M
Wofford College B

South Dakota
Northern State University B

Tennessee
Maryville College B
Rhodes College B
Southern Adventist University B
University of Memphis B
University of Tennessee
  Martin B

Texas
Baylor University M
El Paso Community College C, A
Midwestern State University B
Northwood University: Texas
  Campus A, B
Our Lady of the Lake University of San
  Antonio M
St. Edward's University B
St. Mary's University B
Sam Houston State University B
Southwestern Adventist University B
Stephen F. Austin State University B

Sul Ross State University M
Texas A&M International University M
Texas A&M University
  Kingsville B
  Texarkana B
Texas Christian University B
Texas Tech University B
Trinity University B
University of Dallas M
University of Houston M
University of Texas
  Arlington B
  Dallas B, M, D
  Pan American B, D
  San Antonio M

Utah
Brigham Young University B, M
Utah Valley State College A
Westminster College B

Vermont
Green Mountain College B

Virginia
Bridgewater College B
Christopher Newport University B
Eastern Mennonite University B
Ferrum College B
James Madison University B
Lord Fairfax Community College C
Lynchburg College B
Northern Virginia Community
  College C, A
Shenandoah University B

Washington
City University C, A
Edmonds Community College A
Gonzaga University B
Seattle University B, M
Shoreline Community College C, A
Washington State University B
Western Washington University B
Whitworth College B, M

West Virginia
Bethany College B
Davis and Elkins College B
Wheeling Jesuit University B

Wisconsin
Alverno College B
Cardinal Stritch University B
Carthage College B
Lakeland College B, M
Marian College of Fond du Lac B
Marquette University B
Mount Mary College B
St. Norbert College B
University of Wisconsin
  La Crosse B
  Madison N
Waukesha County Technical College A

International business marketing

Alabama
University of Alabama B

Arkansas
John Brown University B
University of Central Arkansas B

California
Allan Hancock College C, A
Antioch Southern California
  Santa Barbara M
East Los Angeles College A
Sacramento City College C, A

Connecticut
Quinnipiac University B, M
Sacred Heart University B

District of Columbia
American University B, M

Florida
Brevard Community College A
Broward Community College A
Valencia Community College A

Hawaii
Chaminade University of Honolulu M

Illinois
Governors State University B
MacCormac College A
North Central College B
Roosevelt University M

Indiana
Indiana State University B

Iowa
Kirkwood Community College A

Maine
Husson College B
St. Joseph's College B

Maryland
Montgomery College
  Rockville Campus A
  Takoma Park Campus A

Massachusetts
Babson College B
Lasell College B
Newbury College A, B

Michigan
Adrian College B
Central Michigan University B
Detroit College of Business B
Eastern Michigan University B, M
Hillsdale College B
Northwood University B

Minnesota
St. Mary's University of Minnesota B, M
St. Paul Technical College A

Missouri
Lindenwood University M
Missouri Southern State College B
Northwest Missouri State University B

Nevada
University of Nevada
  Las Vegas B

New Hampshire
Franklin Pierce College B

New York
Dominican College of Blauvelt B
Pace University:
  Pleasantville/Briarcliff B, M
Pace University B, M
Rochester Institute of Technology B
Sage Junior College of Albany A
St. Thomas Aquinas College B
State University of New York
  Buffalo D
  College at Brockport B
Wagner College M

Ohio
Muskingum College B
University of Akron B

Oklahoma
Oral Roberts University B

Pennsylvania
Community College of Philadelphia A
Holy Family College B
La Salle University B
St. Joseph's University B, M

Texas
Texas Wesleyan University B

Utah
Brigham Young University B

Vermont
Champlain College A, B

International relations

Washington
City University C, M

International finance

Connecticut
Sacred Heart University B

District of Columbia
American University B, M
Catholic University of America B

Florida
University of Miami B, M

Hawaii
Hawaii Pacific University B

Iowa
Drake University B

Louisiana
Dillard University B

Maine
St. Joseph's College B

Massachusetts
Boston University B, M
Brandeis University M, D
Suffolk University M

Michigan
Ferris State University C, B
Oakland Community College A

Missouri
Washington University B

New York
Daemen College M
Pace University: Pleasantville/Briarcliff M
Pace University M

North Carolina
Brevard College B

Ohio
University of Akron B

Oklahoma
Oklahoma Baptist University B

Pennsylvania
Clarion University of Pennsylvania B
Westminster College B
York College of Pennsylvania B

Texas
Texas A&M International University M
University of Dallas M

West Virginia
Bethany College B

International relations

Alabama
Samford University B
Troy State University Dothan M
Troy State University B
University of Alabama B

Arizona
Northern Arizona University B

Arkansas
Hendrix College B
University of Arkansas Little Rock B
University of Arkansas B

California
Allan Hancock College A
Azusa Pacific University B
California Lutheran University B
California State University
  Bakersfield B
  Chico B
  Fresno M
  Sacramento B, M
Claremont McKenna College B
Dominican University of California B
Las Positas College A
Mills College B
Monterey Institute of International Studies B, M
Occidental College B
Pepperdine University B
Pitzer College B
Pomona College B
Saddleback College A
San Francisco State University B, M
Santa Barbara City College A
Santa Monica College A
Scripps College B
Stanford University B, M
United States International University B, M
University of California
  Davis B
  San Diego D
University of La Verne B
University of Redlands B
University of San Diego B, M
University of Southern California B, M, D
University of the Pacific B
Whittier College B

Colorado
University of Colorado Boulder B, M

Connecticut
Connecticut College B
Fairfield University B
Sacred Heart University B
Trinity College B
University of Bridgeport B
Yale University M

Delaware
University of Delaware B, M

District of Columbia
American University B, M, D
Catholic University of America M
George Washington University B, M
Georgetown University B
Trinity College B

Florida
Bethune-Cookman College B
Eckerd College B
Florida International University B, M, D
Florida State University B, M
Jacksonville University B
Lynn University B
Miami-Dade Community College A
New College of the University of South Florida B
Palm Beach Community College A
Rollins College B
St. Leo University B
Stetson University B
University of Florida M, D
University of Miami M, D
University of North Florida B
University of South Florida B

Georgia
Agnes Scott College B
Berry College B
Brenau University B
Clark Atlanta University M, D
Emory University B
Georgia Institute of Technology B, M
Georgia Southern University B
Kennesaw State University B
Morehouse College B
Oglethorpe University B
Oxford College of Emory University B
State University of West Georgia B
Wesleyan College B

Hawaii
Chaminade University of Honolulu B
Hawaii Pacific University B

Idaho
Albertson College of Idaho B
Northwest Nazarene University B
Ricks College A
University of Idaho B

Illinois
Bradley University B
De Paul University B
Dominican University B
Illinois College B
Knox College B
Lake Forest College B
MacMurray College B
McKendree College B
North Central College B
North Park University B
Northwestern University B
Principia College B
Roosevelt University B
St. Xavier University B
University of Chicago B, M
Wheaton College B

Indiana
Butler University B
St. Joseph's College B
University of Evansville B

Iowa
Cornell College B
Drake University B
Graceland University B
Iowa State University B
Loras College B
Simpson College B
Wartburg College B

Kansas
Tabor College B

Kentucky
Centre College B
Thomas More College A, B

Maine
University of Maine Farmington B
University of Maine B

Maryland
Bowie State University B
College of Notre Dame of Maryland B
Frostburg State University B
Goucher College B
Johns Hopkins University B, M, D
Mount St. Mary's College B
Washington College B

Massachusetts
American International College B
Boston University B, M
Brandeis University M
Bridgewater State College B
Clark University B
Elms College B
Gordon College B
Hampshire College B
Harvard University B
Mount Holyoke College B
Northeastern University B
Simmons College B
Tufts University B, M, D
Wellesley College B
Wheaton College B

Michigan
Adrian College B
Albion College B
Aquinas College B
Calvin College B
Central Michigan University B
Grand Valley State University B
Michigan State University B
University of Detroit Mercy M

Minnesota
Bethel College B
Carleton College B
College of St. Catherine: St. Paul Campus B
Concordia College: Moorhead B
Hamline University B
Macalester College B
Minnesota State University, Mankato B
St. Cloud State University B
University of Minnesota Twin Cities B
University of St. Thomas B
Winona State University A

Missouri
Rockhurst University B
Southwest Missouri State University M
Stephens College B
Washington University M
Webster University B, M
Westminster College B
William Jewell College B
William Woods University B

Montana
Carroll College B

Nebraska
Creighton University B, M
Doane College B
Hastings College B
Nebraska Wesleyan University B
University of Nebraska
  Kearney B
  Lincoln B
  Omaha B

Nevada
University of Nevada Reno B

New Hampshire
University of New Hampshire B

New Jersey
Bloomfield College B
Brookdale Community College A
Felician College B
Seton Hall University B, M

New York
Bard College B
Canisius College B
City University of New York
  City College B, M
  College of Staten Island B
  Hunter College B
Colgate University B
Columbia University
  Graduate School M
  Teachers College M, D
Cornell University M
Elmira College B
Eugene Lang College/New School University B
Hamilton College B
Le Moyne College B
Long Island University
  C. W. Post Campus B, M
Manhattanville College B
Marymount College B
Marymount Manhattan College B
New York University B
St. John's University M
Sarah Lawrence College B
State University of New York
  College at Brockport B
  College at Cortland B
  College at Geneseo B
  New Paltz B
Syracuse University B, M, D
Vassar College B
Wells College B

International relations

North Carolina
Campbell University B
Duke University M
Elon College B
High Point University B
Meredith College B
St. Augustine's College B
Salem College B
Shaw University B

Ohio
Antioch College B
Bowling Green State University B
Capital University B
Case Western Reserve University B
College of Wooster B
Kent State University B
Kenyon College B
Malone College B
Miami University
    Oxford Campus B
Muskingum College B
Ohio Northern University B
Ohio State University
    Columbus Campus B
Ohio Wesleyan University B
Otterbein College B
University of Cincinnati B
University of Toledo B
Wittenberg University B
Wright State University B
Xavier University B

Oklahoma
Oral Roberts University B
University of Central Oklahoma M
University of Tulsa C, B

Oregon
George Fox University B
Lewis & Clark College B
Pacific University B
Portland Community College C
Portland State University B
Southern Oregon University B
Willamette University B

Pennsylvania
Allegheny College B
Bryn Mawr College B
Bucknell University B
California University of Pennsylvania B
College Misericordia B
Dickinson College B
Gettysburg College B
Harrisburg Area Community College A
Immaculata College B
Juniata College B
La Salle University B
Lafayette College B
Lehigh University B
Lincoln University B
Lycoming College B
Muhlenberg College B
Penn State
    University Park B
Point Park College B
St. Joseph's University B
University of Pennsylvania A, B, M, D
University of Pittsburgh M
University of Scranton B
Ursinus College B
West Chester University of
    Pennsylvania B
Westminster College B
Widener University B
Wilkes University B
Wilson College B
York College of Pennsylvania B

Rhode Island
Brown University B
Bryant College B
Salve Regina University M

South Carolina
Newberry College B
University of South Carolina B, M, D

Tennessee
Lambuth University B
Middle Tennessee State University B
Rhodes College B
University of Tennessee
    Martin B

Texas
Abilene Christian University B
Angelo State University M
Austin College B
Baylor University B, M
St. Edward's University B
St. Mary's University B, M
Southern Methodist University B
Southwest Texas State University B
Southwestern Adventist University B
Southwestern University B
Texas A&M University B
Texas Christian University B
University of North Texas M, D
University of Texas
    Arlington B, M
Western Texas College A

Utah
Brigham Young University B, M

Vermont
Marlboro College B
Middlebury College B
Norwich University B

Virginia
Bridgewater College B
Christopher Newport University B
College of William and Mary B
Ferrum College B
George Mason University B, M
James Madison University B
Lynchburg College B
Mary Baldwin College B
Mary Washington College B
Old Dominion University B, M, D
Randolph-Macon College B
Roanoke College B
Sweet Briar College B
University of Virginia B, M, D
Virginia Polytechnic Institute and State
    University B
Virginia Wesleyan College B

Washington
City University B
Eastern Washington University B
Gonzaga University B
Seattle University B
University of Washington B, M
Whitworth College B, T

West Virginia
Bethany College B
Marshall University B
West Virginia Wesleyan College B
Wheeling Jesuit University B

Wisconsin
Beloit College B
Carroll College B
Marquette University B, M
University of Wisconsin
    Madison B, M
    Parkside B, T

Wyoming
University of Wyoming M

International studies

Alabama
Huntingdon College B
Spring Hill College B
Stillman College B
University of Alabama
    Birmingham B

University of Montevallo B
University of South Alabama B

Alaska
University of Alaska
    Fairbanks B

Arizona
Northern Arizona University B

Arkansas
Harding University B
Hendrix College B

California
California Lutheran University B
California State University
    Hayward B
    Long Beach B
    Monterey Bay B
Chabot College A
Las Positas College A
Pepperdine University B
Pitzer College B
University of the Pacific B

Colorado
University of Colorado
    Boulder B
University of Denver B, M

Connecticut
Central Connecticut State
    University B, M
Sacred Heart University B
University of Connecticut M
University of Hartford B
Wesleyan University C

District of Columbia
Trinity College B

Florida
Broward Community College A
Eckerd College B
Jacksonville University B
Lynn University B
University of Miami B
University of Tampa B

Georgia
Berry College B
Brenau University B
Oxford College of Emory University B

Hawaii
Hawaii Pacific University B

Idaho
Ricks College A

Illinois
Benedictine University B
Bradley University B
De Paul University M
Illinois College B
Knox College B
Millikin University B
North Central College B
Northwestern University B
Parkland College A
Trinity International University D
University of Chicago B

Indiana
Butler University B
Earlham College B
Hanover College B
Indiana University--Purdue University
    Indiana University-Purdue
    University Fort Wayne C
Taylor University B
University of Evansville B
Valparaiso University B

Iowa
Central College B
Mount Mercy College B
St. Ambrose University B

Kansas
Tabor College B
University of Kansas B

Kentucky
Bellarmine College B
Northern Kentucky University B

Louisiana
Louisiana State University and
    Agricultural and Mechanical
    College B

Maine
Colby College B
University of Maine
    Farmington B
    Presque Isle B
University of Southern Maine B

Maryland
Frostburg State University B
Goucher College B
Howard Community College A
Towson University B
Washington College B

Massachusetts
Bentley College B
Berkshire Community College A
Clark University B
Hampshire College B
Harvard College B
Massachusetts Bay Community
    College A
Stonehill College B
Western New England College B

Michigan
Hillsdale College B
Kalamazoo Valley Community
    College C, A
Macomb Community College C
Northern Michigan University B
Saginaw Valley State University B
University of Michigan B

Minnesota
Bethel College B
Hamline University B
St. Cloud State University B
University of Minnesota
    Duluth B
Winona State University A

Mississippi
University of Mississippi B
University of Southern Mississippi B

Missouri
Missouri Southern State College B
University of Missouri
    St. Louis C
Washington University B
Webster University B, M
Westminster College B

Montana
Rocky Mountain College B

Nebraska
Hastings College B

New Hampshire
St. Anselm College C
University of New Hampshire B

New Jersey
Brookdale Community College A
College of St. Elizabeth B
Rowan University B
Union County College A

New York
Colgate University B
Concordia College B
Houghton College B
Long Island University
    C. W. Post Campus B
Manhattanville College B

Marymount College *B*
Mohawk Valley Community College *A*
New York University *B, M*
Russell Sage College *B*
St. Francis College *B*
St. Thomas Aquinas College *B*
Sarah Lawrence College *B*
State University of New York
    College at Brockport *B*
    College at Oneonta *B*
Utica College of Syracuse University *B*
Wells College *B*

North Carolina
Campbell University *B*
Elon College *B*
High Point University *B*
Lees-McRae College *B*
Mars Hill College *B*
Shaw University *B*
University of North Carolina
    Chapel Hill *B*

North Dakota
North Dakota State University *B*
University of North Dakota *B*

Ohio
Ashland University *B*
Baldwin-Wallace College *B*
Capital University *B*
Case Western Reserve University *B*
Cedarville College *B*
Denison University *B*
Heidelberg College *B*
John Carroll University *B*
Kent State University *B*
Mount Union College *B*
Muskingum College *B*
Ohio Northern University *B*
Ohio State University
    Columbus Campus *B*
Ohio University *M*
Otterbein College *B*
Tiffin University *B*
University of Dayton *B*
University of Findlay *B*
Wittenberg University *B*

Oklahoma
Southern Nazarene University *B*
University of Oklahoma *B*
University of Tulsa *B*

Oregon
Central Oregon Community College *A*
Oregon State University *B*
Southern Oregon University *B*

Pennsylvania
Chatham College *B*
Chestnut Hill College *C*
Dickinson College *B*
Gettysburg College *B*
Indiana University of Pennsylvania *B*
Juniata College *B*
La Roche College *B*
Lock Haven University of
    Pennsylvania *B, M*
Mansfield University of Pennsylvania *B*
Millersville University of
    Pennsylvania *B*
Muhlenberg College *B*
Neumann College *B*
Point Park College *B*
Susquehanna University *B*
University of Pittsburgh
    Johnstown *C*

Rhode Island
Brown University *B*

South Dakota
Augustana College *B*

Tennessee
Maryville College *B*
Rhodes College *B*

Texas
Abilene Christian University *B*
St. Edward's University *B*
Texas A&M University *B*
Texas Lutheran University *B*
University of St. Thomas *B*

Utah
Salt Lake Community College *A*

Vermont
Bennington College *B*
Marlboro College *B*
Norwich University *B*

Virginia
Christopher Newport University *B*
Hollins University *B*
Mary Baldwin College *B*
Northern Virginia Community College *A*
Randolph-Macon College *B*
Randolph-Macon Woman's College *B*
University of Richmond *B*
Virginia Military Institute *B*

Washington
Clark College *C*
Seattle University *B*
Western Washington University *B*

West Virginia
Marshall University *B*
West Virginia Wesleyan College *B*

Wisconsin
University of Wisconsin
    Madison *B, M, D*
    Milwaukee *B*
    Oshkosh *B*
    Platteville *B*
    Stevens Point *B*
    Superior *B*

Investments/securities

California
Chabot College *A*

Florida
University of Miami *M*
University of South Florida *M*

Illinois
De Paul University *M*
St. Xavier University *C, M*

Iowa
Drake University *B*

Massachusetts
Babson College *B*

Michigan
Ferris State University *C*

Minnesota
Minnesota State University, Mankato *B*
University of St. Thomas *M*

New York
City University of New York
    Baruch College *M*
Pace University:
    Pleasantville/Briarcliff *B, M*
Pace University *B, M*
State University of New York
    Albany *B, M*

Ohio
Kent State University *M*

Pennsylvania
Duquesne University *B*
University of Pennsylvania *M*

Rhode Island
Johnson & Wales University *A, B*

Wisconsin
University of Wisconsin
    Madison *B, M, D*
    Platteville *B*

Islamic studies

California
University of California
    Los Angeles *M, D*

Massachusetts
Harvard College *B*

Michigan
University of Michigan *B*

Missouri
Washington University *B, M*

New York
Columbia University
    Graduate School *M, D*
Sarah Lawrence College *B*

Ohio
Ohio State University
    Columbus Campus *B*

Texas
University of Texas
    Austin *B*

Utah
Brigham Young University *B*

Italian

Arizona
Arizona State University *B*
University of Arizona *B*

California
Cabrillo College *A*
California State University
    Long Beach *C*
Chabot College *A*
Claremont McKenna College *B*
College of the Desert *A*
East Los Angeles College *C*
Long Beach City College *C, A*
Los Angeles Valley College *A*
Loyola Marymount University *B*
Pitzer College *B*
St. Mary's College of California *B*
San Diego City College *A*
San Diego Mesa College *A*
San Francisco State University *B, M*
Santa Clara University *B*
Scripps College *B*
Stanford University *B, M, D*
University of California
    Berkeley *B, M, D*
    Davis *B*
    Los Angeles *B, M, D*
    San Diego *B*
    Santa Barbara *B*
    Santa Cruz *B, D*

Colorado
University of Colorado
    Boulder *B*
University of Denver *B*

Connecticut
Albertus Magnus College *B*
Central Connecticut State University *B*
Connecticut College *B*
Fairfield University *B*
Sacred Heart University *C, A*
Southern Connecticut State University *B*
Trinity College *B*
University of Connecticut *B, M, D*
University of Hartford *B*
Wesleyan University *B*
Yale University *B, M, D*

Delaware
University of Delaware *B, M, T*

District of Columbia
Catholic University of America *M, D*
Georgetown University *B*

Florida
Florida International University *B*
Florida State University *B*
Miami-Dade Community College *A*
University of South Florida *B*

Georgia
Emory University *B*
Oxford College of Emory University *B*
University of Georgia *B*

Illinois
De Paul University *B*
Dominican University *B, T*
Loyola University of Chicago *B*
Northwestern University *B, M, D*
Triton College *A*
University of Chicago *B*
University of Illinois
    Chicago *B*
    Urbana-Champaign *B, M, D*

Indiana
Indiana University
    Bloomington *B, M, D*
University of Notre Dame *B, M*

Iowa
University of Iowa *B, T*

Kentucky
University of Kentucky *B*

Louisiana
Tulane University *B*

Maryland
Johns Hopkins University *B, D*
University of Maryland
    College Park *B*

Massachusetts
Boston College *B, M*
Boston University *B*
Harvard College *B*
Harvard University *D*
Mount Holyoke College *B*
Northeastern University *B*
Smith College *B, M*
Tufts University *B*
University of Massachusetts
    Amherst *B, M*
    Boston *B*
Wellesley College *B*

Michigan
University of Michigan *B, M, D*
Wayne State University *B, M*

Minnesota
University of Minnesota
    Twin Cities *B, M*

Missouri
Washington University *B*

New Hampshire
Dartmouth College *B*

New Jersey
Georgian Court College *T*
Montclair State University *B, T*

Italian

Rutgers
   The State University of New Jersey:
      Douglass College *B, T*
   The State University of New Jersey:
      Livingston College *B, T*
   The State University of New Jersey:
      New Brunswick Graduate
      Campus *M, D, T*
   The State University of New Jersey:
      Newark College of Arts and
      Sciences *B, T*
   The State University of New Jersey:
      Rutgers College *B, T*
   The State University of New Jersey:
      University College New
      Brunswick *B, T*
   The State University of New Jersey:
      University College Newark *T*
Seton Hall University *B, T*

New York
Bard College *B*
Barnard College *B*
City University of New York
   Brooklyn College *B*
   Hunter College *B, M*
   Lehman College *B*
   Queens College *B, M*
   York College *B*
Columbia University
   Columbia College *B*
   Graduate School *M, D*
   School of General Studies *B*
Cornell University *B*
Fordham University *B*
Hofstra University *B*
Iona College *B*
Long Island University
   C. W. Post Campus *B*
Nazareth College of Rochester *B*
New York University *B, M, D*
Pace University:
   Pleasantville/Briarcliff *C*
Pace University *C*
St. John Fisher College *B*
St. John's University *B*
Sarah Lawrence College *B*
State University of New York
   Albany *B*
   Binghamton *B, M*
   Buffalo *B*
   College at Buffalo *B*
   Stony Brook *B, T*
Syracuse University *B*
Vassar College *B*

North Carolina
Duke University *B*
University of North Carolina
   Greensboro *B*

Ohio
College of Wooster *B*
Lake Erie College *B*
Ohio State University
   Columbus Campus *B, M, D*
Youngstown State University *B*

Oklahoma
Tulsa Community College *A*

Oregon
University of Oregon *B, M*

Pennsylvania
Bryn Mawr College *B*
Haverford College *B*
Immaculata College *C, B*
La Salle University *B, T*
Mercyhurst College *B*
Penn State
   University Park *B*
Rosemont College *B*
Temple University *B*
University of Pennsylvania *A, B*
University of Pittsburgh *B, M*

Rhode Island
Brown University *B, M, D*
Providence College *B*
University of Rhode Island *B*

South Carolina
University of South Carolina *B*

Tennessee
University of Tennessee
   Knoxville *B*

Texas
University of Houston *B*
University of Texas
   Austin *B*

Utah
Brigham Young University *B*

Vermont
Marlboro College *B*
Middlebury College *B*

Virginia
Sweet Briar College *B*
University of Virginia *B, M*

Washington
Gonzaga University *B*
University of Washington *B*

Wisconsin
University of Wisconsin
   Madison *B, M, D*
   Milwaukee *B*

Japanese

Alaska
University of Alaska
   Fairbanks *B*

California
Cabrillo College *A*
California State University
   Fullerton *B*
   Long Beach *B*
   Los Angeles *B*
Claremont McKenna College *B*
Foothill College *A*
MiraCosta College *A*
Monterey Institute of International
   Studies *C*
Orange Coast College *A*
Pitzer College *B*
Pomona College *B*
St. Mary's College of California *B*
San Diego State University *B*
San Francisco State University *B, M*
San Jose State University *B*
Scripps College *B*
Stanford University *B, M, D*
University of California
   Berkeley *B, M, D*
   Davis *B*
   Irvine *B*
   Los Angeles *B*
   San Diego *B*
   Santa Barbara *B*
   Santa Cruz *B*
University of San Francisco *C*
University of Southern
   California *B, M, D*
University of the Pacific *B*

Colorado
University of Colorado
   Boulder *B, M*
University of Denver *B*

Connecticut
Connecticut College *B*
Fairfield University *B*
Yale University *B*

District of Columbia
George Washington University *B*

Georgetown University *B*

Georgia
University of Georgia *B*

Hawaii
University of Hawaii
   Hilo *B*
   Manoa *B, M, D*

Illinois
City Colleges of Chicago
   Harold Washington College *A*
Illinois Wesleyan University *B*
North Central College *B*
Parkland College *A*
Richland Community College *A*

Indiana
Indiana University
   Bloomington *M, D*
University of Notre Dame *B*

Iowa
University of Iowa *B, T*

Kansas
Butler County Community College *A*

Louisiana
Dillard University *B*

Maine
Bates College *B*

Maryland
Johns Hopkins University *B*
University of Maryland
   College Park *B*

Massachusetts
Harvard College *B*
Tufts University *B*
University of Massachusetts
   Amherst *B, M*
Wellesley College *B*
Williams College *B*

Michigan
Eastern Michigan University *B*
Hope College *B*
Madonna University *B, T*
University of Michigan *M, D*

Minnesota
Augsburg College *B*
Gustavus Adolphus College *B*
University of Minnesota
   Twin Cities *B, M, D*
Winona State University *A*

Missouri
Washington University *B, M, D*

Montana
University of Montana-Missoula *B*

New Hampshire
Dartmouth College *B*

New Jersey
Seton Hall University *T*

New York
Columbia University
   Graduate School *M, D*
Cornell University *B*
Hamilton College *B*
State University of New York
   Albany *B*
University of Rochester *B*

Ohio
Mount Union College *B*
Ohio State University
   Columbus Campus *B*
University of Findlay *B*

Oklahoma
Tulsa Community College *A*

Oregon
Pacific University *B*
Portland State University *B, T*
University of Oregon *B*

Pennsylvania
Carnegie Mellon University *B*
Gettysburg College *B*
La Salle University *B*
Penn State
   University Park *B*
University of Pittsburgh *B*
Ursinus College *B, T*

Utah
Brigham Young University *B, M*
Snow College *A*
University of Utah *B*

Vermont
Bennington College *B*
Middlebury College *B*

Virginia
George Mason University *B*

Washington
Central Washington University *B*
Everett Community College *A*
Evergreen State College *B*
University of Puget Sound *T*
University of Washington *B*

West Virginia
Salem-Teikyo University *B*

Wisconsin
University of Wisconsin
   Madison *B, M*

Jazz

California
California Institute of the Arts *C, B, M*
California State University
   Long Beach *B, M*
University of Southern California *B, M*

Colorado
Naropa University *C, B*
University of Denver *B*

Connecticut
University of Hartford *B*

District of Columbia
Howard University *B*

Florida
Florida State University *C, M*
Manatee Community College *A*
Palm Beach Community College *A*
University of Miami *B, M*
University of North Florida *B*

Illinois
Augustana College *B*
Benedictine University *B*
De Paul University *B, M*
North Central College *B*
Northwestern University *B*
Roosevelt University *B*

Indiana
Indiana University
   Bloomington *B*
   South Bend *A*

Iowa
University of Iowa *B*

Louisiana
Loyola University New Orleans *B, M*

Maine
University of Maine
   Augusta *A, B*

Massachusetts
Berklee College of Music *B*

Boston Conservatory M
New England Conservatory of
    Music B, M, D
Simon's Rock College of Bard B
Westfield State College B
Michigan
University of Michigan B
Western Michigan University B
Minnesota
University of Minnesota
    Duluth B
Missouri
University of Missouri
    Kansas City B
Webster University B, M
Nevada
University of Nevada
    Las Vegas B
New Jersey
Rowan University B
Rutgers
    The State University of New Jersey:
        Mason Gross School of the
        Arts B, M
    The State University of New Jersey:
        Newark Graduate Campus M
New York
Bard College B
City University of New York
    City College B
Eastman School of Music of the
    University of Rochester B, M
Eugene Lang College/New School
    University B
Five Towns College A, B, M
Ithaca College B
Long Island University
    Brooklyn Campus B
Manhattan School of Music B, M
New York University B
Sarah Lawrence College B
State University of New York
    New Paltz B
University of Rochester B, M
Villa Maria College of Buffalo A
North Carolina
Brevard College B
North Carolina Central University B
Ohio
Bowling Green State University B
Capital University B
Central State University B
Ohio State University
    Columbus Campus B
University of Akron B
University of Cincinnati B
Youngstown State University B
Oregon
University of Oregon M, D
Pennsylvania
Carnegie Mellon University B
University of the Arts B, M
West Chester University of
    Pennsylvania B
Rhode Island
Community College of Rhode Island A
South Carolina
University of South Carolina M
Tennessee
University of Tennessee
    Martin B
Texas
University of North Texas B, M
Vermont
Bennington College B, M
Johnson State College B

Washington
Cornish College of the Arts B
Western Washington University B
Wisconsin
University of Wisconsin
    Madison B, M

Jewish/Judaic studies

Arizona
University of Arizona B
California
San Francisco State University C
University of California
    Berkeley D
    Los Angeles B
    San Diego B, M
University of Judaism B
University of Southern California B
Colorado
University of Denver M
Connecticut
Trinity College B
University of Hartford B
Yale University B
District of Columbia
American University B
George Washington University B
Florida
Florida Atlantic University B
University of Florida B
University of Miami B
Georgia
Emory University B
Oxford College of Emory University A
Illinois
De Paul University B
Moody Bible Institute B
Indiana
Indiana University
    Bloomington B
Louisiana
Tulane University B
Maryland
University of Maryland
    College Park B
Massachusetts
Brandeis University B, M, D
Hampshire College B
Harvard College B
Hebrew College B, M, T
Mount Holyoke College B
Northeastern University B
University of Massachusetts
    Amherst B
Wellesley College B
Michigan
University of Michigan B
Minnesota
University of Minnesota
    Twin Cities B
Missouri
University of Missouri
    Kansas City B
Washington University B, M
New Hampshire
Dartmouth College B
New Jersey
Richard Stockton College of New
    Jersey C

Rutgers
    The State University of New Jersey:
        Douglass College B
    The State University of New Jersey:
        Livingston College B
    The State University of New Jersey:
        Rutgers College B
    The State University of New Jersey:
        University College New
        Brunswick B
New York
Bard College B
City University of New York
    Brooklyn College B, M
    City College B
    Hunter College B
    Lehman College B
    Queens College B
Columbia University
    Graduate School M, D
Hofstra University B
Jewish Theological Seminary of
    America B, M, D
New York University B, D
Sarah Lawrence College B
State University of New York
    Albany B
    Binghamton B
Touro College B, M
Ohio
Oberlin College B
Ohio State University
    Columbus Campus B
University of Cincinnati C, B
Oregon
University of Oregon B
Pennsylvania
Dickinson College B
Penn State
    University Park B
Temple University B
University of Pennsylvania B
University of Pittsburgh C
Rhode Island
Brown University B, M, D
Vermont
Goddard College B
Washington
University of Washington B
Wisconsin
University of Wisconsin
    Madison M, D

Journalism

Alabama
Alabama Agricultural and Mechanical
    University B
Alabama State University B
Auburn University B
James H. Faulkner State Community
    College A
Samford University B
Spring Hill College B
Troy State University B
University of Alabama B, M, D
Alaska
University of Alaska
    Anchorage B
    Fairbanks B
Arizona
Arizona State University B, M
Arizona Western College A
Cochise College A
Grand Canyon University B
Mesa Community College A
Northern Arizona University B
Pima Community College A

University of Arizona B, M
Arkansas
Arkansas State University B, M
Arkansas Tech University B
Harding University B
Henderson State University B
John Brown University A, B
Ouachita Baptist University B, T
University of Arkansas
    Little Rock B, M
University of Arkansas B, M
University of Central Arkansas B
Westark College A
California
Azusa Pacific University B
Bakersfield College A
Butte College C, A
Cabrillo College A
California Baptist University B
California Lutheran University B
California Polytechnic State University:
    San Luis Obispo B
California State University
    Chico B
    Dominguez Hills B
    Fresno B, M
    Fullerton B, M
    Hayward B
    Long Beach B
    Northridge B, M
    Sacramento B
Canada College A
Cerritos Community College A
Chabot College A
Chaffey Community College C
Chapman University B
City College of San Francisco A
College of the Canyons A
College of the Desert A
College of the Redwoods C, A
Compton Community College A
Cuesta College C, A
Cypress College A
Diablo Valley College A
Dominican University of California B
East Los Angeles College A
Fresno City College A
Gavilan Community College A
Glendale Community College A
Golden West College C, A
Grossmont Community College C, A
Humboldt State University B
Imperial Valley College A
Los Angeles Southwest College A
Los Angeles Trade and Technical
    College C, A
Los Angeles Valley College C, A
Los Medanos College A
Merced College A
Modesto Junior College C, A
Mount San Antonio College A
National University B
Ohlone College C, A
Pacific Union College B
Palomar College C, A
Pasadena City College C, A
Pepperdine University B
Point Loma Nazarene University B
Riverside Community College A
Sacramento City College C, A
Saddleback College C, A
San Diego State University B
San Francisco State University B
San Joaquin Delta College A
San Jose State University B, M
Santa Ana College C, A
Santa Monica College A
Santa Rosa Junior College C
Shasta College C, A
Sierra College A
Solano Community College A
Southwestern College A
Taft College A
United States International University B

Journalism

University of California
    Berkeley *B, M*
University of La Verne *B*
University of San Francisco *B*
University of Southern California *B, M*
Ventura College *C, A*
West Hills Community College *A*

Colorado
Colorado Mountain College
    Alpine Campus *A*
Colorado State University *B, M*
Fort Lewis College *B*
Mesa State College *B*
Metropolitan State College of Denver *B*
Trinidad State Junior College *A*
University of Colorado
    Boulder *B, M*
University of Denver *B, M*
University of Northern Colorado *B*
University of Southern Colorado *B*

Connecticut
Central Connecticut State University *B*
Manchester Community-Technical
    College *A*
Norwalk Community-Technical
    College *A*
Quinnipiac University *B, M*
Sacred Heart University *B*
Southern Connecticut State University *B*
University of Bridgeport *B*
University of Connecticut *B*
University of New Haven *C, A*

Delaware
Delaware State University *B*
Delaware Technical and Community
    College
        Owens Campus *A*
University of Delaware *B*

District of Columbia
American University *B, M*
George Washington University *B*
Howard University *B*

Florida
Bethune-Cookman College *B*
Broward Community College *A*
Chipola Junior College *A*
Edward Waters College *B*
Florida Agricultural and Mechanical
    University *B, M*
Florida Southern College *B*
Gulf Coast Community College *A*
Hillsborough Community College *A*
Manatee Community College *A*
Miami-Dade Community College *A*
Palm Beach Community College *A*
Pensacola Junior College *A*
University of Central Florida *B*
University of Florida *B*
University of Miami *B*
University of West Florida *B*

Georgia
Abraham Baldwin Agricultural
    College *A*
Andrew College *A*
Atlanta Metropolitan College *A*
Berry College *B*
Brenau University *B*
Clark Atlanta University *B*
Columbus State University *B*
Dalton State College *A*
Darton College *A*
Floyd College *A*
Fort Valley State University *B*
Gainesville College *A*
Georgia College and State University *B*
Georgia Perimeter College *A*
Georgia Southern University *B*
Georgia State University *B*
Morris Brown College *B*
Paine College *B*
Piedmont College *B*

South Georgia College *A*
State University of West Georgia *B*
Toccoa Falls College *B*
University of Georgia *B, M*

Hawaii
Hawaii Pacific University *B*
University of Hawaii
    Manoa *B*

Idaho
Boise State University *B, T*
Idaho State University *B*
North Idaho College *A*
Ricks College *A*
University of Idaho *B*

Illinois
Black Hawk College
    East Campus *A*
City Colleges of Chicago
    Harold Washington College *A*
    Kennedy-King College *A*
Columbia College *B, M*
Danville Area Community College *A*
Eastern Illinois University *B*
Governors State University *B, M*
Greenville College *B*
Illinois State University *B*
John A. Logan College *A*
Judson College *B*
Kishwaukee College *A*
Lake Land College *A*
Lewis University *B*
Lewis and Clark Community College *A*
Lincoln Land Community College *A*
MacMurray College *B*
North Central College *B*
Northern Illinois University *B*
Northwestern University *B, M*
Olivet Nazarene University *B*
Parkland College *A*
Principia College *B*
Quincy University *A, B*
Rend Lake College *A*
Richland Community College *A*
Roosevelt University *B, M*
Southern Illinois University
    Carbondale *B, M, D*
    Edwardsville *B, M*
Triton College *A*
University of Illinois
    Springfield *M*
    Urbana-Champaign *B, M*
University of St. Francis *B*
Western Illinois University *B*
William Rainey Harper College *A*

Indiana
Anderson University *B*
Ball State University *A, B, M, T*
Bethel College *A*
Butler University *B*
Franklin College *B*
Goshen College *B*
Indiana State University *B, M*
Indiana University
    Bloomington *B, M, D, T*
    South Bend *B*
    Southeast *A*
Indiana University--Purdue University
    Indiana University-Purdue
        University Indianapolis *B*
Manchester College *B*
Purdue University
    Calumet *B*
St. Joseph's College *B*
St. Mary-of-the-Woods College *B*
Taylor University *B*
University of Indianapolis *B*
Valparaiso University *B*
Vincennes University *A*

Iowa
Briar Cliff College *B*
Buena Vista University *B*
Clarke College *B*

Dordt College *B*
Drake University *B, M*
Grand View College *B*
Iowa State University *B, M*
Iowa Wesleyan College *B*
Loras College *B*
Maharishi University of Management *M*
Marshalltown Community College *A*
Morningside College *B*
North Iowa Area Community College *A*
St. Ambrose University *B*
Simpson College *B*
University of Iowa *B, M, D, T*
Waldorf College *A, B*
Wartburg College *B, T*

Kansas
Baker University *B, T*
Benedictine College *B, T*
Bethel College *T*
Butler County Community College *A*
Central Christian College *A*
Coffeyville Community College *A*
Colby Community College *A*
Cowley County Community College *A*
Dodge City Community College *A*
Emporia State University *T*
Garden City Community College *A*
Hutchinson Community College *A*
Independence Community College *A*
Kansas City Kansas Community
    College *A*
Kansas State University *B, M*
Pittsburg State University *B, T*
Pratt Community College *A*
Seward County Community College *A*
University of Kansas *B, M*
Washburn University of Topeka *B*

Kentucky
Asbury College *B*
Campbellsville University *B*
Eastern Kentucky University *B*
Lindsey Wilson College *B*
Murray State University *B, M, T*
Northern Kentucky University *B*
Union College *B*
University of Kentucky *B*
Western Kentucky University *B*

Louisiana
Centenary College of Louisiana *B*
Louisiana State University
    Shreveport *B*
Louisiana State University and
    Agricultural and Mechanical
    College *B, M, D*
Louisiana Tech University *B*
McNeese State University *B*
Nicholls State University *B*
Northwestern State University *B*
Southern University and Agricultural and
    Mechanical College *B, M*
University of Louisiana at Lafayette *B*
University of Louisiana at Monroe *B*
Xavier University of Louisiana *B*

Maine
St. Joseph's College *B*
University of Maine *B*
University of Southern Maine *B*

Maryland
Bowie State University *B*
Charles County Community College *C*
Columbia Union College *B*
Community College of Baltimore County
    Catonsville *A*
Coppin State College *B*
Towson University *B, M*
University of Maryland
    College Park *B, M, D*

Massachusetts
American International College *B*
Boston University *B, M*
Dean College *A*

Emerson College *B, M*
Fitchburg State College *B*
Hampshire College *B*
Massachusetts College of Liberal Arts *B*
Mount Ida College *B*
Newbury College *A*
Northeastern University *B, M*
Salem State College *B*
Suffolk University *B*
University of Massachusetts
    Amherst *B*
Westfield State College *B*

Michigan
Adrian College *B*
Andrews University *B*
Bay de Noc Community College *C*
Calvin College *B*
Central Michigan University *B*
Eastern Michigan University *B*
Grand Valley State University *B*
Kellogg Community College *A*
Lake Michigan College *A*
Lansing Community College *A*
Madonna University *A, B*
Michigan State University *B, M, D*
Northern Michigan University *B*
Oakland Community College *A*
Oakland University *B*
Olivet College *B*
St. Clair County Community College *A*
Schoolcraft College *A*
University of Detroit Mercy *B*
University of Michigan *B, M, D*
Wayne State University *B*
Western Michigan University *B*

Minnesota
Bemidji State University *B*
Bethel College *B*
Concordia College: Moorhead *B*
Minnesota State University, Mankato *B*
Moorhead State University *B*
North Central University *B*
Northland Community & Technical
    College *A*
Northwestern College *B*
Ridgewater College: A Community and
    Technical College *A*
St. Cloud State University *B*
University of Minnesota
    Twin Cities *B, M, D*
University of St. Thomas *B*
Winona State University *B*

Mississippi
Alcorn State University *B*
Coahoma Community College *A*
Delta State University *B*
Hinds Community College *A*
Jackson State University *B*
Mississippi University for Women *B*
Northwest Mississippi Community
    College *A*
Rust College *B*
University of Mississippi *B, M*
University of Southern Mississippi *B*

Missouri
Central Missouri State University *B, M*
College of the Ozarks *B*
Crowder College *A*
Drury University *B*
East Central College *A*
Evangel University *A, B*
Lincoln University *B*
Lindenwood University *B, M*
Missouri Southern State College *B*
Northwest Missouri State University *B*
Southeast Missouri State University *B*
Southwest Missouri State University *B*
St. Louis Community College
    St. Louis Community College at
        Florissant Valley *A*
State Fair Community College *A*
Stephens College *B*

Truman State University *B*
University of Missouri
    Columbia *B, M, D*
    Kansas City *B*
Webster University *B*
William Woods University *B*

Montana
Miles Community College *A*
University of Montana-Missoula *B, M*

Nebraska
Central Community College *C, A*
Creighton University *A, B*
Doane College *B*
Grace University *B*
Hastings College *B, T*
Midland Lutheran College *B, T*
Northeast Community College *A*
Union College *B*
University of Nebraska
    Kearney *B*
    Lincoln *B, M*
    Omaha *B*
Wayne State College *B, T*

Nevada
University of Nevada
    Reno *B, M*

New Hampshire
Franklin Pierce College *B*
Keene State College *B*
Rivier College *B*
University of New Hampshire *B*
White Pines College *B*

New Jersey
Brookdale Community College *A*
Cumberland County College *A*
Essex County College *A*
Fairleigh Dickinson University *B*
Gloucester County College *A*
Middlesex County College *A*
Ocean County College *A*
Rider University *B*
Rowan University *B*
Rutgers
    The State University of New Jersey:
      Cook College *B*
    The State University of New Jersey:
      Douglass College *B*
    The State University of New Jersey:
      Livingston College *B*
    The State University of New Jersey:
      Newark College of Arts and
      Sciences *B*
    The State University of New Jersey:
      Rutgers College *B*
    The State University of New Jersey:
      University College New
      Brunswick *B*
Salem Community College *A*
Sussex County Community College *A*
The College of New Jersey *B*
Thomas Edison State College *B*
Union County College *A*

New Mexico
College of Santa Fe *B*
Eastern New Mexico University *B*
New Mexico Highlands University *B*
New Mexico State University *B*
University of New Mexico *B*

New York
City University of New York
    Baruch College *B*
    Brooklyn College *B*
    Kingsborough Community
      College *A*
Columbia University
    Graduate School *M*
Fordham University *B*
Fulton-Montgomery Community
    College *A*
Hobart and William Smith Colleges *B*
Hofstra University *B*

Iona College *B, M*
Ithaca College *B*
Long Island University
    Brooklyn Campus *B*
Manhattan College *B*
Marist College *B*
Marymount College *B*
Medaille College *B*
Mercy College *B*
Nassau Community College *A*
New York Institute of Technology *M*
New York University *B, M*
Niagara County Community College *A*
Pace University:
    Pleasantville/Briarcliff *B, M*
Pace University *B, M*
Polytechnic University *B, M*
Rochester Institute of Technology *B*
St. Bonaventure University *B*
St. John Fisher College *B*
St. John's University *B*
St. Thomas Aquinas College *B*
State University of New York
    College at Brockport *B*
    College at Buffalo *B*
    College at Old Westbury *B*
    College of Agriculture and
      Technology at Morrisville *A*
    New Paltz *B*
    Oswego *B*
Syracuse University *B, M, D*
Utica College of Syracuse University *B*

North Carolina
Appalachian State University *B*
Barber-Scotia College *B*
Bennett College *B*
Brevard College *B*
Campbell University *B*
East Carolina University *B*
Elon College *B*
Gardner-Webb University *B*
Guilford Technical Community
    College *A*
North Carolina Agricultural and
    Technical State University *B*
North Carolina State University *B*
Sandhills Community College *A*
Shaw University *B*
University of North Carolina
    Asheville *B*
    Chapel Hill *B, M, D*
    Pembroke *B*

North Dakota
Dickinson State University *A*
North Dakota State University *B*

Ohio
Ashland University *B*
Bowling Green State University *B, M, D*
Central State University *B*
Defiance College *B*
Kent State University
    Stark Campus *B*
Kent State University *B, M*
Lorain County Community College *A*
Marietta College *B*
Miami University
    Oxford Campus *B, M*
Mount Union College *B*
Muskingum College *B*
Ohio Northern University *B*
Ohio State University
    Columbus Campus *B, M*
Ohio University
    Southern Campus at Ironton *A*
Ohio University *B, M, D*
Ohio Wesleyan University *B*
Otterbein College *B*
University of Akron *B*
University of Dayton *B*
University of Rio Grande *B*
Wilberforce University *B*
Wilmington College *B*
Wittenberg University *B*

Wright State University *B*
Youngstown State University *B*

Oklahoma
Cameron University *B*
Carl Albert State College *A*
Connors State College *A*
East Central University *B*
Eastern Oklahoma State College *A*
Langston University *B*
Northeastern Oklahoma Agricultural and
    Mechanical College *A*
Northeastern State University *B*
Northwestern Oklahoma State
    University *B*
Oklahoma Baptist University *B*
Oklahoma Christian University of
    Science and Arts *B*
Oklahoma City Community College *A*
Oklahoma City University *B*
Oklahoma State University *B, M*
Rose State College *A*
St. Gregory's University *A, B*
Southeastern Oklahoma State
    University *B*
Southern Nazarene University *B*
Tulsa Community College *A*
University of Central Oklahoma *B*
University of Oklahoma *B, M*
University of Tulsa *C*

Oregon
Chemeketa Community College *A*
Lane Community College *C, A*
Linfield College *B*
Linn-Benton Community College *A*
Mount Hood Community College *A*
Multnomah Bible College *B*
Pacific University *B*
Southern Oregon University *B*
University of Oregon *B, M*
University of Portland *B*
Western Baptist College *B*

Pennsylvania
Bloomsburg University of
    Pennsylvania *B*
Bucks County Community College *A*
California University of Pennsylvania *B*
Carnegie Mellon University *B*
Community College of Allegheny
    County *A*
Delaware County Community College *A*
Duquesne University *B*
Harrisburg Area Community College *A*
Indiana University of Pennsylvania *B*
La Salle University *B*
Lehigh University *B*
Lincoln University *B*
Lock Haven University of
    Pennsylvania *B*
Luzerne County Community College *A*
Mansfield University of
    Pennsylvania *A, B*
Mercyhurst College *B*
Messiah College *B*
Northampton County Area Community
    College *A*
Penn State
    University Park *B, M*
Pennsylvania College of Technology *A*
Point Park College *A, B, M*
Seton Hill College *C, B*
Shippensburg University of
    Pennsylvania *B*
Susquehanna University *B*
Temple University *B, M*
University of Pittsburgh
    Greensburg *B*
    Johnstown *B*
University of the Arts *B*
Widener University *B*

Puerto Rico
Bayamon Central University *B*
Turabo University *B*

University of the Sacred Heart *B*

Rhode Island
University of Rhode Island *B*

South Carolina
Anderson College *B*
Claflin University *B*
Lander University *B*
Morris College *B*
North Greenville College *B*
University of South Carolina
    Aiken *B*
University of South Carolina *B, M, D*
Winthrop University *B*

South Dakota
Augustana College *B*
Black Hills State University *B*
Dakota Wesleyan University *B*
Mount Marty College *B*
South Dakota State University *B, M, T*
University of South Dakota *B, M*

Tennessee
Austin Peay State University *B, M*
Belmont University *B*
Carson-Newman College *B*
Christian Brothers University *B*
Columbia State Community College *A*
David Lipscomb University *B*
East Tennessee State University *B*
Lee University *B*
Middle Tennessee State University *B, M*
Southern Adventist University *B*
Tennessee State University *B*
Tennessee Technological University *B*
Trevecca Nazarene University *B*
Tusculum College *B*
Union University *B*
University of Memphis *B, M*
University of Tennessee
    Knoxville *B*
    Martin *B*

Texas
Abilene Christian University *B, M*
Amarillo College *A*
Angelina College *A*
Angelo State University *B, T*
Baylor University *B, M, T*
College of the Mainland *A*
Del Mar College *A*
El Paso Community College *A*
Hill College *C, A*
Houston Baptist University *B*
Howard College *A*
Jarvis Christian College *B*
Kilgore College *A*
Lee College *A*
Midland College *A*
Midwestern State University *B*
Navarro College *A*
Northeast Texas Community College *A*
Palo Alto College *A*
Paris Junior College *A*
Sam Houston State University *B, T*
San Antonio College *A*
San Jacinto College
    North *A*
South Plains College *A*
Southern Methodist University *B*
Southwest Texas State
    University *B, M, T*
Southwestern Adventist University *B*
Stephen F. Austin State
    University *B, M, T*
Texas A&M University
    Commerce *B*
Texas A&M University *B, M*
Texas Christian University *B, M*
Texas Tech University *B, M*
Texas Wesleyan University *B*
Texas Woman's University *B*
Trinity Valley Community College *A*
Tyler Junior College *A*
University of Houston *B*

Journalism

University of North Texas *B, M*
University of Texas
   Arlington *B*
   Austin *B, M, D*
   El Paso *B*
   Pan American *B, T*
   San Antonio *B*
   Tyler *B*
   of the Permian Basin *B*
Wayland Baptist University *B*
West Texas A&M University *B*
Western Texas College *A*
Wiley College *B*

Utah
Brigham Young University *B*
Dixie State College of Utah *A*
Salt Lake Community College *A*
Snow College *A*
Southern Utah University *B*
University of Utah *B*
Utah State University *B*
Weber State University *B*

Vermont
Castleton State College *B*
College of St. Joseph in Vermont *B*
Green Mountain College *B*
Johnson State College *B*
Lyndon State College *B*
St. Michael's College *B*

Virginia
Averett College *B*
Bluefield College *B*
Hampton University *B*
Liberty University *B*
Longwood College *B*
Norfolk State University *B*
Radford University *B*
Regent University *M*
Southwest Virginia Community College *C*
University of Richmond *B*
University of Virginia's College at Wise *B, T*
Virginia Commonwealth University *B, M*
Virginia Polytechnic Institute and State University *B*
Virginia Union University *B*
Washington and Lee University *B*

Washington
Central Washington University *B*
Centralia College *A*
City University *B*
Eastern Washington University *B, T*
Everett Community College *A*
Evergreen State College *B*
Gonzaga University *B*
Highline Community College *A*
Pacific Lutheran University *B*
Peninsula College *A*
Seattle University *B*
Washington State University *B*
Western Washington University *B*
Whitworth College *B, T*

West Virginia
Concord College *B*
Marshall University *B, M*
Potomac State College of West Virginia University *A*
University of Charleston *B*
West Virginia University Parkersburg *A*
West Virginia University *B, M, T*

Wisconsin
Marian College of Fond du Lac *B*
Marquette University *B, M, T*
University of Wisconsin
   Eau Claire *B*
   Madison *B, M, D*
   Milwaukee *B, M*
   Oshkosh *B*
   River Falls *B, T*
   Superior *B*
   Whitewater *B*

Wyoming
Casper College *A*
Central Wyoming College *A*
Laramie County Community College *A*
Northwest College *A*
University of Wyoming *B*
Western Wyoming Community College *A*

Junior high education

Alabama
Alabama Agricultural and Mechanical University *B, M, T*
Athens State University *B*
Birmingham-Southern College *T*
Faulkner University *B, T*
Huntingdon College *B*
Troy State University Dothan *B, M, T*

Alaska
Alaska Pacific University *B, M*

Arkansas
John Brown University *B*
University of Arkansas *B, M*
University of Central Arkansas *M*
University of the Ozarks *A, B, T*

California
Azusa Pacific University *B, T*
California Lutheran University *B, M*
California State University
   Bakersfield *B, M*
   Hayward *T*
   Long Beach *T*
   Northridge *M*
   San Marcos *T*
Mills College *T*
Mount St. Mary's College *B*
Occidental College *T*
St. Mary's College of California *T*
San Francisco State University *T*
Simpson College *B, T*
Sonoma State University *M*
United States International University *T*
University of California Riverside *T*
University of La Verne *B, M, T*
University of Redlands *B, T*
University of Southern California *T*
Whittier College *T*

Colorado
Adams State College *B, T*
Fort Lewis College *T*
University of Northern Colorado *T*
Western State College of Colorado *T*

Connecticut
Central Connecticut State University *B*
Eastern Connecticut State University *B, T*
Quinnipiac University *B, M*
Sacred Heart University *B, M, T*
St. Joseph College *T*

Delaware
Delaware State University *B*
University of Delaware *B, T*

Florida
Southeastern College of the Assemblies of God *B, T*
University of Florida *B*
University of North Florida *B*
University of West Florida *B, T*

Georgia
Armstrong Atlantic State University *B, M, T*
Augusta State University *B, M*
Berry College *B, M, T*
Brenau University *B, M, T*
Clark Atlanta University *B*
Clayton College and State University *B*
Columbus State University *B, M*
Covenant College *B, T*
Emmanuel College *B*
Fort Valley State University *B, M, T*
Georgia College and State University *B, M, T*
Georgia Southern University *B, M, T*
Georgia Southwestern State University *B, M, T*
Georgia State University *B, M*
Kennesaw State University *B, M*
Mercer University *B, M, T*
Morehouse College *B*
North Georgia College & State University *B, M*
Oglethorpe University *B, M, T*
Paine College *B*
Piedmont College *B, T*
Reinhardt College *B*
Shorter College *B, T*
Thomas College *B*
Toccoa Falls College *B, T*
University of Georgia *B, M, D, T*
Valdosta State University *B, M*
Wesleyan College *B, M, T*

Idaho
Boise State University *T*
Northwest Nazarene University *B*

Illinois
Augustana College *B, T*
Barat College *B*
City Colleges of Chicago Kennedy-King College *A*
Eastern Illinois University *B*
Eureka College *B*
Greenville College *T*
Illinois State University *B, T*
Judson College *B, T*
McKendree College *B, T*
North Park University *B, M*
Quincy University *T*
Rend Lake College *A*
Southwestern Illinois College *A*
Trinity Christian College *T*
University of St. Francis *M, T*

Indiana
Ball State University *M, T*
Butler University *B*
Franklin College *T*
Goshen College *B*
Indiana State University *B, M, T*
Indiana University Northwest *B*
Indiana University--Purdue University Indiana University-Purdue University Fort Wayne *T*
Indiana Wesleyan University *B, M*
Manchester College *B, T*
Tri-State University *B, T*
University of Evansville *B*
University of Indianapolis *T*
Valparaiso University *B, T*
Vincennes University *A*

Iowa
Buena Vista University *M, T*
Central College *T*
Clarke College *B, M, T*
Cornell College *B, T*
Dordt College *B, T*
Faith Baptist Bible College and Theological Seminary *B, T*
Graceland University *T*
Iowa Wesleyan College *B*
Luther College *B*
Morningside College *B, M*
Northwestern College *T*
Simpson College *T*
University of Northern Iowa *B, M*
Upper Iowa University *B, T*
William Penn University *B*

Kansas
Garden City Community College *A*
Independence Community College *A*
McPherson College *B, T*
Newman University *B, T*
Ottawa University *T*
Pittsburg State University *B, T*
Tabor College *B, T*
University of Kansas *B, T*

Kentucky
Alice Lloyd College *B*
Asbury College *B, T*
Bellarmine College *B, T*
Berea College *B, T*
Brescia University *B, T*
Campbellsville University *B*
Cumberland College *B, M, T*
Eastern Kentucky University *B, M*
Kentucky Christian College *B, T*
Kentucky Wesleyan College *B*
Lindsey Wilson College *B, T*
Morehead State University *B, M, T*
Murray State University *B, M, T*
Northern Kentucky University *B, M, T*
Pikeville College *B, T*
Spalding University *B, M, T*
Thomas More College *B*
Transylvania University *B, T*
Union College *B, M, T*
University of Kentucky *B, M, T*
University of Louisville *M, D*
Western Kentucky University *B, M*

Louisiana
Centenary College of Louisiana *B, T*
Dillard University *B, T*
Nicholls State University *B*

Maine
St. Joseph's College *B*
University of Maine Machias *B*
University of New England *T*
University of Southern Maine *T*

Maryland
Goucher College *M*
Morgan State University *M*

Massachusetts
American International College *B, M*
Assumption College *B, T*
Bridgewater State College *B, T*
Eastern Nazarene College *B, M, T*
Fitchburg State College *B*
Gordon College *B*
Lesley College *B, M, T*
Massachusetts College of Liberal Arts *T*
Merrimack College *T*
Simmons College *B, M*
Tufts University *M, T*
Wellesley College *T*
Westfield State College *B, M, T*
Worcester State College *M, T*

Michigan
Adrian College *T*
Calvin College *B, T*
Central Michigan University *M*
Eastern Michigan University *M*
Grand Valley State University *T*
Madonna University *B, T*
Northern Michigan University *B, T*
Saginaw Valley State University *M*
Spring Arbor College *T*
Western Michigan University *B, M, T*

Minnesota
Carleton College *T*

College of St. Catherine: St. Paul Campus B
Concordia University: St. Paul B, T
Minnesota State University, Mankato B, T
Moorhead State University B, T
Northland Community & Technical College A
Ridgewater College: A Community and Technical College A
St. Mary's University of Minnesota B
Winona State University B, M, T

Mississippi
Blue Mountain College B

Missouri
Avila College B, T
Central Missouri State University B, T
College of the Ozarks T
Culver-Stockton College T
East Central College A
Evangel University B, T
Fontbonne College B
Harris Stowe State College B, T
Lindenwood University B
Maryville University of Saint Louis B, M, T
Missouri Baptist College B, T
Missouri Southern State College B, T
Missouri Valley College T
Missouri Western State College B
Northwest Missouri State University B, M, T
Ozark Christian College A
Rockhurst University B
Southwest Baptist University B, T
Southwest Missouri State University B
Truman State University M, T
University of Missouri
   Columbia B
   Kansas City B
   St. Louis T
Washington University B, M, T
Webster University B, T
Westminster College B, T
William Jewell College T
William Woods University B

Montana
Rocky Mountain College B, T

Nebraska
College of Saint Mary B, T
Midland Lutheran College B, T
Nebraska Wesleyan University B
Peru State College B, T
University of Nebraska
   Kearney B, M, T
   Lincoln T

New Hampshire
Antioch New England Graduate School M
Franklin Pierce College T
Plymouth State College of the University System of New Hampshire B

New Jersey
Centenary College T
Rowan University B

Rutgers
   The State University of New Jersey: Camden College of Arts and Sciences T
   The State University of New Jersey: Douglass College T
   The State University of New Jersey: Livingston College T
   The State University of New Jersey: Newark College of Arts and Sciences T
   The State University of New Jersey: Rutgers College T
   The State University of New Jersey: University College Camden T
   The State University of New Jersey: University College New Brunswick T
   The State University of New Jersey: University College Newark T

New Mexico
New Mexico Junior College A
Western New Mexico University B, M

New York
Alfred University T
Bank Street College of Education M
Barnard College T
Canisius College B, M, T
City University of New York
   Brooklyn College B, M, T
   Lehman College M, T
   Queens College B, M, T
College of Mount St. Vincent T
Columbia University
   Teachers College M, D
Concordia College B, T
Dowling College B, M, T
Eugene Lang College/New School University T
Hofstra University T
Long Island University
   Brooklyn Campus B, M
Manhattan College B, T
Manhattanville College M, T
Marymount College B, T
Nazareth College of Rochester T
New York University B, M, T
Russell Sage College B, T
St. Francis College B, T
Sarah Lawrence College M
St. Joseph's College
   St. Joseph's College: Suffolk Campus B, T
   St. Joseph's College B, T
State University of New York
   Buffalo M, D
   College at Cortland M
   College at Fredonia T
   College at Old Westbury T
   College at Oneonta B, M, T
   College at Potsdam B, M, T
   New Paltz B, M, T
   Oswego B
Syracuse University B, M, T
Vassar College T
Wagner College B, T

North Carolina
Appalachian State University B, M, T
Barton College B
Bennett College B
Campbell University B, M, T
Catawba College B, M, T
East Carolina University B, M
Elizabeth City State University B, T
Elon College B, M, T
Fayetteville State University B, M
Gardner-Webb University B
Greensboro College B, T
High Point University B, T
Lees-McRae College T
Lenoir-Rhyne College B, M, T
Mars Hill College B, T
Meredith College T
Methodist College A, B, T
North Carolina Central University B, M
North Carolina State University B
North Carolina Wesleyan College B
University of North Carolina
   Asheville T
   Chapel Hill B, M
   Charlotte B, M
   Greensboro B, M
   Pembroke B, M, T
   Wilmington B, M
Warren Wilson College B, T
Western Carolina University B, M, T
Wingate University B, T
Winston-Salem State University B

North Dakota
Dickinson State University B, T
Mayville State University B, T
Minot State University B, T
North Dakota State University B, T
University of North Dakota B, T

Ohio
Ashland University B, T
Baldwin-Wallace College B
Bluffton College B
Capital University B
Cedarville College B
Central State University B
College of Mount St. Joseph B
College of Wooster B
Defiance College B, T
Hiram College T
Kent State University
   Stark Campus B
Kent State University B, M, D
Malone College B, M
Marietta College B
Mount Union College B, T
Mount Vernon Nazarene College B, T
Notre Dame College of Ohio T
Ohio Northern University B, T
Ohio State University
   Columbus Campus M
Ohio University
   Zanesville Campus B
Ohio University B, D, T
Otterbein College B
Shawnee State University T
University of Akron M
University of Dayton B, M, T
University of Findlay B
University of Rio Grande B, T
Ursuline College B, T
Walsh University B
Wilmington College B
Wittenberg University B
Wright State University M
Youngstown State University B, M

Oklahoma
Northwestern Oklahoma State University T
Oklahoma Christian University of Science and Arts B, T
Oklahoma State University B, M, D, T
Southeastern Oklahoma State University T
Southwestern Oklahoma State University M, T

Oregon
Concordia University B, M, T
Eastern Oregon University B, M
Lewis & Clark College M
Linfield College B, T
Western Baptist College B
Western Oregon University T
Willamette University M

Pennsylvania
California University of Pennsylvania A, B, T
Cedar Crest College B, T
Gettysburg College T
La Salle University B, T
Lock Haven University of Pennsylvania B, T
Mansfield University of Pennsylvania B, T
Reading Area Community College A
St. Vincent College T
Westminster College B, T

Rhode Island
Rhode Island College B, M

South Carolina
Charleston Southern University M
Columbia College B
Erskine College B, T
Lander University B, T
University of South Carolina
   Aiken B, T

South Dakota
Black Hills State University B, T
Dakota State University B, T
Mount Marty College B

Tennessee
Austin Peay State University T
Belmont University B, T
Cumberland University B, T
David Lipscomb University B, T
Freed-Hardeman University T
Johnson Bible College A, B, T
King College T
Lambuth University B, T
Lincoln Memorial University B, T
Tennessee Wesleyan College B, T
Tusculum College B, T
Union University B, T
University of Tennessee
   Chattanooga B
   Knoxville T

Texas
Concordia University at Austin B, T
Texas A&M University
   Commerce B
   Kingsville M
Texas Lutheran University T
Trinity Valley Community College A

Vermont
Castleton State College B, M, T
College of St. Joseph in Vermont B
Goddard College B
Johnson State College B, M
St. Michael's College M
University of Vermont B

Virginia
Bluefield College B
Christopher Newport University T
Eastern Mennonite University T
George Mason University M
Hampton University B
Hollins University T
Longwood College B, T
Mary Baldwin College T
Norfolk State University T
Radford University T
St. Paul's College T
University of Richmond B, T
Virginia Wesleyan College T

Washington
Central Washington University M
Evergreen State College M
Whitworth College B, M, T

West Virginia
Alderson-Broaddus College B
Bluefield State College B
Fairmont State College B
Glenville State College B
Marshall University B, M
West Virginia State College B
Wheeling Jesuit University T

Wisconsin
Alverno College B, T
Beloit College T

Cardinal Stritch University B, T
Carroll College B, T
Carthage College T
Concordia University Wisconsin B, T
Marian College of Fond du Lac B, T
Marquette University B
Mount Senario College B
Northland College T
Ripon College T
St. Norbert College T
Silver Lake College T
University of Wisconsin
    Green Bay T
    La Crosse B, M, T
    Platteville T
    River Falls T
Viterbo University B, T

Wyoming
Eastern Wyoming College A
Western Wyoming Community
    College A

Juridical specialization

Alabama
Samford University D

California
University of San Francisco M

Connecticut
Yale University M, D

District of Columbia
Georgetown University M

Florida
University of Florida M

Illinois
University of Illinois
    Urbana-Champaign M, D

Indiana
Indiana University
    Bloomington M
Valparaiso University D

Maryland
Prince George's Community College A

Massachusetts
Harvard University M, D

Michigan
University of Michigan M, D
Wayne State University M

Minnesota
University of Minnesota
    Twin Cities M

New Jersey
Seton Hall University M

New York
New York University D
Pace University:
    Pleasantville/Briarcliff M
Pace University M

North Carolina
Duke University D

Ohio
Case Western Reserve University M

Virginia
University of Virginia M, D

Labor/personnel relations

Alabama
Wallace State Community College at
    Hanceville A

California
California State University
    Dominguez Hills B
Long Beach City College A
Los Angeles Trade and Technical
    College C, A
Los Medanos College C, A
San Diego City College A
San Francisco State University B
San Jose City College C, A

Connecticut
University of Bridgeport B, M
University of New Haven M

District of Columbia
Southeastern University M

Georgia
Georgia State University M, D
University of Georgia B

Illinois
Barat College B
Black Hawk College C
Kaskaskia College A
Loyola University of Chicago M
Roosevelt University B
University of Illinois
    Springfield B

Indiana
Indiana University
    Bloomington C, A, B
    Kokomo C, A, B
    Northwest C, A, B
    South Bend C, A, B
    Southeast A, B
Indiana University--Purdue University
    Indiana University-Purdue
        University Fort Wayne C, A, B
    Indiana University-Purdue
        University Indianapolis C, A, B
Purdue University
    North Central Campus A, B

Iowa
Iowa State University M
University of Iowa B, D

Kentucky
Northern Kentucky University A, B

Maine
University of Maine B

Massachusetts
University of Massachusetts
    Amherst M
    Boston B

Michigan
Michigan State University M
Wayne State University M

Minnesota
University of Minnesota
    Twin Cities C, M, D
Winona State University B

Missouri
Rockhurst University B

New Hampshire
Antioch New England Graduate
    School M

New Jersey
Rider University B
Rowan University B

Rutgers
    The State University of New Jersey:
        Douglass College B
    The State University of New Jersey:
        Livingston College B
    The State University of New Jersey:
        New Brunswick Graduate
        Campus M, D
    The State University of New Jersey:
        Rutgers College B
    The State University of New Jersey:
        University College New
        Brunswick B
Seton Hall University B
Thomas Edison State College C, B

New York
City University of New York
    Baruch College B, M
Cornell University B, M, D
New York Institute of Technology M
New York University B, M, D
Onondaga Community College A
State University of New York
    College at Old Westbury B
    College at Potsdam B
    Empire State College M

North Carolina
University of North Carolina
    Chapel Hill B

Ohio
Bowling Green State University B
Case Western Reserve University M, D
Cincinnati State Technical and
    Community College C
Cleveland State University B, M, D
Lorain County Community College A
Sinclair Community College C, A
University of Akron M
Youngstown State University A, B

Oregon
University of Oregon M

Pennsylvania
Clarion University of Pennsylvania B
Indiana University of Pennsylvania M
La Salle University B
Penn State
    University Park B, M
St. Francis College M
Temple University B, M, D
University of Pennsylvania B, M, D

Puerto Rico
Inter American University of Puerto Rico
    Metropolitan Campus M
University of Puerto Rico
    Rio Piedras Campus B

Rhode Island
Community College of Rhode Island A
Providence College C, A
Rhode Island College B
University of Rhode Island M

Tennessee
Tennessee Technological University B

Texas
College of the Mainland A
San Antonio College C
University of North Texas B, M, D

Virginia
Norfolk State University B

Washington
Pacific Lutheran University B

West Virginia
West Virginia University M

Wisconsin
Marquette University C
Milwaukee Area Technical College A

University of Wisconsin
    Madison M, D
    Milwaukee M
Western Wisconsin Technical College A

Landscape architecture

Alabama
Auburn University B

Arizona
Arizona State University B
University of Arizona M, D

Arkansas
University of Arkansas
    Little Rock A
University of Arkansas B

California
American River College A
California State Polytechnic University:
    Pomona B, M
City College of San Francisco A
East Los Angeles College A
Los Angeles Pierce College C
MiraCosta College C, A
Modesto Junior College A
Riverside Community College A
San Diego Mesa College C, A
San Joaquin Delta College C, A
Sierra College C, A
Southwestern College C, A
University of California
    Berkeley B, M
    Davis B
University of Southern California M
West Valley College A

Colorado
Colorado State University B
University of Colorado
    Denver M

Connecticut
University of Connecticut B

Florida
Broward Community College A
Florida International University M
Lake City Community College A
University of Florida B, M

Georgia
Middle Georgia College A
University of Georgia B, M

Idaho
University of Idaho B

Illinois
Kishwaukee College A
University of Illinois
    Urbana-Champaign B, M

Indiana
Ball State University B
Purdue University B

Iowa
Iowa State University B, M

Kansas
Kansas State University B, M

Kentucky
Murray State University A
University of Kentucky B

Louisiana
Louisiana State University and
    Agricultural and Mechanical
    College B, M

Maryland
Community College of Baltimore County
    Catonsville C, A
Montgomery College
    Germantown Campus C

Morgan State University *M*
University of Maryland
  College Park *B*
  Eastern Shore *B*

Massachusetts
Conway School of Landscape Design *M*
Endicott College *C, A*
Harvard University *M, D*
University of Massachusetts
  Amherst *B, M*

Michigan
Bay de Noc Community College *A*
Lansing Community College *A*
Michigan State University *B*
University of Michigan *M, D*

Minnesota
University of Minnesota
  Twin Cities *B, M*

Mississippi
Mississippi Gulf Coast Community
  College
    Jefferson Davis Campus *C*
Mississippi State University *B*

Missouri
Washington University *M*

Nevada
University of Nevada
  Las Vegas *B*

New Jersey
Cumberland County College *C*
Rutgers
  The State University of New Jersey:
    Cook College *B*

New Mexico
University of New Mexico *M*

New York
City University of New York
  City College *B*
Cornell University *B, M*
Monroe Community College *A*
Parsons School of Design *B*
State University of New York
  College of Agriculture and
    Technology at Morrisville *A*
  College of Environmental Science
    and Forestry *B, M*
  College of Technology at Delhi *A*

North Carolina
North Carolina Agricultural and
  Technical State University *B*
North Carolina State University *B, M*
Wake Technical Community College *A*

North Dakota
North Dakota State University *B*

Ohio
Central Ohio Technical College *A*
Columbus State Community College *A*
Kent State University *B*
Ohio State University
  Columbus Campus *B, M*

Oklahoma
Oklahoma State University *B*
University of Oklahoma *M*

Oregon
Central Oregon Community College *A*
University of Oregon *B, M*

Pennsylvania
Penn State
  University Park *B, M*
Temple University *B*
University of Pennsylvania *M*

Rhode Island
University of Rhode Island *B*

South Carolina
Clemson University *B*

Texas
Howard College *C*
Texas A&M University *B, M*
Texas Tech University *B, M*
University of Texas
  Arlington *B, M*

Utah
Utah State University *B, M*

Virginia
University of Virginia *M*
Virginia Polytechnic Institute and State
  University *B, M*

Washington
South Seattle Community College *C, A*
University of Washington *B, M*
Washington State University *B*

West Virginia
West Virginia University *B*

Wisconsin
University of Wisconsin
  Madison *M*

Landscaping management

Alabama
James H. Faulkner State Community
  College *C, A*
Shelton State Community College *C*

Arizona
Mesa Community College *A*
Pima Community College *C, A*

California
College of the Redwoods *C*
College of the Sequoias *C*
Foothill College *C, A*
Los Angeles Pierce College *C, A*
Merritt College *C, A*
MiraCosta College *C, A*
Modesto Junior College *C, A*
Mount San Antonio College *C*
San Joaquin Delta College *C*
Santa Rosa Junior College *C*
Southwestern College *C*
Yuba College *C*

Colorado
Colorado State University *B*

Connecticut
Middlesex Community-Technical
  College *C*

Florida
Gulf Coast Community College *A*
Lake City Community College *A*
Pasco-Hernando Community College *C*

Georgia
Floyd College *A*
Gainesville College *C*
University of Georgia *B*

Illinois
College of DuPage *C*
College of Lake County *C, A*
Joliet Junior College *C, A*
Kishwaukee College *C, A*
McHenry County College *C*
Parkland College *A*
Southwestern Illinois College *A*
Triton College *C, A*
William Rainey Harper College *C, A*

Iowa
Iowa Lakes Community College *A*
Northeast Iowa Community College *A*
Western Iowa Tech Community
  College *C*

Maine
Southern Maine Technical College *C, A*
University of Maine
  Augusta *A*

Maryland
University of Maryland
  College Park *B*

Massachusetts
North Shore Community College *A*
Springfield Technical Community
  College *C, A*
University of Massachusetts
  Amherst *A*

Michigan
Bay de Noc Community College *C*
Grand Rapids Community College *A*
Michigan State University *C*
Northwestern Michigan College *A*
Oakland Community College *C, A*

Minnesota
Anoka-Ramsey Community College *A*
Dakota County Technical College *C, A*
Hennepin Technical College *C, A*

Mississippi
Hinds Community College *A*
Mississippi Gulf Coast Community
  College
    Jefferson Davis Campus *C*
    Perkinston *C*
Mississippi State University *B*

Nebraska
Central Community College *C*
Nebraska College of Technical
  Agriculture *A*

Nevada
Community College of Southern
  Nevada *A*

New Hampshire
New Hampshire Technical Institute *C*
University of New Hampshire *A*

New Jersey
Bergen Community College *C*

New Mexico
Dona Ana Branch Community College of
  New Mexico State University *A*

New York
Finger Lakes Community College *C, A*
State University of New York
  College of Agriculture and
    Technology at Cobleskill *A*
  College of Technology at Alfred *A*
  College of Technology at Delhi *A*

North Carolina
Alamance Community College *C*
Blue Ridge Community College *C*
Cape Fear Community College *A*
North Carolina Agricultural and
  Technical State University *B*
Sampson Community College *C*
Sandhills Community College *A*

North Dakota
Minot State University: Bottineau
  Campus *A*

Ohio
Cincinnati State Technical and
  Community College *A*
Clark State Community College *A*
Ohio State University
  Agricultural Technical Institute *A*
  Columbus Campus *B*
Owens Community College
  Toledo *A*

Oregon
Central Oregon Community College *A*
Linn-Benton Community College *C, A*

Portland Community College *C, A*

Pennsylvania
Chatham College *B*
Community College of Allegheny
  County *A*
Delaware Valley College *B*
Penn State
  University Park *C, B*
Temple University *A*

South Carolina
Spartanburg Technical College *A*
Technical College of the Lowcountry *C*
Trident Technical College *C*

South Dakota
South Dakota State University *B*
Southeast Technical Institute *A*

Tennessee
Chattanooga State Technical Community
  College *C*
Tennessee Technological University *B*
University of Tennessee
  Martin *B*

Texas
Collin County Community College
  District *C, A*
Grayson County College *A*
Houston Community College System *C*
Western Texas College *C, A*

Vermont
Vermont Technical College *A*

Virginia
J. Sargeant Reynolds Community
  College *A*
Lord Fairfax Community College *C*
Mountain Empire Community College *C*

Washington
Clark College *C, A*
Edmonds Community College *A*
Pierce College *A*
South Seattle Community College *C, A*

Latin

Alabama
Samford University *B*

California
Loyola Marymount University *B, M*
San Diego State University *B*
Santa Clara University *B*
University of California
  Berkeley *B, M*
  Davis *B*
  Los Angeles *B*
  Santa Cruz *B, D*
University of Southern California *B*

Colorado
University of Denver *B*

Connecticut
Connecticut College *B*
Yale University *B*

Delaware
University of Delaware *B, M, T*

District of Columbia
Catholic University of America *B, M, T*
George Washington University *B*

Florida
Florida State University *B, M*
University of Florida *M*

Georgia
Emory University *B*
Mercer University *B*
Oxford College of Emory University *B*
University of Georgia *B, M*

Latin

Idaho
Idaho State University A
University of Idaho B

Illinois
Augustana College B, T
Concordia University B
Loyola University of Chicago B, M, T
Monmouth College B
Rockford College B
University of Chicago B

Indiana
Butler University B
DePauw University B
Indiana State University B
Indiana University
    Bloomington B, M, D
University of Notre Dame B
Wabash College B

Iowa
Cornell College B, T
Luther College B
University of Iowa B, M, T

Kansas
Wichita State University B

Kentucky
Asbury College B, T
Berea College B, T

Louisiana
Centenary College of Louisiana B
Louisiana State University and
    Agricultural and Mechanical
    College B
Tulane University B, M

Maine
University of Maine B

Maryland
Johns Hopkins University B

Massachusetts
Amherst College B
Boston College B, M
Boston University B
Harvard College B
Smith College B
Tufts University B
Wellesley College B

Michigan
Calvin College B, T
Hope College B
Michigan State University B, M
University of Michigan B, M, D, T
Western Michigan University B

Minnesota
Carleton College B
Concordia College: Moorhead B
Macalester College B
St. Olaf College B, T
University of Minnesota
    Twin Cities B, M, D
University of St. Thomas B

Missouri
Southwest Missouri State University B
Washington University B, M

Montana
University of Montana-Missoula B

Nebraska
Creighton University B
University of Nebraska
    Lincoln B

New Hampshire
Dartmouth College B
St. Anselm College C, B
University of New Hampshire B

New Jersey
Georgian Court College T
Montclair State University B, T
Rutgers
    The State University of New Jersey:
      Douglass College B, T
    The State University of New Jersey:
      Livingston College B, T
    The State University of New Jersey:
      Rutgers College B, T
    The State University of New Jersey:
      University College New
      Brunswick B, T
Seton Hall University T

New York
Bard College B
City University of New York
    Brooklyn College B
    Hunter College B
    Lehman College B
    Queens College B
Colgate University B
College of New Rochelle B, T
Columbia University
    Graduate School M, D
Cornell University B, T
Elmira College B, T
Fordham University B, M, D
Hamilton College B
Hobart and William Smith Colleges B
New York University B
St. Bonaventure University B
Sarah Lawrence College B
State University of New York
    Albany B, M
    Binghamton B
    Buffalo B
Syracuse University B, M
Vassar College B

North Carolina
Duke University B
University of North Carolina
    Chapel Hill B, M, D, T
    Greensboro M
Wake Forest University B

Ohio
Bowling Green State University B
College of Wooster B
John Carroll University B
Kent State University
    Stark Campus B
Kent State University B, M
Miami University
    Oxford Campus B, T
Oberlin College B
Ohio State University
    Columbus Campus B
Ohio University B, T
University of Akron B
University of Cincinnati B, T
University of Toledo B
Wright State University B
Youngstown State University B

Oregon
University of Oregon B

Pennsylvania
Bryn Mawr College B, M, D
Dickinson College B
Duquesne University B
Franklin and Marshall College B
Gettysburg College B
Haverford College B, T
Immaculata College A, B
La Salle University B
Moravian College T
Swarthmore College B
University of Scranton B, T
Ursinus College B, T
West Chester University of
    Pennsylvania B, M
Westminster College B, T

Puerto Rico
Pontifical Catholic University of Puerto
    Rico B

Rhode Island
Brown University B, M, D

South Carolina
Furman University B, T

Tennessee
Rhodes College B
University of Tennessee
    Chattanooga B
    Knoxville B
University of the South B
Vanderbilt University M

Texas
Austin College B
Baylor University B
Rice University B
Southwestern University B, T
Texas Tech University B
University of Dallas B, T
University of North Texas B
University of Texas
    Austin B

Utah
Brigham Young University B

Vermont
Marlboro College B
Middlebury College B
University of Vermont B, M

Virginia
College of William and Mary B
Hampden-Sydney College B
Mary Washington College B
Radford University T
Randolph-Macon College B
Randolph-Macon Woman's College B
Sweet Briar College B
University of Richmond B, T

Washington
Seattle Pacific University B
University of Washington B

West Virginia
Marshall University B

Wisconsin
Lawrence University B, T
University of Wisconsin
    Madison B, M

Latin American studies

Alabama
Samford University B
University of Alabama B, M

Arizona
Prescott College B, M
University of Arizona B, M

California
California State University
    Chico B
    Fullerton B
    Hayward B
    Long Beach C
    Los Angeles B, M
    Monterey Bay B
Chapman University B
Claremont McKenna College B
College of Notre Dame B
Cypress College A
De Anza College C, A
Occidental College B
Pepperdine University B
Pitzer College B
Pomona College B
San Diego City College A
San Diego State University B, M
Scripps College B
Stanford University B, M
University of California
    Berkeley B, M, D
    Los Angeles B, M
    Riverside B
    San Diego B, M
    Santa Barbara B, M
    Santa Cruz B
Whittier College B

Colorado
Fort Lewis College B
University of Colorado
    Boulder B
University of Denver B

Connecticut
Trinity College B
University of Connecticut B
Wesleyan University B
Yale University B

Delaware
University of Delaware B

District of Columbia
American University B
George Washington University B, M
Georgetown University M
Trinity College B

Florida
Flagler College B
Florida Atlantic University B
Florida International University M
Florida State University B
Manatee Community College A
Miami-Dade Community College A
Rollins College B
Stetson University B
University of Florida M
University of Miami B

Georgia
Emory University B
Oxford College of Emory University B

Idaho
University of Idaho B

Illinois
De Paul University B
Illinois Wesleyan University B
Lake Forest College B
University of Chicago M
University of Illinois
    Chicago B
    Urbana-Champaign B

Indiana
Earlham College B
Hanover College B
Indiana University
    Bloomington M

Iowa
Central College B
Cornell College B
Luther College B
University of Northern Iowa B

Kansas
University of Kansas B, M

Kentucky
University of Kentucky B

Louisiana
Tulane University B, M, D

Maine
Colby College B

Maryland
Hood College B
Johns Hopkins University B

Massachusetts
Boston University B
Brandeis University B
College of the Holy Cross B
Hampshire College B

Harvard College *B*
Mount Holyoke College *B*
Northeastern University *B*
Smith College *B*
Tufts University *B, M*
Wellesley College *B*

Michigan
Oakland University *B*
University of Michigan *B*
Western Michigan University *B*

Minnesota
Carleton College *B*
Macalester College *B*
St. Cloud State University *B*
University of Minnesota
    Morris *B*
    Twin Cities *B*

Missouri
University of Missouri
    St. Louis *C*
Washington University *B*

Nebraska
University of Nebraska
    Lincoln *B*

Nevada
University of Nevada
    Las Vegas *B*

New Hampshire
Dartmouth College *B*
St. Anselm College *C*

New Jersey
Richard Stockton College of New
    Jersey *C*
Rutgers
    The State University of New Jersey:
      Douglass College *B*
    The State University of New Jersey:
      Livingston College *B*
    The State University of New Jersey:
      Rutgers College *B*
    The State University of New Jersey:
      University College New
      Brunswick *B*

New Mexico
University of New Mexico *B, M, D*

New York
Adelphi University *B*
Bard College *B*
Barnard College *B*
City University of New York
    Brooklyn College *B*
    City College *B*
    Lehman College *B*
    Queens College *B*
Colgate University *B*
Columbia University
    Columbia College *B*
    Graduate School *M, D*
    School of General Studies *B*
Cornell University *B*
Fordham University *B*
Hobart and William Smith Colleges *B*
New York University *B, M*
St. John's University *M*
Sarah Lawrence College *B*
State University of New York
    Albany *B, M*
    Binghamton *B*
    College at Plattsburgh *B*
    New Paltz *B*
Syracuse University *B*
United States Military Academy *B*
Vassar College *B*

North Carolina
Belmont Abbey College *B*
University of North Carolina
    Chapel Hill *B*
Wake Forest University *M*

Ohio
College of Wooster *B*
Denison University *B*
Kent State University
    Stark Campus *B*
Kent State University *B*
Oberlin College *B*
Ohio State University
    Columbus Campus *B*
Ohio University *B, M*
Pontifical College Josephinum *B*
University of Cincinnati *B*
University of Toledo *B*

Oklahoma
Oklahoma State University *C*

Oregon
Willamette University *B*

Pennsylvania
Bucknell University *B*
Gettysburg College *B*
Lock Haven University of
    Pennsylvania *B*
Penn State
    University Park *B*
St. Joseph's University *C*
Temple University *B*
University of Pennsylvania *B*
University of Pittsburgh *C*

Rhode Island
Brown University *B, M, D*
Providence College *B*
University of Rhode Island *B*

South Carolina
University of South Carolina *B*

Tennessee
Rhodes College *B*
University of Tennessee
    Knoxville *B*
Vanderbilt University *B, M*

Texas
Baylor University *B*
Palo Alto College *A*
Rice University *B*
St. Mary's University *B*
Southern Methodist University *B*
Texas Christian University *B*
Trinity University *B*
University of Texas
    Austin *B, M, D*
    El Paso *B*
    Pan American *B*

Utah
Brigham Young University *B*

Vermont
Goddard College *B*
Marlboro College *B*
Middlebury College *B*
University of Vermont *B*

Virginia
George Mason University *B*
Mary Baldwin College *B*

Washington
Evergreen State College *B*
Gonzaga University *B*
Seattle Pacific University *B*
University of Washington *B*
Western Washington University *B*

Wisconsin
Ripon College *B*
University of Wisconsin
    Eau Claire *B*
    Madison *B, M*

Law (J.D.)

Alabama
Samford University: Cumberland School
    of Law *F*
Thomas Goode Jones School of
    Law--Faulkner University *F*
University of Alabama: School of Law *F*

Arizona
Arizona State University: College of
    Law *F*
University of Arizona: College of Law *F*

Arkansas
University of Arkansas at Little Rock:
    School of Law *F*
University of Arkansas: School of Law *F*

California
California Western School of Law *F*
Golden Gate University: School of
    Law *F*
Humphreys College: School of Law *F*
John F. Kennedy University: School of
    Law *F*
Loyola Marymount University: School of
    Law *F*
McGeorge School of Law: University of
    the Pacific *F*
Pepperdine University: School of Law *F*
Santa Clara University: School of Law *F*
Southwestern University School of
    Law *F*
Stanford University: School of Law *F*
University of California
    Hastings College of the Law *F*
University of California Berkeley: School
    of Law *F*
University of California Davis: School of
    Law *F*
University of California Los Angeles:
    School of Law *F*
University of La Verne College of Law at
    San Fernando Valley *F*
University of La Verne: School of Law *F*
University of San Diego: School of
    Law *F*
University of San Francisco: School of
    Law *F*
University of Southern California: Law
    School *F*
University of West Los Angeles: School
    of Law *F*
Whittier Law School *F*

Colorado
University of Colorado at Boulder:
    School of Law *F*
University of Denver: College of Law *F*

Connecticut
Quinnipiac College: School of Law *F*
University of Connecticut: School of
    Law *F*
Yale Law School *F*

Delaware
Widener University School of Law *F*

District of Columbia
American University: Washington
    College of Law *F*
Catholic University of America: School
    of Law *F*
George Washington University Law
    School *F*
Georgetown University: Law Center *F*
Howard University: School of Law *F*
University of the District of Columbia:
    School of Law *F*

Florida
Florida State University: School of
    Law *F*
Nova Southeastern University of the
    Health Sciences: College of
    Pharmacy *F*
Nova Southeastern University: Shepard
    Broad Law Center *F*
St. Thomas University: School of Law *F*
Stetson University: College of Law *F*
University of Florida: College of Law *F*
University of Miami: School of Law *F*

Georgia
Emory University: School of Law *F*
Georgia State University: College of
    Law *F*
Mercer University: Walter F. George
    School of Law *F*
University of Georgia: School of Law *F*

Hawaii
University of Hawaii William S.
    Richardson: School of Law *F*

Idaho
University of Idaho: College of Law *F*

Illinois
Chicago-Kent College of Law, Illinois
    Institute of Technology *F*
De Paul University: College of Law *F*
John Marshall Law School *F*
Loyola University Chicago: School of
    Law *F*
Northern Illinois University: College of
    Law *F*
Northwestern University: School of
    Law *F*
Southern Illinois University at
    Carbondale: School of Law *F*
University of Chicago: School of Law *F*
University of Illinois at
    Urbana-Champaign: College of Law *F*

Indiana
Indiana University Bloomington: School
    of Law *F*
Indiana University Indianapolis: School
    of Law *F*
University of Notre Dame: School of
    Law *F*
Valparaiso University: School of Law *F*

Iowa
Drake University Law School *F*
University of Iowa: College of Law *F*

Kansas
University of Kansas: School of Law *F*
Washburn University School of Law *F*

Kentucky
Northern Kentucky University: Salmon P.
    Chase School of Law *F*
University of Kentucky: College of
    Law *F*
University of Louisville: School of
    Law *F*

Louisiana
Louisiana State University and
    Agricultural and Mechanical College:
    School of Law *F*
Loyola University: School of Law *F*
Southern University: Law Center *F*
Tulane University: School of Law *F*

Maine
University of Maine: School of Law *F*

Maryland
University of Baltimore: School of
    Law *F*
University of Maryland at Baltimore:
    School of Law *F*

Massachusetts
Boston College: Law School *F*
Boston University: School of Law *F*
Harvard University Law School *F*
New England School of Law *F*

Law (J.D.)

Northeastern University: School of Law F
Suffolk University: Law School F
Western New England College: School of Law F

Michigan
Detroit College of Law F
Thomas M. Cooley Law School F
University of Detroit Mercy: School of Law F
University of Michigan: School of Law F
Wayne State University: School of Law F

Minnesota
Hamline University: School of Law F
University of Minnesota Twin Cities: School of Law F
William Mitchell College of Law: Law Professions F

Mississippi
Mississippi College: School of Law F
University of Mississippi: School of Law F

Missouri
St. Louis University: School of Law F
University of Missouri Columbia: School of Law F
University of Missouri Kansas City: School of Law F
Washington University: School of Law F

Montana
University of Montana: School of Law F

Nebraska
Creighton University: School of Law F
University of Nebraska Lincoln: College of Law F

New Hampshire
Franklin Pierce Law Center F

New Jersey
Rutgers
   The State University of New Jersey: Camden Graduate Campus F
   The State University of New Jersey: Camden School of Law F
   The State University of New Jersey: New Brunswick Graduate Campus F
   The State University of New Jersey: Newark School of Law F
Seton Hall University: School of Law F

New Mexico
University of New Mexico: School of Law F

New York
Albany Law School of Union University F
Benjamin N. Cardozo School of Law F
Brooklyn Law School F
City University of New York School of Law at Queens College F
Columbia University School of Law F
Cornell University: School of Law F
Fordham University: School of Law F
Hofstra University: School of Law F
New York Law School F
New York University: School of Law F
Pace University Westchester: School of Law F
St. John's University: School of Law F
State University of New York at Buffalo: School of Law F
Syracuse University: College of Law F
Touro College: Jacob D. Fuchsberg Law Center F

North Carolina
Campbell University: Norman Adrian Wiggins School of Law F
Duke University: School of Law F
North Carolina Central University: School of Law F
University of North Carolina at Chapel Hill: School of Law F
Wake Forest University: School of Law F

North Dakota
University of North Dakota: School of Law F

Ohio
Capital University: School of Law F
Case Western Reserve University: School of Law F
Cleveland State University: College of Law F
Ohio Northern University: College of Law F
Ohio State University: College of Law F
University of Akron: School of Law F
University of Cincinnati: College of Law F
University of Dayton: School of Law F
University of Toledo: College of Law F

Oklahoma
Oklahoma City University: School of Law F
University of Tulsa: College of Law F

Oregon
Lewis and Clark College: Northwestern School of Law F
University of Oregon: School of Law F
Willamette University: College of Law F

Pennsylvania
Dickinson School of Law F
Duquesne University: School of Law F
Temple University: School of Law F
University of Pennsylvania Law School F
Villanova University: School of Law F

Puerto Rico
Pontifical Catholic University of Puerto Rico: School of Law F
University of Puerto Rico Rio Piedras Campus: School of Law F

South Carolina
University of South Carolina: School of Law F

South Dakota
University of South Dakota: School of Law F

Tennessee
University of Memphis: School of Law F
University of Tennessee College of Law F
Vanderbilt University: School of Law F

Texas
Baylor University: School of Law F
St. Mary's University: School of Law F
South Texas College of Law F
Southern Methodist University: School of Law F
Texas Southern University: Thurgood Marshall School of Law F
Texas Tech University: School of Law F
University of Houston: Law Center F
University of Texas at Austin: School of Law F

Utah
Brigham Young University: School of Law F
University of Utah: College of Law F

Vermont
Vermont Law School F

Virginia
College of William and Mary: School of Law F
George Mason University: School of Law F
Regent University: School of Law F
University of Richmond: The T.C. Williams School of Law F
University of Virginia: School of Law F
Washington and Lee University: School of Law F

Washington
Gonzaga University: School of Law F
Seattle University: School of Law F
University of Washington: School of Law F

West Virginia
West Virginia University: College of Law F

Wisconsin
Marquette University: School of Law F
University of Wisconsin Madison: School of Law F

Wyoming
University of Wyoming: College of Law F

Law enforcement/police science

Alabama
Central Alabama Community College C, A
Community College of the Air Force A
Enterprise State Junior College A
George C. Wallace State Community College Dothan C
Jefferson State Community College A
Wallace State Community College at Hanceville A

Alaska
University of Alaska Southeast C, A

Arizona
Arizona Western College C, A
Central Arizona College C
Cochise College A
Eastern Arizona College C, A
Mohave Community College C, A
Northland Pioneer College C, A
Phoenix College A
Pima Community College C, A
Scottsdale Community College C

Arkansas
Arkansas State University A
Mississippi County Community College C, A
University of Arkansas
   Little Rock A
   Pine Bluff A
Westark College A

California
Allan Hancock College C
American River College A
Bakersfield College A
Barstow College C, A
Butte College A
Cabrillo College C, A
California Lutheran University B
California State University Stanislaus B
Cerritos Community College A
Cerro Coso Community College C, A
Chabot College A
Citrus College C
City College of San Francisco C, A
College of the Desert C, A
College of the Redwoods C
College of the Sequoias C
College of the Siskiyous A
Compton Community College A
Contra Costa College A
Diablo Valley College A
East Los Angeles College C, A
Evergreen Valley College A
Fresno City College C, A
Glendale Community College A
Grossmont Community College C, A
Irvine Valley College C, A
Los Angeles Harbor College C, A
Los Angeles Valley College C, A
Merced College A
MiraCosta College C, A
Modesto Junior College A
Moorpark College A
Mount San Antonio College C, A
Mount San Jacinto College C, A
Napa Valley College C, A
Palomar College C, A
Pasadena City College C, A
Porterville College C, A
Rio Hondo College A
Sacramento City College C, A
San Bernardino Valley College C
San Joaquin Delta College A
Santa Ana College C, A
Santa Monica College A
Santa Rosa Junior College C, A
Shasta College A
Sierra College A
Solano Community College C, A
Southwestern College C
Ventura College A
Victor Valley College C, A
West Hills Community College C, A
Yuba College A

Colorado
Aims Community College C
Arapahoe Community College C
Colorado Mountain College
   Spring Valley Campus C
Pueblo Community College A
Red Rocks Community College C
Trinidad State Junior College A
Western State College of Colorado B

Connecticut
Housatonic Community-Technical College C, A
Three Rivers Community-Technical College A
University of New Haven B
Western Connecticut State University B

Florida
Brevard Community College C
Central Florida Community College C
Daytona Beach Community College C, A
Florida State University C
Hillsborough Community College C, A
Indian River Community College C
Lake City Community College C
Palm Beach Community College C
Pasco-Hernando Community College C
Polk Community College C, A
St. Petersburg Junior College C, A
Santa Fe Community College C
South Florida Community College C
Tallahassee Community College C
Valencia Community College C

Georgia
Abraham Baldwin Agricultural College A
Armstrong Atlantic State University A
Atlanta Metropolitan College A
Dalton State College A
Floyd College A
Georgia Military College A

364

Law enforcement/police science

Gwinnett Technical Institute *A*
Macon State College *C*
Middle Georgia College *A*
South Georgia College *A*

Hawaii
University of Hawaii
    Honolulu Community College *A*

Idaho
College of Southern Idaho *C, A*
Idaho State University *C*
North Idaho College *A*

Illinois
Black Hawk College *C, A*
City Colleges of Chicago
    Harold Washington College *C, A*
    Olive-Harvey College *C*
College of DuPage *A*
College of Lake County *C, A*
Elgin Community College *A*
Illinois Eastern Community Colleges
    Frontier Community College *C*
    Olney Central College *A*
John Wood Community College *A*
Kankakee Community College *A*
Kishwaukee College *C, A*
Lake Land College *A*
McHenry County College *A*
Moraine Valley Community College *A*
Morton College *A*
Oakton Community College *C, A*
Prairie State College *C, A*
Rend Lake College *A*
Richland Community College *A*
Sauk Valley Community College *A*
Southeastern Illinois College *C, A*
Southern Illinois University
    Carbondale *A*
Southwestern Ilinois College *A*
Triton College *A*
Waubonsee Community College *C, A*
William Rainey Harper College *C, A*

Indiana
Indiana State University *M*
Indiana Wesleyan University *A*
Vincennes University *A*

Iowa
Hawkeye Community College *A*
Iowa Central Community College *C, A*
Kirkwood Community College *A*
Marshalltown Community College *A*
North Iowa Area Community College *A*
Wartburg College *B*

Kansas
Allen County Community College *A*
Butler County Community College *C, A*
Garden City Community College *A*
Hutchinson Community College *A*
Johnson County Community
    College *C, A*
Kansas City Kansas Community
    College *C, A*
Seward County Community
    College *C, A*

Kentucky
Ashland Community College *A*
Eastern Kentucky University *B, M*
Hopkinsville Community College *A*
Kentucky State University *B*
Madisonville Community College *A*
Northern Kentucky University *A*
Owensboro Community College *A*
Southeast Community College *A*
Thomas More College *A, B*

Louisiana
Bossier Parish Community College *A*
Delgado Community College *A*
Southeastern Louisiana University *A*
Southern University and Agricultural and
    Mechanical College *A*
University of Louisiana at Lafayette *A*

University of Louisiana at Monroe *A*

Maine
Andover College *A*
Beal College *A*
Southern Maine Technical College *A*

Maryland
Baltimore City Community College *A*
Chesapeake College *C, A*
Community College of Baltimore County
    Essex *C, A*
Frostburg State University *B*
Harford Community College *A*
Montgomery College
    Rockville Campus *A*

Massachusetts
Becker College *B*
Greenfield Community College *A*
Massasoit Community College *A*
Northeastern University *A, B, M*
Springfield Technical Community
    College *A*
Western New England College *B*

Michigan
Delta College *A*
Grand Rapids Community College *A*
Henry Ford Community College *A*
Jackson Community College *C, A*
Kalamazoo Valley Community
    College *C, A*
Kellogg Community College *A*
Kirtland Community College *C, A*
Lake Michigan College *A*
Lansing Community College *A*
Macomb Community College *C, A*
Mid Michigan Community College *A*
North Central Michigan College *C*
Northern Michigan University *C, B*
Northwestern Michigan College *A*
Oakland Community College *C, A*
Schoolcraft College *A*
University of Detroit Mercy *B, M*
Washtenaw Community College *A*

Minnesota
Alexandria Technical College *A*
Century Community and Technical
    College *A*
Fond Du Lac Tribal and Community
    College *A*
Hibbing Community College: A
    Technical and Community College *A*
Inver Hills Community College *A*
Metropolitan State University *B*
Minneapolis Community and Technical
    College *A*
Minnesota State University, Mankato *B*
North Hennepin Community College *A*
Northland Community & Technical
    College *A*
Ridgewater College: A Community and
    Technical College *A*
Vermilion Community College *A*
Winona State University *B*

Mississippi
Jackson State University *B*
Meridian Community College *A*
Southwest Mississippi Community
    College *A*

Missouri
College of the Ozarks *B*
Jefferson College *C, A*
Missouri Southern State College *C*
Missouri Western State College *A*
Moberly Area Community College *C, A*
Penn Valley Community College *C, A*
St. Louis University *B*
Southeast Missouri State University *B*
St. Louis Community College
    St. Louis Community College at
        Florissant Valley *A*
    St. Louis Community College at
        Meramec *C, A*

Three Rivers Community College *A*

Montana
Dawson Community College *C, A*
University of Great Falls *B*

Nebraska
Metropolitan Community College *A*
Northeast Community College *A*
University of Nebraska
    Kearney *B*

Nevada
Community College of Southern
    Nevada *C, A*
Western Nevada Community
    College *C, A*

New Hampshire
Hesser College *A*

New Jersey
Bergen Community College *A*
Burlington County College *A*
Camden County College *A*
County College of Morris *A*
Cumberland County College *C, A*
Essex County College *A*
Gloucester County College *A*
Mercer County Community College *A*
Ocean County College *C, A*
Passaic County Community
    College *C, A*
Rowan University *B*
Union County College *C, A*

New Mexico
New Mexico Junior College *A*
San Juan College *A*

New York
Adirondack Community College *A*
Erie Community College
    North Campus *A*
Jamestown Community College *A*
Monroe Community College *A*
Orange County Community College *A*
Westchester Community College *A*

North Carolina
Asheville Buncombe Technical
    Community College *C, A*
Brunswick Community College *C*
Cape Fear Community College *C*
Carteret Community College *C, A*
Catawba Valley Community College *C*
Central Piedmont Community College *A*
Cleveland Community College *C, A*
College of the Albemarle *C*
Craven Community College *C*
Davidson County Community
    College *C, A*
Durham Technical Community
    College *C*
Gaston College *C*
Guilford Technical Community
    College *A*
Halifax Community College *C*
Johnston Community College *C, A*
Lenoir Community College *C*
Mayland Community College *C*
Mitchell Community College *C, A*
Montgomery Community College *C, A*
Nash Community College *A*
Pfeiffer University *B*
Pitt Community College *A*
Sampson Community College *C*
Sandhills Community College *C*
Southwestern Community College *C*
Vance-Granville Community College *C*
Wake Technical Community College *A*
Wayne Community College *A*
Western Piedmont Community
    College *C*
Wilkes Community College *C, A*

North Dakota
Lake Region State College *C, A*

Ohio
Columbus State Community College *A*
Hocking Technical College *A*
Jefferson Community College *A*
Kent State University
    Stark Campus *B*
    Trumbull Campus *A*
Lakeland Community College *C, A*
Lima Technical College *A*
Lorain County Community College *A*
North Central State College *A*
Ohio University
    Chillicothe Campus *A*
    Southern Campus at Ironton *A*
    Zanesville Campus *A*
Ohio University *A*
Owens Community College
    Findlay Campus *A*
    Toledo *A*
Sinclair Community College *A*
Terra Community College *A*
University of Akron *B*
University of Toledo *A*
Youngstown State University *A*

Oklahoma
Connors State College *C, A*
East Central University *B*
Langston University *B*
Northwestern Oklahoma State
    University *B*
Oklahoma City University *B*
Oklahoma State University
    Oklahoma City *A*
Tulsa Community College *A*
Western Oklahoma State College *A*

Oregon
Chemeketa Community College *A*
Clackamas Community College *C, A*
Lane Community College *C*
Southern Oregon University *B*
Western Oregon University *B*

Pennsylvania
Bucks County Community College *A*
Butler County Community College *A*
Community College of Allegheny
    County *A*
Community College of Beaver County *A*
Community College of Philadelphia *C, A*
Delaware County Community College *A*
Edinboro University of Pennsylvania *A*
Harrisburg Area Community
    College *C, A*
Lackawanna Junior College *A*
Lehigh Carbon Community College *C, A*
Luzerne County Community
    College *C, A*
Mercyhurst College *C, A, B*
Montgomery County Community
    College *A*
Reading Area Community College *A*
Westmoreland County Community
    College *A*
York College of Pennsylvania *A, B*

Puerto Rico
Caribbean University *A*

Rhode Island
Community College of Rhode Island *A*

South Carolina
Greenville Technical College *C*
Tri-County Technical College *A*

South Dakota
Western Dakota Technical Institute *A*

Tennessee
Dyersburg State Community College *A*
Middle Tennessee State University *A*
Nashville State Technical Institute *A*
Roane State Community College *C, A*
Shelby State Community College *C, A*
Walters State Community College *C*

365

Law enforcement/police science

Texas
Alvin Community College C, A
Amarillo College C, A
Angelina College A
Austin Community College C, A
Brazosport College C, A
Central Texas College C
Coastal Bend College A
College of the Mainland A
Del Mar College C, A
Grayson County College A
Hardin-Simmons University B
Hill College C, A
Houston Community College
   System C, A
Kilgore College A
Lee College A
Midland College A
Navarro College A
North Central Texas College A
Northeast Texas Community
   College C, A
Odessa College C, A
St. Mary's University M
Sam Houston State University B
San Antonio College A
San Jacinto College
   North C, A
Southwest Texas State University B
Stephen F. Austin State University B
Tarrant County College C
Temple College A
University of Texas
   Brownsville B
   Pan American B
Vernon Regional Junior College C
Weatherford College C, A
Western Texas College A

Utah
Salt Lake Community College C
Southern Utah University A
Weber State University B

Vermont
Champlain College A, B

Virginia
Dabney S. Lancaster Community
   College C, A
George Mason University B
John Tyler Community College C, A
Lord Fairfax Community College C
Mountain Empire Community College C
Paul D. Camp Community College A
Southwest Virginia Community
   College C
Virginia Highlands Community
   College A
Virginia Western Community College A
Wytheville Community College C, A

Washington
Columbia Basin College A
Green River Community College A
Olympic College A
Spokane Community College A
Whatcom Community College A

West Virginia
Bluefield State College A
Fairmont State College A
West Virginia State College B

Wisconsin
Blackhawk Technical College A
Chippewa Valley Technical College A
Gateway Technical College A
Lakeshore Technical College A
Madison Area Technical College A
Mount Senario College A, B
Nicolet Area Technical College A
Northeast Wisconsin Technical
   College A
University of Wisconsin
   Superior A
Waukesha County Technical College A

Western Wisconsin Technical
   College C, A

Wyoming
Casper College A
Eastern Wyoming College A
Laramie County Community College A
Sheridan College A

Leather/upholstery

Alabama
Gadsden State Community College C
George C. Wallace State Community
   College
   Dothan C
John M. Patterson State Technical
   College C
Northwest-Shoals Community
   College C, A
Shelton State Community College C, A
Southern Union State Community
   College A
Wallace State Community College at
   Hanceville C, A

Alaska
University of Alaska
   Anchorage C, A

California
Sierra College C, A

Colorado
Pikes Peak Community College C

Missouri
Maple Woods Community College A

Nebraska
Mid Plains Community College Area C

North Carolina
Catawba Valley Community College C

North Dakota
North Dakota State College of Science C

Texas
Houston Community College System C
St. Philip's College C
Trinity Valley Community College C

Washington
Pierce College C

Legal administrative assistant

Alabama
George C. Wallace State Community
   College
   Dothan C, A
James H. Faulkner State Community
   College A
Lawson State Community College A
Northwest-Shoals Community College C
Wallace State Community College at
   Hanceville A

Arizona
Central Arizona College C, A
Cochise College A
Northland Pioneer College C, A
Phoenix College C, A
Pima Community College A
Yavapai College C, A

Arkansas
Arkansas State University
   Mountain Home C
Garland County Community College C

California
Allan Hancock College C, A
Butte College C, A
Chabot College A
Chaffey Community College C

City College of San Francisco C, A
Coastline Community College C
College of San Mateo C, A
College of the Redwoods C, A
Columbia College C
Cypress College C, A
East Los Angeles College A
Empire College C, A
Fresno City College C, A
Glendale Community College C, A
Golden West College C, A
Grossmont Community College C, A
Heald Business College
   Fresno C, A
   Santa Rosa C, A
Humphreys College C, A, B
Lake Tahoe Community College C, A
Las Positas College C
Los Angeles Harbor College C, A
Merced College C, A
Pacific Union College A
Palomar College C, A
Pasadena City College A
Porterville College C
Riverside Community College C, A
Sacramento City College C, A
Saddleback College C, A
San Bernardino Valley College C
Santa Rosa Junior College C
Shasta College A
Sierra College C, A
Skyline College C, A
Solano Community College C, A
Southwestern College C, A
Ventura College C, A
Victor Valley College C
Yuba College C

Colorado
Community College of Aurora A
Lamar Community College A
Northeastern Junior College A
Otero Junior College A
Pueblo Community College C, A
Red Rocks Community College C, A
University of Denver M

Connecticut
Briarwood College C, A
Gateway Community College A
Middlesex Community-Technical
   College A
Naugatuck Valley Community-Technical
   College A
Norwalk Community-Technical
   College A
Sacred Heart University A
Teikyo Post University C, A, B
Three Rivers Community-Technical
   College A
Tunxis Community College C, A

Florida
Brevard Community College A
Cooper Career Institute C
Daytona Beach Community College A
Indian River Community College A
Miami-Dade Community College A
Nova Southeastern University B
Pensacola Junior College A
St. Petersburg Junior College C, A
Santa Fe Community College A
Seminole Community College A
Valencia Community College A

Georgia
Athens Area Technical Institute C
DeKalb Technical Institute C
Gainesville College A
Middle Georgia College A

Hawaii
University of Hawaii
   Kapiolani Community College A

Idaho
Boise State University A

Eastern Idaho Technical College C, A
North Idaho College A

Illinois
Black Hawk College A
Career Colleges of Chicago A
College of DuPage C, A
Elgin Community College C, A
John A. Logan College A
John Wood Community College A
Joliet Junior College A
Kankakee Community College A
Kishwaukee College C
Lake Land College A
MacCormac College A
McHenry County College C
Moraine Valley Community College C
Morton College A
Rend Lake College A
Robert Morris College: Chicago C, A
Sauk Valley Community College C, A
Shawnee Community College A
Waubonsee Community College C
William Rainey Harper College C, A

Indiana
Michiana College A
Vincennes University A

Iowa
American Institute of Business A
Des Moines Area Community College A
Iowa Western Community College A
Kirkwood Community College C
North Iowa Area Community
   College C, A
Northeast Iowa Community College A
Western Iowa Tech Community
   College A

Kansas
Dodge City Community College C, A
Independence Community College C, A
Pratt Community College C, A
Seward County Community College C
Washburn University of Topeka C, A

Kentucky
Ashland Community College A
National Business College A
Owensboro Junior College of Business A

Maine
Andover College C, A
Beal College A
Husson College A
Mid-State College A
Thomas College A

Maryland
Allegany College A
Baltimore City Community College A
Community College of Baltimore County
   Catonsville A
Howard Community College C, A
Montgomery College
   Takoma Park Campus C, A
Prince George's Community
   College C, A
Villa Julie College A

Massachusetts
Atlantic Union College A
Bay State College A
Bristol Community College A
Cape Cod Community College C, A
Fisher College A
Holyoke Community College A
Marian Court College C, A
Massasoit Community College A
North Shore Community College A
Roxbury Community College A
Springfield Technical Community
   College A

Michigan
Baker College
    of Auburn Hills *A*
    of Cadillac *A*
    of Jackson *A*
    of Muskegon *A*
    of Owosso *A*
    of Port Huron *A*
Davenport College of Business *A*
Delta College *A*
Detroit College of Business *A*
Gogebic Community College *A*
Grand Rapids Community College *A*
Henry Ford Community College *A*
Kalamazoo Valley Community
    College *C, A*
Kellogg Community College *A*
Kirtland Community College *A*
Lake Michigan College *A*
Lansing Community College *A*
Macomb Community College *C, A*
Mid Michigan Community College *A*
Monroe County Community
    College *C, A*
Montcalm Community College *C, A*
Mott Community College *C, A*
Muskegon Community College *A*
Northern Michigan University *A*
Northwestern Michigan College *C*
Oakland Community College *A*
St. Clair County Community College *A*

Minnesota
Alexandria Technical College *C, A*
Anoka-Ramsey Community College *A*
Hennepin Technical College *C, A*
Hibbing Community College: A
    Technical and Community College *A*
Inver Hills Community College *C, A*
Itasca Community College *A*
Lake Superior College: A Community
    and Technical College *C, A*
Jamestown Business College *A*
Minnesota State College - Southeast
    Technical *C, A*
Ridgewater College: A Community and
    Technical College *C, A*
Rochester Community and Technical
    College *A*
St. Cloud Technical College *C, A*
St. Paul Technical College *C, A*
South Central Technical College *A*
Winona State University *B*

Mississippi
Hinds Community College *A*
Northwest Mississippi Community
    College *A*

Missouri
Crowder College *A*
East Central College *C, A*
Jefferson College *A*
Longview Community College *C*
Maple Woods Community College *C*
Penn Valley Community College *C*
Southeast Missouri State University *C*
St. Louis Community College
    St. Louis Community College at
        Meramec *A*
State Fair Community College *A*

Montana
Flathead Valley Community College *A*
Miles Community College *A*
Montana State University
    College of Technology-Great
        Falls *A*
Montana Tech of the University of
    Montana: College of Technology *A*
Montana Tech of the University of
    Montana *A*
University of Montana-Missoula *A*

Nebraska
Lincoln School of Commerce *C, A*
Midland Lutheran College *A*
Northeast Community College *A*

Nevada
Community College of Southern
    Nevada *C, A*

New Hampshire
Hesser College *A*
McIntosh College *A*
New Hampshire Community Technical
    College
        Nashua *C*

New Jersey
Brookdale Community College *A*
Gloucester County College *A*
Katharine Gibbs School
    Gibbs College *A*
Salem Community College *A*
Warren County Community College *C*

New Mexico
Clovis Community College *A*
Dona Ana Branch Community College of
    New Mexico State University *A*
New Mexico Junior College *C, A*
Western New Mexico University *C, A*

New York
Adelphi University *A*
Briarcliffe College *A*
Bryant & Stratton Business Institute
    Albany *A*
    Syracuse *A*
City University of New York
    Kingsborough Community
        College *A*
    La Guardia Community College *A*
Clinton Community College *C*
Fulton-Montgomery Community
    College *A*
Genesee Community College *C*
Herkimer County Community College *A*
Interboro Institute *A*
Jamestown Business College *A*
Katharine Gibbs School
    New York *C*
Nassau Community College *A*
Pace University:
    Pleasantville/Briarcliff *C, A*
Pace University *C, A*
State University of New York
    College of Technology at Delhi *A*
Trocaire College *A*
Ulster County Community College *C, A*
Westchester Community College *A*

North Carolina
Alamance Community College *C, A*
Carteret Community College *A*
Central Carolina Community College *A*
Central Piedmont Community College *A*
Craven Community College *C, A*
Gaston College *A*
Guilford Technical Community
    College *A*
Lenoir Community College *A*
Nash Community College *A*
Piedmont Community College *A*
Rockingham Community College *A*
South Piedmont Community
    College *C, A*
Wake Technical Community College *A*
Wayne Community College *A*
Western Piedmont Community
    College *A*

North Dakota
Bismarck State College *C, A*
Dickinson State University *A*
Lake Region State College *C, A*
Minot State University: Bottineau
    Campus *A*
North Dakota State College of Science *A*

Ohio
Central Ohio Technical College *A*
Clark State Community College *A*
Columbus State Community College *A*
David N. Myers College *A, B*
Davis College *C, A*
Edison State Community College *A*
Hocking Technical College *C*
Jefferson Community College *A*
Kent State University
    Trumbull Campus *A*
Lima Technical College *A*
Miami-Jacobs College *A*
Northwest State Community College *A*
Northwestern College *A*
Notre Dame College of Ohio *C, B*
Ohio University
    Chillicothe Campus *A*
Sinclair Community College *A*
University of Akron
    Wayne College *A*
University of Akron *A*
University of Cincinnati
    Raymond Walters College *A*
University of Toledo *A*
Youngstown State University *A*

Oklahoma
Eastern Oklahoma State College *A*
Northeastern Oklahoma Agricultural and
    Mechanical College *A*
Oklahoma State University
    Okmulgee *A*
Tulsa Community College *C, A*

Oregon
Chemeketa Community College *A*
Lane Community College *A*
Linn-Benton Community College *C, A*
Mount Hood Community College *A*
Portland Community College *A*

Pennsylvania
Bucks County Community College *A*
Butler County Community College *A*
Cambria-Rowe Business College *A*
Central Pennsylvania College *A*
Churchman Business School *A*
Clarion University of Pennsylvania *A*
Harrisburg Area Community College *A*
Lackawanna Junior College *A*
Laurel Business Institute *A*
Lehigh Carbon Community College *A*
Luzerne County Community College *C*
Manor College *C, A*
Mercyhurst College *C, A*
Montgomery County Community
    College *C, A*
Northampton County Area Community
    College *C*
Pittsburgh Technical Institute *A*
Reading Area Community College *C, A*
Sawyer School *A*
Westmoreland County Community
    College *A*
Yorktowne Business Institute *A*

Puerto Rico
Caribbean University *A*
Colegio Universitario del Este *C*
National College of Business and
    Technology *A*
Universidad Metropolitana *A, B*
University of Puerto Rico
    Bayamon University College *A, B*

Rhode Island
Community College of Rhode
    Island *C, A*

South Carolina
Greenville Technical College *C*
York Technical College *C*

South Dakota
Kilian Community College *A*
Western Dakota Technical Institute *C*

Tennessee
Knoxville Business College *C, A*
Nashville State Technical Institute *A*
Pellissippi State Technical Community
    College *A*

Texas
Alvin Community College *A*
Austin Community College *A*
Blinn College *C*
Brazosport College *C, A*
Brookhaven College *A*
Cedar Valley College *A*
Del Mar College *A*
Eastfield College *A*
El Paso Community College *C*
Grayson County College *C*
Houston Community College
    System *C, A*
Kilgore College *A*
Lamar State College at Port Arthur *C, A*
Midland College *C, A*
North Central Texas College *A*
Northeast Texas Community
    College *C, A*
Richland College *A*
St. Philip's College *A*
San Antonio College *A*
San Jacinto College
    North *C*
Texas A&M University
    Commerce *B*
Texas State Technical College
    Harlingen *A*
Texas Wesleyan University *C*
Trinity Valley Community College *C, A*

Utah
LDS Business College *A*
Mountain West College *C, A*

Vermont
Champlain College *A, B*

Virginia
Blue Ridge Community College *C*
Danville Community College *C*
J. Sargeant Reynolds Community
    College *C*
Lord Fairfax Community College *C*
Mountain Empire Community College *A*
National Business College *C*
New River Community College *C, A*
Southwest Virginia Community
    College *C*
Virginia Highlands Community
    College *C, A*

Washington
Centralia College *C, A*
Clark College *C, A*
Columbia Basin College *C*
Edmonds Community College *A*
Everett Community College *C*
Grays Harbor College *C*
Green River Community College *A*
Lake Washington Technical College *C, A*
Lower Columbia College *A*
Olympic College *A*
Pierce College *C, A*
Renton Technical College *C*
South Puget Sound Community
    College *C, A*
South Seattle Community College *C, A*
Spokane Community College *C, A*
Walla Walla Community College *A*
Wenatchee Valley College *A*
Yakima Valley Community College *C, A*

West Virginia
Bluefield State College *A*
College of West Virginia *A*
West Virginia State College *A*
West Virginia University Institute of
    Technology *A*

Wisconsin
Blackhawk Technical College *A*
Bryant & Stratton College *A*
Gateway Technical College *A*
Madison Area Technical College *C*

Legal administrative assistant

Milwaukee Area Technical College *A*
Moraine Park Technical College *A*
Southwest Wisconsin Technical
    College *A*
Western Wisconsin Technical College *A*

Wyoming

Western Wyoming Community
    College *C, A*

Legal studies

Alabama

Faulkner University *A*
Samford University *D*
University of Alabama *M, D*

Arizona

Arizona State University *D*

Arkansas

University of Arkansas
    Little Rock *D*
University of Arkansas *M*

California

California State University
    Chico *B*
    Long Beach *C*
Chapman University *B*
Claremont McKenna College *B*
Grossmont Community College *C, A*
Mills College *B*
National University *B*
Pepperdine University *M*
Santa Clara University *D*
Scripps College *B*
Stanford University *M, D*
University of California
    Berkeley *B, M, D*
    Riverside *B*
    Santa Barbara *B*
    Santa Cruz *B*
University of San Diego *M*
University of Southern California *D*
University of West Los Angeles *D*

Colorado

United States Air Force Academy *B*
University of Colorado
    Boulder *D*

Connecticut

Quinnipiac University *B, M*
University of Connecticut *M*
University of New Haven *M*
Yale University *M, D*

District of Columbia

American University *M*
Catholic University of America *D*
George Washington University *M, D*
Howard University *M*
Southeastern University *A*

Florida

Manatee Community College *A*
Nova Southeastern University *D*
University of Central Florida *B*
University of Miami *B, M*

Georgia

Georgia State University *D*
University of Georgia *M*

Hawaii

University of Hawaii
    Manoa *D*

Illinois

Black Hawk College *A*
City Colleges of Chicago
    Harold Washington College *A*
    Olive-Harvey College *A*
De Paul University *M*
Illinois Institute of Technology *M, D*
Loyola University of Chicago *M, D*
Roosevelt University *B*

Indiana

Indiana University
    Bloomington *M, D*
Indiana University--Purdue University
    Indiana University-Purdue
        University Fort Wayne *B*
    Indiana University-Purdue
        University Indianapolis *D*
University of Evansville *B*
University of Notre Dame *M, D*

Iowa

University of Iowa *M*

Kansas

University of Kansas *D*

Louisiana

Loyola University New Orleans *D*
Southern University and Agricultural and
    Mechanical College *D*
Tulane University *M, D*

Maine

University of Southern Maine *M*

Maryland

Charles County Community College *A*
University of Baltimore *M*

Massachusetts

Anna Maria College *B*
Bay Path College *B*
Becker College *B*
Boston University *M*
Bridgewater State College *B*
Elms College *B*
Endicott College *B*
Hampshire College *B*
Harvard University *M*
Lasell College *B*
Mount Ida College *B*
Newbury College *B*
Northeastern University *B, M, D*
Simon's Rock College of Bard *B*
Suffolk University *A, B, D*
University of Massachusetts
    Amherst *B*
    Boston *B*
Western New England College *D*

Michigan

Grand Valley State University *B*
Wayne State University *M*

Minnesota

Hamline University *B, M*
Winona State University *B*

Mississippi

Mississippi College *D*

Missouri

Northwest Missouri State University *B*
Park University *B*
University of Missouri
    Columbia *M*
    Kansas City *M, D*
Webster University *B, M*

Nebraska

Creighton University *D*
Lincoln School of Commerce *C*
University of Nebraska
    Lincoln *M, D*

Nevada

University of Nevada
    Las Vegas *D*

New Hampshire

Rivier College *C, A, B*

New Jersey

Ramapo College of New Jersey *B*
The College of New Jersey *B*
Warren County Community College *A*

New Mexico

Albuquerque Technical-Vocational
    Institute *C*
Clovis Community College *A*
University of New Mexico *D*

New York

City University of New York
    John Jay College of Criminal
        Justice *B*
Marymount College *B*
New York University *M, D*
Sage Junior College of Albany *A*
St. John's University *M, D*
State University of New York
    College at Fredonia *B*
Syracuse University *D*
Touro College *M*
United States Military Academy *B*

North Carolina

Duke University *D*
North Carolina Wesleyan College *B*

North Dakota

University of North Dakota *D*

Ohio

Case Western Reserve University *D*
Ohio Dominican College *A*
RETS Tech Center *A*

Oklahoma

University of Oklahoma *D*
University of Tulsa *C, D*

Pennsylvania

Allentown College of St. Francis de
    Sales *B*
Beaver College *B*
Community College of Allegheny
    County *C, A*
Dickinson College *C*
Duquesne University *D*
Pennsylvania College of Technology *B*
Point Park College *B*
St. Joseph's University *A, B*
Temple University *B, M*
University of Pennsylvania *M, D*
University of Pittsburgh *C, B*
Villanova University *M*
Widener University *M, D*
Wilson College *C, A, B*

Puerto Rico

Pontifical Catholic University of Puerto
    Rico *B*
University of Puerto Rico
    Rio Piedras Campus *M*

Rhode Island

Roger Williams University *D*

South Carolina

University of South Carolina *M*

South Dakota

University of South Dakota *D*

Tennessee

Vanderbilt University *D*

Texas

Baylor University *D*
Central Texas College *A*
Schreiner College *B*
Southern Methodist University *M, D*
Texas Tech University *D*
University of Houston *M, D*
University of Texas
    Austin *M*

Utah

University of Utah *M, D*

Virginia

Christopher Newport University *B*
College of William and Mary *M*

Washington

Gonzaga University *M*
Highline Community College *A*
University of Washington *M, D*

West Virginia

College of West Virginia *B*
Marshall University *B*

Wisconsin

Marquette University *D*
University of Wisconsin
    Superior *C, B*

Wyoming

University of Wyoming *D*

Liberal arts/humanities

Alabama

Athens State University *B*
Auburn University at Montgomery *B, M*
Bevill State Community College *A*
Calhoun Community College *A*
Central Alabama Community College *A*
Chattahoochee Valley Community
    College *A*
Enterprise State Junior College *A*
Faulkner University *A, B*
Gadsden State Community College *A*
George C. Wallace State Community
    College
        Dothan *A*
        Selma *A*
Huntingdon College *A*
Jacksonville State University *B, M*
James H. Faulkner State Community
    College *A*
Jefferson Davis Community College *A*
Jefferson State Community College *A*
Lawson State Community College *A*
Lurleen B. Wallace Junior College *A*
Marion Military Institute *A*
Northeast Alabama Community
    College *A*
Northwest-Shoals Community College *A*
Oakwood College *B*
Samford University *A*
Shelton State Community College *A*
Snead State Community College *A*
Spring Hill College *B*
Talladega College *B*
Troy State University
    Dothan *A*
    Montgomery *A, B*
University of Mobile *A, B*
University of North Alabama *B*
University of South Alabama *B*
Wallace State Community College at
    Hanceville *A*

Alaska

Alaska Pacific University *B*
Prince William Sound Community
    College *A*
University of Alaska
    Fairbanks *A*
    Southeast *A, B*

Arizona

Arizona State University *B, M*
Arizona Western College *A*
Central Arizona College *A*
Cochise College *A*
Dine College *A*
Eastern Arizona College *A*
Gateway Community College *A*
Glendale Community College *A*
Grand Canyon University *B*
Mohave Community College *A*
Northern Arizona University *B*
Northland Pioneer College *A*
Paradise Valley Community College *A*
Phoenix College *A*
Pima Community College *A*
Prescott College *B, M*

Liberal arts/humanities

South Mountain Community College *A*
Yavapai College *A*

Arkansas
Arkansas State University
  Beebe Branch *A*
  Mountain Home *A*
Arkansas State University *A, B*
Arkansas Tech University *A, M*
Central Baptist College *A*
Garland County Community College *A*
Henderson State University *A, M*
Hendrix College *B*
John Brown University *B*
Mississippi County Community College *A*
North Arkansas College *A*
Northwest Arkansas Community College *A*
Southern Arkansas University Tech *A*
Southern Arkansas University *A*
University of Arkansas
  Little Rock *A, B*
  Monticello *A*
  Pine Bluff *B*
University of Central Arkansas *A*
University of the Ozarks *B*
Westark College *A*
Williams Baptist College *A, B*

California
Allan Hancock College *A*
American River College *A*
Antioch Southern California
  Los Angeles *B*
  Santa Barbara *B*
Azusa Pacific University *B*
Bakersfield College *A*
Barstow College *A*
Biola University *B*
Butte College *A*
Cabrillo College *A*
California Baptist University *B*
California Institute of Technology *B*
California Lutheran University *B*
California Polytechnic State University: San Luis Obispo *B*
California State Polytechnic University: Pomona *B*
California State University
  Bakersfield *B*
  Chico *B*
  Dominguez Hills *B, M*
  Fullerton *B*
  Hayward *B*
  Long Beach *B*
  Los Angeles *B*
  Monterey Bay *B*
  Northridge *B*
  Sacramento *B*
  San Marcos *B*
  Stanislaus *B*
Canada College *A*
Cerritos Community College *A*
Cerro Coso Community College *A*
Chabot College *A*
Chaffey Community College *A*
Chapman University *B*
Citrus College *A*
City College of San Francisco *A*
Coastline Community College *A*
College of Marin: Kentfield *A*
College of Notre Dame *B*
College of San Mateo *A*
College of the Canyons *A*
College of the Desert *A*
College of the Redwoods *A*
College of the Sequoias *A*
College of the Siskiyous *A*
Columbia College *A*
Compton Community College *A*
Concordia University *B*
Contra Costa College *A*
Crafton Hills College *A*
Cuesta College *A*
Cuyamaca College *A*
Cypress College *A*
De Anza College *A*
Deep Springs College *A*
Diablo Valley College *A*
Dominican University of California *B, M*
Evergreen Valley College *A*
Foothill College *A*
Fresno City College *A*
Fresno Pacific University *A, B*
Gavilan Community College *A*
Glendale Community College *A*
Golden West College *A*
Grossmont Community College *A*
Holy Names College *B*
Hope International University *A*
Humboldt State University *B*
Humphreys College *A*
Imperial Valley College *A*
Irvine Valley College *A*
John F. Kennedy University *B*
Kings River Community College *A*
La Sierra University *B*
Lake Tahoe Community College *A*
Las Positas College *A*
Long Beach City College *A*
Los Angeles Harbor College *A*
Los Angeles Mission College *A*
Los Angeles Pierce College *A*
Los Angeles Southwest College *A*
Los Angeles Trade and Technical College *A*
Los Angeles Valley College *A*
Los Medanos College *A*
Loyola Marymount University *B*
Marymount College *A*
Master's College *B*
Mendocino College *A*
Menlo College *B*
Merced College *A*
Merritt College *A*
Mills College *B, M*
MiraCosta College *A*
Mission College *A*
Modesto Junior College *A*
Monterey Peninsula College *A*
Moorpark College *A*
Mount St. Mary's College *A*
Mount San Antonio College *A*
Mount San Jacinto College *A*
Napa Valley College *A*
National Hispanic University *C, A, B*
National University *A, B*
Occidental College *B*
Ohlone College *A*
Oxnard College *A*
Pacific Union College *A, B*
Palo Verde College *A*
Palomar College *A*
Pasadena City College *C, A*
Patten College *B*
Pepperdine University *B*
Pitzer College *B*
Point Loma Nazarene University *B*
Porterville College *A*
Rio Hondo College *A*
Riverside Community College *A*
Sacramento City College *A*
Saddleback College *A*
St. Mary's College of California *B, M*
San Bernardino Valley College *A*
San Diego City College *A*
San Diego Mesa College *A*
San Diego Miramar College *A*
San Diego State University *B, M*
San Francisco State University *B, M*
San Joaquin Delta College *A*
San Jose City College *A*
San Jose State University *B*
Santa Barbara City College *A*
Santa Clara University *B*
Santa Monica College *A*
Santa Rosa Junior College *A*
Sierra College *A*
Simpson College *A, B*
Skyline College *A*
Solano Community College *A*
Sonoma State University *B*
Southwestern College *A*
Stanford University *B, M, D*
Taft College *A*
Thomas Aquinas College *B*
United States International University *A, B*
University of California
  Berkeley *B, D*
  Irvine *B*
  Riverside *B*
  Santa Barbara *B*
University of Judaism *B*
University of La Verne *B*
University of Redlands *B*
University of San Diego *B*
University of San Francisco *B*
Vanguard University of Southern California *B*
Ventura College *A*
Victor Valley College *A*
West Hills Community College *A*
West Los Angeles College *C, A*
West Valley College *A*
Whittier College *B*
Yuba College *A*

Colorado
Adams State College *A, B*
Aims Community College *A*
Arapahoe Community College *A*
Colorado Christian University *A, B*
Colorado College *B*
Colorado Mountain College
  Alpine Campus *A*
  Spring Valley Campus *A*
  Timberline Campus *A*
Colorado Northwestern Community College *A*
Colorado State University *B*
Community College of Denver *A*
Fort Lewis College *B*
Front Range Community College *A*
Lamar Community College *A*
Mesa State College *A, B*
Morgan Community College *A*
Otero Junior College *A*
Pikes Peak Community College *A*
Pueblo Community College *A*
Red Rocks Community College *A*
Regis University *M*
Trinidad State Junior College *A*
United States Air Force Academy *B*
University of Colorado
  Boulder *B*
  Denver *B, M*
University of Denver *M*

Connecticut
Albertus Magnus College *A, B, M*
Asnuntuck Community-Technical College *A*
Briarwood College *A*
Capital Community College *A*
Charter Oak State College *A, B*
Connecticut College *B*
Eastern Connecticut State University *A, B*
Gateway Community College *A*
Housatonic Community-Technical College *A*
Manchester Community-Technical College *A*
Middlesex Community-Technical College *A*
Mitchell College *A, B*
Naugatuck Valley Community-Technical College *A*
Northwestern Connecticut Community-Technical College *A*
Norwalk Community-Technical College *A*
Quinebaug Valley Community College *A*
Sacred Heart University *A, B*
Southern Connecticut State University *A, B*
Teikyo Post University *A, B*
Three Rivers Community-Technical College *A*
Tunxis Community College *A*
University of Bridgeport *A, B*
University of Connecticut *B*
University of Hartford *A, B*
University of New Haven *A, B, M*
Wesleyan University *B, M*
Western Connecticut State University *A, B*
Yale University *B*

Delaware
University of Delaware *B, M, D*
Wesley College *A, B*
Wilmington College *A, B*

District of Columbia
American University *A, B*
Catholic University of America *B*
George Washington University *B*
Georgetown University *B, M*
Trinity College *B*

Florida
Barry University *B*
Bethune-Cookman College *B*
Broward Community College *A*
Central Florida Community College *A*
Chipola Junior College *A*
Clearwater Christian College *B*
Daytona Beach Community College *A*
Eckerd College *B*
Edison Community College *A*
Florida Agricultural and Mechanical University *A*
Florida Atlantic University *A, B, M*
Florida College *A*
Florida Community College at Jacksonville *A*
Florida Gulf Coast University *A, B*
Florida Institute of Technology *B*
Florida International University *B*
Florida Keys Community College *A*
Florida Southern College *B*
Florida State University *A, B, M, D*
Gulf Coast Community College *A*
Hillsborough Community College *A*
Indian River Community College *A*
Jacksonville University *B*
Lake City Community College *A*
Lake-Sumter Community College *A*
Lynn University *A, B*
Manatee Community College *A*
Miami-Dade Community College *A*
New College of the University of South Florida *B*
Nova Southeastern University *B*
Palm Beach Atlantic College *B*
Palm Beach Community College *A*
Pasco-Hernando Community College *A*
Pensacola Junior College *A*
Polk Community College *A*
Rollins College *M*
St. Leo University *A*
St. Petersburg Junior College *A*
St. Thomas University *B*
Santa Fe Community College *A*
Seminole Community College *A*
South Florida Community College *A*
Stetson University *B*
Tallahassee Community College *A*
University of Central Florida *A, B, M*
University of Florida *B*
University of Miami *B, M*
University of North Florida *A, B*
University of South Florida *B, M*
University of Tampa *A, B*
University of West Florida *A, B*
Valencia Community College *A*
Warner Southern College *A*

Liberal arts/humanities

Georgia
Abraham Baldwin Agricultural College A
Andrew College A
Armstrong Atlantic State University A, B
Atlanta Christian College B
Atlanta Metropolitan College A
Augusta State University A
Bainbridge College A
Brenau University B
Brewton-Parker College A, B
Clark Atlanta University D
Clayton College and State University A
Coastal Georgia Community College A
Columbus State University B
Dalton State College A
Darton College A
East Georgia College A
Emmanuel College A
Emory University A
Floyd College A
Fort Valley State University A
Gainesville College A
Georgia College and State University B
Georgia Military College A
Georgia Perimeter College A
Georgia Southern University B
Georgia State University M
Gordon College A
LaGrange College B
Macon State College A
Mercer University B
Middle Georgia College A
Oglethorpe University B
Oxford College of Emory University B
Reinhardt College A, B
Shorter College B
South Georgia College A
Southern Polytechnic State University A
State University of West Georgia B
Thomas College A, B
Toccoa Falls College A
Truett-McConnell College A
University of Georgia B
Valdosta State University B
Waycross College A
Wesleyan College B
Young Harris College A

Hawaii
Chaminade University of Honolulu A, B
Hawaii Pacific University B
TransPacific Hawaii College B
University of Hawaii
    Hawaii Community College A
    Hilo B
    Honolulu Community College A
    Kapiolani Community College A
    Kauai Community College A
    Leeward Community College C, A
    West Oahu B
    Windward Community College A

Idaho
Boise State University B
College of Southern Idaho A
Idaho State University A, B
Lewis-Clark State College A, B
North Idaho College A
Northwest Nazarene University B
Ricks College A

Illinois
Augustana College B
Barat College B
Black Hawk College
    East Campus A
Black Hawk College C, A
Blackburn College B
Bradley University B, M
City Colleges of Chicago
    Harold Washington College A
    Kennedy-King College A
    Malcolm X College A
    Olive-Harvey College A
    Richard J. Daley College C, A
    Wright College A
College of DuPage A
College of Lake County C, A
Columbia College B
Danville Area Community College A
De Paul University B, M
Eastern Illinois University B
Elgin Community College A
Elmhurst College B
Eureka College B
Governors State University B
Greenville College B
Highland Community College A
Illinois Eastern Community Colleges
    Frontier Community College A
    Lincoln Trail College A
    Olney Central College A
    Wabash Valley College A
Illinois State University B
John A. Logan College A
John Wood Community College A
Joliet Junior College A
Kankakee Community College A
Kaskaskia College A
Kendall College A, B
Kishwaukee College A
Lake Forest College B, M
Lake Land College A
Lewis University B
Lewis and Clark Community College A
Lincoln Land Community College A
McHenry County College A
Monmouth College B
Moraine Valley Community College A
Morton College A
National-Louis University B
North Central College B, M
North Park University B
Northeastern Illinois University B
Northern Illinois University B
Northwestern University M
Oakton Community College A
Olivet Nazarene University B
Parkland College A
Prairie State College A
Quincy University A, B
Rend Lake College A
Richland Community College A
Robert Morris College: Chicago A
Rock Valley College A
Rockford College B
Roosevelt University B, M
St. Augustine College A
St. Xavier University B, M
Sauk Valley Community College A
Shawnee Community College A
Shimer College B
Southern Illinois University
    Carbondale B
    Edwardsville B
Southwestern Ilinois College A
Spoon River College A
Springfield College in Illinois A
Trinity International University B
Triton College A
University of Chicago B, M
University of Illinois
    Chicago B
    Springfield B, M
    Urbana-Champaign B
University of St. Francis B
Waubonsee Community College C, A
Western Illinois University B
William Rainey Harper College A

Indiana
Ancilla College A
Anderson University A
Ball State University A, B
Bethel College A, B
Goshen College B
Holy Cross College A
Indiana State University M
Indiana University
    Bloomington A, B
    East A, B
    Kokomo A, B
    Northwest A, B
    South Bend M
    Southeast A, B, M
Indiana University--Purdue University
    Indiana University-Purdue
        University Fort Wayne A, B, M
    Indiana University-Purdue
        University Indianapolis A, B
Ivy Tech State College
    Central Indiana C
    Columbus C
    Eastcentral C
    Kokomo C
    Lafayette C
    Northcentral C
    Northeast C
    Northwest C
    Southcentral C
    Southeast C
    Southwest C
    Wabash Valley C
    Whitewater C
Manchester College B
Marian College A
Oakland City University A, B
Purdue University
    Calumet B
    North Central Campus B
Purdue University B
Saint Mary's College B
St. Joseph's College B
St. Mary-of-the-Woods College A, B
Taylor University A
University of Indianapolis A
University of Notre Dame B
University of St. Francis B
University of Southern Indiana B, M
Vincennes University A
Wabash College B

Iowa
Briar Cliff College A, B
Central College B
Clarke College A
Clinton Community College A
Des Moines Area Community College A
Dordt College B
Drake University M
Graceland University B
Grand View College A, B
Hawkeye Community College A
Indian Hills Community College A
Iowa Central Community College A
Iowa Lakes Community College A
Iowa State University B, M
Iowa Western Community College A
Kirkwood Community College A
Loras College A
Marshalltown Community College A
Marycrest International University A, B
Mount Mercy College B
Muscatine Community College A
North Iowa Area Community College A
Simpson College B, T
Southeastern Community College
    North Campus A
    South Campus A
Southwestern Community College A
University of Dubuque A, B
University of Iowa B
University of Northern Iowa B
Upper Iowa University A
Waldorf College A, B
Western Iowa Tech Community College A
William Penn University B

Kansas
Baker University M
Barclay College A
Barton County Community College A
Benedictine College B
Bethany College B
Butler County Community College A
Central Christian College A
Coffeyville Community College A
Emporia State University B
Garden City Community College A
Hesston College A
Hutchinson Community College A
Independence Community College A
Johnson County Community College A
Kansas City Kansas Community College A
Kansas State University B
McPherson College B
MidAmerica Nazarene University A
Newman University B
Pittsburg State University B
Pratt Community College A
St. Mary College A, B
Seward County Community College A
Southwestern College B
University of Kansas B
Washburn University of Topeka A, B
Wichita State University A, B, M

Kentucky
Ashland Community College A
Bellarmine College B
Brescia University B
Campbellsville University B
Cumberland College B
Eastern Kentucky University B
Elizabethtown Community College A
Hazard Community College A
Henderson Community College A
Hopkinsville Community College A
Kentucky State University A, B
Lexington Community College A
Lindsey Wilson College A, B
Madisonville Community College A
Maysville Community College A
Midway College B
Morehead State University A, B
Murray State University A
Owensboro Community College A
Paducah Community College A
Prestonsburg Community College A
St. Catharine College A
Southeast Community College A
Spalding University B
Thomas More College A, B
Transylvania University B
University of Louisville B, M
Western Kentucky University A, B

Louisiana
Bossier Parish Community College A
Centenary College of Louisiana B
Delgado Community College A
Louisiana State University
    Alexandria A
    Eunice A
    Shreveport B, M
Louisiana State University and Agricultural and Mechanical College B, M
Louisiana Tech University A, B
Loyola University New Orleans B
McNeese State University A, B
Nicholls State University A, B
Northwestern State University A, B
Nunez Community College A
Our Lady of Holy Cross College B
St. Joseph Seminary College B
Southeastern Louisiana University A, B
Tulane University M
University of Louisiana at Lafayette A, B
University of Louisiana at Monroe A, B
University of New Orleans B

Liberal arts/humanities

Maine
Southern Maine Technical College *A*
Unity College *A, B*
University of Maine
    Augusta *A*
    Fort Kent *A, B*
    Machias *A*
    Presque Isle *A, B*
University of Maine *B, M*
University of New England *B*
University of Southern Maine *A*
Washington County Technical College *A*

Maryland
Allegany College *A*
Anne Arundel Community College *A*
Baltimore City Community College *A*
Carroll Community College *A*
Cecil Community College *A*
Charles County Community College *A*
Chesapeake College *A*
College of Notre Dame of
    Maryland *B, M*
Columbia Union College *A, B*
Community College of Baltimore County
    Catonsville *A*
    Essex *A*
Coppin State College *B*
Frederick Community College *A*
Frostburg State University *B, M*
Hagerstown Community College *A*
Harford Community College *A*
Howard Community College *A*
Johns Hopkins University *D*
Loyola College in Maryland *M*
Montgomery College
    Germantown Campus *A*
    Rockville Campus *A*
Prince George's Community College *A*
St. John's College *B, M*
Salisbury State University *B, T*
Towson University *M*
University of Baltimore *B*
University of Maryland
    Eastern Shore *B*
Villa Julie College *A, B*
Washington College *B*
Western Maryland College *M*
Wor-Wic Community College *A*

Massachusetts
American International College *A, B*
Anna Maria College *B*
Assumption College *A*
Atlantic Union College *B*
Bay Path College *A, B*
Becker College *A, B*
Bentley College *B*
Berkshire Community College *A*
Bristol Community College *A*
Bunker Hill Community College *A*
Cape Cod Community College *A*
Clark University *B, M*
Curry College *B*
Dean College *A*
Eastern Nazarene College *A, B*
Elms College *B*
Emmanuel College *B*
Endicott College *A, B*
Fisher College *C, A*
Fitchburg State College *B*
Framingham State College *B*
Greenfield Community College *A*
Hampshire College *B*
Harvard College *B*
Hellenic College/Holy Cross *B*
Holyoke Community College *A*
Lasell College *A*
Lesley College *A, B, M*
Marian Court College *A*
Massachusetts Bay Community
    College *C, A*
Massachusetts College of Liberal Arts *B*
Massachusetts Institute of Technology *B*
Massasoit Community College *A*
Merrimack College *A, B*
Middlesex Community College *A*
Mount Ida College *A, B*
Mount Wachusett Community College *A*
Newbury College *A*
North Shore Community College *A*
Northern Essex Community College *A*
Pine Manor College *A*
Quincy College *A*
Roxbury Community College *A*
Salem State College *B*
Simon's Rock College of Bard *A, B*
Springfield College *B*
Springfield Technical Community
    College *A*
Stonehill College *B*
Suffolk University *A, B*
Tufts University *B*
University of Massachusetts
    Amherst *B*
    Dartmouth *B*
    Lowell *B*
Western New England College *A, B*
Westfield State College *B*
Wheaton College *B*
Worcester Polytechnic Institute *B*

Michigan
Alma College *B*
Alpena Community College *A*
Andrews University *A, B*
Aquinas College *A, B*
Bay de Noc Community College *A*
Calvin College *B*
Central Michigan University *B, M*
Concordia College *A*
Ferris State University *A*
Glen Oaks Community College *A*
Gogebic Community College *A*
Grace Bible College *A, B*
Grand Rapids Community College *A*
Grand Valley State University *B*
Henry Ford Community College *A*
Jackson Community College *A*
Kalamazoo Valley Community
    College *A*
Kellogg Community College *A*
Kirtland Community College *A*
Lake Michigan College *A*
Lake Superior State University *A*
Lansing Community College *A*
Lawrence Technological University *B*
Marygrove College *A, T*
Michigan State University *B, D*
Michigan Technological University *A, B*
Mid Michigan Community College *A*
Monroe County Community College *A*
Montcalm Community College *A*
Mott Community College *A*
North Central Michigan College *A*
Northern Michigan University *A, B*
Northwestern Michigan College *A*
Oakland Community College *A*
Oakland University *B*
Olivet College *B*
Rochester College *A*
St. Clair County Community College *A*
Schoolcraft College *A*
Siena Heights University *A, B*
Southwestern Michigan College *C, A*
Spring Arbor College *A*
Suomi College *A*
University of Detroit Mercy *B, M*
University of Michigan
    Dearborn *B*
    Flint *B*
University of Michigan *B*
Washtenaw Community College *A*
Wayne County Community College *A*
West Shore Community College *A*
William Tyndale College *A*

Minnesota
Anoka-Ramsey Community College *A*
Augsburg College *B, M*
Bemidji State University *A, B*
Bethany Lutheran College *A*
Bethel College *A, B*
Central Lakes College *A*
Century Community and Technical
    College *A*
College of St. Benedict *B*
College of St. Catherine-Minneapolis *A*
College of St. Scholastica *B*
Concordia College: Moorhead *B*
Concordia University: St. Paul *A, B*
Crown College *A, B*
Fond Du Lac Tribal and Community
    College *A*
Hamline University *M*
Hibbing Community College: A
    Technical and Community College *A*
Inver Hills Community College *A*
Itasca Community College *A*
Lake Superior College: A Community
    and Technical College *A*
Macalester College *B*
Mesabi Range Community and Technical
    College *A*
Metropolitan State University *B*
Minneapolis Community and Technical
    College *A*
Minnesota Bible College *A*
Minnesota State University,
    Mankato *A, B*
Moorhead State University *A, B, M*
North Central University *B*
North Hennepin Community College *A*
Northland Community & Technical
    College *A*
Northwestern College *A*
Ridgewater College: A Community and
    Technical College *A*
Rochester Community and Technical
    College *A*
St. Cloud State University *A, B*
Southwest State University *B*
University of Minnesota
    Duluth *M*
    Morris *B*
    Twin Cities *C, B*
Winona State University *A, B*

Mississippi
Alcorn State University *B*
Belhaven College *B*
Copiah-Lincoln Community College *A*
East Central Community College *A*
Hinds Community College *A*
Holmes Community College *A*
Itawamba Community College *A*
Jones County Junior College *A*
Mary Holmes College *A*
Meridian Community College *A*
Millsaps College *B, M*
Mississippi College *M*
Mississippi Delta Community College *A*
Mississippi Gulf Coast Community
    College
    Jefferson Davis Campus *A*
    Perkinston *A*
Mississippi State University *B*
Northwest Mississippi Community
    College *A*
Rust College *B*
Southwest Mississippi Community
    College *A*
Tougaloo College *B*
University of Mississippi *B*
Wesley College *C*

Missouri
Avila College *B*
Central Methodist College *B*
Columbia College *A, B*
Conception Seminary College *B*
Cottey College *A*
Crowder College *A*
Drury University *B, M*
East Central College *A*
Evangel University *A*
Hannibal-LaGrange College *A, B*
Jefferson College *A*
Lincoln University *B*
Lindenwood University *B*
Longview Community College *A*
Maple Woods Community College *A*
Maryville University of Saint Louis *B*
Mineral Area College *A*
Missouri Southern State College *B*
Missouri Valley College *A, B*
Missouri Western State College *B*
Moberly Area Community College *A*
Northwest Missouri State University *B*
Ozarks Technical Community College *A*
Park University *B*
Penn Valley Community College *A*
Rockhurst University *B*
St. Charles County Community
    College *A*
St. Louis Christian College *A*
St. Louis University *B*
Southeast Missouri State University *B*
Southwest Baptist University *A*
Southwest Missouri State University
    West Plains Campus *A*
Southwest Missouri State University *B*
St. Louis Community College
    St. Louis Community College at
        Florissant Valley *A*
    St. Louis Community College at
        Forest Park *A*
    St. Louis Community College at
        Meramec *A*
State Fair Community College *A*
Stephens College *A, B*
Three Rivers Community College *A*
University of Missouri
    Columbia *B*
    Kansas City *B*
Washington University *M*
Wentworth Military Academy *C, A*

Montana
Dawson Community College *A*
Little Big Horn College *A*
Miles Community College *A*
Montana State University
    Billings *B*
Montana Tech of the University of
    Montana *A, B*
Rocky Mountain College *A, B*
Salish Kootenai College *A*
Stone Child College *A*
University of Great Falls *B*
University of Montana-Missoula *A, B*
Western Montana College of The
    University of Montana *A, B*

Nebraska
Central Community College *C, A*
Chadron State College *B*
College of Saint Mary *A, B*
Dana College *B*
Grace University *B*
Hastings College *B*
Metropolitan Community College *A*
Midland Lutheran College *B*
Northeast Community College *A*
Southeast Community College
    Lincoln Campus *A*
Union College *B*
University of Nebraska
    Kearney *B*
    Lincoln *B*
    Omaha *B*

Nevada
Community College of Southern
    Nevada *A*
University of Nevada
    Las Vegas *B, M*
    Reno *B*
Western Nevada Community College *A*

New Hampshire
Colby-Sawyer College *A*
College for Lifelong Learning *A, B*
Daniel Webster College *A*

Franklin Pierce College *B*
Hesser College *A*
Keene State College *A*
New Hampshire College *A, B*
New Hampshire Community Technical
   College
   Laconia *A*
   Manchester *A*
   Nashua *C, A*
New Hampshire Technical Institute *A*
Notre Dame College *A*
Plymouth State College of the University
   System of New Hampshire *A, B*
Rivier College *A, B*
St. Anselm College *B*
University of New Hampshire
   Manchester *A, B*
University of New Hampshire *B*
White Pines College *A*

New Jersey
Assumption College for Sisters *A*
Atlantic Cape Community College *A*
Bergen Community College *A*
Bloomfield College *B*
Brookdale Community College *A*
Burlington County College *A*
Caldwell College *M*
Camden County College *A*
Centenary College *A*
County College of Morris *A*
Cumberland County College *A*
Drew University *B*
Essex County College *A*
Fairleigh Dickinson University *B*
Felician College *A, B*
Georgian Court College *B*
Gloucester County College *A*
Hudson County Community College *A*
Kean University *M*
Mercer County Community College *A*
Monmouth University *A, M*
Montclair State University *B*
Ocean County College *A*
Passaic County Community College *A*
Ramapo College of New Jersey *B, M*
Raritan Valley Community College *A*
Richard Stockton College of New
   Jersey *B*
Rider University *A, B*
Rowan University *B*
Rutgers
   The State University of New Jersey:
      Camden Graduate Campus *M*
   The State University of New Jersey:
      Newark Graduate Campus *M*
   The State University of New Jersey:
      University College Camden *B*
Salem Community College *A*
Seton Hall University *B*
Sussex County Community College *A*
Thomas Edison State College *A, B*
Union County College *A*
Warren County Community College *A*
William Paterson University of New
   Jersey *B*

New Mexico
Albuquerque Technical-Vocational
   Institute *A*
College of Santa Fe *A, B*
College of the Southwest *B*
Eastern New Mexico University
   Roswell Campus *A*
Eastern New Mexico University *A, B*
New Mexico Institute of Mining and
   Technology *A, B*
New Mexico Junior College *A*
New Mexico Military Institute *A*
New Mexico State University
   Alamogordo *A*
   Carlsbad *A*
Northern New Mexico Community
   College *A*
St. John's College *B, M*
University of New Mexico *B*

Western New Mexico University *B*

New York
Adelphi University *B*
Adirondack Community College *A*
Alfred University *B*
Bard College *B*
Broome Community College *A*
Canisius College *A*
Cayuga County Community College *A*
City University of New York
   Baruch College *B*
   Borough of Manhattan Community
      College *A*
   Bronx Community College *A*
   Brooklyn College *M*
   College of Staten Island *A, B, T*
   Graduate School and University
      Center *M*
   Hostos Community College *A*
   Hunter College *B*
   Kingsborough Community
      College *A*
   La Guardia Community College *A*
   Lehman College *B*
   Medgar Evers College *A*
   New York City Technical
      College *A*
   Queensborough Community
      College *A*
   York College *B*
Clarkson University *B*
Clinton Community College *A*
Colgate University *B*
College of Mount St. Vincent *A, B*
College of New Rochelle
   School of New Resources *B*
College of St. Rose *B, M*
Columbia-Greene Community College *A*
Concordia College *A, B*
Cornell University *B*
Corning Community College *A*
Daemen College *B*
Dominican College of Blauvelt *A, B*
Dowling College *B*
Dutchess Community College *A*
Erie Community College
   City Campus *A*
   North Campus *A*
   South Campus *A*
Eugene Lang College/New School
   University *B*
Finger Lakes Community College *A*
Five Towns College *A*
Fulton-Montgomery Community
   College *C, A*
Genesee Community College *A*
Hamilton College *B*
Herkimer County Community College *A*
Hilbert College *A, B*
Hofstra University *B, M*
Houghton College *A*
Hudson Valley Community College *C*
Iona College *A, B*
Ithaca College *B*
Jamestown Community College *C, A*
Jefferson Community College *A*
Keuka College *A*
Long Island University
   Brooklyn Campus *B*
   C. W. Post Campus *A*
   Southampton College *B*
Manhattanville College *B, M*
Maria College *A*
Marist College *B*
Marymount Manhattan College *B*
Medaille College *A, B*
Mercy College *C, A, B*
Mohawk Valley Community College *A*
Molloy College *A*
Monroe Community College *A*
Mount St. Mary College *B, T*
Nassau Community College *A*
New York Institute of Technology *B*
New York University *A, B, M*

Niagara County Community College *A*
Niagara University *A*
North Country Community College *A*
Nyack College *A, B*
Onondaga Community College *A*
Orange County Community College *A*
Pace University:
   Pleasantville/Briarcliff *B*
Pace University *B*
Polytechnic University *B*
Regents College *A, B, M*
Rensselaer Polytechnic Institute *B*
Roberts Wesleyan College *B*
Rochester Institute of Technology *A*
Rockland Community College *A*
Sage Junior College of Albany *A*
St. John's University *A, B, M*
St. Thomas Aquinas College *B*
Sarah Lawrence College *B*
Schenectady County Community
   College *C, A*
Skidmore College *B, M*
St. Joseph's College
   St. Joseph's College *B*
State University of New York
   Albany *B, M, D*
   Buffalo *A, B, M*
   College at Brockport *M*
   College at Buffalo *B*
   College at Cortland *B*
   College at Old Westbury *B*
   College at Plattsburgh *B, M*
   College of Agriculture and
      Technology at Cobleskill *A*
   College of Agriculture and
      Technology at Morrisville *A*
   College of Technology at Alfred *A*
   College of Technology at Canton *A*
   College of Technology at Delhi *A*
   Empire State College *A, B, M*
   Farmingdale *A*
   Institute of Technology at
      Utica/Rome *B*
   Maritime College *B*
   New Paltz *B*
   Purchase *B*
   Stony Brook *B, M*
Suffolk County Community College *A*
Syracuse University *D*
Tompkins-Cortland Community
   College *C, A*
Touro College *A, B*
Trocaire College *A*
Ulster County Community College *A*
Union College *B*
Utica College of Syracuse University *B*
Vassar College *B*
Villa Maria College of Buffalo *A*
Wadhams Hall Seminary-College *B*
Wagner College *B*
Westchester Community College *A*

North Carolina
Alamance Community College *A*
Appalachian State University *B*
Asheville Buncombe Technical
   Community College *A*
Beaufort County Community College *A*
Belmont Abbey College *B*
Bennett College *B*
Bladen Community College *A*
Blue Ridge Community College *A*
Brevard College *A, B*
Brunswick Community College *A*
Caldwell Community College and
   Technical Institute *A*
Cape Fear Community College *A*
Carteret Community College *A*
Catawba Valley Community College *A*
Central Carolina Community College *A*
Central Piedmont Community College *A*
Chowan College *A, B*
Cleveland Community College *A*
Coastal Carolina Community College *A*
College of the Albemarle *A*

Craven Community College *A*
Davidson County Community College *A*
Duke University *M*
Durham Technical Community
   College *A*
East Carolina University *B*
Edgecombe Community College *A*
Fayetteville Technical Community
   College *A*
Forsyth Technical Community College *A*
Gaston College *C, A*
Guilford College *B*
Guilford Technical Community
   College *A*
Halifax Community College *A*
Haywood Community College *A*
James Sprunt Community College *A*
Johnson C. Smith University *B*
Johnston Community College *A*
Lees-McRae College *B*
Lenoir Community College *A*
Louisburg College *A*
Mars Hill College *B*
Martin Community College *A*
Mayland Community College *A*
Methodist College *A, B*
Mitchell Community College *A*
Montgomery Community College *A*
Montreat College *A*
Mount Olive College *A, B*
Nash Community College *A*
North Carolina School of the Arts *B*
North Carolina State University *B, M*
Peace College *A, B*
Piedmont Community College *A*
Pitt Community College *A*
Randolph Community College *A*
Richmond Community College *A*
Roanoke-Chowan Community College *A*
Rockingham Community College *A*
St. Andrews Presbyterian College *B*
Sandhills Community College *A*
Shaw University *B*
South Piedmont Community College *A*
Southeastern Community College *A*
Southwestern Community College *A*
Surry Community College *A*
Tri-County Community College *A*
University of North Carolina
   Asheville *B, M*
   Chapel Hill *B*
   Charlotte *M*
   Greensboro *B, M*
   Wilmington *M*
Vance-Granville Community College *A*
Wake Forest University *M*
Wake Technical Community College *A*
Warren Wilson College *B*
Wayne Community College *A*
Western Carolina University *B*
Western Piedmont Community
   College *A*
Wilkes Community College *A*
Wilson Technical Community College *A*
Wingate University *B*

North Dakota
Bismarck State College *A*
Dickinson State University *A, B, T*
Lake Region State College *A*
Mayville State University *B*
Minot State University: Bottineau
   Campus *A*
Minot State University *B*
North Dakota State College of Science *A*
North Dakota State University *B*
Trinity Bible College *B*
University of Mary *B*
Valley City State University *B*
Williston State College *A*

Ohio
Antioch College *B*
Ashland University *A*
Bluffton College *B*

Liberal arts/humanities

Bowling Green State University
   Firelands College *A*
Bowling Green State University *B*
Capital University *B*
Chatfield College *A*
Cincinnati State Technical and
   Community College *A*
Clark State Community College *A*
Cleveland State University *B*
College of Mount St. Joseph *A, B*
Columbus State Community College *A*
David N. Myers College *B*
Defiance College *B*
Edison State Community College *A*
Franciscan University of Steubenville *A*
Jefferson Community College *A*
John Carroll University *B, M*
Kent State University
   Ashtabula Regional Campus *A, B*
   East Liverpool Regional Campus *A*
   Stark Campus *A*
   Trumbull Campus *A*
   Tuscarawas Campus *A*
Kent State University *B, M*
Lakeland Community College *A*
Lorain County Community College *A*
Lourdes College *A, B*
Malone College *B*
Marietta College *A, M*
Miami University
   Hamilton Campus *A*
   Middletown Campus *A*
   Oxford Campus *A*
Mount Vernon Nazarene College *A*
Northwest State Community College *A*
Ohio Dominican College *A, B*
Ohio Northern University *B*
Ohio State University
   Columbus Campus *B, M*
   Lima Campus *A*
   Mansfield Campus *A*
   Marion Campus *A*
   Newark Campus *A*
Ohio University
   Chillicothe Campus *A*
   Eastern Campus *A*
   Zanesville Campus *A*
Ohio University *B*
Owens Community College
   Findlay Campus *A*
   Toledo *A*
Pontifical College Josephinum *B*
Shawnee State University *A*
Sinclair Community College *A*
Southern State Community College *A*
Terra Community College *A*
Tiffin University *B*
Union Institute *B, D*
University of Akron
   Wayne College *A*
University of Akron *B*
University of Cincinnati
   Clermont College *A*
   Raymond Walters College *A*
University of Cincinnati *B*
University of Dayton *B, M*
University of Findlay *A*
University of Rio Grande *A*
University of Toledo *A, B, M*
Ursuline College *B*
Walsh University *A, B*
Washington State Community College *A*
Wilberforce University *B*
Wittenberg University *B*
Wright State University *M*
Xavier University *A, B, M*
Youngstown State University *A, B*

Oklahoma
Connors State College *A*
Mid-America Bible College *A*
Murray State College *A*
Northern Oklahoma College *A*
Oklahoma Baptist University *B*
Oklahoma Christian University of
   Science and Arts *B*
Oklahoma City Community College *A*
Oklahoma City University *B, M*
Oklahoma Panhandle State University *A*
Oral Roberts University *B*
Redlands Community College *A*
Rogers State University *A*
Rose State College *A*
St. Gregory's University *A, B*
Seminole State College *A*
University of Central Oklahoma *B*
University of Oklahoma *B, M*
University of Tulsa *B*
Western Oklahoma State College *A*

Oregon
Central Oregon Community College *A*
Chemeketa Community College *A*
Clackamas Community College *A*
Clatsop Community College *A*
Concordia University *A, B*
Eastern Oregon University *A, B*
Lane Community College *A*
Linn-Benton Community College *A*
Marylhurst University *B*
Northwest Christian College *B*
Oregon Institute of Technology *A*
Oregon State University *B*
Pacific University *A*
Portland State University *B*
University of Oregon *B*
Western Baptist College *B*
Western Oregon University *A, B*
Willamette University *B*

Pennsylvania
Allentown College of St. Francis de
   Sales *B*
Alvernia College *B, M*
Beaver College *B, M*
Bloomsburg University of
   Pennsylvania *B*
Bryn Athyn College of the New
   Church *B*
Bucks County Community College *A*
Butler County Community College *A*
Cabrini College *B*
California University of Pennsylvania *B*
Carlow College *B*
Carnegie Mellon University *B*
Cedar Crest College *B*
Chatham College *M*
Clarion University of Pennsylvania *A, B*
College Misericordia *B*
Community College of Allegheny
   County *A*
Community College of Beaver County *A*
Community College of Philadelphia *A*
Delaware County Community College *A*
Drexel University *B*
Duquesne University *B, M*
Eastern College *A*
Edinboro University of
   Pennsylvania *A, B*
Elizabethtown College *C*
Gannon University *A, B*
Gettysburg College *B*
Gwynedd-Mercy College *A*
Harcum College *A*
Harrisburg Area Community College *A*
Holy Family College *B*
Immaculata College *A, B*
Juniata College *B*
Kutztown University of Pennsylvania *B*
La Roche College *B*
La Salle University *A, B*
Lackawanna Junior College *A*
Lebanon Valley College of
   Pennsylvania *A, B*
Lehigh Carbon Community College *A*
Lehigh University *B*
Lock Haven University of
   Pennsylvania *B, M*
Luzerne County Community College *A*
Manor College *A*
Mansfield University of Pennsylvania *B*
Mercyhurst College *C*
Messiah College *B*
Millersville University of
   Pennsylvania *A*
Montgomery County Community
   College *A*
Mount Aloysius College *A, B*
Muhlenberg College *B*
Neumann College *A, B*
Northampton County Area Community
   College *A*
Peirce College *A*
Penn State
   Abington *A, B*
   Altoona *A, B*
   Beaver *A*
   Berks *A*
   Delaware County *A, B*
   Dubois *A, B*
   Erie, The Behrend College *A, B*
   Fayette *A, B*
   Harrisburg *B, M*
   Hazleton *A*
   Lehigh Valley *A*
   McKeesport *A*
   Mont Alto *A*
   New Kensington *A*
   Schuylkill - Capital College *A*
   Shenango *A*
   University Park *C, A, B*
   Wilkes-Barre *A*
   Worthington Scranton *A*
   York *A*
Pennsylvania College of Technology *A*
Point Park College *A, B*
Reading Area Community College *A*
Robert Morris College *A*
Rosemont College *B*
St. Joseph's University *A, B*
St. Vincent College *B*
Seton Hill College *B*
Temple University *A, B, M*
Thiel College *A*
University of Pennsylvania *A, B, M, D*
University of Pittsburgh
   Greensburg *B*
   Johnstown *B*
   Titusville *A*
University of Pittsburgh *B*
Valley Forge Military College *A*
Villanova University *A, B, M*
Waynesburg College *A*
West Chester University of
   Pennsylvania *A, B*
Westmoreland County Community
   College *A*
Widener University *A, B*
Wilkes University *B*
Wilson College *A*
York College of Pennsylvania *A, B*

Puerto Rico
Colegio Universitario del Este *A*
Pontifical Catholic University of Puerto
   Rico *A, B*
Turabo University *B*
University of Puerto Rico
   Aguadilla *A*
   Arecibo Campus *A*
   Bayamon University College *A*
   Carolina Regional College *A*
   Cayey University College *B*
   Humacao University College *A*
   Ponce University College *A*
   Rio Piedras Campus *B*
   Utuado *A*

Rhode Island
Bryant College *A*
Community College of Rhode Island *A*
Providence College *A, B*
Rhode Island College *B*
Salve Regina University *A, B, M, D*
University of Rhode Island *B*

South Carolina
Aiken Technical College *A*
Anderson College *B*
Central Carolina Technical College *A*
Charleston Southern University *B*
Chesterfield-Marlboro Technical
   College *A*
Columbia College *B*
Columbia International University *A, B*
Denmark Technical College *A*
Florence-Darlington Technical College *A*
Francis Marion University *B*
Greenville Technical College *A*
Limestone College *A, B*
Midlands Technical College *A*
Morris College *B*
North Greenville College *A, B*
Orangeburg-Calhoun Technical
   College *A*
Piedmont Technical College *C, A*
Spartanburg Methodist College *A*
Technical College of the Lowcountry *A*
Tri-County Technical College *A*
Trident Technical College *A*
University of South Carolina
   Beaufort *A*
   Salkehatchie Regional Campus *A*
   Sumter *A*
   Union *A*
University of South Carolina *A, B*
Winthrop University *M*
Wofford College *B*
York Technical College *A*

South Dakota
Augustana College *B*
Dakota State University *A*
Dakota Wesleyan University *A*
Kilian Community College *A*
Sinte Gleska University *A*
South Dakota School of Mines and
   Technology *B*
South Dakota State University *B*
University of South Dakota *B, M*

Tennessee
Aquinas College *A*
Austin Peay State University *A*
Belmont University *B*
Bethel College *B*
Carson-Newman College *B*
Chattanooga State Technical Community
   College *A*
Cleveland State Community
   College *C, A*
Columbia State Community College *A*
Crichton College *B*
Cumberland University *B*
David Lipscomb University *B*
Dyersburg State Community College *A*
East Tennessee State University *B, M*
Freed-Hardeman University *B, T*
Hiwassee College *A*
Jackson State Community College *A*
Lambuth University *B*
LeMoyne-Owen College *B*
Lee University *B, M*
Lincoln Memorial University *B, T*
Milligan College *B*
Motlow State Community College *A*
Northeast State Technical Community
   College *A*
Roane State Community College *A*
Shelby State Community College *A*
Southern Adventist University *A*
Tennessee State University *A*
Tennessee Temple University *A, B*
Trevecca Nazarene University *A*
University of Tennessee
   Chattanooga *B*
Vanderbilt University *M*
Volunteer State Community College *A*
Walters State Community College *A*

Texas
Abilene Christian University *B, M*

373

Liberal arts/humanities

Alvin Community College *A*
Amarillo College *A*
Amber University *B*
Angelina College *A*
Blinn College *A*
Brazosport College *A*
Central Texas College *A*
Coastal Bend College *A*
College of the Mainland *A*
Collin County Community College
 District *A*
Concordia University at Austin *A, B*
Dallas Baptist University *A, B, M*
Del Mar College *A*
East Texas Baptist University *A*
Eastfield College *A*
El Paso Community College *A*
Galveston College *A*
Grayson County College *A*
Hill College *C, A*
Houston Baptist University *M*
Houston Community College System *A*
Howard College *A*
Howard Payne University *B*
Huston-Tillotson College *B*
Jacksonville College *A*
Kilgore College *A*
Lamar University *B*
Lee College *A*
Lon Morris College *A*
Lubbock Christian University *B*
Midland College *A*
Navarro College *A*
North Lake College *A*
Northeast Texas Community College *A*
Odessa College *A*
Our Lady of the Lake University of San
 Antonio *B*
Palo Alto College *A*
Panola College *A*
Paris Junior College *A*
Richland College *A*
St. Edward's University *B*
St. Mary's University *B*
St. Philip's College *A*
Sam Houston State University *B*
San Antonio College *C, A*
Schreiner College *A, B*
South Plains College *A*
Southern Methodist University *B, M*
Southwest Texas Junior College *A*
Southwestern Assemblies of God
 University *A*
Stephen F. Austin State University *B*
Tarleton State University *B*
Temple College *A*
Texas A&M International University *B*
Texas A&M University
 Commerce *B*
 Texarkana *A*
Texas A&M University *B, M*
Texas Christian University *B, M*
Trinity Valley Community College *A*
Tyler Junior College *A*
University of Dallas *M*
University of Houston
 Clear Lake *B, M*
 Downtown *B*
University of Mary Hardin-Baylor *B*
University of North Texas *B*
University of St. Thomas *B, M*
University of Texas
 Arlington *M*
 Austin *B*
 Brownsville *B*
 Dallas *B, M, D*
 Pan American *M*
 San Antonio *B*
 Tyler *B, M*
 of the Permian Basin *B*
University of the Incarnate Word *B*
Vernon Regional Junior College *A*
Victoria College *A*
Weatherford College *A*
West Texas A&M University *B*
Western Texas College *A*
Wharton County Junior College *A*

Utah
Brigham Young University *B, M*
College of Eastern Utah *A*
Dixie State College of Utah *A*
LDS Business College *A*
Salt Lake Community College *A*
Utah State University *A, B, M*
Weber State University *A, B*

Vermont
Bennington College *B*
Burlington College *A, B*
Castleton State College *A*
Champlain College *A, B*
College of St. Joseph in Vermont *A, B*
Community College of Vermont *A*
Goddard College *B*
Green Mountain College *B*
Johnson State College *A, B*
Landmark College *A*
Lyndon State College *A, B*
Marlboro College *B*
Middlebury College *B*
Norwich University *B*
Southern Vermont College *A, B*
Trinity College of Vermont *A, B*
University of Vermont *B*

Virginia
Averett College *A, T*
Blue Ridge Community College *A*
Bluefield College *B*
Bridgewater College *B*
Central Virginia Community College *A*
Christendom College *A*
Dabney S. Lancaster Community
 College *A*
Danville Community College *A*
Eastern Mennonite University *C, A, B*
Eastern Shore Community College *A*
Ferrum College *B*
George Mason University *B*
Germanna Community College *A*
Hampden-Sydney College *B*
Hampton University *B*
Hollins University *M*
J. Sargeant Reynolds Community
 College *A*
James Madison University *B*
John Tyler Community College *A*
Liberty University *B, T*
Longwood College *B, T*
Lord Fairfax Community College *A*
Mary Baldwin College *B*
Mary Washington College *M*
Mountain Empire Community College *A*
New River Community College *A*
Northern Virginia Community College *A*
Old Dominion University *M*
Paul D. Camp Community College *A*
Piedmont Virginia Community
 College *C, A*
Radford University *B*
Richard Bland College *A*
Shenandoah University *B*
Southside Virginia Community
 College *A*
Southwest Virginia Community
 College *A*
Thomas Nelson Community College *A*
Tidewater Community College *A*
University of Richmond *C, A, M*
University of Virginia's College at
 Wise *B*
University of Virginia *B*
Virginia Commonwealth University *B*
Virginia Highlands Community
 College *A*
Virginia Intermont College *A, B*
Virginia Polytechnic Institute and State
 University *B*
Virginia State University *B*
Virginia Wesleyan College *B*
Virginia Western Community College *A*
Wytheville Community College *A*

Washington
Antioch University Seattle *B, M*
Bellevue Community College *A*
Big Bend Community College *A*
Centralia College *A*
City University *A, B*
Clark College *A*
Columbia Basin College *A*
Eastern Washington University *B*
Edmonds Community College *A*
Everett Community College *A*
Evergreen State College *B*
Gonzaga University *B*
Grays Harbor College *A*
Green River Community College *A*
Heritage College *A, B*
Highline Community College *A*
North Seattle Community College *A*
Olympic College *A*
Peninsula College *A*
Pierce College *A*
St. Martin's College *A*
Seattle Central Community College *A*
Seattle Pacific University *B, T*
Seattle University *B*
Shoreline Community College *C, A*
Skagit Valley College *A*
South Puget Sound Community
 College *A*
South Seattle Community College *A*
Spokane Community College *A*
Tacoma Community College *A*
University of Washington *B*
Walla Walla College *B*
Walla Walla Community College *A*
Washington State University *B*
Wenatchee Valley College *A*
Western Washington University *B*
Whatcom Community College *A*
Whitworth College *B*
Yakima Valley Community College *A*

West Virginia
Alderson-Broaddus College *A, B*
Bluefield State College *B*
College of West Virginia *B*
Concord College *B*
Fairmont State College *A*
Glenville State College *B*
Marshall University *B, M*
Ohio Valley College *A, B*
Potomac State College of West Virginia
 University *A*
Salem-Teikyo University *A, B*
Shepherd College *A*
Southern West Virginia Community and
 Technical College *A*
University of Charleston *A, B*
West Liberty State College *B*
West Virginia Northern Community
 College *A*
West Virginia State College *A, B*
West Virginia University
 Parkersburg *A*
West Virginia University Institute of
 Technology *A*
West Virginia University *B, M*
West Virginia Wesleyan College *B*
Wheeling Jesuit University *B*

Wisconsin
Alverno College *A*
Beloit College *B*
Cardinal Stritch University *A*
Carroll College *B*
Concordia University Wisconsin *B*
Lawrence University *B*
Madison Area Technical College *A*
Marian College of Fond du Lac *B*
Milwaukee Area Technical College *A*
Mount Senario College *B*
Nicolet Area Technical College *A*
St. Norbert College *B*
Silver Lake College *A*
University of Wisconsin
 Baraboo/Sauk County *A*
 Barron County *A*
 Eau Claire *A*
 Fond du Lac *A*
 Fox Valley *A*
 Green Bay *A, B*
 Manitowoc County *A*
 Marathon County *A*
 Marinette *A*
 Marshfield/Wood County *A*
 Milwaukee *B*
 Oshkosh *B*
 Parkside *B*
 Platteville *B*
 Richland *A*
 Rock County *A*
 Sheboygan County *A*
 Stevens Point *A, B*
 Superior *A, B*
 Washington County *A*
 Waukesha *A*
 Whitewater *A*
Viterbo University *B*

Wyoming
Casper College *A*
Central Wyoming College *A*
Eastern Wyoming College *A*
Laramie County Community College *A*
Northwest College *A*
Sheridan College *A*
Western Wyoming Community
 College *A*

Library assistance

Alabama
Northwest-Shoals Community College *C*

Arizona
Arizona Western College *C*
Mesa Community College *A*
Northland Pioneer College *C, A*

California
Barstow College *C*
Chabot College *A*
Citrus College *C, A*
City College of San Francisco *A*
Cuesta College *C, A*
Foothill College *C, A*
Imperial Valley College *C*
Merced College *A*
Pasadena City College *C, A*
Rio Hondo College *A*
Sacramento City College *C, A*
Sierra College *A*

Colorado
Pueblo Community College *C, A*
University of Denver *M*

Connecticut
Capital Community College *A*
Three Rivers Community-Technical
 College *C*

Florida
Indian River Community College *A*

Illinois
Black Hawk College *C*
City Colleges of Chicago
 Wright College *C, A*
College of DuPage *C, A*
College of Lake County *C, A*
Lewis and Clark Community College *A*

Kansas
Central Christian College *A*
Seward County Community College *A*

Massachusetts
Atlantic Union College *A*

Michigan
Bay de Noc Community College *C*
Oakland Community College *C, A*

New Mexico
Dona Ana Branch Community College of New Mexico State University *A*
Northern New Mexico Community College *C, A*

New York
Syracuse University *M*

Oklahoma
Rose State College *C, A*

Pennsylvania
Northampton County Area Community College *C*

Tennessee
Hiwassee College *A*

Washington
Highline Community College *A*
Lake Washington Technical College *C*

Library science

Alabama
University of Alabama *B, M, D*

Arizona
University of Arizona *M, D*

Arkansas
University of Central Arkansas *M*

California
Cabrillo College *A*
Citrus College *A*
City College of San Francisco *A*
Diablo Valley College *C*
Fresno City College *C, A*
Los Angeles Harbor College *A*
Merced College *A*
Palomar College *C, A*
San Bernardino Valley College *C, A*
San Jose State University *M*
Santa Ana College *C, A*
Sierra College *A*
University of California
    Los Angeles *M, D*

Colorado
University of Colorado
    Denver *M*

Connecticut
Eastern Connecticut State University *B*
Southern Connecticut State University *B, M*

District of Columbia
Catholic University of America *M*

Florida
Florida State University *M, D*
Gulf Coast Community College *A*
University of South Florida *M*

Georgia
Clark Atlanta University *M, D*
Valdosta State University *B*

Hawaii
University of Hawaii
    Manoa *M*

Idaho
College of Southern Idaho *A*

Illinois
Chicago State University *M*
Dominican University *M*
University of Illinois
    Urbana-Champaign *M, D*
University of St. Francis *C*

Indiana
Ball State University *B*
Indiana State University *B, T*
Indiana University
    Bloomington *M, D*
Indiana University--Purdue University
    Indiana University-Purdue
    University Indianapolis *M*
Vincennes University *A*

Iowa
North Iowa Area Community College *A*
University of Iowa *M*
University of Northern Iowa *M*

Kansas
Allen County Community College *A*
Central Christian College *A*
Emporia State University *M, D*

Kentucky
University of Kentucky *M*
Western Kentucky University *B, M, T*

Louisiana
Louisiana State University and Agricultural and Mechanical College *C, M*
Our Lady of Holy Cross College *C*

Maine
University of Maine
    Augusta *A, B*

Maryland
University of Maryland
    College Park *M, D*

Massachusetts
Simmons College *M, D*

Michigan
Central Michigan University *B, M*
University of Michigan *M, D, T*
Wayne State University *C, M*

Minnesota
College of St. Catherine: St. Paul Campus *B, M*
St. Cloud State University *B, M*

Mississippi
University of Southern Mississippi *B, M*

Missouri
Central Missouri State University *M*
East Central College *A*
Missouri Baptist College *T*
Three Rivers Community College *A*

Montana
Western Montana College of The University of Montana *C, T*

Nebraska
Chadron State College *B*
University of Nebraska
    Omaha *B*

New Hampshire
College for Lifelong Learning *C*

New Jersey
Brookdale Community College *A*
Rowan University *M*
Rutgers
    The State University of New Jersey:
    New Brunswick Graduate
    Campus *M, D*

New York
City University of New York
    Queens College *M*
Long Island University
    C. W. Post Campus *M*
Pratt Institute *M*
St. John's University *M*
State University of New York
    Albany *M*
    Buffalo *M, T*
Syracuse University *M*

North Carolina
Appalachian State University *M*
East Carolina University *M, T*
North Carolina Central University *M*
University of North Carolina
    Chapel Hill *C, M, D*
    Greensboro *M*

Ohio
Kent State University *M*
Miami University
    Oxford Campus *T*
Ohio Dominican College *C, A, B, D*

Oklahoma
Northwestern Oklahoma State University *M*
Tulsa Community College *A*
University of Oklahoma *M*

Pennsylvania
Clarion University of Pennsylvania *B, M, T*
Drexel University *M*
Kutztown University of Pennsylvania *B, M, T*
University of Pittsburgh *C, M, D*

Puerto Rico
Inter American University of Puerto Rico
    San German Campus *M*
University of Puerto Rico
    Rio Piedras Campus *M*

Rhode Island
University of Rhode Island *M*

South Carolina
University of South Carolina *M*

South Dakota
Black Hills State University *B, T*

Tennessee
University of Tennessee
    Knoxville *M, T*

Texas
Sam Houston State University *M*
Texas A&M University
    Commerce *B, M*
Texas Woman's University *B, M, D*
University of Houston
    Clear Lake *M*
University of North Texas *B, M, D*
University of Texas
    Austin *M, D*

Virginia
Longwood College *M*
University of Virginia's College at Wise *T*

Washington
University of Washington *M*

West Virginia
Concord College *B, T*
Fairmont State College *B*
Marshall University *B*

Wisconsin
University of Wisconsin
    Madison *M, D*
    Milwaukee *M*

Linguistics

Alaska
University of Alaska
    Fairbanks *B*

Arizona
Northern Arizona University *D*
University of Arizona *B, M, D*

California
California State University
    Bakersfield *B*
    Dominguez Hills *B*
    Fresno *B, M*
    Fullerton *B, M*
    Northridge *B, M*
Foothill College *A*
Pitzer College *B*
Pomona College *B*
San Diego State University *C, B, M*
San Francisco State University *M*
San Jose State University *B, M*
Scripps College *B*
Stanford University *B, M, D*
University of California
    Berkeley *B, M, D*
    Davis *B, M*
    Irvine *B, M, D*
    Los Angeles *B, M, D*
    Riverside *B*
    San Diego *B, M, D*
    Santa Barbara *B, M, D*
    Santa Cruz *B, M, D*
University of Southern California *B, M, D*

Colorado
University of Colorado
    Boulder *B, M, D*

Connecticut
University of Connecticut *B, M, D*
Yale University *B, M, D*

Delaware
University of Delaware *M, D*

District of Columbia
Gallaudet University *M*
Georgetown University *B, M, D*

Florida
Florida Atlantic University *B, M*
Florida International University *M*
Florida State University *B, M, D*
University of Florida *B, M, D*
University of South Florida *M*

Georgia
Morehouse College *B*
University of Georgia *B, M, D*

Hawaii
University of Hawaii
    Hilo *B*
    Manoa *M, D*

Idaho
University of Idaho *B*

Illinois
Judson College *B*
Moody Bible Institute *B*
Northeastern Illinois University *M*
Northwestern University *B, M, D*
Southern Illinois University
    Carbondale *B, M*
University of Chicago *B, M, D*
University of Illinois
    Chicago *M*
    Urbana-Champaign *B, M, D*

Indiana
Ball State University *M*
Indiana University
    Bloomington *B, M, D*

Iowa
Central College *B*
Iowa State University *B*
University of Iowa *B, M, D*

Kansas
University of Kansas *B, M, D*

Kentucky
University of Kentucky *B*
University of Louisville *M*

Linguistics

Louisiana
Louisiana State University and Agricultural and Mechanical College *M, D*
Tulane University *B*

Maine
University of Southern Maine *B*

Maryland
University of Maryland
    Baltimore County *B, M*
    College Park *B, M, D*

Massachusetts
Boston College *B, M*
Boston University *B*
Brandeis University *B*
Hampshire College *B*
Harvard College *B*
Harvard University *M, D*
Massachusetts Institute of Technology *B, D*
Northeastern University *B*
University of Massachusetts
    Amherst *B, M, D*
Wellesley College *B*

Michigan
Eastern Michigan University *B, M*
Michigan State University *B, M, D*
Oakland University *B, M*
University of Michigan *B, M, D*
Wayne State University *B, M*
Western Michigan University *B*

Minnesota
Crown College *B*
Macalester College *B*
St. Cloud State University *B*
University of Minnesota
    Twin Cities *B, M, D*

Mississippi
Jackson State University *B, M*
University of Mississippi *B*

Missouri
Central Missouri State University *M*
University of Missouri
    Columbia *B*

Montana
University of Montana-Missoula *B, M*

New Hampshire
Dartmouth College *B*
University of New Hampshire *B*

New Jersey
Montclair State University *B, M*
Rutgers
    The State University of New Jersey:
      Douglass College *B*
    The State University of New Jersey:
      Livingston College *B*
    The State University of New Jersey:
      New Brunswick Graduate Campus *M, D*
    The State University of New Jersey:
      Rutgers College *B*
    The State University of New Jersey:
      University College New Brunswick *B*

New Mexico
University of New Mexico *B, M, D*

New York
Barnard College *B*
City University of New York
    Brooklyn College *B*
    Graduate School and University Center *M, D*
    Queens College *B, M*
Cornell University *B, M, D*
New York University *B, M, D*

State University of New York
    Albany *B, M*
    Buffalo *B, M, D*
    Oswego *B*
    Stony Brook *B, M, D*
Syracuse University *B, M*
University of Rochester *B, M*

North Carolina
University of North Carolina
    Chapel Hill *B, M, D*

North Dakota
University of North Dakota *M*

Ohio
Cleveland State University *B*
Miami University
    Oxford Campus *B*
Ohio State University
    Columbus Campus *B, M, D*
Ohio University *B, M*
University of Akron *C*
University of Cincinnati *B*
University of Toledo *B*

Oklahoma
University of Oklahoma *B*

Oregon
Portland State University *B, M*
Reed College *B*
University of Oregon *B, M, D*

Pennsylvania
Carnegie Mellon University *B*
Swarthmore College *B*
Temple University *B, M*
University of Pennsylvania *A, B, M, D*
University of Pittsburgh *B, M, D*

Puerto Rico
University of Puerto Rico
    Rio Piedras Campus *M*

Rhode Island
Brown University *B*

South Carolina
University of South Carolina *M, D*

Tennessee
University of Tennessee
    Knoxville *B*

Texas
Baylor University *B*
Navarro College *A*
Rice University *B, M, D*
Texas Tech University *M*
University of Houston *M*
University of Texas
    Arlington *M, D*
    Austin *B, M, D*
    El Paso *B, M*

Utah
Brigham Young University *B, M*
University of Utah *B, M*

Vermont
Marlboro College *B*

Virginia
College of William and Mary *B*
University of Virginia *M*

Washington
Highline Community College *A*
Seattle Pacific University *B*
University of Washington *B, M, D*
Washington State University *B*
Western Washington University *B*

Wisconsin
Lawrence University *B*
University of Wisconsin
    Madison *B, M, D*
    Milwaukee *B*

Logistics/materials management

Alabama
Alabama Agricultural and Mechanical University *B, M*
Auburn University *B*

Alaska
University of Alaska
    Anchorage *B*

Arkansas
University of Arkansas *B, M*

California
California Maritime Academy *B*
California State University
    Hayward *C, M*
Cerritos Community College *A*
Chabot College *A*
College of San Mateo *C, A*
Golden Gate University *M*

Colorado
Arapahoe Community College *A*
Colorado Technical University *B, M*

Delaware
Wilmington College *M*

Florida
Brevard Community College *A*
University of Miami *C*

Georgia
Georgia College and State University *B*
Georgia Southern University *B*

Illinois
Elmhurst College *B*
Kishwaukee College *C*
Parkland College *C*
Prairie State College *C*
Rock Valley College *C, A*
Waubonsee Community College *C, A*
Western Illinois University *B*
William Rainey Harper College *C, A*

Iowa
Iowa State University *B*

Maine
Maine Maritime Academy *B, M*

Massachusetts
Massachusetts Institute of Technology *M*
Massachusetts Maritime Academy *B*
Middlesex Community College *C*
Northeastern University *B*
Northern Essex Community College *C, A*

Michigan
Central Michigan University *B*
Kettering University *B*
Michigan State University *B, M, D*
Western Michigan University *B*

Missouri
University of Missouri
    St. Louis *B*

Nevada
University of Nevada
    Reno *B*

New Jersey
Thomas Edison State College *B*

New York
St. John's University *B*

North Carolina
South Piedmont Community College *A*

Ohio
Bowling Green State University *B*
Columbus State Community College *A*
John Carroll University *B*

Kent State University
    Stark Campus *B*
Ohio State University
    Columbus Campus *B*
Sinclair Community College *A*
University of Akron *B*
University of Toledo *M*
Wright State University *M*

Pennsylvania
Duquesne University *B*
Mercyhurst College *C, A*
Penn State
    University Park *C, B*
Robert Morris College *B*

Puerto Rico
Turabo University *B, M*
University of Puerto Rico
    Bayamon University College *B*

Tennessee
University of Memphis *B*
University of Tennessee
    Knoxville *B*

Texas
Houston Community College
    System *C, A*
Palo Alto College *C, A*
Texas A&M International University *M*
University of Texas
    Arlington *M*

Utah
Salt Lake Community College *A*
Weber State University *B*

Washington
Western Washington University *B*

West Virginia
Salem-Teikyo University *B*

Wisconsin
Chippewa Valley Technical College *A*
Gateway Technical College *A*
Northeast Wisconsin Technical College *A*

Management information systems

Alabama
Auburn University at Montgomery *B*
Auburn University *M*
Central Alabama Community College *C, A*
Community College of the Air Force *A*
Enterprise State Junior College *A*
Spring Hill College *C, A, B*
University of Alabama
    Huntsville *B*
University of North Alabama *B*
University of West Alabama *B*

Alaska
University of Alaska
    Anchorage *B*
    Southeast *C, A*

Arizona
Arizona State University *B*
Central Arizona College *A*
Cochise College *A*
Glendale Community College *C, A*
Northern Arizona University *B*
Phoenix College *C, A*
Pima Community College *A*
Scottsdale Community College *C, A*
University of Arizona *B, M*
University of Phoenix *B*

Arkansas
Arkansas State University *C, A*
Mississippi County Community College *C, A*

Management information systems

Southern Arkansas University
  Tech *C*
University of Arkansas
  Little Rock *B*
Westark College *A*

California
Allan Hancock College *A*
American River College *A*
Armstrong University *M*
Azusa Pacific University *B*
Bakersfield College *A*
Barstow College *A*
Butte College *C, A*
California State Polytechnic University:
  Pomona *A*
California State University
  Bakersfield *B*
  Chico *C, B*
  Dominguez Hills *B*
  Fresno *B*
  Fullerton *B, M*
  Hayward *B, M*
  Northridge *B*
  Stanislaus *B*
Canada College *C, A*
Chabot College *A*
Chaffey Community College *C*
Citrus College *A*
City College of San Francisco *A*
College of Notre Dame *M*
College of San Mateo *C, A*
College of the Canyons *A*
College of the Sequoias *C, A*
College of the Siskiyous *C, A*
Columbia College *C*
Compton Community College *A*
Concordia University *B*
Cypress College *C, A*
Diablo Valley College *A*
Empire College *C*
Evergreen Valley College *A*
Gavilan Community College *C*
Heald Business College
  Fresno *C, A*
Lincoln University *M*
Long Beach City College *C, A*
Los Angeles Harbor College *C, A*
Los Angeles Southwest College *A*
Los Angeles Valley College *C, A*
Master's College *B*
Merced College *A*
Mission College *A*
Modesto Junior College *A*
Moorpark College *A*
Orange Coast College *C, A*
Pacific Union College *B*
Pasadena City College *A*
Point Loma Nazarene University *C, B*
Porterville College *C*
Sacramento City College *C, A*
San Bernardino Valley College *C*
San Diego City College *C, A*
San Diego Mesa College *A*
San Joaquin Delta College *A*
San Jose State University *B*
Shasta College *A*
Taft College *C, A*
University of Redlands *B*
University of San Francisco *B*
Vanguard University of Southern
  California *B*
Ventura College *A*
Victor Valley College *C, A*
West Hills Community College *A*
Yuba College *C*

Colorado
Aims Community College *A*
Arapahoe Community College *C, A*
Colorado Mountain College
  Alpine Campus *C, A*
  Spring Valley Campus *A*
  Timberline Campus *C*
Colorado State University *B*
Colorado Technical University *B, M*

Community College of Aurora *C, A*
Denver Technical College: A Division of
  DeVry University *A*
Front Range Community College *C, A*
Pikes Peak Community College *C, A*
University of Colorado
  Boulder *M*
University of Denver *M*

Connecticut
Albertus Magnus College *B*
Central Connecticut State University *B*
Fairfield University *B*
Manchester Community-Technical
  College *C, A*
Northwestern Connecticut
  Community-Technical College *C, A*
Norwalk Community-Technical
  College *A*
Quinnipiac University *B*
Sacred Heart University *M*
Three Rivers Community-Technical
  College *A*
University of Bridgeport *B, M*
University of Connecticut *B*
University of Hartford *B*
University of New Haven *D*
Western Connecticut State University *B*

Delaware
Delaware Technical and Community
  College
    Terry Campus *A*
Goldey-Beacom College *B*

District of Columbia
American University *M*
Gallaudet University *B*
George Washington University *B, M*
Howard University *B*
Southeastern University *A, B*
University of the District of Columbia *A*

Florida
Barry University *B*
Brevard Community College *A*
Florida Gulf Coast University *B*
Florida Institute of Technology *M*
Florida Memorial College *B*
Florida Southern College *B*
Florida State University *B*
Indian River Community College *A*
Lake-Sumter Community College *A*
Miami-Dade Community College *A*
Northwood University
  Florida Campus *B*
Nova Southeastern University *M*
Palm Beach Community College *A*
Pensacola Junior College *A*
University of Central Florida *B*
University of Miami *M*
University of South Florida *B*
University of Tampa *A, B*
University of West Florida *B*

Georgia
Atlanta Metropolitan College *A*
Bainbridge College *C, A*
Berry College *B*
Clayton College and State University *B*
Coastal Georgia Community
  College *C, A*
Dalton State College *B*
Darton College *C, A*
Georgia College and State University *M*
Georgia Southern University *B*
Georgia Southwestern State University *A*
Kennesaw State University *M*
Mercer University *B, M*
Middle Georgia College *A*
Morris Brown College *B*
Paine College *B*
Savannah Technical Institute *A*
South Georgia College *C, A*
State University of West Georgia *B*
University of Georgia *B*

Hawaii
Brigham Young University
  Hawaii *B*
Hawaii Pacific University *B*
University of Hawaii
  Manoa *B*

Idaho
Boise State University *B, M*
University of Idaho *B*

Illinois
Augustana College *B*
Benedictine University *M*
Bradley University *B*
Chicago State University *B*
City Colleges of Chicago
  Olive-Harvey College *C, A*
Danville Area Community College *C, A*
De Paul University *M*
Eastern Illinois University *B*
Eureka College *B*
Governors State University *B, M*
Highland Community College *A*
Illinois College *B*
Illinois State University *B, M*
John Wood Community College *C, A*
Joliet Junior College *C*
Kishwaukee College *A*
Lewis University *B*
Loyola University of Chicago *B, M*
MacCormac College *C, A*
MacMurray College *B*
Millikin University *B*
North Central College *M*
Northern Illinois University *M*
Parkland College *C*
Richland Community College *A*
Robert Morris College: Chicago *C, A*
Rockford College *B*
Roosevelt University *M*
St. Augustine College *A*
St. Xavier University *M*
Southern Illinois University
  Edwardsville *B*
Southwestern Ilinois College *C, A*
Trinity Christian College *B*
Triton College *C, A*
University of Illinois
  Chicago *B, M, D*
  Springfield *M*
University of St. Francis *B*
Western Illinois University *B*
William Rainey Harper College *C, A*

Indiana
Grace College *B*
Indiana Institute of Technology *A, B*
Indiana State University *B*
Indiana Wesleyan University *A*
Oakland City University *B*
Saint Mary's College *B*
St. Joseph's College *A, B*
Tri-State University *B*
University of Indianapolis *B*
University of Notre Dame *B*
University of Southern Indiana *A*

Iowa
Buena Vista University *B*
Central College *B*
Clarke College *B*
Des Moines Area Community College *A*
Iowa State University *B*
Loras College *B*
Luther College *B*
Morningside College *B*
Northeast Iowa Community College *A*
St. Ambrose University *B*
University of Iowa *B, M, D*
Upper Iowa University *B*

Kansas
Coffeyville Community College *A*
Dodge City Community College *C, A*
Hutchinson Community College *C, A*

Kansas City Kansas Community
  College *C, A*
Newman University *B*
Ottawa University *B*
Southwestern College *B*
Wichita State University *B*

Kentucky
Ashland Community College *A*
Eastern Kentucky University *B*
Henderson Community College *A*
Hopkinsville Community College *A*
Morehead State University *B*
Murray State University *B*
Northern Kentucky University *B*
Owensboro Community College *A*
Paducah Community College *A*
Prestonsburg Community College *A*
Southeast Community College *A*
University of Louisville *B*
Western Kentucky University *B*

Louisiana
Dillard University *B*
Louisiana Tech University *B*
Nicholls State University *A, B*
University of New Orleans *B*

Maine
Husson College *B*
Mid-State College *A*
Thomas College *B*
University of Maine
  Fort Kent *A, B*
  Machias *A*
University of Maine *B*

Maryland
Carroll Community College *C, A*
Chesapeake College *C, A*
Hagerstown Community College *A*
Harford Community College *A*
Howard Community College *A*
Montgomery College
  Germantown Campus *A*
  Takoma Park Campus *A*
Salisbury State University *B*
University of Maryland
  University College *M*
Villa Julie College *B*

Massachusetts
American International College *B*
Babson College *B*
Bay Path College *B*
Berkshire Community College *A*
Boston College *B*
Boston University *B, M*
Bridgewater State College *B*
Greenfield Community College *C*
Massasoit Community College *A*
New England College of Finance *C*
Nichols College *B*
Northeastern University *A, B*
Roxbury Community College *A*
Salem State College *B*
Suffolk University *B*
University of Massachusetts
  Dartmouth *B*
Western New England College *B, M*
Worcester Polytechnic Institute *B, M*

Michigan
Adrian College *B*
Alpena Community College *A*
Baker College
  of Muskegon *A*
  of Owosso *B*
Central Michigan University *B*
Cleary College *A, B*
Cornerstone College and Grand Rapids
  Baptist Seminary *B*
Detroit College of Business *A, B*
Eastern Michigan University *B*
Grand Rapids Community College *C, A*
Kalamazoo Valley Community
  College *A*

Management information systems

Kettering University B
Lake Superior State University A
Lansing Community College A
Macomb Community College C, A
Northern Michigan University A, B
Northwestern Michigan College C, A
Northwood University A
Oakland Community College C, A
Oakland University B
Rochester College B
University of Detroit Mercy B
Wayne State University B
West Shore Community College A
Western Michigan University B

Minnesota
Augsburg College B
College of St. Catherine: St. Paul Campus B
Crown College A
Metropolitan State University B
Minnesota State College - Southeast Technical C, A
Minnesota State University, Mankato B
Moorhead State University B
National American University St. Paul A, B
Northwestern College B
St. Cloud Technical College C
University of Minnesota
   Crookston A, B
   Twin Cities B
University of St. Thomas M
Winona State University B

Mississippi
Delta State University B
Hinds Community College C, A
Meridian Community College A
Mississippi Gulf Coast Community College
   Jackson County Campus A
   Perkinston A
Mississippi State University B
Northwest Mississippi Community College A
University of Mississippi B
University of Southern Mississippi B

Missouri
Avila College B
Central Missouri State University B
East Central College A
Lindenwood University B, M
Maryville University of Saint Louis B, M
Ozarks Technical Community College C, A
St. Louis University B, M, D
Southwest Missouri State University B, M
St. Louis Community College
   St. Louis Community College at Florissant Valley C, A
   St. Louis Community College at Meramec A
Three Rivers Community College A
University of Missouri
   Rolla B
   St. Louis B
William Woods University B

Montana
Flathead Valley Community College C, A
Little Big Horn College A
Montana State University
   Billings B
Rocky Mountain College B
Stone Child College A

Nebraska
Bellevue University B
Creighton University B, M
Doane College B
Metropolitan Community College C, A
Midland Lutheran College B

University of Nebraska
   Omaha B, M

Nevada
Community College of Southern Nevada C, A
University of Nevada
   Las Vegas B
Western Nevada Community College A

New Hampshire
Daniel Webster College B
Franklin Pierce College B
New England College B
New Hampshire Community Technical College
   Nashua C
Rivier College A, B

New Jersey
Atlantic Cape Community College A
Bergen Community College A
Burlington County College A
Camden County College A
County College of Morris A
Cumberland County College C, A
Hudson County Community College C, A
Mercer County Community College C, A
Monmouth University B
Passaic County Community College C, A
Raritan Valley Community College C
Rowan University B
Rutgers
   The State University of New Jersey: Douglass College B
   The State University of New Jersey: Livingston College B
   The State University of New Jersey: Rutgers College B
   The State University of New Jersey: University College New Brunswick B
St. Peter's College A, B, M
Salem Community College A
Seton Hall University B
Stevens Institute of Technology M, D
Union County College C, A

New Mexico
College of Santa Fe B
Eastern New Mexico University B
New Mexico State University
   Alamogordo C, A
Northern New Mexico Community College A
Santa Fe Community College A

New York
Canisius College B
City University of New York
   Baruch College B, M
   Bronx Community College A
   Brooklyn College B
   York College B
Clarkson University B
Dominican College of Blauvelt B
Dowling College B
Fordham University B, M
Fulton-Montgomery Community College A
Hilbert College A
Hofstra University B, M
Iona College B, M
Long Island University
   C. W. Post Campus B, M
Manhattan College B
Nassau Community College A
New York Institute of Technology B, M
New York University B
Pace University:
   Pleasantville/Briarcliff B, M
Pace University B, M
Polytechnic University B, M
Regents College B

Rochester Institute of Technology C, B, M
Sage Junior College of Albany A
St. Francis College A
St. John Fisher College B
St. Thomas Aquinas College B
State University of New York
   Albany B, M
   Buffalo M, D
   College of Technology at Alfred A
   College of Technology at Delhi A
Syracuse University M
Tompkins-Cortland Community College A
Touro College B
Westchester Business Institute C, A

North Carolina
Appalachian State University B
Asheville Buncombe Technical Community College A
Campbell University A, B
Catawba Valley Community College C, A
Central Piedmont Community College C, A
Craven Community College A
East Carolina University B
Guilford Technical Community College A
Montgomery Community College C, A
Mount Olive College B
Nash Community College A
Queens College B
Randolph Community College A
Richmond Community College C, A
University of North Carolina
   Charlotte B
   Wilmington B
Western Carolina University B
Wilkes Community College C, A

North Dakota
Dickinson State University A, B
Jamestown College B
Lake Region State College C, A
North Dakota State College of Science A
North Dakota State University B
University of North Dakota B

Ohio
Ashland University B
Bowling Green State University B, M
Case Western Reserve University M, D
Cedarville College B
Central State University B
Cincinnati State Technical and Community College A
Cleveland State University B, D
David N. Myers College C, B
Defiance College B
Jefferson Community College A
Kent State University
   Stark Campus B
Kent State University B, M, D
Lakeland Community College A
Lima Technical College A
Lorain County Community College A
Miami University
   Oxford Campus B, M
Notre Dame College of Ohio C
Ohio State University
   Columbus Campus B
Ohio University
   Chillicothe Campus A
   Zanesville Campus A
Ohio University B
Shawnee State University B
Stark State College of Technology A
University of Akron
   Wayne College C, A
University of Akron B, M
University of Cincinnati
   Raymond Walters College A
University of Cincinnati B
University of Dayton B

Wright State University B, M
Xavier University C, B, M
Youngstown State University B

Oklahoma
Eastern Oklahoma State College A
Northeastern State University B
Oklahoma Baptist University B
Oklahoma City University B, M
Oklahoma State University B
Oral Roberts University B
Rogers State University A
Southwestern Oklahoma State University B
Tulsa Community College C, A
University of Central Oklahoma B
University of Oklahoma B
University of Tulsa C, B

Oregon
Central Oregon Community College A
Chemeketa Community College A
George Fox University B
Oregon Institute of Technology A
University of Oregon B, M, D
Western Baptist College B

Pennsylvania
Allentown College of St. Francis de Sales B, M
Beaver College C, B
Butler County Community College A
Cabrini College B
California University of Pennsylvania A, B
Carnegie Mellon University B
Chatham College B
College Misericordia B
Community College of Allegheny County C, A
Community College of Beaver County A
Drexel University B
Duquesne University B, M
Eastern College B
Gannon University B
Harrisburg Area Community College C
Indiana University of Pennsylvania B
Lackawanna Junior College A
Luzerne County Community College C, A
Marywood University M
Montgomery County Community College A
Penn State
   Erie, The Behrend College B
   Harrisburg B, M
   University Park C, B
Pennsylvania College of Technology A
Philadelphia University A, B
Reading Area Community College A
Robert Morris College B, M
St. Francis College A, B
St. Joseph's University C, A, B, M
Seton Hill College B
Thiel College A, B
University of Pennsylvania B, M, D
University of Pittsburgh
   Titusville A
University of Pittsburgh M
West Chester University of Pennsylvania M
Widener University B
York College of Pennsylvania A, B

Puerto Rico
Bayamon Central University A, B
Colegio Universitario del Este A, B
Columbia College A
Inter American University of Puerto Rico
   Bayamon Campus B
   Metropolitan Campus B
   San German Campus B
Pontifical Catholic University of Puerto Rico B
Turabo University A, B
Universidad Metropolitana B

University of Puerto Rico
  Mayaguez Campus *B*
  Rio Piedras Campus *B*
University of the Sacred Heart *M*

Rhode Island
Rhode Island College *B, D*
University of Rhode Island *B*

South Carolina
Charleston Southern University *B, M*
Francis Marion University *B*
Furman University *B*

South Dakota
Augustana College *B*
Dakota State University *B*
Huron University *A, B*
Northern State University *B*

Tennessee
Belmont University *B*
Christian Brothers University *B*
Middle Tennessee State University *B*
Pellissippi State Technical Community
  College *A*
Southern Adventist University *B*
University of Memphis *B*
University of Tennessee
  Martin *B*

Texas
Alvin Community College *C*
Baylor University *B, M*
Brookhaven College *A*
Dallas Baptist University *B*
Eastfield College *A*
Lamar University *B*
Midland College *A*
Midwestern State University *B*
Navarro College *A*
Northwood University: Texas Campus *B*
Our Lady of the Lake University of San
  Antonio *B*
Panola College *A*
Prairie View A&M University *B*
Richland College *A*
St. Mary's University *M*
San Antonio College *A*
San Jacinto College
  North *C, A*
Southern Methodist University *B*
Southwest Texas Junior College *A*
Southwest Texas State University *B*
Southwestern Adventist
  University *C, A, B*
Tarleton State University *B*
Texas A&M International
  University *B, M*
Texas A&M University
  Commerce *B*
  Corpus Christi *B*
  Kingsville *B*
  Texarkana *B*
Texas A&M University *M*
Texas State Technical College
  Harlingen *C, A*
Texas Tech University *B*
University of Dallas *M*
University of Houston
  Clear Lake *B, M*
  Downtown *B*
University of Houston *B, M, D*
University of Mary Hardin-Baylor *B*
University of North Texas *B, M, D*
University of St. Thomas *B*
University of Texas
  Arlington *B, M, D*
  Austin *B*
  Dallas *B, M, D*
  El Paso *B*
  San Antonio *B, M*
West Texas A&M University *B*

Utah
Brigham Young University *B, M*
LDS Business College *A*
Salt Lake Community College *C, A*
Utah State University *M, D*
Weber State University *C, A, B*
Westminster College *B*

Vermont
Johnson State College *A, B*

Virginia
Bridgewater College *B*
Central Virginia Community
  College *C, A*
Christopher Newport University *B*
Hampton University *B*
Longwood College *B*
Lord Fairfax Community College *C, A*
Northern Virginia Community College *A*
Old Dominion University *B*
Radford University *B*
University of Virginia *M*
Virginia State University *B*
Virginia Union University *B*
Virginia Western Community College *A*

Washington
City University *M*
Clark College *C, A*
Columbia Basin College *A*
Eastern Washington University *B*
Everett Community College *A*
Gonzaga University *B*
Pacific Lutheran University *B*
Seattle Pacific University *M*
Seattle University *B*
Spokane Community College *B*
Spokane Falls Community College *C, A*
Washington State University *B*
Western Washington University *B*

West Virginia
Alderson-Broaddus College *B*
Fairmont State College *A, B*
Glenville State College *B*
Marshall University *B*
Potomac State College of West Virginia
  University *A*

Wisconsin
Cardinal Stritch University *C, B*
Marquette University *B*
University of Wisconsin
  Eau Claire *B*
  La Crosse *B*
  Madison *B, M*
  Milwaukee *B*
  Oshkosh *B*
Waukesha County Technical College *A*

Wyoming
Central Wyoming College *C, A*
Eastern Wyoming College *A*
Northwest College *A*

Management science

Alabama
Central Alabama Community College *C*
Tuskegee University *B*

Alaska
University of Alaska
  Anchorage *M*
  Southeast *B*

Arizona
Arizona State University *M*
Phoenix College *C, A*

Arkansas
University of Arkansas *M*
University of Central Arkansas *B*

California
Allan Hancock College *A*
California State University
  Dominguez Hills *B*
  Fullerton *B, M*
  Hayward *M*
  Long Beach *B*
  Northridge *B, M*
Canada College *A*
Chabot College *A*
Coastline Community College *C, A*
Cypress College *C, A*
Grossmont Community College *C, A*
Lincoln University *B, M*
Los Angeles Mission College *A*
Los Angeles Pierce College *C, A*
Master's College *B*
Mission College *A*
Palomar College *C, A*
San Diego City College *C, A*
San Francisco State University *B*
San Jose State University *B*
Santa Monica College *C, A*
University of California
  San Diego *B*
Ventura College *A*
Yuba College *C*

Colorado
Colorado State University *B*
Regis University *M*
United States Air Force Academy *B*
University of Denver *B*

Connecticut
Eastern Connecticut State University *B*
Southern Connecticut State University *B*
United States Coast Guard Academy *B*

Delaware
Goldey-Beacom College *A, B*

District of Columbia
Catholic University of America *B, M*
Southeastern University *A, B*
University of the District of Columbia *A*

Florida
Broward Community College *A*
Florida Institute of Technology *M*
Florida State University *B, M*
Lynn University *B*
Miami-Dade Community College *A*
Pensacola Junior College *A*
Stetson University *B*
University of Florida *B, M*
University of Miami *B, M*
University of South Florida *B*

Georgia
Emory University *B*
Georgia Institute of Technology *B*
Georgia Southwestern State University *B*
Savannah State University *B*

Illinois
Benedictine University *M*
Lewis University *B*
Loyola University of Chicago *B*
Northeastern Illinois University *B*
Roosevelt University *B, M*
Shawnee Community College *A*
Southwestern Ilinois College *A*

Indiana
Goshen College *B*
Indiana State University *B*
Indiana Wesleyan University *M*
Oakland City University *M*

Iowa
Buena Vista University *B*
Drake University *B*
Kirkwood Community College *A*
Maharishi University of Management *B*
University of Iowa *B, M, D*

Kansas
Baker University *M*
Southwestern College *B*

Kentucky
Prestonsburg Community College *A*
University of Kentucky *B*

Louisiana
Louisiana State University and
  Agricultural and Mechanical
  College *B, M, D*
Louisiana Tech University *B*
Nicholls State University *B*

Maryland
College of Notre Dame of Maryland *M*
Community College of Baltimore County
  Essex *C*
Coppin State College *B*
Hagerstown Community College *A*
Montgomery College
  Rockville Campus *A*
  Takoma Park Campus *A*

Massachusetts
Babson College *B*
Bay Path College *B*
Bridgewater State College *B*
Cambridge College *M*
Cape Cod Community College *A*
Massachusetts College of Liberal Arts *B*
New England College of Finance *C*
Northeastern University *A, B*
Worcester Polytechnic Institute *B, M*

Michigan
Adrian College *B*
Baker College
  of Auburn Hills *A, B*
  of Mount Clemens *A, B*
  of Muskegon *A, B*
Cornerstone College and Grand Rapids
  Baptist Seminary *B*
Detroit College of Business *B*
Grand Valley State University *B, M*
Henry Ford Community College *A*
Madonna University *B*
Michigan State University *M*
Oakland Community College *A*
University of Michigan
  Dearborn *B*

Minnesota
Concordia University: St. Paul *B*
Minneapolis Community and Technical
  College *C, A*
Minnesota State University, Mankato *B*
Winona State University *B*

Missouri
Central Methodist College *B*
Culver-Stockton College *B*
Rockhurst University *B*
St. Louis University *B, M, D*
University of Missouri
  Columbia *B*
Webster University *B, M, D*

Montana
Montana State University
  Billings *B*
Rocky Mountain College *B*

Nebraska
Creighton University *B*
Grace University *B*
Union College *B*
University of Nebraska
  Lincoln *B*
  Omaha *B*

New Hampshire
Antioch New England Graduate
  School *M*
College for Lifelong Learning *B*
New Hampshire Community Technical
  College
  Manchester *C, A*
Plymouth State College of the University
  System of New Hampshire *B*
Rivier College *A, B*

New Jersey
Caldwell College B, M
Fairleigh Dickinson University B
Kean University B, M
Rider University B
Rowan University B
Rutgers
 The State University of New Jersey:
  Douglass College B
 The State University of New Jersey:
  Livingston College B
 The State University of New Jersey:
  Rutgers College B
 The State University of New Jersey:
  University College New
  Brunswick B

New Mexico
New Mexico State University B

New York
Canisius College B
City University of New York
 Baruch College D
Hofstra University B, M
Iona College M
Pace University:
 Pleasantville/Briarcliff B, M, D
Pace University B, M, D
Polytechnic University M
St. Bonaventure University B
St. John Fisher College B
State University of New York
 Albany B, M
 Binghamton B, M, D
 Buffalo D
 College at Cortland B
 College at Geneseo B
 Institute of Technology at
  Utica/Rome M
 New Paltz B, M
 Oswego B
Suffolk County Community
 College C, A

North Carolina
Alamance Community College C, A
North Carolina Central University B
Wake Forest University B

Ohio
Case Western Reserve University M
Cincinnati State Technical and
 Community College A
David N. Myers College A, B
Heidelberg College B
Kent State University
 Stark Campus B
Miami University
 Oxford Campus B, M
Ohio University B
Southern Ohio College A
University of Akron B, M
University of Cincinnati M, D
University of Dayton M
Wright State University B, M

Oklahoma
Mid-America Bible College B
Northeastern State University B
Oklahoma Baptist University B
Oklahoma Christian University of
 Science and Arts B
Oklahoma State University
 Oklahoma City A
Oklahoma State University B
Oral Roberts University B, M
Western Oklahoma State College A

Oregon
Chemeketa Community College A

Pennsylvania
Drexel University M
Duquesne University B
Gettysburg College B
Harrisburg Area Community College A

Kutztown University of Pennsylvania B
La Salle University B
Lock Haven University of
 Pennsylvania B
Penn State
 Harrisburg M
Shippensburg University of
 Pennsylvania B
University of Pennsylvania B, M, D
University of Scranton B
Westminster College B
Widener University M

Puerto Rico
Bayamon Central University B, M
Inter American University of Puerto Rico
 Arecibo Campus B
 Bayamon Campus B
 San German Campus B

South Carolina
Central Carolina Technical College A
Charleston Southern University B, M
Clemson University D
Greenville Technical College C, A
University of South Carolina B

Tennessee
Belmont University B
Chattanooga State Technical Community
 College A
Christian Brothers University B
Lincoln Memorial University B
Southern Adventist University B
Tennessee Technological University B
Trevecca Nazarene University B
Union University B
University of Tennessee
 Knoxville M, D

Texas
Abilene Christian University B
Angelina College C, A
El Paso Community College C, A
Hardin-Simmons University B
Midland College C, A
North Lake College A
Southern Methodist University B
Southwest Texas State University B, T
Southwestern Adventist University B
Texas A&M University
 Kingsville B
Texas Wesleyan University B
Trinity University B
University of Mary Hardin-Baylor B
University of North Texas M, D
University of Texas
 Arlington B, M
 El Paso B
 San Antonio B, M
 Tyler B
 of the Permian Basin B
University of the Incarnate Word M

Vermont
College of St. Joseph in Vermont B

Virginia
Averett College B
Southside Virginia Community
 College C, A
Thomas Nelson Community College A
Virginia Polytechnic Institute and State
 University B

Washington
Eastern Washington University B
Western Washington University B

West Virginia
Fairmont State College A, B
Wheeling Jesuit University B

Wisconsin
Cardinal Stritch University B, M
Marquette University C
Northland College B

University of Wisconsin
 Green Bay M
 Milwaukee D
Wisconsin Indianhead Technical
 College A

Wyoming
University of Wyoming B

Manufacturing technologies

Alabama
Jacksonville State University B
Northwest-Shoals Community College C
University of West Alabama B

Arizona
Central Arizona College A
Gateway Community College C, A
Yavapai College A

Arkansas
Arkansas State University
 Mountain Home C, A
Southern Arkansas University
 Tech A

California
California State University
 Long Beach B
 Los Angeles B
Cerritos Community College C, A
Don Bosco Technical Institute A
Irvine Valley College C, A
National University M
San Diego City College C, A
Santa Clara University C
University of La Verne C

Colorado
Pueblo Community College C, A

Connecticut
Asnuntuck Community-Technical
 College A
Central Connecticut State University B
Gateway Community College A
Manchester Community-Technical
 College A
Naugatuck Valley Community-Technical
 College C, A
Three Rivers Community-Technical
 College A
University of New Haven A

Florida
Pensacola Junior College A
St. Petersburg Junior College A

Georgia
Columbus Technical Institute C
Georgia Southern University M
Gwinnett Technical Institute A

Illinois
Bradley University B
Illinois Eastern Community Colleges
 Wabash Valley College A
Illinois Institute of Technology B
John Wood Community College A
Kankakee Community College A
Kishwaukee College C, A
Parkland College C, A
Rock Valley College C, A
Western Illinois University B
William Rainey Harper College C, A

Indiana
Ball State University A
ITT Technical Institute
 Fort Wayne A
Indiana University--Purdue University
 Indiana University-Purdue
 University Fort Wayne B

Iowa
Iowa Central Community College A

Kansas
Kansas State University B
Pittsburg State University B

Kentucky
Eastern Kentucky University B, M
Murray State University B
St. Catharine College A

Maine
Kennebec Valley Technical College A
University of Southern Maine B, M

Maryland
Chesapeake College A

Massachusetts
North Shore Community College A
Northeastern University B

Michigan
Eastern Michigan University B
Lake Michigan College C, A
Macomb Community College C, A
Mid Michigan Community College A
Monroe County Community
 College C, A
North Central Michigan College C, A
St. Clair County Community College A
Wayne State University B

Minnesota
Hennepin Technical College C, A
Minnesota State University,
 Mankato B, M
St. Cloud State University B

Missouri
Central Missouri State University A
Mineral Area College C, A

Nebraska
University of Nebraska
 Lincoln A, B

New Hampshire
New Hampshire Community Technical
 College
 Berlin A
 Nashua A
New Hampshire Technical Institute A

New Jersey
Essex County College A
Gloucester County College A
Middlesex County College A
Thomas Edison State College A, B

New Mexico
New Mexico State University
 Carlsbad C, A

New York
Corning Community College A
New York Institute of Technology B
Regents College B
Rochester Institute of Technology B, M
State University of New York
 College of Technology at Canton A
 Farmingdale C, B
Tompkins-Cortland Community
 College A

North Carolina
Central Carolina Community College A
Craven Community College A
Davidson County Community College A
Lenoir Community College A
Mitchell Community College A
Randolph Community College A
Rockingham Community College C
Sandhills Community College C
South Piedmont Community College A
Wake Technical Community College A

Ohio
Bowling Green State University
 Firelands College A
Bowling Green State University B, M

Cincinnati State Technical and
    Community College A
Clark State Community College A
Edison State Community College A
Jefferson Community College A
Kent State University
    Ashtabula Regional Campus C
Kent State University C
Lakeland Community College C, A
Lima Technical College C, A
Sinclair Community College A
Stark State College of Technology A
Terra Community College A
University of Akron
    Wayne College A
University of Akron A
University of Dayton B

Oklahoma
Northeastern State University B
Oklahoma City Community College A

Oregon
Central Oregon Community
    College C, A
Chemeketa Community College A
Portland Community College C, A

Pennsylvania
Butler County Community College C, A
Johnson Technical Institute A
Pennsylvania Institute of Technology A
South Hills School of Business &
    Technology C

Rhode Island
New England Institute of
    Technology A, B

South Carolina
Greenville Technical College A
Trident Technical College C, A
York Technical College C

Tennessee
Jackson State Community College C
Martin Methodist College A

Texas
Richland College A
Sam Houston State University B
Texas A&M University
    Commerce B
Texas State Technical College
    Harlingen A
University of Houston B

Utah
Salt Lake Community College A

Virginia
ECPI College of Technology C, A
John Tyler Community College A
Mountain Empire Community College A

Washington
Clark College A
Everett Community College A
Grays Harbor College A
Western Washington University B

West Virginia
West Virginia University
    Parkersburg A

Wisconsin
Gateway Technical College A

Marine engineering/naval architecture

California
California Maritime Academy B
University of California
    Berkeley M, D

Connecticut
United States Coast Guard Academy B

Florida
Gulf Coast Community College A

Louisiana
University of New Orleans B

Maine
Maine Maritime Academy B

Maryland
United States Naval Academy B

Massachusetts
Massachusetts Institute of
    Technology M, D
Massachusetts Maritime Academy B

Michigan
University of Michigan B, M, D

New York
State University of New York
    Maritime College B
United States Merchant Marine
    Academy B
Webb Institute B

Texas
Texas A&M University
    Galveston B

Marine/aquatic biology

Alabama
Alabama State University B
Auburn University B
Samford University B
Spring Hill College B
Troy State University B
University of Alabama B, M
University of Mobile B
University of North Alabama B
University of West Alabama B

Alaska
University of Alaska
    Fairbanks M
    Southeast B

California
California State University
    Fresno M
    Monterey Bay B, M
    Stanislaus B, M
Diablo Valley College A
Mount San Antonio College A
Oxnard College A
San Francisco State University B, M
San Jose State University B, M
University of California
    San Diego D
    Santa Barbara B, M, D
    Santa Cruz B, M
University of San Diego B, M
University of Southern
    California B, M, D

Connecticut
Mitchell College A
Southern Connecticut State University B

Delaware
University of Delaware M, D

Florida
Barry University B
Eckerd College B
Florida Institute of Technology B, M
Florida Keys Community College A
Gulf Coast Community College A
Jacksonville University B
Manatee Community College A
Nova Southeastern University B, M
Pensacola Junior College A
Stetson University B
University of Miami B, M, D
University of Tampa B
University of West Florida B

Georgia
Savannah State University B
University of Georgia M, D

Hawaii
Hawaii Pacific University B
University of Hawaii
    Hilo B

Idaho
Ricks College A

Indiana
Ball State University B

Iowa
Drake University B

Kansas
Southwestern College B

Louisiana
Nicholls State University B

Maine
College of the Atlantic B
Maine Maritime Academy B
Southern Maine Technical College A
Unity College B
University of Maine
    Machias B
University of Maine B, M, D
University of New England B

Maryland
University of Maryland
    Baltimore County M, D
    Baltimore D
    College Park B, M, D
    Eastern Shore B, M

Massachusetts
Boston University B
Hampshire College B
Harvard College B
Massachusetts Maritime Academy B
Northeastern University B
Salem State College B
Suffolk University B

Minnesota
Bemidji State University B
St. Cloud State University B

Mississippi
Jackson State University B
University of Southern
    Mississippi B, M, D

Missouri
Missouri Southern State College B

New Hampshire
Antioch New England Graduate
    School M
University of New Hampshire B

New Jersey
Fairleigh Dickinson University B
Richard Stockton College of New
    Jersey B
Rider University B
Rutgers
    The State University of New Jersey:
        Cook College B
    The State University of New Jersey:
        Douglass College B
    The State University of New Jersey:
        Livingston College B
    The State University of New Jersey:
        Rutgers College B
    The State University of New Jersey:
        University College New
        Brunswick B

New York
Hofstra University B
Long Island University
    Southampton College B
Sarah Lawrence College B
State University of New York
    College of Environmental Science
        and Forestry B

North Carolina
Brunswick Community College A
Cape Fear Community College A
University of North Carolina
    Chapel Hill M, D
    Wilmington B, M, T

Ohio
Ohio University B
Wittenberg University B

Oklahoma
Northeastern State University B

Oregon
University of Oregon B, M, D

Pennsylvania
East Stroudsburg University of
    Pennsylvania B
Juniata College B
Mansfield University of Pennsylvania B
St. Francis College B
Waynesburg College B

Puerto Rico
University of Puerto Rico
    Humacao University College B

Rhode Island
Brown University B
Roger Williams University A, B
University of Rhode Island B

South Carolina
Coastal Carolina University B
College of Charleston B, M
University of South Carolina B, M, D

Texas
Galveston College A
Lamar University B
Southwest Texas State University B, M
Texas A&M University
    Corpus Christi M
    Galveston B
Texas A&M University B
University of Texas
    Austin B

Utah
Dixie State College of Utah A

Virginia
College of William and Mary M, D

Washington
Western Washington University B

Wisconsin
Lawrence University B, T
University of Wisconsin
    Superior B

Marketing management

Alabama
Community College of the Air Force A
James H. Faulkner State Community
    College A
Troy State University B
Tuskegee University B
University of Alabama M, D
University of Montevallo B

Arizona
Arizona State University B
Central Arizona College A
Northern Arizona University B
Phoenix College A

Arkansas
University of Central Arkansas B

California
Azusa Pacific University B

California Lutheran University *B*
California State Polytechnic University:
  Pomona *B*
California State University
  Bakersfield *B*
  Dominguez Hills *B*
  Fullerton *M*
  Hayward *B, M*
  Long Beach *B*
  Los Angeles *B*
  Northridge *B*
Cerritos Community College *A*
Chabot College *A*
Chapman University *B*
College of San Mateo *C, A*
Cypress College *C, A*
Fresno Pacific University *B*
Glendale Community College *C*
Golden West College *C, A*
La Sierra University *B, M*
Los Angeles Trade and Technical
  College *C, A*
Merced College *A*
Mission College *A*
Mount St. Mary's College *B*
Mount San Antonio College *C, A*
National University *B*
San Diego City College *C, A*
San Diego Mesa College *C, A*
West Valley College *C, A*

Colorado
Colorado State University *B*
Community College of Aurora *A*
Fort Lewis College *B*
Lamar Community College *A*
University of Colorado
  Colorado Springs *B*
University of Southern Colorado *B*

Connecticut
Eastern Connecticut State University *B*
Quinnipiac University *B, M*
Sacred Heart University *B*
Teikyo Post University *A, B*
University of Bridgeport *M*
University of Connecticut *M, D*

Delaware
University of Delaware *B*

District of Columbia
American University *M*
George Washington University *M*
Howard University *B*
Southeastern University *M*
University of the District of Columbia *B*

Florida
Broward Community College *A*
Florida Community College at
  Jacksonville *A*
Florida Gulf Coast University *B*
Florida International University *B*
Florida Southern College *B*
Lynn University *B*
St. Thomas University *B*
Stetson University *B*
Tallahassee Community College *A*
University of Miami *M*

Georgia
Abraham Baldwin Agricultural
  College *C*
Bainbridge College *C, A*
Chattahoochee Technical Institute *C, A*
Clark Atlanta University *B, M*
Columbus State University *B*
Gainesville College *A*
Georgia Southwestern State University *B*
Gwinnett Technical Institute *A*
Kennesaw State University *M*
Morris Brown College *B*
Valdosta State University *B*

Hawaii
University of Hawaii
  Hawaii Community College *C, A*

Idaho
Idaho State University *C, A, B*
Northwest Nazarene University *B*

Illinois
Barat College *B*
Black Hawk College *A*
De Paul University *B, M*
Governors State University *B*
Joliet Junior College *A*
Kaskaskia College *A*
Kishwaukee College *A*
Lewis University *B*
Lincoln Land Community College *A*
MacMurray College *B*
North Central College *B*
North Park University *B*
Northeastern Illinois University *B*
Northwestern University *D*
Parkland College *A*
Rockford College *B*
Southwestern Illinois College *A*
University of St. Francis *M*

Indiana
Butler University *B*
Indiana Institute of Technology *B*
Indiana University
  Southeast *B*
Indiana University--Purdue University
  Indiana University-Purdue
    University Fort Wayne *A*
Saint Mary's College *B*
St. Joseph's College *B*
St. Mary-of-the-Woods College *B*
Tri-State University *B*
University of Indianapolis *B*
Valparaiso University *B*

Iowa
American Institute of Business *A*
Clarke College *B*
Northeast Iowa Community College *A*
University of Iowa *D*

Kansas
Central Christian College *A*
Kansas State University *B*
Pratt Community College *C, A*

Kentucky
Midway College *B*
Northern Kentucky University *B*

Louisiana
Louisiana State University
  Shreveport *B*
McNeese State University *B*
Tulane University *B*

Maine
Husson College *B*
St. Joseph's College *B*
University of Maine
  Machias *A, B*
University of Maine *B*

Maryland
Anne Arundel Community College *C*
Community College of Baltimore County
  Catonsville *C, A*
Montgomery College
  Germantown Campus *C, A*
  Rockville Campus *A*
  Takoma Park Campus *A*
Morgan State University *B*
Prince George's Community
  College *C, A*

Massachusetts
Assumption College *B*
Babson College *B*
Bay Path College *B*
Boston College *B*
Boston University *B*
Bristol Community College *A*
Bunker Hill Community College *C*
Emerson College *M*

Massachusetts College of Liberal Arts *B*
Simmons College *B*
Suffolk University *M*
Westfield State College *B*

Michigan
Baker College
  of Auburn Hills *A*
  of Jackson *B*
  of Mount Clemens *A, B*
  of Owosso *B*
Central Michigan University *B*
Cornerstone College and Grand Rapids
  Baptist Seminary *B*
Jackson Community College *C, A*
Kettering University *B*
Monroe County Community
  College *C, A*
Mott Community College *A*
Northern Michigan University *B*
Saginaw Valley State University *B, M*
Walsh College of Accountancy and
  Business Administration *B*

Minnesota
Concordia University: St. Paul *B*
Metropolitan State University *B*
Southwest State University *A, B*
Winona State University *B*

Mississippi
East Mississippi Community College *A*
Jackson State University *B*
Mississippi Gulf Coast Community
  College
    Perkinston *A*

Missouri
Lindenwood University *M*
Northwest Missouri State University *B*
Southeast Missouri State University *B*
Truman State University *B*
University of Missouri
  St. Louis *C*
Washington University *B*
Webster University *B, M*

Nebraska
Bellevue University *B*
Union College *B*

Nevada
Community College of Southern
  Nevada *A*
University of Nevada
  Las Vegas *B*

New Hampshire
Antioch New England Graduate
  School *M*
Franklin Pierce College *B*
Hesser College *A*

New Jersey
Bloomfield College *B*
Centenary College *B*
Fairleigh Dickinson University *M*
Gloucester County College *A*
Monmouth University *B*
Salem Community College *A*
Thomas Edison State College *C, A, B*

New York
City University of New York
  Baruch College *B, M*
Five Towns College *A*
Fordham University *B, M*
Hudson Valley Community College *A*
Ithaca College *B*
Long Island University
  C. W. Post Campus *B*
Manhattan College *B*
Orange County Community College *A*
Pace University:
  Pleasantville/Briarcliff *B, M*
Pace University *B, M*
Rochester Institute of Technology *B, M*
St. Bonaventure University *B*

St. John's University *B, M*
St. Thomas Aquinas College *B, M*
State University of New York
  Albany *B*
  New Paltz *B*
  Oswego *B*
Syracuse University *B, M*

North Carolina
Appalachian State University *B*
North Carolina Central University *B*

Ohio
Baldwin-Wallace College *B*
Bowling Green State University *B*
Case Western Reserve University *M, D*
Central State University *B*
Defiance College *B*
John Carroll University *B*
Kent State University
  Stark Campus *B*
  Trumbull Campus *A*
Marietta College *B*
Miami University
  Middletown Campus *A*
Mount Vernon Nazarene College *B*
Muskingum Area Technical College *C*
Ohio State University
  Columbus Campus *B*
Ohio University *B*
Otterbein College *B*
Sinclair Community College *A*
Tiffin University *B*
University of Dayton *B*
Youngstown State University *A, B, M*

Oklahoma
Northeastern Oklahoma Agricultural and
  Mechanical College *A*
St. Gregory's University *B*
Southeastern Oklahoma State
  University *B*
Tulsa Community College *C, A*

Oregon
University of Oregon *B*

Pennsylvania
Alvernia College *B*
Beaver College *B*
Cabrini College *B*
Community College of Allegheny
  County *A*
Duquesne University *B*
Eastern College *B*
Grove City College *B*
Holy Family College *C, B*
Indiana University of Pennsylvania *B*
La Salle University *B*
Lehigh University *B*
Mercyhurst College *B*
Penn State
  Harrisburg *B*
Seton Hill College *B*
University of Scranton *M*
Wilson College *A, B*
York College of Pennsylvania *B*

Puerto Rico
Caribbean University *B*
Inter American University of Puerto Rico
  Arecibo Campus *B*
  San German Campus *B, M*
National College of Business and
  Technology *A*
University of Puerto Rico
  Rio Piedras Campus *B, M*
University of the Sacred Heart *B*

Rhode Island
Providence College *B*
Rhode Island College *B*
Roger Williams University *A, B*

South Carolina
Clemson University *B*
Francis Marion University *B*
Spartanburg Technical College *A*

Marketing/distribution

South Dakota
Southeast Technical Institute A

Tennessee
East Tennessee State University B
Hiwassee College A
Lincoln Memorial University B
Tennessee Technological University B
Union University B, T
University of Tennessee
  Knoxville B

Texas
Baylor University B
Houston Baptist University B
Midland College A
Texas A&M University
  Commerce B
  Kingsville B
Texas Wesleyan University B
University of Houston
  Downtown B
University of Texas
  Arlington B
  of the Permian Basin B

Utah
LDS Business College A
Salt Lake Community College A
Snow College C, A

Vermont
Champlain College A, B
Norwich University B

Virginia
Christopher Newport University B
Lynchburg College B
St. Paul's College B
Virginia Commonwealth University B
Virginia Highlands Community
  College A
Virginia Polytechnic Institute and State
  University B

Washington
Bellevue Community College A
Gonzaga University B
Pacific Lutheran University B
Western Washington University B
Yakima Valley Community College C, A

West Virginia
Bethany College B
Concord College B
Davis and Elkins College B
Fairmont State College B
West Virginia State College A
Wheeling Jesuit University B

Wisconsin
Chippewa Valley Technical College A
Marquette University B
Milwaukee Area Technical College A
Northeast Wisconsin Technical
  College A
University of Wisconsin
  La Crosse B
  Madison B, M, D
  Parkside B
  Platteville B
  Superior B
  Whitewater M
Viterbo University B

Marketing research

California
California State University
  Bakersfield B
  Northridge M
Los Angeles Mission College A

Colorado
University of Denver B, M

District of Columbia
Southeastern University B

Georgia
Columbus State University B
DeVry Institute of Technology
  Alpharetta B
University of Georgia M

Hawaii
University of Hawaii
  Hawaii Community College C, A

Idaho
Boise State University B

Illinois
De Paul University M
Southern Illinois University
  Edwardsville M

Kansas
Fort Hays State University B

Maine
Husson College B

Massachusetts
Boston University B
Emerson College M
Mount Ida College A

Minnesota
Winona State University B

Missouri
Lindenwood University M
University of Missouri
  Columbia B

Nebraska
University of Nebraska
  Omaha B

New Hampshire
Antioch New England Graduate
  School M

New York
Canisius College B
City University of New York
  Baruch College M
Fordham University B, M
Ithaca College B
Pace University:
  Pleasantville/Briarcliff B, M
Pace University B, M
State University of New York
  Buffalo D

Ohio
Defiance College B
Kent State University
  Stark Campus B
Tiffin University B
Wright State University M

Oklahoma
Oklahoma Christian University of
  Science and Arts B

Pennsylvania
La Salle University B

Puerto Rico
University of Puerto Rico
  Arecibo Campus A, B

Texas
University of Texas
  Arlington M

Marketing/distribution

Alabama
Alabama Agricultural and Mechanical
  University B, M
Community College of the Air Force A
Enterprise State Junior College A
James H. Faulkner State Community
  College A
Talladega College B
University of South Alabama B
Wallace State Community College at
  Hanceville A

Arizona
Arizona Western College A
Mesa Community College A
Mohave Community College C, A
Northern Arizona University B
Phoenix College C, A
Prescott College B, M

Arkansas
Harding University B
Phillips Community College of the
  University of Arkansas A
University of Central Arkansas B

California
American River College A
Azusa Pacific University B
Barstow College A
California State University
  Bakersfield B
  Fresno B
  Hayward B, M
  Northridge B, M
Cerritos Community College A
Chabot College C, A
City College of San Francisco A
College of San Mateo C, A
College of the Canyons C
College of the Desert A
College of the Sequoias C, A
Compton Community College C, A
Crafton Hills College C, A
Cuesta College C, A
Cypress College C, A
Fashion Institute of Design and
  Merchandising A
Fresno City College C, A
Gavilan Community College C
Glendale Community College C, A
Golden Gate University C, B, M
Grossmont Community College C, A
Imperial Valley College C, A
Lake Tahoe Community College C, A
Las Positas College C, A
Los Angeles Pierce College C, A
Los Angeles Southwest College A
Los Angeles Trade and Technical
  College A
Los Angeles Valley College C, A
Merced College A
MiraCosta College C, A
Mission College A
Modesto Junior College A
Moorpark College A
Napa Valley College C
Ohlone College C, A
Orange Coast College C, A
Pacific Union College B
Pasadena City College C, A
Riverside Community College C, A
Sacramento City College C, A
San Diego City College C
San Diego Mesa College C, A
San Francisco State University B
San Jose City College C, A
San Jose State University B
Santa Ana College C, A
Santa Barbara City College A
Santa Clara University B
Santa Rosa Junior College C
Shasta College A
Sierra College C, A
Solano Community College C, A
Southwestern College C, A
Vanguard University of Southern
  California B
Ventura College A
West Los Angeles College C, A
West Valley College C, A

Yuba College C

Colorado
Adams State College B
Colorado Christian University B
Community College of Aurora C, A
Northeastern Junior College C, A
Red Rocks Community College A
Trinidad State Junior College C, A
University of Denver B, M
University of Southern Colorado B

Connecticut
Asnuntuck Community-Technical
  College C
Briarwood College A
Capital Community College C
Central Connecticut State University B
Manchester Community-Technical
  College C, A
Middlesex Community-Technical
  College A
Naugatuck Valley Community-Technical
  College C, A
Quinnipiac University B, M
Southern Connecticut State University B
Teikyo Post University A, B
Three Rivers Community-Technical
  College C, A
Tunxis Community College C, A
University of Hartford B

Delaware
Delaware State University B
Goldey-Beacom College B
University of Delaware B
Wesley College B

District of Columbia
Howard University B
Southeastern University B

Florida
Barry University B
Broward Community College C, A
Florida Metropolitan University
  Orlando College North A, B
Hillsborough Community College A
Indian River Community College A
International Academy of Merchandising
  and Design A, B
Lake City Community College A
Miami-Dade Community College A
Northwood University
  Florida Campus A, B
Palm Beach Community College A
Pasco-Hernando Community College A
Pensacola Junior College A
Polk Community College A
St. Thomas University B
Santa Fe Community College A
Seminole Community College A
South Florida Community College A
Southeastern College of the Assemblies
  of God B, M
Tallahassee Community College A
University of Miami B
University of Tampa B
University of West Florida B
Valencia Community College A

Georgia
Abraham Baldwin Agricultural
  College A
Albany State University B
Atlanta Metropolitan College A
Chattahoochee Technical Institute C, A
Clayton College and State
  University C, A
Columbus State University B
Dalton State College A
Darton College A
DeKalb Technical Institute C, A
Georgia Southwestern State University B
Georgia State University B
Gwinnett Technical Institute C, A
Kennesaw State University B, M

383

Marketing/distribution

North Georgia College & State University *B*
Savannah State University *B*
South Georgia College *A*
Valdosta State University *B*
Young Harris College *A*

Hawaii
Chaminade University of Honolulu *B*
University of Hawaii
    Hawaii Community College *A*
    Kapiolani Community College *A*

Idaho
Boise State University *A, B*
College of Southern Idaho *A*

Illinois
Barat College *B*
Black Hawk College
    East Campus *A*
Black Hawk College *C, A*
Carl Sandburg College *A*
City Colleges of Chicago
    Harold Washington College *C, A*
College of Lake County *C, A*
De Paul University *B, M*
Governors State University *B*
Greenville College *B*
Illinois Eastern Community Colleges
    Wabash Valley College *A*
John A. Logan College *A*
John Wood Community College *A*
Judson College *B*
Kaskaskia College *A*
Lewis University *B*
McKendree College *B*
Moraine Valley Community College *C, A*
North Central College *B*
Oakton Community College *C, A*
Parkland College *A*
Rend Lake College *A*
Rock Valley College *C, A*
Roosevelt University *B*
Sauk Valley Community College *C, A*
Southwestern Ilinois College *C, A*
Trinity Christian College *B*
Triton College *A*
University of St. Francis *B*
William Rainey Harper College *C, A*

Indiana
Goshen College *B*
Indiana State University *B*
Indiana University--Purdue University
    Indiana University-Purdue University Fort Wayne *A, B*
    Purdue University
      North Central Campus *A*
St. Mary-of-the-Woods College *B*
University of Evansville *B*
Valparaiso University *B*
Vincennes University *A*

Iowa
American Institute of Business *C, A*
Buena Vista University *B*
Clarke College *B*
Des Moines Area Community College *C, A*
Drake University *B*
Grand View College *C*
Hawkeye Community College *A*
Loras College *B*
Marshalltown Community College *C*
Mount Mercy College *B*
Northeast Iowa Community College *C, A*
Simpson College *B*
University of Iowa *B*
Upper Iowa University *B*

Kansas
Allen County Community College *C, A*
Butler County Community College *C, A*
Central Christian College *A*
Coffeyville Community College *A*
Cowley County Community College *A*
Kansas City Kansas Community College *A*
Newman University *B*
Pittsburg State University *B*
Pratt Community College *C, A*
Seward County Community College *C, A*

Kentucky
Campbellsville University *B*
Henderson Community College *C*
Murray State University *B, M*

Louisiana
Our Lady of Holy Cross College *B, T*
Southern University
    Shreveport *A*

Maine
Andover College *A*
Husson College *B*
St. Joseph's College *B*
University of Maine
    Fort Kent *A, B*
    Machias *A, B*

Maryland
Baltimore City Community College *A*
Community College of Baltimore County
    Catonsville *C, A*
Montgomery College
    Germantown Campus *A*
    Rockville Campus *A*
    Takoma Park Campus *A*
Morgan State University *B*
University of Maryland
    Eastern Shore *B*

Massachusetts
American International College *B*
Babson College *B*
Bay Path College *A, B*
Becker College *A*
Bentley College *B*
Bristol Community College *A*
Cape Cod Community College *A*
Elms College *B*
Emerson College *M*
Fitchburg State College *B*
Greenfield Community College *A*
Massasoit Community College *C*
Middlesex Community College *C*
Newbury College *A*
Nichols College *B*
North Shore Community College *A*
Northeastern University *B*
Roxbury Community College *A*
Stonehill College *B*
Suffolk University *B*
Western New England College *B*

Michigan
Adrian College *B*
Alpena Community College *A*
Andrews University *B*
Baker College
    of Auburn Hills *A*
    of Jackson *A*
    of Mount Clemens *A, B*
    of Muskegon *A, B*
    of Owosso *A*
    of Port Huron *A, B*
Ferris State University *C*
Glen Oaks Community College *C*
Grand Rapids Community College *A*
Grand Valley State University *B, M*
Hillsdale College *B*
Kalamazoo Valley Community College *A*
Lansing Community College *A*
Macomb Community College *C, A*
North Central Michigan College *C*
Northern Michigan University *B*
Northwood University *B*
Olivet College *B*

St. Clair County Community College *C, A*
Siena Heights University *A, B*
Southwestern Michigan College *A*
Washtenaw Community College *A*
Western Michigan University *B, T*

Minnesota
Century Community and Technical College *A*
Hennepin Technical College *C, A*
Inver Hills Community College *A*
Lake Superior College: A Community and Technical College *A*
Minnesota State University, Mankato *B*
North Hennepin Community College *A*
Northland Community & Technical College *A*
Ridgewater College: A Community and Technical College *C*
Rochester Community and Technical College *A*
St. Cloud State University *B*
St. Cloud Technical College *C, A*
South Central Technical College *A*
University of Minnesota
    Crookston *A, B*

Mississippi
Holmes Community College *A*
Itawamba Community College *A*
Jackson State University *B*
Meridian Community College *A*
Mississippi Gulf Coast Community College
    Jackson County Campus *A*
    Jefferson Davis Campus *A*
Northwest Mississippi Community College *A*
Southwest Mississippi Community College *A*

Missouri
Avila College *B, M*
College of the Ozarks *B*
Crowder College *A*
Drury University *B, M*
East Central College *A*
Evangel University *B*
Lincoln University *B*
Lindenwood University *M*
Missouri Southern State College *B*
Moberly Area Community College *C, A*
Rockhurst University *B*
Southeast Missouri State University *B*
St. Louis Community College
    St. Louis Community College at Florissant Valley *A*
    St. Louis Community College at Meramec *A*
State Fair Community College *A*
Stephens College *B*
Washington University *B*
Webster University *C, B, M*

Montana
Miles Community College *A*
University of Great Falls *B*

Nebraska
Hastings College *B*
Lincoln School of Commerce *A*
Northeast Community College *A*

Nevada
Community College of Southern Nevada *A*
University of Nevada
    Las Vegas *B*
Western Nevada Community College *C, A*

New Hampshire
Antioch New England Graduate School *M*
Daniel Webster College *C, A*
Franklin Pierce College *B*
Hesser College *A*

McIntosh College *A*
New England College *B*
New Hampshire College *A, B*
New Hampshire Community Technical College
    Manchester *C, A*
New Hampshire Technical Institute *C, A*

New Jersey
Berkeley College *A*
Bloomfield College *B*
Brookdale Community College *A*
Caldwell College *B*
Cumberland County College *A*
Gloucester County College *A*
Middlesex County College *A*
New Jersey City University *B*
Raritan Valley Community College *A*
Rider University *B*
Rowan University *B*
St. Peter's College *A, B*
Thomas Edison State College *C, A, B*
Union County College *A*

New Mexico
Clovis Community College *C*
College of Santa Fe *B*
College of the Southwest *B*
Dona Ana Branch Community College of New Mexico State University *C*
Eastern New Mexico University
    Roswell Campus *C*
New Mexico Highlands University *B*
New Mexico Junior College *A*

New York
Adirondack Community College *A*
Berkeley College of New York City *A, B*
Berkeley College *A, B*
Bryant & Stratton Business Institute
    Syracuse *A*
City University of New York
    Baruch College *B*
    Bronx Community College *A*
    College of Staten Island *A*
    Kingsborough Community College *A*
    New York City Technical College *A*
College of Mount St. Vincent *B*
Dowling College *B*
Elmira College *B*
Fashion Institute of Technology *B*
Herkimer County Community College *A*
Hofstra University *B*
Hudson Valley Community College *A*
Iona College *B, M*
Laboratory Institute of Merchandising *B*
Manhattan College *B*
Nassau Community College *A*
New York University *B, M, D*
Niagara County Community College *A*
Pace University:
    Pleasantville/Briarcliff *B, M*
Pace University *B, M*
Regents College *B*
Rochester Institute of Technology *B, M*
Rockland Community College *A*
Sage Junior College of Albany *A*
St. John's University *B, M*
St. Thomas Aquinas College *B, M*
State University of New York
    College at Brockport *B*
    College of Technology at Alfred *A*
    College of Technology at Delhi *A*
    Farmingdale *C*
Suffolk County Community College *A*
Tompkins-Cortland Community College *A*
Westchester Community College *A*

North Carolina
Alamance Community College *C, A*
Appalachian State University *B*
Barber-Scotia College *B*

Catawba Valley Community
 College *C, A*
Central Carolina Community College *A*
Central Piedmont Community College *A*
Cleveland Community College *A*
Forsyth Technical Community College *A*
Gaston College *A*
Lenoir Community College *C, A*
Mayland Community College *A*
Methodist College *A, B*
North Carolina Agricultural and
 Technical State University *A*
North Carolina Central University *B*
Piedmont Community College *C*
Surry Community College *A*
Wake Technical Community College *A*
Western Piedmont Community
 College *A*
Wilson Technical Community College *C*

North Dakota
Lake Region State College *C, A*
North Dakota State College of Science *A*
North Dakota State University *M*

Ohio
Cedarville College *B*
Cincinnati State Technical and
 Community College *A*
Columbus State Community College *A*
David N. Myers College *A, B*
Edison State Community College *C, A*
Kent State University
 Stark Campus *B*
 Trumbull Campus *A*
Lakeland Community College *C*
Lima Technical College *A*
Lorain County Community College *A*
Marietta College *B*
Miami University
 Middletown Campus *A*
Mount Vernon Nazarene College *B*
Ohio State University
 Columbus Campus *B*
Owens Community College
 Findlay Campus *A*
 Toledo *C, A*
Sinclair Community College *A*
Terra Community College *A*
Tiffin University *B*
University of Akron *C, A*
University of Cincinnati
 Clermont College *C*
University of Cincinnati *B, M, D*
University of Dayton *B*
University of Findlay *B*
Wilberforce University *B*
Wilmington College *B*
Wright State University *M*
Youngstown State University *A, B, M*

Oklahoma
Cameron University *B*
Northeastern State University *B*
Oklahoma City Community College *A*
Oklahoma State University *B, M, D*
Southeastern Oklahoma State
 University *B*
Southern Nazarene University *B*
Southwestern Oklahoma State
 University *B*
Tulsa Community College *A*

Oregon
Central Oregon Community College *A*
Oregon Institute of Technology *C*
Portland Community College *C, A*
Southern Oregon University *B*

Pennsylvania
Allentown College of St. Francis de
 Sales *B*
Butler County Community College *C, A*
California University of
 Pennsylvania *A, B*
Central Pennsylvania College *A*
College Misericordia *B*

Community College of Allegheny
 County *C, A*
Holy Family College *C, B*
La Salle University *A, B*
Mansfield University of Pennsylvania *B*
Montgomery County Community
 College *A*
Neumann College *C, B*
Philadelphia University *B, M*
Robert Morris College *M*
St. Joseph's University *B, M*
South Hills School of Business &
 Technology *A*
Tri-State Business Institute *A*
Waynesburg College *B*
York College of Pennsylvania *B, M*

Puerto Rico
Atlantic College *A, B*
Bayamon Central University *B*
Caribbean University *A, B*
Colegio Universitario del Este *A*
Inter American University of Puerto Rico
 Arecibo Campus *B*
 Bayamon Campus *B*
Technological College of San Juan *A*
University of Puerto Rico
 Bayamon University College *A, B*

Rhode Island
Rhode Island College *B*

South Carolina
Central Carolina Technical College *A*
Charleston Southern University *B*
Coker College *B*
Converse College *B*
Limestone College *B*
South Carolina State University *B*
University of South Carolina
 Aiken *B*

South Dakota
Black Hills State University *B*
Dakota State University *B*
Dakota Wesleyan University *B*
Huron University *B*
Southeast Technical Institute *A*

Tennessee
Chattanooga State Technical Community
 College *A*
Christian Brothers University *B*
Freed-Hardeman University *B*
Lambuth University *B*
Lincoln Memorial University *B*
Tennessee Technological University *B*
Union University *B*

Texas
Alvin Community College *C, A*
Angelina College *C, A*
Angelo State University *B*
Austin Community College *C, A*
Cedar Valley College *A*
Central Texas College *C, A*
Coastal Bend College *A*
El Paso Community College *A*
Hill College *A*
LeTourneau University *B*
Lubbock Christian University *B*
Midland College *A*
Midwestern State University *B*
Navarro College *A*
North Central Texas College *A*
Odessa College *A*
Palo Alto College *C, A*
South Plains College *A*
Southwest Texas State University *B, T*
Temple College *C, A*
Texas A&M University
 Commerce *B*
 Kingsville *B*
Texas A&M University *B, M, D*
Texas Wesleyan University *B*
Trinity Valley Community College *C, A*
University of Houston *B*

University of North Texas *B, M, D*
University of St. Thomas *B*
University of Texas
 Arlington *M*
Western Texas College *A*

Utah
College of Eastern Utah *C*
Dixie State College of Utah *C, A*
LDS Business College *A*
Salt Lake Community College *C, A*

Vermont
Castleton State College *B*
Champlain College *A, B*

Virginia
Averett College *B*
Central Virginia Community College *A*
Danville Community College *A*
Hampton University *B*
Lynchburg College *B*
Mountain Empire Community College *A*
New River Community College *A*
Northern Virginia Community College *A*
Paul D. Camp Community College *A*
Piedmont Virginia Community
 College *C, A*
Thomas Nelson Community College *A*
Virginia Intermont College *B*
Virginia Polytechnic Institute and State
 University *M, D*

Washington
Bellevue Community College *A*
Centralia College *A*
Clark College *A*
Everett Community College *C, A*
Gonzaga University *B*
Highline Community College *A*
Peninsula College *A*
Spokane Community College *A*
Spokane Falls Community College *C, A*
Wenatchee Valley College *A*
Yakima Valley Community College *A*

West Virginia
Alderson-Broaddus College *B*
Bluefield State College *A*
Concord College *B*
Davis and Elkins College *B*
Glenville State College *B*
Marshall University *B*
Potomac State College of West Virginia
 University *A*
West Liberty State College *B*
West Virginia State College *A, B*

Wisconsin
Blackhawk Technical College *A*
Carthage College *B*
Chippewa Valley Technical College *A*
Concordia University Wisconsin *B*
Lakeshore Technical College *A*
Madison Area Technical College *A*
Marian College of Fond du Lac *B*
Moraine Park Technical College *A*
Nicolet Area Technical College *A*
Northeast Wisconsin Technical
 College *A*
Southwest Wisconsin Technical
 College *A*
University of Wisconsin
 Oshkosh *B*
 Superior *B*
 Whitewater *B, M*
Viterbo University *B*
Waukesha County Technical College *A*
Western Wisconsin Technical College *A*

Wyoming
Laramie County Community College *A*
Northwest College *A*
Sheridan College *A*
Western Wyoming Community
 College *A*

Marketing/distribution education

Arkansas
University of Central Arkansas *A*

Colorado
Colorado State University *T*

Florida
Gulf Coast Community College *A*
Palm Beach Community College *A*
University of South Florida *B, M*

Georgia
University of Georgia *B, M*

Hawaii
University of Hawaii
 Manoa *B, T*

Idaho
Ricks College *A*

Indiana
Ball State University *B, M*
Indiana State University *B, T*
Vincennes University *A*

Kansas
Independence Community College *A*

Louisiana
Northwestern State University *B, T*

Michigan
Central Michigan University *B*
Eastern Michigan University *B, T*
Western Michigan University *B*

Minnesota
Northland Community & Technical
 College *A*
Ridgewater College: A Community and
 Technical College *C*
University of Minnesota
 Twin Cities *B, M*

Mississippi
Northwest Mississippi Community
 College *A*

Nebraska
University of Nebraska
 Lincoln *B, T*

New Hampshire
Hesser College *A*

New Jersey
Montclair State University *T*
Rider University *B, T*

New Mexico
College of the Southwest *B, T*
Eastern New Mexico University *B*

New York
Long Island University
 Brooklyn Campus *B, M, T*
Nazareth College of Rochester *T*
New York Institute of Technology *B, T*
Pace University:
 Pleasantville/Briarcliff *B*
Pace University *B*
State University of New York
 College at Buffalo *B, M, T*

North Carolina
Appalachian State University *B, T*
East Carolina University *B*
North Carolina State University *M, T*
University of North Carolina
 Greensboro *B, M, T*

North Dakota
University of North Dakota *B, T*

Ohio
Bowling Green State University *B*
Kent State University *M, T*

Marketing/distribution education

Ohio State University
  Columbus Campus *M, D*
University of Akron *M*
Oklahoma
University of Central Oklahoma *B*
Oregon
Oregon State University *M*
Pennsylvania
Delaware Valley College *T*
Temple University *B, T*
South Dakota
Dakota State University *B, T*
Tennessee
Middle Tennessee State University *B*
Tennessee Temple University *B*
University of Tennessee
  Knoxville *B, T*
Texas
Southwest Texas State University *T*
University of North Texas *M*
Utah
Utah State University *B, M, D*
Washington
Eastern Washington University *B, M, T*
Wisconsin
University of Wisconsin
  Stout *B, T*
  Whitewater *B, T*
Wyoming
Laramie County Community College *A*

Masonry/tile setting

Alabama
Central Alabama Community College *C*
Gadsden State Community College *C*
John M. Patterson State Technical
  College *C*
Lawson State Community College *C*
Reid State Technical College *C*
Shelton State Community College *C*
Sparks State Technical College *C*
Arizona
Central Arizona College *C*
Cochise College *C*
Eastern Arizona College *C*
California
Bakersfield College *A*
Long Beach City College *C, A*
Palomar College *C, A*
Ventura College *A*
Colorado
Red Rocks Community College *C, A*
Florida
Lake City Community College *C*
Illinois
Southwestern Illinois College *C, A*
Indiana
Ivy Tech State College
  Central Indiana *C, A*
  Columbus *C, A*
  Eastcentral *C, A*
  Lafayette *C, A*
  Northcentral *C, A*
  Northeast *C, A*
  Northwest *C, A*
  Southwest *C, A*
  Wabash Valley *C, A*
Oakland City University *C*
Iowa
Kirkwood Community College *C*
Maryland
Cecil Community College *C, A*

Michigan
Lansing Community College *A*
Oakland Community College *C*
Minnesota
Alexandria Technical College *C*
St. Cloud Technical College *C*
St. Paul Technical College *C*
Mississippi
Hinds Community College *C*
Mississippi Delta Community College *C*
Nebraska
Mid Plains Community College Area *C*
Nevada
Western Nevada Community College *A*
New York
State University of New York
  College of Technology at Alfred *A*
  College of Technology at
    Delhi *C, A*
North Carolina
Blue Ridge Community College *C*
Davidson County Community College *C*
Fayetteville Technical Community
  College *C*
Haywood Community College *C*
James Sprunt Community College *C*
Johnston Community College *C*
Lenoir Community College *C*
Piedmont Community College *C*
Pitt Community College *C*
Southeastern Community College *C*
Southwestern Community College *C*
Tri-County Community College *C*
Pennsylvania
Delaware County Community College *C*
Williamson Free School of Mechanical
  Trades *C*
Texas
Howard College *C*
Trinity Valley Community College *C*
Virginia
Piedmont Virginia Community
  College *C*
Wisconsin
Milwaukee Area Technical College *C*
Southwest Wisconsin Technical
  College *C*
Western Wisconsin Technical College *C*
Wisconsin Indianhead Technical
  College *C*

Materials engineering

Alabama
Auburn University *B, M, D*
Tuskegee University *D*
University of Alabama
  Birmingham *B, M, D*
University of Alabama *D*
Arizona
Arizona State University *B*
California
California Polytechnic State University:
  San Luis Obispo *B*
California State University
  Long Beach *B*
  Northridge *B, M*
San Jose State University *B, M*
Stanford University *B, M, D*
University of California
  Berkeley *B*
  Davis *B*
  Irvine *M, D*
  Los Angeles *B, M, D*
  Santa Barbara *M, D*
University of Southern California *M*

Colorado
Colorado School of Mines *M*
University of Denver *D*
Delaware
University of Delaware *M, D*
District of Columbia
George Washington University *M, D*
Howard University *M, D*
Florida
Florida State University *B*
University of Central Florida *M*
University of Florida *B, M, D*
Georgia
Georgia Institute of Technology *B, M, D*
Illinois
Illinois Institute of Technology *B, M, D*
Northwestern University *B, M, D*
University of Illinois
  Chicago *M, D*
Indiana
Purdue University *B, M, D*
Iowa
Iowa State University *B, M, D*
Kentucky
University of Kentucky *B, M, D*
Maryland
Johns Hopkins University *B, M, D*
University of Maryland
  College Park *B, M, D*
Massachusetts
Massachusetts Institute of
  Technology *B, M, D*
Northeastern University *M*
Worcester Polytechnic Institute *B, M, D*
Michigan
University of Michigan *B, M, D*
Wayne State University *M, D*
Western Michigan University *B, M*
Minnesota
University of Minnesota
  Twin Cities *B, M, D*
Winona State University *B*
Missouri
Washington University *M, D*
Montana
Montana Tech of the University of
  Montana *B, M*
New Jersey
New Jersey Institute of Technology *M, D*
Rowan University *B*
Stevens Institute of Technology *M, D*
New Mexico
New Mexico Institute of Mining and
  Technology *B, M, D*
New York
Columbia University
  Fu Foundation School of
    Engineering and Applied
    Science *B, M, D*
Cornell University *B, M, D*
New York State College of Ceramics at
  Alfred University *B, M*
New York University *B*
Rensselaer Polytechnic Institute *B, M, D*
Rochester Institute of Technology *M*
State University of New York
  College of Environmental Science
    and Forestry *B, M, D*
Syracuse University *M*
North Carolina
North Carolina Agricultural and
  Technical State University *B*
North Carolina State University *B, M, D*
St. Augustine's College *B*

Ohio
Case Western Reserve
  University *B, M, D*
Hocking Technical College *A*
Ohio State University
  Columbus Campus *B, M, D*
University of Cincinnati *M, D*
University of Dayton *M, D*
Wright State University *B, M*
Oregon
Oregon Graduate Institute *M, D*
Oregon State University *M*
Pennsylvania
Carnegie Mellon University *B, M, D*
Drexel University *B, M, D*
Lehigh University *B, M, D*
University of Pennsylvania *B, M, D*
University of Pittsburgh *B, M, D*
Wilkes University *B*
Rhode Island
Brown University *B, M, D*
South Carolina
Clemson University *M, D*
South Dakota
South Dakota School of Mines and
  Technology *D*
Tennessee
Vanderbilt University *M, D*
Texas
Rice University *B, M, D*
Southern Methodist University *M*
University of Houston *M, D*
University of Texas
  Arlington *M, D*
  Austin *M, D*
  El Paso *M, D*
Utah
University of Utah *B, M, D*
Virginia
University of Virginia *M, D*
Virginia Polytechnic Institute and State
  University *B, M, D*
Washington
University of Washington *B, M, D*
Washington State University *B, M*
Wisconsin
University of Wisconsin
  Milwaukee *B*

Materials science

Alabama
Alabama Agricultural and Mechanical
  University *D*
University of Alabama
  Birmingham *D*
  Huntsville *M, D*
University of Alabama *D*
Arizona
Arizona State University *D*
University of Arizona *B, M, D*
California
California Institute of Technology *M, D*
University of California
  Davis *B, M*
  San Diego *M, D*
University of Southern California *M, D*
Colorado
Colorado School of Mines *M, D*
National Technological University *M*
University of Denver *D*
Connecticut
University of Connecticut *M, D*

Illinois
Northwestern University B
University of Illinois
  Urbana-Champaign M, D

Iowa
Iowa State University M, D

Maryland
Johns Hopkins University B, M, D

Massachusetts
Harvard College B
Massachusetts Institute of
  Technology B, M, D
Northeastern University M

Michigan
Michigan State University B, M, D
University of Michigan B, M, D
Western Michigan University B, M

Minnesota
University of Minnesota
  Twin Cities B, M, D
Winona State University B

Montana
Montana Tech of the University of
  Montana B

New Jersey
Stevens Institute of Technology M, D

New York
Columbia University
  Fu Foundation School of
    Engineering and Applied
    Science B, M, D
New York State College of Ceramics at
  Alfred University B, M, D
Polytechnic University M
Rochester Institute of Technology M
State University of New York
  Buffalo M, D
  Stony Brook M, D
University of Rochester M, D

North Carolina
University of North Carolina
  Chapel Hill M, D

Ohio
Case Western Reserve
  University B, M, D
Hocking Technical College A
Ohio State University
  Columbus Campus B, M, D
Youngstown State University M

Oregon
Oregon State University M

Pennsylvania
Carnegie Mellon University B, M, D
Lehigh University B, M, D
Penn State
  University Park B
Temple University B

South Dakota
South Dakota School of Mines and
  Technology D

Tennessee
University of Tennessee
  Knoxville B

Texas
Southern Methodist University M
University of Texas
  El Paso B, D

Utah
Salt Lake Community College A

Vermont
University of Vermont M, D

Washington
Washington State University D

Wisconsin
Marquette University M, D
Milwaukee Area Technical College A
University of Wisconsin
  Madison M, D

Mathematics

Alabama
Alabama Agricultural and Mechanical
  University B
Alabama State University B, M
Athens State University B
Auburn University at Montgomery B
Auburn University B, M, D, T
Birmingham-Southern College B, T
Calhoun Community College A
Chattahoochee Valley Community
  College A
Faulkner University B
Huntingdon College B, T
Jacksonville State University B, M
James H. Faulkner State Community
  College A
Lawson State Community College A
Oakwood College B
Samford University B
Shelton State Community College A
Spring Hill College B, T
Stillman College B
Talladega College B
Troy State University
  Dothan B, T
  Montgomery B
Troy State University B
Tuskegee University B, T
University of Alabama
  Birmingham B, M
  Huntsville B, M
University of Alabama B, M, D
University of Mobile B
University of Montevallo B, T
University of North Alabama B
University of South Alabama B, M
University of West Alabama B, T

Alaska
University of Alaska
  Anchorage B
  Fairbanks B, M, D
  Southeast B

Arizona
Arizona State University B, M, D
Arizona Western College A
Eastern Arizona College A
Grand Canyon University B
Mohave Community College A
Northern Arizona University B, M, T
South Mountain Community College A
University of Arizona B, M, D

Arkansas
Arkansas State University
  Beebe Branch A
Arkansas State University B, M
Arkansas Tech University B
Central Baptist College A
Harding University B
Henderson State University B
Hendrix College B
John Brown University B
Lyon College B
Ouachita Baptist University B
Philander Smith College B
Phillips Community College of the
  University of Arkansas A
Southern Arkansas University B
University of Arkansas
  Little Rock B
  Monticello B
  Pine Bluff B
University of Arkansas B, M, D
University of Central Arkansas B, M
University of the Ozarks B

Westark College A

California
Azusa Pacific University B
Bakersfield College A
Barstow College A
Biola University B
Butte College A
Cabrillo College A
California Baptist University B
California Institute of Technology B, D
California Lutheran University B
California Polytechnic State University:
  San Luis Obispo B, M
California State Polytechnic University:
  Pomona B, M
California State University
  Bakersfield B
  Chico B
  Dominguez Hills B
  Fresno B, M
  Fullerton B, M
  Hayward B, M
  Long Beach B, M
  Los Angeles B, M
  Northridge B, M
  Sacramento B, M
  San Marcos B, M
  Stanislaus B
Canada College A
Cerritos Community College A
Chabot College A
Chaffey Community College A
Citrus College A
Claremont McKenna College B
College of Marin: Kentfield A
College of San Mateo A
College of the Canyons A
College of the Desert A
College of the Siskiyous A
Columbia College A
Compton Community College A
Concordia University B
Contra Costa College A
Crafton Hills College A
Cuesta College C, A
Cypress College A
De Anza College A
Diablo Valley College A
East Los Angeles College C
Foothill College A
Fresno City College A
Fresno Pacific University B
Gavilan Community College A
Glendale Community College A
Golden West College A
Grossmont Community College A
Harvey Mudd College B
Humboldt State University B
Imperial Valley College A
Irvine Valley College A
Kings River Community College A
La Sierra University B
Long Beach City College A
Los Angeles Mission College A
Los Angeles Southwest College A
Los Angeles Valley College A
Los Medanos College A
Loyola Marymount University B
Marymount College A
Master's College B
Mendocino College A
Merced College A
Merritt College A
Mills College B
MiraCosta College A
Mission College A
Modesto Junior College A
Monterey Peninsula College A
Moorpark College A
Mount St. Mary's College B
Mount San Jacinto College A
National University B
Occidental College B
Ohlone College C, A

Orange Coast College A
Pacific Union College B
Palomar College A
Pepperdine University B
Pitzer College B
Point Loma Nazarene University B
Pomona College B
Porterville College A
Riverside Community College A
Sacramento City College A
Saddleback College A
St. Mary's College of California B
San Bernardino Valley College A
San Diego City College A
San Diego Mesa College A
San Diego Miramar College A
San Diego State University B, M, T
San Francisco State University B, M
San Joaquin Delta College A
San Jose State University B, M
Santa Ana College A
Santa Barbara City College A
Santa Clara University B
Santa Monica College A
Santa Rosa Junior College A
Scripps College B
Simpson College B
Skyline College A
Solano Community College A
Sonoma State University B
Southwestern College A
Stanford University B, M, D
Taft College A
University of California
  Berkeley B, M, D
  Davis B, M, D
  Irvine B, M, D
  Los Angeles B, M, D
  Riverside B, M, D
  San Diego B, M, D
  Santa Barbara B, M, D
  Santa Cruz B, M, D
University of La Verne B
University of Redlands B
University of San Diego B
University of San Francisco B
University of Southern
  California B, M, D
University of the Pacific B
Vanguard University of Southern
  California B
Ventura College A
Victor Valley College A
West Hills Community College A
West Valley College A
Westmont College B
Whittier College B

Colorado
Adams State College B
Colorado Christian University B
Colorado College B
Colorado Mountain College
  Alpine Campus A
  Timberline Campus A
Colorado School of Mines M, D
Colorado State University B, M, D
Fort Lewis College B
Lamar Community College A
Mesa State College A, B
Metropolitan State College of
  Denver B, T
Otero Junior College A
Regis University B
Trinidad State Junior College A
United States Air Force Academy B
University of Colorado
  Boulder B, M, D
  Colorado Springs B
  Denver B
University of Denver B, M
University of Northern Colorado B, M, T
University of Southern Colorado B, T
Western State College of Colorado B

Mathematics

Connecticut
Albertus Magnus College B
Central Connecticut State
  University B, M
Connecticut College B
Eastern Connecticut State University B
Fairfield University B
Manchester Community-Technical
  College A
Northwestern Connecticut
  Community-Technical College A
Norwalk Community-Technical
  College A
Quinnipiac University B
Sacred Heart University A, B
St. Joseph College B, T
Southern Connecticut State
  University B, M
Trinity College B
University of Bridgeport B
University of Connecticut B, M, D
University of Hartford B
University of New Haven B
Wesleyan University B, M, D
Western Connecticut State
  University B, M
Yale University B, M, D

Delaware
Delaware State University B
University of Delaware B, M, D

District of Columbia
American University B, M
Catholic University of America B, T
Gallaudet University B
George Washington University B, M, D
Georgetown University B
Howard University B, M, D
Trinity College B
University of the District of Columbia B

Florida
Barry University B
Bethune-Cookman College B
Broward Community College A
Chipola Junior College A
Clearwater Christian College B
Eckerd College B
Edward Waters College B
Florida Agricultural and Mechanical
  University B
Florida Atlantic University B, M, D
Florida Gulf Coast University B
Florida International University B
Florida Memorial College B
Florida Southern College B
Florida State University B, M, D
Gulf Coast Community College A
Indian River Community College A
Jacksonville University B
Lake City Community College A
Manatee Community College A
Miami-Dade Community College A
New College of the University of South
  Florida B
Palm Beach Atlantic College B, T
Palm Beach Community College A
Pensacola Junior College A
Polk Community College A
Rollins College B
South Florida Community College A
Stetson University B
University of Central Florida B
University of Florida B, M, D
University of Miami B, M, D
University of North Florida B
University of South Florida B, M, D
University of Tampa A, B, T
University of West Florida B, M

Georgia
Abraham Baldwin Agricultural
  College A
Agnes Scott College B
Albany State University B, M

Andrew College A
Atlanta Metropolitan College A
Augusta State University B
Berry College B, T
Brewton-Parker College A
Clark Atlanta University B, M
Clayton College and State University A
Coastal Georgia Community College A
Columbus State University B
Covenant College B
Dalton State College A
Darton College A
East Georgia College A
Emory University B, M, D
Floyd College A
Fort Valley State University B
Gainesville College A
Georgia College and State University B
Georgia Institute of Technology B, M, D
Georgia Military College A
Georgia Perimeter College A
Georgia Southern University B, M
Georgia Southwestern State University B
Georgia State University B, M
Kennesaw State University B
LaGrange College B
Mercer University B, T
Middle Georgia College A
Morehouse College B
Morris Brown College B
North Georgia College & State
  University B
Oglethorpe University B
Oxford College of Emory University B
Paine College B
Piedmont College B
Savannah State University B
Shorter College B, T
South Georgia College A
Southern Polytechnic State University B
Spelman College B
State University of West Georgia B
University of Georgia B, M, D
Valdosta State University B
Waycross College A
Wesleyan College B, T
Young Harris College A

Hawaii
Brigham Young University
  Hawaii B
Hawaii Pacific University A
University of Hawaii
  Hilo B
  Manoa B, M, D

Idaho
Albertson College of Idaho B
Boise State University B, T
College of Southern Idaho A
Idaho State University A, B, M, D
Lewis-Clark State College B, T
North Idaho College A
Northwest Nazarene University B
Ricks College A
University of Idaho B, M, D

Illinois
Augustana College B, T
Barat College B
Benedictine University B, T
Black Hawk College
  East Campus A
Blackburn College B, T
Bradley University B, T
Chicago State University B, M, T
City Colleges of Chicago
  Harold Washington College A
  Kennedy-King College A
  Olive-Harvey College A
Concordia University B, T
Danville Area Community College A
De Paul University B, M, T
Dominican University B
Eastern Illinois University B, M, T
Elmhurst College B, T

Eureka College B, T
Greenville College B, T
Highland Community College A
Illinois College B
Illinois State University B, M, T
Illinois Wesleyan University B
John A. Logan College A
John Wood Community College A
Joliet Junior College A
Judson College B
Kankakee Community College A
Kishwaukee College A
Knox College B
Lake Forest College B
Lake Land College A
Lewis University B, T
Lewis and Clark Community College A
Lincoln Land Community College A
Loyola University of Chicago B, M
MacMurray College B
McKendree College B, T
Millikin University B, T
Monmouth College B, T
Morton College A
National-Louis University B
North Central College B, T
North Park University B
Northeastern Illinois University B, M
Northern Illinois University B, M, D, T
Northwestern University B, M, D
Olivet Nazarene University B, T
Parkland College A
Principia College B, T
Quincy University A, B, T
Rend Lake College A
Richland Community College A
Rockford College B
Roosevelt University B, M
St. Xavier University B
Sauk Valley Community College A
Southern Illinois University
  Carbondale B, M, D
  Edwardsville B, M
Southwestern Illinois College A
Springfield College in Illinois A
Trinity Christian College B, T
Trinity International University B
Triton College A
University of Chicago B, M, D
University of Illinois
  Chicago B, M, D
  Springfield B, M
  Urbana-Champaign B, M, D
University of St. Francis B
Western Illinois University B, M
Wheaton College B, T
William Rainey Harper College A

Indiana
Ancilla College A
Anderson University B
Ball State University B, M, T
Bethel College B
Butler University B
DePauw University B
Earlham College B
Franklin College B
Goshen College B
Grace College B
Hanover College B
Indiana State University B, M
Indiana University
  Bloomington B, M, D
  East B
  Kokomo B
  Northwest B, T
  South Bend B
  Southeast B
Indiana University--Purdue University
  Indiana University-Purdue
    University Fort Wayne A, B, M
  Indiana University-Purdue
    University Indianapolis B, M
Indiana Wesleyan University B
Manchester College B, T

Marian College B, T
Purdue University
  Calumet B, M
Purdue University B, M, D
Rose-Hulman Institute of Technology B
Saint Mary's College B, T
St. Joseph's College B
St. Mary-of-the-Woods College B
Taylor University B
Tri-State University A, B
University of Evansville B
University of Indianapolis B
University of Notre Dame B, M, D
University of Southern Indiana B
Valparaiso University B, T
Vincennes University A
Wabash College B

Iowa
Briar Cliff College B
Buena Vista University B, T
Central College B, T
Clarke College B, T
Coe College B
Cornell College B, T
Dordt College B
Drake University B
Graceland University B, T
Grinnell College B
Iowa State University B, M, D
Iowa Wesleyan College B
Iowa Western Community College A
Loras College B
Luther College B
Maharishi University of
  Management A, B, M
Marshalltown Community College A
Marycrest International University A, B
Morningside College B
Mount Mercy College B, T
North Iowa Area Community College A
Northwestern College B
St. Ambrose University B
Simpson College B
University of Iowa B, M, D, T
University of Northern Iowa B, M
Upper Iowa University B
Waldorf College A
Wartburg College B, T

Kansas
Allen County Community College A
Baker University B, T
Barton County Community College A
Benedictine College B, T
Bethany College B, T
Bethel College B, T
Butler County Community College A
Central Christian College A
Coffeyville Community College A
Colby Community College A
Cowley County Community College A
Dodge City Community College A
Emporia State University B, M, T
Fort Hays State University B, M
Garden City Community College A
Hutchinson Community College A
Independence Community College A
Kansas City Kansas Community
  College A
Kansas State University B, M, D
Kansas Wesleyan University B, T
McPherson College B, T
MidAmerica Nazarene University B
Newman University B
Ottawa University B
Pittsburg State University B, M, T
Pratt Community College A
St. Mary College B
Seward County Community College A
Southwestern College B
Sterling College B
Tabor College B
University of Kansas B, M, D
Washburn University of Topeka B
Wichita State University B, M, D

Kentucky
Asbury College B, T
Berea College B, T
Campbellsville University B
Centre College B
Cumberland College B, T
Eastern Kentucky University B, M
Georgetown College B
Kentucky Christian College B, T
Kentucky State University B
Kentucky Wesleyan College B, T
Lindsey Wilson College A
Morehead State University B
Murray State University B, M, T
Northern Kentucky University B
Pikeville College B, T
St. Catharine College A
Spalding University B
Thomas More College B
Transylvania University B, T
Union College B
University of Kentucky B, M, D
University of Louisville B, M
Western Kentucky University B, M, T

Louisiana
Centenary College of Louisiana B, T
Dillard University B
Louisiana State University
 Shreveport B
Louisiana State University and
 Agricultural and Mechanical
 College B, M, D
Louisiana Tech University B, M
Loyola University New Orleans B, M
McNeese State University B, M
Nicholls State University B
Northwestern State University B
Southeastern Louisiana University B
Southern University
 New Orleans B
 Shreveport A
Southern University and Agricultural and
 Mechanical College B, M, D
Tulane University B, M, D
University of Louisiana at
 Lafayette B, M, D
University of Louisiana at Monroe B
University of New Orleans B, M
Xavier University of Louisiana B

Maine
Bates College B
Bowdoin College B
Colby College B
St. Joseph's College B
University of Maine
 Farmington B
 Presque Isle B
University of Maine B, M
University of Southern Maine B

Maryland
Allegany College A
Anne Arundel Community College A
Bowie State University B
Charles County Community College A
College of Notre Dame of Maryland B
Columbia Union College B
Community College of Baltimore County
 Essex A
Coppin State College B
Frederick Community College A
Frostburg State University B
Goucher College B
Hagerstown Community College A
Harford Community College A
Hood College B, T
Johns Hopkins University B, D
Loyola College in Maryland B
Montgomery College
 Germantown Campus A
Morgan State University B, M
Mount St. Mary's College B
St. Mary's College of Maryland B
Salisbury State University B, T

Towson University B, T
United States Naval Academy B
University of Maryland
 Baltimore County B
 College Park B, M, D
 Eastern Shore B
Western Maryland College B

Massachusetts
American International College B
Amherst College B
Assumption College B
Atlantic Union College B
Bentley College B
Boston College B, M
Boston University B, M, D
Brandeis University B, M, D
Bridgewater State College B
Cape Cod Community College A
Clark University B
College of the Holy Cross B
Eastern Nazarene College B
Elms College B
Emmanuel College B
Fitchburg State College B
Framingham State College B
Gordon College B
Hampshire College B
Harvard College B, T
Harvard University M, D
Massachusetts College of Liberal Arts B
Massachusetts Institute of
 Technology B, D
Merrimack College B
Mount Holyoke College B
Nichols College B
Northeastern University B, M, D
Regis College B
Roxbury Community College A
Salem State College B, M
Simmons College B
Smith College B
Springfield College B
Springfield Technical Community
 College A
Stonehill College B
Suffolk University B, T
Tufts University B, M, D
University of Massachusetts
 Amherst B, M, D
 Boston B
 Dartmouth B
 Lowell B, M
Wellesley College B
Western New England College B
Westfield State College B
Wheaton College B
Williams College B
Worcester Polytechnic Institute B, M, D
Worcester State College B

Michigan
Adrian College A, B, T
Albion College B, T
Alma College B, T
Andrews University B
Aquinas College B, T
Calvin College B, T
Central Michigan University B, M, D
Concordia College B, T
Cornerstone College and Grand Rapids
 Baptist Seminary B, T
Eastern Michigan University B, M
Gogebic Community College A
Grand Valley State University B
Hillsdale College B
Hope College B, T
Kalamazoo College B, T
Kellogg Community College A
Lake Michigan College A
Lake Superior State University B, T
Lansing Community College A
Lawrence Technological University B
Madonna University A, B, T
Marygrove College B, T
Michigan State University B, M, D

Michigan Technological
 University B, M, D, T
Mid Michigan Community College A
Northern Michigan University B, T
Oakland University B, M
Olivet College B, T
Saginaw Valley State University B
Siena Heights University A, B
Spring Arbor College B
University of Detroit Mercy B, M
University of Michigan
 Dearborn B
 Flint B, T
University of Michigan B, M, D, T
Wayne State University B, M, D
West Shore Community College A
Western Michigan University B, M, T
William Tyndale College B

Minnesota
Augsburg College B
Bemidji State University B
Bethel College B
Carleton College B
College of St. Benedict B
College of St. Catherine: St. Paul
 Campus B
College of St. Scholastica B
Concordia College: Moorhead B
Concordia University: St. Paul B
Gustavus Adolphus College B
Hamline University B
Macalester College B, T
Minnesota State University,
 Mankato B, M
Moorhead State University B
Northland Community & Technical
 College A
Northwestern College B
Ridgewater College: A Community and
 Technical College A
St. Cloud State University B, M
St. John's University B
St. Mary's University of Minnesota B
St. Olaf College B, T
Southwest State University B, T
University of Minnesota
 Duluth B
 Morris B
 Twin Cities C, B, M, D
University of St. Thomas B
Winona State University B, T

Mississippi
Alcorn State University B
Belhaven College B, T
Blue Mountain College B
Delta State University B
East Central Community College A
Hinds Community College A
Holmes Community College A
Jackson State University B
Mary Holmes College A
Millsaps College B, T
Mississippi College B, M
Mississippi Gulf Coast Community
 College
  Jefferson Davis Campus A
Mississippi State University B, M
Mississippi University for Women B, T
Mississippi Valley State University B
Rust College B
Tougaloo College B
University of Mississippi B, M, D, T
University of Southern Mississippi B, M
William Carey College B, T

Missouri
Avila College B
Central Methodist College B
Central Missouri State University B, M
College of the Ozarks B
Crowder College A
Culver-Stockton College B, T
Drury University B, T
East Central College A

Evangel University B
Hannibal-LaGrange College B
Jefferson College A
Lincoln University B
Lindenwood University B
Maryville University of Saint Louis B
Mineral Area College A
Missouri Baptist College B
Missouri Southern State College B, T
Missouri Valley College B
Missouri Western State College B, T
Northwest Missouri State University B
Park University B
Rockhurst University B
St. Louis University B, M, D
Southeast Missouri State
 University B, M
Southwest Baptist University B, T
Southwest Missouri State
 University B, M
St. Louis Community College
 St. Louis Community College at
  Florissant Valley A
 St. Louis Community College at
  Forest Park A
 St. Louis Community College at
  Meramec A
Stephens College B
Three Rivers Community College A
Truman State University B, M
University of Missouri
 Columbia B, M, D
 Kansas City B, M
 Rolla M, D, T
 St. Louis B, M
Washington University B, M, D
Webster University B
Westminster College B
William Jewell College B, T
William Woods University B

Montana
Carroll College B, T
Little Big Horn College A
Miles Community College A
Montana State University
 Billings B
 Bozeman B, M, D, T
Montana Tech of the University of
 Montana A
Rocky Mountain College B, T
University of Great Falls A, B
University of Montana-Missoula B, M, D

Nebraska
Bellevue University B
Chadron State College B
College of Saint Mary B, T
Concordia University B, T
Creighton University A, B, M
Dana College B
Doane College B
Hastings College B
Midland Lutheran College B, T
Nebraska Wesleyan University B
Northeast Community College A
Peru State College B
Union College B
University of Nebraska
 Kearney B, M, T
 Lincoln B, M, D
 Omaha B, M
Wayne State College B, M, T

Nevada
University of Nevada
 Las Vegas B, M
 Reno B, M
Western Nevada Community College A

New Hampshire
Dartmouth College B, D
Franklin Pierce College B
Keene State College B
Plymouth State College of the University
 System of New Hampshire B

Mathematics

Rivier College B, M, T
St. Anselm College B, T
University of New Hampshire B, M, D

New Jersey
Atlantic Cape Community College A
Brookdale Community College A
Caldwell College B
Centenary College B
College of St. Elizabeth B, T
Drew University B
Essex County College A
Fairleigh Dickinson University B, M
Felician College B
Georgian Court College B, M, T
Gloucester County College A
Hudson County Community College A
Kean University B, M
Monmouth University B
Montclair State University B, M, T
New Jersey City University B, M
New Jersey Institute of Technology D
Passaic County Community College A
Princeton University B, M, D
Ramapo College of New Jersey B
Raritan Valley Community College A
Richard Stockton College of New Jersey B
Rider University B
Rowan University B, M
Rutgers
   The State University of New Jersey: Camden College of Arts and Sciences B, T
   The State University of New Jersey: Camden Graduate Campus M
   The State University of New Jersey: Douglass College B, T
   The State University of New Jersey: Livingston College B, T
   The State University of New Jersey: New Brunswick Graduate Campus M, D
   The State University of New Jersey: Newark College of Arts and Sciences B, T
   The State University of New Jersey: Newark Graduate Campus M
   The State University of New Jersey: Rutgers College B, T
   The State University of New Jersey: University College Camden B, T
   The State University of New Jersey: University College New Brunswick B, T
   The State University of New Jersey: University College Newark T
St. Peter's College B
Salem Community College A
Seton Hall University B, M, T
Stevens Institute of Technology M, D
Sussex County Community College A
The College of New Jersey B, T
Thomas Edison State College A, B
William Paterson University of New Jersey B

New Mexico
Clovis Community College A
College of the Southwest B
Eastern New Mexico University B, M
New Mexico Highlands University B
New Mexico Institute of Mining and Technology B, M
New Mexico Junior College A
New Mexico State University B, M, D
San Juan College A
University of New Mexico B, M, D
Western New Mexico University B

New York
Adelphi University B, M, D
Adirondack Community College A
Alfred University B
Bard College B
Barnard College B
Canisius College B
Cayuga County Community College A
City University of New York
   Baruch College B
   Borough of Manhattan Community College A
   Brooklyn College B, M
   City College B, M, T
   College of Staten Island B, T
   Graduate School and University Center D
   Hunter College B, M
   Kingsborough Community College A
   Lehman College B, M
   Queens College B, M
   York College B
Clarkson University B, M, D
Clinton Community College A
Colgate University B
College of Mount St. Vincent B, T
College of New Rochelle B, T
College of St. Rose B
Columbia University
   Columbia College B
   Graduate School M, D
   School of General Studies B
Concordia College B, T
Cornell University B, D
Corning Community College A
Daemen College B, T
Dominican College of Blauvelt B
Dowling College B, T
Dutchess Community College A
Elmira College B, T
Finger Lakes Community College A
Fordham University B, M, D
Fulton-Montgomery Community College A
Hamilton College B
Hartwick College B, T
Herkimer County Community College A
Hobart and William Smith Colleges B
Hofstra University B
Houghton College B
Iona College B, M
Ithaca College B, T
Jefferson Community College A
Keuka College B
Le Moyne College B
Long Island University
   Brooklyn Campus B
   C. W. Post Campus B, M
Manhattan College B
Manhattanville College B
Marist College B, T
Marymount College B, T
Mercy College B
Molloy College B
Monroe Community College A
Mount St. Mary College B, T
Nassau Community College A
Nazareth College of Rochester B
New York Institute of Technology B
New York University B, M, D
Niagara University B
Nyack College B
Orange County Community College A
Pace University:
   Pleasantville/Briarcliff B, T
Pace University B, T
Polytechnic University B, M, D
Regents College B
Rensselaer Polytechnic Institute B, M, D
Roberts Wesleyan College B
Russell Sage College B, T
Sage Junior College of Albany A
St. Bonaventure University B, T
St. Francis College B, T
St. John Fisher College B
St. John's University B, M
St. Lawrence University B, T
St. Thomas Aquinas College B, T
Sarah Lawrence College B
Siena College B, T
Skidmore College B
St. Joseph's College
   St. Joseph's College: Suffolk Campus B, T
   St. Joseph's College B
State University of New York
   Albany B, M, D
   Binghamton B, M, D
   Buffalo B, M, D
   College at Brockport B, M, T
   College at Buffalo B
   College at Cortland B
   College at Fredonia B, T
   College at Geneseo B, T
   College at Old Westbury B, T
   College at Oneonta B
   College at Plattsburgh B
   College at Potsdam B, M, T
   College of Agriculture and Technology at Cobleskill A
   College of Agriculture and Technology at Morrisville A
   College of Technology at Alfred A
   New Paltz B, M, T
   Oswego B
   Purchase B
   Stony Brook B, M, D, T
Suffolk County Community College A
Syracuse University B, M, D
Touro College B
Ulster County Community College A
Union College B
United States Military Academy B
University of Rochester B, M, D
Utica College of Syracuse University B
Vassar College B
Wagner College B, T
Wells College B

North Carolina
Appalachian State University B, M
Barber-Scotia College B
Barton College B
Bennett College B
Brevard College A, B
Caldwell Community College and Technical Institute A
Campbell University B
Catawba College B, T
Chowan College B
Davidson College B
Duke University B
East Carolina University B, M
Elizabeth City State University B
Elon College B, T
Fayetteville State University B
Gardner-Webb University B
Greensboro College B, T
Guilford College B
Guilford Technical Community College A
High Point University B
Johnson C. Smith University B
Lees-McRae College B, T
Lenoir Community College A
Lenoir-Rhyne College B, T
Louisburg College A
Mars Hill College B, T
Meredith College B, T
Methodist College B
Montreat College B
North Carolina Agricultural and Technical State University B, M, T
North Carolina Central University B, M
North Carolina State University B, M, D
North Carolina Wesleyan College B
Pfeiffer University B
Queens College B
St. Andrews Presbyterian College B
St. Augustine's College B
Salem College B
Sandhills Community College A
Shaw University B
University of North Carolina
   Asheville B, T
   Chapel Hill B, M, D, T
   Charlotte B, M, T
   Greensboro B, M, T
   Pembroke B
   Wilmington B, M, T
Wake Forest University B, M
Warren Wilson College B
Western Carolina University B
Wingate University B
Winston-Salem State University B

North Dakota
Dickinson State University B, T
Jamestown College B
Mayville State University B, T
Minot State University: Bottineau Campus A
Minot State University B, T
North Dakota State University B, M, D, T
University of Mary B, T
University of North Dakota B, M, T
Valley City State University B

Ohio
Antioch College B
Ashland University B
Baldwin-Wallace College B, T
Bluffton College B
Bowling Green State University B, M, D
Capital University B
Case Western Reserve University B, M, D
Cedarville College B, T
Central State University B
Cleveland State University B, M, T
College of Mount St. Joseph B, T
College of Wooster B
Defiance College B, T
Denison University B
Franciscan University of Steubenville B
Heidelberg College B
Hiram College B, T
Jefferson Community College A
John Carroll University B, M, T
Kent State University
   Stark Campus B
Kent State University B, M, D, T
Kenyon College B
Lake Erie College B
Lorain County Community College A
Malone College B
Marietta College B
Miami University
   Middletown Campus A
   Oxford Campus B, M, T
Mount Union College B
Mount Vernon Nazarene College B, T
Muskingum College B
Notre Dame College of Ohio B, T
Oberlin College B
Ohio Dominican College B, T
Ohio Northern University B
Ohio State University
   Columbus Campus B, M, D
Ohio University B, M, D
Ohio Wesleyan University B
Otterbein College B
Owens Community College
   Toledo A
Shawnee State University B
University of Akron B, M
University of Cincinnati B, M, D, T
University of Dayton B
University of Findlay B, T
University of Rio Grande B, T
University of Toledo B, M, D
Ursuline College B
Walsh University B
Washington State Community College A
Wilberforce University B
Wilmington College B
Wittenberg University B
Wright State University B, M

Xavier University *B*
Youngstown State University *B, M*

Oklahoma
Cameron University *B*
Carl Albert State College *A*
Connors State College *A*
East Central University *B, T*
Eastern Oklahoma State College *A*
Langston University *B*
Murray State College *A*
Northeastern Oklahoma Agricultural and Mechanical College *A*
Northeastern State University *B*
Northwestern Oklahoma State University *B*
Oklahoma Baptist University *B, T*
Oklahoma Christian University of Science and Arts *B, T*
Oklahoma City Community College *A*
Oklahoma City University *B*
Oklahoma Panhandle State University *B*
Oklahoma State University *B, M, D*
Oral Roberts University *B*
Redlands Community College *A*
Rogers State University *A*
Rose State College *A*
St. Gregory's University *A, B*
Seminole State College *A*
Southeastern Oklahoma State University *B*
Southern Nazarene University *B*
Southwestern Oklahoma State University *B*
Tulsa Community College *A*
University of Central Oklahoma *B*
University of Oklahoma *B, M, D*
University of Science and Arts of Oklahoma *B, T*
Western Oklahoma State College *A*

Oregon
Central Oregon Community College *A*
Chemeketa Community College *A*
Eastern Oregon University *B, T*
George Fox University *B, T*
Lewis & Clark College *B*
Linfield College *B*
Linn-Benton Community College *A*
Oregon State University *B, M, D*
Pacific University *B*
Portland State University *B, D*
Reed College *B*
Southern Oregon University *B, T*
University of Oregon *B, M, D*
University of Portland *B, T*
Western Baptist College *B*
Western Oregon University *B*
Willamette University *B*

Pennsylvania
Albright College *B, T*
Allegheny College *B*
Allentown College of St. Francis de Sales *B*
Alvernia College *B*
Beaver College *B*
Bloomsburg University of Pennsylvania *B, T*
Bryn Mawr College *B, M, D*
Bucknell University *B, M*
Bucks County Community College *A*
Butler County Community College *A*
Cabrini College *B*
California University of Pennsylvania *B*
Carlow College *B*
Carnegie Mellon University *B*
Cedar Crest College *B*
Chatham College *B*
Chestnut Hill College *B*
Cheyney University of Pennsylvania *B*
Clarion University of Pennsylvania *B, T*
College Misericordia *B*
Community College of Allegheny County *A*
Community College of Philadelphia *A*
Delaware Valley College *B*
Dickinson College *B*
Drexel University *B, M, D*
Duquesne University *B*
East Stroudsburg University of Pennsylvania *B*
Eastern College *B*
Edinboro University of Pennsylvania *B, T*
Elizabethtown College *B*
Franklin and Marshall College *B*
Gannon University *B*
Gettysburg College *B*
Grove City College *B*
Gwynedd-Mercy College *B*
Harrisburg Area Community College *A*
Haverford College *B, T*
Holy Family College *B, T*
Immaculata College *B*
Indiana University of Pennsylvania *B, M*
Juniata College *B*
King's College *B, T*
Kutztown University of Pennsylvania *B, M, T*
La Salle University *B, T*
Lafayette College *B*
Lebanon Valley College of Pennsylvania *B, T*
Lehigh Carbon Community College *A*
Lehigh University *B, M, D*
Lincoln University *B, M*
Lock Haven University of Pennsylvania *B*
Luzerne County Community College *A*
Lycoming College *B*
Mansfield University of Pennsylvania *B, T*
Marywood University *B*
Mercyhurst College *B*
Messiah College *B*
Millersville University of Pennsylvania *B, M, T*
Montgomery County Community College *A*
Moravian College *B, T*
Mount Aloysius College *A, B*
Muhlenberg College *B, T*
Northampton County Area Community College *A*
Penn State
    Erie, The Behrend College *B*
    Harrisburg *B*
    University Park *B, M, D*
Rosemont College *B*
St. Francis College *B*
St. Joseph's University *B*
St. Vincent College *B*
Seton Hill College *B, T*
Shippensburg University of Pennsylvania *B, M, T*
Slippery Rock University of Pennsylvania *B, T*
Susquehanna University *B, T*
Swarthmore College *B*
Temple University *B, M, D*
Thiel College *B*
University of Pennsylvania *A, B, M, D*
University of Pittsburgh
    Bradford *B, T*
    Johnstown *B*
University of Pittsburgh *B, M, D*
University of Scranton *A, B, T*
Ursinus College *B, T*
Villanova University *B, M*
Washington and Jefferson College *B*
Waynesburg College *B*
West Chester University of Pennsylvania *B, M*
Westminster College *B*
Widener University *B*
Wilkes University *B, M*
Wilson College *B*
York College of Pennsylvania *B, T*

Puerto Rico
Inter American University of Puerto Rico
    Bayamon Campus *B*
    Metropolitan Campus *B*
    San German Campus *B*
Pontifical Catholic University of Puerto Rico *B*
University of Puerto Rico
    Cayey University College *B*
    Mayaguez Campus *B*
    Ponce University College *B*
    Rio Piedras Campus *B, M*
University of the Sacred Heart *B*

Rhode Island
Brown University *B, M, D*
Providence College *B, T*
Rhode Island College *B, M*
Roger Williams University *A, B*
University of Rhode Island *B, M, D*

South Carolina
Benedict College *B*
Charleston Southern University *B*
Claflin University *B*
Clemson University *B, M, D*
Coker College *B*
College of Charleston *B, M, T*
Columbia College *B*
Converse College *B*
Erskine College *B, T*
Francis Marion University *B*
Furman University *B, T*
Lander University *B, T*
Limestone College *B*
Morris College *B*
Newberry College *B, T*
Presbyterian College *B, T*
South Carolina State University *B*
Southern Wesleyan University *B, T*
The Citadel *B*
University of South Carolina Spartanburg *B*
University of South Carolina *B, M, D*
Voorhees College *B*
Winthrop University *B, M*
Wofford College *B, T*

South Dakota
Augustana College *B, T*
Black Hills State University *B*
Dakota State University *B*
Dakota Wesleyan University *B*
Mount Marty College *B*
Northern State University *B*
South Dakota School of Mines and Technology *B*
South Dakota State University *B, M*
University of South Dakota *B, M*

Tennessee
Austin Peay State University *B*
Belmont University *B, T*
Bethel College *B*
Carson-Newman College *B, T*
Christian Brothers University *B*
Columbia State Community College *A*
Cumberland University *A, B*
David Lipscomb University *B*
Dyersburg State Community College *A*
East Tennessee State University *B, M, T*
Fisk University *B*
Freed-Hardeman University *B, T*
King College *B, T*
Lambuth University *B*
Lane College *B*
LeMoyne-Owen College *B*
Lee University *B*
Lincoln Memorial University *B, T*
Maryville College *B, T*
Middle Tennessee State University *B, M*
Milligan College *B, T*
Rhodes College *B, T*
Roane State Community College *A*
Southern Adventist University *B*
Tennessee State University *B, M*
Tennessee Technological University *B, M, T*
Tennessee Temple University *B*
Tennessee Wesleyan College *B, T*
Trevecca Nazarene University *B*
Union University *B, T*
University of Memphis *B, M, D*
University of Tennessee
    Chattanooga *B, T*
    Knoxville *B, M, D*
    Martin *B*
University of the South *B*
Vanderbilt University *B, M, D*
Walters State Community College *A*

Texas
Abilene Christian University *B*
Alvin Community College *A*
Amarillo College *A*
Angelina College *A*
Angelo State University *B, M, T*
Austin College *B*
Austin Community College *A*
Baylor University *B, M*
Blinn College *A*
Brazosport College *A*
Cedar Valley College *A*
Central Texas College *A*
Coastal Bend College *A*
College of the Mainland *A*
Concordia University at Austin *T*
Dallas Baptist University *B*
Del Mar College *A*
East Texas Baptist University *B*
El Paso Community College *A*
Galveston College *A*
Grayson County College *A*
Hardin-Simmons University *B*
Hill College *A*
Houston Baptist University *B*
Howard College *A*
Howard Payne University *B, T*
Huston-Tillotson College *B*
Jarvis Christian College *B*
Kilgore College *A*
Lamar State College at Orange *A*
Lamar University *B, M*
LeTourneau University *B*
Lee College *A*
Lon Morris College *A*
Lubbock Christian University *B*
McMurry University *B, T*
Midland College *A*
Midwestern State University *B*
Navarro College *A*
Northeast Texas Community College *A*
Odessa College *A*
Our Lady of the Lake University of San Antonio *B*
Panola College *A*
Paris Junior College *A*
Prairie View A&M University *B, M*
Rice University *B, M, D*
St. Edward's University *B, T*
St. Mary's University *B*
St. Philip's College *A*
Sam Houston State University *B, M*
San Jacinto College
    North *A*
Schreiner College *B, T*
Southern Methodist University *B, M, D*
Southwest Texas State University *B, M, T*
Southwestern Adventist University *B, T*
Southwestern University *B, T*
Stephen F. Austin State University *B, M, T*
Sul Ross State University *B*
Tarleton State University *B, M, T*
Texas A&M International University *B, M*

Mathematics

Texas A&M University
  Commerce *B, M*
  Corpus Christi *B, M, T*
  Kingsville *B, M, T*
  Texarkana *B, T*
Texas A&M University *B, M, D*
Texas Christian University *B, M, T*
Texas College *B*
Texas Lutheran University *B*
Texas Southern University *B*
Texas Tech University *B, M, D*
Texas Wesleyan University *B*
Texas Woman's University *B, M, T*
Trinity University *B*
Trinity Valley Community College *A*
Tyler Junior College *A*
University of Dallas *B*
University of Houston
  Clear Lake *B, M*
  Victoria *B, T*
University of Houston *B, M, D*
University of Mary Hardin-Baylor *B, T*
University of North Texas *B, M, D*
University of St. Thomas *B*
University of Texas
  Arlington *B, M*
  Austin *B, M, D*
  Brownsville *B*
  Dallas *B, M*
  El Paso *B, M*
  Pan American *B, M, T*
  San Antonio *B, M*
  Tyler *B, M*
  of the Permian Basin *B*
University of the Incarnate Word *B, M*
Wayland Baptist University *B*
West Texas A&M University *B, M*
Western Texas College *A*
Wharton County Junior College *A*
Wiley College *B*

Utah
Brigham Young University *B, M, D*
Dixie State College of Utah *A*
Snow College *A*
Southern Utah University *B, T*
University of Utah *B, M, D*
Utah State University *B, M*
Weber State University *B*
Westminster College *B*

Vermont
Bennington College *B*
Castleton State College *B*
Johnson State College *B*
Lyndon State College *B*
Marlboro College *B*
Middlebury College *B*
Norwich University *B*
St. Michael's College *B*
University of Vermont *B, M, D*

Virginia
Averett College *B, T*
Bluefield College *B*
Bridgewater College *B*
Christopher Newport University *B*
College of William and Mary *B*
Eastern Mennonite University *B*
Emory & Henry College *B, T*
Ferrum College *B*
George Mason University *B, M*
Hampden-Sydney College *B*
Hampton University *B, M*
Hollins University *B*
James Madison University *B, T*
Liberty University *B, T*
Longwood College *B, T*
Lynchburg College *B*
Mary Baldwin College *B*
Mary Washington College *B*
Mountain Empire Community College *A*
Norfolk State University *B, T*
Northern Virginia Community College *A*
Old Dominion University *B, M*
Piedmont Virginia Community
  College *A*
Radford University *B*
Randolph-Macon College *B*
Randolph-Macon Woman's College *B*
Roanoke College *B, T*
St. Paul's College *B*
Shenandoah University *B*
Sweet Briar College *B*
University of Richmond *B, T*
University of Virginia's College at
  Wise *B, T*
University of Virginia *B, M, D*
Virginia Commonwealth
  University *C, B, M*
Virginia Military Institute *B*
Virginia Polytechnic Institute and State
  University *B, M, D, T*
Virginia State University *B, M*
Virginia Union University *B*
Virginia Wesleyan College *B*
Washington and Lee University *B*

Washington
Central Washington University *B*
Centralia College *A*
Eastern Washington University *B, M, T*
Everett Community College *A*
Evergreen State College *B*
Gonzaga University *B*
Heritage College *B*
Highline Community College *A*
Lower Columbia College *A*
North Seattle Community College *C*
Pacific Lutheran University *B*
St. Martin's College *B*
Seattle Pacific University *B, T*
Seattle University *B*
University of Puget Sound *B, T*
University of Washington *B, M, D*
Walla Walla College *B*
Washington State University *B, M, D*
Western Washington University *B, M, T*
Whitman College *B*
Whitworth College *B, T*

West Virginia
Bethany College *B*
Concord College *B*
Davis and Elkins College *B*
Fairmont State College *B*
Marshall University *B, M*
Potomac State College of West Virginia
  University *A*
Salem-Teikyo University *B*
Shepherd College *B*
West Liberty State College *B*
West Virginia State College *B*
West Virginia University Institute of
  Technology *B*
West Virginia University *B, M, D, T*
West Virginia Wesleyan College *B*
Wheeling Jesuit University *B*

Wisconsin
Alverno College *B, T*
Beloit College *B*
Cardinal Stritch University *B*
Carroll College *B*
Carthage College *B, T*
Concordia University Wisconsin *B, T*
Lakeland College *B*
Lawrence University *B*
Marian College of Fond du Lac *B*
Marquette University *B, M, D, T*
Mount Mary College *B*
Mount Senario College *B, T*
Northland College *B*
Ripon College *B, T*
St. Norbert College *B, T*
Silver Lake College *B, T*
University of Wisconsin
  Eau Claire *B, M*
  Green Bay *B*
  La Crosse *B*
  Madison *B, M, D*
  Milwaukee *B, M, D*
  Oshkosh *B*
  Parkside *B*
  Platteville *B, T*
  River Falls *B*
  Stevens Point *B, T*
  Superior *B, T*
  Whitewater *B, T*
Viterbo University *B, T*
Wisconsin Lutheran College *B*

Wyoming
Casper College *A*
Eastern Wyoming College *A*
Laramie County Community College *A*
Northwest College *A*
Sheridan College *A*
University of Wyoming *B, M, D*
Western Wyoming Community
  College *A*

Mathematics education

Alabama
Alabama Agricultural and Mechanical
  University *B, M*
Athens State University *B*
Auburn University *B*
Birmingham-Southern College *T*
Faulkner University *B, T*
Huntingdon College *T*
Jacksonville State University *B, M, T*
Oakwood College *B*
Talladega College *T*
Troy State University
  Dothan *B, M*
Tuskegee University *B, M*
University of Alabama *B*
University of Mobile *B, T*

Alaska
University of Alaska
  Fairbanks *M*

Arizona
Arizona State University *B, T*
Grand Canyon University *B*
Northern Arizona University *B, M, T*
Prescott College *B, M*
University of Arizona *B, M*

Arkansas
Arkansas State University *B, M, T*
Arkansas Tech University *B, M*
Harding University *B, M, T*
Henderson State University *B, M, T*
John Brown University *B, T*
Ouachita Baptist University *B, T*
Philander Smith College *B*
Southern Arkansas University *B, T*
University of Arkansas
  Pine Bluff *B, M, T*
University of Arkansas *M*
University of Central Arkansas *M, T*
University of the Ozarks *B, T*

California
Azusa Pacific University *T*
California Baptist University *B, T*
California Lutheran University *B, T*
California State Polytechnic University:
  Pomona *T*
California State University
  Bakersfield *B, T*
  Chico *T*
  Dominguez Hills *M, T*
  Fullerton *T*
  Hayward *B, M*
  Long Beach *T*
  Northridge *B, T*
  Sacramento *T*
Concordia University *B, T*
Cuesta College *C, A*
Fresno Pacific University *B, M, T*
Humboldt State University *T*
Los Angeles Southwest College *A*
Loyola Marymount University *M*
Master's College *T*
Mills College *T*
Mount St. Mary's College *T*
Occidental College *T*
Pacific Union College *T*
Saddleback College *A*
San Diego State University *B*
San Francisco State University *B, M, T*
San Jose State University *T*
Sonoma State University *T*
University of California
  Berkeley *D*
University of the Pacific *T*
Westmont College *T*

Colorado
Adams State College *B, T*
Colorado Christian University *B*
Colorado College *M*
Colorado State University *T*
Fort Lewis College *T*
Metropolitan State College of Denver *T*
University of Colorado
  Boulder *T*
  Colorado Springs *T*
University of Denver *B*
University of Northern Colorado *D, T*
University of Southern Colorado *T*
Western State College of Colorado *T*

Connecticut
Central Connecticut State
  University *B, M*
Fairfield University *T*
Quinnipiac University *B, M*
Sacred Heart University *B, M, T*
St. Joseph College *T*
Southern Connecticut State
  University *B, M, T*

Delaware
Delaware State University *B*
University of Delaware *B, T*

District of Columbia
American University *B, D*
Catholic University of America *B*
George Washington University *M, T*
University of the District of Columbia *M*

Florida
Barry University *T*
Bethune-Cookman College *B, T*
Broward Community College *A*
Edward Waters College *B*
Florida Agricultural and Mechanical
  University *B, M, T*
Florida Atlantic University *B*
Florida Institute of
  Technology *B, M, D, T*
Florida International University *B, M, T*
Florida State University *B, M, D, T*
Gulf Coast Community College *A*
Hobe Sound Bible College *B, T*
Nova Southeastern University *M*
Pensacola Junior College *A*
Southeastern College of the Assemblies
  of God *T*
Stetson University *B, T*
University of Central Florida *B, M*
University of Florida *M*
University of North Florida *B, M*
University of South Florida *B, M*
University of West Florida *B, M, T*

Georgia
Agnes Scott College *T*
Armstrong Atlantic State
  University *B, M, T*
Clark Atlanta University *B*
Columbus State University *B, M*

Covenant College B, T
Fort Valley State University B, T
Gainesville College A
Georgia College and State
 University M, T
Georgia Southern University B, M, T
Georgia Southwestern State
 University B, M
Georgia State University M, D
Kennesaw State University B
LaGrange College T
Mercer University M, T
North Georgia College & State
 University B, M
Piedmont College B, T
Shorter College B, T
University of Georgia B, M, D, T
Valdosta State University M, T
Wesleyan College M, T

Hawaii
Brigham Young University
 Hawaii B, T
University of Hawaii
 Manoa B, T

Idaho
Albertson College of Idaho B
Boise State University T
Lewis-Clark State College B, T
Northwest Nazarene University B
University of Idaho M

Illinois
Augustana College B, T
Barat College B
Blackburn College B, T
Chicago State University B
Concordia University M
De Paul University M
Dominican University T
Eastern Illinois University M
Elmhurst College B
Eureka College T
Greenville College B, T
Illinois College T
Illinois State University D
Judson College B, T
Lake Land College A
Lewis University T
Loyola University of Chicago T
MacMurray College B
McKendree College B, T
National-Louis University M
North Central College B, T
North Park University T
Northeastern Illinois University M
Northwestern University B, T
Olivet Nazarene University B, T
Quincy University T
Rockford College T
Roosevelt University B
St. Xavier University B, M, T
Trinity Christian College B, T
Trinity International University B, T
University of Illinois
 Chicago B, M
 Urbana-Champaign B, M, T
Wheaton College T

Indiana
Anderson University B, T
Ball State University T
Bethel College B
Butler University T
Franklin College B, T
Goshen College B
Grace College B
Indiana State University B, M, T
Indiana University
 Bloomington B, T
 Northwest B
 South Bend B, T
 Southeast B

Indiana University--Purdue University
 Indiana University-Purdue
  University Fort Wayne T
Indiana Wesleyan University B, T
Manchester College B, T
Oakland City University B
St. Mary-of-the-Woods College B
Taylor University B
Tri-State University B, T
University of Evansville T
University of Indianapolis B, T
University of Southern Indiana B, T
Valparaiso University B
Vincennes University A

Iowa
Buena Vista University B, T
Central College T
Clarke College B, T
Cornell College B, T
Dordt College B
Drake University M, T
Graceland University T
Grand View College B, T
Iowa State University M, T
Iowa Wesleyan College B
Loras College T
Luther College B
Morningside College B
Northwestern College T
St. Ambrose University B, T
University of Iowa B, M, D, T
University of Northern Iowa M
Wartburg College B
William Penn University B

Kansas
Allen County Community College A
Baker University T
Benedictine College T
Bethany College B
Bethel College T
Colby Community College A
Emporia State University B
Fort Hays State University M
Garden City Community College A
Independence Community College A
McPherson College B, T
MidAmerica Nazarene University B, T
Newman University T
Ottawa University B, T
Pittsburg State University B
St. Mary College T
Southwestern College B, T
Tabor College B, T
University of Kansas B, T
Washburn University of Topeka B

Kentucky
Campbellsville University B
Cumberland College B, T
Kentucky Christian College B
Kentucky State University B
Murray State University B, M, T
Pikeville College B, T
Thomas More College B
Transylvania University B, T
Union College B
Western Kentucky University M

Louisiana
Centenary College of Louisiana B, T
Dillard University B
Louisiana State University
 Shreveport B
Loyola University New Orleans M
McNeese State University T
Nicholls State University B
Northwestern State University B, T
Our Lady of Holy Cross College B
Southeastern Louisiana University B
Southern University and Agricultural and
 Mechanical College B
University of Louisiana at Monroe B
University of New Orleans B
Xavier University of Louisiana B, M, T

Maine
St. Joseph's College B
Thomas College B
University of Maine
 Farmington B
 Presque Isle B
University of New England T
University of Southern Maine T

Maryland
College of Notre Dame of Maryland T
Columbia Union College B
Frederick Community College A
Frostburg State University B, T
Montgomery College
 Germantown Campus A
Morgan State University D
Prince George's Community College A
Salisbury State University B
Towson University M
University of Maryland
 College Park B
 Eastern Shore B

Massachusetts
American International College T
Assumption College T
Boston University B, M, T
Bridgewater State College M, T
Elms College M, T
Fitchburg State College B, M, T
Framingham State College B, M, T
Harvard College T
Merrimack College T
Northeastern University B, M
Salem State College M
Springfield College T
Tufts University M, T
University of Massachusetts
 Dartmouth T
Western New England College T
Westfield State College T
Worcester State College T

Michigan
Albion College B, T
Alma College T
Calvin College B
Central Michigan University B, M
Concordia College B, T
Eastern Michigan University B, T
Ferris State University B
Grand Valley State University T
Lansing Community College A
Michigan State University D
Michigan Technological University T
Northern Michigan University M
Saginaw Valley State University T
University of Detroit Mercy M
University of Michigan
 Dearborn B
Wayne State University B, M, T
Western Michigan University M, D

Minnesota
Augsburg College T
Bemidji State University M, T
Bethel College B
College of St. Benedict T
College of St. Catherine: St. Paul
 Campus B, T
College of St. Scholastica T
Concordia College: Moorhead T
Concordia University: St. Paul B, T
Gustavus Adolphus College T
Minnesota State University,
 Mankato B, M, T
Moorhead State University B, T
Northland Community & Technical
 College A
Northwestern College B
St. Cloud State University M, T
St. John's University T
St. Mary's University of Minnesota B
St. Olaf College T
Southwest State University B, T

University of Minnesota
 Duluth B
 Morris T
 Twin Cities B, M, T
University of St. Thomas T
Winona State University B, T

Mississippi
Blue Mountain College B
Coahoma Community College A
Delta State University B, M
Jackson State University M
Mary Holmes College A
Mississippi College M
Mississippi Gulf Coast Community
 College
 Jefferson Davis Campus A
 Perkinston A
Mississippi State University T
Mississippi Valley State University B, T
Northwest Mississippi Community
 College A
Rust College B
University of Mississippi B, T

Missouri
Avila College T
Central Missouri State
 University B, M, T
College of the Ozarks B, T
Columbia College T
Culver-Stockton College T
Evangel University B
Fontbonne College B
Hannibal-LaGrange College B
Harris Stowe State College T
Lincoln University B, T
Lindenwood University B
Maryville University of Saint
 Louis B, M, T
Missouri Baptist College T
Missouri Southern State College B, T
Missouri Valley College T
Missouri Western State College T
Northwest Missouri State
 University B, M, T
Park University T
Rockhurst University B
Southeast Missouri State University B
Southwest Baptist University T
Southwest Missouri State University B
Truman State University M, T
University of Missouri
 Columbia B, M, D
 St. Louis T
Washington University B, M, T
Webster University M
William Jewell College T
William Woods University B, T

Montana
Montana State University
 Billings B, T
 Bozeman T
 Northern B, T
Rocky Mountain College B, T
University of Great Falls B, T
University of Montana-Missoula T
Western Montana College of The
 University of Montana B, T

Nebraska
Chadron State College M
College of Saint Mary B, T
Concordia University T
Creighton University T
Dana College B
Doane College T
Hastings College B, M, T
Mid Plains Community College Area A
Midland Lutheran College B, T
Peru State College B, T
Union College T

University of Nebraska
    Kearney *B, M, T*
    Lincoln *B, M, T*
    Omaha *M*

Nevada

University of Nevada
    Reno *B*

New Hampshire

Franklin Pierce College *T*
Keene State College *B, T*
Plymouth State College of the University System of New Hampshire *B, M, T*
Rivier College *B, T*
St. Anselm College *T*
University of New Hampshire *B, D, T*

New Jersey

Caldwell College *T*
Centenary College *T*
College of St. Elizabeth *T*
Fairleigh Dickinson University *M*
Kean University *M*
Monmouth University *B, T*
Richard Stockton College of New Jersey *B*
Rider University *B, T*
Rowan University *M, T*
Rutgers
    The State University of New Jersey: Douglass College *T*
    The State University of New Jersey: Livingston College *T*
    The State University of New Jersey: New Brunswick Graduate Campus *M, D, T*
    The State University of New Jersey: Rutgers College *T*
    The State University of New Jersey: University College New Brunswick *T*
St. Peter's College *T*
The College of New Jersey *B, T*

New Mexico

College of the Southwest *B, T*
New Mexico Highlands University *B*
New Mexico Institute of Mining and Technology *B*
Western New Mexico University *B*

New York

Adelphi University *B, M*
Alfred University *M, T*
Bank Street College of Education *M*
Canisius College *B, M, T*
City University of New York
    Brooklyn College *B, M*
    City College *B*
    College of Staten Island *M*
    Hunter College *B, M*
    Lehman College *B, M*
    Queens College *M, T*
    York College *T*
Colgate University *M*
College of St. Rose *B, T*
Columbia University
    Teachers College *M, D*
D'Youville College *M, T*
Dowling College *B*
Elmira College *B, T*
Fordham University *T*
Hofstra University *B, M, T*
Houghton College *B, T*
Ithaca College *B, T*
Keuka College *B, T*
Le Moyne College *T*
Long Island University
    C. W. Post Campus *B, M, T*
Manhattan College *B, T*
Manhattanville College *M, T*
Marist College *B, T*
Marymount College *B, T*
Molloy College *B*
Nazareth College of Rochester *T*
New York Institute of Technology *B, T*
New York University *B, M, D, T*
Niagara University *B, T*
Pace University:
    Pleasantville/Briarcliff *B, M, T*
Pace University *B, M, T*
Rensselaer Polytechnic Institute *B, T*
Roberts Wesleyan College *B, T*
St. Francis College *B, T*
St. John Fisher College *B, T*
St. John's University *B, M, T*
St. Thomas Aquinas College *B, T*
Siena College *T*
St. Joseph's College
    St. Joseph's College *B, T*
State University of New York
    Albany *B, M, T*
    Binghamton *M*
    Buffalo *M, D, T*
    College at Brockport *M*
    College at Buffalo *B, M, T*
    College at Cortland *B, M, T*
    College at Fredonia *B, M, T*
    College at Geneseo *B, M, T*
    College at Old Westbury *B*
    College at Oneonta *B, M, T*
    College at Plattsburgh *B, M*
    College at Potsdam *B, M, T*
    New Paltz *B, M, T*
    Oswego *B, M*
Syracuse University *B, M, D, T*
Utica College of Syracuse University *B*
Vassar College *T*
Wells College *T*

North Carolina

Appalachian State University *B, T*
Barton College *T*
Belmont Abbey College *T*
Bennett College *B, T*
Campbell University *B, T*
Catawba College *T*
Chowan College *B, T*
Davidson College *T*
East Carolina University *B, M*
Elizabeth City State University *B, T*
Elon College *B, T*
Fayetteville State University *B, T*
Gardner-Webb University *B*
Greensboro College *B, T*
Johnson C. Smith University *B*
Lees-McRae College *T*
Lenoir-Rhyne College *B, T*
Louisburg College *A*
Mars Hill College *T*
Meredith College *T*
Methodist College *A, B, T*
North Carolina Agricultural and Technical State University *B, M, T*
North Carolina Central University *B, M*
North Carolina State University *M, D, T*
Queens College *T*
St. Augustine's College *B, T*
Sandhills Community College *A*
Shaw University *B, T*
University of North Carolina
    Chapel Hill *B, M, T*
    Charlotte *B, M*
    Greensboro *B, M, T*
    Pembroke *B, M, T*
    Wilmington *T*
Wake Forest University *M, T*
Western Carolina University *B, M, T*
Wingate University *B, T*
Winston-Salem State University *B*

North Dakota

Dickinson State University *B, T*
Jamestown College *B*
Mayville State University *B, T*
Minot State University *B, M*
North Dakota State University *B, T*
University of Mary *B*
University of North Dakota *B, T*
Valley City State University *B, T*

Ohio

Ashland University *B, T*
Baldwin-Wallace College *T*
Bluffton College *B*
Bowling Green State University *B, M*
Capital University *T*
Case Western Reserve University *T*
Cedarville College *B, T*
Central State University *B*
College of Mount St. Joseph *T*
Defiance College *B, T*
Hiram College *T*
John Carroll University *M*
Kent State University
    Stark Campus *B*
Kent State University *B, M, D, T*
Malone College *T*
Miami University
    Oxford Campus *B, M, T*
Mount Union College *T*
Mount Vernon Nazarene College *B, T*
Ohio Dominican College *D*
Ohio Northern University *T*
Ohio State University
    Columbus Campus *M, D*
Ohio University *B, M, D, T*
Otterbein College *B*
Shawnee State University *B, T*
University of Akron *M*
University of Dayton *B, M, T*
University of Findlay *B, T*
University of Rio Grande *B, T*
University of Toledo *T*
Ursuline College *B, T*
Walsh University *B*
Wilmington College *B*
Wittenberg University *B*
Wright State University *B, M, T*
Xavier University *M, T*
Youngstown State University *B, M*

Oklahoma

Cameron University *B, T*
East Central University *B, T*
Eastern Oklahoma State College *A*
Langston University *B*
Northeastern Oklahoma Agricultural and Mechanical College *A*
Northeastern State University *B*
Northwestern Oklahoma State University *B, T*
Oklahoma Baptist University *B, T*
Oklahoma Christian University of Science and Arts *B, T*
Oklahoma City University *B*
Oklahoma State University *M, D*
Oral Roberts University *B, T*
Rogers State University *A*
Southeastern Oklahoma State University *B, M, T*
Southern Nazarene University *B*
Southwestern Oklahoma State University *B, M, T*
University of Central Oklahoma *B*
University of Oklahoma *B, T*
University of Tulsa *B, T*

Oregon

Concordia University *B, M, T*
George Fox University *B, M, T*
Linfield College *T*
Oregon State University *M, D*
Portland State University *D, T*
Southern Oregon University *T*
University of Portland *T*
Western Baptist College *B*
Western Oregon University *T*

Pennsylvania

Allentown College of St. Francis de Sales *M, T*
Alvernia College *B*
Beaver College *B, M, T*
Bucknell University *T*
Cabrini College *B, T*
California University of Pennsylvania *B, T*
Carlow College *T*
Carnegie Mellon University *T*
Chatham College *M, T*
Chestnut Hill College *T*
Cheyney University of Pennsylvania *T*
Clarion University of Pennsylvania *T*
College Misericordia *B, T*
Delaware Valley College *T*
Dickinson College *T*
Duquesne University *B, M, T*
East Stroudsburg University of Pennsylvania *B, T*
Elizabethtown College *T*
Gannon University *T*
Geneva College *B, T*
Gettysburg College *T*
Grove City College *B, T*
Gwynedd-Mercy College *T*
Holy Family College *B, M, T*
Immaculata College *T*
Indiana University of Pennsylvania *B, M, T*
Juniata College *B, T*
King's College *T*
La Roche College *B*
La Salle University *B, T*
Lebanon Valley College of Pennsylvania *T*
Lincoln University *B, T*
Lock Haven University of Pennsylvania *B, T*
Lycoming College *T*
Mansfield University of Pennsylvania *T*
Marywood University *T*
Mercyhurst College *B*
Messiah College *T*
Millersville University of Pennsylvania *B, M, T*
Moravian College *T*
Penn State
    Harrisburg *B*
Philadelphia College of Bible *B, T*
Point Park College *B*
St. Joseph's University *B*
St. Vincent College *T*
Seton Hill College *B, T*
Shippensburg University of Pennsylvania *T*
Temple University *B, M, T*
Thiel College *B*
University of Pennsylvania *M*
University of Pittsburgh
    Bradford *B*
    Johnstown *B, T*
University of Pittsburgh *T*
Villanova University *T*
Washington and Jefferson College *T*
Waynesburg College *B, T*
West Chester University of Pennsylvania *B, M, T*
Westminster College *T*
Widener University *T*
Wilkes University *M, T*
Wilson College *T*
York College of Pennsylvania *B, T*

Puerto Rico

American University of Puerto Rico *B, T*
Bayamon Central University *B*
Caribbean University *B, T*
Inter American University of Puerto Rico
    Barranquitas Campus *B*
    Metropolitan Campus *B*
Pontifical Catholic University of Puerto Rico *B, T*
Turabo University *B*
Universidad Metropolitana *B*

Rhode Island

Providence College *B*
Rhode Island College *B, M*
Salve Regina University *B*

South Carolina
Coker College B, T
Columbia College B
Furman University T
Lander University B, T
Limestone College B
Morris College B, T
South Carolina State University B, T
The Citadel M
University of South Carolina
  Aiken B, T
Voorhees College B
Wofford College T

South Dakota
Augustana College B, T
Black Hills State University B, T
Dakota State University B, T
Dakota Wesleyan University B, T
Mount Marty College B
Northern State University B, M, T
South Dakota State University B
University of South Dakota B, T

Tennessee
Belmont University T
Christian Brothers University B, M, T
David Lipscomb University B, T
Freed-Hardeman University T
Lambuth University T
Lee University B
Lincoln Memorial University B, T
Maryville College B, T
Middle Tennessee State University M, T
Southern Adventist University B
Tennessee Technological University T
Tennessee Temple University B
Trevecca Nazarene University B, T
Tusculum College B, T
Union University B, T
University of Tennessee
  Chattanooga B, T
  Martin B, T
Vanderbilt University M, D

Texas
Abilene Christian University B, T
Baylor University B, T
Del Mar College A
East Texas Baptist University B
Hardin-Simmons University B, T
Houston Baptist University M, T
Howard Payne University T
Lamar University T
LeTourneau University B
Lubbock Christian University B
McMurry University T
Prairie View A&M University M
St. Mary's University T
Schreiner College T
Southwest Texas State University T
Stephen F. Austin State University M
Tarleton State University M, T
Texas A&M International
  University B, T
Texas A&M University
  Commerce T
  Corpus Christi T
  Kingsville T
Texas Christian University T
Texas Lutheran University B, T
Texas Wesleyan University B, T
University of Dallas T
University of Houston
  Clear Lake T
  Victoria M
University of Houston M, T
University of Mary Hardin-Baylor T
University of Texas
  Arlington T
  Austin M, D
  Dallas M
  Pan American T
  San Antonio M, T
University of the Incarnate Word D
Wayland Baptist University T

West Texas A&M University T

Utah
Brigham Young University B, M
Southern Utah University B
Utah State University B
Weber State University B

Vermont
Castleton State College B, T
Johnson State College B
St. Michael's College M
University of Vermont B, M, T

Virginia
Averett College B, T
Bridgewater College T
Christopher Newport University M
Eastern Mennonite University T
Hampton University T
Hollins University T
Liberty University B
Longwood College B, T
Radford University T
St. Paul's College T
University of Virginia's College at
  Wise T
Virginia Commonwealth University M
Virginia Wesleyan College T

Washington
Central Washington University B, M, T
Heritage College B
Pacific Lutheran University T
Seattle Pacific University B, T
Washington State University T
Western Washington University B, T
Whitworth College B, T

West Virginia
Alderson-Broaddus College T
Concord College B, T
Fairmont State College B
Glenville State College B
Shepherd College T
West Liberty State College B
West Virginia State College B
West Virginia Wesleyan College B
Wheeling Jesuit University T

Wisconsin
Alverno College B, T
Cardinal Stritch University B, T
Carroll College B, T
Carthage College T
Lakeland College T
Lawrence University T
Marian College of Fond du Lac B, T
Mount Mary College B, T
Mount Senario College B, T
Northland College T
St. Norbert College T
University of Wisconsin
  Green Bay T
  La Crosse B, T
  Madison B, M, T
  Oshkosh M, T
  Platteville B
  River Falls T
  Superior B, T
  Whitewater B
Viterbo University B, T

Wyoming
Eastern Wyoming College A

Mathematics/computer science

Alabama
Birmingham-Southern College B
Huntingdon College B
Oakwood College B

Arizona
Northern Arizona University B

Arkansas
Harding University B
Philander Smith College B
University of the Ozarks B

California
California Lutheran University B
Mills College C, B, M
Pepperdine University B
Pomona College B
San Diego State University M
Santa Clara University B
University of California
  San Diego B
  Santa Cruz B, M

Colorado
Colorado School of Mines B
Fort Lewis College B
Metropolitan State College of Denver B
University of Denver D

Connecticut
Quinnipiac University B
Western Connecticut State University B
Yale University B

Delaware
Delaware State University B

Florida
University of Miami B, M

Georgia
Clark Atlanta University B, M
Emory University B
Oglethorpe University B
Piedmont College B

Illinois
Augustana College B
Dominican University B
Eastern Illinois University B
Loyola University of Chicago B
Millikin University B
Parkland College A
Rockford College B
Roosevelt University B
University of Illinois
  Chicago B
  Urbana-Champaign B

Indiana
Anderson University B
Indiana State University B
Indiana University--Purdue University
  Indiana University-Purdue
    University Fort Wayne B
Manchester College B
Purdue University
  Calumet B
Saint Mary's College B, T
St. Joseph's College B
Taylor University B
Valparaiso University B

Iowa
Central College B, T
Coe College B
Morningside College B

Kansas
Central Christian College A
Kansas City Kansas Community
  College A

Kentucky
Berea College T
Brescia University B
Morehead State University B

Louisiana
Southern University and Agricultural and
  Mechanical College M

Maine
Bowdoin College B
St. Joseph's College B

University of Maine
  Farmington B, T
  Fort Kent B

Maryland
Cecil Community College C, A
Community College of Baltimore County
  Catonsville A
Washington College B, T

Massachusetts
Boston University B
Clark University B
Hampshire College B
Harvard College B
Massachusetts Institute of Technology B
Merrimack College B
Salem State College B
Simon's Rock College of Bard B
Stonehill College B
Tufts University B, M, D
Wheaton College B

Michigan
Albion College B, T
Hillsdale College B
Lake Superior State University B
Saginaw Valley State University B
University of Detroit Mercy B

Minnesota
Carleton College B
College of St. Benedict
Concordia College: Moorhead B
Minnesota State University, Mankato M
St. John's University B
University of Minnesota
  Twin Cities M, D
Winona State University B, T

Mississippi
Tougaloo College B

Missouri
Avila College B
Crowder College A
Stephens College B
Washington University B, M, D
William Jewell College B

Montana
University of Montana-Missoula B

New Hampshire
Keene State College B
Rivier College A, B
St. Anselm College B, T

New Jersey
Cumberland County College A
Fairleigh Dickinson University B
Gloucester County College A
Salem Community College A

New Mexico
New Mexico Institute of Mining and
  Technology B, M, D

New York
Adirondack Community College A
Alfred University B
City University of New York
  Brooklyn College B, M
  College of Staten Island B
Colgate University B
College of St. Rose B
Hobart and William Smith Colleges B
Marist College B
New York University B
Onondaga Community College A
Rochester Institute of Technology B
St. Lawrence University B
St. Thomas Aquinas College B
State University of New York
  Binghamton B
University of Rochester B
Vassar College B

North Carolina
Brevard College *B*
Queens College *B*
University of North Carolina
  Pembroke *B*
Wingate University *B*

Ohio
Antioch College *B*
College of Mount St. Joseph *B, T*
Defiance College *B, T*
Hiram College *B*
Jefferson Community College *A*
University of Akron *B, M*
Wittenberg University *B*
Youngstown State University *B*

Oklahoma
Connors State College *A*
Oklahoma Baptist University *B*
Oklahoma Christian University of
  Science and Arts *B*

Oregon
Lewis & Clark College *B*
Southern Oregon University *B*
University of Oregon *B*

Pennsylvania
Carnegie Mellon University *B*
Chestnut Hill College *B*
Dickinson College *B*
Gettysburg College *B*
Grove City College *B*
La Salle University *B*
Lackawanna Junior College *A*
Lock Haven University of
  Pennsylvania *B*
Mount Aloysius College *A, B*
University of Pennsylvania *B*
Ursinus College *B*
Westminster College *B*

Puerto Rico
University of Puerto Rico
  Humacao University College *B*

Rhode Island
Brown University *B*

South Carolina
Charleston Southern University *B*
Claflin University *B*
Furman University *B*
Newberry College *B*
North Greenville College *B*
University of South Carolina
  Aiken *B*

Tennessee
Christian Brothers University *B*
David Lipscomb University *B*
Maryville College *B*
University of the South *B*

Texas
LeTourneau University *B*
McMurry University *B*

Vermont
Castleton State College *B*
Marlboro College *B*

Virginia
Averett College *B, T*
George Mason University *D*
Hampden-Sydney College *B*
Sweet Briar College *B*
University of Richmond *B*
Virginia Wesleyan College *B*

Washington
Evergreen State College *B*
Gonzaga University *B*
Washington State University *B*
Western Washington University *B*

West Virginia
Bethany College *B*
Salem-Teikyo University *B*

Wisconsin
Cardinal Stritch University *B*
Marquette University *B*
St. Norbert College *B*

Wyoming
University of Wyoming *D*

Mechanical engineering

Alabama
Alabama Agricultural and Mechanical
  University *B*
Auburn University *B, M, D*
Tuskegee University *B, M*
University of Alabama
  Birmingham *B, M, D*
  Huntsville *B, M, D*
University of Alabama *B, M, D*
University of South Alabama *B, M*

Alaska
University of Alaska
  Fairbanks *B, M*

Arizona
Arizona State University *B, M, D*
Central Arizona College *A*
Northern Arizona University *B*
University of Arizona *B, M, D*

Arkansas
Arkansas Tech University *B*
John Brown University *B*
University of Arkansas *B, M*

California
California Institute of
  Technology *B, M, D*
California Maritime Academy *B*
California Polytechnic State University:
  San Luis Obispo *B*
California State Polytechnic University:
  Pomona *B*
California State University
  Chico *B*
  Fresno *B*
  Fullerton *B, M*
  Long Beach *B, M*
  Los Angeles *B, M*
  Northridge *B, M*
  Sacramento *B, M*
City College of San Francisco *A*
De Anza College *A*
Loyola Marymount University *B, M*
San Diego State University *B, M*
San Francisco State University *B*
San Joaquin Delta College *C, A*
San Jose State University *B, M*
Santa Clara University *B, M, D*
Stanford University *B, M, D*
University of California
  Berkeley *B, M, D*
  Davis *B*
  Irvine *B, M, D*
  Los Angeles *B, M, D*
  Riverside *B*
  San Diego *B, M, D*
  Santa Barbara *B, M, D*
University of Southern
  California *B, M, D*
University of the Pacific *B*

Colorado
Colorado State University *B, M, D*
United States Air Force Academy *B*
University of Colorado
  Boulder *B, M, D*
  Colorado Springs *B, M*
  Denver *B, M*
University of Denver *B, M*

Connecticut
Fairfield University *B*
Hartford Graduate Center *M*
Trinity College *B*
United States Coast Guard Academy *B*
University of Bridgeport *M*
University of Connecticut *B, M, D*
University of Hartford *B, M*
University of New Haven *A, B, M*
Yale University *B, M, D*

Delaware
University of Delaware *B, M, D*

District of Columbia
Catholic University of America *B, M, D*
George Washington University *B, M*
Howard University *B, M, D*
University of the District of Columbia *B*

Florida
Florida Agricultural and Mechanical
  University *B, M, D*
Florida Atlantic University *B, M, D*
Florida Institute of Technology *B, M, D*
Florida International University *B, M, D*
Florida State University *B, M, D*
Jacksonville University *B*
Miami-Dade Community College *A*
University of Central Florida *B, M, D*
University of Florida *B, M, D*
University of Miami *B, M, D*
University of South Florida *B, M, D*

Georgia
Columbus Technical Institute *A*
Georgia Institute of Technology *B, M, D*
Mercer University *B, M*
Middle Georgia College *A*
Morris Brown College *B*

Hawaii
University of Hawaii
  Manoa *B, M, D*

Idaho
Boise State University *B*
College of Southern Idaho *A*
Ricks College *A*
University of Idaho *B, M, D*

Illinois
Bradley University *B, M*
Dominican University *B*
Illinois Institute of Technology *B, M, D*
Lake Land College *A*
Northern Illinois University *B, M*
Northwestern University *B, M, D*
Parkland College *A*
Southern Illinois University
  Carbondale *B, M*
  Edwardsville *B, M*
University of Illinois
  Chicago *B, M, D*
  Urbana-Champaign *B, M, D*

Indiana
Indiana Institute of Technology *B*
Indiana University--Purdue University
  Indiana University-Purdue
    University Fort Wayne *B*
  Indiana University-Purdue
    University Indianapolis *B, M*
Purdue University
  Calumet *B, T*
Purdue University *B, M, D*
Rose-Hulman Institute of
  Technology *B, M*
Tri-State University *B*
University of Evansville *B*
University of Notre Dame *B, M, D*
Valparaiso University *B*
Vincennes University *A*

Iowa
Dordt College *B*
Iowa State University *B, M, D*
University of Iowa *B, M, D*
William Penn University *B*

Kansas
Kansas State University *B, M, D*
University of Kansas *B, M, D*
Wichita State University *B, M, D*

Kentucky
University of Kentucky *B, M, D*
University of Louisville *B, M*

Louisiana
Louisiana State University and
  Agricultural and Mechanical
  College *B, M, D*
Louisiana Tech University *B*
Southern University and Agricultural and
  Mechanical College *B*
Tulane University *B, M, D*
University of Louisiana at
  Lafayette *B, M*
University of New Orleans *B*

Maine
University of Maine *B, M*

Maryland
Goucher College *B*
Johns Hopkins University *B, M, D*
United States Naval Academy *B*
University of Maryland
  Baltimore County *B, M, D*
  College Park *B, M, D*

Massachusetts
Boston University *B, M, D*
Franklin Institute of Boston *A*
Harvard College *B*
Massachusetts Institute of
  Technology *B, M, D*
Massachusetts Maritime Academy *C*
Northeastern University *B, M, D*
Tufts University *B, M, D*
University of Massachusetts
  Amherst *B, M, D*
  Dartmouth *B, M*
  Lowell *B, M, D*
Wentworth Institute of Technology *A, B*
Western New England College *B, M*
Worcester Polytechnic Institute *B, M, D*

Michigan
Calvin College *B*
Grand Valley State University *B*
Kettering University *B, M*
Lake Superior State University *B*
Lawrence Technological University *B*
Michigan State University *B, M, D*
Michigan Technological
  University *B, M, D, T*
Oakland University *B, M*
Saginaw Valley State University *B*
University of Detroit Mercy *B, M, D*
University of Michigan
  Dearborn *B*
University of Michigan *B, M, D*
Wayne State University *B, M, D*
Western Michigan University *B, M, D*

Minnesota
Concordia College: Moorhead *B*
Minnesota State University, Mankato *B*
University of Minnesota
  Twin Cities *C, B, M, D*
University of St. Thomas *B*
Winona State University *B*

Mississippi
Mississippi State University *B, M*
University of Mississippi *B*

Missouri
Jefferson College *A*
St. Louis University *B*
University of Missouri
  Columbia *B*
  Kansas City *B, M*
  Rolla *B, M, D*
  St. Louis *B*
Washington University *B, M, D*

Montana
Montana State University
  Bozeman *B, M*

Montana Tech of the University of
    Montana *B*

Nebraska

University of Nebraska
    Lincoln *B, M*
    Omaha *B*

Nevada

University of Nevada
    Las Vegas *B, M, D*
    Reno *B, M, D*

New Hampshire

University of New Hampshire *B, M, D*

New Jersey

New Jersey Institute of
    Technology *B, M, D*
Princeton University *B, M, D*
Rowan University *B*
Rutgers
    The State University of New Jersey:
        College of Engineering *B*
    The State University of New Jersey:
        New Brunswick Graduate
        Campus *M, D*
Seton Hall University *B*
Stevens Institute of Technology *B, M, D*

New Mexico

New Mexico State University *B, M*
University of New Mexico *B, M*

New York

Alfred University *B, M*
City University of New York
    City College *B, M, D*
    Graduate School and University
        Center *D*
Clarkson University *B, M, D*
Columbia University
    Fu Foundation School of
        Engineering and Applied
        Science *B, M, D*
Cooper Union for the Advancement of
    Science and Art *B, M*
Cornell University *B, M, D*
Finger Lakes Community College *A*
Hofstra University *B*
Manhattan College *B, M*
New York Institute of Technology *B, M*
New York University *B*
Onondaga Community College *A*
Polytechnic University
    Long Island Campus *B, M, D*
Polytechnic University *B, M, D*
Rensselaer Polytechnic Institute *B, M, D*
Rochester Institute of Technology *B, M*
State University of New York
    Binghamton *B, M, D*
    Buffalo *B, M, D*
    College of Agriculture and
        Technology at Morrisville *A*
    College of Environmental Science
        and Forestry *B, M, D*
    Maritime College *B*
    Stony Brook *B, M, D*
Syracuse University *B, M, D*
Union College *B, M*
United States Military Academy *B*
University of Rochester *B, M, D*

North Carolina

Central Carolina Community College *A*
Duke University *B, M, D*
Edgecombe Community College *A*
North Carolina Agricultural and
    Technical State University *B, M, D*
North Carolina State University *B, M, D*
St. Augustine's College *B*
University of North Carolina
    Charlotte *B, M, D*
Wilson Technical Community College *A*

North Dakota

North Dakota State University *B, M*
University of North Dakota *B, M*

Ohio

Belmont Technical College *A*
Case Western Reserve
    University *B, M, D*
Cedarville College *B*
Cleveland State University *B, M, D*
Columbus State Community College *A*
Edison State Community College *C, A*
Kent State University
    Ashtabula Regional Campus *A*
    Trumbull Campus *A*
Lorain County Community College *A*
Marion Technical College *A*
Northwest State Community College *A*
Ohio Northern University *B*
Ohio State University
    Columbus Campus *B, M, D*
Ohio University *B, M*
Terra Community College *A*
University of Akron *B, M, D*
University of Cincinnati *B, M, D*
University of Dayton *B, M, D*
University of Toledo *B, M*
Washington State Community College *A*
Wilberforce University *B*
Wright State University *B, M*
Youngstown State University *B, M*

Oklahoma

Oklahoma Christian University of
    Science and Arts *B*
Oklahoma State University *B, M, D*
Oral Roberts University *B*
University of Oklahoma *B, M, D*
University of Tulsa *B, M, D*

Oregon

George Fox University *B*
Mount Hood Community College *C, A*
Oregon State University *B, M, D*
Portland State University *B, M, D*
University of Portland *B, M*

Pennsylvania

Bucknell University *B, M*
Carnegie Mellon University *B, M, D*
Drexel University *B, M, D*
Gannon University *B, M*
Geneva College *B*
Gettysburg College *B*
Grove City College *B*
Lafayette College *B*
Lehigh Carbon Community College *A*
Lehigh University *B, M, D*
Lock Haven University of
    Pennsylvania *B*
Penn State
    Erie, The Behrend College *B*
    University Park *B, M, D*
Reading Area Community College *A*
Temple University *B, M*
University of Pennsylvania *B, M, D*
University of Pittsburgh *B, M, D*
Villanova University *B, M*
Widener University *B, M*
Wilkes University *B*
York College of Pennsylvania *B*

Puerto Rico

Inter American University of Puerto Rico
    Bayamon Campus *B*
Turabo University *B*
Universidad Politecnica de Puerto
    Rico *B*
University of Puerto Rico
    Carolina Regional College *A*
    Mayaguez Campus *M*

Rhode Island

Brown University *B, M, D*
Johnson & Wales University *A, B*
University of Rhode Island *B, M, D*

South Carolina

Clemson University *B, M, D*
University of South Carolina *B, M, D*

South Dakota

South Dakota School of Mines and
    Technology *B, M*
South Dakota State University *B*

Tennessee

Chattanooga State Technical Community
    College *A*
Christian Brothers University *B*
Tennessee Technological
    University *B, M, D*
University of Memphis *B, M*
University of Tennessee
    Knoxville *B, M, D*
Vanderbilt University *B, M, D*

Texas

Baylor University *B*
Houston Baptist University *B*
Kilgore College *A*
Lamar University *B*
LeTourneau University *B*
Prairie View A&M University *B*
Rice University *B, M, D*
Southern Methodist University *B, M, D*
Texas A&M University
    Kingsville *B, M*
Texas A&M University *B, M, D*
Texas Tech University *B, M, D*
University of Houston *B, M, D*
University of Texas
    Arlington *B, M, D*
    Austin *B, M, D*
    El Paso *B, M*
    Pan American *B*
    San Antonio *B, M*
    Tyler *B, M*

Utah

Brigham Young University *B, M, D*
Salt Lake Community College *A*
Snow College *A*
Southern Utah University *A*
University of Utah *B, M, D*
Utah State University *B, M, D*

Vermont

Norwich University *B*
University of Vermont *B, M, D*
Vermont Technical College *A*

Virginia

John Tyler Community College *A*
Old Dominion University *B*
Thomas Nelson Community College *A*
University of Virginia *B*
Virginia Commonwealth University *B*
Virginia Military Institute *B*
Virginia Polytechnic Institute and State
    University *B, M, D*

Washington

Gonzaga University *B*
Henry Cogswell College *B*
Lower Columbia College *A*
St. Martin's College *B*
Seattle University *B*
Shoreline Community College *A*
University of Washington *B, M, D*
Walla Walla College *B*
Washington State University *B, M, D*

West Virginia

Potomac State College of West Virginia
    University *A*
West Virginia University Institute of
    Technology *B*
West Virginia University *B, M, D*

Wisconsin

Marquette University *B, M, D*
Milwaukee Area Technical College *A*
Milwaukee School of Engineering *B*
University of Wisconsin
    Madison *B, M, D*
    Milwaukee *B*
    Platteville *B*
Waukesha County Technical College *A*

Wyoming

University of Wyoming *B, M, D*

Mechanical engineering-related technologies

Alabama

Alabama Agricultural and Mechanical
    University *B*
Community College of the Air Force *A*
George C. Wallace State Community
    College
    Dothan *C, A*

Arizona

Mesa Community College *A*
University of Advancing Computer
    Technology *A, B*

Arkansas

Phillips Community College of the
    University of Arkansas *C, A*
University of Arkansas
    Little Rock *A, B*

California

Allan Hancock College *C, A*
California Maritime Academy *B*
Chabot College *A*
City College of San Francisco *C, A*
College of the Redwoods *A*
Compton Community College *C, A*
Don Bosco Technical Institute *A*
East Los Angeles College *A*
Long Beach City College *C, A*
Los Angeles Trade and Technical
    College *C, A*
Los Angeles Valley College *C*
Merced College *A*
Mount San Antonio College *C, A*
Pasadena City College *C, A*
Rio Hondo College *C, A*
Riverside Community College *A*
Saddleback College *C*
San Diego City College *C, A*
University of California
    Riverside *B*
Ventura College *C, A*

Colorado

Arapahoe Community College *C, A*
Metropolitan State College of Denver *B*
University of Southern Colorado *B*

Connecticut

Capital Community College *A*
Central Connecticut State University *B*
Gateway Community College *A*
Naugatuck Valley Community-Technical
    College *A*
Three Rivers Community-Technical
    College *A*
University of Hartford *B*
University of New Haven *A*

Delaware

Delaware Technical and Community
    College
    Owens Campus *A*
    Stanton/Wilmington Campus *A*
    Terry Campus *A*

Florida

Miami-Dade Community College *A*
Santa Fe Community College *C, A*
University of Central Florida *B*

Georgia

Abraham Baldwin Agricultural
    College *A*
Clayton College and State
    University *C, A*
Coastal Georgia Community College *A*
Georgia Southern University *B*
Savannah State University *B*
Southern Polytechnic State University *B*

Mechanical engineering-related technologies

Idaho
Ricks College A

Illinois
Black Hawk College C, A
City Colleges of Chicago
    Wright College C
College of DuPage C, A
College of Lake County C, A
Illinois Eastern Community Colleges
    Lincoln Trail College C, A
John Wood Community College A
Kaskaskia College C
McHenry County College C, A
Moraine Valley Community
    College C, A
Oakton Community College C, A
Parkland College C
Prairie State College C, A
Sauk Valley Community College C, A
Southern Illinois University
    Carbondale B
Waubonsee Community College C, A
William Rainey Harper College A

Indiana
Indiana State University B
Indiana University--Purdue University
    Indiana University-Purdue
        University Fort Wayne A, B
    Indiana University-Purdue
        University Indianapolis A, B
Purdue University
    Calumet B
    North Central Campus A, B
Purdue University A, B
University of Southern Indiana A
Vincennes University A

Iowa
Hawkeye Community College A
Iowa Western Community College A
Kirkwood Community College A
Marshalltown Community College C
Northeast Iowa Community College A
Southeastern Community College
    North Campus A

Kansas
Allen County Community College C, A
Kansas State University A, B
Pittsburg State University B
Pratt Community College C, A

Kentucky
Murray State University A, B
Owensboro Community College A
Western Kentucky University B

Louisiana
Southern University
    Shreveport A
Southern University and Agricultural and
    Mechanical College B

Maine
Central Maine Technical College A
Eastern Maine Technical College C, A
Southern Maine Technical College A

Maryland
Hagerstown Community College C, A
Montgomery College
    Rockville Campus A

Massachusetts
Bristol Community College A
Franklin Institute of Boston A
Massachusetts Bay Community
    College A
Massachusetts Maritime Academy B
Mount Wachusett Community
    College C, A
Northeastern University A, B
Roxbury Community College A
Springfield Technical Community
    College C, A
University of Massachusetts
    Dartmouth B
    Lowell A, B
Wentworth Institute of Technology A, B

Michigan
Andrews University A
Central Michigan University B
Eastern Michigan University B
Ferris State University A, B
Glen Oaks Community College A
Grand Rapids Community College C, A
Kalamazoo Valley Community
    College A
Kirtland Community College C, A
Lake Superior State University A, B
Lansing Community College A
Lawrence Technological University A
Michigan Technological University A, B
Monroe County Community
    College C, A
Mott Community College A
Northwestern Michigan College A
Oakland Community College C, A
Schoolcraft College A
Washtenaw Community College A
Wayne State University B
Western Michigan University B

Minnesota
Alexandria Technical College C
Anoka-Ramsey Community College A
Lake Superior College: A Community
    and Technical College A
Rochester Community and Technical
    College A
South Central Technical College A

Mississippi
Copiah-Lincoln Community
    College C, A
Hinds Community College A
University of Southern Mississippi B

Missouri
Central Missouri State University A, B
Crowder College C, A
Lincoln University A, B
Longview Community College C, A
St. Louis University A, B
Southwest Missouri State University B

Montana
Montana State University
    Bozeman B

Nebraska
Southeast Community College
    Milford Campus A

Nevada
Community College of Southern
    Nevada A

New Hampshire
Keene State College A, B
New Hampshire Community Technical
    College
    Nashua A
New Hampshire Technical Institute A
University of New Hampshire
    Manchester B
University of New Hampshire B

New Jersey
Bergen Community College A
Brookdale Community College A
Burlington County College C
Camden County College A
County College of Morris C, A
Cumberland County College C, A
Gloucester County College A
Middlesex County College A
Thomas Edison State College A, B
Union County College A

New York
Adirondack Community College A
Broome Community College A
City University of New York
    New York City Technical
        College A
    Queensborough Community
        College A
Corning Community College A
Erie Community College
    North Campus A
Finger Lakes Community College A
Fulton-Montgomery Community
    College A
Hudson Valley Community College A
Jamestown Community College A
Mohawk Valley Community College A
Monroe Community College A
New York Institute of Technology A, B
Niagara County Community College A
Onondaga Community College A
Rochester Institute of Technology B
State University of New York
    College at Buffalo B
    College of Agriculture and
        Technology at Morrisville A
    College of Technology at
        Alfred A, B
    College of Technology at Canton A
    College of Technology at
        Farmingdale A
    Institute of Technology at
        Utica/Rome B
Technical Career Institutes C, A
Westchester Community College C, A

North Carolina
Asheville Buncombe Technical
    Community College A
Beaufort County Community College A
Blue Ridge Community College C, A
Cape Fear Community College A
Catawba Valley Community College A
Central Carolina Community College A
Central Piedmont Community College A
Cleveland Community College C, A
Craven Community College C, A
Gaston College A
Lenoir Community College A
Mitchell Community College A
Richmond Community College C, A
South Piedmont Community
    College C, A
University of North Carolina
    Charlotte B
Wake Technical Community College A
Wayne Community College A

North Dakota
North Dakota State College of Science A

Ohio
Bowling Green State University B
Cincinnati State Technical and
    Community College A
Clark State Community College A
Cleveland State University B
Columbus State Community College A
Edison State Community College A
Jefferson Community College A
Kent State University
    Ashtabula Regional Campus A
    Trumbull Campus A
    Tuscarawas Campus A
Lakeland Community College C, A
Lima Technical College A
Lorain County Community College A
Miami University
    Hamilton Campus A, B
    Middletown Campus A, B
    Oxford Campus A
Muskingum Area Technical College A
North Central State College A
Northwest State Community
    College A
Owens Community College
    Findlay Campus A
    Toledo A
Stark State College of Technology A
Terra Community College C, A
University of Akron
    Wayne College A
University of Akron A, B
University of Dayton B
University of Toledo A, B
Washington State Community College A
Youngstown State University A, B

Oklahoma
Northeastern Oklahoma Agricultural and
    Mechanical College A
Oklahoma State University B
Tulsa Community College A

Oregon
Chemeketa Community College A
Oregon Institute of Technology B
Portland Community College C, A

Pennsylvania
Butler County Community College A
California University of Pennsylvania A
Community College of Allegheny
    County C, A
Community College of Philadelphia A
Delaware County Community College A
Harrisburg Area Community
    College A
ICS Center for Degree Studies A
Lehigh Carbon Community College C, A
Luzerne County Community College A
Northampton County Area Community
    College C, A
Penn State
    Altoona A
    Berks A
    Dubois A
    Erie, The Behrend College A, B
    Harrisburg B
    Hazleton A
    Lehigh Valley B
    McKeesport A
    New Kensington A
    Shenango A
    University Park B
    York A
Pennsylvania College of
    Technology A, B
Pennsylvania Institute of Technology A
Point Park College A, B
Temple University A
University of Pittsburgh
    Johnstown A
Westmoreland County Community
    College A

Puerto Rico
University of Puerto Rico
    Bayamon University College A
    Mayaguez Campus B
University of the Sacred Heart B

Rhode Island
Community College of Rhode
    Island C, A
Johnson & Wales University A, B

South Carolina
Florence-Darlington Technical
    College C
Greenville Technical College A
Midlands Technical College A
Orangeburg-Calhoun Technical
    College A
Piedmont Technical College A
South Carolina State University B
Spartanburg Technical College A
Tri-County Technical College A
Trident Technical College A
York Technical College A

South Dakota
Southeast Technical Institute A

Tennessee
Nashville State Technical Institute A
Pellissippi State Technical Community
    College A

Texas
Angelina College C, A
Brookhaven College A
Eastfield College A
Grayson County College A
Hill College C, A
LeTourneau University B
Midland College A
North Central Texas College A
Richland College A
Tarleton State University B
Texas A&M University
  Corpus Christi B
Texas State Technical College
  Harlingen A
  Waco C, A
Texas Tech University B
University of Houston
  Downtown B
University of Houston B
University of North Texas B

Utah
Utah State University B
Weber State University A, B

Vermont
Vermont Technical College A, B

Virginia
Blue Ridge Community College C, A
Central Virginia Community College A
ECPI College of Technology C, A
Germanna Community College A
John Tyler Community College A
Lord Fairfax Community College A
Norfolk State University B
Northern Virginia Community College A
Southside Virginia Community
  College C, A
Tidewater Community College A
Virginia Western Community College A

Washington
Central Washington University B
Clark College A
Columbia Basin College A
Eastern Washington University B
Henry Cogswell College B
Highline Community College A
Lower Columbia College A
Peninsula College A
Shoreline Community College A
Spokane Community College C, A
University of Washington M
Yakima Valley Community College C, A

West Virginia
Bluefield State College A, B
Fairmont State College A, B
West Virginia University
  Parkersburg A
West Virginia University Institute of
  Technology A

Wisconsin
Blackhawk Technical College A
Chippewa Valley Technical College A
Gateway Technical College A
Madison Area Technical College A
Milwaukee School of Engineering A, B
Moraine Park Technical College A
Northeast Wisconsin Technical
  College A
Waukesha County Technical College A

Mechanics/repair

Alabama
Bessemer State Technical College C
Central Alabama Community College C
Enterprise State Junior College A
George C. Wallace State Community
  College
    Selma A

Arkansas
Southern Arkansas University
  Tech A
Westark College C

California
Allan Hancock College C, A
Cerritos Community College C
College of the Redwoods C
Columbia College C
Compton Community College C, A
Fresno City College C, A
Imperial Valley College C, A
Las Positas College C
Modesto Junior College C, A
Palomar College C, A
Riverside Community College C, A
San Jose City College C
Shasta College C, A

Colorado
Otero Junior College C
Red Rocks Community College C, A

Connecticut
Gateway Community College A
Three Rivers Community-Technical
  College A

Florida
Brevard Community College C
Chipola Junior College C
Seminole Community College C

Georgia
Gwinnett Technical Institute C, A

Hawaii
University of Hawaii
  Honolulu Community College C, A

Idaho
Boise State University C
Eastern Idaho Technical College C, A
Idaho State University A
Lewis-Clark State College A
North Idaho College C

Illinois
Black Hawk College C, A
Danville Area Community College A
Kankakee Community College C, A
Moraine Valley Community
  College C, A
Richland Community College A
Southwestern Illinois College C, A
Triton College C

Indiana
Vincennes University A

Iowa
Des Moines Area Community
  College C, A
Iowa Western Community College A
Southeastern Community College
  North Campus A

Kansas
Butler County Community College C, A
Central Christian College A
Kansas City Kansas Community
  College C, A
Pittsburg State University A

Louisiana
Nunez Community College C

Maine
Southern Maine Technical College A
Washington County Technical
  College C, A

Maryland
Cecil Community College C, A

Massachusetts
Franklin Institute of Boston A

Michigan
Bay de Noc Community College C, A
Glen Oaks Community College C
Kirtland Community College C, A
Lansing Community College A
Macomb Community College C
Muskegon Community College C, A
Oakland Community College C, A

Minnesota
Hennepin Technical College C, A
Lake Superior College: A Community
  and Technical College C, A
Mesabi Range Community and Technical
  College A

Mississippi
Northeast Mississippi Community
  College C
Northwest Mississippi Community
  College C

Missouri
Crowder College A

Nebraska
Mid Plains Community College
  Area C, A
Southeast Community College
  Milford Campus A

New Jersey
Raritan Valley Community College A

New York
State University of New York
  College of Technology at Alfred A

North Carolina
Alamance Community College C
Edgecombe Community College C
Forsyth Technical Community College C
Haywood Community College C
James Sprunt Community College C
Johnston Community College C
Mayland Community College C
Pitt Community College A
Rockingham Community College A
Sandhills Community College C

Ohio
Columbus State Community College A
Owens Community College
  Toledo A

Oklahoma
Oklahoma City Community College A

Pennsylvania
Community College of Allegheny
  County C, A
Johnson Technical Institute A

South Carolina
Central Carolina Technical College C
Tri-County Technical College C
Trident Technical College C, A
York Technical College A

South Dakota
Southeast Technical Institute A

Tennessee
Chattanooga State Technical Community
  College C

Texas
Central Texas College C, A
Texas Southern University B
Texas State Technical College
  Waco C, A

Utah
Snow College C, A
Utah Valley State College C, A

Vermont
Community College of Vermont A

Virginia
ECPI College of Technology C
Virginia Highlands Community
  College C

Washington
Olympic College C, A
Pierce College C
Renton Technical College C, A

Wisconsin
Nicolet Area Technical College C
Wisconsin Indianhead Technical
  College C

Wyoming
Casper College C, A
Western Wyoming Community
  College C, A

Medical administrative assistant

Alabama
James H. Faulkner State Community
  College A
Lawson State Community College A
Northwest-Shoals Community College C

Arizona
Central Arizona College C, A
Cochise College A
Gateway Community College C
Yavapai College C, A

Arkansas
Arkansas State University
  Mountain Home C
Garland County Community College A
Phillips Community College of the
  University of Arkansas C

California
Barstow College C
Butte College C, A
Chaffey Community College C
City College of San Francisco A
College of the Redwoods C
Columbia College C
De Anza College C
East Los Angeles College C
Empire College C, A
Fresno City College C, A
Gavilan Community College C
Glendale Community College C, A
Grossmont Community College C, A
Heald Business College
  Santa Rosa C, A
Humphreys College C, A, B
Lake Tahoe Community College C
Los Angeles Harbor College C, A
Merced College C, A
Mount San Antonio College C, A
Ohlone College C, A
Pacific Union College A
Palomar College C, A
Pasadena City College C, A
Riverside Community College C, A
Sacramento City College C, A
Santa Rosa Junior College C
Shasta College C
Sierra College C
Solano Community College C, A
Ventura College C, A
Victor Valley College C
West Hills Community College C, A
Yuba College C

Colorado
Community College of Aurora A
Denver Technical College: A Division of
  DeVry University C
Lamar Community College A
Northeastern Junior College A
Otero Junior College A
Pueblo Community College C, A
Red Rocks Community College C, A

Connecticut
Briarwood College C, A
Gateway Community College A

Medical administrative assistant

Middlesex Community-Technical College *A*
Naugatuck Valley Community-Technical College *A*
Quinebaug Valley Community College *C*
Three Rivers Community-Technical College *A*
Tunxis Community College *C, A*

Delaware
Delaware Technical and Community College
    Owens Campus *A*
    Stanton/Wilmington Campus *A*

Florida
Broward Community College *C*
Cooper Career Institute *C*
Daytona Beach Community College *A*
Lake City Community College *C*
Miami-Dade Community College *A*
Palm Beach Community College *C*
Pasco-Hernando Community College *C*
Pensacola Junior College *A*
Santa Fe Community College *A*
Seminole Community College *A*
South Florida Community College *C, A*
Tallahassee Community College *C*
Valencia Community College *A*

Georgia
Chattahoochee Technical Institute *C*
Dalton State College *A*
Middle Georgia College *A*

Idaho
Eastern Idaho Technical College *C, A*
North Idaho College *A*

Illinois
Black Hawk College *C, A*
Career Colleges of Chicago *A*
College of Lake County *C*
Danville Area Community College *C, A*
Elgin Community College *A*
Illinois Eastern Community Colleges
    Olney Central College *C, A*
John A. Logan College *A*
John Wood Community College *A*
Joliet Junior College *A*
Kankakee Community College *A*
Morton College *C*
Northwestern Business College *A*
Rend Lake College *A*
Sauk Valley Community College *C, A*
Shawnee Community College *A*
Waubonsee Community College *C*
William Rainey Harper College *C, A*

Indiana
International Business College *C, A*
Vincennes University *A*

Iowa
American Institute of Business *A*
Des Moines Area Community College *C, A*
Dordt College *A*
Hawkeye Community College *C*
Iowa Western Community College *A*
Kirkwood Community College *C, A*
North Iowa Area Community College *C, A*
Northeast Iowa Community College *A*
Southeastern Community College
    North Campus *C*
    South Campus *A*
Western Iowa Tech Community College *C, A*

Kansas
Central Christian College *A*
Independence Community College *C, A*
Pratt Community College *C, A*
Washburn University of Topeka *A*

Kentucky
Ashland Community College *A*
National Business College *A*
Owensboro Junior College of Business *C, A*

Louisiana
Nunez Community College *A*

Maine
Andover College *C, A*
Beal College *A*
Husson College *A*
Mid-State College *A*
Thomas College *A*
Washington County Technical College *C*

Maryland
Allegany College *A*
Baltimore City Community College *A*
Community College of Baltimore County
    Catonsville *A*
Howard Community College *C, A*
Montgomery College
    Takoma Park Campus *C, A*
Prince George's Community College *C, A*
Villa Julie College *A*

Massachusetts
Atlantic Union College *A*
Bay State College *A*
Bristol Community College *A*
Cape Cod Community College *C, A*
Endicott College *C*
Fisher College *A*
Holyoke Community College *A*
Marian Court College *C, A*
Mount Wachusett Community College *C*
North Shore Community College *A*
Northern Essex Community College *A*
Roxbury Community College *A*
Springfield Technical Community College *A*

Michigan
Baker College
    of Auburn Hills *C, A*
    of Cadillac *A*
    of Jackson *C, A*
    of Mount Clemens *A*
    of Muskegon *C, A*
    of Owosso *A*
    of Port Huron *C, A*
Davenport College of Business *A*
Detroit College of Business *C, A*
Grand Rapids Community College *A*
Great Lakes College *A*
Kalamazoo Valley Community College *C, A*
Kellogg Community College *A*
Kirtland Community College *C, A*
Lake Michigan College *A*
Lansing Community College *A*
Macomb Community College *C, A*
Mid Michigan Community College *A*
Monroe County Community College *A*
Montcalm Community College *C, A*
Mott Community College *C, A*
Muskegon Community College *A*
Northern Michigan University *A*
Northwestern Michigan College *A*
St. Clair County Community College *A*

Minnesota
Alexandria Technical College *C, A*
Anoka-Ramsey Community College *A*
Central Lakes College *C, A*
Hennepin Technical College *C, A*
Hibbing Community College: A Technical and Community College *A*
Inver Hills Community College *C, A*
Itasca Community College *A*
Lake Superior College: A Community and Technical College *C, A*
Minnesota State College - Southeast Technical *C, A*
Northland Community & Technical College *C, A*
Ridgewater College: A Community and Technical College *C, A*
Rochester Community and Technical College *A*
St. Cloud Technical College *C, A*
St. Paul Technical College *C, A*
South Central Technical College *A*

Mississippi
Mississippi Gulf Coast Community College
    Perkinston *A*
Northwest Mississippi Community College *A*

Missouri
Crowder College *A*
East Central College *C, A*
Jefferson College *A*
Longview Community College *C*
Maple Woods Community College *C*
Northwest Missouri State University *C*
Penn Valley Community College *C*
Southeast Missouri State University *C*
State Fair Community College *A*

Montana
Flathead Valley Community College *A*
Miles Community College *A*
Montana State University
    Billings *A*
    College of Technology-Great Falls *A*
Montana Tech of the University of Montana: College of Technology *A*
Montana Tech of the University of Montana *A*
University of Montana-Missoula *A*

Nebraska
Lincoln School of Commerce *A*
Northeast Community College *A*

Nevada
Western Nevada Community College *C*

New Hampshire
Hesser College *C*
McIntosh College *A*
New Hampshire Community Technical College
    Claremont *C*
    Laconia *C*
    Manchester *C, A*

New Jersey
Essex County College *A*
Gloucester County College *C, A*
Katharine Gibbs School
    Gibbs College *A*
Mercer County Community College *C*
Salem Community College *A*
Sussex County Community College *C*

New Mexico
Clovis Community College *A*
Dona Ana Branch Community College of New Mexico State University *A*
New Mexico State University
    Alamogordo *A*
Western New Mexico University *C, A*

New York
Adirondack Community College *A*
Bryant & Stratton Business Institute
    Syracuse *A*
City University of New York
    Hostos Community College *A*
    Kingsborough Community College *A*
Clinton Community College *C*
Fulton-Montgomery Community College *A*
Genesee Community College *C*
Herkimer County Community College *A*
Hudson Valley Community College *A*
Interboro Institute *A*
Jamestown Business College *C, A*
Nassau Community College *A*
Trocaire College *C*

North Carolina
Alamance Community College *C, A*
Asheville Buncombe Technical Community College *C*
Blue Ridge Community College *C*
Caldwell Community College and Technical Institute *C, A*
Cape Fear Community College *D*
Central Carolina Community College *A*
Central Piedmont Community College *A*
Cleveland Community College *A*
Coastal Carolina Community College *C, A*
College of the Albemarle *A*
Craven Community College *C, A*
Durham Technical Community College *A*
Gaston College *A*
Guilford Technical Community College *A*
Halifax Community College *A*
Johnston Community College *A*
Lenoir Community College *A*
Mayland Community College *A*
Nash Community College *A*
Piedmont Community College *A*
Pitt Community College *A*
Rockingham Community College *A*
Sandhills Community College *A*
South Piedmont Community College *C, A*
Wake Technical Community College *A*
Wayne Community College *A*

North Dakota
Bismarck State College *C, A*
Dickinson State University *A*
Lake Region State College *A*
Minot State University: Bottineau Campus *A*
North Dakota State College of Science *A*

Ohio
Bowling Green State University
    Firelands College *C*
Central Ohio Technical College *A*
Columbus State Community College *A*
Davis College *C, A*
Edison State Community College *A*
Hocking Technical College *C*
Jefferson Community College *A*
Lima Technical College *A*
Marion Technical College *A*
Miami-Jacobs College *A*
Northwest State Community College *A*
Northwestern College *A*
Ohio University
    Chillicothe Campus *A*
Ohio Valley Business College *A*
Owens Community College
    Toledo *A*
Sinclair Community College *C*
Terra Community College *A*
University of Akron
    Wayne College *A*
University of Akron *A*
University of Cincinnati
    Raymond Walters College *C, A*
Youngstown State University *A*

Oklahoma
Eastern Oklahoma State College *A*
Northeastern Oklahoma Agricultural and Mechanical College *A*
Oklahoma State University
    Okmulgee *A*
Tulsa Community College *C, A*

Oregon
Chemeketa Community College *A*
Clackamas Community College *C*
Lane Community College *C*

Linn-Benton Community College *C, A*
Portland Community College *C*

Pennsylvania
Bucks County Community College *A*
Butler County Community College *A*
Cambria-Rowe Business College *C, A*
Central Pennsylvania College *A*
Churchman Business School *A*
Community College of Allegheny
 County *A*
Community College of Beaver County *A*
Lackawanna Junior College *A*
Laurel Business Institute *A*
Lehigh Carbon Community College *A*
Manor College *C, A*
Mercyhurst College *C, A*
Montgomery County Community
 College *C, A*
Northampton County Area Community
 College *A*
Pennsylvania College of Technology *A*
Pennsylvania Institute of Technology *A*
Reading Area Community College *C, A*
Sawyer School *A*
South Hills School of Business &
 Technology *A*
Westmoreland County Community
 College *A*
Yorktowne Business Institute *A*

Puerto Rico
Caribbean University *A*
Colegio Universitario del Este *C*
Turabo University *C*
Universidad Metropolitana *A, B*

Rhode Island
Community College of Rhode
 Island *C, A*
New England Institute of Technology *A*

South Carolina
Aiken Technical College *C*
Florence-Darlington Technical
 College *C*
Greenville Technical College *C*
Orangeburg-Calhoun Technical
 College *C*
Tri-County Technical College *C*
Trident Technical College *C*
York Technical College *C*

South Dakota
Kilian Community College *A*
Southeast Technical Institute *A*
Western Dakota Technical Institute *C*

Tennessee
Knoxville Business College *C, A*
Nashville State Technical Institute *A*
Pellissippi State Technical Community
 College *A*
Roane State Community College *C, A*

Texas
Alvin Community College *A*
Austin Community College *A*
Blinn College *C*
Brazosport College *C, A*
Central Texas College *C*
Coastal Bend College *A*
Collin County Community College
 District *C*
Del Mar College *C, A*
El Paso Community College *C*
Galveston College *A*
Grayson County College *C*
Houston Community College
 System *C, A*
Lamar State College at Port Arthur *C, A*
Northeast Texas Community
 College *C, A*
St. Philip's College *A*
San Jacinto College
 North *C*
Southwestern Adventist University *B*
Temple College *A*

Texas State Technical College
 Sweetwater *C*
Tyler Junior College *C, A*
Vernon Regional Junior College *C*

Utah
LDS Business College *A*
Salt Lake Community College *C*

Vermont
Champlain College *A, B*

Virginia
Blue Ridge Community College *C*
ECPI College of Technology *C, A*
Mountain Empire Community College *A*
National Business College *A*
New River Community College *C, A*

Washington
Centralia College *C, A*
Clark College *C, A*
Columbia Basin College *C*
Edmonds Community College *C*
Everett Community College *C*
Grays Harbor College *C*
Green River Community College *A*
Lake Washington Technical College *C*
Lower Columbia College *A*
Peninsula College *A*
Pierce College *A*
Renton Technical College *C*
Shoreline Community College *C*
South Puget Sound Community
 College *C, A*
Spokane Community College *C, A*
Walla Walla Community College *A*
Wenatchee Valley College *A*
Whatcom Community College *A*
Yakima Valley Community College *C, A*

West Virginia
Bluefield State College *C, A*
College of West Virginia *A*
Potomac State College of West Virginia
 University *A*
West Virginia Northern Community
 College *C*
West Virginia State College *A*
West Virginia University Institute of
 Technology *A*

Wisconsin
Blackhawk Technical College *C, A*
Bryant & Stratton College *C, A*
Chippewa Valley Technical College *C*
Lakeshore Technical College *A*
Madison Area Technical College *A*
Milwaukee Area Technical College *A*
Moraine Park Technical College *C, A*
Northeast Wisconsin Technical
 College *A*
Waukesha County Technical College *C*
Western Wisconsin Technical College *A*
Wisconsin Indianhead Technical
 College *A*

Wyoming
Western Wyoming Community
 College *C, A*

Medical assistant

Alabama
Central Alabama Community College *A*
Community College of the Air Force *A*
Enterprise State Junior College *A*
Faulkner University *A*
George C. Wallace State Community
 College
 Dothan *C, A*
Lawson State Community College *A*
Northwest-Shoals Community College *A*
South College *A*
Wallace State Community College at
 Hanceville *A*

Alaska
University of Alaska
 Anchorage *A*

Arizona
Eastern Arizona College *C*
Northland Pioneer College *C, A*

Arkansas
Arkansas State University
 Mountain Home *C*
Arkansas Tech University *A*
Garland County Community
 College *C, A*

California
Allan Hancock College *C, A*
Barstow College *C*
Butte College *A*
Cabrillo College *C, A*
Cerritos Community College *C, A*
Chabot College *C, A*
Citrus College *C, A*
City College of San Francisco *C, A*
College of San Mateo *C, A*
College of the Redwoods *C*
Compton Community College *A*
Contra Costa College *A*
Cypress College *A*
De Anza College *C, A*
East Los Angeles College *A*
Empire College *A*
Fresno City College *C, A*
Glendale Community College *A*
Lake Tahoe Community College *C, A*
Merced College *A*
Modesto Junior College *A*
Monterey Peninsula College *C, A*
Ohlone College *C, A*
Orange Coast College *C, A*
Palomar College *A*
Pasadena City College *C, A*
Riverside Community College *C, A*
Saddleback College *C, A*
San Diego Mesa College *A*
Santa Ana College *C, A*
Santa Rosa Junior College *C*
Shasta College *C*
Southwestern College *C*
Victor Valley College *C*
West Valley College *C, A*

Colorado
Denver Technical College: A Division of
 DeVry University *C, A*
Morgan Community College *C*

Connecticut
Briarwood College *C, A*
Capital Community College *C, A*
Northwestern Connecticut
 Community-Technical College *A*
Norwalk Community-Technical
 College *C*
Quinebaug Valley Community College *A*

Delaware
Delaware Technical and Community
 College
 Owens Campus *C, A*
 Stanton/Wilmington Campus *C, A*
 Terry Campus *C, A*

Florida
Brevard Community College *C*
Broward Community College *C*
Cooper Career Institute *A*
Florida National College *A*
Indian River Community College *C*
International College *A*
Jones College *A, B*
Keiser College *A*
Miami-Dade Community College *C*
New England Institute of Technology *A*
Pasco-Hernando Community College *C*
Pensacola Junior College *C*
Seminole Community College *C*

South College: Palm Beach Campus *A*

Georgia
Athens Area Technical Institute *C*
Chattahoochee Technical Institute *C*
Clayton College and State University *A*
Columbus Technical Institute *C*
Dalton State College *A*
Darton College *A*
DeKalb Technical Institute *C*
Macon State College *A*

Hawaii
University of Hawaii
 Kapiolani Community
 College *C, A*

Idaho
College of Southern Idaho *C*
Eastern Idaho Technical College *C, A*
Idaho State University *A*
Lewis-Clark State College *A*
North Idaho College *A*

Illinois
Black Hawk College *C*
College of DuPage *C*
Northwestern Business College *A*
Robert Morris College: Chicago *C, A*
Southwestern Ilinois College *C, A*
William Rainey Harper College *C, A*

Indiana
International Business College *C, A*
Ivy Tech State College
 Central Indiana *C, A*
 Columbus *C, A*
 Eastcentral *C, A*
 Kokomo *C, A*
 Lafayette *C, A*
 Northcentral *C, A*
 Northeast *C, A*
 Northwest *C, A*
 Southcentral *C, A*
 Southeast *C*
 Southwest *C, A*
 Wabash Valley *C, A*
 Whitewater *A*
Michiana College *A*

Iowa
Des Moines Area Community College *C*
Hamilton Technical College *C*
Iowa Central Community College *C, A*
Iowa Western Community College *C*
Kirkwood Community College *C, A*
Marshalltown Community College *C*
Southeastern Community College
 North Campus *A*

Kentucky
Eastern Kentucky University *A*
National Business College *A*
Owensboro Junior College of
 Business *C, A*

Louisiana
Bossier Parish Community College *C, A*
Remington College - Education America,
 Inc. *A*
Southern University
 Shreveport *A*

Maine
Andover College *A*
Beal College *A*
Husson College *A*
Kennebec Valley Technical College *A*
Mid-State College *A*
Southern Maine Technical College *C*

Maryland
Allegany College *C*
Anne Arundel Community College *C, A*
Charles County Community College *C*
Montgomery College
 Takoma Park Campus *C, A*
Villa Julie College *A*

Medical assistant

Massachusetts
Bay State College *A*
Bristol Community College *C*
Fisher College *C, A*
Massasoit Community College *C*
Middlesex Community College *C, A*
Newbury College *A*
North Shore Community College *C*
Northern Essex Community College *C*
Springfield Technical Community College *A*

Michigan
Alpena Community College *A*
Baker College
   of Auburn Hills *A*
   of Cadillac *A*
   of Jackson *A*
   of Mount Clemens *A*
   of Muskegon *A*
   of Owosso *A*
   of Port Huron *A*
Bay de Noc Community College *C*
Davenport College of Business *A*
Delta College *A*
Great Lakes College *A*
Henry Ford Community College *C*
Jackson Community College *C, A*
Kalamazoo Valley Community College *A*
Kirtland Community College *A*
Lansing Community College *A*
Macomb Community College *C, A*
Mid Michigan Community College *A*
Muskegon Community College *C*
Northwestern Michigan College *A*
Oakland Community College *C, A*
Schoolcraft College *C*

Minnesota
Dakota County Technical College *C*
Lake Superior College: A Community and Technical College *C*
Ridgewater College: A Community and Technical College *C*
Rochester Community and Technical College *C*

Mississippi
Northeast Mississippi Community College *A*

Montana
Flathead Valley Community College *A*
Montana State University
   College of Technology-Great Falls *A*
University of Montana-Missoula *A*

Nebraska
Central Community College *C, A*
Lincoln School of Commerce *C, A*
Nebraska Methodist College of Nursing and Allied Health *C*
Southeast Community College
   Lincoln Campus *C*

New Hampshire
Hesser College *A*
McIntosh College *A*
New Hampshire Community Technical College
   Claremont *C*
   Manchester *C, A*

New Jersey
Bergen Community College *A*
Hudson County Community College *C, A*
Ocean County College *A*

New Mexico
Eastern New Mexico University
   Roswell Campus *C, A*

New York
Broome Community College *A*
Bryant & Stratton Business Institute
   Albany *A*
   Syracuse *A*
City University of New York
   Bronx Community College *A*
   College of Staten Island *C*
   Queensborough Community College *C*
Erie Community College
   North Campus *C, A*
Mohawk Valley Community College *C*
Niagara County Community College *A*
Rockland Community College *C, A*
State University of New York
   College of Technology at Alfred *A*
Suffolk County Community College *A*
Trocaire College *A*
Wood Tobe-Coburn School *A*

North Carolina
Brunswick Community College *A*
Carteret Community College *C*
Cecils College *A*
Central Carolina Community College *A*
Central Piedmont Community College *A*
Davidson County Community College *C, A*
Edgecombe Community College *A*
Forsyth Technical Community College *A*
Gaston College *A*
Guilford Technical Community College *A*
Haywood Community College *C, A*
James Sprunt Community College *A*
Lenoir Community College *C*
Martin Community College *C, A*
Mitchell Community College *C*
Montgomery Community College *A*
Piedmont Community College *C*
Pitt Community College *A*
Richmond Community College *A*
South Piedmont Community College *C, A*
Tri-County Community College *A*
Vance-Granville Community College *A*
Wake Technical Community College *C, A*
Wayne Community College *A*
Wilkes Community College *C, A*

North Dakota
Minot State University: Bottineau Campus *C, A*

Ohio
Belmont Technical College *A*
Cincinnati State Technical and Community College *C, A*
Columbus State Community College *A*
Davis College *C, A*
Hocking Technical College *C, A*
Jefferson Community College *C, A*
Lakeland Community College *C*
Lorain County Community College *C*
Marion Technical College *C*
Miami-Jacobs College *A*
Muskingum Area Technical College *C, A*
Northwestern College *C, A*
Ohio Institute of Photography and Technology *A*
Ohio University *A*
Ohio Valley Business College *A*
RETS Tech Center *C, A*
Southern Ohio College *A*
Southern State Community College *A*
Stark State College of Technology *A*
University of Akron
   Wayne College *A*
University of Akron *A*
University of Toledo *A*
Youngstown State University *A*

Oklahoma
Northeastern Oklahoma Agricultural and Mechanical College *A*
Tulsa Community College *A*

Oregon
Central Oregon Community College *C*
Clackamas Community College *C*
Linn-Benton Community College *A*
Mount Hood Community College *A*
Portland Community College *C*

Pennsylvania
Bucks County Community College *A*
Butler County Community College *A*
C.H.I/RETS Campus *C*
Central Pennsylvania College *A*
Community College of Allegheny County *C, A*
Community College of Philadelphia *A*
Delaware County Community College *C, A*
Harrisburg Area Community College *A*
Laurel Business Institute *A*
Lehigh Carbon Community College *A*
Median School of Allied Health Careers *C, A*
Mount Aloysius College *A*
Sawyer School *C, A*
Yorktowne Business Institute *A*

Rhode Island
New England Institute of Technology *A*

South Carolina
Central Carolina Technical College *C*
Piedmont Technical College *C*
Technical College of the Lowcountry *C*
Tri-County Technical College *C*
Trident Technical College *C*
York Technical College *C*

Tennessee
Chattanooga State Technical Community College *C*
Draughons Junior College of Business: Nashville *A*
Knoxville Business College *A*
Shelby State Community College *C*

Texas
El Paso Community College *C, A*
Houston Community College System *C*
San Antonio College *A*

Utah
LDS Business College *C*
Mountain West College *C, A*
Salt Lake Community College *C*

Virginia
Dabney S. Lancaster Community College *C*
National Business College *A*

Washington
Clark College *C*
Everett Community College *A*
Highline Community College *A*
Lake Washington Technical College *C, A*
Lower Columbia College *A*
North Seattle Community College *A*
Olympic College *C, A*
Peninsula College *A*
Renton Technical College *C*
Skagit Valley College *C*
South Puget Sound Community College *C, A*
Spokane Community College *C*
Spokane Falls Community College *C, A*
Wenatchee Valley College *C*
Whatcom Community College *C, A*

West Virginia
Bluefield State College *A*
College of West Virginia *A*
Corinthian Schools: National Institute of Technology *A*
West Virginia State College *A*

Wisconsin
Blackhawk Technical College *C*
Bryant & Stratton College *A*
Concordia University Wisconsin *C*
Gateway Technical College *C*
Madison Area Technical College *A*
Nicolet Area Technical College *C*
Northeast Wisconsin Technical College *C*
Southwest Wisconsin Technical College *C*
Waukesha County Technical College *C*
Western Wisconsin Technical College *C*
Wisconsin Indianhead Technical College *C*

Wyoming
Western Wyoming Community College *A*

Medical basic sciences

Alabama
University of Alabama
   Birmingham *M*
University of South Alabama *D*

Arizona
University of Arizona *M, D*

California
University of California
   Riverside *B, M, D*
University of Southern California *M, D*

Connecticut
Yale University *D*

Florida
Nova Southeastern University *M*
University of Florida *M, D*
University of South Florida *M, D*

Georgia
Medical College of Georgia *D*

Hawaii
University of Hawaii
   Manoa *M, D*

Indiana
Indiana University
   Bloomington *M, D*
Indiana University--Purdue University
   Indiana University-Purdue University Indianapolis *M, D*

Kansas
University of Kansas
   Medical Center *M, D*

Kentucky
University of Kentucky *M, D*
University of Louisville *M, D*

Maine
University of New England *B*

Massachusetts
Boston University *M, D*
Harvard University *M, D*
Northeastern University *A, B*

Michigan
Oakland University *B, D*
University of Michigan *B, M, D*
Wayne State University *M, D*

Minnesota
Mayo Graduate School *M*
University of Minnesota
   Twin Cities *M*

Mississippi
University of Mississippi
   Medical Center *M, D*

Missouri
University of Missouri
   Columbia *M, D*

New Jersey
Monmouth University *B*
New Jersey City University *B*

New York
New York University M, D
State University of New York
  Health Science Center at Stony
    Brook M, D

North Carolina
East Carolina University D
University of North Carolina
  Chapel Hill M, D

Ohio
Youngstown State University B

Pennsylvania
Penn State
  University Park D
Temple University M, D
University of Pennsylvania M, D
University of Pittsburgh
  Bradford B
University of Pittsburgh M, D

South Carolina
University of South Carolina M

Tennessee
Southern Adventist University B

Texas
Navarro College A
Texas A&M University B, M, D
Texas Tech University Health Science
  Center M, D
University of Texas
  Southwestern Medical Center at
    Dallas D

Utah
University of Utah B, M, D

West Virginia
Alderson-Broaddus College B
Marshall University B, M
West Virginia University M, D

Medical dietetics

Alabama
University of Alabama
  Birmingham M

Arkansas
University of Central Arkansas B

California
Loma Linda University A, B
University of California
  Berkeley B

Connecticut
Briarwood College A

Florida
Palm Beach Community College A

Illinois
University of Illinois
  Chicago B, M, D

Maine
Southern Maine Technical College A

Massachusetts
Laboure College C, A

Minnesota
College of St. Scholastica B

Ohio
Hocking Technical College C, A
Lima Technical College A
Ohio State University
  Columbus Campus B, M
Owens Community College
  Toledo A

Oregon
Oregon Health Sciences University C

Pennsylvania
Mercyhurst College B

Texas
El Paso Community College A
Tarleton State University B

Utah
Brigham Young University B

Washington
Bastyr University B
Shoreline Community College A

Medical illustrating

California
California State University
  Long Beach B

Georgia
Atlanta Metropolitan College A
Clark Atlanta University B
Medical College of Georgia M
Morris Brown College B

Illinois
University of Illinois
  Chicago M

Iowa
Iowa State University B

Michigan
University of Michigan M

New York
Rochester Institute of Technology B, M

Ohio
Cleveland Institute of Art B
Ohio State University
  Columbus Campus B

Pennsylvania
Beaver College B

Texas
Texas Woman's University B, M
University of Texas
  Southwestern Medical Center at
    Dallas M

Wisconsin
Milwaukee Area Technical College A

Medical laboratory assistant

Alabama
Northwest-Shoals Community College A

California
California State University
  Chico B
De Anza College C

Delaware
Delaware Technical and Community
  College
    Owens Campus C, A

Florida
Broward Community College A

Georgia
Clayton College and State University A

Idaho
North Idaho College A

Illinois
City Colleges of Chicago
  Malcolm X College A
De Paul University B
Oakton Community College A
Southwestern Ilinois College A

Indiana
University of St. Francis A

Iowa
Northeast Iowa Community College A

Kentucky
Somerset Community College A
Southeast Community College A

Maine
Eastern Maine Technical College A
University of New England B

Maryland
University of Maryland
  Eastern Shore B

Massachusetts
Middlesex Community College C

Michigan
Baker College
  of Owosso A
Monroe County Community College C

Minnesota
College of St. Catherine-Minneapolis C
Lake Superior College: A Community
  and Technical College A

Mississippi
Hinds Community College A
Northeast Mississippi Community
  College A

Montana
University of Montana-Missoula A

Nevada
Community College of Southern
  Nevada A

New Jersey
Atlantic Cape Community College A
Brookdale Community College A

New Mexico
New Mexico Junior College A

New York
Long Island University
  Brooklyn Campus B
Marist College B
State University of New York
  College of Agriculture and
    Technology at Cobleskill A
  College of Technology at Canton A

North Carolina
Alamance Community College A
Mars Hill College B
North Carolina State University B
St. Augustine's College B
Western Piedmont Community
  College A

North Dakota
Bismarck State College A

Ohio
Cincinnati State Technical and
  Community College C, A
Columbus State Community College A
Shawnee State University A
Stark State College of Technology A
Washington State Community College A
Youngstown State University A

Oklahoma
Southwestern Oklahoma State
  University B
Tulsa Community College A
Western Oklahoma State College A

Pennsylvania
California University of Pennsylvania B

South Carolina
Aiken Technical College C
Greenville Technical College A
Orangeburg-Calhoun Technical
  College C, A

Tennessee
Hiwassee College A
Roane State Community College A

Texas
Central Texas College C, A
El Paso Community College C
Tarrant County College C
Tyler Junior College A

Virginia
Northern Virginia Community College A
Virginia Highlands Community
  College A

Washington
Pierce College A
Wenatchee Valley College A

Wisconsin
Chippewa Valley Technical College A
Lakeshore Technical College C

Medical laboratory technology

Alabama
Alabama State University B
Faulkner University A
Gadsden State Community College A
James H. Faulkner State Community
  College A
Jefferson State Community College A
Northwest-Shoals Community College A
Wallace State Community College at
  Hanceville A

Alaska
University of Alaska
  Anchorage A

Arkansas
Garland County Community
  College C, A
North Arkansas College A
Southern Arkansas University B
Westark College A

California
California State University
  Bakersfield B
  Dominguez Hills B
  Hayward B
Chabot College A
De Anza College C
Fresno City College C, A
Los Angeles Southwest College A
Mount St. Mary's College B
Pasadena City College C, A
Riverside Community College A

Colorado
Arapahoe Community College A

Connecticut
Central Connecticut State University B
Housatonic Community-Technical
  College A
Manchester Community-Technical
  College A

Delaware
Delaware Technical and Community
  College
    Owens Campus C, A
    Stanton/Wilmington Campus A
University of Delaware B

District of Columbia
George Washington University A

Florida
Barry University B
Bethune-Cookman College B
Brevard Community College A
Broward Community College A
Florida Community College at
  Jacksonville A

Medical laboratory technology

Indian River Community College *A*
Jacksonville University *B*
Keiser College *A*
Lake City Community College *A*
Manatee Community College *A*
Palm Beach Community College *A*
St. Petersburg Junior College *A*
Valencia Community College *A*

Georgia
Clayton College and State University *A*
Coastal Georgia Community College *A*
Dalton State College *A*
Darton College *C, A*
DeKalb Technical Institute *C*
Macon State College *A*
Medical College of Georgia *B, M*
Mercer University *B*
Thomas College *A*
Waycross College *A*

Hawaii
University of Hawaii
    Kapiolani Community College *A*

Idaho
Ricks College *A*
University of Idaho *B*

Illinois
Blackburn College *B*
City Colleges of Chicago
    Malcolm X College *A*
College of Lake County *C, A*
Elgin Community College *C, A*
Finch University of Health Sciences/The Chicago Medical School *B*
John Wood Community College *A*
Kankakee Community College *A*
McKendree College *B*
Moraine Valley Community College *A*
Roosevelt University *B*
Sauk Valley Community College *A*
Southeastern Illinois College *A*
Southwestern Illinois College *A*
University of St. Francis *B*

Indiana
DePauw University *B*
Goshen College *B*
Indiana State University *M*
Indiana University
    East *A*
    Northwest *A*
Indiana University--Purdue University
Indiana University-Purdue
    University Fort Wayne *B*
Ivy Tech State College
    Northcentral *A*
    Wabash Valley *A*
Purdue University
    North Central Campus *A*

Iowa
Des Moines Area Community College *A*
Dordt College *B*
Hawkeye Community College *A*
Iowa Central Community College *A*
Mount Mercy College *B*
Northeast Iowa Community College *A*
Scott Community College *A*

Kansas
Barton County Community College *A*
Central Christian College *A*
Kansas State University *B*
Tabor College *B*
Washburn University of Topeka *B*

Kentucky
Brescia University *B*
Cumberland College *B*
Eastern Kentucky University *A*
Henderson Community College *A*
Madisonville Community College *A*
Murray State University *B*
Pikeville College *B*
Thomas More College *B*

Louisiana
Delgado Community College *A*
Northwestern State University *B*
Southern University
    New Orleans *B*
    Shreveport *A*

Maine
Central Maine Technical College *A*
Eastern Maine Technical College *A*
University of Maine
    Augusta *A*
    Presque Isle *A*

Maryland
Allegany College *A*
Columbia Union College *A, B*
Community College of Baltimore County
    Essex *A*
Howard Community College *A*
Montgomery College
    Takoma Park Campus *A*

Massachusetts
American International College *B*
Bristol Community College *A*
Elms College *B*
Fitchburg State College *B*
Massachusetts College of Liberal Arts *B*
Middlesex Community College *A*
Mount Wachusett Community College *A*
Springfield College *B*
Springfield Technical Community College *A*
Stonehill College *B*

Michigan
Baker College
    of Owosso *A*
Calvin College *B*
Ferris State University *A*
Kellogg Community College *A*
Northern Michigan University *A*

Minnesota
Alexandria Technical College *A*
Hibbing Community College: A Technical and Community College *A*
Lake Superior College: A Community and Technical College *A*
Minnesota State University, Mankato *B*
Moorhead State University *B*
Rochester Community and Technical College *A*
St. Paul Technical College *A*
Winona State University *B*

Mississippi
Blue Mountain College *B*
Copiah-Lincoln Community College *A*
Hinds Community College *A*
Meridian Community College *A*
Mississippi Delta Community College *A*
Mississippi Gulf Coast Community College
    Jackson County Campus *A*
    Perkinston *A*

Missouri
Avila College *B*
Evangel University *B*
Missouri Southern State College *A*
Missouri Western State College *B*
Southwest Baptist University *B*
Three Rivers Community College *A*
Truman State University *B*
University of Missouri
    Kansas City *B*

Nebraska
College of Saint Mary *B*
Dana College *B*
Mid Plains Community College Area *A*
Southeast Community College
    Lincoln Campus *A*

Nevada
Community College of Southern Nevada *A*
Western Nevada Community College *A*

New Hampshire
New Hampshire Community Technical College
    Claremont *A*
University of New Hampshire *B*

New Jersey
Bergen Community College *A*
Bloomfield College *B*
Caldwell College *B*
Camden County College *A*
County College of Morris *A*
Felician College *A*
Mercer County Community College *A*
Middlesex County College *A*
Ocean County College *A*
Rutgers
    The State University of New Jersey: Camden College of Arts and Sciences *B*
    The State University of New Jersey: Douglass College *B*
    The State University of New Jersey: Livingston College *B*
    The State University of New Jersey: Newark College of Arts and Sciences *B*
    The State University of New Jersey: University College Camden *B*
    The State University of New Jersey: University College New Brunswick *B*
Thomas Edison State College *A, B*
University of Medicine and Dentistry of New Jersey
    School of Health Related Professions *A*

New Mexico
Albuquerque Technical-Vocational Institute *A*
New Mexico Junior College *A*
New Mexico State University
    Alamogordo *A*
University of New Mexico *B*
Western New Mexico University *B*

New York
Alfred University *B*
Broome Community College *A*
Canisius College *B*
City University of New York
    Bronx Community College *A*
    College of Staten Island *A*
    Hostos Community College *A*
    Hunter College *B*
    Queensborough Community College *A*
Clinton Community College *A*
Daemen College *C, B*
Dutchess Community College *A*
Erie Community College
    North Campus *A*
Fulton-Montgomery Community College *A*
Hudson Valley Community College *A*
Jamestown Community College *A*
Marist College *B*
Orange County Community College *A*
Rochester Institute of Technology *A, B*
St. John's University *B, M*
State University of New York
    College at Brockport *B*
    College at Fredonia *B*
    College of Agriculture and Technology at Morrisville *A*
    College of Technology at Alfred *A*
    College of Technology at Canton *A*
    Farmingdale *A*
Westchester Community College *A*

North Carolina
Alamance Community College *A*
Appalachian State University *B*
Asheville Buncombe Technical Community College *A*
Barton College *B*
Beaufort County Community College *A*
Bennett College *B*
Coastal Carolina Community College *A*
Davidson County Community College *A*
Halifax Community College *A*
Lees-McRae College *B*
Sandhills Community College *A*
Southeastern Community College *A*
Southwestern Community College *A*
Wake Forest University *B*
Wake Technical Community College *A*

Ohio
Baldwin-Wallace College *B*
Bowling Green State University *B*
Clark State Community College *A*
Columbus State Community College *A*
Defiance College *B*
Jefferson Community College *A*
Kent State University *B*
Lakeland Community College *C, A*
Lorain County Community College *A*
Marion Technical College *A*
Muskingum Area Technical College *A*
Muskingum College *B*
Notre Dame College of Ohio *B*
Ohio State University
    Columbus Campus *B, M*
Shawnee State University *B*
University of Akron *B*
University of Rio Grande *A*
Xavier University *B*
Youngstown State University *A*

Oklahoma
Cameron University *B*
Northeastern Oklahoma Agricultural and Mechanical College *A*
Northeastern State University *B*
Oklahoma State University *B*
Rose State College *A*
Seminole State College *A*
Southeastern Oklahoma State University *B*
Southern Nazarene University *B*
Southwestern Oklahoma State University *B*
Tulsa Community College *A*
University of Oklahoma *B*
University of Science and Arts of Oklahoma *B*

Oregon
Oregon Health Sciences University *B, M*
Portland Community College *A*

Pennsylvania
Allentown College of St. Francis de Sales *B*
Bloomsburg University of Pennsylvania *B*
California University of Pennsylvania *B*
Cedar Crest College *B*
Clarion University of Pennsylvania *B*
Community College of Allegheny County *A*
Community College of Beaver County *A*
Community College of Philadelphia *A*
Edinboro University of Pennsylvania *A, B*
Harcum College *A*
Harrisburg Area Community College *A*
Holy Family College *B*
Kutztown University of Pennsylvania *B*
La Roche College *B*
Lebanon Valley College of Pennsylvania *B*
Lock Haven University of Pennsylvania *B*
MCP Hahnemann University *A, B*

Manor College *A*
Mansfield University of Pennsylvania *B*
Montgomery County Community
    College *A*
Neumann College *C, B*
Penn State
    Dubois *A*
    Hazleton *A*
    New Kensington *A*
    Schuylkill - Capital College *A*
St. Francis College *B*
Seton Hill College *B*
Shippensburg University of
    Pennsylvania *B*
Slippery Rock University of
    Pennsylvania *B*
University of the Sciences in
    Philadelphia *B*
Waynesburg College *B*
York College of Pennsylvania *B*

Puerto Rico

University of Puerto Rico
    Medical Sciences Campus *C, B*
University of the Sacred Heart *C, B*

Rhode Island

Community College of Rhode Island *A*
Rhode Island College *B*

South Carolina

Central Carolina Technical College *C*
Coker College *B*
Erskine College *B*
Florence-Darlington Technical College *A*
Greenville Technical College *A*
Midlands Technical College *A*
Orangeburg-Calhoun Technical
    College *A*
Tri-County Technical College *A*
Trident Technical College *A*
York Technical College *A*

South Dakota

Augustana College *B*
Dakota State University *A*

Tennessee

Cleveland State Community College *A*
Columbia State Community College *A*
David Lipscomb University *B*
Jackson State Community College *A*
Lincoln Memorial University *B*
Roane State Community College *A*
Shelby State Community College *A*
Trevecca Nazarene University *B*
Union University *B*
University of Tennessee
    Memphis *B*

Texas

Amarillo College *A*
Central Texas College *A*
Del Mar College *C, A*
East Texas Baptist University *B*
El Paso Community College *A*
Houston Baptist University *B*
Houston Community College System *A*
McMurry University *B*
St. Philip's College *A*
Southwestern Adventist University *B*
Temple College *A*
Victoria College *A*
Wharton County Junior College *A*

Utah

Dixie State College of Utah *C, A*
Salt Lake Community College *A*
University of Utah *B, M*
Weber State University *A*

Virginia

Bluefield College *A*
Central Virginia Community College *A*
Ferrum College *B*
J. Sargeant Reynolds Community
    College *A*
Northern Virginia Community College *A*
Radford University *B*
Wytheville Community College *A*

Washington

City University *A*
Columbia Basin College *A*
Seattle University *B*
Shoreline Community College *A*
Spokane Community College *A*
Spokane Falls Community College *A*
Walla Walla College *B*
Wenatchee Valley College *A*

West Virginia

Alderson-Broaddus College *B*
Fairmont State College *A*
Marshall University *B*
Southern West Virginia Community and
    Technical College *A*
West Virginia Northern Community
    College *A*

Wisconsin

Carroll College *B*
Chippewa Valley Technical College *A*
Madison Area Technical College *A*
Milwaukee Area Technical College *A*
University of Wisconsin
    La Crosse *B*
    Madison *B*
    Oshkosh *B*
Western Wisconsin Technical College *A*

Medical radiologic technology

Alabama

Central Alabama Community College *A*
Community College of the Air Force *A*
Faulkner University *A*
Gadsden State Community College *A*
George C. Wallace State Community
    College
    Dothan *A*
Jefferson State Community College *A*
Northwest-Shoals Community College *A*
University of Alabama
    Birmingham *B*
University of South Alabama *C, B*
Wallace State Community College at
    Hanceville *A*

Arizona

Gateway Community College *A*
Pima Community College *A*
Scottsdale Community College *A*

Arkansas

Arkansas State University *A, B*
Garland County Community College *A*
North Arkansas College *A*
University of Arkansas
    for Medical Sciences *A, B*
University of Central Arkansas *B*
Westark College *A*

California

Bakersfield College *A*
Cabrillo College *C, A*
California State University
    Long Beach *B*
Canada College *A*
Chaffey Community College *C, A*
City College of San Francisco *C, A*
Compton Community College *A*
Crafton Hills College *A*
Cypress College *C, A*
Foothill College *C, A*
Fresno City College *A*
Loma Linda University *C, A, B*
Long Beach City College *C, A*
Merced College *A*
Merritt College *A*
Moorpark College *C, A*
Mount San Antonio College *C, A*
Orange Coast College *C, A*
Pasadena City College *C, A*
San Diego Mesa College *C, A*
San Joaquin Delta College *A*
Santa Barbara City College *A*
Santa Rosa Junior College *C, A*
Yuba College *A*

Colorado

Aims Community College *A*
Community College of Denver *C, A*
Mesa State College *A*
Pueblo Community College *A*

Connecticut

Capital Community College *A*
Gateway Community College *A*
Middlesex Community-Technical
    College *A*
Naugatuck Valley Community-Technical
    College *A*
Quinnipiac University *B*
University of Hartford *B*

Delaware

Delaware Technical and Community
    College
    Owens Campus *A*
    Stanton/Wilmington Campus *A*

District of Columbia

George Washington University *C, A*
Georgetown University *M*
University of the District of Columbia *A*

Florida

Barry University *B*
Brevard Community College *A*
Broward Community College *A*
Daytona Beach Community College *A*
Edison Community College *A*
Florida Community College at
    Jacksonville *A*
Gulf Coast Community College *A*
Hillsborough Community College *C, A*
Indian River Community College *A*
Keiser College *A*
Manatee Community College *A*
Miami-Dade Community College *A*
Palm Beach Community College *A*
Pensacola Junior College *A*
Polk Community College *A*
St. Petersburg Junior College *A*
Santa Fe Community College *A*
University of Central Florida *B*
Valencia Community College *A*

Georgia

Armstrong Atlantic State University *B*
Athens Area Technical Institute *A*
Atlanta Metropolitan College *A*
Coastal Georgia Community College *A*
Darton College *A*
Floyd College *A*
Gwinnett Technical Institute *A*
Medical College of Georgia *B, M*
Thomas College *A*
Waycross College *A*

Hawaii

University of Hawaii
    Kapiolani Community College *A*

Idaho

Boise State University *A, B*
North Idaho College *A*

Illinois

Barat College *B*
Black Hawk College *A*
City Colleges of Chicago
    Malcolm X College *A*
    Wright College *A*
College of DuPage *A*
College of Lake County *A*
Illinois Eastern Community Colleges
    Olney Central College *A*
John Wood Community College *A*
Kankakee Community College *A*
Kaskaskia College *A*
Kishwaukee College *A*
Lincoln Land Community College *A*
Moraine Valley Community College *A*
National-Louis University *B*
Parkland College *A*
Sauk Valley Community College *A*
Southern Illinois University
    Carbondale *A, B*
Southwestern Illinois College *A*
Triton College *A*
University of St. Francis *B*

Indiana

Ball State University *A*
Indiana University
    Bloomington *B*
    Northwest *A, B*
    South Bend *A*
Indiana University--Purdue University
    Indiana University-Purdue
        University Fort Wayne *A*
    Indiana University-Purdue
        University Indianapolis *A, B*
Ivy Tech State College
    Central Indiana *A*
    Wabash Valley *A*
University of St. Francis *A*
University of Southern Indiana *A*

Iowa

Briar Cliff College *B*
Indian Hills Community College *A*
Iowa Central Community College *A*
Kirkwood Community College *A*
Northeast Iowa Community College *A*
Scott Community College *A*
Southeastern Community College
    North Campus *A*

Kansas

Fort Hays State University *A*
Hutchinson Community College *A*
Johnson County Community College *A*
Newman University *A, B*
Washburn University of Topeka *A*

Kentucky

Hazard Community College *A*
Lexington Community College *A*
Madisonville Community College *A*
Morehead State University *A*
Northern Kentucky University *A*
Owensboro Community College *A*
Southeast Community College *A*
University of Louisville *A*

Louisiana

Delgado Community College *A*
Louisiana State University
    Eunice *A*
Loyola University New Orleans *B*
McNeese State University *B*
Northwestern State University *B*
Our Lady of Holy Cross College *B*
Southern University
    Shreveport *A*
University of Louisiana at Monroe *B*

Maine

Central Maine Technical College *A*
Eastern Maine Technical College *A*
St. Joseph's College *A, B*
Southern Maine Technical College *A*

Maryland

Allegany College *A*
Anne Arundel Community College *A*
Chesapeake College *A*
Community College of Baltimore County
    Essex *A*
Hagerstown Community College *A*
Montgomery College
    Rockville Campus *A*
Prince George's Community College *A*
Wor-Wic Community College *A*

Medical radiologic technology

Massachusetts
Bunker Hill Community College A
Holyoke Community College A
Laboure College A
Massachusetts Bay Community College A
Massachusetts College of Pharmacy and Health Sciences B
Massasoit Community College A
Middlesex Community College A
North Shore Community College A
Northeastern University A
Springfield Technical Community College A
Suffolk University B

Michigan
Andrews University A, B
Baker College of Owosso A
Ferris State University A
Grand Rapids Community College A
Jackson Community College A
Kellogg Community College A
Lake Michigan College A
Lansing Community College A
Marygrove College C, A
Mid Michigan Community College A
Montcalm Community College A
Mott Community College A
Oakland Community College A
Washtenaw Community College A
Wayne State University B

Minnesota
Century Community and Technical College A
College of St. Catherine-Minneapolis A
Lake Superior College: A Community and Technical College A
North Hennepin Community College A
Ridgewater College: A Community and Technical College A
Rochester Community and Technical College A

Mississippi
Copiah-Lincoln Community College A
Meridian Community College A
Mississippi Delta Community College A
Mississippi Gulf Coast Community College
  Jackson County Campus A
  Perkinston A
Northeast Mississippi Community College A
University of Mississippi
  Medical Center C

Missouri
Avila College B
Missouri Southern State College A
Penn Valley Community College A
Southwest Missouri State University B
St. Louis Community College
  St. Louis Community College at Forest Park A
University of Missouri
  Columbia B

Nebraska
Clarkson College A, B
Northeast Community College A
Southeast Community College
  Lincoln Campus A
University of Nebraska
  Kearney B

Nevada
University of Nevada
  Las Vegas C, B

New Hampshire
New Hampshire Technical Institute A

New Jersey
Bergen Community College A
Burlington County College A
Cumberland County College A
Essex County College A
Fairleigh Dickinson University A, B
Mercer County Community College A
Passaic County Community College A
Thomas Edison State College A, B
Union County College A
University of Medicine and Dentistry of New Jersey
  School of Health Related Professions B

New Mexico
Clovis Community College A
Dona Ana Branch Community College of New Mexico State University A
New Mexico Junior College A
Northern New Mexico Community College A
University of New Mexico C, A, B

New York
Broome Community College A
City University of New York
  Bronx Community College A
  Hostos Community College A
  New York City Technical College A
Erie Community College
  City Campus A
Hudson Valley Community College A
Iona College C, A, B
Long Island University
  C. W. Post Campus B
Mohawk Valley Community College A
Nassau Community College A
New York University A
Niagara County Community College A
North Country Community College A
Orange County Community College A
St. Francis College B
State University of New York
  Upstate Medical University A
Trocaire College A
Westchester Community College A

North Carolina
Asheville Buncombe Technical Community College A
Caldwell Community College and Technical Institute A
Cape Fear Community College A
Carteret Community College A
Cleveland Community College A
Edgecombe Community College C, A
Forsyth Technical Community College A
Johnston Community College A
Pitt Community College A
Queens College B
Sandhills Community College A
Southwestern Community College A
University of North Carolina
  Chapel Hill C, B
Vance-Granville Community College A
Wake Technical Community College A

North Dakota
Minot State University B
University of Mary A, B

Ohio
Central Ohio Technical College A
Columbus State Community College A
Jefferson Community College A
Lakeland Community College C, A
Lima Technical College C, A
Marion Technical College A
Miami University
  Oxford Campus C
Muskingum Area Technical College A
North Central State College A
Ohio State University
  Columbus Campus B, M
Shawnee State University A
Sinclair Community College A
University of Akron
  Wayne College A
University of Akron A
University of Cincinnati
  Raymond Walters College A
Xavier University A

Oklahoma
Rose State College A
Tulsa Community College A
Western Oklahoma State College A

Oregon
Oregon Health Sciences University B
Oregon Institute of Technology B
Portland Community College A

Pennsylvania
Bloomsburg University of Pennsylvania B
California University of Pennsylvania B
Clarion University of Pennsylvania A
College Misericordia B
Community College of Allegheny County C, A
Community College of Philadelphia A
Gannon University A
Harrisburg Area Community College A
Holy Family College A, B
La Roche College B
MCP Hahnemann University C, A
Mansfield University of Pennsylvania A
Mount Aloysius College A, B
Northampton County Area Community College A
Pennsylvania College of Technology A
Reading Area Community College A
Robert Morris College A
Widener University A, B

Puerto Rico
Colegio Universitario del Este C, A, B
Inter American University of Puerto Rico
  San German Campus A
University of Puerto Rico
  Medical Sciences Campus A

Rhode Island
Community College of Rhode Island A
Rhode Island College B

South Carolina
Florence-Darlington Technical College A
Greenville Technical College A
Midlands Technical College C, A
Orangeburg-Calhoun Technical College A
Piedmont Technical College A
Spartanburg Technical College A
Trident Technical College C, A
York Technical College A

South Dakota
Mount Marty College B

Tennessee
Austin Peay State University B
Chattanooga State Technical Community College A
Columbia State Community College A
Jackson State Community College A
Roane State Community College A
Shelby State Community College A
Southern Adventist University A
University of Tennessee
  Knoxville B
Volunteer State Community College A

Texas
Amarillo College A
Blinn College A
Del Mar College A
El Paso Community College A
Galveston College C, A
Houston Community College System A
Midland College C, A
Midwestern State University A, B, M
Navarro College A
Odessa College A
St. Philip's College A
South Plains College A
Southwest Texas State University B
Tarrant County College A
Tyler Junior College A
Wharton County Junior College A

Utah
Salt Lake Community College A
Weber State University A, B

Vermont
Champlain College A, B
University of Vermont B

Virginia
Averett College B
Northern Virginia Community College A
Southwest Virginia Community College A
Tidewater Community College A
Virginia Highlands Community College A
Virginia Western Community College A

Washington
Bellevue Community College A
Tacoma Community College C
Wenatchee Valley College A
Yakima Valley Community College A

West Virginia
Alderson-Broaddus College B
Bluefield State College A
Southern West Virginia Community and Technical College A
University of Charleston B
West Virginia Northern Community College A

Wisconsin
Blackhawk Technical College A
Chippewa Valley Technical College A
Concordia University Wisconsin B
Gateway Technical College A
Lakeshore Technical College A
Madison Area Technical College A
Marian College of Fond du Lac B
University of Wisconsin
  Madison B, M, D
Western Wisconsin Technical College A

Wyoming
Casper College A
Laramie County Community College A

Medical records administration

Alabama
Alabama State University B
Shelton State Community College C
University of Alabama
  Birmingham B

Arkansas
Arkansas Tech University B

California
Allan Hancock College C, A
Barstow College C
Chabot College C, A
Chaffey Community College C
City College of San Francisco C, A
Cypress College C, A
Lake Tahoe Community College A
Loma Linda University B
Oxnard College A
Palomar College C, A
San Bernardino Valley College C
Santa Rosa Junior College C

Colorado
Pikes Peak Community College C, A

Delaware
Delaware Technical and Community College
  Stanton/Wilmington Campus C

Florida
Broward Community College *A*
Florida Agricultural and Mechanical University *B*
Florida International University *B*
Gulf Coast Community College *A*
Indian River Community College *A*
Miami-Dade Community College *A*
Pensacola Junior College *A*
Polk Community College *A*
St. Petersburg Junior College *A*
University of Central Florida *B*

Georgia
Atlanta Metropolitan College *A*
Clayton College and State University *A*
Dalton State College *A*
Darton College *A*
Floyd College *A*
Macon State College *B*
Medical College of Georgia *B, M*
Middle Georgia College *A*

Idaho
Boise State University *A, B*

Illinois
Chicago State University *B*
Illinois State University *B*
University of Illinois Chicago *B, M*

Indiana
Indiana University Northwest *B*
Vincennes University *A*

Iowa
North Iowa Area Community College *A*
Northeast Iowa Community College *A*

Kansas
Seward County Community College *C*
University of Kansas Medical Center *B*

Kentucky
Eastern Kentucky University *C, B*

Louisiana
Louisiana Tech University *B*
Southern University Shreveport *A*
University of Louisiana at Lafayette *B*

Maine
Andover College *A*
University of Maine Augusta *A*

Maryland
Baltimore City Community College *A*
Prince George's Community College *C, A*

Massachusetts
Franklin Institute of Boston *C*
Northern Essex Community College *C, A*
Springfield College *B*

Michigan
Baker College
  of Auburn Hills *A*
  of Jackson *A*
Detroit College of Business *B*
Ferris State University *B*
Washtenaw Community College *A*

Minnesota
College of St. Scholastica *B, M*

Mississippi
Mississippi Delta Community College *A*
Mississippi Gulf Coast Community College
  Perkinston *A*
University of Mississippi Medical Center *B*

Missouri
St. Louis University *B*
Stephens College *B*

Montana
Montana State University College of Technology-Great Falls *A*

Nebraska
College of Saint Mary *A, B*

New Jersey
Kean University *B*

New York
Long Island University C. W. Post Campus *B*
Molloy College *A*
Pace University *B*
State University of New York
  Health Science Center at Brooklyn *B*
  Institute of Technology at Utica/Rome *B*

North Carolina
Alamance Community College *A*
Central Piedmont Community College *A*
Durham Technical Community College *C, A*
East Carolina University *B*
Western Carolina University *B*

Ohio
Ohio State University Columbus Campus *B, M*
Owens Community College Toledo *C*

Oklahoma
Southwestern Oklahoma State University *B*

Oregon
Chemeketa Community College *A*
Mount Hood Community College *A*
Portland Community College *A*

Pennsylvania
Duquesne University *B, M*
Gwynedd-Mercy College *B*
Laurel Business Institute *A*
Luzerne County Community College *C*
Mercyhurst College *C, A*
Peirce College *A, B*
Temple University *B*
University of Pittsburgh *B*
Widener University *M, D*

Puerto Rico
Colegio Universitario del Este *A*
Huertas Junior College *A*
Inter American University of Puerto Rico Aguadilla Campus *C*
University of Puerto Rico Medical Sciences Campus *M*

South Dakota
Dakota State University *B*

Tennessee
Chattanooga State Technical Community College *A*
Draughons Junior College of Business: Nashville *A*
Hiwassee College *A*
Tennessee State University *B*
University of Tennessee Memphis *B*

Texas
Howard College *C, A*
St. Philip's College *A*
Southwest Texas State University *A*
Texas A&M University Commerce *B*
University of Texas Medical Branch at Galveston *B*

Virginia
ECPI College of Technology *C, A*
Norfolk State University *B*

Washington
Clark College *C, A*
Columbia Basin College *A*
Renton Technical College *A*

West Virginia
Glenville State College *A*

Wisconsin
Madison Area Technical College *A*
Northeast Wisconsin Technical College *A*
University of Wisconsin Milwaukee *B*

Medical records technology

Alabama
Central Alabama Community College *A*
Chattahoochee Valley Community College *A*
Enterprise State Junior College *A*
Faulkner University *A*
Lawson State Community College *A*
Northwest-Shoals Community College *A*
Shelton State Community College *C*
Wallace State Community College at Hanceville *A*

Arizona
Phoenix College *A*
Pima Community College *A*

Arkansas
Garland County Community College *C, A*
North Arkansas College *C*

California
Allan Hancock College *C, A*
Cerritos Community College *A*
Chabot College *C, A*
City College of San Francisco *C, A*
College of San Mateo *C*
Cypress College *A*
East Los Angeles College *C*
Orange Coast College *C, A*
Santa Rosa Junior College *C*
Ventura College *A*

Colorado
Arapahoe Community College *C, A*

Connecticut
Briarwood College *C, A*
Quinebaug Valley Community College *C*

Delaware
Delaware Technical and Community College
  Terry Campus *C*

Florida
Brevard Community College *C*
Daytona Beach Community College *A*
Florida Community College at Jacksonville *A*
Indian River Community College *A*
International College *A*
Miami-Dade Community College *C, A*
Pasco-Hernando Community College *C*
Pensacola Junior College *A*
Polk Community College *A*
St. Petersburg Junior College *C, A*
Tallahassee Community College *C*
University of Miami *M*

Georgia
Abraham Baldwin Agricultural College *A*
Atlanta Metropolitan College *A*
Clark Atlanta University *B*
Dalton State College *A*
Darton College *A*
Macon State College *A*
Middle Georgia College *A*
Morris Brown College *B*

Idaho
Boise State University *A*
College of Southern Idaho *C*
Idaho State University *C, A*

Illinois
College of DuPage *A*
College of Lake County *A*
John A. Logan College *A*
Moraine Valley Community College *C, A*
Northwestern Business College *A*
Oakton Community College *A*
Robert Morris College: Chicago *A*
Rock Valley College *A*
Shawnee Community College *C, A*
Southeastern Illinois College *A*
Southwestern Ilinois College *A*

Indiana
Indiana University
  Bloomington *B*
  Northwest *A*
Indiana University--Purdue University
  Indiana University-Purdue University Fort Wayne *A*
Purdue University
  Calumet *C, A*
Vincennes University *A*

Iowa
Indian Hills Community College *A*
Kirkwood Community College *A*
Northeast Iowa Community College *A*

Kansas
Central Christian College *A*
Dodge City Community College *C, A*
Hutchinson Community College *C, A*
Johnson County Community College *A*
Washburn University of Topeka *A*

Kentucky
Eastern Kentucky University *A, B*
Henderson Community College *C*
Western Kentucky University *A*

Louisiana
Delgado Community College *A*
Louisiana Tech University *A*
Remington College - Education America, Inc. *A*
Southern University Shreveport *A*

Maine
Andover College *A*

Maryland
Baltimore City Community College *C, A*
Chesapeake College *A*
Montgomery College
  Rockville Campus *A*
  Takoma Park Campus *A*
Prince George's Community College *C, A*

Massachusetts
Bristol Community College *A*
Holyoke Community College *C, A*
Laboure College *C, A*
North Shore Community College *C*
Northern Essex Community College *C*
Springfield Technical Community College *A*

Michigan
Baker College
  of Auburn Hills *A*
  of Jackson *A*
  of Mount Clemens *A*
  of Muskegon *A*
  of Owosso *A*
  of Port Huron *A*

Bay de Noc Community College C
Ferris State University A
Henry Ford Community College A
Schoolcraft College A

Minnesota
College of St.
 Catherine-Minneapolis C, A
Ridgewater College: A Community and
 Technical College A
St. Cloud Technical College C

Mississippi
Hinds Community College A
Meridian Community College A

Missouri
Missouri Western State College C, A
Ozarks Technical Community
 College C, A
St. Charles County Community
 College A

Nebraska
College of Saint Mary C
Mid Plains Community College Area A

Nevada
Community College of Southern
 Nevada A

New Hampshire
McIntosh College C
New Hampshire Community Technical
 College
  Manchester C, A
New Hampshire Technical Institute C

New Jersey
Burlington County College A
Cumberland County College C
Hudson County Community
 College C, A
Passaic County Community College C

New Mexico
Eastern New Mexico University
 Roswell Campus C, A
San Juan College C, A

New York
Adirondack Community College A
Broome Community College A
Bryant & Stratton Business Institute
 Syracuse A
Erie Community College
 North Campus A
Fulton-Montgomery Community
 College C, A
Mohawk Valley Community College A
Monroe Community College A
New York University A
Onondaga Community College A
Rockland Community College A
State University of New York
 College of Technology at Alfred A
Touro College B
Trocaire College A

North Carolina
Brunswick Community College A
Catawba Valley Community College A
Central Piedmont Community
 College C, A
Davidson County Community College A
Edgecombe Community College A
James Sprunt Community College A
Pitt Community College A
Sandhills Community College A
South Piedmont Community
 College C, A
Southwestern Community College A
Wake Technical Community College A
Western Piedmont Community
 College A

North Dakota
North Dakota State College of Science A

Ohio
Bowling Green State University
 Firelands College A
Cincinnati State Technical and
 Community College A
Columbus State Community College A
Davis College C
Hocking Technical College A
Sinclair Community College C, A
Stark State College of Technology A
Youngstown State University A

Oklahoma
East Central University B
Rose State College A

Oregon
Central Oregon Community College C
Lane Community College C

Pennsylvania
Community College of Allegheny
 County C, A
Community College of Philadelphia A
Gwynedd-Mercy College A
Lehigh Carbon Community College C, A
Mercyhurst College C, A, B
South Hills School of Business &
 Technology A
Tri-State Business Institute A
Yorktowne Business Institute A

Puerto Rico
Colegio Universitario del Este A
Huertas Junior College A
Inter American University of Puerto Rico
 San German Campus A

South Carolina
Florence-Darlington Technical College A
Greenville Technical College C
Midlands Technical College A
Piedmont Technical College C

South Dakota
Dakota State University A

Tennessee
Dyersburg State Community College A
Hiwassee College A
Roane State Community College A
Tennessee State University A
University of Tennessee
 Memphis B
Volunteer State Community College A
Walters State Community College C

Texas
Amarillo College A
Central Texas College C
Coastal Bend College A
El Paso Community College C, A
Galveston College C, A
Houston Community College
 System C, A
Howard College C, A
Lee College C, A
Midland College C, A
Paris Junior College A
Richland College A
St. Philip's College C, A
San Jacinto College
 North C, A
South Plains College A
Tarrant County College C, A
Texas State Technical College
 Harlingen A
Tyler Junior College C, A
University of Texas
 Medical Branch at Galveston B
Wharton County Junior College A

Utah
Salt Lake Community College C
University of Utah M, D
Weber State University A

Virginia
ECPI College of Technology C, A

J. Sargeant Reynolds Community
 College C
Northern Virginia Community College A
Tidewater Community College A
Wytheville Community College C

Washington
Centralia College A
Clark College C, A
Renton Technical College A
Shoreline Community College A
Spokane Community College C, A
Spokane Falls Community College C, A
Tacoma Community College C

West Virginia
Bluefield State College A
Fairmont State College A
Potomac State College of West Virginia
 University A

Wisconsin
Chippewa Valley Technical College A
Gateway Technical College A
Moraine Park Technical College A
Western Wisconsin Technical College A

Medical specialties

Connecticut
Yale University D

Illinois
University of Illinois
 Chicago M, D

Michigan
Eastern Michigan University B
Wayne State University M, D

Minnesota
University of Minnesota
 Twin Cities M, D

Missouri
University of Missouri
 Kansas City D

New Hampshire
New Hampshire Community Technical
 College
 Claremont A

New Mexico
University of New Mexico M, D

North Carolina
Durham Technical Community
 College C

Ohio
Wright State University D

Pennsylvania
Butler County Community College C
MCP Hahnemann University M

Puerto Rico
University of Puerto Rico
 Medical Sciences Campus C, D

Texas
University of Texas
 Medical Branch at Galveston M

Virginia
University of Virginia M

West Virginia
Marshall University D

Medical transcription

Alabama
Bevill State Community College A
George C. Wallace State Community
 College
 Dothan C
Shelton State Community College C

Wallace State Community College at
 Hanceville C

Arizona
Eastern Arizona College C
Gateway Community College C
Northland Pioneer College C, A
Phoenix College A

Arkansas
Arkansas State University
 Mountain Home C, A
Arkansas Tech University C
Garland County Community College C
North Arkansas College C

California
California College for Health Sciences A
Chabot College C
Chaffey Community College C
Columbia College C
De Anza College C
Empire College C
Fresno City College C, A
Grossmont Community College C, A
Loma Linda University C
Modesto Junior College C
Riverside Community College C, A
Santa Rosa Junior College C
Shasta College C
Skyline College C, A

Colorado
Denver Technical College: A Division of
 DeVry University C, A

Connecticut
Briarwood College C

Delaware
Delaware Technical and Community
 College
 Owens Campus C, A
 Stanton/Wilmington Campus C
 Terry Campus C, A

Florida
Brevard Community College C
Cooper Career Institute C
Indian River Community College A
Palm Beach Community College C
Pasco-Hernando Community College C
Pensacola Junior College C
Polk Community College A
St. Petersburg Junior College C
Seminole Community College C

Georgia
Chattahoochee Technical Institute C
Dalton State College A
Gwinnett Technical Institute C

Illinois
Black Hawk College C
Career Colleges of Chicago C
College of DuPage C
College of Lake County C
Elgin Community College C, A
Highland Community College C, A
Illinois Eastern Community Colleges
 Olney Central College C
John A. Logan College C
John Wood Community College A
Kishwaukee College C
MacCormac College C, A
McHenry County College C
Moraine Valley Community College C
Oakton Community College C
Parkland College C
Waubonsee Community College C
William Rainey Harper College C

Indiana
Indiana University
 Northwest C
 Southeast C
Michiana College A
Vincennes University A

Iowa
Des Moines Area Community College *C*
Indian Hills Community College *C*
North Iowa Area Community College *A*
Northeast Iowa Community College *C*

Louisiana
Nunez Community College *C*

Maine
Andover College *A*
Beal College *C*
Central Maine Technical College *C*
Mid-State College *C*
Southern Maine Technical College *C*

Maryland
Prince George's Community College *C*

Massachusetts
Bristol Community College *C*
Springfield Technical Community College *C*

Michigan
Baker College
 of Cadillac *A*
 of Jackson *A*
 of Mount Clemens *A*
 of Muskegon *A*
 of Port Huron *A*
Gogebic Community College *A*
Great Lakes College *C*
Henry Ford Community College *C*
Mid Michigan Community College *A*
Mott Community College *C*
North Central Michigan College *C*
Oakland Community College *C, A*
Schoolcraft College *C*
Southwestern Michigan College *C*

Minnesota
College of St. Catherine-Minneapolis *C*

Missouri
St. Charles County Community College *A*

Montana
Montana State University
 College of Technology-Great Falls *A*
University of Montana-Missoula *A*

Nebraska
Metropolitan Community College *C*
Mid Plains Community College Area *C*

New Hampshire
McIntosh College *C*
New Hampshire Community Technical College
 Berlin *C*
 Manchester *C*
 Nashua *C*
New Hampshire Technical Institute *C*

New Jersey
Gloucester County College *C, A*
Hudson County Community College *C*
Passaic County Community College *C*

New Mexico
Eastern New Mexico University
 Roswell Campus *C*
New Mexico State University
 Carlsbad *C*

New York
Herkimer County Community College *C*
State University of New York
 College of Technology at
  Alfred *C, A*
Trocaire College *C*

North Carolina
Alamance Community College *C*
Cape Fear Community College *C*
Carteret Community College *C*
Cecils College *C*

Durham Technical Community College *C*
Edgecombe Community College *C*
Guilford Technical Community College *C*

North Dakota
Minot State University: Bottineau Campus *C*

Ohio
Cincinnati State Technical and Community College *C*
Columbus State Community College *C*
Davis College *C*
Ohio Valley Business College *C*
Stark State College of Technology *C*
University of Akron
 Wayne College *C*

Oregon
Central Oregon Community College *C*
Chemeketa Community College *A*
Linn-Benton Community College *C*

Pennsylvania
Bucks County Community College *C*
Cambria-Rowe Business College *A*
Laurel Business Institute *A*
Lehigh Carbon Community College *C*
Mercyhurst College *C*
Northampton County Area Community College *C*
Tri-State Business Institute *A*

South Carolina
Aiken Technical College *C*
Florence-Darlington Technical College *C*
Greenville Technical College *C*
Tri-County Technical College *C*

South Dakota
Southeast Technical Institute *A*
Western Dakota Technical Institute *A*

Tennessee
Dyersburg State Community College *C*
Roane State Community College *C*
Shelby State Community College *A*
Walters State Community College *C*

Texas
Central Texas College *C*
Collin County Community College District *C*
Galveston College *C*
Houston Community College System *C*
Howard College *C*
Lee College *C*
North Central Texas College *C*
St. Philip's College *C*
Texas State Technical College
 Harlingen *C*
 Sweetwater *C*

Utah
LDS Business College *C*

Vermont
Champlain College *A, B*

Virginia
ECPI College of Technology *C, A*
J. Sargeant Reynolds Community College *C*
Lord Fairfax Community College *C*
Northern Virginia Community College *C*
Tidewater Community College *C*

Washington
Clark College *C*
Columbia Basin College *C, A*
Edmonds Community College *C*
Everett Community College *C*
Green River Community College *C*
Lake Washington Technical College *C*
Pierce College *C*
Renton Technical College *A*

Seattle Central Community College *C*
Shoreline Community College *C*
Skagit Valley College *C*
South Puget Sound Community College *C, A*
Spokane Community College *C*
Tacoma Community College *C*

Wisconsin
Chippewa Valley Technical College *C*
Gateway Technical College *C*
Southwest Wisconsin Technical College *C*
Waukesha County Technical College *C*

Wyoming
Casper College *C, A*

Medicine (M.D.)

Alabama
University of Alabama at Birmingham: School of Medicine *F*
University of South Alabama: School of Medicine *F*

Arizona
University of Arizona: College of Medicine *F*

Arkansas
University of Arkansas for Medical Sciences: College of Medicine *F*

California
Loma Linda University: School of Medicine *F*
Stanford University: School of Medicine *F*
University of California Davis: School of Medicine *F*
University of California Irvine: College of Medicine *F*
University of California Los Angeles: School of Medicine *F*
University of California San Diego: School of Medicine *F*
University of California San Francisco: School of Medicine *F*
University of Southern California: School of Medicine *F*

Colorado
University of Colorado Health Sciences Center: School of Medicine *F*

Connecticut
University of Connecticut Health Center School of Medicine *F*
Yale University: School of Medicine *F*

District of Columbia
George Washington University: School of Medicine and Health Sciences *F*
Georgetown University: School of Medicine *F*
Howard University: School of Medicine *F*

Florida
University of Florida: School of Medicine *F*
University of Miami: School of Medicine *F*
University of South Florida: College of Medicine *F*

Georgia
Emory University: School of Medicine *F*
Medical College of Georgia: School of Medicine *F*
Mercer University: School of Medicine *F*
Morehouse School of Medicine *F*

Hawaii
University of Hawaii at Manoa: John A. Burns School of Medicine *F*

Illinois
Loyola University Chicago: Stritch School of Medicine *F*
Northwestern University: School of Medicine *F*
Rush University: Rush Medical College *F*
Southern Illinois University: School of Medicine *F*
University of Chicago: Pritzker School of Medicine *F*
University of Illinois at Chicago: College of Medicine *F*

Indiana
Indiana University: School of Medicine *F*

Iowa
University of Iowa: College of Medicine *F*

Kansas
University of Kansas Medical Center: School of Medicine *F*

Kentucky
University of Louisville: School of Medicine *F*

Louisiana
Louisiana State University Medical Center: School of Medicine *F*
Louisiana State University: School of Medicine *F*
Tulane University: School of Medicine *F*

Maryland
Johns Hopkins University: School of Medicine *F*
Uniformed Services University of the Health Sciences: School of Medicine *F*
University of Maryland at Baltimore: School of Medicine *F*

Massachusetts
Boston University: School of Medicine *F*
Harvard University: Harvard Medical School *F*
Tufts University: School of Medicine *F*
University of Massachusetts Medical School *F*

Michigan
Michigan State University: College of Human Medicine *F*
University of Michigan: School of Medicine *F*
Wayne State University: School of Medicine *F*

Minnesota
Mayo Medical School *F*
University of Minnesota Medical School *F*

Mississippi
University of Mississippi Medical Center: School of Medicine *F*

Missouri
St. Louis University: School of Medicine *F*
University of Missouri Columbia: School of Medicine *F*
University of Missouri Kansas City: School of Medicine *F*
Washington University: School of Medicine *F*

Nebraska
Creighton University: School of Medicine *F*
University of Nebraska Medical Center: College of Medicine *F*

Medicine (M.D.)

Nevada
University of Nevada: School of Medicine *F*

New Hampshire
Dartmouth College: School of Medicine *F*

New Jersey
University of Medicine and Dentistry of New Jersey
  New Jersey Medical School *F*
  Robert Wood Johnson Medical School at Camden *F*
  Robert Wood Johnson Medical School *F*

New Mexico
University of New Mexico: School of Medicine *F*

New York
Albany Medical College: School of Medicine *F*
Albert Einstein College of Medicine *F*
Columbia University
  College of Physicians and Surgeons *F*
Cornell University Medical College *F*
Mount Sinai School of Medicine of City University of New York *F*
New York Medical College *F*
New York University: School of Medicine *F*
State University of New York Health Science Center at Brooklyn: School of Medicine *F*
State University of New York Health Science Center at Syracuse: School of Medicine *F*
State University of New York Health Sciences Center at Stony Brook: School of Medicine *F*
State University of New York at Buffalo: School of Medicine *F*
University of Rochester: School of Medicine and Dentistry *F*

North Carolina
Duke University: School of Medicine *F*
East Carolina University: School of Medicine *F*
University of North Carolina at Chapel Hill: School of Medicine *F*
Wake Forest University: Bowman Gray School of Medicine *F*

North Dakota
University of North Dakota: School of Medicine *F*

Ohio
Case Western Reserve University: School of Medicine *F*
Medical College of Ohio *F*
Northeastern Ohio Universities College of Medicine *F*
Ohio State University Columbus Campus: College of Medicine *F*
University of Cincinnati: College of Medicine *F*
Wright State University: School of Medicine *F*

Oklahoma
University of Oklahoma Health Sciences Center: College of Medicine *F*

Oregon
Oregon Health Sciences University: School of Medicine *F*

Pennsylvania
Jefferson Medical College of Thomas Jefferson University *F*
Medical College of Pennsylvania and Hahnemann University School of Medicine *F*
Pennsylvania State University College of Medicine *F*
Temple University: School of Medicine *F*
University of Pennsylvania: School of Medicine *F*
University of Pittsburgh: School of Medicine *F*

Puerto Rico
Ponce School of Medicine *F*
Universidad Central del Caribe: Medical School *F*
University of Puerto Rico Medical Sciences Campus: School of Medicine *F*

Rhode Island
Brown University: School of Medicine *F*

South Carolina
Medical University of South Carolina *F*
University of South Carolina: School of Medicine *F*

South Dakota
University of South Dakota: School of Medicine *F*

Tennessee
East Tennessee State University: James H. Quillen College of Medicine *F*
Meharry Medical College: School of Medicine *F*
University of Tennessee Memphis: College of Medicine *F*
Vanderbilt University: School of Medicine *F*

Texas
Baylor College of Medicine *F*
Texas A&M University: Health Science Center College of Medicine *F*
Texas Tech University Health Sciences Center: School of Medicine *F*
University of Texas
  Medical Branch at Galveston: School of Medicine *F*
University of Texas Health Science Center: Medical School *F*
University of Texas Southwestern Medical Center at Dallas Southwestern Medical School *F*
University of Texas-Houston Health Science Center *F*

Utah
University of Utah: School of Medicine *F*

Vermont
University of Vermont: College of Medicine *F*

Virginia
Eastern Virginia Medical School of the Medical College of Hampton Roads: Medical Professions *F*
University of Virginia: School of Medicine *F*
Virginia Commonwealth University: School of Medicine *F*

Washington
University of Washington: School of Medicine *F*

West Virginia
Marshall University: School of Medicine *F*
West Virginia University: School of Medicine *F*

Wisconsin
Medical College of Wisconsin: School of Medicine *F*
University of Wisconsin Madison: School of Medicine *F*

Medieval/renaissance studies

California
California State University Long Beach *C*
University of California
  Davis *B*
  Santa Barbara *B*
  Santa Cruz *B*

Connecticut
Connecticut College *B*
University of Connecticut *M, D*
Wesleyan University *B*
Yale University *M, D*

District of Columbia
Catholic University of America *B, M, D*

Florida
New College of the University of South Florida *B*

Georgia
Emory University *B*
Oxford College of Emory University *B*

Indiana
Hanover College *B*
University of Notre Dame *B, M, D*

Iowa
Cornell College *B*

Louisiana
Tulane University *B*

Massachusetts
Boston College *M*
Hampshire College *B*
Harvard College *B*
Mount Holyoke College *B*
Smith College *B*
Wellesley College *B*

Michigan
University of Michigan *B*
Western Michigan University *M*

Minnesota
College of St. Benedict *B*
St. John's University *B*
St. Olaf College *B*

Missouri
Washington University *B*

Nebraska
University of Nebraska Lincoln *B*

New Hampshire
Plymouth State College of the University System of New Hampshire *B*

New Jersey
Rutgers
  The State University of New Jersey: Douglass College *B*
  The State University of New Jersey: Livingston College *B*
  The State University of New Jersey: Rutgers College *B*
  The State University of New Jersey: University College New Brunswick *B*

New York
Bard College *B*
Barnard College *B*
Columbia University
  Columbia College *B*
  Graduate School *D*
Cornell University *M, D*
New York University *B*
Sarah Lawrence College *B*
State University of New York Binghamton *B*
Syracuse University *B*
Vassar College *B*

North Carolina
Duke University *B*

Ohio
Ohio State University Columbus Campus *B*
Ohio Wesleyan University *B*
University of Toledo *B*

Pennsylvania
Dickinson College *B*
Gettysburg College *B*
Penn State
  University Park *B*
St. Joseph's University *C*
Swarthmore College *B*
University of Pittsburgh *C*

Rhode Island
Brown University *B*

Tennessee
University of Tennessee Knoxville *B*
University of the South *B*

Texas
Southern Methodist University *B, M*
University of Texas
  Austin *D*

Vermont
Marlboro College *B*

Virginia
College of William and Mary *B*
Washington and Lee University *B*

Wisconsin
University of Wisconsin Madison *M, D*

Mental health services

Alabama
Central Alabama Community College *A*
Community College of the Air Force *A*
Wallace State Community College at Hanceville *A*

Alaska
University of Alaska Fairbanks *A*

Arizona
Arizona Western College *C*
Glendale Community College *C*
Pima Community College *C*

California
Allan Hancock College *C, A*
American River College *A*
Cypress College *A*
Los Angeles Trade and Technical College *A*
Mission College *A*
Mount San Antonio College *C, A*
Napa Valley College *C, A*
Pacific Oaks College *M*
Rio Hondo College *A*
Ventura College *A*

Colorado
Community College of Aurora *C*

Connecticut
Naugatuck Valley Community-Technical College *C, A*
Norwalk Community-Technical College *C*

District of Columbia
Gallaudet University *M*

Florida
Daytona Beach Community College *A*
Gulf Coast Community College *A*
Hillsborough Community College *A*

410

Nova Southeastern University *M*
Palm Beach Community College *A*
St. Thomas University *M*
University of Florida *M, D*

Georgia
Atlanta Metropolitan College *A*
Floyd College *A*
Fort Valley State University *M*

Idaho
North Idaho College *A*

Illinois
City Colleges of Chicago
    Kennedy-King College *A*
McHenry County College *C*
Moraine Valley Community College *C*
Roosevelt University *M*

Indiana
Ivy Tech State College
    Central Indiana *A*
    Northeast *A*
    Southcentral *A*
    Wabash Valley *A*

Kentucky
Hopkinsville Community College *A*
Northern Kentucky University *A, B*

Louisiana
Southern University
    Shreveport *A*
Southern University and Agricultural and Mechanical College *M*

Maine
University of Maine
    Augusta *C*

Maryland
Allegany College *A*
Baltimore City Community College *C, A*
Carroll Community College *C, A*
Community College of Baltimore County
    Essex *A*
Harford Community College *A*
Montgomery College
    Rockville Campus *A*
    Takoma Park Campus *A*

Massachusetts
Berkshire Community College *C, A*
Cambridge College *M*
Lesley College *B, M*
Middlesex Community College *A*
North Shore Community College *A*

Michigan
Kellogg Community College *A*
Oakland Community College *A*
University of Michigan *M*
Wayne County Community College *A*
Wayne State University *C, M*

Montana
Montana State University
    Billings *B*

Nebraska
Southeast Community College
    Lincoln Campus *A*

New Hampshire
Antioch New England Graduate School *M, D*
New Hampshire Community Technical College
    Nashua *C, A*
Plymouth State College of the University System of New Hampshire *B*
Rivier College *M*

New Jersey
Essex County College *A*
Thomas Edison State College *B*

New York
City University of New York
    La Guardia Community College *A*
Dutchess Community College *A*
Mohawk Valley Community College *C*
New York Institute of Technology *B*
North Country Community College *C, A*
Nyack College *M*
Orange County Community College *A*

North Carolina
Pitt Community College *A*
South Piedmont Community College *C, A*

Ohio
Belmont Technical College *A*
Columbus State Community College *C, A*
Franciscan University of Steubenville *B*
Franklin University *B*
Muskingum Area Technical College *A*
North Central State College *A*
Ohio University
    Chillicothe Campus *A*
Sinclair Community College *A*
University of Toledo *A*

Oregon
Mount Hood Community College *A*

Pennsylvania
Bucks County Community College *A*
Community College of Allegheny County *C, A*
Community College of Philadelphia *C*
Edinboro University of Pennsylvania *A*
Lackawanna Junior College *A*
MCP Hahnemann University *B, M*
Manor College *A*
Montgomery County Community College *A*
Penn State
    University Park *C*
Pennsylvania College of Technology *A, B*
Reading Area Community College *A*

Puerto Rico
University of Puerto Rico
    Cayey University College *B*

South Dakota
Dakota Wesleyan University *B*
Kilian Community College *A*

Texas
Alvin Community College *C, A*
Austin Community College *C, A*
South Plains College *A*
Vernon Regional Junior College *C*

Vermont
Community College of Vermont *C, A*

Virginia
Blue Ridge Community College *A*
Old Dominion University *B*
Southwest Virginia Community College *A*
Virginia Western Community College *A*

Washington
Edmonds Community College *C, A*

Mental health services technology

Arizona
Arizona Western College *C*
Rio Salado College *C, A*

California
San Joaquin Delta College *A*
Santa Rosa Junior College *C, A*

Colorado
Community College of Denver *C, A*
Pikes Peak Community College *C, A*
Pueblo Community College *C*

Connecticut
Housatonic Community-Technical College *C, A*
Three Rivers Community-Technical College *A*

Delaware
Delaware Technical and Community College
    Owens Campus *C, A*
    Stanton/Wilmington Campus *C, A*
    Terry Campus *C, A*

Idaho
North Idaho College *A*

Illinois
Elgin Community College *C*
Prairie State College *A*
Roosevelt University *M*

Indiana
Ivy Tech State College
    Central Indiana *A*
    Eastcentral *A*
    Northeast *C, A*
    Southcentral *C, A*
    Southeast *C*
    Wabash Valley *A*

Kansas
Kansas City Kansas Community College *C*

Maryland
Chesapeake College *C, A*

Massachusetts
Mount Wachusett Community College *C, A*
Northern Essex Community College *C, A*
Springfield Technical Community College *A*

Missouri
Penn Valley Community College *A*

New Hampshire
New Hampshire Community Technical College
    Nashua *C, A*
New Hampshire Technical Institute *A*

New Jersey
Thomas Edison State College *B*

North Carolina
Pitt Community College *A*
Richmond Community College *A*
Southwestern Community College *A*
Wayne Community College *A*
Wilkes Community College *C, A*

North Dakota
North Dakota State College of Science *A*

Ohio
Columbus State Community College *C, A*
North Central State College *A*

Pennsylvania
Community College of Allegheny County *C, A*
Community College of Philadelphia *A*
Edinboro University of Pennsylvania *B*
Luzerne County Community College *A*
MCP Hahnemann University *A, B*
Westmoreland County Community College *C, A*

Rhode Island
Community College of Rhode Island *A*

Texas
Alvin Community College *C, A*
Blinn College *C, A*
Del Mar College *C, A*
Eastfield College *C, A*
El Paso Community College *A*
Houston Community College System *C, A*
Tarrant County College *A*

Virginia
Virginia Western Community College *A*

Washington
Edmonds Community College *C*
Pierce College *C, A*
Seattle Central Community College *A*

Wisconsin
Madison Area Technical College *A*

Merchant Marine

Maine
Maine Maritime Academy *C*

Massachusetts
Massachusetts Maritime Academy *B*

New York
State University of New York
    Maritime College *B*
United States Merchant Marine Academy *B*

Metal/jewelry arts

Arizona
Arizona State University *B, M*
Mohave Community College *C, A*

California
California College of Arts and Crafts *B, M*
California State University
    Long Beach *B, M*
    Northridge *M*
Monterey Peninsula College *A*
Palomar College *A*
Santa Rosa Junior College *C*

Colorado
Adams State College *B*
Colorado State University *B*
Pueblo Community College *C, A*

Connecticut
Middlesex Community-Technical College *A*

Georgia
Savannah College of Art and Design *B, M*
University of Georgia *B*

Indiana
Ball State University *B*
Indiana University--Purdue University Indiana University-Purdue University Fort Wayne *B*
University of Evansville *B*

Iowa
University of Iowa *B, M*

Kansas
University of Kansas *B, M*

Maine
Maine College of Art *B*

Massachusetts
Bristol Community College *C*
Massachusetts College of Art *B, M*
School of the Museum of Fine Arts *B, M*
Simon's Rock College of Bard *B*
University of Massachusetts
    Dartmouth *B*

Michigan
Center for Creative Studies: College of Art and Design *B*
Cranbrook Academy of Art *M*
Grand Valley State University *B*

Metal/jewelry arts

Northern Michigan University *B*
Siena Heights University *B*
University of Michigan *B*

New Jersey
Rowan University *B*

New York
Parsons School of Design *C, A, B, T*
Pratt Institute *B*
Rochester Institute of
 Technology *A, B, M*
State University of New York
 College at Buffalo *B*
 New Paltz *B, M*

North Carolina
Haywood Community College *A*

Ohio
Bowling Green State University *B*
Cleveland Institute of Art *B*
Kent State University *B*
University of Akron *B*

Oregon
Portland Community College *C, A*
University of Oregon *B, M*

Pennsylvania
Beaver College *B*
Edinboro University of
 Pennsylvania *B, M*
Moore College of Art and Design *B*
Temple University *B, M*
University of the Arts *B*

Rhode Island
Rhode Island College *B*

Texas
Paris Junior College *A*
Sam Houston State University *M*
Texas A&M University
 Commerce *B*
Texas Woman's University *B, M*
University of North Texas *B, M*
University of Texas
 Arlington *B*
 El Paso *B*
Western Texas College *A*

Washington
University of Washington *B, M*

Wisconsin
Northeast Wisconsin Technical
 College *C*
University of Wisconsin
 Madison *B*

Metallurgical engineering

Alabama
University of Alabama *B, M, D*

California
California Polytechnic State University:
 San Luis Obispo *B*

Colorado
Colorado School of Mines *B, M, D*

Connecticut
Hartford Graduate Center *M*
University of Connecticut *M, D*

Idaho
University of Idaho *B, M*

Illinois
Illinois Institute of Technology *B, M, D*
Parkland College *A*
University of Illinois
 Urbana-Champaign *B, M*

Iowa
Iowa State University *B*
Northeast Iowa Community College *A*

Maine
Southern Maine Technical College *A*

Massachusetts
Massachusetts Institute of
 Technology *M, D*

Michigan
Michigan State University *M, D*
Michigan Technological
 University *B, M, D, T*
Monroe County Community
 College *C, A*
University of Michigan *B*
Western Michigan University *B*

Minnesota
Ridgewater College: A Community and
 Technical College *A*

Missouri
East Central College *A*
University of Missouri
 Rolla *B, M, D*

Montana
Montana Tech of the University of
 Montana *B, M*

Nevada
University of Nevada
 Reno *B, M, D*

New Mexico
New Mexico Institute of Mining and
 Technology *B*

New York
Columbia University
 Fu Foundation School of
 Engineering and Applied
 Science *B, M, D*

Ohio
Ohio State University
 Columbus Campus *B*
University of Cincinnati *B, M, D*

Pennsylvania
Carnegie Mellon University *B, M, D*
Lock Haven University of
 Pennsylvania *B*
Penn State
 University Park *B*
University of Pittsburgh *B, M, D*

South Dakota
South Dakota School of Mines and
 Technology *B, M*

Tennessee
University of Tennessee
 Knoxville *M, D*

Texas
University of Texas
 El Paso *B*

Utah
University of Utah *B, M*

Washington
University of Washington *B*

Wisconsin
University of Wisconsin
 Madison *M, D*

Metallurgy

Idaho
University of Idaho *M*

Maine
Southern Maine Technical College *A*

Michigan
Eastern Michigan University *B*

Missouri
University of Missouri
 Rolla *B, M, D*

Montana
Montana Tech of the University of
 Montana *M*

New York
Columbia University
 Fu Foundation School of
 Engineering and Applied
 Science *M, D*

Texas
University of North Texas *M, D*

Utah
University of Utah *M, D*

Meteorology

Alabama
Community College of the Air Force *A*
University of Alabama
 Huntsville *M, D*

Alaska
University of Alaska
 Fairbanks *M, D*

Arizona
University of Arizona *B, M, D*

California
San Jose State University *M*
University of California
 Davis *B, M, D*
 Los Angeles *B, M, D*

Colorado
Colorado State University *M, D*
Metropolitan State College of Denver *B*
United States Air Force Academy *B*
University of Colorado
 Boulder *B, D*

Connecticut
Western Connecticut State University *B*

Delaware
University of Delaware *D*

Florida
Florida Institute of Technology *B, M*
Florida State University *C, B, M, D*
Gulf Coast Community College *A*
Miami-Dade Community College *A*
University of Miami *B, M, D*

Georgia
Georgia Institute of Technology *B, M, D*

Hawaii
University of Hawaii
 Manoa *B, M, D*

Illinois
Northern Illinois University *B*
Parkland College *A*
University of Illinois
 Urbana-Champaign *M, D*

Indiana
Purdue University *B, M, D*
Valparaiso University *B*

Iowa
Iowa State University *B, M, D*

Kansas
University of Kansas *B*

Louisiana
University of Louisiana at Monroe *B*

Maryland
Johns Hopkins University *B*
University of Maryland
 College Park *M, D*

Massachusetts
Harvard College *B*
Harvard University *D*
Massachusetts Institute of
 Technology *M, D*
Massachusetts Maritime Academy *C*

Michigan
University of Michigan *B, M, D*

Minnesota
St. Cloud State University *B*

Mississippi
Jackson State University *B*

Missouri
St. Louis University *B, M, D*
University of Missouri
 Columbia *B, M, D*

Nebraska
Creighton University *B, M*
University of Nebraska
 Lincoln *B*

Nevada
University of Nevada
 Reno *M, D*

New Hampshire
Plymouth State College of the University
 System of New Hampshire *B*

New Jersey
Rutgers
 The State University of New Jersey:
 Cook College *B*
 The State University of New Jersey:
 Douglass College *B*
 The State University of New Jersey:
 New Brunswick Graduate
 Campus *M, D*

New Mexico
New Mexico Institute of Mining and
 Technology *B, M, D*

New York
Columbia University
 Graduate School *M, D*
Cornell University *B*
State University of New York
 Albany *B, M, D*
 College at Brockport *B*
 College at Oneonta *B*
 Maritime College *B*
 Oswego *B*
 Stony Brook *B*

North Carolina
North Carolina State University *B*
University of North Carolina
 Asheville *B*

North Dakota
University of North Dakota *B*

Ohio
Ohio State University
 Columbus Campus *M, D*
Ohio University *B*
Shawnee State University *B*

Oklahoma
University of Oklahoma *B, M, D*

Oregon
Oregon State University *M, D*

Pennsylvania
California University of Pennsylvania *B*
Millersville University of
 Pennsylvania *B*
Penn State
 University Park *B, M, D*

South Dakota
South Dakota School of Mines and
 Technology *M, D*

Texas
Texas A&M University B, M, D
Texas Tech University M

Utah
University of Utah B, M, D
Utah State University M, D

Vermont
Lyndon State College B

Washington
University of Washington B, M, D

Wisconsin
Northland College B
University of Wisconsin
    Madison B, M, D

Wyoming
University of Wyoming M, D

Mexican-American studies

California
California State University
    Dominguez Hills B
    Fresno B
    Fullerton B
    Hayward B
    Los Angeles B, M
    Monterey Bay B
    Northridge B, M
Claremont McKenna College B
East Los Angeles College A
Pomona College B
San Diego City College A
San Diego State University B
San Jose State University M
Santa Ana College A
Scripps College B
Solano Community College A
Southwestern College A
University of California
    Davis B
    Irvine D
    Los Angeles B
    Santa Barbara B
University of Southern California B
Ventura College A

Ohio
Bowling Green State University B

Texas
Concordia University at Austin B
Southern Methodist University B
Sul Ross State University B
University of Texas
    Pan American B

Vermont
Goddard College B

Microbiology/bacteriology

Alabama
Auburn University B, M, D
University of Alabama
    Birmingham D
University of Alabama B

Arizona
Arizona State University B, M, D
Northern Arizona University B
University of Arizona B, M, D

Arkansas
University of Arkansas
    for Medical Sciences M, D
University of Arkansas B

California
Bakersfield College A
California Polytechnic State University:
    San Luis Obispo B
California State Polytechnic University:
    Pomona B
California State University
    Chico B
    Dominguez Hills B
    Fresno B, M
    Long Beach B, M
    Los Angeles B, M
    Northridge B
Cerritos Community College A
Compton Community College A
Crafton Hills College A
Loma Linda University M, D
Oxnard College A
Pitzer College B
Riverside Community College A
San Diego State University B, M
San Francisco State University B, M
San Jose State University M
Southwestern College A
Stanford University M, D
University of California
    Berkeley M, D
    Davis B, M, D
    Irvine D
    Los Angeles B, M, D
    Riverside M, D
    San Diego B
    San Francisco D
    Santa Barbara B
University of Southern California M, D

Colorado
Adams State College B
Colorado State University B, M, D
University of Colorado
    Health Sciences Center D

Connecticut
Quinnipiac University B, M
Southern Connecticut State University B
University of Connecticut M, D

District of Columbia
George Washington University M, D
Georgetown University D
Howard University M, D

Florida
University of Central Florida B, M
University of Florida B, M, D
University of Miami B, M, D
University of South Florida B, M
University of West Florida B

Georgia
Georgia Military College A
University of Georgia B, M, D

Hawaii
University of Hawaii
    Manoa B, M, D

Idaho
College of Southern Idaho A
Idaho State University B, M
Ricks College A
University of Idaho B, M, D

Illinois
Chicago State University B
Finch University of Health Sciences/The
    Chicago Medical School M, D
Northwestern University M, D
Southern Illinois University
    Carbondale B
University of Chicago M, D
University of Illinois
    Chicago M, D
    Urbana-Champaign B, M, D

Indiana
Ball State University B
Indiana University
    Bloomington B, M, D
Indiana University--Purdue University
    Indiana University-Purdue
        University Indianapolis M, D

Iowa
Iowa State University B, M, D
Maharishi University of Management B
University of Iowa B, M, D

Kansas
Central Christian College A
Kansas State University B, M, D
University of Kansas B, M, D

Kentucky
Eastern Kentucky University B
University of Kentucky M, D
University of Louisville M, D

Louisiana
Louisiana State University Medical
    Center M, D
Louisiana State University and
    Agricultural and Mechanical
    College B, M, D
Tulane University M, D
University of Louisiana at Lafayette B
Xavier University of Louisiana B

Maine
University of Maine B, M, D

Maryland
Uniformed Services University of the
    Health Sciences D
University of Maryland
    Baltimore M, D
    College Park B, M, D

Massachusetts
Boston University M, D
Hampshire College B
Tufts University M, D
University of Massachusetts
    Amherst B, M, D

Michigan
Michigan State University B, M, D
Northern Michigan University B
University of Michigan
    Dearborn B
University of Michigan B, M, D
Wayne State University D

Minnesota
Minnesota State University, Mankato B
St. Cloud State University B
University of Minnesota
    Duluth M
    Twin Cities B, M, D

Mississippi
Mississippi State University B
Mississippi University for Women B
University of Mississippi
    Medical Center M, D

Missouri
Missouri Southern State College B
University of Missouri
    Columbia B, M, D
Washington University D

Montana
Montana State University
    Bozeman B, M, D
University of Montana-Missoula B, M

Nebraska
Creighton University M, D

Nevada
University of Nevada
    Reno M, D

New Hampshire
University of New Hampshire B, M, D

New Jersey
Rowan University B
Rutgers
    The State University of New Jersey:
        Camden College of Arts and
        Sciences B
    The State University of New Jersey:
        Cook College B
    The State University of New Jersey:
        Douglass College B
    The State University of New Jersey:
        Livingston College B
    The State University of New Jersey:
        New Brunswick Graduate
        Campus M, D
    The State University of New Jersey:
        Rutgers College B
    The State University of New Jersey:
        University College Camden B
    The State University of New Jersey:
        University College New
        Brunswick B
Seton Hall University M

New Mexico
New Mexico State University B

New York
Albany Medical College M, D
Columbia University
    Graduate School M, D
Cornell University B, M, D
Long Island University
    Brooklyn Campus M
    C. W. Post Campus M
New York University M, D
Rockefeller University D
State University of New York
    Buffalo M, D
    College of Environmental Science
        and Forestry B, M, D
    Health Science Center at Stony
        Brook D
    Upstate Medical University M, D
University of Rochester B, M, D
Wagner College B, M

North Carolina
Duke University M, D
East Carolina University D
North Carolina State University B, M, D
University of North Carolina
    Chapel Hill M, D
Wake Forest University B

North Dakota
North Dakota State University B, M
University of North Dakota M, D

Ohio
Bowling Green State University B
Case Western Reserve University D
Miami University
    Oxford Campus B, M, D
Ohio State University
    Columbus Campus B, M, D
Ohio University B, M, D
Ohio Wesleyan University B
University of Akron B
University of Cincinnati M, D
Wilmington College B
Wright State University M

Oklahoma
Eastern Oklahoma State College A
Oklahoma State University M
University of Oklahoma B, M, D

Oregon
Oregon Health Sciences University M, D
Oregon State University B, M, D

Pennsylvania
Duquesne University B
Juniata College B
MCP Hahnemann University M, D
Penn State
    College of Medicine, Milton S.
        Hershey Medical Center M, D
    University Park B

Thomas Jefferson University: College of
   Health Professions D
University of Pennsylvania M, D
University of Pittsburgh B
University of the Sciences in
   Philadelphia B
West Chester University of
   Pennsylvania B

Puerto Rico
Colegio Universitario del Este B
Inter American University of Puerto Rico
   Arecibo Campus B
   Bayamon Campus B
   San German Campus B
University of Puerto Rico
   Arecibo Campus B
   Humacao University College B
   Mayaguez Campus B
   Medical Sciences Campus M, D

Rhode Island
Brown University M, D
Salve Regina University B
University of Rhode Island B, M, D

South Carolina
Clemson University B, M, D

South Dakota
South Dakota State University B, M
University of South Dakota M, D

Tennessee
East Tennessee State University B, M
University of Memphis B
University of Tennessee
   Knoxville B, M, D
   Memphis M, D
Vanderbilt University M, D

Texas
Southwest Texas State University B
Texas A&M University B, M, D
Texas Tech University Health Science
   Center M, D
Texas Tech University B, M
University of Houston
   Downtown B
University of North Texas M, D
University of Texas
   Arlington B
   Austin B, M, D
   El Paso B
   Medical Branch at Galveston M, D
   Southwestern Medical Center at
      Dallas M, D

Utah
Brigham Young University B, M, D
Snow College A
Weber State University B

Vermont
Bennington College B
University of Vermont B, M, D

Virginia
University of Virginia D
Virginia Commonwealth
   University M, D

Washington
Eastern Washington University B
University of Washington B, D
Washington State University B, M, D

West Virginia
West Liberty State College B
West Virginia University M, D

Wisconsin
Medical College of Wisconsin M, D
University of Wisconsin
   La Crosse B
   Madison B, M, D
   Oshkosh B, M

Wyoming
Sheridan College A

University of Wyoming B

Middle Eastern languages, other

District of Columbia
Catholic University of America M, D

Illinois
University of Chicago M, D

Indiana
Indiana University
   Bloomington B, M, D

Massachusetts
Harvard College B

Michigan
University of Michigan B, M, D
Wayne State University B, M

New Hampshire
Dartmouth College B

New York
Columbia University
   Graduate School M, D
New York University M, D

Texas
University of Texas
   Austin B, M, D

Washington
University of Washington B, M, D

Middle Eastern studies

Arizona
University of Arizona B, M, D

Arkansas
University of Arkansas B

California
University of California
   Berkeley B

Connecticut
Trinity College B
University of Connecticut B

District of Columbia
George Washington University B
Georgetown University M

Georgia
Oxford College of Emory University B

Illinois
University of Chicago M

Maryland
Johns Hopkins University B

Massachusetts
College of the Holy Cross B
Harvard College B
Harvard University M, D
Tufts University B, M
University of Massachusetts
   Amherst B

Michigan
University of Michigan B, M, D

Minnesota
University of Minnesota
   Twin Cities B

Missouri
Washington University B, M

New Hampshire
Dartmouth College B

New Jersey
Princeton University B, M, D

Rutgers
   The State University of New Jersey:
      Douglass College B
   The State University of New Jersey:
      Livingston College B
   The State University of New Jersey:
      Rutgers College B
   The State University of New Jersey:
      University College New
      Brunswick B

New York
Barnard College B
City University of New York
   Queens College B
Columbia University
   Columbia College B
   Graduate School M, D
   School of General Studies B
Cornell University M, D
Fordham University B
New York University B, M, D
Sarah Lawrence College B
United States Military Academy B

Ohio
College of Wooster B
Mount Vernon Nazarene College B
Oberlin College B
Ohio State University
   Columbus Campus B
University of Toledo B

Rhode Island
Brown University B

Texas
Southwest Texas State University B
University of Texas
   Austin B, M

Utah
Brigham Young University B
University of Utah B, M, D

Vermont
Goddard College B
Marlboro College B

Virginia
Emory & Henry College B

Washington
University of Washington M, D

Military technologies

Arizona
Pima Community College C
University of Phoenix A

Colorado
Colorado Mountain College
   Spring Valley Campus A

Georgia
Georgia Military College A

Kansas
Seward County Community College A

Massachusetts
Massachusetts Maritime Academy C

Michigan
Western Michigan University B

Missouri
Webster University B

New York
State University of New York
   College at Brockport B

Puerto Rico
University of Puerto Rico
   Cayey University College B

Utah
Weber State University B

Mining/mineral engineering

Alabama
University of Alabama B, M

Alaska
University of Alaska
   Fairbanks B, M

Arizona
Central Arizona College A
University of Arizona B, M, D

California
University of California
   Berkeley M, D

Colorado
Colorado School of Mines B, M, D

Idaho
North Idaho College A
University of Idaho B, M, D

Illinois
Southern Illinois University
   Carbondale B, M

Kentucky
University of Kentucky B, M, D

Michigan
Michigan Technological
   University C, B, M, D, T

Missouri
University of Missouri
   Rolla B, M, D

Montana
Montana Tech of the University of
   Montana B, M

Nevada
University of Nevada
   Reno B, M

New Mexico
New Mexico Institute of Mining and
   Technology B, M

New York
Columbia University
   Fu Foundation School of
   Engineering and Applied
   Science B, M, D

Oregon
Oregon State University B

Pennsylvania
Penn State
   University Park B, M, D
University of Pittsburgh M

South Dakota
South Dakota School of Mines and
   Technology B, M

Utah
University of Utah B, M, D

Virginia
Virginia Polytechnic Institute and State
   University B, M, D

West Virginia
West Virginia University B, M, D

Wisconsin
University of Wisconsin
   Madison B

Mining/petroleum technologies

Alaska
University of Alaska
   Anchorage C, A
   Fairbanks C

Arizona
Central Arizona College *A*
Eastern Arizona College *A*

California
Long Beach City College *C, A*
Santa Clara University *C*
Sierra College *C, A*
Ventura College *A*

Colorado
Trinidad State Junior College *C*

Illinois
Illinois Eastern Community Colleges Wabash Valley College *C, A*
Lincoln Land Community College *C, A*
Rend Lake College *C, A*

Indiana
Ivy Tech State College Wabash Valley *A*

Louisiana
Nicholls State University *A, B*

Montana
Montana State University Billings *A*
Montana Tech of the University of Montana: College of Technology *A*
Montana Tech of the University of Montana *A*

New Mexico
New Mexico Junior College *A*

Ohio
Hocking Technical College *A*

Texas
Navarro College *A*
Odessa College *C, A*

Utah
College of Eastern Utah *A*

West Virginia
Bluefield State College *B*

Wyoming
Casper College *A*

Ministerial/theological studies

Alabama
Faulkner University *B*
Huntingdon College *B*
Oakwood College *B*
Samford University *M, D*
Spring Hill College *C, B, M*
University of Mobile *B, M*

Alaska
Alaska Bible College *B*

Arizona
American Indian College of the Assemblies of God *B*
Grand Canyon University *B*
Southwestern College *C, A, B*

Arkansas
Harding University *B*
John Brown University *B*
Ouachita Baptist University *B*

California
Azusa Pacific University *D*
Biola University *B, M, D*
California Lutheran University *B*
Concordia University *M*
Fresno Pacific University *B*
Hope International University *C, B, M*
LIFE Bible College *A, B*
Loyola Marymount University *M*
Master's College *B*
Pacific Union College *B*
Pepperdine University *M*
Point Loma Nazarene University *C, B, M*
Simpson College *B, M*
University of San Francisco *B, M*
Vanguard University of Southern California *M*

Colorado
Colorado Christian University *B*

Connecticut
Yale University *M*

District of Columbia
Catholic University of America *M, D*

Florida
Barry University *B, M, D*
Clearwater Christian College *B*
Florida Baptist Theological College *A, B*
Florida Christian College *B*
Hobe Sound Bible College *B*
Palm Beach Atlantic College *B*
Southeastern College of the Assemblies of God *B*
Warner Southern College *B*

Georgia
Atlanta Christian College *B*
Emmanuel College *B*
LaGrange College *B*
Mercer University *M*
Shorter College *B*
Toccoa Falls College *B, M*

Idaho
Boise Bible College *A, B*
Northwest Nazarene University *B, M*

Illinois
Dominican University *C, B*
Greenville College *B, M*
Lincoln Christian College and Seminary *B, M*
Moody Bible Institute *B, M*
North Park University *M, D*
Olivet Nazarene University *M*
Quincy University *A, B*
St. Xavier University *B*
Trinity International University *M, D*
University of St. Francis *B*

Indiana
Anderson University *B, D*
Bethel College *B, M*
Goshen College *B*
Indiana Wesleyan University *B*
Manchester College *A*
Marian College *A, B*
Oakland City University *M, D*
St. Mary-of-the-Woods College *C, A, B, M*
University of Notre Dame *B, M, D*
University of St. Francis *B*

Iowa
Dordt College *B*
Emmaus Bible College *B*
Faith Baptist Bible College and Theological Seminary *B, M*
Loras College *B*
St. Ambrose University *M*
University of Dubuque *M*

Kansas
Barclay College *B*
Central Christian College *A, B*
Hesston College *A*
Manhattan Christian College *A, B*

Kentucky
Brescia University *C, A, B*
Campbellsville University *M*
Kentucky Christian College *A, B*
Kentucky Mountain Bible College *B*
Kentucky Wesleyan College *B*
Thomas More College *A, B*

Louisiana
Loyola University New Orleans *M*
Xavier University of Louisiana *B, M*

Maryland
Mount St. Mary's College *M*
Washington Bible College *B, M*

Massachusetts
Atlantic Union College *B*
Eastern Nazarene College *B, M*
Harvard University *M, D*
Hellenic College/Holy Cross *M*
Merrimack College *A, B*

Michigan
Andrews University *B, M, D*
Cornerstone College and Grand Rapids Baptist Seminary *M, D*
Grace Bible College *B*
Kellogg Community College *A*
Reformed Bible College *A, B*
Rochester College *B*
Spring Arbor College *B*
William Tyndale College *A, B*

Minnesota
College of St. Benedict *B*
College of St. Catherine: St. Paul Campus *B, M*
College of St. Scholastica *B*
Concordia College: Moorhead *B*
Crown College *B, M*
Martin Luther College *B*
Minnesota Bible College *B*
North Central University *B*
Northwestern College *B*
St. John's University *B*
St. Mary's University of Minnesota *B*
University of St. Thomas *M, D*

Mississippi
Blue Mountain College *B*
Magnolia Bible College *B*
Wesley College *B*

Missouri
Baptist Bible College *B*
Berean University *C, A, B, M*
Ozark Christian College *C, A, B*
Rockhurst University *B*
St. Louis Christian College *A, B*
St. Louis University *B, M*
Southwest Baptist University *C, B*

Nebraska
Concordia University *B*
Creighton University *A, B, M*
Grace University *B*
Union College *B*

New Hampshire
Notre Dame College *M*

New Jersey
Caldwell College *B, M*
College of St. Elizabeth *M*
Drew University *M, D*
Seton Hall University *M*

New York
Houghton College *B*
Nyack College *B, M*
Roberts Wesleyan College *B*
St. John's University *C, B, M*

North Carolina
Duke University *M*
John Wesley College *C, A, B*
Lenoir-Rhyne College *B*
Wake Forest University *M*
Wingate University *B*

North Dakota
Trinity Bible College *B*
University of Mary *B*

Ohio
Ashland University *C, M, D*
Cedarville College *B*
Circleville Bible College *A, B*
Franciscan University of Steubenville *A, B, M*
Lourdes College *A, B*
Malone College *B, M*
Mount Vernon Nazarene College *M*
Muskingum College *B*
Notre Dame College of Ohio *A, B*
Pontifical College Josephinum *M*
Walsh University *B*
Xavier University *A, B, M*

Oklahoma
Mid-America Bible College *B*
Oklahoma Baptist University *A*
Oklahoma Christian University of Science and Arts *B*
Oral Roberts University *B, M, D*
Southern Nazarene University *B*
Southwestern College of Christian Ministries *B, M*

Oregon
Concordia University *B*
Eugene Bible College *B*
George Fox University *B*
Multnomah Bible College *B, M*
University of Portland *M*
Western Baptist College *B*

Pennsylvania
Allentown College of St. Francis de Sales *B*
Carlow College *B*
Chestnut Hill College *C, B*
Duquesne University *B, M, D*
Eastern College *B*
Elizabethtown College *B*
Gannon University *B, M*
Immaculata College *A*
King's College *B*
Lancaster Bible College *B, M*
Philadelphia College of Bible *B*
Talmudical Yeshiva of Philadelphia *B*
Valley Forge Christian College *B*

Puerto Rico
Bayamon Central University *M*
Pontifical Catholic University of Puerto Rico *M*

Rhode Island
Providence College *B*

South Carolina
Charleston Southern University *B*
Columbia International University *B, D*
Erskine College *M, D*
Southern Wesleyan University *M*

Tennessee
Carson-Newman College *A*
Crichton College *C, B*
Freed-Hardeman University *M*
Southern Adventist University *B, M*
Tennessee Temple University *B*
Trevecca Nazarene University *B, M*
Union University *B*
University of the South *M, D*
Vanderbilt University *D*

Texas
Abilene Christian University *B, M*
Arlington Baptist College *B*
Baylor University *M*
East Texas Baptist University *B*
Hardin-Simmons University *B, M*
Howard Payne University *C, B*
Institute for Christian Studies *B*
Southern Methodist University *M, D*
Southwestern Adventist University *B*
Southwestern Assemblies of God University *B*
Texas Christian University *C, M, D*

Vermont
St. Michael's College *M*

Ministerial/theological studies

Virginia
Eastern Mennonite University B
Liberty University M, D
Regent University M, D
Shenandoah University C
Virginia Union University M, D

Washington
Puget Sound Christian College B
Seattle University M
Walla Walla College B

West Virginia
Alderson-Broaddus College B
West Virginia Wesleyan College B

Wisconsin
Cardinal Stritch University B
St. Norbert College M
Silver Lake College B

Missionary studies

Alaska
Alaska Bible College B

Arizona
Southwestern College C, A, B

Arkansas
Harding University B
John Brown University B
Ouachita Baptist University B
Williams Baptist College B

California
Biola University D
Fresno Pacific University B
Hope International University A, B, M
Master's College B
San Jose Christian College C, B
Simpson College B, M
Vanguard University of Southern California B

Colorado
Colorado Christian University B

Florida
Florida Christian College B
Hobe Sound Bible College C, A, B
Southeastern College of the Assemblies of God B

Georgia
Covenant College B
Toccoa Falls College B

Idaho
Northwest Nazarene University B

Illinois
Lincoln Christian College and Seminary B, M
Moody Bible Institute B
Wheaton College M

Indiana
Anderson University M

Iowa
Dordt College B
Emmaus Bible College B
Faith Baptist Bible College and Theological Seminary B

Kansas
Barclay College B
Central Christian College A, B
Manhattan Christian College A, B

Kentucky
Asbury College B
Kentucky Mountain Bible College B
Mid-Continent College C, B

Michigan
Cornerstone College and Grand Rapids Baptist Seminary B, M, D
Grace Bible College B

Reformed Bible College B

Minnesota
Concordia University: St. Paul B
Crown College B, M
Northwestern College B

Mississippi
Magnolia Bible College B
Wesley College B

Missouri
Baptist Bible College B, M
Berean University B
Evangel University B
Ozark Christian College B
St. Louis Christian College A, B

Nebraska
Grace University B

New York
Nyack College B, M

North Dakota
Trinity Bible College B

Ohio
Cedarville College B
Circleville Bible College A, B

Oklahoma
Oklahoma Baptist University B
Oklahoma Christian University of Science and Arts B
Oral Roberts University B, M
Southern Nazarene University B
Southwestern College of Christian Ministries B

Oregon
Eugene Bible College B
George Fox University B
Multnomah Bible College B
Western Baptist College B

Pennsylvania
Eastern College B
Lancaster Bible College B
Philadelphia College of Bible B
Valley Forge Christian College B

South Carolina
Columbia International University B, M

Tennessee
Freed-Hardeman University B
Lee University B
Milligan College B
Tennessee Temple University B

Texas
Abilene Christian University B, M
Arlington Baptist College B
Southwestern Assemblies of God University B

Washington
Puget Sound Christian College B

Molecular biology

Alabama
Alabama Agricultural and Mechanical University B, M
Auburn University B

Alaska
University of Alaska Fairbanks M, D

Arizona
Arizona State University B, M, D
University of Arizona M, D

California
California Institute of Technology D
California Lutheran University B

California State University
  Fresno B
  Long Beach B
  Northridge B
Loma Linda University M, D
Los Angeles Southwest College A
Pomona College B
San Diego State University B, D
San Francisco State University M
San Jose State University B
Stanford University D
University of California
  Berkeley B, M, D
  Davis B
  Irvine D
  Los Angeles B, D
  San Diego B
  Santa Barbara B, M, D
  Santa Cruz B, D
University of Southern California B, M, D

Colorado
Colorado State University M, D
Fort Lewis College B
University of Colorado
  Boulder B, M, D

Connecticut
Connecticut College B
Quinnipiac University M
University of New Haven M
Wesleyan University B, D
Yale University B, M, D

District of Columbia
Georgetown University D

Florida
Florida Institute of Technology B, M
Stetson University B
University of Central Florida B
University of Miami B
University of West Florida B

Georgia
Medical College of Georgia D

Idaho
University of Idaho B

Illinois
Benedictine University B
Chicago State University B
Finch University of Health Sciences/The Chicago Medical School M, D
Loyola University of Chicago D
Northwestern University B, M, D
Southern Illinois University Carbondale M, D
University of Chicago M, D

Indiana
Ball State University B
Goshen College B
Indiana University Bloomington D

Iowa
Coe College B
Iowa State University M, D
University of Iowa D

Kansas
University of Kansas M, D

Kentucky
Centre College B

Louisiana
Louisiana State University Medical Center M, D
Tulane University B

Maine
Colby College B
University of Maine B

Maryland
Uniformed Services University of the Health Sciences D
University of Maryland
  Baltimore County M, D
  Baltimore M, D

Massachusetts
Assumption College B
Boston University B, M, D
Brandeis University M, D
Clark University B
Hampshire College B
Harvard College B
Simon's Rock College of Bard B
Tufts University M, D

Michigan
University of Michigan B, M, D
Wayne State University M, D

Minnesota
Mayo Graduate School D
University of Minnesota
  Duluth B
  Twin Cities D
Winona State University B

Mississippi
Mississippi State University D

Missouri
Northwest Missouri State University B
St. Louis University D
University of Missouri
  Kansas City M
Washington University D
William Jewell College B

Montana
Montana State University
  Bozeman M, D
University of Great Falls B

New Hampshire
Dartmouth College B
University of New Hampshire B

New Jersey
Montclair State University B
Princeton University B, M, D
Richard Stockton College of New Jersey B
Rutgers
  The State University of New Jersey: Camden College of Arts and Sciences B
  The State University of New Jersey: Cook College B
  The State University of New Jersey: Douglass College B
  The State University of New Jersey: Livingston College B
  The State University of New Jersey: Rutgers College B
  The State University of New Jersey: University College Camden B
  The State University of New Jersey: University College New Brunswick B

New Mexico
New Mexico State University M, D

New York
Albany Medical College M, D
Bard College B
Clarkson University B
Colgate University B
Columbia University Graduate School M, D
Hamilton College B
Long Island University
  Brooklyn Campus B
Rockefeller University D

State University of New York
    Albany B, M, D
    College of Environmental Science
        and Forestry M, D
    Stony Brook M, D
University of Rochester B
Wells College B

North Carolina
East Carolina University M
Meredith College B
Wake Forest University M, D

North Dakota
North Dakota State University D

Ohio
Case Western Reserve University D
Kent State University M, D
Kenyon College B
Miami University
    Middletown Campus A
Muskingum College B
Ohio Northern University B
Ohio State University
    Columbus Campus M, D
Otterbein College B
University of Cincinnati M, D
Wittenberg University B

Oklahoma
Eastern Oklahoma State College A
Oklahoma State University B, M

Oregon
Oregon Graduate Institute M, D
Oregon Health Sciences University M, D
Oregon State University D
University of Oregon M, D

Pennsylvania
Carnegie Mellon University B
Chestnut Hill College B
Clarion University of Pennsylvania B
Dickinson College B
Grove City College B
Juniata College B
Lehigh University B, M, D
MCP Hahnemann University M, D
Mansfield University of Pennsylvania B
Penn State
    College of Medicine, Milton S.
        Hershey Medical Center M, D
Thomas Jefferson University: College of
    Health Professions D
University of Pennsylvania M, D
University of Pittsburgh B
West Chester University of
    Pennsylvania B
Westminster College B

Puerto Rico
Universidad Metropolitana B

Rhode Island
Brown University B, M, D

Tennessee
Vanderbilt University B, M, D

Texas
Texas A&M University B
Texas Lutheran University B
Texas Tech University B
Texas Woman's University D
University of North Texas M
University of Texas
    Austin B, M, D
    Dallas M, D

Utah
Brigham Young University B, M, D

Vermont
Bennington College B
Johnson State College B
Marlboro College B
Middlebury College B
University of Vermont M, D

Virginia
Hampton University B

Washington
University of Washington M, D
Western Washington University B

West Virginia
Salem-Teikyo University B, M

Wisconsin
Marquette University B
University of Wisconsin
    Eau Claire B
    Madison B, M, D
    Parkside B, M
    Superior B

Wyoming
University of Wyoming B, M, D

Movement therapy

Colorado
Naropa University B, M

Michigan
Oakland Community College C, A

Missouri
Washington University D

New Hampshire
Antioch New England Graduate
    School M

North Carolina
University of North Carolina
    Chapel Hill M, D

Oregon
Oregon State University M

Pennsylvania
MCP Hahnemann University M

Museum studies

California
California State University
    Chico C
    Long Beach C
John F. Kennedy University M
San Francisco State University M
University of Southern California M

Colorado
University of Colorado
    Boulder M

District of Columbia
George Washington University M

Florida
Florida State University C
University of Florida M

Kansas
University of Kansas M

Nebraska
University of Nebraska
    Lincoln M

New Jersey
Seton Hall University M

New Mexico
Institute of American Indian Arts A

New York
Bank Street College of Education M
City University of New York
    City College M
Fashion Institute of Technology M
New York University M
State University of New York
    College at Oneonta M
Syracuse University M

Oklahoma
University of Central Oklahoma B, M
University of Tulsa C

Pennsylvania
University of the Arts M

Tennessee
Rhodes College B
Tusculum College B

Texas
Baylor University B, M
Texas Tech University M

Virginia
Hampton University M
Randolph-Macon Woman's College B

Washington
University of Washington C, M

Wisconsin
University of Wisconsin
    Madison M, D

Music

Alabama
Alabama Agricultural and Mechanical
    University B, M
Alabama State University B, T
Auburn University B, M
Birmingham-Southern College B, T
Calhoun Community College A
Chattahoochee Valley Community
    College A
Community College of the Air Force A
Faulkner University B
Huntingdon College B, T
Jacksonville State University B, M
James H. Faulkner State Community
    College A
Northeast Alabama Community
    College A
Northwest-Shoals Community College A
Stillman College B
Talladega College B
University of Alabama
    Birmingham B
    Huntsville B
University of Alabama B, M
University of Mobile B, T
University of Montevallo B, T
University of North Alabama B
University of South Alabama B
Wallace State Community College at
    Hanceville A

Alaska
University of Alaska
    Anchorage B
    Fairbanks B, M

Arizona
Arizona State University B, M, D
Arizona Western College A
Eastern Arizona College A
Mohave Community College A
Northern Arizona University B, M, T
Pima Community College A
South Mountain Community College A
University of Arizona B

Arkansas
Arkansas State University B
Arkansas Tech University B
Central Baptist College A
Harding University B
Henderson State University B
Hendrix College B
John Brown University B
Lyon College B
Ouachita Baptist University B
Philander Smith College B

University of Arkansas
    Little Rock B
    Monticello B
University of Central Arkansas B, M
University of the Ozarks B
Westark College A

California
Allan Hancock College A
Azusa Pacific University B, M
Bakersfield College A
Barstow College A
Biola University B
Cabrillo College A
California Baptist University B
California Institute of the Arts C, B
California Lutheran University B
California State Polytechnic University:
    Pomona B
California State University
    Bakersfield B
    Chico B, M
    Dominguez Hills B
    Fresno B, M
    Fullerton B
    Hayward B, M
    Long Beach B, M
    Los Angeles B, M
    Monterey Bay B
    Northridge B, M
    Sacramento B, M
    Stanislaus B
Canada College A
Cerritos Community College A
Chabot College A
Chaffey Community College A
Chapman University B
Citrus College A
College of Marin: Kentfield A
College of Notre Dame B
College of San Mateo A
College of the Desert A
College of the Sequoias A
College of the Siskiyous A
Columbia College A
Concordia University B
Contra Costa College A
Crafton Hills College A
Cypress College A
De Anza College A
Diablo Valley College A
Dominican University of California B
East Los Angeles College A
Foothill College C, A
Fresno City College A
Fresno Pacific University B
Gavilan Community College A
Golden West College A
Grossmont Community College A
Holy Names College B, M
Humboldt State University B
Imperial Valley College A
Irvine Valley College A
Kings River Community College A
La Sierra University B
Lake Tahoe Community College A
Las Positas College A
Long Beach City College A
Los Angeles Pierce College C, A
Los Angeles Southwest College A
Los Angeles Valley College A
Los Medanos College A
Loyola Marymount University B
Marymount College A
Master's College B
Mendocino College A
Merced College A
Mills College B, M
MiraCosta College A
Modesto Junior College A
Monterey Peninsula College A
Moorpark College A
Mount St. Mary's College B
Mount San Jacinto College A
Occidental College B

Ohlone College A
Orange Coast College A
Pacific Union College B
Palo Verde College A
Palomar College A
Pasadena City College C, A
Pepperdine University B
Point Loma Nazarene University C, B
Pomona College B
Porterville College A
Riverside Community College A
Sacramento City College A
Saddleback College A
St. Mary's College of California B
San Diego City College A
San Diego Mesa College A
San Diego State University B, M
San Francisco State University B, M
San Joaquin Delta College A
San Jose Christian College C, B
San Jose City College A
San Jose State University B, M
Santa Ana College A
Santa Barbara City College A
Santa Clara University B
Santa Monica College A
Scripps College B
Shasta College A
Skyline College A
Solano Community College A
Sonoma State University B
Southwestern College C, A
Stanford University B, M, D
University of California
  Berkeley B, M, D
  Davis B, M, D
  Irvine B, M
  Los Angeles B, M, D
  Riverside B, M
  San Diego B, M, D
  Santa Barbara B, M, D
  Santa Cruz B
University of La Verne B
University of Redlands B, M
University of San Diego B
University of Southern California B
University of the Pacific B, M
Vanguard University of Southern
  California B
Ventura College C, A
West Hills Community College A
West Los Angeles College C, A
West Valley College A
Westmont College B
Whittier College B

Colorado
Adams State College B
Colorado College B
Colorado State University B, M
Fort Lewis College B
Naropa University C, B
University of Colorado
  Boulder B, M, D
  Denver B
University of Denver B
University of Northern
  Colorado B, M, D, T
University of Southern Colorado B, T
Western State College of Colorado B

Connecticut
Central Connecticut State University B
Connecticut College B, M
Eastern Connecticut State University B
Manchester Community-Technical
  College A
Naugatuck Valley Community-Technical
  College A
Sacred Heart University C, A
Southern Connecticut State University B
Trinity College B
University of Bridgeport B
University of Connecticut B, M, D
University of Hartford B
University of New Haven B

Wesleyan University B, M
Western Connecticut State University B
Yale University B, M, D

Delaware
University of Delaware B

District of Columbia
American University B
Catholic University of America B
George Washington University B
Howard University M
University of the District of
  Columbia A, B

Florida
Barry University B
Bethune-Cookman College B
Broward Community College A
Chipola Junior College A
Clearwater Christian College B
Daytona Beach Community College A
Eckerd College B
Florida Atlantic University B, M
Florida International University B, M
Florida Memorial College B
Florida Southern College B
Florida State University B
Gulf Coast Community College A
Hillsborough Community College A
Indian River Community College A
Jacksonville University B
Manatee Community College A
Miami-Dade Community College A
New College of the University of South
  Florida B
Palm Beach Atlantic College B, T
Palm Beach Community College A
Pensacola Junior College A
Polk Community College A
Rollins College B
Southeastern College of the Assemblies
  of God B
University of Central Florida B
University of Florida B, M, D
University of Miami B, M, D
University of North Florida B
University of Tampa A, B, T
University of West Florida B

Georgia
Abraham Baldwin Agricultural
  College A
Agnes Scott College B
Albany State University B
Armstrong Atlantic State University B, T
Atlanta Metropolitan College A
Augusta State University B
Berry College B
Brewton-Parker College A, B
Clark Atlanta University B
Columbus State University B, M
Covenant College B
Darton College A
Emory University B
Georgia College and State University B
Georgia Military College A
Georgia Perimeter College A
Georgia Southern University B, M
Georgia Southwestern State University B
Kennesaw State University B
LaGrange College B
Macon State College A
Mercer University B, T
Middle Georgia College A
Morehouse College B
Morris Brown College B
North Georgia College & State
  University B
Oxford College of Emory University B
Piedmont College B
Reinhardt College A
Spelman College B
State University of West Georgia M
Thomas College B
Toccoa Falls College B

Truett-McConnell College A
University of Georgia B, M, D
Valdosta State University B
Wesleyan College B
Young Harris College A

Hawaii
Brigham Young University
  Hawaii B
University of Hawaii
  Hilo B
  Manoa B, M, D

Idaho
Albertson College of Idaho B
College of Southern Idaho A
Idaho State University B
North Idaho College A
Northwest Nazarene University B
Ricks College A
University of Idaho B, M

Illinois
Augustana College B
Barat College B
Benedictine University B
Black Hawk College
  East Campus A
Blackburn College B, T
Bradley University B
Chicago State University B
City Colleges of Chicago
  Harold Washington College A
  Kennedy-King College C
  Olive-Harvey College A
College of Lake County A
Columbia College B
Concordia University B, T
De Paul University B, M
Eastern Illinois University B, M, T
Elmhurst College B, T
Greenville College B, T
Highland Community College A
Illinois College B
Illinois State University B
John Wood Community College A
Joliet Junior College A
Judson College B
Kishwaukee College A
Knox College B
Lewis University B, T
Lewis and Clark Community College A
Lincoln Land Community College A
Loyola University of Chicago B
MacMurray College B
McHenry County College A
McKendree College B
Millikin University B
Monmouth College B
North Central College B, T
North Park University B
Northeastern Illinois University B, M
Northern Illinois University B
Olivet Nazarene University B, T
Principia College B
Quincy University A, B
Richland Community College A
Roosevelt University B
St. Xavier University B
Sauk Valley Community College A
Southern Illinois University
  Carbondale B, M
  Edwardsville B, M
Southwestern Ilinois College A
Springfield College in Illinois A
Trinity Christian College B
Trinity International University B
Triton College A
University of Chicago B, M, D
University of Illinois
  Chicago B
  Urbana-Champaign B, M, D
Western Illinois University B, M
Wheaton College B
William Rainey Harper College A

Indiana
Bethel College A, B
Butler University B
DePauw University B
Earlham College B
Goshen College B
Hanover College B
Indiana State University B, M, T
Indiana University
  Bloomington B, M, D
  Southeast B
Indiana University--Purdue University
  Indiana University-Purdue
    University Fort Wayne B
Indiana Wesleyan University B
Manchester College B, T
Marian College A, B, T
Oakland City University B
Saint Mary's College B
St. Joseph's College B
St. Mary-of-the-Woods College B
Taylor University B
University of Evansville B
University of Indianapolis B
University of Notre Dame B, M
Valparaiso University B, T
Vincennes University A
Wabash College B

Iowa
Briar Cliff College B
Buena Vista University B, T
Central College B, T
Clarke College A, B, T
Coe College B
Cornell College B, T
Dordt College B
Drake University B
Graceland University B, T
Grand View College B
Grinnell College B
Iowa State University B
Iowa Western Community College A
Loras College B
Luther College B
Maharishi University of
  Management C, A, B
Marshalltown Community College A
Morningside College B
Mount Mercy College B
North Iowa Area Community College A
Northwestern College B, T
St. Ambrose University B
Simpson College B
University of Iowa B, M, D, T
University of Northern Iowa B, M
Upper Iowa University B
Waldorf College A
Wartburg College B, T

Kansas
Allen County Community College A
Baker University B, T
Benedictine College B, T
Bethany College B, T
Bethel College B, T
Butler County Community College A
Central Christian College A
Coffeyville Community College A
Cowley County Community College A
Dodge City Community College A
Emporia State University B, M, T
Fort Hays State University B, M
Garden City Community College A
Hutchinson Community College A
Independence Community College A
Kansas City Kansas Community
  College A
Kansas State University B, M
Kansas Wesleyan University T
McPherson College B, T
MidAmerica Nazarene University B
Ottawa University B, T
Pittsburg State University B, M, T
Pratt Community College A
Seward County Community College A

Southwestern College B
Sterling College B
Tabor College B
University of Kansas B, M, D
Washburn University of Topeka B
Wichita State University B, M

Kentucky
Asbury College B
Bellarmine College B
Berea College B, T
Campbellsville University B
Centre College B
Cumberland College B, T
Eastern Kentucky University B, M
Georgetown College B
Kentucky State University B
Kentucky Wesleyan College A, B, T
Morehead State University B
Murray State University B, M
Northern Kentucky University B, T
Union College B
University of Kentucky D
University of Louisville B
Western Kentucky University B

Louisiana
Centenary College of Louisiana B
Delgado Community College A
Dillard University B
Louisiana State University and
  Agricultural and Mechanical
  College B, D
Louisiana Tech University B
Loyola University New Orleans B, M
Northwestern State University B
Southern University and Agricultural and
  Mechanical College A
Tulane University B, M
University of Louisiana at Monroe B, M
University of New Orleans B, M
Xavier University of Louisiana B

Maine
Bates College B
Bowdoin College B
Colby College B
University of Maine B, M
University of Southern Maine B

Maryland
Anne Arundel Community College C
Baltimore City Community College A
Charles County Community College A
College of Notre Dame of Maryland B
Columbia Union College B
Community College of Baltimore County
  Essex A
Frostburg State University B
Goucher College B
Howard Community College A
Johns Hopkins University B, M, D
Montgomery College
  Rockville Campus A
Morgan State University B, M
Prince George's Community College A
St. Mary's College of Maryland B
Salisbury State University B, T
Towson University B, M, T
University of Maryland
  Baltimore County
    College Park B, M, D, T
  Eastern Shore B
Washington Bible College A, B
Washington College B
Western Maryland College B

Massachusetts
Amherst College B
Anna Maria College B
Assumption College B
Atlantic Union College B
Berklee College of Music B
Berkshire Community College A
Boston College B
Brandeis University B, M, D
Bridgewater State College B

College of the Holy Cross B
Eastern Nazarene College A, B
Gordon College B
Hampshire College B
Harvard College B
Harvard University M, D
Holyoke Community College A
Massachusetts College of Liberal Arts B
Massachusetts Institute of Technology B
Mount Holyoke College B
New England Conservatory of
  Music B, M
Northeastern University B
Simmons College B
Simon's Rock College of Bard B
Smith College B, M
Springfield Technical Community
  College A
Tufts University B, M
University of Massachusetts
  Amherst B
  Boston B
  Dartmouth B
Wellesley College B
Westfield State College B
Wheaton College B
Williams College B
Worcester Polytechnic Institute B

Michigan
Adrian College A, B, T
Albion College B, T
Alma College B, T
Andrews University B, M
Calvin College B, T
Central Michigan University B
Concordia College B, T
Cornerstone College and Grand Rapids
  Baptist Seminary B, T
Eastern Michigan University B, M
Grace Bible College B
Grand Rapids Community College A
Grand Valley State University B
Henry Ford Community College A
Hillsdale College B
Hope College B, T
Kalamazoo College B
Kellogg Community College A
Lake Michigan College A
Lansing Community College A
Madonna University B, T
Marygrove College T
Mott Community College A
Northern Michigan University B, T
Northwestern Michigan College A
Oakland University B, M
Rochester College B
Saginaw Valley State University B
Schoolcraft College A
Siena Heights University B
Spring Arbor College B
University of Michigan
  Dearborn B
  Flint B
University of Michigan B
Wayne State University B, M, T
Western Michigan University B, M, T
William Tyndale College B

Minnesota
Augsburg College B
Bemidji State University B
Bethel College B
Carleton College B
College of St. Benedict B
College of St. Catherine: St. Paul
  Campus B
College of St. Scholastica B
Concordia College: Moorhead B
Concordia University: St. Paul B
Crown College A, B
Gustavus Adolphus College B
Hamline University B
Macalester College B, T
Minnesota State University,
  Mankato B, M

Moorhead State University B, M
Northland Community & Technical
  College A
Northwestern College B
Ridgewater College: A Community and
  Technical College A
St. Cloud State University B, M
St. John's University B
St. Mary's University of Minnesota B
St. Olaf College B, T
Southwest State University B, T
University of Minnesota
  Duluth B
  Morris B
  Twin Cities B, M, D
University of St. Thomas B
Winona State University B, T

Mississippi
Belhaven College B, T
Blue Mountain College B
Delta State University B
East Central Community College A
Hinds Community College A
Jackson State University B, M
Mary Holmes College A
Millsaps College B, T
Mississippi College B, M
Mississippi Delta Community College A
Mississippi Gulf Coast Community
  College
    Jefferson Davis Campus A
Mississippi University for Women B
Mississippi Valley State University B
Rust College B
Tougaloo College B
University of Mississippi B, M, D, T
University of Southern Mississippi B, M
William Carey College B

Missouri
Avila College B
Baptist Bible College B
Central Missouri State University B, M
College of the Ozarks B
Crowder College A
Culver-Stockton College B, T
Drury University B, T
East Central College A
Evangel University A, B
Jefferson College A
Lindenwood University B, M
Maryville University of Saint Louis B
Missouri Southern State College B, T
Missouri Western State College B
Northwest Missouri State University B
St. Louis University B
Southeast Missouri State University B
Southwest Baptist University B, T
Southwest Missouri State
  University B, M
St. Louis Community College
  St. Louis Community College at
    Florissant Valley A
  St. Louis Community College at
    Forest Park A
  St. Louis Community College at
    Meramec A
Three Rivers Community College A
Truman State University B, M
University of Missouri
  Columbia B, M
  Kansas City B, M
  St. Louis B
Washington University B, M
Webster University B
William Jewell College B

Montana
Montana State University
  Billings B
Rocky Mountain College B
University of Montana-Missoula B, M
Western Montana College of The
  University of Montana B, T

Nebraska
Chadron State College B
Concordia University B
Creighton University B
Dana College B
Doane College B
Hastings College B, T
Midland Lutheran College B, T
Nebraska Wesleyan University B
Northeast Community College A
Peru State College B
Union College B
University of Nebraska
  Kearney B, M, T
  Lincoln B, M, D
  Omaha B, M
Wayne State College B, T

Nevada
University of Nevada
  Las Vegas B, M
  Reno B, M

New Hampshire
Dartmouth College B
Franklin Pierce College B
Keene State College B
Plymouth State College of the University
  System of New Hampshire B
University of New Hampshire B, M

New Jersey
Caldwell College B
College of St. Elizabeth B
Cumberland County College A
Drew University B
Essex County College A
Georgian Court College B, T
Kean University B
Monmouth University B
Montclair State University B, M
New Jersey City University B, T
Princeton University B
Raritan Valley Community College A
Rider University B, M
Rowan University B
Rutgers
  The State University of New Jersey:
    Camden College of Arts and
    Sciences B, T
  The State University of New Jersey:
    Douglass College B
  The State University of New Jersey:
    Livingston College B
  The State University of New Jersey:
    Mason Gross School of the
    Arts B
  The State University of New Jersey:
    New Brunswick Graduate
    Campus M, D, T
  The State University of New Jersey:
    Newark College of Arts and
    Sciences B, T
  The State University of New Jersey:
    Rutgers College B
  The State University of New Jersey:
    University College Camden B, T
  The State University of New Jersey:
    University College New
    Brunswick B
  The State University of New Jersey:
    University College Newark T
Seton Hall University B, T
The College of New Jersey B, M, T
Thomas Edison State College B
Union County College A
William Paterson University of New
  Jersey B

New Mexico
College of Santa Fe B
Eastern New Mexico University B, M
New Mexico Highlands University B
New Mexico Junior College A
New Mexico State University B, M
San Juan College A

Western New Mexico University *B*

New York
Adelphi University *B*
Adirondack Community College *A*
Bard College *B, M*
Barnard College *B*
City University of New York
    Baruch College *B*
    Brooklyn College *B, M*
    City College *B, M*
    College of Staten Island *B*
    Graduate School and University Center *D*
    Hunter College *B, M*
    Kingsborough Community College *A*
    Lehman College *B*
    Queens College *B, M*
    York College *B*
Colgate University *B*
College of St. Rose *B, M*
Columbia University
    Columbia College *B*
    Graduate School *M, D*
    School of General Studies *B*
Concordia College *B*
Cornell University *B, M, D*
Dowling College *B, T*
Eastman School of Music of the University of Rochester *B*
Elmira College *B*
Finger Lakes Community College *A*
Five Towns College *A, B*
Fordham University *B*
Hamilton College *B*
Hartwick College *B*
Hobart and William Smith Colleges *B*
Hofstra University *B*
Houghton College *B*
Ithaca College *B, M, T*
Jewish Theological Seminary of America *M, D*
Long Island University
    Brooklyn Campus *B*
    C. W. Post Campus *B, M*
Manhattanville College *B*
Mercy College *B*
Molloy College *B*
Nazareth College of Rochester *B, T*
New York University *B, M, D*
Niagara County Community College *A*
Nyack College *B*
Onondaga Community College *A*
Roberts Wesleyan College *B*
Rockland Community College *A*
St. Lawrence University *B*
Sarah Lawrence College *B*
Schenectady County Community College *C*
Skidmore College *B*
State University of New York
    Albany *B*
    Binghamton *B*
    Buffalo *B, M, D, T*
    College at Buffalo *B*
    College at Fredonia *B*
    College at Oneonta *B*
    College at Potsdam *B, T*
    New Paltz *B, M*
    Oswego *B*
    Purchase *B, M*
    Stony Brook *B, M, D*
Suffolk County Community College *A*
Syracuse University *B*
University of Rochester *B*
Vassar College *B*
Wells College *B*

North Carolina
Appalachian State University *B*
Barber-Scotia College *B*
Bennett College *B*
Brevard College *A, B*
Caldwell Community College and Technical Institute *A*
Campbell University *B*
Catawba College *B, T*
Central Piedmont Community College *A*
Chowan College *B*
College of the Albemarle *A*
Davidson College *B*
Duke University *B*
Elizabeth City State University *B*
Elon College *B*
Gardner-Webb University *B*
Greensboro College *B, T*
Guilford College *B*
Lenoir-Rhyne College *B, T*
Mars Hill College *B, T*
Meredith College *B, M*
Methodist College *B*
Montreat College *B*
Mount Olive College *A, B*
North Carolina Agricultural and Technical State University *B, T*
North Carolina Central University *B*
Peace College *A*
Pfeiffer University *B*
Queens College *B*
Salem College *B*
Sandhills Community College *A*
Shaw University *B*
Southeastern Community College *A*
University of North Carolina
    Asheville *B*
    Chapel Hill *B*
    Pembroke *B*
    Wilmington *B*
Wake Forest University *B*
Western Carolina University *B, M*
Wilkes Community College *A*
Wingate University *B*
Winston-Salem State University *B*

North Dakota
Dickinson State University *B, T*
Jamestown College *B*
Minot State University: Bottineau Campus *A*
North Dakota State University *B, T*
Trinity Bible College *A, B*
University of Mary *B, T*
University of North Dakota *B, M, T*
Valley City State University *B*

Ohio
Antioch College *B*
Bluffton College *B*
Bowling Green State University *B*
Capital University *B*
Case Western Reserve University *B, M, D*
Cedarville College *B, T*
Cleveland State University *B, M, T*
College of Mount St. Joseph *B, T*
College of Wooster *B*
Denison University *B*
Heidelberg College *B*
Hiram College *B, T*
Kent State University
    Stark Campus *B*
Kent State University *B, M, D*
Kenyon College *B*
Lake Erie College *B*
Lorain County Community College *A*
Lourdes College *A*
Malone College *B*
Marietta College *B*
Miami University
    Oxford Campus *B, T*
Mount Union College *B*
Mount Vernon Nazarene College *B*
Muskingum College *B*
Oberlin College *B*
Ohio Northern University *B*
Ohio State University
    Columbus Campus *B, M, D*
Ohio Wesleyan University *B*
Otterbein College *B*
Shawnee State University *A*
Sinclair Community College *A*
University of Akron *B, M*
University of Cincinnati *B, M, D*
University of Dayton *B*
University of Rio Grande *B*
University of Toledo *B*
Wilberforce University *B*
Wittenberg University *B*
Wright State University *B*
Xavier University *B*
Youngstown State University *B, M*

Oklahoma
Cameron University *B*
Carl Albert State College *A*
Connors State College *A*
East Central University *B*
Eastern Oklahoma State College *A*
Langston University *B*
Northeastern Oklahoma Agricultural and Mechanical College *A*
Northeastern State University *B*
Northwestern Oklahoma State University *B*
Oklahoma Baptist University *B, T*
Oklahoma City Community College *A*
Oklahoma City University *B, M*
Oklahoma Panhandle State University *B*
Oklahoma State University *B*
Oral Roberts University *B*
Rose State College *A*
St. Gregory's University *A*
Southeastern Oklahoma State University *B*
Southern Nazarene University *B*
Southwestern Oklahoma State University *B, M*
Tulsa Community College *A*
University of Central Oklahoma *B*
University of Oklahoma *B*
University of Science and Arts of Oklahoma *B, T*
University of Tulsa *M*
Western Oklahoma State College *A*

Oregon
Chemeketa Community College *A*
Eastern Oregon University *B*
George Fox University *B, T*
Lewis & Clark College *B*
Linfield College *B*
Marylhurst University *B*
Mount Hood Community College *A*
Northwest Christian College *A, B*
Oregon State University *B*
Pacific University *B*
Portland State University *B, M*
Reed College *B*
Southern Oregon University *B, T*
University of Oregon *B, M*
University of Portland *B, M, T*
Western Baptist College *B*
Western Oregon University *B*

Pennsylvania
Allegheny College *B*
Bloomsburg University of Pennsylvania *B*
Bryn Mawr College *B*
Bucknell University *B*
Bucks County Community College *A*
Carnegie Mellon University *B*
Cedar Crest College *B*
Chatham College *B*
Chestnut Hill College *A, B*
Cheyney University of Pennsylvania *B*
Community College of Allegheny County *A*
Community College of Philadelphia *A*
Dickinson College *B*
Drexel University *B*
Eastern College *B*
Edinboro University of Pennsylvania *B, T*
Elizabethtown College *B*
Franklin and Marshall College *B*
Geneva College *B*
Gettysburg College *B*
Grove City College *B*
Haverford College *B*
Immaculata College *B*
Indiana University of Pennsylvania *B, M*
Kutztown University of Pennsylvania *B*
La Salle University *B*
Lebanon Valley College of Pennsylvania *B, T*
Lehigh University *B*
Lincoln University *B*
Lock Haven University of Pennsylvania *B*
Lycoming College *B*
Mansfield University of Pennsylvania *B, M*
Mercyhurst College *B*
Messiah College *B*
Millersville University of Pennsylvania *B*
Moravian College *B, T*
Muhlenberg College *B*
Penn State
    University Park *B, M*
Philadelphia College of Bible *B*
St. Vincent College *B*
Seton Hill College *B, T*
Slippery Rock University of Pennsylvania *B*
Swarthmore College *B*
Temple University *B*
University of Pennsylvania *A, B, M, D*
University of Pittsburgh *B, M, D*
Valley Forge Christian College *B*
West Chester University of Pennsylvania *B, M*
Westminster College *B*
York College of Pennsylvania *B, T*

Puerto Rico
Inter American University of Puerto Rico
    San German Campus *B*
Pontifical Catholic University of Puerto Rico *B*
University of Puerto Rico
    Rio Piedras Campus *B*

Rhode Island
Brown University *B, M*
Community College of Rhode Island *A*
Providence College *B*
Rhode Island College *B*
Salve Regina University *B*
University of Rhode Island *B, M*

South Carolina
Charleston Southern University *B*
Claflin University *B*
Coker College *B, T*
College of Charleston *B*
Columbia College *B*
Converse College *B, M*
Erskine College *B, T*
Furman University *B, T*
Lander University *B, T*
Limestone College *B*
Newberry College *B*
North Greenville College *A, B*
Presbyterian College *B*
Southern Wesleyan University *B*
University of South Carolina *B*
Winthrop University *B, M*

South Dakota
Augustana College *B*
Black Hills State University *B*
Dakota State University *B*
Dakota Wesleyan University *B*
Northern State University *B*
South Dakota State University *B*
University of South Dakota *B*

Tennessee
Austin Peay State University *B, M*
Belmont University *B, T*
Carson-Newman College *B, T*
Columbia State Community College *A*

East Tennessee State University B, T
Fisk University B
Freed-Hardeman University B, T
Hiwassee College A
Lambuth University B
Lane College B
Maryville College B
Middle Tennessee State University B, M
Milligan College B
Rhodes College B, T
Roane State Community College A
Southern Adventist University B
Tennessee State University B
Tennessee Temple University B
Tennessee Wesleyan College B, T
Trevecca Nazarene University B
Union University B
University of Memphis B, M, D
University of Tennessee
    Chattanooga B, M, T
    Knoxville B, M
    Martin B
University of the South B
Walters State Community College A

Texas
Abilene Christian University B
Amarillo College A
Angelina College A
Angelo State University B
Arlington Baptist College B
Austin College B
Austin Community College A
Baylor University B
Blinn College A
Brazosport College A
Central Texas College A
Coastal Bend College A
College of the Mainland A
Dallas Baptist University A, B
East Texas Baptist University B
El Paso Community College A
Galveston College A
Grayson County College A
Hardin-Simmons University B
Hill College A
Houston Baptist University B
Howard College A
Howard Payne University B, T
Huston-Tillotson College B
Jarvis Christian College B
Kilgore College A
Lamar University B, M
Lee College A
Lon Morris College A
Lubbock Christian University B
McMurry University B, T
Midland College A
Midwestern State University B
Navarro College A
Northeast Texas Community College A
Our Lady of the Lake University of San Antonio B
Palo Alto College A
Panola College A
Paris Junior College A
Prairie View A&M University B
Rice University B, M
St. Mary's University B, T
St. Philip's College A
Sam Houston State University B, M
San Jacinto College
    North A
South Plains College A
Southern Methodist University C, B, T
Southwest Texas State University B, M, T
Southwestern Adventist University B, T
Southwestern Assemblies of God University B
Stephen F. Austin State University B, M, T
Sul Ross State University B
Tarleton State University B

Texas A&M University
    Commerce B, M
    Corpus Christi B, T
    Kingsville B, M
Texas Christian University B, T
Texas College B
Texas Lutheran University B
Texas Tech University B, D
Texas Wesleyan University B
Texas Woman's University B, M, T
Trinity University B
Trinity Valley Community College A
University of Houston B, M, D
University of North Texas B, M
University of St. Thomas B
University of Texas
    Arlington B
    Austin B, M, D
    El Paso B
    Pan American B, M, T
    San Antonio B, M
    Tyler B
    of the Permian Basin B
University of the Incarnate Word B
Wayland Baptist University B
West Texas A&M University B, M
Western Texas College A
Wharton County Junior College A
Wiley College B

Utah
Brigham Young University M
Dixie State College of Utah A
Snow College A
Southern Utah University B, T
University of Utah B, M, D
Utah State University B
Weber State University B

Vermont
Bennington College B, M
Castleton State College B
Goddard College B
Johnson State College B
Marlboro College B
Middlebury College B
St. Michael's College B
University of Vermont B

Virginia
Averett College B
Bluefield College B
Bridgewater College B
Christopher Newport University B
College of William and Mary B
Eastern Mennonite University B
Emory & Henry College B
Hollins University B
J. Sargeant Reynolds Community College C, A
Liberty University B
Longwood College B, T
Lynchburg College B
Mary Baldwin College B
Northern Virginia Community College A
Radford University B, M
Randolph-Macon College B
Roanoke College B, T
Shenandoah University B
Sweet Briar College B
University of Richmond B, T
University of Virginia B, M
Virginia Polytechnic Institute and State University B, T
Virginia Union University B
Virginia Wesleyan College B
Washington and Lee University B

Washington
Central Washington University B, M
Centralia College A
Eastern Washington University B, M, T
Everett Community College A
Highline Community College A
Lower Columbia College A
North Seattle Community College C, A

Pacific Lutheran University B
University of Puget Sound B
University of Washington B, M, D
Walla Walla College B
Washington State University B
Western Washington University B, M, T
Whitman College B
Whitworth College B, T

West Virginia
Alderson-Broaddus College B
Bethany College B
Concord College B
Marshall University B, M
Potomac State College of West Virginia University A
Shepherd College B
University of Charleston B
West Virginia University B, M, D, T
West Virginia Wesleyan College B

Wisconsin
Alverno College B
Beloit College B
Cardinal Stritch University B
Carroll College B
Carthage College B, T
Lakeland College B
Lawrence University B
Marian College of Fond du Lac B
Mount Mary College B
Mount Senario College B
Northland College B
Ripon College B, T
St. Norbert College B, T
Silver Lake College C, A, B
University of Wisconsin
    Eau Claire B
    Green Bay B
    La Crosse B
    Madison B, M, D
    Milwaukee B, M
    Oshkosh B
    Parkside B, T
    Platteville B
    River Falls B
    Stevens Point B
    Superior B, M
    Whitewater B, T
Viterbo University B
Wisconsin Lutheran College B

Wyoming
Central Wyoming College A
Eastern Wyoming College A
Laramie County Community College A
Northwest College A
Sheridan College A
University of Wyoming B, M
Western Wyoming Community College A

Music business management

California
Diablo Valley College C, A
Fresno City College A
Los Medanos College C
Point Loma Nazarene University B
Sacramento City College C, A
University of Southern California B
University of the Pacific B

Colorado
Western State College of Colorado B

Connecticut
University of Hartford B
University of New Haven B

District of Columbia
Howard University B

Florida
Florida Southern College B

Jacksonville University B
University of Miami B, M

Georgia
Shorter College B

Idaho
Boise State University B

Illinois
Columbia College B
De Paul University B
Elmhurst College B
Millikin University B
Quincy University A, B
Roosevelt University B

Indiana
Anderson University B
Butler University B
DePauw University B
Grace College B
Indiana State University B
Taylor University B
University of Evansville B
Valparaiso University B

Iowa
Drake University B
Luther College B

Kansas
Benedictine College B
Central Christian College A
Tabor College B

Louisiana
Dillard University B

Massachusetts
Berklee College of Music B
Northeastern University B

Michigan
Ferris State University B
Grace Bible College B

Minnesota
Minnesota State University, Mankato B
Moorhead State University B
St. Mary's University of Minnesota B
Winona State University B

Missouri
Fontbonne College B
University of Missouri
    St. Louis B

Nebraska
Northeast Community College A

New Jersey
Monmouth University B

New York
Concordia College B
Five Towns College A, B
Manhattanville College B
New York University B
Schenectady County Community College A
State University of New York
    College at Fredonia B
    College at Oneonta B
    College at Potsdam B
Syracuse University B
Villa Maria College of Buffalo A

North Carolina
Chowan College A
St. Augustine's College B
Wingate University B

Ohio
Baldwin-Wallace College B
Capital University B
Heidelberg College B
Ohio Northern University B
Otterbein College B

Music business management

Oklahoma
Oklahoma City University *B*
Oklahoma State University *B*
Southwestern Oklahoma State University *B*

Oregon
Southern Oregon University *B*

Pennsylvania
Cheyney University of Pennsylvania *B*
Clarion University of Pennsylvania *B*
Geneva College *B*
Grove City College *B*
Harrisburg Area Community College *A*
Mansfield University of Pennsylvania *B*

South Carolina
South Carolina State University *B*

Tennessee
Belmont University *B*
Middle Tennessee State University *B*
Trevecca Nazarene University *B*

Texas
Collin County Community College District *C, A*
Houston Community College System *C, A*
University of Texas
   Arlington *B*
   San Antonio *B*
University of the Incarnate Word *B*

Vermont
Johnson State College *B*

Virginia
Norfolk State University *B*

Washington
Art Institute of Seattle *A*
Central Washington University *B*
Shoreline Community College *A*
University of Puget Sound *B*

West Virginia
Davis and Elkins College *B*
University of Charleston *B*

Music education

Alabama
Alabama Agricultural and Mechanical University *B, M, T*
Alabama State University *B, M*
Auburn University *B, M, D, T*
Birmingham-Southern College *B, T*
Huntingdon College *B, T*
Jacksonville State University *B, M, T*
Oakwood College *B*
Samford University *B, M, T*
Shelton State Community College *A*
Talladega College *B*
University of Alabama Birmingham *B, T*
University of Alabama *B, M, D*
University of Mobile *B, T*
University of Montevallo *B, M, T*
University of South Alabama *B*

Alaska
University of Alaska
   Anchorage *B*
   Fairbanks *B, M*

Arizona
Arizona State University *B, M*
Grand Canyon University *B*
Northern Arizona University *B, T*
Prescott College *B, M*
South Mountain Community College *C, A*
University of Arizona *B, M, D*

Arkansas
Arkansas State University *B, M, T*
Arkansas Tech University *B, M*
Harding University *B, M, T*
John Brown University *B*
Ouachita Baptist University *B, T*
Southern Arkansas University *B, T*
University of Arkansas Monticello *B*
University of Arkansas *M*
University of Central Arkansas *M, T*
University of the Ozarks *B, T*
Westark College *A*
Williams Baptist College *B*

California
Azusa Pacific University *T*
California Baptist University *B, T*
California Lutheran University *B, T*
California State Polytechnic University: Pomona *T*
California State University
   Bakersfield *B, T*
   Chico *T*
   Dominguez Hills *T*
   Fullerton *B, T*
   Hayward *M*
   Long Beach *M, T*
   Northridge *B, T*
   Sacramento *T*
Chapman University *B*
Concordia University *B*
Fresno Pacific University *B, T*
Holy Names College *C, B, M*
Hope International University *B*
Humboldt State University *T*
La Sierra University *M*
Los Angeles Southwest College *A*
Mount St. Mary's College *T*
Occidental College *T*
Pacific Union College *B, T*
Pepperdine University *B*
Saddleback College *A*
San Diego State University *B*
San Francisco State University *B, T*
San Jose State University *T*
Simpson College *B, T*
Sonoma State University *T*
University of La Verne *T*
University of Redlands *B, T*
University of Southern California *B, M, D*
University of the Pacific *B, T*
Vanguard University of Southern California *B*
Westmont College *T*

Colorado
Adams State College *B, T*
Colorado Christian University *B*
Colorado State University *T*
Fort Lewis College *T*
Metropolitan State College of Denver *B, T*
University of Colorado Boulder *B, M, D*
University of Denver *B*
University of Northern Colorado *B, M, T*
University of Southern Colorado *T*
Western State College of Colorado *T*

Connecticut
Central Connecticut State University *B, M*
University of Connecticut *B*
University of Hartford *B, M, D*
Western Connecticut State University *B, M*

Delaware
Delaware State University *B*
University of Delaware *B, T*

District of Columbia
Catholic University of America *B, M*
George Washington University *M, T*
Howard University *B, M*

Florida
Bethune-Cookman College *B, T*
Broward Community College *A*
Florida Agricultural and Mechanical University *B, T*
Florida Atlantic University *B*
Florida Baptist Theological College *B*
Florida International University *B, M, T*
Florida Southern College *B*
Florida State University *B, M, D, T*
Hobe Sound Bible College *B, T*
Jacksonville University *B, M, T*
Manatee Community College *A*
Palm Beach Atlantic College *B*
Palm Beach Community College *A*
Pensacola Junior College *A*
Southeastern College of the Assemblies of God *B, T*
Stetson University *B, T*
University of Central Florida *B, M*
University of Florida *B, M, D*
University of Miami *B, M, D, T*
University of North Florida *B, M*
University of South Florida *B, M*
University of Tampa *B, T*
University of West Florida *B, T*
Warner Southern College *B*

Georgia
Agnes Scott College *T*
Albany State University *M*
Armstrong Atlantic State University *B, M, T*
Augusta State University *B, M*
Berry College *B, T*
Brenau University *B*
Brewton-Parker College *B*
Columbus State University *B, M*
Fort Valley State University *B, T*
Gainesville College *A*
Georgia College and State University *B*
Georgia Southern University *B, M, T*
Georgia Southwestern State University *B*
Kennesaw State University *B*
Mercer University *B, T*
North Georgia College & State University *B, M*
Paine College *B*
Piedmont College *B, T*
Reinhardt College *B*
Shorter College *B, M, T*
State University of West Georgia *B, M*
Thomas College *B*
Toccoa Falls College *B, T*
University of Georgia *B, M, D, T*
Valdosta State University *B, M*
Young Harris College *A*

Hawaii
Brigham Young University Hawaii *B*
University of Hawaii Manoa *B, T*

Idaho
Boise State University *B, T*
College of Southern Idaho *A*
Idaho State University *B, T*
Northwest Nazarene University *B*
Ricks College *A*
University of Idaho *B*

Illinois
Augustana College *B, T*
Benedictine University *B, T*
Blackburn College *B, T*
Bradley University *B, T*
Chicago State University *B*
College of Lake County *A*
Concordia University *B, M, T*
De Paul University *B, M, T*
Elmhurst College *B*
Eureka College *T*
Greenville College *B, T*
Illinois College *T*
Illinois State University *B, M, T*
Illinois Wesleyan University *B*
Judson College *B, T*
Loyola University of Chicago *T*
MacMurray College *B, T*
Millikin University *B, T*
North Central College *B, T*
North Park University *T*
Northern Illinois University *B, M, T*
Northwestern University *B, M, D, T*
Olivet Nazarene University *B, T*
Quincy University *A, B, T*
Roosevelt University *B, M*
St. Xavier University *B*
Trinity Christian College *B, T*
Trinity International University *B, T*
University of Illinois Urbana-Champaign *B, M, D, T*
VanderCook College of Music *B, M, T*
Wheaton College *B, T*

Indiana
Anderson University *B, T*
Ball State University *T*
Bethel College *B*
Butler University *B, M, T*
DePauw University *B*
Goshen College *B*
Grace College *B*
Indiana State University *B, M, T*
Indiana University
   Bloomington *B, M, D, T*
   South Bend *B, M, T*
Indiana University--Purdue University
   Indiana University-Purdue University Fort Wayne *B, T*
Indiana Wesleyan University *B, T*
Manchester College *B, T*
Oakland City University *B*
St. Mary-of-the-Woods College *B*
Taylor University *B*
University of Evansville *T*
University of Indianapolis *B, T*
Valparaiso University *B, M, T*
Vincennes University *A*

Iowa
Briar Cliff College *B*
Central College *B, T*
Clarke College *B, T*
Cornell College *B, T*
Dordt College *B*
Drake University *M*
Graceland University *T*
Iowa State University *B, T*
Iowa Wesleyan College *B*
Loras College *T*
Luther College *B*
Morningside College *B*
Mount Mercy College *T*
Northwestern College *T*
St. Ambrose University *B, T*
Simpson College *T*
University of Iowa *B, M, D, T*
University of Northern Iowa *B, M*
Wartburg College *B, T*

Kansas
Allen County Community College *A*
Baker University *B, T*
Benedictine College *B, T*
Bethany College *B*
Bethel College *T*
Central Christian College *A*
Colby Community College *A*
Emporia State University *B*
Fort Hays State University *B*
Garden City Community College *A*
Independence Community College *A*
Kansas State University *B, M, T*
McPherson College *B, T*
MidAmerica Nazarene University *B, T*
Ottawa University *B, T*
Pittsburg State University *B*
Southwestern College *B, T*
Sterling College *B*
Tabor College *B, T*

University of Kansas *B, M, D, T*
Washburn University of Topeka *B*
Wichita State University *B, M*

Kentucky
Asbury College *B, T*
Berea College *B, T*
Campbellsville University *B, M*
Cumberland College *B, T*
Eastern Kentucky University *B*
Georgetown College *B*
Kentucky Christian College *B*
Kentucky State University *B*
Morehead State University *B, M*
Murray State University *B, M, T*
Northern Kentucky University *B*
Transylvania University *B, T*
Union College *B, M*
University of Kentucky *B, M*
University of Louisville *M*
Western Kentucky University *B, M*

Louisiana
Centenary College of Louisiana *B, T*
Dillard University *B*
Louisiana State University and Agricultural and Mechanical College *B*
Louisiana Tech University *B*
Loyola University New Orleans *B, M*
McNeese State University *B, M, T*
Nicholls State University *B*
Northwestern State University *B*
Southeastern Louisiana University *B*
Southern University and Agricultural and Mechanical College *B*
University of Louisiana at Lafayette *B*
University of Louisiana at Monroe *B*
University of New Orleans *B*
Xavier University of Louisiana *B*

Maine
University of Maine *B*
University of Southern Maine *B, T*

Maryland
College of Notre Dame of Maryland *T*
Columbia Union College *B*
Community College of Baltimore County Essex *A*
Frederick Community College *A*
Frostburg State University *B, T*
Johns Hopkins University: Peabody Conservatory of Music *B, M*
Montgomery College
 Germantown Campus *A*
 Rockville Campus *A*
St. Mary's College of Maryland *T*
Salisbury State University *B*
Towson University *B, M*
University of Maryland
 College Park *B*
 Eastern Shore *B*
Washington Bible College *B, T*

Massachusetts
Anna Maria College *B, T*
Berklee College of Music *B*
Boston Conservatory *B, M*
Boston University *B, M, D*
Bridgewater State College *T*
Eastern Nazarene College *B, M, T*
Gordon College *B*
New England Conservatory of Music *M*
Northeastern University *B*
Smith College *M*
Tufts University *M*
University of Massachusetts
 Lowell *M*
Westfield State College *B, M, T*

Michigan
Adrian College *B, T*
Albion College *B, T*
Alma College *T*
Andrews University *M, T*
Aquinas College *B, T*
Calvin College *B*
Central Michigan University *B, M*
Concordia College *B, T*
Cornerstone College and Grand Rapids Baptist Seminary *B, T*
Eastern Michigan University *B, T*
Grand Valley State University *B, T*
Hope College *B*
Lansing Community College *A*
Michigan State University *B, M, D*
Northern Michigan University *B, T*
Oakland University *B, T*
Schoolcraft College *C*
University of Michigan
 Flint *B, T*
University of Michigan *B, M, D, T*
Western Michigan University *B, M*

Minnesota
Augsburg College *B, T*
Bemidji State University *T*
Bethel College *B*
College of St. Benedict *T*
College of St. Catherine: St. Paul Campus *B, T*
College of St. Scholastica *T*
Concordia College: Moorhead *T*
Concordia University: St. Paul *B, T*
Crown College *B, T*
Gustavus Adolphus College *T*
Hamline University *B*
Minnesota State University, Mankato *B, M, T*
Moorhead State University *B, M, T*
Northwestern College *B*
Ridgewater College: A Community and Technical College *A*
St. Cloud State University *M, T*
St. John's University *T*
St. Mary's University of Minnesota *B*
St. Olaf College *T*
Southwest State University *B*
University of Minnesota
 Duluth *B*
 Morris *T*
 Twin Cities *B, M*
University of St. Thomas *B, M, T*
Winona State University *B, T*

Mississippi
Alcorn State University *B*
Blue Mountain College *B*
Coahoma Community College *A*
Delta State University *B, M*
Jackson State University *M*
Mississippi College *B, M*
Mississippi Gulf Coast Community College
 Jefferson Davis Campus *A*
Mississippi State University *B, T*
Mississippi University for Women *B, T*
Mississippi Valley State University *B, T*
Northwest Mississippi Community College *A*
Rust College *B*
University of Mississippi *B, T*
University of Southern Mississippi *B, M, D*
William Carey College *B*

Missouri
Avila College *T*
Central Methodist College *B*
Central Missouri State University *B, M, T*
College of the Ozarks *B, T*
Culver-Stockton College *B, T*
Drury University *B, T*
Evangel University *B*
Hannibal-LaGrange College *B*
Lincoln University *B, T*
Lindenwood University *B, M*
Missouri Baptist College *B, T*
Missouri Southern State College *B, T*
Missouri Western State College *B*
Northwest Missouri State University *B, M, T*
St. Louis Christian College *B*
Southeast Missouri State University *B, M*
Southwest Baptist University *B, T*
Southwest Missouri State University *B*
Truman State University *M, T*
University of Missouri
 Columbia *B, M, D*
 Kansas City *B, M*
 St. Louis *B, T*
Washington University *M*
Webster University *B, M*
William Jewell College *B, T*

Montana
Montana State University
 Billings *B, T*
 Bozeman *B, T*
Rocky Mountain College *B, T*
University of Montana-Missoula *T*
Western Montana College of The University of Montana *B, T*

Nebraska
Concordia University *T*
Dana College *B*
Doane College *T*
Grace University *B*
Hastings College *B, M, T*
Mid Plains Community College Area *A*
Midland Lutheran College *B, T*
Nebraska Wesleyan University *B*
Northeast Community College *A*
Peru State College *B, T*
Union College *T*
University of Nebraska
 Kearney *B, M, T*
 Lincoln *B, T*
 Omaha *B, T*

Nevada
University of Nevada
 Reno *B*

New Hampshire
Keene State College *B, T*
Plymouth State College of the University System of New Hampshire *B, T*
University of New Hampshire *B, M, T*

New Jersey
Caldwell College *T*
Essex County College *A*
Kean University *B*
Monmouth University *B, T*
New Jersey City University *M, D, T*
Rider University *B, M*
Rowan University *B*
The College of New Jersey *B, M, T*

New Mexico
Eastern New Mexico University *B*
New Mexico State University *B*
University of New Mexico *B, M*
Western New Mexico University *B*

New York
Adelphi University *B*
City University of New York
 Brooklyn College *B, M*
 City College *B, T*
 Hunter College *B, M*
 Lehman College *M*
 Queens College *M, T*
 York College *T*
College of St. Rose *M, T*
Columbia University
 Teachers College *M, D*
Concordia College *B, T*
Dowling College *B*
Eastman School of Music of the University of Rochester *B, M, D, T*
Five Towns College *B, M*
Fordham University *T*
Hartwick College *B, T*
Hofstra University *B, T*
Houghton College *B, T*
Ithaca College *B, M, T*
Long Island University
 C. W. Post Campus *B, M, T*
Manhattanville College *M, T*
Monroe Community College *A*
Nazareth College of Rochester *M, T*
New York University *B, M, D, T*
Nyack College *B*
Roberts Wesleyan College *B, T*
State University of New York
 Buffalo *M, T*
 College at Fredonia *B, M, T*
 College at Potsdam *B, M, T*
Syracuse University *B, M, T*
University of Rochester *M, D*
Wagner College *T*
Wells College *T*

North Carolina
Appalachian State University *B, M, T*
Bennett College *B, T*
Brevard College *B*
Campbell University *B, T*
Catawba College *B, T*
Chowan College *B*
East Carolina University *B, M*
Elizabeth City State University *B*
Elon College *B, T*
Fayetteville State University *B, T*
Gardner-Webb University *B*
Greensboro College *B, T*
Lenoir-Rhyne College *B, T*
Mars Hill College *B*
Meredith College *B, T*
Methodist College *A, B, T*
North Carolina Agricultural and Technical State University *B, T*
North Carolina Central University *B*
Pfeiffer University *B, T*
St. Augustine's College *B, T*
University of North Carolina
 Chapel Hill *M, T*
 Charlotte *B, M*
 Greensboro *B, M, D, T*
 Pembroke *B, T*
 Wilmington *B*
Western Carolina University *B, T*
Wingate University *B, T*
Winston-Salem State University *B*

North Dakota
Dickinson State University *B, T*
Jamestown College *B*
Minot State University *B, M*
North Dakota State University *B, M, T*
University of Mary *B*
University of North Dakota *B, T*
Valley City State University *B, T*

Ohio
Ashland University *B, T*
Baldwin-Wallace College *B, T*
Bluffton College *B*
Bowling Green State University *B, M*
Capital University *B*
Case Western Reserve University *B, M, D*
Cedarville College *B, T*
Central State University *B*
College of Mount St. Joseph *T*
College of Wooster *B*
Heidelberg College *B*
Hiram College *T*
Kent State University
 Stark Campus *B*
Kent State University *B, M, D, T*
Lorain County Community College *A*
Malone College *B*
Miami University
 Oxford Campus *B, M, T*
Mount Union College *B, T*
Mount Vernon Nazarene College *B, T*
Oberlin College *B, M*
Ohio Northern University *B*

Ohio State University
    Columbus Campus *B*
Ohio University *B, T*
Ohio Wesleyan University *B*
Otterbein College *B*
University of Akron *B, M*
University of Cincinnati *B, M, D, T*
University of Dayton *B, M, T*
University of Rio Grande *B, T*
University of Toledo *B, M, T*
Wilberforce University
Wilmington College *B*
Wittenberg University *B*
Wright State University *B, M, T*
Xavier University *B, M, T*
Youngstown State University *B, M, T*

Oklahoma
Cameron University *B, T*
East Central University *B*
Eastern Oklahoma State College *A*
Langston University *B*
Mid-America Bible College *B*
Northeastern Oklahoma Agricultural and
    Mechanical College *A*
Northeastern State University *B*
Northwestern Oklahoma State
    University *B, T*
Oklahoma Baptist University *B, T*
Oklahoma Christian University of
    Science and Arts *B, T*
Oklahoma City University *B*
Oklahoma State University *B*
Oral Roberts University *B, T*
Southeastern Oklahoma State
    University *B, M, T*
Southern Nazarene University *B*
Southwestern Oklahoma State
    University *B, M, T*
University of Central Oklahoma *B, M*
University of Oklahoma *B, M, D, T*
University of Tulsa *B, M, T*

Oregon
George Fox University *B, M, T*
Linfield College *B, T*
Portland State University *T*
Southern Oregon University *T*
University of Oregon *B, M, D, T*
University of Portland *B, M, T*
Western Baptist College *B*

Pennsylvania
Bucknell University *B, T*
Carnegie Mellon University *B, T*
Chestnut Hill College *B, T*
Clarion University of Pennsylvania *B, T*
Duquesne University *B, M, T*
Edinboro University of
    Pennsylvania *M, T*
Elizabethtown College *T*
Geneva College *B, T*
Gettysburg College *B, T*
Grove City College *B, T*
Immaculata College *T*
Indiana University of
    Pennsylvania *B, M, T*
Lebanon Valley College of
    Pennsylvania *T*
Lincoln University *B, T*
Lycoming College *T*
Mansfield University of
    Pennsylvania *B, M, T*
Marywood University *B, M, T*
Mercyhurst College *B*
Messiah College *B, T*
Millersville University of
    Pennsylvania *B, T*
Moravian College *T*
Penn State
    University Park *B, M, D*
Philadelphia College of Bible *B, T*
St. Vincent College *T*
Seton Hill College *B, T*
Slippery Rock University of
    Pennsylvania *B*
Susquehanna University *B, T*
Temple University *B, M, D, T*
University of the Arts *M*
West Chester University of
    Pennsylvania *B, M, T*
Westminster College *T*
York College of Pennsylvania *B, T*

Puerto Rico
Inter American University of Puerto Rico
    San German Campus *B*
Pontifical Catholic University of Puerto
    Rico *B, T*

Rhode Island
Providence College *B*
Rhode Island College *B, M*
Salve Regina University *B*
University of Rhode Island *B*

South Carolina
Anderson College *B, T*
Charleston Southern University *B*
Claflin University *B*
Coker College *B, T*
Columbia College *B*
Converse College *T*
Furman University *B, T*
Lander University *B, T*
Limestone College *B*
Newberry College *B, T*
North Greenville College *B, T*
Presbyterian College *B, T*
South Carolina State University *B, T*
University of South Carolina *B, M, D*
Winthrop University *B, M, T*

South Dakota
Augustana College *B, T*
Black Hills State University *B, T*
Dakota State University *B, T*
Dakota Wesleyan University *B*
Mount Marty College *B*
Northern State University *B, T*
South Dakota State University *B*
University of South Dakota *B, M, T*

Tennessee
Belmont University *M*
Carson-Newman College *B*
Cumberland University *B*
David Lipscomb University *B, T*
East Tennessee State University *B, T*
Freed-Hardeman University *T*
Hiwassee College *A*
Lambuth University *B, T*
Lee University *B*
Maryville College *B, T*
Milligan College *B*
Roane State Community College *A*
Southern Adventist University *B*
Tennessee Technological University *B, T*
Tennessee Wesleyan College *B, T*
Trevecca Nazarene University *B, T*
Union University *B, T*
University of Tennessee
    Chattanooga *B*
    Knoxville *B, T*
    Martin *B, T*

Texas
Abilene Christian University *B, T*
Amarillo College *A*
Arlington Baptist College *B*
Baylor University *B, M, T*
Dallas Baptist University *B*
Del Mar College *A*
East Texas Baptist University *B*
Hardin-Simmons University *B, M, T*
Houston Baptist University *B*
Howard Payne University *T*
Lamar University *M, T*
Lubbock Christian University *B*
McMurry University *T*
Prairie View A&M University *M*
Sam Houston State University *M, T*
Southern Methodist University *B, M, T*
Southwest Texas State
    University *B, M, T*
Southwestern University *B, T*
Stephen F. Austin State University *M*
Tarleton State University *B, T*
Texas A&M University
    Commerce *M, T*
    Kingsville *B, M, T*
Texas Christian University *B, M, T*
Texas Lutheran University *T*
Texas Tech University *M*
Texas Wesleyan University *B, T*
Texas Woman's University *B, M*
University of Houston *M, D, T*
University of Mary Hardin-Baylor *B, T*
University of North Texas *M, D*
University of Texas
    Arlington *T*
    Austin *M, D*
    El Paso *M*
    Pan American *T*
    San Antonio *M, T*
University of the Incarnate Word *B*
Wayland Baptist University *B, T*
West Texas A&M University *T*

Utah
Brigham Young University *B, M*
Southern Utah University *B*
Utah State University *B*
Weber State University *B*

Vermont
Castleton State College *B, T*
Johnson State College *B*
St. Michael's College *B, M*
University of Vermont *B, T*

Virginia
Bluefield College *B*
Bridgewater College *T*
Christopher Newport University *T*
Eastern Mennonite University *T*
Hampton University *B*
Hollins University *T*
Liberty University *B*
Longwood College *B, T*
Norfolk State University *B*
Old Dominion University *B*
Radford University *T*
Shenandoah University *B, M, D*
Virginia Wesleyan College *T*

Washington
Central Washington University *B, T*
Eastern Washington University *B, M, T*
Gonzaga University *B, T*
North Seattle Community College *C, A*
Pacific Lutheran University *T*
Seattle Pacific University *B, T*
University of Puget Sound *B*
University of Washington *B*
Walla Walla College *B*
Western Washington University *T*
Whitworth College *B, M, T*

West Virginia
Alderson-Broaddus College *B, T*
Concord College *B, T*
Fairmont State College *B*
Glenville State College *B*
Potomac State College of West Virginia
    University *A*
Shepherd College *T*
University of Charleston *B*
West Liberty State College *B*
West Virginia State College *B*
West Virginia Wesleyan College *B*

Wisconsin
Alverno College *B, T*
Cardinal Stritch University *B*
Carroll College *B, T*
Carthage College *B, T*
Concordia University Wisconsin *B, T*
Lakeland College *T*
Lawrence University *B, T*
Marian College of Fond du Lac *B, T*
Mount Mary College *B, T*
Mount Senario College *B*
Northland College *T*
St. Norbert College *B, T*
Silver Lake College *B, M, T*
University of Wisconsin
    Green Bay *T*
    La Crosse *B, T*
    Madison *B, M, T*
    Milwaukee *B, T*
    Oshkosh *B, T*
    Parkside *T*
    River Falls *B, T*
    Stevens Point *B, M*
    Superior *B, T*
    Whitewater *B*
Viterbo University *B, T*

Wyoming
Casper College *A*
Eastern Wyoming College *A*
University of Wyoming *B*
Western Wyoming Community
    College *A*

Music history/literature

Alabama
Birmingham-Southern College *B*
University of Alabama *M*

Arizona
Arizona State University *M*

Arkansas
Ouachita Baptist University *B*

California
California State University
    Fullerton *M*
    Hayward *M*
    Long Beach *M*
    Northridge *B, M*
Mills College *M*
Pepperdine University *B*
San Francisco State University *M*
University of California
    Santa Barbara *D*
University of Redlands *B*
University of Southern California *M, D*
University of the Pacific *B*
Whittier College *B*

Colorado
University of Colorado
    Boulder *M*
University of Denver *M*

Connecticut
Connecticut College *B*
University of Hartford *B, M*
Yale University *M, D*

District of Columbia
Catholic University of America *B, M, D*
Howard University *B*

Florida
Broward Community College *A*
Florida State University *B*

Idaho
University of Idaho *B*

Illinois
Illinois State University *B, M, T*
North Park University *B*
Rockford College *B*
Roosevelt University *B*
University of Illinois
    Urbana-Champaign *B*
Wheaton College *B*

Indiana
Ball State University *M, D*
Butler University *B*
Indiana State University *M*

St. Joseph's College *B*

Iowa
Luther College *B*
Maharishi University of Management *C, B*
University of Iowa *B, M, D*
University of Northern Iowa *M*

Kansas
University of Kansas *B, M, D*

Kentucky
University of Kentucky *B, M, D, T*
University of Louisville *B, M, D*

Maryland
Johns Hopkins University: Peabody Conservatory of Music *M*
Johns Hopkins University *B, M, D*
Western Maryland College *B*

Massachusetts
Assumption College *B*
Berkshire Community College *A*
Boston University *B, M, D*
Hampshire College *B*
Harvard College *B*
Harvard University *D*
Mount Holyoke College *B*
New England Conservatory of Music *B, M*
Northeastern University *B*
Simmons College *B*
Simon's Rock College of Bard *B*
Tufts University *B, M*
Wellesley College *B*

Michigan
Calvin College *B*
Central Michigan University *B*
Michigan State University *M, D*
Northern Michigan University *B, T*
University of Michigan *M, D*
Wayne State University *C*
Western Michigan University *B*

Minnesota
St. Olaf College *B*

Missouri
University of Missouri Kansas City *M*
Washington University *B, M, D*

Montana
University of Montana-Missoula *B*

New Hampshire
Keene State College *B*
University of New Hampshire *B*

New Jersey
Princeton University *M, D*
Seton Hall University *B*

New York
City University of New York Hunter College *B, M*
Queensborough Community College *A*
Columbia University Teachers College *M, D*
Eastman School of Music of the University of Rochester *M, D*
Five Towns College *A, B*
Manhattanville College *B*
Nazareth College of Rochester *B*
Sarah Lawrence College *B*
State University of New York
  Buffalo *M, D*
  College at Fredonia *B*
  College at Potsdam *B, M*
  New Paltz *B*
  Stony Brook *B, M, D*
Syracuse University *M*
University of Rochester *M, D*

North Carolina
Brevard College *B*
Catawba College *B*
University of North Carolina
  Chapel Hill *M, D*
  Greensboro *B, T*

Ohio
Baldwin-Wallace College *B*
Bowling Green State University *B, M*
Case Western Reserve University *M*
Cedarville College *B*
Kent State University *M, D*
Oberlin College *B, M*
Ohio State University Columbus Campus *B*
Ohio University *B, M*
Otterbein College *B*
University of Akron *B, M*
University of Cincinnati *B, M*
Youngstown State University *B, M*

Oklahoma
Connors State College *A*
University of Oklahoma *M*

Oregon
University of Oregon *M, D*

Pennsylvania
Bucknell University *B*
La Salle University *B*
Lafayette College *B*
Penn State University Park *M*
Temple University *B, M*
West Chester University of Pennsylvania *B, M*

South Carolina
Furman University *B*
North Greenville College *A, B*
University of South Carolina *M*

South Dakota
University of South Dakota *M*

Tennessee
Fisk University *B*
Union University *B*

Texas
Baylor University *B, M*
Lon Morris College *A*
McMurry University *T*
Rice University *B, M*
Sam Houston State University *B*
Southern Methodist University *M*
Southwestern University *B*
Texas A&M University Commerce *B*
Texas Christian University *B*
Texas Lutheran University *B*
Texas Tech University *M*
University of Houston *M*
University of North Texas *B*
University of Texas Austin *B*

Vermont
Bennington College *M*
Johnson State College *B*
Marlboro College *B*

Virginia
Christopher Newport University *B*
Mary Baldwin College *B*
Mary Washington College *B*
Randolph-Macon Woman's College *B*
University of Richmond *B*

Washington
University of Washington *B*
Western Washington University *B*

West Virginia
Marshall University *B*

Wisconsin
Lawrence University *B*
University of Wisconsin
  La Crosse *B*
  Madison *B, M, D*
  Stevens Point *B*

Music performance

Alabama
Alabama Agricultural and Mechanical University *B, M*
Alabama State University *B, M*
Huntingdon College *B*
Samford University *B*
Talladega College *B*
University of Alabama *B, M*
University of Montevallo *B, M*
University of South Alabama *B*

Alaska
University of Alaska
  Anchorage *B*
  Fairbanks *B, M*

Arizona
Arizona State University *B, M*
Grand Canyon University *B*
Northern Arizona University *B*
University of Arizona *B, M*

Arkansas
Arkansas State University *B, M*
Henderson State University *B*
Ouachita Baptist University *B*
University of Arkansas *B, M*
University of Central Arkansas *B*

California
Azusa Pacific University *B*
California Institute of the Arts *C, B, M*
California State University
  Chico *B*
  Dominguez Hills *B*
  Fullerton *B, M*
  Hayward *M*
  Long Beach *B, M*
  Los Angeles *B*
  Northridge *B, M*
  Sacramento *B, M*
  Stanislaus *B*
Chabot College *A*
Chapman University *B*
College of Notre Dame *B, M*
Cypress College *C, A*
Dominican University of California *B*
Fresno Pacific University *B*
Gavilan Community College *A*
Golden West College *C, A*
Holy Names College *B, M*
Los Angeles Valley College *C*
Master's College *B*
Mills College *M*
Mount St. Mary's College *B*
Pacific Union College *B*
San Diego State University *B*
San Francisco Conservatory of Music *B, M*
San Francisco State University *B, M*
San Jose State University *B, M*
Sierra College *A*
Simpson College *B*
University of California
  Irvine *B*
  Los Angeles *M*
University of Redlands *B*
University of Southern California *B, M, D*
University of the Pacific *B*

Colorado
Adams State College *B*
Colorado Christian University *B*
Colorado State University *B*
Fort Lewis College *B*
Metropolitan State College of Denver *B*
University of Colorado
  Boulder *B, M, D*
University of Denver *B, M*

Connecticut
University of Connecticut *D*
University of Hartford *B, M, D*
Yale University *M, D*

Delaware
University of Delaware *B, M*

District of Columbia
Catholic University of America *B, M, D*
George Washington University *M*

Florida
Florida Agricultural and Mechanical University *B*
Florida State University *C, B, M, D*
Jacksonville University *B*
Stetson University *B*
University of Central Florida *B*
University of Miami *B, M, D*
University of North Florida *B*
University of South Florida *B, M*
University of Tampa *B*

Georgia
Augusta State University *B*
Berry College *B*
Brenau University *B*
Clayton College and State University *A, B*
Columbus State University *B, M*
Emmanuel College *B*
Gainesville College *A*
Georgia College and State University *B*
Georgia Southern University *B*
Georgia State University *B, M*
Kennesaw State University *B*
Mercer University *B*
Morris Brown College *B*
Piedmont College *B*
Savannah State University *B*
State University of West Georgia *B, M*
Toccoa Falls College *B*
University of Georgia *B*
Valdosta State University *B*

Hawaii
Brigham Young University Hawaii *B*
University of Hawaii Manoa *B, M*

Idaho
Boise State University *B, M*
Idaho State University *B*
North Idaho College *A*
Northwest Nazarene University *B*
University of Idaho *B*

Illinois
Augustana College *B*
Benedictine University *B*
Bradley University *B*
Columbia College *B*
Concordia University *B*
De Paul University *B, M*
Elmhurst College *C*
Eureka College *B*
Illinois State University *B*
Illinois Wesleyan University *B*
Judson College *B*
Millikin University *B*
Moody Bible Institute *B*
North Central College *B*
North Park University *B*
Northern Illinois University *M*
Northwestern University *B*
Olivet Nazarene University *B*
Parkland College *A*
Roosevelt University *B, M*
Trinity Christian College *B*
Trinity International University *B*
University of Illinois Urbana-Champaign *B*
Wheaton College *B*

Music performance

Indiana
Anderson University B
Butler University B, M
DePauw University B
Goshen College B
Grace College B
Indiana State University B, M
Indiana University
    Bloomington B, M, D
    South Bend B, M
Indiana University--Purdue University
    Indiana University-Purdue
      University Fort Wayne B
Indiana Wesleyan University B, T
Manchester College B
Oakland City University B
Saint Mary's College B
St. Mary-of-the-Woods College B
Taylor University B
University of Evansville B
Valparaiso University B, M
Vincennes University A

Iowa
Coe College B
Cornell College B
Luther College B
Morningside College B
Simpson College B
Southwestern Community College A
University of Iowa B, M, D
University of Northern Iowa B, M
Wartburg College B

Kansas
Baker University B
Bethany College B
Central Christian College A
Kansas Wesleyan University B
McPherson College B
MidAmerica Nazarene University B
Pittsburg State University B
Seward County Community College A
Tabor College B
University of Kansas B, M, D

Kentucky
Berea College B, T
Campbellsville University B
Kentucky Christian College B, T
Morehead State University M
Murray State University B
Transylvania University B, T
Union College B
University of Kentucky B, M, T
University of Louisville B, M

Louisiana
Centenary College of Louisiana B, T
Dillard University B
Louisiana State University and
    Agricultural and Mechanical
    College B, M, D
Louisiana Tech University B
Loyola University New Orleans B, M
McNeese State University B
Northwestern State University B
Southeastern Louisiana University B, M
Southern University and Agricultural and
    Mechanical College B
University of Louisiana at
    Lafayette B, M
University of Louisiana at Monroe B
University of New Orleans M
Xavier University of Louisiana B

Maine
University of Maine B, M
University of Southern Maine B

Maryland
College of Notre Dame of Maryland B
Johns Hopkins University: Peabody
    Conservatory of Music B, M, D
Johns Hopkins University B, M, D
University of Maryland
    College Park B

Washington Bible College A, B

Massachusetts
Anna Maria College B
Berklee College of Music B
Berkshire Community College A
Boston Conservatory B, M
Boston University B, M, D
Eastern Nazarene College B
Gordon College B
Greenfield Community College C
Hampshire College B
New England Conservatory of
    Music B, M, D
Northeastern University B
Simmons College B
Simon's Rock College of Bard B
University of Massachusetts
    Amherst B, M, D
    Lowell B, M
Westfield State College B

Michigan
Albion College B
Andrews University B, M
Aquinas College A
Calvin College B
Central Michigan University M
Cornerstone College and Grand Rapids
    Baptist Seminary B, T
Eastern Michigan University B, M
Hope College B
Lansing Community College A
Macomb Community College C
Marygrove College B
Michigan State University B, M, D
Oakland University B, M
University of Michigan
    Flint B
University of Michigan B, M, D, T
Western Michigan University B
William Tyndale College B

Minnesota
Augsburg College B
Bethel College B
College of St. Catherine: St. Paul
    Campus B
Concordia College: Moorhead B
Gustavus Adolphus College B
Hamline University B
Minnesota State University, Mankato B
Moorhead State University B
North Central University B
Northwestern College B
St. Mary's University of Minnesota B
St. Olaf College B
University of Minnesota
    Duluth B, M
    Twin Cities B, M, D
University of St. Thomas B
Winona State University B

Mississippi
Alcorn State University B
Belhaven College B
Jackson State University B
Millsaps College B, T
Mississippi College B, M
University of Southern Mississippi D
William Carey College B

Missouri
Central Methodist College B
Drury University B
Evangel University B
Hannibal-LaGrange College B
Missouri Baptist College B
Southeast Missouri State University B
Southwest Missouri State University B
Truman State University B
University of Missouri
    Kansas City B, M, D
    St. Louis B
Webster University M
William Jewell College B

Montana
Rocky Mountain College B
University of Montana-Missoula B

Nebraska
Hastings College B, T
Northeast Community College A
Union College B
University of Nebraska
    Kearney B
    Omaha B

Nevada
University of Nevada
    Reno B

New Hampshire
Franklin Pierce College B
Keene State College B
University of New Hampshire B

New Jersey
Caldwell College B
Middlesex County College A
Montclair State University B
Rowan University B
Rutgers
    The State University of New Jersey:
      Mason Gross School of the
      Arts B, M, D
    The State University of New Jersey:
      New Brunswick Graduate
      Campus M, D
Seton Hall University B
William Paterson University of New
    Jersey B

New Mexico
University of New Mexico B, M

New York
Bard College B, M
City University of New York
    Brooklyn College B, M
    City College M
    Graduate School and University
      Center D
    Hunter College B, M
    Lehman College B
    Queens College B, M
Columbia University
    School of General Studies B
    Teachers College M, D
Concordia College B
Dutchess Community College C
Eastman School of Music of the
    University of Rochester B, M, D
Five Towns College A, B, M
Houghton College B
Ithaca College B, M, T
Jamestown Community College A
Jewish Theological Seminary of
    America B
Juilliard School B, M, D
Manhattan School of Music B, M, D
Manhattanville College B
Mannes College of Music B, M
Monroe Community College A
Nassau Community College A
Nazareth College of Rochester B
New York University B, M, D
Nyack College B
Sarah Lawrence College B
Schenectady County Community
    College A
State University of New York
    Albany B
    Binghamton B, M
    Buffalo B, M
    College at Fredonia B
    College at Geneseo B
    College at Potsdam B, M
    New Paltz B
    Stony Brook M, D
Syracuse University B, M
University of Rochester M, D
Villa Maria College of Buffalo A

Wagner College B
Westchester Community College A

North Carolina
Appalachian State University B, M
Brevard College A, B
Duke University M
East Carolina University B, M
Elon College B
Gardner-Webb University B
Greensboro College B, T
Lenoir-Rhyne College B
Mars Hill College B
Methodist College B
North Carolina School of the Arts B, M
Peace College B
Queens College B
St. Augustine's College B
Salem College B
University of North Carolina
    Chapel Hill B
    Charlotte B, T
    Greensboro B, M
    Pembroke B
    Wilmington B
Wingate University B

North Dakota
Minot State University B, T
University of North Dakota B

Ohio
Ashland University B
Bowling Green State University B, M
Capital University B
Cedarville College B
Central State University B
Cleveland Institute of Music B, M, D
College of Wooster B
Heidelberg College B
Kent State University
    Stark Campus B
Kent State University B, M
Miami University
    Oxford Campus B, M
Mount Union College B
Mount Vernon Nazarene College B
Ohio Northern University B
Ohio State University
    Columbus Campus B
Ohio University B, M
Ohio Wesleyan University B
Otterbein College B
University of Akron B, M
University of Cincinnati B, M, D
University of Dayton B
University of Toledo M
Wittenberg University B
Wright State University B
Youngstown State University B, M

Oklahoma
Langston University B
Mid-America Bible College B
Northwestern Oklahoma State
    University B
Oklahoma Baptist University B
Oklahoma Christian University of
    Science and Arts B
Oklahoma City University B, M
Oklahoma State University B
Oral Roberts University B
Southwestern Oklahoma State
    University B
University of Central Oklahoma B
University of Oklahoma M, D
University of Tulsa B

Oregon
Lewis & Clark College B
Linfield College B
Pacific University B
Portland Community College C, A
Portland State University B, M
University of Oregon B, M, D
Western Baptist College B
Willamette University B

Music theory/composition

Pennsylvania
Bucknell University B
Carnegie Mellon University B, M
Community College of Philadelphia A
Curtis Institute of Music C, B
Duquesne University B, M
Gettysburg College B
Grove City College B
Indiana University of Pennsylvania B
Lebanon Valley College of
    Pennsylvania B
Lock Haven University of
    Pennsylvania B
Mansfield University of Pennsylvania B
Marywood University B
Mercyhurst College B
Moravian College B
Penn State
    University Park B, M
Philadelphia College of Bible B
St. Vincent College B
Seton Hill College B
Slippery Rock University of
    Pennsylvania B
Susquehanna University B
Temple University C, B, M, D
University of the Arts C, B, M
Valley Forge Christian College B
West Chester University of
    Pennsylvania B, M
Westminster College B
Wilkes University B
York College of Pennsylvania B

Rhode Island
Rhode Island College B
University of Rhode Island B

South Carolina
Anderson College B
Charleston Southern University B
Columbia International University B
Erskine College B
Furman University B
North Greenville College A, B
Southern Wesleyan University B, T
University of South Carolina M, D

South Dakota
Black Hills State University B, T
University of South Dakota B, M

Tennessee
Belmont University B
Carson-Newman College B
Hiwassee College A
Lambuth University B
Lee University B
Maryville College B
Roane State Community College A
Southern Adventist University B
Tennessee Technological University B
Tennessee Temple University B
Union University B
Vanderbilt University B

Texas
Austin Community College A
Baylor University B, M
Del Mar College A
Hardin-Simmons University B, M
Houston Baptist University B
Houston Community College
    System C, A
Lon Morris College A
Midland College A
Navarro College A
Prairie View A&M University B
Rice University B, M
Sam Houston State University B, M
Southern Methodist University B, M
Southwest Texas State University B, M
Southwestern University B
Stephen F. Austin State University B
Texas A&M University
    Commerce B, M
Texas Christian University C, B

Texas Lutheran University B
Texas Tech University B, M
Texas Woman's University B, M
Trinity University B
Tyler Junior College A
University of Houston M, D
University of Mary Hardin-Baylor B, T
University of North Texas B, M, D
University of Texas
    Arlington B, T
    Austin B
    El Paso B, M
    San Antonio B, M
West Texas A&M University B, M

Vermont
Bennington College B, M
Johnson State College B
Marlboro College B
University of Vermont B

Virginia
Bluefield College B
George Mason University B, M
Hampton University B
James Madison University B, M, T
Longwood College B
Mary Baldwin College B
Mary Washington College B
Norfolk State University M, T
Old Dominion University B
Randolph-Macon Woman's College B
Shenandoah University B, M
University of Richmond B
Virginia Commonwealth
    University B, M
Virginia State University B

Washington
Central Washington University B
Cornish College of the Arts B
Eastern Washington University B
Everett Community College A
Gonzaga University B
Pacific Lutheran University B
Seattle Pacific University B, T
Shoreline Community College A
University of Puget Sound B
Walla Walla College B
Washington State University B, M
Western Washington University B
Whitworth College B, T

West Virginia
Alderson-Broaddus College B
Marshall University B

Wisconsin
Alverno College B
Carthage College B, T
Lawrence University B
Mount Senario College T
Northland College B, T
University of Wisconsin
    La Crosse B, T
    Madison B, M, D
    Stevens Point B
    Superior B, M
Viterbo University B

Wyoming
Casper College A
University of Wyoming B

Music theory/composition

Alabama
Birmingham-Southern College B
Huntingdon College B
Samford University B
University of Alabama B, M
University of Montevallo B
University of South Alabama B

Alaska
University of Alaska
    Fairbanks M

Arizona
Arizona State University B, M
University of Arizona M, D

Arkansas
Henderson State University B
Ouachita Baptist University B

California
Azusa Pacific University B, M
California Institute of the Arts C, B, M
California State University
    Dominguez Hills B
    Fullerton B, M
    Hayward M
    Long Beach M
    Northridge B, M
Chapman University B
Fresno Pacific University B
Golden West College C, A
Master's College B
Mills College M
Mount St. Mary's College B
Pepperdine University B
San Francisco Conservatory of
    Music B, M
San Francisco State University M
Solano Community College C
University of Redlands B
University of Southern
    California B, M, D
University of the Pacific B

Colorado
Adams State College B
University of Colorado
    Boulder B, M, D
University of Denver M

Connecticut
Connecticut College B
University of Hartford B, M, D
Western Connecticut State University B
Yale University M, D

Delaware
University of Delaware B

District of Columbia
Catholic University of America B, M, D
Howard University B

Florida
Florida State University B, M, D
Jacksonville University B
Manatee Community College A
Stetson University B
University of Miami B, M, D
University of Tampa B

Georgia
Clayton College and State University B
Columbus State University B, M
Georgia Southern University B
State University of West Georgia B, M
Toccoa Falls College B
University of Georgia B

Idaho
Boise State University B
North Idaho College A
Northwest Nazarene University B
University of Idaho B

Illinois
Bradley University B
Concordia University B
De Paul University B, M
Eureka College B
Moody Bible Institute B
Northwestern University B
Roosevelt University B, M
Trinity International University B
University of Illinois
    Urbana-Champaign B

Wheaton College B

Indiana
Ball State University B
Butler University B, M
DePauw University B
Indiana State University M
Indiana University
    Bloomington B, M, D
    South Bend B
Indiana Wesleyan University B
Valparaiso University B, M
Vincennes University A

Iowa
Coe College B
Drake University B
Luther College B
University of Iowa B, M, D
University of Northern Iowa B, M
Wartburg College B

Kansas
Central Christian College A
University of Kansas B, M, D

Kentucky
Campbellsville University B
University of Louisville B, M

Louisiana
Centenary College of Louisiana B
Loyola University New Orleans B

Maine
University of Maine M

Maryland
College of Notre Dame of Maryland B
Johns Hopkins University: Peabody
    Conservatory of Music B, M, D
Johns Hopkins University B, M, D
Western Maryland College B

Massachusetts
Assumption College B
Berklee College of Music B
Boston Conservatory B
Boston University B, M, D
Brandeis University M, D
Hampshire College B
Harvard College B
Harvard University D
New England Conservatory of
    Music B, M
Simon's Rock College of Bard B
Tufts University B
Westfield State College B

Michigan
Calvin College B
Central Michigan University B
Cornerstone College and Grand Rapids
    Baptist Seminary B, T
Lansing Community College A
Marygrove College B
Michigan State University B, M, D
Oakland University B
University of Michigan B, M
Western Michigan University B

Minnesota
Hamline University B
Minnesota State University, Mankato B
Moorhead State University B
St. Olaf College B

Mississippi
Mississippi College B
Mississippi University for Women B

Missouri
Drury University B
Southeast Missouri State University B
Southwest Missouri State University B
University of Missouri
    Kansas City B, M, D
Washington University B
Webster University B, M

427

Music theory/composition

William Jewell College *B*

Montana
University of Montana-Missoula *B*

Nebraska
University of Nebraska
   Omaha *B*

New Hampshire
Franklin Pierce College *B*
Keene State College *B*
University of New Hampshire *B*

New Jersey
Princeton University *M, D*
Rider University *B, M*
Rowan University *B*

New York
Bard College *B, M*
City University of New York
   Brooklyn College *B, M*
   City College *B, M*
   Graduate School and University
     Center *D*
   Hunter College *B, M*
   Lehman College *B*
   Queens College *B, M*
Columbia University
   Graduate School *M*
   Teachers College *M, D*
Eastman School of Music of the
   University of Rochester *B, M, D*
Five Towns College *A, B, M*
Houghton College *B*
Ithaca College *B, M*
Jewish Theological Seminary of
   America *B*
Juilliard School *B, M, D*
Long Island University
   Brooklyn Campus *B*
Manhattan School of Music *B, M, D*
Manhattanville College *B*
Mannes College of Music *B, M*
Nazareth College of Rochester *B*
New York University *B, M, D*
Nyack College *B*
Sarah Lawrence College *B*
State University of New York
   Albany *B*
   Buffalo *M, D*
   College at Fredonia *B*
   College at Potsdam *B, M*
   New Paltz *B*
   Stony Brook *M, D*
Syracuse University *B, M*
University of Rochester *B, M, D*

North Carolina
Appalachian State University *B*
Brevard College *A, B*
Duke University *M*
East Carolina University *B, M*
Meredith College *B*
University of North Carolina
   Greensboro *B, M*

Ohio
Ashland University *B*
Bowling Green State University *B, M*
Capital University *B*
Cedarville College *B*
Cleveland Institute of Music *B, M, D*
Heidelberg College *B*
Kent State University
   Stark Campus *B*
Kent State University *D*
Miami University
   Oxford Campus *M*
Oberlin College *B*
Ohio Northern University *B*
Ohio State University
   Columbus Campus *B*
Ohio University *B, M*
Otterbein College *B*
University of Akron *B, M*
University of Cincinnati *B, M, D*

University of Dayton *B*
Youngstown State University *B, M*

Oklahoma
Oklahoma Baptist University *B*
Oklahoma City University *B*
Oral Roberts University *B*
Southwestern Oklahoma State
   University *B*
University of Oklahoma *M, D*
University of Tulsa *B*

Oregon
Linfield College *B*
University of Oregon *B, M, D*
Willamette University *B*

Pennsylvania
Bucknell University *B*
Carnegie Mellon University *B, M*
Curtis Institute of Music *C, B*
Duquesne University *M*
Mercyhurst College *B*
Moravian College *B*
Penn State
   University Park *M*
Philadelphia College of Bible *B*
Susquehanna University *B*
Temple University *B, M, D*
University of the Arts *B, M*
West Chester University of
   Pennsylvania *B, M*
Westminster College *B*

Rhode Island
University of Rhode Island *B*

South Carolina
Furman University *B*
Newberry College *B*
North Greenville College *A, B*
University of South Carolina *M, D*

Tennessee
Belmont University *B*
Carson-Newman College *B*
Southern Adventist University *B*
Tennessee Temple University *B*
Union University *B*
University of Tennessee
   Knoxville *B*
Vanderbilt University *B*

Texas
Baylor University *B, M*
Dallas Baptist University *B*
Del Mar College *A*
Hardin-Simmons University *B, M*
Houston Community College
   System *C, A*
Lon Morris College *A*
Rice University *B, M*
Sam Houston State University *B, M*
Southern Methodist University *B, M*
Stephen F. Austin State University *B*
Texas A&M University
   Commerce *B, M*
Texas Christian University *B, M*
Texas Tech University *B, M*
Trinity University *B*
University of Houston *B, M, D*
University of North Texas *B, M, D*
University of Texas
   Arlington *B, T*
   Austin *B*
   El Paso *B*
   San Antonio *B*
West Texas A&M University *B*

Utah
Brigham Young University *M*

Vermont
Bennington College *B, M*
Johnson State College *B*
Marlboro College *B*

Virginia
Christopher Newport University *B*

Randolph-Macon Woman's College *B*
Shenandoah University *B, M*
University of Richmond *B*
Virginia Union University *B*

Washington
Central Washington University *B*
Centralia College *A*
Cornish College of the Arts *B*
Eastern Washington University *B, M*
Pacific Lutheran University *B*
University of Washington *B*
Washington State University *B*
Western Washington University *B*

West Virginia
Marshall University *B*

Wisconsin
Lawrence University *B*
University of Wisconsin
   La Crosse *B*
   Madison *B, M*
   Whitewater *B, T*
Viterbo University *B*

Wyoming
University of Wyoming *B*

Music therapy

Alabama
University of Alabama *B*

Arizona
Arizona State University *B*

California
California State University
   Northridge *M*
Chapman University *B*
University of the Pacific *B*

Colorado
Colorado State University *B*
Naropa University *M*

District of Columbia
Howard University *B*

Florida
Florida State University *C, B, M*
University of Miami *B, M*

Georgia
Georgia College and State University *B*
University of Georgia *B*

Indiana
Indiana University--Purdue University
   Indiana University-Purdue
     University Fort Wayne *B*
St. Mary-of-the-Woods College *B, M*
University of Evansville *B*

Iowa
University of Iowa *B*
Wartburg College *B*

Kansas
Central Christian College *A*
University of Kansas *B, M*

Louisiana
Loyola University New Orleans *B, M*

Massachusetts
Anna Maria College *B*
Berklee College of Music *B*

Michigan
Eastern Michigan University *B, T*
Michigan State University *B, M*
Western Michigan University *B*

Minnesota
Augsburg College *B*
University of Minnesota
   Twin Cities *B*

Mississippi
William Carey College *B*

Missouri
Maryville University of Saint Louis *B*
University of Missouri
   Kansas City *B, M*

New Jersey
Montclair State University *B*

New York
Molloy College *B*
New York University *M, D*
State University of New York
   College at Fredonia *B*
   New Paltz *B*

North Carolina
East Carolina University *B, M*
Queens College *B*

Ohio
Baldwin-Wallace College *B*
College of Wooster *B*
Ohio University *B*
University of Dayton *B*

Oklahoma
Southwestern Oklahoma State
   University *B*

Pennsylvania
Duquesne University *B*
Elizabethtown College *B*
Immaculata College *B, M*
MCP Hahnemann University *M*
Mansfield University of Pennsylvania *B*
Marywood University *B*
Mercyhurst College *B*
Slippery Rock University of
   Pennsylvania *B*
Temple University *B, M*

South Carolina
Charleston Southern University *B*

Tennessee
Tennessee Technological University *B*

Texas
Sam Houston State University *B*
Southern Methodist University *B, M*
Texas Woman's University *B, M*
University of the Incarnate Word *B*
West Texas A&M University *B*

Utah
Utah State University *B, M*

Virginia
Radford University *B*
Shenandoah University *C, B, M*

Wisconsin
Alverno College *B*
University of Wisconsin
   Eau Claire *B*
   Madison *M*
   Oshkosh *B*

Music, piano/organ performance

Alabama
Birmingham-Southern College *B*
Huntingdon College *B*
Samford University *B*

Arizona
Grand Canyon University *B*
Northern Arizona University *B*

Arkansas
John Brown University *B*
Ouachita Baptist University *B*
University of Central Arkansas *B*

Music, voice/choral/opera performance

California
California State University
　Fullerton *B, M*
　Long Beach *B, M*
Fresno City College *A*
Master's College *B*
San Francisco Conservatory of
　Music *B, M*
San Francisco State University *B*
University of Southern
　California *B, M, D*
University of the Pacific *B*

Colorado
University of Colorado
　Boulder *B, M, D*

Connecticut
University of Hartford *B, M*

Delaware
University of Delaware *B*

District of Columbia
Catholic University of America *B, M, D*
Howard University *B*

Florida
Barry University *B*
Florida State University *B, M, D*
Stetson University *B*
University of Miami *B, M, D*

Georgia
Clayton College and State University *C*
Columbus State University *B, M*
Shorter College *B*

Hawaii
Brigham Young University
　Hawaii *B*

Illinois
Augustana College *B*
Benedictine University *B*
Judson College *B*
Millikin University *B*
Moody Bible Institute *B*
North Park University *B*
Northwestern University *B*
Olivet Nazarene University *B*
Roosevelt University *C, B, M*
Trinity Christian College *B*
Trinity International University *B*

Indiana
Ancilla College *C*
Ball State University *B*
Butler University *B, M*
Goshen College *B*
Grace College *B*
Indiana State University *B*
Indiana University
　Bloomington *B*
　South Bend *B*
Indiana University--Purdue University
　Indiana University-Purdue
　　University Fort Wayne *B*
Saint Mary's College *B*
University of Indianapolis *B*
Valparaiso University *M*
Vincennes University *A*

Iowa
Clarke College *B*
Dordt College *B*
Drake University *B*
Luther College *B*
Simpson College *B*
University of Iowa *B*
University of Northern Iowa *M*

Kansas
Central Christian College *A*
MidAmerica Nazarene University *T*
Pittsburg State University *B*
Tabor College *B*
University of Kansas *B, M, D*

Kentucky
Campbellsville University *B*

Louisiana
Centenary College of Louisiana *B, T*
Dillard University *B*
Loyola University New Orleans *B*
Nicholls State University *B*

Maryland
Johns Hopkins University: Peabody
　Conservatory of Music *B, M, D*
Johns Hopkins University *B, M, D*
Washington Bible College *B*

Massachusetts
Anna Maria College *B*
Boston Conservatory *B, M*
Boston University *B, M, D*

Michigan
Calvin College *B*
Northwestern Michigan College *A*
Oakland University *B*
University of Michigan *B, M, T*
William Tyndale College *B*

Minnesota
Bethel College *B*
Concordia College: Moorhead *B*
Minnesota State University, Mankato *B*
Moorhead State University *B*
Northwestern College *B*
St. Mary's University of Minnesota *B*

Mississippi
Blue Mountain College *B*
Mississippi College *B*

Missouri
Hannibal-LaGrange College *B*
University of Missouri
　Kansas City *B, M, D*
Webster University *B*

Nebraska
Concordia University *B*
Hastings College *B*

New Hampshire
Plymouth State College of the University
　System of New Hampshire *B*
University of New Hampshire *B*

New Jersey
Rider University *B, M*

New York
Bard College *B*
City University of New York
　City College *B*
College of St. Rose *C*
Columbia University
　Teachers College *M, D*
Eastman School of Music of the
　University of Rochester *B, M, D*
Five Towns College *A, B, M*
Houghton College *B*
Ithaca College *B, M*
Manhattan School of Music *B, M, D*
Mannes College of Music *B, M*
New York University *B*
Nyack College *B*
Roberts Wesleyan College *B*
Sarah Lawrence College *B*
State University of New York
　College at Fredonia *B*
　New Paltz *B, M*
Syracuse University *B, M*
University of Rochester *M, D*

North Carolina
Brevard College *A, B*
Campbell University *B*
College of the Albemarle *A*
Gardner-Webb University *B*
Lenoir-Rhyne College *B*
Meredith College *B*
Wingate University *B*

Ohio
Baldwin-Wallace College *B*
Bowling Green State University *M*
Capital University *B*
Cedarville College *B*
Kent State University
　Stark Campus *B*
Ohio State University
　Columbus Campus *B*
Ohio University *B*
University of Cincinnati *B, M, D*
Youngstown State University *B, M*

Oklahoma
East Central University *B, T*
Northeastern State University *B*
Northwestern Oklahoma State
　University *B*
Oklahoma Baptist University *B*
Oklahoma Christian University of
　Science and Arts *B*
Oklahoma City University *B*
Oral Roberts University *B*
Southwestern Oklahoma State
　University *B*
University of Central Oklahoma *B*
University of Oklahoma *B, M, D*

Oregon
Western Baptist College *B*
Willamette University *B*

Pennsylvania
Carnegie Mellon University *B*
Gettysburg College *B*
Mansfield University of Pennsylvania *B*
Mercyhurst College *B*
Penn State
　University Park *M*
Seton Hill College *B*
Susquehanna University *B*
Temple University *B, M*
West Chester University of
　Pennsylvania *M*
Westminster College *B*

South Carolina
Coker College *B*
Furman University *B*
North Greenville College *B*
South Carolina State University *B*
Southern Wesleyan University *B*
University of South Carolina *M, D*

Tennessee
Belmont University *B*
David Lipscomb University *B*
Lambuth University *B*
Tennessee Temple University *B*
Union University *B*
University of Tennessee
　Knoxville *B*
　Martin *B*

Texas
Abilene Christian University *B*
Baylor University *M*
Concordia University at Austin *B, T*
Dallas Baptist University *B*
East Texas Baptist University *B*
Howard Payne University *B*
Lon Morris College *A*
McMurry University *B*
Southern Methodist University *B, M*
Stephen F. Austin State University *B*
Texas A&M University
　Commerce *B, M*
Texas Christian University *C, B, M*
University of Mary Hardin-Baylor *B*
University of Texas
　Arlington *B*
　El Paso *B*

Utah
Brigham Young University *M*
Weber State University *B*

Vermont
Bennington College *M*
Johnson State College *B*

Virginia
Shenandoah University *B, M*
Virginia Union University *B*

Washington
Cornish College of the Arts *B*
Eastern Washington University *B*
University of Washington *B, M, D*
Whitworth College *B, T*

Wisconsin
Carthage College *B, T*
Mount Mary College *B*
University of Wisconsin
　Madison *B, M*
Viterbo University *B*

Music, voice/choral/opera performance

Alabama
Birmingham-Southern College *B*
Huntingdon College *B*
Samford University *B*

Arizona
Grand Canyon University *B*
Northern Arizona University *B*

Arkansas
Harding University *B*
Henderson State University *B*
John Brown University *B*
Ouachita Baptist University *B*
University of Central Arkansas *B*

California
California State University
　Fullerton *B, M*
　Long Beach *B*
Fresno City College *A*
Master's College *B*
San Francisco Conservatory of
　Music *B, M*
San Francisco State University *B*
Solano Community College *C*
University of Southern
　California *B, M, D*
University of the Pacific *B*

Colorado
Adams State College *B*
University of Colorado
　Boulder *B, M, D*

Connecticut
University of Hartford *B, M*

Delaware
University of Delaware *B*

District of Columbia
Catholic University of America *B, M, D*
Howard University *B*

Florida
Barry University *B*
Florida State University *B, M, D*
Stetson University *B*
University of Miami *B, M, D*

Georgia
Columbus State University *B, M*
Emory University *M*
Georgia College and State University *B*
Shorter College *B*
State University of West Georgia *B*
Toccoa Falls College *B*

Hawaii
Brigham Young University
　Hawaii *B*

Idaho
University of Idaho *B*

Music, voice/choral/opera performance

Illinois
Augustana College *B*
Benedictine University *B*
Judson College *B*
Millikin University *B*
Monmouth College *T*
Moody Bible Institute *B*
Northwestern University *B*
Olivet Nazarene University *B*
Quincy University *A, B, T*
Roosevelt University *B, M*
St. Xavier University *B*
Trinity Christian College *B*
Trinity International University *B*
University of Illinois
    Urbana-Champaign *B*

Indiana
Ball State University *B*
Butler University *B, M*
Grace College *B*
Indiana State University *B*
Indiana University
    Bloomington *B*
    South Bend *B*
Indiana University--Purdue University
    Indiana University-Purdue
        University Fort Wayne *B*
Indiana Wesleyan University *T*
Saint Mary's College *B*
University of Indianapolis *B*
Valparaiso University *M*
Vincennes University *A*

Iowa
Clarke College *B*
Dordt College *B*
Drake University *M*
Luther College *B*
Simpson College *B*
University of Iowa *B*

Kansas
Allen County Community College *A*
Central Christian College *A*
MidAmerica Nazarene University *T*
Pittsburg State University *B*
Seward County Community College *A*
Tabor College *B*
University of Kansas *B, M, D*

Kentucky
Campbellsville University *B*

Louisiana
Centenary College of Louisiana *B, T*
Dillard University *B*

Maryland
Johns Hopkins University: Peabody
    Conservatory of Music *B, M, D*
Johns Hopkins University *B, M, D*
Washington Bible College *B*

Massachusetts
Anna Maria College *B*
Boston Conservatory *B, M*
Boston University *B, M, D*
Eastern Nazarene College *B*
Emerson College *B*

Michigan
Calvin College *B, T*
Northwestern Michigan College *A*
Oakland University *B*
University of Michigan *B, M*
William Tyndale College *B*

Minnesota
Bethel College *B*
Concordia College: Moorhead *B*
Minnesota State University, Mankato *B*
Moorhead State University *B*
Northwestern College *B*
St. Mary's University of Minnesota *B*

Mississippi
Blue Mountain College *B*
Mississippi College *B*

Missouri
College of the Ozarks *B*
Hannibal-LaGrange College *B*
University of Missouri
    Kansas City *B, M, D*
Washington University *B, M*
Webster University *B*

Nebraska
Concordia University *B*
Hastings College *B*

New Hampshire
Plymouth State College of the University
    System of New Hampshire *B*
University of New Hampshire *B*

New Jersey
Rider University *B, M*

New York
Bard College *B*
City University of New York
    City College *B*
Columbia University
    School of General Studies *B*
    Teachers College *M, D*
Eastman School of Music of the
    University of Rochester *B, M, D*
Five Towns College *A, B, M*
Houghton College *B*
Ithaca College *B, M*
Manhattan School of Music *B, M, D*
Mannes College of Music *B, M*
New York University *B*
Nyack College *B*
Roberts Wesleyan College *B*
Sarah Lawrence College *B*
State University of New York
    Binghamton *M*
    College at Fredonia *B*
    New Paltz *B*
Syracuse University *B, M*
University of Rochester *M, D*

North Carolina
Brevard College *A, B*
Campbell University *B*
College of the Albemarle *A*
Lenoir-Rhyne College *B*
Meredith College *B*
Wingate University *B*

Ohio
Baldwin-Wallace College *B*
Capital University *B*
Cedarville College *B*
Cleveland Institute of Music *B*
Kent State University
    Stark Campus *B*
Oberlin College *B, M*
Ohio State University
    Columbus Campus *B*
Ohio University *B*
University of Cincinnati *B, M, D*
Youngstown State University *B, M*

Oklahoma
East Central University *B, T*
Northeastern State University *B*
Northwestern Oklahoma State
    University *B*
Oklahoma Baptist University *B*
Oklahoma Christian University of
    Science and Arts *B*
Oklahoma City University *B*
Oral Roberts University *B*
Southwestern Oklahoma State
    University *B*
University of Central Oklahoma *B*
University of Oklahoma *B, M, D*
University of Tulsa *B*

Oregon
Western Baptist College *B*
Willamette University *B*

Pennsylvania
Carnegie Mellon University *B*
Clarion University of Pennsylvania *B*
Curtis Institute of Music *M*
Gettysburg College *B*
Mansfield University of Pennsylvania *B*
Mercyhurst College *B*
Penn State
    University Park *M*
Seton Hill College *B*
Susquehanna University *B*
Temple University *C, B, M, D*
University of the Arts *B*
West Chester University of
    Pennsylvania *M*
Westminster College *B*

South Carolina
Anderson College *B*
Charleston Southern University *B*
North Greenville College *B*
South Carolina State University *B*
Southern Wesleyan University *B*
University of South Carolina *M*

South Dakota
Black Hills State University *B*

Tennessee
Belmont University *B*
David Lipscomb University *B*
Hiwassee College *A*
Lambuth University *B*
Tennessee Temple University *B*
Union University *B*
University of Tennessee
    Knoxville *B*
    Martin *B*

Texas
Abilene Christian University *B*
Alvin Community College *A*
Dallas Baptist University *B*
East Texas Baptist University *B*
Howard Payne University *B*
Lamar University *B, M*
Lon Morris College *A*
McMurry University *B, T*
Navarro College *A*
Sam Houston State University *T*
Southern Methodist University *B, M*
Stephen F. Austin State University *B*
Texas A&M University
    Commerce *B, M*
Texas Christian University *B, M*
Trinity University *B*
University of Mary Hardin-Baylor *B*
University of Texas
    Arlington *B*
    El Paso *B*

Utah
Brigham Young University *M*
Weber State University *B*

Vermont
Bennington College *M*
Johnson State College *B*

Virginia
Virginia Union University *B*

Washington
Cornish College of the Arts *B*
Eastern Washington University *B*
University of Washington *B, M, D*
Western Washington University *B*
Whitworth College *B, T*

West Virginia
Davis and Elkins College *B*

Wisconsin
Carthage College *B, T*
Mount Senario College *T*
Northland College *B, T*
University of Wisconsin
    Madison *B, M*
Viterbo University *B*

Musical theater

Alabama
Birmingham-Southern College *B*
Huntingdon College *B*
Northwest-Shoals Community College *C*

Arizona
University of Arizona *B*

Arkansas
Ouachita Baptist University *B, T*
University of Central Arkansas *B*

California
California State University
    Chico *B*
    Fullerton *B*
San Diego City College *A*
San Diego State University *M*
Scripps College *B*
University of Redlands *B*
University of the Pacific *B*

Colorado
University of Northern Colorado *B, M*

Connecticut
University of Hartford *B*

District of Columbia
Catholic University of America *B*
Howard University *B*

Florida
Barry University *B*
Florida State University *B, M*
Jacksonville University *B*
Palm Beach Community College *A*
University of Miami *B, M*

Georgia
Brenau University *B*
Shorter College *B*
Young Harris College *A*

Illinois
Columbia College *B*
Illinois Wesleyan University *B*
Millikin University *B*
North Park University *C*
Rockford College *B*
Roosevelt University *B, M*

Kansas
Central Christian College *A*
Wichita State University *B*

Kentucky
Eastern Kentucky University *B*

Massachusetts
Boston Conservatory *B, M*
Dean College *A*
Emerson College *B*
Hampshire College *B*

Michigan
Lansing Community College *A*
University of Michigan *B*

Minnesota
College of St. Catherine: St. Paul
    Campus *B*
St. Mary's University of Minnesota *B*
University of Minnesota
    Duluth *B*

Missouri
Webster University *B*

Nebraska
University of Nebraska
    Kearney *B*
    Lincoln *B*

Nevada
University of Nevada
    Las Vegas *B*

New Mexico
College of Santa Fe B

New York
City University of New York
  Brooklyn College B, M
Five Towns College B
Ithaca College B
New York University B, M
Sarah Lawrence College B
State University of New York
  Buffalo B
  College at Fredonia B
Syracuse University B
Wagner College B

North Carolina
Brevard College B
College of the Albemarle A
Elon College B
Lees-McRae College B
Mars Hill College B
Meredith College B

Ohio
Baldwin-Wallace College B
Bowling Green State University B
Capital University B
Kent State University B
Ohio Northern University B
Otterbein College B
University of Cincinnati B
Youngstown State University B

Oklahoma
Oklahoma Baptist University B
Oklahoma City University B, M
University of Central Oklahoma B
University of Oklahoma B
University of Tulsa B

Pennsylvania
Carnegie Mellon University B
Dickinson College B
Marywood University B
Mercyhurst College B
Seton Hill College B
University of the Arts B

Rhode Island
Rhode Island College B

South Carolina
Coastal Carolina University B

Tennessee
Belmont University B

Texas
Alvin Community College A
Austin Community College A
Lon Morris College A
Southwest Texas State University B
Texas Wesleyan University B
West Texas A&M University B

Utah
Brigham Young University B
Weber State University B

Virginia
Christopher Newport University B
Longwood College B
Virginia Intermont College B

Washington
Eastern Washington University B
Western Washington University B

Wisconsin
University of Wisconsin
  Stevens Point B
Viterbo University B

Musicology/ethnomusicology

Arizona
University of Arizona M

California
University of California
  Los Angeles B, M, D

Colorado
University of Colorado
  Boulder B, D

Connecticut
Wesleyan University D

Florida
Florida State University M, D
University of Miami M

Illinois
Northwestern University B, D
Roosevelt University M

Indiana
Indiana University
  Bloomington M, D

Iowa
Maharishi University of
  Management C, B
University of Iowa M, D

Kansas
University of Kansas M

Louisiana
Loyola University New Orleans B

Maryland
Johns Hopkins University B, M, D
University of Maryland
  College Park M, D

Massachusetts
Boston University D
Harvard College B
Tufts University B

Michigan
University of Michigan M

Minnesota
Crown College M

Missouri
Washington University M, D

New York
Columbia University
  School of General Studies B
  Teachers College M, D
Eastman School of Music of the
  University of Rochester M, D
New York University M, D
Sarah Lawrence College B
University of Rochester M, D

North Carolina
Duke University M, D

Ohio
Case Western Reserve University D
Kent State University M, D
University of Akron B, M
University of Cincinnati D

Pennsylvania
Marywood University M

Rhode Island
Brown University B, M, D

Texas
Sam Houston State University M
Texas A&M University
  Commerce B
Texas Christian University M
University of North Texas M, D

Utah
Brigham Young University M, D
University of Utah M

Washington
University of Washington B

Native American studies

Alaska
University of Alaska
  Fairbanks A, B

Arizona
Dine College A
Pima Community College A
University of Arizona M, D

California
California State University
  Hayward B
  Long Beach C
De Anza College C, A
Fresno City College A
Humboldt State University B
Palomar College C
Santa Barbara City College A
University of California
  Berkeley B
  Davis B
  Los Angeles M
  Riverside B

Colorado
Fort Lewis College B

Indiana
Indiana University--Purdue University
  Indiana University-Purdue
    University Fort Wayne C

Iowa
Morningside College B

Kansas
University of Kansas M

Massachusetts
Hampshire College B

Minnesota
Bemidji State University B
Fond Du Lac Tribal and Community
  College C
University of Minnesota
  Duluth B
  Twin Cities B

Montana
Little Big Horn College A
Montana State University
  Northern A, B
Salish Kootenai College C, A
Stone Child College A
University of Montana-Missoula B

New Hampshire
Dartmouth College B

New York
Colgate University B
Sarah Lawrence College B

North Carolina
University of North Carolina
  Pembroke B
Western Carolina University M

North Dakota
University of North Dakota B

Oklahoma
Northeastern State University B
Oklahoma State University C
University of Oklahoma B
University of Science and Arts of
  Oklahoma B
University of Tulsa C

South Dakota
Black Hills State University B
University of South Dakota B

Texas
University of the Incarnate Word B

Vermont
Goddard College B

Washington
Evergreen State College B

Wisconsin
Mount Senario College A, B
Northland College B
University of Wisconsin
  Eau Claire B

Wyoming
Central Wyoming College A

Natural resources management

Alaska
University of Alaska
  Fairbanks B, M

Arizona
Prescott College B, M
University of Arizona M, D

California
California State University
  Chico B
  Monterey Bay B
College of the Redwoods C
Columbia College C, A
Humboldt State University B, M
Los Angeles Pierce College A
San Joaquin Delta College C
University of California
  Berkeley B
  Davis B

Colorado
Colorado Mountain College
  Timberline Campus A
Colorado State University B
Pikes Peak Community College C, A
Regis University B

Delaware
Delaware State University B
University of Delaware B

Florida
Pensacola Junior College A
University of Miami B
University of West Florida B

Georgia
Brenau University B

Idaho
University of Idaho B

Illinois
Dominican University B
Southeastern Illinois College A

Indiana
Ball State University B
University of Evansville B

Iowa
Cornell College B
Hawkeye Community College A
Kirkwood Community College A

Kansas
Garden City Community College A

Maine
Unity College B
University of Maine
  Fort Kent B

Maryland
University of Maryland
  College Park B

Massachusetts
Becker College C
Bridgewater State College B
Cape Cod Community College C

Massachusetts Maritime Academy B
North Shore Community College A
University of Massachusetts
 Amherst B
Michigan
Grand Valley State University B
Lake Superior State University A, B
University of Michigan B, M, D
Minnesota
Central Lakes College A
Northland Community & Technical
 College A
University of Minnesota
 Crookston A, B
University of St. Thomas M
Vermilion Community College A
Missouri
Missouri Southern State College B
Webster University M
Montana
Flathead Valley Community College A
University of Montana-Missoula B
Nebraska
Nebraska College of Technical
 Agriculture C, A
University of Nebraska
 Lincoln B
Nevada
University of Nevada
 Las Vegas B, M
 Reno B
New Hampshire
Antioch New England Graduate
 School M
New Hampshire Community Technical
 College
 Berlin A
New Jersey
Rutgers
 The State University of New Jersey:
  Cook College B
New Mexico
Northern New Mexico Community
 College C, A
New York
Cornell University B
Finger Lakes Community College A
Fulton-Montgomery Community
 College A
Rensselaer Polytechnic Institute M, D
State University of New York
 College of Environmental Science
  and Forestry B, M, D
 Purchase C
North Carolina
North Carolina State University M
Western Carolina University B
North Dakota
Minot State University: Bottineau
 Campus A
North Dakota State University B, M
Ohio
Bowling Green State University B
Hocking Technical College A
Kent State University
 Trumbull Campus A
Muskingum Area Technical College A
Ohio State University
 Columbus Campus B, M, D
Otterbein College B
University of Findlay M
Xavier University B
Oklahoma
Northwestern Oklahoma State
 University B

Oklahoma State University
 Oklahoma City A
Southeastern Oklahoma State
 University B
Oregon
Concordia University B
Mount Hood Community College A
Oregon State University B
Portland State University M
Pennsylvania
Duquesne University M
Puerto Rico
Turabo University M
Universidad Metropolitana M
Rhode Island
University of Rhode Island B, M
South Carolina
Central Carolina Technical College A
South Dakota
South Dakota State University B
Tennessee
University of Tennessee
 Martin B
University of the South B
Texas
Hardin-Simmons University M
Stephen F. Austin State University B
Sul Ross State University B
Texas A&M University B
Utah
Brigham Young University B, M
Dixie State College of Utah A
Snow College A
Utah State University M
Vermont
Johnson State College B
Southern Vermont College A, B
Sterling College C, A, B
University of Vermont B, M, D
Virginia
Lord Fairfax Community College A
Virginia Polytechnic Institute and State
 University B
Washington
Central Washington University M
Centralia College A
Grays Harbor College A
Heritage College C, A
Highline Community College A
University of Washington M, D
Washington State University B
Western Washington University B, M
Wisconsin
Milwaukee Area Technical College A
Northland College B
University of Wisconsin
 Green Bay B
 River Falls B
 Stevens Point B, T

Natural sciences

Alabama
Oakwood College B
University of Alabama
 Birmingham B
Alaska
University of Alaska
 Anchorage B
Arizona
Prescott College B, M
California
California State University
 Fresno B

Columbia College A
Lake Tahoe Community College A
Loma Linda University M, D
Loyola Marymount University B
Master's College B
Ohlone College A
Pacific Union College B
Pepperdine University B
Saddleback College A
San Joaquin Delta College A
Santa Rosa Junior College A
Colorado
Colorado Mountain College
 Timberline Campus A
University of Colorado
 Boulder M
Florida
Lynn University B
Georgia
Covenant College B
Reinhardt College A
Hawaii
University of Hawaii
 Hilo B
Idaho
College of Southern Idaho A
Lewis-Clark State College B
Illinois
Black Hawk College
 East Campus A
Concordia University B, T
Shimer College B
Indiana
Ancilla College A
Goshen College B
Tri-State University A
Iowa
Northwestern College T
Kansas
Benedictine College B
Bethel College B
Central Christian College A
Garden City Community College A
Tabor College B
Maine
St. Joseph's College B
University of Southern Maine B
Maryland
St. Mary's College of Maryland B
Massachusetts
Cape Cod Community College A
Hampshire College B
Harvard College B
Michigan
Calvin College B
Concordia College B, T
Marygrove College A, B, T
Siena Heights University A, B
Minnesota
College of St. Benedict B
College of St. Scholastica B
St. John's University B
Missouri
Avila College B
Columbia College B
Park University B
Nebraska
Concordia University B, T
Northeast Community College A
Peru State College B
New Hampshire
Antioch New England Graduate
 School M
Franklin Pierce College B

St. Anselm College B
New Jersey
Warren County Community College A
New Mexico
Clovis Community College A
New York
Alfred University B
City University of New York
 Brooklyn College B, M
Colgate University B
Daemen College B, T
Hofstra University B
Rensselaer Polytechnic Institute M
Roberts Wesleyan College A
State University of New York
 Buffalo M
 College at Geneseo B, T
 College at Plattsburgh M
 College at Potsdam B, T
 College of Agriculture and
  Technology at Cobleskill A
 College of Environmental Science
  and Forestry B
Ohio
Case Western Reserve University B
College of Mount St. Joseph B
Defiance College B
Shawnee State University B
University of Akron B
University of Findlay B
Walsh University B
Xavier University B
Oklahoma
Oklahoma State University M
St. Gregory's University B
University of Science and Arts of
 Oklahoma B, T
Oregon
Marylhurst University B
Pennsylvania
Gettysburg College B
Indiana University of Pennsylvania B
Lehigh Carbon Community College A
Lehigh University B
Lock Haven University of
 Pennsylvania B
University of Pittsburgh
 Titusville A
Puerto Rico
Bayamon Central University B
Colegio Universitario del Este A
Turabo University B
Universidad Metropolitana A, B
University of Puerto Rico
 Ponce University College A
 Rio Piedras Campus B
 Utuado B
University of the Sacred Heart B
South Carolina
Charleston Southern University B, M
University of South Carolina M
Texas
Abilene Christian University T
Lee College A
McMurry University B, T
Our Lady of the Lake University of San
 Antonio B
Vermont
Castleton State College B
Sterling College A, B
Virginia
J. Sargeant Reynolds Community
 College A
Virginia Union University B
Virginia Wesleyan College B
Virginia Western Community College A

Nonprofit/public management

Washington
Everett Community College *A*
Evergreen State College *B*
North Seattle Community College *C*
University of Puget Sound *B*

West Virginia
Alderson-Broaddus College *A*

Wisconsin
Alverno College *B, T*
Silver Lake College *T*

Wyoming
University of Wyoming *B, M*

Navy/Marines

Georgia
Savannah State University *C*

Idaho
University of Idaho *B*

Maine
Maine Maritime Academy *C*

Massachusetts
Massachusetts Maritime Academy *B*

New York
State University of New York
 Maritime College *B*

Pennsylvania
Villanova University *B*
West Chester University of
 Pennsylvania *C*

Virginia
Mary Baldwin College *T*

Wisconsin
University of Wisconsin
 Madison *B*

Neuroscience

Alabama
University of Alabama
 Birmingham *D*

Arizona
University of Arizona *M, D*

California
California Institute of Technology *D*
Pitzer College *B*
Pomona College *B*
Scripps College *B*
Stanford University *M, D*
University of California
 Berkeley *D*
 Davis *B, M, D*
 Los Angeles *B, D*
 Riverside *B, M, D*
 San Diego *B, M, D*
University of Southern California *B, D*
Westmont College *B*

Colorado
Colorado College *B*
Regis University *B*
University of Colorado
 Health Sciences Center *D*

Connecticut
Connecticut College *B*
Fairfield University *B*
Trinity College *B*
University of Hartford *M*
Wesleyan University *B, M*
Yale University *M, D*

Delaware
University of Delaware *D*

District of Columbia
George Washington University *D*

Georgetown University *D*

Florida
Florida State University *D*
University of Miami *D*

Illinois
Finch University of Health Sciences/The
 Chicago Medical School *D*
Loyola University of Chicago *D*
Northwestern University *B, M, D*
University of Chicago *M, D*
University of Illinois
 Urbana-Champaign *D*

Indiana
Indiana University
 Bloomington *D*

Iowa
Iowa State University *M, D*
Maharishi University of Management *D*
University of Iowa *D*

Louisiana
Tulane University *M, D*

Maine
Bates College *B*
Bowdoin College *B*

Maryland
Johns Hopkins University *B*
Uniformed Services University of the
 Health Sciences *D*
University of Maryland
 Baltimore County *D*
 College Park *D*
Washington College *B*

Massachusetts
Amherst College *B*
Boston University *B, M, D*
Brandeis University *B, M, D*
Hampshire College *B*
Harvard College *B*
Mount Holyoke College *B*
Northeastern University *B*
Smith College *B*
Tufts University *M, D*
University of Massachusetts
 Amherst *M, D*

Michigan
Michigan State University *D*
University of Michigan *M, D*
Wayne State University *M*

Minnesota
Macalester College *B*
Mayo Graduate School *D*
University of Minnesota
 Twin Cities *D*

Missouri
St. Louis University *D*
Washington University *B, D*

New Jersey
Rutgers
 The State University of New Jersey:
 New Brunswick Graduate
 Campus *M, D*

New York
Albany Medical College *M, D*
City University of New York
 College of Staten Island *D*
Colgate University *B*
Columbia University
 Columbia College *B*
Cornell University *B*
Hamilton College *B*
New York University *B, M, D*
Rockefeller University *D*
State University of New York
 Albany *M, D*
 Buffalo *M, D*
 Stony Brook *M, D*
Syracuse University *M, D*

University of Rochester *M, D*

North Carolina
Duke University *B, M, D*
University of North Carolina
 Chapel Hill *D*

Ohio
Case Western Reserve University *D*
Kent State University *M, D*
Kenyon College *B*
Muskingum College *B*
Oberlin College *B*
Ohio Wesleyan University *B*

Oregon
University of Oregon *M, D*

Pennsylvania
Allegheny College *B*
Bryn Mawr College *B, M, D*
Cedar Crest College *B*
Chatham College *B*
Franklin and Marshall College *B*
King's College *B*
Lehigh University *B*
MCP Hahnemann University *D*
Penn State
 College of Medicine, Milton S.
 Hershey Medical Center *M, D*
University of Pennsylvania *B, M, D*
University of Pittsburgh *B, M, D*
University of Scranton *B*

Rhode Island
Brown University *B, M, D*

Tennessee
University of Tennessee
 Memphis *D*

Texas
Texas Christian University *B*
University of Texas
 Austin *M, D*
 Dallas *B*
 Medical Branch at Galveston *D*
 San Antonio *M, D*
 Southwestern Medical Center at
 Dallas *M, D*

Utah
University of Utah *D*

Virginia
University of Virginia *D*
Washington and Lee University *B*

Washington
University of Washington *D*
Washington State University *B, M, D*

Wisconsin
Lawrence University *B, T*
University of Wisconsin
 Madison *M, D*

Nonprofit/public management

Alabama
Birmingham-Southern College *M*

California
California State University
 Hayward *C*
Hope International University *M*
Point Loma Nazarene University *C*
University of Judaism *M*

Colorado
Regis University *M*

Connecticut
Central Connecticut State University *B*
Quinnipiac University *B, M*

Florida
Hillsborough Community College *C, A*

Illinois
Barat College *B*
Lake Land College *A*

Indiana
Manchester College *A, B*

Maryland
College of Notre Dame of Maryland *M*

Massachusetts
Boston University *M*
Suffolk University *M*

Michigan
Andrews University *M*
University of Michigan
 Flint *M*

Minnesota
Hamline University *M*
University of St. Thomas *M*

Missouri
Lindenwood University *M*
University of Missouri
 St. Louis *C*

New Hampshire
Antioch New England Graduate
 School *M*

New Jersey
Monmouth University *B*
Seton Hall University *C*

New York
City University of New York
 Baruch College *M*
Medaille College *C*
New York University *M*
Pace University:
 Pleasantville/Briarcliff *B, M*
Pace University *B, M*
State University of New York
 College at Brockport *M*

North Carolina
Brevard College *B*

Ohio
Case Western Reserve University *M*
Franklin University *M*
Kent State University *M*

Pennsylvania
Alvernia College *M*
Eastern College *M*
La Salle University *B*
Penn State
 University Park *C*
Philadelphia College of Bible *M*

South Dakota
Dakota State University *C*

Tennessee
Austin Peay State University *B*
East Tennessee State University *M*
Southern Adventist University *B, M*

Texas
Stephen F. Austin State University *B*
Texas Wesleyan University *C*
University of Texas
 Dallas *D*

Washington
Seattle University *M*

West Virginia
Glenville State College *B*

Wisconsin
University of Wisconsin
 Green Bay *M*
 Madison *M*

Nuclear engineering

Arizona
University of Arizona B, M, D

Arkansas
Arkansas Tech University A

California
University of California
   Berkeley B, M, D
University of Southern California M

Florida
University of Florida B, M, D

Georgia
Georgia Institute of Technology B, M, D

Idaho
Idaho State University M, D
University of Idaho M, D

Illinois
Joliet Junior College C, A
Parkland College A
University of Illinois
   Urbana-Champaign B, M, D

Indiana
Purdue University B, M, D

Louisiana
Louisiana State University and
   Agricultural and Mechanical
   College M

Maryland
University of Maryland
   College Park B, M, D

Massachusetts
Massachusetts Institute of
   Technology B, M, D
Worcester Polytechnic Institute B, M

Michigan
University of Michigan B, M, D

Missouri
East Central College A
University of Missouri
   Columbia M, D
   Rolla B, M, D

New Mexico
University of New Mexico B, M

New York
Columbia University
   Fu Foundation School of
      Engineering and Applied
      Science M, D
Cornell University M, D
Pace University B
Rensselaer Polytechnic Institute B, M, D
United States Military Academy B

North Carolina
North Carolina State University B, M, D

Ohio
Ohio State University
   Columbus Campus M, D
University of Cincinnati B, M, D

Oregon
Oregon State University B, M, D

Pennsylvania
Gettysburg College B
Penn State
   University Park B, M, D

Tennessee
University of Tennessee
   Knoxville B, M, D

Texas
Texas A&M University B, M, D

Utah
University of Utah M, D

Virginia
University of Virginia M, D

Washington
University of Washington M, D

Wisconsin
University of Wisconsin
   Madison B, M, D

Nuclear medical technology

Alabama
Community College of the Air Force A
Enterprise State Junior College A
Faulkner University A
Shelton State Community College A
University of Alabama
   Birmingham B

Arizona
Gateway Community College C, A

Arkansas
University of Arkansas
   for Medical Sciences B
University of Central Arkansas B

California
California State University
   Dominguez Hills B
Loma Linda University C

Connecticut
Gateway Community College A
Middlesex Community-Technical
   College C, A

Delaware
Delaware Technical and Community
   College
      Stanton/Wilmington Campus A

District of Columbia
George Washington University C, A, B

Florida
Barry University B
Broward Community College A
Hillsborough Community College A
Manatee Community College A
Polk Community College A
Santa Fe Community College A
University of Miami B
Valencia Community College A

Georgia
Dalton State College A
Medical College of Georgia B, M

Illinois
Benedictine University B
College of DuPage C
Roosevelt University B
Triton College A
University of St. Francis B

Indiana
Ball State University A
Indiana University
   Bloomington B
Indiana University--Purdue University
   Indiana University-Purdue
      University Indianapolis B

Iowa
University of Iowa B

Kentucky
Lexington Community College A
University of Louisville B

Louisiana
Delgado Community College C

Maryland
Howard Community College A
Prince George's Community
   College C, A

Massachusetts
Bunker Hill Community College A
Laboure College A
Massachusetts College of Pharmacy and
   Health Sciences B
Salem State College B
Springfield Technical Community
   College A
Suffolk University B

Michigan
Ferris State University A, B
Lansing Community College A
Oakland Community College A

Minnesota
St. Cloud State University B
St. Mary's University of Minnesota B

Mississippi
University of Mississippi
   Medical Center C

Missouri
St. Louis University B

Nevada
University of Nevada
   Las Vegas B

New Jersey
Gloucester County College A
Thomas Edison State College B
University of Medicine and Dentistry of
   New Jersey
      School of Health Related
         Professions C, B

New Mexico
University of New Mexico C

New York
City University of New York
   Bronx Community College A
Hudson Valley Community College C
Long Island University
   C. W. Post Campus B
Manhattan College B
Molloy College A
Rochester Institute of Technology C, B
State University of New York
   Buffalo B

North Carolina
Caldwell Community College and
   Technical Institute A
Forsyth Technical Community College A
Pitt Community College A
University of North Carolina
   Chapel Hill C

Ohio
Lorain County Community College A
Notre Dame College of Ohio B
Owens Community College
   Toledo C
University of Cincinnati
   Raymond Walters College A
University of Cincinnati B
University of Findlay C, A, B

Oregon
Oregon Health Sciences University C

Pennsylvania
Cedar Crest College C, B
Community College of Allegheny
   County C, A
Harrisburg Area Community College A
York College of Pennsylvania B

Puerto Rico
University of Puerto Rico
   Medical Sciences Campus B

South Dakota
Southeast Technical Institute A

Tennessee
Chattanooga State Technical Community
   College C

Texas
Amarillo College A
El Paso Community College C
Galveston College C, A
Houston Community College
   System C, A
University of the Incarnate Word B

Utah
Brigham Young University B
Weber State University B

Vermont
University of Vermont B

Virginia
Old Dominion University B

West Virginia
West Virginia State College A
Wheeling Jesuit University B

Wisconsin
University of Wisconsin
   La Crosse B
   Madison B, M, D

Nuclear physics

Iowa
Iowa State University M, D

Massachusetts
Worcester Polytechnic Institute B, M

New York
Columbia University
   Graduate School M, D

Rhode Island
Brown University B, M, D

Texas
University of North Texas M, D
University of Texas
   Arlington M

Nuclear/industrial radiologic technologies

Alabama
Community College of the Air Force A
Northwest-Shoals Community College A

California
Las Positas College C, A

Connecticut
Three Rivers Community-Technical
   College A

Florida
Hillsborough Community College C, A

Massachusetts
Suffolk University B

Michigan
Lake Michigan College A

New Jersey
Thomas Edison State College A, B

New York
City University of New York
   Bronx Community College A
Regents College A, B

Ohio
University of Findlay A
Xavier University A

Oregon
Oregon Institute of Technology *B*

South Carolina
Aiken Technical College *A*

South Dakota
Southeast Technical Institute *A*

Texas
Texas State Technical College
 Waco *C, A*
University of North Texas *B*

Washington
Columbia Basin College *A*

Wisconsin
Lakeshore Technical College *A*

Nursery operations

Alabama
Shelton State Community College *C*

California
College of the Redwoods *C*
College of the Sequoias *C*
Foothill College *C, A*
Los Angeles Pierce College *C*
MiraCosta College *C, A*
Modesto Junior College *C*
Santa Rosa Junior College *C*
Southwestern College *C, A*
Yuba College *C*

Florida
Central Florida Community College *C*
South Florida Community College *C*

Illinois
College of DuPage *C*
Joliet Junior College *C, A*
Kishwaukee College *C, A*
Southwestern Illinois College *A*
William Rainey Harper College *C, A*

Iowa
Indian Hills Community College *C*
Kirkwood Community College *A*

Kansas
Dodge City Community College *C*

Michigan
Northwestern Michigan College *A*

Minnesota
Anoka-Ramsey Community College *A*

Nebraska
Metropolitan Community College *C, A*
Nebraska College of Technical
 Agriculture *A*

New Hampshire
University of New Hampshire *A*

New York
State University of New York
 College of Agriculture and
 Technology at Cobleskill *A*

North Dakota
Minot State University: Bottineau
 Campus *A*

Ohio
Ohio State University
 Agricultural Technical Institute *A*

Pennsylvania
Community College of Allegheny
 County *C*
Penn State
 University Park *C*
Pennsylvania College of Technology *A*

South Dakota
Southeast Technical Institute *A*

Tennessee
Tennessee Technological University *B*

Texas
Western Texas College *C, A*

Washington
Clark College *C*
Edmonds Community College *A*
South Seattle Community College *C, A*
Spokane Community College *A*

Nursing

Alabama
Central Alabama Community College *A*
George C. Wallace State Community
 College
 Selma *A*
Jacksonville State University *B, M*
Northeast Alabama Community
 College *A*
Northwest-Shoals Community College *A*
Oakwood College *A, B*
Shelton State Community College *C*
Spring Hill College *B*
Tuskegee University *B*
University of Alabama *B*
University of Mobile *A, B, M*

Arizona
Arizona State University *B, M*
Arizona Western College *A*
Central Arizona College *C, A*
Cochise College *A*
Gateway Community College *C, A*
Glendale Community College *A*
Grand Canyon University *B*
Phoenix College *A*
Scottsdale Community College *C*
University of Arizona *M, D*
University of Phoenix *B, M*
Yavapai College *A*

Arkansas
Arkansas State University
 Beebe Branch *A*
 Mountain Home *A*
Harding University *B*
Phillips Community College of the
 University of Arkansas *A*
Southern Arkansas University
 Tech *A*
Southern Arkansas University *B*
University of Central Arkansas *B, M*
Westark College *A*

California
Azusa Pacific University *M*
Butte College *C, A*
California State University
 Bakersfield *B, M*
 Dominguez Hills *M*
 Fresno *B, M*
 Fullerton *B*
 Hayward *B, M*
 Long Beach *B, M*
 Los Angeles *B, M*
 Sacramento *B, M*
City College of San Francisco *C, A*
College of the Canyons *A*
College of the Redwoods *C*
Compton Community College *C, A*
Humboldt State University *B*
Loma Linda University *M*
MiraCosta College *C, A*
Modesto Junior College *A*
Moorpark College *C, A*
St. Mary's College of California *B*
Samuel Merritt College *B, M*
San Bernardino Valley College *A*
San Francisco State University *B, M*
San Jose State University *B, M*
Santa Ana College *A*
Shasta College *A*
Sierra College *A*

Southwestern College *A*
University of California
 Los Angeles *B, M, D*
University of Southern California *B, M*
Ventura College *C, A*

Colorado
Community College of Denver *A*
Morgan Community College *A*
Regis University *B*
Trinidad State Junior College *C, A*
University of Colorado
 Colorado Springs *M*
 Health Sciences Center *B, M, D*

Connecticut
Capital Community College *A*
Fairfield University *B, M*
Quinnipiac University *B, M*
Sacred Heart University *B, M*
Southern Connecticut State University *B*
Three Rivers Community-Technical
 College *A*
Western Connecticut State
 University *B, M*
Yale University *M, D*

Delaware
University of Delaware *B, M*
Wesley College *A, M*

District of Columbia
Catholic University of America *B, M, D*
Georgetown University *M*
Howard University *B, M*

Florida
Barry University *B, M, D*
Broward Community College *A*
Daytona Beach Community College *A*
Florida Gulf Coast University *B*
Florida Southern College *B*
Florida State University *B, M*
Gulf Coast Community College *A*
Hillsborough Community College *C, A*
Indian River Community College *A*
Jacksonville University *B*
Lake City Community College *C*
Manatee Community College *A*
Santa Fe Community College *A*
University of Central Florida *B*
University of Miami *B, M, D*
University of South Florida *B, M, D*
University of Tampa *B*

Georgia
Abraham Baldwin Agricultural
 College *A*
Albany State University *M*
Armstrong Atlantic State
 University *A, B, M*
Athens Area Technical Institute *A*
Atlanta Metropolitan College *A*
Brenau University *B, M*
Brewton-Parker College *A*
Clayton College and State
 University *A, B*
Columbus State University *B*
Darton College *A*
East Georgia College *A*
Emory University *B*
Georgia College and State
 University *B, M*
Georgia Military College *A*
Kennesaw State University *B*
LaGrange College *B*
Medical College of Georgia *B, M, D*
Morris Brown College *B*
North Georgia College & State
 University *A, B*
Oxford College of Emory University *B*
Reinhardt College *A*
South Georgia College *A*
State University of West Georgia *B*
Thomas College *B*
Valdosta State University *B, M*
Waycross College *A*

Hawaii
University of Hawaii
 Hawaii Community College *A*
 Hilo *B*
 Kapiolani Community College *A*
 Manoa *M, D*
 Maui Community College *C, A*

Idaho
Idaho State University *M*
Lewis-Clark State College *B*
North Idaho College *A*

Illinois
Black Hawk College
 East Campus *A*
Black Hawk College *C, A*
Bradley University *M*
Chicago State University *B*
City Colleges of Chicago
 Harold Washington College *C*
 Kennedy-King College *A*
 Malcolm X College *A*
 Olive-Harvey College *A*
 Wright College *C*
De Paul University *B, M*
Elmhurst College *B*
Governors State University *M*
Highland Community College *C*
Illinois College *B*
John A. Logan College *A*
Kaskaskia College *A*
Kishwaukee College *C, A*
Lewis University *B, M*
Lincoln Land Community College *A*
Loyola University of Chicago *B, M, D*
MacMurray College *B*
McHenry County College *C*
McKendree College *B*
Moraine Valley Community College *A*
Morton College *A*
North Park University *M*
Northern Illinois University *M*
Olivet Nazarene University *B*
Prairie State College *A*
Quincy University *A, B*
Rend Lake College *C, A*
Rockford College *B*
St. Xavier University *C, M*
Sauk Valley Community College *A*
Shawnee Community College *C, A*
Southwestern Illinois College *A*
Spoon River College *C*
Trinity Christian College *B*
University of Illinois
 Chicago *M*
Wheaton College *B*
William Rainey Harper College *A*

Indiana
Ball State University *A, B*
Goshen College *B*
Indiana State University *A, B, M*
Indiana University
 East *A, B*
 Kokomo *A, B*
Indiana University--Purdue University
 Indiana University-Purdue
 University
 Indianapolis *A, B, M, D*
Indiana Wesleyan University *B, M*
Ivy Tech State College
 Eastcentral *A*
 Lafayette *A*
 Wabash Valley *A*
Marian College *A, B*
Purdue University
 Calumet *B, M*
 North Central Campus *A*
University of Evansville *B*
University of St. Francis *B, M*
University of Southern Indiana *A, B*
Valparaiso University *B, M*

Iowa
Briar Cliff College *B*

Nursing

Clarke College *B, M*
Coe College *B*
Des Moines Area Community College *A*
Graceland University *M*
Grand View College *B*
Iowa Lakes Community College *A*
Marycrest International University *B*
Morningside College *B*
Mount Mercy College *B*
North Iowa Area Community College *A*
Northeast Iowa Community College *A*
St. Ambrose University *B*
Scott Community College *A*
Southeastern Community College
    North Campus *C*
University of Iowa *B, M, D*
Waldorf College *A*

Kansas
Baker University *B*
Butler County Community College *C, A*
Central Christian College *A*
Colby Community College *C*
Emporia State University *B*
Fort Hays State University *B, M*
Hutchinson Community College *A*
Kansas City Kansas Community
    College *A*
MidAmerica Nazarene University *B*
Pittsburg State University *M*
Pratt Community College *A*
Seward County Community
    College *C, A*
University of Kansas
    Medical Center *B, M, D*
Wichita State University *B, M*

Kentucky
Asbury College *B*
Elizabethtown Community College *A*
Henderson Community College *A*
Hopkinsville Community College *A*
Kentucky State University *A*
Kentucky Wesleyan College *B*
Lexington Community College *A*
Madisonville Community College *A*
Morehead State University *B*
Murray State University *M*
Northern Kentucky University *A, B, M*
Paducah Community College *A*
St. Catharine College *A*
Spalding University *B, M, T*
Thomas More College *B*
University of Kentucky *D*

Louisiana
Dillard University *B*
Louisiana State University
    Alexandria *A*
Louisiana State University Medical
    Center *A, B*
Louisiana Tech University *A*
Loyola University New Orleans *B, M*
McNeese State University *M*
Nicholls State University *A, B*
Our Lady of Holy Cross College *B, M*
Southeastern Louisiana University *M*
Southern University and Agricultural and
    Mechanical College *M*
University of Louisiana at Lafayette *M*

Maine
Eastern Maine Technical College *C*
Husson College *B*
Kennebec Valley Technical College *A*
St. Joseph's College *B*
University of Maine
    Augusta *A*
    Fort Kent *B*
University of Maine *B*
University of New England *A, B*
University of Southern Maine *B, M*

Maryland
Anne Arundel Community College *A*
Baltimore City Community College *A*
Cecil Community College *A*
Charles County Community College *A*
College of Notre Dame of Maryland *B*
Coppin State College *B, M*
Johns Hopkins University *M, D*
Montgomery College
    Germantown Campus *A*
    Rockville Campus *A*
    Takoma Park Campus *A*
Salisbury State University *B, M*
Towson University *B*
University of Maryland
    Baltimore *B, M, D*
Villa Julie College *B*

Massachusetts
Anna Maria College *B*
Atlantic Union College *A, B*
Berkshire Community College *A*
Boston College *B, M, D*
Curry College *B*
Elms College *B*
Greenfield Community College *A*
Holyoke Community College *A*
Labouré College *A*
MGH Institute of Health Professions *M*
Northeastern University *B, M*
Regis College *B, M*
Roxbury Community College *A*
Salem State College *B, M*
University of Massachusetts
    Boston *B, M, D*
    Dartmouth *B, M*
    Lowell *M, D*
Worcester State College *B*

Michigan
Andrews University *B, M*
Calvin College *B*
Glen Oaks Community College *C*
Gogebic Community College *A*
Grand Rapids Community College *A*
Grand Valley State University *B, M*
Henry Ford Community College *A*
Kalamazoo Valley Community
    College *C*
Kirtland Community College *C*
Lansing Community College *A*
Macomb Community College *A*
Madonna University *B, M*
Michigan State University *B, M*
Northern Michigan University *B, M*
Oakland Community College *A*
Oakland University *M*
Schoolcraft College *A*
University of Detroit Mercy *B*
University of Michigan
    Flint *B, M*
University of Michigan *M, D*
Wayne State University *C*
West Shore Community College *C*

Minnesota
Augsburg College *B, M*
Bethel College *B, M*
Central Lakes College *A*
College of St. Catherine: St. Paul
    Campus *B, M*
College of St. Scholastica *M*
Hennepin Technical College *C, A*
Metropolitan State University *B, M*
Moorhead State University *B*
Pine Technical College *C, A*
Ridgewater College: A Community and
    Technical College *A*
University of Minnesota
    Twin Cities *B*
Winona State University *B, M*

Mississippi
Alcorn State University *M*
East Central Community College *A*
Hinds Community College *A*
Holmes Community College *A*
Jackson State University *B*
Mary Holmes College *A*
Meridian Community College *A*
Mississippi College *B*
Mississippi Delta Community College *A*
Mississippi Gulf Coast Community
    College
    Jackson County Campus *A*
    Perkinston *C, A*
Mississippi University for
    Women *A, B, M*
Northeast Mississippi Community
    College *A*
Northwest Mississippi Community
    College *A*
University of Mississippi
    Medical Center *B, M, D*
University of Southern Mississippi *D*
William Carey College *B*

Missouri
Central Methodist College *B*
Columbia College *A*
Deaconess College of Nursing *A, B*
Hannibal-LaGrange College *A*
Longview Community College *A*
Maple Woods Community College *A*
Maryville University of Saint Louis *B, M*
Mineral Area College *C*
Ozarks Technical Community College *C*
Research College of Nursing *B, M*
Rockhurst University *B*
Southeast Missouri State
    University *A, B, M*
Southwest Missouri State University *M*
St. Louis Community College
    St. Louis Community College at
        Florissant Valley *A*
    St. Louis Community College at
        Forest Park *A*
    St. Louis Community College at
        Meramec *A*
University of Missouri
    St. Louis *B, M, D*

Montana
Carroll College *B*
Montana State University
    Northern *A, B*

Nebraska
Central Community College *C, A*
Clarkson College *B, M*
College of Saint Mary *A, B*
Creighton University *B, M*
Midland Lutheran College *B*
Nebraska Methodist College of Nursing
    and Allied Health *M*
Union College *B*

Nevada
Community College of Southern
    Nevada *A*

New Hampshire
New Hampshire Community Technical
    College
    Claremont *C, A*
Rivier College *A, B, M*
University of New Hampshire *B, M*

New Jersey
Atlantic Cape Community College *A*
Bloomfield College *B*
Essex County College *A*
Felician College *A, B, M*
Gloucester County College *A*
Kean University *B, M*
Monmouth University *B, M*
New Jersey City University *B*
New Jersey Institute of Technology *B*
Rutgers
    The State University of New Jersey:
        Camden College of Arts and
        Sciences *B*
    The State University of New Jersey:
        College of Nursing *B*
    The State University of New Jersey:
        Newark Graduate Campus *M, D*
    The State University of New Jersey:
        University College Camden *B*
Seton Hall University *C, B, M*
The College of New Jersey *B, M*
Union County College *A*
University of Medicine and Dentistry of
    New Jersey
    School of Nursing *A, B, M*
William Paterson University of New
    Jersey *B, M*

New Mexico
Clovis Community College *C, A*
Dona Ana Branch Community College of
    New Mexico State University *C, A*
Eastern New Mexico University
    Roswell Campus *C, A*
New Mexico Junior College *A*
New Mexico State University
    Alamogordo *C, A*
Northern New Mexico Community
    College *A*
Western New Mexico University *A*

New York
Adelphi University *M, D*
City University of New York
    Borough of Manhattan Community
        College *A*
    College of Staten Island *A*
    Hunter College *M*
    La Guardia Community College *A*
    Lehman College *M*
    Medgar Evers College *A, B*
    New York City Technical
        College *A*
College of Mount St. Vincent *B*
College of New Rochelle *B, M*
Columbia University
    School of Nursing *B, M, D*
Concordia College *B*
D'Youville College *B, M*
Dominican College of Blauvelt *B, M*
Elmira College *B*
Iona College *A*
Long Island University
    Brooklyn Campus *B*
Mercy College *M*
Molloy College *B, M*
Mount St. Mary College *B, M*
New York Institute of Technology *B*
New York University *B, M, D*
Niagara University *B*
North Country Community College *C*
Onondaga Community College *A*
Orange County Community College *A*
Pace University:
    Pleasantville/Briarcliff *B, M, D*
Pace University *B, M, D*
Russell Sage College *B*
St. John Fisher College *B*
St. Joseph's College
    St. Joseph's College *B*
State University of New York
    Binghamton *B, M, D*
    Buffalo *B, M, D*
    College at Brockport *B*
    College at Plattsburgh *B*
    Health Science Center at
        Brooklyn *B*
    Health Science Center at Stony
        Brook *B, M*
    Institute of Technology at
        Utica/Rome *B, M*
    Stony Brook *B, M*
Syracuse University *B, M*
University of Rochester *M, D*

North Carolina
Asheville Buncombe Technical Community College *A*
Barton College *B*
Cape Fear Community College *C, A*
Cleveland Community College *A*
Duke University *M*
East Carolina University *M*
Edgecombe Community College *C*
Gardner-Webb University *A*
Johnston Community College *A*
Louisburg College *A*
Mayland Community College *C*
North Carolina Agricultural and Technical State University *B*
Queens College *M*
Southwestern Community College *A*
Surry Community College *A*
University of North Carolina
   Chapel Hill *B, M, D*
   Charlotte *M*
   Pembroke *B*
Vance-Granville Community College *C*
Wilson Technical Community College *A*
Winston-Salem State University *B*

North Dakota
Dickinson State University *A, B*
University of Mary *B, M*
University of North Dakota *M*

Ohio
Capital University *B, M*
Case Western Reserve University *B, M, D*
Circleville Bible College *A*
Franciscan University of Steubenville *B, M*
Franklin University *B*
Kent State University
   East Liverpool Regional Campus *A*
   Stark Campus *B*
Kent State University *C, B, M*
Lorain County Community College *A*
Malone College *B*
Miami University
   Oxford Campus *A*
Northwest State Community College *C, A*
Ohio State University
   Columbus Campus *B, M, D*
Ohio University
   Chillicothe Campus *A*
   Eastern Campus *B*
   Zanesville Campus *B*
Ohio University *A*
Otterbein College *B*
Sinclair Community College *A*
University of Akron *B, M*
University of Cincinnati
   Raymond Walters College *A*
University of Cincinnati *M, D*
Walsh University *A, B*
Washington State Community College *C*
Wright State University *M*
Xavier University *B*
Youngstown State University *B, M*

Oklahoma
Cameron University *A*
Connors State College *A*
East Central University *B*
Eastern Oklahoma State College *A*
Langston University *B*
Murray State College *A*
Northern Oklahoma College *A*
Oklahoma State University
   Oklahoma City *A*
Southern Nazarene University *B*
Tulsa Community College *A*
University of Central Oklahoma *B*
University of Tulsa *B, M*
Western Oklahoma State College *A*

Oregon
Chemeketa Community College *A*
Eastern Oregon University *B*
Mount Hood Community College *A*
Portland Community College *A*
University of Portland *B, M*

Pennsylvania
Allentown College of St. Francis de Sales *B, M*
Butler County Community College *A*
California University of Pennsylvania *A*
Carlow College *B, M*
Cedar Crest College *B*
College Misericordia *B, M*
Community College of Allegheny County *C, A*
Duquesne University *M, D*
East Stroudsburg University of Pennsylvania *B*
Eastern College *B*
Edinboro University of Pennsylvania *B, M*
Elizabethtown College *B*
Gannon University *B*
Gwynedd-Mercy College *B*
Holy Family College *B, M*
Indiana University of Pennsylvania *B, M*
La Roche College *B, M*
La Salle University *B*
Mansfield University of Pennsylvania *B*
Mercyhurst College *A*
Millersville University of Pennsylvania *B, M, T*
Montgomery County Community College *A*
Neumann College *B, M*
St. Francis College *B*
Seton Hill College *B*
Thiel College *B*
Thomas Jefferson University: College of Health Professions *B*
University of Pittsburgh
   Bradford *B*
University of Pittsburgh *M, D*
Villanova University *M*
Waynesburg College *B*
West Chester University of Pennsylvania *B, M*
Widener University *B*
York College of Pennsylvania *B*

Puerto Rico
Bayamon Central University *A, B*
Caribbean University *B*
Columbia College *A*
Inter American University of Puerto Rico
   Aguadilla Campus *A, B*
   Barranquitas Campus *A, B*
   Guayama Campus *A, B*
   Metropolitan Campus *B*
   San German Campus *B*
Pontifical Catholic University of Puerto Rico *B, M*
Technological College of San Juan *C, A*
Universidad Metropolitana *A, B*
University of Puerto Rico
   Arecibo Campus *A, B*
   Medical Sciences Campus *M*
University of the Sacred Heart *A, B*

Rhode Island
Rhode Island College *B*
Salve Regina University *B*
University of Rhode Island *M, D*

South Carolina
Anderson College *A*
Charleston Southern University *B*
Clemson University *B, M*
South Carolina State University *B*
Technical College of the Lowcountry *C*
University of South Carolina *B, M, D*
York Technical College *A*

South Dakota
Augustana College *B*
Huron University *A, B*
Mount Marty College *B*
South Dakota State University *B, M*

Tennessee
Belmont University *B, M*
Carson-Newman College *B, M*
Chattanooga State Technical Community College *A*
Columbia State Community College *A*
East Tennessee State University *B, M*
Hiwassee College *A*
King College *B*
Maryville College *B*
Milligan College *B*
Motlow State Community College *A*
Roane State Community College *A*
Tennessee State University *A, B, M*
Tennessee Technological University *B*
Tennessee Wesleyan College *B*
Union University *B*
University of Tennessee
   Chattanooga *M*
   Knoxville *B, M, D*
   Memphis *B*

Texas
Alvin Community College *C*
Amarillo College *A*
Angelo State University *A, B, M*
Austin Community College *C, A*
Blinn College *A*
Central Texas College *C, A*
College of the Mainland *A*
Galveston College *A*
Grayson County College *C*
Hill College *C, A*
Houston Community College System *A*
Lee College *A*
Lubbock Christian University *B*
McMurry University *B*
Midland College *A*
Midwestern State University *B, M*
Navarro College *C, A*
North Central Texas College *A*
Odessa College *A*
Paris Junior College *A*
San Antonio College *A*
Temple College *A*
Texas A&M University
   Corpus Christi *B*
Texas Tech University Health Science Center *M, D*
Texas Woman's University *C, M*
Tyler Junior College *C, A*
University of Texas
   Arlington *M*
   El Paso *B, M*
   Medical Branch at Galveston *M*
   Pan American *A, B, M*
   Tyler *B, M*
University of the Incarnate Word *B*
West Texas A&M University *M*

Utah
Brigham Young University *B, M*
College of Eastern Utah *C, A*
Salt Lake Community College *A*
Snow College *A*
Southern Utah University *A*
Utah Valley State College *A*
Westminster College *B, M*

Vermont
Norwich University *B*
Southern Vermont College *A, B*
University of Vermont *B, M*

Virginia
Blue Ridge Community College *A*
Dabney S. Lancaster Community College *A*
Eastern Mennonite University *B*
Eastern Shore Community College *A*
Germanna Community College *A*
Hampton University *B, M*
John Tyler Community College *A*
Liberty University *B*
Lynchburg College *B*
Northern Virginia Community College *A*
Patrick Henry Community College *A*
Radford University *B, M*
Southwest Virginia Community College *C*
Thomas Nelson Community College *A*
Virginia Commonwealth University *C, B, M, D*
Virginia Highlands Community College *A*
Virginia Western Community College *A*
Wytheville Community College *A*

Washington
Clark College *A*
Columbia Basin College *A*
Eastern Washington University *B, M*
Everett Community College *A*
Gonzaga University *B, M*
Highline Community College *A*
Lower Columbia College *A*
Olympic College *A*
Pacific Lutheran University *B, M*
Seattle Central Community College *A*
Seattle Pacific University *M*
Seattle University *B*
Skagit Valley College *C, A*
Spokane Falls Community College *C*
University of Washington *B, M, D*
Wenatchee Valley College *A*
Whatcom Community College *A*
Whitworth College *B, M*

West Virginia
Bluefield State College *B*
College of West Virginia *B*
Glenville State College *B*
Marshall University *B, M*
Shepherd College *B*
Southern West Virginia Community and Technical College *A*
West Liberty State College *B*
West Virginia University Parkersburg *A*
West Virginia University Institute of Technology *B*
Wheeling Jesuit University *B, M*

Wisconsin
Alverno College *B*
Bellin College of Nursing *B*
Cardinal Stritch University *A*
Columbia College of Nursing *B*
Concordia University Wisconsin *B*
Lakeshore Technical College *A*
Marian College of Fond du Lac *B*
Marquette University *B, M*
Milwaukee Area Technical College *A*
Milwaukee School of Engineering *B*
Moraine Park Technical College *C*
Northeast Wisconsin Technical College *A*
University of Wisconsin
   Eau Claire *B, M*
   Green Bay *B*
   Madison *M, D*
Viterbo University *B*

Wyoming
Casper College *A*
Laramie County Community College *A*
Northwest College *C, A*
Sheridan College *C, A*

Nursing (Post-RN)

California
Compton Community College *A*
De Anza College *C*
Holy Names College *B, M*
Loma Linda University *B, M*
National University *B, M*
Samuel Merritt College *C, M*
Solano Community College *A*
Sonoma State University *M*

Nursing (Post-RN)

University of California
Los Angeles *M, D*
San Francisco *M*
University of San Diego *M*
University of Southern California *M*

Colorado
University of Colorado
Colorado Springs *M*

Connecticut
Quinnipiac University *M*

Florida
Indian River Community College *C*
Lynn University *B*
Polk Community College *C*
University of Miami *B*

Georgia
Valdosta State University *B*

Illinois
Benedictine University *B*
Governors State University *B*
McKendree College *B*
Millikin University *B*
Rockford College *B*
St. Xavier University *M*
Southern Illinois University
Edwardsville *M*
University of Illinois
Chicago *M, D*

Indiana
Ball State University *M*
Purdue University
Calumet *B*
St. Joseph's College *B*
University of Indianapolis *B*
University of St. Francis *B*
Valparaiso University *B, M*

Iowa
Graceland University *B*
Hawkeye Community College *C*

Kansas
Kansas Wesleyan University *B*
Newman University *M*
Wichita State University *B, M*

Kentucky
Bellarmine College *B, M*
Eastern Kentucky University *B, M*
Murray State University *M*
University of Kentucky *B, M*
University of Louisville *B, M*
Western Kentucky University *B, M*

Louisiana
Northwestern State University *M*

Maine
Eastern Maine Technical College *A*
Husson College *M*
University of Maine *M*
University of Southern Maine *B*

Massachusetts
Berkshire Community College *A*
Emmanuel College *B*
Framingham State College *B*
MGH Institute of Health Professions *M*
Massachusetts College of Pharmacy and Health Sciences *B, M*
Northeastern University *M*
Salem State College *M*
Worcester State College *B*

Michigan
Great Lakes College *B*
Wayne County Community College *A*
Wayne State University *M*

Minnesota
Bemidji State University *B*
College of St. Scholastica *B*
Minneapolis Community and Technical College *A*

Minnesota State University, Mankato *M*
Winona State University *B, M*

Mississippi
Mississippi University for Women *T*

Missouri
Drury University *B*
Maryville University of Saint Louis *B*
Missouri Baptist College *B*
Southwest Baptist University *B*
Southwest Missouri State University *B*
University of Missouri
Kansas City *B, M, D*
Webster University *B, M*

Nebraska
Clarkson College *B, M*
Midland Lutheran College *B*
Nebraska Wesleyan University *B*
Northeast Community College *A*

New Hampshire
Rivier College *B, M*

New Jersey
College of St. Elizabeth *B*
Ramapo College of New Jersey *B*
Richard Stockton College of New Jersey *B*
St. Peter's College *B, M*
The College of New Jersey *B*
Thomas Edison State College *B*

New York
College of Mount St. Vincent *B*
Columbia University
School of Nursing *B, M, D*
D'Youville College *B, M*
Daemen College *C, B, M*
Long Island University
C. W. Post Campus *B, M*
Southampton College *B*
Molloy College *B, M*
Nazareth College of Rochester *B*
New York University *M, D*
Pace University:
Pleasantville/Briarcliff *B*
Pace University *B*
Roberts Wesleyan College *B*
St. John Fisher College *B*
St. Joseph's College
St. Joseph's College: Suffolk Campus *B*
State University of New York
Health Science Center at Stony Brook *M*
Institute of Technology at Utica/Rome *M*
New Paltz *B, M*
Upstate Medical University *M*

North Carolina
University of North Carolina
Chapel Hill *M, D*

Ohio
Capital University *B*
Case Western Reserve University *M*
Kent State University
Ashtabula Regional Campus *B*
Lourdes College *B*
Miami University
Hamilton Campus *B*
Middletown Campus *B*
Ohio University *B*

Oklahoma
Northeastern Oklahoma Agricultural and Mechanical College *A*
Northeastern State University *B*
Rose State College *A*

Oregon
Eastern Oregon University *B*
Oregon Health Sciences University *M, D*
Southern Oregon University *B*

Pennsylvania
Allentown College of St. Francis de Sales *B, M*
Alvernia College *B*
California University of Pennsylvania *B*
Delaware County Community College *C*
Holy Family College *B, M*
La Salle University *M*
Luzerne County Community College *C*
MCP Hahnemann University *M*
Mansfield University of Pennsylvania *B*
Mount Aloysius College *B*
Penn State
Harrisburg *B*
Thomas Jefferson University: College of Health Professions *M*
University of Pennsylvania *M, D*
University of Pittsburgh *M*

South Carolina
Greenville Technical College *C*
University of South Carolina *M*

Tennessee
Southern Adventist University *B*
University of Tennessee
Knoxville *B*

Texas
East Texas Baptist University *B*
Lamar State College at Orange *A*
Lee College *C*
South Plains College *A*
Texas A&M International University *B*
Texas A&M University
Corpus Christi *M*
University of Texas
Arlington *M*
Medical Branch at Galveston *M*
Pan American *M*

Utah
Brigham Young University *M*

Vermont
University of Vermont *C*

Virginia
J. Sargeant Reynolds Community College *C*
Virginia Commonwealth University *M, D*

West Virginia
Marshall University *M*
Wheeling Jesuit University *B*

Wisconsin
Cardinal Stritch University *M*
Marian College of Fond du Lac *B*
University of Wisconsin
Green Bay *B*
Madison *M, D*

Nursing (RN)

Alabama
Auburn University at Montgomery *B*
Auburn University *B*
Bevill State Community College *A*
Calhoun Community College *A*
Chattahoochee Valley Community College *A*
Gadsden State Community College *A*
Jacksonville State University *B, M*
Jefferson Davis Community College *A*
Jefferson State Community College *A*
Lawson State Community College *A*
Northeast Alabama Community College *A*
Northwest-Shoals Community College *A*
Samford University *A, B, M*
Shelton State Community College *A*
Troy State University *A, B, M*
University of Alabama
Birmingham *B, M, D*
Huntsville *B, M*

University of North Alabama *B*
University of South Alabama *B, M*
University of West Alabama *B*
Wallace State Community College at Hanceville *A*

Alaska
University of Alaska
Anchorage *A, B, M*

Arizona
Arizona Western College *A*
Central Arizona College *C, A*
Cochise College *A*
Eastern Arizona College *A*
Gateway Community College *A*
Glendale Community College *C, A*
Grand Canyon University *B*
Mesa Community College *A*
Mohave Community College *A*
Northern Arizona University *B, M*
Northland Pioneer College *A*
Phoenix College *A*
Pima Community College *A*
Scottsdale Community College *A*
University of Arizona *B*
Yavapai College *A*

Arkansas
Arkansas State University
Mountain Home *A*
Arkansas State University *A, B, M*
Arkansas Tech University *B*
Garland County Community College *A*
Harding University *B*
Henderson State University *B*
Mississippi County Community College *A*
North Arkansas College *A*
Northwest Arkansas Community College *A*
Southern Arkansas University *A*
University of Arkansas
Little Rock *A*
Monticello *B*
Pine Bluff *B*
for Medical Sciences *B, M*
University of Arkansas *B*
Westark College *A*

California
Allan Hancock College *C, A*
American River College *A*
Azusa Pacific University *B*
Bakersfield College *A*
Biola University *B*
Butte College *A*
Cabrillo College *C, A*
California State University
Bakersfield *B*
Chico *B, M*
Dominguez Hills *B*
Fresno *B*
Long Beach *B*
Northridge *B*
Stanislaus *B*
Cerritos Community College *A*
Chabot College *A*
Chaffey Community College *A*
Citrus College *A*
College of San Mateo *A*
College of the Canyons *C*
College of the Desert *A*
College of the Redwoods *C*
College of the Sequoias *A*
Compton Community College *A*
Contra Costa College *A*
Cuesta College *C, A*
Cypress College *A*
De Anza College *A*
Dominican University of California *B*
East Los Angeles College *A*
Evergreen Valley College *A*
Fresno City College *A*
Gavilan Community College *C, A*
Glendale Community College *C, A*

Nursing (RN)

Golden West College C, A
Grossmont Community College A
Imperial Valley College A
Loma Linda University A, B
Long Beach City College C, A
Los Angeles Harbor College A
Los Angeles Pierce College A
Los Angeles Southwest College A
Los Angeles Valley College C, A
Los Medanos College A
Merced College C, A
Merritt College A
Mission College A
Modesto Junior College A
Monterey Peninsula College A
Moorpark College A
Mount St. Mary's College A, B
Mount San Antonio College C, A
Mount San Jacinto College A
Napa Valley College A
Ohlone College A
Pacific Union College A, B
Palomar College A
Pasadena City College C, A
Point Loma Nazarene University B
Rio Hondo College A
Riverside Community College A
Sacramento City College C, A
Saddleback College C, A
Samuel Merritt College B
San Diego City College A
San Diego State University B, M
San Joaquin Delta College C, A
Santa Ana College A
Santa Barbara City College A
Santa Monica College A
Santa Rosa Junior College C, A
Shasta College C, A
Sierra College A
Sonoma State University B
Southwestern College A
University of San Francisco B, M
University of Southern California B, M
Ventura College C, A
Victor Valley College C, A
Yuba College A

Colorado
Arapahoe Community College A
Colorado Mountain College
    Spring Valley Campus A
Community College of Denver A
Front Range Community College A
Mesa State College B
Metropolitan State College of Denver B
Morgan Community College A
Northeastern Junior College A
Otero Junior College A
Pikes Peak Community College A
Pueblo Community College A
University of Colorado
    Colorado Springs B
University of Northern Colorado B, M
University of Southern Colorado B

Connecticut
Central Connecticut State University B
Housatonic Community-Technical
    College A
Naugatuck Valley Community-Technical
    College A
Norwalk Community-Technical
    College A
Quinnipiac University B, M
St. Joseph College B, M
Southern Connecticut State University B
University of Connecticut B, M, D
University of Hartford B
Western Connecticut State University B
Yale University D

Delaware
Delaware State University B

Delaware Technical and Community
    College
    Owens Campus A
    Stanton/Wilmington Campus A
    Terry Campus A
Wilmington College B

District of Columbia
Catholic University of America B
Georgetown University B
University of the District of
    Columbia A, B

Florida
Barry University B
Bethune-Cookman College B
Brevard Community College A
Broward Community College A
Central Florida Community College A
Chipola Junior College A
Edison Community College A
Florida Agricultural and Mechanical
    University B
Florida Atlantic University B, M
Florida Community College at
    Jacksonville A
Florida International University B, M
Florida Keys Community College A
Florida State University B, M
Gulf Coast Community College A
Hillsborough Community College A
Indian River Community College A
Jacksonville University B
Lake City Community College A
Lake-Sumter Community College A
Miami-Dade Community College A
Palm Beach Community College A
Pasco-Hernando Community College A
Pensacola Junior College A
Polk Community College A
St. Petersburg Junior College A
Santa Fe Community College A
Seminole Community College A
South College: Palm Beach Campus B
South Florida Community College A
Tallahassee Community College A
University of Florida B, M, D
University of Miami D
University of North Florida B, M
Valencia Community College A

Georgia
Albany State University B
Augusta State University A
Coastal Georgia Community College A
Columbus State University B
Dalton State College A
Darton College A
Floyd College A
Georgia Baptist College of Nursing B
Georgia Perimeter College A
Georgia Southern University B
Georgia Southwestern State University B
Georgia State University B, M, D
Gordon College A
Kennesaw State University B, M
LaGrange College B
Macon State College A
Middle Georgia College A
North Georgia College & State
    University A, B, M
Piedmont College B
South Georgia College A
State University of West Georgia B

Hawaii
Hawaii Pacific University B, M
University of Hawaii
    Hawaii Community College A
    Kapiolani Community College A
    Kauai Community College A
    Manoa B

Idaho
Boise State University A, B
College of Southern Idaho A
Idaho State University B

Lewis-Clark State College A
North Idaho College A
Northwest Nazarene University B
Ricks College A

Illinois
Black Hawk College A
Blessing-Reiman College of Nursing B
Bradley University B
Carl Sandburg College A
Chicago State University B
City Colleges of Chicago
    Harry S. Truman College A
College of DuPage A
College of Lake County A
Concordia University B
Danville Area Community College A
Elgin Community College A
Highland Community College A
Illinois Eastern Community Colleges
    Olney Central College A
Illinois State University B, M
Illinois Wesleyan University B
John Wood Community College A
Joliet Junior College A
Kankakee Community College A
Kishwaukee College A
Lake Land College A
Lakeview College of Nursing B
Lewis University B
Lewis and Clark Community College A
Moraine Valley Community College A
North Park University B
Northern Illinois University B
Oakton Community College A
Parkland College A
Prairie State College A
Richland Community College A
Rock Valley College A
Rockford College B
St. Xavier University B
Sauk Valley Community College A
Southeastern Illinois College A
Southern Illinois University
    Edwardsville B, M
Southwestern Illinois College A
Trinity Christian College B
Triton College A
University of Illinois
    Chicago B
University of St. Francis B
Waubonsee Community College A
William Rainey Harper College A

Indiana
Anderson University B
Ball State University B
Bethel College A, B
Goshen College B
Indiana State University A, B
Indiana University
    Northwest A, B
    South Bend A, B
    Southeast A
Indiana University--Purdue University
    Indiana University-Purdue
        University Fort Wayne A, B
    Indiana University-Purdue
        University Indianapolis D
Ivy Tech State College
    Central Indiana A
    Columbus A
    Kokomo A
    Lafayette A
    Northcentral A
    Northwest A
    Southcentral A
    Southeast A
    Southwest A
    Whitewater A
Purdue University
    Calumet A, B
Purdue University B
Saint Mary's College B
University of Indianapolis A, B
University of St. Francis A

University of Southern Indiana A, B, M
Valparaiso University B
Vincennes University A

Iowa
Clinton Community College A
Coe College B
Des Moines Area Community College A
Drake University M
Graceland University B
Hawkeye Community College A
Indian Hills Community College A
Iowa Central Community College A
Iowa Wesleyan College B
Iowa Western Community College A
Kirkwood Community College A
Luther College B
Marshalltown Community College A
Marycrest International University B
North Iowa Area Community College A
Northeast Iowa Community College A
Scott Community College A
Southeastern Community College
    North Campus A
    South Campus A
Southwestern Community College A
University of Iowa B
Western Iowa Tech Community
    College A

Kansas
Barton County Community College A
Bethel College B
Butler County Community College C, A
Colby Community College A
Cowley County Community College A
Dodge City Community College A
Garden City Community College A
Hesston College A
Hutchinson Community College A
Johnson County Community College A
Kansas City Kansas Community
    College A
Kansas Wesleyan University A
MidAmerica Nazarene University B
Newman University B
Pittsburg State University B
Seward County Community College A
Southwestern College B
Washburn University of Topeka B

Kentucky
Ashland Community College A
Bellarmine College B, M
Berea College B
Eastern Kentucky University A, B
Hazard Community College A
Kentucky State University A
Maysville Community College A
Morehead State University A, B
Murray State University B
Owensboro Community College A
Pikeville College A
Prestonsburg Community College A
St. Catharine College A
Somerset Community College A
Southeast Community College A
Spalding University B
University of Kentucky B
University of Louisville B
Western Kentucky University A, B

Louisiana
Delgado Community College A
Dillard University B
McNeese State University A, B
Northwestern State University A, B
Southeastern Louisiana University B
Southern University and Agricultural and
    Mechanical College B
University of Louisiana at Lafayette B
University of Louisiana at Monroe B

Maine
Central Maine Medical Center School of
    Nursing A
Central Maine Technical College A

Nursing (RN)

Eastern Maine Technical College *A*
Husson College *B*
Mid-State College *C*
St. Joseph's College *B, M*
Southern Maine Technical College *A*
University of Maine
    Fort Kent *B*
University of Maine *B*
University of New England *A, B*
University of Southern Maine *B, M*

Maryland
Allegany College *A*
Anne Arundel Community College *A*
Baltimore City Community College *A*
Bowie State University *B, M*
Charles County Community College *A*
Chesapeake College *A*
Columbia Union College *B*
Community College of Baltimore County
    Catonsville *A*
    Essex *A*
Frederick Community College *A*
Hagerstown Community College *A*
Harford Community College *A*
Howard Community College *A*
Johns Hopkins University *M, D*
Montgomery College
    Rockville Campus *A*
Prince George's Community College *A*
Wor-Wic Community College *A*

Massachusetts
American International College *B*
Becker College *A*
Berkshire Community College *A*
Boston College *B*
Bristol Community College *A*
Bunker Hill Community College *A*
Cape Cod Community College *A*
Curry College *B*
Endicott College *B*
Fitchburg State College *B*
Greenfield Community College *A*
Labouré College *A*
MGH Institute of Health Professions *M*
Massachusetts Bay Community
    College *A*
Massasoit Community College *A*
Middlesex Community College *A*
Mount Wachusett Community College *A*
North Shore Community College *A*
Northeastern University *B, M*
Northern Essex Community College *A*
Quincy College *A*
Regis College *A*
Salem State College *B*
Simmons College *B, M*
Springfield Technical Community
    College *A*
University of Massachusetts
    Amherst *B, M, D*
    Boston *B*
    Lowell *B*

Michigan
Alpena Community College *A*
Bay de Noc Community College *A*
Delta College *A*
Eastern Michigan University *B, M*
Ferris State University *A, B*
Glen Oaks Community College *A*
Gogebic Community College *A*
Grand Valley State University *B*
Great Lakes College *A*
Henry Ford Community College *A*
Hope College *B*
Jackson Community College *A*
Kalamazoo Valley Community
    College *A*
Kellogg Community College *A*
Kirtland Community College *C, A*
Lake Michigan College *A*
Lake Superior State University *B*
Michigan State University *B, M*
Mid Michigan Community College *A*

Monroe County Community College *A*
Montcalm Community College *A*
Mott Community College *A*
Muskegon Community College *A*
North Central Michigan College *A*
Northern Michigan University *B*
Northwestern Michigan College *A*
Oakland University *B*
Saginaw Valley State University *B*
St. Clair County Community College *A*
Schoolcraft College *A*
Southwestern Michigan College *A*
Suomi College *A*
University of Detroit Mercy *B*
University of Michigan *B*
Washtenaw Community College *A*
Wayne County Community College *A*
Wayne State University *B, D*
West Shore Community College *A*
Western Michigan University *B*

Minnesota
Anoka-Ramsey Community College *A*
Bethel College *B*
Century Community and Technical
    College *A*
College of St. Benedict *B*
College of St. Catherine-Minneapolis *A*
College of St. Catherine: St. Paul
    Campus *B*
College of St. Scholastica *B*
Concordia College: Moorhead *B*
Fond Du Lac Tribal and Community
    College *A*
Gustavus Adolphus College *B*
Hibbing Community College: A
    Technical and Community College *A*
Inver Hills Community College *A*
Lake Superior College: A Community
    and Technical College *A*
Minneapolis Community and Technical
    College *A*
Minnesota State University, Mankato *B*
North Hennepin Community College *A*
Northland Community & Technical
    College *A*
Ridgewater College: A Community and
    Technical College *A*
Rochester Community and Technical
    College *A*
St. John's University *B*
St. Olaf College *B*
University of Minnesota
    Twin Cities *B, M, D*
Winona State University *B, M*

Mississippi
Alcorn State University *A, B*
Delta State University *B, M*
Itawamba Community College *A*
Mississippi Gulf Coast Community
    College
    Jefferson Davis Campus *A*
    Perkinston *A*
University of Southern Mississippi *B*

Missouri
Avila College *B*
Central Missouri State University *B, M*
Crowder College *A*
Culver-Stockton College *B*
Deaconess College of Nursing *A, B*
East Central College *A*
Hannibal-LaGrange College *B*
Jefferson College *A*
Lincoln University *A, B*
Maple Woods Community College *A*
Mineral Area College *A*
Missouri Southern State College *B*
Missouri Western State College *B*
Moberly Area Community College *A*
Park University *A*
Penn Valley Community College *A*
St. Charles County Community
    College *A*
St. Louis University *B, M, D*

St. Luke's College *B*
Southwest Baptist University *A*
Southwest Missouri State University
    West Plains Campus *A*
State Fair Community College *A*
Three Rivers Community College *A*
Truman State University *B*
University of Missouri
    Columbia *B, M, D*
William Jewell College *B*

Montana
Miles Community College *A*
Montana State University
    Bozeman *B, M*
    Northern *A, B*
Montana Tech of the University of
    Montana: College of Technology *A*
Montana Tech of the University of
    Montana *A*
Salish Kootenai College *A, B*

Nebraska
Central Community College *C, A*
Clarkson College *B*
College of Saint Mary *A*
Grace University *B*
Metropolitan Community College *A*
Mid Plains Community College Area *A*
Nebraska Methodist College of Nursing
    and Allied Health *A, B*
Northeast Community College *A*
Southeast Community College
    Lincoln Campus *A*

Nevada
Community College of Southern
    Nevada *A*
University of Nevada
    Las Vegas *B, M*
    Reno *B*
Western Nevada Community College *A*

New Hampshire
Colby-Sawyer College *B*
New Hampshire Community Technical
    College
    Berlin *A*
    Claremont *A*
    Manchester *A*
    Stratham *A*
New Hampshire Technical Institute *A*
Rivier College *A, B*
St. Anselm College *B*
University of New Hampshire
    Manchester *B*

New Jersey
Atlantic Cape Community College *A*
Bergen Community College *A*
Bloomfield College *B*
Brookdale Community College *A*
Burlington County College *A*
Camden County College *A*
County College of Morris *A*
Cumberland County College *A*
Felician College *B*
Gloucester County College *A*
Mercer County Community College *A*
Middlesex County College *A*
Monmouth University *B*
Ocean County College *A*
Passaic County Community College *A*
Ramapo College of New Jersey *B*
Raritan Valley Community College *A*
Richard Stockton College of New
    Jersey *B, M*
Salem Community College *A*
Warren County Community College *A*

New Mexico
Albuquerque Technical-Vocational
    Institute *A*
Dona Ana Branch Community College of
    New Mexico State University *A*
Eastern New Mexico University *B*

New Mexico State University
    Carlsbad *A*
New Mexico State University *B, M*
San Juan College *A*
Santa Fe Community College *A*
University of New Mexico *B, M*

New York
Adelphi University *B*
Adirondack Community College *A*
Broome Community College *A*
Cayuga County Community College *A*
City University of New York
    Bronx Community College *A*
    College of Staten Island *B*
    Hostos Community College *A*
    Hunter College *B*
    Kingsborough Community
        College *A*
    Lehman College *B*
    Queensborough Community
        College *A*
    York College *B*
Clinton Community College *A*
Cochran School of Nursing-St. John's
    Riverside Hospital *A*
Columbia-Greene Community College *A*
Concordia College *A*
Corning Community College *A*
D'Youville College *B, M*
Dominican College of Blauvelt *B*
Dutchess Community College *A*
Elmira College *B*
Erie Community College
    City Campus *A*
    North Campus *A*
Finger Lakes Community College *A*
Fulton-Montgomery Community
    College *A*
Genesee Community College *A*
Hartwick College *B*
Helene Fuld College of Nursing *A*
Hudson Valley Community College *A*
Jamestown Community College *A*
Jefferson Community College *A*
Keuka College *B*
Long Island University
    Brooklyn Campus *M*
Maria College *A*
Mercy College *B*
Mohawk Valley Community College *A*
Molloy College *B, M*
Monroe Community College *C, A*
Nassau Community College *A*
New York Institute of Technology *B*
New York University *B*
Niagara County Community College *A*
Niagara University *B*
North Country Community College *A*
Pace University:
    Pleasantville/Briarcliff *B*
Pace University *B*
Phillips Beth Israel School of Nursing *A*
Regents College *A, B, M*
Roberts Wesleyan College *B*
Rockland Community College *A*
St. John Fisher College *B*
St. Joseph's Hospital Health Center
    School of Nursing *A*
State University of New York
    College of Agriculture and
        Technology at Morrisville *A*
    College of Technology at Alfred *A*
    College of Technology at Canton *A*
    College of Technology at Delhi *A*
    Farmingdale *A*
    Health Science Center at
        Brooklyn *B, M*
    Upstate Medical University *B*
Suffolk County Community College *A*
Syracuse University *B, M*
Tompkins-Cortland Community
    College *A*
Trocaire College *A*
Ulster County Community College *A*

Utica College of Syracuse University *B*
Wagner College *B*
Westchester Community College *A*

North Carolina
Alamance Community College *A*
Asheville Buncombe Technical Community College *A*
Beaufort County Community College *A*
Blue Ridge Community College *A*
Caldwell Community College and Technical Institute *A*
Cape Fear Community College *A*
Catawba Valley Community College *A*
Central Carolina Community College *A*
Cleveland Community College *A*
Coastal Carolina Community College *A*
College of the Albemarle *A*
Craven Community College *A*
Davidson County Community College *C, A*
Durham Technical Community College *A*
East Carolina University *B, M*
Edgecombe Community College *A*
Fayetteville Technical Community College *A*
Forsyth Technical Community College *A*
Gardner-Webb University *B*
Gaston College *A*
Guilford Technical Community College *A*
Halifax Community College *A*
Haywood Community College *A*
James Sprunt Community College *A*
Lenoir Community College *A*
Lenoir-Rhyne College *B*
Mayland Community College *A*
Mitchell Community College *A*
Nash Community College *A*
North Carolina Central University *B*
Piedmont Community College *A*
Pitt Community College *A*
Queens College *B*
Randolph Community College *A*
Richmond Community College *A*
Roanoke-Chowan Community College *A*
Rockingham Community College *A*
Rowan-Cabarrus Community College *A*
Sampson Community College *A*
Sandhills Community College *A*
Southeastern Community College *A*
Surry Community College *A*
Tri-County Community College *A*
University of North Carolina
 Chapel Hill *B*
 Charlotte *B*
 Greensboro *C, B, M*
 Wilmington *B, M*
Vance-Granville Community College *A*
Wake Technical Community College *A*
Wayne Community College *A*
Western Carolina University *B, M*
Western Piedmont Community College *A*
Wilkes Community College *A*
Wilson Technical Community College *A*

North Dakota
Dickinson State University *B*
Jamestown College *B*
Medcenter One College of Nursing *B*
Minot State University *B*
North Dakota State University *B*
University of North Dakota *B*

Ohio
Belmont Technical College *A*
Bowling Green State University Firelands College *A*
Bowling Green State University *B*
Cedarville College *B*
Central Ohio Technical College *A*
Cincinnati State Technical and Community College *A*
Clark State Community College *A*
Cleveland State University *B*
College of Mount St. Joseph *B*
Columbus State Community College *A*
Edison State Community College *A*
Hocking Technical College *A*
Kent State University
 Ashtabula Regional Campus *A*
 East Liverpool Regional Campus *A*
 Stark Campus *A*
 Tuscarawas Campus *A, B*
Kent State University *B*
Lakeland Community College *A*
Lima Technical College *A*
Marion Technical College *A*
Miami University
 Hamilton Campus *A*
 Middletown Campus *A*
 Oxford Campus *B*
North Central State College *A*
Northwest State Community College *A*
Ohio University
 Chillicothe Campus *A, B*
 Southern Campus at Ironton *B*
 Zanesville Campus *A*
Ohio University *A*
Otterbein College *B*
Owens Community College
 Findlay Campus *A*
 Toledo *A*
Shawnee State University *A*
Southern State Community College *A*
Stark State College of Technology *A*
University of Akron *B*
University of Cincinnati *B*
University of Rio Grande *A, B*
University of Toledo *A, B*
Ursuline College *B*
Washington State Community College *A*
Wright State University *B*

Oklahoma
Connors State College *A*
Eastern Oklahoma State College *A*
Northeastern Oklahoma Agricultural and Mechanical College *A*
Northern Oklahoma College *A*
Northwestern Oklahoma State University *B*
Oklahoma Baptist University *B*
Oklahoma City Community College *A*
Oklahoma City University *B*
Oklahoma State University
 Oklahoma City *A*
Oral Roberts University *B*
Redlands Community College *A*
Seminole State College *A*
Southwestern Oklahoma State University *B*
Western Oklahoma State College *A*

Oregon
Central Oregon Community College *A*
Chemeketa Community College *A*
Clackamas Community College *A*
Eastern Oregon University *B*
Lane Community College *A*
Linfield College *B*
Linn-Benton Community College *A*
Oregon Health Sciences University *B*
Southern Oregon University *B*
University of Portland *B, M*

Pennsylvania
Alvernia College *A*
Bloomsburg University of Pennsylvania *B, M*
Bucks County Community College *A*
Clarion University of Pennsylvania *A, B, M*
Community College of Allegheny County *A*
Community College of Beaver County *A*
Community College of Philadelphia *A*
Delaware County Community College *A*
Duquesne University *B*
East Stroudsburg University of Pennsylvania *B*
Edinboro University of Pennsylvania *B*
Gannon University *C, A, B, M*
Gettysburg College *B*
Gwynedd-Mercy College *A*
Harrisburg Area Community College *A*
Immaculata College *B*
Kutztown University of Pennsylvania *B*
La Salle University *B*
Lehigh Carbon Community College *A*
Lock Haven University of Pennsylvania *B*
Luzerne County Community College *A*
Lycoming College *B*
MCP Hahnemann University *B*
Marywood University *B*
Messiah College *B*
Moravian College *B*
Mount Aloysius College *A*
Northampton County Area Community College *A*
Penn State
 Altoona *A, B*
 Fayette *A, B*
 Mont Alto *A, B*
 New Kensington *B*
 Schuylkill - Capital College *B*
 Shenango *A*
 University Park *B, M*
 Worthington Scranton *A, B*
Pennsylvania College of Technology *A*
Reading Area Community College *A*
Seton Hill College *B*
Slippery Rock University of Pennsylvania *B*
Temple University *B, M*
Thomas Jefferson University: College of Health Professions *M*
University of Pennsylvania *B, M, D*
University of Pittsburgh
 Bradford *A*
University of Pittsburgh *B*
University of Scranton *M*
Villanova University *B*
Westmoreland County Community College *A*
Widener University *M*
Wilkes University *B, M*
York College of Pennsylvania *B*

Puerto Rico
Caribbean University *B*
Columbia College *B*
Inter American University of Puerto Rico
 Arecibo Campus *A, B*
 Barranquitas Campus *A, B*
University of Puerto Rico
 Humacao University College *A, B*
 Mayaguez Campus *B*
 Medical Sciences Campus *B*

Rhode Island
Community College of Rhode Island *A*
University of Rhode Island *B*

South Carolina
Central Carolina Technical College *A*
Charleston Southern University *B*
Chesterfield-Marlboro Technical College *C*
Florence-Darlington Technical College *A*
Greenville Technical College *A*
Lander University *B*
Midlands Technical College *A*
Orangeburg-Calhoun Technical College *A*
Piedmont Technical College *C, A*
Technical College of the Lowcountry *A*
Tri-County Technical College *A*
Trident Technical College *A*
University of South Carolina
 Aiken *A, B*
 Spartanburg *A, B*
University of South Carolina *B*
York Technical College *A*

South Dakota
Augustana College *B*
Dakota Wesleyan University *A*
University of South Dakota *A*

Tennessee
Aquinas College *A, B*
Austin Peay State University *B*
Belmont University *B*
Carson-Newman College *B*
Cleveland State Community College *A*
Crichton College *C*
Cumberland University *B*
Dyersburg State Community College *A*
Hiwassee College *A*
Jackson State Community College *A*
King College *B*
Lincoln Memorial University *A, B*
Maryville College *B*
Middle Tennessee State University *B*
Milligan College *B*
Roane State Community College *A*
Shelby State Community College *A*
Southern Adventist University *A*
Tennessee Technological University *B*
Tennessee Wesleyan College *B*
Union University *B*
University of Memphis *B*
University of Tennessee
 Chattanooga *B*
 Knoxville *B*
 Martin *B*
 Memphis *M, D*
Walters State Community College *A*

Texas
Abilene Christian University *B, M*
Alvin Community College *C, A*
Amarillo College *A*
Angelina College *A*
Baylor University *B*
Blinn College *C, A*
Brazosport College *A*
Central Texas College *A*
Coastal Bend College *A*
Collin County Community College District *A*
Del Mar College *A*
East Texas Baptist University *B*
El Paso Community College *A*
Galveston College *C, A*
Grayson County College *A*
Hardin-Simmons University *B, M*
Houston Baptist University *A, B, M*
Houston Community College System *A*
Howard College *A*
Kilgore College *A*
Lamar State College at Port Arthur *A*
Lamar University *A, B, M*
North Central Texas College *A*
Northeast Texas Community College *A*
Odessa College *A*
Panola College *A*
Prairie View A&M University *B*
South Plains College *A*
Southwest Texas Junior College *A*
Southwestern Adventist University *A, B*
Stephen F. Austin State University *B*
Tarleton State University *A, B*
Tarrant County College *A*
Texas A&M International University *B*
Texas Christian University *B*
Texas Woman's University *B, M, D*
Trinity Valley Community College *A*
Tyler Junior College *A*
University of Mary Hardin-Baylor *B*
University of Texas
 Arlington *B, M*
 Austin *B, M, D*
 El Paso *B, M*
 Medical Branch at Galveston *B, M, D*
 Tyler *B*
University of the Incarnate Word *B, M*
Vernon Regional Junior College *A*
Victoria College *A*

Nursing (RN)

West Texas A&M University *B*
Wharton County Junior College *A*

Utah
Dixie State College of Utah *A*
Salt Lake Community College *A*
Snow College *A*
University of Utah *B, M, D*
Weber State University *A, B*

Vermont
Castleton State College *A*
Vermont Technical College *A*

Virginia
Blue Ridge Community College *A*
George Mason University *B, M, D*
Hampton University *B*
J. Sargeant Reynolds Community College *A*
James Madison University *B*
John Tyler Community College *A*
Lord Fairfax Community College *A*
Mountain Empire Community College *A*
Norfolk State University *A, B*
Old Dominion University *B, M*
Piedmont Virginia Community College *A*
Radford University *B, M*
Shenandoah University *A, B*
Southside Virginia Community College *A*
Southwest Virginia Community College *A*
Tidewater Community College *A*
University of Virginia's College at Wise *B*
University of Virginia *B, M, D*
Virginia Commonwealth University *B*
Virginia Highlands Community College *A*

Washington
Bellevue Community College *A*
Big Bend Community College *A*
Clark College *A*
Eastern Washington University *B*
Everett Community College *C, A*
Grays Harbor College *A*
Highline Community College *C, A*
Lower Columbia College *A*
Olympic College *A*
Peninsula College *A*
Seattle Pacific University *B*
Seattle University *B*
Shoreline Community College *A*
Skagit Valley College *A*
Spokane Community College *A*
Spokane Falls Community College *A*
Tacoma Community College *C*
Walla Walla College *B*
Walla Walla Community College *A*
Washington State University *B, M*
Wenatchee Valley College *A*
Yakima Valley Community College *C, A*

West Virginia
Alderson-Broaddus College *B*
Bluefield State College *A*
College of West Virginia *B*
Davis and Elkins College *A*
Fairmont State College *A, B*
Marshall University *B*
Shepherd College *A, B*
University of Charleston *B*
West Virginia Northern Community College *A*
West Virginia University *B, M*
West Virginia Wesleyan College *B*

Wisconsin
Alverno College *B*
Bellin College of Nursing *B*
Beloit College *B*
Blackhawk Technical College *A*
Cardinal Stritch University *A, B*
Carroll College *B*
Chippewa Valley Technical College *A*
Columbia College of Nursing *B*
Concordia University Wisconsin *B*
Gateway Technical College *A*
Madison Area Technical College *A*
Marian College of Fond du Lac *B*
Milwaukee Area Technical College *A*
Moraine Park Technical College *A*
Nicolet Area Technical College *A*
Northeast Wisconsin Technical College *A*
Southwest Wisconsin Technical College *A*
University of Wisconsin
  Madison *B*
  Milwaukee *B, M, D*
  Oshkosh *B, M*
  Parkside *B*
Viterbo University *B, M*
Waukesha County Technical College *A*
Western Wisconsin Technical College *A*
Wisconsin Indianhead Technical College *A*

Wyoming
Casper College *A*
Central Wyoming College *A*
University of Wyoming *B, M*
Western Wyoming Community College *C, A*

Nursing administration

Alabama
University of Mobile *M*

Arizona
University of Phoenix *M*

California
Samuel Merritt College *M*
University of Southern California *M*

Connecticut
Sacred Heart University *M*
Southern Connecticut State University *M*
University of Hartford *M*

Florida
Barry University *M, D*
University of Tampa *M*

Georgia
Armstrong Atlantic State University *M*
Clayton College and State University *B*

Illinois
Bradley University *M*
De Paul University *M*
Loyola University of Chicago *M*
North Park University *M*
St. Xavier University *M*
University of Illinois
  Chicago *M*

Indiana
Indiana University--Purdue University
  Indiana University-Purdue
    University Fort Wayne *M*
  Indiana University-Purdue
    University Indianapolis *M*
University of St. Francis *M*
Valparaiso University *M*

Iowa
University of Iowa *M, D*

Kansas
Newman University *M*

Louisiana
Louisiana State University Medical Center *M, D*

Massachusetts
Northeastern University *M*
Salem State College *M*
University of Massachusetts
  Boston *M*

Michigan
Andrews University *M*
Northern Michigan University *M*
Oakland University *M*
Saginaw Valley State University *M*
University of Michigan *M*
Wayne State University *M*

Minnesota
Winona State University *M*

Mississippi
University of Southern Mississippi *M*

Missouri
Central Methodist College *B*

Nebraska
Clarkson College *M*

Nevada
University of Nevada
  Reno *M*

New Jersey
Seton Hall University *C, M*

New York
College of Mount St. Vincent *M*
College of New Rochelle *M*
Columbia University
  Teachers College *M, D*
D'Youville College *M*
Pace University:
  Pleasantville/Briarcliff *M*
Pace University *M*
St. John Fisher College *B, M*
State University of New York
  Buffalo *M*
  Institute of Technology at Utica/Rome *M*
Wagner College *M*

Ohio
Ashland University *B*
Ohio University
  Chillicothe Campus *B*
Xavier University *M*

Oklahoma
University of Tulsa *M*

Pennsylvania
Duquesne University *M*
Gannon University *M*
Penn State
  University Park *C*
Pennsylvania College of Technology *B*
University of Pennsylvania *B, M, D*
Villanova University *M*

South Carolina
University of South Carolina *M*

Tennessee
Southern Adventist University *M*

Texas
Baylor University *M*
Midwestern State University *M*
Texas A&M University
  Corpus Christi *M*
Texas Woman's University *M*
University of Texas
  Arlington *M*
  El Paso *M*

Utah
Brigham Young University *M*

Virginia
George Mason University *M, D*

Washington
Pacific Lutheran University *M*
Seattle Pacific University *B, M*

West Virginia
College of West Virginia *M*

Wheeling Jesuit University *M*

Wisconsin
University of Wisconsin
  Oshkosh *M*

Nursing anesthesiology

Alabama
University of Alabama
  Birmingham *M*

California
California State University
  Long Beach *M*
Samuel Merritt College *M*
University of California
  Los Angeles *M*
University of Southern California *M*

Florida
Barry University *M*

Illinois
Bradley University *M*
De Paul University *M*
Southern Illinois University
  Edwardsville *M*

Kansas
Newman University *M*
University of Kansas
  Medical Center *M*

Kentucky
Murray State University *M*

Louisiana
Xavier University of Louisiana *M*

Maine
University of New England *M*

Massachusetts
Northeastern University *M*

Michigan
Oakland University *M*
University of Detroit Mercy *M*
University of Michigan
  Flint *M*
Wayne State University *M*

Minnesota
St. Mary's University of Minnesota *M*
University of Minnesota
  Twin Cities *B*

Mississippi
Northwest Mississippi Community College *C, A*

Missouri
Southwest Missouri State University *M*

New York
Albany Medical College *M*
Columbia University
  School of Nursing *M*
State University of New York
  Buffalo *M*

North Carolina
Mayland Community College *C*

North Dakota
University of Mary *M*

Ohio
Case Western Reserve University *M*
Ohio State University
  Columbus Campus *B, M*

Pennsylvania
California University of Pennsylvania *B*
Gannon University *M*
MCP Hahnemann University *M*
St. Joseph's University *M*
University of Pittsburgh *M*

Puerto Rico
Inter American University of Puerto Rico
 Arecibo Campus *M*
Pontifical Catholic University of Puerto
 Rico *M*
University of Puerto Rico
 Medical Sciences Campus *M*

South Carolina
University of South Carolina *M*

South Dakota
Mount Marty College *M*

Texas
Texas Wesleyan University *M*

Virginia
Virginia Commonwealth University *M*

Washington
Gonzaga University *M*

Nursing assistant

Alabama
Bessemer State Technical College *C*
Bevill State Community College *C*
Calhoun Community College *C*
Gadsden State Community College *C*
George C. Wallace State Community
 College
 Selma *C*
Harry M. Ayers State Technical
 College *C*
Northwest-Shoals Community College *C*
Reid State Technical College *C*

Arizona
Arizona Western College *C*
Eastern Arizona College *C*
Gateway Community College *C*
Glendale Community College *A*
Mesa Community College *C*
Northland Pioneer College *C*
Phoenix College *C*
Pima Community College *C*
Scottsdale Community College *C*

Arkansas
Arkansas State University
 Mountain Home *C*
Southern Arkansas University
 Tech *C*

California
Allan Hancock College *C*
Chaffey Community College *C*
College of the Sequoias *C*
Gavilan Community College *C*
Imperial Valley College *C*
Merritt College *C*
MiraCosta College *C*
Modesto Junior College *A*
Pacific Union College *C*
Santa Barbara City College *C*
Santa Rosa Junior College *C, A*
Shasta College *C*
Yuba College *C*

Colorado
Arapahoe Community College *C*
Colorado Mountain College
 Alpine Campus *C*
 Spring Valley Campus *C*
 Timberline Campus *C*
Front Range Community College *C*
Lamar Community College *C*
Morgan Community College *C*
Otero Junior College *C*
Red Rocks Community College *C*
Trinidad State Junior College *C*

Florida
Brevard Community College *C*
Central Florida Community College *C*
Daytona Beach Community College *C*
Indian River Community College *C*
Pasco-Hernando Community College *C*
Pensacola Junior College *C*
Seminole Community College *C*
South Florida Community College *C*
Tallahassee Community College *C*

Georgia
Bainbridge College *C*
Coastal Georgia Community College *C*

Hawaii
University of Hawaii
 Hawaii Community College *C*
 Kapiolani Community College *A*
 Kauai Community College *C*

Idaho
Eastern Idaho Technical College *C*

Illinois
Black Hawk College *C*
City Colleges of Chicago
 Harold Washington College *C*
College of DuPage *C*
College of Lake County *C*
Elgin Community College *C*
Highland Community College *C*
Illinois Eastern Community Colleges
 Frontier Community College *C*
 Lincoln Trail College *C*
 Olney Central College *C*
 Wabash Valley College *C*
John A. Logan College *C*
John Wood Community College *C*
Kankakee Community College *C*
Kaskaskia College *C*
Kishwaukee College *C*
Lewis and Clark Community College *C*
McHenry County College *C*
Morton College *C*
Parkland College *C*
Prairie State College *C*
Rock Valley College *C*
Sauk Valley Community College *C*
Southeastern Illinois College *C*
Southwestern Ilinois College *C*
Spoon River College *C*
Triton College *C*
Waubonsee Community College *C*
William Rainey Harper College *C*

Iowa
Des Moines Area Community College *C*
Hawkeye Community College *C*
Kirkwood Community College *C*
Northeast Iowa Community College *C*

Kansas
Allen County Community College *A*
Barton County Community College *C*
Dodge City Community College *C, A*
Independence Community College *C, A*
Johnson County Community College *C*
Kansas City Kansas Community
 College *C*

Louisiana
Nunez Community College *C*

Maine
Central Maine Medical Center School of
 Nursing *C*
Southern Maine Technical College *C*

Massachusetts
Becker College *C*
Berkshire Community College *C*
Cape Cod Community College *C*
Middlesex Community College *C*
North Shore Community College *C*

Michigan
Delta College *C*
Kellogg Community College *C*
West Shore Community College *A*

Minnesota
Alexandria Technical College *C*
Lake Superior College: A Community
 and Technical College *C*
Mesabi Range Community and Technical
 College *C*
Ridgewater College: A Community and
 Technical College *C*
Rochester Community and Technical
 College *C*
St. Cloud Technical College *C*
St. Paul Technical College *C*
South Central Technical College *C*

Mississippi
Hinds Community College *A*
Itawamba Community College *C*
Mississippi Gulf Coast Community
 College
 Perkinston *C*
Northwest Mississippi Community
 College *C*

Missouri
Mineral Area College *C*

Montana
Montana Tech of the University of
 Montana *C*

Nebraska
Central Community College *C, A*
Mid Plains Community College Area *C*
Nebraska Methodist College of Nursing
 and Allied Health *C*

New Hampshire
Hesser College *A*

New Jersey
Sussex County Community College *C*

New Mexico
Albuquerque Technical-Vocational
 Institute *C*
Clovis Community College *C*
Dona Ana Branch Community College of
 New Mexico State University *C*
Eastern New Mexico University
 Roswell Campus *C*
Northern New Mexico Community
 College *C*

New York
St. Joseph's Hospital Health Center
 School of Nursing *C*
Schenectady County Community
 College *C*
Westchester Community College *C, A*

North Carolina
Beaufort County Community College *C*
Bladen Community College *C*
Brunswick Community College *C*
Carteret Community College *C*
Central Carolina Community College *C*
Central Piedmont Community College *C*
Cleveland Community College *C*
Coastal Carolina Community College *C*
College of the Albemarle *C*
Craven Community College *C*
Edgecombe Community College *C*
Fayetteville Technical Community
 College *C*
Gaston College *C*
Halifax Community College *C*
Haywood Community College *C*
Mitchell Community College *C*
Nash Community College *C*
Richmond Community College *C*
Roanoke-Chowan Community
 College *C*
Sampson Community College *C*
Sandhills Community College *C*
South Piedmont Community College *C*
Southeastern Community College *C, A*
Surry Community College *C*
Tri-County Community College *C*
Vance-Granville Community College *C*
Wilson Technical Community College *C*

Ohio
Central Ohio Technical College *C*
Cincinnati State Technical and
 Community College *C*
Columbus State Community College *C*

Oregon
Central Oregon Community College *C*
Linn-Benton Community College *C*

Pennsylvania
Community College of Allegheny
 County *C*
Community College of Beaver County *C*
Delaware County Community College *C*
Laurel Business Institute *A*

South Carolina
Midlands Technical College *C*
Trident Technical College *C*
York Technical College *C*

South Dakota
Western Dakota Technical Institute *C*

Texas
El Paso Community College *C*
Galveston College *C*
Howard College *C*
Kilgore College *C*
St. Philip's College *C*
South Plains College *A*
Tarrant County College *C*
Texas State Technical College
 Harlingen *C*

Utah
Dixie State College of Utah *C*

Virginia
J. Sargeant Reynolds Community
 College *C*
Southside Virginia Community
 College *C*

Washington
Big Bend Community College *C*
Everett Community College *C*
Lake Washington Technical College *C*
Lower Columbia College *C, A*
North Seattle Community College *A*
Renton Technical College *C*
South Puget Sound Community
 College *C*
Walla Walla Community College *C*

Wisconsin
Chippewa Valley Technical College *C*
Gateway Technical College *C*
Lakeshore Technical College *C*
Madison Area Technical College *C*
Moraine Park Technical College *C*
Nicolet Area Technical College *C*
Northeast Wisconsin Technical
 College *C*
Southwest Wisconsin Technical
 College *C*
Waukesha County Technical College *C*
Western Wisconsin Technical College *C*
Wisconsin Indianhead Technical
 College *C*

Wyoming
Central Wyoming College *C*

Nursing education

Alabama
Lawson State Community College *A*
Shelton State Community College *C, A*

Arkansas
University of Central Arkansas *M*

California
Azusa Pacific University *B, M*
Saddleback College *C, A*
San Jose State University *T*

Nursing education

Colorado
University of Southern Colorado C

Florida
Barry University M, D

Illinois
De Paul University M

Michigan
Northern Michigan University M
Wayne State University C

Minnesota
Ridgewater College: A Community and Technical College C, A
Winona State University M

Nebraska
Northeast Community College A

New Hampshire
New Hampshire Technical Institute C, A
Rivier College M

New York
Columbia University
    Teachers College M, D
D'Youville College M
New York University M

North Carolina
Louisburg College A
Nash Community College A

North Dakota
University of Mary M

Ohio
Otterbein College B

Oklahoma
Eastern Oklahoma State College A

Pennsylvania
Widener University D

Utah
Salt Lake Community College A

Washington
North Seattle Community College C
Olympic College A

Nursing, practical

Alabama
Bessemer State Technical College C
Bevill State Community College C
Calhoun Community College C
Chattahoochee Valley Community College C
Gadsden State Community College C
George C. Wallace State Community College
    Selma C
Harry M. Ayers State Technical College C
J. F. Drake State Technical College C
Northwest-Shoals Community College C
Reid State Technical College C
Shelton State Community College C
Sparks State Technical College C
Wallace State Community College at Hanceville C

Arizona
Arizona Western College C
Central Arizona College C
Gateway Community College C
Mesa Community College C
Mohave Community College C
Northland Pioneer College C
Phoenix College C
Pima Community College C
Scottsdale Community College C

Arkansas
Arkansas State University
    Mountain Home C

North Arkansas College C
Phillips Community College of the University of Arkansas C
Southern Arkansas University Tech C
Westark College C

California
Allan Hancock College C, A
Bakersfield College A
Butte College A
Cabrillo College A
California State University
    Bakersfield B
    Fresno M
Cerritos Community College A
Cerro Coso Community College C, A
Citrus College A
College of the Canyons C
College of the Desert C, A
College of the Siskiyous C, A
Compton Community College C, A
Gavilan Community College A
Glendale Community College A
Imperial Valley College C, A
Los Angeles Trade and Technical College A
Los Medanos College C
Merced College C, A
Merritt College A
MiraCosta College C, A
Mission College A
Modesto Junior College A
Mount San Jacinto College C
Pasadena City College C, A
Porterville College C, A
Rio Hondo College A
Riverside Community College C, A
Sacramento City College C, A
Samuel Merritt College M
Santa Barbara City College C, A
Santa Rosa Junior College C, A
Shasta College C
Sierra College C, A
Southwestern College C, A
Ventura College A

Colorado
Colorado Mountain College
    Spring Valley Campus C
Community College of Denver C
Front Range Community College C
Lamar Community College C
Northeastern Junior College C
Otero Junior College C
Pueblo Community College C

Connecticut
Sacred Heart University M

Delaware
Delaware Technical and Community College
    Owens Campus C
    Terry Campus C
Wilmington College M

District of Columbia
George Washington University C

Florida
Brevard Community College C
Central Florida Community College C
Chipola Junior College C
Daytona Beach Community College C
Indian River Community College C
Lake City Community College C
Pasco-Hernando Community College C
Pensacola Junior College C
Santa Fe Community College C
Seminole Community College C
South Florida Community College C

Georgia
Athens Area Technical Institute C
Bainbridge College C
Chattahoochee Technical Institute C
Coastal Georgia Community College C

Columbus Technical Institute C
Darton College A
DeKalb Technical Institute C
Kennesaw State University M

Hawaii
University of Hawaii
    Hawaii Community College C
    Kapiolani Community College C, A
    Kauai Community College C

Idaho
Boise State University C
College of Southern Idaho C
Eastern Idaho Technical College C
Idaho State University C
North Idaho College C

Illinois
Black Hawk College C
Carl Sandburg College C
City Colleges of Chicago
    Olive-Harvey College C
Danville Area Community College C
Elgin Community College C
Illinois Eastern Community Colleges
    Olney Central College C
John A. Logan College C
John Wood Community College A
Joliet Junior College C
Kankakee Community College C
Kishwaukee College C
Lake Land College C
Lewis and Clark Community College A
Morton College C
Parkland College C
Rend Lake College C, A
Sauk Valley Community College C
Southeastern Illinois College C
Spoon River College C
Triton College C
William Rainey Harper College C

Indiana
Ivy Tech State College
    Central Indiana C
    Columbus C
    Eastcentral C
    Kokomo C
    Lafayette C
    Northcentral C
    Northeast C, A
    Northwest C
    Southcentral C
    Southeast C
    Southwest C
    Wabash Valley C
    Whitewater C
University of St. Francis M
Vincennes University A

Iowa
Clinton Community College C
Des Moines Area Community College C
Hawkeye Community College C
Indian Hills Community College C
Iowa Central Community College C
Iowa Lakes Community College C
Iowa Western Community College C
Kirkwood Community College C
Marshalltown Community College C
Muscatine Community College C
North Iowa Area Community College A
Northeast Iowa Community College C
Scott Community College C
Southeastern Community College
    North Campus C
    South Campus C
Southwestern Community College C
Western Iowa Tech Community College C

Kansas
Barton County Community College C
Butler County Community College C, A
Dodge City Community College C, A

Hutchinson Community College C
Johnson County Community College C
Pratt Community College A
Seward County Community College C, A

Louisiana
Delgado Community College C
Louisiana State University
    Eunice A
Nunez Community College C

Maine
Southern Maine Technical College C

Maryland
Allegany College C
Baltimore City Community College A
Charles County Community College C
Frederick Community College C
Harford Community College C
Howard Community College C
Prince George's Community College C
Wor-Wic Community College C

Massachusetts
Berkshire Community College C
Greenfield Community College C
Massachusetts Bay Community College C
North Shore Community College C
Northern Essex Community College C
Quincy College C

Michigan
Alpena Community College C
Bay de Noc Community College C
Delta College A
Glen Oaks Community College C
Gogebic Community College C
Grand Rapids Community College C
Great Lakes College C
Jackson Community College C
Kalamazoo Valley Community College A
Kellogg Community College C
Kirtland Community College C
Lansing Community College A
Mid Michigan Community College C
Montcalm Community College C
Mott Community College A
Muskegon Community College A
Northern Michigan University C
Northwestern Michigan College C
Oakland Community College C, A
St. Clair County Community College C
Schoolcraft College C
Southwestern Michigan College C
Wayne State University M

Minnesota
Alexandria Technical College C
Central Lakes College C, A
Dakota County Technical College C
Hennepin Technical College C, A
Itasca Community College C
Lake Superior College: A Community and Technical College C
Mesabi Range Community and Technical College C, A
Minnesota State College - Southeast Technical C
Northland Community & Technical College C
Ridgewater College: A Community and Technical College C
St. Cloud Technical College C, A
St. Paul Technical College C
South Central Technical College A

Mississippi
Coahoma Community College C
Copiah-Lincoln Community College C
East Central Community College C
East Mississippi Community College C
Hinds Community College A
Itawamba Community College C
Meridian Community College A

Mississippi Gulf Coast Community
  College
    Jefferson Davis Campus *C*
    Perkinston *C*
Northeast Mississippi Community
  College *A*
Southwest Mississippi Community
  College *C*

Missouri
Jefferson College *C*
Moberly Area Community College *C*
Penn Valley Community College *C*
St. Charles County Community
  College *C*
State Fair Community College *C*

Montana
Montana State University
  Billings *C*
    College of Technology-Great
      Falls *A*
Montana Tech of the University of
  Montana: College of Technology *C*
Montana Tech of the University of
  Montana *A*
University of Montana-Missoula *A*

Nebraska
Central Community College *C*
Metropolitan Community College *C*
Mid Plains Community College Area *C*
Northeast Community College *C*
Southeast Community College
  Lincoln Campus *C*

Nevada
Community College of Southern
  Nevada *C*
Western Nevada Community College *C*

New Hampshire
New Hampshire Community Technical
  College
    Claremont *C*

New Jersey
Raritan Valley Community College *A*
Salem Community College *C*
Union County College *C*

New Mexico
Albuquerque Technical-Vocational
  Institute *C*
Eastern New Mexico University
  Roswell Campus *C*
New Mexico Junior College *C*
New Mexico State University
  Carlsbad *C*
Northern New Mexico Community
  College *C*
Western New Mexico University *A*

New York
City University of New York
  Medgar Evers College *C*
Iona College *C*
Niagara County Community College *C*
State University of New York
  College of Technology at Delhi *C*
Westchester Community College *C*

North Carolina
Alamance Community College *C*
Asheville Buncombe Technical
  Community College *C*
Beaufort County Community College *C*
Bladen Community College *C*
Brunswick Community College *C, D*
Cape Fear Community College *C*
Carteret Community College *C*
Central Carolina Community College *A*
Central Piedmont Community
  College *C, A*
Cleveland Community College *C*
Coastal Carolina Community College *A*
College of the Albemarle *C, D*
Craven Community College *C*
Durham Technical Community
  College *C*
Edgecombe Community College *C*
Fayetteville Technical Community
  College *C*
Forsyth Technical Community College *A*
James Sprunt Community College *C*
Lenoir Community College *C*
Mayland Community College *C*
Montgomery Community College *C*
Nash Community College *A*
Rockingham Community College *C*
Rowan-Cabarrus Community College *D*
Sampson Community College *A*
Sandhills Community College *C*
South Piedmont Community College *C*
Southeastern Community College *C, A*
Surry Community College *C*
Vance-Granville Community College *C*
Wayne Community College *A*
Wilson Technical Community
  College *C, A*

North Dakota
Dickinson State University *A*
North Dakota State College of Science *A*
Williston State College *A*

Ohio
Belmont Technical College *C*
Clark State Community College *C*
Hocking Technical College *C*
Jefferson Community College *C*
Lorain County Community College *C*
North Central State College *C*
Northwest State Community College *C*
Southern State Community College *C*

Oregon
Central Oregon Community College *C*
Clackamas Community College *C*
Lane Community College *C*

Pennsylvania
Harrisburg Area Community College *C*
Lehigh Carbon Community College *C*
Northampton County Area Community
  College *C*
Pennsylvania College of Technology *C*
Reading Area Community College *C, A*
Westmoreland County Community
  College *C*
Widener University *M*

Puerto Rico
Ramirez College of Business and
  Technology *A*

Rhode Island
Community College of Rhode Island *C*

South Carolina
Aiken Technical College *C*
Central Carolina Technical College *C*
Chesterfield-Marlboro Technical
  College *C*
Florence-Darlington Technical
  College *C*
Greenville Technical College *C*
Horry-Georgetown Technical College *C*
Midlands Technical College *C*
Orangeburg-Calhoun Technical
  College *C*
Piedmont Technical College *C*
Spartanburg Technical College *A*
Tri-County Technical College *C*
Trident Technical College *C*

South Dakota
Western Dakota Technical Institute *C*

Tennessee
Chattanooga State Technical Community
  College *C*
Tennessee State University *A*

Texas
Alvin Community College *C*
Amarillo College *C*
Angelina College *A*
Austin Community College *C*
Brazosport College *C*
Central Texas College *C*
Coastal Bend College *C*
College of the Mainland *A*
El Paso Community College *C*
Galveston College *C*
Grayson County College *C*
Hill College *C, A*
Houston Community College System *C*
Howard College *C*
Lamar State College at Orange *C*
Lamar State College at Port Arthur *C*
Midland College *C*
Navarro College *C, A*
Northeast Texas Community College *C*
Panola College *C*
Paris Junior College *A*
St. Philip's College *C*
San Jacinto College
  North *C*
South Plains College *A*
Southwest Texas Junior College *A*
Sul Ross State University *C*
Temple College *C*
Texas A&M University
  Corpus Christi *M*
Texas State Technical College
  Sweetwater *C*
Trinity Valley Community College *C*
Vernon Regional Junior College *C*
Victoria College *C*
Weatherford College *C*
Western Texas College *C*
Wharton County Junior College *C*

Utah
Brigham Young University *M*
Dixie State College of Utah *C*
Salt Lake Community College *C*
Southern Utah University *A*
Utah Valley State College *C*
Weber State University *C*

Vermont
Vermont Technical College *C*

Virginia
Danville Community College *C*
Lord Fairfax Community College *C*
New River Community College *C*
Southside Virginia Community
  College *C*
Wytheville Community College *C*

Washington
Big Bend Community College *C*
Centralia College *C, A*
Clark College *C, A*
Columbia Basin College *A*
Everett Community College *C*
Grays Harbor College *C*
Green River Community College *C*
Lake Washington Technical College *C, A*
Lower Columbia College *A*
North Seattle Community College *A*
Renton Technical College *C*
Skagit Valley College *C*
Spokane Community College *C*
Walla Walla Community College *C*
Wenatchee Valley College *C*

Wisconsin
Chippewa Valley Technical College *C*
Gateway Technical College *C*
Madison Area Technical College *C*
Milwaukee Area Technical College *C*
Northeast Wisconsin Technical
  College *C*
Southwest Wisconsin Technical
  College *C*
Waukesha County Technical College *C*

Wyoming
Western Wyoming Community
  College *C, A*

Nutritional sciences

Alabama
Auburn University *M, D*
Community College of the Air Force *A*
University of Alabama
  Birmingham *D*

Arizona
University of Arizona *B, M, D*

Arkansas
University of Arkansas
  for Medical Sciences *M*

California
Diablo Valley College *A*
Loma Linda University *M*
Pepperdine University *B*
San Diego State University *M*
University of California
  Berkeley *B, M, D*
  Davis *B, M, D*
University of Southern California *M, D*

Connecticut
University of Connecticut *B, M, D*
University of New Haven *M*

Delaware
University of Delaware *B, M*

District of Columbia
Howard University *B, M, D*

Florida
Florida State University *B, M*

Georgia
Clark Atlanta University *B*
Georgia Military College *A*

Hawaii
University of Hawaii
  Manoa *B, M*

Illinois
Benedictine University *B*
University of Chicago *M*
University of Illinois
  Urbana-Champaign *M, D*

Kansas
University of Kansas
  Medical Center *M*

Kentucky
University of Kentucky *D*

Louisiana
Tulane University *M*

Maine
University of Maine *D*

Maryland
University of Maryland
  College Park *M, D*

Massachusetts
Boston University *B, M, D*
Framingham State College *B, M*
Hampshire College *B*
Simmons College *B, M*
Tufts University *M, D*
University of Massachusetts
  Amherst *M*

Michigan
University of Michigan *B, M, D*

Minnesota
College of St. Benedict *B*
St. John's University *B*
University of Minnesota
  Twin Cities *B, M, D*

Mississippi
Mississippi State University *M, D*
University of Southern Mississippi *M*

Missouri
University of Missouri
 Columbia M, D

Nebraska
University of Nebraska
 Lincoln M, D

Nevada
University of Nevada
 Las Vegas B

New Hampshire
University of New Hampshire B

New Jersey
Rutgers
 The State University of New Jersey:
  Cook College B
 The State University of New Jersey:
  Douglass College B
 The State University of New Jersey:
  New Brunswick Graduate
  Campus M, D
 The State University of New Jersey:
  University College New
  Brunswick B

New York
Columbia University
 Graduate School M, D
Cornell University B, M, D
Ithaca College B
Long Island University
 C. W. Post Campus M
Mohawk Valley Community College A
New York Institute of Technology B, M
Russell Sage College B
State University of New York
 Buffalo M
Syracuse University B

North Carolina
North Carolina State University B, M, D
University of North Carolina
 Chapel Hill B, M, D

Ohio
Case Western Reserve
 University B, M, D
Notre Dame College of Ohio B

Oklahoma
Oklahoma State University B, M, D

Pennsylvania
Drexel University B, M, D
Immaculata College B
La Salle University B
MCP Hahnemann University D

South Carolina
Clemson University M, D
South Carolina State University M

Texas
Texas A&M University B, M, D
Texas Woman's University B, M, D
University of Texas
 Austin D
University of the Incarnate Word B, M

Utah
Brigham Young University M
Utah State University M

Vermont
University of Vermont B, M

Virginia
J. Sargeant Reynolds Community
 College C

Washington
Bastyr University B, M
University of Washington M, D
Washington State University D

Wisconsin
Mount Mary College B, M

University of Wisconsin
 Green Bay B
 Madison M, D

Occupational health/industrial hygiene

Alabama
James H. Faulkner State Community
 College C

Alaska
University of Alaska
 Fairbanks C, A

Arkansas
University of Arkansas
 for Medical Sciences M
University of Central Arkansas B

California
California State University
 Fresno B
San Diego Miramar College C, A

Connecticut
University of New Haven C, A, B, M

Hawaii
University of Hawaii
 Honolulu Community College A

Illinois
Illinois State University B

Indiana
Indiana State University B

Iowa
University of Iowa M, D

Kentucky
Murray State University B, M

Maine
Central Maine Technical College C, A

Maryland
Community College of Baltimore County
 Catonsville C, A

Massachusetts
Springfield Technical Community
 College C
University of Massachusetts
 Lowell M, D

Michigan
Calvin College B
Grand Valley State University B
Oakland University B
University of Michigan M, D
Wayne State University M

Missouri
Central Missouri State University M
Southwest Baptist University A, B

Montana
Montana Tech of the University of
 Montana B, M

New York
New York Institute of Technology A, B
Niagara County Community College A

North Carolina
Durham Technical Community
 College A
East Carolina University M
North Carolina Agricultural and
 Technical State University B
St. Augustine's College B

Ohio
Capital University B
Ohio University B
University of Findlay B

Oklahoma
Oklahoma State University
 Oklahoma City A

Pennsylvania
Clarion University of Pennsylvania A
Duquesne University B
Northampton County Area Community
 College C, A
University of Pittsburgh C, M

Puerto Rico
Bayamon Central University B
University of Puerto Rico
 Medical Sciences Campus M

Tennessee
Milligan College M
Roane State Community College C

Texas
North Central Texas College A

Utah
Brigham Young University B

Virginia
Virginia Commonwealth University B

Washington
Central Washington University B

Occupational therapy

Alabama
Alabama State University B
Oakwood College A
Tuskegee University B
University of Alabama
 Birmingham M
University of South Alabama B

Arkansas
University of Central Arkansas B, M

California
Dominican University of California B
East Los Angeles College C
Grossmont Community College A
Loma Linda University C, B, M
Sacramento City College A
Samuel Merritt College M
San Jose State University B, M
University of Southern
 California B, M, D

Colorado
Colorado State University B, M
Pueblo Community College A

Connecticut
Quinnipiac University C, B, M
Sacred Heart University B, M
University of Hartford B

Delaware
Delaware Technical and Community
 College
 Stanton/Wilmington Campus A

District of Columbia
Howard University C, B

Florida
Barry University M
Broward Community College A
Chipola Junior College A
Florida Gulf Coast University B
Florida International University B, M
Gulf Coast Community College A
Hillsborough Community College A
Keiser College A
Miami-Dade Community College A
Nova Southeastern University M, D
Palm Beach Community College A
University of Florida B, M

Georgia
Andrew College A

Atlanta Metropolitan College A
Brenau University B, M
Dalton State College A
Medical College of Georgia B, M

Hawaii
University of Hawaii
 Kapiolani Community College A

Idaho
College of Southern Idaho A
Idaho State University M

Illinois
Chicago State University B
Governors State University M
Illinois College B
McKendree College B
North Park University B
University of Illinois
 Chicago M

Indiana
Indiana University--Purdue University
 Indiana University-Purdue
  University Indianapolis B
Manchester College B
St. Mary-of-the-Woods College B, M
University of Indianapolis M
University of Southern Indiana B
Vincennes University A

Iowa
St. Ambrose University M
Wartburg College B

Kansas
Newman University B
University of Kansas
 Medical Center B, M

Kentucky
Eastern Kentucky University B, M
Murray State University B, M
Spalding University B

Louisiana
Louisiana State University Medical
 Center B, M
University of Louisiana at Monroe B

Maine
Husson College M
University of New England B
University of Southern Maine M

Maryland
Allegany College A
Towson University B, M

Massachusetts
American International College B
Bay Path College B
Becker College A
Boston University B, M
Springfield College M
Worcester State College B, M

Michigan
Eastern Michigan University B, M
Grand Rapids Community College A
Grand Valley State University M
Lansing Community College A
Saginaw Valley State University B
Schoolcraft College A
Wayne State University B, M
Western Michigan University B, M

Minnesota
College of St. Catherine: St. Paul
 Campus B, M
College of St. Scholastica M
Gustavus Adolphus College B
Hamline University B
University of Minnesota
 Twin Cities B

Mississippi
Mississippi Gulf Coast Community College
  Perkinston *A*
University of Mississippi
  Medical Center *B*

Missouri
Maryville University of Saint Louis *B*
Rockhurst University *M*
St. Louis University *M*
University of Missouri
  Columbia *B*
Washington University *M*

Nebraska
College of Saint Mary *B*
Creighton University *D*

New Hampshire
University of New Hampshire *B*

New Jersey
Kean University *B, M*
Richard Stockton College of New Jersey *M*
Seton Hall University *M*

New Mexico
Eastern New Mexico University
  Roswell Campus *A*
University of New Mexico *B, M*
Western New Mexico University *A*

New York
City University of New York
  York College *B*
D'Youville College *B, M*
Dominican College of Blauvelt *B, M*
Ithaca College *B, M*
Keuka College *B*
Long Island University
  Brooklyn Campus *B, M*
Mercy College *B, M*
New York Institute of Technology *B*
New York University *M, D*
Rockland Community College *A*
Russell Sage College *B*
State University of New York
  Buffalo *B, M*
  Health Science Center at Brooklyn *B*
  Health Science Center at Stony Brook *B*
  Stony Brook *B*
Touro College *B, M*
Utica College of Syracuse University *B*

North Carolina
Cape Fear Community College *A*
East Carolina University *B, M*
Lenoir-Rhyne College *B*
Southwestern Community College *A*
University of North Carolina
  Chapel Hill *M*

North Dakota
University of Mary *B*
University of North Dakota *B*

Ohio
Capital University *B*
Cleveland State University *B*
Ohio State University
  Columbus Campus *B, M*
Shawnee State University *B*
Sinclair Community College *A*
University of Findlay *B*
Wittenberg University *B*
Xavier University *C, B*

Oregon
Chemeketa Community College *A*
Pacific University *M*

Pennsylvania
Alvernia College *B*
Chatham College *M*
College Misericordia *M*
Duquesne University *B, M*
Elizabethtown College *B*
Gannon University *B, M*
Mount Aloysius College *B*
Penn State
  Berks *B*
  Dubois *A*
  Mont Alto *A, B*
  Shenango *A*
  University Park *B*
  Worthington Scranton *A*
Philadelphia University *M*
St. Francis College *B, D*
St. Vincent College *B*
Temple University *B, M*
Thomas Jefferson University: College of Health Professions *B, M*
University of Pittsburgh *B*
University of Scranton *B*
University of the Sciences in Philadelphia *B, M*

Puerto Rico
University of Puerto Rico
  Arecibo Campus *T*
  Medical Sciences Campus *B*
  Ponce University College *A*

South Carolina
Florence-Darlington Technical College *A*
Tri-County Technical College *C*

South Dakota
University of South Dakota *M*

Tennessee
Belmont University *M*
Nashville State Technical Institute *C, A*
Southern Adventist University *A*
University of Tennessee
  Chattanooga *B*
  Memphis *B*

Texas
Amarillo College *A*
Texas Woman's University *C, B, M, D*
University of Texas
  El Paso *B*
  Medical Branch at Galveston *B*
  Pan American *B*
  San Antonio *B*

Virginia
J. Sargeant Reynolds Community College *A*
Shenandoah University *M*
Virginia Commonwealth University *B, M*

Washington
University of Puget Sound *B, M*
University of Washington *B*

West Virginia
West Virginia University *M*

Wisconsin
Carthage College *B*
Concordia University Wisconsin *B, M*
Mount Mary College *B, M*
University of Wisconsin
  La Crosse *B*
  Madison *M*
  Milwaukee *B*
  Oshkosh *B*

Wyoming
Casper College *A*
Northwest College *A*

Occupational therapy assistant

Alabama
Central Alabama Community College *A*
Enterprise State Junior College *A*
Faulkner University *A*
Jefferson State Community College *A*
Northwest-Shoals Community College *A*
Wallace State Community College at Hanceville *A*

California
Loma Linda University *A*
Mount St. Mary's College *C, A*
Sacramento City College *C, A*
Santa Ana College *A*

Colorado
Arapahoe Community College *A*
Denver Technical College: A Division of DeVry University *A*
Morgan Community College *A*
Pueblo Community College *A*

Connecticut
Briarwood College *A*
Manchester Community-Technical College *A*

Delaware
Delaware Technical and Community College
  Owens Campus *A*
  Stanton/Wilmington Campus *A*

Florida
Central Florida Community College *A*
Hillsborough Community College *A*
Manatee Community College *A*
Palm Beach Community College *A*
Polk Community College *A*
Tallahassee Community College *C*

Georgia
Brewton-Parker College *A*
Darton College *A*
Middle Georgia College *A*

Hawaii
University of Hawaii
  Kapiolani Community College *A*

Illinois
Black Hawk College *A*
City Colleges of Chicago
  Wright College *A*
College of DuPage *A*
John A. Logan College *A*
Parkland College *A*
Southeastern Illinois College *A*

Indiana
Ivy Tech State College
  Central Indiana *A*
Michiana College *A*
University of St. Francis *A*
University of Southern Indiana *A*

Iowa
Iowa Central Community College *A*
Kirkwood Community College *A*
Waldorf College *A*
Western Iowa Tech Community College *A*

Kansas
Barton County Community College *A*
Johnson County Community College *A*
Kansas City Kansas Community College *A*
Wichita State University *A*

Louisiana
University of Louisiana at Monroe *A*

Maine
Kennebec Valley Technical College *A*

Maryland
Community College of Baltimore County
  Catonsville *A*

Massachusetts
Bay Path College *A, B*
Bay State College *A*
Becker College *A*
Bristol Community College *A*
Greenfield Community College *A*
Lasell College *A*
Massachusetts Bay Community College *A*
Mount Ida College *A*
North Shore Community College *A*
Springfield Technical Community College *A*

Michigan
Baker College
  of Cadillac *A*
  of Muskegon *A*
Lake Michigan College *A*
Macomb Community College *A*
Mott Community College *A*
Schoolcraft College *A*

Minnesota
Anoka-Ramsey Community College *A*
College of St. Catherine-Minneapolis *A*
Lake Superior College: A Community and Technical College *A*

Missouri
Penn Valley Community College *A*
St. Charles County Community College *A*
St. Louis Community College
  St. Louis Community College at Meramec *A*

Montana
Montana State University
  College of Technology-Great Falls *A*

Nebraska
Clarkson College *A*

New Hampshire
Hesser College *A*
New Hampshire Community Technical College
  Claremont *A*

New Jersey
Atlantic Cape Community College *A*
Union County College *A*

New Mexico
Eastern New Mexico University
  Roswell Campus *A*

New York
Adirondack Community College *A*
City University of New York
  La Guardia Community College *A*
Erie Community College
  North Campus *A*
Genesee Community College *A*
Herkimer County Community College *A*
Jamestown Community College *A*
Maria College *A*
Orange County Community College *A*
Rockland Community College *A*
State University of New York
  College of Technology at Canton *A*
Suffolk County Community College *A*
Touro College *A*

North Carolina
Caldwell Community College and Technical Institute *A*
Cape Fear Community College *A*
Davidson County Community College *A*
Durham Technical Community College *A*
Pitt Community College *A*
Rockingham Community College *A*
Southwestern Community College *A*

North Dakota
North Dakota State College of Science *A*

Ohio
Cincinnati State Technical and Community College *A*
Kent State University
  East Liverpool Regional Campus *A*

Occupational therapy assistant

Lima Technical College *A*
Lourdes College *A*
Muskingum Area Technical College *A*
Owens Community College
 Toledo *A*
Shawnee State University *A*
Stark State College of Technology *A*

Oklahoma
Oklahoma City Community College *A*
Tulsa Community College *A*

Oregon
Mount Hood Community College *A*

Pennsylvania
Clarion University of Pennsylvania *A*
Community College of Allegheny
 County *A*
Duquesne University *M*
Harcum College *A*
Lehigh Carbon Community College *A*
Mount Aloysius College *A*
Pennsylvania College of Technology *A*

Puerto Rico
University of Puerto Rico
 Arecibo Campus *T*
 Humacao University College *A*
 Ponce University College *A*

Rhode Island
Community College of Rhode Island *A*

South Carolina
Central Carolina Technical College *C*
Greenville Technical College *A*
Piedmont Technical College *C*
Trident Technical College *A*

Tennessee
Roane State Community College *A*

Texas
Amarillo College *A*
Del Mar College *A*
Houston Community College
 System *C, A*
North Central Texas College *A*
St. Philip's College *A*

Utah
Salt Lake Community College *A*

Vermont
Champlain College *A*

Virginia
J. Sargeant Reynolds Community
 College *A*
Southwest Virginia Community
 College *C*

Washington
Green River Community College *A*
Spokane Falls Community College *A*

West Virginia
College of West Virginia *A*

Wisconsin
Madison Area Technical College *A*
Milwaukee Area Technical College *A*
Wisconsin Indianhead Technical
 College *A*

Wyoming
Casper College *A*

Ocean engineering

California
University of California
 San Diego *M, D*
University of Southern California *D*

Florida
Florida Atlantic University *B, M, D*
Florida Institute of Technology *B, M, D*
Miami-Dade Community College *A*

University of Florida *M, D*

Hawaii
University of Hawaii
 Manoa *M, D*

Maine
Southern Maine Technical College *A*

Maryland
United States Naval Academy *B*

Massachusetts
Massachusetts Institute of
 Technology *B, M, D*
Massachusetts Maritime Academy *B*
Worcester Polytechnic Institute *B, M*

Missouri
East Central College *A*

New Hampshire
University of New Hampshire *B, M*

New Jersey
Stevens Institute of Technology *M, D*

Oregon
Oregon State University *M*

Rhode Island
University of Rhode Island *B, M, D*

Texas
Texas A&M University
 Galveston *B*
Texas A&M University *B, M, D*

Virginia
Virginia Polytechnic Institute and State
 University *B, M*

Wisconsin
University of Wisconsin
 Madison *M*

Oceanography

Alaska
University of Alaska
 Fairbanks *M, D*

Arizona
Arizona Western College *A*

California
California State University
 Monterey Bay *B*
Humboldt State University *B*
Riverside Community College *A*
San Jose State University *B*
Southwestern College *A*
University of California
 San Diego *D*
University of Southern California *M, D*

Connecticut
University of Connecticut *M, D*

Delaware
University of Delaware *M, D*

Florida
Eckerd College *B*
Florida Institute of Technology *B, M, D*
Florida State University *M, D*
Gulf Coast Community College *A*
Nova Southeastern University *D*
Pensacola Junior College *A*
University of Miami *B, M, D*
University of South Florida *M, D*

Hawaii
Hawaii Pacific University *B*
University of Hawaii
 Manoa *M, D*

Louisiana
Louisiana State University and
 Agricultural and Mechanical
 College *M, D*

Maine
Maine Maritime Academy *B*
Southern Maine Technical College *A*
University of Maine *M, D*

Maryland
United States Naval Academy *B*

Massachusetts
Massachusetts Institute of Technology *M*

Michigan
Central Michigan University *B*
Lansing Community College *A*
University of Michigan *B, M, D*

Mississippi
University of Southern Mississippi *M, D*

New Hampshire
University of New Hampshire *M, D*

New Jersey
Rutgers
 The State University of New Jersey:
 New Brunswick Graduate
 Campus *M, D*

New York
Columbia University
 Graduate School *M, D*
 School of General Studies *B*
State University of New York
 Maritime College *B*
 Stony Brook *D*

North Carolina
Cape Fear Community College *A*
University of North Carolina
 Chapel Hill *M, D*
 Wilmington *M*

Oregon
Chemeketa Community College *A*
Oregon State University *M, D*

Pennsylvania
California University of Pennsylvania *B*
Kutztown University of
 Pennsylvania *B, T*
Millersville University of
 Pennsylvania *B*

Rhode Island
University of Rhode Island *M, D*

Texas
Texas A&M University
 Galveston *B*
Texas A&M University *M, D*

Virginia
Old Dominion University *M, D*

Washington
Shoreline Community College *A*
University of Washington *B, M, D*

Wisconsin
University of Wisconsin
 Madison *M, D*

Office supervision/management

Alabama
Alabama Agricultural and Mechanical
 University *B*
Alabama State University *A, B*
Community College of the Air Force *A*
Enterprise State Junior College *A*
Faulkner University *B*
Harry M. Ayers State Technical
 College *A*
Lawson State Community College *A*
Northeast Alabama Community
 College *A*
Northwest-Shoals Community
 College *C, A*

Oakwood College *B*
South College *A*
Southern Union State Community
 College *C, A*
Wallace State Community College at
 Hanceville *A*

Alaska
Prince William Sound Community
 College *C, A*
University of Alaska
 Fairbanks *C, A*

Arizona
Central Arizona College *A*
Cochise College *A*
Gateway Community College *A*
Glendale Community College *A*
Mesa Community College *A*
Mohave Community College *C*
Rio Salado College *C, A*
South Mountain Community College *C*
Yavapai College *C, A*

Arkansas
Arkansas State University
 Beebe Branch *A*
Central Baptist College *A*
Garland County Community
 College *C, A*
Southern Arkansas University
 Tech *A*
University of Central Arkansas *A*

California
Barstow College *C, A*
Cerritos Community College *A*
Cerro Coso Community College *C, A*
Chabot College *A*
Chaffey Community College *C, A*
Coastline Community College *C*
College of the Desert *C, A*
Compton Community College *C*
De Anza College *C*
Glendale Community College *A*
Golden Gate University *C*
Golden West College *C, A*
Imperial Valley College *C, A*
Irvine Valley College *C, A*
Lake Tahoe Community College *C, A*
Las Positas College *A*
Long Beach City College *C, A*
Los Angeles Harbor College *C, A*
Los Angeles Mission College *C, A*
Los Medanos College *C, A*
Merced College *A*
MiraCosta College *C, A*
Mission College *A*
Modesto Junior College *C*
Moorpark College *A*
Napa Valley College *C*
Ohlone College *C, A*
Pacific Union College *B*
Porterville College *C*
Saddleback College *C, A*
San Jose City College *C*
Santa Rosa Junior College *C*
Shasta College *C, A*
Solano Community College *C, A*
Southwestern College *C, A*
Victor Valley College *C*
West Valley College *A*

Colorado
Colorado Northwestern Community
 College *C, A*
Lamar Community College *A*
Mesa State College *A*

Connecticut
Asnuntuck Community-Technical
 College *A*
Central Connecticut State University *B*
Norwalk Community-Technical
 College *C, A*
Quinebaug Valley Community College *A*
Quinnipiac University *B*

Office supervision/management

District of Columbia
University of the District of Columbia *B*

Florida
Brevard Community College *C, A*
Clearwater Christian College *B*
Daytona Beach Community College *A*
Hillsborough Community College *A*
Indian River Community College *A*
Jones College *A, B*
Lake-Sumter Community College *A*
Miami-Dade Community College *C*
New England Institute of Technology *A*
Pasco-Hernando Community College *C, A*
Pensacola Junior College *C, A*
Polk Community College *A*
South Florida Community College *C, A*
Valencia Community College *A*

Georgia
Atlanta Metropolitan College *A*
Chattahoochee Technical Institute *C, A*
Darton College *A*
Emmanuel College *A*
Fort Valley State University *B*
Georgia College and State University *B*
Gwinnett Technical Institute *A*
Herzing College of Business and Technology *C*
Macon State College *C*
South Georgia College *A*

Idaho
Boise State University *A*

Illinois
Black Hawk College *C*
College of DuPage *C, A*
Elgin Community College *C*
Highland Community College *A*
John A. Logan College *A*
Joliet Junior College *C, A*
Kaskaskia College *C, A*
Kishwaukee College *A*
Lincoln Christian College and Seminary *A*
Lincoln Land Community College *A*
MacCormac College *A*
Oakton Community College *C, A*
Sauk Valley Community College *A*
William Rainey Harper College *C, A*

Indiana
Ancilla College *A*
Indiana University--Purdue University
Indiana University-Purdue University Fort Wayne *A*
University of Southern Indiana *B*
Vincennes University *A*

Iowa
Des Moines Area Community College *A*
Hawkeye Community College *A*
Iowa Central Community College *C, A*
Iowa Lakes Community College *A*
Northeast Iowa Community College *A*

Kansas
Allen County Community College *A*
Central Christian College *A, B*
Coffeyville Community College *A*
Dodge City Community College *C, A*
Emporia State University *B*
Fort Hays State University *B*
Kansas City Kansas Community College *C, A*
Pratt Community College *C, A*
Seward County Community College *C, A*
Tabor College *B*
Washburn University of Topeka *A*

Kentucky
Campbellsville University *A, B*
Eastern Kentucky University *B*
Maysville Community College *A*
Murray State University *B*

National Business College *A*
Northern Kentucky University *A, B*
Owensboro Junior College of Business *A*

Louisiana
Bossier Parish Community College *A*
Nunez Community College *A*

Maine
Andover College *A*
Beal College *A*
Eastern Maine Technical College *A*
Husson College *A, B*
Kennebec Valley Technical College *A*
Mid-State College *A*
Southern Maine Technical College *A*
University of Maine
  Augusta *C*
  Machias *A, B*
Washington County Technical College *C, A*

Maryland
Baltimore City Community College *A*
Community College of Baltimore County
  Catonsville *A*
Howard Community College *C, A*
Montgomery College
  Germantown Campus *C*
Prince George's Community College *C, A*
Villa Julie College *A*
Wor-Wic Community College *C, A*

Massachusetts
Atlantic Union College *A, B*
Bay State College *A*
Berkshire Community College *A*
Cape Cod Community College *C, A*
Fisher College *C, A*
Marian Court College *C, A*
Massasoit Community College *A*
Middlesex Community College *A*
Northern Essex Community College *A*
Roxbury Community College *A*
Springfield Technical Community College *A*

Michigan
Andrews University *B*
Baker College
  of Auburn Hills *A*
  of Cadillac *A, B*
  of Jackson *C, A*
  of Mount Clemens *B*
  of Muskegon *A*
  of Owosso *B*
  of Port Huron *A, B*
Central Michigan University *B*
Cornerstone College and Grand Rapids Baptist Seminary *B*
Davenport College of Business *A*
Delta College *A*
Detroit College of Business *B*
Eastern Michigan University *B*
Ferris State University *B*
Gogebic Community College *A*
Grand Rapids Community College *A*
Henry Ford Community College *A*
Lake Superior State University *A*
Lansing Community College *A*
Michigan State University *M*
Northern Michigan University *C*
Oakland Community College *A*

Minnesota
Alexandria Technical College *A*
Concordia College: Moorhead *B*
Inver Hills Community College *A*
Lake Superior College: A Community and Technical College *C, A*
North Hennepin Community College *A*
Winona State University *B*

Mississippi
Delta State University *B*
Hinds Community College *A*
Jackson State University *B*

Mississippi University for Women *B*
Mississippi Valley State University *B*
Rust College *A*

Missouri
Central Missouri State University *B*
Evangel University *A*
Lincoln University *A, B*
Longview Community College *C, A*
Maple Woods Community College *C, A*
Penn Valley Community College *C, A*
Southeast Missouri State University *B*
Southwest Baptist University *A*
St. Louis Community College
  St. Louis Community College at Florissant Valley *C*
  St. Louis Community College at Meramec *C*

Montana
Miles Community College *A*
University of Montana-Missoula *A*

Nebraska
Midland Lutheran College *A, B*
Union College *A*
University of Nebraska
  Kearney *B*
  Lincoln *B*

Nevada
Community College of Southern Nevada *C, A*
Western Nevada Community College *A*

New Hampshire
Antioch New England Graduate School *M*
McIntosh College *A*
New Hampshire Community Technical College
  Laconia *C*
  Manchester *C, A*

New Jersey
Berkeley College *A*
Brookdale Community College *A*
Cumberland County College *C, A*
Gloucester County College *C, A*
Katharine Gibbs School
  Gibbs College *A*
Middlesex County College *A*
Raritan Valley Community College *C*
Salem Community College *A*
Sussex County Community College *C*
Thomas Edison State College *C, A, B*
Union County College *A*
Warren County Community College *C*

New Mexico
Clovis Community College *C, A*
Dona Ana Branch Community College of New Mexico State University *C, A*
New Mexico Junior College *C, A*
Western New Mexico University *C, A*

New York
Berkeley College of New York City *A, B*
Berkeley College *A, B*
Bryant & Stratton Business Institute
  Syracuse *A*
City University of New York
  Borough of Manhattan Community College *A*
  Kingsborough Community College *A*
  Queensborough Community College *A*
Clinton Community College *A*
Columbia-Greene Community College *A*
Erie Community College
  City Campus *A*
  North Campus *A*
  South Campus *A*
Herkimer County Community College *A*
Jamestown Business College *C*
Jefferson Community College *A*
Mohawk Valley Community College *C*

Pace University:
  Pleasantville/Briarcliff *B*
Pace University *B*
Rockland Community College *C*
St. Joseph's College
  St. Joseph's College: Suffolk Campus *C*
State University of New York
  College at Buffalo *B, M*
  College of Agriculture and Technology at Cobleskill *A*
Suffolk County Community College *A*
Trocaire College *A*
Westchester Business Institute *C, A*

North Carolina
Alamance Community College *A*
Central Piedmont Community College *C, A*
Fayetteville State University *A, B*
Halifax Community College *A*

North Dakota
Dickinson State University *A, B*
Lake Region State College *C, A*
Valley City State University *B*

Ohio
Cincinnati State Technical and Community College *A*
Columbus State Community College *C, A*
David N. Myers College *A, B*
DeVry Institute of Technology
  Columbus *B*
Defiance College *B*
Edison State Community College *A*
Hocking Technical College *A*
Kent State University
  Ashtabula Regional Campus *A*
  Trumbull Campus *A*
  Tuscarawas Campus *A*
Lima Technical College *A*
Miami University
  Middletown Campus *C, A*
  Oxford Campus *C, A*
Miami-Jacobs College *C, A*
Mount Vernon Nazarene College *A, B*
Ohio University
  Chillicothe Campus *A*
  Zanesville Campus *A*
Ohio University *A*
Owens Community College
  Toledo *C, A*
Terra Community College *A*
Tiffin University *B*
University of Akron
  Wayne College *A*
University of Akron *A*
University of Cincinnati
  Clermont College *A*
  Raymond Walters College *A*
Youngstown State University *A, B*

Oklahoma
Connors State College *A*
East Central University *B*
Eastern Oklahoma State College *C*
Northern Oklahoma College *A*
Oklahoma State University
  Oklahoma City *C, A*
Seminole State College *A*

Oregon
Chemeketa Community College *C, A*
Clackamas Community College *C, A*
Clatsop Community College *C*
Eugene Bible College *C*
Lane Community College *C, A*
Linn-Benton Community College *C, A*
Portland Community College *A*

Pennsylvania
Bucks County Community College *A*
Cheyney University of Pennsylvania *B*
Churchman Business School *A*
Community College of Beaver County *A*

Office supervision/management

Delaware County Community
  College C, A
Indiana University of Pennsylvania B
Lebanon Valley College of
  Pennsylvania C
Lehigh Carbon Community College A
Marywood University C
Peirce College A, B
Reading Area Community College A
Robert Morris College B
Shippensburg University of
  Pennsylvania B
South Hills School of Business &
  Technology A

Puerto Rico
Colegio Universitario del Este B
Inter American University of Puerto Rico
  Bayamon Campus A
University of Puerto Rico
  Aguadilla A

Rhode Island
Providence College C, A

South Carolina
Chesterfield-Marlboro Technical
  College C
Technical College of the
  Lowcountry C, A
University of South Carolina B

South Dakota
Black Hills State University B
Dakota State University A

Tennessee
Belmont University B
Knoxville Business College A
Lee University B
Middle Tennessee State University B
Pellissippi State Technical Community
  College C
Tennessee Temple University B
University of Memphis B
Walters State Community College A

Texas
Brookhaven College A
Cedar Valley College A
Central Texas College C, A
College of the Mainland A
Eastfield College A
Grayson County College A
Hill College C, A
Houston Community College System A
Lamar University B
North Lake College A
Palo Alto College C, A
Paris Junior College A
San Antonio College A
San Jacinto College
  North C, A
Southwest Texas State University B
Southwestern Adventist University A, B
Stephen F. Austin State University B
Sul Ross State University C, B
Tarleton State University B
Texas A&M University
  Commerce B
Texas Woman's University B
Tyler Junior College A
University of North Texas B

Utah
College of Eastern Utah C
LDS Business College A
Mountain West College C, A
Salt Lake Community College A
Southern Utah University A
Weber State University B

Vermont
Champlain College A, B
Vermont Technical College A

Virginia
Central Virginia Community College C
Dabney S. Lancaster Community
  College C, A
Germanna Community College C
Lord Fairfax Community College A
Mountain Empire Community College A
National Business College A
Norfolk State University B
Northern Virginia Community College A
Paul D. Camp Community College A
Radford University B
St. Paul's College B
Thomas Nelson Community College A
Virginia Commonwealth University B
Virginia Highlands Community
  College C, A
Virginia Intermont College B

Washington
Big Bend Community College C, A
Central Washington University B
Columbia Basin College C, A
Eastern Washington University B
Edmonds Community College C, A
Olympic College A
Peninsula College A
Pierce College A
Renton Technical College C, A
Shoreline Community College C, A
South Seattle Community College C, A
Spokane Community College A
Walla Walla College B
Walla Walla Community College A
Wenatchee Valley College A

West Virginia
College of West Virginia A, B
Concord College A
Davis and Elkins College A, B
Fairmont State College B
West Virginia University Institute of
  Technology A

Wisconsin
Blackhawk Technical College A
Madison Area Technical College A
Milwaukee Area Technical College A
Moraine Park Technical College A
Northeast Wisconsin Technical
  College A

Wyoming
Casper College C, A
Northwest College A
Sheridan College A
Western Wyoming Community
  College A

Operations management/supervision

Alabama
Auburn University B
Community College of the Air Force A
Lawson State Community College A

Arizona
Eastern Arizona College C
Glendale Community College A
University of Arizona B

Arkansas
University of Arkansas B

California
California State Polytechnic University:
  Pomona B
California State University
  Chico B
  Fullerton B
  Hayward M
  Long Beach B
Citrus College C
City College of San Francisco C, A
Cuyamaca College A
DeVry Institute of Technology
  Fremont B
  Long Beach B
  West Hills B
Fashion Institute of Design and
  Merchandising A
Golden Gate University M
National University B
Palomar College C, A
San Diego City College C, A
San Diego State University B
University of La Verne M
University of Southern California M

Colorado
Fort Lewis College B
University of Colorado
  Boulder B

Connecticut
Central Connecticut State University M
Yale University M

Delaware
University of Delaware B

District of Columbia
George Washington University M
Trinity College B

Florida
Florida Southern College B
Florida State University B

Georgia
Dalton State College B
Georgia State University D
Kennesaw State University M
South Georgia College A

Hawaii
University of Hawaii
  Hawaii Community College C, A

Idaho
University of Idaho B

Illinois
Benedictine University M
Carl Sandburg College A
College of DuPage A
De Paul University B, M
DeVry Institute of Technology
  Addison B
  Chicago B
Illinois Institute of Technology M
Kishwaukee College C, A
McHenry County College C, A
Northern Illinois University B
Prairie State College C, A
University of Illinois
  Chicago D
Waubonsee Community College C, A
William Rainey Harper College C, A

Indiana
Indiana Institute of Technology B
Indiana University--Purdue University
  Indiana University-Purdue
    University Fort Wayne C, A, B
  Indiana University-Purdue
    University Indianapolis A, B
Purdue University
  North Central Campus C, A, B
Purdue University A, B
Tri-State University B
University of Southern Indiana M
Valparaiso University B

Iowa
University of Iowa B

Kansas
Barton County Community College C, A
Pratt Community College C, A

Kentucky
Owensboro Junior College of Business A

Louisiana
Louisiana Tech University A, B

Maryland
University of Maryland
  College Park B
  University College M

Massachusetts
Boston College B
Boston University B
Suffolk University M
Worcester Polytechnic Institute B, M

Michigan
Central Michigan University B, M
Ferris State University B
Kettering University M
Lake Michigan College A
Michigan State University B, M, D
Mott Community College A
Oakland Community College A
Saginaw Valley State University B
University of Michigan
  Flint B

Minnesota
Alexandria Technical College A
Minnesota State University, Mankato B
University of St. Thomas B, M
Winona State University B

Mississippi
Hinds Community College A
Mississippi State University B

Missouri
Southeast Missouri State University B
University of Missouri
  St. Louis B
Washington University B
Webster University M

Montana
University of Great Falls A, B

Nebraska
University of Nebraska
  Omaha B

New Hampshire
New Hampshire Community Technical
  College
    Nashua C

New Jersey
Cumberland County College A
Fairleigh Dickinson University M
Thomas Edison State College C, A, B
Warren County Community College C

New Mexico
Western New Mexico University B

New York
City University of New York
  Baruch College B
Daemen College B
Erie Community College
  North Campus C
Iona College M
Pace University:
  Pleasantville/Briarcliff B, M
Pace University B, M
Polytechnic University
  Long Island Campus M
Polytechnic University M
Regents College B
Syracuse University B, M

North Carolina
Asheville Buncombe Technical
  Community College A
Cleveland Community College A
Durham Technical Community
  College C, A
Johnston Community College A
Mitchell Community College A
Pitt Community College A

University of North Carolina
  Asheville C, B
  Chapel Hill D
  Charlotte B
Western Piedmont Community
  College A
Wilson Technical Community College A

Ohio
Bowling Green State University B, M
Case Western Reserve University M, D
Franklin University B
Kent State University B
Lakeland Community College C
Miami University
  Oxford Campus B
North Central State College C, A
Ohio State University
  Columbus Campus B
Ohio University B
Stark State College of Technology A
Terra Community College C
Tiffin University B
University of Akron B
University of Cincinnati
  Raymond Walters College C, A
University of Cincinnati B, M, D
University of Toledo M
Wright State University M
Youngstown State University B

Oklahoma
Carl Albert State College C
East Central University B

Oregon
Chemeketa Community College A

Pennsylvania
Bucks County Community College A
California University of Pennsylvania B
Cheyney University of Pennsylvania B
Community College of Philadelphia A
Delaware County Community College A
Drexel University B
La Salle University B
Lehigh Carbon Community College A
Penn State
  University Park C, B
Reading Area Community College A
Robert Morris College B
Susquehanna University B
University of Pennsylvania B, M
University of Scranton B, M

Rhode Island
Bryant College M

South Carolina
Clemson University M, D

Tennessee
Tennessee Technological University B

Texas
Baylor University B
Del Mar College C, A
El Paso Community College A
Houston Community College
  System C, A
Lamar University M
LeTourneau University B
Sam Houston State University B
Tarrant County College A
Texas A&M University
  Commerce B
Texas State Technical College
  Sweetwater C, A
  Waco A
University of Houston B, M
University of North Texas B, M, D
University of Texas
  Arlington M
  San Antonio B, M
Weatherford College C, A
Wiley College B

Utah
Brigham Young University B

Vermont
College of St. Joseph in Vermont B

Virginia
George Mason University M

Washington
City University C, M
Eastern Washington University B
Seattle Central Community College C
Seattle University B
Western Washington University B

Wisconsin
Blackhawk Technical College A
Chippewa Valley Technical College A
Gateway Technical College A
Marian College of Fond du Lac B
University of Wisconsin
  Madison B
  Milwaukee B
  Oshkosh B

| Operations research |

Arkansas
University of Arkansas
  Little Rock B

California
Stanford University M, D

Colorado
United States Air Force Academy B

Connecticut
Central Connecticut State University B
United States Coast Guard Academy B
University of New Haven B, M

Delaware
University of Delaware B, M, D

District of Columbia
George Washington University M, D

Florida
Florida Institute of Technology M, D

Georgia
Georgia Institute of Technology M

Indiana
Indiana University--Purdue University
  Indiana University-Purdue
    University Fort Wayne B, M

Iowa
Iowa State University M

Kansas
Kansas State University M

Massachusetts
Massachusetts Institute of
  Technology M, D
Northeastern University M

Michigan
Michigan State University M
Wayne State University M
Western Michigan University M

Missouri
St. Louis University M
University of Missouri
  Rolla M

New Jersey
Rutgers
  The State University of New Jersey:
    New Brunswick Graduate
      Campus M, D

New Mexico
New Mexico Institute of Mining and
  Technology M

New York
City University of New York
  Baruch College B, M
Columbia University
  Fu Foundation School of
    Engineering and Applied
    Science B, M, D
New York University B, M, D
Rensselaer Polytechnic Institute M
St. John's University M

North Carolina
University of North Carolina
  Chapel Hill M, D

Ohio
Case Western Reserve University M, D

Pennsylvania
Carnegie Mellon University B
Temple University B, M
University of Pennsylvania M, D

Texas
Southern Methodist University M, D
University of Texas
  Dallas B, M, D

Wisconsin
University of Wisconsin
  Madison B

| Ophthalmic medical assistant |

Alabama
Community College of the Air Force A

Colorado
Pueblo Community College A

Illinois
Triton College A

Louisiana
Delgado Community College C

New York
Rochester Institute of Technology A
Suffolk County Community College A

North Carolina
Durham Technical Community
  College C, A

Oregon
Portland Community College A

Pennsylvania
Central Pennsylvania College A

Puerto Rico
National College of Business and
  Technology A

Tennessee
Volunteer State Community College A

Washington
Spokane Community College A

| Ophthalmic/optometric services |

Colorado
Pueblo Community College A

Connecticut
Middlesex Community-Technical
  College A

Florida
Gulf Coast Community College A
Hillsborough Community College C, A
Miami-Dade Community College A
Polk Community College A

Georgia
DeKalb Technical Institute C, A

Illinois
McHenry County College C

Indiana
Indiana University
  Bloomington A

Louisiana
Louisiana State University Medical
  Center B

Massachusetts
Holyoke Community College C, A
Mount Ida College A

Michigan
Bay de Noc Community College C
Ferris State University A, D

Minnesota
Anoka-Ramsey Community College A

Mississippi
Mississippi Gulf Coast Community
  College
    Perkinston A

New Hampshire
New Hampshire Community Technical
  College
    Nashua C

New Jersey
Camden County College A
Essex County College A
Raritan Valley Community College A

New York
Erie Community College
  North Campus A
Interboro Institute A
Suffolk County Community College A

North Carolina
Durham Technical Community
  College C, A

Ohio
Hocking Technical College A
Lakeland Community College A
Ohio State University
  Columbus Campus M
Owens Community College
  Toledo A

Pennsylvania
Westmoreland County Community
  College C, A

South Carolina
Florence-Darlington Technical
  College C

Tennessee
Roane State Community College A

Texas
El Paso Community College C, A
Tyler Junior College C
University of Houston B, D

Virginia
J. Sargeant Reynolds Community
  College A
Thomas Nelson Community College A

Washington
Spokane Community College C, A

Wisconsin
Madison Area Technical College C

| Optics |

Alabama
Alabama Agricultural and Mechanical
  University D
University of Alabama
  Huntsville B

Arizona
University of Arizona *M, D*
California
Irvine Valley College *C, A*
Florida
University of Central Florida *M, D*
Indiana
Indiana University
  Bloomington *M, D*
Rose-Hulman Institute of
  Technology *B, M*
Vincennes University *A*
Massachusetts
Tufts University *M, D*
Worcester Polytechnic Institute *B, M*
Michigan
Saginaw Valley State University *B*
Missouri
University of Missouri
  St. Louis *M, D*
New Jersey
Stevens Institute of Technology *M, D*
New Mexico
University of New Mexico *D*
New York
Corning Community College *A*
Monroe Community College *A*
University of Rochester *B, M, D*
Ohio
Ohio State University
  Columbus Campus *B, M, D*
Southern Ohio College *A*
Texas
University of North Texas *M*

Optometric/ophthalmic laboratory technology

California
Canada College *A*
Connecticut
Middlesex Community-Technical
  College *A*
Delaware
Delaware Technical and Community
  College
    Owens Campus *A*
Florida
Broward Community College *A*
Georgia
DeKalb Technical Institute *C, A*
Indiana
Indiana University
  Bloomington *A*
Louisiana
Nunez Community College *A*
Minnesota
St. Cloud Technical College *C, A*
New York
Rochester Institute of Technology *C, A*
North Carolina
Duke University *C*
Durham Technical Community
  College *C*
Ohio
Hocking Technical College *A*
Owens Community College
  Toledo *A*
Oregon
Eastern Oregon University *B*

Puerto Rico
University of Puerto Rico
  Medical Sciences Campus *A*
Texas
Tyler Junior College *C, A*
Washington
Seattle Central Community College *C*

Optometry (O.D.)

Alabama
University of Alabama at Birmingham:
  School of Optometry *F*
California
Southern California College of
  Optometry *F*
University of California Berkeley: School
  of Optometry *F*
Florida
Nova Southeastern University Health
  Professions Division: College of
  Optometry *F*
Nova Southeastern University of the
  Health Sciences: College of
  Pharmacy *F*
Illinois
Illinois College of Optometry *F*
Indiana
Indiana University Bloomington: School
  of Optometry *F*
Massachusetts
New England College of Optometry *F*
Michigan
Ferris State University: College of
  Optometry *F*
Missouri
University of Missouri St. Louis: School
  of Optometry *F*
New York
State University of New York College of
  Optometry *F*
Ohio
Ohio State University Columbus
  Campus: College of Optometry *F*
Oklahoma
Northeastern State University: College of
  Optometry *F*
Oregon
Pacific University: School of
  Optometry *F*
Pennsylvania
Pennsylvania College of Optometry *F*
Puerto Rico
Inter American University of Puerto Rico
  School of Optometry *F*
Tennessee
Southern College of Optometry *F*
Texas
University of Houston: College of
  Optometry *F*

Organic chemistry

Colorado
University of Denver *B*
Florida
Florida State University *B, M, D*
Iowa
Iowa State University *M, D*

Maryland
Johns Hopkins University *B*
Massachusetts
Hampshire College *B*
Harvard College *B*
Massachusetts College of Pharmacy and
  Health Sciences *M, D*
Mount Holyoke College *M*
Tufts University *M, D*
Worcester Polytechnic Institute *B, M*
New Jersey
Stevens Institute of Technology *M, D*
New York
Columbia University
  Graduate School *M, D*
Fordham University *M*
Rockefeller University *D*
Sarah Lawrence College *B*
State University of New York
  Albany *D*
  College of Environmental Science
    and Forestry *M, D*
North Carolina
University of North Carolina
  Chapel Hill *M, D*
Oregon
University of Oregon *M, D*
Pennsylvania
University of Scranton *B*
Texas
Texas A&M University
  Commerce *B*
University of North Texas *M, D*
Utah
University of Utah *M, D*
Vermont
Bennington College *B*
Marlboro College *B*
Wisconsin
Marquette University *M, D*
University of Wisconsin
  River Falls *B*

Organizational behavior studies

Arizona
University of Phoenix *M*
California
Antioch Southern California
  Santa Barbara *M*
Chapman University *M*
Claremont McKenna College *B*
Golden Gate University *B*
Pepperdine University *M*
Pitzer College *B*
St. Mary's College of California *M*
Santa Clara University *B*
Scripps College *B*
University of La Verne *B*
University of San Francisco *B*
Colorado
University of Colorado
  Denver *M*
Connecticut
Central Connecticut State University *M*
Eastern Connecticut State University *M*
University of Hartford *M*
District of Columbia
George Washington University *M*
Florida
Warner Southern College *B*
Georgia
Oglethorpe University *B*

Southern Polytechnic State University *B*
Illinois
Benedictine University *B, M*
Greenville College *B*
Loyola University of Chicago *M*
North Park University *B*
Northwestern University *B, M, D*
Trinity International University *M, D*
Indiana
Indiana University
  Bloomington *D*
Oakland City University *B*
Iowa
St. Ambrose University *B*
University of Iowa *D*
Kansas
Newman University *M*
Kentucky
Northern Kentucky University *B*
Louisiana
Loyola University New Orleans *B*
Maine
University of Southern Maine *B*
Maryland
Columbia Union College *B*
Massachusetts
Boston College *D*
Boston University *B*
Emerson College *M*
Harvard University *M, D*
Michigan
Eastern Michigan University *M*
Michigan State University *D*
University of Michigan
  Flint *B*
Wayne State University *B*
Minnesota
Bethel College *B*
Concordia University: St. Paul *B*
Northwestern College *B*
Missouri
St. Louis University *B, D*
St. Louis Community College
  St. Louis Community College at
    Forest Park *C, A*
Nebraska
University of Nebraska
  Omaha *B*
New Hampshire
Antioch New England Graduate
  School *M*
New Jersey
Fairleigh Dickinson University *M*
Rider University *B*
Thomas Edison State College *B*
New York
City University of New York
  Baruch College *M, D*
New York University *B, M, D*
Pace University:
  Pleasantville/Briarcliff *B, M*
Pace University *B, M*
Polytechnic University
  Long Island Campus *M*
Polytechnic University *M*
State University of New York
  Albany *D*
North Carolina
High Point University *B*
Mount Olive College *B*
University of North Carolina
  Chapel Hill *D*
North Dakota
North Dakota State University *M*

Ohio
Bowling Green State University *M*
Case Western Reserve University *M, D*
Miami University
    Oxford Campus *B*
Union Institute *D*
University of Findlay *M*
Youngstown State University *B*

Oregon
University of Oregon *D*

Pennsylvania
La Salle University *B*
University of Pennsylvania *B*
Westminster College *B*

Puerto Rico
University of Puerto Rico
    Mayaguez Campus *B*

Rhode Island
Brown University *B*

South Carolina
Converse College *B*

Texas
Abilene Christian University *M*
Southern Methodist University *B*
University of Houston *B*
University of North Texas *B, D*
University of Texas
    Dallas *B, M, D*

Utah
Brigham Young University *B, M*

Virginia
Bridgewater College *B*
Regent University *D*

Washington
Central Washington University *M*

Wisconsin
Marquette University *B*
Silver Lake College *M*
University of Wisconsin
    Platteville *B*

Ornamental horticulture

Alabama
Bessemer State Technical College *C, A*
Northwest-Shoals Community College *C*

Arkansas
University of Arkansas *B*

California
Bakersfield College *A*
Butte College *C, A*
Cabrillo College *C, A*
California Polytechnic State University:
    San Luis Obispo *B*
Cerritos Community College *A*
City College of San Francisco *C, A*
College of San Mateo *C, A*
College of the Desert *C, A*
College of the Sequoias *C*
Cuyamaca College *A*
Foothill College *C, A*
Las Positas College *C, A*
Los Angeles Pierce College *C, A*
Merced College *C, A*
Modesto Junior College *A*
Monterey Peninsula College *C, A*
Moorpark College *A*
Mount San Antonio College *C*
Orange Coast College *C, A*
Saddleback College *C, A*
San Joaquin Delta College *C, A*
Shasta College *C, A*
Sierra College *C, A*
Solano Community College *C, A*
Ventura College *A*
Victor Valley College *C, A*
Yuba College *C*

Colorado
Northeastern Junior College *C, A*

Delaware
University of Delaware *B, M*

Florida
Central Florida Community College *A*
Florida Agricultural and Mechanical
    University *B*
Florida Southern College *B*
Gulf Coast Community College *A*
Hillsborough Community College *C, A*
Palm Beach Community College *A*
Pensacola Junior College *A*
Santa Fe Community College *A*
Valencia Community College *A*

Georgia
Abraham Baldwin Agricultural
    College *A*
Fort Valley State University *A*

Illinois
College of DuPage *C*
College of Lake County *C, A*
Joliet Junior College *C, A*
Kishwaukee College *C, A*
McHenry County College *C*
Triton College *C, A*
University of Illinois
    Urbana-Champaign *B*
William Rainey Harper College *C, A*

Iowa
Kirkwood Community College *C*

Kentucky
Eastern Kentucky University *B*
Murray State University *B*

Maryland
Prince George's Community College *C*

Massachusetts
North Shore Community College *A*
University of Massachusetts
    Amherst *A*

Michigan
Ferris State University *A*
Michigan State University *C*
Wayne County Community College *C*

Mississippi
Meridian Community College *A*
Mississippi Gulf Coast Community
    College
    Perkinston *A*

Missouri
St. Louis Community College
    St. Louis Community College at
    Meramec *C, A*

Nebraska
Central Community College *C*
Metropolitan Community College *C, A*
Nebraska College of Technical
    Agriculture *A*

Nevada
Community College of Southern
    Nevada *C, A*

New Hampshire
University of New Hampshire *A*

New Jersey
Brookdale Community College *C*
Cumberland County College *C, A*
Mercer County Community College *C, A*

New York
Cornell University *B*
Finger Lakes Community College *C, A*
Niagara County Community College *C*
State University of New York
    College of Agriculture and
      Technology at Cobleskill *A, B*
    College of Technology at Alfred *A*
    College of Technology at Delhi *A*
    Farmingdale *C, A*
Suffolk County Community College *A*

North Carolina
Blue Ridge Community College *C*
Sampson Community College *A*

North Dakota
Minot State University: Bottineau
    Campus *A*

Ohio
Cincinnati State Technical and
    Community College *A*

Oklahoma
Eastern Oklahoma State College *A*
Oklahoma State University
    Oklahoma City *C*

Oregon
Clackamas Community College *C, A*

Pennsylvania
Chatham College *C*
Delaware Valley College *C, B*
Mercyhurst College *C*
Pennsylvania College of Technology *A*

Puerto Rico
Inter American University of Puerto Rico
    Barranquitas Campus *A*

Tennessee
University of Tennessee
    Knoxville *B, M*
Walters State Community College *A*

Texas
Alvin Community College *C*
Austin Community College *C*
Grayson County College *C*
Houston Community College System *C*
Palo Alto College *A*
Southwest Texas State University *B, T*
Tarleton State University *B*
Texas A&M University *B*
Western Texas College *C, A*

Utah
Utah State University *C, A, B*

Vermont
Vermont Technical College *A*

Virginia
Christopher Newport University *B*
J. Sargeant Reynolds Community
    College *C, A*

Washington
Clark College *C, A*
South Puget Sound Community
    College *C, A*
South Seattle Community College *A*
Spokane Community College *C*

Wisconsin
Blackhawk Technical College *C*

Orthotics/prosthetics

California
California State University
    Dominguez Hills *B*

Florida
Florida International University *B*

Iowa
St. Ambrose University *M*

Minnesota
Century Community and Technical
    College *A*

Pennsylvania
Alvernia College *A*
Median School of Allied Health
    Careers *A*

Texas
University of Texas
    Southwestern Medical Center at
      Dallas *B*

Washington
Highline Community College *A*
University of Washington *B*

Osteopathic medicine (D.O.)

California
Western University of Health Sciences *F*

Florida
Nova Southeastern University Health
    Professions Division: College of
    Osteopathic Medicine *F*
Nova Southeastern University of the
    Health Sciences: College of
    Pharmacy *F*

Illinois
Midwestern University: Chicago College
    of Osteopathic Medicine *F*

Iowa
University of Osteopathic Medicine and
    Health Sciences: College of
    Osteopathic Medicine and Surgery *F*

Maine
University of New England: School of
    Osteopathic Medicine *F*

Michigan
Michigan State University: College of
    Osteopathic Medicine *F*

Missouri
Kirksville College of Osteopathic
    Medicine *F*
University of Health Sciences College of
    Osteopathic Medicine *F*

New Jersey
UMDNJ-School of Osteopathic
    Medicine *F*

New York
New York College of Osteopathic
    Medicine of New York Institute of
    Technology *F*

Ohio
Ohio University
    College of Osteopathic Medicine *F*

Oklahoma
Oklahoma State University: College of
    Osteopathic Medicine *F*

Pennsylvania
Lake Erie College of Osteopathic
    Medicine *F*
Philadelphia College of Osteopathic
    Medicine *F*

Texas
University of North Texas Health Science
    Center at Fort Worth: Osteopathic
    Medicine *F*

Pacific area studies

California
Loyola Marymount University *B*
San Jose City College *A*
University of California
    San Diego *M*

Hawaii
Brigham Young University
 Hawaii *B*
University of Hawaii
 Manoa *M*
 West Oahu *B*

Missouri
Northwest Missouri State University *B*

Painting

Alabama
Birmingham-Southern College *B*
University of Alabama *M*

Arizona
Arizona State University *B, M*

Arkansas
Harding University *B*

California
Academy of Art College *C, A, B, M*
Art Center College of Design *B, M*
California College of Arts and
 Crafts *B, M*
California Institute of the Arts *C, B, M*
California State University
 Fullerton *B, M*
 Hayward *B*
 Long Beach *B, M*
 Northridge *B, M*
Chabot College *A*
College of San Mateo *A*
De Anza College *C, A*
Grossmont Community College *A*
Long Beach City College *C, A*
Monterey Peninsula College *A*
Otis College of Art and Design *B, M*
Palomar College *A*
Pasadena City College *A*
San Diego State University *B*
San Francisco Art Institute *B, M*
Santa Rosa Junior College *C*
Solano Community College *A*
University of San Francisco *B*

Colorado
Adams State College *B*
Colorado State University *B*
Naropa University *C, B*
Rocky Mountain College of Art &
 Design *B*

Connecticut
Paier College of Art *C, B*
Sacred Heart University *B*
University of Connecticut *B*
University of Hartford *B, M*

District of Columbia
American University *M*
George Washington University *M*

Florida
Art Institute
 of Fort Lauderdale *A*
Ringling School of Art and Design *B*
University of Miami *B*

Georgia
Atlanta College of Art *B*
Georgia Military College *A*
LaGrange College *B*
Savannah College of Art and
 Design *B, M*
University of Georgia *B*

Illinois
American Academy of Art *A, B*
Barat College *B*
City Colleges of Chicago
 Olive-Harvey College *A*
Rend Lake College *A*
Richland Community College *A*
Rockford College *B*

School of the Art Institute of
 Chicago *B, M*
University of Illinois
 Urbana-Champaign *B*

Indiana
Ball State University *B*
Indiana University--Purdue University
 Indiana University-Purdue
  University Fort Wayne *B*
University of Evansville *B*
Vincennes University *A*

Iowa
Drake University *B, M*
University of Iowa *B, M*

Kansas
Allen County Community College *A*
Central Christian College *A*
Pratt Community College *A*
Seward County Community College *A*
University of Kansas *B, M*

Kentucky
Bellarmine College *B*

Maine
Maine College of Art *B*

Maryland
Maryland Institute College of Art *B, M*

Massachusetts
Boston University *B, M*
Emmanuel College *B*
Hampshire College *B*
Massachusetts College of Art *B, M*
Montserrat College of Art *B*
School of the Museum of Fine Arts *B, M*
Simon's Rock College of Bard *B*
University of Massachusetts
 Dartmouth *B*

Michigan
Center for Creative Studies: College of
 Art and Design *B*
Grand Valley State University *B*
Lansing Community College *A*
Northern Michigan University *B*
Siena Heights University *B*
University of Michigan
 Dearborn *B*
University of Michigan *B*
Western Michigan University *B*

Minnesota
College of Visual Arts *B*
Minneapolis College of Art and
 Design *B*
Minnesota State University, Mankato *B*
Moorhead State University *B*

Mississippi
Mississippi University for Women *B*

Missouri
Kansas City Art Institute *B*
Lindenwood University *B, M*
University of Missouri
 St. Louis *B*
Washington University *B, M*
Webster University *B*

Nebraska
University of Nebraska
 Omaha *B*

New Hampshire
Plymouth State College of the University
 System of New Hampshire *B*
Rivier College *B*
University of New Hampshire *M*

New Jersey
Rowan University *B*
Rutgers
 The State University of New Jersey:
  Mason Gross School of the
  Arts *B, M*

New York
Adelphi University *B*
Bard College *B, M*
City University of New York
 Brooklyn College *M*
 Queens College *B, M*
Columbia University
 School of General Studies *B*
 Teachers College *M, D*
New York Institute of Technology *M*
New York State College of Ceramics at
 Alfred University *B, M, T*
Parsons School of Design *C, A, B, M, T*
Pratt Institute *B, M*
Rochester Institute of
 Technology *A, B, M*
Sarah Lawrence College *B*
School of Visual Arts *B, M*
State University of New York
 Albany *B, M*
 Buffalo *M*
 College at Buffalo *B*
 College at Fredonia *B*
 New Paltz *B*
Syracuse University *B, M*

North Carolina
Brevard College *A, B*

Ohio
Bowling Green State University *B*
Cleveland Institute of Art *B*
Columbus College of Art and Design *B*
Kent State University *B, M*
Lourdes College *A*
Ohio State University
 Columbus Campus *B*
Ohio University *B, M*
Shawnee State University *B*
University of Akron *B*
Wittenberg University *B*
Youngstown State University *B*

Oklahoma
University of Oklahoma *B*

Oregon
Pacific Northwest College of Art *B*
Portland State University *B, M*
University of Oregon *B, M*

Pennsylvania
Beaver College *B*
Carnegie Mellon University *B*
Immaculata College *A*
Mercyhurst College *B*
Moore College of Art and Design *B*
Seton Hill College *B*
Temple University *B, M*
University of the Arts *B, M*

Puerto Rico
Escuela de Artes Plasticas de Puerto
 Rico *B*
University of Puerto Rico
 Rio Piedras Campus *B*

Rhode Island
Providence College *B*
Rhode Island College *B*
Salve Regina University *B*

South Carolina
Anderson College *B*

Tennessee
Carson-Newman College *B*
Union University *B*

Texas
McMurry University *B*
Sam Houston State University *M*
Stephen F. Austin State University *M*
Texas A&M University
 Commerce *B, M*
Texas Woman's University *B, M*
University of Dallas *M, T*
University of Houston *B*
University of North Texas *B, M*

University of Texas
 Arlington *B*
 El Paso *B*
 San Antonio *B, M*
Western Texas College *A*

Utah
Brigham Young University *B, M*
Dixie State College of Utah *A*

Vermont
Bennington College *B, M*
Burlington College *B*
Marlboro College *B*

Virginia
Virginia Commonwealth
 University *B, M*
Virginia Intermont College *B*

Washington
Cornish College of the Arts *B*
North Seattle Community College *C*
University of Washington *B, M*
Western Washington University *B*

West Virginia
Alderson-Broaddus College *B*
Marshall University *B*
West Virginia State College *B*
West Virginia Wesleyan College *B*

Wisconsin
Milwaukee Institute of Art & Design *B*
University of Wisconsin
 Madison *B*

Paleontology

Arkansas
University of Arkansas *D*

California
Loma Linda University *M*

Illinois
Illinois State University *M*

Iowa
University of Northern Iowa *B*

Louisiana
Tulane University *D*

Massachusetts
Harvard College *B*
Harvard University *M, D*

Michigan
University of Michigan *B, M*
Western Michigan University *B*

New York
Columbia University
 Graduate School *M, D*

Ohio
Ohio State University
 Columbus Campus *B, M, D*

Pennsylvania
University of Pittsburgh *B*

South Dakota
South Dakota School of Mines and
 Technology *M*

Texas
Texas Christian University *B*
University of Texas
 Dallas *M, D*

Paralegal/legal assistance

Alabama
Calhoun Community College *A*
Community College of the Air Force *A*
Enterprise State Junior College *A*
Gadsden State Community College *A*

Paralegal/legal assistance

Huntingdon College *A*
James H. Faulkner State Community
  College *A*
Northeast Alabama Community
  College *A*
South College *A*
Spring Hill College *C, A*
Wallace State Community College at
  Hanceville *A*

Alaska
University of Alaska
  Anchorage *C*
  Fairbanks *A*

Arizona
Northland Pioneer College *A*
Phoenix College *C, A*
Pima Community College *C, A*
Yavapai College *C, A*

Arkansas
Westark College *A*

California
American River College *A*
Butte College *C, A*
California State University
  Chico *C*
  Hayward *C*
Canada College *A*
Cerritos Community College *A*
City College of San Francisco *C, A*
Coastline Community College *C*
College of the Redwoods *C, A*
College of the Sequoias *A*
Compton Community College *C, A*
De Anza College *C, A*
Empire College *A*
Fresno City College *C, A*
Glendale Community College *A*
Humphreys College *C, B*
Imperial Valley College *C, A*
Lake Tahoe Community College *C*
Los Angeles Mission College *C, A*
Los Angeles Southwest College *A*
Merritt College *C, A*
Mount San Antonio College *A*
Napa Valley College *C, A*
Palomar College *C, A*
Pasadena City College *C, A*
Saddleback College *C, A*
St. Mary's College of California *C*
San Diego City College *A*
San Diego Miramar College *C, A*
San Francisco State University *C*
Santa Clara University *C*
Shasta College *A*
Skyline College *C, A*
University of La Verne *C, A, B*
University of San Diego *C*
University of West Los Angeles *B*
West Los Angeles College *C, A*
West Valley College *A*

Colorado
Arapahoe Community College *C, A*
Colorado Northwestern Community
  College *A*
Community College of Aurora *C, A*
Community College of Denver *C, A*
Front Range Community College *C*
Pikes Peak Community College *A*
Pueblo Community College *C, A*

Connecticut
Briarwood College *A*
Manchester Community-Technical
  College *C, A*
Naugatuck Valley Community-Technical
  College *A*
Norwalk Community-Technical
  College *C, A*
Quinnipiac University *B*
Sacred Heart University *B*
Teikyo Post University *C, A, B*
University of Bridgeport *A*

University of Hartford *C, A, B*
University of New Haven *C*

Delaware
Delaware Technical and Community
  College
    Owens Campus *C, A*
Wesley College *C, A, B*

District of Columbia
George Washington University *C*
Southeastern University *A*
University of the District of Columbia *A*

Florida
Brevard Community College *A*
Broward Community College *A*
Central Florida Community College *A*
Cooper Career Institute *A*
Daytona Beach Community College *A*
Edison Community College *A*
Florida Community College at
  Jacksonville *A*
Florida Metropolitan University
  Orlando College North *A*
Florida National College *A*
Gulf Coast Community College *A*
Hillsborough Community College *A*
Indian River Community College *A*
International College *A, B*
Jones College *A, B*
Keiser College *A*
Lake-Sumter Community College *A*
Manatee Community College *A*
Miami-Dade Community College *A*
Nova Southeastern University *B*
Palm Beach Community College *A*
Pasco-Hernando Community College *A*
Pensacola Junior College *A*
Polk Community College *A*
Santa Fe Community College *A*
Seminole Community College *A*
South College: Palm Beach
  Campus *A, B*
Tallahassee Community College *A*
Valencia Community College *A*

Georgia
Athens Area Technical Institute *A*
Augusta State University *C*
Brenau University *B*
Darton College *C, A*
Floyd College *A*
Gainesville College *A*
Georgia College and State University *B*
Morris Brown College *B*
Valdosta State University *B*

Hawaii
University of Hawaii
  Kapiolani Community College *A*

Idaho
Eastern Idaho Technical College *C, A*
Idaho State University *A*
Lewis-Clark State College *C, A, B*

Illinois
Black Hawk College
  East Campus *A*
Black Hawk College *A*
Elgin Community College *C, A*
MacCormac College *C, A*
Northwestern Business College *A*
Robert Morris College: Chicago *A*
Rock Valley College *C, A*
Southern Illinois University
  Carbondale *B*
Southwestern Illinois College *C, A*
University of Illinois
  Springfield *B, M*
William Rainey Harper College *A*

Indiana
Ball State University *A, B*
Indiana Wesleyan University *A, B*
International Business College *C, A*

Ivy Tech State College
  Central Indiana *A*
  Eastcentral *A*
  Northeast *A*
St. Mary-of-the-Woods College *C, A, B*
University of Evansville *B*
University of Indianapolis *A*
Vincennes University *A*

Iowa
Des Moines Area Community College *A*
Iowa Lakes Community College *A*
Iowa Western Community College *A*
Kirkwood Community College *A*
Northeast Iowa Community College *C*

Kansas
Central Christian College *A*
Hutchinson Community College *A*
Independence Community College *A*
Johnson County Community
  College *C, A*
Kansas City Kansas Community
  College *A*
Pittsburg State University *C*
Washburn University of Topeka *A*
Wichita State University *A*

Kentucky
Bellarmine College *C*
Eastern Kentucky University *A, B*
Morehead State University *B*
Owensboro Junior College of Business *A*
University of Louisville *A*
Western Kentucky University *A*

Louisiana
Louisiana State University
  Eunice *A*
McNeese State University *A*
Nicholls State University *A*
Northwestern State University *C*
Remington College - Education America,
  Inc. *A*
Southern University
  Shreveport *A*
Tulane University *C*

Maine
Andover College *C, A*
Beal College *C, A*
Husson College *A, B*
Mid-State College *C*
Thomas College *A*
University of Maine
  Augusta *C, A*

Maryland
Anne Arundel Community College *A*
Baltimore City Community College *C, A*
Charles County Community College *A*
Chesapeake College *C, A*
Frederick Community College *C, A*
Hagerstown Community College *C*
Harford Community College *A*
Montgomery College
  Germantown Campus *C, A*
  Rockville Campus *A*
  Takoma Park Campus *C, A*
Prince George's Community
  College *C, A*
Villa Julie College *A, B*

Massachusetts
Anna Maria College *C, A, B*
Assumption College *C*
Atlantic Union College *C, A*
Bay Path College *C, A*
Bay State College *A*
Becker College *C, A*
Boston University *B*
Cape Cod Community College *C*
Elms College *C, A, B*
Fisher College *C, A*
Lasell College *B*
Massachusetts Bay Community
  College *C, A*
Massasoit Community College *A*

Merrimack College *A*
Middlesex Community College *C, A*
Mount Ida College *A*
Mount Wachusett Community College *C*
Newbury College *A, B*
North Shore Community College *A*
Northern Essex Community
  College *C, A*
Quincy College *C, A*
Roxbury Community College *A*
Suffolk University *A, B*

Michigan
Baker College
  of Owosso *A*
Bay de Noc Community College *C*
Davenport College of Business *C, A, B*
Delta College *A*
Eastern Michigan University *B*
Ferris State University *A*
Great Lakes College *A*
Henry Ford Community College *A*
Kellogg Community College *C, A*
Lake Superior State University *A, B*
Lansing Community College *A*
Macomb Community College *A*
Madonna University *A, B*
Montcalm Community College *C, A*
Mott Community College *A*
North Central Michigan College *C, A*
Northern Michigan University *A*
Northwestern Michigan College *C*
Oakland Community College *C, A*
Southwestern Michigan College *A*
University of Detroit Mercy *A, B*

Minnesota
Hamline University *B*
Inver Hills Community College *A*
Itasca Community College *A*
Moorhead State University *B*
North Hennepin Community College *A*
Northland Community & Technical
  College *A*
Winona State University *B*

Mississippi
Hinds Community College *A*
Mississippi College *C, B*
Mississippi Gulf Coast Community
  College
    Jackson County Campus *A*
    Jefferson Davis Campus *A*
    Perkinston *A*
Mississippi University for Women *B*
Northwest Mississippi Community
  College *A*
University of Southern Mississippi *B*

Missouri
Avila College *C, B*
Maryville University of Saint Louis *B*
Mineral Area College *C, A*
Missouri Southern State College *C*
Missouri Western State College *C, A*
Penn Valley Community College *C, A*
Rockhurst University *C*
Southwest Missouri State University
  West Plains Campus *A*
St. Louis Community College
  St. Louis Community College at
    Meramec *C, A*
Webster University *C, B*
William Jewell College *C*
William Woods University *B*

Montana
University of Great Falls *A, B*
University of Montana-Missoula *A*

Nebraska
Central Community College *C, A*
College of Saint Mary *C, A, B*
Lincoln School of Commerce *A*
Metropolitan Community College *A*
Mid Plains Community College Area *A*
Midland Lutheran College *B*

455

Paralegal/legal assistance

Nebraska Wesleyan University *C, B*
Northeast Community College *A*
University of Nebraska
    Omaha *B*

Nevada
Community College of Southern
    Nevada *C, A*
Western Nevada Community College *A*

New Hampshire
College for Lifelong Learning *C*
Hesser College *A*
McIntosh College *A*
New Hampshire Community Technical
    College
    Laconia *C*
    Nashua *C, A*
New Hampshire Technical Institute *C, A*
Notre Dame College *C, B*
Rivier College *C, B*

New Jersey
Atlantic Cape Community College *A*
Bergen Community College *A*
Berkeley College *A*
Brookdale Community College *A*
Burlington County College *A*
Cumberland County College *A*
Essex County College *A*
Fairleigh Dickinson University *C*
Gloucester County College *A*
Hudson County Community College *A*
Mercer County Community College *A*
Middlesex County College *A*
Ocean County College *C*
Raritan Valley Community College *A*
Sussex County Community College *C, A*
Thomas Edison State College *A, B*
Warren County Community College *C, A*

New Mexico
Albuquerque Technical-Vocational
    Institute *A*
Dona Ana Branch Community College of
    New Mexico State University *A*
Eastern New Mexico University
    Roswell Campus *A*
New Mexico Junior College *C, A*
New Mexico State University
    Alamogordo *C, A*
    Carlsbad *C, A*
San Juan College *A*

New York
Berkeley College of New York City *A*
Berkeley College *A*
Broome Community College *C, A*
Bryant & Stratton Business Institute
    Albany *A*
City University of New York
    Bronx Community College *A*
    Hostos Community College *A*
    La Guardia Community College *A*
    New York City Technical
        College *A, B*
Columbia-Greene Community College *C*
Corning Community College *A*
Dutchess Community College *C, A*
Erie Community College
    City Campus *A*
Finger Lakes Community College *A*
Fulton-Montgomery Community
    College *C, A*
Genesee Community College *A*
Herkimer County Community College *A*
Hilbert College *A, B*
Interboro Institute *A*
Jefferson Community College *A*
Long Island University
    Brooklyn Campus *A*
    C. W. Post Campus *C*
Maria College *C, A*
Marist College *C*
Mercy College *B*
Monroe Community College *C*
Nassau Community College *C, A*

New York University *C*
St. John Fisher College *C*
St. John's University *C, A, B*
Schenectady County Community
    College *A*
Suffolk County Community
    College *C, A*
Tompkins-Cortland Community
    College *A*
Westchester Community College *C, A*

North Carolina
Caldwell Community College and
    Technical Institute *A*
Cape Fear Community College *A*
Carteret Community College *A*
Cecils College *A*
Central Carolina Community
    College *C, A*
Coastal Carolina Community College *A*
College of the Albemarle *A*
Davidson County Community
    College *C, A*
Durham Technical Community
    College *A*
Fayetteville Technical Community
    College *A*
Forsyth Technical Community College *A*
Gaston College *A*
Guilford Technical Community
    College *A*
Johnston Community College *A*
Meredith College *C*
Pitt Community College *A*
Rockingham Community College *A*
Rowan-Cabarrus Community College *A*
Sandhills Community College *A*
South Piedmont Community College *A*
Southwestern Community College *A*
Surry Community College *A*
Western Piedmont Community
    College *A*
Wilson Technical Community College *A*

North Dakota
Dickinson State University *A*
Lake Region State College *C, A*

Ohio
Bryant & Stratton College *A*
College of Mount St. Joseph *C, A, B*
Columbus State Community College *A*
David N. Myers College *A, B*
Edison State Community College *A*
Kent State University
    East Liverpool Regional Campus *A*
    Trumbull Campus *C*
Kent State University *C*
Lake Erie College *B*
Lakeland Community College *C, A*
Lima Technical College *A*
Marion Technical College *A*
Muskingum Area Technical College *A*
North Central State College *A*
Northwest State Community College *A*
Northwestern College *A*
Notre Dame College of Ohio *C, B*
RETS Tech Center *A*
Shawnee State University *A*
Sinclair Community College *A*
University of Akron *A*
University of Findlay *C, A*
University of Toledo *C, A*

Oklahoma
East Central University *B*
Northeastern Oklahoma Agricultural and
    Mechanical College *C, A*
Northeastern State University *B*
Oklahoma City University *C*
Rogers State University *A*
Rose State College *A*
Tulsa Community College *A*
University of Tulsa *C*

Oregon
Portland Community College *C, A*

Pennsylvania
Bucks County Community College *C, A*
Central Pennsylvania College *A*
Community College of Allegheny
    County *C, A*
Community College of Philadelphia *A*
Delaware County Community
    College *C, A*
Gannon University *C, A, B*
Harrisburg Area Community
    College *C, A*
Lackawanna Junior College *A*
Lehigh Carbon Community College *A*
Luzerne County Community
    College *C, A*
Manor College *C, A*
Marywood University *A, B*
Mount Aloysius College *A*
Northampton County Area Community
    College *A*
Peirce College *C, A, B*
Penn State
    University Park *C*
Pennsylvania College of Technology *A*
Philadelphia University *A*
Point Park College *A*
Robert Morris College *C*
St. Joseph's University *C*
Tri-State Business Institute *A*
Westmoreland County Community
    College *C, A*
Widener University *C, A*
Yorktowne Business Institute *A*

Puerto Rico
Colegio Universitario del Este *A, B*
Turabo University *C*

Rhode Island
Community College of Rhode Island *A*
Johnson & Wales University *C, A, B*
Providence College *C, A*
Roger Williams University *A, B*

South Carolina
Aiken Technical College *C*
Central Carolina Technical College *A*
Florence-Darlington Technical College *A*
Greenville Technical College *A*
Horry-Georgetown Technical College *C*
Midlands Technical College *C, A*
Orangeburg-Calhoun Technical
    College *A*
Technical College of the Lowcountry *C*
Trident Technical College *C, A*
York Technical College *C*

South Dakota
Western Dakota Technical Institute *A*

Tennessee
Chattanooga State Technical Community
    College *A*
Cleveland State Community College *A*
Draughons Junior College of Business:
    Nashville *A*
Hiwassee College *A*
Knoxville Business College *A*
Pellissippi State Technical Community
    College *A*
Roane State Community College *A*
University of Memphis *C*
University of Tennessee
    Chattanooga *B*
Volunteer State Community College *A*
Walters State Community College *A*

Texas
Alvin Community College *C, A*
Austin Community College *A*
Blinn College *C, A*
Brazosport College *A*
Central Texas College *A*
Collin County Community College
    District *C, A*
Del Mar College *A*
El Paso Community College *C, A*

Grayson County College *A*
Houston Community College System *A*
Howard College *A*
Howard Payne University *B*
Lamar State College at Port Arthur *A*
Lee College *A*
McMurry University *B*
Midland College *C, A*
Navarro College *C*
North Central Texas College *A*
Odessa College *C, A*
St. Philip's College *A*
San Antonio College *A*
San Jacinto College
    North *A*
South Plains College *A*
Southwest Texas State University *C, M*
Stephen F. Austin State University *B*
Tarrant County College *A*
Texas A&M University
    Commerce *B*
Texas Wesleyan University *B*
Texas Woman's University *B*
Trinity Valley Community College *C, A*
Tyler Junior College *A*
University of St. Thomas *B*
Vernon Regional Junior College *A*
Victoria College *C, A*

Utah
Mountain West College *A*
Salt Lake Community College *A*
Utah Valley State College *A*
Westminster College *C*

Vermont
Burlington College *C*
Champlain College *A, B*

Virginia
Blue Ridge Community College *C*
Central Virginia Community College *C*
Dabney S. Lancaster Community
    College *C*
Germanna Community College *C*
Hampton University *C, B*
J. Sargeant Reynolds Community
    College *A*
Mountain Empire Community College *A*
New River Community College *C, A*
Northern Virginia Community College *A*
Thomas Nelson Community College *C*
Tidewater Community College *C, A*
University of Richmond *C, A*
Virginia Highlands Community
    College *C*
Virginia Intermont College *B*

Washington
City University *C, A*
Clark College *C, A*
Columbia Basin College *A*
Edmonds Community College *C, A*
Highline Community College *A*
Lower Columbia College *A*
Pierce College *A*
Skagit Valley College *C, A*
South Puget Sound Community
    College *C, A*
Spokane Community College *C, A*
Spokane Falls Community College *C, A*
Whatcom Community College *A*

West Virginia
Bluefield State College *A*
College of West Virginia *A*
Glenville State College *A*
Shepherd College *A*
University of Charleston *C, A*

Wisconsin
Carthage College *C*
Chippewa Valley Technical College *A*
Concordia University Wisconsin *B*
Lakeshore Technical College *A*
Milwaukee Area Technical College *A*

Northeast Wisconsin Technical
College A
University of Wisconsin
Superior C
Western Wisconsin Technical College A
Wisconsin Indianhead Technical
College C

Wyoming
Casper College A
Laramie County Community College A
Western Wyoming Community
College A

Parasitology

California
University of California
Berkeley M, D

Louisiana
Louisiana State University Medical
Center M, D
Tulane University M, D

New York
New York University M, D
Rockefeller University D
State University of New York
Albany D

North Carolina
University of North Carolina
Chapel Hill M

Oklahoma
Oklahoma State University M, D

Pennsylvania
University of Pennsylvania M, D

Tennessee
East Tennessee State University M

Texas
Texas A&M University M

Virginia
George Mason University M, D

Wisconsin
University of Wisconsin
Madison M, D

Parks/recreation/fitness studies

Alabama
Community College of the Air Force A
Huntingdon College B
Jacksonville State University B
University of North Alabama B, M

Arizona
Arizona State University B, M

Arkansas
Arkansas Tech University B
Garland County Community College A
Henderson State University B
University of Arkansas B

California
Allan Hancock College A
American River College A
Bakersfield College A
California State University
Chico B, M
Hayward B
Northridge B, M
Sacramento M
Cerritos Community College A
Chabot College A
College of the Desert A
Compton Community College C, A
Cypress College A
Fresno City College A
Glendale Community College C, A
Los Angeles Southwest College A
Los Angeles Valley College A
Merritt College A
Modesto Junior College A
Mount San Antonio College A
Pacific Union College B
Palomar College C, A
Pasadena City College A
San Diego Mesa College A
San Jose State University B, M
Santa Barbara City College C, A
Santa Monica College C, A
Santa Rosa Junior College C, A
Southwestern College A

Colorado
Colorado Mountain College
Timberline Campus A
Metropolitan State College of Denver B
University of Southern Colorado B
Western State College of Colorado B

Connecticut
Northwestern Connecticut
Community-Technical College A
Norwalk Community-Technical
College C, A
Southern Connecticut State
University B, M

District of Columbia
University of the District of
Columbia A, B

Florida
Broward Community College A
Central Florida Community College A
Gulf Coast Community College A
Miami-Dade Community College A
Palm Beach Community College A
Polk Community College A

Georgia
Albany State University B
Columbus State University B, M
East Georgia College A
Georgia College and State University B
Georgia Southern University B
Savannah State University B
South Georgia College A
State University of West Georgia B

Hawaii
University of Hawaii
Manoa B

Idaho
Ricks College A
University of Idaho B

Illinois
Moraine Valley Community College A
Rend Lake College A
Southern Illinois University
Carbondale B, M
University of Illinois
Urbana-Champaign B, M, D
University of St. Francis B

Indiana
Franklin College B
Indiana Institute of Technology A, B
Indiana State University M
Indiana University
Bloomington B, M, D
Vincennes University A

Iowa
Graceland University B
Morningside College B
University of Iowa B, M
University of Northern Iowa B
Waldorf College A

Kansas
Central Christian College A
Emporia State University B
Hutchinson Community College A
Kansas State University B
Seward County Community College A

Kentucky
Campbellsville University B
Georgetown College B
Union College B

Louisiana
Southern University and Agricultural and
Mechanical College B, M

Maine
University of Maine
Presque Isle A, B

Maryland
Frostburg State University B, M

Massachusetts
Bridgewater State College B
Gordon College B
Northeastern University B

Michigan
Calvin College B
Central Michigan University B
Grand Valley State University B
Michigan State University B
Northern Michigan University B
Olivet College B, T
University of Michigan B
Wayne State University B, M
Western Michigan University B

Minnesota
Minnesota State University, Mankato B
Northland Community & Technical
College A
Ridgewater College: A Community and
Technical College A
St. Cloud State University B
University of Minnesota
Duluth B
Twin Cities B, M
Vermilion Community College A
Winona State University B

Mississippi
Alcorn State University B
Mississippi University for Women B
University of Mississippi B
University of Southern Mississippi B, M

Missouri
Central Missouri State University B
Northwest Missouri State University B
Southwest Baptist University B
Southwest Missouri State University B
University of Missouri
Columbia B, M

Montana
University of Great Falls A
Western Montana College of The
University of Montana A

Nebraska
Chadron State College B
University of Nebraska
Omaha B

Nevada
University of Nevada
Las Vegas B
Reno B

New Hampshire
Plymouth State College of the University
System of New Hampshire B

New Jersey
Sussex County Community College C, A
Thomas Edison State College A, B

New Mexico
San Juan College C
Santa Fe Community College A
University of New Mexico B, M, T

New York
City University of New York
Kingsborough Community
College A
Houghton College B
Ithaca College B, M
State University of New York
College at Brockport B, M
College at Cortland B
Suffolk County Community College A
Ulster County Community College A

North Carolina
Barber-Scotia College B
Belmont Abbey College B
Brevard College A, B
Catawba College B
East Carolina University B
Fayetteville Technical Community
College A
Louisburg College A
Mount Olive College A, B
North Carolina State University B
Shaw University B
Vance-Granville Community College A

North Dakota
Minot State University: Bottineau
Campus A
North Dakota State University B

Ohio
Ashland University B
Central State University B
Kent State University B
Ohio University B
Youngstown State University B

Oklahoma
East Central University B
Oklahoma Christian University of
Science and Arts B
Oklahoma State University B
Southeastern Oklahoma State
University B
Southwestern Oklahoma State
University B

Oregon
Chemeketa Community College A

Pennsylvania
Lock Haven University of
Pennsylvania B
Messiah College B
Temple University B, M
York College of Pennsylvania B

Puerto Rico
Caribbean University B

South Carolina
Horry-Georgetown Technical College A
Newberry College B
Southern Wesleyan University B

South Dakota
University of South Dakota B

Tennessee
Carson-Newman College B
David Lipscomb University B
Maryville College B
University of Tennessee
Knoxville B, M

Texas
Del Mar College A
Howard Payne University B
Rice University B
Texas Tech University B
University of Mary Hardin-Baylor B
University of North Texas B, M
West Texas A&M University B

Utah
Snow College A
Utah State University B

Vermont
College of St. Joseph in Vermont B
Green Mountain College B
Johnson State College B
University of Vermont B

Virginia
Bluefield College B
Christopher Newport University B
Ferrum College B
George Mason University B
Radford University B, M
Tidewater Community College A
Virginia Commonwealth University B, M
Virginia Wesleyan College B

Washington
Bellevue Community College A
Central Washington University B
Eastern Washington University B
Washington State University B
Western Washington University B
Whitworth College B, T

West Virginia
Alderson-Broaddus College B
Concord College B
Shepherd College B

Wisconsin
Carthage College B
Lakeland College B
Northland College B
University of Wisconsin
    Milwaukee B

Parks/recreational/leisure facilities management

Alabama
Alabama State University B
Enterprise State Junior College A
James H. Faulkner State Community College C
Wallace State Community College at Hanceville A

Alaska
Alaska Pacific University B

Arizona
Northern Arizona University B
Prescott College B, M

Arkansas
Harding University B
University of Arkansas
    Pine Bluff B
University of Arkansas B, M, D

California
Butte College C, A
California Polytechnic State University:
    San Luis Obispo B
California State University
    Dominguez Hills B
    Fresno A
    Hayward B
    Long Beach B, M
    Sacramento B, M
College of the Desert A
Fresno City College A
Humboldt State University B
Mount San Antonio College A
Pacific Union College B
Palomar College C, A
San Diego State University B
San Francisco State University B, M
Santa Rosa Junior College C
Skyline College C
Ventura College C, A
West Valley College C, A

Colorado
Colorado State University B, M, D
University of Northern Colorado B

Connecticut
Mitchell College A
Northwestern Connecticut Community-Technical College A
University of Connecticut B

Delaware
Delaware State University B
University of Delaware B

District of Columbia
Gallaudet University B

Florida
Florida International University B, M
Florida State University B, M
Polk Community College A
Santa Fe Community College A
Tallahassee Community College A
University of Florida B, M

Georgia
Abraham Baldwin Agricultural College A
Atlanta Metropolitan College A
Brewton-Parker College A
Columbus State University B
Georgia Southern University M
Georgia State University B, M
Shorter College B
South Georgia College A
State University of West Georgia B
Thomas College B

Hawaii
University of Hawaii
    Hilo B

Idaho
Northwest Nazarene University B
University of Idaho B, M

Illinois
College of DuPage C
Eastern Illinois University B
Moraine Valley Community College A
Western Illinois University B, M
William Rainey Harper College C, A

Indiana
Bethel College B
Indiana Institute of Technology A, B
Indiana State University B, M
Indiana University
    Bloomington B, M, D
    Southeast A
Indiana Wesleyan University B
Vincennes University A

Iowa
Iowa Lakes Community College A
University of Iowa B, M
Upper Iowa University B
Waldorf College A

Kansas
Bethany College B
Central Christian College A, B
Kansas State University B
Pittsburg State University B

Kentucky
Asbury College B
Eastern Kentucky University B, M
Morehead State University B
Murray State University B, M
Western Kentucky University B, M, T

Maine
Husson College B
Unity College B
University of Maine
    Machias A, B
    Presque Isle A, B
University of Maine B, M

Maryland
Allegany College A
Community College of Baltimore County
    Catonsville C, A

Frederick Community College C, A

Massachusetts
Greenfield Community College C
Springfield College B, M

Michigan
Bay de Noc Community College C
Central Michigan University B, M
Eastern Michigan University B
Ferris State University B
Lake Superior State University B
Lansing Community College A
Michigan State University B, M, D
Northern Michigan University B
Wayne State University B, M
Western Michigan University B

Minnesota
Minnesota State University, Mankato B
Vermilion Community College A
Winona State University B

Mississippi
University of Mississippi M

Missouri
Central Missouri State University B
Culver-Stockton College B
Hannibal-LaGrange College B
Mineral Area College A
Missouri Valley College B
Missouri Western State College B
Southeast Missouri State University B

Nebraska
University of Nebraska
    Kearney B
Wayne State College B

New Hampshire
Franklin Pierce College B
New England College B
University of New Hampshire B

New Jersey
County College of Morris A
Kean University B
Montclair State University B
Sussex County Community College C, A

New Mexico
New Mexico State University B

New York
City University of New York
    Kingsborough Community College A
Dutchess Community College A
Erie Community College
    City Campus B
    South Campus A
Houghton College B
Mohawk Valley Community College A
New York University B, M, D
North Country Community College A
Onondaga Community College A
Orange County Community College A
St. Thomas Aquinas College B
St. Joseph's College
    St. Joseph's College: Suffolk Campus B
State University of New York
    College at Brockport B, M
    College at Cortland M
    College of Agriculture and Technology at Cobleskill A
    College of Environmental Science and Forestry B, M
    College of Technology at Delhi A
Tompkins-Cortland Community College A

North Carolina
Appalachian State University B
Central Piedmont Community College A
East Carolina University B, M
Elon College B
Louisburg College A

Mars Hill College B
North Carolina Agricultural and Technical State University B
North Carolina State University M
Southeastern Community College A
University of North Carolina
    Chapel Hill B, M
    Greensboro B, M
    Pembroke B
    Wilmington B
Wayne Community College A
Western Carolina University B
Wingate University B

North Dakota
Minot State University: Bottineau Campus A
University of North Dakota B

Ohio
Bluffton College B
Bowling Green State University B
Columbus State Community College C, A
Hocking Technical College A
Kent State University
    Stark Campus B
Kent State University B
Ohio State University
    Columbus Campus B
Ohio University B
University of Toledo B

Oklahoma
Eastern Oklahoma State College A
Oklahoma State University B
Oral Roberts University B

Pennsylvania
Butler County Community College A
California University of Pennsylvania B
Cheyney University of Pennsylvania B
East Stroudsburg University of Pennsylvania B
Lock Haven University of Pennsylvania B
Penn State
    Harrisburg M
    University Park C, B, M, D
Slippery Rock University of Pennsylvania B, M
York College of Pennsylvania B

Puerto Rico
Universidad Metropolitana M

Rhode Island
Johnson & Wales University A, B

South Carolina
Clemson University B, M, D
Horry-Georgetown Technical College A
Morris College B

South Dakota
South Dakota State University B

Tennessee
Middle Tennessee State University B
University of Tennessee
    Martin B

Texas
Southwest Texas State University B, M
Texas A&M University B, M, D
Texas Christian University B
Texas Wesleyan University B
University of North Texas B, M
University of Texas
    Pan American B
Western Texas College A

Utah
Brigham Young University B, M
University of Utah B, M, D
Utah State University B, M, D

Vermont
Champlain College A, B

College of St. Joseph in Vermont *B*
Green Mountain College *B*
Lyndon State College *B*
Sterling College *A, B*
University of Vermont *B*

Virginia
Eastern Mennonite University *B*
Northern Virginia Community College *A*
Old Dominion University *B*
Tidewater Community College *A*
Virginia Commonwealth
 University *B, M*
Virginia Wesleyan College *B*

Washington
Eastern Washington University *B*
Skagit Valley College *C*
Spokane Community College *A*
Washington State University *B, M*

West Virginia
Concord College *B*
Glenville State College *A*
Marshall University *B*
Potomac State College of West Virginia
 University *A*
West Virginia State College *B*
West Virginia University *B, M*

Wisconsin
University of Wisconsin
 La Crosse *B, M*
 Madison *B, M*

Wyoming
Northwest College *A*
University of Wyoming *B, M*

Pastoral counseling

Alabama
University of Mobile *B*

Arkansas
Ouachita Baptist University *B*

California
Biola University *M, D*
Holy Names College *C, M*
Master's College *B*
University of San Diego *M*

Colorado
Nazarene Bible College *B*

Florida
Florida Baptist Theological College *B*
Florida Christian College *B*
Southeastern College of the Assemblies
 of God *B*

Hawaii
Chaminade University of Honolulu *M*

Illinois
Lincoln Christian College and
 Seminary *M*
Loyola University of Chicago *M*
Moody Bible Institute *M*
Olivet Nazarene University *M*
St. Xavier University *C*

Indiana
Oakland City University *M*

Iowa
Loras College *M*
Wartburg College *B*

Kansas
Central Christian College *A, B*
Manhattan Christian College *B*
St. Mary College *B*

Kentucky
Kentucky Christian College *B*
Spalding University *A, B, M*

Maryland
Loyola College in Maryland *M, D*
Washington Bible College *B*

Massachusetts
Boston College *M*
Emmanuel College *M*

Michigan
Marygrove College *M*

Minnesota
College of St. Catherine: St. Paul
 Campus *C*
Northwestern College *B*

Mississippi
Magnolia Bible College *B*
Wesley College *B*

Missouri
Baptist Bible College *M*
Berean University *B, M*

Nebraska
Grace University *M*

New Hampshire
Notre Dame College *M*

New Jersey
College of St. Elizabeth *C*
Seton Hall University *C, M*

Ohio
Ashland University *M*
Circleville Bible College *A, B*
College of Mount St. Joseph *B, M*
Malone College *B, M*
University of Dayton *M*

Oklahoma
Mid-America Bible College *B*
Oral Roberts University *B, M*
Southwestern College of Christian
 Ministries *B*

Oregon
Eugene Bible College *B*
George Fox University *M*
Marylhurst University *C*
Western Baptist College *B*

Pennsylvania
Duquesne University *M*
La Salle University *M*
Lancaster Bible College *B*
Moravian College *M*
Neumann College *C, M*
Philadelphia College of Bible *B*
Valley Forge Christian College *B*

Puerto Rico
Bayamon Central University *M*

Rhode Island
Providence College *B*

South Carolina
Morris College *B*

Tennessee
Freed-Hardeman University *M*

Texas
Abilene Christian University *B, M*
Dallas Baptist University *B*
East Texas Baptist University *B*
Hardin-Simmons University *M*
Southwestern Assemblies of God
 University *B*
Texas Christian University *D*
University of Dallas *M*

Virginia
Eastern Mennonite University *M*

Washington
Seattle University *M*
University of Puget Sound *M*

Pathology, human/animal

Alabama
Auburn University *M*
University of Alabama
 Birmingham *D*

Arizona
University of Arizona *M, D*

Arkansas
University of Arkansas
 for Medical Sciences *M*

California
University of California
 Berkeley *M, D*
 Davis *M, D*
 Los Angeles *M, D*
University of Southern California *M, D*

Colorado
Colorado State University *M, D*
University of Colorado
 Health Sciences Center *M, D*

Connecticut
University of Connecticut *B, M, D*
Yale University *M, D*

Illinois
Finch University of Health Sciences/The
 Chicago Medical School *M, D*
Northwestern University *M, D*
University of Chicago *M, D*

Indiana
Indiana University--Purdue University
 Indiana University-Purdue
  University Indianapolis *M, D*

Iowa
University of Iowa *M*

Kansas
Kansas State University *M, D*

Louisiana
Louisiana State University Medical
 Center *M, D*

Maine
University of Maine *B, M*

Maryland
Uniformed Services University of the
 Health Sciences *D*
University of Maryland
 Baltimore *M, D*

Massachusetts
Boston University *D*
Tufts University *M, D*

Michigan
Michigan State University *M, D*
University of Michigan *D*
Wayne State University *D*

Mississippi
Jackson State University *B*
University of Mississippi
 Medical Center *M, D*

Missouri
St. Louis University *M, D*
University of Missouri
 Columbia *M*

New York
Albany Medical College *M, D*
Columbia University
 Graduate School *M, D*
New York University *M, D*
State University of New York
 Buffalo *M, D*
 Health Science Center at Stony
  Brook *D*
 Stony Brook *M, D*
University of Rochester *M, D*

North Carolina
Duke University *M, D*
East Carolina University *D*
University of North Carolina
 Chapel Hill *M, D*

Ohio
Case Western Reserve University *M, D*
Ohio State University
 Columbus Campus *M, D*
University of Cincinnati *M, D*

Pennsylvania
MCP Hahnemann University *M, D*
Penn State
 University Park *M, D*
Thomas Jefferson University: College of
 Health Professions *D*
University of Pennsylvania *M, D*

Tennessee
University of Tennessee
 Memphis *M, D*
Vanderbilt University *M, D*

Texas
Texas A&M University *M, D*
University of Texas
 Medical Branch at Galveston *M, D*

Vermont
University of Vermont *M*

Virginia
Virginia Commonwealth
 University *M, D*

Washington
University of Washington *M, D*

Wisconsin
Medical College of Wisconsin *M, D*
University of Wisconsin
 Madison *M, D*

Wyoming
University of Wyoming *M, D*

Peace/conflict studies

Arizona
Prescott College *B, M*

California
California State University
 Long Beach *C*
Chapman University *B*
San Diego State University *B*
University of California
 Berkeley *B*
 Santa Cruz *B*

Colorado
University of Colorado
 Boulder *C*

District of Columbia
American University *M*

Florida
Nova Southeastern University *M, D*

Illinois
Quincy University *A, B*

Indiana
DePauw University *B*
Earlham College *B*
Goshen College *B*
Indiana University--Purdue University
 Indiana University-Purdue
  University Fort Wayne *C*
Manchester College *B*
University of Notre Dame *M*

Iowa
Clarke College *A, B*
St. Ambrose University *C*

Peace/conflict studies

Massachusetts
Berkshire Community College *A*
College of the Holy Cross *B*
Hampshire College *B*
Tufts University *B*
University of Massachusetts
 Boston *M*
Wellesley College *B*

Michigan
Michigan State University *M*
Wayne State University *C, M*

Minnesota
College of St. Benedict *B*
Hamline University *M*
St. John's University *B*
University of St. Thomas *B*

Missouri
Southwest Missouri State University *M*

New Jersey
Richard Stockton College of New
 Jersey *M*

New York
Colgate University *B*
Manhattan College *B*
Molloy College *B*

North Carolina
University of North Carolina
 Chapel Hill *B*

Ohio
Bluffton College *B*
Kent State University *B*
Ohio State University
 Columbus Campus *B*
Wilmington College *C*

Oregon
Portland Community College *C*

Pennsylvania
Beaver College *M*
Bryn Mawr College *B*
Elizabethtown College *B*
Gettysburg College *B*
Juniata College *B*
La Salle University *B*
University of Pennsylvania *M, D*
West Chester University of
 Pennsylvania *C*

Vermont
Goddard College *B*
Marlboro College *B*
Norwich University *B*

Virginia
Eastern Mennonite University *B, M*
George Mason University *D*

Washington
University of Washington *B*
Whitworth College *B*

Wisconsin
Northland College *B*

Perfusion technology

Connecticut
Quinnipiac University *C*

Florida
Barry University *B*

Massachusetts
Northeastern University *M*

New Jersey
Thomas Edison State College *B*

New York
State University of New York
 Upstate Medical University *B*

Ohio
Ohio State University
 Columbus Campus *B*

Pennsylvania
Carlow College *C*
Duquesne University *B*
MCP Hahnemann University *A, B*

Utah
Brigham Young University *B*

Personal services

California
Chabot College *A*
MiraCosta College *C*

Florida
Manatee Community College *A*

Illinois
College of DuPage *C, A*

Iowa
Northeast Iowa Community College *A*

Massachusetts
Berkshire Community College *C*

Michigan
Baker College
 of Muskegon *A, B*
Southwestern Michigan College *C*

New Hampshire
New Hampshire Community Technical
 College
 Nashua *C*

New Mexico
Northern New Mexico Community
 College *C*

North Carolina
Central Carolina Community College *A*
College of the Albemarle *C*
Piedmont Community College *A*

Oregon
Central Oregon Community
 College *C, A*

South Carolina
Denmark Technical College *C*

Tennessee
Roane State Community College *C*

Petroleum engineering

Alabama
University of Alabama *B*

Alaska
University of Alaska
 Anchorage *B*
 Fairbanks *B, M*

California
California State University
 Bakersfield *B*
Stanford University *B, M, D*
University of California
 Berkeley *B*
University of Southern
 California *M, D, T*

Colorado
Colorado School of Mines *B, M, D*

Kansas
University of Kansas *B, M*

Louisiana
Louisiana State University and
 Agricultural and Mechanical
 College *B, M, D*
University of Louisiana at Lafayette *B*

Missouri
East Central College *A*
University of Missouri
 Rolla *B, M, D*

Montana
Montana Tech of the University of
 Montana *B, M*

New Mexico
New Mexico Institute of Mining and
 Technology *B, M, D*
New Mexico Junior College *A*

Ohio
Marietta College *B*

Oklahoma
University of Oklahoma *B, M, D*
University of Tulsa *B, M, D*

Pennsylvania
Penn State
 University Park *B, M, D*
University of Pittsburgh *M*

Puerto Rico
Caribbean University *B*

Texas
Midland College *A*
Texas A&M University
 Kingsville *B, M*
Texas A&M University *B, M, D*
Texas Tech University *B, M*
University of Houston *M*
University of Texas
 Austin *B, M, D*

Utah
University of Utah *B, M, D*

West Virginia
West Virginia University *B, M*

Wyoming
University of Wyoming *B, M, D*

Pharmaceutical/medicinal chemistry

California
University of California
 San Diego *B*
 San Francisco *D*

Illinois
University of Illinois
 Chicago *M, D*

Indiana
Butler University *M*

Iowa
University of Iowa *M, D*

Kansas
University of Kansas *M, D*

Massachusetts
Massachusetts College of Pharmacy and
 Health Sciences *M, D*
Northeastern University *M*
Worcester Polytechnic Institute *B, M*

Michigan
University of Michigan *B, M, D*
Wayne State University *M, D*

Minnesota
University of Minnesota
 Twin Cities *M, D*

Mississippi
Mississippi College *B*
University of Mississippi *D*

Nebraska
Chadron State College *B*

New Jersey
Rutgers
 The State University of New Jersey:
 New Brunswick Graduate
 Campus *M, D*

New York
Columbia University
 Graduate School *M, D*
State University of New York
 Buffalo *B, M, D*

North Carolina
Campbell University *B*

Ohio
Ohio Northern University *B*
Ohio State University
 Columbus Campus *M, D*
University of Toledo *M, D*

Pennsylvania
Duquesne University *M, D*
University of the Sciences in
 Philadelphia *B, M*

Rhode Island
University of Rhode Island *M, D*

Tennessee
University of Tennessee
 Memphis *M, D*

Virginia
Virginia Commonwealth
 University *M, D*

Washington
University of Washington *M, D*

Wisconsin
University of Wisconsin
 Madison *M, D*

Pharmacology, human/animal

Alabama
Auburn University *M*
University of Alabama
 Birmingham *D*

Arizona
University of Arizona *M, D*

Arkansas
University of Arkansas
 for Medical Sciences *M, D*

California
Loma Linda University *M, D*
Stanford University *M, D*
University of California
 Davis *M, D*
 Irvine *M, D*
 Los Angeles *M, D*
 San Francisco *D*
 Santa Barbara *B*
University of Southern California *M, D*

Colorado
University of Colorado
 Health Sciences Center *D*

Connecticut
Yale University *M, D*

District of Columbia
George Washington University *M, D*
Georgetown University *D*
Howard University *M, D*

Florida
University of Miami *M, D*

Georgia
Medical College of Georgia *D*
University of Georgia *M, D*

Hawaii
University of Hawaii
  Manoa *M, D*

Illinois
Loyola University of Chicago *D*
Northwestern University *M, D*
Southern Illinois University
  Carbondale *M, D*
University of Chicago *M, D*
University of Illinois
  Chicago *M, D*

Indiana
Indiana University--Purdue University
  Indiana University-Purdue
    University Indianapolis *M, D*

Iowa
University of Iowa *M, D*

Kansas
University of Kansas
  Medical Center *M, D*
University of Kansas *M, D*

Kentucky
University of Kentucky *M, D*
University of Louisville *M, D*

Louisiana
Louisiana State University Medical
  Center *M, D*
Tulane University *M, D*

Maryland
Uniformed Services University of the
  Health Sciences *D*
University of Maryland
  Baltimore *M, D*

Massachusetts
Boston University *M, D*
Massachusetts College of Pharmacy and
  Health Sciences *M, D*
Tufts University *M*

Michigan
Michigan State University *M, D*
University of Michigan *M, D*
Wayne State University *M, D*

Minnesota
Mayo Graduate School *D*
University of Minnesota
  Duluth *M*
  Twin Cities *M, D*

Mississippi
University of Mississippi
  Medical Center *M, D*

Missouri
St. Louis University *M, D*
University of Missouri
  Columbia *M, D*

Nebraska
Creighton University *M, D*

Nevada
University of Nevada
  Reno *M, D*

New Hampshire
Antioch New England Graduate
  School *M, D*
Dartmouth College *D*

New Jersey
Rutgers
  The State University of New Jersey:
    New Brunswick Graduate
    Campus *M, D*

New York
Albany Medical College *M, D*
Columbia University
  Graduate School *M, D*
New York University *M, D*
State University of New York
  Buffalo *M, D*
  Health Science Center at
    Brooklyn *D*
  Health Science Center at Stony
    Brook *B, D*
  Stony Brook *B, M, D*
  Upstate Medical University *D*
University of Rochester *M, D*

North Carolina
East Carolina University *D*
University of North Carolina
  Chapel Hill *M, D*
Wake Forest University *D*

North Dakota
North Dakota State University *M, D*
University of North Dakota *M, D*

Ohio
Case Western Reserve University *D*
Kent State University *M, D*
Ohio State University
  Columbus Campus *B, M, D*
University of Cincinnati *D*

Pennsylvania
MCP Hahnemann University *M, D*
Penn State
  College of Medicine, Milton S.
    Hershey Medical Center *M, D*
Thomas Jefferson University: College of
  Health Professions *D*
University of Pennsylvania *M, D*
University of the Sciences in
  Philadelphia *B, M, D*

Puerto Rico
University of Puerto Rico
  Medical Sciences Campus *M, D*

Rhode Island
University of Rhode Island *M, D*

South Dakota
University of South Dakota *M, D*

Tennessee
University of Tennessee
  Memphis *M, D*
Vanderbilt University *D*

Texas
Texas A&M University *M, D*
Texas Tech University Health Science
  Center *M, D*
University of Texas
  Medical Branch at Galveston *M, D*

Vermont
University of Vermont *M, D*

Virginia
University of Virginia *D*
Virginia Commonwealth
  University *C, M, D*

Washington
University of Washington *M, D*

West Virginia
West Virginia University *M, D*

Wisconsin
Medical College of Wisconsin *M, D*
University of Wisconsin
  Madison *M, D*

Pharmacy

Alabama
Auburn University *B, D*

Arkansas
University of Arkansas
  for Medical Sciences *M*
Westark College *A*

California
San Bernardino Valley College *A*
Santa Ana College *C, A*
University of California
  Los Angeles *M, D*
University of the Pacific *M, D*
Westmont College *B*

Colorado
University of Colorado
  Health Sciences Center *M, D*

Connecticut
University of Connecticut *B, M, D*

District of Columbia
Howard University *D*

Florida
Broward Community College *A*
Florida Agricultural and Mechanical
  University *B*
Nova Southeastern University *D*
University of Florida *B, M, D*

Georgia
Thomas College *A*
University of Georgia *B, M, D*

Idaho
College of Southern Idaho *A*
Idaho State University *M, D*

Illinois
City Colleges of Chicago
  Olive-Harvey College *A*
University of Illinois
  Chicago *M, D*

Indiana
Butler University *B, M*
Purdue University *A, B, M*

Iowa
Kirkwood Community College *A*
University of Iowa *M, D, T*

Kansas
University of Kansas *B, M, D*

Kentucky
University of Kentucky *M, D*

Louisiana
University of Louisiana at
  Monroe *B, M, D*

Massachusetts
Holyoke Community College *C, A*
Massachusetts College of Pharmacy and
  Health Sciences *D*
Northeastern University *B, M, D*
Simmons College *B*

Michigan
Ferris State University *B, D*
University of Michigan *B, M, D*
Wayne State University *B, M, D*

Minnesota
University of Minnesota
  Twin Cities *M, D*
Winona State University *A*

Mississippi
University of Mississippi *B*

Missouri
University of Missouri
  Kansas City *D*

Montana
University of Montana-Missoula *B, M, D*

Nebraska
Creighton University *M, D*

New Mexico
Eastern New Mexico University
  Roswell Campus *C*
University of New Mexico *B, M, D*

New York
St. John's University *B, M, D*
State University of New York
  Buffalo *D*

North Carolina
Blue Ridge Community College *C*
Campbell University *B*
Cape Fear Community College *C*
East Carolina University *D*
University of North Carolina
  Chapel Hill *M, D*

North Dakota
North Dakota State University *D*

Ohio
Ohio Northern University *D*
Ohio State University
  Columbus Campus *M, D*
University of Cincinnati *M, D*
University of Toledo *B, M, D*

Oklahoma
Southwestern Oklahoma State
  University *D*

Oregon
Central Oregon Community College *A*
Oregon State University *B*

Pennsylvania
Duquesne University *M, D*
St. Vincent College *D*
Temple University *M, D*
University of the Sciences in
  Philadelphia *D*

Puerto Rico
University of Puerto Rico
  Medical Sciences Campus *B, M*

Rhode Island
University of Rhode Island *M, D*

South Carolina
University of South Carolina *M, D*

South Dakota
South Dakota State University *D*

Tennessee
Draughons Junior College of Business:
  Nashville *A*
Shelby State Community College *C*

Texas
Navarro College *A*
Texas Tech University Health Science
  Center *M, D*
University of Houston *M, D*
University of Texas
  Austin *B, M, D*

Virginia
Virginia Commonwealth
  University *M, D*

Washington
University of Washington *M, D*
Washington State University *D*

West Virginia
West Virginia University *B*

Wisconsin
Milwaukee Area Technical College *C*
University of Wisconsin
  Madison *B, D*

Wyoming
University of Wyoming *D*

Pharmacy assistant

Alabama
Community College of the Air Force *A*
Snead State Community College *C*

Arizona
Arizona Western College A
Pima Community College C, A

California
Imperial Valley College C

Colorado
Arapahoe Community College C
Denver Technical College: A Division of DeVry University A
Front Range Community College C
Otero Junior College A

Connecticut
Gateway Community College C, A

Florida
Manatee Community College A
Pensacola Junior College C

Georgia
Brewton-Parker College A
Darton College A
Macon State College A

Idaho
North Idaho College A

Illinois
Black Hawk College C
Rock Valley College C
William Rainey Harper College C

Indiana
Vincennes University A

Iowa
Clinton Community College C
Muscatine Community College C
Scott Community College C, A
Waldorf College A

Michigan
Baker College
　of Jackson C, A
　of Muskegon A
Bay de Noc Community College C
Henry Ford Community College C
Oakland Community College C, A
St. Clair County Community College C
Southwestern Michigan College C
Washtenaw Community College C
Wayne County Community College C

Minnesota
Century Community and Technical College A
Lake Superior College: A Community and Technical College C
Rochester Community and Technical College C

Mississippi
Mississippi Gulf Coast Community College
　Jefferson Davis Campus A
Northeast Mississippi Community College A

New Jersey
County College of Morris C
Middlesex County College A

New Mexico
Albuquerque Technical-Vocational Institute C

North Carolina
Caldwell Community College and Technical Institute C
Cape Fear Community College C
Davidson County Community College C
Durham Technical Community College C
Fayetteville Technical Community College C
Southeastern Community College C, A

North Dakota
North Dakota State College of Science C, A

Ohio
North Central State College C, A
Northwestern College C, A

Pennsylvania
Community College of Allegheny County A
Harrisburg Area Community College C, A
Johnson Technical Institute A
Lackawanna Junior College C
Mount Aloysius College A
West Chester University of Pennsylvania B

Puerto Rico
Colegio Universitario del Este A
Huertas Junior College A
Inter American University of Puerto Rico Aguadilla Campus C
National College of Business and Technology A

South Carolina
Central Carolina Technical College C
Greenville Technical College C
Midlands Technical College C
Tri-County Technical College C
Trident Technical College C

South Dakota
Western Dakota Technical Institute C

Tennessee
Draughons Junior College of Business: Nashville A
Shelby State Community College C
Walters State Community College C

Texas
Amarillo College C
El Paso Community College C
Houston Community College System C
Lamar State College at Orange C
San Jacinto College
　North C
Tarrant County College C
University of Houston M

Utah
Salt Lake Community College C

Washington
Clark College C
Grays Harbor College C
North Seattle Community College C
Renton Technical College C
Spokane Community College C, A
Spokane Falls Community College C

Wisconsin
Lakeshore Technical College C
Madison Area Technical College C

Philosophy

Alabama
Auburn University B
Birmingham-Southern College B
Samford University B
Spring Hill College B
University of Alabama
　Birmingham B
　Huntsville B
University of Alabama B
University of South Alabama B

Alaska
University of Alaska
　Fairbanks B

Arizona
Arizona State University B, M
Northern Arizona University B
Prescott College M
University of Arizona B, M, D

Arkansas
Arkansas State University B
Hendrix College B
Ouachita Baptist University B
Philander Smith College B
University of Arkansas
　Little Rock B
University of Arkansas B, M, D
University of Central Arkansas B

California
Azusa Pacific University B
Bakersfield College A
Biola University B, M, D
California Baptist University B
California Lutheran University B
California State Polytechnic University: Pomona B
California State University
　Bakersfield B
　Chico B
　Dominguez Hills B
　Fresno B
　Fullerton B
　Hayward B
　Long Beach B, M
　Los Angeles B, M
　Northridge B
　Sacramento B
　Stanislaus B
Canada College A
Cerritos Community College A
Chabot College A
Chaffey Community College A
Chapman University B
Claremont McKenna College B
College of Notre Dame B
College of the Desert A
Compton Community College A
Cypress College A
De Anza College A
East Los Angeles College A
Foothill College A
Gavilan Community College A
Glendale Community College A
Golden West College A
Grossmont Community College A
Humboldt State University B
Irvine Valley College A
Los Angeles Mission College A
Los Angeles Southwest College A
Los Angeles Valley College A
Loyola Marymount University B
Marymount College A
Merced College A
Mills College B
MiraCosta College A
Monterey Peninsula College A
Mount St. Mary's College B
Occidental College B
Ohlone College A
Orange Coast College A
Pepperdine University B
Pitzer College B
Point Loma Nazarene University B
Pomona College B
Riverside Community College A
Saddleback College A
St. John's Seminary College B
St. Mary's College of California B
San Diego City College A
San Diego Mesa College A
San Diego Miramar College A
San Diego State University B, M
San Francisco State University B, M
San Jose State University B, M
Santa Ana College A
Santa Barbara City College A
Santa Clara University B
Scripps College B
Sonoma State University B
Southwestern College A
Stanford University B, M, D

University of California
　Berkeley B, M, D
　Davis B, M, D
　Irvine B, M, D
　Los Angeles B, M, D
　Riverside B, M, D
　San Diego B, M, D
　Santa Barbara B, M, D
　Santa Cruz B
University of La Verne B
University of Redlands B
University of San Diego B
University of San Francisco B
University of Southern California B, M, D
University of the Pacific B
Ventura College A
West Los Angeles College C, A
Westmont College B
Whittier College B

Colorado
Colorado College B
Colorado State University B, M
Fort Lewis College B
Metropolitan State College of Denver B
Regis University B
Trinidad State Junior College A
University of Colorado
　Boulder B, M, D
　Colorado Springs B
　Denver B
University of Denver B, M
University of Northern Colorado B

Connecticut
Central Connecticut State University B
Connecticut College B
Fairfield University B
Sacred Heart University A, B
St. Joseph College B, T
Southern Connecticut State University B
Trinity College B
University of Connecticut B, M, D
University of Hartford B
University of New Haven B
Wesleyan University B
Yale University B, M, D

Delaware
University of Delaware B

District of Columbia
American University B, M
Catholic University of America B, M, D
Gallaudet University B
George Washington University B
Georgetown University B, M, D
Howard University B, M
University of the District of Columbia A, B

Florida
Barry University B
Eckerd College B
Florida Agricultural and Mechanical University B
Florida Atlantic University B
Florida Christian College B
Florida International University B
Florida State University B, M, D
Gulf Coast Community College A
Indian River Community College A
Jacksonville University B
Miami-Dade Community College A
New College of the University of South Florida B
Palm Beach Community College A
Pensacola Junior College A
Rollins College B
St. John Vianney College Seminary B
Stetson University B
University of Central Florida B
University of Florida B, M, D
University of Miami B, M, D
University of North Florida B
University of South Florida B, M

462

University of Tampa *A*
University of West Florida *B*

Georgia
Agnes Scott College *B*
Atlanta Metropolitan College *A*
Clark Atlanta University *B*
Clayton College and State University *A*
Covenant College *B*
Emory University *B, D*
Georgia Perimeter College *A*
Georgia Southern University *B*
Georgia State University *B, M*
Mercer University *B*
Morehouse College *B*
Morris Brown College *B*
Oglethorpe University *B*
Oxford College of Emory University *B*
South Georgia College *A*
Spelman College *B*
State University of West Georgia *B*
Toccoa Falls College *B*
University of Georgia *B, M, D*
Valdosta State University *B*
Wesleyan College *B*

Hawaii
Chaminade University of Honolulu *B*
University of Hawaii
    Hilo *B*
    Manoa *B, M, D*
    West Oahu *B*

Idaho
Albertson College of Idaho *B*
Boise State University *B*
Idaho State University *B*
North Idaho College *A*
Northwest Nazarene University *B*
University of Idaho *B*

Illinois
Augustana College *B*
Barat College *B*
Benedictine University *B*
Bradley University *B*
City Colleges of Chicago
    Harold Washington College *A*
    Olive-Harvey College *A*
Concordia University *B*
De Paul University *B, M, D*
Dominican University *B*
Eastern Illinois University *B*
Elmhurst College *B*
Greenville College *B*
Illinois College *B*
Illinois State University *B*
Illinois Wesleyan University *B*
Judson College *B*
Knox College *B*
Lake Forest College *B*
Lewis University *M*
Lincoln Land Community College *A*
Loyola University of Chicago *B, M, D*
McKendree College *B*
Millikin University *B*
Morton College *A*
North Central College *B*
North Park University *B*
Northeastern Illinois University *B*
Northern Illinois University *B, M*
Northwestern University *B, M, D*
Parkland College *A*
Principia College *B*
Quincy University *A, B*
Richland Community College *A*
Rockford College *B*
Roosevelt University *B*
St. Xavier University *B*
Sauk Valley Community College *A*
Southern Illinois University
    Carbondale *B, M, D*
    Edwardsville *B*
Southwestern Illinois College *A*
Trinity Christian College *B*
Triton College *A*

University of Chicago *B, M, D*
University of Illinois
    Chicago *B, M, D*
    Urbana-Champaign *B, M, D*
Western Illinois University *B*
Wheaton College *B*
William Rainey Harper College *C, A*

Indiana
Anderson University *B*
Ball State University *B*
Butler University *B*
DePauw University *B*
Earlham College *B*
Franklin College *B*
Hanover College *B*
Indiana State University *B, M*
Indiana University
    Bloomington *B, M, D*
    Northwest *B*
    South Bend *A, B*
    Southeast *B*
Indiana University--Purdue University
    Indiana University-Purdue
        University Fort Wayne *B*
    Indiana University-Purdue
        University Indianapolis *B*
Indiana Wesleyan University *A, B*
Manchester College *B*
Marian College *B*
Purdue University
    Calumet *B*
Purdue University *B, M, D*
Saint Mary's College *B*
St. Joseph's College *B*
Taylor University *B*
University of Evansville *B*
University of Indianapolis *B*
University of Notre Dame *B, M, D*
University of Southern Indiana *B*
Valparaiso University *B*
Vincennes University *A*
Wabash College *B*

Iowa
Buena Vista University *B*
Central College *B*
Clarke College *A, B*
Coe College *B*
Cornell College *B*
Dordt College *B*
Drake University *B*
Grinnell College *B*
Iowa State University *B*
Loras College *B*
Luther College *B*
Marycrest International University *A*
Morningside College *B*
Northwestern College *B*
St. Ambrose University *B*
Simpson College *B*
University of Dubuque *B*
University of Iowa *B, M, D*
University of Northern Iowa *B*
Wartburg College *B*

Kansas
Baker University *B*
Benedictine College *B*
Fort Hays State University *B*
Kansas City Kansas Community
    College *A*
Kansas State University *B*
Southwestern College *B*
Tabor College *B*
University of Kansas *B, M, D*
Washburn University of Topeka *B*
Wichita State University *B*

Kentucky
Asbury College *B*
Bellarmine College *B*
Berea College *B*
Centre College *B*
Eastern Kentucky University *B*
Georgetown College *B*

Morehead State University *B*
Murray State University *B*
Northern Kentucky University *B*
Spalding University *B*
Thomas More College *A, B*
Transylvania University *B*
University of Kentucky *B, M, D*
University of Louisville *B, M*
Western Kentucky University *B*

Louisiana
Centenary College of Louisiana *B*
Dillard University *B*
Louisiana State University and
    Agricultural and Mechanical
    College *B, M*
Loyola University New Orleans *B*
Southern University and Agricultural and
    Mechanical College *B*
Tulane University *B, M, D*
University of Louisiana at Lafayette *B*
University of New Orleans *B*
Xavier University of Louisiana *B*

Maine
Bates College *B*
Bowdoin College *B*
Colby College *B*
St. Joseph's College *B*
University of Maine *B*
University of Southern Maine *B*

Maryland
Charles County Community College *A*
College of Notre Dame of Maryland *B*
Community College of Baltimore County
    Essex *A*
Frederick Community College *A*
Frostburg State University *B*
Goucher College *B*
Harford Community College *A*
Hood College *B*
Johns Hopkins University *B, D*
Loyola College in Maryland *B*
Mount St. Mary's College *B*
St. Mary's College of Maryland *B*
Salisbury State University *B*
University of Maryland
    Baltimore County *B, M*
    College Park *B, M, D*
Washington College *B*
Western Maryland College *B*

Massachusetts
American International College *B*
Amherst College *B*
Assumption College *B*
Bentley College *B*
Boston College *B, M, D*
Boston University *B, M, D*
Brandeis University *B*
Bridgewater State College *B*
Cape Cod Community College *A*
Clark University *B*
College of the Holy Cross *B*
Gordon College *B*
Hampshire College *B*
Harvard College *B*
Harvard University *M, D*
Massachusetts College of Liberal Arts *B*
Massachusetts Institute of
    Technology *B, D*
Merrimack College *B*
Mount Holyoke College *B*
Northeastern University *B*
St. John's Seminary College *B*
Simmons College *B*
Simon's Rock College of Bard *B*
Smith College *B, D*
Stonehill College *B*
Suffolk University *B*
Tufts University *B, M*

University of Massachusetts
    Amherst *B, M, D*
    Boston *B*
    Dartmouth *B*
    Lowell *B*
Wellesley College *B*
Wheaton College *B*
Williams College *B*

Michigan
Albion College *B*
Alma College *B*
Aquinas College *B*
Calvin College *B*
Central Michigan University *B*
Eastern Michigan University *B*
Grand Valley State University *B*
Hillsdale College *B*
Hope College *B*
Kalamazoo College *B*
Kellogg Community College *A*
Lake Michigan College *A*
Lansing Community College *A*
Michigan State University *B, M, D*
Northern Michigan University *B*
Oakland University *B*
Siena Heights University *B*
Spring Arbor College *B*
University of Detroit Mercy *B*
University of Michigan
    Dearborn *B*
    Flint *B*
University of Michigan *B, M, D*
Wayne State University *B, M, D*
Western Michigan University *B, M*

Minnesota
Augsburg College *B*
Bemidji State University *B*
Bethel College *B*
Carleton College *B*
College of St. Benedict *B*
College of St. Catherine: St. Paul
    Campus *B*
Concordia College: Moorhead *B*
Gustavus Adolphus College *B*
Hamline University *B*
Macalester College *B*
Metropolitan State University *B*
Minnesota State University, Mankato *B*
Moorhead State University *B*
St. Cloud State University *B*
St. John's University *B*
St. Mary's University of Minnesota *B*
St. Olaf College *B*
Southwest State University *B*
University of Minnesota
    Duluth *B*
    Morris *B*
    Twin Cities *B, M, D*
University of St. Thomas *B*
Winona State University *A*

Mississippi
Belhaven College *B*
Millsaps College *B, T*
Mississippi State University *B*
University of Mississippi *B, M*
University of Southern Mississippi *B, M*

Missouri
Central Methodist College *B*
Drury University *B*
East Central College *A*
Lincoln University *B*
Maryville University of Saint Louis *B*
Northwest Missouri State University *B*
Rockhurst University *B*
St. Louis University *B, M, D*
Southeast Missouri State University *B*
Southwest Missouri State University *B*
Three Rivers Community College *A*

University of Missouri
    Columbia *B, M, D*
    Kansas City *B*
    Rolla *B*
    St. Louis *B*
Washington University *B, M, D*
Webster University *B*
Westminster College *B*
William Jewell College *B*

Montana

Carroll College *B*
Montana State University
    Bozeman *B*
University of Montana-Missoula *B*

Nebraska

Bellevue University *B*
Creighton University *B*
Doane College *B*
Hastings College *B*
Nebraska Wesleyan University *B*
University of Nebraska
    Lincoln *B, M, D*
    Omaha *B*

Nevada

University of Nevada
    Las Vegas *B*
    Reno *B, M*

New Hampshire

Dartmouth College *B*
New England College *B*
Plymouth State College of the University System of New Hampshire *B*
St. Anselm College *B*
Thomas More College of Liberal Arts *B*
University of New Hampshire *B*

New Jersey

Bloomfield College *B*
College of St. Elizabeth *B*
Drew University *B*
Fairleigh Dickinson University *B*
Montclair State University *B*
Princeton University *B, M, D*
Richard Stockton College of New Jersey *B*
Rider University *B*
Rowan University *B*
Rutgers
    The State University of New Jersey: Camden College of Arts and Sciences *B*
    The State University of New Jersey: Douglass College *B*
    The State University of New Jersey: Livingston College *B*
    The State University of New Jersey: New Brunswick Graduate Campus *M, D*
    The State University of New Jersey: Newark College of Arts and Sciences *B*
    The State University of New Jersey: Rutgers College *B*
    The State University of New Jersey: University College Camden *B*
    The State University of New Jersey: University College New Brunswick *B*
    The State University of New Jersey: University College Newark *B*
St. Peter's College *B*
Seton Hall University *B*
Stevens Institute of Technology *B*
Thomas Edison State College *B*
William Paterson University of New Jersey *B*

New Mexico

New Mexico State University *B*
San Juan College *A*
University of New Mexico *B, M, D*

New York

Adelphi University *B*
Alfred University *B*
Audrey Cohen College *A, B*
Bard College *B*
Barnard College *B*
Canisius College *B*
City University of New York
    Baruch College *B*
    Brooklyn College *B*
    City College *B*
    College of Staten Island *B*
    Graduate School and University Center *M, D*
    Hunter College *B*
    Lehman College *B*
    Queens College *B, M*
    York College *B*
Colgate University *B*
College of Mount St. Vincent *B*
College of New Rochelle *B, T*
Columbia University
    Columbia College *B*
    Graduate School *M, D*
    School of General Studies *B*
    Teachers College *M, D*
Cornell University *B, M, D*
D'Youville College *B*
Fordham University *B, M, D*
Hamilton College *B*
Hartwick College *B*
Hobart and William Smith Colleges *B*
Hofstra University *B*
Houghton College *B*
Iona College *B*
Ithaca College *B*
Le Moyne College *B*
Long Island University
    Brooklyn Campus *B*
    C. W. Post Campus *B*
Manhattan College *B*
Manhattanville College *B*
Molloy College *B*
Nazareth College of Rochester *B*
New York University *B, M, D*
Niagara University *B*
Nyack College *B*
Regents College *B*
Rensselaer Polytechnic Institute *B, M*
St. Bonaventure University *B*
St. Francis College *B*
St. John Fisher College *B*
St. John's University *B, M*
St. Lawrence University *B*
St. Thomas Aquinas College *B*
Sarah Lawrence College *B*
Siena College *B*
Skidmore College *B*
State University of New York
    Albany *B, M, D*
    Binghamton *B, M, D*
    Buffalo *B, M, D*
    College at Brockport *B*
    College at Buffalo *B*
    College at Cortland *B*
    College at Fredonia *B*
    College at Geneseo *B*
    College at Oneonta *B*
    College at Plattsburgh *B*
    College at Potsdam *B*
    New Paltz *B*
    Oswego *B*
    Purchase *B*
    Stony Brook *B, M, D*
Syracuse University *B, M, D*
Touro College *B*
Union College *B*
United States Military Academy *B*
University of Rochester *B, M, D*
Utica College of Syracuse University *B*
Vassar College *B*
Wadhams Hall Seminary-College *B*

North Carolina

Appalachian State University *B*
Belmont Abbey College *B*
Brevard College *B*
Davidson College *B*
Duke University *B, M, D*
East Carolina University *B*
Elon College *B*
Guilford College *B*
High Point University *B*
Lenoir-Rhyne College *B*
Methodist College *A, B*
North Carolina State University *B*
St. Andrews Presbyterian College *B*
Salem College *B*
University of North Carolina
    Asheville *B*
    Chapel Hill *B, M, D*
    Charlotte *B*
    Greensboro *B*
Wake Forest University *B*
Western Carolina University *B*
Wingate University *B*

North Dakota

University of North Dakota *B*

Ohio

Antioch College *B*
Ashland University *B*
Baldwin-Wallace College *B*
Bluffton College *B*
Bowling Green State University *B, M, D*
Capital University *B*
Case Western Reserve University *B, M*
Cedarville College *B*
Cleveland State University *B, M*
College of Wooster *B*
Defiance College *B*
Denison University *B*
Franciscan University of Steubenville *B, M*
Hiram College *B*
John Carroll University *B*
Kent State University
    Stark Campus *B*
Kent State University *B, M*
Kenyon College *B*
Lourdes College *A, B*
Marietta College *B*
Miami University
    Middletown Campus *A*
    Oxford Campus *B, M*
Mount Union College *B*
Mount Vernon Nazarene College *B*
Muskingum College *B*
Oberlin College *B*
Ohio Dominican College *B*
Ohio Northern University *B*
Ohio State University
    Columbus Campus *B, M, D*
Ohio University *B, M*
Ohio Wesleyan University *B*
Otterbein College *B*
Pontifical College Josephinum *B*
University of Akron *B*
University of Cincinnati *B, M, D*
University of Dayton *B*
University of Findlay *B*
University of Toledo *B, M*
Ursuline College *B*
Walsh University *B*
Wittenberg University *B*
Wright State University *B*
Xavier University *B*
Youngstown State University *B*

Oklahoma

Oklahoma Baptist University *B*
Oklahoma City University *B*
Oklahoma State University *B, M*
Southern Nazarene University *B*
Tulsa Community College *A*
University of Central Oklahoma *B*
University of Oklahoma *B, M, D*
University of Tulsa *C, B*

Oregon

Chemeketa Community College *A*
Lewis & Clark College *B*
Linfield College *B*
Marylhurst University *B*
Oregon State University *B*
Pacific University *B*
Portland State University *B*
Reed College *B*
University of Oregon *B, M, D*
University of Portland *B*
Willamette University *B*

Pennsylvania

Albright College *B*
Allegheny College *B*
Allentown College of St. Francis de Sales *B*
Beaver College *B*
Bloomsburg University of Pennsylvania *B*
Bryn Mawr College *B*
Bucknell University *B*
Cabrini College *B*
California University of Pennsylvania *B*
Carlow College *B*
Carnegie Mellon University *B, M, D*
Cedar Crest College *B*
Chatham College *B*
Clarion University of Pennsylvania *B*
College Misericordia *B*
Dickinson College *B*
Drexel University *B*
Duquesne University *B, M, D*
East Stroudsburg University of Pennsylvania *B*
Eastern College *B*
Edinboro University of Pennsylvania *B*
Elizabethtown College *B*
Franklin and Marshall College *B*
Gannon University *B*
Geneva College *B*
Gettysburg College *B*
Grove City College *B*
Haverford College *B*
Holy Family College *B*
Indiana University of Pennsylvania *B*
King's College *B*
Kutztown University of Pennsylvania *B*
La Salle University *B*
Lafayette College *B*
Lebanon Valley College of Pennsylvania *B*
Lehigh University *B*
Lincoln University *B*
Lock Haven University of Pennsylvania *B*
Lycoming College *B*
Mansfield University of Pennsylvania *B*
Mercyhurst College *B*
Messiah College *B*
Moravian College *B*
Muhlenberg College *B*
Penn State
    University Park *B, M, D*
Rosemont College *B*
St. Charles Borromeo Seminary - Overbrook *B*
St. Francis College *B*
St. Joseph's University *B*
St. Vincent College *B*
Slippery Rock University of Pennsylvania *B*
Susquehanna University *B*
Swarthmore College *B*
Temple University *B, M, D*
Thiel College *B*
University of Pennsylvania *B, M, D*
University of Pittsburgh *B, M, D*
University of Scranton *B*
Ursinus College *B*
Villanova University *B, M, D*
Washington and Jefferson College *B*
West Chester University of Pennsylvania *B, M*
Westminster College *B*
Wilkes University *B*
York College of Pennsylvania *A*

Puerto Rico
Bayamon Central University *B*
Pontifical Catholic University of Puerto Rico *B*
University of Puerto Rico
    Mayaguez Campus *B*
    Rio Piedras Campus *B, M*

Rhode Island
Brown University *B, M, D*
Providence College *B*
Rhode Island College *B*
Roger Williams University *B*
Salve Regina University *B*
University of Rhode Island *B*

South Carolina
Clemson University *B*
College of Charleston *B*
Furman University *B*
University of South Carolina *B, M, D*
Winthrop University *B*
Wofford College *B*

South Dakota
Augustana College *B*
University of South Dakota *B*

Tennessee
Austin Peay State University *B*
Belmont University *B*
Carson-Newman College *B*
David Lipscomb University *B*
East Tennessee State University *B*
Freed-Hardeman University *B*
Middle Tennessee State University *B*
Rhodes College *B*
University of Memphis *B, M, D*
University of Tennessee
    Knoxville *B, M, D*
    Martin *B*
University of the South *B*
Vanderbilt University *B, M, D*
Walters State Community College *A*

Texas
Austin College *B*
Baylor University *B, M*
Blinn College *A*
Dallas Baptist University *B*
Hardin-Simmons University *B*
Howard Payne University *B*
Lon Morris College *A*
McMurry University *B*
Our Lady of the Lake University of San Antonio *B*
Rice University *B, M, D*
St. Edward's University *B*
St. Mary's University *B*
Sam Houston State University *B*
Schreiner College *B*
Southern Methodist University *B*
Southwest Texas State University *B*
Southwestern University *B*
Texas A&M University *B, M*
Texas Christian University *B*
Texas Lutheran University *B*
Texas Tech University *B, M*
Trinity University *B*
University of Dallas *B, M, D*
University of Houston *B, M*
University of North Texas *B, M*
University of St. Thomas *B, M, D*
University of Texas
    Arlington *B*
    Austin *B, M, D*
    El Paso *B*
    Pan American *B*
    San Antonio *B*
University of the Incarnate Word *B*
Western Texas College *A*

Utah
Brigham Young University *B*
Southern Utah University *B*
University of Utah *B, M, D*
Utah State University *B*

Westminster College *B*

Vermont
Bennington College *B*
Burlington College *B*
Goddard College *B*
Marlboro College *B*
Middlebury College *B*
St. Michael's College *B*
University of Vermont *B*

Virginia
Bluefield College *B*
Christendom College *B*
Christopher Newport University *B*
College of William and Mary *B*
Emory & Henry College *B*
Ferrum College *B*
George Mason University *B*
Hampden-Sydney College *B*
Hollins University *B*
Lynchburg College *B*
Mary Baldwin College *B*
Mary Washington College *B*
Old Dominion University *B*
Randolph-Macon College *B*
Randolph-Macon Woman's College *B*
Roanoke College *B, T*
Sweet Briar College *B*
University of Richmond *B*
University of Virginia *B, M, D*
Virginia Commonwealth University *B*
Virginia Polytechnic Institute and State University *B, M*
Virginia Wesleyan College *B*
Washington and Lee University *B*

Washington
Central Washington University *B*
City University *B*
Eastern Washington University *B*
Everett Community College *A*
Gonzaga University *B, M*
Lower Columbia College *A*
Pacific Lutheran University *B*
St. Martin's College *B*
Seattle Pacific University *B, T*
Seattle University *B*
University of Puget Sound *B*
University of Washington *B, M, D*
Washington State University *B*
Western Washington University *B*
Whitman College *B*
Whitworth College *B*

West Virginia
Bethany College *B*
Marshall University *B*
West Virginia University *B*
West Virginia Wesleyan College *B*
Wheeling Jesuit University *B*

Wisconsin
Alverno College *B*
Carthage College *B*
Lakeland College *B*
Lawrence University *B, T*
Marquette University *B, M, D, T*
Mount Mary College *B*
Ripon College *B*
St. Norbert College *B*
University of Wisconsin
    Eau Claire *B*
    Green Bay *B*
    La Crosse *B*
    Madison *B, M, D*
    Milwaukee *B, M*
    Oshkosh *B*
    Parkside *B*
    Platteville *B*
    Stevens Point *B, T*

Wyoming
University of Wyoming *B, M*

Philosophy/religion

Alabama
Athens State University *B*
Birmingham-Southern College *B*
Huntingdon College *B*
Samford University *B*

Arizona
Prescott College *B, M*

Arkansas
Hendrix College *B*
Lyon College *B*
University of the Ozarks *B*

California
Chapman University *B*
Crafton Hills College *A*
Holy Names College *B*
Long Beach City College *C, A*
Pomona College *B*
San Francisco State University *B*
University of La Verne *B*
University of San Francisco *B*

Colorado
Trinidad State Junior College *A*

Connecticut
Albertus Magnus College *B*

Florida
Bethune-Cookman College *B*
Edward Waters College *B*
Flagler College *B*
Florida Memorial College *B*
New College of the University of South Florida *B*
Palm Beach Atlantic College *B*
Polk Community College *A*
University of West Florida *B*

Georgia
Andrew College *A*
Berry College *B*
Covenant College *B*
Oxford College of Emory University *B*
Paine College *B*
Piedmont College *B*
Toccoa Falls College *B*
Young Harris College *A*

Illinois
Eureka College *B*
Greenville College *B*
Illinois College *B*
Lewis University *B*
Lincoln Christian College and Seminary *M*
MacMurray College *B*
Monmouth College *B*
Olivet Nazarene University *B*

Indiana
Goshen College *B*
Indiana University
    Bloomington *B*
Manchester College *B*
University of Evansville *B*
University of Indianapolis *B*
University of Notre Dame *B*

Iowa
Buena Vista University *B*
Coe College *B*
Graceland University *B*
Morningside College *B*

Kansas
Bethany College *B, T*
Butler County Community College *A*
Central Christian College *A, B*
Cowley County Community College *A*
McPherson College *B*
MidAmerica Nazarene University *B, T*
Southwestern College *B*
Sterling College *B*

Tabor College *B*

Kentucky
Cumberland College *B*
Kentucky Wesleyan College *B*

Louisiana
Centenary College of Louisiana *B*
Loyola University New Orleans *M*

Maine
St. Joseph's College *B*
University of Maine
    Farmington *B*

Maryland
Goucher College *B*
Towson University *B*

Massachusetts
Boston University *B*
Curry College *B*
Hampshire College *B*
Harvard College *B*
Merrimack College *B*
Northeastern University *B*

Michigan
Adrian College *A, B*
Spring Arbor College *B*

Minnesota
Northland Community & Technical College *A*

Missouri
College of the Ozarks *B*
Culver-Stockton College *B*
Missouri Valley College *B*
Ozark Christian College *C, B*
Rockhurst University *B*
St. Louis Christian College *B*
Truman State University *B*
University of Missouri
    St. Louis *B*
Washington University *B, M, D*
William Jewell College *B*

Montana
Miles Community College *A*
Rocky Mountain College *B*

Nebraska
Hastings College *B*
Midland Lutheran College *B*

New Hampshire
University of New Hampshire *B*

New Jersey
Cumberland County College *A*
Kean University *B*
Rowan University *B*
The College of New Jersey *B*

New Mexico
College of Santa Fe *B*

New York
Bard College *B*
Colgate University *B*
Cornell University *B*
Elmira College *B*
Eugene Lang College/New School University *B*
Fordham University *M, D*
Houghton College *B*
Iona College *B*
Ithaca College *B*
Manhattan College *B*
Roberts Wesleyan College *B*
St. John's University *B, M*
St. Thomas Aquinas College *T*
Sarah Lawrence College *B*
State University of New York
    College at Old Westbury *B*

North Carolina
Barton College *B*
Belmont Abbey College *B*
Campbell University *B*

Philosophy/religion

Catawba College *B*
Greensboro College *B*
Louisburg College *A*
Methodist College *A, B*
North Carolina Wesleyan College *B*
Queens College *B*
Sandhills Community College *A*
Shaw University *B*
University of North Carolina
    Pembroke *B*
    Wilmington *B*

North Dakota
Jamestown College *B*

Ohio
Defiance College *B*
Heidelberg College *B*
Ohio Northern University *B*
Otterbein College *B*
Wilmington College *B*
Youngstown State University *B*

Oklahoma
Oklahoma City University *B*

Oregon
Marylhurst University *B*

Pennsylvania
Alvernia College *B*
Duquesne University *M*
Gettysburg College *B*
La Salle University *B*
Millersville University of
    Pennsylvania *B*
Seton Hill College *B*
Ursinus College *B*
Wilson College *B*

Puerto Rico
Inter American University of Puerto Rico
    Metropolitan Campus *D*

South Carolina
Benedict College *B*
Charleston Southern University *B*
Claflin University *B*
Erskine College *B*
Newberry College *B*
Presbyterian College *B*

South Dakota
Mount Marty College *B*

Tennessee
Christian Brothers University *B*
Fisk University *B*
Union University *B*
University of Tennessee
    Chattanooga *B*

Texas
Lon Morris College *A*
Texas Wesleyan University *B*

Vermont
Burlington College *B*
Marlboro College *B*

Virginia
Bridgewater College *B*
Eastern Mennonite University *B*
Ferrum College *B*
Hampden-Sydney College *B*
James Madison University *B*
Lord Fairfax Community College *A*
Radford University *B*
Roanoke College *B*
Virginia Wesleyan College *B*

Washington
Highline Community College *A*

West Virginia
Alderson-Broaddus College *B*
Bethany College *B*
Davis and Elkins College *B*
University of Charleston *B*
West Virginia Wesleyan College *B*

Wisconsin
Beloit College *B*
Northland College *B*

Photography

Alabama
Bessemer State Technical College *C*
Birmingham-Southern College *B*
Calhoun Community College *A*

Arizona
Arizona State University *B*
Northern Arizona University *B*
Prescott College *B, M*

California
Academy of Art College *C, A, B, M*
Allan Hancock College *A*
Art Center College of Design *B*
Bakersfield College *A*
Butte College *A*
California College of Arts and
    Crafts *B, M*
California Institute of the Arts *C, B, M*
California State University
    Fullerton *B, M*
    Hayward *B*
    Long Beach *B*
Cerritos Community College *A*
Chabot College *A*
Chaffey Community College *C, A*
Chapman University *B*
City College of San Francisco *C, A*
College of San Mateo *A*
College of the Siskiyous *A*
Columbia College *A*
Cypress College *C*
De Anza College *A*
East Los Angeles College *A*
Foothill College *C, A*
Fresno City College *C, A*
Glendale Community College *C*
Golden West College *A*
Grossmont Community College *A*
Irvine Valley College *A*
Los Angeles Pierce College *A*
Los Angeles Southwest College *A*
Los Angeles Trade and Technical
    College *C, A*
Merced College *A*
Modesto Junior College *A*
Monterey Peninsula College *C, A*
Moorpark College *A*
Mount San Antonio College *C, A*
Mount San Jacinto College *A*
Orange Coast College *C, A*
Otis College of Art and Design *C, B, M*
Pacific Union College *A*
Palomar College *C, A*
Riverside Community College *C, A*
Saddleback College *A*
San Diego City College *C, A*
San Francisco Art Institute *B, M*
San Joaquin Delta College *A*
San Jose State University *M*
Santa Ana College *C, A*
Santa Monica College *A*
Santa Rosa Junior College *C*
Sierra College *C, A*
Southwestern College *A*
University of California
    Santa Cruz *C, B*
University of San Francisco *B*
University of Southern California *B*
Ventura College *C, A*

Colorado
Adams State College *B*
Art Institute
    of Colorado *A*
Colorado Mountain College
    Spring Valley Campus *C, A*
Colorado State University *B*
Community College of Denver *C, A*

Connecticut
Paier College of Art *C, A*
University of Hartford *B, M*

District of Columbia
Corcoran College of Art and Design *B*
George Washington University *M*

Florida
Art Institute
    of Fort Lauderdale *C, A*
Barry University *B, M*
Brevard Community College *A*
Daytona Beach Community College *A*
Palm Beach Community College *A*
Ringling School of Art and Design *B*
University of Miami *B*

Georgia
Atlanta College of Art *B*
Gwinnett Technical Institute *A*
LaGrange College *B*
Savannah College of Art and
    Design *B, M*
University of Georgia *B*

Idaho
College of Southern Idaho *A*
Ricks College *A*
University of Idaho *B*

Illinois
Barat College *B*
Bradley University *B*
City Colleges of Chicago
    Olive-Harvey College *A*
Columbia College *B, M*
Judson College *B*
Prairie State College *C, A*
School of the Art Institute of
    Chicago *B, M*
Southern Illinois University
    Carbondale *B, M*
Southwestern Ilinois College *A*
University of Illinois
    Chicago *B, M*
    Urbana-Champaign *B*
Western Illinois University *B*

Indiana
Ball State University *B*
Indiana University--Purdue University
    Indiana University-Purdue
    University Fort Wayne *B*
Purdue University *B*

Iowa
Iowa Lakes Community College *A*
Morningside College *B*
University of Iowa *M*

Kansas
Pittsburg State University *B*

Louisiana
Louisiana Tech University *B*

Maine
Maine College of Art *B*
University of Maine
    Augusta *A*

Maryland
Cecil Community College *C, A*
College of Notre Dame of Maryland *B*
Harford Community College *A*
Howard Community College *A*
Maryland Institute College of Art *B, M*
Montgomery College
    Rockville Campus *A*
University of Maryland
    Baltimore County *B*

Massachusetts
Bunker Hill Community College *C*
Fitchburg State College *B*
Hampshire College *B*
Massachusetts College of Art *B, M*
Montserrat College of Art *B*
Northeastern University *B*
Salem State College *B*
School of the Museum of Fine Arts *B, M*
Simon's Rock College of Bard *B*
University of Massachusetts
    Dartmouth *B*

Michigan
Andrews University *B*
Center for Creative Studies: College of
    Art and Design *B*
Cranbrook Academy of Art *M*
Grand Valley State University *B*
Lansing Community College *A*
Macomb Community College *C, A*
Mott Community College *A*
Northern Michigan University *B*
Oakland Community College *C, A*
Siena Heights University *B*
University of Michigan *B*
Washtenaw Community College *A*
Western Michigan University *B*

Minnesota
College of Visual Arts *B*
Minneapolis College of Art and
    Design *B*
Minneapolis Community and Technical
    College *C*
Ridgewater College: A Community and
    Technical College *C*

Missouri
Central Missouri State University *B*
Kansas City Art Institute *B*
St. Louis Community College
    St. Louis Community College at
        Forest Park *A*
    St. Louis Community College at
        Meramec *A*
University of Missouri
    St. Louis *B*
Washington University *B, M*
Webster University *B*

Nebraska
Mid Plains Community College Area *C*

New Hampshire
New Hampshire Community Technical
    College
        Laconia *C*
Rivier College *B*
White Pines College *B*

New Jersey
Brookdale Community College *A*
Camden County College *A*
Rowan University *B*
Rutgers
    The State University of New Jersey:
        Mason Gross School of the
        Arts *B, M*
Thomas Edison State College *B*
Union County College *A*

New York
Adirondack Community College *C, A*
Bard College *B, M*
City University of New York
    Queensborough Community
        College *A*
Fordham University *B*
Herkimer County Community College *A*
Ithaca College *B*
Long Island University
    C. W. Post Campus *B*
Monroe Community College *A*
Nassau Community College *A*
New York State College of Ceramics at
    Alfred University *B, M, T*
New York University *B*
Onondaga Community College *A*
Pace University:
    Pleasantville/Briarcliff *C*
Pace University *C*
Parsons School of Design *C, A, B, T*
Pratt Institute *B, M*

Rochester Institute of
    Technology A, B, M
Sage Junior College of Albany A
St. John's University B
Sarah Lawrence College B
School of Visual Arts B, M
State University of New York
    Albany B, M
    Buffalo B
    College at Buffalo B
    New Paltz B, M
    Purchase B
Syracuse University B, M
Villa Maria College of Buffalo A

North Carolina
Barton College B
Carteret Community College A
Duke University C
Guilford Technical Community
    College C
Randolph Community College A

Ohio
Clark State Community College C
Cleveland Institute of Art B
Columbus College of Art and Design B
Kent State University B
Ohio Institute of Photography and
    Technology C, A
Ohio State University
    Columbus Campus B
Ohio University B, M
University of Akron B
University of Dayton B
Youngstown State University B

Oklahoma
Oklahoma State University
    Okmulgee A
University of Central Oklahoma B
University of Oklahoma B

Oregon
Pacific Northwest College of Art B

Pennsylvania
Antonelli Institute of Art and
    Photography A
Art Institute
    of Philadelphia A
    of Pittsburgh A
Beaver College B
Drexel University B
Harrisburg Area Community
    College C, A
Temple University B, M
University of the Arts B

Rhode Island
Salve Regina University B

South Carolina
Coker College B

Tennessee
Carson-Newman College B
Nashville State Technical Institute C, A
Pellissippi State Technical Community
    College C
Roane State Community College A

Texas
Amarillo College A
El Paso Community College A
St. Edward's University B
Sam Houston State University B, M
Texas A&M University
    Commerce B
Texas Woman's University B, M
Tyler Junior College C
University of Houston B, M
University of North Texas B
University of Texas
    Arlington B
    San Antonio B, M
Western Texas College A

Utah
Brigham Young University B
Dixie State College of Utah A
Weber State University B

Vermont
Bennington College B, M
Burlington College B
Marlboro College B

Virginia
Central Virginia Community College C
J. Sargeant Reynolds Community
    College C
Northern Virginia Community College A
Southwest Virginia Community
    College C
Thomas Nelson Community College A
Tidewater Community College C, A
Virginia Intermont College B

Washington
Cornish College of the Arts B
Everett Community College A
Seattle University B
Shoreline Community College A
University of Washington B, M

West Virginia
Marshall University B
West Virginia State College B

Wisconsin
Milwaukee Area Technical College A
Milwaukee Institute of Art & Design B

Wyoming
Casper College A
Northwest College A
Western Wyoming Community
    College A

Physical education

Alabama
Alabama Agricultural and Mechanical
    University B, M, T
Alabama State University B, M, T
Athens State University B
Auburn University B, M, D, T
Chattahoochee Valley Community
    College A
Faulkner University B, T
Huntingdon College B, T
Jacksonville State University B, M, T
James H. Faulkner State Community
    College A
Lawson State Community College A
Oakwood College B
Samford University B, T
Southern Union State Community
    College A
Tuskegee University B, T
University of Alabama
    Birmingham B, M, T
University of Alabama B, M
University of Mobile B, M, T
University of Montevallo B, M, T
University of South Alabama B, M, T
University of West Alabama B, M, T

Alaska
University of Alaska
    Anchorage B

Arizona
Arizona State University B, M, T
Grand Canyon University B
Northern Arizona University B, T
Prescott College B, M
South Mountain Community College A
University of Arizona B

Arkansas
Arkansas State University B, M, T
Arkansas Tech University B, M
Harding University B, M, T
Henderson State University B, M, T
Hendrix College B
John Brown University B, T
Ouachita Baptist University B, T
Philander Smith College B
Southern Arkansas University B, M, T
University of Arkansas
    Monticello B
    Pine Bluff B, M, T
University of Arkansas B, M
University of Central Arkansas B, M, T
University of the Ozarks B, T
Williams Baptist College B

California
Allan Hancock College A
Azusa Pacific University T
Biola University B, T
Butte College A
California Baptist University B, T
California Lutheran University B, T
California State Polytechnic University:
    Pomona T
California State University
    Bakersfield B, T
    Chico B, M, T
    Dominguez Hills M, T
    Fullerton B, M, T
    Hayward B, M, T
    Long Beach B, M, T
    Los Angeles B, M, T
    Northridge B, T
    Sacramento T
    Stanislaus B
Chaffey Community College C, A
College of the Canyons A
College of the Sequoias A
Columbia College C
Compton Community College A
Concordia University B
Cuesta College C, A
Cypress College C, A
Foothill College C, A
Fresno Pacific University B, T
Golden West College A
Humboldt State University B, M, T
Irvine Valley College A
Kings River Community College A
Master's College B
Mount San Jacinto College A
Pacific Union College B, T
Pepperdine University B
Saddleback College A
San Diego State University B
San Francisco State University B, M, T
Santa Barbara City College A
Sonoma State University M, T
Southwestern College A
Taft College A
University of California
    Berkeley B, M, D
    Davis M
University of La Verne B, T
University of the Pacific T
Vanguard University of Southern
    California B
West Hills Community College A
Westmont College T

Colorado
Adams State College B, M, T
Colorado State University T
Fort Lewis College T
Metropolitan State College of Denver T
Trinidad State Junior College A
University of Northern Colorado M, D, T
University of Southern Colorado B
Western State College of Colorado T

Connecticut
Central Connecticut State
    University B, M
Eastern Connecticut State
    University B, T
Mitchell College A
Southern Connecticut State
    University B, M, T
University of Connecticut B, M, D, T

Delaware
Delaware State University B
University of Delaware B, M, T
Wesley College B

District of Columbia
Gallaudet University B, T
George Washington University A, B, M
Howard University B, M, T
University of the District of Columbia B

Florida
Barry University B, T
Bethune-Cookman College B, T
Clearwater Christian College B
Edward Waters College B
Florida Agricultural and Mechanical
    University B, M, T
Florida International University B, M, T
Florida Memorial College B, T
Florida Southern College B
Florida State University B, M, D, T
Hillsborough Community College A
Jacksonville University B, M, T
Miami-Dade Community College A
Palm Beach Atlantic College B, T
Palm Beach Community College A
Pensacola Junior College A
St. Leo University B, T
University of Central Florida B, M, T
University of Miami M
University of North Florida B
University of South Florida B, M, T
University of Tampa T
University of West Florida B, M, T
Valencia Community College A
Warner Southern College B

Georgia
Albany State University B, M
Armstrong Atlantic State University B, T
Augusta State University B, M
Berry College B, T
Brewton-Parker College A, B
Clark Atlanta University B
Columbus State University B
Fort Valley State University B, T
Gainesville College A
Georgia College and State
    University M, T
Georgia Perimeter College A
Georgia Southern University B, M, T
Georgia Southwestern State
    University B, M
Georgia State University B, M
Kennesaw State University B
Middle Georgia College A
Morehouse College B
Morris Brown College B
North Georgia College & State
    University B, M
Reinhardt College B
South Georgia College A
State University of West Georgia B, M
University of Georgia B, M, D, T
Valdosta State University B, M
Waycross College A

Hawaii
Brigham Young University
    Hawaii B, D
University of Hawaii
    Manoa B, T

Idaho
Albertson College of Idaho B
Boise State University B, M, T
College of Southern Idaho A
Idaho State University B, M, T
Lewis-Clark State College B, T
Northwest Nazarene University B
Ricks College A
University of Idaho B, M, T

Illinois
Augustana College B, T
Blackburn College B, T
Chicago State University B, M
Concordia University B, T
De Paul University B, T
Eastern Illinois University B, M, T
Elmhurst College B
Eureka College T
Greenville College B, T
Illinois College T
Illinois State University B, M, T
John A. Logan College A
Judson College B, T
Kishwaukee College A
Lewis University T
MacMurray College B, T
McKendree College B, T
Millikin University B, T
North Central College B, T
North Park University T
Northeastern Illinois University B
Northern Illinois University B, M, T
Olivet Nazarene University B, T
Quincy University A, B, T
Rockford College B, T
Sauk Valley Community College A
Southern Illinois University
    Carbondale B, M, D
Trinity Christian College B, T
Trinity International University B, T
University of Illinois
    Urbana-Champaign M, T
Western Illinois University B, M
Wheaton College T

Indiana
Anderson University B, T
Ball State University B, M
Bethel College B
Butler University T
Franklin College T
Goshen College B
Grace College B
Hanover College B
Indiana State University B, M, T
Indiana University
    Bloomington B, M, D, T
Indiana University--Purdue University
    Indiana University-Purdue
        University Indianapolis B
Indiana Wesleyan University B, T
Manchester College B, T
Marian College B, T
Oakland City University B
Purdue University B, M, D
St. Joseph's College B
Taylor University B
Tri-State University B, T
University of Evansville T
University of Indianapolis B, T
University of St. Francis C
University of Southern Indiana B, T
Valparaiso University B, T
Vincennes University A

Iowa
Briar Cliff College B
Buena Vista University B, T
Central College B, T
Clarke College B
Cornell College B, T
Dordt College B
Graceland University T
Iowa State University T
Iowa Wesleyan College B
Loras College B
Luther College B
Marshalltown Community College A
Morningside College B
North Iowa Area Community College A
Northwestern College T
St. Ambrose University B
Simpson College B, T
University of Dubuque T
University of Iowa M, D
University of Northern Iowa B, M
Upper Iowa University B
Wartburg College B, T
William Penn University B

Kansas
Baker University B, T
Benedictine College B, T
Bethany College B, T
Bethel College T
Butler County Community College A
Central Christian College A
Coffeyville Community College A
Colby Community College A
Emporia State University B, M, T
Fort Hays State University B, M, T
Garden City Community College A
Independence Community College A
Kansas City Kansas Community
    College A
McPherson College B, T
MidAmerica Nazarene University B, T
Ottawa University B, T
Pittsburg State University B, M, T
Southwestern College B, T
Tabor College B, T
University of Kansas B, M, D, T
Washburn University of Topeka B
Wichita State University B, M

Kentucky
Alice Lloyd College B
Asbury College B, T
Berea College B, T
Campbellsville University B
Cumberland College B, T
Eastern Kentucky University B, M
Kentucky State University B
Lindsey Wilson College B
Morehead State University B, M
Murray State University B, M, T
Northern Kentucky University B
St. Catharine College A
Transylvania University B, T
Union College B
University of Kentucky B
University of Louisville M
Western Kentucky University B, M

Louisiana
Centenary College of Louisiana B, T
Dillard University B
Louisiana State University
    Shreveport B
Louisiana Tech University B, M
McNeese State University T
Nicholls State University B
Northwestern State University B, M, T
Southeastern Louisiana University M
Southern University and Agricultural and
    Mechanical College B
University of Louisiana at Lafayette B
University of Louisiana at Monroe B, M
University of New Orleans B, M
Xavier University of Louisiana B, T

Maine
Husson College B, T
St. Joseph's College B
University of Maine
    Presque Isle B
University of Maine B, M

Maryland
Allegany College A
Bowie State University B
Columbia Union College B
Frederick Community College A
Frostburg State University B, M, T
Hagerstown Community College A
Montgomery College
    Germantown Campus A
    Rockville Campus A
Morgan State University B, M
Prince George's Community College A
Salisbury State University B, T
Towson University B
University of Maryland
    College Park B, M, D, T
    Eastern Shore B
Western Maryland College B, M

Massachusetts
Boston University B, M, T
Bridgewater State College B, M, T
Dean College A
Eastern Nazarene College B, M, T
Northeastern University B
Salem State College B
Springfield College B, M, D, T
University of Massachusetts
    Boston B
Westfield State College B, M, T

Michigan
Adrian College B, T
Albion College B, T
Alma College T
Andrews University M, T
Aquinas College B, T
Calvin College B, T
Central Michigan University B, M
Concordia College B, T
Cornerstone College and Grand Rapids
    Baptist Seminary B, T
Eastern Michigan University B, M, T
Grand Valley State University B, T
Hillsdale College B
Kellogg Community College A
Lansing Community College A
Michigan State University B, M, D
Mid Michigan Community College A
Northern Michigan University B, T
Saginaw Valley State University B, T
Schoolcraft College A
University of Michigan B, M, D
Wayne State University B, M, T
Western Michigan University B, M, T

Minnesota
Augsburg College B, T
Bemidji State University M, T
Bethel College B
College of St. Catherine: St. Paul
    Campus B, T
Concordia College: Moorhead T
Concordia University: St. Paul B, T
Crown College B, T
Gustavus Adolphus College T
Hamline University B
Minnesota State University,
    Mankato B, M, T
Moorhead State University B, T
Northland Community & Technical
    College A
Northwestern College B
Ridgewater College: A Community and
    Technical College A
St. Cloud State University M, T
St. Olaf College T
Southwest State University B, T
University of Minnesota
    Duluth B, T
    Twin Cities B, M, D, T
University of St. Thomas B, T
Winona State University B, M, T

Mississippi
Alcorn State University B
Blue Mountain College B
Delta State University B, M
Hinds Community College A
Jackson State University B, M
Mary Holmes College A
Mississippi Delta Community College A
Mississippi State University B, M, T
Mississippi Valley State University B, T
Northwest Mississippi Community
    College A
University of Southern
    Mississippi B, M, D

Missouri
Central Methodist College B, M
Central Missouri State
    University B, M, T
College of the Ozarks B, T
Crowder College A
Culver-Stockton College B, T
Drury University B, T
Evangel University B
Hannibal-LaGrange College B
Lincoln University B, T
Lindenwood University B
Missouri Baptist College B, T
Missouri Southern State College B, T
Missouri Valley College B
Northwest Missouri State
    University B, M, T
Southeast Missouri State
    University B, M
Southwest Baptist University B, T
Southwest Missouri State University B
Truman State University M, T
University of Missouri
    Kansas City B
    St. Louis B, M, T
Westminster College B, T
William Woods University B, T

Montana
Carroll College B, T
Montana State University
    Billings B, T
    Northern B, T
Rocky Mountain College B, T
University of Great Falls B
University of Montana-Missoula B
Western Montana College of The
    University of Montana B, T

Nebraska
Bellevue University B
Chadron State College B, M
Concordia University T
Dana College B
Doane College B, T
Hastings College B, M, T
Mid Plains Community College Area A
Midland Lutheran College B, T
Nebraska Wesleyan University B
Northeast Community College A
Peru State College B, T
Union College T
University of Nebraska
    Kearney B, M, T
    Lincoln B, M, T
    Omaha B, M, T
Wayne State College B, M

Nevada
University of Nevada
    Las Vegas B
    Reno B, M

New Hampshire
Keene State College B, T
New England College B, T
Plymouth State College of the University
    System of New Hampshire B, T
University of New Hampshire M, T

New Jersey
Essex County College A
Gloucester County College A
Kean University B
Montclair State University B, M, T
Rowan University C, B, M
The College of New Jersey B, M, T
William Paterson University of New
    Jersey B

New Mexico
College of the Southwest B, T
Eastern New Mexico University B, M
New Mexico Highlands University B, M
New Mexico Junior College A
New Mexico State University B
University of New Mexico B, M, D, T
Western New Mexico University B

New York
Adelphi University *M*
Canisius College *B, M, T*
City University of New York
    Brooklyn College *B*
    City College *B, T*
    Hunter College *B, M*
    Lehman College *B*
    Queens College *M, T*
    York College *B, T*
College of Mount St. Vincent *B, T*
Columbia University
    Teachers College *M, D*
Columbia-Greene Community College *A*
Corning Community College *A*
Fulton-Montgomery Community
    College *A*
Herkimer County Community College *A*
Hofstra University *B, M, T*
Houghton College *B*
Hudson Valley Community College *A*
Ithaca College *B, M, T*
Long Island University
    Brooklyn Campus *B, M, T*
    C. W. Post Campus *B, T*
Manhattan College *B, T*
Mohawk Valley Community College *C*
St. Bonaventure University *B, T*
St. Francis College *B, T*
St. Lawrence University *T*
State University of New York
    College at Brockport *B, M, T*
    College at Cortland *B, M, T*
    College of Technology at Delhi *A*
Syracuse University *B, M, T*

North Carolina
Appalachian State University *B, M, T*
Barton College *T*
Brevard College *B*
Campbell University *B, M, T*
Catawba College *B, T*
Chowan College *B, T*
Cleveland Community College *A*
East Carolina University *B, M*
Elizabeth City State University *B*
Elon College *B, T*
Fayetteville State University *B, T*
Gardner-Webb University *B, M*
Greensboro College *B, T*
Guilford College *B, T*
High Point University *B, T*
Johnson C. Smith University *B*
Lenoir Community College *A*
Lenoir-Rhyne College *B, T*
Louisburg College *A*
Mars Hill College *B, T*
Meredith College *B, T*
Methodist College *A, B, T*
North Carolina Agricultural and
    Technical State University *B, M, T*
North Carolina Central University *B, M*
North Carolina Wesleyan College *B*
Pfeiffer University *B*
St. Andrews Presbyterian College *T*
St. Augustine's College *B, T*
Sandhills Community College *A*
University of North Carolina
    Chapel Hill *M*
    Greensboro *B, M, D, T*
    Pembroke *B, T*
    Wilmington *B, T*
Western Carolina University *B, M, T*
Wingate University *B, T*
Winston-Salem State University *B*

North Dakota
Dickinson State University *B, T*
Jamestown College *B*
Mayville State University *B, T*
Minot State University *B, T*
North Dakota State University *B, M, T*
University of Mary *B, T*
University of North Dakota *M, T*
Valley City State University *B, T*

Ohio
Ashland University *B, M, T*
Baldwin-Wallace College *B, T*
Bluffton College *B*
Bowling Green State University *B*
Capital University *B*
Cedarville College *B*
Central State University *B*
Cleveland State University *B, M, T*
College of Mount St. Joseph *B, T*
Defiance College *B, T*
Denison University *B*
Heidelberg College *B*
John Carroll University *B*
Kent State University
    Stark Campus *B*
Kent State University *B, M, D, T*
Malone College *B*
Miami University
    Oxford Campus *B, T*
Mount Union College *B, T*
Mount Vernon Nazarene College *B, T*
Ohio Northern University *T*
Ohio State University
    Columbus Campus *B, M, D*
Ohio University *B*
Ohio Wesleyan University *B*
Otterbein College *B*
Sinclair Community College *A*
University of Akron *M*
University of Dayton *B, M, T*
University of Findlay *B, T*
University of Rio Grande *B, T*
University of Toledo *B, M, D, T*
Walsh University *B*
Wilmington College *B*
Wright State University *B, M, T*
Xavier University *M, T*
Youngstown State University *B, M, T*

Oklahoma
Cameron University *B, T*
Connors State College *A*
East Central University *B, T*
Eastern Oklahoma State College *A*
Langston University *B*
Northeastern Oklahoma Agricultural and
    Mechanical College *A*
Northeastern State University *B*
Northern Oklahoma College *A*
Northwestern Oklahoma State
    University *B, T*
Oklahoma Baptist University *B, T*
Oklahoma Christian University of
    Science and Arts *B, T*
Oklahoma City University *B*
Oklahoma Panhandle State University *B*
Oklahoma State University *M, D*
Oral Roberts University *B, T*
Redlands Community College *A*
Southern Nazarene University *B*
Southwestern Oklahoma State
    University *B, M, T*
Tulsa Community College *A*
University of Central Oklahoma *B*
Western Oklahoma State College *A*

Oregon
Chemeketa Community College *A*
Concordia University *B, M, T*
George Fox University *B, M, T*
Linfield College *T*
Linn-Benton Community College *A*
Oregon State University *M*
University of Portland *B*
Western Baptist College *B*
Western Oregon University *T*

Pennsylvania
Bucks County Community College *A*
Butler County Community College *A*
East Stroudsburg University of
    Pennsylvania *B, M, T*
Edinboro University of
    Pennsylvania *B, M*
Gettysburg College *T*
Indiana University of Pennsylvania *B, T*
Lincoln University *B, T*
Lock Haven University of
    Pennsylvania *B, T*
Marywood University *B, T*
Messiah College *B, T*
Montgomery County Community
    College *A*
Slippery Rock University of
    Pennsylvania *B, M*
Temple University *B, M, D, T*
University of Pittsburgh *B, M, D, T*
Ursinus College *B*
West Chester University of
    Pennsylvania *B, M, T*

Puerto Rico
American University of Puerto Rico *B, T*
Bayamon Central University *B*
Inter American University of Puerto Rico
    Guayama Campus *B*
    Metropolitan Campus *B, M*
    San German Campus *B, M*
Pontifical Catholic University of Puerto
    Rico *B, T*
Turabo University *B*
Universidad Metropolitana *B, M*
University of Puerto Rico
    Cayey University College *B, T*
University of the Sacred Heart *B*

Rhode Island
Rhode Island College *B*
University of Rhode Island *B, M*

South Carolina
Anderson College *B, T*
Charleston Southern University *B*
Claflin University *B*
Coastal Carolina University *B*
Coker College *B, T*
College of Charleston *B, T*
Furman University *T*
Lander University *B, T*
Limestone College *B*
Newberry College *B, T*
South Carolina State University *B, T*
Southern Wesleyan University *B, T*
The Citadel *B, M, T*
University of South Carolina
    Spartanburg *B*
University of South Carolina *B, M*
Voorhees College *B*
Winthrop University *B, M, T*

South Dakota
Augustana College *B, T*
Black Hills State University *B, T*
Dakota State University *B, T*
Dakota Wesleyan University *B, T*
Huron University *B*
Mount Marty College *B*
Northern State University *M, T*
University of South Dakota *B, M, T*

Tennessee
Bethel College *B*
Carson-Newman College *B*
Cumberland University *B*
David Lipscomb University *B, T*
Freed-Hardeman University *T*
Lambuth University *B, T*
Lane College *B*
Lee University *B, T*
Lincoln Memorial University *B, T*
Maryville College *B, T*
Southern Adventist University *B*
Tennessee State University *B*
Tennessee Technological
    University *B, M, T*
Tennessee Wesleyan College *B, T*
Trevecca Nazarene University *B, T*
Tusculum College *B, T*
Union University *B, T*
University of Tennessee
    Knoxville *M, D*
    Martin *B, T*

Texas
Abilene Christian University *B, T*
Alvin Community College *A*
Amarillo College *A*
Angelina College *A*
Angelo State University *T*
Baylor University *B, T*
Brazosport College *A*
Dallas Baptist University *B, T*
Del Mar College *A*
East Texas Baptist University *B*
El Paso Community College *A*
Galveston College *A*
Hardin-Simmons University *B, M, T*
Houston Baptist University *B*
Howard Payne University *B, T*
Huston-Tillotson College *B*
Jarvis Christian College *B*
Lamar University *T*
LeTourneau University *B*
Lubbock Christian University *B*
McMurry University *B, T*
Midland College *A*
Navarro College *A*
Panola College *A*
Prairie View A&M University *M*
St. Edward's University *B, T*
Sam Houston State University *M, T*
Schreiner College *T*
Southwest Texas State University *M, T*
Southwestern Adventist University *T*
Southwestern University *B, T*
Stephen F. Austin State University *M*
Sul Ross State University *M*
Tarleton State University *B, M, T*
Texas A&M International
    University *B, T*
Texas A&M University
    Commerce *B, T*
    Corpus Christi *T*
    Kingsville *B*
Texas A&M University *M, D*
Texas Christian University *B, M, T*
Texas College *B*
Texas Lutheran University *B, T*
Texas Wesleyan University *B, M, T*
University of Houston *B, M, D, T*
University of Mary Hardin-Baylor *B, T*
University of North Texas *B, M, T*
University of Texas
    Arlington *B, T*
    Austin *M, D*
    Pan American *B, M, T*
    San Antonio *M, T*
    Tyler *M, T*
    of the Permian Basin *M*
University of the Incarnate Word *B, M*
Wayland Baptist University *B, T*
West Texas A&M University *T*
Wiley College *B*

Utah
Brigham Young University *B, M*
Dixie State College of Utah *A*
Snow College *A*
Southern Utah University *T*
Utah State University *B, M*
Weber State University *B*

Vermont
Castleton State College *B, T*
Johnson State College *B*
Lyndon State College *B*
Norwich University *B, T*
University of Vermont *B, T*

Virginia
Averett College *B, T*
Bluefield College *B*
Christopher Newport University *M, T*
Eastern Mennonite University *T*
Ferrum College *B*
George Mason University *B, M*
Hampton University *B*
Liberty University *B*
Longwood College *B, T*

Physical education

Lynchburg College B
Norfolk State University B
Old Dominion University B, M
Radford University B, M, T
Roanoke College B, T
Shenandoah University B
University of Richmond T
University of Virginia's College at Wise T
University of Virginia B, M, D
Virginia Commonwealth University B, M
Virginia Intermont College B, T
Virginia State University B

Washington
Central Washington University B, M, T
Eastern Washington University B, M, T
Gonzaga University B, M, T
Pacific Lutheran University T
Seattle Pacific University B, T
Walla Walla College B
Western Washington University B, M, T
Whitworth College B, M, T

West Virginia
Alderson-Broaddus College T
Bethany College B
Concord College B, T
Fairmont State College B
Glenville State College B
Marshall University B, M
Potomac State College of West Virginia University A
Shepherd College T
West Liberty State College B
West Virginia State College B
West Virginia University B, M, D, T
West Virginia Wesleyan College B

Wisconsin
Carroll College B, T
Carthage College B, T
Concordia University Wisconsin B, T
Ripon College T
University of Wisconsin
   La Crosse B, M, T
   Madison B, M, D, T
   Oshkosh B, T
   River Falls B, T
   Stevens Point B, T
   Superior B, T
   Whitewater B, T

Wyoming
Casper College A
Eastern Wyoming College A
Laramie County Community College A
Sheridan College A
University of Wyoming B, M
Western Wyoming Community College A

Physical sciences

Alabama
Auburn University at Montgomery B
Troy State University Dothan B
Troy State University B
University of North Alabama B

Arizona
Arizona Western College A
Grand Canyon University B
Northern Arizona University B, M, T
Pima Community College A
Prescott College B, M

Arkansas
Arkansas State University Beebe Branch A
Arkansas Tech University B
Harding University B
University of Arkansas Monticello B

University of Central Arkansas B, M
University of the Ozarks B
Westark College A

California
Barstow College B
Biola University B
Butte College A
California Baptist University B
California Polytechnic State University: San Luis Obispo B
California State University
   Chico B
   Fresno B
   Hayward B
   Northridge B
   Sacramento B
   Stanislaus B
Canada College A
Cerro Coso Community College A
Chaffey Community College A
Chapman University B
Citrus College A
College of San Mateo A
College of the Siskiyous A
Columbia College A
Compton Community College A
Diablo Valley College A
Fresno City College A
Glendale Community College A
Golden West College A
Imperial Valley College A
Irvine Valley College A
Kings River Community College A
La Sierra University B
Long Beach City College A
Los Angeles Southwest College A
Marymount College A
Master's College B
Mendocino College A
Merced College A
MiraCosta College A
Modesto Junior College A
Mount San Antonio College A
Orange Coast College A
Pacific Union College B, T
Pitzer College B
Pomona College B
Porterville College A
Riverside Community College A
Sacramento City College A
Saddleback College A
San Diego City College A
San Diego Mesa College C, A
San Diego Miramar College A
San Diego State University B
San Francisco State University B, M
San Joaquin Delta College A
San Jose City College A
Santa Monica College A
Santa Rosa Junior College A
Skyline College A
Southwestern College A
Taft College A
University of California
   Berkeley B
   Riverside B
University of Southern California B
University of the Pacific B
Ventura College A
Victor Valley College A
West Hills Community College A
Whittier College B

Colorado
Adams State College B
Colorado State University B
Fort Lewis College B
Lamar Community College A
Mesa State College A, B
Otero Junior College A
Trinidad State Junior College A
University of Colorado Colorado Springs M
University of Southern Colorado B, T

Connecticut
Albertus Magnus College B
Central Connecticut State University B
Connecticut College B
Eastern Connecticut State University B
Mitchell College A
Northwestern Connecticut Community-Technical College A
St. Joseph College B, T
University of Hartford B

District of Columbia
University of the District of Columbia A

Florida
Florida Gulf Coast University B
Palm Beach Community College A
Pensacola Junior College A
Polk Community College A
South Florida Community College A
University of Miami B

Georgia
Abraham Baldwin Agricultural College A
Andrew College A
Armstrong Atlantic State University B
Augusta State University B
Mercer University T
South Georgia College A
Young Harris College A

Hawaii
Brigham Young University Hawaii B
University of Hawaii Hilo B

Idaho
North Idaho College A
University of Idaho M

Illinois
City Colleges of Chicago
   Harold Washington College A
   Richard J. Daley College C, A
Eureka College B
Greenville College B, T
Highland Community College A
Kankakee Community College A
Kishwaukee College A
Lincoln Land Community College A
Morton College A
North Park University B
Northwestern University T
Olivet Nazarene University B, T
Parkland College A
Rend Lake College A
Richland Community College A
Triton College A
Wheaton College B, T
William Rainey Harper College A

Indiana
Goshen College B
Indiana University Bloomington B
Indiana University--Purdue University Indiana University-Purdue University Fort Wayne B
Purdue University A
Tri-State University A, B
University of Indianapolis B
Vincennes University A

Iowa
Buena Vista University B, T
Graceland University B, T
Marshalltown Community College A
William Penn University B

Kansas
Allen County Community College A
Barton County Community College A
Benedictine College T
Bethel College B
Central Christian College A
Cowley County Community College A

Dodge City Community College A
Emporia State University B, M, T
Fort Hays State University B, M
Garden City Community College A
Hutchinson Community College A
Independence Community College A
Kansas City Kansas Community College A
Kansas State University B
McPherson College B
MidAmerica Nazarene University B
Pittsburg State University B, T
Seward County Community College A
Wichita State University T

Kentucky
Alice Lloyd College B
Asbury College B, T
Kentucky Christian College B, T
Pikeville College T
Thomas More College A, B

Maine
St. Joseph's College B

Maryland
Charles County Community College A
Coppin State College B
Frostburg State University B
Howard Community College A
Montgomery College
   Germantown Campus A
   Rockville Campus A
   Takoma Park Campus A
Morgan State University M
Salisbury State University T
United States Naval Academy B
University of Maryland College Park B

Massachusetts
Berkshire Community College A
Boston University B, M
Brandeis University B
Cape Cod Community College A
Clark University B
Hampshire College B
Harvard College B
Harvard University M, D
Middlesex Community College A
Mount Ida College A
Northeastern University B, M, D
Simon's Rock College of Bard B
Westfield State College B
Worcester Polytechnic Institute B, M
Worcester State College B

Michigan
Bay de Noc Community College A
Calvin College B, T
Central Michigan University B
Eastern Michigan University B
Glen Oaks Community College A
Grand Valley State University B
Madonna University A, B
Michigan State University B, M, D
University of Michigan
   Dearborn B
   Flint B
West Shore Community College A
Western Michigan University B, M, D

Minnesota
Concordia University: St. Paul B
Minnesota State University, Mankato B
Northland Community & Technical College A
Ridgewater College: A Community and Technical College A
University of Minnesota Twin Cities B
Winona State University B, T

Mississippi
Hinds Community College A
Mississippi Delta Community College A
Mississippi University for Women B, T

Missouri
Crowder College *A*
Drury University *B, T*
East Central College *A*
Mineral Area College *A*
St. Louis Community College
    St. Louis Community College at
        Forest Park *A*
    St. Louis Community College at
        Meramec *A*
Three Rivers Community College *A*

Montana
Little Big Horn College *A*
Miles Community College *A*

Nebraska
Concordia University *B, D, T*
Doane College *B*
Hastings College *B, T*
Peru State College *B, T*
University of Nebraska
    Kearney *B*

Nevada
Community College of Southern
    Nevada *A*
Western Nevada Community College *A*

New Hampshire
Keene State College *B*

New Jersey
Georgian Court College *T*
Gloucester County College *A*
Montclair State University *T*
Raritan Valley Community College *A*
Rowan University *C, B*
Rutgers
    The State University of New Jersey:
        Cook College *T*
    The State University of New Jersey:
        Douglass College *T*
    The State University of New Jersey:
        Livingston College *T*
    The State University of New Jersey:
        Rutgers College *T*
    The State University of New Jersey:
        University College New
        Brunswick *T*
Sussex County Community College *A*
Union County College *A*

New Mexico
College of Santa Fe *A*
San Juan College *A*
Western New Mexico University *B*

New York
Adirondack Community College *A*
City University of New York
    Brooklyn College *B, M*
Clarkson University *B*
Colgate University *B*
Corning Community College *A*
Finger Lakes Community College *A*
Fulton-Montgomery Community
    College *A*
Hudson Valley Community College *A*
Iona College *B*
Jefferson Community College *A*
St. John's University *B*
Sarah Lawrence College *B*
State University of New York
    College at Brockport *B*
    College of Agriculture and
        Technology at Cobleskill *A*
    College of Environmental Science
        and Forestry *B, M, D*
Suffolk County Community College *A*
Tompkins-Cortland Community
    College *A*
Ulster County Community College *A*
United States Military Academy *B*
Villa Maria College of Buffalo *C*

North Carolina
Brevard College *A, B*

Chowan College *B*
Guilford Technical Community
    College *A*
Johnson C. Smith University *B*
Sandhills Community College *A*

North Dakota
Dickinson State University *B*
Mayville State University *B, T*

Ohio
Ashland University *B, T*
Defiance College *B*
Jefferson Community College *A*
Kent State University *T*
Mount Union College *T*
Notre Dame College of Ohio *B*
Ohio University
    Zanesville Campus *A*
Otterbein College *B*
University of Dayton *B*
Washington State Community College *A*
Wittenberg University *B*
Youngstown State University *B, M*

Oklahoma
Carl Albert State College *A*
Eastern Oklahoma State College *A*
Langston University *B*
Murray State College *A*
Northeastern Oklahoma Agricultural and
    Mechanical College *A*
Oklahoma City University *B*
Redlands Community College *A*
St. Gregory's University *A*
Seminole State College *A*
Tulsa Community College *A*
Western Oklahoma State College *A*

Oregon
Central Oregon Community College *A*
Chemeketa Community College *A*
Pacific University *B*

Pennsylvania
Butler County Community College *A*
Cedar Crest College *B*
Community College of Allegheny
    County *A*
Drexel University *B*
East Stroudsburg University of
    Pennsylvania *B*
Gettysburg College *B*
Harrisburg Area Community College *A*
Juniata College *B*
La Salle University *B*
Lincoln University *B*
Lock Haven University of
    Pennsylvania *B*
Montgomery County Community
    College *A*
Muhlenberg College *B*
Pennsylvania College of Technology *A*
Swarthmore College *B*
University of Pittsburgh
    Bradford *B*
University of Pittsburgh *M, D*
University of Scranton *B*
Villanova University *B*
West Chester University of
    Pennsylvania *B, M*
Widener University *B*
York College of Pennsylvania *B, T*

Puerto Rico
Inter American University of Puerto Rico
    Metropolitan Campus *B*
University of Puerto Rico
    Mayaguez Campus *B*

Rhode Island
Rhode Island College *B*

South Dakota
Black Hills State University *B*

Tennessee
Cumberland University *B*

Freed-Hardeman University *B*
Roane State Community College *A*
Tennessee State University *B*
Tennessee Temple University *B*
Union University *B*

Texas
Alvin Community College *A*
Angelina College *A*
Austin Community College *A*
Central Texas College *A*
Coastal Bend College *A*
Concordia University at Austin *B, T*
Hill College *A*
Howard College *A*
McMurry University *T*
Midland College *A*
Northeast Texas Community College *A*
Odessa College *A*
Paris Junior College *A*
San Jacinto College
    North *A*
Southwestern University *B, T*
Stephen F. Austin State University *T*
Texas A&M International
    University *B, T*
Texas A&M University
    Corpus Christi *T*
Texas Southern University *B*
Trinity Valley Community College *A*
University of Houston
    Clear Lake *B, M*
    Downtown *B*
University of Texas
    Arlington *T*
    Pan American *B, T*
Wayland Baptist University *B*
Western Texas College *A*

Utah
Salt Lake Community College *A*
Snow College *A*
Southern Utah University *B, T*

Vermont
Bennington College *B*
Castleton State College *A, B*
Goddard College *B*
Johnson State College *B*
Lyndon State College *B*
Marlboro College *B*
St. Michael's College *B*
University of Vermont *M*

Virginia
Bridgewater College *B*
Patrick Henry Community College *A*
Radford University *B*
St. Paul's College *B*

Washington
Centralia College *A*
City University *B*
Everett Community College *A*
Evergreen State College *B*
Highline Community College *A*
Lower Columbia College *A*
Whitworth College *B, T*

West Virginia
Marshall University *B, M*

Wisconsin
Alverno College *B, T*
Lawrence University *B*
University of Wisconsin
    Superior *B*

Wyoming
Central Wyoming College *A*
Laramie County Community College *A*
Western Wyoming Community
    College *A*

Physical sciences technologies

Alabama
Northwest-Shoals Community College *A*

California
ITT Technical Institute
    Torrance *A*

Connecticut
Three Rivers Community-Technical
    College *A*
University of New Haven *A*

Delaware
Delaware Technical and Community
    College
    Stanton/Wilmington Campus *A*

District of Columbia
University of the District of Columbia *A*

Illinois
College of Lake County *C, A*

Indiana
Ball State University *A*
ITT Technical Institute
    Indianapolis *A*
Indiana University--Purdue University
    Indiana University-Purdue
        University Fort Wayne *A*
Vincennes University *A*

Kentucky
Western Kentucky University *A*

Michigan
Delta College *A*
Ferris State University *A*
Kalamazoo Valley Community
    College *A*
Kellogg Community College *A*
Lawrence Technological University *A*

Missouri
Maple Woods Community College *C, A*
Southwest Missouri State University *B*

New Jersey
Burlington County College *A*
County College of Morris *A*
Gloucester County College *C, A*

New York
Corning Community College *A*
Erie Community College
    North Campus *A*
Mohawk Valley Community College *A*
Westchester Community College *A*

Pennsylvania
Community College of Allegheny
    County *A*
Community College of Philadelphia *A*
Delaware County Community College *C*
Millersville University of
    Pennsylvania *A*
Northampton County Area Community
    College *A*

Puerto Rico
University of Puerto Rico
    Humacao University College *A*

Rhode Island
Community College of Rhode
    Island *C, A*

South Carolina
Aiken Technical College *C*
Florence-Darlington Technical College *A*
Trident Technical College *A*

South Dakota
Southeast Technical Institute *A*

Physical sciences technologies

Tennessee
Northeast State Technical Community College A
Trevecca Nazarene University B

Texas
Amarillo College A
Houston Community College System A
ITT Technical Institute
   Houston A
Lee College A
Palo Alto College A
Texas State Technical College
   Harlingen A
   Waco A

Utah
Weber State University C, A

Washington
Big Bend Community College C
Columbia Basin College A
Edmonds Community College A
Shoreline Community College A

Physical therapy

Alabama
Alabama State University M
Oakwood College A
University of Alabama
   Birmingham M
University of Mobile M
University of South Alabama B, M

Arizona
Northern Arizona University M

Arkansas
Arkansas State University B
Northwest Arkansas Community College A
University of Central Arkansas A, M, D

California
Azusa Pacific University M
California State University
   Fresno B
   Long Beach M
   Northridge B
   Sacramento B
Chapman University M
Cypress College A
Loma Linda University M, D
Los Angeles Southwest College A
Mount San Antonio College C, A
Riverside Community College A
Samuel Merritt College M
San Francisco State University M
University of California
   San Francisco M
University of Southern California M, D
University of the Pacific M
Whittier College B

Colorado
Adams State College B
Pueblo Community College A
Regis University M
University of Colorado
   Health Sciences Center M

Connecticut
Naugatuck Valley Community-Technical College A
Quinnipiac University B, M
Sacred Heart University B, M
University of Connecticut B
University of Hartford B

Delaware
University of Delaware M

District of Columbia
Howard University C, M

Florida
Broward Community College A
Florida Agricultural and Mechanical University B
Florida Atlantic University M
Florida Gulf Coast University M
Florida International University M
Hillsborough Community College A
Lake City Community College A
Lynn University A
Manatee Community College A
Miami-Dade Community College A
Nova Southeastern University M, D
Palm Beach Community College A
Santa Fe Community College A
University of Central Florida M
University of Florida M
University of Miami B, M, D
University of North Florida M
University of South Florida B

Georgia
Armstrong Atlantic State University B, M
Atlanta Metropolitan College A
Clark Atlanta University B
Columbus State University B
Dalton State College A
Floyd College A
Georgia State University M
Medical College of Georgia M
Morris Brown College B
North Georgia College & State University M
Waycross College A

Idaho
College of Southern Idaho A
Idaho State University M
North Idaho College A
University of Idaho B

Illinois
Bradley University M
Finch University of Health Sciences/The Chicago Medical School M
Governors State University M
North Park University B
Northern Illinois University B
Northwestern University M
University of Illinois
   Chicago M, D

Indiana
Indiana University--Purdue University Indiana University-Purdue University Indianapolis B
Manchester College B
University of Evansville B, M
University of Indianapolis M, D
Vincennes University A

Iowa
Buena Vista University B
Clarke College M
North Iowa Area Community College A
St. Ambrose University M
University of Iowa M, D
University of Osteopathic Medicine and Health Sciences
   Des Moines University - Osteopathic Medical Center B, M
Upper Iowa University B

Kansas
Central Christian College A
Kansas City Kansas Community College A
Pittsburg State University B
Pratt Community College A
University of Kansas
   Medical Center M
Wichita State University M

Kentucky
University of Kentucky B, M

Louisiana
Louisiana State University Medical Center B, M

Maine
Husson College M
University of New England M

Maryland
Allegany College A
Montgomery College
   Rockville Campus A
University of Maryland
   Baltimore M
   Eastern Shore M

Massachusetts
American International College M
Becker College A
Boston University B, M
MGH Institute of Health Professions M
Massasoit Community College A
Northeastern University B, M
Simmons College B, M
Springfield College B, M
University of Massachusetts
   Lowell B

Michigan
Andrews University M
Central Michigan University M
Gogebic Community College A
Grand Valley State University M
Lansing Community College A
Mid Michigan Community College A
Oakland University B, M
University of Michigan
   Flint M
Wayne State University M

Minnesota
College of St. Catherine: St. Paul Campus B, M
College of St. Scholastica M
University of Minnesota
   Twin Cities B, M
Winona State University A

Mississippi
Alcorn State University B
Mississippi Gulf Coast Community College
   Perkinston A
University of Mississippi
   Medical Center B

Missouri
Maryville University of Saint Louis M
Rockhurst University M
St. Louis University M
Southwest Baptist University M
Truman State University B
University of Missouri
   Columbia M
Washington University M

Montana
University of Montana-Missoula M

Nebraska
Creighton University D

Nevada
University of Nevada
   Las Vegas M

New Hampshire
New England College B
Notre Dame College M

New Jersey
Essex County College A
Kean University B, M
Richard Stockton College of New Jersey M
Rutgers
   The State University of New Jersey:
   Camden Graduate Campus M
   The State University of New Jersey:
   Newark Graduate Campus M
Seton Hall University M
University of Medicine and Dentistry of New Jersey
   School of Health Related Professions M

New Mexico
University of New Mexico B, M

New York
City University of New York
   College of Staten Island B, M
   Hunter College B
Clarkson University M
Concordia College B
D'Youville College C, B, M
Daemen College B, M
Dominican College of Blauvelt B, M
Ithaca College B, M
Long Island University
   Brooklyn Campus B, M
Manhattan College B
Mercy College B, M
Nazareth College of Rochester B, M
New York Institute of Technology B, M
New York University M, D
Pace University:
   Pleasantville/Briarcliff B
Pace University B
Russell Sage College B
St. Thomas Aquinas College B
State University of New York
   Buffalo B
   Health Science Center at Brooklyn B
   Health Science Center at Stony Brook B
   Oswego B
   Stony Brook M
   Upstate Medical University B, M
Touro College B, M
Utica College of Syracuse University B

North Carolina
Central Piedmont Community College A
Duke University M
East Carolina University M
Elon College M
Southwestern Community College A
University of North Carolina
   Chapel Hill M
Western Carolina University M
Winston-Salem State University B

North Dakota
University of Mary M
University of North Dakota B, M

Ohio
Bowling Green State University B
Cleveland State University B
College of Mount St. Joseph M
Marion Technical College A
Mount Vernon Nazarene College B
Ohio State University
   Columbus Campus B, M
Ohio University B
Sinclair Community College A
University of Findlay B
University of Toledo B
Youngstown State University B

Oklahoma
Langston University B
Murray State College A
Northeastern Oklahoma Agricultural and Mechanical College A

Oregon
Pacific University M
Willamette University B

Pennsylvania
Beaver College D
Chatham College M
College Misericordia M
Duquesne University B, M
Elizabethtown College B
Gannon University M

Lebanon Valley College of
    Pennsylvania B, M
MCP Hahnemann University M, D
Neumann College M
St. Francis College B, M
St. Vincent College B
Temple University M, D
Thomas Jefferson University: College of
    Health Professions B, M
University of Pittsburgh
    Bradford B
University of Pittsburgh M
University of Scranton B, M
University of the Sciences in
    Philadelphia B, M

Puerto Rico
University of Puerto Rico
    Medical Sciences Campus B

Rhode Island
University of Rhode Island M

South Carolina
University of South Carolina D

South Dakota
Augustana College B
University of South Dakota M

Tennessee
Belmont University M
Carson-Newman College T
Columbia State Community College A
East Tennessee State University M
Hiwassee College A
Jackson State Community College A
University of Tennessee
    Chattanooga B, M
    Memphis B, M

Texas
Amarillo College A
Angelo State University M
Baylor University M
Blinn College A
Del Mar College A
Grayson County College A
Hardin-Simmons University M
San Antonio College A
Southwest Texas State University B, M
Texas Tech University Health Science
    Center M
Texas Woman's University M, D
University of Texas
    El Paso B
    Medical Branch at Galveston B
    San Antonio B
    Southwestern Medical Center at
        Dallas M

Utah
Brigham Young University B, D
Snow College A
University of Utah B

Vermont
University of Vermont M

Virginia
Northern Virginia Community College A
Old Dominion University M
Shenandoah University M
Virginia Commonwealth University M
Wytheville Community College A

Washington
Eastern Washington University M
University of Puget Sound M
University of Washington B, M

West Virginia
Potomac State College of West Virginia
    University A
West Virginia University M
Wheeling Jesuit University M

Wisconsin
Blackhawk Technical College A

Carroll College M
Concordia University Wisconsin B, M
Marquette University M
University of Wisconsin
    La Crosse M
    Madison M

Wyoming
Northwest College A

Physical therapy assistant

Alabama
Central Alabama Community College A
Community College of the Air Force A
Enterprise State Junior College A
Faulkner University A
Jefferson State Community College A
Northwest-Shoals Community College A
South College A
Wallace State Community College at
    Hanceville A

Arizona
Gateway Community College C, A

Arkansas
Arkansas State University A
Northwest Arkansas Community
    College A
University of Central Arkansas A

California
Allan Hancock College A
Cerritos Community College A
De Anza College C
Loma Linda University A
Mount St. Mary's College C, A
Ohlone College A
Sacramento City College C, A
San Diego Mesa College A

Colorado
Arapahoe Community College A
Denver Technical College: A Division of
    DeVry University A
Morgan Community College A
Pueblo Community College A

Connecticut
Housatonic Community-Technical
    College A
Manchester Community-Technical
    College A
Northwestern Connecticut
    Community-Technical College A

Delaware
Delaware Technical and Community
    College
        Stanton/Wilmington Campus A

District of Columbia
George Washington University C

Florida
Brevard Community College A
Broward Community College A
Central Florida Community College A
Florida Community College at
    Jacksonville A
Gulf Coast Community College A
Indian River Community College A
Lake City Community College A
Manatee Community College A
Pasco-Hernando Community College A
Pensacola Junior College A
Polk Community College A
St. Petersburg Junior College A
Seminole Community College A
South College: Palm Beach Campus A

Georgia
Athens Area Technical Institute A
Brewton-Parker College A
Darton College A
Floyd College A
Gwinnett Technical Institute A

Middle Georgia College A
Thomas College A

Hawaii
University of Hawaii
    Kapiolani Community College A

Idaho
Idaho State University A
North Idaho College A

Illinois
Black Hawk College A
College of DuPage A
Elgin Community College A
John Wood Community College A
Kankakee Community College A
Kaskaskia College A
Lake Land College A
Morton College A
Oakton Community College A
Southern Illinois University
    Carbondale A
Southwestern Illinois College A

Indiana
Ivy Tech State College
    Eastcentral A
    Northwest A
Michiana College A
Purdue University
    Calumet A
University of Evansville A
University of Indianapolis A
University of St. Francis A
Vincennes University A

Iowa
Indian Hills Community College A
Iowa Central Community College A
Kirkwood Community College A
North Iowa Area Community College A
Waldorf College A
Western Iowa Tech Community
    College A

Kansas
Central Christian College A
Colby Community College A
Fort Hays State University B
Johnson County Community College A
Kansas City Kansas Community
    College A
Washburn University of Topeka A
Wichita State University A

Kentucky
Ashland Community College A
Hazard Community College A
Madisonville Community College A
Paducah Community College A
Somerset Community College A
Southeast Community College A

Louisiana
Bossier Parish Community College A
Delgado Community College A
Southern University
    Shreveport A

Maine
Kennebec Valley Technical College A

Maryland
Baltimore City Community College A
Carroll Community College A
Charles County Community College A
Chesapeake College A
Montgomery College
    Rockville Campus C

Massachusetts
Bay State College A
Becker College A
Berkshire Community College A
Cape Cod Community College A
Endicott College A
Fisher College C, A
Lasell College A

Massachusetts Bay Community
    College A
Massasoit Community College A
Mount Wachusett Community College A
Newbury College A
North Shore Community College A
Springfield Technical Community
    College A

Michigan
Baker College
    of Cadillac A
    of Muskegon A
Bay de Noc Community College C
Delta College A
Henry Ford Community College A
Kellogg Community College A
Macomb Community College A
Mott Community College A
Oakland Community College A
Suomi College A
University of Michigan
    Flint B

Minnesota
Anoka-Ramsey Community College A
College of St. Catherine-Minneapolis A
Lake Superior College: A Community
    and Technical College A

Mississippi
Meridian Community College A

Missouri
Missouri Western State College A
Ozarks Technical Community College A
Penn Valley Community College A
St. Louis Community College
    St. Louis Community College at
        Meramec A

Montana
Montana State University
    College of Technology-Great
        Falls A

Nebraska
Clarkson College A
Northeast Community College A

Nevada
Community College of Southern
    Nevada A

New Hampshire
Hesser College A
New Hampshire Community Technical
    College
        Claremont A
        Manchester A

New Jersey
Atlantic Cape Community College A
Essex County College A
Fairleigh Dickinson University A
Mercer County Community College A
Union County College A

New Mexico
San Juan College A

New York
Adirondack Community College A
Broome Community College A
City University of New York
    Kingsborough Community
        College A
    La Guardia Community College A
Dutchess Community College A
Genesee Community College A
Herkimer County Community College A
Nassau Community College A
New York University A
Niagara County Community College A
Onondaga Community College A
Orange County Community College A
State University of New York
    College of Technology at Canton A
Suffolk County Community College A

Touro College A
Villa Maria College of Buffalo A
North Carolina
Caldwell Community College and
  Technical Institute A
Davidson County Community College A
Fayetteville Technical Community
  College A
Martin Community College A
North Dakota
Williston State College A
Ohio
Central Ohio Technical College A
Clark State Community College A
Hocking Technical College A
Kent State University
  Ashtabula Regional Campus A
  East Liverpool Regional Campus A
Lima Technical College A
Marion Technical College A
North Central State College A
Owens Community College
  Toledo A
Shawnee State University A
Stark State College of Technology A
Oklahoma
Carl Albert State College A
Northeastern Oklahoma Agricultural and
  Mechanical College A
Oklahoma City Community College A
Rose State College A
Tulsa Community College A
Oregon
Mount Hood Community College A
Pennsylvania
Alvernia College A
Butler County Community College A
Central Pennsylvania College A
Community College of Allegheny
  County A
Harcum College A
Lehigh Carbon Community College A
MCP Hahnemann University A
Mercyhurst College A
Mount Aloysius College A
Penn State
  Dubois A
  Hazleton A
  Mont Alto A
  Shenango A
University of Pittsburgh
  Titusville A
Widener University M
Puerto Rico
University of Puerto Rico
  Arecibo Campus T
  Humacao University College A
  Ponce University College A
Rhode Island
Community College of Rhode Island A
South Carolina
Aiken Technical College C
Central Carolina Technical College C
Florence-Darlington Technical
  College C, A
Greenville Technical College A
Orangeburg-Calhoun Technical
  College C
Piedmont Technical College C
Spartanburg Technical College A
Trident Technical College A
Tennessee
Chattanooga State Technical Community
  College A
Jackson State Community College A
Knoxville Business College A
Roane State Community College A
Shelby State Community College A
Volunteer State Community College A

Walters State Community College A
Texas
Amarillo College A
Angelina College A
Collin County Community College
  District A
Del Mar College A
El Paso Community College A
Houston Community College System A
Howard College A
Kilgore College A
Odessa College A
St. Philip's College A
Tarrant County College A
Wharton County Junior College A
Utah
Brigham Young University B
Salt Lake Community College A
Virginia
John Tyler Community College A
Northern Virginia Community College A
Tidewater Community College A
Virginia Highlands Community
  College A
Washington
Green River Community College A
Spokane Falls Community College A
Whatcom Community College A
West Virginia
College of West Virginia A
Fairmont State College A
Wisconsin
Blackhawk Technical College A
Gateway Technical College A
Milwaukee Area Technical College A
Northeast Wisconsin Technical
  College A
Western Wisconsin Technical College A
Wyoming
Central Wyoming College A

Physical/theoretical chemistry

California
University of Southern California D
Florida
Florida State University B, M, D
Iowa
Iowa State University M, D
Maryland
University of Maryland
  College Park M, D
Massachusetts
Harvard College B
Simon's Rock College of Bard B
Worcester Polytechnic Institute B, M
Michigan
Michigan State University B, M, D
University of Michigan M, D
New Jersey
Stevens Institute of Technology M, D
New York
Columbia University
  Graduate School M, D
Fordham University M
Rockefeller University D
Sarah Lawrence College B
State University of New York
  Albany D
  College of Environmental Science
    and Forestry M, D

North Carolina
University of North Carolina
  Chapel Hill M, D
Oregon
University of Oregon M, D
Pennsylvania
Lehigh University M, D
Puerto Rico
University of Puerto Rico
  Rio Piedras Campus D
Texas
Rice University B, M, D
University of North Texas M, D
Utah
University of Utah M, D
Vermont
Bennington College B
Wisconsin
Marquette University M, D

Physician assistant

Alabama
Central Alabama Community College A
Northwest-Shoals Community College A
Oakwood College A
University of Alabama
  Birmingham B
University of South Alabama M
California
California State University
  Dominguez Hills B
City College of San Francisco A
Foothill College C, A
Samuel Merritt College M
University of Southern California B
Colorado
Otero Junior College A
University of Colorado
  Health Sciences Center C, M
Connecticut
Quinnipiac University B, M
District of Columbia
George Washington University C, B, M
Howard University C, B
Florida
Barry University M
Gulf Coast Community College A
Manatee Community College A
Miami-Dade Community College A
Nova Southeastern University B
University of Florida B, M
Georgia
Dalton State College A
Medical College of Georgia B, M
Waycross College A
Hawaii
University of Hawaii
  Kapiolani Community College A
Idaho
College of Southern Idaho A
Idaho State University B
Illinois
City Colleges of Chicago
  Malcolm X College A
Finch University of Health Sciences/The
  Chicago Medical School M
Southern Illinois University
  Carbondale B
Indiana
Butler University B
University of St. Francis B

Iowa
University of Iowa M
University of Osteopathic Medicine and
  Health Sciences
  Des Moines University -
    Osteopathic Medical Center B
Kansas
Wichita State University B
Kentucky
University of Kentucky B
Louisiana
Louisiana State University Medical
  Center B
Maine
University of New England M
Maryland
Community College of Baltimore County
  Essex C
Loyola College in Maryland M
University of Maryland
  Eastern Shore B
Massachusetts
Massachusetts College of Pharmacy and
  Health Sciences M
North Shore Community College C
Northeastern University M
Springfield College B
Western New England College B, M
Michigan
Grand Valley State University M
Lansing Community College A
Wayne State University M
Western Michigan University M
Minnesota
Augsburg College C, B
Missouri
Rockhurst University B
St. Louis University C, B, M
Montana
Rocky Mountain College B
Nebraska
Metropolitan Community College A
Union College B
New Hampshire
Notre Dame College M
New Jersey
Seton Hall University M
University of Medicine and Dentistry of
  New Jersey
  School of Health Related
    Professions B, M
New Mexico
University of New Mexico B
New York
City University of New York
  City College B
  College of Staten Island B
D'Youville College B
Daemen College B, M
Hudson Valley Community College A
Le Moyne College C
Long Island University
  Brooklyn Campus B
New York Institute of Technology B
Pace University:
  Pleasantville/Briarcliff B
Pace University B
Rochester Institute of Technology B
St. John's University B
State University of New York
  Health Science Center at
    Brooklyn B
  Health Science Center at Stony
    Brook B
  Stony Brook B

Touro College B
Wagner College B

North Carolina
Catawba College B
Duke University M
East Carolina University B
High Point University B
Lenoir-Rhyne College B
Mars Hill College B
Methodist College B
Salem College B
Wake Forest University B

Ohio
University of Findlay B

Oregon
Pacific University M

Pennsylvania
Allentown College of St. Francis de
    Sales B, M
Beaver College M
Chatham College M
Duquesne University B, M
Gannon University B
King's College C, B, M
Lock Haven University of
    Pennsylvania M
MCP Hahnemann University A, B, M
Marywood University B
Philadelphia University B
St. Francis College B, M
Seton Hill College B
University of the Sciences in
    Philadelphia B, M

South Dakota
University of South Dakota B

Tennessee
Bethel College B
Carson-Newman College T
Southern Adventist University A
Trevecca Nazarene University M

Texas
San Antonio College A
University of Texas
    Medical Branch at Galveston B
    Southwestern Medical Center at
        Dallas B

Washington
University of Washington C, B

West Virginia
Alderson-Broaddus College B, M
College of West Virginia B

Wisconsin
Marquette University M
University of Wisconsin
    La Crosse B
    Madison B

Physics

Alabama
Alabama Agricultural and Mechanical
    University B, M, D
Alabama State University B
Athens State University B
Auburn University B, M, D, T
Birmingham-Southern College B, T
Chattahoochee Valley Community
    College A
Jacksonville State University B
Northeast Alabama Community
    College A
Samford University B
Stillman College B
Talladega College B
Tuskegee University B
University of Alabama
    Birmingham B, M, D
    Huntsville B, M, D

University of Alabama B, M, D
University of North Alabama B
University of South Alabama B

Alaska
University of Alaska
    Fairbanks B, M, D

Arizona
Arizona State University B, M, D
Arizona Western College A
Eastern Arizona College A
Northern Arizona University B
South Mountain Community College A
University of Arizona B, M, D

Arkansas
Arkansas State University B
Arkansas Tech University B
Harding University B
Henderson State University B
Hendrix College B
Ouachita Baptist University B
University of Arkansas
    Little Rock B
    Pine Bluff B
University of Arkansas B, M, D
University of Central Arkansas B
University of the Ozarks B
Westark College A

California
Allan Hancock College A
Azusa Pacific University B
Bakersfield College A
Biola University B
Cabrillo College A
California Institute of Technology B, D
California Lutheran University B
California Polytechnic State University:
    San Luis Obispo B
California State Polytechnic University:
    Pomona B
California State University
    Bakersfield B
    Chico B
    Dominguez Hills B
    Fresno B, M
    Fullerton B, M
    Hayward B
    Long Beach B, M
    Los Angeles B, M
    Northridge B, M
    Sacramento B, M
    Stanislaus B
Canada College A
Cerritos Community College A
Chabot College A
Chaffey Community College A
Citrus College A
Claremont McKenna College B
College of San Mateo A
College of the Desert A
College of the Siskiyous A
Columbia College A
Compton Community College A
Contra Costa College A
Crafton Hills College A
Cuesta College C, A
Cypress College A
De Anza College A
Diablo Valley College A
East Los Angeles College A
Foothill College A
Glendale Community College A
Grossmont Community College A
Harvey Mudd College B
Humboldt State University B
Las Positas College A
Long Beach City College C, A
Los Angeles Southwest College A
Los Angeles Valley College A
Loyola Marymount University B
Merced College A
MiraCosta College A
Mission College A

Monterey Peninsula College A
Moorpark College A
Occidental College B
Ohlone College C, A
Orange Coast College A
Pacific Union College B
Pitzer College B
Point Loma Nazarene University B
Pomona College B
Riverside Community College A
Saddleback College A
St. Mary's College of California B
San Bernardino Valley College A
San Diego City College A
San Diego Mesa College C, A
San Diego Miramar College A
San Diego State University B, M
San Francisco State University B, M
San Joaquin Delta College A
San Jose State University B, M
Santa Ana College A
Santa Barbara City College A
Santa Clara University B
Santa Monica College A
Santa Rosa Junior College A
Scripps College B
Solano Community College A
Sonoma State University B
Southwestern College A
Stanford University B, M, D
University of California
    Berkeley B, M, D
    Davis B, M, D
    Irvine B, M, D
    Los Angeles B, M, D
    Riverside B, M, D
    San Diego B, M, D
    Santa Barbara B, M, D
    Santa Cruz B, M, D
University of La Verne B
University of Redlands B
University of San Diego B
University of San Francisco B
University of Southern
    California B, M, D
University of the Pacific B
Ventura College A
West Hills Community College A
West Los Angeles College C, A
West Valley College A
Westmont College B
Whittier College B

Colorado
Adams State College B
Colorado College B
Colorado School of Mines M, D
Colorado State University B, M, D
Fort Lewis College B
Metropolitan State College of Denver B
Red Rocks Community College A
United States Air Force Academy B
University of Colorado
    Boulder B, M, D
    Colorado Springs B, M
    Denver B
University of Denver B, M, D
University of Northern Colorado B, T
University of Southern Colorado B, T
Western State College of Colorado B

Connecticut
Central Connecticut State
    University B, M
Connecticut College B
Fairfield University B
Southern Connecticut State University B
Trinity College B
University of Connecticut B, M, D
University of Hartford B
University of New Haven B
Wesleyan University B, M, D
Yale University B, M, D

Delaware
Delaware State University B, M

University of Delaware B, M, D

District of Columbia
American University B, M
Catholic University of America B, M, D
Gallaudet University B
George Washington University B, M, D
Georgetown University B
Howard University B, M, D
University of the District of Columbia B

Florida
Bethune-Cookman College B
Broward Community College A
Eckerd College B
Florida Agricultural and Mechanical
    University B, M
Florida Atlantic University B, M, D
Florida Institute of Technology B, M, D
Florida International University B, M, D
Florida Southern College B
Florida State University B, M, D
Gulf Coast Community College A
Indian River Community College A
Jacksonville University B
Manatee Community College A
Miami-Dade Community College A
New College of the University of South
    Florida B
Palm Beach Community College A
Pensacola Junior College A
Rollins College B
Stetson University B
University of Central Florida B, M, D
University of Florida B, M, D
University of Miami B, M, D
University of North Florida B
University of South Florida B, M
University of West Florida B

Georgia
Agnes Scott College B
Armstrong Atlantic State University B
Atlanta Metropolitan College A
Augusta State University B
Berry College B, T
Brewton-Parker College A
Clark Atlanta University B, M
Clayton College and State University A
Dalton State College A
Darton College A
Emory University B, M, D
Gainesville College A
Georgia Institute of Technology B, M, D
Georgia Military College A
Georgia Perimeter College A
Georgia Southern University B
Georgia Southwestern State University B
Georgia State University B, M, D
Mercer University B
Middle Georgia College A
Morehouse College B
Morris Brown College B
North Georgia College & State
    University B
Oglethorpe University B
Oxford College of Emory University B
South Georgia College A
Southern Polytechnic State University B
Spelman College B
State University of West Georgia B
University of Georgia B, M, D
Valdosta State University B
Young Harris College A

Hawaii
University of Hawaii
    Hilo B
    Manoa B, M, D

Idaho
Albertson College of Idaho B
Boise State University B, T
College of Southern Idaho A
Idaho State University A, B, M
North Idaho College A
Northwest Nazarene University B

Ricks College *A*
University of Idaho *B, M, D*

Illinois
Augustana College *B, T*
Benedictine University *B, T*
Bradley University *B, T*
Chicago State University *B*
City Colleges of Chicago
    Harold Washington College *A*
    Kennedy-King College *A*
    Olive-Harvey College *A*
De Paul University *B, M, T*
Eastern Illinois University *B, T*
Elmhurst College *B, T*
Greenville College *B, T*
Highland Community College *A*
Illinois College *B*
Illinois Institute of Technology *B, M, D*
Illinois State University *B, T*
Illinois Wesleyan University *B*
John A. Logan College *A*
John Wood Community College *A*
Judson College *B*
Kishwaukee College *A*
Knox College *B*
Lake Forest College *B*
Lewis University *B, T*
Lincoln Land Community College *A*
Loyola University of Chicago *B*
MacMurray College *B*
Millikin University *B*
Monmouth College *B, T*
Morton College *A*
North Central College *B, T*
North Park University *B*
Northeastern Illinois University *B, M*
Northern Illinois University *B, M, T*
Northwestern University *B, M, D*
Parkland College *A*
Principia College *B, T*
Rend Lake College *A*
Roosevelt University *B*
Sauk Valley Community College *A*
Southern Illinois University
    Carbondale *B, M*
    Edwardsville *B, M*
Southwestern Illinois College *A*
Springfield College in Illinois *A*
Triton College *A*
University of Chicago *B, M, D*
University of Illinois
    Chicago *B, M, D*
    Urbana-Champaign *B, M, D*
Western Illinois University *B, M*
Wheaton College *B, T*

Indiana
Anderson University *B*
Ball State University *B, M*
Butler University *B*
DePauw University *B*
Earlham College *B*
Franklin College *B*
Goshen College *B*
Grace College *B*
Hanover College *B*
Indiana State University *B, M, T*
Indiana University
    Bloomington *B, M, D*
    South Bend *B*
Indiana University--Purdue University
    Indiana University-Purdue
        University Fort Wayne *B*
    Indiana University-Purdue
        University Indianapolis *B, M*
Manchester College *B, T*
Marian College *T*
Purdue University
    Calumet *B*
Purdue University *B, M, D*
Rose-Hulman Institute of Technology *B*
Taylor College *B*
University of Evansville *B*
University of Indianapolis *B*
University of Notre Dame *B, M, D*

Valparaiso University *B, T*
Vincennes University *A*
Wabash College *B*

Iowa
Buena Vista University *B, T*
Central College *B, T*
Coe College *B*
Cornell College *B, T*
Dordt College *B*
Drake University *B*
Graceland University *T*
Grinnell College *B*
Iowa State University *B, M, D*
Loras College *B*
Luther College *B*
Maharishi University of
    Management *A, B*
Morningside College *B*
North Iowa Area Community College *A*
Northwestern College *T*
St. Ambrose University *B*
University of Iowa *B, M, D, T*
University of Northern Iowa *B, M*
Wartburg College *B*

Kansas
Allen County Community College *A*
Baker University *B*
Benedictine College *B*
Bethel College *B, T*
Butler County Community College *A*
Central Christian College *A*
Emporia State University *B, T*
Fort Hays State University *B*
Kansas City Kansas Community
    College *A*
Kansas State University *B, M, D*
Kansas Wesleyan University *B, T*
MidAmerica Nazarene University *B*
Pittsburg State University *B, M, T*
Pratt Community College *A*
Seward County Community College *A*
Southwestern College *B*
University of Kansas *B, M, D*
Washburn University of Topeka *B*
Wichita State University *B, M, T*

Kentucky
Berea College *B, T*
Campbellsville University *B*
Centre College *B*
Cumberland College *B, T*
Eastern Kentucky University *B*
Georgetown College *B*
Kentucky Wesleyan College *B, T*
Morehead State University *B*
Murray State University *B, M, T*
Northern Kentucky University *B, T*
Thomas More College *A, B, T*
Transylvania University *B, T*
Union College *B*
University of Kentucky *B, M, D*
University of Louisville *B, M*
Western Kentucky University *B*

Louisiana
Centenary College of Louisiana *B, T*
Dillard University *B*
Louisiana State University
    Shreveport *B*
Louisiana State University and
    Agricultural and Mechanical
    College *B, M, D*
Louisiana Tech University *B, M*
Loyola University New Orleans *B*
McNeese State University *B*
Northwestern State University *B*
Southeastern Louisiana University *B*
Southern University
    New Orleans *B*
Southern University and Agricultural and
    Mechanical College *B, M*
Tulane University *B, M, D*
University of Louisiana at
    Lafayette *B, M*

University of Louisiana at Monroe *B*
University of New Orleans *B, M*
Xavier University of Louisiana *B*

Maine
Bates College *B*
Bowdoin College *B*
Colby College *B*
University of Maine *B, M, D*
University of Southern Maine *B*

Maryland
Allegany College *A*
College of Notre Dame of Maryland *B*
Community College of Baltimore County
    Essex *A*
Frostburg State University *B, T*
Hagerstown Community College *A*
Harford Community College *A*
Johns Hopkins University *B, D*
Loyola College in Maryland *B*
Morgan State University *B*
St. Mary's College of Maryland *B*
Salisbury State University *B, T*
Towson University *B*
United States Naval Academy *B*
University of Maryland
    Baltimore County *B, M, D*
    College Park *B, M, D*
Washington College *B, T*
Western Maryland College *B*

Massachusetts
Amherst College *B*
Boston College *B, M, D*
Boston University *B, M, D*
Brandeis University *B, M, D*
Bridgewater State College *B*
Clark University *B, M, D*
College of the Holy Cross *B*
Curry College *B*
Emmanuel College *M*
Gordon College *B*
Hampshire College *B*
Harvard College *B*
Harvard University *M, D*
Massachusetts College of Liberal Arts *B*
Massachusetts Institute of
    Technology *B, D*
Merrimack College *B*
Mount Holyoke College *B*
Northeastern University *B, M, D*
Simon's Rock College of Bard *B*
Smith College *B*
Suffolk University *B*
Tufts University *B, M, D*
University of Massachusetts
    Amherst *B, M, D*
    Boston *B*
    Dartmouth *B, M*
    Lowell *B, M, D*
Wellesley College *B*
Wheaton College *B*
Williams College *B*
Worcester Polytechnic Institute *B, M, D*

Michigan
Adrian College *A, B, T*
Albion College *B, T*
Alma College *B, T*
Andrews University *B*
Aquinas College *B*
Calvin College *B, T*
Central Michigan University *B, M*
Eastern Michigan University *B, M*
Gogebic Community College *A*
Grand Valley State University *B*
Hillsdale College *B*
Hope College *B, T*
Kalamazoo College *B, T*
Kellogg Community College *A*
Kirtland Community College *A*
Lake Michigan College *A*
Lawrence Technological University *B*
Michigan State University *B, M, D*

Michigan Technological
    University *B, M, D, T*
Northern Michigan University *B, T*
Oakland University *B, M, T*
Saginaw Valley State University *B*
University of Michigan
    Dearborn *B*
    Flint *B, T*
University of Michigan *B, M, D*
Wayne State University *B, M, D*
Western Michigan University *B, M, D, T*

Minnesota
Augsburg College *B*
Bemidji State University *B*
Bethel College *B*
Carleton College *B*
College of St. Benedict *B*
College of St. Catherine: St. Paul
    Campus *B*
Concordia College: Moorhead *B*
Gustavus Adolphus College *B*
Hamline University *B*
Macalester College *B, T*
Minnesota State University,
    Mankato *B, M*
Moorhead State University *B*
St. Cloud State University *B*
St. John's University *B*
St. Mary's University of Minnesota *B*
St. Olaf College *B, T*
University of Minnesota
    Duluth *B, M*
    Morris *B*
    Twin Cities *B, M, D*
University of St. Thomas *B*
Winona State University *B*

Mississippi
Hinds Community College *A*
Jackson State University *B*
Mary Holmes College *A*
Millsaps College *B, T*
Mississippi College *B*
Mississippi State University *B, M*
Tougaloo College *B*
University of Mississippi *B, M, D, T*
University of Southern Mississippi *B, M*

Missouri
Central Methodist College *B*
Central Missouri State University *B*
East Central College *A*
Lincoln University *B*
Missouri Southern State College *B, T*
Northwest Missouri State University *B*
Rockhurst University *B*
St. Louis University *B*
Southeast Missouri State University *B*
Southwest Missouri State University *B*
St. Louis Community College
    St. Louis Community College at
        Florissant Valley *A*
    St. Louis Community College at
        Forest Park *A*
Truman State University *B*
University of Missouri
    Columbia *B, M, D*
    Kansas City *B, M*
    Rolla *B, M, D, T*
    St. Louis *B, M, D*
Washington University *B, M, D*
Westminster College *B*
William Jewell College *B*

Montana
Montana State University
    Bozeman *B, M, D, T*
Rocky Mountain College *B*
University of Montana-Missoula *B, M*

Nebraska
Chadron State College *B*
Concordia University *T*
Creighton University *B, M*
Doane College *B*
Hastings College *B*

Nebraska Wesleyan University B
Northeast Community College A
Union College B
University of Nebraska
    Kearney B, T
    Lincoln B, M, D
    Omaha B

Nevada
University of Nevada
    Las Vegas B, M, D
    Reno B, M, D

New Hampshire
Dartmouth College B, D
University of New Hampshire B, M, D

New Jersey
Brookdale Community College A
Drew University B
Georgian Court College B
Middlesex County College A
Montclair State University B
New Jersey City University B
New Jersey Institute of
    Technology B, M, D
Princeton University B, M, D
Ramapo College of New Jersey B
Richard Stockton College of New
    Jersey B
Rider University B
Rowan University B
Rutgers
    The State University of New Jersey:
        Camden College of Arts and
        Sciences B, T
    The State University of New Jersey:
        Douglass College B
    The State University of New Jersey:
        Livingston College B
    The State University of New Jersey:
        New Brunswick Graduate
        Campus M, D, T
    The State University of New Jersey:
        Newark College of Arts and
        Sciences B
    The State University of New Jersey:
        Rutgers College B
    The State University of New Jersey:
        University College Camden B, T
    The State University of New Jersey:
        University College New
        Brunswick B
St. Peter's College B
Salem Community College A
Seton Hall University B, T
Stevens Institute of Technology M, D
The College of New Jersey B, T
Thomas Edison State College A, B

New Mexico
Eastern New Mexico University B
New Mexico Institute of Mining and
    Technology B, M, D
New Mexico Junior College A
New Mexico State University B, M, D
San Juan College A
University of New Mexico B, M, D

New York
Adelphi University B, M
Adirondack Community College A
Alfred University B
Bard College B
Barnard College B
Canisius College B

City University of New York
    Brooklyn College B, M
    City College B, M, D, T
    College of Staten Island B, T
    Graduate School and University
        Center D
    Hunter College B, M
    Kingsborough Community
        College A
    Lehman College B
    Queens College B, M
    York College B
Clarkson University B, M, D
Colgate University B
College of Mount St. Vincent B
College of New Rochelle B, T
Columbia University
    Columbia College B
    Graduate School M, D
    School of General Studies B
Cornell University B, M, D
Fordham University B, M, D
Hamilton College B
Hartwick College B, T
Hobart and William Smith Colleges B
Hofstra University B
Houghton College B
Iona College B
Ithaca College B, T
Le Moyne College B
Long Island University
    C. W. Post Campus B
Manhattan College B
Manhattanville College B
Monroe Community College A
New York Institute of Technology B
New York University B, M, D
Pace University:
    Pleasantville/Briarcliff B, T
Pace University B, T
Polytechnic University B, M, D
Regents College B
Rensselaer Polytechnic Institute B, M, D
Roberts Wesleyan College B
Rochester Institute of Technology A, B
Rockefeller University D
St. Bonaventure University B, T
St. John Fisher College B
St. John's University B
St. Lawrence University B, T
St. Thomas Aquinas College B, T
Sarah Lawrence College B
Siena College B, T
Skidmore College B
State University of New York
    Albany B, M, D
    Binghamton B, M
    Buffalo B, M, D
    College at Brockport B, T
    College at Buffalo B
    College at Cortland B
    College at Fredonia B, T
    College at Geneseo B, T
    College at Oneonta B
    College at Plattsburgh B
    College at Potsdam B, T
    College of Agriculture and
        Technology at Morrisville A
    New Paltz B, T
    Oswego B
    Stony Brook B, M, D, T
Suffolk County Community College A
Syracuse University B, M, D
Union College B
United States Military Academy B
University of Rochester B, M, D
Utica College of Syracuse University B
Vassar College B
Wagner College B, T
Wells College B

North Carolina
Appalachian State University B
Barber-Scotia College B
Brevard College B

Davidson College B
Duke University B, M, D
East Carolina University B, M
Elizabeth City State University B
Elon College B
Guilford College B
Guilford Technical Community
    College A
Johnson C. Smith University B
Lenoir-Rhyne College B
North Carolina Agricultural and
    Technical State University B, M, T
North Carolina Central University B
North Carolina State University B, M, D
Shaw University B
University of North Carolina
    Asheville B, T
    Chapel Hill B, M, D
    Charlotte B, M, T
    Greensboro B
    Wilmington B, T
Wake Forest University B, M, D
Western Carolina University B

North Dakota
Dickinson State University T
Minot State University B, T
North Dakota State
    University B, M, D, T
University of North Dakota B, M, D

Ohio
Antioch College B
Ashland University B
Baldwin-Wallace College B
Bluffton College B
Bowling Green State University B, M
Case Western Reserve
    University B, M, D
Cedarville College B, T
Cleveland State University B, M, T
College of Wooster B
Denison University B
Heidelberg College B
Hiram College B
Jefferson Community College A
John Carroll University B, M
Kent State University
    Stark Campus B
Kent State University B, M, D, T
Kenyon College B
Lorain County Community College A
Miami University
    Middletown Campus A
    Oxford Campus B, M, T
Mount Union College B
Muskingum College B
Oberlin College B
Ohio Northern University B
Ohio State University
    Columbus Campus B, M, D
Ohio University B, M, D
Ohio Wesleyan University B
Otterbein College B
Terra Community College A
University of Akron B, M
University of Cincinnati B, M, D, T
University of Dayton B
University of Rio Grande B, T
University of Toledo B, M, D
Wittenberg University B
Wright State University B, M
Xavier University B
Youngstown State University B

Oklahoma
Cameron University B
Connors State College A
East Central University B, T
Eastern Oklahoma State College A
Northeastern Oklahoma Agricultural and
    Mechanical College A
Northeastern State University B
Northern Oklahoma College A
Oklahoma Baptist University B
Oklahoma City Community College A

Oklahoma City University B
Oklahoma State University B, M, D
Oral Roberts University B
Rogers State University A
Rose State College A
Southeastern Oklahoma State
    University B
Southern Nazarene University B
Southwestern Oklahoma State
    University B
Tulsa Community College A
University of Central Oklahoma B, M
University of Oklahoma B, M, D
University of Science and Arts of
    Oklahoma B
University of Tulsa B

Oregon
Central Oregon Community College A
Chemeketa Community College A
Eastern Oregon University B, T
Lewis & Clark College B
Linfield College B
Oregon State University B, M, D
Pacific University B
Portland State University B, M
Reed College B
Southern Oregon University B
University of Oregon B, M, D
University of Portland B
Willamette University B

Pennsylvania
Allegheny College B
Bloomsburg University of
    Pennsylvania B, T
Bryn Mawr College B, M, D
Bucknell University B
California University of Pennsylvania B
Carnegie Mellon University B, M, D
Chatham College B
Clarion University of Pennsylvania B, T
Community College of Allegheny
    County A
Dickinson College B
Drexel University B
Duquesne University B
East Stroudsburg University of
    Pennsylvania B
Edinboro University of
    Pennsylvania B, T
Elizabethtown College B
Franklin and Marshall College B
Geneva College B, T
Gettysburg College B
Grove City College B
Haverford College B, T
Immaculata College A
Indiana University of
    Pennsylvania B, M, T
Juniata College B
Kutztown University of
    Pennsylvania B, T
Lafayette College B
Lebanon Valley College of
    Pennsylvania B
Lehigh University B, M, D
Lincoln University B
Lock Haven University of
    Pennsylvania B
Lycoming College B
Mansfield University of
    Pennsylvania B, T
Mercyhurst College B
Messiah College B
Millersville University of
    Pennsylvania B, T
Moravian College B
Muhlenberg College B, T
Northampton County Area Community
    College A
Penn State
    Erie, The Behrend College B
    University Park B, M, D
St. Joseph's University B
St. Vincent College B

Seton Hill College B, T
Shippensburg University of
  Pennsylvania B, T
Slippery Rock University of
  Pennsylvania B, T
Susquehanna University B
Swarthmore College B
Temple University B, M, D
Thiel College B
University of Pennsylvania A, B, M, D
University of Pittsburgh B, M, D
University of Scranton B, T
Ursinus College B, T
Villanova University B
Washington and Jefferson College B
West Chester University of
  Pennsylvania B
Westminster College B
Widener University B
Wilkes University B, M
York College of Pennsylvania A

Puerto Rico
Pontifical Catholic University of Puerto
  Rico B
University of Puerto Rico
  Cayey University College B
  Mayaguez Campus B, M
  Ponce University College A
  Rio Piedras Campus B, M

Rhode Island
Brown University B, M, D
Rhode Island College B
University of Rhode Island B, M, D

South Carolina
Benedict College B
Charleston Southern University B
Clemson University B, M, D
College of Charleston B, T
Erskine College B
Francis Marion University B
Furman University B, T
Presbyterian College B
South Carolina State University B
The Citadel B
University of South Carolina B, M, D
Wofford College B, T

South Dakota
Augustana College B, T
South Dakota School of Mines and
  Technology B
South Dakota State University B, M
University of South Dakota B, M

Tennessee
Austin Peay State University B
Belmont University B, T
Christian Brothers University B
Columbia State Community College A
Cumberland University A
David Lipscomb University B
East Tennessee State University B
Fisk University B, M
Hiwassee College A
King College B, T
Middle Tennessee State University B
Rhodes College B, T
Roane State Community College A
Southern Adventist University B
Tennessee State University B
Tennessee Technological University B, T
Trevecca Nazarene University B
Union University B
University of Memphis B, M
University of Tennessee
  Chattanooga B
  Knoxville B, M, D
University of the South B
Vanderbilt University B, M, D

Texas
Abilene Christian University B
Amarillo College A
Angelina College A
Angelo State University B
Austin College B
Baylor University B, M, D
Blinn College A
Brazosport College A
Central Texas College A
Coastal Bend College A
Del Mar College A
El Paso Community College A
Galveston College A
Grayson County College A
Hardin-Simmons University B
Hill College A
Howard College A
Kilgore College A
Lamar University B
Lon Morris College A
McMurry University B
Midland College A
Midwestern State University B
Navarro College A
Panola College A
Paris Junior College A
Prairie View A&M University B
Rice University B, M, D
St. Mary's University B
Sam Houston State University B, M
San Jacinto College
  North A
Southern Methodist University B, M, D
Southwest Texas State
  University B, M, T
Southwestern Adventist University B, T
Southwestern University B, T
Stephen F. Austin State
  University B, M, T
Tarleton State University B
Texas A&M University
  Commerce B, M
  Kingsville B, M
Texas A&M University B, M, D
Texas Christian University B, M, D, T
Texas Lutheran University B
Texas Tech University B, M, D
Trinity University B
Trinity Valley Community College A
Tyler Junior College A
University of Dallas B
University of Houston B, M, D
University of North Texas B, M, D
University of Texas
  Arlington B, M
  Austin B, M, D
  Dallas B, M, D
  El Paso B, M
  Pan American B
  San Antonio B
West Texas A&M University B
Western Texas College A
Wharton County Junior College A

Utah
Brigham Young University B, M, D
Dixie State College of Utah A
Salt Lake Community College A
Snow College A
University of Utah B, M, D
Utah State University B, M, D
Weber State University B
Westminster College B

Vermont
Bennington College B
Marlboro College B
Middlebury College B
Norwich University B
St. Michael's College B
University of Vermont B, M

Virginia
Bridgewater College B
Christopher Newport University B
College of William and Mary B, M, D
Emory & Henry College B, T
George Mason University B
Hampden-Sydney College B
Hampton University B, M, D
Hollins University B
James Madison University B
Longwood College B, T
Lynchburg College B
Mary Baldwin College B
Mary Washington College B
Norfolk State University B
Old Dominion University B, M, D
Randolph-Macon College B
Randolph-Macon Woman's College B
Roanoke College B, T
Sweet Briar College B
University of Richmond B, T
University of Virginia B, M, D
Virginia Commonwealth
  University B, M
Virginia Military Institute B
Virginia Polytechnic Institute and State
  University B, M, D, T
Virginia State University B, M
Washington and Lee University B

Washington
Central Washington University B
Centralia College A
Eastern Washington University B, T
Everett Community College A
Evergreen State College B
Gonzaga University B
Pacific Lutheran University B
Seattle Pacific University B, T
Seattle University B
University of Puget Sound B, T
University of Washington B, M, D
Walla Walla College B
Washington State University B, M, D
Western Washington University B, T
Whitman College B
Whitworth College B, T

West Virginia
Bethany College B
Marshall University B, M
Potomac State College of West Virginia
  University A
West Virginia State College B
West Virginia University B, M, D, T
West Virginia Wesleyan College B
Wheeling Jesuit University B

Wisconsin
Beloit College B
Carthage College B, T
Lawrence University B
Marquette University B
Northland College T
Ripon College B, T
St. Norbert College B, T
University of Wisconsin
  Eau Claire B
  Green Bay B
  La Crosse B, T
  Madison B, M, D
  Milwaukee B, M, D
  Oshkosh B, M
  Parkside B
  River Falls B
  Stevens Point B, T
  Whitewater B, T

Wyoming
Casper College A
Northwest College A
University of Wyoming B, M, D
Western Wyoming Community
  College A

Physics teacher education

Alabama
Alabama Agricultural and Mechanical
  University B, M
Athens State University B
Birmingham-Southern College T
University of Alabama B

Arizona
Arizona State University B, T
Grand Canyon University B
Northern Arizona University M, T
University of Arizona B, M

Arkansas
Arkansas State University B, T
Harding University B, T
Ouachita Baptist University B, T
Southern Arkansas University B, T
University of Central Arkansas T

California
Azusa Pacific University T
California State Polytechnic University:
  Pomona T
San Diego State University B
San Francisco State University B, T
University of the Pacific T

Colorado
Colorado State University T
Fort Lewis College T
University of Southern Colorado T

Connecticut
Central Connecticut State University B
Southern Connecticut State
  University B, T

Delaware
Delaware State University B, M
University of Delaware B, T

Florida
Bethune-Cookman College B, T
Florida Agricultural and Mechanical
  University T
Florida Institute of Technology B, M
Gulf Coast Community College A
University of West Florida B, T

Georgia
Agnes Scott College T
Armstrong Atlantic State University T

Hawaii
University of Hawaii
  Manoa B, T

Idaho
Boise State University T

Illinois
Augustana College B, T
Elmhurst College B
Greenville College B
Illinois College T
Judson College B, T
Lewis University T
Loyola University of Chicago T
North Park University T
Northwestern University B, T
University of Illinois
  Chicago B
  Urbana-Champaign B, M, T
Wheaton College T

Indiana
Ball State University T
Butler University T
Franklin College T
Indiana State University B, T
Indiana University
  Bloomington B, T
  South Bend B, T
Indiana University--Purdue University
  Indiana University-Purdue
    University Fort Wayne B, T
Manchester College B, T
Purdue University
  Calumet T
Taylor University B
University of Evansville T
University of Indianapolis B, T
Valparaiso University B

Vincennes University A

Iowa
Buena Vista University B, T
Central College T
Cornell College B, T
Dordt College B
Drake University M
Graceland University T
Iowa State University T
Loras College T
Luther College B
Morningside College B
Northwestern College T
St. Ambrose University B, T
University of Iowa B, T
Wartburg College T
William Penn University B

Kansas
Bethel College T
Garden City Community College A
Pittsburg State University B, T
University of Kansas B, T

Kentucky
Campbellsville University B
Cumberland College B, T
Murray State University B, M, T
Transylvania University B, T
Union College M

Louisiana
Dillard University B
Louisiana State University
  Shreveport B
McNeese State University T
Northwestern State University B, T
Southern University and Agricultural and
  Mechanical College B

Maine
St. Joseph's College B
University of Southern Maine T

Massachusetts
Bridgewater State College M, T
Harvard College T
Tufts University T
University of Massachusetts
  Dartmouth T
Worcester State College T

Michigan
Albion College B, T
Alma College T
Andrews University M, T
Calvin College B
Central Michigan University B
Eastern Michigan University B, M, T
Grand Valley State University T
Michigan Technological University T
Northern Michigan University B, T
Western Michigan University B

Minnesota
Augsburg College T
Bethel College B
College of St. Catherine: St. Paul
  Campus T
Concordia College: Moorhead T
Gustavus Adolphus College T
Minnesota State University,
  Mankato B, M, T
Moorhead State University B, T
St. Cloud State University T
St. Olaf College T
University of Minnesota
  Morris T
University of St. Thomas T
Winona State University B, T

Mississippi
Mississippi State University T

Missouri
Central Missouri State University B, T
Maryville University of Saint
  Louis B, M, T

Northwest Missouri State
  University B, T
Rockhurst University B
Southwest Missouri State University B
Truman State University M, T
University of Missouri
  Columbia B
  St. Louis T
Washington University B, M, T

Montana
Montana State University
  Billings B, T
  Bozeman T
Rocky Mountain College A, T
University of Montana-Missoula T

Nebraska
Concordia University T
Doane College T
Hastings College B, M, T
Nebraska Wesleyan University B
Peru State College B, T
Union College T
University of Nebraska
  Kearney B
  Lincoln B, T

New Hampshire
University of New Hampshire T

New Jersey
St. Peter's College T
The College of New Jersey B, T

New Mexico
New Mexico Institute of Mining and
  Technology M

New York
Alfred University M
Canisius College B, M, T
City University of New York
  Brooklyn College B
  City College B
  Queens College T
Colgate University M
Columbia University
  Teachers College M, D
D'Youville College M, T
Fordham University M, T
Hofstra University B, M, T
Houghton College B, T
Ithaca College B, T
Long Island University
  C. W. Post Campus B, T
Manhattan College B, T
New York Institute of Technology B, T
New York University B, M, T
Pace University:
  Pleasantville/Briarcliff B, M
Pace University B, M
St. John Fisher College B, T
St. John's University B, M, T
St. Thomas Aquinas College B, T
State University of New York
  Albany B, M, T
  Binghamton M
  Buffalo T
  College at Brockport M, T
  College at Buffalo B
  College at Fredonia B, T
  College at Geneseo B, M, T
  College at Oneonta B, M, T
  College at Plattsburgh B, M
  College at Potsdam B, M
  Oswego B, M
Syracuse University B, M, T
Vassar College T
Wagner College T
Wells College T

North Carolina
North Carolina Agricultural and
  Technical State University B, T
North Carolina Central University B, M

University of North Carolina
  Greensboro B, M, T
  Wilmington T
Wake Forest University M, T

North Dakota
Minot State University B, T
North Dakota State University B, T
University of North Dakota T

Ohio
Baldwin-Wallace College T
Bluffton College B
Bowling Green State University B, M
Case Western Reserve University T
Cedarville College B, T
Hiram College T
John Carroll University T
Kent State University
  Stark Campus B
Kent State University T
Malone College B
Miami University
  Oxford Campus B, M, T
Mount Union College T
Mount Vernon Nazarene College B, T
Otterbein College B
University of Akron B
University of Dayton B, M, T
University of Rio Grande B, T
University of Toledo B, T
Xavier University B
Youngstown State University B, M

Oklahoma
East Central University T
Eastern Oklahoma State College A
Northeastern State University B
Oklahoma State University M, D
University of Central Oklahoma B
University of Tulsa T

Oregon
Oregon State University M
Portland State University T
University of Portland T

Pennsylvania
Alvernia College B
Bucknell University T
California University of
  Pennsylvania B, T
Chatham College M, T
Clarion University of Pennsylvania B, T
Dickinson College T
Duquesne University B, T
Gettysburg College T
Grove City College B, T
Juniata College B, T
Lebanon Valley College of
  Pennsylvania T
Lock Haven University of
  Pennsylvania B, T
Lycoming College T
Mansfield University of
  Pennsylvania B, T
Moravian College T
St. Vincent College T
Seton Hill College B, T
Thiel College B
University of Pittsburgh
  Johnstown B, T
Washington and Jefferson College T
Westminster College T
Widener University T
Wilkes University M, T

Puerto Rico
University of Puerto Rico
  Mayaguez Campus T

Rhode Island
Rhode Island College B

South Carolina
Furman University T
Wofford College T

South Dakota
Augustana College B, T
Dakota State University B, T
South Dakota State University B
University of South Dakota T

Tennessee
Belmont University T
Christian Brothers University B, M, T
David Lipscomb University B, T
Southern Adventist University B
Trevecca Nazarene University B, T

Texas
Abilene Christian University B, T
Baylor University B, T
Del Mar College A
Hardin-Simmons University B, T
Houston Baptist University T
Lamar University T
St. Mary's University T
Southwest Texas State University T
Texas A&M University
  Commerce T
  Kingsville T
Texas Christian University T
University of Dallas T
University of Houston
  Clear Lake T
University of Houston T
University of Texas
  Arlington T
  San Antonio T
West Texas A&M University T

Utah
Brigham Young University B
Utah State University B
Weber State University B

Vermont
Castleton State College B, T
St. Michael's College B

Virginia
Bridgewater College T
Christopher Newport University T
Hollins University T
Longwood College B, T
Radford University T
Virginia Wesleyan College T

Washington
Central Washington University T
Washington State University T
Western Washington University B, T
Whitworth College B, T

West Virginia
Fairmont State College B
Glenville State College B
Wheeling Jesuit University T

Wisconsin
Carthage College T
Lawrence University T
Northland College T
St. Norbert College T
University of Wisconsin
  Green Bay T
  La Crosse B, T
  River Falls T

Physiology, human/animal

Alabama
University of Alabama
  Birmingham D

Arizona
University of Arizona B, M, D

Arkansas
University of Arkansas
  for Medical Sciences M, D

Physiology, human/animal

California
California State University
 Fresno *B*
 Long Beach *B*
San Francisco State University *B, M*
Stanford University *D*
University of California
 Berkeley *M, D*
 Davis *B, M, D*
 Irvine *D*
 Los Angeles *M, D*
 San Diego *B, M, D*
 San Francisco *D*
 Santa Barbara *B*
University of Southern California *M, D*

Colorado
Colorado State University *M, D*
University of Colorado
 Health Sciences Center *D*

Connecticut
Southern Connecticut State University *B*
University of Connecticut *B, M, D*
Yale University *M, D*

District of Columbia
Georgetown University *M, D*
Howard University *D*

Florida
University of Miami *M, D*

Georgia
Georgia Military College *A*
Medical College of Georgia *D*
University of Georgia *M, D*

Hawaii
University of Hawaii
 Manoa *M, D*

Illinois
Finch University of Health Sciences/The
 Chicago Medical School *M, D*
Loyola University of Chicago *M, D*
Northwestern University *B, M, D*
Southern Illinois University
 Carbondale *B, M, D*
University of Illinois
 Chicago *M, D*
 Urbana-Champaign *B, M, D*

Indiana
Ball State University *M*
Indiana State University *T*
Indiana University--Purdue University
 Indiana University-Purdue
 University Indianapolis *M, D*

Iowa
Iowa State University *M, D*
Maharishi University of
 Management *M, D*
University of Iowa *M, D*

Kansas
Kansas State University *M, D*

Louisiana
Louisiana State University Medical
 Center *M, D*
Tulane University *M, D*

Maryland
Uniformed Services University of the
 Health Sciences *D*
University of Maryland
 Baltimore *M, D*

Massachusetts
Boston University *B, M, D*
Hampshire College *B*
Harvard University *M, D*
Tufts University *M, D*

Michigan
Michigan State University *B, M, D*
Northern Michigan University *B*
University of Michigan *M, D*

Wayne State University *M, D*

Minnesota
Mayo Graduate School *D*
Minnesota State University, Mankato *B*
St. Cloud State University *B*
University of Minnesota
 Duluth *M*
 Twin Cities *B, M, D*

Mississippi
Mississippi State University *M, D*
University of Mississippi
 Medical Center *M, D*

Missouri
St. Louis University *M, D*
University of Missouri
 Columbia *M, D*

New Hampshire
Dartmouth College *D*

New Jersey
Rutgers
 The State University of New Jersey:
  Camden College of Arts and
  Sciences *B*
 The State University of New Jersey:
  Cook College *B*
 The State University of New Jersey:
  Douglass College *B*
 The State University of New Jersey:
  Livingston College *B*
 The State University of New Jersey:
  New Brunswick Graduate
  Campus *M, D*
 The State University of New Jersey:
  Rutgers College *B*
 The State University of New Jersey:
  University College Camden *B*
 The State University of New Jersey:
  University College New
  Brunswick *B*

New York
Albany Medical College *M, D*
Columbia University
 Graduate School *M, D*
Cornell University *M, D*
Long Island University
 Brooklyn Campus *M*
New York University *M, D*
Rockefeller University *D*
State University of New York
 Albany *D*
 Buffalo *M, D*
 College of Environmental Science
  and Forestry *B, M, D*
 Health Science Center at
  Brooklyn *D*
 Health Science Center at Stony
  Brook *D*
 Stony Brook *M, D*
 Upstate Medical University *M, D*
University of Rochester *M, D*

North Carolina
East Carolina University *D*
North Carolina State University *M, D*
University of North Carolina
 Chapel Hill *M, D*

North Dakota
University of North Dakota *M, D*

Ohio
Case Western Reserve University *D*
Kent State University *M, D*
Ohio State University
 Columbus Campus *M, D*
University of Cincinnati *M, D*

Oklahoma
Oklahoma State University *M, D*

Pennsylvania
MCP Hahnemann University *M, D*

Penn State
 College of Medicine, Milton S.
  Hershey Medical Center *M, D*
 University Park *M, D*
University of Pennsylvania *B, D*

Puerto Rico
University of Puerto Rico
 Medical Sciences Campus *M, D*

South Carolina
Clemson University *M, D*

South Dakota
University of South Dakota *M, D*

Tennessee
University of Tennessee
 Memphis *M, D*

Texas
Southwest Texas State University *B*
Texas A&M University *M, D*
Texas Tech University Health Science
 Center *M, D*
University of North Texas *M*

Utah
Brigham Young University *M, D*

Vermont
Marlboro College *B*
University of Vermont *M, D*

Virginia
University of Virginia *D*
Virginia Commonwealth
 University *C, M, D*

West Virginia
West Virginia University *M, D*

Wisconsin
Medical College of Wisconsin *M, D*
University of Wisconsin
 Madison *M, D*

Plant breeding/genetics

Arizona
Prescott College *B, M*

California
University of California
 Riverside *D*

Illinois
University of Illinois
 Urbana-Champaign *M, D*

Minnesota
University of Minnesota
 Twin Cities *M, D*

New York
Cornell University *B, M, D*

North Carolina
North Carolina State University *M, D*

Oklahoma
Oklahoma State University *M, D*

Texas
Texas A&M University *B, M, D*
Texas Tech University *M*

Utah
Brigham Young University *B*

Plant pathology

Alabama
Auburn University *M, D*

Arkansas
University of Arkansas *M*

California
University of California
 Berkeley *M, D*
 Davis *M, D*
 Riverside *M, D*

Colorado
Colorado State University *M, D*

Delaware
University of Delaware *B*

Florida
Manatee Community College *A*
University of Florida *M, D*

Georgia
University of Georgia *B, M, D*

Hawaii
University of Hawaii
 Manoa *M, D*

Illinois
University of Illinois
 Urbana-Champaign *M, D*

Indiana
Purdue University *B, M, D*

Iowa
Iowa State University *B, M, D*

Kansas
Kansas State University *M, D*

Kentucky
University of Kentucky *M, D*

Louisiana
Louisiana State University and
 Agricultural and Mechanical
 College *M, D*

Michigan
Michigan State University *B, M, D*

Minnesota
University of Minnesota
 Twin Cities *M, D*

Mississippi
Mississippi State University *M, D*

Missouri
University of Missouri
 Columbia *M, D*

Montana
Montana State University
 Bozeman *M*

New Jersey
Rutgers
 The State University of New Jersey:
  New Brunswick Graduate
  Campus *M, D*

New York
Cornell University *B, M, D*
State University of New York
 College of Environmental Science
  and Forestry *B, M, D*

North Carolina
North Carolina State University *M, D*

North Dakota
North Dakota State University *M, D*

Ohio
Ohio State University
 Columbus Campus *B, M, D*

Oklahoma
Oklahoma State University *M, D*

Oregon
Oregon State University *M, D*

Pennsylvania
Penn State
 University Park *M, D*

South Carolina
Clemson University *B, M, D*

Texas
Texas A&M University *M, D*

Utah
Dixie State College of Utah *A*

Virginia
Virginia Polytechnic Institute and State University *M, D*

Washington
Washington State University *M, D*

Wisconsin
University of Wisconsin
　Madison *B, M, D*

Plant physiology

Hawaii
University of Hawaii
　Manoa *M, D*

Iowa
Iowa State University *M, D*

Kentucky
University of Kentucky *D*

Nebraska
Peru State College *B*

New Hampshire
University of New Hampshire *B*

New Jersey
Rutgers
　The State University of New Jersey:
　New Brunswick Graduate Campus *M, D*

New York
State University of New York
　Albany *D*
　College of Environmental Science and Forestry *B, M, D*

North Carolina
North Carolina State University *M, D*

North Dakota
North Dakota State University *D*

Pennsylvania
Penn State
　University Park *M, D*

South Carolina
Charleston Southern University *B*
Clemson University *D*

Texas
Texas A&M University *M, D*

Vermont
Marlboro College *B*

Virginia
Virginia Polytechnic Institute and State University *M, D*

Washington
Washington State University *M, D*

Wisconsin
University of Wisconsin
　Madison *M, D*

Plant protection

Arkansas
University of Arkansas *B*

California
College of the Sequoias *C*
San Joaquin Delta College *A*

University of California
　Davis *M*
　Riverside *M*
Ventura College *A*

Georgia
University of Georgia *B, M*

Hawaii
University of Hawaii
　Hilo *B*

Idaho
University of Idaho *B, M, D*

Iowa
Iowa State University *B*

Mississippi
Mississippi State University *B, M*

Nebraska
University of Nebraska
　Lincoln *B*

New York
Cornell University *B, M*
State University of New York
　College of Environmental Science and Forestry *M, D*

North Carolina
North Carolina State University *A*

North Dakota
North Dakota State University *B*

Ohio
Ohio State University
　Columbus Campus *B*

Oklahoma
Northeastern Oklahoma Agricultural and Mechanical College *A*

Puerto Rico
University of Puerto Rico
　Mayaguez Campus *M*
　Utuado *A*

South Carolina
Clemson University *M*

Texas
Texas A&M University *M*
Texas Tech University *B*

Utah
Dixie State College of Utah *A*
Snow College *A*

Washington
Washington State University *B, M*

Plant sciences

Alabama
Alabama Agricultural and Mechanical University *B, M, D*
Tuskegee University *B, M*

Alaska
University of Alaska
　Fairbanks *B*

Arizona
Arizona Western College *A*
University of Arizona *B, M, D*

Arkansas
Arkansas State University *B*
University of Arkansas *D*

California
California Polytechnic State University:
　San Luis Obispo *B*
California State University
　Fresno *B, M*
College of the Desert *A*
College of the Redwoods *C, A*
College of the Sequoias *C*

College of the Siskiyous *A*
Kings River Community College *A*
Mendocino College *C, A*
Modesto Junior College *A*
San Joaquin Delta College *C, A*
Santa Rosa Junior College *C*
University of California
　Berkeley *B*
　Davis *B, M, D*
　Riverside *M*
　Santa Cruz *B, D*
Ventura College *A*
Yuba College *C*

Connecticut
University of Connecticut *M, D*

Delaware
Delaware State University *B*
University of Delaware *B, M, D*

Florida
University of Florida *B*

Georgia
Abraham Baldwin Agricultural College *A*
Fort Valley State University *B*

Idaho
University of Idaho *B, M, D*

Illinois
Southern Illinois University
　Carbondale *B, M*

Iowa
Dordt College *B*
Iowa State University *B*

Louisiana
Louisiana State University and Agricultural and Mechanical College *M, D*
Louisiana Tech University *B*

Maine
Southern Maine Technical College *C, A*
University of Maine *B, M*

Maryland
Howard Community College *C*

Massachusetts
University of Massachusetts
　Amherst *B, M, D*

Michigan
Michigan State University *B, M, D*

Minnesota
University of Minnesota
　Crookston *A*

Mississippi
Northwest Mississippi Community College *A*

Missouri
Southwest Missouri State University *M*
University of Missouri
　Columbia *B*

Montana
Montana State University
　Bozeman *B, M, D*

New Hampshire
University of New Hampshire *B, M, D*

New Jersey
Mercer County Community College *A*
Rutgers
　The State University of New Jersey:
　Cook College *B*
　The State University of New Jersey:
　New Brunswick Graduate Campus *M, D*

New York
Cornell University *B*

State University of New York
　College of Agriculture and Technology at Cobleskill *A, B*
　College of Environmental Science and Forestry *M, D*

North Carolina
North Carolina Agricultural and Technical State University *B*
North Carolina State University *M, D*

North Dakota
North Dakota State University *D*

Ohio
Ohio State University
　Agricultural Technical Institute *A*
　Columbus Campus *B*

Oklahoma
Oklahoma State University *D*

South Carolina
Clemson University *B, M, D*

Tennessee
Hiwassee College *A*
Middle Tennessee State University *B*
University of Tennessee
　Knoxville *B, M, D*

Texas
Prairie View A&M University *B*
Southwest Texas State University *B*
Texas A&M University
　Commerce *B*
　Kingsville *B, M*
Texas A&M University *B, M*
Texas State Technical College
　Waco *A*

Utah
Utah State University *M, D*

Vermont
University of Vermont *B, M, D*
Vermont Technical College *A*

Washington
Washington State University *B*

West Virginia
West Virginia University *B, M*

Wisconsin
University of Wisconsin
　River Falls *B*

Plasma/high-temperature physics

New York
Columbia University
　Graduate School *M, D*

Wisconsin
University of Wisconsin
　Madison *M, D*

Playwriting/screenwriting

California
American Film Institute Center for Advanced Film and Television Studies *M*
Pomona College *B*
University of Southern California *B, M*

Illinois
Columbia College *B*

Iowa
University of Iowa *M*

Massachusetts
Emerson College *B, M*
Hampshire College *B*
Simon's Rock College of Bard *B*
Smith College *M*

Playwriting/screenwriting

Michigan
University of Michigan *B*

Minnesota
Metropolitan State University *B*

New Jersey
Rutgers
  The State University of New Jersey:
    Mason Gross School of the
    Arts *M*
  The State University of New Jersey:
    New Brunswick Graduate
    Campus *M*

New Mexico
University of New Mexico *M*

New York
Bard College *B*
New York University *B, M*
Sarah Lawrence College *B, M*

Ohio
Ohio University *M*

Pennsylvania
University of the Arts *B*

Texas
Texas Tech University *M*

Vermont
Marlboro College *B*

Virginia
Hollins University *M*

Plumbing/pipefitting

Alabama
Bessemer State Technical College *C*
Gadsden State Community College *C*
John M. Patterson State Technical
  College *C*
Lawson State Community College *C*
Shelton State Community College *C*

Arizona
Central Arizona College *C*
Gateway Community College *C, A*

California
Allan Hancock College *C*
Bakersfield College *A*
College of San Mateo *A*
Diablo Valley College *C*
Foothill College *C*
Fresno City College *A*
Long Beach City College *C, A*
Los Angeles Trade and Technical
  College *C, A*
Modesto Junior College *C, A*
Orange Coast College *C, A*
Palomar College *C, A*
San Diego City College *C, A*
Ventura College *A*

Colorado
Red Rocks Community College *C, A*

Florida
Brevard Community College *C*
Indian River Community College *C*
Palm Beach Community College *C*
South Florida Community College *C*
Tallahassee Community College *C*

Indiana
Ivy Tech State College
  Northcentral *C, A*
  Northeast *C, A*
  Northwest *C, A*
  Wabash Valley *C, A*
Oakland City University *C*

Iowa
Northeast Iowa Community College *C*

Western Iowa Tech Community
  College *C*

Maine
Eastern Maine Technical College *C*
Southern Maine Technical College *C*
Washington County Technical College *C*

Michigan
Bay de Noc Community College *C*
Jackson Community College *C, A*
Kellogg Community College *C, A*
Lansing Community College *A*
Macomb Community College *C*
Oakland Community College *C*

Minnesota
St. Cloud Technical College *C, A*
St. Paul Technical College *C*

Mississippi
Mississippi Gulf Coast Community
  College
    Perkinston *C, A*
Northeast Mississippi Community
  College *C*

Missouri
Ranken Technical College *C*

New Mexico
Albuquerque Technical-Vocational
  Institute *C*
Northern New Mexico Community
  College *C, A*

New York
State University of New York
  College of Technology at Alfred *A*
  College of Technology at Canton *C*
  College of Technology at
    Delhi *C, A*

North Carolina
Blue Ridge Community College *C*
Cleveland Community College *C*
Fayetteville Technical Community
  College *C*
Forsyth Technical Community College *C*
Haywood Community College *C*
Johnston Community College *C*
Southeastern Community College *C*
Southwestern Community College *C*
Tri-County Community College *C*
Wake Technical Community College *C*

North Dakota
North Dakota State College of Science *C*

Ohio
Owens Community College
  Toledo *C*

Oregon
Central Oregon Community College *C*

Pennsylvania
Community College of Allegheny
  County *C, A*
Delaware County Community College *C*
Luzerne County Community
  College *C, A*
Pennsylvania College of Technology *C*

Rhode Island
New England Institute of
  Technology *C, A*

South Carolina
Denmark Technical College *C*

Texas
Brazosport College *C, A*
Howard College *C*
Lee College *A*
St. Philip's College *C, A*

Utah
Dixie State College of Utah *C*

Wisconsin
Chippewa Valley Technical College *C*
Gateway Technical College *C*
Western Wisconsin Technical College *C*

Podiatry, podiatric medicine (D.P.M.)

California
California College of Podiatric
  Medicine *C*

Florida
Barry University: School of Graduate
  Medical Sciences *C*
Barry University *C*

Illinois
Dr. William M. Scholl College of
  Podiatric Medicine *C*

Iowa
University of Osteopathic Medicine and
  Health Sciences
    Des Moines University -
    Osteopathic Medical Center *C*
University of Osteopathic Medicine and
  Health Sciences: College of Podiatric
  Medicine and Surgery *C*

New York
New York College of Podiatric
  Medicine *C*

Ohio
Ohio College of Podiatric Medicine *C*

Pennsylvania
Pennsylvania College of Podiatric
  Medicine *C*
Temple University *C*

Political science/government

Alabama
Alabama Agricultural and Mechanical
  University *B*
Alabama State University *B*
Athens State University *B*
Auburn University at Montgomery *B, M*
Auburn University *B, M*
Birmingham-Southern College *B, T*
Huntingdon College *B*
Jacksonville State University *B, M*
Lawson State Community College *A*
Samford University *B*
Spring Hill College *B*
Troy State University
  Montgomery *B*
Troy State University *B*
Tuskegee University *B*
University of Alabama
  Birmingham *B*
  Huntsville *B*
University of Alabama *B, M, D*
University of Mobile *B*
University of Montevallo *B, T*
University of North Alabama *B*
University of South Alabama *B*

Alaska
University of Alaska
  Anchorage *B*
  Fairbanks *B*
  Southeast *B*

Arizona
Arizona State University *B, M, D*
Cochise College *A*
Eastern Arizona College *A*
Grand Canyon University *B*
Northern Arizona University *B, M, D*
Pima Community College *A*
South Mountain Community College *A*
University of Arizona *B, M, D*

Arkansas
Arkansas State University *B, M*
Arkansas Tech University *B*
Harding University *B*
Henderson State University *B*
Hendrix College *B*
Lyon College *B*
Ouachita Baptist University *B*
Philander Smith College *B*
Southern Arkansas University *B*
University of Arkansas
  Little Rock *B*
  Monticello *B*
  Pine Bluff *B*
University of Arkansas *B, M*
University of Central Arkansas *B*
University of the Ozarks *B*
Westark College *A*

California
Azusa Pacific University *B*
Bakersfield College *A*
Cabrillo College *A*
California Baptist University *B*
California Lutheran University *B*
California Polytechnic State University:
  San Luis Obispo *B*
California State Polytechnic University:
  Pomona *B*
California State University
  Bakersfield *B*
  Chico *B, M*
  Dominguez Hills *B*
  Fresno *A*
  Fullerton *B, M*
  Hayward *B*
  Los Angeles *B, M*
  Northridge *B*
  San Marcos *B*
  Stanislaus *B*
Canada College *A*
Cerritos Community College *A*
Chabot College *A*
Chaffey Community College *A*
Chapman University *B*
Claremont McKenna College *B*
College of Notre Dame *B*
College of the Canyons *A*
College of the Desert *A*
Compton Community College *A*
Concordia University *B*
Crafton Hills College *A*
Cypress College *A*
De Anza College *A*
Diablo Valley College *A*
Dominican University of California *B*
East Los Angeles College *A*
Foothill College *A*
Gavilan Community College *A*
Golden Gate University *C, B*
Golden West College *A*
Grossmont Community College *A*
Humboldt State University *B*
Irvine Valley College *A*
La Sierra University *B*
Long Beach City College *C, A*
Los Angeles Southwest College *A*
Los Angeles Valley College *A*
Loyola Marymount University *B*
Master's College *B*
Merced College *A*
Mills College *B*
MiraCosta College *A*
Monterey Peninsula College *A*
Mount St. Mary's College *B*
Occidental College *B*
Ohlone College *A*
Orange Coast College *A*
Pacific Union College *B*
Pepperdine University *B*
Pitzer College *B*
Point Loma Nazarene University *B*
Pomona College *B*
Riverside Community College *A*
Saddleback College *A*

Political science/government

St. Mary's College of California *B*
San Diego City College *A*
San Diego Miramar College *A*
San Diego State University *B, M*
San Francisco State University *B, M*
San Jose State University *B*
Santa Ana College *A*
Santa Barbara City College *A*
Santa Clara University *B*
Santa Monica College *A*
Santa Rosa Junior College *A*
Scripps College *B*
Solano Community College *A*
Sonoma State University *B*
Southwestern College *A*
Stanford University *B, M, D*
United States International University *B*
University of California
   Berkeley *B, M, D*
   Davis *B, M, D*
   Irvine *B, D*
   Los Angeles *B, M, D*
   Riverside *B, M, D*
   San Diego *B, M, D*
   Santa Barbara *B, M, D*
   Santa Cruz *B*
University of Judaism *B*
University of La Verne *B*
University of Redlands *B*
University of San Diego *B*
University of San Francisco *B*
University of Southern California *B, M, D*
University of the Pacific *B*
Vanguard University of Southern California *B*
Ventura College *A*
West Los Angeles College *C, A*
Westmont College *B*
Whittier College *B, M*

Colorado
Colorado Christian University *B*
Colorado College *B*
Colorado State University *B, M, D*
Fort Lewis College *B*
Mesa State College *B*
Metropolitan State College of Denver *B, T*
Otero Junior College *A*
Red Rocks Community College *A*
Regis University *B*
United States Air Force Academy *B*
University of Colorado
   Boulder *B, M, D*
   Colorado Springs *B*
   Denver *B, M*
University of Denver *B*
University of Northern Colorado *B*
University of Southern Colorado *B*
Western State College of Colorado *B*

Connecticut
Albertus Magnus College *B*
Central Connecticut State University *B*
Connecticut College *B*
Eastern Connecticut State University *B*
Fairfield University *B*
Quinnipiac University *B*
Sacred Heart University *A, B*
Southern Connecticut State University *B, M*
Trinity College *B*
United States Coast Guard Academy *B*
University of Connecticut *B, M, D*
University of Hartford *B*
University of New Haven *B*
Wesleyan University *B*
Western Connecticut State University *B*
Yale University *B, M, D*

Delaware
Delaware State University *B*
University of Delaware *B, M, D*
Wesley College *B*

District of Columbia
American University *B, M, D*
Catholic University of America *B, M, D*
Gallaudet University *B*
George Washington University *B, M, D*
Georgetown University *B, M, D*
Howard University *B, M, D*
Trinity College *B*
University of the District of Columbia *B*

Florida
Barry University *B*
Bethune-Cookman College *B*
Broward Community College *A*
Eckerd College *B*
Florida Agricultural and Mechanical University *B*
Florida Atlantic University *B, M*
Florida International University *B, M, D*
Florida Southern College *B*
Florida State University *B, M, D*
Gulf Coast Community College *A*
Jacksonville University *B*
Lynn University *B*
Miami-Dade Community College *A*
New College of the University of South Florida *B*
Palm Beach Atlantic College *B, T*
Palm Beach Community College *A*
Rollins College *B*
St. Leo University *B*
St. Thomas University *B*
Stetson University *B*
University of Central Florida *B, M*
University of Florida *B, M, D*
University of Miami *B, M*
University of North Florida *B*
University of South Florida *B, M*
University of Tampa *A, B*

Georgia
Agnes Scott College *B*
Albany State University *B*
Armstrong Atlantic State University *B, T*
Atlanta Metropolitan College *A*
Augusta State University *B*
Berry College *B*
Brenau University *B*
Brewton-Parker College *A*
Clark Atlanta University *B, M, D*
Clayton College and State University *A*
Columbus State University *B*
Dalton State College *A*
Darton College *A*
East Georgia College *A*
Emmanuel College *B*
Emory University *B, D*
Fort Valley State University *B*
Gainesville College *A*
Georgia College and State University *B, T*
Georgia Military College *A*
Georgia Perimeter College *A*
Georgia Southern University *B, M*
Georgia Southwestern State University *B*
Georgia State University *B, M, D*
Kennesaw State University *B*
LaGrange College *B*
Mercer University *B*
Middle Georgia College *A*
Morehouse College *B*
Morris Brown College *B*
North Georgia College & State University *B*
Oglethorpe University *B*
Oxford College of Emory University *B*
Savannah State University *B*
South Georgia College *A*
Spelman College *B*
State University of West Georgia *B*
Thomas College *B*
University of Georgia *B, M, D*
Valdosta State University *B*
Waycross College *A*

Hawaii
Brigham Young University Hawaii *B*
Chaminade University of Honolulu *B*
Hawaii Pacific University *B*
University of Hawaii
   Hilo *B*
   Manoa *B, M, D*
   West Oahu *B*

Idaho
Albertson College of Idaho *B*
Boise State University *B, T*
College of Southern Idaho *A*
Idaho State University *A, B, M, D*
Lewis-Clark State College *B*
North Idaho College *A*
Northwest Nazarene University *B*
Ricks College *A*
University of Idaho *B, M, D*

Illinois
Augustana College *B, T*
Barat College *B*
Benedictine University *B*
Black Hawk College
   East Campus *A*
Blackburn College *B*
Bradley University *B, T*
Chicago State University *B*
Concordia University *B*
Danville Area Community College *A*
De Paul University *B*
Dominican University *B*
Eastern Illinois University *B, M*
Elmhurst College *B, T*
Eureka College *B*
Governors State University *M*
Highland Community College *A*
Illinois College *B*
Illinois State University *B, M*
Illinois Wesleyan University *B*
John A. Logan College *A*
Joliet Junior College *A*
Judson College *B*
Kendall College *B*
Kishwaukee College *A*
Knox College *B*
Lake Forest College *B*
Lewis University *B*
Lewis and Clark Community College *A*
Lincoln Land Community College *A*
Loyola University of Chicago *B, M, D, T*
MacMurray College *B*
McKendree College *B*
Millikin University *B*
Monmouth College *B, T*
Morton College *A*
North Central College *B*
North Park University *B*
Northeastern Illinois University *B, M*
Northern Illinois University *B, M, D*
Northwestern University *B, M, D*
Olivet Nazarene University *B*
Parkland College *A*
Principia College *B*
Quincy University *A, B*
Rend Lake College *A*
Richland Community College *A*
Rockford College *B*
Roosevelt University *B, M*
St. Xavier University *B*
Sauk Valley Community College *A*
Southern Illinois University
   Carbondale *B, M, D*
   Edwardsville *B*
Southwestern Illinois College *A*
Springfield College in Illinois *A*
Triton College *A*
University of Chicago *B, M, D*
University of Illinois
   Chicago *B, M*
   Springfield *B, M*
   Urbana-Champaign *B, M, D*
University of St. Francis *B*
Western Illinois University *B, M*

Wheaton College *B, T*

Indiana
Anderson University *B*
Ball State University *B, M*
Butler University *B*
DePauw University *B*
Earlham College *B*
Franklin College *B*
Goshen College *B*
Hanover College *B*
Indiana State University *B, M, T*
Indiana University
   Bloomington *B, M, D*
   East *B*
   Northwest *B*
   South Bend *A, B*
   Southeast *B*
Indiana University--Purdue University
   Indiana University-Purdue University Fort Wayne *A, B*
   Indiana University-Purdue University Indianapolis *B*
Indiana Wesleyan University *A, B*
Manchester College *B*
Marian College *T*
Purdue University
   Calumet *B*
Purdue University *B, M, D*
Saint Mary's College *B*
St. Joseph's College *B*
Taylor University *B*
University of Evansville *B*
University of Indianapolis *B*
University of Notre Dame *B, M, D*
University of Southern Indiana *B*
Valparaiso University *B*
Vincennes University *A*
Wabash College *B*

Iowa
Buena Vista University *B, T*
Central College *B, T*
Clarke College *A, B, T*
Coe College *B*
Cornell College *B, T*
Dordt College *B*
Drake University *B*
Graceland University *T*
Grand View College *B*
Grinnell College *B*
Iowa State University *B, M*
Loras College *B*
Luther College *B*
Morningside College *B*
North Iowa Area Community College *A*
Northwestern College *B*
St. Ambrose University *B, T*
Simpson College *B*
University of Iowa *B, M, D, T*
University of Northern Iowa *B, M*
Waldorf College *A*
Wartburg College *B, T*
William Penn University *B*

Kansas
Baker University *B, T*
Benedictine College *B, T*
Bethel College *T*
Butler County Community College *A*
Coffeyville Community College *A*
Emporia State University *B*
Fort Hays State University *B, M*
Independence Community College *A*
Kansas State University *B, M*
Ottawa University *B*
Pittsburg State University *B, T*
Pratt Community College *A*
St. Mary College *B*
Seward County Community College *A*
Sterling College *B*
Tabor College *B*
University of Kansas *B, M, D*
Washburn University of Topeka *B*
Wichita State University *B, M, T*

Political science/government

Kentucky
Bellarmine College B
Berea College B
Campbellsville University B
Centre College B
Cumberland College B, T
Eastern Kentucky University B, M
Georgetown College B, T
Kentucky State University B
Kentucky Wesleyan College B, T
Morehead State University B
Murray State University B, T
Northern Kentucky University B
Pikeville College B
Thomas More College A
Transylvania University B, T
Union College B
University of Kentucky B, M, D
University of Louisville B, M
Western Kentucky University B, T

Louisiana
Centenary College of Louisiana B, T
Dillard University B
Louisiana State University
  Shreveport B
Louisiana State University and
  Agricultural and Mechanical
  College B, M, D
Louisiana Tech University B
Loyola University New Orleans B
McNeese State University B
Nicholls State University B
Southeastern Louisiana University B
Southern University
  New Orleans B
Southern University and Agricultural and
  Mechanical College B, M
Tulane University B, M, D
University of Louisiana at Lafayette B
University of Louisiana at Monroe B
University of New Orleans B, M, D
Xavier University of Louisiana B

Maine
Bates College B
Bowdoin College B
Colby College B
University of Maine
  Presque Isle B
University of Maine B
University of Southern Maine B

Maryland
Allegany College A
Bowie State University B
College of Notre Dame of Maryland B
Community College of Baltimore County
  Essex A
Frederick Community College A
Frostburg State University B
Hood College B
Johns Hopkins University B, D
Loyola College in Maryland B
Morgan State University B
Mount St. Mary's College B
St. Mary's College of Maryland B
Salisbury State University B, T
Towson University B
United States Naval Academy B
University of Baltimore B
University of Maryland
  Baltimore County B
  College Park B, M, D
Washington College B
Western Maryland College B

Massachusetts
American International College B
Amherst College B
Assumption College B
Boston College B, M, D
Boston University B, M, D
Brandeis University B, M, D
Bridgewater State College B
Clark University B
College of the Holy Cross B
Curry College B
Emmanuel College B
Fitchburg State College B
Framingham State College B
Gordon College B
Hampshire College B
Harvard College B
Harvard University M, D
Massachusetts Institute of
  Technology B, M, D
Merrimack College B
Mount Holyoke College B
Northeastern University B, M
Regis College B
Salem State College B
Simmons College B
Simon's Rock College of Bard B
Smith College B
Springfield College B
Stonehill College B
Suffolk University B, M
Tufts University B
University of Massachusetts
  Amherst B, M, D
  Boston B
  Dartmouth B
  Lowell B
Wellesley College B
Westfield State College B
Wheaton College B
Williams College B

Michigan
Adrian College A, B, T
Albion College B, T
Alma College B, T
Andrews University B
Aquinas College B, T
Calvin College B, T
Central Michigan University B, M
Eastern Michigan University B
Grand Valley State University B
Hillsdale College B
Hope College B, T
Kalamazoo College B, T
Kellogg Community College A
Lake Michigan College A
Lake Superior State University B
Lansing Community College A
Marygrove College B, T
Michigan State University B, M, D
Northern Michigan University B, M, T
Oakland University B
Saginaw Valley State University B
University of Detroit Mercy B
University of Michigan
  Dearborn B
  Flint B, T
University of Michigan B, M, D, T
Wayne State University B, M, D
Western Michigan University B, M, D

Minnesota
Augsburg College B
Bemidji State University B
Bethel College B
Carleton College B
College of St. Benedict B
College of St. Catherine: St. Paul
  Campus B
Concordia College: Moorhead B
Concordia University: St. Paul B
Gustavus Adolphus College B
Hamline University B
Macalester College B
Minnesota State University,
  Mankato B, M
Moorhead State University B
Ridgewater College: A Community and
  Technical College A
St. Cloud State University B
St. John's University B
St. Mary's University of Minnesota B
St. Olaf College B
Southwest State University B
University of Minnesota
  Duluth B
  Morris B
  Twin Cities B, M, D
University of St. Thomas B
Winona State University B

Mississippi
Alcorn State University B
Delta State University B
Hinds Community College A
Jackson State University B, M
Millsaps College B, T
Mississippi College B, M
Mississippi State University B, M
Mississippi University for Women B
Mississippi Valley State University B
Rust College B
Tougaloo College B
University of Mississippi B, M, D
University of Southern Mississippi B, M

Missouri
Avila College B
Central Methodist College B
Central Missouri State University B
College of the Ozarks B
Columbia College B
Drury University B, T
East Central College A
Evangel University B
Lincoln University B
Lindenwood University B
Maryville University of Saint Louis B
Missouri Southern State College B, T
Missouri Valley College B
Missouri Western State College B
Northwest Missouri State University B
Park University B
Rockhurst University B
St. Louis University B
Southeast Missouri State University B
Southwest Baptist University B
Southwest Missouri State University B
Stephens College B
Three Rivers Community College A
Truman State University B
University of Missouri
  Columbia B, M, D
  Kansas City B, M
  St. Louis B, M, D
Washington University B, M, D
Webster University B
Westminster College B
William Jewell College B
William Woods University B

Montana
Carroll College B, T
Montana State University
  Bozeman B
Rocky Mountain College B, T
University of Montana-Missoula B, M

Nebraska
Bellevue University B
Chadron State College B
Creighton University B
Doane College B
Hastings College B
Nebraska Wesleyan University B
University of Nebraska
  Kearney B, T
  Lincoln B, M, D
  Omaha B
Wayne State College B, T

Nevada
University of Nevada
  Las Vegas B, M
  Reno B, M, D

New Hampshire
Dartmouth College B
Franklin Pierce College B
Keene State College B
New England College B
New Hampshire College B
Plymouth State College of the University
  System of New Hampshire B
Rivier College B
St. Anselm College B
Thomas More College of Liberal Arts B
University of New Hampshire B, M

New Jersey
Bloomfield College B
Brookdale Community College A
Caldwell College B
Centenary College B
Drew University B
Fairleigh Dickinson University B
Gloucester County College A
Kean University B
Middlesex County College A
Monmouth University B
Montclair State University B
New Jersey City University B
Princeton University B, M, D
Ramapo College of New Jersey B
Richard Stockton College of New
  Jersey B
Rider University B
Rowan University B
Rutgers
  The State University of New Jersey:
    Camden College of Arts and
    Sciences B
  The State University of New Jersey:
    Douglass College B
  The State University of New Jersey:
    Livingston College B
  The State University of New Jersey:
    New Brunswick Graduate
    Campus M, D
  The State University of New Jersey:
    Newark College of Arts and
    Sciences B
  The State University of New Jersey:
    Rutgers College B
  The State University of New Jersey:
    University College Camden B
  The State University of New Jersey:
    University College New
    Brunswick B
  The State University of New Jersey:
    University College Newark B
St. Peter's College B
Salem Community College A
Seton Hall University B, T
The College of New Jersey B
Thomas Edison State College B

New Mexico
College of Santa Fe B
Eastern New Mexico University B
New Mexico Highlands University B
New Mexico State University B, M
San Juan College A
University of New Mexico B, M, D

New York
Adelphi University B
Adirondack Community College A
Alfred University B
Bard College B
Barnard College B
Canisius College B
City University of New York
  Baruch College B
  Brooklyn College B, M
  City College B
  College of Staten Island B
  Graduate School and University
    Center M, D
  Hunter College B
  Lehman College B
  Queens College B, M
  Queensborough Community
    College A
  York College B
Clarkson University B
Colgate University B

Political science/government

College of New Rochelle B, T
Columbia University
    Columbia College B
    Graduate School M, D
    School of General Studies B
Cornell University B, D
Daemen College B
Dowling College B
Elmira College B
Eugene Lang College/New School University B
Fordham University B, M, D
Fulton-Montgomery Community College A
Hamilton College B
Hartwick College B
Hobart and William Smith Colleges B
Hofstra University B
Houghton College B
Iona College B
Ithaca College B
Keuka College B
Le Moyne College B
Long Island University
    Brooklyn Campus B, M
    C. W. Post Campus B, M
    Southampton College B, T
Manhattanville College B
Marist College B
Marymount College B
Marymount Manhattan College B
Medaille College B
Mercy College B
Molloy College B
Monroe Community College A
Nazareth College of Rochester B
New York Institute of Technology B
New York University B, M, D
Niagara University B
Pace University:
    Pleasantville/Briarcliff C, B, T
Pace University C, B, T
Regents College B
Russell Sage College B
St. Bonaventure University B
St. Francis College B
St. John Fisher College B
St. John's University B, M
St. Lawrence University B
Sarah Lawrence College B
Siena College B, T
Skidmore College B
State University of New York
    Albany B, M, D
    Binghamton B, M, D
    Buffalo B, M, D
    College at Brockport B
    College at Buffalo B
    College at Cortland B
    College at Fredonia B
    College at Geneseo B, T
    College at Oneonta B
    College at Plattsburgh B
    College at Potsdam B
    New Paltz B
    Oswego B
    Purchase B
    Stony Brook B, M, D
Suffolk County Community College A
Syracuse University B, M, D
Touro College B
Union College B
United States Military Academy B
University of Rochester B, M, D
Utica College of Syracuse University B
Wagner College B

North Carolina
Appalachian State University B, M
Barber-Scotia College B
Barton College B
Belmont Abbey College B
Bennett College B
Campbell University B
Catawba College B
Davidson College B
Duke University B, M, D
East Carolina University B
Elizabeth City State University B
Elon College B
Fayetteville State University B
Greensboro College B
Guilford College B
High Point University B
Johnson C. Smith University B
Lenoir-Rhyne College B, T
Mars Hill College B
Meredith College B
Methodist College A, B
North Carolina Agricultural and Technical State University B
North Carolina Central University B
North Carolina State University B, M
North Carolina Wesleyan College B
Queens College B
St. Andrews Presbyterian College B
St. Augustine's College B
University of North Carolina
    Asheville B, T
    Chapel Hill B, M, D
    Charlotte B
    Greensboro B, M, T
    Pembroke B
    Wilmington B
Wake Forest University B
Warren Wilson College B
Western Carolina University B
Winston-Salem State University B

North Dakota
Dickinson State University B, T
Jamestown College B
North Dakota State University B, M
University of North Dakota B, M

Ohio
Antioch College B
Ashland University B
Baldwin-Wallace College B
Bluffton College B
Bowling Green State University B, M
Capital University B
Case Western Reserve University B, M, D
Cedarville College B
Central State University B
Cleveland State University B
College of Wooster B
Denison University B
Franciscan University of Steubenville B
Heidelberg College B
Hiram College B
John Carroll University B
Kent State University
    Stark Campus B
Kent State University B, M, D
Kenyon College B
Marietta College B
Miami University
    Middletown Campus A
    Oxford Campus B, M, D
Mount Union College B
Muskingum College B
Notre Dame College of Ohio B, T
Oberlin College B
Ohio Dominican College B, T
Ohio Northern University B
Ohio State University
    Columbus Campus B, M, D
Ohio University B, M
Ohio Wesleyan University B
Otterbein College B
University of Akron B, M
University of Cincinnati B, M, D
University of Dayton B, M
University of Findlay B
University of Toledo B, M
Walsh University B
Wilberforce University B
Wilmington College B
Wittenberg University B
Wright State University B
Xavier University A, B
Youngstown State University B

Oklahoma
Cameron University B
East Central University B
Northeastern Oklahoma Agricultural and Mechanical College A
Northeastern State University B
Northwestern Oklahoma State University B
Oklahoma Baptist University B
Oklahoma City Community College B
Oklahoma City University B
Oklahoma State University
    Oklahoma City A
Oklahoma State University B, M
Oral Roberts University B
Redlands Community College A
Rogers State University A
Rose State College A
St. Gregory's University B
Southern Nazarene University B
Southwestern Oklahoma State University B
Tulsa Community College A
University of Central Oklahoma B, M
University of Oklahoma B, M, D
University of Science and Arts of Oklahoma B
University of Tulsa B
Western Oklahoma State College A

Oregon
Chemeketa Community College A
Eastern Oregon University B
Lewis & Clark College B
Linfield College B
Oregon State University B
Pacific University B
Portland State University B, M
Reed College B
Southern Oregon University B
University of Oregon B, M, D
University of Portland B
Western Oregon University B
Willamette University B

Pennsylvania
Albright College B
Allegheny College B
Allentown College of St. Francis de Sales B
Alvernia College B
Beaver College B
Bloomsburg University of Pennsylvania B
Bryn Mawr College B
Bucknell University B
Cabrini College B
California University of Pennsylvania B
Carnegie Mellon University B
Cedar Crest College B
Chatham College B
Chestnut Hill College B
Cheyney University of Pennsylvania B
Clarion University of Pennsylvania B
Dickinson College B
Duquesne University B, M
East Stroudsburg University of Pennsylvania B, M
Eastern College B
Edinboro University of Pennsylvania B
Elizabethtown College B
Franklin and Marshall College B
Gannon University B
Geneva College B, T
Gettysburg College B
Grove City College B
Haverford College B, T
Immaculata College C, B
Indiana University of Pennsylvania B
Juniata College B
King's College B
Kutztown University of Pennsylvania B
La Salle University B
Lafayette College B
Lebanon Valley College of Pennsylvania B
Lehigh University B, M
Lincoln University B
Lock Haven University of Pennsylvania B
Lycoming College B
Mansfield University of Pennsylvania B, T
Mercyhurst College B
Messiah College B
Millersville University of Pennsylvania B, T
Moravian College B
Muhlenberg College B
Neumann College B, T
Penn State
    Erie, The Behrend College B
    University Park B, M, D
Point Park College B
Rosemont College B
St. Francis College B
St. Joseph's University B
St. Vincent College B
Seton Hill College B
Shippensburg University of Pennsylvania B, T
Slippery Rock University of Pennsylvania B, T
Susquehanna University B
Swarthmore College B
Temple University B, M, D
Thiel College B
University of Pennsylvania A, B, M, D
University of Pittsburgh
    Greensburg B
    Johnstown B
University of Pittsburgh B, M, D
University of Scranton A, B
Ursinus College B
Villanova University B, M
Washington and Jefferson College B
Waynesburg College B
West Chester University of Pennsylvania B
Westminster College B, T
Widener University B
Wilkes University B
Wilson College B
York College of Pennsylvania B

Puerto Rico
Caribbean University A
Inter American University of Puerto Rico
    Metropolitan Campus B
    San German Campus B
Pontifical Catholic University of Puerto Rico B
University of Puerto Rico
    Mayaguez Campus B
    Rio Piedras Campus B

Rhode Island
Brown University B, M, D
Providence College B
Rhode Island College B
Roger Williams University A, B
Salve Regina University B
University of Rhode Island B, M

South Carolina
Benedict College B
Charleston Southern University B
Clemson University B
Coastal Carolina University B
Coker College B
College of Charleston B, T
Converse College B
Francis Marion University B
Furman University B, T
Lander University B, T
Morris College B
Newberry College B
Presbyterian College B

Political science/government

South Carolina State University B
The Citadel B
University of South Carolina
   Aiken B
   Spartanburg B
University of South Carolina B, M, D
Voorhees College B
Winthrop University B
Wofford College B

South Dakota
Augustana College B, T
Black Hills State University B
Northern State University B
South Dakota State University B, T
University of South Dakota B, M

Tennessee
Austin Peay State University B
Belmont University B, T
Carson-Newman College B, T
David Lipscomb University B
East Tennessee State University B
Fisk University B
King College B, T
Lambuth University B
LeMoyne-Owen College B
Lee University B
Maryville College B, T
Middle Tennessee State University B
Rhodes College B
Roane State Community College A
Tennessee State University B
Tennessee Technological University B
Tennessee Temple University B
Trevecca Nazarene University B, T
Union University B
University of Memphis B, M
University of Tennessee
   Chattanooga B
   Knoxville B, M, D
   Martin B
University of the South B
Vanderbilt University B, M, D

Texas
Abilene Christian University B, T
Angelo State University B, T
Austin College B
Baylor University B, M
Coastal Bend College A
College of the Mainland A
Dallas Baptist University B
Del Mar College A
El Paso Community College A
Galveston College A
Hardin-Simmons University B
Houston Baptist University B
Howard Payne University B, T
Huston-Tillotson College B
Lamar University B, M
LeTourneau University B
Lon Morris College A
McMurry University B, T
Midland College A
Midwestern State University B, M
Northeast Texas Community College A
Our Lady of the Lake University of San Antonio B
Palo Alto College A
Panola College A
Paris Junior College A
Prairie View A&M University B
Rice University B, M, D
St. Edward's University B, T
St. Mary's University B, M, T
St. Philip's College A
Sam Houston State University B, M
South Plains College A
Southern Methodist University B
Southwest Texas State University B, M, T
Southwestern University B, T
Stephen F. Austin State University B, T
Sul Ross State University B, M, T
Tarleton State University B, M, T
Texas A&M International University B, M, T
Texas A&M University
   Commerce B, M
   Corpus Christi B, T
   Kingsville B, M, T
Texas A&M University B, M, D
Texas Christian University B, T
Texas College B
Texas Lutheran University B
Texas Southern University B
Texas Tech University B, M, D
Texas Wesleyan University B, T
Texas Woman's University B, M, T
Trinity University B
University of Dallas B, T
University of Houston
   Clear Lake B
University of Houston B, M, D
University of Mary Hardin-Baylor B, T
University of North Texas B, M, D
University of St. Thomas B
University of Texas
   Arlington B, M, T
   Austin B, M, D
   Brownsville B
   Dallas B
   El Paso B, M
   Pan American B
   San Antonio B, M
   Tyler B
   of the Permian Basin B
University of the Incarnate Word B
Wayland Baptist University B
West Texas A&M University B, M, T
Western Texas College A

Utah
Brigham Young University B, M
Dixie State College of Utah A
Snow College A
Southern Utah University B
University of Utah B, M, D
Utah State University B, M
Weber State University B
Westminster College B

Vermont
College of St. Joseph in Vermont B
Johnson State College B
Marlboro College B
Middlebury College B
Norwich University B
St. Michael's College B
University of Vermont B, M

Virginia
Averett College B
Bridgewater College B
Christendom College B
Christopher Newport University B
College of William and Mary B
Emory & Henry College B
Ferrum College B
George Mason University B
Hampden-Sydney College B
Hampton University B
Hollins University B
James Madison University B, T
Liberty University B
Longwood College B, T
Lynchburg College B
Mary Baldwin College B
Mary Washington College B
Norfolk State University B
Old Dominion University B
Radford University B
Randolph-Macon College B
Randolph-Macon Woman's College B
Roanoke College B, T
St. Paul's College B
Sweet Briar College B
University of Richmond B
University of Virginia's College at Wise B, T
University of Virginia B, M, D
Virginia Commonwealth University B
Virginia Intermont College B
Virginia Polytechnic Institute and State University B, M
Virginia State University B
Virginia Union University B
Virginia Wesleyan College B
Washington and Lee University B

Washington
Central Washington University B
City University B
Eastern Washington University B, T
Evergreen State College B
Gonzaga University B
Lower Columbia College A
Pacific Lutheran University B
St. Martin's College B
Seattle Pacific University B, T
Seattle University B
University of Puget Sound B, T
University of Washington B, M, D
Washington State University B, M, D
Western Washington University B, M
Whitman College B
Whitworth College B, T

West Virginia
Bethany College B
Concord College B
Davis and Elkins College B
Fairmont State College B
Marshall University B, M
Potomac State College of West Virginia University A
Shepherd College B
University of Charleston B
West Liberty State College B
West Virginia State College B
West Virginia University B, M, D
West Virginia Wesleyan College B
Wheeling Jesuit University B

Wisconsin
Beloit College B
Carroll College B
Carthage College B
Lawrence University B, T
Marian College of Fond du Lac B
Marquette University B, M, T
Ripon College B
St. Norbert College B, T
University of Wisconsin
   Eau Claire B
   Green Bay B
   La Crosse B, T
   Madison B, M, D
   Milwaukee B, M, D
   Oshkosh B
   Parkside B
   Platteville B, T
   River Falls B, T
   Stevens Point B
   Superior B

Wyoming
Eastern Wyoming College A
Laramie County Community College A
Northwest College A
Sheridan College A
University of Wyoming B, M
Western Wyoming Community College A

Polymer chemistry

California
University of California
   Davis B

Connecticut
University of Connecticut M, D

Georgia
Georgia Institute of Technology B

Massachusetts
Harvard College B
Mount Holyoke College M
Simon's Rock College of Bard B
University of Massachusetts
   Lowell D

Minnesota
Winona State University B

Mississippi
University of Southern Mississippi B, M, D

New Jersey
Stevens Institute of Technology M, D

New York
City University of New York
   College of Staten Island D
Rochester Institute of Technology B
State University of New York
   College of Environmental Science and Forestry B, M, D

North Carolina
North Carolina State University M, D

North Dakota
North Dakota State University B, M, D

Ohio
University of Akron M, D

Pennsylvania
Carnegie Mellon University B
Philadelphia University B

Wisconsin
University of Wisconsin
   River Falls B

Polymer/plastics engineering

California
University of Southern California B

Connecticut
Naugatuck Valley Community-Technical College C
Quinebaug Valley Community College C, A

Hawaii
University of Hawaii
   Honolulu Community College C, A

Louisiana
Nunez Community College A

Massachusetts
Harvard College B
University of Massachusetts
   Amherst M, D
   Lowell B, M, D

Michigan
Eastern Michigan University M
Oakland Community College A
University of Michigan M, D
Wayne State University C

Minnesota
Winona State University B

Missouri
Crowder College A

New Jersey
Stevens Institute of Technology M, D

New York
Polytechnic University M
Rochester Institute of Technology B

North Carolina
Davidson County Community College C, A
Wilson Technical Community College A

Ohio
Case Western Reserve
 University B, M, D
Hocking Technical College A
Kent State University
 Ashtabula Regional Campus C, A
Terra Community College C, A
University of Akron M, D

Pennsylvania
Lehigh University M, D

Tennessee
University of Tennessee
 Knoxville M, D

Texas
Trinity Valley Community College A

Vermont
Vermont Technical College A

Washington
Western Washington University B

Portuguese

California
Chabot College A
University of California
 Berkeley B, D
 Los Angeles B, M
 Santa Barbara B, M

Connecticut
University of Connecticut B
Yale University B, M, D

District of Columbia
Georgetown University B

Florida
Florida International University B
Miami-Dade Community College A
University of Florida B

Illinois
University of Chicago B
University of Illinois
 Urbana-Champaign B, M

Indiana
Indiana University
 Bloomington B, M, D

Iowa
University of Iowa B, T

Louisiana
Dillard University B
Tulane University B, M, D

Massachusetts
Harvard College B
Harvard University D
Smith College B
University of Massachusetts
 Amherst B
 Dartmouth B

Minnesota
University of Minnesota
 Twin Cities B, M

New Jersey
Rutgers
 The State University of New Jersey:
  Douglass College B
 The State University of New Jersey:
  Livingston College B
 The State University of New Jersey:
  Rutgers College B
 The State University of New Jersey:
  University College New
  Brunswick B

New Mexico
University of New Mexico B, M

New York
Columbia University
 School of General Studies B
New York University B, M, D
United States Military Academy B

Ohio
Ohio State University
 Columbus Campus B, M, D

Pennsylvania
University of Pennsylvania B

Rhode Island
Brown University B, M, D

Tennessee
University of Tennessee
 Knoxville B
Vanderbilt University D

Texas
University of Texas
 Austin B, M, D

Utah
Brigham Young University B, M

Wisconsin
University of Wisconsin
 Madison B, M, D

Poultry science

Alabama
Auburn University B, M, D
Northwest-Shoals Community College C
Tuskegee University B, M

Arkansas
University of Arkansas B, M, D

California
California Polytechnic State University:
 San Luis Obispo B
Modesto Junior College A

Delaware
Delaware Technical and Community
 College
  Owens Campus C, A

Florida
University of Florida M

Georgia
Abraham Baldwin Agricultural
 College A
University of Georgia B, M, D

Idaho
University of Idaho B

Maryland
University of Maryland
 College Park M, D

Minnesota
Ridgewater College: A Community and
 Technical College C

Mississippi
Mississippi State University B, M
Northwest Mississippi Community
 College A

Missouri
College of the Ozarks B
Crowder College A

North Carolina
James Sprunt Community College A
North Carolina State University B, M
Wayne Community College A

Ohio
Ohio State University
 Columbus Campus M, D

Oklahoma
Northeastern Oklahoma Agricultural and
 Mechanical College A

Pennsylvania
Penn State
 University Park C

South Carolina
Clemson University B

Texas
Stephen F. Austin State University B
Texas A&M University B, M, D

Utah
Snow College A

Power/electrical transmission

Alabama
Bessemer State Technical College C
Bevill State Community College A
John M. Patterson State Technical
 College C
Lawson State Community College C
Northwest-Shoals Community College C
Shelton State Community College C, A

Arkansas
Phillips Community College of the
 University of Arkansas C

California
Bakersfield College A
Chabot College A
Coastline Community College C
College of the Redwoods C
Foothill College C
Fresno City College C, A
Los Angeles Trade and Technical
 College A
Orange Coast College C, A
Palomar College C, A
San Diego City College C, A
San Joaquin Delta College C, A
San Jose City College A
Santa Ana College C, A

Colorado
Community College of Aurora A
Mesa State College C
Red Rocks Community College C, A

Connecticut
Central Connecticut State University B

Georgia
Chattahoochee Technical Institute C
Clayton College and State University A
Darton College A

Hawaii
University of Hawaii
 Hawaii Community College C, A

Idaho
Boise State University C

Illinois
Black Hawk College A
Illinois Eastern Community Colleges
 Lincoln Trail College C
Kaskaskia College C
Kishwaukee College C
Lincoln Land Community College C
Parkland College C
Southwestern Illinois College C, A

Indiana
Oakland City University C

Iowa
Northeast Iowa Community College A
Western Iowa Tech Community
 College C, A

Kansas
Allen County Community College C
Johnson County Community
 College C, A

Louisiana
Nunez Community College C

Maine
Eastern Maine Technical College A
Southern Maine Technical College A

Massachusetts
Franklin Institute of Boston C

Michigan
Alpena Community College C
Lansing Community College A
Macomb Community College C
Northern Michigan University A

Minnesota
St. Paul Technical College C

Mississippi
Hinds Community College C
Mississippi Delta Community College C
Mississippi Gulf Coast Community
 College
  Perkinston C, A

Montana
Miles Community College A

Nebraska
Central Community College C, A
Metropolitan Community College C, A
Northeast Community College A

New Hampshire
New Hampshire Community Technical
 College
  Berlin A
  Laconia C, A

New Mexico
Albuquerque Technical-Vocational
 Institute C

New York
Erie Community College
 North Campus A
Mohawk Valley Community College C
State University of New York
 College of Technology at
 Delhi C, A

North Carolina
Durham Technical Community
 College C
James Sprunt Community College C
Martin Community College C
Mayland Community College C
Randolph Community College C
Richmond Community College C
Wake Technical Community
 College C, A

North Dakota
Bismarck State College C, A

Ohio
Jefferson Community College A
Ohio State University
 Agricultural Technical Institute A

Pennsylvania
Delaware County Community College C
Penn State
 University Park C
Pennsylvania College of Technology C

South Carolina
Aiken Technical College C
Midlands Technical College C
Technical College of the Lowcountry C

South Dakota
Western Dakota Technical Institute C, A

Power/electrical transmission

Tennessee
Northeast State Technical Community College *A*
Walters State Community College *A*

Texas
Amarillo College *C, A*
Brazosport College *C, A*
Houston Community College System *C*
North Lake College *A*
Texas State Technical College
 Waco *A*

Utah
Salt Lake Community College *A*

Virginia
Piedmont Virginia Community College *C*
Southside Virginia Community College *C*
Tidewater Community College *C*

Washington
Olympic College *C, A*
Spokane Community College *A*

Wisconsin
Chippewa Valley Technical College *C*
Milwaukee Area Technical College *C*
Northeast Wisconsin Technical College *C*
Western Wisconsin Technical College *C*

Prearchitecture

Alabama
Central Alabama Community College *A*

Arizona
University of Arizona *B*

California
Bakersfield College *A*
Canada College *A*
Cerritos Community College *A*
Chabot College *A*
City College of San Francisco *A*
College of Marin: Kentfield *A*
College of San Mateo *A*
College of the Desert *A*
College of the Redwoods *C*
College of the Sequoias *A*
Cuyamaca College *A*
Diablo Valley College *A*
Fresno City College *C, A*
Golden West College *A*
Los Angeles Harbor College *C, A*
Los Angeles Trade and Technical College *C, A*
Orange Coast College *C, A*
San Diego Mesa College *A*
San Joaquin Delta College *C, A*
Santa Monica College *C, A*
Southwestern College *C, A*
Ventura College *A*
West Valley College *A*

Connecticut
Trinity College *B*

Florida
Chipola Junior College *A*
Gulf Coast Community College *A*
Hillsborough Community College *A*
Manatee Community College *A*
Miami-Dade Community College *A*

Hawaii
University of Hawaii
 Honolulu Community College *A*

Illinois
City Colleges of Chicago
 Harold Washington College *A*
 Kennedy-King College *A*
 Olive-Harvey College *A*
Lake Land College *A*

Oakton Community College *C, A*
Rend Lake College *C, A*
Sauk Valley Community College *A*

Iowa
Coe College *B*
Marshalltown Community College *A*

Kansas
Central Christian College *A*
Coffeyville Community College *A*
Dodge City Community College *A*
Independence Community College *C, A*

Kentucky
Lexington Community College *A*

Maryland
Anne Arundel Community College *A*
Montgomery College
 Rockville Campus *A*

Michigan
Calvin College *B*
Grand Rapids Community College *A*
North Central Michigan College *C*
Northern Michigan University *B*
Western Michigan University *B*

Minnesota
Gustavus Adolphus College *B*
St. Cloud Technical College *C, A*

Mississippi
Copiah-Lincoln Community College *A*
Hinds Community College *A*
Mississippi Delta Community College *A*
Mississippi Gulf Coast Community College
 Jefferson Davis Campus *A*
 Perkinston *A*
Northwest Mississippi Community College *A*

Missouri
East Central College *A*
St. Louis Community College
 St. Louis Community College at Meramec *A*
Washington University *B*

Nebraska
Southeast Community College
 Milford Campus *A*

New Jersey
Mercer County Community College *A*

New Mexico
New Mexico Junior College *A*

New York
City University of New York
 College of Staten Island *A*
Fordham University *C*
Institute of Design and Construction *A*
Orange County Community College *A*

North Carolina
Methodist College *B*
Pitt Community College *A*
Roanoke-Chowan Community College *A*
Sandhills Community College *A*

North Dakota
Dickinson State University *A*

Ohio
Case Western Reserve University *B*
Columbus State Community College *A*
Edison State Community College *A*
Sinclair Community College *A*

Oklahoma
Northeastern Oklahoma Agricultural and Mechanical College *A*
University of Oklahoma *B*

Oregon
Central Oregon Community College *A*

Pennsylvania
Butler County Community College *A*
Community College of Beaver County *A*
Harrisburg Area Community College *A*
University of Pennsylvania *B*

Rhode Island
New England Institute of Technology *A, B*

Tennessee
Union University *B*

Texas
Abilene Christian University *A*
Amarillo College *A*
El Paso Community College *A*
Kilgore College *A*
Lon Morris College *A*
Midland College *A*
Panola College *A*
San Antonio College *A*
Weatherford College *A*

Utah
Salt Lake Community College *A*

Virginia
Eastern Shore Community College *C*

Washington
Lower Columbia College *A*
Spokane Falls Community College *C, A*

Wisconsin
University of Wisconsin
 Oshkosh *B*

Precision metal work

Alabama
Bessemer State Technical College *C*
Bevill State Community College *A*
Community College of the Air Force *A*
Gadsden State Community College *C, A*
George C. Wallace State Community College
 Dothan *C, A*
 Selma *A*
Harry M. Ayers State Technical College *A*
J. F. Drake State Technical College *C, A*
Jefferson Davis Community College *C*
John M. Patterson State Technical College *C, A*
Northwest-Shoals Community College *C, A*
Reid State Technical College *C*
Shelton State Community College *C, A*
Southern Union State Community College *A*

Alaska
University of Alaska
 Anchorage *C, A*
 Southeast *C*

Arizona
Arizona Western College *A*
Cochise College *A*
Eastern Arizona College *C, A*
Gateway Community College *C, A*
Northland Pioneer College *C*
Pima Community College *C, A*

Arkansas
North Arkansas College *C*
Phillips Community College of the University of Arkansas *A*
Westark College *C, A*

California
Allan Hancock College *C, A*
American River College *A*
Bakersfield College *A*
Butte College *C, A*
Cerritos Community College *C, A*
Chabot College *A*

Citrus College *C, A*
College of San Mateo *C, A*
College of the Canyons *C*
College of the Desert *C*
College of the Redwoods *C, A*
College of the Sequoias *A*
College of the Siskiyous *A*
Compton Community College *A*
Diablo Valley College *A*
Evergreen Valley College *A*
Gavilan Community College *A*
Glendale Community College *C*
Long Beach City College *C, A*
Los Angeles Pierce College *C, A*
Los Angeles Trade and Technical College *A*
Los Angeles Valley College *C*
Mendocino College *C, A*
Merced College *C, A*
Mount San Antonio College *C, A*
Napa Valley College *A*
Orange Coast College *C*
Palomar College *C, A*
Pasadena City College *C, A*
Porterville College *C, A*
Rio Hondo College *A*
Riverside Community College *C, A*
Sacramento City College *C, A*
San Bernardino Valley College *C, A*
San Diego City College *C, A*
San Joaquin Delta College *C, A*
Santa Monica College *A*
Santa Rosa Junior College *C, A*
Shasta College *A*
Sierra College *A*
Solano Community College *C, A*
University of California
 Santa Cruz *C, B*
Ventura College *C, A*
West Hills Community College *C, A*

Colorado
Aims Community College *C, A*
Arapahoe Community College *C*
Community College of Aurora *A*
Community College of Denver *C*
Front Range Community College *C, A*
Mesa State College *C, A*
Pikes Peak Community College *C, A*
Pueblo Community College *C, A*

Florida
Brevard Community College *C*
Chipola Junior College *C*
South Florida Community College *C*

Georgia
Athens Area Technical Institute *C*
Coastal Georgia Community College *C*
Dalton State College *C*
Darton College *A*
DeKalb Technical Institute *C*
Waycross College *A*

Hawaii
University of Hawaii
 Maui Community College *A*

Idaho
Boise State University *C, A*
Eastern Idaho Technical College *C, A*
Idaho State University *C, A*
North Idaho College *C, A*
Ricks College *A*

Illinois
Black Hawk College *A*
College of DuPage *C*
College of Lake County *C, A*
Elgin Community College *C, A*
Illinois Eastern Community Colleges
 Lincoln Trail College *C*
 Olney Central College *C, A*
 Wabash Valley College *C, A*
Joliet Junior College *C*
Kankakee Community College *C, A*
Kaskaskia College *C, A*

Kishwaukee College C, A
Lincoln Land Community College C
McHenry County College C
Moraine Valley Community College C
Prairie State College C, A
Rend Lake College A
Richland Community College A
Shawnee Community College C
Southeastern Illinois College C, A
Southern Illinois University
    Carbondale A
Southwestern Illinois College C, A
Triton College C, A
Waubonsee Community College C, A
William Rainey Harper College C

Indiana
Ivy Tech State College
    Central Indiana C, A
    Lafayette C, A
    Northcentral C
    Northeast C, A
    Northwest C, A
    Southwest C, A
    Wabash Valley C, A
Oakland City University C, A
Vincennes University A

Iowa
Clinton Community College A
Des Moines Area Community College C
Hawkeye Community College A
Iowa Central Community College C
Iowa Lakes Community College C
Iowa Western Community College A
Kirkwood Community College C, A
Muscatine Community College A
North Iowa Area Community College A
Northeast Iowa Community College C
Scott Community College A
Southeastern Community College
    North Campus C, A
Western Iowa Tech Community
    College C, A

Kansas
Barton County Community College C
Cowley County Community
    College C, A
Hutchinson Community College C, A
Johnson County Community
    College C, A

Louisiana
Delgado Community College C
Nunez Community College C

Maine
Central Maine Technical College C, A
Eastern Maine Technical College C, A
Southern Maine Technical College C, A
Washington County Technical College C

Massachusetts
Northern Essex Community College A

Michigan
Bay de Noc Community College A
Delta College A
Ferris State University A
Glen Oaks Community College C
Grand Rapids Community College C, A
Henry Ford Community College C
Kalamazoo Valley Community
    College C, A
Kellogg Community College C, A
Kirtland Community College C, A
Lansing Community College A
Macomb Community College C, A
Mid Michigan Community College A
Monroe County Community
    College C, A
Muskegon Community College C, A
Oakland Community College C, A
Schoolcraft College C
Southwestern Michigan College A
West Shore Community College C, A

Minnesota
Alexandria Technical College C
Dakota County Technical College C
Dunwoody Institute A
Hennepin Technical College C, A
Lake Superior College: A Community
    and Technical College C
Mesabi Range Community and Technical
    College A
Minnesota State College - Southeast
    Technical C
St. Cloud Technical College C
St. Paul Technical College C

Mississippi
East Mississippi Community College C
Itawamba Community College C
Meridian Community College A
Mississippi Delta Community
    College C, A
Mississippi Gulf Coast Community
    College
        Perkinston C
Northeast Mississippi Community
    College C
Northwest Mississippi Community
    College C

Missouri
Crowder College C
Jefferson College C, A
Maple Woods Community College A
Ozarks Technical Community College A
Ranken Technical College A
State Fair Community College C

Montana
Montana State University
    Billings C
    Northern A

Nebraska
Central Community College C, A
Metropolitan Community College C, A
Mid Plains Community College Area C
Southeast Community College
    Lincoln Campus C, A

Nevada
Community College of Southern
    Nevada A
Western Nevada Community
    College C, A

New Hampshire
New Hampshire Community Technical
    College
        Nashua C, A

New Jersey
Passaic County Community
    College C, A

New Mexico
Albuquerque Technical-Vocational
    Institute C
Eastern New Mexico University
    Roswell Campus C
San Juan College C, A

New York
Corning Community College C
Erie Community College
    North Campus C
Hudson Valley Community College A
Mohawk Valley Community
    College C, A
Rochester Institute of
    Technology A, B, M
Westchester Community College C

North Carolina
Asheville Buncombe Technical
    Community College C, A
Beaufort County Community College C
Blue Ridge Community College C, A
Cape Fear Community College A
Craven Community College C, A
Durham Technical Community
    College C, A
Forsyth Technical Community College C
Halifax Community College A
Haywood Community College C, A
Johnston Community College C, A
Nash Community College C
Piedmont Community College C
Pitt Community College C, A
Randolph Community College C, A
Richmond Community College C
Roanoke-Chowan Community
    College C
South Piedmont Community
    College C
Tri-County Community College C
Wake Technical Community
    College C, A
Wayne Community College A
Wilson Technical Community
    College C, A

North Dakota
Bismarck State College C, A
Lake Region State College C
North Dakota State College of
    Science C, A

Ohio
Lakeland Community College C
North Central State College A
Northwest State Community
    College C, A
Terra Community College C, A

Oklahoma
Northeastern Oklahoma Agricultural and
    Mechanical College A
Tulsa Community College A
Western Oklahoma State College A

Oregon
Chemeketa Community College A
Clackamas Community College C, A
Lane Community College C, A
Linn-Benton Community College C, A
Mount Hood Community College C, A
Portland Community College A

Pennsylvania
Community College of Allegheny
    County C, A
Community College of Beaver County A
Delaware County Community College C
Johnson Technical Institute A
Northampton County Area Community
    College C
Pennsylvania College of
    Technology C, A, B
Reading Area Community College C, A
Triangle Tech
    DuBois Campus A
Westmoreland County Community
    College C, A
Williamson Free School of Mechanical
    Trades C, A

South Carolina
Aiken Technical College C, A
Central Carolina Technical College C
Chesterfield-Marlboro Technical
    College C, A
Denmark Technical College C
Florence-Darlington Technical
    College C, A
Greenville Technical College C, A
Midlands Technical College C, A
Orangeburg-Calhoun Technical
    College C, A
Piedmont Technical College C, A
Spartanburg Technical College A
Trident Technical College C, A
York Technical College C, A

South Dakota
Western Dakota Technical Institute C

Tennessee
Northeast State Technical Community
    College C, A

Texas
Amarillo College C, A
Austin Community College C, A
Brazosport College C, A
Coastal Bend College A
Del Mar College C, A
Eastfield College A
El Paso Community College C
Grayson County College C, A
Hill College C, A
Houston Community College System C
Lee College A
Navarro College A
North Central Texas College A
Northeast Texas Community College C
Odessa College C, A
Panola College C
Paris Junior College A
St. Philip's College C, A
San Jacinto College
    North C, A
Tarrant County College C, A
Texas State Technical College
    Harlingen C, A
    Sweetwater C
    Waco C, A
Vernon Regional Junior College C

Utah
College of Eastern Utah C, A
Salt Lake Community College C, A
Utah State University B
Utah Valley State College C, A
Weber State University A

Virginia
Dabney S. Lancaster Community
    College C
J. Sargeant Reynolds Community
    College C
John Tyler Community College C
New River Community College A
Northern Virginia Community College C
Virginia Highlands Community
    College C
Wytheville Community College C, A

Washington
Big Bend Community College A
Clark College C, A
Everett Community College A
Grays Harbor College A
Green River Community College C, A
Lake Washington Technical College C, A
Renton Technical College C, A
Shoreline Community College C, A
South Seattle Community College C, A
Spokane Community College C, A
Spokane Falls Community College C
Walla Walla Community College C, A

West Virginia
Southern West Virginia Community and
    Technical College C, A
West Virginia University
    Parkersburg C, A

Wisconsin
Gateway Technical College C
Madison Area Technical College C, A
Milwaukee Area Technical College C, A
Moraine Park Technical College C
Nicolet Area Technical College C
Northeast Wisconsin Technical
    College C
Southwest Wisconsin Technical
    College C
Western Wisconsin Technical College C
Wisconsin Indianhead Technical
    College C

Wyoming
Casper College A

Precision metal work

Central Wyoming College C, A
Eastern Wyoming College C, A
Northwest College C
Sheridan College C, A

Precision production trades

Alabama
J. F. Drake State Technical College C, A
Northwest-Shoals Community College C
Shelton State Community College C, A
Wallace State Community College at Hanceville C, A

Arkansas
Southern Arkansas University Tech C, A
Westark College C

California
Cerro Coso Community College C, A
College of San Mateo C, A
Los Angeles Valley College C
Mount San Antonio College C, A
Pacific Union College A, B
Palo Verde College C

Colorado
Red Rocks Community College A
Trinidad State Junior College C, A

Florida
Brevard Community College C

Georgia
Augusta State University A
Columbus Technical Institute C

Illinois
Black Hawk College C, A
College of DuPage C
College of Lake County C
Moraine Valley Community College C
Sauk Valley Community College C
Southwestern Illinois College C, A
William Rainey Harper College C

Indiana
Ivy Tech State College Northcentral A
Vincennes University A

Iowa
Des Moines Area Community College C, A
North Iowa Area Community College A
Southeastern Community College North Campus C, A

Kansas
Kansas City Kansas Community College C, A

Maine
Central Maine Technical College C, A
Eastern Maine Technical College C, A

Michigan
Glen Oaks Community College C
Gogebic Community College A
Grand Rapids Community College C
Lansing Community College A
Macomb Community College C, A
Montcalm Community College C
Muskegon Community College C
North Central Michigan College C, A
Oakland Community College C
St. Clair County Community College C, A
Washtenaw Community College C, A
West Shore Community College A

Minnesota
Hennepin Technical College C, A
Pine Technical College C, A

Mississippi
East Central Community College A

Itawamba Community College C
Meridian Community College C
Mississippi Delta Community College C, A
Mississippi Gulf Coast Community College
  Jackson County Campus A
  Perkinston C
Northeast Mississippi Community College C

Missouri
East Central College C, A
Mineral Area College A
State Fair Community College A

Nebraska
Mid Plains Community College Area C
Southeast Community College
  Lincoln Campus C
  Milford Campus A

New Mexico
Dona Ana Branch Community College of New Mexico State University A
Northern New Mexico Community College C, A

New York
Corning Community College A

North Carolina
Forsyth Technical Community College C
Haywood Community College C

Oregon
Portland Community College C, A

Pennsylvania
Butler County Community College A
Community College of Allegheny County C, A
Williamson Free School of Mechanical Trades A

South Carolina
Horry-Georgetown Technical College A
Tri-County Technical College C, A

Texas
Grayson County College C, A
North Central Texas College A
Texas State Technical College Harlingen C, A

Utah
Salt Lake Community College C

Virginia
Patrick Henry Community College A
Thomas Nelson Community College C

Washington
Renton Technical College C, A
Tacoma Community College C

Wisconsin
Blackhawk Technical College C
Chippewa Valley Technical College C
Lakeshore Technical College C
Nicolet Area Technical College C
Northeast Wisconsin Technical College A

Wyoming
Laramie County Community College A

Predentistry

Alabama
Calhoun Community College A
Faulkner University B
Huntingdon College B
James H. Faulkner State Community College A
Northeast Alabama Community College A
Northwest-Shoals Community College A
Spring Hill College B

University of Alabama B

Arizona
Grand Canyon University B
Northern Arizona University B

Arkansas
Harding University B
Hendrix College B
John Brown University B
Ouachita Baptist University B
University of Central Arkansas B
Westark College A

California
Azusa Pacific University B
Bakersfield College A
California Lutheran University B
California State University Chico B
Chabot College A
Chapman University B
City College of San Francisco A
Claremont McKenna College B
College of Notre Dame B
College of the Siskiyous A
Crafton Hills College C
Cypress College A
Foothill College A
Golden West College A
Marymount College A
Monterey Peninsula College A
Mount St. Mary's College B
Pacific Union College C
Riverside Community College A
University of Southern California B
Ventura College A
West Hills Community College A
Westmont College B
Whittier College B

Colorado
Adams State College B
Fort Lewis College B
Lamar Community College A
Otero Junior College A
Regis University B
Western State College of Colorado B

Connecticut
Quinnipiac University B
Sacred Heart University C
Southern Connecticut State University B
Trinity College B
University of Hartford B
University of New Haven B

Delaware
University of Delaware B

Florida
Barry University B
Broward Community College A
Eckerd College B
Edison Community College A
Florida State University B
Gulf Coast Community College A
Indian River Community College A
Jacksonville University B
Miami-Dade Community College A
Pensacola Junior College A
Santa Fe Community College A
University of Central Florida B
University of Miami B
University of Tampa B

Georgia
Abraham Baldwin Agricultural College A
Andrew College A
Columbus State University B
Darton College A
Georgia Institute of Technology B
Georgia Perimeter College A
Kennesaw State University B
LaGrange College B
Middle Georgia College A
Morehouse College B

Oglethorpe University B
Piedmont College B
South Georgia College A
University of Georgia B
Young Harris College A

Idaho
Boise State University B
College of Southern Idaho A
North Idaho College A
Northwest Nazarene University B
Ricks College A
University of Idaho B

Illinois
Augustana College B
Black Hawk College East Campus A
Blackburn College B
City Colleges of Chicago
  Harold Washington College A
  Kennedy-King College A
De Paul University B
Elmhurst College B
Greenville College B
Judson College B
Kankakee Community College A
Kishwaukee College A
Lewis and Clark Community College A
Lincoln Land Community College A
McKendree College B
Millikin University B
North Park University B
Rend Lake College A
Rockford College B
Roosevelt University B
Sauk Valley Community College A
Springfield College in Illinois A
University of Illinois Chicago B
University of St. Francis B

Indiana
Bethel College B
Goshen College B
Grace College B
Indiana State University B
Indiana University--Purdue University
  Indiana University-Purdue University Fort Wayne B
Indiana Wesleyan University B
Manchester College B
St. Joseph's College B
St. Mary-of-the-Woods College B
University of Evansville B
University of Indianapolis B
University of St. Francis B
Valparaiso University B
Vincennes University A

Iowa
Buena Vista University B
Clarke College B
Coe College B
Cornell College B
Dordt College B
Iowa Wesleyan College B
Kirkwood Community College A
Luther College B
Marshalltown Community College A
Morningside College B
Northwestern College B
Simpson College B
University of Iowa B
Upper Iowa University B
Waldorf College A

Kansas
Coffeyville Community College A
Kansas City Kansas Community College A
Kansas State University B
McPherson College B
Pittsburg State University B
Pratt Community College A
Tabor College B
Washburn University of Topeka B

Predentistry

Kentucky
Campbellsville University B
Centre College B
Cumberland College B
Murray State University B
Thomas More College B
Union College B

Louisiana
Centenary College of Louisiana B
Dillard University B
Nicholls State University B
University of Louisiana at Monroe B

Maine
St. Joseph's College B
University of Maine
    Fort Kent B
University of Southern Maine B

Maryland
Columbia Union College B
Community College of Baltimore County
    Catonsville A
Coppin State College B
Frostburg State College B
Howard Community College A
Montgomery College
    Germantown Campus A
    Rockville Campus A
    Takoma Park Campus A
Morgan State University B
Mount St. Mary's College B
University of Maryland
    Baltimore County B
    Eastern Shore B
Villa Julie College B

Massachusetts
American International College B
Cape Cod Community College A
Eastern Nazarene College B
Elms College B
Framingham State College B
Hampshire College B
Simmons College B
Springfield College B
Springfield Technical Community
    College A
Stonehill College B
University of Massachusetts
    Amherst B
Worcester Polytechnic Institute B

Michigan
Adrian College B
Albion College B
Alma College B
Calvin College B
Cornerstone College and Grand Rapids
    Baptist Seminary B
Ferris State University A
Grand Valley State University B
Hillsdale College B
Kalamazoo College B
Kirtland Community College A
Lansing Community College A
Michigan Technological University B
Northern Michigan University B
Olivet College B
Schoolcraft College A
Siena Heights University A, B
University of Detroit Mercy B
Western Michigan University B

Minnesota
College of St. Benedict B
College of St. Catherine: St. Paul
    Campus B
Concordia College: Moorhead B
Gustavus Adolphus College B
Hamline University B
Minnesota State University, Mankato B
Moorhead State University B
St. Cloud State University B
St. John's University B
St. Mary's University of Minnesota B
St. Olaf College B
University of Minnesota
    Duluth B
    Twin Cities B
Winona State University B

Mississippi
Blue Mountain College B
Coahoma Community College A
East Central Community College A
Holmes Community College A
Itawamba Community College A
Jackson State University B
Mary Holmes College A
Mississippi Delta Community College A
Mississippi Gulf Coast Community
    College
    Jefferson Davis Campus A
Rust College B

Missouri
Central Methodist College B
East Central College A
Evangel University B
Lindenwood University B
Maryville University of Saint Louis B
Missouri Southern State College A
St. Louis Community College
    St. Louis Community College at
        Florissant Valley A
Stephens College B
Truman State University B
University of Missouri
    St. Louis B
Washington University B

Montana
Montana Tech of the University of
    Montana B
University of Great Falls B
University of Montana-Missoula B

Nebraska
College of Saint Mary B
Dana College B
Hastings College B
Mid Plains Community College Area A
Midland Lutheran College B
Northeast Community College A
University of Nebraska
    Lincoln B

New Hampshire
Franklin Pierce College B
Rivier College B
St. Anselm College B
University of New Hampshire B

New Jersey
Bloomfield College B
Georgian Court College B
Rowan University B
Rutgers
    The State University of New Jersey:
        Camden College of Arts and
        Sciences B
    The State University of New Jersey:
        Cook College B
    The State University of New Jersey:
        Douglass College B
    The State University of New Jersey:
        Livingston College B
    The State University of New Jersey:
        Newark College of Arts and
        Sciences B
    The State University of New Jersey:
        Rutgers College B
    The State University of New Jersey:
        University College Camden B
    The State University of New Jersey:
        University College New
        Brunswick B
Stevens Institute of Technology B
Sussex County Community College A

New Mexico
New Mexico Junior College A

New York
Alfred University B
Bard College B
City University of New York
    Brooklyn College B
    College of Staten Island B
    Hunter College B
    Queens College B
Colgate University B
Elmira College B
Fordham University B
Hobart and William Smith Colleges B
Houghton College B
Ithaca College B
Le Moyne College B
Long Island University
    Brooklyn Campus B
Manhattan College B
Marist College B
Molloy College B
New York University B
Rensselaer Polytechnic Institute B
Rochester Institute of Technology B
St. Francis College B
St. John Fisher College B
St. Thomas Aquinas College B
Sarah Lawrence College B
St. Joseph's College
    St. Joseph's College: Suffolk
        Campus B
State University of New York
    College at Brockport B
    College at Geneseo B
    College of Environmental Science
        and Forestry B
    New Paltz B
Syracuse University B
Touro College B
Wagner College B
Wells College B

North Carolina
Appalachian State University B
Barton College B
Belmont Abbey College B
Brevard College A, B
Campbell University B
Catawba College B
Chowan College B
Elon College B
Lees-McRae College B
Mars Hill College B
Meredith College B
Methodist College B
Mitchell Community College A
North Carolina State University B
Pfeiffer University B
St. Andrews Presbyterian College B
Sandhills Community College A
Wingate University B

North Dakota
Dickinson State University B
Mayville State University B
Valley City State University B

Ohio
Ashland University B
Capital University B
Defiance College B
Heidelberg College B
John Carroll University B
Kent State University
    Stark Campus B
Kent State University B
Miami University
    Oxford Campus B
Mount Vernon Nazarene College B
Muskingum College B
Ohio University B
Ohio Wesleyan University B
Otterbein College B
University of Akron B
University of Cincinnati
    Raymond Walters College A
University of Cincinnati B
University of Dayton B
University of Toledo B
Walsh University B
Wittenberg University B
Youngstown State University B

Oklahoma
Connors State College A
East Central University B
Eastern Oklahoma State College A
Northeastern Oklahoma Agricultural and
    Mechanical College A
Oklahoma Christian University of
    Science and Arts B
Oklahoma City University B
Oklahoma State University B
Redlands Community College A

Oregon
Central Oregon Community College A
Chemeketa Community College A
Concordia University B
Eastern Oregon University B
Southern Oregon University B
University of Portland B
Western Baptist College B
Willamette University B

Pennsylvania
Allentown College of St. Francis de
    Sales B
Alvernia College B
California University of Pennsylvania B
College Misericordia B
Elizabethtown College B
Gannon University B
Gettysburg College B
Grove City College B
Holy Family College B
Immaculata College B
Juniata College B
La Salle University B
Lehigh University B
Lock Haven University of
    Pennsylvania B
Mansfield University of Pennsylvania B
Mercyhurst College B
Muhlenberg College B
Reading Area Community College A
Seton Hill College B
Susquehanna University B
University of Pittsburgh
    Bradford B
    Greensburg B
    Johnstown B
Ursinus College B
Villanova University B
Waynesburg College B
Westminster College B
Widener University B
Wilkes University B
York College of Pennsylvania B

Puerto Rico
University of Puerto Rico
    Arecibo Campus T
    Ponce University College A

Rhode Island
Rhode Island College B
Salve Regina University B

South Carolina
Anderson College A
Charleston Southern University B
Clemson University B
Coker College B
College of Charleston B
Erskine College B
Furman University B
North Greenville College B
Spartanburg Technical College A
Wofford College C

South Dakota
Augustana College B
Dakota State University B
Dakota Wesleyan University B

Predentistry

South Dakota School of Mines and Technology *B*

Tennessee
Carson-Newman College *B*
Columbia State Community College *A*
Cumberland University *B*
Freed-Hardeman University *B*
Hiwassee College *A*
Lambuth University *B*
Lincoln Memorial University *B*
Maryville College *B*
Tennessee Technological University *B*
Tennessee Wesleyan College *B*
Union University *B*
University of Tennessee
    Knoxville *B*
    Martin *B*
Walters State Community College *A*

Texas
Abilene Christian University *B*
Amarillo College *A*
Angelina College *A*
Baylor University *B*
Coastal Bend College *A*
Concordia University at Austin *B*
Del Mar College *A*
El Paso Community College *A*
Galveston College *A*
Grayson County College *A*
Howard College *A*
LeTourneau University *B*
Lon Morris College *A*
McMurry University *B*
Midland College *A*
Midwestern State University *B*
Navarro College *A*
Panola College *A*
Paris Junior College *A*
St. Edward's University *B*
St. Philip's College *A*
San Antonio College *A*
South Plains College *A*
Texas A&M University
    Commerce *B*
Texas A&M University *B*
Texas Christian University *B*
Texas Wesleyan University *B*
Trinity Valley Community College *A*
Tyler Junior College *A*
Western Texas College *A*

Utah
Brigham Young University *B*
Dixie State College of Utah *A*
Snow College *A*
University of Utah *B*

Vermont
Castleton State College *B*

Virginia
Averett College *B*
Longwood College *B*
Mountain Empire Community College *A*
Virginia Commonwealth University *B*
Virginia Intermont College *B*
Virginia Wesleyan College *B*

Washington
Centralia College *A*
Eastern Washington University *B*
Everett Community College *A*
Highline Community College *A*
Lower Columbia College *A*
St. Martin's College *B*
Seattle Pacific University *B*
Washington State University *B*
Western Washington University *B*

West Virginia
Alderson-Broaddus College *B*
Concord College *B*
Davis and Elkins College *B*
Marshall University *B*
Potomac State College of West Virginia University *A*
West Virginia Wesleyan College *B*

Wisconsin
Cardinal Stritch University *B*
Lawrence University *B*
Marian College of Fond du Lac *B*
Mount Mary College *B*
Northland College *B*
Ripon College *B*
St. Norbert College *B*
University of Wisconsin
    Madison *B*
    Milwaukee *B*
    Oshkosh *B*
    Parkside *B*
Viterbo University *B*

Wyoming
Casper College *A*
Eastern Wyoming College *A*
Northwest College *A*
Western Wyoming Community College *A*

Preengineering

Alabama
George C. Wallace State Community College
    Selma *A*
Huntingdon College *B*
Northeast Alabama Community College *A*
Northwest-Shoals Community College *A*
Spring Hill College *B*

Arizona
Cochise College *A*
Dine College *A*
South Mountain Community College *C, A*

California
California Baptist University *B*
Chapman University *B*
City College of San Francisco *A*
College of the Canyons *A*
College of the Siskiyous *A*
Crafton Hills College *C*
Las Positas College *A*
MiraCosta College *A*

Colorado
Adams State College *A*
Fort Lewis College *A*
Lamar Community College *A*
Red Rocks Community College *A*
University of Southern Colorado *B*

Connecticut
Asnuntuck Community-Technical College *A*
Quinebaug Valley Community College *A*
University of New Haven *B*

Delaware
Delaware State University *B*

District of Columbia
George Washington University *B*

Florida
Barry University *B*
Indian River Community College *A*
Jacksonville University *B*
Polk Community College *A*
Rollins College *B*
Valencia Community College *A*

Georgia
Columbus State University *B*
Darton College *A*
LaGrange College *B*
Oglethorpe University *B*
South Georgia College *A*
State University of West Georgia *B*
Valdosta State University *B*
Waycross College *A*
Wesleyan College *B*

Hawaii
University of Hawaii
    Honolulu Community College *A*

Idaho
Albertson College of Idaho *B*
Lewis-Clark State College *B*

Illinois
Augustana College *B*
City Colleges of Chicago
    Harold Washington College *A*
    Kennedy-King College *A*
John A. Logan College *A*
Kishwaukee College *A*
Lewis and Clark Community College *A*
Lincoln Land Community College *A*
Millikin University *B*
Rockford College *B*
St. Xavier University *B*
Southwestern Ilinois College *A*
Springfield College in Illinois *A*
Wheaton College *B*

Indiana
DePauw University *B*
Goshen College *B*
St. Joseph's College *B*
Vincennes University *A*

Iowa
Briar Cliff College *A*
Buena Vista University *B*
Clarke College *B*
Coe College *B*
Luther College *B*
Simpson College *B*

Kansas
Butler County Community College *A*

Kentucky
Campbellsville University *B*
Eastern Kentucky University *A*
Institute of Electronic Technology *A*
Kentucky State University *B*
Murray State University *B*
Thomas More College *B*

Louisiana
Dillard University *B*
Loyola University New Orleans *B*
Nicholls State University *A*

Maryland
Frostburg State University *B*

Massachusetts
Framingham State College *C*
North Shore Community College *A*
Springfield Technical Community College *A*

Michigan
Adrian College *B*
Albion College *B*
Alma College *B*
Bay de Noc Community College *A*
Kalamazoo Valley Community College *A*
Northern Michigan University *B*
Oakland Community College *A*
Siena Heights University *A*
Suomi College *A*

Minnesota
Bethel College *B*
Central Lakes College *A*
College of St. Benedict *B*
College of St. Catherine: St. Paul Campus *B*
Gustavus Adolphus College *B*
Hibbing Community College: A Technical and Community College *C*
Itasca Community College *A*
Lake Superior College: A Community and Technical College *A*
Mesabi Range Community and Technical College *A*
Minnesota State University, Mankato *B*
North Hennepin Community College *A*
St. John's University *B*
St. Mary's University of Minnesota *B*
University of Minnesota
    Twin Cities *B*
Winona State University *A*

Mississippi
Meridian Community College *A*
Mississippi Gulf Coast Community College
    Jefferson Davis Campus *A*

Missouri
Central Missouri State University *B*
College of the Ozarks *B*
Lincoln University *B*

Montana
University of Great Falls *B*

Nebraska
Concordia University *B*
Northeast Community College *A*

Nevada
Western Nevada Community College *A*

New Hampshire
St. Anselm College *B*

New Jersey
Salem Community College *A*

New Mexico
New Mexico Junior College *A*
New Mexico State University
    Alamogordo *A*
    Carlsbad *A*
Northern New Mexico Community College *A*
San Juan College *A*
Santa Fe Community College *A*

New York
Bard College *B*
City University of New York
    Kingsborough Community College *A*
    Queensborough Community College *A*
Colgate University *B*
College of Aeronautics *A*
Corning Community College *A*
Jefferson Community College *A*
Le Moyne College *B*
St. John Fisher College *B*
State University of New York
    College at Brockport *B*

North Carolina
Barber-Scotia College *B*
Barton College *B*
Brevard College *A, B*
Coastal Carolina Community College *A*
Methodist College *A, B*
Pfeiffer University *B*
Sandhills Community College *A*

North Dakota
Bismarck State College *A*
Dickinson State University *A, B*
Mayville State University *B*

Ohio
Ashland University *B*
Baldwin-Wallace College *B*
Heidelberg College *B*
Hiram College *B*
Marietta College *B*
Ohio Wesleyan University *B*
Otterbein College *B*
Terra Community College *A*
University of Findlay *B*
University of Rio Grande *B*
Youngstown State University *A, B*

Prelaw

Oklahoma
Eastern Oklahoma State College A
Langston University A
Northeastern Oklahoma Agricultural and Mechanical College A
Northern Oklahoma College A
Oklahoma City Community College A
Rose State College A
Seminole State College A

Oregon
Central Oregon Community College A
Southern Oregon University B

Pennsylvania
California University of Pennsylvania B
Drexel University M
Gettysburg College B
Juniata College B
Mansfield University of Pennsylvania B
Reading Area Community College A
Thiel College B
Waynesburg College B
West Chester University of Pennsylvania B

Puerto Rico
Turabo University B
University of Puerto Rico
    Ponce University College A

Rhode Island
Providence College B

South Carolina
Furman University B
Trident Technical College A

South Dakota
Dakota Wesleyan University B

Tennessee
Bethel College B
Freed-Hardeman University B
Hiwassee College A
Lambuth University B
Maryville College B
Union University B

Texas
Abilene Christian University B
Angelina College A
Brazosport College A
El Paso Community College A
Jarvis Christian College B
Lon Morris College A
McMurry University B
Midwestern State University B
St. Philip's College A

Utah
College of Eastern Utah A
Salt Lake Community College A

Virginia
Emory & Henry College B
Longwood College B
Old Dominion University M

Washington
Centralia College A
Everett Community College A
North Seattle Community College A
Skagit Valley College A

Wisconsin
Carthage College B
Ripon College B
St. Norbert College B
University of Wisconsin
    Oshkosh B

Prelaw

Alabama
Calhoun Community College A
Enterprise State Junior College A
Faulkner University B
Huntingdon College B
Lawson State Community College A
Northwest-Shoals Community College A
Shelton State Community College A
Talladega College B
Wallace State Community College at Hanceville A

Alaska
Alaska Pacific University B
University of Alaska
    Southeast A

Arizona
Arizona State University B
Cochise College A
Eastern Arizona College A
Grand Canyon University B
Northern Arizona University B

Arkansas
Hendrix College B
John Brown University B
Ouachita Baptist University B
University of the Ozarks B
Westark College A

California
Azusa Pacific University B
Bakersfield College A
Biola University B
Butte College C, A
California Lutheran University B
California State University
    Bakersfield B
    Chico B
    Dominguez Hills B
    Stanislaus B
Chabot College A
Chapman University B
Claremont McKenna College B
College of the Siskiyous A
Concordia University B
Crafton Hills College C
Cypress College A
Foothill College A
Golden West College A
Marymount College A
MiraCosta College A
Mount St. Mary's College B
Riverside Community College A
San Diego City College A
San Joaquin Delta College A
University of California
    Riverside B
Ventura College A
Westmont College B
Whittier College B

Colorado
Adams State College B
Colorado Mountain College
    Spring Valley Campus A
    Timberline Campus A
Fort Lewis College B
Lamar Community College A
Otero Junior College A
Regis University B
Trinidad State Junior College A
Western State College of Colorado B

Connecticut
Quinnipiac University B
Sacred Heart University C
Southern Connecticut State University B
Teikyo Post University B
Trinity College B
University of Hartford B

Delaware
University of Delaware B

Florida
Barry University B
Broward Community College A
Chipola Junior College A
Clearwater Christian College B
Eckerd College B
Edward Waters College B
Florida State University B
Gulf Coast Community College A
Indian River Community College A
Jacksonville University B
Lake City Community College A
Manatee Community College A
Miami-Dade Community College A
Nova Southeastern University B
Pensacola Junior College A
St. Thomas University B
University of Central Florida B
University of Miami B
University of Tampa B

Georgia
Abraham Baldwin Agricultural College A
Andrew College A
Coastal Georgia Community College A
Columbus State University B
Emmanuel College B
Georgia Institute of Technology B
Georgia Southwestern State University B
Kennesaw State University B
LaGrange College B
Oglethorpe University B
Piedmont College B
South Georgia College A
State University of West Georgia B
Valdosta State University B
Young Harris College A

Idaho
College of Southern Idaho A
North Idaho College A
Northwest Nazarene University B
Ricks College A

Illinois
Augustana College B
Barat College B
Black Hawk College
    East Campus A
Blackburn College B
City Colleges of Chicago
    Harold Washington College A
    Kennedy-King College A
Danville Area Community College A
De Paul University B
Elmhurst College B
Highland Community College A
Illinois Institute of Technology B
John A. Logan College A
John Wood Community College A
Judson College B
Kishwaukee College A
Lake Land College A
Lewis and Clark Community College A
Lincoln Land Community College A
McKendree College B
Millikin University B
Monmouth College B
Morton College A
Rend Lake College A
Richland Community College A
Rockford College B
Roosevelt University B
St. Xavier University B
Sauk Valley Community College A
Southwestern Illinois College A
Springfield College in Illinois A
University of St. Francis B

Indiana
Anderson University B
Ball State University B
Goshen College B
Grace College B
Indiana State University B
Indiana Wesleyan University B
Manchester College B
Purdue University
    Calumet B
St. Joseph's College B
St. Mary-of-the-Woods College B
University of Evansville B
University of Indianapolis B
University of St. Francis B
Valparaiso University B
Vincennes University A

Iowa
Buena Vista University B
Coe College B
Dordt College B
Grand View College B
Hawkeye Community College A
Iowa Central Community College A
Iowa Wesleyan College B
Loras College B
Luther College B
Maharishi University of Management B
Marshalltown Community College A
Marycrest International University B
Mount Mercy College B
North Iowa Area Community College A
St. Ambrose University C
Simpson College B
University of Iowa B
Upper Iowa University B
Waldorf College A

Kansas
Butler County Community College A
Central Christian College A
Coffeyville Community College A
Colby Community College A
Dodge City Community College A
Garden City Community College A
Independence Community College A
Kansas City Kansas Community College A
McPherson College B
Pittsburg State University B
Pratt Community College A
Seward County Community College A
Tabor College B
Washburn University of Topeka B

Kentucky
Campbellsville University B
Centre College B
Lindsey Wilson College A
Murray State University B
Thomas More College A, B
Union College B

Louisiana
Centenary College of Louisiana B
Dillard University B
Nicholls State University B
University of Louisiana at Lafayette B
University of Louisiana at Monroe B

Maine
St. Joseph's College B
University of Maine
    Fort Kent B
University of Southern Maine B

Maryland
College of Notre Dame of Maryland B
Community College of Baltimore County
    Catonsville A
Frostburg State University B
Morgan State University B
University of Baltimore B
University of Maryland
    Baltimore County B
    Eastern Shore B
Villa Julie College B

Massachusetts
American International College B
Becker College B
Clark University B
Curry College B
Eastern Nazarene College B
Elms College B
Framingham State College B
Massachusetts Institute of Technology B
Newbury College B
Springfield College B

Worcester State College *B*

Michigan
Adrian College *B*
Albion College *B*
Alma College *B*
Bay de Noc Community College *A*
Calvin College *B*
Concordia College *A*
Cornerstone College and Grand Rapids Baptist Seminary *B*
Ferris State University *A*
Gogebic Community College *A*
Hillsdale College *B*
Kalamazoo College *B*
Kellogg Community College *A*
Kirtland Community College *A*
Lansing Community College *A*
Madonna University *B*
Northern Michigan University *B*
Northwestern Michigan College *A*
Olivet College *B*
Schoolcraft College *A*
Siena Heights University *B*
University of Detroit Mercy *B*
West Shore Community College *A*
Western Michigan University *B*
William Tyndale College *B*

Minnesota
College of St. Benedict *B*
College of St. Catherine: St. Paul Campus *B*
Concordia College: Moorhead *B*
Gustavus Adolphus College *B*
Minnesota State University, Mankato *B*
Moorhead State University *B*
Northland Community & Technical College *A*
Ridgewater College: A Community and Technical College *A*
St. Cloud State University *B*
St. John's University *B*
University of Minnesota Twin Cities *B*
Winona State University *B*

Mississippi
Belhaven College *B*
Blue Mountain College *B*
Coahoma Community College *A*
Copiah-Lincoln Community College *A*
Hinds Community College *A*
Jackson State University *B*
Mary Holmes College *A*
Meridian Community College *A*
Mississippi Delta Community College *A*
Mississippi Gulf Coast Community College
    Jefferson Davis Campus *A*
Rust College *B*

Missouri
College of the Ozarks *B*
Evangel University *B*
Fontbonne College *B*
Hannibal-LaGrange College *A*
Lindenwood University *B*
Stephens College *B*
Three Rivers Community College *A*
Truman State University *B*
University of Missouri St. Louis *B*
Washington University *B*
William Woods University *B*

Montana
Miles Community College *A*
Montana Tech of the University of Montana *B*
Rocky Mountain College *B*
University of Montana-Missoula *B*

Nebraska
Creighton University *B*
Dana College *B*
Mid Plains Community College Area *A*
Midland Lutheran College *B*
University of Nebraska Lincoln *B*

New Hampshire
Franklin Pierce College *B*
New England College *B*
Notre Dame College *B*
Rivier College *B*
St. Anselm College *B*

New Jersey
Atlantic Cape Community College *A*
Georgian Court College *B*
Rowan University *B*
Rutgers
    The State University of New Jersey: Camden College of Arts and Sciences *B*
    The State University of New Jersey: Cook College *B*
    The State University of New Jersey: Douglass College *B*
    The State University of New Jersey: Livingston College *B*
    The State University of New Jersey: Newark College of Arts and Sciences *B*
    The State University of New Jersey: Rutgers College *B*
    The State University of New Jersey: University College Camden *B*
    The State University of New Jersey: University College New Brunswick *B*
Stevens Institute of Technology *B*

New Mexico
New Mexico Highlands University *B*
New Mexico Junior College *A*

New York
Alfred University *B*
Audrey Cohen College *A*, *B*
Bard College *B*
City University of New York
    Brooklyn College *B*
    City College *B*
    John Jay College of Criminal Justice *B*
College of New Rochelle *B*
Concordia College *B*
D'Youville College *B*
Elmira College *B*
Fordham University *B*
Ithaca College *B*
Keuka College *B*
Le Moyne College *B*
Long Island University
    Brooklyn Campus *B*
    C. W. Post Campus *B*
    Southampton College *B*
Manhattan College *B*
Marist College *B*
Molloy College *B*
New York University *B*
Pace University *B*
Rensselaer Polytechnic Institute *B*
Rochester Institute of Technology *B*
St. John Fisher College *B*
St. Thomas Aquinas College *B*
Sarah Lawrence College *B*
State University of New York
    College at Fredonia *B*
    College at Geneseo *B*
    College of Environmental Science and Forestry *B*
    New Paltz *B*
    Oswego *B*

North Carolina
Appalachian State University *B*
Barber-Scotia College *B*
Barton College *B*
Belmont Abbey College *B*
Brevard College *B*
Campbell University *B*
Catawba College *B*
Chowan College *B*
College of the Albemarle *A*
Elon College *B*
Gardner-Webb University *B*
Johnson C. Smith University *B*
Lees-McRae College *B*
Lenoir-Rhyne College *B*
Mars Hill College *B*
Methodist College *B*
Mitchell Community College *A*
North Carolina State University *B*
Pfeiffer University *B*
Queens College *B*
St. Andrews Presbyterian College *B*
Sandhills Community College *A*
University of North Carolina Pembroke *B*
Wingate University *B*

North Dakota
Dickinson State University *B*
Jamestown College *B*
Mayville State University *B*
North Dakota State University *B*
Valley City State University *B*

Ohio
Ashland University *B*
Bluffton College *B*
Bowling Green State University *B*
Capital University *B*
Cedarville College *B*
Central State University *B*
Defiance College *B*
Heidelberg College *B*
John Carroll University *B*
Kent State University Stark Campus *B*
Kent State University *B*
Lorain County Community College *A*
Malone College *B*
Miami University Oxford Campus *B*
Muskingum College *B*
Oberlin College *B*
Ohio University *B*
Ohio Wesleyan University *B*
Otterbein College *B*
University of Akron *B*
University of Cincinnati
    Clermont College *A*
    Raymond Walters College *A*
University of Dayton *B*
University of Rio Grande *B*
Ursuline College *B*
Walsh University *B*
Wilmington College *B*
Youngstown State University *B*

Oklahoma
Carl Albert State College *A*
Connors State College *A*
East Central University *B*
Eastern Oklahoma State College *A*
Langston University *B*
Northeastern Oklahoma Agricultural and Mechanical College *A*
Northern Oklahoma College *A*
Northwestern Oklahoma State University *B*
Oklahoma Christian University of Science and Arts *B*
Oklahoma City Community College *A*
Oklahoma City University *B*
Oklahoma State University *B*
Rogers State University *A*
St. Gregory's University *B*
Southern Nazarene University *B*
Western Oklahoma State College *A*

Oregon
Central Oregon Community College *A*
Chemeketa Community College *A*
Eastern Oregon University *B*
Northwest Christian College *B*
Southern Oregon University *B*
Western Baptist College *B*
Willamette University *B*

Pennsylvania
Allentown College of St. Francis de Sales *B*
Alvernia College *B*
California University of Pennsylvania *B*
College Misericordia *B*
Elizabethtown College *B*
Gannon University *B*
Gettysburg College *B*
Grove City College *B*
Holy Family College *B*
Immaculata College *C*
Juniata College *B*
La Salle University *B*
Lock Haven University of Pennsylvania *B*
Mansfield University of Pennsylvania *B*
Marywood University *B*
Mercyhurst College *B*
Mount Aloysius College *B*
Muhlenberg College *B*
Reading Area Community College *A*
Seton Hill College *B*
Susquehanna University *B*
University of Pittsburgh
    Bradford *B*
    Johnstown *B*
Ursinus College *B*
Washington and Jefferson College *B*
Waynesburg College *B*
West Chester University of Pennsylvania *B*
Westminster College *B*
Widener University *B*
York College of Pennsylvania *B*

Puerto Rico
Caribbean University *B*
Pontifical Catholic University of Puerto Rico *B*
University of Puerto Rico Rio Piedras Campus *B*

Rhode Island
Salve Regina University *B*

South Carolina
Charleston Southern University *B*
Clemson University *B*
Coker College *B*
Columbia College *B*
Erskine College *B*
Furman University *B*
Lander University *B*
North Greenville College *B*
Wofford College *C*

South Dakota
Dakota State University *B*
Dakota Wesleyan University *B*
South Dakota School of Mines and Technology *B*

Tennessee
Columbia State Community College *A*
Crichton College *B*
Cumberland University *B*
Hiwassee College *A*
Lambuth University *B*
Lincoln Memorial University *B*
Maryville College *B*
Tennessee Technological University *B*
Tennessee Wesleyan College *B*
Tusculum College *B*
Union University *B*
University of Tennessee Knoxville *B*

Texas
Abilene Christian University *B*
Amarillo College *A*
Angelina College *A*
Baylor University *B*
Central Texas College *A*

Coastal Bend College A
Concordia University at Austin B
Galveston College A
Grayson County College A
Hill College A
Houston Baptist University B
Howard Payne University B
Jarvis Christian College B
Kilgore College A
LeTourneau University B
Lon Morris College A
McMurry University B
Midland College A
Panola College A
Paris Junior College A
St. Edward's University B
Texas A&M University
  Commerce B
Texas Wesleyan University B
Trinity Valley Community College A
Tyler Junior College A
University of Houston
  Clear Lake B
Western Texas College A

Utah
Dixie State College of Utah A
Snow College A
Southern Utah University B
Utah State University B
Westminster College B

Vermont
Castleton State College B
Champlain College A, B
College of St. Joseph in Vermont B
Green Mountain College B
Marlboro College B
Norwich University B

Virginia
Averett College B
Hampton University B
Longwood College B
Mountain Empire Community College C
Virginia Polytechnic Institute and State
  University B
Virginia Wesleyan College B

Washington
Centralia College A
Eastern Washington University B
Everett Community College A
Evergreen State College B
Highline Community College A
Lower Columbia College A
Washington State University B
Western Washington University B

West Virginia
Alderson-Broaddus College B
Concord College B
Marshall University B
Potomac State College of West Virginia
  University A
West Virginia Wesleyan College B

Wisconsin
Cardinal Stritch University B
Carthage College B
Concordia University Wisconsin B
Lawrence University B
Marian College of Fond du Lac B
Mount Mary College B
Mount Senario College B
Northland College B
Ripon College B
St. Norbert College B
University of Wisconsin
  La Crosse B
  Madison B
  Milwaukee B
  Oshkosh B
  Parkside B
  Superior B
  Whitewater B
Viterbo University B

Wyoming
Casper College A
Laramie County Community College A
Northwest College A
Western Wyoming Community
  College A

Premedicine

Alabama
Auburn University B
Calhoun Community College A
Faulkner University B
Huntingdon College B
James H. Faulkner State Community
  College A
Northeast Alabama Community
  College A
Northwest-Shoals Community College A
Spring Hill College B
University of Alabama B

Arizona
Arizona State University B
Eastern Arizona College A
Grand Canyon University B
Northern Arizona University B
Phoenix College A

Arkansas
Harding University B
Hendrix College B
John Brown University B
Ouachita Baptist University B
University of Arkansas B
University of Central Arkansas B
Westark College A

California
Azusa Pacific University B
Bakersfield College A
California Lutheran University B
California State University
  Chico B
Chabot College A
Chapman University B
City College of San Francisco A
Claremont McKenna College B
College of Notre Dame B
College of the Siskiyous A
Compton Community College C, A
Concordia University B
Crafton Hills College C
Cypress College A
Foothill College A
Fresno Pacific University B
Golden West College A
Marymount College A
Mills College C
MiraCosta College A
Monterey Peninsula College A
Mount St. Mary's College B
Riverside Community College A
Scripps College C
Southwestern College A
University of California
  Riverside B
Ventura College A
West Hills Community College A
Westmont College B
Whittier College B

Colorado
Adams State College B
Fort Lewis College B
Otero Junior College A
Regis University B
Western State College of Colorado B

Connecticut
Quinnipiac University B
Sacred Heart University C
Southern Connecticut State University B
Trinity College B
University of New Haven B

Delaware
University of Delaware B

District of Columbia
George Washington University A

Florida
Barry University B
Broward Community College A
Chipola Junior College A
Clearwater Christian College B
Eckerd College B
Edison Community College A
Florida Southern College B
Florida State University B
Gulf Coast Community College A
Hillsborough Community College A
Indian River Community College A
Jacksonville University B
Lynn University B
Miami-Dade Community College A
Nova Southeastern University B
Palm Beach Community College A
Pensacola Junior College A
St. Thomas University B
Santa Fe Community College A
University of Central Florida B
University of Miami B
University of Tampa B

Georgia
Abraham Baldwin Agricultural
  College A
Andrew College A
Clayton College and State University A
Columbus State University B
Darton College A
Floyd College A
Georgia Institute of Technology B
Georgia Perimeter College A
Kennesaw State University B
LaGrange College B
Middle Georgia College A
Morehouse College B
Oglethorpe University B
Piedmont College B
South Georgia College A
State University of West Georgia B
University of Georgia B
Young Harris College A

Hawaii
Hawaii Pacific University B
University of Hawaii
  Hilo B

Idaho
Boise State University B
College of Southern Idaho A
Lewis-Clark State College B
North Idaho College A
Northwest Nazarene University B
Ricks College A
University of Idaho B

Illinois
Augustana College B
Barat College B
Black Hawk College
  East Campus A
Blackburn College B
City Colleges of Chicago
  Harold Washington College A
  Kennedy-King College A
De Paul University B
Elmhurst College B
Greenville College B
Illinois Institute of Technology B
John A. Logan College A
Judson College B
Kankakee Community College A
Kishwaukee College A
Lake Land College A
Lewis and Clark Community College A
Lincoln Land Community College A
MacMurray College B
McKendree College B
Millikin University B
North Park University B
Rend Lake College A
Rockford College B
Roosevelt University B
St. Xavier University B
Sauk Valley Community College A
Southwestern Ilinois College A
Springfield College in Illinois A
University of St. Francis B

Indiana
Ball State University B
Bethel College B
Goshen College B
Grace College B
Indiana State University B
Indiana University--Purdue University
  Indiana University-Purdue
    University Fort Wayne B
  Indiana University-Purdue
    University Indianapolis M
Indiana Wesleyan University B
Manchester College B
Purdue University
  Calumet B
Purdue University B
St. Joseph's College B
St. Mary-of-the-Woods College B
Taylor University B
Tri-State University B
University of Evansville B
University of Indianapolis B
University of Notre Dame B
University of St. Francis B
Valparaiso University B
Vincennes University A

Iowa
Buena Vista University B
Clarke College B
Coe College B
Cornell College B
Dordt College B
Iowa Wesleyan College B
Kirkwood Community College A
Luther College B
Maharishi University of Management B
Marshalltown Community College A
Marycrest International University B
Morningside College B
North Iowa Area Community College A
Northwestern College B
Simpson College B
University of Iowa B
Upper Iowa University B
Waldorf College A

Kansas
Butler County Community College A
Central Christian College B
Coffeyville Community College A
Colby Community College A
Dodge City Community College A
Kansas City Kansas Community
  College A
Kansas State University B
McPherson College B
Pittsburg State University B
Pratt Community College A
Tabor College B
Washburn University of Topeka B

Kentucky
Campbellsville University B
Centre College B
Cumberland College B
Lindsey Wilson College A
Murray State University B
Thomas More College B
Union College B

Louisiana
Centenary College of Louisiana B
Dillard University B
Nicholls State University B
University of Louisiana at Monroe B

Premedicine

Maine
St. Joseph's College *B*
University of Maine
 Fort Kent *B*
University of New England *B*
University of Southern Maine *B*

Maryland
Columbia Union College *B*
Community College of Baltimore County
 Catonsville *A*
Frostburg State University *B*
Howard Community College *A*
Montgomery College
 Germantown Campus *A*
 Rockville Campus *A*
 Takoma Park Campus *A*
Morgan State University *B*
Mount St. Mary's College *B*
University of Maryland
 Baltimore County *B*
 Eastern Shore *B*
Villa Julie College *B*

Massachusetts
American International College *B*
Cape Cod Community College *A*
Eastern Nazarene College *B*
Elms College *B*
Framingham State College *B*
Hampshire College *B*
Harvard College *B*
Simmons College *B*
Simon's Rock College of Bard *B*
Springfield Technical Community
 College *A*
Stonehill College *B*
University of Massachusetts
 Amherst *B*
Worcester Polytechnic Institute *B, M*

Michigan
Adrian College *B*
Albion College *B*
Alma College *B*
Calvin College *B*
Cornerstone College and Grand Rapids
 Baptist Seminary *B*
Delta College *B*
Eastern Michigan University *B*
Grand Valley State University *B*
Hillsdale College *B*
Kalamazoo College *B*
Kellogg Community College *A*
Kirtland Community College *A*
Michigan Technological University *B*
Northern Michigan University *B*
Olivet College *B*
Schoolcraft College *A*
Siena Heights University *B*
University of Detroit Mercy *B*
Washtenaw Community College *A*
Western Michigan University *B*

Minnesota
College of St. Benedict *B*
College of St. Catherine: St. Paul
 Campus *B*
Concordia College: Moorhead *B*
Gustavus Adolphus College *B*
Hamline University *B*
Minnesota State University, Mankato *B*
Moorhead State University *B*
Rochester Community and Technical
 College *A*
St. Cloud State University *B*
St. John's University *B*
St. Mary's University of Minnesota *B*
St. Olaf College *B*
University of Minnesota
 Twin Cities *B*
Winona State University *B*

Mississippi
Blue Mountain College *B*
Coahoma Community College *A*
East Central Community College *A*
Holmes Community College *A*
Jackson State University *B*
Mary Holmes College *A*
Mississippi Gulf Coast Community
 College
 Jefferson Davis Campus *A*
Rust College *B*

Missouri
Avila College *B*
Central Methodist College *B*
East Central College *A*
Evangel University *B*
Lindenwood University *B*
Maryville University of Saint Louis *B*
Missouri Southern State College *A*
St. Louis Community College
 St. Louis Community College at
  Florissant Valley *A*
Stephens College *B*
Three Rivers Community College *A*
Truman State University *B*
University of Missouri
 St. Louis *B*
Washington University *B*
William Woods University *B*

Montana
Montana Tech of the University of
 Montana *B*
Rocky Mountain College *B*
University of Great Falls *B*
University of Montana-Missoula *B*

Nebraska
College of Saint Mary *B*
Dana College *B*
Hastings College *B*
Mid Plains Community College Area *A*
Midland Lutheran College *B*
Northeast Community College *A*
University of Nebraska
 Lincoln *B*

New Hampshire
Franklin Pierce College *B*
New England College *B*
Rivier College *B*
St. Anselm College *B*
University of New Hampshire *B*

New Jersey
Bloomfield College *B*
Essex County College *A*
Georgian Court College *B*
Rowan University *B*
Rutgers
 The State University of New Jersey:
  Camden College of Arts and
  Sciences *B*
 The State University of New Jersey:
  Cook College *B*
 The State University of New Jersey:
  Douglass College *B*
 The State University of New Jersey:
  Livingston College *B*
 The State University of New Jersey:
  Newark College of Arts and
  Sciences *B*
 The State University of New Jersey:
  Rutgers College *B*
 The State University of New Jersey:
  University College Camden *B*
 The State University of New Jersey:
  University College New
  Brunswick *B*
Stevens Institute of Technology *B*
Sussex County Community College *A*

New Mexico
College of Santa Fe *B*
New Mexico Junior College *A*
San Juan College *A*

New York
Alfred University *B*
Bard College *B*
City University of New York
 Brooklyn College *B*
 City College *B*
 College of Staten Island *B*
 Hunter College *B*
 Queens College *B*
Colgate University *B*
Columbia University
 School of General Studies *B*
Concordia College *B*
Cornell University *B*
D'Youville College *B*
Dowling College *C*
Elmira College *B*
Fordham University *B*
Hobart and William Smith Colleges *B*
Houghton College *B*
Ithaca College *B*
Le Moyne College *B*
Long Island University
 Brooklyn Campus *B*
 Southampton College *B*
Manhattan College *B*
Marist College *B*
Marymount College *B*
Molloy College *B*
New York Institute of Technology *B*
New York University *B*
Rensselaer Polytechnic Institute *B*
Rochester Institute of Technology *B*
St. Francis College *B*
St. John Fisher College *B*
St. Thomas Aquinas College *B*
Sarah Lawrence College *B*
St. Joseph's College
 St. Joseph's College: Suffolk
  Campus *B*
State University of New York
 College at Brockport *B*
 College at Geneseo *B*
 College of Environmental Science
  and Forestry *B*
 New Paltz *B*
Syracuse University *B*
Touro College *B*
Wagner College *B*
Wells College *B*

North Carolina
Appalachian State University *B*
Barton College *B*
Belmont Abbey College *B*
Brevard College *A, B*
Campbell University *B*
Catawba College *B*
Chowan College *B*
Elon College *B*
Lees-McRae College *B*
Lenoir-Rhyne College *B*
Louisburg College *A*
Mars Hill College *B*
Meredith College *B*
Methodist College *B*
Mitchell Community College *A*
North Carolina State University *B*
North Carolina Wesleyan College *B*
Pfeiffer University *B*
St. Andrews Presbyterian College *B*
St. Augustine's College *B*
Sandhills Community College *A*
Warren Wilson College *B*
Wingate University *B*

North Dakota
Dickinson State University *B*
Mayville State University *B*
Minot State University *B*
University of North Dakota *B*
Valley City State University *B*

Ohio
Ashland University *B*
Capital University *B*
Defiance College *B*
Heidelberg College *B*
John Carroll University *B*
Kent State University
 Stark Campus *B*
Kent State University *B*
Lorain County Community College *A*
Miami University
 Oxford Campus *B*
Mount Vernon Nazarene College *B*
Muskingum College *B*
Ohio University *B*
Ohio Wesleyan University *B*
Otterbein College *B*
Shawnee State University *B*
University of Akron *B*
University of Cincinnati
 Clermont College *B*
 Raymond Walters College *A*
University of Cincinnati *B*
University of Dayton *B*
University of Findlay *B*
University of Rio Grande *B*
University of Toledo *B*
Ursuline College *B*
Walsh University *B*
Wittenberg University *B*
Xavier University *A*
Youngstown State University *B*

Oklahoma
Connors State College *A*
East Central University *B*
Eastern Oklahoma State College *A*
Northeastern Oklahoma Agricultural and
 Mechanical College *A*
Northern Oklahoma College *A*
Oklahoma Christian University of
 Science and Arts *B*
Oklahoma City University *B*
Oklahoma State University *B*
Redlands Community College *A*
Rogers State University *A*
Rose State College *A*

Oregon
Central Oregon Community College *A*
Chemeketa Community College *A*
Concordia University *B*
Eastern Oregon University *B*
Northwest Christian College *B*
Southern Oregon University *B*
University of Portland *B*
Western Baptist College *B*
Willamette University *B*

Pennsylvania
Albright College *B*
Allentown College of St. Francis de
 Sales *B*
Alvernia College *B*
Cabrini College *B*
California University of Pennsylvania *B*
College Misericordia *B*
East Stroudsburg University of
 Pennsylvania *B*
Elizabethtown College *B*
Gannon University *B*
Gettysburg College *B*
Grove City College *B*
Gwynedd-Mercy College *B*
Holy Family College *B*
Immaculata College *B*
Juniata College *B*
La Salle University *B*
Lehigh University *B*
Lock Haven University of
 Pennsylvania *B*
MCP Hahnemann University *B*
Mansfield University of Pennsylvania *B*
Mercyhurst College *B*
Muhlenberg College *B*
Penn State
 University Park *B*
Philadelphia University *B*
Reading Area Community College *A*
Seton Hill College *B*
Susquehanna University *B*

University of Pittsburgh
  Bradford *B*
  Greensburg *B*
  Johnstown *B*
Ursinus College *B*
Villanova University *B*
Waynesburg College *B*
West Chester University of
  Pennsylvania *B*
Westminster College *B*
Widener University *B*
Wilkes University *B*
York College of Pennsylvania *B*

Puerto Rico
Caribbean University *B*
University of Puerto Rico
  Arecibo Campus *T*
  Mayaguez Campus *B*
  Ponce University College *A*

Rhode Island
Rhode Island College *B*
Salve Regina University *B*

South Carolina
Anderson College *A*
Charleston Southern University *B*
Clemson University *B*
Coker College *B*
College of Charleston *B*
Denmark Technical College *C*
Erskine College *B*
Furman University *B*
Lander University *B*
North Greenville College *B*
Wofford College *C*

South Dakota
Augustana College *B*
Dakota State University *B*
Dakota Wesleyan University *B*
South Dakota School of Mines and
  Technology *B*

Tennessee
Carson-Newman College *B*
Columbia State Community College *A*
Cumberland University *B*
Fisk University *B*
Freed-Hardeman University *B*
Hiwassee College *A*
Lambuth University *B*
Lincoln Memorial University *B*
Maryville College *B*
Tennessee Technological University *B*
Tennessee Wesleyan College *B*
Tusculum College *B*
Union University *B*
University of Tennessee
  Knoxville *B*
  Martin *B*
Walters State Community College *A*

Texas
Abilene Christian University *B*
Amarillo College *A*
Angelina College *A*
Baylor University *B*
Central Texas College *A*
Coastal Bend College *A*
Concordia University at Austin *B*
Del Mar College *A*
El Paso Community College *A*
Galveston College *A*
Grayson County College *A*
Howard College *A*
Howard Payne University *B*
Jarvis Christian College *B*
LeTourneau University *B*
Lon Morris College *A*
McMurry University *B*
Midland College *A*
Midwestern State University *B*
Navarro College *A*
Panola College *A*
Paris Junior College *A*

St. Edward's University *B*
St. Philip's College *A*
South Plains College *A*
Texas A&M University
  Commerce *A*
Texas A&M University *B*
Texas Christian University *B*
Texas Wesleyan University *B*
Trinity Valley Community College *A*
Tyler Junior College *A*
University of Mary Hardin-Baylor *B*
Western Texas College *A*

Utah
Brigham Young University *B*
Dixie State College of Utah *A*
Snow College *A*
University of Utah *B*
Westminster College *B*

Vermont
Castleton State College *B*
Johnson State College *B*

Virginia
Averett College *B*
Longwood College *B*
Mountain Empire Community College *A*
Virginia Commonwealth University *B*
Virginia Intermont College *B*
Virginia Wesleyan College *B*

Washington
Centralia College *A*
Eastern Washington University *B*
Everett Community College *A*
Lower Columbia College *A*
St. Martin's College *B*
Seattle Pacific University *B*
Washington State University *B*
Western Washington University *B*

West Virginia
Alderson-Broaddus College *B*
College of West Virginia *B*
Concord College *B*
Davis and Elkins College *B*
Marshall University *B*
Potomac State College of West Virginia
  University *A*
West Virginia Wesleyan College *B*

Wisconsin
Cardinal Stritch University *B*
Lawrence University *B*
Marian College of Fond du Lac *B*
Mount Mary College *B*
Northland College *B*
Ripon College *B*
St. Norbert College *B*
University of Wisconsin
  Madison *B*
  Milwaukee *B*
  Oshkosh *B*
  Parkside *B*
  Whitewater *B*
Viterbo University *B*

Wyoming
Casper College *A*
Eastern Wyoming College *A*
Northwest College *A*
Western Wyoming Community
  College *A*

Prenursing

Alabama
Calhoun Community College *A*
James H. Faulkner State Community
  College *A*
Northeast Alabama Community
  College *A*
Northwest-Shoals Community
  College *C, A*

California
California State University
  Hayward *B*
Westmont College *B*

Colorado
Red Rocks Community College *A*

Florida
Edison Community College *A*
Pensacola Junior College *A*
South Florida Community College *A*

Georgia
Andrew College *A*
Middle Georgia College *A*
Young Harris College *A*

Illinois
Dominican University *B*
Kishwaukee College *A*
Lewis and Clark Community College *A*
Springfield College in Illinois *A*

Indiana
Ancilla College *A*
DePauw University *B*
Manchester College *A*

Iowa
Dordt College *B*
Marshalltown Community College *A*
Simpson College *B*
University of Iowa *B*

Kansas
Central Christian College *A*
Coffeyville Community College *A*
Colby Community College *A*

Kentucky
Campbellsville University *B*
Henderson Community College *C*

Maryland
Charles County Community
  College *C, A*
Frederick Community College *A*
Frostburg State University *B*
Mount St. Mary's College *B*
University of Maryland
  Baltimore County *A*

Massachusetts
Berkshire Community College *A*
Cape Cod Community College *A*

Michigan
Hillsdale College *B*

Mississippi
Coahoma Community College *A*
Mississippi Gulf Coast Community
  College
  Jefferson Davis Campus *A*

Missouri
College of the Ozarks *B*

Montana
Miles Community College *A*
University of Great Falls *B*
University of Montana-Missoula *B*

New York
Houghton College *B*
Nyack College *A*
St. Thomas Aquinas College *B*
St. Joseph's College
  St. Joseph's College *B*
State University of New York
  College of Agriculture and
  Technology at Morrisville *A*
Villa Maria College of Buffalo *A*

North Carolina
Cape Fear Community College *C*
Chowan College *B*
Mayland Community College *C*
Sandhills Community College *A*

North Dakota
Bismarck State College *A*
Valley City State University *B*

Ohio
Heidelberg College *B*
Miami University
  Hamilton Campus *A*
Muskingum College *B*
University of Findlay *A*
Wittenberg University *B*
Youngstown State University *B*

Oklahoma
Eastern Oklahoma State College *A*
Northeastern State University *B*
Rose State College *A*

Oregon
Chemeketa Community College *A*
Northwest Christian College *A, B*

Pennsylvania
Juniata College *B*

South Carolina
North Greenville College *A*

Tennessee
Freed-Hardeman University *B*
Lambuth University *B*

Texas
Lon Morris College *A*
St. Philip's College *A*
Texas State Technical College
  Harlingen *A*
Trinity Valley Community College *A*

Wisconsin
Ripon College *B*

Preoptometry

Alabama
Faulkner University *B*
Huntingdon College *B*
Northeast Alabama Community
  College *A*
Northwest-Shoals Community College *A*

Arkansas
Hendrix College *B*
Westark College *A*

California
Riverside Community College *A*
Westmont College *B*

Connecticut
University of Hartford *B*

Florida
Barry University *B*
Florida State University *B*
Indian River Community College *A*
Miami-Dade Community College *A*
University of Central Florida *B*

Georgia
LaGrange College *B*
Young Harris College *A*

Idaho
College of Southern Idaho *A*
North Idaho College *A*

Illinois
McKendree College *B*
Millikin University *B*

Indiana
Manchester College *B*
Vincennes University *A*

Iowa
Buena Vista University *B*
Dordt College *B*
Iowa Central Community College *A*
Iowa Wesleyan College *B*

Preoptometry

Marshalltown Community College *A*
Simpson College *B*
University of Iowa *B*

Kansas
Coffeyville Community College *A*
McPherson College *B*
Pittsburg State University *B*

Kentucky
Campbellsville University *B*
Cumberland College *B*
Murray State University *B*
Thomas More College *B*

Louisiana
Dillard University *B*

Maryland
Frostburg State University *B*
Howard Community College *A*
Montgomery College
   Germantown Campus *A*
   Rockville Campus *A*
University of Maryland
   Baltimore County *B*

Michigan
Ferris State University *A*
Hillsdale College *B*
Kalamazoo College *B*
Kirtland Community College *A*
Michigan Technological University *B*
Northern Michigan University *B*
Schoolcraft College *A*

Minnesota
Concordia College: Moorhead *B*
St. Olaf College *B*
University of Minnesota
   Duluth *B*
Winona State University *B*

Mississippi
Coahoma Community College *A*
Mississippi Gulf Coast Community College
   Jefferson Davis Campus *A*
   Perkinston *A*

Missouri
East Central College *A*
St. Louis University *M*
Truman State University *B*

Montana
Rocky Mountain College *B*
University of Great Falls *B*

Nebraska
College of Saint Mary *B*
Dana College *B*
Midland Lutheran College *B*

New Jersey
Bloomfield College *B*

New York
City University of New York
   Hunter College *B*
Houghton College *B*
Ithaca College *B*
Le Moyne College *B*
Marymount College *B*
Pace University:
   Pleasantville/Briarcliff *B*
Pace University *B*
Rochester Institute of Technology *B*
State University of New York
   New Paltz *B*

North Carolina
Belmont Abbey College *B*
Chowan College *B*

North Dakota
Bismarck State College *A*
Dickinson State University *B*
Mayville State University *B*
Valley City State University *B*

Ohio
Ashland University *B*
John Carroll University *B*
Ohio Wesleyan University *B*
Otterbein College *B*
University of Cincinnati
   Clermont College *A*
Walsh University *B*
Wittenberg University *B*
Youngstown State University *B*

Oklahoma
East Central University *B*
Eastern Oklahoma State College *A*
Northeastern Oklahoma Agricultural and Mechanical College *A*
Northeastern State University *B*
Oklahoma Christian University of Science and Arts *B*

Pennsylvania
Beaver College *B*
California University of Pennsylvania *B*
College Misericordia *B*
Gannon University *B*
Gettysburg College *B*
Juniata College *B*
Lehigh University *B*
Mansfield University of Pennsylvania *B*
Seton Hill College *B*
University of Pittsburgh
   Greensburg *B*
   Johnstown *B*
Villanova University *B*
Widener University *B*
Wilkes University *B*

Rhode Island
Rhode Island College *B*

South Carolina
Furman University *B*

South Dakota
Augustana College *B*
Dakota Wesleyan University *B*

Tennessee
Cumberland University *B*
Freed-Hardeman University *B*
Lambuth University *B*
Maryville College *B*
Tennessee Technological University *B*
Tennessee Wesleyan College *B*
Union University *B*

Texas
Amarillo College *A*

Virginia
Virginia Intermont College *B*

West Virginia
Marshall University *B*

Wisconsin
University of Wisconsin
   Oshkosh *B*
Viterbo University *B*

Prepharmacy

Alabama
Calhoun Community College *A*
Huntingdon College *B*
James H. Faulkner State Community College *A*
Northeast Alabama Community College *A*
Northwest-Shoals Community College *A*

Arizona
Eastern Arizona College *A*
Grand Canyon University *B*
Northern Arizona University *B*

Arkansas
Harding University *B*
Hendrix College *B*
John Brown University *B*
Ouachita Baptist University *B*
University of Central Arkansas *B*
Westark College *A*

California
Bakersfield College *A*
California Lutheran University *B*
Chabot College *A*
City College of San Francisco *A*
College of the Siskiyous *A*
Crafton Hills College *C*
Cypress College *A*
Foothill College *A*
Golden West College *A*
Marymount College *A*
Monterey Peninsula College *A*
Riverside Community College *A*
Ventura College *A*
West Hills Community College *A*
Westmont College *B*
Whittier College *B*

Colorado
Adams State College *B*
Fort Lewis College *B*
Lamar Community College *A*
Otero Junior College *A*

Connecticut
Sacred Heart University *C*
Southern Connecticut State University *B*
Trinity College *B*

Delaware
University of Delaware *B*

Florida
Barry University *B*
Broward Community College *A*
Chipola Junior College *A*
Florida State University *B*
Gulf Coast Community College *A*
Indian River Community College *A*
Jacksonville University *B*
Miami-Dade Community College *A*
Nova Southeastern University *B*
Pensacola Junior College *A*
Santa Fe Community College *A*
University of Central Florida *B*
University of Miami *B*

Georgia
Abraham Baldwin Agricultural College *A*
Andrew College *A*
Clayton College and State University *A*
Columbus State University *B*
Darton College *A*
Emmanuel College *A*
Floyd College *A*
Georgia Perimeter College *A*
Kennesaw State University *B*
LaGrange College *B*
Middle Georgia College *A*
North Georgia College & State University *C*
Oglethorpe University *B*
Piedmont College *B*
South Georgia College *A*
State University of West Georgia *B*
Young Harris College *A*

Idaho
College of Southern Idaho *A*
North Idaho College *A*
Ricks College *A*

Illinois
Black Hawk College
   East Campus *A*
City Colleges of Chicago
   Harold Washington College *A*
   Kennedy-King College *A*
De Paul University *B*
Elmhurst College *B*
John A. Logan College *A*
Kankakee Community College *A*
Kishwaukee College *A*
Lake Land College *A*
Lincoln Land Community College *A*
North Park University *B*
Rend Lake College *A*
Rockford College *B*
Roosevelt University *B*
St. Xavier University *B*
Sauk Valley Community College *A*
Southwestern Ilinois College *A*
Springfield College in Illinois *A*

Indiana
Ball State University *B*
Goshen College *B*
Grace College *B*
Indiana State University *B*
Indiana Wesleyan University *B*
Manchester College *B*
Purdue University
   Calumet *B*
St. Mary-of-the-Woods College *B*
University of Evansville *B*
Vincennes University *A*

Iowa
Buena Vista University *B*
Clarke College *B*
Dordt College *B*
Iowa Central Community College *A*
Iowa Wesleyan College *B*
Kirkwood Community College *A*
Luther College *B*
Marshalltown Community College *A*
Morningside College *B*
North Iowa Area Community College *A*
Simpson College *B*
University of Iowa *B*
Upper Iowa University *B*
Waldorf College *A*

Kansas
Coffeyville Community College *A*
Colby Community College *A*
Dodge City Community College *A*
Kansas City Kansas Community College *A*
McPherson College *B*
Pittsburg State University *B*
Pratt Community College *A*
Tabor College *B*
Washburn University of Topeka *B*

Kentucky
Campbellsville University *B*
Centre College *B*
Cumberland College *B*
Murray State University *B*
Thomas More College *B*
Union College *B*

Louisiana
Centenary College of Louisiana *B*
Dillard University *B*
Nicholls State University *A*

Maine
St. Joseph's College *B*
University of Maine
   Fort Kent *B*
University of New England *B*

Maryland
Allegany College *A*
Columbia Union College *B*
Community College of Baltimore County
   Catonsville *A*
Coppin State College *B*
Frederick Community College *A*
Frostburg State University *B*
Howard Community College *A*
Montgomery College
   Germantown Campus *A*
   Rockville Campus *A*
   Takoma Park Campus *A*
Morgan State University *B*

University of Maryland
  Baltimore County *A*
  Eastern Shore *B*
Villa Julie College *B*

Massachusetts
Cape Cod Community College *A*
Eastern Nazarene College *B*
Simmons College *B*
Springfield Technical Community College *A*
Western New England College *B*

Michigan
Adrian College *B*
Calvin College *B*
Delta College *A*
Ferris State University *A*
Grand Valley State University *B*
Hillsdale College *B*
Kellogg Community College *A*
Kirtland Community College *A*
Michigan Technological University *B*
Mid Michigan Community College *A*
Northern Michigan University *B*
Schoolcraft College *A*
Siena Heights University *A, B*
West Shore Community College *A*

Minnesota
College of St. Benedict *B*
College of St. Catherine: St. Paul Campus *B*
Concordia College: Moorhead *B*
Minnesota State University, Mankato *B*
Moorhead State University *B*
St. Cloud State University *B*
St. John's University *B*
St. Mary's University of Minnesota *B*
St. Olaf College *B*
University of Minnesota
  Duluth *B*
  Twin Cities *B*
Winona State University *B*

Mississippi
Blue Mountain College *B*
Coahoma Community College *A*
East Central Community College *A*
Holmes Community College *A*
Jackson State University *B*
Mary Holmes College *A*
Meridian Community College *A*
Mississippi Delta Community College *A*
Mississippi Gulf Coast Community College
  Jefferson Davis Campus *A*
  Perkinston *A*
Rust College *B*

Missouri
Central Methodist College *B*
East Central College *A*
Missouri Southern State College *A*
St. Louis Community College
  St. Louis Community College at Florissant Valley *A*
Stephens College *B*
Three Rivers Community College *A*
Truman State University *B*
University of Missouri
  St. Louis *B*
Washington University *B*

Montana
Montana Tech of the University of Montana *B*
Rocky Mountain College *B*
University of Great Falls *B*
University of Montana-Missoula *B*

Nebraska
College of Saint Mary *B*
Dana College *B*
Hastings College *B*
Mid Plains Community College Area *A*
Midland Lutheran College *B*
Northeast Community College *A*

University of Nebraska
  Lincoln *B*

New Jersey
Bloomfield College *B*
Rowan University *B*
Rutgers
  The State University of New Jersey: Douglass College *B*
Sussex County Community College *A*

New Mexico
New Mexico Junior College *A*

New York
Bard College *B*
City University of New York
  City College *B*
  Hunter College *B*
  Kingsborough Community College *A*
D'Youville College *B*
Fordham University *B*
Ithaca College *B*
Long Island University
  Brooklyn Campus *B*
Mercy College *B*
Rochester Institute of Technology *B*
St. John Fisher College *B*
St. Thomas Aquinas College *B*
State University of New York
  Buffalo *B*
  College at Geneseo *B*
  College of Environmental Science and Forestry *B*
Touro College *B*

North Carolina
Appalachian State University *B*
Barton College *B*
Belmont Abbey College *B*
Brevard College *A, B*
Campbell University *B*
Chowan College *B*
Fayetteville Technical Community College *C*
Guilford Technical Community College *A*
James Sprunt Community College *A*
Lenoir-Rhyne College *B*
Louisburg College *A*
Mars Hill College *B*
Meredith College *B*
Methodist College *B*
Mitchell Community College *A*
North Carolina State University *B*
St. Andrews Presbyterian College *B*
Sandhills Community College *A*
Wingate University *B*

North Dakota
Dickinson State University *A*
Mayville State University *B*
Valley City State University *B*

Ohio
Ashland University *B*
Capital University *B*
Kent State University *B*
Lorain County Community College *A*
Mount Vernon Nazarene College *B*
Ohio University *B*
Otterbein College *B*
Shawnee State University *B*
University of Akron *B*
University of Cincinnati
  Raymond Walters College *A*
University of Cincinnati *B*
Wittenberg University *B*
Xavier University *B*
Youngstown State University *B*

Oklahoma
Connors State College *A*
East Central University *B*
Eastern Oklahoma State College *A*
Northeastern Oklahoma Agricultural and Mechanical College *A*

Northern Oklahoma College *A*
Oklahoma Christian University of Science and Arts *B*
Oklahoma City University *B*
Oklahoma State University *B*
Redlands Community College *A*
Rogers State University *A*
Rose State College *A*

Oregon
Central Oregon Community College *A*
Chemeketa Community College *A*
Eastern Oregon University *B*
Northwest Christian College *B*
Southern Oregon University *B*
Western Baptist College *B*
Willamette University *B*

Pennsylvania
Alvernia College *B*
California University of Pennsylvania *B*
East Stroudsburg University of Pennsylvania *B*
Gannon University *B*
Gettysburg College *B*
Holy Family College *B*
Immaculata College *B*
Juniata College *B*
La Salle University *B*
Lock Haven University of Pennsylvania *B*
Mansfield University of Pennsylvania *B*
Mercyhurst College *B*
Reading Area Community College *A*
University of Pittsburgh
  Greensburg *B*
Westminster College *B*
Wilkes University *B*
York College of Pennsylvania *B*

Puerto Rico
University of Puerto Rico
  Arecibo Campus *T*
Ponce University College *A*

South Carolina
Aiken Technical College *C*
Anderson College *A*
Charleston Southern University *B*
Clemson University *B*
Coker College *B*
Erskine College *B*
Furman University *B*
Lander University *B*
North Greenville College *B*
Wofford College *C*

South Dakota
Augustana College *B*
Dakota State University *B*
Dakota Wesleyan University *B*
South Dakota School of Mines and Technology *B*

Tennessee
Carson-Newman College *B*
Columbia State Community College *A*
Cumberland University *B*
Freed-Hardeman University *B*
Hiwassee College *A*
Lambuth University *B*
Lincoln Memorial University *B*
Maryville College *B*
Tennessee Wesleyan College *B*
Union University *B*
University of Tennessee
  Knoxville *B*
  Martin *B*
Walters State Community College *A*

Texas
Abilene Christian University *B*
Amarillo College *A*
Angelina College *A*
Coastal Bend College *A*
Del Mar College *A*
El Paso Community College *A*
Grayson County College *A*

LeTourneau University *B*
Lon Morris College *A*
McMurry University *B*
Midland College *A*
Midwestern State University *B*
Navarro College *A*
Panola College *A*
Paris Junior College *A*
San Antonio College *A*
South Plains College *A*
Texas A&M University
  Commerce *B*
Texas Southern University *B*
Trinity Valley Community College *A*
Tyler Junior College *A*
University of Houston *B*
Western Texas College *A*

Utah
Dixie State College of Utah *A*
Snow College *A*
University of Utah *B*

Vermont
Castleton State College *B*

Virginia
Averett College *B*
Longwood College *B*
Lord Fairfax Community College *A*
Mountain Empire Community College *A*
Virginia Commonwealth University *B*
Virginia Intermont College *B*
Virginia Wesleyan College *B*

Washington
Centralia College *A*
Eastern Washington University *B*
Everett Community College *A*
Lower Columbia College *A*
St. Martin's College *B*

West Virginia
Alderson-Broaddus College *B*
Concord College *B*
Davis and Elkins College *A*
Marshall University *B*
Potomac State College of West Virginia University *A*
West Virginia Wesleyan College *B*

Wisconsin
Cardinal Stritch University *B*
Lawrence University *B*
Marian College of Fond du Lac *B*
Northland College *B*
Ripon College *B*
University of Wisconsin
  Madison *B*
  Milwaukee *B*
  Oshkosh *B*
  Whitewater *A*
Viterbo University *B*
Wisconsin Indianhead Technical College *C*

Wyoming
Casper College *A*
Eastern Wyoming College *A*
Northwest College *A*
Western Wyoming Community College *A*

Prephysical therapy

Alabama
Faulkner University *B*
Huntingdon College *B*
Northeast Alabama Community College *A*

California
Allan Hancock College *A*
Biola University *B*
California State University
  Hayward *B*
MiraCosta College *A*

Prephysical therapy

Vanguard University of Southern
  California *B*
Westmont College *B*

Colorado
Adams State College *B*
Regis University *B*

Florida
Barry University *B*
Edison Community College *A*
Florida State University *B*
Gulf Coast Community College *A*
Indian River Community College *A*
University of Miami *B*

Georgia
Andrew College *A*
LaGrange College *B*
Waycross College *A*
Young Harris College *A*

Idaho
Lewis-Clark State College *B*

Illinois
Elmhurst College *B*
Kishwaukee College *A*
Millikin University *B*
Rockford College *B*
Springfield College in Illinois *A*

Indiana
Goshen College *B*
Grace College *B*
St. Joseph's College *B*
Valparaiso University *B*
Vincennes University *A*

Iowa
Buena Vista University *B*
Cornell College *B*
Dordt College *B*
Iowa Central Community College *A*
Iowa Wesleyan College *B*
Simpson College *B*
University of Iowa *B*

Kansas
Central Christian College *A*
Coffeyville Community College *A*
Colby Community College *A*
McPherson College *B*
Pittsburg State University *B*
Tabor College *B*

Kentucky
Campbellsville University *B*
Cumberland College *B*
Thomas More College *B*
Union College *B*

Louisiana
Nicholls State University *A*

Maryland
Frostburg State University *B*
Morgan State University *B*
University of Maryland
  Baltimore County *A*
Villa Julie College *B*

Massachusetts
Becker College *B*
Berkshire Community College *A*
Cape Cod Community College *A*
Eastern Nazarene College *B*
Merrimack College *B*

Michigan
Adrian College *B*
Calvin College *B*
Hillsdale College *B*
Kalamazoo College *B*
Michigan Technological University *B*

Minnesota
College of St. Benedict *B*
Concordia College: Moorhead *B*
Gustavus Adolphus College *B*

St. John's University *B*
St. Mary's University of Minnesota *B*
St. Olaf College *B*
Winona State University *B*

Mississippi
Coahoma Community College *A*
Meridian Community College *A*
Mississippi Gulf Coast Community
  College
    Jefferson Davis Campus *A*

Missouri
University of Missouri
  Columbia *B*
Washington University *B*

Montana
Rocky Mountain College *B*
University of Great Falls *B*

Nebraska
Dana College *B*
Hastings College *B*
Midland Lutheran College *B*
Northeast Community College *A*

New Hampshire
Rivier College *B*

New York
City University of New York
  Kingsborough Community
    College *A*
  Queensborough Community
    College *A*
Houghton College *B*
Pace University:
  Pleasantville/Briarcliff *B*
Pace University *B*
State University of New York
  New Paltz *B*
Syracuse University *B*

North Carolina
Barton College *B*
Campbell University *B*
Chowan College *B*
Methodist College *B*
Sandhills Community College *A*

North Dakota
Dickinson State University *A*
Mayville State University *B*
Valley City State University *B*

Ohio
Ashland University *B*
Baldwin-Wallace College *B*
Capital University *B*
Miami University
  Oxford Campus *B*
Muskingum College *B*
Ohio University *B*
Ohio Wesleyan University *B*
Otterbein College *B*
University of Cincinnati
  Raymond Walters College *A*
University of Dayton *B*
University of Findlay *B*
Walsh University *B*
Wittenberg University *B*
Youngstown State University *B*

Oklahoma
Northeastern Oklahoma Agricultural and
  Mechanical College *C, A*

Oregon
Central Oregon Community College *A*
Concordia University *B*
University of Portland *B*

Pennsylvania
Gannon University *B*
Juniata College *B*
Lock Haven University of
  Pennsylvania *B*
Seton Hill College *B*

University of Pittsburgh
  Greensburg *B*
  Johnstown *B*
Ursinus College *B*
Waynesburg College *B*

Puerto Rico
University of Puerto Rico
  Ponce University College *A*

South Carolina
Aiken Technical College *C*
Orangeburg-Calhoun Technical
  College *C*
York Technical College *C*

Tennessee
Columbia State Community College *A*
Freed-Hardeman University *B*
Hiwassee College *A*
Maryville College *B*
Southern Adventist University *A*
Tennessee Technological University *B*
Tennessee Wesleyan College *B*
Union University *B*

Texas
Lon Morris College *A*
Midwestern State University *B*
St. Edward's University *B*

Utah
Salt Lake Community College *A*

Vermont
Castleton State College *M*
Johnson State College *B*

Virginia
Christopher Newport University *B*
Hampton University *B*
Longwood College *B*

West Virginia
Alderson-Broaddus College *B*

Wisconsin
Ripon College *B*
University of Wisconsin
  Oshkosh *B*

Preveterinary medicine

Alabama
Calhoun Community College *A*
Faulkner University *B*
Huntingdon College *B*
James H. Faulkner State Community
  College *A*
Northeast Alabama Community
  College *A*
Northwest-Shoals Community College *A*
Spring Hill College *B*

Arizona
Grand Canyon University *B*
Northern Arizona University *B*
University of Arizona *B*

Arkansas
Harding University *B*
Hendrix College *B*
John Brown University *B*
Ouachita Baptist University *B*
University of Central Arkansas *B*
Westark College *A*

California
Bakersfield College *A*
California Lutheran University *B*
California State University
  Chico *B*
Chabot College *A*
Chapman University *B*
College of Notre Dame *B*
College of the Siskiyous *A*
Crafton Hills College *C*
Cypress College *A*

Foothill College *A*
Golden West College *A*
Los Angeles Pierce College *A*
Marymount College *A*
MiraCosta College *A*
Monterey Peninsula College *A*
Mount St. Mary's College *B*
Pacific Union College *C*
Riverside Community College *A*
Ventura College *A*
Westmont College *B*
Whittier College *B*

Colorado
Adams State College *B*
Fort Lewis College *B*
Lamar Community College *A*
Otero Junior College *A*

Connecticut
Quinnipiac University *B*
Sacred Heart University *C*
Southern Connecticut State University *B*
Trinity College *B*
University of New Haven *B*

Delaware
Delaware State University *B*
University of Delaware *B*

Florida
Barry University *B*
Broward Community College *A*
Chipola Junior College *A*
Eckerd College *B*
Florida State University *B*
Gulf Coast Community College *A*
Indian River Community College *A*
Jacksonville University *B*
Miami-Dade Community College *A*
Pensacola Junior College *A*
St. Thomas University *B*
University of Central Florida *B*
University of Miami *B*
University of Tampa *B*

Georgia
Andrew College *A*
Columbus State University *B*
Floyd College *A*
Georgia Institute of Technology *B*
Kennesaw State University *B*
LaGrange College *B*
Middle Georgia College *A*
North Georgia College & State
  University *C*
Oglethorpe University *B*
Piedmont College *B*
University of Georgia *B*
Young Harris College *A*

Idaho
Boise State University *B*
College of Southern Idaho *A*
North Idaho College *A*
Northwest Nazarene University *B*
Ricks College *A*
University of Idaho *M*

Illinois
Blackburn College *B*
De Paul University *B*
Greenville College *B*
John A. Logan College *B*
Kankakee Community College *A*
Kishwaukee College *A*
Lake Land College *A*
Lincoln Land Community College *A*
MacMurray College *B*
McKendree College *B*
Millikin University *B*
North Park University *B*
Rend Lake College *A*
Rockford College *B*
Roosevelt University *B*
St. Xavier University *B*
Sauk Valley Community College *A*
Southwestern Illinois College *A*

Springfield College in Illinois *A*
University of St. Francis *B*

Indiana
Goshen College *B*
Grace College *B*
Indiana State University *B*
Indiana Wesleyan University *B*
Manchester College *B*
Purdue University
 Calumet *B*
St. Joseph's College *B*
St. Mary-of-the-Woods College *B*
University of Evansville *B*
University of Indianapolis *B*
University of St. Francis *B*
Valparaiso University *B*
Vincennes University *A*

Iowa
Buena Vista University *B*
Clarke College *B*
Coe College *B*
Dordt College *B*
Iowa Central Community College *A*
Iowa Wesleyan College *B*
Kirkwood Community College *A*
Luther College *B*
Marshalltown Community College *A*
Morningside College *B*
Northwestern College *B*
Simpson College *B*
University of Iowa *B*
Upper Iowa University *B*

Kansas
Central Christian College *A*
Coffeyville Community College *A*
Colby Community College *A*
Dodge City Community College *A*
Kansas City Kansas Community
 College *A*
Kansas State University *B*
McPherson College *B*
Pittsburg State University *B*
Pratt Community College *A*
Tabor College *B*
Washburn University of Topeka *B*

Kentucky
Campbellsville University *B*
Centre College *B*
Murray State University *B*
Thomas More College *B*
Union College *B*

Louisiana
Centenary College of Louisiana *B*
Dillard University *B*
Nicholls State University *A*

Maine
St. Joseph's College *B*
University of Maine
 Fort Kent *B*
University of New England *B*
University of Southern Maine *B*

Maryland
Columbia Union College *B*
Community College of Baltimore County
 Catonsville *A*
Frostburg State University *B*
Howard Community College *A*
Mount St. Mary's College *B*
University of Maryland
 Baltimore County *B*
 College Park *B*
 Eastern Shore *B*
Villa Julie College *B*

Massachusetts
American International College *B*
Becker College *B*
Eastern Nazarene College *B*
Elms College *B*
Framingham State College *B*
Hampshire College *B*

Stonehill College *B*
University of Massachusetts
 Amherst *B*
Worcester Polytechnic Institute *B*

Michigan
Adrian College *B*
Albion College *B*
Alma College *B*
Calvin College *B*
Cornerstone College and Grand Rapids
 Baptist Seminary *B*
Delta College *A*
Ferris State University *A*
Grand Valley State University *B*
Hillsdale College *B*
Kalamazoo College *B*
Kellogg Community College *A*
Kirtland Community College *A*
Michigan Technological University *B*
Northern Michigan University *B*
Oakland Community College *A*
Schoolcraft College *A*
Siena Heights University *A*

Minnesota
College of St. Benedict *B*
College of St. Catherine: St. Paul
 Campus *B*
Concordia College: Moorhead *B*
Gustavus Adolphus College *B*
Hamline University *B*
Minnesota State University, Mankato *B*
Moorhead State University *B*
St. Cloud State University *B*
St. John's University *B*
St. Mary's University of Minnesota *B*
St. Olaf College *B*
University of Minnesota
 Duluth *B*
 Twin Cities *B*
Winona State University *B*

Mississippi
Blue Mountain College *B*
Coahoma Community College *A*
East Central Community College *A*
Holmes Community College *A*
Jackson State University *B*
Mary Holmes College *A*
Mississippi Delta Community College *A*
Mississippi Gulf Coast Community
 College
 Jefferson Davis Campus *A*

Missouri
Central Methodist College *B*
East Central College *A*
Evangel University *B*
Lindenwood University *B*
Missouri Southern State College *A*
Northwest Missouri State University *B*
Stephens College *B*
Three Rivers Community College *A*
Truman State University *B*
University of Missouri
 St. Louis *B*
Washington University *B*

Montana
Montana Tech of the University of
 Montana *B*
Rocky Mountain College *B*
University of Great Falls *B*

Nebraska
College of Saint Mary *B*
Dana College *B*
Hastings College *B*
Metropolitan Community College *A*
Mid Plains Community College Area *A*
Midland Lutheran College *B*
Northeast Community College *A*
University of Nebraska
 Lincoln *B*

Nevada
University of Nevada
 Reno *B*

New Hampshire
Franklin Pierce College *B*
Rivier College *B*
University of New Hampshire *B*

New Jersey
Bloomfield College *B*
Georgian Court College *B*
Rowan University *B*
Rutgers
 The State University of New Jersey:
 Camden College of Arts and
 Sciences *B*
 The State University of New Jersey:
 Cook College *B*
 The State University of New Jersey:
 University College Camden *B*

New Mexico
College of Santa Fe *B*

New York
Alfred University *B*
Bard College *B*
City University of New York
 City College *B*
 College of Staten Island *B*
 Hunter College *B*
Colgate University *B*
Cornell University *B*
D'Youville College *B*
Elmira College *B*
Fordham University *B*
Hobart and William Smith Colleges *B*
Houghton College *B*
Ithaca College *B*
Le Moyne College *B*
Long Island University
 C. W. Post Campus *B*
 Southampton College *B*
Manhattan College *B*
Marist College *B*
Molloy College *B*
New York University *B*
Rensselaer Polytechnic Institute *B*
Rochester Institute of Technology *B*
St. Francis College *B*
St. John Fisher College *B*
St. Thomas Aquinas College *B*
St. Joseph's College
 St. Joseph's College: Suffolk
 Campus *B*
State University of New York
 College at Brockport *B*
 College at Geneseo *B*
 College of Environmental Science
 and Forestry *B*
 New Paltz *B*
Syracuse University *B*
Touro College *B*
Wells College *B*

North Carolina
Barton College *B*
Belmont Abbey College *B*
Brevard College *A, B*
Chowan College *B*
Elon College *B*
Lees-McRae College *B*
Mars Hill College *B*
Meredith College *B*
Methodist College *B*
Mitchell Community College *A*
North Carolina State University *B*
Pfeiffer University *B*
St. Andrews Presbyterian College *B*
Sandhills Community College *A*
Warren Wilson College *B*
Wingate University *B*

North Dakota
Dickinson State University *B*
Mayville State University *B*

Minot State University *B*
Valley City State University *B*

Ohio
Ashland University *B*
Defiance College *B*
Heidelberg College *B*
John Carroll University *B*
Kent State University *B*
Lorain County Community College *A*
Muskingum College *B*
Ohio University *B*
Ohio Wesleyan University *B*
Otterbein College *B*
Shawnee State University *B*
University of Akron *B*
University of Cincinnati
 Clermont College *A*
University of Cincinnati *B*
University of Findlay *B*
University of Toledo *B*
Ursuline College *B*
Walsh University *B*
Wittenberg University *B*
Youngstown State University *B*

Oklahoma
Connors State College *A*
East Central University *B*
Eastern Oklahoma State College *A*
Langston University *B*
Murray State College *A*
Oklahoma Christian University of
 Science and Arts *B*
Oklahoma City University *B*
Oklahoma State University *B*

Oregon
Eastern Oregon University *B*
Southern Oregon University *B*
University of Portland *B*
Western Baptist College *B*
Willamette University *B*

Pennsylvania
Allentown College of St. Francis de
 Sales *B*
Alvernia College *B*
California University of Pennsylvania *B*
College Misericordia *B*
Elizabethtown College *B*
Gannon University *B*
Gettysburg College *B*
Grove City College *B*
Gwynedd-Mercy College *B*
Holy Family College *B*
Immaculata College *B*
Juniata College *B*
La Salle University *B*
Lock Haven University of
 Pennsylvania *B*
Mansfield University of Pennsylvania *B*
Mercyhurst College *B*
Muhlenberg College *B*
Penn State
 University Park *B*
Seton Hill College *B*
Susquehanna University *B*
University of Pittsburgh
 Greensburg *B*
 Johnstown *B*
Ursinus College *B*
Waynesburg College *B*
Westminster College *B*
Widener University *B*
Wilkes University *B*
York College of Pennsylvania *B*

Rhode Island
Rhode Island College *B*
Salve Regina University *B*

South Carolina
Clemson University *B*
Erskine College *B*
Furman University *B*
Lander University *B*

Wofford College C

South Dakota
Augustana College B
Dakota State University B
Dakota Wesleyan University B

Tennessee
Cumberland University B
Freed-Hardeman University B
Hiwassee College A
Lincoln Memorial University B
Maryville College B
Tennessee Wesleyan College B
Union University B
University of Tennessee
    Knoxville B
    Martin B
Walters State Community College A

Texas
Abilene Christian University B
Amarillo College A
Angelina College A
Coastal Bend College A
Del Mar College A
El Paso Community College A
Galveston College A
LeTourneau University B
Lon Morris College A
McMurry University B
Midwestern State University B
Navarro College A
Panola College A
Paris Junior College A
San Antonio College A
South Plains College A
Sul Ross State University A
Texas A&M University
    Commerce B
Trinity Valley Community College A
Tyler Junior College A
Western Texas College A

Utah
Dixie State College of Utah A
Utah State University B, M

Vermont
Castleton State College B

Virginia
Averett College B
Longwood College B
Mountain Empire Community College A
Virginia Commonwealth University B
Virginia Intermont College B
Virginia Wesleyan College B

Washington
Centralia College A
Eastern Washington University B
Everett Community College A
Lower Columbia College A
St. Martin's College B
Western Washington University B

West Virginia
Alderson-Broaddus College B
Concord College B
Davis and Elkins College B
Marshall University B
Potomac State College of West Virginia
    University A
West Virginia Wesleyan College B

Wisconsin
Cardinal Stritch University B
Lawrence University B
Marian College of Fond du Lac B
Mount Mary College B
Northland College B
Ripon College B
St. Norbert College B

University of Wisconsin
    Madison B
    Milwaukee B
    Oshkosh B
    Parkside B
    Whitewater B
Viterbo University B

Wyoming
Casper College A
Eastern Wyoming College A
Northwest College A
Western Wyoming Community
    College A

Printmaking

Arizona
Arizona State University B, M

Arkansas
Phillips Community College of the
    University of Arkansas C, A

California
Academy of Art College C, A, B, M
American Film Institute Center for
    Advanced Film and Television
    Studies M
California College of Arts and
    Crafts B, M
California Institute of the Arts C, B, M
California State University
    Fullerton B, M
    Hayward B
    Long Beach B, M
    Northridge B, M
    Stanislaus C
City College of San Francisco C, A
De Anza College C, A
Fresno City College C, A
Monterey Peninsula College A
Otis College of Art and Design B, M
Palomar College A
Pasadena City College C, A
San Diego State University B
San Francisco Art Institute B, M
Santa Rosa Junior College C
University of San Francisco B

Colorado
Adams State College B
Colorado State University B

Connecticut
Capital Community College C
University of Hartford B, M

District of Columbia
American University M
George Washington University M

Florida
Ringling School of Art and Design B
University of Miami B

Georgia
Atlanta College of Art B
University of Georgia B

Illinois
Barat College B
Rockford College B
School of the Art Institute of
    Chicago B, M

Indiana
Ball State University B
Indiana University--Purdue University
    Indiana University-Purdue
        University Fort Wayne B
University of Evansville B
Vincennes University A

Iowa
Drake University B, M
University of Iowa B, M

Kansas
University of Kansas B, M

Maine
Maine College of Art B

Maryland
Maryland Institute College of Art B

Massachusetts
Emmanuel College B
Massachusetts College of Art B, M
Montserrat College of Art B
School of the Museum of Fine Arts B, M
Simon's Rock College of Bard B

Michigan
Center for Creative Studies: College of
    Art and Design B
Cranbrook Academy of Art M
Grand Valley State University B
Northern Michigan University B
University of Michigan B

Minnesota
College of Visual Arts B
Minneapolis College of Art and
    Design B
Moorhead State University B

Mississippi
Mississippi University for Women B

Missouri
Kansas City Art Institute B
Lindenwood University M
University of Missouri
    St. Louis B
Washington University B, M
Webster University B

New Hampshire
New Hampshire Community Technical
    College
        Laconia C
Plymouth State College of the University
    System of New Hampshire B

New Jersey
Rowan University B
Rutgers
    The State University of New Jersey:
        Mason Gross School of the
        Arts B, M

New York
Bard College B
Columbia University
    Teachers College M
New York Institute of Technology M
New York State College of Ceramics at
    Alfred University B, M, T
Parsons School of Design C
Pratt Institute B, M
Sarah Lawrence College B
School of Visual Arts B, M
State University of New York
    College at Buffalo B
    College at Fredonia B
    New Paltz B, M
Syracuse University B, M

Ohio
Bowling Green State University B
Cleveland Institute of Art B
Columbus College of Art and Design B
Kent State University B, M
Lourdes College A
Ohio State University
    Columbus Campus B
Ohio University M
University of Akron B
Wittenberg University B
Youngstown State University B

Oklahoma
University of Oklahoma B

Oregon
Pacific Northwest College of Art B

Portland State University B
University of Oregon B, M

Pennsylvania
Beaver College B
Immaculata College A
Moore College of Art and Design B
Seton Hill College B
Temple University B, M
University of the Arts B, M

Puerto Rico
Escuela de Artes Plasticas de Puerto
    Rico B

Rhode Island
Providence College B

South Carolina
South Carolina State University B

Texas
Sam Houston State University M
Texas A&M University
    Commerce B
University of Dallas M, T
University of Houston B, M
University of North Texas B, M
University of Texas
    Arlington B
    El Paso B
    San Antonio B, M

Utah
Brigham Young University M
Dixie State College of Utah A

Vermont
Bennington College B, M

Virginia
Virginia Commonwealth
    University B, M
Virginia Intermont College B

Washington
Cornish College of the Arts B
University of Washington B, M
Western Washington University B

West Virginia
Marshall University B
West Virginia State College B

Wisconsin
Milwaukee Institute of Art & Design B
University of Wisconsin
    Madison B

Protective services

Alabama
Community College of the Air Force A

Arkansas
Southern Arkansas University
    Tech A

California
American River College A
Bakersfield College A
Chabot College A
Citrus College A
Compton Community College C, A
Fresno City College C, A
Pasadena City College A
San Joaquin Delta College A

Connecticut
Briarwood College C
Capital Community College A

Georgia
Atlanta Metropolitan College A

Illinois
Black Hawk College C, A
Lewis University B
Moraine Valley Community
    College C, A

Richland Community College *A*
Kansas
Hutchinson Community College *A*
Kansas City Kansas Community
College *C, A*
Seward County Community
College *C, A*
Louisiana
Louisiana State University
Eunice *A*
Maryland
Montgomery College
Rockville Campus *A*
Massachusetts
Northeastern University *B, M*
Michigan
Kirtland Community College *C*
Lansing Community College *A*
Michigan State University *B*
Minnesota
Northland Community & Technical
College *A*
New York
Adirondack Community College *A*
City University of New York
John Jay College of Criminal
Justice *A, B*
Hudson Valley Community College *A*
Iona College *M*
Mercy College *B*
State University of New York
College at Brockport *B*
Tompkins-Cortland Community
College *A*
North Carolina
Alamance Community College *A*
Cape Fear Community College *A*
Central Piedmont Community College *A*
Edgecombe Community College *A*
Fayetteville Technical Community
College *A*
Nash Community College *A*
Pitt Community College *C*
Ohio
Ohio University
Chillicothe Campus *A*
Sinclair Community College *A*
Youngstown State University *C, A, B, M*
Pennsylvania
Community College of Allegheny
County *A*
York College of Pennsylvania *B*
South Carolina
Aiken Technical College *A*
Trident Technical College *A*
Tennessee
Cumberland University *B*
Roane State Community College *A*
Texas
Central Texas College *A*
Hill College *C, A*
San Antonio College *A*
San Jacinto College
North *C*
Texas A&M University
Texarkana *B*
Virginia
Germanna Community College *A*
Northern Virginia Community College *A*
Patrick Henry Community College *A*
Piedmont Virginia Community
College *C, A*
Southside Virginia Community
College *C, A*
Virginia Western Community College *A*

Washington
Centralia College *C, A*
Wisconsin
Chippewa Valley Technical College *A*
Milwaukee Area Technical College *A*
Wisconsin Indianhead Technical
College *A*
Wyoming
Sheridan College *A*

Psychobiology/physiological psychology

California
Cuesta College *C, A*
Hope International University *B*
La Sierra University *B*
Occidental College *B*
Pepperdine University *B*
San Francisco State University *M*
Scripps College *B*
University of California
Los Angeles *B*
Riverside *B*
Santa Barbara *B*
Santa Cruz *B*
University of Southern California *B*
Colorado
University of Colorado
Denver *B*
Connecticut
Quinnipiac University *B*
Florida
Florida Atlantic University *B, D*
University of Miami *B, D*
Georgia
Emory University *D*
Illinois
Loyola University of Chicago *D*
Indiana
University of Evansville *B*
Iowa
Luther College *B*
St. Ambrose University *C*
Kentucky
Centre College *B*
Massachusetts
Hampshire College *B*
Harvard College *B*
Pine Manor College *B*
Simmons College *B*
Wellesley College *B*
Wheaton College *B*
Mississippi
William Carey College *M*
Missouri
Northwest Missouri State University *B*
New York
City University of New York
Graduate School and University
Center *D*
Columbia University
School of General Studies *B*
Hamilton College *B*
Long Island University
Southampton College *B*
Medaille College *B*
Sarah Lawrence College *B*
State University of New York
Albany *M, D*
Binghamton *B, D*
New Paltz *B*
Stony Brook *M, D*

Ohio
Hiram College *B*
Oberlin College *B*
Pennsylvania
Albright College *B*
Beaver College *B*
Chatham College *B*
Holy Family College *B*
La Roche College *B*
Lebanon Valley College of
Pennsylvania *B*
Lincoln University *B*
Swarthmore College *B*
University of Pennsylvania *A, B, D*
Texas
Baylor University *B, M, D*
Virginia
Averett College *B*
College of William and Mary *B*
Lynchburg College *B*

Psychology

Alabama
Alabama Agricultural and Mechanical
University *B*
Alabama State University *B*
Athens State University *B*
Auburn University at Montgomery *B, M*
Auburn University *B, M, D*
Birmingham-Southern College *B*
Faulkner University *B*
Huntingdon College *B*
Jacksonville State University *B, M*
Lawson State Community College *A*
Oakwood College *B*
Samford University *B*
Spring Hill College *B*
Talladega College *B*
Troy State University
Dothan *B*
Montgomery *B*
Troy State University *B*
Tuskegee University *B*
University of Alabama
Birmingham *B, M, D*
Huntsville *B, M*
University of Alabama *B, M, D*
University of Mobile *B*
University of Montevallo *B*
University of North Alabama *B*
University of South Alabama *B, M*
University of West Alabama *B*
Alaska
Alaska Pacific University *B*
University of Alaska
Anchorage *B*
Fairbanks *B*
Arizona
Arizona State University *B, M, D*
Cochise College *A*
Dine College *A*
Eastern Arizona College *A*
Grand Canyon University *B*
Mohave Community College *A*
Northern Arizona University *B, M*
Prescott College *B, M*
South Mountain Community College *A*
University of Arizona *B, M, D*
Arkansas
Arkansas State University *B*
Arkansas Tech University *B*
Harding University *B*
Henderson State University *B*
Hendrix College *B*
John Brown University *B*
Lyon College *B*
Ouachita Baptist University *B*
Philander Smith College *B*
Southern Arkansas University *B*

University of Arkansas
Little Rock *B*
Monticello *B*
Pine Bluff *B*
University of Arkansas *B, M, D*
University of Central Arkansas *B*
University of the Ozarks *B*
Westark College *A*
Williams Baptist College *B*
California
Antioch Southern California
Los Angeles *M*
Santa Barbara *M*
Azusa Pacific University *B*
Bakersfield College *A*
Barstow College *A*
Biola University *B, M, D*
Cabrillo College *A*
California Baptist University *B*
California Lutheran University *B*
California State Polytechnic University:
Pomona *B, M*
California State University
Bakersfield *B, M*
Chico *B, M*
Dominguez Hills *B*
Fresno *B, M*
Fullerton *B, M*
Hayward *B*
Long Beach *B, M*
Los Angeles *B, M*
Northridge *B*
Sacramento *B, M*
San Marcos *B, M*
Stanislaus *B, M*
Canada College *A*
Cerritos Community College *A*
Chabot College *A*
Chaffey Community College *A*
Chapman University *B, M*
Citrus College *A*
Claremont McKenna College *B*
College of Notre Dame *B*
College of the Desert *A*
College of the Siskiyous *A*
Compton Community College *A*
Concordia University *B*
Contra Costa College *A*
Crafton Hills College *A*
Cypress College *A*
De Anza College *A*
Dominican University of California *B*
East Los Angeles College *A*
Foothill College *A*
Fresno City College *A*
Fresno Pacific University *B*
Gavilan Community College *A*
Glendale Community College *A*
Golden Gate University *B, M*
Golden West College *A*
Holy Names College *B*
Hope International University *B*
Humboldt State University *B, M*
Imperial Valley College *A*
Irvine Valley College *A*
John F. Kennedy University *B, D*
La Sierra University *B*
Lake Tahoe Community College *A*
Loma Linda University *M, D*
Long Beach City College *C, A*
Los Angeles Harbor College *A*
Los Angeles Mission College *A*
Los Angeles Southwest College *A*
Los Angeles Valley College *A*
Los Medanos College *A*
Loyola Marymount University *B*
Marymount College *A*
Mendocino College *A*
Merced College *A*
Mills College *B*
MiraCosta College *A*
Monterey Peninsula College *A*
Mount St. Mary's College *B*
National University *B*

Occidental College B, M
Ohlone College A
Orange Coast College A
Pacific Graduate School of
  Psychology D
Pacific Union College B
Pasadena City College A
Pepperdine University B, M, D
Pitzer College B
Point Loma Nazarene University B
Pomona College B
Riverside Community College A
Saddleback College A
St. Mary's College of California B, M
San Bernardino Valley College C, A
San Diego City College A
San Diego Mesa College A
San Diego Miramar College A
San Diego State University B, M, D
San Francisco State University B
San Joaquin Delta College A
San Jose City College A
San Jose State University B, M
Santa Ana College A
Santa Barbara City College A
Santa Clara University B
Santa Rosa Junior College A
Saybrook Graduate School and Research
  Center M, D
Scripps College B
Simpson College A, B
Skyline College A
Solano Community College A
Sonoma State University B, M
Southwestern College A
Stanford University B, M, D
United States International
  University C, B, M, D
University of California
  Berkeley B, M, D
  Davis B, D
  Irvine B, D
  Los Angeles B, M, D
  Riverside B, M, D
  San Diego B, M, D
  Santa Barbara B, M, D
  Santa Cruz B, D
University of Judaism M
University of La Verne B
University of Redlands B
University of San Diego B
University of San Francisco B
University of Southern California B, T
University of the Pacific B, M
Vanguard University of Southern
  California B
Ventura College A
West Hills Community College A
West Los Angeles College C, A
West Valley College A
Westmont College B
Whittier College B

Colorado
Adams State College B
Colorado Christian University B
Colorado College B
Colorado Mountain College
  Alpine Campus A
Colorado State University B, M, D
Fort Lewis College B
Lamar Community College A
Mesa State College B
Metropolitan State College of Denver B
Naropa University C, B
Otero Junior College A
Red Rocks Community College A
Regis University B
Trinidad State Junior College A
United States Air Force Academy B
University of Colorado
  Boulder B, M, D
  Colorado Springs B, M
  Denver B, M
University of Denver B, M, D

University of Northern Colorado B, M
University of Southern Colorado B, T
Western State College of Colorado B

Connecticut
Albertus Magnus College B
Central Connecticut State
  University B, M
Connecticut College B, M
Eastern Connecticut State University B
Fairfield University B
Quinnipiac University B
Sacred Heart University A, B
St. Joseph College B
Southern Connecticut State
  University B, M
Teikyo Post University B
Trinity College B
University of Connecticut B, M, D
University of Hartford B, M
University of New Haven B
Wesleyan University B, M
Western Connecticut State University B
Yale University B, M, D

Delaware
Delaware State University B
University of Delaware B, M, D
Wesley College B

District of Columbia
American University B, M, D
Catholic University of America B, M
Gallaudet University B
George Washington University B, M, D
Georgetown University B, D
Howard University B, M, D
Trinity College B
University of the District of Columbia B

Florida
Art Institute
  of Fort Lauderdale A
Barry University B
Bethune-Cookman College B
Broward Community College A
Carlos Albizu University B, M, D
Clearwater Christian College B
Eckerd College B
Edward Waters College B
Embry-Riddle Aeronautical
  University M
Flagler College B
Florida Agricultural and Mechanical
  University B
Florida Atlantic University B, M
Florida Gulf Coast University B
Florida Institute of Technology B, M
Florida International University B, M, D
Florida Memorial College B
Florida Southern College B
Florida State University B, M, D
Gulf Coast Community College A
Indian River Community College A
Jacksonville University B
Lynn University B
Manatee Community College A
Miami-Dade Community College A
New College of the University of South
  Florida B
Nova Southeastern University B
Palm Beach Atlantic College B
Palm Beach Community College A
Pensacola Junior College A
Polk Community College A
Rollins College B
St. Leo University B
St. Thomas University B
South Florida Community College A
Southeastern College of the Assemblies
  of God B
Stetson University B
University of Central Florida B, D
University of Florida B, M, D
University of Miami B, M, D
University of North Florida B, M

University of South Florida B, M, D
University of Tampa A, B
University of West Florida B, M
Warner Southern College B

Georgia
Abraham Baldwin Agricultural
  College A
Agnes Scott College B
Albany State University B
Andrew College B
Armstrong Atlantic State University B
Atlanta Metropolitan College A
Augusta State University B, M
Berry College B
Brenau University B
Brewton-Parker College A, B
Clark Atlanta University B
Clayton College and State University A
Coastal Georgia Community College A
Columbus State University B
Covenant College B
Dalton State College A
Darton College A
East Georgia College A
Emmanuel College B
Emory University B, D
Floyd College A
Fort Valley State University B
Gainesville College A
Georgia College and State
  University B, M
Georgia Institute of Technology B, M, D
Georgia Military College A
Georgia Perimeter College A
Georgia Southern University B, M
Georgia Southwestern State University B
Georgia State University B, M, D
Kennesaw State University B
LaGrange College B
Mercer University B
Middle Georgia College A
Morehouse College B
Morris Brown College B
North Georgia College & State
  University B
Oglethorpe University B
Oxford College of Emory University B
Paine College B
Piedmont College B
Reinhardt College B
Shorter College B
South Georgia College A
Spelman College B
State University of West Georgia B, M
Thomas College B
Toccoa Falls College B
University of Georgia B, M, D
Valdosta State University B, M
Waycross College A
Wesleyan College B
Young Harris College A

Hawaii
Brigham Young University
  Hawaii B
Chaminade University of Honolulu B
Hawaii Pacific University B
University of Hawaii
  Hilo B
  Manoa B, M, D
  West Oahu B

Idaho
Albertson College of Idaho B
Boise State University B
College of Southern Idaho A
Idaho State University B, M
Lewis-Clark State College B
North Idaho College A
Northwest Nazarene University B
Ricks College A
University of Idaho B, M

Illinois
Augustana College B, T

Barat College B
Benedictine University B
Black Hawk College
  East Campus A
Blackburn College B
Bradley University B, T
Chicago State University B
City Colleges of Chicago
  Kennedy-King College A
Concordia University B, M
Danville Area Community College A
De Paul University B
Dominican University B
Eastern Illinois University B, T
Elmhurst College B, T
Eureka College B
Governors State University B, M
Greenville College B
Highland Community College A
Illinois College B
Illinois Institute of Technology B, M, D
Illinois State University B, M
Illinois Wesleyan University B
John A. Logan College A
John Wood Community College A
Joliet Junior College A
Judson College B
Kankakee Community College A
Kendall College B
Kishwaukee College A
Knox College B
Lake Forest College B
Lake Land College A
Lewis University B, T
Lewis and Clark Community College A
Lincoln Land Community College A
Loyola University of Chicago B, T
MacMurray College B
McKendree College B
Millikin University B
Monmouth College B, T
Morton College A
National-Louis University B, M
North Central College B
North Park University B
Northeastern Illinois University B
Northern Illinois University B, M, D
Northwestern University B, M, D
Olivet Nazarene University B, M
Parkland College A
Quincy University A, B
Rend Lake College A
Richland Community College A
Rockford College B
Roosevelt University B, M
St. Augustine College A
St. Xavier University B
Sauk Valley Community College A
Southern Illinois University
  Carbondale B, M, D
  Edwardsville B, M
Southwestern Illinois College A
Springfield College in Illinois A
Trinity Christian College B
Trinity International University B, M
Triton College A
University of Chicago B, M, D
University of Illinois
  Chicago B, M, D
  Springfield B, M
  Urbana-Champaign B, M, D
University of St. Francis B
Western Illinois University B, M
Wheaton College B, T
William Rainey Harper College A

Indiana
Anderson University B
Ball State University B, M
Bethel College B
Butler University B
DePauw University B
Earlham College B
Franklin College B
Goshen College B

Grace College *B*
Hanover College *B*
Indiana State University *M, D*
Indiana University
  Bloomington *B, M, D*
  East *B*
  Kokomo *B*
  Northwest *B*
  South Bend *A, B, M*
  Southeast *B*
Indiana University--Purdue University
  Indiana University-Purdue
    University Fort Wayne *A, B*
  Indiana University-Purdue
    University Indianapolis *B, M*
Indiana Wesleyan University *B, T*
Manchester College *B*
Marian College *B, T*
Purdue University
  Calumet *B*
Purdue University *B, M, D*
Saint Mary's College *B*
St. Joseph's College *B*
St. Mary-of-the-Woods College *B*
Taylor University *B*
Tri-State University *B*
University of Evansville *B*
University of Indianapolis *B*
University of Notre Dame *B, M, D*
University of St. Francis *B, M*
University of Southern Indiana *B*
Valparaiso University *B*
Vincennes University *A*
Wabash College *B*

Iowa
Briar Cliff College *B*
Buena Vista University *B*
Central College *B, T*
Clarke College *B, T*
Coe College *B*
Cornell College *B*
Dordt College *B*
Drake University *B, M*
Graceland University *B, T*
Grand View College *B*
Grinnell College *B*
Iowa Central Community College *A*
Iowa State University *B, M, D*
Iowa Wesleyan College *B*
Iowa Western Community College *A*
Loras College *B, M*
Luther College *B*
Maharishi University of
  Management *A, B, M, D*
Marshalltown Community College *A*
Marycrest International University *A, B*
Morningside College *B*
Mount Mercy College *B*
North Iowa Area Community College *A*
Northwestern College *B*
St. Ambrose University *B, T*
Simpson College *B*
University of Dubuque *B*
University of Iowa *B, D, T*
University of Northern Iowa *B, M*
Upper Iowa University *B*
Waldorf College *A*
Wartburg College *B, T*
William Penn University *B*

Kansas
Baker University *B, T*
Barclay College *B*
Barton County Community College *A*
Benedictine College *B*
Bethany College *B, T*
Bethel College *B, T*
Butler County Community College *A*
Central Christian College *A*
Coffeyville Community College *A*
Colby Community College *A*
Emporia State University *B, M*
Fort Hays State University *B, M*
Garden City Community College *A*
Hutchinson Community College *A*
Independence Community College *A*
Kansas City Kansas Community
  College *A*
Kansas State University *B, M, D*
Kansas Wesleyan University *B*
McPherson College *B, T*
MidAmerica Nazarene University *B, T*
Newman University *B*
Ottawa University *B*
Pittsburg State University *B, M, T*
Pratt Community College *A*
St. Mary College *B, M*
Seward County Community College *A*
Southwestern College *B*
Tabor College *B*
University of Kansas *B, M, D*
Washburn University of Topeka *B*
Wichita State University *B, M, D*

Kentucky
Asbury College *B*
Bellarmine College *B*
Berea College *B*
Brescia University *B*
Campbellsville University *B*
Centre College *B*
Cumberland College *B, T*
Eastern Kentucky University *B*
Georgetown College *B, T*
Kentucky Christian College *B*
Kentucky State University *B*
Kentucky Wesleyan College *B*
Mid-Continent College *B*
Midway College *B*
Morehead State University *B, M*
Murray State University *B, M*
Northern Kentucky University *B*
Pikeville College *B*
Spalding University *B*
Thomas More College *A, B*
Transylvania University *B*
Union College *B*
University of Kentucky *B*
University of Louisville *B, M*
Western Kentucky University *B, M, T*

Louisiana
Centenary College of Louisiana *B, T*
Dillard University *B*
Louisiana State University
  Shreveport *B*
Louisiana State University and
  Agricultural and Mechanical
  College *B, M, D*
Louisiana Tech University *B*
Loyola University New Orleans *B*
McNeese State University *B, M*
Nicholls State University *B*
Northwestern State University *B, M*
Southeastern Louisiana University *B, M*
Southern University
  New Orleans *B*
Southern University and Agricultural and
  Mechanical College *B*
Tulane University *B, M, D*
University of Louisiana at
  Lafayette *B, M*
University of Louisiana at Monroe *B, M*
University of New Orleans *B, M, D*
Xavier University of Louisiana *B*

Maine
Bates College *B*
Bowdoin College *B*
Colby College *B*
St. Joseph's College *B*
University of Maine
  Farmington *B*
  Fort Kent *B*
  Machias *B*
  Presque Isle *B*
University of Maine *B, M, D*
University of New England *B*
University of Southern Maine *B*

Maryland
Allegany College *A*
Bowie State University *B*
Chesapeake College *C, A*
College of Notre Dame of Maryland *B*
Columbia Union College *B*
Community College of Baltimore County
  Essex *A*
Coppin State College *B, M*
Frederick Community College *A*
Frostburg State University *B*
Goucher College *B*
Hood College *B*
Howard Community College *A*
Johns Hopkins University *B, D*
Loyola College in Maryland *B, M*
Morgan State University *B*
Mount St. Mary's College *B*
St. Mary's College of Maryland *B*
Salisbury State University *B, M, T*
Towson University *B, M*
University of Baltimore *B, M*
University of Maryland
  Baltimore County *M, D*
  College Park *B, M, D*
Villa Julie College *B*
Washington College *B, M, T*
Western Maryland College *B*

Massachusetts
Amherst College *B*
Anna Maria College *B, M*
Assumption College *B, M*
Atlantic Union College *B*
Bay Path College *A, B*
Becker College *A, B*
Berkshire Community College *A*
Boston College *B, D*
Boston University *B, M, D*
Brandeis University *B, M, D*
Bridgewater State College *B, M*
Cambridge College *B, M*
Cape Cod Community College *A*
Clark University *B, D*
College of the Holy Cross *B*
Curry College *B*
Eastern Nazarene College *B*
Elms College *B*
Emmanuel College *B*
Endicott College *B*
Fitchburg State College *B*
Framingham State College *B*
Gordon College *B*
Hampshire College *B*
Harvard College *B*
Harvard University *M, D*
Hellenic College/Holy Cross *B*
Lasell College *B*
Massachusetts College of Liberal Arts *B*
Merrimack College *B*
Mount Holyoke College *B, M*
Newbury College *A*
Nichols College *B*
Northeastern University *B, M, D*
Pine Manor College *B*
Regis College *B*
St. John's Seminary College *B*
Salem State College *B*
Simmons College *B*
Simon's Rock College of Bard *B*
Smith College *B*
Springfield College *B*
Stonehill College *B*
Suffolk University *B, M*
Tufts University *B, M, D*
University of Massachusetts
  Amherst *B, M, D*
  Boston *B*
  Dartmouth *B, M*
  Lowell *B*
Wellesley College *B*
Western New England College *B*
Westfield State College *B, M*
Wheaton College *B*
Williams College *B*
Worcester State College *B*

Michigan
Adrian College *A, B, T*
Albion College *B, T*
Alma College *B, T*
Andrews University *B, M, D*
Aquinas College *B, T*
Calvin College *B, T*
Central Michigan University *B, M*
Concordia College *B, T*
Cornerstone College and Grand Rapids
  Baptist Seminary *B*
Eastern Michigan University *B, M*
Gogebic Community College *A*
Grand Valley State University *B, T*
Hillsdale College *B*
Hope College *B, T*
Kalamazoo College *B, T*
Kellogg Community College *A*
Lake Michigan College *A*
Lake Superior State University *B*
Lansing Community College *A*
Madonna University *B*
Marygrove College *B*
Michigan State University *B, M, D*
Mid Michigan Community College *A*
Northern Michigan University *B*
Oakland University *B*
Olivet College *B*
Rochester College *B*
Saginaw Valley State University *B*
Siena Heights University *A, B*
Spring Arbor College *B*
University of Detroit Mercy *B, M*
University of Michigan
  Dearborn *B*
  Flint *B, T*
University of Michigan *B, M, D, T*
Wayne State University *C, B, M, D*
Western Michigan University *B, M, D*
William Tyndale College *B*

Minnesota
Augsburg College *B*
Bemidji State University *B*
Bethel College *B*
Carleton College *B*
College of St. Benedict *B*
College of St. Catherine: St. Paul
  Campus *B*
College of St. Scholastica *B, M*
Concordia College: Moorhead *B*
Concordia University: St. Paul *B*
Crown College *B*
Gustavus Adolphus College *B*
Hamline University *B*
Macalester College *B*
Metropolitan State University *B*
Minnesota State University, Mankato *B*
Moorhead State University *B*
North Central University *B*
Northland Community & Technical
  College *A*
Northwestern College *B*
Ridgewater College: A Community and
  Technical College *A*
St. Cloud State University *B, M*
St. John's University *B*
St. Mary's University of Minnesota *B*
St. Olaf College *B*
Southwest State University *B*
University of Minnesota
  Duluth *B*
  Morris *B*
  Twin Cities *B, M, D*
University of St. Thomas *B*
Winona State University *B*

Mississippi
Belhaven College *B*
Blue Mountain College *B*
Delta State University *B*
East Central Community College *A*
Hinds Community College *A*
Jackson State University *B*

Psychology

Mary Holmes College *A*
Millsaps College *B, T*
Mississippi College *B*
Mississippi Delta Community College *A*
Mississippi Gulf Coast Community College
   Perkinston *A*
Mississippi State University *B, M*
Mississippi University for Women *B*
Tougaloo College *B*
University of Mississippi *B, M, D*
University of Southern Mississippi *B, M, D*
William Carey College *B*

Missouri
Avila College *B*
Central Methodist College *B*
Central Missouri State University *B, M*
College of the Ozarks *B*
Columbia College *B*
Crowder College *A*
Culver-Stockton College *B*
Drury University *B*
East Central College *A*
Evangel University *B*
Hannibal-LaGrange College *B*
Jefferson College *A*
Lincoln University *B*
Lindenwood University *B*
Maryville University of Saint Louis *B*
Mineral Area College *A*
Missouri Baptist College *B*
Missouri Southern State College *B*
Missouri Valley College *B*
Missouri Western State College *B*
Northwest Missouri State University *B*
Park University *B*
Rockhurst University *B*
St. Louis University *B, M, D*
Southeast Missouri State University *B*
Southwest Baptist University *B*
Southwest Missouri State University *B, M*
St. Louis Community College
   St. Louis Community College at Florissant Valley *A*
   St. Louis Community College at Forest Park *A*
Stephens College *B*
Three Rivers Community College *A*
Truman State University *B*
University of Missouri
   Columbia *B, M, D*
   Kansas City *B, M, D*
   Rolla *B, T*
   St. Louis *B, M, D*
Washington University *B, M, D*
Webster University *B*
Westminster College *B*
William Jewell College *B*
William Woods University *B*

Montana
Carroll College *B, T*
Little Big Horn College *A*
Miles Community College *A*
Montana State University
   Billings *B, M*
   Bozeman *B, M*
Rocky Mountain College *B, T*
University of Montana-Missoula *B, M, D*

Nebraska
Bellevue University *B*
Chadron State College *B*
College of Saint Mary *B*
Concordia University *B*
Creighton University *B*
Dana College *B*
Doane College *B*
Hastings College *B, T*
Midland Lutheran College *B*
Nebraska Wesleyan University *B*
Northeast Community College *A*
Peru State College *B, T*
Union College *B*
University of Nebraska
   Kearney *B, T*
   Lincoln *B, M, D*
   Omaha *B, M*
Wayne State College *B, T*

Nevada
University of Nevada
   Las Vegas *B, M, D*
   Reno *B, M, D*

New Hampshire
Antioch New England Graduate School *M, D*
Colby-Sawyer College *B*
Dartmouth College *B, D*
Franklin Pierce College *B*
Hesser College *A*
Keene State College *B*
New England College *B*
New Hampshire College *B*
Notre Dame College *B*
Plymouth State College of the University System of New Hampshire *B*
Rivier College *B*
St. Anselm College *B, T*
University of New Hampshire Manchester *B*
University of New Hampshire *B, M, D*

New Jersey
Atlantic Cape Community College *A*
Bloomfield College *B*
Caldwell College *B*
Centenary College *B*
College of St. Elizabeth *B*
Drew University *B*
Fairleigh Dickinson University *B, M*
Felician College *B*
Georgian Court College *B*
Gloucester County College *A*
Kean University *B, M*
Monmouth University *B*
Montclair State University *B, M, T*
New Jersey City University *B, M*
Ocean County College *A*
Passaic County Community College *A*
Princeton University *B, M, D*
Ramapo College of New Jersey *B*
Richard Stockton College of New Jersey *B*
Rider University *B*
Rowan University *B, M*
Rutgers
   The State University of New Jersey: Camden College of Arts and Sciences *B*
   The State University of New Jersey: Douglass College *B*
   The State University of New Jersey: Livingston College *B*
   The State University of New Jersey: New Brunswick Graduate Campus *D*
   The State University of New Jersey: Newark College of Arts and Sciences *B*
   The State University of New Jersey: Rutgers College *B*
   The State University of New Jersey: University College Camden *B*
   The State University of New Jersey: University College New Brunswick *B*
   The State University of New Jersey: University College Newark *B*
St. Peter's College *B*
Salem Community College *A*
Seton Hall University *B, M*
Sussex County Community College *A*
The College of New Jersey *B*
Thomas Edison State College *B*
William Paterson University of New Jersey *B*

New Mexico
Clovis Community College *A*
College of Santa Fe *B*
College of the Southwest *B*
Eastern New Mexico University *A, B, M*
New Mexico Highlands University *B, M*
New Mexico Institute of Mining and Technology *B*
New Mexico Junior College *A*
New Mexico State University *B, M, D*
San Juan College *A*
University of New Mexico *B, M, D*
Western New Mexico University *B*

New York
Adelphi University *B*
Adirondack Community College *A*
Alfred University *B*
Audrey Cohen College *A, B*
Bard College *B*
Barnard College *B*
Canisius College *B*
City University of New York
   Baruch College *B*
   Brooklyn College *B, M*
   City College *B, M*
   College of Staten Island *B*
   Hunter College *B, M*
   John Jay College of Criminal Justice *B, M*
   Lehman College *B*
   Medgar Evers College *B*
   Queens College *B, M*
   Queensborough Community College *A*
   York College *B*
Clarkson University *B*
Colgate University *B*
College of Mount St. Vincent *A, B*
College of New Rochelle *B, T*
College of St. Rose *B*
Columbia University
   Columbia College *B*
   School of General Studies *B*
   Teachers College *M*
Concordia College *B*
Cornell University *B, D*
Daemen College *B*
Dominican College of Blauvelt *B*
Dowling College *B*
Elmira College *B*
Eugene Lang College/New School University *B*
Fordham University *B, M, D*
Fulton-Montgomery Community College *A*
Hamilton College *B*
Hartwick College *B*
Hilbert College *B*
Hobart and William Smith Colleges *B*
Hofstra University *B*
Houghton College *B*
Iona College *B*
Ithaca College *B*
Keuka College *B*
Le Moyne College *B*
Long Island University
   Brooklyn Campus *B, M*
   C. W. Post Campus *B*
   Southampton College *B*
Manhattan College *B*
Manhattanville College *B*
Marist College *B, M*
Marymount College *B*
Marymount Manhattan College *B*
Medaille College *B*
Mercy College *B*
Molloy College *B*
Mount St. Mary College *B, T*
Nazareth College of Rochester *B*
New York Institute of Technology *B*
New York University *B, M, D*
Niagara University *B*
Nyack College *B*
Pace University:
   Pleasantville/Briarcliff *B, M*
Pace University *B, M*
Regents College *B*
Rensselaer Polytechnic Institute *B, M*
Roberts Wesleyan College *B*
Rochester Institute of Technology *B*
Russell Sage College *B*
St. Bonaventure University *B*
St. Francis College *B*
St. John Fisher College *B*
St. John's University *B*
St. Lawrence University *B*
St. Thomas Aquinas College *B*
Sarah Lawrence College *B, M*
Siena College *B*
Skidmore College *B*
St. Joseph's College
   St. Joseph's College: Suffolk Campus *B*
   St. Joseph's College *B*
State University of New York
   Albany *B, M, D*
   Binghamton *B, M*
   Buffalo *B, M*
   College at Brockport *B, M*
   College at Buffalo *B*
   College at Cortland *B, M*
   College at Fredonia *B*
   College at Geneseo *B, T*
   College at Old Westbury *B*
   College at Oneonta *B*
   College at Plattsburgh *B*
   College at Potsdam *B, T*
   Empire State College *A, B*
   Institute of Technology at Utica/Rome *B*
   New Paltz *B, M*
   Oswego *B*
   Purchase *B*
   Stony Brook *B, M, D*
Suffolk County Community College *A*
Syracuse University *B, M, D*
Touro College *B*
Union College *B*
United States Military Academy *B*
University of Rochester *B, M*
Utica College of Syracuse University *B*
Vassar College *B*
Wagner College *B*
Wells College *B*

North Carolina
Appalachian State University *B*
Barton College *B*
Belmont Abbey College *B*
Bennett College *B*
Campbell University *B*
Catawba College *B*
Chowan College *B*
Davidson College *B*
Duke University *B*
East Carolina University *B, M*
Elizabeth City State University *B*
Elon College *B*
Fayetteville State University *B*
Gardner-Webb University *B*
Gaston College *C*
Greensboro College *B*
Guilford College *B*
High Point University *B*
Johnson C. Smith University *B*
Lees-McRae College *B*
Lenoir Community College *A*
Lenoir-Rhyne College *B*
Louisburg College *A*
Mars Hill College *B*
Meredith College *B*
Methodist College *A, B*
Mount Olive College *B*
North Carolina Agricultural and Technical State University *B*
North Carolina Central University *B, M*
North Carolina State University *B, M, D*
North Carolina Wesleyan College *B*

Peace College B
Pfeiffer University B
Queens College B
St. Andrews Presbyterian College B
St. Augustine's College B
Salem College B
Sandhills Community College A
Shaw University B
University of North Carolina
    Asheville B, T
    Chapel Hill B, M, D
    Charlotte B
    Greensboro B, M, D, T
    Pembroke B
    Wilmington B, M
Wake Forest University B, M
Warren Wilson College B
Western Carolina University B
Wingate University B
Winston-Salem State University B

North Dakota
Dickinson State University B
Jamestown College B
Minot State University B, T
North Dakota State University B, M
University of Mary B
University of North Dakota B, M, D

Ohio
Antioch College B
Ashland University B
Baldwin-Wallace College B
Bluffton College B
Bowling Green State University B, M, D
Capital University B
Case Western Reserve
    University B, M, D
Cedarville College B
Central State University B
Circleville Bible College A, B
Cleveland State University B, M
College of Mount St. Joseph B
College of Wooster B
Defiance College B
Denison University B
Franciscan University of Steubenville B
Heidelberg College B, M
Hiram College B, T
John Carroll University B
Kent State University
    Stark Campus B
Kent State University B
Kenyon College B
Lake Erie College B
Lorain County Community College A
Lourdes College A, B
Malone College B
Marietta College B
Miami University
    Middletown Campus A
    Oxford Campus B, M, D
Mount Union College B
Mount Vernon Nazarene College B
Muskingum College B
Notre Dame College of Ohio C, B, T
Oberlin College B
Ohio Dominican College B, T
Ohio Northern University B
Ohio State University
    Columbus Campus B, M, D
Ohio University
    Southern Campus at Ironton A
Ohio University B
Ohio Wesleyan University B
Otterbein College B
Owens Community College
    Toledo A
Shawnee State University B
Union Institute B, D
University of Akron B, M, D
University of Cincinnati B, M, D
University of Dayton B, M
University of Findlay B
University of Rio Grande A, B
University of Toledo B, M, D

Ursuline College B
Walsh University B
Wilberforce University B
Wilmington College B
Wittenberg University B
Wright State University B
Xavier University A, B, M
Youngstown State University B

Oklahoma
Cameron University B, M
Carl Albert State College A
Connors State College A
East Central University B
Eastern Oklahoma State College A
Langston University B
Mid-America Bible College B
Northeastern Oklahoma Agricultural and
    Mechanical College A
Northeastern State University B
Northwestern Oklahoma State
    University B
Oklahoma Baptist University B
Oklahoma Christian University of
    Science and Arts B
Oklahoma City Community College A
Oklahoma City University B
Oklahoma Panhandle State University B
Oklahoma State University B, M, D
Oral Roberts University B
Redlands Community College A
Rose State College A
St. Gregory's University A, B
Southeastern Oklahoma State
    University B
Southern Nazarene University B
Southwestern Oklahoma State
    University B, M
Tulsa Community College A
University of Central Oklahoma B
University of Oklahoma B, M, D
University of Science and Arts of
    Oklahoma B
University of Tulsa B
Western Oklahoma State College A

Oregon
Central Oregon Community College A
Chemeketa Community College A
Concordia University B
Eastern Oregon University B, T
George Fox University B
Lewis & Clark College B
Linfield College B
Marylhurst University B
Northwest Christian College B
Oregon State University B
Pacific University B, M, D
Portland State University B, M, D
Reed College B
Southern Oregon University B, M
University of Oregon B, M, D
University of Portland B
Western Baptist College B
Western Oregon University B
Willamette University B

Pennsylvania
Albright College B
Allegheny College B
Allentown College of St. Francis de
    Sales B
Alvernia College B
Beaver College B
Bloomsburg University of
    Pennsylvania B
Bryn Mawr College B
Bucknell University B, M
Bucks County Community College A
Butler County Community College A
Cabrini College B
California University of Pennsylvania B
Carlow College B
Carnegie Mellon University B, M, D
Cedar Crest College B
Chatham College B

Chestnut Hill College A, B
Cheyney University of Pennsylvania B
Clarion University of Pennsylvania B
College Misericordia B
Community College of Allegheny
    County A
Delaware County Community College A
Dickinson College B
Drexel University B, M, D, T
Duquesne University B, M, D
East Stroudsburg University of
    Pennsylvania B
Eastern College B
Edinboro University of Pennsylvania B
Elizabethtown College B
Franklin and Marshall College B
Gannon University B
Geneva College B, M
Gettysburg College B
Grove City College B
Gwynedd-Mercy College B
Harrisburg Area Community College A
Haverford College B
Holy Family College B
Immaculata College B
Indiana University of
    Pennsylvania B, M, D
Juniata College B
King's College B
Kutztown University of Pennsylvania B
La Roche College B
La Salle University B, M, D
Lafayette College B
Lebanon Valley College of
    Pennsylvania B
Lehigh University B, M, D
Lincoln University B
Lock Haven University of
    Pennsylvania B
Lycoming College B
Manor College A
Mansfield University of
    Pennsylvania B, T
Marywood University B, M
Mercyhurst College B
Messiah College B
Millersville University of
    Pennsylvania B, M
Moravian College B
Mount Aloysius College B
Muhlenberg College B
Neumann College C, B
Penn State
    Erie, The Behrend College B
    Harrisburg B
    Schuylkill - Capital College B
    University Park B, M, D
Philadelphia University B
Point Park College B
Reading Area Community College A
Rosemont College B
St. Francis College B
St. Joseph's University B, M
St. Vincent College B
Seton Hill College B
Shippensburg University of
    Pennsylvania B, M
Slippery Rock University of
    Pennsylvania B
Susquehanna University B
Swarthmore College B
Temple University B
Thiel College B
University of Pennsylvania A, B, M, D
University of Pittsburgh
    Bradford B
    Greensburg B
    Johnstown B
University of Pittsburgh B, M, D
University of Scranton B
University of the Sciences in
    Philadelphia B, M
Ursinus College B
Villanova University B, M
Washington and Jefferson College B

Waynesburg College B
West Chester University of
    Pennsylvania B, M
Westminster College B
Widener University B
Wilkes University B
Wilson College B
York College of Pennsylvania B

Puerto Rico
Bayamon Central University B, M
Inter American University of Puerto Rico
    Metropolitan Campus B, M
    San German Campus B
Pontifical Catholic University of Puerto
    Rico B
Turabo University B
Universidad Metropolitana B
University of Puerto Rico
    Cayey University College B
    Mayaguez Campus B
    Ponce University College B
    Rio Piedras Campus B, M, D
University of the Sacred Heart B

Rhode Island
Brown University B, M, D
Providence College B
Rhode Island College B, M
Roger Williams University A, B
Salve Regina University B
University of Rhode Island B

South Carolina
Anderson College B
Charleston Southern University B
Clemson University B
Coastal Carolina University B
Coker College B
College of Charleston B
Columbia College B
Columbia International University B
Converse College B
Erskine College B
Francis Marion University B
Furman University B
Lander University B
Limestone College B
Newberry College B
Presbyterian College B, T
South Carolina State University B
Southern Wesleyan University B
The Citadel B
University of South Carolina
    Aiken B
    Spartanburg B
Winthrop University B
Wofford College B

South Dakota
Augustana College B
Black Hills State University B
Dakota Wesleyan University M
Northern State University B
South Dakota State University B, T
University of South Dakota B, M, D

Tennessee
Austin Peay State University B, M
Belmont University B, T
Bethel College B
Carson-Newman College B
Christian Brothers University B
Columbia State Community College A
Crichton College B
Cumberland University B
David Lipscomb University B
Dyersburg State Community College A
East Tennessee State University B, M
Fisk University B, M
Freed-Hardeman University B
Hiwassee College A
King College B
Lambuth University B
Lee University B
Lincoln Memorial University B
Maryville College B

Psychology

Middle Tennessee State University *B, M*
Milligan College *B*
Rhodes College *B*
Roane State Community College *A*
Southern Adventist University *B*
Tennessee State University *B, M*
Tennessee Technological University *B*
Tennessee Temple University *B*
Tennessee Wesleyan College *B*
Trevecca Nazarene University *B*
Tusculum College *B*
Union University *B*
University of Memphis *B, M, D*
University of Tennessee
   Chattanooga *B, M*
   Knoxville *B, M, D*
   Martin *B*
University of the South *B*
Vanderbilt University *B, M, D*
Walters State Community College *A*

Texas
Abilene Christian University *B, M, T*
Amarillo College *A*
Angelina College *A*
Angelo State University *B, M*
Austin College *B*
Baylor University *B*
Blinn College *A*
Brazosport College *A*
Cedar Valley College *A*
Coastal Bend College *A*
College of the Mainland *A*
Concordia University at Austin *T*
Dallas Baptist University *B*
Del Mar College *A*
East Texas Baptist University *B*
El Paso Community College *A*
Galveston College *A*
Grayson County College *A*
Hardin-Simmons University *B, M*
Hill College *A*
Houston Baptist University *B*
Howard College *A*
Howard Payne University *B*
Kilgore College *A*
Lamar University *B*
LeTourneau University *B*
Lon Morris College *A*
Lubbock Christian University *B*
McMurry University *B, T*
Midland College *A*
Midwestern State University *B, M*
Navarro College *A*
Northeast Texas Community College *A*
Odessa College *A*
Our Lady of the Lake University of San Antonio *B*
Palo Alto College *A*
Panola College *A*
Paris Junior College *A*
Prairie View A&M University *B*
Rice University *B, M, D*
St. Edward's University *B, T*
St. Mary's University *B, M, T*
St. Philip's College *A*
Sam Houston State University *B, M*
San Jacinto College
   North *A*
Schreiner College *B*
South Plains College *A*
Southern Methodist University *B*
Southwest Texas State University *B, T*
Southwestern Adventist University *B, T*
Southwestern Assemblies of God University *A*
Southwestern University *B, T*
Stephen F. Austin State University *B, M, T*
Sul Ross State University *B*
Tarleton State University *B*
Texas A&M International University *B, M, T*
Texas A&M University
   Commerce *B, M*
   Corpus Christi *B, M*
   Kingsville *B, M*
   Texarkana *B*
Texas A&M University *B, M, D*
Texas Christian University *B, M, D, T*
Texas Lutheran University *B, T*
Texas Southern University *B, M*
Texas Tech University *B, M, D*
Texas Wesleyan University *B, T*
Texas Woman's University *B, M, T*
Trinity University *B*
Trinity Valley Community College *A*
Tyler Junior College *A*
University of Dallas *B, T*
University of Houston
   Clear Lake *B, M*
   Downtown *B*
   Victoria *B*
University of Houston *B, M, D*
University of Mary Hardin-Baylor *B, M, T*
University of North Texas *B, M, D*
University of St. Thomas *B*
University of Texas
   Arlington *B, M, T*
   Austin *B, M, D*
   Dallas *B*
   El Paso *B, M, D*
   Pan American *B, M, T*
   San Antonio *B, M*
   Tyler *B, M*
   of the Permian Basin *B*
University of the Incarnate Word *B*
Wayland Baptist University *B*
West Texas A&M University *B, M*
Western Texas College *A*
Wharton County Junior College *A*

Utah
Brigham Young University *B, M, D*
Dixie State College of Utah *A*
Snow College *A*
Southern Utah University *B, T*
University of Utah *B, M, D*
Utah State University *B, M, D*
Weber State University *B*
Westminster College *B*

Vermont
Bennington College *B*
Burlington College *B*
Castleton State College *B*
College of St. Joseph in Vermont *B, M*
Goddard College *B, M*
Green Mountain College *B*
Johnson State College *B*
Lyndon State College *B*
Marlboro College *B*
Middlebury College *B*
Norwich University *B*
St. Michael's College *B*
Southern Vermont College *B*
Trinity College of Vermont *B*
University of Vermont *B, M, D*

Virginia
Averett College *B*
Bluefield College *B*
Bridgewater College *B*
Christopher Newport University *B*
College of William and Mary *B, M*
Eastern Mennonite University *B*
Emory & Henry College *B*
Ferrum College *B*
George Mason University *B, M, D*
Hampden-Sydney College *B*
Hampton University *B*
Hollins University *B*
James Madison University *B, M, D*
Liberty University *B*
Longwood College *B, T*
Lynchburg College *B*
Mary Baldwin College *B*
Mary Washington College *B*
Norfolk State University *B*
Northern Virginia Community College *A*
Old Dominion University *B, M*
Radford University *B, M*
Randolph-Macon College *B*
Randolph-Macon Woman's College *B*
Roanoke College *B, T*
Shenandoah University *B*
Sweet Briar College *B*
University of Richmond *B, M*
University of Virginia's College at Wise *B*
University of Virginia *B, M, D*
Virginia Commonwealth University *B, M, D*
Virginia Intermont College *B*
Virginia Military Institute *B*
Virginia Polytechnic Institute and State University *B, M, D, T*
Virginia State University *B, M*
Virginia Union University *B*
Virginia Wesleyan College *B*
Washington and Lee University *B*

Washington
Bastyr University *B*
Central Washington University *B*
Centralia College *A*
City University *B*
Eastern Washington University *B, M, T*
Everett Community College *A*
Evergreen State College *B*
Gonzaga University *B*
Heritage College *B*
Highline Community College *A*
Lower Columbia College *A*
Pacific Lutheran University *B*
St. Martin's College *B*
Seattle Pacific University *B, T*
Seattle University *B, M*
University of Puget Sound *B, T*
University of Washington *B, M, D*
Walla Walla College *B*
Washington State University *B, M, D*
Western Washington University *B, M, T*
Whitman College *B*
Whitworth College *B, T*

West Virginia
Alderson-Broaddus College *B*
Bethany College *B*
Concord College *B*
Davis and Elkins College *A, B*
Fairmont State College *B*
Marshall University *B, M*
Ohio Valley College *B*
Potomac State College of West Virginia University *A*
Shepherd College *B*
University of Charleston *B*
West Liberty State College *B*
West Virginia State College *B*
West Virginia University *B, M, D*
West Virginia Wesleyan College *B*
Wheeling Jesuit University *B*

Wisconsin
Alverno College *B, T*
Beloit College *B*
Cardinal Stritch University *B*
Carroll College *B*
Carthage College *B, T*
Concordia University Wisconsin *B*
Lakeland College *B*
Lawrence University *B*
Marian College of Fond du Lac *B*
Marquette University *B, T*
Mount Senario College *B*
Northland College *B*
Ripon College *B*
St. Norbert College *B, T*
Silver Lake College *B, T*
University of Wisconsin
   Eau Claire *B*
   Green Bay *B*
   La Crosse *B, T*
   Madison *B, M, D*
   Milwaukee *B, M, D*
   Oshkosh *B, M*
   Parkside *B*
   Platteville *B, T*
   River Falls *B, T*
   Stevens Point *B, T*
   Stout *B, M*
   Superior *B*
   Whitewater *B, T*
Viterbo University *B, T*
Wisconsin Lutheran College *B*

Wyoming
Casper College *A*
Central Wyoming College *A*
Eastern Wyoming College *A*
Laramie County Community College *A*
Northwest College *A*
Sheridan College *A*
University of Wyoming *B, M, D*
Western Wyoming Community College *A*

Public administration

Alabama
Auburn University at Montgomery *M, D*
Auburn University *B, M, D*
Huntingdon College *B*
Jacksonville State University *M*
Talladega College *B*
Troy State University Montgomery *M*
University of Alabama
   Birmingham *M*
   Huntsville *M*
University of Alabama *M*
University of South Alabama *M*

Alaska
University of Alaska
   Anchorage *M*
   Southeast *M*

Arizona
Arizona State University *M, D*
Northern Arizona University *M*
Pima Community College *A*
Rio Salado College *C, A*
Scottsdale Community College *C*
University of Arizona *B, M*

Arkansas
Arkansas State University *M*
Harding University *B*
University of Arkansas
   Little Rock *M*
University of Arkansas *B, M*
University of Central Arkansas *M*
University of the Ozarks *B*

California
California Lutheran University *M*
California State University
   Bakersfield *B, M*
   Chico *B, M*
   Dominguez Hills *M*
   Fresno *B, M*
   Fullerton *M*
   Hayward *B, M*
   Long Beach *M*
   Los Angeles *B, M*
   Northridge *M*
College of Notre Dame *M*
Fresno City College *C, A*
Golden Gate University *M, D*
Monterey Institute of International Studies *M*
National University *M*
Palomar College *C, A*
San Diego State University *B, M*

San Francisco State University *M*
San Jose State University *M*
Sonoma State University *M*
United States International University *M*
University of California
    Los Angeles *M*
University of La Verne *B, M, D*
University of San Francisco *B, M*
University of Southern
    California *B, M, D*

Colorado
Red Rocks Community College *C, A*
University of Colorado
    Colorado Springs *M*
    Denver *M, D*
University of Denver *B*

Connecticut
Mitchell College *A*
Three Rivers Community-Technical
    College *A*
University of New Haven *M*

Delaware
University of Delaware *M*

District of Columbia
American University *M, D*
Howard University *M*
Southeastern University *B*
University of the District of Columbia *M*

Florida
Florida Atlantic University *B, M, D*
Florida Gulf Coast University *B*
Florida International University *B, M, D*
Florida Memorial College *B*
Florida Metropolitan University
    Orlando College North *M*
Florida State University *C, M, D*
Nova Southeastern University *M, D*
St. Leo University *B*
Tallahassee Community College *A*
University of Central Florida *B, M, D*
University of Miami *M*
University of North Florida *M*
University of South Florida *M*

Georgia
Albany State University *M*
Augusta State University *M*
Clark Atlanta University *M, D*
Columbus State University *M*
Darton College *A*
Georgia College and State
    University *B, M*
Georgia Southern University *M*
Georgia Southwestern State
    University *B, M*
Georgia State University *M*
Kennesaw State University *M*
Macon State College *A*
Middle Georgia College *A*
North Georgia College & State
    University *B*
Piedmont College *M*
Savannah State University *M*
State University of West Georgia *M*
University of Georgia *M, D*
Valdosta State University *M*

Hawaii
Hawaii Pacific University *B*
University of Hawaii
    Manoa *M*
    West Oahu *B*

Idaho
Boise State University *M*
Idaho State University *M*

Illinois
Augustana College *B*
De Paul University *M*
Governors State University *B, M*
Illinois Institute of Technology *M*
Lewis University *B*
Northern Illinois University *M*
Roosevelt University *C, M*
Southern Illinois University
    Carbondale *M*
    Edwardsville *M*
University of Illinois
    Chicago *M, D*
    Springfield *M*
    Urbana-Champaign *M*

Indiana
Ball State University *M*
Indiana University
    Bloomington *A, B, M, D*
    Northwest *A, B, M*
    South Bend *A, B, M*
Indiana University--Purdue University
    Indiana University-Purdue
      University Fort
      Wayne *C, A, B, M*
    Indiana University-Purdue
      University Indianapolis *A, B, M*
University of Notre Dame *M*

Iowa
Buena Vista University *B*
Drake University *M*
Iowa State University *B, M*
St. Ambrose University *B*
University of Northern Iowa *B*

Kansas
Washburn University of Topeka *B*
Wichita State University *M*

Kentucky
Eastern Kentucky University *M*
Kentucky State University *B, M*
Murray State University *M*
Northern Kentucky University *B, M*
University of Louisville *M*

Louisiana
Louisiana State University and
    Agricultural and Mechanical
    College *M*
Southern University and Agricultural and
    Mechanical College *M*
University of New Orleans *M*

Maine
University of Maine
    Augusta *A, B*
University of Maine *B, M*

Maryland
Anne Arundel Community College *A*
Bowie State University *B*
University of Baltimore *M*
University of Maryland
    College Park *M*

Massachusetts
American International College *B, M*
Bridgewater State College *B, M*
Clark University *B, M*
Harvard University *M, D*
Mount Ida College *A, B*
Northeastern University *B, M*
Stonehill College *B*
Suffolk University *B, M*
University of Massachusetts
    Boston *B, M*

Michigan
Calvin College *B*
Central Michigan University *M*
Eastern Michigan University *B, M*
Ferris State University *C, B*
Grand Valley State University *B*
Lake Superior State University *M*
Michigan State University *B, M*
Northern Michigan University *B, M*
Oakland University *B, M*
Saginaw Valley State University *B*
University of Michigan
    Dearborn *B, M*
    Flint *B, M*
University of Michigan *M, D*
Wayne State University *B, M*
Western Michigan University *B, M, D*

Minnesota
Hamline University *B*
Metropolitan State University *B*
Minnesota State University, Mankato *M*
Moorhead State University *M*
St. Cloud State University *B*
St. Mary's University of Minnesota *B*
Southwest State University *B*
University of Minnesota
    Twin Cities *M*
Winona State University *B*

Mississippi
Belhaven College *C*
Jackson State University *M, D*
Mississippi State University *M, D*
Mississippi Valley State University *B*
University of Mississippi *B*

Missouri
Central Methodist College *B*
East Central College *A*
Lincoln University *B*
Lindenwood University *B*
Northwest Missouri State University *B*
Park University *B, M*
St. Louis University *M*
Southwest Missouri State
    University *B, M*
University of Missouri
    Columbia *M*
    Kansas City *M*
    St. Louis *B, M*
Webster University *M*

Montana
Miles Community College *A*
Montana State University
    Bozeman *M*
University of Montana-Missoula *M*

Nebraska
Doane College *B*
Hastings College *B*
University of Nebraska
    Omaha *B, M*

Nevada
University of Nevada
    Las Vegas *M*
    Reno *M*

New Hampshire
Plymouth State College of the University
    System of New Hampshire *A, B*
University of New Hampshire *M*

New Jersey
Bloomfield College *B*
Brookdale Community College *A*
County College of Morris *A*
Fairleigh Dickinson University *M*
Kean University *B, M*
Princeton University *M, D*
Rutgers
    The State University of New Jersey:
      Camden Graduate Campus *M*
    The State University of New Jersey:
      Newark Graduate Campus *M*
Seton Hall University *M*
The College of New Jersey *B*
Thomas Edison State College *C, A, B*

New Mexico
San Juan College *A*
University of New Mexico *M*

New York
Alfred University *B*
City University of New York
    Baruch College *B, M*
    Hostos Community College *A*
    John Jay College of Criminal
      Justice *A, B*
Columbia University
    Graduate School *M*
Dowling College *M*
Fordham University *B, M*
Long Island University
    Brooklyn Campus *M*
    C. W. Post Campus *B, M*
Marist College *B*
New York University *M, D*
Pace University:
    Pleasantville/Briarcliff *M, D*
Pace University *M, D*
St. John's University *B, M*
State University of New York
    Albany *M, D*
    Binghamton *M*
    College at Brockport *M*
Syracuse University *M, D*
Wagner College *B*

North Carolina
Appalachian State University *M*
Brevard College *B*
Campbell University *B*
East Carolina University *M*
Elon College *B*
Fayetteville State University *B*
Fayetteville Technical Community
    College *A*
North Carolina Central University *M*
North Carolina State University *M, D*
Shaw University *B*
University of North Carolina
    Chapel Hill *M*
    Charlotte *M*
Western Carolina University *M*
Winston-Salem State University *B*

North Dakota
University of North Dakota *B, M*

Ohio
Bowling Green State University *B, M*
Capital University *B*
Cedarville College *B*
David N. Myers College *A, B*
Heidelberg College *B*
Kent State University *M, D*
Miami University
    Oxford Campus *B*
Ohio State University
    Columbus Campus *M, D*
Ohio University *B, M*
University of Akron *M*
University of Cincinnati *M*
University of Toledo *M*
Youngstown State University *B*

Oklahoma
Northeastern State University *B*
University of Oklahoma *B, M*

Oregon
Portland State University *M*
Western Oregon University *B*

Pennsylvania
California University of Pennsylvania *B*
Carnegie Mellon University *B, M, D*
Gannon University *M*
Indiana University of Pennsylvania *M*
Juniata College *B*
Kutztown University of
    Pennsylvania *B, M*
La Salle University *B*
Lincoln University *B*
Marywood University *M*
Mount Aloysius College *A, B*
Penn State
    Harrisburg *M, D*
Point Park College *A, B*
Reading Area Community College *A*
St. Francis College *B*
St. Joseph's University *B*
Seton Hill College *B*
Shippensburg University of
    Pennsylvania *B, M*

Slippery Rock University of
  Pennsylvania *B, M*
University of Pennsylvania *M*
University of Pittsburgh *C, B, M, D*
University of Scranton *B*
Villanova University *M*
Widener University *M*
York College of Pennsylvania *B*

Puerto Rico
Bayamon Central University *B*
Colegio Universitario del Este *B*
Inter American University of Puerto Rico
  Bayamon Campus *B*
  San German Campus *B*
Pontifical Catholic University of Puerto
  Rico *B, D*
Turabo University *A, B*
University of Puerto Rico
  Rio Piedras Campus *M*

Rhode Island
Providence College *C*
Rhode Island College *B*
University of Rhode Island *M*

South Carolina
College of Charleston *M*
University of South Carolina *M*

South Dakota
University of South Dakota *M*

Tennessee
David Lipscomb University *B*
Fisk University *B*
Tennessee State University *M, D*
University of Memphis *M*
University of Tennessee
  Chattanooga *M*
  Knoxville *B, M*
  Martin *B*

Texas
Abilene Christian University *B*
Angelo State University *M*
Baylor University *B, M*
College of the Mainland *A*
Del Mar College *A*
Lamar University *M*
Midwestern State University *M*
Our Lady of the Lake University of San
  Antonio *B*
St. Mary's University *M*
San Antonio College *A*
Southwest Texas State University *M*
Stephen F. Austin State University *B*
Sul Ross State University *M*
Tarrant County College *C, A*
Texas Southern University *B, M*
Texas Tech University *M*
University of Houston
  Clear Lake *M*
University of Houston *M*
University of North Texas *B, M, D*
University of Texas
  Arlington *M, D*
  Dallas *M*
  El Paso *M*
  San Antonio *M*
West Texas A&M University *B*

Utah
University of Utah *C, M*
Utah State University *M*

Vermont
University of Vermont *M*

Virginia
Christopher Newport University *M*
George Mason University *B, M, D*
James Madison University *B, M*
Old Dominion University *M*
Regent University *M*
Shenandoah University *C, B*
Thomas Nelson Community College *A*
Tidewater Community College *A*

University of Virginia's College at
  Wise *B*
Virginia Commonwealth
  University *C, M, D*
Virginia Polytechnic Institute and State
  University *M, D*
Virginia State University *B*

Washington
City University *C, M*
Eastern Washington University *M*
Evergreen State College *B, M*
Seattle University *B, M*
University of Washington *M*
Washington State University *B, M*

West Virginia
West Virginia University *M*

Wisconsin
Carroll College *B*
Lakeland College *B*
Silver Lake College *B*
University of Wisconsin
  Green Bay *B*
  La Crosse *B*
  Madison *M*
  Milwaukee *M*
  Oshkosh *M*
  Stevens Point *B*

Wyoming
University of Wyoming *M*

Public administration/services

Alabama
Alabama State University *M*
Athens State University *B*
Central Alabama Community College *A*
Community College of the Air Force *A*
Huntingdon College *B*
Samford University *B*

Arizona
Pima Community College *C, A*
Prescott College *B, M*

Arkansas
Henderson State University *B*
University of Central Arkansas *B*

California
American River College *B*
California Lutheran University *M*
California State University
  Bakersfield *B, M*
  Dominguez Hills *B*
  Hayward *M*
  Sacramento *B, M*
  Stanislaus *M*
Chabot College *A*
Citrus College *A*
Compton Community College *A*
Fresno City College *C, A*
Gavilan Community College *A*
Moorpark College *A*
Mount San Jacinto College *A*
Pasadena City College *A*
Solano Community College *A*
Southwestern College *A*
University of California
  Irvine *M*
  Riverside *B*
Ventura College *A*

Colorado
Red Rocks Community College *C, A*

Connecticut
Housatonic Community-Technical
  College *A*
University of Connecticut *M*
University of New Haven *M*

District of Columbia
American University *M*

George Washington University *M, D*
Howard University *M*
Southeastern University *B*
Trinity College *B*
University of the District of Columbia *A*

Florida
Broward Community College *A*
Manatee Community College *A*
Miami-Dade Community College *A*
Polk Community College *A*

Georgia
Atlanta Metropolitan College *A*
Clark Atlanta University *D*
Darton College *A*
Georgia Perimeter College *A*
Kennesaw State University *B*

Hawaii
Chaminade University of Honolulu *M*

Idaho
University of Idaho *M*

Illinois
Black Hawk College *A*
Blackburn College *B*
Roosevelt University *B, M*
Southern Illinois University
  Carbondale *M*

Indiana
Ball State University *A*
Indiana State University *M*
Indiana University
  Bloomington *B, M*
  Northwest *A, B, M*
  South Bend *A, B, M*

Iowa
Buena Vista University *B*
Iowa State University *B*

Kansas
Kansas City Kansas Community
  College *A*
Kansas State University *M*
Seward County Community
  College *C, A*
University of Kansas *M*

Kentucky
Murray State University *M*
University of Kentucky *M, D*
Western Kentucky University *M*

Louisiana
Southern University
  Shreveport *C, A*

Massachusetts
Brandeis University *D*
Clark University *B, M*
Framingham State College *M*
Lasell College *B*
Mount Ida College *A, B*
Northeastern University *B, M*
Suffolk University *B, M*
Worcester State College *B*

Michigan
Grand Valley State University *M*
Lansing Community College *A*
Northern Michigan University *B, M*
Schoolcraft College *A*
University of Michigan
  Dearborn *B*
Western Michigan University *M, D*

Minnesota
Hamline University *M, D*
Metropolitan State University *B*
Northland Community & Technical
  College *A*
Winona State University *B*

Missouri
Central Missouri State University *M*
East Central College *A*

Evangel University *B*
Missouri Valley College *B*

Montana
Carroll College *B*
Miles Community College *A*

Nebraska
Doane College *B*
Hastings College *B*
University of Nebraska
  Omaha *B, D*

New Hampshire
Antioch New England Graduate
  School *M*

New Jersey
Caldwell College *C*

New Mexico
College of Santa Fe *A, B*
New Mexico Highlands University *M*
New Mexico State University *M*
Western New Mexico University *A, B*

New York
Alfred University *M*
City University of New York
  Baruch College *B, M*
  John Jay College of Criminal
    Justice *M*
  Medgar Evers College *A, B*
Cornell University *M*
Dominican College of Blauvelt *C*
Hudson Valley Community College *A*
Long Island University
  Brooklyn Campus *B*
Marist College *M*
Medaille College *A, B*
New York University *M*
Pace University:
  Pleasantville/Briarcliff *A*
Pace University *B*
State University of New York
  Albany *B*
  College at Brockport *M*

North Carolina
Western Piedmont Community
  College *A*

Ohio
Cleveland State University *M*
Sinclair Community College *A*
Union Institute *B, D*
University of Akron *M*
University of Dayton *M*
Wright State University *M*
Youngstown State University *B*

Oklahoma
Oklahoma State University
  Oklahoma City *A*

Oregon
Western Oregon University *B*

Pennsylvania
Community College of Allegheny
  County *C, A*
Community College of Beaver County *A*
La Salle University *A, B*
Mansfield University of Pennsylvania *B*
Penn State
  University Park *C*
University of Pittsburgh *M*
University of Scranton *A*
Villanova University *M*
West Chester University of
  Pennsylvania *M*
Widener University *M, D*
York College of Pennsylvania *B*

Puerto Rico
Inter American University of Puerto Rico
  Bayamon Campus *B*

Rhode Island
Providence College *C*

South Carolina
Clemson University *M*

South Dakota
University of South Dakota *M*

Tennessee
Cumberland University *M*
University of Tennessee
　Knoxville *B*

Texas
San Jacinto College
　North *C, A*
Texas A&M University
　Corpus Christi *M*
Texas A&M University *M*
University of Texas
　El Paso *M*
　Pan American *M*
　Tyler *M*

Utah
Brigham Young University *B*
Snow College *A*

Vermont
Champlain College *A, B*
Goddard College *B*

Virginia
Christopher Newport University *B*
University of Virginia's College at
　Wise *B*

Washington
Heritage College *B*
Seattle University *B*

West Virginia
Salem-Teikyo University *B*
West Virginia University Institute of
　Technology *B*

Wisconsin
Marquette University *M*
University of Wisconsin
　Green Bay *B*

Wyoming
Laramie County Community College *C*

Public finance

Alabama
Alabama Agricultural and Mechanical
　University *B*

California
Master's College *B*

Connecticut
Sacred Heart University *B*

Maine
Husson College *B*

Maryland
Morgan State University *B*

Massachusetts
Boston University *M*

New York
City University of New York
　Baruch College *M*
Pace University:
　Pleasantville/Briarcliff *B, M*
Pace University *B, M*

Ohio
Defiance College *B*
Youngstown State University *B*

Rhode Island
Johnson & Wales University *A, B*

Texas
Texas A&M University
　Commerce *B*
University of North Texas *B, M*

Public health

Alabama
University of Alabama
　Birmingham *M, D*

Arizona
University of Arizona *M, D*

Arkansas
University of Central Arkansas *B*

California
California College for Health
　Sciences *M*
California State University
　Fresno *M*
　Long Beach *M*
　Northridge *M*
Loma Linda University *B, M, D*
San Diego State University *M, D*
San Francisco State University *M*
San Jose State University *M*
University of California
　Berkeley *M, D*
　Los Angeles *M, D*

Colorado
University of Colorado
　Health Sciences Center *M*

Connecticut
Southern Connecticut State
　University *B, M*
University of Connecticut *M*
Yale University *M, D*

Delaware
Delaware State University *B*

District of Columbia
George Washington University *M, D*
Trinity College *B*

Florida
Florida International University *M*
Nova Southeastern University *M*
Palm Beach Community College *A*
University of Florida *M*
University of Miami *M*
University of South Florida *M, D*

Georgia
Mercer University *M*
Morris Brown College *B*

Hawaii
University of Hawaii
　Manoa *M, D*

Idaho
Boise State University *M*
Idaho State University *M*

Illinois
Benedictine University *M*
Northern Illinois University *M*
University of Illinois
　Chicago *M, D*
　Springfield *M*

Indiana
Indiana University
　Bloomington *B, M*
Indiana University--Purdue University
　Indiana University-Purdue
　　University Indianapolis *B, M*

Iowa
University of Iowa *M, D*
University of Osteopathic Medicine and
　Health Sciences
　Des Moines University -
　　Osteopathic Medical Center *B*

Kansas
University of Kansas
　Medical Center *M*
Wichita State University *M*

Kentucky
Cumberland College *B*
University of Kentucky *M*

Louisiana
Tulane University *M, D*

Maine
University of Maine
　Presque Isle *B*
University of Southern Maine *M*

Maryland
Morgan State University *M, D*
Uniformed Services University of the
　Health Sciences *M, D*

Massachusetts
Boston University *M*
Harvard University *M, D*
Springfield College *B, M*
University of Massachusetts
　Amherst *M, D*
　Lowell *M*

Michigan
Central Michigan University *B*
University of Michigan *M, D*
Wayne State University *M*

Minnesota
Moorhead State University *B*
University of Minnesota
　Twin Cities *M*

Mississippi
University of Southern Mississippi *B, M*

Missouri
East Central College *A*
St. Louis University *M*
University of Missouri
　Columbia *M*

New Jersey
Richard Stockton College of New
　Jersey *B*
Rutgers
　The State University of New Jersey:
　　Cook College *B*
　The State University of New Jersey:
　　Douglass College *B*
　The State University of New Jersey:
　　Livingston College *B*
　The State University of New Jersey:
　　New Brunswick Graduate
　　Campus *M, D*
　The State University of New Jersey:
　　Rutgers College *B*
　The State University of New Jersey:
　　University College New
　　Brunswick *B*

New Mexico
New Mexico State University *B, M*
University of New Mexico *M*

New York
City University of New York
　Brooklyn College *M*
Columbia University
　Graduate School *M, D*
New York University *M, D*
State University of New York
　Albany *M, D*
　Buffalo *M, D*
University of Rochester *M*

North Carolina
University of North Carolina
　Chapel Hill *B, M, D*
　Greensboro *M*

North Dakota
University of Mary *M*

Ohio
Bowling Green State University *M*
Case Western Reserve University *M*
Kent State University *B, M*

Ohio State University
　Columbus Campus *M*
University of Akron *B*
University of Toledo *M*
Youngstown State University *B*

Oklahoma
Southwestern Oklahoma State
　University *B*

Oregon
Oregon Health Sciences University *M*
Oregon State University *M, D*
Portland State University *M*

Pennsylvania
La Salle University *M*
MCP Hahnemann University *M*
Slippery Rock University of
　Pennsylvania *B, M*
Temple University *M*
University of Pittsburgh *M, D*
West Chester University of
　Pennsylvania *B, M*

Puerto Rico
University of Puerto Rico
　Medical Sciences Campus *M, D*

South Carolina
University of South Carolina *M, D*

Tennessee
East Tennessee State University *M*
University of Tennessee
　Knoxville *M*

Texas
University of Texas
　El Paso *M*

Utah
Snow College *A*
University of Utah *M*
Utah State University *B*

Virginia
Old Dominion University *M*
Virginia Commonwealth University *M*

Washington
Highline Community College *A*
University of Washington *B, M*

West Virginia
West Virginia University *M*

Wisconsin
Milwaukee Area Technical College *C*
University of Wisconsin
　La Crosse *B*
　Madison *M, D*

Wyoming
University of Wyoming *B*

Public health education

Alabama
Northwest-Shoals Community College *A*

Arizona
Northern Arizona University *B*

Arkansas
University of Central Arkansas *B*

California
California State University
　Chico *C, B, T*
　Long Beach *B, M*
Loma Linda University *B, M, D*
University of California
　Los Angeles *M*

Colorado
University of Northern Colorado *B, M*

Georgia
Armstrong Atlantic State University *M*
Darton College *A*

Public health education

Georgia Southern University B, M
Illinois
University of Illinois
  Urbana-Champaign M
Kentucky
Cumberland College B
Maine
University of Maine
  Presque Isle B
Maryland
Johns Hopkins University B
Massachusetts
Springfield College M
Michigan
University of Michigan
  Flint B, M
University of Michigan M, D
Minnesota
Bethel College B
University of St. Thomas B
Winona State University B
Nebraska
University of Nebraska
  Lincoln B
New Hampshire
Plymouth State College of the University
  System of New Hampshire B
New Jersey
Thomas Edison State College B
University of Medicine and Dentistry of
  New Jersey
  School of Health Related
    Professions M
New York
Adelphi University M
City University of New York
  Brooklyn College B, M
Ithaca College B
New York University M, D
North Carolina
East Carolina University B, M
University of North Carolina
  Chapel Hill B, M, D
  Charlotte M
Ohio
Youngstown State University B
Oregon
Oregon State University B
Pennsylvania
Temple University D
University of Pittsburgh M
Puerto Rico
University of Puerto Rico
  Medical Sciences Campus B, M
South Carolina
Coastal Carolina University B
University of South Carolina M, D
Tennessee
University of Tennessee
  Knoxville M
Texas
University of Texas
  Austin M, D
  Medical Branch at Galveston M
Utah
Brigham Young University B
Washington
Eastern Washington University B, T

Wisconsin
University of Wisconsin
  La Crosse B, M
  Madison B, M

Public policy analysis

Alabama
Huntingdon College B
Arkansas
University of Arkansas D
California
California State University
  Hayward B
Pomona College B
Stanford University B
University of California
  Berkeley M, D
  Los Angeles M, D
  San Diego B
University of Southern California M
Connecticut
Three Rivers Community-Technical
  College A
Trinity College B, M
District of Columbia
George Washington University B, M
Georgetown University M
Florida
New College of the University of South
  Florida B
University of Miami B
Georgia
Georgia Institute of Technology B, M, D
Illinois
Olivet Nazarene University B
University of Chicago M, D
University of Illinois
  Chicago D
Indiana
Indiana University
  Bloomington D
  South Bend A, B, M
Indiana University--Purdue University
  Indiana University-Purdue
    University Fort Wayne M
Iowa
University of Northern Iowa M
Louisiana
Southern University and Agricultural and
  Mechanical College M, D
Maine
University of Southern Maine M
Maryland
St. Mary's College of Maryland B
University of Maryland
  Baltimore County M, D
  College Park M, D
Massachusetts
Harvard University M, D
Simmons College B
University of Massachusetts
  Amherst B
  Boston D
Michigan
Albion College B
Michigan Technological University M
University of Michigan M, D
Minnesota
Winona State University B
Missouri
St. Louis University D

New Hampshire
Antioch New England Graduate
  School D
New Jersey
Bloomfield College B
Princeton University B, M
Rutgers
  The State University of New Jersey:
    New Brunswick Graduate
    Campus M
St. Peter's College A, B
New York
Cornell University B
Hamilton College B
Hobart and William Smith Colleges B
Sarah Lawrence College B
State University of New York
  Albany M
Syracuse University B
North Carolina
Duke University B
University of North Carolina
  Chapel Hill B, D
Ohio
Ohio State University
  Columbus Campus M, D
University of Akron
  Wayne College A
Pennsylvania
Carnegie Mellon University B, M, D
Dickinson College B
Duquesne University M
Penn State
  Harrisburg B
  University Park B
St. Vincent College B
University of Pennsylvania B, M, D
Rhode Island
Brown University B
Tennessee
Vanderbilt University M
Texas
San Antonio College A
Southern Methodist University B
University of Texas
  Austin M, D
  Dallas D
Virginia
College of William and Mary B, M
George Mason University D
Virginia Commonwealth University D
Virginia Polytechnic Institute and State
  University B
Washington
Central Washington University B
Wisconsin
Northland College B
University of Wisconsin
  Madison M
  Whitewater B, T

Public relations

Alabama
Alabama State University B
Auburn University B
Spring Hill College B
University of Alabama B, M
Arizona
Glendale Community College A
Grand Canyon University B
Northern Arizona University B
Scottsdale Community College C, A
Arkansas
Harding University B
John Brown University B

California
California Lutheran University B
California State University
  Chico B
  Dominguez Hills B
  Fullerton B, M
  Hayward B
  Long Beach B
  Los Angeles B
Chapman University B
College of Marin: Kentfield A
Golden Gate University M
Golden West College C, A
Master's College B
Pacific Union College B
Pepperdine University B
San Diego State University B
San Jose State University B
University of Southern California B, M
Colorado
Colorado State University M
University of Colorado
  Boulder B
University of Denver M, D
University of Southern Colorado B
Connecticut
Central Connecticut State University B
Manchester Community-Technical
  College C
Quinnipiac University B
Delaware
Delaware State University B
District of Columbia
American University B, M
Florida
Barry University B
Florida Southern College B
Florida State University B
Gulf Coast Community College A
Indian River Community College A
Manatee Community College A
University of Florida B
University of Miami B, M
University of West Florida B
Georgia
Berry College B
Clark Atlanta University B
Columbus State University B
Fort Valley State University B
Georgia Southern University B
Morris Brown College B
Shorter College B
Toccoa Falls College B
University of Georgia B
Valdosta State University B
Hawaii
Hawaii Pacific University B
Idaho
North Idaho College A
University of Idaho B
Illinois
Black Hawk College
  East Campus A
Columbia College B
Greenville College B
Illinois State University B
McKendree College B
Monmouth College B
North Central College B
Quincy University A, B
Richland Community College A
Roosevelt University B
University of St. Francis B
Indiana
Ball State University B, M
Franklin College B
Indiana State University B

Indiana University
   Northwest *B*
   South Bend *B*
Purdue University
   Calumet *B*
Vincennes University *A*

Iowa
Buena Vista University *B*
Clarke College *B*
Dordt College *B*
Drake University *B*
Loras College *B*
Mount Mercy College *B*
North Iowa Area Community College *A*
St. Ambrose University *B*
Simpson College *B*
University of Northern Iowa *B*
Waldorf College *A*
Wartburg College *B*

Kansas
Pittsburg State University *B*

Kentucky
Eastern Kentucky University *B*
Murray State University *B*
Western Kentucky University *B*

Louisiana
University of Louisiana at Lafayette *B*

Maryland
Villa Julie College *A*

Massachusetts
Boston University *B, M*
Emerson College *B, M*
Massachusetts College of Liberal Arts *B*
Northeastern University *B*
Salem State College *B*
Simmons College *B*
Suffolk University *B, M*

Michigan
Andrews University *B*
Central Michigan University *B*
Eastern Michigan University *B*
Ferris State University *C, B*
Grand Valley State University *B*
Kellogg Community College *A*
Michigan State University *M*
Northern Michigan University *B*
University of Detroit Mercy *B*
Wayne State University *B*
Western Michigan University *B*

Minnesota
Metropolitan State University *B*
Minnesota State University, Mankato *B*
Moorhead State University *B*
Northwestern College *B*
St. Cloud State University *B*
St. Cloud Technical College *C, A*
St. Mary's University of Minnesota *B*
Winona State University *B*

Mississippi
Jackson State University *B*
Mississippi University for Women *B*
Northwest Mississippi Community College *A*
University of Southern Mississippi *B*

Missouri
Central Missouri State University *B*
College of the Ozarks *B*
Crowder College *A*
Drury University *B*
East Central College *A*
Fontbonne College *B*
Lindenwood University *B, M*
Northwest Missouri State University *B*
Rockhurst University *B*
St. Louis University *B*
Southeast Missouri State University *B*
St. Louis Community College
   St. Louis Community College at Florissant Valley *A*

Stephens College *B*
University of Missouri
   Columbia *B*
Webster University *B*
William Woods University *B*

Montana
Carroll College *B*
Montana State University
   Billings *B, M*

Nebraska
Doane College *B*
Hastings College *B*
Midland Lutheran College *B*
Union College *B*

Nevada
University of Nevada
   Reno *B*

New Hampshire
Antioch New England Graduate School *M*
Hesser College *A*
New England College *B*
Rivier College *B*

New Jersey
Brookdale Community College *A*
Fairleigh Dickinson University *B*
Rowan University *B, M*
Union County College *A*

New Mexico
Santa Fe Community College *A*

New York
City University of New York
   City College *B*
Cornell University *B*
Elmira College *B*
Iona College *B*
Long Island University
   C. W. Post Campus *B*
Marist College *B*
Medaille College *B*
Mount St. Mary College *C, B*
New York Institute of Technology *M*
Rochester Institute of Technology *C*
State University of New York
   New Paltz *B*
   Oswego *B*
Syracuse University *B, M*
Utica College of Syracuse University *B*

North Carolina
Appalachian State University *B*
Brevard College *B*
Campbell University *B*
Gardner-Webb University *B*
North Carolina Agricultural and Technical State University *B*
North Carolina State University *B*
University of North Carolina
   Pembroke *B*

North Dakota
North Dakota State University *B*

Ohio
Bowling Green State University *B*
Capital University *B*
Defiance College *B*
Franklin University *M*
Heidelberg College *B*
Kent State University
   Stark Campus *B*
Kent State University *B*
Marietta College *B*
Ohio Dominican College *B*
Ohio Northern University *B*
Ohio State University
   Columbus Campus *B, M*
Ohio University *B*
Otterbein College *B*
University of Akron *B*
University of Dayton *B*
University of Rio Grande *A, B*

Ursuline College *B*
Wilmington College *B*
Wright State University *B*
Xavier University *A, B*
Youngstown State University *B*

Oklahoma
Cameron University *B*
Northern Oklahoma College *A*
Northwestern Oklahoma State University *B*
Oklahoma Baptist University *B*
Oklahoma Christian University of Science and Arts *B*
Oklahoma City University *B*
Southeastern Oklahoma State University *B*
University of Central Oklahoma *B*
University of Oklahoma *B*

Oregon
Marylhurst University *C*
Southern Oregon University *B*
University of Oregon *B, M*

Pennsylvania
California University of Pennsylvania *B*
Community College of Beaver County *A*
Duquesne University *B*
La Salle University *B*
Lebanon Valley College of Pennsylvania *C*
Mansfield University of Pennsylvania *B*
Marywood University *B*
Mercyhurst College *B*
Point Park College *B*
Seton Hill College *C, B*
Susquehanna University *B*
University of Pittsburgh
   Bradford *B*
   Greensburg *B*
Westminster College *B*
Widener University *B*
York College of Pennsylvania *B*

Puerto Rico
University of the Sacred Heart *M*

Rhode Island
University of Rhode Island *B*

South Carolina
University of South Carolina *B*
Winthrop University *B*

Tennessee
David Lipscomb University *B*
Freed-Hardeman University *B*
Lambuth University *B*
Lee University *B*
Southern Adventist University *B*
Union University *B*
University of Tennessee
   Martin *B*

Texas
Howard Payne University *B*
Lubbock Christian University *B*
Southern Methodist University *B*
Southwest Texas State University *B*
Texas A&M University
   Commerce *B*
Texas Tech University *B*
Texas Wesleyan University *B*
University of Houston *B, M*
University of North Texas *B*
University of Texas
   Austin *B*
   San Antonio *B*

Utah
Brigham Young University *B*
Salt Lake Community College *A*
Southern Utah University *B*
Weber State University *B*

Vermont
Champlain College *A, B*

Virginia
Hampton University *B*
Mary Baldwin College *B*

Washington
Central Washington University *B*
Eastern Washington University *B*
Edmonds Community College *C*
Gonzaga University *B*
Pacific Lutheran University *B*
Seattle University *B*
Washington State University *B*

West Virginia
Bethany College *B*
Concord College *B*
Marshall University *B, M*
West Virginia Wesleyan College *B*

Wisconsin
Cardinal Stritch University *B*
Carthage College *B*
Marquette University *B*
Mount Mary College *B*
University of Wisconsin
   La Crosse *B*
   Whitewater *B*

Purchasing/procurement/contracts

Alabama
Athens State University *B*
Community College of the Air Force *A*
University of Alabama
   Huntsville *B*

Arizona
Arizona State University *B*

California
California State University
   Hayward *C, B*
Coastline Community College *C*
De Anza College *C, A*
Fresno City College *C, A*
Golden Gate University *M*
San Diego City College *C, A*
Sierra College *A*

District of Columbia
Southeastern University *M*

Florida
Florida Institute of Technology *M*
Hillsborough Community College *A*

Iowa
Des Moines Area Community College *C*
St. Ambrose University *C*

Kansas
Washburn University of Topeka *A*

Kentucky
Elizabethtown Community College *A*

Massachusetts
Middlesex Community College *C*
Northeastern University *A*
Northern Essex Community College *C*
Suffolk University *M*

Michigan
Eastern Michigan University *B*
Kirtland Community College *C, A*
Michigan State University *B, M*

Minnesota
University of St. Thomas *M*

Mississippi
Jackson State University *B*

Missouri
Webster University *M*

Nebraska
Southeast Community College
   Lincoln Campus *A*

Purchasing/procurement/contracts

New Jersey
Thomas Edison State College A, B

New York
Westchester Business Institute C, A

Ohio
Ashland University B, M
Baldwin-Wallace College C
Cincinnati State Technical and
 Community College A
Columbus State Community College A
Miami University
 Oxford Campus B
North Central State College C
Sinclair Community College C, A
Youngstown State University B

Oklahoma
University of Central Oklahoma B

Pennsylvania
Duquesne University C
Luzerne County Community College C
Mercyhurst College C, A
St. Joseph's University C, A, B

Puerto Rico
American University of Puerto Rico B

South Carolina
Horry-Georgetown Technical
 College C, A

South Dakota
Dakota Wesleyan University A, B

Texas
University of Dallas M
University of Houston
 Downtown B

Virginia
Central Virginia Community College C
John Tyler Community College C, A
Northern Virginia Community
 College C, A
Shenandoah University C

Washington
Columbia Basin College A
Shoreline Community College C, A

Wisconsin
Lakeshore Technical College A
Northeast Wisconsin Technical
 College C
University of Wisconsin
 Green Bay A

Quality control/safety technologies

Alabama
Calhoun Community College A
Community College of the Air Force A
Jacksonville State University B

Alaska
Prince William Sound Community
 College A

Arizona
Mesa Community College A
Rio Salado College C, A
University of Arizona B

Arkansas
Arkansas State University
 Beebe Branch A
University of Arkansas
 Little Rock C
Westark College C, A

California
California State University
 Long Beach B
Cerro Coso Community College A
Citrus College C
Coastline Community College A
College of the Canyons C
Las Positas College A
Long Beach City College C, A
Los Angeles Pierce College C, A
Mount San Antonio College C, A
National University B
Palomar College C, A
Rio Hondo College C
San Bernardino Valley College C, A
San Diego City College C, A
San Jose State University M
Southwestern College C, A
University of Southern
 California B, M, D
Ventura College A

Colorado
Lamar Community College C
Pikes Peak Community College C, A

Connecticut
Naugatuck Valley Community-Technical
 College C, A
University of New Haven A, B, M

Delaware
Delaware Technical and Community
 College
 Stanton/Wilmington Campus A

Florida
Brevard Community College A

Georgia
Southern Polytechnic State University M

Illinois
College of Lake County A
Illinois Eastern Community Colleges
 Frontier Community College C, A
 Lincoln Trail College C, A
Kishwaukee College C
Moraine Valley Community
 College C, A
Sauk Valley Community College C
Triton College C
Waubonsee Community College C, A
William Rainey Harper College C, A

Indiana
Indiana State University B
Indiana University
 Bloomington C, A
Indiana University--Purdue University
 Indiana University-Purdue
 University Fort Wayne C
Ivy Tech State College
 Central Indiana C
 Northeast C, A
 Northwest C, A
 Wabash Valley C, A

Iowa
Des Moines Area Community
 College C, A
Muscatine Community College A
Northeast Iowa Community College A
Scott Community College A

Kansas
Cowley County Community College A
Kansas State University A

Kentucky
Eastern Kentucky University A
Elizabethtown Community College A
Murray State University B, M

Louisiana
Delgado Community College A

Maryland
Community College of Baltimore County
 Catonsville C
Prince George's Community College A

Massachusetts
Massachusetts Maritime Academy B
Northeastern University M
Northern Essex Community
 College C, A

Michigan
Baker College
 of Muskegon C, A, B
Bay de Noc Community College C
Eastern Michigan University C
Ferris State University C
Grand Rapids Community College A
Henry Ford Community College A
Jackson Community College C, A
Kalamazoo Valley Community
 College C, A
Lake Michigan College A
Lake Superior State University A
Lansing Community College A
Madonna University A, B
Mott Community College A
Oakland Community College C, A
St. Clair County Community College A
Schoolcraft College C, A
Washtenaw Community College A

Minnesota
Century Community and Technical
 College C, A
University of Minnesota
 Duluth M
Winona State University A, B

Mississippi
Hinds Community College A

Missouri
Central Missouri State University B, M
Longview Community College C, A
St. Louis Community College
 St. Louis Community College at
 Florissant Valley A

Nevada
Community College of Southern
 Nevada A

New Hampshire
Keene State College A, B
New Hampshire Community Technical
 College
 Nashua C
New Hampshire Technical Institute C

New Jersey
Burlington County College A
Gloucester County College C
Salem Community College A

New Mexico
San Juan College A

New York
Broome Community College A
City University of New York
 College of Staten Island C, A
Mercy College C
Monroe Community College A
Rochester Institute of Technology B

North Carolina
Alamance Community College C
Central Carolina Community College C
Guilford Technical Community
 College C, A

North Dakota
University of North Dakota B

Ohio
Cincinnati State Technical and
 Community College C
College of Mount St. Joseph A, B
Columbus State Community College A
Kent State University C
Lakeland Community College A
Lima Technical College A
Lorain County Community College A
Marion Technical College C, A
North Central State College A
Northwest State Community College A
Ohio University
 Chillicothe Campus A
Owens Community College
 Findlay Campus C
 Toledo C, A
Sinclair Community College C, A
Terra Community College C, A
University of Findlay B
University of Toledo A

Oklahoma
Northeastern State University B
Oklahoma State University
 Oklahoma City A
Southeastern Oklahoma State
 University B
Tulsa Community College C, A

Pennsylvania
Butler County Community College A
Indiana University of Pennsylvania B, M
Millersville University of
 Pennsylvania B
Northampton County Area Community
 College C, A
Penn State
 University Park C
Pennsylvania College of Technology A
Slippery Rock University of
 Pennsylvania B
Temple University M

Puerto Rico
University of Puerto Rico
 Aguadilla A, B

South Carolina
Aiken Technical College C
Horry-Georgetown Technical College A
Spartanburg Technical College A
Tri-County Technical College C, A

Tennessee
Pellissippi State Technical Community
 College C
Walters State Community College C

Texas
Amarillo College C, A
Brazosport College C, A
Brookhaven College A
Collin County Community College
 District C, A
El Paso Community College C
Houston Community College
 System C, A
Odessa College C
Palo Alto College A
Richland College A
Tarrant County College A
Temple College A
Texas A&M University M
Texas State Technical College
 Sweetwater C, A
 Waco A

Utah
Utah State University B

Virginia
Central Virginia Community College C

Washington
South Seattle Community College A

West Virginia
Fairmont State College A, B
Marshall University B, M
West Virginia University M

Wisconsin
Gateway Technical College A
Lakeshore Technical College A
Northeast Wisconsin Technical
 College A
University of Wisconsin
 Stout M
Waukesha County Technical College A

Wyoming
Laramie County Community College A

Radiation biology

California
University of California
  Irvine M, D

Colorado
Colorado State University M, D
University of Colorado
  Health Sciences Center M

District of Columbia
George Washington University D

Illinois
Barat College B
University of Chicago M

Iowa
University of Iowa M, D

Massachusetts
Suffolk University B

Ohio
University of Cincinnati M

Pennsylvania
MCP Hahnemann University M, D

Texas
University of Texas
  Southwestern Medical Center at Dallas M, D

Radio/television broadcasting

Alabama
Alabama State University B
Auburn University B
Community College of the Air Force A
Lawson State Community College C, A
Spring Hill College B
Troy State University B
University of Alabama B, M
University of Montevallo B

Arizona
Arizona State University B
Arizona Western College A
Grand Canyon University B
Northern Arizona University B
University of Arizona B, M

Arkansas
Arkansas State University B, M
Harding University B
John Brown University A, B
Southern Arkansas University B
University of the Ozarks B

California
Bakersfield College A
Biola University B
Butte College C, A
California Lutheran University B
California State University
  Bakersfield B
  Chico B
  Fullerton B, M
  Hayward B
  Long Beach B
  Los Angeles B
  Northridge B, M
Chabot College A
Chaffey Community College C, A
City College of San Francisco C, A
College of Marin: Kentfield A
College of San Mateo C, A
College of the Canyons C, A
Cuesta College C, A
Foothill College C, A
Glendale Community College A
Golden West College C, A
Grossmont Community College C, A
Los Angeles Valley College C, A
Master's College B
Modesto Junior College C, A
Moorpark College C, A
Mount San Antonio College C, A
Ohlone College C, A
Orange Coast College C, A
Pasadena City College C, A
Pepperdine University B
Saddleback College C, A
San Diego City College A
San Diego State University B, M
San Francisco State University B, M
San Joaquin Delta College A
San Jose State University B
Santa Ana College C, A
Santa Rosa Junior College C
Southwestern College C, A
University of La Verne B
University of Southern California B, M
Vanguard University of Southern California B

Colorado
Art Institute
  of Colorado A
Colorado Christian University B
Metropolitan State College of Denver B
Pueblo Community College C, A
University of Colorado
  Boulder B
University of Southern Colorado B

Connecticut
Briarwood College A
Central Connecticut State University B
Middlesex Community-Technical College C, A
Quinnipiac University B

Delaware
Delaware State University B

District of Columbia
American University B, M
Gallaudet University B
George Washington University B
Howard University B

Florida
Art Institute
  of Fort Lauderdale A
Barry University B
Brevard Community College A
Broward Community College A
Florida Community College at Jacksonville A
Florida State University B
Gulf Coast Community College A
Manatee Community College A
Miami-Dade Community College C, A
Palm Beach Community College A
Pensacola Junior College A
University of Central Florida B
University of Miami B, M
University of West Florida B

Georgia
Berry College B
Clark Atlanta University B
Georgia Perimeter College A
Georgia Southern University B
Morris Brown College B
Toccoa Falls College B

Hawaii
University of Hawaii
  Leeward Community College C, A

Idaho
Boise State University A
University of Idaho B

Illinois
Chicago State University B
City Colleges of Chicago
  Kennedy-King College C, A
Columbia College B
Governors State University B, M
Illinois Eastern Community Colleges
  Wabash Valley College A
Lake Land College A
Lewis University B
Lewis and Clark Community College A
North Central College B
Northwestern University B, M
Olivet Nazarene University B
Parkland College A
Quincy University A, B
Southern Illinois University
  Carbondale B, M
University of St. Francis B
Western Illinois University M

Indiana
Ball State University B
Franklin College B
Indiana State University B, M
Indiana University
  South Bend
Manchester College A, B
Purdue University
  Calumet B
University of Indianapolis B
Valparaiso University B
Vincennes University A

Iowa
Buena Vista University B
Dordt College B
Drake University B
Grand View College B
Iowa Central Community College A
Iowa Wesleyan College B
St. Ambrose University B
University of Iowa B, M, D
University of Northern Iowa B
Waldorf College A, B
Wartburg College B

Kansas
Coffeyville Community College A
Colby Community College A
Dodge City Community College C, A
Hutchinson Community College A
Independence Community College A
Pittsburg State University B
University of Kansas B

Kentucky
Campbellsville University B
Eastern Kentucky University B
Murray State University B
Northern Kentucky University B
University of Kentucky B
Western Kentucky University B

Louisiana
Southern University and Agricultural and Mechanical College B, M
University of Louisiana at Monroe B

Maine
St. Joseph's College B
University of Southern Maine B

Maryland
Columbia Union College B
Hagerstown Community College A
Montgomery College
  Rockville Campus A
Morgan State University B

Massachusetts
Boston University B, M
Curry College B
Dean College A
Emerson College B
Hampshire College B
Massachusetts College of Liberal Arts B
Mount Wachusett Community College A
Newbury College A
Northeastern University B
Suffolk University B
Westfield State College B

Michigan
Bay de Noc Community College C
Central Michigan University B, M
Cornerstone College and Grand Rapids Baptist Seminary A
Delta College A
Grand Valley State University B
Henry Ford Community College A
Lansing Community College A
Michigan State University B, M
Northern Michigan University B
St. Clair County Community College A
Schoolcraft College A
University of Detroit Mercy B
University of Michigan M
Wayne State University B
Western Michigan University B

Minnesota
Concordia College: Moorhead B
Lake Superior College: A Community and Technical College C
Moorhead State University B
North Central University B
Northland Community & Technical College C, A
Northwestern College A, B
St. Cloud State University B
Southwest State University B
Winona State University B

Mississippi
Coahoma Community College A
Jackson State University B
Mississippi University for Women B
Northwest Mississippi Community College A
Rust College B
University of Mississippi B
University of Southern Mississippi B

Missouri
Central Missouri State University B
College of the Ozarks B
Drury University B
Evangel University A, B
Fontbonne College B
Lindenwood University B, M
Northwest Missouri State University B
Southeast Missouri State University B
Southwest Missouri State University B
St. Louis Community College
  St. Louis Community College at Florissant Valley A
Stephens College B
Webster University B
William Woods University B

Montana
University of Montana-Missoula B

Nebraska
Central Community College C, A
Grace University B
Hastings College B
Northeast Community College A
University of Nebraska
  Kearney B
  Lincoln B
  Omaha B

New Hampshire
Franklin Pierce College B
Hesser College A
Rivier College B

New Jersey
Brookdale Community College A
Cumberland County College A
Essex County College A
Rowan University B
Sussex County Community College A
The College of New Jersey B
Union County College A

Radio/television broadcasting

New Mexico
Eastern New Mexico University *B*

New York
Adirondack Community College *C, A*
Cayuga County Community College *A*
City University of New York
 Brooklyn College *B, M*
 Kingsborough Community
 College *A*
Five Towns College *A, B*
Fordham University *B*
Fulton-Montgomery Community
 College *A*
Herkimer County Community
 College *C, A*
Hofstra University *B*
Ithaca College *B*
Long Island University
 C. W. Post Campus *B*
Manhattan College *B*
Marist College *B*
Medaille College *B*
Mercy College *B*
Nassau Community College *A*
New York Institute of Technology *A, B*
New York University *B*
Onondaga Community College *A*
St. John Fisher College *B*
St. Thomas Aquinas College *B*
State University of New York
 College at Brockport *B*
 College at Buffalo *B*
 College at Cortland *B*
 New Paltz *B*
 Oswego *B*
Suffolk County Community College *A*
Syracuse University *B, M*
Tompkins-Cortland Community
 College *A*

North Carolina
Appalachian State University *B*
Campbell University *B*
Central Carolina Community College *A*
Cleveland Community College *C, A*
Elon College *B*
Gardner-Webb University *B*
Gaston College *A*
North Carolina Agricultural and
 Technical State University *B*
North Carolina State University *B*
University of North Carolina
 Greensboro *B, M*
 Pembroke *B*

North Dakota
Minot State University *B*
North Dakota State University *B*

Ohio
Ashland University *A, B*
Baldwin-Wallace College *B*
Bowling Green State University *B*
Capital University *B*
Cedarville College *B*
Central State University *B*
Kent State University
 Stark Campus *B*
Kent State University *B*
Marietta College *B*
Mount Vernon Nazarene College *B*
Ohio Northern University *B*
Ohio University *A, B, M, D*
Otterbein College *B*
University of Akron *B*
University of Cincinnati *M, T*
University of Dayton *B*
Washington State Community College *A*
Xavier University *A, B*
Youngstown State University *B*

Oklahoma
Cameron University *B*
East Central University *B*
Langston University *B*

Northeastern Oklahoma Agricultural and
 Mechanical College *A*
Northern Oklahoma College *A*
Northwestern Oklahoma State
 University *B*
Oklahoma Baptist University *B*
Oklahoma Christian University of
 Science and Arts *B*
Oklahoma City Community College *A*
Oklahoma City University *B*
Oklahoma State University *B*
Rogers State University *A*
Rose State College *A*
Southeastern Oklahoma State
 University *B*
University of Central Oklahoma *B*
University of Oklahoma *B*

Oregon
George Fox University *B*
Lane Community College *C, A*
Mount Hood Community College *A*
University of Oregon *B, M*

Pennsylvania
Bucks County Community College *A*
California University of Pennsylvania *B*
Geneva College *B*
Kutztown University of
 Pennsylvania *B, M*
La Salle University *B*
Lehigh Carbon Community College *A*
Mansfield University of Pennsylvania *B*
Marywood University *B*
Mercyhurst College *B*
Messiah College *B*
Point Park College *B*
Susquehanna University *B*
Temple University *B, M, D*
University of the Arts *B*
Waynesburg College *B*
Westminster College *B*
York College of Pennsylvania *A, B*

Rhode Island
New England Institute of Technology *A*

South Carolina
Morris College *B*
North Greenville College *B*
Tri-County Technical College *A*
Trident Technical College *A*

Tennessee
Belmont University *B*
Draughons Junior College of Business:
 Nashville *A*
Freed-Hardeman University *B*
Lincoln Memorial University *B*
Trevecca Nazarene University *A*
Union University *B*
University of Tennessee
 Knoxville *B*

Texas
Abilene Christian University *B*
Alvin Community College *C, A*
Amarillo College *A*
Austin Community College *C, A*
Central Texas College *C, A*
Del Mar College *A*
Kilgore College *A*
Midland College *A*
Navarro College *A*
Odessa College *A*
Sam Houston State University *B*
San Antonio College *A*
Southern Methodist University *B, M*
Southwestern Adventist University *B*
Stephen F. Austin State University *B*
Texas A&M University
 Commerce *B*
Texas Christian University *B, M*
Texas Tech University *B*
Texas Wesleyan University *B*
University of North Texas *B, M*

University of Texas
 Arlington *B*
 Austin *B, M, D*
 Pan American *B*

Utah
Brigham Young University *B*
Dixie State College of Utah *A*
Salt Lake Community College *A*
Weber State University *B*

Vermont
Castleton State College *A, B*
Lyndon State College *B*

Virginia
Hampton University *B*
Mary Baldwin College *B*
Regent University *M*
Southwest Virginia Community
 College *C*

Washington
Central Washington University *B*
Centralia College *A*
Columbia Basin College *C*
Eastern Washington University *B*
Gonzaga University *B*
Green River Community College *C*
Pacific Lutheran University *B*
Shoreline Community College *A*
Washington State University *B*
Western Washington University *B*

West Virginia
Alderson-Broaddus College *B*
Bethany College *B*
College of West Virginia *A*
Concord College *B*
Marshall University *B, M*

Wisconsin
Concordia University Wisconsin *B*
Marquette University *B, M*
University of Wisconsin
 Madison *B, M, D*
 Superior *B, M*
 Whitewater *B*
Western Wisconsin Technical College *A*

Wyoming
Central Wyoming College *A*

Range science/management

Arizona
University of Arizona *M, D*

California
California State University
 Chico *B*
College of the Redwoods *C*
University of California
 Berkeley *M*
 Davis *B*

Colorado
Colorado State University *B, M, D*
Lamar Community College *A*

Idaho
College of Southern Idaho *A*
University of Idaho *B, M*

Kansas
Pratt Community College *A*

Montana
Montana State University
 Bozeman *B, M*

Nebraska
Chadron State College *B*
University of Nebraska
 Lincoln *B*

Nevada
University of Nevada
 Reno *B*

New Mexico
New Mexico State University *B, M, D*

North Dakota
North Dakota State University *B, M*

Oklahoma
Northeastern Oklahoma Agricultural and
 Mechanical College *C, A*
Rogers State University *A*
Southeastern Oklahoma State
 University *B*

Oregon
Eastern Oregon University *B*
Oregon State University *B, M, D*

South Dakota
Sinte Gleska University *A*
South Dakota State University *B*

Texas
Abilene Christian University *B*
Angelo State University *B*
Southwest Texas State University *B*
Sul Ross State University *B, M*
Tarleton State University *B*
Texas A&M University
 Kingsville *B, M*
Texas A&M University *B, M, D*
Texas Tech University *B, M, D*

Utah
Brigham Young University *B, M*
Dixie State College of Utah *A*
Utah State University *B, M, D*

Vermont
Sterling College *B*

Washington
Highline Community College *A*
Washington State University *B, M*

Wyoming
Northwest College *A*
University of Wyoming *B, M, D*

Reading education

Alabama
Alabama State University *M*
Auburn University *D, T*
University of Alabama *M*

Arizona
Grand Canyon University *M*
Northern Arizona University *M*
University of Arizona *M, D*

Arkansas
Arkansas State University *M, T*
Harding University *B, M, T*
Southern Arkansas University *M*
University of Arkansas
 Little Rock *M*
University of Central Arkansas *M*

California
Azusa Pacific University *M, T*
California Lutheran University *B, T*
California Polytechnic State University:
 San Luis Obispo *M*
California State University
 Bakersfield *M*
 Chico *M, T*
 Dominguez Hills *M*
 Fresno *M*
 Fullerton *T*
 Hayward *M, T*
 Long Beach *T*
 Los Angeles *M*
Chapman University *M*
Fresno Pacific University *M*
Loyola Marymount University *M*

San Diego State University *M, T*
San Francisco State University *M*
San Jose State University *T*
Sonoma State University *M, T*
University of California
    Berkeley *T*
University of La Verne *M*

Colorado
University of Northern Colorado *M, T*

Connecticut
Central Connecticut State University *M*
Eastern Connecticut State University *M*
Sacred Heart University *B, M*
University of New Haven *M*
Western Connecticut State University *M*

District of Columbia
Howard University *M*
Trinity College *M*
University of the District of Columbia *M*

Florida
Barry University *M*
Florida Agricultural and Mechanical
    University *T*
Florida Atlantic University *M*
Florida International University *M*
Florida State University *M, D*
Miami-Dade Community College *A*
Nova Southeastern University *M*
University of Central Florida *M*
University of Florida *M*
University of Miami *M, D*
University of South Florida *M*

Georgia
Clark Atlanta University *B*
Columbus State University *M*
Georgia Southern University *M, T*
Georgia Southwestern State
    University *B, M*
Georgia State University *M, D*
Mercer University *M*
State University of West Georgia *M*
University of Georgia *M, D*

Illinois
Chicago State University *M, T*
Concordia University *M*
Governors State University *M*
Illinois State University *M, T*
Lewis University *M, T*
National-Louis University *M, D*
North Park University *T*
Northeastern Illinois University *M*
Northern Illinois University *M*
Rockford College *T*
Roosevelt University *M*
St. Xavier University *M*
Western Illinois University *M*

Indiana
Ball State University *M, D, T*
Butler University *M, T*
Franklin College *T*
Indiana State University *M, T*
University of Evansville *T*
University of Indianapolis *T*
University of St. Francis *B, M*

Iowa
Buena Vista University *B, T*
Central College *T*
Clarke College *M*
Dordt College *B*
Drake University *T*
Graceland University *M*
Iowa State University *T*
Iowa Wesleyan College *T*
Luther College *B*
Morningside College *M*
Mount Mercy College *T*
Northwestern College *T*
St. Ambrose University *T*
University of Northern Iowa *B, M*
Upper Iowa University *B*

Wartburg College *T*

Kansas
Garden City Community College *A*
Pittsburg State University *M*
Washburn University of Topeka *M*
Wichita State University *T*

Kentucky
Campbellsville University *B*
Murray State University *B, M, T*
St. Catharine College *A*
Spalding University *M*
Union College *M*
University of Louisville *M*
Western Kentucky University *M*

Louisiana
Centenary College of Louisiana *T*
Dillard University *B*
Loyola University New Orleans *M*
McNeese State University *T*
Northwestern State University *T*
University of Louisiana at Monroe *M*

Maine
University of Maine *M*
University of Southern Maine *B, T*

Maryland
Bowie State University *M*
Frostburg State University *M, T*
Loyola College in Maryland *M*
Towson University *M*
Western Maryland College *M*

Massachusetts
Boston College *M*
Boston University *M, T*
Bridgewater State College *M*
Eastern Nazarene College *M, T*
Elms College *M*
Endicott College *M*
Lesley College *M, T*
Northeastern University *M*
Salem State College *M*
Tufts University *M*
University of Massachusetts
    Lowell *M, D*
Westfield State College *M, T*
Worcester State College *M, T*

Michigan
Andrews University *M, T*
Aquinas College *B, T*
Calvin College *B, M, T*
Central Michigan University *M*
Eastern Michigan University *M*
Marygrove College *M*
Michigan State University *M*
Oakland University *M, D*
Saginaw Valley State University *M*
Wayne State University *M, D*
Western Michigan University *M*

Minnesota
Moorhead State University *B, M, T*
St. Cloud State University *M, T*
University of St. Thomas *M*
Winona State University *B, M, T*

Mississippi
Mississippi State University *T*

Missouri
Central Missouri State University *M, T*
Harris Stowe State College *T*
Lincoln University *M*
Lindenwood University *M*
Missouri Southern State College *B, T*
Northwest Missouri State
    University *M, T*
Southwest Missouri State University *M*
University of Missouri
    Columbia *M, D*
    Kansas City *M*
Webster University *M*

Montana
Carroll College *T*
Montana State University
    Billings *B, M, T*
Western Montana College of The
    University of Montana *T*

Nebraska
Chadron State College *M*
College of Saint Mary *B, T*
Concordia University *M*
Hastings College *M*
University of Nebraska
    Kearney *M, T*
    Omaha *M*

New Hampshire
Plymouth State College of the University
    System of New Hampshire *B, M*
Rivier College *M*
University of New Hampshire *M, T*

New Jersey
Georgian Court College *T*
Kean University *M*
Monmouth University *M*
Montclair State University *M, T*
New Jersey City University *B*
Rider University *M, T*
Rowan University *M*
Rutgers
    The State University of New Jersey:
    New Brunswick Graduate
    Campus *M, D, T*
St. Peter's College *M, T*
The College of New Jersey *M, T*

New Mexico
New Mexico State University *B*
Western New Mexico University *B, M*

New York
Adelphi University *M*
Alfred University *M*
Bank Street College of Education *C, M*
Canisius College *M, T*
City University of New York
    Brooklyn College *B, M*
    Lehman College *M*
    Queens College *M*
College of New Rochelle *M*
College of St. Rose *M, T*
Columbia University
    Teachers College *M, D*
Dowling College *M*
Hofstra University *M, D, T*
Long Island University
    Brooklyn Campus *M*
    C. W. Post Campus *B, M, T*
    Southampton College *M*
Manhattanville College *M, T*
Nazareth College of Rochester *M*
New York University *M, T*
Pace University:
    Pleasantville/Briarcliff *B, M, T*
Pace University *B, M, T*
St. Bonaventure University *M*
St. John's University *M, T*
St. Thomas Aquinas College *C, M*
State University of New York
    Albany *M, D*
    Binghamton *M, T*
    Buffalo *M, D, T*
    College at Brockport *M*
    College at Buffalo *B, M, T*
    College at Cortland *M*
    College at Fredonia *M*
    College at Geneseo *M, T*
    College at Oneonta *M, T*
    College at Plattsburgh *M*
    College at Potsdam *B, M*
    New Paltz *M, T*
    Oswego *M*
Syracuse University *M, D, T*

North Carolina
Appalachian State University *B, M, T*

East Carolina University *M*
Mars Hill College *T*
Meredith College *M*
North Carolina Agricultural and
    Technical State University *M*
University of North Carolina
    Asheville *T*
    Charlotte *M*
    Pembroke *M, T*
    Wilmington *M*
Wingate University *B, T*

North Dakota
Dickinson State University *B, T*
University of Mary *M*
University of North Dakota *M*

Ohio
Ashland University *M, T*
Baldwin-Wallace College *M*
Bowling Green State University *M*
Franciscan University of Steubenville *C*
Hiram College *T*
John Carroll University *M, T*
Kent State University
    Stark Campus *B*
Kent State University *M, T*
Lake Erie College *M*
Malone College *M*
Miami University
    Oxford Campus *M*
Notre Dame College of Ohio *M, T*
Ohio Northern University *T*
Ohio University *D*
Otterbein College *M*
University of Akron *M*
University of Cincinnati *M*
University of Dayton *M, T*
University of Rio Grande *B, T*
Walsh University *B*
Wilmington College *T*
Wittenberg University *B*
Wright State University *M*
Xavier University *M, T*
Youngstown State University *M*

Oklahoma
Northeastern State University *M*
Northwestern Oklahoma State
    University *M*
Southeastern Oklahoma State
    University *M, T*
Southern Nazarene University *M*
University of Central Oklahoma *B, M*
University of Oklahoma *T*

Oregon
University of Portland *T*
Western Oregon University *T*

Pennsylvania
Beaver College *M*
Bloomsburg University of
    Pennsylvania *M*
Bucknell University *M, T*
Cabrini College *T*
California University of Pennsylvania *M*
Clarion University of Pennsylvania *M*
Drexel University *B*
Duquesne University *M*
East Stroudsburg University of
    Pennsylvania *M*
Edinboro University of Pennsylvania *M*
Gannon University *M*
Gwynedd-Mercy College *M*
Holy Family College *M*
Indiana University of Pennsylvania *M*
King's College *M*
Kutztown University of
    Pennsylvania *M, T*
Lincoln University *B, M, T*
Mansfield University of Pennsylvania *C*
Marywood University *M, T*
Millersville University of
    Pennsylvania *M, T*
St. Joseph's University *M*

Reading education

Shippensburg University of
    Pennsylvania *M, T*
Slippery Rock University of
    Pennsylvania *M*
University of Pennsylvania *M, D*
University of Pittsburgh *T*
University of Scranton *M*
West Chester University of
    Pennsylvania *M*
Westminster College *M*
Widener University *M*

Rhode Island
Providence College *M*
Rhode Island College *M*

South Carolina
Clemson University *M*
The Citadel *M*
University of South Carolina *M, D*
Winthrop University *M, T*

South Dakota
Northern State University *T*

Tennessee
Austin Peay State University *M*
East Tennessee State University *M, T*
Middle Tennessee State University *M*
Tennessee Technological
    University *M, T*
Vanderbilt University *M, D*

Texas
Abilene Christian University *B, M, T*
Angelo State University *M*
Baylor University *B, T*
Dallas Baptist University *T*
Del Mar College *A*
Hardin-Simmons University *B, M, T*
Houston Baptist University *M*
Jarvis Christian College *B*
LeTourneau University *B*
McMurry University *T*
Prairie View A&M University *M*
St. Mary's University *B, M, T*
Sam Houston State University *M, T*
Southwest Texas State University *M, T*
Southwestern University *T*
Stephen F. Austin State University *T*
Sul Ross State University *M*
Texas A&M International
    University *B, M, T*
Texas A&M University
    Commerce *M, T*
    Corpus Christi *M, T*
    Kingsville *M, T*
Texas Christian University *T*
Texas Lutheran University *B, T*
Texas Tech University *M*
Texas Wesleyan University *B, M, T*
Texas Woman's University *M, D, T*
University of Houston
    Clear Lake *M, T*
    Victoria *M*
University of Houston *M*
University of Mary Hardin-Baylor *M, T*
University of North Texas *M, D*
University of Texas
    Arlington *T*
    Brownsville *M*
    El Paso *M*
    Pan American *M, T*
    San Antonio *T*
    Tyler *M*
    of the Permian Basin *M*
University of the Incarnate Word *M*
Wayland Baptist University *T*
West Texas A&M University *M, T*

Utah
Brigham Young University *D*

Vermont
Castleton State College *M*
College of St. Joseph in Vermont *M*
Johnson State College *M*
St. Michael's College *M*

University of Vermont *M, T*

Virginia
Averett College *M*
Christopher Newport University *M, T*
George Mason University *M*
James Madison University *M, T*
Longwood College *M, T*
Old Dominion University *M*
Radford University *M, T*
Virginia Commonwealth University *M*

Washington
Central Washington University *M, T*
City University *M*
Eastern Washington University *B, M, T*
Pacific Lutheran University *M, T*
Western Washington University *M*
Whitworth College *B, M, T*

West Virginia
Marshall University *M*
West Virginia University *M, D*

Wisconsin
Cardinal Stritch University *M*
Carthage College *M*
Silver Lake College *T*
University of Wisconsin
    Eau Claire *M*
    La Crosse *M*
    Oshkosh *M*
    Platteville *T*
    River Falls *M, T*
    Superior *B, T*

Real estate

Alabama
Calhoun Community College *A*
Enterprise State Junior College *A*
Northwest-Shoals Community College *C*

Arizona
Arizona State University *B*
Glendale Community College *C, A*
Paradise Valley Community College *C*
Pima Community College *A*
Yavapai College *C*

California
American River College *C, A*
Bakersfield College *A*
Barstow College *C, A*
Butte College *C, A*
Cabrillo College *C, A*
California State University
    Dominguez Hills *B*
    Fresno *B*
    Hayward *B*
    Long Beach *B*
    Los Angeles *B*
    Northridge *B*
Cerritos Community College *C, A*
Chabot College *A*
Citrus College *C*
City College of San Francisco *C, A*
Coastline Community College *C, A*
College of Marin: Kentfield *C, A*
College of San Mateo *C, A*
College of the Canyons *C*
College of the Desert *C, A*
College of the Redwoods *A*
College of the Sequoias *C*
College of the Siskiyous *A*
Compton Community College *A*
Contra Costa College *C, A*
Cuesta College *C, A*
Cuyamaca College *A*
De Anza College *C, A*
Diablo Valley College *C, A*
East Los Angeles College *C, A*
Foothill College *C, A*
Fresno City College *A*
Gavilan Community College *C*
Glendale Community College *C, A*

Golden West College *C, A*
Imperial Valley College *C, A*
Irvine Valley College *C, A*
Lake Tahoe Community College *C, A*
Long Beach City College *C, A*
Los Angeles Harbor College *A*
Los Angeles Mission College *C, A*
Los Angeles Pierce College *C, A*
Los Angeles Southwest College *C, A*
Los Angeles Trade and Technical
    College *C, A*
Los Medanos College *C, A*
Merced College *A*
Merritt College *C, A*
MiraCosta College *C, A*
Mission College *A*
Modesto Junior College *A*
Monterey Peninsula College *C, A*
Moorpark College *A*
Mount San Antonio College *C, A*
Mount San Jacinto College *C, A*
Napa Valley College *C, A*
Ohlone College *C, A*
Palo Verde College *A*
Palomar College *C, A*
Pasadena City College *C, A*
Porterville College *C, A*
Rio Hondo College *A*
Riverside Community College *C, A*
Sacramento City College *C, A*
Saddleback College *C, A*
San Bernardino Valley College *C, A*
San Diego City College *C, A*
San Diego Mesa College *C, A*
San Diego State University *B, M*
San Francisco State University *B*
San Joaquin Delta College *C, A*
San Jose City College *C, A*
Santa Ana College *C, A*
Santa Barbara City College *A*
Santa Monica College *C, A*
Santa Rosa Junior College *C*
Shasta College *C*
Sierra College *C, A*
Solano Community College *C, A*
Southwestern College *C*
University of Southern California *M*
Ventura College *C, A*
Victor Valley College *C, A*
West Hills Community College *A*
West Los Angeles College *C, A*
West Valley College *C, A*
Yuba College *C*

Colorado
Arapahoe Community College *C*
Colorado Mountain College
    Spring Valley Campus *C, A*
    Timberline Campus *C, A*
Colorado State University *B*
University of Colorado
    Boulder *B, M*
University of Denver *B, M*

Connecticut
Manchester Community-Technical
    College *C*
University of Connecticut *B*

District of Columbia
American University *M*
George Washington University *M*

Florida
Brevard Community College *A*
Florida Atlantic University *B*
Florida Community College at
    Jacksonville *A*
Florida International University *B*
Florida State University *B*
Gulf Coast Community College *A*
Miami-Dade Community College *C, A*
Polk Community College *A*
Seminole Community College *C*
University of Florida *B, M*
University of Miami *B*

Georgia
Georgia State University *B, M, D*
State University of West Georgia *B*
University of Georgia *B*

Hawaii
University of Hawaii
    Manoa *B*

Idaho
College of Southern Idaho *A*

Illinois
Black Hawk College *C, A*
City Colleges of Chicago
    Kennedy-King College *C*
    Olive-Harvey College *C*
College of DuPage *C, A*
College of Lake County *C*
Danville Area Community College *C*
Joliet Junior College *C*
Kankakee Community College *A*
Kishwaukee College *C*
Lewis and Clark Community College *A*
Lincoln Land Community College *A*
McHenry County College *C, A*
Morton College *A*
Oakton Community College *C, A*
Prairie State College *C*
Richland Community College *A*
Sauk Valley Community College *C*
Southeastern Illinois College *C*
Southwestern Illinois College *C*
Triton College *C*
Waubonsee Community College *C*
William Rainey Harper College *C, A*

Iowa
Des Moines Area Community College *C*
University of Northern Iowa *B*

Kansas
Dodge City Community College *C*

Kentucky
Ashland Community College *A*
Elizabethtown Community College *A*
Lexington Community College *A*
Morehead State University *B*
Paducah Community College *A*
Prestonsburg Community College *A*
Western Kentucky University *A*

Louisiana
Southern University
    New Orleans *A*
University of New Orleans *B*

Maryland
Community College of Baltimore County
    Catonsville *C, A*
Harford Community College *C*
Villa Julie College *A*

Massachusetts
Babson College *B*
Greenfield Community College *C*
Massachusetts Bay Community
    College *C*
Massachusetts Institute of Technology *M*
Northeastern University *A*

Michigan
Delta College *A*
Eastern Michigan University *B*
Ferris State University *C, A*
Henry Ford Community College *A*
Kirtland Community College *A*
Lansing Community College *A*
Oakland Community College *C*
Western Michigan University *B*

Minnesota
Dakota County Technical College *C, A*
Minnesota State University, Mankato *B*
St. Cloud State University *B*
University of St. Thomas *B, M*

Mississippi
Mississippi State University B
University of Mississippi B

Missouri
Lindenwood University M
St. Louis Community College
  St. Louis Community College at Meramec C, A
University of Missouri
  Columbia B
Webster University B, M

Nebraska
Mid Plains Community College Area C
Northeast Community College A
University of Nebraska
  Omaha B

Nevada
Community College of Southern Nevada C, A
University of Nevada
  Las Vegas B
Western Nevada Community College A

New Hampshire
New Hampshire Community Technical College
  Laconia C
  Manchester C
New Hampshire Technical Institute A

New Jersey
Burlington County College C
Camden County College C
Fairleigh Dickinson University C
Gloucester County College C
Ocean County College C
Raritan Valley Community College C, A
Sussex County Community College C
Thomas Edison State College A, B

New Mexico
New Mexico Junior College A
San Juan College C, A

New York
City University of New York
  Baruch College B
  Lehman College C
Columbia-Greene Community College C, A
Cornell University M
Hudson Valley Community College A
Nassau Community College C
New York University B, M
Orange County Community College A
St. John's University B
Suffolk County Community College C, A

North Carolina
Alamance Community College A
Appalachian State University B
Asheville Buncombe Technical Community College C
Beaufort County Community College C
Bladen Community College A
Blue Ridge Community College C
Brunswick Community College C
Caldwell Community College and Technical Institute C
Cape Fear Community College C
Carteret Community College C
Central Carolina Community College C
Central Piedmont Community College A
Cleveland Community College C
College of the Albemarle C
Craven Community College C
Durham Technical Community College C
Edgecombe Community College C
Fayetteville Technical Community College C
Forsyth Technical Community College C
Guilford Technical Community College C
Haywood Community College C
Pitt Community College C
Rockingham Community College C
Sampson Community College C
Sandhills Community College C
Southwestern Community College C
Surry Community College C
Tri-County Community College C
Western Piedmont Community College C
Wilson Technical Community College C

North Dakota
North Dakota State College of Science A

Ohio
Bowling Green State University
  Firelands College C
Cincinnati State Technical and Community College A
Columbus State Community College A
Davis College C
Edison State Community College A
Franklin University A, B
Hocking Technical College C
Jefferson Community College A
Kent State University
  Trumbull Campus A
Lakeland Community College C
Lorain County Community College A
Marion Technical College A
Miami University
  Hamilton Campus A
Northwest State Community College C
Ohio State University
  Columbus Campus B
Shawnee State University A
Sinclair Community College A
Southern State Community College A
Terra Community College A
University of Akron C
University of Cincinnati
  Clermont College C, A
  Raymond Walters College C, A
University of Cincinnati B, M
University of Toledo A

Oklahoma
Oklahoma City Community College A
Tulsa Community College A
University of Central Oklahoma B
University of Oklahoma B

Oregon
Chemeketa Community College A
Clackamas Community College C
Lane Community College C, A
Portland Community College A

Pennsylvania
Bucks County Community College C
Clarion University of Pennsylvania B
Community College of Philadelphia A
Duquesne University B
Harrisburg Area Community College A
Immaculata College A
Lehigh Carbon Community College C, A
Luzerne County Community College A
Montgomery County Community College C, A
Northampton County Area Community College C
Penn State
  Erie, The Behrend College B
  University Park C, B
Robert Morris College C
St. Francis College A
Shippensburg University of Pennsylvania B
Temple University B, M
University of Pennsylvania B, M
Westmoreland County Community College C

Puerto Rico
Caribbean University A

South Carolina
University of South Carolina B

Tennessee
Northeast State Technical Community College C
University of Memphis B

Texas
Amarillo College C, A
Angelina College C
Baylor University B
Blinn College C
Central Texas College C, A
Coastal Bend College A
College of the Mainland C
Collin County Community College District C, A
Del Mar College A
El Paso Community College C, A
Grayson County College C, A
Hill College A
Houston Community College System C, A
Kilgore College A
Lee College C
Midland College C, A
Navarro College C, A
North Lake College A
Northeast Texas Community College A
Panola College C
Paris Junior College A
Richland College A
San Antonio College A
San Jacinto College
  North C, A
Southern Methodist University B
Tarrant County College C, A
Texas A&M University M
Texas Christian University B
Trinity Valley Community College C
University of North Texas B, M
University of Texas
  Arlington B, M

Utah
Salt Lake Community College C

Virginia
Christopher Newport University B
Eastern Shore Community College C
J. Sargeant Reynolds Community College C
Lord Fairfax Community College C
Northern Virginia Community College C, A
Piedmont Virginia Community College A
Southwest Virginia Community College C
Tidewater Community College A
Virginia Commonwealth University C

Washington
Bellevue Community College C, A
Columbia Basin College A
Green River Community College C, A
North Seattle Community College A
Washington State University B

West Virginia
Davis and Elkins College A
Fairmont State College A

Wisconsin
Chippewa Valley Technical College C
Madison Area Technical College A
Milwaukee Area Technical College A
University of Wisconsin
  Madison B, M
  Milwaukee B
Waukesha County Technical College A

Recreational therapy

Arkansas
University of Central Arkansas B

California
California State University
  Chico B
  Hayward B
San Diego State University B
Skyline College C, A
Whittier College B

Connecticut
Gateway Community College C
Manchester Community-Technical College C
Middlesex Community-Technical College C
Mitchell College A
Northwestern Connecticut Community-Technical College C, A
Norwalk Community-Technical College C, A

District of Columbia
Gallaudet University B
Howard University B

Florida
Broward Community College A

Georgia
Morris Brown College B

Illinois
Moraine Valley Community College A
University of St. Francis B

Indiana
Indiana Institute of Technology A, B
Vincennes University A

Iowa
University of Iowa B

Kansas
Kansas City Kansas Community College A
Pittsburg State University B

Kentucky
Murray State University B

Maine
University of Southern Maine A, B

Massachusetts
Springfield College B, M

Michigan
Calvin College B
Lake Superior State University B

Minnesota
Minnesota State University, Mankato B
Winona State University B

New Hampshire
University of New Hampshire B

New Jersey
Bergen Community College A
Sussex County Community College C

New York
Ithaca College B
Mercy College B
Nazareth College of Rochester B
New York University M, D
Onondaga Community College A
St. Joseph's College
  St. Joseph's College: Suffolk Campus B
State University of New York
  College of Technology at Canton A
Utica College of Syracuse University B

North Carolina
Carteret Community College A
Catawba College B

Recreational therapy

East Carolina University B, M
Vance-Granville Community College A
Western Carolina University B
Western Piedmont Community
 College A
Winston-Salem State University B

Ohio
Ashland University B
College of Mount St. Joseph B
Kent State University B
North Central State College A
Ohio University B
University of Findlay B
University of Toledo B

Pennsylvania
Butler County Community College A
Community College of Allegheny
 County C
Lincoln University B
Lock Haven University of
 Pennsylvania B
Temple University B, M
York College of Pennsylvania B

Utah
Brigham Young University B

Vermont
Green Mountain College B

Virginia
Longwood College B

Washington
Eastern Washington University B
Spokane Community College C, A

West Virginia
Alderson-Broaddus College B
Shepherd College A, B
West Virginia State College B

Wisconsin
Northland College B
University of Wisconsin
 La Crosse B, M

Rehabilitation/therapeutic services

Alabama
Auburn University M, D
Talladega College B
Troy State University B

Arkansas
University of Arkansas M, D
University of Central Arkansas M

California
Imperial Valley College C, A

Colorado
University of Northern
 Colorado B, M, D

Connecticut
Quinebaug Valley Community College A
Three Rivers Community-Technical
 College A

District of Columbia
Gallaudet University M

Florida
Florida State University B, M, D
Polk Community College A
University of Florida D

Georgia
Georgia State University M

Illinois
De Paul University M
Illinois Institute of Technology M
Kaskaskia College C
Southern Illinois University
 Carbondale B, M, D

University of Illinois
 Chicago M, D
 Urbana-Champaign M

Iowa
Iowa Lakes Community College A
Marshalltown Community College A

Louisiana
Louisiana State University Medical
 Center B, M
Southern University and Agricultural and
 Mechanical College B

Maine
University of Maine
 Farmington B

Maryland
University of Maryland
 Eastern Shore B

Massachusetts
Assumption College B
Boston University B, M, D
Northeastern University B, M
Springfield College B, M

Michigan
Central Michigan University B
Michigan State University M
Wayne State University C, M
Western Michigan University M

Minnesota
Minnesota State University, Mankato M

Mississippi
Jackson State University B

Missouri
Maryville University of Saint Louis M

Montana
Montana State University
 Billings A, B, M
University of Great Falls A

New Hampshire
Antioch New England Graduate
 School M, D
Plymouth State College of the University
 System of New Hampshire B

New Jersey
University of Medicine and Dentistry of
 New Jersey
  School of Health Related
   Professions A, B, M, D

New York
City University of New York
 Brooklyn College M
 Hunter College M
Ithaca College B, M
Niagara County Community College C
State University of New York
 Buffalo M, D

North Carolina
East Carolina University B, M
South Piedmont Community
 College C, A

Ohio
Kent State University M

Oregon
Western Oregon University M

Pennsylvania
Community College of Allegheny
 County C
East Stroudsburg University of
 Pennsylvania B
Penn State
 University Park B
University of Pittsburgh B, M, D

Puerto Rico
University of Puerto Rico
 Rio Piedras Campus M

Rhode Island
Community College of Rhode
 Island C, A

South Carolina
South Carolina State University M
University of South Carolina M

South Dakota
Western Dakota Technical Institute C

Texas
Stephen F. Austin State University B
University of North Texas B, M
University of Texas
 Medical Branch at Galveston B
 Pan American B, M
 Southwestern Medical Center at
  Dallas B

Utah
Brigham Young University D

Virginia
Virginia Commonwealth
 University B, M

Washington
University of Washington M

West Virginia
Marshall University M

Wyoming
Central Wyoming College C, A

Religion/religious studies

Alabama
Auburn University B
Birmingham-Southern College B
Faulkner University B
Huntingdon College B
Oakwood College B
Samford University B
Stillman College B
University of Alabama B
University of Mobile B, M
Wallace State Community College at
 Hanceville C

Arizona
Arizona State University B, M
Northern Arizona University B
Prescott College M
Southwestern College C, B
University of Arizona B

Arkansas
Central Baptist College A, B
Harding University B
Hendrix College B
Ouachita Baptist University A, B
Philander Smith College B
University of Central Arkansas B

California
Azusa Pacific University B
Biola University B
California Baptist University B
California Lutheran University B
California State University
 Bakersfield B
 Chico B
 Fresno B
 Fullerton B
 Hayward B
 Long Beach B
 Northridge B
Chaffey Community College A
Chapman University B
Claremont McKenna College B
College of Notre Dame B
Concordia University B
Crafton Hills College C
Dominican University of California B
Hope International University M
Humboldt State University B

LIFE Bible College A, B
La Sierra University B, M
Loma Linda University M
Los Angeles Pierce College A
Loyola Marymount University B, M
Marymount College A
Master's College B
Mount St. Mary's College B, M
Occidental College B
Orange Coast College A
Pacific Union College B
Patten College A, B
Pepperdine University B, M
Pitzer College B
Point Loma Nazarene University B, M
Pomona College B
Queen of the Holy Rosary College A
St. John's Seminary College M
St. Mary's College of California B
San Diego State University B
San Jose Christian College C, B
San Jose State University B
Santa Clara University B, M
Scripps College B
Stanford University B, M, D
University of California
 Berkeley B
 Davis B
 Los Angeles B
 Riverside B
 San Diego B
 Santa Barbara B, M, D
 Santa Cruz B
University of La Verne B
University of Redlands B
University of San Diego B
University of Southern
 California B, M, D
University of the Pacific B
Vanguard University of Southern
 California B
Westmont College B
Whittier College B

Colorado
Colorado College B
Naropa University C, B, M
Nazarene Bible College A
Regis University B
University of Colorado
 Boulder B, M
University of Denver B

Connecticut
Connecticut College B
Fairfield University B
Sacred Heart University A, B, M
St. Joseph College B, T
Trinity College B
University of Bridgeport B
Wesleyan University B
Yale University B, M, D

District of Columbia
American University B, M
Catholic University of America B, M, D
George Washington University B, M
Georgetown University B
Howard University M

Florida
Eckerd College B
Florida Agricultural and Mechanical
 University B
Florida Christian College B
Florida College B
Florida International University B, M
Florida Southern College B
Florida State University B, M, D
Gulf Coast Community College A
Miami-Dade Community College A
New College of the University of South
 Florida B
Palm Beach Atlantic College B
Pensacola Junior College A
Rollins College B

Religion/religious studies

St. John Vianney College Seminary B
St. Leo University B
St. Thomas University B, M
Southeastern College of the Assemblies
   of God B
Stetson University B
University of Florida B, M
University of Miami B
University of South Florida B, M

Georgia
Agnes Scott College B
Brewton-Parker College A, B
Clark Atlanta University B
Emory University B, D
Georgia State University B
LaGrange College B
Mercer University B
Morehouse College B
Morris Brown College B
Oxford College of Emory University B
Shorter College B
Spelman College B
Toccoa Falls College B
University of Georgia B, M
Wesleyan College B

Hawaii
Chaminade University of Honolulu B
University of Hawaii
   Hilo B
   Manoa B, M

Idaho
Albertson College of Idaho B
Northwest Nazarene University B

Illinois
Augustana College B
Bradley University B
De Paul University B
Dominican University B
Elmhurst College B
Greenville College B
Illinois College B
Illinois Wesleyan University B
Judson College B
Lincoln Christian College and
   Seminary C, A, B
Loyola University of Chicago B, M, D
McKendree College B
Millikin University B
Moody Bible Institute B
North Central College B
North Park University B
Northwestern University B, M, D
Olivet Nazarene University B, M
Principia College B
St. Xavier University B
Southern Illinois University
   Carbondale B
Springfield College in Illinois A
Trinity Christian College B
Trinity International University M
University of Chicago M, D
University of Illinois
   Urbana-Champaign B
Wheaton College B

Indiana
Anderson University B
Ball State University B
Bethel College B
Butler University B
DePauw University B
Earlham College B
Franklin College B
Indiana University
   Bloomington B, M, D
Indiana University--Purdue University
   Indiana University-Purdue
      University Indianapolis B
Indiana Wesleyan University A, B
Manchester College A, B
Oakland City University C, A, B
Purdue University B
Saint Mary's College B

St. Joseph's College B
St. Mary-of-the-Woods College B
University of Evansville B
University of Indianapolis B
University of St. Francis B
Wabash College B

Iowa
Briar Cliff College A, B
Buena Vista University B
Central College B
Clarke College A, B
Coe College B
Cornell College B
Dordt College B
Drake University B
Faith Baptist Bible College and
   Theological Seminary M
Graceland University B
Grand View College B
Grinnell College B
Iowa State University B
Loras College B
Luther College B
Morningside College B
Mount Mercy College B
Northwestern College B
Simpson College B
University of Dubuque B, M, D
University of Iowa B, M, D
University of Northern Iowa B
Wartburg College B

Kansas
Baker University B
Barclay College B
Benedictine College B
Bethel College B
Central Christian College A, B
Kansas Wesleyan University B
Manhattan Christian College B
MidAmerica Nazarene University B, T
Ottawa University B
Sterling College B
Tabor College B
University of Kansas B, M
Washburn University of Topeka B

Kentucky
Berea College B
Brescia University A, B
Campbellsville University B
Centre College B
Cumberland College B
Georgetown College B
Kentucky Mountain Bible College A
Midway College B
Pikeville College B
Spalding University B, M
Thomas More College A, B
Transylvania University B
Union College B
Western Kentucky University B

Louisiana
Centenary College of Louisiana B
Loyola University New Orleans B, M

Maine
Bates College B
Bowdoin College B
Colby College B
St. Joseph's College B

Maryland
College of Notre Dame of Maryland B
Columbia Union College B
Goucher College B
Hood College B
Loyola College in Maryland B
St. Mary's College of Maryland B
Western Maryland College B

Massachusetts
Amherst College B
Assumption College B
Atlantic Union College B
Boston University B, M, D

College of the Holy Cross B
Eastern Nazarene College B
Elms College B, M
Hampshire College B
Harvard College B
Harvard University M, D
Merrimack College B
Mount Holyoke College B
Smith College B, M
Stonehill College B
Tufts University B
Wellesley College B
Wheaton College B
Williams College B

Michigan
Adrian College B, T
Albion College B
Alma College B, T
Andrews University B, M
Aquinas College B
Calvin College B, T
Central Michigan University B
Concordia College B
Cornerstone College and Grand Rapids
   Baptist Seminary B
Hillsdale College B
Hope College B, T
Kalamazoo College B
Lansing Community College A
Madonna University A, B
Marygrove College B
Michigan State University B
Siena Heights University B
University of Detroit Mercy B, M
University of Michigan B
Western Michigan University B, M, D
William Tyndale College C, A, B

Minnesota
Augsburg College B
Bethel College B
Carleton College B
College of St. Scholastica B
Concordia College: Moorhead B
Concordia University: St. Paul B
Gustavus Adolphus College B
Hamline University B
Macalester College B
St. Olaf College B
University of Minnesota
   Twin Cities B
University of St. Thomas B

Mississippi
Mary Holmes College A
Millsaps College B, T
Mississippi College B
Wesley College B
William Carey College B

Missouri
Avila College B
Baptist Bible College B
Central Methodist College B
East Central College A
Hannibal-LaGrange College B
Maryville University of Saint Louis B
Missouri Baptist College A, B
Park University M
Southwest Baptist University B
Southwest Missouri State
   University B, M
University of Missouri
   Columbia B, M
   St. Louis C
Washington University B, M
Webster University B
Westminster College B
William Jewell College B

Montana
University of Great Falls A, B

Nebraska
Dana College B
Doane College B

Hastings College B
Midland Lutheran College B
Nebraska Wesleyan University B
Union College B
University of Nebraska
   Omaha B

New Hampshire
Dartmouth College B

New Jersey
Bloomfield College B
Caldwell College B
College of St. Elizabeth B
Drew University B
Georgian Court College B
Montclair State University B
Princeton University B, M, D
Rowan University B
Rutgers
   The State University of New Jersey:
      Douglass College B
   The State University of New Jersey:
      Livingston College B
   The State University of New Jersey:
      Rutgers College B
   The State University of New Jersey:
      University College New
      Brunswick B
St. Peter's College B
Seton Hall University C, B, M
Thomas Edison State College B

New Mexico
College of Santa Fe B
Eastern New Mexico University B
University of New Mexico B

New York
Bard College B
Barnard College B
Canisius College B
City University of New York
   Brooklyn College B
   Hunter College B
   Queens College B
Colgate University B
College of Mount St. Vincent B
College of New Rochelle B, T
College of St. Rose B
Columbia University
   Columbia College B
   Graduate School M, D
   School of General Studies B
Concordia College A, B
Cornell University B
Daemen College B
Fordham University B, M, D
Hamilton College B
Hartwick College B
Hobart and William Smith Colleges B
Houghton College B
Iona College B
Le Moyne College B
Manhattan College B
Manhattanville College B
Nazareth College of Rochester B
New York University B, M
Niagara University B
Nyack College B
St. John Fisher College B
St. John's University C, B, M
St. Lawrence University B
St. Thomas Aquinas College B
Sarah Lawrence College B
Siena College B
Skidmore College B
State University of New York
   Stony Brook B
Syracuse University B, M, D
University of Rochester B
Vassar College B
Wells College B

North Carolina
Appalachian State University B
Belmont Abbey College B

Brevard College *B*
Campbell University *B*
Catawba College *B*
Chowan College *B*
Davidson College *B*
Duke University *B, M, D*
Elon College *B*
Gardner-Webb University *B*
Guilford College *B*
High Point University *B*
Lees-McRae College *B*
Lenoir-Rhyne College *B*
Mars Hill College *B*
Meredith College *B*
Methodist College *A, B, T*
Montreat College *B*
Mount Olive College *A, B*
North Carolina Wesleyan College *B*
Pfeiffer University *B*
St. Andrews Presbyterian College *B*
Salem College *B*
University of North Carolina
    Chapel Hill *B, M, D*
    Charlotte *B*
    Greensboro *B*
Wake Forest University *B, M*
Wingate University *B*

North Dakota
University of North Dakota *B*

Ohio
Ashland University *B*
Baldwin-Wallace College *B*
Bluffton College *B*
Capital University *B*
Case Western Reserve University *B*
Circleville Bible College *A, B*
Cleveland State University *B*
College of Mount St. Joseph *B, M, T*
College of Wooster *B*
Defiance College *B*
Denison University *B*
Heidelberg College *B*
Hiram College *B*
John Carroll University *B, M, T*
Kenyon College *B*
Lourdes College *A, B*
Malone College *M*
Miami University
    Oxford Campus *B, M*
Mount Union College *B*
Mount Vernon Nazarene College *B*
Muskingum College *B*
Oberlin College *B*
Ohio Northern University *B*
Ohio State University
    Columbus Campus *B*
Ohio University *B*
Ohio Wesleyan University *B*
Otterbein College *B*
University of Dayton *B*
University of Findlay *A, B*
Ursuline College *B*
Walsh University *B*
Wittenberg University *B*
Wright State University *B*
Youngstown State University *B*

Oklahoma
Mid-America Bible College *B*
Oklahoma Baptist University *B*
Oklahoma Christian University of
    Science and Arts *B*
Oklahoma City University *B, M*
St. Gregory's University *B*
Southern Nazarene University *B*
Southwestern College of Christian
    Ministries *A, B*
University of Tulsa *B*

Oregon
Concordia University *B*
Eugene Bible College *B*
George Fox University *B*
Lewis & Clark College *B*

Linfield College *B*
Marylhurst University *B*
Reed College *B*
University of Oregon *B*
Western Baptist College *B*
Willamette University *B*

Pennsylvania
Albright College *B*
Allegheny College *B*
Bryn Athyn College of the New
    Church *B*
Bryn Mawr College *B*
Bucknell University *B*
Cabrini College *B*
Chestnut Hill College *C*
Dickinson College *B*
Elizabethtown College *B*
Franklin and Marshall College *B*
Gettysburg College *B*
Grove City College *B*
Haverford College *B*
Holy Family College *B*
Immaculata College *B*
Indiana University of Pennsylvania *B*
Juniata College *B*
La Roche College *B*
La Salle University *B, M*
Lafayette College *B*
Lebanon Valley College of
    Pennsylvania *B*
Lehigh University *B*
Lincoln University *B*
Lycoming College *B*
Marywood University *B*
Mercyhurst College *B*
Messiah College *B*
Moravian College *B*
Muhlenberg College *B*
Neumann College *B*
Penn State
    University Park *B*
Rosemont College *B*
St. Charles Borromeo Seminary -
    Overbrook *C*
St. Francis College *B*
St. Joseph's University *B*
Seton Hill College *B*
Susquehanna University *B*
Swarthmore College *B*
Temple University *B, M, D*
Thiel College *B*
University of Pennsylvania *A, B, M, D*
University of Pittsburgh *B, M, D*
University of Scranton *B, M*
Ursinus College *B*
Villanova University *B, M*
West Chester University of
    Pennsylvania *B*
Westminster College *B*

Puerto Rico
Bayamon Central University *B*

Rhode Island
Brown University *B, M, D*
Providence College *B, M*
Salve Regina University *B*

South Carolina
Anderson College *B*
Charleston Southern University *B*
Coker College *B*
College of Charleston *B*
Columbia College *B*
Converse College *B*
Erskine College *B*
Furman University *B*
North Greenville College *B*
Presbyterian College *B*
Southern Wesleyan University *B*
University of South Carolina *B, M*
Winthrop University *B*
Wofford College *B*

South Dakota
Augustana College *B*

Tennessee
Belmont University *B, T*
Carson-Newman College *B*
David Lipscomb University *B*
King College *B*
Lambuth University *B*
Lane College *B*
Martin Methodist College *B*
Maryville College *B*
Rhodes College *B*
Southern Adventist University *A, B, M*
Trevecca Nazarene University *B*
Union University *B*
University of Tennessee
    Knoxville *B*
University of the South *B*
Vanderbilt University *B, M, D*

Texas
Amarillo College *A*
Arlington Baptist College *B*
Austin College *B*
Baylor University *B, M, D*
Concordia University at Austin *B, T*
East Texas Baptist University *B*
Hardin-Simmons University *M*
Houston Baptist University *B, M*
Howard Payne University *B*
Jarvis Christian College *B*
LeTourneau University *B*
Lon Morris College *A*
McMurry University *B*
Our Lady of the Lake University of San
    Antonio *B*
Rice University *B, M, D*
St. Edward's University *B*
Schreiner College *B*
Southern Methodist University *B, M, D*
Southwestern Adventist University *B*
Southwestern University *B*
Texas Christian University *B*
Texas Lutheran University *B*
Trinity University *B*
University of Dallas *B, M*
University of Mary Hardin-Baylor *B*
University of the Incarnate Word *B, M*
Wayland Baptist University *A, B, M*
Wiley College *B*

Vermont
Burlington College *B*
Goddard College *B*
Marlboro College *B*
Middlebury College *B*
St. Michael's College *B*
University of Vermont *B*

Virginia
Averett College *B*
Bluefield College *B*
Christopher Newport University *B*
College of William and Mary *B*
Emory & Henry College *B*
Ferrum College *B*
Hampden-Sydney College *B*
Hollins University *B*
Liberty University *A, B, M*
Lynchburg College *B*
Mary Baldwin College *B*
Mary Washington College *B*
Randolph-Macon College *B*
Randolph-Macon Woman's College *B*
Regent University *M, D*
Roanoke College *B, T*
Shenandoah University *B*
Sweet Briar College *B*
University of Richmond *B*
University of Virginia *B, M, D*
Virginia Commonwealth University *B*
Virginia Intermont College *B*
Virginia Union University *B*
Virginia Wesleyan College *B*
Washington and Lee University *B*

Washington
Central Washington University *B*

Gonzaga University *B, M*
Pacific Lutheran University *B*
St. Martin's College *B*
Seattle Pacific University *B, T*
Seattle University *B*
University of Puget Sound *B*
University of Washington *B, M*
Walla Walla College *B*
Washington State University *B*
Whitworth College *B*

West Virginia
Alderson-Broaddus College *B*
Bethany College *B*
Marshall University *B*
Ohio Valley College *B*
West Virginia Wesleyan College *B*
Wheeling Jesuit University *B, M*

Wisconsin
Alverno College *B, T*
Cardinal Stritch University *B, M*
Carroll College *B*
Carthage College *B*
Concordia University Wisconsin *B*
Lakeland College *B, M*
Lawrence University *B*
Marquette University *C*
Mount Mary College *B, T*
Northland College *B*
Ripon College *B*
St. Norbert College *B, T*
Silver Lake College *T*
University of Wisconsin
    Eau Claire *B*
    Madison *B, M*
    Oshkosh *B*
Viterbo University *B, T*
Wisconsin Lutheran College *B*

Religious education

Alabama
Faulkner University *B*
Huntingdon College *B*
Oakwood College *B*
Samford University *B*

Alaska
Alaska Bible College *B*

Arizona
Southwestern College *C, A, B*

Arkansas
Central Baptist College *A, B*
Harding University *B*
Ouachita Baptist University *B*
Williams Baptist College *B*

California
Azusa Pacific University *B, M, D*
Biola University *B, M, D*
California Lutheran University *B*
College of Notre Dame *B*
Concordia University *B, M*
Master's College *B*
Mount St. Mary's College *M*
Pacific Union College *B*
Patten College *B*
San Jose Christian College *B*
Simpson College *B, M*
University of San Francisco *M*
Vanguard University of Southern
    California *B*

Colorado
Nazarene Bible College *A, B*

District of Columbia
Catholic University of America *M, D*

Florida
Clearwater Christian College *B*
Florida Baptist Theological College *A, B*
Florida Southern College *B*
St. Thomas University *B*

Southeastern College of the Assemblies of God B
Georgia
Toccoa Falls College B, M
Idaho
Boise Bible College A, B
Northwest Nazarene University B
Illinois
Concordia University M
Lincoln Christian College and Seminary B, M
Loyola University of Chicago M
Moody Bible Institute B, T
North Park University M
Olivet Nazarene University B
Trinity Christian College B
Wheaton College B, M
Indiana
Indiana Wesleyan University A, B
Marian College A, B
St. Mary-of-the-Woods College B
Taylor University B
Iowa
Faith Baptist Bible College and Theological Seminary B
Northwestern College B
Kansas
Barclay College C
Central Christian College A, B
Kansas Wesleyan University B
Manhattan Christian College A, B
MidAmerica Nazarene University A, B
Sterling College B
Kentucky
Asbury College B
Campbellsville University B
Cumberland College B
Kentucky Christian College B
Kentucky Mountain Bible College B
Mid-Continent College C, B
Union College B
Louisiana
Centenary College of Louisiana B
Loyola University New Orleans M
Maryland
Washington Bible College B
Massachusetts
Atlantic Union College B
Boston College M, D
Michigan
Andrews University B, M, D
Aquinas College A
Concordia College B, T
Grace Bible College A, B
Reformed Bible College A, B
Minnesota
College of St. Benedict B
Concordia University: St. Paul B
Crown College C, B
Minnesota Bible College B
North Central University B
Northwestern College B
St. John's University B
St. Mary's University of Minnesota B
University of St. Thomas M
Mississippi
Magnolia Bible College B
Wesley College B
Missouri
Baptist Bible College B
Hannibal-LaGrange College B
Missouri Baptist College B
Ozark Christian College B
St. Louis Christian College B
Southwest Baptist University B

Nebraska
Concordia University B, T
Grace University B
Union College B, T
New Jersey
College of St. Elizabeth C
Felician College M
Seton Hall University B, D
New York
Columbia University Teachers College M, D
Concordia College B
Jewish Theological Seminary of America M
Nyack College B
North Carolina
Duke University M
Lenoir-Rhyne College B
Methodist College A, B, T
Pfeiffer University B, M
North Dakota
Trinity Bible College B
Ohio
Ashland University B, M, T
Capital University B
Cedarville College B
Circleville Bible College A, B
College of Mount St. Joseph B, T
Defiance College B, T
Malone College B
Mount Vernon Nazarene College B
Muskingum College B
Notre Dame College of Ohio C
University of Dayton B
Walsh University B
Oklahoma
Mid-America Bible College B
Oklahoma Baptist University B
Oklahoma Christian University of Science and Arts B
Oklahoma City University M
Oral Roberts University B, M
St. Gregory's University A
Southern Nazarene University B
Southwestern College of Christian Ministries B
Oregon
Eugene Bible College B
George Fox University B
Multnomah Bible College B
University of Portland T
Pennsylvania
Duquesne University M
Gannon University C, A, M
Holy Family College B
Immaculata College B
La Roche College C
La Salle University B, M
Lancaster Bible College B
Mercyhurst College A, B
Messiah College B
Philadelphia College of Bible B, T
St. Vincent College B
Seton Hill College B
Thiel College B
Valley Forge Christian College B
Westminster College B, T
Puerto Rico
Pontifical Catholic University of Puerto Rico M
Rhode Island
Providence College A, M
South Carolina
Columbia College B
Columbia International University B, M
Erskine College B, M
Morris College B
Presbyterian College B

South Dakota
Mount Marty College B
Tennessee
Lee University B
Milligan College B
Southern Adventist University B
Tennessee Temple University B, M
Tennessee Wesleyan College B
Texas
Abilene Christian University M
Arlington Baptist College B
Dallas Baptist University A, B
East Texas Baptist University B
Howard Payne University B
McMurry University B
Southern Methodist University M
Southwestern Assemblies of God University B
Texas Wesleyan University B
Wayland Baptist University B
Virginia
Liberty University M
Washington
Puget Sound Christian College B
Seattle Pacific University B, T
Seattle University M
Wisconsin
Cardinal Stritch University B, T
Marquette University T
Viterbo University B

Religious music

Alabama
Birmingham-Southern College B
Northwest-Shoals Community College C
Samford University B, M
Arizona
Grand Canyon University B
Southwestern College C, A, B
Arkansas
Central Baptist College B
John Brown University B
Ouachita Baptist University B
Williams Baptist College B
California
Azusa Pacific University B
Fresno Pacific University B
Hope International University B, M
Master's College B
Mount St. Mary's College B
Patten College B
Point Loma Nazarene University B
San Jose Christian College B
Santa Clara University M
Simpson College B
University of Southern California M, D
Colorado
Nazarene Bible College A, B
District of Columbia
Catholic University of America M, D
Florida
Bethune-Cookman College B
Clearwater Christian College B
Florida Baptist Theological College A, B
Florida Christian College B
Florida Southern College B
Florida State University C
Hobe Sound Bible College C, B
Jacksonville University B
Southeastern College of the Assemblies of God B
Warner Southern College B
Georgia
Andrew College C
Emory University M

Middle Georgia College A
Piedmont College B
Shorter College B
Toccoa Falls College B
University of Georgia B
Idaho
Boise Bible College A, B
Northwest Nazarene University B
Illinois
Concordia University M
Judson College B
Lincoln Christian College and Seminary B
Millikin University B
Moody Bible Institute B
Olivet Nazarene University B
Indiana
Anderson University B
Bethel College B
Goshen College B
Indiana Wesleyan University A, B
Manchester College B
Oakland City University B
St. Joseph's College C, A, B, M
Iowa
Dordt College B
Drake University B
Faith Baptist Bible College and Theological Seminary B
Wartburg College B
Kansas
Central Christian College A, B
Manhattan Christian College A, B
MidAmerica Nazarene University A, B
Kentucky
Campbellsville University B, M
Cumberland College B
Kentucky Christian College B
Kentucky Mountain Bible College B
Union College B
Louisiana
Centenary College of Louisiana B
Loyola University New Orleans M
Maryland
Washington Bible College B
Massachusetts
Boston University D
Eastern Nazarene College B
Michigan
Aquinas College A, B
Calvin College B
Marygrove College C
Spring Arbor College B
William Tyndale College B
Minnesota
Bethel College B
College of St. Catherine: St. Paul Campus C
Concordia University: St. Paul B
Gustavus Adolphus College B
Minnesota Bible College B
North Central University C, B
St. John's University M
Mississippi
Magnolia Bible College B
Mississippi College B
William Carey College B
Missouri
Baptist Bible College B
Evangel University B
Hannibal-LaGrange College B
Missouri Baptist College B
Ozark Christian College C, B
St. Louis Christian College B
Southwest Baptist University B
William Jewell College B

Religious music

Nebraska
Concordia University B
Grace University B

New Jersey
Rider University B, M

New York
Concordia College B
Jewish Theological Seminary of America B, M, D
Nyack College B

North Carolina
Brevard College A, B
Campbell University B
East Carolina University B
Lenoir-Rhyne College B
North Carolina Central University B
Pfeiffer University B
Wingate University B

Ohio
Cedarville College B
Circleville Bible College A, B
Malone College B
Mount Vernon Nazarene College A, B
Wittenberg University B

Oklahoma
Mid-America Bible College B
Oklahoma Baptist University B
Oral Roberts University B, M
Southern Nazarene University B
Southwestern College of Christian Ministries B
Southwestern Oklahoma State University B

Oregon
Eugene Bible College B
Multnomah Bible College B
Western Baptist College B

Pennsylvania
Duquesne University M
Immaculata College A
Lancaster Bible College B
Marywood University B, M
Philadelphia College of Bible B
St. Charles Borromeo Seminary - Overbrook C
Seton Hill College B
Susquehanna University B
Valley Forge Christian College B

South Carolina
Charleston Southern University B
Columbia International University B
Erskine College M
North Greenville College B

South Dakota
Dakota Wesleyan University B

Tennessee
Belmont University B
Carson-Newman College B
Johnson Bible College A, B
Lambuth University B
Lee University B, M
Tennessee Temple University B
Tennessee Wesleyan College B
Trevecca Nazarene University B
Union University B

Texas
Arlington Baptist College B
Baylor University B, M
Concordia University at Austin B
Dallas Baptist University B
East Texas Baptist University B
Hardin-Simmons University B, M
Houston Baptist University B
Howard Payne University B
McMurry University B
Southern Methodist University M
Southwestern Assemblies of God University B
Southwestern University B
Wayland Baptist University B

Virginia
Bluefield College B

Washington
Pacific Lutheran University B
Puget Sound Christian College B

West Virginia
Alderson-Broaddus College B

Wisconsin
Viterbo University B

Respiratory therapy

Alabama
Central Alabama Community College A
Enterprise State Junior College A
Faulkner University A
George C. Wallace State Community College
  Dothan A
Northwest-Shoals Community College A
University of Alabama
  Birmingham A
University of South Alabama B
Wallace State Community College at Hanceville A

Arizona
Gateway Community College C, A
Pima Community College A

Arkansas
Northwest Arkansas Community College A
University of Arkansas
  for Medical Sciences C, A
University of Central Arkansas B
Westark College A

California
American River College A
Butte College C, A
California College for Health Sciences A
College of the Desert A
Compton Community College A
Crafton Hills College C, A
East Los Angeles College A
Foothill College C, A
Fresno City College A
Grossmont Community College C, A
Los Angeles Southwest College A
Los Angeles Valley College C, A
Modesto Junior College A
Mount San Antonio College C, A
Napa Valley College C, A
Ohlone College A
Orange Coast College C, A
Rio Hondo College A
Santa Monica College A
Skyline College C, A
Victor Valley College C, A

Colorado
Front Range Community College A
Pueblo Community College A

Connecticut
Manchester Community-Technical College A
Naugatuck Valley Community-Technical College A
Norwalk Community-Technical College A
Quinnipiac University B
Sacred Heart University C, A
University of Bridgeport B
University of Hartford B

Delaware
Delaware Technical and Community College
  Owens Campus A
  Stanton/Wilmington Campus A

District of Columbia
University of the District of Columbia A

Florida
Brevard Community College A
Broward Community College A
Daytona Beach Community College A
Edison Community College A
Florida Agricultural and Mechanical University B
Florida Community College at Jacksonville A
Gulf Coast Community College C, A
Hillsborough Community College A
Indian River Community College A
Manatee Community College A
Miami-Dade Community College C, A
Palm Beach Community College C, A
Pensacola Junior College A
Polk Community College A
St. Petersburg Junior College A
Santa Fe Community College A
Seminole Community College A
Tallahassee Community College A
University of Central Florida B
Valencia Community College A

Georgia
Armstrong Atlantic State University B
Athens Area Technical Institute C, A
Brewton-Parker College A
Chattahoochee Technical Institute A
Darton College A
Floyd College A
Georgia State University B
Gwinnett Technical Institute A
Macon State College A
Medical College of Georgia B, M
Thomas College A
Waycross College A

Hawaii
University of Hawaii
  Kapiolani Community College C, A

Idaho
Boise State University A, B
College of Southern Idaho A
North Idaho College A

Illinois
Black Hawk College A
City Colleges of Chicago
  Malcolm X College A
  Olive-Harvey College C
College of DuPage C, A
Kankakee Community College A
Kaskaskia College C
Lincoln Land Community College A
Moraine Valley Community College A
National-Louis University B
Parkland College A
Rock Valley College A
St. Augustine College A
Shawnee Community College A
Southern Illinois University
  Carbondale B
Southwestern Ilinois College C, A
Springfield College in Illinois A
Triton College A
Waubonsee Community College A

Indiana
Ball State University A
Indiana University
  Bloomington B
  Northwest A
Indiana University--Purdue University
  Indiana University-Purdue University Indianapolis A, B
Ivy Tech State College
  Central Indiana A
  Lafayette C, A
  Northeast C, A
  Northwest C, A
University of Southern Indiana A

Vincennes University A

Iowa
Des Moines Area Community College A
Hawkeye Community College C
Kirkwood Community College A
Northeast Iowa Community College A

Kansas
Johnson County Community College C, A
Kansas City Kansas Community College A
Newman University A
Seward County Community College C, A
University of Kansas
  Medical Center B
Washburn University of Topeka A

Kentucky
Ashland Community College A
Lexington Community College A
Madisonville Community College A
Northern Kentucky University A
Southeast Community College A
University of Louisville B

Louisiana
Bossier Parish Community College C, A
Delgado Community College C, A
Louisiana State University
  Eunice A
Louisiana State University Medical Center B, M
Nicholls State University A
Our Lady of Holy Cross College A, B
Southern University
  Shreveport A

Maine
Kennebec Valley Technical College A
Southern Maine Technical College A

Maryland
Allegany College A
Baltimore City Community College A
Columbia Union College A, B
Community College of Baltimore County
  Essex A
Frederick Community College A
Prince George's Community College A
Salisbury State University B

Massachusetts
Berkshire Community College A
Massachusetts Bay Community College C, A
Massasoit Community College A
North Shore Community College A
Northeastern University B
Northern Essex Community College C, A
Springfield Technical Community College A

Michigan
Delta College A
Ferris State University A
Henry Ford Community College A
Kalamazoo Valley Community College A
Lansing Community College A
Macomb Community College A
Marygrove College C, A
Monroe County Community College A
Mott Community College A
Muskegon Community College C, A
Oakland Community College A
Washtenaw Community College A

Minnesota
College of St. Catherine-Minneapolis A
Hibbing Community College: A Technical and Community College A
Lake Superior College: A Community and Technical College A

Rochester Community and Technical
    College *A*
St. Paul Technical College *A*

Mississippi
Hinds Community College *C, A*
Meridian Community College *C*
Mississippi Gulf Coast Community
    College
        Jackson County Campus *A*
        Perkinston *C, A*
Northeast Mississippi Community
    College *A*
Northwest Mississippi Community
    College *A*

Missouri
Ozarks Technical Community College *A*
Penn Valley Community College *A*
Southwest Missouri State University *B*
St. Louis Community College
    St. Louis Community College at
        Forest Park *A*
University of Missouri
    Columbia *B*

Montana
Montana State University
    College of Technology-Great
        Falls *A*
University of Great Falls *B*
University of Montana-Missoula *A*

Nebraska
Metropolitan Community College *C, A*
Midland Lutheran College *A, B*
Nebraska Methodist College of Nursing
    and Allied Health *A, B*
Southeast Community College
    Lincoln Campus *A*
University of Nebraska
    Kearney *B*

New Hampshire
New Hampshire Community Technical
    College
        Claremont *A*

New Jersey
Atlantic Cape Community College *A*
Bergen Community College *A*
Brookdale Community College *A*
Camden County College *A*
County College of Morris *A*
Essex County College *A*
Fairleigh Dickinson University *A*
Gloucester County College *C, A*
Hudson County Community
    College *C, A*
Mercer County Community College *A*
Middlesex County College *A*
Passaic County Community College *A*
Sussex County Community College *A*
Thomas Edison State College *A, B*
Union County College *A*
University of Medicine and Dentistry of
    New Jersey
        School of Health Related
            Professions *C, A, B*

New Mexico
Albuquerque Technical-Vocational
    Institute *A*
Dona Ana Branch Community College of
    New Mexico State University *A*

New York
City University of New York
    Borough of Manhattan Community
        College *A*
Erie Community College
    North Campus *A*
Genesee Community College *A*
Hudson Valley Community College *A*
Long Island University
    Brooklyn Campus *B*
Mohawk Valley Community
    College *C, A*
Molloy College *A*
Nassau Community College *A*
New York University *A*
Onondaga Community College *C, A*
Rockland Community College *A*
State University of New York
    Health Science Center at Stony
        Brook *B*
    Oswego *B*
    Stony Brook *B*
    Upstate Medical University *B*
Westchester Community College *A*

North Carolina
Carteret Community College *A*
Catawba Valley Community College *A*
Central Piedmont Community College *A*
Durham Technical Community
    College *C, A*
Edgecombe Community College *C, A*
Fayetteville Technical Community
    College *A*
Forsyth Technical Community College *A*
Pitt Community College *A*
Rockingham Community College *A*
Sandhills Community College *A*
Southwestern Community College *A*

North Dakota
North Dakota State University *B*
University of Mary *A, B*

Ohio
Bowling Green State University
    Firelands College *A*
Cincinnati State Technical and
    Community College *A*
Columbus State Community College *A*
Jefferson Community College *A*
Lakeland Community College *A*
Lima Technical College *A*
North Central State College *A*
Ohio State University
    Columbus Campus *B, M*
Shawnee State University *A*
Sinclair Community College *A*
Stark State College of Technology *A*
University of Akron
    Wayne College *A*
University of Akron *A*
University of Toledo *C, A, B*
Youngstown State University *B*

Oklahoma
Rose State College *A*
Tulsa Community College *C, A*

Oregon
Lane Community College *A*
Mount Hood Community College *A*

Pennsylvania
Community College of Allegheny
    County *A*
Community College of Philadelphia *A*
Delaware County Community College *A*
Gannon University *A, B*
Gwynedd-Mercy College *A*
Harrisburg Area Community College *A*
Indiana University of Pennsylvania *B*
La Roche College *B*
Lehigh Carbon Community College *A*
Luzerne County Community College *A*
Mansfield University of Pennsylvania *A*
Point Park College *A, B*
Reading Area Community College *A*
University of Pittsburgh
    Johnstown *A*
West Chester University of
    Pennsylvania *A*
York College of Pennsylvania *A, B*

Puerto Rico
Huertas Junior College *A*
Universidad Metropolitana *A, B*

Rhode Island
Community College of Rhode Island *A*

South Carolina
Florence-Darlington Technical
    College *C, A*
Greenville Technical College *C, A*
Midlands Technical College *A*
Orangeburg-Calhoun Technical
    College *C*
Piedmont Technical College *A*
Spartanburg Technical College *A*
Trident Technical College *A*

South Dakota
Dakota State University *A, B*

Tennessee
Chattanooga State Technical Community
    College *A*
Columbia State Community College *A*
East Tennessee State University *C*
Jackson State Community College *A*
Roane State Community College *A*
Southern Adventist University *A*
Volunteer State Community College *C*
Walters State Community College *C*

Texas
Alvin Community College *C, A*
Amarillo College *A*
Austin Community College *C, A*
Collin County Community College
    District *A*
Del Mar College *C, A*
El Paso Community College *A*
Houston Community College
    System *C, A*
Howard College *C, A*
Midland College *A*
Midwestern State University *B*
Odessa College *A*
St. Philip's College *C*
South Plains College *A*
Southwest Texas State University *B*
Tarrant County College *A*
Temple College *A*
Tyler Junior College *A*
University of Texas
    Medical Branch at Galveston *B*
Victoria College *C, A*
Weatherford College *A*

Utah
Weber State University *A, B*

Vermont
Champlain College *A, B*

Virginia
Central Virginia Community College *C*
J. Sargeant Reynolds Community
    College *C, A*
Mountain Empire Community
    College *C, A*
Northern Virginia Community
    College *C, A*
Shenandoah University *A, B*
Southside Virginia Community
    College *A*
Southwest Virginia Community
    College *C*
Tidewater Community College *C, A*

Washington
Seattle Central Community College *A*
Spokane Community College *A*
Tacoma Community College *C*

West Virginia
College of West Virginia *A*
University of Charleston *B*
West Virginia Northern Community
    College *A*
West Virginia University Institute of
    Technology *A*
Wheeling Jesuit University *B*

Wisconsin
Madison Area Technical College *A*
Milwaukee Area Technical College *A*
Northeast Wisconsin Technical
    College *A*
Western Wisconsin Technical College *A*

Wyoming
Western Wyoming Community
    College *C, A*

Retailing/wholesaling

Alabama
Bessemer State Technical College *C, A*
Gadsden State Community College *A*
Jefferson State Community College *A*
Wallace State Community College at
    Hanceville *A*

Arizona
Northern Arizona University *B*
Pima Community College *C, A*

Arkansas
Harding University *B*

California
Chabot College *A*
Chaffey Community College *C, A*
College of the Desert *A*
Columbia College *C*
Fashion Institute of Design and
    Merchandising *A*
Golden West College *C, A*
Las Positas College *A*
Pasadena City College *A*
Santa Clara University *C*
Shasta College *A*
Sierra College *C, A*

Colorado
Community College of Aurora *C, A*

Connecticut
Central Connecticut State University *B*
Gateway Community College *A*
Middlesex Community-Technical
    College *C*
University of New Haven *A, B*

Delaware
Wesley College *B*

Florida
Indian River Community College *A*
Palm Beach Community College *A*

Georgia
Athens Area Technical Institute *C, A*
Savannah Technical Institute *A*

Hawaii
University of Hawaii
    Kapiolani Community
        College *C, A*

Idaho
College of Southern Idaho *C*
Lewis-Clark State College *C*

Illinois
Black Hawk College *C, A*
City Colleges of Chicago
    Wright College *C*
College of DuPage *C, A*
Elgin Community College *C, A*
Illinois Eastern Community Colleges
    Wabash Valley College *C*
John A. Logan College *C*
Joliet Junior College *C*
Kaskaskia College *C*
Kishwaukee College *C*
Lincoln Land Community College *A*
McHenry County College *C, A*
Richland Community College *A*
Southwestern Illinois College *A*
Triton College *C, A*
University of St. Francis *B*
Waubonsee Community College *C, A*
William Rainey Harper College *C, A*

retailing/wholesaling

Indiana
Indiana State University *B*
International Business College *C, A*
Vincennes University *A*

Iowa
Des Moines Area Community College *C, A*
Iowa Western Community College *A*
Kirkwood Community College *C, A*
Muscatine Community College *C*
North Iowa Area Community College *A*
Western Iowa Tech Community College *C, A*

Kansas
Allen County Community College *A*
Barton County Community College *A*
Hutchinson Community College *C, A*
Johnson County Community College *A*

Kentucky
Henderson Community College *C*
Maysville Community College *A*

Maine
Husson College *B*

Maryland
Allegany College *C, A*
Harford Community College *C, A*
Howard Community College *C, A*
Montgomery College
  Germantown Campus *C, A*
  Rockville Campus *A*

Massachusetts
Babson College *B*
Bay Path College *B*
Bay State College *A*
Cape Cod Community College *A*
Middlesex Community College *A*
Newbury College *A*
Roxbury Community College *A*
Simmons College *B*

Michigan
Bay de Noc Community College *C, A*
Cleary College *B*
Davenport College of Business *A*
Delta College *A*
Eastern Michigan University *B*
Ferris State University *C, A, B*
Lansing Community College *A*
Western Michigan University *B*

Minnesota
Alexandria Technical College *C, A*
Dakota County Technical College *C, A*
Lake Superior College: A Community and Technical College *A*
Minnesota State College - Southeast Technical *C, A*
North Hennepin Community College *A*
Ridgewater College: A Community and Technical College *A*
St. Cloud Technical College *C, A*
St. Paul Technical College *C*
University of Minnesota
  Twin Cities *B*

Mississippi
Hinds Community College *C, A*

Missouri
Longview Community College *A*
Maple Woods Community College *A*
Penn Valley Community College *A*

Nebraska
University of Nebraska
  Omaha *B*

Nevada
Community College of Southern Nevada *A*

New Hampshire
Hesser College *A*
New Hampshire College *B*

New Jersey
Atlantic Cape Community College *C*
Bergen Community College *A*
Camden County College *A*
Gloucester County College *A*
Mercer County Community College *C*
Ocean County College *C*
Passaic County Community College *A*
Raritan Valley Community College *C*
Thomas Edison State College *A, B*

New Mexico
Albuquerque Technical-Vocational Institute *C*
Clovis Community College *A*

New York
Bryant & Stratton Business Institute
  Syracuse *A*
City University of New York
  Baruch College *B, M*
Dutchess Community College *A*
Erie Community College
  City Campus *A*
Finger Lakes Community College *C, A*
Genesee Community College *A*
Jefferson Community College *C, A*
Mohawk Valley Community College *A*
Monroe Community College *C, A*
Nassau Community College *A*
Onondaga Community College *A*
Orange County Community College *A*
Suffolk County Community College *A*
Syracuse University *B*
Tompkins-Cortland Community College *A*
Westchester Community College *A*

North Carolina
Alamance Community College *C, A*
Asheville Buncombe Technical Community College *A*
Blue Ridge Community College *A*
Craven Community College *A*
Pitt Community College *A*
Wayne Community College *A*
Western Piedmont Community College *A*

North Dakota
Lake Region State College *C, A*

Ohio
Belmont Technical College *A*
Bowling Green State University
  Firelands College *A*
Columbus State Community College *A*
Edison State Community College *C, A*
Miami University
  Oxford Campus *B*
Muskingum Area Technical College *A*
Northwestern College *C*
Sinclair Community College *A*
University of Akron *A*
University of Toledo *A*
Wilmington College *B*
Youngstown State University *A, B, M*

Oklahoma
Connors State College *C*
East Central University *B*
University of Central Oklahoma *B*

Oregon
Clackamas Community College *C, A*
Lane Community College *C*

Pennsylvania
Bucks County Community College *A*
Central Pennsylvania College *A*
Community College of Beaver County *A*
Community College of Philadelphia *C, A*
Delaware County Community College *A*
Harcum College *A*
Harrisburg Area Community College *C, A*
Philadelphia University *B*
Pittsburgh Technical Institute *A*
Sawyer School *A*
Westmoreland County Community College *A*
York College of Pennsylvania *A*

Puerto Rico
University of Puerto Rico
  Mayaguez Campus *B*

Rhode Island
Community College of Rhode Island *C, A*
Johnson & Wales University *A, B*

South Carolina
Aiken Technical College *A*
Florence-Darlington Technical College *C, A*
Midlands Technical College *C, A*
University of South Carolina *B*

Tennessee
Trevecca Nazarene University *A*

Texas
Alvin Community College *C, A*
Collin County Community College District *C, A*
Lamar University *B*
Sam Houston State University *B*
Tarleton State University *B*
Tarrant County College *A*

Utah
Dixie State College of Utah *C, A*
Weber State University *A*

Vermont
Champlain College *A, B*

Virginia
National Business College *A*
Tidewater Community College *C, A*
Virginia Union University *B*

Washington
Centralia College *C*
Columbia Basin College *A*
Highline Community College *A*
Lake Washington Technical College *C*
Pierce College *C*
Shoreline Community College *A*
Walla Walla Community College *C, A*

West Virginia
Marshall University *B*

Wisconsin
Gateway Technical College *A*
Milwaukee Area Technical College *A*
Moraine Park Technical College *C, A*
Northeast Wisconsin Technical College *A*
Western Wisconsin Technical College *A*
Wisconsin Indianhead Technical College *A*

Robotics

Alabama
Northwest-Shoals Community College *A*

Arkansas
Arkansas State University
  Mountain Home *C*

California
Cerritos Community College *A*
ITT Technical Institute
  West Covina *B*
Orange Coast College *C*
University of California
  San Diego *M, D*

Colorado
Denver Technical College: A Division of DeVry University *A*
Pikes Peak Community College *A*
Red Rocks Community College *C*
University of Southern Colorado *B*

Georgia
Gwinnett Technical Institute *A*

Illinois
Black Hawk College *A*
Kaskaskia College *C*
Oakton Community College *A*
William Rainey Harper College *C*

Indiana
ITT Technical Institute
  Fort Wayne *B*
  Indianapolis *B*
  Newburgh *B*
Indiana University--Purdue University
  Indiana University-Purdue University Indianapolis *A, B*
Ivy Tech State College
  Lafayette *C, A*
  Northcentral *C, A*
  Northeast *C, A*
  Southcentral *C, A*
  Southeast *A*
  Southwest *A*
  Wabash Valley *A*
  Whitewater *A*
Purdue University
  North Central Campus *A*
Purdue University *A, B*
Vincennes University *A*

Iowa
Des Moines Area Community College *A*
Indian Hills Community College *A*
Southeastern Community College
  North Campus *A*

Kansas
Kansas City Kansas Community College *C*

Maine
Central Maine Technical College *C*

Michigan
Mott Community College *A*
Oakland Community College *C, A*

Minnesota
Mesabi Range Community and Technical College *A*

New Hampshire
New Hampshire Community Technical College
  Nashua *A*

New Jersey
Gloucester County College *A*

North Carolina
Central Carolina Community College *A*
Forsyth Technical Community College *A*
Wake Technical Community College *A*

Ohio
Jefferson Community College *A*
Kent State University
  Ashtabula Regional Campus *C*
Kent State University *C*
Lima Technical College *C*
Lorain County Community College *A*
Sinclair Community College *A*
Terra Community College *A*

Oregon
ITT Technical Institute
  Portland *B*

Pennsylvania
Community College of Allegheny County *A*
Electronic Institutes: Middletown *A*
Lehigh Carbon Community College *C, A*
Pennsylvania Institute of Technology *A*

South Carolina
Trident Technical College *A*

Texas
Hill College *A*
Texas State Technical College
  Harlingen *A*
  Sweetwater *A*

Utah
Salt Lake Community College *A*

Virginia
ECPI College of Technology *C, A*
ITT Technical Institute
  Norfolk *B*

Washington
Spokane Community College *A*

Wisconsin
Blackhawk Technical College *A*
Chippewa Valley Technical College *A*
Gateway Technical College *A*

Romance languages, other

Alabama
University of Alabama *M, D*

California
Point Loma Nazarene University *B*
Pomona College *B*
San Francisco State University *B*
University of California
  Los Angeles *M, D*

Colorado
Colorado College *B*

Connecticut
Albertus Magnus College *B*
Connecticut College *B*
Wesleyan University *B*

District of Columbia
Catholic University of America *M, D*

Florida
University of Florida *D*
University of Miami *D*

Illinois
Olivet Nazarene University *B*
University of Chicago *M, D*

Indiana
DePauw University *B*
University of Notre Dame *M*

Louisiana
University of New Orleans *M*

Maine
Bowdoin College *B*

Maryland
University of Maryland
  College Park *B*

Massachusetts
Harvard College *B*
Harvard University *M, D*
Tufts University *B*

Michigan
University of Michigan
  Flint *B*
University of Michigan *M, D*

Minnesota
Carleton College *B*

Missouri
University of Missouri
  Columbia *D*

Nevada
University of Nevada
  Las Vegas *B*

New Hampshire
Dartmouth College *B*

New Mexico
University of New Mexico *D*

New York
City University of New York
  City College *B*
  College of Staten Island *B*
Columbia University
  Graduate School *M*
Cornell University *B*
Dowling College *B, T*
New York University *B, M*
State University of New York
  Stony Brook *M*
Syracuse University *M*

North Carolina
University of North Carolina
  Chapel Hill *B, M, D*

Oklahoma
Cameron University *B*

Oregon
University of Oregon *B, M, D*

Pennsylvania
Haverford College *B, T*
La Salle University *B*
University of Pennsylvania *M, D*

Tennessee
Maryville College *B*
University of Memphis *M*

West Virginia
Wheeling Jesuit University *B*

Wisconsin
Ripon College *B*
University of Wisconsin
  Madison *B, M, D*

Russian

Alabama
University of Alabama *B*
University of South Alabama *B*

Alaska
University of Alaska
  Fairbanks *B*

Arizona
Arizona State University *B*
University of Arizona *B, M*

Arkansas
Ouachita Baptist University *B*

California
Cabrillo College *A*
California State University
  Long Beach *C*
Claremont McKenna College *B*
De Anza College *A*
Monterey Institute of International
  Studies *C*
Pitzer College *B*
Pomona College *B*
San Diego Mesa College *A*
San Diego State University *B*
San Francisco State University *B, M*
Scripps College *B*
Stanford University *M*
University of California
  Berkeley *B, M, D*
  Davis *B, M*
  Los Angeles *B*
  Riverside *B*
  San Diego *B*
  Santa Barbara *B*
  Santa Cruz *B*
University of Southern
  California *B, M, D*

Colorado
Colorado College *B*

University of Colorado
  Boulder *B*
University of Denver *B, M*

Connecticut
Connecticut College *B*
Fairfield University *B*
Trinity College *B*
University of Connecticut *B*
Wesleyan University *B*
Yale University *B*

Delaware
University of Delaware *B, T*

District of Columbia
American University *M*
George Washington University *B*
Georgetown University *B*
Howard University *B*

Florida
Eckerd College *B*
Florida State University *B*
Miami-Dade Community College *A*
New College of the University of South
  Florida *B*
University of Florida *B*
University of South Florida *B*

Georgia
Emory University *B*
Oxford College of Emory University *B*
University of Georgia *B*

Hawaii
University of Hawaii
  Manoa *B, M*

Idaho
Idaho State University *A*
Ricks College *A*

Illinois
Illinois Wesleyan University *B*
Knox College *B*
Northern Illinois University *B*
Parkland College *A*
Principia College *B*
Southern Illinois University
  Carbondale *B*
University of Chicago *B, M, D*
University of Illinois
  Chicago *B*
  Urbana-Champaign *B*

Indiana
Indiana State University *B*
University of Notre Dame *B*

Iowa
Cornell College *B, T*
Grinnell College *B*
Iowa State University *B*
University of Iowa *B, M, T*
University of Northern Iowa *M*

Kansas
University of Kansas *B, M, D*

Kentucky
University of Kentucky *B*
University of Louisville *B*

Louisiana
Loyola University New Orleans *B*
Tulane University *B*

Maine
Bates College *B*
Bowdoin College *B*

Maryland
Goucher College *B*
Johns Hopkins University *B*
University of Maryland
  Baltimore County *B*
  College Park *B, M*

Massachusetts
Amherst College *B*

Boston College *B, M*
Boston University *B*
Brandeis University *B, M, D*
College of the Holy Cross *B*
Harvard College *B*
Harvard University *B*
Mount Holyoke College *B*
Smith College *B*
Tufts University *B*
University of Massachusetts
  Boston *B*
Wellesley College *B*
Wheaton College *B*
Williams College *B*

Michigan
Michigan State University *B, M, D*
Michigan Technological University *C*
Oakland University *B, T*
University of Michigan *B, M, T*
Wayne State University *B*

Minnesota
Augsburg College *B*
Carleton College *B*
Concordia College: Moorhead *T*
Gustavus Adolphus College *B*
Macalester College *B*
St. Cloud State University *B*
St. Olaf College *B*
University of Minnesota
  Twin Cities *B*

Missouri
St. Louis University *B*
Truman State University *B*
University of Missouri
  Columbia *B*
Washington University *B*

Montana
University of Montana-Missoula *B*

Nebraska
University of Nebraska
  Lincoln *B*

New Hampshire
Dartmouth College *B*
University of New Hampshire *B*

New Jersey
Drew University *B*
Montclair State University *T*
Rider University *B*
Rutgers
  The State University of New Jersey:
    Douglass College *B, T*
  The State University of New Jersey:
    Livingston College *B, T*
  The State University of New Jersey:
    Rutgers College *B, T*
  The State University of New Jersey:
    University College New
    Brunswick *B*
Seton Hall University *T*

New Mexico
University of New Mexico *B*

New York
Bard College *B*
Barnard College *B*
City University of New York
  Brooklyn College *B*
  Hunter College *B*
  Lehman College *B*
  Queens College *B*
Colgate University *B*
Columbia University
  Columbia College *B*
  Graduate School *M, D*
  School of General Studies *B*
Cornell University *B, T*
Fordham University *B, M*
Hamilton College *B*
Hobart and William Smith Colleges *B*
Hofstra University *B*

Russian

Marist College *B*
New York University *B*
Sarah Lawrence College *B*
State University of New York
  Albany *B, M*
  Buffalo *B*
  Stony Brook *B, T*
Syracuse University *B*
United States Military Academy *B*
University of Rochester *B*
Vassar College *B*

North Carolina
Duke University *B, M*
Wake Forest University *B*

Ohio
Bowling Green State University *B*
Kent State University
  Stark Campus *B*
Kent State University *B*
Miami University
  Oxford Campus *B, T*
Oberlin College *B*
Ohio State University
  Columbus Campus *B*
Ohio University *B*
Youngstown State University *B*

Oklahoma
Oklahoma State University *B*
Tulsa Community College *A*
University of Oklahoma *B*

Oregon
Portland State University *B, T*
Reed College *B*
University of Oregon *B, M*

Pennsylvania
Bryn Mawr College *B, M, D*
Bucknell University *B*
California University of Pennsylvania *B*
Carnegie Mellon University *B*
Dickinson College *B*
Haverford College *B, T*
Immaculata College *A*
Indiana University of Pennsylvania *B*
Juniata College *B*
Kutztown University of
  Pennsylvania *B, T*
Lafayette College *B*
Lincoln University *B*
Penn State
  University Park *B*
Swarthmore College *B*
Temple University *B*
University of Pennsylvania *A, B, M, D*
University of Pittsburgh *B*
Washington and Jefferson College *T*
West Chester University of
  Pennsylvania *B*

Rhode Island
Brown University *B, M, D*

Tennessee
Rhodes College *B*
University of Tennessee
  Knoxville *B*
University of the South *B*
Vanderbilt University *B*

Texas
Baylor University *B*
Rice University *B*
Southern Methodist University *B*
Texas A&M University *B*
Trinity University *B*
University of Texas
  Arlington *B, T*
  Austin *B*

Utah
Brigham Young University *B, M*
University of Utah *B*

Vermont
Middlebury College *B*

Norwich University *M*
University of Vermont *B*

Virginia
Ferrum College *B*
George Mason University *B*

Washington
Central Washington University *B*
Everett Community College *A*
Evergreen State College *B*
Seattle Pacific University *B*
University of Washington *B, M, D*
Washington State University *B*

Wisconsin
Beloit College *B, T*
Lawrence University *B, T*
University of Wisconsin
  Madison *B, M, D*
  Milwaukee *B*

Wyoming
University of Wyoming *B*

Russian/Slavic studies

Alabama
University of Alabama
  Huntsville *B*

Alaska
University of Alaska
  Fairbanks *B*

California
California State University
  Fullerton *B*
San Diego State University *B*
Stanford University *M*
University of California
  Berkeley *C*
  Riverside *B*
  San Diego *B*
  Santa Cruz *B*

Colorado
University of Colorado
  Boulder *B*
University of Denver *B*

Connecticut
Connecticut College *B*
Trinity College *B*
University of Connecticut *B*
Wesleyan University *B*
Yale University *B, M*

District of Columbia
American University *B*
George Washington University *M*
Georgetown University *M*

Florida
Eckerd College *B*
Florida State University *B, M*
Stetson University *B*

Georgia
Emory University *B*
Oxford College of Emory University *B*

Illinois
Knox College *B*
University of Chicago *M*
University of Illinois
  Urbana-Champaign *B*

Indiana
DePauw University *B*
Indiana University
  Bloomington *M*

Iowa
Cornell College *B*
University of Iowa *B, M*
University of Northern Iowa *B*

Kansas
University of Kansas *B, M*

Kentucky
University of Louisville *B*

Louisiana
Louisiana State University and
  Agricultural and Mechanical
  College *B*
Tulane University *B*

Maine
Colby College *B*
University of Southern Maine *B*

Maryland
University of Maryland
  College Park *B*

Massachusetts
Boston College *M*
Hampshire College *B*
Harvard College *B*
Harvard University *M, D*
Mount Holyoke College *B*
Tufts University *B*
University of Massachusetts
  Amherst *B*
Wellesley College *B*
Wheaton College *B*

Michigan
Grand Valley State University *B*
Oakland University *B*
University of Michigan *B, M*

Minnesota
Carleton College *B*
Concordia College: Moorhead *B*
Gustavus Adolphus College *B*
Hamline University *B*
Macalester College *B*
St. Cloud State University *B*
St. Olaf College *B*
University of Minnesota
  Twin Cities *B, M*
University of St. Thomas *B*

Missouri
University of Missouri
  Columbia *B*
Washington University *B*

New Hampshire
Dartmouth College *B*
St. Anselm College *C*

New Jersey
Drew University *B*
Princeton University *B, M, D*
Rutgers
  The State University of New Jersey:
    Douglass College *B*
  The State University of New Jersey:
    Livingston College *B*
  The State University of New Jersey:
    Rutgers College *B*
  The State University of New Jersey:
    University College New
    Brunswick *B*
Seton Hall University *C*

New Mexico
University of New Mexico *B*

New York
Bard College *B*
Barnard College *B*
City University of New York
  Brooklyn College *B*
  Hunter College *M*
Colgate University *B*
Columbia University
  Columbia College *B*
  Graduate School *M, D*
  School of General Studies *B*
Cornell University *B, M, D*
Fordham University *B*

Hamilton College *B*
Hobart and William Smith Colleges *B*
New York University *B, M*
Sarah Lawrence College *B*
State University of New York
  Albany *B, M*
Syracuse University *B*
United States Military Academy *B*

North Carolina
University of North Carolina
  Chapel Hill *B*

Ohio
Bowling Green State University *B*
College of Wooster *B*
Kent State University *B*
Oberlin College *B*
Ohio State University
  Columbus Campus *B, M*
Wittenberg University *B*

Oklahoma
Oklahoma State University *C*

Pennsylvania
California University of Pennsylvania *B*
Dickinson College *B*
La Salle University *B*
Lehigh University *B*
Muhlenberg College *B*

Rhode Island
Brown University *B, M, D*

Tennessee
Rhodes College *B*
University of Tennessee
  Knoxville *B*
University of the South *B*

Texas
Baylor University *B*
Rice University *B*
Southern Methodist University *B*
Southwest Texas State University *B*
Texas Tech University *B*
University of Houston *B*
University of Texas
  Austin *B, M*

Vermont
Marlboro College *B*
Middlebury College *B*
University of Vermont *B*

Virginia
College of William and Mary *B*
George Mason University *B*
Randolph-Macon Woman's College *B*
Washington and Lee University *B*

Washington
Evergreen State College *B*
University of Washington *B, M*

Scandinavian

California
University of California
  Berkeley *B, M, D*
  Los Angeles *B, M*

Illinois
Augustana College *B*
North Park University *B*
University of Chicago *B*

Iowa
Luther College *B*
Waldorf College *A*

Massachusetts
Harvard College *B*

Minnesota
Augsburg College *B*
Concordia College: Moorhead *B*
Gustavus Adolphus College *B*

St. Olaf College *B*
University of Minnesota
 Twin Cities *B*

Texas
University of Texas
 Austin *B*

Utah
Brigham Young University *B, M*

Washington
Pacific Lutheran University *B*
University of Washington *B, M, D*

Wisconsin
University of Wisconsin
 Madison *B, M, D*

Scandinavian studies

Iowa
Luther College *B*

Massachusetts
Harvard College *B*

Michigan
University of Michigan *B*

Minnesota
Augsburg College *B*
Concordia College: Moorhead *B*
Gustavus Adolphus College *B*
University of Minnesota
 Twin Cities *M, D*

Vermont
Marlboro College *B*

Virginia
College of William and Mary *B*

Washington
Pacific Lutheran University *B*
University of Washington *B*

Wisconsin
University of Wisconsin
 Madison *B, M, D*

School psychology

Alabama
Alabama Agricultural and Mechanical
 University *M*
Auburn University *M, D*
University of Alabama
 Birmingham *M*
University of Alabama *M, D*

Arizona
Northern Arizona University *M*

Arkansas
University of Central Arkansas *M*

California
California State University
 Chico *T*
 Hayward *T*
 Long Beach *M*
 Los Angeles *M*
National University *M*
San Francisco State University *M*
San Jose State University *M*
Stanford University *D*
University of California
 Los Angeles *M, D*

Colorado
University of Denver *M, D*
University of Northern Colorado *D, T*
Western State College of Colorado *B*

Connecticut
Fairfield University *M, T*
University of Hartford *M*

District of Columbia
Gallaudet University *M*
Howard University *M*

Florida
Barry University *M*
Carlos Albizu University *M*
Florida Agricultural and Mechanical
 University *M*
Florida International University *M*
Nova Southeastern University *M*
University of Central Florida *M*
University of Florida *M, D*
University of South Florida *M*
University of West Florida *M*

Georgia
Georgia Southern University *C, M, T*
Georgia State University *M, D*
University of Georgia *M, D*
Valdosta State University *B*

Illinois
Eastern Illinois University *M*
Governors State University *M*
Illinois State University *M, D, T*
Loyola University of Chicago *M, D*
National-Louis University *M, D*
Western Illinois University *M*

Indiana
Ball State University *M, D*
Butler University *M*
Indiana State University *M*
Valparaiso University *M*

Iowa
University of Iowa *D*
University of Northern Iowa *M*

Kansas
Emporia State University *M*
Pittsburg State University *M*
University of Kansas *D*
Wichita State University *M*

Kentucky
Eastern Kentucky University *M*

Louisiana
Nicholls State University *M*

Maine
University of Southern Maine *M*

Massachusetts
Northeastern University *M, D*
University of Massachusetts
 Boston *M*

Michigan
Central Michigan University *M, D*
University of Detroit Mercy *M*
Wayne State University *M*
Western Michigan University *M*

Minnesota
Minnesota State University, Mankato *M*
Moorhead State University *M*

Missouri
Lindenwood University *M*

Montana
University of Montana-Missoula *M*

Nebraska
University of Nebraska
 Kearney *M*
 Omaha *M*

Nevada
University of Nevada
 Las Vegas *M*

New Hampshire
Rivier College *M*

New Jersey
Kean University *M*
New Jersey City University *M*
Rider University *M, T*

Rowan University *M*
Rutgers
 The State University of New Jersey:
  New Brunswick Graduate
  Campus *D*
Seton Hall University *M*

New York
Alfred University *M, D*
City University of New York
 Brooklyn College *M*
 Queens College *M*
College of New Rochelle *M*
College of St. Rose *C, M*
Columbia University
 Teachers College *M, D*
Hofstra University *D*
Marist College *M*
New York University *D*
Pace University:
 Pleasantville/Briarcliff *D*
Pace University *D*
Rochester Institute of Technology *M*
St. John's University *M, D*
State University of New York
 Albany *D*
 Buffalo *M, T*
 College at Plattsburgh *M*
 Oswego *M*
Syracuse University *D*
Touro College *B*

North Carolina
East Carolina University *M, T*
University of North Carolina
 Chapel Hill *M, D*
Western Carolina University *M*

Ohio
Bowling Green State University *M*
John Carroll University *C, M*
Kent State University *M, D*
Miami University
 Oxford Campus *M*
University of Akron *M*
University of Cincinnati *M, D*
University of Dayton *M*
University of Toledo *M*
Wright State University *M*

Oklahoma
Northeastern State University *M*

Pennsylvania
Bucknell University *M*
Eastern College *M*
Edinboro University of Pennsylvania *M*
Immaculata College *B, M*
Indiana University of Pennsylvania *M, D*
Lehigh University *M, D*
Millersville University of
 Pennsylvania *M*
Penn State
 University Park *M, D*
Temple University *M, D*
University of Pennsylvania *D*

Puerto Rico
Inter American University of Puerto Rico
 Metropolitan Campus *M*

Rhode Island
Rhode Island College *M*
University of Rhode Island *M, D*

South Carolina
Francis Marion University *M*
The Citadel *M*
University of South Carolina *M, D*
Winthrop University *M, T*

South Dakota
University of South Dakota *D*

Tennessee
Crichton College *B*
University of Memphis *M*

Texas
Abilene Christian University *M*
Houston Baptist University *M*
Our Lady of the Lake University of San
 Antonio *M*
Sam Houston State University *M*
Southwest Texas State University *M*
Stephen F. Austin State University *M*
Tarleton State University *B, M*
Texas A&M University
 Texarkana *M*
Texas A&M University *M, D*
Texas Woman's University *M, D*
Trinity University *M*
University of Houston
 Clear Lake *M*
University of Mary Hardin-Baylor *M*
University of North Texas *M*
University of Texas
 Tyler *M*

Virginia
James Madison University *M, T*
Radford University *M*
Virginia Union University *B*

Washington
Central Washington University *M, T*
Eastern Washington University *M*
Seattle University *M*
Western Washington University *M*

Wisconsin
Marquette University *M, D*
University of Wisconsin
 La Crosse *M*
 Madison *M, D*
 River Falls *M*
 Stout *M*
 Whitewater *M*

Science education

Alabama
Alabama Agricultural and Mechanical
 University *B, M*
Athens State University *B*
Auburn University *B*
Birmingham-Southern College *T*
Faulkner University *B*
Huntingdon College *T*
Jacksonville State University *B, M, T*
Oakwood College *B*
Samford University *B*
Talladega College *T*
Troy State University
 Dothan *B, M*
Tuskegee University *B, M*
University of Alabama *B*
University of Mobile *T*

Alaska
University of Alaska
 Fairbanks *M*
 Southeast *M*

Arizona
Arizona State University *B, T*
Grand Canyon University *B*
Prescott College *B, M*
University of Arizona *B, M*

Arkansas
Arkansas Tech University *B*
Harding University *B, T*
Philander Smith College *B*
Southern Arkansas University *B, T*
University of Arkansas
 Pine Bluff *B, M, T*
University of Arkansas *B*
University of Central Arkansas *M, T*
University of the Ozarks *B, T*

California
Azusa Pacific University *T*
California Baptist University *B, T*

California Lutheran University *B, T*
California State Polytechnic University:
  Pomona *T*
California State University
  Bakersfield *B, T*
  Chico *T*
  Dominguez Hills *T*
  Fullerton *M, T*
  Long Beach *T*
Concordia University *B*
Fresno Pacific University *M, T*
Humboldt State University *T*
Mills College *T*
Mount St. Mary's College *T*
San Diego State University *T*
San Francisco State University *B, T*
San Jose State University *T*
Sonoma State University *T*
University of California
  Berkeley *D*
University of the Pacific *T*

Colorado
Adams State College *B, T*
Colorado Christian University *B*
Colorado College *M*
Colorado State University *T*
Fort Lewis College *T*
Metropolitan State College of Denver *T*
University of Colorado
  Boulder *T*
  Colorado Springs *T*
University of Denver *T*
University of Southern Colorado *T*

Connecticut
Central Connecticut State University *B*
Eastern Connecticut State University *M*
Fairfield University *T*
Quinnipiac University *B, M*
Sacred Heart University *B, M, T*
St. Joseph College *T*
Southern Connecticut State
  University *B, T*

Delaware
Delaware State University *B, M*
University of Delaware *B, T*
Wesley College *B*

District of Columbia
George Washington University *M, T*

Florida
Broward Community College *A*
Florida Agricultural and Mechanical
  University *B, M, T*
Florida Atlantic University *B*
Florida Institute of
  Technology *B, M, D, T*
Florida International University *B, M, T*
Florida State University *B, M, D, T*
Gulf Coast Community College *A*
Nova Southeastern University *B, M*
Palm Beach Community College *A*
Southeastern College of the Assemblies
  of God *B, T*
University of Central Florida *B, M*
University of Florida *M*
University of North Florida *B, M*
University of South Florida *B, M*
Warner Southern College *B*

Georgia
Albany State University *B, M*
Armstrong Atlantic State
  University *B, M, T*
Columbus State University *B, M*
Covenant College *B, T*
Gainesville College *A*
Georgia College and State University *M*
Georgia Southern University *B, M, T*
Georgia Southwestern State
  University *B, M*
Georgia State University *M, D*
Kennesaw State University *B*
LaGrange College *T*

Mercer University *M, T*
North Georgia College & State
  University *B, M*
State University of West Georgia *B, M*
University of Georgia *B, M, D, T*
Valdosta State University *M, T*
Wesleyan College *M, T*

Hawaii
Brigham Young University
  Hawaii *B, T*
University of Hawaii
  Manoa *B, T*

Idaho
Boise State University *T*
Lewis-Clark State College *B, T*
Northwest Nazarene University *B*
University of Idaho *B, M*

Illinois
Augustana College *B, T*
Blackburn College *B, T*
Chicago State University *T*
Concordia University *B, T*
Eastern Illinois University *M*
Eureka College *T*
Greenville College *T*
Judson College *B, T*
Lewis University *T*
National-Louis University *M*
North Park University *T*
Northwestern University *B, T*
Olivet Nazarene University *B, T*
Southern Illinois University
  Edwardsville *B*
Trinity Christian College *B, T*
University of Illinois
  Urbana-Champaign *B, M, T*

Indiana
Anderson University *B, T*
Ball State University *B, D, T*
Bethel College *B*
Butler University *T*
Calumet College of St. Joseph *B*
Franklin College *T*
Goshen College *B*
Grace College *B*
Indiana State University *B, M, T*
Indiana University
  Bloomington *B, T*
  South Bend *B, T*
  Southeast *B*
Indiana University--Purdue University
  Indiana University-Purdue
    University Fort Wayne *B, T*
Indiana Wesleyan University *B, T*
Manchester College *B, T*
Oakland City University *B*
Purdue University
  Calumet *B*
Saint Mary's College *T*
St. Mary-of-the-Woods College *B*
Taylor University *B*
Tri-State University *B, T*
University of Evansville *T*
University of Indianapolis *B, T*
University of Notre Dame *B*
University of St. Francis *B*
University of Southern Indiana *B, T*
Valparaiso University *B*
Vincennes University *A*

Iowa
Buena Vista University *T*
Central College *T*
Clarke College *B, T*
Cornell College *B, T*
Dordt College *B*
Drake University *M, T*
Graceland University *T*
Iowa State University *T*
Loras College *B*
Luther College *B*
Morningside College *B*
Mount Mercy College *T*

Northwestern College *T*
St. Ambrose University *B, T*
University of Iowa *B, M, D, T*
University of Northern Iowa *B, M*
Upper Iowa University *B*
Wartburg College *T*
William Penn University *B*

Kansas
Benedictine College *T*
Bethany College *T*
Bethel College *T*
Colby Community College *A*
Emporia State University *T*
Garden City Community College *A*
Independence Community College *A*
Kansas Wesleyan University *T*
McPherson College *B, T*
MidAmerica Nazarene University *B, T*
Newman University *T*
Pittsburg State University *B, T*
Southwestern College *B*
Tabor College *B, T*
University of Kansas *B, T*
Washburn University of Topeka *B*

Kentucky
Alice Lloyd College *B*
Campbellsville University *B*
Eastern Kentucky University *B*
Morehead State University *B*
Murray State University *B, M, T*
Northern Kentucky University *B, T*
Spalding University *B*
Thomas More College *B*
Union College *B, M*
University of Kentucky *B*
Western Kentucky University *B*

Louisiana
Centenary College of Louisiana *B, T*
Dillard University *B*
Louisiana State University
  Shreveport *B*
Nicholls State University *B*
Northwestern State University *B, M, T*
Our Lady of Holy Cross College *T*
Southeastern Louisiana University *B*
University of Louisiana at Monroe *B*
University of New Orleans *B, M*
Xavier University of Louisiana *B, T*

Maine
St. Joseph's College *B*
University of Maine
  Farmington *B*
  Presque Isle *B*
University of Maine *M*
University of New England *B, T*
University of Southern Maine *T*

Maryland
Bowie State University *B*
College of Notre Dame of Maryland *T*
Columbia Union College *B*
Montgomery College
  Germantown Campus *A*
  Rockville Campus *A*
  Takoma Park Campus *A*
Morgan State University *D*
Prince George's Community College *A*
Towson University *T*
University of Maryland
  College Park *B*

Massachusetts
American International College *T*
Assumption College *T*
Boston University *B, M, T*
Bridgewater State College *M, T*
Framingham State College *T*
Merrimack College *T*
Smith College *M*
Tufts University *M, T*
Westfield State College *B, M, T*
Worcester State College *T*

Michigan
Albion College *B, T*
Andrews University *M, T*
Aquinas College *B, T*
Calvin College *T*
Central Michigan University *B*
Concordia College *B, T*
Cornerstone College and Grand Rapids
  Baptist Seminary *B, T*
Eastern Michigan University *B, T*
Ferris State University *B*
Grand Valley State University *B, T*
Lansing Community College *A*
Lawrence Technological University *M*
Madonna University *T*
Michigan Technological University *T*
Northern Michigan University *B, T*
Saginaw Valley State University *B, M*
University of Michigan
  Dearborn *T*
University of Michigan *M*
Wayne State University *B, M, T*
Western Michigan University *B*

Minnesota
Augsburg College *T*
Bemidji State University *T*
Bethel College *B*
College of St. Benedict *T*
College of St. Catherine: St. Paul
  Campus *T*
College of St. Scholastica *T*
Concordia College: Moorhead *T*
Concordia University: St. Paul *B, T*
Gustavus Adolphus College *T*
Hamline University *B*
Minnesota State University,
  Mankato *B, M, T*
Moorhead State University *B, T*
Ridgewater College: A Community and
  Technical College *A*
St. Cloud State University *T*
St. John's University *T*
St. Olaf College *T*
Southwest State University *B, T*
University of Minnesota
  Duluth *B*
  Morris *T*
  Twin Cities *M, T*
University of St. Thomas *B, T*
Winona State University *B, M, T*

Mississippi
Blue Mountain College *B*
Coahoma Community College *A*
Delta State University *T*
Jackson State University *M*
Mississippi College *M*
Mississippi Gulf Coast Community
  College
    Perkinston *A*
Mississippi State University *T*
Northwest Mississippi Community
  College *A*
Rust College *B*
University of Mississippi *B*
University of Southern Mississippi *M, D*

Missouri
Avila College *T*
Central Methodist College *B*
Central Missouri State University *B, T*
College of the Ozarks *B, T*
Culver-Stockton College *T*
Evangel University *B*
Hannibal-LaGrange College *B*
Harris Stowe State College *T*
Lincoln University *B, T*
Lindenwood University *M*
Maryville University of Saint
  Louis *B, M, T*
Missouri Baptist College *T*
Missouri Southern State College *B, T*
Missouri Valley College *T*
Northwest Missouri State University *T*
Rockhurst University *B*

Southeast Missouri State University B
Southwest Baptist University T
Southwest Missouri State University B
Truman State University M, T
University of Missouri
   Columbia B, M, D
Washington University B, M, T
Webster University M
William Jewell College T
William Woods University B

Montana
Montana State University
   Billings B, T
   Bozeman M, T
   Northern B, T
Rocky Mountain College B, T
University of Great Falls B, T
University of Montana-Missoula T
Western Montana College of The
   University of Montana B, T

Nebraska
Chadron State College B, M
College of Saint Mary B, T
Concordia University T
Dana College B
Doane College B, T
Hastings College B, M, T
Midland Lutheran College B, T
Nebraska Wesleyan University B
Peru State College B, T
University of Nebraska
   Kearney B, M, T
   Lincoln B, T
Wayne State College B, M

Nevada
University of Nevada
   Reno B

New Hampshire
Antioch New England Graduate
   School M
Franklin Pierce College T
Keene State College B, T
Notre Dame College B, M
Plymouth State College of the University
   System of New Hampshire B, T
Rivier College B, T
St. Anselm College T
University of New Hampshire T

New Jersey
Caldwell College T
College of St. Elizabeth T
Fairleigh Dickinson University M
Monmouth University T
Ramapo College of New Jersey B
Richard Stockton College of New
   Jersey B
Rider University B, T
Rowan University M, T
Rutgers
   The State University of New Jersey:
     Douglass College T
   The State University of New Jersey:
     Livingston College T
   The State University of New Jersey:
     New Brunswick Graduate
     Campus M, D, T
   The State University of New Jersey:
     Newark College of Arts and
     Sciences T
   The State University of New Jersey:
     Rutgers College T
   The State University of New Jersey:
     University College New
     Brunswick T
   The State University of New Jersey:
     University College Newark T
St. Peter's College T
The College of New Jersey T

New Mexico
College of the Southwest B, T
New Mexico Highlands University B

New Mexico Institute of Mining and
   Technology B, M
Western New Mexico University B

New York
Adelphi University B, M
Canisius College B, M, T
City University of New York
   Brooklyn College B, M
   City College B, T
   College of Staten Island M
   Hunter College B, M
   Lehman College M
   Queens College M, T
College of Mount St. Vincent T
College of St. Rose B, T
Columbia University
   Teachers College M, D
Concordia College T
D'Youville College M, T
Dominican College of Blauvelt B
Dowling College B
Elmira College B, T
Fordham University M, T
Houghton College B, T
Ithaca College B, T
Le Moyne College T
Long Island University
   Brooklyn Campus M
   C. W. Post Campus B, T
   Southampton College T
Manhattan College B, T
Manhattanville College M, T
Marymount College B, T
Nazareth College of Rochester T
New York Institute of Technology B, T
New York University B, M, T
Pace University:
   Pleasantville/Briarcliff B, M, T
Pace University B, M, T
Rensselaer Polytechnic Institute B, T
Roberts Wesleyan College B, T
St. Bonaventure University T
St. John Fisher College B, T
St. John's University B, T
St. Lawrence University T
St. Thomas Aquinas College B, T
St. Joseph's College
   St. Joseph's College: Suffolk
     Campus B, T
   St. Joseph's College B, T
State University of New York
   Albany B, M, T
   Buffalo M, D, T
   College at Brockport M, T
   College at Buffalo B, M
   College at Cortland B, M, T
   College at Geneseo B, M, T
   College at Oneonta B, M, T
   College at Plattsburgh M
   College at Potsdam T
   College of Environmental Science
     and Forestry B, T
   New Paltz B, M, T
   Oswego B, M
Syracuse University B, M, D, T
Utica College of Syracuse University B
Vassar College T
Wagner College T
Wells College T

North Carolina
Appalachian State University B, T
Barton College T
Belmont Abbey College T
Bennett College B, T
Catawba College T
East Carolina University B, M
Elizabeth City State University B
Elon College B, T
Forsyth Technical Community College A
Gardner-Webb University B
Lenoir-Rhyne College B, T
Louisburg College A
Mars Hill College T
Meredith College T

North Carolina Central University B, M
North Carolina State University M, D, T
Sandhills Community College A
University of North Carolina
   Chapel Hill M, T
   Greensboro M, T
   Pembroke B, T
Wake Forest University M, T
Western Carolina University B

North Dakota
Dickinson State University B, T
Jamestown College B
Mayville State University B, T
Minot State University B, T
North Dakota State University B, T
University of North Dakota B, T
Valley City State University B, T

Ohio
Ashland University B, T
Baldwin-Wallace College T
Bluffton College B
Bowling Green State University B, M
Capital University T
Cedarville College B
Central State University B
College of Mount St. Joseph T
Defiance College B, T
Hiram College T
Kent State University
   Stark Campus B
Kent State University B, M, T
Malone College B
Miami University
   Oxford Campus B, T
Mount Union College T
Mount Vernon Nazarene College B, T
Ohio Dominican College D
Ohio Northern University T
Ohio University B, T
Otterbein College B
Shawnee State University B, T
University of Akron B
University of Dayton B, M, T
University of Findlay B, T
University of Rio Grande B, T
University of Toledo B, T
Ursuline College B, T
Walsh University B
Wilmington College B
Wittenberg University B
Wright State University B, M, T
Xavier University B
Youngstown State University B, M

Oklahoma
Cameron University B, T
East Central University B
Eastern Oklahoma State College A
Northeastern Oklahoma Agricultural and
   Mechanical College A
Northeastern State University B
Northwestern Oklahoma State
   University B, T
Oklahoma Baptist University B, T
Oklahoma Christian University of
   Science and Arts B, T
Oklahoma City University B
Oklahoma State University B, T
Oral Roberts University B, T
Southeastern Oklahoma State
   University B, M, T
Southern Nazarene University B
Southwestern Oklahoma State
   University B, M, T
University of Central Oklahoma B
University of Oklahoma B, T
University of Tulsa T

Oregon
Concordia University B, M, T
Eastern Oregon University B
Linfield College T
Oregon State University M, D
University of Portland T

Western Baptist College B
Western Oregon University T

Pennsylvania
Albright College T
Allentown College of St. Francis de
   Sales M, T
Beaver College B, M, T
Bloomsburg University of
   Pennsylvania B, T
Bucknell University T
California University of
   Pennsylvania B, T
Carlow College T
Cedar Crest College B, T
Chatham College M, T
Chestnut Hill College T
Cheyney University of Pennsylvania T
Clarion University of Pennsylvania M
Delaware Valley College T
Dickinson College T
Duquesne University B, T
East Stroudsburg University of
   Pennsylvania B, M, T
Elizabethtown College T
Gannon University M, T
Gettysburg College T
Grove City College T
Holy Family College B, T
Immaculata College T
Indiana University of
   Pennsylvania B, M, T
Juniata College B, T
La Roche College B
La Salle University B, T
Lincoln University B, T
Lock Haven University of
   Pennsylvania B, T
Lycoming College T
Marywood University T
Mercyhurst College B
Millersville University of
   Pennsylvania B, T
Moravian College T
St. Joseph's University B
St. Vincent College T
Seton Hill College B, T
Slippery Rock University of
   Pennsylvania M
Susquehanna University T
Temple University B, M, T
Thiel College B
University of Pennsylvania M, D
University of Pittsburgh
   Bradford
   Johnstown B, T
University of Pittsburgh T
University of Scranton T
University of the Sciences in
   Philadelphia T
Ursinus College T
Villanova University T
Waynesburg College B, T
West Chester University of
   Pennsylvania B, M, T
Widener University T
Wilkes University T
York College of Pennsylvania B, T

Puerto Rico
Bayamon Central University B
Caribbean University B, T
Colegio Universitario del Este B
Inter American University of Puerto Rico
   Metropolitan Campus B, M
   San German Campus M
Pontifical Catholic University of Puerto
   Rico B, T
Turabo University T
Universidad Metropolitana B
University of Puerto Rico
   Cayey University College T

Rhode Island
Providence College B
Rhode Island College B, M, T

Science education

South Carolina
Anderson College B, T
Charleston Southern University B, M
Clemson University B
Converse College T
Erskine College B, T
Furman University T
Lander University M
The Citadel M
University of South Carolina
   Aiken B, T

South Dakota
Black Hills State University B, T
Dakota State University B, T
Dakota Wesleyan University B, T
Mount Marty College B
Northern State University M, T
University of South Dakota B, T

Tennessee
Belmont University T
Bethel College B
Cumberland University B
Freed-Hardeman University T
King College T
Lee University B
Lincoln Memorial University B, T
Tennessee Technological University T
Tennessee Temple University B
Tennessee Wesleyan College B, T
Tusculum College B, T
Union University B, T
University of Tennessee
   Chattanooga B, T
   Knoxville T
   Martin B, T
Vanderbilt University M, D

Texas
Abilene Christian University B, T
Angelo State University T
Baylor University B, T
Dallas Baptist University B, T
Del Mar College A
East Texas Baptist University B
Hardin-Simmons University B, T
Howard Payne University T
Lamar University T
LeTourneau University B
Lubbock Christian University B
McMurry University T
Prairie View A&M University M
Southwest Texas State University M, T
Stephen F. Austin State University T
Tarleton State University B, T
Texas A&M University
   Commerce T
   Kingsville T
Texas Christian University T
Texas Woman's University M
University of Houston
   Clear Lake T
University of Houston M, T
University of Mary Hardin-Baylor T
University of Texas
   Arlington T
   Austin M, D
   San Antonio T
University of the Incarnate Word D
Wayland Baptist University T
West Texas A&M University T

Utah
Brigham Young University B, M
University of Utah M
Utah State University B
Weber State University B

Vermont
Castleton State College B, T
Johnson State College
Lyndon State College B
St. Michael's College B, M
University of Vermont B, T

Virginia
Bluefield College B
Christopher Newport University M, T
Eastern Shore Community College A
Liberty University B
Longwood College B, T
Radford University T
University of Virginia's College at
   Wise T
Virginia Wesleyan College T

Washington
Central Washington University B, T
Eastern Washington University M
North Seattle Community College C
Pacific Lutheran University T
Seattle Pacific University B, T
University of Washington B
Washington State University T
Western Washington University B, M, T
Whitworth College B, T

West Virginia
Alderson-Broaddus College T
Concord College B, T
Fairmont State College B
Glenville State College B
Shepherd College B
University of Charleston B
West Liberty State College B
West Virginia State College B
Wheeling Jesuit University T

Wisconsin
Alverno College T
Beloit College B
Cardinal Stritch University B, T
Carroll College T
Carthage College M, T
Concordia University Wisconsin B, T
Lawrence University T
Mount Senario College B, T
Northland College T
Ripon College T
St. Norbert College T
University of Wisconsin
   Eau Claire B
   Green Bay T
   La Crosse B, T
   Madison B, T
   Milwaukee M
   Oshkosh B
   Platteville B, T
   River Falls T
   Superior B, T
   Whitewater B, T
Viterbo University B

Wyoming
Western Wyoming Community
   College A

Science technologies

Alabama
Athens State University B
Community College of the Air Force A
Marion Military Institute A
University of Mobile B

California
American River College A
Bakersfield College A
Barstow College A
Cabrillo College A
Chabot College A
College of the Siskiyous A
Compton Community College A
Los Angeles Harbor College A
Los Angeles Trade and Technical
   College A
Merced College A
Mount San Antonio College A
Pasadena City College A
San Joaquin Delta College A
San Jose City College A
University of La Verne C
Victor Valley College A
West Hills Community College A

Colorado
Red Rocks Community College C, A

Georgia
Abraham Baldwin Agricultural
   College A
Atlanta Metropolitan College A

Illinois
Black Hawk College
   East Campus A
Lake Land College A
Lincoln Land Community College A
Olivet Nazarene University A

Kansas
Central Christian College A
Coffeyville Community College A
Johnson County Community College A

Louisiana
Louisiana State University
   Alexandria A
Southern University
   Shreveport A

Maine
University of Maine
   Fort Kent B

Maryland
Baltimore City Community College A
Charles County Community College A
Chesapeake College A
Harford Community College A
Villa Julie College B

Massachusetts
Mount Wachusett Community College A

Michigan
Henry Ford Community College A
Macomb Community College C, A
Madonna University A, B
Oakland Community College C, A

Minnesota
North Hennepin Community College A

Mississippi
Copiah-Lincoln Community College A

Missouri
St. Louis Community College
   St. Louis Community College at
   Forest Park A

Montana
Little Big Horn College A
Montana State University
   Northern B

Nebraska
Central Community College C, A

New York
Cornell University M, D
Corning Community College A
Herkimer County Community College A
Jefferson Community College A
Niagara County Community College A
Rensselaer Polytechnic Institute M, D
Rochester Institute of
   Technology B, M, D
State University of New York
   College of Technology at Canton A
Suffolk County Community College A

North Carolina
Alamance Community College A

Ohio
Lorain County Community College A
Miami University
   Middletown Campus A
   Oxford Campus A
Ohio State University
   Agricultural Technical Institute A
Wittenberg University B

Oklahoma
Tulsa Community College A

Oregon
Chemeketa Community College A

Pennsylvania
Community College of Allegheny
   County A
Lehigh University B
Reading Area Community College A
Valley Forge Military College A

Tennessee
Cumberland University A
Motlow State Community College A

Texas
College of the Mainland A
Hill College A
Navarro College A
North Central Texas College A
Texas State Technical College
   Waco C, A
University of Mary Hardin-Baylor B

Virginia
Germanna Community College A
Virginia Western Community College A

Washington
Shoreline Community College A

West Virginia
Ohio Valley College A

Science/technology/society

Alabama
Samford University A

Arizona
Arizona Western College A

California
Chaffey Community College A
Pitzer College B
Pomona College B
Scripps College B
Stanford University B
University of California
   Davis B

Connecticut
Wesleyan University B

District of Columbia
George Washington University M

Indiana
Purdue University B

Kansas
Kansas City Kansas Community
   College A

Kentucky
Hazard Community College A

Maryland
Johns Hopkins University B

Massachusetts
Clark University B
Hampshire College B
Harvard College B
Harvard University M, D
Massachusetts Institute of
   Technology B, D
Wellesley College B
Worcester Polytechnic Institute B

Michigan
Eastern Michigan University M
Michigan State University M

Minnesota
University of Minnesota
  Twin Cities *M*

Missouri
Washington University *B, M, D*

Montana
Montana Tech of the University of
  Montana *B*

Nevada
University of Nevada
  Reno *B*

New Hampshire
Antioch New England Graduate
  School *M*

New Jersey
New Jersey Institute of Technology *B*
Rutgers
  The State University of New Jersey:
    Newark College of Arts and
    Sciences *B*

New York
Cornell University *B*
Eugene Lang College/New School
  University *B*
Rensselaer Polytechnic Institute *B, M, D*
Vassar College *B*

North Carolina
Brevard College *B*
North Carolina State University *M*

Pennsylvania
Lehigh University *B*
Slippery Rock University of
  Pennsylvania *B*

Tennessee
Hiwassee College *A*

Virginia
James Madison University *B*
University of Virginia *M*

West Virginia
West Virginia University *M*

Sculpture

Alabama
Birmingham-Southern College *B*
University of Alabama *M*

Arizona
Arizona State University *B, M*

California
Academy of Art College *C, A, B, M*
California College of Arts and
  Crafts *B, M*
California Institute of the Arts *C, B, M*
California State University
  Fullerton *B, M*
  Hayward *B*
  Long Beach *B, M*
  Northridge *B, M*
Chabot College *A*
De Anza College *C, A*
Grossmont Community College *A*
Monterey Peninsula College *A*
Otis College of Art and Design *B, M*
Palomar College *A*
Pasadena City College *A*
San Diego State University *B*
San Francisco Art Institute *B, M*
Santa Rosa Junior College *C*
Solano Community College *A*
University of San Francisco *B*

Colorado
Adams State College *B*
Colorado State University *B*
Rocky Mountain College of Art &
  Design *B*

Connecticut
University of Hartford *B, M*

District of Columbia
American University *M*
George Washington University *M*

Florida
Ringling School of Art and Design *B*
University of Miami *B*

Georgia
Atlanta College of Art *B*
LaGrange College *B*
University of Georgia *B*

Illinois
Barat College *B*
Richland Community College *A*
Rockford College *B*
School of the Art Institute of
  Chicago *B, M*
University of Illinois
  Urbana-Champaign *B*

Indiana
Indiana University--Purdue University
  Indiana University-Purdue
  University Fort Wayne *B*
University of Evansville *B*
Vincennes University *A*

Iowa
Drake University *B*
University of Iowa *B, M*

Kansas
University of Kansas *B, M*

Kentucky
Bellarmine College *B*

Maine
Maine College of Art *B*

Maryland
Maryland Institute College of Art *B, M*

Massachusetts
Boston University *B, M*
Hampshire College *B*
Massachusetts College of Art *B, M*
Montserrat College of Art *B*
School of the Museum of Fine Arts *B, M*
Simon's Rock College of Bard *B*
University of Massachusetts
  Dartmouth *B*

Michigan
Center for Creative Studies: College of
  Art and Design *B*
Cranbrook Academy of Art *M*
Delta College *A*
Grand Valley State University *B*
Northern Michigan University *B*
Siena Heights University *B*
University of Michigan *B*
Western Michigan University *B*

Minnesota
College of Visual Arts *B*
Minneapolis College of Art and
  Design *B*
Minnesota State University, Mankato *B*
Moorhead State University *B*

Mississippi
Mississippi Gulf Coast Community
  College
    Perkinston *A*

Missouri
Kansas City Art Institute *B*
Lindenwood University *M*
Washington University *B, M*
Webster University *B*

New Hampshire
Plymouth State College of the University
  System of New Hampshire *B*

New Jersey
Rowan University *B*
Rutgers
  The State University of New Jersey:
    Mason Gross School of the
    Arts *B, M*

New York
Bard College *B, M*
City University of New York
  Brooklyn College *M*
  Queens College *B, M*
Columbia University
  School of General Studies *B*
  Teachers College *M, D*
New York State College of Ceramics at
  Alfred University *B, M, T*
Parsons School of Design *C, A, B, M, T*
Pratt Institute *B, M*
Rochester Institute of
  Technology *A, B, M*
Sarah Lawrence College *B*
School of Visual Arts *B, M*
State University of New York
  Albany *B, M*
  Buffalo *B*
  College at Buffalo *B*
  College at Fredonia *B*
  New Paltz *B, M*
Syracuse University *B, M*

North Carolina
Brevard College *A, B*

Ohio
Bowling Green State University *B*
Cleveland Institute of Art *B*
Columbus College of Art and Design *B*
Kent State University *B, M*
Lourdes College *A*
Ohio State University
  Columbus Campus *B*
Ohio University *B, M*
University of Akron *B*
Wittenberg University *B*
Youngstown State University *B*

Oregon
Pacific Northwest College of Art *B*
Portland State University *B, M*
University of Oregon *B, M*

Pennsylvania
Carnegie Mellon University *B*
Immaculata College *A*
Lycoming College *B*
Mercyhurst College *B*
Moore College of Art and Design *B*
Seton Hill College *B*
Temple University *B, M*
University of the Arts *B, M*

Puerto Rico
Escuela de Artes Plasticas de Puerto
  Rico *B*
University of Puerto Rico
  Rio Piedras Campus *B*

Rhode Island
Providence College *B*
Rhode Island College *B*

Tennessee
Union University *B*
University of Tennessee
  Knoxville *M*

Texas
Sam Houston State University *M*
Stephen F. Austin State University *M*
Texas A&M University
  Commerce *B, M*
Texas Woman's University *B, M*
University of Dallas *M, T*
University of Houston *B, M*
University of North Texas *B, M*

University of Texas
  Arlington *B*
  El Paso *B*
  San Antonio *B, M*
Western Texas College *A*

Utah
Brigham Young University *M*
Dixie State College of Utah *A*

Vermont
Bennington College *B, M*
Marlboro College *B*

Virginia
Virginia Commonwealth
  University *B, M*
Virginia Intermont College *B*

Washington
Cornish College of the Arts *B*
Pacific Lutheran University *B*
University of Washington *B, M*
Western Washington University *B*

West Virginia
Marshall University *B*
West Virginia State College *B*

Wisconsin
Milwaukee Institute of Art & Design *B*
University of Wisconsin
  Madison *B*

Secondary education

Alabama
Alabama Agricultural and Mechanical
  University *B, M, T*
Alabama State University *B, M, T*
Athens State University *B*
Auburn University at Montgomery *B, M*
Auburn University *M, D, T*
Birmingham-Southern College *T*
Calhoun Community College *A*
Chattahoochee Valley Community
  College *A*
Faulkner University *B, T*
Huntingdon College *B, T*
Jacksonville State University *B, M, T*
James H. Faulkner State Community
  College *A*
Northeast Alabama Community
  College *A*
Northwest-Shoals Community College *A*
Samford University *T*
Shelton State Community College *A*
Spring Hill College *B, M*
Troy State University
  Dothan *B, M, T*
Troy State University *B, M, T*
University of Alabama
  Birmingham *B, M*
University of Alabama *B, M, D*
University of Montevallo *M, T*
University of North Alabama *B, M*
University of South Alabama *B, M, D, T*
University of West Alabama *C, B, M*

Alaska
University of Alaska
  Anchorage *B, T*
  Fairbanks *M*

Arizona
Arizona State University *B, M, D*
Eastern Arizona College *A*
Grand Canyon University *B, M, T*
Northern Arizona University *B, M, T*
Prescott College *B, M*
Southwestern College *B, T*
University of Arizona *B, M*

Arkansas
Arkansas Tech University *B, M*
Harding University *B, M, T*
Hendrix College *B, T*

533

John Brown University *B*
Ouachita Baptist University *B, T*
Philander Smith College *B*
Southern Arkansas University *B, M, T*
University of Arkansas
    Little Rock *M*
    Monticello *B, M*
    Pine Bluff *B, M*
University of Arkansas *M, D*
University of Central Arkansas *T*
University of the Ozarks *B, T*
Westark College *A*

California
Azusa Pacific University *B, T*
Biola University *B, T*
California Baptist University *B, T*
California Lutheran University *B, M*
California State Polytechnic University:
    Pomona *T*
California State University
    Bakersfield *B, M*
    Dominguez Hills *M*
    Fullerton *T*
    Hayward *T*
    Long Beach *M, T*
    Los Angeles *M*
    Northridge *M*
    Sacramento *B, M, T*
    San Marcos *T*
Chapman University *T*
College of Notre Dame *M, T*
Concordia University *B, T*
Cypress College *A*
Holy Names College *T*
Hope International University *B*
Humboldt State University *T*
La Sierra University *M*
Loyola Marymount University *C, M, T*
Master's College *B, T*
Mills College *T*
Mount St. Mary's College *B*
National University *T*
Occidental College *T*
Point Loma Nazarene University *T*
St. Mary's College of California *T*
San Diego State University *M, T*
San Francisco State University *M, T*
San Jose State University *M*
Simpson College *B, T*
Sonoma State University *M*
Stanford University *T*
United States International University *T*
University of California
    Riverside *T*
    Santa Barbara *T*
    Santa Cruz *M*
University of La Verne *B, M, T*
University of Redlands *B, T*
University of San Francisco *T*
University of Southern California *T*
University of the Pacific *B, T*
Vanguard University of Southern
    California *T*
Westmont College *T*
Whittier College *T*

Colorado
Adams State College *B, M, T*
Colorado College *M*
Colorado State University *T*
Fort Lewis College *T*
Metropolitan State College of Denver *T*
Otero Junior College *A*
University of Colorado
    Boulder *T*
    Colorado Springs *T*
University of Denver *B*
University of Southern Colorado *C, T*
Western State College of Colorado *T*

Connecticut
Central Connecticut State University *B*
Connecticut College *M, T*
Fairfield University *C, M*
Quinnipiac University *B, M*

Sacred Heart University *B, M, T*
St. Joseph College *M, T*
Southern Connecticut State
    University *B, M, T*
Trinity College *B, T*
University of Bridgeport *M, T*
University of Connecticut *T*
University of Hartford *B, M, T*
University of New Haven *M*
Western Connecticut State
    University *B, M*

Delaware
University of Delaware *B, M, T*

District of Columbia
American University *M*
Catholic University of America *B, M, T*
Gallaudet University *B, T*
George Washington University *M, T*
Howard University *M*
Trinity College *M*

Florida
Flagler College *B*
Florida Agricultural and Mechanical
    University *M*
Florida Gulf Coast University *B, T*
Florida Southern College *B*
Hillsborough Community College *A*
Indian River Community College *A*
Jacksonville University *B, M, T*
Lynn University *B*
Manatee Community College *A*
Miami-Dade Community College *A*
Nova Southeastern University *B*
Palm Beach Atlantic College *B*
Palm Beach Community College *A*
Rollins College *T*
St. Thomas University *B, T*
Southeastern College of the Assemblies
    of God *B, T*
University of Miami *B, M*
University of North Florida *B, M*
University of Tampa *T*

Georgia
Agnes Scott College *T*
Albany State University *B, M, T*
Armstrong Atlantic State
    University *B, M, T*
Augusta State University *M*
Berry College *B, M, T*
Brewton-Parker College *B*
Clark Atlanta University *B*
Columbus State University *B, M*
Emory University *B*
Fort Valley State University *B, T*
Gainesville College *A*
Georgia College and State
    University *M, T*
Georgia Southwestern State
    University *B, T*
Kennesaw State University *B*
LaGrange College *B*
Macon State College *A*
Middle Georgia College *A*
Morehouse College *B*
North Georgia College & State
    University *B, M*
Oglethorpe University *B, T*
Piedmont College *M, T*
State University of West Georgia *B, M*
Toccoa Falls College *B, T*
Valdosta State University *B, M*
Wesleyan College *T*

Hawaii
Brigham Young University
    Hawaii *B, T*
Chaminade University of Honolulu *B, T*
University of Hawaii
    Hilo *T*
    Manoa *B, M, T*

Idaho
Boise State University *T*

College of Southern Idaho *A*
Idaho State University *B, T*
Lewis-Clark State College *B, T*
North Idaho College *A*
Northwest Nazarene University *B*
University of Idaho *B, M, T*

Illinois
Augustana College *B, T*
Barat College *B*
Benedictine University *T*
Black Hawk College
    East Campus *A*
Bradley University *B*
Chicago State University *B, M, T*
City Colleges of Chicago
    Harold Washington College *A*
Concordia University *B, T*
De Paul University *B, T*
Dominican University *T*
Elmhurst College *B*
Greenville College *T*
Illinois Wesleyan University *B*
John A. Logan College *A*
Joliet Junior College *A*
Judson College *B, T*
Kankakee Community College *A*
Kishwaukee College *A*
Knox College *T*
Lake Forest College *T*
Lewis University *T*
MacMurray College *B, T*
McKendree College *T*
Monmouth College *B, T*
National-Louis University *M, T*
North Central College *B, T*
North Park University *M, T*
Northern Illinois University *M*
Northwestern University *B, T*
Olivet Nazarene University *B, M, T*
Parkland College *A*
Principia College *T*
Quincy University *T*
Rend Lake College *A*
Rockford College *M, T*
Roosevelt University *C, B, M*
St. Xavier University *B*
Sauk Valley Community College *A*
Southern Illinois University
    Edwardsville *M*
Southwestern Illinois College *A*
Springfield College in Illinois *A*
Trinity Christian College *T*
Trinity International University *B, T*
University of Illinois
    Urbana-Champaign *M, D*
University of St. Francis *M, T*
Wheaton College *M, T*

Indiana
Ball State University *B, M, T*
Butler University *B, M*
Franklin College *B*
Goshen College *B*
Grace College *B*
Hanover College *T*
Indiana State University *B, M, D, T*
Indiana University
    Bloomington *B, M, D, T*
    East *T*
    Northwest *B, M, T*
    South Bend *B, M, T*
    Southeast *B, M*
Indiana University--Purdue University
    Indiana University-Purdue
        University Fort Wayne *B, M, T*
    Indiana University-Purdue
        University Indianapolis *B, M, T*
Indiana Wesleyan University *B, M*
Manchester College *B, T*
Marian College *T*
Purdue University
    Calumet *B, M*
Saint Mary's College *T*
St. Joseph's College *B*
St. Mary-of-the-Woods College *B, T*

University of Evansville *B*
University of Indianapolis *A, B, T*
University of St. Francis *B*
University of Southern Indiana *B, M, T*
Valparaiso University *B, T*
Vincennes University *A*

Iowa
Briar Cliff College *B*
Buena Vista University *B, T*
Central College *T*
Clarke College *B, M, T*
Coe College *B*
Cornell College *B, T*
Dordt College *B, T*
Drake University *B, M*
Graceland University *T*
Grand View College *B, T*
Grinnell College *T*
Iowa State University *T*
Iowa Wesleyan College *B*
Loras College *B*
Luther College *B*
Maharishi University of Management *B*
Marshalltown Community College *A*
Marycrest International University *B*
Morningside College *T*
Mount Mercy College *T*
North Iowa Area Community College *A*
Northwestern College *T*
St. Ambrose University *B, T*
Simpson College *B, T*
University of Iowa *B, M, D, T*
Upper Iowa University *B, T*
Waldorf College *A*
Wartburg College *T*
William Penn University *B*

Kansas
Allen County Community College *A*
Benedictine College *M, T*
Bethany College *B, T*
Bethel College *T*
Butler County Community College *A*
Central Christian College *A*
Coffeyville Community College *A*
Colby Community College *A*
Dodge City Community College *A*
Emporia State University *B, M, T*
Fort Hays State University *M*
Garden City Community College *A*
Kansas City Kansas Community
    College *C, A*
Kansas State University *B, M, T*
Kansas Wesleyan University *B, T*
MidAmerica Nazarene University *B, T*
Newman University *B, T*
Pittsburg State University *B, M, T*
Pratt Community College *A*
Southwestern College *B, M, T*
Tabor College *B, T*
University of Kansas *B, T*
Washburn University of Topeka *T*
Wichita State University *B, T*

Kentucky
Alice Lloyd College *B*
Bellarmine College *B, T*
Campbellsville University *B*
Centre College *T*
Cumberland College *B, T*
Eastern Kentucky University *M*
Georgetown College *M*
Kentucky State University *B*
Kentucky Wesleyan College *T*
Midway College *A*
Morehead State University *M*
Murray State University *M*
Northern Kentucky University *B, M, T*
Spalding University *M, T*
Thomas More College *B*
Union College *B, M, T*
University of Kentucky *M*
University of Louisville *M*
Western Kentucky University *M*

Louisiana
Centenary College of Louisiana B, M, T
Dillard University B, T
Louisiana State University and
    Agricultural and Mechanical
    College B
Louisiana Tech University B
Loyola University New Orleans M
McNeese State University B, M, T
Our Lady of Holy Cross College B
Southern University
    New Orleans B
Southern University and Agricultural and
    Mechanical College B, M
University of Louisiana at Lafayette B
University of Louisiana at Monroe M
University of New Orleans B

Maine
St. Joseph's College B
University of Maine
    Farmington B
    Fort Kent B, T
    Machias C
    Presque Isle B
University of Maine B, M
University of New England B, T
University of Southern Maine T

Maryland
Allegany College A
Anne Arundel Community College A
Bowie State University M
Cecil Community College A
Charles County Community College A
Chesapeake College A
College of Notre Dame of Maryland B
Columbia Union College B, T
Community College of Baltimore County
    Catonsville A
    Essex A
Coppin State College B, T
Frostburg State University M
Goucher College T
Harford Community College A
Howard Community College A
Johns Hopkins University M
Montgomery College
    Germantown Campus A
    Takoma Park Campus A
Morgan State University B, T
Prince George's Community College A
St. Mary's College of Maryland T
Salisbury State University T
Towson University M, T
University of Maryland
    Baltimore County B
Washington College T
Western Maryland College M, T

Massachusetts
American International College B, M
Amherst College T
Assumption College B, T
Atlantic Union College B
Boston College B, M, T
Brandeis University T
Clark University M
Eastern Nazarene College M, T
Elms College B, M, T
Emmanuel College B, M, T
Fitchburg State College B, M, T
Framingham State College B, M, T
Hampshire College B
Harvard College T
Massachusetts College of Liberal Arts T
Merrimack College T
Nichols College B
Simmons College B, M
Smith College M
Springfield College B, T
Suffolk University M, T
Tufts University M, T
University of Massachusetts
    Boston M
Wellesley College T
Western New England College T
Westfield State College M
Wheaton College T
Worcester State College M, T

Michigan
Adrian College B
Albion College T
Alma College B
Andrews University M, T
Calvin College B, T
Central Michigan University M
Concordia College B, T
Eastern Michigan University M, T
Ferris State University A, M
Gogebic Community College A
Grace Bible College B
Grand Valley State University M, T
Hillsdale College B
Hope College B, T
Kalamazoo College T
Kellogg Community College A
Lansing Community College A
Madonna University B, T
Marygrove College T
Michigan Technological University T
Mid Michigan Community College A
Northern Michigan University B, M, T
Olivet College T
Saginaw Valley State University M
Siena Heights University B, M, T
Spring Arbor College T
University of Detroit Mercy B, M, T
University of Michigan
    Dearborn B, T
University of Michigan B
Wayne State University M
Western Michigan University B, T

Minnesota
Augsburg College B, T
Bethel College B
Carleton College T
College of St. Benedict B
College of St. Catherine: St. Paul
    Campus B, T
College of St. Scholastica T
Concordia College: Moorhead B, T
Concordia University: St. Paul B, T
Crown College B
Gustavus Adolphus College B
Hamline University B, T
Minnesota State University,
    Mankato B, M, T
Moorhead State University B, T
North Central University B
Northland Community & Technical
    College A
Ridgewater College: A Community and
    Technical College A
St. Cloud State University M, T
St. John's University T
St. Mary's University of Minnesota B
University of Minnesota
    Duluth T
    Morris T
University of St. Thomas M
Winona State University B, M, T

Mississippi
Alcorn State University M
Copiah-Lincoln Community College A
Hinds Community College A
Holmes Community College A
Jackson State University B, M, T
Mary Holmes College A
Millsaps College T
Mississippi College B, M, T
Mississippi Delta Community College A
Mississippi Gulf Coast Community
    College
    Jefferson Davis Campus A
    Perkinston A
Mississippi State University B, M, T
Northwest Mississippi Community
    College A
Rust College B
Tougaloo College B, T
University of Mississippi B

Missouri
Central Methodist College B
Central Missouri State
    University B, M, T
College of the Ozarks B, T
Columbia College T
Crowder College A
Culver-Stockton College T
Drury University B, T
East Central College A
Evangel University B, T
Fontbonne College B
Hannibal-LaGrange College B
Harris Stowe State College B, T
Jefferson College A
Lincoln University M
Lindenwood University B
Maryville University of Saint
    Louis B, M, T
Missouri Baptist College T
Missouri Southern State College B, T
Missouri Valley College B, T
Ozark Christian College A
Park University T
Rockhurst University B
Southeast Missouri State
    University B, M, T
Southwest Baptist University T
Southwest Missouri State
    University B, M
St. Louis Community College
    St. Louis Community College at
        Meramec A
Truman State University M, T
University of Missouri
    Columbia B
    Kansas City B
    St. Louis B, M, T
Washington University B, M, T
Webster University T
Westminster College B, T
William Jewell College T
William Woods University B, T

Montana
Carroll College B
Miles Community College A
Montana State University
    Billings B
    Bozeman B
    Northern B, T
Rocky Mountain College B, T
University of Great Falls B, M, T
Western Montana College of The
    University of Montana B, T

Nebraska
Chadron State College M
College of Saint Mary B, T
Concordia University B, T
Dana College B
Doane College T
Hastings College B, M, T
Mid Plains Community College Area A
Midland Lutheran College B, T
Nebraska Wesleyan University T
Northeast Community College A
Peru State College B, T
Union College B, T
University of Nebraska
    Kearney B, M, T
    Omaha B, M, T

Nevada
University of Nevada
    Las Vegas B, T
    Reno M, T

New Hampshire
Antioch New England Graduate
    School M
Dartmouth College T
Franklin Pierce College T
Keene State College B, T
New England College B, T
New Hampshire College B
Notre Dame College B, M
Plymouth State College of the University
    System of New Hampshire B, M
Rivier College B, M, T
St. Anselm College B
University of New Hampshire
    Manchester T
University of New Hampshire M

New Jersey
Caldwell College T
Centenary College T
College of St. Elizabeth T
Essex County College A
Monmouth University M
Richard Stockton College of New
    Jersey B
Rider University B
Rowan University B, M
Rutgers
    The State University of New Jersey:
        Camden College of Arts and
        Sciences T
    The State University of New Jersey:
        Douglass College T
    The State University of New Jersey:
        Livingston College T
    The State University of New Jersey:
        Newark College of Arts and
        Sciences T
    The State University of New Jersey:
        Rutgers College T
    The State University of New Jersey:
        University College Camden T
    The State University of New Jersey:
        University College New
        Brunswick T
    The State University of New Jersey:
        University College Newark T
St. Peter's College T
Seton Hall University B, M
The College of New Jersey M, T

New Mexico
College of Santa Fe B
College of the Southwest B, T
New Mexico Highlands University B, T
New Mexico Institute of Mining and
    Technology C, M
New Mexico Junior College A
New Mexico State University B
University of New Mexico B, M
Western New Mexico University B, M, T

New York
Adelphi University B, M, T
Alfred University M, T
Barnard College T
Canisius College B, M, T
City University of New York
    Brooklyn College B, M, T
    City College B, M, T
    College of Staten Island M
    Hunter College B, M, T
    Lehman College M, T
    Queens College B, M, T
Colgate University M, T
College of Mount St. Vincent T
College of St. Rose B, M, T
Columbia University
    School of General Studies T
    Teachers College M, D
Concordia College B, T
D'Youville College B, M, T
Dominican College of Blauvelt B, T
Dowling College B, M
Elmira College B, M, T
Eugene Lang College/New School
    University T
Fordham University M, T
Fulton-Montgomery Community
    College A
Hobart and William Smith Colleges T

535

Hofstra University B, M, T
Houghton College B, T
Iona College B, M, T
Ithaca College B, M, T
Le Moyne College M, T
Long Island University
    Brooklyn Campus B, M
    C. W. Post Campus B, M
    Southampton College B, T
Manhattan College B, T
Manhattanville College M, T
Marymount College B, T
Marymount Manhattan College B, T
Molloy College B, M, T
Mount St. Mary College M
Nazareth College of Rochester M, T
New York University B, M, T
Niagara University B, M, T
Nyack College B
Pace University:
    Pleasantville/Briarcliff B, M, T
Pace University B, M, T
Russell Sage College M, T
St. Bonaventure University M
St. Francis College B, T
St. John Fisher College B, T
St. John's University B, M, T
St. Thomas Aquinas College B, M, T
Sarah Lawrence College M
Siena College T
St. Joseph's College
    St. Joseph's College: Suffolk
      Campus B, T
    St. Joseph's College B, T
State University of New York
    Albany B, M, T
    Buffalo M, D
    College at Brockport B, M, T
    College at Buffalo B, M, T
    College at Fredonia B, M, T
    College at Geneseo T
    College at Old Westbury T
    College at Oneonta M, T
    College at Plattsburgh M
    College at Potsdam B, M, T
    New Paltz B, M, T
    Oswego B, M, T
Syracuse University B, M, T
Union College M, T
University of Rochester T
Vassar College T
Wagner College B, T
Wells College T

North Carolina
Appalachian State University B, M, T
Barton College B
Belmont Abbey College B
Brevard College B
Campbell University B
Catawba College T
Chowan College B
Cleveland Community College A
Davidson College T
Duke University M
Elon College B, T
Fayetteville State University B
Gardner-Webb University B, M
Greensboro College T
Guilford College B, T
High Point University B
James Sprunt Community College A
Johnson C. Smith University B, T
Lees-McRae College T
Lenoir-Rhyne College B, M, T
Louisburg College A
Mars Hill College B, T
Martin Community College A
Meredith College T
Methodist College A, B, T
Montreat College T
North Carolina Central University M
North Carolina State University B
North Carolina Wesleyan College T
Pfeiffer University B, T

Pitt Community College A
Queens College T
Salem College T
Sandhills Community College A
Southeastern Community College A
University of North Carolina
    Asheville T
    Charlotte M
    Wilmington M
Warren Wilson College B, T

North Dakota
Dickinson State University B, T
Jamestown College B
Mayville State University B, T
Minot State University B, T
North Dakota State University B
University of Mary B, T
University of North Dakota B, T
Valley City State University B, T

Ohio
Antioch College T
Baldwin-Wallace College B
Bluffton College B
Bowling Green State University
    Firelands College A
Bowling Green State University M
Capital University B
Cedarville College T
Central State University B
College of Mount St. Joseph T
College of Wooster B
Defiance College B, T
Heidelberg College T
Hiram College T
John Carroll University M, T
Kent State University
    Stark Campus B
Kent State University M
Lorain County Community College A
Marietta College B
Miami University
    Oxford Campus M
Mount Union College T
Mount Vernon Nazarene College B, T
Muskingum College B, T
Notre Dame College of Ohio B, T
Ohio Dominican College D
Ohio Northern University B, T
Ohio State University
    Columbus Campus M
Ohio University B, M, D, T
Ohio Wesleyan University B
Otterbein College B
Owens Community College
    Toledo A
Shawnee State University T
University of Akron B, M, D, T
University of Cincinnati
    Clermont College A
University of Cincinnati B, M, D, T
University of Dayton B, M, T
University of Findlay B, T
University of Rio Grande B, T
University of Toledo B, T
Ursuline College B, T
Walsh University B
Washington State Community College A
Wilmington College B
Wittenberg University B
Wright State University M
Xavier University M, T
Youngstown State University B, M

Oklahoma
Cameron University B, T
Carl Albert State College A
Connors State College A
East Central University M, T
Eastern Oklahoma State College A
Langston University B
Mid-America Bible College B
Northeastern Oklahoma Agricultural and
    Mechanical College A
Northeastern State University B

Northern Oklahoma College A
Northwestern Oklahoma State
    University M
Oklahoma Baptist University B, T
Oklahoma Christian University of
    Science and Arts B, T
Oklahoma City Community College A
Oklahoma City University B, M
Oklahoma State University B, M, D, T
Rogers State University A
Rose State College A
St. Gregory's University B
Southeastern Oklahoma State
    University B, M, T
Southern Nazarene University B
Southwestern Oklahoma State
    University M
University of Central Oklahoma B, M
University of Tulsa B, T
Western Oklahoma State College A

Oregon
Chemeketa Community College A
Concordia University B, M, T
Eastern Oregon University B, M
Lewis & Clark College M
Linfield College B, T
Linn-Benton Community College A
Oregon State University M
Portland State University T
Southern Oregon University M, T
University of Portland B, M, T
Western Baptist College B
Western Oregon University B, M, T
Willamette University M

Pennsylvania
Allentown College of St. Francis de
    Sales M, T
Beaver College B, M, T
Bryn Mawr College T
Bucknell University B, M, T
Butler County Community College A
Cedar Crest College B, T
Chatham College M, T
Clarion University of Pennsylvania B
College Misericordia B, T
Delaware Valley College B, T
Dickinson College T
Duquesne University B, M, T
East Stroudsburg University of
    Pennsylvania B, M, T
Eastern College B, T
Elizabethtown College T
Gannon University M, T
Gettysburg College T
Grove City College T
Harrisburg Area Community College A
Holy Family College B, M, T
Immaculata College T
Juniata College B, T
King's College T
Kutztown University of
    Pennsylvania B, M, T
La Roche College B
La Salle University B, M, T
Lebanon Valley College of
    Pennsylvania T
Lehigh University M
Lincoln University B, M, T
Lock Haven University of
    Pennsylvania B, T
Lycoming College T
Mansfield University of
    Pennsylvania B, T
Mercyhurst College B
Millersville University of
    Pennsylvania B, T
Montgomery County Community
    College A
Moravian College B
Muhlenberg College T
Penn State
    University Park B
Point Park College B
Reading Area Community College A

Rosemont College T
St. Francis College B, T
St. Joseph's University B, M
St. Vincent College T
Seton Hill College B, T
Slippery Rock University of
    Pennsylvania B, M
Susquehanna University T
Temple University M
Thiel College T
University of Pittsburgh
    Johnstown B, T
University of Pittsburgh T
University of Scranton B, M
Ursinus College B, T
Villanova University B, M
Washington and Jefferson College T
Waynesburg College C
West Chester University of
    Pennsylvania M
Westminster College B, T
Widener University M
Wilson College T
York College of Pennsylvania B, T

Puerto Rico
American University of Puerto Rico B, T
Bayamon Central University B
Caribbean University B, T
Inter American University of Puerto Rico
    Aguadilla Campus B
    Arecibo Campus B
    Barranquitas Campus B
    Fajardo Campus B, T
    Guayama Campus B
    Metropolitan Campus B
    San German Campus B
Pontifical Catholic University of Puerto
    Rico B
Turabo University B
University of Puerto Rico
    Cayey University College B, T
    Rio Piedras Campus B, M
University of the Sacred Heart B

Rhode Island
Brown University M
Rhode Island College B, M, T
Roger Williams University T
Salve Regina University B
University of Rhode Island B

South Carolina
Anderson College B, T
Charleston Southern University M
Clemson University B, M, T
Coastal Carolina University B, M, T
Converse College M, T
Erskine College B, T
Francis Marion University B, M, T
Furman University M, T
Limestone College B
Presbyterian College B, T
South Carolina State University M
Southern Wesleyan University B
The Citadel M
University of South Carolina
    Aiken B, T
    Spartanburg B, T
University of South Carolina M, D
Winthrop University M, T
Wofford College T

South Dakota
Augustana College B, M, T
Black Hills State University B, T
Dakota State University B, T
Huron University B
Mount Marty College B
Northern State University B, M, T
South Dakota State University B
University of South Dakota M, T

Tennessee
Austin Peay State University T
Belmont University B, T
Bethel College B, T

Carson-Newman College *B*
Christian Brothers University *B, M, T*
Crichton College *B*
Cumberland University *B, T*
David Lipscomb University *B, T*
East Tennessee State University *M, T*
Freed-Hardeman University *B, T*
Hiwassee College *A*
King College *T*
Lambuth University *B, T*
Lane College *B*
Lee University *B, T*
Lincoln Memorial University *B, T*
Maryville College *B, T*
Motlow State Community College *A*
Rhodes College *T*
Roane State Community College *A*
Tennessee State University *B, M, T*
Tennessee Technological
 University *B, M, T*
Tennessee Temple University *B, M, T*
Tennessee Wesleyan College *B, T*
Trevecca Nazarene University *B, T*
Tusculum College *B, T*
Union University *B, T*
University of Tennessee
 Chattanooga *B, M, T*
 Knoxville *T*
University of the South *T*
Vanderbilt University *B, M, T*

Texas
Abilene Christian University *B, M, T*
Angelina College *A*
Angelo State University *B*
Austin College *M*
Baylor University *T*
Brazosport College *A*
Coastal Bend College *A*
College of the Mainland *A*
Concordia University at Austin *B, T*
Dallas Baptist University *B*
East Texas Baptist University *B*
El Paso Community College *A*
Grayson County College *A*
Hardin-Simmons University *B, M, T*
Houston Baptist University *B, M*
Howard Payne University *T*
Huston-Tillotson College *T*
Jarvis Christian College *B*
Lamar University *M, T*
LeTourneau University *B*
Lubbock Christian University *B, M*
McMurry University *B*
Midwestern State University *B*
Navarro College *A*
Our Lady of the Lake University of San
 Antonio *T*
Paul Quinn College *B*
Rice University *M*
St. Edward's University *T*
Sam Houston State University *M, T*
Schreiner College *T*
Southern Methodist University *T*
Southwest Texas State
 University *B, M, T*
Southwestern Assemblies of God
 University *B*
Southwestern University *T*
Stephen F. Austin State University *M*
Sul Ross State University *M*
Tarleton State University *M, T*
Texas A&M International
 University *M, T*
Texas A&M University
 Commerce *M, D, T*
 Corpus Christi *M, T*
 Kingsville *B, M*
 Texarkana *M, T*
Texas Christian University *M, T*
Texas Lutheran University *T*
Texas Tech University *M*
Texas Wesleyan University *B, M, T*
Trinity University *M*
University of Dallas *B, T*
University of Houston
 Victoria *M*
University of Houston *M, T*
University of Mary Hardin-Baylor *T*
University of North Texas *M, D*
University of Texas
 Arlington *M*
 Brownsville *M*
 Pan American *B, M, T*
 of the Permian Basin *M*
University of the Incarnate Word *B*
Wayland Baptist University *T*
West Texas A&M University *M, T*
Wiley College *B*

Utah
Brigham Young University *B*
Dixie State College of Utah *A*
Snow College *A*
Utah State University *B, M, D*
Weber State University *B, M, T*
Westminster College *B, T*

Vermont
Castleton State College *B, M, T*
College of St. Joseph in Vermont *B*
Goddard College *B*
Green Mountain College *B, T*
Johnson State College *B, M*
Middlebury College *T*
Norwich University *T*
St. Michael's College *B, M*
Trinity College of Vermont *B, T*
University of Vermont *B, T*

Virginia
Averett College *B*
Bluefield College *B*
Bridgewater College *T*
Christopher Newport University *T*
College of William and Mary *T*
Eastern Mennonite University *T*
George Mason University *M*
Hampton University *B, M*
Hollins University *T*
James Madison University *M*
Liberty University *B, M*
Longwood College *T*
Mary Baldwin College *T*
Mary Washington College *T*
Norfolk State University *T*
Old Dominion University *M*
Radford University *T*
Randolph-Macon College *T*
Randolph-Macon Woman's College *T*
St. Paul's College *B*
Shenandoah University *C*
University of Richmond *B, T*
University of Virginia's College at
 Wise *T*
Virginia Polytechnic Institute and State
 University *B*
Virginia Wesleyan College *T*

Washington
Central Washington University *M*
Eastern Washington University *M*
Evergreen State College *M*
Gonzaga University *T*
Pacific Lutheran University *B*
St. Martin's College *B, T*
Seattle Pacific University *M*
Walla Walla College *M*
Western Washington University *M*
Whitworth College *B, M, T*

West Virginia
Alderson-Broaddus College *B*
College of West Virginia *A*
Davis and Elkins College *B*
Fairmont State College *B*
Glenville State College *B*
Marshall University *B, M*
Potomac State College of West Virginia
 University *A*
Salem-Teikyo University *B, M, T*
Shepherd College *B, T*
University of Charleston *B*
West Liberty State College *B*
West Virginia State College *B*
West Virginia University *M, T*
West Virginia Wesleyan College *B*
Wheeling Jesuit University *T*

Wisconsin
Alverno College *T*
Beloit College *T*
Cardinal Stritch University *B, T*
Carroll College *T*
Carthage College *T*
Concordia University Wisconsin *B, T*
Lawrence University *T*
Marian College of Fond du Lac *B, T*
Marquette University *T*
Mount Mary College *B, T*
Mount Senario College *B, T*
Northland College *T*
Ripon College *T*
St. Norbert College *T*
University of Wisconsin
 Green Bay *T*
 La Crosse *B, M, T*
 Oshkosh *B, T*
 Parkside *T*
 Platteville *T*
 River Falls *T*
 Stevens Point *B, T*
 Whitewater *B, T*
Viterbo University *B, T*

Wyoming
Central Wyoming College *A*
Eastern Wyoming College *A*
Laramie County Community College *A*
Northwest College *A*
Sheridan College *A*
University of Wyoming *B*
Western Wyoming Community
 College *A*

Secretarial/administrative services

Alabama
Alabama State University *B*
Bessemer State Technical College *C, A*
Central Alabama Community
 College *C, A*
Chattahoochee Valley Community
 College *A*
Community College of the Air Force *A*
Enterprise State Junior College *C, A*
Faulkner University *A*
Gadsden State Community College *C, A*
George C. Wallace State Community
 College
 Dothan *C, A*
J. F. Drake State Technical College *C, A*
James H. Faulkner State Community
 College *C, A*
Jefferson State Community College *C, A*
Lawson State Community College *A*
Northeast Alabama Community
 College *A*
Northwest-Shoals Community College *A*
Reid State Technical College *C*
Snead State Community College *C*
Troy State University *B*

Alaska
University of Alaska
 Fairbanks *C, A*
 Southeast *C, A*

Arizona
Arizona Western College *C, A*
Central Arizona College *C, A*
Cochise College *C, A*
Dine College *C, A*
Eastern Arizona College *C, A*
Gateway Community College *C, A*
Glendale Community College *C*
Mohave Community College *C, A*
Northland Pioneer College *C, A*
Paradise Valley Community
 College *C, A*
Pima Community College *C, A*
Scottsdale Community College *A*
Yavapai College *C, A*

Arkansas
Arkansas State University
 Beebe Branch *A*
 Mountain Home *C, A*
Arkansas State University *C, A, B*
Arkansas Tech University *C*
Garland County Community College *C*
Henderson State University *A*
Mississippi County Community
 College *A*
North Arkansas College *C, A*
Northwest Arkansas Community
 College *A*
Philander Smith College *B*
Phillips Community College of the
 University of Arkansas *C, A*
Southern Arkansas University
 Tech *C*
University of Arkansas
 Monticello *B*
University of Central Arkansas *A, B*
Westark College *C, A*

California
Allan Hancock College *C, A*
American River College *C, A*
Bakersfield College *A*
Barstow College *C, A*
Butte College *C, A*
Canada College *C, A*
Cerritos Community College *A*
Cerro Coso Community College *C, A*
Chabot College *C, A*
Chaffey Community College *C, A*
City College of San Francisco *C, A*
Coastline Community College *C*
College of the Canyons *C*
College of the Desert *C, A*
College of the Redwoods *A*
College of the Sequoias *C, A*
College of the Siskiyous *C, A*
Columbia College *C, A*
Compton Community College *A*
Contra Costa College *C, A*
Crafton Hills College *C, A*
Cypress College *C, A*
De Anza College *C, A*
Diablo Valley College *A*
East Los Angeles College *A*
Empire College *C, A*
Evergreen Valley College *A*
Fresno City College *C, A*
Glendale Community College *C, A*
Golden West College *C, A*
Grossmont Community College *C, A*
Humphreys College *C, A, B*
Imperial Valley College *C, A*
Lake Tahoe Community College *C, A*
Long Beach City College *C, A*
Los Angeles Harbor College *C, A*
Los Angeles Mission College *C, A*
Los Angeles Southwest College *A*
Los Angeles Trade and Technical
 College *C, A*
Los Angeles Valley College *C, A*
Mendocino College *C, A*
Merced College *C, A*
MiraCosta College *C, A*
Mission College *A*
Modesto Junior College *C, A*
Moorpark College *C, A*
Mount San Antonio College *C, A*
Napa Valley College *C, A*
Ohlone College *A*
Orange Coast College *C, A*
Pacific Union College *A*
Palomar College *C, A*
Pasadena City College *C, A*

Secretarial/administrative services

Porterville College A
Rio Hondo College A
Riverside Community College C, A
Sacramento City College C, A
Saddleback College C, A
San Bernardino Valley College C
San Diego City College C, A
San Diego Mesa College C, A
San Diego Miramar College C, A
San Joaquin Delta College A
San Jose City College A
Santa Rosa Junior College C
Shasta College C, A
Sierra College C, A
Skyline College C, A
Solano Community College C, A
Southwestern College C, A
Ventura College C, A
Victor Valley College C, A
West Hills Community College A
West Los Angeles College C, A
West Valley College C, A
Yuba College C

Colorado
Aims Community College C, A
Arapahoe Community College C, A
Community College of Aurora A
Community College of Denver C, A
Front Range Community College C, A
Lamar Community College A
Northeastern Junior College A
Otero Junior College A
Pikes Peak Community College C, A
Pueblo Community College C, A
Red Rocks Community College A

Connecticut
Asnuntuck Community-Technical College A
Briarwood College C, A
Capital Community College C, A
Gateway Community College C, A
Housatonic Community-Technical College C, A
Manchester Community-Technical College C, A
Middlesex Community-Technical College A
Naugatuck Valley Community-Technical College A
Northwestern Connecticut Community-Technical College C, A
Quinebaug Valley Community College C, A
Tunxis Community College C, A

Delaware
Delaware Technical and Community College
    Owens Campus C, A
    Stanton/Wilmington Campus C, A
    Terry Campus C, A

District of Columbia
University of the District of Columbia A

Florida
Brevard Community College A
Central Florida Community College C, A
Clearwater Christian College A
Florida Community College at Jacksonville C, A
Hobe Sound Bible College A
Indian River Community College A
Manatee Community College C, A
Miami-Dade Community College C, A
New England Institute of Technology A
Pensacola Junior College A
Polk Community College A
Santa Fe Community College A
Seminole Community College A
South College: Palm Beach Campus A
South Florida Community College A
Tallahassee Community College C, A
Valencia Community College C, A

Georgia
Athens Area Technical Institute C, A
Atlanta Metropolitan College A
Bainbridge College A
Chattahoochee Technical Institute A
Coastal Georgia Community College C, A
Darton College A
DeKalb Technical Institute C
Floyd College A
Gainesville College A
Gwinnett Technical Institute A
Middle Georgia College A
Morris Brown College B
Savannah Technical Institute A
South Georgia College A
University of Georgia A

Hawaii
University of Hawaii
    Hawaii Community College C, A
    Windward Community College C, A

Idaho
Boise State University A
Eastern Idaho Technical College C, A
ITT Technical Institute
    Boise A
Idaho State University C, A
Lewis-Clark State College A
North Idaho College A
Ricks College C
University of Idaho B

Illinois
Black Hawk College
    East Campus C, A
Black Hawk College C, A
Career Colleges of Chicago C
Carl Sandburg College A
City Colleges of Chicago
    Harold Washington College C, A
    Kennedy-King College C, A
    Malcolm X College C, A
    Olive-Harvey College C, A
    Wright College C, A
College of DuPage A
College of Lake County C, A
Danville Area Community College C, A
Elgin Community College C, A
Illinois Eastern Community Colleges
    Frontier Community College C, A
    Lincoln Trail College C, A
    Olney Central College C, A
    Wabash Valley College C, A
John A. Logan College A
John Wood Community College A
Joliet Junior College C, A
Kankakee Community College A
Kaskaskia College C, A
Lake Land College A
Lincoln Land Community College C, A
MacCormac College A
McHenry County College C, A
Moraine Valley Community College C
Morton College A
Northwestern Business College A
Oakton Community College C
Parkland College C, A
Prairie State College A
Rend Lake College C, A
Robert Morris College: Chicago C, A
Rock Valley College C, A
St. Augustine College C, A
Sauk Valley Community College C, A
Southeastern Illinois College C, A
Southern Illinois University
    Carbondale A
Triton College C, A
Waubonsee Community College C, A
William Rainey Harper College C, A

Indiana
Ancilla College C, A
Ball State University B
Bethel College A
Indiana State University A
International Business College C, A
Ivy Tech State College
    Central Indiana C, A
    Columbus C, A
    Eastcentral C, A
    Kokomo C, A
    Lafayette C, A
    Northcentral C, A
    Northeast C, A
    Northwest C, A
    Southcentral C, A
    Southeast C, A
    Southwest C, A
    Wabash Valley C, A
    Whitewater C, A
Michiana College A
Oakland City University C, A
University of Southern Indiana A
Vincennes University A

Iowa
American Institute of Business C, A
Clinton Community College C, A
Des Moines Area Community College C, A
Faith Baptist Bible College and Theological Seminary A
Indian Hills Community College C
Iowa Central Community College C
Iowa Lakes Community College C
Iowa Western Community College A
Kirkwood Community College C, A
Marshalltown Community College A
Muscatine Community College C, A
North Iowa Area Community College A
Northeast Iowa Community College C
Northwestern College A
Scott Community College C, A
Southeastern Community College
    North Campus C, A
    South Campus A
Southwestern Community College C, A
Western Iowa Tech Community College C, A

Kansas
Allen County Community College A
Barton County Community College C, A
Central Christian College A
Coffeyville Community College A
Fort Hays State University A
Garden City Community College A
Hutchinson Community College C, A
Independence Community College A
Johnson County Community College C, A
Kansas City Kansas Community College C, A
Seward County Community College C, A
Tabor College A, B

Kentucky
Cumberland College B
Eastern Kentucky University A
Elizabethtown Community College A
Henderson Community College A
Hopkinsville Community College A
Kentucky State University A
Lexington Community College A
Lindsey Wilson College A
Morehead State University A, B
Murray State University C, A
National Business College A
Owensboro Community College A
Owensboro Junior College of Business C, A
Paducah Community College A
Prestonsburg Community College A
St. Catharine College A
Southeast Community College A
Western Kentucky University A

Louisiana
Delgado Community College C, A
Louisiana State University
    Eunice C, A
McNeese State University A
Southeastern Louisiana University A
Southern University
    New Orleans A, B
    Shreveport A
University of Louisiana at Monroe A

Maine
Andover College C, A
Beal College C, A
Eastern Maine Technical College A
Husson College A
Mid-State College C, A
Thomas College A

Maryland
Allegany College A
Baltimore City Community College A
Carroll Community College C, A
Cecil Community College A
Chesapeake College C, A
Community College of Baltimore County Catonsville A
Harford Community College C, A
Montgomery College
    Germantown Campus C, A
Prince George's Community College C, A
Villa Julie College A
Wor-Wic Community College C, A

Massachusetts
Atlantic Union College A, B
Bay State College A
Bristol Community College A
Cape Cod Community College C, A
Fisher College C, A
Franklin Institute of Boston C
Greenfield Community College C, A
Holyoke Community College A
Marian Court College C, A
Massasoit Community College C, A
Middlesex Community College C, A
North Shore Community College A
Northern Essex Community College A
Roxbury Community College A
Springfield Technical Community College A

Michigan
Andrews University A, B
Baker College
    of Auburn Hills C, A
    of Cadillac A
    of Jackson C, A
    of Mount Clemens C, A, B
    of Muskegon C, A, B
    of Owosso A, B
    of Port Huron C, A, B
Bay de Noc Community College A
Central Michigan University B
Cleary College A
Davenport College of Business A
Detroit College of Business C, A
Eastern Michigan University B
Ferris State University A
Glen Oaks Community College C
Gogebic Community College A
Grand Rapids Community College C, A
Great Lakes College A
Jackson Community College C, A
Kalamazoo Valley Community College C, A
Kellogg Community College C, A
Kirtland Community College A
Lake Michigan College A
Lansing Community College A
Mid Michigan Community College A
Monroe County Community College C, A
Montcalm Community College A
Mott Community College C, A

Muskegon Community College C, A
North Central Michigan College A
Northern Michigan University A, B, M
Northwestern Michigan College C
Oakland Community College C, A
St. Clair County Community
 College C, A
Schoolcraft College C, A
Southwestern Michigan College C, A
Washtenaw Community College A
West Shore Community College A
Western Michigan University B

Minnesota
Alexandria Technical College C
Anoka-Ramsey Community College A
Century Community and Technical
 College A
Dakota County Technical College C
Fond Du Lac Tribal and Community
 College A
Hibbing Community College: A
 Technical and Community College A
Inver Hills Community College C, A
Itasca Community College A
Lake Superior College: A Community
 and Technical College C, A
Mesabi Range Community and Technical
 College A
Minnesota State College - Southeast
 Technical C, A
North Hennepin Community College A
Northland Community & Technical
 College C, A
Ridgewater College: A Community and
 Technical College C
St. Cloud Technical College C, A
St. Paul Technical College C
South Central Technical College A
University of Minnesota
 Crookston A
Winona State University B, T

Mississippi
Alcorn State University B
Copiah-Lincoln Community College A
Hinds Community College A
Holmes Community College C, A
Jackson State University B, M
Mary Holmes College A
Meridian Community College A
Mississippi Delta Community
 College C, A
Mississippi Gulf Coast Community
 College
  Jackson County Campus C, A
  Jefferson Davis Campus C, A
  Perkinston C, A

Missouri
Baptist Bible College A, B
Central Missouri State University A
Crowder College A
East Central College C, A
Jefferson College A
Longview Community College C, A
Maple Woods Community College C, A
Moberly Area Community College C, A
Ozarks Technical Community
 College C, A
Penn Valley Community College C, A
St. Charles County Community
 College C, A
Southeast Missouri State University B
Southwest Baptist University A
St. Louis Community College
  St. Louis Community College at
   Florissant Valley C, A
  St. Louis Community College at
   Forest Park C, A
  St. Louis Community College at
   Meramec C, A
State Fair Community College A
Three Rivers Community College A

Montana
Dawson Community College C, A
Flathead Valley Community College C
Little Big Horn College C
Miles Community College A
Montana State University
  Billings C, A
  College of Technology-Great
   Falls A
Montana Tech of the University of
 Montana: College of Technology A
Montana Tech of the University of
 Montana A
Salish Kootenai College C, A
Western Montana College of The
 University of Montana A

Nebraska
Central Community College C, A
Lincoln School of Commerce A
Metropolitan Community College C, A
Midland Lutheran College A
Northeast Community College A

Nevada
Community College of Southern
 Nevada A

New Hampshire
Hesser College A
McIntosh College A
New Hampshire Community Technical
 College
  Laconia C
  Manchester C, A
  Stratham C, A

New Jersey
Bergen Community College C, A
Berkeley College C
Brookdale Community College A
Camden County College C
County College of Morris C, A
Cumberland County College C, A
Essex County College A
Gloucester County College C, A
Hudson County Community
 College C, A
Katharine Gibbs School
  Gibbs College C, A
Mercer County Community College C, A
Ocean County College C
Passaic County Community
 College C, A
Salem Community College C, A
Sussex County Community College C, A
Union County College A
Warren County Community College C

New Mexico
Albuquerque Technical-Vocational
 Institute C, A
Clovis Community College C, A
College of Santa Fe A
Dona Ana Branch Community College of
 New Mexico State University C, A
Eastern New Mexico University
 Roswell Campus C, A
New Mexico Junior College C, A
New Mexico State University
  Alamogordo C, A
  Carlsbad A
Northern New Mexico Community
 College C, A
San Juan College C, A
Western New Mexico University C, A

New York
Adirondack Community College C, A
Berkeley College of New York City C
Berkeley College C
Briarcliffe College C, A
Bryant & Stratton Business Institute
  Albany C, A
  Syracuse A
Cayuga County Community
 College C, A
City University of New York
  Borough of Manhattan Community
   College A
  Bronx Community College A
  Hostos Community College A
  La Guardia Community College A
  Lehman College B
  Queensborough Community
   College A
Clinton Community College C, A
Columbia-Greene Community
 College C, A
Concordia College A
Corning Community College C, A
Erie Community College
  City Campus A
  North Campus A
  South Campus A
Finger Lakes Community College C, A
Five Towns College C, A
Fulton-Montgomery Community
 College A
Genesee Community College C, A
Herkimer County Community College A
Hudson Valley Community College A
Interboro Institute A
Jamestown Business College C, A
Katharine Gibbs School
 New York A
Mohawk Valley Community
 College C, A
Monroe College A
Monroe Community College C, A
Nassau Community College A
Niagara County Community College A
Onondaga Community College C, A
Orange County Community
 College A
Pace University:
 Pleasantville/Briarcliff C, A
Pace University A
Rockland Community College A
Sage Junior College of Albany A
St. John's University B
Schenectady County Community
 College A
State University of New York
  College of Agriculture and
   Technology at Morrisville A
  College of Technology at Alfred A
  College of Technology at Delhi A
Suffolk County Community
 College C, A
Technical Career Institutes C, A
Tompkins-Cortland Community
 College C, A
Trocaire College A
Villa Maria College of Buffalo A
Westchester Business Institute C, A
Westchester Community College C, A
Wood Tobe-Coburn School C, A

North Carolina
Alamance Community College A
Asheville Buncombe Technical
 Community College A
Beaufort County Community College A
Blue Ridge Community College C, A
Brunswick Community College A
Caldwell Community College and
 Technical Institute C, A
Cape Fear Community College A
Carteret Community College A
Catawba Valley Community
 College A
Cecils College C, A
Central Carolina Community College A
Central Piedmont Community College A
Cleveland Community College A
Coastal Carolina Community College A
College of the Albemarle A
Craven Community College C
Davidson County Community College A
Durham Technical Community
 College C, A
Edgecombe Community College A
Fayetteville State University A
Gaston College A
Guilford Technical Community
 College A
Haywood Community College C, A
James Sprunt Community College A
Johnston Community College A
Lenoir Community College A
Martin Community College C, A
Mayland Community College A
Mitchell Community College C, A
Montgomery Community College C, A
Nash Community College A
Piedmont Community College A
Pitt Community College A
Randolph Community College A
Richmond Community College C, A
Sampson Community College A
Sandhills Community College A
South Piedmont Community
 College C, A
Southwestern Community College A
Tri-County Community College A
Vance-Granville Community College A
Wake Technical Community College A
Wayne Community College A
Western Piedmont Community
 College A
Wilkes Community College C, A
Wilson Technical Community College A

North Dakota
Bismarck State College C, A
Dickinson State University A, B
Lake Region State College C, A
Mayville State University A, B
Minot State University: Bottineau
 Campus A
North Dakota State College of Science A
Trinity Bible College A, B
Williston State College C, A

Ohio
Bowling Green State University
 Firelands College A
Cedarville College A
Central Ohio Technical College C, A
Cincinnati State Technical and
 Community College A
Clark State Community College C, A
Columbus State Community College A
David N. Myers College A, B
Davis College A
Hocking Technical College A
Kent State University
  Trumbull Campus A
  Tuscarawas Campus A
Lakeland Community College A
Lima Technical College A
Miami University
  Middletown Campus C, A
  Oxford Campus C
Miami-Jacobs College A
Muskingum Area Technical College A
North Central State College A
Northwest State Community
 College C, A
Northwestern College A
Ohio University
  Chillicothe Campus A
  Zanesville Campus A
Ohio Valley Business College C, A
Owens Community College
 Toledo C, A
RETS Tech Center C
Sinclair Community College C, A
Southern State Community College A
Stark State College of Technology A
Terra Community College A
University of Akron
 Wayne College C, A
University of Akron A
University of Cincinnati
  Clermont College C, A
  Raymond Walters College A

Secretarial/administrative services

University of Rio Grande C
University of Toledo A
Youngstown State University A, B

Oklahoma
East Central University B
Eastern Oklahoma State College A
Langston University B
Murray State College A
Oklahoma State University
    Okmulgee A
Redlands Community College A
Rose State College C, A
Tulsa Community College C, A
Western Oklahoma State College A

Oregon
Central Oregon Community
    College C, A
Chemeketa Community College A
Clackamas Community College C
Lane Community College A
Linn-Benton Community College A
Mount Hood Community College C, A
Oregon Institute of Technology A
Portland Community College C, A

Pennsylvania
Bucks County Community College A
Butler County Community College C, A
Cambria-Rowe Business College C, A
Central Pennsylvania College A
Community College of Allegheny
    County C, A
Community College of Beaver County A
Community College of Philadelphia A
Delaware County Community College C
Harrisburg Area Community College A
Lackawanna Junior College A
Laurel Business Institute A
Lehigh Carbon Community College C, A
Luzerne County Community
    College C, A
Manor College C, A
Mercyhurst College C, A
Montgomery County Community
    College C, A
Northampton County Area Community
    College C, A
Peirce College A, B
Penn State
    University Park C
Pennsylvania College of Technology A
Pennsylvania Institute of Technology A
Pittsburgh Technical Institute A
Reading Area Community College C, A
Robert Morris College A
South Hills School of Business &
    Technology A
Westmoreland County Community
    College C, A
Yorktowne Business Institute A

Puerto Rico
American University of Puerto Rico A, B
Atlantic College A, B
Bayamon Central University A, B
Caribbean University A, B
Colegio Universitario del Este A, B
Columbia College A
Huertas Junior College A
Humacao Community College A
ICPR Junior College A
Inter American University of Puerto Rico
    Aguadilla Campus A, B
    Arecibo Campus A, B
    Barranquitas Campus A, B
    Bayamon Campus A, B
    Fajardo Campus A, B
    Guayama Campus A, B
    Metropolitan Campus A, B
    San German Campus A, B
National College of Business and
    Technology A
Pontifical Catholic University of Puerto
    Rico A, B
Ramirez College of Business and
    Technology A
Technological College of San Juan C, A
Turabo University A, B
University of Puerto Rico
    Arecibo Campus A, B
    Carolina Regional College A
    Cayey University College A
    Humacao University College A, B
    Mayaguez Campus B
    Ponce University College A, B
    Rio Piedras Campus B
    Utuado A
University of the Sacred Heart A, B

Rhode Island
Community College of Rhode
    Island C, A
Johnson & Wales University A, B
New England Institute of Technology A

South Carolina
Aiken Technical College C, A
Central Carolina Technical College C, A
Chesterfield-Marlboro Technical
    College C, A
Denmark Technical College C
Florence-Darlington Technical
    College C, A
Greenville Technical College C, A
Horry-Georgetown Technical College A
Midlands Technical College C, A
Orangeburg-Calhoun Technical
    College A
Piedmont Technical College C, A
Technical College of the
    Lowcountry C, A
Tri-County Technical College C, A
Trident Technical College A
York Technical College C, A

South Dakota
Black Hills State University A
Kilian Community College A
Northern State University B
Western Dakota Technical Institute C

Tennessee
Cleveland State Community
    College C, A
Columbia State Community College A
East Tennessee State University B
Hiwassee College A
Jackson State Community College A
Knoxville Business College C, A
Northeast State Technical Community
    College C, A
Pellissippi State Technical Community
    College A
Roane State Community College C, A
Tennessee State University A, B
Tennessee Temple University A, B
Volunteer State Community College C
Walters State Community College A

Texas
Alvin Community College C, A
Amarillo College C, A
Austin Community College A
Blinn College C
Brazosport College C, A
Cedar Valley College A
Central Texas College C, A
Coastal Bend College A
College of the Mainland C, A
Collin County Community College
    District C, A
Del Mar College C, A
Eastfield College C, A
El Paso Community College C, A
Galveston College C, A
Grayson County College A
Hill College C, A
Houston Community College
    System A
Jacksonville College C
Lamar State College at Port Arthur C, A
Lee College C, A
Midland College C, A
Mountain View College A
Navarro College C, A
North Central Texas College A
North Lake College A
Northeast Texas Community
    College C, A
Palo Alto College C, A
Panola College C, A
Paris Junior College A
Richland College A
St. Philip's College C, A
San Antonio College A
Southwest Texas Junior College A
Southwestern Adventist University A, B
Sul Ross State University B
Tarleton State University B, T
Tarrant County College A
Temple College C, A
Texas State Technical College
    Harlingen A
    Sweetwater C, A
Texas Woman's University B
Trinity Valley Community College C, A
Vernon Regional Junior College A
Victoria College A
Weatherford College C, A
Western Texas College C, A

Utah
College of Eastern Utah C, A
Dixie State College of Utah C, A
LDS Business College A
Mountain West College C, A
Salt Lake Community College C, A
Southern Utah University A
Utah State University A
Utah Valley State College C, A
Weber State University A, B

Vermont
Champlain College A, B
Vermont Technical College A

Virginia
Blue Ridge Community College C, A
Central Virginia Community College A
Dabney S. Lancaster Community
    College A
ECPI College of Technology C, A
Germanna Community College C
J. Sargeant Reynolds Community
    College C, A
John Tyler Community College C, A
Lord Fairfax Community College A
New River Community College A
Northern Virginia Community College C
Paul D. Camp Community College A
Southside Virginia Community
    College A
Southwest Virginia Community
    College C, A
Tidewater Community College A
Virginia Commonwealth University B
Virginia Highlands Community
    College A
Virginia Intermont College B
Virginia Western Community College A
Wytheville Community College A

Washington
Bellevue Community College C, A
Clark College A
Edmonds Community College C
Everett Community College C, A
Grays Harbor College C, A
ITT Technical Institute
    Spokane A
Lake Washington Technical College C, A
Lower Columbia College C, A
North Seattle Community College A
Olympic College C, A
Peninsula College A
Pierce College C
Renton Technical College C, A
Seattle Central Community College C, A
Shoreline Community College C, A
Skagit Valley College C, A
South Puget Sound Community
    College C, A
South Seattle Community College C, A
Spokane Community College C, A
Spokane Falls Community College A
Tacoma Community College C
Walla Walla College A
Walla Walla Community College A
Wenatchee Valley College A
Whatcom Community College A
Yakima Valley Community College C, A

West Virginia
College of West Virginia C, A
Concord College A
Fairmont State College A
Potomac State College of West Virginia
    University A
Southern West Virginia Community and
    Technical College C, A
West Virginia Northern Community
    College A
West Virginia State College A
West Virginia University
    Parkersburg C, A

Wisconsin
Blackhawk Technical College C, A
Bryant & Stratton College A
Chippewa Valley Technical College A
Gateway Technical College A
Lakeshore Technical College A
Madison Area Technical College A
Milwaukee Area Technical College A
Moraine Park Technical College C, A
Nicolet Area Technical College A
Northeast Wisconsin Technical
    College A
Southwest Wisconsin Technical
    College C, A
Wisconsin Indianhead Technical
    College C, A

Wyoming
Central Wyoming College C, A
Eastern Wyoming College A
Laramie County Community
    College C, A
Northwest College C, A
Sheridan College C, A
Western Wyoming Community
    College C, A

Security/loss prevention

California
College of the Sequoias C
De Anza College C, A
Long Beach City College C, A
Palomar College C, A
Sierra College A

Florida
Broward Community College A
Florida State University C

Illinois
Black Hawk College C
Lewis University B
Lewis and Clark Community College A
Moraine Valley Community College C
Southwestern Illinois College C, A
Waubonsee Community College C
William Rainey Harper College C

Indiana
Vincennes University A

Iowa
Wartburg College B

Kentucky
Eastern Kentucky University B, M

Maryland
Community College of Baltimore County
 Catonsville *C, A*

Massachusetts
Bristol Community College *C*
Northeastern University *A, B, M*

Michigan
Grand Valley State University *B*
Henry Ford Community College *A*
Macomb Community College *C, A*
Oakland Community College *C, A*
Schoolcraft College *C*

Minnesota
Pine Technical College *A*
Winona State University *B*

Missouri
Central Missouri State University *M*
Webster University *M*

Montana
University of Great Falls *B*

Nevada
Community College of Southern
 Nevada *A*

New Jersey
Essex County College *C*
Gloucester County College *C*
New Jersey City University *B*

New Mexico
San Juan College *A*

New York
Dutchess Community College *C*
Interboro Institute *A*
Long Island University
 C. W. Post Campus *M*
Nassau Community College *A*

North Carolina
Nash Community College *A*

Ohio
Hocking Technical College *C*
Jefferson Community College *A*
Lakeland Community College *C, A*
Ohio University
 Zanesville Campus *A*
Ohio University *A*
Owens Community College
 Toledo *A*
Youngstown State University *B*

Pennsylvania
York College of Pennsylvania *B*

Tennessee
Roane State Community College *A*

Virginia
J. Sargeant Reynolds Community
 College *C*
Northern Virginia Community
 College *C, A*

Washington
Spokane Community College *A*

Sign language interpretation

Arizona
Phoenix College *C, A*
Pima Community College *A*

Arkansas
University of Arkansas
 Little Rock *A*

California
College of the Sequoias *C*
Golden West College *C, A*
Los Angeles Pierce College *A*
Mount San Antonio College *C, A*
Ohlone College *C, A*
Palomar College *C, A*
Riverside Community College *C, A*
Saddleback College *C, A*
San Diego City College *C*
San Diego Mesa College *A*

Colorado
Front Range Community College *A*
Pikes Peak Community College *C, A*

Connecticut
Northwestern Connecticut
 Community-Technical College *C, A*

Delaware
Delaware Technical and Community
 College
 Stanton/Wilmington Campus *A*

District of Columbia
Gallaudet University *M*

Florida
Florida Community College at
 Jacksonville *A*
Hillsborough Community College *A*
Miami-Dade Community College *A*
St. Petersburg Junior College *A*

Georgia
Floyd College *C, A*
Georgia Perimeter College *C, A*

Idaho
College of Southern Idaho *A*
Idaho State University *A, B*

Illinois
Black Hawk College *A*
Columbia College *B*
Waubonsee Community College *C, A*
William Rainey Harper College *C, A*

Indiana
Bethel College *A, B*
Indiana State University *C*
Indiana University--Purdue University
 Indiana University-Purdue
  University Indianapolis *B*
Vincennes University *A*

Iowa
Iowa Western Community College *A*
Kirkwood Community College *A*
Scott Community College *A*

Kansas
Cowley County Community College *A*
Johnson County Community College *A*

Kentucky
Eastern Kentucky University *A, B*

Louisiana
Delgado Community College *C, A*

Maryland
Community College of Baltimore County
 Catonsville *C, A*

Massachusetts
Mount Wachusett Community
 College *C, A*
Northeastern University *B*
Northern Essex Community
 College *C, A*

Michigan
Lansing Community College *A*
Madonna University *C, A, B*
Mott Community College *A*

Minnesota
College of St.
 Catherine-Minneapolis *C, A, B*
St. Cloud Technical College *C*
St. Paul Technical College *C, A*

Mississippi
Hinds Community College *A*
Mississippi Gulf Coast Community
 College
 Jefferson Davis Campus *A*

Missouri
Maple Woods Community College *A*
St. Louis Community College
 St. Louis Community College at
  Florissant Valley *A*
William Woods University *B*

Nebraska
Metropolitan Community College *C*

New Hampshire
New Hampshire Community Technical
 College
 Nashua *C*
University of New Hampshire
 Manchester *B*

New Jersey
Camden County College *A*
Union County College *C, A*

New Mexico
Santa Fe Community College *C*
University of New Mexico *B*

New York
Rochester Institute of Technology *A*
Suffolk County Community College *A*
University of Rochester *B*

North Carolina
Blue Ridge Community College *A*
Central Piedmont Community College *A*
Gardner-Webb University *B*
Wilson Technical Community College *A*

Ohio
Cincinnati State Technical and
 Community College *A*
Columbus State Community
 College *C, A*
Sinclair Community College *A*
Terra Community College *A*
University of Akron *A*

Oklahoma
Oklahoma State University
 Oklahoma City *C, A*
Tulsa Community College *C, A*

Oregon
Portland Community College *C, A*
Western Oregon University *B*

Pennsylvania
Bloomsburg University of
 Pennsylvania *B*
Community College of Allegheny
 County *C, A*
Community College of Philadelphia *C, A*
Mount Aloysius College *A, B*

South Dakota
Southeast Technical Institute *A*

Tennessee
Maryville College *B*

Texas
Blinn College *A*
Collin County Community College
 District *C, A*
Eastfield College *A*
El Paso Community College *C, A*
Houston Community College
 System *C, A*
Howard College *C, A*
Tarrant County College *A*
Tyler Junior College *C, A*
University of Dallas *T*

Utah
Salt Lake Community College *A*

Virginia
J. Sargeant Reynolds Community
 College *C*

Washington
Seattle Central Community College *A*
South Puget Sound Community
 College *C, A*

West Virginia
Fairmont State College *A*

Wisconsin
Gateway Technical College *A*

Slavic languages

California
Stanford University *B, D*
University of California
 Berkeley *B, M, D*
 Los Angeles *B, M, D*
University of Southern California *M, D*

Connecticut
Yale University *M, D*

District of Columbia
George Washington University *B*

Florida
Florida State University *M*

Georgia
Oxford College of Emory University *B*
University of Georgia *B*

Illinois
Northwestern University *B, M, D*
University of Chicago *B, M, D*
University of Illinois
 Chicago *B, M, D*
 Urbana-Champaign *M, D*

Indiana
Indiana University
 Bloomington *B, M, D*

Kansas
University of Kansas *B*

Massachusetts
Harvard College *B*
Harvard University *M, D*

Michigan
University of Michigan *M, D*
Wayne State University *B*

New Jersey
Rutgers
 The State University of New Jersey:
  Newark College of Arts and
  Sciences *B, T*
 The State University of New Jersey:
  University College Newark *T*

New York
Columbia University
 Graduate School *M, D*
 School of General Studies *B*
State University of New York
 Albany *B*
 Stony Brook *M*

North Carolina
Duke University *B*

Ohio
Ohio State University
 Columbus Campus *M, D*

Pennsylvania
California University of Pennsylvania *B*
University of Pittsburgh *B, M, D*

Rhode Island
Brown University *B, M, D*

Texas
University of Texas
 Austin *B, M, D*

Virginia
University of Virginia *B, M, D*

Washington
University of Washington *B, M, D*

Wisconsin
University of Wisconsin
  Madison *B, M, D*

Social psychology

Arizona
Prescott College *B*

California
Los Angeles Southwest College *A*
San Francisco State University *M*
University of California
  Irvine *B*
  Santa Cruz *B, D*

District of Columbia
George Washington University *D*

Florida
Florida Atlantic University *B*

Illinois
Eureka College *B*
Loyola University of Chicago *M, D*

Indiana
Ball State University *M*
Purdue University
  Calumet *B*

Iowa
University of Iowa *D*

Kansas
Pittsburg State University *M*

Louisiana
Our Lady of Holy Cross College *B*

Maryland
Johns Hopkins University *B*

Massachusetts
Hampshire College *B*
Harvard College *B*
Northeastern University *M*
Simon's Rock College of Bard *B*
Suffolk University *B*
Tufts University *B, M, D*
University of Massachusetts
  Lowell *M*

Missouri
Maryville University of Saint Louis *B*
Northwest Missouri State University *B*
University of Missouri
  Columbia *M, D*

Nevada
University of Nevada
  Reno *B, D*

New Hampshire
Antioch New England Graduate
  School *M, D*

New Jersey
Fairleigh Dickinson University *M*
Rutgers
  The State University of New Jersey:
    New Brunswick Graduate
    Campus *D*

New York
Adelphi University *M, D*
Bard College *B*
City University of New York
  Graduate School and University
  Center *D*
Columbia University
  Graduate School *M, D*
  Teachers College *M, D*

Eugene Lang College/New School
  University *B*
Fordham University *M, D*
Long Island University
  Brooklyn Campus *B*
New York University *D*
Sarah Lawrence College *B*
State University of New York
  Albany *M, D*
  Buffalo *D*
  Stony Brook *M, D*
Syracuse University *M, D*
University of Rochester *D*

North Carolina
Duke University *M, D*
University of North Carolina
  Chapel Hill *M, D*

Ohio
Bowling Green State University *M, D*
Miami University
  Oxford Campus *T*
Wright State University *M*

Oklahoma
St. Gregory's University *B*

Pennsylvania
California University of Pennsylvania *M*
Clarion University of Pennsylvania *B*
Moravian College *B*
Penn State
  Abington *B*
  University Park *B*
Temple University *M, D*

South Carolina
Technical College of the Lowcountry *C*

Texas
Our Lady of the Lake University of San
  Antonio *M*
University of the Incarnate Word *B*

Utah
Brigham Young University *B*

Vermont
Bennington College *B*
Burlington College *B*
Marlboro College *B*

Virginia
Longwood College *B*

Wisconsin
University of Wisconsin
  Superior *M*

Social science education

Alabama
Alabama Agricultural and Mechanical
  University *B, M*
Athens State University *B*
Auburn University *B*
Birmingham-Southern College *T*
Huntingdon College *T*
Jacksonville State University *B, M, T*
Oakwood College *B*
Samford University *B, T*
Troy State University
  Dothan *B, M*

Alaska
University of Alaska
  Fairbanks *M*
  Southeast *M*

Arizona
Arizona State University *B, T*
Grand Canyon University *B*
Northern Arizona University *B, T*
Prescott College *B, M*
University of Arizona *B, M*

Arkansas
Arkansas State University *B, M, T*

Arkansas Tech University *B, M*
Henderson State University *B, M, T*
University of Arkansas *B*
University of Central Arkansas *T*

California
Azusa Pacific University *T*
California Baptist University *B, T*
California Lutheran University *B, T*
California Polytechnic State University:
  San Luis Obispo *B, T*
California State Polytechnic University:
  Pomona *T*
California State University
  Bakersfield *B, T*
  Chico *T*
  Dominguez Hills *T*
  Fullerton *T*
  Long Beach *T*
  Northridge *B, T*
  Sacramento *T*
Chapman University *B*
Columbia College *C*
Concordia University *B*
Fresno Pacific University *T*
Hope International University *B*
Humboldt State University *T*
Mills College *T*
Mount St. Mary's College *T*
Occidental College *T*
Pacific Union College *T*
Saddleback College *A*
San Diego State University *B*
San Francisco State University *B, T*
San Jose State University *T*
Simpson College *B, T*
Sonoma State University *T*
University of the Pacific *T*
Westmont College *T*

Colorado
Adams State College *B, T*
Colorado Christian University *B*
Fort Lewis College *T*
Metropolitan State College of Denver *T*
University of Denver *B*
University of Southern Colorado *T*
Western State College of Colorado *T*

Connecticut
Central Connecticut State University *B*
Sacred Heart University *B, M*
St. Joseph College *T*
Southern Connecticut State
  University *B, T*

Delaware
University of Delaware *B*

District of Columbia
George Washington University *T*

Florida
Bethune-Cookman College *B, T*
Flagler College *B*
Florida Agricultural and Mechanical
  University *T*
Florida Atlantic University *B*
Florida International University *B, M, T*
Florida State University *B, M, D, T*
Palm Beach Community College *A*
St. Thomas University *B, T*
Stetson University *B, T*
University of Central Florida *B, M*
University of Florida *M*
University of South Florida *B, M*
Warner Southern College *B*

Georgia
Armstrong Atlantic State
  University *B, M, T*
Clark Atlanta University *B*
Columbus State University *B, M*
Gainesville College *A*
Georgia College and State
  University *B, M*
Georgia Southern University *B, M, T*

Georgia Southwestern State
  University *B, M*
North Georgia College & State
  University *B, M*
Shorter College *M*
State University of West Georgia *B, M*
University of Georgia *B, M, D, T*

Hawaii
Brigham Young University
  Hawaii *B, T*
University of Hawaii
  Manoa *B, T*

Idaho
Boise State University *T*
Lewis-Clark State College *B, T*
Northwest Nazarene University *B*
University of Idaho *M*

Illinois
Augustana College *B, T*
Barat College *B*
Blackburn College *B, T*
Concordia University *B, T*
Dominican University *T*
Eastern Illinois University *B, T*
Lake Land College *A*
Lewis University *T*
McKendree College *B, T*
Millikin University *B, T*
North Park University *T*
Northwestern University *B, T*
Olivet Nazarene University *B, T*
Rockford College *T*
Roosevelt University *B*
University of Illinois
  Chicago *B*
Wheaton College *T*

Indiana
Butler University *T*
Goshen College *B*
Indiana State University *B, M, T*
Manchester College *B, T*
Purdue University
  Calumet *B*
University of Southern Indiana *B, T*
Valparaiso University *B*
Vincennes University *A*

Iowa
Buena Vista University *B, T*
Central College *T*
Clarke College *B, T*
Cornell College *B, T*
Dordt College *B*
Drake University *M, T*
Grand View College *B, T*
Iowa State University *T*
Loras College *T*
Luther College *B*
Morningside College *B*
Northwestern College *T*
St. Ambrose University *B, T*
University of Northern Iowa *B*
Upper Iowa University *B*
Wartburg College *T*
William Penn University *B*

Kansas
Benedictine College *T*
Bethany College *B*
Central Christian College *A*
Emporia State University *B, M, T*
Garden City Community College *A*
Independence Community College *A*
Newman University *T*
Pittsburg State University *B, T*
Tabor College *B, T*
Washburn University of Topeka *B*

Kentucky
Campbellsville University *B*
Murray State University *B, M, T*
Thomas More College *B*
Transylvania University *B, T*
Union College *M*

Louisiana
Dillard University B
Northwestern State University B, T
Xavier University of Louisiana B, T

Maine
University of Maine
    Farmington B
    Presque Isle B
University of New England T
University of Southern Maine T

Maryland
Frostburg State University B, T
Montgomery College
    Germantown Campus A
University of Maryland
    Eastern Shore B

Massachusetts
American International College T
Bridgewater State College M, T
Westfield State College T
Worcester State College T

Michigan
Adrian College B, T
Andrews University M, T
Aquinas College B, T
Central Michigan University B
Cornerstone College and Grand Rapids Baptist Seminary B, T
Eastern Michigan University B, T
Grand Valley State University T
Lansing Community College A
Michigan State University B

Minnesota
College of St. Benedict T
Concordia College: Moorhead T
Crown College A
Gustavus Adolphus College T
Minnesota State University, Mankato B, M, T
St. John's University T
St. Mary's University of Minnesota B
University of Minnesota
    Morris B
Winona State University B, T

Mississippi
Blue Mountain College B
Coahoma Community College A
Delta State University B, M
Jackson State University B
Mary Holmes College A
Mississippi College B, M
Mississippi Gulf Coast Community College
    Jefferson Davis Campus A
Mississippi State University T
Mississippi Valley State University B, T
Northwest Mississippi Community College A
Rust College B
University of Mississippi B, T

Missouri
Avila College T
Fontbonne College B
Lincoln University B, T
Lindenwood University M
Missouri Baptist College T
Missouri Southern State College B, T
Missouri Western State College T
Northwest Missouri State University B, T
Southwest Baptist University B, T
University of Missouri
    St. Louis T
Washington University B, M, T
Webster University M

Montana
Montana State University
    Billings B, T
    Northern B, T
University of Great Falls B, T
University of Montana-Missoula T

Nebraska
Chadron State College M
College of Saint Mary B, T
Concordia University T
Creighton University T
Dana College B
Doane College B, T
Hastings College B, M, T
Midland Lutheran College B, T
Nebraska Wesleyan University B
Peru State College B, T
Union College T
University of Nebraska
    Kearney B, M, T
    Lincoln B, T

Nevada
University of Nevada
    Reno B

New Hampshire
Keene State College B, T
New Hampshire Community Technical College
    Stratham A
Notre Dame College B, M
Rivier College B, T
St. Anselm College T
University of New Hampshire T

New Jersey
Rowan University M
St. Peter's College T
The College of New Jersey B, T

New Mexico
College of the Southwest B, T
Western New Mexico University B

New York
City University of New York
    Hunter College B
Dowling College B
Elmira College B, T
Fordham University M, T
Long Island University
    Brooklyn Campus M
    C. W. Post Campus B, T
    Southampton College T
Manhattan College B, T
Manhattanville College M, T
Marymount College B, T
Pace University:
    Pleasantville/Briarcliff B, T
Pace University B, M
Roberts Wesleyan College B, T
St. John Fisher College B, T
State University of New York
    Binghamton M
    College at Brockport M, T
    College at Oneonta B, M, T
    Oswego B
Vassar College T
Wells College T

North Carolina
Appalachian State University B, M, T
Elon College B, T
Fayetteville State University B, T
Gardner-Webb University B
Johnson C. Smith University B
Lenoir Community College A
Mars Hill College T
North Carolina Agricultural and Technical State University B, M, T
Pfeiffer University B
Sandhills Community College A
University of North Carolina
    Greensboro B, M, T

North Dakota
Dickinson State University B, T
Mayville State University B, T
Minot State University B, T
North Dakota State University B, T
University of Mary B

Valley City State University B, T

Ohio
Bowling Green State University B, M
Cedarville College B
Defiance College B, T
Hiram College T
Kent State University
    Stark Campus B
Kent State University T
Miami University
    Oxford Campus M
Ohio Dominican College D
Shawnee State University B, T
University of Akron B
University of Dayton B, M, T
University of Findlay B, T
University of Rio Grande B, T
Ursuline College B, T
Walsh University B
Wilmington College B
Wittenberg University B
Wright State University M
Xavier University M, T
Youngstown State University B, M

Oklahoma
Eastern Oklahoma State College A
Mid-America Bible College B
Northeastern Oklahoma Agricultural and Mechanical College A
Northwestern Oklahoma State University B
Oklahoma Baptist University B, T
Oklahoma State University B, T
Southwestern Oklahoma State University B, M, T
University of Tulsa T

Oregon
Eastern Oregon University B
Linfield College T
University of Portland T
Western Baptist College B

Pennsylvania
Grove City College T
Holy Family College B, M, T
Immaculata College T
La Salle University B, T
Lock Haven University of Pennsylvania B, T
Mercyhurst College B
Moravian College T
Penn State
    Harrisburg B
Point Park College B
Robert Morris College B
St. Vincent College B
Thiel College B
University of Pittsburgh
    Bradford B
    Johnstown B, T
West Chester University of Pennsylvania B, M, T
Widener University T
Wilson College T

Puerto Rico
Inter American University of Puerto Rico
    Metropolitan Campus B
Turabo University B

South Carolina
Charleston Southern University B, M
Converse College T
Furman University T
The Citadel M
University of South Carolina
    Aiken B, T
Wofford College T

South Dakota
Black Hills State University B, T
Dakota Wesleyan University B, T
Mount Marty College B
Northern State University M, T
University of South Dakota B, T

Tennessee
Belmont University T
Cumberland University B
Lincoln Memorial University B, T
Maryville College B, T
University of Tennessee
    Martin B, T

Texas
Abilene Christian University B, T
Baylor University B, T
Del Mar College A
Hardin-Simmons University B, T
Howard Payne University T
Lamar University T
LeTourneau University B
Lubbock Christian University B
Southwest Texas State University M
Stephen F. Austin State University T
Texas A&M University
    Commerce T
Texas Christian University T
Texas Lutheran University T
Texas Wesleyan University B, M, T
University of Mary Hardin-Baylor T
University of Texas
    San Antonio T

Utah
Weber State University B

Vermont
Castleton State College B, T
Johnson State College B
Lyndon State College B
St. Michael's College B
University of Vermont B, T

Virginia
Averett College B, T
Bridgewater College T
Christopher Newport University T
Eastern Mennonite University T
Liberty University B
Radford University T
University of Virginia's College at Wise T
Virginia Wesleyan College T

Washington
Central Washington University B, T
Eastern Washington University B, M, T
North Seattle Community College C
Pacific Lutheran University T
Seattle Pacific University B, T
Western Washington University B
Whitworth College B, T

West Virginia
Glenville State College B
West Liberty State College B

Wisconsin
Alverno College B, T
Cardinal Stritch University B, T
Carroll College T
Carthage College M, T
Lakeland College B
Lawrence University T
Marquette University B, T
Mount Senario College B, T
Northland College T
Ripon College T
St. Norbert College T
University of Wisconsin
    Green Bay T
    La Crosse B, T
    Madison B, T
    Oshkosh B, T
    Platteville B, T
    River Falls T
    Superior B, T
    Whitewater B, T

Wyoming
Western Wyoming Community College A

Social sciences

Alabama
James H. Faulkner State Community College A
Samford University A
Southern Union State Community College A
Spring Hill College T
Troy State University
    Dothan B, T
    Montgomery A, B
Troy State University B
University of Montevallo B, T

Arizona
Arizona Western College A
Dine College A
Grand Canyon University B
Northern Arizona University B
Prescott College B, M

Arkansas
Arkansas State University
    Beebe Branch A
Harding University B
John Brown University B
Phillips Community College of the University of Arkansas A
University of Arkansas
    Monticello B
University of Central Arkansas M
University of the Ozarks B
Westark College A

California
Allan Hancock College A
Azusa Pacific University B, M
Barstow College A
Biola University B
Butte College A
Cabrillo College A
California Baptist University B
California Institute of Technology B, D
California Polytechnic State University: San Luis Obispo B
California State Polytechnic University: Pomona B
California State University
    Chico B, M
    Fullerton M
    Los Angeles M
    Monterey Bay B
    San Marcos B
    Stanislaus B
Canada College A
Cerro Coso Community College A
Chabot College A
Chaffey Community College A
Chapman University B
Citrus College A
College of San Mateo A
College of the Canyons A
College of the Desert A
College of the Sequoias A
College of the Siskiyous A
Columbia College A
Compton Community College A
Crafton Hills College A
Diablo Valley College C, A
East Los Angeles College A
Foothill College A
Fresno City College A
Fresno Pacific University B
Gavilan Community College A
Glendale Community College A
Golden West College A
Hope International University B
Humboldt State University B, M
Imperial Valley College A
Kings River Community College A
Lake Tahoe Community College A
Las Positas College A
Long Beach City College A
Marymount College A
Mendocino College A
Merced College A
Merritt College A
Mills College A
MiraCosta College A
Mission College A
Modesto Junior College A
Moorpark College A
Mount St. Mary's College B
Mount San Jacinto College A
Napa Valley College A
Ohlone College A
Pacific Oaks College B, M
Pacific Union College B
Pasadena City College A
Pitzer College B
Point Loma Nazarene University B
Pomona College B
Porterville College A
Riverside Community College A
Sacramento City College C, A
Saddleback College A
San Diego City College A
San Diego Mesa College A
San Diego Miramar College A
San Diego State University B
San Francisco State University B, M
San Joaquin Delta College A
San Jose City College A
San Jose State University M
Santa Ana College A
Santa Monica College A
Simpson College B
Solano Community College A
Taft College A
University of California
    Berkeley B
    Irvine B, M, D
University of La Verne B
University of the Pacific B, T
Vanguard University of Southern California B
Ventura College A
West Hills Community College A
West Valley College A
Westmont College B
Yuba College A

Colorado
Adams State College B
Colorado Mountain College
    Alpine Campus A
    Spring Valley Campus A
    Timberline Campus A
Fort Lewis College B
Lamar Community College A
Mesa State College B
United States Air Force Academy B
University of Colorado
    Denver M
University of Denver B
University of Northern Colorado B, M, T
University of Southern Colorado B, T

Connecticut
Albertus Magnus College B
Central Connecticut State University B, M
Connecticut College B
Eastern Connecticut State University B
Northwestern Connecticut Community-Technical College A
Quinnipiac University B
St. Joseph College B, T
Trinity College B
University of Bridgeport B
Western Connecticut State University B

Delaware
Wesley College A

Florida
Flagler College B
Florida Agricultural and Mechanical University M
Florida Atlantic University B
Florida Gulf Coast University B
Florida Southern College B
Florida State University B, M
New College of the University of South Florida B
Palm Beach Community College A
Pensacola Junior College A
Polk Community College A
South Florida Community College A
Stetson University B
Tallahassee Community College A
University of Central Florida B
University of South Florida B
University of Tampa B, T
Warner Southern College B

Georgia
Abraham Baldwin Agricultural College A
Andrew College A
Berry College B, T
Brewton-Parker College A
Clark Atlanta University B
Columbus State University B
Dalton State College A
Darton College A
Floyd College A
Georgia College and State University B
Georgia Military College A
Georgia Southwestern State University B
Mercer University T
Shorter College B, T
South Georgia College A
Thomas College B
Young Harris College A

Hawaii
Hawaii Pacific University B
TransPacific Hawaii College A
University of Hawaii
    West Oahu B

Idaho
Boise State University A, B, T
Lewis-Clark State College B
North Idaho College A
Northwest Nazarene University B
University of Idaho M

Illinois
Barat College B
Benedictine University B, T
City Colleges of Chicago
    Harold Washington College A
    Kennedy-King College A
    Olive-Harvey College A
    Richard J. Daley College C, A
De Paul University B, T
Dominican University B
Eastern Illinois University T
Governors State University B
Greenville College B, T
Highland Community College A
Illinois State University B, T
Kankakee Community College A
Kaskaskia College A
Kendall College B
Kishwaukee College A
Lake Land College A
Lewis University T
McKendree College B
National-Louis University B
North Central College T
North Park University B
Northeastern Illinois University B
Northern Illinois University B, T
Northwestern University T
Olivet Nazarene University B, T
Rend Lake College A
Richland Community College A
Rockford College B
Roosevelt University B
St. Augustine College A
St. Xavier University B
Sauk Valley Community College A
Shimer College B
Southern Illinois University
    Carbondale B
Triton College A
University of Chicago B
William Rainey Harper College A

Indiana
Ancilla College A
Bethel College A, B
Goshen College B
Indiana State University M
Indiana University
    Bloomington B, M
    Kokomo B
Indiana Wesleyan University B
Manchester College B, T
Oakland City University A, B
Purdue University
    Calumet B
Purdue University B, M
St. Joseph's College B
St. Mary-of-the-Woods College B
Tri-State University A, B
University of Southern Indiana A, B
Valparaiso University M, T
Vincennes University A

Iowa
Buena Vista University B, T
Dordt College B
Drake University B
Graceland University B
Grand View College B
Luther College B
Marshalltown Community College A
Marycrest International University A, B
Mount Mercy College T
North Iowa Area Community College A
Upper Iowa University B
Waldorf College A
Wartburg College T
William Penn University B

Kansas
Barton County Community College A
Benedictine College B, T
Bethany College B, T
Bethel College B, T
Central Christian College A
Coffeyville Community College A
Cowley County Community College A
Dodge City Community College A
Emporia State University B, T
Garden City Community College A
Hutchinson Community College A
Independence Community College A
Kansas City Kansas Community College A
Kansas State University B
McPherson College T
MidAmerica Nazarene University B
Pittsburg State University B, M, T
Pratt Community College A
Seward County Community College A
Tabor College B

Kentucky
Asbury College B, T
Brescia University A, B
Campbellsville University A, B, M
Kentucky State University B
Lindsey Wilson College A, B
Mid-Continent College B
Morehead State University B
Pikeville College B
St. Catharine College A
Spalding University B
University of Kentucky B
Western Kentucky University B, T

Louisiana
Loyola University New Orleans B
Northwestern State University B
Our Lady of Holy Cross College B, T
Southern University
    New Orleans B
    Shreveport A

Southern University and Agricultural and Mechanical College *M*
Tulane University *B*

Maine
St. Joseph's College *B*
Unity College *B*
University of Maine
    Augusta *B*
    Fort Kent *B*
    Presque Isle *B*
University of Southern Maine *B*

Maryland
Allegany College *A*
Cecil Community College *A*
Charles County Community College *A*
Chesapeake College *A*
Coppin State College *B*
Frostburg State University *B, T*
Howard Community College *A*
Montgomery College
    Germantown Campus *A*
    Rockville Campus *A*
    Takoma Park Campus *A*
Salisbury State University *T*
Towson University *B*
University of Maryland
    Eastern Shore *B*

Massachusetts
Berkshire Community College *A*
Boston University *M*
Brandeis University *M, D*
Hampshire College *B*
Harvard College *B*
Harvard University *M, D*
Massachusetts Bay Community College *A*
Mount Holyoke College *B*
Northeastern University *B, M, D*
Simon's Rock College of Bard *B*
University of Massachusetts
    Amherst *B*
    Boston *B*

Michigan
Adrian College *B, T*
Andrews University *B*
Aquinas College *B*
Calvin College *B*
Central Michigan University *B, M*
Concordia College *B, T*
Eastern Michigan University *B, M*
Grand Valley State University *B*
Hope College *B, T*
Kalamazoo College *T*
Lake Superior State University *B, T*
Lansing Community College *A*
Madonna University *A, B, T*
Marygrove College *B*
Michigan State University *B, M, D*
Michigan Technological University *C, B, T*
Northern Michigan University *B, T*
Oakland University *B*
Siena Heights University *B*
Spring Arbor College *B*
University of Michigan
    Flint *B, T*
University of Michigan *B, T*
Western Michigan University *B, M, D, T*
William Tyndale College *B*

Minnesota
Augsburg College *B*
Bemidji State University *B*
College of St. Benedict *B*
College of St. Catherine: St. Paul Campus *B*
Concordia University: St. Paul *B*
Hamline University *B*
Macalester College *B*
Metropolitan State University *B*
Moorhead State University *B, T*
Northland Community & Technical College *A*

Northwestern College *B*
Ridgewater College: A Community and Technical College *A*
St. Cloud State University *B*
St. John's University *B*
St. Mary's University of Minnesota *B*
St. Olaf College *T*
University of Minnesota
    Morris *B*
University of St. Thomas *B*
Winona State University *B*

Mississippi
Belhaven College *B*
Blue Mountain College *B*
Delta State University *B*
Jackson State University *B*
Mary Holmes College *A*
Mississippi College *B, M*
Mississippi Delta Community College *A*
Mississippi Gulf Coast Community College
    Jefferson Davis Campus *A*
Mississippi University for Women *B, T*
William Carey College *B, T*

Missouri
Crowder College *A*
Culver-Stockton College *T*
East Central College *A*
Evangel University *A, B*
Fontbonne College *B*
Lincoln University *M*
Mineral Area College *A*
Missouri Baptist College *B*
Missouri Southern State College *B, T*
Rockhurst University *B*
St. Louis University *B*
St. Louis Community College
    St. Louis Community College at Florissant Valley *A*
    St. Louis Community College at Forest Park *A*
    St. Louis Community College at Meramec *A*
Webster University *B*

Montana
Carroll College *B*
Little Big Horn College *A*
Miles Community College *A*
Rocky Mountain College *B, T*
University of Great Falls *B*
Western Montana College of The University of Montana *B*

Nebraska
Bellevue University *B*
Chadron State College *B*
Concordia University *B, T*
Dana College *B*
Doane College *B*
Hastings College *B*
Midland Lutheran College *B, T*
Nebraska Wesleyan University *B*
Northeast Community College *A*
Peru State College *B, T*
Union College *B*
University of Nebraska
    Kearney *B, M, T*
Wayne State College *B, M, T*

Nevada
Community College of Southern Nevada *A*

New Hampshire
Franklin Pierce College *B*
Keene State College *B*
New Hampshire College *B*
Rivier College *B, T*

New Jersey
Atlantic Cape Community College *A*
Brookdale Community College *A*
Caldwell College *B*
Essex County College *A*
Felician College *B*

Monmouth University *B*
Montclair State University *M*
Raritan Valley Community College *A*
Rowan University *B, M*
St. Peter's College *A, B*
Sussex County Community College *A*
Thomas Edison State College *B*
Warren County Community College *A*

New Mexico
College of Santa Fe *B*
College of the Southwest *B*
Eastern New Mexico University *B*
New Mexico Junior College *A*
New Mexico State University
    Carlsbad *A*
Western New Mexico University *B*

New York
Adelphi University *B*
Adirondack Community College *A*
Audrey Cohen College *A, B*
Bard College *B*
Canisius College *A*
Clarkson University *B*
Colgate University *B*
Columbia-Greene Community College *A*
Concordia College *B, T*
Cornell University *B*
Corning Community College *A*
Dominican College of Blauvelt *B*
Dowling College *B*
Elmira College *B, T*
Eugene Lang College/New School University *B*
Finger Lakes Community College *A*
Fulton-Montgomery Community College *A*
Herkimer County Community College *A*
Hofstra University *B*
Hudson Valley Community College *A*
Iona College *B, M*
Ithaca College *B, T*
Jamestown Community College *A*
Long Island University
    Brooklyn Campus *B, M*
    Southampton College *B, T*
Medaille College *B*
Monroe Community College *A*
Mount St. Mary College *B, T*
Nazareth College of Rochester *B*
New York University *B*
Niagara County Community College *A*
Nyack College *B*
Pace University:
    Pleasantville/Briarcliff *B, T*
Pace University *B, T*
Polytechnic University *B*
Rockland Community College *A*
Sage Junior College of Albany *A*
St. Bonaventure University *B*
St. Francis College *B*
St. John's University *B*
St. Thomas Aquinas College *B, T*
Sarah Lawrence College *B*
St. Joseph's College
    St. Joseph's College: Suffolk Campus *B, T*
    St. Joseph's College *B*
State University of New York
    Buffalo *B, M*
    College at Potsdam *T*
    College of Agriculture and Technology at Cobleskill *A*
    College of Agriculture and Technology at Morrisville *A*
    College of Technology at Alfred *A*
    College of Technology at Canton *A*
    College of Technology at Delhi *A*
    Empire State College *A, B*
    Stony Brook *B*
Suffolk County Community College *A*
Syracuse University *M, D*
Tompkins-Cortland Community College *A*
Touro College *B*

Ulster County Community College *A*
United States Military Academy *B*
Utica College of Syracuse University *B*
Westchester Community College *A*

North Carolina
Appalachian State University *B*
Belmont Abbey College *B*
Elizabeth City State University *B*
Elon College *B*
Fayetteville State University *B*
Johnson C. Smith University *B*
Lees-McRae College *B, T*
Louisburg College *A*
Meredith College *T*
North Carolina Agricultural and Technical State University *B, M, T*
North Carolina State University *B*
Sandhills Community College *A*
University of North Carolina
    Greensboro *M*
Western Carolina University *B*
Western Piedmont Community College *A*

North Dakota
Dickinson State University *B, T*
Mayville State University *B, T*
Minot State University: Bottineau Campus *A*
Minot State University *B, T*
North Dakota State University *B, T*
University of Mary *B, T*
University of North Dakota *B, T*
Valley City State University *B*

Ohio
Antioch College *B*
Bowling Green State University
    Firelands College *A*
Cedarville College *B, T*
Cleveland State University *B, M*
Defiance College *B, T*
Heidelberg College *B*
Kent State University *B*
Lake Erie College *B*
Lorain County Community College *A*
Lourdes College *A, B*
Malone College *B*
Notre Dame College of Ohio *B, T*
Ohio Dominican College *B*
Ohio Northern University *B*
Ohio State University
    Columbus Campus *B, M, D*
Ohio University
    Southern Campus at Ironton *A*
Ohio University *A, M*
Shawnee State University *B, T*
Union Institute *B*
University of Akron
    Wayne College *A*
University of Akron *B*
University of Findlay *A, B*
University of Rio Grande *A, B, T*
Wilmington College *B*
Wittenberg University *B*
Youngstown State University *B*

Oklahoma
Connors State College *A*
East Central University *B*
Eastern Oklahoma State College *A*
Langston University *B*
Northeastern Oklahoma Agricultural and Mechanical College *A*
Northern Oklahoma College *A*
Northwestern Oklahoma State University *B*
Oklahoma Baptist University *B, T*
Oklahoma Panhandle State University *B*
St. Gregory's University *B*
Seminole State College *A*
Southern Nazarene University *B*
Tulsa Community College *A*
University of Oklahoma *M*
Western Oklahoma State College *A*

Social sciences

Oregon
Central Oregon Community College A
Concordia University B
Marylhurst University B
Northwest Christian College B
Portland State University M
Southern Oregon University B, T
University of Oregon B
Western Baptist College B

Pennsylvania
Bloomsburg University of Pennsylvania B
Bryn Athyn College of the New Church B
Bucks County Community College A
California University of Pennsylvania B, M
Carlow College B
Carnegie Mellon University B, M, D
Chestnut Hill College A, B
Cheyney University of Pennsylvania B
Clarion University of Pennsylvania B, T
Community College of Allegheny County A
Community College of Beaver County A
Edinboro University of Pennsylvania A, B, M
Gannon University B
Gettysburg College B
Harrisburg Area Community College A
Juniata College B
La Roche College B
La Salle University B, T
Lehigh Carbon Community College A
Lehigh University B, M, D
Lock Haven University of Pennsylvania B
Luzerne County Community College A
Mansfield University of Pennsylvania B
Marywood University B
Montgomery County Community College A
Penn State
 University Park M, D
Reading Area Community College A
Robert Morris College B
Rosemont College B
St. Francis College B
St. Joseph's University B
Seton Hill College B, T
Swarthmore College B
University of Pennsylvania A, B, M, D
University of Pittsburgh
 Bradford B
 Greensburg B
 Johnstown B
University of Pittsburgh B
University of Scranton T
Waynesburg College B
Widener University B
Wilson College B
York College of Pennsylvania B

Puerto Rico
Caribbean University B
Inter American University of Puerto Rico
 Metropolitan Campus B
Pontifical Catholic University of Puerto Rico B
Turabo University A, B
University of Puerto Rico
 Arecibo Campus T
 Carolina Regional College A
 Cayey University College B
 Mayaguez Campus B
 Ponce University College B
 Rio Piedras Campus B
 Utuado A
University of the Sacred Heart B

Rhode Island
Providence College B
Rhode Island College B

South Carolina
Charleston Southern University B
Erskine College B, T
Presbyterian College B, T
Southern Wesleyan University B, T
University of South Carolina M
Wofford College B

South Dakota
Augustana College T
Black Hills State University B
Dakota Wesleyan University B
Sinte Gleska University A, B

Tennessee
Bethel College B
Cumberland University A, B
David Lipscomb University B
Dyersburg State Community College A
East Tennessee State University B
Freed-Hardeman University B, T
Hiwassee College A
LeMoyne-Owen College B
Lee University B
Lincoln Memorial University B, T
Middle Tennessee State University B
Motlow State Community College A
Roane State Community College A
Tennessee State University B
Trevecca Nazarene University B
Union University B, T
University of Tennessee
 Chattanooga B

Texas
Abilene Christian University T
Amarillo College A
Angelina College A
Cedar Valley College A
Central Texas College A
College of the Mainland A
Concordia University at Austin A, B, T
El Paso Community College A
Howard College A
Howard Payne University B, T
Huston-Tillotson College B
Lon Morris College A
McMurry University T
Midland College A
Navarro College A
Odessa College A
Our Lady of the Lake University of San Antonio B
St. Edward's University B
Sam Houston State University B, M
San Jacinto College
 North A
Southern Methodist University B
Southwestern Adventist University B
Southwestern Assemblies of God University A
Southwestern University B, T
Stephen F. Austin State University B
Sul Ross State University B, M, T
Texas A&M International University B
Texas A&M University
 Commerce B, M
Texas Wesleyan University B
Trinity Valley Community College A
Tyler Junior College A
University of Houston
 Downtown B
University of Mary Hardin-Baylor B
University of North Texas B
Wayland Baptist University A, B
West Texas A&M University B
Western Texas College A

Utah
Brigham Young University B
Salt Lake Community College A
Snow College A
Southern Utah University B, T
Utah State University M
Westminster College B

Vermont
Bennington College B
Burlington College B
Castleton State College B
Goddard College B
Johnson State College B
Lyndon State College B
Marlboro College B

Virginia
Averett College B
Bluefield College B
Eastern Mennonite University B
Ferrum College B
Hollins University M
J. Sargeant Reynolds Community College A
James Madison University B, T
Liberty University B, T
Lynchburg College B
Radford University B
St. Paul's College B
University of Virginia's College at Wise T
Virginia Wesleyan College B

Washington
Central Washington University B
Centralia College A
Everett Community College A
Evergreen State College B
Highline Community College A
Lower Columbia College A
Pacific Lutheran University B
Puget Sound Christian College B
University of Washington B
Washington State University B
Whitworth College B, T

West Virginia
Alderson-Broaddus College B
Bluefield State College B
College of West Virginia B
Marshall University B, M
University of Charleston B
West Virginia University
 Parkersburg A
West Virginia Wesleyan College B

Wisconsin
Alverno College B, T
Cardinal Stritch University B
Carthage College B, T
Mount Mary College B
Mount Senario College B, T
Northland College B, T
Silver Lake College B, T
University of Wisconsin
 Milwaukee B
 Platteville B
 River Falls B
 Stevens Point B, T
 Superior B
 Whitewater B
Viterbo University B

Wyoming
Central Wyoming College A
Laramie County Community College A
Sheridan College A
University of Wyoming B
Western Wyoming Community College A

Social studies education

Alabama
Athens State University B
Birmingham-Southern College T
Faulkner University B, T
Huntingdon College T
Lawson State Community College A
Talladega College T
University of Mobile B, T

Arizona
Arizona State University B, T
Prescott College B
University of Arizona B, M

Arkansas
Arkansas Tech University M
Harding University B, M, T
John Brown University B, T
Ouachita Baptist University B, T
Southern Arkansas University B, T
University of Arkansas
 Monticello B
 Pine Bluff B, M, T
University of Arkansas B
University of Central Arkansas T
Williams Baptist College B

California
Azusa Pacific University T
California Baptist University B, T
California Lutheran University B, T
California State University
 Northridge B, T
Concordia University B
Loyola Marymount University M
Master's College T
Mount St. Mary's College T
Occidental College T
University of La Verne B
University of San Francisco T
University of the Pacific T

Colorado
Adams State College B, T
Colorado Christian University B
Colorado State University T
Fort Lewis College T
Metropolitan State College of Denver T
Trinidad State Junior College A
University of Colorado
 Boulder T
 Colorado Springs T
University of Southern Colorado T

Connecticut
Central Connecticut State University B
Fairfield University T
Quinnipiac University B, M
Sacred Heart University B, T
Southern Connecticut State University B, T

Delaware
Delaware State University B
University of Delaware T
Wesley College B

District of Columbia
George Washington University M, T

Florida
Barry University T
Clearwater Christian College B
Flagler College B
Florida Agricultural and Mechanical University B, M
Florida International University B, M, T
Gulf Coast Community College A
Nova Southeastern University M
Southeastern College of the Assemblies of God B, T
University of West Florida B, T

Georgia
Agnes Scott College T
Georgia State University M, D
Kennesaw State University B
LaGrange College T
Mercer University M, T
Valdosta State University M, T

Hawaii
University of Hawaii
 Manoa B, T

Idaho
Albertson College of Idaho B
Boise State University T

546

Illinois
Blackburn College *B, T*
Bradley University *B*
Chicago State University *T*
Concordia University *B, T*
Greenville College *B, T*
Illinois College *T*
Kankakee Community College *A*
Lewis University *T*
North Park University *T*
Northwestern University *B, T*
Olivet Nazarene University *B, T*
Rockford College *T*
Trinity Christian College *B, T*
University of Illinois
   Urbana-Champaign *B, M, T*

Indiana
Anderson University *B, T*
Ball State University *B, T*
Bethel College *B*
Butler University *T*
Franklin College *T*
Indiana State University *B, M, T*
Indiana University
   Bloomington *B, M, T*
   Northwest *B*
   South Bend *B*
   Southeast *B*
Indiana University--Purdue University
Indiana University-Purdue
   University Fort Wayne *B, T*
Indiana University-Purdue
   University Indianapolis *B, T*
Indiana Wesleyan University *B, T*
Manchester College *B, T*
Oakland City University *B*
Purdue University
   Calumet *B*
Saint Mary's College *T*
St. Mary-of-the-Woods College *B*
Taylor University *B*
Tri-State University *B, T*
University of Evansville *T*
University of Indianapolis *B, T*
University of St. Francis *B*
University of Southern Indiana *B, T*
Valparaiso University *B*
Vincennes University *A*

Iowa
Buena Vista University *B, T*
Clarke College *B, T*
Cornell College *B, T*
Dordt College *B*
Drake University *T*
Graceland University *T*
Grand View College *B, T*
Luther College *B*
Northwestern College *T*
St. Ambrose University *T*
University of Iowa *B, M, D, T*
Upper Iowa University *B*
Wartburg College *T*
William Penn University *B*

Kansas
Bethel College *T*
Emporia State University *T*
Garden City Community College *A*
Independence Community College *A*
Kansas Wesleyan University *T*
McPherson College *B, T*
MidAmerica Nazarene University *B, T*
Pittsburg State University *B*
St. Mary College *T*
University of Kansas *B, T*
Washburn University of Topeka *B*

Kentucky
Alice Lloyd College *B*
Brescia University *B*
Campbellsville University *B*
Cumberland College *B, T*
Kentucky State University *B*
Murray State University *B, M, T*
Pikeville College *B, T*
Spalding University *B*
Transylvania University *B, T*
Union College *B, M*

Louisiana
Centenary College of Louisiana *B, T*
Dillard University *B*
Louisiana State University
   Shreveport *B*
McNeese State University *T*
Nicholls State University *B*
Our Lady of Holy Cross College *B, T*
Southeastern Louisiana University *B*
Southern University and Agricultural and
   Mechanical College *B*
University of Louisiana at Monroe *B*
University of New Orleans *B*

Maine
College of the Atlantic *B, T*
St. Joseph's College *B*
University of Maine
   Presque Isle *B*
University of Maine *M*
University of New England *T*
University of Southern Maine *T*

Maryland
College of Notre Dame of Maryland *T*
Montgomery College
   Rockville Campus *A*
   Takoma Park Campus *A*
Mount St. Mary's College *B, T*
University of Maryland
   College Park *B*

Massachusetts
American International College *T*
Assumption College *T*
Boston University *B, M, T*
Bridgewater State College *T*
Elms College *T*
Harvard College *T*
Merrimack College *T*
Northeastern University *B*
Springfield College *T*
Tufts University *M, T*
University of Massachusetts
   Dartmouth *T*
Western New England College *T*
Westfield State College *B, M, T*
Worcester State College *T*

Michigan
Albion College *B, T*
Calvin College *B*
Central Michigan University *B*
Eastern Michigan University *B, T*
Grand Valley State University *T*
Michigan Technological University *T*
Northern Michigan University *B, T*
University of Michigan
   Dearborn *B*
   Flint *B, T*
Wayne State University *B, M, T*

Minnesota
Augsburg College *T*
Bemidji State University *M, T*
Bethel College *B*
College of St. Catherine: St. Paul
   Campus *T*
College of St. Scholastica *B, T*
Concordia University: St. Paul *B, T*
Crown College *B, T*
Gustavus Adolphus College *T*
Minnesota State University,
   Mankato *B, M, T*
Moorhead State University *B, T*
Northwestern College *B*
St. Cloud State University *T*
St. Mary's University of Minnesota *B*
St. Olaf College *T*
Southwest State University *T*
University of Minnesota
   Duluth *B*
   Twin Cities *M, T*
University of St. Thomas *B, T*
Winona State University *B, T*

Mississippi
Mary Holmes College *A*
Mississippi College *B*
Mississippi State University *T*
Northwest Mississippi Community
   College *A*

Missouri
Central Methodist College *B*
Central Missouri State
   University *B, M, T*
College of the Ozarks *B, T*
Columbia College *T*
Evangel University *B*
Fontbonne College *B*
Hannibal-LaGrange College *B*
Harris Stowe State College *T*
Lindenwood University *M*
Missouri Baptist College *T*
Missouri Valley College *B*
Park University *T*
Rockhurst University *B*
Truman State University *M, T*
University of Missouri
   Columbia *B, M, D*
Washington University *B, M, T*
William Jewell College *T*
William Woods University *B, T*

Montana
Montana State University
   Billings *B, T*
   Bozeman *T*
Rocky Mountain College *B, T*
University of Montana-Missoula *T*
Western Montana College of The
   University of Montana *B, T*

Nebraska
Creighton University *T*
Dana College *B*
Hastings College *B, M, T*
Midland Lutheran College *B, T*

Nevada
University of Nevada
   Reno *B*

New Hampshire
Colby-Sawyer College *B, T*
Franklin Pierce College *T*
New England College *B, T*
Plymouth State College of the University
   System of New Hampshire *B, T*
Rivier College *B, T*
St. Anselm College *T*
University of New Hampshire
   Manchester *M*
University of New Hampshire *T*

New Jersey
Caldwell College *T*
Centenary College *T*
College of St. Elizabeth *T*
Fairleigh Dickinson University *M*
Richard Stockton College of New
   Jersey *B*
Rider University *B, T*
Rowan University *T*
Rutgers
   The State University of New Jersey:
    Camden College of Arts and
    Sciences *T*
   The State University of New Jersey:
    New Brunswick Graduate
    Campus *M, D, T*
   The State University of New Jersey:
    Newark College of Arts and
    Sciences *T*
   The State University of New Jersey:
    University College Camden *T*
   The State University of New Jersey:
    University College New
    Brunswick *T*
   The State University of New Jersey:
    University College Newark *T*
St. Peter's College *T*
The College of New Jersey *T*

New Mexico
New Mexico Highlands University *B*
Western New Mexico University *B*

New York
Adelphi University *B, M*
Alfred University *M, T*
Canisius College *B, M, T*
City University of New York
   Brooklyn College *B, M*
   City College *B, T*
   College of Staten Island *M*
   Hunter College *B, M*
   Lehman College *M*
   Queens College *M, T*
   York College *T*
Colgate University *M*
College of Mount St. Vincent *T*
College of St. Rose *B, T*
Columbia University
   Teachers College *M, D*
D'Youville College *B, M, T*
Daemen College *T*
Dowling College *B*
Elmira College *B, T*
Fordham University *T*
Hofstra University *B, M, T*
Houghton College *B, T*
Ithaca College *B, T*
Keuka College *B, T*
Le Moyne College *T*
Long Island University
   Brooklyn Campus *M*
   C. W. Post Campus *M*
   Southampton College *T*
Manhattan College *B, T*
Manhattanville College *M, T*
Marist College *B, T*
Marymount Manhattan College *B, T*
Molloy College *B*
Nazareth College of Rochester *T*
New York Institute of Technology *B, T*
New York University *B, M, T*
Niagara University *B, T*
Pace University:
   Pleasantville/Briarcliff *B, M, T*
Pace University *B, M, T*
Roberts Wesleyan College *B, T*
Russell Sage College *T*
St. Bonaventure University *T*
St. Francis College *B, T*
St. John Fisher College *B, T*
St. John's University *B, M, T*
St. Lawrence University *T*
St. Thomas Aquinas College *B, T*
Siena College *T*
St. Joseph's College
   St. Joseph's College *B, T*

Social studies education

State University of New York
  Albany B, M, T
  Binghamton M
  Buffalo M, T
  College at Brockport M, T
  College at Buffalo B, M, T
  College at Cortland B, M, T
  College at Fredonia B, T
  College at Geneseo B, M, T
  College at Oneonta B, M, T
  College at Plattsburgh B, M
  College at Potsdam B, M, T
  New Paltz B, M, T
  Oswego B, M
  Stony Brook T
Syracuse University B, M, T
Utica College of Syracuse University B
Wagner College T
Wells College T

North Carolina
Appalachian State University M
Barton College T
Belmont Abbey College T
Campbell University B, T
Catawba College T
Davidson College T
East Carolina University B, M
Elizabeth City State University B
Greensboro College T
Lees-McRae College T
Lenoir-Rhyne College B, T
Mars Hill College T
Meredith College T
Methodist College A, B, T
North Carolina State University T
Queens College T
St. Augustine's College B, T
Sandhills Community College A
Shaw University B, T
University of North Carolina
  Greensboro M
  Pembroke B, T
Wake Forest University T
Western Carolina University B, T
Winston-Salem State University B

North Dakota
North Dakota State University B, T
University of North Dakota B, T

Ohio
Ashland University B, T
Baldwin-Wallace College T
Bluffton College B
Bowling Green State University B
Capital University T
Central State University B
College of Mount St. Joseph T
Defiance College B, T
Hiram College T
John Carroll University T
Kent State University
  Stark Campus B
Kent State University B, M, T
Lorain County Community College A
Malone College B
Miami University
  Oxford Campus B, T
Mount Union College T
Mount Vernon Nazarene College B, T
Ohio Dominican College D
Ohio Northern University B, T
Ohio University B, D, T
Otterbein College B
University of Akron B
University of Dayton B, M, T
University of Findlay B, T
University of Toledo T
Ursuline College B, T
Walsh University B
Wilmington College B
Wittenberg University B
Wright State University B, T
Youngstown State University B, M

Oklahoma
Cameron University B, T
East Central University B
Eastern Oklahoma State College A
Langston University B
Northeastern Oklahoma Agricultural and Mechanical College A
Northeastern State University B
Oklahoma Baptist University B, T
Oklahoma Christian University of Science and Arts B, T
Oklahoma City University B
Oklahoma State University B, T
Oral Roberts University B, T
Southeastern Oklahoma State University B, M, T
University of Central Oklahoma B
University of Oklahoma B, T
University of Science and Arts of Oklahoma T
University of Tulsa T
Western Oklahoma State College A

Oregon
Concordia University B, M, T
Eastern Oregon University B
George Fox University B, M, T
Portland State University T
Southern Oregon University T
University of Portland T
Western Baptist College B
Western Oregon University T

Pennsylvania
Albright College T
Allentown College of St. Francis de Sales T
Alvernia College B
Beaver College B, M, T
Bloomsburg University of Pennsylvania B, T
Bucknell University T
Cabrini College B, T
California University of Pennsylvania B, T
Carlow College T
Carnegie Mellon University T
Chatham College M, T
Chestnut Hill College T
Cheyney University of Pennsylvania T
Clarion University of Pennsylvania B, T
Dickinson College T
Duquesne University B, T
East Stroudsburg University of Pennsylvania B, M, T
Edinboro University of Pennsylvania B
Elizabethtown College T
Gannon University B, T
Gettysburg College T
Grove City College B, T
Gwynedd-Mercy College T
Holy Family College B, M, T
Indiana University of Pennsylvania B, M, T
Juniata College B, T
King's College T
Kutztown University of Pennsylvania B, M, T
La Salle University B, T
Lebanon Valley College of Pennsylvania T
Lincoln University B, T
Lock Haven University of Pennsylvania T
Lycoming College T
Mansfield University of Pennsylvania B, T
Marywood University T
Messiah College T
Millersville University of Pennsylvania B, T
Moravian College T
Muhlenberg College T
Philadelphia College of Bible B, T
Robert Morris College B

St. Joseph's University B
St. Vincent College T
Seton Hill College B, T
Susquehanna University T
Temple University B, T
Thiel College B
University of Pennsylvania M
University of Pittsburgh
  Johnstown B, T
University of Pittsburgh T
Ursinus College T
Villanova University T
Washington and Jefferson College T
Waynesburg College B, T
Westminster College B, T
Widener University M
Wilkes University T
York College of Pennsylvania B, T

Puerto Rico
Inter American University of Puerto Rico
  Barranquitas Campus B, T
  Fajardo Campus B, T
  Metropolitan Campus B
Pontifical Catholic University of Puerto Rico B, T

Rhode Island
Providence College B
Rhode Island College B, M

South Carolina
Anderson College B, T
Charleston Southern University B, M
Converse College T
Furman University T
Limestone College B
Morris College B, T
South Carolina State University B, T
The Citadel M
University of South Carolina
  Aiken B, T

South Dakota
Augustana College B, T
Black Hills State University B, T
Dakota State University B, T
Dakota Wesleyan University B, T
Northern State University T

Tennessee
Belmont University T
King College T
Lincoln Memorial University B, T
Tennessee Technological University T
Union University B, T
University of Tennessee
  Chattanooga B, T
  Knoxville T
Vanderbilt University B, M, D

Texas
Abilene Christian University B, T
Angelo State University T
Baylor University B, T
Dallas Baptist University T
East Texas Baptist University B
Hardin-Simmons University B, T
Howard Payne University T
Lamar University T
LeTourneau University B
Lubbock Christian University B
McMurry University T
St. Edward's University B, T
St. Mary's University B, T
Southwest Texas State University T
Texas A&M International University B, T
Texas A&M University
  Commerce T
  Corpus Christi T
  Kingsville T
Texas Christian University T
Texas Lutheran University B, T
Texas Wesleyan University B
University of Dallas T

University of Houston
  Clear Lake T
University of Houston M
University of Texas
  Arlington T
  San Antonio T
West Texas A&M University T

Utah
Weber State University B

Vermont
Castleton State College B, T
College of St. Joseph in Vermont B
Goddard College B
Johnson State College B
St. Michael's College M

Virginia
Bridgewater College T
Christopher Newport University T
Hollins University T
Longwood College B, T
Old Dominion University B, M
St. Paul's College T
University of Richmond T
University of Virginia's College at Wise T
Virginia Intermont College B, T
Virginia Wesleyan College T

Washington
Pacific Lutheran University T
Washington State University T
Western Washington University B, T
Whitworth College B, T

West Virginia
Alderson-Broaddus College T
Concord College B, T
Fairmont State College B
Glenville State College B
Shepherd College T
University of Charleston B
West Virginia State College B
Wheeling Jesuit University T

Wisconsin
Alverno College T
Cardinal Stritch University B, T
Carroll College T
Carthage College T
Concordia University Wisconsin B, T
Marian College of Fond du Lac B, T
Mount Mary College T
Mount Senario College B, T
Northland College T
Ripon College T
St. Norbert College T
University of Wisconsin
  Eau Claire B
  Green Bay T
  La Crosse B, T
  Platteville B, T
  River Falls T
Viterbo University B

Social work

Alabama
Alabama Agricultural and Mechanical University B, M
Alabama State University B
Auburn University B
Community College of the Air Force A
Jacksonville State University B
Lawson State Community College A
Oakwood College B
Shelton State Community College A
Talladega College B
Troy State University B, M
Tuskegee University B
University of Alabama
  Birmingham B
University of Alabama B, M, D
University of Montevallo B

University of North Alabama *B*

Alaska

University of Alaska
    Anchorage *B, M*
    Fairbanks *B*

Arizona

Arizona State University *B, M, D*
Arizona Western College *A*
Cochise College *A*
Glendale Community College *A*
Mohave Community College *A*
Northern Arizona University *B*

Arkansas

Arkansas State University *B*
Harding University *B*
Henderson State University *M*
Southern Arkansas University *B*
University of Arkansas
    Little Rock *M*
    Monticello *B*
    Pine Bluff *B*
University of Arkansas *B*
Westark College *A*

California

Azusa Pacific University *B*
California State University
    Chico *B*
    Fresno *B, M*
    Hayward *B*
    Long Beach *B, M*
    Los Angeles *B, M*
    Sacramento *B, M*
    Stanislaus *M*
Chapman University *B*
College of the Sequoias *C*
Fresno City College *C, A*
Fresno Pacific University *B*
Humboldt State University *B*
La Sierra University *B*
Loma Linda University *M, D*
Long Beach City College *A*
Merced College *A*
Pacific Union College *B*
Point Loma Nazarene University *B*
Riverside Community College *A*
San Bernardino Valley College *C, A*
San Diego State University *B, M*
San Francisco State University *B, M*
San Jose State University *B, M*
Southwestern College *A*
University of California
    Berkeley *M, D*
    Los Angeles *M, D*
University of Southern California *M, D*
Whittier College *B*

Colorado

Colorado State University *B, M*
Lamar Community College *A*
Metropolitan State College of Denver *B*
University of Denver *M, D*

Connecticut

Asnuntuck Community-Technical College *A*
Central Connecticut State University *B*
Eastern Connecticut State University *B*
Naugatuck Valley Community-Technical College *C, A*
Sacred Heart University *B*
St. Joseph College *B*
Southern Connecticut State University *B*
University of Connecticut *M*
Western Connecticut State University *B*

Delaware

Delaware State University *B, M*

District of Columbia

Catholic University of America *B, M, D*
Gallaudet University *B, M*
Howard University *M, D*
University of the District of Columbia *B*

Florida

Barry University *M, D*
Broward Community College *A*
Florida Agricultural and Mechanical University *B*
Florida Atlantic University *B*
Florida Gulf Coast University *M*
Florida International University *B, M, D*
Florida State University *C, B, M, D*
Gulf Coast Community College *A*
Manatee Community College *A*
Miami-Dade Community College *A*
Palm Beach Community College *A*
St. Leo University *B*
University of Central Florida *B, M*
University of South Florida *B, M*
University of West Florida *B*
Warner Southern College *B*

Georgia

Atlanta Metropolitan College *A*
Clark Atlanta University *B, M, D*
Darton College *A*
Fort Valley State University *B*
Gainesville College *A*
Georgia State University *B, M*
Middle Georgia College *A*
Oglethorpe University *B*
Savannah State University *B, M*
Thomas College *B*
University of Georgia *B, M, D*
Valdosta State University *M*

Hawaii

Brigham Young University
    Hawaii *B*
Hawaii Pacific University *B*
University of Hawaii
    Honolulu Community College *A*
    Manoa *B, M, D*

Idaho

Boise State University *B, M*
Idaho State University *B*
Lewis-Clark State College *B*
Northwest Nazarene University *B, M*
Ricks College *A*

Illinois

Bradley University *B*
City Colleges of Chicago
    Harold Washington College *A*
    Kennedy-King College *A*
College of DuPage *C, A*
College of Lake County *C, A*
Concordia University *B*
Elgin Community College *C, A*
Governors State University *B, M*
Greenville College *B*
Illinois Eastern Community Colleges
    Wabash Valley College *A*
Illinois State University *B*
Judson College *B*
Kishwaukee College *A*
Lewis University *B*
Lincoln Land Community College *A*
Loyola University of Chicago *B, M, D*
Northeastern Illinois University *B*
Olivet Nazarene University *B*
Quincy University *A, B*
Rend Lake College *A*
Roosevelt University *B*
St. Augustine College *B*
Southern Illinois University
    Carbondale *B, M*
    Edwardsville *B, M*
Springfield College in Illinois *A*
University of Illinois
    Chicago *B, M, D*
    Springfield *B*
    Urbana-Champaign *M, D*
University of St. Francis *B*
Waubonsee Community College *C, A*
Western Illinois University *B*

Indiana

Anderson University *B*
Ball State University *B*
Goshen College *B*
Grace College *B*
Indiana State University *B*
Indiana University
    East *B*
    Northwest *M*
    South Bend *M*
Indiana University--Purdue University
    Indiana University-Purdue University Indianapolis *B, M, D*
Indiana Wesleyan University *B*
Manchester College *B*
Purdue University
    Calumet *B*
Saint Mary's College *B*
Taylor University *B*
University of Evansville *B*
University of Indianapolis *B*
University of St. Francis *B*
University of Southern Indiana *B, M*
Valparaiso University *B*
Vincennes University *A*

Iowa

Briar Cliff College *B*
Buena Vista University *B*
Clarke College *B*
Dordt College *B*
Hawkeye Community College *A*
Iowa Western Community College *A*
Loras College *B*
Luther College *B*
Marycrest International University *A, B*
North Iowa Area Community College *A*
Northwestern College *B*
St. Ambrose University *M*
University of Iowa *B, M, D*
University of Northern Iowa *B*
Waldorf College *A*
Wartburg College *B*

Kansas

Bethany College *B*
Bethel College *B*
Butler County Community College *A*
Central Christian College *A*
Coffeyville Community College *A*
Colby Community College *A*
Fort Hays State University *B*
Independence Community College *A*
Kansas City Kansas Community College *A*
Kansas State University *B*
Newman University *M*
Pittsburg State University *B*
Seward County Community College *A*
University of Kansas *B, M, D*
Washburn University of Topeka *B, M*
Wichita State University *B*

Kentucky

Asbury College *B*
Brescia University *B*
Campbellsville University *B*
Cumberland College *B*
Eastern Kentucky University *B*
Henderson Community College *A*
Kentucky Christian College *B*
Kentucky State University *B*
Morehead State University *B*
Murray State University *B, M*
Northern Kentucky University *B*
Owensboro Community College *A*
St. Catharine College *A*
Spalding University *B, M*
University of Kentucky *B, M, D*
University of Louisville *M, D*
Western Kentucky University *B*

Louisiana

Dillard University *B*
Louisiana State University and Agricultural and Mechanical College *M, D*
Southeastern Louisiana University *B*
Southern University
    New Orleans *B, M*
Southern University and Agricultural and Mechanical College *B*
Tulane University *M, D*
University of Louisiana at Monroe *B*

Maine

St. Joseph's College *B*
University of Maine
    Augusta *A*
    Fort Kent *A, B*
    Presque Isle *B*
University of Maine *B, M*
University of New England *M*
University of Southern Maine *B, M*

Maryland

Allegany College *A*
Baltimore City Community College *C, A*
Bowie State University *B*
Coppin State College *B*
Frostburg State University *B*
Hood College *B*
Salisbury State University *B*
University of Maryland
    Baltimore County *B*
    Baltimore *M, D*
    Eastern Shore *B*
Western Maryland College *B*

Massachusetts

Anna Maria College *B*
Assumption College *B*
Atlantic Union College *B*
Berkshire Community College *A*
Boston College *M, D*
Boston University *B*
Bridgewater State College *B*
Bunker Hill Community College *A*
Dean College *A*
Eastern Nazarene College *B*
Elms College *B*
Endicott College *B*
Gordon College *B*
Massachusetts College of Liberal Arts *B*
Northern Essex Community College *A*
Regis College *B*
Salem State College *B, M*
Simmons College *M, D*
Smith College *M, D*
Springfield College *M*
Western New England College *B*
Westfield State College *B*
Wheelock College *B*

Michigan

Andrews University *B, M*
Bay de Noc Community College *C*
Calvin College *B*
Central Michigan University *B*
Cornerstone College and Grand Rapids Baptist Seminary *B*
Eastern Michigan University *C, B, M*
Ferris State University *B*
Gogebic Community College *A*
Grand Valley State University *B, M*
Hope College *B*
Kellogg Community College *A*
Lansing Community College *A*
Madonna University *B*
Marygrove College *B*
Michigan State University *B, M*
Mott Community College *A*
Northern Michigan University *B*
Oakland Community College *C, A*
Oakland University *B*
Reformed Bible College *A, B*
Saginaw Valley State University *B*
Schoolcraft College *A*
Siena Heights University *A, B*
Spring Arbor College *B*
University of Detroit Mercy *B*
University of Michigan
    Flint *B*
University of Michigan *M, D*

Wayne State University C, B, M
Western Michigan University B, M

Minnesota
Augsburg College M
Bemidji State University B
Bethel College B
Central Lakes College C, A
College of St. Benedict B
College of St. Catherine: St. Paul Campus B, M
College of St. Scholastica B
Concordia College: Moorhead B
Itasca Community College A
Metropolitan State University B
Minnesota State University, Mankato B
Moorhead State University B
Ridgewater College: A Community and Technical College A
St. Cloud State University B, M
St. John's University B
St. Olaf College B
Southwest State University B
University of Minnesota
  Duluth M
  Twin Cities M, D
University of St. Thomas B, M
Winona State University B

Mississippi
Delta State University B, M
Jackson State University B, M, D
Mississippi College B
Mississippi Delta Community College A
Mississippi Gulf Coast Community College
  Perkinston A
Mississippi State University B
Mississippi Valley State University B, M
Rust College B
University of Mississippi B
University of Southern Mississippi B, M

Missouri
Avila College B
Central Missouri State University B
College of the Ozarks B
Columbia College B
East Central College A
Evangel University A, B
Lindenwood University B
Missouri Western State College B
St. Louis University B, M
Southeast Missouri State University B
Southwest Missouri State University B, M
St. Louis Community College
  St. Louis Community College at Meramec A
University of Missouri
  Columbia B, M
  Kansas City M
  St. Louis B, M
Washington University M, D
William Woods University B

Montana
Carroll College B
Miles Community College A
Salish Kootenai College A
University of Montana-Missoula B

Nebraska
Chadron State College B
Creighton University B
Dana College B
Metropolitan Community College A
Nebraska Wesleyan University B
Union College B
University of Nebraska
  Kearney B
  Omaha B, M

Nevada
University of Nevada
  Las Vegas B, M
  Reno B, M

New Hampshire
Franklin Pierce College B
Keene State College M
New Hampshire Community Technical College
  Laconia C, A
New Hampshire Technical Institute A
Plymouth State College of the University System of New Hampshire B
University of New Hampshire Manchester M
University of New Hampshire B, M

New Jersey
Camden County College A
Cumberland County College A
Essex County College A
Georgian Court College B
Kean University B, M
Monmouth University B
Ocean County College C, A
Ramapo College of New Jersey B
Richard Stockton College of New Jersey B
Rutgers
  The State University of New Jersey: Camden College of Arts and Sciences B
  The State University of New Jersey: Camden Graduate Campus M
  The State University of New Jersey: Livingston College B
  The State University of New Jersey: New Brunswick Graduate Campus M, D
  The State University of New Jersey: Newark College of Arts and Sciences B
  The State University of New Jersey: Newark Graduate Campus M
  The State University of New Jersey: University College Camden B
  The State University of New Jersey: University College Newark B
Seton Hall University B
Thomas Edison State College A, B

New Mexico
Eastern New Mexico University
  Roswell Campus A
New Mexico Highlands University B, M
New Mexico State University
  Alamogordo A
New Mexico State University B, M
Northern New Mexico Community College A
San Juan College C, A
Western New Mexico University B

New York
Adelphi University B, M, D
Audrey Cohen College A, B
City University of New York
  College of Staten Island B
  Graduate School and University Center D
  Hunter College M
  York College B
College of New Rochelle B
College of St. Rose B
Columbia University
  Graduate School M, D
Concordia College B, D
Cornell University B
D'Youville College B
Daemen College B
Dominican College of Blauvelt B
Elmira College B
Fordham University B, M, D
Fulton-Montgomery Community College A
Hofstra University M
Hudson Valley Community College A
Keuka College B
Long Island University
  C. W. Post Campus B
Marist College B
Mercy College B
Molloy College B
Nazareth College of Rochester B
New York University B, M, D
Roberts Wesleyan College B, M
Rochester Institute of Technology B
Siena College B
Skidmore College B
State University of New York
  Albany B, M, D
  Buffalo M, D
  College at Brockport B
  College at Buffalo B
  College at Fredonia B
  College at Plattsburgh B
  Health Science Center at Stony Brook B
  New Paltz B, M
  Stony Brook B, M, D
Syracuse University B, M
Ulster County Community College A

North Carolina
Appalachian State University B
Asheville Buncombe Technical Community College A
Barton College B
Beaufort County Community College A
Bennett College B
Campbell University B
College of the Albemarle A
East Carolina University B, M
Edgecombe Community College A
Elizabeth City State University B
Gaston College A
Guilford Technical Community College A
Halifax Community College A
Johnson C. Smith University B
Lenoir Community College A
Louisburg College A
Mars Hill College B
Martin Community College A
Meredith College B, T
Methodist College A, B
North Carolina Agricultural and Technical State University B, M
North Carolina Central University B
North Carolina State University B
Piedmont Community College A
Richmond Community College A
Sandhills Community College A
Shaw University B
South Piedmont Community College A
University of North Carolina
  Chapel Hill M, D
  Charlotte B
  Greensboro B, M
  Pembroke B
  Wilmington B
Warren Wilson College B
Western Carolina University B

North Dakota
Dickinson State University B
Minot State University B
University of Mary B
University of North Dakota B, M

Ohio
Ashland University B
Bluffton College B
Bowling Green State University B
Capital University B
Case Western Reserve University M, D
Cedarville College B
Central State University B
Clark State Community College A
Cleveland State University B, M
College of Mount St. Joseph B
College of Wooster B
Defiance College C, B
Franciscan University of Steubenville B
Lourdes College A, B
Malone College B
Miami University
  Oxford Campus B
Mount Vernon Nazarene College B
Muskingum Area Technical College A
Northwest State Community College A
Ohio Dominican College B
Ohio State University
  Columbus Campus B, M, D
Ohio University
  Chillicothe Campus A
Ohio University B, M
Sinclair Community College A
Union Institute B
University of Akron B, M
University of Cincinnati
  Clermont College A
  Raymond Walters College A
University of Cincinnati B, M
University of Dayton B
University of Findlay B
University of Rio Grande A, B
University of Toledo B
Ursuline College B
Wilmington College B
Wright State University B
Xavier University B
Youngstown State University A, B

Oklahoma
Connors State College A
East Central University B
Northeastern Oklahoma Agricultural and Mechanical College A
Northeastern State University B
Northwestern Oklahoma State University B
Oklahoma Baptist University B
Oral Roberts University B
Southwestern Oklahoma State University B
University of Oklahoma B, M

Oregon
Chemeketa Community College A
Concordia University B
George Fox University B
Pacific University B
Portland State University M, D
University of Portland B

Pennsylvania
Allentown College of St. Francis de Sales B
Alvernia College B
Bloomsburg University of Pennsylvania B
Bryn Mawr College M, D
Bucks County Community College A
Cabrini College B
California University of Pennsylvania B
Carlow College B
Cedar Crest College B
Chatham College B
College Misericordia B
Community College of Allegheny County C, A
Eastern College B
Edinboro University of Pennsylvania A, B, M
Elizabethtown College B
Gannon University B
Harrisburg Area Community College A
Holy Family College B
Immaculata College B
Juniata College B
Kutztown University of Pennsylvania B
La Salle University B
Lock Haven University of Pennsylvania B
Mansfield University of Pennsylvania A, B
Marywood University B, M
Mercyhurst College B
Messiah College B
Millersville University of Pennsylvania B

Muhlenberg College *B*
Northampton County Area Community
    College *A*
Philadelphia College of Bible *B*
Reading Area Community College *A*
St. Francis College *B*
Seton Hill College *B*
Shippensburg University of
    Pennsylvania *B*
Slippery Rock University of
    Pennsylvania *B*
Temple University *B, M*
University of Pennsylvania *M, D*
University of Pittsburgh *B, M, D*
West Chester University of
    Pennsylvania *B, M*
Westminster College *B*
Widener University *B, M*

Puerto Rico
Bayamon Central University *B*
Caribbean University *A, B*
Colegio Universitario del Este *A, B*
Inter American University of Puerto Rico
    Arecibo Campus *B*
    Metropolitan Campus *B, M*
Pontifical Catholic University of Puerto
    Rico *B, D*
Turabo University *B*
University of Puerto Rico
    Humacao University College *B*
    Rio Piedras Campus *B, M*
University of the Sacred Heart *B*

Rhode Island
Community College of Rhode Island *A*
Providence College *B*
Rhode Island College *B, M*
Salve Regina University *B*

South Carolina
Aiken Technical College *A*
Benedict College *B*
Coker College *B, T*
Columbia College *B*
Florence-Darlington Technical College *A*
Limestone College *B*
Midlands Technical College *A*
Orangeburg-Calhoun Technical
    College *C*
Piedmont Technical College *A*
South Carolina State University *B*
University of South Carolina *M, D*
Winthrop University *B*

South Dakota
Augustana College *B*

Tennessee
Austin Peay State University *B*
Belmont University *B, T*
East Tennessee State University *B*
Freed-Hardeman University *B*
LeMoyne-Owen College *B*
Lincoln Memorial University *B*
Maryville College *B*
Middle Tennessee State University *B*
Southern Adventist University *B*
Tennessee State University *B*
Trevecca Nazarene University *B*
Union University *B*
University of Memphis *B*
University of Tennessee
    Chattanooga *B*
    Knoxville *B, M, D*
    Martin *B*

Texas
Abilene Christian University *B*
Amarillo College *A*
Angelina College *A*
Baylor University *B, M*
College of the Mainland *A*
Del Mar College *A*
Eastfield College *A*
Galveston College *C, A*
Hardin-Simmons University *B*

Howard Payne University *B*
Lamar University *B*
Lubbock Christian University *B*
Midland College *A*
Midwestern State University *B*
Our Lady of the Lake University of San
    Antonio *B, M*
Panola College *A*
Prairie View A&M University *B*
St. Edward's University *B*
Southwest Texas State University *B, M*
Southwestern Adventist University *B*
Stephen F. Austin State University *B*
Tarleton State University *B*
Texas A&M University
    Commerce *B, M*
Texas Christian University *B*
Texas College *B*
Texas Lutheran University *B*
Texas Southern University *B*
Texas Tech University *B*
Texas Woman's University *B*
Tyler Junior College *A*
University of Houston *M, D*
University of Mary Hardin-Baylor *B*
University of North Texas *B*
University of Texas
    Arlington *B, M, D*
    Austin *B, M, D*
    El Paso *B*
    Pan American *B, M*
West Texas A&M University *B*

Utah
Brigham Young University *B, M*
Dixie State College of Utah *A*
Salt Lake Community College *A*
Snow College *A*
University of Utah *M, D*
Utah State University *B*
Weber State University *B*

Vermont
Castleton State College *B*
Champlain College *A, B*
Goddard College *B*
Southern Vermont College *B*
Trinity College of Vermont *B*
University of Vermont *B, M*

Virginia
Christopher Newport University *B*
Eastern Mennonite University *B*
Ferrum College *B*
George Mason University *B*
James Madison University *B*
Longwood College *B*
Mary Baldwin College *B*
Norfolk State University *B, M, D*
Radford University *B, M*
Thomas Nelson Community College *A*
Virginia Commonwealth
    University *B, M, D*
Virginia Highlands Community
    College *C, A*
Virginia Intermont College *B*
Virginia State University *B*
Virginia Union University *B*

Washington
Eastern Washington University *B, M*
Heritage College *B*
Pacific Lutheran University *B*
Seattle University *B*
University of Washington *B, M, D*
Walla Walla College *B, M*
Washington State University *B*

West Virginia
Bethany College *B*
College of West Virginia *B*
Concord College *B*
Fairmont State College *B*
Marshall University *B*
Potomac State College of West Virginia
    University *A*
Shepherd College *B*

West Virginia State College *A, B*
West Virginia University
    Parkersburg *C, A*
West Virginia University *B, M*

Wisconsin
Beloit College *B*
Carroll College *B*
Carthage College *B*
Concordia University Wisconsin *B*
Marian College of Fond du Lac *B*
Marquette University *B*
Mount Mary College *B*
Mount Senario College *B*
University of Wisconsin
    Eau Claire *B*
    Madison *B, M, D*
    Milwaukee *B, M*
    Oshkosh *B*
    River Falls *B*
    Superior *B*
    Whitewater *B, T*
Viterbo University *B*

Wyoming
Casper College *A*
Sheridan College *A*
University of Wyoming *B, M*

Social/philosophical foundations of education

Alabama
Troy State University
    Dothan *M*
Troy State University *M*

Arizona
Arizona State University *M*
University of Arizona *M, D*

California
California State University
    Long Beach *M*
    Los Angeles *M*
    Northridge *M*
Hope International University *M*
Stanford University *M, D*

Colorado
University of Colorado
    Boulder *M, D*

Connecticut
Central Connecticut State University *M*
University of Connecticut *D, T*

Florida
Florida Atlantic University *M*
Florida State University *M, D*
University of Florida *M, D*

Georgia
Georgia State University *M, D*
University of Georgia *M, D*

Hawaii
University of Hawaii
    Manoa *M, D*

Illinois
Loyola University of Chicago *M, D*
Northern Illinois University *M*
University of Illinois
    Urbana-Champaign *M, D*
Western Illinois University *M*

Indiana
Indiana University
    Bloomington *M, D*

Iowa
Iowa State University *M*
University of Iowa *M, D*
University of Northern Iowa *M*

Kansas
University of Kansas *M*

Kentucky
University of Kentucky *M*

Maryland
Loyola College in Maryland *M*

Massachusetts
Tufts University *M*

Michigan
Eastern Michigan University *M*
Wayne State University *M, D*

Minnesota
University of Minnesota
    Twin Cities *B, M*

Missouri
Washington University *B*

New Jersey
Rutgers
    The State University of New Jersey:
    New Brunswick Graduate
    Campus *M, D*

New Mexico
University of New Mexico *D*

New York
Columbia University
    Teachers College *M, D*
Eugene Lang College/New School
    University *B*
Fordham University *M*
Hofstra University *M, T*
New York University *M, D*
State University of New York
    Buffalo *D*
Syracuse University *M, D*

North Carolina
University of North Carolina
    Chapel Hill *D*

Ohio
University of Akron *M*
University of Cincinnati *M, D*
University of Toledo *M*
Youngstown State University *M*

Oklahoma
University of Oklahoma *M, D*

Pennsylvania
Penn State
    University Park *M, D*
University of Pennsylvania *M, D*

South Carolina
University of South Carolina *D*

Texas
University of Houston *M, D*
University of Texas
    San Antonio *M*

Utah
University of Utah *M, D*

Washington
Eastern Washington University *M*
Western Washington University *B*

Wisconsin
University of Wisconsin
    Milwaukee *M*
    Whitewater *M*

Sociology

Alabama
Alabama Agricultural and Mechanical
    University *B*
Alabama State University *B*
Athens State University *B*
Auburn University at Montgomery *B*
Auburn University *B*
Birmingham-Southern College *B*
Jacksonville State University *B*

Lawson State Community College A
Samford University B
Stillman College B
Talladega College B
Troy State University
   Dothan B
Troy State University B
Tuskegee University B
University of Alabama
   Birmingham B, M
   Huntsville B
University of Alabama B
University of Mobile B
University of Montevallo B, T
University of North Alabama B
University of South Alabama B, M
University of West Alabama B

Alaska

University of Alaska
   Anchorage B
   Fairbanks B

Arizona

Arizona State University B, M, D
Eastern Arizona College A
Gateway Community College A
Grand Canyon University B
Mohave Community College A
Northern Arizona University B, M
Pima Community College A
Prescott College B, M
South Mountain Community College A
University of Arizona B, M, D

Arkansas

Arkansas State University
   Beebe Branch A
Arkansas State University B, M
Arkansas Tech University B
Harding University B
Henderson State University B
Hendrix College B
Ouachita Baptist University B
Philander Smith College B
Southern Arkansas University B
University of Arkansas
   Little Rock B
   Pine Bluff B
University of Arkansas B, M
University of Central Arkansas B, M
University of the Ozarks B
Westark College A

California

Azusa Pacific University B
Bakersfield College A
Biola University B
Cabrillo College A
California Lutheran University B
California State Polytechnic University:
   Pomona B
California State University
   Bakersfield B
   Chico B
   Dominguez Hills B
   Fullerton B, M
   Hayward B, M
   Long Beach B
   Los Angeles B, M
   Northridge B
   Sacramento B, M
   San Marcos B, M
   Stanislaus B
Cerritos Community College A
Chabot College A
Chaffey Community College A
Chapman University B
College of Notre Dame B
College of the Desert A
Compton Community College A
Contra Costa College A
Crafton Hills College A
Cypress College A
De Anza College A
Diablo Valley College A

East Los Angeles College A
Foothill College A
Fresno City College A
Gavilan Community College A
Glendale Community College A
Golden West College A
Holy Names College B
Humboldt State University B, M
Irvine Valley College A
La Sierra University B
Las Positas College A
Long Beach City College C, A
Los Angeles Southwest College A
Los Angeles Valley College A
Los Medanos College A
Loyola Marymount University B
Marymount College A
Merced College A
Mills College B
MiraCosta College A
Monterey Peninsula College A
Mount St. Mary's College B
Occidental College B
Ohlone College C, A
Orange Coast College A
Pepperdine University B
Pitzer College B
Point Loma Nazarene University B
Pomona College B
Riverside Community College A
Saddleback College A
St. Mary's College of California B
San Diego Mesa College A
San Diego Miramar College A
San Diego State University B, M
San Francisco State University B
San Jose State University B, M
Santa Ana College A
Santa Barbara City College A
Santa Clara University B
Santa Rosa Junior College A
Scripps College B
Sonoma State University B
Southwestern College A
Stanford University B, M, D
United States International University B
University of California
   Berkeley B, M, D
   Davis B, M, D
   Irvine B
   Los Angeles B, M, D
   Riverside B, M, D
   San Diego B, M, D
   San Francisco D
   Santa Barbara B, M, D
   Santa Cruz B, D
University of La Verne B
University of Redlands B
University of San Diego B
University of San Francisco B
University of Southern
   California B, M, D
University of the Pacific B
Vanguard University of Southern
   California B
Ventura College A
West Los Angeles College C, A
West Valley College A
Westmont College B
Whittier College B

Colorado

Adams State College B
Colorado College B
Colorado State University B, M, D
Fort Lewis College B
Mesa State College B
Metropolitan State College of
   Denver B, T
Red Rocks Community College A
Regis University B
University of Colorado
   Boulder B, M, D
   Colorado Springs B, M
   Denver B, M

University of Denver B, M
University of Northern Colorado B
University of Southern Colorado B
Western State College of Colorado B

Connecticut

Albertus Magnus College B
Central Connecticut State University B
Connecticut College B
Eastern Connecticut State University B
Fairfield University B
Quinnipiac University B
Sacred Heart University A, B
St. Joseph College B
Southern Connecticut State
   University B, M
Teikyo Post University B
Trinity College B
University of Connecticut B, M, D
University of Hartford B
University of New Haven B
Wesleyan University B
Western Connecticut State University B
Yale University B, M, D

Delaware

Delaware State University B
University of Delaware B, M, D

District of Columbia

American University B, M, D
Catholic University of America B, M, D
Gallaudet University B
George Washington University B, M
Georgetown University B
Howard University B, M, D
Trinity College B
University of the District of Columbia B

Florida

Barry University B
Bethune-Cookman College B
Broward Community College A
Eckerd College B
Edward Waters College B
Florida Agricultural and Mechanical
   University B
Florida Atlantic University B, M
Florida International University B, M, D
Florida Memorial College B
Florida Southern College B
Florida State University B, M, D
Gulf Coast Community College A
Jacksonville University B
Miami-Dade Community College A
New College of the University of South
   Florida B
Palm Beach Community College A
Pensacola Junior College A
Rollins College B
St. Leo University B
St. Thomas University B
Stetson University B
University of Central Florida B, M
University of Florida B, M, D
University of Miami B, M, D
University of North Florida B
University of South Florida B, M, D
University of Tampa A, B
University of West Florida B

Georgia

Abraham Baldwin Agricultural
   College A
Agnes Scott College B
Albany State University B
Andrew College A
Atlanta Metropolitan College A
Augusta State University B
Berry College B
Brewton-Parker College A, B
Clark Atlanta University B, M
Clayton College and State University A
Columbus State University B
Covenant College B
Dalton State College A
Darton College A

East Georgia College A
Emory University B, D
Fort Valley State University B
Gainesville College A
Georgia College and State University B
Georgia Military College A
Georgia Perimeter College A
Georgia Southern University B, M
Georgia Southwestern State University B
Georgia State University B, M, D
Kennesaw State University B
LaGrange College B
Mercer University B
Middle Georgia College A
Morehouse College B
Morris Brown College B
North Georgia College & State
   University B
Oglethorpe University B
Oxford College of Emory University B
Paine College B
Piedmont College B
Savannah State University B
Shorter College B
South Georgia College A
Spelman College B
State University of West Georgia B, M
Thomas College B
University of Georgia B, M, D
Valdosta State University B, M
Waycross College A

Hawaii

Hawaii Pacific University B
University of Hawaii
   Hilo B
   Manoa B, M, D
   West Oahu B

Idaho

Albertson College of Idaho B
Boise State University A, B, T
College of Southern Idaho A
Idaho State University B
Lewis-Clark State College B
North Idaho College A
Northwest Nazarene University B
Ricks College A
University of Idaho B

Illinois

Augustana College B, T
Barat College B
Benedictine University B, T
Black Hawk College
   East Campus A
Bradley University B, T
Chicago State University B
Concordia University B
Danville Area Community College A
De Paul University B, M
Dominican University B
Eastern Illinois University B
Elmhurst College B, T
Greenville College B
Highland Community College A
Illinois College B
Illinois State University B, M
Illinois Wesleyan University B
John Wood Community College A
Joliet Junior College A
Judson College B
Kishwaukee College A
Knox College B
Lake Forest College B
Lewis University B, T
Lewis and Clark Community College A
Lincoln Land Community College A
Loyola University of Chicago B, M, D, T
McKendree College B
Millikin University B
Monmouth College B, T
Morton College A
North Central College B
North Park University B
Northeastern Illinois University B

Northern Illinois University *B, M*
Northwestern University *B, M, D*
Olivet Nazarene University *B*
Principia College *B*
Quincy University *A, B*
Rend Lake College *A*
Richland Community College *A*
Rockford College *B*
Roosevelt University *B, M*
St. Xavier University *B*
Sauk Valley Community College *A*
Shimer College *B*
Southern Illinois University
    Carbondale *B, M, D*
    Edwardsville *B, M*
Southwestern Illinois College *A*
Springfield College in Illinois *A*
Trinity Christian College *B*
Trinity International University *B*
University of Chicago *B, M, D*
University of Illinois
    Chicago *B, M, D*
    Springfield *B, M*
    Urbana-Champaign *B, M, D*
Western Illinois University *B, M*
Wheaton College *B*

Indiana
Anderson University *B*
Ball State University *B*
Bethel College *B*
Butler University *B*
DePauw University *B*
Earlham College *B*
Franklin College *B*
Goshen College *B*
Grace College *B*
Hanover College *B*
Indiana State University *B, M, T*
Indiana University
    Bloomington *B, M, D*
    East *B*
    Kokomo *B*
    Northwest *B*
    South Bend *A, B*
    Southeast *B*
Indiana University--Purdue University
    Indiana University-Purdue
        University Fort Wayne *B, M*
    Indiana University-Purdue
        University Indianapolis *B*
Indiana Wesleyan University *A, B*
Manchester College *B*
Marian College *B, T*
Purdue University
    Calumet *B*
Purdue University *B, M, D*
Saint Mary's College *B*
St. Joseph's College *B*
Taylor University *B*
University of Evansville *B*
University of Indianapolis *B, M*
University of Notre Dame *B, M, D*
University of Southern Indiana *B*
Valparaiso University *B, M, T*
Vincennes University *A*

Iowa
Briar Cliff College *B*
Central College *B, T*
Clarke College *A, B*
Coe College *B*
Cornell College *B, T*
Drake University *B*
Graceland University *B, T*
Grinnell College *B*
Iowa State University *B, M, D*
Iowa Wesleyan College *B*
Loras College *B*
Luther College *B*
Morningside College *B*
Mount Mercy College *B*
North Iowa Area Community College *A*
Northwestern College *B*
St. Ambrose University *B, T*
Simpson College *B*

University of Dubuque *B, T*
University of Iowa *B, M, D, T*
University of Northern Iowa *B, M*
Upper Iowa University *B*
Waldorf College *A*
Wartburg College *B, T*
William Penn University *B*

Kansas
Allen County Community College *A*
Baker University *B, T*
Benedictine College *B*
Bethany College *B*
Bethel College *T*
Central Christian College *A*
Coffeyville Community College *A*
Colby Community College *A*
Dodge City Community College *A*
Emporia State University *B*
Fort Hays State University *B*
Independence Community College *A*
Kansas City Kansas Community
    College *A*
Kansas State University *B, M, D*
Kansas Wesleyan University *B*
McPherson College *B, T*
MidAmerica Nazarene University *B*
Newman University *B*
Ottawa University *B*
Pittsburg State University *B, T*
Pratt Community College *A*
St. Mary College *B*
Seward County Community College *A*
Tabor College *B*
University of Kansas *B, M, D*
Washburn University of Topeka *B*
Wichita State University *B, M, T*

Kentucky
Asbury College *B*
Bellarmine College *B*
Berea College *B*
Campbellsville University *B*
Centre College *B*
Eastern Kentucky University *B*
Georgetown College *B, T*
Kentucky State University *B*
Kentucky Wesleyan College *B*
Morehead State University *B, M*
Murray State University *B*
Northern Kentucky University *B*
Pikeville College *B*
Spalding University *B*
Thomas More College *A, B*
Transylvania University *B*
Union College *B*
University of Kentucky *B, M, D*
University of Louisville *B, M*
Western Kentucky University *B, M, T*

Louisiana
Centenary College of Louisiana *B*
Dillard University *B*
Louisiana State University
    Shreveport *B*
Louisiana State University and
    Agricultural and Mechanical
    College *B, M, D*
Louisiana Tech University *B*
Loyola University New Orleans *B*
McNeese State University *B*
Nicholls State University *B*
Southeastern Louisiana University *B*
Southern University
    New Orleans *B*
    Shreveport *B*
Southern University and Agricultural and
    Mechanical College *B, M*
Tulane University *B, M, D*
University of Louisiana at Lafayette *B*
University of Louisiana at Monroe *B*
University of New Orleans *B, M*
Xavier University of Louisiana *B*

Maine
Bates College *B*

Bowdoin College *B*
Colby College *B*
St. Joseph's College *B*
University of Maine
    Fort Kent *B*
    Presque Isle *B*
University of Maine *B*
University of Southern Maine *B*

Maryland
Allegany College *A*
Community College of Baltimore County
    Essex *A*
Frederick Community College *A*
Frostburg State University *B*
Goucher College *B*
Harford Community College *A*
Hood College *B*
Johns Hopkins University *B, D*
Loyola College in Maryland *B*
Morgan State University *B, M*
Mount St. Mary's College *B*
St. Mary's College of Maryland *B*
Salisbury State University *B*
Towson University *B*
University of Maryland
    Baltimore County *B, M*
    College Park *B, M, D*
    Eastern Shore *B*
Washington College *B*
Western Maryland College *B*

Massachusetts
American International College *B*
Amherst College *B*
Assumption College *B*
Boston College *B, M, D*
Boston University *B, M, D*
Brandeis University *B, M, D*
Bridgewater State College *B*
Cape Cod Community College *A*
Clark University *B*
College of the Holy Cross *B*
Curry College *B*
Eastern Nazarene College *B*
Elms College *B*
Emmanuel College *B*
Fitchburg State College *B*
Framingham State College *B*
Gordon College *B*
Hampshire College *B*
Harvard College *B*
Harvard University *M, D*
Lasell College *B*
Massachusetts College of Liberal Arts *B*
Merrimack College *B*
Mount Holyoke College *B*
Newbury College *A*
Northeastern University *B, M, D*
Regis College *B*
St. John's Seminary College *B*
Salem State College *B*
Simmons College *B*
Simon's Rock College of Bard *B*
Smith College *B*
Springfield College *B*
Stonehill College *B*
Suffolk University *B*
Tufts University *B*
University of Massachusetts
    Amherst *B, M, D*
    Boston *B, M*
    Dartmouth *B*
    Lowell *B*
Wellesley College *B*
Western New England College *B*
Westfield State College *B*
Wheaton College *B*
Williams College *B*
Worcester State College *B*

Michigan
Adrian College *B, T*
Albion College *B*
Alma College *B, T*
Andrews University *B*

Aquinas College *B, T*
Calvin College *B*
Central Michigan University *B, M*
Concordia College *B, T*
Cornerstone College and Grand Rapids
    Baptist Seminary *B*
Eastern Michigan University *B, M*
Grand Valley State University *B*
Hillsdale College *B*
Hope College *B, T*
Kalamazoo College *B, T*
Kellogg Community College *A*
Lake Michigan College *A*
Lake Superior State University *B*
Lansing Community College *A*
Madonna University *B, T*
Michigan State University *B, M, D*
Mid Michigan Community College *A*
Northern Michigan University *B, T*
Oakland University *B*
Olivet College *B*
Saginaw Valley State University *B*
Spring Arbor College *B*
University of Detroit Mercy *B*
University of Michigan
    Dearborn *B*
    Flint *B*
University of Michigan *B, M, D, T*
Wayne State University *B, M, D*
Western Michigan University *B, M, D*

Minnesota
Augsburg College *B*
Bemidji State University *B*
Carleton College *B*
College of St. Benedict *B*
College of St. Catherine: St. Paul
    Campus *B*
Concordia College: Moorhead *B*
Concordia University: St. Paul *B*
Gustavus Adolphus College *B*
Hamline University *B*
Macalester College *B*
Minnesota State University,
    Mankato *B, M*
Moorhead State University *B*
Ridgewater College: A Community and
    Technical College *A*
St. Cloud State University *B*
St. John's University *B*
St. Mary's University of Minnesota *B*
St. Olaf College *B*
Southwest State University *B*
University of Minnesota
    Duluth *B*
    Morris *B*
    Twin Cities *B, M, D*
University of St. Thomas *B*
Winona State University *B*

Mississippi
Alcorn State University *B*
Hinds Community College *A*
Jackson State University *B, M*
Millsaps College *B, T*
Mississippi College *B, M*
Mississippi Delta Community College *A*
Mississippi State University *B, M, D*
Mississippi Valley State University *B*
Rust College *B*
Tougaloo College *B*
University of Mississippi *B, M*
University of Southern Mississippi *B*

Missouri
Avila College *B*
Central Methodist College *B*
Central Missouri State University *B, M*
College of the Ozarks *B*
Columbia College *B*
Culver-Stockton College *B*
Drury University *B*
East Central College *A*
Evangel University *B*
Lincoln University *B, M*
Lindenwood University *B*

Sociology

Maryville University of Saint Louis B
Missouri Southern State College B, T
Missouri Valley College B
Northwest Missouri State University B
Park University B
Rockhurst University B
St. Louis University B
Southeast Missouri State University B
Southwest Baptist University B
Southwest Missouri State University B
Three Rivers Community College A
Truman State University B
University of Missouri
    Columbia B, M, D
    Kansas City B, M
    St. Louis B, M
Webster University B
Westminster College B

Montana
Carroll College B
Montana State University
    Billings B
    Bozeman B
Rocky Mountain College B, T
University of Great Falls B, T
University of Montana-Missoula B, M

Nebraska
Bellevue University B
Chadron State College B
Creighton University B
Dana College B
Doane College B
Hastings College B
Midland Lutheran College B
Nebraska Wesleyan University B
Peru State College B, T
University of Nebraska
    Kearney B
    Lincoln B, M, D
    Omaha B, M
Wayne State College B, T

Nevada
University of Nevada
    Las Vegas B, M, D
    Reno B, M

New Hampshire
Dartmouth College B
Franklin Pierce College B
Keene State College B
New England College B
Plymouth State College of the University System of New Hampshire B
Rivier College B
St. Anselm College B, T
University of New Hampshire B, M, D

New Jersey
Atlantic Cape Community College A
Bloomfield College B
Brookdale Community College A
Caldwell College B
Centenary College B
College of St. Elizabeth B
Drew University B
Fairleigh Dickinson University B
Felician College B
Georgian Court College B
Gloucester County College A
Kean University B
Middlesex County College A
Montclair State University B
New Jersey City University B
Passaic County Community College A
Princeton University B, M, D
Ramapo College of New Jersey B
Richard Stockton College of New Jersey B
Rider University B
Rowan University B
Rutgers
    The State University of New Jersey: Camden College of Arts and Sciences B
    The State University of New Jersey: Douglass College B
    The State University of New Jersey: Livingston College B
    The State University of New Jersey: New Brunswick Graduate Campus M, D
    The State University of New Jersey: Newark College of Arts and Sciences B
    The State University of New Jersey: Rutgers College B
    The State University of New Jersey: University College Camden B
    The State University of New Jersey: University College New Brunswick B
    The State University of New Jersey: University College Newark B
St. Peter's College B
Salem Community College A
Seton Hall University B, T
The College of New Jersey B
Thomas Edison State College B
William Paterson University of New Jersey B, M

New Mexico
Eastern New Mexico University B
New Mexico Highlands University B
New Mexico State University B, M
San Juan College A
University of New Mexico B, M, D
Western New Mexico University B

New York
Adelphi University B
Adirondack Community College A
Alfred University B
Audrey Cohen College A, B
Bard College B
Barnard College B
City University of New York
    Baruch College B
    Brooklyn College B, M
    City College B, M
    College of Staten Island B
    Graduate School and University Center D
    Hunter College B
    Lehman College B
    Queens College B, M
    Queensborough Community College A
    York College B
Clarkson University B
Colgate University B
College of Mount St. Vincent B
College of New Rochelle B, T
College of St. Rose B
Columbia University
    Columbia College B
    Graduate School M, D
    School of General Studies B
    Teachers College M, D
Cornell University B, M, D
D'Youville College B
Dowling College B
Elmira College B
Eugene Lang College/New School University B
Fordham University B, M, D
Fulton-Montgomery Community College A
Hamilton College B
Hartwick College B
Hobart and William Smith Colleges B
Hofstra University B
Houghton College B
Iona College B
Ithaca College B
Keuka College B
Le Moyne College B
Long Island University
    Brooklyn Campus B, M
    C. W. Post Campus B
    Southampton College B
Manhattan College B
Manhattanville College B
Marymount College B
Marymount Manhattan College B
Mercy College B
Molloy College B
Mount St. Mary College B, T
Nazareth College of Rochester B
New York University B, M, D
Niagara University B
Pace University:
    Pleasantville/Briarcliff B, T
Pace University B, T
Regents College B
Roberts Wesleyan College B
Russell Sage College B
St. Bonaventure University B
St. Francis College B
St. John Fisher College B
St. John's University B, M
St. Lawrence University B
Sarah Lawrence College B
Siena College B, T
Skidmore College B
St. Joseph's College
    St. Joseph's College: Suffolk Campus B
    St. Joseph's College B
State University of New York
    Albany B, M, D
    Binghamton B, M, D
    Buffalo B, M, D
    College at Brockport B
    College at Buffalo B
    College at Cortland B
    College at Fredonia B
    College at Geneseo B, T
    College at Old Westbury B
    College at Oneonta B
    College at Plattsburgh B
    College at Potsdam B
    Institute of Technology at Utica/Rome B
    New Paltz B, M
    Oswego B
    Purchase B
    Stony Brook B, M, D
Syracuse University B, M, D
Touro College B
Union College B
United States Military Academy B
Utica College of Syracuse University B
Vassar College B
Wagner College B
Wells College B

North Carolina
Appalachian State University B, M
Barber-Scotia College B
Belmont Abbey College B
Bennett College B
Catawba College B
Davidson College B
Duke University B, M, D
East Carolina University B, M
Elizabeth City State University B
Elon College B
Fayetteville State University B
Greensboro College B
Guilford College B
High Point University B
Johnson C. Smith University B
Lees-McRae College B
Louisburg College A
Mars Hill College B, T
Meredith College B
Methodist College A, B
North Carolina Agricultural and Technical State University B
North Carolina Central University B, M
North Carolina State University B, M, D
North Carolina Wesleyan College B
Pfeiffer University B
Queens College B
St. Augustine's College B
Salem College B
Shaw University B
University of North Carolina
    Asheville B, T
    Chapel Hill B, M, D
    Charlotte B, M
    Greensboro B, M, T
    Pembroke B
    Wilmington B
Wake Forest University B
Western Carolina University B
Wingate University B
Winston-Salem State University B

North Dakota
Minot State University B, T
North Dakota State University B, M, T
University of North Dakota B, M

Ohio
Antioch College B
Ashland University B
Baldwin-Wallace College B
Bluffton College B
Bowling Green State University B, M, D
Capital University B
Case Western Reserve University B, M, D
Cedarville University B
Central State University B
Cleveland State University B, M
College of Mount St. Joseph B
College of Wooster B
Denison University B
Franciscan University of Steubenville B
Hiram College B
John Carroll University B
Kent State University
    Stark Campus B
Kent State University B, M, D
Kenyon College B
Lake Erie College B
Lourdes College A, B
Miami University
    Middletown Campus A
    Oxford Campus B
Mount Union College B
Mount Vernon Nazarene College B
Muskingum College B
Notre Dame College of Ohio B, T
Oberlin College B
Ohio Dominican College B, T
Ohio Northern University B
Ohio State University
    Columbus Campus B, M, D
Ohio University B, M
Ohio Wesleyan University B
Otterbein College B
Owens Community College
    Toledo A
University of Akron B, M, D
University of Cincinnati B, M, D
University of Dayton B
University of Findlay B
University of Rio Grande A
University of Toledo B, M
Ursuline College B
Walsh University B
Wilberforce University B
Wilmington College B
Wittenberg University B
Wright State University B
Xavier University A, B
Youngstown State University B

Oklahoma
Cameron University B
Carl Albert State College A
Connors State College A
East Central University B
Eastern Oklahoma State College A

Langston University *B*
Northeastern Oklahoma Agricultural and Mechanical College *A*
Northeastern State University *B*
Northwestern Oklahoma State University *B*
Oklahoma Baptist University *B*
Oklahoma City University *B*
Oklahoma State University *B, M, D*
Redlands Community College *A*
Rose State College *A*
Southeastern Oklahoma State University *B*
Southern Nazarene University *B*
Southwestern Oklahoma State University *B*
Tulsa Community College *A*
University of Central Oklahoma *B*
University of Oklahoma *B, M, D*
University of Science and Arts of Oklahoma
University of Tulsa *B*
Western Oklahoma State College *A*

Oregon
Central Oregon Community College *A*
Chemeketa Community College *A*
Eastern Oregon University *B, T*
George Fox University *B*
Lewis & Clark College *B*
Linfield College *B*
Oregon State University *B*
Pacific University *B*
Portland State University *B, M, D*
Reed College *B*
Southern Oregon University *B*
University of Oregon *B, M, D*
University of Portland *B*
Western Oregon University *B*
Willamette University *B*

Pennsylvania
Beaver College *B*
Bloomsburg University of Pennsylvania *B*
Bryn Mawr College *B*
Bucknell University *B*
Cabrini College *B*
California University of Pennsylvania *B*
Carlow College *B*
Cedar Crest College *B*
Chestnut Hill College *A, B*
Cheyney University of Pennsylvania *B*
Clarion University of Pennsylvania *B*
Community College of Allegheny County *A*
Delaware County Community College *A*
Dickinson College *B*
Drexel University *B*
Duquesne University *B, M*
East Stroudsburg University of Pennsylvania *B*
Eastern College *B*
Edinboro University of Pennsylvania *B*
Elizabethtown College *B*
Franklin and Marshall College *B*
Geneva College *B, T*
Gettysburg College *B*
Grove City College *B*
Gwynedd-Mercy College *B*
Haverford College *B, T*
Holy Family College *B*
Immaculata College *B*
Indiana University of Pennsylvania *B, M*
Juniata College *B*
King's College *B*
Kutztown University of Pennsylvania *B*
La Roche College *B*
La Salle University *B*
Lafayette College *B*
Lebanon Valley College of Pennsylvania *B*
Lehigh University *B, M*
Lincoln University *B*
Lock Haven University of Pennsylvania *B*
Lycoming College *B*
Mansfield University of Pennsylvania *B, T*
Mercyhurst College *B*
Messiah College *B*
Millersville University of Pennsylvania *B, T*
Moravian College *B*
Penn State
    Harrisburg *B*
    Shenango *A*
    University Park *A, B, M, D*
Rosemont College *B*
St. Francis College *B*
St. Joseph's University *B*
St. Vincent College *B*
Seton Hill College *B*
Shippensburg University of Pennsylvania *B*
Slippery Rock University of Pennsylvania *B, T*
Susquehanna University *B*
Temple University *B, M, D*
Thiel College *B*
University of Pennsylvania *A, B, M, D*
University of Pittsburgh Johnstown *B*
University of Pittsburgh *B, M, D*
University of Scranton *A, B*
Ursinus College *B*
Villanova University *B*
Washington and Jefferson College *B*
Waynesburg College *B*
West Chester University of Pennsylvania *B*
Westminster College *B, T*
Widener University *B*
Wilkes University *B*
Wilson College *B*
York College of Pennsylvania *B*

Puerto Rico
Inter American University of Puerto Rico
    Metropolitan Campus *B*
    San German Campus *B*
Pontifical Catholic University of Puerto Rico *B*
Turabo University *B*
University of Puerto Rico
    Cayey University College *B*
    Mayaguez Campus *B*
    Rio Piedras Campus *B, M*

Rhode Island
Brown University *B, M, D*
Providence College *B*
Rhode Island College *B*
Salve Regina University *B*
University of Rhode Island *B*

South Carolina
Charleston Southern University *B*
Claflin University *B*
Clemson University *B, M*
Coastal Carolina University *B*
Coker College *B*
College of Charleston *B, T*
Converse College *B*
Francis Marion University *B*
Furman University *B, T*
Lander University *B*
Morris College *B*
Newberry College *B*
Presbyterian College *B*
South Carolina State University *B*
University of South Carolina
    Aiken *B*
    Spartanburg *B*
University of South Carolina *B, M, D*
Voorhees College *B*
Winthrop University *B*
Wofford College *B*

South Dakota
Augustana College *B, T*
Black Hills State University *B*
Dakota Wesleyan University *B*
Northern State University *B*
South Dakota State University *B, M, D, T*
University of South Dakota *B, M*

Tennessee
Austin Peay State University *B*
Belmont University *B, T*
Carson-Newman College *B*
Columbia State Community College *A*
East Tennessee State University *B, M*
Fisk University *B, M*
Hiwassee College *A*
Lambuth University *B*
Lane College *B*
LeMoyne-Owen College *B*
Lee University *B*
Maryville College *B*
Middle Tennessee State University *B, M*
Milligan College *B*
Rhodes College *B, T*
Roane State Community College *A*
Tennessee State University *B*
Tennessee Technological University *B*
Trevecca Nazarene University *B*
Union University *B, T*
University of Memphis *B, M*
University of Tennessee
    Knoxville *B, M, D*
    Martin *B*
Vanderbilt University *B, M, D*

Texas
Abilene Christian University *B, T*
Angelo State University *B*
Austin College *B*
Baylor University *B, M, D*
Brazosport College *A*
Coastal Bend College *A*
College of the Mainland *A*
Concordia University at Austin *T*
Dallas Baptist University *B*
Del Mar College *A*
East Texas Baptist University *B*
El Paso Community College *A*
Galveston College *A*
Grayson County College *A*
Hardin-Simmons University *B*
Houston Baptist University *B*
Howard Payne University *B*
Huston-Tillotson College *B*
Jarvis Christian College *B*
Kilgore College *A*
Lamar State College at Orange *A*
Lamar University *B*
Lon Morris College *A*
McMurry University *B*
Midland College *A*
Midwestern State University *B*
Northeast Texas Community College *A*
Our Lady of the Lake University of San Antonio *B*
Palo Alto College *A*
Panola College *A*
Paris Junior College *A*
Prairie View A&M University *B, M*
Rice University *B*
St. Edward's University *B, T*
St. Mary's University *B, T*
St. Philip's College *A*
Sam Houston State University *B, M*
San Jacinto College
    North *A*
Southern Methodist University *B*
Southwest Texas State University *B, M, T*
Southwestern University *B*
Stephen F. Austin State University *B, T*
Tarleton State University *B*
Texas A&M International University *B, M*
Texas A&M University
    Commerce *B, M*
    Corpus Christi *B*
    Kingsville *B, M*
Texas A&M University *B, M, D*
Texas Christian University *B*
Texas College *B*
Texas Southern University *B, M*
Texas Tech University *B, M*
Texas Woman's University *B, M, D, T*
Trinity University *B*
Trinity Valley Community College *A*
Tyler Junior College *A*
University of Houston
    Clear Lake *B, M*
University of Houston *B, M*
University of Mary Hardin-Baylor *B, T*
University of North Texas *B, M, D*
University of Texas
    Arlington *B, M, T*
    Austin *B, M, D*
    Brownsville *B*
    Dallas *B*
    El Paso *B, M*
    Pan American *B, M*
    San Antonio *B, M*
    Tyler *B*
    of the Permian Basin *B*
University of the Incarnate Word *B*
Weatherford College *A*
West Texas A&M University *B*
Western Texas College *A*
Wharton County Junior College *A*
Wiley College *B*

Utah
Brigham Young University *B, M, D*
Dixie State College of Utah *A*
Snow College *A*
Southern Utah University *B*
University of Utah *B, M, D*
Utah State University *B, M, D*
Weber State University *B*
Westminster College *B*

Vermont
Castleton State College *B*
Johnson State College *B*
Marlboro College *B*
Middlebury College *B*
St. Michael's College *B*
University of Vermont *B*

Virginia
Bluefield College *B*
Bridgewater College *B*
Christopher Newport University *B*
College of William and Mary *B*
Eastern Mennonite University *B*
Emory & Henry College *B*
George Mason University *B, M*
Hampton University *B*
Hollins University *B*
James Madison University *B*
Longwood College *B, M, T*
Lynchburg College *B*
Mary Baldwin College *B*
Mary Washington College *B*
Norfolk State University *B, M*
Old Dominion University *B, M*
Radford University *B*
Randolph-Macon College *B*
Randolph-Macon Woman's College *B*
Roanoke College *B, T*
St. Paul's College *B*
Shenandoah University *B*
Sweet Briar College *B*
University of Richmond *B*
University of Virginia's College at Wise *B, T*
University of Virginia *B, M, D*
Virginia Commonwealth University *C, B, M*
Virginia Polytechnic Institute and State University *B, M, D*
Virginia State University *B*
Virginia Union University *B*
Virginia Wesleyan College *B*
Washington and Lee University *B*

Sociology

Washington
Central Washington University *B*
Centralia College *A*
City University *B*
Eastern Washington University *B, T*
Everett Community College *A*
Gonzaga University *B*
Heritage College *B*
Highline Community College *A*
Lower Columbia College *A*
Pacific Lutheran University *B*
Seattle Pacific University *B, T*
Seattle University *B*
University of Puget Sound *B, T*
University of Washington *B, M, D*
Walla Walla College *B*
Washington State University *B, M, D*
Western Washington University *B, T*
Whitman College *B*
Whitworth College *B, T*

West Virginia
Concord College *B*
Davis and Elkins College *B*
Fairmont State College *B*
Marshall University *B, M*
Potomac State College of West Virginia University *A*
Shepherd College *B*
West Liberty State College *B*
West Virginia State College *B*
West Virginia University *B, M*
West Virginia Wesleyan College *B*

Wisconsin
Beloit College *B*
Cardinal Stritch University *B*
Carroll College *B*
Carthage College *B, T*
Lakeland College *B*
Marquette University *B, T*
Northland College *B, T*
Ripon College *B*
St. Norbert College *B, T*
University of Wisconsin
 Eau Claire *B*
 La Crosse *B, T*
 Madison *B, M, D*
 Milwaukee *B, M*
 Oshkosh *B*
 Parkside *B*
 Platteville *B*
 River Falls *B, T*
 Stevens Point *B, T*
 Superior *B*
 Whitewater *B, T*
Viterbo University *B*

Wyoming
Casper College *A*
Eastern Wyoming College *A*
Laramie County Community College *A*
Northwest College *A*
Sheridan College *A*
University of Wyoming *B, M*
Western Wyoming Community College *A*

Software engineering

Arizona
Phoenix College *A*
University of Advancing Computer Technology *A, B*

Arkansas
Westark College *C*

California
California State University
 Hayward *B*
Cogswell Polytechnical College *B*
Foothill College *C, A*
San Jose City College *C, A*
Santa Clara University *C, M*

Colorado
Colorado Technical University *B, M, D*
National Technological University *M*
Technical Trades Institute *A*

District of Columbia
Catholic University of America *M*
George Washington University *M*

Florida
Embry-Riddle Aeronautical University *B*
Florida Institute of Technology *M*
Florida State University *M*
Tallahassee Community College *A*

Georgia
Mercer University *M*
Southern Polytechnic State University *M*

Illinois
De Paul University *M*

Indiana
Indiana University--Purdue University
Indiana University-Purdue University Fort Wayne *C*

Iowa
University of Iowa *M*

Maryland
Harford Community College *C*
University of Maryland
 University College *M*

Massachusetts
Northeastern University *M*

Michigan
Andrews University *M*
Oakland University *M*

Minnesota
Lake Superior College: A Community and Technical College *C*
St. Paul Technical College *C, A*
University of St. Thomas *M*

Montana
Carroll College *B*
Montana Tech of the University of Montana *B*

Nevada
University of Nevada
 Las Vegas *B*

New Jersey
Essex County College *C*
Monmouth University *M*
Stevens Institute of Technology *B, M*

New York
College of Aeronautics *A*
Polytechnic University *C*
Rochester Institute of Technology *B*
State University of New York
 Buffalo *M, D*
Westchester Business Institute *C, A*

Ohio
Bowling Green State University *B*
Miami-Jacobs College *C, A*
Shawnee State University *B*
Stark State College of Technology *A*

Oklahoma
Oklahoma Baptist University *B*

Oregon
Oregon Graduate Institute *M, D*
Oregon Institute of Technology *A, B*
Portland Community College *C, A*
Portland State University *M*
University of Oregon *B*

Pennsylvania
Carnegie Mellon University *M*
Drexel University *M*
Gannon University *B*

South Dakota
South Dakota School of Mines and Technology *B*

Texas
Southern Methodist University *M*
University of Houston
 Clear Lake *M*

Vermont
Vermont Technical College *A, B*

Virginia
J. Sargeant Reynolds Community College *C*

Washington
Grays Harbor College *C*
Henry Cogswell College *C*
North Seattle Community College *C, A*
Seattle University *M*
Walla Walla Community College *C*

Wisconsin
Carroll College *B*
Milwaukee School of Engineering *B*

Soil sciences

Alabama
Alabama Agricultural and Mechanical University *B, M, D, T*
Auburn University *B, M, D*
Tuskegee University *B, M*

Alaska
University of Alaska
 Fairbanks *B*

Arizona
Prescott College *B, M*
University of Arizona *B, M, D*

California
California Polytechnic State University:
 San Luis Obispo *B*
California State Polytechnic University:
 Pomona *B*
Merced College *A*
Modesto Junior College *A*
San Joaquin Delta College *A*
University of California
 Berkeley *B*
 Davis *B, M, D*
 Riverside *M, D*
Ventura College *A*
West Hills Community College *A*

Colorado
Colorado Mountain College
 Timberline Campus *A*

Delaware
Delaware State University *B*
University of Delaware *B, M, D*

Florida
University of Florida *B, M, D*

Georgia
University of Georgia *B*

Hawaii
University of Hawaii
 Hilo *B*
 Manoa *B, M, D*

Idaho
University of Idaho *B, M, D*

Illinois
University of Illinois
 Urbana-Champaign *B*

Iowa
Iowa State University *M, D*

Kentucky
University of Kentucky *D*

Maine
Southern Maine Technical College *C, A*
University of Maine *B*

Minnesota
Fond Du Lac Tribal and Community College *A*
Ridgewater College: A Community and Technical College *C*
University of Minnesota
 Crookston *A, B*
 Twin Cities *M, D*

Missouri
Crowder College *A*

Nebraska
University of Nebraska
 Lincoln *B*

New Hampshire
Antioch New England Graduate School *M*
University of New Hampshire *B, M*

New Jersey
Rutgers
 The State University of New Jersey:
 Cook College *B*

New Mexico
New Mexico State University *B*

New York
Cornell University *B*
State University of New York
 College of Agriculture and Technology at Cobleskill *A*
 College of Environmental Science and Forestry *M, D*

North Carolina
North Carolina State University *B, M, D*

North Dakota
North Dakota State University *B, M, D*

Ohio
Ohio State University
 Agricultural Technical Institute *A*
 Columbus Campus *B, D*

Oklahoma
Eastern Oklahoma State College *A*
Oklahoma State University *B, M, D*

Oregon
Eastern Oregon University *B*
Oregon State University *M, D*

Pennsylvania
Penn State
 Lehigh Valley *B*
 University Park *B, M, D*

Puerto Rico
University of Puerto Rico
 Mayaguez Campus *M*

South Carolina
Clemson University *B*

Tennessee
Hiwassee College *A*
Middle Tennessee State University *B*
Tennessee Technological University *B*
University of Tennessee
 Knoxville *B, M, D*

Texas
Prairie View A&M University *M*
Southwest Texas State University *B*
Tarleton State University *B*
Texas A&M University
 Commerce *B*
 Kingsville *M*
Texas A&M University *B, M, D*
Texas Tech University *M*

Utah
Brigham Young University *B, M*
Dixie State College of Utah *A*

Utah State University B, M, D
Vermont
University of Vermont B, M, D
Virginia
Mountain Empire Community College A
Virginia Polytechnic Institute and State
 University B, M, D
Washington
Highline Community College A
Spokane Community College A
Washington State University B, M, D
Wisconsin
University of Wisconsin
 Madison B, M
 River Falls B
 Stevens Point B
Wyoming
Northwest College A
University of Wyoming M, D

Solid-state/low-temperature physics

Massachusetts
Tufts University M, D
Worcester Polytechnic Institute B, M
New Jersey
Stevens Institute of Technology M, D
New York
Columbia University
 Graduate School M, D
State University of New York
 Albany M, D
Texas
University of North Texas M, D
Wisconsin
University of Wisconsin
 Madison M, D

South Asian languages

Illinois
University of Chicago B
Massachusetts
Harvard College B
Minnesota
University of Minnesota
 Twin Cities M, D
New Hampshire
Dartmouth College B
New York
Columbia University
 Graduate School M, D
Washington
University of Washington B
Wisconsin
University of Wisconsin
 Madison B, M, D

South Asian studies

California
University of California
 Berkeley B, M, D
 Santa Cruz B
Illinois
University of Chicago M
Massachusetts
Harvard College B

Michigan
Oakland University B
University of Michigan B
Minnesota
Hamline University B
University of Minnesota
 Twin Cities M, D
Missouri
University of Missouri
 Columbia B
New York
Columbia University
 Graduate School M, D
Sarah Lawrence College B
Ohio
College of Wooster B
Pennsylvania
University of Pennsylvania B, M, D
Rhode Island
Brown University B
Vermont
Marlboro College B
Virginia
Mary Baldwin College B
Washington
University of Washington B, M
Wisconsin
University of Wisconsin
 Madison B, M

Southeast Asian studies

California
University of California
 Berkeley B, M, D
 Los Angeles B, D
 Santa Cruz B
Massachusetts
Hampshire College B
Harvard College B
Michigan
University of Michigan B, M
Minnesota
Hamline University B
Ohio
Ohio State University
 Columbus Campus B, M
Ohio University M
Vermont
Marlboro College B
Virginia
Mary Baldwin College B
Washington
University of Washington B

Spanish

Alabama
Alabama State University B
Auburn University B, M
Birmingham-Southern College B, T
Huntingdon College B
Jacksonville State University B
Oakwood College B
Samford University B
Spring Hill College B, T
University of Alabama
 Birmingham B
 Huntsville B
University of Alabama B, M
University of Mobile B, T
University of Montevallo B

University of South Alabama B
Arizona
Arizona State University B, M, D
Arizona Western College A
Cochise College A
Northern Arizona University B, T
Prescott College B, M
University of Arizona B, M, D
Arkansas
Arkansas State University B
Harding University B
Henderson State University B
Hendrix College B
Lyon College B
Ouachita Baptist University B
Southern Arkansas University B
University of Arkansas
 Little Rock B
University of Arkansas B, M
University of Central Arkansas B
California
Allan Hancock College A
Azusa Pacific University B
Bakersfield College A
Biola University B
Cabrillo College A
California Lutheran University B
California State Polytechnic University:
 Pomona B
California State University
 Bakersfield B
 Chico B
 Dominguez Hills B
 Fresno B, M
 Fullerton B, M
 Hayward B
 Long Beach B, M
 Los Angeles B, M
 Monterey Bay B
 Northridge B, M
 Sacramento B, M
 San Marcos B
 Stanislaus B
Canada College A
Cerritos Community College A
Chabot College A
Chaffey Community College A
Chapman University B
Citrus College A
Claremont McKenna College B
College of San Mateo A
College of the Desert A
College of the Siskiyous A
Compton Community College A
Crafton Hills College A
Cypress College A
De Anza College A
Foothill College A
Fresno City College A
Fresno Pacific University B
Gavilan Community College A
Glendale Community College A
Golden West College A
Grossmont Community College C, A
Holy Names College B
Humboldt State University B
Imperial Valley College A
Irvine Valley College A
La Sierra University B
Lake Tahoe Community College A
Long Beach City College C, A
Los Angeles Mission College A
Los Angeles Southwest College A
Los Angeles Valley College A
Loyola Marymount University B
Mendocino College A
Merced College A
Merritt College A
Mills College B
MiraCosta College A
Modesto Junior College A
Monterey Institute of International
 Studies C

Mount St. Mary's College B
Occidental College B
Ohlone College A
Orange Coast College A
Pacific Union College B
Pepperdine University B
Pitzer College B
Point Loma Nazarene University C, B
Pomona College B
Riverside Community College A
St. John's Seminary College B
St. Mary's College of California B
San Diego City College A
San Diego Mesa College A
San Diego Miramar College A
San Diego State University B, M
San Francisco State University B, M
San Joaquin Delta College A
San Jose State University B, M
Santa Barbara City College A
Santa Clara University B
Santa Monica College A
Scripps College B
Skyline College A
Solano Community College A
Sonoma State University B
Southwestern College A
Stanford University B, M, D
University of California
 Berkeley B, D
 Davis B, M, D
 Irvine B, M, D
 Los Angeles B, M
 Riverside B, M, D
 San Diego B, M
 Santa Barbara B, M
 Santa Cruz B, D
University of La Verne B
University of Redlands B
University of San Diego B
University of San Francisco B
University of Southern
 California B, M, D
University of the Pacific B
Vanguard University of Southern
 California B
Ventura College A
West Los Angeles College C, A
Westmont College B
Whittier College B
Colorado
Adams State College B
Colorado College B
Colorado State University B
Fort Lewis College B
Metropolitan State College of
 Denver B, T
Red Rocks Community College A
Regis University B
Trinidad State Junior College A
University of Colorado
 Boulder B, M, D
 Colorado Springs B
 Denver B
University of Denver B
University of Northern Colorado B, T
University of Southern Colorado B, T
Western State College of Colorado B
Connecticut
Albertus Magnus College B
Central Connecticut State
 University B, M
Connecticut College B
Eastern Connecticut State University B
Fairfield University B
Quinnipiac University B
Sacred Heart University A, B
St. Joseph College B, T
Southern Connecticut State University B
Trinity College B
University of Connecticut B, M, D
University of Hartford B
Wesleyan University B
Western Connecticut State University B

Yale University *B, M, D*

Delaware
Delaware State University *B*
University of Delaware *B, M, T*

District of Columbia
American University *B, M*
Catholic University of
   America *B, M, D, T*
Gallaudet University *B*
George Washington University *B*
Georgetown University *B, M, D*
Howard University *B, M, D*
Trinity College *B*
University of the District of Columbia *B*

Florida
Barry University *B*
Eckerd College *B*
Flagler College *B*
Florida Agricultural and Mechanical
   University *B*
Florida Atlantic University *B, M*
Florida Gulf Coast University *B*
Florida International University *B, M, D*
Florida Southern College *B*
Florida State University *B, M, D*
Jacksonville University *B*
Manatee Community College *A*
Miami-Dade Community College *A*
New College of the University of South
   Florida *B*
Rollins College *B*
Stetson University *B*
University of Central Florida *B, M*
University of Florida *B, M*
University of Miami *B, M, D*
University of North Florida *B*
University of South Florida *B, M*
University of Tampa *A, B*

Georgia
Agnes Scott College *B*
Albany State University *B*
Armstrong Atlantic State University *B, T*
Augusta State University *B*
Berry College *B, T*
Clark Atlanta University *B*
Clayton College and State University *A*
Emory University *B, D*
Georgia College and State
   University *B, T*
Georgia Southern University *B*
Georgia Southwestern State University *B*
Georgia State University *B, M*
Kennesaw State University *B*
LaGrange College *B*
Mercer University *B*
Morehouse College *B*
Morris Brown College *B*
North Georgia College & State
   University *B*
Oxford College of Emory University *B*
Piedmont College *B*
Shorter College *B, T*
South Georgia College *A*
Spelman College *B*
State University of West Georgia *B*
University of Georgia *B, M*
Valdosta State University *B*
Wesleyan College *B*
Young Harris College *A*

Hawaii
University of Hawaii
   Manoa *B, M*

Idaho
Albertson College of Idaho *B*
Boise State University *B*
Idaho State University *A, B*
Ricks College *A*
University of Idaho *B, M*

Illinois
Augustana College *B, T*
Benedictine University *B, T*
Blackburn College *B*
Bradley University *B, T*
Chicago State University *B*
City Colleges of Chicago
   Harold Washington College *A*
De Paul University *B*
Dominican University *B*
Elmhurst College *B, T*
Greenville College *B*
Illinois College *B*
Illinois State University *B, T*
Illinois Wesleyan University *B*
John Wood Community College *A*
Kishwaukee College *A*
Knox College *B*
Lake Forest College *B*
Loyola University of Chicago *B, M*
MacMurray College *B*
Millikin University *B, T*
Monmouth College *B, T*
North Central College *B, T*
North Park University *B*
Northeastern Illinois University *B*
Northern Illinois University *B, M, T*
Northwestern University *B, M, D*
Olivet Nazarene University *B, T*
Parkland College *A*
Principia College *B, T*
Rend Lake College *A*
Richland Community College *A*
Rockford College *B*
Roosevelt University *B, M*
St. Xavier University *B*
Southern Illinois University
   Carbondale *B*
Springfield College in Illinois *A*
Trinity Christian College *B, T*
Triton College *A*
University of Chicago *B*
University of Illinois
   Chicago *B, D*
   Urbana-Champaign *B, M, D*
Western Illinois University *B*
Wheaton College *B*

Indiana
Anderson University *B*
Ball State University *B, M, T*
Butler University *B*
DePauw University *B*
Earlham College *B*
Franklin College *B*
Goshen College *B*
Grace College *B*
Hanover College *B*
Indiana State University *B, M*
Indiana University
   Bloomington *B, M, D*
   Northwest *B*
   South Bend *A, B*
Indiana University--Purdue University
   Indiana University-Purdue
      University Fort Wayne *A, B*
   Indiana University-Purdue
      University Indianapolis *B*
Indiana Wesleyan University *B*
Manchester College *B, T*
Marian College *B, T*
Purdue University
   Calumet *B*
Saint Mary's College *B, T*
St. Mary-of-the-Woods College *B*
Taylor University *B*
University of Evansville *B*
University of Indianapolis *B*
University of Notre Dame *B, M*
University of Southern Indiana *B*
Valparaiso University *B, T*
Vincennes University *A*
Wabash College *B*

Iowa
Briar Cliff College *B*
Buena Vista University *B, T*
Central College *B*
Clarke College *B, T*
Coe College *B*
Cornell College *B, T*
Dordt College *B*
Drake University *B*
Graceland University *B, T*
Grinnell College *B*
Iowa State University *B*
Loras College *B*
Luther College *B*
Maharishi University of Management *A*
Marshalltown Community College *A*
Marycrest International University *B*
Morningside College *B*
Northwestern College *B, T*
St. Ambrose University *B, T*
Simpson College *B*
University of Iowa *B, M, D, T*
University of Northern Iowa *B, M*
Waldorf College *A*
Wartburg College *B, T*

Kansas
Baker University *B, T*
Benedictine College *B, T*
Bethel College *B, T*
Butler County Community College *A*
Independence Community College *A*
Kansas Wesleyan University *B, T*
McPherson College *B, T*
MidAmerica Nazarene University *B*
Pittsburg State University *B, T*
Pratt Community College *A*
Southwestern College *B*
University of Kansas *B, M, D*
Washburn University of Topeka *B*
Wichita State University *B, M*

Kentucky
Asbury College *B, T*
Berea College *B, T*
Brescia University *B*
Centre College *B*
Eastern Kentucky University *B*
Georgetown College *B, T*
Kentucky Wesleyan College *B*
Morehead State University *B*
Murray State University *B, T*
Northern Kentucky University *B*
Thomas More College *A*
Transylvania University *B*
University of Kentucky *B, M, D*
University of Louisville *B, M*
Western Kentucky University *B, M, T*

Louisiana
Centenary College of Louisiana *B, T*
Dillard University *B*
Louisiana State University
   Shreveport *B*
Louisiana State University and
   Agricultural and Mechanical
   College *B, M*
Louisiana Tech University *B*
Loyola University New Orleans *B*
McNeese State University *B*
Southeastern Louisiana University *B*
Southern University
   New Orleans *B*
Southern University and Agricultural and
   Mechanical College *B*
Tulane University *B, M, D*
University of Louisiana at Monroe *B*
University of New Orleans *B*
Xavier University of Louisiana *B*

Maine
Bates College *B*
Bowdoin College *B*
Colby College *B*
University of Maine *B*

Maryland
Allegany College *A*
College of Notre Dame of Maryland *B*
Community College of Baltimore County
   Catonsville *A*
Frostburg State University *T*
Goucher College *B*
Hood College *B, T*
Johns Hopkins University *B, D*
Loyola College in Maryland *B*
Mount St. Mary's College *B*
Salisbury State University *B, T*
Towson University *B, T*
University of Maryland
   Baltimore County *B*
   College Park *B, M, D*
Washington College *B, T*
Western Maryland College *B*

Massachusetts
Amherst College *B*
Anna Maria College *B*
Assumption College *B*
Atlantic Union College *B*
Boston College *B, M, D*
Boston University *B, M, D*
Brandeis University *B, M, D*
Bridgewater State College *B, T*
Clark University *B*
College of the Holy Cross *B*
Eastern Nazarene College *B*
Elms College *B, M, T*
Emmanuel College *B*
Framingham State College *B*
Gordon College *B*
Harvard College *B*
Harvard University *D*
Mount Holyoke College *B*
Northeastern University *B*
Regis College *B*
Simmons College *B, M*
Simon's Rock College of Bard *B*
Smith College *B*
Tufts University *B*
University of Massachusetts
   Amherst *B, M, D*
   Boston *B*
   Dartmouth *B*
Wellesley College *B*
Wheaton College *B*
Williams College *B*
Worcester State College *B*

Michigan
Adrian College *A, B, T*
Albion College *B, T*
Alma College *B, T*
Andrews University *B*
Aquinas College *B, T*
Calvin College *B, T*
Central Michigan University *B*
Eastern Michigan University *B, M*
Grand Valley State University *B*
Hillsdale College *B*
Hope College *B, T*
Kalamazoo College *B, T*
Lansing Community College *A*
Madonna University *B, T*
Michigan State University *B, M, D*
Michigan Technological University *C*
Northern Michigan University *B, T*
Oakland University *B, T*
Saginaw Valley State University *B*
Siena Heights University *B*
Spring Arbor College *B*
University of Michigan
   Dearborn *B*
   Flint *B, T*
University of Michigan *B, M, D*
Wayne State University *B, M*
Western Michigan University *B, M, T*

Minnesota
Augsburg College *B*
Bemidji State University *B*
Bethel College *B*
Carleton College *B*
College of St. Benedict *B*
College of St. Catherine: St. Paul
   Campus *B*
Concordia College: Moorhead *B, T*
Gustavus Adolphus College *B*

Hamline University *B*
Macalester College *B, T*
Minnesota State University,
 Mankato *B, M*
Moorhead State University *B*
Northland Community & Technical
 College *A*
Northwestern College *B*
St. Cloud State University *B*
St. John's University *B*
St. Mary's University of Minnesota *B*
St. Olaf College *B, T*
Southwest State University *B*
University of Minnesota
 Duluth *B*
 Morris *B*
 Twin Cities *B, M, D*
University of St. Thomas *B*
Winona State University *B*

Mississippi
Blue Mountain College *B*
Millsaps College *B, T*
Mississippi College *B*
Mississippi University for Women *B, T*
University of Mississippi *B, M, T*

Missouri
Central Methodist College *B*
Central Missouri State University *B, T*
College of the Ozarks *B*
Crowder College *A*
Drury University *B, T*
East Central College *A*
Evangel University *B*
Lindenwood University *B*
Missouri Southern State College *B*
Missouri Western State College *B, T*
Northwest Missouri State University *B*
Rockhurst University *B*
St. Louis University *B, M*
Southeast Missouri State University *B*
Southwest Baptist University *B, T*
Southwest Missouri State University *B*
Truman State University *B*
University of Missouri
 Columbia *B, M*
 Kansas City *B*
 St. Louis *B*
Washington University *B, M, D*
Webster University *B*
Westminster College *B*
William Jewell College *B*
William Woods University *B*

Montana
Carroll College *B, T*
Montana State University
 Billings *B*
University of Montana-Missoula *B, M*

Nebraska
Bellevue University *B*
Concordia University *B, T*
Creighton University *B*
Dana College *B*
Doane College *B*
Hastings College *B*
Midland Lutheran College *B*
Nebraska Wesleyan University *B*
Union College *B*
University of Nebraska
 Kearney *B, M, T*
 Lincoln *B*
 Omaha *B*
Wayne State College *B, T*

Nevada
University of Nevada
 Las Vegas *B, M*
 Reno *B*

New Hampshire
Dartmouth College *B*
Keene State College *B*
Plymouth State College of the University
 System of New Hampshire *B*

Rivier College *B, M, T*
St. Anselm College *B*
University of New Hampshire *B, M*

New Jersey
Bloomfield College *B*
Caldwell College *B*
College of St. Elizabeth *B, T*
Drew University *B*
Fairleigh Dickinson University *B*
Georgian Court College *B, T*
Kean University *B*
Montclair State University *B, M, T*
New Jersey City University *B*
Richard Stockton College of New
 Jersey *B*
Rider University *B*
Rowan University *B*
Rutgers
 The State University of New Jersey:
  Camden College of Arts and
  Sciences *B, T*
 The State University of New Jersey:
  Douglass College *B, T*
 The State University of New Jersey:
  Livingston College *B, T*
 The State University of New Jersey:
  New Brunswick Graduate
  Campus *M, D, T*
 The State University of New Jersey:
  Newark College of Arts and
  Sciences *B, T*
 The State University of New Jersey:
  Rutgers College *B, T*
 The State University of New Jersey:
  University College Camden *B, T*
 The State University of New Jersey:
  University College New
  Brunswick *B, T*
 The State University of New Jersey:
  University College Newark *T*
St. Peter's College *B*
Seton Hall University *B, T*
The College of New Jersey *B*
William Paterson University of New
 Jersey *B*

New Mexico
Eastern New Mexico University *B*
New Mexico Highlands University *B*
New Mexico Junior College *A*
New Mexico State University *M*
University of New Mexico *B, M, D*
Western New Mexico University *B*

New York
Adelphi University *B*
Alfred University *B*
Bard College *B*
Barnard College *B*
Canisius College *B*
City University of New York
 Baruch College *B*
 Brooklyn College *B, M*
 City College *B, T*
 College of Staten Island *B*
 Graduate School and University
  Center *D*
 Hunter College *B, M*
 Lehman College *B*
 Queens College *B, M*
 York College *B*
Colgate University *B*
College of Mount St. Vincent *B, T*
College of New Rochelle *B, T*
College of St. Rose *B*
Columbia University
 Columbia College *B*
 Graduate School *M, D*
 School of General Studies *B*
Cornell University *B, T*
Daemen College *B, T*
Dominican College of Blauvelt *B*
Elmira College *B, T*
Fordham University *B, M*
Hamilton College *B*

Hartwick College *B, T*
Hobart and William Smith Colleges *B*
Hofstra University *B*
Houghton College *B*
Iona College *B, M*
Ithaca College *B, T*
Le Moyne College *B*
Long Island University
 C. W. Post Campus *B, M*
Manhattan College *B*
Manhattanville College *B*
Marist College *B, T*
Marymount College *B, T*
Mercy College *B*
Molloy College *B*
Nazareth College of Rochester *B*
New York University *B, M, D*
Niagara University *B*
Orange County Community College *A*
Pace University:
 Pleasantville/Briarcliff *C, T*
Pace University *C, B, T*
Russell Sage College *B, T*
St. Bonaventure University *B*
St. John Fisher College *B*
St. John's University *B, M*
St. Lawrence University *B, T*
St. Thomas Aquinas College *B*
Sarah Lawrence College *B*
Siena College *B, T*
Skidmore College *B*
State University of New York
 Albany *B, M, D*
 Binghamton *B, M*
 Buffalo *B, M, D*
 College at Brockport *B, T*
 College at Buffalo *B*
 College at Cortland *B*
 College at Fredonia *B, T*
 College at Geneseo *B, T*
 College at Old Westbury *C, B, T*
 College at Oneonta *B*
 College at Plattsburgh *B*
 College at Potsdam *B, T*
 New Paltz *B, T*
 Oswego *B*
 Stony Brook *B, M, D, T*
Syracuse University *B, M, D*
United States Military Academy *B*
University of Rochester *B, M*
Wagner College *B*
Wells College *B*

North Carolina
Appalachian State University *B*
Barton College *B, T*
Campbell University *B*
Catawba College *B*
Davidson College *B*
Duke University *B, M, D*
East Carolina University *B*
Elon College *B*
Gardner-Webb University *B*
Greensboro College *B, T*
Guilford College *B, T*
High Point University *B*
Lenoir-Rhyne College *B, T*
Mars Hill College *B*
Meredith College *B*
Methodist College *A, B, T*
North Carolina Central University *B*
North Carolina State University *B*
Peace College *B*
Queens College *B*
St. Augustine's College *B*
Salem College *B*
University of North Carolina
 Asheville *B, T*
 Chapel Hill *T*
 Charlotte *B*
 Greensboro *B, T*
 Wilmington *B, T*
Wake Forest University *B*
Western Carolina University *B*
Wingate University *B*

Winston-Salem State University *B*

North Dakota
Dickinson State University *B, T*
Minot State University *B, T*
North Dakota State University *B*
University of North Dakota *B, T*
Valley City State University *B*

Ohio
Ashland University *B*
Baldwin-Wallace College *B, T*
Bluffton College *B*
Bowling Green State University *B, M*
Capital University *B*
Case Western Reserve University *B*
Cedarville College *B, T*
Cleveland State University *B, M*
College of Wooster *B*
Denison University *B*
Franciscan University of Steubenville *B*
Heidelberg College *B*
Hiram College *B, T*
John Carroll University *B*
Kent State University
 Stark Campus
Kent State University *B, M*
Kenyon College *B*
Lake Erie College *B*
Lourdes College *A*
Malone College *B*
Marietta College *B*
Miami University
 Middletown Campus *A*
 Oxford Campus *B, M, T*
Mount Union College *B*
Mount Vernon Nazarene College *B*
Muskingum College *B*
Notre Dame College of Ohio *B, T*
Oberlin College *B*
Ohio Dominican College *B*
Ohio Northern University *B*
Ohio State University
 Columbus Campus *B, M, D*
Ohio University *B, M*
Ohio Wesleyan University *B*
Otterbein College *B*
Owens Community College
 Toledo *A*
University of Akron *B, M*
University of Cincinnati *B, M, D, T*
University of Dayton *B*
University of Findlay *B, T*
University of Toledo *B, M*
Walsh University *B*
Wilmington College *B*
Wittenberg University *B*
Wright State University *B*
Xavier University *A, B*
Youngstown State University *B*

Oklahoma
Northeastern State University *B*
Oklahoma Baptist University *B, T*
Oklahoma Christian University of
 Science and Arts *B*
Oklahoma City University *B*
Oklahoma State University *B*
Oral Roberts University *B*
Southern Nazarene University *B*
Tulsa Community College *A*
University of Central Oklahoma *B*
University of Oklahoma *B, M, D*
University of Tulsa *B*
Western Oklahoma State College *A*

Oregon
George Fox University *B*
Lewis & Clark College *B*
Linfield College *B*
Oregon State University *B*
Pacific University *B*
Portland State University *B, M*
Reed College *B*
Southern Oregon University *B*
University of Oregon *B, M*

Spanish

University of Portland B, T
Western Oregon University B, T
Willamette University B

Pennsylvania
Albright College B, T
Allegheny College B
Allentown College of St. Francis de Sales B
Beaver College B
Bloomsburg University of Pennsylvania B, T
Bryn Mawr College B
Bucknell University B
Cabrini College B
California University of Pennsylvania B
Carnegie Mellon University B
Cedar Crest College B
Chatham College B
Chestnut Hill College A, B
Cheyney University of Pennsylvania B
Clarion University of Pennsylvania B, T
Dickinson College B
Duquesne University B
East Stroudsburg University of Pennsylvania B
Eastern College B
Edinboro University of Pennsylvania B, T
Elizabethtown College B
Franklin and Marshall College B
Geneva College B, T
Gettysburg College B
Grove City College B, T
Haverford College B, T
Holy Family College B, T
Immaculata College C, A, B
Indiana University of Pennsylvania B, M
Juniata College B
King's College B, T
Kutztown University of Pennsylvania B, T
La Salle University B, T
Lafayette College B
Lebanon Valley College of Pennsylvania B, T
Lehigh University B
Lincoln University B
Lock Haven University of Pennsylvania B
Lycoming College B
Mansfield University of Pennsylvania B, T
Marywood University B
Mercyhurst College B
Messiah College B
Millersville University of Pennsylvania B, M, T
Moravian College B, T
Muhlenberg College B, T
Penn State
 University Park B, M, D
Rosemont College B
St. Francis College B
St. Joseph's University B
St. Vincent College B
Seton Hill College B, T
Shippensburg University of Pennsylvania B, T
Slippery Rock University of Pennsylvania B, T
Susquehanna University B, T
Swarthmore College B
Temple University B, M, D
Thiel College B
University of Pennsylvania A, B, D
University of Pittsburgh B, M, D
University of Scranton B, T
Villanova University B
Washington and Jefferson College B
West Chester University of Pennsylvania B, M
Westminster College B
Widener University B
Wilkes University B
York College of Pennsylvania B

Puerto Rico
Bayamon Central University B
Caribbean University B
Inter American University of Puerto Rico
 Metropolitan Campus B, M
 San German Campus B
Pontifical Catholic University of Puerto Rico B, M
University of Puerto Rico
 Cayey University College B
 Mayaguez Campus B, M
 Rio Piedras Campus B, M, D
University of the Sacred Heart B

Rhode Island
Brown University B, M, D
Providence College B, T
Rhode Island College B, M
Salve Regina University B
University of Rhode Island B, M

South Carolina
Charleston Southern University B
Clemson University B
Coker College B
College of Charleston B, T
Columbia College B
Converse College B
Erskine College B
Francis Marion University B
Furman University B, T
Lander University B, T
Newberry College B
Presbyterian College B, T
South Carolina State University B
The Citadel B
University of South Carolina
 Spartanburg B
University of South Carolina B, M
Winthrop University M
Wofford College B

South Dakota
Augustana College B, T
Black Hills State University B
Northern State University B
South Dakota State University B
University of South Dakota B

Tennessee
Austin Peay State University B
Belmont University B, T
Carson-Newman College B, T
David Lipscomb University B
Fisk University B
King College B, T
Lee University B
Maryville College B, T
Milligan College B
Rhodes College B, T
Tennessee State University B
Tennessee Technological University B, T
Union University B, T
University of Tennessee
 Chattanooga B
 Knoxville B, M
 Martin B
University of the South B
Vanderbilt University B, M, D

Texas
Abilene Christian University B
Angelo State University B, T
Austin College B
Baylor University B, M
Blinn College A
Coastal Bend College A
Concordia University at Austin B, T
East Texas Baptist University B
Galveston College A
Hardin-Simmons University B
Houston Baptist University B
Howard Payne University B, T
Kilgore College B
Lamar University B
Lon Morris College A
McMurry University B, T
Midland College A
Midwestern State University B
Our Lady of the Lake University of San Antonio B
Paris Junior College A
Prairie View A&M University B
Rice University B, M
St. Edward's University B, T
St. Mary's University B
St. Philip's College A
Sam Houston State University B
South Plains College A
Southern Methodist University B
Southwest Texas State University B, M, T
Southwestern University B, T
Stephen F. Austin State University B, T
Sul Ross State University B
Tarleton State University B, T
Texas A&M International University B, M, T
Texas A&M University
 Commerce B
 Corpus Christi B, T
 Kingsville B, M
Texas A&M University B, M
Texas Christian University B, T
Texas Lutheran University B
Texas Tech University B, M, D
Texas Wesleyan University B
Texas Woman's University B, T
Trinity University B
Trinity Valley Community College A
University of Dallas B
University of Houston B, M
University of Mary Hardin-Baylor B
University of North Texas B, M
University of St. Thomas B
University of Texas
 Arlington B, M
 Austin B, M, D
 Brownsville B, M
 El Paso B, M
 Pan American B, M, T
 San Antonio B, M
 Tyler B
 of the Permian Basin B
University of the Incarnate Word B
Wayland Baptist University B
West Texas A&M University B
Wharton County Junior College A

Utah
Brigham Young University B, M
Snow College A
Southern Utah University B
University of Utah B, M, D
Utah State University B
Weber State University B

Vermont
Bennington College B
Castleton State College B
Marlboro College B
Middlebury College B
St. Michael's College B
University of Vermont B

Virginia
Bridgewater College B
Christopher Newport University B
College of William and Mary B
Eastern Mennonite University B
Emory & Henry College B, T
Ferrum College B
George Mason University B
Hampden-Sydney College B
Hollins University B
Longwood College B, T
Lynchburg College B
Mary Baldwin College B
Mary Washington College B
Norfolk State University T
Randolph-Macon College B
Randolph-Macon Woman's College B
Roanoke College B, T
Sweet Briar College B
University of Richmond B, T
University of Virginia's College at Wise B, T
University of Virginia B, M, D
Virginia Wesleyan College B
Washington and Lee University B

Washington
Central Washington University B
Centralia College A
Eastern Washington University B, T
Everett Community College A
Evergreen State College B
Gonzaga University B
Heritage College B
Pacific Lutheran University B
Seattle Pacific University B
Seattle University B
University of Puget Sound B, T
University of Washington B
Walla Walla College B
Washington State University B
Western Washington University B, T
Whitman College B
Whitworth College B, T

West Virginia
Bethany College B
Davis and Elkins College B
Marshall University B
Potomac State College of West Virginia University A
Wheeling Jesuit University B

Wisconsin
Alverno College T
Beloit College B
Cardinal Stritch University B
Carroll College B
Carthage College B, T
Lakeland College B
Lawrence University B
Marian College of Fond du Lac B, T
Marquette University B, M, D
Mount Mary College B, T
Ripon College B, T
St. Norbert College B, T
Silver Lake College T
University of Wisconsin
 Eau Claire B
 Green Bay B
 La Crosse B
 Madison B, M, D
 Milwaukee B
 Oshkosh B
 Parkside B
 Platteville B
 River Falls B
 Stevens Point B, T
 Whitewater B, T
Viterbo University B
Wisconsin Lutheran College B

Wyoming
Casper College A
Sheridan College A
University of Wyoming B, M
Western Wyoming Community College A

Spanish language teacher education

Alabama
Birmingham-Southern College T
University of Alabama B

Arizona
Arizona State University B, T
Northern Arizona University B, T
Prescott College B, M
University of Arizona B, M

Spanish language teacher education

Arkansas
Arkansas State University B, T
Ouachita Baptist University B, T
Southern Arkansas University B, T

California
Azusa Pacific University T
California State University
   Chico T
   Dominguez Hills T
   Fullerton T
   Long Beach T
Humboldt State University T
Pacific Union College T
San Diego State University B
San Francisco State University B, T
San Jose State University T
University of the Pacific T

Colorado
Adams State College B, T
Colorado State University T
Fort Lewis College T
Metropolitan State College of Denver T
University of Colorado
   Colorado Springs T
University of Southern Colorado T
Western State College of Colorado T

Connecticut
Central Connecticut State University B
Fairfield University T
Quinnipiac University B, M
St. Joseph College T
Southern Connecticut State
   University B, T

Delaware
Delaware State University B
University of Delaware B, T

District of Columbia
Catholic University of America B

Florida
Barry University T
Flagler College B
St. Thomas University B, T
Stetson University B, T

Georgia
Agnes Scott College T
Armstrong Atlantic State University T
Georgia Southern University B, M, T
Georgia Southwestern State
   University B, M, T
Kennesaw State University B
Piedmont College B, T
Valdosta State University T

Hawaii
University of Hawaii
   Manoa B, T

Idaho
Boise State University T

Illinois
Augustana College B, T
Dominican University T
Elmhurst College B
Greenville College B
Illinois College B
Loyola University of Chicago T
MacMurray College B, T
North Central College B, T
North Park University T
Northwestern University B, T
Olivet Nazarene University B, T
Rockford College T
Roosevelt University B
Trinity Christian College B, T
University of Illinois
   Chicago B
   Urbana-Champaign B, M, T
Wheaton College T

Indiana
Anderson University B, T
Ball State University T
Franklin College B, T
Grace College B
Indiana State University B, T
Indiana University
   Bloomington B, T
   Northwest B
   South Bend B, T
Indiana University--Purdue University
   Indiana University-Purdue
      University Fort Wayne B, T
   Indiana University-Purdue
      University Indianapolis B, T
Indiana Wesleyan University T
Manchester College B, T
St. Mary-of-the-Woods College B
Taylor University B
University of Evansville T
University of Indianapolis B, T
University of Southern Indiana B, T
Valparaiso University B
Vincennes University A

Iowa
Buena Vista University B, T
Central College T
Clarke College B, T
Cornell College B, T
Dordt College B
Drake University M, T
Graceland University T
Iowa State University T
Loras College T
Luther College B
Morningside College B
Northwestern College T
St. Ambrose University B, T
University of Iowa B, T
Wartburg College T

Kansas
Baker University T
Benedictine College T
Bethel College T
McPherson College B, T
MidAmerica Nazarene University B, T
Pittsburg State University B, T
St. Mary College T

Kentucky
Murray State University B, M, T

Louisiana
Centenary College of Louisiana B, T
Dillard University B
Southeastern Louisiana University B
Southern University and Agricultural and
   Mechanical College B

Maryland
Salisbury State University B
Towson University T

Massachusetts
Assumption College T
Bridgewater State College T
Elms College T
Framingham State College B, M, T
Harvard College T
Tufts University T
University of Massachusetts
   Dartmouth T
Westfield State College T
Worcester State College T

Michigan
Albion College B, T
Alma College T
Calvin College B
Central Michigan University B
Concordia College B, T
Eastern Michigan University B, T
Grand Valley State University T
Michigan State University M
Northern Michigan University B, M, T
University of Michigan M, D
Western Michigan University B

Minnesota
Augsburg College T
Bemidji State University T
Bethel College B
College of St. Benedict T
College of St. Catherine: St. Paul
   Campus T
Concordia College: Moorhead T
Gustavus Adolphus College T
Minnesota State University,
   Mankato B, M, T
Moorhead State University B, T
St. Cloud State University T
St. John's University T
St. Mary's University of Minnesota B
St. Olaf College T
University of Minnesota
   Duluth B
   Morris T
University of St. Thomas T
Winona State University B, T

Mississippi
Blue Mountain College B
Mississippi State University T
University of Mississippi B, T

Missouri
Central Missouri State
   University B, M, T
College of the Ozarks B, T
Lindenwood University M
Missouri Western State College B
Northwest Missouri State
   University B, T
Rockhurst University B
Southwest Missouri State University B
Truman State University M, T
University of Missouri
   Columbia B
   St. Louis T
Washington University B, M, T
William Jewell College T
William Woods University B, T

Montana
Montana State University
   Billings T
University of Montana-Missoula T

Nebraska
Concordia University T
Creighton University T
Dana College B
Doane College T
Hastings College B, M, T
Midland Lutheran College B, T
University of Nebraska
   Lincoln B, T

New Hampshire
Franklin Pierce College T
Keene State College B, T
Plymouth State College of the University
   System of New Hampshire B, T
Rivier College B, M, T
St. Anselm College T
University of New Hampshire T

New Jersey
Monmouth University B, T
Rider University B
Rowan University T
St. Peter's College T
The College of New Jersey B, T

New Mexico
Western New Mexico University B

New York
Alfred University T
Canisius College B, M, T
City University of New York
   Brooklyn College B
   City College B
   Kingsborough Community
      College A
   Lehman College M
   Queens College T
   York College T
College of St. Rose B, T
Columbia University
   Teachers College M, D
D'Youville College M, T
Dowling College B
Elmira College B, T
Fordham University M, T
Hofstra University B, M, T
Houghton College B, T
Ithaca College B, T
Long Island University
   C. W. Post Campus B, M, T
Manhattan College B, T
Marist College B, T
Marymount College B, T
Molloy College B
New York University B, M, T
Niagara University B, T
St. Bonaventure University T
St. John Fisher College B, T
St. John's University B, M, T
St. Thomas Aquinas College B, T
Siena College T
State University of New York
   Albany B, M, T
   Binghamton M
   Buffalo T
   College at Brockport B
   College at Buffalo B
   College at Fredonia B, T
   College at Geneseo B, M, T
   College at Oneonta B, T
   College at Plattsburgh B, M
   College at Potsdam B, M
   New Paltz B, M, T
   Oswego B
Vassar College T
Wells College T

North Carolina
Appalachian State University M
Campbell University B, T
Davidson College T
East Carolina University B
Greensboro College B, T
Meredith College T
North Carolina Central University B, M
Queens College T
Salem College T
University of North Carolina
   Charlotte B
   Greensboro B, M, T
Wake Forest University M, T
Western Carolina University B, T
Wilson Technical Community College A
Wingate University B, T

North Dakota
Dickinson State University B, T
Minot State University B, T
North Dakota State University B, T
University of North Dakota B, T
Valley City State University B, T

Ohio
Ashland University B, T
Baldwin-Wallace College T
Bluffton College B
Bowling Green State University B, M
Cedarville College B
Hiram College T
Kent State University
   Stark Campus B
Kent State University B, T
Malone College B
Miami University
   Oxford Campus B, T
Mount Union College T

Mount Vernon Nazarene College *B, T*
Ohio University *B*
University of Akron *B*
University of Dayton *B, M, T*
University of Findlay *B, T*
University of Toledo *B, T*
Xavier University *M, T*
Youngstown State University *B, M, T*

Oklahoma
Northeastern State University *B*
Northwestern Oklahoma State
  University *B, T*
Oklahoma Baptist University *B, T*
Oklahoma City University *B*
Oral Roberts University *B, T*
Southeastern Oklahoma State
  University *B, T*
Southern Nazarene University *B*
Southwestern Oklahoma State
  University *T*
University of Central Oklahoma *B*
University of Tulsa *T*

Oregon
Eastern Oregon University *B, T*
Linfield College *T*
Portland State University *T*
University of Portland *T*
Western Oregon University *T*

Pennsylvania
Allentown College of St. Francis de
  Sales *T*
Bucknell University *T*
Cabrini College *B*
California University of
  Pennsylvania *B, T*
Carnegie Mellon University *T*
Chestnut Hill College *T*
Clarion University of Pennsylvania *B, T*
Dickinson College *T*
Duquesne University *B, T*
Gettysburg College *T*
Grove City College *B, T*
Holy Family College *B, M, T*
Juniata College *B, T*
King's College *T*
La Roche College *B*
La Salle University *B, T*
Lebanon Valley College of
  Pennsylvania *T*
Lock Haven University of
  Pennsylvania *B, T*
Lycoming College *T*
Mansfield University of
  Pennsylvania *B, T*
Marywood University *T*
Messiah College *T*
Moravian College *T*
St. Vincent College *T*
Seton Hill College *B, T*
Thiel College *B*
Villanova University *T*
Washington and Jefferson College *T*
Westminster College *T*
Widener University *T*
Wilson College *T*

Puerto Rico
American University of Puerto Rico *B, T*
Bayamon Central University *B*
Inter American University of Puerto Rico
  Arecibo Campus *B*
  Barranquitas Campus *B, T*
  Fajardo Campus *B, T*
  Metropolitan Campus *B, T*
Turabo University *B*
Universidad Metropolitana *B*

Rhode Island
Providence College *B*
Rhode Island College *B*
Salve Regina University *B*

South Carolina
Charleston Southern University *B*

Coker College *B, T*
Furman University *T*
South Carolina State University *B, T*
Wofford College *T*

South Dakota
Augustana College *B, T*
Black Hills State University *B, T*
South Dakota State University *B*
University of South Dakota *T*

Tennessee
Belmont University *T*
David Lipscomb University *B, T*
Lee University *B*
Maryville College *B, T*
Union University *B, T*
University of Tennessee
  Martin *B, T*

Texas
Abilene Christian University *B, T*
Baylor University *B, T*
East Texas Baptist University *B*
Hardin-Simmons University *B, T*
Houston Baptist University *T*
Howard Payne University *T*
Lamar University *T*
Lubbock Christian University *B*
McMurry University *T*
St. Mary's University *T*
Southwest Texas State University *M, T*
Texas A&M International
  University *B, T*
Texas A&M University
  Commerce *T*
  Kingsville *T*
Texas Christian University *T*
Texas Lutheran University *T*
Texas Wesleyan University *B, T*
University of Dallas *T*
University of Houston *T*
University of Mary Hardin-Baylor *T*
University of Texas
  Arlington *M, T*
  Pan American *T*
  San Antonio *T*
Wayland Baptist University *T*
West Texas A&M University *T*

Utah
Brigham Young University *B*
Weber State University *B*

Vermont
Castleton State College *B, T*
St. Michael's College *B*

Virginia
Bridgewater College *T*
Christopher Newport University *T*
Eastern Mennonite University *T*
Hollins University *T*
Longwood College *B, T*
Radford University *T*
University of Virginia's College at
  Wise *T*
Virginia Wesleyan College *T*

Washington
Central Washington University *B, T*
Heritage College *B*
Western Washington University *B, T*
Whitworth College *B, T*

West Virginia
Wheeling Jesuit University *T*

Wisconsin
Alverno College *T*
Cardinal Stritch University *B, T*
Carroll College *B, T*
Carthage College *T*
Lawrence University *T*
Marian College of Fond du Lac *B, T*
Mount Mary College *B, T*
St. Norbert College *T*

University of Wisconsin
  Green Bay *T*
  La Crosse *B, T*
  Platteville *B, T*
  River Falls *T*
  Whitewater *B*
Viterbo University *B*

Special education

Alabama
Alabama Agricultural and Mechanical
  University *B, M, T*
Alabama State University *B, M, T*
Auburn University *B, M, D, T*
Birmingham-Southern College *B*
Jacksonville State University *B, M, T*
University of Alabama
  Birmingham *B, M*
University of Alabama *B, M, D*
University of North Alabama *B, M*
University of South Alabama *B, M, T*
University of West Alabama *B, M, T*

Alaska
University of Alaska
  Anchorage *C, M*

Arizona
Arizona State University *B, M*
Central Arizona College *A*
Grand Canyon University *B, T*
Northern Arizona University *B, M, T*
Prescott College *B, M*
University of Arizona *B, M, D*

Arkansas
Arkansas State University *B, M, T*
Harding University *B, M, T*
Henderson State University *M*
John Brown University *T*
Philander Smith College *B*
Southern Arkansas University *B, M, T*
University of Arkansas
  Little Rock *M*
  Monticello *B*
  Pine Bluff *B*
University of Arkansas *B, M, D*
University of Central Arkansas *B, M*
University of the Ozarks *B*
Westark College *A*

California
Azusa Pacific University *M*
California Baptist University *M, T*
California Lutheran University *B, M*
California State University
  Bakersfield *M*
  Chico *T*
  Dominguez Hills *M*
  Fresno *M*
  Fullerton *M*
  Hayward *M, T*
  Long Beach *M, T*
  Los Angeles *M, D*
  Northridge *M*
  Sacramento *M*
  San Marcos *M*
Cerritos Community College *A*
Chapman University *M, T*
Compton Community College *A*
Cuesta College *C, A*
Fresno City College *C*
Fresno Pacific University *M, T*
Holy Names College *M*
La Sierra University *B, M*
Long Beach City College *C, A*
Loyola Marymount University *C, M*
Master's College *B*
Mount St. Mary's College *M*
National University *M, T*
Pacific Oaks College *T*
Point Loma Nazarene University *M*
Sacramento City College *C, A*
St. Mary's College of California *M*

San Diego State University *M, T*
San Francisco State University *M, D, T*
San Jose State University *M*
Santa Clara University *M*
Simpson College *T*
University of California
  Berkeley *D, T*
  Los Angeles *D*
  Riverside *M, D, T*
University of La Verne *M, T*
University of San Diego *M, T*
University of San Francisco *M*
University of the Pacific *D*

Colorado
Adams State College *M, T*
Metropolitan State College of Denver *T*
University of Colorado
  Colorado Springs *M*
  Denver *M*
University of Denver *M, D*
University of Northern Colorado *M, D, T*

Connecticut
Central Connecticut State
  University *B, M*
Fairfield University *C, M*
Gateway Community College *C, A*
St. Joseph College *B, M, T*
Southern Connecticut State University *M*
Three Rivers Community-Technical
  College *C, A*
University of Connecticut *B, M, D, T*
University of Hartford *B, M, T*
Western Connecticut State University *M*

Delaware
Delaware State University *B, M*
University of Delaware *B, M, T*
Wilmington College *M*

District of Columbia
American University *M, T*
George Washington University *M*
Howard University *M*
Trinity College *M*
University of the District of Columbia *M*

Florida
Barry University *B, M*
Bethune-Cookman College *B, T*
Broward Community College *A*
Clearwater Christian College *B*
Edward Waters College *B*
Florida Atlantic University *B, M, D*
Florida Gulf Coast University *B, M, T*
Florida International University *M, D*
Florida State University *C, D*
Gulf Coast Community College *A*
Jacksonville University *B, M, T*
Nova Southeastern University *B, M*
Pensacola Junior College *A*
St. Leo University *B*
Southeastern College of the Assemblies
  of God *B, T*
University of Central Florida *B, M*
University of Florida *B, M, D*
University of Miami *B, M, D*
University of North Florida *B, M*
University of South Florida *B, M*
Warner Southern College *B*

Georgia
Armstrong Atlantic State
  University *B, M, T*
Augusta State University *B, M*
Brenau University *B, T*
Columbus State University *B, M*
Georgia College and State
  University *B, M, T*
Georgia Southern University *B, M, T*
Georgia Southwestern State
  University *B, M, T*
Georgia State University *D*
North Georgia College & State
  University *B, M*
Piedmont College *B, T*

562

Special education

State University of West Georgia B, M
University of Georgia B, M, D, T
Valdosta State University B, M

Hawaii
Brigham Young University
    Hawaii B, T
University of Hawaii
    Manoa B, M, T

Idaho
Boise State University T
Idaho State University B, M
Lewis-Clark State College B, T
Northwest Nazarene University M
Ricks College A
University of Idaho B, M, D, T

Illinois
Barat College B
Benedictine University B, M, T
Chicago State University B
Dominican University M
Eastern Illinois University B, M
Elmhurst College B
Governors State University M, T
Greenville College B, T
Illinois State University B, M, D, T
John A. Logan College C, A
Joliet Junior College A
Kishwaukee College A
Lewis University M
Loyola University of Chicago B, M, T
Monmouth College B, T
National-Louis University M
Northeastern Illinois University B, M
Northern Illinois University B, M, D
Parkland College A
Quincy University A, B, T
Rend Lake College A
Sauk Valley Community College A
Southern Illinois University
    Carbondale B, M, D
    Edwardsville B, M
Trinity Christian College B, T
University of Illinois
    Chicago M, D
    Urbana-Champaign B, M, D, T
Western Illinois University B, M

Indiana
Ball State University B, M, D
Butler University M
Indiana State University B, M, T
Indiana University
    Bloomington B, M, D, T
    South Bend B, M
    Southeast B
Indiana University--Purdue University
    Indiana University-Purdue
        University Fort Wayne T
    Indiana University-Purdue
        University Indianapolis M
Manchester College B, T
Marian College T
Purdue University
    Calumet B
Purdue University B
St. Mary-of-the-Woods College B
University of Evansville B
University of St. Francis B, M, T
Valparaiso University M, D
Vincennes University A

Iowa
Buena Vista University B, T
Clarke College B, M, T
Dordt College B
Drake University M
Iowa State University M, T
Loras College B
Morningside College B, M
Mount Mercy College T
St. Ambrose University M, T
University of Dubuque C, T
University of Iowa M, D
University of Northern Iowa B, M

Upper Iowa University B, T
Waldorf College A
William Penn University B

Kansas
Benedictine College B, T
Bethel College T
Emporia State University M, T
Fort Hays State University M
Kansas City Kansas Community
    College A
Kansas State University M, D
Kansas Wesleyan University T
McPherson College B, T
Pittsburg State University B, M, T
Tabor College B, T
University of Kansas M, D
Washburn University of Topeka M
Wichita State University M

Kentucky
Bellarmine College B, M, T
Brescia University B, T
Cumberland College B, M
Eastern Kentucky University B, M
Morehead State University B, M
Murray State University B, M, T
Northern Kentucky University B, M, T
Union College B
University of Kentucky B, M, D, T
University of Louisville M, D
Western Kentucky University B, M

Louisiana
Dillard University B
Louisiana State University
    Shreveport B
Louisiana Tech University B
McNeese State University B, T
Nicholls State University B
Northwestern State University M
Our Lady of Holy Cross College B, T
Southeastern Louisiana University B, M
Southern University and Agricultural and
    Mechanical College B, M, D
University of Louisiana at Lafayette B
University of Louisiana at Monroe B, M
University of New Orleans M, D
Xavier University of Louisiana B

Maine
University of Maine
    Farmington B
University of Maine M
University of Southern Maine M

Maryland
Baltimore City Community College C
Bowie State University M
College of Notre Dame of Maryland B
Coppin State College B, M, T
Goucher College B
Hood College B
Loyola College in Maryland M
Towson University B
University of Maryland
    Baltimore County T
    College Park B, M, D, T
    Eastern Shore B, M, T
Western Maryland College M

Massachusetts
American International College B, M
Assumption College M
Atlantic Union College M
Becker College C, A
Boston University B, M, D, T
Bridgewater State College B, M, T
Curry College B
Eastern Nazarene College B, M, T
Elms College B, M, T
Endicott College M
Fitchburg State College B, M, T
Framingham State College M
Gordon College B
Lasell College B
Lesley College B, M, T

Northeastern University M
Simmons College B, M
Springfield College B
University of Massachusetts
    Boston M
Westfield State College B, T
Wheelock College B, M

Michigan
Aquinas College B
Calvin College B, T
Central Michigan University M
Eastern Michigan University M
Gogebic Community College A
Grand Valley State University B, M, T
Kellogg Community College A
Lansing Community College A
Marygrove College B, M, T
Michigan State University B, M, D
Northern Michigan University B
Oakland University M
Saginaw Valley State University B, T
Schoolcraft College A
University of Detroit Mercy B, M
Wayne State University B, M, D, T
Western Michigan University M, D

Minnesota
Bemidji State University M
Minnesota State University, Mankato M
Moorhead State University B, M, T
Northland Community & Technical
    College A
St. Cloud State University B, M, T
University of Minnesota
    Duluth T
    Twin Cities M
University of St. Thomas M
Winona State University B, M, T

Mississippi
Alcorn State University B
Delta State University B, M
Jackson State University B, M
Mary Holmes College A
Millsaps College T
Mississippi College B, M
Mississippi Delta Community College A
Mississippi Gulf Coast Community
    College
        Jefferson Davis Campus A
Mississippi State University B, M, T
Mississippi University for Women B, T
Mississippi Valley State University M
Northwest Mississippi Community
    College A
University of Mississippi B, T
University of Southern Mississippi B, M
William Carey College M

Missouri
Avila College B
Central Missouri State
    University B, M, D
Culver-Stockton College T
East Central College A
Evangel University B
Fontbonne College B
Lincoln University B, T
Lindenwood University B, M
Missouri Baptist College T
Missouri Southern State College B, T
Missouri Valley College B
St. Louis University M
Southeast Missouri State
    University B, M
Southwest Missouri State University M
Stephens College B
Truman State University M
University of Missouri
    Columbia M, D
    Kansas City M
    St. Louis B, M, T
Webster University B, M, T
William Woods University B

Montana
Carroll College T
Montana State University
    Billings A, B, M, T
    Northern M
University of Great Falls B
Western Montana College of The
    University of Montana T

Nebraska
College of Saint Mary B, T
Concordia University B, T
Dana College B
Doane College B
Hastings College B, M, T
Nebraska Wesleyan University B
Peru State College B, T
University of Nebraska
    Kearney B, M, T
    Lincoln B, M
    Omaha B
Wayne State College B, M

Nevada
University of Nevada
    Las Vegas B, M, D, T
    Reno B, M, T

New Hampshire
Keene State College B, M, T
New England College B, T
Notre Dame College B, M
Plymouth State College of the University
    System of New Hampshire B
Rivier College D, T
University of New Hampshire M

New Jersey
College of St. Elizabeth T
Felician College B, T
Georgian Court College B, M, T
Gloucester County College A
Kean University B, M
Monmouth University B, M
New Jersey City University B, M
Rowan University C, B, M
Rutgers
    The State University of New Jersey:
        Douglass College T
    The State University of New Jersey:
        Livingston College T
    The State University of New Jersey:
        New Brunswick Graduate
        Campus M, D, T
    The State University of New Jersey:
        Rutgers College T
    The State University of New Jersey:
        University College New
        Brunswick T
Seton Hall University B, T
The College of New Jersey B, M, T
William Paterson University of New
    Jersey B, M

New Mexico
College of Santa Fe M
College of the Southwest B, T
Eastern New Mexico University B, M
New Mexico Highlands University B, M
New Mexico State University B
University of New Mexico B, M, D, T
Western New Mexico University B, M, T

New York
Adelphi University M
Bank Street College of Education M
Canisius College B, M, D
City University of New York
    Brooklyn College B, M
    College of Staten Island M
    Hunter College B, M
    Medgar Evers College B, T
    Queens College M
    York College T
College of Mount St. Vincent B, T
College of New Rochelle M
College of St. Rose B, M, T

Special education

Columbia University
    Teachers College *M, D*
D'Youville College *B, M, T*
Daemen College *B, M, T*
Dominican College of Blauvelt *B, T*
Dowling College *B, M, T*
Fordham University *B*
Hobart and William Smith Colleges *T*
Hofstra University *M*
Keuka College *B, T*
Le Moyne College *T*
Long Island University
    Brooklyn Campus *M*
    C. W. Post Campus *B, M*
Manhattan College *B, M, T*
Manhattanville College *M, T*
Marist College *B, T*
Marymount College *B, T*
Marymount Manhattan College *B, T*
Mercy College *T*
Molloy College *B, T*
Mount St. Mary College *B, M, T*
Nazareth College of Rochester *M, T*
New York University *B, M, T*
Niagara University *B*
Pace University:
    Pleasantville/Briarcliff *B, M*
Pace University *B, M*
St. Bonaventure University *M*
St. John's University *B, M, T*
St. Thomas Aquinas College *C, B, M, T*
St. Joseph's College
    St. Joseph's College: Suffolk
      Campus *B, T*
    St. Joseph's College *B, T*
State University of New York
    Albany *M*
    Binghamton *M*
    Buffalo *D*
    College at Buffalo *M*
    College at Geneseo *B, M, T*
    College at Old Westbury *B, T*
    College at Plattsburgh *B, M*
    College at Potsdam *M*
    New Paltz *B, M, T*
    Oswego *M*
Syracuse University *B, M, D, T*
Touro College *B, M*
Wagner College *B, M, T*

North Carolina
Appalachian State University *M*
Barton College *B*
Bennett College *B*
East Carolina University *M*
Elizabeth City State University *B, T*
Elon College *B*
Fayetteville State University *M*
Greensboro College *B, T*
High Point University *B*
Lenoir-Rhyne College *M*
Martin Community College *A*
Methodist College *A, B, T*
North Carolina Agricultural and
    Technical State University *B*
North Carolina Central University *M*
North Carolina State University *M*
Pfeiffer University *B*
Roanoke-Chowan Community College *A*
St. Augustine's College *B, T*
Shaw University *B, T*
University of North Carolina
    Chapel Hill *M, D*
    Charlotte *M*
    Greensboro *M*
    Pembroke *B, T*
    Wilmington *B, M*
Western Carolina University *B*
Winston-Salem State University *B*

North Dakota
Jamestown College *B*
University of Mary *B, M*
University of North Dakota *M*

Ohio
Ashland University *B, M, T*
Bluffton College *B*
Bowling Green State University *B, M*
Cedarville College *B*
Central State University *B*
Cleveland State University *B, T*
College of Mount St. Joseph *B*
Defiance College *B*
Kent State University *M, D*
Miami University
    Oxford Campus *B, M*
Muskingum College *B, T*
Ohio Dominican College *B, D*
Ohio State University
    Columbus Campus *B, M*
Ohio University
    Southern Campus at Ironton *M*
Ohio University *B, M*
Otterbein College *B*
Sinclair Community College *A*
University of Akron *B, M, T*
University of Cincinnati *M, D*
University of Dayton *B, T*
University of Findlay *B, M, T*
University of Rio Grande *B, T*
University of Toledo *B, M, T*
Wright State University *M*
Xavier University *B, M, T*
Youngstown State University *B, M*

Oklahoma
East Central University *B, M, T*
Langston University *B*
Northeastern State University *B, M*
Northwestern Oklahoma State
    University *B*
Oklahoma Baptist University *B, T*
Oklahoma Christian University of
    Science and Arts *B, T*
Oral Roberts University *B, T*
Southeastern Oklahoma State
    University *B*
Southwestern Oklahoma State
    University *B*
University of Central Oklahoma *B, M*
University of Oklahoma *B, M, D, T*

Oregon
Eastern Oregon University *T*
Portland Community College *C*
Portland State University *M, T*
Southern Oregon University *T*
University of Oregon *M, D, T*
University of Portland *T*
Western Oregon University *T*

Pennsylvania
Beaver College *B, M, T*
Bloomsburg University of
    Pennsylvania *B, M, T*
Cabrini College *B, T*
California University of
    Pennsylvania *B, M, T*
Carlow College *B, T*
Chatham College *M, T*
Cheyney University of
    Pennsylvania *B, M, T*
Clarion University of
    Pennsylvania *B, M*
College Misericordia *B*
Duquesne University *B, M, T*
East Stroudsburg University of
    Pennsylvania *B, M, T*
Edinboro University of
    Pennsylvania *A, B, M, T*
Gannon University *B*
Gwynedd-Mercy College *B, T*
Holy Family College *B, T*
Immaculata College *T*
Indiana University of Pennsylvania *B, T*
Juniata College *B, T*
King's College *B*
Kutztown University of Pennsylvania *B*
La Roche College *C*
La Salle University *B, T*
Lebanon Valley College of
    Pennsylvania *T*
Lehigh University *M, D*
Lock Haven University of
    Pennsylvania *B, T*
Mansfield University of
    Pennsylvania *B, M, T*
Marywood University *B, M*
Mercyhurst College *B, M, T*
Millersville University of
    Pennsylvania *B, M, T*
Penn State
    University Park *B, M, D*
Rosemont College *T*
St. Joseph's University *C*
Seton Hill College *B, M, T*
Shippensburg University of
    Pennsylvania *M, T*
Slippery Rock University of
    Pennsylvania *B, M, T*
University of Pennsylvania *M, D*
University of Scranton *B*
West Chester University of
    Pennsylvania *B, M*

Puerto Rico
American University of Puerto Rico *B, T*
Bayamon Central University *B, M*
Caribbean University *B, T*
Inter American University of Puerto Rico
    Arecibo Campus *B*
    Metropolitan Campus *B, M*
    San German Campus *B, M*
Pontifical Catholic University of Puerto
    Rico *B*
Turabo University *B, M*
Universidad Metropolitana *B, M*
University of Puerto Rico
    Rio Piedras Campus *M*

Rhode Island
Community College of Rhode Island *A*
Providence College *B, M*
Rhode Island College *B, M*
Salve Regina University *B*

South Carolina
Clemson University *B, M*
College of Charleston *B, M, T*
Columbia College *B, T*
Converse College *B, M, T*
Erskine College *B, T*
Francis Marion University *M*
Furman University *B, M, T*
Lander University *B, T*
Newberry College *B*
Presbyterian College *B, T*
South Carolina State University *B, M, T*
Southern Wesleyan University *B, T*
University of South Carolina *M, D*
Winthrop University *B, M, T*

South Dakota
Augustana College *B, M, T*
Black Hills State University *B, T*
Dakota State University *B, T*
Dakota Wesleyan University *B*
Northern State University *B, T*
Sinte Gleska University *A, B*
University of South Dakota *B, M*

Tennessee
Austin Peay State University *B, T*
Bethel College *B, M, T*
Carson-Newman College *B, T*
Cumberland University *B*
East Tennessee State University *B, M, T*
Freed-Hardeman University *B, T*
Hiwassee College *A*
Johnson Bible College *A, B, T*
Lambuth University *B, T*
Lee University *B*
Middle Tennessee State
    University *B, M, T*
Milligan College *T*
Roane State Community College *A*
Southern Adventist University *M*
Tennessee State University *B, M, T*
Tennessee Technological
    University *B, M, T*
Tusculum College *B, T*
Union University *B, T*
University of Memphis *B*
University of Tennessee
    Chattanooga *B, M, T*
    Knoxville *M, T*
    Martin *B, T*
Vanderbilt University *B, M, D, T*

Texas
Abilene Christian University *B, T*
Angelo State University *M, T*
Baylor University *B, T*
Del Mar College *A*
Eastfield College *C*
El Paso Community College *A*
Houston Baptist University *B*
Jarvis Christian College *B*
Lamar University *M, T*
Our Lady of the Lake University of San
    Antonio *B, M*
Prairie View A&M University *M*
Sam Houston State University *M, T*
Southwest Texas State University *M, T*
Southwestern University *T*
Stephen F. Austin State University *M, T*
Sul Ross State University *M*
Texas A&M International
    University *B, M, T*
Texas A&M University
    Commerce *B, M, D, T*
    Corpus Christi *M, T*
    Kingsville *M*
    Texarkana *M, T*
Texas Christian University *B, M, T*
Texas Southern University *M*
Texas Tech University *M, D*
Texas Woman's University *M, D, T*
University of Houston
    Clear Lake *T*
    Victoria *M*
University of Houston *M, D*
University of Mary Hardin-Baylor *T*
University of North Texas *M, D*
University of Texas
    Austin *M, D*
    Dallas *M*
    El Paso *T*
    Pan American *B, M, T*
    San Antonio *M, T*
    Tyler *T*
    of the Permian Basin *T*
University of the Incarnate Word *M*
West Texas A&M University *M, T*

Utah
Brigham Young University *B, M*
Snow College *A*
University of Utah *M, D*
Utah State University *B, M, D*
Westminster College *B, T*

Vermont
Castleton State College *B, M, T*
College of St. Joseph in Vermont *B, M*
Green Mountain College *T*
Johnson State College *M*
Lyndon State College *B, M*
St. Michael's College *M*
Trinity College of Vermont *B, T*
University of Vermont *M, T*

Virginia
Averett College *M*
Bridgewater College *T*
Eastern Mennonite University *T*
George Mason University *M*
Hampton University *B, M*
James Madison University *M, T*
Liberty University *M*
Longwood College *B, M, T*
Lynchburg College *M*
Norfolk State University *B, T*

Old Dominion University *M*
Radford University *B, M, T*
University of Virginia's College at
 Wise *T*
University of Virginia *M, D*
Virginia Commonwealth University *M*
Virginia Intermont College *B, T*

Washington
Central Washington University *B, M, T*
City University *M*
Eastern Washington University *M, T*
Gonzaga University *B, M, T*
Heritage College *M*
Pacific Lutheran University *B, M*
St. Martin's College *B, T*
Shoreline Community College *A*
University of Washington *M, D*
Walla Walla College *M*
Western Washington University *B, M, T*
Whitworth College *B, M, T*

West Virginia
Alderson-Broaddus College *B*
Bethany College *B*
Glenville State College *B*
Marshall University *B, M*
West Liberty State College *B*
West Virginia State College *B*
West Virginia University *M, D*

Wisconsin
Cardinal Stritch University *B, M*
Carthage College *B, T*
University of Wisconsin
 Eau Claire *B, M*
 La Crosse *M*
 Madison *M, D*
 Milwaukee *M, T*
 Oshkosh *B*
 Superior *M*
 Whitewater *B, T*

Wyoming
Eastern Wyoming College *A*
Northwest College *A*
University of Wyoming *B*

Speech pathology

Alabama
Alabama Agricultural and Mechanical
 University *M*
University of Alabama *M*
University of Montevallo *B, M, T*

Arizona
Scottsdale Community College *C*

Arkansas
Arkansas State University *M*
Harding University *B*
Ouachita Baptist University *B*
University of Central Arkansas *B*

California
California State University
 Fresno *M*
 Northridge *B*
Loma Linda University *M*
San Diego State University *C*
Stanford University *D*

Colorado
University of Colorado
 Boulder *B, M, D*
University of Northern Colorado *B, M*

District of Columbia
University of the District of Columbia *B*

Florida
Gulf Coast Community College *A*
Nova Southeastern University *M, D*
Polk Community College *A*

Georgia
Armstrong Atlantic State
 University *B, M*

Idaho
Idaho State University *M*

Illinois
Eastern Illinois University *B, M, T*
Elmhurst College *B, T*
Governors State University *B, M, T*
Northwestern University *B*
Parkland College *A*
St. Xavier University *B, M*

Indiana
Ball State University *M*
Butler University *B*
Indiana State University *B, M*

Iowa
University of Northern Iowa *B, M*

Kansas
University of Kansas *M, D*

Kentucky
Murray State University *M*

Louisiana
Louisiana State University Medical
 Center *M*
Xavier University of Louisiana *B*

Maine
University of Maine
 Farmington *B*

Maryland
University of Maryland
 College Park *B, M, D*

Massachusetts
Becker College *A*
Boston University *M, D*
Elms College *B*
Emerson College *B, M*
MGH Institute of Health Professions *M*
North Shore Community College *C*
Northeastern University *B, M*
Worcester State College *M*

Michigan
Baker College
 of Muskegon *A*
Calvin College *B*
Central Michigan University *M*
Northern Michigan University *B, M*
Wayne State University *B*

Minnesota
Minnesota State University, Mankato *M*
Moorhead State University *B*

Mississippi
Mississippi Delta Community College *A*
Mississippi University for Women *B, M*

Missouri
Central Missouri State University *B, T*
East Central College *A*
Fontbonne College *B*
St. Louis University *B*
Southeast Missouri State University *B*

Nebraska
University of Nebraska
 Kearney *B, M, T*

Nevada
University of Nevada
 Reno *B, D*

New Hampshire
University of New Hampshire *B*

New Jersey
Montclair State University *T*
Seton Hall University *M*
The College of New Jersey *M*
William Paterson University of New
 Jersey *B*

New York
Adelphi University *B*
Columbia University
 Teachers College *M, D*
Hofstra University *B, M*
Ithaca College *M*
Long Island University
 C. W. Post Campus *M*
Nazareth College of Rochester *B, M, T*
New York University *M*
Pace University:
 Pleasantville/Briarcliff *B*
Pace University *B*
State University of New York
 Buffalo *M*
 College at Buffalo *B*
 College at Fredonia *M*
 College at Geneseo *B*
 College at Plattsburgh *M*
 New Paltz *B*
Touro College *M*

North Carolina
Catawba Valley Community College *A*
Davidson County Community College *A*
Forsyth Technical Community College *A*
Sandhills Community College *A*
Southwestern Community College *A*
Tri-County Community College *A*
University of North Carolina
 Chapel Hill *M*
Wilkes Community College *A*

North Dakota
Minot State University *B*
University of North Dakota *M*

Ohio
Case Western Reserve University *M, D*
Kent State University
 Stark Campus *B*
Kent State University *M, D*
Miami University
 Oxford Campus *B*
University of Akron *M*
University of Toledo *B*

Oklahoma
Northeastern State University *B, M*
Oklahoma State University *B, M*
University of Central Oklahoma *M*
University of Science and Arts of
 Oklahoma *B*
University of Tulsa *B, M, T*

Oregon
Portland State University *M*

Pennsylvania
Duquesne University *B, M*
Edinboro University of Pennsylvania *M*
Geneva College *B*

Puerto Rico
University of Puerto Rico
 Medical Sciences Campus *B, M*

Rhode Island
University of Rhode Island *M*

South Carolina
University of South Carolina *M*

South Dakota
Northern State University *B, T*

Tennessee
Lambuth University *B*
Southern Adventist University *A*
University of Tennessee
 Knoxville *B, M*

Texas
Lamar University *M*
Richland College *A*
Stephen F. Austin State University *M, T*
Texas A&M University
 Kingsville *B*
Texas Woman's University *M*

University of Houston *M*
University of North Texas *M*
University of Texas
 El Paso *M*

Utah
Brigham Young University *B, M*
University of Utah *M*

Vermont
University of Vermont *B, T*

Virginia
James Madison University *B, M, T*

Washington
Washington State University *B, M*

West Virginia
Marshall University *B*

Wisconsin
Marquette University *M*
Northeast Wisconsin Technical
 College *A*
University of Wisconsin
 Oshkosh *M*
 Whitewater *B, T*

Speech pathology/audiology

Alabama
Auburn University *B, M*
University of Alabama *B*
University of South Alabama *B, M, D*

Arizona
Arizona State University *M*
Northern Arizona University *M*

Arkansas
Arkansas State University *B*
Harding University *B*
University of Arkansas
 Little Rock *B, M*
 for Medical Sciences *M*
University of Arkansas *B, M*
University of Central Arkansas *B, M*

California
California State University
 Fullerton *B, M*
 Hayward *B, M*
 Los Angeles *B, M*
 Northridge *M*
 Sacramento *B, M*
 Stanislaus *B*
Loma Linda University *C, B*
San Francisco State University *B, M*
San Jose State University *B, M*
Santa Ana College *C*
University of California
 Santa Barbara *B, M, D*
University of Redlands *B, M*

Colorado
University of Colorado
 Boulder *M, D*

Connecticut
Southern Connecticut State University *M*
University of Connecticut *M, D*

District of Columbia
Gallaudet University *M*
George Washington University *B, M*
University of the District of Columbia *M*

Florida
Florida Atlantic University *M*
Florida State University *B, M, D*
University of Central Florida *B, M*
University of Florida *B, M, D*
University of South Florida *M*

Hawaii
University of Hawaii
 Manoa *B, M*

Speech pathology/audiology

Idaho
Idaho State University B
North Idaho College A

Illinois
Augustana College B
Illinois State University B, M, T
Northwestern University B, D
Southern Illinois University
 Edwardsville B
University of Illinois
 Urbana-Champaign B, M, D

Indiana
Ball State University B
Indiana State University M
Indiana University
 Bloomington B, M, D
Purdue University B, M, D

Iowa
University of Iowa M, D

Kansas
Fort Hays State University M
Wichita State University B, M, D

Kentucky
Brescia University B
University of Kentucky B, M
University of Louisville M
Western Kentucky University B, M, T

Louisiana
Louisiana State University
 Shreveport B
Louisiana State University Medical
 Center M
Louisiana State University and
 Agricultural and Mechanical
 College B, M, D
Louisiana Tech University B, M
Southern University and Agricultural and
 Mechanical College B
University of Louisiana at
 Lafayette B, M
University of Louisiana at Monroe B, M
Xavier University of Louisiana B

Maine
University of Maine B, M

Maryland
Loyola College in Maryland B, M
Towson University B, M

Massachusetts
Boston University M, D
Elms College B
Emerson College B
North Shore Community College A
Worcester State College B, M

Michigan
Andrews University B
Calvin College B
Central Michigan University B
Michigan State University B, M, D
University of Michigan B
Wayne State University B, M
Western Michigan University B, M

Minnesota
Moorhead State University B, M
St. Cloud State University B
University of Minnesota
 Twin Cities B

Mississippi
Delta State University B
University of Mississippi B, M
University of Southern Mississippi B, M

Missouri
Central Missouri State University M
Fontbonne College M
St. Louis University B, M
Southwest Missouri State
 University B, M

University of Missouri
 Columbia B, M

Nebraska
University of Nebraska
 Lincoln B, M

Nevada
University of Nevada
 Reno B, M

New Hampshire
University of New Hampshire M

New Jersey
Richard Stockton College of New
 Jersey B
William Paterson University of New
 Jersey M

New Mexico
Eastern New Mexico University B, M
University of New Mexico B, M

New York
Adelphi University M, D
City University of New York
 Brooklyn College B, M
 Graduate School and University
  Center D
 Hunter College M
 Lehman College B
 Queens College B, M
College of St. Rose B, M, T
Columbia University
 Teachers College M, D
Elmira College B
Ithaca College B, T
Long Island University
 Brooklyn Campus B
 C. W. Post Campus B
Marymount Manhattan College B
Mercy College B
Molloy College B
St. John's University B, M
State University of New York
 Buffalo B, M, D, T
 College at Cortland B
 College at Fredonia B, M, T
 College at Geneseo B, T
 College at Plattsburgh B, M
 New Paltz B, M
Syracuse University B, M, D

North Carolina
Appalachian State University B
Cape Fear Community College A
East Carolina University B, M, D
North Carolina Central University M
Randolph Community College A
Shaw University B
University of North Carolina
 Chapel Hill M
 Greensboro B, M

North Dakota
Minot State University B, M
University of North Dakota B

Ohio
College of Wooster B
Kent State University
 Stark Campus B
Kent State University B, M, D
Miami University
 Oxford Campus B, M, T
Ohio State University
 Columbus Campus B, M, D
Ohio University M, D
University of Akron B, M
University of Cincinnati B, M, D

Oklahoma
University of Central Oklahoma B

Oregon
University of Oregon B, M, D

Pennsylvania
California University of
 Pennsylvania B, M
Clarion University of Pennsylvania B, M
East Stroudsburg University of
 Pennsylvania B
Indiana University of Pennsylvania M
Marywood University B, M
Penn State
 University Park B, M, D
Temple University B, M, D
University of Pittsburgh M, D
West Chester University of
 Pennsylvania B, M

Puerto Rico
Inter American University of Puerto Rico
 Barranquitas Campus B

South Carolina
South Carolina State University B, M
University of South Carolina D

South Dakota
Augustana College B
Northern State University B, T

Tennessee
East Tennessee State University B, M
Tennessee State University B
University of Memphis M, D
Vanderbilt University M, D

Texas
Abilene Christian University B
Baylor University M
Hardin-Simmons University B
Howard College C, A
Lamar University B
Southwest Texas State University B, M
Stephen F. Austin State University B
Texas Christian University B, M, T
Texas Tech University Health Science
 Center M
Texas Woman's University B
University of Houston M
University of North Texas B, M
University of Texas
 Dallas B, M
 El Paso B, M

Utah
Brigham Young University M
University of Utah M, D
Utah State University B, M, D

Vermont
University of Vermont M

Virginia
Hampton University B, M
Old Dominion University B, M
Radford University M
University of Virginia B, M

Washington
Eastern Washington University B, T
University of Washington B, M, D
Western Washington University B, M

West Virginia
Marshall University B, M
West Virginia University B, M

Wisconsin
Marquette University B
University of Wisconsin
 Eau Claire B, M
 Madison B, M, D
 Stevens Point B, M, T
 Whitewater M

Wyoming
University of Wyoming B, M

Speech teacher education

Alabama
Huntingdon College T

Arizona
Grand Canyon University B
Northern Arizona University B, T
University of Arizona B, M

Arkansas
Arkansas Tech University B
Harding University B, T
Ouachita Baptist University B, T
University of Arkansas
 Monticello B

California
California State University
 Hayward B, M, T
San Diego State University B
San Francisco State University B, T

Colorado
Adams State College B, T
Colorado State University T
Metropolitan State College of Denver T

Georgia
North Georgia College & State
 University B

Hawaii
University of Hawaii
 Manoa B, T

Idaho
Boise State University T
Lewis-Clark State College B, T

Illinois
Augustana College B, T
Greenville College B
Lewis University T
North Park University T
University of Illinois
 Urbana-Champaign B, M, T

Indiana
Ball State University T
Indiana State University M, T
Indiana University
 Bloomington B, T
Indiana University--Purdue University
 Indiana University-Purdue
  University Fort Wayne B, T
 Indiana University-Purdue
  University Indianapolis B, T
University of Indianapolis B, T
Vincennes University A

Iowa
Central College T
Dordt College B
Graceland University T
Loras College T
Luther College B
Northwestern College T
St. Ambrose University T
University of Iowa B, M, T
Wartburg College T

Kansas
Baker University T
Benedictine College T
Coffeyville Community College A
Emporia State University B, T
McPherson College B, T
Pittsburg State University B, T

Kentucky
Murray State University B, M, T

Louisiana
Louisiana Tech University B
McNeese State University T
Northwestern State University B, T
Southeastern Louisiana University B
University of Louisiana at Monroe B

University of New Orleans B
Xavier University of Louisiana B

Maryland
University of Maryland
   College Park B

Massachusetts
Bridgewater State College M
Emerson College B, M
Northeastern University B

Michigan
Alma College T
Central Michigan University B
Concordia College B, T
Lansing Community College A
Michigan State University D
Northern Michigan University B, M, T
University of Michigan M, D

Minnesota
Augsburg College T
Concordia College: Moorhead T
Minnesota State University,
   Mankato B, M
Moorhead State University B, T
St. Cloud State University T
St. Olaf College T
Southwest State University B, T
Winona State University B, T

Mississippi
Mississippi Delta Community College A
Mississippi State University T

Missouri
Central Missouri State
   University B, M, T
Culver-Stockton College B, T
Lindenwood University M
Missouri Southern State College B, T
Southwest Baptist University T
William Jewell College T

Nebraska
Creighton University T
Dana College B
Hastings College B, T
Midland Lutheran College B, T
Nebraska Wesleyan University B
Peru State College B, T
University of Nebraska
   Kearney B, M, T
   Lincoln B

New Jersey
Kean University B
Monmouth University B
The College of New Jersey B, M

New York
City University of New York
   Brooklyn College B
   Lehman College M
   York College T
Columbia University
   Teachers College M, D
Elmira College B, T
Ithaca College B, T
Long Island University
   C. W. Post Campus M
Marymount Manhattan College B, T
Nazareth College of Rochester T
Pace University:
   Pleasantville/Briarcliff B, M, T
Pace University B, M, T
State University of New York
   College at Fredonia B, M, T
   College at Plattsburgh M
   New Paltz B, M, T
Syracuse University B

North Carolina
North Carolina Agricultural and
   Technical State University B, T
University of North Carolina
   Greensboro B, T

North Dakota
Dickinson State University B, T
North Dakota State University B, T
University of North Dakota B, T

Ohio
Baldwin-Wallace College T
Bluffton College B
Bowling Green State University B
Cedarville College B, T
Defiance College B, T
Hiram College T
Kent State University
   Stark Campus B
Kent State University B, T
Malone College B
Miami University
   Oxford Campus B, T
Mount Union College T
Ohio University B
University of Akron B
University of Rio Grande B, T
Youngstown State University B, M

Oklahoma
East Central University B, T
Eastern Oklahoma State College A
Northeastern State University B
Oklahoma Christian University of
   Science and Arts B, T
Southeastern Oklahoma State
   University B, M, T
Southern Nazarene University B
Southwestern Oklahoma State
   University T

Oregon
Portland State University T
Southern Oregon University T
University of Portland T
Western Oregon University T

Pennsylvania
California University of Pennsylvania M

South Carolina
Lander University B, T

South Dakota
Augustana College B
Black Hills State University B, T
South Dakota State University B
University of South Dakota B, T

Texas
Abilene Christian University B, T
Baylor University B, T
East Texas Baptist University B
Hardin-Simmons University B, T
Howard Payne University T
Lamar University T
McMurry University T
Southwest Texas State University T
Texas A&M University
   Commerce T
   Corpus Christi T
   Kingsville T
Texas Christian University B, T
University of Texas
   Pan American B, T
West Texas A&M University T

Vermont
Johnson State College M

Virginia
University of Virginia's College at
   Wise T

Washington
Washington State University T
Western Washington University T
Whitworth College B, T

West Virginia
Concord College B, T
Fairmont State College B
Glenville State College B

Wisconsin
Cardinal Stritch University T
Lakeland College B
St. Norbert College T
University of Wisconsin
   Green Bay T
   Platteville B, T
   River Falls T
   Whitewater B, T

Speech/rhetorical studies

Alabama
Alabama State University B
Huntingdon College B, T
Samford University B
Troy State University B
University of Alabama
   Huntsville B
University of Alabama B, M
University of Montevallo B, T
University of North Alabama B

Alaska
University of Alaska
   Fairbanks B

Arizona
Arizona Western College A
Northern Arizona University B, T
Pima Community College A

Arkansas
Arkansas State University
   Beebe Branch A
Arkansas State University B, M
Arkansas Tech University B
Henderson State University B
University of Arkansas
   Monticello B
   Pine Bluff B
University of Central Arkansas B
Westark College A

California
Cabrillo College A
California Lutheran University B
California Polytechnic State University:
   San Luis Obispo B
California State University
   Chico B
   Fresno M
   Fullerton B, M
   Hayward B, M
   Long Beach B, M
   Los Angeles B, M
   Northridge B, M
Cerritos Community College A
Chabot College A
College of San Mateo A
College of the Desert A
Columbia College A
Compton Community College A
Cypress College A
Foothill College A
Fresno City College A
Golden West College A
Grossmont Community College A
Humboldt State University B
Irvine Valley College A
Las Positas College A
Long Beach City College A
Master's College B
Mendocino College A
Merced College A
Modesto Junior College C, A
Ohlone College C, A
Orange Coast College A
Palomar College A
Pasadena City College C, A
Pepperdine University B
Point Loma Nazarene University B
Riverside Community College A
Saddleback College A
San Diego City College A
San Diego Miramar College A
San Francisco State University B, M
San Joaquin Delta College A
Santa Rosa Junior College C
Skyline College A
Southwestern College A
University of California
   Berkeley B, M, D
   Davis B, M
Ventura College A
West Los Angeles College C, A
West Valley College A

Colorado
Colorado State University B, M
Metropolitan State College of Denver B
University of Southern Colorado B

Delaware
Delaware State University B

District of Columbia
Catholic University of America M, D

Florida
Florida Atlantic University B, M
Gulf Coast Community College A
Miami-Dade Community College A
Stetson University B
University of Central Florida B
University of South Florida B, M, D

Georgia
Atlanta Metropolitan College A
Berry College B
Clark Atlanta University B
Clayton College and State University A
Darton College A
Georgia Southern University B
Georgia State University B
Morris Brown College B
University of Georgia B, M, D
Young Harris College A

Hawaii
Brigham Young University
   Hawaii A
University of Hawaii
   Hilo B
   Manoa B, M

Idaho
College of Southern Idaho A
Northwest Nazarene University B

Illinois
Augustana College B
Blackburn College B
Bradley University B, T
Chicago State University B
City Colleges of Chicago
   Harold Washington College A
Eastern Illinois University B, M, T
Illinois College T
Illinois State University B, T
Judson College B
Lake Land College A
Lewis University T
Monmouth College B, T
North Central College B
Northeastern Illinois University B, M
Northern Illinois University B, M
Northwestern University B
Rend Lake College A
Richland Community College A
Roosevelt University B
Southern Illinois University
   Carbondale B, M, D
   Edwardsville B
Southwestern Ilinois College A
Triton College A
University of Illinois
   Chicago B, M
   Urbana-Champaign B, M, D

Indiana
Ball State University M
Butler University B

Indiana State University M
Indiana University
    East A
    South Bend A, B
Vincennes University A
Wabash College B

Iowa
Drake University B
Graceland University B, T
Iowa State University B
Mount Mercy College B, T
Simpson College B
University of Dubuque B
University of Iowa B, M, D, T
University of Northern Iowa B, M
Wartburg College T

Kansas
Baker University B, T
Bethany College B
Butler County Community College A
Coffeyville Community College A
Kansas Wesleyan University B, T
Pratt Community College A
University of Kansas B, M, D
Washburn University of Topeka B

Kentucky
Asbury College B
Eastern Kentucky University B
Morehead State University B
Murray State University B, T
Northern Kentucky University B
University of Kentucky B
Western Kentucky University B, T

Louisiana
Centenary College of Louisiana B
Louisiana State University
    Shreveport B
Louisiana State University and
    Agricultural and Mechanical
    College B, M, D
Louisiana Tech University B, M
McNeese State University B
Northwestern State University B
Southern University and Agricultural and
    Mechanical College B
University of Louisiana at Monroe B

Maine
Bates College B
University of Maine B, M

Maryland
Bowie State University B
Frederick Community College A
Frostburg State University B, T
Morgan State University B
Mount St. Mary's College B
University of Maryland
    College Park B

Massachusetts
Emerson College B, M
Northeastern University B

Michigan
Albion College B
Calvin College B
Central Michigan University B, M
Concordia College B, T
Cornerstone College and Grand Rapids
    Baptist Seminary B, T
Eastern Michigan University B, M
Hillsdale College B
Lake Michigan College A
Mid Michigan Community College A
Northern Michigan University B, T
Spring Arbor College B
University of Detroit Mercy B
University of Michigan
    Flint B, T
University of Michigan B, D, T

Minnesota
Augsburg College B
Metropolitan State University B
Minnesota State University,
    Mankato B, M
Moorhead State University B
St. Cloud State University B
St. Olaf College B
Southwest State University B
University of Minnesota
    Morris B
    Twin Cities B, M, D
Winona State University B

Mississippi
Blue Mountain College B
Hinds Community College A
Jackson State University B
Mississippi Valley State University B

Missouri
Central Missouri State University B, M
East Central College A
Evangel University B
Missouri Western State College B, T
Southwest Baptist University T
St. Louis Community College
    St. Louis Community College at
        Florissant Valley A
Three Rivers Community College A
Truman State University B
William Jewell College B

Montana
Miles Community College A

Nebraska
Chadron State College B
Creighton University B
Doane College B
Hastings College B, T
Nebraska Wesleyan University B
Northeast Community College A
University of Nebraska
    Kearney B, M, T
    Omaha B

New Jersey
Rutgers
    The State University of New Jersey:
        Camden College of Arts and
        Sciences T
    The State University of New Jersey:
        University College Camden T

New Mexico
Eastern New Mexico University B
New Mexico State University D
University of New Mexico B, M, D

New York
City University of New York
    Brooklyn College B, M
    York College B
Hofstra University B
Ithaca College B, T
Long Island University
    Brooklyn Campus B
Mercy College B
New York University M
Pace University:
    Pleasantville/Briarcliff B
Pace University B
Rensselaer Polytechnic Institute M, D
St. John's University B
St. Joseph's College
    St. Joseph's College B
State University of New York
    Albany B, M
    College at Cortland B
    College at Oneonta B
    College at Potsdam B
Syracuse University B, M
Touro College B
Utica College of Syracuse University B

North Carolina
Appalachian State University B
Fayetteville State University B
Meredith College B
Methodist College A, B
North Carolina Agricultural and
    Technical State University B
North Carolina State University B
University of North Carolina
    Greensboro B, M, T
    Wilmington B

North Dakota
North Dakota State University B, M

Ohio
Bowling Green State University B
Defiance College B, T
Denison University B
Kent State University
    Stark Campus B
Kent State University B, M, D
Miami University
    Oxford Campus B, M, T
Ohio University M, D
University of Akron B, M
Youngstown State University B

Oklahoma
Connors State College A
East Central University B
Northeastern Oklahoma Agricultural and
    Mechanical College A
Northeastern State University B
Northwestern Oklahoma State
    University B
Oklahoma Baptist University B, T
Oklahoma Christian University of
    Science and Arts B
Oklahoma Panhandle State University B
Oklahoma State University B, M
Redlands Community College A
Rose State College A
Southern Nazarene University B
Tulsa Community College A
Western Oklahoma State College A

Oregon
Chemeketa Community College A
Multnomah Bible College B
Oregon State University B
Portland State University B, M
Southern Oregon University B, T
Western Oregon University B
Willamette University B

Pennsylvania
Bloomsburg University of
    Pennsylvania B
California University of Pennsylvania B
Carnegie Mellon University D
Clarion University of Pennsylvania B, T
Community College of Philadelphia A
Duquesne University D
East Stroudsburg University of
    Pennsylvania B
Geneva College B
Kutztown University of Pennsylvania B
La Salle University B
Lock Haven University of
    Pennsylvania B
Mansfield University of Pennsylvania B
Penn State
    Delaware County B
    University Park B, M, D
Shippensburg University of
    Pennsylvania B, T
Temple University B, M
University of Pittsburgh C, B, M, D
West Chester University of
    Pennsylvania B
York College of Pennsylvania B

South Carolina
Anderson College B

South Dakota
Augustana College T
Black Hills State University B, T
Dakota Wesleyan University B
University of South Dakota B, M

Tennessee
Belmont University B
Carson-Newman College B
David Lipscomb University B
East Tennessee State University B
Fisk University B
Trevecca Nazarene University B
Union University B, T

Texas
Abilene Christian University B, M
Amarillo College A
Angelina College A
Baylor University B
Blinn College A
Brazosport College A
Coastal Bend College A
Del Mar College A
East Texas Baptist University B
El Paso Community College A
Galveston College A
Grayson County College A
Houston Baptist University B
Howard Payne University B
Lamar University B, M
Lon Morris College A
Midland College A
Navarro College A
Northeast Texas Community College A
Panola College A
St. Philip's College A
Sam Houston State University B
San Jacinto College
    North A
Southwest Texas State
    University B, M, T
Stephen F. Austin State University B, M
Sul Ross State University B
Tarleton State University B
Texas A&M University
    Commerce B, M
Texas A&M University B, M, D
Texas Tech University B, M
Texas Woman's University D
Trinity University B
Trinity Valley Community College A
Tyler Junior College A
University of Houston
    Victoria B
University of Mary Hardin-Baylor B
University of North Texas B, M
University of Texas
    Arlington B
    Austin B, M, D
    Pan American B, M, T
    Tyler B
    of the Permian Basin B
University of the Incarnate Word B
Weatherford College A
West Texas A&M University B

Utah
Southern Utah University B
University of Utah B
Utah State University B

Virginia
George Mason University B
Old Dominion University B
University of Richmond B
University of Virginia's College at
    Wise T

Washington
Eastern Washington University T
Gonzaga University B
University of Washington B, M, D

West Virginia
Alderson-Broaddus College B
Marshall University B, M
West Virginia Wesleyan College B

Wisconsin
Beloit College B
Ripon College B

University of Wisconsin
   Madison *B, M, D*
   River Falls *B, M*
   Superior *B, M*
   Whitewater *B*

Wyoming

Laramie County Community College *A*

Speech/theater education

Alabama

Alabama Agricultural and Mechanical University *B, M*
Birmingham-Southern College *T*
University of Alabama
   Birmingham *M*

Alaska

University of Alaska
   Southeast *M*

Arizona

Arizona State University *B, T*
Grand Canyon University *B*

Arkansas

Arkansas State University *B, T*
Harding University *M*
Ouachita Baptist University *B, T*

California

California Lutheran University *B, T*
California State University
   Bakersfield *B, T*
   Northridge *B, T*
Chapman University *B*
San Francisco State University *B*
San Jose State University *M*
University of the Pacific *T*
Whittier College *B, T*

Colorado

Front Range Community College *C*

District of Columbia

George Washington University *M, T*
Howard University *B*

Florida

St. Thomas University *M*

Georgia

Columbus State University *B*
Piedmont College *B, T*
University of Georgia *M, D*

Idaho

Boise State University *T*
Lewis-Clark State College *B, T*
Northwest Nazarene University *B*

Illinois

Augustana College *B, T*
Bradley University *B, D*
Elmhurst College *B*
Greenville College *T*
Illinois College *B*
North Park University *T*
Wheaton College *T*

Indiana

Anderson University *B, T*
Franklin College *T*
Indiana State University *B, T*
Indiana University--Purdue University
   Indiana University-Purdue
     University Fort Wayne *B, T*
St. Mary-of-the-Woods College *B*
Taylor University *B*
University of Evansville *T*
University of Indianapolis *B, T*
Vincennes University *A*

Iowa

Buena Vista University *B, T*
Central College *T*
Cornell College *B, T*
Drake University *M, T*
Graceland University *T*
Iowa State University *T*
Loras College *T*
Luther College *B*
St. Ambrose University *B, T*
University of Iowa *B, M, T*
Wartburg College *T*
William Penn University *B*

Kansas

Baker University *T*
Benedictine College *T*
Bethel College *T*
McPherson College *B, T*
MidAmerica Nazarene University *B, T*
Pittsburg State University *B, T*
Washburn University of Topeka *B*
Wichita State University *T*

Kentucky

Cumberland College *B, T*
Murray State University *B, M, T*

Louisiana

Centenary College of Louisiana *B, T*

Maine

University of Southern Maine *T*

Massachusetts

Boston University *B, M*
Bridgewater State College *B*
Emerson College *B, M*
Westfield State College *B, T*

Michigan

Alma College *T*
Cornerstone College and Grand Rapids Baptist Seminary *B*
Northern Michigan University *B, M, T*

Minnesota

Augsburg College *T*
College of St. Catherine: St. Paul Campus *T*
Concordia College: Moorhead *T*
Minnesota State University,
   Mankato *B, M*
Moorhead State University *B, T*
St. Mary's University of Minnesota *B*
St. Olaf College *T*
University of St. Thomas *T*
Winona State University *B, T*

Mississippi

Mississippi College *B*
Mississippi Delta Community College *A*
Northwest Mississippi Community College *A*

Missouri

Avila College *T*
Central Missouri State University *B, T*
Culver-Stockton College *T*
Hannibal-LaGrange College *B*
Missouri Southern State College *B, T*
Missouri Valley College *T*
Missouri Western State College *B*
Southeast Missouri State University *B*
Southwest Baptist University *T*
Southwest Missouri State University *B*
Truman State University *M, T*
University of Missouri
   St. Louis *T*
Webster University *M*
William Jewell College *T*

Montana

Montana State University
   Billings *T*
Rocky Mountain College *B, T*

Nebraska

Concordia University *T*
Creighton University *T*
Dana College *B*
Doane College *T*
Hastings College *B, M, T*
Midland Lutheran College *B, T*
University of Nebraska
   Kearney *B, M, T*
   Lincoln *B*

Nevada

University of Nevada
   Reno *B*

New Hampshire

Keene State College *B*

New Jersey

Richard Stockton College of New Jersey *C*
The College of New Jersey *B, M*

New York

Adelphi University *B, M*
City University of New York
   Brooklyn College *B*
Fulton-Montgomery Community College *A*
Ithaca College *B, T*
New York University *B, M, D*
St. Joseph's College
   St. Joseph's College *B, T*
State University of New York
   Buffalo *T*

North Carolina

Mars Hill College *B*
Meredith College *B, T*
North Carolina Agricultural and Technical State University *B, T*
Sandhills Community College *A*

North Dakota

Dickinson State University *B, T*
Minot State University *B, T*
North Dakota State University *B, T*

Ohio

Baldwin-Wallace College *T*
Bowling Green State University *B*
Cedarville College *B*
Defiance College *B, T*
Hiram College *T*
Kent State University
   Stark Campus *B*
Kent State University *B, T*
Miami University
   Oxford Campus *B*
Mount Union College *T*
Muskingum College *B*
Ohio Dominican College *D*
Ohio State University
   Columbus Campus *D*
Otterbein College *B*
University of Findlay *B, T*
Youngstown State University *B, M*

Oklahoma

East Central University *B, T*
Eastern Oklahoma State College *A*
Northeastern Oklahoma Agricultural and Mechanical College *A*
Northwestern Oklahoma State University *B, T*
Oklahoma Baptist University *B, T*
Oklahoma Christian University of Science and Arts *B, T*
Oklahoma City University *B*
Oklahoma State University *B, T*
Oral Roberts University *B, T*
Southern Nazarene University *M*
Southwestern Oklahoma State University *T*
University of Central Oklahoma *B*

Pennsylvania

Allentown College of St. Francis de Sales *T*
Bucknell University *T*
California University of Pennsylvania *B, T*
Clarion University of Pennsylvania *B, T*
East Stroudsburg University of Pennsylvania *B, T*
Juniata College *B, T*
Lycoming College *T*
Marywood University *B, T*
Point Park College *B*
Robert Morris College *B*
University of Pittsburgh
   Johnstown *B, T*
Villanova University *T*
York College of Pennsylvania *B, T*

Rhode Island

Rhode Island College *B*
Salve Regina University *B*

South Carolina

Lander University *B, T*

South Dakota

Augustana College *B, T*
Black Hills State University *B, T*
Mount Marty College *B*
South Dakota State University *B*
University of South Dakota *T*

Tennessee

Freed-Hardeman University *T*
University of Tennessee
   Knoxville *B*

Texas

Abilene Christian University *B, T*
Blinn College *A*
Houston Baptist University *T*
Howard Payne University *T*
Lubbock Christian University *B*
McMurry University *T*
Texas A&M University
   Commerce *T*
Texas Christian University *T*
Texas Lutheran University *T*
University of Texas
   Arlington *T*
   San Antonio *T*
Wayland Baptist University *T*
West Texas A&M University *T*

Utah

Weber State University *B*

Vermont

Johnson State College *B*

Virginia

Averett College *B, T*
Bridgewater College *T*
Longwood College *B, T*
University of Virginia's College at Wise *T*
Virginia Commonwealth University *B*
Virginia Highlands Community College *A*

Washington

Pacific Lutheran University *B*
Western Washington University *B, T*
Whitworth College *B, T*

West Virginia

Fairmont State College *B*

Wisconsin

Alverno College *T*
Cardinal Stritch University *B, T*
Carthage College *T*
Lakeland College *T*
Ripon College *T*
St. Norbert College *T*
University of Wisconsin
   Madison *B, M, T*
   Platteville *B, T*
   River Falls *T*
   Superior *B, M, T*
Viterbo University *B*

Sports medicine/athletic training

Alabama
Huntingdon College C
Northwest-Shoals Community College A
Samford University B
Troy State University B
University of Alabama B
University of Mobile B
University of West Alabama B
Wallace State Community College at Hanceville A

Arizona
Grand Canyon University B

Arkansas
John Brown University B

California
California Lutheran University B
California State University
    Fullerton T
    Hayward B
    Northridge M
    Stanislaus B
Chapman University M
Fresno Pacific University B
Hope International University B
Master's College B
Orange Coast College C, A
Pepperdine University B
San Bernardino Valley College C
San Diego State University B
San Francisco State University B
Santa Barbara City College A
University of the Pacific B
Whittier College B

Colorado
Adams State College B
Denver Technical College: A Division of DeVry University A
University of Southern Colorado B

Connecticut
Central Connecticut State University B
Mitchell College A
Quinnipiac University B
Sacred Heart University B

Delaware
University of Delaware B

Florida
Barry University B, M
Broward Community College A
Florida Southern College B
Florida State University C
Stetson University B
University of Miami B
University of West Florida B, M

Georgia
Abraham Baldwin Agricultural College A
Georgia Southern University B
Georgia State University M
Valdosta State University B

Hawaii
University of Hawaii
    Manoa B

Idaho
Boise State University B, M
Northwest Nazarene University B

Illinois
McKendree College B
Millikin University B
North Central College B
Quincy University A, B
St. Xavier University C
Sauk Valley Community College A
Trinity International University B

Indiana
Anderson University B
Ball State University B
DePauw University B
Franklin College B
Grace College B
Indiana State University B
Indiana Wesleyan University B
Taylor University B
University of Evansville B
University of Indianapolis B
Valparaiso University B
Vincennes University A

Iowa
Coe College B
Dordt College B
Graceland University B
Morningside College B
North Iowa Area Community College A
Northwestern College C
St. Ambrose University B
Simpson College C
University of Iowa B, M
Upper Iowa University B

Kansas
Benedictine College C
Central Christian College C
Coffeyville Community College A
Dodge City Community College A
Garden City Community College A
Pittsburg State University B
Seward County Community College A
Southwestern College C
Tabor College B

Kentucky
Campbellsville University B
Murray State University C
Union College B

Maine
University of New England C
University of Southern Maine B

Maryland
Towson University B

Massachusetts
Boston University B
Dean College A
Eastern Nazarene College B
Endicott College B
Lasell College B
Merrimack College B
Northeastern University B
Springfield College B, M
Westfield State College B

Michigan
Aquinas College B
Central Michigan University B
Eastern Michigan University B
Hope College B
Madonna University C
Northern Michigan University B
Olivet College B
University of Michigan B, D

Minnesota
Bethel College B
Gustavus Adolphus College B
Hamline University B
Minnesota State University, Mankato B
Northland Community & Technical College A
Northwestern College B
Ridgewater College: A Community and Technical College A
Winona State University B

Mississippi
Belhaven College B

Missouri
Central Methodist College B
Missouri Baptist College B
Park University B
Southeast Missouri State University B
Southwest Missouri State University B
William Woods University B

Montana
Rocky Mountain College B

Nebraska
Midland Lutheran College B

Nevada
University of Nevada
    Las Vegas B

New Hampshire
Colby-Sawyer College B
Keene State College B
New England College B
Plymouth State College of the University System of New Hampshire B
Rivier College B
University of New Hampshire B

New Jersey
Rowan University B

New Mexico
College of the Southwest B
New Mexico Junior College A
New Mexico State University B

New York
Alfred University B
Canisius College B
Concordia College B
Dominican College of Blauvelt B
Finger Lakes Community College A
Hofstra University B
Ithaca College B
Long Island University
    Brooklyn Campus M
Russell Sage College B
State University of New York
    College at Brockport B

North Carolina
Appalachian State University B
Barton College B
Campbell University B
Catawba College B
Chowan College B
East Carolina University B
Elon College B
Greensboro College B
Guilford College B
High Point University B
Lenoir-Rhyne College B
Louisburg College A
Mars Hill College B
Methodist College B
Pfeiffer University B
St. Andrews Presbyterian College B
University of North Carolina
    Pembroke B
    Wilmington B
Wingate University B

North Dakota
Mayville State University B
North Dakota State University B
University of Mary B
University of North Dakota B

Ohio
Ashland University B
Baldwin-Wallace College B
Capital University B
Cedarville College B
College of Mount St. Joseph B
Defiance College C, B
Heidelberg College B
Lorain County Community College A
Marietta College B
Miami University
    Oxford Campus B
Mount Union College B
Ohio Northern University B
Ohio University B, M
Otterbein College B
Shawnee State University C, B
University of Akron B, M
University of Findlay B
Xavier University B
Youngstown State University B

Oklahoma
East Central University B
Northeastern Oklahoma Agricultural and Mechanical College A
Northeastern State University B
Oklahoma Baptist University B
Oklahoma City University B
Oklahoma State University B
Southern Nazarene University B
University of Tulsa B

Oregon
Concordia University B
George Fox University B
Linfield College B
Southern Oregon University B

Pennsylvania
Alvernia College C, B
California University of Pennsylvania B, M
Duquesne University B
East Stroudsburg University of Pennsylvania B
King's College B
Lock Haven University of Pennsylvania B
Marywood University B
Mercyhurst College B
Messiah College B
University of Pittsburgh
    Bradford B
Waynesburg College B
West Chester University of Pennsylvania B, M

Puerto Rico
University of Puerto Rico
    Ponce University College B

South Carolina
Anderson College B
Charleston Southern University C
Erskine College B
Limestone College B
Newberry College B

South Dakota
Augustana College B
Dakota Wesleyan University B
Mount Marty College B
South Dakota State University B

Tennessee
Carson-Newman College B
David Lipscomb University B
Lambuth University B
Lincoln Memorial University B
Middle Tennessee State University B
Tennessee Wesleyan College B
Tusculum College B
Union University B
University of Tennessee
    Chattanooga M
    Martin B

Texas
Howard College A
Howard Payne University B
McMurry University T
St. Edward's University B, T
South Plains College A
Southwest Texas State University B, T
Texas A&M University
    Commerce B
Texas Christian University T
Texas Lutheran University B
Texas Tech University B, M
Texas Wesleyan University B
Texas Woman's University M

Utah
Brigham Young University B, M
Weber State University B

Vermont
Castleton State College B
Johnson State College B
Lyndon State College C, B
Norwich University B

Virginia
Averett College B
Bluefield College B
Bridgewater College B
Liberty University B
Longwood College B
Lynchburg College B

Washington
Eastern Washington University B
Pacific Lutheran University B
Washington State University B
Western Washington University B
Whitworth College B

West Virginia
Alderson-Broaddus College B
Marshall University B, M
Salem-Teikyo University B
University of Charleston B
West Virginia Wesleyan College B

Wisconsin
Carroll College B
Carthage College B
Concordia University Wisconsin B
University of Wisconsin
    La Crosse B
    Madison C
    Stevens Point B

Sports/fitness administration

Alabama
Faulkner University B
Huntingdon College B
Shelton State Community College A

Arizona
Grand Canyon University B

Arkansas
Harding University B

California
California State University
    Hayward C
Concordia University B
Fresno Pacific University B
Mendocino College A
San Francisco State University B, M
University of San Francisco M
University of the Pacific B

Colorado
University of Southern Colorado B

Connecticut
Eastern Connecticut State University B
Mitchell College A
Teikyo Post University B
University of New Haven B

Delaware
Delaware State University B
University of Delaware B
Wilmington College B

District of Columbia
American University M

Florida
Barry University B, M
Flagler College B
Florida State University B
Lynn University B, M
Manatee Community College A
St. Leo University B
St. Petersburg Junior College C
St. Thomas University B, M
Stetson University B
University of Miami B
Warner Southern College B

Georgia
Georgia Southern University B, M
Georgia State University M
South Georgia College A
University of Georgia B

Idaho
Albertson College of Idaho B

Illinois
Elmhurst College B
Greenville College B
Judson College B
Millikin University B
North Central College B
Principia College B
Quincy University A, B

Indiana
Goshen College B
Indiana Institute of Technology A, B
Indiana State University B, M
Indiana Wesleyan University B
Marian College B
Taylor University B
Tri-State University B
University of Evansville B
Valparaiso University B
Vincennes University A

Iowa
Graceland University B
Iowa Wesleyan College B
Loras College B
St. Ambrose University B
Simpson College B
University of Iowa B, M, D
Wartburg College B
William Penn University B

Kansas
Central Christian College A
St. Mary College B
Southwestern College B
Wichita State University B, M

Kentucky
Kentucky Wesleyan College B
Union College B
University of Louisville B

Louisiana
Tulane University B

Maine
Husson College B
Thomas College B
University of New England B

Maryland
Community College of Baltimore County
    Essex A
Towson University B

Massachusetts
Becker College A, B
Dean College A
Endicott College B
Holyoke Community College A
Mount Ida College A
Nichols College B
North Shore Community College C
Northeastern University M
Northern Essex Community College A
Salem State College B
Springfield College B, M
University of Massachusetts
    Amherst B, M, D
Western New England College B

Michigan
Aquinas College B
Central Michigan University M
Concordia College B
Northern Michigan University B
Oakland Community College A
University of Michigan B
Wayne State University M

Minnesota
Crown College B
Minnesota State University, Mankato B
Northwestern College B
St. Cloud State University M
Winona State University B

Mississippi
Belhaven College B
University of Southern Mississippi M

Missouri
Missouri Baptist College B
Southeast Missouri State University B
Southwest Baptist University B

Montana
Montana State University
    Billings B, M
    Bozeman B

Nebraska
Bellevue University B
Chadron State College M
Concordia University B
Dana College B
Hastings College B
Nebraska Wesleyan University B
Union College B
University of Nebraska
    Kearney B
Wayne State College B

Nevada
University of Nevada
    Las Vegas M

New Hampshire
Colby-Sawyer College B
Daniel Webster College B
Franklin Pierce College B
Hesser College A
Keene State College B
New England College B
New Hampshire College B
New Hampshire Technical Institute A
Plymouth State College of the University
    System of New Hampshire B

New Jersey
Rowan University B
Seton Hall University C, B
The College of New Jersey B

New York
Canisius College M
City University of New York
    Kingsborough Community
        College A
Herkimer County Community College A
Ithaca College B
Medaille College C, B
New York University B
St. John's University C, B
St. Thomas Aquinas College B
State University of New York
    College at Brockport B
    College of Technology at Alfred A

North Carolina
Barton College B
Campbell University B
Chowan College B
Elon College B
Greensboro College B
Guilford College B
High Point University B
Meredith College B
Methodist College B
Pfeiffer University B
Western Carolina University B
Wingate University B

Ohio
Baldwin-Wallace College B
Bowling Green State University B
Cedarville College B
Central State University B
Cincinnati State Technical and
    Community College C
Columbus State Community College A
Kent State University
    Stark Campus B
Kent State University M
Miami University
    Oxford Campus B, M
Mount Union College B
Mount Vernon Nazarene College A, B
Ohio Northern University B
Ohio University B, M
Otterbein College B
University of Dayton B
University of Rio Grande B
Xavier University B, M
Youngstown State University B

Oklahoma
University of Tulsa B

Oregon
Concordia University B
George Fox University B
Portland Community College C
Southern Oregon University B
Western Baptist College B

Pennsylvania
Allentown College of St. Francis de
    Sales B
Butler County Community College A
College Misericordia B
Lock Haven University of
    Pennsylvania B
Mercyhurst College B
Millersville University of
    Pennsylvania M
Neumann College B, M
Robert Morris College B, M
Slippery Rock University of
    Pennsylvania B
University of Pittsburgh
    Bradford B
West Chester University of
    Pennsylvania M
Widener University B
York College of Pennsylvania B

South Carolina
Anderson College B
Erskine College B
Limestone College B
North Greenville College B
Technical College of the Lowcountry C
University of South Carolina B
Winthrop University B

South Dakota
Dakota State University B
Huron University B
Northern State University B

Tennessee
Southern Adventist University B
Tennessee Wesleyan College B
Tusculum College B
Union University B
University of Memphis B
University of Tennessee
    Knoxville B
    Martin B

Texas
Baylor University B
Hardin-Simmons University M
LeTourneau University B
Midwestern State University B
Texas Lutheran University B
University of Houston B
University of the Incarnate Word B

Utah
Brigham Young University B, D

Vermont
Champlain College A, B
Johnson State College B

Virginia
Averett College B
Hampton University B
Liberty University B
Longwood College B
Lynchburg College B
Virginia Intermont College B

Washington
Central Washington University B
Lake Washington Technical College C
Washington State University B

West Virginia
Bethany College B
Davis and Elkins College B
Marshall University B
Salem-Teikyo University B

Wisconsin
Carroll College B
Marian College of Fond du Lac B
University of Wisconsin
    La Crosse B, M

Stationary energy sources mechanics

Alabama
Community College of the Air Force A

Illinois
Triton College C, A

Kansas
Barton County Community College A

Massachusetts
Massachusetts Maritime Academy C

Michigan
Oakland Community College C, A

Pennsylvania
Johnson Technical Institute A

Wisconsin
Gateway Technical College C
Northeast Wisconsin Technical
    College C

Statistics

Alabama
Auburn University M, T
University of Alabama M, D
University of South Alabama B

Alaska
University of Alaska
    Fairbanks B

Arizona
Arizona State University M
Northern Arizona University B

Arkansas
University of Arkansas M

California
California Polytechnic State University:
    San Luis Obispo B
California State University
    Chico B
    Hayward B, M
    Long Beach B
    Northridge B
    Stanislaus B
Chabot College A
Master's College B
Pomona College B

San Diego State University B, M
San Francisco State University B
San Jose State University B
Stanford University M, D
University of California
    Berkeley B, M, D
    Davis B, M, D
    Riverside B, M, D
    San Diego M
    Santa Barbara B, M, D
University of Southern California M

Colorado
Colorado State University B, M, D
Fort Lewis College B
University of Denver B

Connecticut
Central Connecticut State University B
University of Connecticut B, M, D
Yale University M, D

Delaware
University of Delaware B, M, D

District of Columbia
American University B, M, D
George Washington University B, M, D

Florida
Florida International University B
Florida State University B, M, D
Manatee Community College A
University of Central Florida B, M
University of Florida B, M, D
University of Miami M
University of North Florida B
University of West Florida B, M

Georgia
Georgia Institute of Technology M
Georgia Military College A
Oxford College of Emory University B
University of Georgia B, M, D

Idaho
University of Idaho M

Illinois
Loyola University of Chicago B
Northern Illinois University M
Northwestern University B, M, D
Roosevelt University B
Southern Illinois University
    Carbondale M
University of Chicago B, M, D
University of Illinois
    Chicago B
    Urbana-Champaign B, M, D

Indiana
Ball State University M
Indiana University--Purdue University
    Indiana University-Purdue
        University Fort Wayne B
Purdue University B, M, D

Iowa
Iowa State University B, M, D
Luther College B
University of Iowa B, M, D

Kansas
Independence Community College A
Kansas State University B, M, D

Kentucky
Eastern Kentucky University B
University of Kentucky M, D

Louisiana
Louisiana State University and
    Agricultural and Mechanical
    College B
Tulane University M
Xavier University of Louisiana B

Maine
University of Southern Maine M

Maryland
University of Maryland
    Baltimore County M, D
    College Park M, D

Massachusetts
Hampshire College B
Harvard College B
Harvard University M, D

Michigan
Central Michigan University B
Eastern Michigan University B, M
Grand Valley State University B
Michigan State University B, M, D
Oakland University B, M
University of Michigan B, M, D
Wayne State University M
Western Michigan University B, M, D

Minnesota
Minnesota State University, Mankato M
St. Cloud State University B
University of Minnesota
    Twin Cities B, M, D
Winona State University B

Mississippi
Mississippi State University M

Missouri
Northwest Missouri State University B
University of Missouri
    Columbia B, M, D
    Kansas City B, M
    Rolla D
Washington University B, M

Montana
Montana State University
    Bozeman M, D
University of Montana-Missoula B

Nebraska
University of Nebraska
    Kearney B
    Lincoln M, D

New Hampshire
Plymouth State College of the University
    System of New Hampshire B

New Jersey
Montclair State University M
New Jersey Institute of Technology B
Rutgers
    The State University of New Jersey:
        Douglass College B
    The State University of New Jersey:
        Livingston College B
    The State University of New Jersey:
        New Brunswick Graduate
        Campus M, D
    The State University of New Jersey:
        Rutgers College B
    The State University of New Jersey:
        University College New
        Brunswick B
Stevens Institute of Technology B, M
The College of New Jersey B

New Mexico
New Mexico State University M
University of New Mexico B, M, D

New York
Barnard College B
Canisius College B
City University of New York
    Baruch College B, M
    Hunter College B
    Queens College M
Columbia University
    Columbia College B
    Graduate School M, D
    School of General Studies B
Cornell University M, D
New York University B, M, D
Rensselaer Polytechnic Institute M

Rochester Institute of
    Technology A, B, M
State University of New York
    Buffalo B, M
    College at Oneonta B
Syracuse University M
University of Rochester B, M

North Carolina
Appalachian State University B
North Carolina State University B, M, D
University of North Carolina
    Chapel Hill M, D
    Charlotte M

North Dakota
North Dakota State University B, M, D

Ohio
Bowling Green State University B, M
Case Western Reserve
    University B, M, D
Miami University
    Oxford Campus B, M
Ohio Northern University B
Ohio State University
    Columbus Campus M, D
University of Akron B, M
Wright State University M

Oklahoma
Oklahoma State University B, M, D
University of Central Oklahoma B

Oregon
Oregon State University M, D
Portland State University M

Pennsylvania
Carnegie Mellon University B
La Salle University B
Lehigh University B, M
Penn State
    University Park B, M, D
Temple University B, M, D
University of Pennsylvania B, M, D
University of Pittsburgh C, B, M, D
Villanova University B

Puerto Rico
University of Puerto Rico
    Mayaguez Campus M

Rhode Island
Brown University B
University of Rhode Island M

South Carolina
University of South Carolina B, M, D

South Dakota
Dakota State University B

Texas
Baylor University M, D
Rice University B, M, D
Southern Methodist University B, M, D
Stephen F. Austin State University M
Texas A&M University M, D
Texas Tech University M
University of Houston
    Clear Lake M
University of Texas
    Austin M
    Dallas B, M, D
    El Paso M
    San Antonio B, M

Utah
Brigham Young University B, M
Snow College A
University of Utah M
Utah State University B, M

Vermont
University of Vermont B, M

Virginia
University of Virginia M, D
Virginia Commonwealth University C

Virginia Polytechnic Institute and State
  University B, M, D

Washington
University of Washington M, D
Washington State University M

West Virginia
West Virginia University B, M

Wisconsin
University of Wisconsin
  La Crosse B
  Madison B, M, D

Wyoming
Eastern Wyoming College A
University of Wyoming B, M, D

Studio arts

Alabama
Auburn University B, M
Huntingdon College B
Spring Hill College B
University of Alabama
  Birmingham B
University of Alabama B, M
University of North Alabama B
University of South Alabama B

Alaska
University of Alaska
  Fairbanks B

Arizona
Arizona State University B
Grand Canyon University B
Northern Arizona University B
University of Arizona B

Arkansas
Henderson State University B
Ouachita Baptist University B, T
University of Central Arkansas B
Williams Baptist College B

California
Art Center College of Design B
Biola University B
Cabrillo College A
California Institute of the Arts C, B, M
California State University
  Chico B
  Fullerton B, M
  Hayward B
  Long Beach B, M
  Stanislaus B
Chabot College A
Chapman University B
College of Notre Dame B
Dominican University of California B
Foothill College C, A
Gavilan Community College A
John F. Kennedy University M
Loyola Marymount University B
Mills College B, M
Monterey Peninsula College A
Orange Coast College A
Otis College of Art and Design B, M
Pasadena City College A
Pitzer College B
Pomona College B
Porterville College C, A
San Diego City College A
San Diego Miramar College A
San Diego State University B, M
San Francisco Art Institute B, M
San Francisco State University M
Santa Barbara City College C, A
Santa Clara University B
Scripps College B
Sonoma State University B

University of California
  Davis B
  Irvine B, M
  Riverside B
  San Diego B
  Santa Barbara B, M
  Santa Cruz C, B
University of San Francisco B
University of Southern California B, M
University of the Pacific B
West Hills Community College A

Colorado
Colorado College B
Colorado Mountain College
  Alpine Campus A
Colorado State University B
Fort Lewis College B
University of Colorado
  Boulder B
  Colorado Springs B
University of Denver B, M

Connecticut
Albertus Magnus College B
Capital Community College C
Connecticut College B
Naugatuck Valley Community-Technical
  College C
Northwestern Connecticut
  Community-Technical College A
Norwalk Community-Technical
  College A
Paier College of Art C, B
Quinebaug Valley Community College A
Trinity College B
University of Connecticut B, M
Wesleyan University B

Delaware
University of Delaware B

District of Columbia
American University B
Gallaudet University B
Georgetown University B
University of the District of Columbia B

Florida
Florida Atlantic University M
Florida Gulf Coast University B
Florida International University B, M
Florida Southern College B
Florida State University B, M
Jacksonville University B
Palm Beach Atlantic College B
Ringling School of Art and Design B
Rollins College B
University of Central Florida B
University of Florida M
University of North Florida B
University of West Florida B

Georgia
Atlanta College of Art B
Berry College B
Brenau University B
Gainesville College A
Georgia Southern University M
Piedmont College B
University of Georgia B
Wesleyan College B

Hawaii
University of Hawaii
  Manoa B, M

Idaho
North Idaho College A
Northwest Nazarene University B

Illinois
American Academy of Art A, B
Augustana College B
Barat College B
Blackburn College B, T
Bradley University B, M, T
Columbia College B

De Paul University B
Dominican University B
Illinois College B
Illinois State University B, M
Judson College B
Lake Forest College B
Loyola University of Chicago B
Monmouth College B
North Central College B
North Park University B
Northeastern Illinois University B
Northern Illinois University B, M
Northwestern University B
Principia College B
Rockford College B
School of the Art Institute of
  Chicago B, M
Southern Illinois University
  Carbondale B, M
  Edwardsville M
Trinity Christian College B
University of Illinois
  Chicago B, M
  Urbana-Champaign M
Western Illinois University B

Indiana
Anderson University B
DePauw University B
Goshen College B
Indiana State University B
Indiana University
  Bloomington B, M
  Northwest B
  South Bend B
Indiana University--Purdue University
  Indiana University-Purdue
    University Fort Wayne B
Indiana Wesleyan University B
Oakland City University B
Saint Mary's College B
University of Notre Dame B, M
University of St. Francis B
Valparaiso University B

Iowa
Clarke College A, B
Graceland University B, T
Loras College B
Maharishi University of
  Management B, M
Morningside College B
St. Ambrose University B
University of Iowa B, M
University of Northern Iowa B

Kansas
Baker University B
Fort Hays State University M
Independence Community College A
Kansas Wesleyan University B, T
Pittsburg State University B
Seward County Community College A
University of Kansas B, M
Wichita State University B, M

Kentucky
Asbury College B
Berea College B, T
Campbellsville University B
Kentucky State University B
Lindsey Wilson College A
Morehead State University B, M
Murray State University B, M, T
Northern Kentucky University B
St. Catharine College A
Spalding University B
Thomas More College A, B, T
Transylvania University B, T
University of Kentucky B, M, T
University of Louisville B, M
Western Kentucky University B

Louisiana
Centenary College of Louisiana B

Louisiana State University and
  Agricultural and Mechanical
  College B, M
Loyola University New Orleans B
Tulane University B
University of New Orleans B, M

Maine
Colby College B
Maine College of Art B
University of Maine
  Farmington B
University of Maine B
University of Southern Maine B

Maryland
College of Notre Dame of Maryland B
Maryland College of Art and Design A
Montgomery College
  Rockville Campus A
  Takoma Park Campus A
Prince George's Community College A
University of Maryland
  College Park B
Western Maryland College B

Massachusetts
Anna Maria College B
Assumption College B
Atlantic Union College B
Berkshire Community College A
Boston College B
Boston University M
Bristol Community College C
Clark University B
College of the Holy Cross B
Emmanuel College B
Endicott College B
Framingham State College B
Gordon College B
Hampshire College B
Harvard College B
Massachusetts College of Art B, M
Massachusetts College of Liberal Arts B
Middlesex Community College C, A
Montserrat College of Art B
Mount Holyoke College B
Salem State College B
School of the Museum of Fine Arts B, M
Simon's Rock College of Bard B
Smith College B
Stonehill College B
Tufts University M
University of Massachusetts
  Amherst B, M
  Dartmouth B, M
Wellesley College B
Wheaton College B
Williams College B

Michigan
Andrews University B
Aquinas College B
Calvin College B
Center for Creative Studies: College of
  Art and Design B
Eastern Michigan University B, M
Grand Valley State University B
Hope College B, T
Kendall College of Art and Design B
Marygrove College B
Michigan State University B, M
Monroe County Community College A
Northwestern Michigan College A
Saginaw Valley State University B
Siena Heights University B
Suomi College B
University of Michigan
  Flint B
University of Michigan B, M

Minnesota
Bethel College B
Carleton College B
College of St. Catherine: St. Paul
  Campus B
College of Visual Arts B

Concordia College: Moorhead *B*
Hamline University *B*
Macalester College *B*
Minneapolis College of Art and Design *B*
Minnesota State University, Mankato *B*
Moorhead State University *M*
Northwestern College *B*
Ridgewater College: A Community and Technical College *A*
St. Cloud State University *B, M*
St. Mary's University of Minnesota *B*
University of Minnesota
    Duluth *B*
    Morris *B*
Winona State University *B*

Mississippi
Millsaps College *B, T*

Missouri
Central Missouri State University *B*
Drury University *B, T*
Evangel University *B*
Fontbonne College *B*
Lindenwood University *B, M*
Maryville University of Saint Louis *B*
Missouri Southern State College *B, T*
Missouri Western State College *B*
St. Louis University *B*
St. Louis Community College
    St. Louis Community College at Florissant Valley *A*
Truman State University *B*
University of Missouri
    Kansas City *B, M*
    St. Louis *B*
Washington University *B, M*
Webster University *B*
William Woods University *B*

Montana
Montana State University
    Bozeman *B, M*

Nebraska
Bellevue University *B*
College of Saint Mary *B*
Concordia University *B*
Hastings College *B*
Metropolitan Community College *A*
Union College *B*

New Hampshire
Dartmouth College *B*
Franklin Pierce College *B*
Plymouth State College of the University System of New Hampshire *B*
Rivier College *B*
University of New Hampshire
    Manchester *A*
University of New Hampshire *B*

New Jersey
Atlantic Cape Community College *A*
Caldwell College *B*
Drew University *B*
Fairleigh Dickinson University *B*
Kean University *B*
Middlesex County College *A*
Raritan Valley Community College *A*
Rider University *B*
Rowan University *B*
Rutgers
    The State University of New Jersey: Mason Gross School of the Arts *M*

New York
Bard College *B, M*
City University of New York
    Brooklyn College *B, M*
    City College *B, M*
    Hunter College *B, M*
    Lehman College *B, M*
    Queens College *B*
    York College *B*
Colgate University *B*

College of New Rochelle *B, M, T*
College of St. Rose *B*
Columbia University
    Columbia College *B*
Cornell University *B*
Daemen College *B*
Eugene Lang College/New School University *B*
Finger Lakes Community College *A*
Fordham University *B*
Hamilton College *B*
Hobart and William Smith Colleges *B*
Houghton College *B*
Ithaca College *B*
Jamestown Community College *A*
Long Island University
    C. W. Post Campus *B*
    Southampton College *B*
Manhattanville College *B*
Marymount College *B*
Marymount Manhattan College *B*
Nazareth College of Rochester *B, T*
New York Institute of Technology *M*
New York State College of Ceramics at Alfred University *B, M, T*
New York University *B, M*
Parsons School of Design *C, A, B, T*
Pratt Institute *M*
Rochester Institute of Technology *B, M*
St. Thomas Aquinas College *B*
Sarah Lawrence College *B*
School of Visual Arts *B, M*
Skidmore College *B*
State University of New York
    Albany *B, M*
    Binghamton *B*
    Buffalo *B*
    College at Brockport *B*
    College at Buffalo *B*
    College at Cortland *B*
    College at Fredonia *B*
    College at Geneseo *B*
    College at Oneonta *B*
    College at Potsdam *B*
    Oswego *M*
    Purchase *B, M*
    Stony Brook *B, M*
Syracuse University *B*
Union College *B*
University of Rochester *B*
Utica College of Syracuse University *B*
Vassar College *B*
Villa Maria College of Buffalo *A*
Wagner College *B*
Wells College *B*
Westchester Community College *C, A*

North Carolina
Appalachian State University *B*
Barton College *B*
Brevard College *A, B*
Campbell University *B*
Chowan College *B*
East Carolina University *B, M*
Greensboro College *B*
Meredith College *B*
North Carolina Central University *B*
Queens College *B*
Randolph Community College *A*
Salem College *B*
University of North Carolina
    Asheville *B*
    Chapel Hill *B, M*
    Charlotte *B*
    Greensboro *B, T*
    Pembroke *B*
    Wilmington *B*
Wake Forest University *B*
Western Carolina University *B, M*

North Dakota
Jamestown College *B*

Ohio
Ashland University *B*
Baldwin-Wallace College *B*

Capital University *B*
Central State University *B*
College of Wooster *B*
Columbus College of Art and Design *B*
Denison University *B*
Hiram College *B, T*
Kent State University
    Stark Campus *B*
Kent State University *B, M*
Lourdes College *A*
Marietta College *B*
Oberlin College *B*
Ohio University *B*
Ohio Wesleyan University *B*
University of Akron *B*
University of Findlay *B*
Youngstown State University *B*

Oklahoma
Oklahoma Baptist University *B*
Oklahoma City Community College *A*
Oklahoma State University *B*
Oral Roberts University *B*
University of Oklahoma *B*

Oregon
Portland State University *B*
Willamette University *B*

Pennsylvania
Allegheny College *B*
Bloomsburg University of Pennsylvania *B, M*
Bryn Mawr College *B*
Bucknell University *B*
Cabrini College *B*
Carnegie Mellon University *B*
Chestnut Hill College *A, B*
Duquesne University *B*
Edinboro University of Pennsylvania *B*
Franklin and Marshall College *B*
Gettysburg College *B*
Immaculata College *C, A*
Juniata College *B*
Lehigh Carbon Community College *A*
Lock Haven University of Pennsylvania *B*
Mansfield University of Pennsylvania *B*
Marywood University *C, B, M*
Mercyhurst College *B*
Moore College of Art and Design *B*
Moravian College *B*
Muhlenberg College *B*
Northampton County Area Community College *A*
Rosemont College *B*
St. Vincent College *B*
Seton Hill College *B*
Swarthmore College *B*
University of Pittsburgh *B*
West Chester University of Pennsylvania *B*
Westminster College *B*

Rhode Island
Brown University *B*
Providence College *B*
Rhode Island College *B, M*
Roger Williams University *A, B*
Salve Regina University *B*

South Carolina
Coastal Carolina University *B*
College of Charleston *B*
Converse College *B*
Furman University *B*
Limestone College *B*
North Greenville College *A*
University of South Carolina
    Aiken *B*
University of South Carolina *B, M*

South Dakota
Dakota State University *B*
University of South Dakota *B, M*

Tennessee
Belmont University *B, T*

David Lipscomb University *B*
Lambuth University *B*
Rhodes College *B*
Roane State Community College *A*
Union University *B*
University of Tennessee
    Knoxville *B*

Texas
Abilene Christian University *B*
Baylor University *B*
Coastal Bend College *A*
College of the Mainland *A*
El Paso Community College *C, A*
Hardin-Simmons University *B*
Howard Payne University *B*
Lamar University *B*
Lon Morris College *A*
Palo Alto College *A*
Rice University *B, M*
Sam Houston State University *B, M*
Southern Methodist University *B, M*
Southwest Texas State University *B, T*
Southwestern University *B*
Texas A&M University
    Commerce *M*
    Corpus Christi *B*
Texas Christian University *B, M*
Texas Tech University *B*
Texas Woman's University *B, M*
University of Dallas *B*
University of Houston *B, M*
University of Texas
    Arlington *B*
    Austin *B, M*
    El Paso *B, M*
    San Antonio *M*
West Texas A&M University *B, M*

Utah
Brigham Young University *M*

Vermont
Bennington College *B, M*
Burlington College *B*
Green Mountain College *B*
Johnson State College *B, M*
Marlboro College *B*
Middlebury College *B*
St. Michael's College *B*
University of Vermont *B*

Virginia
George Mason University *B*
Hollins University *B*
Longwood College *B*
Mary Baldwin College *B*
Mary Washington College *B*
Northern Virginia Community College *A*
Piedmont Virginia Community College *A*
Randolph-Macon College *B*
Randolph-Macon Woman's College *B*
Sweet Briar College *B*
Thomas Nelson Community College *A*
University of Richmond *B, T*
Virginia Commonwealth University *B*
Virginia Western Community College *A*
Washington and Lee University *B*

Washington
Cornish College of the Arts *B*
Eastern Washington University *B*
Gonzaga University *B*
Lower Columbia College *A*
North Seattle Community College *A*
Pacific Lutheran University *B*
Seattle University *B*
Western Washington University *B*
Whitman College *B*

West Virginia
Concord College *B*

Wisconsin
Beloit College *B*
Cardinal Stritch University *B*
Carthage College *B*

Lawrence University *B*
Mount Senario College *B*
Northland College *B*
University of Wisconsin
   Madison *B, M*
   River Falls *B*
   Superior *B, M*
Viterbo University *B*

Surgical/operating room technology

Alabama
Community College of the Air Force *A*

Arizona
Gateway Community College *C, A*

Arkansas
North Arkansas College *C, A*
University of Arkansas
   for Medical Sciences *C, A*
Westark College *C, A*

California
Saddleback College *C, A*
Southwestern College *C*

Colorado
Community College of Denver *C*
Pueblo Community College *C*

Connecticut
Manchester Community-Technical
   College *A*

Florida
Brevard Community College *C*
Central Florida Community College *C*
Daytona Beach Community College *C*
Santa Fe Community College *C*

Georgia
Athens Area Technical Institute *C*
Chattahoochee Technical Institute *C*
Coastal Georgia Community College *C*
Columbus Technical Institute *C*
Darton College *A*
DeKalb Technical Institute *C*
Macon State College *A*
Savannah Technical Institute *A*
Thomas College *A*
Waycross College *A*

Idaho
Boise State University *C*
College of Southern Idaho *A*
Eastern Idaho Technical College *C*

Illinois
College of DuPage *C, A*
Elgin Community College *C*
John Wood Community College *C*
Parkland College *C*
Prairie State College *C*
Richland Community College *C*
Southeastern Illinois College *C*
Triton College *C*

Indiana
Ivy Tech State College
   Central Indiana *A*
   Lafayette *A*
   Northwest *A*
   Southwest *A*
   Wabash Valley *A*
University of St. Francis *A*
Vincennes University *C*

Iowa
Kirkwood Community College *C, A*
Marshalltown Community College *A*
Western Iowa Tech Community
   College *C*

Kansas
Hutchinson Community College *C*
Johnson County Community College *A*
Seward County Community College *C*

Louisiana
Bossier Parish Community College *C*
Delgado Community College *C*
Southern University
   Shreveport *A*

Maine
Southern Maine Technical College *A*

Maryland
Baltimore City Community College *C*
Frederick Community College *C*

Massachusetts
Massachusetts Bay Community
   College *C*
North Shore Community College *C*
Quincy College *C*
Springfield Technical Community
   College *C, A*

Michigan
Baker College
   of Cadillac *A*
   of Jackson *A*
   of Mount Clemens *A*
   of Muskegon *A*
Delta College *A*
Kalamazoo Valley Community
   College *C*
Lansing Community College *A*
Northern Michigan University *C*
Washtenaw Community College *C*

Minnesota
Lake Superior College: A Community
   and Technical College *C, A*
Rochester Community and Technical
   College *A*
St. Cloud Technical College *C, A*

Mississippi
Hinds Community College *C, A*
Itawamba Community College *C, A*

Missouri
Ozarks Technical Community
   College *C, A*
Penn Valley Community College *C*
St. Louis Community College
   St. Louis Community College at
     Forest Park *A*
Three Rivers Community College *C*

Nebraska
Metropolitan Community College *C, A*
Northeast Community College *A*
Southeast Community College
   Lincoln Campus *C, A*

New Hampshire
New Hampshire Community Technical
   College
     Manchester *A*
     Stratham *A*

New Jersey
Bergen Community College *C*
University of Medicine and Dentistry of
   New Jersey
     School of Health Related
       Professions *C*

New Mexico
Albuquerque Technical-Vocational
   Institute *C*

New York
Nassau Community College *A*
Niagara County Community College *C*
Onondaga Community College *C*
Trocaire College *A*

North Carolina
Blue Ridge Community College *C, A*
Catawba Valley Community College *A*
Coastal Carolina Community College *A*
College of the Albemarle *C*
Edgecombe Community College *C*
Fayetteville Technical Community
   College *C*
Guilford Technical Community
   College *C*
Lenoir Community College *C*
Rockingham Community College *C*
Sandhills Community College *C, A*
Wilson Technical Community College *C*

North Dakota
Bismarck State College *A*

Ohio
Cincinnati State Technical and
   Community College *A*
Columbus State Community College *A*
Owens Community College
   Toledo *A*
Sinclair Community College *A*
University of Akron
   Wayne College *A*
University of Akron *A*

Oklahoma
Northeastern Oklahoma Agricultural and
   Mechanical College *C*

Oregon
Mount Hood Community College *A*

Pennsylvania
Carlow College *C*
Community College of Allegheny
   County *C, A*
Delaware County Community College *A*
Lehigh Carbon Community College *A*
Luzerne County Community
   College *C, A*
Mount Aloysius College *C, A*
Pennsylvania College of Technology *C*
University of Pittsburgh
   Johnstown *A*
Westmoreland County Community
   College *C*

Rhode Island
New England Institute of Technology *A*

South Carolina
Central Carolina Technical College *A*
Florence-Darlington Technical
   College *C*
Greenville Technical College *C*
Midlands Technical College *C*
Piedmont Technical College *C*
Tri-County Technical College *C*
York Technical College *C*

South Dakota
Southeast Technical Institute *A*

Tennessee
East Tennessee State University *A*
Nashville State Technical Institute *C*
Northeast State Technical Community
   College *C*

Texas
Amarillo College *C, A*
Collin County Community College
   District *C*
Del Mar College *C, A*
El Paso Community College *A*
Houston Community College System *C*
Kilgore College *C*
Lamar State College at Port Arthur *C, A*
Odessa College *A*
St. Philip's College *C*
South Plains College *A*
Tarrant County College *A*
Temple College *C*
Texas State Technical College
   Harlingen *C*
Trinity Valley Community College *C*

Utah
Salt Lake Community College *A*

Washington
Renton Technical College *A*
Seattle Central Community College *C*
Spokane Community College *A*

West Virginia
West Virginia Northern Community
   College *C*

Wisconsin
Gateway Technical College *C*
Madison Area Technical College *C*
Milwaukee Area Technical College *C, A*
Northeast Wisconsin Technical
   College *C*
Waukesha County Technical College *A*
Western Wisconsin Technical College *C*

Wyoming
Central Wyoming College *A*

Surveying

Alabama
Northwest-Shoals Community College *A*

Alaska
University of Alaska
   Anchorage *A, B*

Arkansas
University of Arkansas
   Little Rock *B*

California
California State University
   Fresno *B*
Chabot College *A*
City College of San Francisco *C*
Coastline Community College *C*
Cuyamaca College *A*
Palomar College *C, A*
Santa Ana College *C, A*
Shasta College *A*
Sierra College *A*

Colorado
Metropolitan State College of Denver *B*

Delaware
Delaware Technical and Community
   College
     Terry Campus *C, A*

Florida
Miami-Dade Community College *A*
Palm Beach Community College *A*
University of Florida *B*
Valencia Community College *A*

Georgia
Middle Georgia College *A*
Southern Polytechnic State University *B*

Illinois
Lincoln Land Community College *C*

Indiana
Purdue University *B*
Vincennes University *A*

Kansas
Kansas State University *A, B*

Kentucky
Murray State University *A*

Maine
University of Maine *B, M, D*

Maryland
Community College of Baltimore County
   Catonsville *C, A*

Massachusetts
Northeastern University *A*

Michigan
Ferris State University *A, B*
Michigan Technological University *B*

Surveying

Minnesota
St. Cloud State University *B*

Missouri
East Central College *A*
Longview Community College *A*

Montana
Flathead Valley Community College *A*

New Hampshire
New Hampshire Community Technical
   College
      Berlin *A*
University of New Hampshire *A*

New Jersey
Burlington County College *A*
County College of Morris *C*
Essex County College *A*
Gloucester County College *A*
Middlesex County College *A*
Ocean County College *A*
Thomas Edison State College *A, B*

New Mexico
New Mexico State University *B*

New York
Mohawk Valley Community
   College *C, A*
Orange County Community College *C*
State University of New York
   College of Environmental Science
      and Forestry *A*
   College of Technology at
      Alfred *A, B*

North Carolina
Asheville Buncombe Technical
   Community College *A*
Central Carolina Community College *A*
Guilford Technical Community
   College *C, A*
Johnston Community College *A*
Sandhills Community College *A*
Wake Technical Community College *A*

Ohio
Cincinnati State Technical and
   Community College *A*
Columbus State Community College *C*
Lakeland Community College *C*
Ohio State University
   Columbus Campus *B, M, D*
Sinclair Community College *C*
Stark State College of Technology *A*
Terra Community College *C, A*
University of Akron *A*

Oklahoma
Oklahoma State University
   Oklahoma City *C, A*

Oregon
Chemeketa Community College *C*
Oregon Institute of Technology *B*

Pennsylvania
Community College of Allegheny
   County *A*
Penn State
   University Park *B*
   Wilkes-Barre *A, B*
Pennsylvania College of Technology *A*
Temple University *A*

Puerto Rico
Universidad Politecnica de Puerto
   Rico *B*
University of Puerto Rico
   Mayaguez Campus *B*

South Carolina
Piedmont Technical College *A*
Trident Technical College *C*

South Dakota
Southeast Technical Institute *A*

Texas
Houston Community College System *A*
Lamar University *B*
Southwest Texas State University *B, M*
Texas A&M University
   Corpus Christi *B*
Tyler Junior College *C, A*

Utah
Salt Lake Community College *C, A*

Virginia
J. Sargeant Reynolds Community
   College *C*
John Tyler Community College *C*

Washington
Centralia College *A*
Grays Harbor College *C, A*
Renton Technical College *C*

Wisconsin
Nicolet Area Technical College *A*

Wyoming
Sheridan College *A*

Systems engineering

Arizona
University of Arizona *B, M, D*

California
California State University
   Northridge *M*
San Jose State University *B, M*
University of California
   San Diego *B, M, D*
University of Southern California *B*

Colorado
National Technological University *M*
University of Southern Colorado *M*

District of Columbia
Howard University *B, M*

Florida
Florida Atlantic University *M*
Florida International University *B*
University of Florida *B, M, D*
University of West Florida *M*

Idaho
University of Idaho *M*

Iowa
Iowa State University *M*

Louisiana
Louisiana Tech University *M*

Maine
Maine Maritime Academy *B*

Maryland
Johns Hopkins University *M, D*
United States Naval Academy *B*
University of Maryland
   College Park *M*

Massachusetts
Boston University *B, M, D*
Harvard College *B*
Northeastern University *B, M*
Worcester Polytechnic Institute *B, M*

Michigan
Oakland University *B, M, D*

Minnesota
University of St. Thomas *B, M*

Missouri
Washington University *B, M, D*

Montana
Montana Tech of the University of
   Montana *B*

New Jersey
Rutgers
   The State University of New Jersey:
      New Brunswick Graduate
      Campus *M, D*

New York
Polytechnic University
   Long Island Campus *M*
Rensselaer Polytechnic Institute *B, M, D*
Rochester Institute of Technology *M*
State University of New York
   Binghamton *M, D*
   College of Environmental Science
      and Forestry *M, D*
United States Merchant Marine
   Academy *B*
United States Military Academy *B*

Ohio
Case Western Reserve
   University *B, M, D*
Jefferson Community College *A*
Ohio State University
   Columbus Campus *B, M, D*

Pennsylvania
Lehigh University *M*
University of Pennsylvania *B, M, D*
University of Pittsburgh *M*

Puerto Rico
University of Puerto Rico
   Mayaguez Campus *M*

Rhode Island
Providence College *B*

Texas
St. Mary's University *M*
Southern Methodist University *M*
Texas A&M University *B*
University of Houston *M, D*

Virginia
George Mason University *M*
University of Virginia *B, M, D*
Virginia Polytechnic Institute and State
   University *M*

Systems science/theory

California
University of Southern California *B, M*

Connecticut
Yale University *B, M, D*

Idaho
Idaho State University *M*

Indiana
Indiana University
   Bloomington *B, D*

Kansas
University of Kansas *B*

Massachusetts
Harvard College *B*

Missouri
Washington University *B*

Oregon
Portland State University *D*

Pennsylvania
Kutztown University of Pennsylvania *B*

Texas
Mountain View College *C, A*

West Virginia
Marshall University *B*

Taxation

Alabama
University of Alabama *M*

Arizona
Arizona State University *M*

California
California State University
   Fullerton *M*
   Hayward *C, M*
   Northridge *M*
De Anza College *C, A*
Golden Gate University *M*
National University *M*
San Diego State University *M*
San Jose State University *M*
Santa Rosa Junior College *C*
University of San Diego *M*
University of Southern California *M*

Colorado
University of Colorado
   Boulder *M*

Connecticut
Manchester Community-Technical
   College *C*
University of Hartford *M*
University of New Haven *M*

District of Columbia
American University *M*
Southeastern University *M*

Florida
Florida Atlantic University *M*
Florida International University *M*
Florida State University *M*
University of Central Florida *M*
University of Miami *M*

Georgia
Georgia State University *M*
Mercer University *M*

Illinois
De Paul University *M*
St. Xavier University *M*

Louisiana
University of New Orleans *M*

Maine
Thomas College *M*

Maryland
University of Baltimore *M*

Massachusetts
Bentley College *M*
Boston University *M*
Northeastern University *M*
Suffolk University *M*

Michigan
Grand Valley State University *M*
Walsh College of Accountancy and
   Business Administration *M*
Washtenaw Community College *C*
Wayne State University *M*

Minnesota
St. Cloud Technical College *C, A*
University of Minnesota
   Twin Cities *M*

Mississippi
Mississippi State University *M*
University of Mississippi *M*

Missouri
University of Missouri
   St. Louis *C*

New Hampshire
McIntosh College *A*

New Jersey
Fairleigh Dickinson University *M*

Seton Hall University *C, M*

New York
City University of New York
  Baruch College *M*
Hofstra University *M*
Long Island University
  Brooklyn Campus *M*
  C. W. Post Campus *M*
New York University *M*
Pace University:
  Pleasantville/Briarcliff *M*
Pace University *M*
St. John Fisher College *M*
St. John's University *M*
State University of New York
  Albany *B, M*

Ohio
Capital University *M*
University of Akron *M*
University of Toledo *M*
Xavier University *M*

Oklahoma
University of Tulsa *M*

Pennsylvania
Drexel University *M*
Duquesne University *M*
King's College *M*
Penn State
  University Park *C*
Philadelphia University *M*
Robert Morris College *M*
Temple University *T*
Villanova University *M*
Widener University *M*

Puerto Rico
University of the Sacred Heart *M*

Rhode Island
Bryant College *M*

South Carolina
University of South Carolina *M*

Texas
Baylor University *M*
Navarro College *A*
Southern Methodist University *M*
University of Houston *M*
University of North Texas *M*
University of Texas
  Arlington *M, D*
  San Antonio *M*

Virginia
ECPI College of Technology *C, A*
George Mason University *M*
Old Dominion University *M*
Virginia Commonwealth University *M*

Teacher assistance

Arizona
Cochise College *C*
Dine College *C*
Mesa Community College *A*

California
American River College *A*
Barstow College *C, A*
Cerritos Community College *A*
Chabot College *A*
Chaffey Community College *C*
City College of San Francisco *C, A*
Compton Community College *C, A*
Contra Costa College *A*
Long Beach City College *C, A*
Los Angeles Mission College *C, A*
Los Angeles Southwest College *A*
Mount St. Mary's College *A*
Shasta College *A*
Sierra College *C, A*
Solano Community College *A*
Victor Valley College *A*

Colorado
Otero Junior College *A*

Connecticut
Manchester Community-Technical
  College *C, A*
Quinebaug Valley Community College *C*

Florida
Florida Community College at
  Jacksonville *A*
South Florida Community College *A*

Georgia
Atlanta Metropolitan College *A*
Macon State College *C*

Illinois
City Colleges of Chicago
  Harold Washington College *C, A*
  Malcolm X College *A*
Elgin Community College *C*
Illinois Eastern Community Colleges
  Frontier Community College *C*
  Lincoln Trail College *A*
John A. Logan College *A*
Joliet Junior College *C, A*
Kaskaskia College *C, A*
Lincoln Land Community College *C*
Moraine Valley Community College *C*
Prairie State College *C*
Rend Lake College *A*

Iowa
Dordt College *A*
Kirkwood Community College *A*

Kansas
Butler County Community College *A*

Louisiana
Southern University
  Shreveport *A*

Maine
Kennebec Valley Technical College *A*
University of Maine
  Fort Kent *A*

Massachusetts
Atlantic Union College *A*
Greenfield Community College *C*
North Shore Community College *C*

Michigan
Baker College
  of Cadillac *A*
Bay de Noc Community College *C*
Kirtland Community College *C*

Minnesota
Concordia University: St. Paul *A*
St. Cloud Technical College *C, A*

Mississippi
Mississippi Gulf Coast Community
  College
  Jefferson Davis Campus *C*

Missouri
St. Louis Community College
  St. Louis Community College at
    Florissant Valley *A*
  St. Louis Community College at
    Forest Park *A*

New Hampshire
New Hampshire Technical Institute *A*

New Jersey
Middlesex County College *A*
Ocean County College *C*

New Mexico
Clovis Community College *A*
Eastern New Mexico University
  Roswell Campus *A*
New Mexico Highlands University *A*
New Mexico State University
  Alamogordo *A*
New Mexico State University *A*

University of New Mexico *A*

New York
City University of New York
  Bronx Community College *A*
  Kingsborough Community
    College *A*
Fulton-Montgomery Community
  College *C*
Herkimer County Community
  College *C, A*
Maria College *A*
St. John Fisher College *C*
St. John's University *A*

North Carolina
Brunswick Community College *C, A*
Carteret Community College *A*
College of the Albemarle *C*
Craven Community College *A*
Guilford Technical Community
  College *C*
Halifax Community College *C, A*
Lenoir Community College *A*
Nash Community College *A*
Pitt Community College *C*
Roanoke-Chowan Community College *A*
Sandhills Community College *A*
Vance-Granville Community College *A*

Ohio
Lourdes College *A*
University of Akron *A*

Oregon
Chemeketa Community College *A*
Clackamas Community College *C*
Portland Community College *C*

Pennsylvania
Bucks County Community College *A*
Cedar Crest College *C*
Delaware County Community College *A*
Laurel Business Institute *A*
Montgomery County Community
  College *A*
Reading Area Community College *C*

Puerto Rico
Pontifical Catholic University of Puerto
  Rico *A*
Universidad Metropolitana *C*

South Dakota
Sinte Gleska University *A*

Tennessee
Hiwassee College *A*
Johnson Bible College *A*

Texas
Angelina College *A*
Midland College *A*
Odessa College *A*
Richland College *A*
St. Philip's College *C, A*

Virginia
Central Virginia Community College *C*
John Tyler Community College *C*
Tidewater Community College *A*

Washington
Big Bend Community College *C, A*
Edmonds Community College *C*
Green River Community College *C*
North Seattle Community College *A*
Renton Technical College *C, A*
Shoreline Community College *C*
Spokane Falls Community College *A*
Tacoma Community College *A*
Walla Walla Community College *C, A*
Whatcom Community College *A*

Wisconsin
Alverno College *A*
Southwest Wisconsin Technical
  College *A*
Waukesha County Technical College *C*

Wyoming
Western Wyoming Community
  College *C*

Teacher education, multiple levels

Alabama
Huntingdon College *B, T*
Lawson State Community College *A*
Troy State University *B, M, T*
University of North Alabama *B, M*

Alaska
University of Alaska
  Anchorage *M*

Arizona
Prescott College *B, M*

California
Azusa Pacific University *B, T*
California State Polytechnic University:
  Pomona *T*
California State University
  Sacramento *T*
College of Notre Dame *M*
Concordia University *B, T*
Fresno City College *C, A*
Glendale Community College *C, A*
Mills College *M*
National University *T*
Occidental College *M, T*
Pepperdine University *T*
San Diego State University *M, T*
United States International University *T*
University of California
  Berkeley *T*
  Los Angeles *M, D*
University of San Diego *M*
University of San Francisco *M*
University of the Pacific *B, T*
Whittier College *T*

Colorado
Adams State College *B, T*
Fort Lewis College *T*
Western State College of Colorado *T*

Connecticut
Central Connecticut State University *B*
Quinnipiac University *B, M*
Sacred Heart University *B, M*

District of Columbia
George Washington University *M*
Howard University *M*

Florida
Edward Waters College *T*
Flagler College *B*
Nova Southeastern University *M*

Georgia
Atlanta Metropolitan College *A*
Darton College *A*
East Georgia College *A*
Floyd College *A*
North Georgia College & State
  University *B, M*

Hawaii
Chaminade University of Honolulu *M*
University of Hawaii
  Manoa *M, D*

Idaho
Boise State University *T*

Illinois
Chicago State University *B*
Concordia University *B, M, T*
Dominican University *M*
Judson College *B*
Kankakee Community College *A*
Lewis and Clark Community College *A*
Monmouth College *B, T*
North Central College *B, T*

North Park University *B, M*
Northwestern University *T*
Quincy University *A, B, T*
Roosevelt University *B*

Indiana
Ball State University *T*
Indiana State University *B, T*
Indiana University
    Bloomington *B, T*
Manchester College *B, T*
Purdue University
    Calumet *B*
University of Evansville *B*
University of Indianapolis *T*
University of Notre Dame *M*
Vincennes University *A*

Iowa
Buena Vista University *B, T*
Loras College *B*
Morningside College *B*
University of Iowa *B*

Kansas
Bethany College *T*
Central Christian College *A*
Coffeyville Community College *A*
Tabor College *B*

Kentucky
Cumberland College *M, T*
Midway College *B*
Murray State University *B, M*

Louisiana
Xavier University of Louisiana *B, T*

Maine
University of Maine
    Farmington *B*
    Fort Kent *B, T*
University of New England *T*

Maryland
Baltimore City Community College *A*
Carroll Community College *A*
Frederick Community College *A*
Goucher College *M*
Harford Community College *A*
Morgan State University *B, T*

Massachusetts
Anna Maria College *B, T*
Merrimack College *T*
Northeastern University *B*
Smith College *M*
University of Massachusetts
    Dartmouth *M*

Michigan
Adrian College *B*
Central Michigan University *B, M*
Lake Superior State University *B, T*
Lawrence Technological University *M*
University of Michigan *B*
Wayne State University *T*
Western Michigan University *T*

Minnesota
Martin Luther College *B*
Minnesota State University, Mankato *M*
Moorhead State University *B, T*
Ridgewater College: A Community and Technical College *A*
St. Mary's University of Minnesota *M*
Winona State University *B, M, T*

Mississippi
Mississippi Gulf Coast Community College
    Perkinston *A*

Missouri
Central Missouri State University *T*
Culver-Stockton College *T*
Fontbonne College *B*
Harris Stowe State College *B, T*
Lindenwood University *B, M*

Missouri Southern State College *B, T*
Washington University *T*
William Jewell College *T*

Montana
Rocky Mountain College *B, T*

Nebraska
Dana College *B*
Midland Lutheran College *B*
University of Nebraska
    Lincoln *T*
Wayne State College *M*

New Hampshire
Antioch New England Graduate School *M*
Keene State College *T*
Plymouth State College of the University System of New Hampshire *M*

New Jersey
College of St. Elizabeth *T*
Cumberland County College *C, A*
Felician College *M*
Gloucester County College *A*
Richard Stockton College of New Jersey *A*
St. Peter's College *M*

New Mexico
New Mexico State University *M*
Western New Mexico University *M*

New York
Bank Street College of Education *M*
City University of New York
    Medgar Evers College *A*
College of St. Rose *M, T*
Columbia University
    Teachers College *M, D*
D'Youville College *M, T*
Dowling College *B, M*
Genesee Community College *A*
Ithaca College *B, M, T*
Jewish Theological Seminary of America *M, D*
Mount St. Mary College *B, M, T*
New York University *B, M, T*
St. Bonaventure University *M*
St. Thomas Aquinas College *B, M, T*
Sarah Lawrence College *M*
State University of New York
    New Paltz *M*
University of Rochester *M*
Wagner College *B, T*

North Carolina
Cleveland Community College *A*
Gardner-Webb University *B*
Halifax Community College *C, A*
North Carolina State University *B*
University of North Carolina
    Greensboro *B, T*
Western Piedmont Community College *A*
Winston-Salem State University *B*

North Dakota
Jamestown College *B*
Minot State University *B, T*
North Dakota State University *M*
University of North Dakota *M*

Ohio
Central State University *B*
Defiance College *B*
John Carroll University *M, T*
Kent State University
    Stark Campus *B*
Marietta College *B*
Mount Union College *T*
Ohio Wesleyan University *B*
Otterbein College *B*
Shawnee State University *B, T*
University of Findlay *B*
University of Rio Grande *B, T*
Ursuline College *M*

Wilmington College *B*
Wright State University *M*
Youngstown State University *B, M*

Oklahoma
Oklahoma City Community College *A*
Oklahoma State University *B, M, D, T*
Oral Roberts University *M*
Southeastern Oklahoma State University *B, M, T*
Southwestern Oklahoma State University *M*
University of Central Oklahoma *B*

Oregon
Concordia University *B, M, T*
George Fox University *B, M, T*
Lewis & Clark College *M*
Western Baptist College *B*
Western Oregon University *T*

Pennsylvania
Bucknell University *T*
Community College of Allegheny County *A*
Edinboro University of Pennsylvania *M*
Gettysburg College *T*
La Salle University *B, T*
Mansfield University of Pennsylvania *B, T*
Mercyhurst College *B*
Moravian College *T*
Northampton County Area Community College *A*
Westminster College *B, T*

Puerto Rico
Inter American University of Puerto Rico
    Metropolitan Campus *B*

Rhode Island
Rhode Island College *B*

South Carolina
Columbia College *B*
Furman University *T*
University of South Carolina *M*
Winthrop University *T*

South Dakota
Dakota State University *B, T*

Tennessee
Cumberland University *B, M*
Southern Adventist University *M*
Tennessee Wesleyan College *B, T*
University of Tennessee
    Knoxville *M*
    Martin *M, T*

Texas
Abilene Christian University *B, M, T*
East Texas Baptist University *B*
Hardin-Simmons University *B, T*
Howard Payne University *B, T*
LeTourneau University *B*
Lubbock Christian University *B*
McMurry University *B*
St. Edward's University *T*
St. Mary's University *B, T*
Southwest Texas State University *M, T*
Texas A&M International University *M, T*
Texas A&M University
    Commerce *B*
Texas Wesleyan University *B, T*
University of Mary Hardin-Baylor *M, T*
West Texas A&M University *T*

Vermont
College of St. Joseph in Vermont *B*
Goddard College *M*
Johnson State College *B, M*

Virginia
Longwood College *B, T*
Virginia Union University *B*

Washington
Antioch University Seattle *M, T*
City University *T*
Evergreen State College *M*
Heritage College *B*
University of Puget Sound *M*
University of Washington *M*
Washington State University *M, D*
Western Washington University *C, B, M*
Whitworth College *B, M, T*

West Virginia
Alderson-Broaddus College *B*
Glenville State College *B*

Wisconsin
Beloit College *T*
Cardinal Stritch University *B, T*
University of Wisconsin
    Green Bay *T*
    La Crosse *B, M, T*
    Superior *B, M, T*
Viterbo University *B*

Technical education

Alabama
Auburn University *B, M, D, T*
Northeast Alabama Community College *A*
Tuskegee University *B, M*

Arizona
Northern Arizona University *B, T*
Prescott College *B*

Colorado
Colorado State University *M, D, T*

Connecticut
Central Connecticut State University *B, M*
University of Connecticut *D, T*

Delaware
Delaware Technical and Community College
    Owens Campus *C*
    Stanton/Wilmington Campus *C*
    Terry Campus *C*

Florida
Palm Beach Community College *A*
University of South Florida *B*
University of West Florida *M*

Georgia
University of Georgia *M, D, T*
Valdosta State University *B*

Hawaii
University of Hawaii
    Honolulu Community College *A*

Idaho
Idaho State University *B, T*
University of Idaho *M*

Illinois
City Colleges of Chicago
    Kennedy-King College *A*
Eastern Illinois University *B, T*
University of Illinois
    Urbana-Champaign *B, M, D, T*

Indiana
Indiana State University *B, T*
Vincennes University *A*

Kansas
Independence Community College *A*
Pittsburg State University *B, M, T*

Kentucky
Eastern Kentucky University *A*
Murray State University *A, B, T*
Western Kentucky University *A*

Maine
University of Southern Maine B, T

Maryland
University of Maryland
  Eastern Shore B

Michigan
Andrews University M, T
Ferris State University B, M
Kellogg Community College A
Wayne State University B, M, D, T

Minnesota
Bemidji State University B
Minnesota State University,
  Mankato B, T
Ridgewater College: A Community and
  Technical College A

Mississippi
Mississippi State University B, M, T

Missouri
University of Missouri
  Columbia B, M, D

Nebraska
Chadron State College M
Peru State College B, T
University of Nebraska
  Lincoln B

New Hampshire
Keene State College B, T

New Jersey
College of St. Elizabeth M

New Mexico
New Mexico Highlands University B
University of New Mexico M, D, T

New York
New York Institute of
  Technology A, B, T
State University of New York
  College at Buffalo B, M, T
  Oswego B, T

North Carolina
East Carolina University M
North Carolina State University M, D, T

North Dakota
Lake Region State College A
Valley City State University B

Ohio
Kent State University
  Stark Campus B
Ohio State University
  Columbus Campus M, D
University of Akron B, M, T
University of Findlay M

Oklahoma
Oklahoma State University B, T

Oregon
Oregon State University M

Pennsylvania
Pittsburgh Institute of Aeronautics A
Temple University M
West Chester University of
  Pennsylvania M

Rhode Island
Rhode Island College B

South Carolina
Florence-Darlington Technical College A
Piedmont Technical College A
Trident Technical College A

Tennessee
Middle Tennessee State University M

Texas
Texas A&M University
  Commerce T
  Corpus Christi M
Texas A&M University M
University of North Texas M, D
University of Texas
  Tyler T

Utah
Brigham Young University B
Utah State University B, M

Washington
Pacific Lutheran University B
Renton Technical College C, A
Walla Walla College B

West Virginia
Marshall University M
West Virginia University D

Wisconsin
University of Wisconsin
  Platteville B, T
  Stout B

Wyoming
University of Wyoming B

Technical theater/design/stagecraft

Arizona
University of Arizona B

California
Allan Hancock College C
California Institute of the Arts M
California State University
  Hayward B
  Long Beach B, M
Chapman University B
Cypress College C, A
Foothill College C, A
Fresno City College C, A
Gavilan Community College A
Glendale Community College A
Grossmont Community College C, A
Humboldt State University M
Irvine Valley College A
MiraCosta College C, A
Palomar College C
Pepperdine University B
San Diego State University M
San Francisco State University M
Santa Barbara City College A
Santa Rosa Junior College C
University of California
  Santa Cruz C, B

Colorado
Pikes Peak Community College C, A

Connecticut
University of Connecticut B

Delaware
University of Delaware B

District of Columbia
Howard University B

Florida
Barry University B
Florida Community College at
  Jacksonville A
Florida State University B

Idaho
Ricks College A

Illinois
Barat College B
Columbia College B
De Paul University B, M
Millikin University B
Rockford College B

Indiana
Indiana University
  Bloomington A
University of Evansville B
Vincennes University A

Iowa
University of Iowa M
University of Northern Iowa B

Kansas
Central Christian College A
University of Kansas B

Louisiana
Centenary College of Louisiana B
Dillard University B

Maryland
Howard Community College A
Montgomery College
  Rockville Campus A

Massachusetts
Boston University B, M
Emerson College B
Fitchburg State College B
Hampshire College B
Salem State College B
Simon's Rock College of Bard B

Michigan
Calvin College B
Eastern Michigan University B
University of Michigan B
Western Michigan University B

Minnesota
Central Lakes College A
Minnesota State University, Mankato B
Moorhead State University B
University of Minnesota
  Duluth B

Missouri
University of Missouri
  Kansas City M
Webster University B
William Woods University B

Montana
Rocky Mountain College B

New Hampshire
Franklin Pierce College B
Plymouth State College of the University
  System of New Hampshire B

New Jersey
Essex County College A
Rowan University B
Rutgers
  The State University of New Jersey:
    Mason Gross School of the
    Arts B, M
  The State University of New Jersey:
    New Brunswick Graduate
    Campus M

New Mexico
College of Santa Fe A

New York
City University of New York
  New York City Technical
    College B
Fordham University B
Ithaca College B
New York University B, M
Sarah Lawrence College B, M
State University of New York
  College at Fredonia B
  New Paltz B
  Purchase B, M
Syracuse University B, M
Wagner College B

North Carolina
Greensboro College B
North Carolina School of the Arts B, M

North Dakota
Dickinson State University B

Ohio
Clark State Community College A
Kent State University
  Stark Campus B
Kent State University B, M
Ohio University B, M
Otterbein College B
Sinclair Community College A
University of Akron B
University of Cincinnati B, M
University of Findlay B
Wright State University B
Youngstown State University B

Oklahoma
Oklahoma City Community College A
Oral Roberts University B
Southeastern Oklahoma State
  University B

Oregon
Chemeketa Community College A

Pennsylvania
Allentown College of St. Francis de
  Sales B
California University of Pennsylvania B
Carnegie Mellon University B
Dickinson College B
Seton Hill College B

Rhode Island
Rhode Island College B

Texas
Baylor University B
Lon Morris College A
Southern Methodist University M
Texas Tech University B, M
Trinity University B

Vermont
Bennington College B
Johnson State College A, B
Marlboro College B

Virginia
Virginia Commonwealth University B

Washington
Cornish College of the Arts B
Eastern Washington University B
North Seattle Community College C
Shoreline Community College A

West Virginia
Marshall University B

Wisconsin
University of Wisconsin
  Madison B, M
Viterbo University B

Wyoming
Casper College A

Technical/business writing

Alabama
Spring Hill College B
University of Alabama
  Huntsville C

Alaska
University of Alaska
  Fairbanks M

Arkansas
University of Arkansas
  Little Rock B, M

California
California State University
  Chico C
  Long Beach C
De Anza College C, A

Orange Coast College A
San Francisco State University C, B

Colorado
Colorado State University M
University of Colorado
 Denver M

Connecticut
University of Hartford B

Florida
Barry University B
University of West Florida B

Georgia
Kennesaw State University B
Southern Polytechnic State
 University B, M

Idaho
Boise State University M, D

Illinois
Black Hawk College C, A
Chicago State University B
College of Lake County C, A
Dominican University B
Illinois Institute of Technology M

Iowa
Marycrest International University A, B

Kansas
Independence Community College A
Pittsburg State University B

Maryland
Montgomery College
 Rockville Campus C
Towson University M

Massachusetts
Clark University M
Fitchburg State College B
North Shore Community College C
Northeastern University M
University of Massachusetts
 Dartmouth M
Worcester Polytechnic Institute B

Michigan
Grand Valley State University B
Madonna University B
Washtenaw Community College A

Minnesota
Metropolitan State University B
St. Mary's University of Minnesota B

Missouri
Southwest Missouri State
 University B, M
St. Louis Community College
 St. Louis Community College at
  Florissant Valley A
 St. Louis Community College at
  Meramec C

Montana
Miles Community College A
Montana Tech of the University of
 Montana B, M

New Hampshire
Plymouth State College of the University
 System of New Hampshire B

New Jersey
Essex County College A
New Jersey Institute of Technology M, D

New Mexico
College of Santa Fe B
New Mexico Institute of Mining and
 Technology B

New York
Clarkson University B
New York Institute of Technology C, B
Rensselaer Polytechnic Institute M
Rochester Institute of Technology B

State University of New York
 College of Agriculture and
  Technology at Morrisville A
 Institute of Technology at
  Utica/Rome B

North Carolina
North Carolina State University M

Ohio
Bowling Green State University B
Capital University B
Cedarville College B
Cincinnati State Technical and
 Community College C, A
Edison State Community College C, A
Miami University
 Oxford Campus M
Terra Community College A
University of Findlay C, B
Youngstown State University B

Oklahoma
East Central University B
Oklahoma State University B

Oregon
Oregon State University M, D
Portland Community College C
Portland State University M

Pennsylvania
California University of Pennsylvania B
Carlow College B
Carnegie Mellon University B, M
Drexel University B, M
Immaculata College B
La Salle University B
Mansfield University of Pennsylvania A
Penn State
 University Park C
Pennsylvania College of Technology B
University of the Sciences in
 Philadelphia B

South Carolina
Winthrop University B

Tennessee
Chattanooga State Technical Community
 College A
Tennessee Technological University B

Texas
Houston Community College System A
Southwest Texas State University M
Texas Tech University M, D
University of Houston
 Downtown B
University of Texas
 El Paso M

Utah
Weber State University B

Virginia
James Madison University B, M
Longwood College B, T
Northern Virginia Community College C

Washington
Clark College A
Eastern Washington University M
Everett Community College A

West Virginia
Alderson-Broaddus College B
West Virginia State College B

Wisconsin
Gateway Technical College A
Milwaukee School of Engineering B
Mount Mary College B

Technology/industrial arts education

Alabama
Alabama Agricultural and Mechanical
 University B, M, T
Community College of the Air Force A

Arizona
Eastern Arizona College A
Northern Arizona University B, M, T
Prescott College B

Arkansas
Arkansas State University A, T
University of Arkansas
 Pine Bluff T
University of Central Arkansas A, M

California
California State University
 Chico B
Cypress College A
Long Beach City College C, A
Pacific Union College B, T
San Francisco State University B, T

Colorado
Colorado State University M, T
Western State College of Colorado T

Connecticut
Central Connecticut State
 University B, M

Florida
Hillsborough Community College A
Miami-Dade Community College A

Georgia
Georgia Southern University B, M, T
University of Georgia B, M

Hawaii
University of Hawaii
 Honolulu Community College A
 Manoa B

Idaho
Ricks College A
University of Idaho B, M, T

Illinois
Chicago State University B

Indiana
Ball State University B, M
Indiana State University B, M, T
Purdue University B, M, D
Vincennes University A

Iowa
Iowa State University B, M, D, T
University of Northern Iowa B
William Penn University B

Kansas
Central Christian College A
Fort Hays State University B
Independence Community College A
McPherson College B, T
Pittsburg State University B, M, T

Kentucky
Berea College B, T
Eastern Kentucky University B, M
Morehead State University B
Murray State University B, M, T

Louisiana
Northwestern State University B, T

Maine
University of Southern Maine B, T

Maryland
University of Maryland
 Eastern Shore B

Massachusetts
Fitchburg State College B, T

Westfield State College B, T

Michigan
Andrews University M
Central Michigan University B, M
Eastern Michigan University B, M, T
Michigan State University M, D
Northern Michigan University B, T
Wayne State University M

Minnesota
Bemidji State University M, T
Minnesota State University,
 Mankato B, M, T
Moorhead State University B, T
St. Cloud State University M
University of Minnesota
 Twin Cities B, M, D, T

Mississippi
Alcorn State University B
Mississippi Gulf Coast Community
 College
  Jefferson Davis Campus A
Mississippi State University T
University of Southern Mississippi B

Missouri
Central Missouri State
 University B, M, T
College of the Ozarks B
Southwest Missouri State University B

Montana
Montana State University
 Billings T
 Bozeman B, T
 Northern B
Western Montana College of The
 University of Montana B, T

Nebraska
Chadron State College M
Concordia University T
University of Nebraska
 Kearney B
 Lincoln B, T

Nevada
University of Nevada
 Reno B

New Hampshire
Keene State College T

New Jersey
Kean University B
Montclair State University B, M, T
The College of New Jersey B, T

New Mexico
University of New Mexico B
Western New Mexico University B

New York
College of St. Rose C, B
New York Institute of Technology B, T
State University of New York
 College at Buffalo B, M, T
 Oswego M, T

North Carolina
Appalachian State University B, T
East Carolina University M
North Carolina Agricultural and
 Technical State University B, M, T
North Carolina State University M, D
Western Carolina University B, T

North Dakota
University of North Dakota B, T
Valley City State University B, T

Ohio
Bowling Green State University B
Kent State University
 Stark Campus B
Kent State University B, M, T
Ohio Northern University B, T

Ohio State University
  Columbus Campus B
Ohio University B, M, T

Oklahoma
East Central University B
Langston University B
Northeastern State University B
Northwestern Oklahoma State
  University B, T
Oklahoma State University B, M, T
Rogers State University A
Southwestern Oklahoma State
  University B, M, T
University of Central Oklahoma B

Oregon
Chemeketa Community College C, A

Pennsylvania
California University of
  Pennsylvania B, M, T
Millersville University of
  Pennsylvania B, M, T
Pittsburgh Institute of Aeronautics A

Rhode Island
Rhode Island College B, M

South Carolina
South Carolina State University B, T

South Dakota
Black Hills State University B
Northern State University M, T

Tennessee
Middle Tennessee State University B
University of Tennessee
  Knoxville M, D, T

Texas
Abilene Christian University B, T
El Paso Community College A
Prairie View A&M University B
Sam Houston State University M, T
Southwest Texas State University M, T
Sul Ross State University M
Texas A&M University
  Commerce M, T
  Kingsville M
University of Texas
  San Antonio M
  Tyler T

Utah
Brigham Young University B, M
Utah State University B

Washington
Central Washington University B, T
Eastern Washington University B, M, T
South Seattle Community College C
Western Washington University B, T

West Virginia
Fairmont State College B
Marshall University M

Wisconsin
University of Wisconsin
  Platteville B, T
  Stout B, M, T

Wyoming
University of Wyoming B

Telecommunications

Alabama
Calhoun Community College A
Northwest-Shoals Community College A

Alaska
Alaska Pacific University C, M

Arizona
Pima Community College C, A
Yavapai College A

California
Butte College C, A
California Institute of the Arts B, M
California State University
  Hayward C, B, M
  Monterey Bay B
Chabot College A
City College of San Francisco C
College of the Canyons C, A
Compton Community College A
Golden Gate University C, A, B, M
ITT Technical Institute
  Hayward B
  Oxnard B
Moorpark College A
Pepperdine University B
San Diego State University B
Santa Ana College C, A
Skyline College C, A

Colorado
Colorado Christian University B
Lamar Community College A
University of Colorado
  Boulder M
University of Denver M

Connecticut
Quinnipiac University B

Delaware
Delaware Technical and Community
  College
  Terry Campus A

District of Columbia
George Washington University M
University of the District of
  Columbia C, B

Florida
Broward Community College A
Daytona Beach Community College A
Seminole Community College A

Georgia
Atlanta College of Art B
Dalton State College A
Gwinnett Technical Institute A
Morris Brown College B
Valdosta State University B

Hawaii
University of Hawaii
  Leeward Community College A

Illinois
De Paul University M
Illinois Eastern Community Colleges
  Lincoln Trail College C, A
John Wood Community College A
Judson College B
Lake Land College C, A
Lincoln Land Community College A
Richland Community College A
Roosevelt University C, B, M

Indiana
Ball State University B
Butler University B
Franklin College B
Goshen College B
Indiana University
  Bloomington B, M
Purdue University
  Calumet B
Vincennes University A

Iowa
Des Moines Area Community College A
Loras College B
Maharishi University of
  Management A, B

Kansas
Butler County Community College C, A
Kansas City Kansas Community
  College C, A
Seward County Community
  College C, A

Kentucky
Hazard Community College A
Murray State University B, M

Louisiana
Bossier Parish Community College C, A
Our Lady of Holy Cross College T
University of Louisiana at Lafayette M

Maryland
Baltimore City Community College C, A
University of Maryland
  College Park M

Massachusetts
Dean College A
Massachusetts Bay Community
  College A
Massasoit Community College A
Middlesex Community College A
North Shore Community College A
Salem State College B
Suffolk University B
Wentworth Institute of Technology A
Worcester Polytechnic Institute M

Michigan
Calvin College B
Ferris State University M
Henry Ford Community College A
Northern Michigan University A, B
Oakland Community College A
University of Michigan
  Dearborn M
University of Michigan M
Washtenaw Community College A
Western Michigan University B

Minnesota
Dakota County Technical College C, A
Ridgewater College: A Community and
  Technical College C
St. Mary's University of Minnesota B, M
University of St. Thomas B
Winona State University B

Mississippi
Meridian Community College A

Missouri
DeVry Institute of Technology
  Kansas City B
Jefferson College A
Northwest Missouri State University B
St. Charles County Community
  College A
St. Louis Community College
  St. Louis Community College at
    Florissant Valley A
  St. Louis Community College at
    Meramec C
University of Missouri
  Kansas City B
Webster University M

Montana
Miles Community College A
University of Great Falls B
University of Montana-Missoula B

Nebraska
College of Saint Mary C, A

New Hampshire
Franklin Pierce College B
McIntosh College A
New Hampshire Community Technical
  College
  Nashua C, A

New Jersey
Atlantic Cape Community College A
Brookdale Community College A
DeVry Institute A
Middlesex County College A
Rider University B
Rowan University B
Stevens Institute of Technology M
Union County College A

New Mexico
College of Santa Fe B
New Mexico Highlands University B

New York
Briarcliffe College A
Broome Community College A
Cayuga County Community College A
City University of New York
  Bronx Community College A
  New York City Technical
    College A, B
Cornell University B
Dominican College of Blauvelt C, B
Dutchess Community College A
Five Towns College A, B
Herkimer County Community College A
Ithaca College B
Manhattan College B
Marist College B
Monroe Community College C
Nassau Community College A
New York Institute of Technology B
New York University M
Niagara County Community College A
Onondaga Community College A
Pace University:
  Pleasantville/Briarcliff M
Pace University M
Polytechnic University M
Pratt Institute B, M
Rochester Institute of Technology B, M
St. John's University C, A, B
Schenectady County Community
  College A
State University of New York
  College at Fredonia B
  College of Agriculture and
    Technology at Cobleskill A
  Institute of Technology at
    Utica/Rome B, M
Syracuse University M
Utica College of Syracuse University B
Westchester Community College C, A

North Carolina
Central Carolina Community College C
Elizabeth City State University B
Gardner-Webb University B
Halifax Community College A
Johnson C. Smith University B
Lenoir-Rhyne College B
Wake Technical Community College A
Winston-Salem State University B

Ohio
Bowling Green State University B
Defiance College B
Edison State Community College C, A
Hocking Technical College A
Kent State University
  Stark Campus B
Kent State University B
Marietta College B
Ohio Northern University B
Ohio State University
  Columbus Campus B
Ohio University
  Zanesville Campus A
Ohio University B, M
University of Cincinnati
  Raymond Walters College A
Youngstown State University B

Oklahoma
Cameron University B
Carl Albert State College A
Oklahoma Baptist University B
Oklahoma State University M
Oral Roberts University B
Tulsa Community College A

Oregon
Chemeketa Community College A
Southern Oregon University B

Pennsylvania
Bucks County Community College C, A
California University of
 Pennsylvania A, B
Carnegie Mellon University B
Delaware County Community
 College C, A
Drexel University B, M
ICS Center for Degree Studies A
Kutztown University of Pennsylvania M
La Salle University B, M
Marywood University B
Penn State
 University Park B
University of Pittsburgh C, M

Puerto Rico
Inter American University of Puerto Rico
 Bayamon Campus A
University of the Sacred Heart B

Rhode Island
New England Institute of
 Technology A, B

South Carolina
York Technical College C

Tennessee
Lee University B
Lincoln Memorial University B

Texas
Amarillo College A
Baylor University B
Central Texas College C, A
DeVry Institute of Technology
 Irving B
Del Mar College A
El Paso Community College A
Hill College C, A
Howard College C, A
Midland College A
South Plains College A
Southern Methodist University B, M
Texas A&M University
 Commerce B
 Corpus Christi B, T
Tyler Junior College C, A
University of North Texas B
Western Texas College A

Utah
Brigham Young University B
Salt Lake Community College A
Southern Utah University B
Utah Valley State College C, A, B

Vermont
Champlain College A, B
Vermont Technical College A

Virginia
ECPI College of Technology C, A
Germanna Community College A
J. Sargeant Reynolds Community
 College C
Patrick Henry Community College A
Piedmont Virginia Community
 College C, A
Southwest Virginia Community
 College C

Washington
Clark College A
Everett Community College C, A
Evergreen State College B
Gonzaga University B
Lower Columbia College A
Seattle Pacific University C
Shoreline Community College C, A
Skagit Valley College C, A
Tacoma Community College A
Western Washington University B

West Virginia
Concord College B
University of Charleston A, B

Wisconsin
University of Wisconsin
 La Crosse B
Waukesha County Technical College A

Textile sciences/engineering

Alabama
Auburn University B

California
Shasta College C, A

Georgia
Georgia Institute of Technology B, M, D

Massachusetts
University of Massachusetts
 Dartmouth B, M

Michigan
Western Michigan University B

New York
Cornell University B, M, D

North Carolina
North Carolina State University B, M

Pennsylvania
Philadelphia University B, M

South Carolina
Clemson University B, M, D

Tennessee
Hiwassee College A

Texas
Texas Tech University B

Virginia
Institute of Textile Technology M

Theater history/criticism

Alabama
Spring Hill College B

California
Chapman University B, M
College of the Desert A
Mills College B
San Francisco State University M
San Jose State University M
Scripps College B
Whittier College B

Connecticut
Naugatuck Valley Community-Technical
 College A

Delaware
University of Delaware B

District of Columbia
George Washington University B
Howard University B

Florida
Manatee Community College A

Georgia
Oxford College of Emory University B

Illinois
De Paul University C, B

Indiana
Valparaiso University B

Iowa
University of Northern Iowa B

Kansas
Seward County Community College A

Louisiana
Dillard University B
Tulane University M

Maryland
Washington College B

Massachusetts
Boston University B
Brandeis University B
Emerson College M
Hampshire College B
Harvard College B
Simon's Rock College of Bard B
Tufts University B, M, D

Michigan
Calvin College B

Minnesota
Moorhead State University B
St. Olaf College B

Missouri
Washington University B, M

New Jersey
Rowan University B

New York
Bard College B
Columbia University
 Columbia College B
Cornell University M, D
Eugene Lang College/New School
 University B
Marymount College B
New York University B
Sarah Lawrence College B, M

North Carolina
Appalachian State University B

Ohio
Kent State University
 Stark Campus B
Kenyon College B
Ohio University M

Oklahoma
Western Oklahoma State College A

Pennsylvania
Allentown College of St. Francis de
 Sales B
Moravian College B

Tennessee
Fisk University B

Texas
Lon Morris College A
University of Dallas B, T

Utah
Snow College A

Vermont
Burlington College B
Marlboro College B

Virginia
Mary Baldwin College B
Virginia Wesleyan College B

Washington
Whitworth College B, T

Wisconsin
University of Wisconsin
 Madison M, D
 Whitewater B, T
Viterbo University B

Theological professions (B.Div., M.Div., Rabbinical, or Talmudical)

Alabama
Beeson Divinity School at Samford
 University F
Southern Christian University F

California
American Baptist Seminary of the
 West F
Azusa Pacific University: School of
 Theology F
Church Divinity School of the Pacific F
Claremont School of Theology F
Dominican School of Philosophy and
 Theology F
Franciscan School of Theology F
Fuller Theological Seminary F
Golden Gate Baptist Theological
 Seminary F
Hebrew Union College-Jewish Institute
 of Religion F
International School of Theology F
Jesuit School of Theology at Berkeley:
 Professional F
Mennonite Brethren Biblical Seminary F
Pacific Lutheran Theological
 Seminary F
Pacific School of Religion F
St. John's Seminary F
St. Patrick's Seminary F
San Francisco Theological Seminary F
Starr King School for the Ministry F
Talbot School of Theology of Biola
 University F
Westminster Theological Seminary in
 California F

Colorado
Denver Conservative Baptist Seminary F
Iliff School of Theology F
Yeshiva Toras Chaim Talmudical
 Seminary F

Connecticut
Beth Benjamin Academy of
 Connecticut F
Holy Apostles College and Seminary F
Yale University: Divinity School F

District of Columbia
Catholic University of America: School
 of Theology F
Dominican House of Studies F
Howard University: Divinity School F
Washington Theological Union F
Wesley Theological Seminary F

Florida
St. Vincent De Paul Regional
 Seminary F

Georgia
Candler School of Theology F
Columbia Theological Seminary F
Interdenominational Theological
 Center F

Illinois
Bethany Theological Seminary F
Brisk Rabbinical College F
Catholic Theological Union F
Chicago Theological Seminary F
Garrett-Evangelical Theological
 Seminary F
Hebrew Theological College F
Lincoln Christian Seminary F
Lutheran School of Theology at
 Chicago F
McCormick Theological Seminary F
Meadville-Lombard Theological
 School F
North Park Theological Seminary F
Northern Baptist Theological
 Seminary F

Seabury-Western Theological Seminary F
Trinity Evangelical Divinity School F
University of Chicago: Divinity School F
University of St. Mary of the Lake--Mundelein Seminary F

Indiana
Anderson University: School of Theology F
Associated Mennonite Biblical Seminary F
Christian Theological Seminary F
Concordia Theological Seminary F
Earlham School of Religion F
St. Meinrad School of Theology F
University of Notre Dame: School of Theology F

Iowa
Faith Baptist Theological Seminary F
University of Dubuque: School of Theology F
Wartburg Theological Seminary F

Kansas
Central Baptist Theological Seminary F

Kentucky
Asbury Theological Seminary F
Lexington Theological Seminary F
Louisville Presbyterian Theological Seminary F
Southern Baptist Theological Seminary F

Louisiana
New Orleans Baptist Theological Seminary F
Notre Dame Seminary School of Theology F

Maine
Bangor Theological Seminary F

Maryland
Capital Bible Seminary F
Mount St. Mary's College: Seminary F
Ner Israel Rabbinical College F
St. Mary's Seminary and University F

Massachusetts
Andover Newton Theological School F
Boston University: School of Theology F
Episcopal Divinity School F
Gordon-Conwell Theological Seminary F
Harvard University: Divinity School F
Holy Cross Greek Orthodox School of Theology F
Pope John XXIII National Seminary F
St. John's Seminary F
Weston Jesuit School of Theology F

Michigan
Andrews University Seminary F
Calvin Theological Seminary F
Grand Rapids Baptist Seminary F
Sacred Heart Major Seminary F
Western Theological Seminary F

Minnesota
Bethel Theological Seminary F
Luther Seminary: Theological Professions F
St. John's University: School of Theology F
United Theological Seminary of the Twin Cities F
University of St. Thomas: School of Divinity F

Mississippi
Reformed Theological Seminary F
Wesley Biblical Seminary F

Missouri
Aquinas Institute of Theology F
Assemblies of God Theological Seminary F
Concordia Seminary F
Covenant Theological Seminary F
Eden Theological Seminary F
Kenrick-Glennon Seminary F
Midwestern Baptist Theological Seminary F
Nazarene Theological Seminary F
St. Paul School of Theology F

New Jersey
Drew University: School of Theology F
Immaculate Conception Seminary of Seton Hall University F
New Brunswick Theological Seminary F
Princeton Theological Seminary F

New York
Alliance Theological Seminary F
Central Yeshiva Tomchei Tmimim Lubavitz F
Christ The King Seminary F
Colgate Rochester Divinity School-Bexley Crozer Theological Seminary F
General Theological Seminary F
Kehilath Yakov Rabbinical Seminary F
Kol Yaakov Torah Center F
Mesivta Eastern Parkway Rabbinical Seminary F
Mirrer Yeshiva Central Institute F
New York Theological Seminary F
Ohr Hameir Theological Seminary F
Rabbinical College Beth Shraga F
Rabbinical Seminary M'Kor Chaim F
St. Bernard's Institute F
St. Joseph's Seminary and College F
St. Vladimir's Orthodox Theological Seminary F
Seminary of the Immaculate Conception F
Yeshiva of Nitra Rabbinical College F

North Carolina
Duke University: Divinity School F
Hood Theological Seminary F

Ohio
Ashland Theological Seminary F
Athenaeum of Ohio F
Hebrew Union College-Jewish Institute of Religion F
Methodist Theological School in Ohio F
St. Mary Seminary F
Trinity Lutheran Seminary F
United Theological Seminary F
Winebrenner Seminary F

Oklahoma
Oral Roberts University: School of Theology and Missions F
Phillips Theological Seminary F

Oregon
Mount Angel Seminary F
Multnomah Biblical Seminary F
Western Conservative Baptist Seminary F
Western Evangelical Seminary F

Pennsylvania
Academy of the New Church F
Baptist Bible College and Seminary of Pennsylvania F
Biblical Theological Seminary F
Eastern Baptist Theological Seminary F
Evangelical School of Theology F
Lancaster Theological Seminary F
Lutheran Theological Seminary at Gettysburg F
Lutheran Theological Seminary at Philadelphia F
Moravian Theological Seminary F
Pittsburgh Theological Seminary F
Reformed Presbyterian Theological Seminary F
St. Charles Borromeo Seminary-Overbrook F
St. Vincent Seminary F
Trinity Episcopal School for Ministry F
Westminster Theological Seminary F

Puerto Rico
Evangelical Seminary of Puerto Rico F

South Carolina
Columbia Biblical Seminary and Graduate School of Missions F
Erskine Theological Seminary F
Lutheran Theological Southern Seminary F

South Dakota
North American Baptist Seminary F

Tennessee
Church of God School of Theology F
Emmanuel School of Religion F
Harding University Graduate School of Religion F
Memphis Theological Seminary F
Mid-America Baptist Theological Seminary F
Temple Baptist Seminary: Theological Professions F
University of the South: School of Theology F
Vanderbilt University: The Divinity School F

Texas
Abilene Christian University: College of Biblical and Family Studies F
Austin Presbyterian Theological Seminary F
Baptist Missionary Association Theological Seminary F
Episcopal Theological Seminary of the Southwest F
Houston Graduate School of Theology F
Oblate School of Theology F
Southern Methodist University: Perkins School of Theology F
Texas Christian University: Brite Divinity School F
University of St. Thomas: School of Theology F

Virginia
Eastern Mennonite Seminary F
Liberty Baptist Theological Seminary F
Protestant Episcopal Theological Seminary in Virginia F
Regent University: School of Divinity F
Union Theological Seminary in Virginia F
Virginia Union University: School of Theology F

Washington
Gonzaga University: Department of Religious Studies F
Seattle University: School of Theology and Ministry F

Wisconsin
Nashotah House F
Sacred Heart School of Theology F
St. Francis Seminary F

Theological studies

Arkansas
John Brown University B
Ouachita Baptist University B

California
Azusa Pacific University B
Concordia University B
LIFE Bible College B
Loyola Marymount University B, M
Master's College B
Mount St. Mary's College M
Patten College B
Queen of the Holy Rosary College A
St. John's Seminary College B
San Jose Christian College B
Simpson College B, M
University of San Francisco M
Vanguard University of Southern California M

Colorado
University of Denver B, M, D

Delaware
Wesley College C

District of Columbia
Catholic University of America M
Trinity College B

Florida
Florida Baptist Theological College A, B
St. John Vianney College Seminary B
St. Thomas University M

Georgia
Atlanta Christian College B
Young Harris College A

Illinois
Concordia University B, M
Lincoln Christian College and Seminary C, A, B, M
MacMurray College B
North Park University M
Quincy University A, B
Trinity Christian College B
Trinity International University M, D
University of Chicago M, D
Wheaton College M

Indiana
Anderson University B
Earlham College M
Hanover College B
Indiana Wesleyan University M
University of Evansville B
University of St. Francis C, B
Valparaiso University B, M

Iowa
Dordt College B
Faith Baptist Bible College and Theological Seminary M
Loras College B, M
St. Ambrose University B, M

Kansas
Barclay College B
Manhattan Christian College A, B
Newman University B
St. Mary College B

Kentucky
Bellarmine College B
Thomas More College A, B

Maryland
Columbia Union College B
Morgan State University B
Mount St. Mary's College B
Washington Bible College C, A, B, M

Massachusetts
Assumption College B
Boston College B, M, D
Boston University M, D
Elms College B, M
Hellenic College/Holy Cross B, M
St. John's Seminary College B

Michigan
Calvin College B
Cornerstone College and Grand Rapids Baptist Seminary M
Grace Bible College A, B
Reformed Bible College B
William Tyndale College A, B

Theological studies

Minnesota
College of St. Benedict *B*
Concordia University: St. Paul *B*
Crown College *B*
Martin Luther College *B*
Minnesota Bible College *B*
North Central University *B*
St. John's University *B, M*
St. Mary's University of Minnesota *B, M*
St. Olaf College *B*

Mississippi
Magnolia Bible College *B*

Missouri
Baptist Bible College *M*
Berean University *C, A, B*
Conception Seminary College *C*
Ozark Christian College *B*
St. Louis Christian College *B*
Southwest Baptist University *B*

Montana
Carroll College *B*
University of Great Falls *A, B*

Nebraska
Concordia University *B, D*
Midland Lutheran College *B*

New Hampshire
Notre Dame College *B, M*
St. Anselm College *B*

New Jersey
Assumption College for Sisters *C, A*
Felician College *B*
Georgian Court College *M*
Seton Hall University *C*

New Mexico
College of Santa Fe *B*

New York
Concordia College *B*
Fordham University *B, M, D*
Houghton College *B*
Jewish Theological Seminary of America *M, D*
Molloy College *B*
Nyack College *C, A, B*
St. Bonaventure University *M*
St. John's University *C, B, M*

North Carolina
Belmont Abbey College *B*
Lenoir-Rhyne College *B*
Mount Olive College *B*
Shaw University *C, M*

Ohio
Cedarville College *B*
Circleville Bible College *B*
Defiance College *B*
Notre Dame College of Ohio *A, B*
Ohio Dominican College *C, A, B*
Ohio Wesleyan University *B*
University of Dayton *M, D*
University of Findlay *B*
Ursuline College *M*

Oklahoma
Oklahoma Baptist University *B*
Oklahoma Christian University of Science and Arts *M*
St. Gregory's University *B*

Oregon
Concordia University *B*
George Fox University *B*
Marylhurst University *M*
Multnomah Bible College *M*
University of Portland *B*
Western Baptist College *A, B*

Pennsylvania
Elizabethtown College *B*
Geneva College *A, B*
Immaculata College *C*
Moravian College *M*

St. Charles Borromeo Seminary - Overbrook *M*
Seton Hill College *B*
Talmudical Yeshiva of Philadelphia *B*
Villanova University *B, M*
Waynesburg College *B*

Puerto Rico
Pontifical Catholic University of Puerto Rico *B*

South Carolina
Anderson College *B*
Charleston Southern University *B*
Columbia International University *M*
Erskine College *M*
North Greenville College *B*

Tennessee
Martin Methodist College *B*
Southern Adventist University *B*
Tennessee Wesleyan College *B*
Trevecca Nazarene University *B, M*
Union University *B*
University of the South *M, D*

Texas
Houston Baptist University *M*
St. Mary's University *M*
Southwestern Assemblies of God University *B*
Texas Lutheran University *B*
University of St. Thomas *B, M*

Virginia
Christendom College *B, M*

Washington
Puget Sound Christian College *B*
Seattle University *M*

West Virginia
Alderson-Broaddus College *B*
Ohio Valley College *B*

Wisconsin
Concordia University Wisconsin *B*
Marquette University *B, M, D*

Theoretical/mathematical physics

Alabama
Southern Union State Community College *A*

Arkansas
University of Arkansas *M*

Colorado
University of Colorado Boulder *D*

Georgia
Oxford College of Emory University *B*

Indiana
Indiana University Bloomington *D*

Massachusetts
Hampshire College *B*
Harvard College *B*

Minnesota
Winona State University *B*

New Mexico
New Mexico Institute of Mining and Technology *D*

Texas
Southwestern Adventist University *B*

Wisconsin
University of Wisconsin Madison *M, D*

Tourism/travel management

Alabama
Shelton State Community College *C*

Alaska
Alaska Pacific University *C, A*

Arizona
Phoenix College *C, A*
Pima Community College *C, A*

Arkansas
Arkansas State University *B*

California
Canada College *C, A*
Chabot College *A*
City College of San Francisco *A*
Coastline Community College *C*
College of the Redwoods *C*
Empire College *C*
MiraCosta College *C, A*
Mount St. Mary's College *A*
Saddleback College *C, A*
San Diego Mesa College *C, A*
San Joaquin Delta College *C*
Southwestern College *C, A*

Colorado
Fort Lewis College *B*
Mesa State College *A*
Metropolitan State College of Denver *B*
Northeastern Junior College *C, A*
Pueblo Community College *C, A*
University of Colorado Boulder *A*
University of Denver *B, M*

Connecticut
Briarwood College *A*
Three Rivers Community-Technical College *C, A*
University of New Haven *A, B, M*

District of Columbia
Southeastern University *B*

Florida
Broward Community College *A*
Daytona Beach Community College *A*
Florida National College *A*
Lynn University *B*
Miami-Dade Community College *C, A*
St. Thomas University *B*
Valencia Community College *A*

Georgia
American InterContinental University *C, A*
Gwinnett Technical Institute *C, A*

Hawaii
Brigham Young University Hawaii *A, B*
Hawaii Pacific University *B*
University of Hawaii Maui Community College *A*

Idaho
College of Southern Idaho *A*

Illinois
City Colleges of Chicago Harold Washington College *C, A*
Danville Area Community College *C*
John A. Logan College *C, A*
MacCormac College *C, A*
Northwestern Business College *A*
Parkland College *C*
Robert Morris College: Chicago *C, A*
Roosevelt University *B*

Indiana
Indiana University--Purdue University Indiana University-Purdue University Indianapolis *B*
University of Indianapolis *A, B*

Iowa
Iowa Lakes Community College *A*
Northeast Iowa Community College *C*

Louisiana
Southern University Shreveport *A*

Maine
Andover College *C, A*
Mid-State College *C, A*
University of Maine Machias *B*

Maryland
Villa Julie College *A*

Massachusetts
Bay Path College *C, A*
Becker College *B*
Berkshire Community College *C*
Cape Cod Community College *C*
Fisher College *C, A*
Lasell College *B*
Marian Court College *C, A*
Middlesex Community College *C*
Mount Ida College *A*
Newbury College *A*
North Shore Community College *A*
Northern Essex Community College *C, A*
Quincy College *A*

Michigan
Baker College
 of Mount Clemens *A*
 of Muskegon *A*
Grand Valley State University *B*
Lansing Community College *A*
Michigan State University *B*
Northern Michigan University *B*
Western Michigan University *B*

Mississippi
Mississippi Gulf Coast Community College Jefferson Davis Campus *A*

Missouri
East Central College *C, A*
St. Louis Community College St. Louis Community College at Forest Park *A*

Montana
Western Montana College of The University of Montana *A*

Nebraska
Lincoln School of Commerce *C*
University of Nebraska Kearney *B*

New Hampshire
McIntosh College *C, A*
New Hampshire College *B*
New Hampshire Technical Institute *C, A*
University of New Hampshire *B*

New Jersey
Atlantic Cape Community College *C, A*
Cumberland County College *C, A*
Essex County College *A*
Mercer County Community College *C*
Sussex County Community College *C, A*

New Mexico
Albuquerque Technical-Vocational Institute *C, A*
New Mexico State University *B*

New York
Adirondack Community College *A*
Broome Community College *A*
Bryant & Stratton Business Institute Syracuse *A*
City University of New York Kingsborough Community College *A*
Corning Community College *C, A*

Daemen College *B*
Dowling College *B*
Finger Lakes Community College *A*
Herkimer County Community College *A*
Jefferson Community College *A*
Monroe Community College *A*
New York University *B, M*
Niagara University *B*
Rochester Institute of
 Technology *A, B, M*
Rockland Community College *A*
St. John's University *B*
State University of New York
 College of Agriculture and
  Technology at Cobleskill *A*
 College of Agriculture and
  Technology at Morrisville *A*
 College of Technology at Delhi *A*
Suffolk County Community College *A*
Westchester Community College *C, A*

North Carolina
Blue Ridge Community College *A*
College of the Albemarle *A*

Ohio
Columbus State Community College *A*
Davis College *A*
Hocking Technical College *C, A*
Kent State University *B*
Lakeland Community College *A*
Lorain County Community College *A*
Muskingum Area Technical College *A*
Northwestern College *C, A*
Ohio University
 Southern Campus at Ironton *A*
Ohio University
RETS Tech Center *C*
Sinclair Community College *A*
Tiffin University *B*
University of Akron *A*
Youngstown State University *A, B*

Oklahoma
Northeastern State University *B*
Oklahoma City Community College *A*
Tulsa Community College *C, A*

Oregon
Central Oregon Community College *A*
Chemeketa Community College *A*
Mount Hood Community College *C, A*

Pennsylvania
Central Pennsylvania College *A*
Mansfield University of
 Pennsylvania *A, B*
Mercyhurst College *C, A, B*
Peirce College *A, B*
Robert Morris College *B*
South Hills School of Business &
 Technology *C*
University of Pennsylvania *B, M*
Westmoreland County Community
 College *A*

Puerto Rico
Colegio Universitario del Este *C, A, B*
Huertas Junior College *C*
Inter American University of Puerto Rico
 Fajardo Campus *A*
National College of Business and
 Technology *A*
Pontifical Catholic University of Puerto
 Rico *A, B*
Technological College of San Juan *C*

Rhode Island
Johnson & Wales University *A, B*

South Carolina
Clemson University *B*

South Dakota
Black Hills State University *A, B*

Tennessee
Pellissippi State Technical Community
 College *A*

Texas
Amarillo College *C*
Collin County Community College
 District *C*
El Paso Community College *C, A*
Houston Community College
 System *C, A*
Richland College *A*
Tarrant County College *C, A*
University of Texas
 San Antonio *B*

Utah
Mountain West College *C, A*
Salt Lake Community College *C*

Vermont
Champlain College *A, B*
Johnson State College *B*

Virginia
National Business College *A*
Northern Virginia Community
 College *C, A*
Virginia Highlands Community
 College *C*

Washington
Spokane Falls Community College *C, A*
Yakima Valley Community College *C, A*

West Virginia
College of West Virginia *C, A*
Concord College *B*
Davis and Elkins College *B*
West Liberty State College *B*
West Virginia Northern Community
 College *A*

Wisconsin
Madison Area Technical College *A*
Northeast Wisconsin Technical
 College *A*
Wisconsin Indianhead Technical
 College *C*

Tourism/travel marketing

Alabama
Community College of the Air Force *A*
Shelton State Community College *C*

Alaska
University of Alaska
 Southeast *C, A*

Arizona
Phoenix College *C, A*

California
Butte College *C, A*
City College of San Francisco *A*
Coastline Community College *A*
Cypress College *C, A*
Empire College *C*
Foothill College *C, A*
Los Medanos College *C, A*
Palomar College *C, A*
Pasadena City College *C, A*
Saddleback College *C*
San Diego City College *C, A*
San Francisco State University *B*
Santa Ana College *A*
United States International University *B*

Colorado
Arapahoe Community College *C*
Community College of Aurora *C*
Community College of Denver *C*
Fort Lewis College *B*
Metropolitan State College of Denver *B*
Pikes Peak Community College *C*
Pueblo Community College *C, A*
Red Rocks Community College *C, A*

Connecticut
University of New Haven *A, B*

District of Columbia
George Washington University *B, M*

Florida
Florida National College *A*
Lynn University *B*
Miami-Dade Community College *C, A*
St. Thomas University *B*

Georgia
Gwinnett Technical Institute *C, A*

Illinois
College of DuPage *C, A*
Danville Area Community College *A*
Elgin Community College *C*
MacCormac College *C, A*
Moraine Valley Community
 College *C, A*
Parkland College *C*
Waubonsee Community College *C, A*

Indiana
Indiana University--Purdue University
 Indiana University-Purdue
  University Fort Wayne *A*
International Business College *C, A*

Iowa
American Institute of Business *A*
Des Moines Area Community College *C*
Iowa Lakes Community College *A*
Northeast Iowa Community College *C*

Maine
Andover College *C, A*
Beal College *A*
Mid-State College *C, A*
University of Maine
 Machias *A, B*

Maryland
Chesapeake College *A*
Villa Julie College *A*

Massachusetts
Bay Path College *A, B*
Bay State College *A*
Becker College *A*
Berkshire Community College *A*
Bristol Community College *C*
Fisher College *A*
Massasoit Community College *C, A*
Mount Ida College *A, B*
Newbury College *A*
Northern Essex Community College *A*

Michigan
Baker College
 of Muskegon *A*
 of Port Huron *A*
Eastern Michigan University *B*
Grand Valley State University *B*
Lansing Community College *A*
Western Michigan University *B*

Minnesota
Central Lakes College *C*
Dakota County Technical College *C*

Mississippi
Hinds Community College *A*
Mississippi Gulf Coast Community
 College
  Jefferson Davis Campus *A*

Missouri
Central Missouri State University *B*
East Central College *C, A*
Mineral Area College *A*
St. Louis University *A, B*

Montana
Western Montana College of The
 University of Montana *A*

Nebraska
Lincoln School of Commerce *C*
Midland Lutheran College *A*

New Hampshire
Hesser College *A*
New Hampshire Technical Institute *C, A*
Plymouth State College of the University
 System of New Hampshire *B*
University of New Hampshire *B*

New Jersey
Bergen Community College *C, A*
Raritan Valley Community College *C*
Sussex County Community College *C, A*

New York
Adirondack Community College *A*
Broome Community College *A*
Bryant & Stratton Business Institute
 Syracuse *C, A*
City University of New York
 Kingsborough Community
  College *A*
 La Guardia Community College *A*
Corning Community College *A*
Dowling College *B*
Dutchess Community College *A*
Finger Lakes Community College *A*
Genesee Community College *C, A*
Jefferson Community College *C, A*
Marymount Manhattan College *C*
Monroe Community College *A*
Rochester Institute of Technology *B, M*
St. John Fisher College *C*
Schenectady County Community
 College *C, A*
State University of New York
 College of Agriculture and
  Technology at Cobleskill *A*
 College of Agriculture and
  Technology at Morrisville *A*
 College of Technology at Delhi *A*
Suffolk County Community
 College *C, A*
Tompkins-Cortland Community
 College *A*
Westchester Community College *C, A*
Wood Tobe-Coburn School *C*

North Carolina
Blue Ridge Community College *A*
Cecils College *C*
Central Piedmont Community College *A*
College of the Albemarle *A*

Ohio
Columbus State Community College *A*
Davis College *A*
Kent State University
 Trumbull Campus *A*
Muskingum Area Technical College *A*
RETS Tech Center *C*
Sinclair Community College *A*
University of Akron *A*
Youngstown State University *A, B*

Oklahoma
Oklahoma City Community College *A*

Pennsylvania
Butler County Community College *C*
California University of Pennsylvania *B*
Central Pennsylvania College *A*
Community College of Allegheny
 County *C, A*
Community College of Beaver
 County *C, A*
Harcum College *A*
Harrisburg Area Community
 College *C, A*
Lehigh Carbon Community College *A*
Luzerne County Community College *A*
Mansfield University of
 Pennsylvania *A, B*
Northampton County Area Community
 College *C, A*
Reading Area Community College *A*
Robert Morris College *M*
Yorktowne Business Institute *A*

Puerto Rico
Colegio Universitario del Este *C*
University of the Sacred Heart *A, B*

Rhode Island
Johnson & Wales University *A, B*

Texas
Amarillo College *A*
Central Texas College *C, A*
El Paso Community College *C, A*
Texas A&M University *B*

Utah
Brigham Young University *B*
Dixie State College of Utah *C, A*
Salt Lake Community College *C*

Vermont
Champlain College *A, B*

Virginia
J. Sargeant Reynolds Community College *C*

Washington
Art Institute of Seattle *A*
Columbia Basin College *C*
Edmonds Community College *C, A*
Yakima Valley Community College *A*

West Virginia
Bluefield State College *A*
College of West Virginia *C, A*
Concord College *B*
West Liberty State College *B*

Wisconsin
Gateway Technical College *C*
University of Wisconsin
  Madison *B, M*

Toxicology

Arizona
University of Arizona *M, D*

Arkansas
University of Arkansas for Medical Sciences *M, D*

California
San Diego State University *M*
San Jose State University *M*
University of California
  Davis *M, D*
  Irvine *M, D*
  Riverside *M, D*
University of Southern California *M, D*

Colorado
University of Colorado
  Health Sciences Center *D*

District of Columbia
American University *M*
George Washington University *M, D*

Florida
University of Miami *B*

Georgia
University of Georgia *M, D*

Indiana
Indiana University--Purdue University
  Indiana University-Purdue University Indianapolis *M, D*

Iowa
Iowa State University *M, D*

Kentucky
University of Kentucky *M, D*

Louisiana
University of Louisiana at Monroe *B*

Maryland
University of Maryland
  Baltimore County *M, D*
  Baltimore *M, D*
  College Park *M, D*
  Eastern Shore *D*

Massachusetts
Massachusetts Institute of Technology *M, D*
Northeastern University *B*

Michigan
Michigan State University *D*
University of Michigan *M, D*
Wayne State University *M, D*

Minnesota
Minnesota State University, Mankato *B*
University of Minnesota
  Duluth *M*
  Twin Cities *M, D*

Mississippi
Mississippi State University *D*

New Hampshire
Antioch New England Graduate School *M*

New Jersey
Bloomfield College *B*
College of St. Elizabeth *B*
Felician College *B*
Monmouth University *B*
Rutgers
  The State University of New Jersey:
    New Brunswick Graduate Campus *M, D*
St. Peter's College *B*
University of Medicine and Dentistry of New Jersey
  School of Health Related Professions *C, B*

New York
Albany Medical College *M, D*
Clarkson University *B*
Cornell University *B*
St. John's University *B, M*
State University of New York
  Albany *M, D*
  Buffalo *M, D*
  College of Environmental Science and Forestry *B, M, D*
University of Rochester *M, D*

North Carolina
North Carolina State University *M, D*
University of North Carolina
  Chapel Hill *M, D*

Ohio
Ashland University *B*
Case Western Reserve University *M*
Wright State University *M*

Oregon
Oregon State University *M, D*

Pennsylvania
Duquesne University *M, D*
Penn State
  College of Medicine, Milton S. Hershey Medical Center *M, D*
University of the Sciences in Philadelphia *B, M*

South Carolina
Clemson University *B, M*

Texas
Prairie View A&M University *M*
Texas A&M University *M, D*
Texas Tech University *M*
University of Texas
  Medical Branch at Galveston *D*
  San Antonio *M*

Utah
Utah State University *M, D*

Virginia
Virginia Commonwealth University *M, D*

West Virginia
West Virginia University *M, D*

Wisconsin
Medical College of Wisconsin *M, D*
University of Wisconsin
  Madison *M, D*

Trade/industrial education

Alabama
Alabama Agricultural and Mechanical University *B, M*
Athens State University *B*
Lawson State Community College *C*

Alaska
University of Alaska
  Anchorage *M*

Arkansas
University of Arkansas
  Pine Bluff *B, T*
University of Arkansas *B, M, D*
University of Central Arkansas *M*

California
California Polytechnic State University:
  San Luis Obispo *M*
California State University
  Los Angeles *T*
Humboldt State University *B, T*

Colorado
Colorado State University *T*
University of Southern Colorado *T*

Delaware
Delaware State University *B*

Florida
Florida Agricultural and Mechanical University *B, M*
Florida International University *B, M, T*
Florida State University *D*
University of Central Florida *B, M*
University of North Florida *B*
University of South Florida *B, M*

Georgia
Darton College *A*
Valdosta State University *B*

Hawaii
University of Hawaii
  Manoa *B, T*

Illinois
Southern Illinois University
  Carbondale *B, M, D*
Western Illinois University *B*

Indiana
Ball State University *T*
Indiana State University *B, M, T*
Purdue University *A*

Iowa
Iowa State University *B, T*
University of Northern Iowa *B*
William Penn University *B*

Kansas
Central Christian College *A*
Fort Hays State University *B, T*
Pittsburg State University *B, T*

Kentucky
Eastern Kentucky University *B, M*
Morehead State University *B*
Murray State University *B, T*
Northern Kentucky University *B, T*
University of Kentucky *B, M*

University of Louisville *B, M*
Western Kentucky University *B*

Louisiana
Louisiana State University and Agricultural and Mechanical College *B, M, D*
Northwestern State University *B, T*

Massachusetts
Fitchburg State College *M*

Michigan
Andrews University *M, T*
Lansing Community College *A*
Madonna University *T*
Western Michigan University *B*

Minnesota
St. Cloud State University *T*

Mississippi
Hinds Community College *A*
Mississippi Gulf Coast Community College
  Jefferson Davis Campus *A*
  Perkinston *A*

Missouri
Lincoln University *B, T*

Nebraska
Metropolitan Community College *A*
University of Nebraska
  Kearney *B*
  Lincoln *B, T*

Nevada
University of Nevada
  Reno *B*

New Jersey
Rutgers
  The State University of New Jersey:
    New Brunswick Graduate Campus *M, D, T*

New Mexico
New Mexico Highlands University *B*

New York
New York Institute of Technology *A, B, T*
State University of New York
  Albany *B, M, T*
  College at Buffalo *B, M, T*
  Oswego *B, M, T*

North Carolina
Guilford Technical Community College *A*
North Carolina Agricultural and Technical State University *B, T*
North Carolina State University *T*
Southwestern Community College *A*

North Dakota
University of North Dakota *M*
Valley City State University *B, T*

Ohio
Bowling Green State University *B*
Kent State University *B, M, T*
Ohio State University
  Columbus Campus *B, M*
Ohio University *B*

Oklahoma
East Central University *B*
Oklahoma Panhandle State University *B*
Oklahoma State University *B, M, T*
University of Central Oklahoma *B*

Pennsylvania
Indiana University of Pennsylvania *B, T*
Penn State
  University Park *B*
Temple University *B*

Rhode Island
Rhode Island College *B*

South Carolina
Clemson University *B, M*
South Carolina State University *B, T*

South Dakota
Black Hills State University *B, T*
South Dakota State University *M*

Tennessee
University of Tennessee
 Knoxville *B, T*

Texas
Sam Houston State University *M*
Southwest Texas State University *M, T*
Texas A&M University
 Commerce *M, T*
Texas A&M University *D, T*
University of Houston *B, M*
University of North Texas *M, D*
Wayland Baptist University *B*

Utah
Brigham Young University *B, M*
Southern Utah University *B, T*

Virginia
Norfolk State University *B*
Virginia Polytechnic Institute and State
 University *M, D*
Virginia State University *B, M*

Washington
Central Washington University *B, T*
Renton Technical College *C, A*
South Seattle Community College *C, A*
Western Washington University *M*

West Virginia
Fairmont State College *B*
Marshall University *M*

Wisconsin
University of Wisconsin
 Stout *M*

Wyoming
University of Wyoming *B*
Western Wyoming Community
 College *A*

Transportation management

Arizona
Gateway Community College *C*

Colorado
University of Colorado
 Boulder *B*

Florida
University of North Florida *B*

Illinois
Triton College *C, A*

Iowa
Iowa State University *B, M*

Maine
Maine Maritime Academy *B, M*

Maryland
University of Maryland
 College Park *B*

Massachusetts
Massachusetts Maritime Academy *C*
Northeastern University *A*

Michigan
Henry Ford Community College *A*

New Jersey
Middlesex County College *A*
Monmouth University *B*

New York
City University of New York
 Queensborough Community
  College *A*
Daemen College *C, B*
Dowling College *B*
Polytechnic University *M*
State University of New York
 Maritime College *B, M*
Syracuse University *M*
United States Merchant Marine
 Academy *B*

Ohio
Sinclair Community College *C, A*

Tennessee
University of Tennessee
 Knoxville *B*

Texas
Texas A&M International University *M*
Texas Southern University *B*

Utah
Salt Lake Community College *A*

Washington
Spokane Falls Community College *A*

West Virginia
Marshall University *B*

Transportation/materials moving

Alabama
Calhoun Community College *A*
Community College of the Air Force *A*

California
California State University
 Dominguez Hills *M*
 Long Beach *C*
Compton Community College *C*
Don Bosco Technical Institute *A*
Fresno City College *C, A*

Illinois
Black Hawk College *C*
John Wood Community College *C*
Northwestern University *M*
Richland Community College *A*
Triton College *C, A*

Iowa
Des Moines Area Community College *C*
Indian Hills Community College *C*
Northeast Iowa Community College *C*

Maryland
Morgan State University *M*

Massachusetts
Holyoke Community College *C*
Massachusetts Maritime Academy *C*

Michigan
Henry Ford Community College *A*

Mississippi
East Mississippi Community College *C*

Missouri
Crowder College *C*

Nebraska
Southeast Community College
 Lincoln Campus *C*

Nevada
University of Nevada
 Las Vegas *M*

New York
Nassau Community College *A*
Niagara University *B*

North Dakota
Lake Region State College *A*

Ohio
Columbus State Community College *A*
John Carroll University *B*
University of Akron
 Wayne College *A*
University of Akron *A*
University of Toledo *A*

Pennsylvania
Community College of Allegheny
 County *A*

Texas
Brookhaven College *A*
Texas Southern University *B*

Virginia
Central Virginia Community College *C*
J. Sargeant Reynolds Community
 College *C*
University of Richmond *C, A*

Washington
Green River Community College *C, A*
Highline Community College *A*
Spokane Falls Community College *A*

Wisconsin
Northeast Wisconsin Technical
 College *A*
University of Wisconsin
 Superior *B*

Turf management

Arizona
Northland Pioneer College *C, A*

California
Butte College *C*
College of the Desert *C, A*
Los Angeles Pierce College *C*
MiraCosta College *C, A*
Monterey Peninsula College *C*
Mount San Antonio College *C*

Florida
Edison Community College *C*
Florida Southern College *B*
Indian River Community College *A*
Lake City Community College *C*

Georgia
University of Georgia *B*

Illinois
College of DuPage *C*
College of Lake County *A*
Danville Area Community College *C*
Joliet Junior College *C, A*
Kishwaukee College *C*
Lewis and Clark Community College *A*
Lincoln Land Community College *C*
Rend Lake College *C*
Southwestern Illinois College *A*
William Rainey Harper College *C, A*

Iowa
Des Moines Area Community College *C*
Kirkwood Community College *A*
Western Iowa Tech Community
 College *A*

Maine
University of Maine *B*

Maryland
University of Maryland
 College Park *B*

Massachusetts
University of Massachusetts
 Amherst *A*

Michigan
Michigan State University *C*
Northwestern Michigan College *A*

Minnesota
Anoka-Ramsey Community College *A*

Mississippi
Mississippi Gulf Coast Community
 College
  Perkinston *A*

Missouri
Longview Community College *A*

Nebraska
Central Community College *C*
Nebraska College of Technical
 Agriculture *A*
Northeast Community College *A*

New Jersey
Rutgers
 The State University of New Jersey:
  Cook College *B*

New York
State University of New York
 College of Agriculture and
  Technology at Cobleskill *A*
 College of Technology at Delhi *A*

North Carolina
Blue Ridge Community College *C*
Brunswick Community College *A*
Catawba Valley Community College *A*
North Carolina State University *A, B*
Sandhills Community College *A*
Wayne Community College *A*

North Dakota
Minot State University: Bottineau
 Campus *A*

Ohio
Cincinnati State Technical and
 Community College *C*
Clark State Community College *A*
Ohio State University
 Agricultural Technical Institute *A*
 Columbus Campus *B*
Owens Community College
 Toledo *A*

Oregon
Central Oregon Community College *A*

Pennsylvania
Community College of Allegheny
 County *A*
Delaware Valley College *B*
Penn State
 University Park *B*
Westmoreland County Community
 College *A*

South Carolina
Clemson University *B*
Greenville Technical College *C*
Technical College of the Lowcountry *C*
Trident Technical College *C*

South Dakota
Southeast Technical Institute *A*

Tennessee
Chattanooga State Technical Community
 College *C*
Walters State Community College *A*

Texas
Grayson County College *A*
Texas State Technical College
 Waco *C, A*
Western Texas College *C, A*

Virginia
J. Sargeant Reynolds Community
 College *A*
Northern Virginia Community College *C*

Washington
Spokane Community College *A*
Walla Walla Community College *C, A*

Urban studies

Alabama
Alabama Agricultural and Mechanical University B, M
Lawson State Community College A

California
California State University
    Long Beach C
    Northridge B
Loyola Marymount University B
San Diego State University B
San Francisco State University B
San Jose State University M
Stanford University B
University of California
    San Diego B
Whittier College B

Connecticut
Connecticut College B
Trinity College B
University of Connecticut B

Delaware
University of Delaware M, D

District of Columbia
University of the District of Columbia A, B

Florida
New College of the University of South Florida B
University of Tampa B

Georgia
Atlanta Metropolitan College A
Clayton College and State University A
Floyd College A
Georgia Perimeter College A
Georgia State University B, M
Morehouse College B
Morris Brown College B

Illinois
De Paul University B
Elmhurst College B
North Park University B
Northwestern University B, M
Rockford College B
Roosevelt University B, M
Wheaton College C

Indiana
Indiana State University M
Indiana University--Purdue University
    Indiana University-Purdue University Fort Wayne C

Iowa
Mount Mercy College B
University of Iowa M

Kansas
MidAmerica Nazarene University B

Kentucky
University of Louisville D

Louisiana
Dillard University B
Tulane University B
University of New Orleans M, D

Maryland
Towson University B
University of Maryland
    College Park M

Massachusetts
Boston University B
Hampshire College B
Harvard College B
Harvard University M, D
Massachusetts Institute of Technology M, D
Tufts University M

Westfield State College B
Worcester State College B

Michigan
Aquinas College B

Minnesota
Macalester College B
Minnesota State University, Mankato B, M
Ridgewater College: A Community and Technical College A
St. Cloud State University B
University of Minnesota
    Duluth B
    Twin Cities B
Winona State University B

Mississippi
Jackson State University B

Missouri
St. Louis University B, M
University of Missouri
    Kansas City B

Nebraska
Bellevue University B
University of Nebraska
    Omaha B, M

Nevada
University of Nevada
    Reno M

New Jersey
Rutgers
    The State University of New Jersey: Camden College of Arts and Sciences B
    The State University of New Jersey: Douglass College B
    The State University of New Jersey: Livingston College B
    The State University of New Jersey: Rutgers College B
    The State University of New Jersey: University College Camden B
    The State University of New Jersey: University College New Brunswick B
St. Peter's College A, B

New York
Audrey Cohen College A, B
Barnard College B
Canisius College B
City University of New York
    Brooklyn College B
    Hunter College B, M
    Queens College B, M
College of Mount St. Vincent B
Columbia University
    Columbia College B
    School of General Studies B
Daemen College C
Eugene Lang College/New School University B
Fordham University B
Hobart and William Smith Colleges B
Iona College B
Long Island University
    Brooklyn Campus M
New York University B
Sarah Lawrence College B
State University of New York
    Albany B
    Buffalo M
Vassar College B

Ohio
Cleveland State University B, M, D
College of Wooster B
Malone College B
Oberlin College B
Ohio State University
    Columbus Campus B
Ohio Wesleyan University B

University of Akron M
University of Cincinnati
    Clermont College A
    Raymond Walters College A
University of Cincinnati B
University of Toledo B
Wittenberg University B
Wright State University B, M

Oklahoma
Langston University B
University of Central Oklahoma B, M

Oregon
Portland State University B, M, D

Pennsylvania
Bryn Mawr College B
California University of Pennsylvania B
Haverford College B
Lehigh University B
Shippensburg University of Pennsylvania B
Temple University B, M, D
University of Pennsylvania A, B, M
University of Pittsburgh B

Puerto Rico
University of the Sacred Heart B

Rhode Island
Brown University B
Community College of Rhode Island A
Rhode Island College B

South Carolina
College of Charleston B
Furman University B

Tennessee
David Lipscomb University B
Rhodes College B
University of Tennessee
    Knoxville B
Vanderbilt University B

Texas
Baylor University B
St. Philip's College A
Trinity University B
University of Texas
    Arlington M

Utah
University of Utah B

Virginia
Norfolk State University M
Old Dominion University M, D
University of Richmond B
Virginia Commonwealth University C, B, M, D
Virginia Polytechnic Institute and State University M

Wisconsin
Marquette University B
University of Wisconsin
    Green Bay B
    Madison M, D
    Milwaukee B, M, D
    Oshkosh B

Urban/community/regional planning

Alabama
Alabama Agricultural and Mechanical University B, M
Auburn University M
University of Alabama B

Arizona
Arizona State University B, M
Northern Arizona University B
University of Arizona B, M

California
California Polytechnic State University: San Luis Obispo B, M
California State Polytechnic University: Pomona B, M
California State University
    Chico B, M
East Los Angeles College A
Modesto Junior College A
San Diego State University M
San Jose State University M
University of California
    Berkeley M, D
    Davis B, M
    Irvine M
    Los Angeles M, D
University of Southern California B, M, D

Colorado
University of Colorado
    Boulder B
    Denver M

Connecticut
Central Connecticut State University B

District of Columbia
University of the District of Columbia A, B, M

Florida
Florida Atlantic University B, M
Florida State University M, D
University of Florida M
University of Miami M

Georgia
Georgia Institute of Technology M
Morris Brown College B

Hawaii
University of Hawaii
    Manoa M

Illinois
University of Illinois
    Chicago M
    Urbana-Champaign B, M, D

Indiana
Ball State University B, M
Indiana State University M
Indiana University--Purdue University
    Indiana University-Purdue University Indianapolis M

Iowa
Iowa State University B, M
University of Iowa M

Kansas
Kansas State University M
University of Kansas M

Louisiana
University of New Orleans M

Maine
University of Southern Maine M

Maryland
University of Maryland
    College Park M

Massachusetts
Bridgewater State College B
Conway School of Landscape Design M
Harvard College B
Harvard University D
Massachusetts Institute of Technology B, M, D
Tufts University M
University of Massachusetts
    Amherst M, D
Westfield State College B

Michigan
Eastern Michigan University B, M
Grand Valley State University B

Michigan State University *B, M*
University of Michigan *M, D*
Wayne State University *M*
Minnesota
Minnesota State University, Mankato *B*
St. Cloud State University *B*
Mississippi
Jackson State University *B, M, D*
University of Southern Mississippi *B*
Missouri
St. Louis University *M*
Southwest Missouri State
  University *B, M*
Washington University *M*
Nebraska
University of Nebraska
  Lincoln *M*
Nevada
University of Nevada
  Las Vegas *B*
New Hampshire
Plymouth State College of the University
  System of New Hampshire *B*
University of New Hampshire *B*
New Jersey
Rutgers
  The State University of New Jersey:
  New Brunswick Graduate
  Campus *M, D*
New Mexico
New Mexico State University *B*
University of New Mexico *M*
New York
City University of New York
  City College *M*
  Hunter College *M*
Cornell University *B, M, D*
New York Institute of Technology *M*
New York University *M*
Pratt Institute *M*
State University of New York
  Albany *M*
  College at Buffalo *B*
  College of Environmental Science
    and Forestry *B, M*
North Carolina
Appalachian State University *B*
East Carolina University *B*
University of North Carolina
  Chapel Hill *M, D*
Ohio
Miami University
  Oxford Campus *B*
Ohio State University
  Columbus Campus *B, M, D*
Ohio University *B*
University of Akron *C, M*
University of Cincinnati *B, M*
Wittenberg University *B*
Oklahoma
University of Oklahoma *M*
Oregon
Portland State University *B, M*
University of Oregon *M*
Pennsylvania
Art Institute
  of Pittsburgh *C*
Bryn Mawr College *B*
Indiana University of Pennsylvania *B*
Mansfield University of Pennsylvania *B*
Penn State
  University Park *M, D*
University of Pennsylvania *M, D*
West Chester University of
  Pennsylvania *M*

Puerto Rico
University of Puerto Rico
  Rio Piedras Campus *B*
Rhode Island
University of Rhode Island *M*
South Carolina
Clemson University *M*
Tennessee
University of Memphis *M*
University of Tennessee
  Knoxville *M*
Texas
Rice University *M*
Southwest Texas State University *B*
Texas A&M University *M, D*
University of North Texas *B*
University of Texas
  Arlington *B*
  Austin *M, D*
Utah
Utah State University *M*
Virginia
University of Virginia *B, M*
Virginia Polytechnic Institute and State
  University *M*
Washington
Eastern Washington University *B, M*
University of Washington *B, M, D*
Washington State University *M*
Western Washington University *B*
Wisconsin
Northland College *B*
University of Wisconsin
  Madison *M, D*
  Milwaukee *M*
Wyoming
University of Wyoming *M*

Vehicle/equipment operation

Alabama
Bevill State Community College *C*
Community College of the Air Force *A*
Reid State Technical College *C*
Arizona
Central Arizona College *C, A*
Cochise College *C*
Arkansas
North Arkansas College *C*
California
City College of San Francisco *C*
College of the Redwoods *C*
Merced College *C*
Colorado
Community College of Denver *C*
Connecticut
University of New Haven *A*
Delaware
Delaware Technical and Community
  College
    Owens Campus *C, A*
Florida
Brevard Community College *C*
Central Florida Community College *C*
Tallahassee Community College *C*
Illinois
Black Hawk College *C*
Elgin Community College *C*
Illinois Eastern Community Colleges
  Wabash Valley College *C*
Sauk Valley Community College *C*
Southeastern Illinois College *C*

Iowa
Des Moines Area Community College *C*
Hawkeye Community College *C*
Scott Community College *C*
Kansas
Johnson County Community
  College *C, A*
Maine
Washington County Technical College *C*
Maryland
Charles County Community College *C*
Michigan
Kirtland Community College *C, A*
Lansing Community College *A*
Oakland Community College *C*
Minnesota
Alexandria Technical College *C*
Central Lakes College *C*
Minnesota State College - Southeast
  Technical *C*
Mississippi
Mississippi Gulf Coast Community
  College
    Perkinston *C*
Northwest Mississippi Community
  College *C*
Nebraska
Central Community College *C*
Northeast Community College *C*
Nevada
Western Nevada Community College *A*
New Mexico
Albuquerque Technical-Vocational
  Institute *C*
North Carolina
Cape Fear Community College *C*
Johnston Community College *C, A*
North Dakota
North Dakota State College of
  Science *C, A*
South Carolina
Greenville Technical College *C*
South Dakota
Southeast Technical Institute *A*
Texas
Amarillo College *C*
Brazosport College *C, A*
Cedar Valley College *A*
Coastal Bend College *C*
Virginia
Southside Virginia Community
  College *C*
Washington
Big Bend Community College *C*
Skagit Valley College *C, A*

Vehicle/mobile equipment mechanics

Alabama
Bessemer State Technical College *C, A*
Bevill State Community College *A*
Central Alabama Community College *C*
Community College of the Air Force *A*
Harry M. Ayers State Technical
  College *C*
J. F. Drake State Technical College *C*
Northwest-Shoals Community College *C*
Shelton State Community College *C, A*

Alaska
University of Alaska
  Anchorage *C, A*
  Fairbanks *C*
  Southeast *C, A*
Arizona
Arizona Western College *C, A*
Central Arizona College *A*
Gateway Community College *C, A*
Mesa Community College *A*
Mohave Community College *C, A*
Pima Community College *C, A*
Yavapai College *C, A*
Arkansas
Southern Arkansas University
  Tech *A*
Westark College *C, A*
California
American River College *A*
Barstow College *C, A*
Butte College *C, A*
Citrus College *C, A*
College of the Desert *C, A*
College of the Redwoods *C, A*
Fresno City College *C, A*
Glendale Community College *C, A*
Golden West College *C, A*
Kings River Community College *C*
Long Beach City College *C, A*
Palomar College *C, A*
Sacramento City College *C, A*
Saddleback College *C*
San Diego Miramar College *C, A*
Shasta College *A*
Sierra College *A*
Ventura College *C, A*
Victor Valley College *C, A*
Yuba College *C*
Colorado
Aims Community College *C, A*
Community College of Aurora *A*
Mesa State College *C, A*
Pikes Peak Community College *A*
Trinidad State Junior College *C, A*
Delaware
Delaware Technical and Community
  College
    Owens Campus *C, A*
    Stanton/Wilmington Campus *A*
Florida
Daytona Beach Community
  College *C, A*
Hillsborough Community College *A*
Seminole Community College *C, A*
Georgia
Athens Area Technical Institute *C*
Bainbridge College *A*
Columbus Technical Institute *C*
Dalton State College *C, A*
Darton College *A*
DeKalb Technical Institute *C*
Hawaii
University of Hawaii
  Honolulu Community College *C, A*
Idaho
Boise State University *C*
Eastern Idaho Technical College *C*
Idaho State University *C, A*
Lewis-Clark State College *A*
North Idaho College *C, A*
Ricks College *A*
Illinois
Black Hawk College
  East Campus *A*
Black Hawk College *C, A*
Carl Sandburg College *C, A*
College of Lake County *C, A*
Danville Area Community College *C, A*

Vehicle/mobile equipment mechanics

Illinois
Eastern Community Colleges
    Olney Central College *C, A*
John A. Logan College *C*
Kankakee Community College *C, A*
Kaskaskia College *C, A*
Kishwaukee College *C, A*
Lake Land College *A*
Lincoln Land Community College *C, A*
Moraine Valley Community
    College *C, A*
Rend Lake College *C, A*
Rock Valley College *A*
Sauk Valley Community College *A*
Shawnee Community College *C, A*
Southern Illinois University
    Carbondale *B*

Indiana
Ivy Tech State College
    Northcentral *C*
    Southcentral *C*

Iowa
Hawkeye Community College *A*
Iowa Western Community College *A*
Kirkwood Community College *C, A*
North Iowa Area Community College *A*
Northeast Iowa Community
    College *C, A*

Kansas
Barton County Community College *A*
Central Christian College *A*
Cowley County Community
    College *C, A*
Garden City Community College *A*
Pratt Community College *C, A*

Louisiana
Nunez Community College *C*

Maine
Eastern Maine Technical College *C, A*
Southern Maine Technical College *A*

Maryland
Allegany College *C, A*
Harford Community College *C, A*
Montgomery College
    Rockville Campus *C*

Massachusetts
Franklin Institute of Boston *A*

Michigan
Andrews University *B*
Bay de Noc Community College *A*
Ferris State University *A*
Grand Rapids Community College *C, A*
Henry Ford Community College *A*
Jackson Community College *C, A*
Kirtland Community College *C, A*
Mid Michigan Community College *C, A*
Monroe County Community
    College *C, A*
Northern Michigan University *A*
Northwestern Michigan College *A*
Oakland Community College *C, A*
Southwestern Michigan College *C, A*
Washtenaw Community College *C, A*

Minnesota
Alexandria Technical College *C*
Hennepin Technical College *C, A*
Lake Superior College: A Community
    and Technical College *C, A*
St. Cloud Technical College *C, A*
St. Paul Technical College *C*

Mississippi
Coahoma Community College *A*
Hinds Community College *C*
Mississippi Delta Community
    College *C, A*
Mississippi Gulf Coast Community
    College
        Jackson County Campus *A*
        Perkinston *C, A*
Northwest Mississippi Community
    College *C*

Missouri
Crowder College *C, A*
East Central College *C, A*
Jefferson College *C, A*
Longview Community College *C, A*
St. Louis Community College
    St. Louis Community College at
        Forest Park *A*
State Fair Community College *A*

Montana
Miles Community College *C, A*
Montana State University
    Northern *A, B*
Montana Tech of the University of
    Montana: College of Technology *A*
Montana Tech of the University of
    Montana *A*

Nebraska
Central Community College *C, A*
Metropolitan Community College *A*
Mid Plains Community College Area *C*
Southeast Community College
    Lincoln Campus *C, A*
    Milford Campus *A*

New Hampshire
New Hampshire Community Technical
    College
        Laconia *A*

New Jersey
Sussex County Community College *C*

New Mexico
Albuquerque Technical-Vocational
    Institute *C, A*
Clovis Community College *C, A*
Dona Ana Branch Community College of
    New Mexico State University *C, A*
Eastern New Mexico University
    Roswell Campus *A*
New Mexico Junior College *C, A*
Northern New Mexico Community
    College *C, A*

New York
City University of New York
    Bronx Community College *C, A*
Hudson Valley Community College *A*
State University of New York
    College of Technology at
        Delhi *C, A*

North Carolina
Alamance Community College *C, A*
Cape Fear Community College *A*
Catawba Valley Community College *C*
Central Carolina Community College *A*
Central Piedmont Community College *C*
Coastal Carolina Community
    College *C, A*
Durham Technical Community
    College *C, A*
Gaston College *C, A*
Halifax Community College *C*
Haywood Community College *C, A*
Lenoir Community College *A*
Mitchell Community College *C*
Pitt Community College *C, A*
Randolph Community College *C*
Roanoke-Chowan Community
    College *C*
South Piedmont Community
    College *C, A*
Tri-County Community College *A*
Vance-Granville Community College *C*
Wake Technical Community
    College *C, A*
Wayne Community College *A*
Wilson Technical Community College *C*

North Dakota
Lake Region State College *C, A*

North Dakota State College of
    Science *C, A*

Ohio
Columbus State Community College *A*
Northwestern College *C, A*
Sinclair Community College *C, A*
University of Cincinnati
    Raymond Walters College *C, A*
Washington State Community College *A*

Oklahoma
Northeastern Oklahoma Agricultural and
    Mechanical College *A*

Pennsylvania
Community College of Beaver County *A*
Johnson Technical Institute *A*
Montgomery County Community
    College *A*
Pennsylvania College of
    Technology *C, A, B*
Reading Area Community College *A*

Puerto Rico
University of Puerto Rico
    Carolina Regional College *A*

Rhode Island
New England Institute of
    Technology *C, A*

South Carolina
Aiken Technical College *C, A*
Greenville Technical College *C, A*
Horry-Georgetown Technical College *A*
Midlands Technical College *C*
Orangeburg-Calhoun Technical
    College *A*
Piedmont Technical College *A*
Trident Technical College *C*
York Technical College *A*

Texas
Alvin Community College *C*
Austin Community College *C*
Brookhaven College *A*
Cedar Valley College *A*
Central Texas College *C, A*
Coastal Bend College *C, A*
College of the Mainland *C*
Del Mar College *C, A*
Eastfield College *C, A*
El Paso Community College *C, A*
Hill College *C, A*
Houston Community College
    System *C, A*
Kilgore College *C*
Midland College *A*
North Central Texas College *A*
Northeast Texas Community
    College *C, A*
Odessa College *C, A*
Tarrant County College *C, A*
Temple College *A*
Texas State Technical College
    Sweetwater *C*
    Waco *C, A*
Vernon Regional Junior College *C, A*
Western Texas College *C, A*

Utah
College of Eastern Utah *C, A*
Salt Lake Community College *A*
Southern Utah University *A*
Weber State University *C, A, B*

Virginia
Danville Community College *A*
Northern Virginia Community College *A*
Southside Virginia Community
    College *C*
Thomas Nelson Community
    College *A*
Tidewater Community College *C, A*

Washington
Big Bend Community College *A*
Clark College *C, A*

Columbia Basin College *C, A*
Green River Community College *C, A*
Lake Washington Technical College *C, A*
Lower Columbia College *C*
Peninsula College *A*
Shoreline Community College *C, A*
Skagit Valley College *A*
South Puget Sound Community
    College *C, A*
South Seattle Community College *C, A*
Spokane Community College *C, A*
Walla Walla College *C, A*
Walla Walla Community College *C, A*
Western Washington University *B*

West Virginia
Southern West Virginia Community and
    Technical College *C, A*

Wisconsin
Blackhawk Technical College *C, A*
Chippewa Valley Technical College *C*
Gateway Technical College *C*
Madison Area Technical College *C, A*
Northeast Wisconsin Technical
    College *C*
Waukesha County Technical
    College *C, A*
Western Wisconsin Technical College *C*
Wisconsin Indianhead Technical
    College *C*

Wyoming
Central Wyoming College *C, A*
Laramie County Community
    College *C, A*

Vehicle/petroleum products marketing

Iowa
Iowa Western Community College *C*

Michigan
Northwood University *A, B*
Oakland Community College *C, A*
Western Michigan University *B*

Mississippi
Hinds Community College *C*
Mississippi Gulf Coast Community
    College
        Perkinston *C*

Montana
Dawson Community College *C, A*

Nebraska
Central Community College *C, A*

Oregon
Clackamas Community College *C*

Veterinarian assistant

Alabama
Snead State Community College *A*

California
Foothill College *C, A*
San Diego Mesa College *A*

Colorado
Bel-Rea Institute of Animal
    Technology *A*
Colorado Mountain College
    Spring Valley Campus *A*
Otero Junior College *A*

Connecticut
Northwestern Connecticut
    Community-Technical College *A*
Quinnipiac University *B*

Delaware
Delaware Technical and Community College
  Owens Campus *A*

Florida
Manatee Community College *A*
Pensacola Junior College *A*
St. Petersburg Junior College *A*

Georgia
Brewton-Parker College *A*
Fort Valley State University *A, B*
Gwinnett Technical Institute *C*

Illinois
Joliet Junior College *A*
Parkland College *A*

Indiana
Purdue University *A, B*

Iowa
Des Moines Area Community College *C*
Kirkwood Community College *A*
Waldorf College *A*

Kansas
Colby Community College *A*
Johnson County Community College *A*

Kentucky
Morehead State University *A*
Murray State University *B*

Louisiana
Northwestern State University *A*

Maine
University of Maine
  Augusta *A*

Maryland
Community College of Baltimore County
  Essex *A*

Massachusetts
Becker College *A, B*
Berkshire Community College *C*
Holyoke Community College *A*
Mount Ida College *A, B*
North Shore Community College *A*

Michigan
Bay de Noc Community College *C*
Macomb Community College *C*
Michigan State University *C, B*

Minnesota
Ridgewater College: A Community and Technical College *A*

Mississippi
Hinds Community College *A*
Mississippi Gulf Coast Community College
  Perkinston *A*

Missouri
Jefferson College *A*
Maple Woods Community College *A*

Nebraska
Nebraska College of Technical Agriculture *A*
Northeast Community College *A*
University of Nebraska
  Lincoln *B*

New Hampshire
New Hampshire Community Technical College
  Manchester *A*

New Jersey
Camden County College *A*
County College of Morris *A*
Thomas Edison State College *A, B*

New York
City University of New York
  La Guardia Community College *A*
Medaille College *A*
Mercy College *B*
State University of New York
  College of Technology at Canton *A*
  College of Technology at Delhi *A*
Suffolk County Community College *A*

North Carolina
Central Carolina Community College *A*

North Dakota
North Dakota State University *B*

Ohio
Columbus State Community College *A*
University of Cincinnati
  Raymond Walters College *A*

Oklahoma
Oklahoma State University
  Oklahoma City *A*

Oregon
Portland Community College *A*

Pennsylvania
Harcum College *A*
Johnson Technical Institute *A*
Lehigh Carbon Community College *A*
Manor College *A*
Median School of Allied Health Careers *C*
Northampton County Area Community College *A*
Wilson College *A*

Puerto Rico
University of Puerto Rico
  Medical Sciences Campus *B*

South Carolina
Tri-County Technical College *A*

Tennessee
Columbia State Community College *A*
Lincoln Memorial University *A, B*

Texas
Houston Community College System *C*
Midland College *A*
Sul Ross State University *A*

Utah
Snow College *A*

Vermont
Vermont Technical College *A*

Virginia
Blue Ridge Community College *C, A*
Northern Virginia Community College *A*

Washington
Pierce College *A*
Yakima Valley Community College *A*

West Virginia
Fairmont State College *A*

Wisconsin
Madison Area Technical College *A*

Wyoming
Eastern Wyoming College *A*

Veterinary medicine (D.V.M.)

Alabama
Auburn University: College of Veterinary Medicine *F*
Tuskegee University: School of Veterinary Medicine *F*

California
University of California Davis: School of Veterinary Medicine *F*

Colorado
Colorado State University: College of Veterinary Medicine and Biomedical Sciences *F*

Florida
University of Florida: College of Veterinary Medicine *F*

Georgia
University of Georgia: College of Veterinary Medicine *F*

Illinois
University of Illinois at Urbana-Champaign: College of Veterinary Medicine *F*

Indiana
Purdue University: School of Veterinary Medicine *F*

Iowa
Iowa State University: College of Veterinary Medicine *F*

Kansas
Kansas State University: College of Veterinary Medicine *F*

Louisiana
Louisiana State University and Agricultural and Mechanical College: School of Veterinary Medicine *F*

Massachusetts
Tufts University: School of Veterinary Medicine *F*

Michigan
Michigan State University: School of Veterinary Medicine *F*

Minnesota
University of Minnesota Twin Cities: College of Veterinary Medicine *F*

Mississippi
Mississippi State University: College of Veterinary Medicine *F*

Missouri
University of Missouri Columbia: School of Veterinary Medicine *F*

New York
Cornell University: College of Veterinary Medicine *F*

North Carolina
North Carolina State University: College of Veterinary Medicine *F*

Ohio
Ohio State University Columbus Campus: College of Veterinary Medicine *F*

Oklahoma
Oklahoma State University: College of Veterinary Medicine *F*

Oregon
Oregon State University: College of Veterinary Medicine *F*

Pennsylvania
University of Pennsylvania: School of Veterinary Medicine *F*

Tennessee
University of Tennessee Knoxville: College of Veterinary Medicine *F*

Texas
Texas A&M University: College of Veterinary Medicine *F*

Virginia
Virginia Polytechnic Institute: Virginia-Maryland Regional College of Veterinary Medicine *F*

Washington
Washington State University: School of Veterinary Medicine *F*

Wisconsin
University of Wisconsin Madison: School of Veterinary Medicine *F*

Veterinary specialties

Alabama
Auburn University *M, D*
Tuskegee University *M*

California
University of California Davis *M*

Colorado
Colorado State University *M, D*

Florida
Brevard Community College *A*
University of Florida *M, D*

Georgia
University of Georgia *M, D*

Idaho
University of Idaho *M*

Illinois
University of Illinois Urbana-Champaign *M, D*

Indiana
Purdue University *M, D*

Iowa
Iowa State University *M, D*

Kansas
Kansas State University *M, D*

Kentucky
University of Kentucky *M, D*

Louisiana
Louisiana State University and Agricultural and Mechanical College *M, D*

Massachusetts
Becker College *B*

Minnesota
University of Minnesota Twin Cities *M, D*

Mississippi
Mississippi Gulf Coast Community College
  Perkinston *A*
Mississippi State University *M, D*

Missouri
University of Missouri Columbia *M, D*

Nebraska
University of Nebraska Lincoln *B, M*

New Hampshire
New Hampshire Community Technical College
  Stratham *A*

North Dakota
Minot State University: Bottineau Campus *A*
North Dakota State University *B*

Oregon
Oregon State University *M, D*

Pennsylvania
Wilson College *B*

Tennessee
Lincoln Memorial University *B*

Veterinary specialties

University of Tennessee
  Knoxville D
Texas
Texas A&M University B, M, D
Virginia
Virginia Polytechnic Institute and State University M, D
Washington
Washington State University B, M, D
Wisconsin
University of Wisconsin
  Madison M, D

Virology

Illinois
University of Chicago M, D
Massachusetts
Harvard University M, D
New York
Albany Medical College M, D
Ohio
Case Western Reserve University D
Ohio State University
  Columbus Campus M, D
Pennsylvania
Thomas Jefferson University: College of Health Professions D
Utah
Brigham Young University M

Visual/performing arts

Alabama
Alabama Agricultural and Mechanical University B
Birmingham-Southern College B
Chattahoochee Valley Community College A
Faulkner University B
James H. Faulkner State Community College A
Shelton State Community College C, A
University of Alabama
  Birmingham B
Arizona
Arizona Western College A
Prescott College B, M
University of Arizona B
Arkansas
Arkansas Tech University B
Southern Arkansas University
  Tech A
California
Cabrillo College A
California Baptist University B
California Institute of the Arts C, B, M
California Lutheran University B
California State University
  Bakersfield B
  Los Angeles B, M
  Monterey Bay B
  San Marcos B
Chapman University B
Cypress College C, A
Diablo Valley College A
Fashion Institute of Design and Merchandising
  San Francisco A
Fashion Institute of Design and Merchandising A
Fresno City College C, A
Glendale Community College A
Irvine Valley College A
Long Beach City College A
Marymount College A
Merced College A
Modesto Junior College C, A
Moorpark College A
Otis College of Art and Design B, M
Pacific Union College B
Pomona College B
Porterville College A
Sacramento City College A
St. Mary's College of California B
San Diego City College A
San Joaquin Delta College A
Skyline College A
Sonoma State University B
University of California
  San Diego M
  Santa Barbara B, M, D
University of La Verne B

Colorado
Art Institute
  of Colorado A
Colorado Mountain College
  Alpine Campus A
  Spring Valley Campus A
Fort Lewis College B
Mesa State College A, B
Naropa University C, B
Pikes Peak Community College C, A
Regis University B

Connecticut
Albertus Magnus College B
Asnuntuck Community-Technical College A
Connecticut College B
Fairfield University B
Trinity College B
Tunxis Community College C, A
University of Connecticut B
University of Hartford B, M, D

Delaware
University of Delaware M

District of Columbia
Catholic University of America M, D
Gallaudet University B
George Washington University B, M
Howard University B

Florida
Flagler College B
Florida Agricultural and Mechanical University B
International Fine Arts College B
Lynn University B
Manatee Community College A
Palm Beach Community College A
Ringling School of Art and Design B
South Florida Community College A
University of South Florida B, M
University of Tampa B

Georgia
Abraham Baldwin Agricultural College A
Andrew College A
Atlanta College of Art B
Darton College A
Emmanuel College A, B
Kennesaw State University B
LaGrange College B
Mercer University B
Savannah College of Art and Design B, M
Young Harris College A

Hawaii
Brigham Young University
  Hawaii B

Illinois
American Academy of Art A, B
Barat College B
Black Hawk College A
City Colleges of Chicago
  Kennedy-King College A
Columbia College B
Highland Community College A
Kaskaskia College A
Kishwaukee College A
Moraine Valley Community College A
North Central College B
Northwestern University B
Parkland College A
Rend Lake College A
Richland Community College A
Rockford College B
Roosevelt University B, M
School of the Art Institute of Chicago B, M
Southern Illinois University
  Carbondale M
University of St. Francis B
William Rainey Harper College A

Indiana
Goshen College B
Indiana State University M
Indiana University
  Bloomington B, M
Ivy Tech State College
  Northcentral A
  Southwest A
University of Evansville B
Vincennes University A

Iowa
Graceland University B
Iowa State University B
Maharishi University of Management A, B, M
Marshalltown Community College A
North Iowa Area Community College A
Waldorf College A

Kansas
Barton County Community College A
Central Christian College A
Coffeyville Community College A
Colby Community College A
Cowley County Community College A
Garden City Community College A
Hutchinson Community College A
Kansas City Kansas Community College A
MidAmerica Nazarene University B, T
Pratt Community College A
St. Mary College B
Seward County Community College A
Southwestern College B
Washburn University of Topeka B
Wichita State University B

Kentucky
Western Kentucky University B, T

Louisiana
Loyola University New Orleans B
Southern University
  New Orleans B
University of Louisiana at Lafayette B

Maine
Bowdoin College B
University of Maine
  Machias B

Maryland
Frostburg State University B
Montgomery College
  Rockville Campus A
University of Maryland
  Baltimore County B
Villa Julie College A

Massachusetts
Berkshire Community College A
Boston University B, M
Cape Cod Community College A
Clark University B
Curry College B
Emerson College B, M
Hampshire College B
Harvard College B
Holyoke Community College A
Massachusetts College of Liberal Arts B
Middlesex Community College A
Northeastern University B
Pine Manor College A, B
Simon's Rock College of Bard B
Springfield Technical Community College A
Suffolk University B
Tufts University M

Michigan
Albion College B, T
Andrews University B
Calvin College B
Lansing Community College A
Mid Michigan Community College A
Oakland University B
Olivet College B, T
University of Michigan
  Flint B
Western Michigan University M

Minnesota
Concordia University: St. Paul B
Hamline University B
Minneapolis College of Art and Design B
Minnesota State University, Mankato B
Northland Community & Technical College A
St. Olaf College B, T
Winona State University B

Mississippi
Delta State University B, T
Mississippi State University B

Missouri
Drury University B, T
Fontbonne College B
Mineral Area College A
St. Louis Community College
  St. Louis Community College at Florissant Valley A
Stephens College B
Washington University B, M

Montana
Miles Community College A
Western Montana College of The University of Montana B

Nebraska
Hastings College B
University of Nebraska
  Kearney B, M, T
  Omaha B

New Hampshire
Franklin Pierce College B
Keene State College B

New Jersey
Bloomfield College B
Brookdale Community College A
Fairleigh Dickinson University B
Mercer County Community College A
Montclair State University B
Richard Stockton College of New Jersey B
Rowan University B
Rutgers
  The State University of New Jersey: Mason Gross School of the Arts B, M
  The State University of New Jersey: Newark College of Arts and Sciences B
Seton Hall University B, T
The College of New Jersey B
William Paterson University of New Jersey M

New Mexico
College of Santa Fe B
New Mexico Highlands University B

Northern New Mexico Community
  College A

New York
Adirondack Community College A
Bard College B, M
City University of New York
  Brooklyn College B, M
  City College B, M
  Queens College B
  Queensborough Community
    College A
Columbia University
  Columbia College B
  School of General Studies B
Cornell University B, M
Dowling College B
Eugene Lang College/New School
  University B
Five Towns College A, B
Fulton-Montgomery Community
  College A
Hofstra University B
Ithaca College B, M
Juilliard School B
Long Island University
  Brooklyn Campus B
New York State College of Ceramics at
  Alfred University B, M, T
New York University M, D
Niagara County Community College A
Pace University:
  Pleasantville/Briarcliff B
Pace University B
St. Bonaventure University B
Sarah Lawrence College B
School of Visual Arts B, M
State University of New York
  College at Brockport B, M
  College at Buffalo B
  College at Old Westbury B
  New Paltz B
Wells College B
Westchester Community College A

North Carolina
Bennett College B
Brevard College A, B
Carteret Community College A
Central Piedmont Community College A
Fayetteville State University B
Guilford Technical Community
  College A
Methodist College B
North Carolina Agricultural and
  Technical State University B
St. Andrews Presbyterian College B
Shaw University B
Western Piedmont Community
  College A

North Dakota
University of North Dakota B

Ohio
Antioch College B
Cleveland Institute of Art B
Kent State University
  Stark Campus A
Kent State University B, M
Lorain County Community College A
Mount Union College T
Notre Dame College of Ohio B, T
Ohio University D
Otterbein College B
Sinclair Community College A
University of Dayton B
Wittenberg University B
Youngstown State University B

Oklahoma
Oklahoma City University B, M
St. Gregory's University A
Southern Nazarene University B

Oregon
Central Oregon Community College A

Concordia University B
Oregon State University B
Pacific Northwest College of Art B
Pacific University B

Pennsylvania
Art Institute
  of Pittsburgh A
Beaver College B
Bucks County Community College A
Cedar Crest College B
Chatham College B
Community College of Allegheny
  County C, A
Duquesne University B, M
East Stroudsburg University of
  Pennsylvania B
Edinboro University of Pennsylvania B
Gettysburg College B
Harrisburg Area Community College A
Kutztown University of Pennsylvania B
Marywood University B
Moore College of Art and Design B
St. Joseph's University B
Seton Hill College B
Swarthmore College B
University of the Arts C, B, M
York College of Pennsylvania A, B

Puerto Rico
Escuela de Artes Plasticas de Puerto
  Rico B
Inter American University of Puerto Rico
  San German Campus B
Ramirez College of Business and
  Technology A
University of Puerto Rico
  Rio Piedras Campus B
University of the Sacred Heart B

Rhode Island
Brown University B
University of Rhode Island B

South Carolina
Charleston Southern University B
Lander University B
Presbyterian College B, T

Tennessee
Carson-Newman College B
Lincoln Memorial University B, T
Maryville College B
Milligan College B
Roane State Community College A
Tusculum College B
University of Tennessee
  Martin B
University of the South B

Texas
Angelina College A
Coastal Bend College A
College of the Mainland A
Hill College A
Howard College A
Lon Morris College A
Mountain View College C
Rice University B, M
Texas A&M University
  Commerce B
  Corpus Christi B
Texas Lutheran University B
Texas Tech University D
Texas Wesleyan University B, T
Trinity Valley Community College A
Tyler Junior College A
University of Texas
  Austin B
  Dallas B

Utah
Weber State University B

Vermont
Bennington College B
Burlington College A, B
Castleton State College B

Goddard College B
Green Mountain College B
Johnson State College B
Marlboro College B
Norwich University M

Virginia
George Mason University M
Longwood College B, T
Norfolk State University M
Old Dominion University M
Regent University M
Shenandoah University B
Virginia State University B

Washington
Centralia College A
Columbia Basin College A
Everett Community College A
Evergreen State College B
Highline Community College A
North Seattle Community College C, A
Seattle Pacific University B, T
Western Washington University B
Whitworth College B, T

West Virginia
Bethany College B
Marshall University B
West Virginia University M

Wisconsin
Cardinal Stritch University B
Carroll College B
Mount Senario College B
University of Wisconsin
  Green Bay B
  Milwaukee M
  Stevens Point B
  Superior B, M, T

Wyoming
Casper College A
University of Wyoming B
Western Wyoming Community
  College A

Vocational home economics

Alabama
Alabama State University A

Arkansas
Harding University B
Southern Arkansas University
  Tech C, A

Colorado
Colorado State University T

Florida
Polk Community College A

Georgia
East Georgia College A

Illinois
Black Hawk College C, A
College of Lake County C

Indiana
Ball State University B, T
Vincennes University A

Kansas
Coffeyville Community College A
Pittsburg State University B

Louisiana
Nicholls State University B
Northwestern State University B

Michigan
Delta College C, A

Mississippi
Alcorn State University B

Missouri
College of the Ozarks B
Penn Valley Community College A

Nebraska
Concordia University T
University of Nebraska
  Lincoln M, D

Ohio
Kent State University B, T
Mount Vernon Nazarene College B, T
Youngstown State University A, B

Oklahoma
Connors State College A
East Central University B, T
University of Central Oklahoma B

Pennsylvania
Community College of Allegheny
  County C, A

Tennessee
Carson-Newman College B, T
Tennessee Technological University B

Texas
Abilene Christian University B, T
Southwest Texas State University T
Stephen F. Austin State University T
Texas Tech University B, M

Utah
Snow College A

West Virginia
Fairmont State College B

Vocational rehabilitation counseling

Alabama
University of Alabama M

Arkansas
University of Arkansas
  Little Rock M
University of Arkansas M, D

California
California State University
  Fresno B, M

Colorado
University of Northern Colorado M

Florida
University of Florida M
University of South Florida M

Georgia
Fort Valley State University M
Georgia State University M
University of Georgia M

Illinois
Southern Illinois University
  Carbondale B, M, D

Kansas
Emporia State University B, M

Kentucky
University of Kentucky M

Massachusetts
Assumption College M
Boston University M, D
Springfield College M

Michigan
Wayne State University M

Mississippi
Jackson State University M

New Jersey
Seton Hall University M

University of Medicine and Dentistry of
   New Jersey
      School of Health Related
         Professions *M*

New York
Hofstra University *M*

North Carolina
East Carolina University *B, M*
University of North Carolina
   Chapel Hill *M*

Ohio
Bowling Green State University *M*
University of Cincinnati *M*
Wright State University *B*

Oklahoma
East Central University *B*

Pennsylvania
Edinboro University of Pennsylvania *M*

Tennessee
University of Memphis *B*
University of Tennessee
   Knoxville *M*

Texas
Stephen F. Austin State University *M*
University of Texas
   Southwestern Medical Center at
      Dallas *M*

Virginia
Virginia Commonwealth
   University *C, M*

Washington
Edmonds Community College *A*

West Virginia
West Virginia University *M*

Wisconsin
University of Wisconsin
   Stout *B, M*

Wyoming
Central Wyoming College *C, A*

Water transportation

Alaska
University of Alaska
   Southeast *C, A*

California
California Maritime Academy *B*

Idaho
North Idaho College *C*

Maine
Maine Maritime Academy *A, B, M*

Massachusetts
Massachusetts Maritime Academy *B*

Mississippi
Mississippi Gulf Coast Community
   College
      Perkinston *C*

New York
United States Merchant Marine
   Academy *B*

North Carolina
Cape Fear Community College *A*

Texas
Texas A&M University
   Galveston *B*
Texas A&M University *B*

Washington
Seattle Central Community College *A*

Wisconsin
Wisconsin Indianhead Technical
   College *C*

Western European studies

District of Columbia
American University *B*
Georgetown University *M*

Illinois
Illinois Wesleyan University *B*
Knox College *B*

Indiana
Indiana University
   Bloomington *M*
Vincennes University *A*

Iowa
Central College *B*

Kansas
Central Christian College *A, B*

Maryland
Johns Hopkins University *B*
St. John's College *B, M*

Massachusetts
Harvard College *B*
Tufts University *B, M*

Michigan
University of Michigan *B*

New York
Bard College *B*
City University of New York
   Brooklyn College *B*
Columbia University
   Graduate School *M, D*
Eugene Lang College/New School
   University *B*
New York University *M*
St. Francis College *B*
United States Military Academy *B*

Ohio
College of Wooster *B*
Denison University *B*
Ohio State University
   Columbus Campus *B*

Vermont
Marlboro College *B*

Virginia
Sweet Briar College *B*

Washington
Seattle University *B*
Western Washington University *B*

Wildlife/wildlands management

Alabama
Auburn University *B, M, D*

Alaska
Alaska Pacific University *B, M*
University of Alaska
   Fairbanks *B, M*

Arizona
Prescott College *B, M*
University of Arizona *B*

Arkansas
Arkansas State University *B*
Arkansas Tech University *B*
University of Arkansas
   Monticello *B*
Westark College *A*

California
Cerritos Community College *A*
Humboldt State University *B*
Modesto Junior College *C, A*
Napa Valley College *C, A*
San Joaquin Delta College *A*
University of California
   Berkeley *M, D*
   Davis *B*

Colorado
Colorado State University *B, M, D*

Delaware
Delaware State University *B*
University of Delaware *B*

District of Columbia
University of the District of Columbia *A*

Florida
University of Florida *B, M, D*
University of Miami *B*

Georgia
Abraham Baldwin Agricultural
   College *A*
University of Georgia *B*

Idaho
College of Southern Idaho *A*
North Idaho College *A*
Ricks College *A*
University of Idaho *B, M*

Illinois
Lake Land College *A*
Shawnee Community College *A*
Southeastern Illinois College *A*

Indiana
Purdue University *B, M, D*

Iowa
Iowa State University *M, D*

Kansas
Colby Community College *A*
Garden City Community College *A*
Pittsburg State University *B*
Pratt Community College *A*

Kentucky
Eastern Kentucky University *B*
Murray State University *B*

Louisiana
Louisiana State University and
   Agricultural and Mechanical
   College *B, M, D*
McNeese State University *B*

Maine
Unity College *B*
University of Maine *B, M*

Maryland
Frederick Community College *A*
Frostburg State University *B, M*

Massachusetts
University of Massachusetts
   Amherst *B, M, D*

Michigan
Bay de Noc Community College *C*
Lake Superior State University *B*
Michigan State University *B, M, D*
Northern Michigan University *M*
University of Michigan *B, M*

Minnesota
St. Cloud State University *B*
University of Minnesota
   Twin Cities *B, M, D*
Vermilion Community College *A*

Mississippi
Mississippi State University *B, M*

Missouri
East Central College *A*
Northwest Missouri State University *B*
Southwest Missouri State University *B*

Montana
Miles Community College *A*
Montana State University
   Bozeman *M, D*
University of Montana-Missoula *B, M*
Western Montana College of The
   University of Montana *B*

Nebraska
University of Nebraska
   Lincoln *B, M*

Nevada
University of Nevada
   Reno *B*

New Hampshire
Antioch New England Graduate
   School *M*
University of New Hampshire *B, M*

New Jersey
Rowan University *B*
Rutgers
   The State University of New Jersey:
      Cook College *B*

New Mexico
Eastern New Mexico University *B*
New Mexico State University *B, M*
Western New Mexico University *B*

New York
State University of New York
   College of Agriculture and
      Technology at Cobleskill *A*
   College of Environmental Science
      and Forestry *B, M, D*

North Carolina
Haywood Community College *A*
North Carolina State University *B, M*

North Dakota
Minot State University: Bottineau
   Campus *A*
North Dakota State University *B*
University of North Dakota *B*

Ohio
Hocking Technical College *A*
Ohio State University
   Columbus Campus *B*
University of Findlay *B*

Oklahoma
Eastern Oklahoma State College *A*
Northeastern Oklahoma Agricultural and
   Mechanical College *C, A*
Oklahoma State University *B, M, D*
Southeastern Oklahoma State
   University *B*
Western Oklahoma State College *A*

Oregon
Central Oregon Community College *A*
Oregon State University *B, M, D*

Pennsylvania
California University of Pennsylvania *B*
Muhlenberg College *B*
Penn State
   Dubois *A*
   University Park *B*

Puerto Rico
University of Puerto Rico
   Humacao University College *B*

South Dakota
South Dakota State University *B, M*

Tennessee
Lincoln Memorial University *B*
Tennessee Technological University *B*
University of Tennessee
   Martin *B*

Texas
Southwest Texas State University *B*
Stephen F. Austin State University *B*

Sul Ross State University *B, M*
Texas A&M University
  Commerce *B*
  Kingsville *B, M, D*
Texas A&M University *B, M, D*
Texas Tech University *B, M, D*

Utah
Brigham Young University *B, M, D*
Dixie State College of Utah *A*
Snow College *A*
Utah State University *B, M, D*

Vermont
Sterling College *A, B*
University of Vermont *B, M*

Virginia
Virginia Polytechnic Institute and State University *B, M, D*

Washington
Grays Harbor College *A*
Highline Community College *A*
Spokane Community College *A*
University of Washington *B*
Washington State University *B*

West Virginia
West Virginia University *B, M*

Wisconsin
Northland College *B*
University of Wisconsin
  Madison *B, M, D*
  Stevens Point *B*

Wyoming
Casper College *A*
Eastern Wyoming College *A*
Northwest College *A*
University of Wyoming *B*
Western Wyoming Community College *A*

Women's studies

Alabama
University of Alabama *M*

Arizona
Arizona State University *B*
Prescott College *B, M*
University of Arizona *B, M*

California
California State University
  Fresno *B*
  Long Beach *C, B*
  Monterey Bay *B*
  San Marcos *B*
Compton Community College *A*
Diablo Valley College *C*
Fresno City College *A*
Irvine Valley College *A*
Loyola Marymount University *B*
Mills College *B*
Monterey Peninsula College *A*
Occidental College *B*
Pitzer College *B*
Pomona College *B*
Riverside Community College *A*
Sacramento City College *A*
Saddleback College *A*
St. Mary's College of California *B*
San Diego State University *B, M*
San Francisco State University *B, M*
Santa Ana College *A*
Scripps College *B*
Southwestern College *A*
Stanford University *B*
University of California
  Berkeley *B*
  Davis *B*
  Irvine *B*
  Los Angeles *B*
  Riverside *B*
  San Diego *B*
  Santa Barbara *B*
  Santa Cruz *B*
University of Southern California *B*
West Valley College *A*

Colorado
Colorado College *B*
University of Colorado
  Boulder *B*
University of Denver *B*

Connecticut
Connecticut College *B*
Manchester Community-Technical College *A*
Southern Connecticut State University *M*
Trinity College *B*
University of Connecticut *B*
University of Hartford *B*
Wesleyan University *B*
Yale University *B*

Delaware
University of Delaware *B*

District of Columbia
American University *B*
George Washington University *M*
Georgetown University *B*

Florida
Eckerd College *B*
Florida Atlantic University *M*
Florida International University *B*
Florida State University *B*
Manatee Community College *A*
University of Miami *B*
University of South Florida *B, M*

Georgia
Agnes Scott College *B*
Emory University *B, D*
Oxford College of Emory University *A*
University of Georgia *C, B*

Illinois
De Paul University *C, B*
Knox College *B*
Northwestern University *B*
Roosevelt University *C, B, M*

Indiana
DePauw University *B*
Earlham College *B*
Goshen College *B*
Indiana University
  Bloomington *B*
  South Bend *B*
Indiana University--Purdue University
  Indiana University-Purdue University Fort Wayne *A, B*
Manchester College *B*

Iowa
Cornell College *B*
Iowa State University *B*
St. Ambrose University *C*
University of Iowa *D*
University of Northern Iowa *M*

Kansas
Kansas City Kansas Community College *C, A*
Pittsburg State University *C*
University of Kansas *B*
Wichita State University *B*

Kentucky
University of Louisville *B*

Louisiana
Tulane University *B*

Maine
Bates College *B*
Bowdoin College *B*
Colby College *B*
University of Maine *B*
University of Southern Maine *B*

Maryland
Goucher College *B*
Johns Hopkins University *B*
Towson University *B, M*
University of Maryland
  College Park *B, M, D*

Massachusetts
Amherst College *B*
Brandeis University *M*
Clark University *D*
Hampshire College *B*
Harvard College *B*
Mount Holyoke College *B*
Northeastern University *B*
Simmons College *B*
Simon's Rock College of Bard *B*
Smith College *B*
Suffolk University *B*
Tufts University *B*
University of Massachusetts
  Amherst *B*
  Boston *C, B*
Wellesley College *B*
Wheaton College *B*

Michigan
Albion College *C*
Eastern Michigan University *B, M*
Henry Ford Community College *A*
Michigan State University *B*
University of Michigan *B*
Western Michigan University *B*

Minnesota
Augsburg College *B*
Carleton College *B*
College of St. Catherine: St. Paul Campus *B*
Hamline University *B*
Macalester College *B*
Metropolitan State University *B*
Minnesota State University, Mankato *B, M*
St. Olaf College *B*
University of Minnesota
  Duluth *B*
  Twin Cities *B*
University of St. Thomas *B*
Winona State University *A*

Missouri
Drury University *B*
Washington University *B*

Montana
University of Montana-Missoula *B*

Nebraska
Nebraska Wesleyan University *B*
University of Nebraska
  Lincoln *B*

Nevada
University of Nevada
  Las Vegas *B*
  Reno *B*

New Hampshire
Dartmouth College *B*
University of New Hampshire *B*

New Jersey
Bloomfield College *B*
Caldwell College *C*
Drew University *B, M, D*
Richard Stockton College of New Jersey *C*
Rowan University *B*
Rutgers
  The State University of New Jersey: Douglass College *B*
  The State University of New Jersey: Livingston College *B*
  The State University of New Jersey: New Brunswick Graduate Campus *M*
  The State University of New Jersey: Newark College of Arts and Sciences *B*
  The State University of New Jersey: Rutgers College *B*
  The State University of New Jersey: University College New Brunswick *B*

New Mexico
University of New Mexico *B*

New York
Barnard College *B*
Canisius College *C*
City University of New York
  Brooklyn College *B*
  College of Staten Island *B*
  Hunter College *B*
  Queens College *B*
Colgate University *B*
College of New Rochelle *B*
Columbia University
  Columbia College *B*
  School of General Studies *B*
Cornell University *B*
Eugene Lang College/New School University *B*
Fordham University *B*
Hamilton College *B*
Hobart and William Smith Colleges *B*
New York University *B*
Sarah Lawrence College *B, M*
Skidmore College *B*
State University of New York
  Albany *B*
  Buffalo *B*
  College at Brockport *B*
  New Paltz *B*
  Oswego *B*
  Stony Brook *B*
Suffolk County Community College *A*
Syracuse University *B*
Tompkins-Cortland Community College *A*
Union College *B*
University of Rochester *B*
Vassar College *B*
Wells College *B*

North Carolina
Duke University *B*
East Carolina University *B*
Guilford College *B*
University of North Carolina
  Chapel Hill *B*
  Greensboro *B*

Ohio
Antioch College *B*
Bowling Green State University *B*
Case Western Reserve University *B*
College of Wooster *B*
Denison University *B*
Lourdes College *C*
Oberlin College *B*
Ohio State University
  Columbus Campus *B, M*
Ohio University *C*
Ohio Wesleyan University *B*
Owens Community College
  Toledo *A*
University of Cincinnati
  Raymond Walters College *C*
University of Toledo *B*

Oklahoma
Oklahoma State University *C*
University of Oklahoma *B*

Women's studies

University of Tulsa C

Oregon
Portland State University B
University of Oregon B

Pennsylvania
Allegheny College B
Bryn Mawr College B
Bucknell University B
Chatham College B
Gettysburg College B
Penn State
 University Park B
Rosemont College B
Temple University B
University of Pennsylvania B
University of Pittsburgh C

Rhode Island
Brown University B
Providence College B
Rhode Island College B
University of Rhode Island B

South Carolina
University of South Carolina B

Tennessee
University of Tennessee
 Knoxville B

Texas
El Paso Community College A
Rice University B
Southwestern University B
Texas Woman's University M

Utah
University of Utah B

Vermont
Bennington College B
Burlington College B
Goddard College B
Marlboro College B
Middlebury College B
University of Vermont B

Virginia
College of William and Mary B
Hollins University B
Mary Baldwin College B
Old Dominion University B
Randolph-Macon College B
University of Richmond B

Washington
Gonzaga University B
North Seattle Community College C, A
Pacific Lutheran University B
University of Washington B, M, D
Washington State University B
Western Washington University B

Wisconsin
Beloit College B
Carthage College B
Lawrence University B
Marquette University B
Ripon College B
University of Wisconsin
 Whitewater B

Wyoming
Casper College A
University of Wyoming B

Woodworking

Alabama
Gadsden State Community College C
George C. Wallace State Community
 College
  Dothan C
Northwest-Shoals Community
 College C, A
Shelton State Community College C, A

Sparks State Technical College C
Wallace State Community College at
 Hanceville C, A

Alaska
University of Alaska
 Anchorage C, A

California
Bakersfield College A
College of the Redwoods C
Compton Community College C, A
Long Beach City College C, A
Merced College C, A
Palomar College C, A
Saddleback College C
San Joaquin Delta College C, A
Sierra College C, A

Colorado
Red Rocks Community College C, A

Georgia
Gwinnett Technical Institute A

Idaho
College of Southern Idaho C, A

Illinois
Illinois Eastern Community Colleges
 Olney Central College A

Indiana
Ivy Tech State College
 Central Indiana C, A
 Northcentral C, A
 Northwest C, A
 Southwest C, A

Iowa
Des Moines Area Community College A
Maharishi University of Management C
North Iowa Area Community College C
Western Iowa Tech Community
 College A

Kansas
Allen County Community College A
Central Christian College A
Pittsburg State University A, B

Maine
Southern Maine Technical College A

Michigan
Bay de Noc Community College C
Kendall College of Art and Design B
Northern Michigan University B
Oakland Community College A

Minnesota
Hennepin Technical College C, A
St. Paul Technical College C

Mississippi
East Central Community College C
Northwest Mississippi Community
 College C

Nebraska
Mid Plains Community College
 Area C, A

New Mexico
Northern New Mexico Community
 College C, A

New York
Rochester Institute of
 Technology A, B, M

North Carolina
Haywood Community College C, A
Mayland Community College C
Rockingham Community College A
Tri-County Community College C

Ohio
University of Rio Grande A

Pennsylvania
Bucks County Community College A

Johnson Technical Institute A
Pennsylvania College of Technology A
University of the Arts B

South Dakota
Western Dakota Technical Institute C

Texas
San Jacinto College
 North C

Washington
Peninsula College C, A
Seattle Central Community College A

Wisconsin
Madison Area Technical College C
Northeast Wisconsin Technical
 College C
Western Wisconsin Technical College C
Wisconsin Indianhead Technical
 College C

Zoology

Alabama
Alabama Agricultural and Mechanical
 University B, M
Auburn University B, M, D

Alaska
University of Alaska
 Fairbanks M, D

Arizona
Arizona State University B, M, D
Northern Arizona University B

Arkansas
Arkansas State University
 Beebe Branch A
Arkansas State University B
University of Arkansas B

California
California State Polytechnic University:
 Pomona B
California State University
 Stanislaus B
Cerritos Community College A
Citrus College A
East Los Angeles College C
Humboldt State University B
Palomar College C, A
Riverside Community College A
San Diego State University B
San Francisco State University B
San Joaquin Delta College A
San Jose State University B
Southwestern College A
University of California
 Davis B
 Santa Barbara B, M
Ventura College A

Colorado
Adams State College B
Colorado State University B, M, D

Connecticut
Connecticut College B, M
Southern Connecticut State University B
University of Connecticut M, D

District of Columbia
George Washington University M, D

Florida
Palm Beach Community College A
Pensacola Junior College A
University of Florida B, M, D
University of Miami D
University of South Florida B, M, T

Hawaii
University of Hawaii
 Manoa B, M, D

Idaho
College of Southern Idaho A
Idaho State University B
North Idaho College A
Ricks College A
University of Idaho B, M, D

Illinois
Black Hawk College
 East Campus A
Olivet Nazarene University B
Rend Lake College A
Southern Illinois University
 Carbondale B, M, D

Indiana
Ball State University B
Indiana State University T
Indiana University
 Bloomington M, D
Vincennes University A

Iowa
Iowa State University B, M, D
Marshalltown Community College A

Kansas
Independence Community College A
Pratt Community College A
Seward County Community College A

Louisiana
Louisiana State University and
 Agricultural and Mechanical
 College M, D

Maine
College of the Atlantic B
University of Maine B, M, D

Maryland
Uniformed Services University of the
 Health Sciences D
University of Maryland
 College Park B, M, D

Massachusetts
Harvard College B

Michigan
Andrews University B
Michigan State University B, M, D
Northern Michigan University B
University of Michigan B, D

Minnesota
Minnesota State University, Mankato B
St. Cloud State University B
University of Minnesota
 Twin Cities M, D

Mississippi
Mary Holmes College A

Missouri
East Central College A
Northwest Missouri State University B

Montana
University of Montana-Missoula B

New Hampshire
University of New Hampshire B, M, D

New Jersey
New Jersey Institute of Technology B
Rowan University B
Rutgers
 The State University of New Jersey:
  Camden College of Arts and
  Sciences B
 The State University of New Jersey:
  Newark College of Arts and
  Sciences B
 The State University of New Jersey:
  University College Camden B

New Mexico
Western New Mexico University B

Zoology

New York
Cornell University B, M, D
State University of New York
    College of Environmental Science
        and Forestry B, M, D
    Oswego B

North Carolina
Duke University D
Mars Hill College B
Methodist College A, B
North Carolina State University B, M, D

North Dakota
North Dakota State University B, M, D

Ohio
Kent State University
    Stark Campus B
Kent State University B
Miami University
    Middletown Campus A
    Oxford Campus B, M, D
Ohio State University
    Columbus Campus B
Ohio University B, M, D
Ohio Wesleyan University B
University of Akron B
Wittenberg University B

Oklahoma
Langston University B
Northern Oklahoma College A
Oklahoma State University B, M, D
Redlands Community College A
Southeastern Oklahoma State
    University B
University of Oklahoma B, M, D

Oregon
Chemeketa Community College A
Oregon State University B, M, D

Pennsylvania
Juniata College B

Rhode Island
University of Rhode Island B, M, D

South Carolina
Clemson University M, D

Tennessee
Bethel College B
University of Tennessee
    Knoxville B, M, D

Texas
Hill College A
South Plains College A
Southwest Texas State University B
Tarleton State University B, T
Texas A&M University B, M, D
Texas Tech University B, M, D
Texas Woman's University B
University of Texas
    Austin B, M, D

Utah
Brigham Young University B, M, D
Dixie State College of Utah A
Snow College A
Southern Utah University B
Weber State University B

Vermont
Marlboro College B

Washington
Centralia College A
Eastern Washington University B
University of Washington B, M, D
Washington State University B, M, D

Wisconsin
University of Wisconsin
    Madison B, M, D

Wyoming
Sheridan College A

University of Wyoming B, M, D

Special academic programs

Accelerated program

Alabama
Alabama Agricultural and Mechanical University
Auburn University
Auburn University at Montgomery
Bevill State Community College
Birmingham-Southern College
Calhoun Community College
Chattahoochee Valley Community College
Community College of the Air Force
George C. Wallace State Community College
    Dothan
    Selma
Jacksonville State University
James H. Faulkner State Community College
Jefferson State Community College
Lawson State Community College
Lurleen B. Wallace Junior College
Northeast Alabama Community College
Northwest-Shoals Community College
Shelton State Community College
Snead State Community College
Spring Hill College
University of Alabama
University of Alabama Huntsville
University of Mobile
University of Montevallo
University of South Alabama
University of West Alabama
Wallace State Community College at Hanceville

Alaska
Alaska Pacific University
University of Alaska
    Fairbanks

Arizona
Arizona State University
Arizona Western College
DeVry Institute of Technology
    Phoenix
Gateway Community College
Northern Arizona University
Paradise Valley Community College
Pima Community College
Rio Salado College
University of Advancing Computer Technology
University of Arizona
University of Phoenix
Yavapai College

Arkansas
Arkansas State University
Arkansas State University
    Beebe Branch
University of Arkansas
    Little Rock
University of Central Arkansas

California
Allan Hancock College
American River College
Antioch Southern California
    Los Angeles
Armstrong University
Azusa Pacific University
Barstow College
Biola University
California Baptist University
California Lutheran University
California State University
    Bakersfield
    Dominguez Hills
    Fresno
    Fullerton
    Hayward
    Los Angeles
    Stanislaus
Chaffey Community College
Chapman University
City College of San Francisco
Claremont McKenna College
Coastline Community College
College of Notre Dame
Compton Community College
DeVry Institute of Technology
    Fremont
    Pomona
    West Hills
Diablo Valley College
East Los Angeles College
Empire College
Evergreen Valley College
Fresno City College
Fresno Pacific University
Golden Gate University
Golden West College
Grossmont Community College
Heald Business College
    Santa Rosa
Holy Names College
Hope International University
Irvine Valley College
John F. Kennedy University
La Sierra University
Las Positas College
Long Beach City College
Los Angeles Harbor College
Los Angeles Mission College
Los Angeles Southwest College
Mendocino College
Menlo College
Mount St. Mary's College
National University
Occidental College
Pacific Oaks College
Pasadena City College
Patten College
Pepperdine University
Sacramento City College
St. Mary's College of California
San Diego City College
San Diego Mesa College
San Diego Miramar College
San Francisco Art Institute
San Francisco College of Mortuary Science
San Francisco Conservatory of Music
San Jose Christian College
San Jose City College
San Jose State University
Santa Clara University
Santa Monica College
Scripps College
Simpson College
Sonoma State University
Southern California Institute of Architecture
University of California
    Berkeley
    Davis
    Riverside
    San Diego
    Santa Barbara
University of Judaism
University of La Verne
University of San Francisco
University of Southern California
University of West Los Angeles
University of the Pacific
Vista Community College
Westmont College
Whittier College

Colorado
Adams State College
Colorado School of Mines
Colorado State University
Colorado Technical University
Community College of Denver
Fort Lewis College
Metropolitan State College of Denver
Pueblo Community College
Red Rocks Community College
Regis University
Technical Trades Institute
Trinidad State Junior College
University of Colorado
    Boulder
University of Denver
University of Southern Colorado

Connecticut
Albertus Magnus College
Capital Community College
Connecticut College
Quinebaug Valley Community College
Sacred Heart University
Southern Connecticut State University
Teikyo Post University
Trinity College
University of Bridgeport
University of New Haven
Wesleyan University
Western Connecticut State University
Yale University

Delaware
Delaware State University
Goldey-Beacom College
University of Delaware
Wilmington College

District of Columbia
American University
Catholic University of America
Gallaudet University
George Washington University
Howard University
Southeastern University

Florida
Barry University
Bethune-Cookman College
Brevard Community College
Broward Community College
Chipola Junior College
Eckerd College
Edison Community College
Edward Waters College
Florida Agricultural and Mechanical University
Florida Atlantic University
Florida Community College at Jacksonville
Florida Institute of Technology
Florida International University
Florida Metropolitan University
    Orlando College North
Florida State University
Gulf Coast Community College
Hillsborough Community College
International Academy of Merchandising and Design
International College
Jacksonville University
Jones College
Keiser College
Lynn University
Manatee Community College
Miami-Dade Community College
New College of the University of South Florida
Northwood University
    Florida Campus
Nova Southeastern University
Pasco-Hernando Community College
Pensacola Junior College
Polk Community College
Rollins College
St. Petersburg Junior College
St. Thomas University
Seminole Community College
South College: Palm Beach Campus
South Florida Community College
Stetson University
Tampa Technical Institute
University of Florida
University of Miami
University of North Florida
University of South Florida
University of West Florida

Georgia
Agnes Scott College
American InterContinental University
Clark Atlanta University
Columbus State University
DeVry Institute of Technology
    Alpharetta
    Atlanta
Emory University
Georgia College and State University
Georgia Institute of Technology
Georgia Perimeter College
Georgia Southwestern State University
Mercer University
Middle Georgia College
Morris Brown College
North Georgia College & State University
Piedmont College
State University of West Georgia
Thomas College
Toccoa Falls College
Truett-McConnell College
University of Georgia
Valdosta State University

Hawaii
Brigham Young University
    Hawaii
Chaminade University of Honolulu
Hawaii Pacific University
University of Hawaii
    Manoa
    West Oahu

Idaho
Lewis-Clark State College
Northwest Nazarene University
Ricks College

Illinois
American Academy of Art
Augustana College
Benedictine University
Black Hawk College
Blackburn College
Bradley University
Chicago State University
City Colleges of Chicago
    Malcolm X College
College of DuPage

Accelerated program

College of Lake County
De Paul University
DeVry Institute of Technology
    Addison
    Chicago
Dominican University
Elgin Community College
Elmhurst College
Greenville College
Illinois State University
Illinois Wesleyan University
Judson College
Lewis University
Lincoln Land Community College
Loyola University of Chicago
McHenry County College
McKendree College
National-Louis University
North Central College
North Park University
Northwestern University
Olivet Nazarene University
Parkland College
Robert Morris College: Chicago
Rockford College
Roosevelt University
Shimer College
Southern Illinois University
    Carbondale
    Edwardsville
Southwestern Illinois College
Trinity International University
University of Chicago
University of Illinois
    Chicago
    Urbana-Champaign
University of St. Francis

Indiana
Anderson University
Ball State University
Bethel College
Butler University
Calumet College of St. Joseph
Earlham College
Goshen College
Indiana Institute of Technology
Indiana State University
Indiana University
    Bloomington
    Northwest
    South Bend
    Southeast
Indiana University--Purdue University
    Indiana University-Purdue
        University Fort Wayne
Indiana Wesleyan University
Marian College
Michiana College
Oakland City University
Purdue University
Rose-Hulman Institute of Technology
Saint Mary's College
St. Joseph's College
St. Mary-of-the-Woods College
University of Indianapolis
University of Notre Dame
Valparaiso University

Iowa
American Institute of Business
Buena Vista University
Clarke College
Clinton Community College
Coe College
Cornell College
Graceland University
Grand View College
Grinnell College
Iowa Central Community College
Iowa State University
Kirkwood Community College
Maharishi University of Management
Marycrest International University

Morningside College
Mount Mercy College
Muscatine Community College
Northwestern College
St. Ambrose University
Scott Community College
Simpson College
University of Dubuque
University of Iowa
Upper Iowa University
Waldorf College
William Penn University

Kansas
Baker University
Barton County Community College
Bethany College
Butler County Community College
Emporia State University
Fort Hays State University
Kansas City Kansas Community College
Kansas State University
MidAmerica Nazarene University
Ottawa University
St. Mary College
Southwestern College
Sterling College
Tabor College
University of Kansas
Wichita State University

Kentucky
Bellarmine College
Campbellsville University
Cumberland College
Kentucky State University
Mid-Continent College
Morehead State University
Spalding University
Thomas More College
Union College
University of Kentucky
University of Louisville

Louisiana
Louisiana State University and
    Agricultural and Mechanical College
Loyola University New Orleans
McNeese State University
Northwestern State University
Nunez Community College
Tulane University
University of Louisiana at Lafayette
University of Louisiana at Monroe
Xavier University of Louisiana

Maine
Andover College
Bates College
Beal College
Bowdoin College
College of the Atlantic
Mid-State College
Unity College
University of Maine
University of Maine
    Farmington
    Presque Isle

Maryland
Baltimore International College
Bowie State University
College of Notre Dame of Maryland
Coppin State College
Frostburg State University
Goucher College
Hagerstown Community College
Hood College
Howard Community College
Johns Hopkins University
Loyola College in Maryland
Maryland College of Art and Design
Maryland Institute College of Art

Montgomery College
    Germantown Campus
    Rockville Campus
    Takoma Park Campus
Salisbury State University
Sojourner-Douglass College
Towson University
University of Baltimore
University of Maryland
    College Park
    Eastern Shore
    University College
Villa Julie College
Western Maryland College

Massachusetts
American International College
Anna Maria College
Atlantic Union College
Bay Path College
Bentley College
Berklee College of Music
Boston College
Boston University
College of the Holy Cross
Elms College
Emmanuel College
Endicott College
Fitchburg State College
Gordon College
Harvard College
Hebrew College
Laboure College
Lesley College
Massachusetts Bay Community College
Massachusetts College of Pharmacy and
    Health Sciences
Middlesex Community College
New England College of Finance
North Shore Community College
Northeastern University
Northern Essex Community College
Pine Manor College
Quincy College
Simmons College
Simon's Rock College of Bard
Smith College
University of Massachusetts
    Boston
    Dartmouth
    Lowell
Wheaton College
Williams College
Worcester Polytechnic Institute

Michigan
Albion College
Alma College
Andrews University
Aquinas College
Baker College
    of Auburn Hills
    of Cadillac
    of Jackson
    of Mount Clemens
    of Muskegon
    of Owosso
    of Port Huron
Central Michigan University
Cleary College
Concordia College
Cornerstone College and Grand Rapids
    Baptist Seminary
Davenport College of Business
Detroit College of Business
Eastern Michigan University
Ferris State University
Glen Oaks Community College
Great Lakes College
Hillsdale College
Jackson Community College
Kalamazoo College
Kellogg Community College
Kettering University

Kirtland Community College
Lansing Community College
Michigan State University
Monroe County Community College
Northwood University
Oakland University
Olivet College
Reformed Bible College
Rochester College
Saginaw Valley State University
Schoolcraft College
Southwestern Michigan College
University of Michigan
University of Michigan
    Dearborn
Walsh College of Accountancy and
    Business Administration
Wayne State University
Western Michigan University
William Tyndale College

Minnesota
Bemidji State University
Carleton College
Century Community and Technical
    College
College of St. Benedict
College of St. Scholastica
Concordia College: Moorhead
Concordia University: St. Paul
Crown College
Dakota County Technical College
Inver Hills Community College
Minneapolis Community and Technical
    College
Minnesota State College - Southeast
    Technical
National American University
    St. Paul
St. Mary's University of Minnesota
Southwest State University
University of Minnesota
    Duluth
    Morris
    Twin Cities
Winona State University

Mississippi
Belhaven College
Blue Mountain College
Hinds Community College
Meridian Community College
Mississippi Gulf Coast Community
    College
    Jefferson Davis Campus
    Perkinston
Mississippi State University
Northwest Mississippi Community
    College
Tougaloo College
University of Mississippi
University of Southern Mississippi
William Carey College

Missouri
Avila College
Central Methodist College
College of the Ozarks
Columbia College
DeVry Institute of Technology
    Kansas City
Drury University
Fontbonne College
Hannibal-LaGrange College
Lincoln University
Lindenwood University
Longview Community College
Maryville University of Saint Louis
Missouri Baptist College
Missouri Southern State College
Park University
Research College of Nursing
Rockhurst University
St. Louis University

Southeast Missouri State University
St. Louis Community College
    St. Louis Community College at Meramec
Stephens College
University of Missouri
    Columbia
    Rolla
Washington University
Webster University
Wentworth Military Academy
Westminster College
William Woods University

Montana
Montana State University
    Billings
    Northern
Rocky Mountain College
University of Montana-Missoula

Nebraska
Bellevue University
Central Community College
Chadron State College
Clarkson College
Concordia University
Creighton University
Dana College
Doane College
Grace University
Midland Lutheran College
Northeast Community College
University of Nebraska
    Kearney
    Lincoln
    Omaha

New Hampshire
Colby-Sawyer College
College for Lifelong Learning
Daniel Webster College
Franklin Pierce College
Hesser College
New Hampshire College
New Hampshire Community Technical College
    Claremont
    Laconia
    Stratham
Notre Dame College
University of New Hampshire

New Jersey
Bloomfield College
Caldwell College
College of St. Elizabeth
Cumberland County College
DeVry Institute
Drew University
Fairleigh Dickinson University
Felician College
Monmouth University
Montclair State University
New Jersey Institute of Technology
Ramapo College of New Jersey
Raritan Valley Community College
Richard Stockton College of New Jersey
Rider University
Rowan University
Rutgers
    The State University of New Jersey: Newark College of Arts and Sciences
    The State University of New Jersey: Rutgers College
St. Peter's College
Stevens Institute of Technology
Thomas Edison State College
Union County College
University of Medicine and Dentistry of New Jersey
    School of Health Related Professions
    School of Nursing
William Paterson University of New Jersey

New Mexico
College of Santa Fe
Eastern New Mexico University
New Mexico Institute of Mining and Technology
New Mexico State University
University of New Mexico

New York
Alfred University
Audrey Cohen College
Bard College
Barnard College
Bryant & Stratton Business Institute Syracuse
Cayuga County Community College
City University of New York
    Brooklyn College
    City College
    Hunter College
    Kingsborough Community College
    Lehman College
    Queens College
Clarkson University
Colgate University
College of Aeronautics
College of Insurance
College of New Rochelle
College of New Rochelle
    School of New Resources
College of St. Rose
Columbia University
    Fu Foundation School of Engineering and Applied Science
    School of General Studies
    School of Nursing
Concordia College
Cornell University
D'Youville College
DeVry Institute of Technology
    New York
Dominican College of Blauvelt
Dowling College
Elmira College
Eugene Lang College/New School University
Fulton-Montgomery Community College
Hamilton College
Hartwick College
Hobart and William Smith Colleges
Hofstra University
Hudson Valley Community College
Iona College
Ithaca College
Juilliard School
Katharine Gibbs School
    New York
Keuka College
Le Moyne College
Long Island University
    C. W. Post Campus
    Southampton College
Manhattan College
Manhattanville College
Marist College
Marymount Manhattan College
Medaille College
Mercy College
Molloy College
Monroe Community College
Mount St. Mary College
New York Institute of Technology
New York University
Niagara University
Ohr Somayach Tanenbaum Education Center
Pace University
Pace University: Pleasantville/Briarcliff
Phillips Beth Israel School of Nursing
Polytechnic University
Polytechnic University
    Long Island Campus
Pratt Institute
Regents College
Rensselaer Polytechnic Institute
Rochester Institute of Technology
Russell Sage College
St. Francis College
St. John Fisher College
St. John's University
St. Thomas Aquinas College
Skidmore College
St. Joseph's College
    St. Joseph's College
State University of New York
    Binghamton
    Buffalo
    College at Brockport
    College at Plattsburgh
    Empire State College
    Institute of Technology at Utica/Rome
    New Paltz
Syracuse University
Touro College
Union College
Utica College of Syracuse University
Wells College
Westchester Business Institute

North Carolina
Barton College
Bennett College
Brevard College
Campbell University
Cecils College
Cleveland Community College
Craven Community College
Duke University
East Carolina University
Elon College
Fayetteville State University
Greensboro College
Guilford College
High Point University
John Wesley College
Johnson C. Smith University
Lenoir-Rhyne College
Mars Hill College
Meredith College
Methodist College
Montreat College
Mount Olive College
North Carolina State University
Pfeiffer University
Queens College
St. Augustine's College
Shaw University
Surry Community College
University of North Carolina
    Charlotte
    Greensboro
    Wilmington
Wake Forest University
Wayne Community College
Western Carolina University

North Dakota
North Dakota State University
University of Mary
University of North Dakota

Ohio
Ashland University
Baldwin-Wallace College
Bowling Green State University
Case Western Reserve University
Cedarville College
Cleveland State University
College of Mount St. Joseph
Columbus College of Art and Design
David N. Myers College
DeVry Institute of Technology
    Columbus
Defiance College
Franciscan University of Steubenville
Franklin University
Heidelberg College
Hiram College
Hocking Technical College
John Carroll University
Kent State University
Kenyon College
Lourdes College
Marietta College
Miami-Jacobs College
Mount Union College
Muskingum College
Ohio State University
    Columbus Campus
Ohio University
Ohio University
    Eastern Campus
Otterbein College
Pontifical College Josephinum
Terra Community College
University of Akron
University of Cincinnati
University of Dayton
University of Findlay
University of Rio Grande
University of Toledo
Ursuline College
Walsh University
Wittenberg University
Wright State University
Youngstown State University

Oklahoma
Northeastern Oklahoma Agricultural and Mechanical College
Oklahoma Baptist University
Oklahoma Christian University of Science and Arts
Oklahoma City Community College
Oklahoma City University
Oklahoma State University
Oral Roberts University
Redlands Community College
Rose State College
St. Gregory's University
Southeastern Oklahoma State University
Southwestern Oklahoma State University
University of Central Oklahoma
University of Oklahoma
University of Science and Arts of Oklahoma
University of Tulsa

Oregon
Chemeketa Community College
Clackamas Community College
Concordia University
Eastern Oregon University
George Fox University
Lane Community College
Lewis & Clark College
Mount Hood Community College
Northwest Christian College
Oregon Institute of Technology
Pacific University
Portland State University
Reed College
Southern Oregon University
University of Portland
Western Baptist College

Pennsylvania
Albright College
Allegheny College
Allentown College of St. Francis de Sales
Bryn Mawr College
Bucknell University
Cabrini College

Accelerated program

California University of Pennsylvania
Cambria-Rowe Business College
Carlow College
Carnegie Mellon University
Cedar Crest College
Chatham College
Clarion University of Pennsylvania
College Misericordia
Delaware County Community College
Dickinson College
Drexel University
Duquesne University
Eastern College
Edinboro University of Pennsylvania
Elizabethtown College
Franklin and Marshall College
Gannon University
Geneva College
Grove City College
Gwynedd-Mercy College
Haverford College
Holy Family College
Immaculata College
King's College
La Roche College
La Salle University
Lafayette College
Lebanon Valley College of Pennsylvania
Lincoln University
Lycoming College
Manor College
Mansfield University of Pennsylvania
Marywood University
Mercyhurst College
Messiah College
Millersville University of Pennsylvania
Moore College of Art and Design
Muhlenberg College
Neumann College
Northampton County Area Community College
Peirce College
Pennsylvania College of Technology
Philadelphia College of Bible
Philadelphia University
Point Park College
Rosemont College
St. Charles Borromeo Seminary - Overbrook
St. Francis College
St. Joseph's University
St. Vincent College
Sawyer School
Seton Hill College
Shippensburg University of Pennsylvania
Slippery Rock University of Pennsylvania
Susquehanna University
Temple University
University of Pennsylvania
University of Pittsburgh
University of Pittsburgh Johnstown
University of Scranton
University of the Arts
Ursinus College
Valley Forge Christian College
Villanova University
Washington and Jefferson College
Waynesburg College
West Chester University of Pennsylvania
Westminster College
Widener University
Wilkes University

Puerto Rico
Colegio Universitario del Este
Columbia College
Inter American University of Puerto Rico
    Guayama Campus
    Metropolitan Campus
    San German Campus
Pontifical Catholic University of Puerto Rico
Turabo University

Universidad Metropolitana
University of Puerto Rico
    Cayey University College

Rhode Island
Brown University
Johnson & Wales University
New England Institute of Technology
Roger Williams University
Salve Regina University
University of Rhode Island

South Carolina
Anderson College
Benedict College
Charleston Southern University
Claflin University
Coastal Carolina University
College of Charleston
Converse College
Francis Marion University
Greenville Technical College
Lander University
Limestone College
Presbyterian College
Trident Technical College
University of South Carolina
University of South Carolina
    Aiken
    Spartanburg
Wofford College

South Dakota
Augustana College
Black Hills State University
Mount Marty College
South Dakota State University
University of South Dakota

Tennessee
Belmont University
Bethel College
Carson-Newman College
Chattanooga State Technical Community College
Christian Brothers University
Crichton College
David Lipscomb University
East Tennessee State University
Freed-Hardeman University
Johnson Bible College
King College
Knoxville Business College
Lane College
Lincoln Memorial University
Milligan College
Northeast State Technical Community College
Rhodes College
Roane State Community College
Tennessee Technological University
Trevecca Nazarene University
Tusculum College
Union University
University of Memphis
University of Tennessee
    Knoxville
    Memphis
University of the South
Vanderbilt University

Texas
Angelina College
Baylor University
Collin County Community College District
Concordia University at Austin
Dallas Baptist University
DeVry Institute of Technology Irving
Del Mar College
East Texas Baptist University
Lamar University
McMurry University

Mountain View College
North Lake College
Northwood University: Texas Campus
Paris Junior College
Prairie View A&M University
Rice University
St. Philip's College
San Jacinto College
    North
Schreiner College
Southern Methodist University
Southwestern Adventist University
Southwestern University
Stephen F. Austin State University
Tarleton State University
Texas A&M University
Texas A&M University Commerce
Texas Christian University
Texas Tech University
Texas Wesleyan University
Texas Woman's University
Trinity University
Tyler Junior College
University of Houston
University of Mary Hardin-Baylor
University of North Texas
University of Texas
    Austin
    Dallas
    El Paso
    San Antonio
University of the Incarnate Word
Wayland Baptist University

Utah
Brigham Young University
University of Utah
Utah State University
Utah Valley State College
Weber State University
Westminster College

Vermont
Champlain College
College of St. Joseph in Vermont
Johnson State College
Marlboro College
Middlebury College
New England Culinary Institute
Norwich University
Southern Vermont College

Virginia
Averett College
Blue Ridge Community College
Bluefield College
Bridgewater College
Christopher Newport University
Danville Community College
George Mason University
Germanna Community College
Hampden-Sydney College
Hampton University
Hollins University
James Madison University
Liberty University
Longwood College
Mary Baldwin College
Mountain Empire Community College
Norfolk State University
Old Dominion University
Radford University
Randolph-Macon College
Randolph-Macon Woman's College
Richard Bland College
Roanoke College
St. Paul's College
Southwest Virginia Community College
Sweet Briar College
Thomas Nelson Community College
University of Richmond
University of Virginia
University of Virginia's College at Wise

Virginia Commonwealth University
Virginia Intermont College
Virginia Military Institute
Virginia Polytechnic Institute and State University

Washington
Central Washington University
City University
Grays Harbor College
Henry Cogswell College
Highline Community College
Pacific Lutheran University
St. Martin's College
Seattle University
University of Washington
Wenatchee Valley College

West Virginia
Alderson-Broaddus College
Bethany College
College of West Virginia
Davis and Elkins College
Glenville State College
Potomac State College of West Virginia University
Salem-Teikyo University
University of Charleston
West Liberty State College
West Virginia Northern Community College
West Virginia University
West Virginia Wesleyan College

Wisconsin
Bellin College of Nursing
Blackhawk Technical College
Cardinal Stritch University
Carthage College
Concordia University Wisconsin
Lakeshore Technical College
Madison Area Technical College
Marian College of Fond du Lac
Milwaukee Area Technical College
Moraine Park Technical College
Mount Mary College
Mount Senario College
Northeast Wisconsin Technical College
Northland College
Ripon College
Silver Lake College
University of Wisconsin
    Eau Claire
    Madison
    Parkside
    River Falls
    Stout
Waukesha County Technical College
Western Wisconsin Technical College
Wisconsin Indianhead Technical College

Wyoming
Northwest College
University of Wyoming

Combined bachelor's/graduate program in accounting

Alabama
Alabama State University
Jacksonville State University

Arkansas
University of Central Arkansas

California
San Diego State University

Colorado
University of Colorado
    Boulder

Georgia
Georgia Southern University

Idaho
Albertson College of Idaho

Iowa
Drake University
Grand View College
University of Dubuque

Kansas
Wichita State University

Kentucky
Murray State University

Maine
Husson College

Massachusetts
Babson College
Bentley College
Stonehill College

Michigan
Baker College
    of Muskegon
Saginaw Valley State University

Missouri
University of Missouri
    Columbia
Webster University

Montana
University of Great Falls

New Jersey
Caldwell College
Kean University

New York
City University of New York
    Medgar Evers College
College of St. Rose
Fordham University
Long Island University
    Southampton College
St. John Fisher College
St. John's University
State University of New York
    College at Oneonta

North Carolina
Meredith College
Wake Forest University

Ohio
Case Western Reserve University

Oklahoma
Oklahoma State University
University of Oklahoma

Pennsylvania
Grove City College
King's College
Lock Haven University of Pennsylvania
Philadelphia University

Puerto Rico
Atlantic College
University of Puerto Rico
    Aguadilla

South Carolina
Newberry College

Tennessee
University of Memphis

Texas
Baylor University
Houston Baptist University
Southwestern Adventist University
Texas A&M University
Texas A&M University
    Texarkana
Trinity University
University of Houston
    Clear Lake
University of St. Thomas
University of Texas
    Arlington

Virginia
Randolph-Macon College
Virginia Polytechnic Institute and State
    University

Washington
Heritage College
Washington State University

West Virginia
University of Charleston

Combined bachelor's/graduate program in architecture

Georgia
Agnes Scott College
Georgia Institute of Technology

Indiana
Earlham College

Michigan
University of Michigan

New York
New York Institute of Technology

Ohio
Kent State University

Texas
University of Dallas

Vermont
Norwich University

Virginia
Hollins University
Virginia Polytechnic Institute and State
    University

Washington
University of Washington
Washington State University

Combined bachelor's/graduate program in business administration

Alabama
Jacksonville State University
Samford University
Spring Hill College
University of Alabama
University of Mobile

Arkansas
Harding University
University of Arkansas
    Monticello
University of Central Arkansas

California
California State University
    Stanislaus
Holy Names College
John F. Kennedy University
Monterey Institute of International
    Studies
San Francisco State University
Scripps College
Sonoma State University
University of California
    Irvine
    Santa Cruz
University of Judaism

Colorado
Regis University
University of Southern Colorado
Western State College of Colorado

Connecticut
Quinnipiac University
Sacred Heart University
St. Joseph College

Florida
Florida Institute of Technology
Florida Southern College
Nova Southeastern University
Palm Beach Atlantic College
Rollins College
University of South Florida

Hawaii
Hawaii Pacific University

Idaho
Albertson College of Idaho
Northwest Nazarene University

Illinois
Dominican University
Illinois Institute of Technology
Lewis University
University of Illinois
    Urbana-Champaign
University of St. Francis

Indiana
Earlham College
Indiana Institute of Technology
University of St. Francis
University of Southern Indiana

Iowa
Morningside College
University of Dubuque
Upper Iowa University
Wartburg College

Kansas
Wichita State University

Kentucky
Bellarmine College
Murray State University
Thomas More College
University of Kentucky

Louisiana
Louisiana Tech University
Tulane University
Xavier University of Louisiana

Maine
Husson College

University of Maine
University of Southern Maine

Maryland
Loyola College in Maryland
University of Baltimore

Massachusetts
Babson College
Becker College
Bentley College
Clark University
College of the Holy Cross
Massachusetts Maritime Academy
Nichols College
Suffolk University
University of Massachusetts
    Boston
Wheaton College
Worcester Polytechnic Institute

Michigan
Baker College
    of Muskegon
Eastern Michigan University
Lawrence Technological University
University of Michigan
    Flint

Minnesota
St. Cloud State University

Mississippi
Millsaps College

Missouri
Avila College
Culver-Stockton College
Drury University
Maryville University of Saint Louis
Missouri Valley College
Northwest Missouri State University
St. Louis University
University of Missouri
    Kansas City
Washington University

Montana
University of Great Falls

Nebraska
Hastings College

New Hampshire
New Hampshire College
University of New Hampshire

New Jersey
College of St. Elizabeth
Fairleigh Dickinson University
Rider University
Rutgers
    The State University of New Jersey:
        College of Engineering
    The State University of New Jersey:
        Cook College
    The State University of New Jersey:
        Douglass College
    The State University of New Jersey:
        Livingston College
    The State University of New Jersey:
        Newark College of Arts and
        Sciences
    The State University of New Jersey:
        Rutgers College
    The State University of New Jersey:
        University College New
        Brunswick
    The State University of New Jersey:
        University College Newark
Seton Hall University

Combined bachelor's/graduate program in business administration

New Mexico
College of Santa Fe

New York
Alfred University
Bard College
Canisius College
Clarkson University
College of Insurance
College of St. Rose
Cornell University
Dowling College
Elmira College
Fordham University
Hartwick College
Hobart and William Smith Colleges
Iona College
Ithaca College
Long Island University
   C. W. Post Campus
Manhattan College
Marymount College
Marymount Manhattan College
Molloy College
New York Institute of Technology
New York State College of Ceramics at
   Alfred University
Nyack College
Pace University
Pace University: Pleasantville/Briarcliff
Rensselaer Polytechnic Institute
Rochester Institute of Technology
Russell Sage College
St. Bonaventure University
St. John Fisher College
St. John's University
St. Lawrence University
Siena College
Skidmore College
State University of New York
   Binghamton
   Buffalo
   College at Cortland
   College at Fredonia
   College at Geneseo
   College at Oneonta
   College at Plattsburgh
   College at Potsdam
   Maritime College
   Oswego
Syracuse University
Touro College
Union College
University of Rochester
Wells College

North Carolina
Campbell University
Pfeiffer University
University of North Carolina
   Chapel Hill
   Greensboro

North Dakota
North Dakota State University

Ohio
Case Western Reserve University
Central State University
David N. Myers College
Franciscan University of Steubenville
Franklin University
John Carroll University
Kent State University
Otterbein College
University of Findlay
Xavier University

Oklahoma
Cameron University
Southern Nazarene University

Oregon
Portland State University
University of Portland
Willamette University

Pennsylvania
Duquesne University
Gannon University
Geneva College
Kutztown University of Pennsylvania
Lehigh University
Philadelphia University
Point Park College
St. Vincent College
University of Pennsylvania
University of the Sciences in
   Philadelphia
Waynesburg College
Widener University

Puerto Rico
Turabo University
Universidad Metropolitana

Rhode Island
Salve Regina University

South Carolina
Lander University

South Dakota
University of South Dakota

Tennessee
Maryville College

Texas
Angelo State University
Baylor University
Dallas Baptist University
Midwestern State University
Rice University
Sam Houston State University
Southwestern Adventist University
Texas A&M University
   Commerce
Texas Christian University
Texas Tech University
Texas Wesleyan University
University of Dallas
University of St. Thomas
University of Texas
   Arlington
   Dallas
West Texas A&M University

Utah
Westminster College

Vermont
Castleton State College
Champlain College
St. Michael's College

Virginia
Liberty University
Old Dominion University
Virginia Polytechnic Institute and State
   University

Washington
Seattle University
University of Washington
Washington State University

West Virginia
University of Charleston
Wheeling Jesuit University

Wisconsin
University of Wisconsin
   La Crosse

Combined bachelor's/graduate program in chemistry

Alabama
Jacksonville State University

Connecticut
Sacred Heart University
Wesleyan University

Florida
Florida Institute of Technology

Georgia
Georgia Institute of Technology

Idaho
Idaho State University

Iowa
University of Northern Iowa

Kansas
Wichita State University

Kentucky
Murray State University

Massachusetts
Boston University
University of Massachusetts
   Dartmouth

Missouri
University of Missouri
   Rolla

Montana
University of Great Falls

New Jersey
Caldwell College

New York
Rochester Institute of Technology
St. John's University

Oregon
Southern Oregon University

Pennsylvania
Bucknell University
Carlow College
Duquesne University
Lock Haven University of Pennsylvania

South Carolina
Newberry College

Texas
University of Texas
   Arlington

Virginia
Virginia Polytechnic Institute and State
   University

Washington
Washington State University

Combined bachelor's/graduate program in dentistry

California
University of Southern California
University of the Pacific

Colorado
University of Colorado
   Health Sciences Center
Western State College of Colorado

District of Columbia
Howard University

Florida
Nova Southeastern University
University of North Florida

Illinois
Southern Illinois University
   Edwardsville

Iowa
Buena Vista University
Luther College
University of Iowa
Wartburg College

Kansas
McPherson College

Kentucky
Murray State University

Maryland
Bowie State University
Salisbury State University
University of Maryland
   College Park

Massachusetts
Boston University

Michigan
University of Michigan

Minnesota
College of St. Benedict
St. John's University

Missouri
Missouri Valley College
University of Missouri
   Kansas City

Nebraska
Hastings College
University of Nebraska
   Lincoln

New Jersey
Fairleigh Dickinson University
New Jersey Institute of Technology
Richard Stockton College of New Jersey
Stevens Institute of Technology

New York
Alfred University
Barnard College
Canisius College
City University of New York
   Queens College
Le Moyne College
New York University
Rensselaer Polytechnic Institute
St. Francis College
St. John Fisher College
St. John's University
Siena College
Wagner College

North Carolina
University of North Carolina
   Chapel Hill

North Dakota
Valley City State University

Ohio
Case Western Reserve University
Ohio State University
 Columbus Campus

Oregon
Eastern Oregon University
Portland State University

Pennsylvania
Juniata College
Lehigh University
St. Francis College
University of Pittsburgh
Villanova University

Tennessee
University of Tennessee
 Martin

Texas
McMurry University
Texas A&M University
 Commerce
University of Texas
 Arlington

Washington
University of Washington

Wisconsin
University of Wisconsin
 Green Bay

Combined bachelor's/graduate program in education

Alabama
Alabama State University
Jacksonville State University

Alaska
University of Alaska
 Southeast

Arkansas
University of Central Arkansas

California
California State University
 Stanislaus
Holy Names College
Occidental College

Connecticut
Quinnipiac University
Sacred Heart University

Florida
Nova Southeastern University

Georgia
Piedmont College

Idaho
Albertson College of Idaho

Indiana
Earlham College
Oakland City University
University of St. Francis

Iowa
Emmaus Bible College
Grand View College

Morningside College
St. Ambrose University

Kansas
Wichita State University

Kentucky
Murray State University

Maine
University of Southern Maine

Maryland
College of Notre Dame of Maryland
Maryland Institute College of Art

Massachusetts
Boston College
Boston University
Simmons College
Wheelock College

Michigan
Albion College
Alma College
Baker College
 of Cadillac
Reformed Bible College

Minnesota
Minnesota Bible College

Mississippi
Mississippi Valley State University

Missouri
Maryville University of Saint Louis
Truman State University

Montana
University of Great Falls

New Hampshire
University of New Hampshire

New Jersey
Caldwell College
Rutgers
 The State University of New Jersey:
  Douglass College
 The State University of New Jersey:
  Livingston College
 The State University of New Jersey:
  Rutgers College
 The State University of New Jersey:
  University College New
  Brunswick

New York
City University of New York
 Medgar Evers College
Fordham University
Hobart and William Smith Colleges
St. John Fisher College
St. John's University
Sarah Lawrence College
Utica College of Syracuse University

Ohio
Otterbein College

Oklahoma
Cameron University

Oregon
Pacific University
Southern Oregon University

Pennsylvania
Beaver College
Carlow College

Duquesne University
Gwynedd-Mercy College
Lehigh University
Lock Haven University of Pennsylvania

Puerto Rico
Turabo University
Universidad Metropolitana
University of Puerto Rico
 Aguadilla

South Carolina
Anderson College
Newberry College

Texas
Trinity University

Utah
Westminster College

Vermont
Bennington College

Virginia
Liberty University
University of Virginia
Virginia Polytechnic Institute and State
 University

Washington
Heritage College
Puget Sound Christian College
Washington State University
Whitman College

Wisconsin
Carroll College

Combined bachelor's/graduate program in engineering

Alabama
Huntingdon College

California
Harvey Mudd College
Occidental College
San Francisco State University
Santa Clara University
Scripps College
University of California
 Santa Cruz
University of San Francisco
Westmont College
Whittier College

Colorado
Regis University
University of Colorado
 Boulder
 Denver
Western State College of Colorado

Connecticut
Fairfield University
Trinity College
University of Bridgeport
Yale University

Florida
Florida Institute of Technology
Florida Southern College

Georgia
Berry College
Georgia Institute of Technology
Mercer University

Idaho
Albertson College of Idaho

Illinois
Augustana College
Dominican University
Finch University of Health Sciences/The
 Chicago Medical School
Illinois Wesleyan University
Knox College
MacMurray College
University of Illinois
 Urbana-Champaign

Indiana
Anderson University
Earlham College
Goshen College
Taylor University

Iowa
Cornell College
Grand View College
Iowa State University
Northwestern College
Simpson College
Wartburg College

Kansas
Bethany College
Wichita State University

Kentucky
Murray State University
University of Kentucky
University of Louisville

Louisiana
Dillard University
Tulane University
University of Louisiana at Lafayette

Maine
Bates College
Colby College

Maryland
Johns Hopkins University
University of Maryland
 Baltimore County

Massachusetts
Boston University
Massachusetts Institute of Technology
Massachusetts Maritime Academy
Mount Holyoke College
Northeastern University
Regis College
Tufts University
University of Massachusetts
 Lowell
Wheaton College
Williams College
Worcester Polytechnic Institute

Michigan
Albion College
Kettering University
Lawrence Technological University

Minnesota
Bethel College
Hamline University
University of St. Thomas

Mississippi
Belhaven College
Mississippi University for Women

Missouri
Drury University
Missouri Valley College

Combined bachelor's/graduate program in engineering

University of Missouri
Rolla
Washington University
Westminster College

Montana
Montana Tech of the University of Montana
University of Great Falls

Nebraska
Hastings College
Nebraska Wesleyan University

New Jersey
Fairleigh Dickinson University
Richard Stockton College of New Jersey
Stevens Institute of Technology

New York
Canisius College
Clarkson University
College of St. Rose
Cornell University
Fordham University
Hartwick College
Hobart and William Smith Colleges
Ithaca College
Manhattan College
New York Institute of Technology
Polytechnic University
Rochester Institute of Technology
St. Lawrence University
Siena College
Skidmore College
State University of New York
Albany
College at Geneseo
College at Oneonta
Union College
University of Rochester
Vassar College
Wells College

North Carolina
Elon College
Wake Forest University

North Dakota
Jamestown College
North Dakota State University
University of North Dakota
Valley City State University

Ohio
Hiram College
John Carroll University
Wittenberg University
Xavier University

Oklahoma
Oklahoma Baptist University

Oregon
Eastern Oregon University
George Fox University
Pacific University
Portland State University
Reed College
Willamette University

Pennsylvania
Allegheny College
Beaver College
Bryn Mawr College
Bucknell University
Carlow College
Dickinson College
Drexel University
Gettysburg College
Juniata College
Lock Haven University of Pennsylvania
Millersville University of Pennsylvania
Slippery Rock University of Pennsylvania
Thiel College
Washington and Jefferson College
West Chester University of Pennsylvania

Puerto Rico
Inter American University of Puerto Rico
Barranquitas Campus

South Carolina
Furman University
Lander University
Newberry College
The Citadel
University of South Carolina

South Dakota
Augustana College
South Dakota School of Mines and Technology

Tennessee
King College
Rhodes College

Texas
Jarvis Christian College
McMurry University
Paul Quinn College
Prairie View A&M University
Rice University
Southwestern University
Texas A&M University
Commerce
University of Dallas
University of St. Thomas
University of Texas
Arlington
Dallas

Utah
Westminster College

Vermont
Castleton State College

Virginia
Emory & Henry College
Hampden-Sydney College
Randolph-Macon College
University of Virginia
Virginia Polytechnic Institute and State University

Washington
Washington State University

West Virginia
West Virginia University Institute of Technology

Wisconsin
Beloit College
Milwaukee School of Engineering
University of Wisconsin
La Crosse
Platteville
Superior

Combined bachelor's/graduate program in environmental studies

California
Monterey Institute of International Studies
San Francisco State University
University of San Francisco

Colorado
Western State College of Colorado

Connecticut
University of New Haven
Wesleyan University

Florida
Florida Institute of Technology
Nova Southeastern University

Georgia
Georgia Institute of Technology

Illinois
Augustana College
Illinois Institute of Technology

Iowa
Cornell College

Kansas
McPherson College

Kentucky
Murray State University

Louisiana
Southern University and Agricultural and Mechanical College

Maryland
Johns Hopkins University
Towson University

Massachusetts
Boston University
Clark University

Michigan
Albion College
Lawrence Technological University

Mississippi
Mississippi Valley State University

New Jersey
Caldwell College

New Mexico
College of Santa Fe

New York
Bard College
Canisius College
City University of New York
College of Staten Island
Medgar Evers College
New York Institute of Technology
Rochester Institute of Technology

Ohio
Miami University
Oxford Campus
Ohio State University
Columbus Campus
Wittenberg University

Oregon
Pacific University
Portland State University
Southern Oregon University

Pennsylvania
Beaver College
Carlow College
Duquesne University
Gettysburg College
Lebanon Valley College of Pennsylvania
St. Francis College

Rhode Island
University of Rhode Island

South Carolina
Furman University

Texas
McMurry University
Prairie View A&M University
Rice University
University of Texas
Dallas

Vermont
Sterling College

Virginia
Christopher Newport University
Virginia Polytechnic Institute and State University

Washington
Heritage College
Washington State University

Wisconsin
Milwaukee School of Engineering
University of Wisconsin
Platteville

Combined bachelor's/graduate program in fine arts

Alabama
Samford University

California
Academy of Art College
John F. Kennedy University
San Francisco State University
University of California
Santa Cruz

Colorado
Western State College of Colorado

Indiana
University of St. Francis

Kansas
Wichita State University

Maryland
Maryland Institute College of Art
University of Maryland
Baltimore County

Massachusetts
Wheaton College

Minnesota
Minnesota State University, Mankato

Missouri
Northwest Missouri State University

New York
City University of New York
Queens College

North Carolina
University of North Carolina
Chapel Hill

Ohio
Kent State University

Oregon
Portland State University

Pennsylvania
Edinboro University of Pennsylvania

South Dakota
University of South Dakota

Virginia
Virginia Polytechnic Institute and State University

Washington
University of Washington
Washington State University

Wisconsin
University of Wisconsin Madison

Combined bachelor's/graduate program in forestry

Arkansas
University of Arkansas Monticello

Colorado
Western State College of Colorado

Florida
Florida Southern College

Idaho
Albertson College of Idaho

Illinois
Augustana College
Knox College

Iowa
Cornell College

Louisiana
Southern University and Agricultural and Mechanical College

Michigan
Albion College

New York
Bard College
Canisius College
State University of New York College at Geneseo

North Carolina
High Point University
Wake Forest University

North Dakota
North Dakota State University

Ohio
Miami University Oxford Campus
Ohio State University Columbus Campus
Xavier University

Oregon
Portland State University
Willamette University

Pennsylvania
Gettysburg College
Lebanon Valley College of Pennsylvania
Moravian College
St. Francis College

South Carolina
Furman University

Vermont
Sterling College

Virginia
Christopher Newport University
Emory & Henry College
James Madison University
Randolph-Macon College
Virginia Polytechnic Institute and State University

Washington
Washington State University

West Virginia
Marshall University

Combined bachelor's/graduate program in law

Alabama
Samford University

California
Humphreys College
John F. Kennedy University
Occidental College
University of La Verne
University of San Francisco
University of West Los Angeles
Whittier College

Colorado
Western State College of Colorado

Connecticut
Quinnipiac University

District of Columbia
Catholic University of America

Florida
Nova Southeastern University
Stetson University

Idaho
Albertson College of Idaho
University of Idaho

Illinois
Illinois Institute of Technology
Knox College
Roosevelt University

Iowa
Drake University

Kansas
McPherson College

Louisiana
Southern University and Agricultural and Mechanical College
Tulane University

Maine
Bowdoin College
University of Southern Maine

Maryland
University of Baltimore
University of Maryland College Park

Massachusetts
Becker College
Northeastern University
Suffolk University
University of Massachusetts Dartmouth
Western New England College
Worcester Polytechnic Institute

Michigan
Siena Heights University

Missouri
Avila College
Central Missouri State University
Drury University
University of Missouri Kansas City

Montana
University of Great Falls

Nebraska
Creighton University
Hastings College
University of Nebraska Lincoln

New Jersey
Rutgers The State University of New Jersey: Newark College of Arts and Sciences
Seton Hall University
Stevens Institute of Technology
The College of New Jersey

New York
Barnard College
City University of New York City College
College of St. Rose
Eugene Lang College/New School University
Fordham University
Hartwick College
New York Institute of Technology
Pace University
Pace University: Pleasantville/Briarcliff
Rensselaer Polytechnic Institute
Russell Sage College
St. John's University
Skidmore College
State University of New York Albany
Syracuse University
Union College

North Carolina
Campbell University
University of North Carolina Chapel Hill

North Dakota
Valley City State University

Ohio
Ohio Northern University

Oklahoma
University of Tulsa

Oregon
Portland State University
Willamette University

Pennsylvania
Dickinson College
Duquesne University
Gannon University
Juniata College
Kutztown University of Pennsylvania
St. Francis College
St. Vincent College
Seton Hill College
Slippery Rock University of Pennsylvania
Temple University
University of Pennsylvania
Villanova University
Washington and Jefferson College
Waynesburg College

Rhode Island
Roger Williams University
University of Rhode Island

South Carolina
Voorhees College

South Dakota
University of South Dakota

Tennessee
Lambuth University

Texas
Texas A&M University Commerce

Vermont
University of Vermont

Virginia
Old Dominion University
Virginia Union University
Washington and Lee University

Washington
Whitman College

Wisconsin
University of Wisconsin Green Bay

Combined bachelor's/graduate program in mathematics

Alabama
Alabama State University
Jacksonville State University

Arkansas
University of Central Arkansas

California
University of Southern California

Connecticut
Wesleyan University
Yale University

Florida
Florida Institute of Technology

Georgia
Clark Atlanta University
Georgia Institute of Technology

Iowa
Grand View College

Kansas
Wichita State University

Combined bachelor's/graduate program in mathematics

Kentucky
Murray State University

Massachusetts
Boston University

Missouri
University of Missouri
    Rolla

Montana
University of Great Falls

New Jersey
Caldwell College

New York
City University of New York
    City College
New York University
Rochester Institute of Technology
St. John's University
State University of New York
    College at Potsdam

Oregon
Southern Oregon University

Pennsylvania
Bucknell University
Carlow College
Duquesne University
Lock Haven University of Pennsylvania
University of Pittsburgh

South Dakota
South Dakota School of Mines and
    Technology

Virginia
Virginia Polytechnic Institute and State
    University

Washington
Heritage College
Washington State University

Combined bachelor's/graduate program in medicine

California
University of California
    Riverside
University of Southern California

Colorado
University of Colorado
    Health Sciences Center
Western State College of Colorado

District of Columbia
Howard University

Florida
University of Miami
University of South Florida

Georgia
Mercer University

Illinois
Bradley University
Illinois Institute of Technology
Knox College
Loyola University of Chicago
Northwestern University

Iowa
University of Iowa

Kentucky
Murray State University

Louisiana
Tulane University

Maryland
University of Maryland
    College Park

Massachusetts
Boston University
Tufts University

Michigan
University of Michigan

Missouri
Central Missouri State University
Drury University
University of Missouri
    Kansas City

Nebraska
Hastings College
University of Nebraska
    Lincoln

New Jersey
Fairleigh Dickinson University
New Jersey Institute of Technology
Ramapo College of New Jersey
Richard Stockton College of New Jersey
Rutgers
    The State University of New Jersey:
        Camden College of Arts and
        Sciences
    The State University of New Jersey:
        College of Engineering
    The State University of New Jersey:
        Cook College
    The State University of New Jersey:
        Douglass College
    The State University of New Jersey:
        Livingston College
    The State University of New Jersey:
        Newark College of Arts and
        Sciences
    The State University of New Jersey:
        Rutgers College
    The State University of New Jersey:
        University College New
        Brunswick
Stevens Institute of Technology
The College of New Jersey

New York
Canisius College
City University of New York
    Brooklyn College
    City College
    Queens College
New York University
Rensselaer Polytechnic Institute
St. John Fisher College
Siena College
Union College
University of Rochester

North Carolina
University of North Carolina
    Chapel Hill

North Dakota
Valley City State University

Ohio
Kent State University
Ohio State University
    Columbus Campus

Oregon
Eastern Oregon University
Portland State University

Pennsylvania
Drexel University
Edinboro University of Pennsylvania
Gannon University
Juniata College
Lehigh University
MCP Hahnemann University
Rosemont College
Temple University
University of Pittsburgh
University of the Sciences in
    Philadelphia
Villanova University
Washington and Jefferson College
Widener University

Rhode Island
Brown University

South Carolina
Voorhees College

South Dakota
University of South Dakota

Tennessee
Lambuth University
University of Tennessee
    Martin

Texas
Lubbock Christian University
McMurry University
Rice University
Texas A&M University
    Commerce
University of Texas
    Arlington

Virginia
Hampden-Sydney College
Old Dominion University
Virginia Commonwealth University

Washington
University of Washington

Wisconsin
University of Wisconsin
    Green Bay
    Madison

Combined bachelor's/graduate program in nursing

Alabama
Birmingham-Southern College
Jacksonville State University

Arkansas
Harding University
University of Central Arkansas

California
Holy Names College
San Francisco State University

Colorado
University of Colorado
    Health Sciences Center

Connecticut
Quinnipiac University
Sacred Heart University
St. Joseph College

Florida
Barry University

Georgia
Armstrong Atlantic State University
Berry College

Hawaii
Hawaii Pacific University

Illinois
St. Xavier University

Indiana
Earlham College
Purdue University
    North Central Campus
University of St. Francis

Iowa
Graceland University
Grand View College

Kansas
Pittsburg State University
Wichita State University

Kentucky
Murray State University

Louisiana
Southern University and Agricultural and
    Mechanical College
University of Louisiana at Lafayette

Maine
Husson College
St. Joseph's College
University of Southern Maine

Maryland
Johns Hopkins University
Salisbury State University
Towson University

Massachusetts
Massachusetts College of Pharmacy and
    Health Sciences
Mount Holyoke College
Northeastern University
Regis College

Michigan
Albion College
University of Michigan

Minnesota
Minnesota Bible College

Missouri
Culver-Stockton College
St. Luke's College
University of Missouri
    Rolla
Webster University

Montana
University of Great Falls

Nebraska
Clarkson College
Grace University

New Jersey
Fairleigh Dickinson University

Felician College
Ramapo College of New Jersey
Richard Stockton College of New Jersey

New York
City University of New York
    Medgar Evers College
College of Mount St. Vincent
Concordia College
Daemen College
Molloy College
New York University
Pace University
Pace University: Pleasantville/Briarcliff
Regents College
Russell Sage College
St. John Fisher College
State University of New York
    Buffalo

North Carolina
University of North Carolina
    Chapel Hill

North Dakota
Dickinson State University
Valley City State University

Ohio
College of Mount St. Joseph
John Carroll University
Otterbein College
Wittenberg University

Oregon
Portland State University
Southern Oregon University

Pennsylvania
Allegheny College
Carlow College
Drexel University
Edinboro University of Pennsylvania
Gwynedd-Mercy College
Juniata College
Lock Haven University of Pennsylvania
MCP Hahnemann University
Thomas Jefferson University: College of Health Professions
University of Pennsylvania

Puerto Rico
Inter American University of Puerto Rico
    Barranquitas Campus

South Carolina
Furman University

Tennessee
David Lipscomb University
Maryville College

Texas
Jarvis Christian College
McMurry University
Southwestern Adventist University
Texas A&M University
    Commerce

Utah
Westminster College

Washington
Washington State University

Wisconsin
Beloit College

Combined bachelor's/graduate program in occupational therapy

Alabama
Alabama State University

Arkansas
University of Central Arkansas

California
Loma Linda University

Connecticut
Quinnipiac University
Sacred Heart University

Florida
Barry University
Nova Southeastern University

Georgia
Columbus State University

Illinois
Augustana College
Illinois College

Indiana
University of Southern Indiana

Iowa
St. Ambrose University
Wartburg College

Maine
Husson College
University of Southern Maine

Maryland
Towson University
Villa Julie College

Massachusetts
Boston University

Michigan
Alma College
Calvin College

Minnesota
College of St. Scholastica

Missouri
Avila College
Culver-Stockton College
Rockhurst University
Stephens College
Washington University

Nebraska
Hastings College

New Jersey
Seton Hall University

New York
D'Youville College
Dominican College of Blauvelt
Ithaca College
Juilliard School
Long Island University
    Brooklyn Campus
Marymount College
Russell Sage College
Touro College

North Carolina
University of North Carolina
    Chapel Hill

North Dakota
Valley City State University

Ohio
University of Findlay
Wittenberg University

Oregon
Pacific University
Portland State University

Pennsylvania
Bloomsburg University of Pennsylvania
College Misericordia
Gannon University
Juniata College
Lebanon Valley College of Pennsylvania
Moravian College
St. Francis College
University of Scranton
University of the Sciences in
    Philadelphia
Villanova University

South Dakota
University of South Dakota

Virginia
Virginia Commonwealth University

West Virginia
West Virginia University

Wisconsin
Carthage College
Concordia University Wisconsin
Lawrence University
University of Wisconsin
    Green Bay
    La Crosse
    Madison

Combined bachelor's/graduate program in optometry

Colorado
Western State College of Colorado

Florida
Nova Southeastern University

Kansas
McPherson College

Kentucky
Murray State University

Maryland
Salisbury State University

Massachusetts
Assumption College
Wheaton College

New Jersey
The College of New Jersey

New York
Canisius College
Ithaca College
Le Moyne College
Marymount College
St. John's University
Siena College
State University of New York
    Binghamton
    College at Oneonta
    College at Plattsburgh
    College at Potsdam
    New Paltz
    Oswego

North Dakota
Valley City State University

Ohio
Ohio State University
    Columbus Campus

Oregon
Eastern Oregon University
Pacific University
Portland State University

Pennsylvania
Beaver College
Gannon University
Gettysburg College
Juniata College
Lehigh University
Millersville University of Pennsylvania
Villanova University
Washington and Jefferson College
Widener University

Tennessee
University of Tennessee
    Martin

Texas
Texas A&M University
    Commerce

Vermont
University of Vermont

Wisconsin
University of Wisconsin
    Green Bay

Combined bachelor's/graduate program in osteopathic medicine

California
Pitzer College

Florida
Nova Southeastern University

Kansas
McPherson College

Kentucky
Pikeville College

Maryland
Salisbury State University

New Jersey
New Jersey Institute of Technology
Richard Stockton College of New Jersey

New York
Marymount College
New York Institute of Technology
St. John Fisher College
State University of New York
    New Paltz
Touro College

Combined bachelor's/graduate program in osteopathic medicine

Oregon
Portland State University

Pennsylvania
Gannon University
Juniata College
Kutztown University of Pennsylvania
Temple University
Widener University

Tennessee
University of Tennessee
    Martin

Combined bachelor's/graduate program in pharmacy

Alabama
Samford University

Colorado
University of Colorado
    Health Sciences Center

Florida
Nova Southeastern University

Indiana
Butler University

Iowa
University of Iowa
Wartburg College

Kansas
McPherson College
University of Kansas

Kentucky
Murray State University

Maryland
Washington College

Massachusetts
Massachusetts College of Pharmacy and
    Health Sciences
Northeastern University
Western New England College

Michigan
University of Michigan

Montana
University of Montana-Missoula

Nebraska
Hastings College
University of Nebraska
    Lincoln

New Jersey
Rutgers
    The State University of New Jersey:
    Camden College of Arts and
    Sciences

New York
Canisius College
Long Island University
    Brooklyn Campus
St. John Fisher College

North Carolina
Campbell University
University of North Carolina
    Chapel Hill

North Dakota
North Dakota State University
Valley City State University

Ohio
Ohio Northern University
Ohio State University
    Columbus Campus
Xavier University

Oklahoma
Southwestern Oklahoma State University

Oregon
Portland State University

Pennsylvania
Gannon University
St. Vincent College
University of Pittsburgh
Wilkes University

South Carolina
Furman University

South Dakota
South Dakota State University

Tennessee
Fisk University
Lambuth University
University of Tennessee
    Martin

Texas
Texas A&M University
    Commerce

Virginia
Virginia Commonwealth University

Washington
University of Washington
Washington State University

West Virginia
West Virginia University

Wisconsin
University of Wisconsin
    Green Bay
    Madison

Wyoming
University of Wyoming

Combined bachelor's/graduate program in physical therapy

Alabama
Alabama State University

Arkansas
University of Central Arkansas

California
Loma Linda University
San Francisco State University

Colorado
University of Colorado
    Health Sciences Center
Western State College of Colorado

Connecticut
Quinnipiac University
Sacred Heart University

Florida
Nova Southeastern University
University of Central Florida
University of Miami
University of North Florida

Georgia
Armstrong Atlantic State University
Brenau University
Columbus State University

Illinois
Bradley University
Millikin University

Iowa
Clarke College
St. Ambrose University

Kansas
McPherson College
Pittsburg State University

Maine
Husson College

Maryland
University of Maryland
    College Park

Massachusetts
Boston University
Simmons College

Michigan
Grand Valley State University

Minnesota
College of St. Catherine: St. Paul
    Campus
College of St. Scholastica

Missouri
Avila College
Maryville University of Saint Louis
Rockhurst University

Nebraska
Hastings College

New Hampshire
Notre Dame College

New Jersey
Kean University
Richard Stockton College of New Jersey
Seton Hall University

New York
City University of New York
    College of Staten Island
Concordia College
D'Youville College
Daemen College
Dominican College of Blauvelt
Ithaca College
Juilliard School
Long Island University
    Brooklyn Campus
Marymount College
Nazareth College of Rochester
New York Institute of Technology
Russell Sage College
St. Francis College
St. Thomas Aquinas College
State University of New York
    Upstate Medical University
Touro College
Utica College of Syracuse University

North Carolina
University of North Carolina
    Chapel Hill
Winston-Salem State University

North Dakota
University of North Dakota
Valley City State University

Ohio
College of Mount St. Joseph
University of Findlay

Oregon
Pacific University
Portland State University

Pennsylvania
Beaver College
Bloomsburg University of Pennsylvania
Cabrini College
Drexel University
Duquesne University
Elizabethtown College
Gettysburg College
Juniata College
Lebanon Valley College of Pennsylvania
MCP Hahnemann University
Moravian College
St. Francis College
Temple University
Thomas Jefferson University: College of
    Health Professions
University of Scranton
University of the Sciences in
    Philadelphia
Villanova University
Widener University

South Carolina
Furman University

South Dakota
University of South Dakota

Tennessee
University of Tennessee
    Chattanooga

Texas
Angelo State University
Hardin-Simmons University
McMurry University
Texas A&M University
    Commerce
Texas Woman's University

Vermont
University of Vermont

West Virginia
West Virginia University

Wisconsin
Carroll College
Concordia University Wisconsin
Marquette University
University of Wisconsin
    Green Bay
    Madison

Combined bachelor's/graduate program in podiatry

Connecticut
Quinnipiac University

District of Columbia
Howard University

Florida
Barry University

Maryland
Salisbury State University

Massachusetts
Assumption College

New Jersey
Bloomfield College
Richard Stockton College of New Jersey

New York
Canisius College
Le Moyne College
Rensselaer Polytechnic Institute
St. John Fisher College
Siena College
St. Joseph's College
    St. Joseph's College: Suffolk Campus

Oregon
Portland State University

Pennsylvania
Chestnut Hill College
Juniata College
Millersville University of Pennsylvania
St. Francis College
St. Vincent College
Washington and Jefferson College
Widener University

Tennessee
University of Tennessee
    Martin

Texas
Prairie View A&M University

Combined bachelor's/graduate program in psychology

Arkansas
University of Central Arkansas

Colorado
University of Colorado
    Boulder

Connecticut
Wesleyan University
Yale University

Florida
Florida Institute of Technology
Nova Southeastern University

Georgia
Georgia Institute of Technology

Iowa
Grand View College
Iowa State University

Kansas
Wichita State University

Kentucky
Murray State University

Maryland
Johns Hopkins University

Massachusetts
Boston University

Montana
University of Great Falls

New Jersey
Caldwell College
Kean University

New York
City University of New York
    City College

Oregon
Southern Oregon University

Pennsylvania
Bryn Mawr College
Geneva College
Lock Haven University of Pennsylvania
Rosemont College

Vermont
Burlington College

Virginia
Virginia Polytechnic Institute and State University

Washington
Heritage College
Washington State University

Combined bachelor's/graduate program in social work

Alabama
Alabama State University
Jacksonville State University

California
California State University
    Stanislaus
San Francisco State University

Indiana
Grace College
University of St. Francis

Kansas
Manhattan Christian College
Wichita State University

Kentucky
Brescia University
Murray State University

Louisiana
Tulane University

Maine
University of Southern Maine

Maryland
University of Maryland
    Baltimore County

Massachusetts
Boston College
Northeastern University

Minnesota
St. Cloud State University

Mississippi
Mississippi Valley State University

Missouri
Avila College
Maryville University of Saint Louis
University of Missouri
    Rolla
Washington University

Montana
University of Great Falls

New York
Bard College
Concordia College
Fordham University
Marymount College
Molloy College
State University of New York
    Buffalo
    New Paltz

North Carolina
University of North Carolina
    Chapel Hill

North Dakota
Dickinson State University
Valley City State University

Ohio
Cedarville College
College of Mount St. Joseph

Oregon
Portland State University

Pennsylvania
Bryn Mawr College
Lock Haven University of Pennsylvania

South Dakota
University of South Dakota

Texas
Prairie View A&M University
St. Edward's University
Southwestern Adventist University

Virginia
Virginia Commonwealth University

Washington
Heritage College
Walla Walla College

Wisconsin
University of Wisconsin
    Superior

Combined bachelor's/graduate program in veterinary medicine

Colorado
Western State College of Colorado

Kansas
McPherson College

Maryland
Salisbury State University

Mississippi
Mississippi State University

Missouri
Southwest Missouri State University

Nebraska
Grace University

New York
Wells College

North Dakota
Valley City State University

Ohio
Kent State University

Tennessee
Lambuth University
University of Tennessee
    Martin

Texas
Texas A&M University
    Commerce

Virginia
Bridgewater College
Virginia Polytechnic Institute and State University

Washington
Washington State University

Combined liberal arts/career program in accounting

Alabama
Birmingham-Southern College
Calhoun Community College
Jacksonville State University

Alaska
Alaska Pacific University
University of Alaska
    Southeast

Arizona
Phoenix College

Arkansas
Garland County Community College
University of Arkansas
    Monticello
    Pine Bluff
University of Central Arkansas
University of the Ozarks

California
California State University
    Chico
    Hayward
    Sacramento
Chaffey Community College
Chapman University
Columbia College
Cypress College
Diablo Valley College
Heald Business College
    Fresno
    Santa Rosa
Hope International University
Long Beach City College
Modesto Junior College
Ohlone College
Orange Coast College
Pacific Union College
Pasadena City College
San Diego City College
Santa Clara University
University of La Verne

Colorado
Community College of Denver
Fort Lewis College
Pueblo Community College
Trinidad State Junior College

Combined liberal arts/career program in accounting

Western State College of Colorado

Connecticut
Briarwood College
Norwalk Community-Technical College
Quinnipiac University
Sacred Heart University
Teikyo Post University
University of Bridgeport

Delaware
Wesley College

Florida
Edison Community College
Edward Waters College
Hillsborough Community College
Northwood University
    Florida Campus
St. Leo University
Tallahassee Community College
University of West Florida

Georgia
Floyd College
Morehouse College
Waycross College

Hawaii
Brigham Young University
    Hawaii

Idaho
Albertson College of Idaho

Illinois
Benedictine University
Black Hawk College
City Colleges of Chicago
    Harold Washington College
Dominican University
MacMurray College
McHenry County College
McKendree College

Indiana
Franklin College
Goshen College
Indiana Institute of Technology
Marian College
Oakland City University
St. Joseph's College
University of St. Francis

Iowa
Central College
Grand View College
Iowa State University
Marycrest International University
Morningside College
Northwestern College
Simpson College
University of Dubuque
Upper Iowa University
Wartburg College

Kansas
Allen County Community College
Butler County Community College
Coffeyville Community College
Manhattan Christian College
Tabor College
Wichita State University

Kentucky
Asbury College
Henderson Community College
Murray State University
Transylvania University

Louisiana
Centenary College of Louisiana
Dillard University
Louisiana State University
    Eunice

Maine
University of Southern Maine

Maryland
Baltimore City Community College
Frederick Community College
Harford Community College
Morgan State University
Mount St. Mary's College
Prince George's Community College
Towson University
Wor-Wic Community College

Massachusetts
Babson College
Becker College
Curry College
Fisher College
Lasell College
Massachusetts College of Liberal Arts

Michigan
Adrian College
Alma College
Baker College
    of Muskegon
    of Owosso
    of Port Huron
Cornerstone College and Grand Rapids Baptist Seminary
Delta College
Glen Oaks Community College
Hope College
Kellogg Community College
Mid Michigan Community College
Rochester College

Minnesota
Century Community and Technical College
College of St. Scholastica
Minnesota State University, Mankato
Northwestern College

Missouri
Avila College
Central Missouri State University
Culver-Stockton College
Drury University
East Central College
Jefferson College
Mineral Area College
Missouri Baptist College
St. Louis Community College
    St. Louis Community College at Forest Park
Stephens College
Washington University
Westminster College
William Jewell College

Montana
Rocky Mountain College
University of Great Falls

Nebraska
Bellevue University
Midland Lutheran College
Northeast Community College
Peru State College

New Hampshire
Franklin Pierce College
New England College
New Hampshire Community Technical College
    Laconia

New Jersey
Atlantic Cape Community College
Bloomfield College
Caldwell College
College of St. Elizabeth
County College of Morris
Ocean County College
Passaic County Community College
Rowan University
The College of New Jersey
Warren County Community College

New Mexico
San Juan College

New York
Clarkson University
Clinton Community College
College of St. Rose
Dominican College of Blauvelt
Hartwick College
Herkimer County Community College
Interboro Institute
Long Island University
    Southampton College
Mohawk Valley Community College
Molloy College
Mount St. Mary College
New York Institute of Technology
New York State College of Ceramics at Alfred University
New York University
St. Francis College
St. Joseph's College
    St. Joseph's College: Suffolk Campus
State University of New York
    College at Brockport
    Oswego
Tompkins-Cortland Community College
Utica College of Syracuse University

North Carolina
Beaufort County Community College
Belmont Abbey College
Coastal Carolina Community College
Elizabeth City State University
Elon College
Lees-McRae College
Lenoir Community College
Methodist College
Nash Community College
Pfeiffer University
Queens College
Sampson Community College

North Dakota
Dickinson State University
University of North Dakota

Ohio
Ashland University
Bluffton College
Capital University
Cedarville College
Circleville Bible College
Clark State Community College
College of Mount St. Joseph
Columbus State Community College
David N. Myers College
Davis College
Lima Technical College
Mount Vernon Nazarene College
Otterbein College
University of Akron
    Wayne College

Oklahoma
Cameron University
Carl Albert State College
Oklahoma Panhandle State University
Oral Roberts University
Redlands Community College

Oregon
Clackamas Community College
Concordia University
Eastern Oregon University
Lane Community College
Pacific University
Southern Oregon University

Pennsylvania
Beaver College
Bucknell University
Cedar Crest College
Chatham College
Elizabethtown College
Geneva College
Gwynedd-Mercy College
Immaculata College
Lehigh University
Lock Haven University of Pennsylvania
Moravian College
Philadelphia University
Point Park College
Rosemont College
Seton Hill College
Temple University
University of Pittsburgh
    Greensburg
Waynesburg College

Puerto Rico
Atlantic College
Colegio Universitario del Este
Turabo University
Universidad Metropolitana
University of Puerto Rico
    Aguadilla
    Arecibo Campus

Rhode Island
Salve Regina University

South Carolina
Anderson College
Chesterfield-Marlboro Technical College
Columbia International University
Converse College
Florence-Darlington Technical College
Limestone College
Newberry College
Orangeburg-Calhoun Technical College

Tennessee
Christian Brothers University
Cleveland State Community College
Dyersburg State Community College
Lambuth University
Lincoln Memorial University
Tennessee Technological University
University of Tennessee
    Knoxville

Texas
Blinn College
Coastal Bend College
Midwestern State University
St. Edward's University
Sam Houston State University
South Plains College
Southwestern Adventist University
Texas A&M International University
Texas A&M University
    Texarkana
University of St. Thomas

Utah
Westminster College

Vermont
Champlain College
College of St. Joseph in Vermont
Lyndon State College
Norwich University
Southern Vermont College

Virginia
Northern Virginia Community College
University of Virginia's College at Wise
Virginia Polytechnic Institute and State University

Washington
Big Bend Community College
Gonzaga University
Lower Columbia College
Pacific Lutheran University
St. Martin's College
University of Washington
Walla Walla College
Washington State University

West Virginia
Concord College
Fairmont State College
Glenville State College
West Virginia University Institute of Technology
Wheeling Jesuit University

Wisconsin
Carroll College
Mount Mary College
Mount Senario College
University of Wisconsin Green Bay
Viterbo University

Combined liberal arts/career program in architecture

Arizona
Phoenix College

California
California College of Arts and Crafts
Chaffey Community College
Long Beach City College
Modesto Junior College
Orange Coast College
San Joaquin Delta College
San Joaquin Valley College Inc.
Santa Rosa Junior College
United States International University
University of San Francisco

Colorado
Arapahoe Community College
Western State College of Colorado

Florida
University of South Florida

Georgia
Agnes Scott College
Georgia Institute of Technology
Southern Polytechnic State University

Illinois
City Colleges of Chicago
    Harold Washington College
Knox College
Monmouth College
Principia College

Indiana
Earlham College

Iowa
Coe College

Kansas
Allen County Community College
Central Christian College
Kansas State University

Louisiana
Louisiana Tech University
Southern University and Agricultural and Mechanical College
Tulane University
University of Louisiana at Lafayette

Maryland
Frederick Community College
Howard Community College
Morgan State University

Massachusetts
Boston Architectural Center
Franklin Institute of Boston
Wellesley College

Michigan
Adrian College
Delta College
Lawrence Technological University
University of Michigan

Minnesota
Carleton College
Macalester College

Mississippi
Hinds Community College
Mississippi State University

Missouri
Drury University
East Central College
University of Missouri St. Louis
Washington University

New Jersey
Mercer County Community College
Union County College

New York
Colgate University
Erie Community College
    City Campus
    North Campus
    South Campus
Hobart and William Smith Colleges
New York Institute of Technology
Parsons School of Design
State University of New York
    College of Technology at Alfred
    College of Technology at Canton
    Maritime College

North Carolina
Coastal Carolina Community College
North Carolina State University

North Dakota
North Dakota State University

Ohio
Columbus State Community College
Kent State University
    Stark Campus
Ohio State University
    Columbus Campus

Pennsylvania
Lehigh University
Philadelphia University
Temple University

Puerto Rico
University of Puerto Rico
    Rio Piedras Campus

Tennessee
University of Tennessee Knoxville

Texas
Baylor University
Coastal Bend College
Rice University
University of Dallas
University of Texas Austin

Vermont
Norwich University

Virginia
Virginia Polytechnic Institute and State University

Washington
University of Washington
Washington State University

West Virginia
Fairmont State College

Wisconsin
Milwaukee Area Technical College
University of Wisconsin Platteville

Combined liberal arts/career program in aviation

California
Chaffey Community College
Cypress College
Long Beach City College
Orange Coast College
Pacific Union College

Colorado
Community College of Denver

Illinois
Moraine Valley Community College

Indiana
Indiana Institute of Technology

Iowa
University of Dubuque

Kansas
Central Christian College
Hesston College
Wichita State University

Maryland
Frederick Community College

Michigan
Baker College of Muskegon
Delta College

Minnesota
Minnesota State University, Mankato
North Central University

Missouri
Central Missouri State University
St. Louis Community College
    St. Louis Community College at Forest Park

Montana
Rocky Mountain College

New Hampshire
Daniel Webster College

New Jersey
County College of Morris

New Mexico
San Juan College

New York
College of Aeronautics
St. Francis College

North Carolina
College of the Albemarle
Lenoir Community College

North Dakota
University of North Dakota

Ohio
Columbus State Community College

Oregon
Lane Community College
Multnomah Bible College

Pennsylvania
Geneva College

Utah
Westminster College

Washington
Big Bend Community College

West Virginia
Fairmont State College

Combined liberal arts/career program in business administration

Alabama
Alabama State University
Birmingham-Southern College
Calhoun Community College
Chattahoochee Valley Community College
Community College of the Air Force
Concordia College
Faulkner University
Jacksonville State University
Northwest-Shoals Community College
Samford University
Shelton State Community College
Spring Hill College
University of Alabama
University of Mobile

Alaska
Alaska Pacific University
University of Alaska Southeast

Arizona
Gateway Community College
Mohave Community College
Northern Arizona University

Arkansas
Garland County Community College
Harding University
Philander Smith College
University of Arkansas
    Monticello
    Pine Bluff
University of Central Arkansas
University of the Ozarks

Combined liberal arts/career program in business administration

California
Antioch Southern California
    Santa Barbara
Biola University
California College for Health Sciences
California State University
    Chico
    Hayward
    Monterey Bay
    Sacramento
    San Marcos
    Stanislaus
Chaffey Community College
Chapman University
Columbia College
Concordia University
Cypress College
Diablo Valley College
Dominican University of California
Heald Business College
    Santa Rosa
Holy Names College
Hope International University
Long Beach City College
Modesto Junior College
Occidental College
Ohlone College
Orange Coast College
Pacific Union College
Pasadena City College
San Diego City College
San Francisco State University
San Joaquin Delta College
San Joaquin Valley College Inc.
Santa Clara University
Santa Rosa Junior College
United States International University
University of La Verne
University of Redlands
Westmont College
Whittier College

Colorado
Colorado Mountain College
    Alpine Campus
    Timberline Campus
Community College of Aurora
Community College of Denver
Fort Lewis College
Metropolitan State College of Denver
Pueblo Community College
Trinidad State Junior College
University of Colorado
    Denver
Western State College of Colorado

Connecticut
Asnuntuck Community-Technical College
Briarwood College
Quinnipiac University
Sacred Heart University
St. Joseph College
Teikyo Post University
United States Coast Guard Academy
University of Bridgeport

Delaware
Wesley College

Florida
Clearwater Christian College
Daytona Beach Community College
Edison Community College
Edward Waters College
Florida Institute of Technology
Florida Southern College
Hillsborough Community College
Northwood University
    Florida Campus
Palm Beach Atlantic College
Rollins College
St. Leo University
South College: Palm Beach Campus
Southeastern College of the Assemblies of God
Stetson University
Tallahassee Community College
University of South Florida
University of West Florida

Georgia
Atlanta Christian College
Clayton College and State University
Emory University
Floyd College
Georgia Institute of Technology
Georgia Southwestern State University
LaGrange College
Morehouse College
Paine College
Reinhardt College
Southern Polytechnic State University
Waycross College

Hawaii
Brigham Young University
    Hawaii

Idaho
Albertson College of Idaho
Northwest Nazarene University
University of Idaho

Illinois
Barat College
Benedictine University
Black Hawk College
Blackburn College
Bradley University
City Colleges of Chicago
    Harold Washington College
    Harry S. Truman College
Dominican University
Illinois State University
Lewis University
MacMurray College
McHenry County College
McKendree College
Monmouth College
Moraine Valley Community College
North Central College
Olivet Nazarene University
University of Illinois
    Springfield
University of St. Francis

Indiana
Earlham College
Franklin College
Goshen College
Grace College
Indiana Institute of Technology
Indiana Wesleyan University
Marian College
Oakland City University
St. Joseph's College
University of St. Francis
University of Southern Indiana
Valparaiso University

Iowa
Briar Cliff College
Central College
Dordt College
Graceland University
Grand View College
Iowa State University
Marycrest International University
Morningside College
North Iowa Area Community College
Northwestern College
Simpson College
Southeastern Community College
    South Campus
Southwestern Community College
University of Dubuque
Upper Iowa University
Waldorf College
Wartburg College
William Penn University

Kansas
Allen County Community College
Baker University
Barclay College
Bethany College
Butler County Community College
Central Christian College
Coffeyville Community College
Colby Community College
Hesston College
Kansas State University
Manhattan Christian College
McPherson College
Newman University
Ottawa University
Pittsburg State University
Tabor College
Wichita State University

Kentucky
Asbury College
Ashland Community College
Bellarmine College
Brescia University
Elizabethtown Community College
Henderson Community College
Kentucky Christian College
Midway College
Murray State University
Pikeville College
Southeast Community College
Thomas More College
Transylvania University

Louisiana
Centenary College of Louisiana
Dillard University
Louisiana State University
    Eunice
Louisiana Tech University
Southern University and Agricultural and Mechanical College
Tulane University
University of Louisiana at Lafayette

Maine
Maine Maritime Academy
St. Joseph's College
University of Maine
University of Maine
    Fort Kent
    Presque Isle
University of Southern Maine
Washington County Technical College

Maryland
Allegany College
Baltimore City Community College
College of Notre Dame of Maryland
Community College of Baltimore County
    Essex
Coppin State College
Frederick Community College
Frostburg State University
Hagerstown Community College
Harford Community College
Howard Community College
Morgan State University
Mount St. Mary's College
Prince George's Community College
Towson University
Western Maryland College
Wor-Wic Community College

Massachusetts
Anna Maria College
Babson College
Becker College
Bentley College
Boston University
Clark University
Curry College
Fisher College
Framingham State College
Lasell College
Lesley College
Massachusetts College of Liberal Arts
Massachusetts Maritime Academy
Nichols College
Simmons College
Suffolk University

Michigan
Adrian College
Alma College
Baker College
    of Auburn Hills
    of Muskegon
    of Owosso
    of Port Huron
Cornerstone College and Grand Rapids Baptist Seminary
Delta College
Glen Oaks Community College
Hope College
Kellogg Community College
Lawrence Technological University
Mid Michigan Community College
Reformed Bible College
Rochester College
Wayne State University

Minnesota
Augsburg College
Bemidji State University
Central Lakes College
Century Community and Technical College
College of St. Catherine: St. Paul Campus
College of St. Scholastica
Gustavus Adolphus College
Minnesota State University, Mankato
North Central University
Northwestern College
St. Cloud State University
St. Olaf College

Mississippi
Hinds Community College
Millsaps College
Mississippi State University

Missouri
Avila College
Central Missouri State University
Columbia College
Culver-Stockton College
Drury University
East Central College
Jefferson College
Mineral Area College
Missouri Baptist College
Missouri Valley College
Northwest Missouri State University
St. Louis Community College
    St. Louis Community College at Forest Park
Stephens College
Three Rivers Community College
Washington University
Westminster College
William Jewell College

Montana
Carroll College
Montana State University
    College of Technology-Great Falls
Rocky Mountain College
University of Great Falls
University of Montana-Missoula

Nebraska
Bellevue University
Clarkson College
Dana College
Midland Lutheran College
Northeast Community College
Peru State College
Southeast Community College
    Lincoln Campus

New Hampshire
Colby-Sawyer College
Daniel Webster College
Franklin Pierce College
Keene State College
New England College
New Hampshire College
New Hampshire Community Technical College
    Laconia
Notre Dame College

New Jersey
Atlantic Cape Community College
Bloomfield College
Caldwell College
Camden County College
College of St. Elizabeth
County College of Morris
Fairleigh Dickinson University
Kean University
Mercer County Community College
New Jersey City University
Ocean County College
Passaic County Community College
Richard Stockton College of New Jersey
Rowan University
Seton Hall University
Union County College
Warren County Community College

New Mexico
College of Santa Fe
Eastern New Mexico University
    Roswell Campus
New Mexico State University
    Alamogordo
San Juan College

New York
City University of New York
    College of Staten Island
    Medgar Evers College
    Queens College
Clarkson University
Clinton Community College
College of Insurance
College of St. Rose
Concordia College
D'Youville College
Dominican College of Blauvelt
Dowling College
Erie Community College
    City Campus
    North Campus
    South Campus
Hartwick College
Herkimer County Community College
Hobart and William Smith Colleges
Houghton College
Interboro Institute
Iona College
Juilliard School
Keuka College
Long Island University
    Southampton College
Marist College
Marymount College
Marymount Manhattan College
Medaille College
Mohawk Valley Community College
Molloy College
Mount St. Mary College
Nazareth College of Rochester
New York Institute of Technology
New York State College of Ceramics at Alfred University
New York University
Niagara University
Onondaga Community College
Roberts Wesleyan College
Russell Sage College
Sage Junior College of Albany
St. Bonaventure University
St. Francis College
St. John Fisher College
Schenectady County Community College
Skidmore College
St. Joseph's College
    St. Joseph's College: Suffolk Campus
State University of New York
    Binghamton
    Buffalo
    College at Brockport
    College at Geneseo
    College at Plattsburgh
    College at Potsdam
    College of Technology at Alfred
    College of Technology at Canton
    Institute of Technology at Utica/Rome
    Maritime College
    Oswego
Tompkins-Cortland Community College
Utica College of Syracuse University
Villa Maria College of Buffalo
Wagner College
Westchester Community College

North Carolina
Beaufort County Community College
Belmont Abbey College
Bladen Community College
Cleveland Community College
Coastal Carolina Community College
College of the Albemarle
Elizabeth City State University
Elon College
James Sprunt Community College
Lees-McRae College
Lenoir Community College
Mayland Community College
Methodist College
Nash Community College
North Carolina State University
Peace College
Pfeiffer University
Queens College
Randolph Community College
St. Augustine's College
Sampson Community College
Sandhills Community College
Southeastern Community College
University of North Carolina
    Asheville
    Chapel Hill
Wilson Technical Community College

North Dakota
Dickinson State University
Mayville State University
North Dakota State University
Trinity Bible College
University of North Dakota
Valley City State University

Ohio
Antioch College
Ashland University
Bluffton College
Capital University
Cedarville College
Circleville Bible College
Cleveland State University
College of Mount St. Joseph
Columbus State Community College
David N. Myers College
Davis College
Defiance College
Franciscan University of Steubenville
Kent State University
    Ashtabula Regional Campus
    Stark Campus
Lima Technical College
Lourdes College
Miami University
    Middletown Campus
Mount Vernon Nazarene College
Muskingum College
Ohio Northern University
Ohio State University
    Columbus Campus
Ohio Valley Business College
Ohio Wesleyan University
Otterbein College
Southern State Community College
University of Akron
    Wayne College
Walsh University
Wilmington College
Wittenberg University

Oklahoma
Cameron University
Carl Albert State College
Mid-America Bible College
Oklahoma Panhandle State University
Oral Roberts University
Redlands Community College
Southern Nazarene University
Southwestern Oklahoma State University
Western Oklahoma State College

Oregon
Clackamas Community College
Concordia University
Eastern Oregon University
Lane Community College
Pacific University
Southern Oregon University

Pennsylvania
Allentown College of St. Francis de Sales
Beaver College
Bucknell University
Cedar Crest College
Chatham College
Community College of Allegheny County
Delaware Valley College
Dickinson College
Edinboro University of Pennsylvania
Elizabethtown College
Geneva College
Gettysburg College
Gwynedd-Mercy College
Immaculata College
La Roche College
Lafayette College
Lehigh University
Lock Haven University of Pennsylvania
Mercyhurst College
Moravian College
Philadelphia College of Bible
Philadelphia University
Point Park College
Rosemont College
Seton Hill College
Temple University
Thiel College
University of Pittsburgh
University of Pittsburgh
    Greensburg
    Johnstown
Widener University

Puerto Rico
Atlantic College
Colegio Universitario del Este
Inter American University of Puerto Rico
    Bayamon Campus
Turabo University
Universidad Metropolitana
University of Puerto Rico
    Aguadilla
    Arecibo Campus
    Rio Piedras Campus
University of the Sacred Heart

Rhode Island
Salve Regina University

South Carolina
Anderson College
Chesterfield-Marlboro Technical College
Coker College
College of Charleston
Columbia International University
Converse College
Erskine College
Florence-Darlington Technical College
Lander University
Limestone College
Midlands Technical College
Newberry College

South Dakota
University of South Dakota

Tennessee
Bethel College
Christian Brothers University
Cleveland State Community College
Cumberland University
Draughons Junior College of Business:
    Nashville
Dyersburg State Community College
Freed-Hardeman University
King College
Lambuth University
Lane College
LeMoyne-Owen College
Lee University
Lincoln Memorial University
Roane State Community College
Shelby State Community College
Tennessee Technological University
Tennessee Temple University
Tennessee Wesleyan College
Union University
University of Memphis
University of Tennessee
    Knoxville
Volunteer State Community College
Walters State Community College

Texas
Blinn College
Coastal Bend College
Collin County Community College District
Concordia University at Austin
Hardin-Simmons University
Houston Community College System
Howard Payne University
Jarvis Christian College
McMurry University
Midland College
Midwestern State University
Northwood University: Texas Campus
Paul Quinn College
Rice University
St. Edward's University
Sam Houston State University
Schreiner College
South Plains College
Southwestern Adventist University
Texas A&M International University
Texas A&M University
    Texarkana
Texas Lutheran University
Texas Tech University
Trinity University
University of Dallas
University of St. Thomas

Combined liberal arts/career program in business administration

University of Texas
    Austin
University of the Incarnate Word
Weatherford College

Utah
Utah Valley State College
Westminster College

Vermont
Castleton State College
Champlain College
College of St. Joseph in Vermont
Community College of Vermont
Green Mountain College
Lyndon State College
Norwich University
St. Michael's College
Southern Vermont College
Trinity College of Vermont

Virginia
Liberty University
Mary Baldwin College
Old Dominion University
University of Virginia's College at Wise
Virginia Commonwealth University
Virginia Polytechnic Institute and State University
Virginia Union University

Washington
Clark College
Everett Community College
Gonzaga University
Lower Columbia College
North Seattle Community College
Pacific Lutheran University
Peninsula College
St. Martin's College
University of Washington
Walla Walla College
Walla Walla Community College
Washington State University

West Virginia
Concord College
Fairmont State College
Glenville State College
University of Charleston
West Virginia University Institute of Technology
Wheeling Jesuit University

Wisconsin
Alverno College
Carroll College
Carthage College
Milwaukee Area Technical College
Mount Mary College
Mount Senario College
University of Wisconsin
    Green Bay
    La Crosse
    Parkside
    Superior
Viterbo University

Wyoming
Northwest College

Combined liberal arts/career program in computer science

Alabama
Alabama State University
Birmingham-Southern College
Calhoun Community College
Chattahoochee Valley Community College
Community College of the Air Force
Faulkner University
Jacksonville State University
Northwest-Shoals Community College
Samford University
University of Mobile

Arizona
Gateway Community College
Mohave Community College

Arkansas
Garland County Community College
Northwest Arkansas Community College
Philander Smith College
University of Arkansas
University of Arkansas
    Pine Bluff
University of Central Arkansas
University of the Ozarks

California
Biola University
California State University
    Chico
    Hayward
    Monterey Bay
    Sacramento
    San Marcos
    Stanislaus
Chaffey Community College
Chapman University
Columbia College
Cypress College
Diablo Valley College
Heald Business College
    Fresno
    Santa Rosa
Hope International University
Long Beach City College
Modesto Junior College
Mount San Antonio College
Occidental College
Ohlone College
Orange Coast College
Pacific Union College
Pasadena City College
Pepperdine University
San Diego City College
San Francisco State University
San Joaquin Delta College
San Joaquin Valley College Inc.
Santa Clara University
Santa Rosa Junior College
Sonoma State University
United States International University
University of La Verne
University of Redlands

Colorado
Colorado College
Community College of Aurora
Community College of Denver
Fort Lewis College
Metropolitan State College of Denver
Pueblo Community College
Technical Trades Institute
Trinidad State Junior College
Western State College of Colorado

Connecticut
Asnuntuck Community-Technical College
Quinnipiac University
Sacred Heart University
Teikyo Post University
University of Bridgeport

Florida
Daytona Beach Community College
Edison Community College
Florida Institute of Technology
Florida Southern College
Hillsborough Community College
Northwood University
    Florida Campus
Palm Beach Atlantic College
St. Leo University
South College: Palm Beach Campus
Stetson University
Tallahassee Community College
University of South Florida
University of West Florida

Georgia
Emory University
Georgia Institute of Technology
Georgia Perimeter College
Georgia Southwestern State University
LaGrange College
Morehouse College
Paine College
Southern Polytechnic State University
Waycross College

Hawaii
Brigham Young University
    Hawaii

Idaho
Albertson College of Idaho
Northwest Nazarene University
University of Idaho

Illinois
Barat College
Benedictine University
Blackburn College
City Colleges of Chicago
    Harold Washington College
    Harry S. Truman College
Dominican University
Illinois State University
Illinois Wesleyan University
Lewis University
MacMurray College
McHenry County College
McKendree College
Monmouth College
Moraine Valley Community College
North Central College
Olivet Nazarene University
University of Illinois
    Springfield
University of St. Francis

Indiana
Goshen College
Indiana Wesleyan University
Oakland City University
St. Joseph's College

Iowa
Briar Cliff College
Central College
Dordt College
Graceland University
Grand View College
Iowa State University
Marycrest International University
Morningside College
North Iowa Area Community College
Northwestern College
St. Ambrose University
Simpson College
Southwestern Community College
University of Dubuque
Upper Iowa University
Waldorf College
Wartburg College
William Penn University

Kansas
Allen County Community College
Baker University
Butler County Community College
Central Christian College
Coffeyville Community College
Colby Community College
Hesston College
Kansas State University
Manhattan Christian College
McPherson College
Newman University
Ottawa University
Pittsburg State University
Tabor College
Wichita State University

Kentucky
Asbury College
Bellarmine College
Brescia University
Elizabethtown Community College
Henderson Community College
Midway College
Murray State University
Pikeville College
Southeast Community College
Thomas More College
Transylvania University

Louisiana
Dillard University
Grantham College of Engineering
Louisiana State University
    Eunice
Louisiana Tech University
Southern University and Agricultural and Mechanical College
Tulane University
University of Louisiana at Lafayette

Maine
St. Joseph's College
University of Maine
University of Maine
    Fort Kent
University of Southern Maine
Washington County Technical College

Maryland
Allegany College
Baltimore City Community College
College of Notre Dame of Maryland
Community College of Baltimore County
    Essex
Coppin State College
Frederick Community College
Frostburg State University
Hagerstown Community College
Harford Community College
Howard Community College
Johns Hopkins University
Morgan State University
Mount St. Mary's College
Prince George's Community College
Towson University
University of Maryland
    Baltimore County
Wor-Wic Community College

Massachusetts
Becker College
Curry College
Framingham State College
Franklin Institute of Boston
Massachusetts College of Liberal Arts
Middlesex Community College
Simmons College
Suffolk University
Wellesley College
Western New England College

Michigan
Alma College

Baker College
    of Muskegon
    of Owosso
    of Port Huron
Cornerstone College and Grand Rapids Baptist Seminary
Delta College
Glen Oaks Community College
Hope College
Kellogg Community College
Mid Michigan Community College
Reformed Bible College
Rochester College

Minnesota
Augsburg College
Bemidji State University
Central Lakes College
College of St. Scholastica
Gustavus Adolphus College
Hamline University
Minnesota State University, Mankato
Northwestern College
St. Cloud State University
St. Olaf College

Mississippi
Hinds Community College
Millsaps College
Mississippi State University
Mississippi Valley State University

Missouri
Avila College
Central Missouri State University
Columbia College
Culver-Stockton College
Drury University
East Central College
Jefferson College
Missouri Valley College
Northwest Missouri State University
St. Louis Community College
    St. Louis Community College at Forest Park
University of Missouri
    Rolla
Washington University
William Jewell College

Montana
Carroll College
Rocky Mountain College
Stone Child College
University of Great Falls
University of Montana-Missoula

Nebraska
Bellevue University
Dana College
Midland Lutheran College
Northeast Community College
Peru State College
Southeast Community College
    Lincoln Campus

New Hampshire
Daniel Webster College
Franklin Pierce College
Keene State College
New Hampshire College
New Hampshire Community Technical College
    Laconia

New Jersey
Atlantic Cape Community College
Bloomfield College
Caldwell College
Camden County College
College of St. Elizabeth
County College of Morris
Fairleigh Dickinson University

Kean University
Mercer County Community College
New Jersey City University
Ocean County College
Passaic County Community College
Richard Stockton College of New Jersey
Rowan University
Thomas Edison State College
Union County College
Warren County Community College

New Mexico
College of Santa Fe
Eastern New Mexico University
    Roswell Campus
New Mexico State University
    Alamogordo
San Juan College

New York
City University of New York
    College of Staten Island
    Medgar Evers College
    Queens College
Clinton Community College
College of St. Rose
Dominican College of Blauvelt
Dowling College
Erie Community College
    City Campus
    North Campus
    South Campus
Hartwick College
Herkimer County Community College
Houghton College
Interboro Institute
Iona College
Jamestown Community College
Marist College
Marymount College
Medaille College
Mohawk Valley Community College
Molloy College
Mount St. Mary College
New York Institute of Technology
New York State College of Ceramics at Alfred University
New York University
Onondaga Community College
Roberts Wesleyan College
Russell Sage College
Sage Junior College of Albany
St. Francis College
St. John Fisher College
Schenectady County Community College
Skidmore College
St. Joseph's College
    St. Joseph's College: Suffolk Campus
State University of New York
    Binghamton
    College at Brockport
    College at Plattsburgh
    College at Potsdam
    College of Technology at Alfred
    College of Technology at Canton
    Institute of Technology at Utica/Rome
    Maritime College
    Oswego
    Purchase
Tompkins-Cortland Community College
Utica College of Syracuse University
Villa Maria College of Buffalo
Wagner College
Westchester Community College

North Carolina
Beaufort County Community College
Belmont Abbey College
Bladen Community College
Carteret Community College
Cleveland Community College
Coastal Carolina Community College

College of the Albemarle
Elizabeth City State University
Elon College
Methodist College
Nash Community College
North Carolina State University
Pfeiffer University
St. Augustine's College
University of North Carolina
    Asheville
    Chapel Hill
Wilson Technical Community College

North Dakota
Dickinson State University
North Dakota State University
University of North Dakota
Valley City State University

Ohio
Ashland University
Bluffton College
Capital University
Cedarville College
Cleveland State University
College of Mount St. Joseph
Columbus State Community College
Davis College
Defiance College
Franciscan University of Steubenville
Kent State University
    Ashtabula Regional Campus
    Stark Campus
Lima Technical College
Miami University
    Middletown Campus
Mount Vernon Nazarene College
Muskingum College
Ohio Northern University
Ohio State University
    Columbus Campus
Ohio Valley Business College
Ohio Wesleyan University
Otterbein College
Southern State Community College
University of Akron
    Wayne College
Walsh University
Wilmington College
Wittenberg University

Oklahoma
Cameron University
Carl Albert State College
Oklahoma City Community College
Oklahoma Panhandle State University
Oral Roberts University
Redlands Community College
Southern Nazarene University
Southwestern Oklahoma State University
Western Oklahoma State College

Oregon
Clackamas Community College
Eastern Oregon University
Lane Community College
Pacific University
Reed College
Southern Oregon University

Pennsylvania
Allentown College of St. Francis de Sales
Beaver College
Bucknell University
Cedar Crest College
Delaware Valley College
Dickinson College
Duquesne University
Edinboro University of Pennsylvania
Elizabethtown College
Geneva College
Gettysburg College
Gwynedd-Mercy College
Immaculata College

La Roche College
Lafayette College
Lehigh University
Lock Haven University of Pennsylvania
Mercyhurst College
Moravian College
Philadelphia College of Bible
Philadelphia University
Point Park College
Seton Hill College
Temple University
University of Pittsburgh
    Johnstown
Widener University

Puerto Rico
Atlantic College
Colegio Universitario del Este
Inter American University of Puerto Rico
    Barranquitas Campus
    Bayamon Campus
Turabo University
Universidad Metropolitana
University of Puerto Rico
    Aguadilla
    Arecibo Campus
    Rio Piedras Campus
University of the Sacred Heart

Rhode Island
Salve Regina University

South Carolina
Anderson College
Chesterfield-Marlboro Technical College
College of Charleston
Columbia International University
Converse College
Florence-Darlington Technical College
Lander University
Limestone College
Midlands Technical College
Newberry College
Orangeburg-Calhoun Technical College

South Dakota
University of South Dakota

Tennessee
Bethel College
Christian Brothers University
Cleveland State Community College
Draughons Junior College of Business: Nashville
Dyersburg State Community College
Freed-Hardeman University
Lambuth University
Lane College
Tennessee Technological University
Tennessee Temple University
Union University
University of Memphis
University of Tennessee
    Knoxville
Volunteer State Community College
Walters State Community College

Texas
Blinn College
Coastal Bend College
Collin County Community College District
Concordia University at Austin
Hardin-Simmons University
Houston Community College System
Jarvis Christian College
McMurry University
Midland College
Midwestern State University
Northwood University: Texas Campus
Paul Quinn College
Rice University
St. Edward's University

Combined liberal arts/career program in computer science

St. Mary's University
Sam Houston State University
South Plains College
Southwestern Adventist University
Texas A&M University
    Commerce
Texas Lutheran University
Weatherford College

Utah
Utah Valley State College
Westminster College

Vermont
Castleton State College
Champlain College
College of St. Joseph in Vermont
Community College of Vermont
Norwich University
St. Michael's College

Virginia
Liberty University
Longwood College
University of Virginia's College at Wise
Virginia Commonwealth University
Virginia Polytechnic Institute and State University

Washington
Big Bend Community College
Clark College
Everett Community College
Gonzaga University
Lower Columbia College
North Seattle Community College
Pacific Lutheran University
Peninsula College
St. Martin's College
University of Washington
Walla Walla College
Walla Walla Community College
Washington State University
Whitman College

West Virginia
Concord College
Fairmont State College
Glenville State College
Shepherd College
West Virginia University Institute of Technology
Wheeling Jesuit University

Wisconsin
Carroll College
Carthage College
Milwaukee Area Technical College
University of Wisconsin
    Green Bay
    La Crosse
    Parkside
    Superior
Viterbo University

Combined liberal arts/career program in criminal justice

Alabama
Alabama State University
Calhoun Community College
Chattahoochee Valley Community College
Community College of the Air Force
Faulkner University
Jacksonville State University
Northwest-Shoals Community College

Arizona
Gateway Community College

Mohave Community College
Northern Arizona University

Arkansas
Garland County Community College
Harding University
Northwest Arkansas Community College
University of Arkansas
University of Arkansas
    Monticello
    Pine Bluff

California
California State University
    Chico
    Hayward
    Sacramento
    Stanislaus
Chapman University
Imperial Valley College
Long Beach City College
Loyola Marymount University
Modesto Junior College
Mount San Antonio College
Ohlone College
Pacific Union College
Pasadena City College
San Francisco State University
San Joaquin Delta College
San Joaquin Valley College Inc.
Santa Rosa Junior College
Sonoma State University
University of La Verne

Colorado
Community College of Aurora
Metropolitan State College of Denver
Pueblo Community College
Trinidad State Junior College
Western State College of Colorado

Connecticut
Asnuntuck Community-Technical College
Briarwood College
Quinnipiac University
Sacred Heart University
Teikyo Post University

Florida
Daytona Beach Community College
Edison Community College
Edward Waters College
Florida Southern College
Hillsborough Community College
St. Leo University
Tallahassee Community College
University of South Florida
University of West Florida

Georgia
Clark Atlanta University
LaGrange College
Macon State College
Reinhardt College
Waycross College

Illinois
Benedictine University
Blackburn College
City Colleges of Chicago
    Harold Washington College
    Harry S. Truman College
Danville Area Community College
Dominican University
Illinois State University
Lewis University
MacMurray College
McHenry County College
McKendree College
Moraine Valley Community College
North Central College
Olivet Nazarene University

University of Illinois
    Springfield

Indiana
Grace College
Indiana Wesleyan University
Oakland City University
St. Joseph's College
University of St. Francis

Iowa
Briar Cliff College
Graceland University
Grand View College
Morningside College
North Iowa Area Community College
Northwestern College
Simpson College
Southeastern Community College
    South Campus
University of Dubuque
Upper Iowa University
Wartburg College
William Penn University

Kansas
Allen County Community College
Bethany College
Butler County Community College
Central Christian College
Colby Community College
Kansas State University
Manhattan Christian College
Newman University
Pittsburg State University
Wichita State University

Kentucky
Murray State University
Pikeville College
Thomas More College

Louisiana
Dillard University
Louisiana State University
    Eunice
Southern University and Agricultural and Mechanical College
University of Louisiana at Lafayette

Maine
St. Joseph's College
University of Maine
    Fort Kent

Maryland
Allegany College
Baltimore City Community College
Community College of Baltimore County
    Essex
Coppin State College
Frostburg State University
Hagerstown Community College
Harford Community College
Howard Community College
Prince George's Community College
Wor-Wic Community College

Massachusetts
Anna Maria College
Becker College
Curry College
Fisher College
Framingham State College
Lasell College
Suffolk University
Western New England College

Michigan
Adrian College
Baker College
    of Muskegon
Bay de Noc Community College

Cornerstone College and Grand Rapids
    Baptist Seminary
Delta College
Glen Oaks Community College
Jackson Community College
Kellogg Community College
Mid Michigan Community College

Minnesota
Bemidji State University
Century Community and Technical College
Gustavus Adolphus College
Minnesota State University, Mankato
Northwestern College
St. Cloud State University

Mississippi
Hinds Community College
Mississippi State University
Mississippi Valley State University

Missouri
Central Missouri State University
Columbia College
Culver-Stockton College
Drury University
East Central College
Jefferson College
Mineral Area College
Missouri Baptist College
Missouri Valley College
St. Louis Community College
    St. Louis Community College at Forest Park
Three Rivers Community College

Montana
University of Great Falls
University of Montana-Missoula

Nebraska
Bellevue University
Dana College
Midland Lutheran College
Northeast Community College
Peru State College

New Hampshire
Franklin Pierce College
New England College
New Hampshire Community Technical College
    Laconia
Notre Dame College

New Jersey
Atlantic Cape Community College
Bloomfield College
Caldwell College
Camden County College
County College of Morris
Fairleigh Dickinson University
Kean University
Mercer County Community College
New Jersey City University
Ocean County College
Passaic County Community College
Richard Stockton College of New Jersey
Rowan University
Union County College
Warren County Community College

New Mexico
Eastern New Mexico University
    Roswell Campus
New Mexico State University
    Alamogordo
San Juan College

New York
City University of New York
    John Jay College of Criminal Justice
Clinton Community College
College of St. Rose
Erie Community College
    City Campus
    North Campus
    South Campus
Herkimer County Community College
Iona College
Jamestown Community College
Keuka College
Marist College
Medaille College
Mohawk Valley Community College
Molloy College
Mount St. Mary College
New York Institute of Technology
New York State College of Ceramics at Alfred University
Onondaga Community College
Roberts Wesleyan College
Russell Sage College
Sage Junior College of Albany
St. Francis College
St. Thomas Aquinas College
Schenectady County Community College
State University of New York
    Binghamton
    College at Brockport
    College at Plattsburgh
    College at Potsdam
    College of Technology at Canton
    Oswego
Tompkins-Cortland Community College
Utica College of Syracuse University
Westchester Community College

North Carolina
Beaufort County Community College
Belmont Abbey College
Bladen Community College
Brunswick Community College
Carteret Community College
Cleveland Community College
Coastal Carolina Community College
College of the Albemarle
Elizabeth City State University
Elon College
James Sprunt Community College
Lees-McRae College
Lenoir Community College
Mayland Community College
Methodist College
Nash Community College
North Carolina State University
Pfeiffer University
Randolph Community College
St. Augustine's College
Sampson Community College
Southeastern Community College
Wilson Technical Community College

North Dakota
North Dakota State University
University of North Dakota

Ohio
Ashland University
Bluffton College
Capital University
Cedarville College
Clark State Community College
Columbus State Community College
David N. Myers College
Defiance College
Kent State University
    Ashtabula Regional Campus
    Stark Campus
Lourdes College
Ohio Northern University
Ohio State University
    Columbus Campus
Ohio Valley Business College
University of Akron
    Wayne College
Wilmington College

Oklahoma
Cameron University
Carl Albert State College
Mid-America Bible College
Redlands Community College
Southwestern Oklahoma State University
Western Oklahoma State College

Oregon
Clackamas Community College
Lane Community College
Southern Oregon University

Pennsylvania
Allentown College of St. Francis de Sales
California University of Pennsylvania
Delaware Valley College
Edinboro University of Pennsylvania
Elizabethtown College
Geneva College
La Roche College
Lock Haven University of Pennsylvania
Mercyhurst College
Moravian College
Point Park College
Seton Hill College
Temple University
University of Pittsburgh
    Greensburg
Widener University

Puerto Rico
Colegio Universitario del Este
Inter American University of Puerto Rico
    Barranquitas Campus
Turabo University
Universidad Metropolitana
University of the Sacred Heart

Rhode Island
Salve Regina University

South Carolina
Chesterfield-Marlboro Technical College
Coker College
Columbia International University
Florence-Darlington Technical College
Lander University
Midlands Technical College
Newberry College
Orangeburg-Calhoun Technical College
Spartanburg Methodist College

South Dakota
University of South Dakota

Tennessee
Cleveland State Community College
Cumberland University
Draughons Junior College of Business: Nashville
Dyersburg State Community College
Lambuth University
Lane College
Shelby State Community College
Volunteer State Community College
Walters State Community College

Texas
Blinn College
Coastal Bend College
Hardin-Simmons University
Houston Community College System
Jarvis Christian College
McMurry University
Midland College
Midwestern State University
Northwood University: Texas Campus
Paul Quinn College
St. Edward's University
Sam Houston State University
South Plains College
Southwestern Adventist University
Texas A&M International University
Texas A&M University
    Commerce
    Texarkana
Texas Lutheran University
Weatherford College

Vermont
Castleton State College
Champlain College
Community College of Vermont
Norwich University
Southern Vermont College
Trinity College of Vermont

Virginia
Longwood College
University of Virginia's College at Wise
Virginia Commonwealth University
Virginia Union University

Washington
Everett Community College
Gonzaga University
Lower Columbia College
Peninsula College
St. Martin's College
Walla Walla Community College
Washington State University

West Virginia
Fairmont State College
Glenville State College
Shepherd College
Wheeling Jesuit University

Wisconsin
Carroll College
Carthage College
Mount Senario College
University of Wisconsin
    Parkside
    Superior
Viterbo University

Combined liberal arts/career program in education

Alabama
Alabama State University
Birmingham-Southern College
Calhoun Community College
Community College of the Air Force
Concordia College
Jacksonville State University

Alaska
Alaska Pacific University
University of Alaska
    Southeast

Arkansas
Philander Smith College
University of Arkansas
    Monticello
    Pine Bluff
University of Central Arkansas
University of the Ozarks

California
California State University
    Chico
    Monterey Bay
    Sacramento
Cypress College
Fresno Pacific University
Hope International University
National University
Occidental College
Ohlone College
Pacific Union College
Santa Clara University
Sonoma State University
United States International University

Colorado
Colorado College
Colorado Mountain College
    Alpine Campus
Community College of Denver
Fort Lewis College
Trinidad State Junior College
Western State College of Colorado

Connecticut
Quinnipiac University
Sacred Heart University
University of Bridgeport

Delaware
Wesley College

Florida
Clearwater Christian College
Edward Waters College
Florida Baptist Theological College
Florida Institute of Technology
St. Leo University
Tallahassee Community College
University of West Florida

Georgia
LaGrange College
Morehouse College
Piedmont College
Waycross College

Hawaii
Brigham Young University
    Hawaii

Idaho
Albertson College of Idaho
University of Idaho

Illinois
Barat College
Benedictine University
Blackburn College
City Colleges of Chicago
    Harold Washington College
Danville Area Community College
Dominican University
MacMurray College
McKendree College
Monmouth College

Indiana
Franklin College
Goshen College
Marian College
Oakland City University
St. Joseph's College
University of St. Francis

Iowa
Central College
Grand View College
Marycrest International University
Morningside College
Northwestern College

St. Ambrose University
Simpson College
University of Dubuque
Upper Iowa University
Wartburg College
William Penn University

Kansas
Allen County Community College
Baker University
Bethany College
Coffeyville Community College
Hesston College
Manhattan Christian College
Tabor College
Wichita State University

Kentucky
Asbury College
Henderson Community College
Kentucky Christian College
Murray State University
Pikeville College

Louisiana
Centenary College of Louisiana
Louisiana State University
　Eunice
University of Louisiana at Lafayette
Xavier University of Louisiana

Maine
Washington County Technical College

Maryland
Baltimore City Community College
College of Notre Dame of Maryland
Coppin State College
Harford Community College
Howard Community College
Mount St. Mary's College
Towson University
University of Maryland
　Baltimore County

Massachusetts
Becker College
Boston University
Curry College
Fisher College
Fitchburg State College
Framingham State College
Greenfield Community College
Lasell College
Massachusetts College of Liberal Arts
Middlesex Community College
Mount Holyoke College
Nichols College
Simmons College
Springfield Technical Community
　College
Suffolk University
Western New England College

Michigan
Adrian College
Alma College
Baker College
　of Muskegon
Delta College
Hope College
Kalamazoo Valley Community College
Kellogg Community College
Mid Michigan Community College
Reformed Bible College
Rochester College

Minnesota
College of St. Catherine: St. Paul
　Campus
College of St. Scholastica
Minnesota State University, Mankato
North Central University

Northwestern College
St. Olaf College

Mississippi
Mississippi State University
Mississippi Valley State University

Missouri
Avila College
Central Missouri State University
Columbia College
Culver-Stockton College
Drury University
East Central College
Jefferson College
Missouri Baptist College
St. Louis Christian College
St. Louis Community College
　St. Louis Community College at
　　Forest Park
Stephens College
University of Missouri
　Kansas City
Washington University
Westminster College
William Jewell College

Montana
Flathead Valley Community College
Rocky Mountain College
University of Great Falls
University of Montana-Missoula

Nebraska
Creighton University
Dana College
Midland Lutheran College
Northeast Community College
Peru State College

New Hampshire
Colby-Sawyer College
Franklin Pierce College
Keene State College
New England College
Notre Dame College

New Jersey
Atlantic Cape Community College
Bloomfield College
Caldwell College
County College of Morris
Ocean County College

New Mexico
New Mexico State University
　Alamogordo
San Juan College

New York
City University of New York
　Queens College
Clinton Community College
College of St. Rose
Dominican College of Blauvelt
Herkimer County Community College
Hobart and William Smith Colleges
Long Island University
　Southampton College
Marymount College
Medaille College
Mohawk Valley Community College
Molloy College
New York Institute of Technology
New York State College of Ceramics at
　Alfred University
New York University
St. Francis College
Skidmore College
St. Joseph's College
　St. Joseph's College: Suffolk
　　Campus

State University of New York
　Oswego
Utica College of Syracuse University
Wagner College

North Carolina
Belmont Abbey College
College of the Albemarle
Elizabeth City State University
Elon College
Lees-McRae College
Lenoir Community College
Methodist College
Nash Community College
Peace College
Pfeiffer University
Queens College
Sampson Community College
Sandhills Community College

North Dakota
Dickinson State University
North Dakota State University
University of North Dakota

Ohio
Ashland University
Capital University
Cedarville College
College of Mount St. Joseph
Lourdes College
Mount Vernon Nazarene College
Muskingum College
Otterbein College
University of Akron
　Wayne College
Wittenberg University

Oklahoma
Cameron University
Carl Albert State College
Mid-America Bible College
Oklahoma Panhandle State University
Oral Roberts University
Redlands Community College

Oregon
Concordia University
Eastern Oregon University
Eugene Bible College
Multnomah Bible College
Pacific University
Southern Oregon University

Pennsylvania
Allegheny College
Allentown College of St. Francis de Sales
Beaver College
Bucknell University
Cedar Crest College
Elizabethtown College
Geneva College
Gwynedd-Mercy College
Immaculata College
Lehigh University
Lock Haven University of Pennsylvania
Moravian College
Point Park College
Rosemont College
Slippery Rock University of
　Pennsylvania
Temple University

Puerto Rico
Atlantic College
Turabo University
Universidad Metropolitana
University of Puerto Rico
　Aguadilla
　Arecibo Campus
　Rio Piedras Campus

Rhode Island
Salve Regina University

South Carolina
Anderson College
Chesterfield-Marlboro Technical College
Converse College
Erskine College
Limestone College
Newberry College

Tennessee
Christian Brothers University
Dyersburg State Community College
Freed-Hardeman University
Lambuth University
Lane College
Lincoln Memorial University
Shelby State Community College
Tennessee Technological University
Tennessee Temple University
Tennessee Wesleyan College
University of Memphis
University of Tennessee
　Knoxville
Volunteer State Community College

Texas
Coastal Bend College
Jarvis Christian College
Midwestern State University
Navarro College
St. Edward's University
Sam Houston State University
South Plains College
Southwestern Adventist University
Texas A&M International University

Utah
Westminster College

Vermont
Champlain College
College of St. Joseph in Vermont
Green Mountain College
Trinity College of Vermont

Virginia
Longwood College
Northern Virginia Community College
Randolph-Macon College
University of Virginia's College at Wise
Virginia Polytechnic Institute and State
　University

Washington
Big Bend Community College
Everett Community College
Gonzaga University
Lower Columbia College
Pacific Lutheran University
Puget Sound Christian College
St. Martin's College
University of Washington
Walla Walla College
Washington State University
Whitman College

West Virginia
Bethany College
Concord College
Fairmont State College
Glenville State College
University of Charleston
West Virginia University Institute of
　Technology

Wisconsin
Alverno College
Beloit College
Carroll College
Mount Mary College
Mount Senario College

University of Wisconsin
　　Green Bay
Viterbo University

Combined liberal arts/career program in engineering

Alabama
Alabama State University
Auburn University
Birmingham-Southern College
Calhoun Community College
Huntingdon College
Northwest-Shoals Community College
Samford University
Spring Hill College
Tuskegee University

Alaska
University of Alaska
　　Southeast

Arkansas
Harding University
University of the Ozarks

California
Biola University
California Institute of Technology
California Lutheran University
California State University
　　Chico
　　Hayward
　　Sacramento
　　Stanislaus
Chaffey Community College
Cypress College
Diablo Valley College
Modesto Junior College
Occidental College
Ohlone College
Pomona College
St. Mary's College of California
San Francisco State University
San Joaquin Delta College
San Joaquin Valley College Inc.
Santa Clara University
Scripps College
University of Southern California
Westmont College

Colorado
Colorado College
Fort Lewis College
Metropolitan State College of Denver
Pueblo Community College
Trinidad State Junior College
University of Colorado
　　Denver
Western State College of Colorado

Connecticut
Fairfield University
Norwalk Community-Technical College
Trinity College
United States Coast Guard Academy
University of Bridgeport
Wesleyan University

Florida
Daytona Beach Community College
Florida Institute of Technology
Florida Southern College
Hillsborough Community College
Jacksonville University
Rollins College
Tallahassee Community College
University of South Florida
University of West Florida

Georgia
Agnes Scott College
Albany State University
Armstrong Atlantic State University
Clark Atlanta University
Columbus State University
Covenant College
Emory University
Georgia Institute of Technology
Georgia Southwestern State University
LaGrange College
Oxford College of Emory University
Paine College
Southern Polytechnic State University
Waycross College

Idaho
Albertson College of Idaho
Northwest Nazarene University

Illinois
Augustana College
Barat College
Benedictine University
Blackburn College
City Colleges of Chicago
　　Harold Washington College
　　Harry S. Truman College
Dominican University
Eastern Illinois University
Elmhurst College
Greenville College
Illinois Wesleyan University
Knox College
Lake Forest College
MacMurray College
McHenry County College
Monmouth College
Olivet Nazarene University
Principia College
Quincy University
University of Illinois
　　Urbana-Champaign
University of St. Francis
Wheaton College

Indiana
Anderson University
Butler University
Earlham College
Goshen College
Indiana Institute of Technology
Manchester College
St. Joseph's College
Wabash College

Iowa
Briar Cliff College
Buena Vista University
Clarke College
Coe College
Dordt College
Drake University
Grand View College
Luther College
North Iowa Area Community College
St. Ambrose University
University of Northern Iowa
Wartburg College
William Penn University

Kansas
Allen County Community College
Baker University
Bethany College
Bethel College
Butler County Community College
Central Christian College
Colby Community College
Emporia State University
Kansas State University
Pittsburg State University
Southwestern College
Wichita State University

Kentucky
Asbury College
Berea College
Brescia University
Centre College
Georgetown College
Murray State University
Transylvania University

Louisiana
Centenary College of Louisiana
Dillard University
Grantham College of Engineering
Louisiana Tech University
Southern University and Agricultural and
　　Mechanical College
Tulane University
University of Louisiana at Lafayette

Maine
Bates College
Bowdoin College
Maine Maritime Academy
University of Maine
University of Southern Maine

Maryland
Allegany College
Baltimore City Community College
Bowie State University
College of Notre Dame of Maryland
Columbia Union College
Community College of Baltimore County
　　Essex
Coppin State College
Frederick Community College
Frostburg State University
Goucher College
Hagerstown Community College
Harford Community College
Hood College
Howard Community College
Johns Hopkins University
Morgan State University
Towson University
University of Maryland
　　Baltimore County
Western Maryland College

Massachusetts
Assumption College
Boston College
Boston University
College of the Holy Cross
Framingham State College
Franklin Institute of Boston
Massachusetts Maritime Academy
Mount Holyoke College
Regis College
Stonehill College
Suffolk University
Tufts University
Wellesley College

Michigan
Adrian College
Albion College
Alma College
Delta College
Glen Oaks Community College
Hope College
Kellogg Community College
Lawrence Technological University
Michigan Technological University
Olivet College
University of Michigan
Wayne State University

Minnesota
Augsburg College
Carleton College
Central Lakes College
Century Community and Technical
　　College
College of St. Benedict
Gustavus Adolphus College
Macalester College
Minnesota State University, Mankato
Northwestern College
St. Cloud State University
St. John's University
St. Olaf College

Mississippi
Hinds Community College
Millsaps College
Mississippi State University
Mississippi University for Women

Missouri
Central Missouri State University
College of the Ozarks
Culver-Stockton College
Drury University
East Central College
Fontbonne College
Jefferson College
Lindenwood University
Maryville University of Saint Louis
Missouri Baptist College
Missouri Southern State College
Northwest Missouri State University
Southwest Baptist University
St. Louis Community College
　　St. Louis Community College at
　　　　Forest Park
University of Missouri
　　Rolla
　　St. Louis
Washington University
William Jewell College

Montana
Carroll College
University of Great Falls

Nebraska
Dana College

New Hampshire
Daniel Webster College
Keene State College
St. Anselm College

New Jersey
Camden County College
County College of Morris
Fairleigh Dickinson University
Mercer County Community College
New Jersey Institute of Technology
Ocean County College
Passaic County Community College
Richard Stockton College of New Jersey
Rowan University
Rutgers
　　The State University of New Jersey:
　　　　Camden College of Arts and
　　　　Sciences
　　The State University of New Jersey:
　　　　College of Engineering
　　The State University of New Jersey:
　　　　Cook College
　　The State University of New Jersey:
　　　　Douglass College
　　The State University of New Jersey:
　　　　Livingston College
　　The State University of New Jersey:
　　　　Newark College of Arts and
　　　　Sciences
　　The State University of New Jersey:
　　　　Rutgers College
Union County College

Combined liberal arts/career program in engineering

New Mexico
Eastern New Mexico University
    Roswell Campus
New Mexico State University
    Alamogordo
San Juan College

New York
Alfred University
Bard College
City University of New York
    Brooklyn College
    College of Staten Island
Clarkson University
Colgate University
College of Mount St. Vincent
College of St. Rose
Elmira College
Erie Community College
    City Campus
    North Campus
    South Campus
Hamilton College
Hartwick College
Hobart and William Smith Colleges
Houghton College
Ithaca College
Jamestown Community College
Le Moyne College
Mohawk Valley Community College
New York Institute of Technology
New York State College of Ceramics at
    Alfred University
New York University
Onondaga Community College
Pace University
Pace University: Pleasantville/Briarcliff
Russell Sage College
St. Bonaventure University
St. John Fisher College
St. John's University
St. Thomas Aquinas College
Siena College
Skidmore College
State University of New York
    Binghamton
    College at Brockport
    College at Buffalo
    College at Cortland
    College at Geneseo
    College at Potsdam
    College of Technology at Alfred
    Maritime College
    Oswego
Syracuse University
Union College
University of Rochester

North Carolina
Beaufort County Community College
Bennett College
Coastal Carolina Community College
College of the Albemarle
Elon College
Lenoir Community College
Methodist College
North Carolina State University
Pfeiffer University
St. Augustine's College
University of North Carolina
    Asheville
    Greensboro
Warren Wilson College
Wilson Technical Community College

North Dakota
Jamestown College
North Dakota State University
University of North Dakota
Valley City State University

Ohio
Ashland University
Case Western Reserve University
Cedarville College
Clark State Community College
Cleveland State University
Columbus State Community College
Denison University
Franciscan University of Steubenville
Heidelberg College
Kent State University
    Ashtabula Regional Campus
Lake Erie College
Lima Technical College
Miami University
    Middletown Campus
Muskingum College
Ohio Northern University
Ohio State University
    Columbus Campus
Ohio Wesleyan University
Otterbein College
Southern State Community College
University of Akron
    Wayne College
Walsh University

Oklahoma
Carl Albert State College
Oklahoma Baptist University
Oral Roberts University

Oregon
Eastern Oregon University
George Fox University
Lewis & Clark College
Linfield College
Pacific University
Reed College
Southern Oregon University

Pennsylvania
Allegheny College
Beaver College
Bloomsburg University of Pennsylvania
Bryn Mawr College
Bucknell University
California University of Pennsylvania
Cedar Crest College
Chatham College
Clarion University of Pennsylvania
Duquesne University
Edinboro University of Pennsylvania
Elizabethtown College
Franklin and Marshall College
Geneva College
Gettysburg College
Haverford College
Lafayette College
Lebanon Valley College of Pennsylvania
Lehigh University
Lock Haven University of Pennsylvania
Mansfield University of Pennsylvania
Millersville University of Pennsylvania
Moravian College
Muhlenberg College
Philadelphia University
Point Park College
Rosemont College
St. Francis College
St. Vincent College
Slippery Rock University of
    Pennsylvania
Susquehanna University
Swarthmore College
Temple University
Thiel College
University of Pittsburgh
University of Pittsburgh
    Johnstown
Waynesburg College
Widener University

Puerto Rico
Inter American University of Puerto Rico
    Barranquitas Campus
    Bayamon Campus
Turabo University
University of Puerto Rico
    Aguadilla
University of the Sacred Heart

Rhode Island
University of Rhode Island

South Carolina
College of Charleston
Erskine College
Florence-Darlington Technical College
Furman University
Lander University
Newberry College
Presbyterian College
Voorhees College
Winthrop University
Wofford College

Tennessee
Bethel College
Christian Brothers University
Freed-Hardeman University
King College
Lane College
LeMoyne-Owen College
Lincoln Memorial University
Maryville College
Tennessee Technological University
Union University
University of Tennessee
    Knoxville
University of the South
Volunteer State Community College
Walters State Community College

Texas
Austin College
Coastal Bend College
Huston-Tillotson College
Jarvis Christian College
McMurry University
Midwestern State University
Paul Quinn College
Rice University
St. Mary's University
Sam Houston State University
Schreiner College
Southwestern Adventist University
Southwestern University
Texas A&M University
    Commerce
Texas Lutheran University
Texas Tech University
Texas Wesleyan University
Trinity University
University of Dallas

Utah
Westminster College

Vermont
Castleton State College
Norwich University
St. Michael's College

Virginia
Eastern Mennonite University
Emory & Henry College
Longwood College
Mary Baldwin College
Randolph-Macon College
Roanoke College
Virginia Commonwealth University
Virginia Polytechnic Institute and State
    University
Washington and Lee University

Washington
Big Bend Community College
Everett Community College
Gonzaga University
Lower Columbia College
Pacific Lutheran University
Peninsula College
St. Martin's College
University of Puget Sound
University of Washington
Walla Walla College
Walla Walla Community College
Washington State University
Whitman College

West Virginia
Bethany College
West Virginia University Institute of
    Technology
Wheeling Jesuit University

Wisconsin
Carthage College
Lawrence University
University of Wisconsin
    La Crosse
    Parkside
    Superior

Wyoming
Northwest College

Combined liberal arts/career program in environmental studies

Alabama
Birmingham-Southern College
Northwest-Shoals Community College
Samford University
University of Mobile

Alaska
Alaska Pacific University
University of Alaska
    Southeast

Arizona
Northern Arizona University

Arkansas
University of Central Arkansas
University of the Ozarks

California
California State University
    Chico
    Hayward
    Monterey Bay
    Sacramento
    Stanislaus
Chaffey Community College
Chapman University
Dominican University of California
Hope International University
Occidental College
Pitzer College
San Francisco State University
Sonoma State University
United States International University
University of La Verne
University of Redlands
Westmont College
Whittier College

Colorado
Colorado Mountain College
    Spring Valley Campus
    Timberline Campus
Fort Lewis College
Metropolitan State College of Denver
Western State College of Colorado

Connecticut
Briarwood College

Combined liberal arts/career program in environmental studies

Sacred Heart University
Teikyo Post University
United States Coast Guard Academy

Delaware
Wesley College

Florida
Florida Institute of Technology
Florida Southern College
Hillsborough Community College
Rollins College
St. Leo University
Stetson University
Tallahassee Community College
University of South Florida
University of West Florida

Georgia
Georgia Institute of Technology
Waycross College

Idaho
University of Idaho

Illinois
Augustana College
Benedictine University
Dominican University
Illinois State University
Illinois Wesleyan University
Monmouth College
Olivet Nazarene University
University of Illinois
    Springfield
University of St. Francis

Indiana
Goshen College
Marian College
St. Joseph's College
University of St. Francis

Iowa
Central College
Dordt College
Iowa State University
Marycrest International University
Northwestern College
St. Ambrose University
Simpson College
University of Dubuque
Upper Iowa University

Kansas
Kansas State University
McPherson College
Tabor College
Wichita State University

Kentucky
Midway College
Murray State University

Louisiana
Centenary College of Louisiana
Louisiana Tech University
Southern University and Agricultural and
    Mechanical College
Tulane University

Maine
St. Joseph's College
Unity College
University of Maine
University of Maine
    Fort Kent
University of Southern Maine

Maryland
Frostburg State University
Harford Community College

Howard Community College
Johns Hopkins University
Towson University
University of Maryland
    Baltimore County

Massachusetts
Anna Maria College
Curry College
Framingham State College
Greenfield Community College
Massachusetts Maritime Academy
Mount Holyoke College
Simmons College
Wellesley College

Michigan
Adrian College
Alma College
Baker College
    of Owosso
Delta College
Glen Oaks Community College
Lawrence Technological University
Mid Michigan Community College
University of Michigan

Minnesota
Bemidji State University
Gustavus Adolphus College
Minnesota State University, Mankato
St. Cloud State University
St. Olaf College

Mississippi
Hinds Community College
Mississippi State University
Mississippi Valley State University

Missouri
Columbia College
Drury University
Mineral Area College
Northwest Missouri State University
Stephens College
University of Missouri
    Rolla
Washington University
Westminster College

Montana
Carroll College
Rocky Mountain College
University of Montana-Missoula

Nebraska
Dana College
Midland Lutheran College
Southeast Community College
    Lincoln Campus

New Hampshire
Colby-Sawyer College
Franklin Pierce College
Keene State College
New England College

New Jersey
Bloomfield College
Caldwell College
Fairleigh Dickinson University
Kean University
Richard Stockton College of New Jersey
Rowan University
Thomas Edison State College
Warren County Community College

New Mexico
College of Santa Fe

New York
Alfred University

City University of New York
    College of Staten Island
    Queens College
College of St. Rose
Erie Community College
    City Campus
    North Campus
    South Campus
Hartwick College
Herkimer County Community College
Le Moyne College
Marist College
Molloy College
New York Institute of Technology
New York State College of Ceramics at
    Alfred University
St. John Fisher College
Siena College
Skidmore College
State University of New York
    Binghamton
    College at Brockport
    College at Cortland
    College at Plattsburgh
    College at Potsdam
    College of Agriculture and
       Technology at Cobleskill
    Maritime College
    New Paltz
    Purchase
Tompkins-Cortland Community College

North Carolina
Beaufort County Community College
Elon College
Lenoir Community College
North Carolina State University
Pfeiffer University
Queens College
University of North Carolina
    Asheville
    Chapel Hill

North Dakota
North Dakota State University
University of North Dakota

Ohio
Antioch College
Ashland University
Baldwin-Wallace College
Capital University
Cedarville College
Columbus State Community College
Defiance College
Denison University
Kent State University
    Ashtabula Regional Campus
    Stark Campus
Muskingum College
Ohio Northern University
Ohio State University
    Columbus Campus
Ohio Wesleyan University
Otterbein College
Wittenberg University

Oklahoma
Southern Nazarene University

Oregon
Concordia University
Eastern Oregon University
Pacific University
Southern Oregon University

Pennsylvania
Allentown College of St. Francis de Sales
Beaver College
Bucknell University
Cedar Crest College
Chatham College
Delaware Valley College

Dickinson College
Edinboro University of Pennsylvania
Elizabethtown College
Franklin and Marshall College
Gettysburg College
Immaculata College
Lafayette College
Lehigh University
Lock Haven University of Pennsylvania
Lycoming College
Philadelphia University
Rosemont College
Susquehanna University
Temple University
University of Pittsburgh
    Greensburg
    Johnstown

Puerto Rico
Inter American University of Puerto Rico
    Barranquitas Campus
Universidad Metropolitana
University of Puerto Rico
    Rio Piedras Campus

Rhode Island
Salve Regina University

South Carolina
Lander University
Midlands Technical College
Newberry College
Presbyterian College

Tennessee
Lincoln Memorial University
Tennessee Technological University
University of Tennessee
    Knoxville

Texas
Coastal Bend College
Concordia University at Austin
Houston Community College System
McMurry University
Midland College
Midwestern State University
Rice University
Sam Houston State University
Texas Lutheran University
University of St. Thomas
University of the Incarnate Word

Utah
Utah Valley State College
Westminster College

Vermont
Castleton State College
Green Mountain College
Norwich University
St. Michael's College
Southern Vermont College
Sterling College

Virginia
University of Virginia's College at Wise
Virginia Polytechnic Institute and State
    University

Washington
Everett Community College
Gonzaga University
North Seattle Community College
Pacific Lutheran University
University of Washington
Walla Walla College
Washington State University
Whitman College

West Virginia
College of West Virginia

Combined liberal arts/career program in environmental studies

Glenville State College
Shepherd College
University of Charleston
Wheeling Jesuit University

Wisconsin
Alverno College
Carroll College
Lawrence University
University of Wisconsin
   Green Bay
   Parkside

Combined liberal arts/career program in forestry

Alabama
Birmingham-Southern College
Chattahoochee Valley Community
   College
Northwest-Shoals Community College

Arkansas
Garland County Community College
University of Arkansas
   Monticello

California
Chaffey Community College
Columbia College
Modesto Junior College
Mount San Antonio College

Colorado
Fort Lewis College
Western State College of Colorado

Florida
Florida Southern College
Rollins College
Stetson University
Tallahassee Community College

Georgia
Waycross College

Idaho
Albertson College of Idaho

Illinois
Augustana College
Illinois Wesleyan University

Indiana
Butler University

Iowa
Iowa Wesleyan College
University of Dubuque

Kansas
Baker University
Colby Community College
Kansas State University
Manhattan Christian College
Pittsburg State University

Louisiana
Louisiana Tech University
Southern University and Agricultural and
   Mechanical College

Maine
Unity College
University of Maine
University of Maine
   Fort Kent

Maryland
Allegany College
Western Maryland College

Michigan
Delta College
Michigan Technological University
University of Michigan

Minnesota
Central Lakes College

Mississippi
Hinds Community College
Mississippi State University

Missouri
East Central College
William Jewell College

Montana
University of Montana-Missoula

New York
Clinton Community College
Erie Community College
   City Campus
   North Campus
   South Campus
Fulton-Montgomery Community College
Herkimer County Community College
Jamestown Community College
Le Moyne College
Mohawk Valley Community College
St. John Fisher College
Siena College
State University of New York
   College at Cortland
   College at Geneseo
   College at Oneonta
   College of Agriculture and
      Technology at Cobleskill
   College of Agriculture and
      Technology at Morrisville
   College of Technology at Alfred
   New Paltz

North Carolina
Catawba College
High Point University
Lees-McRae College
Mayland Community College
North Carolina State University
University of North Carolina
   Asheville
Warren Wilson College

North Dakota
North Dakota State University

Ohio
Baldwin-Wallace College
Denison University
Ohio State University
   Columbus Campus
Wittenberg University

Oklahoma
Western Oklahoma State College

Oregon
Eastern Oregon University
Reed College

Pennsylvania
Allegheny College
Elizabethtown College
Franklin and Marshall College
Gettysburg College
Lycoming College
Moravian College
Muhlenberg College
St. Francis College
Susquehanna University
Thiel College

South Carolina
Newberry College
Presbyterian College

Tennessee
University of Tennessee
   Knoxville

Texas
Baylor University

Vermont
Sterling College

Virginia
Bridgewater College
Emory & Henry College
Randolph-Macon College
Virginia Polytechnic Institute and State
   University
Washington and Lee University

Washington
Peninsula College
University of Washington
Washington State University
Whitman College

West Virginia
Glenville State College

Wisconsin
Beloit College
Lawrence University
University of Wisconsin
   Platteville

Combined liberal arts/career program in medical technology

Arkansas
Garland County Community College
University of Arkansas
University of Central Arkansas

California
California State University
   Chico
Chaffey Community College
Columbia College
Cypress College
Diablo Valley College
Heald Business College
   Santa Rosa
Long Beach City College
Modesto Junior College
Pacific Union College
Sonoma State University

Colorado
Community College of Denver
Pueblo Community College

Connecticut
Quinnipiac University
University of Bridgeport

Delaware
Wesley College

Florida
University of West Florida

Georgia
Georgia Perimeter College
Waycross College

Illinois
Benedictine University
Danville Area Community College
Dominican University
Eastern Illinois University
Illinois State University
McKendree College
Monmouth College

Indiana
Goshen College
St. Joseph's College
University of St. Francis

Iowa
Dordt College
Iowa Wesleyan College
Morningside College
Northwestern College
University of Northern Iowa
Wartburg College

Kansas
Allen County Community College
Coffeyville Community College
Tabor College
Wichita State University

Kentucky
Henderson Community College
Murray State University
Pikeville College

Maryland
Howard Community College
University of Maryland
   College Park

Massachusetts
Massachusetts College of Liberal Arts

Michigan
Glen Oaks Community College

Minnesota
College of St. Scholastica
Minnesota State University, Mankato

Mississippi
Mississippi State University
University of Mississippi
   Medical Center

Missouri
Avila College
Central Missouri State University
Culver-Stockton College
East Central College
Mineral Area College
St. Louis Community College
   St. Louis Community College at
      Forest Park
William Jewell College

Nebraska
Dana College

New Jersey
Atlantic Cape Community College
Bloomfield College
Caldwell College
County College of Morris
Passaic County Community College

New Mexico
New Mexico State University
   Alamogordo
San Juan College

New York
College of St. Rose
Genesee Community College
Mount St. Mary College
New York Institute of Technology
State University of New York
 College at Brockport
 College at Oneonta
 Oswego

North Carolina
Belmont Abbey College
College of the Albemarle
Elon College
Greensboro College
High Point University
Lees-McRae College
Lenoir Community College
Peace College

North Dakota
University of North Dakota

Ohio
Ashland University
College of Mount St. Joseph
Columbus State Community College

Oklahoma
Cameron University
Oklahoma Panhandle State University

Oregon
Eastern Oregon University
Lane Community College

Pennsylvania
Allentown College of St. Francis de Sales
Cedar Crest College
Geneva College
Gwynedd-Mercy College
La Roche College
Lebanon Valley College of Pennsylvania
Lock Haven University of Pennsylvania
Moravian College
St. Francis College
Seton Hill College
University of the Sciences in
 Philadelphia
Waynesburg College

Puerto Rico
University of Puerto Rico
 Aguadilla
 Arecibo Campus
University of the Sacred Heart

Rhode Island
Salve Regina University

South Carolina
Anderson College
Columbia International University
Florence-Darlington Technical College
Newberry College
Orangeburg-Calhoun Technical College
Southern Wesleyan University

South Dakota
South Dakota School of Mines and
 Technology

Tennessee
David Lipscomb University
Lincoln Memorial University
Roane State Community College
University of Tennessee
 Knoxville

Texas
Sam Houston State University
Southwestern Adventist University

Vermont
Norwich University

Virginia
Northern Virginia Community College
University of Virginia's College at Wise

Washington
Pacific Lutheran University
University of Washington

West Virginia
Concord College

Wisconsin
Beloit College
Carroll College

Combined liberal arts/career program in natural resource management

Alaska
Alaska Pacific University

California
California State University
 Chico
Chaffey Community College
Columbia College
Modesto Junior College
Mount San Antonio College
San Joaquin Delta College
San Joaquin Valley College Inc.
Santa Rosa Junior College

Colorado
Colorado Mountain College
 Timberline Campus
Trinidad State Junior College
Western State College of Colorado

Florida
Florida Institute of Technology
Rollins College

Georgia
Reinhardt College
Waycross College

Idaho
Albertson College of Idaho

Iowa
Luther College
Northwestern College
Upper Iowa University

Kansas
Kansas State University
Manhattan Christian College

Kentucky
Murray State University

Louisiana
Louisiana Tech University

Maine
Unity College
University of Maine

Massachusetts
Gordon College
Greenfield Community College

Michigan
University of Michigan

Minnesota
Central Lakes College
Minnesota State University, Mankato

Mississippi
Hinds Community College

Missouri
Northwest Missouri State University
William Jewell College

Montana
University of Montana-Missoula

New Hampshire
Franklin Pierce College

New Jersey
Mercer County Community College
Richard Stockton College of New Jersey
Rowan University

New York
Erie Community College
 City Campus
 North Campus
 South Campus
Iona College
Jamestown Community College

North Carolina
Lenoir Community College
North Carolina State University
University of North Carolina
 Asheville

North Dakota
North Dakota State University

Ohio
Denison University
Muskingum College
Ohio State University
 Columbus Campus
University of Akron
 Wayne College

Oklahoma
Cameron University

Oregon
Eastern Oregon University

Pennsylvania
Delaware Valley College
Edinboro University of Pennsylvania
Elizabethtown College
Gettysburg College
Moravian College

Puerto Rico
University of Puerto Rico
 Rio Piedras Campus

South Carolina
Newberry College

Tennessee
Tennessee Technological University
University of Memphis
University of Tennessee
 Knoxville
Volunteer State Community College

Texas
Coastal Bend College

Vermont
Sterling College

Virginia
Virginia Polytechnic Institute and State
 University

Washington
Everett Community College
University of Washington
Washington State University

Wisconsin
Northland College

Combined liberal arts/career program in nursing

Alabama
Birmingham-Southern College
Calhoun Community College
Chattahoochee Valley Community
 College
Jacksonville State University
Northwest-Shoals Community College
Samford University
Shelton State Community College
University of Mobile

Alaska
University of Alaska
 Southeast

Arizona
Gateway Community College
Mohave Community College
Phoenix College

Arkansas
Garland County Community College
Harding University
Northwest Arkansas Community College
University of Arkansas
University of Arkansas
 Monticello
 Pine Bluff
University of Central Arkansas

California
Biola University
California State University
 Chico
 Hayward
 Sacramento
 Stanislaus
Chabot College
Chaffey Community College
City College of San Francisco
Cypress College
Dominican University of California
Holy Names College
Imperial Valley College
Loma Linda University
Long Beach City College
Modesto Junior College
Ohlone College
Pacific Union College
Pasadena City College
St. Mary's College of California
San Diego City College
San Francisco State University
San Joaquin Delta College
San Joaquin Valley College Inc.
Santa Rosa Junior College
Sonoma State University

Colorado
Community College of Denver
Metropolitan State College of Denver
Morgan Community College
Pueblo Community College
Trinidad State Junior College

Combined liberal arts/career program in nursing

University of Colorado
    Health Sciences Center

Connecticut
Quinnipiac University
Sacred Heart University
St. Joseph College

Florida
Daytona Beach Community College
Edison Community College
Florida Southern College
Hillsborough Community College
South College: Palm Beach Campus
Tallahassee Community College
University of South Florida
University of Tampa
University of West Florida

Georgia
Armstrong Atlantic State University
Covenant College
Emory University
Georgia Baptist College of Nursing
Georgia Southwestern State University
LaGrange College
Macon State College
Paine College
Waycross College

Idaho
North Idaho College

Illinois
Benedictine University
Black Hawk College
Blackburn College
City Colleges of Chicago
    Harold Washington College
    Harry S. Truman College
Danville Area Community College
Dominican University
Greenville College
Illinois State University
Illinois Wesleyan University
Knox College
Lewis University
MacMurray College
Monmouth College
Moraine Valley Community College
Olivet Nazarene University
St. Xavier University
University of St. Francis
Wheaton College

Indiana
Earlham College
Franklin College
Goshen College
Indiana Wesleyan University
Marian College
St. Joseph's College
University of St. Francis
University of Southern Indiana

Iowa
Briar Cliff College
Graceland University
Grand View College
Marycrest International University
Morningside College
North Iowa Area Community College
Northwestern College
St. Ambrose University
Southeastern Community College
    South Campus
Southwestern Community College
University of Northern Iowa
Wartburg College

Kansas
Allen County Community College
Baker University
Butler County Community College
Central Christian College
Colby Community College
Hesston College
Kansas State University
Pittsburg State University
Wichita State University

Kentucky
Asbury College
Bellarmine College
Elizabethtown Community College
Georgetown College
Henderson Community College
Midway College
Murray State University
Pikeville College
Southeast Community College
Thomas More College

Louisiana
Dillard University
Louisiana State University
    Eunice
Louisiana Tech University
Southern University and Agricultural and Mechanical College
University of Louisiana at Lafayette

Maine
Central Maine Medical Center School of Nursing
St. Joseph's College
University of Maine
University of Maine
    Fort Kent
University of Southern Maine

Maryland
Allegany College
Baltimore City Community College
College of Notre Dame of Maryland
Community College of Baltimore County Essex
Coppin State College
Frederick Community College
Hagerstown Community College
Harford Community College
Howard Community College
Johns Hopkins University
Mount St. Mary's College
Prince George's Community College
Towson University
University of Maryland
    College Park
Wor-Wic Community College

Massachusetts
Becker College
Curry College
Gordon College
Labouré College
Massachusetts College of Pharmacy and Health Sciences
Mount Holyoke College
Regis College
Simmons College

Michigan
Albion College
Bay de Noc Community College
Delta College
Glen Oaks Community College
Hope College
Jackson Community College
Kellogg Community College
Mid Michigan Community College

Minnesota
Bemidji State University
Central Lakes College
Century Community and Technical College
College of St. Catherine: St. Paul Campus
College of St. Scholastica
Concordia College: Moorhead
Gustavus Adolphus College
Macalester College
Minnesota Bible College
Minnesota State University, Mankato
North Central University
St. Olaf College

Mississippi
Hinds Community College
University of Mississippi
    Medical Center

Missouri
Avila College
Central Missouri State University
College of the Ozarks
Columbia College
Culver-Stockton College
East Central College
Fontbonne College
Jefferson College
Mineral Area College
Missouri Baptist College
Northwest Missouri State University
Rockhurst University
St. Louis Community College
    St. Louis Community College at Forest Park
Three Rivers Community College
William Jewell College

Montana
Carroll College
University of Great Falls
University of Montana-Missoula

Nebraska
Clarkson College
Creighton University
Mid Plains Community College Area
Midland Lutheran College
Northeast Community College
Southeast Community College
    Lincoln Campus

New Hampshire
Colby-Sawyer College

New Jersey
Atlantic Cape Community College
Bloomfield College
Camden County College
College of St. Elizabeth
County College of Morris
Fairleigh Dickinson University
Kean University
Mercer County Community College
New Jersey City University
Ocean County College
Passaic County Community College
Richard Stockton College of New Jersey
Union County College
Warren County Community College

New Mexico
Eastern New Mexico University
    Roswell Campus
New Mexico State University
    Alamogordo
San Juan College

New York
City University of New York
    College of Staten Island
    Medgar Evers College
Clinton Community College
Cochran School of Nursing-St. John's Riverside Hospital
Concordia College
D'Youville College
Dominican College of Blauvelt
Erie Community College
    City Campus
    North Campus
    South Campus
Hartwick College
Herkimer County Community College
Jamestown Community College
Juilliard School
Keuka College
Manhattanville College
Mohawk Valley Community College
Molloy College
Nazareth College of Rochester
New York Institute of Technology
New York University
Phillips Beth Israel School of Nursing
Roberts Wesleyan College
Russell Sage College
St. John Fisher College
St. Joseph's Hospital Health Center
    School of Nursing
State University of New York
    Binghamton
    College at Brockport
    College at Oneonta
    College at Plattsburgh
    College of Technology at Alfred
    Institute of Technology at Utica/Rome
Tompkins-Cortland Community College
University of Rochester
Utica College of Syracuse University
Wagner College
Westchester Community College

North Carolina
Beaufort County Community College
Bennett College
Bladen Community College
Carteret Community College
Cleveland Community College
Coastal Carolina Community College
College of the Albemarle
Gardner-Webb University
Lenoir Community College
Nash Community College
Peace College
Queens College
Randolph Community College
Sampson Community College
Sandhills Community College
Southeastern Community College
University of North Carolina
    Asheville
    Chapel Hill
Wilson Technical Community College

North Dakota
North Dakota State University
University of North Dakota
Valley City State University

Ohio
Bowling Green State University
    Firelands College
Capital University
Cedarville College
Circleville Bible College
Cleveland State University
College of Mount St. Joseph
Columbus State Community College
Heidelberg College
Kent State University
    Ashtabula Regional Campus
    Stark Campus
Lima Technical College
Lourdes College
Miami University
    Middletown Campus
Mount Vernon Nazarene College
Muskingum College

Ohio State University
    Columbus Campus
Otterbein College
Southern State Community College
University of Findlay
Walsh University
Wittenberg University

Oklahoma
Cameron University
Carl Albert State College
Oklahoma Panhandle State University
Oral Roberts University
Redlands Community College
Southern Nazarene University
Southwestern Oklahoma State University
Western Oklahoma State College

Oregon
Clackamas Community College
Eastern Oregon University
Lane Community College
Southern Oregon University

Pennsylvania
Allegheny College
Allentown College of St. Francis de Sales
Beaver College
Cabrini College
California University of Pennsylvania
Cedar Crest College
Clarion University of Pennsylvania
Community College of Allegheny
    County
Edinboro University of Pennsylvania
Elizabethtown College
Geneva College
Gettysburg College
Gwynedd-Mercy College
Immaculata College
La Roche College
Lebanon Valley College of Pennsylvania
Lock Haven University of Pennsylvania
Moravian College
Rosemont College
Seton Hill College
Temple University
Thiel College

Puerto Rico
Inter American University of Puerto Rico
    Barranquitas Campus
Universidad Metropolitana
University of Puerto Rico
    Aguadilla
University of the Sacred Heart

Rhode Island
Salve Regina University

South Carolina
Chesterfield-Marlboro Technical College
Columbia International University
Florence-Darlington Technical College
Lander University
Midlands Technical College
Newberry College
Orangeburg-Calhoun Technical College
Voorhees College
Wofford College

South Dakota
South Dakota School of Mines and
    Technology
University of South Dakota

Tennessee
Bethel College
Cumberland University
Dyersburg State Community College
Fisk University
King College
LeMoyne-Owen College

Lincoln Memorial University
Maryville College
Roane State Community College
Shelby State Community College
Tennessee Technological University
Tennessee Wesleyan College
Union University
University of Memphis
University of Tennessee
    Knoxville
Volunteer State Community College
Walters State Community College

Texas
Blinn College
Central Texas College
Coastal Bend College
Collin County Community College
    District
Hardin-Simmons University
Houston Community College System
Jarvis Christian College
McMurry University
Midland College
Midwestern State University
South Plains College
Southwestern Adventist University
Texas A&M International University
Texas State Technical College
    Harlingen
Trinity Valley Community College
University of the Incarnate Word

Utah
Utah Valley State College
Westminster College

Vermont
Castleton State College
Norwich University
Southern Vermont College

Virginia
Liberty University
Mary Baldwin College
Randolph-Macon Woman's College
University of Virginia's College at Wise
Virginia Commonwealth University

Washington
Big Bend Community College
Clark College
Everett Community College
Gonzaga University
Lower Columbia College
North Seattle Community College
Pacific Lutheran University
Peninsula College
University of Washington
Walla Walla College
Walla Walla Community College
Washington State University

West Virginia
Fairmont State College
Glenville State College
Shepherd College
University of Charleston
West Virginia University Institute of
    Technology
Wheeling Jesuit University

Wisconsin
Alverno College
Beloit College
Carroll College
Milwaukee Area Technical College
University of Wisconsin
    Green Bay
    Parkside
    Platteville
Viterbo University

Wyoming
Northwest College

Combined liberal arts/career program in occupational therapy

Alabama
Alabama State University
Community College of the Air Force
Northwest-Shoals Community College

Arizona
Gateway Community College

Arkansas
Garland County Community College
University of Arkansas
University of Central Arkansas

California
Dominican University of California
Loma Linda University

Colorado
Pueblo Community College

Connecticut
Briarwood College
Quinnipiac University
Sacred Heart University

Florida
Daytona Beach Community College
Hillsborough Community College
Tallahassee Community College

Georgia
Columbus State University

Illinois
Augustana College
MacMurray College
McKendree College
Monmouth College
Moraine Valley Community College

Indiana
Franklin College
University of St. Francis
University of Southern Indiana

Iowa
Dordt College
St. Ambrose University
Wartburg College

Kansas
Allen County Community College
Kansas State University
Manhattan Christian College

Kentucky
Murray State University

Louisiana
Centenary College of Louisiana
Dillard University

Maryland
Allegany College
Towson University

Massachusetts
Becker College
Boston University
Gordon College

Michigan
Alma College
Baker College
    of Muskegon

Minnesota
College of St. Catherine: St. Paul
    Campus
College of St. Scholastica
Gustavus Adolphus College

Mississippi
Hinds Community College
University of Mississippi
    Medical Center

Missouri
Culver-Stockton College
Drury University
Northwest Missouri State University
St. Louis Community College
    St. Louis Community College at
        Forest Park
Stephens College
Washington University
William Jewell College

Montana
Rocky Mountain College

Nebraska
Clarkson College
Creighton University
Dana College

New Hampshire
Keene State College
New England College

New Jersey
Atlantic Cape Community College
Kean University
Seton Hall University
Union County College

New Mexico
Eastern New Mexico University
    Roswell Campus

New York
College of Mount St. Vincent
D'Youville College
Dominican College of Blauvelt
Erie Community College
    City Campus
    North Campus
    South Campus
Jamestown Community College
Juilliard School
Keuka College
Marymount College
New York Institute of Technology
Russell Sage College
St. Francis College
State University of New York
    College of Agriculture and
        Technology at Cobleskill
    College of Technology at Canton
Touro College
Utica College of Syracuse University

North Carolina
University of North Carolina
    Chapel Hill

North Dakota
University of North Dakota
Valley City State University

Ohio
Cleveland State University
Denison University

Combined liberal arts/career program in occupational therapy

Lima Technical College
Lourdes College
Ohio State University
    Columbus Campus
Ohio Wesleyan University
Wittenberg University

Oregon
Pacific University
Southern Oregon University

Pennsylvania
Allegheny College
Cabrini College
Elizabethtown College
Lebanon Valley College of Pennsylvania
Moravian College
St. Vincent College
Temple University
Tri-State Business Institute
University of Scranton
University of the Sciences in
    Philadelphia

Puerto Rico
University of Puerto Rico
    Aguadilla
    Arecibo Campus

South Carolina
Florence-Darlington Technical College
Newberry College
Tri-County Technical College

South Dakota
University of South Dakota

Tennessee
Bethel College
King College
Union University
University of Tennessee
    Knoxville

Texas
Coastal Bend College
Houston Community College System

Vermont
Champlain College

Virginia
Liberty University
Longwood College
Virginia Commonwealth University

Washington
University of Washington

Wisconsin
Carthage College
Lawrence University
Mount Mary College
University of Wisconsin
    La Crosse
    Platteville

Combined liberal arts/career program in pharmacy

Alabama
Community College of the Air Force

Arkansas
University of Arkansas

California
Chaffey Community College

Colorado
Trinidad State Junior College

Illinois
Benedictine University

Indiana
Goshen College

Iowa
Dordt College
Wartburg College

Kansas
Allen County Community College

Maryland
Coppin State College
Howard Community College
University of Maryland
    College Park

Massachusetts
Massachusetts College of Pharmacy and
    Health Sciences
Simmons College
Western New England College

Michigan
Baker College
    of Muskegon
Kellogg Community College

Minnesota
Century Community and Technical
    College

Montana
University of Great Falls
University of Montana-Missoula

Nebraska
Creighton University

New Jersey
County College of Morris

North Dakota
Valley City State University

Ohio
Ohio Northern University

Oklahoma
Carl Albert State College

Oregon
Southern Oregon University

Pennsylvania
Cabrini College
Temple University
University of the Sciences in
    Philadelphia

Puerto Rico
Colegio Universitario del Este
University of Puerto Rico
    Aguadilla
    Arecibo Campus

South Carolina
Columbia International University
Florence-Darlington Technical College
Newberry College
Voorhees College

Tennessee
Draughons Junior College of Business:
    Nashville

King College
Lambuth University
University of Tennessee
    Knoxville

Virginia
Northern Virginia Community College

Washington
University of Washington
Washington State University

Combined liberal arts/career program in physical therapy

Alabama
Alabama State University
Birmingham-Southern College
Northwest-Shoals Community College

Arizona
Gateway Community College

Arkansas
Harding University
Northwest Arkansas Community College
University of Arkansas
University of Central Arkansas

California
Biola University
Chaffey Community College
Chapman University
Hope International University
Loma Linda University
Ohlone College
San Francisco State University
Sonoma State University
Whittier College

Colorado
Pueblo Community College
Trinidad State Junior College
University of Colorado
    Health Sciences Center
Western State College of Colorado

Connecticut
Quinnipiac University
Sacred Heart University

Florida
Daytona Beach Community College
Edison Community College
Florida Southern College
Hillsborough Community College
Stetson University
Tallahassee Community College
University of Central Florida
University of South Florida

Georgia
Albany State University
Covenant College
Georgia Perimeter College
Georgia Southwestern State University
Waycross College

Illinois
Black Hawk College
Monmouth College

Indiana
Franklin College
Goshen College
Indiana Wesleyan University

Iowa
Briar Cliff College

Dordt College
Northwestern College
St. Ambrose University

Kansas
Allen County Community College
Central Christian College
Colby Community College
Kansas State University
Manhattan Christian College
Pittsburg State University
Tabor College
Wichita State University

Kentucky
Ashland Community College
Southeast Community College

Louisiana
Centenary College of Louisiana
Dillard University
Louisiana State University
    Eunice

Maryland
Allegany College
Coppin State College
Howard Community College
University of Maryland
    College Park
Villa Julie College

Massachusetts
Becker College
Boston University
Simmons College

Michigan
Baker College
    of Muskegon
Delta College

Minnesota
College of St. Catherine: St. Paul
    Campus
College of St. Scholastica

Mississippi
Hinds Community College
University of Mississippi
    Medical Center

Missouri
Columbia College
Drury University
Northwest Missouri State University
St. Louis Community College
    St. Louis Community College at
        Forest Park

Montana
University of Montana-Missoula

Nebraska
Clarkson College
Creighton University
Dana College

New Hampshire
New England College
Notre Dame College

New Jersey
Atlantic Cape Community College
Fairleigh Dickinson University
Kean University
Mercer County Community College
Union County College

New Mexico
San Juan College

New York
City University of New York
    College of Staten Island
College of Mount St. Vincent
Concordia College
D'Youville College
Dominican College of Blauvelt
Juilliard School
Marist College
Marymount College
Mount St. Mary College
Nazareth College of Rochester
New York Institute of Technology
Russell Sage College
St. Francis College
St. Thomas Aquinas College
State University of New York
    College at Oneonta
    College of Agriculture and
      Technology at Cobleskill
    New Paltz
    Oswego
Touro College
Utica College of Syracuse University

North Carolina
Greensboro College
Nash Community College
University of North Carolina
    Chapel Hill

North Dakota
University of North Dakota
Valley City State University

Ohio
Cleveland State University
College of Mount St. Joseph
Kent State University
    Ashtabula Regional Campus
Lima Technical College
Ohio Wesleyan University
Walsh University

Oklahoma
Carl Albert State College

Oregon
Pacific University
Southern Oregon University

Pennsylvania
Allegheny College
Beaver College
Cabrini College
Elizabethtown College
Gettysburg College
Lebanon Valley College of Pennsylvania
Moravian College
St. Vincent College
Susquehanna University
Temple University
University of Scranton
University of the Sciences in
    Philadelphia
Waynesburg College

Puerto Rico
University of Puerto Rico
    Aguadilla
    Arecibo Campus

Rhode Island
Salve Regina University

South Carolina
Florence-Darlington Technical College
Newberry College

South Dakota
South Dakota School of Mines and
    Technology
Southeast Technical Institute
University of South Dakota

Tennessee
Bethel College
King College
Lambuth University
Roane State Community College
Shelby State Community College
Union University
University of Memphis
University of Tennessee
    Knoxville
Volunteer State Community College
Walters State Community College

Texas
Blinn College
Coastal Bend College
Collin County Community College
    District
Houston Community College System
McMurry University
South Plains College
Texas Woman's University

Vermont
Lyndon State College

Virginia
Longwood College
Virginia Commonwealth University

Washington
University of Washington

West Virginia
Wheeling Jesuit University

Wisconsin
University of Wisconsin
    Platteville

Combined liberal arts/career program in physician assistant

Alabama
Northwest-Shoals Community College

Arizona
Gateway Community College

Arkansas
University of Arkansas

California
Chaffey Community College
Foothill College
Mount San Antonio College
San Diego City College

Colorado
University of Colorado
    Health Sciences Center

Connecticut
Quinnipiac University

Florida
Daytona Beach Community College
Tallahassee Community College

Georgia
Georgia Southwestern State University
Waycross College

Illinois
Black Hawk College

Indiana
University of St. Francis

Iowa
Briar Cliff College
Dordt College

Kansas
Allen County Community College
Central Christian College
Colby Community College
Kansas State University
Wichita State University

Louisiana
Centenary College of Louisiana
Dillard University

Maryland
Community College of Baltimore County
    Essex
University of Maryland
    College Park

Massachusetts
Massachusetts College of Pharmacy and
    Health Sciences
Western New England College

Michigan
Wayne State University

Minnesota
Augsburg College

Mississippi
Hinds Community College

Missouri
Drury University

Montana
Rocky Mountain College

Nebraska
Dana College

New Hampshire
Notre Dame College

New York
City University of New York
    College of Staten Island
D'Youville College
Juilliard School
Le Moyne College
Marist College
Marymount College
New York Institute of Technology
St. Francis College
Villa Maria College of Buffalo
Wagner College

North Carolina
Greensboro College
High Point University
Methodist College
University of North Carolina
    Chapel Hill

North Dakota
University of North Dakota

Ohio
Davis College
Lima Technical College

Oregon
Pacific University
Southern Oregon University

Pennsylvania
Allentown College of St. Francis de Sales
Beaver College
Lock Haven University of Pennsylvania
Philadelphia University
St. Vincent College
Seton Hill College
University of the Sciences in
    Philadelphia

Puerto Rico
University of Puerto Rico
    Aguadilla

South Dakota
University of South Dakota

Tennessee
Bethel College
Draughons Junior College of Business:
    Nashville
Union University
University of Memphis

Texas
Coastal Bend College
South Plains College

Washington
University of Washington

Wisconsin
University of Wisconsin
    La Crosse
    Platteville

Combined liberal arts/career program in radiology technician

Alabama
Community College of the Air Force
Northwest-Shoals Community College

Arizona
Gateway Community College

Arkansas
Garland County Community College
University of Arkansas

California
Chaffey Community College
Cypress College
Foothill College
Loma Linda University
Long Beach City College
Orange Coast College
San Joaquin Delta College
Santa Rosa Junior College

Colorado
Community College of Denver
Pueblo Community College

Connecticut
Quinnipiac University

Florida
Daytona Beach Community College
Edison Community College
Hillsborough Community College
Tallahassee Community College

Georgia
Floyd College
Georgia Perimeter College
Waycross College

Combined liberal arts/career program in radiology technician

Illinois
Black Hawk College
Danville Area Community College
Moraine Valley Community College

Indiana
University of St. Francis
University of Southern Indiana

Iowa
Briar Cliff College
Dordt College

Kansas
Allen County Community College
Kansas State University
Newman University

Kentucky
Southeast Community College

Maine
St. Joseph's College
University of Southern Maine

Maryland
Allegany College
College of Notre Dame of Maryland
Community College of Baltimore County
    Essex
Hagerstown Community College
Prince George's Community College
Wor-Wic Community College

Massachusetts
Massachusetts College of Pharmacy and
    Health Sciences

Michigan
Baker College
    of Owosso
Delta College
Glen Oaks Community College
Mid Michigan Community College

Minnesota
Century Community and Technical
    College

Mississippi
Hinds Community College
University of Mississippi
    Medical Center

Missouri
Avila College
Drury University
Jefferson College
St. Louis Community College
    St. Louis Community College at
        Forest Park

Nebraska
Clarkson College
Dana College
Northeast Community College
Southeast Community College
    Lincoln Campus

New Jersey
Fairleigh Dickinson University
Mercer County Community College
Passaic County Community College
Union County College

New York
Erie Community College
    City Campus
    North Campus
    South Campus
Iona College

Mohawk Valley Community College
Molloy College
St. Francis College
Westchester Community College

North Carolina
Carteret Community College
Greensboro College
Lenoir Community College
University of North Carolina
    Chapel Hill

North Dakota
Jamestown College

Ohio
Columbus State Community College
Ohio State University
    Columbus Campus
University of Akron
    Wayne College

Oklahoma
Western Oklahoma State College

Pennsylvania
La Roche College
Lebanon Valley College of Pennsylvania

Puerto Rico
Colegio Universitario del Este

South Carolina
Columbia International University
Florence-Darlington Technical College
Orangeburg-Calhoun Technical College

Tennessee
Roane State Community College
Shelby State Community College
Volunteer State Community College

Texas
Blinn College
Coastal Bend College
Houston Community College System
Midland College
Midwestern State University
South Plains College
University of the Incarnate Word

Vermont
Champlain College

West Virginia
University of Charleston
West Virginia Northern Community
    College

Wisconsin
Marian College of Fond du Lac
Milwaukee Area Technical College
University of Wisconsin
    La Crosse

Combined liberal arts/career program in social work

Alabama
Alabama State University
Jacksonville State University

Arizona
Mohave Community College
Northern Arizona University

Arkansas
Harding University
Philander Smith College

University of Arkansas
University of Arkansas
    Monticello
    Pine Bluff

California
California State University
    Chico
    Monterey Bay
    Sacramento
    San Marcos
    Stanislaus
Chaffey Community College
Chapman University
Cypress College
Hope International University
Long Beach City College
Modesto Junior College
Pacific Union College
San Francisco State University
United States International University
Whittier College

Colorado
Community College of Denver
Metropolitan State College of Denver

Connecticut
Sacred Heart University
St. Joseph College

Florida
Daytona Beach Community College
St. Leo University
Southeastern College of the Assemblies
    of God
Tallahassee Community College
University of South Florida
University of West Florida

Georgia
LaGrange College

Hawaii
Brigham Young University
    Hawaii

Idaho
Northwest Nazarene University

Illinois
Barat College
Benedictine University
City Colleges of Chicago
    Harold Washington College
Illinois State University
Lewis University
MacMurray College
McKendree College
Monmouth College
Northeastern Illinois University
Olivet Nazarene University
Quincy University
St. Augustine College
University of Illinois
    Springfield
University of St. Francis

Indiana
Goshen College
Grace College
Indiana Wesleyan University
St. Joseph's College
University of St. Francis
University of Southern Indiana

Iowa
Briar Cliff College
Dordt College
Marycrest International University
Northwestern College
Upper Iowa University

Wartburg College

Kansas
Allen County Community College
Bethany College
Butler County Community College
Central Christian College
Colby Community College
Kansas State University
Manhattan Christian College
Pittsburg State University
Wichita State University

Kentucky
Asbury College
Brescia University
Henderson Community College
Murray State University

Louisiana
Dillard University
Southern University and Agricultural and
    Mechanical College

Maine
St. Joseph's College
University of Maine
University of Maine
    Fort Kent
University of Southern Maine

Maryland
Allegany College
Coppin State College
Frostburg State University
Morgan State University
University of Maryland
    Baltimore County
Western Maryland College

Massachusetts
Curry College
Lasell College
Massachusetts College of Liberal Arts
Western New England College
Wheelock College

Michigan
Bay de Noc Community College
Cornerstone College and Grand Rapids
    Baptist Seminary
Delta College
Hope College
Kellogg Community College
Reformed Bible College
Rochester College
Wayne State University

Minnesota
Augsburg College
Bemidji State University
Central Lakes College
College of St. Catherine: St. Paul
    Campus
College of St. Scholastica
Minnesota State University, Mankato
St. Cloud State University
St. Olaf College

Mississippi
Hinds Community College
Mississippi State University
Mississippi Valley State University

Missouri
Avila College
Central Missouri State University
Columbia College
Culver-Stockton College
Drury University
East Central College
Fontbonne College

Maryville University of Saint Louis
Missouri Baptist College
St. Louis Community College
    St. Louis Community College at
      Forest Park
Washington University

Montana
Carroll College
University of Great Falls
University of Montana-Missoula

Nebraska
Bellevue University
Dana College

New Hampshire
Franklin Pierce College
New England College
New Hampshire Community Technical
    College
      Laconia

New Jersey
Kean University
Mercer County Community College
Ocean County College
Passaic County Community College
Richard Stockton College of New Jersey
Rowan University

New Mexico
New Mexico State University
    Alamogordo
San Juan College

New York
City University of New York
    College of Staten Island
Clinton Community College
College of St. Rose
D'Youville College
Dowling College
Erie Community College
    City Campus
    North Campus
    South Campus
Iona College
Jamestown Community College
Juilliard School
Keuka College
Marist College
Marymount College
Molloy College
Nazareth College of Rochester
New York University
Onondaga Community College
Roberts Wesleyan College
St. Francis College
Schenectady County Community College
Skidmore College
State University of New York
    Binghamton
    Buffalo
    College at Brockport
    College at Plattsburgh
    New Paltz

North Carolina
Beaufort County Community College
Elizabeth City State University
Elon College
Lenoir Community College
Methodist College
Pfeiffer University
University of North Carolina
    Chapel Hill

North Dakota
University of North Dakota
Valley City State University

Ohio
Ashland University
Bluffton College
Capital University
Cedarville College
Clark State Community College
Cleveland State University
College of Mount St. Joseph
Defiance College
Franciscan University of Steubenville
Kent State University
    Ashtabula Regional Campus
Lima Technical College
Lourdes College
Mount Vernon Nazarene College
Ohio State University
    Columbus Campus
University of Akron
    Wayne College
Wilmington College

Oklahoma
Carl Albert State College
Oral Roberts University

Oregon
Concordia University
Eastern Oregon University
Pacific University

Pennsylvania
Allentown College of St. Francis de Sales
Cedar Crest College
Chatham College
Edinboro University of Pennsylvania
Elizabethtown College
Gwynedd-Mercy College
Lock Haven University of Pennsylvania
Mansfield University of Pennsylvania
Mercyhurst College
Philadelphia College of Bible
Rosemont College
Seton Hill College
Temple University
Widener University

Puerto Rico
Colegio Universitario del Este
Turabo University
Universidad Metropolitana
University of Puerto Rico
    Arecibo Campus
    Rio Piedras Campus
University of the Sacred Heart

Rhode Island
Salve Regina University

South Carolina
Coker College
Florence-Darlington Technical College
Lander University
Limestone College

South Dakota
South Dakota School of Mines and
    Technology
University of South Dakota

Tennessee
Bethel College
Cleveland State Community College
Dyersburg State Community College
Freed-Hardeman University
Lincoln Memorial University
Tennessee Technological University
Tennessee Wesleyan College
Union University
University of Memphis
University of Tennessee
    Knoxville
Volunteer State Community College
Walters State Community College

Texas
Blinn College
Coastal Bend College
Hardin-Simmons University
Howard Payne University
Midwestern State University
Prairie View A&M University
St. Edward's University
Southwestern Adventist University
Texas A&M International University
Texas Lutheran University

Vermont
Castleton State College
Champlain College
Lyndon State College
Southern Vermont College
Trinity College of Vermont

Virginia
Mary Baldwin College
Virginia Union University

Washington
Pacific Lutheran University
St. Martin's College
University of Washington
Walla Walla College

West Virginia
Concord College
Shepherd College
West Virginia University Institute of
    Technology

Wisconsin
Carroll College
Carthage College
Mount Mary College
Mount Senario College
University of Wisconsin
    Green Bay
    Parkside
    Superior
Viterbo University

Cooperative education

Alabama
Alabama Agricultural and Mechanical
    University
Alabama State University
Athens State University
Auburn University
Auburn University at Montgomery
Bessemer State Technical College
Bevill State Community College
Calhoun Community College
Central Alabama Community College
Faulkner University
Gadsden State Community College
George C. Wallace State Community
    College
    Dothan
Harry M. Ayers State Technical College
J. F. Drake State Technical College
Jacksonville State University
James H. Faulkner State Community
    College
John M. Patterson State Technical
    College
Lurleen B. Wallace Junior College
Northwest-Shoals Community College
Oakwood College
Sparks State Technical College
Stillman College
Talladega College
Troy State University
    Dothan
Tuskegee University
University of Alabama

University of Alabama
    Birmingham
    Huntsville
University of Montevallo
University of North Alabama
University of South Alabama
Wallace State Community College at
    Hanceville

Alaska
University of Alaska
    Anchorage
    Fairbanks
    Southeast

Arizona
Arizona State University
Arizona Western College
Cochise College
DeVry Institute of Technology
    Phoenix
Dine College
Eastern Arizona College
Embry-Riddle Aeronautical University
    Prescott Campus
Gateway Community College
Glendale Community College
Mesa Community College
Northern Arizona University
Northland Pioneer College
Paradise Valley Community College
Phoenix College
Pima Community College
Rio Salado College
Scottsdale Community College
South Mountain Community College
University of Arizona

Arkansas
Arkansas State University
Arkansas State University
    Mountain Home
Garland County Community College
Harding University
Philander Smith College
University of Arkansas
University of Arkansas
    Little Rock
    Pine Bluff
University of Central Arkansas
Westark College

California
Allan Hancock College
American River College
Antioch Southern California
    Los Angeles
Barstow College
Biola University
Brooks College
Butte College
California Lutheran University
California Maritime Academy
California Polytechnic State University:
    San Luis Obispo
California State Polytechnic University:
    Pomona
California State University
    Bakersfield
    Chico
    Dominguez Hills
    Fresno
    Fullerton
    Hayward
    Long Beach
    Los Angeles
    Monterey Bay
    Northridge
    Sacramento
    Stanislaus
Canada College
Cerritos Community College
Cerro Coso Community College
Chabot College

Cooperative education

Chaffey Community College
Chapman University
Citrus College
City College of San Francisco
Coastline Community College
College of San Mateo
College of the Canyons
College of the Desert
College of the Redwoods
College of the Siskiyous
Columbia College
Compton Community College
Crafton Hills College
Cuesta College
De Anza College
DeVry Institute of Technology
    Fremont
    Long Beach
    Pomona
    West Hills
Diablo Valley College
Don Bosco Technical Institute
East Los Angeles College
Evergreen Valley College
Foothill College
Glendale Community College
Golden Gate University
Golden West College
Heald Business College
    Santa Rosa
Humboldt State University
Humphreys College
Irvine Valley College
Kings River Community College
Long Beach City College
Los Angeles Harbor College
Los Angeles Mission College
Los Angeles Pierce College
Los Angeles Southwest College
Los Angeles Trade and Technical College
Los Angeles Valley College
Los Medanos College
Master's College
Mendocino College
Merritt College
MiraCosta College
Mission College
Modesto Junior College
Monterey Peninsula College
Mount San Jacinto College
Napa Valley College
Ohlone College
Orange Coast College
Otis College of Art and Design
Pacific Union College
Palomar College
Riverside Community College
Sacramento City College
Saddleback College
San Diego City College
San Diego State University
San Francisco Art Institute
San Joaquin Delta College
San Joaquin Valley College Inc.
San Jose City College
San Jose State University
Santa Ana College
Santa Barbara City College
Santa Clara University
Santa Monica College
Santa Rosa Junior College
Shasta College
Sierra College
Skyline College
Solano Community College
Southwestern College
United States International University
University of California
    Berkeley
    Irvine
    Riverside
    San Diego
    Santa Cruz
University of Southern California
University of the Pacific
Victor Valley College
West Hills Community College
West Los Angeles College
Westmont College
Yuba College

Colorado
Aims Community College
Arapahoe Community College
Colorado School of Mines
Colorado State University
Colorado Technical University
Community College of Aurora
Community College of Denver
Fort Lewis College
Front Range Community College
Lamar Community College
Mesa State College
Metropolitan State College of Denver
Northeastern Junior College
Pueblo Community College
Red Rocks Community College
Trinidad State Junior College
University of Colorado
    Boulder
    Denver
    Health Sciences Center
University of Denver
University of Northern Colorado
University of Southern Colorado
Western State College of Colorado

Connecticut
Central Connecticut State University
Eastern Connecticut State University
Housatonic Community-Technical College
Manchester Community-Technical College
Naugatuck Valley Community-Technical College
Northwestern Connecticut Community-Technical College
Norwalk Community-Technical College
Sacred Heart University
Southern Connecticut State University
Teikyo Post University
Three Rivers Community-Technical College
University of Bridgeport
University of Connecticut
University of Hartford
University of New Haven
Western Connecticut State University

Delaware
Delaware State University
Delaware Technical and Community College
    Owens Campus
    Stanton/Wilmington Campus
    Terry Campus
Goldey-Beacom College
University of Delaware

District of Columbia
American University
Gallaudet University
George Washington University
Howard University
Southeastern University
Trinity College
University of the District of Columbia

Florida
Bethune-Cookman College
Brevard Community College
Broward Community College
Carlos Albizu University
Central Florida Community College
Chipola Junior College
Daytona Beach Community College
Edison Community College
Edward Waters College
Embry-Riddle Aeronautical University
Florida Agricultural and Mechanical University
Florida Atlantic University
Florida Institute of Technology
Florida International University
Florida Keys Community College
Florida Memorial College
Florida Metropolitan University
    Orlando College North
Florida National College
Florida State University
Gulf Coast Community College
Lake City Community College
Lake-Sumter Community College
Manatee Community College
Miami-Dade Community College
Nova Southeastern University
Palm Beach Community College
Pasco-Hernando Community College
Pensacola Junior College
St. Leo University
Santa Fe Community College
Seminole Community College
South Florida Community College
Tallahassee Community College
University of Central Florida
University of Florida
University of North Florida
University of South Florida
University of West Florida
Valencia Community College

Georgia
Albany State University
Armstrong Atlantic State University
Atlanta Metropolitan College
Augusta State University
Berry College
Brenau University
Clark Atlanta University
Columbus State University
Darton College
DeVry Institute of Technology
    Alpharetta
    Atlanta
Floyd College
Fort Valley State University
Georgia College and State University
Georgia Institute of Technology
Georgia Southern University
Georgia Southwestern State University
Georgia State University
Gordon College
Gwinnett Technical Institute
Kennesaw State University
Mercer University
Middle Georgia College
Morehouse College
Morris Brown College
North Georgia College & State University
Oglethorpe University
Paine College
Reinhardt College
Savannah State University
Southern Polytechnic State University
State University of West Georgia
University of Georgia
Valdosta State University

Hawaii
Brigham Young University
    Hawaii
Hawaii Pacific University
University of Hawaii
    Hawaii Community College
    Honolulu Community College
    Kauai Community College
    Manoa
    Maui Community College
    Windward Community College

Idaho
College of Southern Idaho
Lewis-Clark State College
University of Idaho

Illinois
Augustana College
Barat College
Black Hawk College
Black Hawk College
    East Campus
Blackburn College
Bradley University
Chicago State University
City Colleges of Chicago
    Harold Washington College
    Harry S. Truman College
    Kennedy-King College
    Malcolm X College
    Olive-Harvey College
    Richard J. Daley College
College of DuPage
College of Lake County
De Paul University
DeVry Institute of Technology
    Addison
    Chicago
Elgin Community College
Elmhurst College
Greenville College
Illinois Institute of Technology
Illinois State University
John A. Logan College
Joliet Junior College
Judson College
Kaskaskia College
Lake Land College
Lewis University
Lewis and Clark Community College
Lexington College
Lincoln Land Community College
North Central College
Northeastern Illinois University
Northern Illinois University
Northwestern University
Parkland College
Rend Lake College
Robert Morris College: Chicago
Rock Valley College
St. Augustine College
Sauk Valley Community College
School of the Art Institute of Chicago
Southern Illinois University
    Carbondale
    Edwardsville
Trinity International University
Triton College
University of Illinois
    Chicago
    Urbana-Champaign
University of St. Francis
William Rainey Harper College

Indiana
Ancilla College
Anderson University
Ball State University
Butler University
Calumet College of St. Joseph
Franklin College
Goshen College
Indiana State University
Indiana University
    Bloomington
    East
    Northwest
Indiana University--Purdue University
    Indiana University-Purdue University Fort Wayne
    Indiana University-Purdue University Indianapolis

Ivy Tech State College
  Central Indiana
  Southcentral
  Southwest
Oakland City University
Purdue University
Purdue University
  Calumet
Rose-Hulman Institute of Technology
Tri-State University
University of Evansville
University of Indianapolis
University of Southern Indiana
Valparaiso University

Iowa
Clarke College
Clinton Community College
Des Moines Area Community College
Grand View College
Indian Hills Community College
Iowa Central Community College
Iowa Lakes Community College
Iowa State University
Iowa Western Community College
Kirkwood Community College
Maharishi University of Management
Marshalltown Community College
Marycrest International University
Muscatine Community College
North Iowa Area Community College
Northeast Iowa Community College
St. Ambrose University
Scott Community College
Simpson College
Southwestern Community College
University of Dubuque
University of Iowa
University of Northern Iowa
Waldorf College

Kansas
Allen County Community College
Barton County Community College
Benedictine College
Bethel College
Butler County Community College
Central Christian College
Cloud County Community College
Colby Community College
Cowley County Community College
Emporia State University
Garden City Community College
Hesston College
Hutchinson Community College
Johnson County Community College
Kansas City Kansas Community College
Kansas State University
McPherson College
Newman University
Pittsburg State University
Seward County Community College
University of Kansas
Wichita State University

Kentucky
Ashland Community College
Cumberland College
Eastern Kentucky University
Georgetown College
Henderson Community College
Kentucky Christian College
Kentucky State University
Lexington Community College
Madisonville Community College
Maysville Community College
Morehead State University
Murray State University
Northern Kentucky University
Owensboro Community College
Owensboro Junior College of Business
Prestonsburg Community College
Somerset Community College
Thomas More College

Union College
University of Kentucky
University of Louisville
Western Kentucky University

Louisiana
Delgado Community College
Louisiana State University and
  Agricultural and Mechanical College
Louisiana Tech University
McNeese State University
Nunez Community College
Southern University and Agricultural and
  Mechanical College
Southern University
  New Orleans
Tulane University
University of Louisiana at Monroe
University of New Orleans
Xavier University of Louisiana

Maine
Andover College
Husson College
Maine Maritime Academy
Unity College
University of Maine
University of Maine
  Machias
University of Southern Maine
Washington County Technical College

Maryland
Anne Arundel Community College
Baltimore City Community College
Baltimore International College
Bowie State University
Cecil Community College
Charles County Community College
Chesapeake College
Columbia Union College
Community College of Baltimore County
  Catonsville
  Essex
Coppin State College
Frederick Community College
Hagerstown Community College
Harford Community College
Howard Community College
Johns Hopkins University
Maryland College of Art and Design
Montgomery College
  Germantown Campus
  Rockville Campus
  Takoma Park Campus
Morgan State University
Mount St. Mary's College
Prince George's Community College
Sojourner-Douglass College
University of Baltimore
University of Maryland
  Baltimore County
  College Park
  Eastern Shore
  University College
Villa Julie College

Massachusetts
Atlantic Union College
Bay Path College
Becker College
Boston University
Bristol Community College
Cape Cod Community College
Gordon College
Holyoke Community College
Lasell College
Massachusetts Bay Community College
Massachusetts Institute of Technology
Massachusetts Maritime Academy
Merrimack College
Middlesex Community College
Mount Wachusett Community College
Nichols College

Northeastern University
Northern Essex Community College
Springfield College
Springfield Technical Community
  College
Suffolk University
University of Massachusetts
  Amherst
  Boston
  Dartmouth
  Lowell
Wentworth Institute of Technology
Westfield State College
Worcester Polytechnic Institute

Michigan
Adrian College
Andrews University
Aquinas College
Baker College
  of Auburn Hills
  of Cadillac
  of Jackson
  of Mount Clemens
  of Muskegon
  of Owosso
  of Port Huron
Bay de Noc Community College
Calvin College
Central Michigan University
Cleary College
Davenport College of Business
Delta College
Detroit College of Business
Eastern Michigan University
Ferris State University
Gogebic Community College
Grand Rapids Community College
Grand Valley State University
Henry Ford Community College
Kalamazoo Valley Community College
Kellogg Community College
Kettering University
Kirtland Community College
Lake Michigan College
Lake Superior State University
Lansing Community College
Lawrence Technological University
Macomb Community College
Madonna University
Marygrove College
Michigan State University
Michigan Technological University
Mid Michigan Community College
Monroe County Community College
Montcalm Community College
Mott Community College
Muskegon Community College
North Central Michigan College
Northwestern Michigan College
Oakland Community College
Oakland University
Olivet College
Saginaw Valley State University
St. Clair County Community College
Schoolcraft College
Siena Heights University
Southwestern Michigan College
University of Detroit Mercy
University of Michigan
University of Michigan
  Dearborn
  Flint
Washtenaw Community College
Wayne County Community College
Wayne State University
Western Michigan University

Minnesota
Augsburg College
Bemidji State University
Concordia College: Moorhead
Concordia University: St. Paul
Crown College

Fond Du Lac Tribal and Community
  College
Gustavus Adolphus College
Inver Hills Community College
Itasca Community College
Lake Superior College: A Community
  and Technical College
Macalester College
Minneapolis College of Art and Design
Minnesota State College - Southeast
  Technical
Ridgewater College: A Community and
  Technical College
St. Mary's University of Minnesota
Southwest State University
University of Minnesota
  Twin Cities
Vermilion Community College

Mississippi
Alcorn State University
Delta State University
Hinds Community College
Holmes Community College
Jackson State University
Jones County Junior College
Mary Holmes College
Meridian Community College
Mississippi College
Mississippi Gulf Coast Community
  College
  Jackson County Campus
  Jefferson Davis Campus
  Perkinston
Mississippi State University
Mississippi University for Women
Mississippi Valley State University
Tougaloo College
University of Mississippi
University of Southern Mississippi

Missouri
Avila College
DeVry Institute of Technology
  Kansas City
Fontbonne College
Kansas City Art Institute
Lincoln University
Lindenwood University
Longview Community College
Maryville University of Saint Louis
Moberly Area Community College
Ozarks Technical Community College
Rockhurst University
St. Louis University
Southeast Missouri State University
Southwest Baptist University
Southwest Missouri State University
St. Louis Community College
  St. Louis Community College at
    Florissant Valley
University of Missouri
  Columbia
  Kansas City
  Rolla
  St. Louis
Washington University
Webster University
William Jewell College
William Woods University

Montana
Carroll College
Dull Knife Memorial College
Miles Community College
Montana State University
  Billings
  Northern
Montana Tech of the University of
  Montana
Montana Tech of the University of
  Montana: College of Technology
Rocky Mountain College
Salish Kootenai College

Stone Child College
University of Great Falls
University of Montana-Missoula
Western Montana College of The
  University of Montana

Nebraska

Central Community College
Chadron State College
Clarkson College
College of Saint Mary
Concordia University
Doane College
Metropolitan Community College
Northeast Community College
Peru State College
Southeast Community College
  Lincoln Campus
  Milford Campus
University of Nebraska
  Lincoln
  Omaha
Wayne State College

Nevada

Western Nevada Community College

New Hampshire

Daniel Webster College
Hesser College
Keene State College
New Hampshire College
New Hampshire Community Technical
  College
    Claremont
    Laconia
    Manchester

New Jersey

Atlantic Cape Community College
Bergen Community College
Berkeley College
Bloomfield College
Brookdale Community College
Burlington County College
Camden County College
County College of Morris
DeVry Institute
Essex County College
Fairleigh Dickinson University
Felician College
Gloucester County College
Kean University
Mercer County Community College
Middlesex County College
Monmouth University
Montclair State University
New Jersey City University
New Jersey Institute of Technology
Passaic County Community College
Princeton University
Ramapo College of New Jersey
Raritan Valley Community College
Rider University
Rowan University
Rutgers
  The State University of New Jersey:
    College of Engineering
  The State University of New Jersey:
    Cook College
St. Peter's College
Salem Community College
Seton Hall University
Stevens Institute of Technology
Warren County Community College

New Mexico

Dona Ana Branch Community College of
  New Mexico State University
Eastern New Mexico University
New Mexico Highlands University
New Mexico Institute of Mining and
  Technology
New Mexico Junior College

New Mexico State University
New Mexico State University
  Alamogordo
  Carlsbad
San Juan College
Santa Fe Community College
University of New Mexico
Western New Mexico University

New York

Alfred University
Audrey Cohen College
Berkeley College
Berkeley College of New York City
Broome Community College
Bryant & Stratton Business Institute
  Syracuse
City University of New York
  Borough of Manhattan Community
    College
  Bronx Community College
  City College
  College of Staten Island
  Hostos Community College
  John Jay College of Criminal
    Justice
  La Guardia Community College
  Lehman College
  Queens College
  Queensborough Community
    College
  York College
Clarkson University
College of Insurance
College of New Rochelle
Columbia-Greene Community College
Concordia College
Cornell University
Daemen College
DeVry Institute of Technology
  New York
Dominican College of Blauvelt
Dowling College
Dutchess Community College
Erie Community College
  City Campus
  North Campus
Finger Lakes Community College
Fulton-Montgomery Community College
Genesee Community College
Hilbert College
Hudson Valley Community College
Iona College
Jamestown Community College
Jefferson Community College
Katharine Gibbs School
  New York
Keuka College
Laboratory Institute of Merchandising
Long Island University
  Brooklyn Campus
  C. W. Post Campus
  Southampton College
Manhattan College
Marist College
Mercy College
Molloy College
Monroe College
Monroe Community College
Mount St. Mary College
Nassau Community College
New York Institute of Technology
New York State College of Ceramics at
  Alfred University
Niagara County Community College
Niagara University
Onondaga Community College
Orange County Community College
Pace University
Pace University: Pleasantville/Briarcliff
Polytechnic University
Polytechnic University
  Long Island Campus
Rensselaer Polytechnic Institute
Rochester Institute of Technology

Russell Sage College
Sage Junior College of Albany
St. Thomas Aquinas College
State University of New York
  College at Brockport
  College at Buffalo
  College at Cortland
  College at Fredonia
  College at Plattsburgh
  College at Potsdam
  College of Technology at Alfred
  Maritime College
  New Paltz
Suffolk County Community College
Syracuse University
Technical Career Institutes
Tompkins-Cortland Community College
Ulster County Community College
Union College
Utica College of Syracuse University
Westchester Business Institute
Westchester Community College

North Carolina

Alamance Community College
Appalachian State University
Asheville Buncombe Technical
  Community College
Barton College
Beaufort County Community College
Blue Ridge Community College
Caldwell Community College and
  Technical Institute
Campbell University
Cape Fear Community College
Catawba Valley Community College
Central Piedmont Community College
Cleveland Community College
Coastal Carolina Community College
College of the Albemarle
Craven Community College
Davidson County Community College
Durham Technical Community College
East Carolina University
Edgecombe Community College
Elizabeth City State University
Fayetteville State University
Fayetteville Technical Community
  College
Forsyth Technical Community College
Gaston College
Guilford Technical Community College
Haywood Community College
James Sprunt Community College
Johnson C. Smith University
Lenoir Community College
Lenoir-Rhyne College
Louisburg College
Mars Hill College
Martin Community College
Mayland Community College
Meredith College
Mitchell Community College
Mount Olive College
North Carolina Agricultural and
  Technical State University
North Carolina Central University
North Carolina State University
North Carolina Wesleyan College
Pfeiffer University
Piedmont Community College
Pitt Community College
Randolph Community College
Richmond Community College
Roanoke-Chowan Community College
Rockingham Community College
Rowan-Cabarrus Community College
St. Augustine's College
Sampson Community College
Sandhills Community College
South Piedmont Community College
Southwestern Community College
Surry Community College

University of North Carolina
  Charlotte
  Pembroke
  Wilmington
Vance-Granville Community College
Wake Technical Community College
Wayne Community College
Western Carolina University
Western Piedmont Community College
Wilkes Community College
Wilson Technical Community College
Winston-Salem State University

North Dakota

Bismarck State College
Jamestown College
Lake Region State College
Mayville State University
Minot State University
Minot State University: Bottineau
  Campus
North Dakota State College of Science
North Dakota State University
Sitting Bull College
University of Mary
University of North Dakota
Valley City State University
Williston State College

Ohio

Antioch College
Bowling Green State University
Bryant & Stratton College
Case Western Reserve University
Central Ohio Technical College
Central State University
Cincinnati State Technical and
  Community College
Clark State Community College
Cleveland State University
College of Mount St. Joseph
Columbus College of Art and Design
Columbus State Community College
David N. Myers College
DeVry Institute of Technology
  Columbus
Defiance College
Franklin University
Hocking Technical College
John Carroll University
Kent State University
Lakeland Community College
Lima Technical College
Lorain County Community College
Malone College
Marion Technical College
Miami University
  Hamilton Campus
  Middletown Campus
  Oxford Campus
Mount Union College
Mount Vernon Nazarene College
Northwest State Community College
Northwestern College
Notre Dame College of Ohio
Ohio Northern University
Ohio State University
  Agricultural Technical Institute
  Columbus Campus
  Mansfield Campus
  Marion Campus
  Newark Campus
Ohio University
Owens Community College
  Toledo
Sinclair Community College
Southern Ohio College
Stark State College of Technology
University of Akron
University of Akron
  Wayne College
University of Cincinnati
University of Cincinnati
  Raymond Walters College

University of Dayton
University of Findlay
University of Rio Grande
University of Toledo
Wilberforce University
Wright State University
Xavier University
Youngstown State University

Oklahoma
Carl Albert State College
Eastern Oklahoma State College
Langston University
Mid-America Bible College
Northeastern State University
Oklahoma Baptist University
Oklahoma Panhandle State University
Oklahoma State University
Oklahoma State University
    Okmulgee
Oral Roberts University
Redlands Community College
Rogers State University
University of Oklahoma
University of Science and Arts of
    Oklahoma

Oregon
Central Oregon Community College
Chemeketa Community College
Clackamas Community College
Clatsop Community College
Eastern Oregon University
George Fox University
Lane Community College
Linfield College
Linn-Benton Community College
Mount Hood Community College
Oregon Institute of Technology
Oregon State University
Pacific Northwest College of Art
Pacific University
Portland State University
Reed College
Southern Oregon University
University of Oregon

Pennsylvania
Alvernia College
Beaver College
Bloomsburg University of Pennsylvania
Bryn Athyn College of the New Church
Bucks County Community College
Butler County Community College
Cabrini College
California University of Pennsylvania
Carnegie Mellon University
Chatham College
Chestnut Hill College
Cheyney University of Pennsylvania
College Misericordia
Community College of Allegheny
    County
Delaware County Community College
Delaware Valley College
Drexel University
Duquesne University
Education America
    Vale Technical Institute
Gannon University
Geneva College
Gwynedd-Mercy College
Holy Family College
Indiana University of Pennsylvania
La Salle University
Lackawanna Junior College
Laurel Business Institute
Lehigh Carbon Community College
Lehigh University
Lincoln University
Mansfield University of Pennsylvania
Mercyhurst College
Millersville University of Pennsylvania
Moore College of Art and Design

Neumann College
Northampton County Area Community
    College
Peirce College
Penn State
    Erie, The Behrend College
    University Park
Pennsylvania College of Technology
Pennsylvania Institute of Technology
Philadelphia University
Reading Area Community College
Robert Morris College
St. Francis College
St. Joseph's University
St. Vincent College
Sawyer School
Shippensburg University of Pennsylvania
South Hills School of Business &
    Technology
Temple University
Thiel College
University of Pittsburgh
University of Pittsburgh
    Greensburg
    Johnstown
Westmoreland County Community
    College
Widener University
Wilkes University
Williamson Free School of Mechanical
    Trades
York College of Pennsylvania

Puerto Rico
American University of Puerto Rico
Huertas Junior College
Inter American University of Puerto Rico
    Arecibo Campus
    Bayamon Campus
    Guayama Campus
    San German Campus
Technological College of San Juan
Universidad Politecnica de Puerto Rico
University of Puerto Rico
    Arecibo Campus
    Bayamon University College
    Mayaguez Campus
    Rio Piedras Campus
University of the Sacred Heart

Rhode Island
Bryant College
Community College of Rhode Island
Johnson & Wales University
New England Institute of Technology
Providence College
Roger Williams University
University of Rhode Island

South Carolina
Aiken Technical College
Central Carolina Technical College
Clemson University
Coastal Carolina University
Coker College
College of Charleston
Denmark Technical College
Florence-Darlington Technical College
Francis Marion University
Furman University
Greenville Technical College
Lander University
Midlands Technical College
Morris College
Newberry College
Orangeburg-Calhoun Technical College
South Carolina State University
Southern Wesleyan University
Spartanburg Technical College
Technical College of the Lowcountry
Tri-County Technical College
Trident Technical College
University of South Carolina

University of South Carolina
    Aiken
    Beaufort
Voorhees College
Winthrop University
York Technical College

South Dakota
Black Hills State University
Dakota State University
South Dakota School of Mines and
    Technology
South Dakota State University

Tennessee
Austin Peay State University
Belmont University
Chattanooga State Technical Community
    College
Cleveland State Community College
Crichton College
Cumberland University
Dyersburg State Community College
East Tennessee State University
Fisk University
Freed-Hardeman University
Jackson State Community College
Johnson Bible College
LeMoyne-Owen College
Middle Tennessee State University
Motlow State Community College
Nashville State Technical Institute
Northeast State Technical Community
    College
Pellissippi State Technical Community
    College
Roane State Community College
Shelby State Community College
Tennessee State University
Tennessee Technological University
University of Memphis
University of Tennessee
    Chattanooga
    Knoxville
    Martin
Vanderbilt University

Texas
Abilene Christian University
Angelo State University
Brazosport College
Brookhaven College
Cedar Valley College
Coastal Bend College
College of the Mainland
Collin County Community College
    District
DeVry Institute of Technology
    Irving
Eastfield College
El Paso Community College
Hill College
Houston Community College System
Huston-Tillotson College
Jarvis Christian College
Kilgore College
Lamar State College at Port Arthur
Lamar University
LeTourneau University
Lee College
McMurry University
Midland College
Mountain View College
Northeast Texas Community College
Palo Alto College
Paul Quinn College
Prairie View A&M University
Rice University
Richland College
St. Mary's University
St. Philip's College
Sam Houston State University
San Antonio College
Schreiner College

Southern Methodist University
Southwestern Adventist University
Stephen F. Austin State University
Texas A&M International University
Texas A&M University
Texas A&M University
    Commerce
    Corpus Christi
    Kingsville
Texas College
Texas Southern University
Texas State Technical College
    Harlingen
    Sweetwater
    Waco
Texas Tech University
Texas Woman's University
Tyler Junior College
University of Houston
University of Houston
    Clear Lake
    Downtown
University of North Texas
University of St. Thomas
University of Texas
    Arlington
    Austin
    Brownsville
    Dallas
    El Paso
    Pan American
    San Antonio
University of the Incarnate Word
Vernon Regional Junior College
Weatherford College
West Texas A&M University

Utah
Brigham Young University
College of Eastern Utah
Dixie State College of Utah
LDS Business College
Salt Lake Community College
Snow College
Southern Utah University
University of Utah
Utah State University
Utah Valley State College
Weber State University
Westminster College

Vermont
Castleton State College
Lyndon State College
Sterling College
University of Vermont

Virginia
Central Virginia Community College
Christopher Newport University
Dabney S. Lancaster Community College
Ferrum College
George Mason University
Hampton University
J. Sargeant Reynolds Community
    College
James Madison University
Lord Fairfax Community College
New River Community College
Norfolk State University
Northern Virginia Community College
Old Dominion University
Patrick Henry Community College
Piedmont Virginia Community College
St. Paul's College
Southwest Virginia Community College
Thomas Nelson Community College
Tidewater Community College
University of Virginia
University of Virginia's College at Wise
Virginia Commonwealth University
Virginia Highlands Community College
Virginia Polytechnic Institute and State
    University

Cooperative education

Virginia State University
Virginia Union University
Virginia Wesleyan College
Virginia Western Community College

Washington
Big Bend Community College
Central Washington University
Centralia College
Clark College
Eastern Washington University
Edmonds Community College
Everett Community College
Grays Harbor College
Green River Community College
Highline Community College
Lake Washington Technical College
Lower Columbia College
North Seattle Community College
Olympic College
Pacific Lutheran University
Pierce College
Renton Technical College
St. Martin's College
Seattle Central Community College
Seattle Pacific University
Shoreline Community College
Skagit Valley College
South Puget Sound Community College
Spokane Community College
Spokane Falls Community College
University of Puget Sound
University of Washington
Walla Walla College
Walla Walla Community College
Washington State University
Wenatchee Valley College
Whatcom Community College
Whitworth College

West Virginia
College of West Virginia
Concord College
Corinthian Schools: National Institute of Technology
Davis and Elkins College
Glenville State College
Marshall University
Shepherd College
University of Charleston
West Virginia State College
West Virginia University
West Virginia University Institute of Technology
West Virginia University
    Parkersburg

Wisconsin
Bryant & Stratton College
Cardinal Stritch University
Carthage College
Lakeshore Technical College
Marian College of Fond du Lac
Marquette University
Milwaukee Area Technical College
Milwaukee Institute of Art & Design
Milwaukee School of Engineering
Mount Senario College
Northland College
St. Norbert College
University of Wisconsin
    Eau Claire
    La Crosse
    Madison
    Milwaukee
    Platteville
    River Falls
    Stevens Point
    Stout
Viterbo University
Waukesha County Technical College
Western Wisconsin Technical College

Wyoming
Central Wyoming College
Laramie County Community College
Northwest College
Western Wyoming Community College

Distance learning

Alabama
Alabama Agricultural and Mechanical University
Athens State University
Auburn University
Auburn University at Montgomery
Bevill State Community College
Calhoun Community College
Community College of the Air Force
Enterprise State Junior College
Gadsden State Community College
Jacksonville State University
James H. Faulkner State Community College
Jefferson Davis Community College
Jefferson State Community College
Northwest-Shoals Community College
Snead State Community College
Spring Hill College
Troy State University
Troy State University
    Dothan
    Montgomery
University of Alabama
University of Alabama
    Huntsville
University of North Alabama

Alaska
Alaska Pacific University
Prince William Sound Community College
University of Alaska
    Anchorage
    Fairbanks
    Southeast

Arizona
Arizona State University
Arizona Western College
Central Arizona College
Cochise College
Embry-Riddle Aeronautical University
    Prescott Campus
Gateway Community College
Glendale Community College
Grand Canyon University
Mesa Community College
Northern Arizona University
Paradise Valley Community College
Phoenix College
Pima Community College
Rio Salado College
Scottsdale Community College
University of Advancing Computer Technology
University of Arizona
University of Phoenix
Yavapai College

Arkansas
Arkansas State University
Arkansas Tech University
Garland County Community College
Henderson State University
Mississippi County Community College
North Arkansas College
Northwest Arkansas Community College
Phillips Community College of the University of Arkansas
Southern Arkansas University
Southern Arkansas University Tech
University of Arkansas
University of Arkansas
    Monticello
    Pine Bluff
    for Medical Sciences
University of Central Arkansas
Westark College

California
Allan Hancock College
Barstow College
Butte College
California College for Health Sciences
California Lutheran University
California Maritime Academy
California Polytechnic State University:
    San Luis Obispo
California State University
    Bakersfield
    Chico
    Fresno
    Fullerton
    Hayward
    Long Beach
    Los Angeles
    Monterey Bay
    Northridge
    Sacramento
    Stanislaus
Canada College
Cerritos Community College
Cerro Coso Community College
Chabot College
Citrus College
City College of San Francisco
Coastline Community College
Cogswell Polytechnical College
College of San Mateo
College of the Canyons
College of the Desert
College of the Siskiyous
Concordia University
Crafton Hills College
Cuesta College
Cypress College
De Anza College
Diablo Valley College
East Los Angeles College
Evergreen Valley College
Foothill College
Fresno City College
Fresno Pacific University
Gavilan Community College
Glendale Community College
Golden Gate University
Golden West College
Grossmont Community College
Holy Names College
Hope International University
Humboldt State University
Irvine Valley College
LIFE Bible College
La Sierra University
Lake Tahoe Community College
Las Positas College
Loma Linda University
Long Beach City College
Los Angeles Harbor College
Los Angeles Pierce College
Mendocino College
Merritt College
MiraCosta College
Modesto Junior College
Monterey Peninsula College
Mount San Antonio College
Napa Valley College
National University
Ohlone College
Orange Coast College
Oxnard College
Pacific Oaks College
Palomar College
Pasadena City College
Riverside Community College
Sacramento City College
Saddleback College
San Diego Mesa College
San Diego State University
San Francisco State University
San Joaquin Delta College
San Jose State University
Santa Ana College
Santa Barbara City College
Santa Monica College
Santa Rosa Junior College
Shasta College
Sierra College
Simpson College
Solano Community College
Sonoma State University
Southwestern College
Taft College
University of California
    Berkeley
    Los Angeles
    Riverside
    Santa Barbara
University of La Verne
University of San Francisco
University of Southern California
Victor Valley College
Yuba College

Colorado
Adams State College
Arapahoe Community College
Colorado Christian University
Colorado Mountain College
    Alpine Campus
    Spring Valley Campus
    Timberline Campus
Colorado Northwestern Community College
Colorado State University
Community College of Aurora
Community College of Denver
Fort Lewis College
Front Range Community College
Mesa State College
Metropolitan State College of Denver
Morgan Community College
Nazarene Bible College
Northeastern Junior College
Pikes Peak Community College
Pueblo Community College
Red Rocks Community College
Trinidad State Junior College
University of Colorado
    Boulder
    Colorado Springs
    Denver
    Health Sciences Center
University of Northern Colorado
University of Southern Colorado

Connecticut
Asnuntuck Community-Technical College
Capital Community College
Central Connecticut State University
Charter Oak State College
Eastern Connecticut State University
Gateway Community College
Housatonic Community-Technical College
Manchester Community-Technical College
Naugatuck Valley Community-Technical College
Northwestern Connecticut Community-Technical College
Quinebaug Valley Community College
Sacred Heart University
Southern Connecticut State University
Teikyo Post University
Tunxis Community College
University of Bridgeport
University of Connecticut
University of Hartford
Western Connecticut State University

Distance learning

Delaware
Delaware State University
Delaware Technical and Community College
  Owens Campus
    Stanton/Wilmington Campus
    Terry Campus
Goldey-Beacom College
University of Delaware
Wilmington College

District of Columbia
Gallaudet University
George Washington University
Howard University

Florida
Barry University
Bethune-Cookman College
Brevard Community College
Broward Community College
Central Florida Community College
Chipola Junior College
Daytona Beach Community College
Edison Community College
Embry-Riddle Aeronautical University
Florida Atlantic University
Florida Baptist Theological College
Florida Christian College
Florida Community College at Jacksonville
Florida Gulf Coast University
Florida Institute of Technology
Florida International University
Florida Keys Community College
Florida State University
Gulf Coast Community College
Hillsborough Community College
Indian River Community College
Jacksonville University
Jones College
Lake City Community College
Lake-Sumter Community College
Manatee Community College
Miami-Dade Community College
Northwood University
  Florida Campus
Nova Southeastern University
Palm Beach Community College
Pasco-Hernando Community College
Pensacola Junior College
Polk Community College
St. Leo University
St. Petersburg Junior College
St. Thomas University
Santa Fe Community College
Seminole Community College
South Florida Community College
Tallahassee Community College
University of Central Florida
University of Florida
University of Miami
University of North Florida
University of South Florida
Valencia Community College

Georgia
American InterContinental University
Armstrong Atlantic State University
Athens Area Technical Institute
Atlanta Metropolitan College
Augusta State University
Bainbridge College
Brenau University
Chattahoochee Technical Institute
Clayton College and State University
Columbus State University
Darton College
East Georgia College
Emmanuel College
Floyd College
Gainesville College
Georgia College and State University
Georgia Institute of Technology
Georgia Perimeter College
Georgia Southern University
Georgia Southwestern State University
Georgia State University
Macon State College
Medical College of Georgia
Middle Georgia College
North Georgia College & State University
Piedmont College
South Georgia College
Southern Polytechnic State University
State University of West Georgia
University of Georgia
Valdosta State University

Hawaii
Chaminade University of Honolulu
Hawaii Pacific University
University of Hawaii
  Hawaii Community College
  Hilo
  Honolulu Community College
  Kapiolani Community College
  Kauai Community College
  Leeward Community College
  Manoa
  West Oahu
  Windward Community College

Idaho
Boise State University
College of Southern Idaho
Eastern Idaho Technical College
Idaho State University
Lewis-Clark State College
North Idaho College
Northwest Nazarene University
Ricks College
University of Idaho

Illinois
Benedictine University
Black Hawk College
Black Hawk College
  East Campus
Bradley University
City Colleges of Chicago
  Harold Washington College
  Kennedy-King College
  Malcolm X College
  Olive-Harvey College
  Richard J. Daley College
  Wright College
College of DuPage
College of Lake County
Concordia University
Danville Area Community College
De Paul University
Dominican University
Elgin Community College
Finch University of Health Sciences/The Chicago Medical School
Governors State University
Highland Community College
Illinois Eastern Community Colleges
  Frontier Community College
  Lincoln Trail College
  Olney Central College
  Wabash Valley College
Illinois Institute of Technology
John A. Logan College
John Wood Community College
Joliet Junior College
Kankakee Community College
Kaskaskia College
Kishwaukee College
Lake Land College
Lakeview College of Nursing
Lewis University
Lewis and Clark Community College
Lincoln Christian College and Seminary
Lincoln Land Community College
McHenry County College
Moody Bible Institute
Morton College
National-Louis University
Northeastern Illinois University
Northern Illinois University
Northwestern Business College
Oakton Community College
Olivet Nazarene University
Parkland College
Prairie State College
Quincy University
Rend Lake College
Richland Community College
Robert Morris College: Chicago
Sauk Valley Community College
Shawnee Community College
Southeastern Illinois College
Southern Illinois University
  Carbondale
  Edwardsville
Southwestern Ilinois College
Spoon River College
Springfield College in Illinois
Triton College
University of Illinois
  Chicago
  Springfield
University of St. Francis
Waubonsee Community College
Western Illinois University
William Rainey Harper College

Indiana
Ball State University
Calumet College of St. Joseph
Goshen College
Grace College
Indiana State University
Indiana University
  Bloomington
  East
  Kokomo
  Northwest
  South Bend
Indiana University--Purdue University
  Indiana University-Purdue University Fort Wayne
  Indiana University-Purdue University Indianapolis
Indiana Wesleyan University
Ivy Tech State College
  Central Indiana
  Columbus
  Eastcentral
  Kokomo
  Lafayette
  Northcentral
  Northeast
  Northwest
  Southcentral
  Southeast
  Southwest
  Wabash Valley
  Whitewater
Oakland City University
Purdue University
Purdue University
  North Central Campus
St. Mary-of-the-Woods College
University of Indianapolis
University of Southern Indiana
Vincennes University

Iowa
Buena Vista University
Clarke College
Clinton Community College
Des Moines Area Community College
Drake University
Graceland University
Grand View College
Hawkeye Community College
Iowa Central Community College
Iowa Lakes Community College
Iowa State University
Iowa Wesleyan College
Iowa Western Community College
Kirkwood Community College
Maharishi University of Management
Marshalltown Community College
Marycrest International University
Morningside College
Muscatine Community College
North Iowa Area Community College
Northeast Iowa Community College
St. Ambrose University
Scott Community College
Southeastern Community College
  North Campus
  South Campus
Southwestern Community College
University of Iowa
University of Northern Iowa
Western Iowa Tech Community College
William Penn University

Kansas
Allen County Community College
Barclay College
Barton County Community College
Bethel College
Butler County Community College
Coffeyville Community College
Colby Community College
Dodge City Community College
Emporia State University
Fort Hays State University
Garden City Community College
Hutchinson Community College
Independence Community College
Johnson County Community College
Kansas City Kansas Community College
Kansas State University
Newman University
Pittsburg State University
Pratt Community College
St. Mary College
Seward County Community College
University of Kansas
University of Kansas
  Medical Center
Washburn University of Topeka
Wichita State University

Kentucky
Ashland Community College
Campbellsville University
Cumberland College
Elizabethtown Community College
Henderson Community College
Hopkinsville Community College
Kentucky State University
Lexington Community College
Madisonville Community College
Maysville Community College
Midway College
Morehead State University
Murray State University
Northern Kentucky University
Owensboro Community College
Paducah Community College
Prestonsburg Community College
Somerset Community College
Southeast Community College
University of Kentucky
University of Louisville
Western Kentucky University

Louisiana
Bossier Parish Community College
Centenary College of Louisiana
Delgado Community College
Louisiana State University and Agricultural and Mechanical College
Louisiana State University
  Alexandria
  Eunice
  Shreveport

Louisiana Tech University
Loyola University New Orleans
McNeese State University
Nicholls State University
Northwestern State University
Nunez Community College
Our Lady of Holy Cross College
Southeastern Louisiana University
Southern University and Agricultural and Mechanical College
University of Louisiana at Monroe
University of New Orleans
Xavier University of Louisiana

Maine
Husson College
Southern Maine Technical College
University of Maine
University of Maine
    Augusta
    Farmington
    Fort Kent
    Machias
    Presque Isle
University of New England
University of Southern Maine

Maryland
Allegany College
Anne Arundel Community College
Baltimore City Community College
Bowie State University
Carroll Community College
Cecil Community College
Charles County Community College
Chesapeake College
Columbia Union College
Community College of Baltimore County
    Catonsville
    Essex
Coppin State College
Frederick Community College
Frostburg State University
Hagerstown Community College
Harford Community College
Howard Community College
Maryland Institute College of Art
Montgomery College
    Germantown Campus
    Rockville Campus
    Takoma Park Campus
Prince George's Community College
Towson University
University of Baltimore
University of Maryland
    Baltimore
    Baltimore County
    College Park
    Eastern Shore
    University College
Wor-Wic Community College

Massachusetts
Atlantic Union College
Becker College
Bentley College
Berkshire Community College
Bridgewater State College
Bristol Community College
Bunker Hill Community College
Cape Cod Community College
Endicott College
Fisher College
Fitchburg State College
Framingham State College
Greenfield Community College
Hebrew College
Holyoke Community College
Lesley College
Massachusetts Bay Community College
Massachusetts College of Liberal Arts
Massachusetts Institute of Technology
Massasoit Community College
Middlesex Community College
Mount Wachusett Community College
Nichols College
North Shore Community College
Northeastern University
Northern Essex Community College
Suffolk University
University of Massachusetts
    Amherst
    Boston
    Dartmouth
    Lowell
Worcester State College

Michigan
Alpena Community College
Andrews University
Aquinas College
Baker College
    of Auburn Hills
    of Cadillac
    of Jackson
    of Mount Clemens
    of Muskegon
    of Owosso
    of Port Huron
Bay de Noc Community College
Central Michigan University
Cleary College
Concordia College
Davenport College of Business
Delta College
Eastern Michigan University
Ferris State University
Glen Oaks Community College
Gogebic Community College
Grand Rapids Community College
Grand Valley State University
Great Lakes College
Henry Ford Community College
Jackson Community College
Kalamazoo Valley Community College
Kellogg Community College
Kettering University
Kirtland Community College
Lake Michigan College
Lake Superior State University
Lansing Community College
Lawrence Technological University
Macomb Community College
Madonna University
Michigan State University
Michigan Technological University
Mid Michigan Community College
Montcalm Community College
Mott Community College
Muskegon Community College
Northern Michigan University
Northwestern Michigan College
Northwood University
Oakland Community College
Oakland University
Reformed Bible College
Saginaw Valley State University
St. Clair County Community College
Schoolcraft College
Southwestern Michigan College
Suomi College
University of Michigan
University of Michigan
    Dearborn
Walsh College of Accountancy and Business Administration
Washtenaw Community College
Wayne County Community College
Wayne State University
West Shore Community College
Western Michigan University

Minnesota
Alexandria Technical College
Anoka-Ramsey Community College
Bemidji State University
Central Lakes College
College of St. Scholastica
Concordia University: St. Paul
Crown College
Fond Du Lac Tribal and Community College
Hamline University
Hennepin Technical College
Hibbing Community College: A Technical and Community College
Inver Hills Community College
Lake Superior College: A Community and Technical College
Metropolitan State University
Minneapolis College of Art and Design
Minneapolis Community and Technical College
Moorhead State University
National American University
    St. Paul
North Central University
North Hennepin Community College
Northwestern College
Pine Technical College
Ridgewater College: A Community and Technical College
Rochester Community and Technical College
St. Cloud State University
St. Cloud Technical College
Southwest State University
University of Minnesota
    Crookston
    Duluth
    Morris
    Twin Cities
Winona State University

Mississippi
Alcorn State University
Coahoma Community College
East Central Community College
East Mississippi Community College
Hinds Community College
Holmes Community College
Meridian Community College
Mississippi Delta Community College
Mississippi Gulf Coast Community College
    Jackson County Campus
    Jefferson Davis Campus
    Perkinston
Mississippi State University
Mississippi University for Women
University of Mississippi
University of Southern Mississippi

Missouri
Avila College
Baptist Bible College
Berean University
Central Missouri State University
Crowder College
East Central College
Fontbonne College
Jefferson College
Longview Community College
Maple Woods Community College
Mineral Area College
Missouri Southern State College
Moberly Area Community College
Ozarks Technical Community College
Park University
Penn Valley Community College
Rockhurst University
St. Charles County Community College
St. Louis University
Southwest Missouri State University
Southwest Missouri State University West Plains Campus
St. Louis Community College
    St. Louis Community College at Florissant Valley
    St. Louis Community College at Meramec
State Fair Community College
Stephens College
Three Rivers Community College
University of Missouri
    Columbia
    Rolla
    St. Louis
Webster University

Montana
Dawson Community College
Flathead Valley Community College
Little Big Horn College
Miles Community College
Montana State University
    Billings
    Bozeman
    College of Technology-Great Falls
    Northern
Montana Tech of the University of Montana
Rocky Mountain College
Stone Child College
University of Great Falls
University of Montana-Missoula
Western Montana College of The University of Montana

Nebraska
Bellevue University
Central Community College
Chadron State College
Clarkson College
Concordia University
Creighton University
Metropolitan Community College
Mid Plains Community College Area
Midland Lutheran College
Nebraska College of Technical Agriculture
Northeast Community College
Peru State College
Southeast Community College
    Lincoln Campus
University of Nebraska
    Kearney
    Lincoln
    Omaha
Wayne State College

Nevada
Community College of Southern Nevada
University of Nevada
    Las Vegas
    Reno
Western Nevada Community College

New Hampshire
College for Lifelong Learning
Hesser College
New Hampshire College
New Hampshire Community Technical College
    Berlin
    Laconia
    Nashua
New Hampshire Technical Institute
Notre Dame College
University of New Hampshire

New Jersey
Atlantic Cape Community College
Bergen Community College
Berkeley College
Bloomfield College
Brookdale Community College
Burlington County College
Camden County College
College of St. Elizabeth
County College of Morris
Cumberland County College
Fairleigh Dickinson University
Felician College
Georgian Court College
Gloucester County College

Hudson County Community College
Kean University
Mercer County Community College
New Jersey City University
New Jersey Institute of Technology
Ocean County College
Passaic County Community College
Ramapo College of New Jersey
Raritan Valley Community College
Richard Stockton College of New Jersey
Rutgers
- The State University of New Jersey: Camden College of Arts and Sciences
- The State University of New Jersey: College of Engineering
- The State University of New Jersey: College of Nursing
- The State University of New Jersey: Cook College
- The State University of New Jersey: Douglass College
- The State University of New Jersey: Livingston College
- The State University of New Jersey: Mason Gross School of the Arts
- The State University of New Jersey: Newark College of Arts and Sciences
- The State University of New Jersey: Rutgers College
- The State University of New Jersey: University College Camden
- The State University of New Jersey: University College New Brunswick
- The State University of New Jersey: University College Newark

Salem Community College
Sussex County Community College
Thomas Edison State College
Union County College
University of Medicine and Dentistry of New Jersey
- School of Health Related Professions

Warren County Community College
William Paterson University of New Jersey

New Mexico

Albuquerque Technical-Vocational Institute
Clovis Community College
College of Santa Fe
Eastern New Mexico University
Eastern New Mexico University Roswell Campus
New Mexico Highlands University
New Mexico Institute of Mining and Technology
New Mexico Junior College
New Mexico State University
New Mexico State University
- Alamogordo
- Carlsbad

Northern New Mexico Community College
San Juan College
Santa Fe Community College
University of New Mexico

New York

Adelphi University
Berkeley College
Berkeley College of New York City
Bryant & Stratton Business Institute Albany
City University of New York
- Borough of Manhattan Community College
- Hunter College
- Medgar Evers College
- Queens College

Clinton Community College
College of Aeronautics
College of Insurance
Columbia-Greene Community College
Concordia College
Cornell University
Corning Community College
Dutchess Community College
Erie Community College
- City Campus
- North Campus
- South Campus

Eugene Lang College/New School University
Fashion Institute of Technology
Finger Lakes Community College
Fulton-Montgomery Community College
Genesee Community College
Herkimer County Community College
Hudson Valley Community College
Iona College
Jamestown Community College
Jefferson Community College
Jewish Theological Seminary of America
Long Island University
- C. W. Post Campus
- Southampton College

Manhattan College
Marist College
Marymount College
Marymount Manhattan College
Mercy College
Mohawk Valley Community College
Monroe Community College
Nassau Community College
New York Institute of Technology
New York State College of Ceramics at Alfred University
New York University
North Country Community College
Nyack College
Onondaga Community College
Pace University
Pace University: Pleasantville/Briarcliff
Polytechnic University
Polytechnic University
- Long Island Campus

Regents College
Rensselaer Polytechnic Institute
Rochester Institute of Technology
Rockland Community College
St. John's University
St. Joseph's College
- St. Joseph's College: Suffolk Campus

State University of New York
- Albany
- Binghamton
- Buffalo
- College at Brockport
- College at Buffalo
- College at Cortland
- College at Fredonia
- College at Oneonta
- College at Plattsburgh
- College at Potsdam
- College of Agriculture and Technology at Cobleskill
- College of Agriculture and Technology at Morrisville
- College of Technology at Alfred
- College of Technology at Canton
- College of Technology at Delhi
- Institute of Technology at Utica/Rome
- New Paltz
- Oswego
- Purchase

Suffolk County Community College
Syracuse University
Technical Career Institutes
Tompkins-Cortland Community College
Touro College
Ulster County Community College
Westchester Community College

North Carolina

Appalachian State University
Asheville Buncombe Technical Community College
Beaufort County Community College
Bladen Community College
Blue Ridge Community College
Brunswick Community College
Caldwell Community College and Technical Institute
Cape Fear Community College
Carteret Community College
Catawba Valley Community College
Central Carolina Community College
Central Piedmont Community College
Cleveland Community College
Coastal Carolina Community College
College of the Albemarle
Craven Community College
Davidson County Community College
Duke University
Durham Technical Community College
East Carolina University
Edgecombe Community College
Fayetteville State University
Forsyth Technical Community College
Gaston College
Guilford Technical Community College
Haywood Community College
James Sprunt Community College
Johnston Community College
Lenoir Community College
Lenoir-Rhyne College
Mars Hill College
Martin Community College
Mayland Community College
Mitchell Community College
Montgomery Community College
Nash Community College
North Carolina Agricultural and Technical State University
North Carolina State University
Piedmont Community College
Pitt Community College
Randolph Community College
Richmond Community College
Roanoke-Chowan Community College
Rockingham Community College
Rowan-Cabarrus Community College
Sampson Community College
Sandhills Community College
Shaw University
South Piedmont Community College
Southeastern Community College
Surry Community College
University of North Carolina
- Asheville
- Chapel Hill
- Charlotte
- Greensboro
- Pembroke
- Wilmington

Vance-Granville Community College
Wake Technical Community College
Wayne Community College
Western Carolina University
Western Piedmont Community College
Wilkes Community College
Wilson Technical Community College
Winston-Salem State University

North Dakota

Bismarck State College
Dickinson State University
Lake Region State College
Mayville State University
Minot State University
Minot State University: Bottineau Campus
North Dakota State College of Science
North Dakota State University
University of Mary
University of North Dakota
Williston State College

Ohio

Bowling Green State University
Bowling Green State University Firelands College
Bryant & Stratton College
Cedarville College
Cincinnati State Technical and Community College
Cleveland State University
College of Mount St. Joseph
Columbus State Community College
David N. Myers College
Defiance College
Edison State Community College
Franciscan University of Steubenville
Franklin University
Hocking Technical College
Kent State University
Kent State University
- Ashtabula Regional Campus
- East Liverpool Regional Campus
- Stark Campus
- Trumbull Campus
- Tuscarawas Campus

Lakeland Community College
Lima Technical College
Lorain County Community College
Miami University
- Hamilton Campus
- Middletown Campus

Miami-Jacobs College
North Central State College
Northwest State Community College
Northwestern College
Ohio State University
- Columbus Campus

Ohio University
Ohio University
- Chillicothe Campus

Owens Community College
- Findlay Campus
- Toledo

Sinclair Community College
Union Institute
University of Akron
University of Akron
- Wayne College

University of Cincinnati
University of Cincinnati
- Raymond Walters College

University of Findlay
University of Rio Grande
University of Toledo
Youngstown State University

Oklahoma

Cameron University
Carl Albert State College
Connors State College
East Central University
Eastern Oklahoma State College
Mid-America Bible College
Northeastern Oklahoma Agricultural and Mechanical College
Northeastern State University
Northern Oklahoma College
Northwestern Oklahoma State University
Oklahoma City Community College
Oklahoma State University
Oklahoma State University
- Oklahoma City
- Okmulgee

Oral Roberts University
Redlands Community College
Rogers State University
Rose State College
Southeastern Oklahoma State University
Southwestern Oklahoma State University
Tulsa Community College
University of Central Oklahoma
University of Oklahoma
University of Science and Arts of Oklahoma
Western Oklahoma State College

Oregon

Central Oregon Community College
Chemeketa Community College
Clackamas Community College
Clatsop Community College
Concordia University
Eastern Oregon University
Eugene Bible College
Lane Community College
Linfield College
Linn-Benton Community College
Marylhurst University
Mount Hood Community College
Oregon Institute of Technology
Oregon State University
Portland Community College
Portland State University
Southern Oregon University
Western Baptist College
Western Oregon University

Pennsylvania

Allentown College of St. Francis de Sales
Bloomsburg University of Pennsylvania
Bucks County Community College
Butler County Community College
Cabrini College
California University of Pennsylvania
Carlow College
Cheyney University of Pennsylvania
Clarion University of Pennsylvania
College Misericordia
Community College of Allegheny County
Community College of Beaver County
Community College of Philadelphia
Duquesne University
Edinboro University of Pennsylvania
Gannon University
Harcum College
Harrisburg Area Community College
ICS Center for Degree Studies
Indiana University of Pennsylvania
Juniata College
King's College
Kutztown University of Pennsylvania
La Roche College
Lackawanna Junior College
Lafayette College
Lehigh Carbon Community College
Lehigh University
Luzerne County Community College
MCP Hahnemann University
Manor College
Mansfield University of Pennsylvania
Marywood University
Millersville University of Pennsylvania
Montgomery County Community College
Mount Aloysius College
Neumann College
Northampton County Area Community College
Peirce College
Penn State
   Abington
   Altoona
   Beaver
   Delaware County
   Dubois
   Erie, The Behrend College
   Fayette
   Harrisburg
   Hazleton
   McKeesport
   Mont Alto
   New Kensington
   Schuylkill - Capital College
   Shenango
   University Park
   Wilkes-Barre
   Worthington Scranton
   York
Pennsylvania College of Technology
Philadelphia University
Point Park College
Reading Area Community College
St. Francis College
Seton Hill College
Shippensburg University of Pennsylvania
Temple University
University of Pennsylvania
University of Pittsburgh
University of Pittsburgh
   Bradford
   Greensburg
   Johnstown
   Titusville
University of Scranton
Valley Forge Christian College
Waynesburg College
West Chester University of Pennsylvania
Westmoreland County Community College
Wilkes University
York College of Pennsylvania

Puerto Rico

Colegio Universitario del Este
Huertas Junior College
Inter American University of Puerto Rico San German Campus
Turabo University
Universidad Metropolitana

Rhode Island

Community College of Rhode Island
University of Rhode Island

South Carolina

Aiken Technical College
Central Carolina Technical College
Charleston Southern University
Chesterfield-Marlboro Technical College
Clemson University
Coastal Carolina University
Columbia International University
Florence-Darlington Technical College
Greenville Technical College
Lander University
Limestone College
Midlands Technical College
Newberry College
Orangeburg-Calhoun Technical College
Piedmont Technical College
South Carolina State University
Southern Wesleyan University
Spartanburg Technical College
Technical College of the Lowcountry
Tri-County Technical College
Trident Technical College
University of South Carolina
University of South Carolina
   Beaufort
   Spartanburg
   Sumter
   Union
Winthrop University
York Technical College

South Dakota

Black Hills State University
Dakota State University
Northern State University
South Dakota State University
University of South Dakota

Tennessee

Austin Peay State University
Chattanooga State Technical Community College
Cleveland State Community College
Columbia State Community College
Dyersburg State Community College
East Tennessee State University
Johnson Bible College
LeMoyne-Owen College
Lee University
Middle Tennessee State University
Motlow State Community College
Nashville State Technical Institute
Northeast State Technical Community College
Pellissippi State Technical Community College
Roane State Community College
Shelby State Community College
Tennessee Technological University
Union University
University of Memphis
University of Tennessee
   Chattanooga
   Knoxville
   Martin
   Memphis
Volunteer State Community College
Walters State Community College

Texas

Alvin Community College
Amarillo College
Amber University
Angelina College
Arlington Baptist College
Blinn College
Brazosport College
Cedar Valley College
Central Texas College
Coastal Bend College
College of the Mainland
Collin County Community College District
Concordia University at Austin
Dallas Baptist University
Del Mar College
Eastfield College
El Paso Community College
Galveston College
Grayson County College
Hill College
Houston Baptist University
Houston Community College System
Jarvis Christian College
Kilgore College
Lamar State College at Orange
Lamar State College at Port Arthur
Lamar University
LeTourneau University
Lee College
Midland College
Midwestern State University
Mountain View College
Navarro College
North Central Texas College
North Lake College
Northwood University: Texas Campus
Odessa College
Palo Alto College
Paul Quinn College
Prairie View A&M University
Richland College
St. Mary's University
St. Philip's College
Sam Houston State University
San Antonio College
San Jacinto College
   North
Schreiner College
Southern Methodist University
Southwest Texas State University
Southwestern Adventist University
Stephen F. Austin State University
Sul Ross State University
Tarleton State University
Tarrant County College
Temple College
Texas A&M University
Texas A&M University
   Commerce
   Corpus Christi
   Kingsville
   Texarkana
Texas Southern University
Texas State Technical College
   Harlingen
   Sweetwater
   Waco
Texas Tech University
Texas Wesleyan University
Texas Woman's University
Trinity Valley Community College
Tyler Junior College
University of Dallas
University of Houston
University of Houston
   Clear Lake
   Downtown
   Victoria
University of North Texas
University of Texas
   Arlington
   Austin
   Dallas
   Pan American
   San Antonio
   of the Permian Basin
Vernon Regional Junior College
Wayland Baptist University
Weatherford College
West Texas A&M University
Western Texas College
Wharton County Junior College

Utah

Brigham Young University
College of Eastern Utah
Dixie State College of Utah
Salt Lake Community College
Southern Utah University
University of Utah
Utah State University
Utah Valley State College
Weber State University

Vermont

Burlington College
Champlain College
Community College of Vermont
Goddard College
Johnson State College
Norwich University
Southern Vermont College
University of Vermont
Vermont Technical College

Virginia

Averett College
Blue Ridge Community College
Central Virginia Community College
Christopher Newport University
Dabney S. Lancaster Community College
Danville Community College
Eastern Shore Community College
George Mason University
J. Sargeant Reynolds Community College
James Madison University
John Tyler Community College
Liberty University
Longwood College
Lord Fairfax Community College
Mountain Empire Community College
New River Community College
Norfolk State University
Northern Virginia Community College
Old Dominion University
Patrick Henry Community College
Paul D. Camp Community College
Piedmont Virginia Community College
Radford University
Southside Virginia Community College
Southwest Virginia Community College
Thomas Nelson Community College
Tidewater Community College
University of Virginia's College at Wise
Virginia Highlands Community College

Virginia Polytechnic Institute and State University
Wytheville Community College

Washington

Bellevue Community College
Big Bend Community College
Central Washington University
Centralia College
City University
Clark College
Columbia Basin College
Eastern Washington University
Edmonds Community College
Everett Community College
Gonzaga University
Grays Harbor College
Green River Community College
Highline Community College
Lake Washington Technical College
Lower Columbia College
North Seattle Community College
Olympic College
Peninsula College
Pierce College
Renton Technical College
Seattle Central Community College
Seattle Pacific University
Shoreline Community College
Skagit Valley College
South Puget Sound Community College
South Seattle Community College
Spokane Community College
Spokane Falls Community College
Tacoma Community College
University of Washington
Walla Walla College
Walla Walla Community College
Washington State University
Wenatchee Valley College
Whatcom Community College
Yakima Valley Community College

West Virginia

Alderson-Broaddus College
Bluefield State College
College of West Virginia
Glenville State College
Marshall University
Potomac State College of West Virginia University
Southern West Virginia Community and Technical College
West Virginia Northern Community College
West Virginia State College
West Virginia University
West Virginia University Parkersburg
West Virginia Wesleyan College

Wisconsin

Blackhawk Technical College
Bryant & Stratton College
Cardinal Stritch University
Chippewa Valley Technical College
Concordia University Wisconsin
Gateway Technical College
Lakeshore Technical College
Madison Area Technical College
Marian College of Fond du Lac
Marquette University
Milwaukee Area Technical College
Milwaukee School of Engineering
Moraine Park Technical College
Nicolet Area Technical College
Northeast Wisconsin Technical College
Northland College
St. Norbert College
Southwest Wisconsin Technical College
University of Wisconsin
 Baraboo/Sauk County
 Eau Claire
 Fond du Lac
 Green Bay
 La Crosse
 Marinette
 Milwaukee
 Oshkosh
 Parkside
 Richland
 River Falls
 Rock County
 Sheboygan County
 Stevens Point
 Stout
 Superior
 Washington County
 Waukesha
 Whitewater
Waukesha County Technical College
Western Wisconsin Technical College
Wisconsin Indianhead Technical College

Wyoming

Casper College
Central Wyoming College
Eastern Wyoming College
Laramie County Community College
Northwest College
Sheridan College
University of Wyoming
Western Wyoming Community College

Double major

Alabama

Alabama Agricultural and Mechanical University
Alabama State University
Athens State University
Auburn University
Auburn University at Montgomery
Birmingham-Southern College
Calhoun Community College
Community College of the Air Force
Faulkner University
George C. Wallace State Community College
 Selma
Huntingdon College
Jacksonville State University
James H. Faulkner State Community College
Lawson State Community College
Northeast Alabama Community College
Oakwood College
Samford University
Shelton State Community College
South College
Spring Hill College
Stillman College
Talladega College
Troy State University
Troy State University
 Dothan
 Montgomery
Tuskegee University
University of Alabama
University of Alabama
 Birmingham
 Huntsville
University of Mobile
University of Montevallo
University of North Alabama
University of South Alabama
University of West Alabama
Wallace State Community College at Hanceville

Alaska

Alaska Bible College
Alaska Pacific University
University of Alaska
 Anchorage
 Fairbanks
 Southeast

Arizona

American Indian College of the Assemblies of God
Arizona State University
Cochise College
DeVry Institute of Technology
 Phoenix
Dine College
Eastern Arizona College
Embry-Riddle Aeronautical University
 Prescott Campus
Gateway Community College
Grand Canyon University
Northern Arizona University
Pima Community College
Prescott College
Rio Salado College
University of Advancing Computer Technology
University of Arizona

Arkansas

Arkansas State University
Arkansas State University
 Beebe Branch
Arkansas Tech University
Garland County Community College
Harding University
Hendrix College
Lyon College
Mississippi County Community College
Ouachita Baptist University
Southern Arkansas University
Southern Arkansas University Tech
University of Arkansas
University of Arkansas
 Little Rock
 Monticello
 Pine Bluff
University of Central Arkansas
University of the Ozarks
Williams Baptist College

California

Allan Hancock College
Antioch Southern California
 Los Angeles
 Santa Barbara
Armstrong University
Art Institutes International
 San Francisco
Bakersfield College
Biola University
Butte College
California Baptist University
California College of Arts and Crafts
California Institute of Technology
California Lutheran University
California Maritime Academy
California Polytechnic State University:
 San Luis Obispo
California State Polytechnic University:
 Pomona
California State University
 Bakersfield
 Chico
 Dominguez Hills
 Fresno
 Fullerton
 Hayward
 Long Beach
 Los Angeles
 Northridge
 Sacramento
 San Marcos
 Stanislaus
Canada College
Cerro Coso Community College
Chabot College
Chapman University
Claremont McKenna College
College of Notre Dame
College of San Mateo
College of the Desert
College of the Redwoods
Columbia College
Concordia University
Cuesta College
Cuyamaca College
DeVry Institute of Technology
 Fremont
 Long Beach
 Pomona
 West Hills
Dominican University of California
East Los Angeles College
Empire College
Evergreen Valley College
Fresno City College
Fresno Pacific University
Golden West College
Grossmont Community College
Harvey Mudd College
Heald Business College
 Santa Rosa
Holy Names College
Hope International University
Humboldt State University
Humphreys College
Imperial Valley College
Irvine Valley College
John F. Kennedy University
Kings River Community College
La Sierra University
Lake Tahoe Community College
Los Angeles Harbor College
Los Angeles Southwest College
Loyola Marymount University
Master's College
Mendocino College
Menlo College
Mills College
MiraCosta College
Modesto Junior College
Monterey Peninsula College
Mount St. Mary's College
Mount San Antonio College
Mount San Jacinto College
Napa Valley College
National University
Occidental College
Ohlone College
Pacific Oaks College
Pacific Union College
Patten College
Pepperdine University
Pitzer College
Pomona College
Porterville College
Sacramento City College
Saddleback College
St. John's Seminary College
St. Mary's College of California
Samuel Merritt College
San Bernardino Valley College
San Diego City College
San Diego Mesa College
San Diego State University
San Francisco Art Institute
San Francisco State University
San Jose Christian College
San Jose State University
Santa Ana College
Santa Barbara City College
Santa Clara University
Scripps College
Shasta College
Sierra College
Simpson College
Solano Community College
Sonoma State University
Southwestern College
Stanford University

University of California
- Berkeley
- Davis
- Irvine
- Los Angeles
- Riverside
- San Diego
- Santa Barbara
- Santa Cruz

University of La Verne
University of Redlands
University of San Diego
University of San Francisco
University of Southern California
University of the Pacific
Vanguard University of Southern California
Victor Valley College
West Valley College
Westmont College
Whittier College

Colorado
Adams State College
Aims Community College
Colorado Christian University
Colorado College
Colorado School of Mines
Colorado State University
Colorado Technical University
Community College of Denver
Denver Technical College: A Division of DeVry University
Fort Lewis College
Front Range Community College
Mesa State College
Metropolitan State College of Denver
Morgan Community College
Naropa University
Nazarene Bible College
Pikes Peak Community College
Pueblo Community College
Red Rocks Community College
Regis University
Rocky Mountain College of Art & Design
Trinidad State Junior College
United States Air Force Academy
University of Colorado
- Boulder
- Colorado Springs
- Denver

University of Denver
University of Northern Colorado
University of Southern Colorado
Western State College of Colorado

Connecticut
Albertus Magnus College
Asnuntuck Community-Technical College
Briarwood College
Capital Community College
Central Connecticut State University
Connecticut College
Eastern Connecticut State University
Fairfield University
Housatonic Community-Technical College
Manchester Community-Technical College
Naugatuck Valley Community-Technical College
Northwestern Connecticut Community-Technical College
Norwalk Community-Technical College
Quinebaug Valley Community College
Quinnipiac University
Sacred Heart University
St. Joseph College
Southern Connecticut State University
Teikyo Post University
Three Rivers Community-Technical College
Trinity College
Tunxis Community College
United States Coast Guard Academy
University of Bridgeport
University of Connecticut
University of Hartford
University of New Haven
Wesleyan University
Western Connecticut State University
Yale University

Delaware
Delaware State University
Delaware Technical and Community College
- Owens Campus
- Stanton/Wilmington Campus
- Terry Campus

University of Delaware
Wesley College
Wilmington College

District of Columbia
American University
Catholic University of America
Gallaudet University
George Washington University
Georgetown University
Howard University
Trinity College
University of the District of Columbia

Florida
Barry University
Bethune-Cookman College
Brevard Community College
Clearwater Christian College
Eckerd College
Edward Waters College
Embry-Riddle Aeronautical University
Flagler College
Florida Agricultural and Mechanical University
Florida Atlantic University
Florida Baptist Theological College
Florida Christian College
Florida Community College at Jacksonville
Florida International University
Florida Keys Community College
Florida Memorial College
Florida Metropolitan University
- Orlando College North

Florida Southern College
Florida State University
Hillsborough Community College
Hobe Sound Bible College
International College
Jacksonville University
Jones College
Lynn University
New College of the University of South Florida
New England Institute of Technology
Northwood University
- Florida Campus

Palm Beach Atlantic College
Palm Beach Community College
Pasco-Hernando Community College
Pensacola Junior College
Polk Community College
Rollins College
St. Leo University
St. Thomas University
South College: Palm Beach Campus
South Florida Community College
Southeastern College of the Assemblies of God
Stetson University
University of Central Florida
University of Florida
University of Miami
University of North Florida
University of South Florida
University of Tampa
University of West Florida
Valencia Community College
Warner Southern College

Georgia
Agnes Scott College
Albany State University
American InterContinental University
Armstrong Atlantic State University
Atlanta Christian College
Augusta State University
Bainbridge College
Berry College
Brenau University
Brewton-Parker College
Clark Atlanta University
Clayton College and State University
Coastal Georgia Community College
Covenant College
DeVry Institute of Technology
- Alpharetta

East Georgia College
Emory University
Floyd College
Georgia College and State University
Georgia Institute of Technology
Georgia Military College
Georgia Perimeter College
Georgia Southern University
Georgia Southwestern State University
Georgia State University
Gwinnett Technical Institute
Kennesaw State University
LaGrange College
Mercer University
Middle Georgia College
Morehouse College
Morris Brown College
North Georgia College & State University
Oglethorpe University
Oxford College of Emory University
Piedmont College
Reinhardt College
Savannah College of Art and Design
Savannah State University
Shorter College
Spelman College
State University of West Georgia
Thomas College
Toccoa Falls College
University of Georgia
Valdosta State University
Wesleyan College

Hawaii
Brigham Young University
- Hawaii

Chaminade University of Honolulu
Hawaii Pacific University
University of Hawaii
- Hawaii Community College
- Hilo
- Kapiolani Community College
- Manoa
- Maui Community College
- West Oahu
- Windward Community College

Idaho
Albertson College of Idaho
Boise Bible College
Boise State University
Idaho State University
Lewis-Clark State College
Northwest Nazarene University
Ricks College
University of Idaho

Illinois
Augustana College
Barat College
Benedictine University
Black Hawk College
- East Campus

Blackburn College
Blessing-Reiman College of Nursing
Bradley University
Chicago State University
City Colleges of Chicago
- Harold Washington College
- Malcolm X College

College of DuPage
Concordia University
Danville Area Community College
De Paul University
DeVry Institute of Technology
- Addison
- Chicago

Dominican University
Eastern Illinois University
Elgin Community College
Elmhurst College
Eureka College
Greenville College
Illinois College
Illinois Eastern Community Colleges
- Frontier Community College
- Lincoln Trail College
- Olney Central College
- Wabash Valley College

Illinois Institute of Technology
Illinois Wesleyan University
International Academy of Merchandising and Design
Judson College
Kaskaskia College
Kishwaukee College
Knox College
Lake Forest College
Lewis University
Lewis and Clark Community College
Lincoln Christian College and Seminary
Loyola University of Chicago
MacMurray College
McKendree College
Millikin University
Monmouth College
Moody Bible Institute
Moraine Valley Community College
Morton College
North Central College
Northern Illinois University
Northwestern Business College
Northwestern University
Olivet Nazarene University
Parkland College
Principia College
Quincy University
Rockford College
Roosevelt University
St. Augustine College
St. Xavier University
Sauk Valley Community College
School of the Art Institute of Chicago
Shimer College
Southeastern Illinois College
Southern Illinois University
- Carbondale
- Edwardsville

Southwestern Ilinois College
Springfield College in Illinois
Trinity Christian College
Trinity International University
University of Chicago
University of Illinois
- Chicago
- Springfield
- Urbana-Champaign

University of St. Francis
Western Illinois University
Wheaton College

Indiana
Ancilla College
Anderson University
Ball State University
Bethel College

Butler University
Calumet College of St. Joseph
DePauw University
Earlham College
Franklin College
Goshen College
Grace College
Hanover College
Indiana Institute of Technology
Indiana State University
Indiana University
    Bloomington
    East
    Northwest
    South Bend
    Southeast
Indiana University--Purdue University
    Indiana University-Purdue
      University Fort Wayne
    Indiana University-Purdue
      University Indianapolis
Indiana Wesleyan University
Ivy Tech State College
    Southcentral
Manchester College
Marian College
Michiana College
Oakland City University
Purdue University
Rose-Hulman Institute of Technology
Saint Mary's College
St. Joseph's College
St. Mary-of-the-Woods College
Tri-State University
University of Evansville
University of Indianapolis
University of Notre Dame
University of St. Francis
University of Southern Indiana
Valparaiso University
Vincennes University
Wabash College

Iowa
American Institute of Business
Briar Cliff College
Buena Vista University
Central College
Clarke College
Clinton Community College
Coe College
Cornell College
Dordt College
Drake University
Emmaus Bible College
Faith Baptist Bible College and
    Theological Seminary
Graceland University
Grand View College
Grinnell College
Iowa State University
Iowa Wesleyan College
Loras College
Luther College
Maharishi University of Management
Marycrest International University
Morningside College
Mount Mercy College
Muscatine Community College
Northeast Iowa Community College
Northwestern College
St. Ambrose University
Scott Community College
Simpson College
Southwestern Community College
University of Dubuque
University of Iowa
University of Northern Iowa
Upper Iowa University
Wartburg College
Western Iowa Tech Community College
William Penn University

Kansas
Allen County Community College
Baker University
Barclay College
Benedictine College
Bethany College
Bethel College
Central Christian College
Coffeyville Community College
Cowley County Community College
Dodge City Community College
Emporia State University
Fort Hays State University
Hutchinson Community College
Independence Community College
Johnson County Community College
Kansas City Kansas Community College
Kansas State University
Kansas Wesleyan University
Manhattan Christian College
McPherson College
MidAmerica Nazarene University
Newman University
Ottawa University
Pittsburg State University
St. Mary College
Seward County Community College
Southwestern College
Sterling College
Tabor College
University of Kansas
Washburn University of Topeka
Wichita State University

Kentucky
Alice Lloyd College
Asbury College
Bellarmine College
Berea College
Brescia University
Campbellsville University
Centre College
Cumberland College
Eastern Kentucky University
Georgetown College
Henderson Community College
Kentucky Christian College
Kentucky State University
Kentucky Wesleyan College
Madisonville Community College
Mid-Continent College
Midway College
Morehead State University
Murray State University
National Business College
Northern Kentucky University
Owensboro Community College
Owensboro Junior College of Business
Pikeville College
Spalding University
Thomas More College
Transylvania University
Union College
University of Kentucky
University of Louisville
Western Kentucky University

Louisiana
Bossier Parish Community College
Centenary College of Louisiana
Delgado Community College
Dillard University
Louisiana State University and
    Agricultural and Mechanical College
Louisiana State University
    Shreveport
Louisiana Tech University
Loyola University New Orleans
McNeese State University
Northwestern State University
Nunez Community College
Our Lady of Holy Cross College
Southeastern Louisiana University
Southern University and Agricultural and
    Mechanical College
Tulane University
University of Louisiana at Lafayette
University of Louisiana at Monroe
University of New Orleans
Xavier University of Louisiana

Maine
Andover College
Bates College
Beal College
Bowdoin College
Colby College
Husson College
Maine College of Art
Mid-State College
St. Joseph's College
Southern Maine Technical College
Unity College
University of Maine
University of Maine
    Farmington
    Fort Kent
    Machias
    Presque Isle
University of New England
University of Southern Maine
Washington County Technical College

Maryland
Anne Arundel Community College
Baltimore City Community College
Baltimore International College
Bowie State University
Cecil Community College
College of Notre Dame of Maryland
Columbia Union College
Coppin State College
Frostburg State University
Goucher College
Harford Community College
Hood College
Howard Community College
Johns Hopkins University
Johns Hopkins University: Peabody
    Conservatory of Music
Loyola College in Maryland
Maryland Institute College of Art
Montgomery College
    Germantown Campus
    Rockville Campus
    Takoma Park Campus
Mount St. Mary's College
Prince George's Community College
St. Mary's College of Maryland
Salisbury State University
Towson University
United States Naval Academy
University of Maryland
    Baltimore County
    College Park
    Eastern Shore
Villa Julie College
Washington Bible College
Washington College
Western Maryland College
Wor-Wic Community College

Massachusetts
American International College
Amherst College
Anna Maria College
Assumption College
Atlantic Union College
Babson College
Berklee College of Music
Boston College
Boston Conservatory
Boston University
Brandeis University
Bridgewater State College
Bunker Hill Community College
Clark University
College of the Holy Cross
Curry College
Eastern Nazarene College
Elms College
Emerson College
Emmanuel College
Fisher College
Fitchburg State College
Framingham State College
Gordon College
Harvard College
Hellenic College/Holy Cross
Lasell College
Lesley College
Marian Court College
Massachusetts Bay Community College
Massachusetts College of Art
Massachusetts College of Liberal Arts
Massachusetts College of Pharmacy and
    Health Sciences
Massachusetts Institute of Technology
Massachusetts Maritime Academy
Merrimack College
Montserrat College of Art
Mount Holyoke College
New England Conservatory of Music
Newbury College
Nichols College
Northeastern University
Northern Essex Community College
Pine Manor College
Regis College
Roxbury Community College
St. John's Seminary College
Salem State College
Simmons College
Smith College
Springfield College
Stonehill College
Suffolk University
Tufts University
University of Massachusetts
    Amherst
    Boston
    Dartmouth
    Lowell
Wellesley College
Wentworth Institute of Technology
Western New England College
Westfield State College
Wheaton College
Wheelock College
Williams College
Worcester Polytechnic Institute
Worcester State College

Michigan
Adrian College
Albion College
Alma College
Alpena Community College
Andrews University
Aquinas College
Baker College
    of Auburn Hills
    of Cadillac
    of Jackson
    of Mount Clemens
    of Muskegon
    of Owosso
    of Port Huron
Calvin College
Center for Creative Studies: College of
    Art and Design
Central Michigan University
Concordia College
Cornerstone College and Grand Rapids
    Baptist Seminary
Delta College
Detroit College of Business
Eastern Michigan University
Ferris State University
Glen Oaks Community College
Gogebic Community College
Grace Bible College

Grand Valley State University
Great Lakes College
Hillsdale College
Hope College
Kalamazoo College
Kellogg Community College
Kendall College of Art and Design
Kettering University
Kirtland Community College
Lake Superior State University
Lansing Community College
Lawrence Technological University
Madonna University
Marygrove College
Michigan State University
Michigan Technological University
Mott Community College
Muskegon Community College
Northern Michigan University
Northwood University
Oakland University
Olivet College
Reformed Bible College
Rochester College
Saginaw Valley State University
St. Clair County Community College
Siena Heights University
Southwestern Michigan College
Spring Arbor College
Suomi College
University of Detroit Mercy
University of Michigan
University of Michigan
   Dearborn
   Flint
Walsh College of Accountancy and
   Business Administration
Wayne State University
Western Michigan University
William Tyndale College

Minnesota
Augsburg College
Bemidji State University
Bethel College
Carleton College
College of St. Benedict
College of St. Catherine: St. Paul
   Campus
College of St. Scholastica
Concordia College: Moorhead
Concordia University: St. Paul
Crown College
Gustavus Adolphus College
Hamline University
Hennepin Technical College
Lake Superior College: A Community
   and Technical College
Macalester College
Martin Luther College
Metropolitan State University
Minnesota Bible College
Minnesota State University, Mankato
Moorhead State University
NEI College of Technology
National American University
   St. Paul
North Central University
Northwestern College
St. Cloud State University
St. John's University
St. Mary's University of Minnesota
St. Olaf College
Southwest State University
University of Minnesota
   Crookston
   Duluth
   Morris
   Twin Cities
University of St. Thomas
Winona State University

Mississippi
Alcorn State University
Belhaven College
Blue Mountain College
Delta State University
Hinds Community College
Jackson State University
Millsaps College
Mississippi College
Mississippi State University
Mississippi University for Women
Mississippi Valley State University
Rust College
Tougaloo College
University of Mississippi
University of Southern Mississippi
Wesley College
William Carey College

Missouri
Avila College
Central Methodist College
Central Missouri State University
College of the Ozarks
Columbia College
Conception Seminary College
Crowder College
Culver-Stockton College
DeVry Institute of Technology
   Kansas City
Drury University
Evangel University
Fontbonne College
Hannibal-LaGrange College
Harris Stowe State College
Jefferson College
Kansas City Art Institute
Lincoln University
Lindenwood University
Maryville University of Saint Louis
Missouri Baptist College
Missouri Southern State College
Missouri Valley College
Missouri Western State College
Northwest Missouri State University
Ozark Christian College
Park University
Research College of Nursing
Rockhurst University
St. Charles County Community College
St. Louis Christian College
St. Louis University
Southeast Missouri State University
Southwest Baptist University
Southwest Missouri State University
St. Louis Community College
   St. Louis Community College at
      Forest Park
Stephens College
Truman State University
University of Missouri
   Columbia
   Kansas City
   Rolla
   St. Louis
Washington University
Webster University
Westminster College
William Jewell College
William Woods University

Montana
Carroll College
Dawson Community College
Dull Knife Memorial College
Montana State University
   Billings
   Bozeman
   Northern
Montana Tech of the University of
   Montana
Rocky Mountain College
Salish Kootenai College
Stone Child College
University of Great Falls
University of Montana-Missoula
Western Montana College of The
   University of Montana

Nebraska
Bellevue University
Central Community College
Chadron State College
Clarkson College
College of Saint Mary
Concordia University
Creighton University
Dana College
Doane College
Grace University
Hastings College
Lincoln School of Commerce
Metropolitan Community College
Midland Lutheran College
Nebraska Wesleyan University
Peru State College
Union College
University of Nebraska
   Kearney
   Lincoln
   Omaha
Wayne State College

Nevada
Community College of Southern Nevada
University of Nevada
   Las Vegas
   Reno
Western Nevada Community College

New Hampshire
Colby-Sawyer College
College for Lifelong Learning
Daniel Webster College
Dartmouth College
Franklin Pierce College
Hesser College
Keene State College
McIntosh College
New England College
New Hampshire College
New Hampshire Community Technical
   College
   Berlin
   Claremont
   Laconia
   Stratham
New Hampshire Technical Institute
Notre Dame College
Plymouth State College of the University
   System of New Hampshire
Rivier College
University of New Hampshire
University of New Hampshire
   Manchester

New Jersey
Atlantic Cape Community College
Bloomfield College
Burlington County College
Caldwell College
Centenary College
College of St. Elizabeth
County College of Morris
Cumberland County College
DeVry Institute
Drew University
Essex County College
Fairleigh Dickinson University
Felician College
Georgian Court College
Kean University
Mercer County Community College
Middlesex County College
Monmouth University
Montclair State University
New Jersey City University
New Jersey Institute of Technology
Passaic County Community College
Ramapo College of New Jersey
Raritan Valley Community College
Richard Stockton College of New Jersey
Rider University
Rowan University
Rutgers
   The State University of New Jersey:
      Camden College of Arts and
      Sciences
   The State University of New Jersey:
      College of Engineering
   The State University of New Jersey:
      Cook College
   The State University of New Jersey:
      Douglass College
   The State University of New Jersey:
      Livingston College
   The State University of New Jersey:
      Newark College of Arts and
      Sciences
   The State University of New Jersey:
      Rutgers College
   The State University of New Jersey:
      University College Camden
   The State University of New Jersey:
      University College New
      Brunswick
   The State University of New Jersey:
      University College Newark
St. Peter's College
Salem Community College
Seton Hall University
Stevens Institute of Technology
Sussex County Community College
The College of New Jersey
Thomas Edison State College
University of Medicine and Dentistry of
   New Jersey
   School of Nursing
Warren County Community College
William Paterson University of New
   Jersey

New Mexico
Clovis Community College
College of Santa Fe
Dona Ana Branch Community College of
   New Mexico State University
Eastern New Mexico University
Institute of American Indian Arts
New Mexico Highlands University
New Mexico Institute of Mining and
   Technology
New Mexico State University
New Mexico State University
   Alamogordo
   Carlsbad
University of New Mexico
Western New Mexico University

New York
Adelphi University
Alfred University
Bard College
Barnard College
Broome Community College
Bryant & Stratton Business Institute
   Albany
   Syracuse
Canisius College
Cayuga County Community College
City University of New York
   Brooklyn College
   College of Staten Island
   Hunter College
   Lehman College
   Queens College
   York College
Clarkson University
Colgate University
College of Aeronautics
College of Mount St. Vincent
College of New Rochelle
College of St. Rose

Columbia University
    Columbia College
    Fu Foundation School of
      Engineering and Applied Science
    School of General Studies
    School of Nursing
Concordia College
Cornell University
Corning Community College
D'Youville College
Daemen College
DeVry Institute of Technology
    New York
Dowling College
Eastman School of Music of the
    University of Rochester
Elmira College
Erie Community College
    City Campus
    North Campus
    South Campus
Finger Lakes Community College
Fordham University
Fulton-Montgomery Community College
Genesee Community College
Hamilton College
Hartwick College
Hobart and William Smith Colleges
Hofstra University
Houghton College
Hudson Valley Community College
Institute of Design and Construction
Iona College
Ithaca College
Jamestown Community College
Jefferson Community College
Jewish Theological Seminary of America
Juilliard School
Keuka College
Le Moyne College
Long Island University
    Brooklyn Campus
    C. W. Post Campus
    Southampton College
Manhattan College
Manhattanville College
Mannes College of Music
Marist College
Marymount College
Marymount Manhattan College
Medaille College
Mercy College
Mohawk Valley Community College
Molloy College
Mount St. Mary College
Nazareth College of Rochester
New York Institute of Technology
New York State College of Ceramics at
    Alfred University
New York University
Niagara County Community College
Niagara University
North Country Community College
Nyack College
Onondaga Community College
Pace University
Pace University: Pleasantville/Briarcliff
Polytechnic University
Polytechnic University
    Long Island Campus
Pratt Institute
Rensselaer Polytechnic Institute
Roberts Wesleyan College
Rochester Institute of Technology
Rockland Community College
Russell Sage College
St. Bonaventure University
St. Francis College
St. John Fisher College
St. John's University
St. Lawrence University
St. Thomas Aquinas College
Sarah Lawrence College
School of Visual Arts
Siena College
Skidmore College
State University of New York
    Albany
    Binghamton
    Buffalo
    College at Brockport
    College at Buffalo
    College at Cortland
    College at Fredonia
    College at Geneseo
    College at Old Westbury
    College at Oneonta
    College at Plattsburgh
    College at Potsdam
    College of Agriculture and
      Technology at Morrisville
    College of Technology at Delhi
    Empire State College
    Farmingdale
    Health Science Center at Stony
      Brook
    Institute of Technology at Utica/
      Rome
    New Paltz
    Oswego
    Purchase
    Stony Brook
Syracuse University
Ulster County Community College
Union College
United States Merchant Marine Academy
United States Military Academy
University of Rochester
Utica College of Syracuse University
Vassar College
Wagner College
Webb Institute
Wells College
Westchester Business Institute
Westchester Community College

North Carolina

Alamance Community College
Appalachian State University
Asheville Buncombe Technical
    Community College
Barber-Scotia College
Barton College
Beaufort County Community College
Belmont Abbey College
Bennett College
Bladen Community College
Blue Ridge Community College
Brevard College
Campbell University
Carteret Community College
Catawba College
Catawba Valley Community College
Cecils College
Central Piedmont Community College
Chowan College
Cleveland Community College
College of the Albemarle
Craven Community College
Davidson College
Duke University
East Carolina University
Edgecombe Community College
Elizabeth City State University
Elon College
Fayetteville State University
Forsyth Technical Community College
Gardner-Webb University
Gaston College
Greensboro College
Guilford College
High Point University
James Sprunt Community College
John Wesley College
Johnson C. Smith University
Johnston Community College
Lenoir-Rhyne College
Mars Hill College
Mayland Community College
Meredith College
Methodist College
Montgomery Community College
Mount Olive College
Nash Community College
North Carolina Agricultural and
    Technical State University
North Carolina Central University
North Carolina State University
North Carolina Wesleyan College
Peace College
Pfeiffer University
Piedmont Community College
Pitt Community College
Queens College
Randolph Community College
Richmond Community College
Robeson Community College
St. Andrews Presbyterian College
Salem College
Sandhills Community College
Shaw University
South Piedmont Community College
Southwestern Community College
Surry Community College
Tri-County Community College
University of North Carolina
    Asheville
    Chapel Hill
    Charlotte
    Greensboro
    Pembroke
    Wilmington
Vance-Granville Community College
Wake Forest University
Wake Technical Community College
Warren Wilson College
Wayne Community College
Western Carolina University
Wilkes Community College
Wilson Technical Community College
Wingate University
Winston-Salem State University

North Dakota

Dickinson State University
Jamestown College
Mayville State University
Minot State University
Minot State University: Bottineau
    Campus
North Dakota State University
Trinity Bible College
University of Mary
University of North Dakota
Valley City State University
Williston State College

Ohio

Antioch College
Ashland University
Baldwin-Wallace College
Belmont Technical College
Bluffton College
Bowling Green State University
Bowling Green State University
    Firelands College
Bryant & Stratton College
Capital University
Case Western Reserve University
Cedarville College
Central Ohio Technical College
Central State University
Cincinnati State Technical and
    Community College
Circleville Bible College
Clark State Community College
Cleveland Institute of Music
Cleveland State University
College of Mount St. Joseph
College of Wooster
Columbus College of Art and Design
Columbus State Community College
David N. Myers College
DeVry Institute of Technology
    Columbus
Defiance College
Denison University
Edison State Community College
Franciscan University of Steubenville
Franklin University
Heidelberg College
Hiram College
Hocking Technical College
Jefferson Community College
John Carroll University
Kent State University
Kent State University
    Ashtabula Regional Campus
    East Liverpool Regional Campus
    Stark Campus
    Trumbull Campus
    Tuscarawas Campus
Kenyon College
Lake Erie College
Lima Technical College
Lourdes College
Malone College
Marietta College
Marion Technical College
Miami University
    Hamilton Campus
    Middletown Campus
    Oxford Campus
Miami-Jacobs College
Mount Union College
Mount Vernon Nazarene College
Muskingum College
Northwestern College
Notre Dame College of Ohio
Oberlin College
Ohio Dominican College
Ohio Institute of Photography and
    Technology
Ohio Northern University
Ohio State University
    Agricultural Technical Institute
    Columbus Campus
    Marion Campus
Ohio University
Ohio University
    Chillicothe Campus
    Lancaster Campus
    Zanesville Campus
Ohio Valley Business College
Ohio Wesleyan University
Otterbein College
Owens Community College
    Findlay Campus
    Toledo
Pontifical College Josephinum
Shawnee State University
Stark State College of Technology
Terra Community College
Tiffin University
Union Institute
University of Akron
University of Cincinnati
University of Cincinnati
    Clermont College
    Raymond Walters College
University of Dayton
University of Findlay
University of Rio Grande
University of Toledo
Ursuline College
Walsh University
Washington State Community College
Wilmington College
Wittenberg University
Wright State University
Xavier University
Youngstown State University

Oklahoma

Cameron University
East Central University
Langston University
Mid-America Bible College

Double major

Northeastern State University
Northwestern Oklahoma State University
Oklahoma Baptist University
Oklahoma Christian University of Science and Arts
Oklahoma City Community College
Oklahoma City University
Oklahoma Panhandle State University
Oklahoma State University
Oklahoma State University
   Oklahoma City
   Okmulgee
Oral Roberts University
Rose State College
St. Gregory's University
Southeastern Oklahoma State University
Southern Nazarene University
Southwestern College of Christian Ministries
Southwestern Oklahoma State University
University of Central Oklahoma
University of Oklahoma
University of Science and Arts of Oklahoma
University of Tulsa

Oregon
Central Oregon Community College
Chemeketa Community College
Clatsop Community College
Concordia University
Eastern Oregon University
George Fox University
Lane Community College
Lewis & Clark College
Linfield College
Marylhurst University
Mount Hood Community College
Multnomah Bible College
Northwest Christian College
Oregon Institute of Technology
Oregon State University
Pacific Northwest College of Art
Pacific University
Portland Community College
Portland State University
Reed College
Southern Oregon University
University of Oregon
University of Portland
Western Baptist College
Western Oregon University
Willamette University

Pennsylvania
Albright College
Allegheny College
Allentown College of St. Francis de Sales
Alvernia College
Beaver College
Bloomsburg University of Pennsylvania
Bryn Mawr College
Bucknell University
Butler County Community College
Cabrini College
California University of Pennsylvania
Carlow College
Carnegie Mellon University
Cedar Crest College
Central Pennsylvania College
Chatham College
Chestnut Hill College
Cheyney University of Pennsylvania
Clarion University of Pennsylvania
College Misericordia
Community College of Beaver County
Curtis Institute of Music
Delaware County Community College
Delaware Valley College
Dickinson College
Drexel University
Duquesne University
East Stroudsburg University of Pennsylvania
Edinboro University of Pennsylvania
Elizabethtown College
Franklin and Marshall College
Gannon University
Geneva College
Gettysburg College
Grove City College
Gwynedd-Mercy College
Harcum College
Harrisburg Area Community College
Haverford College
Holy Family College
Immaculata College
Indiana University of Pennsylvania
Juniata College
King's College
Kutztown University of Pennsylvania
La Roche College
La Salle University
Lackawanna Junior College
Lafayette College
Lancaster Bible College
Laurel Business Institute
Lebanon Valley College of Pennsylvania
Lincoln University
Lock Haven University of Pennsylvania
Luzerne County Community College
Lycoming College
Manor College
Mansfield University of Pennsylvania
Marywood University
Mercyhurst College
Messiah College
Millersville University of Pennsylvania
Moore College of Art and Design
Moravian College
Muhlenberg College
Neumann College
Peirce College
Penn State
   Abington
   Altoona
   Beaver
   Delaware County
   Dubois
   Erie, The Behrend College
   Fayette
   Harrisburg
   Hazleton
   McKeesport
   Mont Alto
   New Kensington
   Schuylkill - Capital College
   Shenango
   University Park
   Wilkes-Barre
   Worthington Scranton
   York
Pennsylvania College of Technology
Pennsylvania Institute of Technology
Philadelphia College of Bible
Philadelphia University
Point Park College
Robert Morris College
Rosemont College
St. Francis College
St. Joseph's University
St. Vincent College
Seton Hill College
Shippensburg University of Pennsylvania
Slippery Rock University of Pennsylvania
South Hills School of Business & Technology
Susquehanna University
Swarthmore College
Temple University
Thiel College
University of Pennsylvania
University of Pittsburgh
University of Pittsburgh
   Bradford
   Greensburg
   Johnstown
University of Scranton
University of the Arts
University of the Sciences in Philadelphia
Ursinus College
Valley Forge Christian College
Valley Forge Military College
Villanova University
Washington and Jefferson College
Waynesburg College
West Chester University of Pennsylvania
Westminster College
Westmoreland County Community College
Widener University
Wilkes University
Wilson College
York College of Pennsylvania
Yorktowne Business Institute

Puerto Rico
Bayamon Central University
Inter American University of Puerto Rico
   Fajardo Campus
   Guayama Campus
   Metropolitan Campus
   San German Campus
Pontifical Catholic University of Puerto Rico
Technological College of San Juan
University of Puerto Rico
   Bayamon University College
   Mayaguez Campus
   Rio Piedras Campus
University of the Sacred Heart

Rhode Island
Brown University
Bryant College
Community College of Rhode Island
Johnson & Wales University
New England Institute of Technology
Providence College
Rhode Island College
Roger Williams University
Salve Regina University
University of Rhode Island

South Carolina
Aiken Technical College
Benedict College
Charleston Southern University
Claflin University
Clemson University
Coastal Carolina University
Coker College
College of Charleston
Columbia College
Columbia International University
Converse College
Erskine College
Francis Marion University
Furman University
Lander University
Limestone College
Morris College
Newberry College
North Greenville College
Orangeburg-Calhoun Technical College
Piedmont Technical College
Presbyterian College
South Carolina State University
Southern Wesleyan University
Spartanburg Technical College
Technical College of the Lowcountry
The Citadel
Tri-County Technical College
Trident Technical College
University of South Carolina
University of South Carolina
   Aiken
   Spartanburg
Winthrop University
Wofford College
York Technical College

South Dakota
Augustana College
Black Hills State University
Dakota State University
Dakota Wesleyan University
Huron University
Kilian Community College
Mount Marty College
Northern State University
Sinte Gleska University
South Dakota School of Mines and Technology
South Dakota State University
Southeast Technical Institute
University of South Dakota

Tennessee
Austin Peay State University
Belmont University
Bethel College
Carson-Newman College
Chattanooga State Technical Community College
Christian Brothers University
Crichton College
Cumberland University
David Lipscomb University
Draughons Junior College of Business: Nashville
East Tennessee State University
Fisk University
Freed-Hardeman University
Johnson Bible College
King College
Knoxville Business College
Lambuth University
LeMoyne-Owen College
Lee University
Lincoln Memorial University
Maryville College
Middle Tennessee State University
Milligan College
Motlow State Community College
Nashville State Technical Institute
Northeast State Technical Community College
Pellissippi State Technical Community College
Rhodes College
Roane State Community College
Southern Adventist University
Tennessee Technological University
Tennessee Temple University
Tennessee Wesleyan College
Trevecca Nazarene University
Tusculum College
Union University
University of Memphis
University of Tennessee
   Chattanooga
   Knoxville
   Martin
University of the South
Vanderbilt University
Volunteer State Community College

Texas
Abilene Christian University
Angelo State University
Arlington Baptist College
Austin College
Baylor University
College of the Mainland
Concordia University at Austin
Dallas Baptist University
DeVry Institute of Technology Irving
East Texas Baptist University
El Paso Community College
Hardin-Simmons University
Houston Baptist University
Howard Payne University
Huston-Tillotson College
Jarvis Christian College

Lamar State College at Port Arthur
Lamar University
LeTourneau University
Lubbock Christian University
McMurry University
Midwestern State University
Northwood University: Texas Campus
Our Lady of the Lake University of San Antonio
Prairie View A&M University
Rice University
St. Mary's University
St. Philip's College
Sam Houston State University
San Antonio College
Schreiner College
Southern Methodist University
Southwest Texas State University
Southwestern Adventist University
Southwestern Assemblies of God University
Southwestern University
Stephen F. Austin State University
Tarleton State University
Texas A&M International University
Texas A&M University
Texas A&M University
   Commerce
   Corpus Christi
   Galveston
   Kingsville
Texas Christian University
Texas College
Texas Lutheran University
Texas Southern University
Texas Tech University
Texas Wesleyan University
Texas Woman's University
Trinity University
University of Dallas
University of Houston
University of Houston
   Clear Lake
   Downtown
   Victoria
University of Mary Hardin-Baylor
University of North Texas
University of St. Thomas
University of Texas
   Arlington
   Austin
   Brownsville
   Dallas
   El Paso
   Pan American
   San Antonio
   Tyler
   of the Permian Basin
University of the Incarnate Word
Wayland Baptist University
West Texas A&M University

Utah
Brigham Young University
College of Eastern Utah
LDS Business College
Salt Lake Community College
Southern Utah University
University of Utah
Utah State University
Weber State University
Westminster College

Vermont
Bennington College
Burlington College
Castleton State College
Champlain College
College of St. Joseph in Vermont
Community College of Vermont
Goddard College
Green Mountain College
Johnson State College
Lyndon State College
Marlboro College
Middlebury College
Norwich University
St. Michael's College
Southern Vermont College
Trinity College of Vermont
University of Vermont
Vermont Technical College

Virginia
Bluefield College
Bridgewater College
Christendom College
Christopher Newport University
College of William and Mary
Dabney S. Lancaster Community College
Danville Community College
ECPI College of Technology
Eastern Mennonite University
Emory & Henry College
Ferrum College
George Mason University
Germanna Community College
Hampden-Sydney College
Hollins University
J. Sargeant Reynolds Community College
James Madison University
Liberty University
Longwood College
Lord Fairfax Community College
Lynchburg College
Mary Baldwin College
Mary Washington College
Mountain Empire Community College
National Business College
Norfolk State University
Northern Virginia Community College
Old Dominion University
Patrick Henry Community College
Radford University
Randolph-Macon College
Randolph-Macon Woman's College
Roanoke College
St. Paul's College
Shenandoah University
Southside Virginia Community College
Southwest Virginia Community College
Sweet Briar College
Tidewater Community College
University of Richmond
University of Virginia
University of Virginia's College at Wise
Virginia Commonwealth University
Virginia Highlands Community College
Virginia Intermont College
Virginia Military Institute
Virginia Polytechnic Institute and State University
Virginia State University
Virginia Wesleyan College
Washington and Lee University

Washington
Bastyr University
Central Washington University
Centralia College
City University
Eastern Washington University
Gonzaga University
Henry Cogswell College
Heritage College
Highline Community College
Pacific Lutheran University
Peninsula College
Pierce College
Puget Sound Christian College
St. Martin's College
Seattle Pacific University
Seattle University
University of Puget Sound
University of Washington
Walla Walla College
Washington State University
Wenatchee Valley College
Western Washington University
Whitman College
Whitworth College

West Virginia
Alderson-Broaddus College
Bethany College
Bluefield State College
College of West Virginia
Concord College
Davis and Elkins College
Fairmont State College
Glenville State College
Marshall University
Ohio Valley College
Potomac State College of West Virginia University
Salem-Teikyo University
Shepherd College
University of Charleston
West Liberty State College
West Virginia Northern Community College
West Virginia State College
West Virginia University
West Virginia University Institute of Technology
West Virginia University Parkersburg
West Virginia Wesleyan College
Wheeling Jesuit University

Wisconsin
Alverno College
Beloit College
Bryant & Stratton College
Cardinal Stritch University
Carroll College
Carthage College
Chippewa Valley Technical College
Concordia University Wisconsin
Lakeland College
Lakeshore Technical College
Lawrence University
Marian College of Fond du Lac
Marquette University
Milwaukee Area Technical College
Milwaukee Institute of Art & Design
Milwaukee School of Engineering
Moraine Park Technical College
Mount Mary College
Mount Senario College
Nicolet Area Technical College
Northeast Wisconsin Technical College
Northland College
Ripon College
St. Norbert College
Silver Lake College
Southwest Wisconsin Technical College
University of Wisconsin
   Eau Claire
   Green Bay
   La Crosse
   Madison
   Milwaukee
   Oshkosh
   Parkside
   Platteville
   River Falls
   Stevens Point
   Stout
   Superior
   Whitewater
Viterbo University
Waukesha County Technical College
Western Wisconsin Technical College
Wisconsin Indianhead Technical College
Wisconsin Lutheran College

Wyoming
Northwest College
Sheridan College
University of Wyoming

Dual enrollment

Alabama
Alabama Agricultural and Mechanical University
Athens State University
Auburn University
Auburn University at Montgomery
Bevill State Community College
Birmingham-Southern College
Calhoun Community College
Central Alabama Community College
Chattahoochee Valley Community College
Enterprise State Junior College
Gadsden State Community College
George C. Wallace State Community College
   Dothan
   Selma
Harry M. Ayers State Technical College
Huntingdon College
J. F. Drake State Technical College
Jacksonville State University
James H. Faulkner State Community College
Jefferson Davis Community College
John M. Patterson State Technical College
Lurleen B. Wallace Junior College
Marion Military Institute
Northeast Alabama Community College
Northwest-Shoals Community College
Reid State Technical College
Samford University
Shelton State Community College
Snead State Community College
Spring Hill College
Stillman College
University of Alabama
University of Alabama
   Birmingham
   Huntsville
University of Montevallo
University of North Alabama
University of South Alabama
University of West Alabama
Wallace State Community College at Hanceville

Alaska
Prince William Sound Community College
University of Alaska
   Anchorage
   Fairbanks
   Southeast

Arizona
Arizona State University
Arizona Western College
Central Arizona College
Cochise College
Eastern Arizona College
Embry-Riddle Aeronautical University
   Prescott Campus
Gateway Community College
Glendale Community College
Grand Canyon University
Mesa Community College
Mohave Community College
Northern Arizona University
Northland Pioneer College
Paradise Valley Community College
Phoenix College
Pima Community College
Rio Salado College
Scottsdale Community College
South Mountain Community College
University of Arizona
Yavapai College

Arkansas
Arkansas State University
Arkansas State University
    Beebe Branch
Arkansas Tech University
Garland County Community College
Harding University
Lyon College
Mississippi County Community College
North Arkansas College
Northwest Arkansas Community College
Ouachita Baptist University
Phillips Community College of the
    University of Arkansas
Southern Arkansas University
    Tech
University of Arkansas
University of Arkansas
    Little Rock
    Monticello
    Pine Bluff
University of Central Arkansas
University of the Ozarks
Westark College
Williams Baptist College

California
Academy of Art College
Allan Hancock College
Art Institutes International
    San Francisco
Bakersfield College
Barstow College
Butte College
Cabrillo College
California Baptist University
California Polytechnic State University:
    San Luis Obispo
California State Polytechnic University:
    Pomona
California State University
    Chico
    Dominguez Hills
    Fresno
    Fullerton
    Hayward
    Long Beach
    Los Angeles
    Monterey Bay
    Northridge
    Stanislaus
Canada College
Cerritos Community College
Cerro Coso Community College
Chabot College
Chaffey Community College
Citrus College
City College of San Francisco
Coastline Community College
College of Notre Dame
College of San Mateo
College of the Canyons
College of the Desert
College of the Redwoods
College of the Sequoias
College of the Siskiyous
Concordia University
Contra Costa College
Crafton Hills College
Cuyamaca College
Cypress College
De Anza College
Diablo Valley College
Dominican University of California
Don Bosco Technical Institute
East Los Angeles College
Evergreen Valley College
Fresno City College
Gavilan Community College
Glendale Community College
Golden West College
Grossmont Community College
Hope International University
Humboldt State University
Imperial Valley College
Irvine Valley College
LIFE Bible College
La Sierra University
Lake Tahoe Community College
Las Positas College
Los Angeles Harbor College
Los Angeles Mission College
Los Angeles Pierce College
Los Angeles Southwest College
Los Angeles Trade and Technical College
Los Angeles Valley College
Loyola Marymount University
Marymount College
Mendocino College
Menlo College
Merced College
Merritt College
MiraCosta College
Mission College
Modesto Junior College
Monterey Peninsula College
Mount St. Mary's College
Mount San Antonio College
Mount San Jacinto College
Napa Valley College
Ohlone College
Oxnard College
Pacific Union College
Palo Verde College
Palomar College
Pasadena City College
Patten College
Porterville College
Rio Hondo College
Riverside Community College
Sacramento City College
Saddleback College
Samuel Merritt College
San Bernardino Valley College
San Diego City College
San Diego Mesa College
San Diego Miramar College
San Diego State University
San Francisco State University
San Joaquin Delta College
San Jose City College
San Jose State University
Santa Ana College
Santa Barbara City College
Santa Monica College
Santa Rosa Junior College
Shasta College
Sierra College
Skyline College
Solano Community College
Southwestern College
Taft College
University of California
    Berkeley
    Davis
    Riverside
    Santa Barbara
    Santa Cruz
University of San Francisco
University of Southern California
Ventura College
Victor Valley College
Vista Community College
West Hills Community College
West Los Angeles College
West Valley College
Yuba College

Colorado
Adams State College
Aims Community College
Arapahoe Community College
Colorado Mountain College
    Alpine Campus
    Spring Valley Campus
    Timberline Campus
Colorado Northwestern Community
    College
Colorado School of Mines
Community College of Denver
Fort Lewis College
Front Range Community College
Lamar Community College
Mesa State College
Metropolitan State College of Denver
Morgan Community College
Naropa University
Northeastern Junior College
Otero Junior College
Pikes Peak Community College
Red Rocks Community College
Regis University
Trinidad State Junior College
University of Colorado
    Boulder
    Colorado Springs
University of Northern Colorado
University of Southern Colorado
Western State College of Colorado

Connecticut
Albertus Magnus College
Briarwood College
Capital Community College
Connecticut College
Gateway Community College
Housatonic Community-Technical
    College
Manchester Community-Technical
    College
Middlesex Community-Technical
    College
Mitchell College
Naugatuck Valley Community-Technical
    College
Northwestern Connecticut
    Community-Technical College
Norwalk Community-Technical College
Quinebaug Valley Community College
Sacred Heart University
St. Joseph College
Teikyo Post University
Three Rivers Community-Technical
    College
Tunxis Community College
University of Bridgeport
University of Connecticut
University of Hartford
University of New Haven
Wesleyan University
Western Connecticut State University

Delaware
Delaware State University
Delaware Technical and Community
    College
        Owens Campus
        Stanton/Wilmington Campus
        Terry Campus
Goldey-Beacom College
University of Delaware
Wesley College

District of Columbia
Catholic University of America
Gallaudet University
George Washington University
Howard University
Southeastern University
University of the District of Columbia

Florida
Barry University
Brevard Community College
Broward Community College
Central Florida Community College
Chipola Junior College
Clearwater Christian College
Daytona Beach Community College
Edison Community College
Embry-Riddle Aeronautical University
Florida Agricultural and Mechanical
    University
Florida Atlantic University
Florida Baptist Theological College
Florida Christian College
Florida Community College at
    Jacksonville
Florida Institute of Technology
Florida International University
Florida Keys Community College
Florida Memorial College
Florida National College
Florida State University
Gulf Coast Community College
Hillsborough Community College
Hobe Sound Bible College
Indian River Community College
Lake City Community College
Lake-Sumter Community College
Manatee Community College
Miami-Dade Community College
New England Institute of Technology
Northwood University
    Florida Campus
Nova Southeastern University
Palm Beach Atlantic College
Palm Beach Community College
Pasco-Hernando Community College
Pensacola Junior College
Polk Community College
Ringling School of Art and Design
Rollins College
St. Petersburg Junior College
St. Thomas University
Santa Fe Community College
Seminole Community College
South College: Palm Beach Campus
South Florida Community College
Southeastern College of the Assemblies
    of God
Stetson University
Tallahassee Community College
University of Central Florida
University of Florida
University of Miami
University of North Florida
University of South Florida
University of Tampa
University of West Florida
Valencia Community College
Warner Southern College

Georgia
Abraham Baldwin Agricultural College
Agnes Scott College
Albany State University
Andrew College
Athens Area Technical Institute
Atlanta Christian College
Atlanta College of Art
Atlanta Metropolitan College
Augusta State University
Bainbridge College
Berry College
Brewton-Parker College
Chattahoochee Technical Institute
Clark Atlanta University
Coastal Georgia Community College
Columbus State University
Columbus Technical Institute
Darton College
DeKalb Technical Institute
East Georgia College
Emmanuel College
Emory University
Floyd College
Fort Valley State University
Gainesville College
Georgia College and State University
Georgia Institute of Technology
Georgia Perimeter College
Georgia Southwestern State University
Gordon College
Gwinnett Technical Institute
Kennesaw State University
LaGrange College
Macon State College
Mercer University

Middle Georgia College
Morehouse College
North Georgia College & State University
Oxford College of Emory University
Paine College
Piedmont College
Savannah State University
South Georgia College
Spelman College
State University of West Georgia
Thomas College
Toccoa Falls College
Truett-McConnell College
University of Georgia
Valdosta State University
Waycross College
Wesleyan College
Young Harris College

Hawaii
Chaminade University of Honolulu
Hawaii Pacific University
University of Hawaii
    Hawaii Community College
    Hilo
    Honolulu Community College
    Kapiolani Community College
    Kauai Community College
    Leeward Community College
    Maui Community College
    Windward Community College

Idaho
Albertson College of Idaho
College of Southern Idaho
Eastern Idaho Technical College
Lewis-Clark State College
North Idaho College
Northwest Nazarene University
University of Idaho

Illinois
Barat College
Benedictine University
Black Hawk College
Black Hawk College
    East Campus
Blackburn College
Carl Sandburg College
Chicago State University
City Colleges of Chicago
    Harold Washington College
    Harry S. Truman College
    Kennedy-King College
    Malcolm X College
    Olive-Harvey College
    Richard J. Daley College
College of DuPage
College of Lake County
Danville Area Community College
Dominican University
Elgin Community College
Elmhurst College
Eureka College
Governors State University
Highland Community College
Illinois Eastern Community Colleges
    Frontier Community College
    Lincoln Trail College
    Olney Central College
    Wabash Valley College
John A. Logan College
John Wood Community College
Judson College
Kankakee Community College
Kaskaskia College
Kishwaukee College
Knox College
Lake Land College
Lewis University
Lewis and Clark Community College
Lincoln Land Community College
Loyola University of Chicago
MacMurray College
McHenry County College
Moody Bible Institute
Morton College
Northeastern Illinois University
Northern Illinois University
Oakton Community College
Parkland College
Prairie State College
Quincy University
Rend Lake College
Richland Community College
Robert Morris College: Chicago
Rock Valley College
Roosevelt University
Sauk Valley Community College
School of the Art Institute of Chicago
Shawnee Community College
Shimer College
Southeastern Illinois College
Southern Illinois University
    Carbondale
Southwestern Illinois College
Spoon River College
Springfield College in Illinois
Triton College
University of Illinois
    Chicago
    Urbana-Champaign
Waubonsee Community College
Western Illinois University
William Rainey Harper College

Indiana
Ancilla College
Ball State University
Butler University
Calumet College of St. Joseph
DePauw University
Earlham College
Goshen College
Grace College
Indiana Institute of Technology
Indiana University
    Bloomington
    East
    Kokomo
    Northwest
    Southeast
Indiana University--Purdue University
    Indiana University-Purdue University Fort Wayne
    Indiana University-Purdue University Indianapolis
Indiana Wesleyan University
Ivy Tech State College
    Central Indiana
    Columbus
    Eastcentral
    Kokomo
    Lafayette
    Northcentral
    Northeast
    Northwest
    Southeast
    Southwest
    Wabash Valley
    Whitewater
Manchester College
Marian College
Oakland City University
Purdue University
Purdue University
    Calumet
    North Central Campus
St. Joseph's College
University of Evansville
University of Indianapolis
University of St. Francis
Valparaiso University
Vincennes University

Iowa
American Institute of Business
Buena Vista University
Central College
Clinton Community College
Coe College
Des Moines Area Community College
Drake University
Grand View College
Hawkeye Community College
Indian Hills Community College
Iowa Central Community College
Iowa Lakes Community College
Iowa State University
Iowa Wesleyan College
Iowa Western Community College
Kirkwood Community College
Loras College
Luther College
Marshalltown Community College
Marycrest International University
Mount Mercy College
Muscatine Community College
Northeast Iowa Community College
Scott Community College
Southeastern Community College
    North Campus
    South Campus
Southwestern Community College
University of Dubuque
University of Iowa
University of Northern Iowa
Upper Iowa University
Waldorf College
Western Iowa Tech Community College
William Penn University

Kansas
Allen County Community College
Baker University
Barton County Community College
Bethany College
Bethel College
Butler County Community College
Cloud County Community College
Coffeyville Community College
Colby Community College
Cowley County Community College
Dodge City Community College
Emporia State University
Fort Hays State University
Garden City Community College
Hutchinson Community College
Independence Community College
Johnson County Community College
Kansas City Kansas Community College
Manhattan Christian College
McPherson College
MidAmerica Nazarene University
Newman University
Ottawa University
Pittsburg State University
Pratt Community College
St. Mary College
Seward County Community College
Southwestern College
Sterling College
Tabor College
University of Kansas
Washburn University of Topeka

Kentucky
Ashland Community College
Bellarmine College
Campbellsville University
Eastern Kentucky University
Elizabethtown Community College
Georgetown College
Henderson Community College
Hopkinsville Community College
Kentucky State University
Lindsey Wilson College
Madisonville Community College
Maysville Community College
Mid-Continent College
Morehead State University
Murray State University
Northern Kentucky University
Owensboro Junior College of Business
Paducah Community College
Pikeville College
Prestonsburg Community College
St. Catharine College
Somerset Community College
Southeast Community College
Spalding University
Thomas More College
Union College
University of Kentucky
University of Louisville
Western Kentucky University

Louisiana
Bossier Parish Community College
Centenary College of Louisiana
Delgado Community College
Dillard University
Louisiana State University and Agricultural and Mechanical College
Louisiana State University
    Alexandria
    Eunice
    Shreveport
Louisiana Tech University
Loyola University New Orleans
McNeese State University
Nicholls State University
Northwestern State University
Nunez Community College
Our Lady of Holy Cross College
St. Joseph Seminary College
Southern University and Agricultural and Mechanical College
University of Louisiana at Lafayette
University of Louisiana at Monroe
University of New Orleans

Maine
Andover College
Bates College
Colby College
Thomas College
Unity College
University of Maine
    Augusta
    Farmington
    Fort Kent
    Presque Isle

Maryland
Allegany College
Anne Arundel Community College
Baltimore City Community College
Bowie State University
Carroll Community College
Cecil Community College
Charles County Community College
Chesapeake College
College of Notre Dame of Maryland
Community College of Baltimore County
    Catonsville
    Essex
Coppin State College
Frederick Community College
Frostburg State University
Goucher College
Hagerstown Community College
Harford Community College
Hood College
Howard Community College
Johns Hopkins University
Maryland College of Art and Design
Maryland Institute College of Art
Montgomery College
    Germantown Campus
    Rockville Campus
    Takoma Park Campus
Morgan State University
Prince George's Community College
St. Mary's College of Maryland

Salisbury State University
Towson University
University of Maryland
- College Park
- Eastern Shore
- University College
Villa Julie College
Washington College
Western Maryland College

Massachusetts

American International College
Atlantic Union College
Berkshire Community College
Boston University
Bridgewater State College
Bristol Community College
Bunker Hill Community College
Cape Cod Community College
Curry College
Eastern Nazarene College
Emerson College
Fitchburg State College
Framingham State College
Greenfield Community College
Hebrew College
Holyoke Community College
Lesley College
Massachusetts Bay Community College
Massachusetts College of Liberal Arts
Massachusetts Maritime Academy
Middlesex Community College
Montserrat College of Art
Mount Holyoke College
Mount Wachusett Community College
New England College of Finance
North Shore Community College
Northern Essex Community College
Quincy College
Roxbury Community College
Salem State College
Simon's Rock College of Bard
Springfield Technical Community College
Stonehill College
Suffolk University
University of Massachusetts
- Amherst
- Boston
- Dartmouth
- Lowell
Wentworth Institute of Technology
Western New England College
Wheaton College
Worcester Polytechnic Institute
Worcester State College

Michigan

Alma College
Alpena Community College
Andrews University
Aquinas College
Baker College
- of Auburn Hills
- of Cadillac
- of Jackson
- of Mount Clemens
- of Muskegon
- of Owosso
- of Port Huron
Bay de Noc Community College
Calvin College
Central Michigan University
Cleary College
Concordia College
Cornerstone College and Grand Rapids Baptist Seminary
Davenport College of Business
Delta College
Detroit College of Business
Ferris State University
Glen Oaks Community College
Gogebic Community College
Grace Bible College

Grand Rapids Community College
Grand Valley State University
Great Lakes College
Henry Ford Community College
Hillsdale College
Hope College
Jackson Community College
Kalamazoo College
Kalamazoo Valley Community College
Kellogg Community College
Kendall College of Art and Design
Kirtland Community College
Lake Michigan College
Lake Superior State University
Lansing Community College
Lawrence Technological University
Macomb Community College
Madonna University
Michigan State University
Michigan Technological University
Mid Michigan Community College
Monroe County Community College
Montcalm Community College
Mott Community College
Muskegon Community College
North Central Michigan College
Northern Michigan University
Northwestern Michigan College
Northwood University
Oakland Community College
Olivet College
Reformed Bible College
Rochester College
Saginaw Valley State University
St. Clair County Community College
Schoolcraft College
Siena Heights University
Southwestern Michigan College
Spring Arbor College
Suomi College
University of Michigan
University of Michigan
- Dearborn
- Flint
Washtenaw Community College
Wayne County Community College
Wayne State University
West Shore Community College
Western Michigan University
William Tyndale College

Minnesota

Anoka-Ramsey Community College
Augsburg College
Bemidji State University
Bethany Lutheran College
Carleton College
Central Lakes College
Century Community and Technical College
College of St. Catherine: St. Paul Campus
College of St. Scholastica
Concordia College: Moorhead
Concordia University: St. Paul
Crown College
Gustavus Adolphus College
Hennepin Technical College
Hibbing Community College: A Technical and Community College
Inver Hills Community College
Itasca Community College
Lake Superior College: A Community and Technical College
Martin Luther College
Mesabi Range Community and Technical College
Minneapolis Community and Technical College
Minnesota Bible College
Minnesota State University, Mankato
Moorhead State University
NEI College of Technology
North Hennepin Community College
Pine Technical College

Ridgewater College: A Community and Technical College
Rochester Community and Technical College
St. Cloud State University
St. Cloud Technical College
St. John's University
Southwest State University
University of Minnesota
- Crookston
- Duluth
- Morris
- Twin Cities
Vermilion Community College
Winona State University

Mississippi

Belhaven College
Blue Mountain College
Copiah-Lincoln Community College
Delta State University
East Central Community College
East Mississippi Community College
Hinds Community College
Holmes Community College
Jones County Junior College
Meridian Community College
Mississippi College
Mississippi Gulf Coast Community College
- Jackson County Campus
- Jefferson Davis Campus
- Perkinston
Mississippi State University
Mississippi University for Women
Mississippi Valley State University
Southwest Mississippi Community College
University of Southern Mississippi
Wesley College
William Carey College

Missouri

Avila College
Central Methodist College
Central Missouri State University
College of the Ozarks
Columbia College
Cottey College
Culver-Stockton College
Drury University
East Central College
Evangel University
Fontbonne College
Hannibal-LaGrange College
Harris Stowe State College
Jefferson College
Lincoln University
Lindenwood University
Longview Community College
Maple Woods Community College
Maryville University of Saint Louis
Mineral Area College
Missouri Baptist College
Missouri Southern State College
Missouri Valley College
Missouri Western State College
Moberly Area Community College
Northwest Missouri State University
Ozarks Technical Community College
Park University
Penn Valley Community College
Research College of Nursing
Rockhurst University
St. Charles County Community College
St. Louis Christian College
St. Louis University
Southeast Missouri State University
Southwest Baptist University
Southwest Missouri State University
Southwest Missouri State University West Plains Campus

St. Louis Community College
St. Louis Community College at Florissant Valley
St. Louis Community College at Forest Park
St. Louis Community College at Meramec
State Fair Community College
Stephens College
Three Rivers Community College
Truman State University
University of Missouri
- Columbia
- Kansas City
- Rolla
- St. Louis
Washington University
Webster University
William Jewell College
William Woods University

Montana

Carroll College
Dawson Community College
Flathead Valley Community College
Miles Community College
Montana State University
- Billings
- College of Technology-Great Falls
- Northern
Montana Tech of the University of Montana
Montana Tech of the University of Montana: College of Technology
Rocky Mountain College
Salish Kootenai College
Stone Child College
University of Great Falls
University of Montana-Missoula

Nebraska

Bellevue University
Central Community College
Chadron State College
Clarkson College
Concordia University
Creighton University
Dana College
Doane College
Grace University
Metropolitan Community College
Mid Plains Community College Area
Midland Lutheran College
Northeast Community College
Peru State College
Southeast Community College
- Lincoln Campus
Union College
University of Nebraska
- Kearney
- Lincoln
- Omaha
Wayne State College

Nevada

Community College of Southern Nevada
University of Nevada
- Las Vegas
Western Nevada Community College

New Hampshire

Colby-Sawyer College
Daniel Webster College
Franklin Pierce College
Hesser College
New England College
New Hampshire Community Technical College
- Nashua
- Stratham
Notre Dame College
St. Anselm College

New Jersey

Atlantic Cape Community College
Brookdale Community College
Burlington County College
Camden County College
College of St. Elizabeth
County College of Morris
Cumberland County College
Essex County College
Felician College
Gloucester County College
Hudson County Community College
Kean University
Mercer County Community College
Middlesex County College
Monmouth University
New Jersey City University
New Jersey Institute of Technology
Ocean County College
Raritan Valley Community College
Richard Stockton College of New Jersey
Rutgers
   The State University of New Jersey:
      Camden College of Arts and
      Sciences
   The State University of New Jersey:
      College of Engineering
   The State University of New Jersey:
      College of Nursing
   The State University of New Jersey:
      Cook College
   The State University of New Jersey:
      Douglass College
   The State University of New Jersey:
      Livingston College
   The State University of New Jersey:
      Newark College of Arts and
      Sciences
   The State University of New Jersey:
      Rutgers College
   The State University of New Jersey:
      University College Camden
   The State University of New Jersey:
      University College Newark
St. Peter's College
Salem Community College
Seton Hall University
Stevens Institute of Technology
Sussex County Community College
The College of New Jersey
Union County College
University of Medicine and Dentistry of
   New Jersey
     School of Health Related
     Professions
Warren County Community College
William Paterson University of New
   Jersey

New Mexico

Albuquerque Technical-Vocational
   Institute
Clovis Community College
Dona Ana Branch Community College of
   New Mexico State University
Eastern New Mexico University
Eastern New Mexico University
   Roswell Campus
New Mexico Highlands University
New Mexico Institute of Mining and
   Technology
New Mexico Junior College
New Mexico Military Institute
New Mexico State University
   Alamogordo
   Carlsbad
Northern New Mexico Community
   College
San Juan College
Santa Fe Community College
University of New Mexico
Western New Mexico University

New York

Alfred University
Bard College
Broome Community College
Canisius College
Cayuga County Community College
City University of New York
   Borough of Manhattan Community
     College
   Bronx Community College
   Brooklyn College
   City College
   Hostos Community College
   Hunter College
   John Jay College of Criminal
     Justice
   Kingsborough Community College
   La Guardia Community College
   Lehman College
   New York City Technical College
   Queens College
   Queensborough Community
     College
Clinton Community College
College of St. Rose
Columbia-Greene Community College
Corning Community College
Daemen College
Dominican College of Blauvelt
Dutchess Community College
Elmira College
Erie Community College
   City Campus
   North Campus
   South Campus
Finger Lakes Community College
Five Towns College
Fulton-Montgomery Community College
Genesee Community College
Herkimer County Community College
Hilbert College
Hudson Valley Community College
Ithaca College
Jamestown Community College
Jefferson Community College
Jewish Theological Seminary of America
Long Island University
   Brooklyn Campus
   C. W. Post Campus
   Southampton College
Maria College
Marist College
Marymount Manhattan College
Mohawk Valley Community College
Monroe College
Monroe Community College
Mount St. Mary College
New York Institute of Technology
New York State College of Ceramics at
   Alfred University
Niagara County Community College
Niagara University
North Country Community College
Onondaga Community College
Orange County Community College
Pace University
Pace University: Pleasantville/Briarcliff
Parsons School of Design
Phillips Beth Israel School of Nursing
Polytechnic University
Polytechnic University
   Long Island Campus
Rensselaer Polytechnic Institute
Roberts Wesleyan College
Rockland Community College
Sage Junior College of Albany
St. Francis College
St. John's University
St. Thomas Aquinas College
Schenectady County Community College
State University of New York
   Albany
   Binghamton
   Buffalo
   College at Brockport
   College at Buffalo
   College at Cortland
   College at Fredonia
   College at Potsdam
   College of Agriculture and
     Technology at Cobleskill
   College of Agriculture and
     Technology at Morrisville
   College of Technology at Canton
   College of Technology at Delhi
   Empire State College
   Maritime College
   New Paltz
   Oswego
   Stony Brook
Suffolk County Community College
Syracuse University
Tompkins-Cortland Community College
Touro College
Trocaire College
Ulster County Community College
Union College
University of Rochester
Utica College of Syracuse University
Villa Maria College of Buffalo

North Carolina

Alamance Community College
Appalachian State University
Asheville Buncombe Technical
   Community College
Barton College
Beaufort County Community College
Belmont Abbey College
Bladen Community College
Blue Ridge Community College
Brevard College
Brunswick Community College
Caldwell Community College and
   Technical Institute
Cape Fear Community College
Carteret Community College
Catawba College
Catawba Valley Community College
Central Carolina Community College
Central Piedmont Community College
Chowan College
Cleveland Community College
Coastal Carolina Community College
College of the Albemarle
Davidson County Community College
Durham Technical Community College
East Carolina University
Edgecombe Community College
Fayetteville Technical Community
   College
Forsyth Technical Community College
Gardner-Webb University
Gaston College
Greensboro College
Guilford Technical Community College
Halifax Community College
Haywood Community College
High Point University
James Sprunt Community College
John Wesley College
Johnston Community College
Lenoir Community College
Louisburg College
Mars Hill College
Martin Community College
Mayland Community College
Meredith College
Methodist College
Mitchell Community College
Montgomery Community College
Montreat College
Mount Olive College
Nash Community College
North Carolina School of the Arts
North Carolina State University
Peace College
Pfeiffer University
Piedmont Community College
Pitt Community College
Queens College
Randolph Community College
Richmond Community College
Roanoke-Chowan Community College
Robeson Community College
Rockingham Community College
Rowan-Cabarrus Community College
St. Andrews Presbyterian College
St. Augustine's College
Salem College
Sampson Community College
Sandhills Community College
Shaw University
South Piedmont Community College
Southeastern Community College
Southwestern Community College
Surry Community College
Tri-County Community College
University of North Carolina
   Asheville
   Chapel Hill
   Charlotte
   Greensboro
   Pembroke
Vance-Granville Community College
Wake Forest University
Wake Technical Community College
Warren Wilson College
Wayne Community College
Western Carolina University
Western Piedmont Community College
Wilkes Community College
Wilson Technical Community College
Wingate University

North Dakota

Bismarck State College
Dickinson State University
Jamestown College
Lake Region State College
Mayville State University
Minot State University
Minot State University: Bottineau
   Campus
North Dakota State University
University of Mary
Williston State College

Ohio

Ashland University
Belmont Technical College
Bluffton College
Bowling Green State University
Bowling Green State University
   Firelands College
Case Western Reserve University
Cedarville College
Central Ohio Technical College
Chatfield College
Clark State Community College
Cleveland State University
Columbus State Community College
Defiance College
Edison State Community College
Franklin University
Heidelberg College
Hiram College
Hocking Technical College
Jefferson Community College
John Carroll University
Kent State University
Kent State University
   Ashtabula Regional Campus
   East Liverpool Regional Campus
   Stark Campus
   Trumbull Campus
   Tuscarawas Campus
Kenyon College
Lake Erie College

Lakeland Community College
Lima Technical College
Lorain County Community College
Lourdes College
Malone College
Marion Technical College
Miami University
    Hamilton Campus
    Middletown Campus
Miami-Jacobs College
Muskingum College
North Central State College
Northwest State Community College
Oberlin College
Ohio Dominican College
Ohio Northern University
Ohio State University
    Agricultural Technical Institute
    Columbus Campus
    Lima Campus
    Mansfield Campus
    Marion Campus
    Newark Campus
Ohio University
    Chillicothe Campus
    Eastern Campus
    Southern Campus at Ironton
    Zanesville Campus
Otterbein College
Owens Community College
    Findlay Campus
    Toledo
Sinclair Community College
Southern State Community College
Stark State College of Technology
Terra Community College
Tiffin University
University of Akron
University of Akron
    Wayne College
University of Cincinnati
    Clermont College
    Raymond Walters College
University of Dayton
University of Findlay
University of Rio Grande
University of Toledo
Ursuline College
Walsh University
Washington State Community College
Wilmington College
Wittenberg University
Wright State University
Xavier University

Oklahoma
Cameron University
Carl Albert State College
Connors State College
East Central University
Eastern Oklahoma State College
Langston University
Mid-America Bible College
Northeastern Oklahoma Agricultural and Mechanical College
Northeastern State University
Northern Oklahoma College
Northwestern Oklahoma State University
Oklahoma Baptist University
Oklahoma Christian University of Science and Arts
Oklahoma City Community College
Oklahoma City University
Oklahoma Panhandle State University
Oklahoma State University
Oklahoma State University
    Oklahoma City
    Okmulgee
Redlands Community College
Rogers State University
Rose State College
St. Gregory's University
Seminole State College
Southeastern Oklahoma State University
Southern Nazarene University
Southwestern College of Christian Ministries
Southwestern Oklahoma State University
Tulsa Community College
University of Central Oklahoma
University of Oklahoma
University of Science and Arts of Oklahoma
University of Tulsa
Western Oklahoma State College

Oregon
Central Oregon Community College
Chemeketa Community College
Clackamas Community College
Clatsop Community College
Concordia University
Eastern Oregon University
George Fox University
Lane Community College
Lewis & Clark College
Linn-Benton Community College
Mount Hood Community College
Oregon State University
Pacific Northwest College of Art
Portland Community College
Reed College
Southern Oregon University

Pennsylvania
Albright College
Allegheny College
Allentown College of St. Francis de Sales
Alvernia College
Bloomsburg University of Pennsylvania
Bryn Mawr College
Bucks County Community College
Cabrini College
California University of Pennsylvania
Chatham College
Chestnut Hill College
College Misericordia
Community College of Allegheny County
Community College of Beaver County
Community College of Philadelphia
Curtis Institute of Music
Delaware Valley College
Duquesne University
Edinboro University of Pennsylvania
Elizabethtown College
Geneva College
Grove City College
Harrisburg Area Community College
Holy Family College
Kutztown University of Pennsylvania
La Roche College
La Salle University
Lehigh Carbon Community College
Lincoln University
Lock Haven University of Pennsylvania
Luzerne County Community College
Manor College
Mansfield University of Pennsylvania
Marywood University
Mercyhurst College
Millersville University of Pennsylvania
Moore College of Art and Design
Moravian College
Northampton County Area Community College
Penn State
    Beaver
    Delaware County
    Dubois
    Fayette
    Harrisburg
    Hazleton
    McKeesport
    Mont Alto
    New Kensington
    Shenango
    Wilkes-Barre
    Worthington Scranton
    York
Reading Area Community College
St. Vincent College
Shippensburg University of Pennsylvania
Slippery Rock University of Pennsylvania
South Hills School of Business & Technology
Susquehanna University
Swarthmore College
Temple University
University of Pennsylvania
University of Pittsburgh
University of Pittsburgh
    Bradford
    Greensburg
University of Scranton
University of the Arts
Ursinus College
Valley Forge Christian College
Valley Forge Military College
Villanova University
Washington and Jefferson College
Waynesburg College
Westminster College
Widener University
Wilkes University
York College of Pennsylvania

Puerto Rico
Huertas Junior College
Inter American University of Puerto Rico
    Aguadilla Campus
    Fajardo Campus
    Guayama Campus
    San German Campus
Pontifical Catholic University of Puerto Rico
University of Puerto Rico
    Ponce University College
    Utuado
University of the Sacred Heart

Rhode Island
Community College of Rhode Island
Roger Williams University
University of Rhode Island

South Carolina
Aiken Technical College
Anderson College
Benedict College
Central Carolina Technical College
Charleston Southern University
Claflin University
Clemson University
Coker College
College of Charleston
Columbia College
Erskine College
Florence-Darlington Technical College
Francis Marion University
Greenville Technical College
Lander University
Midlands Technical College
Newberry College
North Greenville College
Orangeburg-Calhoun Technical College
Piedmont Technical College
Presbyterian College
South Carolina State University
Southern Wesleyan University
Spartanburg Methodist College
Spartanburg Technical College
Technical College of the Lowcountry
The Citadel
Tri-County Technical College
Trident Technical College
University of South Carolina
University of South Carolina
    Aiken
    Beaufort
    Salkehatchie Regional Campus
    Sumter
    Union
Wofford College
York Technical College

South Dakota
Augustana College
Black Hills State University
Dakota State University
Dakota Wesleyan University
Kilian Community College
Mount Marty College
Northern State University
Sinte Gleska University
South Dakota School of Mines and Technology
South Dakota State University
University of South Dakota
Western Dakota Technical Institute

Tennessee
Carson-Newman College
Chattanooga State Technical Community College
Cleveland State Community College
Columbia State Community College
Crichton College
David Lipscomb University
Dyersburg State Community College
East Tennessee State University
Freed-Hardeman University
Hiwassee College
Jackson State Community College
King College
Knoxville Business College
LeMoyne-Owen College
Lee University
Martin Methodist College
Maryville College
Middle Tennessee State University
Motlow State Community College
Nashville State Technical Institute
Northeast State Technical Community College
Pellissippi State Technical Community College
Rhodes College
Roane State Community College
Shelby State Community College
Tennessee Technological University
Tennessee Temple University
Tennessee Wesleyan College
Trevecca Nazarene University
Union University
University of Memphis
University of Tennessee
    Chattanooga
    Knoxville
    Martin
Vanderbilt University
Volunteer State Community College
Walters State Community College

Texas
Abilene Christian University
Alvin Community College
Amarillo College
Angelina College
Angelo State University
Arlington Baptist College
Austin Community College
Blinn College

Brazosport College
Brookhaven College
Cedar Valley College
Central Texas College
Coastal Bend College
College of the Mainland
Collin County Community College District
Concordia University at Austin
Dallas Baptist University
Del Mar College
East Texas Baptist University
El Paso Community College
Galveston College
Grayson County College
Hill College
Houston Baptist University
Houston Community College System
Howard College
Howard Payne University
Institute for Christian Studies
Jacksonville College
Jarvis Christian College
Kilgore College
Lamar State College at Port Arthur
Lamar University
Lee College
Lon Morris College
Lubbock Christian University
McMurry University
Midland College
Midwestern State University
Mountain View College
Navarro College
North Central Texas College
North Lake College
Northeast Texas Community College
Northwood University: Texas Campus
Odessa College
Our Lady of the Lake University of San Antonio
Palo Alto College
Panola College
Paris Junior College
Prairie View A&M University
Rice University
Richland College
St. Philip's College
Sam Houston State University
San Antonio College
San Jacinto College
   North
South Plains College
Southwest Texas Junior College
Southwest Texas State University
Southwestern Assemblies of God University
Southwestern University
Stephen F. Austin State University
Tarleton State University
Tarrant County College
Temple College
Texas A&M International University
Texas A&M University
Texas A&M University
   Commerce
   Galveston
Texas Lutheran University
Texas State Technical College
   Harlingen
   Sweetwater
   Waco
Texas Tech University
Texas Wesleyan University
Texas Woman's University
Trinity Valley Community College
Tyler Junior College
University of Houston
University of Houston
   Clear Lake
   Downtown
University of Mary Hardin-Baylor
University of North Texas

University of Texas
   Arlington
   Austin
   Brownsville
   El Paso
   San Antonio
Vernon Regional Junior College
Victoria College
Wayland Baptist University
Weatherford College
Western Texas College

Utah

Brigham Young University
College of Eastern Utah
Dixie State College of Utah
LDS Business College
Salt Lake Community College
University of Utah
Utah State University
Utah Valley State College
Weber State University
Westminster College

Vermont

Burlington College
Castleton State College
Champlain College
College of St. Joseph in Vermont
Community College of Vermont
Johnson State College
Lyndon State College
Marlboro College
Vermont Technical College

Virginia

Blue Ridge Community College
Bluefield College
Central Virginia Community College
Christopher Newport University
College of William and Mary
Dabney S. Lancaster Community College
Danville Community College
ECPI College of Technology
Eastern Mennonite University
Eastern Shore Community College
Emory & Henry College
Ferrum College
George Mason University
Germanna Community College
J. Sargeant Reynolds Community College
John Tyler Community College
Liberty University
Lord Fairfax Community College
Lynchburg College
Mary Baldwin College
Mountain Empire Community College
New River Community College
Northern Virginia Community College
Old Dominion University
Patrick Henry Community College
Paul D. Camp Community College
Piedmont Virginia Community College
Radford University
Randolph-Macon College
Randolph-Macon Woman's College
Richard Bland College
Roanoke College
Southside Virginia Community College
Southwest Virginia Community College
Thomas Nelson Community College
Tidewater Community College
University of Virginia's College at Wise
Virginia Commonwealth University
Virginia Highlands Community College
Virginia Intermont College
Virginia Polytechnic Institute and State University
Virginia State University
Virginia Western Community College
Wytheville Community College

Washington

Bellevue Community College
Big Bend Community College
Central Washington University
Centralia College
City University
Clark College
Columbia Basin College
Edmonds Community College
Everett Community College
Gonzaga University
Grays Harbor College
Green River Community College
Highline Community College
Lake Washington Technical College
Lower Columbia College
North Seattle Community College
Northwest Indian College
Olympic College
Pacific Lutheran University
Pierce College
Puget Sound Christian College
Renton Technical College
St. Martin's College
Seattle Central Community College
Shoreline Community College
Skagit Valley College
South Puget Sound Community College
South Seattle Community College
Spokane Community College
Spokane Falls Community College
Tacoma Community College
University of Washington
Walla Walla College
Walla Walla Community College
Wenatchee Valley College
Whatcom Community College
Whitman College
Whitworth College
Yakima Valley Community College

West Virginia

Alderson-Broaddus College
Bethany College
College of West Virginia
Concord College
Davis and Elkins College
Fairmont State College
Potomac State College of West Virginia University
Salem-Teikyo University
Shepherd College
Southern West Virginia Community and Technical College
University of Charleston
West Virginia Northern Community College
West Virginia State College
West Virginia University
West Virginia University Institute of Technology
West Virginia University Parkersburg
West Virginia Wesleyan College

Wisconsin

Alverno College
Beloit College
Blackhawk Technical College
Cardinal Stritch University
Carthage College
Chippewa Valley Technical College
Concordia University Wisconsin
Gateway Technical College
Lakeland College
Madison Area Technical College
Marian College of Fond du Lac
Marquette University
Milwaukee Area Technical College
Milwaukee Institute of Art & Design
Milwaukee School of Engineering
Moraine Park Technical College
Mount Mary College
Nicolet Area Technical College
Silver Lake College
Southwest Wisconsin Technical College
University of Wisconsin
   Baraboo/Sauk County
   Barron County
   Eau Claire
   Fond du Lac
   Fox Valley
   Green Bay
   La Crosse
   Madison
   Manitowoc County
   Marathon County
   Marinette
   Marshfield/Wood County
   Oshkosh
   Parkside
   Platteville
   Richland
   River Falls
   Rock County
   Sheboygan County
   Stevens Point
   Stout
   Superior
   Washington County
   Waukesha
Viterbo University
Waukesha County Technical College
Wisconsin Lutheran College

Wyoming

Casper College
Central Wyoming College
Eastern Wyoming College
Laramie County Community College
Northwest College
Sheridan College
University of Wyoming
Western Wyoming Community College

ESL program

Alabama

Auburn University
Auburn University at Montgomery
Enterprise State Junior College
Gadsden State Community College
Jacksonville State University
Spring Hill College
Troy State University
University of Alabama
University of Alabama Huntsville
University of Mobile
University of North Alabama
University of South Alabama

Alaska

University of Alaska
   Anchorage

Arizona

Arizona Western College
Cochise College
Embry-Riddle Aeronautical University Prescott Campus
Gateway Community College
Glendale Community College
Grand Canyon University
Mesa Community College
Mohave Community College
Northern Arizona University
Pima Community College
Rio Salado College
Scottsdale Community College
South Mountain Community College
University of Arizona
Yavapai College

Arkansas

Arkansas State University

John Brown University
Ouachita Baptist University
University of Arkansas
    Little Rock
University of Central Arkansas

California
Academy of Art College
Allan Hancock College
Biola University
Brooks College
Butte College
California Maritime Academy
California Polytechnic State University:
  San Luis Obispo
California State Polytechnic University:
  Pomona
California State University
  Bakersfield
  Chico
  Dominguez Hills
  Fresno
  Fullerton
  Hayward
  Long Beach
  Monterey Bay
  Northridge
  Sacramento
Cerro Coso Community College
Chabot College
Chaffey Community College
City College of San Francisco
Coastline Community College
College of Notre Dame
College of San Mateo
College of the Canyons
College of the Desert
College of the Redwoods
College of the Sequoias
College of the Siskiyous
Columbia College
Concordia University
Cuesta College
Cypress College
De Anza College
Diablo Valley College
Dominican University of California
East Los Angeles College
Evergreen Valley College
Foothill College
Fresno Pacific University
Gavilan Community College
Glendale Community College
Golden Gate University
Golden West College
Grossmont Community College
Holy Names College
Hope International University
Humboldt State University
Irvine Valley College
La Sierra University
Lake Tahoe Community College
Las Positas College
Lincoln University
Loma Linda University
Long Beach City College
Los Angeles Harbor College
Los Angeles Southwest College
Marymount College
Menlo College
MiraCosta College
Modesto Junior College
Monterey Institute of International
  Studies
Monterey Peninsula College
Mount San Antonio College
Napa Valley College
National University
Ohlone College
Orange Coast College
Otis College of Art and Design
Pacific Union College
Palomar College
Pitzer College
Point Loma Nazarene University
Queen of the Holy Rosary College
Riverside Community College
Sacramento City College
Saddleback College
St. John's Seminary College
San Diego State University
San Francisco Art Institute
San Francisco State University
San Joaquin Delta College
Santa Ana College
Santa Barbara City College
Santa Monica College
Santa Rosa Junior College
Shasta College
Sierra College
Skyline College
Sonoma State University
Southwestern College
United States International University
University of California
  Davis
  Irvine
  Los Angeles
  Santa Barbara
  Santa Cruz
University of La Verne
University of Redlands
University of San Francisco
University of Southern California
University of the Pacific
Ventura College

Colorado
Arapahoe Community College
Colorado College
Colorado School of Mines
Community College of Aurora
Fort Lewis College
Lamar Community College
Morgan Community College
Northeastern Junior College
Pikes Peak Community College
Red Rocks Community College
Trinidad State Junior College
United States Air Force Academy
University of Colorado
  Boulder
University of Denver
University of Northern Colorado
University of Southern Colorado

Connecticut
Albertus Magnus College
Briarwood College
Capital Community College
Housatonic Community-Technical
  College
Manchester Community-Technical
  College
Middlesex Community-Technical
  College
Naugatuck Valley Community-Technical
  College
Northwestern Connecticut
  Community-Technical College
Norwalk Community-Technical College
Quinebaug Valley Community College
Sacred Heart University
Teikyo Post University
Three Rivers Community-Technical
  College
Tunxis Community College
University of Bridgeport
University of Connecticut
University of Hartford
University of New Haven
Western Connecticut State University

Delaware
Delaware State University
Delaware Technical and Community
  College
    Stanton/Wilmington Campus
University of Delaware
Wesley College

District of Columbia
American University
Catholic University of America
Gallaudet University
George Washington University
Georgetown University
Trinity College
University of the District of Columbia

Florida
Art Institute
  of Fort Lauderdale
Barry University
Central Florida Community College
Daytona Beach Community College
Eckerd College
Embry-Riddle Aeronautical University
Florida Atlantic University
Florida Community College at
  Jacksonville
Florida Institute of Technology
Florida Keys Community College
Florida National College
Florida State University
Hillsborough Community College
Hobe Sound Bible College
International College
International Fine Arts College
Jacksonville University
Lynn University
Miami-Dade Community College
Palm Beach Atlantic College
Palm Beach Community College
Pensacola Junior College
St. John Vianney College Seminary
St. Petersburg Junior College
St. Thomas University
Santa Fe Community College
Seminole Community College
South Florida Community College
Tallahassee Community College
University of Central Florida
University of Florida
University of Miami
University of North Florida
University of Tampa
University of West Florida
Valencia Community College

Georgia
American InterContinental University
Andrew College
Brenau University
Brewton-Parker College
Chattahoochee Technical Institute
DeKalb Technical Institute
Emory University
Gainesville College
Georgia College and State University
Georgia Institute of Technology
Georgia Perimeter College
Georgia Southern University
Georgia Southwestern State University
Georgia State University
LaGrange College
Mercer University
Morehouse College
Savannah College of Art and Design
Savannah Technical Institute
State University of West Georgia
Toccoa Falls College
University of Georgia

Hawaii
Brigham Young University
  Hawaii
Chaminade University of Honolulu
Hawaii Pacific University
TransPacific Hawaii College
University of Hawaii
  Hawaii Community College
  Honolulu Community College
  Kapiolani Community College
  Kauai Community College
  Manoa
  Maui Community College

Idaho
College of Southern Idaho
Eastern Idaho Technical College
Idaho State University
Lewis-Clark State College
North Idaho College

Illinois
Benedictine University
Black Hawk College
Carl Sandburg College
City Colleges of Chicago
  Harold Washington College
  Wright College
College of DuPage
College of Lake County
Columbia College
Danville Area Community College
De Paul University
DeVry Institute of Technology
  Chicago
Dominican University
Eastern Illinois University
Elgin Community College
Highland Community College
Illinois Eastern Community Colleges
  Wabash Valley College
Illinois State University
John Wood Community College
Joliet Junior College
Kendall College
Kishwaukee College
Lake Land College
Lewis University
Lincoln Land Community College
Loyola University of Chicago
MacCormac College
McHenry County College
Moraine Valley Community College
National-Louis University
North Central College
North Park University
Northeastern Illinois University
Parkland College
Prairie State College
Quincy University
Rockford College
Roosevelt University
St. Augustine College
Sauk Valley Community College
School of the Art Institute of Chicago
Southern Illinois University
  Carbondale
  Edwardsville
Southwestern Ilionois College
University of Illinois
  Urbana-Champaign
Western Illinois University
William Rainey Harper College

Indiana
Ball State University
Butler University
DePauw University
Goshen College
Indiana Institute of Technology
Indiana State University
Indiana University
  Bloomington
  South Bend
Indiana University--Purdue University
  Indiana University-Purdue
    University Fort Wayne
  Indiana University-Purdue
    University Indianapolis

Ivy Tech State College
    Central Indiana
    Northeast
University of Evansville
University of Indianapolis
University of Southern Indiana
Valparaiso University
Vincennes University

Iowa
Buena Vista University
Clarke College
Clinton Community College
Coe College
Cornell College
Dordt College
Drake University
Graceland University
Iowa State University
Iowa Wesleyan College
Kirkwood Community College
Loras College
Maharishi University of Management
Marshalltown Community College
Morningside College
Muscatine Community College
Northeast Iowa Community College
Northwestern College
Scott Community College
Simpson College
University of Dubuque
University of Iowa
University of Northern Iowa
Waldorf College
Wartburg College
Western Iowa Tech Community College
William Penn University

Kansas
Baker University
Barton County Community College
Benedictine College
Butler County Community College
Coffeyville Community College
Dodge City Community College
Fort Hays State University
Garden City Community College
Hesston College
Hutchinson Community College
Independence Community College
Kansas City Kansas Community College
Kansas State University
Kansas Wesleyan University
MidAmerica Nazarene University
Ottawa University
University of Kansas
University of Kansas
    Medical Center
Washburn University of Topeka
Wichita State University

Kentucky
Campbellsville University
Kentucky State University
Murray State University
Thomas More College
University of Kentucky
University of Louisville
Western Kentucky University

Louisiana
Delgado Community College
Louisiana State University and
    Agricultural and Mechanical College
Louisiana Tech University
Loyola University New Orleans
Nicholls State University
Nunez Community College
St. Joseph Seminary College
Tulane University
University of Louisiana at Monroe
University of New Orleans

Maine
Husson College
University of Maine
University of New England
University of Southern Maine

Maryland
Baltimore City Community College
Cecil Community College
Chesapeake College
College of Notre Dame of Maryland
Community College of Baltimore County
    Catonsville
Frederick Community College
Hood College
Montgomery College
    Germantown Campus
    Rockville Campus
    Takoma Park Campus
Mount St. Mary's College
Prince George's Community College
Towson University
University of Maryland
    Baltimore County
    College Park
Washington Bible College
Wor-Wic Community College

Massachusetts
American International College
Anna Maria College
Atlantic Union College
Bay Path College
Bay State College
Bentley College
Berkshire Community College
Boston Conservatory
Boston University
Bridgewater State College
Bristol Community College
Bunker Hill Community College
Cape Cod Community College
Clark University
Curry College
Dean College
Elms College
Emmanuel College
Endicott College
Fisher College
Framingham State College
Franklin Institute of Boston
Greenfield Community College
Holyoke Community College
Lasell College
Massachusetts College of Pharmacy and
    Health Sciences
Massachusetts Institute of Technology
Massasoit Community College
Merrimack College
Middlesex Community College
Montserrat College of Art
Mount Ida College
Mount Wachusett Community College
New England Conservatory of Music
Newbury College
North Shore Community College
Northeastern University
Northern Essex Community College
Pine Manor College
Roxbury Community College
Salem State College
Springfield College
Suffolk University
University of Massachusetts
    Amherst
    Boston
Wentworth Institute of Technology
Worcester Polytechnic Institute
Worcester State College

Michigan
Adrian College
Alma College
Andrews University
Aquinas College
Calvin College
Central Michigan University
Davenport College of Business
Eastern Michigan University
Ferris State University
Grand Rapids Community College
Grand Valley State University
Kalamazoo Valley Community College
Kirtland Community College
Macomb Community College
Madonna University
Michigan State University
Mott Community College
Northwood University
Oakland Community College
Saginaw Valley State University
Southwestern Michigan College
Spring Arbor College
Suomi College
University of Detroit Mercy
University of Michigan
Washtenaw Community College
Wayne State University
Western Michigan University

Minnesota
Augsburg College
Bemidji State University
Century Community and Technical
    College
College of St. Benedict
Concordia College: Moorhead
Concordia University: St. Paul
Crown College
Dakota County Technical College
Hamline University
Hennepin Technical College
Lake Superior College: A Community
    and Technical College
Minneapolis Community and Technical
    College
Minnesota State College - Southeast
    Technical
Minnesota State University, Mankato
North Hennepin Community College
Northwestern College
St. Cloud Technical College
St. John's University
St. Mary's University of Minnesota
St. Paul Technical College
Southwest State University
University of Minnesota
    Twin Cities
University of St. Thomas

Mississippi
Belhaven College
Mississippi State University
Mississippi University for Women
University of Mississippi
University of Southern Mississippi

Missouri
Avila College
Central Methodist College
Central Missouri State University
Columbia College
Conception Seminary College
Crowder College
Drury University
East Central College
Fontbonne College
Maryville University of Saint Louis
Missouri Southern State College
Missouri Valley College
Ozarks Technical Community College
Penn Valley Community College
St. Louis University
Southwest Missouri State University
St. Louis Community College
    St. Louis Community College at
        Florissant Valley
Stephens College
Truman State University
University of Missouri
    Columbia
    Rolla
Washington University
Webster University
Wentworth Military Academy
Westminster College
William Woods University

Montana
Carroll College
Miles Community College
Montana State University
    Bozeman
Rocky Mountain College
University of Montana-Missoula

Nebraska
Bellevue University
Central Community College
Concordia University
Creighton University
Dana College
Doane College
Metropolitan Community College
Northeast Community College
Union College
University of Nebraska
    Kearney
    Lincoln
    Omaha

Nevada
Community College of Southern Nevada
University of Nevada
    Las Vegas
    Reno
Western Nevada Community College

New Hampshire
Colby-Sawyer College
Franklin Pierce College
Keene State College
New Hampshire College
New Hampshire Community Technical
    College
    Nashua
New Hampshire Technical Institute
Rivier College
University of New Hampshire
University of New Hampshire
    Manchester
White Pines College

New Jersey
Assumption College for Sisters
Atlantic Cape Community College
Bergen Community College
Bloomfield College
Brookdale Community College
Burlington County College
Caldwell College
Camden County College
Centenary College
College of St. Elizabeth
County College of Morris
Essex County College
Fairleigh Dickinson University
Georgian Court College
Hudson County Community College
Kean University
Mercer County Community College
Middlesex County College
Monmouth University
Montclair State University
New Jersey City University
New Jersey Institute of Technology
Ocean County College
Passaic County Community College
Ramapo College of New Jersey
Rowan University

Rutgers
    The State University of New Jersey: Camden College of Arts and Sciences
    The State University of New Jersey: College of Engineering
    The State University of New Jersey: College of Nursing
    The State University of New Jersey: Cook College
    The State University of New Jersey: Douglass College
    The State University of New Jersey: Livingston College
    The State University of New Jersey: Mason Gross School of the Arts
    The State University of New Jersey: Newark College of Arts and Sciences
    The State University of New Jersey: Rutgers College
    The State University of New Jersey: University College Camden
    The State University of New Jersey: University College New Brunswick
    The State University of New Jersey: University College Newark
Salem Community College
Seton Hall University
Sussex County Community College
Union County College
Warren County Community College
William Paterson University of New Jersey

New Mexico

Albuquerque Technical-Vocational Institute
Clovis Community College
Dona Ana Branch Community College of New Mexico State University
New Mexico Highlands University
New Mexico Junior College
New Mexico State University Carlsbad
San Juan College
Santa Fe Community College
University of New Mexico

New York

Berkeley College
Berkeley College of New York City
Canisius College
City University of New York
    Baruch College
    Borough of Manhattan Community College
    Bronx Community College
    Brooklyn College
    City College
    College of Staten Island
    Hostos Community College
    John Jay College of Criminal Justice
    Kingsborough Community College
    New York City Technical College
    Queens College
    Queensborough Community College
    York College
Clarkson University
Clinton Community College
College of Aeronautics
College of Insurance
Concordia College
Cornell University
Dowling College
Dutchess Community College
Eastman School of Music of the University of Rochester
Elmira College
Erie Community College
    City Campus
    North Campus
    South Campus
Eugene Lang College/New School University
Finger Lakes Community College
Fordham University
Fulton-Montgomery Community College
Genesee Community College
Hamilton College
Herkimer County Community College
Hofstra University
Jamestown Community College
Long Island University
    C. W. Post Campus
    Southampton College
Manhattan College
Manhattan School of Music
Manhattanville College
Mannes College of Music
Marist College
Marymount College
Marymount Manhattan College
Mercy College
Mohawk Valley Community College
Molloy College
Monroe Community College
Nassau Community College
New York Institute of Technology
New York University
Nyack College
Onondaga Community College
Orange County Community College
Pace University
Pace University: Pleasantville/Briarcliff
Parsons School of Design
Polytechnic University
    Long Island Campus
Pratt Institute
Rensselaer Polytechnic Institute
Roberts Wesleyan College
Rochester Institute of Technology
Rockland Community College
St. John's University
St. Thomas Aquinas College
School of Visual Arts
State University of New York
    Binghamton
    Buffalo
    College at Buffalo
    College at Old Westbury
    College at Plattsburgh
    College of Agriculture and Technology at Cobleskill
    College of Agriculture and Technology at Morrisville
    Institute of Technology at Utica/Rome
    New Paltz
    Purchase
    Stony Brook
Suffolk County Community College
Syracuse University
Technical Career Institutes
Tompkins-Cortland Community College
Touro College
Union College
University of Rochester
Utica College of Syracuse University
Wagner College
Westchester Community College

North Carolina

Asheville Buncombe Technical Community College
Beaufort County Community College
Blue Ridge Community College
Brevard College
Brunswick Community College
Cleveland Community College
College of the Albemarle
Durham Technical Community College
Elon College
Forsyth Technical Community College
Gaston College
High Point University
James Sprunt Community College
Lenoir-Rhyne College
Mars Hill College
Methodist College
North Carolina State University
Randolph Community College
Richmond Community College
Rowan-Cabarrus Community College
Sandhills Community College
Shaw University
Surry Community College
University of North Carolina
    Charlotte
    Wilmington
Wake Technical Community College
Warren Wilson College
Wilkes Community College

North Dakota

Lake Region State College
North Dakota State University
University of North Dakota

Ohio

Ashland University
Baldwin-Wallace College
Capital University
Case Western Reserve University
Cedarville College
Central Ohio Technical College
Cincinnati State Technical and Community College
Cleveland State University
College of Mount St. Joseph
Columbus College of Art and Design
Columbus State Community College
Franklin University
Hiram College
Hocking Technical College
Kent State University
Marietta College
Mount Union College
Muskingum College
Ohio Dominican College
Ohio State University
    Columbus Campus
Ohio University
Otterbein College
Pontifical College Josephinum
Sinclair Community College
University of Akron
University of Cincinnati
University of Dayton
University of Findlay
University of Rio Grande
University of Toledo
Wright State University
Xavier University
Youngstown State University

Oklahoma

Oklahoma City Community College
Oklahoma City University
Oklahoma State University
Oral Roberts University
Tulsa Community College
University of Central Oklahoma
University of Oklahoma
University of Tulsa

Oregon

Central Oregon Community College
Chemeketa Community College
Clackamas Community College
Concordia University
George Fox University
Lane Community College
Lewis & Clark College
Linfield College
Linn-Benton Community College
Marylhurst University
Pacific University
Portland Community College
Portland State University
Southern Oregon University
University of Portland
Western Oregon University

Pennsylvania

Albright College
Beaver College
Cabrini College
Carnegie Mellon University
Cedar Crest College
Chatham College
Chestnut Hill College
Community College of Philadelphia
Delaware Valley College
Drexel University
Duquesne University
Gannon University
Geneva College
Gwynedd-Mercy College
Harcum College
Harrisburg Area Community College
Immaculata College
Indiana University of Pennsylvania
Juniata College
King's College
La Roche College
Lackawanna Junior College
Lehigh Carbon Community College
Lehigh University
Manor College
Marywood University
Montgomery County Community College
Northampton County Area Community College
Penn State
    Abington
    Altoona
    Beaver
    Delaware County
    University Park
    York
Philadelphia College of Bible
Philadelphia University
Point Park College
Rosemont College
St. Joseph's University
Seton Hill College
Temple University
Thiel College
University of Pennsylvania
University of Pittsburgh
University of the Arts
University of the Sciences in Philadelphia
Valley Forge Christian College
Valley Forge Military College
Villanova University
Waynesburg College
Widener University
Wilson College

Puerto Rico

Huertas Junior College
Inter American University of Puerto Rico
    Fajardo Campus
    Metropolitan Campus
    San German Campus
National College of Business and Technology
Pontifical Catholic University of Puerto Rico
University of Puerto Rico
    Arecibo Campus
    Bayamon University College
    Humacao University College
    Mayaguez Campus
    Rio Piedras Campus

Rhode Island

Bryant College
Community College of Rhode Island

Johnson & Wales University
New England Institute of Technology
Roger Williams University
Salve Regina University

South Carolina
Anderson College
Coker College
College of Charleston
Limestone College
North Greenville College
Spartanburg Methodist College
The Citadel
Tri-County Technical College
Trident Technical College
University of South Carolina
University of South Carolina
    Aiken
    Sumter

South Dakota
Dakota State University
Huron University
Northern State University
University of South Dakota

Tennessee
Carson-Newman College
Chattanooga State Technical Community
    College
Hiwassee College
Johnson Bible College
King College
Lambuth University
Lee University
Lincoln Memorial University
Martin Methodist College
Maryville College
Milligan College
Nashville State Technical Institute
Pellissippi State Technical Community
    College
Southern Adventist University
Tennessee State University
Tennessee Wesleyan College
Tusculum College
Union University
University of Memphis
University of Tennessee
    Chattanooga
    Knoxville
    Martin
Vanderbilt University
Volunteer State Community College

Texas
Abilene Christian University
Alvin Community College
Amarillo College
Angelo State University
Baylor University
Blinn College
Central Texas College
Collin County Community College
    District
Concordia University at Austin
Dallas Baptist University
Del Mar College
East Texas Baptist University
Eastfield College
El Paso Community College
Houston Baptist University
Houston Community College System
Howard College
Howard Payne University
Kilgore College
Lamar State College at Port Arthur
Lamar University
Lee College
Lon Morris College
Midland College
Midwestern State University
Mountain View College
Navarro College

North Lake College
Northeast Texas Community College
Our Lady of the Lake University of San
    Antonio
Palo Alto College
Prairie View A&M University
Rice University
St. Mary's University
St. Philip's College
San Jacinto College
    North
Southern Methodist University
Southwest Texas State University
Southwestern Adventist University
Stephen F. Austin State University
Tarrant County College
Texas A&M International University
Texas A&M University
Texas A&M University
    Commerce
    Kingsville
Texas Christian University
Texas Lutheran University
Texas State Technical College
    Harlingen
Texas Tech University
Texas Wesleyan University
Tyler Junior College
University of Dallas
University of Houston
University of Houston
    Downtown
University of Mary Hardin-Baylor
University of North Texas
University of St. Thomas
University of Texas
    Arlington
    Austin
    San Antonio
University of the Incarnate Word
Weatherford College
West Texas A&M University

Utah
Brigham Young University
College of Eastern Utah
Dixie State College of Utah
Salt Lake Community College
Snow College
Southern Utah University
University of Utah
Utah State University
Utah Valley State College
Weber State University

Vermont
Champlain College
College of St. Joseph in Vermont
Community College of Vermont
Green Mountain College
Johnson State College
Landmark College
St. Michael's College
Vermont Technical College

Virginia
Blue Ridge Community College
Christopher Newport University
Eastern Mennonite University
Eastern Shore Community College
Emory & Henry College
George Mason University
J. Sargeant Reynolds Community
    College
James Madison University
Liberty University
Mary Baldwin College
Northern Virginia Community College
Old Dominion University
Piedmont Virginia Community College
Radford University
Shenandoah University
Thomas Nelson Community College
Tidewater Community College

University of Richmond
Virginia Commonwealth University
Virginia Polytechnic Institute and State
    University

Washington
Art Institute of Seattle
Central Washington University
Centralia College
City University
Clark College
Columbia Basin College
Eastern Washington University
Edmonds Community College
Everett Community College
Gonzaga University
Grays Harbor College
Green River Community College
Highline Community College
Lake Washington Technical College
Lower Columbia College
North Seattle Community College
Olympic College
Pacific Lutheran University
Peninsula College
Pierce College
Renton Technical College
St. Martin's College
Seattle Pacific University
Seattle University
Shoreline Community College
Skagit Valley College
South Puget Sound Community College
South Seattle Community College
Spokane Community College
Spokane Falls Community College
University of Washington
Walla Walla College
Wenatchee Valley College
Western Washington University
Whatcom Community College
Whitworth College
Yakima Valley Community College

West Virginia
Bethany College
Concord College
Davis and Elkins College
Fairmont State College
Glenville State College
Marshall University
Salem-Teikyo University
West Virginia University
West Virginia Wesleyan College
Wheeling Jesuit University

Wisconsin
Beloit College
Cardinal Stritch University
Chippewa Valley Technical College
Concordia University Wisconsin
Gateway Technical College
Lakeland College
Lakeshore Technical College
Madison Area Technical College
Milwaukee Area Technical College
Milwaukee School of Engineering
Moraine Park Technical College
Mount Senario College
Nicolet Area Technical College
St. Norbert College
Silver Lake College
Southwest Wisconsin Technical College
University of Wisconsin
    Eau Claire
    Green Bay
    La Crosse
    Marinette
    Milwaukee
    Parkside
    Stevens Point
    Stout
Western Wisconsin Technical College

Wyoming
Eastern Wyoming College
Sheridan College
Western Wyoming Community College

External degree

Alabama
Troy State University
    Montgomery
University of Alabama

Arizona
Northern Arizona University
Prescott College
University of Phoenix

Arkansas
Arkansas Tech University
John Brown University

California
Biola University
California Polytechnic State University:
    San Luis Obispo
California State University
    Bakersfield
    Long Beach
    Northridge
Cogswell Polytechnical College
LIFE Bible College
Oxnard College
Pacific Union College
St. Mary's College of California
San Diego State University
Sonoma State University
University of San Francisco
Westmont College

Colorado
Metropolitan State College of Denver
University of Northern Colorado
University of Southern Colorado

Connecticut
Charter Oak State College

Florida
Embry-Riddle Aeronautical University
Florida Baptist Theological College
Florida Gulf Coast University
Hobe Sound Bible College
South Florida Community College
University of Florida

Georgia
Abraham Baldwin Agricultural College
Fort Valley State University
Georgia College and State University
Georgia Military College
State University of West Georgia

Hawaii
University of Hawaii
    Kapiolani Community College

Idaho
Idaho State University

Illinois
Governors State University
Greenville College
Moody Bible Institute
Roosevelt University
Western Illinois University

Indiana
Indiana Institute of Technology

External degree

Indiana University
   Bloomington
   East
   Kokomo
   Northwest
   South Bend
   Southeast
Indiana University--Purdue University
   Indiana University-Purdue University Indianapolis
Indiana Wesleyan University
Oakland City University
St. Mary-of-the-Woods College
Vincennes University

Iowa
Graceland University
Hawkeye Community College
Iowa Central Community College
Iowa State University
Kirkwood Community College
University of Iowa
Upper Iowa University

Kansas
Kansas City Kansas Community College
Pittsburg State University
Seward County Community College

Kentucky
Murray State University
Union College
University of Louisville

Louisiana
Loyola University New Orleans

Maine
Eastern Maine Technical College
St. Joseph's College
University of Maine
University of Maine
   Fort Kent
   Machias

Maryland
Columbia Union College
Coppin State College
Howard Community College
University of Maryland
   College Park
   University College
Washington College

Massachusetts
Atlantic Union College
Bunker Hill Community College
Framingham State College
Lesley College
Massachusetts College of Art

Michigan
Baker College
   of Auburn Hills
   of Cadillac
   of Jackson
   of Mount Clemens
   of Muskegon
   of Owosso
   of Port Huron
Central Michigan University
Ferris State University
Northwood University
Siena Heights University
Spring Arbor College
University of Michigan
Western Michigan University

Minnesota
Bemidji State University
Bethel College
Metropolitan State University
Moorhead State University

St. Mary's University of Minnesota
St. Olaf College
Southwest State University
University of Minnesota
   Morris
   Twin Cities
Winona State University

Missouri
Berean University
Hannibal-LaGrange College
Lindenwood University
Stephens College
University of Missouri
   Columbia

Nebraska
Chadron State College
Clarkson College
Doane College
University of Nebraska
   Lincoln

New Hampshire
Hesser College
University of New Hampshire
University of New Hampshire
   Manchester

New Jersey
Caldwell College
County College of Morris
Mercer County Community College
Thomas Edison State College

New Mexico
San Juan College

New York
City University of New York
   Bronx Community College
Fulton-Montgomery Community College
Regents College
Russell Sage College
Skidmore College
State University of New York
   Empire State College
Utica College of Syracuse University

North Carolina
Lenoir-Rhyne College
North Carolina State University
Shaw University
University of North Carolina
   Charlotte

North Dakota
Minot State University
University of Mary

Ohio
David N. Myers College
Ohio University
   Chillicothe Campus
   Eastern Campus
Union Institute
University of Findlay
University of Toledo
Walsh University

Oklahoma
Mid-America Bible College
Oklahoma City University
Oral Roberts University
Southern Nazarene University
University of Oklahoma

Oregon
Eastern Oregon University
George Fox University
Linfield College

Pennsylvania
Community College of Allegheny County
Elizabethtown College
ICS Center for Degree Studies
Luzerne County Community College
Marywood University
Peirce College
Penn State
   Abington
   University Park
St. Francis College
University of Pittsburgh
University of Pittsburgh
   Bradford
   Greensburg

Puerto Rico
Inter American University of Puerto Rico
   Guayama Campus
University of Puerto Rico
   Rio Piedras Campus
University of the Sacred Heart

Rhode Island
Johnson & Wales University
Roger Williams University

South Carolina
Benedict College
Southern Wesleyan University
University of South Carolina

South Dakota
Northern State University
University of South Dakota

Tennessee
Lee University
Tennessee Temple University
University of Memphis

Texas
Concordia University at Austin
Lamar State College at Port Arthur
Northwood University: Texas Campus
Southwestern Adventist University
Southwestern Assemblies of God University
Texas A&M University
   Commerce
Wayland Baptist University

Utah
Brigham Young University
Utah State University
Weber State University

Vermont
Burlington College
Community College of Vermont
Goddard College
Johnson State College
Norwich University

Virginia
George Mason University
Liberty University
Mary Baldwin College
Virginia Western Community College

Washington
City University
Clark College
Seattle Pacific University
Skagit Valley College
Walla Walla Community College
Washington State University

West Virginia
Alderson-Broaddus College
West Liberty State College

West Virginia State College
West Virginia University

Wisconsin
Cardinal Stritch University
Chippewa Valley Technical College
Madison Area Technical College
Mount Senario College
University of Wisconsin
   Green Bay
   Platteville
   River Falls
   Stout
   Superior
   Whitewater

Wyoming
Western Wyoming Community College

Honors program

Alabama
Alabama Agricultural and Mechanical University
Alabama State University
Auburn University
Auburn University at Montgomery
Bevill State Community College
Birmingham-Southern College
Chattahoochee Valley Community College
Enterprise State Junior College
George C. Wallace State Community College
   Dothan
Huntingdon College
Jacksonville State University
James H. Faulkner State Community College
Jefferson Davis Community College
Jefferson State Community College
Lurleen B. Wallace Junior College
Northeast Alabama Community College
Oakwood College
Samford University
Shelton State Community College
Spring Hill College
Stillman College
Troy State University
Troy State University
   Montgomery
Tuskegee University
University of Alabama
University of Alabama
   Birmingham
   Huntsville
University of Mobile
University of Montevallo
University of West Alabama

Alaska
Prince William Sound Community College
University of Alaska
   Anchorage
   Fairbanks

Arizona
Arizona State University
Arizona Western College
Central Arizona College
Cochise College
Gateway Community College
Glendale Community College
Grand Canyon University
Mesa Community College
Northern Arizona University
Northland Pioneer College
Paradise Valley Community College
Phoenix College
Pima Community College
Rio Salado College

Scottsdale Community College
South Mountain Community College
University of Arizona

Arkansas

Arkansas State University
Arkansas State University Beebe Branch
Arkansas Tech University
Garland County Community College
Harding University
Henderson State University
Hendrix College
John Brown University
North Arkansas College
Northwest Arkansas Community College
Ouachita Baptist University
Phillips Community College of the University of Arkansas
Southern Arkansas University Tech
University of Arkansas
University of Arkansas
    Little Rock
    Monticello
    Pine Bluff
University of Central Arkansas
Westark College

California

Academy of Art College
Azusa Pacific University
Barstow College
Biola University
Butte College
Cabrillo College
California Polytechnic State University: San Luis Obispo
California State University
    Bakersfield
    Chico
    Dominguez Hills
    Fresno
    Fullerton
    Hayward
    Long Beach
    Los Angeles
    Monterey Bay
    Northridge
    San Marcos
    Stanislaus
Cerro Coso Community College
Chaffey Community College
Chapman University
Claremont McKenna College
College of San Mateo
College of the Canyons
College of the Desert
College of the Redwoods
College of the Sequoias
Compton Community College
Concordia University
Contra Costa College
Cuesta College
Cypress College
De Anza College
Deep Springs College
Diablo Valley College
Dominican University of California
East Los Angeles College
Evergreen Valley College
Foothill College
Fresno City College
Glendale Community College
Golden West College
Hope International University
Humboldt State University
Humphreys College
Imperial Valley College
Kings River Community College
La Sierra University
Long Beach City College
Los Angeles Harbor College
Los Angeles Pierce College
Los Angeles Southwest College
Los Angeles Valley College
Loyola Marymount University
Marymount College
Menlo College
Merced College
Merritt College
MiraCosta College
Mission College
Modesto Junior College
Monterey Institute of International Studies
Mount St. Mary's College
Mount San Antonio College
Mount San Jacinto College
Napa Valley College
Occidental College
Orange Coast College
Otis College of Art and Design
Oxnard College
Pacific Union College
Pasadena City College
Pepperdine University
Rio Hondo College
Riverside Community College
Sacramento City College
Saddleback College
St. John's Seminary College
St. Mary's College of California
San Bernardino Valley College
San Diego City College
San Diego Mesa College
San Diego Miramar College
San Diego State University
San Joaquin Delta College
San Jose City College
San Jose State University
Santa Ana College
Santa Barbara City College
Santa Clara University
Santa Monica College
Scripps College
Shasta College
Solano Community College
Sonoma State University
Southwestern College
Stanford University
United States International University
University of California
    Berkeley
    Davis
    Irvine
    Los Angeles
    Riverside
    San Diego
    San Francisco
    Santa Barbara
    Santa Cruz
University of Judaism
University of La Verne
University of Redlands
University of San Diego
University of San Francisco
University of Southern California
University of the Pacific
Ventura College
Victor Valley College
West Hills Community College
West Los Angeles College
West Valley College
Westmont College

Colorado

Arapahoe Community College
Colorado School of Mines
Colorado State University
Fort Lewis College
Front Range Community College
Metropolitan State College of Denver
Regis University
University of Colorado
    Boulder
    Denver
University of Denver
University of Northern Colorado
University of Southern Colorado
Western State College of Colorado

Connecticut

Albertus Magnus College
Central Connecticut State University
Connecticut College
Eastern Connecticut State University
Fairfield University
Housatonic Community-Technical College
Manchester Community-Technical College
Northwestern Connecticut Community-Technical College
Norwalk Community-Technical College
Quinnipiac University
Sacred Heart University
St. Joseph College
Southern Connecticut State University
Teikyo Post University
Trinity College
United States Coast Guard Academy
University of Bridgeport
University of Connecticut
University of Hartford
University of New Haven
Wesleyan University
Western Connecticut State University
Yale University

Delaware

Delaware State University
Goldey-Beacom College
University of Delaware

District of Columbia

American University
Catholic University of America
Gallaudet University
George Washington University
Georgetown University
Howard University
Southeastern University
Trinity College
University of the District of Columbia

Florida

Art Institute of Fort Lauderdale
Barry University
Bethune-Cookman College
Brevard Community College
Broward Community College
Central Florida Community College
Chipola Junior College
Daytona Beach Community College
Eckerd College
Edison Community College
Florida Agricultural and Mechanical University
Florida Atlantic University
Florida Community College at Jacksonville
Florida Gulf Coast University
Florida International University
Florida Memorial College
Florida Southern College
Florida State University
Gulf Coast Community College
Hillsborough Community College
Jacksonville University
Lynn University
Manatee Community College
Miami-Dade Community College
Northwood University Florida Campus
Palm Beach Atlantic College
Palm Beach Community College
Pasco-Hernando Community College
Pensacola Junior College
Rollins College
St. Leo University
St. Petersburg Junior College
St. Thomas University
Santa Fe Community College
Seminole Community College
South Florida Community College
Stetson University
Tallahassee Community College
University of Central Florida
University of Florida
University of Miami
University of North Florida
University of South Florida
University of Tampa
University of West Florida
Valencia Community College

Georgia

Abraham Baldwin Agricultural College
Albany State University
Andrew College
Armstrong Atlantic State University
Atlanta Metropolitan College
Augusta State University
Berry College
Brenau University
Brewton-Parker College
Chattahoochee Technical Institute
Clark Atlanta University
Clayton College and State University
Columbus State University
Columbus Technical Institute
Darton College
East Georgia College
Emory University
Fort Valley State University
Gainesville College
Georgia College and State University
Georgia Institute of Technology
Georgia Perimeter College
Georgia Southern University
Georgia Southwestern State University
Georgia State University
Kennesaw State University
Macon State College
Mercer University
Morehouse College
Morris Brown College
North Georgia College & State University
Oglethorpe University
Paine College
Piedmont College
Reinhardt College
Savannah State University
Shorter College
Spelman College
State University of West Georgia
Thomas College
Toccoa Falls College
Truett-McConnell College
University of Georgia
Valdosta State University
Wesleyan College

Hawaii

Brigham Young University Hawaii
Hawaii Pacific University
University of Hawaii
    Hawaii Community College
    Hilo
    Kapiolani Community College
    Leeward Community College
    Manoa

Idaho

Albertson College of Idaho
Boise State University
College of Southern Idaho
Idaho State University
Lewis-Clark State College
Northwest Nazarene University
Ricks College
University of Idaho

Illinois
Augustana College
Benedictine University
Black Hawk College
Blackburn College
Bradley University
Carl Sandburg College
Chicago State University
City Colleges of Chicago
    Harry S. Truman College
    Kennedy-King College
    Malcolm X College
    Olive-Harvey College
    Richard J. Daley College
    Wright College
College of DuPage
College of Lake County
Concordia University
De Paul University
Dominican University
Eastern Illinois University
Elgin Community College
Elmhurst College
Eureka College
Governors State University
Greenville College
Illinois Eastern Community Colleges
    Frontier Community College
    Lincoln Trail College
    Olney Central College
    Wabash Valley College
Illinois State University
Illinois Wesleyan University
Joliet Junior College
Judson College
Kankakee Community College
Knox College
Lake Forest College
Lake Land College
Lewis University
Lincoln Land Community College
Loyola University of Chicago
MacMurray College
McHenry County College
McKendree College
Millikin University
Monmouth College
National-Louis University
North Central College
North Park University
Northeastern Illinois University
Northern Illinois University
Northwestern University
Oakton Community College
Parkland College
Prairie State College
Principia College
Quincy University
Rend Lake College
Richland Community College
Robert Morris College: Chicago
Rockford College
Roosevelt University
St. Xavier University
Sauk Valley Community College
Shawnee Community College
Southern Illinois University
    Carbondale
    Edwardsville
Spoon River College
Trinity Christian College
Trinity International University
Triton College
University of Illinois
    Chicago
    Urbana-Champaign
Waubonsee Community College
Western Illinois University
William Rainey Harper College

Indiana
Anderson University
Ball State University
Butler University
Calumet College of St. Joseph
DePauw University
Goshen College
Indiana State University
Indiana University
    Bloomington
    Kokomo
    Northwest
    South Bend
Indiana University--Purdue University
    Indiana University-Purdue
        University Fort Wayne
    Indiana University-Purdue
        University Indianapolis
Indiana Wesleyan University
Manchester College
Marian College
Oakland City University
Purdue University
Purdue University
    Calumet
St. Joseph's College
Taylor University
University of Evansville
University of Indianapolis
University of Notre Dame
University of St. Francis
University of Southern Indiana
Valparaiso University
Vincennes University

Iowa
Buena Vista University
Central College
Clarke College
Clinton Community College
Coe College
Des Moines Area Community College
Drake University
Graceland University
Grand View College
Indian Hills Community College
Iowa Central Community College
Iowa Lakes Community College
Iowa State University
Kirkwood Community College
Loras College
Luther College
Morningside College
Mount Mercy College
Muscatine Community College
North Iowa Area Community College
Northwestern College
Scott Community College
Simpson College
University of Dubuque
University of Iowa
University of Northern Iowa
Waldorf College
Wartburg College
Western Iowa Tech Community College

Kansas
Baker University
Bethany College
Butler County Community College
Coffeyville Community College
Colby Community College
Emporia State University
Hutchinson Community College
Johnson County Community College
Kansas City Kansas Community College
Kansas State University
Pittsburg State University
Pratt Community College
St. Mary College
Southwestern College
Sterling College
Tabor College
University of Kansas
Washburn University of Topeka
Wichita State University

Kentucky
Ashland Community College
Bellarmine College
Berea College
Brescia University
Campbellsville University
Cumberland College
Eastern Kentucky University
Elizabethtown Community College
Georgetown College
Hazard Community College
Henderson Community College
Hopkinsville Community College
Kentucky State University
Madisonville Community College
Midway College
Morehead State University
Murray State University
National Business College
Northern Kentucky University
Owensboro Community College
Owensboro Junior College of Business
Paducah Community College
Somerset Community College
Thomas More College
University of Kentucky
University of Louisville
Western Kentucky University

Louisiana
Delgado Community College
Dillard University
Louisiana State University Medical Center
Louisiana State University and Agricultural and Mechanical College
Louisiana State University
    Eunice
    Shreveport
Louisiana Tech University
Loyola University New Orleans
McNeese State University
Nicholls State University
Northwestern State University
Nunez Community College
Southeastern Louisiana University
Southern University and Agricultural and Mechanical College
Tulane University
University of Louisiana at Lafayette
University of Louisiana at Monroe
University of New Orleans
Xavier University of Louisiana

Maine
Bates College
Colby College
St. Joseph's College
University of Maine
University of Maine
    Augusta
    Farmington
    Fort Kent
    Machias
    Presque Isle
University of New England
University of Southern Maine

Maryland
Allegany College
Anne Arundel Community College
Baltimore City Community College
Baltimore International College
Bowie State University
Carroll Community College
Chesapeake College
College of Notre Dame of Maryland
Community College of Baltimore County
    Catonsville
    Essex
Coppin State College
Frederick Community College
Frostburg State University
Goucher College
Hagerstown Community College
Hood College
Howard Community College
Johns Hopkins University
Loyola College in Maryland
Montgomery College
    Germantown Campus
    Rockville Campus
    Takoma Park Campus
Morgan State University
Mount St. Mary's College
Prince George's Community College
St. Mary's College of Maryland
Salisbury State University
Sojourner-Douglass College
Towson University
United States Naval Academy
University of Baltimore
University of Maryland
    Baltimore County
    College Park
    Eastern Shore
Villa Julie College
Western Maryland College
Wor-Wic Community College

Massachusetts
American International College
Amherst College
Assumption College
Atlantic Union College
Babson College
Bay Path College
Bentley College
Berkshire Community College
Boston College
Boston University
Bridgewater State College
Bunker Hill Community College
College of the Holy Cross
Curry College
Dean College
Eastern Nazarene College
Elms College
Emerson College
Emmanuel College
Endicott College
Fitchburg State College
Framingham State College
Gordon College
Greenfield Community College
Harvard College
Holyoke Community College
Marian Court College
Massachusetts Bay Community College
Massachusetts College of Liberal Arts
Massasoit Community College
Merrimack College
Middlesex Community College
Mount Ida College
Mount Wachusett Community College
New England Conservatory of Music
Newbury College
North Shore Community College
Northeastern University
Northern Essex Community College
Pine Manor College
Regis College
Roxbury Community College
Salem State College
Simmons College
Smith College
Springfield College
Springfield Technical Community College
Stonehill College
Suffolk University
University of Massachusetts
    Amherst
    Boston
    Dartmouth
    Lowell
Wellesley College
Wentworth Institute of Technology
Western New England College
Westfield State College
Wheaton College

Williams College
Worcester State College

Michigan
Adrian College
Albion College
Alma College
Andrews University
Aquinas College
Calvin College
Central Michigan University
Delta College
Eastern Michigan University
Ferris State University
Gogebic Community College
Grand Valley State University
Henry Ford Community College
Hillsdale College
Kalamazoo Valley Community College
Kellogg Community College
Kettering University
Kirtland Community College
Lake Michigan College
Lake Superior State University
Lansing Community College
Marygrove College
Michigan State University
Michigan Technological University
Mid Michigan Community College
Mott Community College
Muskegon Community College
Northern Michigan University
Northwestern Michigan College
Northwood University
Oakland University
Olivet College
Saginaw Valley State University
St. Clair County Community College
Schoolcraft College
Siena Heights University
Southwestern Michigan College
Spring Arbor College
University of Detroit Mercy
University of Michigan
University of Michigan
    Dearborn
    Flint
Washtenaw Community College
Wayne County Community College
Wayne State University
Western Michigan University

Minnesota
Augsburg College
Bemidji State University
Bethany Lutheran College
Bethel College
Century Community and Technical College
College of St. Benedict
College of St. Catherine: St. Paul Campus
College of St. Scholastica
Concordia College: Moorhead
Crown College
Gustavus Adolphus College
Hamline University
Hibbing Community College: A Technical and Community College
Inver Hills Community College
Macalester College
Minneapolis Community and Technical College
Minnesota State University, Mankato
Moorhead State University
NEI College of Technology
North Hennepin Community College
Rochester Community and Technical College
St. Cloud State University
St. John's University
St. Mary's University of Minnesota
Southwest State University
University of Minnesota
    Morris
    Twin Cities
University of St. Thomas
Vermilion Community College
Winona State University

Mississippi
Alcorn State University
Belhaven College
Blue Mountain College
Copiah-Lincoln Community College
Delta State University
East Central Community College
East Mississippi Community College
Hinds Community College
Jackson State University
Mary Holmes College
Millsaps College
Mississippi College
Mississippi Gulf Coast Community College
    Jackson County Campus
    Jefferson Davis Campus
    Perkinston
Mississippi State University
Mississippi University for Women
Mississippi Valley State University
Rust College
Tougaloo College
University of Mississippi
University of Southern Mississippi
William Carey College

Missouri
Central Methodist College
Central Missouri State University
College of the Ozarks
Columbia College
Crowder College
Culver-Stockton College
Drury University
East Central College
Fontbonne College
Hannibal-LaGrange College
Jefferson College
Lincoln University
Lindenwood University
Longview Community College
Maple Woods Community College
Maryville University of Saint Louis
Mineral Area College
Missouri Southern State College
Missouri Western State College
Park University
Penn Valley Community College
Research College of Nursing
Rockhurst University
St. Louis University
Southeast Missouri State University
Southwest Baptist University
Southwest Missouri State University
St. Louis Community College
    St. Louis Community College at Florissant Valley
    St. Louis Community College at Forest Park
    St. Louis Community College at Meramec
Stephens College
Truman State University
University of Missouri
    Columbia
    Kansas City
    Rolla
    St. Louis
William Jewell College
William Woods University

Montana
Carroll College
Montana State University
    Bozeman
    College of Technology-Great Falls
Rocky Mountain College
University of Montana-Missoula
Western Montana College of The University of Montana

Nebraska
Central Community College
Chadron State College
Concordia University
Creighton University
Dana College
Doane College
Lincoln School of Commerce
Metropolitan Community College
Northeast Community College
Peru State College
Union College
University of Nebraska
    Kearney
    Lincoln
    Omaha
Wayne State College

Nevada
Community College of Southern Nevada
University of Nevada
    Las Vegas
    Reno
Western Nevada Community College

New Hampshire
Colby-Sawyer College
Dartmouth College
Franklin Pierce College
Hesser College
Keene State College
New England College
New Hampshire College
New Hampshire Community Technical College
    Laconia
Plymouth State College of the University System of New Hampshire
Rivier College
St. Anselm College
University of New Hampshire

New Jersey
Bergen Community College
Bloomfield College
Brookdale Community College
Caldwell College
Camden County College
Centenary College
College of St. Elizabeth
County College of Morris
Cumberland County College
Essex County College
Fairleigh Dickinson University
Felician College
Kean University
Monmouth University
Montclair State University
New Jersey City University
New Jersey Institute of Technology
Ocean County College
Passaic County Community College
Princeton University
Ramapo College of New Jersey
Richard Stockton College of New Jersey
Rider University
Rowan University
Rutgers
    The State University of New Jersey: Camden College of Arts and Sciences
    The State University of New Jersey: College of Engineering
    The State University of New Jersey: College of Nursing
    The State University of New Jersey: Cook College
    The State University of New Jersey: Douglass College
    The State University of New Jersey: Livingston College
    The State University of New Jersey: Mason Gross School of the Arts
    The State University of New Jersey: Newark College of Arts and Sciences
    The State University of New Jersey: Rutgers College
    The State University of New Jersey: University College Camden
    The State University of New Jersey: University College New Brunswick
    The State University of New Jersey: University College Newark
St. Peter's College
Salem Community College
Seton Hall University
Stevens Institute of Technology
Sussex County Community College
The College of New Jersey
Union County College
William Paterson University of New Jersey

New Mexico
Clovis Community College
Eastern New Mexico University
New Mexico Highlands University
New Mexico Junior College
New Mexico State University
New Mexico State University Carlsbad
San Juan College
Santa Fe Community College
University of New Mexico
Western New Mexico University

New York
Adelphi University
Alfred University
Barnard College
Broome Community College
Bryant & Stratton Business Institute Syracuse
Canisius College
Cayuga County Community College
City University of New York
    Baruch College
    Borough of Manhattan Community College
    Bronx Community College
    Brooklyn College
    City College
    College of Staten Island
    Hunter College
    John Jay College of Criminal Justice
    Kingsborough Community College
    Lehman College
    Medgar Evers College
    Queens College
    York College
Clarkson University
Clinton Community College
Colgate University
College of Mount St. Vincent
College of New Rochelle

Columbia University
    Columbia College
    Fu Foundation School of
        Engineering and Applied Science
    School of General Studies
Columbia-Greene Community College
Concordia College
Cooper Union for the Advancement of
    Science and Art
Cornell University
Corning Community College
D'Youville College
Dominican College of Blauvelt
Dowling College
Dutchess Community College
Elmira College
Erie Community College
    City Campus
    North Campus
    South Campus
Fashion Institute of Technology
Finger Lakes Community College
Fordham University
Fulton-Montgomery Community College
Genesee Community College
Hartwick College
Herkimer County Community College
Hilbert College
Hobart and William Smith Colleges
Hofstra University
Houghton College
Iona College
Ithaca College
Jamestown Community College
Jefferson Community College
Jewish Theological Seminary of America
Juilliard School
Keuka College
Le Moyne College
Long Island University
    Brooklyn Campus
    C. W. Post Campus
    Southampton College
Manhattan College
Manhattanville College
Marist College
Marymount College
Marymount Manhattan College
Mercy College
Mohawk Valley Community College
Monroe Community College
Mount St. Mary College
Nassau Community College
Nazareth College of Rochester
New York Institute of Technology
New York State College of Ceramics at
    Alfred University
New York University
Niagara County Community College
Niagara University
Nyack College
Orange County Community College
Pace University
Pace University: Pleasantville/Briarcliff
Parsons School of Design
Polytechnic University
Polytechnic University
    Long Island Campus
Rensselaer Polytechnic Institute
Roberts Wesleyan College
Rockland Community College
Russell Sage College
Sage Junior College of Albany
St. Bonaventure University
St. Francis College
St. John Fisher College
St. John's University
St. Thomas Aquinas College
Schenectady County Community College
Skidmore College
St. Joseph's College
    St. Joseph's College

State University of New York
    Albany
    Binghamton
    Buffalo
    College at Brockport
    College at Buffalo
    College at Cortland
    College at Fredonia
    College at Geneseo
    College at Oneonta
    College at Plattsburgh
    College at Potsdam
    College of Agriculture and
        Technology at Cobleskill
    College of Agriculture and
        Technology at Morrisville
    College of Environmental Science
        and Forestry
    College of Technology at Alfred
    College of Technology at Delhi
    Farmingdale
    New Paltz
    Oswego
    Stony Brook
Suffolk County Community College
Syracuse University
Technical Career Institutes
Tompkins-Cortland Community College
Touro College
Ulster County Community College
Union College
United States Military Academy
University of Rochester
Utica College of Syracuse University
Wagner College
Westchester Business Institute
Westchester Community College

North Carolina
Appalachian State University
Barber-Scotia College
Barton College
Belmont Abbey College
Bennett College
Brevard College
Campbell University
Catawba College
Central Carolina Community College
Central Piedmont Community College
Cleveland Community College
Davidson College
Duke University
East Carolina University
Elizabeth City State University
Elon College
Fayetteville State University
Forsyth Technical Community College
Gardner-Webb University
Greensboro College
Guilford College
High Point University
Johnson C. Smith University
Lees-McRae College
Lenoir-Rhyne College
Mars Hill College
Meredith College
Methodist College
Montreat College
Mount Olive College
North Carolina Agricultural and
    Technical State University
North Carolina Central University
North Carolina State University
North Carolina Wesleyan College
Peace College
Pfeiffer University
Queens College
St. Andrews Presbyterian College
St. Augustine's College
Salem College
Sandhills Community College
Shaw University

University of North Carolina
    Asheville
    Chapel Hill
    Charlotte
    Greensboro
    Pembroke
    Wilmington
Wake Forest University
Warren Wilson College
Western Carolina University
Wilkes Community College
Wingate University
Winston-Salem State University

North Dakota
Jamestown College
Minot State University
North Dakota State University
University of North Dakota

Ohio
Ashland University
Baldwin-Wallace College
Bluffton College
Bowling Green State University
Capital University
Case Western Reserve University
Cedarville College
Central Ohio Technical College
Central State University
Cincinnati State Technical and
    Community College
Clark State Community College
Cleveland Institute of Art
College of Mount St. Joseph
Columbus State Community College
Defiance College
Denison University
Franciscan University of Steubenville
Heidelberg College
Jefferson Community College
John Carroll University
Kent State University
Kent State University
    Stark Campus
    Trumbull Campus
    Tuscarawas Campus
Kenyon College
Marietta College
Miami University
    Hamilton Campus
    Oxford Campus
Mount Union College
Mount Vernon Nazarene College
Oberlin College
Ohio Dominican College
Ohio Northern University
Ohio State University
    Agricultural Technical Institute
    Columbus Campus
    Lima Campus
    Mansfield Campus
    Marion Campus
    Newark Campus
Ohio University
Ohio Wesleyan University
Otterbein College
Owens Community College
    Findlay Campus
    Toledo
Shawnee State University
Sinclair Community College
University of Akron
University of Akron
    Wayne College
University of Cincinnati
University of Dayton
University of Findlay
University of Rio Grande
University of Toledo
Walsh University
Wilberforce University
Wilmington College
Wittenberg University

Wright State University
Xavier University
Youngstown State University

Oklahoma
Cameron University
Carl Albert State College
East Central University
Eastern Oklahoma State College
Langston University
Murray State College
Northeastern Oklahoma Agricultural and
    Mechanical College
Northeastern State University
Oklahoma Baptist University
Oklahoma Christian University of
    Science and Arts
Oklahoma City Community College
Oklahoma City University
Oklahoma State University
Oklahoma State University
    Oklahoma City
Oral Roberts University
Redlands Community College
Rose State College
St. Gregory's University
Seminole State College
Southeastern Oklahoma State University
Tulsa Community College
University of Central Oklahoma
University of Oklahoma
University of Science and Arts of
    Oklahoma
University of Tulsa
Western Oklahoma State College

Oregon
Clackamas Community College
George Fox University
Lewis & Clark College
Linfield College
Mount Hood Community College
Oregon State University
Pacific University
Portland State University
Southern Oregon University
University of Oregon
University of Portland
Western Baptist College
Western Oregon University

Pennsylvania
Albright College
Alvernia College
Beaver College
Bloomsburg University of Pennsylvania
Bucknell University
Bucks County Community College
Cabrini College
California University of Pennsylvania
Carlow College
Carnegie Mellon University
Cedar Crest College
Chestnut Hill College
Clarion University of Pennsylvania
College Misericordia
Community College of Allegheny
    County
Community College of Philadelphia
Delaware Valley College
Dickinson College
Drexel University
Duquesne University
East Stroudsburg University of
    Pennsylvania
Eastern College
Edinboro University of Pennsylvania
Elizabethtown College
Franklin and Marshall College
Gannon University
Geneva College
Gettysburg College
Grove City College
Gwynedd-Mercy College

Harrisburg Area Community College
Immaculata College
Indiana University of Pennsylvania
Juniata College
King's College
Kutztown University of Pennsylvania
La Roche College
La Salle University
Lafayette College
Lehigh University
Lincoln University
Lock Haven University of Pennsylvania
Luzerne County Community College
Lycoming College
Mansfield University of Pennsylvania
Marywood University
Mercyhurst College
Messiah College
Millersville University of Pennsylvania
Montgomery County Community College
Moravian College
Muhlenberg College
Neumann College
Peirce College
Penn State
    Abington
    Altoona
    Beaver
    Berks
    Delaware County
    Dubois
    Erie, The Behrend College
    Fayette
    Harrisburg
    Hazleton
    Lehigh Valley
    McKeesport
    Mont Alto
    New Kensington
    Shenango
    University Park
    Wilkes-Barre
    Worthington Scranton
    York
Philadelphia College of Bible
Philadelphia University
Point Park College
Robert Morris College
Rosemont College
St. Francis College
St. Joseph's University
St. Vincent College
Seton Hill College
Shippensburg University of Pennsylvania
Slippery Rock University of Pennsylvania
Susquehanna University
Swarthmore College
Temple University
Thiel College
University of Pennsylvania
University of Pittsburgh
University of Scranton
Ursinus College
Valley Forge Christian College
Valley Forge Military College
Villanova University
Washington and Jefferson College
Waynesburg College
West Chester University of Pennsylvania
Westminster College
Westmoreland County Community College
Widener University
Wilkes University
Wilson College
York College of Pennsylvania

Puerto Rico
American University of Puerto Rico
Atlantic College
Caribbean University
Colegio Universitario del Este
Inter American University of Puerto Rico
    Aguadilla Campus
    Arecibo Campus
    Bayamon Campus
    Fajardo Campus
    Guayama Campus
    Metropolitan Campus
    San German Campus
Pontifical Catholic University of Puerto Rico
Technological College of San Juan
Turabo University
Universidad Metropolitana
University of Puerto Rico
    Aguadilla
    Arecibo Campus
    Bayamon University College
    Cayey University College
    Humacao University College
    Mayaguez Campus
    Medical Sciences Campus
    Ponce University College
    Rio Piedras Campus
University of the Sacred Heart

Rhode Island
Brown University
Bryant College
Community College of Rhode Island
Johnson & Wales University
Providence College
Rhode Island College
Roger Williams University
Salve Regina University
University of Rhode Island

South Carolina
Anderson College
Benedict College
Charleston Southern University
Claflin University
Clemson University
Coastal Carolina University
Coker College
College of Charleston
Columbia College
Converse College
Francis Marion University
Lander University
Limestone College
Morris College
Newberry College
North Greenville College
Presbyterian College
South Carolina State University
Southern Wesleyan University
The Citadel
University of South Carolina
University of South Carolina
    Aiken
    Sumter
Voorhees College
Winthrop University
York Technical College

South Dakota
Dakota State University
Dakota Wesleyan University
Mount Marty College
Northern State University
South Dakota State University
University of South Dakota

Tennessee
Austin Peay State University
Belmont University
Bethel College
Carson-Newman College
Chattanooga State Technical Community College
Christian Brothers University
Cleveland State Community College
Columbia State Community College
Cumberland University
David Lipscomb University
East Tennessee State University
Fisk University
Freed-Hardeman University
Hiwassee College
King College
Lambuth University
Lane College
LeMoyne-Owen College
Lee University
Lincoln Memorial University
Martin Methodist College
Maryville College
Middle Tennessee State University
Motlow State Community College
Nashville State Technical Institute
Northeast State Technical Community College
Pellissippi State Technical Community College
Rhodes College
Roane State Community College
Shelby State Community College
Southern Adventist University
Tennessee State University
Tennessee Technological University
Tennessee Temple University
Tennessee Wesleyan College
Union University
University of Memphis
University of Tennessee
    Chattanooga
    Knoxville
    Martin
University of the South
Vanderbilt University
Volunteer State Community College
Walters State Community College

Texas
Abilene Christian University
Alvin Community College
Amarillo College
Austin College
Baylor University
Brazosport College
Brookhaven College
Collin County Community College District
Del Mar College
East Texas Baptist University
Eastfield College
El Paso Community College
Galveston College
Grayson County College
Hill College
Houston Baptist University
Howard Payne University
Huston-Tillotson College
Jarvis Christian College
Lamar State College at Port Arthur
Lamar University
LeTourneau University
Lee College
McMurry University
Midland College
Midwestern State University
Mountain View College
Navarro College
Northwood University: Texas Campus
Palo Alto College
Panola College
Paul Quinn College
Prairie View A&M University
Rice University
Richland College
St. Edward's University
St. Mary's University
St. Philip's College
Sam Houston State University
San Antonio College
San Jacinto College
    North
Schreiner College
Southern Methodist University
Southwest Texas State University
Southwestern Adventist University
Southwestern University
Stephen F. Austin State University
Sul Ross State University
Tarleton State University
Tarrant County College
Temple College
Texas A&M International University
Texas A&M University
Texas A&M University
    Commerce
Texas Christian University
Texas College
Texas Lutheran University
Texas Southern University
Texas Tech University
Texas Woman's University
Trinity University
Trinity Valley Community College
Tyler Junior College
University of Houston
University of Houston
    Downtown
University of Mary Hardin-Baylor
University of North Texas
University of St. Thomas
University of Texas
    Arlington
    Austin
    Brownsville
    Dallas
    El Paso
    Pan American
    San Antonio
    Tyler
Wayland Baptist University
Weatherford College
Western Texas College
Wiley College

Utah
Brigham Young University
Dixie State College of Utah
Snow College
Southern Utah University
University of Utah
Utah State University
Utah Valley State College
Weber State University
Westminster College

Vermont
Castleton State College
Champlain College
Green Mountain College
Johnson State College
Lyndon State College
Middlebury College
Norwich University
St. Michael's College
Southern Vermont College
University of Vermont
Vermont Technical College

Virginia
Averett College
Blue Ridge Community College
Bluefield College
Bridgewater College
Christendom College
Christopher Newport University
College of William and Mary
Danville Community College
Eastern Mennonite University
George Mason University
Germanna Community College
Hampden-Sydney College
Hampton University
James Madison University
Liberty University
Longwood College
Lord Fairfax Community College
Lynchburg College

Mary Baldwin College
Norfolk State University
Northern Virginia Community College
Old Dominion University
Paul D. Camp Community College
Piedmont Virginia Community College
Radford University
Randolph-Macon College
Randolph-Macon Woman's College
Roanoke College
St. Paul's College
Southside Virginia Community College
Southwest Virginia Community College
Sweet Briar College
Thomas Nelson Community College
Tidewater Community College
University of Virginia
University of Virginia's College at Wise
Virginia Commonwealth University
Virginia Military Institute
Virginia Polytechnic Institute and State University
Virginia State University
Virginia Union University
Virginia Wesleyan College
Washington and Lee University
Wytheville Community College

Washington
Central Washington University
Centralia College
Clark College
Eastern Washington University
Edmonds Community College
Gonzaga University
Highline Community College
Olympic College
Pacific Lutheran University
Peninsula College
Seattle Pacific University
Seattle University
Skagit Valley College
Spokane Falls Community College
University of Puget Sound
University of Washington
Walla Walla College
Walla Walla Community College
Washington State University
Western Washington University
Whatcom Community College
Whitman College
Whitworth College

West Virginia
Alderson-Broaddus College
Bethany College
Concord College
Davis and Elkins College
Fairmont State College
Glenville State College
Marshall University
Ohio Valley College
Potomac State College of West Virginia University
Shepherd College
West Liberty State College
West Virginia State College
West Virginia University
West Virginia Wesleyan College
Wheeling Jesuit University

Wisconsin
Cardinal Stritch University
Carroll College
Carthage College
Columbia College of Nursing
Lakeland College
Lakeshore Technical College
Lawrence University
Marian College of Fond du Lac
Marquette University
Milwaukee Area Technical College
Mount Mary College
Northland College
St. Norbert College
University of Wisconsin
   Eau Claire
   Fond du Lac
   Fox Valley
   La Crosse
   Madison
   Marathon County
   Milwaukee
   Oshkosh
   Parkside
   Platteville
   River Falls
   Sheboygan County
   Stout
   Superior
   Washington County
   Waukesha
   Whitewater

Wyoming
Central Wyoming College
Northwest College
University of Wyoming
Western Wyoming Community College

Independent study

Alabama
Athens State University
Auburn University
Auburn University at Montgomery
Birmingham-Southern College
Central Alabama Community College
Chattahoochee Valley Community College
Community College of the Air Force
Concordia College
Faulkner University
Harry M. Ayers State Technical College
Huntingdon College
Jacksonville State University
James H. Faulkner State Community College
Jefferson Davis Community College
Jefferson State Community College
John M. Patterson State Technical College
Northeast Alabama Community College
Northwest-Shoals Community College
Snead State Community College
Spring Hill College
Stillman College
Talladega College
Troy State University
Troy State University
   Dothan
   Montgomery
Tuskegee University
University of Alabama
University of Alabama
   Birmingham
   Huntsville
University of Mobile
University of Montevallo
University of North Alabama
University of South Alabama

Alaska
Alaska Pacific University
Prince William Sound Community College
University of Alaska
   Anchorage
   Fairbanks
   Southeast

Arizona
American Indian College of the Assemblies of God
Arizona State University
Arizona Western College
Central Arizona College
Cochise College
Dine College
Eastern Arizona College
Embry-Riddle Aeronautical University Prescott Campus
Gateway Community College
Glendale Community College
Grand Canyon University
Mesa Community College
Mohave Community College
Northern Arizona University
Northland Pioneer College
Paradise Valley Community College
Phoenix College
Pima Community College
Prescott College
Rio Salado College
South Mountain Community College
University of Arizona
University of Phoenix
Yavapai College

Arkansas
Arkansas State University
Arkansas State University Beebe Branch
Arkansas Tech University
Garland County Community College
Harding University
Hendrix College
John Brown University
Lyon College
North Arkansas College
Northwest Arkansas Community College
Philander Smith College
Phillips Community College of the University of Arkansas
Southern Arkansas University Tech
University of Arkansas
University of Arkansas
   Little Rock
   Monticello
   Pine Bluff
   for Medical Sciences
University of Central Arkansas
University of the Ozarks
Williams Baptist College

California
Academy of Art College
Allan Hancock College
American River College
Antioch Southern California
   Los Angeles
   Santa Barbara
Armstrong University
Art Center College of Design
Barstow College
Biola University
Butte College
Cabrillo College
California Baptist University
California College of Arts and Crafts
California Institute of Technology
California Institute of the Arts
California Lutheran University
California Polytechnic State University: San Luis Obispo
California State University
   Bakersfield
   Dominguez Hills
   Fresno
   Fullerton
   Hayward
   Long Beach
   Los Angeles
   Monterey Bay
   Northridge
   Sacramento
   Stanislaus
Canada College
Cerro Coso Community College
Chabot College
Chaffey Community College
Chapman University
City College of San Francisco
Claremont McKenna College
Coastline Community College
Cogswell Polytechnical College
College of Notre Dame
College of San Mateo
College of the Canyons
College of the Desert
College of the Redwoods
College of the Sequoias
College of the Siskiyous
Columbia College
Concordia University
Contra Costa College
Cuesta College
Cuyamaca College
Cypress College
De Anza College
Deep Springs College
Diablo Valley College
Dominican University of California
Don Bosco Technical Institute
East Los Angeles College
Evergreen Valley College
Fashion Institute of Design and Merchandising
Foothill College
Fresno City College
Fresno Pacific University
Glendale Community College
Golden West College
Grossmont Community College
Harvey Mudd College
Holy Names College
Hope International University
Humboldt State University
Humphreys College
Imperial Valley College
Irvine Valley College
John F. Kennedy University
Kings River Community College
LIFE Bible College
La Sierra University
Las Positas College
Long Beach City College
Los Angeles Harbor College
Los Angeles Mission College
Los Angeles Southwest College
Los Angeles Trade and Technical College
Los Angeles Valley College
Los Medanos College
Loyola Marymount University
Marymount College
Master's College
Mendocino College
Menlo College
Merritt College
Mills College
MiraCosta College
Mission College
Modesto Junior College
Monterey Institute of International Studies
Monterey Peninsula College
Moorpark College
Mount St. Mary's College
Mount San Jacinto College
Napa Valley College
National University
Occidental College
Ohlone College
Orange Coast College
Otis College of Art and Design
Oxnard College
Pacific Oaks College
Pacific Union College
Palo Verde College
Pasadena City College
Patten College
Pepperdine University
Pitzer College
Pomona College

Queen of the Holy Rosary College
Rio Hondo College
Sacramento City College
Saddleback College
St. John's Seminary College
St. Mary's College of California
Samuel Merritt College
San Diego City College
San Diego Mesa College
San Diego Miramar College
San Diego State University
San Francisco Art Institute
San Francisco Conservatory of Music
San Francisco State University
San Joaquin Delta College
San Joaquin Valley College Inc.
San Jose Christian College
San Jose City College
San Jose State University
Santa Ana College
Santa Barbara City College
Santa Clara University
Santa Monica College
Santa Rosa Junior College
Scripps College
Shasta College
Sierra College
Solano Community College
Sonoma State University
Southern California Institute of
   Architecture
Southwestern College
Stanford University
Taft College
United States International University
University of California
   Berkeley
   Davis
   Irvine
   Los Angeles
   Riverside
   San Diego
   Santa Barbara
   Santa Cruz
University of Judaism
University of La Verne
University of Redlands
University of San Diego
University of San Francisco
University of Southern California
University of West Los Angeles
University of the Pacific
Vanguard University of Southern
   California
Ventura College
Victor Valley College
Vista Community College
West Hills Community College
West Los Angeles College
West Valley College
Westmont College
Whittier College

Colorado
Adams State College
Aims Community College
Arapahoe Community College
Colorado College
Colorado Mountain College
   Alpine Campus
   Spring Valley Campus
   Timberline Campus
Colorado Northwestern Community
   College
Colorado School of Mines
Colorado State University
Community College of Denver
Fort Lewis College
Front Range Community College
Lamar Community College
Mesa State College
Metropolitan State College of Denver
Morgan Community College
Northeastern Junior College
Pikes Peak Community College

Pueblo Community College
Red Rocks Community College
Regis University
Trinidad State Junior College
United States Air Force Academy
University of Colorado
   Boulder
   Colorado Springs
   Denver
   Health Sciences Center
University of Denver
University of Northern Colorado
University of Southern Colorado
Western State College of Colorado

Connecticut
Albertus Magnus College
Asnuntuck Community-Technical
   College
Briarwood College
Capital Community College
Central Connecticut State University
Charter Oak State College
Connecticut College
Eastern Connecticut State University
Fairfield University
Gateway Community College
Housatonic Community-Technical
   College
Manchester Community-Technical
   College
Middlesex Community-Technical
   College
Naugatuck Valley Community-Technical
   College
Northwestern Connecticut
   Community-Technical College
Paier College of Art
Quinebaug Valley Community College
Quinnipiac University
Sacred Heart University
St. Joseph College
Southern Connecticut State University
Teikyo Post University
Three Rivers Community-Technical
   College
Trinity College
Tunxis Community College
United States Coast Guard Academy
University of Bridgeport
University of Connecticut
University of Hartford
University of New Haven
Wesleyan University
Western Connecticut State University
Yale University

Delaware
Delaware State University
University of Delaware
Wesley College
Wilmington College

District of Columbia
American University
Catholic University of America
Gallaudet University
George Washington University
Georgetown University
Howard University
Southeastern University
Trinity College
University of the District of Columbia

Florida
Art Institute
   of Fort Lauderdale
Barry University
Bethune-Cookman College
Brevard Community College
Broward Community College
Carlos Albizu University
Central Florida Community College
Chipola Junior College

Daytona Beach Community College
Eckerd College
Edward Waters College
Embry-Riddle Aeronautical University
Flagler College
Florida Agricultural and Mechanical
   University
Florida Atlantic University
Florida Baptist Theological College
Florida College
Florida Community College at
   Jacksonville
Florida Gulf Coast University
Florida International University
Florida Keys Community College
Florida Metropolitan University
   Orlando College North
Florida Southern College
Florida State University
Gulf Coast Community College
Jacksonville University
Jones College
Lake City Community College
Lake-Sumter Community College
Manatee Community College
Miami-Dade Community College
New College of the University of South
   Florida
Northwood University
   Florida Campus
Palm Beach Atlantic College
Palm Beach Community College
Pasco-Hernando Community College
Pensacola Junior College
Polk Community College
Rollins College
St. John Vianney College Seminary
St. Leo University
St. Petersburg Junior College
St. Thomas University
Santa Fe Community College
Seminole Community College
South Florida Community College
Southeastern College of the Assemblies
   of God
Stetson University
Tallahassee Community College
University of Central Florida
University of Florida
University of Miami
University of North Florida
University of South Florida
University of Tampa
Valencia Community College
Warner Southern College

Georgia
Abraham Baldwin Agricultural College
Agnes Scott College
American InterContinental University
Art Institute
   of Atlanta
Atlanta Christian College
Atlanta College of Art
Augusta State University
Brenau University
Brewton-Parker College
Clark Atlanta University
Coastal Georgia Community College
Columbus State University
Covenant College
Dalton State College
Darton College
East Georgia College
Emmanuel College
Emory University
Floyd College
Georgia Baptist College of Nursing
Georgia College and State University
Georgia Institute of Technology
Georgia Military College
Georgia Southern University
Georgia Southwestern State University
Georgia State University
Kennesaw State University

LaGrange College
Mercer University
Morris Brown College
Oglethorpe University
Oxford College of Emory University
Paine College
Piedmont College
Reinhardt College
Savannah College of Art and Design
Savannah State University
Shorter College
South Georgia College
Southern Polytechnic State University
Spelman College
State University of West Georgia
Toccoa Falls College
University of Georgia
Valdosta State University
Waycross College
Wesleyan College

Hawaii
Brigham Young University
   Hawaii
Chaminade University of Honolulu
Hawaii Pacific University
TransPacific Hawaii College
University of Hawaii
   Hawaii Community College
   Hilo
   Honolulu Community College
   Kapiolani Community College
   Leeward Community College
   Manoa
   Maui Community College
   West Oahu
   Windward Community College

Idaho
Albertson College of Idaho
Boise Bible College
Boise State University
Idaho State University
Lewis-Clark State College
North Idaho College
Northwest Nazarene University
University of Idaho

Illinois
American Academy of Art
Augustana College
Barat College
Benedictine University
Black Hawk College
Black Hawk College
   East Campus
Blackburn College
Bradley University
Carl Sandburg College
Chicago State University
City Colleges of Chicago
   Harold Washington College
   Harry S. Truman College
   Kennedy-King College
   Malcolm X College
   Olive-Harvey College
   Richard J. Daley College
   Wright College
College of DuPage
College of Lake County
Columbia College
Concordia University
Danville Area Community College
De Paul University
Dominican University
Eastern Illinois University
Elgin Community College
Elmhurst College
Eureka College
Governors State University
Greenville College
Highland Community College
Illinois College

Illinois Eastern Community Colleges
  Frontier Community College
  Lincoln Trail College
  Olney Central College
  Wabash Valley College
Illinois Institute of Technology
Illinois State University
Illinois Wesleyan University
International Academy of Merchandising
  and Design
John A. Logan College
John Wood Community College
Joliet Junior College
Judson College
Kankakee Community College
Kaskaskia College
Kendall College
Kishwaukee College
Knox College
Lake Forest College
Lake Land College
Lakeview College of Nursing
Lewis University
Lincoln Christian College and Seminary
Lincoln Land Community College
Loyola University of Chicago
MacMurray College
McHenry County College
McKendree College
Millikin University
Monmouth College
Moody Bible Institute
Moraine Valley Community College
National-Louis University
North Central College
North Park University
Northeastern Illinois University
Northern Illinois University
Northwestern University
Oakton Community College
Olivet Nazarene University
Parkland College
Prairie State College
Principia College
Quincy University
Rend Lake College
Richland Community College
Rock Valley College
Rockford College
Roosevelt University
St. Augustine College
St. Xavier University
Sauk Valley Community College
School of the Art Institute of Chicago
Shawnee Community College
Shimer College
Southeastern Illinois College
Southern Illinois University
  Carbondale
  Edwardsville
Southwestern Ilinois College
Springfield College in Illinois
Trinity Christian College
Trinity International University
Triton College
University of Chicago
University of Illinois
  Chicago
  Springfield
  Urbana-Champaign
University of St. Francis
VanderCook College of Music
Waubonsee Community College
Western Illinois University
Wheaton College
William Rainey Harper College

Indiana
Ancilla College
Anderson University
Ball State University
Bethel College
Butler University
Calumet College of St. Joseph
DePauw University

Earlham College
Franklin College
Goshen College
Hanover College
Indiana Institute of Technology
Indiana State University
Indiana University
  Bloomington
  East
  Kokomo
  Northwest
  Southeast
Indiana University--Purdue University
  Indiana University-Purdue
    University Fort Wayne
  Indiana University-Purdue
    University Indianapolis
Indiana Wesleyan University
International Business College
Ivy Tech State College
  Kokomo
  Southwest
  Whitewater
Manchester College
Marian College
Michiana College
Oakland City University
Purdue University
Purdue University
  North Central Campus
Rose-Hulman Institute of Technology
Saint Mary's College
St. Joseph's College
St. Mary-of-the-Woods College
Taylor University
University of Evansville
University of Indianapolis
University of Notre Dame
University of St. Francis
University of Southern Indiana
Valparaiso University
Vincennes University
Wabash College

Iowa
Briar Cliff College
Buena Vista University
Central College
Clarke College
Clinton Community College
Coe College
Cornell College
Des Moines Area Community College
Dordt College
Drake University
Graceland University
Grand View College
Grinnell College
Indian Hills Community College
Iowa Central Community College
Iowa State University
Iowa Wesleyan College
Iowa Western Community College
Kirkwood Community College
Loras College
Luther College
Maharishi University of Management
Marshalltown Community College
Marycrest International University
Morningside College
Mount Mercy College
Muscatine Community College
North Iowa Area Community College
Northeast Iowa Community College
Northwestern College
St. Ambrose University
Scott Community College
Simpson College
Southeastern Community College
  North Campus
  South Campus
Southwestern Community College
University of Dubuque
University of Iowa
University of Northern Iowa

Upper Iowa University
Waldorf College
Wartburg College
Western Iowa Tech Community College
William Penn University

Kansas
Allen County Community College
Baker University
Barclay College
Barton County Community College
Benedictine College
Bethany College
Bethel College
Butler County Community College
Central Christian College
Coffeyville Community College
Colby Community College
Cowley County Community College
Dodge City Community College
Emporia State University
Fort Hays State University
Hesston College
Hutchinson Community College
Independence Community College
Johnson County Community College
Kansas City Kansas Community College
Kansas State University
Kansas Wesleyan University
McPherson College
MidAmerica Nazarene University
Newman University
Pittsburg State University
St. Mary College
Southwestern College
Sterling College
Tabor College
University of Kansas
University of Kansas
  Medical Center
Washburn University of Topeka
Wichita State University

Kentucky
Alice Lloyd College
Asbury College
Bellarmine College
Berea College
Brescia University
Campbellsville University
Centre College
Cumberland College
Eastern Kentucky University
Georgetown College
Henderson Community College
Kentucky Christian College
Kentucky State University
Kentucky Wesleyan College
Lexington Community College
Lindsey Wilson College
Madisonville Community College
Maysville Community College
Midway College
Morehead State University
Murray State University
Northern Kentucky University
Owensboro Community College
Owensboro Junior College of Business
Pikeville College
Prestonsburg Community College
St. Catharine College
Somerset Community College
Spalding University
Thomas More College
Transylvania University
Union College
University of Kentucky
University of Louisville
Western Kentucky University

Louisiana
Centenary College of Louisiana
Delgado Community College
Dillard University

Grantham College of Engineering
Louisiana State University Medical
  Center
Louisiana State University and
  Agricultural and Mechanical College
Louisiana State University
  Eunice
  Shreveport
Louisiana Tech University
Loyola University New Orleans
Nicholls State University
Nunez Community College
Our Lady of Holy Cross College
Remington College - Education America,
  Inc.
Southeastern Louisiana University
Southern University and Agricultural and
  Mechanical College
Tulane University
University of Louisiana at Lafayette
University of New Orleans
Xavier University of Louisiana

Maine
Andover College
Bates College
Beal College
Bowdoin College
Central Maine Technical College
Colby College
College of the Atlantic
Husson College
Maine College of Art
St. Joseph's College
Thomas College
Unity College
University of Maine
University of Maine
  Augusta
  Farmington
  Fort Kent
  Machias
  Presque Isle
University of New England
University of Southern Maine
Washington County Technical College

Maryland
Allegany College
Anne Arundel Community College
Baltimore City Community College
Bowie State University
Carroll Community College
Cecil Community College
Chesapeake College
College of Notre Dame of Maryland
Columbia Union College
Community College of Baltimore County
  Catonsville
  Essex
Coppin State College
Frostburg State University
Goucher College
Hagerstown Community College
Harford Community College
Hood College
Howard Community College
Johns Hopkins University
Loyola College in Maryland
Maryland College of Art and Design
Maryland Institute College of Art
Montgomery College
  Germantown Campus
  Rockville Campus
  Takoma Park Campus
Morgan State University
Mount St. Mary's College
Prince George's Community College
St. Mary's College of Maryland
Salisbury State University
Sojourner-Douglass College
Towson University
United States Naval Academy
University of Baltimore

University of Maryland
  Baltimore County
  College Park
  Eastern Shore
Villa Julie College
Washington Bible College
Washington College
Western Maryland College

Massachusetts
American International College
Amherst College
Anna Maria College
Assumption College
Atlantic Union College
Babson College
Bay Path College
Bay State College
Bentley College
Berkshire Community College
Boston Architectural Center
Boston College
Boston Conservatory
Boston University
Brandeis University
Bridgewater State College
Bristol Community College
Bunker Hill Community College
Cape Cod Community College
Clark University
College of the Holy Cross
Curry College
Dean College
Eastern Nazarene College
Elms College
Emerson College
Emmanuel College
Endicott College
Fitchburg State College
Framingham State College
Gordon College
Greenfield Community College
Hampshire College
Harvard College
Hebrew College
Hellenic College/Holy Cross
Holyoke Community College
Laboure College
Lasell College
Lesley College
Marian Court College
Massachusetts Bay Community College
Massachusetts College of Art
Massachusetts College of Liberal Arts
Massachusetts College of Pharmacy and Health Sciences
Massachusetts Institute of Technology
Massasoit Community College
Merrimack College
Middlesex Community College
Montserrat College of Art
Mount Holyoke College
Mount Ida College
Mount Wachusett Community College
New England College of Finance
New England Conservatory of Music
Newbury College
Nichols College
North Shore Community College
Northeastern University
Pine Manor College
Quincy College
Regis College
Roxbury Community College
St. John's Seminary College
Salem State College
Simmons College
Simon's Rock College of Bard
Smith College
Springfield College
Springfield Technical Community College
Stonehill College
Suffolk University
Tufts University

University of Massachusetts
  Amherst
  Boston
  Dartmouth
Wellesley College
Wentworth Institute of Technology
Western New England College
Westfield State College
Wheaton College
Wheelock College
Williams College
Worcester Polytechnic Institute

Michigan
Adrian College
Albion College
Alma College
Aquinas College
Baker College
  of Auburn Hills
  of Cadillac
  of Jackson
  of Mount Clemens
  of Muskegon
  of Owosso
  of Port Huron
Calvin College
Center for Creative Studies: College of Art and Design
Central Michigan University
Cleary College
Concordia College
Cornerstone College and Grand Rapids Baptist Seminary
Davenport College of Business
Delta College
Detroit College of Business
Eastern Michigan University
Glen Oaks Community College
Gogebic Community College
Grace Bible College
Grand Rapids Community College
Grand Valley State University
Great Lakes College
Henry Ford Community College
Hillsdale College
Jackson Community College
Kalamazoo College
Kalamazoo Valley Community College
Kellogg Community College
Kendall College of Art and Design
Kettering University
Kirtland Community College
Lake Superior State University
Lansing Community College
Lawrence Technological University
Macomb Community College
Madonna University
Marygrove College
Michigan State University
Monroe County Community College
Montcalm Community College
Mott Community College
Muskegon Community College
North Central Michigan College
Northern Michigan University
Northwestern Michigan College
Northwood University
Oakland University
Olivet College
Reformed Bible College
Rochester College
Saginaw Valley State University
Schoolcraft College
Siena Heights University
Southwestern Michigan College
Spring Arbor College
Suomi College
University of Detroit Mercy
University of Michigan
University of Michigan
  Dearborn
  Flint
Washtenaw Community College
Wayne County Community College
Wayne State University
West Shore Community College
Western Michigan University
William Tyndale College

Minnesota
Alexandria Technical College
Anoka-Ramsey Community College
Augsburg College
Bemidji State University
Bethany Lutheran College
Bethel College
Carleton College
Central Lakes College
College of St. Benedict
College of St. Catherine: St. Paul Campus
College of St. Scholastica
College of Visual Arts
Concordia College: Moorhead
Concordia University: St. Paul
Crown College
Dunwoody Institute
Gustavus Adolphus College
Hamline University
Hennepin Technical College
Hibbing Community College: A Technical and Community College
Itasca Community College
Lake Superior College: A Community and Technical College
Macalester College
Martin Luther College
Mesabi Range Community and Technical College
Metropolitan State University
Minneapolis College of Art and Design
Minneapolis Community and Technical College
Minnesota Bible College
Minnesota State University, Mankato
Moorhead State University
National American University St. Paul
North Central University
North Hennepin Community College
Northwestern College
Pine Technical College
Rochester Community and Technical College
St. Cloud State University
St. Cloud Technical College
St. John's University
St. Mary's University of Minnesota
St. Olaf College
Southwest State University
University of Minnesota
  Duluth
  Morris
  Twin Cities
University of St. Thomas
Vermilion Community College
Winona State University

Mississippi
Alcorn State University
Belhaven College
Delta State University
Hinds Community College
Jackson State University
Mary Holmes College
Meridian Community College
Millsaps College
Mississippi College
Mississippi State University
Mississippi Valley State University
Northwest Mississippi Community College
Rust College
Tougaloo College
University of Mississippi
Wesley College
William Carey College

Missouri
Avila College
Berean University
Central Methodist College
College of the Ozarks
Columbia College
Conception Seminary College
Cottey College
Culver-Stockton College
Drury University
East Central College
Fontbonne College
Hannibal-LaGrange College
Jefferson College
Kansas City Art Institute
Lincoln University
Lindenwood University
Longview Community College
Maryville University of Saint Louis
Mineral Area College
Missouri Baptist College
Missouri Southern State College
Missouri Valley College
Northwest Missouri State University
Ozarks Technical Community College
Park University
Research College of Nursing
Rockhurst University
St. Charles County Community College
St. Louis University
Southeast Missouri State University
Southwest Baptist University
Southwest Missouri State University
St. Louis Community College
  St. Louis Community College at Florissant Valley
  St. Louis Community College at Forest Park
  St. Louis Community College at Meramec
Stephens College
Three Rivers Community College
Truman State University
University of Missouri
  Columbia
  Rolla
  St. Louis
Washington University
Webster University
Wentworth Military Academy
Westminster College
William Jewell College
William Woods University

Montana
Carroll College
Dawson Community College
Flathead Valley Community College
Miles Community College
Montana State University
  Billings
  Bozeman
  College of Technology-Great Falls
  Northern
Montana Tech of the University of Montana
Rocky Mountain College
Stone Child College
University of Great Falls
University of Montana-Missoula
Western Montana College of The University of Montana

Nebraska
Bellevue University
Central Community College
Chadron State College
Clarkson College
College of Saint Mary
Concordia University
Creighton University
Dana College
Doane College
Grace University

Hastings College
Lincoln School of Commerce
Metropolitan Community College
Mid Plains Community College Area
Midland Lutheran College
Nebraska Methodist College of Nursing and Allied Health
Nebraska Wesleyan University
Northeast Community College
Peru State College
Southeast Community College
    Lincoln Campus
Union College
University of Nebraska
    Kearney
    Omaha
Wayne State College

Nevada
Community College of Southern Nevada
University of Nevada
    Las Vegas
    Reno
Western Nevada Community College

New Hampshire
Colby-Sawyer College
College for Lifelong Learning
Daniel Webster College
Dartmouth College
Franklin Pierce College
Hesser College
Keene State College
New England College
New Hampshire College
New Hampshire Community Technical College
    Berlin
    Claremont
    Laconia
    Manchester
    Nashua
    Stratham
Notre Dame College
Plymouth State College of the University System of New Hampshire
Rivier College
St. Anselm College
Thomas More College of Liberal Arts
University of New Hampshire
University of New Hampshire
    Manchester
White Pines College

New Jersey
Assumption College for Sisters
Atlantic Cape Community College
Bloomfield College
Brookdale Community College
Burlington County College
Caldwell College
Camden County College
Centenary College
College of St. Elizabeth
Cumberland County College
Drew University
Essex County College
Fairleigh Dickinson University
Felician College
Georgian Court College
Hudson County Community College
Kean University
Mercer County Community College
Middlesex County College
Monmouth University
Montclair State University
New Jersey City University
New Jersey Institute of Technology
Ocean County College
Passaic County Community College
Princeton University
Ramapo College of New Jersey
Raritan Valley Community College
Richard Stockton College of New Jersey
Rider University
Rowan University
Rutgers
    The State University of New Jersey: Camden College of Arts and Sciences
    The State University of New Jersey: Cook College
    The State University of New Jersey: Douglass College
    The State University of New Jersey: Livingston College
    The State University of New Jersey: Newark College of Arts and Sciences
    The State University of New Jersey: Rutgers College
    The State University of New Jersey: University College Camden
    The State University of New Jersey: University College New Brunswick
    The State University of New Jersey: University College Newark
St. Peter's College
Salem Community College
Seton Hall University
Stevens Institute of Technology
Sussex County Community College
The College of New Jersey
Thomas Edison State College
University of Medicine and Dentistry of New Jersey
    School of Health Related Professions
    School of Nursing
Warren County Community College
William Paterson University of New Jersey

New Mexico
College of Santa Fe
Dona Ana Branch Community College of New Mexico State University
Eastern New Mexico University
Eastern New Mexico University
    Roswell Campus
Institute of American Indian Arts
New Mexico Highlands University
New Mexico Institute of Mining and Technology
New Mexico State University
New Mexico State University
    Alamogordo
    Carlsbad
San Juan College
Santa Fe Community College
University of New Mexico
Western New Mexico University

New York
Adelphi University
Adirondack Community College
Alfred University
Bard College
Barnard College
Briarcliffe College
Broome Community College
Bryant & Stratton Business Institute
    Albany
Canisius College
City University of New York
    Baruch College
    Borough of Manhattan Community College
    Bronx Community College
    Brooklyn College
    City College
    College of Staten Island
    Hunter College
    John Jay College of Criminal Justice
    Kingsborough Community College
    La Guardia Community College
    Lehman College
    Medgar Evers College
    New York City Technical College
    Queens College
    Queensborough Community College
    York College
Clarkson University
Clinton Community College
Colgate University
College of Mount St. Vincent
College of New Rochelle
College of New Rochelle
    School of New Resources
College of St. Rose
Columbia University
    Columbia College
    School of General Studies
    School of Nursing
Columbia-Greene Community College
Concordia College
Cooper Union for the Advancement of Science and Art
Cornell University
Corning Community College
D'Youville College
Daemen College
Dominican College of Blauvelt
Dowling College
Dutchess Community College
Elmira College
Erie Community College
    City Campus
    North Campus
    South Campus
Eugene Lang College/New School University
Finger Lakes Community College
Five Towns College
Fordham University
Fulton-Montgomery Community College
Genesee Community College
Hamilton College
Hartwick College
Herkimer County Community College
Hilbert College
Hobart and William Smith Colleges
Hofstra University
Houghton College
Interboro Institute
Iona College
Ithaca College
Jamestown Community College
Jefferson Community College
Jewish Theological Seminary of America
Keuka College
Laboratory Institute of Merchandising
Le Moyne College
Long Island University
    Brooklyn Campus
    C. W. Post Campus
    Southampton College
Manhattan College
Manhattanville College
Maria College
Marist College
Marymount College
Marymount Manhattan College
Medaille College
Mercy College
Mohawk Valley Community College
Molloy College
Monroe Community College
Mount St. Mary College
Nazareth College of Rochester
New York Institute of Technology
New York School of Interior Design
New York State College of Ceramics at Alfred University
New York University
Niagara County Community College
Niagara University
Nyack College
Ohr Somayach Tanenbaum Education Center
Onondaga Community College
Orange County Community College
Pace University
Pace University: Pleasantville/Briarcliff
Parsons School of Design
Pratt Institute
Regents College
Rensselaer Polytechnic Institute
Roberts Wesleyan College
Rochester Institute of Technology
Rockland Community College
Russell Sage College
Sage Junior College of Albany
St. Bonaventure University
St. Francis College
St. John Fisher College
St. John's University
St. Lawrence University
St. Thomas Aquinas College
Sarah Lawrence College
Schenectady County Community College
School of Visual Arts
Siena College
Skidmore College
St. Joseph's College
    St. Joseph's College
    St. Joseph's College: Suffolk Campus
State University of New York
    Albany
    Binghamton
    Buffalo
    College at Brockport
    College at Buffalo
    College at Cortland
    College at Fredonia
    College at Geneseo
    College at Old Westbury
    College at Oneonta
    College at Plattsburgh
    College at Potsdam
    College of Agriculture and Technology at Cobleskill
    College of Environmental Science and Forestry
    College of Technology at Alfred
    College of Technology at Canton
    College of Technology at Delhi
    Empire State College
    Health Science Center at Stony Brook
    Institute of Technology at Utica/Rome
    Maritime College
    New Paltz
    Oswego
    Purchase
    Stony Brook
    Upstate Medical University
Suffolk County Community College
Syracuse University
Technical Career Institutes
Tompkins-Cortland Community College
Touro College
Trocaire College
Ulster County Community College
Union College
United States Merchant Marine Academy
United States Military Academy
University of Rochester
Utica College of Syracuse University
Vassar College

Wagner College
Wells College
Westchester Community College

North Carolina

Alamance Community College
Appalachian State University
Asheville Buncombe Technical Community College
Barton College
Beaufort County Community College
Belmont Abbey College
Bennett College
Bladen Community College
Brevard College
Caldwell Community College and Technical Institute
Campbell University
Catawba College
Catawba Valley Community College
Central Carolina Community College
Central Piedmont Community College
Chowan College
Cleveland Community College
Coastal Carolina Community College
College of the Albemarle
Craven Community College
Davidson College
Davidson County Community College
Duke University
East Carolina University
Edgecombe Community College
Elizabeth City State University
Elon College
Fayetteville State University
Forsyth Technical Community College
Gardner-Webb University
Gaston College
Greensboro College
Guilford College
Guilford Technical Community College
Halifax Community College
Haywood Community College
High Point University
John Wesley College
Johnson C. Smith University
Lenoir-Rhyne College
Louisburg College
Mars Hill College
Mayland Community College
Meredith College
Methodist College
Mitchell Community College
Montgomery Community College
Montreat College
Mount Olive College
North Carolina Agricultural and Technical State University
North Carolina Central University
North Carolina School of the Arts
North Carolina State University
North Carolina Wesleyan College
Peace College
Pfeiffer University
Piedmont Community College
Queens College
Richmond Community College
Roanoke-Chowan Community College
Rockingham Community College
St. Andrews Presbyterian College
St. Augustine's College
Salem College
Sampson Community College
Sandhills Community College
Shaw University
South Piedmont Community College
Southeastern Community College
Southwestern Community College
Surry Community College
Tri-County Community College
University of North Carolina
  Asheville
  Charlotte
  Greensboro
  Pembroke
  Wilmington
Vance-Granville Community College
Wake Forest University
Warren Wilson College
Western Carolina University
Wilkes Community College
Wilson Technical Community College
Wingate University
Winston-Salem State University

North Dakota

Dickinson State University
Jamestown College
Minot State University
Minot State University: Bottineau Campus
North Dakota State University
Sitting Bull College
Trinity Bible College
University of Mary
University of North Dakota

Ohio

Antioch College
Ashland University
Baldwin-Wallace College
Bluffton College
Bowling Green State University
Bowling Green State University Firelands College
Bryant & Stratton College
Capital University
Case Western Reserve University
Cedarville College
Central State University
Chatfield College
Cincinnati State Technical and Community College
Circleville Bible College
Cleveland Institute of Art
Cleveland Institute of Electronics
Cleveland Institute of Music
Cleveland State University
College of Mount St. Joseph
College of Wooster
Columbus College of Art and Design
Columbus State Community College
David N. Myers College
Defiance College
Denison University
Edison State Community College
Franciscan University of Steubenville
Franklin University
Heidelberg College
Hiram College
Hocking Technical College
Jefferson Community College
John Carroll University
Kent State University
Kent State University
  Ashtabula Regional Campus
  East Liverpool Regional Campus
  Stark Campus
  Trumbull Campus
  Tuscarawas Campus
Kenyon College
Lake Erie College
Lakeland Community College
Lima Technical College
Lorain County Community College
Lourdes College
Malone College
Marietta College
Marion Technical College
Miami University
  Hamilton Campus
  Middletown Campus
  Oxford Campus
Miami-Jacobs College
Mount Union College
Mount Vernon Nazarene College
Muskingum College
North Central State College
Northwest State Community College
Notre Dame College of Ohio
Oberlin College
Ohio Dominican College
Ohio Institute of Photography and Technology
Ohio Northern University
Ohio State University
  Agricultural Technical Institute
  Columbus Campus
  Lima Campus
  Mansfield Campus
  Marion Campus
  Newark Campus
Ohio University
Ohio University
  Chillicothe Campus
  Eastern Campus
  Lancaster Campus
  Zanesville Campus
Ohio Wesleyan University
Otterbein College
Owens Community College Toledo
Pontifical College Josephinum
Shawnee State University
Sinclair Community College
Southern Ohio College
Stark State College of Technology
Terra Community College
Tiffin University
Union Institute
University of Akron
University of Akron Wayne College
University of Cincinnati
University of Cincinnati
  Clermont College
  Raymond Walters College
University of Dayton
University of Findlay
University of Rio Grande
University of Toledo
Ursuline College
Walsh University
Washington State Community College
Wilmington College
Wittenberg University
Wright State University
Xavier University

Oklahoma

Cameron University
Carl Albert State College
East Central University
Mid-America Bible College
Northwestern Oklahoma State University
Oklahoma Baptist University
Oklahoma Christian University of Science and Arts
Oklahoma City Community College
Oklahoma City University
Oklahoma Panhandle State University
Oklahoma State University
Oklahoma State University Oklahoma City
Oral Roberts University
Redlands Community College
Rogers State University
Rose State College
Southeastern Oklahoma State University
Southern Nazarene University
Southwestern College of Christian Ministries
Southwestern Oklahoma State University
Tulsa Community College
University of Central Oklahoma
University of Oklahoma
University of Science and Arts of Oklahoma
University of Tulsa

Oregon

Art Institute of Portland
Central Oregon Community College
Chemeketa Community College
Clackamas Community College
Concordia University
Eastern Oregon University
Eugene Bible College
George Fox University
Lane Community College
Lewis & Clark College
Linfield College
Marylhurst University
Mount Hood Community College
Oregon Institute of Technology
Oregon State University
Pacific Northwest College of Art
Pacific University
Portland State University
Reed College
Southern Oregon University
University of Oregon
University of Portland
Western Baptist College
Western Oregon University
Willamette University

Pennsylvania

Albright College
Allegheny College
Allentown College of St. Francis de Sales
Alvernia College
Art Institute of Philadelphia
Beaver College
Bloomsburg University of Pennsylvania
Bryn Athyn College of the New Church
Bryn Mawr College
Bucknell University
Bucks County Community College
Butler County Community College
Cabrini College
California University of Pennsylvania
Carlow College
Carnegie Mellon University
Cedar Crest College
Chatham College
Chestnut Hill College
Cheyney University of Pennsylvania
Clarion University of Pennsylvania
College Misericordia
Community College of Allegheny County
Delaware County Community College
Delaware Valley College
Dickinson College
Drexel University
Duquesne University
Eastern College
Edinboro University of Pennsylvania
Elizabethtown College
Franklin and Marshall College
Gannon University
Geneva College
Gettysburg College
Grove City College
Gwynedd-Mercy College
Harcum College
Harrisburg Area Community College
Haverford College
Holy Family College
ICS Center for Degree Studies
Immaculata College
Indiana University of Pennsylvania
Juniata College
King's College
Kutztown University of Pennsylvania
La Roche College
La Salle University
Lafayette College
Lancaster Bible College
Lebanon Valley College of Pennsylvania
Lehigh Carbon Community College
Lehigh University

Lincoln University
Lock Haven University of Pennsylvania
Luzerne County Community College
Lycoming College
Manor College
Mansfield University of Pennsylvania
Marywood University
Mercyhurst College
Messiah College
Millersville University of Pennsylvania
Montgomery County Community College
Moore College of Art and Design
Moravian College
Mount Aloysius College
Muhlenberg College
Neumann College
Peirce College
Penn State
    Abington
    Altoona
    Beaver
    Berks
    Delaware County
    Dubois
    Erie, The Behrend College
    Fayette
    Harrisburg
    Hazleton
    Lehigh Valley
    McKeesport
    Mont Alto
    New Kensington
    Schuylkill - Capital College
    Shenango
    University Park
    Wilkes-Barre
    Worthington Scranton
    York
Pennsylvania Institute of Technology
Philadelphia College of Bible
Philadelphia University
Point Park College
Reading Area Community College
Robert Morris College
Rosemont College
St. Charles Borromeo Seminary - Overbrook
St. Francis College
St. Joseph's University
St. Vincent College
Seton Hill College
Shippensburg University of Pennsylvania
Slippery Rock University of Pennsylvania
Susquehanna University
Swarthmore College
Temple University
Thiel College
Thomas Jefferson University: College of Health Professions
University of Pennsylvania
University of Pittsburgh
University of Pittsburgh
    Bradford
    Greensburg
    Johnstown
    Titusville
University of Scranton
University of the Arts
Ursinus College
Valley Forge Christian College
Villanova University
Washington and Jefferson College
Waynesburg College
West Chester University of Pennsylvania
Westminster College
Westmoreland County Community College
Widener University
Wilkes University
Wilson College
York College of Pennsylvania

Puerto Rico
American University of Puerto Rico
Bayamon Central University
Colegio Universitario del Este
Columbia College
Huertas Junior College
Inter American University of Puerto Rico
    Aguadilla Campus
    Arecibo Campus
    Bayamon Campus
    Fajardo Campus
    Guayama Campus
    Metropolitan Campus
    San German Campus
National College of Business and Technology
Pontifical Catholic University of Puerto Rico
Turabo University
Universidad Metropolitana
University of the Sacred Heart

Rhode Island
Brown University
Bryant College
Johnson & Wales University
Providence College
Rhode Island College
Roger Williams University
Salve Regina University
University of Rhode Island

South Carolina
Aiken Technical College
Anderson College
Central Carolina Technical College
Chesterfield-Marlboro Technical College
Claflin University
Coastal Carolina University
Coker College
College of Charleston
Columbia College
Columbia International University
Converse College
Denmark Technical College
Erskine College
Florence-Darlington Technical College
Francis Marion University
Furman University
Horry-Georgetown Technical College
Lander University
Limestone College
Newberry College
North Greenville College
Orangeburg-Calhoun Technical College
Piedmont Technical College
Presbyterian College
Southern Wesleyan University
Spartanburg Methodist College
Spartanburg Technical College
Technical College of the Lowcountry
Trident Technical College
University of South Carolina
University of South Carolina
    Aiken
    Beaufort
    Salkehatchie Regional Campus
    Spartanburg
    Union
Voorhees College
Winthrop University
Wofford College

South Dakota
Augustana College
Black Hills State University
Dakota State University
Dakota Wesleyan University
Kilian Community College
Mount Marty College
Northern State University
Sinte Gleska University
South Dakota School of Mines and Technology
South Dakota State University
University of South Dakota

Tennessee
Austin Peay State University
Belmont University
Bethel College
Carson-Newman College
Chattanooga State Technical Community College
Christian Brothers University
Crichton College
Cumberland University
David Lipscomb University
Dyersburg State Community College
East Tennessee State University
Fisk University
Freed-Hardeman University
Hiwassee College
Johnson Bible College
King College
Lambuth University
Lane College
Lee University
Lincoln Memorial University
Martin Methodist College
Maryville College
Middle Tennessee State University
Milligan College
Motlow State Community College
Pellissippi State Technical Community College
Rhodes College
Roane State Community College
Shelby State Community College
Southern Adventist University
Tennessee State University
Tennessee Technological University
Tennessee Temple University
Tennessee Wesleyan College
Tusculum College
Union University
University of Memphis
University of Tennessee
    Chattanooga
    Knoxville
    Martin
University of the South
Vanderbilt University
Volunteer State Community College

Texas
Abilene Christian University
Amber University
Arlington Baptist College
Austin College
Austin Community College
Central Texas College
College of the Mainland
Concordia University at Austin
Dallas Baptist University
Del Mar College
East Texas Baptist University
Eastfield College
El Paso Community College
Houston Baptist University
Lamar State College at Port Arthur
Lamar University
LeTourneau University
Lee College
Lon Morris College
Lubbock Christian University
McMurry University
Midwestern State University
Mountain View College
Navarro College
Northwood University: Texas Campus
Prairie View A&M University
Rice University
St. Mary's University
Sam Houston State University
Schreiner College
Southern Methodist University
Southwest Texas State University
Southwestern Adventist University
Southwestern Assemblies of God University
Southwestern University
Stephen F. Austin State University
Sul Ross State University
Texas A&M International University
Texas A&M University
Texas A&M University
    Commerce
    Corpus Christi
    Galveston
    Texarkana
Texas Christian University
Texas College
Texas Lutheran University
Texas State Technical College
    Harlingen
Texas Tech University
Texas Wesleyan University
Trinity University
University of Dallas
University of Houston
University of Houston
    Clear Lake
    Downtown
    Victoria
University of Mary Hardin-Baylor
University of North Texas
University of St. Thomas
University of Texas
    Arlington
    Austin
    Brownsville
    Dallas
    El Paso
    San Antonio
    Southwestern Medical Center at Dallas
    Tyler
    of the Permian Basin
University of the Incarnate Word
West Texas A&M University
Western Texas College

Utah
Brigham Young University
Snow College
Southern Utah University
University of Utah
Weber State University
Westminster College

Vermont
Bennington College
Burlington College
Castleton State College
Champlain College
College of St. Joseph in Vermont
Community College of Vermont
Goddard College
Green Mountain College
Johnson State College
Lyndon State College
Marlboro College
Middlebury College
Norwich University
St. Michael's College
Southern Vermont College
Sterling College
Trinity College of Vermont
University of Vermont
Vermont Technical College

Virginia
Averett College
Blue Ridge Community College
Bridgewater College
Central Virginia Community College
Christendom College
Christopher Newport University
College of William and Mary
Dabney S. Lancaster Community College
Danville Community College

ECPI College of Technology
Eastern Mennonite University
Emory & Henry College
Ferrum College
George Mason University
Germanna Community College
Hampden-Sydney College
Hampton University
Hollins University
J. Sargeant Reynolds Community College
James Madison University
Liberty University
Longwood College
Lord Fairfax Community College
Lynchburg College
Mary Baldwin College
Mary Washington College
Mountain Empire Community College
Norfolk State University
Northern Virginia Community College
Old Dominion University
Patrick Henry Community College
Paul D. Camp Community College
Piedmont Virginia Community College
Radford University
Randolph-Macon College
Randolph-Macon Woman's College
Roanoke College
St. Paul's College
Shenandoah University
Southwest Virginia Community College
Sweet Briar College
Thomas Nelson Community College
Tidewater Community College
University of Richmond
University of Virginia
University of Virginia's College at Wise
Virginia Commonwealth University
Virginia Highlands Community College
Virginia Intermont College
Virginia Military Institute
Virginia Polytechnic Institute and State University
Virginia State University
Virginia Union University
Virginia Wesleyan College
Virginia Western Community College
Washington and Lee University
Wytheville Community College

Washington

Antioch University Seattle
Central Washington University
Centralia College
City University
Clark College
Eastern Washington University
Edmonds Community College
Everett Community College
Evergreen State College
Gonzaga University
Grays Harbor College
Green River Community College
Henry Cogswell College
Heritage College
Highline Community College
Lower Columbia College
North Seattle Community College
Northwest Indian College
Olympic College
Pacific Lutheran University
Pierce College
St. Martin's College
Seattle Central Community College
Seattle Pacific University
Seattle University
Shoreline Community College
Skagit Valley College
South Puget Sound Community College
South Seattle Community College
Spokane Community College
Spokane Falls Community College
University of Puget Sound
University of Washington

Walla Walla College
Walla Walla Community College
Washington State University
Wenatchee Valley College
Western Washington University
Whatcom Community College
Whitman College
Whitworth College

West Virginia

Alderson-Broaddus College
Bethany College
College of West Virginia
Davis and Elkins College
Marshall University
Ohio Valley College
Salem-Teikyo University
Shepherd College
Southern West Virginia Community and Technical College
University of Charleston
West Liberty State College
West Virginia Northern Community College
West Virginia University
West Virginia University Parkersburg
West Virginia Wesleyan College
Wheeling Jesuit University

Wisconsin

Bellin College of Nursing
Beloit College
Blackhawk Technical College
Cardinal Stritch University
Carroll College
Carthage College
Chippewa Valley Technical College
Columbia College of Nursing
Concordia University Wisconsin
Gateway Technical College
Lakeland College
Lakeshore Technical College
Lawrence University
Marian College of Fond du Lac
Marquette University
Milwaukee Area Technical College
Milwaukee Institute of Art & Design
Milwaukee School of Engineering
Moraine Park Technical College
Mount Mary College
Nicolet Area Technical College
Northland College
St. Norbert College
Silver Lake College
University of Wisconsin
    Baraboo/Sauk County
    Eau Claire
    Fond du Lac
    Fox Valley
    Green Bay
    Madison
    Manitowoc County
    Marathon County
    Marinette
    Marshfield/Wood County
    Milwaukee
    Oshkosh
    Parkside
    Platteville
    Richland
    River Falls
    Rock County
    Sheboygan County
    Stevens Point
    Stout
    Superior
    Washington County
    Waukesha
    Whitewater
Viterbo University
Waukesha County Technical College
Western Wisconsin Technical College
Wisconsin Lutheran College

Wyoming

Central Wyoming College
Eastern Wyoming College
Northwest College
Sheridan College
University of Wyoming
Western Wyoming Community College

Internship

Alabama

Alabama Agricultural and Mechanical University
Alabama State University
Auburn University
Auburn University at Montgomery
Bessemer State Technical College
Birmingham-Southern College
Calhoun Community College
Community College of the Air Force
Enterprise State Junior College
Faulkner University
Harry M. Ayers State Technical College
Huntingdon College
J. F. Drake State Technical College
Jacksonville State University
James H. Faulkner State Community College
Jefferson State Community College
John M. Patterson State Technical College
Lawson State Community College
Northwest-Shoals Community College
Samford University
Snead State Community College
South College
Spring Hill College
Stillman College
Talladega College
Troy State University
Troy State University Dothan
Tuskegee University
University of Alabama
University of Alabama Birmingham
    Huntsville
University of Mobile
University of Montevallo
University of South Alabama
Wallace State Community College at Hanceville

Alaska

Alaska Bible College
Alaska Pacific University
Prince William Sound Community College
University of Alaska
    Anchorage
    Fairbanks
    Southeast

Arizona

American Indian College of the Assemblies of God
Arizona State University
Arizona Western College
Central Arizona College
Cochise College
Dine College
Embry-Riddle Aeronautical University Prescott Campus
Gateway Community College
Glendale Community College
Grand Canyon University
Mesa Community College
Northern Arizona University
Paradise Valley Community College
Phoenix College
Prescott College
Rio Salado College
Scottsdale Community College

Southwestern College
University of Advancing Computer Technology
University of Arizona

Arkansas

Arkansas State University
Arkansas Tech University
Central Baptist College
Garland County Community College
Harding University
Henderson State University
Hendrix College
John Brown University
Lyon College
Mississippi County Community College
Northwest Arkansas Community College
Ouachita Baptist University
Philander Smith College
Phillips Community College of the University of Arkansas
Southern Arkansas University
Southern Arkansas University Tech
University of Arkansas
University of Arkansas
    Little Rock
    Monticello
    Pine Bluff
University of Central Arkansas
University of the Ozarks
Westark College
Williams Baptist College

California

Academy of Art College
Allan Hancock College
Antioch Southern California
    Los Angeles
    Santa Barbara
Armstrong University
Art Center College of Design
Art Institutes International
    San Francisco
Azusa Pacific University
Barstow College
Biola University
Brooks College
Cabrillo College
California Baptist University
California College of Arts and Crafts
California Institute of Technology
California Institute of the Arts
California Lutheran University
California Maritime Academy
California Polytechnic State University: San Luis Obispo
California State Polytechnic University: Pomona
California State University
    Bakersfield
    Chico
    Dominguez Hills
    Fresno
    Fullerton
    Hayward
    Long Beach
    Los Angeles
    Monterey Bay
    Northridge
    Sacramento
    San Marcos
    Stanislaus
Canada College
Cerro Coso Community College
Chabot College
Chaffey Community College
Chapman University
City College of San Francisco
Claremont McKenna College
Cogswell Polytechnical College
College of Notre Dame
College of the Sequoias
College of the Siskiyous

Columbia College
Concordia University
Cuyamaca College
Cypress College
De Anza College
Diablo Valley College
Dominican University of California
Evergreen Valley College
Fashion Institute of Design and Merchandising
Fashion Institute of Design and Merchandising
   San Francisco
Foothill College
Fresno City College
Fresno Pacific University
Gavilan Community College
Glendale Community College
Golden Gate University
Grossmont Community College
Harvey Mudd College
Heald Business College
   Santa Rosa
Holy Names College
Hope International University
Humboldt State University
Humphreys College
John F. Kennedy University
LIFE Bible College
La Sierra University
Lake Tahoe Community College
Las Positas College
Lincoln University
Long Beach City College
Loyola Marymount University
Marymount College
Master's College
Menlo College
Merced College
Mills College
MiraCosta College
Modesto Junior College
Monterey Institute of International Studies
Moorpark College
Mount St. Mary's College
Mount San Jacinto College
Napa Valley College
National University
Occidental College
Ohlone College
Orange Coast College
Otis College of Art and Design
Pacific Oaks College
Pacific Union College
Pasadena City College
Pepperdine University
Pitzer College
Point Loma Nazarene University
Pomona College
Queen of the Holy Rosary College
Riverside Community College
Sacramento City College
Saddleback College
St. Mary's College of California
San Bernardino Valley College
San Diego City College
San Diego Mesa College
San Diego State University
San Francisco Art Institute
San Francisco State University
San Joaquin Delta College
San Joaquin Valley College Inc.
San Jose Christian College
San Jose City College
San Jose State University
Santa Ana College
Santa Barbara City College
Santa Clara University
Santa Monica College
Santa Rosa Junior College
Shasta College
Sierra College
Simpson College
Solano Community College

Sonoma State University
Southern California Institute of Architecture
Southwestern College
Stanford University
United States International University
University of California
   Berkeley
   Davis
   Irvine
   Los Angeles
   Riverside
   San Diego
   Santa Barbara
   Santa Cruz
University of Judaism
University of La Verne
University of Redlands
University of San Diego
University of San Francisco
University of Southern California
University of West Los Angeles
University of the Pacific
Vanguard University of Southern California
Westmont College
Whittier College
Yuba College

Colorado
Adams State College
Aims Community College
Arapahoe Community College
Art Institute
   of Colorado
Bel-Rea Institute of Animal Technology
Colorado Mountain College
   Alpine Campus
   Spring Valley Campus
   Timberline Campus
Colorado Northwestern Community College
Colorado School of Mines
Colorado State University
Colorado Technical University
Community College of Aurora
Community College of Denver
Denver Technical College: A Division of DeVry University
Fort Lewis College
Front Range Community College
Lamar Community College
Mesa State College
Metropolitan State College of Denver
Morgan Community College
Naropa University
Nazarene Bible College
Northeastern Junior College
Pikes Peak Community College
Pueblo Community College
Red Rocks Community College
Regis University
Rocky Mountain College of Art & Design
University of Colorado
   Boulder
   Denver
   Health Sciences Center
University of Denver
University of Northern Colorado
University of Southern Colorado
Western State College of Colorado

Connecticut
Albertus Magnus College
Asnuntuck Community-Technical College
Briarwood College
Capital Community College
Central Connecticut State University
Connecticut College
Eastern Connecticut State University
Fairfield University
Gateway Community College

Housatonic Community-Technical College
Middlesex Community-Technical College
Mitchell College
Naugatuck Valley Community-Technical College
Northwestern Connecticut Community-Technical College
Norwalk Community-Technical College
Paier College of Art
Quinebaug Valley Community College
Quinnipiac University
Sacred Heart University
St. Joseph College
Southern Connecticut State University
Teikyo Post University
Three Rivers Community-Technical College
Trinity College
Tunxis Community College
United States Coast Guard Academy
University of Bridgeport
University of Connecticut
University of Hartford
University of New Haven
Wesleyan University
Western Connecticut State University

Delaware
Delaware State University
Delaware Technical and Community College
   Owens Campus
   Stanton/Wilmington Campus
   Terry Campus
Goldey-Beacom College
University of Delaware
Wesley College
Wilmington College

District of Columbia
American University
Catholic University of America
Corcoran College of Art and Design
Gallaudet University
George Washington University
Georgetown University
Howard University
Trinity College
University of the District of Columbia

Florida
Art Institute
   of Fort Lauderdale
Barry University
Bethune-Cookman College
Brevard Community College
Broward Community College
Central Florida Community College
Clearwater Christian College
Daytona Beach Community College
Eckerd College
Edison Community College
Edward Waters College
Embry-Riddle Aeronautical University
Flagler College
Florida Agricultural and Mechanical University
Florida Atlantic University
Florida Baptist Theological College
Florida Christian College
Florida Gulf Coast University
Florida Institute of Technology
Florida International University
Florida Memorial College
Florida Metropolitan University
   Orlando College North
Florida Southern College
Florida State University
Gulf Coast Community College
Hillsborough Community College
Hobe Sound Bible College

International Academy of Merchandising and Design
International Fine Arts College
Jacksonville University
Jones College
Lake City Community College
Lake-Sumter Community College
Lynn University
Miami-Dade Community College
New College of the University of South Florida
New England Institute of Technology
Northwood University
   Florida Campus
Nova Southeastern University
Palm Beach Atlantic College
Palm Beach Community College
Pasco-Hernando Community College
Pensacola Junior College
Polk Community College
Ringling School of Art and Design
Rollins College
St. Leo University
St. Petersburg Junior College
St. Thomas University
South College: Palm Beach Campus
South Florida Community College
Southeastern College of the Assemblies of God
Stetson University
University of Central Florida
University of Florida
University of Miami
University of North Florida
University of South Florida
University of Tampa
University of West Florida
Valencia Community College
Warner Southern College

Georgia
Abraham Baldwin Agricultural College
Agnes Scott College
Albany State University
American InterContinental University
Armstrong Atlantic State University
Art Institute
   of Atlanta
Athens Area Technical Institute
Atlanta Christian College
Atlanta College of Art
Atlanta Metropolitan College
Augusta State University
Berry College
Brenau University
Brewton-Parker College
Chattahoochee Technical Institute
Clark Atlanta University
Clayton College and State University
Columbus State University
Columbus Technical Institute
Covenant College
Dalton State College
DeKalb Technical Institute
Emmanuel College
Emory University
Fort Valley State University
Georgia College and State University
Georgia Institute of Technology
Georgia Perimeter College
Georgia Southern University
Georgia Southwestern State University
Georgia State University
Gwinnett Technical Institute
Herzing College of Business and Technology
Kennesaw State University
LaGrange College
Macon State College
Medical College of Georgia
Mercer University
Morehouse College
Morris Brown College
North Georgia College & State University

Oglethorpe University
Oxford College of Emory University
Paine College
Piedmont College
Reinhardt College
Savannah College of Art and Design
Savannah State University
Savannah Technical Institute
Shorter College
Southern Polytechnic State University
Spelman College
State University of West Georgia
Thomas College
Toccoa Falls College
University of Georgia
Valdosta State University
Wesleyan College
Young Harris College

Hawaii
Brigham Young University
    Hawaii
Chaminade University of Honolulu
Hawaii Pacific University
University of Hawaii
    Hilo
    Honolulu Community College
    Kapiolani Community College
    Kauai Community College
    Leeward Community College
    Manoa
    West Oahu

Idaho
Albertson College of Idaho
Boise Bible College
Boise State University
College of Southern Idaho
Eastern Idaho Technical College
Idaho State University
Lewis-Clark State College
North Idaho College
Northwest Nazarene University
Ricks College
University of Idaho

Illinois
American Academy of Art
Augustana College
Barat College
Benedictine University
Black Hawk College
Black Hawk College
    East Campus
Blackburn College
Bradley University
Career Colleges of Chicago
Carl Sandburg College
Chicago State University
City Colleges of Chicago
    Harold Washington College
    Harry S. Truman College
    Kennedy-King College
    Malcolm X College
    Olive-Harvey College
    Richard J. Daley College
    Wright College
College of DuPage
College of Lake County
Columbia College
Concordia University
Danville Area Community College
De Paul University
Dominican University
Eastern Illinois University
Elgin Community College
Elmhurst College
Eureka College
Finch University of Health Sciences/The
    Chicago Medical School
Governors State University
Greenville College
Highland Community College
Illinois College
Illinois Eastern Community Colleges
    Lincoln Trail College
    Olney Central College
    Wabash Valley College
Illinois Institute of Technology
Illinois State University
Illinois Wesleyan University
International Academy of Merchandising
    and Design
John A. Logan College
John Wood Community College
Joliet Junior College
Judson College
Kankakee Community College
Kaskaskia College
Kendall College
Kishwaukee College
Knox College
Lake Forest College
Lake Land College
Lewis University
Lewis and Clark Community College
Lexington College
Lincoln Christian College and Seminary
Lincoln Land Community College
Loyola University of Chicago
MacCormac College
MacMurray College
McHenry County College
McKendree College
Millikin University
Monmouth College
Moody Bible Institute
Moraine Valley Community College
Morton College
National-Louis University
North Central College
North Park University
Northeastern Illinois University
Northern Illinois University
Northwestern Business College
Northwestern University
Oakton Community College
Olivet Nazarene University
Parkland College
Prairie State College
Principia College
Quincy University
Rend Lake College
Robert Morris College: Chicago
Rock Valley College
Rockford College
Roosevelt University
St. Augustine College
St. Xavier University
Sauk Valley Community College
School of the Art Institute of Chicago
Shawnee Community College
Shimer College
Southeastern Illinois College
Southern Illinois University
    Carbondale
    Edwardsville
Southwestern Ilinois College
Spoon River College
Trinity Christian College
Trinity International University
University of Chicago
University of Illinois
    Chicago
    Springfield
    Urbana-Champaign
University of St. Francis
VanderCook College of Music
Waubonsee Community College
Western Illinois University
Wheaton College
William Rainey Harper College

Indiana
Anderson University
Ball State University
Bethel College
Butler University
Calumet College of St. Joseph
DePauw University
Earlham College
Franklin College
Goshen College
Grace College
Hanover College
Indiana Institute of Technology
Indiana State University
Indiana University
    Bloomington
    East
    Kokomo
    Northwest
    South Bend
    Southeast
Indiana University--Purdue University
    Indiana University-Purdue
        University Fort Wayne
    Indiana University-Purdue
        University Indianapolis
Indiana Wesleyan University
International Business College
Ivy Tech State College
    Central Indiana
    Columbus
    Eastcentral
    Kokomo
    Lafayette
    Northcentral
    Northeast
    Northwest
    Southcentral
    Southeast
    Southwest
    Wabash Valley
    Whitewater
Manchester College
Marian College
Michiana College
Oakland City University
Purdue University
Purdue University
    Calumet
    North Central Campus
Saint Mary's College
St. Joseph's College
St. Mary-of-the-Woods College
Taylor University
Tri-State University
University of Evansville
University of Indianapolis
University of St. Francis
University of Southern Indiana
Valparaiso University
Vincennes University
Wabash College

Iowa
American Institute of Business
Briar Cliff College
Buena Vista University
Central College
Clarke College
Coe College
Cornell College
Des Moines Area Community College
Dordt College
Drake University
Faith Baptist Bible College and
    Theological Seminary
Graceland University
Grand View College
Grinnell College
Hawkeye Community College
Indian Hills Community College
Iowa Central Community College
Iowa Lakes Community College
Iowa State University
Iowa Wesleyan College
Iowa Western Community College
Kirkwood Community College
Loras College
Luther College
Maharishi University of Management
Marshalltown Community College
Marycrest International University
Morningside College
Mount Mercy College
Muscatine Community College
Northeast Iowa Community College
Northwestern College
St. Ambrose University
Scott Community College
Simpson College
Southeastern Community College
    North Campus
Southwestern Community College
University of Dubuque
University of Iowa
University of Northern Iowa
Upper Iowa University
Waldorf College
Wartburg College
Western Iowa Tech Community College
William Penn University

Kansas
Allen County Community College
Baker University
Barclay College
Barton County Community College
Benedictine College
Bethany College
Bethel College
Butler County Community College
Central Christian College
Cloud County Community College
Coffeyville Community College
Colby Community College
Cowley County Community College
Dodge City Community College
Emporia State University
Fort Hays State University
Garden City Community College
Hesston College
Hutchinson Community College
Independence Community College
Johnson County Community College
Kansas City Kansas Community College
Kansas State University
Kansas Wesleyan University
Manhattan Christian College
McPherson College
MidAmerica Nazarene University
Newman University
Ottawa University
Pittsburg State University
Pratt Community College
St. Mary College
Seward County Community College
Southwestern College
Tabor College
University of Kansas
University of Kansas
    Medical Center
Washburn University of Topeka
Wichita State University

Kentucky
Alice Lloyd College
Asbury College
Ashland Community College
Bellarmine College
Berea College
Brescia University
Campbellsville University
Centre College
Cumberland College
Eastern Kentucky University
Elizabethtown Community College
Georgetown College
Kentucky Christian College
Kentucky Mountain Bible College
Kentucky State University
Kentucky Wesleyan College
Lexington Community College
Lindsey Wilson College
Madisonville Community College
Maysville Community College

Midway College
Morehead State University
Murray State University
National Business College
Northern Kentucky University
Owensboro Junior College of Business
Pikeville College
St. Catharine College
Somerset Community College
Southeast Community College
Spalding University
Thomas More College
Transylvania University
Union College
University of Kentucky
University of Louisville
Western Kentucky University

Louisiana

Bossier Parish Community College
Centenary College of Louisiana
Delgado Community College
Dillard University
Louisiana State University Medical Center
Louisiana State University and Agricultural and Mechanical College
Louisiana State University Shreveport
Louisiana Tech University
Loyola University New Orleans
McNeese State University
Nicholls State University
Northwestern State University
Nunez Community College
Our Lady of Holy Cross College
Southeastern Louisiana University
Southern University and Agricultural and Mechanical College
Southern University
   New Orleans
   Shreveport
Tulane University
University of Louisiana at Lafayette
University of Louisiana at Monroe
University of New Orleans
Xavier University of Louisiana

Maine

Andover College
Bates College
Central Maine Medical Center School of Nursing
Central Maine Technical College
Colby College
College of the Atlantic
Eastern Maine Technical College
Husson College
Maine College of Art
Maine Maritime Academy
Mid-State College
St. Joseph's College
Southern Maine Technical College
Thomas College
Unity College
University of Maine
University of Maine
   Augusta
   Farmington
   Fort Kent
   Machias
   Presque Isle
University of New England
University of Southern Maine
Washington County Technical College

Maryland

Allegany College
Anne Arundel Community College
Baltimore City Community College
Baltimore International College
Bowie State University
Carroll Community College
Cecil Community College

Chesapeake College
College of Notre Dame of Maryland
Columbia Union College
Community College of Baltimore County
   Essex
Coppin State College
Frederick Community College
Frostburg State University
Goucher College
Hagerstown Community College
Harford Community College
Hood College
Howard Community College
Johns Hopkins University
Johns Hopkins University: Peabody Conservatory of Music
Loyola College in Maryland
Maryland College of Art and Design
Maryland Institute College of Art
Montgomery College
   Germantown Campus
   Rockville Campus
   Takoma Park Campus
Morgan State University
Mount St. Mary's College
St. Mary's College of Maryland
Salisbury State University
Sojourner-Douglass College
Towson University
University of Baltimore
University of Maryland
   Baltimore County
   College Park
   Eastern Shore
Villa Julie College
Washington Bible College
Washington College
Western Maryland College
Wor-Wic Community College

Massachusetts

American International College
Anna Maria College
Assumption College
Atlantic Union College
Babson College
Bay Path College
Bay State College
Becker College
Bentley College
Berklee College of Music
Berkshire Community College
Boston Architectural Center
Boston College
Boston Conservatory
Boston University
Brandeis University
Bridgewater State College
Bristol Community College
Bunker Hill Community College
Cape Cod Community College
Clark University
College of the Holy Cross
Curry College
Dean College
Eastern Nazarene College
Elms College
Emerson College
Emmanuel College
Endicott College
Fisher College
Fitchburg State College
Framingham State College
Gordon College
Greenfield Community College
Hampshire College
Harvard College
Hebrew College
Hellenic College/Holy Cross
Holyoke Community College
Lasell College
Lesley College
Marian Court College
Massachusetts Bay Community College
Massachusetts College of Art

Massachusetts College of Liberal Arts
Massachusetts College of Pharmacy and Health Sciences
Massachusetts Institute of Technology
Massachusetts Maritime Academy
Merrimack College
Middlesex Community College
Montserrat College of Art
Mount Holyoke College
Mount Ida College
Mount Wachusett Community College
New England Conservatory of Music
Newbury College
Nichols College
North Shore Community College
Northeastern University
Northern Essex Community College
Pine Manor College
Quincy College
Regis College
Roxbury Community College
Salem State College
Simmons College
Simon's Rock College of Bard
Smith College
Springfield College
Stonehill College
Suffolk University
Tufts University
University of Massachusetts
   Amherst
   Boston
   Dartmouth
   Lowell
Wellesley College
Western New England College
Westfield State College
Wheaton College
Wheelock College
Williams College
Worcester Polytechnic Institute
Worcester State College

Michigan

Adrian College
Albion College
Alma College
Alpena Community College
Andrews University
Aquinas College
Baker College
   of Auburn Hills
   of Cadillac
   of Jackson
   of Mount Clemens
   of Muskegon
   of Owosso
   of Port Huron
Bay de Noc Community College
Calvin College
Center for Creative Studies: College of Art and Design
Central Michigan University
Cleary College
Concordia College
Cornerstone College and Grand Rapids Baptist Seminary
Davenport College of Business
Delta College
Detroit College of Business
Eastern Michigan University
Ferris State University
Glen Oaks Community College
Gogebic Community College
Grace Bible College
Grand Rapids Community College
Grand Valley State University
Great Lakes College
Hillsdale College
Hope College
Jackson Community College
Kalamazoo College
Kalamazoo Valley Community College
Kellogg Community College
Kendall College of Art and Design

Kirtland Community College
Lake Superior State University
Lansing Community College
Lawrence Technological University
Macomb Community College
Madonna University
Marygrove College
Michigan State University
Michigan Technological University
Mid Michigan Community College
Montcalm Community College
Mott Community College
Muskegon Community College
North Central Michigan College
Northern Michigan University
Northwestern Michigan College
Northwood University
Oakland Community College
Oakland University
Olivet College
Reformed Bible College
Rochester College
Saginaw Valley State University
St. Clair County Community College
Schoolcraft College
Siena Heights University
Southwestern Michigan College
Spring Arbor College
Suomi College
University of Detroit Mercy
University of Michigan
University of Michigan
   Dearborn
   Flint
Walsh College of Accountancy and Business Administration
Washtenaw Community College
Wayne County Community College
Wayne State University
West Shore Community College
Western Michigan University
William Tyndale College

Minnesota

Alexandria Technical College
Anoka-Ramsey Community College
Augsburg College
Bemidji State University
Bethel College
Carleton College
Central Lakes College
Century Community and Technical College
College of St. Benedict
College of St. Catherine-Minneapolis
College of St. Catherine: St. Paul Campus
College of St. Scholastica
College of Visual Arts
Concordia College: Moorhead
Concordia University: St. Paul
Crown College
Dakota County Technical College
Dunwoody Institute
Gustavus Adolphus College
Hamline University
Hennepin Technical College
Inver Hills Community College
Itasca Community College
Lake Superior College: A Community and Technical College
Macalester College
Martin Luther College
Mesabi Range Community and Technical College
Metropolitan State University
Minneapolis College of Art and Design
Minneapolis Community and Technical College
Minnesota Bible College
Minnesota State College - Southeast Technical
Minnesota State University, Mankato
Moorhead State University
NEI College of Technology

National American University
    St. Paul
North Central University
North Hennepin Community College
Northland Community & Technical
    College
Northwestern College
Pine Technical College
Ridgewater College: A Community and
    Technical College
Rochester Community and Technical
    College
St. Cloud State University
St. Cloud Technical College
St. John's University
St. Mary's University of Minnesota
St. Olaf College
St. Paul Technical College
South Central Technical College
Southwest State University
University of Minnesota
    Crookston
    Duluth
    Morris
    Twin Cities
University of St. Thomas
Vermilion Community College
Winona State University

Mississippi
Alcorn State University
Belhaven College
Blue Mountain College
Delta State University
Hinds Community College
Holmes Community College
Jackson State University
Mary Holmes College
Meridian Community College
Millsaps College
Mississippi College
Mississippi Gulf Coast Community
    College
    Jefferson Davis Campus
Mississippi State University
Mississippi University for Women
Mississippi Valley State University
Rust College
Tougaloo College
University of Mississippi
Wesley College
William Carey College

Missouri
Avila College
Central Methodist College
Central Missouri State University
College of the Ozarks
Columbia College
Crowder College
Culver-Stockton College
Drury University
East Central College
Evangel University
Fontbonne College
Hannibal-LaGrange College
Harris Stowe State College
Jefferson College
Kansas City Art Institute
Lincoln University
Lindenwood University
Longview Community College
Maple Woods Community College
Maryville University of Saint Louis
Mineral Area College
Missouri Baptist College
Missouri Southern State College
Missouri Valley College
Missouri Western State College
Moberly Area Community College
Northwest Missouri State University
Ozark Christian College
Ozarks Technical Community College
Park University

Penn Valley Community College
Rockhurst University
St. Charles County Community College
St. Louis Christian College
St. Louis University
Southeast Missouri State University
Southwest Baptist University
Southwest Missouri State University
St. Louis Community College
    St. Louis Community College at
        Florissant Valley
    St. Louis Community College at
        Meramec
State Fair Community College
Stephens College
Three Rivers Community College
Truman State University
University of Missouri
    Columbia
    Rolla
    St. Louis
Washington University
Webster University
Westminster College
William Jewell College
William Woods University

Montana
Blackfeet Community College
Carroll College
Dawson Community College
Dull Knife Memorial College
Flathead Valley Community College
Little Big Horn College
Miles Community College
Montana State University
    Billings
    Bozeman
    College of Technology-Great Falls
    Northern
Montana Tech of the University of
    Montana
Rocky Mountain College
Salish Kootenai College
University of Great Falls
University of Montana-Missoula
Western Montana College of The
    University of Montana

Nebraska
Bellevue University
Central Community College
Chadron State College
Clarkson College
College of Saint Mary
Concordia University
Creighton University
Dana College
Doane College
Grace University
Hastings College
Lincoln School of Commerce
Metropolitan Community College
Mid Plains Community College Area
Midland Lutheran College
Nebraska College of Technical
    Agriculture
Nebraska Methodist College of Nursing
    and Allied Health
Nebraska Wesleyan University
Northeast Community College
Peru State College
Southeast Community College
    Lincoln Campus
    Milford Campus
Union College
University of Nebraska
    Kearney
    Lincoln
    Omaha
Wayne State College

Nevada
Community College of Southern Nevada

University of Nevada
    Las Vegas
    Reno
Western Nevada Community College

New Hampshire
Colby-Sawyer College
College for Lifelong Learning
Daniel Webster College
Dartmouth College
Franklin Pierce College
Hesser College
Keene State College
McIntosh College
New England College
New Hampshire College
New Hampshire Community Technical
    College
    Berlin
    Claremont
    Laconia
    Manchester
    Nashua
    Stratham
New Hampshire Technical Institute
Notre Dame College
Plymouth State College of the University
    System of New Hampshire
Rivier College
St. Anselm College
University of New Hampshire
University of New Hampshire
    Manchester
White Pines College

New Jersey
Atlantic Cape Community College
Bergen Community College
Berkeley College
Bloomfield College
Brookdale Community College
Burlington County College
Caldwell College
Camden County College
Centenary College
College of St. Elizabeth
County College of Morris
Drew University
Essex County College
Fairleigh Dickinson University
Felician College
Georgian Court College
Hudson County Community College
Katharine Gibbs School
    Gibbs College
Kean University
Mercer County Community College
Middlesex County College
Monmouth University
Montclair State University
New Jersey City University
New Jersey Institute of Technology
Passaic County Community College
Princeton University
Ramapo College of New Jersey
Richard Stockton College of New Jersey
Rider University
Rowan University

Rutgers
    The State University of New Jersey:
        Camden College of Arts and
        Sciences
    The State University of New Jersey:
        College of Engineering
    The State University of New Jersey:
        College of Nursing
    The State University of New Jersey:
        Cook College
    The State University of New Jersey:
        Douglass College
    The State University of New Jersey:
        Livingston College
    The State University of New Jersey:
        Mason Gross School of the Arts
    The State University of New Jersey:
        Newark College of Arts and
        Sciences
    The State University of New Jersey:
        Rutgers College
    The State University of New Jersey:
        University College Camden
    The State University of New Jersey:
        University College New
        Brunswick
    The State University of New Jersey:
        University College Newark
St. Peter's College
Salem Community College
Seton Hall University
Stevens Institute of Technology
Sussex County Community College
The College of New Jersey
Union County College
University of Medicine and Dentistry of
    New Jersey
    School of Health Related
        Professions
Warren County Community College
William Paterson University of New
    Jersey

New Mexico
Albuquerque Technical-Vocational
    Institute
Clovis Community College
College of Santa Fe
College of the Southwest
Dona Ana Branch Community College of
    New Mexico State University
Eastern New Mexico University
Eastern New Mexico University
    Roswell Campus
Institute of American Indian Arts
New Mexico Highlands University
New Mexico Institute of Mining and
    Technology
New Mexico Junior College
New Mexico State University
New Mexico State University
    Carlsbad
Northern New Mexico Community
    College
San Juan College
Santa Fe Community College
University of New Mexico
Western New Mexico University

New York
Adelphi University
Adirondack Community College
Alfred University
Audrey Cohen College
Bard College
Barnard College
Berkeley College
Berkeley College of New York City
Briarcliffe College
Broome Community College
Bryant & Stratton Business Institute
    Albany
    Syracuse
Canisius College

City University of New York
  Baruch College
  Borough of Manhattan Community College
  Bronx Community College
  Brooklyn College
  City College
  College of Staten Island
  Hostos Community College
  Hunter College
  John Jay College of Criminal Justice
  Kingsborough Community College
  La Guardia Community College
  Lehman College
  Medgar Evers College
  New York City Technical College
  Queens College
  Queensborough Community College
  York College
Clinton Community College
Colgate University
College of Aeronautics
College of Insurance
College of Mount St. Vincent
College of New Rochelle
College of New Rochelle School of New Resources
College of St. Rose
Columbia University
  Columbia College
  Fu Foundation School of Engineering and Applied Science
  School of General Studies
Columbia-Greene Community College
Concordia College
Cooper Union for the Advancement of Science and Art
Cornell University
Corning Community College
Culinary Institute of America
D'Youville College
Daemen College
Dominican College of Blauvelt
Dowling College
Dutchess Community College
Eastman School of Music of the University of Rochester
Elmira College
Erie Community College
  City Campus
  North Campus
  South Campus
Eugene Lang College/New School University
Fashion Institute of Technology
Finger Lakes Community College
Five Towns College
Fordham University
Fulton-Montgomery Community College
Genesee Community College
Hamilton College
Hartwick College
Herkimer County Community College
Hilbert College
Hobart and William Smith Colleges
Hofstra University
Houghton College
Hudson Valley Community College
Interboro Institute
Iona College
Ithaca College
Jamestown Community College
Jefferson Community College
Jewish Theological Seminary of America
Katharine Gibbs School New York
Keuka College
Laboratory Institute of Merchandising
Le Moyne College
Long Island University
  Brooklyn Campus
  C. W. Post Campus
  Southampton College

Manhattan College
Manhattanville College
Maria College
Marist College
Marymount College
Marymount Manhattan College
Medaille College
Mercy College
Mohawk Valley Community College
Molloy College
Monroe College
Monroe Community College
Mount St. Mary College
Nassau Community College
Nazareth College of Rochester
New York Institute of Technology
New York State College of Ceramics at Alfred University
New York University
Niagara County Community College
Niagara University
North Country Community College
Nyack College
Onondaga Community College
Orange County Community College
Pace University
Pace University: Pleasantville/Briarcliff
Parsons School of Design
Polytechnic University
Polytechnic University Long Island Campus
Pratt Institute
Rensselaer Polytechnic Institute
Roberts Wesleyan College
Rochester Institute of Technology
Rockland Community College
Russell Sage College
Sage Junior College of Albany
St. Bonaventure University
St. Francis College
St. John Fisher College
St. John's University
St. Lawrence University
St. Thomas Aquinas College
Sarah Lawrence College
Schenectady County Community College
School of Visual Arts
Siena College
Skidmore College
St. Joseph's College
  St. Joseph's College
  St. Joseph's College: Suffolk Campus
State University of New York
  Albany
  Binghamton
  Buffalo
  College at Brockport
  College at Buffalo
  College at Cortland
  College at Fredonia
  College at Geneseo
  College at Old Westbury
  College at Oneonta
  College at Plattsburgh
  College at Potsdam
  College of Agriculture and Technology at Cobleskill
  College of Agriculture and Technology at Morrisville
  College of Environmental Science and Forestry
  College of Technology at Alfred
  College of Technology at Canton
  College of Technology at Delhi
  Empire State College
  Health Science Center at Stony Brook
  Institute of Technology at Utica/Rome
  Maritime College
  New Paltz
  Oswego
  Purchase
  Stony Brook

Suffolk County Community College
Syracuse University
Technical Career Institutes
Tompkins-Cortland Community College
Touro College
Trocaire College
Ulster County Community College
Union College
United States Merchant Marine Academy
University of Rochester
Utica College of Syracuse University
Vassar College
Villa Maria College of Buffalo
Wagner College
Webb Institute
Wells College
Westchester Business Institute
Westchester Community College
Wood Tobe-Coburn School

North Carolina

Alamance Community College
Appalachian State University
Asheville Buncombe Technical Community College
Barber-Scotia College
Barton College
Beaufort County Community College
Belmont Abbey College
Bennett College
Blue Ridge Community College
Brevard College
Brunswick Community College
Campbell University
Cape Fear Community College
Carteret Community College
Catawba College
Cecils College
Central Carolina Community College
Central Piedmont Community College
Chowan College
Cleveland Community College
Coastal Carolina Community College
Craven Community College
Duke University
Durham Technical Community College
East Carolina University
Elizabeth City State University
Elon College
Fayetteville State University
Forsyth Technical Community College
Gardner-Webb University
Gaston College
Greensboro College
Guilford College
Guilford Technical Community College
Halifax Community College
Haywood Community College
High Point University
James Sprunt Community College
John Wesley College
Johnson C. Smith University
Johnston Community College
Lees-McRae College
Lenoir-Rhyne College
Mars Hill College
Martin Community College
Mayland Community College
Meredith College
Methodist College
Montgomery Community College
Montreat College
Mount Olive College
North Carolina Agricultural and Technical State University
North Carolina Central University
North Carolina School of the Arts
North Carolina State University
North Carolina Wesleyan College
Peace College
Pfeiffer University
Piedmont Community College
Pitt Community College
Queens College
Randolph Community College

Richmond Community College
Roanoke-Chowan Community College
St. Andrews Presbyterian College
St. Augustine's College
Salem College
Sampson Community College
Sandhills Community College
Shaw University
South Piedmont Community College
Southeastern Community College
Southwestern Community College
Surry Community College
Tri-County Community College
University of North Carolina
  Asheville
  Chapel Hill
  Charlotte
  Greensboro
  Pembroke
  Wilmington
Vance-Granville Community College
Wake Forest University
Warren Wilson College
Wayne Community College
Western Carolina University
Wilkes Community College
Wilson Technical Community College
Wingate University
Winston-Salem State University

North Dakota

Bismarck State College
Dickinson State University
Jamestown College
Lake Region State College
Mayville State University
Minot State University
Minot State University: Bottineau Campus
North Dakota State College of Science
North Dakota State University
Trinity Bible College
University of Mary
University of North Dakota
Valley City State University
Williston State College

Ohio

Antioch College
Ashland University
Baldwin-Wallace College
Belmont Technical College
Bluffton College
Bowling Green State University
Bowling Green State University Firelands College
Bryant & Stratton College
Capital University
Case Western Reserve University
Cedarville College
Central Ohio Technical College
Central State University
Chatfield College
Cincinnati College of Mortuary Science
Cincinnati State Technical and Community College
Circleville Bible College
Clark State Community College
Cleveland Institute of Art
Cleveland State University
College of Mount St. Joseph
College of Wooster
Columbus College of Art and Design
Columbus State Community College
David N. Myers College
Davis College
Defiance College
Denison University
Edison State Community College
Franciscan University of Steubenville
Franklin University
Heidelberg College
Hiram College
Hocking Technical College

Jefferson Community College
John Carroll University
Kent State University
Kent State University
    Ashtabula Regional Campus
    East Liverpool Regional Campus
    Trumbull Campus
    Tuscarawas Campus
Kenyon College
Lake Erie College
Lima Technical College
Lourdes College
Malone College
Marietta College
Marion Technical College
Miami University
    Hamilton Campus
    Middletown Campus
    Oxford Campus
Miami-Jacobs College
Mount Union College
Mount Vernon Nazarene College
Muskingum Area Technical College
Muskingum College
North Central State College
Northwest State Community College
Notre Dame College of Ohio
Oberlin College
Ohio Dominican College
Ohio Institute of Photography and Technology
Ohio Northern University
Ohio State University
    Agricultural Technical Institute
    Columbus Campus
Ohio University
Ohio University
    Chillicothe Campus
    Lancaster Campus
Ohio Valley Business College
Ohio Wesleyan University
Otterbein College
Owens Community College
    Findlay Campus
    Toledo
RETS Tech Center
Shawnee State University
Sinclair Community College
Southern Ohio College
Southern State Community College
Stark State College of Technology
Terra Community College
Tiffin University
University of Akron
University of Cincinnati
University of Cincinnati
    Clermont College
    Raymond Walters College
University of Dayton
University of Findlay
University of Rio Grande
University of Toledo
Ursuline College
Walsh University
Washington State Community College
Wilberforce University
Wilmington College
Wittenberg University
Wright State University
Xavier University
Youngstown State University

Oklahoma
Cameron University
Connors State College
East Central University
Eastern Oklahoma State College
Langston University
Mid-America Bible College
Northeastern State University
Northwestern Oklahoma State University
Oklahoma Baptist University
Oklahoma Christian University of Science and Arts
Oklahoma City Community College
Oklahoma City University
Oklahoma Panhandle State University
Oklahoma State University
Oklahoma State University
    Okmulgee
Oral Roberts University
Redlands Community College
Rose State College
St. Gregory's University
Southeastern Oklahoma State University
Southern Nazarene University
Southwestern College of Christian Ministries
Southwestern Oklahoma State University
Tulsa Community College
University of Central Oklahoma
University of Oklahoma
University of Science and Arts of Oklahoma
University of Tulsa

Oregon
Art Institute
    of Portland
Central Oregon Community College
Clackamas Community College
Concordia University
Eastern Oregon University
Eugene Bible College
George Fox University
Lane Community College
Lewis & Clark College
Linfield College
Linn-Benton Community College
Marylhurst University
Mount Hood Community College
Multnomah Bible College
Northwest Christian College
Oregon Institute of Technology
Oregon State University
Pacific Northwest College of Art
Pacific University
Portland Community College
Portland State University
Reed College
Southern Oregon University
University of Oregon
University of Portland
Western Baptist College
Western Oregon University
Willamette University

Pennsylvania
Albright College
Allegheny College
Allentown College of St. Francis de Sales
Alvernia College
Art Institute
    of Philadelphia
    of Pittsburgh
Beaver College
Bloomsburg University of Pennsylvania
Bradley Academy for the Visual Arts
Bryn Athyn College of the New Church
Bryn Mawr College
Bucknell University
Bucks County Community College
Butler County Community College
Cabrini College
California University of Pennsylvania
Carlow College
Carnegie Mellon University
Cedar Crest College
Central Pennsylvania College
Chatham College
Chestnut Hill College
Cheyney University of Pennsylvania
Clarion University of Pennsylvania
College Misericordia
Community College of Allegheny County
Community College of Beaver County
Community College of Philadelphia
Delaware County Community College
Delaware Valley College
Dickinson College
Drexel University
Duquesne University
East Stroudsburg University of Pennsylvania
Eastern College
Edinboro University of Pennsylvania
Electronic Institutes: Middletown
Elizabethtown College
Franklin and Marshall College
Gannon University
Geneva College
Gettysburg College
Grove City College
Gwynedd-Mercy College
Harcum College
Harrisburg Area Community College
Holy Family College
Immaculata College
Indiana University of Pennsylvania
Johnson Technical Institute
Juniata College
King's College
Kutztown University of Pennsylvania
La Roche College
La Salle University
Lackawanna Junior College
Lafayette College
Lancaster Bible College
Laurel Business Institute
Lebanon Valley College of Pennsylvania
Lehigh Carbon Community College
Lehigh University
Lincoln University
Lock Haven University of Pennsylvania
Luzerne County Community College
Lycoming College
MCP Hahnemann University
Manor College
Mansfield University of Pennsylvania
Marywood University
Median School of Allied Health Careers
Mercyhurst College
Messiah College
Millersville University of Pennsylvania
Montgomery County Community College
Moore College of Art and Design
Moravian College
Mount Aloysius College
Muhlenberg College
Neumann College
Northampton County Area Community College
Peirce College
Penn State
    Abington
    Altoona
    Beaver
    Berks
    Delaware County
    Dubois
    Erie, The Behrend College
    Fayette
    Harrisburg
    Hazleton
    Lehigh Valley
    McKeesport
    Mont Alto
    New Kensington
    Schuylkill - Capital College
    Shenango
    University Park
    Wilkes-Barre
    Worthington Scranton
    York
Pennsylvania College of Technology
Pennsylvania Institute of Culinary Arts
Pennsylvania Institute of Technology
Philadelphia College of Bible
Philadelphia University
Pittsburgh Technical Institute
Point Park College
Reading Area Community College
Robert Morris College
Rosemont College
St. Francis College
St. Joseph's University
St. Vincent College
Sawyer School
Seton Hill College
Shippensburg University of Pennsylvania
Slippery Rock University of Pennsylvania
South Hills School of Business & Technology
Susquehanna University
Swarthmore College
Temple University
Thiel College
Thomas Jefferson University: College of Health Professions
Tri-State Business Institute
University of Pennsylvania
University of Pittsburgh
University of Pittsburgh
    Bradford
    Greensburg
    Johnstown
    Titusville
University of Scranton
University of the Arts
University of the Sciences in Philadelphia
Ursinus College
Valley Forge Christian College
Villanova University
Washington and Jefferson College
Waynesburg College
West Chester University of Pennsylvania
Westminster College
Westmoreland County Community College
Widener University
Wilkes University
Williamson Free School of Mechanical Trades
Wilson College
York College of Pennsylvania

Puerto Rico
American University of Puerto Rico
Atlantic College
Colegio Universitario del Este
Huertas Junior College
Humacao Community College
Inter American University of Puerto Rico
    Aguadilla Campus
    Arecibo Campus
    Barranquitas Campus
    Fajardo Campus
    Metropolitan Campus
    San German Campus
National College of Business and Technology
Pontifical Catholic University of Puerto Rico
Turabo University
Universidad Metropolitana
University of Puerto Rico
    Arecibo Campus
    Bayamon University College
    Humacao University College
    Mayaguez Campus
    Medical Sciences Campus
    Ponce University College
    Rio Piedras Campus
    Utuado
University of the Sacred Heart

Rhode Island
Brown University
Bryant College
Community College of Rhode Island
Johnson & Wales University
New England Institute of Technology
Providence College
Rhode Island College

Roger Williams University
Salve Regina University
University of Rhode Island

South Carolina

Aiken Technical College
Anderson College
Benedict College
Central Carolina Technical College
Charleston Southern University
Claflin University
Coastal Carolina University
Coker College
College of Charleston
Columbia College
Columbia International University
Converse College
Denmark Technical College
Erskine College
Florence-Darlington Technical College
Francis Marion University
Furman University
Horry-Georgetown Technical College
Lander University
Limestone College
Morris College
Newberry College
North Greenville College
Piedmont Technical College
Presbyterian College
South Carolina State University
Southern Wesleyan University
Technical College of the Lowcountry
The Citadel
Tri-County Technical College
Trident Technical College
University of South Carolina
University of South Carolina
    Aiken
    Spartanburg
    Union
Voorhees College
Winthrop University
Wofford College

South Dakota

Augustana College
Black Hills State University
Dakota State University
Dakota Wesleyan University
Kilian Community College
Mount Marty College
Northern State University
Sinte Gleska University
South Dakota School of Mines and Technology
South Dakota State University
University of South Dakota
Western Dakota Technical Institute

Tennessee

Austin Peay State University
Belmont University
Bethel College
Carson-Newman College
Chattanooga State Technical Community College
Christian Brothers University
Cleveland State Community College
Crichton College
Cumberland University
David Lipscomb University
Draughons Junior College of Business: Nashville
Dyersburg State Community College
East Tennessee State University
Fisk University
Freed-Hardeman University
Hiwassee College
Jackson State Community College
Johnson Bible College
King College
Knoxville Business College
Lambuth University

Lane College
LeMoyne-Owen College
Lee University
Lincoln Memorial University
Maryville College
Middle Tennessee State University
Milligan College
Nashville State Technical Institute
O'More College of Design
Pellissippi State Technical Community College
Rhodes College
Roane State Community College
Shelby State Community College
Southern Adventist University
Tennessee Technological University
Tennessee Temple University
Tennessee Wesleyan College
Trevecca Nazarene University
Tusculum College
Union University
University of Memphis
University of Tennessee
    Chattanooga
    Knoxville
    Martin
    Memphis
University of the South
Vanderbilt University

Texas

Abilene Christian University
Alvin Community College
Angelina College
Angelo State University
Austin College
Austin Community College
Baylor University
Brazosport College
Central Texas College
Coastal Bend College
College of the Mainland
Collin County Community College District
Concordia University at Austin
Dallas Baptist University
Del Mar College
East Texas Baptist University
El Paso Community College
Galveston College
Grayson County College
Hill College
Houston Baptist University
Houston Community College System
Howard Payne University
Huston-Tillotson College
Institute for Christian Studies
Jarvis Christian College
Kilgore College
Lamar State College at Port Arthur
Lamar University
LeTourneau University
Lee College
Lubbock Christian University
McMurry University
Midland College
Midwestern State University
Navarro College
North Lake College
Northwood University: Texas Campus
Odessa College
Our Lady of the Lake University of San Antonio
Palo Alto College
Paul Quinn College
Prairie View A&M University
Rice University
Richland College
St. Edward's University
St. Mary's University
St. Philip's College
Sam Houston State University
San Antonio College
San Jacinto College
    North

Schreiner College
Southern Methodist University
Southwest Texas State University
Southwestern Adventist University
Southwestern Assemblies of God University
Southwestern University
Stephen F. Austin State University
Sul Ross State University
Tarleton State University
Texas A&M International University
Texas A&M University
Texas A&M University
    Commerce
    Corpus Christi
    Galveston
    Kingsville
    Texarkana
Texas Christian University
Texas College
Texas Lutheran University
Texas Southern University
Texas State Technical College
    Harlingen
    Sweetwater
Texas Tech University
Texas Wesleyan University
Texas Woman's University
Trinity University
Trinity Valley Community College
Tyler Junior College
University of Dallas
University of Houston
University of Houston
    Clear Lake
    Downtown
    Victoria
University of Mary Hardin-Baylor
University of North Texas
University of St. Thomas
University of Texas
    Arlington
    Austin
    Brownsville
    Dallas
    El Paso
    Medical Branch at Galveston
    Pan American
    San Antonio
    Southwestern Medical Center at Dallas
    Tyler
    of the Permian Basin
University of the Incarnate Word
Vernon Regional Junior College
Wayland Baptist University
Weatherford College
West Texas A&M University
Western Texas College
Wiley College

Utah

Brigham Young University
Dixie State College of Utah
LDS Business College
Mountain West College
Salt Lake Community College
Southern Utah University
University of Utah
Utah State University
Weber State University
Westminster College

Vermont

Bennington College
Burlington College
Castleton State College
Champlain College
College of St. Joseph in Vermont
Community College of Vermont
Goddard College
Green Mountain College
Johnson State College
Landmark College

Lyndon State College
Marlboro College
Middlebury College
New England Culinary Institute
Norwich University
St. Michael's College
Southern Vermont College
Sterling College
Trinity College of Vermont
University of Vermont
Vermont Technical College

Virginia

Averett College
Blue Ridge Community College
Bluefield College
Bridgewater College
Central Virginia Community College
Christendom College
Christopher Newport University
College of William and Mary
Dabney S. Lancaster Community College
Danville Community College
ECPI College of Technology
Eastern Mennonite University
Emory & Henry College
Ferrum College
George Mason University
Hampden-Sydney College
Hampton University
Hollins University
J. Sargeant Reynolds Community College
James Madison University
Liberty University
Longwood College
Lynchburg College
Mary Baldwin College
Mary Washington College
Mountain Empire Community College
National Business College
Norfolk State University
Northern Virginia Community College
Old Dominion University
Patrick Henry Community College
Paul D. Camp Community College
Radford University
Randolph-Macon College
Randolph-Macon Woman's College
Roanoke College
St. Paul's College
Shenandoah University
Southside Virginia Community College
Southwest Virginia Community College
Sweet Briar College
Thomas Nelson Community College
Tidewater Community College
University of Richmond
University of Virginia
University of Virginia's College at Wise
Virginia Commonwealth University
Virginia Highlands Community College
Virginia Intermont College
Virginia Military Institute
Virginia Polytechnic Institute and State University
Virginia State University
Virginia Union University
Virginia Wesleyan College
Virginia Western Community College
Washington and Lee University
Wytheville Community College

Washington

Art Institute of Seattle
Central Washington University
Centralia College
Clark College
Columbia Basin College
Cornish College of the Arts
Eastern Washington University
Edmonds Community College
Everett Community College
Evergreen State College

Gonzaga University
Grays Harbor College
Green River Community College
Henry Cogswell College
Heritage College
Highline Community College
Lake Washington Technical College
North Seattle Community College
Northwest Indian College
Pacific Lutheran University
Peninsula College
Pierce College
Puget Sound Christian College
Renton Technical College
St. Martin's College
Seattle Central Community College
Seattle Pacific University
Seattle University
Shoreline Community College
Skagit Valley College
South Puget Sound Community College
Spokane Community College
Spokane Falls Community College
Tacoma Community College
University of Puget Sound
University of Washington
Walla Walla College
Walla Walla Community College
Washington State University
Wenatchee Valley College
Western Washington University
Whatcom Community College
Whitman College
Whitworth College
Yakima Valley Community College

West Virginia
Alderson-Broaddus College
Bethany College
Bluefield State College
College of West Virginia
Davis and Elkins College
Glenville State College
Marshall University
Salem-Teikyo University
Shepherd College
Southern West Virginia Community and Technical College
University of Charleston
West Liberty State College
West Virginia Northern Community College
West Virginia State College
West Virginia University
West Virginia University Institute of Technology
West Virginia University Parkersburg
West Virginia Wesleyan College
Wheeling Jesuit University

Wisconsin
Alverno College
Beloit College
Blackhawk Technical College
Bryant & Stratton College
Cardinal Stritch University
Carroll College
Carthage College
Chippewa Valley Technical College
Concordia University Wisconsin
Gateway Technical College
Lakeland College
Lakeshore Technical College
Lawrence University
Madison Area Technical College
Marian College of Fond du Lac
Marquette University
Milwaukee Area Technical College
Milwaukee Institute of Art & Design
Milwaukee School of Engineering
Moraine Park Technical College
Mount Mary College
Mount Senario College
Nicolet Area Technical College
Northeast Wisconsin Technical College
Northland College
Ripon College
St. Norbert College
Silver Lake College
Southwest Wisconsin Technical College
University of Wisconsin
    Barron County
    Eau Claire
    Green Bay
    La Crosse
    Madison
    Marathon County
    Marinette
    Marshfield/Wood County
    Milwaukee
    Oshkosh
    Parkside
    Platteville
    River Falls
    Stevens Point
    Stout
    Superior
    Washington County
    Whitewater
Viterbo University
Western Wisconsin Technical College
Wisconsin Indianhead Technical College
Wisconsin Lutheran College

Wyoming
Casper College
Eastern Wyoming College
Laramie County Community College
Northwest College
Sheridan College
University of Wyoming
Western Wyoming Community College

Semester at sea

Alabama
Birmingham-Southern College

Arizona
University of Arizona

California
California State University Monterey Bay
Chapman University
Marymount College
University of California San Diego
University of San Diego
Westmont College
Whittier College

Colorado
Colorado College
Colorado State University
University of Colorado
    Boulder
    Denver
University of Northern Colorado
Western State College of Colorado

Connecticut
Connecticut College
Fairfield University
Manchester Community-Technical College
Trinity College
University of Connecticut
Wesleyan University

Delaware
Goldey-Beacom College

Florida
Barry University
Eckerd College
Flagler College
University of Florida
University of Miami

Georgia
Agnes Scott College
Emory University
Morehouse College
Oxford College of Emory University

Illinois
Barat College

Indiana
DePauw University
Indiana University Bloomington
University of Indianapolis
Wabash College

Iowa
Cornell College
Drake University

Kentucky
Murray State University

Maine
Bates College
Bowdoin College
Colby College
College of the Atlantic
Maine Maritime Academy
Unity College
University of Maine

Maryland
Hood College
Salisbury State University
University of Maryland College Park

Massachusetts
Babson College
Boston University
College of the Holy Cross
Massachusetts Maritime Academy
Mount Holyoke College
Northeastern University
Pine Manor College
Simmons College
Smith College
Tufts University
Wellesley College

Michigan
Albion College
Central Michigan University

Minnesota
Hamline University

Missouri
Culver-Stockton College
Maryville University of Saint Louis
Stephens College
Westminster College
William Woods University

Nebraska
Dana College

New Hampshire
Colby-Sawyer College
Dartmouth College
Keene State College
University of New Hampshire
University of New Hampshire Manchester

New Jersey
Drew University
Richard Stockton College of New Jersey
Rowan University
The College of New Jersey

New York
Alfred University
Bard College
Colgate University
Cornell University
Hobart and William Smith Colleges
Long Island University
    C. W. Post Campus
    Southampton College
Manhattanville College
New York State College of Ceramics at Alfred University
Skidmore College
State University of New York Maritime College

Ohio
Case Western Reserve University
Denison University
Heidelberg College
Kenyon College
Mount Union College
Ohio State University Columbus Campus
Otterbein College
University of Dayton
Wittenberg University

Oklahoma
Oklahoma State University

Oregon
Linfield College
University of Oregon
Willamette University

Pennsylvania
Allegheny College
Drexel University
Franklin and Marshall College
Gettysburg College
Lafayette College
Moravian College
St. Francis College
Susquehanna University
University of Pittsburgh
University of Pittsburgh
    Bradford
    Greensburg
    Johnstown
    Titusville
University of Scranton
Ursinus College
Westminster College

Puerto Rico
University of the Sacred Heart

Rhode Island
Roger Williams University
Salve Regina University

South Carolina
College of Charleston
Presbyterian College

Tennessee
University of the South

Texas
St. Edward's University
Southern Methodist University
Texas A&M University Galveston
Texas Christian University
Trinity University

University of Houston

Utah
University of Utah
Weber State University

Vermont
Middlebury College
St. Michael's College
Southern Vermont College

Virginia
College of William and Mary
Hampden-Sydney College
Mary Baldwin College
University of Richmond
Virginia Commonwealth University

Washington
Western Washington University

West Virginia
West Virginia University

Wisconsin
Viterbo University

Student designed major

Alabama
Auburn University at Montgomery
Birmingham-Southern College
Huntingdon College
Lawson State Community College
Snead State Community College
Spring Hill College
University of Alabama
University of Alabama
　Birmingham
University of South Alabama

Alaska
Alaska Pacific University
University of Alaska
　Anchorage
　Fairbanks
　Southeast

Arizona
Central Arizona College
Pima Community College
Prescott College
University of Arizona

Arkansas
Garland County Community College
Harding University
Hendrix College
John Brown University
Lyon College
North Arkansas College
University of Arkansas
University of Arkansas
　Little Rock

California
Academy of Art College
Antioch Southern California
　Los Angeles
　Santa Barbara
Biola University
California College of Arts and Crafts
California Institute of Technology
California Institute of the Arts
California Lutheran University
California State University
　Bakersfield
　Chico
　Dominguez Hills
　Fresno
　Fullerton
　Hayward
　Long Beach
　Los Angeles
　Monterey Bay
　Northridge
　Sacramento
　San Marcos
　Stanislaus
Chabot College
Claremont McKenna College
College of Notre Dame
College of the Sequoias
College of the Siskiyous
Concordia University
Cuesta College
Cuyamaca College
Dominican University of California
Fresno Pacific University
Grossmont Community College
Harvey Mudd College
Holy Names College
Hope International University
Humboldt State University
John F. Kennedy University
La Sierra University
Las Positas College
Los Angeles Pierce College
Loyola Marymount University
Mendocino College
Menlo College
Mills College
MiraCosta College
Mount St. Mary's College
Occidental College
Orange Coast College
Pacific Oaks College
Pacific Union College
Pepperdine University
Pitzer College
Pomona College
Saddleback College
St. Mary's College of California
San Diego City College
San Diego Mesa College
San Diego State University
San Francisco State University
San Joaquin Delta College
San Jose State University
Santa Clara University
Scripps College
Simpson College
Sonoma State University
Stanford University
University of California
　Berkeley
　Davis
　Los Angeles
　Riverside
　San Diego
　Santa Barbara
　Santa Cruz
University of Judaism
University of La Verne
University of Redlands
University of San Francisco
University of Southern California
University of the Pacific
West Los Angeles College
Westmont College
Whittier College

Colorado
Adams State College
Colorado College
Colorado Northwestern Community
　College
Fort Lewis College
Lamar Community College
Mesa State College
Metropolitan State College of Denver
Morgan Community College
Naropa University
Regis University
United States Air Force Academy
University of Colorado
　Boulder
　Denver
University of Denver
University of Northern Colorado
Western State College of Colorado

Connecticut
Albertus Magnus College
Central Connecticut State University
Connecticut College
Eastern Connecticut State University
Manchester Community-Technical
　College
Middlesex Community-Technical
　College
Naugatuck Valley Community-Technical
　College
Quinnipiac University
Sacred Heart University
St. Joseph College
Southern Connecticut State University
Teikyo Post University
Trinity College
University of Bridgeport
University of Connecticut
University of Hartford
University of New Haven
Wesleyan University
Western Connecticut State University
Yale University

Delaware
Delaware State University
University of Delaware

District of Columbia
American University
George Washington University
Georgetown University
Howard University
Trinity College

Florida
Brevard Community College
Eckerd College
Florida Atlantic University
Florida Christian College
Florida National College
Jacksonville University
Jones College
New College of the University of South
　Florida
Palm Beach Atlantic College
Rollins College
Stetson University
University of Florida
University of South Florida
Valencia Community College

Georgia
Agnes Scott College
Atlanta College of Art
Berry College
Clayton College and State University
Covenant College
Fort Valley State University
Georgia College and State University
Georgia Institute of Technology
Georgia Southern University
Georgia State University
Mercer University
Oglethorpe University
Oxford College of Emory University
Shorter College
Spelman College
Toccoa Falls College
University of Georgia
Wesleyan College

Hawaii
Brigham Young University
　Hawaii
Chaminade University of Honolulu
Hawaii Pacific University
University of Hawaii
　Hilo
　Honolulu Community College
　Manoa
　West Oahu

Idaho
Albertson College of Idaho
Boise State University
Idaho State University
Northwest Nazarene University
University of Idaho

Illinois
Barat College
Blackburn College
Bradley University
Carl Sandburg College
Chicago State University
City Colleges of Chicago
　Olive-Harvey College
College of DuPage
College of Lake County
Columbia College
Dominican University
Eureka College
Governors State University
Greenville College
Highland Community College
Illinois Eastern Community Colleges
　Frontier Community College
　Lincoln Trail College
　Olney Central College
　Wabash Valley College
Illinois State University
Illinois Wesleyan University
John Wood Community College
Judson College
Kaskaskia College
Kendall College
Knox College
Lake Forest College
Lewis University
Lewis and Clark Community College
McKendree College
Millikin University
Monmouth College
Morton College
North Central College
North Park University
Northeastern Illinois University
Northern Illinois University
Northwestern University
Olivet Nazarene University
Principia College
Quincy University
Rock Valley College
Rockford College
Roosevelt University
St. Xavier University
Sauk Valley Community College
School of the Art Institute of Chicago
Southeastern Illinois College
Southern Illinois University
　Edwardsville
University of Chicago
University of Illinois
　Chicago
　Springfield
　Urbana-Champaign
University of St. Francis
Western Illinois University
Wheaton College

Indiana
Anderson University
Ball State University
Calumet College of St. Joseph
DePauw University

Student designed major

Earlham College
Goshen College
Indiana University
    Bloomington
    Northwest
Indiana University--Purdue University
    Indiana University-Purdue
        University Fort Wayne
Indiana Wesleyan University
Manchester College
Purdue University
Saint Mary's College
St. Joseph's College
St. Mary-of-the-Woods College
Taylor University
University of Indianapolis
University of Notre Dame
Valparaiso University
Vincennes University

Iowa
Briar Cliff College
Buena Vista University
Central College
Clarke College
Coe College
Cornell College
Dordt College
Drake University
Graceland University
Grand View College
Grinnell College
Iowa State University
Iowa Wesleyan College
Kirkwood Community College
Loras College
Luther College
Marycrest International University
Morningside College
Mount Mercy College
Northeast Iowa Community College
Northwestern College
St. Ambrose University
Simpson College
University of Dubuque
University of Iowa
University of Northern Iowa
Upper Iowa University
Wartburg College

Kansas
Allen County Community College
Baker University
Benedictine College
Bethany College
Central Christian College
Coffeyville Community College
Cowley County Community College
Emporia State University
Garden City Community College
Kansas Wesleyan University
McPherson College
Newman University
Ottawa University
Pittsburg State University
St. Mary College
Southwestern College
Sterling College
Tabor College
University of Kansas
Washburn University of Topeka

Kentucky
Berea College
Brescia University
Centre College
Eastern Kentucky University
Georgetown College
Kentucky State University
Midway College
Morehead State University
Thomas More College
Transylvania University
University of Kentucky

University of Louisville
Western Kentucky University

Louisiana
Centenary College of Louisiana
Delgado Community College
Louisiana State University and
   Agricultural and Mechanical College
Loyola University New Orleans
Northwestern State University
Nunez Community College
Tulane University
University of Louisiana at Lafayette
University of New Orleans

Maine
Bates College
Bowdoin College
Colby College
College of the Atlantic
Eastern Maine Technical College
Husson College
Maine College of Art
Unity College
University of Maine
    Farmington
    Fort Kent
    Presque Isle
University of New England
University of Southern Maine
Washington County Technical College

Maryland
Anne Arundel Community College
Chesapeake College
College of Notre Dame of Maryland
Columbia Union College
Goucher College
Hood College
Johns Hopkins University
Maryland Institute College of Art
Montgomery College
    Germantown Campus
    Rockville Campus
    Takoma Park Campus
Mount St. Mary's College
St. Mary's College of Maryland
Salisbury State University
Towson University
University of Baltimore
University of Maryland
    Baltimore County
    College Park
Villa Julie College
Washington College
Western Maryland College

Massachusetts
Amherst College
Anna Maria College
Assumption College
Babson College
Berklee College of Music
Berkshire Community College
Boston College
Boston University
Brandeis University
Bristol Community College
Clark University
College of the Holy Cross
Curry College
Dean College
Elms College
Emerson College
Emmanuel College
Fitchburg State College
Gordon College
Hampshire College
Harvard College
Hebrew College
Holyoke Community College
Lasell College
Lesley College
Massachusetts College of Art

Massachusetts College of Liberal Arts
Merrimack College
Montserrat College of Art
Mount Holyoke College
Mount Ida College
New England College of Finance
Northeastern University
Pine Manor College
Regis College
Salem State College
Simmons College
Simon's Rock College of Bard
Smith College
Stonehill College
Tufts University
University of Massachusetts
    Amherst
    Boston
    Dartmouth
Wellesley College
Wentworth Institute of Technology
Western New England College
Westfield State College
Wheaton College
Williams College
Worcester Polytechnic Institute

Michigan
Adrian College
Albion College
Alma College
Andrews University
Aquinas College
Calvin College
Central Michigan University
Concordia College
Delta College
Eastern Michigan University
Gogebic Community College
Grand Valley State University
Hope College
Lake Superior State University
Marygrove College
Michigan State University
Northern Michigan University
Oakland University
Olivet College
Saginaw Valley State University
Siena Heights University
Southwestern Michigan College
Spring Arbor College
University of Michigan
University of Michigan
    Dearborn
    Flint
Wayne State University
Western Michigan University

Minnesota
Augsburg College
Bethel College
Carleton College
Century Community and Technical
   College
College of St. Benedict
College of St. Catherine: St. Paul
   Campus
College of St. Scholastica
Gustavus Adolphus College
Hamline University
Macalester College
Metropolitan State University
Minnesota Bible College
Moorhead State University
North Central University
Ridgewater College: A Community and
   Technical College
St. Cloud State University
St. John's University
St. Mary's University of Minnesota
St. Olaf College
Southwest State University

University of Minnesota
    Duluth
    Morris
    Twin Cities
University of St. Thomas
Winona State University

Mississippi
Mississippi State University
Tougaloo College

Missouri
Central Methodist College
Central Missouri State University
College of the Ozarks
Columbia College
Culver-Stockton College
Drury University
Fontbonne College
Hannibal-LaGrange College
Lincoln University
Lindenwood University
Missouri Baptist College
Missouri Valley College
Park University
St. Louis University
Southwest Missouri State University
Stephens College
University of Missouri
    Columbia
    Kansas City
    St. Louis
Washington University
Webster University
Westminster College
William Jewell College
William Woods University

Montana
Carroll College
Miles Community College
Montana State University
    Billings
    Bozeman
Montana Tech of the University of
   Montana
Rocky Mountain College

Nebraska
Chadron State College
Clarkson College
Dana College
Doane College
Hastings College
Lincoln School of Commerce
Midland Lutheran College
Union College
University of Nebraska
    Lincoln
    Omaha
Wayne State College

Nevada
Community College of Southern Nevada
University of Nevada
    Las Vegas

New Hampshire
Colby-Sawyer College
College for Lifelong Learning
Dartmouth College
Franklin Pierce College
Hesser College
Keene State College
New England College
New Hampshire Community Technical
   College
    Manchester
    Nashua
Plymouth State College of the University
   System of New Hampshire
University of New Hampshire

Student designed major

University of New Hampshire
   Manchester

New Jersey
Bloomfield College
Caldwell College
Centenary College
College of St. Elizabeth
Drew University
Fairleigh Dickinson University
Felician College
Monmouth University
Princeton University
Ramapo College of New Jersey
Richard Stockton College of New Jersey
Rutgers
   The State University of New Jersey:
     Camden College of Arts and
     Sciences
   The State University of New Jersey:
     College of Engineering
   The State University of New Jersey:
     Cook College
   The State University of New Jersey:
     Douglass College
   The State University of New Jersey:
     Livingston College
   The State University of New Jersey:
     Newark College of Arts and
     Sciences
   The State University of New Jersey:
     Rutgers College
   The State University of New Jersey:
     University College Camden
   The State University of New Jersey:
     University College New
     Brunswick
   The State University of New Jersey:
     University College Newark
St. Peter's College
Union County College

New Mexico
College of Santa Fe
Eastern New Mexico University
New Mexico Institute of Mining and
   Technology
New Mexico State University
New Mexico State University
   Carlsbad
University of New Mexico
Western New Mexico University

New York
Alfred University
Bard College
Barnard College
Broome Community College
Canisius College
City University of New York
   Baruch College
   Hunter College
   La Guardia Community College
   Lehman College
   Queens College
Clarkson University
Colgate University
College of Mount St. Vincent
College of New Rochelle
College of New Rochelle
   School of New Resources
College of St. Rose
Columbia University
   Columbia College
   School of General Studies
Columbia-Greene Community College
Concordia College
Cooper Union for the Advancement of
   Science and Art
Cornell University
Daemen College
Eastman School of Music of the
   University of Rochester
Elmira College

Erie Community College
   City Campus
   North Campus
   South Campus
Eugene Lang College/New School
   University
Fordham University
Fulton-Montgomery Community College
Hamilton College
Hartwick College
Hobart and William Smith Colleges
Hofstra University
Hudson Valley Community College
Ithaca College
Jefferson Community College
Jewish Theological Seminary of America
Keuka College
Long Island University
   Brooklyn Campus
   C. W. Post Campus
   Southampton College
Manhattanville College
Marist College
Marymount College
Medaille College
Mercy College
Mohawk Valley Community College
Molloy College
New York Institute of Technology
New York State College of Ceramics at
   Alfred University
New York University
Niagara County Community College
North Country Community College
Pratt Institute
Rensselaer Polytechnic Institute
Rochester Institute of Technology
Rockland Community College
Russell Sage College
Sage Junior College of Albany
St. Bonaventure University
St. Lawrence University
Sarah Lawrence College
Skidmore College
State University of New York
   Albany
   Binghamton
   Buffalo
   College at Brockport
   College at Cortland
   College at Fredonia
   College at Plattsburgh
   College at Potsdam
   College of Agriculture and
     Technology at Morrisville
   College of Technology at Alfred
   College of Technology at Canton
   College of Technology at Delhi
   Empire State College
   Maritime College
   New Paltz
   Purchase
   Stony Brook
Syracuse University
Touro College
Ulster County Community College
Union College
University of Rochester
Vassar College
Wells College
Westchester Community College

North Carolina
Appalachian State University
Bennett College
Brevard College
Catawba College
Catawba Valley Community College
Craven Community College
Davidson College
Duke University
Elon College
Greensboro College
Guilford College
High Point University

Lees-McRae College
Lenoir-Rhyne College
Mars Hill College
Meredith College
Methodist College
North Carolina State University
Queens College
Richmond Community College
Rockingham Community College
St. Andrews Presbyterian College
Salem College
Shaw University
Surry Community College
University of North Carolina
   Asheville
   Chapel Hill
   Greensboro
Warren Wilson College
Western Carolina University

North Dakota
Dickinson State University
Jamestown College
Mayville State University
North Dakota State College of Science
North Dakota State University
Valley City State University
Williston State College

Ohio
Antioch College
Baldwin-Wallace College
Belmont Technical College
Bluffton College
Bowling Green State University
Bowling Green State University
   Firelands College
Capital University
Case Western Reserve University
Cincinnati State Technical and
   Community College
Circleville Bible College
Clark State Community College
Cleveland State University
College of Wooster
Columbus State Community College
David N. Myers College
Defiance College
Denison University
Edison State Community College
Franklin University
Heidelberg College
Hiram College
Hocking Technical College
John Carroll University
Kent State University
Kent State University
   Ashtabula Regional Campus
   East Liverpool Regional Campus
   Stark Campus
   Trumbull Campus
   Tuscarawas Campus
Kenyon College
Lake Erie College
Lima Technical College
Lourdes College
Malone College
Marietta College
Marion Technical College
Miami University
   Hamilton Campus
   Middletown Campus
   Oxford Campus
Mount Union College
Muskingum Area Technical College
Muskingum College
North Central State College
Northwest State Community College
Notre Dame College of Ohio
Oberlin College
Ohio Dominican College

Ohio State University
   Agricultural Technical Institute
   Columbus Campus
   Marion Campus
   Newark Campus
Ohio University
Ohio University
   Chillicothe Campus
   Eastern Campus
   Lancaster Campus
   Southern Campus at Ironton
   Zanesville Campus
Ohio Wesleyan University
Otterbein College
Owens Community College
   Findlay Campus
   Toledo
Shawnee State University
Sinclair Community College
Southern State Community College
Stark State College of Technology
Terra Community College
Union Institute
University of Akron
University of Akron
   Wayne College
University of Cincinnati
   Raymond Walters College
University of Findlay
University of Rio Grande
University of Toledo
Ursuline College
Washington State Community College
Wilmington College
Wittenberg University
Wright State University
Youngstown State University

Oklahoma
Cameron University
Oklahoma Baptist University
Oklahoma City Community College
Oklahoma City University
Oklahoma State University
Oral Roberts University
St. Gregory's University
Southern Nazarene University
University of Oklahoma
University of Science and Arts of
   Oklahoma
University of Tulsa

Oregon
Central Oregon Community College
Clatsop Community College
Eastern Oregon University
George Fox University
Lewis & Clark College
Linfield College
Marylhurst University
Oregon State University
Pacific Northwest College of Art
Reed College
Southern Oregon University
University of Portland
Western Oregon University
Willamette University

Pennsylvania
Albright College
Allegheny College
Alvernia College
Beaver College
Bryn Mawr College
Bucknell University
Bucks County Community College
Cabrini College
California University of Pennsylvania
Carlow College
Carnegie Mellon University
Cedar Crest College
Chatham College
Chestnut Hill College
College Misericordia

Delaware County Community College
Dickinson College
Duquesne University
East Stroudsburg University of Pennsylvania
Eastern College
Edinboro University of Pennsylvania
Franklin and Marshall College
Geneva College
Gettysburg College
Grove City College
Harrisburg Area Community College
Haverford College
Juniata College
King's College
Kutztown University of Pennsylvania
La Salle University
Lafayette College
Lebanon Valley College of Pennsylvania
Lock Haven University of Pennsylvania
Lycoming College
Mansfield University of Pennsylvania
Marywood University
Mercyhurst College
Messiah College
Montgomery County Community College
Moore College of Art and Design
Moravian College
Mount Aloysius College
Muhlenberg College
Neumann College
Northampton County Area Community College
Penn State
   Abington
   Altoona
   Beaver
   Delaware County
   Dubois
   Fayette
   Hazleton
   McKeesport
   Mont Alto
   New Kensington
   Shenango
   University Park
   Wilkes-Barre
   Worthington Scranton
   York
Pennsylvania College of Technology
Point Park College
Reading Area Community College
Rosemont College
St. Francis College
St. Joseph's University
Seton Hill College
Susquehanna University
Swarthmore College
Temple University
University of Pennsylvania
University of Pittsburgh
University of Pittsburgh
   Bradford
   Greensburg
   Johnstown
Ursinus College
Washington and Jefferson College
West Chester University of Pennsylvania
Westminster College
Westmoreland County Community College
Widener University
Wilkes University
Wilson College

Puerto Rico
Atlantic College

Rhode Island
Brown University
New England Institute of Technology
Providence College
Rhode Island College
Roger Williams University
University of Rhode Island

South Carolina
Anderson College
Coastal Carolina University
Coker College
Columbia College
Furman University
Lander University
Limestone College
Newberry College
North Greenville College
Tri-County Technical College
University of South Carolina
University of South Carolina
   Aiken
   Beaufort
   Salkehatchie Regional Campus
   Spartanburg
   Sumter
   Union
Wofford College

South Dakota
Augustana College
Dakota State University
Dakota Wesleyan University
Mount Marty College
Northern State University
University of South Dakota

Tennessee
Bethel College
Carson-Newman College
Chattanooga State Technical Community College
Crichton College
Fisk University
Freed-Hardeman University
Lambuth University
LeMoyne-Owen College
Maryville College
Middle Tennessee State University
Nashville State Technical Institute
Rhodes College
Tennessee Wesleyan College
Tusculum College
University of Memphis
University of Tennessee
   Knoxville
   Martin
University of the South
Vanderbilt University

Texas
Abilene Christian University
Austin College
Baylor University
Jarvis Christian College
McMurry University
Midland College
Rice University
Schreiner College
Southern Methodist University
Southwestern Adventist University
Southwestern University
Stephen F. Austin State University
Texas A&M University
   Texarkana
Texas Christian University
Texas Lutheran University
Texas Tech University
University of Dallas
University of Houston
   Clear Lake
University of North Texas
University of Texas
   Arlington
   Austin
   Dallas
   Tyler
West Texas A&M University

Utah
University of Utah
Utah State University
Weber State University
Westminster College

Vermont
Bennington College
Burlington College
Castleton State College
Community College of Vermont
Goddard College
Green Mountain College
Marlboro College
Middlebury College
Norwich University
St. Michael's College
Southern Vermont College
Trinity College of Vermont
University of Vermont

Virginia
Averett College
Bluefield College
Christopher Newport University
College of William and Mary
Emory & Henry College
Ferrum College
George Mason University
Hollins University
Liberty University
Mary Baldwin College
Mary Washington College
Mountain Empire Community College
Northern Virginia Community College
Old Dominion University
Radford University
Randolph-Macon Woman's College
St. Paul's College
Sweet Briar College
University of Richmond
University of Virginia
University of Virginia's College at Wise
Virginia Commonwealth University
Virginia Polytechnic Institute and State University
Virginia Wesleyan College
Washington and Lee University

Washington
Antioch University Seattle
Central Washington University
Centralia College
Eastern Washington University
Everett Community College
Evergreen State College
Gonzaga University
Heritage College
Highline Community College
Northwest Indian College
Pacific Lutheran University
Pierce College
Renton Technical College
Seattle Pacific University
Spokane Community College
University of Puget Sound
University of Washington
Wenatchee Valley College
Western Washington University
Whatcom Community College
Whitman College
Whitworth College

West Virginia
Bethany College
College of West Virginia
Concord College
Davis and Elkins College
Glenville State College
Marshall University
University of Charleston
West Liberty State College
West Virginia University
West Virginia University Institute of Technology
West Virginia Wesleyan College
Wheeling Jesuit University

Wisconsin
Beloit College
Blackhawk Technical College
Cardinal Stritch University
Carroll College
Carthage College
Chippewa Valley Technical College
Concordia University Wisconsin
Lakeshore Technical College
Lawrence University
Marian College of Fond du Lac
Mount Mary College
Nicolet Area Technical College
Northland College
Ripon College
St. Norbert College
Silver Lake College
University of Wisconsin
   Green Bay
   Madison
   Milwaukee
   Oshkosh
   Platteville
   River Falls
   Stevens Point
   Superior
   Whitewater
Viterbo University
Wisconsin Lutheran College

Wyoming
Central Wyoming College
University of Wyoming

Study abroad

Alabama
Auburn University
Auburn University at Montgomery
Birmingham-Southern College
Huntingdon College
Northeast Alabama Community College
Oakwood College
Samford University
Spring Hill College
Talladega College
Troy State University
University of Alabama
University of Alabama Birmingham
University of Mobile
University of Montevallo
University of South Alabama

Alaska
Alaska Pacific University
University of Alaska
   Anchorage
   Fairbanks
   Southeast

Arizona
Arizona State University
Arizona Western College
Embry-Riddle Aeronautical University Prescott Campus
Gateway Community College
Glendale Community College
Grand Canyon University
Mesa Community College
Northern Arizona University
Phoenix College
Scottsdale Community College
University of Arizona

Arkansas
Arkansas State University

Arkansas Tech University
Garland County Community College
Harding University
Hendrix College
John Brown University
Lyon College
Ouachita Baptist University
Philander Smith College
Southern Arkansas University
University of Arkansas
University of Arkansas
    Little Rock
University of Central Arkansas
University of the Ozarks
Williams Baptist College

California
Allan Hancock College
Antioch Southern California
    Los Angeles
    Santa Barbara
Azusa Pacific University
Biola University
Butte College
Cabrillo College
California Baptist University
California College of Arts and Crafts
California Institute of Technology
California Institute of the Arts
California Lutheran University
California Polytechnic State University:
    San Luis Obispo
California State Polytechnic University:
    Pomona
California State University
    Bakersfield
    Chico
    Dominguez Hills
    Fresno
    Fullerton
    Hayward
    Long Beach
    Los Angeles
    Monterey Bay
    Northridge
    Sacramento
    San Marcos
    Stanislaus
Canada College
Cerro Coso Community College
Chabot College
Chaffey Community College
Chapman University
Citrus College
City College of San Francisco
Claremont McKenna College
Coastline Community College
College of Notre Dame
College of San Mateo
College of the Canyons
College of the Sequoias
College of the Siskiyous
Cuesta College
Cypress College
De Anza College
Diablo Valley College
Dominican University of California
East Los Angeles College
Fashion Institute of Design and
    Merchandising
Fashion Institute of Design and
    Merchandising
    San Francisco
Foothill College
Fresno City College
Fresno Pacific University
Gavilan Community College
Glendale Community College
Golden West College
Grossmont Community College
Harvey Mudd College
Holy Names College
Hope International University
Humboldt State University
Irvine Valley College

Kings River Community College
La Sierra University
Los Angeles Harbor College
Los Angeles Pierce College
Los Angeles Southwest College
Los Angeles Trade and Technical College
Los Medanos College
Loyola Marymount University
Marymount College
Master's College
Menlo College
Merced College
Mills College
MiraCosta College
Modesto Junior College
Monterey Institute of International
    Studies
Moorpark College
Mount St. Mary's College
Mount San Antonio College
Napa Valley College
Occidental College
Ohlone College
Orange Coast College
Otis College of Art and Design
Oxnard College
Pacific Union College
Palomar College
Pasadena City College
Pepperdine University
Pitzer College
Point Loma Nazarene University
Pomona College
Rio Hondo College
Riverside Community College
Sacramento City College
Saddleback College
St. Mary's College of California
San Diego City College
San Diego Mesa College
San Diego State University
San Francisco Art Institute
San Francisco State University
San Joaquin Delta College
San Jose State University
Santa Ana College
Santa Barbara City College
Santa Clara University
Santa Monica College
Santa Rosa Junior College
Scripps College
Sierra College
Simpson College
Skyline College
Sonoma State University
Southern California Institute of
    Architecture
Southwestern College
Stanford University
United States International University
University of California
    Berkeley
    Davis
    Irvine
    Los Angeles
    Riverside
    San Diego
    San Francisco
    Santa Barbara
    Santa Cruz
University of Judaism
University of La Verne
University of Redlands
University of San Diego
University of San Francisco
University of Southern California
University of the Pacific
Vanguard University of Southern
    California
Ventura College
Victor Valley College
West Hills Community College
West Los Angeles College
Westmont College
Whittier College

Yuba College

Colorado
Adams State College
Arapahoe Community College
Art Institute
    of Colorado
Colorado College
Colorado Mountain College
    Alpine Campus
    Spring Valley Campus
    Timberline Campus
Colorado School of Mines
Colorado State University
Community College of Aurora
Community College of Denver
Fort Lewis College
Front Range Community College
Metropolitan State College of Denver
Naropa University
Red Rocks Community College
Regis University
United States Air Force Academy
University of Colorado
    Boulder
    Colorado Springs
    Denver
University of Denver
University of Northern Colorado
University of Southern Colorado
Western State College of Colorado

Connecticut
Albertus Magnus College
Central Connecticut State University
Connecticut College
Eastern Connecticut State University
Fairfield University
Naugatuck Valley Community-Technical
    College
Quinebaug Valley Community College
Quinnipiac University
Sacred Heart University
St. Joseph College
Southern Connecticut State University
Teikyo Post University
Three Rivers Community-Technical
    College
Trinity College
University of Bridgeport
University of Connecticut
University of Hartford
University of New Haven
Wesleyan University
Western Connecticut State University
Yale University

Delaware
University of Delaware
Wesley College

District of Columbia
American University
Catholic University of America
Corcoran College of Art and Design
Gallaudet University
George Washington University
Georgetown University
Howard University
Trinity College

Florida
Barry University
Bethune-Cookman College
Brevard Community College
Broward Community College
Central Florida Community College
Clearwater Christian College
Daytona Beach Community College
Eckerd College
Edison Community College
Embry-Riddle Aeronautical University
Flagler College
Florida Atlantic University

Florida Community College at
    Jacksonville
Florida Gulf Coast University
Florida International University
Florida Southern College
Florida State University
Hillsborough Community College
International Academy of Merchandising
    and Design
International Fine Arts College
Jacksonville University
Lake City Community College
Lynn University
Miami-Dade Community College
New College of the University of South
    Florida
Northwood University
    Florida Campus
Nova Southeastern University
Palm Beach Atlantic College
Palm Beach Community College
Pensacola Junior College
Ringling School of Art and Design
Rollins College
St. Leo University
St. Thomas University
Seminole Community College
Stetson University
Tallahassee Community College
University of Central Florida
University of Florida
University of Miami
University of North Florida
University of South Florida
University of Tampa
University of West Florida
Valencia Community College

Georgia
Abraham Baldwin Agricultural College
Agnes Scott College
American InterContinental University
Armstrong Atlantic State University
Art Institute
    of Atlanta
Atlanta Christian College
Atlanta College of Art
Augusta State University
Berry College
Brenau University
Clark Atlanta University
Clayton College and State University
Coastal Georgia Community College
Columbus State University
Covenant College
Darton College
East Georgia College
Emory University
Floyd College
Fort Valley State University
Gainesville College
Georgia College and State University
Georgia Institute of Technology
Georgia Perimeter College
Georgia Southern University
Georgia Southwestern State University
Georgia State University
Gordon College
Kennesaw State University
LaGrange College
Macon State College
Mercer University
Middle Georgia College
Morehouse College
Morris Brown College
North Georgia College & State
    University
Oglethorpe University
Oxford College of Emory University
Paine College
Piedmont College
Savannah College of Art and Design
Shorter College
South Georgia College
Southern Polytechnic State University

Spelman College
State University of West Georgia
Toccoa Falls College
Truett-McConnell College
University of Georgia
Valdosta State University
Waycross College
Wesleyan College
Young Harris College

Hawaii
Chaminade University of Honolulu
Hawaii Pacific University
University of Hawaii
   Hilo
   Kapiolani Community College
   Kauai Community College
   Manoa

Idaho
Albertson College of Idaho
Boise Bible College
Boise State University
Idaho State University
Northwest Nazarene University
University of Idaho

Illinois
American Academy of Art
Augustana College
Barat College
Benedictine University
Black Hawk College
Black Hawk College
   East Campus
Blackburn College
Bradley University
Carl Sandburg College
Chicago State University
City Colleges of Chicago
   Olive-Harvey College
College of DuPage
College of Lake County
Columbia College
Concordia University
De Paul University
Dominican University
Eastern Illinois University
Elgin Community College
Elmhurst College
Eureka College
Governors State University
Greenville College
Harrington Institute of Interior Design
Highland Community College
Illinois College
Illinois Eastern Community Colleges
   Frontier Community College
   Lincoln Trail College
   Olney Central College
   Wabash Valley College
Illinois Institute of Technology
Illinois State University
Illinois Wesleyan University
International Academy of Merchandising and Design
John A. Logan College
John Wood Community College
Joliet Junior College
Judson College
Kankakee Community College
Kaskaskia College
Kendall College
Kishwaukee College
Knox College
Lake Forest College
Lake Land College
Lincoln Land Community College
Loyola University of Chicago
MacMurray College
McHenry County College
McKendree College
Millikin University
Monmouth College

Moody Bible Institute
Moraine Valley Community College
North Central College
North Park University
Northeastern Illinois University
Northern Illinois University
Northwestern University
Oakton Community College
Olivet Nazarene University
Parkland College
Prairie State College
Principia College
Quincy University
Rend Lake College
Robert Morris College: Chicago
Rock Valley College
Rockford College
Roosevelt University
St. Xavier University
Sauk Valley Community College
School of the Art Institute of Chicago
Shimer College
Southeastern Illinois College
Southern Illinois University
   Carbondale
   Edwardsville
Southwestern Illinois College
Springfield College in Illinois
Trinity Christian College
Trinity International University
University of Chicago
University of Illinois
   Chicago
   Urbana-Champaign
University of St. Francis
Waubonsee Community College
Western Illinois University
Wheaton College
William Rainey Harper College

Indiana
Anderson University
Ball State University
Bethel College
Butler University
Calumet College of St. Joseph
DePauw University
Earlham College
Franklin College
Goshen College
Grace College
Hanover College
Indiana State University
Indiana University
   Bloomington
   Kokomo
   Northwest
   South Bend
   Southeast
Indiana University--Purdue University
   Indiana University-Purdue University Fort Wayne
   Indiana University-Purdue University Indianapolis
Indiana Wesleyan University
Manchester College
Marian College
Purdue University
Rose-Hulman Institute of Technology
Saint Mary's College
St. Joseph's College
St. Mary-of-the-Woods College
Taylor University
Tri-State University
University of Evansville
University of Indianapolis
University of Notre Dame
University of St. Francis
University of Southern Indiana
Valparaiso University
Wabash College

Iowa
Briar Cliff College

Buena Vista University
Central College
Clarke College
Clinton Community College
Coe College
Cornell College
Des Moines Area Community College
Dordt College
Drake University
Graceland University
Grand View College
Grinnell College
Iowa Central Community College
Iowa State University
Iowa Wesleyan College
Kirkwood Community College
Loras College
Luther College
Maharishi University of Management
Marycrest International University
Morningside College
Mount Mercy College
Muscatine Community College
Northeast Iowa Community College
Northwestern College
St. Ambrose University
Scott Community College
Simpson College
University of Dubuque
University of Iowa
University of Northern Iowa
Waldorf College
Wartburg College

Kansas
Baker University
Benedictine College
Bethany College
Bethel College
Emporia State University
Johnson County Community College
Kansas State University
McPherson College
MidAmerica Nazarene University
Newman University
Pittsburg State University
St. Mary College
Southwestern College
Tabor College
University of Kansas
Washburn University of Topeka
Wichita State University

Kentucky
Alice Lloyd College
Asbury College
Bellarmine College
Berea College
Brescia University
Campbellsville University
Centre College
Cumberland College
Eastern Kentucky University
Georgetown College
Kentucky Christian College
Kentucky State University
Kentucky Wesleyan College
Mid-Continent College
Midway College
Morehead State University
Murray State University
Northern Kentucky University
Spalding University
Thomas More College
Transylvania University
Union College
University of Kentucky
University of Louisville
Western Kentucky University

Louisiana
Centenary College of Louisiana
Dillard University

Louisiana State University and Agricultural and Mechanical College
Louisiana State University Shreveport
Louisiana Tech University
Loyola University New Orleans
Nicholls State University
Northwestern State University
Our Lady of Holy Cross College
Southeastern Louisiana University
Southern University and Agricultural and Mechanical College
Tulane University
University of Louisiana at Lafayette
University of Louisiana at Monroe
University of New Orleans
Xavier University of Louisiana

Maine
Bates College
Bowdoin College
Colby College
College of the Atlantic
Maine College of Art
Maine Maritime Academy
St. Joseph's College
Thomas College
University of Maine
University of Maine
   Farmington
   Fort Kent
   Machias
   Presque Isle
University of New England
University of Southern Maine

Maryland
Baltimore City Community College
Baltimore International College
Bowie State University
Charles County Community College
College of Notre Dame of Maryland
Columbia Union College
Community College of Baltimore County
   Catonsville
Frostburg State University
Goucher College
Hood College
Johns Hopkins University
Loyola College in Maryland
Maryland Institute College of Art
Montgomery College
   Germantown Campus
   Rockville Campus
   Takoma Park Campus
Mount St. Mary's College
St. Mary's College of Maryland
Salisbury State University
Towson University
University of Baltimore
University of Maryland
   Baltimore County
   College Park
Villa Julie College
Washington Bible College
Washington College
Western Maryland College

Massachusetts
American International College
Amherst College
Anna Maria College
Atlantic Union College
Babson College
Bay Path College
Becker College
Bentley College
Berklee College of Music
Boston College
Boston University
Brandeis University
Bridgewater State College
Bunker Hill Community College
Cape Cod Community College

Study abroad

Clark University
College of the Holy Cross
Curry College
Dean College
Eastern Nazarene College
Elms College
Emerson College
Emmanuel College
Endicott College
Fitchburg State College
Framingham State College
Gordon College
Hampshire College
Harvard College
Hellenic College/Holy Cross
Holyoke Community College
Lasell College
Lesley College
Massachusetts Bay Community College
Massachusetts College of Art
Massachusetts College of Liberal Arts
Massachusetts Institute of Technology
Merrimack College
Middlesex Community College
Montserrat College of Art
Mount Holyoke College
Mount Ida College
Mount Wachusett Community College
Newbury College
Nichols College
North Shore Community College
Northeastern University
Northern Essex Community College
Pine Manor College
Regis College
St. John's Seminary College
Salem State College
School of the Museum of Fine Arts
Simmons College
Simon's Rock College of Bard
Smith College
Springfield College
Stonehill College
Suffolk University
Tufts University
University of Massachusetts
    Amherst
    Boston
    Dartmouth
    Lowell
Wellesley College
Wentworth Institute of Technology
Western New England College
Westfield State College
Wheaton College
Wheelock College
Williams College
Worcester Polytechnic Institute
Worcester State College

Michigan
Adrian College
Albion College
Alma College
Andrews University
Aquinas College
Calvin College
Center for Creative Studies: College of Art and Design
Central Michigan University
Concordia College
Cornerstone College and Grand Rapids Baptist Seminary
Davenport College of Business
Delta College
Eastern Michigan University
Grand Rapids Community College
Grand Valley State University
Hillsdale College
Hope College
Kalamazoo College
Kendall College of Art and Design
Kettering University
Lansing Community College
Lawrence Technological University
Macomb Community College
Madonna University
Marygrove College
Michigan State University
Michigan Technological University
Mott Community College
Northern Michigan University
Northwestern Michigan College
Northwood University
Oakland University
Olivet College
Reformed Bible College
Saginaw Valley State University
Siena Heights University
Spring Arbor College
Suomi College
University of Detroit Mercy
University of Michigan
University of Michigan
    Dearborn
    Flint
Wayne State University
Western Michigan University

Minnesota
Anoka-Ramsey Community College
Augsburg College
Bemidji State University
Bethel College
Carleton College
Central Lakes College
College of St. Benedict
College of St. Catherine: St. Paul Campus
College of St. Scholastica
College of Visual Arts
Concordia College: Moorhead
Concordia University: St. Paul
Crown College
Gustavus Adolphus College
Hamline University
Inver Hills Community College
Itasca Community College
Macalester College
Martin Luther College
Mesabi Range Community and Technical College
Minneapolis College of Art and Design
Minnesota State University, Mankato
Moorhead State University
North Central University
North Hennepin Community College
Northwestern College
Ridgewater College: A Community and Technical College
St. Cloud State University
St. John's University
St. Mary's University of Minnesota
St. Olaf College
Southwest State University
University of Minnesota
    Crookston
    Duluth
    Morris
    Twin Cities
University of St. Thomas
Winona State University

Mississippi
Belhaven College
Hinds Community College
Millsaps College
Mississippi College
Mississippi State University
Mississippi University for Women
Northeast Mississippi Community College
Rust College
Tougaloo College
University of Mississippi
University of Southern Mississippi
William Carey College

Missouri
Central Methodist College
Central Missouri State University
College of the Ozarks
Columbia College
Crowder College
Culver-Stockton College
Drury University
East Central College
Evangel University
Fontbonne College
Hannibal-LaGrange College
Kansas City Art Institute
Lindenwood University
Maryville University of Saint Louis
Missouri Baptist College
Missouri Southern State College
Moberly Area Community College
Northwest Missouri State University
Research College of Nursing
Rockhurst University
St. Charles County Community College
St. Louis University
Southeast Missouri State University
Southwest Baptist University
Southwest Missouri State University
St. Louis Community College
    St. Louis Community College at Florissant Valley
    St. Louis Community College at Forest Park
    St. Louis Community College at Meramec
Stephens College
Truman State University
University of Missouri
    Columbia
    Kansas City
    Rolla
    St. Louis
Washington University
Webster University
Westminster College
William Jewell College
William Woods University

Montana
Carroll College
Montana State University
    Bozeman
Rocky Mountain College
University of Montana-Missoula
Western Montana College of The University of Montana

Nebraska
Bellevue University
Chadron State College
Clarkson College
Concordia University
Creighton University
Dana College
Doane College
Grace University
Hastings College
Midland Lutheran College
Peru State College
Union College
University of Nebraska
    Kearney
    Lincoln
    Omaha

Nevada
University of Nevada
    Las Vegas
    Reno

New Hampshire
Colby-Sawyer College
Dartmouth College
Franklin Pierce College
Keene State College
New England College
New Hampshire College
Notre Dame College
Plymouth State College of the University System of New Hampshire
Rivier College
St. Anselm College
Thomas More College of Liberal Arts
University of New Hampshire
University of New Hampshire Manchester

New Jersey
Bergen Community College
Berkeley College
Bloomfield College
Brookdale Community College
Caldwell College
Centenary College
College of St. Elizabeth
County College of Morris
Drew University
Fairleigh Dickinson University
Felician College
Georgian Court College
Kean University
Middlesex County College
Monmouth University
Montclair State University
New Jersey City University
New Jersey Institute of Technology
Ocean County College
Princeton University
Ramapo College of New Jersey
Richard Stockton College of New Jersey
Rider University
Rowan University
Rutgers
    The State University of New Jersey: Camden College of Arts and Sciences
    The State University of New Jersey: College of Engineering
    The State University of New Jersey: Cook College
    The State University of New Jersey: Douglass College
    The State University of New Jersey: Livingston College
    The State University of New Jersey: Mason Gross School of the Arts
    The State University of New Jersey: Newark College of Arts and Sciences
    The State University of New Jersey: Rutgers College
    The State University of New Jersey: University College Camden
    The State University of New Jersey: University College New Brunswick
    The State University of New Jersey: University College Newark
St. Peter's College
Seton Hall University
Stevens Institute of Technology
The College of New Jersey
William Paterson University of New Jersey

New Mexico
College of Santa Fe
Eastern New Mexico University
New Mexico Institute of Mining and Technology
New Mexico State University
University of New Mexico

New York
Adelphi University
Adirondack Community College
Alfred University
Audrey Cohen College
Bard College
Barnard College

Berkeley College
Berkeley College of New York City
Broome Community College
Canisius College
Cayuga County Community College
City University of New York
    Borough of Manhattan Community College
    Brooklyn College
    City College
    College of Staten Island
    Hostos Community College
    Hunter College
    John Jay College of Criminal Justice
    Lehman College
    Medgar Evers College
    New York City Technical College
    Queens College
    York College
Clarkson University
Colgate University
College of Insurance
College of Mount St. Vincent
College of New Rochelle
College of St. Rose
Columbia University
    Columbia College
    School of General Studies
Concordia College
Cooper Union for the Advancement of Science and Art
Cornell University
Corning Community College
D'Youville College
Daemen College
Dutchess Community College
Elmira College
Erie Community College
    City Campus
    North Campus
    South Campus
Eugene Lang College/New School University
Fashion Institute of Technology
Fordham University
Fulton-Montgomery Community College
Genesee Community College
Hamilton College
Hartwick College
Hobart and William Smith Colleges
Hofstra University
Houghton College
Iona College
Ithaca College
Jamestown Community College
Jewish Theological Seminary of America
Juilliard School
Keuka College
Laboratory Institute of Merchandising
Le Moyne College
Long Island University
    C. W. Post Campus
    Southampton College
Manhattan College
Manhattanville College
Marist College
Marymount College
Marymount Manhattan College
Mercy College
Mohawk Valley Community College
Molloy College
Mount St. Mary College
Nassau Community College
Nazareth College of Rochester
New York Institute of Technology
New York School of Interior Design
New York State College of Ceramics at Alfred University
New York University
Niagara County Community College
Niagara University
Nyack College
Ohr Somayach Tanenbaum Education Center
Onondaga Community College
Pace University
Pace University: Pleasantville/Briarcliff
Parsons School of Design
Pratt Institute
Rensselaer Polytechnic Institute
Roberts Wesleyan College
Rochester Institute of Technology
Rockland Community College
Russell Sage College
Sage Junior College of Albany
St. Bonaventure University
St. Francis College
St. John Fisher College
St. John's University
St. Lawrence University
St. Thomas Aquinas College
Sarah Lawrence College
School of Visual Arts
Siena College
Skidmore College
State University of New York
    Albany
    Binghamton
    Buffalo
    College at Brockport
    College at Buffalo
    College at Cortland
    College at Fredonia
    College at Geneseo
    College at Old Westbury
    College at Oneonta
    College at Plattsburgh
    College at Potsdam
    College of Agriculture and Technology at Cobleskill
    College of Agriculture and Technology at Morrisville
    College of Environmental Science and Forestry
    Empire State College
    Farmingdale
    New Paltz
    Oswego
    Purchase
    Stony Brook
Syracuse University
Tompkins-Cortland Community College
Touro College
Union College
United States Military Academy
University of Rochester
Utica College of Syracuse University
Vassar College
Villa Maria College of Buffalo
Wagner College
Wells College

North Carolina
Appalachian State University
Barton College
Belmont Abbey College
Brevard College
Campbell University
Catawba College
Chowan College
Davidson College
Duke University
East Carolina University
Elon College
Gardner-Webb University
Greensboro College
Guilford College
High Point University
John Wesley College
Johnson C. Smith University
Lees-McRae College
Lenoir Community College
Lenoir-Rhyne College
Mars Hill College
Meredith College
Methodist College
Montreat College
North Carolina Agricultural and Technical State University
North Carolina State University
Peace College
Pfeiffer University
Queens College
St. Andrews Presbyterian College
St. Augustine's College
Salem College
Shaw University
University of North Carolina
    Asheville
    Chapel Hill
    Charlotte
    Greensboro
    Pembroke
    Wilmington
Wake Forest University
Warren Wilson College
Western Carolina University
Wingate University

North Dakota
Dickinson State University
Mayville State University
Minot State University
North Dakota State University
University of Mary
University of North Dakota

Ohio
Antioch College
Ashland University
Baldwin-Wallace College
Bluffton College
Bowling Green State University
Capital University
Case Western Reserve University
Cedarville College
Central State University
Cleveland State University
College of Mount St. Joseph
College of Wooster
Columbus State Community College
Defiance College
Denison University
Franciscan University of Steubenville
Franklin University
Heidelberg College
Hiram College
John Carroll University
Kent State University
Kenyon College
Lake Erie College
Lorain County Community College
Malone College
Marietta College
Miami University
    Hamilton Campus
    Middletown Campus
    Oxford Campus
Mount Union College
Mount Vernon Nazarene College
Muskingum College
Notre Dame College of Ohio
Oberlin College
Ohio Dominican College
Ohio Northern University
Ohio State University
    Columbus Campus
Ohio University
Ohio University
    Chillicothe Campus
    Zanesville Campus
Ohio Wesleyan University
Otterbein College
Terra Community College
Tiffin University
University of Akron
University of Cincinnati
University of Cincinnati
    Raymond Walters College
University of Dayton
University of Findlay
University of Toledo
Walsh University
Wilberforce University
Wilmington College
Wittenberg University
Wright State University
Xavier University
Youngstown State University

Oklahoma
Oklahoma Baptist University
Oklahoma Christian University of Science and Arts
Oklahoma City University
Oklahoma State University
Oral Roberts University
St. Gregory's University
Southern Nazarene University
University of Oklahoma
University of Tulsa

Oregon
Central Oregon Community College
Chemeketa Community College
Clackamas Community College
Concordia University
Eastern Oregon University
George Fox University
Lane Community College
Lewis & Clark College
Linfield College
Mount Hood Community College
Northwest Christian College
Oregon Institute of Technology
Oregon State University
Pacific Northwest College of Art
Pacific University
Portland Community College
Portland State University
Reed College
Southern Oregon University
University of Oregon
University of Portland
Western Baptist College
Western Oregon University
Willamette University

Pennsylvania
Albright College
Allegheny College
Allentown College of St. Francis de Sales
Alvernia College
Beaver College
Bloomsburg University of Pennsylvania
Bryn Mawr College
Bucknell University
Cabrini College
California University of Pennsylvania
Carlow College
Carnegie Mellon University
Cedar Crest College
Chatham College
Chestnut Hill College
Clarion University of Pennsylvania
College Misericordia
Community College of Allegheny County
Delaware County Community College
Dickinson College
Drexel University
Duquesne University
Edinboro University of Pennsylvania
Elizabethtown College
Franklin and Marshall College
Gannon University
Geneva College
Gettysburg College
Grove City College
Harcum College
Harrisburg Area Community College
Haverford College
Holy Family College
Immaculata College
Indiana University of Pennsylvania
Juniata College
King's College

Kutztown University of Pennsylvania
La Roche College
Lafayette College
Lancaster Bible College
Lebanon Valley College of Pennsylvania
Lehigh Carbon Community College
Lehigh University
Lincoln University
Lock Haven University of Pennsylvania
Lycoming College
Mansfield University of Pennsylvania
Marywood University
Mercyhurst College
Messiah College
Millersville University of Pennsylvania
Moore College of Art and Design
Moravian College
Muhlenberg College
Neumann College
Northampton County Area Community College
Penn State
    Abington
    Altoona
    Berks
    Delaware County
    Erie, The Behrend College
    Harrisburg
    Lehigh Valley
    Schuylkill - Capital College
    University Park
Philadelphia College of Bible
Philadelphia University
Point Park College
Robert Morris College
Rosemont College
St. Francis College
St. Joseph's University
St. Vincent College
Seton Hill College
Shippensburg University of Pennsylvania
Slippery Rock University of Pennsylvania
Susquehanna University
Swarthmore College
Temple University
Thiel College
Thomas Jefferson University: College of Health Professions
University of Pennsylvania
University of Pittsburgh
University of Pittsburgh
    Bradford
    Greensburg
    Johnstown
    Titusville
University of Scranton
Ursinus College
Valley Forge Christian College
Villanova University
Washington and Jefferson College
Waynesburg College
West Chester University of Pennsylvania
Westminster College
Westmoreland County Community College
Widener University
Wilkes University
Wilson College
York College of Pennsylvania

Puerto Rico
Inter American University of Puerto Rico
    Guayama Campus
    Metropolitan Campus
    San German Campus
Pontifical Catholic University of Puerto Rico
Technological College of San Juan
University of Puerto Rico
    Cayey University College
    Humacao University College
    Mayaguez Campus
    Rio Piedras Campus

Rhode Island
Brown University
Bryant College
Community College of Rhode Island
Johnson & Wales University
Providence College
Rhode Island College
Roger Williams University
Salve Regina University
University of Rhode Island

South Carolina
Anderson College
Charleston Southern University
Claflin University
Clemson University
Coastal Carolina University
Coker College
College of Charleston
Columbia College
Columbia International University
Converse College
Erskine College
Furman University
Lander University
Newberry College
Presbyterian College
South Carolina State University
Southern Wesleyan University
Spartanburg Methodist College
Tri-County Technical College
University of South Carolina
University of South Carolina
    Aiken
    Beaufort
    Salkehatchie Regional Campus
    Spartanburg
Winthrop University
Wofford College

South Dakota
Augustana College
Dakota State University
Dakota Wesleyan University
Northern State University
South Dakota School of Mines and Technology
South Dakota State University
University of South Dakota

Tennessee
Austin Peay State University
Belmont University
Carson-Newman College
Christian Brothers University
David Lipscomb University
East Tennessee State University
Fisk University
Freed-Hardeman University
King College
Lambuth University
LeMoyne-Owen College
Lee University
Martin Methodist College
Maryville College
Middle Tennessee State University
Milligan College
Southern Adventist University
Tennessee State University
Tennessee Technological University
Tennessee Wesleyan College
Tusculum College
Union University
University of Memphis
University of Tennessee
    Chattanooga
    Knoxville
    Martin
University of the South
Vanderbilt University

Texas
Abilene Christian University
Alvin Community College
Angelo State University
Austin College
Austin Community College
Baylor University
Brookhaven College
Collin County Community College District
Concordia University at Austin
Dallas Baptist University
East Texas Baptist University
Hardin-Simmons University
Houston Baptist University
Howard Payne University
Lamar University
LeTourneau University
McMurry University
Midland College
Midwestern State University
North Lake College
Northwood University: Texas Campus
Rice University
Richland College
St. Edward's University
St. Mary's University
San Antonio College
Schreiner College
Southern Methodist University
Southwest Texas State University
Southwestern Adventist University
Southwestern University
Texas A&M International University
Texas A&M University
Texas A&M University
    Commerce
    Kingsville
Texas Christian University
Texas Lutheran University
Texas Tech University
Texas Wesleyan University
Trinity University
University of Dallas
University of Houston
University of Houston
    Clear Lake
    Downtown
University of Mary Hardin-Baylor
University of North Texas
University of St. Thomas
University of Texas
    Arlington
    Austin
    Dallas
    El Paso
    Pan American
    San Antonio
    Tyler
University of the Incarnate Word

Utah
Brigham Young University
Salt Lake Community College
University of Utah
Utah State University
Weber State University

Vermont
Bennington College
Burlington College
Castleton State College
Champlain College
College of St. Joseph in Vermont
Goddard College
Green Mountain College
Johnson State College
Landmark College
Lyndon State College
Marlboro College
Middlebury College
New England Culinary Institute
Norwich University
St. Michael's College
Southern Vermont College
Sterling College
Trinity College of Vermont
University of Vermont

Virginia
Averett College
Blue Ridge Community College
Bluefield College
Bridgewater College
Christendom College
Christopher Newport University
College of William and Mary
Eastern Mennonite University
Emory & Henry College
Ferrum College
George Mason University
Hampden-Sydney College
Hampton University
Hollins University
James Madison University
Liberty University
Longwood College
Lynchburg College
Mary Baldwin College
Mary Washington College
Norfolk State University
Northern Virginia Community College
Old Dominion University
Radford University
Randolph-Macon College
Randolph-Macon Woman's College
Roanoke College
Shenandoah University
Southside Virginia Community College
Sweet Briar College
Tidewater Community College
University of Richmond
University of Virginia
University of Virginia's College at Wise
Virginia Commonwealth University
Virginia Intermont College
Virginia Military Institute
Virginia Polytechnic Institute and State University
Virginia Wesleyan College
Washington and Lee University

Washington
Antioch University Seattle
Central Washington University
Centralia College
Clark College
Eastern Washington University
Edmonds Community College
Everett Community College
Evergreen State College
Gonzaga University
Grays Harbor College
Green River Community College
Lower Columbia College
North Seattle Community College
Olympic College
Pacific Lutheran University
Peninsula College
Seattle Central Community College
Seattle Pacific University
Seattle University
Shoreline Community College
Skagit Valley College
South Puget Sound Community College
South Seattle Community College
Spokane Community College
Spokane Falls Community College
University of Puget Sound
University of Washington
Walla Walla College
Washington State University
Western Washington University
Whatcom Community College
Whitman College
Whitworth College

West Virginia
Alderson-Broaddus College
Bethany College
College of West Virginia

Davis and Elkins College
Fairmont State College
Marshall University
Potomac State College of West Virginia University
Salem-Teikyo University
University of Charleston
West Virginia University
West Virginia Wesleyan College
Wheeling Jesuit University

Wisconsin

Alverno College
Beloit College
Cardinal Stritch University
Carroll College
Carthage College
Columbia College of Nursing
Concordia University Wisconsin
Lakeland College
Lawrence University
Marian College of Fond du Lac
Marquette University
Milwaukee Institute of Art & Design
Milwaukee School of Engineering
Mount Mary College
Northland College
Ripon College
St. Norbert College
University of Wisconsin
   Baraboo/Sauk County
   Eau Claire
   Green Bay
   La Crosse
   Madison
   Marathon County
   Milwaukee
   Oshkosh
   Parkside
   Platteville
   River Falls
   Sheboygan County
   Stevens Point
   Stout
   Superior
   Washington County
   Waukesha
   Whitewater
Viterbo University
Wisconsin Lutheran College

Wyoming

Northwest College
University of Wyoming

Teacher certification

Alabama

Alabama Agricultural and Mechanical University
Alabama State University
Athens State University
Auburn University
Auburn University at Montgomery
Birmingham-Southern College
Faulkner University
Huntingdon College
Jacksonville State University
Samford University
Sparks State Technical College
Spring Hill College
Stillman College
Talladega College
Troy State University
Troy State University
   Dothan
   Montgomery
Tuskegee University
University of Alabama
University of Alabama
   Birmingham
   Huntsville
University of Mobile
University of Montevallo
University of North Alabama
University of South Alabama
University of West Alabama

Alaska

Alaska Pacific University
University of Alaska
   Anchorage
   Fairbanks
   Southeast

Arizona

American Indian College of the Assemblies of God
Arizona State University
Arizona Western College
Cochise College
Grand Canyon University
Northern Arizona University
Prescott College
Southwestern College
University of Arizona
University of Phoenix
Yavapai College

Arkansas

Arkansas State University
Arkansas Tech University
Harding University
Henderson State University
Hendrix College
John Brown University
Lyon College
Ouachita Baptist University
Philander Smith College
Southern Arkansas University
University of Arkansas
University of Arkansas
   Little Rock
   Monticello
   Pine Bluff
University of Central Arkansas
University of the Ozarks

California

Academy of Art College
Antioch Southern California
   Santa Barbara
Azusa Pacific University
Biola University
California Baptist University
California Lutheran University
California Polytechnic State University: San Luis Obispo
California State Polytechnic University: Pomona
California State University
   Bakersfield
   Chico
   Dominguez Hills
   Fresno
   Fullerton
   Hayward
   Long Beach
   Los Angeles
   Monterey Bay
   Northridge
   Sacramento
   San Marcos
   Stanislaus
Chapman University
College of Notre Dame
Concordia University
Dominican University of California
Fresno Pacific University
Holy Names College
Hope International University
Humboldt State University
John F. Kennedy University
La Sierra University
Loyola Marymount University
Master's College
Mills College
Mount St. Mary's College
National University
Occidental College
Pacific Oaks College
Pacific Union College
Patten College
Pepperdine University
Point Loma Nazarene University
Pomona College
St. Mary's College of California
San Diego City College
San Diego Mesa College
San Diego State University
San Francisco State University
San Jose State University
Santa Clara University
Simpson College
Sonoma State University
United States International University
University of California
   Berkeley
   Davis
   Irvine
   Los Angeles
   Riverside
   San Diego
   Santa Barbara
   Santa Cruz
University of La Verne
University of Redlands
University of San Diego
University of San Francisco
University of Southern California
University of the Pacific
Vanguard University of Southern California
West Valley College
Westmont College
Whittier College

Colorado

Adams State College
Colorado Christian University
Colorado College
Colorado State University
Fort Lewis College
Mesa State College
Metropolitan State College of Denver
Morgan Community College
Regis University
University of Colorado
   Boulder
   Colorado Springs
   Denver
University of Northern Colorado
University of Southern Colorado
Western State College of Colorado

Connecticut

Central Connecticut State University
Connecticut College
Eastern Connecticut State University
Fairfield University
Quinnipiac University
Sacred Heart University
St. Joseph College
Southern Connecticut State University
Trinity College
University of Bridgeport
University of Connecticut
University of Hartford
Western Connecticut State University
Yale University

Delaware

Delaware State University
University of Delaware
Wesley College
Wilmington College

District of Columbia

American University
Catholic University of America
Gallaudet University
George Washington University
Howard University
Trinity College
University of the District of Columbia

Florida

Barry University
Bethune-Cookman College
Central Florida Community College
Clearwater Christian College
Edward Waters College
Embry-Riddle Aeronautical University
Flagler College
Florida Agricultural and Mechanical University
Florida Atlantic University
Florida Baptist Theological College
Florida Christian College
Florida Gulf Coast University
Florida Institute of Technology
Florida International University
Florida Memorial College
Florida Southern College
Florida State University
Gulf Coast Community College
Hillsborough Community College
Hobe Sound Bible College
Jacksonville University
Lynn University
Nova Southeastern University
Palm Beach Atlantic College
Rollins College
St. Leo University
St. Thomas University
Seminole Community College
Southeastern College of the Assemblies of God
Stetson University
University of Central Florida
University of Florida
University of Miami
University of North Florida
University of South Florida
University of Tampa
University of West Florida
Warner Southern College

Georgia

Agnes Scott College
Albany State University
Armstrong Atlantic State University
Augusta State University
Berry College
Brenau University
Brewton-Parker College
Clark Atlanta University
Clayton College and State University
Coastal Georgia Community College
Columbus State University
Covenant College
Emmanuel College
Emory University
Fort Valley State University
Georgia College and State University
Georgia Institute of Technology
Georgia Southern University
Georgia Southwestern State University
Georgia State University
LaGrange College
Mercer University
Morris Brown College
North Georgia College & State University
Oglethorpe University
Paine College
Piedmont College
Shorter College
Spelman College
State University of West Georgia
Toccoa Falls College
University of Georgia
Valdosta State University
Wesleyan College

Teacher certification

Hawaii
Brigham Young University
    Hawaii
Chaminade University of Honolulu
Hawaii Pacific University
University of Hawaii
    Hilo
    Kapiolani Community College
    Manoa

Idaho
Albertson College of Idaho
Boise State University
Idaho State University
Lewis-Clark State College
Northwest Nazarene University
University of Idaho

Illinois
Augustana College
Barat College
Benedictine University
Blackburn College
Bradley University
Chicago State University
Columbia College
Concordia University
De Paul University
Dominican University
Eastern Illinois University
Elmhurst College
Eureka College
Governors State University
Greenville College
Illinois College
Illinois Eastern Community Colleges
    Frontier Community College
Illinois State University
Judson College
Kankakee Community College
Kendall College
Knox College
Lake Forest College
Lewis University
Lincoln Christian College and Seminary
Loyola University of Chicago
MacMurray College
McKendree College
Millikin University
Monmouth College
Moody Bible Institute
National-Louis University
North Central College
North Park University
Northeastern Illinois University
Northern Illinois University
Northwestern University
Olivet Nazarene University
Principia College
Quincy University
Rockford College
Roosevelt University
St. Xavier University
School of the Art Institute of Chicago
Southern Illinois University
    Carbondale
    Edwardsville
Trinity Christian College
Trinity International University
University of Illinois
    Chicago
    Springfield
    Urbana-Champaign
University of St. Francis
VanderCook College of Music
Western Illinois University
Wheaton College

Indiana
Anderson University
Ball State University
Bethel College
Butler University
Calumet College of St. Joseph
DePauw University
Franklin College
Goshen College
Grace College
Hanover College
Indiana State University
Indiana University
    Bloomington
    East
    Kokomo
    Northwest
    South Bend
    Southeast
Indiana University--Purdue University
    Indiana University-Purdue
        University Fort Wayne
    Indiana University-Purdue
        University Indianapolis
Indiana Wesleyan University
Manchester College
Marian College
Oakland City University
Purdue University
Purdue University
    Calumet
    North Central Campus
Saint Mary's College
St. Joseph's College
St. Mary-of-the-Woods College
Taylor University
Tri-State University
University of Evansville
University of Indianapolis
University of Notre Dame
University of St. Francis
University of Southern Indiana
Valparaiso University
Wabash College

Iowa
Briar Cliff College
Buena Vista University
Central College
Clarke College
Coe College
Cornell College
Dordt College
Drake University
Emmaus Bible College
Faith Baptist Bible College and
    Theological Seminary
Graceland University
Grand View College
Grinnell College
Iowa State University
Iowa Wesleyan College
Loras College
Luther College
Maharishi University of Management
Marycrest International University
Morningside College
Mount Mercy College
Northwestern College
St. Ambrose University
Simpson College
University of Dubuque
University of Iowa
University of Northern Iowa
Upper Iowa University
Wartburg College
William Penn University

Kansas
Baker University
Barclay College
Benedictine College
Bethany College
Bethel College
Cloud County Community College
Cowley County Community College
Emporia State University
Fort Hays State University
Kansas City Kansas Community College
Kansas State University
Kansas Wesleyan University
McPherson College
MidAmerica Nazarene University
Newman University
Ottawa University
Pittsburg State University
St. Mary College
Southwestern College
Sterling College
Tabor College
University of Kansas
Washburn University of Topeka
Wichita State University

Kentucky
Alice Lloyd College
Asbury College
Bellarmine College
Berea College
Brescia University
Campbellsville University
Centre College
Cumberland College
Eastern Kentucky University
Georgetown College
Kentucky Christian College
Kentucky State University
Kentucky Wesleyan College
Lindsey Wilson College
Midway College
Morehead State University
Murray State University
Northern Kentucky University
Pikeville College
Spalding University
Thomas More College
Transylvania University
Union College
University of Kentucky
University of Louisville
Western Kentucky University

Louisiana
Centenary College of Louisiana
Dillard University
Louisiana State University and
    Agricultural and Mechanical College
Louisiana State University
    Shreveport
Louisiana Tech University
Loyola University New Orleans
McNeese State University
Nicholls State University
Northwestern State University
Our Lady of Holy Cross College
Southeastern Louisiana University
Southern University and Agricultural and
    Mechanical College
Tulane University
University of Louisiana at Lafayette
University of Louisiana at Monroe
University of New Orleans
Xavier University of Louisiana

Maine
Andover College
Bates College
Bowdoin College
Colby College
College of the Atlantic
Husson College
Maine College of Art
St. Joseph's College
Thomas College
University of Maine
University of Maine
    Farmington
    Fort Kent
    Machias
    Presque Isle
University of New England
University of Southern Maine

Maryland
Baltimore City Community College
Bowie State University
Cecil Community College
Chesapeake College
College of Notre Dame of Maryland
Columbia Union College
Coppin State College
Frederick Community College
Frostburg State University
Goucher College
Hood College
Johns Hopkins University
Johns Hopkins University: Peabody
    Conservatory of Music
Loyola College in Maryland
Maryland Institute College of Art
Morgan State University
Mount St. Mary's College
Prince George's Community College
St. Mary's College of Maryland
Salisbury State University
Towson University
University of Maryland
    Baltimore County
    College Park
    Eastern Shore
Villa Julie College
Washington Bible College
Washington College
Western Maryland College

Massachusetts
American International College
Amherst College
Anna Maria College
Assumption College
Atlantic Union College
Bay Path College
Becker College
Berklee College of Music
Boston College
Boston Conservatory
Boston University
Brandeis University
Bridgewater State College
Clark University
College of the Holy Cross
Curry College
Eastern Nazarene College
Elms College
Emerson College
Emmanuel College
Endicott College
Fitchburg State College
Framingham State College
Gordon College
Harvard College
Hebrew College
Holyoke Community College
Lasell College
Lesley College
Massachusetts College of Art
Massachusetts College of Liberal Arts
Merrimack College
Montserrat College of Art
Mount Holyoke College
Mount Ida College
New England Conservatory of Music
Nichols College
Northeastern University
Pine Manor College
Regis College
Salem State College
Simmons College
Smith College
Springfield College
Stonehill College
Suffolk University
Tufts University
University of Massachusetts
    Amherst
    Boston
    Dartmouth
Wellesley College

Western New England College
Westfield State College
Wheaton College
Wheelock College
Williams College
Worcester Polytechnic Institute
Worcester State College

Michigan
Adrian College
Albion College
Alma College
Andrews University
Aquinas College
Calvin College
Central Michigan University
Concordia College
Cornerstone College and Grand Rapids Baptist Seminary
Eastern Michigan University
Ferris State University
Grand Valley State University
Hillsdale College
Hope College
Kalamazoo College
Lake Superior State University
Lansing Community College
Madonna University
Marygrove College
Michigan State University
Michigan Technological University
Northern Michigan University
Oakland University
Olivet College
Saginaw Valley State University
Siena Heights University
Spring Arbor College
University of Detroit Mercy
University of Michigan
University of Michigan
   Dearborn
   Flint
Wayne State University
Western Michigan University

Minnesota
Augsburg College
Bemidji State University
Bethel College
Carleton College
College of St. Benedict
College of St. Catherine: St. Paul Campus
College of St. Scholastica
Concordia College: Moorhead
Concordia University: St. Paul
Crown College
Gustavus Adolphus College
Hamline University
Macalester College
Martin Luther College
Minnesota State University, Mankato
Moorhead State University
North Central University
Northwestern College
St. Cloud State University
St. John's University
St. Mary's University of Minnesota
St. Olaf College
Southwest State University
University of Minnesota
   Duluth
   Morris
   Twin Cities
University of St. Thomas
Winona State University

Mississippi
Alcorn State University
Belhaven College
Blue Mountain College
Delta State University
Jackson State University
Millsaps College
Mississippi College
Mississippi State University
Mississippi University for Women
Mississippi Valley State University
Rust College
Tougaloo College
University of Mississippi
University of Southern Mississippi
William Carey College

Missouri
Avila College
Central Methodist College
Central Missouri State University
College of the Ozarks
Columbia College
Culver-Stockton College
Drury University
Evangel University
Fontbonne College
Hannibal-LaGrange College
Harris Stowe State College
Lincoln University
Lindenwood University
Maryville University of Saint Louis
Missouri Baptist College
Missouri Southern State College
Missouri Valley College
Missouri Western State College
Northwest Missouri State University
Park University
Rockhurst University
St. Louis University
Southeast Missouri State University
Southwest Baptist University
Southwest Missouri State University
St. Louis Community College
   St. Louis Community College at Florissant Valley
Stephens College
Truman State University
University of Missouri
   Columbia
   Kansas City
   Rolla
   St. Louis
Washington University
Webster University
Westminster College
William Jewell College
William Woods University

Montana
Carroll College
Montana State University
   Billings
   Bozeman
   Northern
Rocky Mountain College
University of Great Falls
University of Montana-Missoula
Western Montana College of The University of Montana

Nebraska
Chadron State College
College of Saint Mary
Concordia University
Creighton University
Dana College
Doane College
Grace University
Hastings College
Midland Lutheran College
Nebraska Wesleyan University
Peru State College
Union College
University of Nebraska
   Kearney
   Lincoln
   Omaha
Wayne State College

Nevada
University of Nevada
   Las Vegas
   Reno

New Hampshire
Colby-Sawyer College
Dartmouth College
Franklin Pierce College
Keene State College
New England College
New Hampshire College
Notre Dame College
Plymouth State College of the University System of New Hampshire
Rivier College
St. Anselm College
University of New Hampshire
University of New Hampshire Manchester

New Jersey
Bloomfield College
Caldwell College
Centenary College
College of St. Elizabeth
Drew University
Essex County College
Fairleigh Dickinson University
Felician College
Georgian Court College
Kean University
Monmouth University
Montclair State University
New Jersey City University
Princeton University
Ramapo College of New Jersey
Richard Stockton College of New Jersey
Rider University
Rutgers
   The State University of New Jersey: Camden College of Arts and Sciences
   The State University of New Jersey: Cook College
   The State University of New Jersey: Douglass College
   The State University of New Jersey: Livingston College
   The State University of New Jersey: Mason Gross School of the Arts
   The State University of New Jersey: Newark College of Arts and Sciences
   The State University of New Jersey: Rutgers College
   The State University of New Jersey: University College Camden
   The State University of New Jersey: University College New Brunswick
   The State University of New Jersey: University College Newark
St. Peter's College
Seton Hall University
The College of New Jersey
William Paterson University of New Jersey

New Mexico
College of Santa Fe
College of the Southwest
Eastern New Mexico University
New Mexico Highlands University
New Mexico Institute of Mining and Technology
New Mexico State University
University of New Mexico
Western New Mexico University

New York
Adelphi University
Alfred University
Barnard College
Canisius College
City University of New York
   Brooklyn College
   City College
   College of Staten Island
   Hunter College
   Lehman College
   Medgar Evers College
   Queens College
   York College
Colgate University
College of Mount St. Vincent
College of New Rochelle
College of St. Rose
Columbia University
   Columbia College
   School of General Studies
Concordia College
Cornell University
D'Youville College
Daemen College
Dominican College of Blauvelt
Dowling College
Eastman School of Music of the University of Rochester
Elmira College
Erie Community College
   City Campus
   North Campus
   South Campus
Eugene Lang College/New School University
Five Towns College
Fordham University
Hamilton College
Hartwick College
Hobart and William Smith Colleges
Hofstra University
Houghton College
Iona College
Ithaca College
Keuka College
Le Moyne College
Long Island University
   Brooklyn Campus
   C. W. Post Campus
   Southampton College
Manhattan College
Manhattanville College
Maria College
Marist College
Marymount College
Marymount Manhattan College
Medaille College
Mercy College
Mohawk Valley Community College
Molloy College
Mount St. Mary College
Nazareth College of Rochester
New York Institute of Technology
New York State College of Ceramics at Alfred University
New York University
Niagara University
Nyack College
Ohr Somayach Tanenbaum Education Center
Pace University
Pace University: Pleasantville/Briarcliff
Parsons School of Design
Pratt Institute
Rensselaer Polytechnic Institute
Roberts Wesleyan College
Rochester Institute of Technology
Russell Sage College
St. Bonaventure University
St. Francis College
St. John Fisher College
St. John's University
St. Lawrence University
St. Thomas Aquinas College
Sarah Lawrence College
Schenectady County Community College
School of Visual Arts
Siena College

Skidmore College
St. Joseph's College
St. Joseph's College
St. Joseph's College: Suffolk Campus
State University of New York
Albany
Binghamton
Buffalo
College at Brockport
College at Buffalo
College at Cortland
College at Fredonia
College at Geneseo
College at Old Westbury
College at Oneonta
College at Plattsburgh
College at Potsdam
College of Environmental Science and Forestry
New Paltz
Oswego
Stony Brook
Syracuse University
Touro College
Union College
University of Rochester
Utica College of Syracuse University
Vassar College
Wagner College
Wells College

North Carolina
Appalachian State University
Barber-Scotia College
Barton College
Belmont Abbey College
Bennett College
Brevard College
Campbell University
Catawba College
Catawba Valley Community College
Chowan College
Davidson College
Duke University
East Carolina University
Elizabeth City State University
Elon College
Fayetteville State University
Greensboro College
Guilford College
High Point University
John Wesley College
Johnson C. Smith University
Lees-McRae College
Lenoir-Rhyne College
Mars Hill College
Meredith College
Methodist College
Montreat College
Mount Olive College
North Carolina Agricultural and Technical State University
North Carolina Central University
North Carolina State University
North Carolina Wesleyan College
Pfeiffer University
Queens College
Richmond Community College
Rowan-Cabarrus Community College
St. Andrews Presbyterian College
St. Augustine's College
Salem College
Shaw University
University of North Carolina
Asheville
Chapel Hill
Charlotte
Greensboro
Pembroke
Wilmington
Wake Forest University
Warren Wilson College
Western Carolina University
Wingate University
Winston-Salem State University

North Dakota
Dickinson State University
Jamestown College
Mayville State University
Minot State University
North Dakota State University
Trinity Bible College
University of Mary
University of North Dakota
Valley City State University

Ohio
Antioch College
Ashland University
Baldwin-Wallace College
Bluffton College
Bowling Green State University
Bowling Green State University Firelands College
Capital University
Case Western Reserve University
Cedarville College
Central State University
Cleveland Institute of Music
Cleveland State University
College of Mount St. Joseph
College of Wooster
Columbus State Community College
Defiance College
Denison University
Franciscan University of Steubenville
Heidelberg College
Hiram College
John Carroll University
Kent State University
Lake Erie College
Lourdes College
Malone College
Marietta College
Miami University
Hamilton Campus
Middletown Campus
Oxford Campus
Mount Union College
Mount Vernon Nazarene College
Muskingum College
Notre Dame College of Ohio
Oberlin College
Ohio Dominican College
Ohio Northern University
Ohio State University
Columbus Campus
Lima Campus
Mansfield Campus
Marion Campus
Newark Campus
Ohio University
Ohio University
Chillicothe Campus
Eastern Campus
Southern Campus at Ironton
Zanesville Campus
Ohio Wesleyan University
Otterbein College
Shawnee State University
University of Akron
University of Cincinnati
University of Cincinnati Raymond Walters College
University of Dayton
University of Findlay
University of Rio Grande
University of Toledo
Ursuline College
Walsh University
Wilmington College
Wittenberg University
Wright State University
Xavier University
Youngstown State University

Oklahoma
Cameron University
East Central University
Langston University
Mid-America Bible College
Northeastern State University
Northwestern Oklahoma State University
Oklahoma Baptist University
Oklahoma Christian University of Science and Arts
Oklahoma City University
Oklahoma Panhandle State University
Oklahoma State University
Oral Roberts University
Southeastern Oklahoma State University
Southern Nazarene University
Southwestern Oklahoma State University
University of Central Oklahoma
University of Oklahoma
University of Science and Arts of Oklahoma
University of Tulsa

Oregon
Concordia University
Eastern Oregon University
George Fox University
Linfield College
Northwest Christian College
Oregon State University
Pacific University
Portland State University
Southern Oregon University
University of Oregon
University of Portland
Western Baptist College
Western Oregon University
Willamette University

Pennsylvania
Albright College
Allegheny College
Allentown College of St. Francis de Sales
Alvernia College
Beaver College
Bloomsburg University of Pennsylvania
Bryn Athyn College of the New Church
Bryn Mawr College
Bucknell University
Cabrini College
California University of Pennsylvania
Carlow College
Carnegie Mellon University
Cedar Crest College
Chatham College
Chestnut Hill College
Cheyney University of Pennsylvania
Clarion University of Pennsylvania
College Misericordia
Delaware Valley College
Dickinson College
Drexel University
Duquesne University
East Stroudsburg University of Pennsylvania
Eastern College
Edinboro University of Pennsylvania
Elizabethtown College
Gannon University
Geneva College
Gettysburg College
Grove City College
Gwynedd-Mercy College
Haverford College
Holy Family College
Immaculata College
Indiana University of Pennsylvania
Juniata College
King's College
Kutztown University of Pennsylvania
La Roche College
La Salle University
Lancaster Bible College
Lebanon Valley College of Pennsylvania
Lincoln University
Lock Haven University of Pennsylvania
Lycoming College
Mansfield University of Pennsylvania
Marywood University
Mercyhurst College
Messiah College
Millersville University of Pennsylvania
Montgomery County Community College
Moore College of Art and Design
Moravian College
Muhlenberg College
Neumann College
Penn State
Erie, The Behrend College
Harrisburg
University Park
Philadelphia College of Bible
Point Park College
Robert Morris College
Rosemont College
St. Francis College
St. Joseph's University
St. Vincent College
Seton Hill College
Shippensburg University of Pennsylvania
Slippery Rock University of Pennsylvania
Susquehanna University
Swarthmore College
Temple University
Thiel College
University of Pennsylvania
University of Pittsburgh
University of Pittsburgh
Bradford
Greensburg
Johnstown
University of Scranton
University of the Arts
University of the Sciences in Philadelphia
Ursinus College
Valley Forge Christian College
Villanova University
Washington and Jefferson College
Waynesburg College
West Chester University of Pennsylvania
Westminster College
Widener University
Wilkes University
Wilson College
York College of Pennsylvania

Puerto Rico
Bayamon Central University
Caribbean University
Escuela de Artes Plasticas de Puerto Rico
Inter American University of Puerto Rico
Aguadilla Campus
Arecibo Campus
San German Campus
University of Puerto Rico
Aguadilla
Arecibo Campus
Cayey University College
Humacao University College
Mayaguez Campus
Utuado
University of the Sacred Heart

Rhode Island
Brown University
Johnson & Wales University
Providence College
Rhode Island College
Roger Williams University
Salve Regina University
University of Rhode Island

South Carolina
Anderson College
Benedict College

Charleston Southern University
Claflin University
Clemson University
Coastal Carolina University
Coker College
College of Charleston
Columbia College
Columbia International University
Converse College
Erskine College
Francis Marion University
Furman University
Greenville Technical College
Lander University
Limestone College
Morris College
Newberry College
North Greenville College
Presbyterian College
South Carolina State University
Southern Wesleyan University
The Citadel
University of South Carolina
University of South Carolina
   Aiken
   Spartanburg
   Sumter
Winthrop University
Wofford College

South Dakota
Augustana College
Black Hills State University
Dakota State University
Dakota Wesleyan University
Huron University
Mount Marty College
Northern State University
South Dakota State University
University of South Dakota

Tennessee
Aquinas College
Austin Peay State University
Belmont University
Bethel College
Carson-Newman College
Christian Brothers University
Crichton College
Cumberland University
David Lipscomb University
East Tennessee State University
Fisk University
Freed-Hardeman University
Johnson Bible College
King College
Lambuth University
Lane College
LeMoyne-Owen College
Lee University
Lincoln Memorial University
Maryville College
Middle Tennessee State University
Milligan College
Rhodes College
Roane State Community College
Southern Adventist University
Tennessee State University
Tennessee Technological University
Tennessee Temple University
Tennessee Wesleyan College
Trevecca Nazarene University
Tusculum College
Union University
University of Memphis
University of Tennessee
   Chattanooga
   Knoxville
   Martin
University of the South
Vanderbilt University

Texas
Abilene Christian University
Angelo State University
Austin College
Baylor University
Concordia University at Austin
Dallas Baptist University
East Texas Baptist University
El Paso Community College
Hardin-Simmons University
Houston Baptist University
Howard Payne University
Huston-Tillotson College
Jarvis Christian College
Lamar University
LeTourneau University
Lubbock Christian University
McMurry University
Midwestern State University
Our Lady of the Lake University of San Antonio
Paul Quinn College
Prairie View A&M University
Rice University
St. Edward's University
St. Mary's University
St. Philip's College
Sam Houston State University
Schreiner College
Southern Methodist University
Southwest Texas State University
Southwestern Adventist University
Southwestern Assemblies of God University
Southwestern University
Stephen F. Austin State University
Sul Ross State University
Tarleton State University
Texas A&M International University
Texas A&M University
Texas A&M University
   Commerce
   Corpus Christi
   Kingsville
   Texarkana
Texas Christian University
Texas College
Texas Lutheran University
Texas Southern University
Texas Tech University
Texas Wesleyan University
Texas Woman's University
Trinity University
University of Dallas
University of Houston
University of Houston
   Clear Lake
   Downtown
   Victoria
University of Mary Hardin-Baylor
University of North Texas
University of St. Thomas
University of Texas
   Arlington
   Austin
   Dallas
   El Paso
   Pan American
   San Antonio
   Tyler
   of the Permian Basin
University of the Incarnate Word
Wayland Baptist University
West Texas A&M University

Utah
Brigham Young University
Dixie State College of Utah
Snow College
Southern Utah University
University of Utah
Utah State University
Weber State University
Westminster College

Vermont
Bennington College
Castleton State College
Champlain College
College of St. Joseph in Vermont
Goddard College
Green Mountain College
Johnson State College
Lyndon State College
Middlebury College
Norwich University
St. Michael's College
Trinity College of Vermont
University of Vermont

Virginia
Averett College
Bluefield College
Bridgewater College
Christopher Newport University
College of William and Mary
Eastern Mennonite University
Emory & Henry College
Ferrum College
George Mason University
Hampton University
Hollins University
James Madison University
Liberty University
Longwood College
Lynchburg College
Mary Baldwin College
Mary Washington College
New River Community College
Norfolk State University
Old Dominion University
Patrick Henry Community College
Radford University
Randolph-Macon College
Randolph-Macon Woman's College
Roanoke College
St. Paul's College
Shenandoah University
Sweet Briar College
University of Richmond
University of Virginia
University of Virginia's College at Wise
Virginia Commonwealth University
Virginia Intermont College
Virginia Military Institute
Virginia Polytechnic Institute and State University
Virginia State University
Virginia Union University
Virginia Wesleyan College
Washington and Lee University

Washington
Antioch University Seattle
Central Washington University
City University
Eastern Washington University
Evergreen State College
Gonzaga University
Grays Harbor College
Heritage College
Pacific Lutheran University
St. Martin's College
Seattle Pacific University
Seattle University
South Seattle Community College
University of Puget Sound
University of Washington
Walla Walla College
Washington State University
Western Washington University
Whitman College
Whitworth College

West Virginia
Alderson-Broaddus College
Bethany College
Bluefield State College
Concord College
Davis and Elkins College
Fairmont State College
Glenville State College
Marshall University
Ohio Valley College
Shepherd College
Southern West Virginia Community and Technical College
University of Charleston
West Liberty State College
West Virginia State College
West Virginia University
West Virginia University Parkersburg
West Virginia Wesleyan College
Wheeling Jesuit University

Wisconsin
Alverno College
Beloit College
Cardinal Stritch University
Carroll College
Carthage College
Concordia University Wisconsin
Lakeland College
Lawrence University
Marian College of Fond du Lac
Marquette University
Milwaukee Institute of Art & Design
Mount Mary College
Mount Senario College
Northland College
Ripon College
St. Norbert College
Silver Lake College
University of Wisconsin
   Eau Claire
   Green Bay
   La Crosse
   Madison
   Milwaukee
   Oshkosh
   Parkside
   Platteville
   Richland
   River Falls
   Stevens Point
   Stout
   Superior
   Whitewater
Viterbo University
Wisconsin Lutheran College

Wyoming
Northwest College
University of Wyoming

United Nations semester

Alabama
Spring Hill College

Arkansas
University of Arkansas

California
Mount St. Mary's College
Occidental College
Point Loma Nazarene University
Scripps College
University of the Pacific

Connecticut
Sacred Heart University
Trinity College

Florida
Barry University
Eckerd College
Florida Southern College

United Nations semester

Georgia
Agnes Scott College

Illinois
Illinois Wesleyan University
Lincoln Land Community College
Millikin University
North Central College
Rockford College

Indiana
DePauw University
Franklin College
Hanover College
Indiana University Bloomington
University of Indianapolis
Valparaiso University

Iowa
Drake University
Morningside College
Simpson College

Kansas
Fort Hays State University

Maryland
Western Maryland College

Minnesota
Hamline University

Mississippi
Millsaps College

Missouri
Park University
Westminster College
William Jewell College
William Woods University

Nebraska
Dana College
Nebraska Wesleyan University

New Hampshire
Keene State College

New Jersey
College of St. Elizabeth
Drew University

New York
Alfred University
College of New Rochelle
Elmira College
Fordham University
Hobart and William Smith Colleges
Long Island University
    Brooklyn Campus
    C. W. Post Campus
Marist College
New York State College of Ceramics at Alfred University
State University of New York New Paltz
Wagner College

North Carolina
Guilford College
Lenoir-Rhyne College
Meredith College
Salem College

Ohio
Baldwin-Wallace College
College of Wooster
Muskingum College
Ohio Wesleyan University
University of Dayton

Pennsylvania
Gettysburg College
Lycoming College
Seton Hill College
Susquehanna University
Thiel College
University of Scranton
Ursinus College
Wilson College

South Carolina
Winthrop University

Texas
Schreiner College
Trinity University

Utah
Weber State University

Virginia
Hollins University
Randolph-Macon College

West Virginia
Bethany College

Wisconsin
Carroll College
University of Wisconsin Milwaukee

Wyoming
University of Wyoming

Urban semester

California
Westmont College

Colorado
Colorado College

Connecticut
Trinity College
University of Connecticut
Wesleyan University

Idaho
Ricks College

Illinois
Greenville College
Illinois Wesleyan University
Knox College
Lake Forest College
Millikin University
Monmouth College
Wheaton College

Indiana
Bethel College
DePauw University
Goshen College
Manchester College
Valparaiso University
Wabash College

Iowa
Briar Cliff College
Coe College
Cornell College
Grinnell College
University of Dubuque
Wartburg College

Kansas
Bethany College
McPherson College
Southwestern College

Maine
Bates College

Massachusetts
Gordon College
Worcester State College

Michigan
Albion College
Alma College
Calvin College
Kalamazoo College
Spring Arbor College

Minnesota
Carleton College
College of St. Benedict
Concordia College: Moorhead
Macalester College
Northwestern College
St. John's University
St. Mary's University of Minnesota
St. Olaf College
University of St. Thomas

Missouri
Westminster College

Nebraska
Dana College
Nebraska Wesleyan University

New York
Colgate University
Cornell University
Eugene Lang College/New School University
Hartwick College
Hobart and William Smith Colleges
New York State College of Ceramics at Alfred University

Ohio
Ohio Wesleyan University
University of Dayton
Wittenberg University
Xavier University

Oklahoma
Southern Nazarene University

Oregon
Linfield College
Willamette University

Pennsylvania
Albright College
Allegheny College
Allentown College of St. Francis de Sales
East Stroudsburg University of Pennsylvania
Juniata College
Lafayette College
Lehigh University
Messiah College
Moravian College
Susquehanna University

South Dakota
Augustana College

Texas
Trinity University

Virginia
Virginia Commonwealth University

Washington
Whitman College

Wisconsin
Beloit College
Lawrence University
Mount Senario College
Ripon College
St. Norbert College

Visiting/exchange student program

Alabama
Alabama Agricultural and Mechanical University
Auburn University at Montgomery
Birmingham-Southern College
University of Alabama

Alaska
Alaska Pacific University
University of Alaska
    Anchorage
    Fairbanks
    Southeast

Arizona
Arizona State University
Glendale Community College
Grand Canyon University
Northern Arizona University
University of Arizona

Arkansas
Arkansas Tech University
Hendrix College
Ouachita Baptist University
University of Arkansas
    Little Rock

California
Azusa Pacific University
Biola University
California Baptist University
California College of Arts and Crafts
California Lutheran University
California Polytechnic State University: San Luis Obispo
California State Polytechnic University: Pomona
California State University
    Bakersfield
    Chico
    Dominguez Hills
    Fresno
    Hayward
    Los Angeles
    Northridge
    San Marcos
    Stanislaus
Chapman University
Claremont McKenna College
College of Notre Dame
College of the Siskiyous
Concordia University
Dominican University of California
Fashion Institute of Design and Merchandising
Fashion Institute of Design and Merchandising San Francisco
Foothill College
Harvey Mudd College
Holy Names College
Humboldt State University
Mills College
MiraCosta College
Mount St. Mary's College
Occidental College
Otis College of Art and Design
Pitzer College
Pomona College
St. Mary's College of California
San Diego State University

San Francisco Art Institute
San Francisco State University
San Jose State University
Santa Clara University
Scripps College
Sonoma State University
Southern California Institute of
    Architecture
University of California
    Berkeley
    Los Angeles
    Riverside
    San Diego
    Santa Barbara
    Santa Cruz
University of La Verne
University of Redlands
University of San Diego
University of San Francisco
University of Southern California
Vanguard University of Southern
    California
Westmont College
Whittier College

Colorado
Colorado State University
Fort Lewis College
Mesa State College
United States Air Force Academy
University of Colorado
    Boulder
University of Northern Colorado
University of Southern Colorado
Western State College of Colorado

Connecticut
Central Connecticut State University
Connecticut College
Eastern Connecticut State University
Fairfield University
Southern Connecticut State University
Trinity College
United States Coast Guard Academy
University of Bridgeport
University of Hartford
Wesleyan University
Yale University

Delaware
Delaware State University
Wesley College

District of Columbia
American University
Catholic University of America
Corcoran College of Art and Design
Gallaudet University
Howard University
Trinity College

Florida
Broward Community College
Eckerd College
Flagler College
Florida Atlantic University
Florida International University
Lake City Community College
New College of the University of South
    Florida
Ringling School of Art and Design
Rollins College
St. Petersburg Junior College
Stetson University
University of Central Florida
University of Florida
University of South Florida
University of West Florida

Georgia
Agnes Scott College
Atlanta College of Art
Augusta State University

Brewton-Parker College
Clark Atlanta University
Covenant College
Emory University
Georgia College and State University
Morehouse College
Reinhardt College
Savannah State University
Spelman College
State University of West Georgia
University of Georgia
Valdosta State University
Wesleyan College

Hawaii
Brigham Young University
    Hawaii
University of Hawaii
    Hilo
    Kapiolani Community College
    Manoa

Idaho
Albertson College of Idaho
Boise State University
Idaho State University
University of Idaho

Illinois
Barat College
Benedictine University
Chicago State University
Concordia University
Illinois Institute of Technology
Illinois State University
Illinois Wesleyan University
Judson College
Lake Forest College
Millikin University
North Central College
North Park University
Northeastern Illinois University
Oakton Community College
St. Xavier University
School of the Art Institute of Chicago
Trinity International University
University of Chicago
University of Illinois
    Chicago
    Urbana-Champaign
Wheaton College

Indiana
Ball State University
DePauw University
Earlham College
Indiana University--Purdue University
    Indiana University-Purdue
    University Fort Wayne
Purdue University
St. Mary-of-the-Woods College
University of Evansville
University of Indianapolis
University of Notre Dame
Valparaiso University
Wabash College

Iowa
Buena Vista University
Cornell College
Drake University
Graceland University
Grinnell College
Iowa State University
Iowa Wesleyan College
Kirkwood Community College
Maharishi University of Management
Morningside College
University of Iowa
University of Northern Iowa

Kansas
Bethany College

Emporia State University
Fort Hays State University
Johnson County Community College
Kansas State University
McPherson College
Pittsburg State University
St. Mary College
Southwestern College

Kentucky
Berea College
Campbellsville University
Kentucky State University
Morehead State University
Murray State University
Union College
University of Kentucky
University of Louisville
Western Kentucky University

Louisiana
Centenary College of Louisiana
Louisiana State University and
    Agricultural and Mechanical College
Loyola University New Orleans
Nicholls State University
Northwestern State University
Our Lady of Holy Cross College
Southeastern Louisiana University
Southern University and Agricultural and
    Mechanical College
Tulane University
University of Louisiana at Lafayette
University of New Orleans
Xavier University of Louisiana

Maine
Bates College
Bowdoin College
Colby College
College of the Atlantic
Maine College of Art
Thomas College
University of Maine
University of Maine
    Farmington
    Presque Isle
University of Southern Maine

Maryland
Bowie State University
Maryland Institute College of Art
St. Mary's College of Maryland
Salisbury State University
Towson University
University of Baltimore
University of Maryland
    College Park
    Eastern Shore
Washington College
Western Maryland College

Massachusetts
Amherst College
Anna Maria College
Boston College
College of the Holy Cross
Eastern Nazarene College
Elms College
Emmanuel College
Framingham State College
Gordon College
Harvard College
Hellenic College/Holy Cross
Lesley College
Massachusetts College of Art
Massachusetts College of Liberal Arts
Middlesex Community College
Montserrat College of Art
Mount Holyoke College
Northeastern University
Northern Essex Community College
Pine Manor College
Regis College

Salem State College
School of the Museum of Fine Arts
Simmons College
Simon's Rock College of Bard
Smith College
Suffolk University
Tufts University
University of Massachusetts
    Amherst
    Boston
Wellesley College
Westfield State College
Williams College
Worcester Polytechnic Institute
Worcester State College

Michigan
Albion College
Alma College
Aquinas College
Center for Creative Studies: College of
    Art and Design
Cleary College
Concordia College
Grand Valley State University
Kalamazoo College
Kendall College of Art and Design
Lansing Community College
Michigan State University
Michigan Technological University
Northern Michigan University
Siena Heights University
University of Michigan
Wayne State University
Western Michigan University

Minnesota
Bethel College
College of St. Catherine: St. Paul
    Campus
Concordia College: Moorhead
Concordia University: St. Paul
Gustavus Adolphus College
Hamline University
Minneapolis College of Art and Design
Minnesota State University, Mankato
Moorhead State University
North Central University
Northwestern College
St. Cloud State University
Southwest State University
University of Minnesota
    Morris
    Twin Cities
University of St. Thomas
Winona State University

Mississippi
Jackson State University
Mississippi State University
Tougaloo College

Missouri
Avila College
Central Missouri State University
Drury University
Fontbonne College
Kansas City Art Institute
Lindenwood University
Maple Woods Community College
Northwest Missouri State University
Research College of Nursing
Rockhurst University
St. Louis University
Southeast Missouri State University
Southwest Missouri State University
St. Louis Community College
    St. Louis Community College at
        Florissant Valley
Truman State University
University of Missouri
    Columbia
    St. Louis
Washington University

Westminster College
William Jewell College
William Woods University

Montana
Little Big Horn College
Montana State University
    Bozeman
Rocky Mountain College
University of Montana-Missoula

Nebraska
College of Saint Mary
Creighton University
Doane College
Hastings College
University of Nebraska
    Kearney
    Lincoln
    Omaha

Nevada
University of Nevada
    Las Vegas
    Reno

New Hampshire
Colby-Sawyer College
Dartmouth College
Franklin Pierce College
Keene State College
New England College
New Hampshire College
Notre Dame College
Plymouth State College of the University System of New Hampshire
University of New Hampshire
University of New Hampshire
    Manchester

New Jersey
College of St. Elizabeth
County College of Morris
Drew University
Montclair State University
Rutgers
    The State University of New Jersey: Camden College of Arts and Sciences
    The State University of New Jersey: Rutgers College
St. Peter's College
Stevens Institute of Technology
The College of New Jersey
William Paterson University of New Jersey

New Mexico
College of Santa Fe
Eastern New Mexico University
Institute of American Indian Arts
New Mexico Institute of Mining and Technology
New Mexico State University
University of New Mexico

New York
Alfred University
Bard College
Barnard College
Canisius College
City University of New York
    Baruch College
    Borough of Manhattan Community College
    Brooklyn College
    City College
    Hunter College
    John Jay College of Criminal Justice
    Lehman College
Colgate University
College of Mount St. Vincent

College of New Rochelle
College of St. Rose
Columbia University
    Columbia College
Concordia College
Cooper Union for the Advancement of Science and Art
Cornell University
D'Youville College
Elmira College
Erie Community College
    City Campus
    North Campus
    South Campus
Eugene Lang College/New School University
Fashion Institute of Technology
Fordham University
Hartwick College
Hobart and William Smith Colleges
Houghton College
Juilliard School
Keuka College
Long Island University
    Brooklyn Campus
    C. W. Post Campus
    Southampton College
Manhattan College
Manhattanville College
Marymount College
Marymount Manhattan College
Monroe Community College
Mount St. Mary College
Nazareth College of Rochester
New York State College of Ceramics at Alfred University
New York University
Niagara University
Parsons School of Design
Pratt Institute
Rensselaer Polytechnic Institute
Rochester Institute of Technology
Russell Sage College
St. Lawrence University
St. Thomas Aquinas College
Sarah Lawrence College
Skidmore College
State University of New York
    Albany
    Binghamton
    Buffalo
    College at Buffalo
    College at Cortland
    College at Fredonia
    College at Geneseo
    College at Old Westbury
    College at Plattsburgh
    College at Potsdam
    New Paltz
    Oswego
    Stony Brook
United States Military Academy
University of Rochester
Utica College of Syracuse University
Vassar College
Wagner College

North Carolina
Bennett College
Campbell University
Davidson College
Duke University
East Carolina University
Elon College
Forsyth Technical Community College
Johnson C. Smith University
Lenoir-Rhyne College
Mars Hill College
Meredith College
Methodist College
North Carolina State University
Queens College
St. Andrews Presbyterian College
Salem College

University of North Carolina
    Charlotte
    Wilmington
Wake Forest University
Warren Wilson College

Ohio
Baldwin-Wallace College
Bluffton College
Bowling Green State University
Cleveland State University
College of Wooster
Defiance College
Denison University
John Carroll University
Kenyon College
Malone College
Marietta College
Miami University
    Oxford Campus
Muskingum College
Notre Dame College of Ohio
Oberlin College
Ohio State University
    Columbus Campus
Ohio Wesleyan University
Otterbein College
University of Rio Grande
University of Toledo
Walsh University
Wittenberg University
Wright State University
Xavier University
Youngstown State University

Oklahoma
East Central University
Oklahoma Baptist University
Oklahoma City University
Oklahoma State University
University of Oklahoma
University of Tulsa

Oregon
Concordia University
Eastern Oregon University
George Fox University
Linfield College
Mount Hood Community College
Oregon Health Sciences University
Oregon State University
Pacific Northwest College of Art
Portland State University
Reed College
Southern Oregon University
University of Oregon
Willamette University

Pennsylvania
Albright College
Allegheny College
Bryn Mawr College
Cabrini College
California University of Pennsylvania
Carnegie Mellon University
Chatham College
Chestnut Hill College
Clarion University of Pennsylvania
College Misericordia
Dickinson College
Duquesne University
East Stroudsburg University of Pennsylvania
Edinboro University of Pennsylvania
Franklin and Marshall College
Gettysburg College
Haverford College
Indiana University of Pennsylvania
Juniata College
La Salle University
Lebanon Valley College of Pennsylvania
Lehigh University
Lincoln University
Mansfield University of Pennsylvania

Messiah College
Muhlenberg College
Penn State
    University Park
Rosemont College
St. Francis College
St. Joseph's University
Seton Hill College
Slippery Rock University of Pennsylvania
Susquehanna University
Swarthmore College
Temple University
University of Pennsylvania
University of Scranton
University of the Arts
West Chester University of Pennsylvania
Westminster College
Wilson College

Puerto Rico
Inter American University of Puerto Rico
    Aguadilla Campus
    Guayama Campus
Pontifical Catholic University of Puerto Rico
Technological College of San Juan
University of Puerto Rico
    Arecibo Campus
    Bayamon University College
    Cayey University College
    Humacao University College
    Mayaguez Campus
    Medical Sciences Campus
    Rio Piedras Campus
University of the Sacred Heart

Rhode Island
Brown University
Rhode Island College
Salve Regina University
University of Rhode Island

South Carolina
Clemson University
Coker College
College of Charleston
Columbia College
Horry-Georgetown Technical College
Lander University
Presbyterian College
South Carolina State University
University of South Carolina
University of South Carolina
    Spartanburg
Winthrop University

South Dakota
Black Hills State University
Huron University
South Dakota State University
University of South Dakota

Tennessee
Carson-Newman College
East Tennessee State University
LeMoyne-Owen College
Lee University
Tennessee State University
Union University
University of Memphis
University of Tennessee
    Knoxville
    Martin
    Memphis

Texas
Angelo State University
Austin College
Cedar Valley College
Houston Community College System
Rice University
Southern Methodist University

Southwestern University
Texas Christian University
Texas Wesleyan University
University of North Texas
University of the Incarnate Word

Utah
University of Utah
Utah State University
Weber State University

Vermont
Goddard College
Green Mountain College
Johnson State College
Marlboro College
Middlebury College
St. Michael's College
University of Vermont

Virginia
Christopher Newport University
College of William and Mary
George Mason University
Hampden-Sydney College
Hollins University
Mary Baldwin College
Radford University
Randolph-Macon College
Randolph-Macon Woman's College
St. Paul's College
Southside Virginia Community College
Sweet Briar College
University of Richmond
Virginia Commonwealth University
Virginia Military Institute
Virginia Polytechnic Institute and State University
Virginia State University
Washington and Lee University

Washington
Central Washington University
Edmonds Community College
Everett Community College
Gonzaga University
Pacific Lutheran University
Seattle Pacific University
Seattle University
University of Washington
Washington State University
Western Washington University
Whitman College
Whitworth College

West Virginia
Alderson-Broaddus College
West Virginia University
West Virginia Wesleyan College
Wheeling Jesuit University

Wisconsin
Alverno College
Beloit College
Carroll College
Concordia University Wisconsin
Marquette University
Milwaukee Institute of Art & Design
Northland College
Ripon College
University of Wisconsin
    Eau Claire
    Green Bay
    La Crosse
    Parkside
    Platteville
    River Falls
    Sheboygan County
    Stout
    Superior

Wyoming
University of Wyoming

Washington semester

Alabama
Alabama Agricultural and Mechanical University
Birmingham-Southern College
Huntingdon College
Spring Hill College
University of Alabama

Arizona
Arizona State University
Grand Canyon University
Northern Arizona University

Arkansas
Hendrix College
John Brown University

California
Azusa Pacific University
Biola University
California Baptist University
California Lutheran University
California State University
    Long Beach
Chapman University
Claremont McKenna College
Fresno Pacific University
Loyola Marymount University
Master's College
Mills College
Mount St. Mary's College
Occidental College
Orange Coast College
Pepperdine University
Point Loma Nazarene University
Pomona College
Santa Clara University
Scripps College
Stanford University
University of California
    Davis
    Irvine
    Riverside
    San Diego
    Santa Barbara
    Santa Cruz
University of Redlands
University of Southern California
University of the Pacific
Vanguard University of Southern California
Westmont College
Whittier College

Colorado
Colorado Christian University
Colorado College
Mesa State College
Metropolitan State College of Denver

Connecticut
Albertus Magnus College
Connecticut College
Eastern Connecticut State University
Fairfield University
Quinnipiac University
Trinity College
University of Bridgeport
University of Hartford
Wesleyan University

Delaware
University of Delaware

District of Columbia
American University
Catholic University of America
Georgetown University
Trinity College

Florida
Barry University
Eckerd College
Florida Community College at Jacksonville
Florida Gulf Coast University
Florida Southern College
New College of the University of South Florida
Palm Beach Atlantic College
Rollins College
Stetson University
University of Miami
University of Tampa
University of West Florida

Georgia
Agnes Scott College
Berry College
Columbus State University
Covenant College
Emory University
Oglethorpe University
Oxford College of Emory University
Spelman College
State University of West Georgia
University of Georgia

Idaho
Northwest Nazarene University

Illinois
Blackburn College
Bradley University
Dominican University
Elmhurst College
Eureka College
Greenville College
Illinois College
Illinois State University
Illinois Wesleyan University
Judson College
Knox College
Lake Forest College
Loyola University of Chicago
MacMurray College
McKendree College
Millikin University
Monmouth College
North Central College
North Park University
Northwestern University
Olivet Nazarene University
Rockford College
Southern Illinois University Carbondale
Trinity Christian College
Trinity International University
University of Illinois Urbana-Champaign
University of St. Francis
Wheaton College

Indiana
Ball State University
Bethel College
DePauw University
Franklin College
Hanover College
Indiana University
    Bloomington
    Northwest
Indiana University--Purdue University
    Indiana University-Purdue University Fort Wayne
Saint Mary's College
St. Joseph's College
Taylor University
University of Indianapolis
University of Notre Dame
Valparaiso University
Wabash College

Iowa
Briar Cliff College
Central College
Coe College
Cornell College
Dordt College
Drake University
Grand View College
Iowa State University
Luther College
Morningside College
Northwestern College
Simpson College
University of Iowa
University of Northern Iowa
Wartburg College
William Penn University

Kansas
Bethany College
MidAmerica Nazarene University
Southwestern College
Sterling College
Tabor College
University of Kansas
Wichita State University

Kentucky
Asbury College
Bellarmine College
Campbellsville University
Kentucky Wesleyan College
Morehead State University
Transylvania University
Western Kentucky University

Louisiana
Centenary College of Louisiana
Louisiana State University Shreveport
Loyola University New Orleans
Tulane University
University of Louisiana at Lafayette
University of New Orleans

Maine
Bates College
Bowdoin College
Colby College
St. Joseph's College
Unity College
University of Southern Maine

Maryland
Columbia Union College
Hood College
Johns Hopkins University
Mount St. Mary's College
Salisbury State University
Washington College
Western Maryland College

Massachusetts
American International College
Anna Maria College
Assumption College
Bay Path College
Boston College
Boston University
Brandeis University
Clark University
College of the Holy Cross
Eastern Nazarene College
Elms College
Emmanuel College
Framingham State College
Gordon College
Lesley College
Massachusetts College of Liberal Arts
Massachusetts Institute of Technology
Merrimack College
Mount Holyoke College
Nichols College

Pine Manor College
Regis College
Simmons College
Smith College
Stonehill College
Suffolk University
Tufts University
University of Massachusetts
 Dartmouth
Wellesley College
Western New England College
Westfield State College
Wheaton College
Worcester Polytechnic Institute
Worcester State College

Michigan
Adrian College
Albion College
Alma College
Calvin College
Central Michigan University
Cornerstone College and Grand Rapids
 Baptist Seminary
Eastern Michigan University
Grand Valley State University
Hillsdale College
Hope College
Lake Superior State University
Northern Michigan University
Spring Arbor College
University of Detroit Mercy
University of Michigan
University of Michigan
 Dearborn

Minnesota
Bethel College
College of St. Catherine: St. Paul
 Campus
Concordia College: Moorhead
Gustavus Adolphus College
Hamline University
Macalester College
Moorhead State University
Northwestern College
St. Mary's University of Minnesota
St. Olaf College
University of Minnesota
 Morris
University of St. Thomas

Mississippi
Millsaps College
Mississippi State University
Tougaloo College

Missouri
Avila College
Drury University
Evangel University
Lindenwood University
Maryville University of Saint Louis
Northwest Missouri State University
Park University
Research College of Nursing
Rockhurst University
Southwest Baptist University
Stephens College
University of Missouri
 Columbia
Washington University
Westminster College
William Jewell College
William Woods University

Nebraska
Creighton University
Doane College
Nebraska Wesleyan University

Nevada
University of Nevada
 Las Vegas

New Hampshire
Colby-Sawyer College
Dartmouth College
Franklin Pierce College
Keene State College
St. Anselm College
University of New Hampshire
University of New Hampshire
 Manchester

New Jersey
Caldwell College
College of St. Elizabeth
Drew University
Kean University
Monmouth University
Montclair State University
New Jersey City University
Richard Stockton College of New Jersey
Rutgers
 The State University of New Jersey:
  Douglass College
 The State University of New Jersey:
  Livingston College
 The State University of New Jersey:
  Newark College of Arts and
  Sciences
 The State University of New Jersey:
  Rutgers College
 The State University of New Jersey:
  University College New
  Brunswick
St. Peter's College
Seton Hall University

New Mexico
University of New Mexico

New York
Alfred University
Bard College
Canisius College
City University of New York
 Brooklyn College
 Lehman College
Colgate University
College of New Rochelle
Cornell University
Daemen College
Elmira College
Hamilton College
Hartwick College
Hilbert College
Hobart and William Smith Colleges
Hofstra University
Houghton College
Jamestown Community College
Keuka College
Le Moyne College
Long Island University
 C. W. Post Campus
 Southampton College
Manhattan College
Manhattanville College
Marist College
Molloy College
Nazareth College of Rochester
New York State College of Ceramics at
 Alfred University
New York University
Niagara University
Nyack College
Roberts Wesleyan College
St. Bonaventure University
St. John Fisher College
St. Lawrence University
St. Thomas Aquinas College
Siena College
Skidmore College
State University of New York
 Albany
 Binghamton
 Buffalo
 College at Brockport
 College at Buffalo
 College at Cortland
 College at Fredonia
 College at Geneseo
 College at Oneonta
 Oswego
 Stony Brook
Union College
United States Military Academy
University of Rochester
Utica College of Syracuse University
Vassar College
Wagner College
Wells College

North Carolina
Barton College
Bennett College
Campbell University
Catawba College
Chowan College
Davidson College
Duke University
Elon College
Guilford College
Johnson C. Smith University
Lenoir-Rhyne College
Meredith College
Methodist College
Montreat College
Pfeiffer University
Queens College
St. Andrews Presbyterian College
Salem College
University of North Carolina
 Asheville
 Greensboro
 Pembroke

Ohio
Ashland University
Baldwin-Wallace College
Bluffton College
Bowling Green State University
Capital University
Case Western Reserve University
College of Wooster
Denison University
Heidelberg College
Hiram College
John Carroll University
Kent State University
Kenyon College
Malone College
Marietta College
Mount Union College
Mount Vernon Nazarene College
Muskingum College
Oberlin College
Ohio Dominican College
Ohio Northern University
Ohio Wesleyan University
Otterbein College
University of Cincinnati
University of Dayton
University of Findlay
Wilmington College
Wittenberg University
Xavier University

Oklahoma
Oklahoma City University
Oral Roberts University
Southern Nazarene University
University of Oklahoma
University of Tulsa

Oregon
George Fox University
Lewis & Clark College
Linfield College
Pacific University
Portland State University
University of Portland
Western Baptist College
Willamette University

Pennsylvania
Albright College
Allegheny College
Allentown College of St. Francis de Sales
Alvernia College
Beaver College
Bucknell University
Carnegie Mellon University
Cedar Crest College
Chatham College
Dickinson College
Duquesne University
Eastern College
Elizabethtown College
Franklin and Marshall College
Gannon University
Geneva College
Gettysburg College
Grove City College
Indiana University of Pennsylvania
Juniata College
King's College
La Roche College
Lafayette College
Lebanon Valley College of Pennsylvania
Lehigh University
Lycoming College
Mansfield University of Pennsylvania
Mercyhurst College
Messiah College
Moravian College
Muhlenberg College
Rosemont College
St. Francis College
St. Joseph's University
Seton Hill College
Shippensburg University of Pennsylvania
Susquehanna University
Thiel College
University of Pittsburgh
University of Pittsburgh
 Greensburg
University of Scranton
Ursinus College
Villanova University
Washington and Jefferson College
Westminster College
Wilson College

Puerto Rico
Inter American University of Puerto Rico
 Aguadilla Campus
 Barranquitas Campus
 Fajardo Campus
University of Puerto Rico
 Rio Piedras Campus

Rhode Island
Providence College
Roger Williams University
Salve Regina University
University of Rhode Island

South Carolina
College of Charleston
Columbia College
Furman University
Presbyterian College
Southern Wesleyan University
Wofford College

South Dakota
Augustana College
Northern State University

Tennessee
Belmont University
Carson-Newman College
King College
Lee University
Maryville College
Milligan College
Rhodes College
Tennessee Temple University
Union University
University of the South
Vanderbilt University

Texas
Austin College
Dallas Baptist University
East Texas Baptist University
LeTourneau University
Midland College
St. Mary's University
Southern Methodist University
Southwest Texas State University
Southwestern University
Texas Christian University
Texas Lutheran University
Trinity University
University of Dallas
University of Houston

Utah
Brigham Young University
University of Utah
Weber State University

Vermont
Middlebury College
St. Michael's College
Trinity College of Vermont
University of Vermont

Virginia
Eastern Mennonite University
Hampden-Sydney College
Hollins University
James Madison University
Liberty University
Randolph-Macon College
Randolph-Macon Woman's College
Roanoke College
Sweet Briar College
University of Richmond
Virginia Commonwealth University
Virginia Polytechnic Institute and State University
Washington and Lee University

Washington
Gonzaga University
St. Martin's College
Seattle Pacific University
University of Washington
Western Washington University
Whitman College
Whitworth College

West Virginia
Bethany College
Davis and Elkins College
Marshall University
Shepherd College
University of Charleston
West Virginia University
West Virginia Wesleyan College
Wheeling Jesuit University

Wisconsin
Beloit College
Carroll College
Carthage College
Lakeland College
Lawrence University
Marquette University
Mount Mary College
Ripon College
St. Norbert College
University of Wisconsin
    Milwaukee

Wyoming
University of Wyoming

Weekend college

Alabama
Alabama Agricultural and Mechanical University
Athens State University
Auburn University at Montgomery
Bessemer State Technical College
Bevill State Community College
Calhoun Community College
Enterprise State Junior College
Gadsden State Community College
George C. Wallace State Community College
    Dothan
Harry M. Ayers State Technical College
Northwest-Shoals Community College
Shelton State Community College
Troy State University
    Dothan
University of Alabama
University of Alabama
    Birmingham
University of South Alabama
Wallace State Community College at Hanceville

Arizona
Arizona Western College
Cochise College
DeVry Institute of Technology
    Phoenix
Glendale Community College
Mesa Community College
Mohave Community College
Northern Arizona University
Paradise Valley Community College
Pima Community College
Rio Salado College
Yavapai College

Arkansas
Arkansas Tech University
Mississippi County Community College
North Arkansas College
University of Arkansas
    Little Rock

California
Barstow College
Biola University
Chabot College
Chaffey Community College
City College of San Francisco
Coastline Community College
College of San Mateo
Crafton Hills College
Cuesta College
Cuyamaca College
De Anza College
DeVry Institute of Technology
    Fremont
    Long Beach
    Pomona
    West Hills
Deep Springs College
Diablo Valley College
Dominican University of California
East Los Angeles College
Evergreen Valley College
Foothill College
Fresno City College
Golden West College
Holy Names College
John F. Kennedy University
Long Beach City College
Los Angeles Harbor College
Los Angeles Southwest College
Marymount College
MiraCosta College
Mission College
Modesto Junior College
Monterey Peninsula College
Mount St. Mary's College
Mount San Jacinto College
Napa Valley College
Ohlone College
Orange Coast College
Pacific Oaks College
Palomar College
Patten College
Rio Hondo College
Riverside Community College
Sacramento City College
Saddleback College
St. Mary's College of California
San Diego City College
San Diego Miramar College
San Joaquin Delta College
San Jose City College
Santa Ana College
Santa Monica College
Shasta College
Sierra College
Simpson College
University of La Verne

Colorado
Aims Community College
Arapahoe Community College
Colorado Christian University
Community College of Aurora
Community College of Denver
Denver Technical College: A Division of DeVry University
Front Range Community College
Metropolitan State College of Denver
Morgan Community College
Pikes Peak Community College
Red Rocks Community College
University of Denver
University of Southern Colorado

Connecticut
Capital Community College
Eastern Connecticut State University
Housatonic Community-Technical College
Manchester Community-Technical College
Norwalk Community-Technical College
Quinebaug Valley Community College
Sacred Heart University
St. Joseph College
Teikyo Post University
University of Bridgeport

Delaware
Wilmington College

District of Columbia
Southeastern University
Trinity College
University of the District of Columbia

Florida
Bethune-Cookman College
Broward Community College
Daytona Beach Community College
Edward Waters College
Florida Agricultural and Mechanical University
Florida Atlantic University
Florida Baptist Theological College
Florida Community College at Jacksonville
Florida International University
Gulf Coast Community College
Hillsborough Community College
Indian River Community College
Jacksonville University
Jones College
Miami-Dade Community College
Northwood University
    Florida Campus
Palm Beach Community College
Pasco-Hernando Community College
Pensacola Junior College
St. Leo University
St. Petersburg Junior College
Santa Fe Community College
Seminole Community College
University of Florida
University of North Florida
University of South Florida
Valencia Community College

Georgia
Albany State University
Armstrong Atlantic State University
Atlanta Metropolitan College
Bainbridge College
Brenau University
Brewton-Parker College
Clayton College and State University
Darton College
DeVry Institute of Technology
    Alpharetta
    Atlanta
Georgia Perimeter College
Georgia Southern University
Gwinnett Technical Institute
Middle Georgia College
Shorter College
State University of West Georgia

Hawaii
Hawaii Pacific University
University of Hawaii
    Kapiolani Community College
    Leeward Community College
    Maui Community College
    West Oahu

Idaho
Boise State University
Eastern Idaho Technical College
Lewis-Clark State College

Illinois
Benedictine University
Black Hawk College
City Colleges of Chicago
    Harry S. Truman College
    Kennedy-King College
    Malcolm X College
    Richard J. Daley College
    Wright College
College of DuPage
De Paul University
DeVry Institute of Technology
    Addison
    Chicago
Elgin Community College
Governors State University
Illinois Eastern Community Colleges
    Frontier Community College
    Lincoln Trail College
    Olney Central College
    Wabash Valley College
International Academy of Merchandising and Design
John A. Logan College
Kaskaskia College
Lincoln Land Community College
Moraine Valley Community College
North Central College
Oakton Community College
Parkland College
Prairie State College
Roosevelt University
St. Xavier University

Weekend college

Shimer College
Southeastern Illinois College
Southern Illinois University
    Edwardsville
Southwestern Illinois College
Triton College
University of Illinois
    Springfield
University of St. Francis
Waubonsee Community College
Western Illinois University
William Rainey Harper College

Indiana

Bethel College
Calumet College of St. Joseph
Indiana University
    East
    Northwest
    South Bend
    Southeast
Indiana University--Purdue University
    Indiana University-Purdue
        University Fort Wayne
    Indiana University-Purdue
        University Indianapolis
Ivy Tech State College
    Central Indiana
    Kokomo
    Northwest
    Southeast
    Wabash Valley
    Whitewater
Purdue University
    Calumet
    North Central Campus
St. Mary-of-the-Woods College
University of Indianapolis
University of St. Francis
Vincennes University

Iowa

Briar Cliff College
Buena Vista University
Des Moines Area Community College
Drake University
Grand View College
Iowa Lakes Community College
Iowa State University
Iowa Western Community College
Kirkwood Community College
Marycrest International University
Mount Mercy College
Simpson College
University of Dubuque

Kansas

Allen County Community College
Butler County Community College
Johnson County Community College
Kansas City Kansas Community College
Pratt Community College
St. Mary College
Wichita State University

Kentucky

Ashland Community College
Brescia University
Clear Creek Baptist Bible College
Elizabethtown Community College
Hazard Community College
Henderson Community College
Kentucky State University
Lexington Community College
Madisonville Community College
Morehead State University
Paducah Community College
St. Catharine College
Spalding University
Thomas More College
University of Kentucky

Louisiana

Delgado Community College
Loyola University New Orleans
Nunez Community College
University of New Orleans

Maine

Husson College
University of Southern Maine

Maryland

Anne Arundel Community College
Baltimore City Community College
Baltimore International College
Bowie State University
Carroll Community College
Cecil Community College
Charles County Community College
Chesapeake College
College of Notre Dame of Maryland
Community College of Baltimore County
    Catonsville
Coppin State College
Frederick Community College
Frostburg State University
Harford Community College
Howard Community College
Montgomery College
    Germantown Campus
    Rockville Campus
    Takoma Park Campus
Morgan State University
Mount St. Mary's College
Prince George's Community College
University of Baltimore
University of Maryland
    University College
Villa Julie College

Massachusetts

American International College
Anna Maria College
Bay Path College
Becker College
Curry College
Elms College
Emmanuel College
Lesley College
Marian Court College
Middlesex Community College
Mount Wachusett Community College
Newbury College
Northeastern University
Northern Essex Community College
Wentworth Institute of Technology

Michigan

Baker College
    of Auburn Hills
    of Cadillac
    of Mount Clemens
Bay de Noc Community College
Central Michigan University
Cleary College
Cornerstone College and Grand Rapids
    Baptist Seminary
Davenport College of Business
Delta College
Eastern Michigan University
Grand Rapids Community College
Jackson Community College
Kalamazoo Valley Community College
Kellogg Community College
Lake Michigan College
Lake Superior State University
Lansing Community College
Macomb Community College
Mott Community College
Northern Michigan University
Northwood University
Rochester College
St. Clair County Community College
Schoolcraft College
Siena Heights University
Southwestern Michigan College
Spring Arbor College
University of Detroit Mercy
University of Michigan
Washtenaw Community College
Wayne State University
Western Michigan University
William Tyndale College

Minnesota

Anoka-Ramsey Community College
Augsburg College
Century Community and Technical
    College
College of St. Catherine: St. Paul
    Campus
Crown College
Inver Hills Community College
Lake Superior College: A Community
    and Technical College
Metropolitan State University
Minneapolis Community and Technical
    College
North Central University
North Hennepin Community College

Mississippi

Belhaven College
Blue Mountain College
Jackson State University
Meridian Community College
Mississippi Gulf Coast Community
    College
    Jackson County Campus
    Jefferson Davis Campus
    Perkinston
Mississippi University for Women
Northwest Mississippi Community
    College
Tougaloo College

Missouri

Avila College
Central Missouri State University
Crowder College
DeVry Institute of Technology
    Kansas City
Drury University
East Central College
Fontbonne College
Hannibal-LaGrange College
Longview Community College
Maryville University of Saint Louis
Missouri Southern State College
Missouri Western State College
Northwest Missouri State University
Park University
Penn Valley Community College
St. Louis Community College
    St. Louis Community College at
        Florissant Valley
    St. Louis Community College at
        Forest Park
Stephens College
University of Missouri
    Kansas City
William Woods University

Montana

Rocky Mountain College

Nebraska

Bellevue University
Central Community College
College of Saint Mary
Doane College
Metropolitan Community College
Southeast Community College
    Lincoln Campus

Nevada

Community College of Southern Nevada

New Hampshire

Hesser College
New Hampshire College
New Hampshire Community Technical
    College
    Nashua
Notre Dame College

New Jersey

Bloomfield College
Brookdale Community College
Burlington County College
Caldwell College
Camden County College
College of St. Elizabeth
County College of Morris
DeVry Institute
Fairleigh Dickinson University
Felician College
Hudson County Community College
Katharine Gibbs School
    Gibbs College
Mercer County Community College
Montclair State University
New Jersey City University
Passaic County Community College
Rider University
Union County College
Warren County Community College

New Mexico

Clovis Community College
New Mexico Junior College
New Mexico State University
New Mexico State University
    Alamogordo
    Carlsbad
Santa Fe Community College
University of New Mexico

New York

Adelphi University
Audrey Cohen College
Broome Community College
City University of New York
    Borough of Manhattan Community
        College
    Bronx Community College
    Brooklyn College
    College of Staten Island
    John Jay College of Criminal
        Justice
    Lehman College
    New York City Technical College
    Queens College
    York College
College of St. Rose
D'Youville College
Daemen College
DeVry Institute of Technology
    New York
Dominican College of Blauvelt
Dowling College
Erie Community College
    City Campus
    North Campus
    South Campus
Hofstra University
Iona College
Jamestown Community College
Jefferson Community College
Long Island University
    C. W. Post Campus
Maria College
Marist College
Marymount College
Medaille College
Mercy College
Molloy College
Monroe Community College
New York Institute of Technology
New York University
Orange County Community College
Rochester Institute of Technology
Rockland Community College
Sage Junior College of Albany

St. John Fisher College
St. John's University
St. Joseph's Hospital Health Center School of Nursing
St. Joseph's College
   St. Joseph's College
      St. Joseph's College: Suffolk Campus
State University of New York
   Buffalo
   College at Brockport
   College of Agriculture and Technology at Cobleskill
   College of Agriculture and Technology at Morrisville
   College of Technology at Alfred
   College of Technology at Delhi
Tompkins-Cortland Community College
Trocaire College
Utica College of Syracuse University
Westchester Business Institute

North Carolina
Alamance Community College
Barton College
Belmont Abbey College
Bladen Community College
Caldwell Community College and Technical Institute
Central Piedmont Community College
Durham Technical Community College
East Carolina University
Edgecombe Community College
Elizabeth City State University
Fayetteville State University
Fayetteville Technical Community College
Gaston College
Greensboro College
John Wesley College
Lenoir Community College
Louisburg College
Methodist College
Pfeiffer University
Piedmont Community College
Queens College
Randolph Community College
Sampson Community College
Shaw University
Surry Community College
University of North Carolina Charlotte
Wayne Community College
Wilkes Community College
Wilson Technical Community College

Ohio
Ashland University
Baldwin-Wallace College
Central Ohio Technical College
Clark State Community College
College of Mount St. Joseph
Columbus State Community College
David N. Myers College
DeVry Institute of Technology Columbus
Defiance College
Franklin University
Heidelberg College
Hiram College
Hocking Technical College
Kent State University
Kent State University
   East Liverpool Regional Campus
   Tuscarawas Campus
Lake Erie College
Lakeland Community College
Lorain County Community College
Lourdes College
Malone College
Marion Technical College
Miami-Jacobs College
North Central State College
Northwest State Community College
Northwestern College
Notre Dame College of Ohio
Ohio Dominican College
Ohio State University
   Agricultural Technical Institute
   Mansfield Campus
   Marion Campus
   Newark Campus
Ohio University
   Eastern Campus
Otterbein College
Owens Community College
   Findlay Campus
   Toledo
Sinclair Community College
Southern State Community College
Terra Community College
Tiffin University
University of Akron
   Wayne College
University of Cincinnati
University of Cincinnati
   Clermont College
University of Findlay
University of Toledo
Wittenberg University
Xavier University
Youngstown State University

Oklahoma
Mid-America Bible College
Northeastern State University
Oklahoma City Community College
Oral Roberts University
Redlands Community College
Southwestern Oklahoma State University
Tulsa Community College

Oregon
Chemeketa Community College
Eastern Oregon University
Lane Community College
Marylhurst University
Mount Hood Community College
Oregon State University
Portland Community College
Western Baptist College

Pennsylvania
Allentown College of St. Francis de Sales
Alvernia College
Beaver College
Bucks County Community College
Cabrini College
California University of Pennsylvania
Carlow College
Cedar Crest College
Chestnut Hill College
College Misericordia
Community College of Philadelphia
Duquesne University
Gannon University
Gwynedd-Mercy College
Harrisburg Area Community College
Indiana University of Pennsylvania
Lebanon Valley College of Pennsylvania
Luzerne County Community College
Mercyhurst College
Montgomery County Community College
Mount Aloysius College
Neumann College
Peirce College
Penn State
   Fayette
   Harrisburg
   York
Pennsylvania College of Technology
Philadelphia College of Bible
Point Park College
Reading Area Community College
Robert Morris College
St. Joseph's University
Seton Hill College
University of Pittsburgh
Valley Forge Christian College
Widener University
Wilkes University

Puerto Rico
Colegio Universitario del Este
Inter American University of Puerto Rico Aguadilla Campus
Turabo University
University of Puerto Rico Arecibo Campus

Rhode Island
Community College of Rhode Island
Johnson & Wales University

South Carolina
Benedict College
Claflin University
Greenville Technical College
Lander University
Midlands Technical College
Piedmont Technical College
University of South Carolina
Voorhees College
York Technical College

South Dakota
Southeast Technical Institute
University of South Dakota

Tennessee
Aquinas College
Carson-Newman College
Chattanooga State Technical Community College
LeMoyne-Owen College
Northeast State Technical Community College
Pellissippi State Technical Community College
Roane State Community College
Shelby State Community College
Tennessee State University
Volunteer State Community College
Walters State Community College

Texas
Alvin Community College
Amber University
Brookhaven College
College of the Mainland
Dallas Baptist University
DeVry Institute of Technology Irving
Del Mar College
El Paso Community College
Galveston College
Houston Community College System
Huston-Tillotson College
Lamar State College at Port Arthur
Lee College
Midland College
Mountain View College
Northwood University: Texas Campus
Our Lady of the Lake University of San Antonio
Palo Alto College
Prairie View A&M University
Richland College
St. Philip's College
San Antonio College
San Jacinto College
   North
Schreiner College
Texas State Technical College
   Harlingen
Texas Wesleyan University
Trinity Valley Community College
Tyler Junior College
University of Houston
   Clear Lake
   Downtown
University of North Texas
University of Texas
   Dallas
   Pan American
Weatherford College

Utah
Salt Lake Community College
Southern Utah University
Utah State University
Utah Valley State College
Westminster College

Vermont
Burlington College
Community College of Vermont
Johnson State College
Norwich University
Southern Vermont College
Trinity College of Vermont

Virginia
Bluefield College
Germanna Community College
J. Sargeant Reynolds Community College
John Tyler Community College
Northern Virginia Community College
Old Dominion University
Patrick Henry Community College
Piedmont Virginia Community College
Tidewater Community College
Virginia Western Community College

Washington
City University
Columbia Basin College
Eastern Washington University
Edmonds Community College
North Seattle Community College
Pierce College
Seattle Pacific University
South Puget Sound Community College
Spokane Falls Community College
University of Washington
Yakima Valley Community College

West Virginia
Fairmont State College
Ohio Valley College
Shepherd College
West Virginia State College
West Virginia University

Wisconsin
Alverno College
Carroll College
Carthage College
Concordia University Wisconsin
Lakeshore Technical College
Milwaukee Area Technical College
Moraine Park Technical College
University of Wisconsin
   Oshkosh
   Parkside
   Rock County
Western Wisconsin Technical College

Colleges in this book

Alabama
Alabama Agricultural and Mechanical University, Normal 35762
Alabama State University, Montgomery 36101
Athens State University, Athens 35611
Auburn University, Auburn 36849
Auburn University at Montgomery, Montgomery 36124-4023
Auburn University: College of Veterinary Medicine, Auburn 36849
Auburn University: School of Pharmacy, Auburn 36849
Beeson Divinity School at Samford University, Birmingham 35229
Bessemer State Technical College, Bessemer 35021
Bevill State Community College, Sumiton 35148
Birmingham-Southern College, Birmingham 35254
Calhoun Community College, Decatur 35609
Central Alabama Community College, Alexander City 35011
Chattahoochee Valley Community College, Phenix City 36869
Community College of the Air Force, Maxwell AFB 36112-6613
Concordia College, Selma 36701
Enterprise State Junior College, Enterprise 36331
Faulkner University, Montgomery 36109
Gadsden State Community College, Gadsden 35902-0227
George C. Wallace State Community College at Dothan, Dothan 36303-9234
George C. Wallace State Community College at Selma, Selma 36702
Harry M. Ayers State Technical College, Anniston 36202
Huntingdon College, Montgomery 36106-2148
ITT Technical Institute: Birmingham, Birmingham 35242
J. F. Drake State Technical College, Huntsville 35811
Jacksonville State University, Jacksonville 36265-1602
James H. Faulkner State Community College, Bay Minette 36507
Jefferson Davis Community College, Brewton 36427
Jefferson State Community College, Birmingham 35215
John M. Patterson State Technical College, Montgomery 36116-2699
Lawson State Community College, Birmingham 35221
Lurleen B. Wallace Junior College, Andalusia 36420
Marion Military Institute, Marion 36756
Northeast Alabama Community College, Rainsville 35986
Northwest-Shoals Community College, Muscle Shoals 35662
Oakwood College, Huntsville 35896
Reid State Technical College, Evergreen 36401
Samford University, Birmingham 35229
Samford University: Cumberland School of Law, Birmingham 35229
Samford University: McWhorter School of Pharmacy, Birmingham 35229
Shelton State Community College, Tuscaloosa 35405
Snead State Community College, Boaz 35957
South College, Montgomery 36104
Southern Christian University, Montgomery 36117
Southern Union State Community College, Wadley 36276
Sparks State Technical College, Eufaula 36072-0580
Spring Hill College, Mobile 36608
Stillman College, Tuscaloosa 35403
Talladega College, Talladega 35160
Thomas Goode Jones School of Law--Faulkner University, Montgomery 36109
Troy State University, Troy 36082
Troy State University Dothan, Dothan 36304
Troy State University in Montgomery, Montgomery 36103-4419
Tuskegee University, Tuskegee 36088
Tuskegee University: School of Veterinary Medicine, Tuskegee 36088
University of Alabama, Tuscaloosa 35487-0100
University of Alabama at Birmingham, Birmingham 35294
University of Alabama at Birmingham: School of Dentistry, Birmingham 35294
University of Alabama at Birmingham: School of Medicine, Birmingham 35294
University of Alabama at Birmingham: School of Optometry, Birmingham 35294
University of Alabama in Huntsville, Huntsville 35899
University of Alabama: School of Law, Tuscaloosa 35487
University of Mobile, Mobile 36663-0220
University of Montevallo, Montevallo 35115
University of North Alabama, Florence 35632
University of South Alabama, Mobile 36688-2000
University of South Alabama: School of Medicine, Mobile 36688
University of West Alabama, Livingston 35470
Wallace State Community College at Hanceville, Hanceville 35077

Alaska
Alaska Bible College, Glennallen 99588-0289
Alaska Pacific University, Anchorage 99508
Prince William Sound Community College, Valdez 99686
University of Alaska Anchorage, Anchorage 99508
University of Alaska Fairbanks, Fairbanks 99775-7480
University of Alaska Southeast, Juneau 99801

Arizona
American Indian College of the Assemblies of God, Phoenix 85021
Arizona Institute of Business and Technology, Phoenix 85019
Arizona State University, Tempe 85287
Arizona State University: College of Law, Tempe 85287
Arizona Western College, Yuma 85366
Central Arizona College, Coolidge 85228
Cochise College, Douglas 85607
DeVry Institute of Technology: Phoenix, Phoenix 85201
Dine College, Tsaile 86556
Eastern Arizona College, Thatcher 85552
Embry-Riddle Aeronautical University: Prescott Campus, Prescott 86301-3720
Gateway Community College, Phoenix 85034
Glendale Community College, Glendale 85302
Grand Canyon University, Phoenix 85017
ITT Technical Institute: Phoenix, Phoenix 85008
ITT Technical Institute: Tucson, Tucson 85704
Mesa Community College, Mesa 85202
Mohave Community College, Kingman 86401
Northern Arizona University, Flagstaff 86011-4084
Northland Pioneer College, Holbrook 86025
Paradise Valley Community College, Phoenix 85032
Phoenix College, Phoenix 85013
Pima Community College, Tucson 85709-1010
Prescott College, Prescott 86301
Rio Salado College, Tempe 85281
Scottsdale Community College, Scottsdale 85256
South Mountain Community College, Phoenix 85040
Southwestern College, Phoenix 85032
Thunderbird, The American Graduate School of International Management, Glendale 85306
Universal Technical Institute, Phoenix 85017
University of Advancing Computer Technology, Tempe 85283-1042
University of Arizona, Tucson 85721-0040
University of Arizona: College of Law, Tucson 85721
University of Arizona: College of Medicine, Tucson 85724
University of Arizona: College of Pharmacy, Tucson 85721
University of Phoenix, Phoenix 85040
Yavapai College, Prescott 86301

Arkansas
Arkansas State University, State Univ 72467
Arkansas State University: Beebe Branch, Beebe 72012
Arkansas State University: Mountain Home, Mountain Home 72653
Arkansas Tech University, Russellville 72801
Central Baptist College, Conway 72032
Garland County Community College, Hot Springs 71913
Harding University, Searcy 72149
Henderson State University, Arkadelphia 71999-0001
Hendrix College, Conway 72032
ITT Technical Institute: Little Rock, Little Rock 72204
John Brown University, Siloam Springs 72761-2121
Lyon College, Batesville 72503-2317
Mississippi County Community College, Blytheville 72316
North Arkansas College, Harrison 72601
Northwest Arkansas Community College, Bentonville 72712
Ouachita Baptist University, Arkadelphia 71998
Philander Smith College, Little Rock 72202-3718
Phillips Community College of the University of Arkansas, Helena 72342
Southern Arkansas University, Magnolia 71753
Southern Arkansas University Tech, Camden 71701
University of Arkansas, Fayetteville 72701
University of Arkansas at Little Rock, Little Rock 72204-1099
University of Arkansas at Little Rock: School of Law, Little Rock 72202
University of Arkansas at Monticello, Monticello 71656
University of Arkansas at Pine Bluff, Pine Bluff 71601
University of Arkansas for Medical Sciences, Little Rock 72205
University of Arkansas for Medical Sciences: College of Medicine, Little Rock 72205
University of Arkansas for Medical Sciences: College of Pharmacy, Little Rock 72205
University of Arkansas: School of Law, Fayetteville 72701
University of Central Arkansas, Conway 72035
University of the Ozarks, Clarksville 72830
Westark College, Fort Smith 72913-3649
Williams Baptist College, Walnut Ridge 72476

California
Academy of Art College, San Francisco 94105
Allan Hancock College, Santa Maria 93454-6399
American Baptist Seminary of the West, Berkeley 94704
American Conservatory Theater, San Francisco 94108
American Film Institute Center for Advanced Film and Television Studies, Los Angeles 90027
American River College, Sacramento 95841
Antioch Southern California at Los Angeles, Marina Del Rey 90292
Antioch Southern California at Santa Barbara, Santa Barbara 93101-1581
Armstrong University, Oakland 94612
Art Center College of Design, Pasadena 91103
Art Institutes International San Francisco, San Francisco 94102
Azusa Pacific University, Azusa 91702
Azusa Pacific University: School of Theology, Azusa 91702
Bakersfield College, Bakersfield 93305
Barstow College, Barstow 92311
Biola University, La Mirada 90639
Brooks College, Long Beach 90804
Butte College, Oroville 95965
Cabrillo College, Aptos 95003
California Baptist University, Riverside 92504
California College for Health Sciences, National City 91950
California College of Arts and Crafts, San Francisco 94107
California College of Podiatric Medicine, San Francisco 94115
California Institute of Technology, Pasadena 91125

Colleges in this book

California Institute of the Arts, Valencia 91355
California Lutheran University, Thousand Oaks 91360
California Maritime Academy, Vallejo 94590
California Polytechnic State University: San Luis Obispo, San Luis Obispo 93407
California School of Professional Psychology at Alameda, Alameda 94501
California School of Professional Psychology at San Diego, San Diego 92121
California State Polytechnic University: Pomona, Pomona 91768
California State University: Bakersfield, Bakersfield 93311
California State University: Chico, Chico 95929-0722
California State University: Dominguez Hills, Carson 90747
California State University: Fresno, Fresno 93740-8027
California State University: Fullerton, Fullerton 92834-6900
California State University: Hayward, Hayward 94542
California State University: Long Beach, Long Beach 90840
California State University: Los Angeles, Los Angeles 90032
California State University: Monterey Bay, Seaside 93955
California State University: Northridge, Northridge 91330
California State University: Sacramento, Sacramento 95819
California State University: San Marcos, San Marcos 92096
California State University: Stanislaus, Turlock 95382
California Western School of Law, San Diego 92101
Canada College, Redwood City 94061
Cerritos Community College, Norwalk 90650
Cerro Coso Community College, Ridgecrest 93555
Chabot College, Hayward 94545
Chaffey Community College, Rancho Cucamnga 91737
Chapman University, Orange 92866
Church Divinity School of the Pacific, Berkeley 94709
Citrus College, Glendora 91741
City College of San Francisco, San Francisco 94112
Claremont McKenna College, Claremont 9171-6425
Claremont School of Theology, Claremont 91711
Cleveland Chiropractic College of Los Angeles, Los Angeles 90004
Coastline Community College, Fountain Valley 92708
Cogswell Polytechnical College, Sunnyvale 94089
College of Marin: Kentfield, Kentfield 94904
College of Notre Dame, Belmont 94002
College of Oceaneering, Wilmington 90744
College of San Mateo, San Mateo 94402-3784
College of the Canyons, Valencia 91355
College of the Desert, Palm Desert 92260
College of the Redwoods, Eureka 95501-9300
College of the Sequoias, Visalia 93277
College of the Siskiyous, Weed 96094
Columbia College, Sonora 95370
Compton Community College, Compton 90221
Concordia University, Irvine 92612-3299
Contra Costa College, San Pablo 94806
Crafton Hills College, Yucaipa 92399
Cuesta College, San Luis Obispo 93403
Cuyamaca College, El Cajon 92019
Cypress College, Cypress 90630
De Anza College, Cupertino 95014
DeVry Institute of Technology: Fremont, Fremont 94555
DeVry Institute of Technology: Long Beach, Long Beach 90806
DeVry Institute of Technology: Pomona, Pomona 91768
DeVry Institute of Technology: West Hills, West Hills 91304
Deep Springs College, Dyer 89010
Diablo Valley College, Pleasant Hill 94523
Dominican School of Philosophy and Theology, Berkeley 94709
Dominican University of California, San Rafael 94901-2298
Don Bosco Technical Institute, Rosemead 91770-4299
East Los Angeles College, Monterey Park 91754
Empire College, Santa Rosa 95403
Evergreen Valley College, San Jose 95135

Fashion Institute of Design and Merchandising, Los Angeles 90015
Fashion Institute of Design and Merchandising: San Francisco, San Francisco 94108
Fielding Institute, Santa Barbara 93105
Foothill College, Los Altos Hills 94022
Franciscan School of Theology, Berkeley 94709
Fresno City College, Fresno 93741
Fresno Pacific University, Fresno 93702
Fuller Theological Seminary, Pasadena 91182
Gavilan Community College, Gilroy 95020
Glendale Community College, Glendale 91208
Golden Gate Baptist Theological Seminary, Mill Valley 94941
Golden Gate University, San Francisco 94105
Golden Gate University: School of Law, San Francisco 94105
Golden West College, Huntington Beach 92647
Grossmont Community College, El Cajon 92020
Harvey Mudd College, Claremont 91711
Heald Business College: Fresno, Fresno 93704-1706
Heald Business College: Santa Rosa, Santa Rosa 95403
Hebrew Union College-Jewish Institute of Religion, Los Angeles 90007
Holy Names College, Oakland 94619
Hope International University, Fullerton 92831
Humboldt State University, Arcata 95521-8299
Humphreys College, Stockton 95207
Humphreys College: School of Law, Stockton 95207
ITT Technical Institute: Anaheim, Anaheim 92801
ITT Technical Institute: Hayward, Hayward 94545
ITT Technical Institute: Lathrop, Lathrop 95330
ITT Technical Institute: Oxnard, Oxnard 93030
ITT Technical Institute: Rancho Cordova, Rancho Cordova 95670
ITT Technical Institute: San Bernardino, San Bernardino 92408
ITT Technical Institute: San Diego, San Diego 92123
ITT Technical Institute: Santa Clara, Santa Clara 95054
ITT Technical Institute: Sylmar, Sylmar 91342
ITT Technical Institute: Torrance, Torrance 90502
ITT Technical Institute: West Covina, West Covina 91790
Imperial Valley College, Imperial 92251
International School of Theology, San Bernardino 92414
Irvine Valley College, Irvine 92618-4399
Jesuit School of Theology at Berkeley: Professional, Berkeley 94709
John F. Kennedy University, Orinda 94563
John F. Kennedy University: School of Law, Orinda 94563
Kings River Community College, Reedley 93654
LIFE Bible College, San Dimas 91773
La Sierra University, Riverside 92515
Lake Tahoe Community College, South Lake Tahoe 96150
Las Positas College, Livermore 94550
Life Chiropractic College West, San Lorenzo 94580
Lincoln University, Oakland 94612
Loma Linda University, Loma Linda 92350
Loma Linda University: School of Dentistry, Loma Linda 92350
Loma Linda University: School of Medicine, Loma Linda 92350
Long Beach City College, Long Beach 90808
Los Angeles College of Chiropractic, Whittier 90604
Los Angeles Harbor College, Wilmington 90744
Los Angeles Mission College, Sylmar 91342
Los Angeles Pierce College, Woodland Hills 91371
Los Angeles Southwest College, Los Angeles 90047
Los Angeles Trade and Technical College, Los Angeles 90015
Los Angeles Valley College, Van Nuys 91401
Los Medanos College, Pittsburg 94565
Loyola Marymount University, Los Angeles 90045
Loyola Marymount University: School of Law, Los Angeles 90015
Marymount College, Rancho Palos Verdes 90275
Master's College, Santa Clarita 91321
McGeorge School of Law: University of the Pacific, Sacramento 95817
Mendocino College, Ukiah 95482
Menlo College, Atherton 94027
Mennonite Brethren Biblical Seminary, Fresno 93727

Merced College, Merced 95348
Merritt College, Oakland 94619
Mills College, Oakland 94613
MiraCosta College, Oceanside 92056
Mission College, Santa Clara 95054
Modesto Junior College, Modesto 95350
Monterey Institute of International Studies, Monterey 93940
Monterey Peninsula College, Monterey 93940
Moorpark College, Moorpark 93021
Mount St. Mary's College, Los Angeles 90049
Mount San Antonio College, Walnut 91789
Mount San Jacinto College, San Jacinto 92583
Napa Valley College, Napa 94558
National Hispanic University, San Jose 95127
National University, La Jolla 92037
Occidental College, Los Angeles 90041
Ohlone College, Fremont 94539
Orange Coast College, Costa Mesa 92628-5005
Otis College of Art and Design, Los Angeles 90045
Oxnard College, Oxnard 93033
Pacific Graduate School of Psychology, Palo Alto 94303
Pacific Lutheran Theological Seminary, Berkeley 94708
Pacific Oaks College, Pasadena 91103
Pacific School of Religion, Berkeley 94709
Pacific Union College, Angwin 94508
Palmer College of Chiropractic-West, San Jose 95134
Palo Verde College, Blythe 92225
Palomar College, San Marcos 92069
Pasadena City College, Pasadena 91106
Patten College, Oakland 94601
Pepperdine University, Malibu 90263
Pepperdine University: School of Law, Malibu 90263
Phillips Graduate Institute, Encino 91316-1509
Pitzer College, Claremont 91711
Point Loma Nazarene University, San Diego 92106-2899
Pomona College, Claremont 91711
Porterville College, Porterville 93257
Queen of the Holy Rosary College, Fremont 94539
Rio Hondo College, Whittier 90601
Riverside Community College, Riverside 92506
Sacramento City College, Sacramento 95822
Saddleback College, Mission Viejo 92692
St. John's Seminary, Camarillo 93012
St. John's Seminary College, Camarillo 93012
St. Mary's College of California, Moraga 94556
St. Patrick's Seminary, Menlo Park 94025
Samuel Merritt College, Oakland 94609
San Bernardino Valley College, San Bernardino 92410
San Diego City College, San Diego 92101
San Diego Mesa College, San Diego 92111
San Diego Miramar College, San Diego 92126
San Diego State University, San Diego 92182-7455
San Francisco Art Institute, San Francisco 94133
San Francisco College of Mortuary Science, San Francisco 94110-4927
San Francisco Conservatory of Music, San Francisco 94122
San Francisco State University, San Francisco 94132
San Francisco Theological Seminary, San Anselmo 94960
San Joaquin Delta College, Stockton 95207
San Joaquin Valley College Inc., Visalia 93291
San Jose Christian College, San Jose 95112
San Jose City College, San Jose 95128
San Jose State University, San Jose 95112-0001
Santa Ana College, Santa Ana 92706
Santa Barbara City College, Santa Barbara 93109
Santa Clara University, Santa Clara 95053
Santa Clara University: School of Law, Santa Clara 95053
Santa Monica College, Santa Monica 90405
Santa Rosa Junior College, Santa Rosa 95401
Saybrook Graduate School and Research Center, San Francisco 94133
Scripps College, Claremont 91711
Shasta College, Redding 96049-6006
Sierra College, Rocklin 95677
Simpson College, Redding 96003
Skyline College, San Bruno 94066
Solano Community College, Suisun City 94585-3197
Sonoma State University, Rohnert Park 94928
Southern California College of Optometry, Fullerton 92631

Southern California Institute of Architecture, Los Angeles 90066
Southwestern College, Chula Vista 91910
Southwestern University School of Law, Los Angeles 90005
Stanford University, Stanford 94305
Stanford University: School of Law, Stanford 94305
Stanford University: School of Medicine, Stanford 94304
Starr King School for the Ministry, Berkeley 94709
Taft College, Taft 93268
Talbot School of Theology of Biola University, La Mirada 90639
Thomas Aquinas College, Santa Paula 93060
United States International University, San Diego 92131-1799
University of California Berkeley: School of Law, Berkeley 94720
University of California Berkeley: School of Optometry, Berkeley 94720
University of California Davis: School of Law, Davis 95616
University of California Davis: School of Medicine, Davis 95616
University of California Davis: School of Veterinary Medicine, Davis 95616
University of California Hastings College of the Law, San Francisco 94102
University of California Irvine: College of Medicine, Irvine 92697
University of California Los Angeles: School of Dentistry, Los Angeles 90095
University of California Los Angeles: School of Law, Los Angeles 90095
University of California Los Angeles: School of Medicine, Los Angeles 90095
University of California San Diego: School of Medicine, La Jolla 92093
University of California San Francisco: School of Dentistry, San Francisco 94143
University of California San Francisco: School of Medicine, San Francisco 94143
University of California San Francisco: School of Pharmacy, San Francisco 94143
University of California: Berkeley, Berkeley 94720
University of California: Davis, Davis 95616
University of California: Irvine, Irvine 92697
University of California: Los Angeles, Los Angeles 90095
University of California: Riverside, Riverside 92521
University of California: San Diego, La Jolla 92093
University of California: San Francisco, San Francisco 94143
University of California: Santa Barbara, Santa Barbara 93106-3500
University of California: Santa Cruz, Santa Cruz 95064
University of Judaism, Bel Air 90077
University of La Verne, La Verne 91750
University of La Verne College of Law at San Fernando Valley, Woodland Hills 91367
University of La Verne: School of Law, La Verne 91750
University of Redlands, Redlands 92373-0999
University of San Diego, San Diego 92110
University of San Diego: School of Law, San Diego 92110
University of San Francisco, San Francisco 94117
University of San Francisco: School of Law, San Francisco 94117
University of Southern California, Los Angeles 90089
University of Southern California: Law School, Los Angeles 90089
University of Southern California: School of Dentistry, Los Angeles 90089
University of Southern California: School of Medicine, Los Angeles 90033
University of Southern California: School of Pharmacy, Los Angeles 90033
University of West Los Angeles, Inglewood 90301
University of West Los Angeles: School of Law, Inglewood 90301
University of the Pacific, Stockton 95211
University of the Pacific: School of Dentistry, San Francisco 94115
University of the Pacific: School of Pharmacy, Stockton 95211

Vanguard University of Southern California, Costa Mesa 92626
Ventura College, Ventura 93003
Victor Valley College, Victorville 92392
Vista Community College, Berkeley 94704
West Hills Community College, Coalinga 93210
West Los Angeles College, Culver City 90230-3500
West Valley College, Saratoga 95070
Western University of Health Sciences, Pomona 91766
Westminster Theological Seminary in California, Escondido 92027
Westmont College, Santa Barbara 93108
Whittier College, Whittier 90608
Whittier Law School, Los Angeles 90020
Wright Institute, Berkeley 94704
Yuba College, Marysville 95901

Colorado

Adams State College, Alamosa 81102
Aims Community College, Greeley 80632
Arapahoe Community College, Littleton 80160
Art Institute of Colorado, Denver 80203
Bel-Rea Institute of Animal Technology, Denver 80231
Colorado Christian University, Lakewood 80226
Colorado College, Colorado Springs 80903
Colorado Mountain College: Alpine Campus, Steamboat Springs 80487
Colorado Mountain College: Spring Valley Campus, Glenwood Springs 81601
Colorado Mountain College: Timberline Campus, Leadville 80461
Colorado Northwestern Community College, Rangely 81648
Colorado School of Mines, Golden 80401
Colorado State University, Fort Collins 80523
Colorado State University: College of Veterinary Medicine and Biomedical Sciences, Fort Collins 80523
Colorado Technical University, Colorado Springs 80907
Community College of Aurora, Aurora 80011
Community College of Denver, Denver 80217
Denver Conservative Baptist Seminary, Denver 80250
Denver Technical College: A Division of DeVry University, Denver 80224
Fort Lewis College, Durango 81301
Front Range Community College, Westminster 80030
ITT Technical Institute: Thornton, Thornton 80229
Iliff School of Theology, Denver 80210
Lamar Community College, Lamar 81052
Mesa State College, Grand Junction 81502-2647
Metropolitan State College of Denver, Denver 80217-3662
Morgan Community College, Fort Morgan 80701
Naropa University, Boulder 80302
National Technological University, Fort Collins 80526
Nazarene Bible College, Colorado Springs 80910
Northeastern Junior College, Sterling 80751
Otero Junior College, La Junta 81050
Pikes Peak Community College, Colorado Springs 80906-5498
Pueblo Community College, Pueblo 81004
Red Rocks Community College, Lakewood 80228-1255
Regis University, Denver 80221
Rocky Mountain College of Art & Design, Denver 80224
Technical Trades Institute, Colorado Springs 80909
Trinidad State Junior College, Trinidad 81082
United States Air Force Academy, USAF Academy 80840
University of Colorado Health Sciences Center, Denver 80262
University of Colorado Health Sciences Center: College of Pharmacy, Denver 80262
University of Colorado Health Sciences Center: School of Dentistry, Denver 80262
University of Colorado Health Sciences Center: School of Medicine, Denver 80262
University of Colorado at Boulder, Boulder 80309-0026
University of Colorado at Boulder: School of Law, Boulder 80309
University of Colorado at Colorado Springs, Colorado Springs 80933-7150
University of Colorado at Denver, Denver 80217
University of Denver, Denver 80208
University of Denver: College of Law, Denver 80220

University of Northern Colorado, Greeley 80639
University of Southern Colorado, Pueblo 81001
Western State College of Colorado, Gunnison 81231
Westwood College of Aviation Technology, Broomfield 80021
Yeshiva Toras Chaim Talmudical Seminary, Denver 80204

Connecticut

Albertus Magnus College, New Haven 06511-1189
Asnuntuck Community-Technical College, Enfield 06082
Beth Benjamin Academy of Connecticut, Stamford 06901
Briarwood College, Southington 06489
Capital Community College, Hartford 06105-2354
Central Connecticut State University, New Britain 06050
Charter Oak State College, New Britain 06053-2142
Connecticut College, New London 06320
Eastern Connecticut State University, Willimantic 06226
Fairfield University, Fairfield 06430-5195
Gateway Community College, New Haven 06511
Hartford Graduate Center, Hartford 06120
Holy Apostles College and Seminary, Cromwell 06416
Housatonic Community-Technical College, Bridgeport 06604
Manchester Community-Technical College, Manchester 06045-1046
Middlesex Community-Technical College, Middletown 06457
Mitchell College, New London 06320
Naugatuck Valley Community-Technical College, Waterbury 06708
Northwestern Connecticut Community-Technical College, Winsted 06098
Norwalk Community-Technical College, Norwalk 06854
Paier College of Art, Hamden 06514-3902
Quinebaug Valley Community College, Danielson 06239
Quinnipiac College: School of Law, Hamden 06518
Quinnipiac University, Hamden 06518
Sacred Heart University, Fairfield 06432-1000
St. Joseph College, West Hartford 06117
Southern Connecticut State University, New Haven 06515
Teikyo Post University, Waterbury 06723-2540
Three Rivers Community-Technical College, Norwich 06360
Trinity College, Hartford 06106
Tunxis Community College, Farmington 06032
United States Coast Guard Academy, New London 06320
University of Bridgeport, Bridgeport 06601
University of Bridgeport College of Chiropractic, Bridgeport 06601
University of Connecticut, Storrs 06269
University of Connecticut Health Center School of Medicine, Farmington 06032
University of Connecticut: School of Dentistry, Farmington 06030
University of Connecticut: School of Law, Hartford 06105
University of Connecticut: School of Pharmacy, Storrs 06269
University of Hartford, Whartford 06117
University of New Haven, West Haven 06516
Wesleyan University, Middletown 06459
Western Connecticut State University, Danbury 06810
Yale Law School, New Haven 06520
Yale University, New Haven 06520
Yale University: Divinity School, New Haven 06511
Yale University: School of Medicine, New Haven 06510

Delaware

Delaware State University, Dover 19901
Delaware Technical and Community College: Owens Campus, Georgetown 19947
Delaware Technical and Community College: Stanton/Wilmington Campus, Newark 19713
Delaware Technical and Community College: Terry Campus, Dover 19901

Colleges in this book

Goldey-Beacom College, Wilmington 19808
University of Delaware, Newark 19716
Wesley College, Dover 19901-3875
Widener University School of Law, Wilmington 19803
Wilmington College, New Castle 19720

District of Columbia
American University, Washington 20016
American University: Washington College of Law, Washington 20016
Catholic University of America, Washington 20064
Catholic University of America: School of Law, Washington 20064
Catholic University of America: School of Theology, Washington 20064
Corcoran College of Art and Design, Washington 20006-4804
Dominican House of Studies, Washington 20017
Gallaudet University, Washington 20002
George Washington University, Washington 20052
George Washington University Law School, Washington 20052
George Washington University: School of Medicine and Health Sciences, Washington 20037
Georgetown University, Washington 20057
Georgetown University: Law Center, Washington 20001
Georgetown University: School of Medicine, Washington 20007
Howard University, Washington 20059
Howard University: College of Dentistry, Washington 20059
Howard University: Divinity School, Washington 20017
Howard University: School of Law, Washington 20008
Howard University: School of Medicine, Washington 20059
Howard University: School of Pharmacy, Washington 20059
Southeastern University, Washington 20024
Trinity College, Washington 20017
University of the District of Columbia, Washington 20008
University of the District of Columbia: School of Law, Washington 20008
Washington Theological Union, Washington 20012
Wesley Theological Seminary, Washington 20016

Florida
Art Institute of Fort Lauderdale, Ft. Lauderdale 33316
Barry University, Miami Shores 33161-6695
Barry University: School of Graduate Medical Sciences, Miami Shores 33161
Bethune-Cookman College, Daytona Beach 32114
Brevard Community College, Cocoa 32922-9987
Broward Community College, Ft. Lauderdale 33301
Carlos Albizu University, Miami 33172
Central Florida Community College, Ocala 34478
Chipola Junior College, Marianna 32446
Clearwater Christian College, Clearwater 33759-4595
Cooper Career Institute, West Palm Beach 32409
Daytona Beach Community College, Daytona Beach 32120
Eckerd College, St. Petersbrg 33711
Edison Community College, Fort Myers 33906-6210
Edward Waters College, Jacksonville 32209
Embry-Riddle Aeronautical University, Daytona Beach 32114-3900
Flagler College, St. Augustine 32085-1027
Florida Agricultural and Mechanical University, Tallahassee 32307
Florida Agricultural and Mechanical University: School of Pharmacy, Tallahassee 32307
Florida Atlantic University, Boca Raton 33431
Florida Baptist Theological College, Graceville 32440
Florida Christian College, Kissimmee 34744
Florida College, Temple Terrace 33617
Florida Community College at Jacksonville, Jacksonville 32202
Florida Gulf Coast University, Ft. Myers 33965-6565
Florida Institute of Technology, Melbourne 32901-6975
Florida International University, Miami 33199
Florida Keys Community College, Key West 33040
Florida Memorial College, Miami 33054
Florida Metropolitan University: Orlando College North, Orlando 32810
Florida National College, Hialeah 33012

Florida Southern College, Lakeland 33801-5698
Florida State University, Tallahassee 32306-2400
Florida State University: School of Law, Tallahassee 32306
Gulf Coast Community College, Panama City 32401
Hillsborough Community College, Tampa 33631-3127
Hobe Sound Bible College, Hobe Sound 33475
ITT Technical Institute: Ft. Lauderdale, Ft. Lauderdale 33328
ITT Technical Institute: Jacksonville, Jacksonville 32244
ITT Technical Institute: Maitland, Maitland 32751
ITT Technical Institute: Miami, Miami 33126
ITT Technical Institute: Tampa, Tampa 33634
Indian River Community College, Fort Pierce 34981-5599
International Academy of Merchandising and Design, Tampa 33634
International College, Naples 34112
International Fine Arts College, Miami 33132
Jacksonville University, Jacksonville 32211
Jones College, Jacksonville 32211
Keiser College, Ft. Lauderdale 33309
Lake City Community College, Lake City 32025
Lake-Sumter Community College, Leesburg 34788
Lynn University, Boca Raton 33431
Manatee Community College, Bradenton 34207
Miami-Dade Community College, Miami 33132
New College of the University of South Florida, Sarasota 34243-2197
New England Institute of Technology, West Palm Beach 33407
Northwood University: Florida Campus, West Palm Beach 33409
Nova Southeastern University, Ft. Lauderdale 33314
Nova Southeastern University Health Professions Division: College of Optometry, Fort Lauderdale 33328
Nova Southeastern University Health Professions Division: College of Osteopathic Medicine, Fort Lauderdale 33314
Nova Southeastern University of the Health Sciences: College of Pharmacy, Fort Lauderdale 33314
Nova Southeastern University: Shepard Broad Law Center, Fort Lauderdale 33314
Palm Beach Atlantic College, West Palm Beach 33416-4708
Palm Beach Community College, Lake Worth 33461
Pasco-Hernando Community College, New Port Richey 34654-5199
Pensacola Junior College, Pensacola 32504-8998
Polk Community College, Winter Haven 33881
Ringling School of Art and Design, Sarasota 34234
Rollins College, Winter Park 32789-4499
St. John Vianney College Seminary, Miami 33165
St. Leo University, St. Leo 33574-6665
St. Petersburg Junior College, St. Petersbrg 33733
St. Thomas University, Miami 33054
St. Thomas University: School of Law, Miami 33054
St. Vincent De Paul Regional Seminary, Boynton Beach 33436
Santa Fe Community College, Gainesville 32606
Seminole Community College, Sanford 32773
South College: Palm Beach Campus, West Palm Beach 33409
South Florida Community College, Avon Park 33825
Southeastern College of the Assemblies of God, Lakeland 33801
Stetson University, DeLand 32720
Stetson University: College of Law, St. Petersburg 33707
Tallahassee Community College, Tallahassee 32304-2895
Tampa Technical Institute, Tampa 33612
University of Central Florida, Orlando 32816
University of Florida, Gainesville 32611
University of Florida: College of Dentistry, Gainesville 32610
University of Florida: College of Law, Gainesville 32611
University of Florida: College of Pharmacy, Gainesville 32610
University of Florida: College of Veterinary Medicine, Gainesville 32610

University of Florida: School of Medicine, Gainesville 32610
University of Miami, Coral Gables 33124-4616
University of Miami: School of Law, Coral Gables 33124
University of Miami: School of Medicine, Miami 33101
University of North Florida, Jacksonville 32224-2645
University of South Florida, Tampa 33620-9951
University of South Florida: College of Medicine, Tampa 33612
University of Tampa, Tampa 33606-1490
University of West Florida, Pensacola 32514
Valencia Community College, Orlando 32802-3028
Warner Southern College, Lake Wales 33853-8725

Georgia
Abraham Baldwin Agricultural College, Tifton 31794
Agnes Scott College, Atlanta 30030
Albany State University, Albany 31705
American InterContinental University, Atlanta 30326-1019
Andrew College, Cuthbert 31740
Armstrong Atlantic State University, Savannah 31419
Art Institute of Atlanta, Atlanta 30328
Athens Area Technical Institute, Athens 30601-1500
Atlanta Christian College, East Point 30344
Atlanta College of Art, Atlanta 30309
Atlanta Metropolitan College, Atlanta 30310
Augusta State University, Augusta 30904-2200
Bainbridge College, Bainbridge 31717
Berry College, Mount Berry 30149
Brenau University, Gainesville 30501
Brewton-Parker College, Mount Vernon 30445
Candler School of Theology, Atlanta 30322
Chattahoochee Technical Institute, Marietta 30060
Clark Atlanta University, Atlanta 30314
Clayton College and State University, Morrow 30260-0285
Coastal Georgia Community College, Brunswick 31520
Columbia Theological Seminary, Decatur 30031
Columbus State University, Columbus 31907
Columbus Technical Institute, Columbus 31904
Covenant College, Lookout Mountain 30750
Dalton State College, Dalton 30720
Darton College, Albany 31707-3098
DeKalb Technical Institute, Clarkston 30021
DeVry Institute of Technology: Alpharetta, Alpharetta 30004
DeVry Institute of Technology: Atlanta, Decatur 30030
East Georgia College, Swainsboro 30401-2699
Emmanuel College, Franklin Springs 30639
Emory University, Atlanta 30322
Emory University: School of Law, Atlanta 30322
Emory University: School of Medicine, Atlanta 30322
Floyd College, Rome 30162
Fort Valley State University, Fort Valley 31030-4313
Gainesville College, Gainesville 30503
Georgia Baptist College of Nursing, Atlanta 30312
Georgia College and State University, Milledgeville 31061
Georgia Institute of Technology, Atlanta 30332-0001
Georgia Military College, Milledgeville 31061
Georgia Perimeter College, Decatur 30034
Georgia Southern University, Statesboro 30460
Georgia Southwestern State University, Americus 31709-4693
Georgia State University, Atlanta 30303
Georgia State University: College of Law, Atlanta 30303
Gordon College, Barnesville 30204
Gupton Jones College of Funeral Service, Decatur 30035
Gwinnett Technical Institute, Lawrenceville 30046
Herzing College of Business and Technology, Atlanta 30326
Interdenominational Theological Center, Atlanta 30314
Kennesaw State University, Kennesaw 30144-5591
LaGrange College, LaGrange 30240
Life College, Marietta 30060
Macon State College, Macon 31206-5144
Medical College of Georgia, Augusta 30912
Medical College of Georgia: School of Dentistry, Augusta 30912
Medical College of Georgia: School of Medicine, Augusta 30912

Mercer University, Macon 31207
Mercer University Southern School of Pharmacy, Atlanta 30341
Mercer University: School of Medicine, Macon 31207
Mercer University: Walter F. George School of Law, Macon 31207
Middle Georgia College, Cochran 31014
Morehouse College, Atlanta 30314
Morehouse School of Medicine, Atlanta 30310
Morris Brown College, Atlanta 30314
North Georgia College & State University, Dahlonega 30597
Oglethorpe University, Atlanta 30319
Oxford College of Emory University, Oxford 30054-1418
Paine College, Augusta 30901-3182
Piedmont College, Demorest 30535
Reinhardt College, Waleska 30183
Savannah College of Art and Design, Savannah 31402
Savannah State University, Savannah 31404
Savannah Technical Institute, Savannah 31405
Shorter College, Rome 30165
South Georgia College, Douglas 31533
Southern Polytechnic State University, Marietta 30060-2896
Spelman College, Atlanta 30314
State University of West Georgia, Carrollton 30118-0001
Thomas College, Thomasville 31792-7499
Toccoa Falls College, Toccoa Falls 30598
Truett-McConnell College, Cleveland 30528
University of Georgia, Athens 30602
University of Georgia: College of Pharmacy, Athens 30602
University of Georgia: College of Veterinary Medicine, Athens 30602
University of Georgia: School of Law, Athens 30602
Valdosta State University, Valdosta 31698
Waycross College, Waycross 31503
Wesleyan College, Macon 31210
Young Harris College, Young Harris 30582

Hawaii

Brigham Young University-Hawaii, Laie 96762
Chaminade University of Honolulu, Honolulu 96816-1578
Hawaii Pacific University, Honolulu 96813
TransPacific Hawaii College, Honolulu 96821
University of Hawaii William S. Richardson: School of Law, Honolulu 96822
University of Hawaii at Hilo, Hilo 96720
University of Hawaii at Manoa, Honolulu 96822
University of Hawaii at Manoa: John A. Burns School of Medicine, Honolulu 96822
University of Hawaii: Hawaii Community College, Hilo 96720
University of Hawaii: Honolulu Community College, Honolulu 96817
University of Hawaii: Kapiolani Community College, Honolulu 96816
University of Hawaii: Kauai Community College, Lihue 96766
University of Hawaii: Leeward Community College, Pearl City 96782
University of Hawaii: Maui Community College, Kahului 96732
University of Hawaii: West Oahu, Pearl City 96782
University of Hawaii: Windward Community College, Kaneohe 96817

Idaho

Albertson College of Idaho, Caldwell 83605
Boise Bible College, Boise 83714
Boise State University, Boise 83725
College of Southern Idaho, Twin Falls 83303
Eastern Idaho Technical College, Idaho Falls 83404
ITT Technical Institute: Boise, Boise 83713
Idaho State University, Pocatello 83209
Idaho State University: College of Pharmacy, Pocatello 83209
Lewis-Clark State College, Lewiston 83501
North Idaho College, Coeur d'Alene 83814
Northwest Nazarene University, Nampa 83686-5897
Ricks College, Rexburg 83460
University of Idaho, Moscow 83844-4140
University of Idaho: College of Law, Moscow 83844

Illinois

Adler School of Professional Psychology, Chicago 60601
American Academy of Art, Chicago 60604
Augustana College, Rock Island 61201
Barat College, Lake Forest 60045
Benedictine University, Lisle 60532
Bethany Theological Seminary, Richmond 47374
Black Hawk College, Moline 61265
Black Hawk College: East Campus, Kewanee 61443-0630
Blackburn College, Carlinville 62626
Blessing-Reiman College of Nursing, Quincy 62305
Bradley University, Peoria 61625
Brisk Rabbinical College, Chicago 60659
Career Colleges of Chicago, Chicago 60603
Carl Sandburg College, Galesburg 61401
Catholic Theological Union, Chicago 60615
Chicago School of Professional Psychology, Chicago 60605
Chicago State University, Chicago 60628
Chicago Theological Seminary, Chicago 60637
Chicago-Kent College of Law, Illinois Institute of Technology, Chicago 60661
City Colleges of Chicago: Harold Washington College, Chicago 60601
City Colleges of Chicago: Harry S. Truman College, Chicago 60640
City Colleges of Chicago: Kennedy-King College, Chicago 60621
City Colleges of Chicago: Malcolm X College, Chicago 60612
City Colleges of Chicago: Olive-Harvey College, Chicago 60628
City Colleges of Chicago: Richard J. Daley College, Chicago 60652
City Colleges of Chicago: Wright College, Chicago 60634
College of DuPage, Glen Ellyn 60137-6599
College of Lake County, Grayslake 60030
Columbia College, Chicago 60605
Concordia University, River Forest 60305-1499
Danville Area Community College, Danville 61832
De Paul University, Chicago 60604-2287
De Paul University: College of Law, Chicago 60604
DeVry Institute of Technology: Addison, Addison 60101
DeVry Institute of Technology: Chicago, Chicago 60618
Dominican University, River Forest 60305
Dr. William M. Scholl College of Podiatric Medicine, Chicago 60610
Eastern Illinois University, Charleston 61920-3099
Elgin Community College, Elgin 60123-7193
Elmhurst College, Elmhurst 60126
Eureka College, Eureka 61530
Finch University of Health Sciences/The Chicago Medical School, North Chicago 60064
Garrett-Evangelical Theological Seminary, Evanston 60201
Governors State University, University Park 60466
Greenville College, Greenville 62246-0159
Harrington Institute of Interior Design, Chicago 60605
Hebrew Theological College, Skokie 60077
Highland Community College, Freeport 61032-9341
ITT Technical Institute: Burr Ridge, Burr Ridge 60521
ITT Technical Institute: Hoffman Estates, Hoffman Estates 60195
ITT Technical Institute: Matteson, Matteson 60443
Illinois College, Jacksonville 62650
Illinois College of Optometry, Chicago 60616
Illinois Eastern Community Colleges: Frontier Community College, Fairfield 62837
Illinois Eastern Community Colleges: Lincoln Trail College, Robinson 62454
Illinois Eastern Community Colleges: Olney Central College, Olney 62450
Illinois Eastern Community Colleges: Wabash Valley College, Mount Carmel 62863
Illinois Institute of Technology, Chicago 60616
Illinois State University, Normal 61761
Illinois Wesleyan University, Bloomington 61702
International Academy of Merchandising and Design, Chicago 60602
John A. Logan College, Carterville 62918
John Marshall Law School, Chicago 60604
John Wood Community College, Quincy 62301
Joliet Junior College, Joliet 60431
Judson College, Elgin 60123
Kankakee Community College, Kankakee 60901
Kaskaskia College, Centralia 62801
Kendall College, Evanston 60201-2899
Kishwaukee College, Malta 60150
Knowledge Systems Institute, Skokie 60076
Knox College, Galesburg 61401
Lake Forest College, Lake Forest 60045
Lake Forest Graduate School of Management, Lake Forest 60045
Lake Land College, Mattoon 61938
Lakeview College of Nursing, Danville 61832
Lewis University, Romeoville 60446
Lewis and Clark Community College, Godfrey 62035
Lexington College, Chicago 60643
Lincoln Christian College and Seminary, Lincoln 62656
Lincoln Christian Seminary, Lincoln 62656
Lincoln Land Community College, Springfield 62794-9256
Loyola University Chicago: School of Law, Chicago 60611
Loyola University Chicago: Stritch School of Medicine, Maywood 60153
Loyola University of Chicago, Chicago 60611
Lutheran School of Theology at Chicago, Chicago 60615
MacCormac College, Chicago 60605
MacMurray College, Jacksonville 62650
McCormick Theological Seminary, Chicago 60637
McHenry County College, Crystal Lake 60012-2761
McKendree College, Lebanon 62254
Meadville-Lombard Theological School, Chicago 60637
Midwestern University: Chicago College of Osteopathic Medicine, Downers Grove 60515
Midwestern University: Chicago College of Pharmacy, Downers Grove 60515
Millikin University, Decatur 62522-2084
Monmouth College, Monmouth 61462
Moody Bible Institute, Chicago 60610
Moraine Valley Community College, Palos Hills 60465-0937
Morton College, Cicero 60804
National College of Chiropractic: Chiropractic Professions, Lombard 60148
National-Louis University, Evanston 60201
North Central College, Naperville 60566
North Park Theological Seminary, Chicago 60625
North Park University, Chicago 60625-4895
Northeastern Illinois University, Chicago 60625
Northern Baptist Theological Seminary, Lombard 60148
Northern Illinois University, DeKalb 60115
Northern Illinois University: College of Law, DeKalb 60115
Northwestern Business College, Chicago 60630
Northwestern University, Evanston 60208
Northwestern University: Dental School, Chicago 60611
Northwestern University: School of Law, Chicago 60611
Northwestern University: School of Medicine, Chicago 60611
Oakton Community College, Des Plaines 60016
Olivet Nazarene University, Bourbonnais 60914
Parkland College, Champaign 61821-1899
Prairie State College, Chicago Heights 60411
Principia College, Elsah 62028-9799
Quincy University, Quincy 62301
Rend Lake College, Ina 62846
Richland Community College, Decatur 62521
Robert Morris College: Chicago, Chicago 60605
Rock Valley College, Rockford 61114-5699
Rockford College, Rockford 61108
Roosevelt University, Chicago 60605-1394
Rush University: Rush Medical College, Chicago 60612
St. Augustine College, Chicago 60640
St. Xavier University, Chicago 60655
Sauk Valley Community College, Dixon 61021
School of the Art Institute of Chicago, Chicago 60603
Seabury-Western Theological Seminary, Evanston 60201
Shawnee Community College, Ullin 62992

Colleges in this book

Shimer College, Waukegan 60079
Southeastern Illinois College, Harrisburg 62946
Southern Illinois University at Carbondale, Carbondale 62901
Southern Illinois University at Carbondale: School of Law, Carbondale 62901
Southern Illinois University at Edwardsville, Edwardsville 62026
Southern Illinois University: School of Dentistry, Alton 62002
Southern Illinois University: School of Medicine, Springfield 62794
Southwestern Ilinois College, Belleville 62221-5899
Spoon River College, Canton 61520
Springfield College in Illinois, Springfield 62702-2694
Telshe Yeshiva-Chicago, Chicago 60625
Trinity Christian College, Palos Heights 60463
Trinity Evangelical Divinity School, Deerfield 60015
Trinity International University, Deerfield 60015
Triton College, River Grove 60171
University of Chicago, Chicago 60637
University of Chicago: Divinity School, Chicago 60637
University of Chicago: Pritzker School of Medicine, Chicago 60637
University of Chicago: School of Law, Chicago 60637
University of Illinois at Chicago, Chicago 60607
University of Illinois at Chicago: College of Dentistry, Chicago 60612
University of Illinois at Chicago: College of Medicine, Chicago 60612
University of Illinois at Chicago: College of Pharmacy, Chicago 60612
University of Illinois at Urbana-Champaign, Urbana 61801
University of Illinois at Urbana-Champaign: College of Law, Champaign 61820
University of Illinois at Urbana-Champaign: College of Veterinary Medicine, Urbana 61801
University of Illinois: Springfield, Springfield 62794
University of St. Francis, Joliet 60435
University of St. Mary of the Lake--Mundelein Seminary, Mundelein 60060
VanderCook College of Music, Chicago 60616-3731
Waubonsee Community College, Sugar Grove 60554-9799
Western Illinois University, Macomb 61455
Wheaton College, Wheaton 60187
William Rainey Harper College, PaLatine 60067

Indiana

Ancilla College, Donaldson 46513
Anderson University, Anderson 46012
Anderson University: School of Theology, Anderson 46012
Associated Mennonite Biblical Seminary, Elkhart 46517
Ball State University, Muncie 47306
Bethel College, Mishawaka 46545
Butler University, Indianapolis 46208
Butler University: College of Pharmacy, Indianapolis 46208
Calumet College of St. Joseph, Whiting 46394
Christian Theological Seminary, Indianapolis 46208
Concordia Theological Seminary, Fort Wayne 46825
DePauw University, Greencastle 46135
Earlham College, Richmond 47374
Earlham School of Religion, Richmond 47374
Franklin College, Franklin 46131
Goshen College, Goshen 46526
Grace College, Winona Lake 46590
Hanover College, Hanover 47243-0108
Holy Cross College, Notre Dame 46556-0308
ITT Technical Institute: Fort Wayne, Fort Wayne 46825
ITT Technical Institute: Indianapolis, Indianapolis 46268
ITT Technical Institute: Newburgh, Newburgh 47630
Indiana Institute of Technology, Fort Wayne 46803-1297
Indiana State University, Terre Haute 47809
Indiana University Bloomington, Bloomington 47405
Indiana University Bloomington: School of Law, Bloomington 47405
Indiana University Bloomington: School of Optometry, Bloomington 47405
Indiana University East, Richmond 47374-1289
Indiana University Indianapolis: School of Law, Indianapolis 46202
Indiana University Kokomo, Kokomo 46904-9003
Indiana University Northwest, Gary 46408
Indiana University School of Dentistry, Indianapolis 46202
Indiana University South Bend, South Bend 46634-7111
Indiana University Southeast, New Albany 47150-6405
Indiana University-Purdue University Fort Wayne, Fort Wayne 46805-1499
Indiana University-Purdue University Indianapolis, Indianapolis 46202
Indiana University: School of Medicine, Indianapolis 46202
Indiana Wesleyan University, Marion 46953
International Business College, Fort Wayne 46804
Ivy Tech State College: Central Indiana, Indianapolis 46208
Ivy Tech State College: Columbus, Columbus 47203
Ivy Tech State College: Eastcentral, Muncie 47302
Ivy Tech State College: Kokomo, Kokomo 46903
Ivy Tech State College: Lafayette, Lafayette 47903
Ivy Tech State College: Northcentral, South Bend 46619
Ivy Tech State College: Northeast, Fort Wayne 46805
Ivy Tech State College: Northwest, Gary 46409
Ivy Tech State College: Southcentral, Sellersburg 47172
Ivy Tech State College: Southeast, Madison 47250
Ivy Tech State College: Southwest, Evansville 47710
Ivy Tech State College: Wabash Valley, Terre Haute 47802
Ivy Tech State College: Whitewater, Richmond 47374
Manchester College, North Manchester 46962
Marian College, Indianapolis 46222
Michiana College, South Bend 46617
Oakland City University, Oakland City 47660
Purdue University, West Lafayette 47907
Purdue University: Calumet, Hammond 46323
Purdue University: North Central Campus, Westville 46391
Purdue University: School of Pharmacy, West Lafayette 47907
Purdue University: School of Veterinary Medicine, West Lafayette 47907
Rose-Hulman Institute of Technology, Terre Haute 47803-3999
Saint Mary's College, Notre Dame 46556
St. Joseph's College, Rensselaer 47978
St. Mary-of-the-Woods College, St. Mary-of-the-Woods 47876
St. Meinrad School of Theology, St. Meinrad 47577
Taylor University, Upland 46989
Tri-State University, Angola 46703
University of Evansville, Evansville 47722
University of Indianapolis, Indianapolis 46227-3697
University of Notre Dame, Notre Dame 46556
University of Notre Dame: School of Law, Notre Dame 46556
University of Notre Dame: School of Theology, Notre Dame 46556
University of St. Francis, Fort Wayne 46808
University of Southern Indiana, Evansville 47712
Valparaiso University, Valparaiso 46383-6493
Valparaiso University: School of Law, Valparaiso 46383
Vincennes University, Vincennes 47591
Wabash College, Crawfordsville 47933

Iowa

American Institute of Business, Des Moines 50321
Briar Cliff College, Sioux City 51104
Buena Vista University, Storm Lake 50588
Central College, Pella 50219
Clarke College, Dubuque 52001
Clinton Community College, Clinton 52732
Coe College, Cedar Rapids 52402
Cornell College, Mount Vernon 52314
Des Moines Area Community College, Ankeny 50021
Des Moines University - Osteopathic Medical Center, Des Moines 50312
Dordt College, Sioux Center 51250
Drake University, Des Moines 50311
Drake University Law School, Des Moines 50311
Drake University: College of Pharmacy, Des Moines 50311
Emmaus Bible College, Dubuque 52001
Faith Baptist Bible College and Theological Seminary, Ankeny 50021
Faith Baptist Theological Seminary, Ankeny 50021
Graceland University, Lamoni 50140
Grand View College, Des Moines 50316
Grinnell College, Grinnell 50112
Hamilton Technical College, Davenport 52807
Hawkeye Community College, Waterloo 50704-8015
Indian Hills Community College, Ottumwa 52501
Iowa Central Community College, Fort Dodge 50501
Iowa Lakes Community College, Estherville 51334-2725
Iowa State University, Ames 50011
Iowa State University: College of Veterinary Medicine, Ames 50011
Iowa Wesleyan College, Mt. Pleasant 52641-1398
Iowa Western Community College, Council Bluffs 51502
Kirkwood Community College, Cedar Rapids 52404
Loras College, Dubuque 52001
Luther College, Decorah 52101
Maharishi University of Management, Fairfield 52557
Marshalltown Community College, Marshalltown 50158
Marycrest International University, Davenport 52804
Morningside College, Sioux City 51106
Mount Mercy College, Cedar Rapids 52402
Muscatine Community College, Muscatine 52761
North Iowa Area Community College, Mason City 50401
Northeast Iowa Community College, Calmar 52132
Northwestern College, Orange City 51041
Palmer College of Chiropractic, Davenport 52803
St. Ambrose University, Davenport 52803
Scott Community College, Bettendorf 52722
Simpson College, Indianola 50125
Southeastern Community College: North Campus, West Burlington 52655
Southeastern Community College: South Campus, Keokuk 62354
Southwestern Community College, Creston 50801
University of Dubuque, Dubuque 52001
University of Dubuque: School of Theology, Dubuque 52001
University of Iowa, Iowa City 52242
University of Iowa College of Dentistry, Iowa City 52242
University of Iowa: College of Law, Iowa City 52242
University of Iowa: College of Medicine, Iowa City 52242
University of Iowa: College of Pharmacy, Iowa City 52242
University of Northern Iowa, Cedar Falls 50614
University of Osteopathic Medicine and Health Sciences: College of Osteopathic Medicine and Surgery, Des Moines 50312
University of Osteopathic Medicine and Health Sciences: College of Podiatric Medicine and Surgery, Des Moines 50312
Upper Iowa University, Fayette 52142-1859
Waldorf College, Forest City 50436
Wartburg College, Waverly 50677
Wartburg Theological Seminary, Dubuque 52003
Western Iowa Tech Community College, Sioux City 51102
William Penn University, Oskaloosa 52577

Kansas

Allen County Community College, Iola 66749
Baker University, Baldwin City 66006
Barclay College, Haviland 67059
Barton County Community College, Great Bend 67530
Benedictine College, Atchison 66002
Bethany College, Lindsborg 67456-1897
Bethel College, North Newton 67117
Butler County Community College, Eldorado 67042
Central Baptist Theological Seminary, Kansas City 66102
Central Christian College, McPherson 67460
Cloud County Community College, Concordia 66901
Coffeyville Community College, Coffeyville 67337
Colby Community College, Colby 67701
Cowley County Community College, Arkansas City 67005

Dodge City Community College, Dodge City 67801-2399
Emporia State University, Emporia 66801
Fort Hays State University, Hays 67601
Garden City Community College, Garden City 67846
Hesston College, Hesston 67062
Hutchinson Community College, Hutchinson 67501
Independence Community College, Independence 67301
Johnson County Community College, Overland Prk 66210
Kansas City Kansas Community College, Kansas City 66112
Kansas State University, Manhattan 66506
Kansas State University: College of Veterinary Medicine, Manhattan 66506
Kansas Wesleyan University, Salina 67401
Manhattan Christian College, Manhattan 66502
McPherson College, McPherson 67460-1402
MidAmerica Nazarene University, Olathe 66062
Newman University, Wichita 67213
Ottawa University, Ottawa 66067-3399
Pittsburg State University, Pittsburg 66762
Pratt Community College, Pratt 67124
St. Mary College, Leavenworth 66048
Seward County Community College, Liberal 67905
Southwestern College, Winfield 67156
Sterling College, Sterling 67579
Tabor College, Hillsboro 67063
University of Kansas, Lawrence 66045
University of Kansas Medical Center, Kansas City 66160
University of Kansas Medical Center: School of Medicine, Kansas City 66160
University of Kansas: School of Law, Lawrence 66045
Washburn University School of Law, Topeka 66621
Washburn University of Topeka, Topeka 66621
Wichita State University, Wichita 67260

Kentucky
Alice Lloyd College, Pippa Passes 41844
Asbury College, Wilmore 40390
Asbury Theological Seminary, Wilmore 40390
Ashland Community College, Ashland 41101
Bellarmine College, Louisville 40205
Berea College, Berea 40404
Brescia University, Owensboro 42301
Campbellsville University, Campbellsville 42718
Centre College, Danville 40422
Clear Creek Baptist Bible College, Pineville 40977-9754
Cumberland College, Williamsburg 40769
Eastern Kentucky University, Richmond 40475
Elizabethtown Community College, Elizabethtown 42701
Georgetown College, Georgetown 40324
Hazard Community College, Hazard 41701
Henderson Community College, Henderson 42420
Hopkinsville Community College, Hopkinsville 42241-2100
ITT Technical Institute: Louisville, Louisville 40223
Institute of Electronic Technology, Paducah 42001
Kentucky Christian College, Grayson 41143
Kentucky Mountain Bible College, Vancleve 41385
Kentucky State University, Frankfort 40601
Kentucky Wesleyan College, Owensboro 42301
Lexington Community College, Lexington 40506
Lexington Theological Seminary, Lexington 40508
Lindsey Wilson College, Columbia 42728
Louisville Presbyterian Theological Seminary, Louisville 40205
Madisonville Community College, Madisonville 42431
Maysville Community College, Maysville 41056
Mid-Continent College, Mayfield 42066-0357
Midway College, Midway 40347
Morehead State University, Morehead 40351
Murray State University, Murray 42071
National Business College, Lexington 40508
Northern Kentucky University, Highland Heights 41099
Northern Kentucky University: Salmon P. Chase School of Law, Highland Heights 41099
Owensboro Community College, Owensboro 42303
Owensboro Junior College of Business, Owensboro 42304
Paducah Community College, Paducah 42002-7380
Pikeville College, Pikeville 41501
Prestonsburg Community College, Prestonsburg 41653
RETS Medical and Business Institute, Hopkinsville 42240
St. Catharine College, St. Catharine 40061
Somerset Community College, Somerset 42501
Southeast Community College, Cumberland 40823
Southern Baptist Theological Seminary, Louisville 40280
Spalding University, Louisville 40203-2188
Thomas More College, Crestview Hills 41017
Transylvania University, Lexington 40508-1797
Union College, Barbourville 40906
University of Kentucky, Lexington 40506
University of Kentucky: College of Dentistry, Lexington 40536
University of Kentucky: College of Law, Lexington 40506
University of Kentucky: College of Medicine, Lexington 40536
University of Louisville, Louisville 40292
University of Louisville: School of Dentistry, Louisville 40292
University of Louisville: School of Law, Louisville 40292
University of Louisville: School of Medicine, Louisville 40202
Western Kentucky University, Bowling Green 42101-3576

Louisiana
Bossier Parish Community College, Bossier City 71111
Centenary College of Louisiana, Shreveport 71134
Delgado Community College, New Orleans 70119
Dillard University, New Orleans 70122-3097
Grantham College of Engineering, Slidell 70469
ITT Technical Institute: St. Rose, St. Rose 70087
Louisiana State University Medical Center, New Orleans 70112
Louisiana State University Medical Center: School of Dentistry, New Orleans 70119
Louisiana State University Medical Center: School of Medicine, New Orleans 70112
Louisiana State University and Agricultural and Mechanical College, Baton Rouge 70803
Louisiana State University and Agricultural and Mechanical College: School of Law, Baton Rouge 70803
Louisiana State University and Agricultural and Mechanical College: School of Veterinary Medicine, Baton Rouge 70803
Louisiana State University at Alexandria, Alexandria 71302
Louisiana State University at Eunice, Eunice 70535
Louisiana State University in Shreveport, Shreveport 71115
Louisiana State University: School of Medicine, Shreveport 71130
Louisiana Tech University, Ruston 71272
Loyola University New Orleans, New Orleans 70118-6195
Loyola University: School of Law, New Orleans 70118
McNeese State University, Lake Charles 70609
New Orleans Baptist Theological Seminary, New Orleans 70126
Nicholls State University, Thibodaux 70310
Northeast Louisiana University School of Pharmacy, Monroe 71209
Northwestern State University, Natchitoches 71497
Notre Dame Seminary School of Theology, New Orleans 70118
Nunez Community College, Chalmette 70043
Our Lady of Holy Cross College, New Orleans 70131
Remington College - Education America, Inc., Lafayette 70508
St. Joseph Seminary College, St. Benedict 70457
Southeastern Louisiana University, Hammond 70402
Southern University and Agricultural and Mechanical College, Baton Rouge 70813
Southern University at New Orleans, New Orleans 70126
Southern University in Shreveport, Shreveport 71107
Southern University: Law Center, Baton Rouge 70813
Tulane University, New Orleans 70118
Tulane University: School of Law, New Orleans 70118
Tulane University: School of Medicine, New Orleans 70112
University of Louisiana at Lafayette, Lafayette 70504
University of Louisiana at Monroe, Monroe 71209
University of New Orleans, New Orleans 70148
Xavier University of Louisiana, New Orleans 70125
Xavier University of Louisiana: College of Pharmacy, New Orleans 70125

Maine
Andover College, Portland 04103
Bangor Theological Seminary, Bangor 04401
Bates College, Lewiston 04240
Beal College, Bangor 04401
Bowdoin College, Brunswick 04011
Central Maine Medical Center School of Nursing, Lewiston 04240
Central Maine Technical College, Auburn 04210
Colby College, Waterville 04901
College of the Atlantic, Bar Harbor 04609
Eastern Maine Technical College, Bangor 04401
Husson College, Bangor 04401
Kennebec Valley Technical College, Fairfield 04937
Maine College of Art, Portland 04101
Maine Maritime Academy, Castine 04420
Mid-State College, Auburn 04210
St. Joseph's College, Standish 04084-5263
Southern Maine Technical College, South Portland 04106
Thomas College, Waterville 04901
Unity College, Unity 04988
University of Maine, Orono 04469
University of Maine at Augusta, Augusta 04330
University of Maine at Farmington, Farmington 04938
University of Maine at Fort Kent, Fort Kent 04743
University of Maine at Machias, Machias 04654
University of Maine at Presque Isle, Presque Isle 04769
University of Maine: School of Law, Portland 04102
University of New England, Biddeford 04005
University of New England: School of Osteopathic Medicine, Biddeford 04005
University of Southern Maine, Gorham 04038
Washington County Technical College, Calais 04619

Maryland
Allegany College, Cumberland 21502
Anne Arundel Community College, Arnold 21012
Baltimore City Community College, Baltimore 21215
Baltimore International College, Baltimore 21202-3230
Bowie State University, Bowie 20715
Capital Bible Seminary, Lanham 20706
Carroll Community College, Westminster 21157
Cecil Community College, North East 21901
Charles County Community College, La Plata 20646-0910
Chesapeake College, Wye Mills 21679
College of Notre Dame of Maryland, Baltimore 21210-2476
Columbia Union College, Takoma Park 20912
Community College of Baltimore County - Catonsville, Catonsville 21228
Community College of Baltimore County - Essex, Baltimore 21237
Coppin State College, Baltimore 21216-3698
Frederick Community College, Frederick 21702
Frostburg State University, Frostburg 21532
Goucher College, Baltimore 21204
Hagerstown Community College, Hagerstown 21742-6590
Harford Community College, Bel Air 21015
Hood College, Frederick 21701-8575
Howard Community College, Columbia 21044
Johns Hopkins University, Baltimore 21218
Johns Hopkins University: Peabody Conservatory of Music, Baltimore 21202
Johns Hopkins University: School of Medicine, Baltimore 21205
Loyola College in Maryland, Baltimore 21210
Maryland College of Art and Design, Silver Springs 20902-4111
Maryland Institute College of Art, Baltimore 21217
Montgomery College: Germantown Campus, Germantown 20876
Montgomery College: Rockville Campus, Rockville 20850

Colleges in this book

Montgomery College: Takoma Park Campus, Takoma Park 20912
Morgan State University, Baltimore 21251
Mount St. Mary's College, Emmitsburg 21727
Mount St. Mary's College: Seminary, Emmitsburg 21727
Ner Israel Rabbinical College, Baltimore 21208
Prince George's Community College, Largo 20774
St. John's College, Annapolis 21404
St. Mary's College of Maryland, St. Mary's City 20686-3001
St. Mary's Seminary and University, Baltimore 21210
Salisbury State University, Salisbury 21801
Sojourner-Douglass College, Baltimore 21205
Towson University, Towson 21252-0001
Uniformed Services University of the Health Sciences, Bethesda 20814
Uniformed Services University of the Health Sciences: School of Medicine, Bethesda 20814
United States Naval Academy, Annapolis 21402
University of Baltimore, Baltimore 21201
University of Baltimore: School of Law, Baltimore 21201
University of Maryland at Baltimore: School of Dentistry, Baltimore 21201
University of Maryland at Baltimore: School of Law, Baltimore 21201
University of Maryland at Baltimore: School of Medicine, Baltimore City 21201
University of Maryland at Baltimore: School of Pharmacy, Baltimore 21201
University of Maryland: Baltimore, Baltimore 21201
University of Maryland: Baltimore County, Baltimore 21250
University of Maryland: College Park, College Park 20742
University of Maryland: Eastern Shore, Princess Anne 21853
University of Maryland: University College, College Park 20742
Villa Julie College, Stevenson 21153
Washington Bible College, Lanham 20706
Washington College, Chestertown 21620
Western Maryland College, Westminster 21157-4390
Wor-Wic Community College, Salisbury 21804

Massachusetts

American International College, Springfield 01109
Amherst College, Amherst 01002
Andover Newton Theological School, Newton Centre 02159
Anna Maria College, Paxton 01612
Assumption College, Worcester 01609
Atlantic Union College, South Lancaster 01561
Babson College, Babson Park 02457-0310
Bay Path College, Longmeadow 01106
Bay State College, Boston 02116
Becker College, Worcester 01609
Bentley College, Waltham 02452-4705
Berklee College of Music, Boston 02215
Berkshire Community College, Pittsfield 02101
Boston Architectural Center, Boston 02115
Boston College, Chestnut Hill 02467
Boston College: Law School, Newton 02159
Boston Conservatory, Boston 02215
Boston University, Boston 02215
Boston University Goldman School of Dental Medicine, Boston 02118
Boston University: School of Law, Boston 02215
Boston University: School of Medicine, Boston 02118
Boston University: School of Theology, Boston 02215
Brandeis University, Waltham 02454-9110
Bridgewater State College, Bridgewater 02325
Bristol Community College, Fall River 02720
Bunker Hill Community College, Boston 02129
Cambridge College, Cambridge 02138
Cape Cod Community College, West Barnstable 02668
Clark University, Worcester 01610-1477
College of the Holy Cross, Worcester 01610-2395
Conway School of Landscape Design, Conway 01341-0179
Curry College, Milton 02186
Dean College, Franklin 02038
Eastern Nazarene College, Quincy 02170
Elms College, Chicopee 01013
Emerson College, Boston 02116-1596
Emmanuel College, Boston 02115
Endicott College, Beverly 01915
Episcopal Divinity School, Cambridge 02138
Fisher College, Boston 02116
Fitchburg State College, Fitchburg 01420-2697
Framingham State College, Framingham 01701-9101
Franklin Institute of Boston, Boston 02116
Gordon College, Wenham 01984
Gordon-Conwell Theological Seminary, South Hamilton 01982
Greenfield Community College, Greenfield 01301
Hampshire College, Amherst 01002
Harvard College, Cambridge 02138
Harvard School of Dental Medicine, Boston 02115
Harvard University, Cambridge 02138
Harvard University Law School, Cambridge 02138
Harvard University: Divinity School, Cambridge 02138
Harvard University: Harvard Medical School, Boston 02115
Hebrew College, Brookline 02446
Hellenic College/Holy Cross, Brookline 02445
Holy Cross Greek Orthodox School of Theology, Brookline 02146
Holyoke Community College, Holyoke 01040
ITT Technical Institute: Framingham, Framingham 01702
Laboure College, Boston 02124
Lasell College, Newton 02466
Lesley College, Cambridge 02138
MGH Institute of Health Professions, Boston 02114
Marian Court College, Swampscott 01907
Massachusetts Bay Community College, Wellesley Hills 02481
Massachusetts College of Art, Boston 02115
Massachusetts College of Liberal Arts, North Adams 01247
Massachusetts College of Pharmacy and Allied Health Sciences: School of Pharmacy, Boston 02115
Massachusetts College of Pharmacy and Health Sciences, Boston 02115
Massachusetts Institute of Technology, Cambridge 02139
Massachusetts Maritime Academy, Buzzards Bay 02532
Massachusetts School of Professional Psychology, Boston 02132
Massasoit Community College, Brockton 02302
Merrimack College, North Andover 01845
Middlesex Community College, Bedford 01730
Montserrat College of Art, Beverly 01915
Mount Holyoke College, South Hadley 01075
Mount Ida College, Newton Centre 02459
Mount Wachusett Community College, Gardner 01440-1000
New England College of Finance, Boston 02111
New England College of Optometry, Boston 02115
New England Conservatory of Music, Boston 02115
New England School of Law, Boston 02116
Newbury College, Brookline 02445
Nichols College, Dudley 01571
North Shore Community College, Danvers 01923
Northeastern University, Boston 02115
Northeastern University: Bouve College of Pharmacy and Health Sciences, Boston 02115
Northeastern University: School of Law, Boston 02115
Northern Essex Community College, Haverhill 01830
Pine Manor College, Chestnut Hill 02467
Pope John XXIII National Seminary, Weston 02193
Quincy College, Quincy 02169
Regis College, Weston 02493-1571
Roxbury Community College, Roxbury Crossing 02120-3400
St. John's Seminary, Brighton 02135
St. John's Seminary College, Brighton 02135
Salem State College, Salem 01970
School of the Museum of Fine Arts, Boston 02115
Simmons College, Boston 02115-5898
Simon's Rock College of Bard, Great Barrington 01230
Smith College, Northampton 01063
Springfield College, Springfield 01109
Springfield Technical Community College, Springfield 01105
Stonehill College, Easton 02357
Suffolk University, Boston 02108
Suffolk University: Law School, Boston 02114
Tufts University, Medford 02155
Tufts University: School of Dental Medicine, Boston 02111
Tufts University: School of Medicine, Boston 02111
Tufts University: School of Veterinary Medicine, North Grafton 01536
University of Massachusetts Amherst, Amherst 01003-8190
University of Massachusetts Boston, Boston 02125-3393
University of Massachusetts Dartmouth, North Dartmouth 02747
University of Massachusetts Lowell, Lowell 01854-2882
University of Massachusetts Medical School, Worcester 01655
Wellesley College, Wellesley 02481
Wentworth Institute of Technology, Boston 02115
Western New England College, Springfield 01119-2688
Western New England College: School of Law, Springfield 01119
Westfield State College, Westfield 01086-1630
Weston Jesuit School of Theology, Cambridge 02138
Wheaton College, Norton 02766
Wheelock College, Boston 02215
Williams College, Williamstown 01267
Worcester Polytechnic Institute, Worcester 01609
Worcester State College, Worcester 01602

Michigan

Adrian College, Adrian 49221
Albion College, Albion 49224
Alma College, Alma 48801
Alpena Community College, Alpena 49707
Andrews University, Berrien Sprs 49104
Andrews University Seminary, Berrien Springs 49104
Aquinas College, Grand Rapids 49506
Baker College of Auburn Hills, Auburn Hills 48326
Baker College of Cadillac, Cadillac 49601
Baker College of Jackson, Jackson 49202
Baker College of Mount Clemens, Clinton Township 48035
Baker College of Muskegon, Muskegon 49442
Baker College of Owosso, Owosso 48867
Baker College of Port Huron, Port Huron 48060-2597
Bay de Noc Community College, Escanaba 49829
Calvin College, Grand Rapids 49546
Calvin Theological Seminary, Grand Rapids 49546
Center for Creative Studies: College of Art and Design, Detroit 48202
Center for Humanistic Studies, Detroit 48202
Central Michigan University, Mt. Pleasant 48859
Cleary College, Howell 48843
Concordia College, Ann Arbor 48105
Cornerstone College and Grand Rapids Baptist Seminary, Grand Rapids 49525
Cranbrook Academy of Art, Bloomfield Hills 48303-801
Davenport College of Business, Grand Rapids 49503
Delta College, University Center 48710
Detroit College of Business, Dearborn 48126
Detroit College of Law, Detroit 48201
Eastern Michigan University, Ypsilanti 48197
Ferris State University, Big Rapids 49307
Ferris State University College of Pharmacy, Big Rapids 49307
Ferris State University: College of Optometry, Big Rapids 49307
Glen Oaks Community College, Centreville 49032-9719
Gogebic Community College, Ironwood 49938
Grace Bible College, Grand Rapids 49509
Grand Rapids Baptist Seminary, Grand Rapids 49505
Grand Rapids Community College, Grand Rapids 49503-3295
Grand Valley State University, Allendale 49401
Great Lakes College, Midland 48642
Henry Ford Community College, Dearborn 48128
Hillsdale College, Hillsdale 49242
Hope College, Holland 49422-9000
ITT Technical Institute: Grand Rapids, Grand Rapids 49546
ITT Technical Institute: Troy, Troy 48083-1905
Jackson Community College, Jackson 49201
Kalamazoo College, Kalamazoo 49006

Kalamazoo Valley Community College, Kalamazoo 49003
Kellogg Community College, Battle Creek 49016
Kendall College of Art and Design, Grand Rapids 49503
Kettering University, Flint 48504
Kirtland Community College, Roscommon 48653
Lake Michigan College, Benton Harbr 49022
Lake Superior State University, Sault St Marie 49783-1699
Lansing Community College, Lansing 48901
Lawrence Technological University, Southfield 48075
Macomb Community College, Warren 48093
Madonna University, Livonia 48150
Marygrove College, Detroit 48221
Michigan State University, East Lansing 48824-1046
Michigan State University: College of Human Medicine, East Lansing 48824
Michigan State University: College of Osteopathic Medicine, East Lansing 48824
Michigan State University: School of Veterinary Medicine, East Lansing 48824
Michigan Technological University, Houghton 49931
Mid Michigan Community College, Harrison 48625
Monroe County Community College, Monroe 48161
Montcalm Community College, Sidney 48885
Mott Community College, Flint 48503
Muskegon Community College, Muskegon 49442
North Central Michigan College, Petoskey 49770
Northern Michigan University, Marquette 49855
Northwestern Michigan College, Traverse City 49686
Northwood University, Midland 48640
Oakland Community College, Bloomfield Hills 48304
Oakland University, Rochester 48309-4401
Olivet College, Olivet 49076
Reformed Bible College, Grand Rapids 49525
Rochester College, Rochester Hlls 48307
Sacred Heart Major Seminary, Detroit 48206
Saginaw Valley State University, University Center 48710
St. Clair County Community College, Port Huron 48061-5015
Schoolcraft College, Livonia 48152
Siena Heights University, Adrian 49221-1796
Southwestern Michigan College, Dowagiac 49047
Spring Arbor College, Spring Arbor 49283-9799
Suomi College, Hancock 49930
Thomas M. Cooley Law School, Lansing 48901
University of Detroit Mercy, Detroit 48219
University of Detroit Mercy: School of Dentistry, Detroit 48219-0900
University of Detroit Mercy: School of Law, Detroit 48226
University of Michigan, Ann Arbor 48109-1070
University of Michigan: College of Pharmacy, Ann Arbor 48109
University of Michigan: Dearborn, Dearborn 48128
University of Michigan: Flint, Flint 48502-1950
University of Michigan: School of Dentistry, Ann Arbor 48109
University of Michigan: School of Law, Ann Arbor 48109
University of Michigan: School of Medicine, Ann Arbor 48109
Walsh College of Accountancy and Business Administration, Troy 48007-7706
Washtenaw Community College, Ann Arbor 48106
Wayne County Community College, Detroit 48226
Wayne State University, Detroit 48202
Wayne State University: College of Pharmacy and Allied Health, Detroit 48202
Wayne State University: School of Law, Detroit 48202
Wayne State University: School of Medicine, Detroit 48201
West Shore Community College, Scottville 49454-0277
Western Michigan University, Kalamazoo 49008
Western Theological Seminary, Holland 49419
William Tyndale College, Farmington Hills 48331

Minnesota

Alexandria Technical College, Alexandria 56308
Anoka-Ramsey Community College, Coon Rapids 55433
Augsburg College, Minneapolis 55454
Bemidji State University, Bemidji 56601
Bethany Lutheran College, Mankato 56001
Bethel College, St. Paul 55112
Bethel Theological Seminary, St. Paul 55112
Carleton College, Northfield 55057
Central Lakes College, Brainerd 56401
Century Community and Technical College, White Bear Lake 55110
College of St. Benedict, St. Joseph 56374
College of St. Catherine-Minneapolis, Minneapolis 55454
College of St. Catherine: St. Paul Campus, St. Paul 55105
College of St. Scholastica, Duluth 55811
College of Visual Arts, St. Paul 55102
Concordia College: Moorhead, Moorhead 56562
Concordia University: St. Paul, St. Paul 55104
Crown College, St. Bonifacius 55375-9002
Dakota County Technical College, Rosemount 55068
Dunwoody Institute, Minneapolis 55403
Fond Du Lac Tribal and Community College, Cloquet 55720
Gustavus Adolphus College, St. Peter 56082
Hamline University, St. Paul 55104-1284
Hamline University: School of Law, St. Paul 55104
Hennepin Technical College, Brooklyn Park 55445
Hibbing Community College: A Technical and Community College, Hibbing 55746
Inver Hills Community College, Inver Grove Heights 55076
Itasca Community College, Grand Rapids 55744
Lake Superior College: A Community and Technical College, Duluth 55811
Luther Seminary: Theological Professions, St. Paul 55108
Macalester College, St. Paul 55105
Martin Luther College, New Ulm 56073-3965
Mayo Graduate School, Rochester 55905
Mayo Medical School, Rochester 55905
Mesabi Range Community and Technical College, Virginia and Eveleth 55792
Metropolitan State University, St. Paul 55106
Minneapolis College of Art and Design, Minneapolis 55404
Minneapolis Community and Technical College, Minneapolis 55403
Minnesota Bible College, Rochester 55902
Minnesota State College - Southeast Technical, Winona 55987
Minnesota State University, Mankato, Mankato 56001
Moorhead State University, Moorhead 56563
NEI College of Technology, Columbia Heights 55421
National American University: St. Paul, St. Paul 55108
North Central University, Minneapolis 55404
North Hennepin Community College, Minneapolis 55445
Northland Community & Technical College, Thief River Falls 56701
Northwestern College, St. Paul 55113
Northwestern College of Chiropractic, Bloomington 55431
Pine Technical College, Pine City 55063
Ridgewater College: A Community and Technical College, Willmar 56201
Rochester Community and Technical College, Rochester 55904
St. Cloud State University, St. Cloud 56301
St. Cloud Technical College, St. Cloud 56303
St. John's University, Collegeville 56321
St. John's University: School of Theology, Collegeville 56321
St. Mary's University of Minnesota, Winona 55987
St. Olaf College, Northfield 55057
St. Paul Technical College, St. Paul 55102
South Central Technical College, North Mankato 56003
Southwest State University, Marshall 56258
United Theological Seminary of the Twin Cities, New Brighton 55112
University of Minnesota Medical School, Minneapolis 55455
University of Minnesota Twin Cities: College of Veterinary Medicine, St. Paul 55108
University of Minnesota Twin Cities: School of Dentistry, Minneapolis 55455
University of Minnesota Twin Cities: School of Law, Minneapolis 55455
University of Minnesota: Crookston, Crookston 56716
University of Minnesota: Duluth, Duluth 55812
University of Minnesota: Morris, Morris 56267
University of Minnesota: Twin Cities, Minneapolis-St. Paul 55455-0213
University of St. Thomas, St. Paul 55105-1096
University of St. Thomas: School of Divinity, St. Paul 55105
Vermilion Community College, Ely 55731
William Mitchell College of Law: Law Professions, St. Paul 55105
Winona State University, Winona 55987

Mississippi

Alcorn State University, Alcorn State 39096
Belhaven College, Jackson 39202
Blue Mountain College, Blue Mountain 38610-0160
Coahoma Community College, Clarksdale 38614
Copiah-Lincoln Community College, Wesson 39191
Delta State University, Cleveland 38733
East Central Community College, Decatur 39327
East Mississippi Community College, Scooba 39358
Hinds Community College, Raymond 39154
Holmes Community College, Goodman 39079
Itawamba Community College, Fulton 38843
Jackson State University, Jackson 39217
Jones County Junior College, Ellisville 39437
Magnolia Bible College, Kosciusko 39090
Mary Holmes College, West Point 39773
Meridian Community College, Meridian 39307
Millsaps College, Jackson 39210
Mississippi College, Clinton 39058
Mississippi College: School of Law, Jackson 39201
Mississippi Delta Community College, Moorhead 38761
Mississippi Gulf Coast Community College: Jackson County Campus, Gautier 39553
Mississippi Gulf Coast Community College: Jefferson Davis Campus, Gulfport 39507
Mississippi Gulf Coast Community College: Perkinston, Perkinston 39573
Mississippi State University, Miss. State 39762
Mississippi State University: College of Veterinary Medicine, Mississippi University 39762
Mississippi University for Women, Columbus 39701
Mississippi Valley State University, Itta Bena 38941-1400
Northeast Mississippi Community College, Booneville 38829
Northwest Mississippi Community College, Senatobia 38668
Reformed Theological Seminary, Jackson 39209
Rust College, Holly Springs 38635
Southwest Mississippi Community College, Summit 39666
Tougaloo College, Tougaloo 39174
University of Mississippi, University 38677
University of Mississippi Medical Center, Jackson 39216
University of Mississippi Medical Center: School of Dentistry, Jackson 39216
University of Mississippi Medical Center: School of Medicine, Jackson 39216
University of Mississippi: School of Law, University 38677
University of Mississippi: School of Pharmacy, University 38677
University of Southern Mississippi, Hattiesburg 39406-5011
Wesley Biblical Seminary, Jackson 39286
Wesley College, Florence 39073
William Carey College, Hattiesburg 39401

Missouri

Aquinas Institute of Theology, St. Louis 63108
Assemblies of God Theological Seminary, Springfield 65802
Avila College, Kansas City 64145-1698
Baptist Bible College, Springfield 65803
Berean University, Springfield 65802
Central Methodist College, Fayette 65248
Central Missouri State University, Warrensburg 64093
Cleveland Chiropractic College of Kansas City, Kansas City 64131
College of the Ozarks, Point Lookout 65726

Columbia College, Columbia 65216
Conception Seminary College, Conception 64433
Concordia Seminary, Clayton 63105
Cottey College, Nevada 64772
Covenant Theological Seminary, St. Louis 63141
Crowder College, Neosho 64850
Culver-Stockton College, Canton 63435
DeVry Institute of Technology: Kansas City, Kansas City 64131
Deaconess College of Nursing, St. Louis 63139
Drury University, Springfield 65802
East Central College, Union 63084
Eden Theological Seminary, Webster Groves 63119
Evangel University, Springfield 65802
Fontbonne College, St. Louis 63105
Hannibal-LaGrange College, Hannibal 63401-1999
Harris Stowe State College, St. Louis 63103-2199
ITT Technical Institute: Arnold, Arnold 63010
ITT Technical Institute: Earth City, Earth City 63045
Jefferson College, Hillsboro 63050
Kansas City Art Institute, Kansas City 64111
Kenrick-Glennon Seminary, St. Louis 63119
Kirksville College of Osteopathic Medicine, Kirksville 63501
Lincoln University, Jefferson City 65102
Lindenwood University, St. Charles 63301
Logan College of Chiropractic, Chesterfield 63006
Longview Community College, Lee's Summit 64081
Maple Woods Community College, Kansas City 64156-1299
Maryville University of Saint Louis, St. Louis 63141-7299
Midwestern Baptist Theological Seminary, Kansas City 64118
Mineral Area College, Park Hills 63601-1000
Missouri Baptist College, St. Louis 63141
Missouri Southern State College, Joplin 64801-1595
Missouri Valley College, Marshall 65340
Missouri Western State College, St. Joseph 64507
Moberly Area Community College, Moberly 65270
Nazarene Theological Seminary, Kansas City 64131
Northwest Missouri State University, Maryville 64468
Ozark Christian College, Joplin 64801
Ozarks Technical Community College, Springfield 65801
Park University, Parkville 64152
Penn Valley Community College, Kansas City 64111-2429
Ranken Technical College, St. Louis 63113
Research College of Nursing, Kansas City 64132
Rockhurst University, Kansas City 64110
St. Charles County Community College, St. Peters 63376
St. Louis Christian College, Florissant 63033
St. Louis College of Pharmacy, St. Louis 63110
St. Louis Community College at Florissant Valley, St. Louis 63135
St. Louis Community College at Forest Park, St. Louis 63110
St. Louis Community College at Meramec, St. Louis 63122-5799
St. Louis University, St. Louis 63103
St. Louis University: School of Law, St. Louis 63108
St. Louis University: School of Medicine, St. Louis 63104
St. Luke's College, Kansas City 64111
St. Paul School of Theology, Kansas City 64127
Southeast Missouri State University, Cape Girardeau 63701
Southwest Baptist University, Bolivar 65613
Southwest Missouri State University, Springfield 65804-0094
Southwest Missouri State University: West Plains Campus, West Plains 65775
State Fair Community College, Sedalia 65301-2199
Stephens College, Columbia 65215
Three Rivers Community College, Poplar Bluff 63901
Truman State University, Kirksville 63501
University of Health Sciences College of Osteopathic Medicine, Kansas City 64124
University of Missouri Columbia: School of Law, Columbia 65211
University of Missouri Columbia: School of Medicine, Columbia 65212
University of Missouri Columbia: School of Veterinary Medicine, Columbia 65211
University of Missouri Kansas City: School of Dentistry, Kansas City 64108
University of Missouri Kansas City: School of Law, Kansas City 64110
University of Missouri Kansas City: School of Medicine, Kansas City 64108
University of Missouri St. Louis: School of Optometry, St. Louis 63121
University of Missouri: Columbia, Columbia 65211-1210
University of Missouri: Kansas City, Kansas City 64110
University of Missouri: Rolla, Rolla 65409
University of Missouri: St. Louis, St. Louis 63121-4499
Washington University, St. Louis 63130-4899
Washington University: School of Law, St. Louis 63130
Washington University: School of Medicine, St. Louis 63110
Webster University, Webster Groves 63119
Wentworth Military Academy, Lexington 64067
Westminster College, Fulton 65251
William Jewell College, Liberty 64068
William Woods University, Fulton 65251

Montana

Blackfeet Community College, Browning 59417
Carroll College, Helena 59625
Dawson Community College, Glendive 59330
Dull Knife Memorial College, Lame Deer 59043
Flathead Valley Community College, Kalispell 59901
Little Big Horn College, Crow Agency 59022
Miles Community College, Miles City 59301
Montana State University College of Technology-Great Falls, Great Falls 59405
Montana State University: Billings, Billings 59101
Montana State University: Bozeman, Bozeman 59717-2190
Montana State University: Northern, Havre 59501
Montana Tech of the University of Montana, Butte 59701
Montana Tech of the University of Montana: College of Technology, Butte 59701
Rocky Mountain College, Billings 59102-1796
Salish Kootenai College, Pablo 59855
Stone Child College, Box Elder 59521-9796
University of Great Falls, Great Falls 59405
University of Montana School of Pharmacy and Allied Health Sciences, Missoula 59812
University of Montana-Missoula, Missoula 59812
University of Montana: School of Law, Missoula 59812
Western Montana College of The University of Montana, Dillon 59725-3598

Nebraska

Bellevue University, Bellevue 68005
Central Community College, Grand Island 68802
Chadron State College, Chadron 69337
Clarkson College, Omaha 68131
College of Saint Mary, Omaha 68124
Concordia University, Seward 68434
Creighton University, Omaha 68178
Creighton University: School of Dentistry, Omaha 68178
Creighton University: School of Law, Omaha 68178
Creighton University: School of Medicine, Omaha 68178
Dana College, Blair 68008
Doane College, Crete 68333
Grace University, Omaha 68108
Hastings College, Hastings 68901-7696
ITT Technical Institute: Omaha, Omaha 68127
Lincoln School of Commerce, Lincoln 68501
Metropolitan Community College, Omaha 68103
Mid Plains Community College Area, North Platte 69101
Midland Lutheran College, Fremont 68025
Nebraska College of Technical Agriculture, Curtis 69025
Nebraska Methodist College of Nursing and Allied Health, Omaha 68114
Nebraska Wesleyan University, Lincoln 68504
Northeast Community College, Norfolk 68702-0469
Peru State College, Peru 68421
Southeast Community College: Lincoln Campus, Lincoln 68520
Southeast Community College: Milford Campus, Milford 68405-8498
Union College, Lincoln 68506
University of Nebraska - Kearney, Kearney 68849
University of Nebraska - Lincoln, Lincoln 68588
University of Nebraska - Omaha, Omaha 68182
University of Nebraska Lincoln: College of Law, Lincoln 68583
University of Nebraska Medical Center: College of Dentistry, Lincoln 68583
University of Nebraska Medical Center: College of Medicine, Omaha 68134
University of Nebraska Medical Center: College of Pharmacy, Omaha 68198
Wayne State College, Wayne 68787

Nevada

Community College of Southern Nevada, North Las Vegas 89030
ITT Technical Institute: Henderson, Henderson 89014
University of Nevada: Las Vegas, Las Vegas 89154
University of Nevada: Reno, Reno 89557
University of Nevada: School of Medicine, Reno 89557
Western Nevada Community College, Carson City 89703-7399

New Hampshire

Antioch New England Graduate School, Keene 03431-3516
Colby-Sawyer College, New London 03257
College for Lifelong Learning, Concord 03301
Daniel Webster College, Nashua 03063
Dartmouth College, Hanover 03755
Dartmouth College: School of Medicine, Hanover 03755
Franklin Pierce College, Rindge 03461-0060
Franklin Pierce Law Center, Concord 03301
Hesser College, Manchester 03103
Keene State College, Keene 03435
McIntosh College, Dover 03820
New England College, Henniker 03242
New Hampshire College, Manchester 03106
New Hampshire Community Technical College: Berlin, Berlin 03570
New Hampshire Community Technical College: Claremont, Claremont 03743
New Hampshire Community Technical College: Laconia, Laconia 03246
New Hampshire Community Technical College: Manchester, Manchester 03102
New Hampshire Community Technical College: Nashua, Nashua 03061
New Hampshire Community Technical College: Stratham, Stratham 03885
New Hampshire Technical Institute, Concord 03301
Notre Dame College, Manchester 03104
Plymouth State College of the University System of New Hampshire, Plymouth 03264
Rivier College, Nashua 03060
St. Anselm College, Manchester 03102-1310
Thomas More College of Liberal Arts, Merrimack 03054
University of New Hampshire, Durham 03824
University of New Hampshire at Manchester, Manchester 03102
White Pines College, Chester 03036

New Jersey

Assumption College for Sisters, Mendham 07945-0800
Atlantic Cape Community College, Mays Landing 08330
Bergen Community College, Paramus 07652
Berkeley College, West Paterson 07424
Bloomfield College, Bloomfield 07003
Brookdale Community College, Lincroft 07738
Burlington County College, Pemberton 08068
Caldwell College, Caldwell 07006-6195
Camden County College, Blackwood 08012
Centenary College, Hackettstown 07840
College of St. Elizabeth, Morristown 07960-6989
County College of Morris, Randolph 07869
Cumberland County College, Vineland 08362-0517
DeVry Institute, North Brunswick 08902

Colleges in this book

Drew University, Madison 07940-1493
Drew University: School of Theology, Madison 07940
Essex County College, Newark 07102
Fairleigh Dickinson University, Teaneck 07666-1996
Felician College, Lodi 07644
Georgian Court College, Lakewood 08701
Gibbs College, Montclair 07042
Gloucester County College, Sewell 08080
Hudson County Community College, Jersey City 07306
Immaculate Conception Seminary of Seton Hall University, South Orange 07079
Kean University, Union 07083
Mercer County Community College, Trenton 08690-0182
Middlesex County College, Edison 08818-3050
Monmouth University, West Long Branch 07764-1898
Montclair State University, Upper Montclair 07043
New Brunswick Theological Seminary, New Brunswick 08901
New Jersey City University, Jersey City 07305-1597
New Jersey Institute of Technology, Newark 07102-1982
Ocean County College, Toms River 08754
Passaic County Community College, Paterson 07505-1179
Princeton Theological Seminary, Princeton 08542
Princeton University, Princeton 08544
Ramapo College of New Jersey, Mahwah 07430-1680
Raritan Valley Community College, Somerville 08876-1265
Richard Stockton College of New Jersey, Pomona 08240
Rider University, Lawrenceville 08648-3001
Rowan University, Glassboro 08028
Rutgers, The State University of New Jersey: Camden College of Arts and Sciences, Camden 08102
Rutgers, The State University of New Jersey: Camden Graduate Campus, Camden 08102
Rutgers, The State University of New Jersey: Camden School of Law, Camden 08102
Rutgers, The State University of New Jersey: College of Engineering, Piscataway 08854-8097
Rutgers, The State University of New Jersey: College of Nursing, Newark 07102-1896
Rutgers, The State University of New Jersey: College of Pharmacy, New Brunswick 08903
Rutgers, The State University of New Jersey: Cook College, Piscataway 08854-8097
Rutgers, The State University of New Jersey: Douglass College, Piscataway 08854-8097
Rutgers, The State University of New Jersey: Livingston College, Piscataway 08854
Rutgers, The State University of New Jersey: Mason Gross School of the Arts, Piscataway 08854-8097
Rutgers, The State University of New Jersey: New Brunswick Graduate Campus, New Brunswick 08901-1103
Rutgers, The State University of New Jersey: Newark College of Arts and Sciences, Newark 07102-1896
Rutgers, The State University of New Jersey: Newark Graduate Campus, Camden 08102
Rutgers, The State University of New Jersey: Newark School of Law, Newark 07102
Rutgers, The State University of New Jersey: Rutgers College, Piscataway 08854-8097
Rutgers, The State University of New Jersey: University College Camden, Camden 08102
Rutgers, The State University of New Jersey: University College New Brunswick, New Brunswick 08903
Rutgers, The State University of New Jersey: University College Newark, Newark 07102-1896
St. Peter's College, Jersey City 07306
Salem Community College, Carneys Point 08069-2799
Seton Hall University, South Orange 07079
Seton Hall University: School of Law, Newark 07102
Stevens Institute of Technology, Hoboken 07030
Sussex County Community College, Newton 07860
The College of New Jersey, Ewing 08628
Thomas Edison State College, Trenton 08608
UMDNJ-School of Osteopathic Medicine, Stratford 08084
Union County College, Cranford 07016
University of Medicine and Dentistry of New Jersey: New Jersey Medical School, Newark 07103
University of Medicine and Dentistry of New Jersey: Robert Wood Johnson Medical School at Camden, Camden 08103
University of Medicine and Dentistry of New Jersey: New Jersey Dental School, Newark 07103
University of Medicine and Dentistry of New Jersey: Robert Wood Johnson Medical School, Piscataway 08854
University of Medicine and Dentistry of New Jersey: School of Health Related Professions, Newark 07107
University of Medicine and Dentistry of New Jersey: School of Nursing, Newark 07107
Warren County Community College, Washington 07882-4343
William Paterson University of New Jersey, Wayne 07470

New Mexico

Albuquerque Technical-Vocational Institute, Albuquerque 87106
Clovis Community College, Clovis 88101-8381
College of Santa Fe, Santa Fe 87505
College of the Southwest, Hobbs 88240
Dona Ana Branch Community College of New Mexico State University, Las Cruces 88003
Eastern New Mexico University, Portales 88130
Eastern New Mexico University: Roswell Campus, Roswell 88202
ITT Technical Institute: Albuquerque, Albuquerque 87109
Institute of American Indian Arts, Santa Fe 87504
New Mexico Highlands University, Las Vegas 87701
New Mexico Institute of Mining and Technology, Socorro 87801
New Mexico Junior College, Hobbs 88240
New Mexico Military Institute, Roswell 88201
New Mexico State University, Las Cruces 88003-8001
New Mexico State University at Alamogordo, Alamogordo 88310
New Mexico State University at Carlsbad, Carlsbad 88220
Northern New Mexico Community College, Espanola 87532
St. John's College, Santa Fe 87501
San Juan College, Farmington 87402
Santa Fe Community College, Santa Fe 87505
University of New Mexico, Albuquerque 87131-2046
University of New Mexico College of Pharmacy, Albuquerque 87131
University of New Mexico: School of Law, Albuquerque 87131
University of New Mexico: School of Medicine, Albuquerque 87131
Western New Mexico University, Silver City 88062

New York

Adelphi University, Garden City 11530
Adirondack Community College, Queensbury 12804
Albany College of Pharmacy, Albany 12208
Albany Law School of Union University, Albany 12208
Albany Medical College, Albany 12208
Albany Medical College: School of Medicine, Albany 12208
Albert Einstein College of Medicine, Bronx 10461
Alfred University, Alfred 14802
Alliance Theological Seminary, Nyack 10960
American Academy McAllister Institute of Funeral Service, New York 10019
American Academy of Dramatic Arts, New York 10016
Audrey Cohen College, New York 10013
Bank Street College of Education, New York 10025
Bard College, Annandale-on-Hudson 12504
Barnard College, New York 10027
Benjamin N. Cardozo School of Law, New York 10003
Berkeley College, White Plains 10604
Berkeley College of New York City, New York 10017
Briarcliffe College, Bethpage 11714
Brooklyn Law School, Brooklyn 11201
Broome Community College, Binghamton 13902
Bryant & Stratton Business Institute: Albany, Albany 12205
Bryant & Stratton Business Institute: Syracuse, Syracuse 13203
Canisius College, Buffalo 14208
Cayuga County Community College, Auburn 13021
Central Yeshiva Tomchei Tmimim Lubavitz, Brooklyn 11230
Christ The King Seminary, East Aurora 14052
City University of New York Graduate School and University Center, New York 10036
City University of New York: Baruch College, New York 10010-5285
City University of New York: Borough of Manhattan Community College, New York 10007
City University of New York: Bronx Community College, Bronx 10453
City University of New York: Brooklyn College, Brooklyn 11210
City University of New York: City College, New York 10031
City University of New York: College of Staten Island, Staten Island 10314
City University of New York: Hostos Community College, Bronx 10451
City University of New York: Hunter College, New York 10021
City University of New York: John Jay College of Criminal Justice, New York 10019
City University of New York: Kingsborough Community College, Brooklyn 11235
City University of New York: La Guardia Community College, Long Island City 11101
City University of New York: Lehman College, Bronx 10468
City University of New York: Medgar Evers College, Brooklyn 11225
City University of New York: New York City Technical College, Brooklyn 11201
City University of New York: Queens College, Flushing 11367
City University of New York: Queensborough Community College, Bayside 11364
City University of New York: School of Law at Queens College, Flushing 11367
City University of New York: York College, Jamaica 11451
Clarkson University, Potsdam 13699
Clinton Community College, Plattsburgh 12901
Cochran School of Nursing-St. John's Riverside Hospital, Yonkers 10701
Colgate Rochester Divinity School-Bexley Crozer Theological Seminary, Rochester 14620
Colgate University, Hamilton 13346
College of Aeronautics, Flushing 11369
College of Insurance, New York 10007-2165
College of Mount St. Vincent, Riverdale 10471
College of New Rochelle, New Rochelle 10805
College of New Rochelle: School of New Resources, New Rochelle 10805
College of St. Rose, Albany 12203
Columbia University: College of Physicians and Surgeons, New York 10032
Columbia University: Columbia College, New York 10027
Columbia University: Fu Foundation School of Engineering and Applied Science, New York 10027
Columbia University: Graduate School, New York 10027
Columbia University: School of Dental and Oral Surgery, New York 10032
Columbia University: School of General Studies, New York 10027
Columbia University: School of Law, New York 10027
Columbia University: School of Nursing, New York 10032
Columbia University: Teachers College, New York 10027
Columbia-Greene Community College, Hudson 12534
Concordia College, Bronxville 10708
Cooper Union for the Advancement of Science and Art, New York 10003
Cornell University, Ithaca 14850
Cornell University Medical College, New York 10021
Cornell University: College of Veterinary Medicine, Ithaca 14853
Cornell University: School of Law, Ithaca 14853
Corning Community College, Corning 14830
Culinary Institute of America, Hyde Park 12538
D'Youville College, Buffalo 14201
Daemen College, Amherst 14226

Colleges in this book

DeVry Institute of Technology: New York, Long Island City 11101
Dominican College of Blauvelt, Orangeburg 10962
Dowling College, Oakdale 11769
Dutchess Community College, Poughkeepsie 12601
Eastman School of Music of the University of Rochester, Rochester 14604
Elmira College, Elmira 14901
Erie Community College: City Campus, Buffalo 14203-2698
Erie Community College: North Campus, Williamsville 14221-7095
Erie Community College: South Campus, Orchard Park 14127-2199
Eugene Lang College/New School University, New York 10003
Fashion Institute of Technology, New York 10001
Finger Lakes Community College, Canandaigua 14424
Five Towns College, Dix Hills 11746
Fordham University, Bronx 10458
Fordham University: School of Law, New York 10023
Fulton-Montgomery Community College, Johnstown 12095-3790
General Theological Seminary, New York 10011
Genesee Community College, Batavia 14020-9704
Hamilton College, Clinton 13323
Hartwick College, Oneonta 13820-4020
Helene Fuld College of Nursing, New York 10035
Herkimer County Community College, Herkimer 13350
Hilbert College, Hamburg 14075-1597
Hobart and William Smith Colleges, Geneva 14456
Hofstra University, Hempstead 11549
Hofstra University: School of Law, Hempstead 11550
Houghton College, Houghton 14744
Hudson Valley Community College, Troy 12180
ITT Technical Institute: Albany, Albany 12205
ITT Technical Institute: Getzville, Getzville 14068
ITT Technical Institute: Liverpool, Liverpool 13088
Institute of Design and Construction, Brooklyn 11201
Interboro Institute, New York 10019
Iona College, New Rochelle 10801-1890
Ithaca College, Ithaca 14850-7020
Jamestown Business College, Jamestown 14701
Jamestown Community College, Jamestown 14702-0020
Jefferson Community College, Watertown 13601
Jewish Theological Seminary of America, New York 10027
Juilliard School, New York 10023-6588
Katharine Gibbs School: New York, New York 10166
Kehilath Yakov Rabbinical Seminary, Brooklyn 11211
Keuka College, Keuka Park 14478
Kol Yaakov Torah Center, Monsey 10952
Laboratory Institute of Merchandising, New York 10022
Le Moyne College, Syracuse 13214-1399
Long Island University: Brooklyn Campus, Brooklyn 11201
Long Island University: C. W. Post Campus, Brookville 11548-1300
Long Island University: Southampton College, Southampton 11968
Long Island University: Arnold and Marie Schwartz College of Pharmacy and Health Sciences, Brooklyn 11201
Manhattan College, Riverdale 10471
Manhattan School of Music, New York 10027
Manhattanville College, Purchase 10577
Mannes College of Music, New York 10024
Maria College, Albany 12208
Marist College, Poughkeepsie 12601
Marymount College, Tarrytown 10591
Marymount Manhattan College, New York 10021-4597
Medaille College, Buffalo 14214
Mercy College, Dobbs Ferry 10522
Mesivta Eastern Parkway Rabbinical Seminary, Brooklyn 11218
Mesivta Tifereth Jerusalem of America, New York 10002
Mirrer Yeshiva Central Institute, Brooklyn 11223
Mohawk Valley Community College, Utica 13501
Molloy College, Rockville Center 11570
Monroe College, Bronx 10468
Monroe Community College, Rochester 14623
Mount St. Mary College, Newburgh 12550

Mount Sinai School of Medicine of City University of New York, New York 10029
Nassau Community College, Garden City 11530
Nazareth College of Rochester, Rochester 14618
New York Chiropractic College, Seneca Falls 13148
New York College of Osteopathic Medicine of New York Institute of Technology, Old Westbury 11568
New York College of Podiatric Medicine, New York 10035
New York Institute of Technology, Old Westbury 11568
New York Law School, New York 10013
New York Medical College, Valhalla 10595
New York School of Interior Design, New York 10021
New York State College of Ceramics at Alfred University, Alfred 14802
New York Theological Seminary, New York 10001
New York University, New York 10003
New York University: College of Dentistry, New York 10010
New York University: School of Law, New York 10012
New York University: School of Medicine, New York 10016
Niagara County Community College, Sanborn 14132
Niagara University, Niagara University 14109
North Country Community College, Saranac Lake 12983-0089
Nyack College, Nyack 10960-3698
Ohr Hameir Theological Seminary, Peekskill 10566
Ohr Somayach Institutions: School of Theology, Monsey 10952
Ohr Somayach Tanenbaum Education Center, Monsey 10952
Onondaga Community College, Syracuse 13215
Orange County Community College, Middletown 10940
Pace University, New York 10038
Pace University Westchester: School of Law, White Plains 10603
Pace University: Pleasantville/Briarcliff, Pleasantville 10570
Parsons School of Design, New York 10011
Phillips Beth Israel School of Nursing, New York 10010
Polytechnic University, Brooklyn 11201
Polytechnic University: Long Island Campus, Farmingdale 11735
Pratt Institute, Brooklyn 11205
Rabbi Isaac Elchanan Theological Seminary, New York 10033
Rabbinical College Beth Shraga, Monsey 10952
Rabbinical College Bobover Yeshiva B'nei Zion, Brooklyn 11219
Rabbinical Seminary M'Kor Chaim, Brooklyn 11219
Regents College, Albany 12203
Rensselaer Polytechnic Institute, Troy 12180
Roberts Wesleyan College, Rochester 14624
Rochester Institute of Technology, Rochester 14623
Rockefeller University, New York 10021
Rockland Community College, Suffern 10901
Russell Sage College, Troy 12180
Sage Junior College of Albany, Albany 12208
St. Bernard's Institute, Rochester 14620
St. Bonaventure University, St. Bonaventure 14778
St. Francis College, Brooklyn Heights 11201
St. John Fisher College, Rochester 14618-3597
St. John's University, Jamaica 11439
St. John's University: College of Pharmacy and Allied Health Professions, Jamaica 11439
St. John's University: School of Law, Jamaica 11439
St. Joseph's College, Brooklyn 11205
St. Joseph's College: Suffolk Campus, Patchogue 11772
St. Joseph's Hospital Health Center School of Nursing, Syracuse 13203
St. Joseph's Seminary and College, Yonkers 10704
St. Lawrence University, Canton 13617
St. Thomas Aquinas College, Sparkill 10976
St. Vladimir's Orthodox Theological Seminary, Crestwood 10707
Sarah Lawrence College, Bronxville 10708
Schenectady County Community College, Schenectady 12305
School of Visual Arts, New York 10010
Seminary of the Immaculate Conception, Huntington 11743
Sh'or Yoshuv Rabbinical College, Far Rockaway 11691
Siena College, Loudonville 12211

Skidmore College, Saratoga Springs 12866
State University of New York College at Brockport, Brockport 14420
State University of New York College at Buffalo, Buffalo 14222
State University of New York College at Cortland, Cortland 13045
State University of New York College at Fredonia, Fredonia 14063
State University of New York College at Geneseo, Geneseo 14454-1471
State University of New York College at Old Westbury, Old Westbury 11568-0210
State University of New York College at Oneonta, Oneonta 13820-4015
State University of New York College at Plattsburgh, Plattsburgh 12901
State University of New York College at Potsdam, Potsdam 13676
State University of New York College of Agriculture and Technology at Cobleskill, Cobleskill 12043
State University of New York College of Agriculture and Technology at Morrisville, Morrisville 13408
State University of New York College of Environmental Science and Forestry, Syracuse 13210
State University of New York College of Optometry, New York 10010
State University of New York College of Technology at Alfred, Alfred 14802
State University of New York College of Technology at Canton, Canton 13617
State University of New York College of Technology at Delhi, Delhi 13753
State University of New York Empire State College, Saratoga Springs 12866
State University of New York Health Science Center at Brooklyn, Brooklyn 11203
State University of New York Health Science Center at Brooklyn: School of Medicine, Brooklyn 11203
State University of New York Health Science Center at Stony Brook, Stony Brook 11794
State University of New York Health Science Center at Syracuse: School of Medicine, Syracuse 13210
State University of New York Health Sciences Center at Stony Brook: School of Dentistry, Stony Brook 11794
State University of New York Health Sciences Center at Stony Brook: School of Medicine, Stony Brook 11794
State University of New York Institute of Technology at Utica/Rome, Utica 13504
State University of New York Maritime College, Throggs Neck 10465
State University of New York Upstate Medical University, Syracuse 13210
State University of New York at Albany, Albany 12222
State University of New York at Binghamton, Binghamton 13902-6000
State University of New York at Buffalo, Buffalo 14260-1608
State University of New York at Buffalo: School of Dentistry, Buffalo 14214
State University of New York at Buffalo: School of Law, Buffalo 14260
State University of New York at Buffalo: School of Medicine, Buffalo 14214
State University of New York at Buffalo: School of Pharmacy, Buffalo 14260
State University of New York at Farmingdale, Farmingdale 11735
State University of New York at New Paltz, New Paltz 12561-2443
State University of New York at Oswego, Oswego 13126-3599
State University of New York at Purchase, Purchase 10577
State University of New York at Stony Brook, Stony Brook 11794
Suffolk County Community College, Selden 11784
Syracuse University, Syracuse 13244
Syracuse University: College of Law, Syracuse 13244
Technical Career Institutes, New York 10001
Tompkins-Cortland Community College, Dryden 13053-0139
Touro College, New York 10010

Touro College: Jacob D. Fuchsberg Law Center, Huntington 11743
Trocaire College, Buffalo 14220
Ulster County Community College, Stone Ridge 12484
Union College, Schenectady 12308
Union Theological Seminary: Theological Professions, New York 10027
United States Merchant Marine Academy, Kings Point 11024-1699
United States Military Academy, West Point 10996-5000
University of Rochester, Rochester 14627
University of Rochester: School of Medicine and Dentistry, Rochester 14642
Utica College of Syracuse University, Utica 13502-4892
Vassar College, Poughkeepsie 12604
Villa Maria College of Buffalo, Buffalo 14225
Wadhams Hall Seminary-College, Ogdensburg 13669
Wagner College, Staten Island 10301
Webb Institute, Glen Cove 11542
Wells College, Aurora 13026
Westchester Business Institute, White Plains 10602
Westchester Community College, Valhalla 10595
Wood Tobe-Coburn School, New York 10016-0190
Yeshiva Karlin Stolin Beth Aron Y'Israel Rabbinical Institute, Brooklyn 11204
Yeshiva of Nitra Rabbinical College, Mt. Kisco 11211
Yeshivat Mikdash Melech, Brooklyn 11230

North Carolina
Alamance Community College, Graham 27253
Appalachian State University, Boone 28608
Asheville Buncombe Technical Community College, Asheville 28801
Barber-Scotia College, Concord 28025
Barton College, Wilson 27893
Beaufort County Community College, Washington 27889
Belmont Abbey College, Belmont 28012
Bennett College, Greensboro 27401-3239
Bladen Community College, Dublin 28332
Blue Ridge Community College, Flat Rock 28731
Brevard College, Brevard 28712
Brunswick Community College, Supply 28462
Caldwell Community College and Technical Institute, Hudson 28638
Campbell University, Buies Creek 27506
Campbell University: Norman Adrian Wiggins School of Law, Buies Creek 27506
Campbell University: School of Pharmacy, Buies Creek 27506
Cape Fear Community College, Wilmington 28401
Carolinas College of Health Sciences, Charlotte 28232
Carteret Community College, Morehead City 28557
Catawba College, Salisbury 28144-2488
Catawba Valley Community College, Hickory 28602
Cecils College, Asheville 28806
Central Carolina Community College, Sanford 27330
Central Piedmont Community College, Charlotte 28235
Chowan College, Murfreesboro 27855
Cleveland Community College, Shelby 28152
Coastal Carolina Community College, Jacksonville 28546
College of the Albemarle, Elizabth City 27906-2327
Craven Community College, New Bern 28562
Davidson College, Davidson 28036
Davidson County Community College, Lexington 27293-1287
Duke University, Durham 27708
Duke University: Divinity School, Durham 27708
Duke University: School of Law, Durham 27708
Duke University: School of Medicine, Durham 27710
Durham Technical Community College, Durham 27703
East Carolina University, Greenville 27858
East Carolina University: School of Medicine, Greenville 27858
Edgecombe Community College, Tarboro 27886
Elizabeth City State University, Elizabth City 27909
Elon College, Elon College 27244
Fayetteville State University, Fayetteville 28301
Fayetteville Technical Community College, Fayetteville 28303
Forsyth Technical Community College, Winston-Salem 27103
Gardner-Webb University, Boiling Springs 28017
Gaston College, Dallas 28034-1499
Greensboro College, Greensboro 27401-1875
Guilford College, Greensboro 27410
Guilford Technical Community College, Jamestown 27282
Halifax Community College, Weldon 27890
Haywood Community College, Clyde 28721
High Point University, High Point 27262-3598
Hood Theological Seminary, Salisbury 28144
James Sprunt Community College, Kenansville 28349
John Wesley College, High Point 27265-3197
Johnson C. Smith University, Charlotte 28216-5398
Johnston Community College, Smithfield 27577
Lees-McRae College, Banner Elk 28604
Lenoir Community College, Kinston 28502
Lenoir-Rhyne College, Hickory 28603
Louisburg College, Louisburg 27549
Mars Hill College, Mars Hill 28754
Martin Community College, Williamston 27892
Mayland Community College, Spruce Pine 28777
Meredith College, Raleigh 27607-5298
Methodist College, Fayetteville 28311
Mitchell Community College, Statesville 28677
Montgomery Community College, Troy 27371
Montreat College, Montreat 28757
Mount Olive College, Mount Olive 28365
Nash Community College, Rocky Mount 27804
North Carolina Agricultural and Technical State University, Greensboro 27411
North Carolina Central University, Durham 27707
North Carolina Central University: School of Law, Durham 27707
North Carolina School of the Arts, Winston-Salem 27127
North Carolina State University, Raleigh 27695-7103
North Carolina State University: College of Veterinary Medicine, Raleigh 27606
North Carolina Wesleyan College, Rocky Mount 27804
Peace College, Raleigh 27604
Pfeiffer University, Misenheimer 28109
Piedmont Community College, Roxboro 27573-1197
Pitt Community College, Greenville 27835
Queens College, Charlotte 28274
Randolph Community College, Asheboro 27204
Richmond Community College, Hamlet 28345
Roanoke-Chowan Community College, Ahoskie 27910
Robeson Community College, Lumberton 28359
Rockingham Community College, Wentworth 27375
Rowan-Cabarrus Community College, Salisbury 28145
St. Andrews Presbyterian College, Laurinburg 28352
St. Augustine's College, Raleigh 27610
Salem College, Winston-Salem 27108
Sampson Community College, Clinton 28329
Sandhills Community College, Pinehurst 28374
Shaw University, Raleigh 27601
South Piedmont Community College, Polkton 28135
Southeastern Baptist Theological Seminary: Theological Professions, Wake Forest 27588
Southeastern Community College, Whiteville 28472
Southwestern Community College, Sylva 28779
Surry Community College, Dobson 27017
Tri-County Community College, Murphy 28906
University of North Carolina at Asheville, Asheville 28804
University of North Carolina at Chapel Hill, Chapel Hill 27599
University of North Carolina at Chapel Hill: School of Dentistry, Chapel Hill 27599
University of North Carolina at Chapel Hill: School of Law, Chapel Hill 27599
University of North Carolina at Chapel Hill: School of Medicine, Chapel Hill 27599
University of North Carolina at Chapel Hill: School of Pharmacy, Chapel Hill 27599
University of North Carolina at Charlotte, Charlotte 28223
University of North Carolina at Greensboro, Greensboro 27402-6170
University of North Carolina at Pembroke, Pembroke 28377
University of North Carolina at Wilmington, Wilmington 28403-3297
Vance-Granville Community College, Henderson 27536
Wake Forest University, Winston-Salem 27109
Wake Forest University: Bowman Gray School of Medicine, Winston-Salem 27157
Wake Forest University: School of Law, Winston-Salem 27109
Wake Technical Community College, Raleigh 27603
Warren Wilson College, Asheville 28815
Wayne Community College, Goldsboro 27533
Western Carolina University, Cullowhee 28723
Western Piedmont Community College, Morganton 28655
Wilkes Community College, Wilkesboro 28697
Wilson Technical Community College, Wilson 27893
Wingate University, Wingate 28174
Winston-Salem State University, Winston-Salem 27110

North Dakota
Bismarck State College, Bismarck 58506
Dickinson State University, Dickinson 58601-4896
Jamestown College, Jamestown 58405
Lake Region State College, Devils Lake 58301
Mayville State University, Mayville 58257
Medcenter One College of Nursing, Bismarck 58501
Minot State University, Minot 58707-5002
Minot State University: Bottineau Campus, Bottineau 58318
North Dakota State College of Science, Wahpeton 58076
North Dakota State University, Fargo 58105
North Dakota State University: College of Pharmacy, Fargo 58105
Sitting Bull College, Fort Yates 58538
Trinity Bible College, Ellendale 58436
United Tribes Technical College, Bismarck 58504
University of Mary, Bismarck 58504
University of North Dakota, Grand Forks 58202
University of North Dakota: School of Law, Grand Forks 58202
University of North Dakota: School of Medicine, Grand Forks 58202
Valley City State University, Valley City 58072
Williston State College, Williston 58802-1326

Ohio
Academy of Court Reporting, Cleveland 44113
Antioch College, Yellow Springs 45387
Ashland Theological Seminary, Ashland 44805
Ashland University, Ashland 44805
Athenaeum of Ohio, Cincinnati 45230
Baldwin-Wallace College, Berea 44017
Belmont Technical College, St. Clairsville 43950
Bluffton College, Bluffton 45817-1196
Bowling Green State University, Bowling Green 43403
Bowling Green State University: Firelands College, Huron 44839
Bryant & Stratton College, Cleveland 44114
Capital University, Columbus 43209
Capital University: School of Law, Columbus 43215
Case Western Reserve University, Cleveland 44106
Case Western Reserve University: School of Dentistry, Cleveland 44106
Case Western Reserve University: School of Law 44106
Case Western Reserve University: School of Medicine, Cleveland 44106
Cedarville College, Cedarville 45314
Central Ohio Technical College, Newark 43055
Central State University, Wilberforce 45384-3002
Chatfield College, St. Martin 45118
Cincinnati College of Mortuary Science, Cincinnati 45224-1428
Cincinnati State Technical and Community College, Cincinnati 45223-2690
Circleville Bible College, Circleville 43113
Clark State Community College, Springfield 45501
Cleveland Institute of Art, Cleveland 44106
Cleveland Institute of Electronics, Cleveland 44114
Cleveland Institute of Music, Cleveland 44106
Cleveland State University, Cleveland 44115
Cleveland State University: College of Law, Cleveland 44115
College of Mount St. Joseph, Cincinnati 45233
College of Wooster, Wooster 44691
Columbus College of Art and Design, Columbus 43215
Columbus State Community College, Columbus 43215
David N. Myers College, Cleveland 44115
Davis College, Toledo 43623

Colleges in this book

DeVry Institute of Technology: Columbus, Columbus 43209
Defiance College, Defiance 43512
Denison University, Granville 43023
Edison State Community College, Piqua 45356
Franciscan University of Steubenville, Steubenville 43952-1763
Franklin University, Columbus 43215-5399
Hebrew Union College-Jewish Institute of Religion, Cincinnati 45220
Heidelberg College, Tiffin 44883-2462
Hiram College, Hiram 44234
Hocking Technical College, Nelsonville 45764
ITT Technical Institute: Dayton, Dayton 45414
ITT Technical Institute: Norwood, Norwood 45212
ITT Technical Institute: Strongsville, Strongsville 44136
ITT Technical Institute: Youngstown, Youngstown 44509
Jefferson Community College, Steubenville 43952
John Carroll University, University Heights 44118
Kent State University, Kent 44242-0001
Kent State University: Ashtabula Regional Campus, Ashtabula 44004
Kent State University: East Liverpool Regional Campus, East Liverpool 43920
Kent State University: Stark Campus, Canton 44720-7599
Kent State University: Trumbull Campus, Warren 44483
Kent State University: Tuscarawas Campus, New Philadelphia 44663
Kenyon College, Gambier 43022
Lake Erie College, Painesville 44077
Lakeland Community College, Kirtland 44094
Lima Technical College, Lima 45804-3597
Lorain County Community College, Elyria 44035
Lourdes College, Sylvania 43560
Malone College, Canton 44709-3897
Marietta College, Marietta 45750
Marion Technical College, Marion 43302
Medical College of Ohio, Toledo 43699
Methodist Theological School in Ohio, Delaware 43015
Miami University: Hamilton Campus, Hamilton 45011
Miami University: Middletown Campus, Middletown 45042
Miami University: Oxford Campus, Oxford 45056
Miami-Jacobs College, Dayton 45401
Mount Union College, Alliance 44601
Mount Vernon Nazarene College, Mount Vernon 43050
Muskingum Area Technical College, Zanesville 43701
Muskingum College, New Concord 43762
North Central State College, Mansfield 44901
Northeastern Ohio Universities College of Medicine, Rootstown 44272
Northwest State Community College, Archbold 43502-9542
Northwestern College, Lima 45805
Notre Dame College of Ohio, Cleveland 44121-4293
Oberlin College, Oberlin 44074
Ohio College of Podiatric Medicine, Cleveland 44106
Ohio Dominican College, Columbus 43219
Ohio Institute of Photography and Technology, Dayton 45439
Ohio Northern University, Ada 45810
Ohio Northern University: College of Law, Ada 45810
Ohio Northern University: College of Pharmacy, Ada 45810
Ohio State University Agricultural Technical Institute, Wooster 44691
Ohio State University Columbus Campus: College of Dentistry, Columbus 43210
Ohio State University Columbus Campus: College of Medicine, Columbus 43210
Ohio State University Columbus Campus: College of Optometry, Columbus 43210
Ohio State University Columbus Campus: College of Pharmacy, Columbus 43210
Ohio State University Columbus Campus: College of Veterinary Medicine, Columbus 43210
Ohio State University: College of Law, Columbus 43210
Ohio State University: Columbus Campus, Columbus 43210
Ohio State University: Lima Campus, Lima 45804
Ohio State University: Mansfield Campus, Mansfield 44905

Ohio State University: Marion Campus, Marion 43302
Ohio State University: Newark Campus, Newark 43055
Ohio University, Athens 45701
Ohio University: Chillicothe Campus, Chillicothe 45601
Ohio University: College of Osteopathic Medicine, Athens 45701
Ohio University: Eastern Campus, St. Clairsville 43950
Ohio University: Lancaster Campus, Lancaster 43130
Ohio University: Southern Campus at Ironton, Ironton 45638
Ohio University: Zanesville Campus, Zanesville 43701
Ohio Valley Business College, East Lvrpool 43920
Ohio Wesleyan University, Delaware 43015
Otterbein College, Westerville 43081
Owens Community College: Findlay Campus, Findlay 45840
Owens Community College: Toledo, Toledo 43699-1947
Pontifical College Josephinum, Columbus 43235
RETS Tech Center, Centerville 45459
St. Mary Seminary, Wickliffe 44092
Shawnee State University, Portsmouth 45662
Sinclair Community College, Dayton 45402
Southern Ohio College, Cincinnati 45215
Southern State Community College, Hillsboro 45133
Stark State College of Technology, Canton 44720
Terra Community College, Fremont 43420
Tiffin University, Tiffin 44883
Trinity Lutheran Seminary, Columbus 43209
Union Institute, Cincinnati 45206
United Theological Seminary, Dayton 45406
University of Akron, Akron 44325
University of Akron: School of Law, Akron 44325
University of Akron: Wayne College, Orrville 44667-9758
University of Cincinnati, Cincinnati 45221
University of Cincinnati: Clermont College, Batavia 45103
University of Cincinnati: College of Law, Cincinnati 45221
University of Cincinnati: College of Medicine, Cincinnati 45267
University of Cincinnati: College of Pharmacy, Cincinnati 45267
University of Cincinnati: Raymond Walters College, Cincinnati 45236
University of Dayton, Dayton 45469
University of Dayton: School of Law, Dayton 45469
University of Findlay, Findlay 45840
University of Rio Grande, Rio Grande 45674
University of Toledo, Toledo 43606
University of Toledo: College of Law, Toledo 43606
University of Toledo: College of Pharmacy, Toledo 43606
Ursuline College, Pepper Pike 44124
Walsh University, North Canton 44720
Washington State Community College, Marietta 45750
Wilberforce University, Wilberforce 45384-1091
Wilmington College, Wilmington 45177
Winebrenner Seminary, Findlay 45839
Wittenberg University, Springfield 45501
Wright State University, Dayton 45435
Wright State University: School of Medicine, Dayton 45401
Xavier University, Cincinnati 45207
Youngstown State University, Youngstown 44555

Oklahoma

Cameron University, Lawton 73505
Carl Albert State College, Poteau 74953
Connors State College, Warner 74469
East Central University, Ada 74820
Eastern Oklahoma State College, Wilburton 74578
Langston University, Langston 73050
Mid-America Bible College, Oaklahoma City 73170
Murray State College, Tishomingo 73460
Northeastern Oklahoma Agricultural and Mechanical College, Miami 74354-6497
Northeastern State University, Tahlequah 74464-2399
Northeastern State University: College of Optometry, Tahlequah 74464
Northern Oklahoma College, Tonkawa 74653
Northwestern Oklahoma State University, Alva 73717
Oklahoma Baptist University, Shawnee 74804

Oklahoma Christian University of Science and Arts, Oaklahoma City 73136
Oklahoma City Community College, Okalhoma City 73159
Oklahoma City University, Oklahoma City 73106
Oklahoma City University: School of Law, Oklahoma City 73146
Oklahoma Panhandle State University, Goodwell 73939-0430
Oklahoma State University, Stillwater 74078
Oklahoma State University: College of Osteopathic Medicine, Tulsa 74107
Oklahoma State University: College of Veterinary Medicine, Stillwater 74078
Oklahoma State University: Oklahoma City, Okalhoma City 73107
Oklahoma State University: Okmulgee, Okmulgee 74447
Oral Roberts University, Tulsa 74171
Oral Roberts University: School of Theology and Missions, Tulsa 74171
Phillips Theological Seminary, Enid 73702
Redlands Community College, El Reno 73036
Rogers State University, Claremore 74017
Rose State College, Midwest City 73110
St. Gregory's University, Shawnee 74804
Seminole State College, Seminole 74818
Southeastern Oklahoma State University, Durant 74701-0609
Southern Nazarene University, Bethany 73008
Southwestern College of Christian Ministries, Bethany 73008
Southwestern Oklahoma State University, Weatherford 73096-3098
Southwestern Oklahoma State University School of Pharmacy, Weatherford 73096
Tulsa Community College, Tulsa 74135-6198
University of Central Oklahoma, Edmond 73034
University of Oklahoma, Norman 73019
University of Oklahoma College of Pharmacy, Oklahoma City 73190
University of Oklahoma Health Sciences Center: College of Dentistry, Oklahoma City 73117
University of Oklahoma Health Sciences Center: College of Medicine, Oklahoma City 73104
University of Oklahoma: College of Law, Norman 73019
University of Science and Arts of Oklahoma, Chickasha 73018
University of Tulsa, Tulsa 74104-3189
University of Tulsa: College of Law, Tulsa 74104
Western Oklahoma State College, Altus 73521

Oregon

Art Institute of Portland, Portland 97201
Central Oregon Community College, Bend 97701
Chemeketa Community College, Salem 97309
Clackamas Community College, Oregon City 97045
Clatsop Community College, Astoria 97103
Concordia University, Portland 97211
Eastern Oregon University, LaGrande 97850
Eugene Bible College, Eugene 97405
George Fox University, Newberg 97132
ITT Technical Institute: Portland, Portland 97218
Lane Community College, Eugene 97405
Lewis & Clark College, Portland 97219-7899
Lewis and Clark College: Northwestern School of Law, Portland 97219
Linfield College, McMinnville 97128
Linn-Benton Community College, Albany 97321
Marylhurst University, Marylhurst 97036
Mount Angel Seminary, St. Benedict 97373
Mount Hood Community College, Gresham 97030
Multnomah Bible College, Portland 97220
Multnomah Biblical Seminary, Portland 97220
Northwest Christian College, Eugene 97401
Oregon Graduate Institute, Portland 97291
Oregon Health Sciences University, Portland 97201
Oregon Health Sciences University: School of Dentistry, Portland 97201
Oregon Health Sciences University: School of Medicine, Portland 97201
Oregon Institute of Technology, Klamath Falls 97601
Oregon State University, Corvallis 97331

Oregon State University: College of Pharmacy, Corvallis 97331
Oregon State University: College of Veterinary Medicine, Corvallis 97331
Pacific Northwest College of Art, Portland 97209
Pacific University, Forest Grove 97116
Pacific University: School of Optometry, Forest Grove 97116
Portland Community College, Portland 97280-0990
Portland State University, Portland 97207
Reed College, Portland 97202-8199
Southern Oregon University, Ashland 97520
University of Oregon, Eugene 97403-1217
University of Oregon: School of Law, Eugene 97403
University of Portland, Portland 97203-5798
Western Baptist College, Salem 97301
Western Conservative Baptist Seminary, Portland 97215
Western Evangelical Seminary, Tigard 97281
Western Oregon University, Monmouth 97361
Western States Chiropractic College, Portland 97230
Willamette University, Salem 97301-3922
Willamette University: College of Law, Salem 97301

Pennsylvania

Academy of the New Church, Bryn Athyn 19009
Albright College, Reading 19612
Allegheny College, Meadville 16335
Allentown College of St. Francis de Sales, Center Valley 18034-9568
Alvernia College, Reading 19607
American College, Bryn Mawr 19010
Antonelli Institute of Art and Photography, Erdenheim 19038
Art Institute of Philadelphia, Philadelphia 19103
Art Institute of Pittsburgh, Pittsburgh 15222
Baptist Bible College and Seminary of Pennsylvania, Clarks Summit 18411
Beaver College, Glenside 19038-3295
Biblical Theological Seminary, Hatfield 19440
Bloomsburg University of Pennsylvania, Bloomsburg 17815
Bradley Academy for the Visual Arts, York 17402
Bryn Athyn College of the New Church, Bryn Athyn 19009
Bryn Mawr College, Bryn Mawr 19010-2899
Bucknell University, Lewisburg 17837
Bucks County Community College, Newtown 18940
Butler County Community College, Butler 16003-1203
C.H.I/RETS Campus, Broomall 19008
Cabrini College, Radnor 19087-3698
California University of Pennsylvania, California 15419
Cambria-Rowe Business College, Johnstown 15902
Carlow College, Pittsburgh 15213
Carnegie Mellon University, Pittsburgh 15213
Cedar Crest College, Allentown 18104-6196
Central Pennsylvania College, Summerdale 17093
Chatham College, Pittsburgh 15232
Chestnut Hill College, Philadelphia 19118-2693
Cheyney University of Pennsylvania, Cheyney 19319
Churchman Business School, Easton 18042
Clarion University of Pennsylvania, Clarion 16214
College Misericordia, Dallas 18612
Community College of Allegheny County, Pittsburgh 15233
Community College of Beaver County, Monaca 15061
Community College of Philadelphia, Philadelphia 19130
Curtis Institute of Music, Philadelphia 19103
Delaware County Community College, Media 19063-1094
Delaware Valley College, Doylestown 18901
Dickinson College, Carlisle 17013
Dickinson School of Law, Carlisle 17013
Drexel University, Philadelphia 19104-2875
Duquesne University, Pittsburgh 15282-0201
Duquesne University: School of Law, Pittsburgh 15282
East Stroudsburg University of Pennsylvania, East Stroudsburg 18301-2999
Eastern Baptist Theological Seminary, Wynnewood 19096
Eastern College, St. Davids 19087-3696
Edinboro University of Pennsylvania, Edinboro 16444
Education America: Vale Technical Institute, Blairsville 15717
Electronic Institutes: Middletown, Middletown 17057

Elizabethtown College, Elizabethtown 17022
Evangelical School of Theology, Myerstown 17067
Franklin and Marshall College, Lancaster 17604-3003
Gannon University, Erie 16541
Geneva College, Beaver Falls 15010
Gettysburg College, Gettysburg 17325
Grove City College, Grove City 16127
Gwynedd-Mercy College, Gwynedd Valley 19437
Harcum College, Bryn Mawr 19010-3476
Harrisburg Area Community College, Harrisburg 17110
Haverford College, Haverford 19041
Holy Family College, Philadelphia 19114-2094
ICS Center for Degree Studies, Scranton 18515
ITT Technical Institute: Mechanicsburg, Mechanicsburg 17055
ITT Technical Institute: Monroeville, Monroeville 15146
ITT Technical Institute: Pittsburgh, Pittsburgh 15220
Immaculata College, Immaculata 19345
Indiana University of Pennsylvania, Indiana 15705-1088
Jefferson Medical College of Thomas Jefferson University, Philadelphia 19107
Johnson Technical Institute, Scranton 18508
Juniata College, Huntingdon 16652
King's College, Wilkes-Barre 18711
Kutztown University of Pennsylvania, Kutztown 19530
La Roche College, Pittsburgh 15237
La Salle University, Philadelphia 191410-1199
Lackawanna Junior College, Scranton 18509
Lafayette College, Easton 18042
Lake Erie College of Osteopathic Medicine, Erie 16509
Lancaster Bible College, Lancaster 17608
Lancaster Theological Seminary, Lancaster 17603
Laurel Business Institute, Uniontown 15401
Lebanon Valley College of Pennsylvania, Annville 17003
Lehigh Carbon Community College, Schnecksville 18078
Lehigh University, Bethlehem 18015
Lincoln University, Lincoln University 19352
Lock Haven University of Pennsylvania, Lock Haven 17745
Lutheran Theological Seminary at Gettysburg, Gettysburg 17325
Lutheran Theological Seminary at Philadelphia, Philadelphia 19119
Luzerne County Community College, Nanticoke 18634
Lycoming College, Williamsport 17701
MCP Hahnemann University, Philadelphia 19102-1192
Manor College, Jenkintown 19046
Mansfield University of Pennsylvania, Mansfield 16933
Marywood University, Scranton 18509
Median School of Allied Health Careers, Pittsburgh 15222
Medical College of Pennsylvania and Hahnemann University School of Medicine, Philadelphia 19129
Mercyhurst College, Erie 16546
Messiah College, Grantham 17027
Millersville University of Pennsylvania, Millersville 17551-0302
Montgomery County Community College, Blue Bell 19422
Moore College of Art and Design, Philadelphia 19103
Moravian College, Bethlehem 18018
Moravian Theological Seminary, Bethlehem 18018
Mount Aloysius College, Cresson 16630
Muhlenberg College, Allentown 18104
Neumann College, Aston 19014-1928
Newport Business Institute, Lower Burrell 15068
Northampton County Area Community College, Bethlehem 18020
Peirce College, Philadelphia 19102
Penn State Abington, Abington 19001
Penn State Altoona, Altoona 16601-3760
Penn State Beaver, Monaca 15061
Penn State Berks, Reading 19610-6009
Penn State College of Medicine, Milton S. Hershey Medical Center, Hershey 17033-2390
Penn State Delaware County, Media 19063
Penn State Dubois, DuBois 15801
Penn State Erie, The Behrend College, Erie 16563
Penn State Fayette, Uniontown 15401
Penn State Great Valley Graduate Center, Malvern 19355

Penn State Harrisburg, Middletown 17057-4898
Penn State Hazleton, Hazleton 18201
Penn State Lehigh Valley, Fogelsville 18051-9999
Penn State McKeesport, McKeesport 15132
Penn State Mont Alto, Mont Alto 17237-9703
Penn State New Kensington, New Kensington 15068-1798
Penn State Schuylkill - Capital College, Schuylkill Haven 17972
Penn State Shenango, Sharon 16146
Penn State University Park, University Park 16802
Penn State Wilkes-Barre, Lehman 18627-0217
Penn State Worthington Scranton, Dunmore 18512-1699
Penn State York, York 17403
Pennsylvania College of Optometry, Philadelphia 19141
Pennsylvania College of Podiatric Medicine, Philadelphia 19107
Pennsylvania College of Technology, Williamsport 17701
Pennsylvania Institute of Culinary Arts, Pittsburgh 15222
Pennsylvania Institute of Technology, Media 19063
Pennsylvania State University College of Medicine, Hershey 17033
Philadelphia College of Bible, Langhorne 19047
Philadelphia College of Osteopathic Medicine, Philadelphia 19131
Philadelphia College of Pharmacy and Science: School of Pharmacy, Philadelphia 19104
Philadelphia University, Philadelphia 19144
Pittsburgh Institute of Aeronautics, Pittsburgh 15236
Pittsburgh Institute of Mortuary Science, Pittsburgh 15206-3706
Pittsburgh Technical Institute, Pittsburgh 15222
Pittsburgh Theological Seminary, Pittsburgh 15206
Point Park College, Pittsburgh 15222
Reading Area Community College, Reading 19603
Reformed Presbyterian Theological Seminary, Pittsburgh 15208
Robert Morris College, Moon Township 15108
Rosemont College, Rosemont 19010
St. Charles Borromeo Seminary - Overbrook, Wynnewood 19096
St. Charles Borromeo Seminary-Overbrook, Wynnewood 19096
St. Francis College, Loretto 15940
St. Joseph's University, Philadelphia 19131
St. Vincent College, Latrobe 15650-2690
St. Vincent Seminary, Latrobe 15650
Sawyer School, Pittsburgh 15222
Seton Hill College, Greensburg 15601
Shippensburg University of Pennsylvania, Shippensburg 17257-2299
Slippery Rock University of Pennsylvania, Slippery Rock 16057
South Hills School of Business & Technology, State Coll 16801-4516
Susquehanna University, Selinsgrove 17870-1001
Swarthmore College, Swarthmore 19081
Talmudical Yeshiva of Philadelphia, Philadelphia 19131
Temple University, Philadelphia 19122-6096
Temple University: School of Dentistry, Philadelphia 19140
Temple University: School of Law, Philadelphia 19122
Temple University: School of Medicine, Philadelphia 19122
Temple University: School of Pharmacy, Philadelphia 19104
Thiel College, Greenville 16125
Thomas Jefferson University: College of Health Professions, Philadelphia 19107
Tri-State Business Institute, Erie 16506
Triangle Tech: DuBois Campus, DuBois 15801
Triangle Tech: Pittsburgh Campus, Pittsburgh 15214
Trinity Episcopal School for Ministry, Ambridge 15003
University of Pennsylvania, Philadelphia 19104
University of Pennsylvania Law School, Philadelphia 19104
University of Pennsylvania: School of Dental Medicine, Philadelphia 19104
University of Pennsylvania: School of Medicine, Philadelphia 19104
University of Pennsylvania: School of Veterinary Medicine, Philadelphia 19104

Colleges in this book

University of Pittsburgh, Pittsburgh 15260
University of Pittsburgh at Bradford, Bradford 16701
University of Pittsburgh at Greensburg, Greensburg 15601
University of Pittsburgh at Johnstown, Johnstown 15904
University of Pittsburgh at Titusville, Titusville 16354
University of Pittsburgh: School of Dental Medicine, Pittsburgh 15261
University of Pittsburgh: School of Law, Pittsburgh 15260
University of Pittsburgh: School of Medicine, Pittsburgh 15261
University of Pittsburgh: School of Pharmacy, Pittsburgh 15261
University of Scranton, Scranton 18510
University of the Arts, Philadelphia 19102
University of the Sciences in Philadelphia, Philadelphia 19104
Ursinus College, Collegeville 19426
Valley Forge Christian College, Phoenixville 19460
Valley Forge Military College, Wayne 19087
Villanova University, Villanova 19085
Villanova University: School of Law, Villanova 19085
Washington and Jefferson College, Washington 15301
Waynesburg College, Waynesburg 15370
West Chester University of Pennsylvania, West Chester 19383
Westminster College, New Wilmington 16172
Westminster Theological Seminary, Philadelphia 19118
Westmoreland County Community College, Youngwood 15697-1895
Widener University, Chester 19013
Widener University School of Law, Harrisburg 17106
Wilkes University, Wilkes-Barre 18766
Williamson Free School of Mechanical Trades, Media 19063
Wilson College, Chambersburg 17201
York College of Pennsylvania, York 17405
Yorktowne Business Institute, York 17404

Puerto Rico

American University of Puerto Rico, Bayamon 00960
Atlantic College, Guaynabo 00970
Bayamon Central University, Bayamon 00960-1725
Caribbean University, Bayamon 00960
Colegio Universitario del Este, Carolina 00984
Columbia College, Caguas 00726
Escuela de Artes Plasticas de Puerto Rico, San Juan 00902-1112
Evangelical Seminary of Puerto Rico, San Juan 00925
Huertas Junior College, Caguas 00726
Humacao Community College, Humacao 00792
ICPR Junior College, San Juan 00919-0304
Inter American University of Puerto Rico School of Optometry, San Juan 00919
Inter American University of Puerto Rico: Aguadilla Campus, Aguadilla 00605
Inter American University of Puerto Rico: Arecibo Campus, Arecibo 00614
Inter American University of Puerto Rico: Barranquitas Campus, Barranquitas 00794-0517
Inter American University of Puerto Rico: Bayamon Campus, Bayamon 00957
Inter American University of Puerto Rico: Fajardo Campus, Fajardo 00738
Inter American University of Puerto Rico: Guayama Campus, Guayama 00785
Inter American University of Puerto Rico: Metropolitan Campus, San Juan 191293
Inter American University of Puerto Rico: San German Campus, San German 00683
Inter American University of Puerto Rico: School of Law, San Juan 00936
National College of Business and Technology, Bayamon 00960
Ponce School of Medicine, Ponce 00732
Pontifical Catholic University of Puerto Rico, Ponce 00731
Pontifical Catholic University of Puerto Rico: School of Law, Ponce 00731
Ramirez College of Business and Technology, San Juan 00910
Technological College of San Juan, San Juan 00918
Turabo University, Gurabo 00778

Universidad Central del Caribe: Medical School, Bayamon 00960
Universidad Metropolitana, Rio Piedras 00928
Universidad Politecnica de Puerto Rico, Hato Rey 00919
University of Puerto Rico Medical Sciences Campus: School of Dentistry, Rio Piedras 00936
University of Puerto Rico Medical Sciences Campus: School of Medicine, Rio Piedras 00936
University of Puerto Rico Medical Sciences Campus: School of Pharmacy, San Juan 00936
University of Puerto Rico Rio Piedras Campus: School of Law, Rio Piedras 00931
University of Puerto Rico at Utuado, Utuado 00641
University of Puerto Rico: Aguadilla, Aguadilla 00604-0160
University of Puerto Rico: Arecibo Campus, Arecibo 00613
University of Puerto Rico: Bayamon University College, Bayamon 00959
University of Puerto Rico: Carolina Regional College, Carolina 00984-4800
University of Puerto Rico: Cayey University College, Cayey 00736
University of Puerto Rico: Humacao University College, Humacao 00791
University of Puerto Rico: Mayaguez Campus, Mayaguez 00681
University of Puerto Rico: Medical Sciences Campus, San Juan 00936-5067
University of Puerto Rico: Ponce University College, Ponce 00732
University of Puerto Rico: Rio Piedras Campus, San Juan 00931-3344
University of the Sacred Heart, Santurce 00914

Rhode Island

Brown University, Providence 02912
Brown University: School of Medicine, Providence 02912
Bryant College, Smithfield 02917-1284
Community College of Rhode Island, Warwick 02886
Johnson & Wales University, Providence 02903-3703
New England Institute of Technology, Warwick 02886
Providence College, Providence 02918-0001
Rhode Island College, Providence 02908
Roger Williams University, Bristol 02809
Salve Regina University, Newport 02840
University of Rhode Island, Kingston 02881-2020
University of Rhode Island: College of Pharmacy, Kingston 02881

South Carolina

Aiken Technical College, Aiken 29802
Anderson College, Anderson 29621
Benedict College, Columbia 29204
Central Carolina Technical College, Sumter 29150
Charleston Southern University, Charleston 29423
Chesterfield-Marlboro Technical College, Cheraw 29520
Claflin University, Orangeburg 29115
Clemson University, Clemson 29634-5124
Coastal Carolina University, Conway 29528-6054
Coker College, Hartsville 29550
College of Charleston, Charleston 29424-0001
Columbia Biblical Seminary and Graduate School of Missions, Columbia 29230
Columbia College, Columbia 29203
Columbia International University, Columbia 29230-3122
Converse College, Spartanburg 29302
Denmark Technical College, Denmark 29042
Erskine College, Due West 29639
Erskine Theological Seminary, Due West 29639
Florence-Darlington Technical College, Florence 29501-0548
Francis Marion University, Florence 29501-0547
Furman University, Greenville 29613
Greenville Technical College, Greenville 29606
Horry-Georgetown Technical College, Conway 29526-1966
ITT Technical Institute: Greenville, Greenville 29615
Lander University, Greenwood 29649
Limestone College, Gaffney 29340-3799

Lutheran Theological Southern Seminary, Columbia 29203
Medical University of South Carolina, Charleston 29425
Medical University of South Carolina: College of Dental Medicine, Charleston 29425
Medical University of South Carolina: College of Pharmacy, Charleston 29425
Midlands Technical College, Columbia 29202
Morris College, Sumter 29150-3599
Newberry College, Newberry 29108
North Greenville College, Tigerville 29688
Orangeburg-Calhoun Technical College, Orangeburg 29118
Piedmont Technical College, Greenwood 29648
Presbyterian College, Clinton 29325
Sherman College of Straight Chiropractic, Spartanburg 29304
South Carolina State University, Orangeburg 29117
Southern Wesleyan University, Central 29630
Spartanburg Methodist College, Spartanburg 29301
Spartanburg Technical College, Spartanburg 29305
Technical College of the Lowcountry, Beaufort 29902
The Citadel, Charleston 29409
Tri-County Technical College, Pendleton 29670
Trident Technical College, Charleston 29423
University of South Carolina, Columbia 29208
University of South Carolina at Aiken, Aiken 29801
University of South Carolina at Beaufort, Beaufort 29902
University of South Carolina at Spartanburg, Spartanburg 29303
University of South Carolina at Sumter, Sumter 29150
University of South Carolina at Union, Union 29379
University of South Carolina: Salkehatchie Regional Campus, Allendale 29810
University of South Carolina: School of Law, Columbia 29208
University of South Carolina: School of Medicine, Columbia 29208
University of South Carolina: School of Pharmacy, Columbia 29208
Voorhees College, Denmark 29042-0678
Winthrop University, Rock Hill 29733
Wofford College, Spartanburg 29303-3663
York Technical College, Rock Hill 29730

South Dakota

Augustana College, Sioux Falls 57197
Black Hills State University, Spearfish 57799
Dakota State University, Madison 57042
Dakota Wesleyan University, Mitchell 57301
Huron University, Huron 57350
Kilian Community College, Sioux Falls 57104
Mount Marty College, Yankton 57078
North American Baptist Seminary, Sioux Falls 57105
Northern State University, Aberdeen 57401-7198
Sinte Gleska University, Rosebud 57570
South Dakota School of Mines and Technology, Rapid City 57701
South Dakota State University, Brookings 57007
South Dakota State University: College of Pharmacy, Brookings 57007
Southeast Technical Institute, Sioux Falls 57107
University of South Dakota, Vermillion 57069
University of South Dakota: School of Law, Vermillion 57069
University of South Dakota: School of Medicine, Vermillion 57069
Western Dakota Technical Institute, Rapid City 57703

Tennessee

Aquinas College, Nashville 37205
Austin Peay State University, Clarksville 37040
Belmont University, Nashville 37212
Bethel College, McKenzie 38201
Carson-Newman College, Jefferson City 37760
Chattanooga State Technical Community College, Chattanooga 37406
Christian Brothers University, Memphis 38104
Church of God School of Theology, Cleveland 37320
Cleveland State Community College, Cleveland 37320
Columbia State Community College, Columbia 38402
Crichton College, Memphis 38175
Cumberland University, Lebanon 37087

David Lipscomb University, Nashville 37204-3951
Draughons Junior College of Business: Nashville, Nashville 37217
Dyersburg State Community College, Dyersburg 38024
East Tennessee State University, Johnson City 37614-0734
East Tennessee State University: James H. Quillen College of Medicine, Johnson City 37614
Emmanuel School of Religion, Johnson City 37601
Fisk University, Nashville 37208-3051
Freed-Hardeman University, Henderson 38340
Harding University Graduate School of Religion, Memphis 38117
Hiwassee College, Madisonville 37354
ITT Technical Institute: Knoxville, Knoxville 37932
ITT Technical Institute: Memphis, Memphis 38119
ITT Technical Institute: Nashville, Nashville 37214
Jackson State Community College, Jackson 38301
John A. Gupton College, Nashville 37203
Johnson Bible College, Knoxville 37998
King College, Bristol 37620
Knoxville Business College, Knoxville 37917
Lambuth University, Jackson 38301
Lane College, Jackson 38301
LeMoyne-Owen College, Memphis 38126
Lee University, Cleveland 37320
Lincoln Memorial University, Harrogate 37752
Martin Methodist College, Pulaski 38478
Maryville College, Maryville 37804
Meharry Medical College: School of Dentistry, Nashville 37208
Meharry Medical College: School of Medicine, Nashville 37208
Memphis Theological Seminary, Memphis 38104
Mid-America Baptist Theological Seminary, Germantown 38138
Middle Tennessee State University, Murfreesboro 37132
Milligan College, Milligan College 37682
Motlow State Community College, Tullahoma 37388
Nashville State Technical Institute, Nashville 37209
Northeast State Technical Community College, Blountville 37617
O'More College of Design, Franklin 37064
Pellissippi State Technical Community College, Knoxville 37933
Rhodes College, Memphis 38112
Roane State Community College, Harriman 37748
Shelby State Community College, Memphis 38174-0568
Southern Adventist University, Collegedale 37315-0370
Southern College of Optometry, Memphis 38104
Temple Baptist Seminary: Theological Professions, Chattanooga 37404
Tennessee State University, Nashville 37209-1561
Tennessee Technological University, Cookeville 38505
Tennessee Temple University, Chattanooga 37404
Tennessee Wesleyan College, Athens 37371
Trevecca Nazarene University, Nashville 37210
Tusculum College, Greeneville 37743-9997
Union University, Jackson 38305
University of Memphis, Memphis 38152
University of Memphis: School of Law, Memphis 38152
University of Tennessee College of Law, Knoxville 37996
University of Tennessee Knoxville: College of Veterinary Medicine, Knoxville 37901
University of Tennessee Memphis: College of Dentistry, Memphis 38163
University of Tennessee Memphis: College of Medicine, Memphis 38163
University of Tennessee Memphis: College of Pharmacy, Memphis 38163
University of Tennessee: Chattanooga, Chattanooga 37403
University of Tennessee: Knoxville, Knoxville 37996
University of Tennessee: Martin, Martin 38238
University of Tennessee: Memphis, Memphis 38163
University of the South, Sewanee 37383
University of the South: School of Theology, Sewanee 37383
Vanderbilt University, Nashville 37240
Vanderbilt University: School of Law, Nashville 37240
Vanderbilt University: School of Medicine, Nashville 37232
Vanderbilt University: The Divinity School, Nashville 37240
Volunteer State Community College, GalLatin 37066
Walters State Community College, Morristown 37813-6899

Texas

Abilene Christian University, Abilene 79699
Abilene Christian University: College of Biblical and Family Studies, Abilene 79699
Alvin Community College, Alvin 77511
Amarillo College, Amarillo 79178
Amber University, Garland 75041
Angelina College, Lufkin 75902
Angelo State University, San Angelo 76909
Arlington Baptist College, Arlington 76012
Austin College, Sherman 75090-4400
Austin Community College, Austin 78752
Austin Presbyterian Theological Seminary, Austin 78705
Baptist Missionary Association Theological Seminary, Jacksonville 75766
Baylor College of Medicine, Houston 77030
Baylor University, Waco 76798
Baylor University: School of Law, Waco 76798
Blinn College, Brenham 77833
Brazosport College, Lake Jackson 77566
Brookhaven College, Farmers Birch 75244
Cedar Valley College, Lancaster 75134
Central Texas College, Killeen 76540
Coastal Bend College, Beeville 78102
College of the Mainland, Texas City 77591
Collin County Community College District, Plano 75093
Commonwealth Institute of Funeral Service, Houston 77090
Concordia University at Austin, Austin 78705
Dallas Baptist University, Dallas 75211-9299
DeVry Institute of Technology: Irving, Dallas 75063-2440
Del Mar College, Corpus Christi 78404
East Texas Baptist University, Marshall 75670
Eastfield College, Mesquite 75150
El Paso Community College, El Paso 79998
Episcopal Theological Seminary of the Southwest, Austin 78768
Galveston College, Galveston 77550
Grayson County College, Denison 75020
Hardin-Simmons University, Abilene 79698
Hill College, Hillsboro 76645
Houston Baptist University, Houston 77074
Houston Community College System, Houston 77270
Houston Graduate School of Theology, Houston 77004
Howard College, Big Spring 79720
Howard Payne University, Brownwood 76801
Huston-Tillotson College, Austin 78702
ITT Technical Institute: Arlington, Arlington 76017
ITT Technical Institute: Austin, Austin 78723
ITT Technical Institute: Houston, Houston 77063
ITT Technical Institute: Houston North, Houston 77090-5818
ITT Technical Institute: Houston South, Houston 77058
ITT Technical Institute: Richardson, Richardson 75080
ITT Technical Institute: San Antonio, San Antonio 78249
Institute for Christian Studies, Austin 78705
Jacksonville College, Jacksonville 75766
Jarvis Christian College, Hawkins 75765-1470
Kilgore College, Kilgore 75662
Lamar State College at Orange, Orange 77630
Lamar State College at Port Arthur, Port Arthur 77641-0310
Lamar University, Beaumont 77710
LeTourneau University, Longview 75607
Lee College, Baytown 77522
Lon Morris College, Jacksonville 75766
Lubbock Christian University, Lubbock 79407
McMurry University, Abilene 79697
Midland College, Midland 79705
Midwestern State University, Wichita Falls 76308
Mountain View College, Dallas 75211
Navarro College, Corsicana 75110
North Central Texas College, Gainesville 76240
North Lake College, Irving 75038
Northeast Texas Community College, Mt. Pleasant 75456
Northwood University: Texas Campus, Cedar Hill 75104
Oblate School of Theology, San Antonio 78216
Odessa College, Odessa 79764
Our Lady of the Lake University of San Antonio, San Antonio 78207-4689
Palo Alto College, San Antonio 78224
Panola College, Carthage 75633
Paris Junior College, Paris 75460
Parker College of Chiropractic, Dallas 75229
Paul Quinn College, Dallas 75241
Prairie View A&M University, Prairie View 77446
Rice University, Houston 77251-1892
Richland College, Dallas 75243-2199
St. Edward's University, Austin 78704
St. Mary's University, San Antonio 78228
St. Mary's University: School of Law, San Antonio 78228
St. Philip's College, San Antonio 78203
Sam Houston State University, Huntsville 77341
San Antonio College, San Antonio 78212
San Jacinto College: North, Houston 77049
Schreiner College, Kerrville 78028
South Plains College, Levelland 79336
South Texas College of Law, Houston 77002
Southern Methodist University, Dallas 75275-0296
Southern Methodist University: Perkins School of Theology, Dallas 75275
Southern Methodist University: School of Law, Dallas 75275
Southwest Texas Junior College, Uvalde 78801
Southwest Texas State University, San Marcos 78666
Southwestern Adventist University, Keene 76059
Southwestern Assemblies of God University, Waxahachie 75165
Southwestern Baptist Theological Seminary: Theological Professions, Fort Worth 76115
Southwestern University, Georgetown 78626
Stephen F. Austin State University, Nacogdoches 75962
Sul Ross State University, Alpine 79832
Tarleton State University, Stephenville 76402
Tarrant County College, Fort Worth 76102
Temple College, Temple 76504
Texas A&M International University, Laredo 78041-1900
Texas A&M University, College Station 77843
Texas A&M University-Commerce, Commerce 75429
Texas A&M University-Corpus Christi, Corpus Christi 78412
Texas A&M University-Galveston, Galveston 77553
Texas A&M University-Kingsville, Kingsville 78363
Texas A&M University-Texarkana, Texarkana 75505
Texas A&M University: Baylor College of Dentistry, Dallas 75266
Texas A&M University: College of Veterinary Medicine, College Station 77843
Texas A&M University: Health Science Center College of Medicine, College Station 77843
Texas Chiropractic College, Pasadena 77505
Texas Christian University, Fort Worth 76129
Texas Christian University: Brite Divinity School, Fort Worth 76129
Texas College, Tyler 75712-4500
Texas Lutheran University, Seguin 78155-5999
Texas Southern University, Houston 77004
Texas Southern University: College of Pharmacy and Health Sciences, Houston 77004
Texas Southern University: Thurgood Marshall School of Law, Houston 77004
Texas State Technical College: Harlingen, Harlingen 78550-3697
Texas State Technical College: Sweetwater, Sweetwater 79556
Texas State Technical College: Waco, Waco 76705
Texas Tech University, Lubbock 79409
Texas Tech University Health Science Center, Lubbock 79430
Texas Tech University Health Sciences Center: School of Medicine, Lubbock 79430
Texas Tech University: School of Law, Lubbock 79409
Texas Wesleyan University, Fort Worth 76105-1536
Texas Woman's University, Denton 76204-5587
Trinity University, San Antonio 78212-7200

Colleges in this book

Trinity Valley Community College, Athens 75751
Tyler Junior College, Tyler 75711
University of Dallas, Irving 75062
University of Houston, Houston 77004
University of Houston: Clear Lake, Houston 77058-1080
University of Houston: College of Optometry, Houston 77204
University of Houston: College of Pharmacy, Houston 77204
University of Houston: Downtown, Houston 77002
University of Houston: Law Center, Houston 77204
University of Houston: Victoria, Victoria 77901
University of Mary Hardin-Baylor, Belton 76513
University of North Texas, Denton 76203-1070
University of North Texas Health Science Center at Fort Worth: Osteopathic Medicine, Fort Worth 76107
University of St. Thomas, Houston 77006-4696
University of St. Thomas: School of Theology, Houston 77024
University of Texas Health Science Center: Dental School, San Antonio 78284
University of Texas Health Science Center: Medical School, San Antonio 78284
University of Texas Health Sciences Center-Dental Branch, Houston 77030
University of Texas Medical Branch at Galveston, Galveston 77555
University of Texas Medical Branch at Galveston: School of Medicine, Galveston 77555
University of Texas Southwestern Medical Center at Dallas, Dallas 75390
University of Texas Southwestern Medical Center at Dallas Southwestern Medical School, Dallas 75235
University of Texas at Arlington, Arlington 76019
University of Texas at Austin, Austin 78712
University of Texas at Austin: College of Pharmacy, Austin 78712
University of Texas at Austin: School of Law, Austin 78714
University of Texas at Brownsville, Brownsville 78520
University of Texas at Dallas, Richardson 75083
University of Texas at El Paso, El Paso 79968
University of Texas at San Antonio, San Antonio 78249
University of Texas at Tyler, Tyler 75799
University of Texas of the Permian Basin, Odessa 79762
University of Texas-Houston Health Science Center, Houston 77225
University of Texas: Pan American, Edinburg 78539
University of the Incarnate Word, San Antonio 78209-6397
Vernon Regional Junior College, Vernon 76384
Victoria College, Victoria 77901
Wayland Baptist University, Plainview 79072
Weatherford College, Weatherford 76086
West Texas A&M University, Canyon 79016
Western Texas College, Snyder 79549
Wharton County Junior College, Wharton 77488
Wiley College, Marshall 75670

Utah
Brigham Young University, Provo 84602
Brigham Young University: School of Law, Provo 84602
College of Eastern Utah, Price 84501
Dixie State College of Utah, St. George 84770
ITT Technical Institute: Murray, Murray 84123
LDS Business College, Salt Lake City 84111-1392
Mountain West College, Salt Lake City 84106
Salt Lake Community College, Salt Lake City 84130
Snow College, Ephraim 84627
Southern Utah University, Cedar City 84720
University of Utah, Salt Lake City 84112
University of Utah: College of Law, Salt Lake City 84112
University of Utah: College of Pharmacy, Salt Lake City 84112
University of Utah: School of Medicine, Salt Lake City 84132
Utah State University, Logan 84322
Utah Valley State College, Orem 84058
Weber State University, Ogden 84408
Westminster College, Salt Lake City 84105-3697

Vermont
Bennington College, Bennington 05201
Burlington College, Burlington 05401
Castleton State College, Castleton 05735
Champlain College, Burlington 05402
College of St. Joseph in Vermont, Rutland 05701-3899
Community College of Vermont, Waterbury 05676
Goddard College, Plainfield 05667
Green Mountain College, Poultney 05764
Johnson State College, Johnson 05656
Landmark College, Putney 05346
Lyndon State College, Lyndonville 05851
Marlboro College, Marlboro 05344
Middlebury College, Middlebury 05753
New England Culinary Institute, Montpelier 05602
Norwich University, Northfield 05663
St. Michael's College, Colchester 05439
Southern Vermont College, Bennington 05201
Sterling College, Craftsbury Common 05827
Trinity College of Vermont, Burlington 05401
University of Vermont, Burlington 05405-0160
University of Vermont: College of Medicine, Burlington 05405
Vermont Law School, South Royalton 05068
Vermont Technical College, Randolph Center 05061

Virginia
Averett College, Danville 24541
Blue Ridge Community College, Weyers Cave 24486
Bluefield College, Bluefield 24605
Bridgewater College, Bridgewater 22812
Central Virginia Community College, Lynchburg 24502
Christendom College, Front Royal 22630
Christopher Newport University, Newport News 23606
College of William and Mary, Williamsburg 23187-8795
College of William and Mary: School of Law, Williamsburg 23187
Dabney S. Lancaster Community College, Clifton Forge 24422
Danville Community College, Danville 24541
ECPI College of Technology, Virginia Beach 23462
Eastern Mennonite Seminary, Harrisonburg 22801
Eastern Mennonite University, Harrisonburg 22802
Eastern Shore Community College, Melfa 23410
Eastern Virginia Medical School of the Medical College of Hampton Roads, Norfolk 23501
Eastern Virginia Medical School of the Medical College of Hampton Roads: Medical Professions, Norfolk 23501
Emory & Henry College, Emory 24327
Ferrum College, Ferrum 24088
George Mason University, Fairfax 22030
George Mason University: School of Law, Arlington 22201
Germanna Community College, Locust Grove 22508-2102
Hampden-Sydney College, Hampden-Sydney 23943
Hampton University, Hampton 23668
Hollins University, Roanoke 24020
ITT Technical Institute: Norfolk, Norfolk 23502
ITT Technical Institute: Richmond, Richmond 23235
Institute of Textile Technology, Charlottesville 22903
J. Sargeant Reynolds Community College, Richmond 23285-5622
James Madison University, Harrisonburg 22807
John Tyler Community College, Chester 23831
Liberty Baptist Theological Seminary, Lynchburg 24502
Liberty University, Lynchburg 24502
Longwood College, Farmville 23909
Lord Fairfax Community College, Middletown 22645
Lynchburg College, Lynchburg 24501
Mary Baldwin College, Staunton 24401
Mary Washington College, Fredericksburg 22401
Mountain Empire Community College, Big Stone Gap 24219
National Business College, Roanoke 24017
New River Community College, Dublin 24084
Norfolk State University, Norfolk 23504
Northern Virginia Community College, Annandale 22003
Old Dominion University, Norfolk 23529
Patrick Henry Community College, Martinsville 24115
Paul D. Camp Community College, Franklin 23851

Piedmont Virginia Community College, Charlottesville 22902-7589
Protestant Episcopal Theological Seminary in Virginia, Alexandria 22304
Radford University, Radford 24142
Randolph-Macon College, Ashland 23005
Randolph-Macon Woman's College, Lynchburg 24503
Regent University, Virginia Beach 23464-9800
Regent University: School of Divinity, Virginia Beach 23464
Regent University: School of Law, Virginia Beach 23464
Richard Bland College, Petersburg 23805
Roanoke College, Salem 24153
St. Paul's College, Lawrenceville 23868
Shenandoah University, Winchester 22601
Southside Virginia Community College, Alberta 23821
Southwest Virginia Community College, Richlands 24641
Sweet Briar College, Sweet Briar 24595
Thomas Nelson Community College, Hampton 23670
Tidewater Community College, Norfolk 23510
Union Theological Seminary in Virginia, Richmond 23227
University of Richmond, University of Richmond 23173
University of Richmond: The T.C. Williams School of Law, University of Richmond 23173
University of Virginia, Charlottesville 22903
University of Virginia's College at Wise, Wise 24293
University of Virginia: School of Law, Charlottesville 22903
University of Virginia: School of Medicine, Charlottesville 22908
Virginia Commonwealth University, Richmond 23284-9005
Virginia Commonwealth University: School of Dentistry, Richmond 23298
Virginia Commonwealth University: School of Medicine, Richmond 23298
Virginia Highlands Community College, Abingdon 24210
Virginia Intermont College, Bristol 24201
Virginia Military Institute, Lexington 24450-0304
Virginia Polytechnic Institute and State University, Blacksburg 24061
Virginia Polytechnic Institute: Virginia-Maryland Regional College of Veterinary Medicine, Blacksburg 24061
Virginia State University, Petersburg 23806
Virginia Union University, Richmond 23220
Virginia Union University: School of Theology, Richmond 23220
Virginia Wesleyan College, Norfolk 23502-5599
Virginia Western Community College, Roanoke 24038
Washington and Lee University, Lexington 24450-0303
Washington and Lee University: School of Law, Lexington 24450
Wytheville Community College, Wytheville 24382

Washington
Antioch University Seattle, Seattle 98121
Art Institute of Seattle, Seattle 98121
Bastyr University, Kenmore 98028
Bellevue Community College, Bellevue 98007
Big Bend Community College, Moses Lake 98837-3299
Central Washington University, Ellensburg 98926-7500
Centralia College, Centralia 98531
City University, Bellevue 98004
Clark College, Vancouver 98663-3598
Columbia Basin College, Pasco 99301
Cornish College of the Arts, Seattle 98102
Eastern Washington University, Cheney 99004
Edmonds Community College, Lynnwood 98036-5999
Everett Community College, Everett 98201-1352
Evergreen State College, Olympia 98505
Gonzaga University, Spokane 99258-0001
Gonzaga University: Department of Religious Studies, Spokane 99258
Gonzaga University: School of Law, Spokane 99220
Grays Harbor College, Aberdeen 98520
Green River Community College, Auburn 98092
Henry Cogswell College, Everett 98201
Heritage College, Toppenish 98948
Highline Community College, Des Moines 98198

ITT Technical Institute: Bothell, Bothell 98021
ITT Technical Institute: Seattle, Seattle 98168
ITT Technical Institute: Spokane, Spokane 99212
Lake Washington Technical College, Kirkland 98034
Lower Columbia College, Longview 98632-0310
North Seattle Community College, Seattle 98103
Northwest Indian College, Bellingham 98226
Olympic College, Bremerton 98337-1699
Pacific Lutheran University, Tacoma 98447-0003
Peninsula College, Port Angeles 98362
Pierce College, Lakewood 98498-1999
Puget Sound Christian College, Edmonds 98020-3171
Renton Technical College, Renton 98056-4195
St. Martin's College, Lacey 98503
Seattle Central Community College, Seattle 98122
Seattle Pacific University, Seattle 98119-1997
Seattle University, Seattle 98122
Seattle University: School of Law, Tacoma 98402
Seattle University: School of Theology and Ministry, Seattle 98122
Shoreline Community College, Seattle 98133
Skagit Valley College, Mount Vernon 98273
South Puget Sound Community College, Olympia 98512-6218
South Seattle Community College, Seattle 98106-1499
Spokane Community College, Spokane 99217-5399
Spokane Falls Community College, Spokane 99224
Tacoma Community College, Tacoma 98466
University of Puget Sound, Tacoma 98416
University of Washington, Seattle 98195
University of Washington: School of Dentistry, Seattle 98195
University of Washington: School of Law, Seattle 98105
University of Washington: School of Medicine, Seattle 98195
Walla Walla College, College Place 99324
Walla Walla Community College, Walla Walla 99362-9270
Washington State University, Pullman 99164
Washington State University: College of Pharmacy, Pullman 99164
Washington State University: School of Veterinary Medicine, Pullman 99164
Wenatchee Valley College, Wenatchee 98801-1799
Western Washington University, Bellingham 98225
Whatcom Community College, Bellingham 98226
Whitman College, Walla Walla 99362-2083
Whitworth College, Spokane 99251
Yakima Valley Community College, Yakima 98907-2520

West Virginia

Alderson-Broaddus College, Philippi 26416
Bethany College, Bethany 26032
Bluefield State College, Bluefield 24701
College of West Virginia, Beckley 25802
Concord College, Athens 24712
Corinthian Schools: National Institute of Technology, Cross Lanes 25313
Davis and Elkins College, Elkins 26241
Fairmont State College, Fairmont 26554
Glenville State College, Glenville 26351
Marshall University, Huntington 25755
Marshall University: School of Medicine, Huntington 25704
Ohio Valley College, Parkersburg 26101
Potomac State College of West Virginia University, Keyser 26726
Salem-Teikyo University, Salem 26426
Shepherd College, Shepherdstown 25443-3210
Southern West Virginia Community and Technical College, Mount Gay 25637
University of Charleston, Charleston 25304
West Liberty State College, West Liberty 26074-0295
West Virginia Northern Community College, Wheeling 26003
West Virginia School of Osteopathic Medicine, Lewisburg 24901
West Virginia State College, Institute 25112-1000
West Virginia University, Morgantown 26506-6201
West Virginia University Institute of Technology, Montgomery 25136
West Virginia University at Parkersburg, Parkersburg 26101

West Virginia University: College of Law, Morgantown 26506
West Virginia University: School of Dentistry, Morgantown 26506
West Virginia University: School of Medicine, Morgantown 26506
West Virginia University: School of Pharmacy, Morgantown 26506
West Virginia Wesleyan College, Buckhannon 26201
Wheeling Jesuit University, Wheeling 26003

Wisconsin

Alverno College, Milwaukee 53234-3922
Bellin College of Nursing, Green Bay 54305
Beloit College, Beloit 53511
Blackhawk Technical College, Janesville 53547
Bryant & Stratton College, Milwaukee 53202
Cardinal Stritch University, Milwaukee 53217
Carroll College, Waukesha 53186
Carthage College, Kenosha 53140
Chippewa Valley Technical College, Eau Claire 54701
Columbia College of Nursing, Milwaukee 53211
Concordia University Wisconsin, Mequon 53097
Gateway Technical College, Kenosha 53144
Herzing College, Madison 53704
ITT Technical Institute: Greenfield, Greenfield 53220-4612
Lakeland College, Sheboygan 53082
Lakeshore Technical College, Cleveland 53015
Lawrence University, Appleton 54912-0599
Madison Area Technical College, Madison 53704
Marian College of Fond du Lac, Fond du Lac 54935
Marquette University, Milwaukee 53201-1881
Marquette University: School of Dentistry, Milwaukee 53201
Marquette University: School of Law, Milwaukee 53233
Medical College of Wisconsin, Milwaukee 53226
Medical College of Wisconsin: School of Medicine, Milwaukee 53226
Milwaukee Area Technical College, Milwaukee 53233
Milwaukee Institute of Art & Design, Milwaukee 53202
Milwaukee School of Engineering, Milwaukee 53202-3109
Moraine Park Technical College, Fond du Lac 54935
Mount Mary College, Milwaukee 53222
Mount Senario College, Ladysmith 54848
Nashotah House, Nashotah 53058
Nicolet Area Technical College, Rhinelander 54501
Northeast Wisconsin Technical College, Green Bay 54307-9042
Northland College, Ashland 54806
Ripon College, Ripon 54971
Sacred Heart School of Theology, Hales Corners 53130
St. Francis Seminary, St. Francis 53235
St. Norbert College, De Pere 54115-2099
Silver Lake College, Manitowoc 54220
Southwest Wisconsin Technical College, Fennimore 53809
University of Wisconsin Madison: School of Law, Madison 53706
University of Wisconsin Madison: School of Medicine, Madison 53706
University of Wisconsin Madison: School of Pharmacy, Madison 53706
University of Wisconsin Madison: School of Veterinary Medicine, Madison 53706
University of Wisconsin-Baraboo/Sauk County, Baraboo 53913
University of Wisconsin-Barron County, Rice Lake 54868
University of Wisconsin-Eau Claire, Eau Claire 54701
University of Wisconsin-Fond du Lac, Fond du Lac 54935
University of Wisconsin-Fox Valley, Menasha 54952
University of Wisconsin-Green Bay, Green Bay 54311-7001
University of Wisconsin-La Crosse, La Crosse 54601
University of Wisconsin-Madison, Madison 53706-1400
University of Wisconsin-Manitowoc County, Manitowoc 54220
University of Wisconsin-Marathon County, Wausau 54401
University of Wisconsin-Marinette, Marinette 54143

University of Wisconsin-Marshfield/Wood County, Marshfield 54449
University of Wisconsin-Milwaukee, Milwaukee 53201
University of Wisconsin-Oshkosh, Oshkosh 54901
University of Wisconsin-Parkside, Kenosha 53141-2000
University of Wisconsin-Platteville, Platteville 53818
University of Wisconsin-Richland, Richland Center 53581
University of Wisconsin-River Falls, River Falls 54022
University of Wisconsin-Rock County, Janesville 53546
University of Wisconsin-Sheboygan County, Sheboygan 53081
University of Wisconsin-Stevens Point, Stevens Point 54481
University of Wisconsin-Stout, Menomonie 54751
University of Wisconsin-Superior, Superior 54880
University of Wisconsin-Washington County, West Bend 53095
University of Wisconsin-Waukesha, Waukesha 53188
University of Wisconsin-Whitewater, Whitewater 53190
Viterbo University, La Crosse 54601
Waukesha County Technical College, Pewaukee 53072
Western Wisconsin Technical College, La Crosse 54602-0908
Wisconsin Indianhead Technical College, Shell Lake 54871
Wisconsin Lutheran College, Milwaukee 53226

Wyoming

Casper College, Casper 82601
Central Wyoming College, Riverton 82501
Eastern Wyoming College, Torrington 82240
Laramie County Community College, Cheyenne 82007
Northwest College, Powell 82435
Sheridan College, Sheridan 82801
University of Wyoming, Laramie 82071
University of Wyoming: College of Law, Laramie 82071
University of Wyoming: School of Pharmacy, Laramie 82071
Western Wyoming Community College, Rock Springs 82902-0428

Alphabetical index of majors

Accounting 49
Acting/directing 55
Actuarial science 56
Acupuncture/Oriental medicine 56
Administration of special education 56
Adult/continuing education administration 56
Adult/continuing teacher education 57
Advertising 57
Aerospace/aeronautical/astronautical engineering 58
African studies 59
African-American studies 59
Agribusiness operations 60
Agricultural animal breeding/genetics 60
Agricultural animal health 60
Agricultural animal nutrition 60
Agricultural animal physiology 61
Agricultural business 61
Agricultural economics 62
Agricultural education 62
Agricultural engineering 63
Agricultural food processing 63
Agricultural mechanization 63
Agricultural plant pathology 64
Agricultural plant physiology 64
Agricultural production 64
Agricultural sciences 64
Agricultural supplies 65
Agronomy/crop science 65
Air Force 66
Air traffic control 66
Air transportation 66
Aircraft mechanics 67
American literature 67
American studies 68
Analytical chemistry 69
Anatomy 69
Animal sciences 69
Anthropology 70
Applied mathematics 72
Applied physics 73
Arabic 74
Archaeology 74
Architectural engineering 74
Architectural engineering technology 74
Architecture 75
Architecture/related programs 76
Area studies 77
Area/ethnic/cultural studies 77
Army 77
Art 78
Art education 81
Art history/criticism/conservation 83
Art therapy 85
Arts management 85
Asian studies 86
Asian-American studies 86
Astronomy 86
Astrophysics 87
Audiology/hearing sciences 87
Auto body repair 88
Automotive technology 89
Aviation management 90
Banking/financial support services 90
Behavioral sciences 91
Bible studies 92
Biblical languages/literature 92
Bilingual/bicultural education 93
Biochemistry 93
Bioengineering/biomedical engineering 95
Biological immunology 96
Biological technology 96
Biological/life sciences 96
Biological/physical sciences 97
Biology 99
Biology teacher education 104
Biomedical sciences/technologies 106
Biometrics 106
Biophysics 107
Biopsychology 107
Biostatistics 107
Biotechnology research 107
Blood bank technology 108
Botany 108
Business 109
Business administration/management 113
Business communications 119
Business computer facilities operation 120
Business computer programming 120
Business economics 121
Business education 123
Business marketing/marketing management 124
Business quantitative methods/management science 127
Business statistics 127
Business systems analysis/design 127
Business systems networking/telecommunications 128
Business/personal services marketing 129
CAD-CAM/drafting 129
Canadian studies 132
Cardiovascular technology 132
Caribbean studies 132
Carpentry 132
Cell biology 133
Ceramic sciences/engineering 134
Ceramics 134
Chemical engineering 134
Chemical/atomic physics 135
Chemistry 136
Chemistry teacher education 140
Child care/guidance 142
Chinese 144
Chiropractic (D.C.) 144
Civil engineering 145
Civil engineering/civil technology 146
Classical/ancient Near Eastern languages 147
Classics 147
Clerical/general office 148
Clinical laboratory science 150
Clinical psychology 152
Clinical/medical social work 152
Clothing/apparel/textile studies 153
Clothing/textile products and services 153
Coast Guard 154
Cognitive psychology/psycholinguistics 154
College counseling 154
Commercial photography 154
Communication disorders 155
Communications 155
Communications technologies 159
Community health services 160
Community organization/resources/services 160
Community psychology 161
Community/junior college administration 161
Comparative literature 161
Comparative/international education 162
Computer engineering 162
Computer graphics 163
Computer programming 164
Computer science 166
Computer systems analysis 169
Computer teacher education 170
Computer/information sciences 170
Conducting 176
Conservation/renewable resources 176
Construction 177
Construction management 178
Construction trades 178
Construction/building science 179
Construction/building technologies 179
Consumer resource management 180
Corrections administration 180
Cosmetic services 181
Counseling psychology 182
Counselor education 183
Court reporter 184
Crafts/folk art/artisanry 185
Creative writing 185
Criminal justice studies 186
Criminal justice/corrections 188
Criminal justice/law enforcement administration 190
Criminology 191
Culinary arts/related services 192
Curriculum/instruction 193
Custodial/home services 195
Cytotechnology 195
Dairy science 195
Dance 195
Dance therapy 196
Data entry/information processing 196
Data processing technology 198
Demography/population studies 200
Dental assistant 200
Dental hygiene studies 201
Dental laboratory technology 202
Dental specialties 202
Dentistry (D.D.S. or D.M.D.) 202
Design/visual communications 203
Developmental/child psychology 204
Diagnostic medical sonography 204
Diesel mechanics 205
Dietetics 205
Drama/dance teacher education 206
Drama/theater arts 207
Drawing 210
Driver/safety education 211
Drug/alcohol abuse counseling 211
Early childhood education 212
Earth/planetary sciences 215
East Asian studies 216
East European languages 217
East/Southeast Asian languages 217
Eastern European studies 217
Ecology 217
Economics 218
Education 221
Education administration/K-12 224
Education administration/supervision 225
Education of autistic 227
Education of blind/visually handicapped 227
Education of deaf/hearing impaired 227
Education of emotionally handicapped 228
Education of gifted/talented 228
Education of learning disabled 229
Education of mentally handicapped 230
Education of multiple handicapped 230
Education of physically handicapped 231
Education of speech impaired 231
Education/instructional media design 231
Educational evaluation/research 232
Educational psychology 232
Educational statistics/research methods 233
Educational supervision 233
Educational testing/measurement 234
Electrical/electronic engineering-related technologies 234
Electrical/electronics/communications engineering 237
Electrician 239
Electrocardiograph technology 239
Electrodiagnostic technologies 239
Electroencephalograph technology 240
Electromechanical instrumentation 240
Electronics/electrical equipment repair 241
Elementary education 242
Elementary particle physics 246
Emergency medical technology 247
Engineering 248
Engineering design 250
Engineering mechanics 250
Engineering physics 250
Engineering science 251
Engineering-related technologies 252
Engineering/industrial management 253
English 254
English composition 259
English education 259
English literature 262
Enterprise management/operations 263
Entomology 263
Entrepreneurship 264
Environmental control technologies 264
Environmental design 265
Environmental health 266
Environmental health engineering 266
Environmental science/conservation 267
Environmental studies 269
Epidemiology 270
Equestrian/equine studies 270
ESL teacher education 270
Ethnic/cultural studies 271
European studies 272
Evolutionary biology 272
Exercise sciences 272
Experimental psychology 273
Family/community studies 274
Family/individual development 274
Farm/ranch management 275
Fashion design/illustration 275
Fashion/apparel marketing 276
Fiber arts 277
Film/cinema studies 277
Film/video/cinematography/production 278
Finance/banking 278
Financial management/services 281
Financial planning 282
Financial services marketing 282

Alphabetical index of majors

Fine arts 282
Fire protection 284
Fire protection/safety
  technology 284
Fire services administration 285
Firefighting/fire science 285
Fisheries/fishing 286
Flight attendant 287
Floristry marketing 287
Food management 287
Food products retailing/
  wholesaling 287
Food sciences/technology 287
Food/nutrition studies 288
Foreign language/translation 289
Foreign languages education 289
Foreign languages/literatures 291
Forensic technologies 292
Forest production/processing 292
Forestry 292
French 293
Funeral services/mortuary
  science 296
Gaming/sports officiating 297
Genetics, plant/animal 297
Geochemistry 297
Geography 297
Geological engineering 299
Geology 299
Geophysical engineering 301
Geophysics/seismology 301
German 302
German language teacher
  education 304
Germanic languages 305
Gerontology 305
Global studies 306
Graphic design/commercial
  art/illustration 306
Graphic/printing equipment
  operation 308
Greek, ancient 309
Greek, modern 310
Greenhouse management 310
Health education 310
Health occupations teacher
  education 312
Health physics/radiologic
  health 312
Health products/services
  marketing 312
Health professions/related
  sciences 312
Health system administration 314
Health/medical biostatistics 315
Health/medical laboratory
  technologies 315
Health/physical fitness 316
Heating/air conditioning/
  refrigeration mechanics 317
Hebrew 319
Hematology technology 319
Higher education
  administration 319
Hispanic-American studies 319
Historic preservation/
  conservation 320
History 320
History teacher education 325
Home economics 326
Home economics business
  services 327
Home economics education 328
Home furnishings/equipment 328
Home/office products
  marketing 329
Horticultural services 329
Horticulture science 329
Hospitality administration/
  management 330
Hospitality/recreation
  marketing 331
Hotel/motel/restaurant
  management 332
Housing studies 333

Human resources management 333
Human services 335
Industrial design 336
Industrial equipment
  maintenance/repair 336
Industrial production
  technologies 337
Industrial/manufacturing
  engineering 339
Industrial/organizational
  psychology 340
Information sciences/systems 340
Inorganic chemistry 343
Institutional food production 343
Insurance marketing 344
Insurance/risk management 344
Interdisciplinary studies 344
Interior architecture 346
Interior design 347
Intermedia 348
International agriculture 348
International business 348
International business
  marketing 350
International finance 351
International relations 351
International studies 352
Investments/securities 353
Islamic studies 353
Italian 353
Japanese 354
Jazz 354
Jewish/Judaic studies 355
Journalism 355
Junior high education 358
Juridical specialization 360
Labor/personnel relations 360
Landscape architecture 360
Landscaping management 361
Latin 361
Latin American studies 362
Law (J.D.) 363
Law enforcement/police
  science 364
Leather/upholstery 366
Legal administrative assistant 366
Legal studies 368
Liberal arts/humanities 368
Library assistance 374
Library science 375
Linguistics 375
Logistics/materials
  management 376
Management information
  systems 376
Management science 379
Manufacturing technologies 380
Marine engineering/naval
  architecture 381
Marine/aquatic biology 381
Marketing management 381
Marketing research 383
Marketing/distribution 383
Marketing/distribution
  education 385
Masonry/tile setting 386
Materials engineering 386
Materials science 386
Mathematics 387
Mathematics education 392
Mathematics/computer science 395
Mechanical engineering 396
Mechanical engineering-related
  technologies 397
Mechanics/repair 399
Medical administrative
  assistant 399
Medical assistant 401
Medical basic sciences 402
Medical dietetics 403
Medical illustrating 403
Medical laboratory assistant 403
Medical laboratory technology 403
Medical radiologic technology 405
Medical records administration 406

Medical records technology 407
Medical specialties 408
Medical transcription 408
Medicine (M.D.) 409
Medieval/renaissance studies 410
Mental health services 410
Mental health services
  technology 411
Merchant Marine 411
Metal/jewelry arts 411
Metallurgical engineering 412
Metallurgy 412
Meteorology 412
Mexican-American studies 413
Microbiology/bacteriology 413
Middle Eastern languages,
  other 414
Middle Eastern studies 414
Military technologies 414
Mining/mineral engineering 414
Mining/petroleum technologies 414
Ministerial/theological studies 415
Missionary studies 416
Molecular biology 416
Movement therapy 417
Museum studies 417
Music 417
Music business management 421
Music education 422
Music history/literature 424
Music performance 425
Music theory/composition 427
Music therapy 428
Music, piano/organ
  performance 428
Music, voice/choral/opera
  performance 429
Musical theater 430
Musicology/ethnomusicology 431
Native American studies 431
Natural resources management 431
Natural sciences 432
Navy/Marines 433
Neuroscience 433
Nonprofit/public management 433
Nuclear engineering 434
Nuclear medical technology 434
Nuclear physics 434
Nuclear/industrial radiologic
  technologies 434
Nursery operations 435
Nursing 435
Nursing (Post-RN) 437
Nursing (RN) 438
Nursing administration 442
Nursing anesthesiology 442
Nursing assistant 443
Nursing education 443
Nursing, practical 444
Nutritional sciences 445
Occupational health/industrial
  hygiene 446
Occupational therapy 446
Occupational therapy assistant 447
Ocean engineering 448
Oceanography 448
Office supervision/management 448
Operations management/
  supervision 450
Operations research 451
Ophthalmic medical assistant 451
Ophthalmic/optometric
  services 451
Optics 451
Optometric/ophthalmic
  laboratory technology 452
Optometry (O.D.) 452
Organic chemistry 452
Organizational behavior
  studies 452
Ornamental horticulture 453
Orthotics/prosthetics 453
Osteopathic medicine (D.O.) 453
Pacific area studies 453
Painting 454

Paleontology 454
Paralegal/legal assistance 454
Parasitology 457
Parks/recreation/fitness studies 457
Parks/recreational/leisure
  facilities management 458
Pastoral counseling 459
Pathology, human/animal 459
Peace/conflict studies 459
Perfusion technology 460
Personal services 460
Petroleum engineering 460
Pharmaceutical/medicinal
  chemistry 460
Pharmacology, human/animal 460
Pharmacy 461
Pharmacy assistant 461
Philosophy 462
Philosophy/religion 465
Photography 466
Physical education 467
Physical sciences 470
Physical sciences technologies 471
Physical therapy 472
Physical therapy assistant 473
Physical/theoretical chemistry 474
Physician assistant 474
Physics 475
Physics teacher education 478
Physiology, human/animal 479
Plant breeding/genetics 480
Plant pathology 480
Plant physiology 481
Plant protection 481
Plant sciences 481
Plasma/high-temperature
  physics 481
Playwriting/screenwriting 481
Plumbing/pipefitting 482
Podiatry, podiatric medicine
  (D.P.M.) 482
Political science/government 482
Polymer chemistry 486
Polymer/plastics engineering 486
Portuguese 487
Poultry science 487
Power/electrical transmission 487
Prearchitecture 488
Precision metal work 488
Precision production trades 490
Predentistry 490
Preengineering 492
Prelaw 493
Premedicine 495
Prenursing 497
Preoptometry 497
Prepharmacy 498
Prephysical therapy 499
Preveterinary medicine 500
Printmaking 502
Protective services 502
Psychobiology/physiological
  psychology 503
Psychology 503
Public administration 508
Public administration/services 510
Public finance 511
Public health 511
Public health education 511
Public policy analysis 512
Public relations 512
Purchasing/procurement/
  contracts 513
Quality control/safety
  technologies 514
Radiation biology 515
Radio/television broadcasting 515
Range science/management 516
Reading education 516
Real estate 518
Recreational therapy 519
Rehabilitation/therapeutic
  services 520
Religion/religious studies 520
Religious education 522

Religious music 523
Respiratory therapy....................524
Retailing/wholesaling 525
Robotics 526
Romance languages, other............527
Russian.......................................527
Russian/Slavic studies 528
Scandinavian..............................528
Scandinavian studies....................529
School psychology......................529
Science education 529
Science technologies...................532
Science/technology/society 532
Sculpture 533
Secondary education...................533
Secretarial/administrative
  services 537
Security/loss prevention 540
Sign language interpretation........541
Slavic languages 541
Social psychology......................542
Social science education..............542
Social sciences............................544
Social studies education 546
Social work 548
Social/philosophical
  foundations of education 551
Sociology 551
Software engineering...................556
Soil sciences 556
Solid-state/low-temperature
  physics 557
South Asian languages 557
South Asian studies 557
Southeast Asian studies 557
Spanish.......................................557
Spanish language teacher
  education 560
Special education........................562
Speech pathology........................565
Speech pathology/audiology 565
Speech teacher education 566
Speech/rhetorical studies.............567
Speech/theater education.............569
Sports medicine/athletic
  training 570
Sports/fitness administration 571
Stationary energy sources
  mechanics...............................572
Statistics.....................................572
Studio arts 573
Surgical/operating room
  technology 575
Surveying 575
Systems engineering....................576
Systems science/theory................576
Taxation......................................576
Teacher assistance.......................577
Teacher education, multiple
  levels......................................577
Technical education 578
Technical theater/design/
  stagecraft 579
Technical/business writing 579
Technology/industrial arts
  education 580
Telecommunications 581
Textile sciences/engineering..........582
Theater history/criticism...............582
Theological professions
  (B.Div., M.Div., Rabbinical, or
  Talmudical)..............................582
Theological studies 583
Theoretical/mathematical
  physics 584
Tourism/travel management..........584
Tourism/travel marketing 585
Toxicology 586
Trade/industrial education 586
Transportation management 587
Transportation/materials
  moving...................................587
Turf management........................587
Urban studies 588

Urban/community/regional
  planning 588
Vehicle/equipment operation.........589
Vehicle/mobile equipment
  mechanics 589
Vehicle/petroleum products
  marketing...............................590
Veterinarian assistant 590
Veterinary medicine (D.V.M.).......591
Veterinary specialties...................591
Virology 592
Visual/performing arts 592
Vocational home economics..........593
Vocational rehabilitation
  counseling..............................593
Water transportation.....................594
Western European studies 594
Wildlife/wildlands
  management...........................594
Women's studies..........................595
Woodworking..............................596
Zoology 596

Selected Books and Software from the College Board

Annual college directories

The College Board Scholarship Handbook with *FUND FINDER*™ CD-ROM, 2001. Over 2,300 *real* scholarships, grants, internships, and loans for undergraduate students. 600 pages, paperbound. **Item# 006488** — $24.95

The College Board College Handbook with *College Explorer*® CD-ROM, 2001. Over 2 million copies sold. The only one-volume guide to all U.S. two- and four-year colleges. 1,700 pages, paperbound. **Item# 006445** — $25.95

The College Board College Cost & Financial Aid Handbook, 2001. Detailed cost and financial aid information at 3,100 two- and four-year institutions; includes indexed information on college scholarships. 700 pages, paperbound. **Item# 006461** — $21.95

The College Board Index of Majors and Graduate Degrees, 2001. "A comprehensive, no-nonsense guide" — *The New York Times*. Covers 600 major fields of study at all degree levels: undergraduate, graduate, and professional, including law, medicine, and dentistry. 680 pages, paperbound. **Item# 006453** — $21.95

The College Board International Student Handbook of U.S. Colleges, 2001. Provides students with information they need to apply for study at 3,000 U.S. colleges, including costs, required tests, financial aid, ESL programs. 360 pages, paperbound. **Item# 006496** — $25.95

Test prep for College Board programs

10 Real SAT®s, Second Edition. From the College Board, official source of the SAT: 10 real, complete SATs for student practice, including two new tests administered in 2000. With test-taking tips from the test makers themselves. 700 pages, paperbound. **Item# 006542** — $18.95

Real SAT II: Subject Tests. The only source of real SAT II practice questions from cover to cover—in a newly revised updated edition. 700 pages paperbound. **Item# 005996** — $17.95

AP® CD-ROM in Calculus AB, 2000. This valuable study tool, designed to complement the materials provided in the classroom, includes practice tests. **Item# 201907** — $49.00

AP CD-ROM in U.S. History, 1998. This valuable study tool, designed to complement the written preparation materials provided in the classroom, includes essay tutorials and practice tests. **Item # 201865** — $49.00

AP CD-ROM in European History, 1999. This valuable study tool, designed to complement the written preparation materials provided in the classroom, includes essay tutorials and practice tests. **Item # 201891** — $49.00

AP CD-ROM in English Language, 1999. This valuable study tool, designed to complement the written preparation materials provided in the classroom, includes essay tutorials and practice tests. **Item # 201889** — $49.00

AP CD-ROM in English Literature, 1998. This valuable study tool, designed to complement the written preparation materials provided in the classroom, includes essay tutorials and practice tests. **Item # 201864** — $49.00

One-on-One with the SAT™. (Version 2.0) New release! Valuable advice and test-taking strategies from the SAT test makers, plus the opportunity to take a real, complete SAT and hundreds of additional practice questions on computer. Get a free diagnostic test and predicted SAT score at www.collegeboard.com. (Home version— Windows® and Macintosh®) **Item# 006534** — $29.95

The Official Study Guide for the CLEP® Examinations 2001. Passing scores on CLEP exams can earn credit at over 2,800 colleges. Only guide to cover all 34 CLEP exams with sample questions for all tests. 500 pages, paperbound. **Item# 006437** — $18.00

General guidance for students and parents

The College Application Essay, Sarah Myers McGinty. Application essay policies of more than 180 institutions, types of questions asked, plus 40 actual questions and analyses of 6 essays. 131 pages, paperbound. **Item# 005759** — $12.95

Campus Visits and College Interviews, Zola Dincin Schneider. "…must reading for students and parents." — *The Book Report*. Why they are important, when to visit, what to look for, questions usually asked, much more. 126 pages, paperbound. **Item# 002601** — $9.95

The College Board Guide to 150 Popular College Majors. One-of-a-kind reference to majors in 17 fields, with related information on typical courses, high school preparation, much more. 377 pages, paperbound. **Item# 004000** — $16.00

The College Board Guide to Jobs and Career Planning, Second Edition, Joyce Slayton Mitchell. Detailed descriptions of more than 100 occupations, with educational requirements, income range, more. 331 pages, paperbound. **Item# 004671** — $14.00

The Parents' Guide to Paying for College, Gerald Krefetz. Expert advice from a well-known investment analyst and financial consultant on covering college costs, with case studies. 158 pages, paperbound. **Item# 006046** — $14.95

Order Form

Dept. GSX0100A

Mail order form to: College Board Publications, Dept. GSX0100A, Two College Way, Forrester Center, WV 25438 *(payment must accompany all orders)*
or phone: 800 323-7155, M–F, 8 am–11 pm Eastern Time *(credit card orders only)*
or fax 24 hours, 7 days a week to: 800 525-5562 *(purchase orders above $25 and credit card orders)*
or online through the College Board Store at www.collegeboard.com *(credit card orders only)*

Item No.	Title	Price	Amount
	Annual college directories		
006488	Scholarship Handbook with FUND FINDER™ CD-ROM, 2001	$24.95	
006445	The College Handbook, with College Explorer® CD-ROM, 2001	$25.95	
006461	College Cost & Financial Aid Handbook, 2001	$21.95	
006453	Index of Majors and Graduate Degrees, 2001	$21.95	
006496	International Student Handbook of U.S. Colleges, 2001	$25.95	
988215	2001 Scholarship 3-book set: College Handbook, Scholarship Handbook, College Cost & Financial Aid Handbook	$49.00	
988213	2001 International 3-book set: International Student Handbook, College Handbook, Index of Majors	$49.00	
	Test prep for College Board programs		
201907	AP® CD-ROM in Calculus AB, 2000	$49.00	
201864	AP CD-ROM in English Literature, 1998	$49.00	
201865	AP CD-ROM in U.S. History, 1998	$49.00	
201891	AP CD-ROM in European History, 1999	$49.00	
201889	AP CD-ROM in English Language, 1999	$49.00	
006542	10 Real SAT®s, 2nd Edition	$18.95	
006534	One-on-One with the SAT™ (Home version, Windows®/Macintosh®)	$29.95	
006437	The Official Study Guide for the CLEP® Examinations, 2001	$18.00	
005996	Real SAT II: Subject Tests	$17.95	
	General guidance for students and parents		
005759	The College Application Essay	$12.95	
002601	Campus Visits and College Interviews	$ 9.95	
004000	College Board Guide to 150 Popular College Majors	$16.00	
004671	College Board Guide to Jobs and Career Planning	$14.00	
006046	The Parents' Guide to Paying for College	$14.95	

Subtotal $ _____
Shipping and handling $ _____
Total $ _____
Sales Tax: $ _____
(IL, CA, FL, GA, PA, DC, MA, TX, VA, WV, Can.)
Grand Total $ _____

Shipping and Handling
$0 – $20.00 = $4.00
$20.01 – $40.00 = $5.00
$40.01 – $60.00 = $6.00
$60.01+ = 10% of dollar value of order

☐ Enclosed is my check or money order made payable to the **College Board**   ☐ Enclosed is my purchase order
☐ Please charge my   ☐ MasterCard   ☐ Visa   ☐ American Express   ☐ Discover

☐☐☐☐ ☐☐☐☐ ☐☐☐☐ ☐☐☐☐   exp. date: _____ / _____
card number   month   year   cardholder's signature

Allow two weeks from receipt of order for delivery.

SHIP TO:

_____   _____
Name   Street Address (no P. O. Box numbers, please)

_____   _____ _____   (_____) _____
City   State   Zip   Telephone